MATCH OF THE
BBC SPORT

FOOTBALL YEARBOOK

2004/2005

BBC

BOOKS

First published 2004

Data collation by Warner Leach Ltd

ISBN 0 563 52135 X

Published by BBC Books, BBC Worldwide Ltd,
Woodlands, 80 Wood Lane, London W12 0TT

Commissioning editor: Ben Dunn
Author: Terry Pratt
Data interpretation: Tony Warner
Data management: Peter Watts, John Haines
Design: John-Paul Warner
Picture and data research: Stephen Hall

Printed and bound in Great Britain by Butler & Tanner Ltd, Frome

From left to right: Henrik Larsson of Celtic by Lee Smith; David Beckham of England by Darren Walsh; Paolo Maldini of AC Milan by Andrew Budd; Zinedine Zidane of France by Alex Morton; Frank Lampard of Chelsea by Darren Walsh; Thierry Henry of Arsenal by Alex Morton; Fernando Morientes of Monaco by Darren Walsh; Tim Howard of Manchester United by Darren Walsh

The *real* footballing clash

INDESIT
Didier Drogba

You can't argue with the league table, they say! Who are they trying to kid? Most fans can show how it's a travesty of mathematics over undeniable truth and plain bad luck. But then supporters will debate anything…

- Playing with style or getting the result?
- Galacticos versus team ethic?
- Keep tinkering or have a clear first XI?
- Hit the transfer market or promote from youth?

It's a never-ending discussion and you can't have too much ammunition to hand. And now it's a squad game and the argument extends to whether you'd even pick the same XI as your manager.

The *Match of the Day Football Yearbook* fills the wide chasm between the endless subjective opinion we all delight in and the bare league table. It puts your club and its players into a context of the best (and worst) in Europe. All the key facts are present, only here they are organised into charts and lists that compare players

- within their own club,
- against others in the same division and, ultimately,
- across the top six leagues on the Continent.

You'll be familiar with these new-style stats; they form the nuggets behind many a newspaper article and adorn informed game commentary. They tell the story behind the rising and falling beat of the league table. They resonate because they spotlight the players; combinations and selections that make a real difference.

They will regularly surprise, sometimes shock and eventually seduce you. Best of all, they give you the ammunition to back up what you already believe.The charts highlight the most- and least-effective players. There will be list-topping defenders you want to deny, goal-scorers whose Strike Rates you can't believe and *always* results you'd love to change.

EDCOM
Fernando Morientes

Before long, though, you will find support for your views on who should be playing regularly and who's got to go. And then they help you to ransack Europe's elite for the up-and-coming stars to replace them. Last year you might have spotted a certain **Didier Drogba** flying high in the charts (lifting unfashionable Guingamp to a late surge) before Marseilles snaffled him. Or you may have noticed that although **Fernando Morientes** was barely playing for Real, he had the best strike-rate at the club.

- Your team needs a midfield enforcer…find players whose defence tightens up when they play.
- As Madrid's Galacticos fade, who's going to replace them?
- Run the rule over that French defender that transfer speculation links with your team.

And start planning to win the big prize with your fantasy XI.

Our charts are signposts to information you'll want to dip deeper into. They put facts – rather than a calculator – at your fingertips. They will give a new and wider perspective on your favourite pastime, challenge your opinions and arm you for every season's biggest footballing clash – your views versus the opinions of friends and colleagues.

Thanks again go to Tony Warner, Peter Watts, Steve Hall, John-Paul Warner and John Haines, plus the photographers of Action Images plc for making it all possible in an impossible time-scale.

Terry Pratt

Contents

Leagues

Clubs

Cups

Charts explained...

	PLAYER	LGE	FAC	LC	Euro	TOT	AVE
1	Hasselbaink	12	1	2	2	17	166
2	Crespo	10	0	0	2	12	114
3	Lampard	10	1	0	4	15	338
4	Mutu	6	3	0	1	10	292
5	Gudjohnsen	6	2	2	3	13	260
6	Duff	5	0	0	1	6	
7	Johnson	3	0	0	1	4	
8	Gronkjaer	2	0	0	1	3	82
9	Terry	2	1	0	0	3	
10	Melchiot	2	0	0	0	2	
11	Bridge	1	0	0	2	3	

Goals chart – Chelsea
The Chelsea Goals list shows the main sources of the club's goals. Hasselbaink tops it with 12 league goals. Cup goals are also noted but it's league goals that determine the order. The Ave. column shows the average number of minutes between goals, the Strike Rate of the featured scorers, even (as with Crespo) if they have not played many games.

Contribution to Attacking Power – Average number of minutes between League team goals while on pitch	71
Player Strike Rate – Average number of minutes between League goals scored by player	183
Club Strike Rate – Average minutes between League goals scored by club	73

	PLAYER	GOALS LGE	GOALS ALL	ASSISTS	POWER	S RATE
1	Jermain Defoe	7	7	0	71	183 mins
2	Robbie Keane	14	16	3	68	206 mins
3	Frederic Kanoute	7	12	1	76	262 mins
4	Simon Davies	2	2	1	57	780 mins
5	Darren Anderton	1	3	4	62	1436 mins

Key Players Goalscorers – Spurs chart
Defoe tops the Spurs Key Goalscorers chart as he has the best Strike Rate. It shows 183 minutes, which is the average time between his seven league goals. The lower it is, the more regularly he scores. Keane is the second most reliable scorer with a goal every 206 minutes, on average. Davies takes the fourth place in the chart, despite being a midfielder. He also has the best Attacking Power, which shows that Spurs are more likely to score when he is on the pitch – a team goal every 57 minutes. Anderton has the most assists with four.

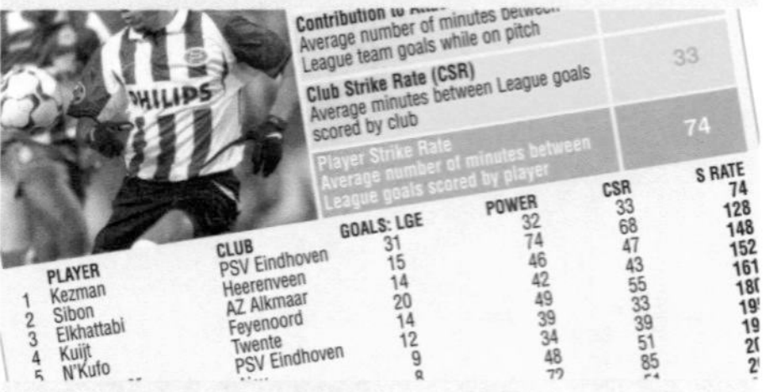

Club Strike Rate (CSR) – Average minutes between League goals scored by club	33
Player Strike Rate – Average number of minutes between League goals scored by player	74

	PLAYER	CLUB	GOALS: LGE	POWER	CSR	S RATE
1	Kezman	PSV Eindhoven	31	32	33	74
2	Sibon	Heerenveen	15	74	68	128
3	Elkhattabi	AZ Alkmaar	14	46	47	148
4	Kuijt	Feyenoord	20	42	43	152
5	N'Kufo	Twente	14	49	55	161
		PSV Eindhoven	12	39	33	

Chart topping Goalscorers list – Holland
Kezman is the most reliable goalscorer in Dutch football. His Strike Rate is a league goal every 74 minutes, on average, for PSV. The Top Goalscorers table lists the 20 best strikers in the division by Strike Rate. To qualify for the chart they must have played at least 17 league games – that's half the Dutch season.

Measuring the Bergkamp effect

Start with *your* club

Blinkers come as part of the football fan's primary equipment. Much as we love the beautiful game, it's definitely more attractive when our team's winning. So the best place to start this book is with those who drive your obsession – your team.

Of course you know the top-scorer but how often is he scoring? Who in your division nets more often? Does anyone score a higher percentage of their team's goals? Who's providing most of the assists? Then there's that Bergkamp-style player who's rarely on the score-sheet but always sparks the attack into life when he's playing – how often does the team score when he's on the pitch?

These nuggets are slipped out now and again during the season – but only here will you find the complete collection.

It only takes a second to score a goal...

...but if you're averaging one an hour, that's phenomenal. A full list of your club's top scorers is in the Goals chart, but our Goalscorers chart shows who hits the net most reliably. The player with the best **Strike Rate** tops it.

The **Strike Rate** shows how many minutes a player averages between league goals. If he scores 10 goals and plays 900 minutes over the season then his **Strike Rate** is 90, or a goal a game. He needn't be a striker to top the chart but he must have played a minimum number of games. This chart also shows how often his team scores when he's on the pitch – his **Attacking Power**. It's a measure of his wider contribution; adding goals to the runs, passes and support play which make him so dangerous. So a team may average a goal every 50 minutes during the league season but scores every 45 minutes when this star is playing. Premier club charts will also note the number of assists.

Is there anyone better than Henry?

The Arsenal forward has won a league championship, hit a hat-trick against Italian giants in their own backyard, taken the Premiership Golden Boot and UEFA's Golden Shoe...but is anyone netting more regularly? We compare all the scorers in a division in our Chart-Topping Goalscorers list on the pages that round up the highest rated clubs and players across each division. This ranks the players from one to 20 on their **Strike Rate** in league games.

Players must have played more regularly to make this list (at least 17 league games) so some irregular players may not feature, despite having good **Strike Rates**. If you think we have been too harsh with our 17-game hurdle, the information is there to make up your own list.

What happened in January?

It's not a question of whether you will suffer a blip during the season but how long it lasts. Even Arsenal fans have their 'if onlys' from this record-busting season. For Premiership sides, and the Celtic and Rangers duo in Scotland, we have detailed the highs and lows over the season against results and chart position. We use the images that filled the newspaper back pages, illustrating the action, or the elation and despair on the face behind the headline. The result is a graphic biorhythm that shows how small incidents can turn into an irrepressible tide of confidence, or how missing a chance or a key player starts a slump where you can't buy a result – ask Man City fans.

Refs go out looking for him

Our Disciplinary Records chart those who attract the referee's attention. We show how often they receive a card on average. So a **Disciplinary Average** of 180 minutes means the player has averaged a card every two games. Small wonder the refs are after him – but which refs? The Premier Round-up pages keep a tally of their records too.

He's worth 15 points a season to us

However, your goalie rarely gets the headline unless he's committed a howler. Managers tend to stick with their keepers, so the Chart-topping Goalkeepers round-up often mirrors the league's 'Against' column. We chart keepers by the average number of minutes between conceding goals. So 36 goals conceded in 2,520 minutes on the pitch means they let in a goal every 70 minutes. This is their **Defensive Rating**, which we can compare against any defender in any division.

In the Premiership we also note their **Goals to Shots Ratio**, which divides the number of **Shots on Target** against the goals conceded, and highlights a good shot-stopper behind a porous defence.

It's his positional play

Like keepers, defenders are measured by their **Defensive Rating** – how regularly the team concedes a league goal when they are playing. Our Defenders chart also notes the number of **Clean Sheets** recorded in games when they have played at least 70 minutes.

Managers start to get sub-happy with 20 minutes to go, particularly if they feel the result is already decided. Fantasy games recognise this and often feature a cut-off point around 60–70 minutes, after which the player is worth more fantasy points to you. If a player has played as least 70 minutes we call it a **Counting Game** and a **Clean Sheet** is recorded in our defender's stats.

He's a box-to-box player

Games can be controlled by a dominant midfield, snuffing out opposition attacks and launching raids of their own. In the Midfielders chart we measure each player's contribution both to scoring and to keeping it tight at the back. Bolton's Okocha has gone through the season without scoring a league goal but, with seven assists, is still considered invaluable to Bolton. When he is on the pitch they score on average every 74 minutes. So 74 is his **Attacking Power**.

We also want to know how often Bolton concede when Okocha's playing. Is he doing his bit to protect the defence? His **Defensive Rating** is a goal conceded every 66 minutes – obviously the higher it is, the fewer goals the opposition have scored. The simple way to measure his overall contribution is to compare how often the team scores with how often it concedes when Okocha plays. Take his **Attacking Power** (74) away from his **Defensive Rating** (66) and you get minus 8. This is like his personal 'goal difference' so we've called it his **Scoring Difference**. This is how we chart midfielders. Positive figures show more goals scored than conceded, minus results show the reverse.

It's a squad game

How a manager uses key players tells you a lot about them. Bergkamp is a key figure for Arsenal; scoring only a handful of goals but a constant danger. His threat is clear in his low Attacking Power score of 42 – better than Henry's! Bergkamp usually starts a game but is substituted around the 70-minute mark – by which time it's often won!

Charts explained...

All competitions Red

League Average 173 mins between cards

	PLAYER	LEAGUE Y	LEAGUE R	TOTAL Y	TOTAL R	AVE
		5 Y	0 R	6 Y	0 R	173
1	Thompson	9	0	9	0	264
2	Flitcroft	3	0	3	0	285
3	Andresen	6	0	6	0	314
4	Gresko	3	0	3	0	330
5	Amoruso					370

Disciplinary – Blackburn
Thompson tops Blackburn's Bookings chart. He doesn't have the most cards – and Neill picked up two reds – but Thompson was picking up his cards at a rate of one every two games – twice as fast as the sixth-placed Neill.

Goals Conceded in all competitions	48
Clean Sheets In games when he played at least 70 mins	17
Goals to Shots Ratio The average number of shots on target per each League goal conceded	5
Defensive Rating Ave number of mins between League goals conceded while on the pitch	95

Goalkeepers – Sunderland
Poom conceded 40 league goals but he played in 43 games for Sunderland. Some of his colleagues may have conceded less in fewer games, but the key figure is Poom's Defensive Rating of 95 – averaging less than a goal a game. He has kept 17 clean sheets and saved five shots for every goal conceded in his Goals to Shots Ratio.

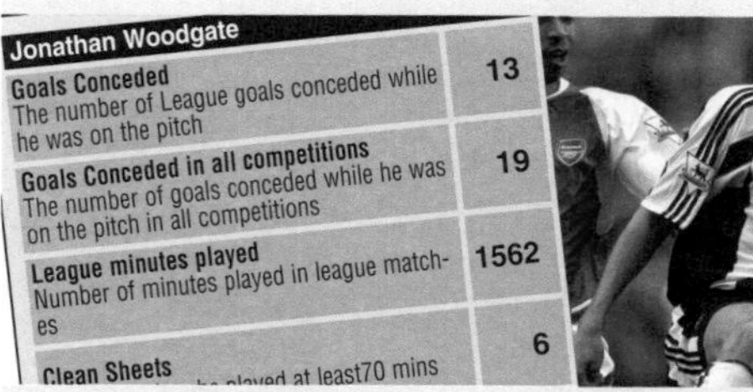

Jonathan Woodgate	
Goals Conceded The number of League goals conceded while he was on the pitch	13
Goals Conceded in all competitions The number of goals conceded while he was on the pitch in all competitions	19
League minutes played Number of minutes played in league matches	1562
Clean Sheets ... played at least70 mins	6

Defenders table – Newcastle
Woodgate makes a huge difference to Newcastle. Like keepers, we measure defenders by how regularly the team concedes when they play. His Defensive Rating is 120 – way ahead of his colleagues. The club concedes a goal every 86 minutes on average. Woodgate's games included six clean sheets.

Charts explained...

Assists League goals scored by team-mates where he delivered the final pass	1
Defensive Rating Average number of mins between League goals conceded while he was on the pitch	69
Contribution to Attacking Power Average number of minutes between League team goals while on pitch	67
Scoring Difference Defensive Rating minus Contribution to Attacking Power	2

	PLAYER	GOALS LGE	GOALS ALL	ASSISTS	DEF RATE	POWER	SC DIFF
1	Osvaldo Juninho Paulista	8	9	1	69	67	2 mins
2	Gaizka Mendieta	2	3	5	74	78	-4 mins
	Boudewijn Zenden	4	7	5	79	86	-7 mins

Midfield table – Boro

Juninho tops a midfield of big names at Boro. He has the only positive Scoring Difference meaning Boro are more likely to score than concede when he plays – just! We take his Attacking Power of 67 away from his Defensive Rating of 69 leaving a difference of two. Individual goals are noted but don't impact the Scoring Difference as that measures Juninho's impact on the team's effectiveness.

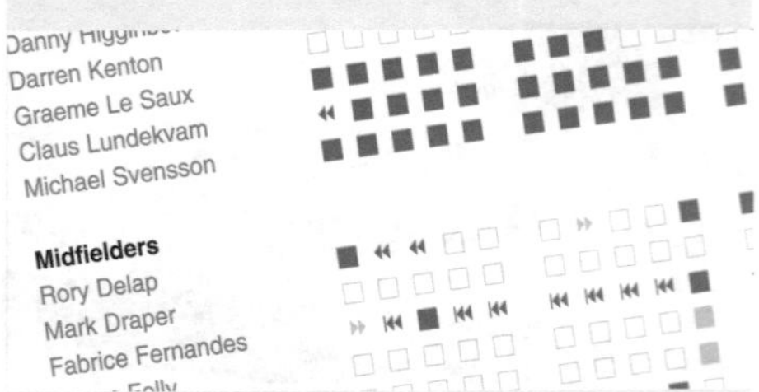
Darren Kenton
Graeme Le Saux
Claus Lundekvam
Michael Svensson
Midfielders
Rory Delap
Mark Draper
Fabrice Fernandes

Squad Appearance cut-out – Saints

Southampton's Squad Appearances chart gets into the nitty-gritty of the season, showing who played when. Here Michael Svensson has five dark green squares, meaning he played every minute of their first five games. Dark green means 'started the game' so there will be 11 dark greens for every game. Rory Delap started the second game but the arrow shows he was substituted. Fabrice Fernandes started the first game on the bench (light green) but came on.

	HOME	AWAY	TOTAL	AVE
shots on target	164	128	292	7.7
shots off target	136	87	223	5.9
TOTAL	300	215	515	13.6

Ratio of goals to shots Average number of shots on target per League goal scored	5.3
Accuracy rating	56.7

Goal attempts – Man City

This Goal Attempts chart supports Keegan's claim that his team were playing well but not getting the breaks. City struck more Shots on Target (and have more Total Shots) than even Chelsea. They averaged over 13 shots a game. They were less deadly though, needing over five shots to notch a goal (Chelsea only 3). The Accuracy Rating turns Shots 'On' versus 'Off' Target into a percentage rating. With 57% on target, City are performing close to Arsenal's level.

The Squad Appearances table is a visual interpretation of the way a squad is used. The game numbers run along the top; the players (divided into their positions) down the side. Dark green shows a starting player and light green a player on the bench. A full square shows they stayed put – either on the pitch or on the bench; arrows mean a player was subbed on or off; and a small vertical line by the arrow shows a **Counting Game** which means they were on for 70 minutes or more.

How come he's not been capped...?

...he must be French! The League Appearances table rounds off a player's information: it gives his age on the first of July 2004 and totals his appearances in the squad, on the pitch, in minutes and in **Counting Games**.

Internationally, we have looked at the registrations of all players in the top divisions to discover the 20 countries that supply most players, and added the four home countries to this list. These are the 24 international teams we follow in the book to show where capped players play their club football. These inevitably include the top international sides. For all top division players we give their nationality and *if they play for one of our 24 countries*, we give their caps this season (to indicate they are current internationals). The summer FIFA Ranking for these 24 countries is also shown.

He's got to hit the target from there

The Goal Attempts For table looks at each club's attack. This gives a figure for both **Shots on Target** and **Shots off Target** and charts the total.The number of their shots on target that ended in a goal are revealed in the **Goals to Shots Ratio**, while the percentage of the club's shots that are on target is displayed in the **Accuracy Rating** figure. Houllier used evidence of Liverpool's high number of shots as proof of the team's attacking prowess – but it didn't save his job. The Goal Attempts Against table is the defensive equivalent, showing how much they are under the cosh.

Need a good holding midfield player?

He'll have to be cheap, ideally in his early twenties, perhaps just winning his first caps. Start looking on the Continent or in the lower divisions in their Divisional Round-up pages. Club Defences might be a good starting point to look for a team that is defensively punching above its league table rating. Hunt through the Top Midfielders, which details the players in a division by **Scoring Difference**, and look for good **Defensive Ratings** (the higher it is, the fewer the number of goals conceded) with unfashionable or mid-table sides. You can follow up possible candidates in their own club pages.

He's got to be a winner

Another way to check your selection is to see if their teams' points tally goes up when they're playing. The Chart Topping Point Earners is led by players who net the highest figure in **Average Points per Game**. The top teams dominate this chart, but the Badly Missed Players list compares players with their team's average points and picks out those with the most positive difference. Team of the Season fills a 4-4-2 formation with the top players. Its keeper and defenders are rated by their **Defensive Rating**; the midfield four by their **Scoring Difference** but the two strikers are chosen differently. The first by the leading **Strike Rate**, and the second by the top striker's Attacking Power. Those with 12 **Counting Games** are chosen first. We asterisk (*) low numbers of games.

To qualify for a Divisional XI they have to have played at least 17 **Counting Games**. We only allow a maximum of one player per club in each position, i.e. one keeper, one defender, one midfield player and one striker is the most a club can have.

The best in Europe

Finally, the major divisions in Europe are amalgamated into four round-up pages with the best of the best compared. This is where the use of averages comes into its own as teams play differing numbers of games but can be compared on their league averages. Because of the small number of clubs and the dominance of the Old Firm, performances from Scotland can distort the table, so we have elected to leave the Scottish Premier sides out of these charts. However, the information is there for you to make the comparison.

For the pan-European charts' Team of the Season, we also work on 17 **Counting Games** and have the same rule of only one player per club per area of the team.

A top Fantasy XI

Well over a million teams will be entered into fantasy leagues for the 2004/5 season. The information in this book provides unparalleled help in determining players' fantasy potential. Most of the key factors among Premiership players are assessed for you: with goals scored by defenders; midfield players and strikers noted; defenders and keepers conceding goals are there and players who play regularly and play for the significant portion of the game. This all goes to make the *Match of the Day Football Yearbook* the best place to check your selections.

Turn to page 6 to find your club…

Thierry Henry

Charts explained...

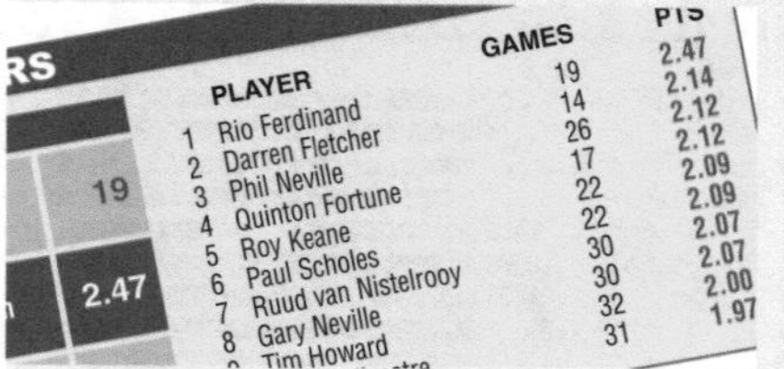

	PLAYER	GAMES	PTS
1	Rio Ferdinand	19	2.47
2	Darren Fletcher	14	2.14
3	Phil Neville	26	2.12
4	Quinton Fortune	17	2.12
5	Roy Keane	22	2.09
6	Paul Scholes	22	2.09
7	Ruud van Nistelrooy	30	2.07
8	Gary Neville	30	2.07
9	Tim Howard	32	2.00

Top Point Earners – Man United
Rio limped off to suspension against Wolves and United's season fell apart. Their Top Point Earners chart illustrates the damage. With Ferdinand United averaged 2.47 points – higher than Arsenal – over 19 games. The non-Ferdinand games dropped to a 1.47 average, bringing the overall Club Average points down to 1.97.

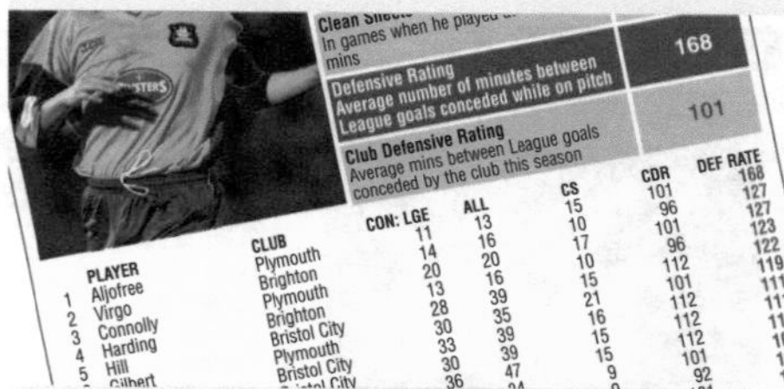

Defensive Rating: Average number of minutes between League goals conceded while on pitch — 168
Club Defensive Rating: Average mins between League goals conceded by the club this season — 101

	PLAYER	CLUB	CON: LGE	ALL	CS	CDR	DEF RATE
1	Aljofree	Plymouth	11	13	15	101	168
2	Virgo	Brighton	14	16	10	96	127
3	Connolly	Plymouth	20	20	17	101	127
4	Harding	Brighton	13	16	10	96	123
5	Hill	Bristol City	28	39	15	112	122

Chart 11 Chart-topping Defenders - Division 3
Good defenders win titles. Plymouth prove the point with Aljofree heading the Nationwide Third Division Chart-Topping Defenders list. His Defensive Rating of 168 is way ahead of his colleagues and the rest of the division. To qualify these top 20 players must have played at least 17 Counting Games.

	PLAYER	POS	AGE	CAPS	MINS	GOALS	CARDS (Y)	CARDS (R)	CLUB SIDE
1	Lilian Thuram	DEF	31	9	663	0	0	0	Juventus
2	Bixente Lizarazu	DEF	34	8	597	0	0	0	Bayern Munich
3	David Trezeguet	ATT	26	8	564	6	0	0	Juventus
4	Marcel Desailly	DEF	35	7	552	0	0	0	Chelsea
5	Fabien Barthez	GK	33	6	540	0	0	0	Marseille
6	Mikael Silvestre	DEF	26	7	529	0	0	0	Man Utd
7	Thierry Henry	ATT	26	7	513	3	0	0	Arsenal

International Appearances – France
We follow 24 International countries. They are the 20 international teams whose players feature most prominently in the top six European divisions plus the four home countries. At club level we note the caps for these. We also turn it around and show where these international sides' players are performing. The top of the French chart shows how the game of football has changed. Only Barthez of their top 15 is playing his club football in France.

THE PREMIERSHIP ROUND-UP

STADIUM CAPACITY AND HOME CROWDS

	TEAM	CAPACITY	AVE	HIGH	LOW
1	Portsmouth	20200	99.53	20140	20024
2	Man Utd	68174	99.22	67758	67346
3	Arsenal	38500	98.91	38419	37677
4	Newcastle	52200	98.54	52165	42155
5	Wolverhampton	29400	98.21	29396	27327
6	Charlton	26875	97.83	26768	25206
7	Man City	48000	97.57	47304	44307
8	Southampton	32551	97.44	32151	30513
9	Chelsea	42449	97.14	41932	40491
10	Birmingham	30009	96.9	29588	27225
11	Everton	40228	96.54	40228	35775
12	Tottenham	36214	96.31	36137	30016
13	Liverpool	45000	94.84	44374	34663
14	Leicester	32500	93.87	32148	23044
15	Bolton	28723	93.29	28353	23098
16	Leeds	40205	91.2	40153	30544
17	Middlesbrough	34820	87.3	34738	26721
18	Fulham	18800	86.93	18306	13981
19	Aston Villa	43275	84.63	42573	28625
20	Blackburn	30475	79.99	30074	19939

Key: Average. The percentage of each stadium filled in League games over the season (AVE), the stadium capacity and the highest and lowest crowds recorded.

AWAY ATTENDANCE

	TEAM	AVE	HIGH	LOW
1	Liverpool	98.53	67647	17682
2	Man Utd	97.21	52165	18306
3	Arsenal	96.74	67639	18102
4	Newcastle	96.24	67622	16506
5	Chelsea	96.18	67609	18244
6	Leeds	95.8	67744	17104
7	Wolverhampton	95.37	67648	17031
8	Tottenham	95.33	67634	17024
9	Man City	95.13	67645	16124
10	Aston Villa	94.71	67621	16153
11	Blackburn	93.9	67748	13981
12	Everton	93.88	67642	17103
13	Birmingham	93	67633	14667
14	Southampton	92.8	67758	16767
15	Middlesbrough	92.7	67346	14546
16	Leicester	92.41	67749	14562
17	Bolton	92.24	67647	14393
18	Portsmouth	92.17	67639	15624
19	Fulham	91.74	67727	20065
20	Charlton	90.09	67477	16585

Key: Average. How close each club has come to filling grounds in its away league matches (AVE) and the highest and lowest crowds recorded.

CLUB STRIKE FORCE

O2
O2

Pires and Henry - a striking pair

Goals scored in the League	73
Goals scored in all competions	114
Shots on target (SoT) Shots on target hit by the team recorded in League games	273

1 Arsenal

Club Strike Rate (CSR) Average number of minutes between League goals scored by club	47

	CLUB	LGE	ALL	SoT	CSR
1	Arsenal	73	114	273	47
2	Chelsea	67	102	244	51
3	Man Utd	64	98	284	53
4	Liverpool	55	80	300	62
5	Man City	55	83	292	62
6	Fulham	52	61	221	66
7	Newcastle	52	82	262	66
8	Blackburn	51	56	238	67
9	Charlton	51	57	200	67
10	Aston Villa	48	64	228	71
11	Bolton	48	64	286	71
12	Leicester	48	52	209	71
13	Portsmouth	47	63	217	73
14	Tottenham	47	62	235	73
15	Everton	45	54	215	76
16	Middlesbrough	44	56	251	78
17	Southampton	44	50	265	78
18	Birmingham	43	49	183	80
19	Leeds	40	45	185	86
20	Wolverhampton	38	47	191	90

TOTAL: LEAGUE: 1012 AL COMPS: 1339

CLUB DEFENCES

1 Arsenal

Club Defensive Rate (CDR) Average number of minutes between League goals conceded by club	132

	CLUB	LGE	ALL	CS	SoT	CDR
1	Arsenal	26	48	15	164	132
2	Chelsea	30	48	21	156	114
3	Man Utd	35	49	14	196	98
4	Liverpool	37	53	15	183	92
5	Newcastle	40	54	11	204	86
6	Aston Villa	44	52	12	231	78
7	Southampton	45	50	12	296	76
8	Fulham	46	52	15	250	74
9	Birmingham	48	52	15	230	71
10	Charlton	51	59	10	300	67
11	Middlesbrough	52	60	14	258	66
12	Man City	54	71	7	210	63
13	Portsmouth	54	68	8	242	63
14	Bolton	56	68	10	220	61
15	Everton	57	61	10	259	60
16	Tottenham	57	64	8	287	60
17	Blackburn	59	71	8	249	58
18	Leicester	65	71	9	256	53
19	Wolverhampton	77	86	7	285	44
20	Leeds	79	88	3	303	43

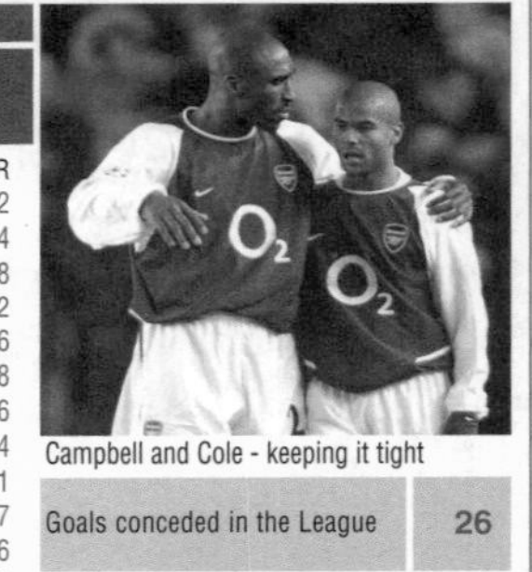

O2
O2

Campbell and Cole - keeping it tight

Goals conceded in the League	26
Goals conceded in all competions	48
Clean Sheets (CS) Number of league games where no goals were conceded	15
Shots on Target Against (SoT) Shots on Target conceded by team in League games	164

CLUB GOAL ATTEMPTS FOR

1 Liverpool

Total shots	558

	CLUB	SoT	Soff	Tot	SG	AR
1	Liverpool	300	258	558	5.5	53.8
2	Bolton	286	247	533	6	53.7
3	Man City	292	223	515	5.3	56.7
4	Man Utd	284	210	494	4.4	57.5
5	Chelsea	244	237	481	3.6	50.7
6	Arsenal	273	198	471	3.7	58.0
7	Blackburn	238	219	457	4.7	52.1
8	Middlesbrough	251	206	457	5.7	54.9
9	Southampton	265	192	457	6	58.0
10	Newcastle	262	186	448	5	58.5
11	Aston Villa	228	210	438	4.8	52.1
12	Everton	215	215	430	4.8	50.0
13	Tottenham	235	186	421	5	55.8
14	Fulham	221	181	402	4.3	55.0
15	Portsmouth	217	185	402	4.6	54.0
16	Wolverhampton	191	207	398	5	48.0
17	Charlton	200	184	384	3.9	52.1
18	Leeds	185	182	367	4.6	50.4
19	Leicester	209	157	366	4.4	57.1
20	Birmingham	183	152	335	4.3	54.6

Carlsberg
10
Reebo

Owen shoots on target

Shots on target	300
Shots off target	258
Ratio of shots on target to goals	5.5
Accuracy Rating	53.8

CLUB GOAL ATTEMPTS AGAINST

1 Arsenal

Total shots against	340

	CLUB	SoT	Soff	Tot	SG	AR
1	Chelsea	156	184	340	5.2	45.9
2	Arsenal	164	192	356	6.3	46.1
3	Birmingham	230	144	374	4.8	61.5
4	Newcastle	204	189	393	5.1	51.9
5	Liverpool	183	213	396	4.9	46.2
6	Man City	210	196	406	3.9	51.7
7	Bolton	220	186	406	3.9	54.2
8	Aston Villa	231	188	419	5.3	55.1
9	Portsmouth	242	189	431	4.5	56.1
10	Fulham	250	182	432	5.4	57.9
11	Leicester	256	182	438	3.9	58.4
12	Everton	259	181	440	4.5	58.9
13	Man Utd	196	246	442	5.6	44.3
14	Blackburn	249	202	451	4.2	55.2
15	Wolverhampton	285	175	460	3.7	62.0
16	Middlesbrough	258	204	462	5	55.8
17	Tottenham	287	194	481	5	59.7
18	Charlton	300	187	487	5.9	61.6
19	Leeds	303	189	492	3.8	61.6
20	Southampton	296	214	510	6.6	58.0

Cudicini - fewest shots to save

Shots on target	156
Shots off target	184
Ratio of shots on target to goals	5.2
Accuracy Rating	45.9

CLUB DISCIPLINARY RECORDS

Mark Viduka of Leeds receiving a red card

League Yellow	53
League Red	3
League Total	56
All Competitions Yellow	75
All Competitions Red	5
TOTAL	80

1 Leeds

Cards Average in League
Average number of minutes between a card being shown of either colour: **61**

	CLUB	LEAGUE		TOTAL		AVE
1	Leeds	72 Y	5 R	80 Y	5 R	44
2	Leicester	61	7	64	7	50
3	Wolverhampton	67	2	76	2	50
4	Bolton	66	0	79	0	52
5	Fulham	63	3	71	3	52
6	Blackburn	61	3	65	4	53
7	Portsmouth	62	3	73	4	53
8	Tottenham	62	1	70	2	54
9	Everton	55	3	61	3	59
10	Middlesbrough	57	1	70	2	59
11	Arsenal	53	3	75	5	61
12	Aston Villa	53	3	65	4	61
13	Southampton	53	3	57	3	61
14	Birmingham	46	5	47	5	67
15	Newcastle	48	3	68	3	67
16	Man City	47	3	64	4	68
17	Chelsea	46	3	80	5	70
18	Liverpool	48	1	58	2	70
19	Man Utd	45	3	67	5	71
20	Charlton	38	3	39	3	83
	TOTAL	1103	58	1329	71	

FINAL LEAGUE TABLE

		HOME					AWAY					TOTAL			
	P	W	D	L	F	A	W	D	L	F	A	F	A	DIF	PTS
Arsenal	38	15	4	0	40	14	11	8	0	33	12	73	26	47	90
Chelsea	38	12	4	3	34	13	12	3	4	33	17	67	30	37	79
Man Utd	38	12	4	3	37	15	11	2	6	27	20	64	35	29	75
Liverpool	38	10	4	5	29	15	6	8	5	26	22	55	37	18	60
Newcastle	38	11	5	3	33	14	2	12	5	19	26	52	40	12	56
Aston Villa	38	9	6	4	24	19	6	5	8	24	25	48	44	4	56
Charlton	38	7	6	6	29	29	7	5	7	22	22	51	51	0	53
Bolton	38	6	8	5	24	21	8	3	8	24	35	48	56	-8	53
Fulham	38	9	4	6	29	21	5	6	8	23	25	52	46	6	52
Birmingham	38	8	5	6	26	24	4	9	6	17	24	43	48	-5	50
Middlesbrough	38	8	4	7	25	23	5	5	9	19	29	44	52	-8	48
Southampton	38	8	6	5	24	17	4	5	10	20	28	44	45	-1	47
Portsmouth	38	10	4	5	35	19	2	5	12	12	35	47	54	-7	45
Tottenham	38	9	4	6	33	27	4	2	13	14	30	47	57	-10	45
Blackburn	38	5	4	10	25	31	7	4	8	26	28	51	59	-8	44
Man City	38	5	9	5	31	24	4	5	10	24	30	55	54	1	41
Everton	38	8	5	6	27	20	1	7	11	18	37	45	57	-12	39
Leicester City	38	3	10	6	19	28	3	5	11	29	37	48	65	-17	33
Leeds United	38	5	7	7	25	31	3	2	14	15	48	40	79	-39	33
Wolverhampton	38	7	5	7	23	35	0	7	12	15	42	38	77	-39	33

PLAYER DISCIPLINARY RECORD

HUTH
29

League Yellow	8
League Red	1
League Total	9
All Competitions Yellow	8
All Competitions Red	1
TOTAL ALL COMPETITIONS	9

1 Robert Huth - Chelsea

Cards Average
Average number of minutes between a card being shown of either colour: **88**

	PLAYER		LEAGUE		TOTAL		AVE
1	Huth	Chelsea	8Y	1R	8Y	1R	88
2	Cisse	Birmingham	5	0	5	0	108
3	Sherwood	Portsmouth	6	0	6	0	108
4	Dugarry	Birmingham	6	1	6	1	140
5	Diouf	Liverpool	11	1	13	1	141
6	Inamoto	Fulham	8	0	8	0	161
7	Domi	Leeds	5	0	5	0	162
8	Ferguson	Everton	6	1	6	1	168
9	Thompson	Blackburn	5	0	6	0	173
10	Ince	Wolves	15	1	15	1	178
11	Parlour	Arsenal	8	0	8	0	189
12	McCann	Southampton	4	0	4	0	200
13	Konchesky	Tottenham	4	0	4	0	207
14	Batty	Leeds	4	0	5	0	208
15	Rae	Wolves	11	1	11	1	210
16	Vieira	Arsenal	11	1	14	1	211
17	Redknapp	Tottenham	6	0	6	0	212
18	Marsden	Southampton	4	0	4	0	213
19	Schemmel	Portsmouth	5	0	5	0	214
20	Ganea	Wolves	3	0	3	0	215

(Playing a minimum of 500 minutes in in the League)

REFEREES

Games	19
Yellow	72
Yellow/Red	6
Straight red	5
Rescinded red cards	1

1 Robert Styles

Cards Average
Average number of cards per match of either colour: **4.37**

	REF	Games	Y	Y/R	R	Resc	AVE
1	R. Styles	19	72	6	5	1	4.37
2	A. G. Wiley	20	82	0	3	0	4.25
3	B. Knight	12	41	1	4	0	3.83
4	P. Dowd	17	63	1	1	1	3.82
5	M. A. Riley	21	74	2	2	0	3.71
6	M. D. Messias	17	59	2	0	0	3.59
7	N. S. Barry	20	64	0	2	0	3.30
8	S. G. Bennett	20	56	7	3	0	3.30
9	S. W. Dunn	19	57	3	2	0	3.26
10	U. D. Rennie	17	55	0	0	0	3.24
11	A. P. D'Urso	21	64	1	1	0	3.14
12	G. Poll	24	68	0	1	0	2.88
13	M. L. Dean	22	58	1	2	0	2.77
14	G. P. Barber	21	54	1	2	0	2.71
15	C. J. Foy	8	21	0	0	0	2.63
16	H. M. Webb	8	16	1	0	0	2.13
17	D. J. Gallagher	19	39	1	0	0	2.11
18	M. R. Halsey	24	47	1	1	0	2.04
19	P. A. Durkin	24	46	0	1	0	1.96
20	J. T. Winter	22	38	0	0	0	1.73
21	P. Walton	5	6	0	0	0	1.20
	TOTAL	380	1080	28	30	2	2.99

PLAYER NATIONALITIES

Overseas country with the most player appearances in the Premiership - FRANCE

In the squad	1102	Percentage of League action	9.41
Appearances in League games	962	Caps for France this season	65
Most appearances	Henry	Percentage of time on pitch	97.4

	COUNTRY	PLAYERS	IN SQUAD	LGE APP	% LGE ACT	CAPS	MOST APP	APP
1	England	284	4871	4005	39.70	151	Jlloyd Samuel	100.0
2	France	53	1102	962	9.41	65	Thierry Henry	97.4
3	Rep of Ireland	36	769	686	7.34	104	Shay Given	100.0
4	Scotland	27	466	382	3.58	70	Paul Telfer	88.9
5	Holland	17	425	332	3.39	42	Edwin Van der Sar	97.4
6	Wales	18	351	258	2.72	93	Gary Speed	96.3
7	Germany	9	240	223	2.40	10	Jens Lehmann	100.0
8	Australia	8	222	213	2.28	26	Mark Schwarzer	89.5
9	USA	10	203	167	1.76		Kasey Keller	100.0
10	Sweden	9	211	179	1.68	35	Olof Mellberg	85.3
11	Denmark	8	189	169	1.62	21	Thomas Sorensen	97.5
12	N Ireland	10	213	146	1.57	30	Damien Johnson	89.8
13	Brazil	9	195	164	1.52	17	Gilberto Silva	74.4
14	Finland	7	173	138	1.50	21	Sami Hyypia	100.0
15	Nigeria	6	140	123	1.33		Ayegbeni Yakubu	91.1
16	Norway	8	159	135	1.29		Claus Lundekvam	73.5
17	Italy	9	171	135	1.22	0	Carlo Cudicini	68.4
18	Iceland	7	137	108	1.12		Jussi Jaaskelainen	100.0
19	Senegal	6	139	118	1.08	24	Henri Camara	75.6
20	Cameroon	5	120	108	1.03	9	Bisan Etame Lauren	80.4

CLUB MAKE-UP – HOME AND OVERSEAS PLAYERS

1 Arsenal

Overseas players in the squad	24	Home country players	13
Percent of overseas players	64.9	Percent of League action	78.9
Most appearances	Lehmann	Appearance percentage	100.0

	CLUB	OVERSEAS	HOME	% OVERSEAS	% LGE ACT	MOST APP	APP %
1	Arsenal	24	13	64.9	78.9	Jens Lehmann	100.0
2	Fulham	19	15	55.9	71.9	Edwin Van der Sar	97.4
3	Portsmouth	21	17	55.3	68.2	Arjan De Zeeuw	94.7
4	Bolton	18	16	52.9	65.9	Jussi Jaaskelainen	100.0
5	Liverpool	17	12	58.6	61.6	Sami Hyypia	100.0
6	Middlesbrough	13	19	40.6	60.2	George Boateng	91.2
7	Chelsea	21	11	65.6	60.1	Claude Makelele	70.2
8	Man City	18	15	54.5	54.9	Sylvain Distin	97.4
9	Blackburn	14	18	43.8	52.9	Brad Friedel	94.7
10	Aston Villa	12	13	48.0	45.4	Thomas Sorensen	97.5
11	Man Utd	11	22	33.3	43.6	Tim Howard	84.2
12	Charlton	10	19	34.5	39.6	Hermann Hreidarsson	86.8
13	Southampton	10	23	30.3	32.8	Antti Niemi	73.7
14	Everton	7	21	25.0	32.3	Tomasz Radzinski	74.7
15	Tottenham	12	21	36.4	31.3	Kasey Keller	100.0
16	Birmingham	9	21	30.0	23.8	Mikael Forssell	81.7
17	Leeds	9	25	26.5	22.0	Mark Viduka	74.0
18	Newcastle	6	23	20.7	19.2	Oliver Bernard	91.6
19	Leicester	6	26	18.8	19.2	Mustafa Izzet	75.1
20	Wolverhampton	9	25	26.5	15.8	Henri Camara	75.6

CHART-TOPPING MIDFIELDERS

1 Fredrik Ljungberg - Arsenal	
Goals scored in the League	4
Assists in league games	5
Defensive Rating Av number of mins between League goals conceded while on the pitch	158
Contribution to Attacking Power Average number of minutes between League team goals while on pitch	47
Scoring Difference Defensive Rating minus Contribution to Attacking Power	111

	PLAYER	CLUB	GOALS	ASS	DEF R	POWER	SCORE DIFF
1	Ljungberg	Arsenal	4	5	158	47	111 mins
2	Vieira	Arsenal	4	4	149	47	102 mins
3	Pires	Arsenal	14	9	142	42	100 mins
4	Keane	Man Utd	3	3	129	51	78 mins
5	Silva	Arsenal	4	3	116	45	71 mins
6	Lampard	Chelsea	10	5	116	51	65 mins
7	Makelele	Chelsea	0	0	114	51	63 mins
8	Neville, P	Man Utd	0	2	114	56	58 mins
9	Giggs	Man Utd	7	10	101	55	46 mins
10	Fortune	Man Utd	0	2	90	45	45 mins
11	Dyer	Newcastle	1	5	103	58	45 mins
12	Hamann	Liverpool	2	2	101	62	39 mins
13	Scholes	Man Utd	9	5	88	49	39 mins
14	Kewell	Liverpool	7	2	94	60	34 mins
15	Geremi	Chelsea	1	4	92	60	32 mins
16	Murphy	Liverpool	4	3	99	67	32 mins
17	Gerrard	Liverpool	4	8	94	63	31 mins
18	Jenas	Newcastle	2	2	95	68	27 mins
19	Robert	Newcastle	6	7	92	66	26 mins
20	Parker	Charlton	2	3	84	61	23 mins

The Divisional Round-up charts combine the records of chart-topping keepers, defenders, midfield players and forwards, from every club in the division.. The one above is for **the Chart-topping Midfielders**. The players are ranked by their Scoring Difference although other attributes are shown for you to compare.

CHART-TOPPING GOALSCORERS

1 Thierry Henry - Arsenal	
Goals scored in the League (GL)	30
Goals scored in all competitions (GA)	39
Contribution to Attacking Power (AP) Average number of minutes between League team goals while on pitch	46
Player Strike Rate Average number of minutes between League goals scored by player	111
Club Strike Rate (CSR) Average minutes between League goals scored by club	47

	PLAYER	CLUB	GOALS: LGE	ALL	POWER	CSR	S RATE
1	Henry	Arsenal	30	39	46	47	111 mins
2	Saha	Fulham	13	15	60	66	131 mins
3	van Nistelrooy	Man Utd	20	30	50	53	138 mins
4	Shearer	Newcastle	22	28	63	66	151 mins
5	Forssell	Birmingham	18	20	68	80	155 mins
6	Owen	Liverpool	16	19	61	62	157 mins
7	Hasselbaink	Chelsea	12	17	49	51	166 mins
8	Anelka	Man City	16	24	62	62	171 mins
9	Angel	Aston Villa	16	23	78	71	172 mins
10	Yakubu	Portsmouth	16	19	69	73	195 mins
11	Phillips	Southampton	13	14	83	78	199 mins
12	Pires	Arsenal	14	19	41	47	202 mins
13	Keane	Tottenham	14	16	68	73	206 mins
14	Beattie	Southampton	14	17	74	78	212 mins
15	Euell	Charlton	10	10	61	67	222 mins
16	Djorkaeff	Bolton	9	10	68	71	228 mins
17	Dickov	Leicester	11	13	64	71	229 mins
18	Viduka	Leeds	11	12	79	86	230 mins
19	Cole	Blackburn	11	12	65	67	238 mins
20	Scholes	Man Utd	9	14	48	53	243 mins

The Chart-topping Goalscorers measures the players by Strike Rate. They are most likely to be Forwards but Midfield players and even Defenders do come through the club tables. It is not a measure of the number of League goals scored - although that is also noted - but how often on average they have scored.

CHART-TOPPING DEFENDERS

1 William Gallas - Chelsea	
Goals Conceded in the League The number of League goals conceded while he was on the pitch	11
Goals Conceded in all competitions The number of goals conceded while he was on the pitch in all competitions	24
Clean Sheets In games when he played at least 70 mins	16
Defensive Rating Average number of minutes between League goals conceded while on pitch	191
Club Defensive Rating Average mins between League goals conceded by the club this season	114

	PLAYER	CLUB	CON: LGE	ALL	CS	CDR	DEF RATE1
1	Gallas	Chelsea	11	24	16	114	191 mins
2	Campbell	Arsenal	22	39	14	132	140 mins
3	Toure	Arsenal	23	42	14	132	135 mins
4	Ferdinand	Man Utd	13	16	9	98	135 mins
5	Cole	Arsenal	21	38	12	132	134 mins
6	Woodgate	Newcastle	13	19	6	86	120 mins
7	Neville, G	Man Utd	23	31	12	98	117 mins
8	Melchiot	Chelsea	16	26	11	114	115 mins
9	Lauren	Arsenal	24	40	10	132	114 mins
10	Bridge	Chelsea	26	38	18	114	114 mins
11	Carragher	Liverpool	17	25	12	92	112 mins
12	Dodd	Southampton	22	28	12	76	108 mins
13	Terry	Chelsea	28	42	17	114	106 mins
14	Svensson, M	Southampton	23	29	11	76	102 mins
15	Johnson	Chelsea	15	21	9	114	100 mins
16	Silvestre	Man Utd	29	35	11	98	98 mins
17	Le Saux	Southampton	16	17	7	76	98 mins
18	Riise	Liverpool	23	32	9	92	93 mins
19	Hyypia	Liverpool	37	48	15	92	92 mins
20	O'Brien	Newcastle	27	37	6	86	87 mins

The Chart-topping Defenders are resolved by their Defensive Rating, how often their team concedes a goal while they are playing. All these rightly favour players at the best performing clubs because good players win matches. However, good players in lower-table clubs will chart where they have lifted the team's performance.

CHART-TOPPING GOALKEEPERS

1 Jens Lehmann - Arsenal	
Goals conceded in the League (CL)	26
Goals conceded in all comps (CA)	43
Counting Games League games when he played at least 70 minutes	38
Clean Sheets In games when he played at least 70 mins	15
Goals to Shots Ratio (GSR) The average number of shots on target per each League goal conceded	6.3
Defensive Rating Average number of minutes between League goals conceded while on pitch	132

	PLAYER	CLUB	CG	CON: LGE	ALL	CS	GSR	DEF RATE
1	Lehmann	Arsenal	38	26	43	15	6.3	132 mins
2	Cudicini	Chelsea	26	20	26	14	4.7	117 mins
3	Dudek	Liverpool	30	28	37	13	5.5	96 mins
4	Howard	Man Utd	32	31	41	12	5.3	93 mins
5	Given	Newcastle	38	40	52	11	5.1	86 mins
6	Taylor, Maik	Birmingham	34	37	41	13	5.8	80 mins
7	Sorensen	Aston Villa	38	42	50	12	5.5	79 mins
8	Van der Sar	Fulham	37	44	49	15	5.5	76 mins
9	Niemi	Southampton	28	34	39	8	6.6	74 mins
10	James	Man City	17	22	22	3	4.3	70 mins
11	Kiely	Charlton	37	48	56	10	6.1	69 mins
12	Hislop	Portsmouth	29	39	46	6	4.9	67 mins
13	Seaman	Man City	19	24	29	4	4.7	66 mins
14	Martyn	Everton	33	47	51	10	4.7	63 mins
15	Jaaskelainen	Bolton	38	56	62	10	3.9	61 mins
16	Schwarzer	Middlesbrough	34	51	59	11	4.8	60 mins
17	Keller	Tottenham	38	57	64	8	5	60 mins
18	Friedel	Blackburn	36	57	69	8	4.1	57 mins
19	Walker	Leicester	37	62	67	9	4	53 mins
20	Oakes	Wolverhampton	21	39	43	4	3.8	48 mins
21	Robinson	Leeds	35	76	85	2	3.8	41 mins

The Chart-topping Goalkeepers are positioned by their Defensive Rating. We also show Clean Sheets where the team has not conceded and the Keeper has played all or most (at least 70 minutes) of the game. Now teams use several keepers in a season, not every team will necessarily chart on this page.

GOALS

	PLAYER	TEAM	LGE	SR
1	Henry	Arsenal	30	111
2	Shearer	Newcastle	22	151
3	van Nistelrooy	Man Utd	20	138
4	Forssell	Birmingham	18	155
5	Owen	Liverpool	16	157
6	Anelka	Man City	16	171
7	Angel	Aston Villa	16	172
8	Yakubu	Portsmouth	16	195
9	Keane	Tottenham	14	206
10	Beattie	Southampton	14	212
11	Saha	Fulham	13	131
12	Phillips	Southampton	13	199
13	Ferdinand	Leicester	12	129
14	Hasselbaink	Chelsea	12	166
15	Dickov	Leicester	11	229
16	Viduka	Leeds	11	230
17	Cole	Blackburn	11	238
18	Crespo	Chelsea	10	114
19	Euell	Charlton	10	222
20	Sheringham	Portsmouth	9	246
21	Vassell	Aston Villa	9	253
22	Rooney	Everton	9	271
23	Bent, M	Leicester	9	277
24	Boa Morte	Fulham	9	309
25	Smith	Leeds	9	349

GOALS – MIDFIELDERS

	PLAYER	TEAM	LGE	SR
1	Pires	Arsenal	14	202
2	Lampard	Chelsea	10	338
3	Djorkaeff	Bolton	9	228
4	Scholes	Man Utd	9	243
5	Nolan	Bolton	9	345
6	Giggs	Man Utd	7	362
7	Wright-Phillips	Man City	7	416
8	Kewell	Liverpool	7	445
9	Robert	Newcastle	6	427
10	Malbranque	Fulham	6	552
11	Holland	Charlton	6	568
12	Duff	Chelsea	5	292
13	Berger	Portsmouth	5	337
14	Watson	Everton	5	343
15	Sibierski	Man City	5	349
16	Davis, S	Fulham	5	394
17	Scowcroft	Leicester	5	596

GOALS – DEFENDERS

	PLAYER	TEAM	LGE	ALL
1	Hyypia	Liverpool	4	855
2	Amoruso	Blackburn	3	331
3	Johnson	Chelsea	3	501
4	Duberry	Leeds	3	570
5	Babbel	Blackburn	3	679
6	Unsworth	Everton	3	685
7	Stefanovic	Portsmouth	3	941

TEAM OF THE SEASON

LEHMANN
Arsenal
CG 38 DR 132

GALLAS
Chelsea
CG 22 DR 191

CAMPBELL
Arsenal
CG 34 DR 140

FERDINAND
Man Utd
CG 19 DR 135

WOODGATE
Newcastle
CG 17 DR 120

LJUNGBERG
Arsenal
CG 26 SD +111

LAMPARD
Chelsea
CG 37 SD +65

KEANE
Man Utd
CG 22 SD +78

DYER
Newcastle
CG 23 SD +45

HASSELBAINK
Chelsea
CG 19 AP 49

HENRY
Arsenal
CG 37 SR 111

The Premiership Team of the Season shows a 4-4-2 of the best players in the Premiership based upon the selection criteria used for the chart-toppers. The players selected are taken from the lists for each club except that to get into a Divisional Team of the Season you must have played at least 17 Counting Games in the league (roughly half the league season) and not 12 as is the case in the club lists. The other restriction is that we are only allowing one player from each club in each position. So the maximum number of players one club can have in the divisional team is four.

- **The Divisional team's goalkeeper** is the player with the highest Defensive Rating
- **The Divisional team's defenders** are also tested by Defensive Rating, i.e. the average number of minutes between league goals conceded while on the pitch.
- **The Divisional team's midfield** are selected on their Scoring Difference, i.e.their Defensive Rating minus their Contribution to Attacking Power (average number of minutes between league goals scored while on the pitch. It takes no account of assists.
- **The Divisional team strikeforce** is made up of the striker with the highest Strike Rate (his average number of minutes between league goals scored while on the pitch) together with the striker with the highest Contribution to Attacking Power.

ASSISTS

	PLAYER	TEAM	LGE ASSISTS
1	Izzet	Leicester	14
2	Di Canio	Charlton	12
3	Emerton	Blackburn	12
4	Giggs	Man Utd	10
5	Malbranque	Fulham	10
6	Barry	Aston Villa	10
7	Pires	Arsenal	9
8	Duff	Chelsea	9
9	Davies	Bolton	8
10	Gerrard	Liverpool	8
11	Robert	Newcastle	7
12	Bergkamp	Arsenal	7
13	Tugay	Blackburn	7
14	Henry	Arsenal	6
15	Beattie	Southampton	6
16	Boa Morte	Fulham	6
17	Hitzlsperger	Aston Villa	6
18	Pennant	Leeds	6
19	Cole	Chelsea	6
20	Hasselbaink	Chelsea	5
21	Cole	Blackburn	5
22	Scholes	Man Utd	5
23	Mutu	Chelsea	5
24	Radzinski	Everton	5
25	Berger	Portsmouth	5

SHARE OF GOALS

	PLAYER	TEAM	% LGE GOALS
1	Shearer	Newcastle	42.31
2	Forssell	Birmingham	41.86
3	Henry	Arsenal	41.10
4	Yakubu	Portsmouth	34.04
5	Angel	Aston Villa	33.33
6	Beattie	Southampton	31.82
7	van Nistelrooy	Man Utd	31.25
8	Keane	Tottenham	29.79
9	Phillips	Southampton	29.55
10	Owen	Liverpool	29.09
11	Anelka	Man City	29.09
12	Viduka	Leeds	27.50
13	Saha	Fulham	25.00
14	Ferdinand	Leicester	25.00
15	Dickov	Leicester	22.92
16	Smith	Leeds	22.50
17	Cole	Blackburn	21.57
18	Rooney	Everton	20.00
19	Euell	Charlton	19.61
20	Sheringham	Portsmouth	19.15
21	Vassell	Aston Villa	18.75
22	Bent, M	Leicester	18.75
23	Hasselbaink	Chelsea	17.91
24	Boa Morte	Fulham	17.31
25	Crespo	Chelsea	14.93

PREMIERSHIP CHART-TOPPING POINT EARNERS

	PLAYER	TEAM	GAMES	POINTS	AVE
1	Pires	Arsenal	32	80	2.50
2	Ferdinand	Man Utd	19	47	2.47
3	Gallas	Chelsea	22	54	2.45
4	Toure	Arsenal	34	82	2.41
5	Henry	Arsenal	37	89	2.41
6	Lehmann	Arsenal	38	90	2.37
7	Hasselbaink	Chelsea	19	42	2.21
8	Cudicini	Chelsea	26	56	2.15
9	Lampard	Chelsea	37	79	2.14
10	Neville, P	Man Utd	26	55	2.12
11	van Nistelrooy	Man Utd	30	62	2.07
12	Howard	Man Utd	32	64	2.00
13	Vassell	Aston Villa	20	36	1.80
14	Hamann	Liverpool	24	42	1.75
15	Kishishev	Charlton	25	43	1.72
16	Woodgate	Newcastle	17	29	1.71
17	Owen	Liverpool	28	47	1.68
18	McCann	Aston Villa	27	45	1.67
19	Djorkaeff	Bolton	20	33	1.65
20	Parker	Charlton	20	33	1.65

For the Top Point Earners we have applied the same rule of only allowing one player per position for each club, the same as the Team of the Season. The most one club can have in the top 20 is four players, one keeper, one defender, one midfielder and a forward.

O2

1 Robert Pires - Arsenal

Counting Games Played at least 70mins.	32
Total Points Taken in Counting Games	80
Average Taken in Counting Games	2.50

PREMIERSHIP MOST MISSED PLAYERS

	PLAYER	TEAM	AVERAGE	CLUB	DIFF
1	Ferdinand	Man Utd	2.47	1.97	0.50
2	Davies	Tottenham	1.65	1.18	0.47
3	Unsworth	Everton	1.45	1.03	0.42
4	Gallas	Chelsea	2.45	2.08	0.37
5	Linderoth	Everton	1.39	1.03	0.36
6	Vassell	Aston Villa	1.80	1.47	0.33
7	Kishishev	Charlton	1.72	1.39	0.33
8	Dodd	Southampton	1.56	1.24	0.32
9	Gresko	Blackburn	1.47	1.16	0.31
10	Stubbs	Everton	1.30	1.03	0.27
11	Neill	Blackburn	1.42	1.16	0.26
12	Djorkaeff	Bolton	1.65	1.39	0.26
13	Parker	Charlton	1.65	1.39	0.26
14	Stone	Portsmouth	1.44	1.18	0.26
15	Perry	Charlton	1.64	1.39	0.25
16	Melchiot	Chelsea	2.32	2.08	0.24
17	Woodgate	Newcastle	1.71	1.47	0.24
18	Taylor	Portsmouth	1.41	1.18	0.23
19	Cameron	Wolves	1.09	0.87	0.22
20	Viduka	Leeds	1.08	0.87	0.21

The Most Missed Players we have applied the same rule of only allowing one player per position for each club, the same as the Team of the Season. The most one club can have in the top 20 is four players, one keeper, one defender, one midfielder and a forward.

vodafone

1 Rio Ferdinand- Manchester Utd

Average points	2.47
Club average	1.97
Difference	0.50

ARSENAL

Thierry Henry ends the debate. By adding a striker's hunger for goal to all his other qualities he hit 41% of Arsenal's championship goals – up from 28% the previous year.

The Assists Table tells the same story. Last year Henry served up 21 assists for colleagues, nearly double his nearest challenger. This season he has a mere six assists but his supporting act is delivering.

Robert Pires is the most dangerous midfielder in the division. He leads the Attacking Power list with the team averaging a goal every 41 minutes when he is on the pitch.

Second only to Pires, **Dennis Bergkamp** may not play many full games but he often decides them, helping to conjure a team goal every 42 minutes.

NICKNAME: THE GUNNERS

KEY: Won, Drawn, Lost

	Comp	Opponent	H/A	Res	Score	Scorers
1	fa cs	Man Utd	A	L	3-4*	Henry 20 (*on penalties)
2	prem	Everton	H	W	2-1	Henry 35 pen; Pires 58
3	prem	Middlesbrough	A	W	4-0	Henry 5; Silva 13; Wiltord 22,60
4	prem	Aston Villa	H	W	2-0	Campbell 57; Henry 90
5	prem	Man City	A	W	2-1	Wiltord 48; Ljungberg 72
6	prem	Portsmouth	H	D	1-1	Henry 40 pen
7	cl gb	Inter Milan	H	L	0-3	
8	prem	Man Utd	A	D	0-0	
9	prem	Newcastle	H	W	3-2	Henry 18,80 pen; Silva 67
10	cl gb	L Moscow	A	D	0-0	
11	prem	Liverpool	A	W	2-1	Hyypia 31 og; Pires 68
12	prem	Chelsea	H	W	2-1	Edu 5; Henry 75
13	cl gb	Dinamo Kiev	A	L	1-2	Henry 80
14	prem	Charlton	A	D	1-1	Henry 40
15	ccr3	Rotherham	H	D	9-8*	Aliadiere 11 (*on penalties)
16	prem	Leeds	A	W	4-1	Henry 8,33; Pires 17; Silva 50
17	cl gb	Dinamo Kiev	H	W	1-0	Cole 88
18	prem	Tottenham	H	W	2-1	Pires 69; Ljungberg 79
19	prem	Birmingham	A	W	3-0	Ljungberg 4; Bergkamp 80; Pires 88
20	cl gb	Inter Milan	A	W	5-1	Henry 25,85; Ljungberg 49; Edu 87; Pires 89
21	prem	Fulham	H	D	0-0	
22	ccr4	Wolves	H	W	5-1	Aliadiere 24,71; Kanu 68; Wiltord 79; Fabregas 88
23	prem	Leicester	A	D	1-1	Silva 60
24	cl gb	L Moscow	H	W	2-0	Pires 12; Ljungberg 67
25	prem	Blackburn	H	W	1-0	Bergkamp 11
26	ccqf	West Brom	A	W	2-0	Kanu 25; Aliadiere 57
27	prem	Bolton	A	D	1-1	Pires 57
28	prem	Wolves	H	W	3-0	Vieira 16; Henry 24,89
29	prem	Southampton	A	W	1-0	Pires 35
30	facr3	Leeds	A	W	4-1	Henry 26; Edu 33; Pires 87; Toure 90
31	prem	Everton	A	D	1-1	Kanu 30
32	prem	Middlesbrough	H	W	4-1	Henry 38 pen; Queudrue 44 og; Pires 57; Ljungberg 68
33	prem	Aston Villa	A	W	2-0	Henry 29,53 pen
34	ccsfl1	Middlesbrough	H	L	0-1	
35	facr4	Middlesbrough	H	W	4-1	Bergkamp 19; Ljungberg 28,68; Bentley 90
36	prem	Man City	H	W	2-1	Tarnat 37 og; Henry 83
37	ccsfl2	Middlesbrough	A	L	1-2	Edu 77
38	prem	Wolverhampton	A	W	3-1	Bergkamp 9; Henry 58; Toure 63
39	prem	Southampton	H	W	2-0	Henry 31,90
40	facr5	Chelsea	H	W	2-1	Reyes 56,61
41	prem	Chelsea	A	W	2-1	Vieira 15; Edu 21
42	cl rl1	Celta Vigo	A	W	3-2	Edu 18,58; Pires 80
43	prem	Charlton	H	W	2-1	Pires 2; Henry 4
44	facqf	Portsmouth	A	W	5-1	Henry 25,50; Ljungberg 43,57; Toure 45
45	cl rl2	Celta Vigo	H	W	2-0	Henry 14,34
46	prem	Blackburn	A	W	2-0	Henry 57; Pires 87
47	prem	Bolton	H	W	2-1	Pires 16; Bergkamp 24
48	cl qfl1	Chelsea	A	D	1-1	Pires 59
49	prem	Man Utd	H	D	1-1	Henry 50
50	facsf	Man Utd	H	L	0-1	
51	cl qfl2	Chelsea	H	L	1-2	Reyes 45
52	prem	Liverpool	H	W	4-2	Henry 31,50,78; Pires 49
53	prem	Newcastle	A	D	0-0	
54	prem	Leeds	H	W	5-0	Pires 6; Henry 27,33 pen,50,67
55	prem	Tottenham	A	D	2-2	Vieira 3; Pires 35
56	prem	Birmingham	H	D	0-0	
57	prem	Portsmouth	A	D	1-1	Reyes 49
58	prem	Fulham	A	W	1-0	Reyes 9
59	prem	Leicester	H	W	2-1	Henry 47 pen; Vieira 66

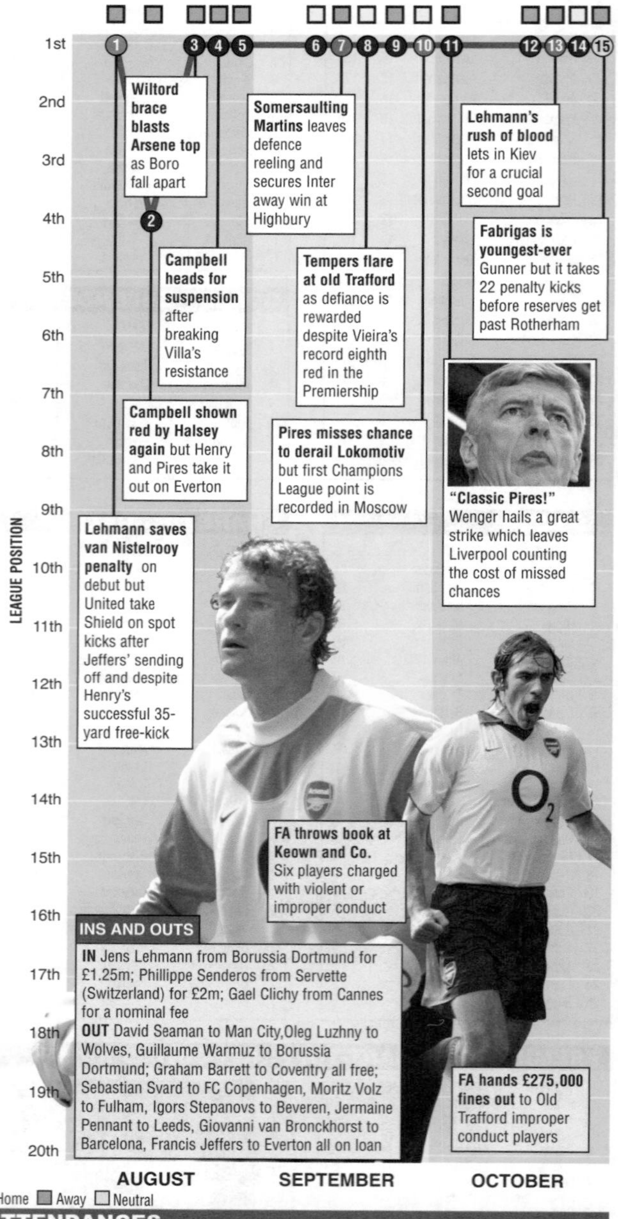

LEAGUE POSITION: 1st, 2nd, 3rd, 4th, 5th, 6th, 7th, 8th, 9th, 10th, 11th, 12th, 13th, 14th, 15th, 16th, 17th, 18th, 19th, 20th

AUGUST · SEPTEMBER · OCTOBER

Wiltord brace blasts Arsene top as Boro fall apart

Somersaulting Martins leaves defence reeling and secures Inter away win at Highbury

Lehmann's rush of blood lets in Kiev for a crucial second goal

Campbell heads for suspension after breaking Villa's resistance

Tempers flare at old Trafford as defiance is rewarded despite Vieira's record eighth red in the Premiership

Fabrigas is youngest-ever Gunner but it takes 22 penalty kicks before reserves get past Rotherham

Campbell shown red by Halsey again but Henry and Pires take it out on Everton

Pires misses chance to derail Lokomotiv but first Champions League point is recorded in Moscow

"Classic Pires!" Wenger hails a great strike which leaves Liverpool counting the cost of missed chances

Lehmann saves van Nistelrooy penalty on debut but United take Shield on spot kicks after Jeffers' sending off and despite Henry's successful 35-yard free-kick

FA throws book at Keown and Co. Six players charged with violent or improper conduct

FA hands £275,000 fines out to Old Trafford improper conduct players

INS AND OUTS

IN Jens Lehmann from Borussia Dortmund for £1.25m; Phillippe Senderos from Servette (Switzerland) for £2m; Gael Clichy from Cannes for a nominal fee

OUT David Seaman to Man City, Oleg Luzhny to Wolves, Guillaume Warmuz to Borussia Dortmund; Graham Barrett to Coventry all free; Sebastian Svard to FC Copenhagen, Moritz Volz to Fulham, Igors Stepanovs to Beveren, Jermaine Pennant to Leeds, Giovanni van Bronckhorst to Barcelona, Francis Jeffers to Everton all on loan

Home · Away · Neutral

ATTENDANCES

HOME GROUND: HIGHBURY **CAPACITY:** 38500 **AVERAGE LEAGUE AT HOME:** 38078

20	Inter Milan	85400	43	Charlton	38137	28	Wolves	38003	3	Middlesboro	29450
13	Dinamo Kiev	80000	40	Chelsea	38136	25	Blackburn	37677	38	Wolves	29392
8	Man Utd	67639	52	Liverpool	38119	35	Middlesboro	37256	37	Middlesboro	28781
1	Man Utd	59293	32	Middlesboro	38117	16	Leeds	36491	46	Blackburn	28627
53	Newcastle	52141	9	Newcastle	38112	55	Tottenham	36097	22	Wolves	28161
5	Man City	46436	36	Man City	38103	51	Chelsea	35486	27	Bolton	28003
11	Liverpool	44374	18	Tottenham	38101	45	Celta Vigo	35402	15	Rotherham	27451
41	Chelsea	41847	54	Leeds	38094	24	L Moscow	35343	14	Charlton	26660
48	Chelsea	40778	21	Fulham	38063	17	Dinamo Kiev	34419	10	L Moscow	24000
50	Man Utd	39939	56	Birmingham	38061	7	Inter Milan	34393	42	Celta Vigo	21000
33	Aston Villa	39380	47	Bolton	38053	29	Southampton	32151	26	West Brom	20369
31	Everton	38726	6	Portsmouth	38052	23	Leicester	32108	57	Portsmouth	20140
59	Leicester	38419	2	Everton	38014	30	Leeds	31207	44	Portsmouth	20137
49	Man Utd	38184	4	Aston Villa	38010	34	Middlesboro	31070	58	Fulham	18102
12	Chelsea	38172	39	Southampton	38007	19	Birmingham	29588			

Undefeated! Undeniably the best

Final Position: **1st**

KEY: ● League ● Champions Lge ● UEFA Cup ● FA Cup ○ League Cup ● Other

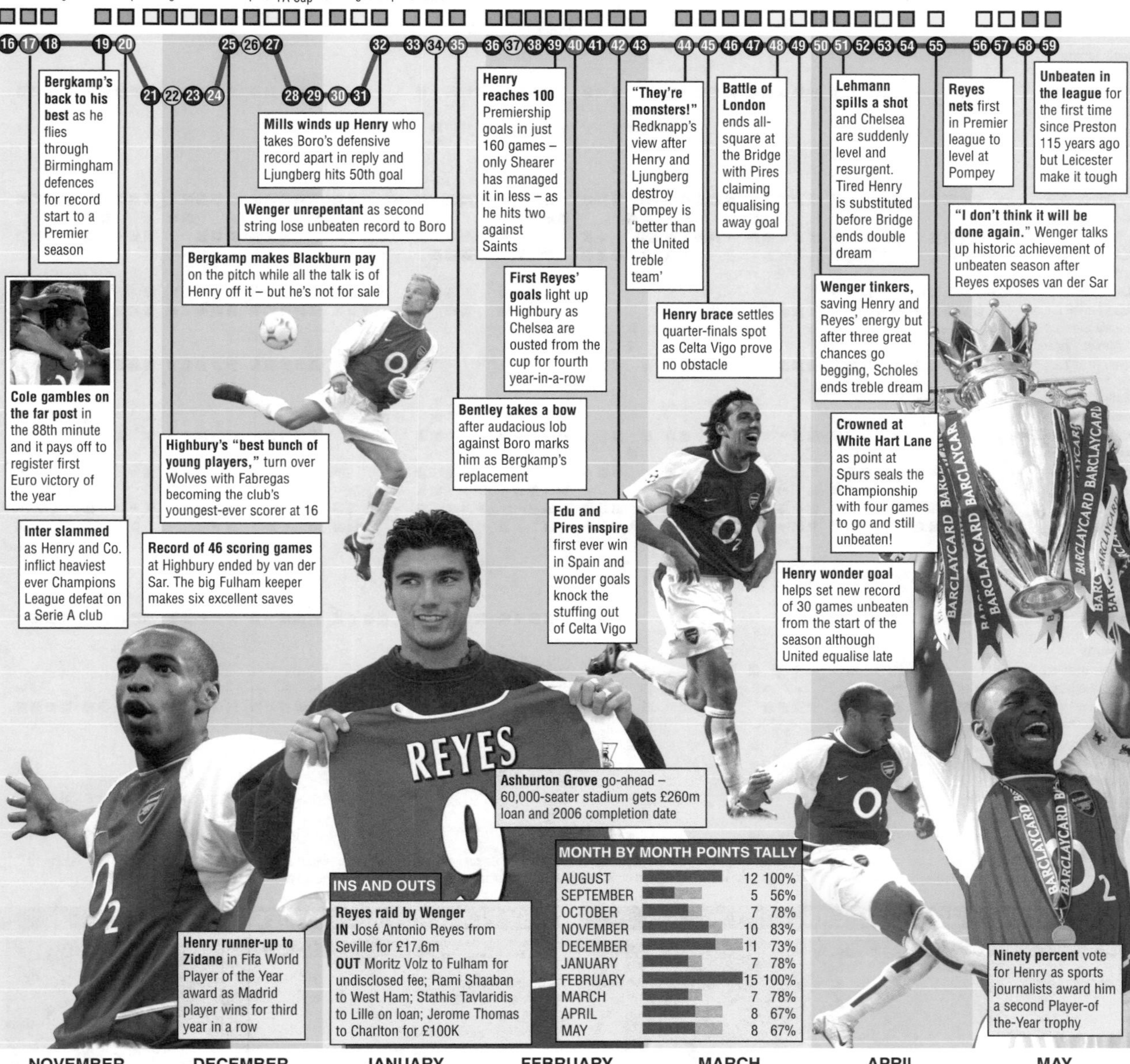
16 17 18 19 20 21 22 23 24 25 26 27 28 29 30 31 32 33 34 35 36 37 38 39 40 41 42 43 44 45 46 47 48 49 50 51 52 53 54 55 56 57 58 59
REYES
9

Bergkamp's back to his best as he flies through Birmingham defences for record start to a Premier season

Cole gambles on the far post in the 88th minute and it pays off to register first Euro victory of the year

Inter slammed as Henry and Co. inflict heaviest ever Champions League defeat on a Serie A club

Record of 46 scoring games at Highbury ended by van der Sar. The big Fulham keeper makes six excellent saves

Highbury's "best bunch of young players," turn over Wolves with Fabregas becoming the club's youngest-ever scorer at 16

Bergkamp makes Blackburn pay on the pitch while all the talk is of Henry off it – but he's not for sale

Mills winds up Henry who takes Boro's defensive record apart in reply and Ljungberg hits 50th goal

Wenger unrepentant as second string lose unbeaten record to Boro

Henry reaches 100 Premiership goals in just 160 games – only Shearer has managed it in less – as he hits two against Saints

First Reyes' goals light up Highbury as Chelsea are ousted from the cup for fourth year-in-a-row

Bentley takes a bow after audacious lob against Boro marks him as Bergkamp's replacement

Edu and Pires inspire first ever win in Spain and wonder goals knock the stuffing out of Celta Vigo

"They're monsters!" Redknapp's view after Henry and Ljungberg destroy Pompey is 'better than the United treble team'

Battle of London ends all-square at the Bridge with Pires claiming equalising away goal

Henry brace settles quarter-finals spot as Celta Vigo prove no obstacle

Lehmann spills a shot and Chelsea are suddenly level and resurgent. Tired Henry is substituted before Bridge ends double dream

Wenger tinkers, saving Henry and Reyes' energy but after three great chances go begging, Scholes ends treble dream

Crowned at White Hart Lane as point at Spurs seals the Championship with four games to go and still unbeaten!

Henry wonder goal helps set new record of 30 games unbeaten from the start of the season although United equalise late

Reyes nets first in Premier league to level at Pompey

Unbeaten in the league for the first time since Preston 115 years ago but Leicester make it tough

"I don't think it will be done again." Wenger talks up historic achievement of unbeaten season after Reyes exposes van der Sar

Ashburton Grove go-ahead – 60,000-seater stadium gets £260m loan and 2006 completion date

Henry runner-up to Zidane in Fifa World Player of the Year award as Madrid player wins for third year in a row

Ninety percent vote for Henry as sports journalists award him a second Player-of the-Year trophy

INS AND OUTS

Reyes raid by Wenger
IN José Antonio Reyes from Seville for £17.6m
OUT Moritz Volz to Fulham for undisclosed fee; Rami Shaaban to West Ham; Stathis Tavlaridis to Lille on loan; Jerome Thomas to Charlton for £100K

MONTH BY MONTH POINTS TALLY

Month	Points	%
AUGUST	12	100%
SEPTEMBER	5	56%
OCTOBER	7	78%
NOVEMBER	10	83%
DECEMBER	11	73%
JANUARY	7	78%
FEBRUARY	15	100%
MARCH	7	78%
APRIL	8	67%
MAY	8	67%

NOVEMBER DECEMBER JANUARY FEBRUARY MARCH APRIL MAY

GOAL ATTEMPTS

FOR – Goal attempts recorded in League games

	HOME	AWAY	TOTAL	AVE
shots on target	151	122	273	7.2
shots off target	109	89	198	5.2
TOTAL	260	211	471	12.4

Ratio of goals to shots Average number of shots on target per League goal scored: **3.7**

Accuracy rating Average percentage of total goal attempts which were on target: **58**

AGAINST – Goal attempts recorded in League games

	HOME	AWAY	TOTAL	AVE
shots on target	66	98	164	4.3
shots off target	70	122	192	5.1
TOTAL	136	220	356	9.4

Ratio of goals to shots Average number of shots on target per League goal scored: **6.3**

Accuracy rating Average percentage of total goal attempts which were on target: **46.1**

GOALS

Thierry Henry

League	30
FA Cup	3
League Cup	0
Europe	5
Other	1
TOTAL	39

League Average **111** mins between goals

	PLAYER	LGE	FAC	LC	Euro	TOT	AVE
1	Henry	30	3	0	5	39	111
2	Pires	14	1	0	4	19	202
3	Vieira	4	0	0	0	4	634
4	Ljungberg	4	4	0	2	10	554
5	Silva	4	0	0	0	4	636
6	Bergkamp	4	1	0	0	5	439
7	Wiltord	3	0	1	0	4	215
8	Edu	2	1	1	3	7	745
9	Reyes	2	2	0	1	5	327
10	Kanu	1	0	2	0	3	428
11	Toure	1	2	0	0	3	3094
12	Campbell	1	0	0	0	1	3085
13	Fabregas	0	0	1	0	1	
14	Bentley	0	1	0	0	1	
15	Aliadiere	0	0	4	0	4	
	Other	3	0	0	1	4	
	TOTAL	73	15	9	16	114	

SQUAD APPEARANCES

	1	2	3	4	5	6	7	8	9	10	11	12	13	14	15	16	17	18	19	20	21	22	23	24	25	26	27	28	29	30	31	32	33	34	35	36	37	38	39	40	41	42	43	44	45	46	47	48	49	50	51	52	53	54	55	56	57	58	59
Venue	A	H	A	H	A	H	H	A	H	A	A	H	A	A	H	A	H	H	A	A	H	H	A	H	H	A	A	H	A	A	A	H	A	H	H	H	A	A	H	H	A	A	H	A	H	A	H	A	H	H	H	H	A	H	A	H	A	A	H
Competition	O	L	L	L	L	L	C	L	L	C	L	L	C	L	W	L	C	L	L	C	L	W	L	C	L	W	L	L	L	F	L	L	L	W	F	L	W	L	L	F	L	C	L	F	O	L	L	C	L	F	C	L	L	L	L	L	L	L	L
Result	L	W	W	W	W	D	L	D	W	D	W	W	L	D	D	W	W	W	W	W	D	W	D	W	W	W	D	W	W	W	D	W	W	L	W	W	L	W	W	W	W	W	W	W	W	W	W	D	D	L	L	W	D	W	D	D	D	W	W

Goalkeepers
Craig Holloway
Jens Lehmann
Rami Shaaban
Graham Stack
Stuart Taylor

Defenders
Sol Campbell
Gael Clichy
Ashley Cole
Pascal Cygan
Justin Hoyte
Martin Keown
Bisan Mayer Lauren
Frankie Simek
Efstathios Tavlaridis
Habib Kolo Toure

Midfielders
David Bentley
Eduardo Cesar Gaspar
Francesco Fabregas
Fredrik Ljungberg
Ray Parlour
Robert Pires
Gilberto Silva
Olafur Ingi Skulason
Ryan Smith
John Spicer
Giovanni Van Bronckhorst
Patrick Vieira

Forwards
Jeremie Aliadiere
Dennis Bergkamp
Thierry Henry
Francis Jeffers
Nwankwo Kanu
Quincy Owusu-Abeyie
Michal Papadopoulos
Jose Antonio Reyes
Jerome Thomas
Sylvain Wiltord

KEY: On all match · On bench · Subbed or sent off (Counting game) · Subbed or sent off (playing less than 70 mins) · Subbed on from bench (Counting Game) · Subbed on (playing less than 70 mins) · Subbed on and then subbed or sent off (Counting Game) · Subbed on and then subbed or sent off (playing less than 70 mins) · Not in 16

KEY PLAYERS - GOALSCORERS

Thierry Henry

Goals in the League	30
Goals in all competitions	39
Assists League goals scored by team-mates where he delivered the final pass	6
Contribution to Attacking Power Average number of minutes between League team goals while on pitch	46
Player Strike Rate Average number of minutes between League goals scored by player	111
Club Strike Rate Average minutes between League goals scored by club	47

	PLAYER	GOALS LGE	GOALS ALL	ASSISTS	POWER	S RATE
1	Thierry Henry	30	39	6	46	111 mins
2	Robert Pires	14	19	9	41	202 mins
3	Dennis Bergkamp	4	5	7	42	439 mins
4	Fredrik Ljungberg	4	10	5	47	554 mins
5	Patrick Vieira	4	4	4	46	634 mins

KEY PLAYERS - MIDFIELDERS

Fredrik Ljungberg

Goals in the League	4
Goals in all competitions	10
Assists League goals scored by team-mates where he delivered the final pass	5
Defensive Rating Average number of mins between League goals conceded while he was on the pitch	158
Contribution to Attacking Power Average number of minutes between League team goals while on pitch	47
Scoring Difference Defensive Rating minus Contribution to Attacking Power	111

	PLAYER	GOALS LGE	GOALS ALL	ASSISTS	DEF RATE	POWER	SC DIFF
1	Fredrik Ljungberg	4	10	5	158	47	111 mins
2	Patrick Vieira	4	4	4	149	47	102 mins
3	Robert Pires	14	19	9	142	42	100 mins
4	Gilberto Silva	4	4	3	116	45	71 mins
5	Ray Parlour	0	0	0	109	58	51 mins

PLAYER APPEARANCES

	AGE (on 01/07/04)	IN NAMED 16	APPEARANCES	COUNTING GAMES	MINUTES ON PITCH	APPEARANCES	MINUTES ON PITCH	THIS SEASON	HOME COUNTRY
Goalkeepers									
Craig Holloway	19	0	0	0	0	0	0	-	England
Jens Lehmann	34	38	38	38	3420	54	4860	5	Germany (9)
Rami Shaaban	29	5	0	0	0	0	0	-	Sweden
Graham Stack	22	28	0	0	0	5	480	-	England
Stuart Taylor	23	5	0	0	0	0	0	-	England
Defenders									
Sol Campbell	29	35	35	34	3085	50	4435	4	England (12)
Gael Clichy	18	17	12	6	660	22	1352	-	France
Ashley Cole	23	32	32	31	2823	48	4293	6	England (12)
Pascal Cygan	30	26	18	10	995	23	1356	-	France
Justin Hoyte	19	3	1	0	1	3	171	-	England
Martin Keown	37	23	10	3	345	16	763	-	England
Bisan Lauren	27	32	32	30	2744	47	4094	-	Cameroon
Frankie Simek	19	0	0	0	0	1	90	-	United States
Efstathios Tavlaridis	24	1	0	0	0	3	300	-	Greece
Habib Kolo Toure	23	36	36	34	3094	54	4634	-	Ivory Coast
Midfielders									
David Bentley	19	4	1	0	61	8	408	-	England
Eduardo	26	34	30	12	1489	48	2863	-	Brazil
Francesco Fabregas	17	0	0	0	0	3	192	-	Spain
Fredrik Ljungberg	27	30	30	26	2216	44	3312	1	Sweden (21)
Ray Parlour	31	28	25	13	1519	37	2325	-	England
Robert Pires	30	37	36	32	2830	51	3973	8	France (2)
Gilberto Silva	27	32	32	25	2544	45	3428	7	Brazil (1)
Olafur Ingi Skulason	21	0	0	0	0	1	36	-	Iceland
Ryan Smith	17	0	0	0	0	3	79	-	England
John Spicer	20	0	0	0	0	1	4	-	England
G Van Bronckhorst	29	0	0	0	0	1	26	7	Holland (4)
Patrick Vieira	28	29	29	28	2535	44	3790	6	France (2)
Forwards									
Jeremie Aliadiere	21	14	10	1	264	15	596	-	France
Dennis Bergkamp	35	30	28	18	1757	38	2427	-	Holland
Thierry Henry	26	37	37	37	3330	51	4458	7	France (2)
Francis Jeffers	23	1	0	0	0	1	14	-	England
Nwankwo Kanu	27	20	10	3	428	24	1107	-	Nigeria
Quincy Owusu-Abeyie	18	0	0	0	0	3	109	-	Holland
Michal Papadopoulos	19	0	0	0	0	1	8	-	Czech Republic
Jose Antonio Reyes	20	16	13	7	654	20	1137	5	Spain (3)
Jerome Thomas	21	1	1	1	90	4	199	-	England
Sylvain Wiltord	30	14	12	5	645	20	1269	7	France (2)

KEY: LEAGUE ALL COMPS CAPS (FIFA RANKING)

TEAM OF THE SEASON

Lehmann

CG 38 DR 132

Lauren

CG 30 DR 114

Campbell

CG 34 DR 140

Toure

CG 34 DR 135

Cole

CG 31 DR 134

LJUNGBERG

CG 26 SD +111

VIEIRA

CG 28 SD +102

GILBERTO

CG 25 SD +71

PIRES

CG 32 SD +100

BERGKAMP

CG 18 AP 42

HENRY

CG 37 SR 111

KEY: DR = Diffensive Rate, SD = Scoring Difference AP = Attacking Power SR = Strike Rate, CG=Counting games – League games playing at least 70 minutes

TOP POINT EARNERS

Robert Pires

Counting Games League games when he played at least 70 minutes	32
Average points Average League points taken in Counting games	2.50
Club Average points Average points taken in League games	2.37

	PLAYER	GAMES	PTS
1	Robert Pires	32	2.50
2	Gilberto Silva	25	2.44
3	Habib Kolo Toure	34	2.41
4	Thierry Henry	37	2.41
5	Bisan Etame Mayer Lauren	30	2.40
6	Jens Lehmann	38	2.37
7	Patrick Vieira	28	2.36
8	Sol Campbell	34	2.35
9	Ashley Cole	31	2.35
10	Fredrik Ljungberg	26	2.31

KEY PLAYERS - DEFENDERS

Sol Campbell

Goals Conceded The number of League goals conceded while he was on the pitch	22
Goals Conceded in all competitions The number of goals conceded while he was on the pitch in all competitions	39
League minutes played Number of minutes played in league matches	3085
Clean Sheets In games when he played at least70 mins	14
Defensive Rating Average number of mins between League goals conceded while he was on the pitch	140
Club Defensive Rating Average number of mins between League goals conceded by the club this season	132

	PLAYER	CON LGE	CON ALL	GAMES	C SHEETS	DEF RATE
1	Sol Campbell	22	39	3085	14	140 mins
2	Habib Kolo Toure	23	42	3094	14	135 mins
3	Ashley Cole	21	38	2823	12	134 mins
4	Bisan Etame Mayer Lauren	24	40	2744	10	114 mins

KEY GOALKEEPER

Jens Lehmann

Goals Conceded in the League The number of League goals conceded while he was on the pitch	26
Goals Conceded in all competitions Number of goals conceded while he was on the pitch in all competitions	43
League minutes played Number of minutes played in league matches	3420
Clean Sheets In games when he played at least 70 mins	15
Goals to Shots Ratio The average number of shots on target per each League goal conceded	6.3
Defensive Rating Ave mins between League goals conceded while on the pitch	132

BOOKINGS

Ray Parlour

League Yellow	8
League Red	0
All competitions Yellow	8
All competitions Red	0

League Average 189 mins between cards

	PLAYER	LEAGUE		TOTAL		AVE
1	Parlour	8 Y	0 R	8 Y	0 R	189
2	Vieira	11	1	14	1	211
3	Cole	5	1	6	1	470
4	Edu	3	0	5	0	496
5	Lauren	5	0	6	0	548
6	Clichy	1	0	1	0	660
7	Toure	4	0	6	0	773
8	Bergkamp	2	0	2	0	878
9	Cygan	1	0	2	0	995
10	Campbell	2	1	4	1	1028
11	Ljungberg	2	0	2	0	1108
12	Henry	3	0	4	0	1110
13	Silva	2	0	5	0	1272
14	Lehmann	2	0	3	0	1710
	Other	2	0	7	2	
	TOTAL	53	3	75	5	

CHELSEA

William Gallas heads the list of player successes; most of which date from **Claudio Ranieri's** pre-**Roman Abramovich** era. The Frenchman leads the Premiership Defenders' table. His Defensive Rating is an astonishing 191 minutes which means that Chelsea concede less than a goal every two league games when he plays.
Frank Lampard's ten league scores put him second in the Midfield Goals chart. Add his five assists to the goals and only four midfielders have a better combined total.
Wayne Bridge and **John Terry** are first and second respectively when it comes to notching clean sheets in the division and **Jimmy-Floyd Hasselbaink** ended his in-and-out season with the club's best Strike Rate, averaging a goal every 166 minutes.

NICKNAME: THE BLUES

KEY: Won / Drawn / Lost

#	Comp	Opponent	Venue	Res	Score	Scorers
1	cl3ql1	**Zilina**	A	W	2-0	Gudjohnsen 42; Drahno 75 og
2	prem	**Liverpool**	A	W	2-1	Veron 27; Hasselbaink 88
3	prem	**Leicester**	H	W	2-1	Nalis 3 og; Mutu 45
4	cl3ql2	**Zilina**	H	W	3-0	Johnson 32; Huth 67; Hasselbaink 78
5	prem	**Blackburn**	H	D	2-2	Mutu 45; Hasselbaink 63 pen
6	prem	**Tottenham**	H	W	4-2	Lampard 35; Mutu 37,75; Hasselbaink 90
7	cl gg	**Sparta Prague**	A	W	1-0	Gallas 85
8	prem	**Wolves**	A	W	5-0	Lampard 17; Hasselbaink 36; Duff 52; Crespo 67,90
9	prem	**Aston Villa**	H	W	1-0	Hasselbaink 43
10	cl gg	**Besiktas**	H	L	0-2	
11	prem	**Middlesbrough**	A	W	2-1	Gudjohnsen 17; Crespo 88
12	prem	**Birmingham**	A	D	0-0	
13	prem	**Arsenal**	A	L	1-2	Crespo 8
14	cl gg	**Lazio**	H	W	2-1	Lampard 57; Mutu 65
15	prem	**Man City**	H	W	1-0	Hasselbaink 34
16	ccr3	**Notts County**	H	W	4-2	Hasselbaink 14; Gudjohnsen 36,65 pen; Cole, J 87
17	prem	**Everton**	A	W	1-0	Mutu 49
18	cl gg	**Lazio**	A	W	4-0	Crespo 15; Gudjohnsen 70; Duff 75; Lampard 80
19	prem	**Newcastle**	H	W	5-0	Johnson 25; Crespo 39; Lampard 42 pen; Duff 76; Gudjohnsen 84
20	prem	**Southampton**	A	W	1-0	Melchiot 47
21	cl gg	**Sparta Prague**	H	D	0-0	
22	prem	**Man Utd**	H	W	1-0	Lampard 29 pen
23	ccr4	**Reading**	A	W	1-0	Hasselbaink 57
24	prem	**Leeds**	A	D	1-1	Duff 70
25	cl gg	**Besiktas**	A	W	2-0	Hasselbaink 77; Bridge 85
26	prem	**Bolton**	H	L	1-2	Crespo 22
27	ccqf	**Aston Villa**	A	L	1-2	Cole, J 69
28	prem	**Fulham**	A	W	1-0	Crespo 62
29	prem	**Charlton**	A	L	2-4	Terry 10; Gudjohnsen 72
30	prem	**Portsmouth**	H	W	3-0	Bridge 65; Lampard 73; Geremi 82
31	facr3	**Watford**	A	D	2-2	Gudjohnsen 33 pen; Lampard 41
32	prem	**Liverpool**	H	L	0-1	
33	prem	**Leicester**	A	W	4-0	Hasselbaink 12; Dabizas 44 og; Mutu 88; Babayaro 90
34	facr3r	**Watford**	H	W	4-0	Mutu 7,76; Hasselbaink 34; Gudjohnsen 84
35	prem	**Birmingham**	H	D	0-0	
36	facr4	**Scarborough**	A	W	1-0	Terry 10
37	prem	**Blackburn**	A	W	3-2	Lampard 25,36; Johnson 88
38	prem	**Charlton**	H	W	1-0	Hasselbaink 28 pen
39	prem	**Portsmouth**	A	W	2-0	Parker 17; Crespo 78
40	facr5	**Arsenal**	A	L	1-2	Mutu 40
41	prem	**Arsenal**	H	L	1-2	Gudjohnsen 1
42	cl rl1	**Stuttgart**	A	W	1-0	Meira 12 og
43	prem	**Man City**	A	W	1-0	Gudjohnsen 82
44	cl rl2	**Stuttgart**	H	D	0-0	
45	prem	**Bolton**	A	W	2-0	Terry 71; Duff 74
46	prem	**Fulham**	H	W	2-1	Gudjohnsen 7; Duff 30
47	cl qfl1	**Arsenal**	H	D	1-1	Gudjohnsen 53
48	prem	**Wolves**	H	W	5-2	Melchiot 4; Lampard 70; Hasselbaink 77,87,90
49	prem	**Tottenham**	A	W	1-0	Hasselbaink 38
50	cl qfl2	**Arsenal**	A	W	2-1	Lampard 51; Bridge 87
51	prem	**Middlesbrough**	H	D	0-0	
52	prem	**Aston Villa**	A	L	2-3	Crespo 11,90
53	prem	**Everton**	H	D	0-0	
54	cl sfl1	**Monaco**	A	L	1-3	Crespo 23
55	prem	**Newcastle**	A	L	1-2	Cole, J 5
56	prem	**Southampton**	H	W	4-0	Crainey 59 og; Lampard 75,83; Johnson 85
57	cl sfl2	**Monaco**	H	D	2-2	Gronkjaer 22; Lampard 44
58	prem	**Man Utd**	A	D	1-1	Gronkjaer 19
59	prem	**Leeds**	H	W	1-0	Gronkjaer 20

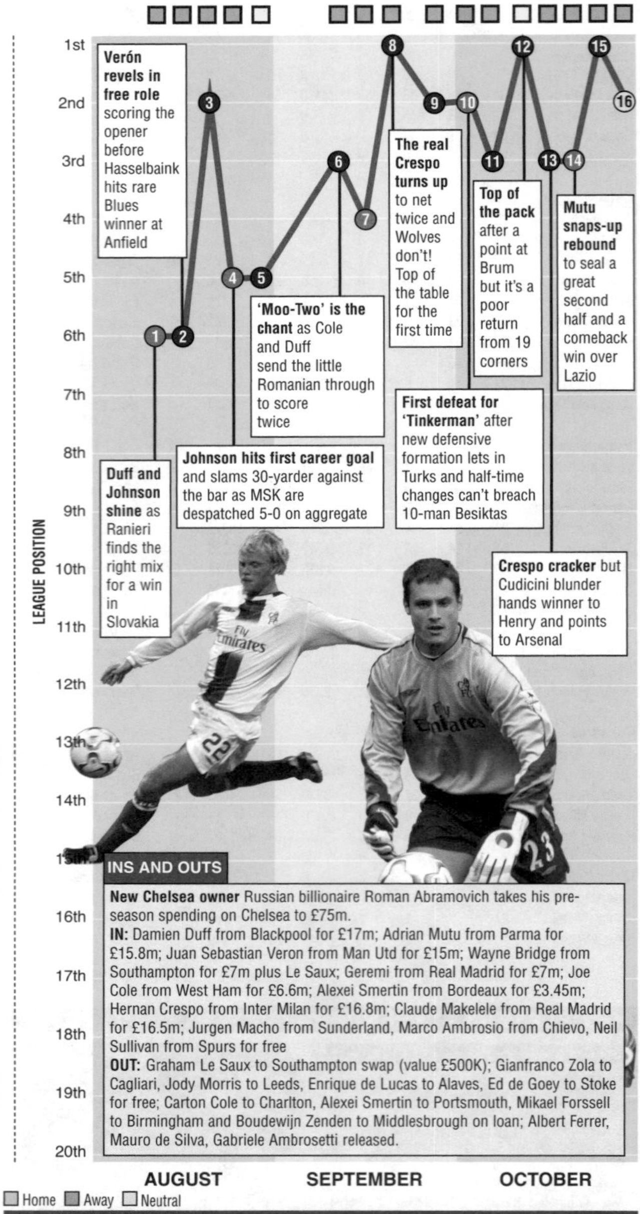

LEAGUE POSITION
1st
2nd
3rd
4th
5th
6th
7th
8th
9th
10th
11th
12th
13th
14th
15th
16th
17th
18th
19th
20th
Verón revels in free role scoring the opener before Hasselbaink hits rare Blues winner at Anfield
Duff and Johnson shine as Ranieri finds the right mix for a win in Slovakia
Johnson hits first career goal and slams 30-yarder against the bar as MSK are despatched 5-0 on aggregate
'Moo-Two' is the chant as Cole and Duff send the little Romanian through to score twice
The real Crespo turns up to net twice and Wolves don't! Top of the table for the first time
First defeat for 'Tinkerman' after new defensive formation lets in Turks and half-time changes can't breach 10-man Besiktas
Top of the pack after a point at Brum but it's a poor return from 19 corners
Crespo cracker but Cudicini blunder hands winner to Henry and points to Arsenal
Mutu snaps-up rebound to seal a great second half and a comeback win over Lazio
AUGUST
SEPTEMBER
OCTOBER
Home
Away
Neutral

INS AND OUTS

New Chelsea owner Russian billionaire Roman Abramovich takes his pre-season spending on Chelsea to £75m.
IN: Damien Duff from Blackpool for £17m; Adrian Mutu from Parma for £15.8m; Juan Sebastian Veron from Man Utd for £15m; Wayne Bridge from Southampton for £7m plus Le Saux; Geremi from Real Madrid for £7m; Joe Cole from West Ham for £6.6m; Alexei Smertin from Bordeaux for £3.45m; Hernan Crespo from Inter Milan for £16.8m; Claude Makelele from Real Madrid for £16.5m; Jurgen Macho from Sunderland, Marco Ambrosio from Chievo, Neil Sullivan from Spurs for free
OUT: Graham Le Saux to Southampton swap (value £500K); Gianfranco Zola to Cagliari, Jody Morris to Leeds, Enrique de Lucas to Alaves, Ed de Goey to Stoke for free; Carton Cole to Charlton, Alexei Smertin to Portsmouth, Mikael Forssell to Birmingham and Boudewijn Zenden to Middlesbrough on loan; Albert Ferrer, Mauro de Silva, Gabriele Ambrosetti released.

ATTENDANCES

HOME GROUND: STAMFORD BRIDGE **CAPACITY:** 42449 **AVERAGE LEAGUE AT HOME:** 41234

#	Opponent	Att	#	Opponent	Att	#	Opponent	Att	#	Opponent	Att
58	Man Utd	67609	48	Wolves	41215	21	Sparta Prague	40152	8	Wolves	29208
25	Besiktas	55350	9	Aston Villa	41182	34	Watford	38763	11	Middlesboro	29170
55	Newcastle	52016	53	Everton	41169	13	Arsenal	38172	29	Charlton	26768
18	Lazio	50000	46	Fulham	41169	40	Arsenal	38136	45	Bolton	26717
42	Stuttgart	50000	6	Tottenham	41165	57	Monaco	37132	37	Blackburn	24867
43	Man City	47304	52	Aston Villa	41112	44	Stuttgart	36657	23	Reading	24107
2	Liverpool	44082	3	Leicester	41073	24	Leeds	36305	4	Zilina	23408
22	Man Utd	41932	35	Birmingham	41073	49	Tottenham	36101	31	Watford	21121
41	Arsenal	41847	5	Blackburn	41066	16	Notts County	35997	39	Portsmouth	20140
30	Portsmouth	41552	15	Man City	41040	50	Arsenal	35486	7	Sparta Prague	18997
32	Liverpool	41420	51	Middlesboro	40873	10	Besiktas	32957	28	Fulham	18244
19	Newcastle	41332	47	Arsenal	40778	20	Southampton	32149	54	Monaco	15000
56	Southampton	41321	26	Bolton	40491	33	Leicester	31547	1	Zilina	6160
59	Leeds	41276	14	Lazio	40405	27	Aston Villa	30414	36	Scarborough	5379
38	Charlton	41255	17	Everton	40189	12	Birmingham	29460			

Tinkerman wins hearts but no trophies

Final Position: **2nd**

KEY: ● League ● Champions Lge ● UEFA Cup ● FA Cup ○ League Cup ● Other

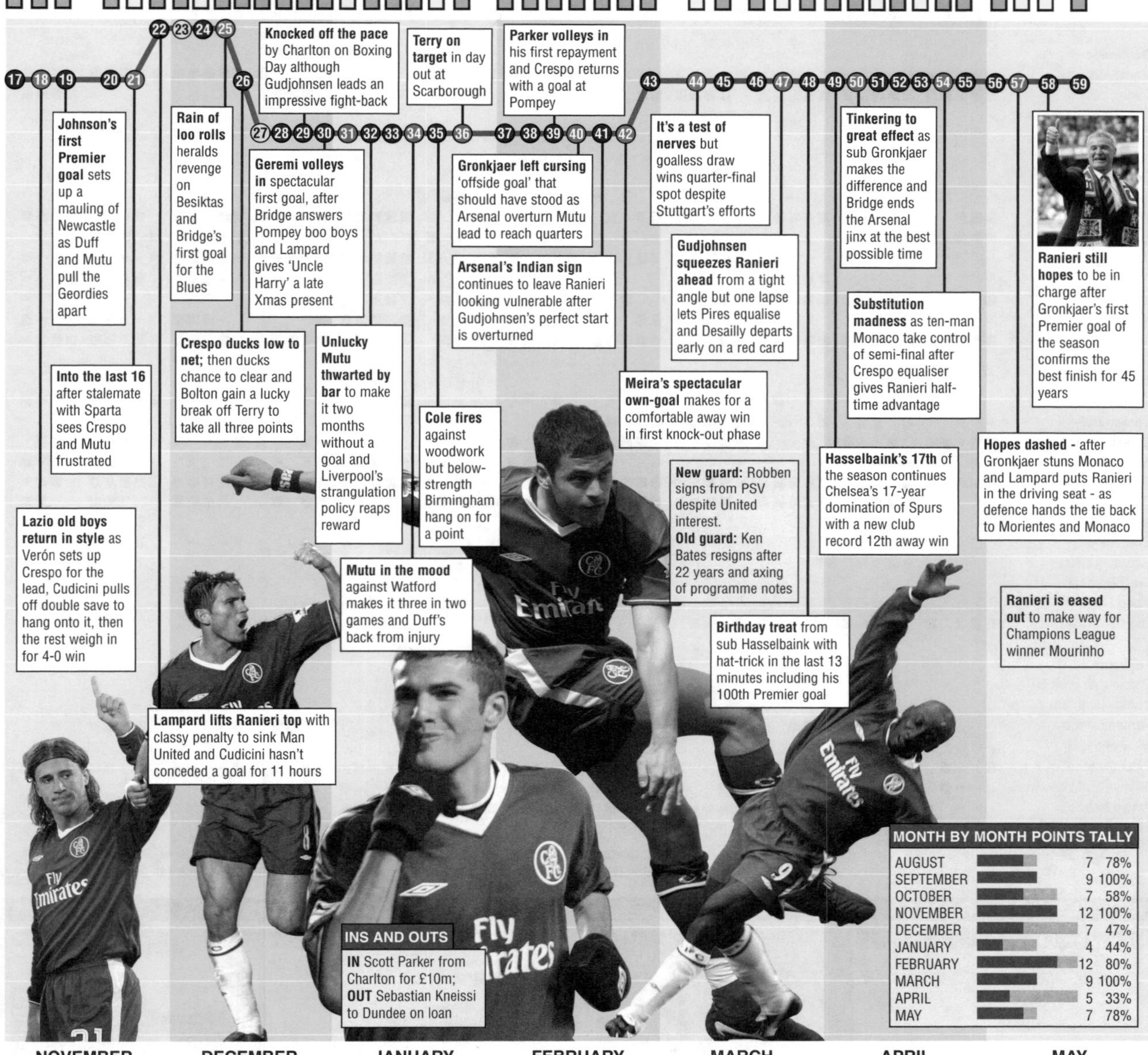

17 18 19 20 21 22 23 24 25 26 27 28 29 30 31 32 33 34 35 36 37 38 39 40 41 42 43 44 45 46 47 48 49 50 51 52 53 54 55 56 57 58 59
Johnson's first Premier goal sets up a mauling of Newcastle as Duff and Mutu pull the Geordies apart
Into the last 16 after stalemate with Sparta sees Crespo and Mutu frustrated
Lazio old boys return in style as Verón sets up Crespo for the lead, Cudicini pulls off double save to hang onto it, then the rest weigh in for 4-0 win
Lampard lifts Ranieri top with classy penalty to sink Man United and Cudicini hasn't conceded a goal for 11 hours
Rain of loo rolls heralds revenge on Besiktas and Bridge's first goal for the Blues
Crespo ducks low to net; then ducks chance to clear and Bolton gain a lucky break off Terry to take all three points
Knocked off the pace by Charlton on Boxing Day although Gudjohnsen leads an impressive fight-back
Geremi volleys in spectacular first goal, after Bridge answers Pompey boo boys and Lampard gives 'Uncle Harry' a late Xmas present
Unlucky Mutu thwarted by bar to make it two months without a goal and Liverpool's strangulation policy reaps reward
Mutu in the mood against Watford makes it three in two games and Duff's back from injury
Cole fires against woodwork but below-strength Birmingham hang on for a point
Terry on target in day out at Scarborough
Parker volleys in his first repayment and Crespo returns with a goal at Pompey
Gronkjaer left cursing 'offside goal' that should have stood as Arsenal overturn Mutu lead to reach quarters
Arsenal's Indian sign continues to leave Ranieri looking vulnerable after Gudjohnsen's perfect start is overturned
Meira's spectacular own-goal makes for a comfortable away win in first knock-out phase
It's a test of nerves but goalless draw wins quarter-final spot despite Stuttgart's efforts
Gudjohnsen squeezes Ranieri ahead from a tight angle but one lapse lets Pires equalise and Desailly departs early on a red card
New guard: Robben signs from PSV despite United interest.
Old guard: Ken Bates resigns after 22 years and axing of programme notes
Birthday treat from sub Hasselbaink with hat-trick in the last 13 minutes including his 100th Premier goal
Tinkering to great effect as sub Gronkjaer makes the difference and Bridge ends the Arsenal jinx at the best possible time
Substitution madness as ten-man Monaco take control of semi-final after Crespo equaliser gives Ranieri half-time advantage
Hasselbaink's 17th of the season continues Chelsea's 17-year domination of Spurs with a new club record 12th away win
Ranieri still hopes to be in charge after Gronkjaer's first Premier goal of the season confirms the best finish for 45 years
Hopes dashed - after Gronkjaer stuns Monaco and Lampard puts Ranieri in the driving seat - as defence hands the tie back to Morientes and Monaco
Ranieri is eased out to make way for Champions League winner Mourinho

INS AND OUTS

IN Scott Parker from Charlton for £10m; **OUT** Sebastian Kneissi to Dundee on loan

MONTH BY MONTH POINTS TALLY

Month	Points	%
AUGUST	7	78%
SEPTEMBER	9	100%
OCTOBER	7	58%
NOVEMBER	12	100%
DECEMBER	7	47%
JANUARY	4	44%
FEBRUARY	12	80%
MARCH	9	100%
APRIL	5	33%
MAY	7	78%

NOVEMBER DECEMBER JANUARY FEBRUARY MARCH APRIL MAY

GOAL ATTEMPTS

FOR — Goal attempts recorded in League games

	HOME	AWAY	TOTAL	AVE
shots on target	122	122	244	6.4
shots off target	132	105	237	6.2
TOTAL	254	227	481	12.7

Ratio of goals to shots — Average number of shots on target per League goal scored: **3.6**

Accuracy rating — Average percentage of total goal attempts which were on target: **50.7**

AGAINST — Goal attempts recorded in League games

	HOME	AWAY	TOTAL	AVE
shots on target	52	104	156	4.1
shots off target	62	122	184	4.8
TOTAL	114	226	340	8.9

Ratio of goals to shots — Average number of shots on target per League goal scored: **5.2**

Accuracy rating — Average percentage of total goal attempts which were on target: **45.9**

GOALS

Jimmy-Floyd Hasselbaink

League	12
FA Cup	1
League Cup	2
Europe	2
Other	0
TOTAL	17

League Average **166** mins between goals

	PLAYER	LGE	FAC	LC	Euro	TOT	AVE
1	Hasselbaink	12	1	2	2	17	166
2	Crespo	10	0	0	2	12	114
3	Lampard	10	1	0	4	15	338
4	Mutu	6	3	0	1	10	292
5	Gudjohnsen	6	2	2	3	13	260
6	Duff	5	0	0	1	6	292
7	Johnson	3	0	0	1	4	501
8	Gronkjaer	2	0	0	1	3	825
9	Terry	2	1	0	0	3	1482
10	Melchiot	2	0	0	0	2	920
11	Bridge	1	0	0	2	3	2963
12	Geremi	1	0	0	0	1	1746
13	Parker	1	0	0	0	1	602
14	Cole, J	1	0	2	0	3	1651
15	Veron	1	0	0	0	1	484
	Other	4	0	0	4	8	
	TOTAL	67	8	6	21	102	

SQUAD APPEARANCES

Match	1 2 3 4 5	6 7 8 9 10	11 12 13 14 15	16 17 18 19 20	21 22 23 24 25	26 27 28 29 30	31 32 33 34 35	36 37 38 39 40	41 42 43 44 45	46 47 48 49 50	51 52 53 54 55	56 57 58 59
Venue	A A H H H	H A A H H	A A A H H	H A A H A	H H A A A	H A A A H	A H A H H	A A H A A	H A A H A	H H H A A	H A H A A	H H A H
Competition	C L L C L	L C L L C	L L L C L	W L C L L	C L W L C	L W L L L	F L L F L	F L L L F	L C L C L	L C L L C	L L L C L	L C L L
Result	W W W W D	W W W W L	W D L W W	W W W W W	D W W D W	L L W L W	D L W W D	W W W W L	L W W D W	W D W W W	D L D L L	W D D W

Goalkeepers
Marco Ambrosio
Carlo Cudicini
Yves Makaba-Makalamby
Neil Sullivan

Defenders
Celestine Babayaro
Wayne Bridge
Marcel Desailly
William Gallas
Robert Huth
Glen Johnson
Mario Melchiot
John Terry

Midfielders
Joe Cole
Damien Duff
Geremi Sorele Nitjap Fotso
Jesper Gronkjaer
Frank Lampard
Claude Makelele
Alexis Nicolas
Scott Parker
Emmanuel Petit
Craig Rocastle
Mario Stanic
Juan Sebastian Veron

Forwards
Gabriele Ambrosetti
Carlton Cole
Hernan Crespo
Mikael Forssell
Eidur Gudjohnsen
Jimmy-Floyd Hasselbaink
Adrian Mutu
Filipe Oliveira

KEY: On all match · On bench · Subbed or sent off (Counting game) · Subbed or sent off (playing less than 70 mins) · Subbed on from bench (Counting Game) · Subbed on (playing less than 70 mins) · Subbed on and then subbed or sent off (Counting Game) · Subbed on and then subbed or sent off (playing less than 70 mins) · Not in 16

KEY PLAYERS - GOALSCORERS

Jimmy-Floyd Hasselbaink

Goals in the League	12
Goals in all competitions	17
Assists League goals scored by team-mates where he delivered the final pass	5
Contribution to Attacking Power Average number of minutes between League team goals while on pitch	49
Player Strike Rate Average number of minutes between League goals scored by player	166
Club Strike Rate Average minutes between League goals scored by club	51

	PLAYER	GOALS LGE	GOALS ALL	ASSISTS	POWER	S RATE
1	Jimmy-Floyd Hasselbaink	12	17	5	49	166 mins
2	Eidur Gudjohnsen	6	13	2	52	260 mins
3	Adrian Mutu	6	10	5	51	292 mins
4	Damien Duff	5	6	9	44	292 mins
5	Frank Lampard	10	15	5	51	338 mins

KEY PLAYERS - MIDFIELDERS

Damien Duff

Goals in the League	5
Goals in all competitions	6
Assists League goals scored by team-mates where he delivered the final pass	9
Defensive Rating Average number of mins between League goals conceded while he was on the pitch	112
Contribution to Attacking Power Average number of minutes between League team goals while on pitch	44
Scoring Difference Defensive Rating minus Contribution to Attacking Power	68

	PLAYER	GOALS LGE	GOALS ALL	ASSISTS	DEF RATE	POWER	SC DIFF
1	Damien Duff	5	6	9	112	44	68 mins
2	Frank Lampard	10	15	5	116	51	65 mins
3	Claude Makelele	0	0	0	114	51	63 mins
4	Geremi Sorele Nitjap Fotso	1	1	4	92	60	32 mins

PLAYER APPEARANCES

	AGE (on 01/07/04)	IN NAMED 16	APPEARANCES	COUNTING GAMES	MINUTES ON PITCH	APPEARANCES	MINUTES ON PITCH	THIS SEASON	HOME COUNTRY
Goalkeepers									
Marco Ambrosio	31	30	8	8	720	12	1080	-	Italy
Carlo Cudicini	30	26	26	26	2340	40	3569	-	Italy
Yves M-Makalamby	18	1	0	0	0	0	0	-	Belgium
Neil Sullivan	34	19	4	4	360	8	661	-	Scotland
Defenders									
Celestine Babayaro	25	7	6	5	439	14	1083	-	Nigeria
Wayne Bridge	23	33	33	33	2963	48	4209	7	England (12)
Marcel Desailly	35	21	15	15	1330	25	2168	7	France (2)
William Gallas	26	32	29	22	2097	45	3528	5	France (2)
Robert Huth	19	23	16	8	797	20	945	-	Germany
Glen Johnson	19	22	19	17	1502	32	2512	1	England (12)
Mario Melchiot	27	27	23	19	1840	33	2599	1	Holland (4)
John Terry	23	34	33	33	2964	51	4584	7	England (12)
Midfielders									
Joe Cole	22	36	35	12	1651	50	2331	7	England (12)
Damien Duff	25	24	23	15	1459	37	2327	6	Rep of Ireland (15)
Geremi Nitjap Fotso	25	27	25	17	1746	39	2775	4	Cameroon (12)
Jesper Gronkjaer	26	32	31	11	1649	48	2690	-	Holland
Frank Lampard	26	38	38	37	3375	58	5040	7	England (12)
Claude Makelele	31	30	30	25	2401	46	3751	6	France (2)
Alexis Nicolas	21	4	2	1	91	3	157	-	England
Scott Parker	23	11	11	5	602	17	958	2	England (12)
Emmanuel Petit	33	5	4	2	260	7	395	-	France
Craig Rocastle	22	1	0	0	0	0	0	-	England
Mario Stanic	32	5	2	0	26	5	113	-	Croatia
Juan Seb Veron	29	7	7	5	484	14	1027	4	Argentina (5)
Forwards									
Gabriele Ambrosetti	30	0	0	0	0	0	0	-	Italy
Carlton Cole	20	0	0	0	0	0	0	-	England
Hernan Crespo	29	23	19	9	1143	31	1840	7	Argentina (5)
Mikael Forssell	23	1	0	0	0	1	57	4	Finland (42)
Eidur Gudjohnsen	25	29	26	15	1561	41	2618	-	Iceland
J-Floyd Hasselbaink	32	31	30	19	1988	44	2883	2	Holland (4)
Adrian Mutu	25	26	25	16	1750	36	2397	-	Romania
Filipe Oliveira	20	3	1	0	12	2	36	-	Portugal

KEY: LEAGUE ALL COMPS CAPS (FIFA RANKING)

TEAM OF THE SEASON

Cudicini

CG 26 DR 117

Melchiot

CG 19 DR 115

Gallas

CG 22 DR 191

Terry

CG 33 DR 106

Bridge

CG 33 DR 114

Geremi

CG 17 SD +32

Makelele

CG 25 SD +63

Lampard

CG 37 SD +65

Duff

CG 15 SD +68

Gudjohnsen

CG 15 AP 52

Hasselbaink

CG 19 SR 166

KEY: DR = Diffensive Rate, SD = Scoring Difference AP = Attacking Power SR = Strike Rate, CG=Counting games – League games playing at least 70 minutes

TOP POINT EARNERS

William Gallas

Counting Games League games when he played at least 70 minutes	22
Average points Average League points taken in Counting games	2.45
Club Average points Average points taken in League games	2.08

	PLAYER	GAMES	PTS
1	William Gallas	22	2.45
2	Mario Melchiot	19	2.32
3	Damien Duff	15	2.27
4	Jimmy-Floyd Hasselbaink	19	2.21
5	Eidur Gudjohnsen	15	2.20
6	John Terry	33	2.15
7	Carlo Cudicini	26	2.15
8	Frank Lampard	37	2.14
9	Wayne Bridge	33	2.00
10	Claude Makelele	25	1.96

KEY PLAYERS - DEFENDERS

William Gallas

Goals Conceded The number of League goals conceded while he was on the pitch	11
Goals Conceded in all competitions The number of goals conceded while he was on the pitch in all competitions	24
League minutes played Number of minutes played in league matches	2097
Clean Sheets In games when he played at least70 mins	16
Defensive Rating Average number of mins between League goals conceded while he was on the pitch	191
Club Defensive Rating Average number of mins between League goals conceded by the club this season	114

	PLAYER	CON LGE	CON ALL	MINS	C SHEETS	DEF RATE
1	William Gallas	11	24	2097	16	191 mins
2	Mario Melchiot	16	28	1840	11	115 mins
3	Wayne Bridge	26	38	2963	18	114 mins
4	John Terry	28	42	2964	17	106 mins
5	Glen Johnson	15	21	1502	9	100 mins

KEY GOALKEEPER

Carlo Cudicini

Goals Conceded in the League The number of League goals conceded while he was on the pitch	20
Goals Conceded in all competitions Number of goals conceded while he was on the pitch in all competitions	26
League minutes played Number of minutes played in league matches	2340
Clean Sheets In games when he played at least 70 mins	14
Goals to Shots Ratio The average number of shots on target per each League goal conceded	4.7
Defensive Rating Ave mins between League goals conceded while on the pitch	117

BOOKINGS

Robert Huth

League Yellow	8
League Red	1
All competitions Yellow	8
All competitions Red	1
League Average 88 mins between cards	

	PLAYER	LEAGUE		TOTAL		AVE
		8 Y	1 R	8 Y	1 R	
1	Huth	8 Y	1 R	8 Y	1 R	88
2	Parker	2	0	2	0	301
3	Gronkjaer	5	0	6	0	329
4	Hasselbaink	6	0	9	0	331
5	Mutu	4	0	7	0	437
6	Gudjohnsen	2	1	2	1	520
7	Cole, J	3	0	4	0	550
8	Crespo	2	0	2	0	571
9	Terry	5	0	8	0	592
10	Johnson	2	0	5	1	751
11	Lampard	3	0	4	0	1125
12	Makelele	2	0	7	0	1200
13	Geremi	0	1	0	1	1746
14	Melchiot	1	0	4	0	1840
15	Gallas	1	0	3	0	2097
	Other	0	0	6	1	
	TOTAL	46	3	77	5	

MANCHESTER UNITED

United's season came apart when **Rio Ferdinand** accepted his banishment. Until then they were enjoying their best ever start to a season, averaging nearly 2.4 points a game – just higher than Arsenal's average – and rarely conceding a goal. Over the last 17 games they only managed 1.47 points per game.

Ferdinand has the third best Defensive Rating of the season, conceding one league goal on average for every 135 minutes on the park.

Roy Carroll missed the 12 Counting Games hurdle. He was on course to lead the goalkeepers' chart with both his Defensive Rating of 135 and Goals-to-Shots Ratio of 8.3 shots for every goal conceded. **Ryan Giggs**' combined total of goals scored plus assists was second only to Pires among Premier midfielders.

NICKNAME: RED DEVILS

KEY: Won / Drawn / Lost

No	Comp	Opponent	Venue	Result	Score	Scorers
1	fa cs	**Arsenal**	H	W	4-3*	Silvestre 15 (*on penalties)
2	prem	**Bolton**	H	W	4-0	Giggs 35,73; Scholes 77; van Nistelrooy 87
3	prem	**Newcastle**	A	W	2-1	van Nistelrooy 50; Scholes 59
4	prem	**Wolves**	H	W	1-0	O'Shea 10
5	prem	**Southampton**	A	L	0-1	
6	prem	**Charlton**	A	W	2-0	van Nistelrooy 62,81
7	cl ge	**Panathinaikos**	H	W	5-0	Silvestre 14; Fortune 15; Solskjaer 33; Butt 40; Djemba-Djemba 83
8	prem	**Arsenal**	H	D	0-0	
9	prem	**Leicester**	A	W	4-1	Keane 15; van Nistelrooy 16,45,52
10	cl ge	**Stuttgart**	A	L	1-2	van Nistelrooy 67 pen
11	prem	**Birmingham**	H	W	3-0	van Nistelrooy 36 pen; Scholes 57; Giggs 82
12	prem	**Leeds**	A	W	1-0	Keane 81
13	cl ge	**Rangers**	A	W	1-0	Neville, P 5
14	prem	**Fulham**	H	L	1-3	Forlan 45
15	ccr3	**Leeds**	A	W	3-2	Bellion 78; Forlan 108; Djemba-Djemba 117
16	prem	**Portsmouth**	H	W	3-0	Forlan 37; Ronaldo 80; Keane 82
17	cl ge	**Rangers**	H	W	3-0	Forlan 6; van Nistelrooy 43,60
18	prem	**Liverpool**	A	W	2-1	Giggs 59,70
19	prem	**Blackburn**	H	W	2-1	van Nistelrooy 24; Kleberson 38
20	cl ge	**Panathinaikos**	A	W	1-0	Forlan 85
21	prem	**Chelsea**	A	L	0-1	
22	ccr4	**West Brom**	A	L	0-2	
23	prem	**Aston Villa**	H	W	4-0	van Nistelrooy 16,45; Forlan 90,90
24	cl ge	**Stuttgart**	H	W	2-0	van Nistelrooy 45; Giggs 58
25	prem	**Man City**	H	W	3-1	Scholes 7,73; van Nistelrooy 34
26	prem	**Tottenham**	A	W	2-1	O'Shea 15; van Nistelrooy 25
27	prem	**Everton**	H	W	3-2	Butt 9; Kleberson 44; Bellion 68
28	prem	**Middlesbrough**	A	W	1-0	Mills 14 og
29	facr3	**Aston Villa**	A	W	2-1	Scholes 64,68
30	prem	**Bolton**	A	W	2-1	Scholes 24; van Nistelrooy 39
31	prem	**Newcastle**	H	D	0-0	
32	prem	**Wolves**	A	L	0-1	
33	facr4	**Northampton**	A	W	3-0	Silvestre 34; Hargreaves 47 og; Forlan 68
34	prem	**Southampton**	H	W	3-2	Saha 18; Scholes 37; van Nistelrooy 60
35	prem	**Everton**	A	W	4-3	Saha 9,29; van Nistelrooy 24,89
36	prem	**Middlesbrough**	H	L	2-3	van Nistelrooy 45; Giggs 63
37	facr5	**Man City**	H	W	4-2	Scholes 34; van Nistelrooy 71,80; Ronaldo 73
38	prem	**Leeds**	H	D	1-1	Scholes 64
39	cl rl1	**Porto**	A	L	1-2	Fortune 14
40	prem	**Fulham**	A	D	1-1	Saha 14
41	facqf	**Fulham**	H	W	2-1	van Nistelrooy 24,62
42	cl rl2	**Porto**	H	D	1-1	Scholes 32
43	prem	**Man City**	A	L	1-4	Scholes 35
44	prem	**Tottenham**	H	W	3-0	Giggs 30; Ronaldo 89; Bellion 90
45	prem	**Arsenal**	A	D	1-1	Saha 86
46	facsf	**Arsenal**	A	W	1-0	Scholes 32
47	prem	**Birmingham**	A	W	2-1	Ronaldo 60; Saha 78
48	prem	**Leicester**	H	W	1-0	Neville, G 56
49	prem	**Portsmouth**	A	L	0-1	
50	prem	**Charlton**	H	W	2-0	Saha 28; Neville, G 65
51	prem	**Liverpool**	H	L	0-1	
52	prem	**Blackburn**	A	L	0-1	
53	prem	**Chelsea**	H	D	1-1	van Nistelrooy 77
54	prem	**Aston Villa**	A	W	2-0	Ronaldo 4; van Nistelrooy 10
55	facf	**Millwall**	H	W	3-0	Ronaldo 44; van Nistelrooy 65 pen,81

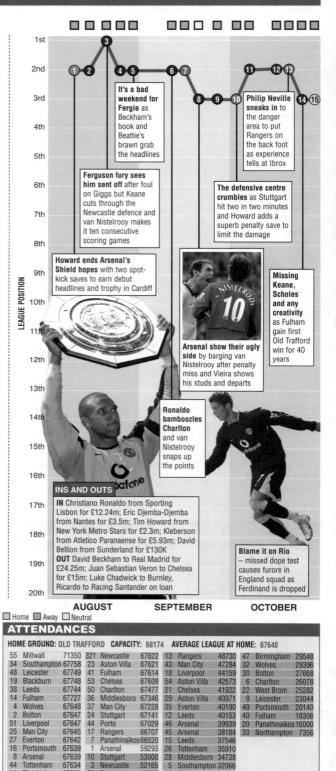

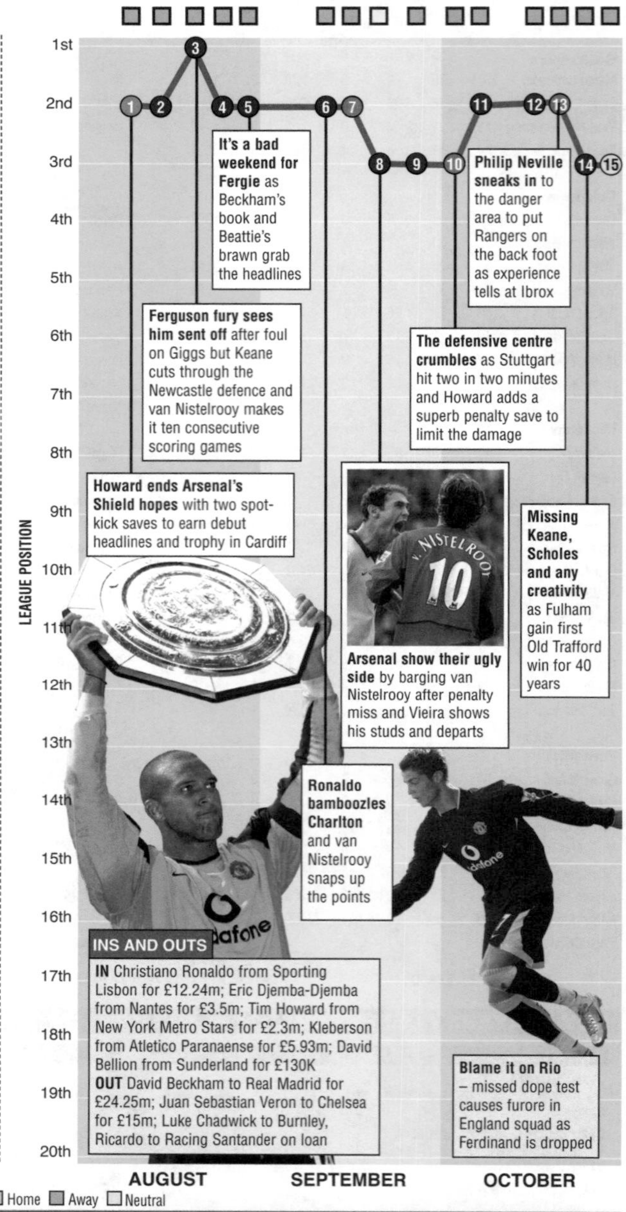

LEAGUE POSITION
1st
2nd
3rd
4th
5th
6th
7th
8th
9th
10th
11th
12th
13th
14th
15th
16th
17th
18th
19th
20th
AUGUST
SEPTEMBER
OCTOBER
It's a bad weekend for Fergie as Beckham's book and Beattie's brawn grab the headlines
Philip Neville sneaks in to the danger area to put Rangers on the back foot as experience tells at Ibrox
Ferguson fury sees him sent off after foul on Giggs but Keane cuts through the Newcastle defence and van Nistelrooy makes it ten consecutive scoring games
The defensive centre crumbles as Stuttgart hit two in two minutes and Howard adds a superb penalty save to limit the damage
Howard ends Arsenal's Shield hopes with two spot-kick saves to earn debut headlines and trophy in Cardiff
Missing Keane, Scholes and any creativity as Fulham gain first Old Trafford win for 40 years
Arsenal show their ugly side by barging van Nistelrooy after penalty miss and Vieira shows his studs and departs
Ronaldo bamboozles Charlton and van Nistelrooy snaps up the points
Blame it on Rio – missed dope test causes furore in England squad as Ferdinand is dropped

INS AND OUTS

IN Christiano Ronaldo from Sporting Lisbon for £12.24m; Eric Djemba-Djemba from Nantes for £3.5m; Tim Howard from New York Metro Stars for £2.3m; Kleberson from Atletico Paranaense for £5.93m; David Bellion from Sunderland for £130K
OUT David Beckham to Real Madrid for £24.25m; Juan Sebastian Veron to Chelsea for £15m; Luke Chadwick to Burnley, Ricardo to Racing Santander on loan

Home / Away / Neutral

ATTENDANCES

HOME GROUND: OLD TRAFFORD **CAPACITY:** 68174 **AVERAGE LEAGUE AT HOME:** 67640

No	Opponent	Att	No	Opponent	Att	No	Opponent	Att	No	Opponent	Att
55	Millwall	71350	321	Newcastle	67622	13	Rangers	48730	47	Birmingham	29548
34	Southampton	67758	23	Aston Villa	67621	43	Man City	47284	32	Wolves	29396
48	Leicester	67749	41	Fulham	67614	18	Liverpool	44159	30	Bolton	27668
19	Blackburn	67748	53	Chelsea	67609	54	Aston Villa	42573	6	Charlton	26078
38	Leeds	67744	50	Charlton	67477	21	Chelsea	41932	22	West Brom	25282
14	Fulham	67727	36	Middlesboro	67346	29	Aston Villa	40371	9	Leicester	23044
4	Wolves	67648	37	Man City	67228	35	Everton	40190	49	Portsmouth	20140
2	Bolton	67647	24	Stuttgart	67141	12	Leeds	40153	40	Fulham	18306
51	Liverpool	67647	44	Porto	67029	46	Arsenal	39939	20	Panathinaikos	16000
25	Man City	67645	17	Rangers	66707	45	Arsenal	38184	33	Northampton	7356
27	Everton	67642	7	Panathinaikos	66520	15	Leeds	37546			
16	Portsmouth	67639	1	Arsenal	59293	26	Tottenham	35910			
8	Arsenal	67639	10	Stuttgart	53000	28	Middlesboro	34738			
44	Tottenham	67634	3	Newcastle	52165	5	Southampton	32066			
11	Birmingham	67633	39	Porto	49977	52	Blackburn	29616			

Missing Rio but rediscovering the Cup

Final Position: **3rd**

KEY: ● League ● Champions Lge ● UEFA Cup ● FA Cup ○ League Cup ● Other

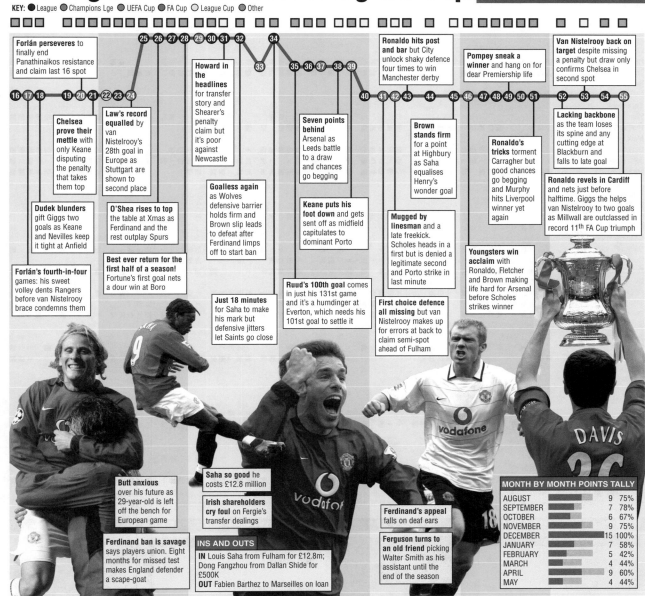

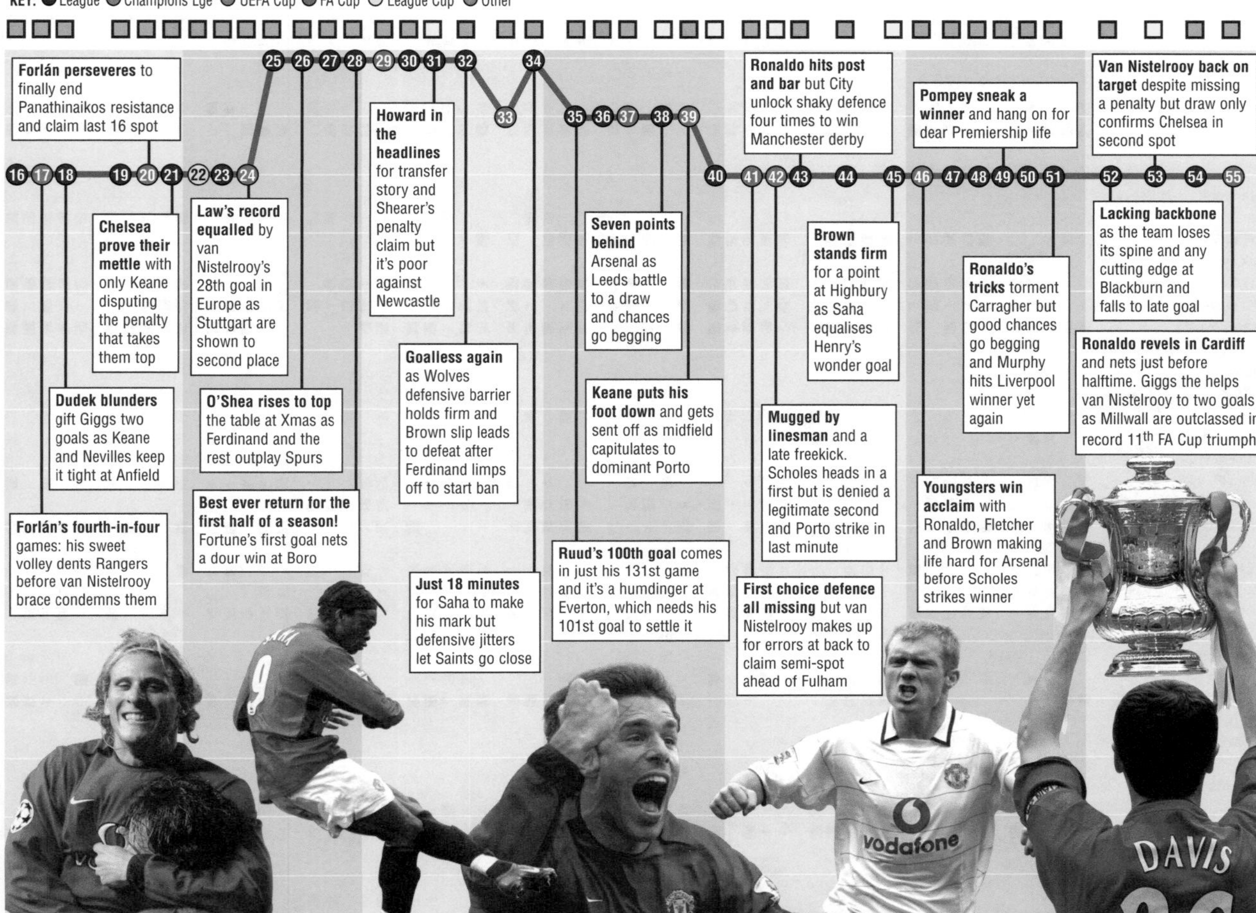

16 17 18 19 20 21 22 23 24 25 26 27 28 29 30 31 32 33 34 35 36 37 38 39 40 41 42 43 44 45 46 47 48 49 50 51 52 53 54 55
DAVIS
vodafone

Forlán perseveres to finally end Panathinaikos resistance and claim last 16 spot

Chelsea prove their mettle with only Keane disputing the penalty that takes them top

Dudek blunders gift Giggs two goals as Keane and Nevilles keep it tight at Anfield

Forlán's fourth-in-four games: his sweet volley dents Rangers before van Nistelrooy brace condemns them

Law's record equalled by van Nistelrooy's 28th goal in Europe as Stuttgart are shown to second place

O'Shea rises to top the table at Xmas as Ferdinand and the rest outplay Spurs

Best ever return for the first half of a season! Fortune's first goal nets a dour win at Boro

Howard in the headlines for transfer story and Shearer's penalty claim but it's poor against Newcastle

Goalless again as Wolves defensive barrier holds firm and Brown slip leads to defeat after Ferdinand limps off to start ban

Just 18 minutes for Saha to make his mark but defensive jitters let Saints go close

Seven points behind Arsenal as Leeds battle to a draw and chances go begging

Keane puts his foot down and gets sent off as midfield capitulates to dominant Porto

Ruud's 100th goal comes in just his 131st game and it's a humdinger at Everton, which needs his 101st goal to settle it

Ronaldo hits post and bar but City unlock shaky defence four times to win Manchester derby

Brown stands firm for a point at Highbury as Saha equalises Henry's wonder goal

Mugged by linesman and a late freekick. Scholes heads in a first but is denied a legitimate second and Porto strike in last minute

First choice defence all missing but van Nistelrooy makes up for errors at back to claim semi-spot ahead of Fulham

Pompey sneak a winner and hang on for dear Premiership life

Ronaldo's tricks torment Carragher but good chances go begging and Murphy hits Liverpool winner yet again

Youngsters win acclaim with Ronaldo, Fletcher and Brown making life hard for Arsenal before Scholes strikes winner

Van Nistelrooy back on target despite missing a penalty but draw only confirms Chelsea in second spot

Lacking backbone as the team loses its spine and any cutting edge at Blackburn and falls to late goal

Ronaldo revels in Cardiff and nets just before halftime. Giggs the helps van Nistelrooy to two goals as Millwall are outclassed in record 11th FA Cup triumph

Butt anxious over his future as 29-year-old is left off the bench for European game

Ferdinand ban is savage says players union. Eight months for missed test makes England defender a scape-goat

Saha so good he costs £12.8 million

Irish shareholders cry foul on Fergie's transfer dealings

Ferdinand's appeal falls on deaf ears

Ferguson turns to an old friend picking Walter Smith as his assistant until the end of the season

INS AND OUTS

IN Louis Saha from Fulham for £12.8m; Dong Fangzhou from Dallan Shide for £500K
OUT Fabien Barthez to Marseilles on loan

MONTH BY MONTH POINTS TALLY

Month	Points	%
AUGUST	9	75%
SEPTEMBER	7	78%
OCTOBER	6	67%
NOVEMBER	9	75%
DECEMBER	15	100%
JANUARY	7	58%
FEBRUARY	5	42%
MARCH	4	44%
APRIL	9	60%
MAY	4	44%

NOVEMBER DECEMBER JANUARY FEBRUARY MARCH APRIL MAY

GOAL ATTEMPTS

FOR — Goal attempts recorded in League games

	HOME	AWAY	TOTAL	AVE
shots on target	142	142	284	7.5
shots off target	117	93	210	5.5
TOTAL	259	235	494	13

Ratio of goals to shots Average number of shots on target per League goal scored: **4.4**

Accuracy rating Average percentage of total goal attempts which were on target: **57.5**

AGAINST — Goal attempts recorded in League games

	HOME	AWAY	TOTAL	AVE
shots on target	88	108	196	5.2
shots off target	104	142	246	6.5
TOTAL	192	250	442	11.6

Ratio of goals to shots Average number of shots on target per League goal scored: **5.6**

Accuracy rating Average percentage of total goal attempts which were on target: **44.3**

GOALS

Ruud van Nistelrooy

League	20
FA Cup	6
League Cup	0
Europe	4
Other	0
TOTAL	30

League Average **138** mins between goals

	PLAYER	LGE	FAC	LC	Euro	TOT	AVE
1	van Nistelrooy	20	6	0	4	30	138
2	Scholes	9	4	0	1	14	243
3	Saha	7	0	0	0	7	123
4	Giggs	7	0	0	1	8	362
5	Forlan	4	1	1	2	8	269
6	Ronaldo	4	2	0	0	6	389
7	Keane	3	0	0	0	3	731
8	Kleberson	2	0	0	0	2	394
9	Bellion	2	0	1	0	3	233
10	O'Shea	2	0	0	0	2	1408
11	Neville, G	2	0	0	0	2	1345
12	Butt	1	0	0	1	2	1109
13	Neville, P	0	0	0	1	1	
14	Solskjaer	0	0	0	1	1	
15	Fortune	0	0	0	2	2	
	Other	1	2	1	2	7	
	TOTAL	64	15	3	15	98	

SQUAD APPEARANCES

Match	1 2 3 4 5	6 7 8 9 10	11 12 13 14 15	16 17 18 19 20	21 22 23 24 25	26 27 28 29 30	31 32 33 34 35	36 37 38 39 40	41 42 43 44 45	46 47 48 49 50	51 52 53 54 55
Venue	H H A H A	A H H A A	H A A H A	H H A H A	A A H H H	A H A A A	H A A H A	H H H A A	H H A H A	A A H A H	H A H A H
Competition	O L L L L	L C L L C	L L C L W	L C L L C	L W L C L	L L L F L	L L F L L	L F L C L	F C L L L	F L L L L	L L L L F
Result	W W W W L	W W D W L	W W W L W	W W W W W	L L W W W	W W W W W	D L W W W	L W D L D	W D L W D	W W W L W	L L D W W

Goalkeepers
Roy Carroll
Tim Howard
Ben Williams

Defenders
Wes Brown
Rio Ferdinand
Mark Lynch
Gary Neville
John O'Shea
Mikael Silvestre

Midfielders
Phillip Bardsley
Nicky Butt
Eric Djemba-Djemba
Chris Eagles
Darren Fletcher
Quinton Fortune
Ryan Giggs
David Jones
Roy Keane
Jose Pereira Kleberson
Phil Neville
Danny Pugh
Keiron Richardson
Christiano Ronaldo
Paul Scholes
Paul Tierney
Neil Wood

Forwards
David Bellion
Diego Forlan
Eddie Johnson
Daniel Nardiello
Louis Saha
Ole Gunnar Solskjaer
Ruud van Nistelrooy

KEY: On all match · On bench · Subbed or sent off (Counting game) · Subbed or sent off (playing less than 70 mins) · Subbed on from bench (Counting Game) · Subbed on (playing less than 70 mins) · Subbed on and then subbed or sent off (Counting Game) · Subbed on and then subbed or sent off (playing less than 70 mins) · Not in 16

KEY PLAYERS - GOALSCORERS

Ruud van Nistelrooy

Goals in the League	20
Goals in all competitions	30
Assists League goals scored by team-mates where he delivered the final pass	2
Contribution to Attacking Power Average number of minutes between League team goals while on pitch	50
Player Strike Rate Average number of minutes between League goals scored by player	138
Club Strike Rate Average minutes between League goals scored by club	53

	PLAYER	GOALS LGE	GOALS ALL	ASSISTS	POWER	S RATE
1	Ruud van Nistelrooy	20	30	2	50	138 mins
2	Paul Scholes	9	14	5	48	243 mins
3	Ryan Giggs	7	8	10	55	362 mins
4	Christiano Ronaldo	4	6	3	48	389 mins
5	Roy Keane	3	3	3	51	731 mins

KEY PLAYERS - MIDFIELDERS

Roy Keane

Goals in the League	3
Goals in all competitions	3
Assists League goals scored by team-mates where he delivered the final pass	3
Defensive Rating Average number of mins between League goals conceded while he was on the pitch	129
Contribution to Attacking Power Average number of minutes between League team goals while on pitch	51
Scoring Difference Defensive Rating minus Contribution to Attacking Power	78

	PLAYER	GOALS LGE	GOALS ALL	ASSISTS	DEF RATE	POWER	SC DIFF
1	Roy Keane	3	3	3	129	51	78 mins
2	Christiano Ronaldo	4	6	3	111	49	62 mins
3	Phil Neville	0	1	2	114	56	58 mins
4	Ryan Giggs	7	8	10	101	55	46 mins
5	Quinton Fortune	0	2	2	90	45	45 mins

PLAYER APPEARANCES

	AGE (on 01/07/04)	IN NAMED 16	APPEARANCES	COUNTING GAMES	MINUTES ON PITCH	APPEARANCES	MINUTES ON PITCH	THIS SEASON	HOME COUNTRY
Goalkeepers									
Roy Carroll	26	37	6	6	540	12	1027	2	N Ireland (114)
Tim Howard	25	38	32	32	2880	44	3953	-	United States
Ben Williams	21	0	0	0	0	0	0	-	England
Defenders									
Wes Brown	24	18	17	14	1413	25	2044	-	England
Rio Ferdinand	25	20	20	19	1759	27	2380	1	England (12)
Mark Lynch	22	1	0	0	0	0	0	-	England
Gary Neville	29	30	30	30	2689	42	3748	5	England (12)
John O'Shea	23	37	33	30	2815	49	4053	6	Rep of Ireland (15)
Mikael Silvestre	26	34	34	31	2848	46	3909	7	France (2)
Midfielders									
Phillip Bardsley	19	0	0	0	0	2	109	-	England
Nicky Butt	29	33	21	11	1109	34	1991	7	England (12)
Eric Djemba-Djemba	23	22	15	8	881	22	1139	4	Cameroon (12)
Chris Eagles	18	0	0	0	0	2	71	-	England
Darren Fletcher	20	29	22	14	1451	35	2298	8	Scotland (63)
Quinton Fortune	27	25	23	17	1620	35	2640	-	South Africa
Ryan Giggs	30	34	33	26	2531	47	3744	8	Wales (66)
David Jones	19	0	0	0	0	0	0	-	England
Roy Keane	32	28	28	22	2194	38	3021	1	Rep of Ireland (15)
Kleberson	25	18	12	6	787	16	1059	2	Brazil (1)
Phil Neville	27	34	31	26	2503	43	3499	8	England (12)
Danny Pugh	21	1	0	0	0	2	92	-	England
Keiron Richardson	19	0	0	0	0	3	172	-	England
Christiano Ronaldo	19	33	29	13	1555	40	2356	-	Portugal
Paul Scholes	29	28	28	22	2190	40	3239	4	England (12)
Paul Tierney	21	0	0	0	0	1	90	-	England
Neil Wood	21	0	0	0	0	0	0	-	England
Forwards									
David Bellion	21	18	14	4	466	22	879	-	France
Diego Forlan	25	30	24	9	1077	32	1539	7	Uruguay (25)
Eddie Johnson	19	0	0	0	0	1	9	-	England
Daniel Nardiello	21	0	0	0	0	1	14	-	England
Louis Saha	25	12	12	8	861	14	981	3	France (2)
Ole Gunnar Solskjaer	31	15	13	5	654	19	881	-	Norway
Ruud van Nistelrooy	28	33	32	30	2751	44	3743	7	Holland (4)

KEY: LEAGUE ALL COMPS CAPS (FIFA RANKING)

TEAM OF THE SEASON

Howard

CG 32 DR 93

Gary Neville

CG 30 DR 117

Ferdinand

CG 19 DR 135

Silvestre

CG 31 DR 98

O'Shea

CG 30 DR 83

Ronaldo

CG 13 SD +62

Keane

CG 22 SD +78

Phil Neville

CG 26 SD +58

Giggs

CG 26 SD +46

Scholes

CG 22 AP 48

Nistelrooy
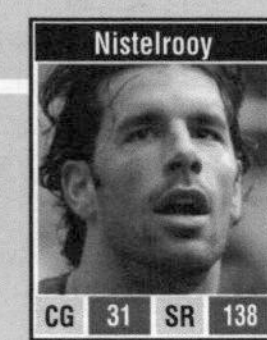
CG 31 SR 138

KEY: DR = Diffensive Rate, SD = Scoring Difference AP = Attacking Power SR = Strike Rate, CG=Counting games – League games playing at least 70 minutes

TOP POINT EARNERS

Rio Ferdinand

Counting Games League games when he played at least 70 minutes	19
Average points Average League points taken in Counting games	2.47
Club Average points Average points taken in League games	1.97

	PLAYER	GAMES	PTS
1	Rio Ferdinand	19	2.47
2	Darren Fletcher	14	2.14
3	Phil Neville	26	2.12
4	Quinton Fortune	17	2.12
5	Roy Keane	22	2.09
6	Paul Scholes	22	2.09
7	Ruud van Nistelrooy	30	2.07
8	Gary Neville	30	2.07
9	Tim Howard	32	2.00
10	Mikael Silvestre	31	1.97

KEY PLAYERS - DEFENDERS

Rio Ferdinand

Goals Conceded The number of League goals conceded while he was on the pitch	13
Goals Conceded in all competitions The number of goals conceded while he was on the pitch in all competitions	16
League minutes played Number of minutes played in league matches	1759
Clean Sheets In games when he played at least70 mins	9
Defensive Rating Average number of mins between League goals conceded while he was on the pitch	135
Club Defensive Rating Average number of mins between League goals conceded by the club this season	98

	PLAYER	CON LGE	CON ALL	MINS	C SHEETS	DEF RATE
1	Rio Ferdinand	13	16	1759	9	135 mins
2	Gary Neville	23	31	2689	12	117 mins
3	Mikael Silvestre	29	35	2848	11	98 mins
4	John O'Shea	34	46	2815	8	83 mins
5	Wes Brown	20	25	1413	4	71 mins

KEY GOALKEEPER

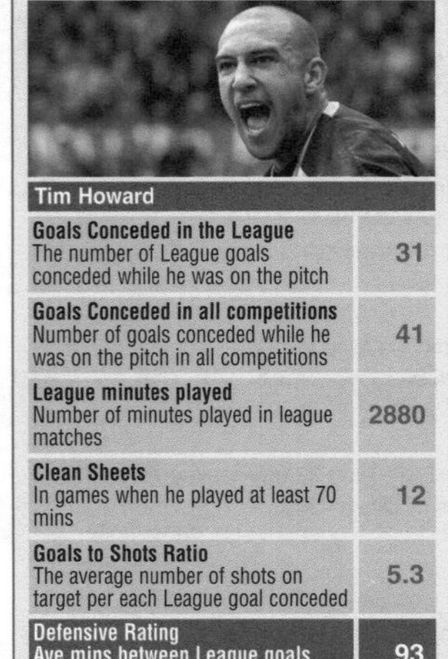

Tim Howard

Goals Conceded in the League The number of League goals conceded while he was on the pitch	31
Goals Conceded in all competitions Number of goals conceded while he was on the pitch in all competitions	41
League minutes played Number of minutes played in league matches	2880
Clean Sheets In games when he played at least 70 mins	12
Goals to Shots Ratio The average number of shots on target per each League goal conceded	5.3
Defensive Rating Ave mins between League goals conceded while on the pitch	93

BOOKINGS

Darren Fletcher

League Yellow	4
League Red	2
All competitions Yellow	4
All competitions Red	2

League Average 241 mins between cards

	PLAYER	LEAGUE Y	LEAGUE R	TOTAL Y	TOTAL R	AVE
1	Fletcher	4 Y	2 R	4 Y	2 R	241
2	Ronaldo	5	0	5	0	311
3	Solskjaer	2	0	2	0	327
4	Scholes	5	0	10	0	438
5	Neville, G	5	0	8	1	537
6	Forlan	2	0	2	0	538
7	Butt	2	0	3	0	554
8	van Nistelrooy	4	0	4	0	687
9	Kleberson	1	0	1	0	787
10	Fortune	2	0	5	0	810
11	Neville, P	3	0	7	0	834
12	Giggs	3	0	3	0	843
13	Djemba-Djemba	1	0	1	0	881
14	Keane	2	0	3	1	1097
15	Brown	1	0	1	0	1413
	Other	3	0	8	0	
	TOTAL	45	2	67	4	

LIVERPOOL

The Champions League berth secured, **Gerard Houllier** fell on his sword. It may have been a lack of cutting edge to his midfield that caused the fans to desert him.

Liverpool had four players charting in the top 20 midfield Defensive Ratings – **Dietmar Hamann** was highest showing the team conceded only one goal for every 101 minutes that he played – but not one got into the top 20 for Attacking Power.

Steven Gerrard did feature in an attacking chart through his combination of eight assists and four league goals, which was among the top ten in the division.

For the second season **Michael Owen** was sixth in the divisional Strike Rate table. He averaged a goal every 157 minutes, compared to 149 last year.

NICKNAME: THE REDS

KEY: Won Drawn Lost

1	prem	**Chelsea**	H	L	1-2	Owen 79 pen
2	prem	**Aston Villa**	A	D	0-0	
3	prem	**Tottenham**	H	D	0-0	
4	prem	**Everton**	A	W	3-0	Owen 39,52; Kewell 80
5	prem	**Blackburn**	A	W	3-1	Owen 12 pen,68; Kewell 90
6	prem	**Leicester**	H	W	2-1	Owen 20 pen; Heskey 75
7	ucr1l1	**O Ljubljana**	A	D	1-1	Owen 78
8	prem	**Charlton**	A	L	2-3	Smicer 15; Owen 52 pen
9	prem	**Arsenal**	H	L	1-2	Kewell 14
10	ucr1l2	**O Ljubljana**	H	W	3-0	Le Tallec 30; Heskey 37; Kewell 47
11	prem	**Portsmouth**	A	L	0-1	
12	prem	**Leeds**	H	W	3-1	Owen 35; Murphy 57; Sinama-Pongolle 84
13	ccr3	**Blackburn**	A	W	4-3	Murphy 41 pen; Heskey 49,61; Kewell 79
14	prem	**Fulham**	A	W	2-1	Heskey 17; Murphy 89 pen
15	ucr2l1	**S Bucharest**	A	D	1-1	Traore 23
16	prem	**Man Utd**	H	L	1-2	Kewell 76
17	prem	**Middlesbrough**	A	D	0-0	
18	ucr2l2	**S Bucharest**	H	W	1-0	Kewell 49
19	prem	**Birmingham**	H	W	3-1	Gerrard 35 pen; Kewell 69; Heskey 78
20	ccr4	**Bolton**	H	L	2-3	Murphy 66; Smicer 88
21	prem	**Newcastle**	A	D	1-1	Murphy 6
22	prem	**Southampton**	H	L	1-2	Heskey 75
23	prem	**Bolton**	H	W	3-1	Hyypia 30; Sinama-Pongolle 47; Smicer 54
24	prem	**Man City**	A	D	2-2	Smicer 66; Hamann 80
25	facr3	**Yeovil**	A	W	2-0	Heskey 70; Murphy 77 pen
26	prem	**Chelsea**	A	W	1-0	Cheyrou 33
27	prem	**Aston Villa**	H	W	1-0	Delaney 36 og
28	prem	**Tottenham**	A	L	1-2	Kewell 75
29	prem	**Wolverhampton**	A	D	1-1	Cheyrou 42
30	facr4	**Newcastle**	H	W	2-1	Cheyrou 2,61
31	prem	**Everton**	H	D	0-0	
32	prem	**Bolton**	A	D	2-2	Hyypia 51; Gerrard 69
33	prem	**Man City**	H	W	2-1	Owen 3; Gerrard 51
34	facr5	**Portsmouth**	H	D	1-1	Owen 2
35	facr5r	**Portsmouth**	A	L	0-1	
36	ucr3l1	**Levski Sofia**	H	W	2-0	Gerrard 67; Kewell 70
37	prem	**Leeds**	A	D	2-2	Kewell 21; Baros 42
38	ucr3l2	**Levski Sofia**	A	W	4-2	Gerrard 7; Owen 11; Hamann 43; Hyypia 67
39	ucr4l1	**Marseille**	H	D	1-1	Baros 55
40	prem	**Southampton**	A	L	0-2	
41	prem	**Portsmouth**	H	W	3-0	Hamann 6; Owen 28,58
42	prem	**Wolves**	H	W	1-0	Hyypia 90
43	ucr4l2	**Marseille**	A	L	1-2	Heskey 15
44	prem	**Leicester**	A	D	0-0	
45	prem	**Blackburn**	H	W	4-0	Owen 7,24; Todd 22 og; Heskey 79
46	prem	**Arsenal**	A	L	2-4	Hyypia 5; Owen 42
47	prem	**Charlton**	H	L	0-1	
48	prem	**Fulham**	H	D	0-0	
49	prem	**Man Utd**	A	W	1-0	Murphy 63 pen
50	prem	**Middlesbrough**	H	W	2-0	Murphy 49 pen; Heskey 53
51	prem	**Birmingham**	A	W	3-0	Owen 29; Heskey 51; Gerrard 86
52	prem	**Newcastle**	H	D	1-1	Owen 67

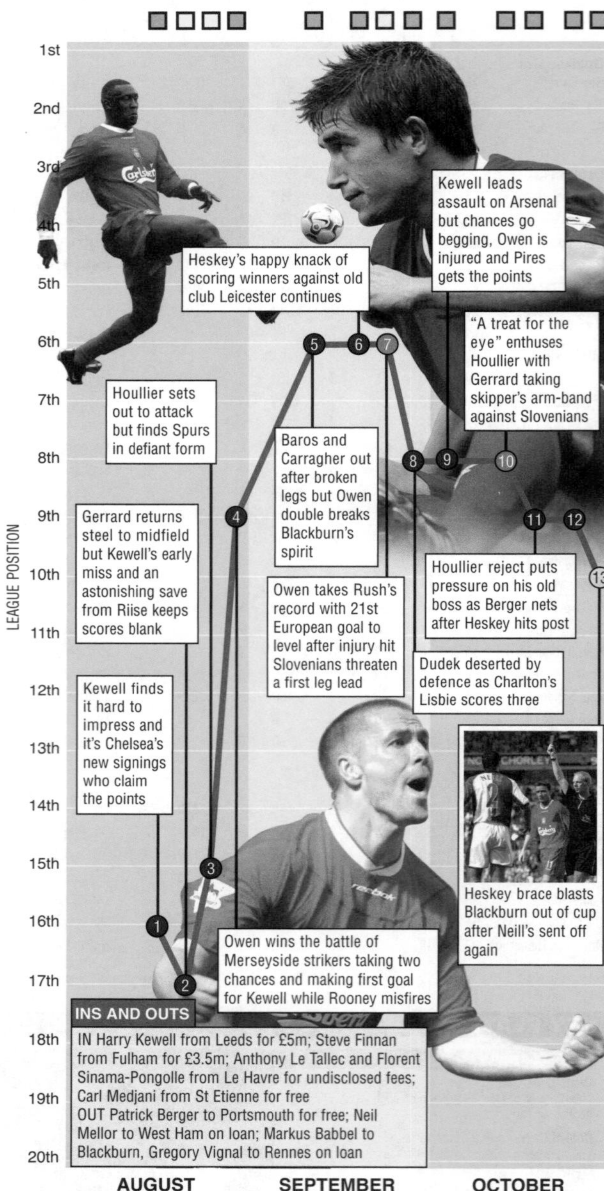

1st
2nd
3rd
4th
5th
6th
7th
8th
9th
10th
11th
12th
13th
14th
15th
16th
17th
18th
19th
20th
LEAGUE POSITION
Kewell leads assault on Arsenal but chances go begging, Owen is injured and Pires gets the points
Heskey's happy knack of scoring winners against old club Leicester continues
"A treat for the eye" enthuses Houllier with Gerrard taking skipper's arm-band against Slovenians
Houllier sets out to attack but finds Spurs in defiant form
Baros and Carragher out after broken legs but Owen double breaks Blackburn's spirit
Gerrard returns steel to midfield but Kewell's early miss and an astonishing save from Riise keeps scores blank
Houllier reject puts pressure on his old boss as Berger nets after Heskey hits post
Owen takes Rush's record with 21st European goal to level after injury hit Slovenians threaten a first leg lead
Dudek deserted by defence as Charlton's Lisbie scores three
Kewell finds it hard to impress and it's Chelsea's new signings who claim the points
Heskey brace blasts Blackburn out of cup after Neill's sent off again
Owen wins the battle of Merseyside strikers taking two chances and making first goal for Kewell while Rooney misfires
INS AND OUTS
IN Harry Kewell from Leeds for £5m; Steve Finnan from Fulham for £3.5m; Anthony Le Tallec and Florent Sinama-Pongolle from Le Havre for undisclosed fees; Carl Medjani from St Etienne for free
OUT Patrick Berger to Portsmouth for free; Neil Mellor to West Ham on loan; Markus Babbel to Blackburn, Gregory Vignal to Rennes on loan
AUGUST
SEPTEMBER
OCTOBER

Home Away Neutral

ATTENDANCES

HOME GROUND: ANFIELD CAPACITY: 45000 AVERAGE LEAGUE AT HOME: 42677

49	Man Utd	67647	12	Leeds	43599	39	Marseille	41270	44	Leicester	32013
21	Newcastle	52151	33	Man City	43257	38	Levski Sofia	40281	5	Blackburn	30074
43	Marseille	50000	23	Bolton	42987	4	Everton	40200	51	Birmingham	29553
24	Man City	47201	10	O Ljubljana	42880	47	Charlton	40003	29	Wolves	29380
9	Arsenal	44374	18	S Bucharest	42837	37	Leeds	39932	32	Bolton	27552
52	Newcastle	44172	19	Birmingham	42683	36	Levski Sofia	39149	8	Charlton	26508
16	Man Utd	44159	2	Aston Villa	42573	46	Arsenal	38119	15	S Bucharest	25000
6	Leicester	44094	48	Fulham	42042	28	Tottenham	36104	11	Portsmouth	20123
1	Chelsea	44082	50	Middlesboro	42031	34	Portsmouth	34669	35	Portsmouth	19529
31	Everton	44056	22	Southampton	41762	41	Portsmouth	34663	14	Fulham	17682
42	Wolves	43795	45	Blackburn	41559	17	Middlesboro	34268	13	Blackburn	16918
3	Tottenham	43778	26	Chelsea	41420	20	Bolton	33185	7	O Ljubljana	10000
27	Aston Villa	43771	30	Newcastle	41365	40	Southampton	32056	25	Yeovil	5348

Fourth's not enough for Owen and Co.

Final Position: **4th**

KEY: League, Champions Lge, UEFA Cup, FA Cup, League Cup, Other

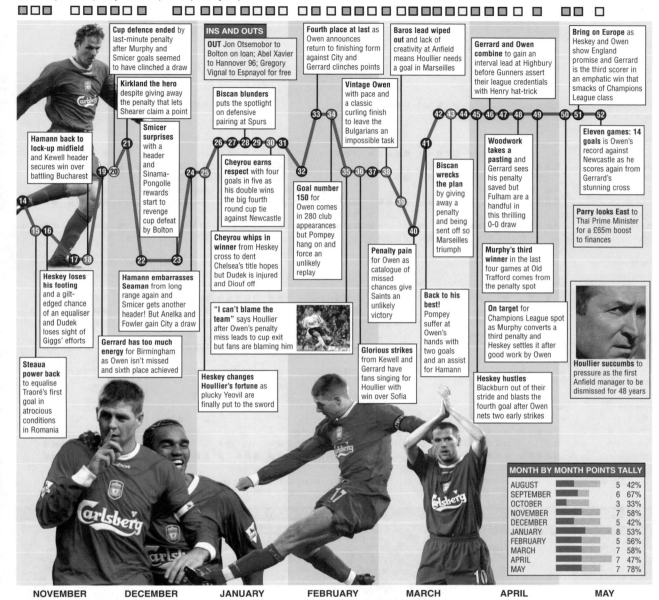

Hamann back to lock-up midfield and Kewell header secures win over battling Bucharest

Steaua power back to equalise Traoré's first goal in atrocious conditions in Romania

Heskey loses his footing and a gilt-edged chance of an equaliser and Dudek loses sight of Giggs' efforts

Cup defence ended by last-minute penalty after Murphy and Smicer goals seemed to have clinched a draw

Kirkland the hero despite giving away the penalty that lets Shearer claim a point

Gerrard has too much energy for Birmingham as Owen isn't missed and sixth place achieved

Smicer surprises with a header and Sinama-Pongolle rewards start to revenge cup defeat by Bolton

Hamann embarrasses Seaman from long range again and Smicer gets another header! But Anelka and Fowler gain City a draw

Heskey changes Houllier's fortune as plucky Yeovil are finally put to the sword

INS AND OUTS

OUT Jon Otsemobor to Bolton on loan; Abel Xavier to Hannover 96; Gregory Vignal to Espnayol for free

Biscan blunders puts the spotlight on defensive pairing at Spurs

Cheyrou earns respect with four goals in five as his double wins the big fourth round cup tie against Newcastle

Cheyrou whips in winner from Heskey cross to dent Chelsea's title hopes but Dudek is injured and Diouf off

"I can't blame the team" says Houllier after Owen's penalty miss leads to cup exit but fans are blaming him

Fourth place at last as Owen announces return to finishing form against City and Gerrard clinches points

Goal number 150 for Owen comes in 280 club appearances but Pompey hang on and force an unlikely replay

Vintage Owen with pace and a classic curling finish to leave the Bulgarians an impossible task

Glorious strikes from Kewell and Gerrard have fans singing for Houllier with win over Sofia

Penalty pain for Owen as catalogue of missed chances give Saints an unlikely victory

Baros lead wiped out and lack of creativity at Anfield means Houllier needs a goal in Marseilles

Back to his best! Pompey suffer at Owen's hands with two goals and an assist for Hamann

Biscan wrecks the plan by giving away a penalty and being sent off so Marseilles triumph

Gerrard and Owen combine to gain an interval lead at Highbury before Gunners assert their league credentials with Henry hat-trick

Woodwork takes a pasting and Gerrard sees his penalty saved but Fulham are a handful in this thrilling 0-0 draw

Heskey hustles Blackburn out of their stride and blasts the fourth goal after Owen nets two early strikes

Murphy's third winner in the last four games at Old Trafford comes from the penalty spot

On target for Champions League spot as Murphy converts a third penalty and Heskey settles it after good work by Owen

Bring on Europe as Heskey and Owen show England promise and Gerrard is the third scorer in an emphatic win that smacks of Champions League class

Eleven games: 14 goals is Owen's record against Newcastle as he scores again from Gerrard's stunning cross

Parry looks East to Thai Prime Minister for a £65m boost to finances

Houllier succumbs to pressure as the first Anfield manager to be dismissed for 48 years

NOVEMBER DECEMBER JANUARY FEBRUARY MARCH APRIL MAY

MONTH BY MONTH POINTS TALLY

Month	Points	%
AUGUST	5	42%
SEPTEMBER	6	67%
OCTOBER	3	33%
NOVEMBER	7	58%
DECEMBER	5	42%
JANUARY	8	53%
FEBRUARY	5	56%
MARCH	7	58%
APRIL	7	47%
MAY	7	78%

GOAL ATTEMPTS

FOR
Goal attempts recorded in League games

	HOME	AWAY	TOTAL	AVE
shots on target	156	144	300	7.9
shots off target	148	110	258	6.8
TOTAL	304	254	558	14.7

Ratio of goals to shots Average number of shots on target per League goal scored: 5.5

Accuracy rating Average percentage of total goal attempts which were on target: 53.8

AGAINST
Goal attempts recorded in League games

	HOME	AWAY	TOTAL	AVE
shots on target	82	101	183	4.8
shots off target	69	144	213	5.6
TOTAL	151	245	396	10.4

Ratio of goals to shots Average number of shots on target per League goal scored: 4.9

Accuracy rating Average percentage of total goal attempts which were on target: 46.2

GOALS

Michael Owen

League	16
FA Cup	1
League Cup	0
Europe	2
Other	0
TOTAL	19

League Average 157 mins between goals

	PLAYER	LGE	FAC	LC	Euro	TOT	AVE
1	Owen	16	1	0	2	19	157
2	Kewell	7	0	1	3	11	445
3	Heskey	7	1	2	2	12	340
4	Hyypia	4	0	0	1	5	855
5	Gerrard	4	0	0	2	6	751
6	Murphy	4	1	2	0	7	470
7	Smicer	3	0	1	0	4	412
8	Hamann	2	0	0	1	3	1108
9	Cheyrou	2	2	0	0	4	348
10	Baros	1	0	0	1	2	608
11	Sinama-Pongolle	1	0	0	0	1	398
12	Le Tallec	0	0	0	1	1	
13	Traore	0	0	0	1	1	
	Other	4	0	0	0	4	
	TOTAL	55	5	6	14	80	

SQUAD APPEARANCES

Match	1 2 3 4 5	6 7 8 9 10	11 12 13 14 15	16 17 18 19 20	21 22 23 24 25	26 27 28 29 30	31 32 33 34 35	36 37 38 39 40	41 42 43 44 45	46 47 48 49 50	51 52
Venue	H A H A A	H A A H H	A H A A A	H A H H H	A H H A A	A H A A H	H A H H A	H A A H A	H H A A H	A H H A H	A H
Competition	L L L L L	L E L L E	L L W L E	L L E L W	L L L L F	L L L L F	L L L F F	E L E E L	L L E L L	L L L L L	L L
Result	L D D W W	W D L L W	L W W W D	L D W W L	D L W D W	W W L D W	D D W D L	W D W D L	W W L D W	L L D W W	W D

Goalkeepers
Patrice Luzi Bernardi
Jerzy Dudek
Paul Harrison
Paul Jones
Chris Kirkland
Patrice Luzi

Defenders
Igor Biscan
Jamie Carragher
Steve Finnan
Stephane Henchoz
Sami Hyypia
Jon Otsemobor
John Arne Riise
Djimi Traore

Midfielders
Bruno Cheyrou
Salif Diao
Steven Gerrard
Dietmar Hamann
Harry Kewell
Anthony Le Tallec
Danny Murphy
Darren Potter
Vladimir Smicer
John Welsh

Forwards
Milan Baros
El Hadji Diouf
Emile Heskey
Michael Owen
Florent Sinama-Pongolle

KEY: On all match | On bench | Subbed or sent off (Counting game) | Subbed or sent off (playing less than 70 mins) | Subbed on from bench (Counting Game) | Subbed on (playing less than 70 mins) | Subbed on and then subbed or sent off (Counting Game) | Subbed on and then subbed or sent off (playing less than 70 mins) | Not in 16

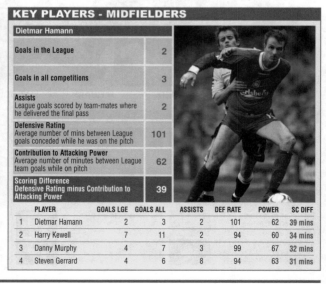

KEY PLAYERS - GOALSCORERS

Michael Owen

Goals in the League	16
Goals in all competitions	19
Assists League goals scored by team-mates where he delivered the final pass	3
Contribution to Attacking Power Average number of minutes between League team goals while on pitch	61
Player Strike Rate Average number of minutes between League goals scored by player	157
Club Strike Rate Average minutes between League goals scored by club	62

	PLAYER	GOALS LGE	GOALS ALL	ASSISTS	POWER	S RATE
1	Michael Owen	16	19	3	61	157 mins
2	Emile Heskey	7	12	5	59	340 mins
3	Harry Kewell	7	11	2	59	445 mins
4	Danny Murphy	4	7	3	67	470 mins
5	Steven Gerrard	4	6	8	62	751 mins

KEY PLAYERS - MIDFIELDERS

Dietmar Hamann

Goals in the League	2
Goals in all competitions	3
Assists League goals scored by team-mates where he delivered the final pass	2
Defensive Rating Average number of mins between League goals conceded while he was on the pitch	101
Contribution to Attacking Power Average number of minutes between League team goals while on pitch	62
Scoring Difference Defensive Rating minus Contribution to Attacking Power	39

	PLAYER	GOALS LGE	GOALS ALL	ASSISTS	DEF RATE	POWER	SC DIFF
1	Dietmar Hamann	2	3	2	101	62	39 mins
2	Harry Kewell	7	11	2	94	60	34 mins
3	Danny Murphy	4	7	3	99	67	32 mins
4	Steven Gerrard	4	6	8	94	63	31 mins

PLAYER APPEARANCES

	AGE (on 01/07/04)	IN NAMED 16	APPEARANCES	COUNTING GAMES	MINUTES ON PITCH	APPEARANCES	MINUTES ON PITCH	THIS SEASON	HOME COUNTRY
Goalkeepers									
Patrice Bernardi	23	18	1	0	14	1	14	-	France
Jerzy Dudek	31	35	30	30	2686	38	3406	-	Poland
Paul Harrison	19	1	0	0	0	0	0	-	England
Paul Jones	37	3	2	2	180	2	180	7	Wales (66)
Chris Kirkland	23	16	6	6	540	12	1080	2	England (12)
Patrice Luzi	23	4	0	0	0	0	0	-	France
Defenders									
Igor Biscan	26	33	29	24	2323	39	3024	-	Croatia
Jamie Carragher	26	23	22	21	1906	29	2536	3	England (12)
Steve Finnan	28	23	22	17	1726	31	2433	-	England
Stephane Henchoz	29	27	19	14	1421	28	2165	-	Switzerland
Sami Hyypia	30	38	38	38	3420	51	4545	4	Finland (42)
Jon Otsemobor	21	4	4	3	297	5	387	-	England
John Arne Riise	23	33	28	23	2140	35	2725	-	Norway
Djimi Traore	24	15	7	5	576	11	912	-	France
Midfielders									
Bruno Cheyrou	26	20	12	6	696	19	1049	1	France (2)
Salif Diao	27	10	3	2	216	7	478	6	Senegal (31)
Steven Gerrard	24	34	34	33	3004	47	4070	5	England (12)
Dietmar Hamann	30	26	25	24	2216	35	3036	4	Germany (9)
Harry Kewell	25	36	36	33	3117	49	4151	2	Australia (89)
Anthony Le Tallec	19	22	12	2	415	22	869	-	France
Danny Murphy	27	35	30	19	1880	41	2616	2	England (12)
Darren Potter	19	0	0	0	0	0	0	-	England
Vladimir Smicer	31	22	20	10	1235	25	1584	3	Czech Republic (10)
John Welsh	20	2	1	0	8	2	12	-	England
Forwards									
Milan Baros	22	18	13	5	608	18	883	4	Czech Republic (10)
El Hadji Diouf	23	28	26	15	1698	33	2153	5	Senegal (31)
Emile Heskey	26	35	34	22	2383	46	3174	8	England (12)
Michael Owen	24	30	29	28	2514	38	3293	5	England (12)
F Sinama-Pongolle	19	18	14	1	398	22	648	-	France

KEY: LEAGUE ALL COMPS CAPS (FIFA RANKING)

TEAM OF THE SEASON

Dudek
CG 30 DR 96
Carragher
CG 21 DR 112
Henchoz
CG 14 DR 102
Hyypia
CG 38 DR 92
Riise
CG 23 DR 93
Murphy
CG 19 SD +32
Gerrard
CG 33 SD +31
Hamann
CG 24 SD +39
Kewell
CG 33 SD +34
Heskey
CG 22 AP 59
Owen
CG 28 SR 157

KEY: DR = Diffensive Rate, SD = Scoring Difference AP = Attacking Power SR = Strike Rate, CG=Counting games – League games playing at least 70 minutes

TOP POINT EARNERS

Dietmar Hamann

Counting Games League games when he played at least 70 minutes	24
Average points Average League points taken in Counting games	1.75
Club Average points Average points taken in League games	1.58

	PLAYER	GAMES	PTS
1	Dietmar Hamann	24	1.75
2	Danny Murphy	19	1.74
3	Michael Owen	28	1.68
4	El Hadji Diouf	15	1.67
5	John Arne Riise	23	1.65
6	Emile Heskey	22	1.64
7	Steven Gerrard	33	1.61
8	Jerzy Dudek	30	1.60
9	Steve Finnan	17	1.59
10	Igor Biscan	24	1.58

KEY PLAYERS - DEFENDERS

Jamie Carragher

Goals Conceded The number of League goals conceded while he was on the pitch	17
Goals Conceded in all competitions The number of goals conceded while he was on the pitch in all competitions	25
League minutes played Number of minutes played in league matches	1906
Clean Sheets In games when he played at least70 mins	12
Defensive Rating Average number of mins between League goals conceded while he was on the pitch	112
Club Defensive Rating Average number of mins between League goals conceded by the club this season	92

	PLAYER	CON LGE	CON ALL	MINS	C SHEETS	DEF RATE
1	Jamie Carragher	17	25	1906	12	112 mins
2	Stephane Henchoz	14	23	1421	6	102 mins
3	John Arne Riise	23	32	2140	9	93 mins
4	Sami Hyypia	37	48	3420	15	92 mins
5	Steve Finnan	20	27	1726	4	86 mins

KEY GOALKEEPER

Jerzy Dudek

Goals Conceded in the League The number of League goals conceded while he was on the pitch	28
Goals Conceded in all competitions Number of goals conceded while he was on the pitch in all competitions	37
League minutes played Number of minutes played in league matches	2686
Clean Sheets In games when he played at least 70 mins	13
Goals to Shots Ratio The average number of shots on target per each League goal conceded	5.5
Defensive Rating Ave mins between League goals conceded while on the pitch	96

BOOKINGS

El Hadji Diouf

League Yellow	11
League Red	1
All competitions Yellow	12
All competitions Red	1

League Average **141** mins between cards

	PLAYER	LEAGUE		TOTAL		AVE
1	El Hadji Diouf	11 Y	1 R	12 Y	1 R	141
2	Baros	2	0	2	0	304
3	Hamann	6	0	6	0	369
4	Finnan	4	0	4	0	431
5	Kewell	6	0	6	0	519
6	Kirkland	1	0	1	0	540
7	Biscan	4	0	4	1	580
8	Henchoz	2	0	3	0	710
9	Murphy	2	0	2	0	940
10	Carragher	2	0	2	0	953
11	Smicer	1	0	2	0	1235
12	Gerrard	2	0	2	0	1502
13	Heskey	1	0	1	0	2383
14	Hyypia	1	0	1	0	3420
	Other	3	0	5	0	
	TOTAL	48	1	53	2	

NEWCASTLE UNITED

Injuries at crucial times cost the Magpies their dream of UEFA Cup glory. **Jonathan Woodgate** claimed the fifth best Defensive Rating in the division, conceding one team goal on average for every 120 minutes played. But he played less than half a season.

Olivier Bernard was next highest and a full 30 minutes worse.

Even when they missed youth and pace they still had **Gary Speed** in midfield, while **Shola Ameobi** deputised for **Craig Bellamy** up front, scoring seven goals in the process- one every 222 minutes. **Alan Shearer** still seems evergreen and irreplaceable enjoying the fourth best Strike Rate in the division with a goal every 151 minutes – up from 180 minutes last year.

Laurent Robert was in the division's top 10 midfielders for his combined league goals and assists total.

NICKNAME: THE MAGPIES KEY: Won Drawn Lost

1	ecql1	**Partizan**	A	W	1-0	Solano 39
2	prem	**Leeds**	A	D	2-2	Shearer 20 pen,88
3	prem	**Man Utd**	H	L	1-2	Shearer 26
4	ecql2	**Partizan**	H	L	3-4*	(*on penalties)
5	prem	**Birmingham**	H	L	0-1	
6	prem	**Everton**	A	D	2-2	Shearer 59 pen,82 pen
7	prem	**Bolton**	H	D	0-0	
8	ucr1l1	**NAC Breda**	H	W	5-0	Bellamy 30,37; Bramble 59; Shearer 77; Ambrose 88
9	prem	**Arsenal**	A	L	2-3	Robert 26; Bernard 71
10	prem	**Southampton**	H	W	1-0	Shearer 44
11	ucr1l2	**NAC Breda**	A	W	1-0	Robert 86
12	prem	**Middlesbrough**	A	W	1-0	Ameobi 21
13	prem	**Fulham**	A	W	3-2	Robert 16; Shearer 51 pen,56
14	prem	**Portsmouth**	H	W	3-0	Speed 17; Shearer 28 pen; Ameobi 61
15	ccr3	**West Brom**	H	L	1-2	Robert 65
16	prem	**Aston Villa**	H	D	1-1	Robert 45
17	ucr2l1	**Basel**	A	W	3-2	Robert 14; Bramble 38; Ameobi 75
18	prem	**Chelsea**	A	L	0-5	
19	prem	**Man City**	H	W	3-0	Ameobi 57; Shearer 77,85
20	ucr2l2	**Basel**	H	W	1-0	Smiljanic 14 og
21	prem	**Wolves**	A	D	1-1	Shearer 31
22	prem	**Liverpool**	H	D	1-1	Shearer 62 pen
23	prem	**Tottenham**	H	W	4-0	Robert 35,55; Shearer 59,66
24	prem	**Charlton**	A	D	0-0	
25	prem	**Leicester**	A	D	1-1	Ambrose 90
26	prem	**Blackburn**	H	L	0-1	
27	facr3	**Southampton**	A	W	3-0	Dyer 24,67; Robert 39
28	prem	**Leeds**	H	W	1-0	Shearer 4
29	prem	**Man Utd**	A	D	0-0	
30	prem	**Fulham**	H	W	3-1	O'Brien 4; Speed 41; Robert 54
31	facr4	**Liverpool**	A	L	1-2	Robert 4
32	prem	**Birmingham**	A	D	1-1	Speed 37
33	prem	**Leicester**	H	W	3-1	Ameobi 30; Taggart 37 og; Jenas 59
34	prem	**Blackburn**	A	D	1-1	Bellamy 52
35	prem	**Middlesbrough**	H	W	2-1	Bellamy 63; Shearer 83 pen
36	ucr3l1	**Valerenga**	A	D	1-1	Bellamy 39
37	prem	**Portsmouth**	A	D	1-1	Bellamy 34
38	ucr3l2	**Valerenga**	H	W	3-1	Shearer 19; Ameobi 47,89
39	ucr4l1	**Mallorca**	H	W	4-1	Bellamy 67; Shearer 71; Robert 74; Bramble 84
40	prem	**Tottenham**	A	L	0-1	
41	prem	**Charlton**	H	W	3-1	Shearer 1,77; Jenas 35
42	ucr4l2	**Mallorca**	A	W	3-0	Shearer 46,89; Bellamy 78
43	prem	**Bolton**	A	L	0-1	
44	prem	**Everton**	H	W	4-2	Bellamy 5; Dyer 21; Shearer 52,90
45	ucqfl1	**PSV Eindhoven**	A	D	1-1	Jenas 45
46	prem	**Arsenal**	H	D	0-0	
47	ucqfl2	**PSV Eindhoven**	H	W	2-1	Shearer 9; Speed 66
48	prem	**Aston Villa**	A	D	0-0	
49	ucsfl1	**Marseille**	H	D	0-0	
50	prem	**Chelsea**	H	W	2-1	Ameobi 44; Shearer 48
51	prem	**Man City**	A	L	0-1	
52	ucsfl2	**Marseille**	A	L	0-2	
53	prem	**Wolves**	H	D	1-1	Bowyer 38
54	prem	**Southampton**	A	D	3-3	Ameobi 7; Bowyer 35; Ambrose 90
55	prem	**Liverpool**	A	D	1-1	Ameobi 25

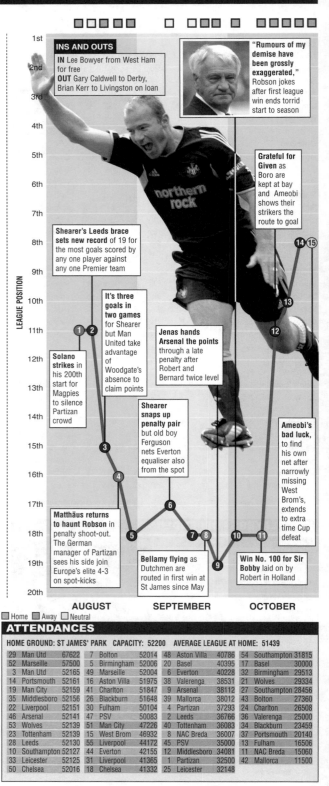

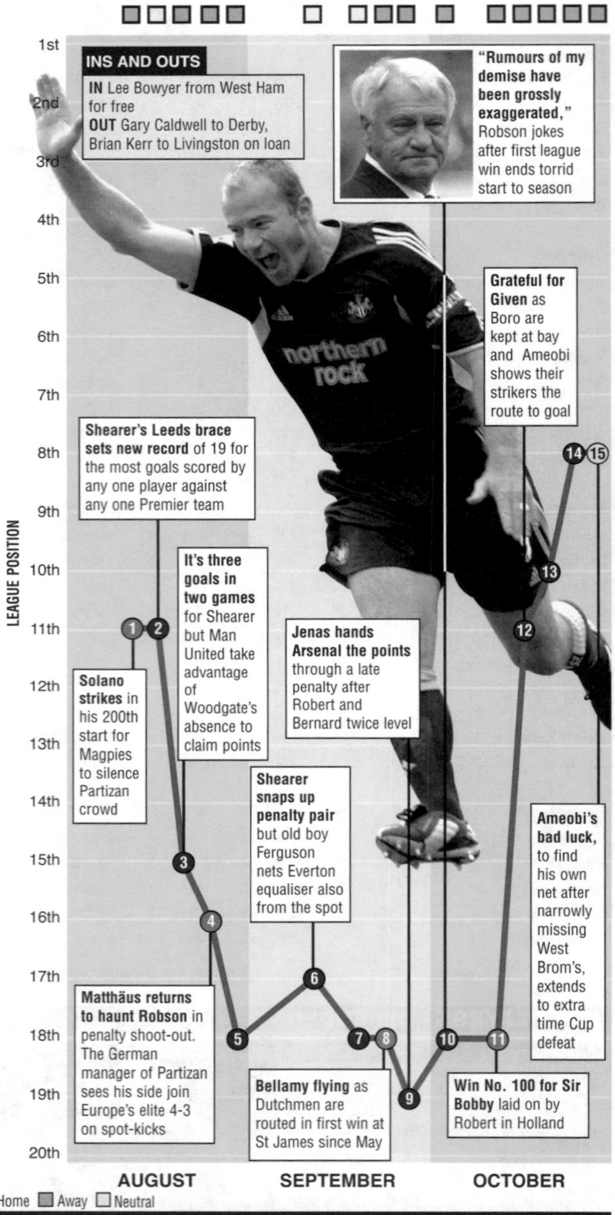

1st 2nd 3rd 4th 5th 6th 7th 8th 9th 10th 11th 12th 13th 14th 15th 16th 17th 18th 19th 20th

LEAGUE POSITION

INS AND OUTS

IN Lee Bowyer from West Ham for free

OUT Gary Caldwell to Derby, Brian Kerr to Livingston on loan

"Rumours of my demise have been grossly exaggerated," Robson jokes after first league win ends torrid start to season

Grateful for Given as Boro are kept at bay and Ameobi shows their strikers the route to goal

Shearer's Leeds brace sets new record of 19 for the most goals scored by any one player against any one Premier team

It's three goals in two games for Shearer but Man United take advantage of Woodgate's absence to claim points

Jenas hands Arsenal the points through a late penalty after Robert and Bernard twice level

Solano strikes in his 200th start for Magpies to silence Partizan crowd

Shearer snaps up penalty pair but old boy Ferguson nets Everton equaliser also from the spot

Ameobi's bad luck, to find his own net after narrowly missing West Brom's, extends to extra time Cup defeat

Matthäus returns to haunt Robson in penalty shoot-out. The German manager of Partizan sees his side join Europe's elite 4-3 on spot-kicks

Bellamy flying as Dutchmen are routed in first win at St James since May

Win No. 100 for Sir Bobby laid on by Robert in Holland

AUGUST SEPTEMBER OCTOBER

Home Away Neutral

ATTENDANCES

HOME GROUND: ST JAMES' PARK CAPACITY: 52200 AVERAGE LEAGUE AT HOME: 51439

29	Man Utd	67622	7	Bolton	52014	48	Aston Villa	40786	54	Southampton	31815
52	Marseille	57500	5	Birmingham	52006	20	Basel	40395	17	Basel	30000
3	Man Utd	52165	49	Marseille	52004	6	Everton	40228	32	Birmingham	29513
14	Portsmouth	52161	16	Aston Villa	51975	38	Valerenga	38531	21	Wolves	29334
19	Man City	52159	41	Charlton	51847	9	Arsenal	38112	27	Southampton	28456
35	Middlesboro	52156	26	Blackburn	51648	39	Mallorca	38012	43	Bolton	27360
22	Liverpool	52151	30	Fulham	50104	4	Partizan	37293	24	Charlton	26508
46	Arsenal	52141	47	PSV	50083	2	Leeds	36766	36	Valerenga	25000
53	Wolves	52139	51	Man City	47226	40	Tottenham	36083	34	Blackburn	23459
23	Tottenham	52139	15	West Brom	46932	8	NAC Breda	36007	37	Portsmouth	20140
28	Leeds	52130	55	Liverpool	44172	45	PSV	35000	13	Fulham	16506
10	Southampton	52127	44	Everton	42155	12	Middlesboro	34081	11	NAC Breda	15060
33	Leicester	52125	31	Liverpool	41365	1	Partizan	32500	42	Mallorca	11500
50	Chelsea	52016	18	Chelsea	41332	25	Leicester	32148			

Injuries cost Shearer's UEFA hopes

Final Position: 5th

KEY: League · Champions Lge · UEFA Cup · FA Cup · League Cup · Other

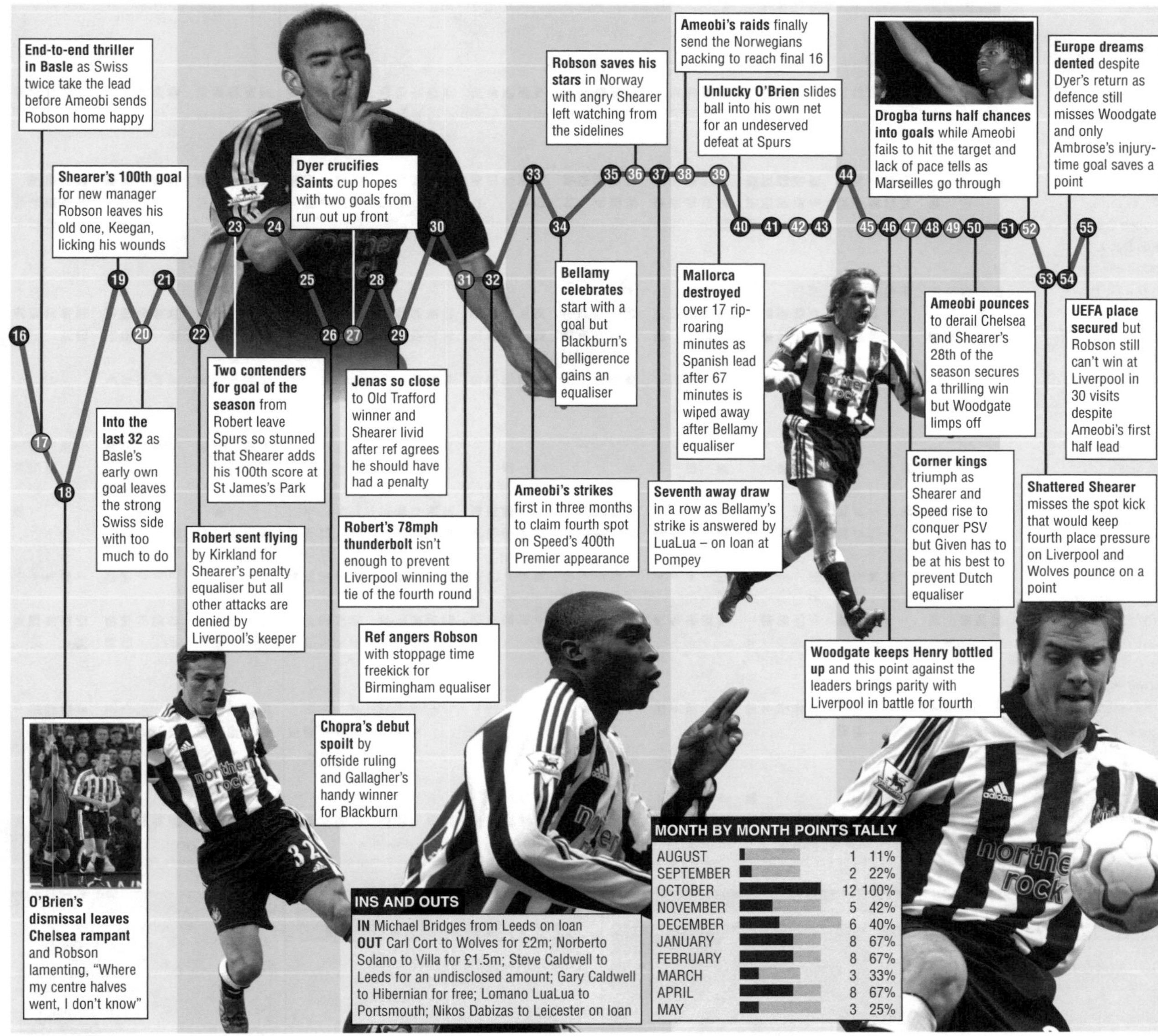

End-to-end thriller in Basle as Swiss twice take the lead before Ameobi sends Robson home happy
O'Brien's dismissal leaves Chelsea rampant and Robson lamenting, "Where my centre halves went, I don't know"
Shearer's 100th goal for new manager Robson leaves his old one, Keegan, licking his wounds
Into the last 32 as Basle's early own goal leaves the strong Swiss side with too much to do
Robert sent flying by Kirkland for Shearer's penalty equaliser but all other attacks are denied by Liverpool's keeper
Two contenders for goal of the season from Robert leave Spurs so stunned that Shearer adds his 100th score at St James's Park
Dyer crucifies Saints cup hopes with two goals from run out up front
Chopra's debut spoilt by offside ruling and Gallagher's handy winner for Blackburn
Jenas so close to Old Trafford winner and Shearer livid after ref agrees he should have had a penalty
Robert's 78mph thunderbolt isn't enough to prevent Liverpool winning the tie of the fourth round
Ref angers Robson with stoppage time freekick for Birmingham equaliser
Ameobi's strikes first in three months to claim fourth spot on Speed's 400th Premier appearance
Bellamy celebrates start with a goal but Blackburn's belligerence gains an equaliser
Robson saves his stars in Norway with angry Shearer left watching from the sidelines
Seventh away draw in a row as Bellamy's strike is answered by LuaLua – on loan at Pompey
Ameobi's raids finally send the Norwegians packing to reach final 16
Mallorca destroyed over 17 rip-roaring minutes as Spanish lead after 67 minutes is wiped away after Bellamy equaliser
Unlucky O'Brien slides ball into his own net for an undeserved defeat at Spurs
Woodgate keeps Henry bottled up and this point against the leaders brings parity with Liverpool in battle for fourth
Corner kings triumph as Shearer and Speed rise to conquer PSV but Given has to be at his best to prevent Dutch equaliser
Drogba turns half chances into goals while Ameobi fails to hit the target and lack of pace tells as Marseilles go through
Ameobi pounces to derail Chelsea and Shearer's 28th of the season secures a thrilling win but Woodgate limps off
Shattered Shearer misses the spot kick that would keep fourth place pressure on Liverpool and Wolves pounce on a point
Europe dreams dented despite Dyer's return as defence still misses Woodgate and only Ambrose's injury-time goal saves a point
UEFA place secured but Robson still can't win at Liverpool in 30 visits despite Ameobi's first half lead
NOVEMBER
DECEMBER
JANUARY
FEBRUARY
MARCH
APRIL
MAY

INS AND OUTS

IN Michael Bridges from Leeds on loan
OUT Carl Cort to Wolves for £2m; Norberto Solano to Villa for £1.5m; Steve Caldwell to Leeds for an undisclosed amount; Gary Caldwell to Hibernian for free; Lomano LuaLua to Portsmouth; Nikos Dabizas to Leicester on loan

MONTH BY MONTH POINTS TALLY

Month	Points	%
AUGUST	1	11%
SEPTEMBER	2	22%
OCTOBER	12	100%
NOVEMBER	5	42%
DECEMBER	6	40%
JANUARY	8	67%
FEBRUARY	8	67%
MARCH	3	33%
APRIL	8	67%
MAY	3	25%

GOAL ATTEMPTS

FOR – Goal attempts recorded in League games

	HOME	AWAY	TOTAL	AVE
shots on target	166	96	262	6.9
shots off target	114	72	186	4.9
TOTAL	280	168	448	11.8

Ratio of goals to shots – Average number of shots on target per League goal scored: **5**

Accuracy rating – Average percentage of total goal attempts which were on target: **58.5**

AGAINST – Goal attempts recorded in League games

	HOME	AWAY	TOTAL	AVE
shots on target	86	118	204	5.4
shots off target	93	96	189	5
TOTAL	179	214	393	10.3

Ratio of goals to shots – Average number of shots on target per League goal scored: **5.1**

Accuracy rating – Average percentage of total goal attempts which were on target: **51.9**

GOALS

Alan Shearer

League	22
FA Cup	0
League Cup	0
Europe	6
Other	0
TOTAL	28

League Average **151** mins between goals

	PLAYER	LGE	FAC	LC	Euro	TOT	AVE
1	Shearer	22	0	0	6	28	151
2	Ameobi	7	0	0	1	8	222
3	Robert	6	2	1	3	12	427
4	Bellamy	4	0	0	4	8	303
5	Speed	3	0	0	1	4	1098
6	Ambrose	2	0	0	0	2	484
7	Jenas	2	0	0	1	3	1193
8	Bowyer	2	0	0	0	2	806
9	O'Brien	1	0	0	0	1	2346
10	Bernard	1	0	0	0	1	3132
11	Dyer	1	2	0	0	3	2156
12	Solano	0	0	0	1	1	
13	Bramble	0	0	0	3	3	
	Other	1	0	0	5	6	
	TOTAL	52	4	1	25	82	

SQUAD APPEARANCES

Match	1 2 3 4 5	6 7 8 9 10	11 12 13 14 15	16 17 18 19 20	21 22 23 24 25	26 27 28 29 30	31 32 33 34 35	36 37 38 39 40	41 42 43 44 45	46 47 48 49 50	51 52 53 54 55
Venue	A A H H H	A H H A H	A A A H H	H A A H H	A H H A A	H A H A H	A A H A H	A A H H A	H A A H A	H H A H H	A A H A A
Competition	C L L C L	L L E L L	E L L L W	L E L L E	L L L L L	L F L L L	F L L L L	E L E E L	L E L L E	L E L E L	L E L L L
Result	W D L L L	D D W L W	W W W W L	D W L W W	D D W D D	L W W D W	L D W D W	D D W W L	W W L W D	D W D D W	L L D D D

Goalkeepers

Tony Caig
Shay Given
Steve Harper

Defenders

Oliver Bernard
Titus Bramble
Stephen Caldwell
Nikos Dabizas
Robbie Elliott
Andrew Griffin
Aaron Hughes
Andy O'Brien
Steven Taylor
Jonathan Woodgate

Midfielders

Darren Ambrose
Lee Bowyer
Martin Brittain
Kieron Dyer
Jermaine Jenas
Bradley Orr
Laurent Robert
Nolberto Solano
Gary Speed
Hugo Viana

Forwards

Shola Ameobi
Craig Bellamy
Michael Bridges
Michael Chopra
Lomana Tresor LuaLua
Alan Shearer

KEY: On all match · On bench · Subbed or sent off (Counting game) · Subbed or sent off (playing less than 70 mins) · Subbed on from bench (Counting Game) · Subbed on (playing less than 70 mins) · Subbed on and then subbed or sent off (Counting Game) · Subbed on and then subbed or sent off (playing less than 70 mins) · Not in 16

KEY PLAYERS - GOALSCORERS

Alan Shearer

Goals in the League	22
Goals in all competitions	28
Assists League goals scored by team-mates where he delivered the final pass	3
Contribution to Attacking Power Average number of minutes between League team goals while on pitch	63
Player Strike Rate Average number of minutes between League goals scored by player	151
Club Strike Rate Average minutes between League goals scored by club	66

	PLAYER	GOALS LGE	GOALS ALL	ASSISTS	POWER	S RATE
1	Alan Shearer	22	28	3	63	151 mins
2	Shola Ameobi	7	8	3	48	222 mins
3	Craig Bellamy	4	8	0	80	303 mins
4	Laurent Robert	6	12	7	65	427 mins
5	Lee Bowyer	2	2	1	67	806 mins

KEY PLAYERS - MIDFIELDERS

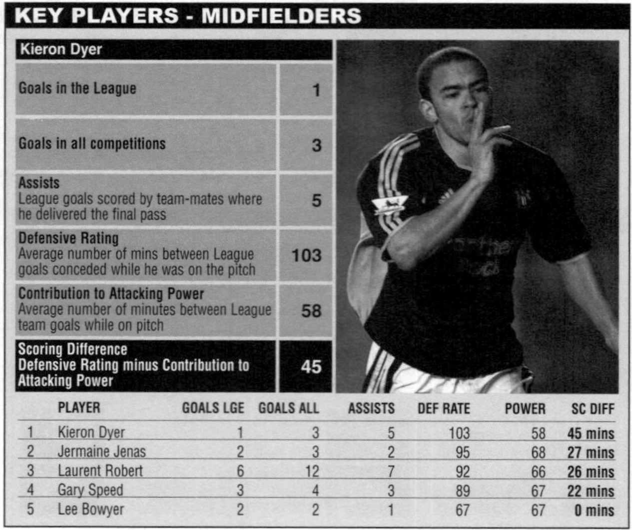

Kieron Dyer

Goals in the League	1
Goals in all competitions	3
Assists League goals scored by team-mates where he delivered the final pass	5
Defensive Rating Average number of mins between League goals conceded while he was on the pitch	103
Contribution to Attacking Power Average number of minutes between League team goals while on pitch	58
Scoring Difference Defensive Rating minus Contribution to Attacking Power	45

	PLAYER	GOALS LGE	GOALS ALL	ASSISTS	DEF RATE	POWER	SC DIFF
1	Kieron Dyer	1	3	5	103	58	45 mins
2	Jermaine Jenas	2	3	2	95	68	27 mins
3	Laurent Robert	6	12	7	92	66	26 mins
4	Gary Speed	3	4	3	89	67	22 mins
5	Lee Bowyer	2	2	1	67	67	0 mins

PLAYER APPEARANCES

	AGE (on 01/07/04)	IN NAMED 16	APPEARANCES	COUNTING GAMES	MINUTES ON PITCH	APPEARANCES	MINUTES ON PITCH	THIS SEASON	HOME COUNTRY
Goalkeepers									
Tony Caig	30	3	0	0	0	0	0	-	England
Shay Given	28	38	38	38	3420	53	4800	8	Rep of Ireland (15)
Steve Harper	30	35	0	0	0	2	210	-	England
Defenders									
Oliver Bernard	24	36	35	35	3132	51	4625	-	France
Titus Bramble	22	31	28	26	2397	41	3571	-	England
Stephen Caldwell	23	10	5	3	328	7	461	6	Scotland (63)
Nikos Dabizas	30	1	0	0	0	0	0	-	Greece
Robbie Elliott	30	5	0	0	0	0	0	-	England
Andrew Griffin	25	13	5	5	438	8	738	-	England
Aaron Hughes	24	37	34	32	2962	47	4162	4	N Ireland (114)
Andy O'Brien	25	30	28	25	2346	42	3549	6	Rep of Ireland (15)
Steven Taylor	18	3	1	1	90	2	100	-	England
Jonathan Woodgate	24	21	18	17	1562	27	2402	1	England (12)
Midfielders									
Darren Ambrose	20	28	24	10	968	37	1552	-	England
Lee Bowyer	27	26	25	18	1612	26	1638	-	England
Martin Brittain	19	2	1	0	17	2	32	-	England
Kieron Dyer	25	25	25	23	2156	34	2901	6	England (12)
Jermaine Jenas	21	31	31	25	2385	46	3624	3	England (12)
Bradley Orr	21	0	0	0	0	0	0	-	England
Laurent Robert	29	35	35	29	2562	52	3903	-	France
Nolberto Solano	29	14	12	7	712	20	1303	-	Peru
Gary Speed	34	38	38	37	3294	54	4704	7	Wales (66)
Hugo Viana	21	31	16	3	552	27	1036	3	Portugal (20)
Forwards									
Shola Ameobi	22	32	26	16	1554	41	2506	-	England
Craig Bellamy	24	16	16	12	1210	24	1801	5	Wales (66)
Michael Bridges	25	7	6	0	72	9	178	-	England
Michael Chopra	20	10	6	1	135	6	135	-	England
Lomana LuaLua	23	13	7	2	226	11	377	-	Congo DR
Alan Shearer	34	37	37	37	3311	52	4623	-	England

KEY: LEAGUE ALL COMPS CAPS (FIFA RANKING)

TEAM OF THE SEASON

Given CG 38 DR 86

Hughes CG 32 DR 85

Woodgate CG 17 DR 120

O'Brien CG 25 DR 87

Bernard CG 35 DR 87

Dyer CG 23 SD +45

Speed CG 37 SD +22

Jenas CG 25 SD +27

Robert CG 29 SD +26

Bellamy CG 12 AP 80

Shearer CG 37 SR 151

KEY: DR = Diffensive Rate, SD = Scoring Difference AP = Attacking Power SR = Strike Rate, CG=Counting games – League games playing at least 70 minutes

TOP POINT EARNERS

Shola Ameobi

Counting Games League games when he played at least 70 minutes	16
Average points Average League points taken in Counting games	1.81
Club Average points Average points taken in League games	1.47

	PLAYER	GAMES	PTS
1	Shola Ameobi	16	**1.81**
2	Jonathan Woodgate	17	**1.71**
3	Kieron Dyer	23	**1.57**
4	Oliver Bernard	35	**1.57**
5	Aaron Hughes	32	**1.56**
6	Jermaine Jenas	25	**1.56**
7	Alan Shearer	37	**1.51**
8	Gary Speed	37	**1.51**
9	Andy O'Brien	25	**1.48**
10	Shay Given	38	**1.47**

KEY PLAYERS - DEFENDERS

Jonathan Woodgate

Goals Conceded The number of League goals conceded while he was on the pitch	13
Goals Conceded in all competitions The number of goals conceded while he was on the pitch in all competitions	19
League minutes played Number of minutes played in league matches	1562
Clean Sheets In games when he played at least70 mins	6
Defensive Rating Average number of mins between League goals conceded while he was on the pitch	120
Club Defensive Rating Average number of mins between League goals conceded by the club this season	86

	PLAYER	CON LGE	CON ALL	MINS	C SHEETS	DEF RATE
1	Jonathan Woodgate	13	19	1562	6	**120 mins**
2	Andy O'Brien	27	37	2346	6	**87 mins**
3	Oliver Bernard	36	49	3132	11	**87 mins**
4	Aaron Hughes	35	47	2962	10	**85 mins**
5	Titus Bramble	33	44	2397	6	**73 mins**

KEY GOALKEEPER

Shay Given

Goals Conceded in the League The number of League goals conceded while he was on the pitch	40
Goals Conceded in all competitions Number of goals conceded while he was on the pitch in all competitions	52
League minutes played Number of minutes played in league matches	3420
Clean Sheets In games when he played at least 70 mins	11
Goals to Shots Ratio The average number of shots on target per each League goal conceded	5.1
Defensive Rating Ave mins between League goals conceded while on the pitch	86

BOOKINGS

Hugo Viana

League Yellow	2
League Red	0
All competitions Yellow	3
All competitions Red	0

League Average 276 mins between cards

	PLAYER	LEAGUE		TOTAL		AVE
1	Viana	2 Y	0 R	3 Y	0 R	276
2	Ambrose	3	0	3	0	322
3	Bowyer	5	0	6	0	322
4	Bramble	7	0	9	0	342
5	Bellamy	3	0	4	0	403
6	Woodgate	3	0	3	0	520
7	Speed	6	0	6	0	549
8	O'Brien	2	2	5	2	586
9	Robert	3	1	3	1	640
10	Bernard	4	0	7	0	783
11	Jenas	3	0	5	0	795
12	Dyer	1	0	2	0	2156
13	Shearer	1	0	3	0	3311
14	Given	1	0	1	0	3420
	Other	4	0	8	0	
	TOTAL	**48**	**3**	**68**	**3**	

ASTON VILLA

From relegation scrap to within goal-difference of Europe is the measure of **David O'Leary's** achievement.

His team were in the bottom three in late November yet (briefly) fourth by early May.

Juan Pablo Ángel barely played any full games under Graham Taylor the previous season with only five Counting Games where he was able to influence affairs on the pitch for 70 minutes.

He scored just one league goal and was branded an expensive flop. But for O'Leary he netted 16 (a third of Villa's total) and his 23 in all competitions is the fourth highest in the division.

Gareth Barry's success in midfield is underlined by adding his three goals to his ten assists. The combined total of 13 is the eighth best in the Premiership.

NICKNAME: THE VILLANS KEY: Won Drawn Lost

1	prem	**Portsmouth**	A	L	1-2	Barry 84 pen
2	prem	**Liverpool**	H	D	0-0	
3	prem	**Arsenal**	A	L	0-2	
4	prem	**Leicester**	H	W	3-1	Thatcher 8 og; Angel 10,16
5	prem	**Man City**	A	L	1-4	Angel 31
6	prem	**Charlton**	H	W	2-1	Alpay 37; Samuel 55
7	ccr2	**Wycombe**	A	W	5-0	Whittingham 14; Angel 31,50 pen,55; Vassell 86 pen
8	prem	**Chelsea**	A	L	0-1	
9	prem	**Bolton**	H	D	1-1	Angel 58
10	prem	**Birmingham**	A	D	0-0	
11	prem	**Everton**	H	D	0-0	
12	ccr3	**Leicester**	H	W	1-0	Hitzlsperger 75
13	prem	**Newcastle**	A	D	1-1	Dublin 11
14	prem	**Middlesbrough**	H	L	0-2	
15	prem	**Tottenham**	A	L	1-2	Allback 66
16	prem	**Southampton**	H	W	1-0	Dublin 45
17	ccr4	**Crystal Palace**	H	W	3-0	Symons 22 og; McCann 70; Angel 79
18	prem	**Man Utd**	A	L	0-4	
19	prem	**Wolves**	H	W	3-2	Angel 21,24; Barry 48
20	ccqf	**Chelsea**	H	W	2-1	Angel 16; McCann 78
21	prem	**Blackburn**	A	W	2-0	Moore 62; Angel 75
22	prem	**Leeds**	A	D	0-0	
23	prem	**Fulham**	H	W	3-0	Angel 33; Vassell 67,82
24	facr3	**Man Utd**	H	L	1-2	Barry 19
25	prem	**Portsmouth**	H	W	2-1	Angel 22; Vassell 84
26	prem	**Liverpool**	A	L	0-1	
27	prem	**Arsenal**	H	L	0-2	
28	ccsfl1	**Bolton**	A	L	2-5	Angel 20,56
29	ccsfl2	**Bolton**	H	W	2-0	Hitzlsperger 10; Samuel 88
30	prem	**Leicester**	A	W	5-0	Vassell 50,60; Crouch 57,68; Dublin 64
31	prem	**Leeds**	H	W	2-0	Angel 45 pen; Johnsen 59
32	prem	**Fulham**	A	W	2-1	Angel 13; Vassell 32
33	prem	**Birmingham**	H	D	2-2	Vassell 21; Hitzlsperger 47
34	prem	**Everton**	A	L	0-2	
35	prem	**Wolves**	A	W	4-0	Hitzlsperger 7; Mellberg 18; Angel 24,59
36	prem	**Blackburn**	H	L	0-2	
37	prem	**Charlton**	A	W	2-1	Vassell 24; Samuel 54
38	prem	**Man City**	H	D	1-1	Angel 26
39	prem	**Bolton**	A	D	2-2	Crouch 18; Hendrie 53
40	prem	**Chelsea**	H	W	3-2	Vassell 39 pen; Hitzlsperger 49; Hendrie 52
41	prem	**Newcastle**	H	D	0-0	
42	prem	**Middlesbrough**	A	W	2-1	Barry 45; Crouch 89
43	prem	**Tottenham**	H	W	1-0	Angel 5
44	prem	**Southampton**	A	D	1-1	Angel 39 pen
45	prem	**Man Utd**	H	L	0-2	

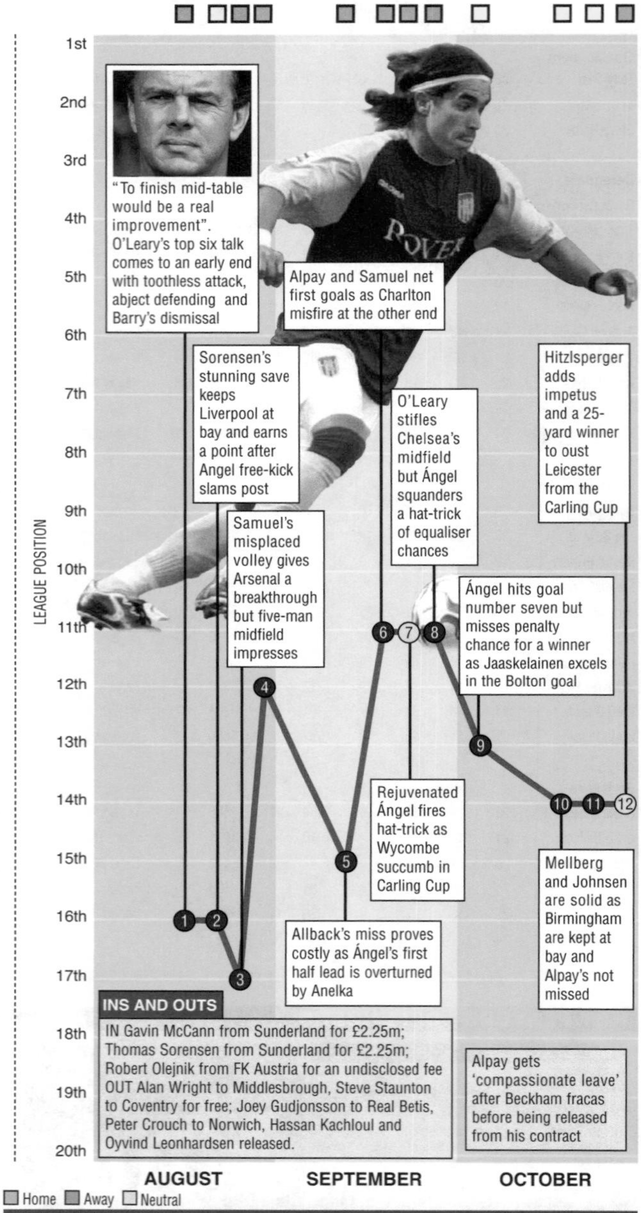

LEAGUE POSITION

1st 2nd 3rd 4th 5th 6th 7th 8th 9th 10th 11th 12th 13th 14th 15th 16th 17th 18th 19th 20th

"To finish mid-table would be a real improvement". O'Leary's top six talk comes to an early end with toothless attack, abject defending and Barry's dismissal

Sorensen's stunning save keeps Liverpool at bay and earns a point after Angel free-kick slams post

Samuel's misplaced volley gives Arsenal a breakthrough but five-man midfield impresses

Alpay and Samuel net first goals as Charlton misfire at the other end

Allback's miss proves costly as Ángel's first half lead is overturned by Anelka

Rejuvenated Ángel fires hat-trick as Wycombe succumb in Carling Cup

O'Leary stifles Chelsea's midfield but Ángel squanders a hat-trick of equaliser chances

Ángel hits goal number seven but misses penalty chance for a winner as Jaaskelainen excels in the Bolton goal

Hitzlsperger adds impetus and a 25-yard winner to oust Leicester from the Carling Cup

Mellberg and Johnsen are solid as Birmingham are kept at bay and Alpay's not missed

Alpay gets 'compassionate leave' after Beckham fracas before being released from his contract

INS AND OUTS

IN Gavin McCann from Sunderland for £2.25m; Thomas Sorensen from Sunderland for £2.25m; Robert Olejnik from FK Austria for an undisclosed fee OUT Alan Wright to Middlesbrough, Steve Staunton to Coventry for free; Joey Gudjonsson to Real Betis, Peter Crouch to Norwich, Hassan Kachloul and Oyvind Leonhardsen released.

AUGUST SEPTEMBER OCTOBER

Home Away Neutral

ATTENDANCES

HOME GROUND: VILLA PARK CAPACITY: 43275 AVERAGE LEAGUE AT HOME: 36621

18	Man Utd	67621	27	Arsenal	39380	4	Leicester	32274	12	Leicester	26729
13	Newcastle	51975	34	Everton	39353	44	Southampton	32054	39	Bolton	26374
5	Man City	46687	31	Leeds	39171	6	Charlton	31410	37	Charlton	26250
26	Liverpool	43771	22	Leeds	38513	42	Middlesboro	31322	17	Crystal Palace	24258
45	Man Utd	42573	3	Arsenal	38010	16	Southampton	31285	21	Blackburn	20722
2	Liverpool	42573	38	Man City	37602	30	Leicester	31056	1	Portsmouth	20101
43	Tottenham	42573	36	Blackburn	37532	20	Chelsea	30414	28	Bolton	16302
8	Chelsea	41182	19	Wolves	36964	9	Bolton	30229	32	Fulham	16153
40	Chelsea	41112	29	Bolton	36883	14	Middlesboro	29898	7	Wycombe	6072
41	Newcastle	40786	11	Everton	36146	10	Birmingham	29546			
24	Man Utd	40371	23	Fulham	35617	35	Wolves	29386			
33	Birmingham	40061	15	Tottenham	33140	25	Portsmouth	28625			

O'Leary's faith in Ángel is rewarded

Final Position: **6th**

KEY: League, Champions Lge, UEFA Cup, FA Cup, League Cup, Other

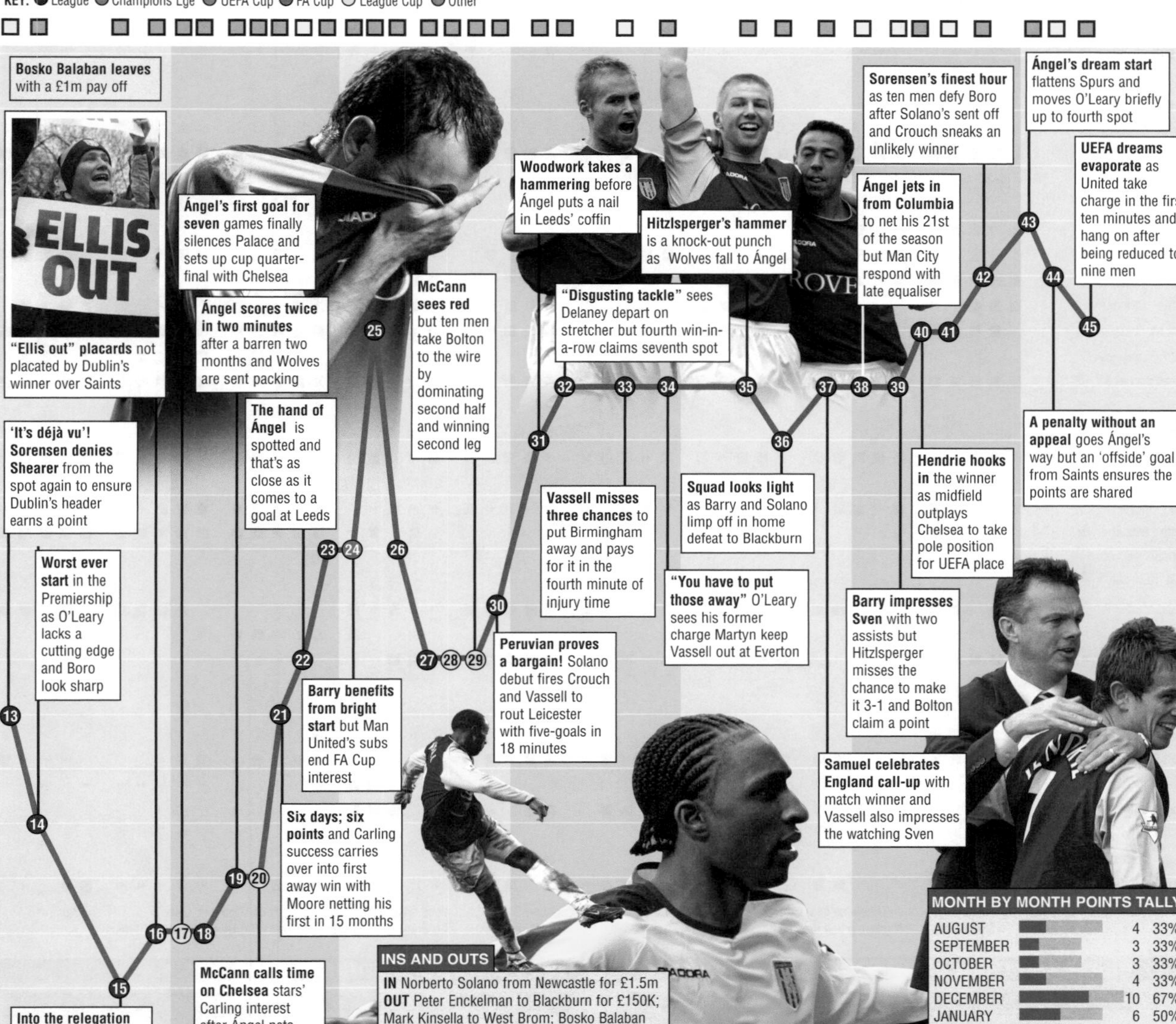

Bosko Balaban leaves with a £1m pay off
ELLIS OUT
"Ellis out" placards not placated by Dublin's winner over Saints
'It's déjà vu'! Sorensen denies Shearer from the spot again to ensure Dublin's header earns a point
Worst ever start in the Premiership as O'Leary lacks a cutting edge and Boro look sharp
Into the relegation zone after Allbäck's header only serves to wake up Spurs and Keane hits the winner
Ángel's first goal for seven games finally silences Palace and sets up cup quarter-final with Chelsea
Ángel scores twice in two minutes after a barren two months and Wolves are sent packing
The hand of Ángel is spotted and that's as close as it comes to a goal at Leeds
McCann calls time on Chelsea stars' Carling interest after Ángel nets 11th of the season
Six days; six points and Carling success carries over into first away win with Moore netting his first in 15 months
Barry benefits from bright start but Man United's subs end FA Cup interest
McCann sees red but ten men take Bolton to the wire by dominating second half and winning second leg
Woodwork takes a hammering before Ángel puts a nail in Leeds' coffin
Peruvian proves a bargain! Solano debut fires Crouch and Vassell to rout Leicester with five-goals in 18 minutes
"Disgusting tackle" sees Delaney depart on stretcher but fourth win-in-a-row claims seventh spot
Vassell misses three chances to put Birmingham away and pays for it in the fourth minute of injury time
Hitzlsperger's hammer is a knock-out punch as Wolves fall to Ángel
Squad looks light as Barry and Solano limp off in home defeat to Blackburn
"You have to put those away" O'Leary sees his former charge Martyn keep Vassell out at Everton
Sorensen's finest hour as ten men defy Boro after Solano's sent off and Crouch sneaks an unlikely winner
Ángel jets in from Columbia to net his 21st of the season but Man City respond with late equaliser
Hendrie hooks in the winner as midfield outplays Chelsea to take pole position for UEFA place
Barry impresses Sven with two assists but Hitzlsperger misses the chance to make it 3-1 and Bolton claim a point
Samuel celebrates England call-up with match winner and Vassell also impresses the watching Sven
Ángel's dream start flattens Spurs and moves O'Leary briefly up to fourth spot
UEFA dreams evaporate as United take charge in the first ten minutes and hang on after being reduced to nine men
A penalty without an appeal goes Ángel's way but an 'offside' goal from Saints ensures the points are shared
INS AND OUTS
IN Norberto Solano from Newcastle for £1.5m
OUT Peter Enckelman to Blackburn for £150K; Mark Kinsella to West Brom; Bosko Balaban Club Brugge for free; Mustapha Hadji to Espanyol on loan
MONTH BY MONTH POINTS TALLY
AUGUST 4 33%
SEPTEMBER 3 33%
OCTOBER 3 33%
NOVEMBER 4 33%
DECEMBER 10 67%
JANUARY 6 50%
FEBRUARY 7 58%
MARCH 6 67%
APRIL 9 60%
MAY 4 44%
NOVEMBER
DECEMBER
JANUARY
FEBRUARY
MARCH
APRIL
MAY

GOAL ATTEMPTS

FOR — Goal attempts recorded in League games

	HOME	AWAY	TOTAL	AVE
shots on target	130	98	228	6
shots off target	110	100	210	5.5
TOTAL	240	198	438	11.5

Ratio of goals to shots — Average number of shots on target per League goal scored: **4.8**

Accuracy rating — Average percentage of total goal attempts which were on target: **52.1**

AGAINST — Goal attempts recorded in League games

	HOME	AWAY	TOTAL	AVE
shots on target	93	138	231	6.1
shots off target	90	98	188	4.9
TOTAL	183	236	419	11

Ratio of goals to shots — Average number of shots on target per League goal scored: **5.3**

Accuracy rating — Average percentage of total goal attempts which were on target: **55.1**

GOALS

Juan Pablo Angel

League	16
FA Cup	0
League Cup	7
Europe	0
Other	0
TOTAL	23

League Average: 172 mins between goals

	PLAYER	LGE	FAC	LC	Euro	TOT	AVE
1	Angel	16	0	7	0	23	172
2	Vassell	9	0	1	0	10	253
3	Crouch	4	0	0	0	4	147
4	Hitzlsperger	3	0	2	0	5	744
5	Barry	3	1	0	0	4	1002
6	Dublin	3	0	0	0	3	393
7	Samuel	2	0	1	0	3	1710
8	Hendrie	2	0	0	0	2	1293
9	Allback	1	0	0	0	1	754
10	Johnsen	1	0	0	0	1	1875
11	Alpay	1	0	0	0	1	428
12	Mellberg	1	0	0	0	1	2916
13	Whittingham	0	0	1	0	1	
14	McCann	0	0	2	0	2	
	Other	2	0	1	0	3	
	TOTAL	48	1	15	0	64	

SQUAD APPEARANCES

Match	1	2	3	4	5	6	7	8	9	10	11	12	13	14	15	16	17	18	19	20	21	22	23	24	25	26	27	28	29	30	31	32	33	34	35	36	37	38	39	40	41	42	43	44	45
Venue	A	H	A	H	A	H	A	A	H	A	H	H	A	H	A	H	H	A	H	H	A	A	H	H	H	A	H	A	H	A	H	A	H	A	A	H	A	H	A	H	H	A	H	A	H
Competition	L	L	L	L	L	L	W	L	L	L	L	W	L	L	L	L	W	L	L	W	L	L	L	F	L	L	L	W	W	L	L	L	L	L	L	L	L	L	L	L	L	L	L	L	L
Result	L	D	L	W	L	W	W	L	D	D	D	W	D	L	L	W	W	L	W	W	W	D	W	L	W	L	L	L	W	W	W	W	D	L	W	L	W	D	D	W	D	W	W	D	L

Goalkeepers

Stefan Postma
Thomas Sorensen

Defenders

Alpay Ozalan
Ulises De La Cruz
Mark Delaney
Ronny Johnsen
Olof Mellberg
Liam Ridgewell
Jlloyd Samuel

Midfielders

Gareth Barry
Moustapha Hadji
Lee Hendrie
Tomas Hitzlsperger
Hassan Kachloul
Mark Kinsella
Gavin McCann
Nolberto Solano
Peter Whittingham

Forwards

Marcus Allback
Juan Pablo Angel
Peter Crouch
Dion Dublin
Luke Moore
Stefan Moore
Darius Vassell

KEY: On all match · On bench · Subbed or sent off (Counting game) · Subbed or sent off (playing less than 70 mins) · Subbed on from bench (Counting Game) · Subbed on (playing less than 70 mins) · Subbed on and then subbed or sent off (Counting Game) · Subbed on and then subbed or sent off (playing less than 70 mins) · Not in 16

KEY PLAYERS - GOALSCORERS

Juan Pablo Angel

Goals in the League	16
Goals in all competitions	23
Assists League goals scored by team-mates where he delivered the final pass	2
Contribution to Attacking Power Average number of minutes between League team goals while on pitch	78
Player Strike Rate Average number of minutes between League goals scored by player	172
Club Strike Rate Average minutes between League goals scored by club	71

	PLAYER	GOALS LGE	GOALS ALL	ASSISTS	POWER	S RATE
1	Juan Pablo Angel	16	23	2	78	172 mins
2	Darius Vassell	9	10	2	56	253 mins
3	Tomas Hitzlsperger	3	5	6	57	744 mins
4	Gareth Barry	3	4	10	69	1002 mins
5	Lee Hendrie	2	2	3	73	1293 mins

KEY PLAYERS - MIDFIELDERS

Gareth Barry

Goals in the League	3
Goals in all competitions	4
Assists League goals scored by team-mates where he delivered the final pass	10
Defensive Rating Average number of mins between League goals conceded while he was on the pitch	84
Contribution to Attacking Power Average number of minutes between League team goals while on pitch	70
Scoring Difference Defensive Rating minus Contribution to Attacking Power	14

	PLAYER	GOALS LGE	GOALS ALL	ASSISTS	DEF RATE	POWER	SC DIFF
1	Gareth Barry	3	4	10	84	70	14 mins
2	Gavin McCann	0	2	1	79	66	13 mins
3	Tomas Hitzlsperger	3	5	6	70	57	13 mins
4	Lee Hendrie	2	2	3	70	74	-4 mins
5	Peter Whittingham	0	1	3	72	122	-50 mins

PLAYER APPEARANCES

	AGE (on 01/07/04)	IN NAMED 16	APPEARANCES	COUNTING GAMES	MINUTES ON PITCH	APPEARANCES	MINUTES ON PITCH	THIS SEASON	HOME COUNTRY
Goalkeepers									
Stefan Postma	27	38	2	0	85	2	85	-	Holland
Thomas Sorensen	28	38	38	36	3335	45	3965	8	Denmark (14)
Defenders									
Alpay Ozalan	31	8	6	4	428	6	428	-	Turkey
Ulises De La Cruz	29	33	28	19	1846	32	2172	-	Ecuador
Mark Delaney	28	28	25	22	2040	30	2490	7	Wales (66)
Ronny Johnsen	35	28	23	19	1875	27	2182	-	Norway
Olof Mellberg	26	34	33	32	2916	39	3413	7	Sweden (21)
Liam Ridgewell	19	22	11	5	500	13	526	-	England
Jlloyd Samuel	23	38	38	38	3420	45	4050	-	England
Midfielders									
Gareth Barry	23	36	36	32	3006	43	3583	-	England
Moustapha Hadji	32	1	1	0	25	1	25	-	Morocco
Lee Hendrie	27	32	32	26	2585	37	2910	-	England
Tomas Hitzlsperger	22	36	32	22	2233	38	2539	-	Germany
Hassan Kachloul	31	1	0	0	0	0	0	-	Morocco
Mark Kinsella	31	8	2	0	104	2	104	7	Rep of Ireland (15)
Gavin McCann	26	28	28	27	2449	35	3028	-	England
Nolberto Solano	29	10	10	7	799	10	799	-	Peru
Peter Whittingham	19	36	32	16	1957	39	2470	-	England
Forwards									
Marcus Allback	31	19	15	5	754	19	895	6	Sweden (21)
Juan Pablo Angel	28	33	33	29	2758	39	3261	-	Colombia
Peter Crouch	23	21	16	3	588	18	686	-	England
Dion Dublin	35	31	23	11	1178	28	1533	-	England
Luke Moore	18	7	7	0	146	7	146	-	England
Stefan Moore	20	10	8	0	260	12	421	-	England
Darius Vassell	24	32	32	20	2277	39	2732	3	England (12)

KEY: LEAGUE ALL COMPS CAPS (FIFA RANKING)

TEAM OF THE SEASON

Sorensen — CG 36 DR 79

De La Cruz — CG 19 DR 84
Mellberg — CG 32 DR 86
Johnsen — CG 19 DR 82
Samuel — CG 38 DR 78

Hendrie — CG 26 SD -4
Hitzlsperger — CG 22 SD +13
McCann — CG 27 SD +13
Barry — CG 32 SD +14

Vassell — CG 20 AP 56
Angel — CG 29 SR 172

KEY: DR = Diffensive Rate, SD = Scoring Difference AP = Attacking Power SR = Strike Rate, CG=Counting games – League games playing at least 70 minutes

TOP POINT EARNERS

Darius Vassell

Counting Games League games when he played at least 70 minutes	20
Average points Average League points taken in Counting games	1.80
Club Average points Average points taken in League games	1.47

	PLAYER	GAMES	PTS
1	Darius Vassell	20	1.80
2	Gavin McCann	27	1.67
3	Tomas Hitzlsperger	22	1.64
4	Olof Mellberg	32	1.59
5	Ulises De La Cruz	19	1.58
6	Gareth Barry	32	1.53
7	Juan Pablo Angel	29	1.48
8	Jlloyd Samuel	38	1.47
9	Thomas Sorensen	36	1.44
10	Ronny Johnsen	19	1.42

KEY PLAYERS - DEFENDERS

Olof Mellberg

Goals Conceded The number of League goals conceded while he was on the pitch	34
Goals Conceded in all competitions The number of goals conceded while he was on the pitch in all competitions	40
League minutes played Number of minutes played in league matches	2916
Clean Sheets In games when he played at least70 mins	12
Defensive Rating Average number of mins between League goals conceded while he was on the pitch	86
Club Defensive Rating Average number of mins between League goals conceded by the club this season	78

	PLAYER	CON LGE	CON ALL	GAMES	C SHEETS	DEF RATE
1	Olof Mellberg	34	40	2916	12	86 mins
2	Ulises De La Cruz	22	24	1846	6	84 mins
3	Ronny Johnsen	23	28	1875	5	82 mins
4	Jlloyd Samuel	44	52	3420	12	78 mins
5	Mark Delaney	27	33	2040	6	76 mins

KEY GOALKEEPER

Thomas Sorensen

Goals Conceded in the League The number of League goals conceded while he was on the pitch	42
Goals Conceded in all competitions Number of goals conceded while he was on the pitch in all competitions	50
League minutes played Number of minutes played in league matches	3335
Clean Sheets In games when he played at least 70 mins	12
Goals to Shots Ratio The average number of shots on target per each League goal conceded	5.5
Defensive Rating Ave mins between League goals conceded while on the pitch	79

BOOKINGS

Lee Hendrie

League Yellow	9
League Red	0
All competitions Yellow	10
All competitions Red	0

League Average **287** mins between cards

	PLAYER	LEAGUE Y	LEAGUE R	TOTAL Y	TOTAL R	AVE
1	Hendrie	9	0	10	0	287
2	McCann	6	1	9	2	349
3	Solano	1	1	1	1	399
4	Whittingham	4	0	4	0	489
5	Delaney	4	0	5	0	510
6	Hitzlsperger	4	0	5	0	558
7	Samuel	6	0	7	0	570
8	Crouch	1	0	1	0	588
9	Johnsen	3	0	4	0	625
10	Mellberg	4	0	4	0	729
11	Barry	3	1	3	1	751
12	Angel	3	0	3	0	919
13	De La Cruz	2	0	2	0	923
14	Dublin	1	0	2	0	1178
15	Sorensen	1	0	2	0	3335
	Other	1	0	3	0	
	TOTAL	53	3	65	4	

CHARLTON ATHLETIC

The departure of **Scott Parker**, ending his successful partnership with **Matt Holland** in midfield, disrupted Charlton's season but they still enjoyed their highest-ever finish.

A look at the Midfielders chart shows Parker way ahead of his colleagues with a Scoring Difference of +23. Before the midfielder left for Chelsea on January 31st, the club was averaging 1.7 points a game and conceding barely a goal a game; afterwards it was just one point a game with a far worse defensive record.

Alan Curbishly made a shrewd addition in **Paulo di Canio** whose guile made him the highest striker on the Assists Table with 12.

Dean Kiely had most shots on target to deal with, 293. He made 6.1 saves for every goal he conceded.

NICKNAME: THE ADDICKS

KEY: Won · Drawn · Lost

#	Comp	Opponent	Venue	Res	Score	Scorers
1	prem	Man City	H	L	0-3	
2	prem	Wolves	A	W	4-0	Euell 5; Jensen 15; Bartlett 25,33
3	prem	Everton	H	D	2-2	Euell 25 pen,49 pen
4	prem	Bolton	A	D	0-0	
5	prem	Man Utd	H	L	0-2	
6	prem	Aston Villa	A	L	1-2	Lisbie 86
7	ccr2	Luton	H	W	8-7*	Parker 41; Lisbie 58; di Canio 90; Jensen 95 (*on penalties)
8	prem	Liverpool	H	W	3-2	Lisbie 31,43,83
9	prem	Portsmouth	A	W	2-1	Fortune 77; Bartlett 90
10	prem	Blackburn	A	W	1-0	Hreidarsson 33
11	prem	Arsenal	H	D	1-1	di Canio 27 pen
12	ccr3	Everton	A	L	0-1	
13	prem	Birmingham	A	W	2-1	Holland 11,58
14	prem	Fulham	H	W	3-1	Stuart 10; Johansson 69,76
15	prem	Leicester	A	D	1-1	di Canio 84 pen
16	prem	Leeds	H	L	0-1	
17	prem	Southampton	A	L	2-3	Parker 46,65
18	prem	Middlesbrough	A	D	0-0	
19	prem	Newcastle	H	D	0-0	
20	prem	Chelsea	H	W	4-2	Hreidarsson 1; Holland 35; Johansson 48; Euell 53
21	prem	Tottenham	A	W	1-0	Cole, C 69
22	facr3	Gillingham	A	L	2-3	Cox 1 og; Cole, C 90
23	prem	Man City	A	D	1-1	di Canio 84
24	prem	Wolverhampton	H	W	2-0	Euell 38,79
25	prem	Everton	A	W	1-0	Stuart 41
26	prem	Bolton	H	L	1-2	Johansson 12
27	prem	Chelsea	A	L	0-1	
28	prem	Tottenham	H	L	2-4	Stuart 51; Perry 81
29	prem	Blackburn	H	W	3-2	Cole, C 10; Euell 36; Jensen 90
30	prem	Arsenal	A	L	1-2	Jensen 59
31	prem	Middlesbrough	H	W	1-0	Holland 25
32	prem	Newcastle	A	L	1-3	Jensen 54
33	prem	Aston Villa	H	L	1-2	Cole, C 8
34	prem	Portsmouth	H	D	1-1	Bartlett 8
35	prem	Liverpool	A	W	1-0	Bartlett 63
36	prem	Birmingham	H	D	1-1	Holland 86
37	prem	Man Utd	A	L	0-2	
38	prem	Fulham	A	L	0-2	
39	prem	Leicester	H	D	2-2	Fortune 53; di Canio 75 pen
40	prem	Leeds	A	D	3-3	Holland 11; Euell 76 pen,79
41	prem	Southampton	H	W	2-1	Euell 36; Cole, C 53

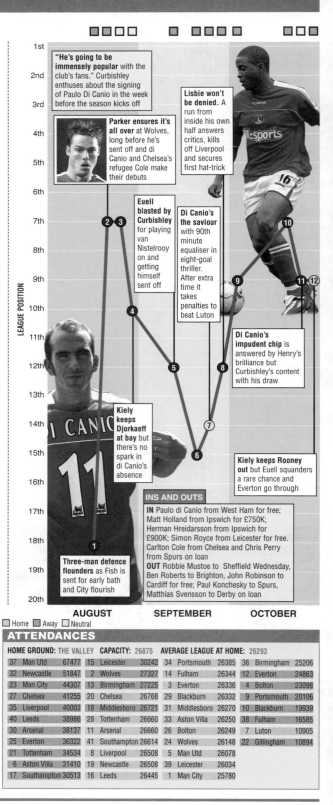

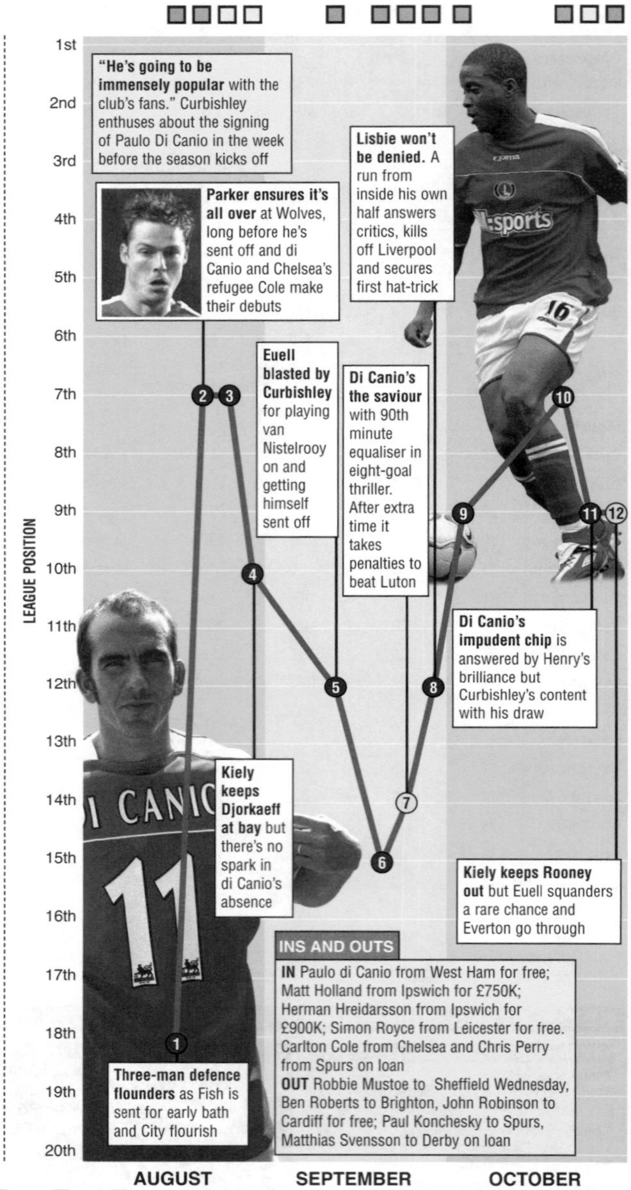

LEAGUE POSITION (1st–20th) — AUGUST · SEPTEMBER · OCTOBER

"He's going to be **immensely popular** with the club's fans." Curbishley enthuses about the signing of Paulo Di Canio in the week before the season kicks off

Three-man defence flounders as Fish is sent for early bath and City flourish

Parker ensures it's all over at Wolves, long before he's sent off and di Canio and Chelsea's refugee Cole make their debuts

Euell blasted by Curbishley for playing van Nistelrooy on and getting himself sent off

Kiely keeps Djorkaeff at bay but there's no spark in di Canio's absence

Di Canio's the saviour with 90th minute equaliser in eight-goal thriller. After extra time it takes penalties to beat Luton

Lisbie won't be denied. A run from inside his own half answers critics, kills off Liverpool and secures first hat-trick

Di Canio's impudent chip is answered by Henry's brilliance but Curbishley's content with his draw

Kiely keeps Rooney out but Euell squanders a rare chance and Everton go through

Home · Away · Neutral

INS AND OUTS

IN Paulo di Canio from West Ham for free; Matt Holland from Ipswich for £750K; Herman Hreidarsson from Ipswich for £900K; Simon Royce from Leicester for free. Carlton Cole from Chelsea and Chris Perry from Spurs on loan

OUT Robbie Mustoe to Sheffield Wednesday, Ben Roberts to Brighton, John Robinson to Cardiff for free; Paul Konchesky to Spurs, Matthias Svensson to Derby on loan

ATTENDANCES

HOME GROUND: THE VALLEY **CAPACITY:** 26875 **AVERAGE LEAGUE AT HOME:** 26293

#	Opponent	Att	#	Opponent	Att	#	Opponent	Att	#	Opponent	Att
37	Man Utd	67477	15	Leicester	30242	34	Portsmouth	26385	36	Birmingham	25206
32	Newcastle	51847	2	Wolves	27327	14	Fulham	26344	12	Everton	24863
23	Man City	44307	13	Birmingham	27225	3	Everton	26336	4	Bolton	23098
27	Chelsea	41255	20	Chelsea	26768	29	Blackburn	26332	9	Portsmouth	20106
35	Liverpool	40003	18	Middlesboro	26721	31	Middlesboro	26270	10	Blackburn	19939
40	Leeds	38986	28	Tottenham	26660	33	Aston Villa	26250	38	Fulham	16585
30	Arsenal	38137	11	Arsenal	26660	26	Bolton	26249	7	Luton	10905
25	Everton	36322	41	Southampton	26614	24	Wolves	26148	22	Gillingham	10894
21	Tottenham	34534	8	Liverpool	26508	5	Man Utd	26078			
6	Aston Villa	31410	19	Newcastle	26508	39	Leicester	26034			
17	Southampton	30513	16	Leeds	26445	1	Man City	25780			

Highest finish despite Parker's exit

Final Position: **7th**

KEY: ● League ● Champions Lge ● UEFA Cup ● FA Cup ○ League Cup ● Other

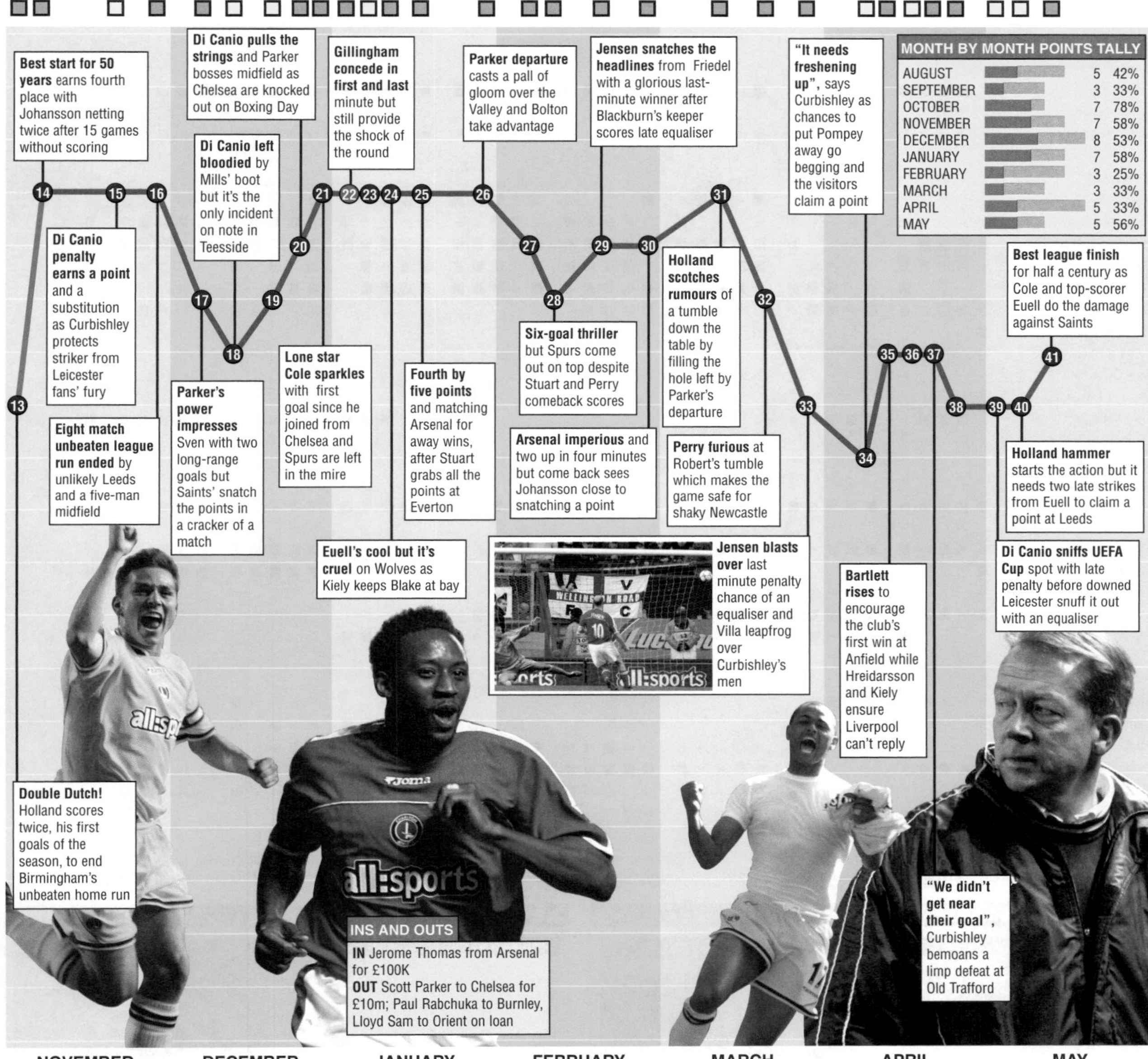

Best start for 50 years earns fourth place with Johansson netting twice after 15 games without scoring
Di Canio pulls the strings and Parker bosses midfield as Chelsea are knocked out on Boxing Day
Gillingham concede in first and last minute but still provide the shock of the round
Parker departure casts a pall of gloom over the Valley and Bolton take advantage
Jensen snatches the headlines from Friedel with a glorious last-minute winner after Blackburn's keeper scores late equaliser
"It needs freshening up", says Curbishley as chances to put Pompey away go begging and the visitors claim a point
Di Canio left bloodied by Mills' boot but it's the only incident on note in Teesside
Di Canio penalty earns a point and a substitution as Curbishley protects striker from Leicester fans' fury
Holland scotches rumours of a tumble down the table by filling the hole left by Parker's departure
Best league finish for half a century as Cole and top-scorer Euell do the damage against Saints
Six-goal thriller but Spurs come out on top despite Stuart and Perry comeback scores
Lone star Cole sparkles with first goal since he joined from Chelsea and Spurs are left in the mire
Fourth by five points and matching Arsenal for away wins, after Stuart grabs all the points at Everton
Parker's power impresses Sven with two long-range goals but Saints' snatch the points in a cracker of a match
Eight match unbeaten league run ended by unlikely Leeds and a five-man midfield
Arsenal imperious and two up in four minutes but come back sees Johansson close to snatching a point
Perry furious at Robert's tumble which makes the game safe for shaky Newcastle
Holland hammer starts the action but it needs two late strikes from Euell to claim a point at Leeds
Euell's cool but it's cruel on Wolves as Kiely keeps Blake at bay
Jensen blasts over last minute penalty chance of an equaliser and Villa leapfrog over Curbishley's men
Bartlett rises to encourage the club's first win at Anfield while Hreidarsson and Kiely ensure Liverpool can't reply
Di Canio sniffs UEFA Cup spot with late penalty before downed Leicester snuff it out with an equaliser
Double Dutch! Holland scores twice, his first goals of the season, to end Birmingham's unbeaten home run
"We didn't get near their goal", Curbishley bemoans a limp defeat at Old Trafford
INS AND OUTS
IN Jerome Thomas from Arsenal for £100K
OUT Scott Parker to Chelsea for £10m; Paul Rabchuka to Burnley, Lloyd Sam to Orient on loan
NOVEMBER
DECEMBER
JANUARY
FEBRUARY
MARCH
APRIL
MAY

MONTH BY MONTH POINTS TALLY		
AUGUST	5	42%
SEPTEMBER	3	33%
OCTOBER	7	78%
NOVEMBER	7	58%
DECEMBER	8	53%
JANUARY	7	58%
FEBRUARY	3	25%
MARCH	3	33%
APRIL	5	33%
MAY	5	56%

GOAL ATTEMPTS

FOR – Goal attempts recorded in League games

	HOME	AWAY	TOTAL	AVE
shots on target	116	84	200	5.3
shots off target	100	84	184	4.8
TOTAL	216	168	384	10.1

Ratio of goals to shots Average number of shots on target per League goal scored: 3.9

Accuracy rating Average percentage of total goal attempts which were on target: 52.1

AGAINST – Goal attempts recorded in League games

	HOME	AWAY	TOTAL	AVE
shots on target	139	161	300	7.9
shots off target	103	84	187	4.9
TOTAL	242	245	487	12.8

Ratio of goals to shots Average number of shots on target per League goal scored: 5.9

Accuracy rating Average percentage of total goal attempts which were on target: 61.6

GOALS

Jason Euell

League	10
FA Cup	0
League Cup	0
Europe	0
Other	0
TOTAL	10

League Average 222 mins between goals

	PLAYER	LGE	FAC	LC	Euro	TOT	AVE
1	Euell	10	0	0	0	10	222
2	Holland	6	0	0	0	6	568
3	Bartlett	5	0	0	0	5	218
4	di Canio	4	0	1	0	5	502
5	Jensen	4	0	1	0	5	591
6	Johansson	4	0	0	0	4	356
7	Lisbie	4	0	1	0	5	113
8	Cole, C	4	1	0	0	5	244
9	Stuart	3	0	0	0	3	674
10	Hreidarsson	2	0	0	0	2	1484
11	Parker	2	0	1	0	3	883
12	Fortune	2	0	0	0	2	1014
13	Perry	1	0	0	0	1	2312
	Other	0	1	0	0	1	
	TOTAL	51	2	4	0	57	

SQUAD APPEARANCES

Match	1	2	3	4	5	6	7	8	9	10	11	12	13	14	15	16	17	18	19	20	21	22	23	24	25	26	27	28	29	30	31	32	33	34	35	36	37	38	39	40	41
Venue	H	A	H	A	H	A	H	H	A	A	H	A	A	H	A	H	A	A	H	H	A	A	A	H	A	H	A	H	H	A	H	A	H	H	A	H	A	A	H	A	H
Competition	L	L	L	L	L	L	W	L	L	L	L	W	L	L	L	L	L	L	L	L	L	F	L	L	L	L	L	L	L	L	L	L	L	L	L	L	L	L	L	L	L
Result	L	W	D	D	L	L	W	W	W	W	D	L	W	W	D	L	L	D	D	W	W	L	D	W	W	L	L	L	W	L	W	L	L	D	W	D	L	L	D	D	W

Goalkeepers
Dean Kiely
Sergio Leite
Simon Royce

Defenders
Mark Fish
Jonathan Fortune
Hermann Hreidarsson
Radostin Kishishev
Chris Perry
Chris Powell
Gary Rowett
Richard Rufus
Osei Sankofa
Michael Turner
Luke Young

Midfielders
Jamal Campbell-Ryce
Matt Holland
Stephen Hughes
Claus Jensen
Paul Konchesky
Kevin Lisbie
Scott Parker
Graham Stuart

Forwards
Shaun Bartlett
Carlton Cole
Paolo di Canio
Jason Euell
Jonatan Johansson
Mathias Svensson
Jerome Thomas

KEY: On all match; On bench; Subbed or sent off (Counting game); Subbed or sent off (playing less than 70 mins); Subbed on from bench (Counting Game); Subbed on (playing less than 70 mins); Subbed on and then subbed or sent off (Counting Game); Subbed on and then subbed or sent off (playing less than 70 mins); Not in 16

KEY PLAYERS - GOALSCORERS

Jason Euell

Goals in the League	10
Goals in all competitions	10
Assists League goals scored by team-mates where he delivered the final pass	3
Contribution to Attacking Power Average number of minutes between League team goals while on pitch	61
Player Strike Rate Average number of minutes between League goals scored by player	222
Club Strike Rate Average minutes between League goals scored by club	67

	PLAYER	GOALS LGE	GOALS ALL	ASSISTS	POWER	S RATE
1	Jason Euell	10	10	3	61	222 mins
2	Jonatan Johansson	4	4	1	67	356 mins
3	Paolo di Canio	4	5	12	69	502 mins
4	Matt Holland	6	6	2	66	568 mins
5	Claus Jensen	4	5	5	81	591 mins

KEY PLAYERS - MIDFIELDERS

Scott Parker

Goals in the League	2
Goals in all competitions	3
Assists League goals scored by team-mates where he delivered the final pass	3
Defensive Rating Average number of mins between League goals conceded while he was on the pitch	84
Contribution to Attacking Power Average number of minutes between League team goals while on pitch	61
Scoring Difference Defensive Rating minus Contribution to Attacking Power	23

	PLAYER	GOALS LGE	GOALS ALL	ASSISTS	DEF RATE	POWER	SC DIFF
1	Scott Parker	2	3	3	84	61	23 mins
2	Matt Holland	6	6	2	68	67	1 min
3	Graham Stuart	3	3	1	61	61	0 mins
4	Claus Jensen	4	5	5	66	82	-16 mins
5	Paul Konchesky	0	0	1	55	93	-38 mins

PLAYER APPEARANCES

	AGE (on 01/07/04)	IN NAMED 16	APPEARANCES	COUNTING GAMES	MINUTES ON PITCH	APPEARANCES	MINUTES ON PITCH	THIS SEASON	HOME COUNTRY
Goalkeepers									
Dean Kiely	33	37	37	37	3330	40	3630	-	Rep of Ireland
Sergio Leite	24	4	0	0	0	0	0	-	Portugal
Simon Royce	32	35	1	1	90	1	90	-	England
Defenders									
Mark Fish	30	26	23	20	1857	25	2022	-	South Africa
Jonathan Fortune	23	37	28	22	2028	31	2283	-	England
Hermann Hreidarsson	29	33	33	33	2968	35	3148	-	Iceland
Radostin Kishishev	29	36	33	25	2578	35	2731	-	Bulgaria
Chris Perry	31	32	29	25	2312	31	2458	-	England
Chris Powell	34	28	16	10	965	17	1047	-	England
Gary Rowett	30	1	1	1	90	1	90	-	England
Richard Rufus	29	0	0	0	0	0	0	-	England
Osei Sankofa	19	2	0	0	0	0	0	-	England
Michael Turner	20	5	0	0	0	0	0	-	England
Luke Young	24	25	24	20	1913	25	2033	-	England
Midfielders									
Jamal Campbell-Ryce	21	3	2	0	35	4	77	-	England
Matt Holland	30	38	38	38	3406	41	3697	-	England
Stephen Hughes	27	5	0	0	0	0	0	-	England
Claus Jensen	27	33	31	25	2365	34	2665	7	Denmark (14)
Paul Konchesky	23	22	21	15	1482	22	1572	-	England
Kevin Lisbie	25	9	9	4	452	10	539	-	Jamaica
Scott Parker	23	20	20	20	1765	22	1975	2	England (12)
Graham Stuart	33	30	28	21	2021	31	2249	-	England
Forwards									
Shaun Bartlett	31	20	19	9	1090	19	1090	-	South Africa
Carlton Cole	20	24	21	7	975	22	1065	-	England
Paolo di Canio	36	32	31	19	2009	33	2163	-	Italy
Jason Euell	27	31	31	21	2222	34	2377	-	England
Jonatan Johansson	28	32	26	13	1423	29	1656	5	Finland (42)
Mathias Svensson	29	4	3	1	136	4	155	-	Sweden
Jerome Thomas	21	3	1	0	45	1	45	-	England

KEY: LEAGUE ALL COMPS CAPS (FIFA RANKING)

TEAM OF THE SEASON

Kiely

CG 37 DR 69

Kishishev

CG 25 DR 78

Perry

CG 25 DR 70

Fish

CG 20 DR 81

Hreidarsson

CG 33 DR 71

Stuart

CG 21 SD 0

Holland

CG 38 SD +1

Parker

CG 20 SD +23

Jensen

CG 25 SD -16

Johansson

CG 13 AP 67

Euell

CG 21 SR 222

KEY: DR = Diffensive Rate, SD = Scoring Difference AP = Attacking Power SR = Strike Rate, CG=Counting games – League games playing at least 70 minutes

TOP POINT EARNERS

Radostin Kishishev

Counting Games League games when he played at least 70 minutes	25
Average points Average League points taken in Counting games	1.72
Club Average points Average points taken in League games	1.39

	PLAYER	GAMES	PTS
1	Radostin Kishishev	25	1.72
2	Scott Parker	20	1.65
3	Chris Perry	25	1.64
4	Jonatan Johansson	13	1.62
5	Mark Fish	20	1.55
6	Graham Stuart	21	1.52
7	Jason Euell	21	1.43
8	Dean Kiely	37	1.43
9	Hermann Hreidarsson	33	1.42
10	Matt Holland	38	1.39

KEY PLAYERS - DEFENDERS

Mark Fish

Goals Conceded The number of League goals conceded while he was on the pitch	23
Goals Conceded in all competitions The number of goals conceded while he was on the pitch in all competitions	28
League minutes played Number of minutes played in league matches	1857
Clean Sheets In games when he played at least70 mins	7
Defensive Rating Average number of mins between League goals conceded while he was on the pitch	81
Club Defensive Rating Average number of mins between League goals conceded by the club this season	67

	PLAYER	CON LGE	CON ALL	GAMES	C SHEETS	DEF RATE
1	Mark Fish	23	28	1857	7	81 mins
2	Radostin Kishishev	33	37	2578	10	78 mins
3	Hermann Hreidarsson	42	46	2968	10	71 mins
4	Chris Perry	33	37	2312	7	70 mins
5	Jonathan Fortune	33	40	2028	5	61 mins

KEY GOALKEEPER

Dean Kiely

Goals Conceded in the League The number of League goals conceded while he was on the pitch	48
Goals Conceded in all competitions Number of goals conceded while he was on the pitch in all competitions	56
League minutes played Number of minutes played in league matches	3330
Clean Sheets In games when he played at least 70 mins	10
Goals to Shots Ratio The average number of shots on target per each League goal conceded	6.1
Defensive Rating Ave mins between League goals conceded while on the pitch	69

BOOKINGS

Scott Parker

League Yellow	6
League Red	1
All competitions Yellow	7
All competitions Red	1

League Average 252 mins between cards

	PLAYER	LEAGUE Y	LEAGUE R	TOTAL Y	TOTAL R	AVE
1	Parker	6Y	1R	7Y	1R	252
2	Euell	5	1	5	1	370
3	Young	5	0	5	0	382
4	Perry	5	0	5	0	462
5	Konchesky	3	0	3	0	494
6	Kishishev	4	0	4	0	644
7	Fish	1	1	1	1	928
8	Powell	1	0	1	0	965
9	Hreidarsson	3	0	3	0	989
10	Fortune	2	0	2	0	1014
11	Bartlett	1	0	1	0	1090
12	di Canio	1	0	1	0	2009
13	Jensen	1	0	1	0	2365
	Other	0	0	0	0	
	TOTAL	38	3	39	3	

BOLTON WANDERERS

Striking from midfield proves Bolton's forte. **Kevin Nolan** and **Youri Djorkaeff** are both prolific behind **Kevin Davies'** selfless running and finish third equal in the division's Midfield Goals chart with nine apiece.

Davies also scored nine. His Strike Rate, averaging a goal every 367 minutes, wasn't among the top 40 in the division but he delivered an impressive eight assists – the second highest striker.

Jay Jay Okocha must be the unluckiest player not to net a league goal. His long range strikes damaged plenty of woodwork and he also claimed seven assists.

The formula led Bolton to a place in the Carling Cup final and their highest-ever Premiership finish. **Sam Allardyce** enjoying the luxury of a 20 point gap between his side and the drop zone.

NICKNAME: THE TROTTERS

KEY: Won Drawn Lost

1	prem	**Man Utd**	A	L	0-4	
2	prem	**Blackburn**	H	D	2-2	Djorkaeff 3 pen; Davies 25
3	prem	**Portsmouth**	A	L	0-4	
4	prem	**Charlton**	H	D	0-0	
5	prem	**Middlesbrough**	H	W	2-0	Davies 23; N'Gotty 81
6	prem	**Newcastle**	A	D	0-0	
7	ccr2	**Walsall**	H	W	3-1	Jardel 15,80; Nolan 69
8	prem	**Wolves**	H	D	1-1	Davies 85
9	prem	**Aston Villa**	A	D	1-1	Nolan 46
10	prem	**Man City**	A	L	2-6	Nolan 25; Campo 60
11	prem	**Birmingham**	H	L	0-1	
12	ccr3	**Gillingham**	H	W	2-0	Giannakopoulos 25; Pedersen 66
13	prem	**Tottenham**	A	W	1-0	Nolan 73
14	prem	**Southampton**	H	D	0-0	
15	prem	**Leeds**	A	W	2-0	Davies 16; Giannakopoulos 17
16	prem	**Everton**	H	W	2-0	Frandsen 26; Djorkaeff 46
17	ccr4	**Liverpool**	A	W	3-2	Jardel 3; Okocha 79; Djorkaeff 90
18	prem	**Fulham**	A	L	1-2	Davies 53
19	prem	**Chelsea**	A	W	2-1	N'Gotty 39; Terry 90 og
20	ccqf	**Southampton**	H	D	1-0	Pedersen 115 (aet)
21	prem	**Arsenal**	H	D	1-1	Pedersen 83
22	prem	**Liverpool**	A	L	1-3	Pedersen 85
23	prem	**Leicester**	H	D	2-2	Thatcher 35 og; Campo 54
24	facr3	**Tranmere**	A	D	1-1	Nolan 78
25	prem	**Man Utd**	H	L	1-2	Djorkaeff 89
26	prem	**Blackburn**	A	W	4-3	Nolan 1,78; Djorkaeff 43; Giannakopoulos 73
27	facr3r	**Tranmere**	H	L	1-2	Shakes 90
28	prem	**Portsmouth**	H	W	1-0	Davies 53
29	ccsfl1	**Aston Villa**	H	W	5-2	Okocha 2,80; Nolan 9; Giannakopoulos 17; N'Gotty 74
30	ccsfl2	**Aston Villa**	A	L	0-2	
31	prem	**Charlton**	A	W	2-1	Pedersen 1; Nolan 78
32	prem	**Liverpool**	H	D	2-2	Hunt 11; Djorkaeff 58
33	prem	**Leicester**	A	D	1-1	Walker 32 og
34	prem	**Man City**	H	L	1-3	Nolan 22
35	cccf	**Middlesbrough**	H	L	1-2	Davies 21
36	prem	**Birmingham**	A	L	0-2	
37	prem	**Chelsea**	H	L	0-2	
38	prem	**Arsenal**	A	L	1-2	Campo 41
39	prem	**Newcastle**	H	W	1-0	Pedersen 4
40	prem	**Middlesbrough**	A	L	0-2	
41	prem	**Aston Villa**	H	D	2-2	Pedersen 48; Davies 86
42	prem	**Wolves**	A	W	2-1	Pedersen 43; Davies 90
43	prem	**Tottenham**	H	W	2-0	Campo 7; Pedersen 65
44	prem	**Southampton**	A	W	2-1	Nolan 77; Davies 78
45	prem	**Leeds**	H	W	4-1	Djorkaeff 47,54; Harte 55 og; Nolan 78
46	prem	**Everton**	A	W	2-1	Djorkaeff 14,87
47	prem	**Fulham**	H	L	0-2	

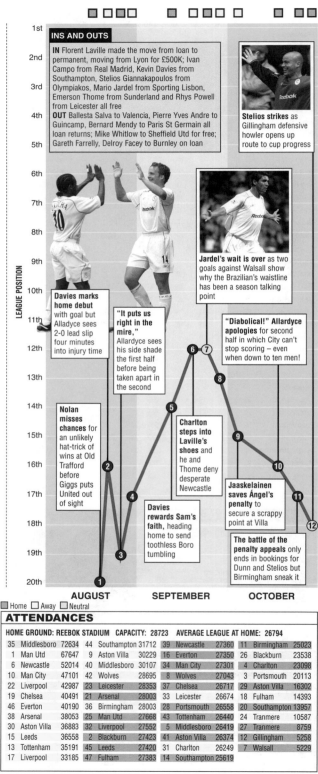

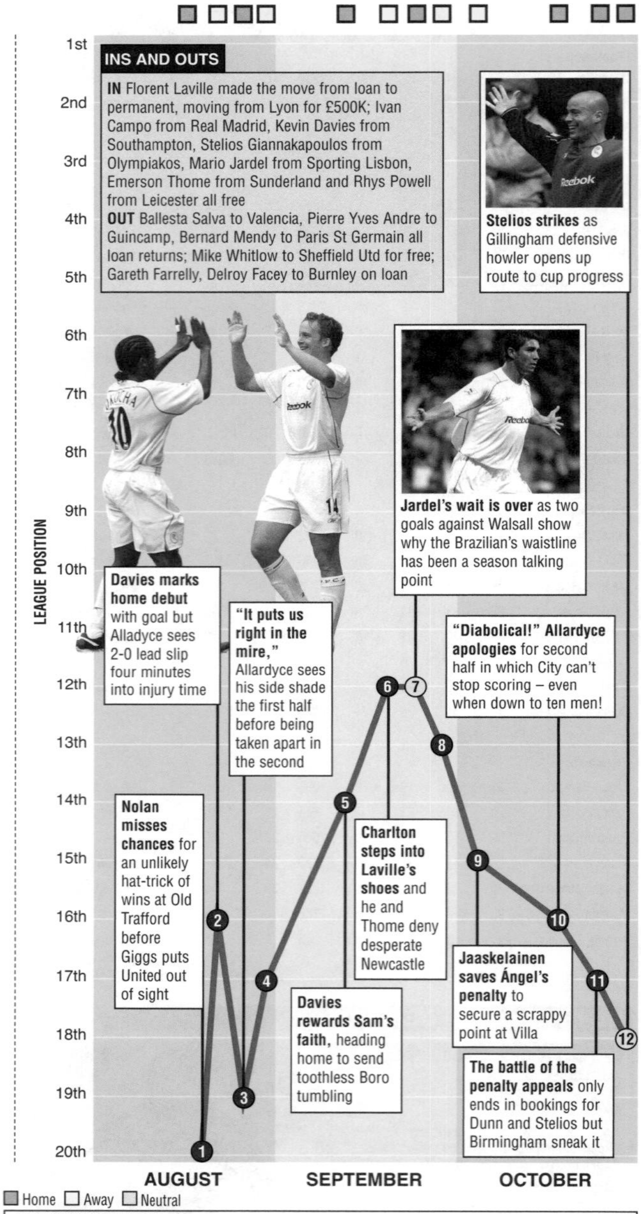

INS AND OUTS

IN Florent Laville made the move from loan to permanent, moving from Lyon for £500K; Ivan Campo from Real Madrid, Kevin Davies from Southampton, Stelios Giannakapoulos from Olympiakos, Mario Jardel from Sporting Lisbon, Emerson Thome from Sunderland and Rhys Powell from Leicester all free
OUT Ballesta Salva to Valencia, Pierre Yves Andre to Guincamp, Bernard Mendy to Paris St Germain all loan returns; Mike Whitlow to Sheffield Utd for free; Gareth Farrelly, Delroy Facey to Burnley on loan

Stelios strikes as Gillingham defensive howler opens up route to cup progress

Jardel's wait is over as two goals against Walsall show why the Brazilian's waistline has been a season talking point

Davies marks home debut with goal but Alladyce sees 2-0 lead slip four minutes into injury time

"It puts us right in the mire," Allardyce sees his side shade the first half before being taken apart in the second

"Diabolical!" Allardyce apologies for second half in which City can't stop scoring – even when down to ten men!

Nolan misses chances for an unlikely hat-trick of wins at Old Trafford before Giggs puts United out of sight

Charlton steps into Laville's shoes and he and Thome deny desperate Newcastle

Davies rewards Sam's faith, heading home to send toothless Boro tumbling

Jaaskelainen saves Ángel's penalty to secure a scrappy point at Villa

The battle of the penalty appeals only ends in bookings for Dunn and Stelios but Birmingham sneak it

LEAGUE POSITION: 1st 2nd 3rd 4th 5th 6th 7th 8th 9th 10th 11th 12th 13th 14th 15th 16th 17th 18th 19th 20th

AUGUST SEPTEMBER OCTOBER

Home Away Neutral

ATTENDANCES

HOME GROUND: REEBOK STADIUM CAPACITY: 28723 AVERAGE LEAGUE AT HOME: 26794

35	Middlesboro	72634	44	Southampton	31712	39	Newcastle	27360	11	Birmingham	25023
1	Man Utd	67647	9	Aston Villa	30229	16	Everton	27350	26	Blackburn	23538
6	Newcastle	52014	40	Middlesboro	30107	34	Man City	27301	4	Charlton	23098
10	Man City	47101	42	Wolves	28695	8	Wolves	27043	3	Portsmouth	20113
22	Liverpool	42987	23	Leicester	28353	37	Chelsea	26717	29	Aston Villa	16302
19	Chelsea	40491	21	Arsenal	28003	33	Leicester	26674	18	Fulham	14393
46	Everton	40190	36	Birmingham	28003	28	Portsmouth	26558	20	Southampton	13957
38	Arsenal	38053	25	Man Utd	27668	43	Tottenham	26440	24	Tranmere	10587
30	Aston Villa	36883	32	Liverpool	27552	5	Middlesboro	26419	27	Tranmere	8759
15	Leeds	36558	2	Blackburn	27423	41	Aston Villa	26374	12	Gillingham	5258
13	Tottenham	35191	45	Leeds	27420	31	Charlton	26249	7	Walsall	5229
17	Liverpool	33185	47	Fulham	27383	14	Southampton	25619			

Midfield flair nets new league high

Final Position **8th**

KEY: ● League ● Champions Lge ● UEFA Cup ● FA Cup ○ League Cup ● Other

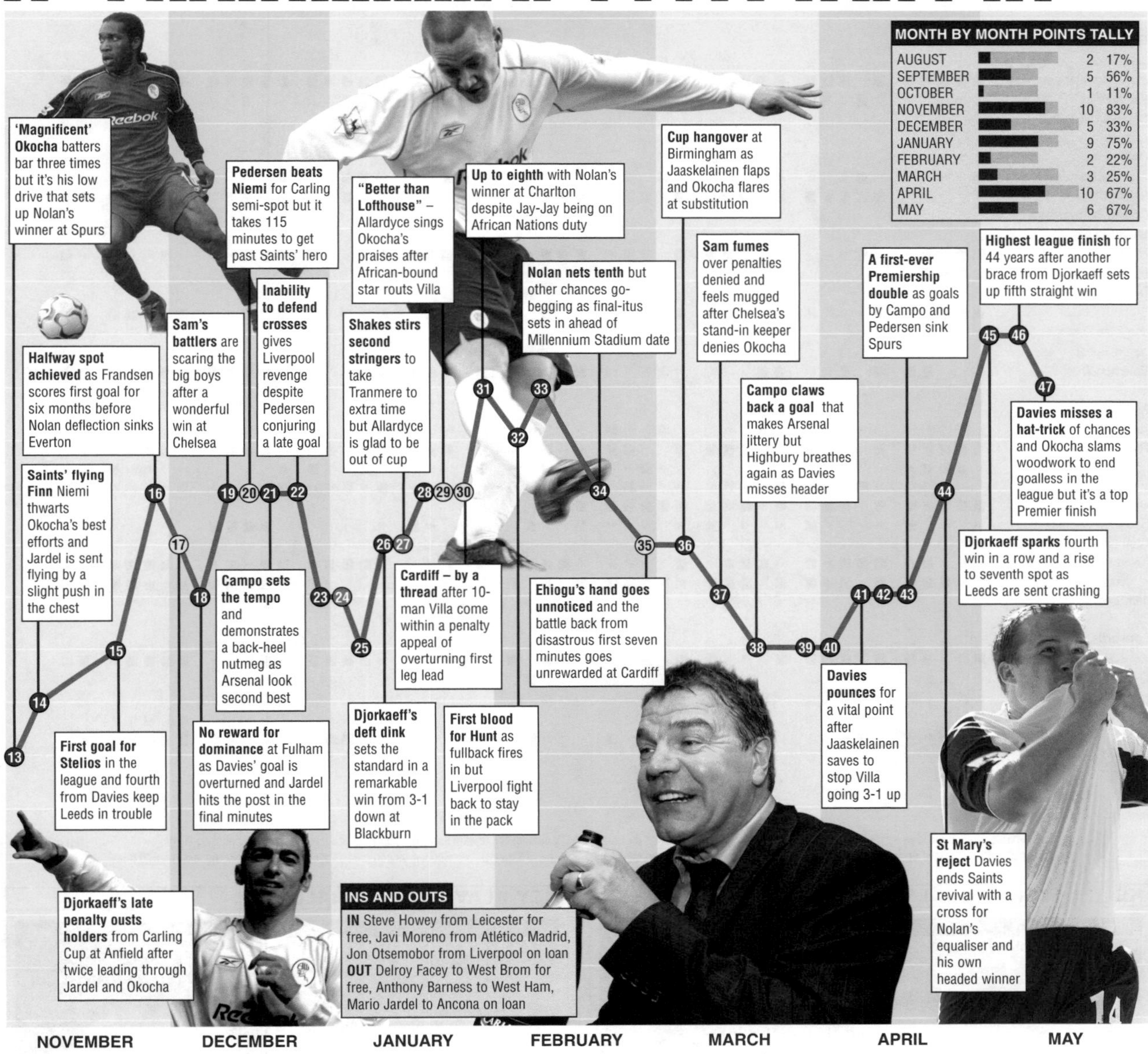

MONTH BY MONTH POINTS TALLY
AUGUST 2 17%
SEPTEMBER 5 56%
OCTOBER 1 11%
NOVEMBER 10 83%
DECEMBER 5 33%
JANUARY 9 75%
FEBRUARY 2 22%
MARCH 3 25%
APRIL 10 67%
MAY 6 67%
'Magnificent' Okocha batters bar three times but it's his low drive that sets up Nolan's winner at Spurs
Saints' flying Finn Niemi thwarts Okocha's best efforts and Jardel is sent flying by a slight push in the chest
First goal for Stelios in the league and fourth from Davies keep Leeds in trouble
Halfway spot achieved as Frandsen scores first goal for six months before Nolan deflection sinks Everton
Djorkaeff's late penalty ousts holders from Carling Cup at Anfield after twice leading through Jardel and Okocha
Sam's battlers are scaring the big boys after a wonderful win at Chelsea
No reward for dominance at Fulham as Davies' goal is overturned and Jardel hits the post in the final minutes
Pedersen beats Niemi for Carling semi-spot but it takes 115 minutes to get past Saints' hero
Campo sets the tempo and demonstrates a back-heel nutmeg as Arsenal look second best
Inability to defend crosses gives Liverpool revenge despite Pedersen conjuring a late goal
"Better than Lofthouse" – Allardyce sings Okocha's praises after African-bound star routs Villa
Djorkaeff's deft dink sets the standard in a remarkable win from 3-1 down at Blackburn
Shakes stirs second stringers to take Tranmere to extra time but Allardyce is glad to be out of cup
Cardiff – by a thread after 10-man Villa come within a penalty appeal of overturning first leg lead
Up to eighth with Nolan's winner at Charlton despite Jay-Jay being on African Nations duty
First blood for Hunt as fullback fires in but Liverpool fight back to stay in the pack
Nolan nets tenth but other chances go-begging as final-itus sets in ahead of Millennium Stadium date
Ehiogu's hand goes unnoticed and the battle back from disastrous first seven minutes goes unrewarded at Cardiff
Cup hangover at Birmingham as Jaaskelainen flaps and Okocha flares at substitution
Sam fumes over penalties denied and feels mugged after Chelsea's stand-in keeper denies Okocha
Campo claws back a goal that makes Arsenal jittery but Highbury breathes again as Davies misses header
Davies pounces for a vital point after Jaaskelainen saves to stop Villa going 3-1 up
A first-ever Premiership double as goals by Campo and Pedersen sink Spurs
St Mary's reject Davies ends Saints revival with a cross for Nolan's equaliser and his own headed winner
Djorkaeff sparks fourth win in a row and a rise to seventh spot as Leeds are sent crashing
Highest league finish for 44 years after another brace from Djorkaeff sets up fifth straight win
Davies misses a hat-trick of chances and Okocha slams woodwork to end goalless in the league but it's a top Premier finish
INS AND OUTS
IN Steve Howey from Leicester for free, Javi Moreno from Atlético Madrid, Jon Otsemobor from Liverpool on loan
OUT Delroy Facey to West Brom for free, Anthony Barness to West Ham, Mario Jardel to Ancona on loan
NOVEMBER
DECEMBER
JANUARY
FEBRUARY
MARCH
APRIL
MAY

GOAL ATTEMPTS

FOR – Goal attempts recorded in League games

	HOME	AWAY	TOTAL	AVE
shots on target	177	109	286	7.5
shots off target	133	114	247	6.5
TOTAL	**310**	**223**	**533**	**14**

Ratio of goals to shots Average number of shots on target per League goal scored	6
Accuracy rating Average percentage of total goal attempts which were on target	53.7

AGAINST – Goal attempts recorded in League games

	HOME	AWAY	TOTAL	AVE
shots on target	94	126	220	5.8
shots off target	77	109	186	4.9
TOTAL	**171**	**235**	**406**	**10.7**

Ratio of goals to shots Average number of shots on target per League goal scored	3.9
Accuracy rating Average percentage of total goal attempts which were on target	54.2

GOALS

Kevin Davies

League	9
FA Cup	0
League Cup	1
Europe	0
Other	0
TOTAL	10

League Average
367
mins between goals

	PLAYER	LGE	FAC	LC	Euro	TOT	AVE
1	Davies	**9**	0	1	0	10	367
2	Nolan	**9**	1	2	0	12	345
3	Djorkaeff	**9**	0	1	0	10	228
4	Pedersen	**7**	0	2	0	9	250
5	Campo	**4**	0	0	0	4	799
6	Giannakopoulos	**2**	0	2	0	4	782
7	N'Gotty	**2**	0	1	0	3	1444
8	Hunt	**1**	0	0	0	1	2564
9	Frandsen	**1**	0	0	0	1	1915
10	Shakes	**0**	1	0	0	1	
11	Jardel	**0**	0	3	0	3	
12	Okocha	**0**	0	3	0	3	
	Other	4	0	0	0	4	
	TOTAL	**48**	**2**	**15**	**0**	**65**	

SQUAD APPEARANCES

Match	1 2 3 4 5	6 7 8 9 10	11 12 13 14 15	16 17 18 19 20	21 22 23 24 25	26 27 28 29 30	31 32 33 34 35	36 37 38 39 40	41 42 43 44 45	46 47
Venue	A H A H H	A H H A A	H H A H A	H A A A H	H A H A H	A H H H A	A H A H H	A H A H A	H A H A H	A H
Competition	L L L L L	L W L L L	L W L L L	L W L L W	L L L F L	L F L W W	L L L L W	L L L L L	L L L L L	L L
Result	L D L D W	D W D D L	L W W D W	W W L W D	D L D D L	W L W W L	W D D L L	L L L W L	D W W W W	W L

Goalkeepers
Jeremy Bon
Jussi Jaaskelainen
Kevin Poole
Donovan Ricketts

Defenders
Anthony Barness
Simon Charlton
Charlie Comyn-Platt
Steve Howey
Nicky Hunt
Florent Laville
Danny Livesey
Bruno N'Gotty
Jon Otsemobor
Jason Talbot
Emerson Thome

Midfielders
Ibrahim Ba
Ramos Ivan Campo
Youri Djorkaeff
Per Frandsen
Ricardo Gardner
Stylianos Giannakopoulos
Glen Little
Kevin Nolan
Augustine Okocha
Jeff Smith

Forwards
Kevin Davies
Delroy Facey
Mario Jardel
Javi Moreno
Henrik Pedersen
Dwight Pezzarossi
Ricky Shakes
Cleveland Taylor
Ricardo Vaz Te

KEY: On all match · On bench · Subbed or sent off (Counting game) · Subbed or sent off (playing less than 70 mins) · Subbed on from bench (Counting Game) · Subbed on (playing less than 70 mins) · Subbed on and then subbed or sent off (Counting Game) · Subbed on and then subbed or sent off (playing less than 70 mins) · Not in 16

KEY PLAYERS - GOALSCORERS

Youri Djorkaeff

Goals in the League	9
Goals in all competitions	10
Assists League goals scored by team-mates where he delivered the final pass	4
Contribution to Attacking Power Average number of minutes between League team goals while on pitch	68
Player Strike Rate Average number of minutes between League goals scored by player	228
Club Strike Rate Average minutes between League goals scored by club	71

	PLAYER	GOALS LGE	GOALS ALL	ASSISTS	POWER	S RATE
1	Youri Djorkaeff	9	10	4	68	**228 mins**
2	Henrik Pedersen	7	9	0	72	**250 mins**
3	Kevin Nolan	9	12	1	72	**345 mins**
4	Kevin Davies	9	10	8	70	**367 mins**
5	Stylianos Giannakopoulos	2	4	3	67	**782 mins**

KEY PLAYERS - MIDFIELDERS

Stelios Giannakopoulos

Goals in the League	2
Goals in all competitions	4
Assists League goals scored by team-mates where he delivered the final pass	3
Defensive Rating Average number of mins between League goals conceded while he was on the pitch	63
Contribution to Attacking Power Average number of minutes between League team goals while on pitch	68
Scoring Difference Defensive Rating minus Contribution to Attacking Power	-5

	PLAYER	GOALS LGE	GOALS ALL	ASSISTS	DEF RATE	POWER	SC DIFF
1	Stelios Giannakopoulos	2	4	3	63	68	**-5 mins**
2	Kevin Nolan	9	12	1	65	72	**-7 mins**
3	Augustine Okocha	0	3	7	66	74	**-8 mins**
4	Youri Djorkaeff	9	10	4	57	68	**-11 mins**
5	Per Frandsen	1	1	0	58	71	**-13 mins**

PLAYER APPEARANCES

	AGE (on 01/07/04)	IN NAMED 16	APPEARANCES	COUNTING GAMES	MINUTES ON PITCH	APPEARANCES	MINUTES ON PITCH	THIS SEASON	HOME COUNTRY
Goalkeepers									
Jeremy Bon	19	0	0	0	0	1	90	-	France
Jussi Jaaskelainen	29	38	38	38	3420	41	3690	-	Iceland
Kevin Poole	40	36	0	0	0	6	600	-	England
Donovan Ricketts	27	2	0	0	0	0	0	-	Jamaica
Defenders									
Anthony Barness	32	27	15	9	987	23	1562	-	England
Simon Charlton	32	35	31	25	2524	38	3017	-	England
Charlie Comyn-Platt	18	0	0	0	0	3	220	-	England
Ricardo Gardner	25	22	22	19	1778	26	2074	-	Jamaica
Steve Howey	32	5	3	2	225	3	225	-	England
Nicky Hunt	20	34	31	27	2564	38	3165	-	England
Florent Laville	30	5	5	4	386	5	386	-	France
Danny Livesey	19	0	0	0	0	2	210	-	England
Bruno N'Gotty	33	34	33	31	2887	39	3439	-	France
Jon Otsemobor	21	3	1	0	68	1	68	-	England
Jason Talbot	18	0	0	0	0	0	0	-	England
Emerson Thome	32	29	26	25	2257	32	2797	-	Brazil
Midfielders									
Ibrahim Ba	30	14	9	1	212	16	697	-	France
Ramos Ivan Campo	30	38	38	33	3197	43	3677	-	Spain
Youri Djorkaeff	36	28	27	20	2048	32	2418	-	France
Per Frandsen	34	36	33	16	1915	38	2319	-	Denmark
Stelios	29	34	31	14	1563	39	2083	-	Greece
Glen Little	28	4	4	0	34	4	34	-	England
Kevin Nolan	22	38	37	33	3105	44	3550	-	England
Augustine Okocha	30	35	35	31	2964	41	3424	-	Nigeria
Jeff Smith	24	0	0	0	0	2	174	-	England
Cleveland Taylor	20	0	0	0	0	1	42	-	England
Forwards									
Kevin Davies	27	38	38	34	3300	43	3676	-	England
Delroy Facey	24	2	1	0	15	3	183	-	England
Mario Jardel	30	14	7	0	166	12	495	-	Brazil
Javi Moreno	29	14	8	0	232	10	248	-	Spain
Henrik Pedersen	29	36	33	13	1749	42	2412	-	Denmark
Dwight Pezzarossi	24	2	0	0	0	0	0	-	Guatemala
Ricky Shakes	19	0	0	0	0	1	35	-	England
Ricardo Vaz Te	17	5	1	0	24	3	180	-	Portugal

KEY: LEAGUE ALL COMPS CAPS (FIFA RANKING)

TEAM OF THE SEASON

Jaaskelainen CG 38 DR 61

Hunt CG 27 DR 69

Thome CG 25 DR 64

N'Gotty CG 31 DR 61

Gardner CG 19 DR 61

Stelios CG 14 SD -5

Nolan CG 33 SD -7

Okocha CG 31 SD -8

Djorkaeff CG 20 SD -11

Davies CG 34 AP 70

Pedersen CG 13 SR 250

KEY: DR = Diffensive Rate, SD = Scoring Difference AP = Attacking Power SR = Strike Rate, CG=Counting games – League games playing at least 70 minutes

TOP POINT EARNERS

Youri Djorkaeff

Counting Games League games when he played at least 70 minutes	20
Average points Average League points taken in Counting games	1.65
Club Average points Average points taken in League games	1.39

	PLAYER	GAMES	PTS
1	Youri Djorkaeff	20	**1.65**
2	Nicky Hunt	27	**1.56**
3	Ramos Ivan Campo	33	**1.55**
4	Kevin Nolan	33	**1.48**
5	Augustine Okocha	31	**1.45**
6	Bruno N'Gotty	31	**1.45**
7	Kevin Davies	34	**1.44**
8	Emerson Thome	25	**1.40**
9	Jussi Jaaskelainen	38	**1.39**
10	Simon Charlton	25	**1.36**

KEY PLAYERS - DEFENDERS

Nicky Hunt

Goals Conceded The number of League goals conceded while he was on the pitch	37
Goals Conceded in all competitions The number of goals conceded while he was on the pitch in all competitions	44
League minutes played Number of minutes played in league matches	2564
Clean Sheets In games when he played at least70 mins	8
Defensive Rating Average number of mins between League goals conceded while he was on the pitch	69
Club Defensive Rating Average number of mins between League goals conceded by the club this season	61

	PLAYER	CON LGE	CON ALL	MINS	C SHEETS	DEF RATE
1	Nicky Hunt	37	44	2564	8	**69 mins**
2	Emerson Thome	35	44	2257	6	**64 mins**
3	Bruno N'Gotty	47	55	2887	7	**61 mins**
4	Ricardo Gardner	29	32	1778	7	**61 mins**
5	Simon Charlton	44	49	2524	7	**57 mins**

KEY GOALKEEPER

Jussi Jaaskelainen

Goals Conceded in the League The number of League goals conceded while he was on the pitch	56
Goals Conceded in all competitions Number of goals conceded while he was on the pitch in all competitions	62
League minutes played Number of minutes played in league matches	3420
Clean Sheets In games when he played at least 70 mins	10
Goals to Shots Ratio The average number of shots on target per each League goal conceded	3.9
Defensive Rating Ave mins between League goals conceded while on the pitch	61

BOOKINGS

Emerson Thome

League Yellow	7
League Red	0
All competitions Yellow	8
All competitions Red	0
League Average 322 mins between cards	

	PLAYER	LEAGUE		TOTAL		AVE
1	Thome	7 Y	0 R	8 Y	0 R	322
2	Gardner	5	0	6	0	355
3	Campo	9	0	11	0	355
4	Davies	9	0	11	0	366
5	Frandsen	5	0	6	0	383
6	Nolan	8	0	9	0	388
7	Giannakopoulos	4	0	5	0	390
8	Hunt	6	0	8	0	427
9	Okocha	4	0	4	0	741
10	N'Gotty	3	0	3	0	962
11	Pedersen	1	0	1	0	1749
12	Djorkaeff	1	0	1	0	2048
13	Charlton	1	0	1	0	2524
14	Jaaskelainen	1	0	1	0	3420
	Other	2	0	4	0	
	TOTAL	**66**	**0**	**79**	**0**	

FULHAM

When Louis Saha played his last game for Fulham in early January he had a Strike Rate second only to Henry.

He averaged a goal every 131 minutes and had scored 40% of Fulham's league goals. Although he had played only 12 Counting Games the previous year he had still achieved a respectable rate of 231. But he beat that by 100 minutes.

Post Saha **Chris Coleman** changed the system, kept morale high and claimed a best-ever Premiership placing. A little more weight fell on **Steed Malbranque** whose combination of six goals added to ten league assists is bettered by only two other Premier midfielders.

Edwin van der Sar was on good form (apart from one laughable lapse) and boasts the best record of Clean Sheets among the division's keepers.

NICKNAME: THE COTTAGERS

KEY: Won / Drawn / Lost

1	prem	**Middlesbrough**	H	W	3-2	Marlet 18; Inamoto 56; Saha 70
2	prem	**Everton**	A	L	1-3	Hayles 69
3	prem	**Tottenham**	A	W	3-0	Hayles 23,67; Boa Morte 71
4	prem	**Birmingham**	A	D	2-2	Saha 1; Boa Morte 78
5	prem	**Man City**	H	D	2-2	Malbranque 73; Saha 79
6	ccr2	**Wigan**	A	L	0-1	
7	prem	**Blackburn**	A	W	2-0	Boa Morte 5; Saha 55
8	prem	**Leicester**	H	W	2-0	Boa Morte 36,73
9	prem	**Wolves**	H	D	0-0	
10	prem	**Newcastle**	H	L	2-3	Clark 6; Saha 8
11	prem	**Man Utd**	A	W	3-1	Clark 3; Malbranque 66; Inamoto 79
12	prem	**Liverpool**	H	L	1-2	Saha 39
13	prem	**Charlton**	A	L	1-3	Davis, S 89
14	prem	**Portsmouth**	H	W	2-0	Saha 30,33
15	prem	**Arsenal**	A	D	0-0	
16	prem	**Bolton**	H	W	2-1	Davis, S 75; Sava 76
17	prem	**Leeds**	A	L	2-3	Saha 48,85
18	prem	**Chelsea**	H	L	0-1	
19	prem	**Southampton**	H	W	2-0	Saha 19,63 pen
20	prem	**Aston Villa**	A	L	0-3	
21	facr3	**Cheltenham**	H	W	2-1	Saha 13,90
22	prem	**Middlesbrough**	A	L	1-2	Hayles 90
23	prem	**Everton**	H	W	2-1	Saha 45 pen; Malbranque 46
24	prem	**Newcastle**	A	L	1-3	Davis, S 74
25	facr4	**Everton**	A	D	1-1	Davis, S 49
26	prem	**Tottenham**	H	W	2-1	Malbranque 45 pen; McBride 67
27	facr4r	**Everton**	H	W	2-1	Inamoto 57; Malbranque 102
28	prem	**Southampton**	A	D	0-0	
29	prem	**Aston Villa**	H	L	1-2	Boa Morte 1
30	facr5	**West Ham**	H	D	0-0	
31	prem	**Wolves**	A	L	1-2	Malbranque 84
32	facr5r	**West Ham**	A	W	3-0	McBride 76; Hayles 79; Boa Morte 90
33	prem	**Man Utd**	H	D	1-1	Boa Morte 64
34	facqf	**Man Utd**	A	L	1-2	Malbranque 23 pen
35	prem	**Leeds**	H	W	2-0	Davis, S 71; Boa Morte 83
36	prem	**Chelsea**	A	L	1-2	Pembridge 19
37	prem	**Man City**	A	D	0-0	
38	prem	**Birmingham**	H	D	0-0	
39	prem	**Leicester**	A	W	2-0	John 66,89
40	prem	**Blackburn**	H	L	3-4	Bocanegra 26; John 45; Boa Morte 60
41	prem	**Liverpool**	A	D	0-0	
42	prem	**Charlton**	H	W	2-0	Malbranque 18 pen; Davis, S 64
43	prem	**Portsmouth**	A	D	1-1	McBride 85
44	prem	**Arsenal**	H	L	0-1	
45	prem	**Bolton**	A	W	2-0	McBride 45,78

LEAGUE POSITION
1st
2nd
3rd
4th
5th
6th
7th
8th
9th
10th
11th
12th
13th
14th
15th
16th
17th
18th
19th
20th
"We're no longer the spoilt rich kids," says Coleman after 'Boro win shows steel in addition to technique and ability
Hayles shows what might have been as second-half sub scores and unsettles Everton but he can't pull back three
Target Reyna chooses Man City and Marlet makes a break for Marseille
Saha picks Purse's pocket after just 36 seconds but Birmingham twice come from behind for a draw
Marlet's not missed as Hayles leads the line with two goals and an assist at Spurs
Saha so good as lone striker scores for the third game running to claim seventh spot
Coleman matches his mentor Keegan after Saha's pacey strike is only equalised in the 93rd minute
Malbranque's craft sets up two goals for Boa Morte and lifts Coleman to fourth spot
Saha fluffs and scuffs and ultimately Van der Sar needs to be on top form to keep Wolves at bay
Clark gets things rolling against his old club and Saha makes it 2-0 after eight minutes but then it comes off the rails
First win at Old Trafford for 40 years and it's deserved as Malbranque pulls strings and Goma snuffs out van Nistelrooy
dabs.com
AUGUST
SEPTEMBER
OCTOBER
Home
Away
Neutral

INS AND OUTS

IN Mark Crossley from Middlesbrough for £500K; Mark Pembridge from Everton for £500K; Jerome Bonnissel from Rangers for free; Moritz Volz from Arsenal on loan
OUT Steve Finnan to Liverpool for £3.5m; Maik Taylor to Birmingham, Pierre Wome to Bologna on loan; Bjarne Goldbaek released; John Collins retired. Steve Marlet to Marseille on loan

ATTENDANCES

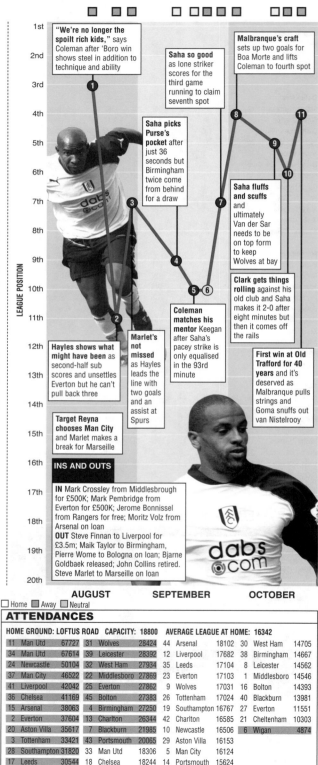

HOME GROUND: LOFTUS ROAD **CAPACITY:** 18800 **AVERAGE LEAGUE AT HOME:** 16342

11	Man Utd	67727	31	Wolves	28424	44	Arsenal	18102	30	West Ham	14705
34	Man Utd	67614	39	Leicester	28392	12	Liverpool	17682	38	Birmingham	14667
24	Newcastle	50104	32	West Ham	27934	35	Leeds	17104	8	Leicester	14562
37	Man City	46522	22	Middlesboro	27869	23	Everton	17103	1	Middlesboro	14546
41	Liverpool	42042	25	Everton	27862	9	Wolves	17031	16	Bolton	14393
36	Chelsea	41169	45	Bolton	27383	26	Tottenham	17024	40	Blackburn	13981
15	Arsenal	38063	4	Birmingham	27250	19	Southampton	16767	27	Everton	11551
2	Everton	37604	13	Charlton	26344	42	Charlton	16585	21	Cheltenham	10303
20	Aston Villa	35617	7	Blackburn	21985	10	Newcastle	16506	6	Wigan	4874
3	Tottenham	33421	43	Portsmouth	20065	29	Aston Villa	16153			
28	Southampton	31820	33	Man Utd	18306	5	Man City	16124			
17	Leeds	30544	18	Chelsea	18244	14	Portsmouth	15624			

Coleman salvages top finish post Saha

Final Position: **9th**

KEY: ● League ● Champions Lge ● UEFA Cup ● FA Cup ○ League Cup ● Other

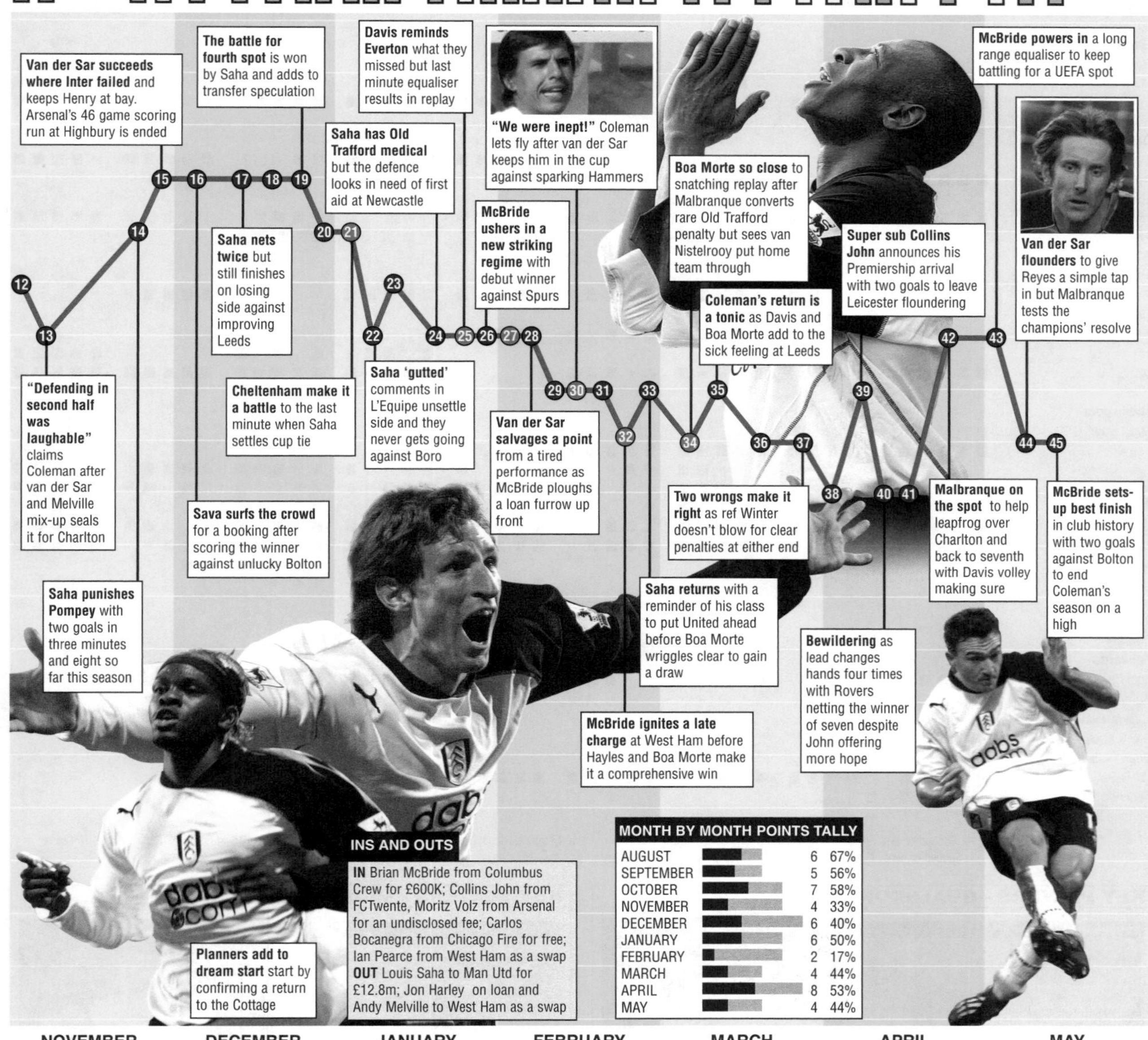

Van der Sar succeeds where Inter failed and keeps Henry at bay. Arsenal's 46 game scoring run at Highbury is ended
The battle for fourth spot is won by Saha and adds to transfer speculation
Davis reminds Everton what they missed but last minute equaliser results in replay
Saha has Old Trafford medical but the defence looks in need of first aid at Newcastle
"We were inept!" Coleman lets fly after van der Sar keeps him in the cup against sparking Hammers
McBride ushers in a new striking regime with debut winner against Spurs
Boa Morte so close to snatching replay after Malbranque converts rare Old Trafford penalty but sees van Nistelrooy put home team through
McBride powers in a long range equaliser to keep battling for a UEFA spot
Super sub Collins John announces his Premiership arrival with two goals to leave Leicester floundering
Van der Sar flounders to give Reyes a simple tap in but Malbranque tests the champions' resolve
Saha nets twice but still finishes on losing side against improving Leeds
Coleman's return is a tonic as Davis and Boa Morte add to the sick feeling at Leeds
"Defending in second half was laughable" claims Coleman after van der Sar and Melville mix-up seals it for Charlton
Cheltenham make it a battle to the last minute when Saha settles cup tie
Saha 'gutted' comments in L'Equipe unsettle side and they never gets going against Boro
Van der Sar salvages a point from a tired performance as McBride ploughs a loan furrow up front
Two wrongs make it right as ref Winter doesn't blow for clear penalties at either end
Malbranque on the spot to help leapfrog over Charlton and back to seventh with Davis volley making sure
McBride sets-up best finish in club history with two goals against Bolton to end Coleman's season on a high
Sava surfs the crowd for a booking after scoring the winner against unlucky Bolton
Saha punishes Pompey with two goals in three minutes and eight so far this season
Saha returns with a reminder of his class to put United ahead before Boa Morte wriggles clear to gain a draw
Bewildering as lead changes hands four times with Rovers netting the winner of seven despite John offering more hope
McBride ignites a late charge at West Ham before Hayles and Boa Morte make it a comprehensive win
Planners add to dream start start by confirming a return to the Cottage
NOVEMBER
DECEMBER
JANUARY
FEBRUARY
MARCH
APRIL
MAY

INS AND OUTS

IN Brian McBride from Columbus Crew for £600K; Collins John from FCTwente, Moritz Volz from Arsenal for an undisclosed fee; Carlos Bocanegra from Chicago Fire for free; Ian Pearce from West Ham as a swap **OUT** Louis Saha to Man Utd for £12.8m; Jon Harley on loan and Andy Melville to West Ham as a swap

MONTH BY MONTH POINTS TALLY

Month	Points	%
AUGUST	6	67%
SEPTEMBER	5	56%
OCTOBER	7	58%
NOVEMBER	4	33%
DECEMBER	6	40%
JANUARY	6	50%
FEBRUARY	2	17%
MARCH	4	44%
APRIL	8	53%
MAY	4	44%

GOAL ATTEMPTS

FOR — Goal attempts recorded in League games

	HOME	AWAY	TOTAL	AVE
shots on target	118	103	221	5.8
shots off target	95	86	181	4.8
TOTAL	213	189	402	10.6

Ratio of goals to shots Average number of shots on target per League goal scored	4.3
Accuracy rating Average percentage of total goal attempts which were on target	55

AGAINST — Goal attempts recorded in League games

	HOME	AWAY	TOTAL	AVE
shots on target	97	153	250	6.6
shots off target	79	103	182	4.8
TOTAL	176	256	432	11.4

Ratio of goals to shots Average number of shots on target per League goal scored	5.4
Accuracy rating Average percentage of total goal attempts which were on target	57.9

GOALS

Louis Saha

League	13
FA Cup	2
League Cup	0
Europe	0
Other	0
TOTAL	15

League Average **131** mins between goals

	PLAYER	LGE	FAC	LC	Euro	TOT	AVE
1	Saha	13	2	0	0	15	131
2	Boa Morte	9	1	0	0	10	309
3	Malbranque	6	2	0	0	8	552
4	Davis, S	5	1	0	0	6	394
5	Hayles	4	1	0	0	5	258
6	McBride	4	1	0	0	5	165
7	John	3	0	0	0	3	108
8	Inamoto	2	1	0	0	3	648
9	Clark	2	0	0	0	2	1090
10	Sava	1	0	0	0	1	114
11	Pembridge	1	0	0	0	1	697
12	Marlet	1	0	0	0	1	89
13	Bocanegra	1	0	0	0	1	1321
	Other	0	0	0	0	0	
	TOTAL	52	9	0	0	61	

SQUAD APPEARANCES

Match	1	2	3	4	5	6	7	8	9	10	11	12	13	14	15	16	17	18	19	20	21	22	23	24	25	26	27	28	29	30	31	32	33	34	35	36	37	38	39	40	41	42	43	44	45
Venue	H	A	A	A	H	A	A	H	H	H	A	H	A	H	A	H	A	H	H	A	H	A	H	A	A	H	H	A	H	H	A	A	H	A	H	A	A	H	A	H	A	H	A	H	A
Competition	L	L	L	L	L	W	L	L	L	L	L	L	L	L	L	L	L	L	L	L	F	L	L	L	F	L	F	L	L	F	L	F	L	F	L	L	L	L	L	L	L	L	L	L	L
Result	W	L	W	D	D	L	W	W	D	L	W	L	L	W	D	W	L	L	W	L	W	L	W	L	D	W	W	D	L	D	L	W	D	L	W	L	D	D	W	L	D	W	D	L	W

Goalkeepers
Dave Beasant
Mark Crossley
Edwin Van der Sar

Defenders
Carlos Bocanegra
Jerome Bonnissel
Tom Davis
Alain Goma
Adam Green
Jon Harley
Mark Hudson
Zatyiah Knight
Dean Leacock
Andy Melville
Ian Pearce
Moritz Volz

Midfielders
Malik Buari
Lee Clark
Sean Davis
Martin Djetou
Junichi Inamoto
Sylvain Legwinski
Steed Malbranque
Mark Pembridge
Bobby Petta
Darren Pratley
Zeshan Rehman

Forwards
Luis Boa Morte
Barry Hayles
Collins John
Steve Marlet
Brian McBride
Louis Saha
Facundo Sava
Andrejs Stolcers

KEY: On all match · On bench · Subbed or sent off (Counting game) · Subbed or sent off (playing less than 70 mins) · Subbed on from bench (Counting Game) · Subbed on (playing less than 70 mins) · Subbed on and then subbed or sent off (Counting Game) · Subbed on and then subbed or sent off (playing less than 70 mins) · Not in 16

KEY PLAYERS - GOALSCORERS

Louis Saha

Goals in the League	13
Goals in all competitions	15
Assists League goals scored by team-mates where he delivered the final pass	4
Contribution to Attacking Power Average number of minutes between League team goals while on pitch	60
Player Strike Rate Average number of minutes between League goals scored by player	131
Club Strike Rate Average minutes between League goals scored by club	66

	PLAYER	GOALS LGE	GOALS ALL	ASSISTS	POWER	S RATE
1	Louis Saha	13	15	4	60	131 mins
2	Luis Boa Morte	9	10	6	69	309 mins
3	Sean Davis	5	6	2	70	394 mins
4	Steed Malbranque	6	8	10	66	552 mins
5	Lee Clark	2	2	2	58	090 mins

KEY PLAYERS - MIDFIELDERS

Steed Malbranque

Goals in the League	6
Goals in all competitions	8
Assists League goals scored by team-mates where he delivered the final pass	10
Defensive Rating Average number of mins between League goals conceded while he was on the pitch	75
Contribution to Attacking Power Average number of minutes between League team goals while on pitch	66
Scoring Difference Defensive Rating minus Contribution to Attacking Power	9

	PLAYER	GOALS LGE	GOALS ALL	ASSISTS	DEF RATE	POWER	SC DIFF
1	Steed Malbranque	6	8	10	75	66	9 mins
2	Sean Davis	5	6	2	76	70	6 mins
3	Sylvain Legwinski	0	0	1	70	65	5 mins
4	Lee Clark	2	2	2	62	59	3 mins
5	Martin Djetou	0	0	0	73	73	0 mins

PLAYER APPEARANCES

	AGE (on 01/07/04)	IN NAMED 16	APPEARANCES	COUNTING GAMES	MINUTES ON PITCH	APPEARANCES	MINUTES ON PITCH	THIS SEASON	HOME COUNTRY
Goalkeepers									
Dave Beasant	45	3	0	0	0	0	0	-	England
Mark Crossley	35	36	1	1	90	2	180	7	Wales (66)
Edwin Van der Sar	33	37	37	37	3330	43	3900	11	Holland (4)
Defenders									
Carlos Bocanegra	25	15	15	15	1321	19	1711	-	United States
Jerome Bonnissel	31	16	16	15	1354	16	1354	-	France
Tom Davis	20	0	0	0	0	0	0	-	England
Alain Goma	31	28	23	23	2070	29	2595	-	France
Adam Green	20	7	4	4	360	7	630	-	England
Jon Harley	24	4	4	2	316	4	316	-	England
Mark Hudson	22	4	0	0	0	0	0	-	England
Zatyiah Knight	24	34	31	30	2718	37	3241	-	England
Dean Leacock	20	5	4	3	305	5	395	-	England
Andy Melville	35	18	9	9	810	11	945	6	Wales (66)
Ian Pearce	30	15	13	12	1096	13	1096	-	England
Moritz Volz	21	34	33	31	2880	38	3360	-	Germany
Midfielders									
Malik Buari	20	6	3	0	82	4	147	-	Ghana
Lee Clark	31	25	25	23	2179	27	2349	-	England
Sean Davis	24	24	24	21	1969	30	2538	-	England
Martin Djetou	29	36	26	17	1762	31	2199	-	France
Junichi Inamoto	24	31	22	8	1295	25	1504	-	Japan
Sylvain Legwinski	30	33	32	26	2583	37	3006	-	France
Steed Malbranque	24	38	38	36	3313	44	3883	-	France
Mark Pembridge	33	12	12	6	697	15	815	4	Wales (66)
Bobby Petta	29	17	9	1	322	14	542	-	Holland
Darren Pratley	19	2	1	0	18	2	26	-	England
Zeshan Rehman	20	3	1	0	2	2	36	-	England
Forwards									
Luis Boa Morte	26	33	33	31	2785	39	3266	6	Portugal (20)
Barry Hayles	32	30	26	5	1032	32	1361	-	Jamaica
Collins John	18	8	8	2	325	8	325	-	Holland
Steve Marlet	30	1	1	1	89	1	89	5	France (2)
Brian McBride	32	16	16	5	659	19	901	-	United States
Louis Saha	25	21	21	19	1699	22	1789	3	France (2)
Facundo Sava	30	15	6	0	114	9	254	-	Argentina
Andrejs Stolcers	29	0	0	0	0	1	82	-	Latvia

KEY: LEAGUE　ALL COMPS　CAPS (FIFA RANKING)

TEAM OF THE SEASON

Van der Sar
CG 37 DR 76
Volz
CG 31 DR 76
Knight
CG 30 DR 72
Goma
CG 23 DR 80
Bocanegra
CG 15 DR 83
Malbranque
CG 36 SD +9
Davis
CG 21 SD +6
Legwinski
CG 26 SD +5
Clark
CG 23 SD +3
Boa Morte
CG 31 AP 69
Saha
CG 19 SR 131

KEY: DR = Diffensive Rate, SD = Scoring Difference AP = Attacking Power SR = Strike Rate, CG=Counting games – League games playing at least 70 minutes

TOP POINT EARNERS

Jerome Bonnissel

Counting Games League games when he played at least 70 minutes	15
Average points Average League points taken in Counting games	1.67
Club Average points Average points taken in League games	1.37

	PLAYER	GAMES	PTS
1	Jerome Bonnissel	15	**1.67**
2	Alain Goma	23	**1.52**
3	Lee Clark	23	**1.48**
4	Martin Djetou	17	**1.47**
5	Sylvain Legwinski	26	**1.42**
6	Edwin Van der Sar	37	**1.41**
7	Steed Malbranque	36	**1.39**
8	Moritz Volz	31	**1.35**
9	Zatyiah Knight	30	**1.33**
10	Louis Saha	19	**1.32**

KEY PLAYERS - DEFENDERS

Carlos Bocanegra

Goals Conceded The number of League goals conceded while he was on the pitch	16
Goals Conceded in all competitions The number of goals conceded while he was on the pitch in all competitions	18
League minutes played Number of minutes played in league matches	1321
Clean Sheets In games when he played at least70 mins	7
Defensive Rating Average number of mins between League goals conceded while he was on the pitch	83
Club Defensive Rating Average number of mins between League goals conceded by the club this season	74

	PLAYER	CON LGE	CON ALL	MINS	C SHEETS	DEF RATE
1	Carlos Bocanegra	16	18	1321	7	**83 mins**
2	Alain Goma	26	31	2070	11	**80 mins**
3	Moritz Volz	38	42	2880	12	**76 mins**
4	Zatyiah Knight	38	43	2718	12	**72 mins**
5	Jerome Bonnissel	19	19	1354	6	**71 mins**

KEY GOALKEEPER

Edwin van der Sar

Goals Conceded in the League The number of League goals conceded while he was on the pitch	44
Goals Conceded in all competitions Number of goals conceded while he was on the pitch in all competitions	49
League minutes played Number of minutes played in league matches	3330
Clean Sheets In games when he played at least 70 mins	15
Goals to Shots Ratio The average number of shots on target per each League goal conceded	5.5
Defensive Rating Ave mins between League goals conceded while on the pitch	76

BOOKINGS

Junichi Inamoto

League Yellow	8
League Red	0
All competitions Yellow	8
All competitions Red	0

League Average 161 mins between cards

	PLAYER	LEAGUE Y	LEAGUE R	TOTAL Y	TOTAL R	AVE
1	Inamoto	8	0	8	0	161
2	Legwinski	9	1	9	1	258
3	Boa Morte	9	1	9	1	278
4	Davis, S	5	0	5	0	393
5	Goma	5	0	7	0	414
6	Bocanegra	2	1	3	1	440
7	Hayles	2	0	5	0	516
8	Volz	5	0	6	0	576
9	Djetou	3	0	3	0	587
10	Knight	4	0	4	0	679
11	Pembridge	1	0	1	0	697
12	Clark	2	0	2	0	1089
13	Malbranque	3	0	4	0	1104
14	Saha	1	0	1	0	1699
	Other	4	0	4	0	
	TOTAL	**63**	**3**	**71**	**3**	

BIRMINGHAM CITY

"Chelsea's best striker is Mikael Forssell," claimed the London club's former chairman Ken Bates, and the figures prove him right.

The on-loan Finn's Strike Rate is the fifth highest in the division, averaging a goal every 155 minutes, eclipsing Hasselbaink and Gudjohnsen. He netted 42% of Birmingham's goals, which is the second highest share of club goals in the Premiership.

It is Forssell's second season out on loan. Last year he lifted Borussia Monchengladbach up the table after a move in January. **Steve Bruce** might have noticed that he had a Strike Rate better than 200 minutes despite playing only half a season in Germany.

Keeper **Maik Taylor** claims the fifth highest Goals to Shots Ratio, saving nearly six shots for every goal he concedes.

NICKNAME: THE BLUES

KEY: Won / Drawn / Lost

1	prem	**Tottenham**	H	W	1-0	Dunn 36 pen
2	prem	**Southampton**	A	D	0-0	
3	prem	**Newcastle**	A	W	1-0	Dunn 61
4	prem	**Fulham**	H	D	2-2	Forssell 45,82
5	prem	**Leeds**	A	W	2-0	Savage 79 pen; Forssell 84
6	ccr2	**Blackpool**	A	L	0-1	
7	prem	**Portsmouth**	H	W	2-0	Clemence 21; Lazaridis 50
8	prem	**Man Utd**	A	L	0-3	
9	prem	**Chelsea**	H	D	0-0	
10	prem	**Aston Villa**	H	D	0-0	
11	prem	**Bolton**	A	W	1-0	Forssell 31
12	prem	**Charlton**	H	L	1-2	Dugarry 64
13	prem	**Wolves**	A	D	1-1	Forssell 49
14	prem	**Arsenal**	H	L	0-3	
15	prem	**Liverpool**	A	L	1-3	Forssell 33
16	prem	**Blackburn**	H	L	0-4	
17	prem	**Leicester**	A	W	2-0	Morrison 42; Forssell 66
18	prem	**Man City**	H	W	2-1	Kenna 81; Forssell 87
19	prem	**Everton**	A	L	0-1	
20	facr3	**Blackburn**	H	W	4-0	Morrison 23; Clemence 36; Forssell 78; Hughes, B 84
21	prem	**Tottenham**	A	L	1-4	Savage 68 pen
22	prem	**Southampton**	H	W	2-1	Clemence 16; Kenna 67
23	prem	**Chelsea**	A	D	0-0	
24	facr4	**Wimbledon**	H	W	1-0	Hughes, B 4
25	prem	**Newcastle**	H	D	1-1	John 90
26	prem	**Man City**	A	D	0-0	
27	prem	**Everton**	H	W	3-0	Johnson, D 8; Lazaridis 39; Forssell 49
28	facr5	**Sunderland**	A	D	1-1	Forssell 28
29	prem	**Aston Villa**	A	D	2-2	Forssell 60; John 90
30	facr5r	**Sunderland**	H	L	0-2	
31	prem	**Middlesbrough**	H	W	3-1	Forssell 23,79; Savage 57
32	prem	**Bolton**	H	W	2-0	Forssell 24; Hughes, B 69
33	prem	**Leicester**	H	L	0-1	
34	prem	**Middlesbrough**	A	L	3-5	Forssell 23,59; Morrison 45
35	prem	**Leeds**	H	W	4-1	Hughes, B 12,67; Forssell 69,81 pen
36	prem	**Fulham**	A	D	0-0	
37	prem	**Man Utd**	H	L	1-2	Grainger 39
38	prem	**Portsmouth**	A	L	1-3	John 67
39	prem	**Charlton**	A	D	1-1	Morrison 84
40	prem	**Wolves**	H	D	2-2	Forssell 34; Morrison 41
41	prem	**Arsenal**	A	D	0-0	
42	prem	**Liverpool**	H	L	0-3	
43	prem	**Blackburn**	A	D	1-1	John 83

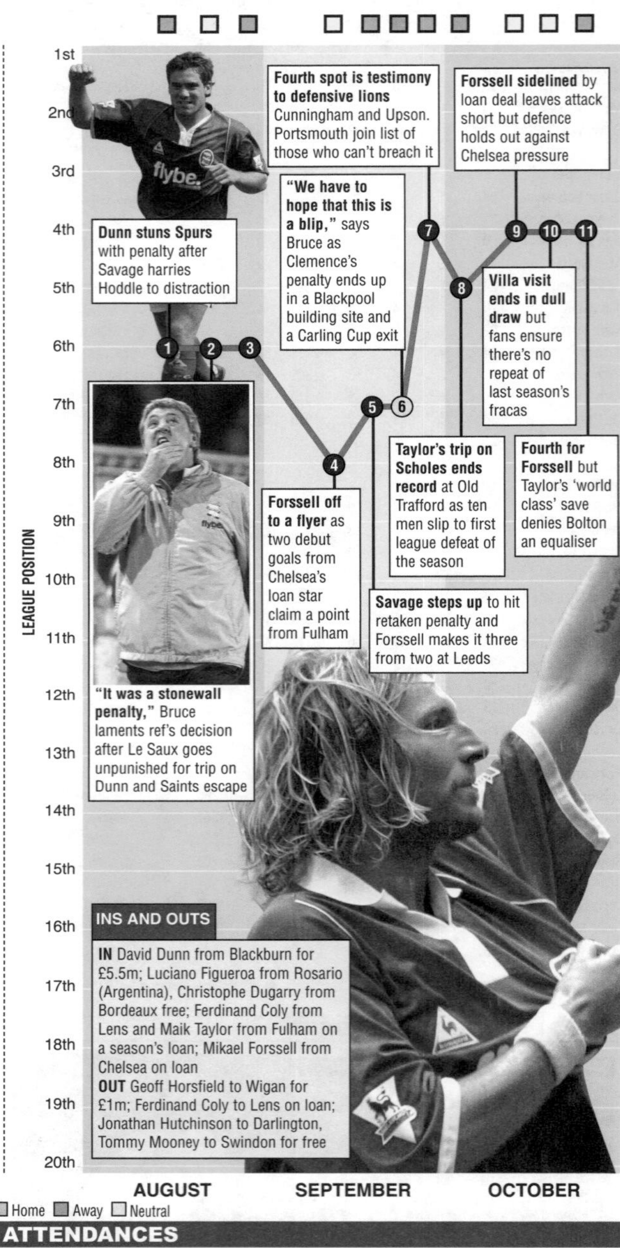
LEAGUE POSITION
1st
2nd
3rd
4th
5th
6th
7th
8th
9th
10th
11th
12th
13th
14th
15th
16th
17th
18th
19th
20th
AUGUST
SEPTEMBER
OCTOBER
flybe.
Dunn stuns Spurs with penalty after Savage harries Hoddle to distraction
"It was a stonewall penalty," Bruce laments ref's decision after Le Saux goes unpunished for trip on Dunn and Saints escape
Forssell off to a flyer as two debut goals from Chelsea's loan star claim a point from Fulham
Savage steps up to hit retaken penalty and Forssell makes it three from two at Leeds
"We have to hope that this is a blip," says Bruce as Clemence's penalty ends up in a Blackpool building site and a Carling Cup exit
Fourth spot is testimony to defensive lions Cunningham and Upson. Portsmouth join list of those who can't breach it
Taylor's trip on Scholes ends record at Old Trafford as ten men slip to first league defeat of the season
Forssell sidelined by loan deal leaves attack short but defence holds out against Chelsea pressure
Villa visit ends in dull draw but fans ensure there's no repeat of last season's fracas
Fourth for Forssell but Taylor's 'world class' save denies Bolton an equaliser
Home
Away
Neutral

INS AND OUTS

IN David Dunn from Blackburn for £5.5m; Luciano Figueroa from Rosario (Argentina), Christophe Dugarry from Bordeaux free; Ferdinand Coly from Lens and Maik Taylor from Fulham on a season's loan; Mikael Forssell from Chelsea on loan

OUT Geoff Horsfield to Wigan for £1m; Ferdinand Coly to Lens on loan; Jonathan Hutchinson to Darlington, Tommy Mooney to Swindon for free

ATTENDANCES

HOME GROUND: ST ANDREWS **CAPACITY:** 30009 **AVERAGE LEAGUE AT HOME:** 29077

8	Man Utd	67633	34	Middlesboro	30244	31	Middlesboro	29369	43	Blackburn	26070
3	Newcastle	52006	21	Tottenham	30016	1	Tottenham	29358	30	Sunderland	25645
26	Man City	46967	14	Arsenal	29588	16	Blackburn	29354	39	Charlton	25206
15	Liverpool	42683	42	Liverpool	29553	22	Southampton	29071	11	Bolton	25023
23	Chelsea	41073	37	Man Utd	29548	35	Leeds	29069	28	Sunderland	24966
29	Aston Villa	40061	10	Aston Villa	29546	7	Portsmouth	29057	24	Wimbledon	22159
19	Everton	39631	18	Man City	29520	27	Everton	29004	38	Portsmouth	20104
41	Arsenal	38061	25	Newcastle	29513	13	Wolves	28831	20	Blackburn	18688
5	Leeds	34305	40	Wolves	29494	32	Bolton	28003	36	Fulham	14667
2	Southampton	31656	33	Leicester	29491	4	Fulham	27250	6	Blackpool	7370
17	Leicester	30639	9	Chelsea	29460	12	Charlton	27225			

Forssell fires Bruce to the top half

Final Position: **10th**

KEY: ● League ● Champions Lge ● UEFA Cup ● FA Cup ○ League Cup ● Other

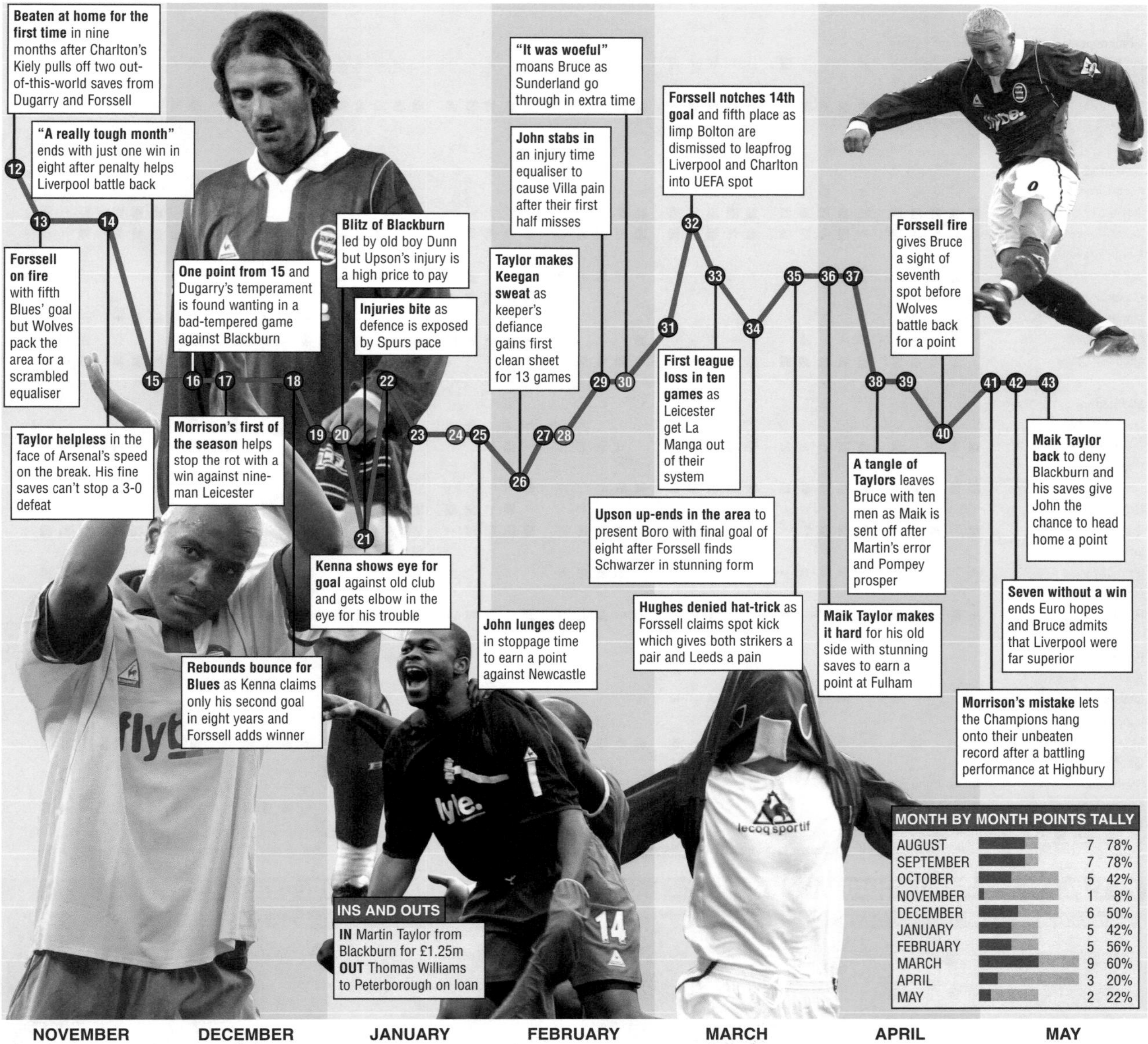

Beaten at home for the first time in nine months after Charlton's Kiely pulls off two out-of-this-world saves from Dugarry and Forssell

"A really tough month" ends with just one win in eight after penalty helps Liverpool battle back

Forssell on fire with fifth Blues' goal but Wolves pack the area for a scrambled equaliser

Taylor helpless in the face of Arsenal's speed on the break. His fine saves can't stop a 3-0 defeat

One point from 15 and Dugarry's temperament is found wanting in a bad-tempered game against Blackburn

Morrison's first of the season helps stop the rot with a win against nine-man Leicester

Rebounds bounce for Blues as Kenna claims only his second goal in eight years and Forssell adds winner

Blitz of Blackburn led by old boy Dunn but Upson's injury is a high price to pay

Injuries bite as defence is exposed by Spurs pace

Kenna shows eye for goal against old club and gets elbow in the eye for his trouble

John lunges deep in stoppage time to earn a point against Newcastle

Taylor makes Keegan sweat as keeper's defiance gains first clean sheet for 13 games

"It was woeful" moans Bruce as Sunderland go through in extra time

John stabs in an injury time equaliser to cause Villa pain after their first half misses

Forssell notches 14th goal and fifth place as limp Bolton are dismissed to leapfrog Liverpool and Charlton into UEFA spot

First league loss in ten games as Leicester get La Manga out of their system

Upson up-ends in the area to present Boro with final goal of eight after Forssell finds Schwarzer in stunning form

Hughes denied hat-trick as Forssell claims spot kick which gives both strikers a pair and Leeds a pain

Maik Taylor makes it hard for his old side with stunning saves to earn a point at Fulham

A tangle of Taylors leaves Bruce with ten men as Maik is sent off after Martin's error and Pompey prosper

Forssell fire gives Bruce a sight of seventh spot before Wolves battle back for a point

Maik Taylor back to deny Blackburn and his saves give John the chance to head home a point

Seven without a win ends Euro hopes and Bruce admits that Liverpool were far superior

Morrison's mistake lets the Champions hang onto their unbeaten record after a battling performance at Highbury

INS AND OUTS

IN Martin Taylor from Blackburn for £1.25m
OUT Thomas Williams to Peterborough on loan

MONTH BY MONTH POINTS TALLY

Month	Points	%
AUGUST	7	78%
SEPTEMBER	7	78%
OCTOBER	5	42%
NOVEMBER	1	8%
DECEMBER	6	50%
JANUARY	5	42%
FEBRUARY	5	56%
MARCH	9	60%
APRIL	3	20%
MAY	2	22%

NOVEMBER DECEMBER JANUARY FEBRUARY MARCH APRIL MAY

GOAL ATTEMPTS

FOR — Goal attempts recorded in League games

	HOME	AWAY	TOTAL	AVE
shots on target	113	70	183	4.8
shots off target	79	73	152	4
TOTAL	192	143	335	8.8

Ratio of goals to shots — Average number of shots on target per League goal scored: **4.3**

Accuracy rating — Average percentage of total goal attempts which were on target: **54.6**

AGAINST — Goal attempts recorded in League games

	HOME	AWAY	TOTAL	AVE
shots on target	103	127	230	6.1
shots off target	74	70	144	3.8
TOTAL	177	197	374	9.8

Ratio of goals to shots — Average number of shots on target per League goal scored: **4.8**

Accuracy rating — Average percentage of total goal attempts which were on target: **61.5**

GOALS

Mikael Forssell

League	18
FA Cup	2
League Cup	0
Europe	0
Other	0
TOTAL	20

League Average: 155 mins between goals

	PLAYER	LGE	FAC	LC	Euro	TOT	AVE
1	Forssell	18	2	0	0	20	155
2	Morrison	4	1	0	0	5	450
3	John	4	0	0	0	4	212
4	Savage	3	0	0	0	3	889
5	Hughes, B	3	2	0	0	5	561
6	Lazaridis	2	0	0	0	2	1060
7	Clemence	2	1	0	0	3	1360
8	Dunn	2	0	0	0	2	893
9	Kenna	2	0	0	0	2	600
10	Grainger	1	0	0	0	1	250
11	Dugarry	1	0	0	0	1	981
12	Johnson, D	1	0	0	0	1	3072
	Other	0	0	0	0	0	
	TOTAL	43	6	0	0	49	

SQUAD APPEARANCES

Match	1	2	3	4	5	6	7	8	9	10	11	12	13	14	15	16	17	18	19	20	21	22	23	24	25	26	27	28	29	30	31	32	33	34	35	36	37	38	39	40	41	42	43
Venue	H	A	A	H	A	A	H	A	H	H	A	H	A	H	A	H	A	H	A	H	A	H	A	H	H	A	H	A	A	H	H	H	H	A	H	A	H	A	A	H	A	H	A
Competition	L	L	L	L	L	W	L	L	L	L	L	L	L	L	L	L	L	L	L	F	L	L	L	F	L	L	L	F	L	F	L	L	L	L	L	L	L	L	L	L	L	L	L
Result	W	D	W	D	W	L	W	L	D	D	W	L	D	L	L	L	W	W	L	W	L	W	D	W	D	D	W	D	D	L	W	W	L	L	W	D	L	L	D	D	D	L	D

Goalkeepers
Ian Bennett
Colin Doyle
Maik Taylor
Nico Vaesen

Defenders
Aliou Cisse
Jamie Clapham
Kenny Cunningham
Martin Grainger
Jeff Kenna
Darren Purse
Martin Taylor
Olivier Tebily
Matthew Upson

Midfielders
Darren Carter
Stephen Clemence
Paul Devlin
David Dunn
Bryan Hughes
Damien Johnson
Jovan Kirovski
Stan Lazaridis
Carl Motteram
Robbie Savage

Forwards
Andrew Barrowman
Christophe Dugarry
Luciano Figueroa
Mikael Forssell
Geoff Horsfield
Stern John
Clinton Morrison

KEY: On all match | On bench | Subbed or sent off (Counting game) | Subbed or sent off (playing less than 70 mins) | Subbed on from bench (Counting Game) | Subbed on (playing less than 70 mins) | Subbed on and then subbed or sent off (Counting Game) | Subbed on and then subbed or sent off (playing less than 70 mins) | Not in 16

KEY PLAYERS - GOALSCORERS

Mikael Forssell

Goals in the League	18
Goals in all competitions	20
Assists League goals scored by team-mates where he delivered the final pass	3
Contribution to Attacking Power Average number of minutes between League team goals while on pitch	68
Player Strike Rate Average number of minutes between League goals scored by player	155
Club Strike Rate Average minutes between League goals scored by club	80

	PLAYER	GOALS LGE	GOALS ALL	ASSISTS	POWER	S RATE
1	Mikael Forssell	18	20	3	68	155 mins
2	Clinton Morrison	4	5	5	62	450 mins
3	Bryan Hughes	3	5	0	64	561 mins
4	Jeff Kenna	2	2	0	99	600 mins
5	Robbie Savage	3	3	5	86	889 mins

KEY PLAYERS - MIDFIELDERS

Bryan Hughes

Goals in the League	3
Goals in all competitions	5
Assists League goals scored by team-mates where he delivered the final pass	0
Defensive Rating Average number of mins between League goals conceded while he was on the pitch	73
Contribution to Attacking Power Average number of minutes between League team goals while on pitch	65
Scoring Difference Defensive Rating minus Contribution to Attacking Power	8

	PLAYER	GOALS LGE	GOALS ALL	ASSISTS	DEF RATE	POWER	SC DIFF
1	Bryan Hughes	3	5	0	73	65	8 mins
2	Stan Lazaridis	2	2	5	85	82	3 mins
3	Robbie Savage	3	3	5	86	86	0 mins
4	Damien Johnson	1	1	4	70	79	-9 mins
5	Stephen Clemence	2	3	1	68	80	-12 mins

PLAYER APPEARANCES

	AGE (on 01/07/04)	IN NAMED 16	APPEARANCES	COUNTING GAMES	MINUTES ON PITCH	APPEARANCES	MINUTES ON PITCH	THIS SEASON	HOME COUNTRY
Goalkeepers									
Ian Bennett	32	38	6	4	461	6	461	-	England
Colin Doyle	18	2	0	0	0	0	0	-	England
Maik Taylor	32	34	34	32	2959	39	3439	7	N Ireland (114)
Nico Vaesen	34	2	0	0	0	0	0	-	Belgium
Defenders									
Aliou Cisse	28	26	15	3	543	17	616	4	Senegal (31)
Jamie Clapham	28	26	25	21	2015	27	2128	-	England
Kenny Cunningham	33	37	36	35	3210	41	3684	8	Rep of Ireland (15)
Martin Grainger	31	4	4	2	250	4	250	-	England
Jeff Kenna	33	20	17	13	1199	21	1589	-	Rep of Ireland
Darren Purse	27	13	9	9	802	12	1102	-	England
Martin Taylor	24	15	12	11	993	12	993	-	England
Olivier Tebily	28	34	27	14	1557	29	1717	-	Ivory Coast
Matthew Upson	25	31	30	30	2685	33	2877	5	England (12)
Midfielders									
Darren Carter	20	10	5	0	76	8	147	-	England
Stephen Clemence	26	35	35	26	2719	38	2985	-	England
Paul Devlin	32	2	2	0	22	2	22	3	Scotland (63)
David Dunn	24	21	21	19	1786	25	2024	-	England
Bryan Hughes	28	27	26	16	1683	30	2060	-	Wales
Damien Johnson	25	35	35	34	3072	40	3552	4	N Ireland (114)
Jovan Kirovski	28	7	6	0	74	8	95	-	United States
Stan Lazaridis	31	31	30	22	2119	33	2344	5	Australia (89)
Carl Motteram	19	2	0	0	0	0	0	-	England
Robbie Savage	29	31	31	28	2668	35	3048	6	Wales (66)
Forwards									
Andrew Barrowman	19	4	1	0	4	1	4	-	Scotland
Christophe Dugarry	32	14	14	10	981	15	1009	-	France
Luciano Figueroa	23	2	1	0	4	2	31	-	Argentina
Mikael Forssell	23	32	32	32	2795	37	3156	4	Finland (42)
Geoff Horsfield	30	3	3	0	146	3	146	-	England
Stern John	27	34	29	5	846	32	1018	-	Trinidad & Tobago
Clinton Morrison	25	36	32	16	1798	37	2250	9	Rep of Ireland (15)

KEY: LEAGUE ALL COMPS CAPS (FIFA RANKING)

TEAM OF THE SEASON

TAYLOR
CG 32 DR 80

KENNA
CG 13 DR 92

UPSON
CG 30 DR 77

CUNNINGHAM
CG 35 DR 73

TEBILY
CG 14 DR 74

JOHNSON
CG 34 SD -9

SAVAGE
CG 28 SD 0

HUGHES
CG 16 SD +8

LAZARIDIS
CG 22 SD +3

MORRISON
CG 16 AP 62

FORSSELL
CG 32 SR 155

KEY: DR = Diffensive Rate, SD = Scoring Difference AP = Attacking Power SR = Strike Rate, CG=Counting games – League games playing at least 70 minutes

TOP POINT EARNERS

Jeff Kenna

Counting Games League games when he played at least 70 minutes	13
Average points Average League points taken in Counting games	1.54
Club Average points Average points taken in League games	1.32

	PLAYER	GAMES	PTS
1	Jeff Kenna	13	1.54
2	Maik Taylor	32	1.50
3	Stephen Clemence	26	1.46
4	Clinton Morrison	16	1.44
5	David Dunn	19	1.42
6	Damien Johnson	34	1.38
7	Bryan Hughes	16	1.38
8	Kenny Cunningham	35	1.37
9	Matthew Upson	30	1.33
10	Robbie Savage	28	1.32

KEY PLAYERS - DEFENDERS

Jeff Kenna

Goals Conceded The number of League goals conceded while he was on the pitch	13
Goals Conceded in all competitions The number of goals conceded while he was on the pitch in all competitions	16
League minutes played Number of minutes played in league matches	1199
Clean Sheets In games when he played at least70 mins	6
Defensive Rating Average number of mins between League goals conceded while he was on the pitch	92
Club Defensive Rating Average number of mins between League goals conceded by the club this season	71

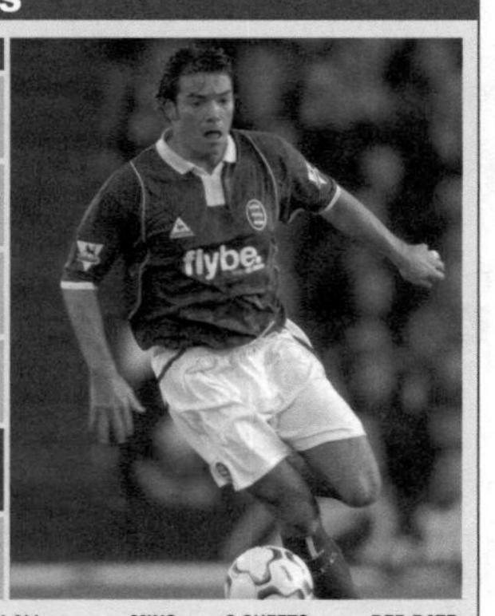
flybe

	PLAYER	CON LGE	CON ALL	MINS	C SHEETS	DEF RATE
1	Jeff Kenna	13	16	1199	6	92 mins
2	Matthew Upson	35	37	2685	12	77 mins
3	Olivier Tebily	21	21	1557	6	74 mins
4	Kenny Cunningham	44	48	3210	15	73 mins
5	Jamie Clapham	29	30	2015	10	69 mins

KEY GOALKEEPER

Maik Taylor

Goals Conceded in the League The number of League goals conceded while he was on the pitch	37
Goals Conceded in all competitions Number of goals conceded while he was on the pitch in all competitions	41
League minutes played Number of minutes played in league matches	2959
Clean Sheets In games when he played at least 70 mins	13
Goals to Shots Ratio The average number of shots on target per each League goal conceded	5.8
Defensive Rating Ave mins between League goals conceded while on the pitch	80

BOOKINGS

Aliou Cisse

League Yellow	5
League Red	0
All competitions Yellow	5
All competitions Red	0
League Average 108 mins between cards	

	PLAYER	LEAGUE Y	LEAGUE R	TOTAL Y	TOTAL R	AVE
1	Cisse	5	0	5	0	108
2	Dugarry	6	1	6	1	140
3	Savage	12	0	12	0	222
4	Tebily	4	0	4	0	389
5	Johnson, D	6	0	6	0	512
6	Clemence	4	0	4	0	679
7	Purse	0	1	1	1	802
8	Dunn	2	0	2	0	893
9	Cunningham	2	1	2	1	1070
10	Kenna	1	0	1	0	1199
11	Upson	2	0	2	0	1342
12	Taylor, Maik	0	2	0	2	1479
13	Morrison	1	0	1	0	1798
14	Forssell	1	0	1	0	2795
	Other	0	0	0	0	
	TOTAL	46	5	47	5	

MIDDLESBROUGH

Steve McClaren has given chairman **Steve Gibson** his first silverware with the Carling Cup to polish. They also enjoyed a secure mid-table finish.

Colin Cooper stepped in to salvage Boro's reputation for being tight at the back. He enjoyed the fifth highest Defensive Rating in the Premiership, playing 120 minutes on average for every goal conceded by the team.

While **Ugo Ehiogu** and **Gareth Southgate** were dogged by injury and **Danny Mills** haunted by Henry, **Franck Queudrue** was on hand to achieve 12 clean sheets.

Tight at the back but starved up front where five supposedly Premiership attackers rotated to poor affect and **Juninho** topped the club Goalscorers table with eight goals hit at a Strike Rate of one every 287 minutes. But that cup makes it the best-ever season.

NICKNAME: BORO

KEY: Won Drawn Lost

No	Comp	Opponent			Score	Scorers
1	prem	**Fulham**	A	L	2-3	Marinelli 10; Nemeth 81
2	prem	**Arsenal**	H	L	0-4	
3	prem	**Leicester**	A	D	0-0	
4	prem	**Leeds**	H	L	2-3	Nemeth 60; Juninho 63
5	prem	**Bolton**	A	L	0-2	
6	prem	**Everton**	H	W	1-0	Job 6
7	ccr2	**Brighton**	H	W	1-0	Christie 94
8	prem	**Southampton**	A	W	1-0	Christie 13
9	prem	**Chelsea**	H	L	1-2	Nemeth 46
10	prem	**Newcastle**	H	L	0-1	
11	prem	**Tottenham**	A	D	0-0	
12	ccr3	**Wigan**	A	W	2-1	Maccarone 36; Mendieta 66
13	prem	**Wolves**	H	W	2-0	Mendieta 73; Juninho 83
14	prem	**Aston Villa**	A	W	2-0	Zenden 30; Ricketts 49 pen
15	prem	**Liverpool**	H	D	0-0	
16	prem	**Man City**	A	W	1-0	Sun Jihai 30 og
17	ccr4	**Everton**	H	D	0-0	
18	prem	**Portsmouth**	H	D	0-0	
19	prem	**Charlton**	H	D	0-0	
20	ccqf	**Tottenham**	A	W	5-4*	Ricketts 86 (*on penalties)
21	prem	**Blackburn**	A	D	2-2	Juninho 31,51
22	prem	**Man Utd**	H	L	0-1	
23	facr3	**Notts County**	H	W	2-0	Richardson 25 og; Zenden 64
24	prem	**Fulham**	H	W	2-1	Job 15; Nemeth 67
25	prem	**Arsenal**	A	L	1-4	Maccarone 86 pen
26	prem	**Leicester**	H	D	3-3	Juninho 8; Maccarone 90; Curtis 90 og
27	ccsfl1	**Arsenal**	A	W	1-0	Juninho 53
28	facr4	**Arsenal**	A	L	1-4	Job 23
29	prem	**Leeds**	A	W	3-0	Zenden 53; Job 77; Ricketts 89 pen
30	ccsfl2	**Arsenal**	H	W	2-1	Zenden 69; Reyes 85 og
31	prem	**Blackburn**	H	L	0-1	
32	prem	**Man Utd**	A	W	3-2	Juninho 34,38; Job 80
33	prem	**Newcastle**	A	L	1-2	Zenden 33
34	cccf	**Bolton**	A	W	2-1	Job 2; Zenden 7 pen
35	prem	**Birmingham**	A	L	1-3	Nemeth 75
36	prem	**Tottenham**	H	W	1-0	Nemeth 73
37	prem	**Charlton**	A	L	0-1	
38	prem	**Birmingham**	H	W	5-3	Mendieta 5; Maccarone 21,45; Southgate 30; Nemeth 90
39	prem	**Everton**	A	D	1-1	Yobo 83 og
40	prem	**Bolton**	H	W	2-0	Nolan 8 og; Greening 51
41	prem	**Chelsea**	A	D	0-0	
42	prem	**Southampton**	H	W	3-1	Juninho 23; Nemeth 32; Maccarone 49
43	prem	**Wolves**	A	L	0-2	
44	prem	**Aston Villa**	H	L	1-2	Job 41
45	prem	**Liverpool**	A	L	0-2	
46	prem	**Man City**	H	W	2-1	Maccarone 8; Nemeth 32
47	prem	**Portsmouth**	A	L	1-5	Zenden 27

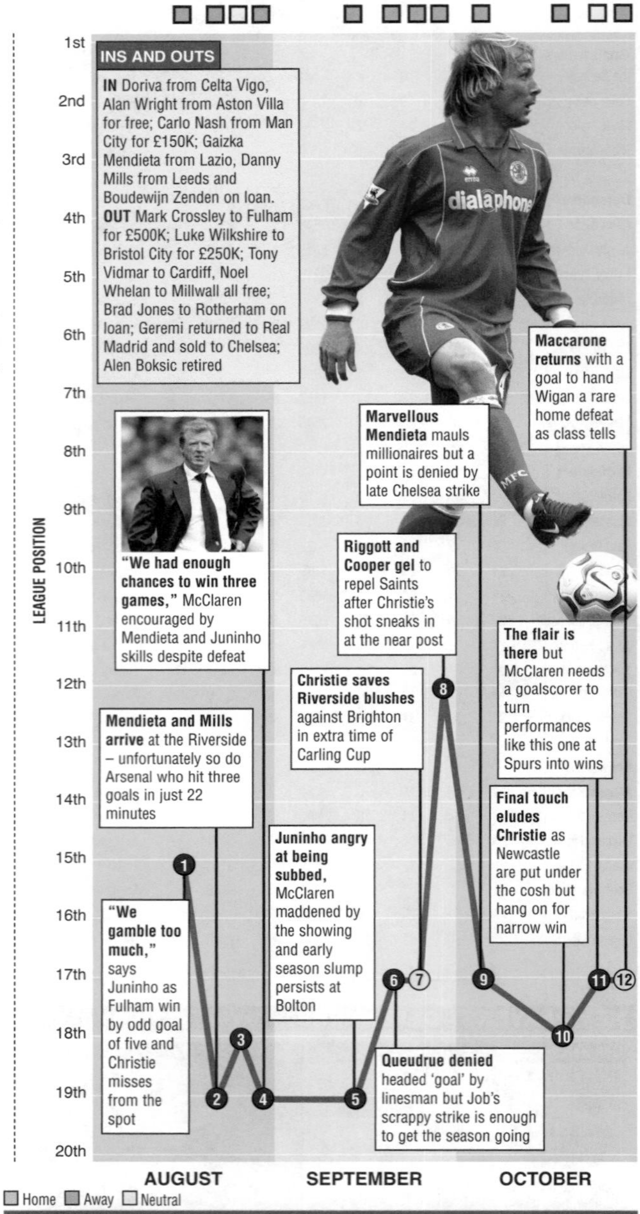

INS AND OUTS

IN Doriva from Celta Vigo, Alan Wright from Aston Villa for free; Carlo Nash from Man City for £150K; Gaizka Mendieta from Lazio, Danny Mills from Leeds and Boudewijn Zenden on loan. **OUT** Mark Crossley to Fulham for £500K; Luke Wilkshire to Bristol City for £250K; Tony Vidmar to Cardiff, Noel Whelan to Millwall all free; Brad Jones to Rotherham on loan; Geremi returned to Real Madrid and sold to Chelsea; Alen Boksic retired

LEAGUE POSITION: 1st 2nd 3rd 4th 5th 6th 7th 8th 9th 10th 11th 12th 13th 14th 15th 16th 17th 18th 19th 20th

AUGUST SEPTEMBER OCTOBER

Home Away Neutral

"We had enough chances to win three games," McClaren encouraged by Mendieta and Juninho skills despite defeat

Mendieta and Mills arrive at the Riverside – unfortunately so do Arsenal who hit three goals in just 22 minutes

"We gamble too much," says Juninho as Fulham win by odd goal of five and Christie misses from the spot

Juninho angry at being subbed, McClaren maddened by the showing and early season slump persists at Bolton

Christie saves Riverside blushes against Brighton in extra time of Carling Cup

Riggott and Cooper gel to repel Saints after Christie's shot sneaks in at the near post

Marvellous Mendieta mauls millionaires but a point is denied by late Chelsea strike

Queudrue denied headed 'goal' by linesman but Job's scrappy strike is enough to get the season going

The flair is there but McClaren needs a goalscorer to turn performances like this one at Spurs into wins

Final touch eludes Christie as Newcastle are put under the cosh but hang on for narrow win

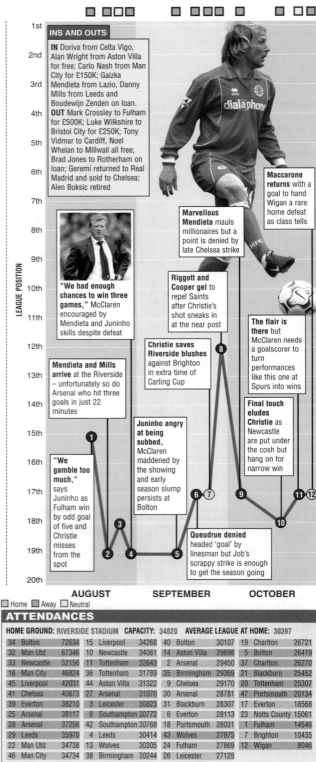

Maccarone returns with a goal to hand Wigan a rare home defeat as class tells

ATTENDANCES

HOME GROUND: RIVERSIDE STADIUM **CAPACITY:** 34820 **AVERAGE LEAGUE AT HOME:** 30397

34	Bolton	72634	15	Liverpool	34268	40	Bolton	30107	19	Charlton	26721
32	Man Utd	67346	10	Newcastle	34081	14	Aston Villa	29898	5	Bolton	26419
33	Newcastle	52156	11	Tottenham	32643	2	Arsenal	29450	37	Charlton	26270
16	Man City	46824	36	Tottenham	31789	35	Birmingham	29369	21	Blackburn	25452
45	Liverpool	42031	44	Aston Villa	31322	9	Chelsea	29170	20	Tottenham	25307
41	Chelsea	40873	27	Arsenal	31070	30	Arsenal	28781	47	Portsmouth	20134
39	Everton	38210	3	Leicester	30823	31	Blackburn	28307	17	Everton	18568
25	Arsenal	38117	8	Southampton	30772	6	Everton	28113	23	Notts County	15061
28	Arsenal	37256	42	Southampton	30768	18	Portsmouth	28031	1	Fulham	14546
29	Leeds	35970	4	Leeds	30414	43	Wolves	27975	7	Brighton	10435
22	Man Utd	34738	13	Wolves	30305	24	Fulham	27869	12	Wigan	8046
46	Man City	34734	38	Birmingham	30244	26	Leicester	27125			

Strikerless season has silver lining

Final Position: 11th

KEY: ● League ● Champions Lge ● UEFA Cup ● FA Cup ○ League Cup ● Other

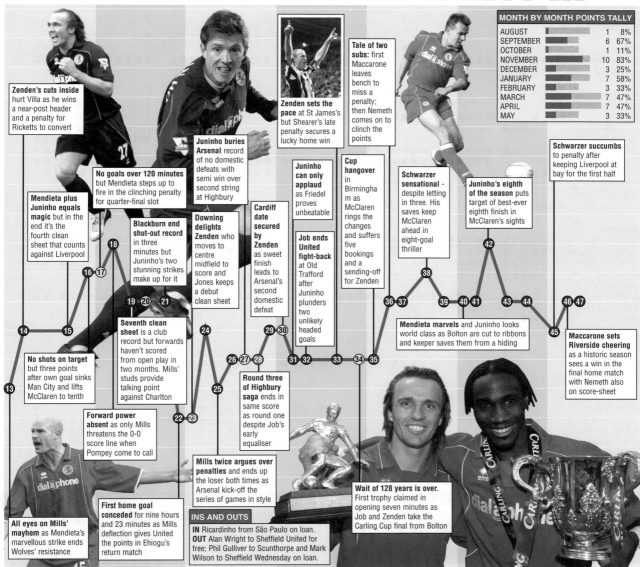

Zenden's cuts inside hurt Villa as he wins a near-post header and a penalty for Ricketts to convert

All eyes on Mills' mayhem as Mendieta's marvellous strike ends Wolves' resistance

No shots on target but three points after own goal sinks Man City and lifts McClaren to tenth

Mendieta plus Juninho equals magic but in the end it's the fourth clean sheet that counts against Liverpool

No goals over 120 minutes but Mendieta steps up to fire in the clinching penalty for quarter-final slot

Forward power absent as only Mills threatens the 0-0 score line when Pompey come to call

Blackburn end shut-out record in three minutes but Juninho's two stunning strikes make up for it

Seventh clean sheet is a club record but forwards haven't scored from open play in two months. Mills' studs provide talking point against Charlton

First home goal conceded for nine hours and 23 minutes as Mills deflection gives United the points in Ehiogu's return match

Juninho buries Arsenal record of no domestic defeats with semi win over second string at Highbury

Downing delights Zenden who moves to centre midfield to score and Jones keeps a debut clean sheet

Mills twice argues over penalties and ends up the loser both times as Arsenal kick-off the series of games in style

Round three of Highbury saga ends in same score as round one despite Job's early equaliser

Cardiff date secured by Zenden as sweet finish leads to Arsenal's second domestic defeat

Zenden sets the pace at St James's but Shearer's late penalty secures a lucky home win

Juninho can only applaud as Friedel proves unbeatable

Job ends United fight-back at Old Trafford after Juninho plunders two unlikely headed goals

Tale of two subs: first Maccarone leaves bench to miss a penalty; then Nemeth comes on to clinch the points

Cup hangover in Birmingham as McClaren rings the changes and suffers five bookings and a sending-off for Zenden

Wait of 128 years is over. First trophy claimed in opening seven minutes as Job and Zenden take the Carling Cup final from Bolton

Schwarzer sensational - despite letting in three. His saves keep McClaren ahead in eight-goal thriller

Mendieta marvels and Juninho looks world class as Bolton are cut to ribbons and keeper saves them from a hiding

Juninho's eighth of the season puts target of best-ever eighth finish in McClaren's sights

Schwarzer succumbs to penalty after keeping Liverpool at bay for the first half

Maccarone sets Riverside cheering as a historic season sees a win in the final home match with Nemeth also on score-sheet

NOVEMBER DECEMBER JANUARY FEBRUARY MARCH APRIL MAY

MONTH BY MONTH POINTS TALLY

Month	Points	%
AUGUST	1	8%
SEPTEMBER	6	67%
OCTOBER	1	11%
NOVEMBER	10	83%
DECEMBER	3	25%
JANUARY	7	58%
FEBRUARY	3	33%
MARCH	7	47%
APRIL	7	47%
MAY	3	33%

INS AND OUTS

IN Ricardinho from São Paulo on loan.
OUT Alan Wright to Sheffield United for free; Phil Gulliver to Scunthorpe and Mark Wilson to Sheffield Wednesday on loan.

GOAL ATTEMPTS

FOR – Goal attempts recorded in League games

	HOME	AWAY	TOTAL	AVE
shots on target	145	106	251	6.6
shots off target	112	94	206	5.4
TOTAL	257	200	457	12

Ratio of goals to shots – Average number of shots on target per League goal scored: 5.7

Accuracy rating – Average percentage of total goal attempts which were on target: 54.9

AGAINST – Goal attempts recorded in League games

	HOME	AWAY	TOTAL	AVE
shots on target	102	156	258	6.8
shots off target	98	106	204	5.4
TOTAL	200	262	462	12.2

Ratio of goals to shots – Average number of shots on target per League goal scored: 5

Accuracy rating – Average percentage of total goal attempts which were on target: 55.8

GOALS

Szilard Nemeth

League	9
FA Cup	0
League Cup	0
Europe	0
Other	0
TOTAL	9

League Average 180 mins between goals

	PLAYER	LGE	FAC	LC	Euro	TOT	AVE
1	Nemeth	9	0	0	0	9	180
2	Juninho	8	0	1	0	9	287
3	Maccarone	6	0	1	0	7	204
4	Job	5	1	1	0	7	315
5	Zenden	4	1	2	0	7	688
6	Ricketts	2	0	1	0	3	394
7	Mendieta	2	0	1	0	3	1329
8	Southgate	1	0	0	0	1	2430
9	Marinelli	1	0	0	0	1	54
10	Christie	1	0	1	0	2	663
11	Greening	1	0	0	0	1	1592
	Other	4	1	1	0	6	
	TOTAL	44	3	9	0	56	

SQUAD APPEARANCES

Match	1	2	3	4	5	6	7	8	9	10	11	12	13	14	15	16	17	18	19	20	21	22	23	24	25	26	27	28	29	30	31	32	33	34	35	36	37	38	39	40	41	42	43	44	45	46	47
Venue	A	H	A	H	A	H	H	A	H	H	A	A	H	A	H	A	H	H	H	A	A	H	H	H	A	H	A	A	A	H	H	A	A	A	A	H	A	H	A	H	A	H	A	H	A	H	A
Competition	L	L	L	L	L	L	W	L	L	L	L	W	L	L	L	L	W	L	L	W	L	L	F	L	L	L	W	F	L	W	L	L	L	W	L	L	L	L	L	L	L	L	L	L	L	L	L
Result	L	L	D	L	L	W	W	W	L	L	D	W	W	W	D	W	D	D	D	W	D	L	W	W	L	D	W	L	W	W	L	W	L	W	L	W	L	W	D	W	D	W	L	L	L	W	L

Goalkeepers
Bradley Jones
Carlo Nash
Mark Schwarzer
Ross Turnbull

Defenders
Jamie Bates
Colin Cooper
Andrew Davies
Ugo Ehiogu
Danny Mills
Franck Queudrue
Chris Riggott
Gareth Southgate
Robbie Stockdale
Alan Wright

Midfielders
George Boateng
Guidoni Junior Doriva
Jonathan Greening
Osvaldo Juninho Paulista
Carlos Marinelli
Gaizka Mendieta
James Morrison
Stuart Parnaby
Ricardo Luis Pozzi
Gerard Robinson
Mark Wilson
Boudewijn Zenden

Forwards
Malcolm Christie
Stewart Downing
Joseph-Desire Job
Massimo Maccarone
Szilard Nemeth
Michael Ricketts

KEY: ■ On all match ■ On bench ⏮ Subbed or sent off (Counting game) « Subbed or sent off (playing less than 70 mins) ⏭ Subbed on from bench (Counting Game) » Subbed on (playing less than 70 mins) Subbed on and then subbed or sent off (Counting Game) Subbed on and then subbed or sent off (playing less than 70 mins) □ Not in 16

KEY PLAYERS - GOALSCORERS

Osvaldo Juninho Paulista

Goals in the League	8
Goals in all competitions	9
Assists League goals scored by team-mates where he delivered the final pass	1
Contribution to Attacking Power Average number of minutes between League team goals while on pitch	67
Player Strike Rate Average number of minutes between League goals scored by player	287
Club Strike Rate Average minutes between League goals scored by club	78

	PLAYER	GOALS LGE	GOALS ALL	ASSISTS	POWER	S RATE
1	Osvaldo Juninho Paulista	8	9	1	67	287 mins
2	Joseph-Desire Job	5	7	2	65	315 mins
3	Boudewijn Zenden	4	7	5	85	688 mins
4	Gaizka Mendieta	2	3	5	78	1329 mins
5	Jonathan Greening	1	1	0	88	1592 mins

KEY PLAYERS - MIDFIELDERS

Osvaldo Juninho Paulista

Goals in the League	8
Goals in all competitions	9
Assists League goals scored by team-mates where he delivered the final pass	1
Defensive Rating Average number of mins between League goals conceded while he was on the pitch	69
Contribution to Attacking Power Average number of minutes between League team goals while on pitch	67
Scoring Difference Defensive Rating minus Contribution to Attacking Power	2

	PLAYER	GOALS LGE	GOALS ALL	ASSISTS	DEF RATE	POWER	SC DIFF
1	Osvaldo Juninho Paulista	8	9	1	69	67	2 mins
2	Gaizka Mendieta	2	3	5	74	78	-4 mins
3	Boudewijn Zenden	4	7	5	79	86	-7 mins
4	Guidoni Junior Doriva	0	0	2	64	73	-9 mins
5	George Boateng	0	0	1	68	89	-21 mins

PLAYER APPEARANCES

	AGE (on 01/07/04)	IN NAMED 16	APPEARANCES	COUNTING GAMES	MINUTES ON PITCH	APPEARANCES	MINUTES ON PITCH	THIS SEASON	HOME COUNTRY
Goalkeepers									
Bradley Jones	22	21	1	1	90	2	180	-	United States
Carlo Nash	30	16	1	1	90	1	90	-	England
Mark Schwarzer	31	34	34	34	3060	42	3870	5	Australia (89)
Ross Turnbull	19	3	0	0	0	0	0	-	England
Defenders									
Jamie Bates	17	6	0	0	0	0	0	-	England
Colin Cooper	37	22	19	15	1439	21	1638	-	England
Andrew Davies	19	15	10	6	722	10	722	-	England
Ugo Ehiogu	31	18	16	15	1395	19	1654	-	England
Danny Mills	27	28	28	28	2501	37	3401	3	England (12)
Franck Queudrue	25	31	31	30	2696	40	3596	-	France
Chris Riggott	23	28	17	12	1271	24	1865	-	England
Gareth Southgate	33	27	27	27	2430	34	3047	2	England (12)
Robbie Stockdale	24	4	2	0	84	2	84	-	Scotland
Alan Wright	32	2	2	2	180	2	180	-	England
Midfielders									
George Boateng	28	35	35	35	3119	43	3927	-	Holland
Doriva	32	26	21	13	1525	26	1949	-	Brazil
Jonathan Greening	25	28	25	16	1592	29	1984	-	England
Juninho Paulista	31	33	31	24	2292	38	2846	-	Brazil
Carlos Marinelli	22	1	1	0	54	1	54	-	Argentina
Gaizka Mendieta	30	31	31	28	2658	38	3318	-	Spain
James Morrison	18	2	1	0	29	2	57	-	England
Stuart Parnaby	21	16	13	6	814	16	943	-	England
Ricardo	28	1	0	0	0	0	0	-	Brazil
Gerard Robinson	22	3	2	2	180	2	180	-	Rep of Ireland
Mark Wilson	25	2	0	0	0	0	0	-	England
Boudewijn Zenden	27	31	31	30	2750	39	3459	8	Holland (4)
Forwards									
Malcolm Christie	25	10	10	7	663	11	719	-	England
Stewart Downing	19	22	20	5	780	24	1081	-	England
Joseph-Desire Job	26	24	24	12	1575	29	1808	-	Cameroon
Massimo Maccarone	24	29	23	9	1222	30	1664	-	Italy
Szilard Nemeth	25	34	32	11	1618	38	1967	-	Slovakia
Michael Ricketts	25	25	23	6	788	30	1232	-	England

KEY: LEAGUE ALL COMPS CAPS (FIFA RANKING)

TEAM OF THE SEASON

SCHWARZER CG 34 DR 60

MILLS CG 28 DR 61

COOPER CG 15 DR 120

SOUTHGATE CG 27 DR 71

QUEDRUE CG 30 DR 73

MENDIETA CG 28 SD -4

DORIVA CG 13 SD -9

JUNINHO CG 24 SD +2

ZENDEN CG 30 SD -7

JOB CG 12 AP 65

NEMETH CG 11* SR 180

KEY: DR = Diffensive Rate, SD = Scoring Difference AP = Attacking Power SR = Strike Rate, CG=Counting games – League games playing at least 70 minutes

TOP POINT EARNERS

Guidoni Junior Doriva

Counting Games League games when he played at least 70 minutes	13
Average points Average League points taken in Counting games	1.54
Club Average points Average points taken in League games	1.26

	PLAYER	GAMES	PTS
1	Guidoni Junior Doriva	13	1.54
2	Colin Cooper	15	1.53
3	Franck Queudrue	30	1.47
4	Boudewijn Zenden	30	1.40
5	Osvaldo Juninho Paulista	24	1.38
6	Gaizka Mendieta	28	1.36
7	Danny Mills	28	1.32
8	Ugo Ehiogu	15	1.27
9	Gareth Southgate	27	1.26
10	George Boateng	35	1.20

KEY PLAYERS - DEFENDERS

Colin Cooper

Goals Conceded The number of League goals conceded while he was on the pitch	12
Goals Conceded in all competitions The number of goals conceded while he was on the pitch in all competitions	13
League minutes played Number of minutes played in league matches	1439
Clean Sheets In games when he played at least70 mins	9
Defensive Rating Average number of mins between League goals conceded while he was on the pitch	120
Club Defensive Rating Average number of mins between League goals conceded by the club this season	66

	PLAYER	CON LGE	CON ALL	GAMES	C SHEETS	DEF RATE
1	Colin Cooper	12	13	1439	9	120 mins
2	Franck Queudrue	37	45	2696	12	73 mins
3	Gareth Southgate	34	38	2430	11	71 mins
4	Danny Mills	41	49	2501	8	61 mins
5	Ugo Ehiogu	26	27	1395	3	54 mins

KEY GOALKEEPER

Mark Schwarzer

Goals Conceded in the League The number of League goals conceded while he was on the pitch	51
Goals Conceded in all competitions Number of goals conceded while he was on the pitch in all competitions	59
League minutes played Number of minutes played in league matches	3060
Clean Sheets In games when he played at least 70 mins	11
Goals to Shots Ratio The average number of shots on target per each League goal conceded	4.8
Defensive Rating Ave mins between League goals conceded while on the pitch	60

BOOKINGS

Guidoni Junior Doriva

League Yellow	6
League Red	0
All competitions Yellow	6
All competitions Red	0

League Average 254 mins between cards

	PLAYER	LEAGUE		TOTAL		AVE
1	Doriva	6 Y	0 R	6 Y	0 R	254
2	Mills	8	0	10	0	312
3	Greening	5	0	5	0	318
4	Ricketts	2	0	4	0	394
5	Zenden	5	1	6	1	458
6	Ehiogu	3	0	3	0	465
7	Cooper	3	0	3	0	479
8	Boateng	6	0	8	1	519
9	Maccarone	2	0	2	0	611
10	Riggott	2	0	3	0	635
11	Christie	1	0	1	0	663
12	Queudrue	4	0	6	0	674
13	Nemeth	2	0	2	0	809
14	Parnaby	1	0	3	0	814
15	Mendieta	3	0	3	0	886
	Other	4	0	5	0	
	TOTAL	57	1	70	2	

SOUTHAMPTON

Antti Niemi is the shot-stopper supreme. The Finn tops the Goalkeepers' Goals-to-Shots Ratio for the second season running. He faced 6.6 Goal Attempts for every goal conceded, even better than last year when he led with an average of 6.2.

Saints passed from **Gordon Strachan** to **Paul Sturrock**, keeping a Scottish accent and a collection of 's', 't', 'r's and 'c's in the managers' names so no-one would notice.

The loss of **Jason Dodd** through injury hurt as the fullback had a top 12 Defensive Rating. When he played the team averaged a goal conceded every 108 minutes – less than one a game.

The **Kevin Phillips** and **James Beattie** partnership finally gelled as one of the most potent in the division with Strike Rates of 199 and 212 respectively.

NICKNAME: THE SAINTS

KEY: Won, Drawn, Lost

1	prem	**Leicester**	A	D	2-2	Phillips 76; Beattie 80
2	prem	**Birmingham**	H	D	0-0	
3	prem	**Leeds**	A	D	0-0	
4	prem	**Man Utd**	H	W	1-0	Beattie 88
5	prem	**Wolves**	H	W	2-0	Beattie 37 pen,52
6	prem	**Tottenham**	A	W	3-1	Beattie 3,43; Phillips 60 og
7	ucr1l1	**S Bucharest**	H	D	1-1	Phillips 52
8	prem	**Middlesbrough**	H	L	0-1	
9	prem	**Newcastle**	A	L	0-1	
10	ucr1l2	**S Bucharest**	A	L	0-1	
11	prem	**Everton**	A	D	0-0	
12	prem	**Blackburn**	H	W	2-0	Beattie 59; Griffit 87
13	ccr3	**Bristol City**	A	W	3-0	Beattie 31; Ormerod 67; Le Saux 89
14	prem	**Man City**	H	L	0-2	
15	prem	**Bolton**	A	D	0-0	
16	prem	**Chelsea**	H	L	0-1	
17	prem	**Aston Villa**	A	L	0-1	
18	ccr4	**Portsmouth**	H	W	2-0	Beattie 33,90 pen
19	prem	**Charlton**	H	W	3-2	Svensson, M 6; Ormerod 45,86
20	prem	**Liverpool**	A	W	2-1	Ormerod 2; Svensson, M 64
21	ccqf	**Bolton**	A	D	0-1	(After extra time)
22	prem	**Portsmouth**	H	W	3-0	Schemmel 34 og; Pahars 68; Beattie 90
23	prem	**Fulham**	A	L	0-2	
24	prem	**Arsenal**	H	L	0-1	
25	facr3	**Newcastle**	H	L	0-3	
26	prem	**Leicester**	H	D	0-0	
27	prem	**Birmingham**	A	L	1-2	Ormerod 6
28	prem	**Leeds**	H	W	2-1	Ormerod 36; Phillips 43
29	prem	**Man Utd**	A	L	2-3	Phillips 38,53
30	prem	**Fulham**	H	D	0-0	
31	prem	**Arsenal**	A	L	0-2	
32	prem	**Everton**	H	D	3-3	Phillips 58; Beattie 82 pen; Fernandes 90
33	prem	**Blackburn**	A	D	1-1	Phillips 5
34	prem	**Liverpool**	H	W	2-0	Beattie 51; Phillips 85
35	prem	**Portsmouth**	A	L	0-1	
36	prem	**Tottenham**	H	W	1-0	Delap 64
37	prem	**Wolves**	A	W	4-1	Beattie 25; Lundekvam 58; Phillips 89,90
38	prem	**Middlesbrough**	A	L	1-3	Beattie 70
39	prem	**Man City**	A	W	3-1	Beattie 34; Phillips 55,81
40	prem	**Bolton**	H	L	1-2	Pahars 21
41	prem	**Chelsea**	A	L	0-4	
42	prem	**Aston Villa**	H	D	1-1	Phillips 45
43	prem	**Newcastle**	H	D	3-3	Beattie 19; Bramble 39 og; Griffit 89
44	prem	**Charlton**	A	L	1-2	Prutton 64

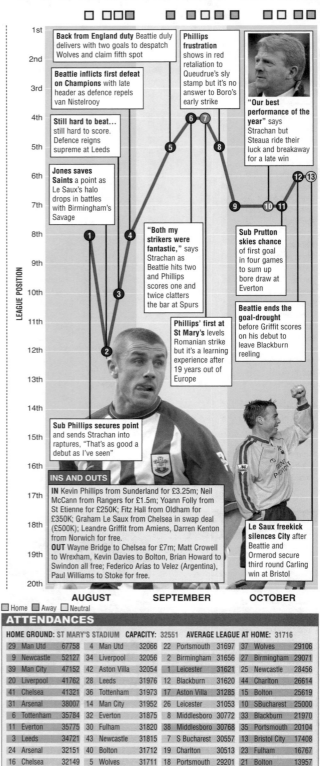

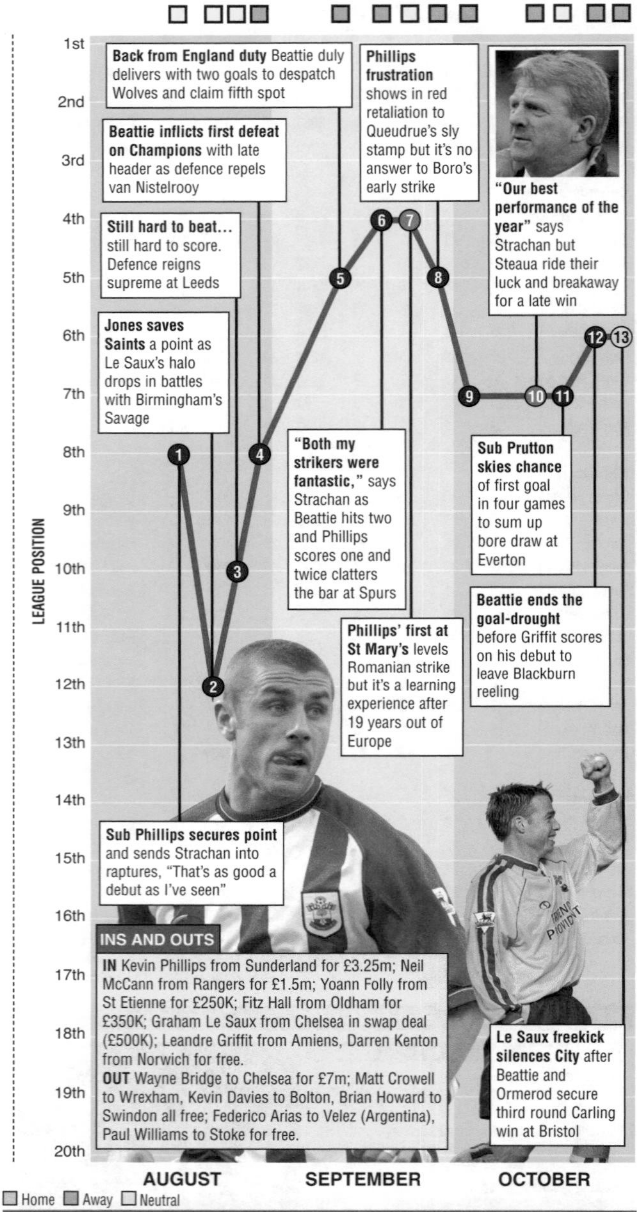

1st
2nd
3rd
4th
5th
6th
7th
8th
9th
10th
11th
12th
13th
14th
15th
16th
17th
18th
19th
20th
LEAGUE POSITION
Back from England duty Beattie duly delivers with two goals to despatch Wolves and claim fifth spot
Phillips frustration shows in red retaliation to Queudrue's sly stamp but it's no answer to Boro's early strike
"Our best performance of the year" says Strachan but Steaua ride their luck and breakaway for a late win
Beattie inflicts first defeat on Champions with late header as defence repels van Nistelrooy
Still hard to beat... still hard to score. Defence reigns supreme at Leeds
Jones saves Saints a point as Le Saux's halo drops in battles with Birmingham's Savage
"Both my strikers were fantastic," says Strachan as Beattie hits two and Phillips scores one and twice clatters the bar at Spurs
Sub Prutton skies chance of first goal in four games to sum up bore draw at Everton
Beattie ends the goal-drought before Griffit scores on his debut to leave Blackburn reeling
Phillips' first at St Mary's levels Romanian strike but it's a learning experience after 19 years out of Europe
Sub Phillips secures point and sends Strachan into raptures, "That's as good a debut as I've seen"
Le Saux freekick silences City after Beattie and Ormerod secure third round Carling win at Bristol
AUGUST
SEPTEMBER
OCTOBER
Home Away Neutral

INS AND OUTS

IN Kevin Phillips from Sunderland for £3.25m; Neil McCann from Rangers for £1.5m; Yoann Folly from St Etienne for £250K; Fitz Hall from Oldham for £350K; Graham Le Saux from Chelsea in swap deal (£500K); Leandre Griffit from Amiens, Darren Kenton from Norwich for free.

OUT Wayne Bridge to Chelsea for £7m; Matt Crowell to Wrexham, Kevin Davies to Bolton, Brian Howard to Swindon all free; Federico Arias to Velez (Argentina), Paul Williams to Stoke for free.

ATTENDANCES

HOME GROUND: ST MARY'S STADIUM **CAPACITY:** 32551 **AVERAGE LEAGUE AT HOME:** 31716

29	Man Utd	67758	4	Man Utd	32066	22	Portsmouth	31697	37	Wolves	29106
9	Newcastle	52127	34	Liverpool	32056	2	Birmingham	31656	27	Birmingham	29071
39	Man City	47152	42	Aston Villa	32054	1	Leicester	31621	25	Newcastle	28456
20	Liverpool	41762	28	Leeds	31976	12	Blackburn	31620	44	Charlton	26614
41	Chelsea	41321	36	Tottenham	31973	17	Aston Villa	31285	15	Bolton	25619
31	Arsenal	38007	14	Man City	31952	26	Leicester	31053	10	SBucharest	25000
6	Tottenham	35784	32	Everton	31875	8	Middlesboro	30772	33	Blackburn	21970
11	Everton	35775	30	Fulham	31820	38	Middlesboro	30768	35	Portsmouth	20104
3	Leeds	34721	43	Newcastle	31815	7	S Bucharest	30557	13	Bristol City	17408
24	Arsenal	32151	40	Bolton	31712	19	Charlton	30513	23	Fulham	16767
16	Chelsea	32149	5	Wolves	31711	18	Portsmouth	29201	21	Bolton	13957

Managers come and go but Niemi stops

Final Position: **12th**

KEY: ● League ● Champions Lge ● UEFA Cup ● FA Cup ○ League Cup ● Other

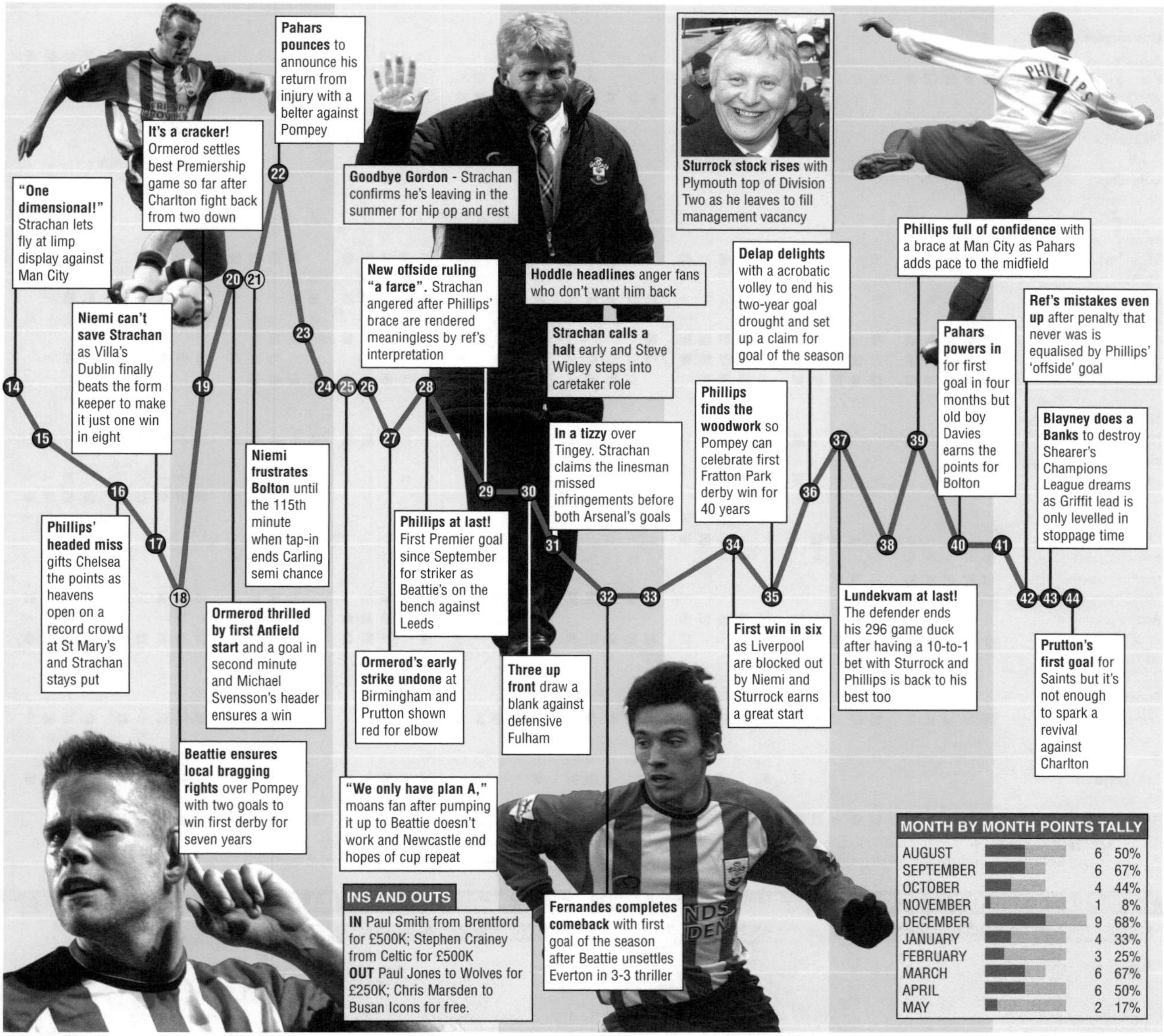

"One dimensional!" Strachan lets fly at limp display against Man City

Niemi can't save Strachan as Villa's Dublin finally beats the form keeper to make it just one win in eight

Phillips' headed miss gifts Chelsea the points as heavens open on a record crowd at St Mary's and Strachan stays put

It's a cracker! Ormerod settles best Premiership game so far after Charlton fight back from two down

Beattie ensures local bragging rights over Pompey with two goals to win first derby for seven years

Ormerod thrilled by first Anfield start and a goal in second minute and Michael Svensson's header ensures a win

Niemi frustrates Bolton until the 115th minute when tap-in ends Carling semi chance

Pahars pounces to announce his return from injury with a belter against Pompey

"We only have plan A," moans fan after pumping it up to Beattie doesn't work and Newcastle end hopes of cup repeat

Ormerod's early strike undone at Birmingham and Prutton shown red for elbow

Goodbye Gordon - Strachan confirms he's leaving in the summer for hip op and rest

Phillips at last! First Premier goal since September for striker as Beattie's on the bench against Leeds

New offside ruling "a farce". Strachan angered after Phillips' brace are rendered meaningless by ref's interpretation

Three up front draw a blank against defensive Fulham

Hoddle headlines anger fans who don't want him back

Strachan calls a halt early and Steve Wigley steps into caretaker role

In a tizzy over Tingey. Strachan claims the linesman missed infringements before both Arsenal's goals

Fernandes completes comeback with first goal of the season after Beattie unsettles Everton in 3-3 thriller

Sturrock stock rises with Plymouth top of Division Two as he leaves to fill management vacancy

Phillips finds the woodwork so Pompey can celebrate first Fratton Park derby win for 40 years

First win in six as Liverpool are blocked out by Niemi and Sturrock earns a great start

Delap delights with a acrobatic volley to end his two-year goal drought and set up a claim for goal of the season

Lundekvam at last! The defender ends his 296 game duck after having a 10-to-1 bet with Sturrock and Phillips is back to his best too

Phillips full of confidence with a brace at Man City as Pahars adds pace to the midfield

Pahars powers in for first goal in four months but old boy Davies earns the points for Bolton

Ref's mistakes even up after penalty that never was is equalised by Phillips' 'offside' goal

Blayney does a Banks to destroy Shearer's Champions League dreams as Griffit lead is only levelled in stoppage time

Prutton's first goal for Saints but it's not enough to spark a revival against Charlton

INS AND OUTS

IN Paul Smith from Brentford for £500K; Stephen Crainey from Celtic for £500K
OUT Paul Jones to Wolves for £250K; Chris Marsden to Busan Icons for free.

MONTH BY MONTH POINTS TALLY

Month	Points	%
AUGUST	6	50%
SEPTEMBER	6	67%
OCTOBER	4	44%
NOVEMBER	1	8%
DECEMBER	9	68%
JANUARY	4	33%
FEBRUARY	3	25%
MARCH	6	67%
APRIL	6	50%
MAY	2	17%

NOVEMBER DECEMBER JANUARY FEBRUARY MARCH APRIL MAY

GOAL ATTEMPTS

FOR – Goal attempts recorded in League games

	HOME	AWAY	TOTAL	AVE
shots on target	145	120	265	7
shots off target	104	88	192	5.1
TOTAL	249	208	457	12

Ratio of goals to shots – Average number of shots on target per League goal scored: **6**

Accuracy rating – Average percentage of total goal attempts which were on target: **58**

AGAINST – Goal attempts recorded in League games

	HOME	AWAY	TOTAL	AVE
shots on target	148	148	296	7.8
shots off target	94	120	214	5.6
TOTAL	242	268	510	13.4

Ratio of goals to shots – Average number of shots on target per League goal scored: **6.6**

Accuracy rating – Average percentage of total goal attempts which were on target: **58**

GOALS

James Beattie

League	14
FA Cup	0
League Cup	3
Europe	0
Other	0
TOTAL	17

League Average **212** mins between goals

	PLAYER	LGE	FAC	LC	Euro	TOT	AVE
1	Beattie	14	0	3	0	17	212
2	Phillips	13	0	0	1	14	199
3	Ormerod	5	0	1	0	6	241
4	Pahars	2	0	0	0	2	294
5	Svensson, M	2	0	0	0	2	1168
6	Griffit	2	0	0	0	2	75
7	Lundekvam	1	0	0	0	1	2513
8	Prutton	1	0	0	0	1	2055
9	Fernandes	1	0	0	0	1	1747
10	Delap	1	0	0	0	1	2127
11	Le Saux	0	0	1	0	1	
	Other	2	0	0	0	2	
	TOTAL	44	0	5	1	50	

SQUAD APPEARANCES

Match	1	2	3	4	5	6	7	8	9	10	11	12	13	14	15	16	17	18	19	20	21	22	23	24	25	26	27	28	29	30	31	32	33	34	35	36	37	38	39	40	41	42	43	44
Venue	A	H	A	H	H	A	H	H	A	A	A	H	A	H	A	H	A	H	H	A	A	H	A	H	H	H	A	H	A	H	A	H	A	H	A	H	A	A	A	H	A	H	H	A
Competition	L	L	L	L	L	L	E	L	L	E	L	L	W	L	L	L	L	W	L	L	W	L	L	L	F	L	L	L	L	L	L	L	L	L	L	L	L	L	L	L	L	L	L	L
Result	D	D	D	W	W	W	D	L	L	L	D	W	W	L	D	L	L	W	W	W	D	W	L	L	L	D	L	W	L	D	L	D	D	W	L	W	W	L	W	L	L	D	D	L

Goalkeepers
Alan Blayney
Paul Jones
Antti Niemi
Michael Poke
Paul Smith

Defenders
Chris Baird
Stephen Crainey
Martin Cranie
Jason Dodd
Fitz Hall
Danny Higginbotham
Darren Kenton
Graeme Le Saux
Claus Lundekvam
Michael Svensson

Midfielders
Rory Delap
Mark Draper
Fabrice Fernandes
Yoann Folly
Leandre Griffit
Chris Marsden
Neil McCann
Matthew Oakley
David Prutton
Anders Svensson
Paul Telfer
Jo Tessem

Forwards
James Beattie
Dextor Blackstock
Augustin Delgado
Brett Ormerod
Marian Pahars
Kevin Phillips

KEY: On all match | On bench | Subbed or sent off (Counting game) | Subbed or sent off (playing less than 70 mins) | Subbed on from bench (Counting Game) | Subbed on (playing less than 70 mins) | Subbed on and then subbed or sent off (Counting Game) | Subbed on and then subbed or sent off (playing less than 70 mins) | Not in 16

KEY PLAYERS - GOALSCORERS

Kevin Phillips

Goals in the League	13
Goals in all competitions	14
Assists League goals scored by team-mates where he delivered the final pass	4
Contribution to Attacking Power Average number of minutes between League team goals while on pitch	83
Player Strike Rate Average number of minutes between League goals scored by player	199
Club Strike Rate Average minutes between League goals scored by club	78

	PLAYER	GOALS LGE	GOALS ALL	ASSISTS	POWER	S RATE
1	Kevin Phillips	13	14	4	83	199 mins
2	James Beattie	14	17	6	74	212 mins
3	Michael Svensson	2	2	1	86	1168 mins
4	Fabrice Fernandes	1	1	2	72	1747 mins
5	David Prutton	1	1	3	64	2055 mins

KEY PLAYERS - MIDFIELDERS

Rory Delap

Goals in the League	1
Goals in all competitions	1
Assists League goals scored by team-mates where he delivered the final pass	3
Defensive Rating Average number of mins between League goals conceded while he was on the pitch	76
Contribution to Attacking Power Average number of minutes between League team goals while on pitch	71
Scoring Difference Defensive Rating minus Contribution to Attacking Power	5

	PLAYER	GOALS LGE	GOALS ALL	ASSISTS	DEF RATE	POWER	SC DIFF
1	Rory Delap	1	1	3	76	71	5 mins
2	David Prutton	1	1	3	64	64	0 mins
3	Fabrice Fernandes	1	1	2	67	73	-6 mins
4	Paul Telfer	0	0	2	74	80	-6 mins

PLAYER APPEARANCES

	AGE (on 01/07/04)	IN NAMED 16	APPEARANCES	COUNTING GAMES	MINUTES ON PITCH	APPEARANCES	MINUTES ON PITCH	THIS SEASON	HOME COUNTRY
Goalkeepers									
Alan Blayney	22	11	2	2	180	2	180	-	N Ireland
Paul Jones	37	19	8	8	720	10	855	7	Wales (66)
Antti Niemi	32	32	28	28	2520	33	2955	4	Finland (42)
Michael Poke	18	2	0	0	0	0	0	-	England
Paul Smith	24	12	0	0	0	0	0	-	England
Defenders									
Chris Baird	22	6	4	1	191	4	191	7	N Ireland (114)
Stephen Crainey	23	7	5	5	439	5	439	2	Scotland (63)
Martin Cranie	17	2	1	0	62	1	62	-	England
Jason Dodd	33	28	28	25	2371	34	2934	-	England
Fitz Hall	23	20	11	8	753	12	873	-	England
Danny Higginbotham	25	36	27	25	2290	31	2680	-	England
Darren Kenton	25	9	7	3	366	7	366	-	England
Graeme Le Saux	35	19	19	17	1562	21	1742	-	England
Claus Lundekvam	31	31	31	26	2513	36	2963	-	Norway
Michael Svensson	28	26	26	26	2336	32	2906	5	Sweden (21)
Midfielders									
Rory Delap	28	26	26	22	2127	31	2494	3	Rep of Ireland (15)
Mark Draper	33	1	1	0	49	1	49	-	England
Fabrice Fernandes	24	31	27	16	1747	31	2080	-	France
Yoann Folly	19	10	9	9	810	9	810	-	France
Leandre Griffit	20	9	5	0	150	5	150	-	France
Chris Marsden	35	14	13	8	853	17	1138	-	England
Neil McCann	29	18	18	6	801	21	897	6	Scotland (63)
Matthew Oakley	26	7	7	7	630	8	720	-	England
David Prutton	22	29	27	22	2055	30	2281	-	England
Anders Svensson	27	32	30	12	1532	34	1892	8	Sweden (21)
Paul Telfer	32	37	37	33	3039	43	3466	-	Scotland
Jo Tessem	32	4	3	1	97	3	97	-	Norway
Forwards									
James Beattie	26	37	37	32	2966	42	3416	3	England (12)
Dextor Blackstock	18	3	0	0	0	0	0	-	England
Augustin Delgado	29	6	4	0	58	6	130	-	Ecuador
Brett Ormerod	27	32	22	10	1204	26	1522	-	England
Marian Pahars	27	17	14	5	587	16	720	-	Latvia
Kevin Phillips	30	35	34	28	2588	37	2858	-	England

KEY: LEAGUE   ALL COMPS   CAPS (FIFA RANKING)

TEAM OF THE SEASON

NIEMI

CG 28 DR 74

DODD

CG 25 DR 108

M SVENSSON

CG 26 DR 102

LUNDEKVAM

CG 26 DR 81

LE SAUX

CG 17 DR 98

FERNANDES

CG 16 SD -6

TELFER

CG 33 SD -6

DELAP

CG 22 SD +5

PRUTTON

CG 22 SD 0

BEATTIE

CG 32 AP 74

PHILLIPS

CG 28 SR 199

KEY: DR = Diffensive Rate, SD = Scoring Difference AP = Attacking Power SR = Strike Rate, CG=Counting games – League games playing at least 70 minutes

TOP POINT EARNERS

Jason Dodd

Counting Games League games when he played at least 70 minutes	25
Average points Average League points taken in Counting games	1.56
Club Average points Average points taken in League games	1.24

	PLAYER	GAMES	PTS
1	Jason Dodd	25	1.56
2	Fabrice Fernandes	16	1.44
3	Claus Lundekvam	26	1.38
4	Michael Svensson	26	1.38
5	David Prutton	22	1.36
6	Rory Delap	22	1.36
7	James Beattie	32	1.31
8	Graeme Le Saux	17	1.29
9	Paul Telfer	33	1.27
10	Antti Niemi	28	1.21

KEY PLAYERS - DEFENDERS

Jason Dodd

Goals Conceded The number of League goals conceded while he was on the pitch	22
Goals Conceded in all competitions The number of goals conceded while he was on the pitch in all competitions	28
League minutes played Number of minutes played in league matches	2371
Clean Sheets In games when he played at least70 mins	12
Defensive Rating Average number of mins between League goals conceded while he was on the pitch	108
Club Defensive Rating Average number of mins between League goals conceded by the club this season	76

FRIENDS PROVIDENT

	PLAYER	CON LGE	CON ALL	GAMES	C SHEETS	DEF RATE
1	Jason Dodd	22	28	2371	12	108 mins
2	Michael Svensson	23	29	2336	11	102 mins
3	Graeme Le Saux	16	17	1562	7	98 mins
4	Claus Lundekvam	31	36	2513	10	81 mins
5	Danny Higginbotham	33	38	2290	5	69 mins

KEY GOALKEEPER

Antti Niemi

Goals Conceded in the League The number of League goals conceded while he was on the pitch	34
Goals Conceded in all competitions Number of goals conceded while he was on the pitch in all competitions	39
League minutes played Number of minutes played in league matches	2520
Clean Sheets In games when he played at least 70 mins	8
Goals to Shots Ratio The average number of shots on target per each League goal conceded	6.6
Defensive Rating Ave mins between League goals conceded while on the pitch	74

BOOKINGS

Neil McCann

League Yellow	4
League Red	0
All competitions Yellow	4
All competitions Red	0
League Average 200 mins between cards	

	PLAYER	LEAGUE Y	LEAGUE R	TOTAL Y	TOTAL R	AVE
1	McCann	4Y	0R	4Y	0R	200
2	Marsden	4	0	4	0	213
3	Svensson, A	6	0	6	0	255
4	Svensson, M	8	1	8	1	259
5	Oakley	2	0	2	0	315
6	Le Saux	4	0	4	0	390
7	Prutton	4	1	5	1	411
8	Higginbotham	3	0	3	0	763
9	Folly	1	0	1	0	810
10	Phillips	2	1	2	1	862
11	Beattie	3	0	4	0	988
12	Telfer	3	0	3	0	1013
13	Dodd	2	0	2	0	1185
14	Ormerod	1	0	2	0	1204
15	Lundekvam	2	0	3	0	1256
	Other	4	0	4	0	
	TOTAL	53	3	57	3	

PORTSMOUTH

Harry Redknapp shored up an injury-ravaged side with his usual dealing flair and wheeled Pompey to mid-table respectability.

Persuading Newcastle to loan out **LuaLua** was a key stroke. It helped spark **Yakubu Ayegbeni** into life. The Nigerian had five goals in 23 league games and was playing second fiddle to **Teddy Sheringham** until LuaLua's debut on the 7th of February. He then hit 11 in 14 to match Owen's league and season totals.

His Strike Rate of a goal every 195 minutes was one of only 12 under 200.

Arjan De Zeeuw was the rock on which the defence was built, playing in all bar two league games when he was suspended. They were both bad losses and led to Harry's famously miserable Xmas.

NICKNAME: POMPEY

KEY: Won / Drawn / Lost

No	Comp	Opponent	H/A	Res	Score	Scorers
1	prem	**Aston Villa**	H	W	2-1	Sheringham 42; Berger 63
2	prem	**Man City**	A	D	1-1	Yakubu 24
3	prem	**Bolton**	H	W	4-0	Stone 48; Sheringham 57,88,90 pen
4	prem	**Wolves**	A	D	0-0	
5	prem	**Arsenal**	A	D	1-1	Sheringham 26
6	prem	**Blackburn**	H	L	1-2	De Zeeuw 57
7	ccr2	**Northampton**	H	W	5-2	Sherwood 13,83; Roberts 17,60; Taylor 41
8	prem	**Birmingham**	A	L	0-2	
9	prem	**Charlton**	H	L	1-2	Sheringham 34
10	prem	**Liverpool**	H	W	1-0	Berger 4
11	prem	**Newcastle**	A	L	0-3	
12	ccr3	**Nottm Forest**	A	W	4-2	Walker 57 og; Yakubu 64,108; Roberts, J 101
13	prem	**Man Utd**	A	L	0-3	
14	prem	**Leeds**	H	W	6-1	Stefanovic 17; O'Neil 45,71; Foxe 63; Berger 75; Yakubu 86
15	prem	**Fulham**	A	L	0-2	
16	prem	**Leicester**	H	L	0-2	
17	ccr4	**Southampton**	A	L	0-2	
18	prem	**Middlesbrough**	A	D	0-0	
19	prem	**Everton**	H	L	1-2	Roberts 15
20	prem	**Southampton**	A	L	0-3	
21	prem	**Tottenham**	H	W	2-0	Berger 52,68
22	prem	**Chelsea**	A	L	0-3	
23	facr3	**Blackpool**	H	W	2-1	Schemmel 36; Yakubu 90
24	prem	**Aston Villa**	A	L	1-2	Yakubu 49
25	prem	**Man City**	H	W	4-2	Stefanovic 19; Yakubu 52,77; Sheringham 58
26	prem	**Bolton**	A	L	0-1	
27	facr4	**Scunthorpe**	H	W	2-1	Taylor 35,66
28	prem	**Wolves**	H	D	0-0	
29	prem	**Tottenham**	A	L	3-4	Berkovic 39; LuaLua 73; Mornar 84
30	prem	**Chelsea**	H	L	0-2	
31	facr5	**Liverpool**	A	D	1-1	Taylor 77
32	facr5r	**Liverpool**	H	W	1-0	Hughes, R 72
33	prem	**Newcastle**	H	D	1-1	LuaLua 89
34	facqf	**Arsenal**	H	L	1-5	Sheringham 90
35	prem	**Everton**	A	L	0-1	
36	prem	**Liverpool**	A	L	0-3	
37	prem	**Southampton**	H	W	1-0	Yakubu 68
38	prem	**Blackburn**	A	W	2-1	Sheringham 17; Yakubu 82
39	prem	**Charlton**	A	D	1-1	Yakubu 65
40	prem	**Birmingham**	H	W	3-1	Stefanovic 45; LuaLua 62; Yakubu 73 pen
41	prem	**Man Utd**	H	W	1-0	Stone 36
42	prem	**Leeds**	A	W	2-1	Yakubu 9; LuaLua 51
43	prem	**Fulham**	H	D	1-1	Yakubu 80
44	prem	**Arsenal**	H	D	1-1	Yakubu 30
45	prem	**Leicester**	A	L	1-3	Quashie 66
46	prem	**Middlesbrough**	H	W	5-1	Yakubu 4,14 pen,31,83; Sheringham 80

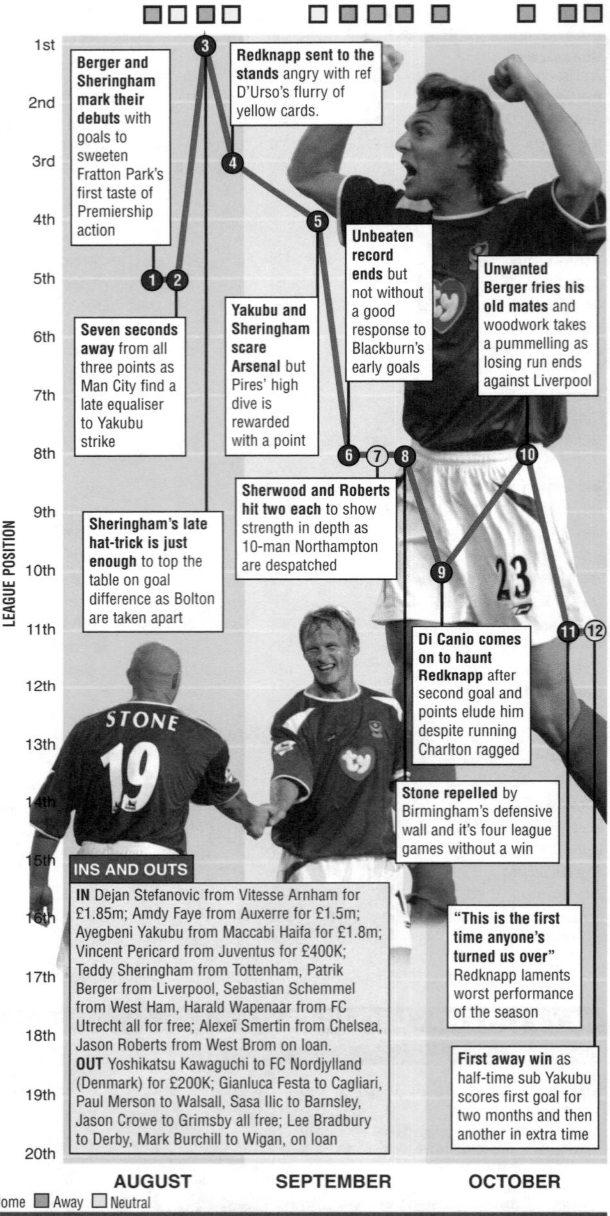

LEAGUE POSITION: 1st – 20th

AUGUST · SEPTEMBER · OCTOBER

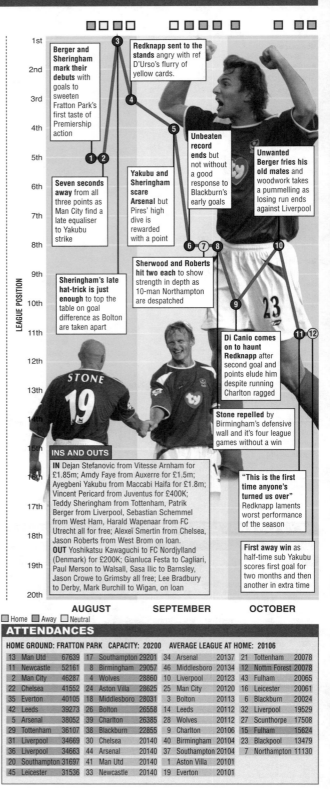

Berger and Sheringham mark their debuts with goals to sweeten Fratton Park's first taste of Premiership action

Redknapp sent to the stands angry with ref D'Urso's flurry of yellow cards.

Unbeaten record ends but not without a good response to Blackburn's early goals

Unwanted Berger fries his old mates and woodwork takes a pummelling as losing run ends against Liverpool

Seven seconds away from all three points as Man City find a late equaliser to Yakubu strike

Yakubu and Sheringham scare Arsenal but Pires' high dive is rewarded with a point

Sherwood and Roberts hit two each to show strength in depth as 10-man Northampton are despatched

Sheringham's late hat-trick is just enough to top the table on goal difference as Bolton are taken apart

Di Canio comes on to haunt Redknapp after second goal and points elude him despite running Charlton ragged

Stone repelled by Birmingham's defensive wall and it's four league games without a win

"This is the first time anyone's turned us over" Redknapp laments worst performance of the season

First away win as half-time sub Yakubu scores first goal for two months and then another in extra time

INS AND OUTS

IN Dejan Stefanovic from Vitesse Arnham for £1.85m; Amdy Faye from Auxerre for £1.5m; Ayegbeni Yakubu from Maccabi Haifa for £1.8m; Vincent Pericard from Juventus for £400K; Teddy Sheringham from Tottenham, Patrik Berger from Liverpool, Sebastian Schemmel from West Ham, Harald Wapenaar from FC Utrecht all for free; Alexeï Smertin from Chelsea, Jason Roberts from West Brom on loan.

OUT Yoshikatsu Kawaguchi to FC Nordjylland (Denmark) for £200K; Gianluca Festa to Cagliari, Paul Merson to Walsall, Sasa Ilic to Barnsley, Jason Crowe to Grimsby all free; Lee Bradbury to Derby, Mark Burchill to Wigan, on loan

Home / Away / Neutral

ATTENDANCES

HOME GROUND: FRATTON PARK CAPACITY: 20200 AVERAGE LEAGUE AT HOME: 20106

13	Man Utd	67639	17	Southampton	29201	34	Arsenal	20137	21	Tottenham	20078
11	Newcastle	52161	8	Birmingham	29057	46	Middlesboro	20134	12	Nottm Forest	20078
2	Man City	46287	4	Wolves	28860	10	Liverpool	20123	43	Fulham	20065
22	Chelsea	41552	24	Aston Villa	28625	25	Man City	20120	16	Leicester	20061
35	Everton	40105	18	Middlesboro	28031	3	Bolton	20113	6	Blackburn	20024
42	Leeds	39273	26	Bolton	26558	14	Leeds	20112	32	Liverpool	19529
5	Arsenal	38052	39	Charlton	26385	28	Wolves	20112	27	Scunthorpe	17508
29	Tottenham	36107	38	Blackburn	22855	9	Charlton	20106	15	Fulham	15624
31	Liverpool	34669	30	Chelsea	20140	40	Birmingham	20104	23	Blackpool	13479
36	Liverpool	34663	44	Arsenal	20140	37	Southampton	20104	7	Northampton	11130
20	Southampton	31697	41	Man Utd	20140	1	Aston Villa	20101			
45	Leicester	31536	33	Newcastle	20140	19	Everton	20101			

Harry and Jim coax more from Yakubu

Final Position: 13th

KEY: ● League ● Champions Lge ● UEFA Cup ● FA Cup ○ League Cup ● Other

De Zeeuw despatched by ref after trip on Beattie. Saints gain a penalty and route to Carling Cup quarters
INS AND OUTS
IN Ivica Mornar from Anderlecht for £400K; John Curtis from Leicester for a nominal fee; Eyal Berkovic from Man City for free; Petri Pesanen from Ajax, Lomano LuaLua from Newcastle on loan.
OUT Boris Zivkovic to VfB Stuttgart for free; Carl Robinson to Sheffield Utd on loan.
MONTH BY MONTH POINTS TALLY
AUGUST 8 67%
SEPTEMBER 1 11%
OCTOBER 3 33%
NOVEMBER 3 25%
DECEMBER 4 27%
JANUARY 4 33%
FEBRUARY 1 11%
MARCH 6 50%
APRIL 10 83%
MAY 5 42%
Abusive Berger is sent off for ranting at ref after penalty claim turned down. It all goes wrong after a bright start at Fulham
Berkovic uses bitterness to good effect with debut performance which damages Keegan and inspires Yakubu
LuaLua leaves it late to impress his main employers as he volleys equaliser in draw with Newcastle
Yakubu fires against the Gunners before Reyes nets his League first to keep record intact
Hughes scores first goal to knock out Liverpool after Hislop ensures penalty justice is done
First league win over Saints for 16 years as Yakubu converts Stone's cross
Stone's first goal for eight months in his 50th game claims three vital points against Man United
Redknapp makes up with Mandaric over coach row in time to see Sheringham sign off in style with one goal and Yakubu hit four!
Yakubu gives Ferdinand the run around but late subs make it safe for United
Yakubu leaves it late before final minute goal saves replay trip to Blackpool
Todorov returns briefly after pre-season injury but looks rusty compared to Liverpool's two-goal Owen
Yakubu steers home winner after LuaLua's fine run at Blackburn for first away victory of the season to break out of bottom three
Yakubu's fifth goal in six and LuaLua's fourth on loan ensure 40 points marker is reached at Leeds' expense
Explosive Berger blasts Spurs apart from two free-kicks to pick up three points
LuaLua's constant threat wounds Birmingham who succumb to goals by the striker, Stefanovic and Yakubu
Volley gives O'Neil dream start to Premiership career and he adds a second as rout of Leeds has Harry purring
Harry curses Xmas in the relegation zone after Saints turn his injury-struck side over
Arsenal hit five – a quarter of the goals conceded at Fratton Park this season
Taylor return is two goals as Sheringham guile sinks Scunthorpe
Taylor fires in a reply to Liverpool's fiery start and Hislop hangs in there to claim a home replay
"I need to rest people really," says Redknapp after a tired display and a bad deflection against Leicester
Stone's harsh treatment ends in sending off but run of three defeats is also ended at Boro
Stefanovic sent off at Bolton and Redknapp's thin squad is further threatened by his suspension
New signings double away tally to six goals but Spurs have the last word in best of seven thriller
Berkovic passes his way around Goodison but it's another pointless away trip for fans
Sub Berkovic takes control at the Valley to eclipse a poor first half and claim a point courtesy of Yakubu
The form team with 17 points out of a possible 21 as Yakubu continues scoring to gain a draw with Fulham
NOVEMBER
DECEMBER
JANUARY
FEBRUARY
MARCH
APRIL
MAY

GOAL ATTEMPTS

FOR – Goal attempts recorded in League games

	HOME	AWAY	TOTAL	AVE
shots on target	134	83	217	5.7
shots off target	101	84	185	4.9
TOTAL	**235**	**167**	**402**	**10.6**

Ratio of goals to shots Average number of shots on target per League goal scored	4.6
Accuracy rating Average percentage of total goal attempts which were on target	54

AGAINST – Goal attempts recorded in League games

	HOME	AWAY	TOTAL	AVE
shots on target	105	137	242	6.4
shots off target	106	83	189	5
TOTAL	**211**	**220**	**431**	**11.3**

Ratio of goals to shots Average number of shots on target per League goal scored	4.5
Accuracy rating Average percentage of total goal attempts which were on target	56.1

GOALS

Ayegbeni Yakubu

League	16
FA Cup	1
League Cup	2
Europe	0
Other	0
TOTAL	19

League Average 195 mins between goals

	PLAYER	LGE	FAC	LC	Euro	TOT	AVE
1	Yakubu	**16**	1	2	0	19	195
2	Sheringham	**9**	1	0	0	10	246
3	Berger	**5**	0	0	0	5	337
4	LuaLua	**4**	0	0	0	4	232
5	Stefanovic	**3**	0	0	0	3	941
6	O'Neil	**2**	0	0	0	2	117
7	Stone	**2**	0	0	0	2	1269
8	Roberts, J	**1**	0	3	0	4	485
9	Quashie	**1**	0	0	0	1	1602
10	Berkovic	**1**	0	0	0	1	813
11	Foxe	**1**	0	0	0	1	720
12	Mornar	**1**	0	0	0	1	358
13	De Zeeuw	**1**	0	0	0	1	3240
14	Taylor	**0**	3	1	0	4	
15	Sherwood	**0**	0	2	0	2	
	Other	0	2	1	0	3	
	TOTAL	**47**	**7**	**9**	**0**	**63**	

SQUAD APPEARANCES

Match	Venue	Competition	Result
1	H	L	W
2	A	L	D
3	H	L	W
4	A	L	D
5	A	L	D
6	H	L	L
7	H	W	W
8	A	L	L
9	H	L	L
10	H	L	W
11	A	L	L
12	A	W	W
13	A	L	L
14	H	L	W
15	A	L	L
16	H	L	L
17	A	W	L
18	A	L	D
19	H	L	L
20	A	L	L
21	H	L	W
22	A	L	L
23	H	F	W
24	A	L	L
25	H	L	W
26	A	L	L
27	H	F	W
28	H	L	D
29	A	L	L
30	H	L	L
31	A	F	D
32	H	F	W
33	H	L	D
34	H	F	L
35	A	L	L
36	A	L	L
37	H	L	W
38	A	L	W
39	A	L	D
40	H	L	W
41	H	L	W
42	A	L	W
43	H	L	D
44	H	L	D
45	A	L	L
46	H	L	W

Goalkeepers
Shaka Hislop
Alan Knight
Pavel Srnicek
Harald Wapenaar

Defenders
John Curtis
Arjan De Zeeuw
Richard Duffy
Petri Pasanen
Linvoy Primus
Sebastien Schemmel
Dejan Stefanovic
Matthew Taylor
Jamie Vincent
Boris Zivkovic

Midfielders
Patrik Berger
Eyal Berkovic
Shaun Cooper
Amdy Faye
Hayden Foxe
Kevin Harper
Richard Hughes
Warren Hunt
Gary O'Neil
Anthony Pulis
Nigel Quashie
Carl Robinson
Tim Sherwood
Alexei Smertin
Steve Stone

Forwards
Deon Burton
Lomana Tresor LuaLua
Ivica Mornar
Sebastian Olszar
Vincent Pericard
Jason Roberts
Teddy Sheringham
Svetoslav Todorov
Ayegbeni Yakubu

KEY: On all match · On bench · Subbed or sent off (Counting game) · Subbed or sent off (playing less than 70 mins) · Subbed on from bench (Counting Game) · Subbed on (playing less than 70 mins) · Subbed on and then subbed or sent off (Counting Game) · Subbed on and then subbed or sent off (playing less than 70 mins) · Not in 16

KEY PLAYERS - GOALSCORERS

Ayegbeni Yakubu

Goals in the League	16
Goals in all competitions	19
Assists League goals scored by team-mates where he delivered the final pass	3
Contribution to Attacking Power Average number of minutes between League team goals while on pitch	69
Player Strike Rate Average number of minutes between League goals scored by player	195
Club Strike Rate Average minutes between League goals scored by club	73

	PLAYER	GOALS LGE	GOALS ALL	ASSISTS	POWER	S RATE
1	Ayegbeni Yakubu	16	19	3	69	195 mins
2	Teddy Sheringham	9	10	4	76	246 mins
3	Patrik Berger	5	5	5	73	337 mins
4	Dejan Stefanovic	3	3	0	67	941 mins
5	Steve Stone	2	2	5	68	1269 mins

KEY PLAYERS - MIDFIELDERS

Steve Stone

Goals in the League	2
Goals in all competitions	2
Assists League goals scored by team-mates where he delivered the final pass	5
Defensive Rating Average number of mins between League goals conceded while he was on the pitch	77
Contribution to Attacking Power Average number of minutes between League team goals while on pitch	69
Scoring Difference Defensive Rating minus Contribution to Attacking Power	8

	PLAYER	GOALS LGE	GOALS ALL	ASSISTS	DEF RATE	POWER	SC DIFF
1	Steve Stone	2	2	5	77	69	8 mins
2	Patrik Berger	5	5	5	77	73	4 mins
3	Alexei Smertin	0	0	0	67	71	-4 mins
4	Nigel Quashie	1	1	0	64	70	-6 mins
5	Amdy Faye	0	0	0	74	92	-18 mins

PLAYER APPEARANCES

	AGE (on 01/07/04)	IN NAMED 16	APPEARANCES	COUNTING GAMES	MINUTES ON PITCH	APPEARANCES	MINUTES ON PITCH	THIS SEASON	HOME COUNTRY
Goalkeepers									
Shaka Hislop	35	29	29	29	2610	33	2970	-	Trinidad & Tobago
Alan Knight	43	1	0	0	0	0	0	-	England
Pavel Srnicek	36	8	3	3	270	4	360	-	Czech Republic
Harald Wapenaar	34	37	5	5	450	7	630	-	Holland
Defenders									
John Curtis	25	12	6	5	495	6	495	-	England
Arjan De Zeeuw	34	36	36	36	3240	42	3810	-	Holland
Richard Duffy	18	3	1	1	69	1	69	-	Wales
Petri Pasanen	23	13	12	9	941	16	1301	-	Finland
Linvoy Primus	30	26	20	16	1516	25	1966	-	England
Sebastien Schemmel	29	18	14	11	1073	18	1379	-	France
Dejan Stefanovic	29	32	32	31	2823	38	3273	2	Serbia & M'negro (45)
Matthew Taylor	22	32	29	17	1793	37	2474	-	England
Jamie Vincent	29	0	0	0	0	1	120	-	England
Boris Zivkovic	28	20	18	17	1552	20	1724	9	Croatia (25)
Midfielders									
Patrik Berger	30	21	20	18	1683	23	1905	-	Czech Republic
Eyal Berkovic	32	14	11	8	813	15	1107	-	Israel
Shaun Cooper	20	0	0	0	0	0	0	-	England
Amdy Faye	27	27	27	23	2288	31	2575	1	Senegal (31)
Hayden Foxe	27	14	9	6	720	12	938	1	Australia (89)
Kevin Harper	28	13	8	1	153	10	330	-	England
Richard Hughes	25	15	11	7	700	15	946	2	Scotland (63)
Warren Hunt	20	0	0	0	0	0	0	-	England
Gary O'Neil	21	8	3	2	233	5	334	-	England
Anthony Pulis	19	1	0	0	0	0	0	-	England
Nigel Quashie	25	22	21	17	1602	25	1896	-	England
Carl Robinson	27	4	1	0	6	3	10	8	Wales (66)
Tim Sherwood	35	14	12	5	652	15	878	-	England
Alexei Smertin	29	27	26	21	2066	33	2663	-	Russia
Steve Stone	32	33	32	27	2537	36	2819	-	England
Forwards									
Deon Burton	27	6	1	0	18	2	108	-	Jamaica
Lomana LuaLua	23	15	15	8	926	15	926	-	Congo DR
Ivica Mornar	30	11	8	2	358	10	489	8	Croatia (25)
Sebastian Olszar	22	0	0	0	0	1	35	-	Poland
Vincent Pericard	21	7	7	1	154	8	244	-	France
Jason Roberts	26	14	10	4	485	12	695	-	Grenada
Teddy Sheringham	38	36	32	23	2215	38	2698	-	England
Svetoslav Todorov	25	2	1	0	45	1	45	-	Bulgaria
Ayegbeni Yakubu	21	37	37	35	3114	43	3638	-	Nigeria

KEY: LEAGUE ALL COMPS CAPS (FIFA RANKING)

TEAM OF THE SEASON

HISLOP — CG 29 DR 67

ZIVKOVIC — CG 17 DR 65
PRIMUS — CG 16 DR 69
DE ZEEUW — CG 36 DR 66
TAYLOR — CG 17 DR 62

STONE — CG 27 SD +8
QUASHIE — CG 17 SD -6
SMERTIN — CG 21 SD -4
BERGER — CG 18 SD +4

SHERINGHAM — CG 23 AP 76
YAKUBU — CG 35 SR 195

KEY: DR = Diffensive Rate, SD = Scoring Difference AP = Attacking Power SR = Strike Rate, CG=Counting games – League games playing at least 70 minutes

TOP POINT EARNERS

Steve Stone

Counting Games League games when he played at least 70 minutes	27
Average points Average League points taken in Counting games	1.44
Club Average points Average points taken in League games	1.18

	PLAYER	GAMES	PTS
1	Steve Stone	27	**1.44**
2	Matthew Taylor	17	**1.41**
3	Amdy Faye	23	**1.39**
4	Shaka Hislop	29	**1.38**
5	Alexei Smertin	21	**1.38**
6	Linvoy Primus	16	**1.31**
7	Dejan Stefanovic	31	**1.26**
8	Ayegbeni Yakubu	35	**1.26**
9	Teddy Sheringham	23	**1.26**
10	Arjan De Zeeuw	36	**1.25**

KEY PLAYERS - DEFENDERS

Linvoy Primus

Goals Conceded The number of League goals conceded while he was on the pitch	22
Goals Conceded in all competitions The number of goals conceded while he was on the pitch in all competitions	31
League minutes played Number of minutes played in league matches	1516
Clean Sheets In games when he played at least70 mins	4
Defensive Rating Average number of mins between League goals conceded while he was on the pitch	69
Club Defensive Rating Average number of mins between League goals conceded by the club this season	63

	PLAYER	CON LGE	CON ALL	MINS	C SHEETS	DEF RATE
1	Linvoy Primus	22	31	1516	4	69 mins
2	Arjan De Zeeuw	49	60	3240	8	66 mins
3	Boris Zivkovic	24	26	1552	5	65 mins
4	Matthew Taylor	29	42	1793	4	62 mins
5	Dejan Stefanovic	46	52	2823	5	61 mins

KEY GOALKEEPER

Shaka Hislop

Goals Conceded in the League The number of League goals conceded while he was on the pitch	39
Goals Conceded in all competitions Number of goals conceded while he was on the pitch in all competitions	46
League minutes played Number of minutes played in league matches	2610
Clean Sheets In games when he played at least 70 mins	6
Goals to Shots Ratio The average number of shots on target per each League goal conceded	4.9
Defensive Rating Ave mins between League goals conceded while on the pitch	67

BOOKINGS

Tim Sherwood

League Yellow	6
League Red	0
All competitions Yellow	6
All competitions Red	0

League Average **108** mins between cards

	PLAYER	LEAGUE		TOTAL		AVE
1	Sherwood	6 Y	0 R	6 Y	0 R	108
2	Schemmel	5	0	5	0	214
3	Quashie	5	0	7	0	320
4	Foxe	2	0	2	0	360
5	Faye	6	0	6	0	381
6	Berkovic	2	0	2	0	406
7	Berger	3	1	3	1	420
8	Sheringham	5	0	5	0	443
9	De Zeeuw	7	0	7	1	462
10	Stone	4	1	4	1	507
11	Zivkovic	3	0	3	0	517
12	Hughes	1	0	3	0	700
13	Stefanovic	3	1	4	1	705
14	Taylor	2	0	2	0	896
15	LuaLua	1	0	1	0	926
	Other	7	0	13	0	
	TOTAL	62	3	73	4	

TOTTENHAM HOTSPUR

David Pleat stood down as caretaker and director leaving memories of underachievement but an exciting striking trio.

Spurs are the only club with three forwards in the top 30 Goalscorers list. **Jermain Defoe** only scored seven goals but did so in short order and is highest placed at 10th with a Strike Rate of a goal every 183 minutes.

Robbie Keane's rate is 206 and holds 14th place, while **Frederic Kanouté** nets every 262 minutes on average. However, none feature prominently in the Assists Table which could be a problem in deciding on a partnership.

Kasey Keller was one of four keepers in the division to play every league game. He had the worst clean sheets record of the four but faced more shots, 285.

NICKNAME: SPURS

KEY: Won Drawn Lost

No	Comp	Opponent	Venue	Result	Score	Scorers
1	prem	**Birmingham**	A	L	0-1	
2	prem	**Leeds**	H	W	2-1	Taricco 41; Kanoute 71
3	prem	**Liverpool**	A	D	0-0	
4	prem	**Fulham**	H	L	0-3	
5	prem	**Chelsea**	A	L	2-4	Kanoute 25,87
6	prem	**Southampton**	H	L	1-3	Kanoute 62
7	ccr2	**Coventry**	A	W	3-0	Kanoute 14; Keane 23; Ricketts 85
8	prem	**Man City**	A	D	0-0	
9	prem	**Everton**	H	W	3-0	Kanoute 43; Poyet 46; Keane 49
10	prem	**Leicester**	A	W	2-1	Mabizela 79; Kanoute 90
11	prem	**Middlesbrough**	H	D	0-0	
12	ccr3	**West Ham**	H	W	1-0	Zamora 91
13	prem	**Bolton**	H	L	0-1	
14	prem	**Arsenal**	A	L	1-2	Anderton 5
15	prem	**Aston Villa**	H	W	2-1	Ricketts 78; Keane 81
16	prem	**Blackburn**	A	L	0-1	
17	ccr4	**Man City**	H	W	3-1	Anderton 9; Postiga 30; Kanoute 90
18	prem	**Wolves**	H	W	5-2	Keane 29,75,83; Kanoute 50; Dalmat 90
19	prem	**Newcastle**	A	L	0-4	
20	ccqf	**Middlesbrough**	H	L	4-5*	Anderton 2 (*on penalties)
21	prem	**Man Utd**	H	L	1-2	Poyet 63
22	prem	**Portsmouth**	A	L	0-2	
23	prem	**Charlton**	H	L	0-1	
24	facr3	**Crystal Palace**	H	W	3-0	Kanoute 15,20,48
25	prem	**Birmingham**	H	W	4-1	Dalmat 10,24; Davies 39; Keane 79
26	prem	**Leeds**	A	W	1-0	Keane 56
27	prem	**Liverpool**	H	W	2-1	Keane 25 pen; Postiga 54
28	facr4	**Man City**	A	D	1-1	Doherty 57
29	prem	**Fulham**	A	L	1-2	Keane 18 pen
30	facr4r	**Man City**	H	L	3-4	King 2; Keane 19; Ziege 43
31	prem	**Portsmouth**	H	W	4-3	Defoe 13; Keane 42,79; Poyet 89
32	prem	**Charlton**	A	W	4-2	Davies 10; Defoe 43; King 46; Jackson 85
33	prem	**Leicester**	H	D	4-4	Brown 6; Defoe 13,89; Keane 28
34	prem	**Middlesbrough**	A	L	0-1	
35	prem	**Newcastle**	H	W	1-0	O'Brien 86 og
36	prem	**Man Utd**	A	L	0-3	
37	prem	**Southampton**	A	L	0-1	
38	prem	**Chelsea**	H	L	0-1	
39	prem	**Everton**	A	L	1-3	Carr 75
40	prem	**Man City**	H	D	1-1	Defoe 52
41	prem	**Bolton**	A	L	0-2	
42	prem	**Arsenal**	H	D	2-2	Redknapp 62; Keane 90 pen
43	prem	**Aston Villa**	A	L	0-1	
44	prem	**Blackburn**	H	W	1-0	Defoe 18
45	prem	**Wolves**	A	W	2-0	Keane 34; Defoe 57

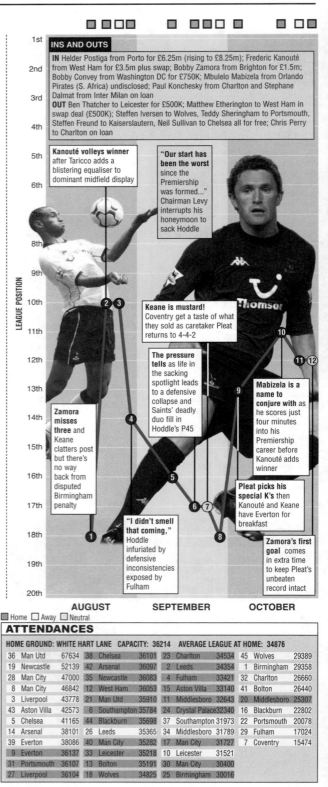

INS AND OUTS

IN Helder Postiga from Porto for £6.25m (rising to £8.25m); Frederic Kanouté from West Ham for £3.5m plus swap; Bobby Zamora from Brighton for £1.5m; Bobby Convey from Washington DC for £750K; Mbulelo Mabizela from Orlando Pirates (S. Africa) undisclosed; Paul Konchesky from Charlton and Stephane Dalmat from Inter Milan on loan

OUT Ben Thatcher to Leicester for £500K; Matthew Etherington to West Ham in swap deal (£500K); Steffen Iversen to Wolves, Teddy Sheringham to Portsmouth, Steffen Freund to Kaiserslautern, Neil Sullivan to Chelsea all for free; Chris Perry to Charlton on loan

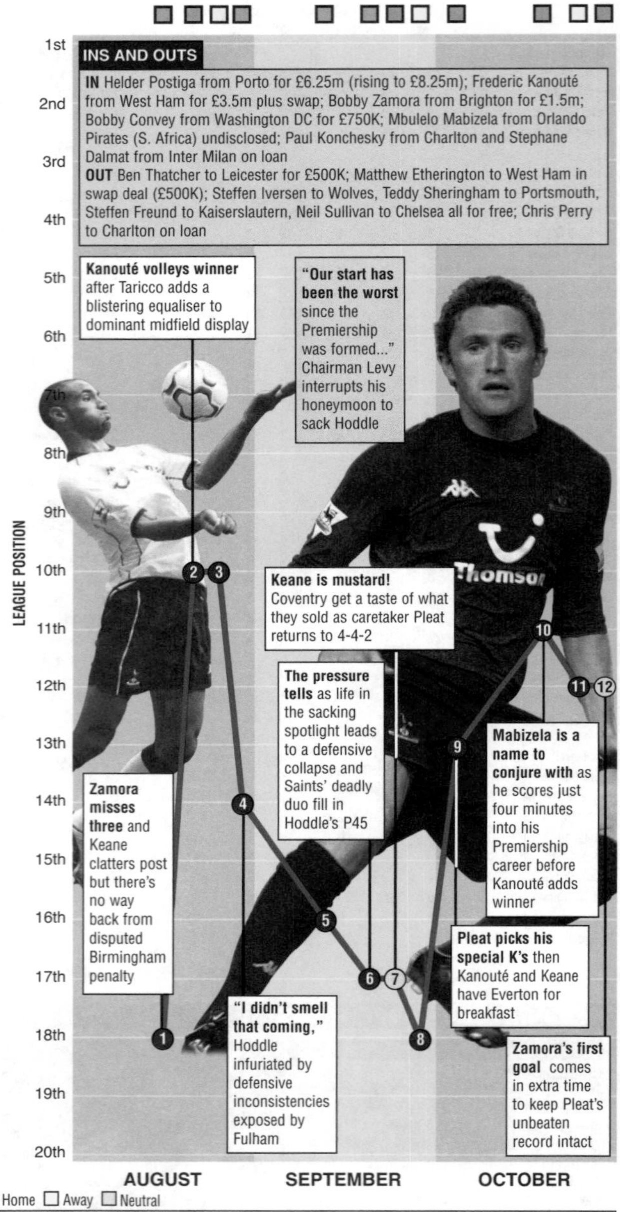

1st
2nd
3rd
4th
5th
6th
7th
8th
9th
10th
11th
12th
13th
14th
15th
16th
17th
18th
19th
20th
LEAGUE POSITION
Kanouté volleys winner after Taricco adds a blistering equaliser to dominant midfield display
"Our start has been the worst since the Premiership was formed..." Chairman Levy interrupts his honeymoon to sack Hoddle
Keane is mustard! Coventry get a taste of what they sold as caretaker Pleat returns to 4-4-2
The pressure tells as life in the sacking spotlight leads to a defensive collapse and Saints' deadly duo fill in Hoddle's P45
Mabizela is a name to conjure with as he scores just four minutes into his Premiership career before Kanouté adds winner
Zamora misses three and Keane clatters post but there's no way back from disputed Birmingham penalty
Pleat picks his special K's then Kanouté and Keane have Everton for breakfast
"I didn't smell that coming," Hoddle infuriated by defensive inconsistencies exposed by Fulham
Zamora's first goal comes in extra time to keep Pleat's unbeaten record intact
AUGUST
SEPTEMBER
OCTOBER
Home Away Neutral

ATTENDANCES

HOME GROUND: WHITE HART LANE **CAPACITY:** 36214 **AVERAGE LEAGUE AT HOME:** 34876

36	Man Utd	67634	38	Chelsea	36101	23	Charlton	34534	45	Wolves	29389
19	Newcastle	52139	42	Arsenal	36097	2	Leeds	34354	1	Birmingham	29358
28	Man City	47000	35	Newcastle	36083	4	Fulham	33421	32	Charlton	26660
8	Man City	46842	12	West Ham	36053	15	Aston Villa	33140	41	Bolton	26440
3	Liverpool	43778	21	Man Utd	35910	11	Middlesboro	32643	20	Middlesboro	25307
43	Aston Villa	42573	6	Southampton	35784	24	Crystal Palace	32340	16	Blackburn	22802
5	Chelsea	41165	44	Blackburn	35698	37	Southampton	31973	22	Portsmouth	20078
14	Arsenal	38101	26	Leeds	35365	34	Middlesboro	31789	29	Fulham	17024
39	Everton	38086	40	Man City	35282	17	Man City	31727	7	Coventry	15474
9	Everton	36137	33	Leicester	35218	10	Leicester	31521			
31	Portsmouth	36107	13	Bolton	35191	30	Man City	30400			
27	Liverpool	36104	18	Wolves	34825	25	Birmingham	30016			

Two managers out but striking trio in

Final Position: 14th

KEY: ● League ● Champions Lge ● UEFA Cup ● FA Cup ○ League Cup ● Other

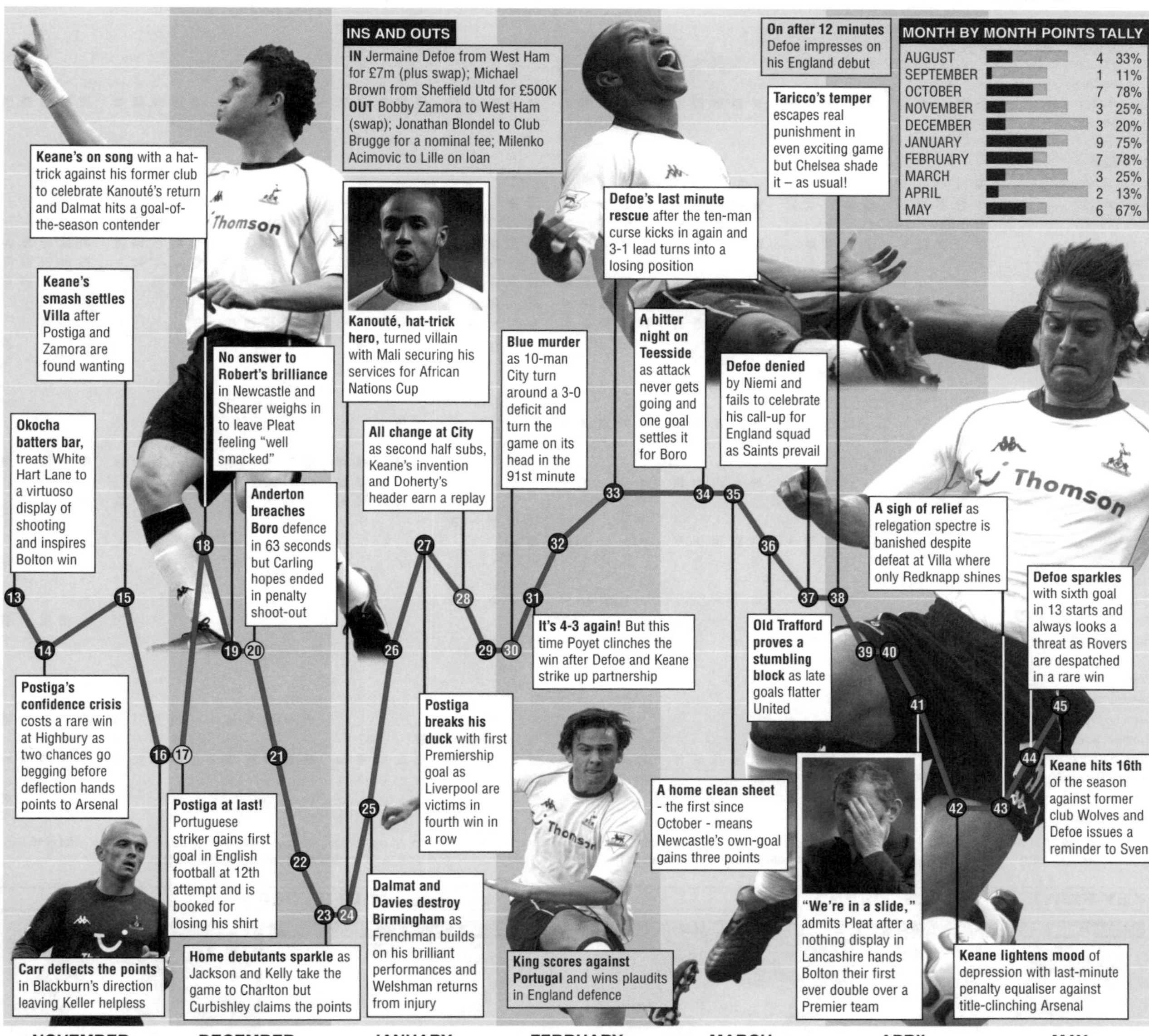

INS AND OUTS
IN Jermaine Defoe from West Ham for £7m (plus swap); Michael Brown from Sheffield Utd for £500K
OUT Bobby Zamora to West Ham (swap); Jonathan Blondel to Club Brugge for a nominal fee; Milenko Acimovic to Lille on loan
MONTH BY MONTH POINTS TALLY
AUGUST 4 33%
SEPTEMBER 1 11%
OCTOBER 7 78%
NOVEMBER 3 25%
DECEMBER 3 20%
JANUARY 9 75%
FEBRUARY 7 78%
MARCH 3 25%
APRIL 2 13%
MAY 6 67%
Okocha batters bar, treats White Hart Lane to a virtuoso display of shooting and inspires Bolton win
Postiga's confidence crisis costs a rare win at Highbury as two chances go begging before deflection hands points to Arsenal
Keane's smash settles Villa after Postiga and Zamora are found wanting
Carr deflects the points in Blackburn's direction leaving Keller helpless
Postiga at last! Portuguese striker gains first goal in English football at 12th attempt and is booked for losing his shirt
Keane's on song with a hat-trick against his former club to celebrate Kanouté's return and Dalmat hits a goal-of-the-season contender
No answer to Robert's brilliance in Newcastle and Shearer weighs in to leave Pleat feeling "well smacked"
Anderton breaches Boro defence in 63 seconds but Carling hopes ended in penalty shoot-out
Home debutants sparkle as Jackson and Kelly take the game to Charlton but Curbishley claims the points
Kanouté, hat-trick hero, turned villain with Mali securing his services for African Nations Cup
Dalmat and Davies destroy Birmingham as Frenchman builds on his brilliant performances and Welshman returns from injury
All change at City as second half subs, Keane's invention and Doherty's header earn a replay
Postiga breaks his duck with first Premiership goal as Liverpool are victims in fourth win in a row
Blue murder as 10-man City turn around a 3-0 deficit and turn the game on its head in the 91st minute
It's 4-3 again! But this time Poyet clinches the win after Defoe and Keane strike up partnership
King scores against Portugal and wins plaudits in England defence
Defoe's last minute rescue after the ten-man curse kicks in again and 3-1 lead turns into a losing position
A bitter night on Teesside as attack never gets going and one goal settles it for Boro
On after 12 minutes Defoe impresses on his England debut
Defoe denied by Niemi and fails to celebrate his call-up for England squad as Saints prevail
A home clean sheet - the first since October - means Newcastle's own-goal gains three points
Old Trafford proves a stumbling block as late goals flatter United
Taricco's temper escapes real punishment in even exciting game but Chelsea shade it – as usual!
"We're in a slide," admits Pleat after a nothing display in Lancashire hands Bolton their first ever double over a Premier team
A sigh of relief as relegation spectre is banished despite defeat at Villa where only Redknapp shines
Keane lightens mood of depression with last-minute penalty equaliser against title-clinching Arsenal
Defoe sparkles with sixth goal in 13 starts and always looks a threat as Rovers are despatched in a rare win
Keane hits 16th of the season against former club Wolves and Defoe issues a reminder to Sven
NOVEMBER
DECEMBER
JANUARY
FEBRUARY
MARCH
APRIL
MAY

GOAL ATTEMPTS

FOR – Goal attempts recorded in League games

	HOME	AWAY	TOTAL	AVE
shots on target	142	93	235	6.2
shots off target	108	78	186	4.9
TOTAL	**250**	**171**	**421**	**11.1**

Ratio of goals to shots Average number of shots on target per League goal scored	5
Accuracy rating Average percentage of total goal attempts which were on target	55.8

AGAINST – Goal attempts recorded in League games

	HOME	AWAY	TOTAL	AVE
shots on target	126	161	287	7.6
shots off target	101	93	194	5.1
TOTAL	**227**	**254**	**481**	**12.7**

Ratio of goals to shots Average number of shots on target per League goal scored	5
Accuracy rating Average percentage of total goal attempts which were on target	59.7

GOALS

Robbie Keane

League	14
FA Cup	1
League Cup	1
Europe	0
Other	0
TOTAL	16

League Average **206** mins between goals

	PLAYER	LGE	FAC	LC	Euro	TOT	AVE
1	Keane	**14**	1	1	0	16	206
2	Kanoute	**7**	3	2	0	12	262
3	Defoe	**7**	0	0	0	7	183
4	Poyet	**3**	0	0	0	3	318
5	Dalmat	**3**	0	0	0	3	375
6	Davies	**2**	0	0	0	2	780
7	Redknapp	**1**	0	0	0	1	1273
8	Mabizela	**1**	0	0	0	1	106
9	Jackson	**1**	0	0	0	1	733
10	King	**1**	1	0	0	2	2349
11	Anderton	**1**	0	2	0	3	1436
12	Carr	**1**	0	0	0	1	2808
13	Brown	**1**	0	0	0	1	1492
14	Postiga	**1**	0	1	0	2	889
15	Ricketts	**1**	0	1	0	2	1161
	Other	2	2	1	0	5	
	TOTAL	**47**	**7**	**8**	**0**	**62**	

SQUAD APPEARANCES

Match	1	2	3	4	5	6	7	8	9	10	11	12	13	14	15	16	17	18	19	20	21	22	23	24	25	26	27	28	29	30	31	32	33	34	35	36	37	38	39	40	41	42	43	44	45
Venue	A	H	A	H	A	H	A	A	H	A	H	H	H	A	H	A	H	H	A	H	H	A	H	H	H	A	H	A	A	H	H	A	H	A	H	A	A	H	A	H	A	H	A	H	A
Competition	L	L	L	L	L	L	W	L	L	L	L	W	L	L	L	L	W	L	L	W	L	L	L	F	L	L	L	F	L	F	L	L	L	L	L	L	L	L	L	L	L	L	L	L	L
Result	L	W	D	L	L	L	W	D	W	W	D	W	L	L	W	L	W	W	L	L	L	L	L	W	W	W	W	D	L	L	W	W	D	L	W	L	L	L	L	D	L	D	L	W	W

Goalkeepers
Robert Burch
Lars Hirschfeld
Kasey Keller
Neil Sullivan

Defenders
Goran Bunjevcevic
Stephen Carr
Gary Doherty
Anthony Gardner
Stephen Kelly
Ledley King
Dean Richards
Mauricio Taricco
Christian Ziege

Midfielders
Milenko Acimovic
Darren Anderton
Jonathan Blondel
Michael Brown
Stephane Dalmat
Simon Davies
Johnnie Jackson
Paul Konchesky
Mbulelo Mabizela
Dean Marney
Gustavo Poyet
Jamie Redknapp
Rohan Ricketts

Forwards
Lee Barnard
Jermain Defoe
Frederic Kanoute
Robbie Keane
Manuel Helder Postiga
Mark Yeates
Bobby Zamora

KEY: On all match; On bench; Subbed or sent off (Counting game); Subbed or sent off (playing less than 70 mins); Subbed on from bench (Counting Game); Subbed on (playing less than 70 mins); Subbed on and then subbed or sent off (Counting Game); Subbed on and then subbed or sent off (playing less than 70 mins); Not in 16

KEY PLAYERS - GOALSCORERS

Jermain Defoe

Goals in the League	7
Goals in all competitions	7
Assists League goals scored by team-mates where he delivered the final pass	0
Contribution to Attacking Power Average number of minutes between League team goals while on pitch	71
Player Strike Rate Average number of minutes between League goals scored by player	183
Club Strike Rate Average minutes between League goals scored by club	73

Thomson

	PLAYER	GOALS LGE	GOALS ALL	ASSISTS	POWER	S RATE
1	Jermain Defoe	7	7	0	71	183 mins
2	Robbie Keane	14	16	3	68	206 mins
3	Frederic Kanoute	7	12	1	76	262 mins
4	Simon Davies	2	2	1	57	780 mins
5	Darren Anderton	1	3	4	62	1436 mins

KEY PLAYERS - MIDFIELDERS

Simon Davies

Goals in the League	2
Goals in all competitions	2
Assists League goals scored by team-mates where he delivered the final pass	1
Defensive Rating Average number of mins between League goals conceded while he was on the pitch	62
Contribution to Attacking Power Average number of minutes between League team goals while on pitch	58
Scoring Difference Defensive Rating minus Contribution to Attacking Power	4

Thomson
29

	PLAYER	GOALS LGE	GOALS ALL	ASSISTS	DEF RATE	POWER	SC DIFF
1	Simon Davies	2	2	1	62	58	4 mins
2	Ledley King	1	2	1	56	57	1 mins
3	Darren Anderton	1	3	4	62	62	0 mins
4	Michael Brown	1	1	1	55	68	-13 mins

PLAYER APPEARANCES

	AGE (on 01/07/04)	IN NAMED 16	APPEARANCES	COUNTING GAMES	MINUTES ON PITCH	APPEARANCES	MINUTES ON PITCH	THIS SEASON	HOME COUNTRY
Goalkeepers									
Robert Burch	20	21	0	0	0	0	0	-	England
Lars Hirschfeld	25	14	0	0	0	0	0	-	Canada
Kasey Keller	34	38	38	38	3420	45	4110	-	United States
Neil Sullivan	34	3	0	0	0	0	0	-	Scotland
Defenders									
Goran Bunjevcevic	31	19	8	1	329	9	419	2	Serbia & M'tenegro (45)
Stephen Carr	27	32	32	31	2808	39	3498	5	Rep of Ireland (15)
Gary Doherty	24	30	17	16	1452	22	1917	9	Rep of Ireland (15)
Anthony Gardner	23	33	33	33	2970	40	3660	1	England (12)
Stephen Kelly	20	17	11	7	737	11	737	-	Rep of Ireland
Dean Richards	30	23	23	23	2070	26	2295	-	England
Mauricio Taricco	31	32	32	24	2527	37	2962	-	Argentina
Christian Ziege	32	8	8	5	565	10	684	1	Germany (9)
Midfielders									
Milenko Acimovic	27	2	0	0	0	0	0	-	Slovenia
Darren Anderton	32	20	20	14	1436	24	1738	-	England
Jonathan Blondel	20	1	1	0	28	3	149	2	Belgium (17)
Michael Brown	27	17	17	17	1492	19	1672	-	England
Stephane Dalmat	25	24	23	8	1126	29	1439	-	France
Simon Davies	24	18	18	17	1559	21	1768	4	Wales (66)
Johnnie Jackson	21	14	11	5	733	14	881	-	England
Ledley King	23	28	28	25	2349	34	2920	2	England (12)
Paul Konchesky	23	12	12	8	829	15	1090	-	England
Mbulelo Mabizela	23	10	6	0	106	7	169	-	South Africa
Dean Marney	20	5	3	0	90	3	90	-	England
Gustavo Poyet	36	23	19	8	954	24	1332	-	Uruguay
Jamie Redknapp	31	17	17	12	1273	17	1273	-	England
Rohan Ricketts	21	26	24	9	1161	28	1430	-	England
Forwards									
Lee Barnard	19	1	0	0	0	0	0	-	England
Jermain Defoe	21	15	15	14	1278	15	1278	2	England (12)
Frederic Kanoute	26	27	27	18	1833	31	2147	-	France
Robbie Keane	23	34	34	31	2880	41	3558	7	Rep of Ireland (15)
Helder Postiga	21	25	18	7	889	23	1119	-	Portugal
Mark Yeates	2005	2	1	1	90	1	90	-	Rep of Ireland
Bobby Zamora	23	17	16	2	624	18	762	-	England

KEY: LEAGUE ALL COMPS CAPS (FIFA RANKING)

TEAM OF THE SEASON

KELLER — CG 38 DR 60

CARR — CG 31 DR 55
DOHERTY — CG 16 DR 61
GARDNER — CG 33 DR 62
TARICCO — CG 24 DR 62

DAVIS — CG 17 SD +4
KING — CG 25 SD +1
BROWN — CG 17 SD -13
ANDERTON — CG 14 SD 0

KEANE — CG 31 AP 68
DEFOE — CG 14 SR 183

KEY: DR = Diffensive Rate, SD = Scoring Difference AP = Attacking Power SR = Strike Rate, CG=Counting games – League games playing at least 70 minutes

TOP POINT EARNERS

Simon Davies

Counting Games League games when he played at least 70 minutes	17
Average points Average League points taken in Counting games	1.65
Club Average points Average points taken in League games	1.18

	PLAYER	GAMES	PTS
1	Simon Davies	17	**1.65**
2	Darren Anderton	14	**1.64**
3	Mauricio Taricco	24	**1.33**
4	Robbie Keane	31	**1.29**
5	Gary Doherty	16	**1.25**
6	Michael Brown	17	**1.24**
7	Jermain Defoe	14	**1.21**
8	Ledley King	25	**1.20**
9	Stephen Carr	31	**1.19**
10	Kasey Keller	38	**1.18**

KEY PLAYERS - DEFENDERS

Mauricio Taricco

Goals Conceded The number of League goals conceded while he was on the pitch	41
Goals Conceded in all competitions The number of goals conceded while he was on the pitch in all competitions	44
League minutes played Number of minutes played in league matches	2527
Clean Sheets In games when he played at least70 mins	6
Defensive Rating Average number of mins between League goals conceded while he was on the pitch	62
Club Defensive Rating Average number of mins between League goals conceded by the club this season	60

	PLAYER	CON LGE	CON ALL	MINS	C SHEETS	DEF RATE
1	Mauricio Taricco	41	44	2527	6	**62 mins**
2	Anthony Gardner	48	55	2970	8	**62 mins**
3	Gary Doherty	24	27	1452	2	**61 mins**
4	Ledley King	42	49	2349	4	**56 mins**
5	Stephen Carr	51	58	2808	6	**55 mins**

KEY GOALKEEPER

Kasey Keller

Goals Conceded in the League The number of League goals conceded while he was on the pitch	57
Goals Conceded in all competitions Number of goals conceded while he was on the pitch in all competitions	64
League minutes played Number of minutes played in league matches	3420
Clean Sheets In games when he played at least 70 mins	8
Goals to Shots Ratio The average number of shots on target per each League goal conceded	5
Defensive Rating Ave mins between League goals conceded while on the pitch	60

BOOKINGS

Paul Konchesky

League Yellow	4
League Red	0
All competitions Yellow	4
All competitions Red	0

League Average **207** mins between cards

	PLAYER	LEAGUE Y	LEAGUE R	TOTAL Y	TOTAL R	AVE
1	Konchesky	4	0	4	0	207
2	Redknapp	6	0	6	0	212
3	Carr	10	1	12	1	255
4	Ziege	2	0	2	0	282
5	Taricco	8	0	8	0	315
6	Anderton	4	0	5	0	359
7	Gardner	8	0	9	0	371
8	Doherty	3	0	4	0	484
9	Dalmat	2	0	2	0	563
10	Zamora	1	0	1	0	624
11	Richards	3	0	3	0	690
12	Davies	2	0	2	0	779
13	Postiga	1	0	2	0	889
14	Poyet	1	0	1	1	954
15	Ricketts	1	0	1	0	1161
	Other	6	0	8	0	
	TOTAL	**62**	**1**	**70**	**2**	

BLACKBURN ROVERS

The emergence of **Jonathan Stead** fired a late charge up the table in a season of serious injuries and sour expressions from **Graeme Souness**.

Stead's Strike Rate is an impressive goal every 180 minutes although he narrowly misses the 12 Counting Games hurdle needed to impact the Premier charts but hits the Division Three charts with a rate of 144.

The other bright spot is **Brett Emerton**'s impact on the Assists Table where his total of 12 is second highest.

Emerton scored on his debut but added only one other league goal. It shouldn't have been a surprise to Souness as the Aussie played all but one game for Feyenoord last year but scored only three goals for a prolific team and was eclipsed by Japan's Ono and Arsenal-bound van Persie.

NICKNAME: ROVERS

KEY: Won, Drawn, Lost

No	Comp	Opponent	Venue	Result	Score	Scorers
1	prem	**Wolves**	H	W	5-1	Amoruso 17; Thompson 29; Emerton 53; Cole 79,87
2	prem	**Bolton**	A	D	2-2	Jansen 50; Yorke 90
3	prem	**Man City**	H	L	2-3	Sinclair 44 og; Amoruso 61
4	prem	**Chelsea**	A	D	2-2	Cole 1,57
5	prem	**Liverpool**	H	L	1-3	Jansen 8
6	prem	**Portsmouth**	A	W	2-1	Neill 35; Cole 43
7	uc1rl1	**Genclerbirligi**	A	L	1-3	Emerton 57
8	prem	**Fulham**	H	L	0-2	
9	prem	**Leeds**	A	L	1-2	Baggio 86
10	uc1rl2	**Genclerbirligi**	H	D	1-1	Jansen 65
11	prem	**Charlton**	H	L	0-1	
12	prem	**Southampton**	A	L	0-2	
13	ccr3	**Liverpool**	H	L	3-4	Cole 35; Ferguson, B 81; Yorke 90
14	prem	**Leicester**	A	L	0-2	
15	prem	**Everton**	H	W	2-1	Babbel 6; Yorke 13
16	prem	**Man Utd**	A	L	1-2	Emerton 62
17	prem	**Tottenham**	H	W	1-0	Carr 78 og
18	prem	**Birmingham**	A	W	4-0	Ferguson, B 66; Neill 68; Tugay 83; Gallagher 88
19	prem	**Arsenal**	A	L	0-1	
20	prem	**Aston Villa**	H	L	0-2	
21	prem	**Middlesbrough**	H	D	2-2	Babbel 3,90
22	prem	**Newcastle**	A	W	1-0	Gallagher 72
23	facr3	**Birmingham**	A	L	0-4	
24	prem	**Wolves**	A	D	2-2	Cole 14; Yorke 78
25	prem	**Bolton**	H	L	3-4	Gresko 2; Yorke 24; Cole 34
26	prem	**Man City**	A	D	1-1	Flitcroft 55
27	prem	**Chelsea**	H	L	2-3	Flitcroft 3; Gallagher 87
28	prem	**Middlesbrough**	A	W	1-0	Stead 39
29	prem	**Newcastle**	H	D	1-1	Stead 85
30	prem	**Charlton**	A	L	2-3	Cole 74; Friedel 90
31	prem	**Southampton**	H	D	1-1	Cole 52
32	prem	**Arsenal**	H	L	0-2	
33	prem	**Aston Villa**	A	W	2-0	Flitcroft 26; Stead 36
34	prem	**Portsmouth**	H	L	1-2	Taylor 37 og
35	prem	**Liverpool**	A	L	0-4	
36	prem	**Leeds**	H	L	1-2	Short 90
37	prem	**Fulham**	A	W	4-3	Cole 23; Douglas 48; Amoruso 51; Stead 75
38	prem	**Leicester**	H	W	1-0	Dabizas 42 og
39	prem	**Everton**	A	W	1-0	Stead 81
40	prem	**Man Utd**	H	W	1-0	Stead 85
41	prem	**Tottenham**	A	L	0-1	
42	prem	**Birmingham**	H	D	1-1	Cole 24

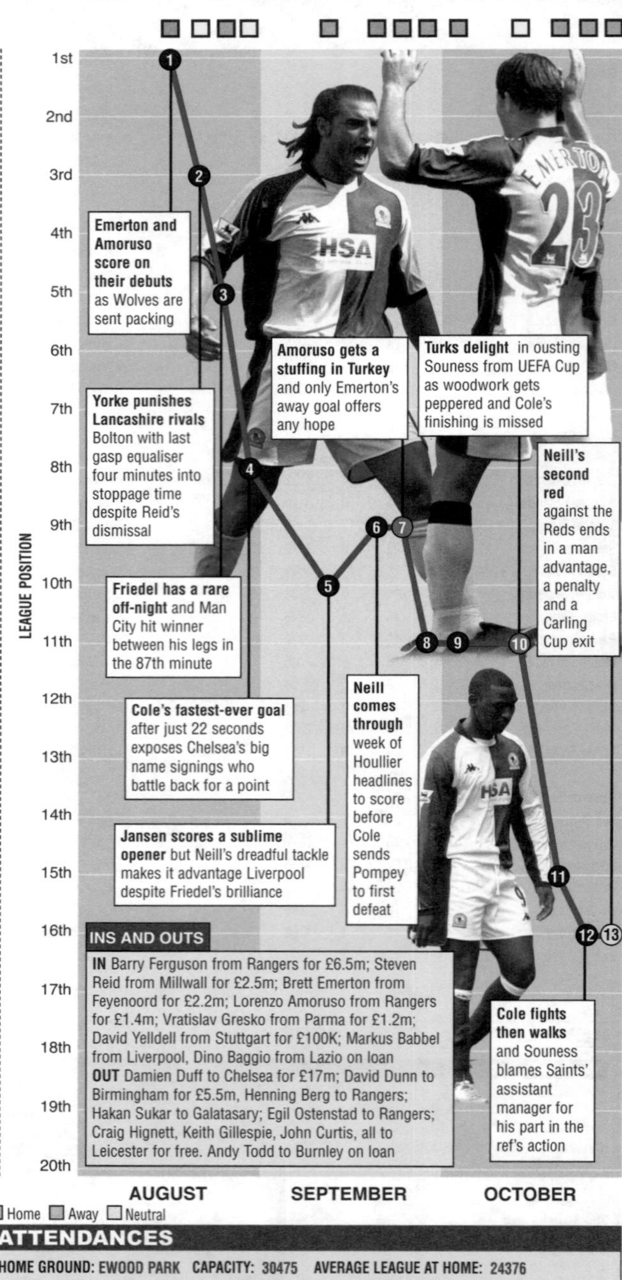

1st
2nd
3rd
4th
5th
6th
7th
8th
9th
10th
11th
12th
13th
14th
15th
16th
17th
18th
19th
20th
LEAGUE POSITION
Emerton and Amoruso score on their debuts as Wolves are sent packing
Yorke punishes Lancashire rivals Bolton with last gasp equaliser four minutes into stoppage time despite Reid's dismissal
Friedel has a rare off-night and Man City hit winner between his legs in the 87th minute
Cole's fastest-ever goal after just 22 seconds exposes Chelsea's big name signings who battle back for a point
Jansen scores a sublime opener but Neill's dreadful tackle makes it advantage Liverpool despite Friedel's brilliance
Amoruso gets a stuffing in Turkey and only Emerton's away goal offers any hope
Neill comes through week of Houllier headlines to score before Cole sends Pompey to first defeat
Turks delight in ousting Souness from UEFA Cup as woodwork gets peppered and Cole's finishing is missed
Neill's second red against the Reds ends in a man advantage, a penalty and a Carling Cup exit
Cole fights then walks and Souness blames Saints' assistant manager for his part in the ref's action
AUGUST
SEPTEMBER
OCTOBER
Home
Away
Neutral

INS AND OUTS

IN Barry Ferguson from Rangers for £6.5m; Steven Reid from Millwall for £2.5m; Brett Emerton from Feyenoord for £2.2m; Lorenzo Amoruso from Rangers for £1.4m; Vratislav Gresko from Parma for £1.2m; David Yelldell from Stuttgart for £100K; Markus Babbel from Liverpool, Dino Baggio from Lazio on loan
OUT Damien Duff to Chelsea for £17m; David Dunn to Birmingham for £5.5m, Henning Berg to Rangers; Hakan Sukar to Galatasary; Egil Ostenstad to Rangers; Craig Hignett, Keith Gillespie, John Curtis, all to Leicester for free. Andy Todd to Burnley on loan

ATTENDANCES

HOME GROUND: EWOOD PARK **CAPACITY:** 30475 **AVERAGE LEAGUE AT HOME:** 24376

16	Man Utd	67748	14	Leicester	30975	42	Birmingham	26070	31	Southampton	21970
22	Newcastle	51648	5	Liverpool	30074	21	Middlesboro	25452	20	Aston Villa	20722
26	Man City	47090	40	Man Utd	29616	27	Chelsea	24867	6	Portsmouth	20024
35	Liverpool	41559	18	Birmingham	29354	25	Bolton	23538	11	Charlton	19939
4	Chelsea	41066	32	Arsenal	28627	29	Newcastle	23459	23	Birmingham	18688
39	Everton	38884	28	Middlesboro	28307	3	Man City	23361	7	Genclerbirligi	18000
19	Arsenal	37677	2	Bolton	27423	34	Portsmouth	22855	13	Liverpool	16918
33	Aston Villa	37532	24	Wolves	27393	17	Tottenham	22802	10	Genclerbirligi	14573
41	Tottenham	35698	36	Leeds	26611	38	Leicester	22749	37	Fulham	13981
9	Leeds	35039	30	Charlton	26332	15	Everton	22179			
12	Southampton	31620	1	Wolves	26270	8	Fulham	21985			

Stead's goals secure the late escape

Final Position: **15th**

KEY: ● League ● Champions Lge ● UEFA Cup ● FA Cup ○ League Cup ● Other

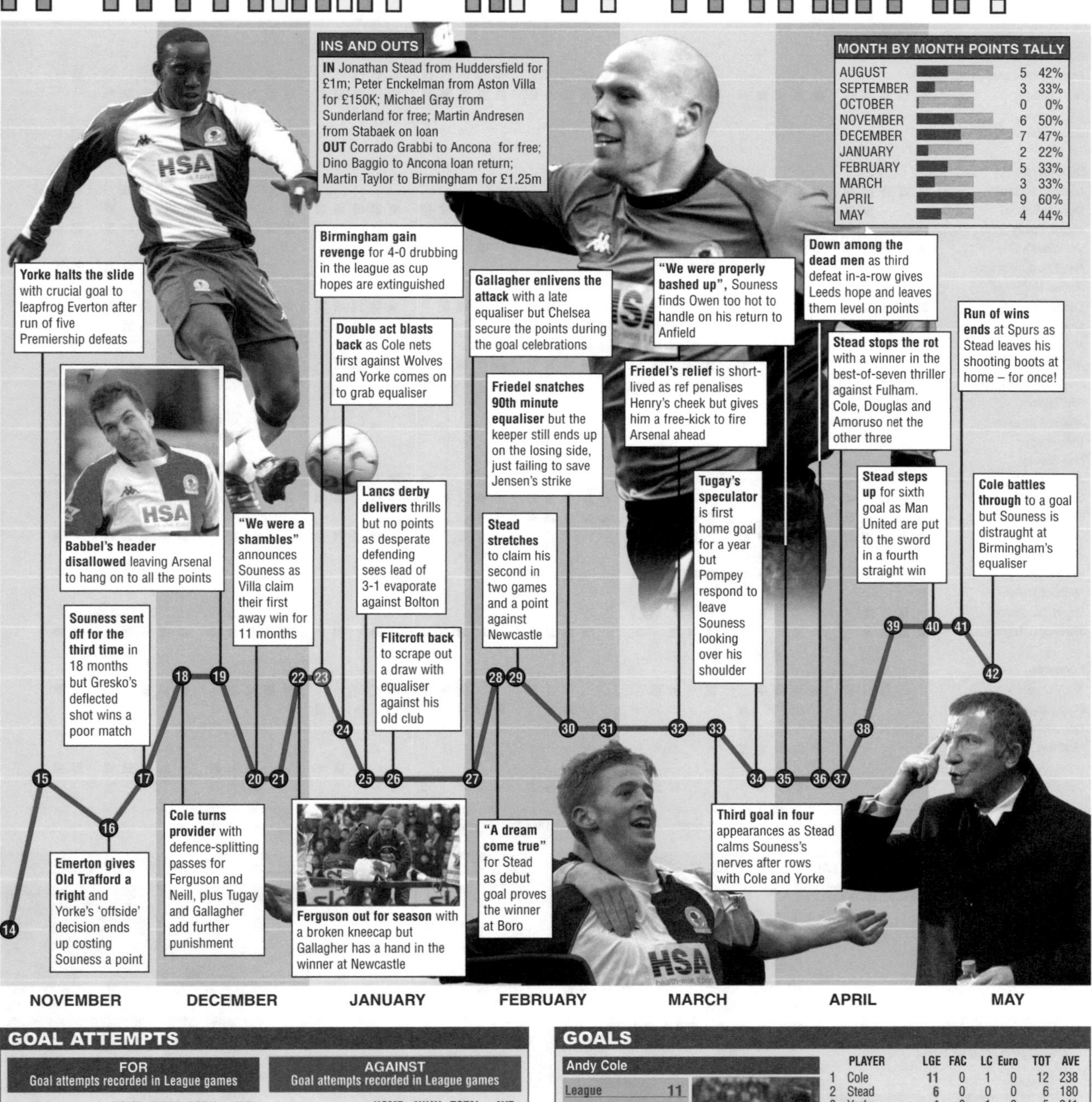

INS AND OUTS
IN Jonathan Stead from Huddersfield for £1m; Peter Enckelman from Aston Villa for £150K; Michael Gray from Sunderland for free; Martin Andresen from Stabaek on loan
OUT Corrado Grabbi to Ancona for free; Dino Baggio to Ancona loan return; Martin Taylor to Birmingham for £1.25m
MONTH BY MONTH POINTS TALLY
AUGUST 5 42%
SEPTEMBER 3 33%
OCTOBER 0 0%
NOVEMBER 6 50%
DECEMBER 7 47%
JANUARY 2 22%
FEBRUARY 5 33%
MARCH 3 33%
APRIL 9 60%
MAY 4 44%
Yorke halts the slide with crucial goal to leapfrog Everton after run of five Premiership defeats
Babbel's header disallowed leaving Arsenal to hang on to all the points
Souness sent off for the third time in 18 months but Gresko's deflected shot wins a poor match
Emerton gives Old Trafford a fright and Yorke's 'offside' decision ends up costing Souness a point
Cole turns provider with defence-splitting passes for Ferguson and Neill, plus Tugay and Gallagher add further punishment
"We were a shambles" announces Souness as Villa claim their first away win for 11 months
Birmingham gain revenge for 4-0 drubbing in the league as cup hopes are extinguished
Double act blasts back as Cole nets first against Wolves and Yorke comes on to grab equaliser
Lancs derby delivers thrills but no points as desperate defending sees lead of 3-1 evaporate against Bolton
Flitcroft back to scrape out a draw with equaliser against his old club
Ferguson out for season with a broken kneecap but Gallagher has a hand in the winner at Newcastle
Gallagher enlivens the attack with a late equaliser but Chelsea secure the points during the goal celebrations
Friedel snatches 90th minute equaliser but the keeper still ends up on the losing side, just failing to save Jensen's strike
Stead stretches to claim his second in two games and a point against Newcastle
"A dream come true" for Stead as debut goal proves the winner at Boro
"We were properly bashed up", Souness finds Owen too hot to handle on his return to Anfield
Friedel's relief is short-lived as ref penalises Henry's cheek but gives him a free-kick to fire Arsenal ahead
Tugay's speculator is first home goal for a year but Pompey respond to leave Souness looking over his shoulder
Third goal in four appearances as Stead calms Souness's nerves after rows with Cole and Yorke
Down among the dead men as third defeat in-a-row gives Leeds hope and leaves them level on points
Stead stops the rot with a winner in the best-of-seven thriller against Fulham. Cole, Douglas and Amoruso net the other three
Stead steps up for sixth goal as Man United are put to the sword in a fourth straight win
Run of wins ends at Spurs as Stead leaves his shooting boots at home – for once!
Cole battles through to a goal but Souness is distraught at Birmingham's equaliser
NOVEMBER
DECEMBER
JANUARY
FEBRUARY
MARCH
APRIL
MAY

GOAL ATTEMPTS

FOR – Goal attempts recorded in League games

	HOME	AWAY	TOTAL	AVE
shots on target	141	97	238	6.3
shots off target	115	104	219	5.8
TOTAL	256	201	457	12

Ratio of goals to shots Average number of shots on target per League goal scored	4.7
Accuracy rating Average percentage of total goal attempts which were on target	52.1

AGAINST – Goal attempts recorded in League games

	HOME	AWAY	TOTAL	AVE
shots on target	104	145	249	6.6
shots off target	105	97	202	5.3
TOTAL	209	242	451	11.9

Ratio of goals to shots Average number of shots on target per League goal scored	4.2
Accuracy rating Average percentage of total goal attempts which were on target	55.2

GOALS

Andy Cole

League	11
FA Cup	0
League Cup	1
Europe	0
Other	0
TOTAL	12

League Average **238** mins between goals

	PLAYER	LGE	FAC	LC	Euro	TOT	AVE
1	Cole	11	0	1	0	12	238
2	Stead	6	0	0	0	6	180
3	Yorke	4	0	1	0	5	341
4	Gallagher	3	0	0	0	3	373
5	Babbel	3	0	0	0	3	679
6	Amoruso	3	0	0	0	3	331
7	Flitcroft	3	0	0	0	3	793
8	Neill	2	0	0	0	2	1297
9	Jansen	2	0	0	1	3	423
10	Emerton	2	0	0	1	3	1436
11	Friedel	1	0	0	0	1	3240
12	Short	1	0	0	0	1	1617
13	Gresko	1	0	0	0	1	1884
15	Baggio	1	0	0	0	1	172
	Other	8	0	1	0	9	
	TOTAL	51	0	3	2	56	

SQUAD APPEARANCES

Match	1	2	3	4	5	6	7	8	9	10	11	12	13	14	15	16	17	18	19	20	21	22	23	24	25	26	27	28	29	30	31	32	33	34	35	36	37	38	39	40	41	42
Venue	H	A	H	A	H	A	A	H	A	H	H	A	H	A	H	A	H	A	A	H	H	A	A	A	H	A	H	A	H	A	H	H	A	H	A	H	A	H	A	H	A	H
Competition	L	L	L	L	L	L	E	L	L	E	L	L	W	L	L	L	L	L	L	L	L	L	F	L	L	L	L	L	L	L	L	L	L	L	L	L	L	L	L	L	L	L
Result	W	D	L	D	L	W	L	L	L	D	L	L	L	L	W	L	W	W	L	L	D	W	L	D	L	D	L	W	D	L	D	L	W	L	L	L	W	W	W	W	L	D

Goalkeepers
Peter Enckelman
Brad Friedel
Alan Kelly
David Yelldell

Defenders
Lorenzo Amoruso
Markus Babbel
Michael Gray
Vratislav Gresko
Nils-Eric Johansson
James McEveley
Lucas Neill
Craig Short
Martin Taylor
Andy Todd

Midfielders
Martin Andresen
Dino Baggio
Neil Danns
Jonathan Douglas
Brett Emerton
Barry Ferguson
Garry Flitcroft
Alan Mahon
Steven Reid
Michael Taylor
David Thompson
Kerimoglu Tugay

Forwards
Andy Cole
Paul Gallagher
Corrado Grabbi
Matthew Jansen
John Stead
Dwight Yorke

KEY: On all match — Subbed or sent off (Counting game) — Subbed on from bench (Counting Game) — Subbed on and then subbed or sent off (Counting Game) — Not in 16
On bench — Subbed or sent off (playing less than 70 mins) — Subbed on (playing less than 70 mins) — Subbed on and then subbed or sent off (playing less than 70 mins)

KEY PLAYERS - GOALSCORERS

Andy Cole

Goals in the League	11
Goals in all competitions	12
Assists League goals scored by team-mates where he delivered the final pass	5
Contribution to Attacking Power Average number of minutes between League team goals while on pitch	65
Player Strike Rate Average number of minutes between League goals scored by player	238
Club Strike Rate Average minutes between League goals scored by club	67

	PLAYER	GOALS LGE	GOALS ALL	ASSISTS	POWER	S RATE
1	Andy Cole	11	12	5	65	238 mins
2	Markus Babbel	3	3	2	67	679 mins
3	Garry Flitcroft	3	3	1	67	793 mins
4	Lucas Neill	2	2	0	55	1297 mins
5	Brett Emerton	2	3	12	68	1436 mins

KEY PLAYERS - MIDFIELDERS

Kerimoglu Tugay

Goals in the League	1
Goals in all competitions	1
Assists League goals scored by team-mates where he delivered the final pass	7
Defensive Rating Average number of mins between League goals conceded while he was on the pitch	60
Contribution to Attacking Power Average number of minutes between League team goals while on pitch	64
Scoring Difference Defensive Rating minus Contribution to Attacking Power	-4

	PLAYER	GOALS LGE	GOALS ALL	ASSISTS	DEF RATE	POWER	SC DIFF
1	Kerimoglu Tugay	1	1	7	60	64	-4 mins
2	Brett Emerton	2	3	12	55	68	-13 mins
3	Garry Flitcroft	3	3	1	54	68	-14 mins
4	Barry Ferguson	1	2	2	64	86	-22 mins

PLAYER APPEARANCES

	AGE (on 01/07/04)	IN NAMED 16	APPEARANCES	COUNTING GAMES	MINUTES ON PITCH	APPEARANCES	MINUTES ON PITCH	THIS SEASON	HOME COUNTRY
Goalkeepers									
Peter Enckelman	27	25	2	2	180	2	180	-	Finland
Brad Friedel	33	36	36	36	3240	40	3600	-	United States
Alan Kelly	35	8	0	0	0	0	0	-	Rep of Ireland
David Yelldell	22	6	0	0	0	0	0	-	United States
Defenders									
Lorenzo Amoruso	33	13	12	11	992	14	1172	-	Italy
Markus Babbel	31	26	25	22	2036	28	2306	-	Germany
Michael Gray	29	14	14	14	1249	14	1249	-	England
Vratislav Gresko	26	25	24	19	1884	28	2208	-	Slovakia
Nils-Eric Johansson	24	27	14	5	763	15	770	-	Sweden
James McEveley	18	0	0	0	0	0	0	-	England
Lucas Neill	26	32	32	26	2593	35	2813	4	Australia (89)
Craig Short	36	19	19	17	1617	20	1668	-	England
Martin Taylor	24	12	7	6	547	7	547	-	England
Andy Todd	29	22	19	18	1671	21	1837	-	England
Midfielders									
Martin Andresen	27	14	11	8	857	11	857	-	Norway
Dino Baggio	32	11	9	0	172	12	316	-	Italy
Neil Danns	21	2	1	0	17	1	17	-	England
Jonathan Douglas	22	14	14	11	1127	14	1127	1	Rep of Ireland (15)
Brett Emerton	25	37	37	30	2872	40	3084	4	Australia (89)
Barry Ferguson	26	15	15	12	1209	16	1299	6	Scotland (63)
Garry Flitcroft	31	32	31	23	2379	33	2559	-	England
Alan Mahon	26	4	3	1	170	4	215	-	Rep of Ireland
Steven Reid	23	21	16	4	804	19	997	4	Rep of Ireland (15)
Michael Taylor	21	6	4	4	360	7	503	-	England
David Thompson	26	11	11	9	868	14	1106	-	England
Kerimoglu Tugay	33	37	36	28	2799	40	3159	-	Turkey
Forwards									
Andy Cole	32	35	34	26	2623	37	2848	-	England
Paul Gallagher	19	27	26	5	1120	28	1187	-	England
Corrado Grabbi	28	7	5	0	79	7	160	-	Italy
Matthew Jansen	26	28	19	5	846	21	981	-	England
John Stead	21	13	13	11	1080	13	1080	-	England
Dwight Yorke	32	28	23	10	1362	27	1581	-	Trinidad & Tobago

KEY: LEAGUE ALL COMPS CAPS (FIFA RANKING)

TEAM OF THE SEASON

FRIEDEL

CG 36 DR 57

NEILL

CG 26 DR 59

SHORT

CG 17 DR 70

TODD

CG 18 DR 64

GRAY

CG 14 DR 62

EMERTON
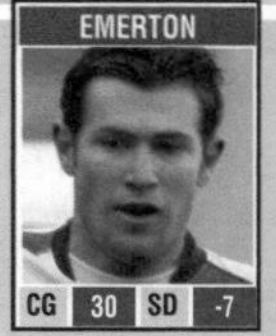
CG 30 SD -7

TUGAY

CG 28 SD -4

FLITCROFT

CG 23 SD -14

FERGUSON

CG 12 SD -22

STEAD

CG 11* AP 83

COLE

CG 26 SR 238

KEY: DR = Diffensive Rate, SD = Scoring Difference AP = Attacking Power SR = Strike Rate, CG=Counting games – League games playing at least 70 minutes * = Played less than 12 counting games

TOP POINT EARNERS

Vratislav Gresko

Counting Games League games when he played at least 70 minutes	19
Average points Average League points taken in Counting games	1.47
Club Average points Average points taken in League games	1.16

	PLAYER	GAMES	PTS
1	Vratislav Gresko	19	1.47
2	Lucas Neill	26	1.42
3	Craig Short	17	1.35
4	Garry Flitcroft	23	1.30
5	Markus Babbel	22	1.23
6	Kerimoglu Tugay	28	1.21
7	Brad Friedel	36	1.19
8	Andy Todd	18	1.11
9	Michael Gray	14	1.07
10	Andy Cole	26	1.04

KEY PLAYERS - DEFENDERS

Craig Short

Goals Conceded The number of League goals conceded while he was on the pitch	23
Goals Conceded in all competitions The number of goals conceded while he was on the pitch in all competitions	25
League minutes played Number of minutes played in league matches	1617
Clean Sheets In games when he played at least70 mins	6
Defensive Rating Average number of mins between League goals conceded while he was on the pitch	70
Club Defensive Rating Average number of mins between League goals conceded by the club this season	58

HSA

	PLAYER	CON LGE	CON ALL	MINS	C SHEETS	DEF RATE
1	Craig Short	23	25	1617	6	70 mins
2	Andy Todd	26	31	1671	5	64 mins
3	Michael Gray	20	20	1249	4	62 mins
4	Lucas Neill	44	51	2593	6	59 mins
5	Markus Babbel	37	48	2036	5	55 mins

KEY GOALKEEPER

Brad Friedel

Goals Conceded in the League The number of League goals conceded while he was on the pitch	57
Goals Conceded in all competitions Number of goals conceded while he was on the pitch in all competitions	69
League minutes played Number of minutes played in league matches	3240
Clean Sheets In games when he played at least 70 mins	8
Goals to Shots Ratio The average number of shots on target per each League goal conceded	4.1
Defensive Rating Ave mins between League goals conceded while on the pitch	57

BOOKINGS

David Thompson

League Yellow	5
League Red	0
All competitions Yellow	6
All competitions Red	0

League Average 173 mins between cards

	PLAYER	LEAGUE		TOTAL		AVE
1	Thompson	5 Y	0 R	6 Y	0 R	173
2	Flitcroft	9	0	9	0	264
3	Andresen	3	0	3	0	285
4	Gresko	6	0	6	0	314
5	Amoruso	3	0	3	0	330
6	Neill	6	1	6	2	370
7	Douglas	3	0	3	0	375
8	Reid	1	1	1	1	402
9	Ferguson, B	3	0	3	0	403
10	Todd	4	0	5	0	417
11	Gallagher	2	0	2	0	560
12	Cole	3	1	3	1	655
13	Tugay	4	0	5	0	699
14	Emerton	4	0	5	0	718
15	Babbel	2	0	2	0	1018
	Other	3	0	3	0	
	TOTAL	61	3	65	4	

MANCHESTER CITY

Was it bad luck or just bad team selections that dogged **Kevin Keegan** through the season?

Antoine Sibierski was only an occasional starter but had an Attacking Power equal to Lampard. City would average a goal every 51 minutes when he played. He started nearly every game for Lens the previous year and top-scored with 12 goals and a respectable Strike Rate of 240.

Like Sibierski, **Claudio Reyna** and the other leading midfielders had a positive Scoring Difference (rare in midfielders in the last third of the table); meaning City scored more than they conceded when the top four were on the park.

Nicolas Anelka hit 23 goals in total. His 16 scored in the league placed him eighth in the Premiership Top Goalscorer list with a Strike Rate of a goal every 171 minutes.

NICKNAME: BLUES/CITIZENS

KEY: Won Drawn Lost

No.	Comp	Opponent	Venue	Result	Score	Scorers
1	ucql1	**TNS**	H	W	5-0	Sinclair 14; Wright-Phillips 51; Sun Jihai 60; Sommeil 74; Anelka 87
2	prem	**Charlton**	A	W	3-0	Anelka 14 pen; Sibierski 23; Sun Jihai 83
3	prem	**Portsmouth**	H	D	1-1	Sommeil 90
4	prem	**Blackburn**	A	W	3-2	Tarnat 4 fk; Barton 59; Anelka 87
5	ucq12	**TNS**	A	W	2-0	Negouai 43; Huckerby 81
6	prem	**Arsenal**	H	L	1-2	Lauren 11 og
7	prem	**Aston Villa**	H	W	4-1	Anelka 48 pen,68 pen,83; Tarnat 50
8	prem	**Fulham**	A	D	2-2	Knight 46 og; Wanchope 90
9	uc1rl1	**Lokeren**	H	W	3-2	Sibierski 8; Fowler 77; Anelka 80 pen
10	prem	**Tottenham**	H	D	0-0	
11	prem	**Wolves**	A	L	0-1	
12	uc1rl2	**Lokeren**	A	W	1-0	Anelka 19 pen
13	prem	**Bolton**	H	W	6-2	Wright-Phillips 27,56; Distin 48; Anelka 58,72; Reyna 84
14	prem	**Chelsea**	A	L	0-1	
15	ccr3	**QPR**	A	W	3-0	Wright-Phillips 22,77; Macken 79
16	prem	**Southampton**	A	W	2-0	Fowler 4; Wanchope 85
17	uc2rl1	**G Grodzisk**	H	D	1-1	Anelka 6
18	prem	**Leicester**	H	L	0-3	
19	prem	**Newcastle**	A	L	0-3	
20	uc2rl2	**G Grodzisk**	A	D	0-0	
21	prem	**Middlesbrough**	H	L	0-1	
22	ccr4	**Tottenham**	A	L	1-3	Fowler 80
23	prem	**Everton**	A	D	0-0	
24	prem	**Man Utd**	A	L	1-3	Wright-Phillips 52
25	prem	**Leeds**	H	D	1-1	Sibierski 82
26	prem	**Birmingham**	A	L	1-2	Fowler 15
27	prem	**Liverpool**	H	D	2-2	Anelka 30 pen; Fowler 90
28	facr3	**Leicester**	H	D	2-2	Anelka 27 pen,69
29	prem	**Charlton**	H	D	1-1	Fowler 39
30	prem	**Portsmouth**	A	L	2-4	Anelka 21; Sibierski 45
31	facr3r	**Leicester**	A	W	3-1	Sibierski 12; Anelka 90; Macken 90
32	prem	**Blackburn**	H	D	1-1	Anelka 50
33	facr4	**Tottenham**	H	D	1-1	Anelka 10
34	prem	**Arsenal**	A	L	1-2	Anelka 89
35	facr4r	**Tottenham**	A	W	4-3	Distin 48; Bosvelt 61; Wright-Phillips 79; Macken 90
36	prem	**Birmingham**	H	D	0-0	
37	prem	**Liverpool**	A	L	1-2	Wright-Phillips 50
38	facr5	**Man Utd**	A	L	2-4	Tarnat 78; Fowler 86
39	prem	**Bolton**	A	W	3-1	Fowler 27,31; Charlton 50 og
40	prem	**Chelsea**	H	L	0-1	
41	prem	**Man Utd**	H	W	4-1	Fowler 3; Macken 32; Sinclair 73; Wright-Phillips 90
42	prem	**Leeds**	A	L	1-2	Anelka 43
43	prem	**Fulham**	H	D	0-0	
44	prem	**Aston Villa**	A	D	1-1	Distin 82
45	prem	**Wolves**	H	D	3-3	Anelka 25; Sibierski 39; Wright-Phillips 90
46	prem	**Tottenham**	A	D	1-1	Anelka 25
47	prem	**Southampton**	H	L	1-3	Anelka 78
48	prem	**Leicester**	A	D	1-1	Tarnat 45
49	prem	**Newcastle**	H	W	1-0	Wanchope 59
50	prem	**Middlesbrough**	A	L	1-2	Wanchope 35
51	prem	**Everton**	H	W	5-1	Wanchope 16,30; Anelka 41; Sibierski 89; Wright-Phillips 90

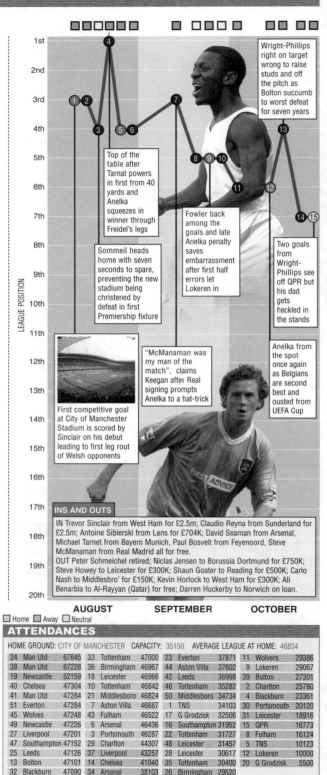

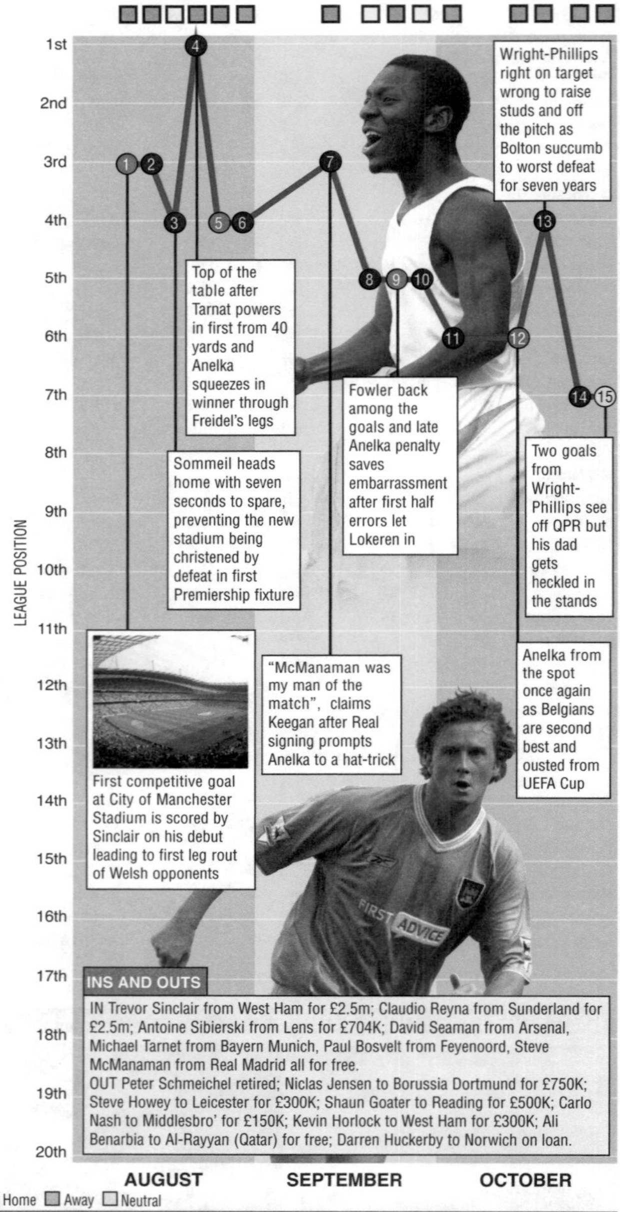

LEAGUE POSITION
1st
2nd
3rd
4th
5th
6th
7th
8th
9th
10th
11th
12th
13th
14th
15th
16th
17th
18th
19th
20th
AUGUST
SEPTEMBER
OCTOBER
Home Away Neutral
Wright-Phillips right on target wrong to raise studs and off the pitch as Bolton succumb to worst defeat for seven years
Top of the table after Tarnat powers in first from 40 yards and Anelka squeezes in winner through Freidel's legs
Fowler back among the goals and late Anelka penalty saves embarrassment after first half errors let Lokeren in
Two goals from Wright-Phillips see off QPR but his dad gets heckled in the stands
Sommeil heads home with seven seconds to spare, preventing the new stadium being christened by defeat in first Premiership fixture
"McManaman was my man of the match", claims Keegan after Real signing prompts Anelka to a hat-trick
Anelka from the spot once again as Belgians are second best and ousted from UEFA Cup
First competitive goal at City of Manchester Stadium is scored by Sinclair on his debut leading to first leg rout of Welsh opponents
FIRST ADVICE

INS AND OUTS

IN Trevor Sinclair from West Ham for £2.5m; Claudio Reyna from Sunderland for £2.5m; Antoine Sibierski from Lens for £704K; David Seaman from Arsenal, Michael Tarnet from Bayern Munich, Paul Bosvelt from Feyenoord, Steve McManaman from Real Madrid all for free.

OUT Peter Schmeichel retired; Niclas Jensen to Borussia Dortmund for £750K; Steve Howey to Leicester for £300K; Shaun Goater to Reading for £500K; Carlo Nash to Middlesbro' for £150K; Kevin Horlock to West Ham for £300K; Ali Benarbia to Al-Rayyan (Qatar) for free; Darren Huckerby to Norwich on loan.

ATTENDANCES

HOME GROUND: CITY OF MANCHESTER CAPACITY: 35150 AVERAGE LEAGUE AT HOME: 46834

24	Man Utd	67645	33	Tottenham	47000	23	Everton	37871	11	Wolvers	29386
38	Man Utd	67228	36	Birmingham	46967	44	Aston Villa	37602	9	Lokeren	29067
19	Newcastle	52159	18	Leicester	46966	42	Leeds	36998	39	Bolton	27301
40	Chelsea	47304	10	Tottenham	46842	46	Tottenham	35282	2	Charlton	25780
41	Man Utd	47284	21	Middlesboro	46824	50	Middlesboro	34734	4	Blackburn	23361
51	Everton	47284	7	Aston Villa	46687	1	TNS	34103	30	Portsmouth	20120
45	Wolves	47248	43	Fulham	46522	17	G Grodzisk	32506	31	Leicester	18916
49	Newcastle	47226	6	Arsenal	46436	16	Southampton	31952	15	QPR	16773
27	Liverpool	47201	3	Portsmouth	46287	22	Tottenham	31727	8	Fulham	16124
47	Southampton	47152	29	Charlton	44307	48	Leicester	31457	5	TNS	10123
25	Leeds	47126	37	Liverpool	43257	28	Leicester	30617	12	Lokeren	10000
13	Bolton	47101	14	Chelsea	41040	35	Tottenham	30400	20	G Grodzisk	5500
32	Blackburn	47090	34	Arsenal	38103	26	Birmingham	29520			

Attacking and scoring but not winning

Final Position: **16th**

KEY: League, Champions Lge, UEFA Cup, FA Cup, League Cup, Other

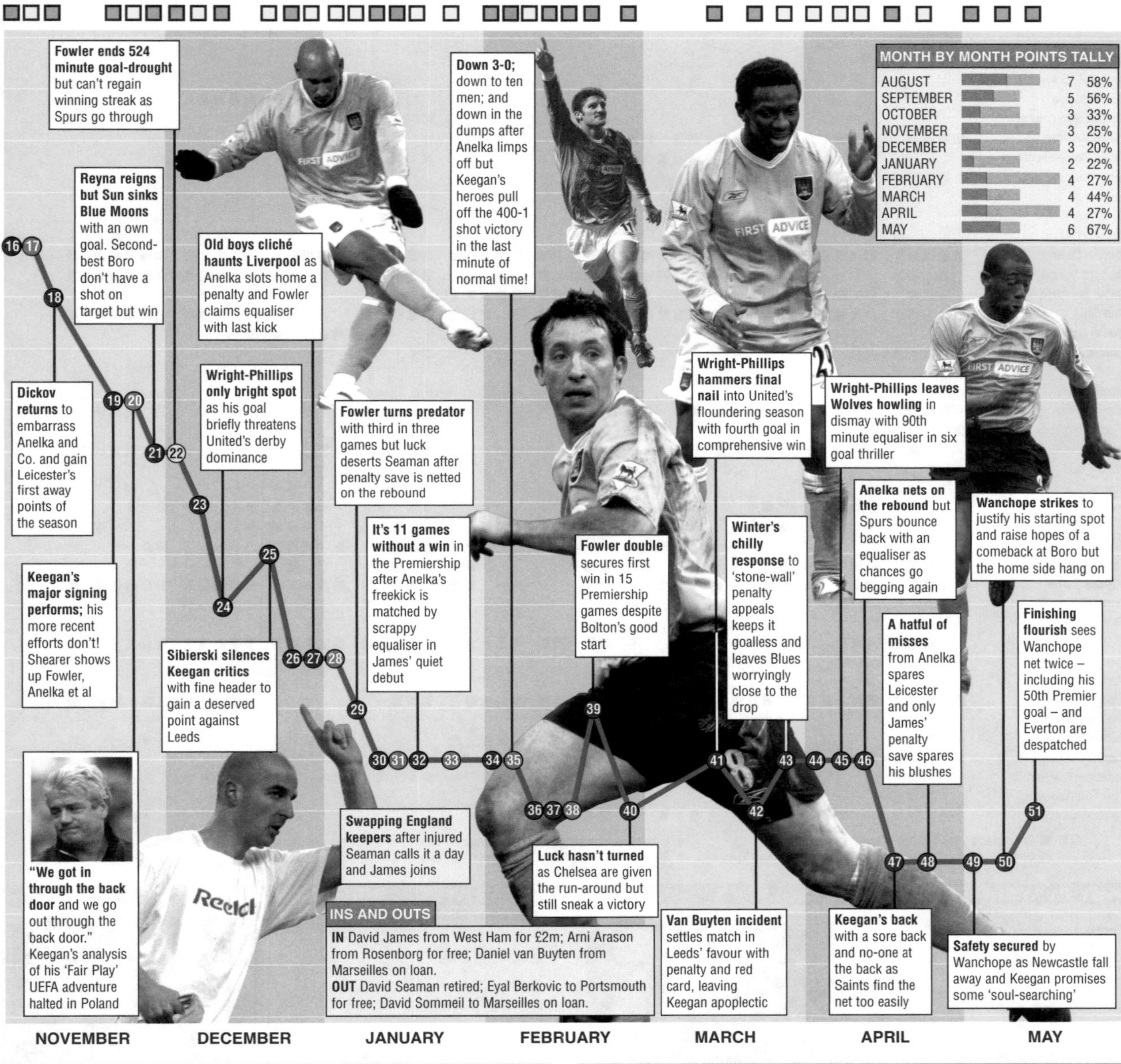

MONTH BY MONTH POINTS TALLY
AUGUST 7 58%
SEPTEMBER 5 56%
OCTOBER 3 33%
NOVEMBER 3 25%
DECEMBER 3 20%
JANUARY 2 22%
FEBRUARY 4 27%
MARCH 4 44%
APRIL 4 27%
MAY 6 67%
Dickov returns to embarrass Anelka and Co. and gain Leicester's first away points of the season
Reyna reigns but Sun sinks Blue Moons with an own goal. Second-best Boro don't have a shot on target but win
Keegan's major signing performs; his more recent efforts don't! Shearer shows up Fowler, Anelka et al
"We got in through the back door and we go out through the back door." Keegan's analysis of his 'Fair Play' UEFA adventure halted in Poland
Fowler ends 524 minute goal-drought but can't regain winning streak as Spurs go through
Old boys cliché haunts Liverpool as Anelka slots home a penalty and Fowler claims equaliser with last kick
Wright-Phillips only bright spot as his goal briefly threatens United's derby dominance
Sibierski silences Keegan critics with fine header to gain a deserved point against Leeds
Fowler turns predator with third in three games but luck deserts Seaman after penalty save is netted on the rebound
It's 11 games without a win in the Premiership after Anelka's freekick is matched by scrappy equaliser in James' quiet debut
Swapping England keepers after injured Seaman calls it a day and James joins
Down 3-0; down to ten men; and down in the dumps after Anelka limps off but Keegan's heroes pull off the 400-1 shot victory in the last minute of normal time!
Fowler double secures first win in 15 Premiership games despite Bolton's good start
Luck hasn't turned as Chelsea are given the run-around but still sneak a victory
INS AND OUTS
IN David James from West Ham for £2m; Arni Arason from Rosenborg for free; Daniel van Buyten from Marseilles on loan.
OUT David Seaman retired; Eyal Berkovic to Portsmouth for free; David Sommeil to Marseilles on loan.
Wright-Phillips hammers final nail into United's floundering season with fourth goal in comprehensive win
Winter's chilly response to 'stone-wall' penalty appeals keeps it goalless and leaves Blues worryingly close to the drop
Van Buyten incident settles match in Leeds' favour with penalty and red card, leaving Keegan apoplectic
Wright-Phillips leaves Wolves howling in dismay with 90th minute equaliser in six goal thriller
Anelka nets on the rebound but Spurs bounce back with an equaliser as chances go begging again
A hatful of misses from Anelka spares Leicester and only James' penalty save spares his blushes
Keegan's back with a sore back and no-one at the back as Saints find the net too easily
Wanchope strikes to justify his starting spot and raise hopes of a comeback at Boro but the home side hang on
Finishing flourish sees Wanchope net twice – including his 50th Premier goal – and Everton are despatched
Safety secured by Wanchope as Newcastle fall away and Keegan promises some 'soul-searching'
NOVEMBER
DECEMBER
JANUARY
FEBRUARY
MARCH
APRIL
MAY

GOAL ATTEMPTS

FOR – Goal attempts recorded in League games

	HOME	AWAY	TOTAL	AVE
shots on target	164	128	292	7.7
shots off target	136	87	223	5.9
TOTAL	300	215	515	13.6

Ratio of goals to shots Average number of shots on target per League goal scored: **5.3**

Accuracy rating Average percentage of total goal attempts which were on target: **56.7**

AGAINST – Goal attempts recorded in League games

	HOME	AWAY	TOTAL	AVE
shots on target	81	129	210	5.5
shots off target	68	128	196	5.2
TOTAL	149	257	406	10.7

Ratio of goals to shots Average number of shots on target per League goal scored: **3.9**

Accuracy rating Average percentage of total goal attempts which were on target: **51.7**

GOALS

Nicolas Anelka

League	16
FA Cup	4
League Cup	0
Europe	3
Other	0
TOTAL	23

League Average: 171 mins between goals

	PLAYER	LGE	FAC	LC	Euro	TOT	AVE
1	Anelka	16	4	0	3	23	171
2	Fowler	7	1	1	1	10	273
3	Wright-Phillips	7	1	2	0	10	416
4	Wanchope	6	0	0	0	6	200
5	Sibierski	5	1	0	1	7	349
6	Tarnat	3	1	0	0	4	953
7	Distin	2	1	0	0	3	1665
8	Macken	1	2	1	0	4	596
9	Sinclair	1	0	0	0	1	1996
10	Barton	1	0	0	0	1	2186
11	Sun Jihai	1	0	0	0	1	2637
12	Sommeil	1	0	0	0	1	1620
13	Reyna	1	0	0	0	1	1560
14	Bosvelt	0	1	0	0	1	
	Other	3	0	0	2	5	
	TOTAL	55	12	4	7	78	

SQUAD APPEARANCES

Match	1 2 3 4 5	6 7 8 9 10	11 12 13 14 15	16 17 18 19 20	21 22 23 24 25	26 27 28 29 30	31 32 33 34 35	36 37 38 39 40	41 42 43 44 45	46 47 48 49 50	51
Venue	H A H A A	H H A H H	A A H A A	A H H A A	H A A A H	A H H H A	A H H A A	H A A A H	H A H A H	A H A H A	H
Competition	E L L L E	L L L E L	L E L L W	L E L L E	L W L L L	L L F L L	F L F L F	L L F L L	L L L L L	L L L L L	L
Result	W W D W W	L W D W D	L W W L W	W D L L D	L L D L D	L D D D L	W D D L W	D L L W L	W L D D D	D L D W L	W

Goalkeepers
Arni Gautur Arason
David James
Kasper Schmeichel
David Seaman
Kevin Stuhr-Ellegaard
Nicky Weaver

Defenders
Mikkel Bischoff
Sylvain Distin
Richard Dunne
David Sommeil
Sun Jihai
Daniel Van Buyten
Gerard Wiekens

Midfielders
Joey Barton
Eyal Berkovic
Paul Bosvelt
Willo Flood
Stephen Jordan
Steve McManaman
Claudio Reyna
Antoine Sibierski
Trevor Sinclair
Michael Tarnat
Danny Tiatto
Glenn Whelan
Shaun Wright-Phillips

Forwards
Nicolas Anelka
Stephen Elliot
Robbie Fowler
Darren Huckerby
Jonathan Macken
Christian Negouai
Paulo Wanchope

KEY: On all match | On bench | Subbed or sent off (Counting game) | Subbed or sent off (playing less than 70 mins) | Subbed on from bench (Counting Game) | Subbed on (playing less than 70 mins) | Subbed on and then subbed or sent off (Counting Game) | Subbed on and then subbed or sent off (playing less than 70 mins) | Not in 16

KEY PLAYERS - GOALSCORERS

Nicolas Anelka

Goals in the League	16
Goals in all competitions	24
Assists League goals scored by team-mates where he delivered the final pass	4
Contribution to Attacking Power Average number of minutes between League team goals while on pitch	62
Player Strike Rate Average number of minutes between League goals scored by player	171
Club Strike Rate Average minutes between League goals scored by club	62

	PLAYER	GOALS LGE	GOALS ALL	ASSISTS	POWER	S RATE
1	Nicolas Anelka	16	24	4	62	171 mins
2	Robbie Fowler	7	10	1	65	273 mins
3	Antoine Sibierski	5	7	3	51	349 mins
4	Shaun Wright-Phillips	7	11	3	62	416 mins
5	Michael Tarnat	3	4	5	58	953 mins

KEY PLAYERS - MIDFIELDERS

Claudio Reyna

Goals in the League	1
Goals in all competitions	1
Assists League goals scored by team-mates where he delivered the final pass	1
Defensive Rating Average number of mins between League goals conceded while he was on the pitch	74
Contribution to Attacking Power Average number of minutes between League team goals while on pitch	65
Scoring Difference Defensive Rating minus Contribution to Attacking Power	9

	PLAYER	GOALS LGE	GOALS ALL	ASSISTS	DEF RATE	POWER	SC DIFF
1	Claudio Reyna	1	1	1	74	65	9 mins
2	Antoine Sibierski	5	7	3	58	51	7 mins
3	Michael Tarnat	3	4	5	65	58	7 mins
4	Shaun Wright-Phillips	7	11	3	68	62	6 mins
5	Trevor Sinclair	1	2	2	59	62	-3 mins

PLAYER APPEARANCES

	AGE (on 01/07/04)	IN NAMED 16	APPEARANCES	COUNTING GAMES	MINUTES ON PITCH	APPEARANCES	MINUTES ON PITCH	THIS SEASON	HOME COUNTRY
Goalkeepers									
Arni Gautur Arason	29	16	0	0	0	2	180	-	Iceland
David James	33	17	17	17	1530	17	1530	8	England (12)
Kasper Schmeichel	17	1	0	0	0	0	0	-	Denmark
David Seaman	40	19	19	17	1593	26	2223	-	England
Kevin Stuhr-Ellegaard	21	14	4	3	297	7	567	-	Denmark
Nicky Weaver	25	9	0	0	0	1	90	-	England
Defenders									
Mikkel Bischoff	22	1	0	0	0	1	90	-	Denmark
Sylvain Distin	26	37	37	37	3330	49	4410	-	France
Richard Dunne	24	36	30	28	2591	41	3513	3	Rep of Ireland (15)
David Sommeil	29	22	18	18	1620	25	2250	-	France
Sun Jihai	26	36	33	28	2637	42	3447	-	China PR
Daniel Van Buyten	26	5	5	5	435	6	525	4	Belgium (17)
Gerard Wiekens	31	5	0	0	0	1	90	-	Holland
Midfielders									
Joey Barton	21	33	28	24	2186	39	2821	-	England
Eyal Berkovic	32	8	4	1	144	7	319	-	Israel
Paul Bosvelt	34	28	25	20	1908	35	2692	6	Holland (4)
Willo Flood	19	0	0	0	0	1	90	-	Rep of Ireland
Stephen Jordan	22	5	2	0	10	2	10	-	England
Steve McManaman	32	25	22	16	1609	30	2108	-	England
Claudio Reyna	30	26	23	16	1560	31	2059	-	United States
Antoine Sibierski	29	37	33	15	1746	40	2146	-	France
Trevor Sinclair	31	31	29	21	1996	38	2708	1	England (12)
Michael Tarnat	34	34	32	32	2860	41	3639	-	Germany
Danny Tiatto	24	8	5	1	152	9	348	2	Australia (89)
Glenn Whelan	20	0	0	0	0	1	18	-	Rep of Ireland
Shaun Wright-Phillips	22	34	34	32	2914	45	3749	-	England
Forwards									
Nicolas Anelka	25	32	32	30	2736	43	3627	-	France
Stephen Elliot	2005	3	2	0	20	2	20	-	Rep of Ireland
Robbie Fowler	29	34	31	17	1908	41	2726	-	England
Darren Huckerby	28	0	0	0	0	1	90	-	England
Jonathan Macken	26	26	15	5	596	21	897	-	England
Christian Negouai	26	1	0	0	0	1	90	-	France
Paulo Wanchope	28	25	22	10	1199	26	1330	-	Costa Rica

KEY: LEAGUE ALL COMPS CAPS (FIFA RANKING)

TEAM OF THE SEASON

JAMES — CG 17 DR 70

SUN JIHAI — CG 28 DR 66

DISTIN — CG 37 DR 63

SOMMEIL — CG 18 DR 63

DUNNE — CG 28 DR 60

WRIGHT-PHILLIPS — CG 32 SD +6

REYNA — CG 16 SD +9

SIBIERSKI — CG 15 SD +7

TARNAT — CG 32 SD +7

FOWLER — CG 17 AP 65

ANELKA — CG 30 SR 171

KEY: DR = Diffensive Rate, SD = Scoring Difference AP = Attacking Power SR = Strike Rate, CG=Counting games – League games playing at least 70 minutes

TOP POINT EARNERS

David Seaman

Counting Games League games when he played at least 70 minutes	17
Average points Average League points taken in Counting games	1.24
Club Average points Average points taken in League games	1.08

	PLAYER	GAMES	PTS
1	David Seaman	17	1.24
2	Antoine Sibierski	15	1.20
3	Trevor Sinclair	21	1.19
4	Michael Tarnat	32	1.19
5	Joey Barton	24	1.17
6	Sun Jihai	28	1.14
7	David James	17	1.12
8	Sylvain Distin	37	1.11
9	David Sommeil	18	1.06
10	Steve McManaman	16	1.06

KEY PLAYERS - DEFENDERS

Sun Jihai

Goals Conceded The number of League goals conceded while he was on the pitch	40
Goals Conceded in all competitions The number of goals conceded while he was on the pitch in all competitions	49
League minutes played Number of minutes played in league matches	2637
Clean Sheets In games when he played at least70 mins	6
Defensive Rating Average number of mins between League goals conceded while he was on the pitch	66
Club Defensive Rating Average number of mins between League goals conceded by the club this season	63

	PLAYER	CON LGE	CON ALL	GAMES	C SHEETS	DEF RATE
1	Sun Jihai	40	49	2637	6	66 mins
2	Sylvain Distin	53	70	3330	7	63 mins
3	David Sommeil	26	34	1620	3	62 mins
4	Richard Dunne	43	58	2591	4	60 mins

KEY GOALKEEPER

David James

Goals Conceded in the League The number of League goals conceded while he was on the pitch	22
Goals Conceded in all competitions Number of goals conceded while he was on the pitch in all competitions	22
League minutes played Number of minutes played in league matches	1530
Clean Sheets In games when he played at least 70 mins	3
Goals to Shots Ratio The average number of shots on target per each League goal conceded	4.3
Defensive Rating Ave mins between League goals conceded while on the pitch	70

BOOKINGS

Joey Barton

League Yellow	7
League Red	0
All competitions Yellow	11
All competitions Red	1

League Average **312** mins between cards

	PLAYER	LEAGUE Y	LEAGUE R	TOTAL Y	TOTAL R	AVE
1	Barton	7	0	11	1	312
2	Sun Jihai	8	0	9	0	329
3	Dunne	5	0	5	0	518
4	Sommeil	3	0	4	0	540
5	Bosvelt	3	0	6	0	636
6	Distin	5	0	5	0	666
7	Tarnat	4	0	5	0	715
8	Wright-Phillips	3	1	4	1	728
9	Fowler	2	0	3	0	954
10	Sinclair	2	0	2	0	998
11	Wanchope	1	0	2	0	1199
12	Anelka	1	1	2	1	1368
13	McManaman	1	0	1	0	1609
14	Sibierski	1	0	1	0	1746
	Other	1	1	2	1	
	TOTAL	47	3	62	4	

EVERTON

It could be argued that Everton's season is not much worse than last year's. The fine dividing line between success and failure is illustrated by the fact that they scored only one goal less and conceded only one more than in finishing sixth last year.

The key differences are 11 league places and the level of expectation built around the nous of **David Moyes** and promise of **Wayne Rooney**.

Rooney tops the club scoring charts with a similar Strike Rate to last year, averaging a goal every 271 minutes – just sneaking into the best 30 in the division.

Nigel Martyn has possibly won more plaudits than anyone. His Goals to Shots Ratio shows 4.7 shots on target for every one conceded.

NICKNAME: THE TOFFEES

KEY: Won Drawn Lost

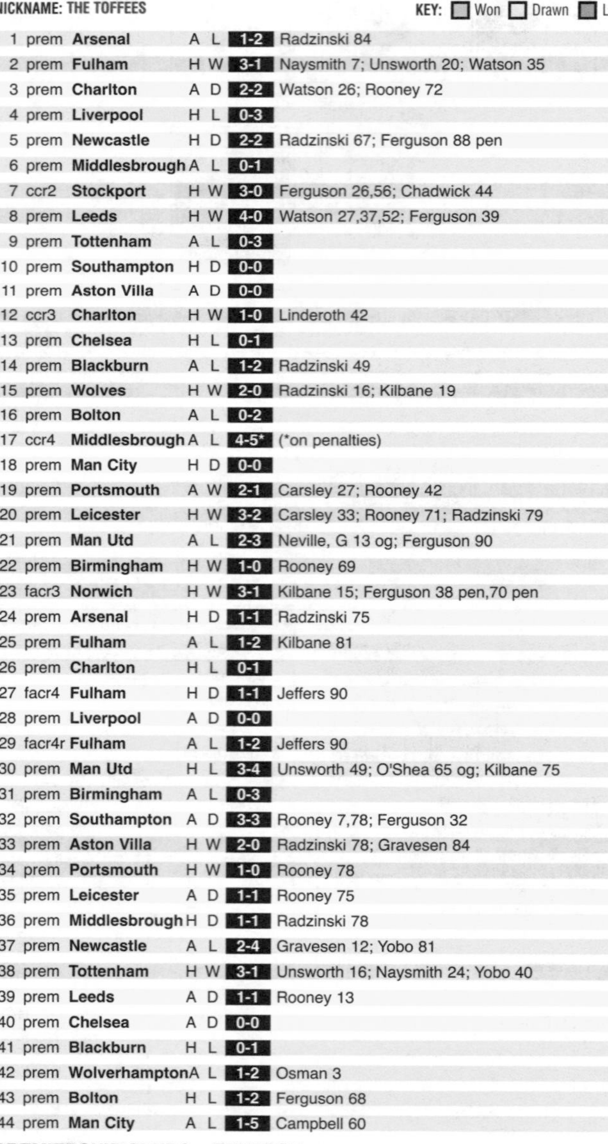

1	prem	**Arsenal**	A	L	1-2	Radzinski 84
2	prem	**Fulham**	H	W	3-1	Naysmith 7; Unsworth 20; Watson 35
3	prem	**Charlton**	A	D	2-2	Watson 26; Rooney 72
4	prem	**Liverpool**	H	L	0-3	
5	prem	**Newcastle**	H	D	2-2	Radzinski 67; Ferguson 88 pen
6	prem	**Middlesbrough**	A	L	0-1	
7	ccr2	**Stockport**	H	W	3-0	Ferguson 26,56; Chadwick 44
8	prem	**Leeds**	H	W	4-0	Watson 27,37,52; Ferguson 39
9	prem	**Tottenham**	A	L	0-3	
10	prem	**Southampton**	H	D	0-0	
11	prem	**Aston Villa**	A	D	0-0	
12	ccr3	**Charlton**	H	W	1-0	Linderoth 42
13	prem	**Chelsea**	H	L	0-1	
14	prem	**Blackburn**	A	L	1-2	Radzinski 49
15	prem	**Wolves**	H	W	2-0	Radzinski 16; Kilbane 19
16	prem	**Bolton**	A	L	0-2	
17	ccr4	**Middlesbrough**	A	L	4-5*	(*on penalties)
18	prem	**Man City**	H	D	0-0	
19	prem	**Portsmouth**	A	W	2-1	Carsley 27; Rooney 42
20	prem	**Leicester**	H	W	3-2	Carsley 33; Rooney 71; Radzinski 79
21	prem	**Man Utd**	A	L	2-3	Neville, G 13 og; Ferguson 90
22	prem	**Birmingham**	H	W	1-0	Rooney 69
23	facr3	**Norwich**	H	W	3-1	Kilbane 15; Ferguson 38 pen,70 pen
24	prem	**Arsenal**	H	D	1-1	Radzinski 75
25	prem	**Fulham**	A	L	1-2	Kilbane 81
26	prem	**Charlton**	H	L	0-1	
27	facr4	**Fulham**	H	D	1-1	Jeffers 90
28	prem	**Liverpool**	A	D	0-0	
29	facr4r	**Fulham**	A	L	1-2	Jeffers 90
30	prem	**Man Utd**	H	L	3-4	Unsworth 49; O'Shea 65 og; Kilbane 75
31	prem	**Birmingham**	A	L	0-3	
32	prem	**Southampton**	A	D	3-3	Rooney 7,78; Ferguson 32
33	prem	**Aston Villa**	H	W	2-0	Radzinski 78; Gravesen 84
34	prem	**Portsmouth**	H	W	1-0	Rooney 78
35	prem	**Leicester**	A	D	1-1	Rooney 75
36	prem	**Middlesbrough**	H	D	1-1	Radzinski 78
37	prem	**Newcastle**	A	L	2-4	Gravesen 12; Yobo 81
38	prem	**Tottenham**	H	W	3-1	Unsworth 16; Naysmith 24; Yobo 40
39	prem	**Leeds**	A	D	1-1	Rooney 13
40	prem	**Chelsea**	A	D	0-0	
41	prem	**Blackburn**	H	L	0-1	
42	prem	**Wolverhampton**	A	L	1-2	Osman 3
43	prem	**Bolton**	H	L	1-2	Ferguson 68
44	prem	**Man City**	A	L	1-5	Campbell 60

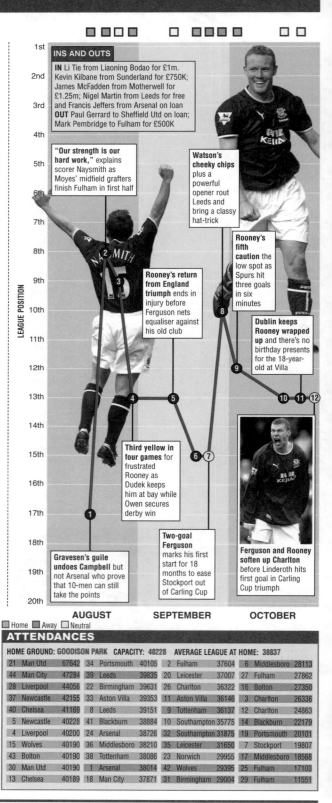

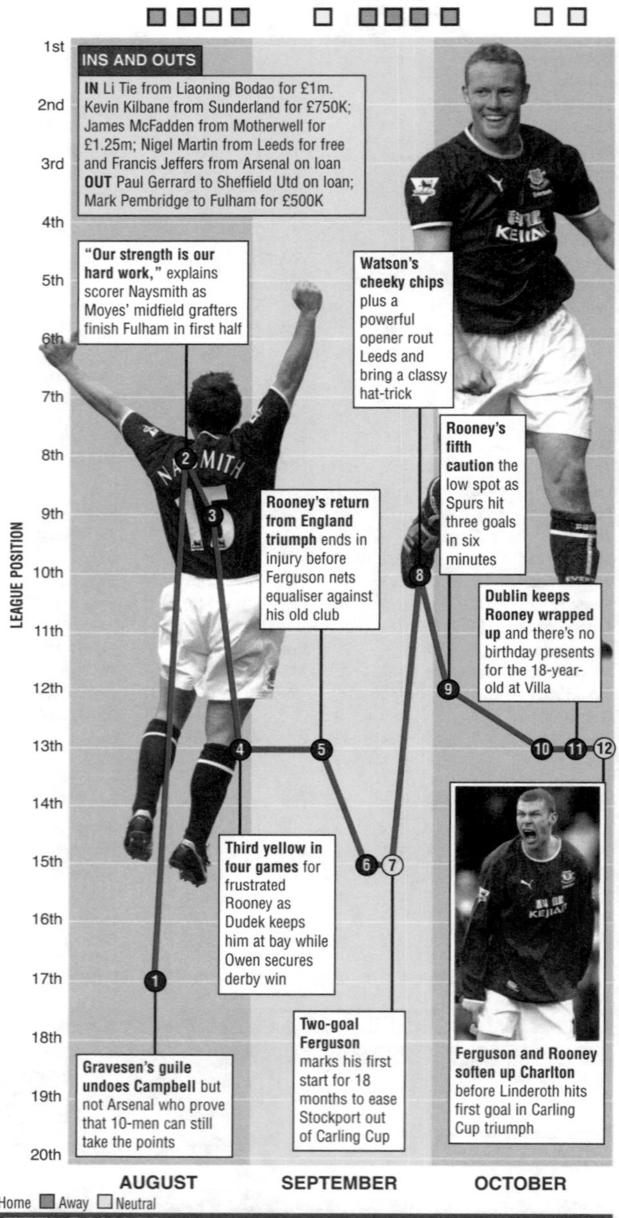

LEAGUE POSITION

1st 2nd 3rd 4th 5th 6th 7th 8th 9th 10th 11th 12th 13th 14th 15th 16th 17th 18th 19th 20th

AUGUST SEPTEMBER OCTOBER

Home Away Neutral

INS AND OUTS

IN Li Tie from Liaoning Bodao for £1m. Kevin Kilbane from Sunderland for £750K; James McFadden from Motherwell for £1.25m; Nigel Martin from Leeds for free and Francis Jeffers from Arsenal on loan **OUT** Paul Gerrard to Sheffield Utd on loan; Mark Pembridge to Fulham for £500K

"Our strength is our hard work," explains scorer Naysmith as Moyes' midfield grafters finish Fulham in first half

Watson's cheeky chips plus a powerful opener rout Leeds and bring a classy hat-trick

Rooney's fifth caution the low spot as Spurs hit three goals in six minutes

Rooney's return from England triumph ends in injury before Ferguson nets equaliser against his old club

Dublin keeps Rooney wrapped up and there's no birthday presents for the 18-year-old at Villa

Third yellow in four games for frustrated Rooney as Dudek keeps him at bay while Owen secures derby win

Two-goal Ferguson marks his first start for 18 months to ease Stockport out of Carling Cup

Gravesen's guile undoes Campbell but not Arsenal who prove that 10-men can still take the points

Ferguson and Rooney soften up Charlton before Linderoth hits first goal in Carling Cup triumph

ATTENDANCES

HOME GROUND: GOODISON PARK **CAPACITY:** 40228 **AVERAGE LEAGUE AT HOME:** 38837

21	Man Utd	67642	34	Portsmouth	40105	2	Fulham	37604	6	Middlesboro	28113
44	Man City	47284	39	Leeds	39835	20	Leicester	37007	27	Fulham	27862
28	Liverpool	44056	22	Birmingham	39631	26	Charlton	36322	16	Bolton	27350
37	Newcastle	42155	33	Aston Villa	39353	11	Aston Villa	36146	3	Charlton	26336
40	Chelsea	41169	8	Leeds	39151	9	Tottenham	36137	12	Charlton	24863
5	Newcastle	40228	41	Blackburn	38884	10	Southampton	35775	14	Blackburn	22179
4	Liverpool	40200	24	Arsenal	38726	32	Southampton	31875	19	Portsmouth	20101
15	Wolves	40190	36	Middlesboro	38210	35	Leicester	31650	7	Stockport	19807
43	Bolton	40190	38	Tottenham	38086	23	Norwich	29955	17	Middlesboro	18568
30	Man Utd	40190	1	Arsenal	38014	42	Wolves	29395	25	Fulham	17103
13	Chelsea	40189	18	Man City	37871	31	Birmingham	29004	29	Fulham	11551

Odd goals cost Moyes eleven places

Final Position: 17th

KEY: ● League ● Champions Lge ● UEFA Cup ● FA Cup ○ League Cup ● Other

Rooney and McFadden strike. Pair on target for England and Scotland respectively
Nyarko's bar-slammer, Rooney's chip, Kilbane's and Jeffers' headers and Radzinski's two gilt-edged chances, all go begging while Mutu snatches points with his hand
Radzinski's third of the season is only consolation after lifeless performance at Blackburn slips Moyes into the relegation zone
Kilbane's first goal loops in and ends Wolves' resistance after Radzinski's strike from distance
No goals at Boro over 120 minutes but sub Osman misses fifth penalty and home side go through
Gravesen so close to grabbing a winner against Man City but Rooney's subbed early again
Rooney comes on as sub, scores, walks off... and is brought back by ref after pushing incident in win at Pompey
In front; behind; then back in front as back-to-back wins regain mid-table spot
Rooney writes the headlines for the right reasons scoring third from last four games after Ferguson unsettles Birmingham
Ferguson on a roll as two calm penalties ends Norwich's interest in the cup
Wenger out-foxed as lone star Jeffers causes havoc in the box and Moyes have-a-go policy earns a draw
Moyes plays two forward lines and still the chances go begging at Fulham
Jeffers pounces on a cup life-line in the 89th minute to deny Fulham
Dudek denies Stubbs but Martyn is "a colossus" in Merseyside draw
Sub Rooney inspires a thrilling comeback after first half horror show but United still snatch the points
Jeffers strikes again in final minute to force extra time but Fulham have the last laugh
Rooney wins praise for giving Saints hell but they redeem themselves with late goals in a 3-3 thriller
Martyn keeps Villa out before Radzinski earns the lead and Gravesen seals first win in seven
Seventh goal of the season and Rooney makes them count with a tight win over Pompey
Ferguson's headlock red card lets Moyes down and lets Leicester back in
Radzinski strikes but Boro conjure a scrappy equaliser and Rooney suffers double injury to threaten England appearance
"Youth team defending," rails Moyes as Unsworth and Yobo make it too easy for Shearer and Co.
Martyn frustrates his old team with a string of saves that earn a draw after Leeds equalise Rooney's fifth in six games
Only lost one in last nine as Martyn's luck holds at Chelsea although Rooney tests Ambrosio
Defenders turn scorers in Rooney and Ferguson's absence with Unsworth, Naysmith and Yobo netting against Spurs
"A lack of energy" lets Blackburn in to win game that had 0-0 written all over it
Ferguson equaliser in vain as Bolton look the form team in a deserved win at Goodison
Lowest top-flight points total since 1889 and a finish just above the relegation slots as Man City hand out a hammering
Radzinski fails to build on Osman's start and Wolves reply in second half
NOVEMBER
DECEMBER
JANUARY
FEBRUARY
MARCH
APRIL
MAY

INS AND OUTS

IN none
OUT Leon Osman to Derby on loan

MONTH BY MONTH POINTS TALLY

Month	Points	%
AUGUST	4	33%
SEPTEMBER	4	44%
OCTOBER	2	22%
NOVEMBER	3	25%
DECEMBER	10	67%
JANUARY	2	17%
FEBRUARY	4	33%
MARCH	5	56%
APRIL	5	33%
MAY	0	0%

GOAL ATTEMPTS

FOR — Goal attempts recorded in League games

	HOME	AWAY	TOTAL	AVE
shots on target	137	78	215	5.7
shots off target	125	90	215	5.7
TOTAL	**262**	**168**	**430**	**11.3**

Ratio of goals to shots Average number of shots on target per League goal scored: **4.8**

Accuracy rating Average percentage of total goal attempts which were on target: **50**

AGAINST — Goal attempts recorded in League games

	HOME	AWAY	TOTAL	AVE
shots on target	112	147	259	6.8
shots off target	103	78	181	4.8
TOTAL	**215**	**225**	**440**	**11.6**

Ratio of goals to shots Average number of shots on target per League goal scored: **4.5**

Accuracy rating Average percentage of total goal attempts which were on target: **58.9**

GOALS

Wayne Rooney

League	9
FA Cup	0
League Cup	0
Europe	0
Other	0
TOTAL	9

League Average **271** mins between goals

	PLAYER	LGE	FAC	LC	Euro	TOT	AVE
1	Rooney	**9** Y	0 R	0 Y	0 R	9	271
2	Radzinski	**8**	0	0	0	8	320
3	Ferguson	**5**	2	2	0	9	236
4	Watson	**5**	0	0	0	5	343
5	Kilbane	**3**	1	0	0	4	786
6	Unsworth	**3**	0	0	0	3	685
7	Gravesen	**2**	0	0	0	2	1273
8	Naysmith	**2**	0	0	0	2	1215
9	Yobo	**2**	0	0	0	2	1218
10	Carsley	**2**	0	0	0	2	704
11	Osman	**1**	0	0	0	1	279
12	Campbell	**1**	0	0	0	1	762
13	Linderoth	**0**	0	1	0	1	
14	Chadwick	**0**	0	1	0	1	
15	Jeffers	**0**	2	0	0	2	
	Other	2	0	0	0	2	
	TOTAL	**45**	**5**	**4**	**0**	**54**	

SQUAD APPEARANCES

Match	1	2	3	4	5	6	7	8	9	10	11	12	13	14	15	16	17	18	19	20	21	22	23	24	25	26	27	28	29	30	31	32	33	34	35	36	37	38	39	40	41	42	43	44
Venue	A	H	A	H	H	A	H	H	A	H	A	H	H	A	H	A	A	H	A	H	A	H	H	H	A	H	H	A	A	H	A	A	H	H	A	H	A	H	A	A	H	A	H	A
Competition	L	L	L	L	L	L	W	L	L	L	L	W	L	L	L	L	W	L	L	L	L	L	F	L	L	L	F	L	F	L	L	L	L	L	L	L	L	L	L	L	L	L	L	L
Result	L	W	D	L	D	L	W	W	L	D	D	W	L	L	W	L	D	D	W	W	L	W	W	D	L	L	D	D	L	L	L	D	W	W	D	D	L	W	D	D	L	L	L	L

Goalkeepers
Nigel Martyn
Steve Simonsen
Iain Turner
Richard Wright

Defenders
Peter Clarke
Tony Hibbert
Gary Naysmith
Alessandro Pistone
Alan Stubbs
David Unsworth
David Weir
Joseph Yobo

Midfielders
Lee Carsley
Thomas Gravesen
Kevin Kilbane
Li Tie
Tobias Linderoth
James McFadden
Alex Nyarko
Leon Osman
Mark Pembridge
Steve Watson

Forwards
Kevin Campbell
Nick Chadwick
Duncan Ferguson
Francis Jeffers
Tomasz Radzinski
Wayne Rooney

KEY: On all match; On bench; Subbed or sent off (Counting game); Subbed or sent off (playing less than 70 mins); Subbed on from bench (Counting Game); Subbed on (playing less than 70 mins); Subbed on and then subbed or sent off (Counting Game); Subbed on and then subbed or sent off (playing less than 70 mins); Not in 16

KEY PLAYERS - GOALSCORERS

Wayne Rooney

Goals in the League	9
Goals in all competitions	9
Assists League goals scored by team-mates where he delivered the final pass	4
Contribution to Attacking Power Average number of minutes between League team goals while on pitch	78
Player Strike Rate Average number of minutes between League goals scored by player	271
Club Strike Rate Average minutes between League goals scored by club	76

	PLAYER	GOALS LGE	GOALS ALL	ASSISTS	POWER	S RATE
1	Wayne Rooney	9	9	4	78	271 mins
2	Tomasz Radzinski	8	8	5	65	320 mins
3	Steve Watson	5	5	3	71	343 mins
4	David Unsworth	3	3	0	55	685 mins
5	Kevin Kilbane	3	4	1	84	786 mins

KEY PLAYERS - MIDFIELDERS

Tobias Linderoth

Goals in the League	0
Goals in all competitions	1
Assists League goals scored by team-mates where he delivered the final pass	3
Defensive Rating Average number of mins between League goals conceded while he was on the pitch	63
Contribution to Attacking Power Average number of minutes between League team goals while on pitch	69
Scoring Difference Defensive Rating minus Contribution to Attacking Power	-6

	PLAYER	GOALS LGE	GOALS ALL	ASSISTS	DEF RATE	POWER	SC DIFF
1	Tobias Linderoth	0	1	3	63	69	-6 mins
2	Thomas Gravesen	2	2	2	64	75	-11 mins
3	Kevin Kilbane	3	4	1	67	84	-17 mins
4	Steve Watson	5	5	3	50	71	-21 mins

PLAYER APPEARANCES

	AGE (on 01/07/04)	IN NAMED 16	APPEARANCES	COUNTING GAMES	MINUTES ON PITCH	APPEARANCES	MINUTES ON PITCH	THIS SEASON	HOME COUNTRY
Goalkeepers									
Nigel Martyn	37	33	33	32	2946	39	3546	-	England
Steve Simonsen	25	21	1	1	90	1	90	-	England
Iain Turner	20	4	0	0	0	0	0	-	Scotland
Richard Wright	26	17	4	3	294	4	294	-	England
Defenders									
Peter Clarke	22	4	1	1	90	2	120	-	England
Tony Hibbert	23	29	25	23	2178	31	2748	-	England
Gary Naysmith	25	31	29	25	2429	34	2882	7	Scotland (63)
Alessandro Pistone	28	23	21	16	1623	24	1917	-	Italy
Alan Stubbs	32	28	27	23	2218	31	2520	-	England
David Unsworth	30	30	26	20	2054	31	2471	-	England
David Weir	34	17	10	8	808	12	988	-	Scotland
Joseph Yobo	23	30	28	27	2436	31	2631	-	Nigeria
Midfielders									
Lee Carsley	30	23	21	12	1408	25	1828	3	Rep of Ireland (15)
Thomas Gravesen	28	30	30	28	2546	36	3069	6	Denmark (14)
Kevin Kilbane	27	30	30	24	2359	33	2659	7	Rep of Ireland (15)
Li Tie	26	11	5	3	324	7	440	-	China PR
Tobias Linderoth	25	34	28	18	2009	30	2104	8	Sweden (21)
James McFadden	21	29	23	5	1076	27	1423	10	Scotland (63)
Alex Nyarko	30	16	11	4	644	14	883	-	Ghana
Leon Osman	23	5	4	3	279	5	293	-	England
Mark Pembridge	33	4	4	3	336	4	336	4	Wales (66)
Steve Watson	30	24	24	16	1714	26	1863	-	England
Forwards									
Kevin Campbell	34	19	17	5	762	18	770	-	England
Nick Chadwick	21	6	3	1	127	4	217	-	England
Duncan Ferguson	32	20	20	10	1181	24	1533	-	Scotland
Francis Jeffers	23	21	18	2	609	22	806	-	England
Tomasz Radzinski	30	35	34	24	2556	38	2747	-	Canada
Wayne Rooney	18	34	34	23	2440	40	2958	7	England (12)

KEY: LEAGUE | ALL COMPS | CAPS (FIFA RANKING)

TEAM OF THE SEASON

MARTYN	CG	32	DR	63
HIBBERT	CG	23	DR	57
STUBBS	CG	23	DR	63
YOBO	CG	27	DR	61
NAYSMITH	CG	25	DR	76
WATSON	CG	16	SD	-21
GRAVESEN	CG	28	SD	-11
LINDEROTH	CG	18	SD	-6
KILBANE	CG	24	SD	-17
RADZINSKI	CG	24	AP	65
ROONEY	CG	23	SR	271

KEY: DR = Diffensive Rate, SD = Scoring Difference AP = Attacking Power SR = Strike Rate, CG=Counting games – League games playing at least 70 minutes

TOP POINT EARNERS

David Unsworth

Counting Games League games when he played at least 70 minutes	20
Average points Average League points taken in Counting games	1.45
Club Average points Average points taken in League games	1.03

	PLAYER	GAMES	PTS
1	David Unsworth	20	1.45
2	Tobias Linderoth	18	1.39
3	Alan Stubbs	23	1.30
4	Tomasz Radzinski	24	1.21
5	Kevin Kilbane	24	1.21
6	Gary Naysmith	25	1.12
7	Thomas Gravesen	28	1.11
8	Steve Watson	16	1.06
9	Joseph Yobo	27	1.00
10	Alessandro Pistone	16	1.00

KEY PLAYERS - DEFENDERS

Gary Naysmith

Goals Conceded The number of League goals conceded while he was on the pitch	32
Goals Conceded in all competitions The number of goals conceded while he was on the pitch in all competitions	35
League minutes played Number of minutes played in league matches	2429
Clean Sheets In games when he played at least70 mins	7
Defensive Rating Average number of mins between League goals conceded while he was on the pitch	76
Club Defensive Rating Average number of mins between League goals conceded by the club this season	60

KEJIAN

	PLAYER	CON LGE	CON ALL	GAMES	C SHEETS	DEF RATE
1	Gary Naysmith	32	35	2429	7	76 mins
2	Alan Stubbs	35	37	2218	7	63 mins
3	Joseph Yobo	40	40	2436	7	61 mins
4	Tony Hibbert	38	42	2178	8	57 mins
5	Alessandro Pistone	29	32	1623	2	56 mins

KEY GOALKEEPER

Nigel Martyn

Goals Conceded in the League The number of League goals conceded while he was on the pitch	47
Goals Conceded in all competitions Number of goals conceded while he was on the pitch in all competitions	51
League minutes played Number of minutes played in league matches	2946
Clean Sheets In games when he played at least 70 mins	10
Goals to Shots Ratio The average number of shots on target per each League goal conceded	4.7
Defensive Rating Ave mins between League goals conceded while on the pitch	63

BOOKINGS

Duncan Ferguson

League Yellow	6
League Red	1
All competitions Yellow	6
All competitions Red	1

League Average **168** mins between cards

	PLAYER	LEAGUE 6Y	LEAGUE 1R	TOTAL 6Y	TOTAL 1R	AVE
1	Ferguson	6Y	1R	6Y	1R	168
2	Rooney	11	0	12	0	221
3	Jeffers	2	0	2	0	304
4	Carsley	4	0	5	0	352
5	McFadden	3	0	3	0	358
6	Watson	4	0	4	0	428
7	Linderoth	4	0	4	0	502
8	Gravesen	5	0	5	0	509
9	Nyarko	1	0	1	0	644
10	Unsworth	3	0	3	0	684
11	Campbell	1	0	1	0	762
12	Weir	1	0	1	0	808
13	Naysmith	2	1	4	1	809
14	Stubbs	2	0	2	0	1109
15	Radzinski	2	0	2	0	1278
	Other	4	1	6	1	
	TOTAL	55	3	61	3	

LEICESTER CITY

The Assists Table is one topped by Leicester. **Muzzy Izzet** capped a season of hard graft in midfield with a total of 14 assists, a remarkable achievement in a relegated club, making Izzet one of very few players to enhance their reputation in a relegation season.

Another player to have managed that achievement was **Paul Dickov**. The striker put the allegations of La Manga behind him to become the highest-charting striker in the three relegated clubs. He pipped the higher-profile Leeds pair with a Strike Rate of a goal every 229 minutes.

Micky Adams' management style won respect over the season and while his side were six points adrift of Everton in 17th, Leicester also had a far better goal difference than the two lower sides.

NICKNAME: THE FOXES

KEY: Won / Drawn / Lost

1	prem	**Southampton**	H	D	2-2	Dickov 5 pen; Ferdinand 10
2	prem	**Chelsea**	A	L	1-2	Scowcroft 40
3	prem	**Middlesbrough**	H	D	0-0	
4	prem	**Aston Villa**	A	L	1-3	Izzet 53
5	prem	**Leeds**	H	W	4-0	Nalis 20; Dickov 23,83; Scowcroft 90
6	prem	**Liverpool**	A	L	1-2	Bent, M 90
7	ccr2	**Crewe**	H	W	1-0	Dickov 82 pen
8	prem	**Man Utd**	H	L	1-4	Sinclair 73
9	prem	**Fulham**	A	L	0-2	
10	prem	**Tottenham**	H	L	1-2	Dickov 38
11	prem	**Wolves**	A	L	3-4	Ferdinand 12,15; Scimeca 35
12	ccr3	**Aston Villa**	A	L	0-1	
13	prem	**Blackburn**	H	W	2-0	Bent, M 75; Howey 82
14	prem	**Man City**	A	W	3-0	Stewart 12; Dickov 53 pen; Bent, M 58
15	prem	**Charlton**	H	D	1-1	Ferdinand 39
16	prem	**Portsmouth**	A	W	2-0	Ferdinand 31; Bent, M 59
17	prem	**Arsenal**	H	D	1-1	Hignett 90
18	prem	**Birmingham**	H	L	0-2	
19	prem	**Everton**	A	L	2-3	Ferdinand 45; Scowcroft 58
20	prem	**Newcastle**	H	D	1-1	Dickov 67
21	prem	**Bolton**	A	D	2-2	Bent, M 18; Ferdinand 90
22	facr3	**Man City**	A	D	2-2	Dickov 4; Bent, M 66
23	prem	**Southampton**	A	D	0-0	
24	prem	**Chelsea**	H	L	0-4	
25	facr3r	**Man City**	H	L	1-3	Ferdinand 73
26	prem	**Middlesbrough**	A	D	3-3	Dickov 49,65; Bent, M 76
27	prem	**Aston Villa**	H	L	0-5	
28	prem	**Newcastle**	A	L	1-3	Ferdinand 80
29	prem	**Bolton**	H	D	1-1	Ferdinand 16
30	prem	**Tottenham**	A	D	4-4	Doherty 9 og; Ferdinand 51; Thatcher 72; Bent, M 77
31	prem	**Wolves**	H	D	0-0	
32	prem	**Birmingham**	A	W	1-0	Ferdinand 53
33	prem	**Everton**	H	D	1-1	Bent, M 90
34	prem	**Liverpool**	H	D	0-0	
35	prem	**Leeds**	A	L	2-3	Dickov 77; Izzet 79
36	prem	**Fulham**	H	L	0-2	
37	prem	**Man Utd**	A	L	0-1	
38	prem	**Blackburn**	A	L	0-1	
39	prem	**Man City**	H	D	1-1	Scowcroft 66
40	prem	**Charlton**	A	D	2-2	Bent, M 5; Ferdinand 88
41	prem	**Portsmouth**	H	W	3-1	Taylor 6 og; Dickov 27; Scowcroft 71
42	prem	**Arsenal**	A	L	1-2	Dickov 26

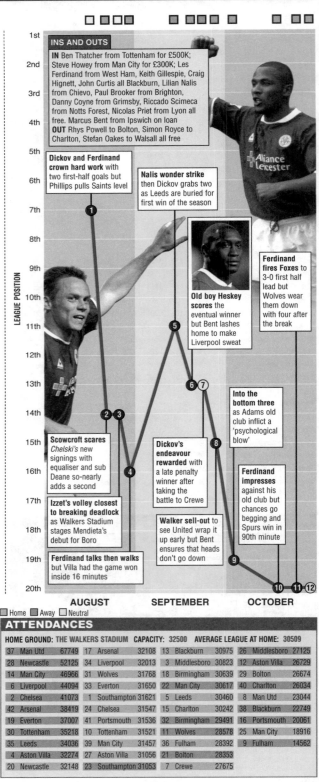

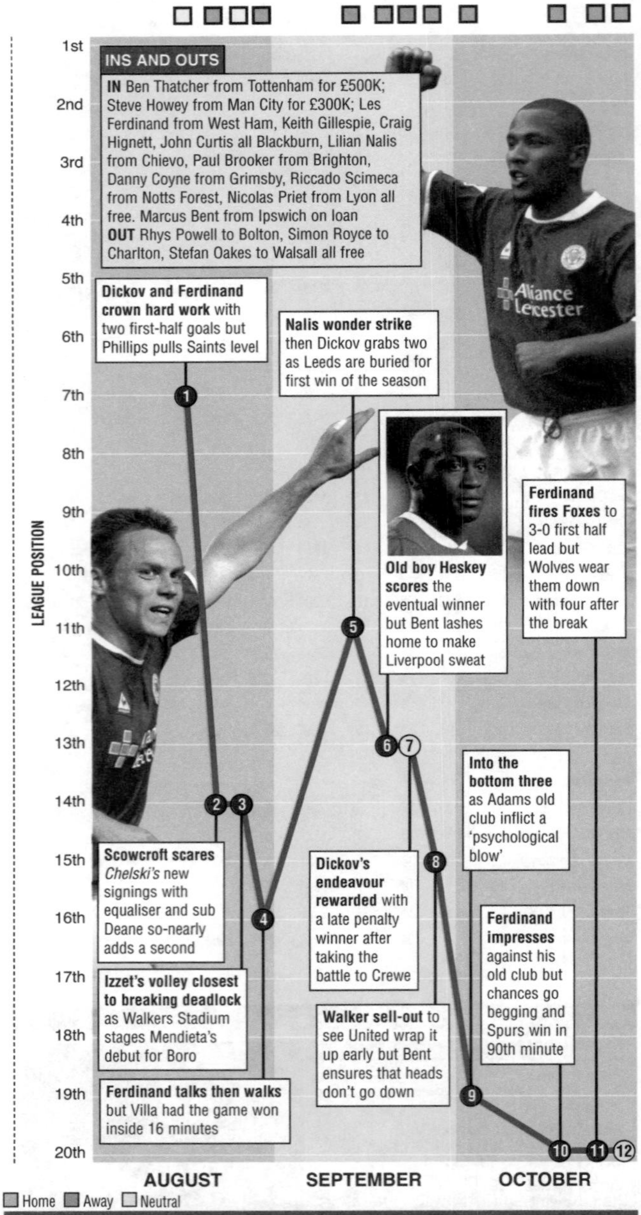

INS AND OUTS

IN Ben Thatcher from Tottenham for £500K; Steve Howey from Man City for £300K; Les Ferdinand from West Ham, Keith Gillespie, Craig Hignett, John Curtis all Blackburn, Lilian Nalis from Chievo, Paul Brooker from Brighton, Danny Coyne from Grimsby, Riccado Scimeca from Notts Forest, Nicolas Priet from Lyon all free. Marcus Bent from Ipswich on loan
OUT Rhys Powell to Bolton, Simon Royce to Charlton, Stefan Oakes to Walsall all free

LEAGUE POSITION: 1st, 2nd, 3rd, 4th, 5th, 6th, 7th, 8th, 9th, 10th, 11th, 12th, 13th, 14th, 15th, 16th, 17th, 18th, 19th, 20th

AUGUST — SEPTEMBER — OCTOBER

1. **Dickov and Ferdinand crown hard work** with two first-half goals but Phillips pulls Saints level
2. **Scowcroft scares** *Chelski's* new signings with equaliser and sub Deane so-nearly adds a second
3. **Izzet's volley closest to breaking deadlock** as Walkers Stadium stages Mendieta's debut for Boro
4. **Ferdinand talks then walks** but Villa had the game won inside 16 minutes
5. **Nalis wonder strike** then Dickov grabs two as Leeds are buried for first win of the season
6. **Old boy Heskey scores** the eventual winner but Bent lashes home to make Liverpool sweat
7. **Dickov's endeavour rewarded** with a late penalty winner after taking the battle to Crewe
8. **Walker sell-out** to see United wrap it up early but Bent ensures that heads don't go down
9. **Into the bottom three** as Adams old club inflict a 'psychological blow'
10. **Ferdinand impresses** against his old club but chances go begging and Spurs win in 90th minute
11. **Ferdinand fires Foxes** to 3-0 first half lead but Wolves wear them down with four after the break

Home / Away / Neutral

ATTENDANCES

HOME GROUND: THE WALKERS STADIUM **CAPACITY:** 32500 **AVERAGE LEAGUE AT HOME:** 30509

37	Man Utd	67749	17	Arsenal	32108	13	Blackburn	30975	26	Middlesboro	27125
28	Newcastle	52125	34	Liverpool	32013	3	Middlesboro	30823	12	Aston Villa	26729
14	Man City	46966	31	Wolves	31768	18	Birmingham	30639	29	Bolton	26674
6	Liverpool	44094	33	Everton	31650	22	Man City	30617	40	Charlton	26034
2	Chelsea	41073	1	Southampton	31621	5	Leeds	30460	8	Man Utd	23044
42	Arsenal	38419	24	Chelsea	31547	15	Charlton	30242	38	Blackburn	22749
19	Everton	37007	41	Portsmouth	31536	32	Birmingham	29491	16	Portsmouth	20061
30	Tottenham	35218	10	Tottenham	31521	11	Wolves	28578	25	Man City	18916
35	Leeds	34036	39	Man City	31457	36	Fulham	28392	9	Fulham	14562
4	Aston Villa	32274	27	Aston Villa	31056	21	Bolton	28353			
20	Newcastle	32148	23	Southampton	31053	7	Crewe	27675			

Down as forecast but never a pushover

Final Position: 18th

KEY: League, Champions Lge, UEFA Cup, FA Cup, League Cup, Other

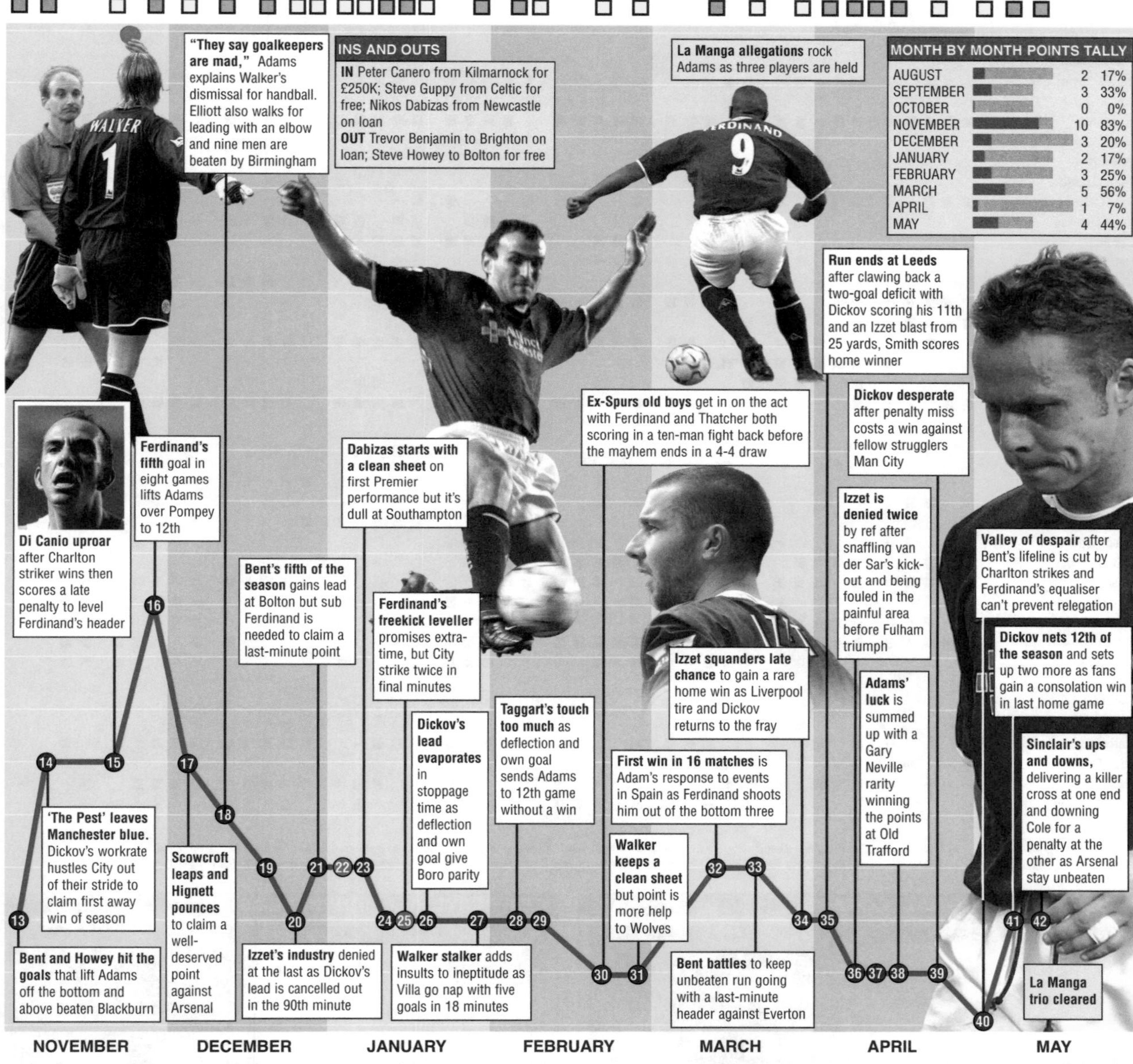

"They say goalkeepers are mad," Adams explains Walker's dismissal for handball. Elliott also walks for leading with an elbow and nine men are beaten by Birmingham
INS AND OUTS
IN Peter Canero from Kilmarnock for £250K; Steve Guppy from Celtic for free; Nikos Dabizas from Newcastle on loan
OUT Trevor Benjamin to Brighton on loan; Steve Howey to Bolton for free
La Manga allegations rock Adams as three players are held
MONTH BY MONTH POINTS TALLY
AUGUST 2 17%
SEPTEMBER 3 33%
OCTOBER 0 0%
NOVEMBER 10 83%
DECEMBER 3 20%
JANUARY 2 17%
FEBRUARY 3 25%
MARCH 5 56%
APRIL 1 7%
MAY 4 44%
Run ends at Leeds after clawing back a two-goal deficit with Dickov scoring his 11th and an Izzet blast from 25 yards, Smith scores home winner
Ex-Spurs old boys get in on the act with Ferdinand and Thatcher both scoring in a ten-man fight back before the mayhem ends in a 4-4 draw
Dickov desperate after penalty miss costs a win against fellow strugglers Man City
Di Canio uproar after Charlton striker wins then scores a late penalty to level Ferdinand's header
Ferdinand's fifth goal in eight games lifts Adams over Pompey to 12th
Dabizas starts with a clean sheet on first Premier performance but it's dull at Southampton
Izzet is denied twice by ref after snaffling van der Sar's kick-out and being fouled in the painful area before Fulham triumph
Valley of despair after Bent's lifeline is cut by Charlton strikes and Ferdinand's equaliser can't prevent relegation
Bent's fifth of the season gains lead at Bolton but sub Ferdinand is needed to claim a last-minute point
Ferdinand's freekick leveller promises extra-time, but City strike twice in final minutes
Dickov nets 12th of the season and sets up two more as fans gain a consolation win in last home game
Izzet squanders late chance to gain a rare home win as Liverpool tire and Dickov returns to the fray
Adams' luck is summed up with a Gary Neville rarity winning the points at Old Trafford
Dickov's lead evaporates in stoppage time as deflection and own goal give Boro parity
Taggart's touch too much as deflection and own goal sends Adams to 12th game without a win
Sinclair's ups and downs, delivering a killer cross at one end and downing Cole for a penalty at the other as Arsenal stay unbeaten
First win in 16 matches is Adam's response to events in Spain as Ferdinand shoots him out of the bottom three
'The Pest' leaves Manchester blue. Dickov's workrate hustles City out of their stride to claim first away win of season
Scowcroft leaps and Hignett pounces to claim a well-deserved point against Arsenal
Walker keeps a clean sheet but point is more help to Wolves
Bent and Howey hit the goals that lift Adams off the bottom and above beaten Blackburn
Izzet's industry denied at the last as Dickov's lead is cancelled out in the 90th minute
Walker stalker adds insults to ineptitude as Villa go nap with five goals in 18 minutes
Bent battles to keep unbeaten run going with a last-minute header against Everton
La Manga trio cleared
NOVEMBER
DECEMBER
JANUARY
FEBRUARY
MARCH
APRIL
MAY

GOAL ATTEMPTS

FOR — Goal attempts recorded in League games

	HOME	AWAY	TOTAL	AVE
shots on target	124	85	209	5.5
shots off target	88	69	157	4.1
TOTAL	212	154	366	9.6

Ratio of goals to shots Average number of shots on target per League goal scored	4.4
Accuracy rating Average percentage of total goal attempts which were on target	57.1

AGAINST — Goal attempts recorded in League games

	HOME	AWAY	TOTAL	AVE
shots on target	104	152	256	6.7
shots off target	97	85	182	4.8
TOTAL	201	237	438	11.5

Ratio of goals to shots Average number of shots on target per League goal scored	3.9
Accuracy rating Average percentage of total goal attempts which were on target	58.4

GOALS

Les Ferdinand

League	12
FA Cup	1
League Cup	0
Europe	0
Other	0
TOTAL	13

League Average 129 mins between goals

	PLAYER	LGE	FAC	LC	Euro	TOT	AVE
1	Ferdinand	12	1	0	0	13	129
2	Dickov	11	1	1	0	13	229
3	Bent, M	9	1	0	0	10	277
4	Scowcroft	5	0	0	0	5	596
5	Izzet	2	0	0	0	2	1284
6	Stewart	1	0	0	0	1	1580
7	Scimeca	1	0	0	0	1	2534
8	Nalis	1	0	0	0	1	1034
9	Howey	1	0	0	0	1	965
10	Sinclair	1	0	0	0	1	990
11	Hignett	1	0	0	0	1	295
12	Thatcher	1	0	0	0	1	2480
	Other	2	0	0	0	2	
	TOTAL	48	3	1	0	52	

SQUAD APPEARANCES

Match	1	2	3	4	5	6	7	8	9	10	11	12	13	14	15	16	17	18	19	20	21	22	23	24	25	26	27	28	29	30	31	32	33	34	35	36	37	38	39	40	41	42
Venue	H	A	H	A	H	A	H	H	A	H	A	A	H	A	H	A	H	H	A	H	A	A	A	H	H	A	H	A	H	A	H	A	H	H	A	H	A	A	H	A	H	A
Competition	L	L	L	L	L	L	W	L	L	L	L	W	L	L	L	L	L	L	L	L	L	F	L	L	F	L	L	L	L	L	L	L	L	L	L	L	L	L	L	L	L	L
Result	D	L	D	L	W	L	W	L	L	L	L	L	W	W	D	W	D	L	L	D	D	D	D	L	L	D	L	L	D	D	D	W	D	D	L	L	L	L	D	D	W	L

Goalkeepers
Danny Coyne
Paul Murphy
Ian Walker

Defenders
Peter Canero
John Curtis
Nikos Dabizas
Callum Davidson
Matt Elliott
Matt Heath
Steve Howey
Alan Rogers
Riccardo Scimeca
Frank Sinclair
Gerry Taggart
Ben Thatcher

Midfielders
Paul Brooker
Steffen Freund
Keith Gillespie
Steve Guppy
Craig Hignett
Andrew Impey
Mustafa Izzet
Billy McKinlay
Lilian Nalis
James Scowcroft
Jordan Stewart

Forwards
Trevor Benjamin
Marcus Bent
Brian Deane
Paul Dickov
Les Ferdinand
Nicolas Priet

KEY: On all match · On bench · Subbed or sent off (Counting game) · Subbed or sent off (playing less than 70 mins) · Subbed on from bench (Counting Game) · Subbed on (playing less than 70 mins) · Subbed on and then subbed or sent off (Counting Game) · Subbed on and then subbed or sent off (playing less than 70 mins) · Not in 16

KEY PLAYERS - GOALSCORERS

Paul Dickov

Goals in the League	11
Goals in all competitions	13
Assists League goals scored by team-mates where he delivered the final pass	4
Contribution to Attacking Power Average number of minutes between League team goals while on pitch	64
Player Strike Rate Average number of minutes between League goals scored by player	229
Club Strike Rate Average minutes between League goals scored by club	71

	PLAYER	GOALS LGE	GOALS ALL	ASSISTS	POWER	S RATE
1	Paul Dickov	11	13	4	64	229 mins
2	Marcus Bent	9	10	2	80	277 mins
3	James Scowcroft	5	5	3	70	596 mins
4	Mustafa Izzet	2	2	14	73	1284 mins
5	Jordan Stewart	1	1	2	58	1580 mins

KEY PLAYERS - MIDFIELDERS

Jordan Stewart

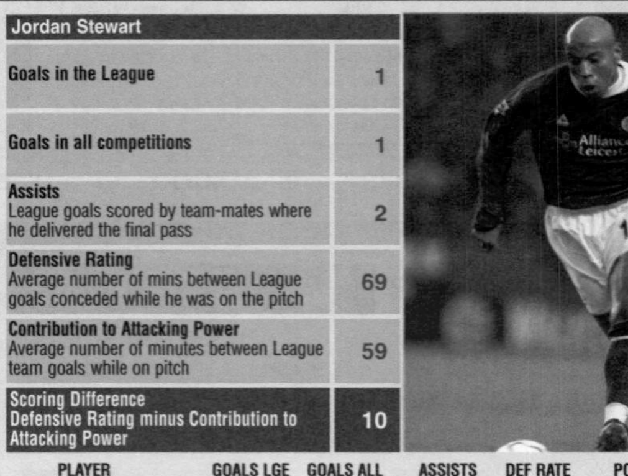

Goals in the League	1
Goals in all competitions	1
Assists League goals scored by team-mates where he delivered the final pass	2
Defensive Rating Average number of mins between League goals conceded while he was on the pitch	69
Contribution to Attacking Power Average number of minutes between League team goals while on pitch	59
Scoring Difference Defensive Rating minus Contribution to Attacking Power	10

	PLAYER	GOALS LGE	GOALS ALL	ASSISTS	DEF RATE	POWER	SC DIFF
1	Jordan Stewart	1	1	2	69	59	10 mins
2	Billy McKinlay	0	0	1	73	63	10 mins
3	Mustafa Izzet	2	2	14	64	73	-9 mins
4	James Scowcroft	5	5	3	49	71	-22 mins

PLAYER APPEARANCES

	AGE (on 01/07/04)	IN NAMED 16	APPEARANCES	COUNTING GAMES	MINUTES ON PITCH	APPEARANCES	MINUTES ON PITCH	THIS SEASON	HOME COUNTRY
Goalkeepers									
Danny Coyne	25	31	4	1	159	5	249	-	Wales
Paul Murphy	21	0	0	0	0	0	0	-	Rep of Ireland
Ian Walker	32	37	37	35	3261	40	3531	2	England (12)
Defenders									
Peter Canero	23	10	7	2	245	7	245	-	Scotland
John Curtis	25	15	15	13	1205	17	1385	-	England
Nikos Dabizas	30	17	17	17	1502	17	1502	-	Greece
Callum Davidson	28	15	14	9	912	16	1092	-	Scotland
Matt Elliott	35	13	7	3	379	8	387	-	Scotland
Matt Heath	23	16	13	13	1157	15	1337	-	England
Steve Howey	32	15	13	9	965	15	1145	-	England
Alan Rogers	27	8	8	7	675	8	675	-	England
Riccardo Scimeca	29	29	29	28	2534	31	2678	-	England
Frank Sinclair	32	16	14	10	990	17	1260	-	Jamaica
Gerry Taggart	33	11	9	7	734	9	734	-	N Ireland
Ben Thatcher	28	29	29	27	2480	29	2480	-	England
Midfielders									
Paul Brooker	28	3	3	0	57	6	231	-	England
Steffen Freund	34	15	14	11	1082	14	1082	-	Germany
Keith Gillespie	29	22	12	4	616	13	643	6	N Ireland (114)
Steve Guppy	35	17	15	8	885	15	885	-	England
Craig Hignett	34	22	13	2	295	15	448	-	England
Andrew Impey	32	18	14	11	1104	17	1374	-	England
Mustafa Izzet	29	29	29	28	2567	32	2712	-	Turkey
Billy McKinlay	35	21	16	12	1262	19	1522	-	Scotland
Lilian Nalis	32	24	20	8	1034	22	1214	-	France
James Scowcroft	30	35	35	31	2979	39	3214	-	England
Jordan Stewart	22	30	25	16	1580	29	1849	-	England
Forwards									
Trevor Benjamin	25	6	4	1	132	4	132	-	England
Marcus Bent	26	34	33	25	2489	35	2663	-	England
Brian Deane	36	6	4	0	98	6	225	-	England
Paul Dickov	31	35	35	26	2514	39	2845	-	England
Les Ferdinand	37	29	29	9	1551	31	1662	-	England
Nicolas Priet	21	0	0	0	0	1	2	-	France

KEY: LEAGUE ALL COMPS CAPS (FIFA RANKING)

TEAM OF THE SEASON

WALKER

CG 35 DR 53

SCIMECA
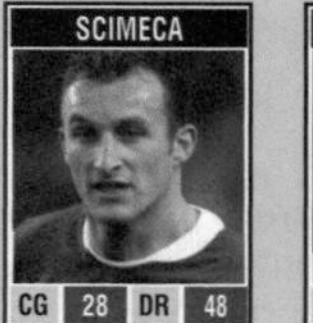
CG 28 DR 48

DABIZAS

CG 17 DR 56

THATCHER

CG 27 DR 58

HEATH

CG 13 DR 72

MCKINLAY

CG 12 SD +10

IZZET

CG 28 SD -9

STEWART

CG 16 SD +10

SCOWCROFT

CG 31 SD -22

BENT

CG 25 AP 80

DICKOV

CG 26 SR 229

KEY: DR = Diffensive Rate, SD = Scoring Difference AP = Attacking Power SR = Strike Rate, CG=Counting games – League games playing at least 70 minutes

TOP POINT EARNERS

Jordan Stewart

Counting Games League games when he played at least 70 minutes	16
Average points Average League points taken in Counting games	1.19
Club Average points Average points taken in League games	0.87

	PLAYER	GAMES	PTS
1	Jordan Stewart	16	1.19
2	Marcus Bent	25	1.04
3	Matt Heath	13	0.92
4	Ian Walker	35	0.91
5	Ben Thatcher	27	0.89
6	Mustafa Izzet	28	0.89
7	Nikos Dabizas	17	0.88
8	John Curtis	13	0.85
9	James Scowcroft	31	0.84
10	Paul Dickov	26	0.81

KEY PLAYERS - DEFENDERS

Matt Heath

Goals Conceded The number of League goals conceded while he was on the pitch	16
Goals Conceded in all competitions The number of goals conceded while he was on the pitch in all competitions	21
League minutes played Number of minutes played in league matches	1157
Clean Sheets In games when he played at least70 mins	3
Defensive Rating Average number of mins between League goals conceded while he was on the pitch	72
Club Defensive Rating Average number of mins between League goals conceded by the club this season	53

	PLAYER	CON LGE	CON ALL	GAMES	C SHEETS	DEF RATE
1	Matt Heath	16	21	1157	3	72 mins
2	Ben Thatcher	43	43	2480	7	58 mins
3	Nikos Dabizas	27	27	1502	4	56 mins
4	Riccardo Scimeca	53	54	2534	6	48 mins
5	John Curtis	28	31	1205	3	43 mins

KEY GOALKEEPER

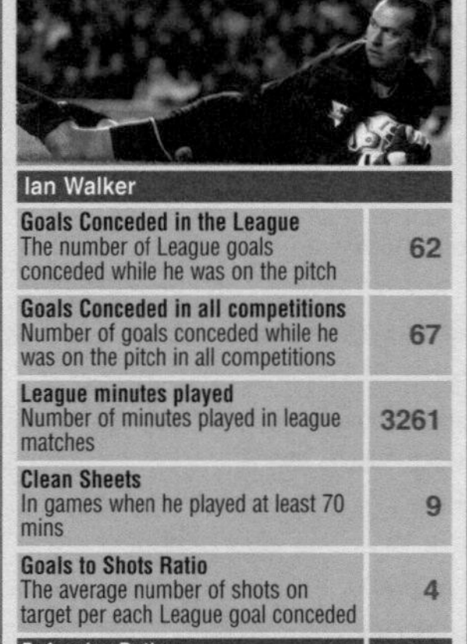

Ian Walker

Goals Conceded in the League The number of League goals conceded while he was on the pitch	62
Goals Conceded in all competitions Number of goals conceded while he was on the pitch in all competitions	67
League minutes played Number of minutes played in league matches	3261
Clean Sheets In games when he played at least 70 mins	9
Goals to Shots Ratio The average number of shots on target per each League goal conceded	4
Defensive Rating Ave mins between League goals conceded while on the pitch	53

BOOKINGS

Nikos Dabizas

League Yellow	5
League Red	1
All competitions Yellow	5
All competitions Red	1

League Average **250** mins between cards

	PLAYER	LEAGUE		TOTAL		AVE
		5 Y	1 R	5 Y	1 R	
1	Dabizas	5 Y	1 R	5 Y	1 R	250
2	McKinlay	5	0	5	0	252
3	Gillespie	2	0	2	0	308
4	Scimeca	7	1	7	1	316
5	Thatcher	7	0	7	0	354
6	Dickov	7	0	8	0	359
7	Izzet	7	0	7	0	366
8	Ferdinand	3	1	3	1	387
9	Davidson	2	0	2	0	456
10	Howey	2	0	2	0	482
11	Sinclair	2	0	3	0	495
12	Rogers	0	1	0	1	675
13	Taggart	1	0	1	0	734
14	Bent, M	3	0	3	0	829
15	Scowcroft	2	1	3	1	993
	Other	6	2	6	2	
	TOTAL	**61**	**7**	**64**	**7**	

LEEDS UNITED

The real struggle at Leeds is the on-going financial battle for the club. **Peter Reid's** collection of on-loan players was replaced by **Eddie Gray's** return to Yorkshire grit.

With defenders regularly having to perform in midfield, **Paul Robinson** was under the cosh and had to deal with the second highest total of Shots on Target in the division.

Jermaine Pennant looked the best of the loan players and managed six assists.

Mark Viduka inevitably found it harder to score. His Strike Rate dropped to an average of a goal every 230 minutes – compared to his 129 the previous year – a fall from second to 20th in the division. And **Alan Smith's** nine goals came at a rate of one every 349 minutes.

NICKNAME: UNITED

KEY: Won / Drawn / Lost

1	prem	**Newcastle**	H	D	2-2	Viduka 24; Smith 57
2	prem	**Tottenham**	A	L	1-2	Smith 5
3	prem	**Southampton**	H	D	0-0	
4	prem	**Middlesbrough**	A	W	3-2	Sakho 16; Camara 77; Viduka 89
5	prem	**Leicester**	A	L	0-4	
6	prem	**Birmingham**	H	L	0-2	
7	ccr2	**Swindon**	H	W	4-3*	Harte 77; Robinson 90 (*on penalties)
8	prem	**Everton**	A	L	0-4	
9	prem	**Blackburn**	H	W	2-1	Johnson, Seth 11,27
10	prem	**Man Utd**	H	L	0-1	
11	prem	**Liverpool**	A	L	1-3	Smith 42
12	ccr3	**Man Utd**	H	L	2-3	Roque Junior 49,113
13	prem	**Arsenal**	H	L	1-4	Smith 64
14	prem	**Portsmouth**	A	L	1-6	Smith 19
15	prem	**Bolton**	H	L	0-2	
16	prem	**Charlton**	A	W	1-0	Milner 9
17	prem	**Chelsea**	H	D	1-1	Pennant 18
18	prem	**Fulham**	H	W	3-2	Duberry 41; Viduka 46; Matteo 88
19	prem	**Man City**	A	D	1-1	Viduka 24
20	prem	**Aston Villa**	H	D	0-0	
21	prem	**Wolves**	A	L	1-3	Duberry 3
22	facr3	**Arsenal**	H	L	1-4	Viduka 8
23	prem	**Newcastle**	A	L	0-1	
24	prem	**Tottenham**	H	L	0-1	
25	prem	**Southampton**	A	L	1-2	Kilgallon 75
26	prem	**Middlesbrough**	H	L	0-3	
27	prem	**Aston Villa**	A	L	0-2	
28	prem	**Wolves**	H	W	4-1	Smith 14; Matteo 41; Milner 61; Viduka 90
29	prem	**Man Utd**	A	D	1-1	Smith 67
30	prem	**Liverpool**	H	D	2-2	Bakke 29; Viduka 34
31	prem	**Fulham**	A	L	0-2	
32	prem	**Man City**	H	W	2-1	McPhail 23; Viduka 76 pen
33	prem	**Birmingham**	A	L	1-4	Viduka 3
34	prem	**Leicester**	H	W	3-2	Duberry 11; Viduka 13; Smith 86
35	prem	**Blackburn**	A	W	2-1	Caldwell 2; Viduka 89
36	prem	**Everton**	H	D	1-1	Milner 50
37	prem	**Arsenal**	A	L	0-5	
38	prem	**Portsmouth**	H	L	1-2	Harte 83 pen
39	prem	**Bolton**	A	L	1-4	Viduka 27 pen
40	prem	**Charlton**	H	D	3-3	Kilgallon 29; Pennant 41; Smith 69 pen
41	prem	**Chelsea**	A	L	0-1	

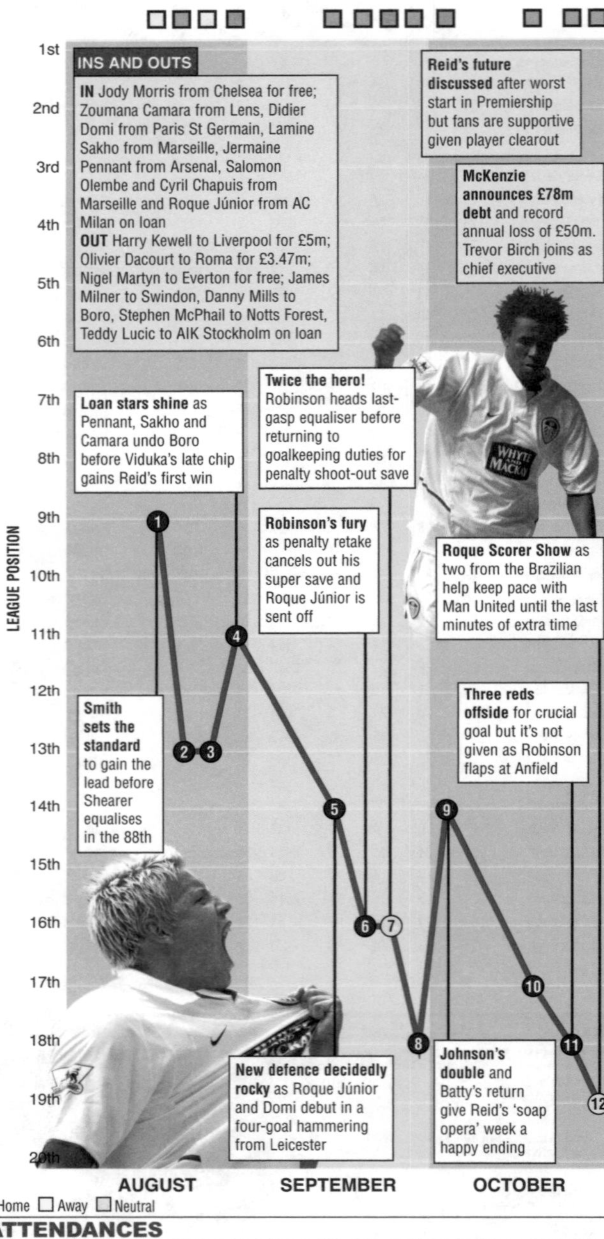

1st
2nd
3rd
4th
5th
6th
7th
8th
9th
10th
11th
12th
13th
14th
15th
16th
17th
18th
19th
20th
LEAGUE POSITION
INS AND OUTS
IN Jody Morris from Chelsea for free; Zoumana Camara from Lens, Didier Domi from Paris St Germain, Lamine Sakho from Marseille, Jermaine Pennant from Arsenal, Salomon Olembe and Cyril Chapuis from Marseille and Roque Júnior from AC Milan on loan
OUT Harry Kewell to Liverpool for £5m; Olivier Dacourt to Roma for £3.47m; Nigel Martyn to Everton for free; James Milner to Swindon, Danny Mills to Boro, Stephen McPhail to Notts Forest, Teddy Lucic to AIK Stockholm on loan
Reid's future discussed after worst start in Premiership but fans are supportive given player clearout
McKenzie announces £78m debt and record annual loss of £50m. Trevor Birch joins as chief executive
Loan stars shine as Pennant, Sakho and Camara undo Boro before Viduka's late chip gains Reid's first win
Twice the hero! Robinson heads last-gasp equaliser before returning to goalkeeping duties for penalty shoot-out save
Robinson's fury as penalty retake cancels out his super save and Roque Júnior is sent off
Roque Scorer Show as two from the Brazilian help keep pace with Man United until the last minutes of extra time
Smith sets the standard to gain the lead before Shearer equalises in the 88th
Three reds offside for crucial goal but it's not given as Robinson flaps at Anfield
New defence decidedly rocky as Roque Júnior and Domi debut in a four-goal hammering from Leicester
Johnson's double and Batty's return give Reid's 'soap opera' week a happy ending
1
2
3
4
5
6
7
8
9
10
11
12
AUGUST
SEPTEMBER
OCTOBER

Home / Away / Neutral

ATTENDANCES

HOME GROUND: ELLAND ROAD **CAPACITY:** 40205 **AVERAGE LEAGUE AT HOME:** 36666

29	Man Utd	67744	40	Charlton	38986	24	Tottenham	35365	7	Swindon	29211
23	Newcastle	52130	20	Aston Villa	38513	9	Blackburn	35039	21	Wolves	29139
19	Man City	47126	37	Arsenal	38094	3	Southampton	34721	33	Birmingham	29069
11	Liverpool	43599	12	Man Utd	37546	2	Tottenham	34354	39	Bolton	27420
41	Chelsea	41276	32	Man City	36998	6	Birmingham	34305	35	Blackburn	26611
10	Man Utd	40153	28	Wolves	36867	34	Leicester	34036	16	Charlton	26445
30	Liverpool	39932	1	Newcastle	36766	25	Southampton	31976	14	Portsmouth	20112
36	Everton	39835	15	Bolton	36558	22	Arsenal	31207	31	Fulham	17104
38	Portsmouth	39273	13	Arsenal	36491	18	Fulham	30544			
27	Aston Villa	39171	17	Chelsea	36305	5	Leicester	30460			
8	Everton	39151	26	Middlesboro	35970	4	Middlesboro	30414			

Survival comes at the price of relegation

19th

KEY: ● League ● Champions Lge ● UEFA Cup ● FA Cup ○ League Cup ● Other

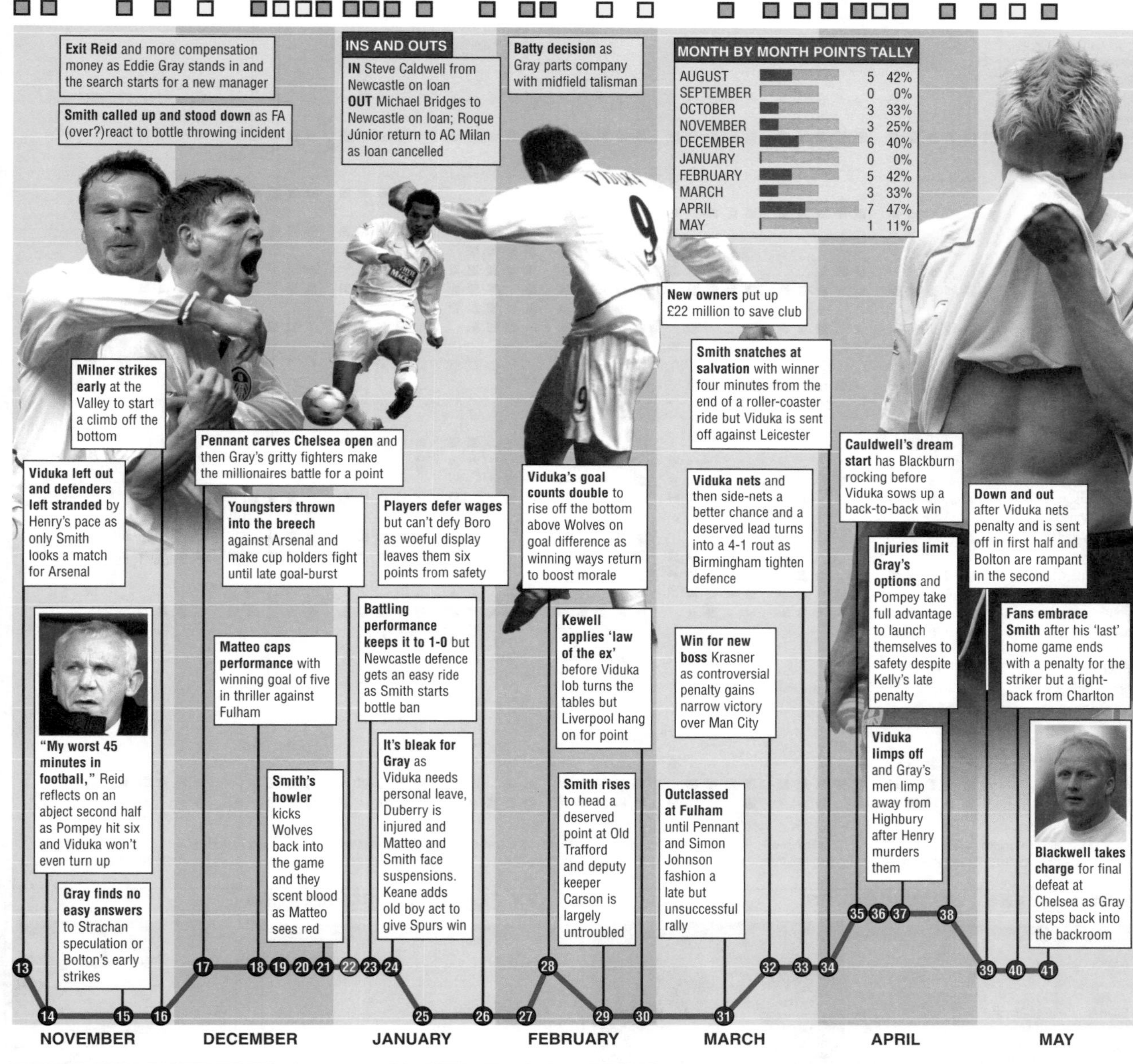
Exit Reid and more compensation money as Eddie Gray stands in and the search starts for a new manager
Smith called up and stood down as FA (over?)react to bottle throwing incident
INS AND OUTS
IN Steve Caldwell from Newcastle on loan
OUT Michael Bridges to Newcastle on loan; Roque Júnior return to AC Milan as loan cancelled
Batty decision as Gray parts company with midfield talisman
MONTH BY MONTH POINTS TALLY
AUGUST 5 42%
SEPTEMBER 0 0%
OCTOBER 3 33%
NOVEMBER 3 25%
DECEMBER 6 40%
JANUARY 0 0%
FEBRUARY 5 42%
MARCH 3 33%
APRIL 7 47%
MAY 1 11%
New owners put up £22 million to save club
Smith snatches at salvation with winner four minutes from the end of a roller-coaster ride but Viduka is sent off against Leicester
Milner strikes early at the Valley to start a climb off the bottom
Pennant carves Chelsea open and then Gray's gritty fighters make the millionaires battle for a point
Viduka left out and defenders left stranded by Henry's pace as only Smith looks a match for Arsenal
Youngsters thrown into the breech against Arsenal and make cup holders fight until late goal-burst
Players defer wages but can't defy Boro as woeful display leaves them six points from safety
Viduka's goal counts double to rise off the bottom above Wolves on goal difference as winning ways return to boost morale
Viduka nets and then side-nets a better chance and a deserved lead turns into a 4-1 rout as Birmingham tighten defence
Cauldwell's dream start has Blackburn rocking before Viduka sows up a back-to-back win
Down and out after Viduka nets penalty and is sent off in first half and Bolton are rampant in the second
Injuries limit Gray's options and Pompey take full advantage to launch themselves to safety despite Kelly's late penalty
Fans embrace Smith after his 'last' home game ends with a penalty for the striker but a fight-back from Charlton
"My worst 45 minutes in football," Reid reflects on an abject second half as Pompey hit six and Viduka won't even turn up
Matteo caps performance with winning goal of five in thriller against Fulham
Battling performance keeps it to 1-0 but Newcastle defence gets an easy ride as Smith starts bottle ban
Kewell applies 'law of the ex' before Viduka lob turns the tables but Liverpool hang on for point
Win for new boss Krasner as controversial penalty gains narrow victory over Man City
Gray finds no easy answers to Strachan speculation or Bolton's early strikes
Smith's howler kicks Wolves back into the game and they scent blood as Matteo sees red
It's bleak for Gray as Viduka needs personal leave, Duberry is injured and Matteo and Smith face suspensions. Keane adds old boy act to give Spurs win
Smith rises to head a deserved point at Old Trafford and deputy keeper Carson is largely untroubled
Outclassed at Fulham until Pennant and Simon Johnson fashion a late but unsuccessful rally
Viduka limps off and Gray's men limp away from Highbury after Henry murders them
Blackwell takes charge for final defeat at Chelsea as Gray steps back into the backroom
13 14 15 16 17 18 19 20 21 22 23 24 25 26 27 28 29 30 31 32 33 34 35 36 37 38 39 40 41
NOVEMBER
DECEMBER
JANUARY
FEBRUARY
MARCH
APRIL
MAY

GOAL ATTEMPTS

FOR Goal attempts recorded in League games	HOME	AWAY	TOTAL	AVE
shots on target	111	74	185	4.9
shots off target	107	75	182	4.8
TOTAL	218	149	367	9.7
Ratio of goals to shots Average number of shots on target per League goal scored				4.6
Accuracy rating Average percentage of total goal attempts which were on target				50.4

AGAINST Goal attempts recorded in League games	HOME	AWAY	TOTAL	AVE
shots on target	143	160	303	8
shots off target	115	74	189	5
TOTAL	258	234	492	12.9
Ratio of goals to shots Average number of shots on target per League goal scored				3.8
Accuracy rating Average percentage of total goal attempts which were on target				61.6

GOALS

Mark Viduka	
League	11
FA Cup	1
League Cup	0
Europe	0
Other	0
TOTAL	12

League Average 230 mins between goals

	PLAYER	LGE	FAC	LC	Euro	TOT	AVE
1	Viduka	11	1	0	0	12	230
2	Smith	9	0	0	0	9	349
3	Milner	3	0	0	0	3	791
4	Duberry	3	0	0	0	3	570
5	Kilgallon	2	0	0	0	2	316
6	Pennant	2	0	0	0	2	1479
7	Johnson, Seth	2	0	0	0	2	981
8	Matteo	2	0	0	0	2	1442
9	McPhail	1	0	0	0	1	772
10	Camara	1	0	0	0	1	1170
11	Sakho	1	0	0	0	1	776
12	Harte	1	0	1	0	2	1909
13	Bakke	1	0	0	0	1	720
14	Roque Junior	0	0	2	0	2	
15	Robinson	0	0	1	0	1	
	Other	1	0	0	0	1	
	TOTAL	40	1	4	0	45	

SQUAD APPEARANCES

Match	1	2	3	4	5	6	7	8	9	10	11	12	13	14	15	16	17	18	19	20	21	22	23	24	25	26	27	28	29	30	31	32	33	34	35	36	37	38	39	40	41
Venue	H	A	H	A	A	H	H	A	H	H	A	H	H	A	H	A	H	H	A	H	A	H	A	H	A	H	A	H	A	H	A	H	A	H	A	H	A	H	A	H	A
Competition	L	L	L	L	L	L	W	L	L	L	L	W	L	L	L	L	L	L	L	L	L	F	L	L	L	L	L	L	L	L	L	L	L	L	L	L	L	L	L	L	L
Result	D	L	D	W	L	L	W	L	W	L	L	L	L	L	L	W	D	W	D	D	L	L	L	L	L	L	L	W	D	D	L	W	L	W	W	D	L	L	L	D	L

Goalkeepers
Shaun Allaway
Scott Carson
Nigel Martyn
Paul Robinson

Defenders
Stephen Caldwell
Zoumana Camara
Didier Domi
Michael Duberry
Ian Harte
Gary Kelly
Matthew Kilgallon
Dominic Matteo
Lucas Radebe
Frazer Richardson
Jose Vitor Roque Junior

Midfielders
Eirik Bakke
Nick Barmby
David Batty
Seth Johnson
Simon Johnson
Stephen McPhail
James Milner
Jody Morris
Salomon Olembe
Jermaine Pennant
Jason Wilcox

Forwards
Michael Bridges
Cyril Chapuis
Paul Keegan
Aaron Lennon
Lamine Sakho
Alan Smith
Mark Viduka
Jamie Winter

KEY: On all match | On bench | Subbed or sent off (Counting game) | Subbed or sent off (playing less than 70 mins) | Subbed on from bench (Counting Game) | Subbed on (playing less than 70 mins) | Subbed on and then subbed or sent off (Counting Game) | Subbed on and then subbed or sent off (playing less than 70 mins) | Not in 16

KEY PLAYERS - GOALSCORERS

Mark Viduka

Goals in the League	11
Goals in all competitions	12
Assists League goals scored by team-mates where he delivered the final pass	3
Contribution to Attacking Power Average number of minutes between League team goals while on pitch	79
Player Strike Rate Average number of minutes between League goals scored by player	230
Club Strike Rate Average minutes between League goals scored by club	86

	PLAYER	GOALS LGE	GOALS ALL	ASSISTS	POWER	S RATE
1	Mark Viduka	11	12	3	79	230 mins
2	Alan Smith	9	9	4	78	349 mins
3	Michael Duberry	3	3	2	90	570 mins
4	James Milner	3	3	0	76	791 mins
5	Seth Johnson	2	2	3	75	981 mins

KEY PLAYERS - MIDFIELDERS

James Milner

Goals in the League	3
Goals in all competitions	3
Assists League goals scored by team-mates where he delivered the final pass	0
Defensive Rating Average number of mins between League goals conceded while he was on the pitch	48
Contribution to Attacking Power Average number of minutes between League team goals while on pitch	77
Scoring Difference Defensive Rating minus Contribution to Attacking Power	-29

	PLAYER	GOALS LGE	GOALS ALL	ASSISTS	DEF RATE	POWER	SC DIFF
1	James Milner	3	3	0	48	77	-29 mins
2	Seth Johnson	2	2	3	41	75	-34 mins
3	Jermaine Pennant	2	2	6	46	80	-34 mins

PLAYER APPEARANCES

	AGE (on 01/07/04)	IN NAMED 16	APPEARANCES	COUNTING GAMES	MINUTES ON PITCH	APPEARANCES	MINUTES ON PITCH	THIS SEASON	HOME COUNTRY
Goalkeepers									
Shaun Allaway	21	2	0	0	0	0	0	-	England
Scott Carson	18	34	3	2	182	3	182	-	England
Nigel Martyn	37	4	0	0	0	0	0	-	England
Paul Robinson	24	35	35	35	3148	38	3478	7	England (12)
Defenders									
Stephen Caldwell	23	13	13	13	1170	13	1170	6	Scotland (63)
Zoumana Camara	25	14	13	13	1170	15	1410	-	France
Didier Domi	26	14	12	7	813	14	938	-	France
Michael Duberry	28	20	19	19	1710	20	1800	-	England
Ian Harte	26	32	23	21	1909	26	2239	8	Rep of Ireland (15)
Gary Kelly	30	37	37	37	3312	39	3469	-	Rep of Ireland
Matthew Kilgallon	20	12	8	7	631	9	721	-	England
Dominic Matteo	30	33	33	31	2884	34	2974	-	Scotland
Lucas Radebe	35	22	14	11	960	15	1043	-	South Africa
Frazer Richardson	21	13	5	3	275	6	365	-	England
Roque Junior	27	8	5	5	407	7	647	8	Brazil (1)
Midfielders									
Eirik Bakke	26	10	10	7	720	11	789	-	Norway
Nick Barmby	30	11	6	0	153	6	153	-	England
David Batty	35	16	12	8	834	14	1044	-	England
Seth Johnson	25	26	25	19	1961	26	2081	-	England
Simon Johnson	21	9	5	1	177	5	177	-	England
Stephen McPhail	24	18	12	6	772	12	772	3	Rep of Ireland (15)
James Milner	18	32	30	24	2373	32	2576	-	England
Jody Morris	25	16	12	9	938	12	938	-	England
Salomon Olembe	23	15	12	7	841	14	1019	1	Cameroon (12)
Jermaine Pennant	21	36	36	31	2958	36	2958	-	England
Jason Wilcox	32	7	6	1	237	7	282	-	England
Forwards									
Michael Bridges	25	13	10	0	283	12	415	-	England
Cyril Chapuis	25	2	1	0	45	3	144	-	France
Paul Keegan	20	1	0	0	0	0	0	-	Rep of Ireland
Aaron Lennon	17	19	11	0	224	14	413	-	England
Lamine Sakho	26	18	17	4	776	19	876	2	Senegal (31)
Alan Smith	23	35	35	35	3140	38	3470	2	England (12)
Mark Viduka	28	30	30	26	2531	31	2621	3	Australia (89)
Jamie Winter	18	1	0	0	0	0	0	-	Scotland

KEY: LEAGUE | ALL COMPS | CAPS (FIFA RANKING)

TEAM OF THE SEASON

ROBINSON

CG 38 DR 41

KELLY

CG 37 DR 44

DUBERRY

CG 19 DR 44

MATTEO

CG 31 DR 46

HARTE

CG 21 DR 52

PENNANT

CG 31 SD -34

MORRIS

CG 9* SD -59

JOHNSON

CG 19 SD -34

MILNER

CG 24 SD -29

SMITH

CG 35 AP 78

VIDUKA

CG 26 SR 230

KEY: DR = Diffensive Rate, SD = Scoring Difference AP = Attacking Power SR = Strike Rate, CG=Counting games – League games playing at least 70 minutes

TOP POINT EARNERS

Stephen Caldwell

Counting Games League games when he played at least 70 minutes	13
Average points Average League points taken in Counting games	1.15
Club Average points Average points taken in League games	0.87

	PLAYER	GAMES	PTS
1	Stephen Caldwell	13	1.15
2	Mark Viduka	26	1.08
3	Dominic Matteo	31	1.03
4	Jermaine Pennant	31	1.03
5	Seth Johnson	19	1.00
6	James Milner	24	1.00
7	Alan Smith	35	0.94
8	Gary Kelly	37	0.89
9	Paul Robinson	35	0.89
10	Michael Duberry	19	0.89

KEY PLAYERS - DEFENDERS

Ian Harte

Goals Conceded The number of League goals conceded while he was on the pitch	37
Goals Conceded in all competitions The number goals conceded while he was on the pitch in all competitions	46
League minutes played Number of minutes played in league matches	1909
Clean Sheets In games when he played at least70 mins	3
Defensive Rating Average number of mins between League goals conceded while he was on the pitch	52
Club Defensive Rating Average number of mins between League goals conceded by the club this season	43

	PLAYER	CON LGE	CON ALL	GAMES	C SHEETS	DEF RATE
1	Ian Harte	37	46	1909	3	52 mins
2	Dominic Matteo	63	67	2884	2	46 mins
3	Michael Duberry	39	43	1710	2	44 mins
4	Gary Kelly	75	78	3312	3	44 mins
5	Stephen Caldwell	28	28	1170	0	42 mins

KEY GOALKEEPER

Paul Robinson

Goals Conceded in the League The number of League goals conceded while he was on the pitch	76
Goals Conceded in all competitions Number of goals conceded while he was on the pitch in all competitions	85
League minutes played Number of minutes played in league matches	3148
Clean Sheets In games when he played at least 70 mins	2
Goals to Shots Ratio The average number of shots on target per each League goal conceded	3.8
Defensive Rating Ave mins between League goals conceded while on the pitch	41

BOOKINGS

Didier Domi

League Yellow	5
League Red	0
All competitions Yellow	5
All competitions Red	0

League Average **162** mins between cards

	PLAYER	LEAGUE		TOTAL		AVE
1	Domi	5 Y	0 R	5 Y	0 R	162
2	Batty	4	0	5	0	208
3	Sakho	3	0	3	0	258
4	Matteo	10	1	10	1	262
5	Olembe	3	0	4	0	280
6	Viduka	6	2	6	2	316
7	Bakke	2	0	3	0	360
8	McPhail	2	0	2	0	386
9	Camara	3	0	4	0	390
10	Johnson, Seth	5	0	5	0	392
11	Morris	2	0	2	0	469
12	Radebe	2	0	3	0	480
13	Pennant	5	0	5	0	591
14	Smith	5	0	8	0	628
15	Duberry	2	0	2	0	855
	Other	13	2	13	2	
	TOTAL	**72**	**5**	**80**	**5**	

WOLVERHAMPTON WANDERERS

By March 26th – some 35 games into Wolves season – **Henri Camara** had scored just once.

It was a dreadful return from the former Sedan striker who had been their leading scorer, hitting 14 goals for a bottom of the table French side at a Strike Rate of 189.

Then he went on a run of four in four games during which he was teamed with **Carl Cort** signed from Newcastle. Cort hit five in 13 games and with Camara's six in eight, Dave Jones had a strike partnership – but too late!

The defence was more settled with **Lee Naylor** and **Paul Butler** two of the hardest worked defenders in the Premiership.

Two keepers shared 37 games for Wolves and ended with nearly identical records. **Paul Jones** and **Michael Oakes** both had a Defensive Rating in the mid-40s and shared the same Goals-to-Shots Ratio of 3.8.

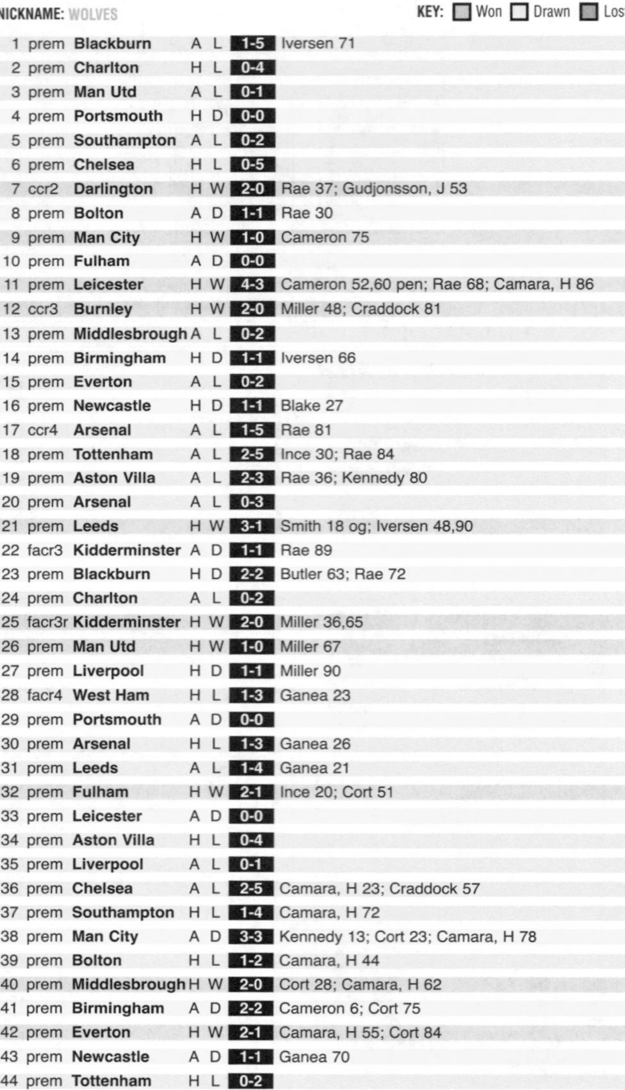

NICKNAME: WOLVES

KEY: Won / Drawn / Lost

1	prem	**Blackburn**	A	L	1-5	Iversen 71
2	prem	**Charlton**	H	L	0-4	
3	prem	**Man Utd**	A	L	0-1	
4	prem	**Portsmouth**	H	D	0-0	
5	prem	**Southampton**	A	L	0-2	
6	prem	**Chelsea**	H	L	0-5	
7	ccr2	**Darlington**	H	W	2-0	Rae 37; Gudjonsson, J 53
8	prem	**Bolton**	A	D	1-1	Rae 30
9	prem	**Man City**	H	W	1-0	Cameron 75
10	prem	**Fulham**	A	D	0-0	
11	prem	**Leicester**	H	W	4-3	Cameron 52,60 pen; Rae 68; Camara, H 86
12	ccr3	**Burnley**	H	W	2-0	Miller 48; Craddock 81
13	prem	**Middlesbrough**	A	L	0-2	
14	prem	**Birmingham**	H	D	1-1	Iversen 66
15	prem	**Everton**	A	L	0-2	
16	prem	**Newcastle**	H	D	1-1	Blake 27
17	ccr4	**Arsenal**	A	L	1-5	Rae 81
18	prem	**Tottenham**	A	L	2-5	Ince 30; Rae 84
19	prem	**Aston Villa**	A	L	2-3	Rae 36; Kennedy 80
20	prem	**Arsenal**	A	L	0-3	
21	prem	**Leeds**	H	W	3-1	Smith 18 og; Iversen 48,90
22	facr3	**Kidderminster**	A	D	1-1	Rae 89
23	prem	**Blackburn**	H	D	2-2	Butler 63; Rae 72
24	prem	**Charlton**	A	L	0-2	
25	facr3r	**Kidderminster**	H	W	2-0	Miller 36,65
26	prem	**Man Utd**	H	W	1-0	Miller 67
27	prem	**Liverpool**	H	D	1-1	Miller 90
28	facr4	**West Ham**	H	L	1-3	Ganea 23
29	prem	**Portsmouth**	A	D	0-0	
30	prem	**Arsenal**	H	L	1-3	Ganea 26
31	prem	**Leeds**	A	L	1-4	Ganea 21
32	prem	**Fulham**	H	W	2-1	Ince 20; Cort 51
33	prem	**Leicester**	A	D	0-0	
34	prem	**Aston Villa**	H	L	0-4	
35	prem	**Liverpool**	A	L	0-1	
36	prem	**Chelsea**	A	L	2-5	Camara, H 23; Craddock 57
37	prem	**Southampton**	H	L	1-4	Camara, H 72
38	prem	**Man City**	A	D	3-3	Kennedy 13; Cort 23; Camara, H 78
39	prem	**Bolton**	H	L	1-2	Camara, H 44
40	prem	**Middlesbrough**	H	W	2-0	Cort 28; Camara, H 62
41	prem	**Birmingham**	A	D	2-2	Cameron 6; Cort 75
42	prem	**Everton**	H	W	2-1	Camara, H 55; Cort 84
43	prem	**Newcastle**	A	D	1-1	Ganea 70
44	prem	**Tottenham**	H	L	0-2	

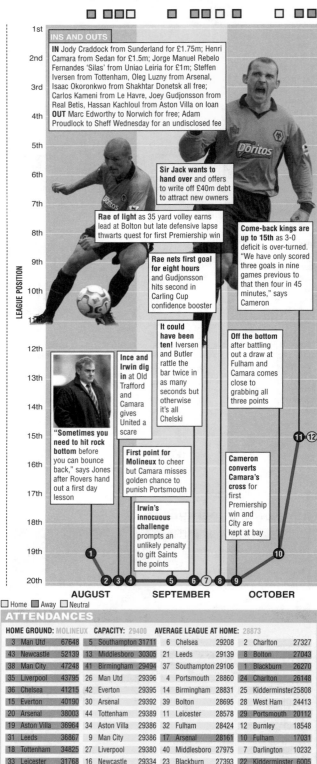

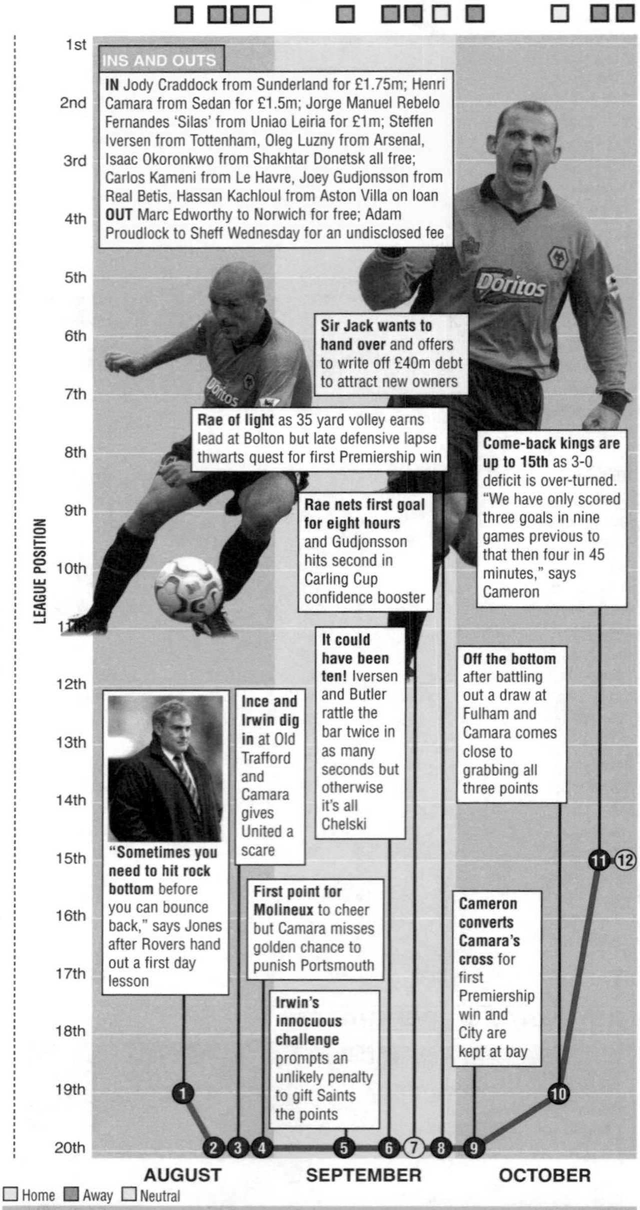

LEAGUE POSITION

1st 2nd 3rd 4th 5th 6th 7th 8th 9th 10th 11th 12th 13th 14th 15th 16th 17th 18th 19th 20th

INS AND OUTS

IN Jody Craddock from Sunderland for £1.75m; Henri Camara from Sedan for £1.5m; Jorge Manuel Rebelo Fernandes 'Silas' from Uniao Leiria for £1m; Steffen Iversen from Tottenham, Oleg Luzny from Arsenal, Isaac Okoronkwo from Shakhtar Donetsk all free; Carlos Kameni from Le Havre, Joey Gudjonsson from Real Betis, Hassan Kachloul from Aston Villa on loan **OUT** Marc Edworthy to Norwich for free; Adam Proudlock to Sheff Wednesday for an undisclosed fee

Sir Jack wants to hand over and offers to write off £40m debt to attract new owners

Rae of light as 35 yard volley earns lead at Bolton but late defensive lapse thwarts quest for first Premiership win

Come-back kings are up to 15th as 3-0 deficit is over-turned. "We have only scored three goals in nine games previous to that then four in 45 minutes," says Cameron

Rae nets first goal for eight hours and Gudjonsson hits second in Carling Cup confidence booster

It could have been ten! Iversen and Butler rattle the bar twice in as many seconds but otherwise it's all Chelski

Off the bottom after battling out a draw at Fulham and Camara comes close to grabbing all three points

Ince and Irwin dig in at Old Trafford and Camara gives United a scare

"Sometimes you need to hit rock bottom before you can bounce back," says Jones after Rovers hand out a first day lesson

First point for Molineux to cheer but Camara misses golden chance to punish Portsmouth

Cameron converts Camara's cross for first Premiership win and City are kept at bay

Irwin's innocuous challenge prompts an unlikely penalty to gift Saints the points

1 2 3 4 5 6 7 8 9 10 11 12

AUGUST SEPTEMBER OCTOBER

Home / Away / Neutral

ATTENDANCES

HOME GROUND: MOLINEUX **CAPACITY:** 29400 **AVERAGE LEAGUE AT HOME:** 28873

3	Man Utd	67648	5	Southampton	31711	6	Chelsea	29208	2	Charlton	27327
43	Newcastle	52139	13	Middlesboro	30305	21	Leeds	29139	8	Bolton	27043
38	Man City	47248	41	Birmingham	29494	37	Southampton	29106	1	Blackburn	26270
35	Liverpool	43795	26	Man Utd	29396	4	Portsmouth	28860	24	Charlton	26148
36	Chelsea	41215	42	Everton	29395	14	Birmingham	28831	25	Kidderminster	25808
15	Everton	40190	30	Arsenal	29392	39	Bolton	28695	28	West Ham	24413
20	Arsenal	38003	44	Tottenham	29389	11	Leicester	28578	29	Portsmouth	20112
19	Aston Villa	36964	34	Aston Villa	29386	32	Fulham	28424	12	Burnley	18548
31	Leeds	36867	9	Man City	29386	17	Arsenal	28161	10	Fulham	17031
18	Tottenham	34825	27	Liverpool	29380	40	Middlesboro	27975	7	Darlington	10232
33	Leicester	31768	16	Newcastle	29334	23	Blackburn	27393	22	Kidderminster	6005

Cort and Camara get together too late

Final Position: **20th**

KEY: ● League ● Champions Lge ● UEFA Cup ● FA Cup ○ League Cup ● Other

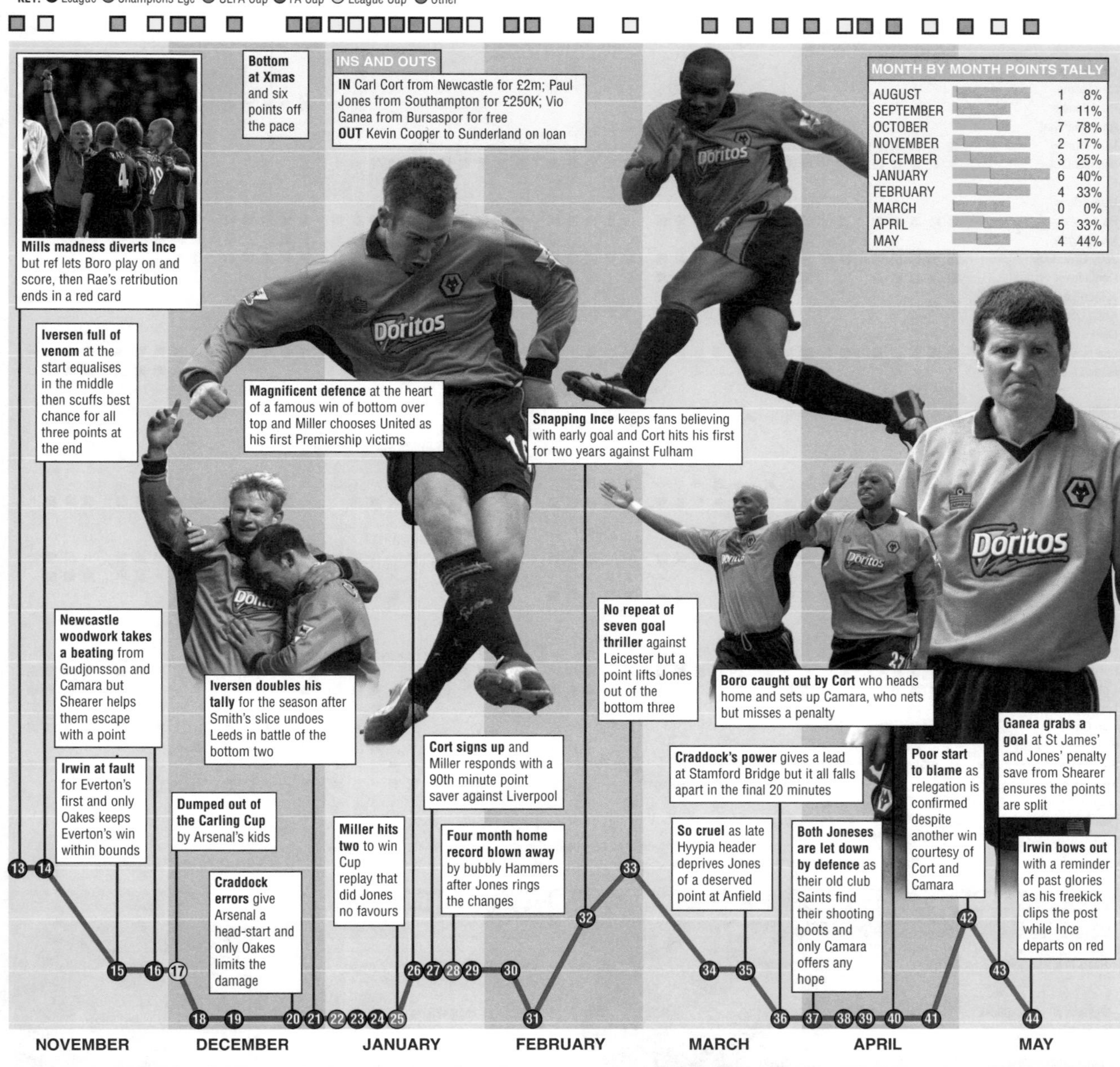
Bottom at Xmas and six points off the pace
INS AND OUTS
IN Carl Cort from Newcastle for £2m; Paul Jones from Southampton for £250K; Vio Ganea from Bursaspor for free
OUT Kevin Cooper to Sunderland on loan
MONTH BY MONTH POINTS TALLY
AUGUST 1 8%
SEPTEMBER 1 11%
OCTOBER 7 78%
NOVEMBER 2 17%
DECEMBER 3 25%
JANUARY 6 40%
FEBRUARY 4 33%
MARCH 0 0%
APRIL 5 33%
MAY 4 44%
Mills madness diverts Ince but ref lets Boro play on and score, then Rae's retribution ends in a red card
Iversen full of venom at the start equalises in the middle then scuffs best chance for all three points at the end
Magnificent defence at the heart of a famous win of bottom over top and Miller chooses United as his first Premiership victims
Snapping Ince keeps fans believing with early goal and Cort hits his first for two years against Fulham
Newcastle woodwork takes a beating from Gudjonsson and Camara but Shearer helps them escape with a point
Iversen doubles his tally for the season after Smith's slice undoes Leeds in battle of the bottom two
No repeat of seven goal thriller against Leicester but a point lifts Jones out of the bottom three
Boro caught out by Cort who heads home and sets up Camara, who nets but misses a penalty
Irwin at fault for Everton's first and only Oakes keeps Everton's win within bounds
Dumped out of the Carling Cup by Arsenal's kids
Cort signs up and Miller responds with a 90th minute point saver against Liverpool
Craddock's power gives a lead at Stamford Bridge but it all falls apart in the final 20 minutes
Ganea grabs a goal at St James' and Jones' penalty save from Shearer ensures the points are split
Poor start to blame as relegation is confirmed despite another win courtesy of Cort and Camara
Miller hits two to win Cup replay that did Jones no favours
Four month home record blown away by bubbly Hammers after Jones rings the changes
So cruel as late Hyypia header deprives Jones of a deserved point at Anfield
Both Joneses are let down by defence as their old club Saints find their shooting boots and only Camara offers any hope
Craddock errors give Arsenal a head-start and only Oakes limits the damage
Irwin bows out with a reminder of past glories as his freekick clips the post while Ince departs on red
NOVEMBER
DECEMBER
JANUARY
FEBRUARY
MARCH
APRIL
MAY

GOAL ATTEMPTS

FOR – Goal attempts recorded in League games

	HOME	AWAY	TOTAL	AVE
shots on target	102	89	191	5
shots off target	108	99	207	5.4
TOTAL	210	188	398	10.5

Ratio of goals to shots – Average number of shots on target per League goal scored: **5**

Accuracy rating – Average percentage of total goal attempts which were on target: **48**

AGAINST – Goal attempts recorded in League games

	HOME	AWAY	TOTAL	AVE
shots on target	118	167	285	7.5
shots off target	86	89	175	4.6
TOTAL	204	256	460	12.1

Ratio of goals to shots – Average number of shots on target per League goal scored: **3.7**

Accuracy rating – Average percentage of total goal attempts which were on target: **62**

GOALS

Henri Camara

League	7
FA Cup	0
League Cup	0
Europe	0
Other	0
TOTAL	7

League Average **369** mins between goals

	PLAYER	LGE	FAC	LC	Euro	TOT	AVE
1	Camara	7	0	0	0	7	369
2	Rae	5	1	2	0	8	506
3	Cort	5	0	0	0	5	230
4	Cameron	4	0	0	0	4	555
5	Iversen	4	0	0	0	4	220
6	Ganea	3	1	0	0	4	216
7	Miller	2	2	1	0	5	711
8	Kennedy	2	0	0	0	2	1267
9	Ince	2	0	0	0	2	1429
10	Blake	1	0	0	0	1	1002
11	Butler	1	0	0	0	1	3330
12	Craddock	1	0	1	0	2	2792
13	Gudjonsson	0	0	1	0	1	
	Other	1	0	0	0	1	
	TOTAL	38	4	5	0	47	

SQUAD APPEARANCES

Match	1	2	3	4	5	6	7	8	9	10	11	12	13	14	15	16	17	18	19	20	21	22	23	24	25	26	27	28	29	30	31	32	33	34	35	36	37	38	39	40	41	42	43	44
Venue	A	H	A	H	A	H	H	A	H	A	H	H	A	H	A	H	A	A	A	A	H	A	H	A	H	H	H	H	A	H	A	H	A	H	A	A	H	A	H	H	A	H	A	H
Competition	L	L	L	L	L	L	W	L	L	L	L	W	L	L	L	L	W	L	L	L	L	F	L	L	F	L	L	F	L	L	L	L	L	L	L	L	L	L	L	L	L	L	L	L
Result	L	L	L	D	L	L	W	D	W	D	W	W	L	D	L	D	L	L	L	L	W	D	D	L	W	W	D	L	D	L	L	W	D	L	L	L	L	D	L	W	D	W	D	L

Goalkeepers
Carl Ikeme
Paul Jones
Andy Marshall
Matt Murray
Michael Oakes

Defenders
Paul Butler
Mark Clyde
Jody Craddock
Denis Irwin
Joleon Lescott
Keith Lowe
Oleg Luzhny
Lee Naylor
Isaac Okoronkwo

Midfielders
Keith Andrews
Sammy Clingan
Kevin Cooper
Johannes Gudjonsson
Paul Ince
Ivar Ingimarsson
Hassan Kachloul
Mark Kennedy
Shaun Newton
Alex Rae

Forwards
Nathan Blake
Henri Camara
Colin Cameron
Leon Clarke
Carl Cort
Ioan Vlorel Ganea
Steffen Iversen
Kenny Miller
Jorge Manuel Silas
Dean Sturridge

KEY: On all match · On bench · Subbed or sent off (Counting game) · Subbed or sent off (playing less than 70 mins) · Subbed on from bench (Counting Game) · Subbed on (playing less than 70 mins) · Subbed on and then subbed or sent off (Counting Game) · Subbed on and then subbed or sent off (playing less than 70 mins) · Not in 16

KEY PLAYERS - GOALSCORERS

Henri Camara

Goals in the League	7
Goals in all competitions	7
Assists League goals scored by team-mates where he delivered the final pass	3
Contribution to Attacking Power Average number of minutes between League team goals while on pitch	80
Player Strike Rate Average number of minutes between League goals scored by player	369
Club Strike Rate Average minutes between League goals scored by club	90

	PLAYER	GOALS LGE	GOALS ALL	ASSISTS	POWER	S RATE
1	Henri Camara	7	7	3	80	369 mins
2	Alex Rae	5	8	3	101	506 mins
3	Colin Cameron	4	4	0	79	555 mins
4	Mark Kennedy	2	2	5	90	1267 mins
5	Paul Ince	2	2	1	98	1429 mins

KEY PLAYERS - MIDFIELDERS

Shaun Newton

Goals in the League	0
Goals in all competitions	0
Assists League goals scored by team-mates where he delivered the final pass	2
Defensive Rating Average number of mins between League goals conceded while he was on the pitch	43
Contribution to Attacking Power Average number of minutes between League team goals while on pitch	75
Scoring Difference Defensive Rating minus Contribution to Attacking Power	-32

	PLAYER	GOALS LGE	GOALS ALL	ASSISTS	DEF RATE	POWER	SC DIFF
1	Shaun Newton	0	0	2	43	75	-32 mins
2	Mark Kennedy	2	2	5	44	91	-47 mins
3	Alex Rae	5	8	3	52	101	-49 mins
4	Paul Ince	2	2	1	45	99	-54 mins

PLAYER APPEARANCES

	AGE (on 01/07/04)	IN NAMED 16	APPEARANCES	COUNTING GAMES	MINUTES ON PITCH	APPEARANCES	MINUTES ON PITCH	THIS SEASON	HOME COUNTRY
Goalkeepers									
Carl Ikeme	18	6	0	0	0	0	0	-	England
Paul Jones	37	16	16	16	1440	16	1440	7	Wales (66)
Andy Marshall	29	6	0	0	0	1	90	-	England
Matt Murray	23	10	1	1	90	2	135	-	England
Michael Oakes	30	38	21	21	1890	26	2295	-	England
Defenders									
Paul Butler	31	37	37	37	3330	41	3690	-	Rep of Ireland
Mark Clyde	21	19	10	4	525	13	795	-	N Ireland
Jody Craddock	28	34	32	31	2792	38	3287	-	England
Ivar Ingimarsson	26	1	0	0	0	0	0	-	Iceland
Denis Irwin	38	34	32	27	2654	33	2744	-	Rep of Ireland
Joleon Lescott	21	0	0	0	0	1	90	-	England
Keith Lowe	-	1	0	0	0	0	0	-	England
Oleg Luzhny	35	14	6	3	392	9	617	-	Ukraine
Lee Naylor	24	38	38	35	3207	43	3657	-	England
Isaac Okoronkwo	26	11	7	7	630	8	720	-	Nigeria
Midfielders									
Keith Andrews	23	1	1	1	90	3	247	-	Rep of Ireland
Sammy Clingan	20	1	0	0	0	0	0	-	N Ireland
Kevin Cooper	29	2	0	0	0	0	0	-	England
Johannes Gudjonsson	24	20	11	4	455	16	830	-	Iceland
Paul Ince	36	32	32	31	2857	35	3082	-	England
Hassan Kachloul	31	6	4	0	72	4	72	-	Morocco
Mark Kennedy	28	31	31	28	2534	36	2909	-	Rep of Ireland
Shaun Newton	28	30	28	16	1722	32	1930	-	England
Alex Rae	34	35	33	26	2529	37	2844	-	Scotland
Forwards									
Nathan Blake	32	13	13	9	1002	14	1092	6	Wales (66)
Henri Camara	27	30	30	29	2586	32	2748	6	Senegal (31)
Colin Cameron	31	33	30	22	2218	33	2488	7	Scotland (63)
Leon Clarke	19	0	0	0	0	3	44	-	England
Carl Cort	26	16	16	11	1152	16	1152	-	England
Ioan Vlorel Ganea	30	19	16	5	647	19	837	-	Romania
Steffen Iversen	28	24	16	7	878	20	1147	-	Norway
Kenny Miller	24	28	25	10	1421	30	1789	7	Scotland (63)
Jorge Manuel Silas	27	14	9	1	284	14	543	-	Portugal
Dean Sturridge	30	8	5	1	200	6	223	-	England

KEY: LEAGUE ALL COMPS CAPS (FIFA RANKING)

TEAM OF THE SEASON

OAKES — CG 21 DR 48

IRWIN — CG 27 DR 45
BUTLER — CG 37 DR 44
CRADDOCK — CG 31 DR 42
NAYLOR — CG 35 DR 45

NEWTON — CG 16 SD -32
INCE — CG 31 SD -54
RAE — CG 26 SD -49
KENNEDY — CG 28 SD -47

CAMERON — CG 22 AP 79
CAMARA — CG 29 SR 369

KEY: DR = Diffensive Rate, SD = Scoring Difference AP = Attacking Power SR = Strike Rate, CG=Counting games – League games playing at least 70 minutes

TOP POINT EARNERS

Shaun Newton

Counting Games League games when he played at least 70 minutes	16
Average points Average League points taken in Counting games	1.25
Club Average points Average points taken in League games	0.87

	PLAYER	GAMES	PTS
1	Shaun Newton	16	1.25
2	Colin Cameron	22	1.09
3	Henri Camara	29	0.93
4	Lee Naylor	35	0.91
5	Michael Oakes	21	0.90
6	Paul Butler	37	0.89
7	Paul Jones	16	0.88
8	Paul Ince	31	0.87
9	Alex Rae	26	0.81
10	Mark Kennedy	28	0.79

KEY PLAYERS - DEFENDERS

Lee Naylor

Goals Conceded The number of League goals conceded while he was on the pitch	72
Goals Conceded in all competitions The number of goals conceded while he was on the pitch in all competitions	81
League minutes played Number of minutes played in league matches	3207
Clean Sheets In games when he played at least70 mins	7
Defensive Rating Average number of mins between League goals conceded while he was on the pitch	45
Club Defensive Rating Average number of mins between League goals conceded by the club this season	44

	PLAYER	CON LGE	CON ALL	GAMES	C SHEETS	DEF RATE
1	Lee Naylor	72	81	3207	7	45 mins
2	Denis Irwin	59	60	2654	5	45 mins
3	Paul Butler	75	83	3330	7	44 mins
4	Jody Craddock	66	72	2792	6	42 mins

KEY GOALKEEPER

Michael Oakes

Goals Conceded in the League The number of League goals conceded while he was on the pitch	39
Goals Conceded in all competitions Number of goals conceded while he was on the pitch in all competitions	43
League minutes played Number of minutes played in league matches	1890
Clean Sheets In games when he played at least 70 mins	4
Goals to Shots Ratio The average number of shots on target per each League goal conceded	3.8
Defensive Rating Ave mins between League goals conceded while on the pitch	48

BOOKINGS

Paul Ince

League Yellow	15
League Red	1
All competitions Yellow	15
All competitions Red	1

League Average 178 mins between cards

	PLAYER	LEAGUE		TOTAL		AVE
		15 Y	1 R	15 Y	1 R	178
1	Ince	15 Y	1 R	15 Y	1 R	178
2	Rae	11	1	11	1	210
3	Ganea	3	0	3	0	215
4	Okoronkwo	2	0	2	0	315
5	Blake	3	0	3	0	334
6	Cameron	5	0	6	0	443
7	Gudjonsson	1	0	3	0	455
8	Miller	3	0	3	0	473
9	Butler	7	0	8	0	475
10	Naylor	5	0	5	0	641
11	Irwin	4	0	5	0	663
12	Iversen	1	0	1	0	878
13	Camara	2	0	2	0	1293
14	Craddock	2	0	3	0	1396
15	Newton	1	0	1	0	1722
	Other	2	0	5	0	
	TOTAL	67	2	76	2	

THE AXA FA CUP

1ST ROUND

Accrington (0) 1 Huddersfield (0) 0
Gouck 90 — 3,129

Barnet (2) 2 Stalybridge (1) 2
Gamble 4 — Keeling 45
Beadle 30 — Eastwood 77 pen
1,736

Blackpool (2) 4 Boreham W (0) 0
Taylor 12,89 — 3,969
Coid 14
Burns 90

Bournemouth (1) 1 Bristol Rovers (0) 0
Elliott 37 — 7,200

Bradford PA (2) 2 Bristol City (2) 5
Hayward 5 — Amankwaah 6,8
Clist 13 og — Stansfield 55
1,945 — Wilkshire 67
Matthews 83

Brentford (1) 7 Gainsborough (0) 1
Harrold 45,65,86 — Smith 81
Rougier 47 — 3,041
Purkiss 50 og
Frampton 55
O'Connor 76

Bury (0) 1 Rochdale (1) 2
Porter 71 — Bertos 27
5,464 — Townson 50

Cheltenham (1) 3 Hull City (0) 1
Spencer 6 — Price 46
Yates 48 — 3,624
Brayson 90

Chester (0) 0 Gravesend (1) 1
2,251 — Skinner 39 pen

Colchester (1) 1 Oxford (0) 0
McGleish 38 — 3,672

Farnborough (0) 0 Weston SM (1) 1
936 — Clark 5

Grantham (1) 1 Leyton Orient (1) 2
Wilkin 4 — Purser 17
2,792 — Alexander 90

Grays Ath (0) 1 Aldershot (0) 2
Griffiths 55 — D'Sane 73 pen,78
1,500

Grimsby (0) 1 QPR (0) 0
Boulding 80 — 4,144

Hartlepool (2) 4 Whitby (0) 0
Gabbiadini 25,30 — 5,294
Humphreys 51
Brackstone 68

Hornchurch (1) 2 Darlington (0) 0
West 43 pen — 2,186
John 61

Kidderminster (1) 2 Northwich (0) 1
Bennett 39,84 — Thompson 87
2,052

Lancaster (1) 1 Cambridge (1) 2
Hughes 34 pen — Kitson 16
1,864 — Guttridge 90

Lincoln (2) 3 Brighton (0) 1
Mayo 13 pen — McPhee 83
Bloomer 37 — 4,425
Yeo 60

Macclesfield (1) 3 Boston (0) 0
Carruthers 20,61 — 2,059
Little 90

Mansfield (4) 6 Bishops S (0) 0
MacKenzie 12,43,51 — 4,679
Junior Mendes 15
Larkin 42
Curtis 78

Northampton (1) 3 Plymouth (1) 2
Walker 37 — Friio 32
Hargreaves 60 — Stonebridge 62
Asamoah 83 — 4,385

Notts County (3) 7 Shildon (0) 2
Fenton 7 — Middleton 55
Platt 14,18 — Barnes 63 pen
Nicholson 64 — 4,016
Richardson 69
Barras 84
Heffernan 88

Oldham (2) 3 Carlisle (0) 0
Zola 35 — 4,391
Cooksey 37,78

Peterborough (0) 2 Hereford (0) 0
Willock 53 — 4,479
Logan 58

Port Vale (0) 2 Ford Utd (1) 2
McPhee 60 — Abraham 20
Burns 64 — Fiddes 74
4,016

Scarborough (0) 1 Doncaster (0) 0
Rose 79 — 3,497

Scunthorpe (1) 2 Shrewsbury (0) 1
Hayes 9,90 — Quinn 87
3,232

Sheff Wed (1) 4 Salisbury (0) 0
Proudlock 32 pen,47,64 — 11,419
Owusu 70

Southend (1) 1 Canvey I (1) 1
Gower 2 — Chenery 7
9,234

Stevenage (2) 2 Stockport (0) 1
Maamria 29,37 — Goodwin 69 pen
2,538

Swansea (1) 3 Rushden & D (0) 0
Trundle 38 — 5,031
Nugent 58
Durkan 88

Telford (0) 3 Crawley (2) 2
Lavery 58 — Armstrong 8
Ricketts 72 — Gregory 28
Murphy 90 — 1,581

Thurrock (0) 1 Luton (1) 1
Bowes 80 — Boyce 39
1,551

Torquay (0) 1 Burton (1) 2
Benfield 55 — Woods 10 og
2,790 — Talbot 71

Tranmere (1) 3 Chesterfield (0) 2
Dadi 4 — Davies 51
Hulme 80 — Evatt 83
Mellon 87 pen — 5,633

Woking (3) 3 Histon (1) 1
Selley 23,39 pen — Cambridge 2
Sharpling 45 — 2,217

Wycombe (1) 4 Swindon (0) 1
Thomson 44 — Gurney 71 pen
Currie 64,85 — 4,738
McSporran 87

Yeovil (1) 4 Wrexham (0) 1
Gall 39 — Armstrong 88
Williams 46 — 5,049
Pluck 59, — Edwards, J 66

York (1) 1 Barnsley (1) 2
Nogan 36 — Rankin 38
5,658 — Betsy 82

1st Round replays

Luton (1) 3 Thurrock (0) 1
Forbes 39,76,87 pen — Akurang 49
3,667

Stalybridge (0) 0 Barnet (1) 2
1,549 — Grazioli 27,84

Canvey I (2) 2 Southend (1) 3
Boylan 10 — Bramble 23
Minton 45 — Smith 46,90
2,731

Ford Utd (0) 1 Port Vale (1) 2
Poole 90 — Paynter 38
1,324 — Chandler 114 og
After Extra Time

2ND ROUND

FA Cup 2nd Round

Bournemouth (0) 1 Accrington (1) 1
Browning 56 — Mullin 9
7,551

Bristol City (0) 0 Barnsley (0) 0
6,741

Burton (0) 0 Hartlepool (0) 1
3,132 — Porter 70

Cheltenham (2) 3 Leyton Orient (0) 1
McCann 18 pen,34 — Lockwood 69
Taylor 60 — 3,959

Colchester (0) 1 Aldershot (0) 0
Vine 83 — 4,255

Gravesend (1) 1 Notts County (0) 2
Perkins 42 — Fenton 69
2,998 — Platt 90

Hornchurch (0) 0 Tranmere (1) 1
3,500 — Jones 26

Macclesfield (1) 1 Cambridge (1) 1
Tipton 22 pen — Turner, J 23
2,182

Northampton (1) 4 Weston SM (0) 1
Smith, M 36 pen — Clark 80
Low 64, Richards 77,90 — 3,948

Oldham (0) 2 Blackpool (3) 5
Eyre, J 61 — Taylor 2,20,57
Johnson 90 — Southern 25
6,143 — Richardson 73

Peterborough (1) 3 Grimsby (1) 2
Clarke, A 22 — Jevons 24
Thomson 47 — Cas 84
Newton 65 — 4,836

Port Vale (0) 0 Scarborough (0) 1
4,651 — Sestanovich 80

Rochdale (0) 0 Luton (1) 2
2,807 — Robinson 20 pen
Mansell 77

Scunthorpe (1) 2 Sheff Wed (0) 2
Torpey 33,71 — N'dumbu 84
7,418 — Holt 90

Southend (1) 3 Lincoln (0) 0
Bramble 39 — 4,258
Gower 64, Corbett 89

Swansea (1) 2 Stevenage (0) 1
Nugent 23 — Elding 49
Trundle 51 — 6,125

Telford (1) 3 Brentford (0) 0
Moore 26,58,80 pen — 2,996

Woking (0) 0 Kidderminster (1) 3
3,484 — Bennett 6,64, Burton 74

Wycombe (0) 1 Mansfield (0) 1
Holligan 53 — Christie 61
3,212

Yeovil (3) 5 Barnet (1) 1
Pluck 9 — Beadle 10
Williams 18 pen,27 — 5,973
Crittenden 74, Edwards, J 78

2nd Round replays

Accrington (0) 0 Bournemouth (0) 0
2,585
Accrington win 5-3 on penalties

Barnsley (2) 2 Bristol City (0) 1
Kay 24 — Roberts 65
Monk 43 — 5,434

Cambridge (0) 2 Macclesfield (1) 2
Turner 66 — Miles 26, Tipton 101
Tann 119 — 2,545
Macclesfield win 4-2 on penalties

Mansfield (1) 3 Wycombe (0) 2
Lawrence 14,72 pen,90 pen — McSporran 56,59
5,512

Sheff Wed (0) 0 Scunthorpe (0) 0
11,722
Scunthorpe win 3-1 on penalties

3RD ROUND

Accrington (0) 0 Colchester (0) 0
4,368

Aston Villa (1) 1 Man Utd (0) 2
Barry 19 — Scholes 64,68
40,371

Barnsley (0) 0 Scunthorpe (0) 0
10,839

Birmingham (2) 4 Blackburn (0) 0
Morrison 23 — 18,688
Clemence 36
Forssell 78
Hughes, B 84

Bradford (0) 1 Luton (1) 2
Gray 83 pen — Forbes 22,48
8,222

Cardiff (0) 0 Sheff Utd (0) 1
10,525 — Allison 74

Coventry (0) 2 Peterborough (0) 1
McSheffrey 59 — Clarke, A 79
Joachim 61 — 11,400

Crewe (0) 0 Telford (1) 1
7,085 — Mills 2

Everton (2) 3 Norwich (1) 1
Kilbane 15 — Brennan 27
Ferguson 38 pen,70 pen — 29,955

Fulham (1) 2 Cheltenham (1) 1
Saha 13,90 — McCann 5
10,303

Gillingham (3) 3 Charlton (1) 2
Johnson, T 17 — Cox 1 og
Sidibe 19 — Cole, C 90
Smith 34 — 10,894

SEAFRANCE

Triple save from fourth-choice keeper helps Gillingham through against in-form Charlton. Bossu only plays because of injuries but his 6'6" frame denies three Premier strikers five minutes from time

Ipswich (0) 3 Derby (0) 0
Naylor 54 — 16,159
Miller, T 69
Kuqi 89

Kidderminster (0) 1 Wolves (0) 1
Williams, J 77 — Rae 89
6,005

Leeds (1) 1 Arsenal (2) 4
Viduka 8 — Henry 26
31,207 — Edu 33
Pires 87
Toure 90

Man City (1) 2 Leicester (1) 2
Anelka 27 pen,69 — Dickov 4
30,617 — Bent, M 66

Mansfield (0) 0 Burnley (1) 2
8,290 — Moore, I 30,73

Middlesbro (1) 2 Notts County (0) 0
Richardson 25 og 15,061
Zenden 64

Millwall (2) 2 Walsall (1) 1
Baltacha 33 Leitao 12
Cahill 45 6,977

Northampton (0) 1 Rotherham (0) 1
Smith, M 63 Barker, R 55
5,741

Nottm Forest (0) 1 West Brom (0) 0
King 54 pen 11,843

Portsmouth (1) 2 Blackpool (1) 1
Schemmel 36 Taylor 43
Yakubu 90 13,479

Preston (3) 3 Reading (3) 3
O'Neil, B 9 Goater 7
Fuller 32,45 Jackson, Mi 13 og
9,428 Davis 37 og

Southampton (0) 0 Newcastle (2) 3
28,456 Dyer 24,67
Robert 39

Southend (1) 1 Scarborough (0) 1
Smith 9 6,902

Sunderland (0) 1 Hartlepool (0) 0
Arca 53 40,816

Swansea (1) 2 Macclesfield (0) 1
Trundle 44,70 Tipton 65
8,112

Tottenham (2) 3 Crystal P (0) 0
Kanoute 15,20,48 32,340

Tranmere (0) 1 Bolton (0) 1
Haworth, S 51 Nolan 78
10,587

Watford (2) 2 Chelsea (2) 2
Helguson 5 Gudjohnsen 33 pen
Mahon 35 Lampard 41
21,121

Wigan (0) 1 West Ham (0) 2
Quinn 90 og Mullins 80
11,793 Connolly 85

The Hammers almost drop a clanger when a shocking own goal by Quinn gives hard-working Wigan chances of snatching a replay. However, West Ham hold out for the win after Mullins and Connolly put them on top.

Wimbledon (0) 1 Stoke (1) 1
Nowland 73 Eustace 12
3,609

Yeovil (0) 0 Liverpool (0) 2
5,348 Heskey 70
Murphy 77 pen

3rd Round replays

Bolton (0) 1 Tranmere (0) 2
Shakes 90 Dadi 82
8,759 Hulme 91
After Extra Time

Chelsea (2) 4 Watford (0) 0
Mutu 7,76 38,763
Hasselbaink 34
Gudjohnsen 84

Colchester (1) 2 Accrington (0) 1
Keith 11,84 Mullin 89
5,611

Leicester (0) 1 Man City (1) 3
Ferdinand 73 Sibierski 12
18,916 Anelka 90, Macken 90

Reading (0) 1 Preston (1) 2
Goater 84 Cresswell 28
9,314 Koumantarakis 47

Six goals before half-time with Preston's Fuller twice pulling the home side level from own goals conceded

Rotherham (1) 1 Northampton (1) 2
Hurst 19 Walker 36
9,405 Smith, M 54

Scarborough (0) 1 Southend (0) 0
Quayle 83 4,859

Scunthorpe (1) 2 Barnsley (0) 0
Torpey 14 6,293
McCombe 74

Stoke (0) 0 Wimbledon (1) 1
6,463 Nowland 32

Wolves (1) 2 Kidderminster (0) 0
Miller 36,65 25,808

Rae thwarts Kidderminster in the 89th minute after the third division side, managed by ex-Liverpool midfielder Molby, look on course for the fourth round with Williams' late goal against Wolves

4TH ROUND

Arsenal (2) 4 Middlesbro (1) 1
Bergkamp 19 Job 23
Ljungberg 28,68 37,256
Bentley 90

Birmingham (1) 1 Wimbledon (0) 0
Hughes, B 4 22,159

Burnley (2) 3 Gillingham (0) 1
Moore, I 30 Henderson 71
Blake 33,64 9,735

Coventry (1) 1 Colchester (1) 1
Joachim 33 Adebola 30 og
15,341

Everton (0) 1 Fulham (0) 1
Jeffers 90 Davis, S 49
27,862

Ipswich (0) 1 Sunderland (1) 2
Reuser 89 Smith 45
21,406 Arca 68

Liverpool (1) 2 Newcastle (1) 1
Cheyrou 2,61 Robert 4
41,365

Luton (0) 0 Tranmere (0) 1
8,767 Mellon 81

Man City (1) 1 Tottenham (0) 1
Anelka 10 Doherty 57
47,000

Northampton (0) 0 Man Utd (1) 3
7,356 Silvestre 34
Hargreaves 47 og
Forlan 68

Nottm Forest (0) 0 Sheff Utd (1) 3
17,306 Lester 33 pen
Morgan 79
Allison 90

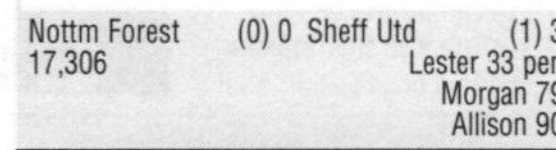

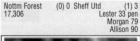

Lester reminds Forest how to score converting a penalty against his old club who have now gone over ten hours without a goal from open play. From this start the Blades fashion a flattering win

Portsmouth (1) 2 Scunthorpe (0) 1
Taylor 35,66 Parton 88
17,508

Scarborough (0) 0 Chelsea (1) 1
5,379 Terry 10

Swansea (0) 2 Preston (0) 1
Robinson 80 Etuhu 58
Trundle 82 10,200

Trundle gives Preston the elbow after receiving one himself which will require an operation. The Swansea striker nets the winner as his side comes from behind with two goals in the last ten minutes

Telford (0) 0 Millwall (1) 2
5,589 Ifill 37, Wise 83

Wolves (1) 1 West Ham (3) 3
Ganea 23 Deane 4
24,413 Harewood 21
Connolly 32

4th Round replays

Colchester (2) 3 Coventry (1) 1
Vine 12,43,57 Joachim 25
5,530

Fulham (0) 2 Everton (0) 1
Inamoto 57 Jeffers 90
Malbranque 102 11,551
After Extra Time

Tottenham (3) 3 Man City (0) 4
King 2 Distin 48
Keane 19 Bosvelt 61
Ziege 43 Wright-Phillips 79
30,400 Macken 90

Macken completes stunning comeback as City turn around a 3-0 halftime deficit with only ten men and no Anelka, who limps off injured. Reserve keeper Arason also earns rave reviews with a wonderful double save

5TH ROUND

Arsenal (0) 2 Chelsea (1) 1
Reyes 56,61 — Mutu 40
38,136

Wenger's striker is pacy, talented and netting goals but it's not Henry, who is rested to allow Reyes to torment Chelsea with two goals. He preserves Arsenal's 15 game undefeated run against Chelsea.

Fulham (0) 0 West Ham (0) 0
14,705

Liverpool (1) 1 Portsmouth (0) 1
Owen 2 — Taylor 77
34,669

Man Utd (1) 4 Man City (0) 2
Scholes 34 — Tarnat 78
van Nistelrooy 71,80 — Fowler 86
Ronaldo 73
67,228

Van Nistelrooy poaches vital goals while City squander chances as the red half of Manchester celebrates despite Gary Neville's sending off

Sheff Utd (0) 1 Colchester (0) 0
Peschisolido 61
17,074

Sunderland (1) 1 Birmingham (1) 1
Kyle 39 — Forssell 28
24,966

Tranmere (1) 2 Swansea (1) 1
Taylor 24 pen — Robinson 16
Hulme 59
12,215

Millwall (0) 1 Burnley (0) 0
Dichio 72
10,420

5th Round replays

Birmingham (0) 0 Sunderland (0) 2
25,645 — Smith 99,115
After Extra Time

Portsmouth (0) 1 Liverpool (0) 0
Hughes, R 72
19,529

West Ham (0) 0 Fulham (0) 3
27,934 — McBride 76
Hayles 79, Boa Morte 90

McBride makes Hammers pay by converting the crucial first goal while Harewood and the other West Ham strikers are letting Fulham off the hook at the other end

QUARTER-FINALS

Man Utd (1) 2 Fulham (1) 1
van Nistelrooy 24,62 — Malbranque 23 pen
67,614

Keane blunders at the back to make life difficult for makeshift United defence. Fulham's Malbranque becomes the first player to score a domestic penalty at Old Trafford for 10 years before youngsters Fletcher and Ronaldo set up the second of a brace for van Nistelrooy

vodafone
vodafone

Millwall (0) 0 Tranmere (0) 0
16,404

Achterberg foils Muscat in the only incident of note at the New Den.
Millwall's defender takes penalty responsibility and fires too close to Tranmere's Dutch keeper

Quarter-final replay

Tranmere (1) 1 Millwall (2) 2
Jones 41 — Cahill 11
15,510 — Harris 16

Dichio unlocks Tranmere twice in the first 16 minutes for Cahill and Harris to score the goals that earn a semi-final tie against Sunderland at Old Trafford

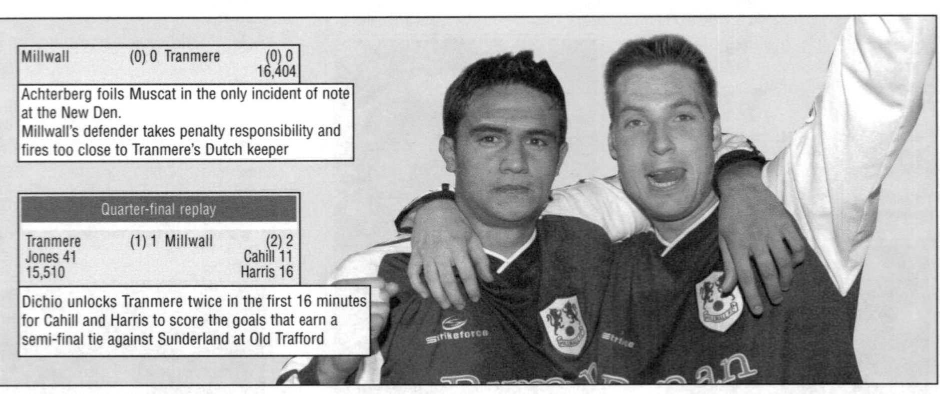

Portsmouth (0) 1 Arsenal (3) 5
Sheringham 90 — Henry 25,50
20,137 — Ljungberg 43,57
Toure 45

"They all work, they all run, they've all got ability" Redknapp delivers his verdict on Arsenal after seeing his Portsmouth team dismissed 5-1.
Henry and Ljungberg collect two apiece in a stunning team display that wraps up the tie long before sub Sheringham adds a consolation goal

Sunderland (1) 1 Sheff Utd (0) 0
Smith 15
37,115

Smith sets Stadium of Light roaring with an early goal and Sheffield United can't repeat last season's semi-final foray.
"We were wimps," complains Blades' manager Warnock as Poom has an easy time in the Sunderland goal

SEMI-FINALS

Arsenal	(0) 0	Man Utd	(1) 1
39,939			Scholes 32

Scholes settles it as United youngsters out-scrap Arsenal in a riveting match.
Wenger rests Henry and Reyes and Bergkamp and Edu come so close to proving him right in the first few minutes of the game. After that Brown locks the United defence up tight, Fletcher bosses the midfield and Ronaldo torments Clichy as Ferguson's tactics prove good enough to end Arsenal's treble chance

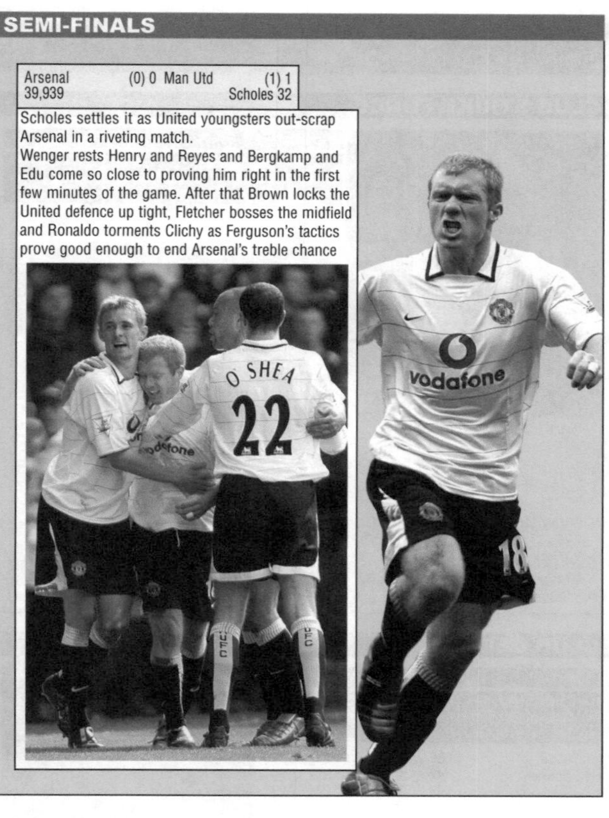

Sunderland	(0) 0	Millwall	(1) 1
56,112			Cahill 25

Wise celebrates Millwall's first FA Cup final appearance after Cahill's goal proves enough to beat Sunderland.
The Aussie midfielder nets after 26 minutes and his well-taken finish is the difference over a 90 minutes where the Wearsiders have the bulk of the chances.
Kyle, Arca and McCartney all shoot poorly before an ill-tempered game sees McAteer sent off. Millwall have a place in the UEFA Cup and a shot at one of the great upsets if they can beat United

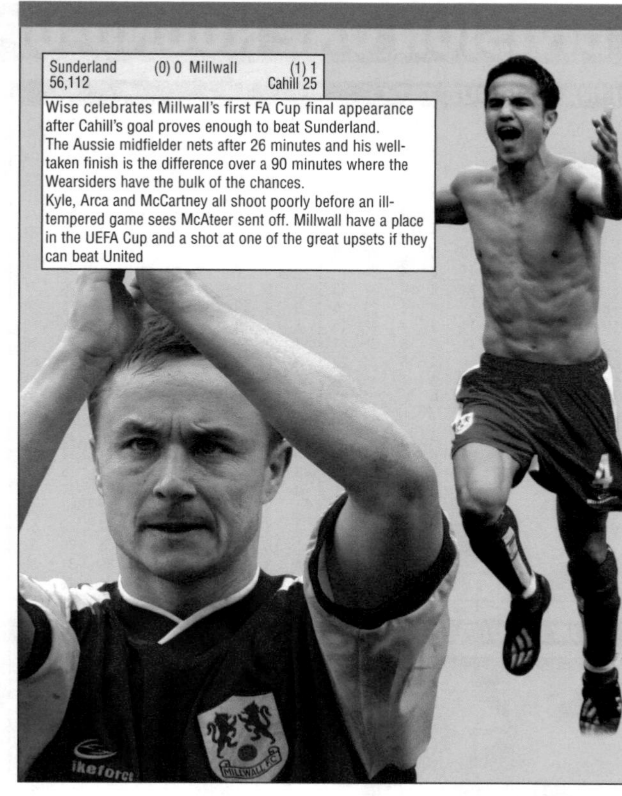

FINAL

Man Utd	(1) 3	Millwall	(0) 0
Ronaldo 44			71,350
van Nistelrooy 65 pen,81			

Ronaldo roasts Millwall on both flanks as United register a record 11th FA Cup final win.
The Portuguese wonder goes through an astonishing repertoire of ball skills to undermine defenders' confidence and earn the spite of the underdog's player-manager Wise.
With Millwall's lone striker Harris unable to register a notable attack in a one-sided final it's a question of how many United will score.
After fine saves by Marshall from Keane's pin-point 30-yarder and Ronaldo's low strike from the left, a Gary Neville cross is headed home by the Portuguese winger, to give United a half-time lead.
The second half starts with Fletcher drifting past a number of Millwall tackles before hitting a tame shot. Then Giggs punishes the first division side with two fine runs, slaloming in from the right to earn a penalty converted by van Nistelrooy and whipping in a cross from the left to the same end.
Keane, becoming the first player to play in six cup finals, picks up the trophy but Millwall supporters are the real stars of the final in their sheer delight at just being present.

DIVISION ONE ROUND-UP

FINAL LEAGUE TABLE

		HOME					AWAY					TOTAL			
	P	W	D	L	F	A	W	D	L	F	A	F	A	DIF	PTS
Norwich	46	18	3	2	44	15	10	7	6	35	24	79	39	40	94
West Brom	46	14	5	4	34	16	11	6	6	30	26	64	42	22	86
Sunderland	46	13	8	2	33	15	9	5	9	29	30	62	45	17	79
West Ham	46	12	7	4	42	20	7	10	6	25	25	67	45	22	74
Ipswich	46	12	3	8	49	36	9	7	7	35	36	84	72	12	73
Crystal Palace	46	10	8	5	34	25	11	2	10	38	36	72	61	11	73
Wigan	46	11	8	4	29	16	7	9	7	31	29	60	45	15	71
Sheff Utd	46	11	6	6	37	25	9	5	9	28	31	65	56	9	71
Reading	46	11	6	6	29	25	9	4	10	26	32	55	57	-2	70
Millwall	46	11	8	4	28	15	7	7	9	27	33	55	48	7	69
Stoke	46	11	7	5	35	24	7	5	11	23	31	58	55	3	66
Coventry	46	9	9	5	34	22	8	5	10	33	32	67	54	13	65
Cardiff	46	10	6	7	40	25	7	8	8	28	33	68	58	10	65
Nottm Forest	46	8	9	6	33	25	7	6	10	28	33	61	58	3	60
Preston	46	11	7	5	43	29	4	7	12	26	42	69	71	-2	59
Watford	46	9	8	6	31	28	6	4	13	23	40	54	68	-14	57
Rotherham	46	8	8	7	31	27	5	7	11	22	34	53	61	-8	54
Crewe	46	11	3	9	33	26	3	8	12	24	40	57	66	-9	53
Burnley	46	9	6	8	37	32	4	8	11	23	45	60	77	-17	53
Derby	46	11	5	7	39	33	2	8	13	14	34	53	67	-14	52
Gillingham	46	10	1	12	28	34	4	8	11	20	33	48	67	-19	51
Walsall	46	8	7	8	29	31	5	5	13	16	34	45	65	-20	51
Bradford	46	6	3	14	23	35	4	3	16	15	34	38	69	-31	36
Wimbledon	46	3	4	16	21	40	5	1	17	20	49	41	89	-48	29

CLUB STRIKE FORCE

Kuqi and Magilton strike for Ipswich

Goals scored in the League	84
Goals scored in all competitions	90
Shots on target (SoT) Shots on target hit by the team recorded in League games	337

1 Ipswich

Club Strike Rate (CSR) Average number of minutes between League goals scored by club	49

	CLUB	LGE	ALL	SoT	CSR
1	Ipswich	84	90	337	49
2	Norwich	79	80	319	52
3	Crystal Palace	72	83	271	58
4	Preston	69	75	344	60
5	Cardiff	68	74	325	61
6	Coventry	67	73	350	62
7	West Ham	67	80	309	62
8	Sheff Utd	65	72	282	64
9	West Brom	64	74	270	65
10	Sunderland	62	77	323	67
11	Nottm Forest	61	64	247	68
12	Burnley	60	68	231	69
13	Wigan	60	65	309	69
14	Stoke	58	61	264	71
15	Crewe	57	59	237	73
16	Millwall	55	63	237	75
17	Reading	55	66	238	75
18	Watford	54	56	250	77
19	Derby	53	54	321	78
20	Rotherham	53	59	217	78
21	Gillingham	48	56	254	86
22	Walsall	45	49	205	92
23	Wimbledon	41	43	209	101
24	Bradford	38	39	244	109

CLUB DISCIPLINARY RECORDS

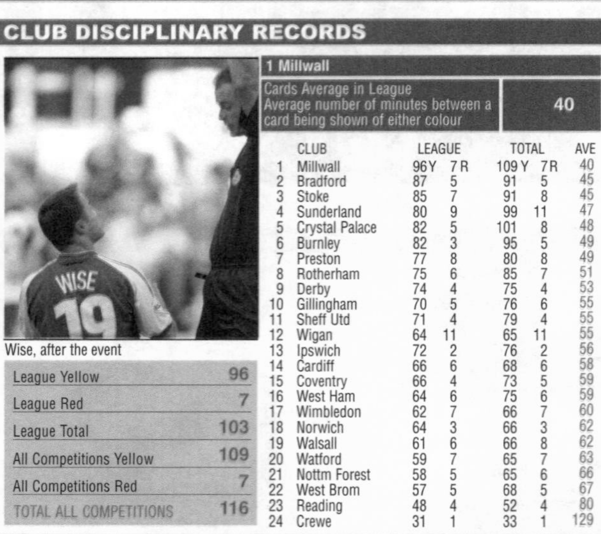

Wise, after the event

League Yellow	96
League Red	7
League Total	103
All Competitions Yellow	109
All Competitions Red	7
TOTAL ALL COMPETITIONS	116

1 Millwall

Cards Average in League Average number of minutes between a card being shown of either colour	40

	CLUB	LEAGUE		TOTAL		AVE
1	Millwall	96Y	7R	109Y	7R	40
2	Bradford	87	5	91	5	45
3	Stoke	85	7	91	8	45
4	Sunderland	80	9	99	11	47
5	Crystal Palace	82	5	101	8	48
6	Burnley	82	3	95	5	49
7	Preston	77	8	80	8	49
8	Rotherham	75	6	85	7	51
9	Derby	74	4	75	4	53
10	Gillingham	70	5	76	6	55
11	Sheff Utd	71	4	79	4	55
12	Wigan	64	11	65	11	55
13	Ipswich	72	2	76	2	56
14	Cardiff	66	6	68	6	58
15	Coventry	66	4	73	5	59
16	West Ham	64	6	75	6	59
17	Wimbledon	62	7	66	7	60
18	Norwich	64	3	66	3	62
19	Walsall	61	6	66	8	62
20	Watford	59	7	65	7	63
21	Nottm Forest	58	5	65	6	66
22	West Brom	57	5	68	5	67
23	Reading	48	4	52	4	80
24	Crewe	31	1	33	1	129

CLUB DEFENCES

1 Norwich

Club Defensive Rate (CDR) Average number of minutes between League goals conceded by club	106

	CLUB	LGE	ALL	CS	SoT	CDR
1	Norwich	42	43	18	319	99
2	West Brom	42	47	19	206	99
3	Sunderland	45	57	18	213	92
4	West Ham	45	56	17	210	92
5	Wigan	45	49	17	226	92
6	Millwall	48	54	16	253	86
7	Coventry	54	62	13	212	77
8	Stoke	55	60	14	308	75
9	Sheff Utd	56	60	15	272	74
10	Reading	57	65	13	277	73
11	Cardiff	58	63	14	274	71
12	Nottm Forest	58	65	11	294	71
13	Crystal Palace	61	74	13	273	68
14	Rotherham	61	66	15	272	68
15	Walsall	65	71	10	317	64
16	Crewe	66	68	11	434	63
17	Derby	67	72	10	256	62
18	Gillingham	67	75	13	286	62
19	Watford	68	75	9	267	61
20	Bradford	69	71	7	316	60
21	Preston	71	77	11	269	58
22	Ipswich	72	78	6	273	58
23	Burnley	77	83	10	267	54
24	Wimbledon	89	93	5	299	47

Mulryne tackling for Norwich

Goals conceded in the League	39
Goals conceded in all competitions	43
Clean Sheets (CS) Number of league games where no goals were conceded	18
Shots on Target Against (SoT) Shots on Target conceded by team in League games	319

STADIUM CAPACITY AND HOME CROWDS

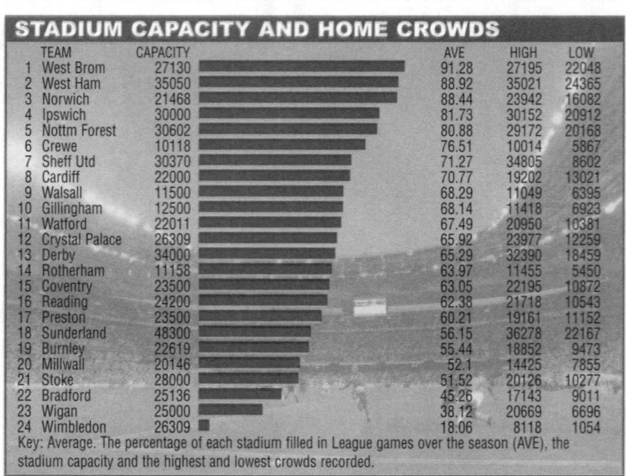

	TEAM	CAPACITY	AVE	HIGH	LOW
1	West Brom	27130	91.28	27195	22048
2	West Ham	35050	88.92	35021	24365
3	Norwich	21468	88.44	23942	16082
4	Ipswich	30000	81.73	30152	20912
5	Nottm Forest	30602	80.88	29172	20168
6	Crewe	10118	76.51	10014	5867
7	Sheff Utd	30370	71.27	34805	8602
8	Cardiff	22000	70.77	19202	13021
9	Walsall	11500	68.29	11049	6395
10	Gillingham	12500	68.14	11418	6923
11	Watford	22011	67.49	20950	10381
12	Crystal Palace	26309	65.92	23977	12259
13	Derby	34000	65.29	32390	18459
14	Rotherham	11158	63.97	11455	5450
15	Coventry	23500	63.05	22195	10872
16	Reading	24200	62.38	21718	10543
17	Preston	23500	60.21	19161	11152
18	Sunderland	48300	56.15	36278	22167
19	Burnley	22619	55.44	18852	9473
20	Millwall	20146	52.1	14425	7855
21	Stoke	28000	51.52	20126	10277
22	Bradford	25136	45.26	17143	9011
23	Wigan	25000	38.12	20669	6696
24	Wimbledon	26309	18.06	8118	1054

Key: Average. The percentage of each stadium filled in League games over the season (AVE), the stadium capacity and the highest and lowest crowds recorded.

AWAY ATTENDANCE

	TEAM	AVE	HIGH	LOW
1	West Ham	79.25	29679	8118
2	West Brom	73.28	34805	6376
3	Sunderland	71.77	30329	4800
4	Norwich	69.22	35174	7368
5	Nottm Forest	68.09	32390	6317
6	Wigan	66.89	34375	1054
7	Sheff Utd	66.34	28972	6016
8	Crystal Palace	65.72	31861	6001
9	Derby	65.57	30838	6509
10	Burnley	64.58	31474	5639
11	Ipswich	64.11	35021	6389
12	Stoke	63.41	28758	3623
13	Preston	62.94	28777	2866
14	Gillingham	62.34	34551	5049
15	Cardiff	62.3	31858	5056
16	Rotherham	62.24	34483	3061
17	Walsall	61.98	36278	3315
18	Wimbledon	61.26	29818	5777
19	Coventry	61.06	27890	5524
20	Reading	60.97	32634	2066
21	Watford	60.8	34685	6115
22	Millwall	59.33	31626	3037
23	Bradford	59.3	30370	3334
24	Crewe	58.45	31158	1145

Key: Average. How close each club has come to filling grounds in its away league matches (AVE) and the highest and lowest crowds recorded.

CHART-TOPPING MIDFIELDERS

1 McVeigh - Norwich	
Goals scored in the League	5
Defensive Rating Av number of mins between League goals conceded while on the pitch	121
Contribution to Attacking Power Average number of minutes between League team goals while on pitch	57
Scoring Difference Defensive Rating minus Contribution to Attacking Power	64

	PLAYER	CLUB	GOALS	DEF RATE	POWER	S DIFF
1	McVeigh	Norwich	5	121	57	64
2	Holt	Norwich	1	106	52	54
3	Robinson	West Brom	0	112	61	51
4	Johnson	West Brom	2	105	55	50
5	Gray	Crystal Palace	3	94	46	48
6	Francis	Norwich	7	94	51	43
7	Horlock	West Ham	1	103	61	42
8	Thirlwell	Sunderland	0	83	51	32
9	Oster	Sunderland	5	94	64	30
10	Liddell	Wigan	9	95	66	29
11	Gregan	West Brom	1	92	65	27
12	Etherington	West Ham	5	85	59	26
13	Koumas	West Brom	10	96	71	25
14	Jarrett	Wigan	1	86	63	23
15	Bullard	Wigan	2	92	69	23

CHART-TOPPING GOALSCORERS

1 Johnson - Crystal Palace	
Goals scored in the League (GL)	27
Goals scored in all competitions (GA)	32
Contribution to Attacking Power (AP) Average number of minutes between League team goals while on pitch	55
Player Strike Rate Average number of minutes between League goals scored by player	128
Club Strike Rate (CSR) Average minutes between League goals scored by club	58

	PLAYER	CLUB	GOALS: LGE	ALL	POWER	CSR	S RATE
1	Johnson	Crystal Palace	27	32	55	58	128 mins
2	Thorne	Cardiff	13	13	49	61	132
3	Harewood	Nottm Forest	12	12	53	68	142
4	Defoe	West Ham	11	14	60	62	143
5	Freedman	Crystal Palace	13	15	63	58	157
6	Healy	Preston	15	15	58	60	172
7	Harewood	West Ham	13	14	55	62	179
8	Lester	Sheff Utd	12	15	63	64	180
9	Earnshaw	Cardiff	21	26	65	61	182
10	"Bent, D"	Ipswich	16	17	55	49	183
11	Fuller	Preston	18	20	57	60	184
12	Stewart	Sunderland	14	16	65	67	187
13	Akinbiyi	Stoke	10	10	68	71	197
14	Ashton	Crewe	19	20	73	73	202
15	Butler	Rotherham	15	15	72	78	202

CHART-TOPPING DEFENDERS

1 Taggart - Stoke	
Goals Conceded in the League The number of League goals conceded while he was on the pitch	14
Goals Conceded in all competitions The number of goals conceded while he was on the pitch in all competitions	14
Clean Sheets In games when he played at least 70 mins	10
Defensive Rating Average number of minutes between League goals conceded while on pitch	128
Club Defensive Rating Average mins between League goals conceded by the club this season	75

	PLAYER	CLUB	CON: LGE	ALL	CS	CDR	DEF RATE
1	Taggart	Stoke	14	14	10	75	128
2	Williams	Sunderland	18	23	8	92	122
3	Gaardsoe	West Brom	38	42	19	99	107
4	Edworthy	Norwich	35	39	17	106	106
5	Fleming	Norwich	39	43	18	106	106
6	Mackay	Norwich	38	42	18	106	106
7	Drury	Norwich	36	40	15	106	103
8	Breen	Sunderland	27	33	14	92	102
9	Ryan	Millwall	23	26	10	86	101
10	Muscat	Millwall	24	26	10	86	99
11	Dailly	West Ham	38	48	16	92	99
12	Breckin	Wigan	41	45	17	92	96
13	Jackson	Wigan	21	24	8	92	95
14	Babb	Sunderland	21	28	8	92	94
15	Pearce	West Ham	23	26	9	92	93

CHART-TOPPING GOALKEEPERS

1 Green - Norwich	
Goals conceded in the League (CL)	39
Goals conceded in all comps (CA)	43
Counting Games League games when he played at least 70 minutes	46
Clean Sheets In games when he played at least 70 mins	18
Goals to Shots Ratio (GSR) The average number of shots on target per each League goal conceded	8.2
Defensive Rating Average number of minutes between League goals conceded while on pitch	106

	PLAYER	CLUB	CG	CON: LGE	ALL	CS	GSR	DEF RATE
1	Green	Norwich	46	39	43	18	8.2	106
2	Hoult	West Brom	44	39	44	19	5.1	100
3	James	West Ham	27	25	30	10	5.1	97
4	Filan	Wigan	45	42	44	17	5.3	96
5	Poom	Sunderland	43	40	48	17	5	95
6	Warner	Millwall	28	27	29	12	6.1	93
7	Bywater	West Ham	17	18	24	6	4	84
8	Kenny	Sheff Utd	27	30	32	9	5.3	79
9	Margetson	Cardiff	22	25	30	6	5.1	78
10	Walker	Walsall	42	52	58	10	5.5	73
11	de Goey	Stoke	36	45	46	11	5.8	70
12	Combe	Bradford	21	27	29	3	5	68
13	Shearer	Coventry	30	39	42	10	3.5	68
14	Ward	Nottm Forest	32	42	49	6	4.9	68
15	Hahnemann	Reading	36	47	55	10	4.4	68

PLAYER DISCIPLINARY RECORD

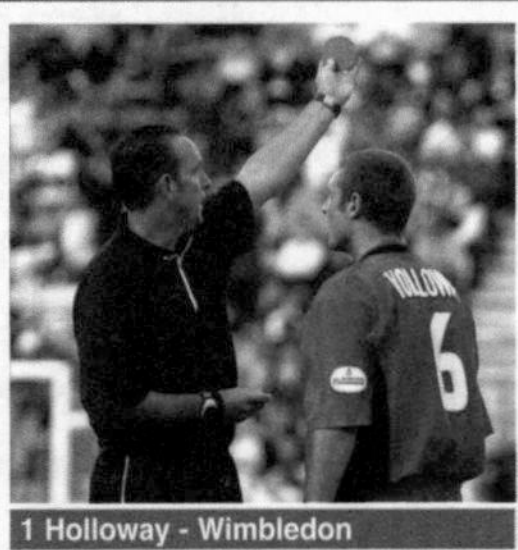

1 Holloway - Wimbledon	
Cards Average mins between cards	104
League Yellow	4
League Red	2
TOTAL	6

	PLAYER		LY	LR	TOT	AVE
1	Holloway	Wimbledon	4	2	6	104
2	Gnohere	Burnley	6	2	8	137
3	Thornton	Sunderland	8	1	9	148
4	Johnson	Gillingham	4	0	4	153
5	Baird	Walsall	3	2	5	169
6	Cahill	Millwall	18	2	20	176
7	Mullins	Crystal Palace	5	0	5	180
8	Whitlow	Sheff Utd	7	0	7	180
9	H'nthaler	Gillingham	12	1	13	189
10	Defoe	West Ham	5	3	8	196
11	Roberts	Wigan	4	2	6	197
12	Bradbury	Derby	3	0	3	198
13	Branston	Rotherham	2	1	3	202
14	Byfield	Sunderland	4	0	4	203
15	Dichio	Millwall	5	1	6	205
16	Harper	Norwich	2	1	3	206
17	Talbot	Rotherham	7	1	8	206
18	Eustace	Stoke	9	1	10	217
19	Kennedy	Wigan	3	1	4	218
20	B-Williams	Ipswich	9	0	9	220
21	Kamara	Wimbledon	7	0	7	222
22	Dinning	Wigan	4	0	4	223
23	Black	Crystal Palace	4	1	5	224
24	Mahon	Ipswich	3	0	3	228

TEAM OF THE SEASON

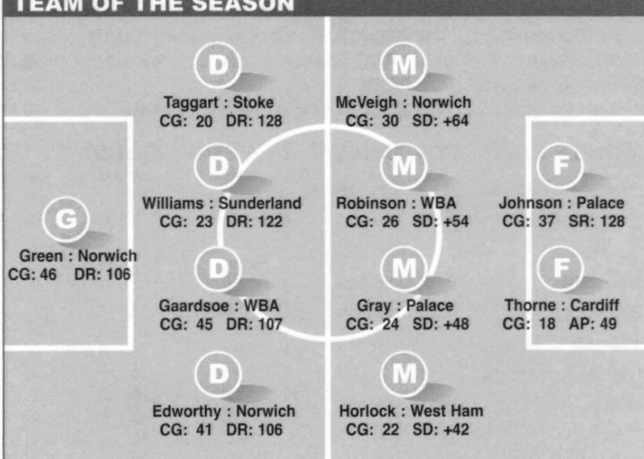

D
Taggart : Stoke
CG: 20 DR: 128
M
McVeigh : Norwich
CG: 30 SD: +64
D
Williams : Sunderland
CG: 23 DR: 122
M
Robinson : WBA
CG: 26 SD: +54
F
Johnson : Palace
CG: 37 SR: 128
G
Green : Norwich
CG: 46 DR: 106
D
Gaardsoe : WBA
CG: 45 DR: 107
M
Gray : Palace
CG: 24 SD: +48
F
Thorne : Cardiff
CG: 18 AP: 49
D
Edworthy : Norwich
CG: 41 DR: 106
M
Horlock : West Ham
CG: 22 SD: +42

NORWICH CITY

Final Position: **1ST**

NICKNAME: THE CANARIES   KEY: Won / Drawn / Lost

							Attendance
1	div1	**Bradford**	A	D	2-2	Rivers 44 pen; Easton 47	13,159
2	ccr1	**Northampton**	A	L	0-1		5,476
3	div1	**Rotherham**	H	W	2-0	Easton 9; Rivers 30	16,263
4	div1	**Sheff Utd**	A	L	0-1		24,285
5	div1	**Wimbledon**	H	W	3-2	Francis 10; Rivers 27 pen,56	16,082
6	div1	**Nottm Forest**	A	L	0-2		21,058
7	div1	**Burnley**	H	W	2-0	Crouch 58; Roberts 90	16,407
8	div1	**Gillingham**	A	W	2-1	Francis 28; Crouch 67	8,022
9	div1	**Stoke**	A	D	1-1	Huckerby 67	10,672
10	div1	**Crystal Palace**	H	W	2-1	Huckerby 38 pen; Mackay 89	16,425
11	div1	**Reading**	H	W	2-1	Huckerby 17; McVeigh 87	16,387
12	div1	**Wigan**	A	D	1-1	Roberts 63	9,346
13	div1	**West Ham**	A	D	1-1	Crouch 63	31,308
14	div1	**West Brom**	A	L	0-1		24,966
15	div1	**Derby**	H	W	2-1	Roberts 81 pen; Mulryne 90	16,346
16	div1	**Sunderland**	H	W	1-0	Francis 33	16,427
17	div1	**Walsall**	A	W	3-1	Henderson 52; McVeigh 60; Crouch 64	8,331
18	div1	**Millwall**	H	W	3-1	McVeigh 12; Henderson 15,30	16,423
19	div1	**Watford**	H	L	1-2	Jarvis 88	16,420
20	div1	**Preston**	A	D	0-0		14,775
21	div1	**Coventry**	H	D	1-1	Henderson 35	16,414
22	div1	**Crewe**	H	W	1-0	Huckerby 39	16,367
23	div1	**Millwall**	A	D	0-0		9,850
24	div1	**Cardiff**	H	W	4-1	Huckerby 34; Roberts 54; Fleming 71; Vidmar 79 og	16,428
25	div1	**Ipswich**	A	W	2-0	McKenzie 37,76	30,152
26	div1	**Nottm Forest**	H	W	1-0	Svensson 14	16,429
27	div1	**Derby**	A	W	4-0	Fleming 51; Mackay 78; McVeigh 81; McKenzie 88 pen	23,783
28	facr3	**Everton**	A	L	1-3	Brennan 27	29,955
29	div1	**Bradford**	H	L	0-1		16,360
30	div1	**Rotherham**	A	D	4-4	Roberts 29; McKenzie 33; Huckerby 45 pen; Francis 89	7,448
31	div1	**Sheff Utd**	H	W	1-0	Roberts 59	18,977
32	div1	**Wimbledon**	A	W	1-0	Huckerby 16	7,368
33	div1	**Coventry**	A	W	2-0	Holt 38; Brennan 85	15,757
34	div1	**West Ham**	H	D	1-1	Huckerby 76	23,940
35	div1	**West Brom**	H	D	0-0		23,223
36	div1	**Ipswich**	H	W	3-1	Mackay 50,59; Huckerby 88	23,942
37	div1	**Cardiff**	A	L	1-2	McKenzie 55	16,317
38	div1	**Gillingham**	H	W	3-0	Pouton 63 og; Mulryne 65; McVeigh 67	23,198
39	div1	**Crystal Palace**	A	L	0-1		23,798
40	div1	**Stoke**	H	W	1-0	Svensson 45	23,565
41	div1	**Burnley**	A	W	5-3	Svensson 14,62; Huckerby 32,89; McKenzie 51	12,417
42	div1	**Wigan**	H	W	2-0	Svensson 55; Huckerby 72	23,446
43	div1	**Reading**	A	W	1-0	Mulryne 86	18,460
44	div1	**Walsall**	H	W	5-0	Francis 2; McKenzie 45; Svensson 51,86; Huckerby 73	23,558
45	div1	**Watford**	A	W	2-1	Francis 29; McKenzie 48	19,290
46	div1	**Preston**	H	W	3-2	McKenzie 2; Francis 28; Huckerby 84	23,673
47	div1	**Sunderland**	A	L	0-1		35,174
48	div1	**Crewe**	A	W	3-1	Fleming 28; Roberts 31,88 pen	9,833

MONTHLY POINTS TALLY

AUGUST	7	47%
SEPTEMBER	13	87%
OCTOBER	8	53%
NOVEMBER	11	61%
DECEMBER	13	87%
JANUARY	4	44%
FEBRUARY	7	78%
MARCH	10	56%
APRIL	15	100%
MAY	6	67%

LEAGUE GOALS

	PLAYER	LGE	FAC	LC	Oth	TOT
1	Huckerby	**14**	0	0	0	14
2	McKenzie	**9**	0	0	0	9
3	Roberts	**8**	0	0	0	8
4	Francis	**7**	0	0	0	7
5	Svensson	**7**	0	0	0	7
6	McVeigh	**5**	0	0	0	5
7	Rivers	**4**	0	0	0	4
8	Mackay	**4**	0	0	0	4
9	Henderson	**4**	0	0	0	4
10	Crouch	**4**	0	0	0	4
11	Fleming	**3**	0	0	0	3
	Other	10	1	0	0	11
	TOTAL	79	1	0	0	80

KEY PLAYERS - GOALSCORERS

Mathias Svensson

Goals in the League	7
Goals in all competitions	7
Contribution to Attacking Power Average number of minutes between League team goals while on pitch	44
Player Strike Rate The total number of minutes he was on the pitch for every League goal scored	201
Club Strike Rate Average number of minutes between League goals scored by club	52

	PLAYER	GOALS LGE	GOALS ALL	POWER	S RATE
1	Mathias Svensson	7	7	44	201 mins
2	Darren Huckerby	14	14	51	224 mins
3	Peter Crouch	4	4	73	294 mins
4	Damian Francis	7	7	51	482 mins
5	Phillip Mulryne	3	3	48	545 mins

KEY PLAYERS - MIDFIELDERS

Phillip Mulryne

Goals in the League	3
Goals in all competitions	3
Defensive Rating Average number of mins between League goals conceded while on the pitch	117
Contribution to Attacking Power Average number of minutes between League team goals while on pitch	48
Scoring Difference Defensive Rating minus Contribution to Attacking Power	69

	PLAYER	GOALS LGE	GOALS ALL	DEF RATE	ATT POWER	SCORE DIFF
1	Phillip Mulryne	3	3	117	48	69 mins
2	Paul McVeigh	5	5	121	57	64 mins
3	Gary Holt	1	1	106	52	54 mins
4	Damian Francis	7	7	94	51	43 mins

KEY PLAYERS - DEFENDERS

Marc Edworthy

Goals Conceded in League	35
Goals Conceded in all competitions	39
Clean Sheets In League games when he played at least 70 mins	17
Defensive Rating Ave number of mins between League goals conceded while on the pitch	106
Club Defensive Rating Average number of mins between League goals conceded by the club this season	106

	PLAYER	CON LGE	CON ALL	CLN SHEETS	DEF RATE
1	Marc Edworthy	35	39	17	106 mins
2	Craig Fleming	39	43	18	106 mins
3	Malcolm Mackay	38	42	18	106 mins
4	Adam Drury	36	40	15	103 mins

KEY GOALKEEPER

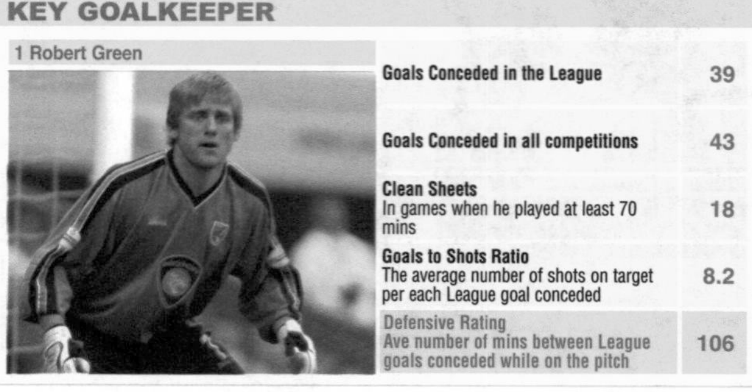

1 Robert Green

Goals Conceded in the League	39
Goals Conceded in all competitions	43
Clean Sheets In games when he played at least 70 mins	18
Goals to Shots Ratio The average number of shots on target per each League goal conceded	8.2
Defensive Rating Ave number of mins between League goals conceded while on the pitch	106

DISCIPLINARY RECORDS

	PLAYER	YELLOW	RED	AVE
1	Harper	2	1	206
2	Crouch	4	1	235
3	Henderson	4	0	280
4	Rivers	2	0	284
5	Cooper	2	0	303
6	Mulryne	4	0	408
7	Roberts	3	0	441
8	Svensson	3	0	470
9	McKenzie	2	0	523
10	Huckerby	5	0	626
11	Mackay	5	1	673
12	Francis	5	0	674
13	Easton	1	0	735
	Other	22	0	
	TOTAL	64	3	

TOP POINT EARNERS

	PLAYER	GAMES	AV PTS
1	Mathias Svensson	16	**2.44**
2	Peter Crouch	14	**2.29**
3	Damian Francis	35	**2.14**
4	Paul McVeigh	30	**2.10**
5	Darren Huckerby	34	**2.09**
6	Adam Drury	40	**2.08**
7	Marc Edworthy	41	**2.05**
8	Gary Holt	46	**2.04**
9	Robert Green	46	**2.04**
10	Craig Fleming	46	**2.04**
	CLUB AVERAGE:		**2.04**

LEAGUE APPEARANCES AND BOOKINGS

	AGE (on 01/07/04)	IN NAMED 16	APPEARANCES	COUNTING GAMES	MINUTES ON PITCH	Yellow	Red
Goalkeepers							
Paul Crichton	35	39	0	0	0	0	0
Robert Green	24	46	46	46	4140	1	0
Joe Lewis	16	7	0	0	0	0	0
Defenders							
Jim Brennan	27	24	15	5	718	0	0
Keith Briggs	22	5	3	0	96	0	0
Adam Drury	25	42	42	40	3717	3	0
Marc Edworthy	31	42	42	41	3723	5	0
Craig Fleming	32	46	46	46	4140	3	0
Malcolm Mackay	32	45	45	45	4038	5	1
Midfielders							
Kevin Cooper	29	10	10	4	606	2	0
Clint Easton	26	17	11	5	735	1	0
Damian Francis	25	46	41	35	3371	5	0
Kevin Harper	28	9	9	6	620	2	1
Gary Holt	31	46	46	46	4131	5	0
Paul McVeigh	26	44	44	30	3137	4	0
Phillip Mulryne	26	44	34	14	1635	4	0
Mark Rivers	28	16	12	3	569	2	0
Jason Shackell	20	10	6	4	395	0	0
Forwards							
Zema Abbey	27	3	3	0	72	0	0
Peter Crouch	23	15	15	14	1176	4	1
Elvis Hammond	23	4	4	0	110	0	0
Ian Henderson	19	30	19	9	1121	4	0
Darren Huckerby	28	36	36	34	3134	5	0
Ryan Jarvis	17	18	12	0	121	0	0
Leon McKenzie	26	22	18	11	1047	2	0
David Nielsen	27	2	2	2	175	1	0
Alex Notman	24	4	1	0	21	0	0
Iwan Roberts	36	43	41	9	1324	3	0
Mathias Svensson	29	21	20	16	1410	3	0

TEAM OF THE SEASON

G — Robert Green, CG: 46 DR: 106

D — Marc Edworthy, CG: 41 DR: 106
D — Craig Fleming, CG: 46 DR: 106
D — Malcolm Mackay, CG: 45 DR: 106
D — Adam Drury, CG: 40 DR: 103

M — Phillip Mulryne, CG: 14 SD: 69
M — Paul McVeigh, CG: 30 SD: 64
M — Gary Holt, CG: 46 SD: 54
M — Damian Francis, CG: 35 SD: 43

F — Mathias Svensson, CG: 16 SR: 201
F — Darren Huckerby, CG: 34 SR: 224

SQUAD APPEARANCES

Match	1	2	3	4	5	6	7	8	9	10	11	12	13	14	15	16	17	18	19	20	21	22	23	24	25	26	27	28	29	30	31	32	33	34	35	36	37	38	39	40	41	42	43	44	45	46	47	48
Venue	A	A	H	A	H	A	H	A	A	H	H	A	A	A	H	H	A	H	H	A	H	H	A	H	A	H	A	A	H	A	H	A	A	H	H	H	A	H	A	H	A	H	A	H	A	H	A	A
Competition	L	W	L	L	L	L	L	L	L	L	L	L	L	L	L	L	L	L	L	L	L	L	L	L	L	L	L	F	L	L	L	L	L	L	L	L	L	L	L	L	L	L	L	L	L	L	L	L
Result	D	L	W	L	W	L	W	W	D	W	W	D	D	L	W	W	W	W	L	D	D	W	D	W	W	W	W	L	L	D	W	W	W	D	D	W	L	W	L	W	W	W	W	W	W	W	L	W

Goalkeepers
Paul Crichton
Robert Green
Joe Lewis

Defenders
Jim Brennan
Keith Briggs
Adam Drury
Marc Edworthy
Craig Fleming
Malcolm Mackay

Midfielders
Kevin Cooper
Clint Easton
Damian Francis
Kevin Harper
Gary Holt
Paul McVeigh
Phillip Mulryne
Mark Rivers
Jason Shackell

Forwards
Zema Abbey
Peter Crouch
Elvis Hammond
Ian Henderson
Darren Huckerby
Ryan Jarvis
Leon McKenzie
David Nielsen
Alex Notman
Iwan Roberts
Mathias Svensson

KEY: ■ On all match; ■ On bench; ⏮ Subbed or sent off (Counting game); « Subbed or sent off (playing less than 70 minutes); ⏭ Subbed on from bench (Counting Game); » Subbed on (playing less than 70 minutes); Subbed on and then subbed or sent off (Counting Game); Subbed on and then subbed or sent off (playing less than 70 minutes); □ Not in 16

WEST BROMWICH ALBION

Final Position: **2nd**

NICKNAME: BAGGIES KEY: Won Drawn Lost

					Score	Scorers	Attendance
1	div1	Walsall	A	L	1-4	Koumas 70	11,030
2	ccR1	Brentford	H	W	4-0	Hulse 18,76; Haas 74; Dobie 90	10,440
3	div1	Burnley	H	W	4-1	Sakiri 31; Hulse 59; Hughes 88,89	22,489
4	div1	Watford	A	W	1-0	Hughes 56	15,023
5	div1	Preston	H	W	1-0	Hughes 45 pen	24,402
6	div1	Derby	A	W	1-0	Hulse 76	21,499
7	div1	Ipswich	H	W	4-1	Gaardsoe 11; Hulse 16,57; Diallo 86	24,954
8	div1	Wigan	A	L	0-1		12,874
9	div1	Crystal Palace	A	D	2-2	Hulse 52; Koumas 89	17,477
10	ccR2	Hartlepool	A	W	2-1	Clement 61; Hulse 81	5,265
11	div1	Stoke	H	W	1-0	Dobie 59	24,297
12	div1	Millwall	H	W	2-1	Koumas 5; Dobie 24	22,909
13	div1	Gillingham	A	W	2-0	Dobie 26; Clement 29	8,883
14	div1	Sheff Utd	H	L	0-2		27,195
15	div1	Norwich	H	W	1-0	Koumas 35	24,966
16	div1	Wimbledon	H	L	0-1		22,048
17	div1	Rotherham	A	W	3-0	Barker, S 39 og; Hulse 49,65	7,815
18	ccR3	Newcastle	A	W	2-1	Ameobi 29 og; Hughes 101	46,932
19	div1	Sunderland	H	D	0-0		26,135
20	div1	West Ham	A	W	4-3	Hulse 25,40; Deane 66 og; Hughes 77	30,359
21	div1	Reading	H	D	0-0		22,839
22	div1	Cardiff	A	D	1-1	Koumas 49	17,678
23	div1	Nottm Forest	A	W	3-0	Koumas 38,90; Louis-Jean 44 og	27,331
24	ccR4	Man Utd	H	W	2-0	Haas 6; Dobie 56	25,282
25	div1	West Ham	H	D	1-1	Mullins 80 og	26,194
26	div1	Bradford	A	W	1-0	Dobie 88	11,198
27	div1	Crewe	H	D	2-2	Haas 7; Gregan 72	22,825
28	ccQF	Arsenal	H	L	0-2		20,369
29	div1	Coventry	A	L	0-1		17,616
30	div1	Derby	H	D	1-1	Gaardsoe 90	26,412
31	div1	Wimbledon	A	D	0-0		6,376
32	facr3	Nottm Forest	A	L	0-1		11,843
33	div1	Walsall	H	W	2-0	Koumas 62; Horsfield 72	24,558
34	div1	Burnley	A	D	1-1	Horsfield 73	13,106
35	div1	Watford	H	W	3-1	Horsfield 41,66; Hughes 61	23,958
36	div1	Preston	A	L	0-3		16,569
37	div1	Cardiff	H	W	2-1	Clement 55; Hughes 85	25,196
38	div1	Sheff Utd	A	W	2-1	Moore 70; Gaardsoe 85	34,805
39	div1	Rotherham	H	L	0-1		24,104
40	div1	Norwich	A	D	0-0		23,223
41	div1	Coventry	H	W	3-0	Horsfield 23; Hughes 53; Kinsella 79	25,414
42	div1	Crewe	A	W	2-1	Johnson 69; Hughes 73	8,335
43	div1	Wigan	H	W	2-1	Hughes 77 pen; Gaardsoe 90	26,215
44	div1	Crystal Palace	H	W	2-0	Moore 81; Dyer 86	24,990
45	div1	Ipswich	A	W	3-2	Koumas 71; Dyer 73; Horsfield 90	24,608
46	div1	Gillingham	H	W	1-0	Hughes 79	24,524
47	div1	Millwall	A	D	1-1	Johnson 55	13,304
48	div1	Sunderland	A	W	1-0	Koumas 90	32,201
49	div1	Bradford	H	W	2-0	Horsfield 55; Hughes 60	26,143
50	div1	Reading	A	L	0-1		20,619
51	div1	Stoke	A	L	1-4	Dobie 50	18,352
52	div1	Nottm Forest	H	L	0-2		26,821

KEY PLAYERS - GOALSCORERS

Lee Hughes

Goals in the League	11
Goals in all competitions	12
Contribution to Attacking Power Average number of minutes between League team goals while on pitch	56
Player Strike Rate The total number of minutes he was on the pitch for every League goal scored	170
Club Strike Rate Average number of minutes between League goals scored by club	65

	PLAYER	GOALS LGE	GOALS ALL	POWER	S RATE
1	Lee Hughes	11	12	56	170 mins
2	Geoff Horsfield	7	7	73	231 mins
3	Robert Hulse	9	12	62	257 mins
4	Jason Koumas	10	10	70	325 mins
5	Darren Moore	2	2	67	875 mins

KEY PLAYERS - MIDFIELDERS

Paul Robinson

WEST BROMWICH
BUILDING SOCIETY

Goals in the League	0
Goals in all competitions	0
Defensive Rating Average number of mins between League goals conceded while on the pitch	112
Contribution to Attacking Power Average number of minutes between League team goals while on pitch	61
Scoring Difference Defensive Rating minus Contribution to Attacking Power	51

	PLAYER	GOALS LGE	GOALS ALL	DEF RATE	ATT POWER	SCORE DIFF
1	Paul Robinson	0	0	112	61	51 mins
2	Andy Johnson	2	2	105	55	50 mins
3	Sean Gregan	1	1	92	65	27 mins
4	Jason Koumas	10	10	96	71	25 mins
5	James O'Connor	0	0	93	75	18 mins

KEY PLAYERS - DEFENDERS

Phil Gilchrist

WEST BROMWICH
BUILDING SOCIETY

Goals Conceded in League	12
Goals Conceded in all competitions	14
Clean Sheets In League games when he played at least 70 mins	7
Defensive Rating Ave number of mins between League goals conceded while on the pitch	116
Club Defensive Rating Average number of mins between League goals conceded by the club this season	99

	PLAYER	CON LGE	CON ALL	CLN SHEETS	DEF RATE
1	Phil Gilchrist	12	14	7	116 mins
2	Thomas Gaardsoe	38	42	19	107 mins
3	Neil Clement	27	31	8	89 mins
4	Bernt Haas	36	41	13	89 mins
5	Darren Moore	21	22	6	83 mins

MONTHLY POINTS TALLY

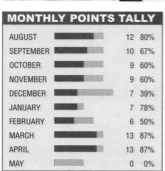

AUGUST	12	80%
SEPTEMBER	10	67%
OCTOBER	9	60%
NOVEMBER	9	60%
DECEMBER	7	39%
JANUARY	7	78%
FEBRUARY	6	50%
MARCH	13	87%
APRIL	13	87%
MAY	0	0%

LEAGUE GOALS

	PLAYER	LGE	FAC	LC	Oth	TOT
1	Hughes	11	0	1	0	12
2	Koumas	10	0	0	0	10
3	Hulse	9	0	3	0	12
4	Horsfield	7	0	0	0	7
5	Dobie	5	0	2	0	7
6	Gaardsoe	4	0	0	0	4
7	Clement	2	0	1	0	3
8	Dyer	2	0	0	0	2
9	Johnson	2	0	0	0	2
10	Moore	2	0	0	0	2
11	Kinsella	1	0	0	0	1
	Other	9	0	3	0	12
	TOTAL	**64**	**0**	**10**	**0**	**74**

KEY GOALKEEPER

1 Russell Hoult

Goals Conceded in the League	39
Goals Conceded in all competitions	44
Clean Sheets In games when he played at least 70 mins	19
Goals to Shots Ratio The average number of shots on target per each League goal conceded	5.1
Defensive Rating Ave number of mins between League goals conceded while on the pitch	100

DISCIPLINARY RECORDS

	PLAYER	YELLOW	RED	AVE
1	Haas	8	0	401
2	Koumas	5	2	463
3	Hughes	4	0	467
4	Gregan	7	0	511
5	Robinson	5	0	513
6	Kinsella	2	0	535
7	O'Connor	4	0	560
8	Hulse	3	1	579
9	Gaardsoe	5	1	675
10	Dobie	2	0	795
11	Horsfield	2	0	807
12	Volmer	1	0	952
13	Johnson	2	1	979
	Other	7	0	
	TOTAL	57	5	

TOP POINT EARNERS

	PLAYER	GAMES	AV PTS
1	Lee Hughes	13	**2.31**
2	Paul Robinson	26	**2.08**
3	Andy Johnson	31	**2.06**
4	Robert Hulse	20	**2.00**
5	Neil Clement	24	**1.92**
6	Thomas Gaardsoe	45	**1.91**
7	Darren Moore	19	**1.89**
8	James O'Connor	21	**1.86**
9	Bernt Haas	36	**1.83**
10	Sean Gregan	37	**1.81**
	CLUB AVERAGE:		**1.87**

TEAM OF THE SEASON

G	Russell Hoult	CG: 43 DR: 100
D	Phil Gilchrist	CG: 15 DR: 116
D	Thomas Gaardsoe	CG: 45 DR: 107
D	Neil Clement	CG: 24 DR: 89
D	Bernt Haas	CG: 36 DR: 89
M	Paul Robinson	CG: 26 SD: 51
M	Andy Johnson	CG: 31 SD: 50
M	Sean Gregan	CG: 37 SD: 27
M	Jason Koumas	CG: 33 SD: 25
F	Lee Hughes	CG: 13 SR: 170
F	Geoff Horsfield	CG: 16 SR: 231

LEAGUE APPEARANCES AND BOOKINGS

	AGE (on 01/07/04)	IN NAMED 16	APPEARANCES	COUNTING GAMES	MINUTES ON PITCH	Yellow	Red
Goalkeepers							
Russell Hoult	31	44	44	43	3915	0	0
Joe Murphy	23	46	4	2	262	0	0
Kevin Pressman	36	2	0	0	0	0	0
Defenders							
Sehou Berthe	26	4	3	2	216	0	0
James Chambers	23	22	13	11	992	1	0
Neil Clement	25	45	35	24	2398	1	0
Thomas Gaardsoe	24	45	45	45	4050	5	1
Phil Gilchrist	30	20	17	15	1392	1	0
Bernt Haas	26	38	36	36	3215	8	0
Darren Moore	30	23	22	19	1750	1	0
Alassane Ndour	22	5	2	1	155	0	0
Larus Sigurdsson	31	5	5	3	337	2	0
Joost Volmer	30	20	15	9	952	1	0
Ronnie Wallwork	26	8	5	2	324	1	0
Midfielders							
Adam Chambers	23	4	4	2	231	0	0
Lloyd Dyer	21	20	17	2	548	0	0
Sean Gregan	30	43	43	37	3579	7	0
Andy Johnson	30	38	37	31	2937	2	1
Mark Kinsella	31	18	18	8	1070	2	0
Jason Koumas	24	42	42	33	3247	5	2
James O'Connor	24	32	30	21	2240	4	0
Paul Robinson	25	31	31	26	2566	5	0
Artim Sakiri	30	31	25	1	883	0	0
Forwards							
Danny Dichio	29	13	11	1	397	0	0
Scott Dobie	25	31	31	9	1590	2	0
Delroy Facey	24	12	9	0	274	0	0
Geoff Horsfield	30	20	20	16	1614	2	0
Lee Hughes	28	36	32	13	1869	4	0
Robert Hulse	24	35	33	20	2317	3	1
Morten Skoubo	24	3	2	0	24	0	0

SQUAD APPEARANCES

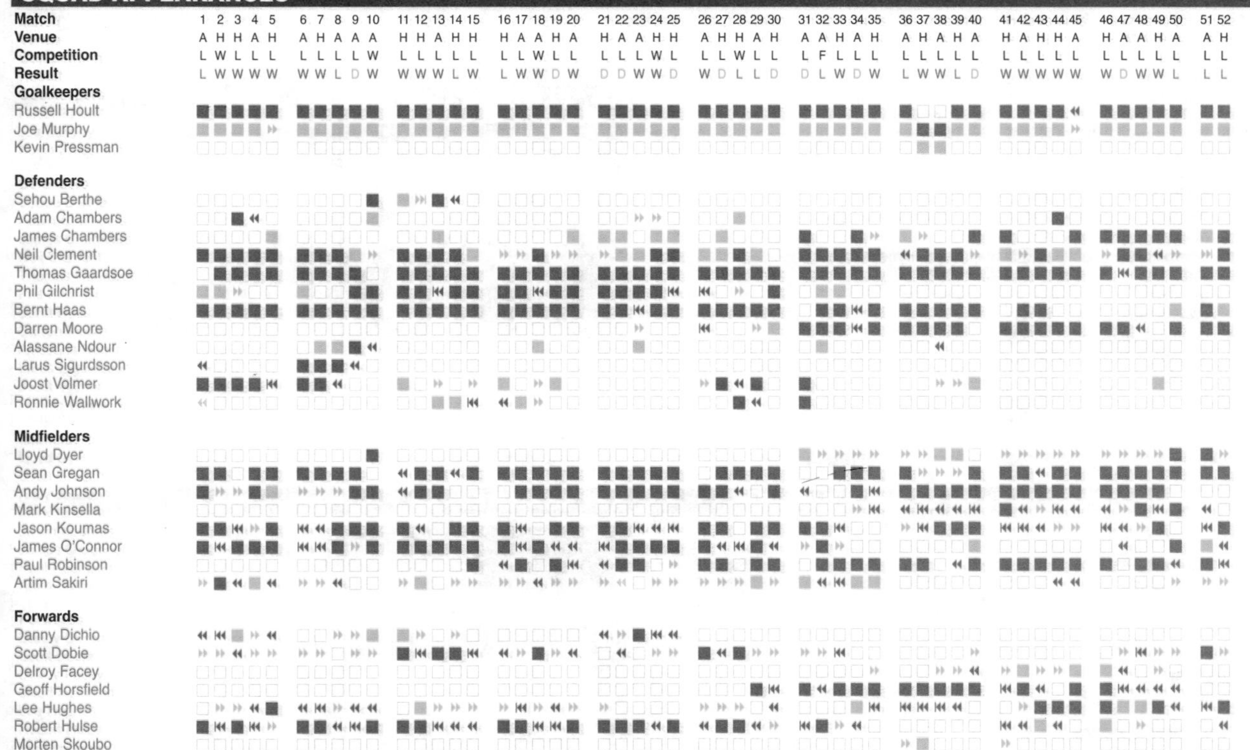
Match 1 2 3 4 5 6 7 8 9 10 11 12 13 14 15 16 17 18 19 20 21 22 23 24 25 26 27 28 29 30 31 32 33 34 35 36 37 38 39 40 41 42 43 44 45 46 47 48 49 50 51 52
Venue A H H A H A H A A A H H A H H H A A H A H A A H H A H H A H A A H A H H A H A A H A H H A H A A H A A H
Competition L W L L L L L L L W L L L L L L L W L L L L L W L L L W L L L F L L L L L L L L L L L L L L L L L L L L
Result L W W W W W W L D W W W W L W L W W D W D D W W D W D L L D D L W D W L W W L D W W W W W W D W W L L L
Goalkeepers
Russell Hoult
Joe Murphy
Kevin Pressman
Defenders
Sehou Berthe
Adam Chambers
James Chambers
Neil Clement
Thomas Gaardsoe
Phil Gilchrist
Bernt Haas
Darren Moore
Alassane Ndour
Larus Sigurdsson
Joost Volmer
Ronnie Wallwork
Midfielders
Lloyd Dyer
Sean Gregan
Andy Johnson
Mark Kinsella
Jason Koumas
James O'Connor
Paul Robinson
Artim Sakiri
Forwards
Danny Dichio
Scott Dobie
Delroy Facey
Geoff Horsfield
Lee Hughes
Robert Hulse
Morten Skoubo

KEY: On all match; On bench; Subbed or sent off (Counting game); Subbed or sent off (playing less than 70 minutes); Subbed on from bench (Counting Game); Subbed on (playing less than 70 minutes); Subbed on and then subbed or sent off (Counting Game); Subbed on and then subbed or sent off (playing less than 70 minutes); Not in 16

SUNDERLAND

Final Position: **3rd**

NICKNAME: MACKEMS/BLACKCATS   KEY: ☐ Won ☐ Drawn ☐ Lost

							Attendance
1	div1	Nottm Forest	A	L	0-2		23,529
2	ccR1	Mansfield	A	W	2-1	Artell 18 og; Kyle 90	5,665
3	div1	Millwall	H	L	0-1		24,877
4	div1	Preston	A	W	2-0	Thornton 4; Stewart 41	14,018
5	div1	Watford	H	W	2-0	Stewart 40 pen; Wright 67	23,600
6	div1	Bradford	A	W	4-0	Breen 10; Stewart 15; Arca 31; Thornton 76	14,116
7	div1	Crystal Palace	H	W	2-1	Kyle 46; Stewart 90 pen	27,324
8	div1	Stoke	A	L	1-3	Kyle 54	15,005
9	div1	Derby	A	D	1-1	Poom 90	22,535
10	ccR2	Huddersfield	H	L	2-4	Kyle 25,90	13,516
11	div1	Reading	H	W	2-0	Arca 28; Oster 32	22,420
12	div1	Ipswich	H	W	3-2	Breen 44; Oster 49; Kyle 85	24,840
13	div1	Sheff Utd	A	W	1-0	Kyle 68	27,008
14	div1	Cardiff	H	D	0-0		26,835
15	div1	Walsall	H	W	1-0	Stewart 42	36,278
16	div1	Rotherham	H	D	0-0		24,506
17	div1	Norwich	A	L	0-1		16,427
18	div1	West Brom	A	D	0-0		26,135
19	div1	Gillingham	A	W	3-1	Downing 45; Oster 58; Stewart 72	9,066
20	div1	Coventry	H	D	0-0		27,247
21	div1	Crewe	A	L	0-3		9,807
22	div1	Burnley	H	D	1-1	Kyle 39	29,852
23	div1	Wigan	H	D	1-1	Downing 82 pen	22,167
24	div1	Coventry	A	D	1-1	Downing 8	12,913
25	div1	West Ham	A	L	2-3	McAteer 4; Oster 30	30,329
26	div1	Wimbledon	H	W	2-1	Stewart 27 pen; Proctor 90	22,334
27	div1	Bradford	H	W	3-0	McAteer 43; Smith 67; Kyle 82	29,639
28	div1	Rotherham	A	W	2-0	Stewart 30,41 pen	11,455
29	facr3	Hartlepool	H	W	1-0	Arca 53	40,816
30	div1	Nottm Forest	H	W	1-0	Arca 38	26,340
31	div1	Millwall	A	L	1-2	Stewart 30	13,048
32	facr4	Ipswich	A	W	2-1	Smith 45; Arca 68	21,406
33	div1	Watford	A	D	2-2	Stewart 76; Byfield 86	16,798
34	facr5	Birmingham	H	D	1-1	Kyle 39	24,966
35	div1	Cardiff	A	L	0-4		17,337
36	facr5r	Birmingham	A	W	2-0	Smith 99,115	25,645
37	div1	Walsall	A	W	3-1	Arca 18; Kyle 54; Stewart 81	7,185
38	facqf	Sheff Utd	H	W	1-0	Smith 15	37,115
39	div1	Preston	H	D	3-3	Mears 25 og; Thornton 70; Stewart 84 pen	27,181
40	div1	West Ham	H	W	2-0	Kyle 61; Whitley 76	29,533
41	div1	Stoke	H	D	1-1	Byfield 69	24,510
42	div1	Reading	A	W	2-0	Byfield 73; Smith 74	18,019
43	div1	Gillingham	H	W	2-1	Thornton 11; Byfield 53	23,262
44	div1	Derby	H	W	2-1	Oster 31; Smith 50	30,838
45	facsf	Millwall	H	L	0-1		56,112
46	div1	Wimbledon	A	W	2-1	Stewart 45; Byfield 73	4,800
47	div1	Sheff Utd	H	W	3-0	Smith 7; Breen 65; Kyle 90	27,472
48	div1	Ipswich	A	L	0-1		26,801
49	div1	West Brom	H	L	0-1		32,201
50	div1	Crystal Palace	A	L	0-3		18,291
51	div1	Wigan	A	D	0-0		11,380
52	div1	Crewe	H	D	1-1	Whitley 25	25,311
53	div1	Norwich	H	W	1-0	Robinson 44	35,174
54	div1	Burnley	A	W	2-1	Breen 37; Kyle 66	18,852
55	d1po1	Crystal Palace	A	L	2-3	Stewart 51 pen; Kyle 85	25,287
56	d1po2	Crystal Palace	H	L	4-5*	Kyle 42; Stewart 45 (*on penalties)	34,536

MONTHLY POINTS TALLY

Month	Points	%
AUGUST	9	60%
SEPTEMBER	10	67%
OCTOBER	8	53%
NOVEMBER	6	40%
DECEMBER	11	61%
JANUARY	3	50%
FEBRUARY	1	17%
MARCH	17	81%
APRIL	7	39%
MAY	7	78%

LEAGUE GOALS

	PLAYER	LGE	FAC	LC	Oth	TOT
1	Stewart	14	0	0	2	16
2	Kyle	10	1	3	2	16
3	Oster	5	0	0	0	5
4	Byfield	5	0	0	0	5
5	Thornton	4	0	0	0	4
6	Breen	4	0	0	0	4
7	Arca	4	2	0	0	6
8	Smith	4	4	0	0	8
9	Downing	3	0	0	0	3
10	McAteer	2	0	0	0	2
11	Whitley	2	0	0	0	2
	Other	5	0	1	0	6
	TOTAL	62	7	4	4	77

KEY PLAYERS - GOALSCORERS

Marcus Stewart

Goals in the League	14
Goals in all competitions	16
Contribution to Attacking Power Average number of minutes between League team goals while on pitch	65
Player Strike Rate The total number of minutes he was on the pitch for every League goal scored	187
Club Strike Rate Average number of minutes between League goals scored by club	67

	PLAYER	GOALS LGE	GOALS ALL	POWER	S RATE
1	Marcus Stewart	14	16	65	187 mins
2	Sean Thornton	4	4	53	335 mins
3	Kevin Kyle	10	16	68	336 mins
4	Tommy Smith	4	8	64	464 mins
5	John Oster	5	5	64	604 mins

KEY PLAYERS - MIDFIELDERS

Sean Thornton

Goals in the League	4
Goals in all competitions	4
Defensive Rating Average number of mins between League goals conceded while on the pitch	112
Contribution to Attacking Power Average number of minutes between League team goals while on pitch	54
Scoring Difference Defensive Rating minus Contribution to Attacking Power	58

	PLAYER	GOALS LGE	GOALS ALL	DEF RATE	ATT POWER	SCORE DIFF
1	Sean Thornton	4	4	112	54	58 mins
2	Paul Thirlwell	0	0	83	51	32 mins
3	John Oster	5	5	94	64	30 mins
4	Julio Arca	4	6	88	68	20 mins
5	Colin Healy	0	0	108	89	19 mins

KEY PLAYERS - DEFENDERS

Darren Williams

Goals Conceded in League	18
Goals Conceded in all competitions	23
Clean Sheets In League games when he played at least 70 mins	8
Defensive Rating Ave number of mins between League goals conceded while on the pitch	122
Club Defensive Rating Average number of mins between League goals conceded by the club this season	92

	PLAYER	CON LGE	CON ALL	CLN SHEETS	DEF RATE
1	Darren Williams	18	23	8	122 mins
2	Gary Breen	27	33	14	102 mins
3	Phil Babb	21	28	8	94 mins
4	Joachim Bjorklund	20	26	6	92 mins
5	George McCartney	39	50	14	89 mins

KEY GOALKEEPER

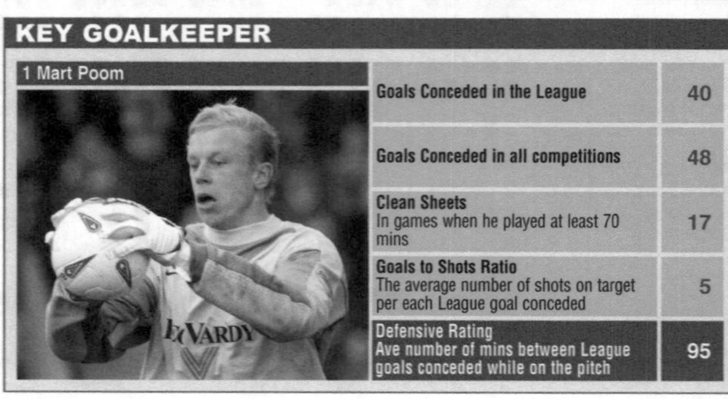

1 Mart Poom

Goals Conceded in the League	40
Goals Conceded in all competitions	48
Clean Sheets In games when he played at least 70 mins	17
Goals to Shots Ratio The average number of shots on target per each League goal conceded	5
Defensive Rating Ave number of mins between League goals conceded while on the pitch	95

DISCIPLINARY RECORDS

	PLAYER	YELLOW	RED	AVE
1	Thornton	8	1	148
2	Byfield	4	0	203
3	Arca	7	2	302
4	Whitley	7	2	318
5	Williams	6	0	365
6	Kyle	8	1	372
7	Thirlwell	5	0	380
8	McAteer	4	0	399
9	Wright	4	0	439
10	Babb	4	0	495
11	Breen	5	0	551
12	Butler	1	0	592
13	Bjorklund	2	1	616
	Other	15	2	
	TOTAL	80	9	

TOP POINT EARNERS

	PLAYER	GAMES	AV PTS
1	Sean Thornton	14	**2.21**
2	Paul Thirlwell	18	**2.00**
3	John Oster	29	**1.93**
4	Gary Breen	30	**1.93**
5	Marcus Stewart	27	**1.93**
6	Phil Babb	22	**1.86**
7	George McCartney	38	**1.79**
8	Mart Poom	42	**1.74**
9	Darren Williams	23	**1.70**
10	Julio Arca	30	**1.67**
	CLUB AVERAGE:		**1.72**

LEAGUE APPEARANCES AND BOOKINGS

	AGE (on 01/07/04)	IN NAMED 16	APPEARANCES	COUNTING GAMES	MINUTES ON PITCH	Yellow	Red
Goalkeepers							
Ben Alnwick	-	4	0	0	0	0	0
Michael Ingham	23	31	0	0	0	0	0
Ewan McLean	18	1	0	0	0	0	0
Thomas Myhre	30	13	4	4	339	0	0
Mart Poom	32	43	43	42	3800	1	1
Defenders							
Phil Babb	33	26	22	22	1980	4	0
Joachim Bjorklund	33	34	25	19	1849	2	1
Gary Breen	30	32	32	30	2758	5	0
Ben Clark	21	11	5	1	150	0	0
Michael Gray	29	1	1	0	24	0	0
Craig James	21	2	1	0	62	0	0
George McCartney	23	40	40	38	3483	5	0
Simon Ramsden	22	2	0	0	0	0	0
Darren Williams	27	38	29	23	2194	6	0
Stephen Wright	24	25	22	18	1758	4	0
Midfielders							
Julio Arca	23	31	31	30	2725	7	2
Chris Black	21	1	1	0	8	0	0
Thomas Butler	23	15	12	5	592	1	0
Kevin Cooper	29	7	4	0	35	0	0
Colin Healy	24	20	20	15	1513	1	0
Kevin Kilbane	27	5	5	4	415	0	0
Grant Leadbitter	18	2	0	0	0	0	0
Jason McAteer	33	19	19	16	1597	4	0
John Oster	25	40	38	29	3022	2	1
Alan Quinn	25	9	6	2	329	0	0
Carl Robinson	27	8	7	5	534	0	0
Paul Thirlwell	25	32	29	18	1902	5	0
Sean Thornton	21	27	22	14	1340	8	1
Jeff Whitley	25	35	33	30	2862	7	2
Forwards							
Darren Byfield	27	18	17	6	812	4	0
Stewart Downing	19	7	7	7	629	0	0
Tore Andre Flo	31	0	0	0	0	0	0
Kevin Kyle	23	44	44	32	3355	8	1
Matthew Piper	22	10	9	1	366	0	0
Mike Proctor	23	25	17	1	368	0	0
Tommy Smith	24	37	34	14	1856	2	0
Marcus Stewart	31	41	40	27	2622	4	0
Neil Taggart	19	0	0	0	0	0	0

TEAM OF THE SEASON

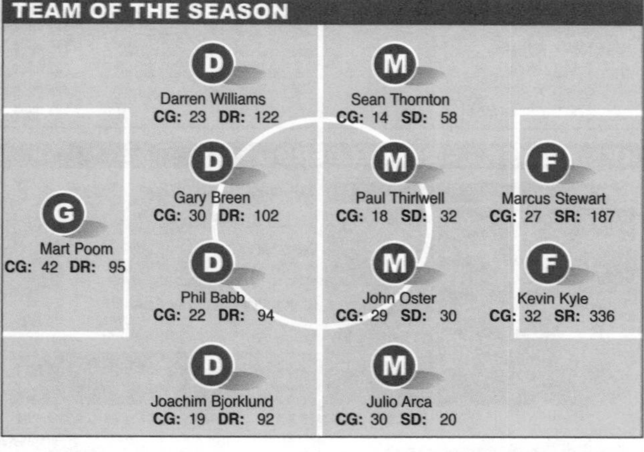

D
Darren Williams
CG: 23 DR: 122
D
Gary Breen
CG: 30 DR: 102
D
Phil Babb
CG: 22 DR: 94
D
Joachim Bjorklund
CG: 19 DR: 92
G
Mart Poom
CG: 42 DR: 95
M
Sean Thornton
CG: 14 SD: 58
M
Paul Thirlwell
CG: 18 SD: 32
M
John Oster
CG: 29 SD: 30
M
Julio Arca
CG: 30 SD: 20
F
Marcus Stewart
CG: 27 SR: 187
F
Kevin Kyle
CG: 32 SR: 336

SQUAD APPEARANCES

Match	1 2 3 4 5	6 7 8 9 10	11 12 13 14 15	16 17 18 19 20	21 22 23 24 25	26 27 28 29 30	31 32 33 34 35	36 37 38 39 40	41 42 43 44 45	46 47 48 49 50	51 52 53 54 55	56
Venue	A A H A H	A H A A H	H H A H H	H A A A H	A H H A A	H H A H H	A A A H A	A A H H H	H A H H H	A H A H A	A H H A A	H
Competition	L W L L L	L L L L W	L L L L L	L L L L L	L L L L L	L L L F L	L F L F L	F L F L L	L L L L F	L L L L L	L L L L O	O
Result	L W L W W	W W L D L	W W W D W	D L D W D	L D D D L	W W W W W	L W D D L	W W W D W	D W W W L	W W L L L	D D W W L	L

Goalkeepers
Ben Alnwick
Michael Ingham
Ewan McLean
Thomas Myhre
Mart Poom

Defenders
Phil Babb
Joachim Bjorklund
Gary Breen
Ben Clark
Michael Gray
Craig James
George McCartney
Simon Ramsden
Darren Williams
Stephen Wright

Midfielders
Julio Arca
Chris Black
Thomas Butler
Kevin Cooper
Colin Healy
Kevin Kilbane
Grant Leadbitter
Jason McAteer
John Oster
Alan Quinn
Carl Robinson
Paul Thirlwell
Sean Thornton
Jeff Whitley

Forwards

KEY: On all match; On bench; Subbed or sent off (Counting game); Subbed or sent off (playing less than 70 minutes); Subbed on from bench (Counting Game); Subbed on (playing less than 70 minutes); Subbed on and then subbed or sent off (Counting Game); Subbed on and then subbed or sent off (playing less than 70 minutes); Not in 16

WEST HAM UNITED

Final Position: **4th**

NICKNAME: THE HAMMERS

KEY: Won / Drawn / Lost

							Attendance
1	div1	**Preston**	A	W	2-1	Defoe 5; Connolly 69	18,246
2	ccr1	**Rushden & D**	H	W	3-1	Defoe 9; Connolly 14,78	13,715
3	div1	**Sheff Utd**	H	D	0-0		28,972
4	div1	**Rotherham**	A	L	0-1		8,739
5	div1	**Bradford**	H	W	1-0	Defoe 32	30,370
6	div1	**Ipswich**	A	W	2-1	Defoe 21; Connolly 47	29,679
7	div1	**Reading**	H	W	1-0	Dailly 17	32,634
8	div1	**Crewe**	A	W	3-0	Connolly 16,21; Etherington 25	9,575
9	div1	**Gillingham**	A	L	0-2		11,418
10	ccr2	**Cardiff**	A	W	3-2	Defoe 45 pen,88; Dailly 64	10,724
11	div1	**Millwall**	H	D	1-1	Connolly 25	31,626
12	div1	**Crystal Palace**	H	W	3-0	Defoe 19; Mellor 32,56	31,861
13	div1	**Derby**	A	W	1-0	Hutchison 90	22,810
14	div1	**Norwich**	H	D	1-1	Edworthy 6 og	31,308
15	div1	**Burnley**	H	D	2-2	Connolly 20; Hutchison 86	31,474
16	div1	**Nottm Forest**	H	D	1-1	Defoe 56	29,544
17	div1	**Cardiff**	A	D	0-0		19,202
18	ccr3	**Tottenham**	A	L	0-1		36,053
19	div1	**Coventry**	A	D	1-1	Defoe 15	19,126
20	div1	**West Brom**	H	L	3-4	Defoe 1; Deane 10,18	30,359
21	div1	**Watford**	A	D	0-0		20,950
22	div1	**Wimbledon**	A	D	1-1	Deane 51	8,118
23	div1	**Wigan**	H	W	4-0	Horlock 4; Jarrett 17 og; Harewood 55,75	34,375
24	div1	**West Brom**	A	D	1-1	Deane 68	26,194
25	div1	**Stoke**	H	L	0-1		24,365
26	div1	**Sunderland**	H	W	3-2	Defoe 55,61; Pearce 80	30,329
27	div1	**Walsall**	A	D	1-1	Harewood 10	9,272
28	div1	**Ipswich**	H	L	1-2	Defoe 49	35,021
29	div1	**Nottm Forest**	A	W	2-0	Harewood 7; Defoe 84	27,491
30	facr3	**Wigan**	A	W	2-1	Mullins 80; Connolly 85	11,793
31	div1	**Preston**	H	L	1-2	Connolly 19	28,777
32	div1	**Sheff Utd**	A	D	3-3	Carrick 19; Harley 22; Harewood 37	22,787
33	facr4	**Wolverhampton**	A	W	3-1	Deane 4; Harewood 21; Connolly 32	24,413
34	div1	**Rotherham**	H	W	2-1	Deane 15; Dailly 59	34,483
35	div1	**Bradford**	A	W	2-1	Zamora 65; Harewood 78	13,078
36	facr5	**Fulham**	A	D	0-0		14,705
37	div1	**Norwich**	A	D	1-1	Harewood 61	23,940
38	facr5r	**Fulham**	H	L	0-3		27,934
39	div1	**Cardiff**	H	W	1-0	Zamora 73	31,858
40	div1	**Burnley**	A	D	1-1	Connolly 36 pen	12,440
41	div1	**Walsall**	H	D	0-0		33,177
42	div1	**Wimbledon**	H	W	5-0	Etherington 37,49,70; Zamora 40; Reo-Coker 62	29,818
43	div1	**Sunderland**	A	L	0-2		29,533
44	div1	**Crewe**	H	W	4-2	Harewood 6,20; Reo-Coker 35; McAnuff 41	31,158
45	div1	**Millwall**	A	L	1-4	Harewood 49 pen	14,055
46	div1	**Gillingham**	H	W	2-1	Zamora 3; Etherington 76	34,551
47	div1	**Reading**	A	L	0-2		21,718
48	div1	**Derby**	H	D	0-0		28,207
49	div1	**Crystal Palace**	A	L	0-1		23,977
50	div1	**Coventry**	H	W	2-0	Zamora 37; Connolly 71 pen	27,890
51	div1	**Stoke**	A	W	2-0	Connolly 39; Harewood 59	18,227
52	div1	**Watford**	H	W	4-0	Hutchison 17; Dailly 44; Harewood 63 pen,90	34,685
53	div1	**Wigan**	A	D	1-1	Deane 90	20,669
54	d1po1	**Ipswich**	A	L	0-1		28,435
55	d1po2	**Ipswich**	H	W	2-0	Etherington 50; Dailly 71	34,002
56	d1pof	**Crystal Palace**	A	L	0-1		72,523

MONTHLY POINTS TALLY

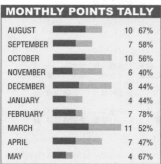

AUGUST	10	67%
SEPTEMBER	7	58%
OCTOBER	10	56%
NOVEMBER	6	40%
DECEMBER	8	44%
JANUARY	4	44%
FEBRUARY	7	78%
MARCH	11	52%
APRIL	7	47%
MAY	4	67%

LEAGUE GOALS

	PLAYER	LGE	FAC	LC	Oth	TOT
1	Harewood	**13**	1	0	0	14
2	Defoe	**11**	0	3	0	14
3	Connolly	**10**	2	2	0	14
4	Deane	**6**	1	0	0	7
5	Zamora	**5**	0	0	0	5
6	Etherington	**5**	0	0	1	6
7	Dailly	**3**	0	1	1	5
8	Hutchison	**3**	0	0	0	3
9	Mellor	**2**	0	0	0	2
10	Reo-Coker	**2**	0	0	0	2
11	Harley	**1**	0	0	0	1
	Other	6	1	0	0	7
	TOTAL	**67**	**5**	**6**	**2**	**80**

KEY PLAYERS - GOALSCORERS

Jermain Defoe

Goals in the League	11
Goals in all competitions	14
Contribution to Attacking Power Average number of minutes between League team goals while on pitch	60
Player Strike Rate The total number of minutes he was on the pitch for every League goal scored	143
Club Strike Rate Average number of minutes between League goals scored by club	62

	PLAYER	GOALS LGE	GOALS ALL	POWER	S RATE
1	Jermain Defoe	11	14	60	**143 mins**
2	Marlon Harewood	13	14	55	**179 mins**
3	Bobby Zamora	5	5	59	**262 mins**
4	David Connolly	10	14	60	**308 mins**
5	Matthew Etherington	5	6	59	**580 mins**

KEY PLAYERS - MIDFIELDERS

Kevin Horlock

Goals in the League	1
Goals in all competitions	1
Defensive Rating Average number of mins between League goals conceded while on the pitch	103
Contribution to Attacking Power Average number of minutes between League team goals while on pitch	61
Scoring Difference Defensive Rating minus Contribution to Attacking Power	42

	PLAYER	GOALS LGE	GOALS ALL	DEF RATE	ATT POWER	SCORE DIFF
1	Kevin Horlock	1	1	103	61	**42 mins**
2	Matthew Etherington	5	6	85	59	**26 mins**
3	Michael Carrick	1	1	85	63	**22 mins**
4	Wayne Quinn	0	0	85	66	**19 mins**

KEY PLAYERS - DEFENDERS

Christian Dailly

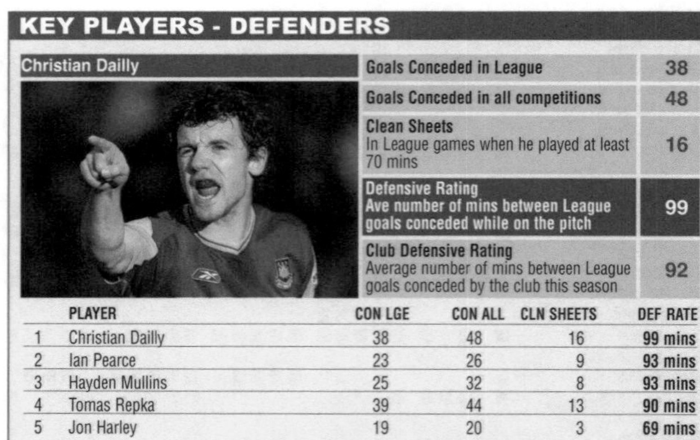

Goals Conceded in League	38
Goals Conceded in all competitions	48
Clean Sheets In League games when he played at least 70 mins	16
Defensive Rating Ave number of mins between League goals conceded while on the pitch	99
Club Defensive Rating Average number of mins between League goals conceded by the club this season	92

	PLAYER	CON LGE	CON ALL	CLN SHEETS	DEF RATE
1	Christian Dailly	38	48	16	**99 mins**
2	Ian Pearce	23	26	9	**93 mins**
3	Hayden Mullins	25	32	8	**93 mins**
4	Tomas Repka	39	44	13	**90 mins**
5	Jon Harley	19	20	3	**69 mins**

KEY GOALKEEPER

1 David James

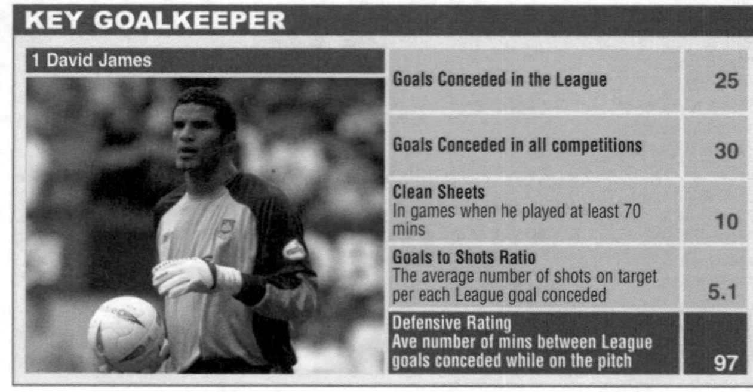

Goals Conceded in the League	25
Goals Conceded in all competitions	30
Clean Sheets In games when he played at least 70 mins	10
Goals to Shots Ratio The average number of shots on target per each League goal conceded	5.1
Defensive Rating Ave number of mins between League goals conceded while on the pitch	97

DISCIPLINARY RECORDS

	PLAYER	YELLOW	RED	AVE
1	Defoe	5	3	196
2	Repka	12	0	293
3	Horlock	7	0	295
4	Connolly	8	1	342
5	Hutchison	3	0	388
6	Stockdale	1	0	451
7	Deane	2	0	485
8	Reo-Coker	2	0	571
9	Zamora	2	0	654
10	Etherington	3	1	724
11	Quinn	2	0	891
12	Ferdinand	1	0	905
13	Melville	1	0	1034
	Other	15	1	
	TOTAL	**64**	**6**	

TOP POINT EARNERS

	PLAYER	GAMES	AV PTS
1	Stephen Bywater	16	**2.00**
2	Jermain Defoe	17	**1.76**
3	David Connolly	29	**1.76**
4	Bobby Zamora	13	**1.69**
5	Kevin Horlock	22	**1.68**
6	Christian Dailly	42	**1.67**
7	Matthew Etherington	31	**1.65**
8	Marlon Harewood	26	**1.62**
9	Tomas Repka	38	**1.58**
10	Hayden Mullins	25	**1.52**
	CLUB AVERAGE:		**1.61**

LEAGUE APPEARANCES AND BOOKINGS

	AGE (on 01/07/04)	IN NAMED 16	APPEARANCES	COUNTING GAMES	MINUTES ON PITCH	Yellow	Red
Goalkeepers							
Stephen Bywater	23	44	18	16	1510	0	1
David Forde	24	2	0	0	0	0	0
David James	33	27	27	27	2430	0	0
Rami Shaaban	29	3	0	0	0	0	0
Pavel Srnicek	36	16	3	2	209	0	0
Defenders							
Rufus Brevett	34	2	2	1	119	1	0
Shaun Byrne	23	5	0	0	0	0	0
Christian Dailly	30	42	42	42	3780	3	0
Anton Ferdinand	19	34	20	7	905	1	0
Jon Harley	24	15	15	14	1306	1	0
Matthew Kilgallon	20	15	3	1	183	0	0
Andy Melville	35	19	14	11	1034	1	0
Hayden Mullins	25	28	27	25	2322	2	0
Ian Pearce	30	24	24	24	2149	2	0
Tomas Repka	30	41	40	38	3520	12	0
Robbie Stockdale	24	10	7	5	451	1	0
Midfielders							
Niclas Alexandersson	32	8	8	5	509	0	0
Sebastien Carole	21	2	1	0	4	0	0
Michael Carrick	22	35	35	33	3072	1	0
Chris Cohen	-	11	7	0	189	2	0
Matthew Etherington	22	35	35	31	2898	3	1
Kevin Horlock	31	30	26	22	2065	7	0
Don Hutchison	33	26	24	7	1165	3	0
Robert Lee	38	16	16	9	1068	0	0
Steve Lomas	30	5	5	5	450	0	0
Jobi McAnuff	22	15	12	1	410	1	0
Daryl McMahon	21	0	0	0	0	0	0
David Noble	22	6	3	0	29	0	0
Mark Noble	-	0	0	0	0	0	0
Wayne Quinn	27	23	22	18	1782	2	0
Nigel Reo-Coker	20	16	15	12	1143	2	0
Forwards							
David Connolly	27	40	40	29	3078	8	1
Brian Deane	36	28	26	5	971	2	0
Jermain Defoe	21	19	19	17	1572	5	3
Richard Garcia	22	13	7	1	323	0	0
Marlon Harewood	24	28	28	26	2323	1	0
Neil Mellor	21	19	15	5	694	0	0
Adam Nowland	23	13	11	0	326	1	0
Youssef Sofiane	19	4	1	0	18	0	0
Bobby Zamora	23	17	17	13	1308	2	0

TEAM OF THE SEASON

G — David James, CG: 27 DR: 97

D — Christian Dailly, CG: 42 DR: 99

D — Hayden Mullins, CG: 25 DR: 93

D — Ian Pearce, CG: 24 DR: 93

D — Tomas Repka, CG: 38 DR: 90

M — Kevin Horlock, CG: 22 SD: 42

M — Matthew Etherington, CG: 31 SD: 26

M — Michael Carrick, CG: 33 SD: 22

M — Wayne Quinn, CG: 18 SD: 19

F — Jermain Defoe, CG: 17 SR: 143

F — Marlon Harewood, CG: 26 SR: 179

SQUAD APPEARANCES

Match	1	2	3	4	5	6	7	8	9	10	11	12	13	14	15	16	17	18	19	20	21	22	23	24	25	26	27	28	29	30	31	32	33	34	35	36	37	38	39	40	41	42	43	44	45	46	47	48	49	50	51	52	53	54	55	56
Venue	A	H	H	A	H	A	H	A	A	A	H	H	A	H	H	H	A	A	A	H	A	A	H	A	H	H	A	H	A	A	H	A	A	H	A	A	A	H	H	A	H	H	A	H	A	H	A	H	A	H	A	H	A	A	H	A
Competition	L	W	L	L	L	L	L	L	L	W	L	L	L	L	L	L	L	W	L	L	L	L	L	L	L	L	L	L	L	F	L	L	F	L	L	F	L	F	L	L	L	L	L	L	L	L	L	L	L	L	L	L	L	O	O	O
Result	W	W	D	L	W	W	W	W	L	W	D	W	W	D	D	D	D	L	D	L	D	D	W	D	L	W	D	L	W	W	L	D	W	W	W	D	D	L	W	D	D	W	L	W	L	W	L	D	L	W	W	W	D	L	W	L

Goalkeepers
Stephen Bywater
David Forde
David James
Rami Shaaban
Pavel Srnicek

Defenders
Rufus Brevett
Shaun Byrne
Christian Dailly
Anton Ferdinand
Jon Harley
Matthew Kilgallon
Andy Melville
Hayden Mullins
Ian Pearce
Tomas Repka
Robbie Stockdale

Midfielders
Niclas Alexandersson
Sebastien Carole
Michael Carrick
Chris Cohen
Matthew Etherington
Kevin Horlock
Don Hutchison
Robert Lee
Steve Lomas
Jobi McAnuff
Daryl McMahon
David Noble
Mark Noble
Wayne Quinn
Nigel Reo-Coker

Forwards
David Connolly
Brian Deane
Jermain Defoe
Richard Garcia
Marlon Harewood
Neil Mellor
Adam Nowland
Youssef Sofiane
Bobby Zamora

KEY: On all match · On bench · Subbed or sent off (Counting game) · Subbed or sent off (playing less than 70 minutes) · Subbed on from bench (Counting Game) · Subbed on (playing less than 70 minutes) · Subbed on and then subbed or sent off (Counting Game) · Subbed on and then subbed or sent off (playing less than 70 minutes) · Not in 16

IPSWICH TOWN

Final Position: **5th**

NICKNAME: TRACTOR BOYS

KEY: Won Drawn Lost

							Attendance
1	div1	**Reading**	H	D	1-1	Miller, T 90 pen	24,830
2	ccR1	**Kidderminster**	H	D	0-0		11,118
3	div1	**Crewe**	A	L	0-1		6,982
4	div1	**Coventry**	H	D	1-1	Bent, M 17	22,419
5	div1	**Wigan**	A	L	0-1		8,292
6	div1	**West Ham**	H	L	1-2	Wright 65	29,679
7	div1	**West Brom**	A	L	1-4	Naylor 63	24,954
8	div1	**Walsall**	H	W	2-1	Armstrong 13 pen; Bent, D 67	20,912
9	div1	**Wimbledon**	H	W	4-1	Armstrong 24; Naylor 26; Bent, D 68; Counago 81 pen	23,428
10	ccR2	**Notts County**	A	L	1-2	Counago 6 pen	4,059
11	div1	**Watford**	A	W	2-1	Kuqi 52; Magilton 82	15,350
12	div1	**Sunderland**	A	L	2-3	Bent, D 36; Naylor 51	24,840
13	div1	**Rotherham**	H	W	2-1	Counago 53,70 pen	21,859
14	div1	**Bradford**	A	W	1-0	Mahon 42	10,229
15	div1	**Burnley**	H	W	6-1	Counago 20,22; Wright 29; Bart-Williams 31; Chaplow 40; Kuqi 90	22,048
16	div1	**Stoke**	H	W	1-0	Richards 43	22,122
17	div1	**Crystal Palace**	A	W	4-3	Naylor 26,45; Counago 78; Kuqi 89	15,483
18	div1	**Preston**	A	D	1-1	Collins 64	14,863
19	div1	**Gillingham**	H	L	3-4	Westlake 18; Counago 60; Miller, T 74	24,788
20	div1	**Derby**	A	D	2-2	Miller, T 56 pen; Bent, D 65	19,976
21	div1	**Sheff Utd**	H	W	3-0	Kuqi 43 pen; Westlake 67; Bent, D 90	25,004
22	div1	**Cardiff**	A	W	3-2	Miller, T 29 pen; Santos 33; Bart-Williams 82	17,833
23	div1	**Nottm Forest**	A	D	1-1	Bent, D 62	21,558
24	div1	**Derby**	H	W	2-1	Bent, D 1; Mawene 69 og	25,018
25	div1	**Millwall**	A	D	0-0		9,829
26	div1	**Norwich**	H	L	0-2		30,152
27	div1	**West Ham**	A	W	2-1	Counago 70 pen,79	35,021
28	div1	**Crystal Palace**	H	L	1-3	Wright 11	27,629
29	facr3	**Derby**	H	W	3-0	Naylor 54; Miller, T 69; Kuqi 89	16,159
30	div1	**Reading**	A	D	1-1	McGreal 72	17,362
31	div1	**Crewe**	H	W	6-4	Miller, T 3,9; Kuqi 55,88; Reuser 72; Counago 74	22,071
32	facr4	**Sunderland**	H	L	1-2	Reuser 89	21,406
33	div1	**Coventry**	A	D	1-1	Westlake 58	14,441
34	div1	**Wigan**	H	L	1-3	Kuqi 60	22,093
35	div1	**Bradford**	H	W	3-1	Kuqi 28; Westlake 45; Bent, D 52	21,478
36	div1	**Burnley**	A	L	2-4	Miller, T 65; Reuser 88	12,418
37	div1	**Preston**	H	W	2-0	Miller, T 72; Westlake 90	23,359
38	div1	**Stoke**	A	L	0-2		11,435
39	div1	**Norwich**	A	L	1-3	Miller, T 88 pen	23,942
40	div1	**Millwall**	H	L	1-3	Bent, D 52	23,582
41	div1	**Walsall**	A	W	3-1	Bent, D 48,59,90	6,562
42	div1	**Watford**	H	W	4-1	Bowditch 5,24,61; Wright 90	23,524
43	div1	**Wimbledon**	A	W	2-1	Bent, D 72; Kuqi 73	6,389
44	div1	**West Brom**	H	L	2-3	Miller, T 43; Bent, D 78	24,608
45	div1	**Rotherham**	A	W	3-1	Wright 67; Bent, D 88; Kuqi 90	6,561
46	div1	**Sunderland**	H	W	1-0	Miller, T 45	26,801
47	div1	**Gillingham**	A	W	2-1	Reuser 62; Bent, D 67	9,641
48	div1	**Nottm Forest**	H	L	1-2	Bowditch 34	27,848
49	div1	**Sheff Utd**	A	D	1-1	Westlake 71	24,184
50	div1	**Cardiff**	H	D	1-1	Kuqi 26	28,703
51	d1po1	**West Ham**	H	W	1-0	Bent, D 57	28,435
52	d1po2	**West Ham**	A	L	0-2		34,002

MONTHLY POINTS TALLY

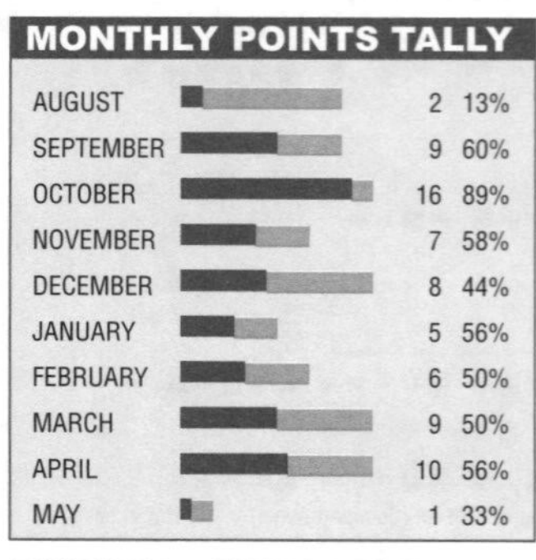

AUGUST 2 13%
SEPTEMBER 9 60%
OCTOBER 16 89%
NOVEMBER 7 58%
DECEMBER 8 44%
JANUARY 5 56%
FEBRUARY 6 50%
MARCH 9 50%
APRIL 10 56%
MAY 1 33%

LEAGUE GOALS

	PLAYER	LGE	FAC	LC	Oth	TOT
1	Bent, D	16	0	0	1	17
2	Miller, T	11	1	0	0	12
3	Kuqi	11	1	0	0	12
4	Counago	10	0	1	0	11
5	Westlake	6	0	0	0	6
6	Naylor	5	1	0	0	6
7	Wright	5	0	0	0	5
8	Bowditch	4	0	1	0	5
9	Reuser	3	1	0	0	4
10	Bart-Williams	2	0	0	0	2
11	Armstrong	2	0	0	0	2
	Other	9	0	0	0	9
	TOTAL	84	4	2	1	91

KEY PLAYERS - GOALSCORERS

Darren Bent

Goals in the League	16
Goals in all competitions	17
Contribution to Attacking Power Average number of minutes between League team goals while on pitch	55
Player Strike Rate The total number of minutes he was on the pitch for every League goal scored	183
Club Strike Rate Average number of minutes between League goals scored by club	49

	PLAYER	GOALS LGE	GOALS ALL	POWER	S RATE
1	Darren Bent	16	17	55	183 mins
2	Tommy Miller	11	12	52	220 mins
3	Shefki Kuqi	11	12	42	221 mins
4	Ian Westlake	6	6	51	455 mins
5	Richard Naylor	5	6	44	582 mins

KEY PLAYERS - MIDFIELDERS

Chris Bart-Williams

Goals in the League	2
Goals in all competitions	2
Defensive Rating Average number of mins between League goals conceded while on the pitch	58
Contribution to Attacking Power Average number of minutes between League team goals while on pitch	44
Scoring Difference Defensive Rating minus Contribution to Attacking Power	14

	PLAYER	GOALS LGE	GOALS ALL	DEF RATE	ATT POWER	SCORE DIFF
1	Chris Bart-Williams	2	2	58	44	14 mins
2	Jermaine Wright	5	5	57	47	10 mins
3	Ian Westlake	6	6	59	51	8 mins
4	Jim Magilton	1	1	56	52	4 mins
5	Tommy Miller	11	12	54	53	1 mins

KEY PLAYERS - DEFENDERS

John McGreal

Goals Conceded in League	23
Goals Conceded in all competitions	25
Clean Sheets In League games when he played at least 70 mins	3
Defensive Rating Ave number of mins between League goals conceded while on the pitch	68
Club Defensive Rating Average number of mins between League goals conceded by the club this season	58

	PLAYER	CON LGE	CON ALL	CLN SHEETS	DEF RATE
1	John McGreal	23	25	3	68 mins
2	Fabian Wilnis	59	65	6	59 mins
3	Matthew Richards	65	71	6	58 mins
4	Georges Santos	41	43	4	56 mins

KEY GOALKEEPER

1 Kelvin Davis

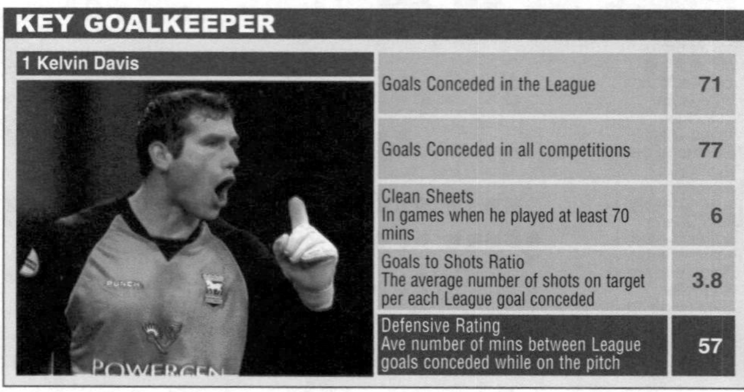

Goals Conceded in the League	71
Goals Conceded in all competitions	77
Clean Sheets In games when he played at least 70 mins	6
Goals to Shots Ratio The average number of shots on target per each League goal conceded	3.8
Defensive Rating Ave number of mins between League goals conceded while on the pitch	57

DISCIPLINARY RECORDS

	PLAYER	YELLOW	RED	AVE
1	Bart-Williams	9	0	220
2	Mahon	3	0	228
3	Diallo	4	1	255
4	Santos	8	1	255
5	Naylor	8	0	363
6	Counago	4	0	424
7	Elliott	2	0	450
8	Kuqi	5	0	487
9	Wilnis	7	0	499
10	Reuser	1	0	603
11	Bowditch	1	0	675
12	Richards	5	0	752
13	McGreal	2	0	786
	Other	13	0	
	TOTAL	72	2	

TOP POINT EARNERS

	PLAYER	GAMES	AV PTS
1	Chris Bart-Williams	18	2.17
2	John McGreal	17	2.00
3	Shefki Kuqi	21	1.95
4	Matthew Richards	40	1.78
5	Georges Santos	21	1.76
6	Jermaine Wright	42	1.69
7	Darren Bent	29	1.66
8	Ian Westlake	25	1.64
9	Richard Naylor	28	1.61
10	Kelvin Davis	45	1.56
	CLUB AVERAGE:		1.59

LEAGUE APPEARANCES AND BOOKINGS

	AGE (on 01/07/04)	IN NAMED 16	APPEARANCES	COUNTING GAMES	MINUTES ON PITCH	Yellow	Red
Goalkeepers							
Nathan Abbey	25	4	0	0	0	0	0
Kelvin Davis	27	45	45	45	4050	1	0
Andy Marshall	29	1	0	0	0	0	0
Lewis Price	19	41	1	1	90	0	0
Defenders							
Scott Barron	18	1	0	0	0	0	0
Aidan Collins	17	1	0	0	0	0	0
Drissa Diallo	31	22	19	11	1276	4	1
Matt Elliott	35	10	10	10	900	2	0
Christopher Makin	37	5	5	4	427	2	0
John McGreal	32	22	18	17	1572	2	0
Gerard Nash	17	8	1	0	15	0	0
Matthew Richards	19	45	44	40	3764	5	0
Georges Santos	33	42	34	21	2302	8	1
Fabian Wilnis	33	42	41	38	3498	7	0
Midfielders							
Chris Bart-Williams	30	28	26	18	1987	9	0
Matt Bloomfield	20	1	0	0	0	0	0
Dean Bowditch	18	35	16	3	675	1	0
Jim Magilton	35	46	46	43	3913	4	0
Alan Mahon	26	12	11	7	684	3	0
Tommy Miller	25	36	34	22	2416	2	0
Scott Mitchell	18	8	2	0	10	0	0
Antonio Murray	19	1	0	0	0	0	0
Martijn Reuser	29	25	17	1	603	1	0
Ian Westlake	20	43	39	25	2729	3	0
Jermaine Wright	28	46	45	42	3881	0	0
Forwards							
Alun Armstrong	29	16	7	3	370	0	0
Darren Bent	20	37	37	29	2922	1	0
Marcus Bent	26	4	4	4	360	0	0
Pablo Gonzalez Counago	24	32	29	11	1698	4	0
Shefki Kuqi	27	37	36	21	2436	5	0
Sam Morrow	19	0	0	0	0	0	0
Richard Naylor	27	40	39	28	2909	8	0

TEAM OF THE SEASON

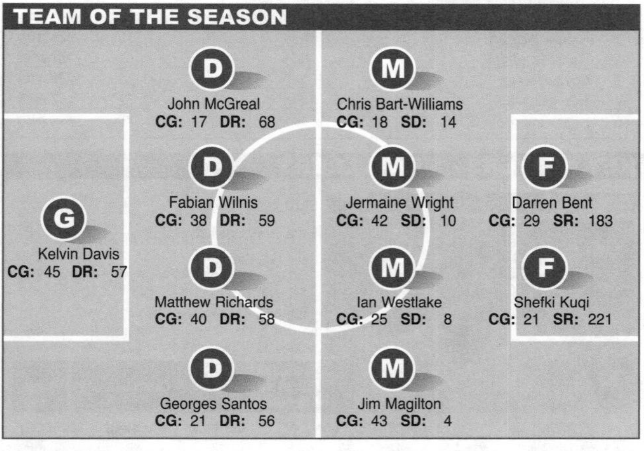

D
John McGreal
CG: 17 DR: 68
M
Chris Bart-Williams
CG: 18 SD: 14
D
Fabian Wilnis
CG: 38 DR: 59
M
Jermaine Wright
CG: 42 SD: 10
F
Darren Bent
CG: 29 SR: 183
G
Kelvin Davis
CG: 45 DR: 57
D
Matthew Richards
CG: 40 DR: 58
M
Ian Westlake
CG: 25 SD: 8
F
Shefki Kuqi
CG: 21 SR: 221
D
Georges Santos
CG: 21 DR: 56
M
Jim Magilton
CG: 43 SD: 4

SQUAD APPEARANCES

Match	1 2 3 4 5	6 7 8 9 10	11 12 13 14 15	16 17 18 19 20	21 22 23 24 25	26 27 28 29 30	31 32 33 34 35	36 37 38 39 40	41 42 43 44 45	46 47 48 49 50	51 52
Venue	H H A H A	H A H H A	A A H A H	H A A H A	H A A H A	H A H H A	H H A H H	A H A A H	A H A H A	H A H A H	H A
Competition	L W L L L	L L L L W	L L L L L	L L L L L	L L L L L	L L L F L	L F L L L	L L L L L	L L L L L	L L L L L	O O
Result	D D L D L	L L W W L	W L W W W	W W D L D	W W D W D	L W L W D	W L D L W	L W L L L	W W W L W	W W L D D	W L

Goalkeepers
Nathan Abbey
Kelvin Davis
Andy Marshall
Lewis Price

Defenders
Scott Barron
Aidan Collins
Drissa Diallo
Matt Elliott
Christopher Makin
John McGreal
Gerard Nash
Matthew Richards
Georges Santos
Fabian Wilnis

Midfielders
Chris Bart-Williams
Matt Bloomfield
Dean Bowditch
Jim Magilton
Alan Mahon
Tommy Miller
Scott Mitchell
Antonio Murray
Martijn Reuser
Ian Westlake
Jermaine Wright

Forwards
Alun Armstrong
Darren Bent
Marcus Bent
Pablo Gonzalez Counago
Shefki Kuqi
Sam Morrow
Richard Naylor

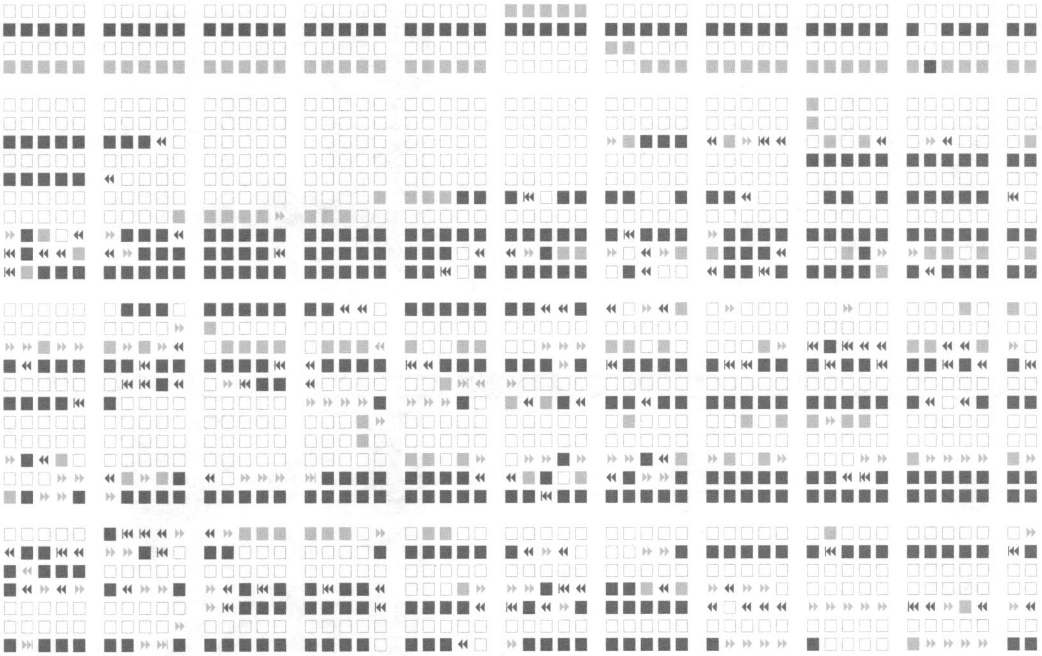

KEY: ■ On all match | ■ On bench | ⏮ Subbed or sent off (Counting game) | « Subbed or sent off (playing less than 70 minutes) | ⏭ Subbed on from bench (Counting Game) | » Subbed on (playing less than 70 minutes) | ⏭ Subbed on and then subbed or sent off (Counting Game) | » Subbed on and then subbed or sent off (playing less than 70 minutes) | □ Not in 16

CRYSTAL PALACE

PROMOTED VIA PLAY-OFFS Final Position: **6th**

NICKNAME: THE EAGLES KEY: Won / Drawn / Lost

No	Comp	Opponent	H/A	Res	Score	Scorers	Attendance
1	div1	Burnley	A	W	3-2	Freedman 6 pen,32,67	12,976
2	ccR1	Torquay	A	D	3-1*	Freedman 29 (*on penalties)	3,366
3	div1	Watford	H	W	1-0	Shipperley 14	15,333
4	div1	Wimbledon	A	W	3-1	Butterfield 59; Freedman 65 pen; Hughes, M 90	6,113
5	div1	Sheff Utd	H	L	1-2	Johnson 76 pen	15,466
6	div1	Millwall	A	D	1-1	Watson 67	14,425
7	div1	Sunderland	A	L	1-2	Johnson 89	27,324
8	div1	Bradford	H	L	0-1		13,514
9	div1	West Brom	H	D	2-2	Freedman 59; Johnson 90	17,477
10	ccR2	Doncaster	H	W	2-1	Johnson 17 pen,25 pen	4,904
11	div1	Norwich	A	L	1-2	Derry 2	16,425
12	div1	West Ham	A	L	0-3		31,861
13	div1	Cardiff	H	W	2-1	Routledge 45; Shipperley 47	16,160
14	div1	Derby	H	D	1-1	Butterfield 45	14,344
15	div1	Rotherham	H	D	1-1	Freedman 57	18,715
16	div1	Ipswich	H	L	3-4	Johnson 5; Freedman 16,88 pen	15,483
17	div1	Gillingham	A	L	0-1		8,889
18	ccR3	Blackpool	A	W	3-1	Johnson 24,87; Freedman 62 pen	6,010
19	div1	Wigan	A	L	0-5		6,796
20	div1	Preston	H	D	1-1	Johnson 84	14,608
21	div1	Walsall	A	D	0-0		6,910
22	div1	Stoke	A	W	1-0	Johnson 27	10,277
23	div1	Coventry	H	D	1-1	Edwards 9	14,622
24	ccR4	Aston Villa	A	L	0-3		24,258
25	div1	Preston	A	L	1-4	Derry 71	12,836
26	div1	Crewe	H	L	1-3	Butterfield 78	12,259
27	div1	Nottm Forest	H	W	1-0	Johnson 12	16,935
28	div1	Reading	A	W	3-0	Johnson 40,90; Routledge 43	12,743
29	div1	Millwall	H	L	0-1		19,737
30	div1	Ipswich	A	W	3-1	Johnson 61,86; Gray 65	27,629
31	facr3	Tottenham	A	L	0-3		32,340
32	div1	Burnley	H	D	0-0		15,276
33	div1	Watford	A	W	5-1	Johnson 9,45 pen; Routledge 39; Gray 73; Freedman 90	15,017
34	div1	Bradford	A	W	2-1	Johnson 13; Shipperley 15	10,310
35	div1	Wimbledon	H	W	3-1	Johnson 32,89; Granville 59	20,552
36	div1	Sheff Utd	A	W	3-0	Johnson 42; Popovic 57; Shipperley 87	23,816
37	div1	Stoke	H	W	6-3	Johnson 5,9 pen,33 pen; Hughes, M 45; Shipperley 55; Routledge 90	16,715
38	div1	Derby	A	L	1-2	Hughes, M 16	21,856
39	div1	Gillingham	H	W	1-0	Butterfield 53	17,485
40	div1	Reading	H	D	2-2	Freedman 33; Johnson 44	17,853
41	div1	Nottm Forest	A	L	2-3	Shipperley 58; Granville 76	28,306
42	div1	Norwich	H	W	1-0	Routledge 41	23,798
43	div1	West Brom	A	L	0-2		24,990
44	div1	Rotherham	A	W	2-1	Gray 11; Shipperley 27	6,001
45	div1	Cardiff	A	W	2-0	Johnson 55; Routledge 87	16,656
46	div1	West Ham	H	W	1-0	Freedman 66	23,977
47	div1	Wigan	H	D	1-1	Granville 79	18,799
48	div1	Sunderland	H	W	3-0	Johnson 24 pen; Shipperley 63; Freedman 80	18,291
49	div1	Crewe	A	W	3-2	Johnson 30,36,56 pen	8,136
50	div1	Walsall	H	W	1-0	Johnson 88	21,518
51	div1	Coventry	A	L	1-2	Freedman 64	22,195
52	d1po1	Sunderland	H	W	3-2	Shipperley 52; Butterfield 64; Johnson 87	25,287
53	d1po2	Sunderland	A	W	5-4*	Powell 90 (*on penalties)	34,536
54	d1pof	West Ham	H	W	1-0	Shipperley 62	72,523

MONTHLY POINTS TALLY

Month	Points	%
AUGUST	10	67%
SEPTEMBER	1	8%
OCTOBER	5	28%
NOVEMBER	6	40%
DECEMBER	9	50%
JANUARY	10	83%
FEBRUARY	9	75%
MARCH	4	33%
APRIL	16	89%
MAY	3	50%

LEAGUE GOALS

	PLAYER	LGE	FAC	LC	Oth	TOT
1	Johnson	27	0	4	1	32
2	Freedman	13	0	2	0	15
3	Shipperley	8	0	0	2	10
4	Routledge	6	0	0	0	6
5	Butterfield	4	0	0	1	5
6	Granville	3	0	0	0	3
7	Gray	3	0	0	0	3
8	Hughes, M	3	0	0	0	3
9	Derry	2	0	0	0	2
10	Edwards	1	0	0	0	1
11	Popovic	1	0	0	0	1
	Other	1	0	0	1	2
	TOTAL	72	0	6	5	83

KEY PLAYERS - GOALSCORERS

Andrew Johnson

Goals in the League	27
Goals in all competitions	32
Contribution to Attacking Power Average number of minutes between League team goals while on pitch	55
Player Strike Rate The total number of minutes he was on the pitch for every League goal scored	128
Club Strike Rate Average number of minutes between League goals scored by club	58

	PLAYER	GOALS LGE	GOALS ALL	POWER	S RATE
1	Andrew Johnson	27	32	55	128 mins
2	Dougie Freedman	13	15	63	157 mins
3	Neil Shipperley	8	10	55	429 mins
4	Wayne Routledge	6	6	52	512 mins
5	Danny Granville	3	3	46	619 mins

KEY PLAYERS - MIDFIELDERS

Julian Gray

Goals in the League	3
Goals in all competitions	3
Defensive Rating Average number of mins between League goals conceded while on the pitch	94
Contribution to Attacking Power Average number of minutes between League team goals while on pitch	46
Scoring Difference Defensive Rating minus Contribution to Attacking Power	48

	PLAYER	GOALS LGE	GOALS ALL	DEF RATE	ATT POWER	SCORE DIFF
1	Julian Gray	3	3	94	46	48 mins
2	Wayne Routledge	6	6	73	52	21 mins
3	Michael Hughes	3	3	77	60	17 mins
4	Aki Riihilahti	0	0	63	50	13 mins
5	Shaun Derry	2	2	51	64	-13 mins

KEY PLAYERS - DEFENDERS

Mark Hudson

Goals Conceded in League	14
Goals Conceded in all competitions	14
Clean Sheets In League games when he played at least 70 mins	4
Defensive Rating Ave number of mins between League goals conceded while on the pitch	87
Club Defensive Rating Average number of mins between League goals conceded by the club this season	68

	PLAYER	CON LGE	CON ALL	CLN SHEETS	DEF RATE
1	Mark Hudson	14	14	4	87 mins
2	Danny Granville	25	29	8	74 mins
3	Tony Popovic	41	52	13	73 mins
4	Gary Borrowdale	21	28	5	72 mins
5	Danny Butterfield	60	73	13	67 mins

KEY GOALKEEPER

1 Thomas Myhre

churchill

Goals Conceded in the League	19
Goals Conceded in all competitions	20
Clean Sheets In games when he played at least 70 mins	5
Goals to Shots Ratio The average number of shots on target per each League goal conceded	6.1
Defensive Rating Ave number of mins between League goals conceded while on the pitch	71

DISCIPLINARY RECORDS

	PLAYER	YELLOW	RED	AVE
1	Mullins	5	0	180
2	Black	4	1	224
3	Hughes, M	12	0	249
4	Powell	2	1	252
5	Derry	7	1	286
6	Popovic	10	0	301
7	Riihilahti	7	0	304
8	Smith	3	0	365
9	Fleming	3	0	389
10	Watson	2	0	411
11	Borrowdale	3	0	501
12	Symons	2	0	504
13	Edwards	1	0	551
	Other	21	2	
	TOTAL	**82**	**5**	

TOP POINT EARNERS

	PLAYER	GAMES	AV PTS
1	Mark Hudson	13	**2.23**
2	Julian Gray	24	**2.13**
3	Danny Granville	20	**2.10**
4	Aki Riihilahti	20	**2.00**
5	Wayne Routledge	30	**1.80**
6	Tony Popovic	33	**1.73**
7	Gary Borrowdale	13	**1.69**
8	Andrew Johnson	37	**1.68**
9	Danny Butterfield	44	**1.64**
10	Michael Hughes	33	**1.64**
	CLUB AVERAGE:		**1.59**

TEAM OF THE SEASON

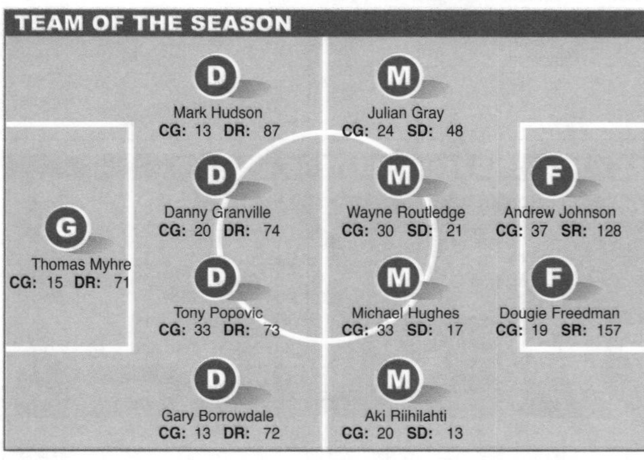

D
Mark Hudson
CG: 13 DR: 87
M
Julian Gray
CG: 24 SD: 48
D
Danny Granville
CG: 20 DR: 74
M
Wayne Routledge
CG: 30 SD: 21
F
Andrew Johnson
CG: 37 SR: 128
G
Thomas Myhre
CG: 15 DR: 71
D
Tony Popovic
CG: 33 DR: 73
M
Michael Hughes
CG: 33 SD: 17
F
Dougie Freedman
CG: 19 SR: 157
D
Gary Borrowdale
CG: 13 DR: 72
M
Aki Riihilahti
CG: 20 SD: 13

LEAGUE APPEARANCES AND BOOKINGS

	AGE (on 01/07/04)	IN NAMED 16	APPEARANCES	COUNTING GAMES	MINUTES ON PITCH	Yellow	Red
Goalkeepers							
Cedric Berthelin	27	44	17	17	1530	0	0
Matt Clarke	30	4	4	4	360	0	0
Lance Cronin	18	12	0	0	0	0	0
Thomas Myhre	30	15	15	15	1350	0	0
Nico Vaesen	34	10	10	10	900	0	0
Defenders							
Gary Borrowdale	18	39	23	13	1503	3	0
Danny Butterfield	24	45	45	44	3996	3	0
Rob Edwards	21	7	7	6	551	1	0
Curtis Fleming	35	22	17	12	1169	3	0
Danny Granville	29	25	21	20	1856	3	0
Mark Hudson	22	14	14	13	1218	0	1
Mikele Leigertwood	21	16	12	6	652	1	0
Hayden Mullins	25	10	10	10	900	5	0
Tony Popovic	31	34	34	33	3010	10	0
Darren Powell	28	10	10	8	756	2	1
Jamie Smith	29	18	15	10	1097	3	0
Kit Symons	33	28	15	10	1008	2	0
Sam Togwell	19	1	0	0	0	0	0
Midfielders							
Thomas Black	27	41	25	10	1120	4	1
Shaun Derry	26	42	37	21	2288	7	1
Julian Gray	24	24	24	24	2159	3	0
Gavin Heeroo	19	1	1	0	1	0	0
Michael Hughes	32	36	34	33	2990	12	0
Tariq Nabil	17	0	0	0	0	0	0
Aki Riihilahti	27	35	30	20	2133	7	0
Wayne Routledge	19	45	44	30	3070	1	1
Tom Soares	17	6	3	0	3	0	0
Ben Watson	18	23	16	5	822	2	0
Forwards							
Dougie Freedman	29	42	35	19	2036	1	0
Andrew Johnson	23	42	41	37	3454	4	0
Neil Shipperley	29	40	40	37	3435	5	0
Gareth Williams	21	5	0	0	0	0	0

SQUAD APPEARANCES

Match	1	2	3	4	5	6	7	8	9	10	11	12	13	14	15	16	17	18	19	20	21	22	23	24	25	26	27	28	29	30	31	32	33	34	35	36	37	38	39	40	41	42	43	44	45	46	47	48	49	50	51	52	53	54
Venue	A	A	H	A	H	A	A	H	H	H	A	A	H	H	H	H	A	A	A	H	A	A	H	A	A	H	H	A	H	A	A	H	A	A	H	A	H	A	H	H	A	H	A	A	A	H	H	H	A	H	A	H	A	H
Competition	L	W	L	L	L	L	L	L	L	W	L	L	L	L	L	L	L	W	L	L	L	L	L	W	L	L	L	L	L	L	F	L	L	L	L	L	L	L	L	L	L	L	L	L	L	L	L	L	L	L	L	O	O	O
Result	W	D	W	W	L	D	L	L	D	W	L	L	W	D	D	L	L	W	L	D	D	W	D	L	L	L	W	W	L	W	L	D	W	W	W	W	W	L	W	D	L	W	L	W	W	W	D	W	W	W	L	W	W	W

Goalkeepers
Cedric Berthelin
Matt Clarke
Lance Cronin
Thomas Myhre
Nico Vaesen

Defenders
Gary Borrowdale
Danny Butterfield
Rob Edwards
Curtis Fleming
Danny Granville
Mark Hudson
Mikele Leigertwood
Hayden Mullins
Tony Popovic
Darren Powell
Jamie Smith
Kit Symons
Sam Togwell

Midfielders
Thomas Black
Shaun Derry
Julian Gray
Gavin Heeroo
Michael Hughes
Tariq Nabil
Aki Riihilahti
Wayne Routledge
Tom Soares
Ben Watson

Forwards
Dougie Freedman
Andrew Johnson
Neil Shipperley
Gareth Williams

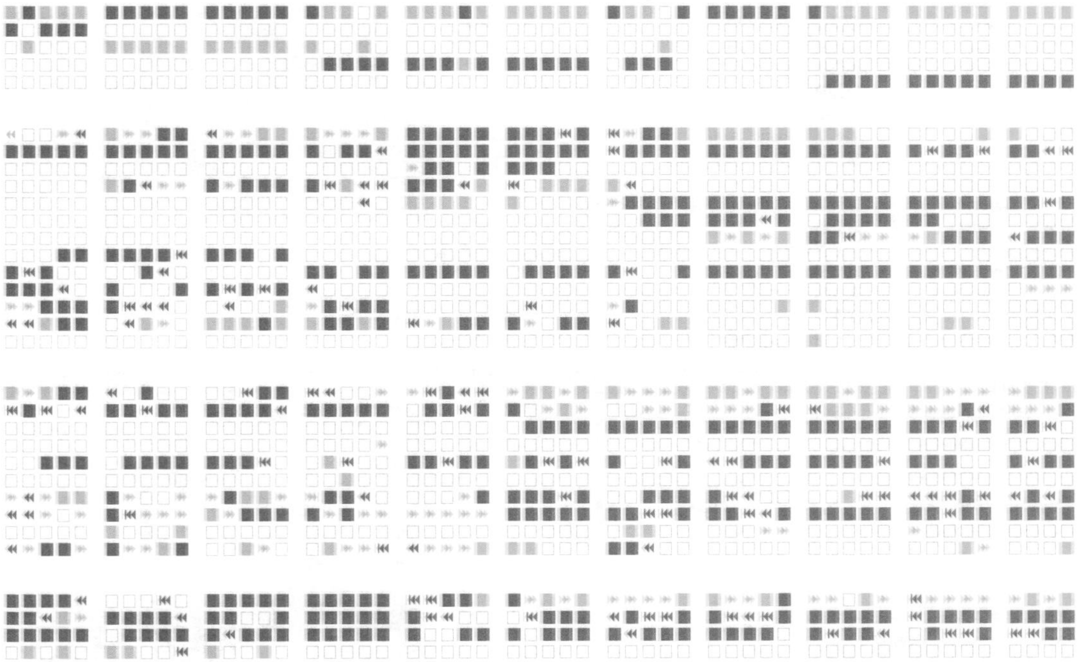

KEY: On all match · On bench · Subbed or sent off (Counting game) · Subbed or sent off (playing less than 70 minutes) · Subbed on from bench (Counting Game) · Subbed on (playing less than 70 minutes) · Subbed on and then subbed or sent off (Counting Game) · Subbed on and then subbed or sent off (playing less than 70 minutes) · Not in 16

WIGAN ATHLETIC

Final Position: **7th**

NICKNAME: THE LATICS — KEY: ☐ Won ☐ Drawn ☐ Lost

#	Comp	Opponent	H/A	Res	Score	Scorers	Attendance
1	div1	**Millwall**	A	L	0-2		10,898
2	ccR1	**Hull City**	H	W	2-0	McCulloch 7; Jarrett 87	3,295
3	div1	**Preston**	H	D	1-1	McCulloch 89	12,073
4	div1	**Burnley**	A	W	2-0	Kennedy 13; Ellington 77	13,231
5	div1	**Ipswich**	H	W	1-0	Ellington 57	8,292
6	div1	**Rotherham**	A	W	3-0	Jarrett 53; Ellington 59; Roberts 72	6,660
7	div1	**Wimbledon**	A	W	4-2	Bullard 21; Liddell 29; Horsfield 33; Ellington 55	1,054
8	div1	**West Brom**	H	W	1-0	Horsfield 45	12,874
9	div1	**Watford**	H	W	1-0	McCulloch 11	9,211
10	ccR2	**Fulham**	H	W	1-0	Ellington 73	4,874
11	div1	**Coventry**	A	D	1-1	Jackson 90	14,862
12	div1	**Cardiff**	A	D	0-0		15,143
13	div1	**Norwich**	H	D	1-1	Liddell 25	9,346
14	div1	**Derby**	A	D	2-2	Liddell 5,31	19,151
15	div1	**Stoke**	H	W	2-1	Horsfield 56,69	7,678
16	div1	**Gillingham**	H	W	1-0	Liddell 53 pen	6,696
17	div1	**Sheff Utd**	H	D	1-1	Horsfield 4	12,032
18	div1	**Walsall**	A	L	0-2		7,041
19	ccR3	**Middlesbrough**	H	L	1-2	Bullard 75	8,046
20	div1	**Crystal Palace**	H	W	5-0	Liddell 10,50 pen; Horsfield 31; Ellington 56,69	6,796
21	div1	**Reading**	A	L	0-1		13,819
22	div1	**Nottm Forest**	H	D	2-2	Ellington 44; Liddell 71	10,403
23	div1	**West Ham**	A	L	0-4		34,375
24	div1	**Sunderland**	A	D	1-1	De Vos 70	22,167
25	div1	**Reading**	H	L	0-2		7,512
26	div1	**Bradford**	H	W	1-0	Horsfield 85	7,256
27	div1	**Crewe**	A	W	3-2	McCulloch 8; De Vos 20; Bullard 80	7,873
28	div1	**Rotherham**	H	L	1-2	Ellington 90	9,235
29	div1	**Sheff Utd**	A	D	1-1	Ellington 24	26,056
30	facr3	**West Ham**	H	L	1-2	Quinn 90 og	11,793
31	div1	**Millwall**	H	D	0-0		7,047
32	div1	**Preston**	A	W	4-2	Roberts, J 1; Ellington 45,80; Teale 72	19,161
33	div1	**Burnley**	H	D	0-0		11,147
34	div1	**Ipswich**	A	W	3-1	Roberts, J 18; Ellington 33; Teale 53	22,093
35	div1	**Derby**	H	W	2-0	Ellington 45; McCulloch 78	9,146
36	div1	**Stoke**	A	D	1-1	Ellington 84	14,927
37	div1	**Walsall**	H	W	1-0	Ellington 81	7,593
38	div1	**Crewe**	H	L	2-3	McCulloch 30,36	8,367
39	div1	**Bradford**	A	D	0-0		11,744
40	div1	**West brom**	A	L	1-2	Liddell 73 pen	26,215
41	div1	**Coventry**	H	W	2-1	Roberts, J 16,22	8,784
42	div1	**Watford**	A	D	1-1	Roberts, J 13	13,382
43	div1	**Wimbledon**	H	L	0-1		7,622
44	div1	**Gillingham**	A	W	3-0	Ellington 33; Roberts, J 42; Mahon 67	7,410
45	div1	**Norwich**	A	L	0-2		23,446
46	div1	**Cardiff**	H	W	3-0	Roberts, J 36,58; Ellington 54	8,052
47	div1	**Crystal Palace**	A	D	1-1	Ellington 45	18,799
48	div1	**Sunderland**	H	D	0-0		11,380
49	div1	**Nottm Forest**	A	L	0-1		29,172
50	div1	**West Ham**	H	D	1-1	Roberts, N 34	20,669

KEY PLAYERS - GOALSCORERS

Jason Roberts

Goals in the League	8
Goals in all competitions	8
Contribution to Attacking Power Average number of minutes between League team goals while on pitch	62
Player Strike Rate The total number of minutes he was on the pitch for every League goal scored	148
Club Strike Rate Average number of minutes between League goals scored by club	69

	PLAYER	GOALS LGE	GOALS ALL	POWER	S RATE
1	Jason Roberts	8	8	62	148 mins
2	Geoff Horsfield	7	7	60	182 mins
3	Nathan Ellington	18	19	65	203 mins
4	Andy Liddell	9	9	66	338 mins
5	Lee McCulloch	6	7	63	454 mins

KEY PLAYERS - MIDFIELDERS

Andy Liddell

Goals in the League	9
Goals in all competitions	9
Defensive Rating Average number of mins between League goals conceded while on the pitch	95
Contribution to Attacking Power Average number of minutes between League team goals while on pitch	66
Scoring Difference Defensive Rating minus Contribution to Attacking Power	29

	PLAYER	GOALS LGE	GOALS ALL	DEF RATE	ATT POWER	SCORE DIFF
1	Andy Liddell	9	9	95	66	29 mins
2	Jason Jarrett	1	2	86	63	23 mins
3	Jimmy Bullard	2	3	92	69	23 mins
4	Lee McCulloch	6	7	76	63	13 mins

KEY PLAYERS - DEFENDERS

Ian Breckin

Goals Conceded in League	41
Goals Conceded in all competitions	45
Clean Sheets In League games when he played at least 70 mins	17
Defensive Rating Ave number of mins between League goals conceded while on the pitch	96
Club Defensive Rating Average number of mins between League goals conceded by the club this season	92

	PLAYER	CON LGE	CON ALL	CLN SHEETS	DEF RATE
1	Ian Breckin	41	45	17	96 mins
2	Matt Jackson	21	24	8	95 mins
3	Leighton Baines	22	25	7	92 mins
4	Nicky Eaden	45	49	16	91 mins
5	Jason De Vos	25	27	9	90 mins

MONTHLY POINTS TALLY

Month	Points	%
AUGUST	10	67%
SEPTEMBER	11	73%
OCTOBER	9	50%
NOVEMBER	4	33%
DECEMBER	8	44%
JANUARY	5	56%
FEBRUARY	10	83%
MARCH	5	33%
APRIL	8	44%
MAY	1	17%

LEAGUE GOALS

	PLAYER	LGE	FAC	LC	Oth	TOT
1	Ellington	**18**	0	1	0	19
2	Liddell	**9**	0	0	0	9
3	Roberts, J	**8**	0	0	0	8
4	Horsfield	**7**	0	0	0	7
5	McCulloch	**6**	0	1	0	7
6	Teale	**2**	0	0	0	2
7	Roberts, N	**2**	0	0	0	2
8	Bullard	**2**	0	1	0	3
9	De Vos	**2**	0	0	0	2
10	Jarrett	**1**	0	1	0	2
11	Kennedy	**1**	0	0	0	1
	Other	2	1	0	0	3
	TOTAL	**60**	**1**	**4**	**0**	**65**

KEY GOALKEEPER

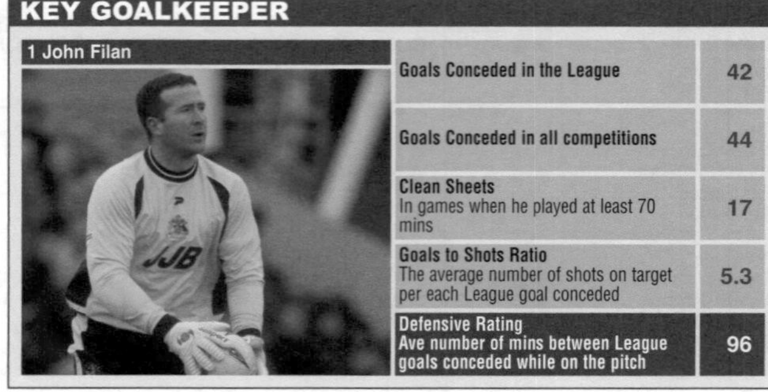

1 John Filan

Goals Conceded in the League	42
Goals Conceded in all competitions	44
Clean Sheets In games when he played at least 70 mins	17
Goals to Shots Ratio The average number of shots on target per each League goal conceded	5.3
Defensive Rating Ave number of mins between League goals conceded while on the pitch	96

DISCIPLINARY RECORDS

	PLAYER	YELLOW	RED	AVE
1	Roberts, J	4	2	197
2	Kennedy	3	1	218
3	Dinning	4	0	223
4	Baines	7	1	251
5	Jarrett	9	1	301
6	McCulloch	7	1	340
7	De Vos	2	2	560
8	McMillan	2	0	561
9	Roberts, N	2	0	586
10	Horsfield	2	0	638
11	Jackson	2	1	665
12	Eaden	6	0	681
13	Filan	3	2	807
	Other	11	0	
	TOTAL	**64**	**11**	

TOP POINT EARNERS

	PLAYER	GAMES	AV PTS
1	Jason Roberts	13	**2.00**
2	Matt Jackson	20	**1.85**
3	Geoff Horsfield	13	**1.85**
4	Andy Liddell	30	**1.67**
5	Jason Jarrett	31	**1.61**
6	Nathan Ellington	40	**1.58**
7	Jimmy Bullard	45	**1.58**
8	John Filan	45	**1.58**
9	Ian Breckin	43	**1.56**
10	Nicky Eaden	45	**1.56**
	CLUB AVERAGE:		**1.54**

TEAM OF THE SEASON

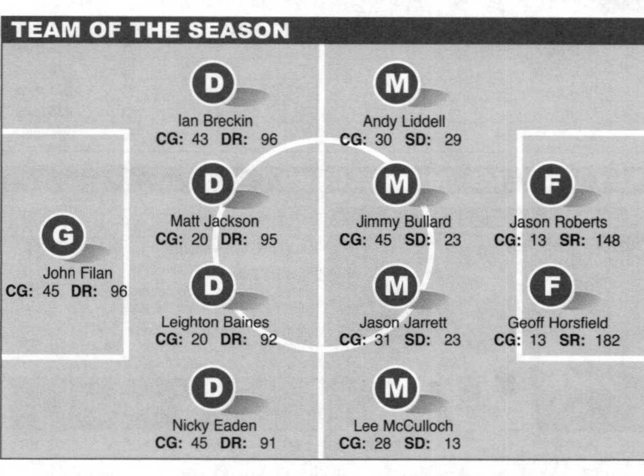
D
Ian Breckin
CG: 43 DR: 96
M
Andy Liddell
CG: 30 SD: 29
D
Matt Jackson
CG: 20 DR: 95
M
Jimmy Bullard
CG: 45 SD: 23
F
Jason Roberts
CG: 13 SR: 148
G
John Filan
CG: 45 DR: 96
D
Leighton Baines
CG: 20 DR: 92
M
Jason Jarrett
CG: 31 SD: 23
F
Geoff Horsfield
CG: 13 SR: 182
D
Nicky Eaden
CG: 45 DR: 91
M
Lee McCulloch
CG: 28 SD: 13

LEAGUE APPEARANCES AND BOOKINGS

	AGE (on 01/07/04)	IN NAMED 16	APPEARANCES	COUNTING GAMES	MINUTES ON PITCH	Yellow	Red
Goalkeepers							
John Filan	34	45	45	45	4035	3	2
James Salisbury	20	1	0	0	0	0	0
Gary Walsh	36	45	3	1	106	0	0
Ryan Yeomans	18	1	0	0	0	0	0
Defenders							
Leighton Baines	19	28	26	20	2013	7	1
Ian Breckin	28	45	45	43	3945	3	0
Jason De Vos	30	28	27	23	2240	2	2
Nicky Eaden	32	46	46	45	4086	6	0
Matt Jackson	32	35	24	20	1996	2	1
Peter Kennedy	30	17	11	10	872	3	1
Steven McMillan	28	18	15	12	1123	2	0
Paul Mitchell	22	34	12	1	361	1	0
Alan Rogers	27	5	5	3	341	2	0
Midfielders							
Jimmy Bullard	25	46	46	45	4050	2	0
Tony Dinning	29	16	13	9	892	4	0
Gareth Farrelly	28	12	7	2	260	0	0
Jason Jarrett	24	43	41	31	3017	9	1
Jamie Lawrence	34	6	4	0	86	0	0
Andy Liddell	31	42	40	30	3043	1	0
Alan Mahon	26	14	14	11	1078	0	0
Lee McCulloch	26	41	41	28	2721	7	1
Forwards							
Mark Burchill	23	6	4	0	94	1	0
Nathan Ellington	23	44	44	40	3658	1	0
Michael Flynn	23	13	8	1	160	0	0
Geoff Horsfield	30	16	16	13	1277	2	0
David Moore	18	0	0	0	0	0	0
Jason Roberts	26	14	14	13	1184	4	2
Neil Roberts	26	35	27	10	1172	2	0
Gary Teale	25	38	28	13	1523	0	0
Magno Silva Vieira	19	2	0	0	0	0	0

SQUAD APPEARANCES

Match	1	2	3	4	5	6	7	8	9	10	11	12	13	14	15	16	17	18	19	20	21	22	23	24	25
Venue	A	H	H	A	H	A	A	H	H	H	A	A	H	A	H	H	H	A	H	H	A	H	A	A	H
Competition	L	W	L	L	L	L	L	L	L	W	L	L	L	L	L	L	L	L	W	L	L	L	L	L	L
Result	L	D	D	W	W	W	W	W	W	W	D	D	D	D	W	W	D	L	L	W	L	D	L	D	L

Match	26	27	28	29	30	31	32	33	34	35	36	37	38	39	40	41	42	43	44	45	46	47	48	49	50
Venue	H	A	H	A	H	H	A	H	A	H	A	H	H	A	A	H	A	H	A	A	H	A	H	A	H
Competition	L	L	L	L	F	L	L	L	L	L	L	L	L	L	L	L	L	L	L	L	L	L	L	L	L
Result	W	W	L	D	L	D	W	D	W	W	D	W	L	D	L	W	D	L	W	L	W	D	D	L	D

Goalkeepers
John Filan
James Salisbury
Gary Walsh
Ryan Yeomans

Defenders
Leighton Baines
Ian Breckin
Jason De Vos
Nicky Eaden
Matt Jackson
Peter Kennedy
Steven McMillan
Paul Mitchell
Alan Rogers

Midfielders
Jimmy Bullard
Tony Dinning
Gareth Farrelly
Jason Jarrett
Jamie Lawrence
Andy Liddell
Alan Mahon
Lee McCulloch

Forwards
Mark Burchill
Nathan Ellington
Michael Flynn
Geoff Horsfield
David Moore
Jason Roberts
Neil Roberts
Gary Teale
Magno Silva Vieira

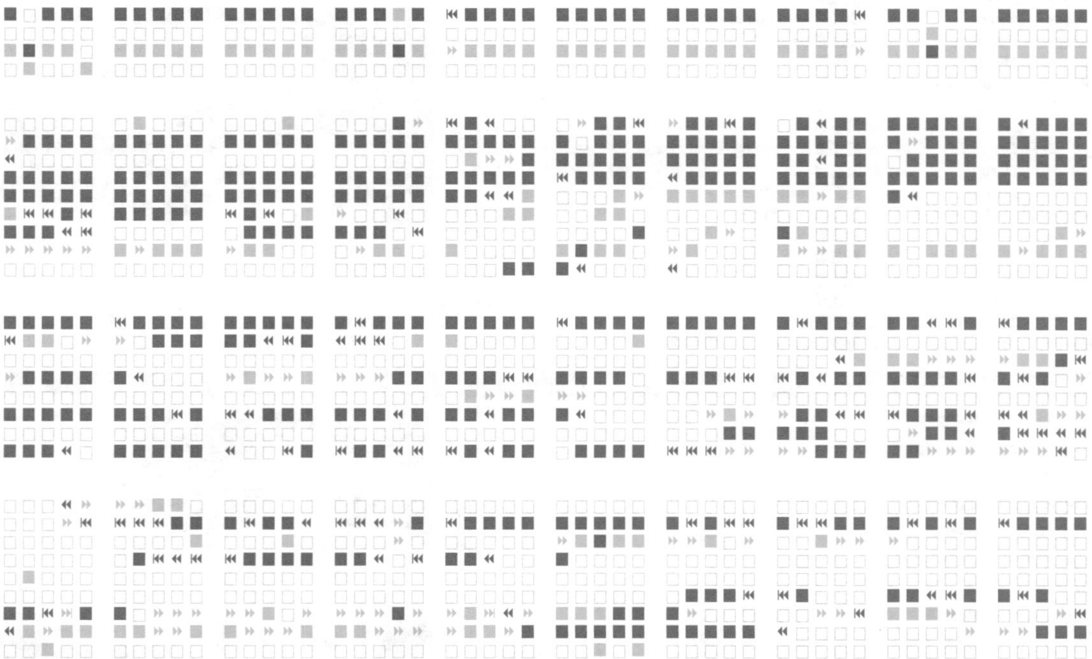

KEY: ■ On all match ■ On bench ⏮ Subbed or sent off (Counting game) « Subbed or sent off (playing less than 70 minutes) ⏭ Subbed on from bench (Counting Game) » Subbed on (playing less than 70 minutes) ⏭ Subbed on and then subbed or sent off (Counting Game) » Subbed on and then subbed or sent off (playing less than 70 minutes) □ Not in 16

SHEFFIELD UNITED

Final Position: **8th**

NICKNAME: THE BLADES

KEY: Won Drawn Lost

							Attendance
1	div1	Gillingham	H	D	0-0		21,569
2	ccR1	Macclesfield	A	W	2-1	Lester 35,82 pen	2,764
3	div1	West Ham	A	D	0-0		28,972
4	div1	Norwich	H	W	1-0	Page 23	24,285
5	div1	Crystal Palace	A	W	2-1	Ndlovu 18; Allison 45	15,466
6	div1	Coventry	H	W	2-1	Brown 42 pen; Lester 87	20,102
7	div1	Nottm Forest	A	L	1-3	Ndlovu 54	25,209
8	div1	Rotherham	H	W	5-0	Tonge 12; Peschisolido 23,57; Ndlovu 61,83	22,572
9	div1	Cardiff	H	W	5-3	Tonge 53; Ndlovu 62,78 pen,89 pen; Lester 85	21,323
10	ccR2	QPR	H	L	0-2		9,578
11	div1	Bradford	A	W	2-1	Ndlovu 29; McCall 54	11,067
12	div1	Wimbledon	A	W	2-1	Ward 62; Peschisolido 68	6,016
13	div1	Sunderland	H	L	0-1		27,008
14	div1	West Brom	A	W	2-0	Tonge 9; Ward 37	27,195
15	div1	Millwall	A	L	0-2		10,046
16	div1	Wigan	A	D	1-1	Lester 86	12,032
17	div1	Reading	H	L	1-2	Ward 10	20,651
18	div1	Stoke	A	D	2-2	Kozluk 53; Lester 90 pen	14,217
19	div1	Crewe	H	W	2-0	Armstrong 21; Lester 74 pen	17,396
20	div1	Burnley	H	W	1-0	Tonge 45	20,967
21	div1	Ipswich	A	L	0-3		25,004
22	div1	Preston	H	W	2-0	Brown 31 pen; McCall 75	21,003
23	div1	Burnley	A	L	2-3	Montgomery 24; Whitlow 31	11,452
24	div1	Walsall	H	W	2-0	Peschisolido 41; Montgomery 52	8,602
25	div1	Watford	H	D	2-2	Jagielka 52; Lester 85 pen	18,637
26	div1	Coventry	A	W	1-0	Lester 56 pen	21,132
27	div1	Wigan	H	D	1-1	Lester 23	26,056
28	facr3	Cardiff	A	W	1-0	Allison 74	10,525
29	div1	Gillingham	A	W	3-0	Peschisolido 38,58,66	8,353
30	div1	West Ham	H	D	3-3	Peschisolido 5; Shaw 72; Jagielka 90	22,787
31	facr4	Nottm Forest	A	W	3-0	Lester 33 pen; Morgan 79; Allison 90	17,306
32	div1	Derby	A	L	0-2		23,603
33	div1	Norwich	A	L	0-1		18,977
34	div1	Crystal Palace	H	L	0-3		23,816
35	facr5	Colchester	H	W	1-0	Peschisolido 61	17,074
36	div1	West Brom	H	L	1-2	Moore 57 og	34,805
37	div1	Crewe	A	W	1-0	Montgomery 85	6,525
38	div1	Reading	A	L	1-2	Gray 10	15,545
39	div1	Millwall	H	W	2-1	Ward 58; Gray 62	19,579
40	facqf	Sunderland	A	L	0-1		37,115
41	div1	Watford	A	W	2-0	Lester 42; Gray 90	13,861
42	div1	Rotherham	A	D	1-1	Lester 48 pen	9,793
43	div1	Bradford	H	W	2-0	Morgan 60; Lester 62	20,052
44	div1	Derby	H	D	1-1	Gray 21	21,351
45	div1	Cardiff	A	L	1-2	Ndlovu 25	13,666
46	div1	Nottm Forest	H	L	1-2	Wright 59	22,339
47	div1	Sunderland	A	L	0-3		27,472
48	div1	Wimbledon	H	W	2-1	Gray 50,67	19,391
49	div1	Stoke	H	L	0-1		19,372
50	div1	Walsall	A	W	1-0	Lester 49 pen	7,873
51	div1	Ipswich	H	D	1-1	Gray 63 pen	24,184
52	div1	Preston	A	D	3-3	Jagielka 21; Gray 38,77	16,612

KEY PLAYERS - GOALSCORERS

Andy Gray

Goals in the League	9
Goals in all competitions	9
Contribution to Attacking Power Average number of minutes between League team goals while on pitch	71
Player Strike Rate The total number of minutes he was on the pitch for every League goal scored	135
Club Strike Rate Average number of minutes between League goals scored by club	64

	PLAYER	GOALS LGE	GOALS ALL	POWER	S RATE
1	Andy Gray	9	9	71	135 mins
2	Jack Lester	12	15	63	180 mins
3	Peter Ndlovu	9	9	62	277 mins
4	Ashley Ward	4	4	64	436 mins
5	Nick Montgomery	3	3	63	888 mins

KEY PLAYERS - MIDFIELDERS

Stuart McCall

Goals in the League	2
Goals in all competitions	2
Defensive Rating Average number of mins between League goals conceded while on the pitch	79
Contribution to Attacking Power Average number of minutes between League team goals while on pitch	57
Scoring Difference Defensive Rating minus Contribution to Attacking Power	22

	PLAYER	GOALS LGE	GOALS ALL	DEF RATE	ATT POWER	SCORE DIFF
1	Stuart McCall	2	2	79	57	22 mins
2	Michael Tonge	4	4	74	63	11 mins
3	Andy Gray	9	9	76	71	5 mins
4	Nick Montgomery	3	3	65	63	2 mins

KEY PLAYERS - DEFENDERS

Robert Page

Goals Conceded in League	32
Goals Conceded in all competitions	34
Clean Sheets In League games when he played at least 70 mins	10
Defensive Rating Ave number of mins between League goals conceded while on the pitch	82
Club Defensive Rating Average number of mins between League goals conceded by the club this season	74

	PLAYER	CON LGE	CON ALL	CLN SHEETS	DEF RATE
1	Robert Page	32	34	10	82 mins
2	Robert Kozluk	48	52	13	76 mins
3	Chris Morgan	37	39	11	75 mins
4	Philip Jagielka	52	56	15	74 mins
5	Alan Wright	25	25	6	71 mins

MONTHLY POINTS TALLY

AUGUST	11	73%
SEPTEMBER	12	80%
OCTOBER	4	27%
NOVEMBER	10	67%
DECEMBER	8	53%
JANUARY	4	33%
FEBRUARY	3	25%
MARCH	11	61%
APRIL	7	39%
MAY	1	33%

LEAGUE GOALS

	PLAYER	LGE	FAC	LC	Oth	TOT
1	Lester	12	1	2	0	15
2	Ndlovu	9	0	0	0	9
3	Gray	9	0	0	0	9
4	Peschisolido	8	1	0	0	9
5	Ward	4	0	0	0	4
6	Tonge	4	0	0	0	4
7	Montgomery	3	0	0	0	3
8	Jagielka, P	3	0	0	0	3
9	Brown	2	0	0	0	2
10	McCall	2	0	0	0	2
11	Wright	1	0	0	0	1
	Other	8	3	0	0	11
	TOTAL	65	5	2	0	72

KEY GOALKEEPER

1 Patrick Kenny

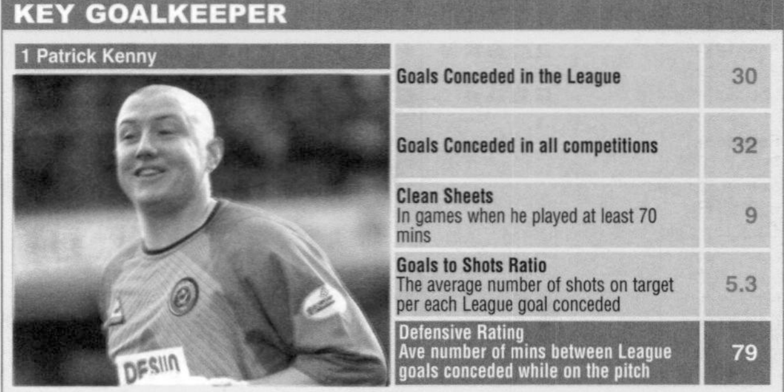

Goals Conceded in the League	30
Goals Conceded in all competitions	32
Clean Sheets In games when he played at least 70 mins	9
Goals to Shots Ratio The average number of shots on target per each League goal conceded	5.3
Defensive Rating Ave number of mins between League goals conceded while on the pitch	79

DISCIPLINARY RECORDS

	PLAYER	YELLOW	RED	AVE
1	Whitlow	7	0	180
2	Ward	7	0	248
3	Morgan	6	1	396
4	Brown	1	2	399
5	Lester	5	0	432
6	Page	6	0	439
7	Kozluk	7	1	456
8	Montgomery	5	0	533
9	Kenny	3	0	794
10	Tonge	5	0	823
11	Ndlovu	3	0	829
12	Wright	2	0	886
13	McCall	3	0	1023
	Other	11	0	
	TOTAL	71	4	

TOP POINT EARNERS

	PLAYER	GAMES	AV PTS
1	Jack Lester	21	**1.81**
2	Paul Gerrard	16	**1.81**
3	Ashley Ward	16	**1.75**
4	Stuart McCall	34	**1.74**
5	Peter Ndlovu	23	**1.61**
6	Robert Kozluk	40	**1.60**
7	Philip Jagielka	43	**1.58**
8	Robert Page	29	**1.55**
9	Michael Tonge	46	**1.54**
10	Chris Morgan	30	**1.50**
	CLUB AVERAGE:		**1.54**

TEAM OF THE SEASON

G
Patrick Kenny
CG: 26 **DR:** 79

D
Robert Page
CG: 29 **DR:** 82

D
Robert Kozluk
CG: 40 **DR:** 76

D
Chris Morgan
CG: 30 **DR:** 75

D
Philip Jagielka
CG: 43 **DR:** 74

M
Stuart McCall
CG: 34 **SD:** 22

M
Michael Tonge
CG: 46 **SD:** 11

M
Andy Gray
CG: 13 **SD:** 5

M
Nick Montgomery
CG: 24 **SD:** 2

F
Jack Lester
CG: 21 **SR:** 180

F
Peter Ndlovu
CG: 23 **SR:** 277

LEAGUE APPEARANCES AND BOOKINGS

	AGE (on 01/07/04)	IN NAMED 16	APPEARANCES	COUNTING GAMES	MINUTES ON PITCH	Yellow	Red
Goalkeepers							
Lee Baxter	28	1	1	0	45	0	0
Alan Fettis	33	3	3	2	225	0	0
Paul Gerrard	31	16	16	16	1440	0	0
Patrick Kenny	25	27	27	26	2384	3	0
Kristian Rogers	23	0	0	0	0	0	0
Defenders							
Chris Armstrong	21	17	12	4	580	0	0
Simon Francis	19	8	5	4	357	1	0
Jon Harley	24	5	5	4	398	2	0
Philip Jagielka	21	45	43	43	3870	2	0
Robert Kozluk	26	44	42	40	3652	7	1
Chris Morgan	26	32	32	30	2775	6	1
Robert Page	29	31	30	29	2636	6	0
Ashley Sestanovich	-	2	2	0	54	0	0
Michael Whitlow	36	32	17	13	1261	7	0
Alan Wright	32	24	20	19	1772	2	0
Midfielders							
Michael Brown	27	15	15	12	1198	1	2
Colin Cryan	23	6	1	0	21	0	0
Andy Gray	26	14	14	13	1213	1	0
Kevan Hurst	18	0	0	0	0	0	0
Stuart McCall	40	39	37	34	3070	3	0
Nick Montgomery	23	42	36	24	2665	5	0
Mark Rankine	34	29	12	5	557	0	0
Carl Robinson	27	6	5	4	341	0	0
Ian Ross	18	1	0	0	0	0	0
Michael Tonge	21	46	46	46	4117	5	0
Danny Wood	20	1	1	1	90	0	0
Forwards							
Wayne Allison	35	44	39	12	1520	1	0
Dries Boussatta	31	13	6	1	242	0	0
Jonathan Forte	17	10	7	1	203	0	0
Steve Kabba	23	2	1	0	31	0	0
Jack Lester	28	36	32	21	2162	5	0
Izale McLeod	19	10	6	1	180	2	0
Peter Ndlovu	31	38	36	23	2489	3	0
Andy Parkinson	25	18	7	3	272	1	0
Paul Peschisolido	33	33	27	8	1255	1	0
Paul Shaw	30	19	13	3	442	0	0
Dean Sturridge	30	4	4	0	138	0	0
Ashley Ward	33	23	23	16	1742	7	0

SQUAD APPEARANCES

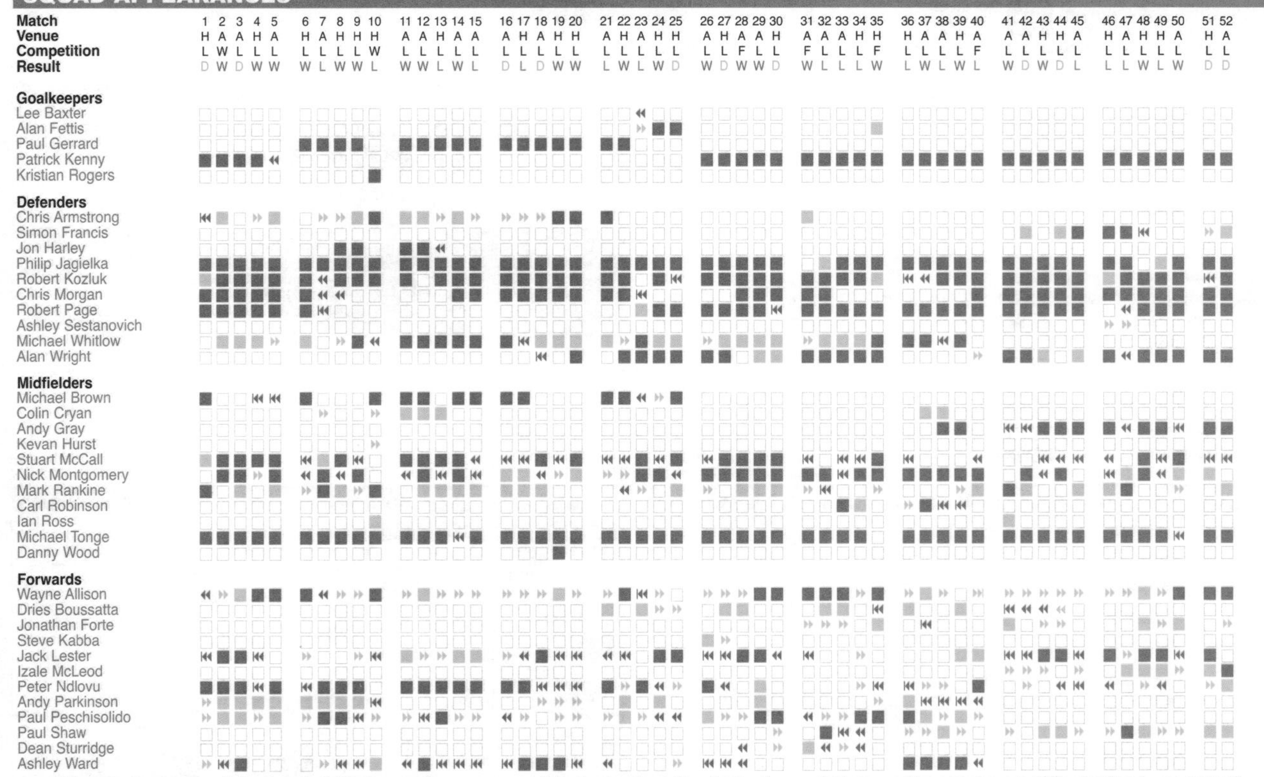

Match 1 2 3 4 5 6 7 8 9 10 11 12 13 14 15 16 17 18 19 20 21 22 23 24 25 26 27 28 29 30 31 32 33 34 35 36 37 38 39 40 41 42 43 44 45 46 47 48 49 50 51 52
Venue H A A H A H A H H H A A H A A A H A H H A H A H H A H A A H A A A H H H A A H A A A H H A H A H H A H A
Competition L W L L L L L L L W L L L L L L L L L L L L L L L L L F L L F L L L F L L L L F L L L L L L L L L L L L
Result D W D W W W L W W L W W L W L D L D W W L W L W D W D W W D W L L L W L W L W L W D W D L L L W L W D D
Goalkeepers
Lee Baxter
Alan Fettis
Paul Gerrard
Patrick Kenny
Kristian Rogers
Defenders
Chris Armstrong
Simon Francis
Jon Harley
Philip Jagielka
Robert Kozluk
Chris Morgan
Robert Page
Ashley Sestanovich
Michael Whitlow
Alan Wright
Midfielders
Michael Brown
Colin Cryan
Andy Gray
Kevan Hurst
Stuart McCall
Nick Montgomery
Mark Rankine
Carl Robinson
Ian Ross
Michael Tonge
Danny Wood
Forwards
Wayne Allison
Dries Boussatta
Jonathan Forte
Steve Kabba
Jack Lester
Izale McLeod
Peter Ndlovu
Andy Parkinson
Paul Peschisolido
Paul Shaw
Dean Sturridge
Ashley Ward
KEY: On all match
On bench
Subbed or sent off (Counting game)
Subbed or sent off (playing less than 70 minutes)
Subbed on from bench (Counting Game)
Subbed on (playing less than 70 minutes)
Subbed on and then subbed or sent off (Counting Game)
Subbed on and then subbed or sent off (playing less than 70 minutes)
Not in 16

READING

Final Position: **9th**

NICKNAME: THE ROYALS

KEY: Won / Drawn / Lost

							Attendance
1	div1	**Ipswich**	A	D	1-1	Sidwell 59	24,830
2	ccR1	**Boston**	A	W	3-1	Forster 16,87; Sidwell 83	2,055
3	div1	**Nottm Forest**	H	W	3-0	Sidwell 49; Murray 59; Goater 79	16,833
4	div1	**Derby**	A	W	3-2	Goater 3; Murray 30,36	18,970
5	div1	**Rotherham**	H	D	0-0		14,047
6	div1	**Wimbledon**	A	W	3-0	Goater 12,59; Hughes 53	2,066
7	div1	**West Ham**	A	L	0-1		32,634
8	div1	**Cardiff**	H	W	2-1	Forster 62; Sidwell 79	15,810
9	div1	**Coventry**	H	L	1-2	Forster 21	15,371
10	ccR2	**Oxford**	A	W	3-1	Salako 52; Forster 66; Harper 90	9,870
11	div1	**Sunderland**	A	L	0-2		22,420
12	div1	**Norwich**	A	L	1-2	Forster 25	16,387
13	div1	**Bradford**	H	D	2-2	Sidwell 5; Hughes 78	12,594
14	div1	**Gillingham**	H	W	2-1	Murray 54; Sidwell 85	13,011
15	div1	**Preston**	H	W	3-2	Goater 39 pen; Mackie 82; Forster 90	13,130
16	div1	**Walsall**	H	L	0-1		11,225
17	div1	**Sheff Utd**	A	W	2-1	Williams 7; Forster 43	20,651
18	ccR3	**Huddersfield**	H	W	1-0	Forster 83	11,892
19	div1	**Crewe**	A	L	0-1		7,091
20	div1	**Wigan**	H	W	1-0	Hughes 69	13,819
21	div1	**Millwall**	H	W	1-0	Salako 23	14,090
22	div1	**West Brom**	A	D	0-0		22,839
23	div1	**Burnley**	A	L	0-3		9,473
24	div1	**Watford**	H	W	2-1	Cox 59 og; Sidwell 88	14,521
25	ccR4	**Chelsea**	H	L	0-1		24,107
26	div1	**Wigan**	A	W	2-0	Forster 55,89	7,512
27	div1	**Stoke**	A	L	0-3		11,212
28	div1	**Crystal Palace**	H	L	0-3		12,743
29	div1	**Wimbledon**	H	L	0-3		14,486
30	div1	**Walsall**	A	D	1-1	Shorey 72	8,089
31	facr3	**Preston**	A	D	3-3	Goater 7; Jackson, Mi 13 og; Davis 37 og	9,428
32	div1	**Ipswich**	H	D	1-1	Owusu 62	17,362
33	facr3r	**Preston**	H	L	1-2	Goater 84	9,314
34	div1	**Nottm Forest**	A	W	1-0	Murray 41	23,116
35	div1	**Derby**	H	W	3-1	Goater 2,51; Sidwell 41	14,382
36	div1	**Rotherham**	A	L	1-5	Goater 20 pen	6,405
37	div1	**Gillingham**	A	W	1-0	Goater 8	8,600
38	div1	**Burnley**	H	D	2-2	Owusu 19; Harper 90	10,543
39	div1	**Sheff Utd**	H	W	2-1	Shorey 25; Goater 34 pen	15,545
40	div1	**Preston**	A	L	1-2	Salako 82	11,745
41	div1	**Crystal Palace**	A	D	2-2	Owusu 14,56	17,853
42	div1	**Stoke**	H	D	0-0		14,132
43	div1	**Cardiff**	A	W	3-2	Ingimarsson 39; Kitson 45; Morgan 90	14,051
44	div1	**Sunderland**	H	L	0-2		18,019
45	div1	**Coventry**	A	W	2-1	Salako 10; Goater 54	15,811
46	div1	**West Ham**	H	W	2-0	Kitson 35,52	21,718
47	div1	**Bradford**	A	L	1-2	Kitson 25	10,287
48	div1	**Norwich**	H	L	0-1		18,460
49	div1	**Crewe**	H	D	1-1	Kitson 10	14,729
50	div1	**Millwall**	A	W	1-0	Goater 16	12,535
51	div1	**West Brom**	H	W	1-0	Sidwell 88	20,619
52	div1	**Watford**	A	L	0-1		17,979

KEY PLAYERS - GOALSCORERS

Shaun Goater

Goals in the League	12
Goals in all competitions	14
Contribution to Attacking Power Average number of minutes between League team goals while on pitch	63
Player Strike Rate The total number of minutes he was on the pitch for every League goal scored	205
Club Strike Rate Average number of minutes between League goals scored by club	75

	PLAYER	GOALS LGE	GOALS ALL	POWER	S RATE
1	Shaun Goater	12	14	63	**205 mins**
2	Nick Forster	7	11	82	**365 mins**
3	Scott Murray	5	5	69	**445 mins**
4	Steven Sidwell	8	9	72	**474 mins**
5	John Salako	3	4	83	**867 mins**

KEY PLAYERS - MIDFIELDERS

Steven Sidwell

Goals in the League	8
Goals in all competitions	9
Defensive Rating Average number of mins between League goals conceded while on the pitch	74
Contribution to Attacking Power Average number of minutes between League team goals while on pitch	73
Scoring Difference Defensive Rating minus Contribution to Attacking Power	1

	PLAYER	GOALS LGE	GOALS ALL	DEF RATE	ATT POWER	SCORE DIFF
1	Steven Sidwell	8	9	74	73	**1 mins**
2	James Harper	1	2	82	82	**0 mins**
3	Scott Murray	5	5	70	70	**0 mins**
4	Andrew Hughes	3	3	73	75	**-2 mins**
5	Ricky Newman	0	0	70	78	**-8 mins**

KEY PLAYERS - DEFENDERS

Graeme Murty

Goals Conceded in League	42
Goals Conceded in all competitions	49
Clean Sheets In League games when he played at least 70 mins	13
Defensive Rating Ave number of mins between League goals conceded while on the pitch	80
Club Defensive Rating Average number of mins between League goals conceded by the club this season	73

	PLAYER	CON LGE	CON ALL	CLN SHEETS	DEF RATE
1	Graeme Murty	42	49	13	**80 mins**
2	Adrian Williams	39	46	7	**74 mins**
3	Steve Brown	23	28	4	**71 mins**
4	Nicky Shorey	44	52	10	**71 mins**
5	Ivar Ingimarsson	31	34	7	**69 mins**

MONTHLY POINTS TALLY

AUGUST	11	73%
SEPTEMBER	3	20%
OCTOBER	10	67%
NOVEMBER	10	56%
DECEMBER	4	27%
JANUARY	7	78%
FEBRUARY	7	58%
MARCH	8	44%
APRIL	7	47%
MAY	3	50%

LEAGUE GOALS

	PLAYER	LGE	FAC	LC	Oth	TOT
1	Goater	**12**	2	0	0	14
2	Sidwell	**8**	0	1	0	9
3	Forster	**7**	0	4	0	11
4	Murray	**5**	0	0	0	5
5	Kitson	**5**	0	0	0	5
6	Owusu	**4**	0	0	0	4
7	Hughes	**3**	0	0	0	3
8	Salako	**3**	0	1	0	4
9	Shorey	**2**	0	0	0	2
10	Ingimarsson	**1**	0	0	0	1
11	Harper	**1**	0	1	0	2
	Other	4	2	0	0	6
	TOTAL	**55**	**4**	**7**	**0**	**66**

KEY GOALKEEPER

1 Marcus Hahnemann

Goals Conceded in the League	47
Goals Conceded in all competitions	55
Clean Sheets In games when he played at least 70 mins	10
Goals to Shots Ratio The average number of shots on target per each League goal conceded	4.4
Defensive Rating Ave number of mins between League goals conceded while on the pitch	68

DISCIPLINARY RECORDS

	PLAYER	YELLOW	RED	AVE
1	Savage	2	0	302
2	Newman	7	0	322
3	Brown	5	0	327
4	Sidwell	10	1	344
5	Owusu	1	1	499
6	Murray	4	0	556
7	Williams	5	0	580
8	Mackie	1	0	652
9	Hughes	4	0	862
10	Kitson	1	0	1014
11	Ingimarsson	1	1	1076
12	Forster	2	0	1276
13	Goater	1	0	2458
	Other	4	1	
	TOTAL	48	4	

TOP POINT EARNERS

	PLAYER	GAMES	AV PTS
1	Shaun Goater	23	**1.91**
2	Ricky Newman	22	**1.73**
3	James Harper	31	**1.65**
4	John Salako	25	**1.60**
5	Graeme Murty	37	**1.59**
6	Andrew Hughes	35	**1.57**
7	Ivar Ingimarsson	23	**1.52**
8	Marcus Hahnemann	35	**1.51**
9	Steven Sidwell	41	**1.51**
10	Steve Brown	17	**1.47**
	CLUB AVERAGE:		**1.52**

TEAM OF THE SEASON

G — Marcus Hahnemann CG: 35 DR: 68

D — Graeme Murty CG: 37 DR: 80

D — Adrian Williams CG: 32 DR: 74

D — Steve Brown CG: 17 DR: 71

D — Nicky Shorey CG: 35 DR: 71

M — Steven Sidwell CG: 41 SD: 1

M — James Harper CG: 31 SD: 0

M — Scott Murray CG: 20 SD: 0

M — Andrew Hughes CG: 35 SD: -2

F — Shaun Goater CG: 23 SR: 205

F — Nick Forster CG: 28 SR: 365

LEAGUE APPEARANCES AND BOOKINGS

	AGE (on 01/07/04)	IN NAMED 16	APPEARANCES	COUNTING GAMES	MINUTES ON PITCH	Yellow	Red
Goalkeepers							
Jamie Ashdown	23	27	10	10	900	0	0
Marcus Hahnemann	32	38	36	35	3205	1	0
Jamie Young	19	27	1	0	35	0	0
Defenders							
Steve Brown	32	21	19	17	1635	5	0
Dean Gordon	31	5	3	0	77	0	0
Ivar Ingimarsson	26	28	25	23	2152	1	1
John Mackie	28	19	9	6	652	1	0
Graeme Murty	29	38	38	37	3360	1	0
Nicky Shorey	23	35	35	35	3138	0	1
Adrian Williams	32	34	33	32	2900	5	0
Midfielders							
Andre Boucaud	19	2	0	0	0	0	0
Paul Brooker	28	14	11	3	497	0	0
Omar Daley	23	7	5	0	98	0	0
James Harper	23	43	39	31	3102	1	0
Andrew Hughes	26	43	43	35	3449	4	0
Scott Murray	30	36	34	20	2226	4	0
Ricky Newman	33	38	30	22	2254	7	0
John Salako	35	39	37	25	2602	0	0
Steven Sidwell	21	43	43	41	3789	10	1
Kevin Watson	30	29	22	7	1010	0	0
Forwards							
Martin Butler	29	4	3	0	59	0	0
Andre Fashanu	20	0	0	0	0	0	0
Nick Forster	30	30	30	28	2552	2	0
Shaun Goater	34	38	34	23	2458	1	0
Darius Henderson	22	3	1	0	13	1	0
David Kitson	24	19	17	10	1014	1	0
Dean Morgan	20	17	13	2	454	0	0
Lloyd Owusu	27	19	16	8	998	1	1
Basir Savage	22	24	15	3	604	2	0
Nathan Tyson	22	16	8	0	189	0	0

SQUAD APPEARANCES

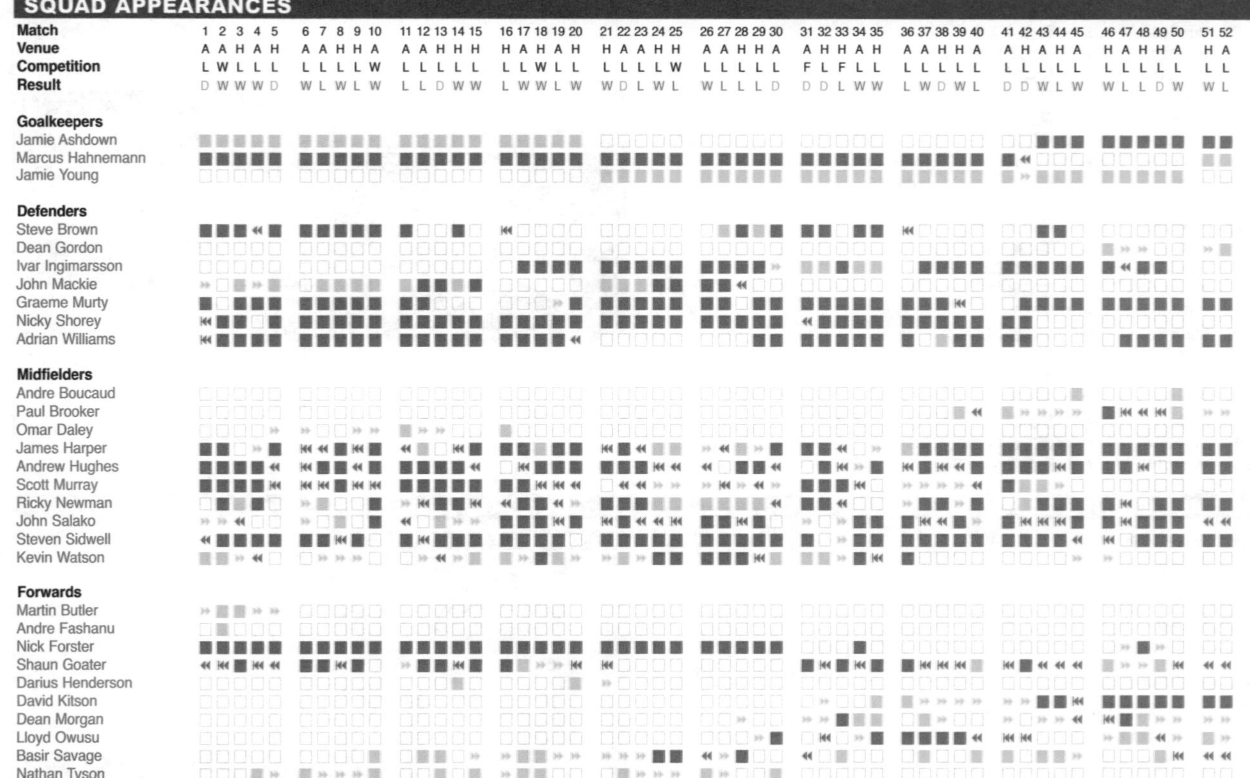

Match 1 2 3 4 5 6 7 8 9 10 11 12 13 14 15 16 17 18 19 20 21 22 23 24 25 26 27 28 29 30 31 32 33 34 35 36 37 38 39 40 41 42 43 44 45 46 47 48 49 50 51 52
Venue A A H A H A A H H A A A H H H H A H A H H A A H H A A H H A A H H A H A A H H A A H A H A H A H H A H A
Competition L W L L L L L L L W L L L L L L L W L L L L L L W L L L L L F L F L L L L L L L L L L L L L L L L L L L
Result D W W W D W L W L W L L D W W L W W L W W D L W L W L L L D D D L W W L W D W L D D W L W W L L D W W L
Goalkeepers
Jamie Ashdown
Marcus Hahnemann
Jamie Young
Defenders
Steve Brown
Dean Gordon
Ivar Ingimarsson
John Mackie
Graeme Murty
Nicky Shorey
Adrian Williams
Midfielders
Andre Boucaud
Paul Brooker
Omar Daley
James Harper
Andrew Hughes
Scott Murray
Ricky Newman
John Salako
Steven Sidwell
Kevin Watson
Forwards
Martin Butler
Andre Fashanu
Nick Forster
Shaun Goater
Darius Henderson
David Kitson
Dean Morgan
Lloyd Owusu
Basir Savage
Nathan Tyson
KEY: On all match
On bench
Subbed or sent off (Counting game)
Subbed or sent off (playing less than 70 minutes)
Subbed on from bench (Counting Game)
Subbed on (playing less than 70 minutes)
Subbed on and then subbed or sent off (Counting Game)
Subbed on and then subbed or sent off (playing less than 70 minutes)
Not in 16

MILLWALL

Final Position: **10th**

NICKNAME: THE LIONS

KEY: □ Won □ Drawn □ Lost

							Attendance
1	div1	**Wigan**	H	W	2-0	Wise 53; Cahill 74	10,898
2	ccR1	**Oxford**	H	L	0-1		4,781
3	div1	**Sunderland**	A	W	1-0	Whelan 7	24,877
4	div1	**Crewe**	H	D	1-1	Whelan 90	9,504
5	div1	**Stoke**	A	D	0-0		13,087
6	div1	**Crystal Palace**	H	D	1-1	Peeters 90	14,425
7	div1	**Gillingham**	A	L	3-4	Ifill 11; Peeters 61,69	8,237
8	div1	**Watford**	A	L	1-3	Ifill 34	11,305
9	div1	**Wimbledon**	H	W	2-0	Harris 44 pen; Whelan 90	7,855
10	div1	**Walsall**	H	W	2-1	Ward 16; Harris 80 pen	9,262
11	div1	**West Ham**	A	D	1-1	Cahill 73	31,626
12	div1	**West Brom**	A	L	1-2	Nethercott 45	22,909
13	div1	**Coventry**	H	W	2-1	Ifill 63; Harris 85	9,849
14	div1	**Rotherham**	A	D	0-0		5,461
15	div1	**Preston**	H	L	0-1		8,015
16	div1	**Sheff Utd**	H	W	2-0	Harris 54 pen; Ifill 66	10,046
17	div1	**Burnley**	A	D	1-1	Whelan 53	10,435
18	div1	**Nottm Forest**	H	W	1-0	Braniff 45	9,635
19	div1	**Norwich**	A	L	1-3	Ward 90	16,423
20	div1	**Reading**	A	L	0-1		14,090
21	div1	**Derby**	H	D	0-0		10,308
22	div1	**Bradford**	A	L	2-3	Cahill 19; Chadwick 24	10,107
23	div1	**Norwich**	H	D	0-0		9,850
24	div1	**Ipswich**	H	D	0-0		9,829
25	div1	**Cardiff**	A	W	3-1	Roberts 5; Cahill 65; Sweeney 84	14,610
26	div1	**Crystal Palace**	A	W	1-0	Harris 18	19,737
27	div1	**Gillingham**	H	L	1-2	Chadwick 56	12,084
28	facr3	**Walsall**	H	W	2-1	Baltacha 33; Cahill 45	6,977
29	div1	**Wigan**	A	D	0-0		7,047
30	div1	**Sunderland**	H	W	2-1	Dichio 39,62	13,048
31	div1	**Crewe**	A	W	2-1	Dichio 44,90	6,685
32	div1	**Stoke**	H	D	1-1	Dichio 23	9,034
33	facr4	**Telford**	A	W	2-0	Ifill 37; Wise 83	5,589
34	facr5	**Burnley**	H	W	1-0	Dichio 72	10,420
35	div1	**Preston**	A	W	2-1	Ifill 45; Cahill 77	12,903
36	div1	**Rotherham**	H	W	2-1	Harris 38; Cahill 90	8,254
37	div1	**Burnley**	H	W	2-0	Ifill 12; Sweeney 52	10,148
38	div1	**Sheff Utd**	A	L	1-2	Ifill 69	19,579
39	facqf	**Tranmere**	H	D	0-0		16,404
40	div1	**Ipswich**	A	W	3-1	Harris 30,48; Ward 37	23,582
41	facqfr	**Tranmere**	A	W	2-1	Cahill 11; Harris 16	15,510
42	div1	**West Ham**	H	W	4-1	Dailly 34 og; Cahill 46,56; Chadwick 80	14,055
43	div1	**Wimbledon**	A	W	1-0	Cahill 43	3,037
44	div1	**Walsall**	A	D	1-1	Ifill 88	6,486
45	facsf	**Sunderland**	A	W	1-0	Cahill 25	56,112
46	div1	**Cardiff**	H	D	0-0		9,584
47	div1	**Coventry**	A	L	0-4		12,546
48	div1	**West Brom**	H	D	1-1	Dichio 19	13,304
49	div1	**Nottm Forest**	A	D	2-2	Livermore 46; Chadwick 84	22,263
50	div1	**Watford**	H	L	1-2	Dichio 16	10,263
51	div1	**Reading**	H	L	0-1		12,535
52	div1	**Derby**	A	L	0-2		26,056
53	div1	**Bradford**	H	W	1-0	Harris 58 pen	9,635
54	facf	**Man Utd**	A	L	0-3		71,350

KEY PLAYERS - GOALSCORERS

Neil Harris

Goals in the League	9
Goals in all competitions	10
Contribution to Attacking Power Average number of minutes between League team goals while on pitch	62
Player Strike Rate The total number of minutes he was on the pitch for every League goal scored	265
Club Strike Rate Average number of minutes between League goals scored by club	75

	PLAYER	GOALS LGE	GOALS ALL	POWER	S RATE
1	Neil Harris	9	10	62	**265 mins**
2	Paul Ifill	8	9	64	**320 mins**
3	Tim Cahill	9	12	73	**392 mins**
4	Peter Sweeney	2	2	88	**969 mins**
5	Darren Ward	3	3	75	**1380 mins**

KEY PLAYERS - MIDFIELDERS

Tim Cahill

Goals in the League	9
Goals in all competitions	12
Defensive Rating Average number of mins between League goals conceded while on the pitch	93
Contribution to Attacking Power Average number of minutes between League team goals while on pitch	74
Scoring Difference Defensive Rating minus Contribution to Attacking Power	19

	PLAYER	GOALS LGE	GOALS ALL	DEF RATE	ATT POWER	SCORE DIFF
1	Tim Cahill	9	12	93	74	**19 mins**
2	Dennis Wise	1	2	91	73	**18 mins**
3	Andy Roberts	1	1	87	74	**13 mins**
4	David Livermore	1	1	78	82	**-4 mins**
5	Peter Sweeney	2	2	75	88	**-13 mins**

KEY PLAYERS - DEFENDERS

Robert Ryan

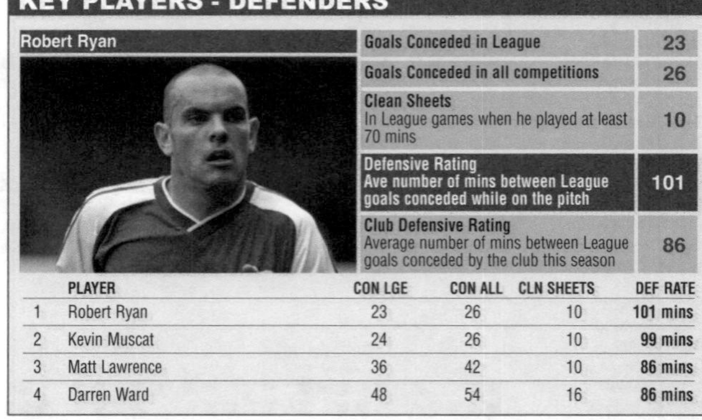

Goals Conceded in League	23
Goals Conceded in all competitions	26
Clean Sheets In League games when he played at least 70 mins	10
Defensive Rating Ave number of mins between League goals conceded while on the pitch	101
Club Defensive Rating Average number of mins between League goals conceded by the club this season	86

	PLAYER	CON LGE	CON ALL	CLN SHEETS	DEF RATE
1	Robert Ryan	23	26	10	**101 mins**
2	Kevin Muscat	24	26	10	**99 mins**
3	Matt Lawrence	36	42	10	**86 mins**
4	Darren Ward	48	54	16	**86 mins**

MONTHLY POINTS TALLY

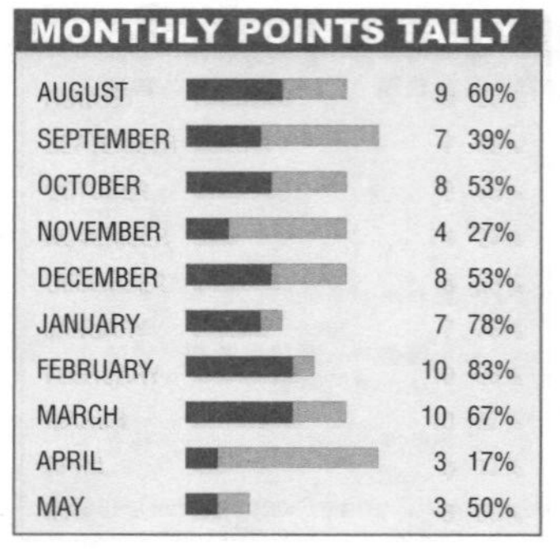

AUGUST	9	60%
SEPTEMBER	7	39%
OCTOBER	8	53%
NOVEMBER	4	27%
DECEMBER	8	53%
JANUARY	7	78%
FEBRUARY	10	83%
MARCH	10	67%
APRIL	3	17%
MAY	3	50%

LEAGUE GOALS

	PLAYER	LGE	FAC	LC	Oth	TOT
1	Harris	**9**	1	0	0	10
2	Cahill	**9**	3	0	0	12
3	Ifill	**8**	1	0	0	9
4	Dichio	**7**	1	0	0	8
5	Chadwick	**4**	0	0	0	4
6	Whelan	**4**	0	0	0	4
7	Ward	**3**	0	0	0	3
8	Peeters	**3**	0	0	0	3
9	Sweeney	**2**	0	0	0	2
10	Wise	**1**	1	0	0	2
11	Nethercott	**1**	0	0	0	1
	Other	4	1	0	0	5
	TOTAL	**55**	**8**	**0**	**0**	**63**

KEY GOALKEEPER

1 Tony Warner

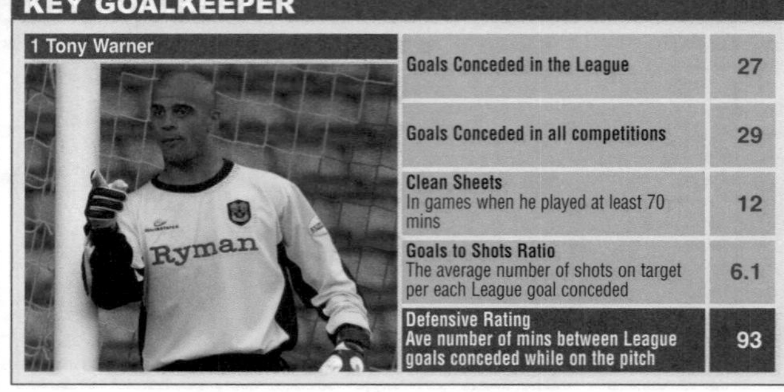
Ryman

Goals Conceded in the League	27
Goals Conceded in all competitions	29
Clean Sheets In games when he played at least 70 mins	12
Goals to Shots Ratio The average number of shots on target per each League goal conceded	6.1
Defensive Rating Ave number of mins between League goals conceded while on the pitch	93

DISCIPLINARY RECORDS

	PLAYER	YELLOW	RED	AVE
1	Cahill	18	2	176
2	Dichio	5	1	205
3	Fofana	3	0	275
4	Wise	8	1	282
5	Peeters	4	0	291
6	Livermore	9	1	295
7	Craig	2	0	317
8	Braniff	2	0	338
9	Muscat	5	2	339
10	Nethercott	3	0	368
11	Whelan	2	0	403
12	Harris	5	0	476
13	Lawrence	6	0	514
	Other	24	0	
	TOTAL	96	7	

TOP POINT EARNERS

	PLAYER	GAMES	AV PTS
1	Neil Harris	17	**2.06**
2	Robert Ryan	24	**1.75**
3	Kevin Muscat	26	**1.62**
4	Andy Roberts	24	**1.58**
5	Dennis Wise	28	**1.57**
6	Tim Cahill	38	**1.55**
7	Darren Ward	46	**1.50**
8	David Livermore	31	**1.48**
9	Matt Lawrence	33	**1.48**
10	Paul Ifill	26	**1.46**
	CLUB AVERAGE:		**1.50**

TEAM OF THE SEASON

G Tony Warner — **CG:** 28 **DR:** 93

D Robert Ryan — **CG:** 24 **DR:** 101

D Kevin Muscat — **CG:** 26 **DR:** 99

D Matt Lawrence — **CG:** 33 **DR:** 86

D Darren Ward — **CG:** 46 **DR:** 86

M Tim Cahill — **CG:** 38 **SD:** 19

M Dennis Wise — **CG:** 28 **SD:** 18

M Andy Roberts — **CG:** 24 **SD:** 13

M David Livermore — **CG:** 31 **SD:** -4

F Neil Harris — **CG:** 17 **SR:** 265

F Paul Ifill — **CG:** 26 **SR:** 320

LEAGUE APPEARANCES AND BOOKINGS

	AGE (on 01/07/04)	IN NAMED 16	APPEARANCES	COUNTING GAMES	MINUTES ON PITCH	Yellow	Red
Goalkeepers							
Willy Gueret	30	44	2	2	180	0	0
Andy Marshall	29	18	16	16	1440	0	0
Tony Warner	30	30	28	28	2520	4	0
Defenders							
Tony Craig	19	10	9	6	635	2	0
Joe Dolan	24	1	1	0	35	0	0
Alan Dunne	21	11	8	2	399	1	0
Maldondo-Duarte Juan	22	4	3	1	155	0	0
Matt Lawrence	30	39	36	33	3087	6	0
Kevin Muscat	30	27	27	26	2376	5	2
Stuart Nethercott	31	22	14	12	1105	3	0
Marcus Phillips	21	0	0	0	0	0	0
Paul Robinson	22	14	10	6	634	0	0
Robert Ryan	27	31	30	24	2333	3	0
Darren Ward	25	46	46	46	4140	5	0
Midfielders							
Tim Cahill	24	40	40	38	3530	18	2
Barry Cogan	18	3	3	0	78	0	0
Marvin Elliot	19	27	21	12	1331	1	0
Aboubaka Fofana	21	19	16	6	825	3	0
Charlie Hearn	20	16	7	2	286	1	0
David Livermore	24	37	35	31	2958	9	1
Andy Roberts	30	40	33	24	2522	3	0
Peter Sweeney	19	33	29	16	1938	2	0
Curt Weston	17	1	1	0	27	0	0
Dennis Wise	37	39	31	28	2538	8	1
Forwards							
Kevin Braniff	21	24	16	3	676	2	0
Nick Chadwick	21	16	15	10	1041	1	0
Danny Dichio	29	15	15	12	1234	5	1
Neil Harris	26	38	38	17	2382	5	0
Paul Ifill	24	33	33	26	2563	3	0
Mark McCammon	25	12	7	1	276	0	0
Bob Peeters	30	22	20	8	1164	4	0
Mark Quigley	18	1	1	0	3	0	0
Richard Sadlier	25	2	2	0	34	0	0
John Sutton	20	5	4	1	197	0	0
Noel Whelan	29	16	15	5	807	2	0

SQUAD APPEARANCES

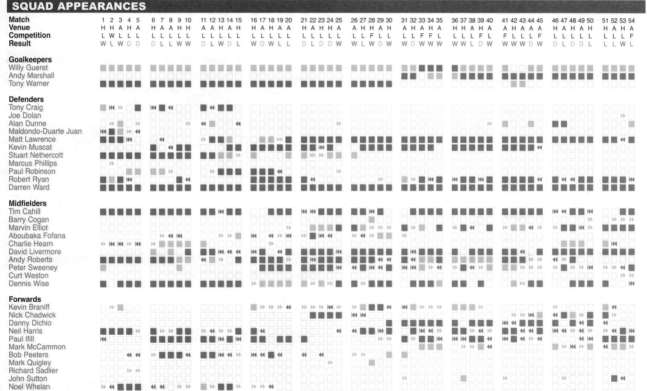

Match	1	2	3	4	5	6	7	8	9	10	11	12	13	14	15	16	17	18
Venue	H	H	A	H	A	H	A	A	H	H	A	A	H	A	H	H	A	H
Competition	L	W	L	L	L	L	L	L	L	L	L	L	L	L	L	L	L	L
Result	W	L	W	D	D	D	L	L	W	W	D	L	W	D	L	W	D	W

Match	19	20	21	22	23	24	25	26	27	28	29	30	31	32	33	34	35	36
Venue	A	A	H	A	H	H	A	A	H	H	A	H	A	H	A	H	A	H
Competition	L	L	L	L	L	L	L	L	L	F	L	L	L	L	F	F	L	L
Result	L	L	D	L	D	D	W	W	L	W	D	W	W	D	W	W	W	W

Match	37	38	39	40	41	42	43	44	45	46	47	48	49	50	51	52	53	54
Venue	H	A	H	A	A	H	A	A	A	H	A	H	A	H	H	A	H	A
Competition	L	L	F	L	F	L	L	L	F	L	L	L	L	L	L	L	L	F
Result	W	L	D	W	W	W	W	D	W	D	L	D	D	L	L	L	W	L

Goalkeepers
Willy Gueret
Andy Marshall
Tony Warner

Defenders
Tony Craig
Joe Dolan
Alan Dunne
Maldondo-Duarte Juan
Matt Lawrence
Kevin Muscat
Stuart Nethercott
Marcus Phillips
Paul Robinson
Robert Ryan
Darren Ward

Midfielders
Tim Cahill
Barry Cogan
Marvin Elliot
Aboubaka Fofana
Charlie Hearn
David Livermore
Andy Roberts
Peter Sweeney
Curt Weston
Dennis Wise

Forwards
Kevin Braniff
Nick Chadwick
Danny Dichio
Neil Harris
Paul Ifill
Mark McCammon
Bob Peeters
Mark Quigley
Richard Sadlier
John Sutton
Noel Whelan

KEY: On all match · On bench · Subbed or sent off (Counting game) · Subbed or sent off (playing less than 70 minutes) · Subbed on from bench (Counting Game) · Subbed on (playing less than 70 minutes) · Subbed on and then subbed or sent off (Counting Game) · Subbed on and then subbed or sent off (playing less than 70 minutes) · Not in 16

STOKE CITY

Final Position: **11th**

NICKNAME: THE POTTERS KEY: ☐ Won ☐ Drawn ☐ Lost

	Comp	Opponent	H/A	Res	Score	Scorers	Attendance
1	div1	**Derby**	A	W	3-0	Noel-Williams 15; Greenacre 20; Neal 90	21,517
2	div1	**Wimbledon**	H	W	2-1	Asaba 26 pen; Thomas 90	12,550
3	ccR1	**Rochdale**	H	W	2-1	Iwelumo 13; Goodfellow 90	4,687
4	div1	**Walsall**	A	D	1-1	Asaba 33	9,033
5	div1	**Millwall**	H	D	0-0		13,087
6	div1	**Preston**	A	L	0-1		12,965
7	div1	**Burnley**	H	L	1-2	Asaba 53	14,876
8	div1	**Coventry**	A	L	2-4	Asaba 45; Thomas 78	13,982
9	div1	**Sunderland**	H	W	3-1	Noel-Williams 24; Russell 37,39	15,005
10	div1	**Norwich**	H	D	1-1	Noel-Williams 36	10,672
11	ccR2	**Gillingham**	H	L	0-2		4,607
12	div1	**West Brom**	A	L	0-1		24,297
13	div1	**Rotherham**	A	L	0-3		5,450
14	div1	**Nottm Forest**	H	W	2-1	Thomas 6; Asaba 31	13,755
15	div1	**Wigan**	A	L	1-2	Williams 40	7,678
16	div1	**Ipswich**	A	L	0-1		22,122
17	div1	**Crewe**	H	D	1-1	Greenacre 90	17,569
18	div1	**Sheff Utd**	H	D	2-2	Noel-Williams 4; Akinbiyi 18	14,217
19	div1	**Cardiff**	A	L	1-3	Commons 59	15,227
20	div1	**Bradford**	H	W	1-0	Eustace 11	11,661
21	div1	**Crystal Palace**	H	L	0-1		10,277
22	div1	**Gillingham**	A	L	1-3	Eustace 77	7,888
23	div1	**Cardiff**	H	L	2-3	Eustace 38; Akinbiyi 74	12,208
24	div1	**West Ham**	A	W	1-0	Richardson 33	24,365
25	div1	**Reading**	H	W	3-0	Hoekstra 18,26,87 pen	11,212
26	div1	**Watford**	A	W	3-1	Taggart 15; Akinbiyi 55,72	13,732
27	div1	**Preston**	H	D	1-1	Eustace 90 pen	20,126
28	div1	**Burnley**	A	W	1-0	Akinbiyi 52	12,812
29	facr3	**Wimbledon**	A	D	1-1	Eustace 12	3,609
30	div1	**Derby**	H	W	2-1	Akinbiyi 29; Taggart 53	16,402
31	facr3r	**Wimbledon**	H	L	0-1		6,463
32	div1	**Wimbledon**	A	W	1-0	Noel-Williams 54	3,623
33	div1	**Walsall**	H	W	3-2	Russell 8; Asaba 37,56	18,035
34	div1	**Millwall**	A	D	1-1	Clarke 4	9,034
35	div1	**Crystal Palace**	A	L	3-6	Eustace 6; Clarke 45; Asaba 83 pen	16,715
36	div1	**Wigan**	H	D	1-1	Akinbiyi 45	14,927
37	div1	**Ipswich**	H	W	2-0	Hoekstra 37 pen; Akinbiyi 68	11,435
38	div1	**Watford**	H	W	3-1	Akinbiyi 18,43; Noel-Williams 20	13,108
39	div1	**Reading**	A	D	0-0		14,132
40	div1	**Sunderland**	A	D	1-1	Svard 13	24,510
41	div1	**Crewe**	A	L	0-2		10,014
42	div1	**Norwich**	A	L	0-1		23,565
43	div1	**Coventry**	H	W	1-0	Commons 41	12,855
44	div1	**Nottm Forest**	A	D	0-0		28,758
45	div1	**Rotherham**	H	L	0-2		11,978
46	div1	**Sheff Utd**	A	W	1-0	Clarke 45	19,372
47	div1	**West Ham**	H	L	0-2		18,227
48	div1	**Bradford**	A	W	2-0	Noel-Williams 2,46	10,147
49	div1	**West Brom**	H	W	4-1	Russell 45; Commons 62,73; Noel-Williams 86	18,352
50	div1	**Gillingham**	H	D	0-0		19,240

KEY PLAYERS - GOALSCORERS

Adeola Akinbiyi

Goals in the League	10
Goals in all competitions	10
Contribution to Attacking Power Average number of minutes between League team goals while on pitch	68
Player Strike Rate The total number of minutes he was on the pitch for every League goal scored	197
Club Strike Rate Average number of minutes between League goals scored by club	71

	PLAYER	GOALS LGE	GOALS ALL	POWER	S RATE
1	Adeola Akinbiyi	10	10	68	197 mins
2	Carl Asaba	8	8	77	312 mins
3	Gifton Noel-Williams	9	9	69	384 mins
4	John Eustace	5	6	62	436 mins
5	Kristian Commons	4	4	73	440 mins

KEY PLAYERS - MIDFIELDERS

John Eustace

Goals in the League	5
Goals in all competitions	6
Defensive Rating Average number of mins between League goals conceded while on the pitch	66
Contribution to Attacking Power Average number of minutes between League team goals while on pitch	62
Scoring Difference Defensive Rating minus Contribution to Attacking Power	4

	PLAYER	GOALS LGE	GOALS ALL	DEF RATE	ATT POWER	SCORE DIFF
1	John Eustace	5	6	66	62	4 mins
2	Darel Russell	4	4	75	71	4 mins
3	Kristian Commons	4	4	73	73	0 mins
4	Keith Andrews	0	0	66	78	-12 mins
5	Karl Henry	0	0	82	119	-37 mins

KEY PLAYERS - DEFENDERS

Gerry Taggart

Goals Conceded in League	14
Goals Conceded in all competitions	14
Clean Sheets In League games when he played at least 70 mins	10
Defensive Rating Ave number of mins between League goals conceded while on the pitch	128
Club Defensive Rating Average number of mins between League goals conceded by the club this season	75

	PLAYER	CON LGE	CON ALL	CLN SHEETS	DEF RATE
1	Gerry Taggart	14	14	10	128 mins
2	John Halls	35	37	12	86 mins
3	Wayne Thomas	41	44	13	83 mins
4	Clive Clarke	44	49	13	82 mins
5	Marcus Hall	39	43	11	75 mins

MONTHLY POINTS TALLY

Month	Points	%
AUGUST	8	53%
SEPTEMBER	4	22%
OCTOBER	4	33%
NOVEMBER	4	27%
DECEMBER	13	72%
JANUARY	9	100%
FEBRUARY	2	22%
MARCH	8	44%
APRIL	7	47%
MAY	7	78%

LEAGUE GOALS

	PLAYER	LGE	FAC	LC	Oth	TOT
1	Akinbiyi	**10**	0	0	0	10
2	Noel-Williams	**9**	0	0	0	9
3	Asaba	**8**	0	0	0	8
4	Eustace	**5**	1	0	0	6
5	Commons	**4**	0	0	0	4
6	Hoekstra	**4**	0	0	0	4
7	Russell	**4**	0	0	0	4
8	Thomas	**3**	0	0	0	3
9	Clarke	**3**	0	0	0	3
10	Greenacre	**2**	0	0	0	2
11	Taggart	**2**	0	0	0	2
	Other	4	0	2	0	6
	TOTAL	**58**	**1**	**2**	**0**	**61**

KEY GOALKEEPER

1 Ed de Goey

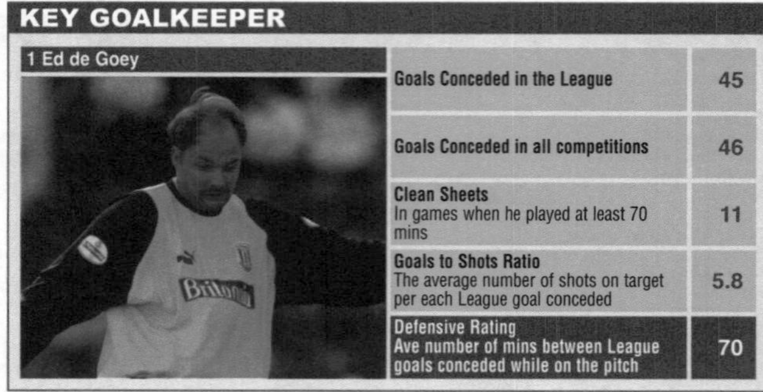

Goals Conceded in the League	45
Goals Conceded in all competitions	46
Clean Sheets In games when he played at least 70 mins	11
Goals to Shots Ratio The average number of shots on target per each League goal conceded	5.8
Defensive Rating Ave number of mins between League goals conceded while on the pitch	70

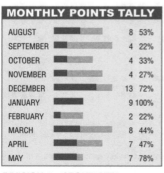

DISCIPLINARY RECORDS

	PLAYER	YELLOW	RED	AVE
1	Eustace	9	1	217
2	Andrews	5	0	279
3	Asaba	7	1	311
4	Hall	7	2	326
5	Taggart	5	0	358
6	Neal	2	0	375
7	Thomas	8	1	376
8	Akinbiyi	5	0	394
9	Hill	2	0	401
10	Halls	6	1	430
11	Henry	3	0	438
12	Clarke	7	0	513
13	Greenacre	1	0	662
	Other	18	1	
	TOTAL	85	7	

TOP POINT EARNERS

	PLAYER	GAMES	AV PTS
1	Gerry Taggart	20	**1.90**
2	John Eustace	23	**1.65**
3	Gifton Noel-Williams	37	**1.65**
4	John Halls	33	**1.61**
5	Clive Clarke	39	**1.56**
6	Kristian Commons	13	**1.54**
7	Adeola Akinbiyi	20	**1.50**
8	Marcus Hall	31	**1.45**
9	Darel Russell	45	**1.44**
10	Wayne Thomas	36	**1.44**
	CLUB AVERAGE:		**1.43**

TEAM OF THE SEASON

G Ed de Goey — CG: 34 DR: 70

D Gerry Taggart — CG: 20 DR: 128

D John Halls — CG: 33 DR: 86

D Wayne Thomas — CG: 36 DR: 83

D Clive Clarke — CG: 39 DR: 82

M John Eustace — CG: 23 SD: 4

M Darel Russell — CG: 45 SD: 4

M Kristian Commons — CG: 13 SD: 0

M Keith Andrews — CG: 15 SD: -12

F Adeola Akinbiyi — CG: 20 SR: 197

F Carl Asaba — CG: 25 SR: 312

LEAGUE APPEARANCES AND BOOKINGS

	AGE (on 01/07/04)	IN NAMED 16	APPEARANCES	COUNTING GAMES	MINUTES ON PITCH	Yellow	Red
Goalkeepers							
Neil Cutler	27	41	13	10	980	1	0
Ed de Goey	37	40	37	34	3160	2	0
Ben Foster	21	7	0	0	0	0	0
Defenders							
Clive Clarke	24	44	42	39	3592	7	0
Brynjar Gunnarsson	28	9	3	0	93	1	0
Marcus Hall	28	38	35	31	2940	7	2
John Halls	22	34	34	33	3010	6	1
Clinton Hill	25	24	13	8	803	2	0
Gareth Owen	21	6	3	1	116	0	0
Frazer Richardson	21	7	7	7	606	0	0
Sebastian Svard	21	18	13	7	830	0	0
Gerry Taggart	33	21	21	20	1793	5	0
Wayne Thomas	25	39	39	36	3389	8	1
Andy Wilkinson	19	8	3	1	119	0	0
Paul Williams	33	19	19	15	1469	2	0
Brian Wilson	21	4	2	0	14	0	0
Midfielders							
Keith Andrews	23	16	16	15	1395	5	0
Kristian Commons	20	44	33	13	1758	1	0
Jay Denny	-	1	0	0	0	0	0
John Eustace	24	26	26	23	2179	9	1
Marc Goodfellow	22	6	4	0	88	0	0
Karl Henry	21	23	20	14	1314	3	0
Peter Hoekstra	31	26	23	11	1441	1	0
Richard Johnson	30	8	7	2	302	0	1
Petur Marteinsson	30	5	3	2	238	0	0
Lewis Neal	22	23	19	5	751	2	0
Darel Russell	23	45	45	45	4037	6	0
Forwards							
Adeola Akinbiyi	29	30	30	20	1974	5	0
Carl Asaba	31	40	37	25	2493	7	1
Chris Greenacre	26	19	13	4	662	1	0
Chris Iwelumo	25	17	9	1	278	1	0
Gifton Noel-Williams	24	42	42	37	3456	3	0
Jermaine Palmer	-	6	3	0	53	0	0

SQUAD APPEARANCES

Match	1	2	3	4	5	6	7	8	9	10	11	12	13	14	15	16	17	18	19	20	21	22	23	24	25	26	27	28	29	30	31	32	33	34	35	36	37	38	39	40	41	42	43	44	45	46	47	48	49	50
Venue	A	H	H	A	H	A	H	A	H	H	H	A	A	H	A	A	H	H	A	H	H	A	H	A	H	A	H	A	A	H	H	A	H	A	A	H	H	H	A	A	A	A	H	A	H	A	H	A	H	H
Competition	L	L	W	L	L	L	L	L	L	L	W	L	L	L	L	L	L	L	L	L	L	L	L	L	L	L	L	L	F	L	F	L	L	L	L	L	L	L	L	L	L	L	L	L	L	L	L	L	L	L
Result	W	W	W	D	D	L	L	L	W	D	L	L	L	W	L	L	D	D	L	W	L	L	L	W	W	W	D	W	D	W	L	W	W	D	L	D	W	W	D	D	L	L	W	D	L	W	L	W	W	D

Goalkeepers
Neil Cutler
Ed de Goey
Ben Foster

Defenders
Clive Clarke
Brynjar Gunnarsson
Marcus Hall
John Halls
Clinton Hill
Gareth Owen
Frazer Richardson
Sebastian Svard
Gerry Taggart
Wayne Thomas
Andy Wilkinson
Paul Williams
Brian Wilson

Midfielders
Keith Andrews
Kristian Commons
Jay Denny
John Eustace
Marc Goodfellow
Karl Henry
Peter Hoekstra
Richard Johnson
Petur Marteinsson
Lewis Neal
Darel Russell

Forwards
Adeola Akinbiyi
Carl Asaba
Chris Greenacre
Chris Iwelumo
Gifton Noel-Williams
Jermaine Palmer

KEY: On all match | On bench | Subbed or sent off (Counting game) | Subbed or sent off (playing less than 70 minutes) | Subbed on from bench (Counting Game) | Subbed on (playing less than 70 minutes) | Subbed on and then subbed or sent off (Counting Game) | Subbed on and then subbed or sent off (playing less than 70 minutes) | Not in 16

COVENTRY CITY

Final Position: **12th**

NICKNAME: THE SKY BLUES

KEY: ☐ Won ☐ Drawn ☐ Lost

		Opponent			Score	Scorers	Attendance
1	ccR1	**Peterborough**	H	W	2-0	Barrett 63; Adebola 67	8,280
2	div1	**Walsall**	H	D	0-0		15,377
3	div1	**Ipswich**	A	D	1-1	Doyle 31	22,419
4	div1	**Nottm Forest**	H	L	1-3	Whing 46	17,586
5	div1	**Sheff Utd**	A	L	1-2	Suffo 67	20,102
6	div1	**Stoke**	H	W	4-2	Suffo 5; Barrett 10; Adebola 58; Morrell 75	13,982
7	div1	**Preston**	A	L	2-4	Staunton 42 pen; Morrell 77	11,886
8	div1	**Reading**	A	W	2-1	Adebola 35; Morrell 76	15,371
9	ccR2	**Tottenham**	H	L	0-3		15,474
10	div1	**Wigan**	H	D	1-1	Morrell 90	14,862
11	div1	**Crewe**	H	W	2-0	McAllister 49; Morrell 73	11,557
12	div1	**Millwall**	A	L	1-2	Staunton 72 pen	9,849
13	div1	**Wimbledon**	H	W	1-0	Pead 63	10,872
14	div1	**Cardiff**	H	L	1-3	Doyle 11	11,767
15	div1	**Watford**	A	D	1-1	Staunton 90	13,487
16	div1	**Derby**	A	W	3-1	Warnock 11; Suffo 38,80	21,641
17	div1	**West Ham**	H	D	1-1	Barrett 38	19,126
18	div1	**Bradford**	H	D	0-0		11,862
19	div1	**Sunderland**	A	D	0-0		27,247
20	div1	**Gillingham**	H	D	2-2	Joachim 55,90	13,432
21	div1	**Norwich**	A	D	1-1	McAllister 49 pen	16,414
22	div1	**Crystal Palace**	A	D	1-1	Jackson 90	14,622
23	div1	**Rotherham**	A	L	0-2		5,524
24	div1	**Sunderland**	H	D	1-1	McAllister 21 pen	12,913
25	div1	**Burnley**	A	W	2-1	Suffo 8; Weller 40 og	10,358
26	div1	**West Brom**	H	W	1-0	Jackson 89	17,616
27	div1	**Sheff Utd**	H	L	0-1		21,132
28	div1	**Bradford**	A	L	0-1		11,432
29	facr3	**Peterborough**	H	W	2-1	McSheffrey 59; Joachim 61	11,400
30	div1	**Watford**	H	D	0-0		12,226
31	div1	**Walsall**	A	W	6-1	Morrell 6,57; McSheffrey 48,82; Joachim 70; Roper 76 og	8,264
32	facr4	**Colchester**	H	D	1-1	Joachim 33	15,341
33	div1	**Ipswich**	H	D	1-1	Warnock 45	14,441
34	facr4r	**Colchester**		L	1-3	Joachim 25	5,530
35	div1	**Nottm Forest**	A	W	1-0	Suffo 4	23,075
36	div1	**Norwich**	H	L	0-2		15,757
37	div1	**Wimbledon**	A	W	3-0	Joachim 9; Suffo 40; Gudjonsson, B 63	5,905
38	div1	**Derby**	H	W	2-0	McSheffrey 20; Joachim 33	16,042
39	div1	**Cardiff**	A	W	1-0	McSheffrey 71 pen	14,376
40	div1	**West Brom**	A	L	0-3		25,414
41	div1	**Burnley**	H	W	4-0	Joachim 10; McSheffrey 33,39 pen; Konjic 78	12,953
42	div1	**Preston**	H	W	4-1	Gudjonsson, B 2,27; Doyle 8; McSheffrey 11	13,142
43	div1	**Wigan**	A	L	1-2	Warnock 72	8,784
44	div1	**Reading**	H	L	1-2	McSheffrey 67	15,811
45	div1	**Stoke**	A	L	0-1		12,855
46	div1	**Millwall**	H	W	4-0	Joachim 6,58; Deloumeaux 12; McSheffrey 87 pen	12,546
47	div1	**Crewe**	A	L	1-3	Lowe 83	7,475
48	div1	**West Ham**	A	L	0-2		27,890
49	div1	**Rotherham**	H	D	1-1	Morrell 56	13,572
50	div1	**Gillingham**	A	W	5-2	Doyle 8; Morrell 24; McSheffrey 31,85; Shaw 90	10,388
51	div1	**Crystal Palace**	H	W	2-1	Konjic 4; Doyle 27	22,195

MONTHLY POINTS TALLY

Month	Points	%
AUGUST	2	17%
SEPTEMBER	7	58%
OCTOBER	10	56%
NOVEMBER	6	33%
DECEMBER	7	39%
JANUARY	5	56%
FEBRUARY	9	75%
MARCH	9	50%
APRIL	4	27%
MAY	6	100%

LEAGUE GOALS

	PLAYER	LGE	FAC	LC	Oth	TOT
1	McSheffrey	**11**	1	0	0	12
2	Morrell	**9**	0	0	0	9
3	Joachim	**8**	3	0	0	11
4	Suffo	**7**	0	0	0	7
5	Doyle	**5**	0	0	0	5
6	Staunton	**3**	0	0	0	3
7	Gudjonsson, B	**3**	0	0	0	3
8	McAllister	**3**	0	0	0	3
9	Warnock	**3**	0	0	0	3
10	Konjic	**2**	0	0	0	2
11	Barrett	**2**	0	1	0	3
	Other	11	0	1	0	12
	TOTAL	**67**	**4**	**2**	**0**	**73**

KEY PLAYERS - GOALSCORERS

Gary McSheffrey

Goals in the League	11
Goals in all competitions	12
Contribution to Attacking Power Average number of minutes between League team goals while on pitch	49
Player Strike Rate The total number of minutes he was on the pitch for every League goal scored	131
Club Strike Rate Average number of minutes between League goals scored by club	62

	PLAYER	GOALS LGE	GOALS ALL	POWER	S RATE
1	Gary McSheffrey	11	12	49	**131 mins**
2	Andy Morrell	9	9	53	**203 mins**
3	Patrick Kenge Suffo	7	7	67	**262 mins**
4	Julian Joachim	8	11	64	**299 mins**
5	Bjarni Gudjonsson	3	3	47	**462 mins**

KEY PLAYERS - MIDFIELDERS

Bjarni Gudjonsson

Goals in the League	3
Goals in all competitions	3
Defensive Rating Average number of mins between League goals conceded while on the pitch	87
Contribution to Attacking Power Average number of minutes between League team goals while on pitch	48
Scoring Difference Defensive Rating minus Contribution to Attacking Power	39

	PLAYER	GOALS LGE	GOALS ALL	DEF RATE	ATT POWER	SCORE DIFF
1	Bjarni Gudjonsson	3	3	87	48	**39 mins**
2	Youssef Safri	0	0	79	67	**12 mins**
3	Michael Doyle	5	5	70	61	**9 mins**
4	Graham Barrett	2	3	78	72	**6 mins**

KEY PLAYERS - DEFENDERS

Andrew Whing

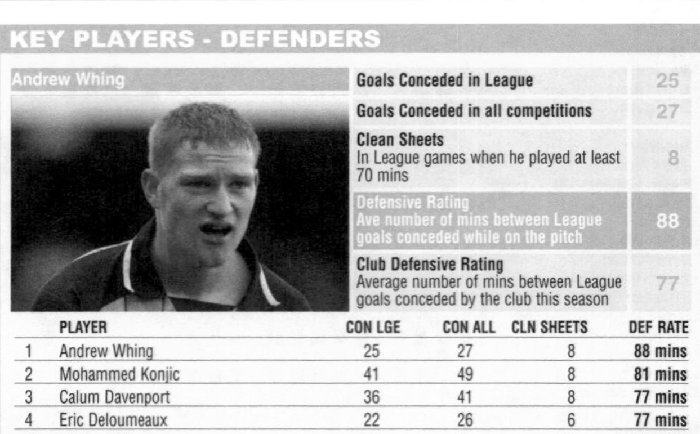

Goals Conceded in League	25
Goals Conceded in all competitions	27
Clean Sheets In League games when he played at least 70 mins	8
Defensive Rating Ave number of mins between League goals conceded while on the pitch	88
Club Defensive Rating Average number of mins between League goals conceded by the club this season	77

	PLAYER	CON LGE	CON ALL	CLN SHEETS	DEF RATE
1	Andrew Whing	25	27	8	**88 mins**
2	Mohammed Konjic	41	49	8	**81 mins**
3	Calum Davenport	36	41	8	**77 mins**
4	Eric Deloumeaux	22	26	6	**77 mins**
5	Stephen Warnock	47	52	11	**77 mins**

KEY GOALKEEPER

1 Scott Shearer

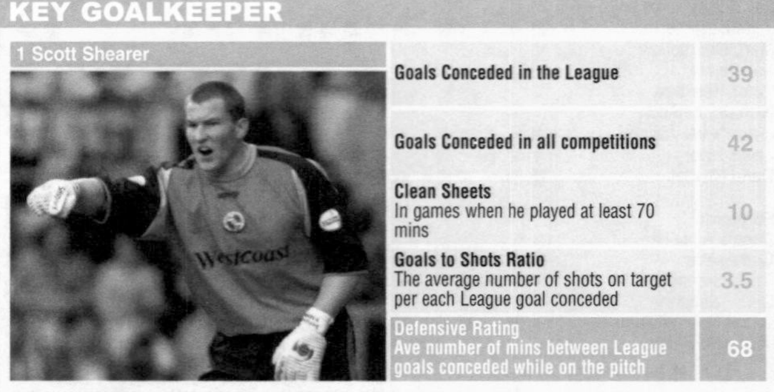
Westcoast

Goals Conceded in the League	39
Goals Conceded in all competitions	42
Clean Sheets In games when he played at least 70 mins	10
Goals to Shots Ratio The average number of shots on target per each League goal conceded	3.5
Defensive Rating Ave number of mins between League goals conceded while on the pitch	68

DISCIPLINARY RECORDS

	PLAYER	YELLOW	RED	AVE
1	Shaw	4	0	301
2	Grainger	2	0	315
3	Safri	7	1	335
4	Doyle	8	1	374
5	Suffo	3	1	458
6	McSheffrey	3	0	479
7	Warnock	7	0	515
8	Davenport	5	0	555
9	Deloumeaux	3	0	562
10	Barrett	3	0	600
11	Morrell	3	0	609
12	Konjic	5	0	661
13	Adebola	2	0	703
	Other	11	1	
	TOTAL	66	4	

TOP POINT EARNERS

	PLAYER	GAMES	AV PTS
1	Bjarni Gudjonsson	14	**1.86**
2	Andy Morrell	18	**1.78**
3	Eric Deloumeaux	19	**1.68**
4	Gary McSheffrey	14	**1.64**
5	Graham Barrett	16	**1.56**
6	Michael Doyle	36	**1.50**
7	Stephen Warnock	39	**1.49**
8	Scott Shearer	29	**1.48**
9	Youssef Safri	29	**1.48**
10	Patrick Kenge Suffo	19	**1.37**
	CLUB AVERAGE:		**1.41**

LEAGUE APPEARANCES AND BOOKINGS

	AGE (on 01/07/04)	IN NAMED 16	APPEARANCES	COUNTING GAMES	MINUTES ON PITCH	Yellow	Red
Goalkeepers							
Pegguy Arphexad	31	15	5	4	405	0	0
Richard Brush	19	4	0	0	0	0	0
Scott Shearer	23	46	30	29	2655	0	0
Gavin Ward	34	27	12	12	1080	0	0
Defenders							
Peter Clarke	22	6	5	4	363	0	1
Calum Davenport	21	40	33	30	2775	5	0
Eric Deloumeaux	31	19	19	19	1688	3	0
Dean Gordon	31	7	5	3	334	1	0
Martin Grainger	31	7	7	7	630	2	0
Claus Jorgensen	28	16	8	3	357	0	0
Mohammed Konjic	34	44	42	35	3308	5	0
Richard Shaw	35	33	19	12	1204	4	0
Steve Staunton	35	35	34	30	2861	3	0
Stephen Warnock	22	44	44	39	3606	7	0
Andrew Whing	19	36	28	23	2200	2	0
Midfielders							
Graham Barrett	22	35	31	16	1802	3	0
Michael Doyle	22	42	40	36	3368	8	1
Stuart Giddings	18	1	1	0	1	0	0
Bjarni Gudjonsson	25	18	18	14	1386	1	0
Andrew Hall	18	0	0	0	0	0	0
Johnnie Jackson	21	7	5	2	245	0	0
Avun Jephcott	20	2	0	0	0	0	0
Brian Kerr	22	9	9	3	446	0	0
Yazid Mansouri	26	17	14	5	740	1	0
Gary McAllister	39	15	14	12	1174	0	0
Isaac Osbourne	18	2	0	0	0	0	0
Craig Pead	22	24	17	5	726	0	0
David Pipe	20	1	0	0	0	0	0
Courtney Pitt	22	1	1	1	75	1	0
Youssef Safri	27	31	31	29	2684	7	1
Eddie Stanford	19	1	1	1	90	0	0
Forwards							
Dele Adebola	29	32	28	12	1406	2	0
Julian Joachim	29	29	29	25	2388	2	0
Onandi Lowe	29	2	2	1	120	0	0
Gary McSheffrey	22	20	19	14	1437	3	0
Andy Morrell	29	32	30	18	1827	3	0
Keith O'Neill	28	1	1	0	7	0	0
Sebastian Olszar	22	6	5	1	186	0	0
Patrick Kenge Suffo	26	29	27	19	1835	3	1

TEAM OF THE SEASON

D
Andrew Whing
CG: 23 DR: 88
M
Bjarni Gudjonsson
CG: 14 SD: 39
D
Mohammed Konjic
CG: 35 DR: 81
M
Youssef Safri
CG: 29 SD: 12
F
Gary McSheffrey
CG: 14 SR: 131
G
Scott Shearer
CG: 29 DR: 68
D
Calum Davenport
CG: 30 DR: 77
M
Michael Doyle
CG: 36 SD: 9
F
Andy Morrell
CG: 18 SR: 203
D
Eric Deloumeaux
CG: 19 DR: 77
M
Graham Barrett
CG: 16 SD: 6

SQUAD APPEARANCES

Match	1	2	3	4	5	6	7	8	9	10	11	12	13	14	15	16	17	18	19	20	21	22	23	24	25	26	27	28	29	30	31	32	33	34	35	36	37	38	39	40	41	42	43	44	45	46	47	48	49	50	51
Venue	H	H	A	H	A	H	A	A	H	H	H	A	H	H	A	A	H	H	A	H	A	A	A	H	A	H	H	A	H	H	A	H	H	A	H	A	H	A	A	H	H	A	H	A	H	A	A	H	A	H	
Competition	W	L	L	L	L	L	L	L	W	L	L	L	L	L	L	L	L	L	L	L	L	L	L	L	L	L	L	L	F	L	L	F	L	F	L	L	L	L	L	L	L	L	L	L	L	L	L	L	L	L	L
Result	W	D	D	L	L	W	L	W	L	D	W	L	W	L	D	W	D	D	D	D	D	D	L	D	W	W	L	L	W	D	W	D	D	L	W	L	W	W	W	L	W	W	L	L	L	W	L	L	D	W	W

Goalkeepers
Pegguy Arphexad
Richard Brush
Scott Shearer
Gavin Ward

Defenders
Peter Clarke
Calum Davenport
Eric Deloumeaux
Dean Gordon
Martin Grainger
Mohammed Konjic
Richard Shaw
Steve Staunton
Stephen Warnock
Andrew Whing

Midfielders
Graham Barrett
Michael Doyle
Stuart Giddings
Bjarni Gudjonsson
Andrew Hall
Johnnie Jackson
Avun Jephcott
Claus Jorgensen
Brian Kerr
Yazid Mansouri
Gary McAllister
Isaac Osbourne
Craig Pead
David Pipe
Courtney Pitt
Youssef Safri
Eddie Stanford

Forwards
Dele Adebola
Julian Joachim
Onandi Lowe
Gary McSheffrey
Andy Morrell
Keith O'Neill
Sebastian Olszar
Patrick Kenge Suffo

KEY: On all match; On bench; Subbed or sent off (Counting game); Subbed or sent off (playing less than 70 minutes); Subbed on from bench (Counting Game); Subbed on (playing less than 70 minutes); Subbed on and then subbed or sent off (Counting Game); Subbed on and then subbed or sent off (playing less than 70 minutes); Not in 16

CARDIFF CITY

Final Position: **13th**

NICKNAME: THE BLUEBIRDS

KEY: Won Drawn Lost

							Attendance
1	div1	Rotherham	A	D	0-0		8,176
2	ccR1	Leyton Orient	H	W	4-1	Earnshaw 39,40,55; Campbell 56	4,503
3	div1	Bradford	H	L	0-2		16,421
4	div1	Nottm Forest	A	W	2-1	Earnshaw 2; Kavanagh 7	23,407
5	div1	Derby	H	W	4-1	Lee 30; Kavanagh 40 pen; Earnshaw 55; Collins 70	15,091
6	div1	Walsall	A	D	1-1	Whalley 90	8,974
7	div1	Gillingham	H	W	5-0	Thorne 18; Earnshaw 21,35,45,74	15,057
8	div1	Reading	A	L	1-2	Thorne 12	15,810
9	div1	Sheff Utd	A	L	3-5	Earnshaw 46,64; Langley 69	21,323
10	ccR2	West Ham	H	L	2-3	Earnshaw 12,25	10,724
11	div1	Crewe	H	W	3-0	Thorne 44,85; Earnshaw 52	14,385
12	div1	Wigan	H	D	0-0		15,143
13	div1	Crystal Palace	A	L	1-2	Kavanagh 60	16,160
14	div1	Sunderland	A	D	0-0		26,835
15	div1	Coventry	A	W	3-1	Whalley 27; Gordon 32; Earnshaw 40 pen	11,767
16	div1	West Ham	H	D	0-0		19,202
17	div1	Watford	H	W	3-0	Earnshaw 32; Vidmar 77; Kavanagh 87	14,011
18	div1	Burnley	A	D	1-1	Earnshaw 76	10,886
19	div1	Stoke	H	W	3-1	Earnshaw 24,71; Gabbidon 81	15,227
20	div1	Wimbledon	A	W	1-0	Collins 15	5,056
21	div1	West Brom	H	D	1-1	Earnshaw 65 pen	17,678
22	div1	Ipswich	H	L	2-3	Earnshaw 58 pen; Thorne 86	17,833
23	div1	Stoke	A	W	3-2	Thorne 33,40,72	12,208
24	div1	Preston	H	D	2-2	Langley 63; Thorne 90	13,703
25	div1	Norwich	A	L	1-4	Thorne 59	16,428
26	div1	Millwall	H	L	1-3	Thorne 30	14,610
27	div1	Walsall	H	L	0-1		17,531
28	div1	Watford	A	L	1-2	Thorne 53	15,512
29	facr3	Sheff Utd	H	L	0-1		10,525
30	div1	Rotherham	H	W	3-2	Thorne 24; Kavanagh 38; Earnshaw 45	13,021
31	div1	Bradford	A	W	1-0	Langley 72	11,132
32	div1	Nottm Forest	H	D	0-0		17,913
33	div1	Derby	A	D	2-2	Earnshaw 60; Kavanagh 62	20,958
34	div1	West Brom	A	L	1-2	Lee 80	25,196
35	div1	Sunderland	H	W	4-0	Kavanagh 19; Langley 27; Gabbidon 47; Lee 80	17,337
36	div1	West Ham	A	L	0-1		31,858
37	div1	Coventry	H	L	0-1		14,376
38	div1	Norwich	H	W	2-1	Parry 17; Earnshaw 20	16,317
39	div1	Reading	H	L	2-3	Earnshaw 42; Bullock 72	14,051
40	div1	Crewe	A	W	1-0	Williams 70 og	6,650
41	div1	Sheff Utd	H	W	2-1	Langley 45; Robinson 63	13,666
42	div1	Gillingham	A	W	2-1	Earnshaw 36; Bullock 86	7,852
43	div1	Millwall	A	D	0-0		9,584
44	div1	Crystal Palace	H	L	0-2		16,656
45	div1	Wigan	A	L	0-3		8,052
46	div1	Burnley	H	W	2-0	Langley 78 pen; Campbell 80	13,525
47	div1	Preston	A	D	2-2	Campbell 51; Gabbidon 56	11,972
48	div1	Wimbledon	H	D	1-1	Robinson 82	15,337
49	div1	Ipswich	A	D	1-1	Bullock 41	28,703

KEY PLAYERS - GOALSCORERS

Peter Thorne

Goals in the League	13
Goals in all competitions	13
Contribution to Attacking Power Average number of minutes between League team goals while on pitch	49
Player Strike Rate The total number of minutes he was on the pitch for every League goal scored	132
Club Strike Rate Average number of minutes between League goals scored by club	61

	PLAYER	GOALS LGE	GOALS ALL	POWER	S RATE
1	Peter Thorne	13	13	49	132 mins
2	Robert Earnshaw	21	26	65	182 mins
3	Graham Kavanagh	7	7	61	341 mins
4	Alan Lee	3	3	70	519 mins
5	Richard Langley	6	6	60	596 mins

KEY PLAYERS - MIDFIELDERS

John Robinson

Goals in the League	2
Goals in all competitions	2
Defensive Rating Average number of mins between League goals conceded while on the pitch	78
Contribution to Attacking Power Average number of minutes between League team goals while on pitch	56
Scoring Difference Defensive Rating minus Contribution to Attacking Power	22

	PLAYER	GOALS LGE	GOALS ALL	DEF RATE	ATT POWER	SCORE DIFF
1	John Robinson	2	2	78	56	22 mins
2	Graham Kavanagh	7	7	82	61	21 mins
3	Mark Bonner	0	0	80	61	19 mins
4	Richard Langley	6	6	72	61	11 mins
5	Willie Boland	0	0	67	60	7 mins

KEY PLAYERS - DEFENDERS

Gary Croft

Goals Conceded in League	25
Goals Conceded in all competitions	25
Clean Sheets In League games when he played at least 70 mins	6
Defensive Rating Ave number of mins between League goals conceded while on the pitch	83
Club Defensive Rating Average number of mins between League goals conceded by the club this season	71

	PLAYER	CON LGE	CON ALL	CLN SHEETS	DEF RATE
1	Gary Croft	25	25	6	83 mins
2	Daniel Gabbidon	46	51	13	78 mins
3	Tony Vidmar	55	60	14	74 mins
4	James Collins	20	21	4	70 mins
5	Christopher Barker	47	51	10	66 mins

MONTHLY POINTS TALLY

AUGUST	8	53%
SEPTEMBER	7	47%
OCTOBER	8	53%
NOVEMBER	8	53%
DECEMBER	4	22%
JANUARY	7	78%
FEBRUARY	4	33%
MARCH	9	60%
APRIL	8	44%
MAY	2	33%

LEAGUE GOALS

	PLAYER	LGE	FAC	LC	Oth	TOT
1	Earnshaw	21	0	5	0	26
2	Thorne	13	0	0	0	13
3	Kavanagh	7	0	0	0	7
4	Langley	6	0	0	0	6
5	Lee	3	0	0	0	3
6	Bullock	3	0	0	0	3
7	Gabbidon	3	0	0	0	3
8	Campbell	2	0	1	0	3
9	Robinson	2	0	0	0	2
10	Whalley	2	0	0	0	2å
11	Vidmar	1	0	0	0	1
	Other	5	0	0	0	5
	TOTAL	68	0	6	0	74åˇ

KEY GOALKEEPER

1 Martyn Margetson

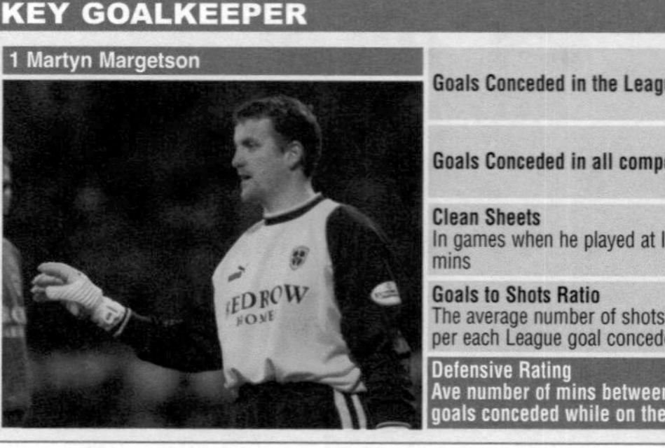

Goals Conceded in the League	25
Goals Conceded in all competitions	30
Clean Sheets In games when he played at least 70 mins	6
Goals to Shots Ratio The average number of shots on target per each League goal conceded	5.1
Defensive Rating Ave number of mins between League goals conceded while on the pitch	78

DISCIPLINARY RECORDS

	PLAYER	YELLOW	RED	AVE
1	Lee	5	1	259
2	Bullock	2	0	266
3	Kavanagh	8	0	298
4	Gordon	2	0	349
5	Campbell	1	1	389
6	Langley	9	0	397
7	Vidmar	8	1	449
8	Weston	4	0	476
9	Gray	1	0	495
10	Croft	3	1	519
11	Thorne	3	0	572
12	Robinson	4	0	627
13	Collins	2	0	698
	Other	14	2	
	TOTAL	66	6	

TOP POINT EARNERS

	PLAYER	GAMES	AV PTS
1	Gary Croft	20	**1.80**
2	Mark Bonner	13	**1.62**
3	John Robinson	27	**1.56**
4	James Collins	15	**1.53**
5	Alan Lee	16	**1.50**
6	Richard Langley	38	**1.47**
7	Neil Alexander	24	**1.46**
8	Martyn Margetson	21	**1.43**
9	Tony Vidmar	45	**1.42**
10	Daniel Gabbidon	39	**1.41**
	CLUB AVERAGE:		**1.41**

LEAGUE APPEARANCES AND BOOKINGS

	AGE (on 01/07/04)	IN NAMED 16	APPEARANCES	COUNTING GAMES	MINUTES ON PITCH	Yellow	Red
Goalkeepers							
Neil Alexander	26	45	25	24	2182	1	0
Arran Lee-Barrett	24	2	1	0	7	0	0
Martyn Margetson	32	45	22	21	1958	0	1
Defenders							
Christopher Barker	24	45	39	34	3123	2	0
James Collins	20	25	20	15	1396	2	0
Gary Croft	30	35	27	20	2076	3	1
Daniel Gabbidon	24	41	41	39	3577	4	0
Spencer Prior	33	30	7	5	427	0	0
Tony Vidmar	34	45	45	45	4045	8	1
Rhys Weston	23	24	24	19	1905	4	0
Midfielders							
Willie Boland	28	37	37	30	2863	3	1
Mark Bonner	30	26	20	13	1275	1	0
Jason Bowen	31	6	2	0	19	0	0
Lee Bullock	23	11	10	5	533	2	0
Julian Gray	24	10	9	5	495	1	0
Graham Kavanagh	30	27	27	26	2386	8	0
Richard Langley	24	44	44	38	3576	9	0
Leyton Maxwell	24	2	1	0	6	0	0
John Robinson	32	34	34	27	2509	4	0
Gareth Whalley	30	27	22	15	1459	0	0
Forwards							
Andy Campbell	25	36	25	4	778	1	1
Robert Earnshaw	23	46	46	42	3824	3	0
Stuart Fleetwood	18	4	2	0	18	0	0
Gavin Gordon	25	24	15	6	699	2	0
Alan Lee	25	24	23	16	1556	5	1
Paul Parry	23	17	17	8	1018	0	0
Peter Thorne	31	24	23	18	1717	3	0

TEAM OF THE SEASON

G: Martyn Margetson CG: 21 DR: 78

D: Gary Croft CG: 20 DR: 83

D: Daniel Gabbidon CG: 39 DR: 78

D: Tony Vidmar CG: 45 DR: 74

D: James Collins CG: 15 DR: 70

M: John Robinson CG: 27 SD: 22

M: Graham Kavanagh CG: 26 SD: 21

M: Mark Bonner CG: 13 SD: 19

M: Richard Langley CG: 38 SD: 11

F: Peter Thorne CG: 18 SR: 132

F: Robert Earnshaw CG: 42 SR: 182

SQUAD APPEARANCES

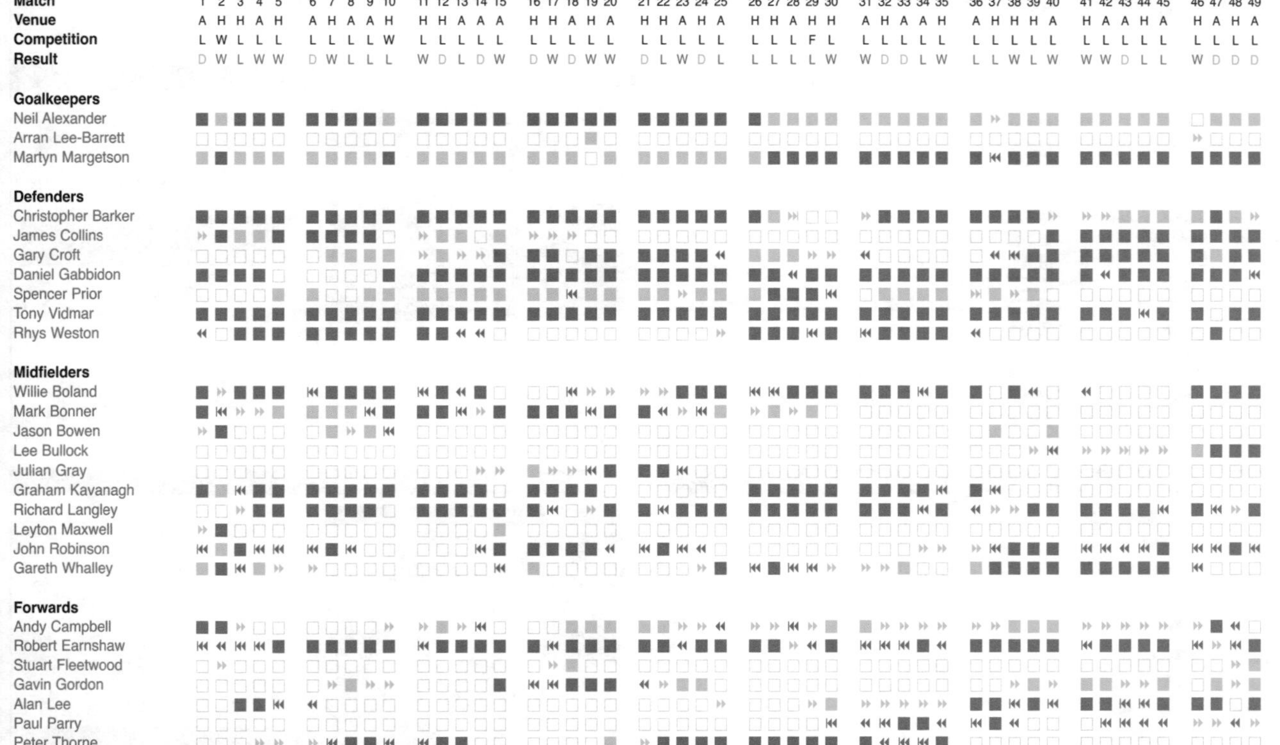

Match 1 2 3 4 5 6 7 8 9 10 11 12 13 14 15 16 17 18 19 20 21 22 23 24 25 26 27 28 29 30 31 32 33 34 35 36 37 38 39 40 41 42 43 44 45 46 47 48 49
Venue A H H A H A H A A H H H A A A H H A H A H H A H A H H A H H A H A A H A H H H A H A A H A H A H A
Competition L W L L L L L L L W L L L L L L L L L L L L L L L L L L F L L L L L L L L L L L L L L L L L L L L
Result D W L W W D W L L L W D L D W D W D W W D L W D L L L L L W W D D L W L L W L W W W D L L W D D D
Goalkeepers
Neil Alexander
Arran Lee-Barrett
Martyn Margetson
Defenders
Christopher Barker
James Collins
Gary Croft
Daniel Gabbidon
Spencer Prior
Tony Vidmar
Rhys Weston
Midfielders
Willie Boland
Mark Bonner
Jason Bowen
Lee Bullock
Julian Gray
Graham Kavanagh
Richard Langley
Leyton Maxwell
John Robinson
Gareth Whalley
Forwards
Andy Campbell
Robert Earnshaw
Stuart Fleetwood
Gavin Gordon
Alan Lee
Paul Parry
Peter Thorne
KEY: On all match
On bench
Subbed or sent off (Counting game)
Subbed or sent off (playing less than 70 minutes)
Subbed on from bench (Counting Game)
Subbed on (playing less than 70 minutes)
Subbed on and then subbed or sent off (Counting Game)
Subbed on and then subbed or sent off (playing less than 70 minutes)
Not in 16

NOTTINGHAM FOREST

Final Position: **14th**

NICKNAME: THE REDS

KEY: ☐Won ☐Drawn ☐Lost

							Attendance
1	div1	**Sunderland**	H	W	2-0	Harewood 19; Louis-Jean 41	23,529
2	ccR1	**Port Vale**	A	D	2-3*	(*on penalties)	4,950
3	div1	**Reading**	A	L	0-3		16,833
4	div1	**Cardiff**	H	L	1-2	Harewood 70	23,407
5	div1	**Coventry**	A	W	3-1	Reid 19,61; Johnson 65	17,586
6	div1	**Norwich**	H	W	2-0	Johnson 30; Harewood 51 pen	21,058
7	div1	**Sheff Utd**	H	W	3-1	Harewood 30 pen,56; Reid 71	25,209
8	div1	**Burnley**	A	W	3-0	Harewood 7; Reid 76; Taylor 82	12,530
9	div1	**Crewe**	A	L	1-3	Harewood 54	8,685
10	ccR2	**Tranmere**	A	W	4-1*	(*on penalties)	4,477
11	div1	**Derby**	H	D	1-1	Reid 28	29,059
12	div1	**Preston**	H	L	0-1		22,278
13	div1	**Stoke**	A	L	1-2	Williams 90	13,755
14	div1	**Rotherham**	H	D	2-2	Harewood 31,37	20,168
15	div1	**Wimbledon**	H	W	6-0	Harewood 24 pen,37; Reid 45; Taylor 62; Dawson 65; Morgan 81	23,500
16	div1	**West Ham**	A	D	1-1	Reid 5	29,544
17	div1	**Bradford**	A	W	2-1	Jess 78; Reid 90	11,654
18	ccR3	**Portsmouth**	H	L	2-4	Bopp 42,67	20,078
19	div1	**Millwall**	A	L	0-1		9,635
20	div1	**Walsall**	A	L	1-4	Reid 42	7,321
21	div1	**Watford**	H	D	1-1	Bopp 54	21,229
22	div1	**Wigan**	A	D	2-2	Thompson 51; Harewood 67	10,403
23	div1	**West Brom**	H	L	0-3		27,331
24	div1	**Ipswich**	H	D	1-1	Morgan 68	21,558
25	div1	**Watford**	A	D	1-1	Reid 89	14,988
26	div1	**Crystal Palace**	A	L	0-1		16,935
27	div1	**Norwich**	A	L	0-1		16,429
28	div1	**West Ham**	H	L	0-2		27,491
29	facr3	**West Brom**	H	W	1-0	King 54 pen	11,843
30	div1	**Sunderland**	A	L	0-1		26,340
31	div1	**Reading**	H	L	0-1		23,116
32	facr4	**Sheff Utd**	H	L	0-3		17,306
33	div1	**Cardiff**	A	D	0-0		17,913
34	div1	**Coventry**	H	L	0-1		23,075
35	div1	**Walsall**	H	D	3-3	Impey 3; King 56; Taylor 90	25,012
36	div1	**Rotherham**	A	D	1-1	Jess 89	9,046
37	div1	**Gillingham**	H	D	0-0		26,473
38	div1	**Bradford**	H	W	2-1	Reid 9; Taylor 90	26,021
39	div1	**Wimbledon**	A	W	1-0	Taylor 4	6,317
40	div1	**Gillingham**	A	L	1-2	Barmby 27	9,096
41	div1	**Crystal Palace**	H	W	3-2	Williams 4,74; Reid 13	28,306
42	div1	**Burnley**	H	D	1-1	Taylor 80	26,885
43	div1	**Derby**	A	L	2-4	Taylor 45; Williams 67	32,390
44	div1	**Crewe**	H	W	2-0	King 8,20	24,347
45	div1	**Sheff Utd**	A	W	2-1	King 24; Taylor 74	22,339
46	div1	**Stoke**	H	D	0-0		28,758
47	div1	**Preston**	A	D	2-2	King 4; Williams 45	15,117
48	div1	**Millwall**	H	D	2-2	Reid 55; Johnson 70	22,263
49	div1	**Ipswich**	A	W	2-1	Johnson 12,55	27,848
50	div1	**Wigan**	H	W	1-0	Johnson 58	29,172
51	div1	**West Brom**	A	W	2-0	Williams 4; Johnson 90	26,821

MONTHLY POINTS TALLY

Month	Points	%
AUGUST	9	60%
SEPTEMBER	7	58%
OCTOBER	8	44%
NOVEMBER	2	13%
DECEMBER	2	13%
JANUARY	1	11%
FEBRUARY	6	40%
MARCH	10	56%
APRIL	9	60%
MAY	6	100%

LEAGUE GOALS

	PLAYER	LGE	FAC	LC	Oth	TOT
1	Reid	13	0	0	0	13
2	Harewood	12	0	0	0	12
3	Taylor	8	0	0	0	8
4	Johnson	7	0	0	0	7
5	Williams	6	0	0	0	6
6	King	5	0	0	0	5
7	Morgan	2	0	0	0	2
8	Jess	2	0	0	0	2
9	Impey	1	0	0	0	1
10	Dawson	1	0	0	0	1
11	Bopp	1	0	2	0	3
	Other	3	1	0	0	4
	TOTAL	61	1	2	0	64

KEY PLAYERS - GOALSCORERS

Marlon Harewood

Goals in the League	12
Goals in all competitions	12
Contribution to Attacking Power Average number of minutes between League team goals while on pitch	53
Player Strike Rate The total number of minutes he was on the pitch for every League goal scored	142
Club Strike Rate Average number of minutes between League goals scored by club	68

	PLAYER	GOALS LGE	GOALS ALL	POWER	S RATE
1	Marlon Harewood	12	12	53	142 mins
2	Andrew Reid	13	13	68	315 mins
3	Gareth Taylor	8	8	67	328 mins
4	Marlon King	5	5	75	333 mins
5	Gareth Williams	6	6	66	558 mins

KEY PLAYERS - MIDFIELDERS

Andrew Impey

Goals in the League	1
Goals in all competitions	1
Defensive Rating Average number of mins between League goals conceded while on the pitch	78
Contribution to Attacking Power Average number of minutes between League team goals while on pitch	63
Scoring Difference Defensive Rating minus Contribution to Attacking Power	15

	PLAYER	GOALS LGE	GOALS ALL	DEF RATE	ATT POWER	SCORE DIFF
1	Andrew Impey	1	1	78	63	15 mins
2	Danny Sonner	0	0	70	65	5 mins
3	Gareth Williams	6	6	71	67	4 mins
4	Andrew Reid	13	13	71	68	3 mins
5	Eoin Jess	2	2	60	60	0 mins

KEY PLAYERS - DEFENDERS

Michael Dawson

Goals Conceded in League	32
Goals Conceded in all competitions	32
Clean Sheets In League games when he played at least 70 mins	9
Defensive Rating Ave number of mins between League goals conceded while on the pitch	82
Club Defensive Rating Average number of mins between League goals conceded by the club this season	71

	PLAYER	CON LGE	CON ALL	CLN SHEETS	DEF RATE
1	Michael Dawson	32	32	9	82 mins
2	Matthieu Louis-Jean	47	54	8	70 mins
3	Des Walker	30	35	7	70 mins
4	Wes Morgan	41	45	5	66 mins
5	John Thompson	37	41	4	64 mins

KEY GOALKEEPER

1 Darren Ward

Goals Conceded in the League	42
Goals Conceded in all competitions	49
Clean Sheets In games when he played at least 70 mins	6
Goals to Shots Ratio The average number of shots on target per each League goal conceded	4.9
Defensive Rating Ave number of mins between League goals conceded while on the pitch	68

DISCIPLINARY RECORDS

	PLAYER	YELLOW	RED	AVE
1	Morgan	7	2	298
2	Bopp	3	0	305
3	Evans	2	0	360
4	McPhail	3	0	377
5	Dawson	6	0	435
6	Sonner	4	0	436
7	Taylor	5	0	524
8	Robertson	2	0	540
9	King	2	1	555
10	Thompson	3	1	594
11	Louis-Jean	5	0	655
12	Reid	5	0	820
13	Stewart	1	0	931
	Other	10	1	
	TOTAL	58	5	

TOP POINT EARNERS

	PLAYER	GAMES	AV PTS
1	Michael Dawson	28	1.75
2	Andrew Impey	14	1.71
3	Marlon King	18	1.50
4	Gareth Williams	37	1.38
5	Marlon Harewood	19	1.37
6	Matthieu Louis-Jean	35	1.31
7	Andrew Reid	46	1.30
8	Danny Sonner	17	1.29
9	Eoin Jess	21	1.24
10	Wes Morgan	29	1.21
	CLUB AVERAGE:		1.30

LEAGUE APPEARANCES AND BOOKINGS

	AGE (on 01/07/04)	IN NAMED 16	APPEARANCES	COUNTING GAMES	MINUTES ON PITCH	Yellow	Red
Goalkeepers							
Pascal Foreman	21	6	0	0	0	0	0
Paul Gerrard	31	8	8	7	678	0	0
Barry Roche	22	46	8	6	608	0	0
Darren Ward	30	32	32	31	2854	0	0
Defenders							
James Biggins	19	0	0	0	0	0	0
Michael Dawson	20	31	30	28	2611	6	0
Chris Doig	23	23	10	7	723	0	0
Brynjar Gunnarsson	28	28	13	5	748	0	0
Matthieu Louis-Jean	28	38	38	35	3276	5	0
Wes Morgan	20	34	32	29	2686	7	2
Davy Oyen	28	5	4	4	360	0	0
James Perch	18	0	0	0	0	0	0
Gregor Robertson	20	25	16	11	1080	2	0
Alan Rogers	27	12	12	11	1042	0	1
David Tarka	21	1	0	0	0	0	0
John Thompson	23	35	32	25	2378	3	1
Des Walker	38	32	25	22	2099	2	0
Midfielders							
Nick Barmby	30	6	6	4	424	1	0
James Beaumont	19	1	0	0	0	0	0
Eugen Bopp	20	20	15	9	917	3	0
Brian Cash	21	5	1	0	7	0	0
Paul Evans	29	8	8	8	720	2	0
Ross Gardner	18	5	2	1	104	0	0
Andrew Impey	32	16	16	14	1318	1	0
Eoin Jess	33	46	34	21	2027	2	0
Stephen McPhail	24	14	14	11	1133	3	0
Andrew Reid	21	46	46	46	4101	5	0
Danny Sonner	32	42	27	17	1744	4	0
Michael Stewart	23	17	13	9	931	1	0
Gareth Williams	22	42	39	37	3349	2	0
Forwards							
Michael Chopra	20	7	5	2	241	0	0
Marlon Harewood	24	19	19	19	1708	0	0
Richard Jeffery	20	4	4	4	360	0	0
David Johnson	27	17	17	9	939	1	0
Marlon King	24	20	20	18	1667	2	1
Gareth Taylor	31	34	34	28	2622	5	0
Craig Westcarr	19	13	3	0	27	1	0

TEAM OF THE SEASON

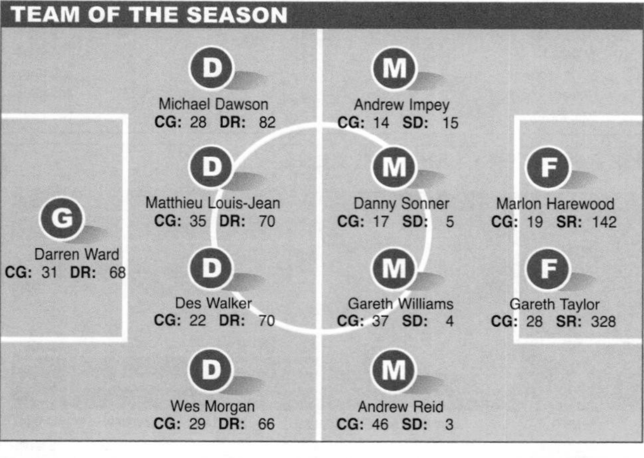

G
Darren Ward
CG: 31 DR: 68
D
Michael Dawson
CG: 28 DR: 82
D
Matthieu Louis-Jean
CG: 35 DR: 70
D
Des Walker
CG: 22 DR: 70
D
Wes Morgan
CG: 29 DR: 66
M
Andrew Impey
CG: 14 SD: 15
M
Danny Sonner
CG: 17 SD: 5
M
Gareth Williams
CG: 37 SD: 4
M
Andrew Reid
CG: 46 SD: 3
F
Marlon Harewood
CG: 19 SR: 142
F
Gareth Taylor
CG: 28 SR: 328

SQUAD APPEARANCES

Match	1	2	3	4	5	6	7	8	9	10	11	12	13	14	15	16	17	18	19	20	21	22	23	24	25	26	27	28	29	30	31	32	33	34	35	36	37	38	39	40	41	42	43	44	45	46	47	48	49	50	51
Venue	H	A	A	H	A	H	H	A	A	A	H	H	A	H	H	A	A	H	A	A	H	A	H	H	A	A	A	H	H	A	H	H	A	H	H	A	H	H	A	A	H	H	A	H	A	H	A	H	A	H	A
Competition	L	W	L	L	L	L	L	L	L	W	L	L	L	L	L	L	L	W	L	L	L	L	L	L	L	L	L	L	F	L	L	F	L	L	L	L	L	L	L	L	L	L	L	L	L	L	L	L	L	L	L
Result	W	D	L	L	W	W	W	W	L	W	D	L	L	D	W	D	W	L	L	L	D	D	L	D	D	L	L	L	W	L	L	L	D	L	D	D	D	W	W	L	W	D	L	W	W	D	D	D	W	W	W

Goalkeepers
Pascal Foreman
Paul Gerrard
Barry Roche
Darren Ward

Defenders
James Biggins
Michael Dawson
Chris Doig
Brynjar Gunnarsson
Matthieu Louis-Jean
Wes Morgan
Davy Oyen
James Perch
Gregor Robertson
Alan Rogers
David Tarka
John Thompson
Des Walker

Midfielders
Nick Barmby
James Beaumont
Eugen Bopp
Brian Cash
Paul Evans
Ross Gardner
Andrew Impey
Eoin Jess
Stephen McPhail
Andrew Reid
Danny Sonner
Michael Stewart
Gareth Williams

Forwards
Michael Chopra
Marlon Harewood
Richard Jeffery
David Johnson
Marlon King
Gareth Taylor
Craig Westcarr

KEY: On all match · On bench · Subbed or sent off (Counting game) · Subbed or sent off (playing less than 70 minutes) · Subbed on from bench (Counting Game) · Subbed on (playing less than 70 minutes) · Subbed on and then subbed or sent off (Counting Game) · Subbed on and then subbed or sent off (playing less than 70 minutes) · Not in 16

PRESTON NORTH END 15th

NICKNAME: THE LILYWHITES   KEY: ☐ Won ☐ Drawn ☐ Lost

							Attendance
1	div1	West Ham	H	L	1-2	Lewis 2	18,246
2	ccR1	Notts County	H	D	6-7*	(*on penalties)	5,016
3	div1	Wigan	A	D	1-1	Fuller 87	12,073
4	div1	Sunderland	H	L	0-2		14,018
5	div1	West Brom	A	L	0-1		24,402
6	div1	Stoke	H	W	1-0	McKenna 19	12,965
7	div1	Bradford	A	L	1-2	Fuller 10	11,243
8	div1	Coventry	H	W	4-2	Fuller 35,45; Cresswell 66; Keane 88	11,886
9	div1	Rotherham	H	W	4-1	Cresswell 11; Fuller 55; Alexander 65 pen; O'Neil, B 73	12,340
10	div1	Walsall	A	L	1-2	Fuller 62	6,981
11	div1	Nottm Forest	A	W	1-0	Abbott 36	22,278
12	div1	Wimbledon	H	W	1-0	Fuller 29	13,801
13	div1	Millwall	A	W	1-0	McKenna 51	8,015
14	div1	Reading	A	L	2-3	Fuller 20; Alexander 53 pen	13,130
15	div1	Crewe	A	L	1-2	Etuhu 90	7,012
16	div1	Ipswich	H	D	1-1	Healy 21	14,863
17	div1	Derby	H	W	3-0	Alexander 22 pen; Healy 68; Fuller 72	12,839
18	div1	Watford	H	W	2-1	Abbott 51; Healy 90	11,152
19	div1	Crystal Palace	A	D	1-1	Healy 51	14,608
20	div1	Norwich	H	D	0-0		14,775
21	div1	Sheff Utd	A	L	0-2		21,003
22	div1	Crystal Palace	H	W	4-1	Fuller 48; Alexander 50; Lewis 79; Healy 90	12,836
23	div1	Cardiff	A	D	2-2	Fuller 52; Healy 84	13,703
24	div1	Gillingham	A	W	1-0	Fuller 3	7,602
25	div1	Burnley	H	W	5-3	Fuller 18,71,82; Lewis 60; Healy 88	18,802
26	div1	Stoke	A	D	1-1	Healy 66	20,126
27	div1	Crewe	H	D	0-0		15,830
28	facr3	Reading	H	D	3-3	O'Neil, B 9; Fuller 32,45	9,428
29	div1	West Ham	A	W	2-1	Fuller 64; Healy 67	28,777
30	facr3r	Reading	A	W	2-1	Cresswell 28; Koumantarakis 47	9,314
31	div1	Wigan	H	L	2-4	Etuhu 30; Alexander 86	19,161
32	facr4	Swansea	A	L	1-2	Etuhu 58	10,200
33	div1	West Brom	H	W	3-0	Lewis 33; Healy 75; Alexander 87 pen	16,569
34	div1	Watford	A	L	0-2		12,675
35	div1	Millwall	H	L	1-2	Davis 70	12,903
36	div1	Ipswich	A	L	0-2		23,359
37	div1	Reading	H	W	2-1	Healy 35,89	11,745
38	div1	Burnley	A	D	1-1	Alexander 58 pen	15,837
39	div1	Sunderland	A	D	3-3	Healy 43; Mears 79; Lewis 90	27,181
40	div1	Gillingham	H	D	0-0		13,111
41	div1	Coventry	A	L	1-4	Fuller 48	13,142
42	div1	Walsall	H	L	1-2	Alexander 53	11,551
43	div1	Rotherham	A	L	0-1		6,268
44	div1	Bradford	H	W	1-0	Gemmill 50	12,367
45	div1	Wimbledon	A	D	3-3	McKenna 25; Lynch 43; Koumantarakis 84	2,866
46	div1	Nottm Forest	H	D	2-2	Lucketti 34; McKenna 77	15,117
47	div1	Derby	A	L	1-5	Mawene 55 og	24,162
48	div1	Cardiff	H	D	2-2	Lewis 15; McKenna 46	11,972
49	div1	Norwich	A	L	2-3	McKenna 5; Healy 48	23,673
50	div1	Sheff Utd	H	D	3-3	Alexander 24; Healy 54; Fuller 79	16,612

MONTHLY POINTS TALLY

Month	Points	%
AUGUST	4	27%
SEPTEMBER	6	50%
OCTOBER	10	56%
NOVEMBER	8	53%
DECEMBER	12	67%
JANUARY	3	50%
FEBRUARY	3	25%
MARCH	6	29%
APRIL	6	40%
MAY	1	17%

LEAGUE GOALS

	PLAYER	LGE	FAC	LC	Oth	TOT
1	Fuller	**18**	2	0	0	20
2	Healy	**15**	0	0	0	15
3	Alexander	**9**	0	0	0	9
4	McKenna	**6**	0	0	0	6
5	Lewis	**6**	0	0	0	6
6	Cresswell	**2**	1	0	0	3
7	Abbott	**2**	0	0	0	2
8	Etuhu	**2**	1	0	0	3
9	Davis	**1**	0	0	0	1
10	Lynch	**1**	0	0	0	1
11	Gemmill	**1**	0	0	0	1
	Other	6	2	0	0	8
	TOTAL	**69**	**6**	**0**	**0**	**75**

KEY PLAYERS - GOALSCORERS

David Healy

Goals in the League	15
Goals in all competitions	15
Contribution to Attacking Power Average number of minutes between League team goals while on pitch	58
Player Strike Rate The total number of minutes he was on the pitch for every League goal scored	172
Club Strike Rate Average number of minutes between League goals scored by club	60

	PLAYER	GOALS LGE	GOALS ALL	POWER	S RATE
1	David Healy	15	15	58	**172 mins**
2	Ricardo Fuller	18	20	57	**184 mins**
3	Eddie Lewis	6	6	60	**390 mins**
4	Graham Alexander	9	9	59	**442 mins**
5	Paul McKenna	6	6	53	**553 mins**

KEY PLAYERS - MIDFIELDERS

Michael Keane

Goals in the League	1
Goals in all competitions	1
Defensive Rating Average number of mins between League goals conceded while on the pitch	70
Contribution to Attacking Power Average number of minutes between League team goals while on pitch	65
Scoring Difference Defensive Rating minus Contribution to Attacking Power	5

	PLAYER	GOALS LGE	GOALS ALL	DEF RATE	ATT POWER	SCORE DIFF
1	Michael Keane	1	1	70	65	**5 mins**
2	Eddie Lewis	6	6	65	60	**5 mins**
3	Paul McKenna	6	6	55	54	**1 mins**
4	Graham Alexander	9	9	59	59	**0 mins**
5	Dickson Etuhu	2	3	54	65	**-11 mins**

KEY PLAYERS - DEFENDERS

Brian O'Neil

Goals Conceded in League	31
Goals Conceded in all competitions	37
Clean Sheets In League games when he played at least 70 mins	6
Defensive Rating Ave number of mins between League goals conceded while on the pitch	74
Club Defensive Rating Average number of mins between League goals conceded by the club this season	58

	PLAYER	CON LGE	CON ALL	CLN SHEETS	DEF RATE
1	Brian O'Neil	31	37	6	**74 mins**
2	Marlon Broomes	41	43	8	**63 mins**
3	Chris Lucketti	55	58	9	**60 mins**
4	Michael Jackson	61	64	9	**59 mins**
5	Rob Edwards	25	26	2	**54 mins**

KEY GOALKEEPER

1 Jonathan Gould

Goals Conceded in the League	55
Goals Conceded in all competitions	61
Clean Sheets In games when he played at least 70 mins	9
Goals to Shots Ratio The average number of shots on target per each League goal conceded	4.2
Defensive Rating Ave number of mins between League goals conceded while on the pitch	60

DISCIPLINARY RECORDS

	PLAYER	YELLOW	RED	AVE
1	Broomes	7	2	287
2	Lynch	2	0	324
3	Keane	6	0	325
4	Fuller	8	2	331
5	Cresswell	9	1	361
6	Healy	7	0	369
7	Lewis	6	0	390
8	Alexander	8	1	442
9	Jackson, Mi	5	1	596
10	Gemmill	1	0	614
11	Davis	2	0	644
12	Edwards	2	0	676
13	O'Neil, B	3	0	766
	Other	11	1	
	TOTAL	77	8	

TOP POINT EARNERS

	PLAYER	GAMES	AV PTS
1	Brian O'Neil	23	**1.48**
2	Chris Lucketti	36	**1.47**
3	Marlon Broomes	28	**1.43**
4	Paul McKenna	36	**1.42**
5	Jonathan Gould	36	**1.39**
6	Graham Alexander	44	**1.34**
7	Ricardo Fuller	36	**1.31**
8	David Healy	26	**1.31**
9	Dickson Etuhu	17	**1.29**
10	Michael Keane	16	**1.25**
	CLUB AVERAGE:		**1.28**

LEAGUE APPEARANCES AND BOOKINGS

	AGE (on 01/07/04)	IN NAMED 16	APPEARANCES	COUNTING GAMES	MINUTES ON PITCH	Yellow	Red
Goalkeepers							
Jonathan Gould	35	40	37	36	3280	1	1
Andrew Lonergan	20	27	8	8	720	0	0
David Lucas	26	24	2	1	138	0	0
Defenders							
Kyle Armstrong	-	2	0	0	0	0	0
Lee Briscoe	28	7	2	1	104	0	0
Marlon Broomes	26	31	31	28	2587	7	2
Claude Davis	25	29	21	12	1289	2	0
Rob Edwards	31	30	24	13	1353	2	0
David Elebert	-	1	0	0	0	0	0
Michael Jackson	30	43	42	39	3579	5	1
Chris Lucketti	32	38	37	36	3284	3	0
Tyrone Mears	21	15	12	10	960	1	0
Brian O'Neil	31	29	29	23	2300	3	0
Midfielders							
Graham Alexander	32	45	45	44	3978	8	1
Craig Burley	32	4	4	1	124	0	0
Lee Cartwright	31	20	12	2	341	1	0
Dickson Etuhu	22	34	31	17	1947	1	0
Scot Gemmill	33	7	7	7	614	1	0
Michael Keane	21	32	30	16	1952	6	0
Eddie Lewis	30	33	33	21	2340	6	0
Alan McCormack	20	12	5	2	251	1	0
Paul McKenna	26	39	39	36	3317	3	0
Eric Skora	22	4	2	0	39	0	0
Jeff Smith	24	10	5	0	130	0	0
Forwards							
Pawel Abbott	22	15	9	1	230	0	0
Richard Cresswell	26	45	45	40	3616	9	1
Ricardo Fuller	24	38	38	36	3313	8	2
David Healy	24	42	38	26	2583	7	0
Mark Jackson	-	3	2	1	95	0	0
George Koumantarakis	30	8	7	0	228	0	0
Simon Lynch	22	27	18	6	649	2	0

TEAM OF THE SEASON

G – Jonathan Gould – CG: 36 DR: 60

D – Brian O'Neil – CG: 23 DR: 74
D – Marlon Broomes – CG: 28 DR: 63
D – Chris Lucketti – CG: 36 DR: 60
D – Michael Jackson – CG: 39 DR: 59

M – Michael Keane – CG: 16 SD: 5
M – Eddie Lewis – CG: 21 SD: 5
M – Paul McKenna – CG: 36 SD: 1
M – Graham Alexander – CG: 44 SD: 0

F – David Healy – CG: 26 SR: 172
F – Ricardo Fuller – CG: 36 SR: 184

SQUAD APPEARANCES

Match	1	2	3	4	5	6	7	8	9	10	11	12	13	14	15	16	17	18	19	20	21	22	23	24	25
Venue	H	H	A	H	A	H	A	H	H	A	A	H	A	A	A	H	H	H	A	H	A	H	A	A	H
Competition	L	W	L	L	L	L	L	L	L	L	L	L	L	L	L	L	L	L	L	L	L	L	L	L	L
Result	L	D	D	L	L	W	L	W	W	L	W	W	W	L	L	D	W	W	D	D	L	W	D	W	W

Match	26	27	28	29	30	31	32	33	34	35	36	37	38	39	40	41	42	43	44	45	46	47	48	49	50
Venue	A	H	H	A	A	H	A	H	A	H	A	H	A	A	H	A	H	A	H	A	H	A	H	A	H
Competition	L	L	F	L	F	L	F	L	L	L	L	L	L	L	L	L	L	L	L	L	L	L	L	L	L
Result	D	D	D	W	W	L	L	W	L	L	L	W	D	D	D	L	L	L	W	D	D	L	D	L	D

Goalkeepers
Jonathan Gould
Andrew Lonergan
David Lucas

Defenders
Kyle Armstrong
Lee Briscoe
Marlon Broomes
Claude Davis
Rob Edwards
David Elebert
Michael Jackson
Chris Lucketti
Tyrone Mears
Brian O'Neil

Midfielders
Graham Alexander
Craig Burley
Lee Cartwright
Dickson Etuhu
Scot Gemmill
Michael Keane
Eddie Lewis
Alan McCormack
Paul McKenna
Eric Skora
Jeff Smith

Forwards
Pawel Abbott
Richard Cresswell
Ricardo Fuller
David Healy
Mark Jackson
George Koumantarakis
Simon Lynch

KEY: On all match; On bench; Subbed or sent off (Counting game); Subbed or sent off (playing less than 70 minutes); Subbed on from bench (Counting Game); Subbed on (playing less than 70 minutes); Subbed on and then subbed or sent off (Counting Game); Subbed on and then subbed or sent off (playing less than 70 minutes); Not in 16

WATFORD

Final Position: **16th**

NICKNAME: THE HORNETS

KEY: ☐Won ☐Drawn ☐Lost

							Attendance
1	ccR1	Bournemouth	H	D	0-0		9,561
2	div1	Crystal Palace	A	L	0-1		15,333
3	div1	West Brom	H	L	0-1		15,023
4	div1	Sunderland	A	L	0-2		23,600
5	div1	Gillingham	H	D	2-2	Helguson 7; Webber 54	12,793
6	div1	Millwall	H	W	3-1	Dyer 8; Cox 45 pen; Young 90	11,305
7	div1	Derby	A	L	2-3	Gayle 37; Young 81	18,459
8	div1	Wigan	A	L	0-1		9,211
9	ccR2	Bristol City	A	L	0-1		5,213
10	div1	Ipswich	H	L	1-2	Fitzgerald 49	15,350
11	div1	Burnley	H	D	1-1	Fitzgerald 45	11,573
12	div1	Crewe	A	W	1-0	Webber 61	7,055
13	div1	Walsall	H	D	1-1	Baird 61 og	12,231
14	div1	Bradford	H	W	1-0	Fitzgerald 61	10,381
15	div1	Coventry	H	D	1-1	Fitzgerald 83	13,487
16	div1	Wimbledon	A	W	3-1	Devlin 22; Webber 33; Fitzgerald 67	6,115
17	div1	Cardiff	A	L	0-3		14,011
18	div1	Rotherham	H	W	1-0	Webber 47	18,067
19	div1	Preston	A	L	1-2	Webber 64	11,152
20	div1	Nottm Forest	A	D	1-1	Cook 84	21,229
21	div1	Norwich	A	W	2-1	Fitzgerald 24; Cox 81 pen	16,420
22	div1	West Ham	H	D	0-0		20,950
23	div1	Reading	A	L	1-2	Cook 60	14,521
24	div1	Nottm Forest	H	D	1-1	Fitzgerald 73	14,988
25	div1	Sheff Utd	A	D	2-2	Smith, J 64; Helguson 65	18,637
26	div1	Stoke	H	L	1-3	Helguson 4	13,732
27	div1	Gillingham	A	L	0-1		8,971
28	div1	Cardiff	H	W	2-1	Fitzgerald 61; Cook 88	15,512
29	facr3	Chelsea	H	D	2-2	Helguson 5; Mahon 35	21,121
30	div1	Coventry	A	D	0-0		12,226
31	facr3r	Chelsea	A	L	0-4		38,763
32	div1	Crystal Palace	H	L	1-5	Helguson 58 pen	15,017
33	div1	West Brom	A	L	1-3	Fitzgerald 77	23,958
34	div1	Sunderland	H	D	2-2	Mahon 7; Cox 68 pen	16,798
35	div1	Preston	H	W	2-0	Bouazza 36; Devlin 80	12,675
36	div1	Walsall	A	W	1-0	Cook 15	6,684
37	div1	Wimbledon	H	W	4-0	Cook 5; Cox 39 pen; Smith, J 63; Ardley 77	15,323
38	div1	Stoke	A	L	1-3	Helguson 36	13,108
39	div1	Bradford	A	L	0-2		17,143
40	div1	Sheff Utd	H	L	0-2		13,861
41	div1	Derby	H	W	2-1	Helguson 19; Mahon 53	13,931
42	div1	Ipswich	A	L	1-4	Fitzgerald 45	23,524
43	div1	Wigan	H	D	1-1	Helguson 24	13,382
44	div1	Crewe	H	W	2-1	Hyde 31; Wright 62 og	18,041
45	div1	Burnley	A	W	3-2	Devlin 34 pen; Helguson 55; Cook 84	11,413
46	div1	Rotherham	A	D	1-1	Dyer 24	7,221
47	div1	Millwall	A	W	2-1	Dyer 53; Cook 71	10,263
48	div1	Norwich	H	L	1-2	Blizzard 78	19,290
49	div1	West Ham	A	L	0-4		34,685
50	div1	Reading	H	W	1-0	Young 43	17,979

MONTHLY POINTS TALLY

AUGUST	1	8%
SEPTEMBER	4	27%
OCTOBER	11	61%
NOVEMBER	8	44%
DECEMBER	5	33%
JANUARY	1	11%
FEBRUARY	10	83%
MARCH	4	22%
APRIL	10	67%
MAY	3	50%

LEAGUE GOALS

	PLAYER	LGE	FAC	LC	Oth	TOT
1	Fitzgerald	**10**	0	1	0	11
2	Helguson	**8**	1	0	0	9
3	Cook	**7**	0	0	0	7
4	Webber	**5**	0	0	0	5
5	Cox	**4**	0	0	0	4
6	Young	**3**	0	0	0	3
7	Devlin	**3**	0	0	0	3
8	Dyer	**3**	0	0	0	3
9	Mahon	**2**	1	0	0	3
10	Smith, J	**2**	0	0	0	2
11	Blizzard	**1**	0	0	0	1
	Other	6	0	0	0	6
	TOTAL	**54**	**2**	**1**	**0**	**57**

KEY PLAYERS - GOALSCORERS

Heidar Helguson

Goals in the League	8
Goals in all competitions	9
Contribution to Attacking Power Average number of minutes between League team goals while on pitch	81
Player Strike Rate The total number of minutes he was on the pitch for every League goal scored	225
Club Strike Rate Average number of minutes between League goals scored by club	77

	PLAYER	GOALS LGE	GOALS ALL	POWER	S RATE
1	Heidar Helguson	8	9	81	225 mins
2	Scott Fitzgerald	10	11	69	258 mins
3	Lee Cook	7	7	57	286 mins
4	Danny Webber	5	5	90	396 mins
5	Bruce Dyer	3	3	126	504 mins

KEY PLAYERS - MIDFIELDERS

Lee Cook

Goals in the League	7
Goals in all competitions	7
Defensive Rating Average number of mins between League goals conceded while on the pitch	51
Contribution to Attacking Power Average number of minutes between League team goals while on pitch	57
Scoring Difference Defensive Rating minus Contribution to Attacking Power	-6

	PLAYER	GOALS LGE	GOALS ALL	DEF RATE	ATT POWER	SCORE DIFF
1	Lee Cook	7	7	51	57	-6 mins
2	Paolo Vernazza	0	0	74	87	-13 mins
3	Paul Devlin	3	3	60	74	-14 mins
4	Micah Hyde	1	1	61	78	-17 mins
5	Gavin Mahon	2	3	56	76	-20 mins

KEY PLAYERS - DEFENDERS

Stephen Kelly

Goals Conceded in League	16
Goals Conceded in all competitions	16
Clean Sheets In League games when he played at least 70 mins	3
Defensive Rating Ave number of mins between League goals conceded while on the pitch	73
Club Defensive Rating Average number of mins between League goals conceded by the club this season	61

	PLAYER	CON LGE	CON ALL	CLN SHEETS	DEF RATE
1	Stephen Kelly	16	16	3	73 mins
2	Jack Smith	21	27	6	68 mins
3	Neil Cox	45	50	9	66 mins
4	Neal Ardley	50	56	9	63 mins
5	Marcus Gayle	46	52	4	62 mins

KEY GOALKEEPER

1 Lenny Pidgeley

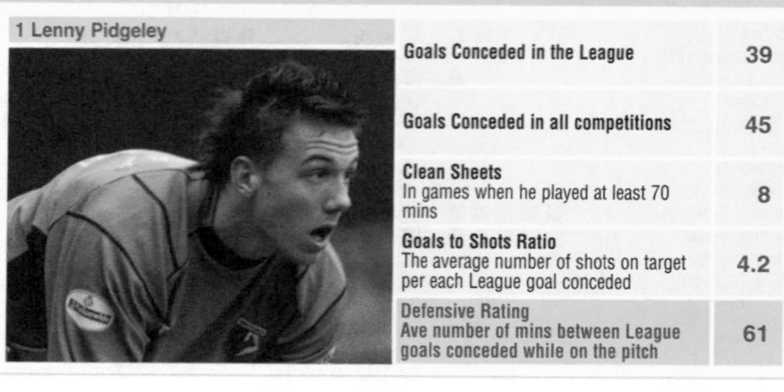

Goals Conceded in the League	39
Goals Conceded in all competitions	45
Clean Sheets In games when he played at least 70 mins	8
Goals to Shots Ratio The average number of shots on target per each League goal conceded	4.2
Defensive Rating Ave number of mins between League goals conceded while on the pitch	61

DISCIPLINARY RECORDS

	PLAYER	YELLOW	RED	AVE
1	Bouazza	2	0	245
2	Helguson	6	1	256
3	Hand	4	0	316
4	Cox	7	1	373
5	Vernazza	3	1	390
6	Hyde	6	0	427
7	Robinson	2	0	450
8	Devlin	6	1	493
9	Cook	4	0	500
10	Brown	2	0	525
11	Kelly	2	0	585
12	Fitzgerald	4	0	645
13	Dyer	2	0	756
	Other	9	3	
	TOTAL	59	7	

TOP POINT EARNERS

	PLAYER	GAMES	AV PTS
1	Lee Cook	17	**1.82**
2	Scott Fitzgerald	24	**1.58**
3	Jack Smith	16	**1.50**
4	Stephen Kelly	13	**1.46**
5	Paolo Vernazza	15	**1.40**
6	Sean Dyche	22	**1.32**
7	Micah Hyde	26	**1.31**
8	Neil Cox	32	**1.31**
9	Paul Mayo	14	**1.29**
10	Paul Devlin	38	**1.29**
	CLUB AVERAGE:		**1.24**

TEAM OF THE SEASON

D
Stephen Kelly
CG: 13 DR: 73
M
Lee Cook
CG: 17 SD: -6
D
Jack Smith
CG: 16 DR: 68
M
Paolo Vernazza
CG: 15 SD: -13
F
Heidar Helguson
CG: 20 SR: 225
G
Lenny Pidgeley
CG: 26 DR: 61
D
Neil Cox
CG: 32 DR: 66
M
Paul Devlin
CG: 38 SD: -14
F
Scott Fitzgerald
CG: 24 SR: 258
D
Neal Ardley
CG: 34 DR: 63
M
Micah Hyde
CG: 26 SD: -17

LEAGUE APPEARANCES AND BOOKINGS

	AGE (on 01/07/04)	IN NAMED 16	APPEARANCES	COUNTING GAMES	MINUTES ON PITCH	Yellow	Red
Goalkeepers							
Alec Chamberlain	40	45	21	19	1761	0	1
Kevin Hitchcock	41	1	0	0	0	0	0
Richard Lee	21	6	0	0	0	0	0
Lenny Pidgeley	19	40	27	26	2378	0	1
Defenders							
Neal Ardley	31	42	38	34	3137	2	1
Chris Baird	22	6	6	6	540	0	0
Wayne Brown	26	15	12	11	1051	2	0
Neil Cox	32	35	34	32	2985	7	1
Lloyd Doyley	21	24	9	6	645	0	0
Sean Dyche	33	43	25	22	2040	0	0
Marcus Gayle	33	33	32	31	2834	1	0
Jerel Ifil	22	11	10	9	823	0	0
Stephen Kelly	20	13	13	13	1170	2	0
Paul Mayo	22	14	14	14	1260	0	0
Jack Smith	20	21	17	16	1423	1	0
Midfielders							
Dominic Blizzard	20	2	2	1	119	0	0
Lee Cook	21	46	41	17	2003	4	0
Paul Devlin	32	39	39	38	3457	6	1
Gary Fisken	22	3	1	0	25	0	0
Jamie Hand	20	27	21	9	1266	4	0
Micah Hyde	29	33	33	26	2563	6	0
Richard Johnson	30	0	0	0	0	0	0
Gavin Mahon	27	32	32	31	2809	3	0
Anthony McNamee	20	2	2	0	45	0	0
Paul Robinson	25	10	10	10	900	2	0
Paolo Vernazza	24	34	29	15	1562	3	1
Ashley Young	18	9	5	1	160	0	0
Forwards							
Hameur Bouazza	19	10	9	3	491	2	0
Bruce Dyer	29	45	31	13	1512	2	0
Scott Fitzgerald	24	44	44	24	2582	4	0
Heidar Helguson	26	22	22	20	1796	6	1
Danny Webber	22	29	27	21	1982	2	0

SQUAD APPEARANCES

Match	1	2	3	4	5	6	7	8	9	10	11	12	13	14	15	16	17	18	19	20	21	22	23	24	25
Venue	H	A	H	A	H	H	A	A	A	H	H	A	H	H	H	A	A	H	A	A	A	H	A	H	A
Competition	W	L	L	L	L	L	L	L	W	L	L	L	L	L	L	L	L	L	L	L	L	L	L	L	L
Result	D	L	L	L	D	W	L	L	L	L	D	W	D	W	D	W	L	W	L	D	W	D	L	D	D

Match	26	27	28	29	30	31	32	33	34	35	36	37	38	39	40	41	42	43	44	45	46	47	48	49	50
Venue	H	A	H	H	A	A	H	A	H	H	A	H	A	A	H	H	A	H	H	A	A	A	H	A	H
Competition	L	L	L	F	L	F	L	L	L	L	L	L	L	L	L	L	L	L	L	L	L	L	L	L	L
Result	L	L	W	D	D	L	L	L	D	W	W	W	L	L	L	W	L	D	W	W	D	W	L	L	W

Goalkeepers
Alec Chamberlain
Kevin Hitchcock
Richard Lee
Lenny Pidgeley

Defenders
Neal Ardley
Chris Baird
Wayne Brown
Neil Cox
Lloyd Doyley
Sean Dyche
Marcus Gayle
Stephen Kelly
Paul Mayo
Jack Smith

Midfielders
Dominic Blizzard
Lee Cook
Paul Devlin
Gary Fisken
Jamie Hand
Micah Hyde
Jerel Ifil
Richard Johnson
Gavin Mahon
Anthony McNamee
Paul Robinson
Paolo Vernazza
Ashley Young

Forwards
Hameur Bouazza
Bruce Dyer
Scott Fitzgerald
Heidar Helguson
Danny Webber

KEY: On all match — On bench — Subbed or sent off (Counting game) — Subbed or sent off (playing less than 70 minutes) — Subbed on from bench (Counting Game) — Subbed on (playing less than 70 minutes) — Subbed on and then subbed or sent off (Counting Game) — Subbed on and then subbed or sent off (playing less than 70 minutes) — Not in 16

ROTHERHAM UNITED

Final Position: **17th**

NICKNAME: THE MERRY MILLERS

KEY: ☐Won ☐Drawn ☐Lost

							Attendance
1	div1	Cardiff	H	D	0-0		8,176
2	ccR1	York	H	W	2-1	Swailes 2; Sedgwick 43	2,919
3	div1	Norwich	A	L	0-2		16,263
4	div1	West Ham	H	W	1-0	Byfield 14	8,739
5	div1	Reading	A	D	0-0		14,047
6	div1	Wigan	H	L	0-3		6,660
7	div1	Crewe	H	L	0-2		5,495
8	div1	Sheff Utd	A	L	0-5		22,572
9	div1	Preston	A	L	1-4	Byfield 45	12,340
10	ccR2	Colchester	H	W	1-0	Sedgwick 22	2,474
11	div1	Gillingham	H	D	1-1	Byfield 80 pen	5,501
12	div1	Stoke	H	W	3-0	Byfield 45 pen; Butler 51,90	5,450
13	div1	Ipswich	A	L	1-2	Butler 59	21,859
14	div1	Millwall	H	D	0-0		5,461
15	div1	Nottm Forest	A	D	2-2	Byfield 51; Butler 56	20,168
16	div1	Crystal Palace	A	D	1-1	Swailes 32	18,715
17	div1	Sunderland	A	D	0-0		24,506
18	div1	West Brom	H	L	0-3		7,815
19	ccR3	Arsenal	A	D	8-9*	Byfield 90 (*on penalties)	27,451
20	div1	Watford	A	L	0-1		18,067
21	div1	Wimbledon	H	W	3-1	Butler 34; Swailes 38; McIntosh 54	5,777
22	div1	Burnley	A	D	1-1	Mullin 51	12,928
23	div1	Walsall	H	W	2-0	Swailes 67; Butler 80	6,101
24	div1	Coventry	H	W	2-0	Byfield 14; Barker, S 39	5,524
25	div1	Wimbledon	A	W	2-1	Barker, S 45; McIntosh 67	3,061
26	div1	Derby	H	D	0-0		7,320
27	div1	Bradford	A	W	2-0	Byfield 16 pen; Mullin 90	10,923
28	div1	Wigan	A	W	2-1	Hoskins 81,83	9,235
29	div1	Sunderland	H	L	0-2		11,455
30	facr3	Northampton	A	D	1-1	Barker, R 55	5,741
31	div1	Cardiff	A	L	2-3	Talbot 3; Mullin 9	13,021
32	facr3r	Northampton	H	L	1-2	Hurst 19	9,405
33	div1	Norwich	H	D	4-4	Butler 28,42,65; Mullin 75	7,448
34	div1	West Ham	A	L	1-2	Repka 23 og	34,483
35	div1	Reading	H	W	5-1	Pollitt 24 pen; Monkhouse 36; Butler 47; Proctor 79; Barker, R 90	6,405
36	div1	Nottm Forest	H	D	1-1	Monkhouse 65	9,046
37	div1	Millwall	A	L	1-2	Proctor 90 pen	8,254
38	div1	West Brom	A	W	1-0	Sedgwick 73	24,104
39	div1	Bradford	H	L	1-2	Hurst 74	6,796
40	div1	Derby	A	L	0-1		21,741
41	div1	Sheff Utd	H	D	1-1	Monkhouse 52	9,793
42	div1	Gillingham	A	L	0-2		8,047
43	div1	Preston	H	W	1-0	Butler 30	6,268
44	div1	Crewe	A	D	0-0		6,749
45	div1	Crystal Palace	H	L	1-2	Proctor 85	6,001
46	div1	Ipswich	H	L	1-3	Sedgwick 24	6,561
47	div1	Stoke	A	W	2-0	Morris 22; Butler 68	11,978
48	div1	Watford	H	D	1-1	Butler 4	7,221
49	div1	Coventry	A	D	1-1	Butler 75	13,572
50	div1	Burnley	H	W	3-0	Butler 19; Stockdale 39; Proctor 85 pen	9,157
51	div1	Walsall	A	L	2-3	Proctor 55 pen; Warne 90 pen	11,049

KEY PLAYERS - GOALSCORERS

Martin Butler

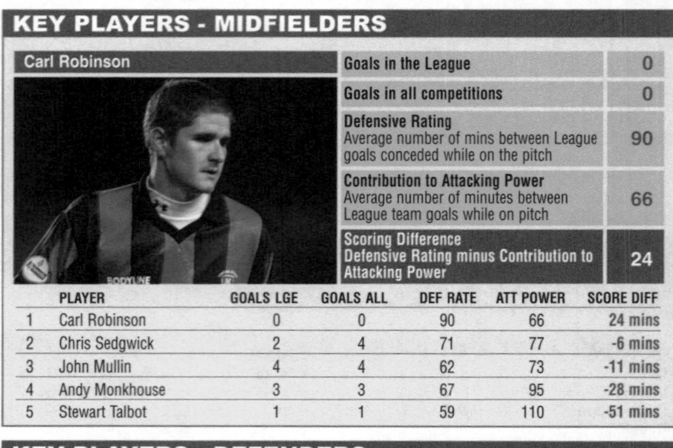

Goals in the League	15
Goals in all competitions	15
Contribution to Attacking Power Average number of minutes between League team goals while on pitch	72
Player Strike Rate The total number of minutes he was on the pitch for every League goal scored	202
Club Strike Rate Average number of minutes between League goals scored by club	78

	PLAYER	GOALS LGE	GOALS ALL	POWER	S RATE
1	Martin Butler	15	15	72	202 mins
2	Mike Proctor	5	5	67	269 mins
3	Darren Byfield	7	8	85	319 mins
4	Andy Monkhouse	3	3	94	537 mins
5	Martin McIntosh	2	2	81	770 mins

KEY PLAYERS - MIDFIELDERS

Carl Robinson

Goals in the League	0
Goals in all competitions	0
Defensive Rating Average number of mins between League goals conceded while on the pitch	90
Contribution to Attacking Power Average number of minutes between League team goals while on pitch	66
Scoring Difference Defensive Rating minus Contribution to Attacking Power	24

	PLAYER	GOALS LGE	GOALS ALL	DEF RATE	ATT POWER	SCORE DIFF
1	Carl Robinson	0	0	90	66	24 mins
2	Chris Sedgwick	2	4	71	77	-6 mins
3	John Mullin	4	4	62	73	-11 mins
4	Andy Monkhouse	3	3	67	95	-28 mins
5	Stewart Talbot	1	1	59	110	-51 mins

KEY PLAYERS - DEFENDERS

Martin McIntosh

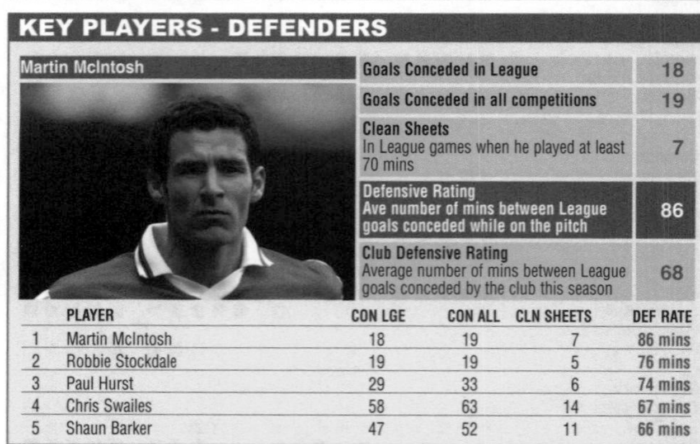

Goals Conceded in League	18
Goals Conceded in all competitions	19
Clean Sheets In League games when he played at least 70 mins	7
Defensive Rating Ave number of mins between League goals conceded while on the pitch	86
Club Defensive Rating Average number of mins between League goals conceded by the club this season	68

	PLAYER	CON LGE	CON ALL	CLN SHEETS	DEF RATE
1	Martin McIntosh	18	19	7	86 mins
2	Robbie Stockdale	19	19	5	76 mins
3	Paul Hurst	29	33	6	74 mins
4	Chris Swailes	58	63	14	67 mins
5	Shaun Barker	47	52	11	66 mins

MONTHLY POINTS TALLY

AUGUST	5	33%
SEPTEMBER	4	27%
OCTOBER	4	22%
NOVEMBER	7	58%
DECEMBER	13	72%
JANUARY	1	11%
FEBRUARY	7	58%
MARCH	4	27%
APRIL	6	33%
MAY	3	50%

LEAGUE GOALS

	PLAYER	LGE	FAC	LC	Oth	TOT
1	Butler	15	0	0	0	15
2	Byfield	7	0	1	0	8
3	Proctor	5	0	0	0	5
4	Mullin	4	0	0	0	4
5	Monkhouse	3	0	0	0	3
6	Swailes	3	0	1	0	4
7	McIntosh	2	0	0	0	2
8	Sedgwick	2	0	2	0	4
9	Barker, S	2	0	0	0	2
10	Pollitt	1	0	0	0	1
11	Warne	1	0	0	0	1
	Other	8	2	0	0	10
	TOTAL	53	2	4	0	59

KEY GOALKEEPER

1 Mike Pollitt

Goals Conceded in the League	59
Goals Conceded in all competitions	64
Clean Sheets In games when he played at least 70 mins	14
Goals to Shots Ratio The average number of shots on target per each League goal conceded	4.4
Defensive Rating Ave number of mins between League goals conceded while on the pitch	66

DISCIPLINARY RECORDS

	PLAYER	YELLOW	RED	AVE
1	Branston	2	1	202
2	Talbot	7	1	206
3	Monkhouse	7	0	230
4	McIntosh	3	2	308
5	Scott	2	0	366
6	Butler	8	0	379
7	Sedgwick	8	0	423
8	Warne	5	0	428
9	Swailes	9	0	430
10	Minto	5	0	526
11	Mullin	6	0	536
12	Byfield	4	0	557
13	Barker, S	4	1	621
	Other	5	1	
	TOTAL	75	6	

TOP POINT EARNERS

	PLAYER	GAMES	AV PTS
1	Martin McIntosh	16	**1.50**
2	Carl Robinson	14	**1.50**
3	Mike Proctor	13	**1.46**
4	Paul Hurst	22	**1.45**
5	Paul Warne	20	**1.45**
6	Shaun Barker	33	**1.30**
7	John Mullin	35	**1.29**
8	Chris Sedgwick	36	**1.28**
9	Martin Butler	33	**1.27**
10	Chris Swailes	43	**1.23**
	CLUB AVERAGE:		**1.17**

LEAGUE APPEARANCES AND BOOKINGS

	AGE (on 01/07/04)	IN NAMED 16	APPEARANCES	COUNTING GAMES	MINUTES ON PITCH	Yellow	Red
Goalkeepers							
Bradley Jones	22	8	0	0	0	0	0
Gary Montgomery	21	38	4	3	274	0	0
Mike Pollitt	32	43	43	43	3870	1	0
Defenders							
Shaun Barker	21	38	36	33	3107	4	1
Julien Baudet	25	21	11	7	688	0	1
Guy Branston	25	9	8	6	608	2	1
Phil Gilchrist	30	10	10	9	826	0	0
Paul Hurst	29	40	28	22	2134	0	0
Martin McIntosh	33	19	18	16	1540	3	2
Scott Minto	32	43	32	27	2630	5	0
Craig Mudd	17	1	0	0	0	0	0
Rob Scott	30	11	10	7	732	2	0
Robbie Stockdale	24	16	16	16	1440	0	0
Chris Swailes	33	43	43	43	3870	9	0
Midfielders							
Nick Daws	34	21	9	7	660	0	0
Darren Garner	32	14	13	8	855	1	0
Andy Monkhouse	23	36	27	14	1610	7	0
Jody Morris	25	5	5	5	450	0	0
John Mullin	28	40	38	35	3218	6	0
Carl Robinson	27	14	14	14	1260	1	0
Chris Sedgwick	24	40	40	36	3390	8	0
Stewart Talbot	31	28	23	16	1653	7	1
Forwards							
Richard Barker	29	44	31	10	1474	1	0
Martin Butler	29	37	37	33	3034	8	0
Darren Byfield	27	28	28	22	2230	4	0
William Hoskins	17	8	3	0	40	0	0
Alan Lee	25	1	1	1	90	0	0
Mike Proctor	23	17	17	13	1346	1	0
Mark Robins	34	18	9	1	237	0	0
Paul Warne	31	43	35	20	2141	5	0

TEAM OF THE SEASON

G — Mike Pollitt — **CG:** 43 **DR:** 66

D — Martin McIntosh — **CG:** 16 **DR:** 86

D — Paul Hurst — **CG:** 22 **DR:** 74

D — Chris Swailes — **CG:** 43 **DR:** 67

D — Robbie Stockdale — **CG:** 16 **DR:** 76

M — Chris Sedgwick — **CG:** 36 **SD:** -6

M — John Mullin — **CG:** 35 **SD:** -11

M — Andy Monkhouse — **CG:** 14 **SD:** -28

M — Stewart Talbot — **CG:** 16 **SD:** -51

F — Martin Butler — **CG:** 33 **SR:** 202

F — Mike Proctor — **CG:** 13 **SR:** 269

SQUAD APPEARANCES

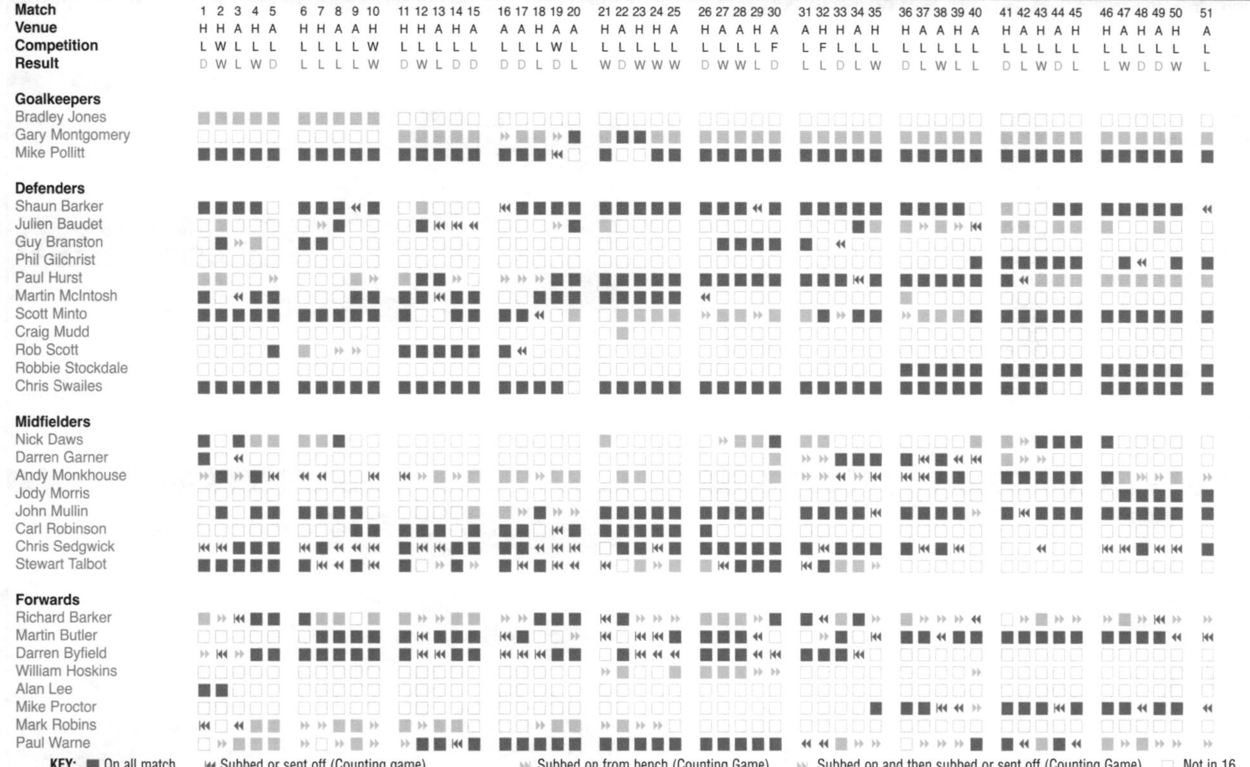

Match 1 2 3 4 5 6 7 8 9 10 11 12 13 14 15 16 17 18 19 20 21 22 23 24 25 26 27 28 29 30 31 32 33 34 35 36 37 38 39 40 41 42 43 44 45 46 47 48 49 50 51
Venue H H A H A H H A A H H H A H A A A H A A H A H H A H A A H A A H H A H H A A H A H A H A H H A H A H A
Competition L W L L L L L L L W L L L L L L L L W L L L L L L L L L L F L F L L L L L L L L L L L L L L L L L L L
Result D W L W D L L L L W D W L D D D D L D L W D W W W D W W L D L L D L W D L W L L D L W D L L W D D W L
Goalkeepers
Bradley Jones
Gary Montgomery
Mike Pollitt
Defenders
Shaun Barker
Julien Baudet
Guy Branston
Phil Gilchrist
Paul Hurst
Martin McIntosh
Scott Minto
Craig Mudd
Rob Scott
Robbie Stockdale
Chris Swailes
Midfielders
Nick Daws
Darren Garner
Andy Monkhouse
Jody Morris
John Mullin
Carl Robinson
Chris Sedgwick
Stewart Talbot
Forwards
Richard Barker
Martin Butler
Darren Byfield
William Hoskins
Alan Lee
Mike Proctor
Mark Robins
Paul Warne
KEY: On all match
On bench
Subbed or sent off (Counting game)
Subbed or sent off (playing less than 70 minutes)
Subbed on from bench (Counting Game)
Subbed on (playing less than 70 minutes)
Subbed on and then subbed or sent off (Counting Game)
Subbed on and then subbed or sent off (playing less than 70 minutes)
Not in 16

CREWE ALEXANDRA

Final Position: **18th**

NICKNAME: THE RAILWAYMEN KEY: ☐ Won ☐ Drawn ☐ Lost

							Attendance
1	div1	Wimbledon	A	L	1-3	Brammer 8	1,145
2	ccR1	Wrexham	H	W	2-0	Ashton 54 pen; Jones 88	3,152
3	div1	Ipswich	H	W	1-0	Lunt 69	6,982
4	div1	Millwall	A	D	1-1	Ashton 58	9,504
5	div1	Walsall	H	W	1-0	Jones 66	7,026
6	div1	Burnley	A	L	0-1		11,495
7	div1	Rotherham	A	W	2-0	Ashton 45 pen; Walker 57	5,495
8	div1	West Ham	H	L	0-3		9,575
9	div1	Nottm Forest	H	W	3-1	Lunt 64; Ashton 74; Jones 88	8,685
10	ccR2	Leicester	A	L	0-1		27,675
11	div1	Cardiff	A	L	0-3		14,385
12	div1	Coventry	A	L	0-2		11,557
13	div1	Watford	H	L	0-1		7,055
14	div1	Bradford	H	D	2-2	Jones 46; Ashton 49	5,867
15	div1	Derby	H	W	3-0	Barrowman 10; Ashton 24; Rix 78	8,656
16	div1	Preston	H	W	2-1	Lunt 10; Foster 28	7,012
17	div1	Stoke	A	D	1-1	Jones, S 53	17,569
18	div1	Reading	H	W	1-0	Jones, S 15	7,091
19	div1	Sheff Utd	A	L	0-2		17,396
20	div1	Gillingham	A	L	0-2		6,923
21	div1	Sunderland	H	W	3-0	Ashton 53; Jones, S 55,63	9,807
22	div1	Norwich	A	L	0-1		16,367
23	div1	Gillingham	H	D	1-1	Jones, S 11	6,271
24	div1	Crystal Palace	A	W	3-1	Ashton 8,86; Varney 16	12,259
25	div1	West Brom	A	D	2-2	Jones, S 18; Wright 45	22,825
26	div1	Wigan	H	L	2-3	Jones, B 10; Jones, S 17	7,873
27	div1	Burnley	H	W	3-1	Ashton 37; Jones, S 55,90	9,512
28	div1	Preston	A	D	0-0		15,830
29	facr3	Telford	H	L	0-1		7,085
30	div1	Wimbledon	H	W	1-0	Jones, S 62	6,234
31	div1	Ipswich	A	L	4-6	Ashton 35; McGreal 48 og; Richards 66 og; Robinson 82	22,071
32	div1	Millwall	H	L	1-2	Roberts 65 og	6,685
33	div1	Walsall	A	D	1-1	Foster 85	6,871
34	div1	Bradford	A	L	1-2	Rix 66	9,935
35	div1	Sheff Utd	H	L	0-1		6,525
36	div1	Derby	A	D	0-0		19,861
37	div1	Wigan	A	W	3-2	Ashton 20 pen,26 pen,90	8,367
38	div1	West Brom	H	L	1-2	Ashton 63	8,335
39	div1	West Ham	A	L	2-4	Jones, S 61,72	31,158
40	div1	Cardiff	H	L	0-1		6,650
41	div1	Stoke	H	W	2-0	Lunt 25,61	10,014
42	div1	Nottm Forest	A	L	0-2		24,347
43	div1	Rotherham	H	D	0-0		6,749
44	div1	Watford	A	L	1-2	Ashton 61 pen	18,041
45	div1	Coventry	H	W	3-1	Higdon 46; Symes 64; Ashton 90 pen	7,475
46	div1	Reading	A	D	1-1	Lunt 39	14,729
47	div1	Crystal Palace	H	L	2-3	Ashton 47; Lunt 73	8,136
48	div1	Sunderland	A	D	1-1	Ashton 76	25,311
49	div1	Norwich	H	L	1-3	Ashton 82	9,833

KEY PLAYERS - GOALSCORERS

Dean Ashton

Goals in the League	19
Goals in all competitions	20
Contribution to Attacking Power Average number of minutes between League team goals while on pitch	73
Player Strike Rate The total number of minutes he was on the pitch for every League goal scored	202
Club Strike Rate Average number of minutes between League goals scored by club	73

	PLAYER	GOALS LGE	GOALS ALL	POWER	S RATE
1	Dean Ashton	19	20	73	202 mins
2	Steve Jones	14	15	68	279 mins
3	Kenny Lunt	7	7	72	559 mins
4	Ben Rix	2	2	70	815 mins
5	David Brammer	1	1	68	1378 mins

KEY PLAYERS - MIDFIELDERS

Justin Cochrane

Goals in the League	0
Goals in all competitions	0
Defensive Rating Average number of mins between League goals conceded while on the pitch	74
Contribution to Attacking Power Average number of minutes between League team goals while on pitch	74
Scoring Difference Defensive Rating minus Contribution to Attacking Power	0

	PLAYER	GOALS LGE	GOALS ALL	DEF RATE	ATT POWER	SCORE DIFF
1	Justin Cochrane	0	0	74	74	0 mins
2	David Brammer	1	1	60	69	-9 mins
3	Ben Rix	2	2	60	71	-11 mins
4	Kenny Lunt	7	7	60	73	-13 mins
5	David Vaughan	0	0	65	87	-22 mins

KEY PLAYERS - DEFENDERS

Chris McCready

Goals Conceded in League	20
Goals Conceded in all competitions	20
Clean Sheets In League games when he played at least 70 mins	4
Defensive Rating Ave number of mins between League goals conceded while on the pitch	70
Club Defensive Rating Average number of mins between League goals conceded by the club this season	63

	PLAYER	CON LGE	CON ALL	CLN SHEETS	DEF RATE
1	Chris McCready	20	20	4	70 mins
2	Adrian Moses	20	20	3	69 mins
3	David Wright	52	54	9	67 mins
4	Billy Jones	32	33	6	63 mins
5	Steve Foster	65	67	11	62 mins

MONTHLY POINTS TALLY

AUGUST	7	47%
SEPTEMBER	6	50%
OCTOBER	8	44%
NOVEMBER	6	40%
DECEMBER	9	50%
JANUARY	3	33%
FEBRUARY	1	11%
MARCH	7	33%
APRIL	5	33%
MAY	1	17%

LEAGUE GOALS

	PLAYER	LGE	FAC	LC	Oth	TOT
1	Ashton	19	0	1	0	20
2	Jones, S	14	0	1	0	15
3	Lunt	7	0	0	0	7
4	Foster	2	0	0	0	2
5	Rix	2	0	0	0	2
6	Walker	1	0	0	0	1
7	Barrowman	1	0	0	0	1
8	Higdon	1	0	0	0	1
9	Robinson	1	0	0	0	1
10	Varney	1	0	0	0	1
11	Jones, B	1	0	0	0	1
	Other	7	0	0	0	7
	TOTAL	**57**	**0**	**2**	**0**	**59**

KEY GOALKEEPER

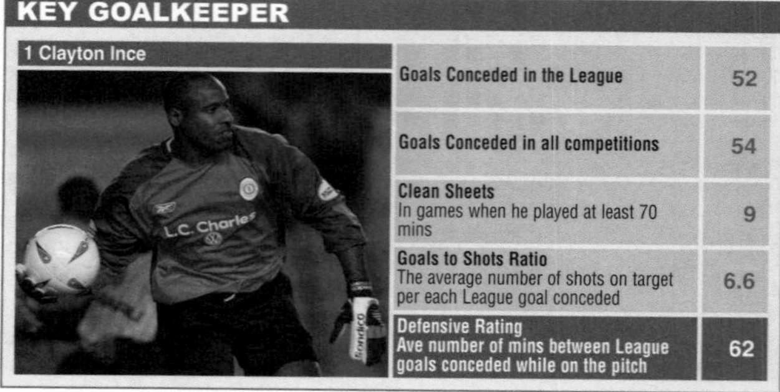

1 Clayton Ince

Goals Conceded in the League	52
Goals Conceded in all competitions	54
Clean Sheets In games when he played at least 70 mins	9
Goals to Shots Ratio The average number of shots on target per each League goal conceded	6.6
Defensive Rating Ave number of mins between League goals conceded while on the pitch	62

DISCIPLINARY RECORDS

	PLAYER	YELLOW	RED	AVE
1	Brammer	3	0	459
2	Walker	3	0	498
3	Jones, B	3	0	672
4	Cochrane	4	0	772
5	Lunt	4	1	783
6	Hignett	1	0	959
7	Foster	4	0	1012
8	McCready	1	0	1401
9	Rix	1	0	1629
10	Wright	2	0	1732
11	Tonkin	1	0	1920
12	Jones, S	2	0	1951
13	Vaughan	1	0	2518
	Other	1	0	
	TOTAL	31	1	

TOP POINT EARNERS

	PLAYER	GAMES	AV PTS
1	Richard Walker	15	**1.40**
2	Ben Rix	15	**1.40**
3	Chris McCready	13	**1.38**
4	Justin Cochrane	33	**1.30**
5	Billy Jones	21	**1.29**
6	Clayton Ince	36	**1.22**
7	Steve Jones	43	**1.21**
8	David Brammer	15	**1.20**
9	Dean Ashton	43	**1.16**
10	Steve Foster	45	**1.16**
	CLUB AVERAGE:		**1.15**

TEAM OF THE SEASON

G — Clayton Ince — **CG:** 36 **DR:** 62

D — Chris McCready — **CG:** 13 **DR:** 70

D — Adrian Moses — **CG:** 14 **DR:** 69

D — David Wright — **CG:** 38 **DR:** 67

D — Billy Jones — **CG:** 21 **DR:** 63

M — Justin Cochrane — **CG:** 33 **SD:** 0

M — David Brammer — **CG:** 15 **SD:** -9

M — Ben Rix — **CG:** 15 **SD:** -11

M — Kenny Lunt — **CG:** 43 **SD:** -13

F — Dean Ashton — **CG:** 43 **SR:** 202

F — Steve Jones — **CG:** 43 **SR:** 279

LEAGUE APPEARANCES AND BOOKINGS

	AGE (on 01/07/04)	IN NAMED 16	APPEARANCES	COUNTING GAMES	MINUTES ON PITCH		
Goalkeepers							
Ademola Bankole	34	34	0	0	0	0	0
Clayton Ince	31	38	36	36	3235	0	0
Stuart Tomlinson	20	10	1	0	5	0	0
Ben Williams	21	10	10	10	900	0	0
Defenders							
Tom Betts	21	0	0	0	0	0	0
Steve Foster	23	45	45	45	4050	4	0
Billy Jones	17	31	27	21	2018	3	0
Chris McCready	23	27	22	13	1401	1	0
Adrian Moses	29	23	21	14	1379	0	0
Mark Roberts	20	4	2	0	9	0	0
Anthony Tonkin	24	31	26	20	1920	1	0
Richard Walker	23	25	20	15	1496	3	0
David Wright	24	40	40	38	3465	2	0
Adam Yates	21	1	0	0	0	0	0
Midfielders							
Lee Bell	20	8	3	0	38	0	0
David Brammer	29	17	16	15	1378	3	0
Justin Cochrane	22	40	39	33	3089	4	0
Michael Higdon	20	17	10	7	653	0	0
Craig Hignett	34	15	15	10	959	1	0
Ian Jeffs	21	0	0	0	0	0	0
Kenny Lunt	24	45	45	43	3915	4	1
Ben Rix	20	28	25	15	1629	1	0
James Robinson	21	20	8	1	162	0	0
Neil Sorvel	31	34	31	24	2401	0	0
David Vaughan	21	32	31	27	2518	1	0
Forwards							
Dean Ashton	20	44	44	43	3834	1	0
Andrew Barrowman	19	6	4	3	232	0	0
Paul Edwards	21	19	10	2	294	0	0
Steve Jones	27	45	45	43	3902	2	0
Allan Smart	30	17	5	0	49	0	0
Michael Symes	20	5	4	1	109	0	0
Luke Varney	21	16	8	5	492	0	0
Jonathan Walters	20	2	0	0	0	0	0
Eamon Zayed	20	1	0	0	0	0	0

SQUAD APPEARANCES

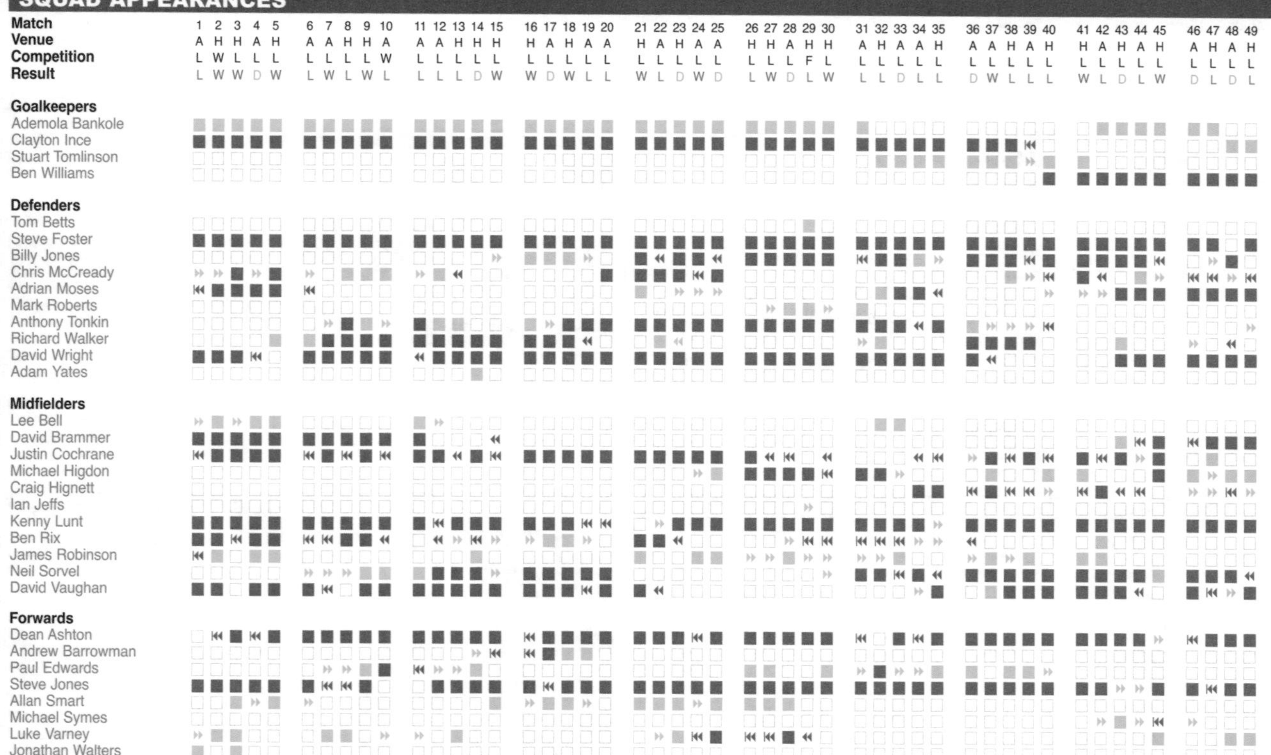
Match
Venue
Competition
Result
Goalkeepers
Ademola Bankole
Clayton Ince
Stuart Tomlinson
Ben Williams
Defenders
Tom Betts
Steve Foster
Billy Jones
Chris McCready
Adrian Moses
Mark Roberts
Anthony Tonkin
Richard Walker
David Wright
Adam Yates
Midfielders
Lee Bell
David Brammer
Justin Cochrane
Michael Higdon
Craig Hignett
Ian Jeffs
Kenny Lunt
Ben Rix
James Robinson
Neil Sorvel
David Vaughan
Forwards
Dean Ashton
Andrew Barrowman
Paul Edwards
Steve Jones
Allan Smart
Michael Symes
Luke Varney
Jonathan Walters
Eamon Zayed

KEY: On all match · On bench · Subbed or sent off (Counting game) · Subbed or sent off (playing less than 70 minutes) · Subbed on from bench (Counting Game) · Subbed on (playing less than 70 minutes) · Subbed on and then subbed or sent off (Counting Game) · Subbed on and then subbed or sent off (playing less than 70 minutes) · Not in 16

BURNLEY

Final Position: **19th**

NICKNAME: THE CLARETS — KEY: Won Drawn Lost

							Attendance
1	div1	Crystal Palace	H	L	2-3	Blake 11; Roche 19	12,976
2	ccR1	Chesterfield	A	D	3-2*	(*on penalties)	2,928
3	div1	West Brom	A	L	1-4	Blake 28	22,489
4	div1	Wigan	H	L	0-2		13,231
5	div1	Gillingham	A	W	3-0	Moore, I 27; West 30; Blake 77	7,645
6	div1	Crewe	H	W	1-0	Chaplow 52	11,495
7	div1	Stoke	A	W	2-1	May 18; Chadwick 27	14,876
8	div1	Norwich	A	L	0-2		16,407
9	div1	Nottm Forest	H	L	0-3		12,530
10	div1	Bradford	H	W	4-0	Moore, I 43; Chadwick 54,60; Blake 68	12,719
11	ccR2	Scunthorpe	A	W	3-2	Chadwick 22; Blake 42; Moore, I 77	2,915
12	div1	Wimbledon	A	D	2-2	Blake 21,37	5,639
13	div1	Watford	A	D	1-1	Chadwick 54	11,573
14	div1	Walsall	H	W	3-1	Facey 4,82,87	10,532
15	div1	Ipswich	A	L	1-6	Facey 49	22,048
16	div1	West Ham	A	D	2-2	Facey 38; Moore, I 82	31,474
17	div1	Millwall	H	D	1-1	Moore, I 60	10,435
18	ccR3	Wolverhampton	A	L	0-2		18,548
19	div1	Cardiff	H	D	1-1	Chaplow 52	10,886
20	div1	Sheff Utd	A	L	0-1		20,967
21	div1	Derby	A	L	0-2		21,960
22	div1	Rotherham	H	D	1-1	Blake 35	12,928
23	div1	Reading	H	W	3-0	Blake 5; Chaplow 47; Chadwick 54	9,473
24	div1	Sunderland	A	D	1-1	Moore, I 72	29,852
25	div1	Sheff Utd	H	W	3-2	Blake 17,45 pen; Moore, I 34	11,452
26	div1	Coventry	H	L	1-2	Blake 53	10,358
27	div1	Preston	A	L	3-5	Moore, I 24; Gnohere 64; Blake 78 pen	18,802
28	div1	Crewe	A	L	1-3	Blake 89 pen	9,512
29	div1	Stoke	H	L	0-1		12,812
30	facr3	Mansfield	A	W	2-0	Moore, I 30,73	8,290
31	div1	Crystal Palace	A	D	0-0		15,276
32	div1	West Brom	H	D	1-1	Blake 68	13,106
33	facr4	Gillingham	H	W	3-1	Moore, I 30; Blake 33,64	9,735
34	div1	Wigan	A	D	0-0		11,147
35	div1	Gillingham	H	W	1-0	Little 83	10,400
36	facr5	Millwall	A	L	0-1		10,420
37	div1	Ipswich	H	W	4-2	Little 26; May 28; Chaplow 61; Blake 90	12,418
38	div1	Reading	A	D	2-2	Moore, I 23; May 67	10,543
39	div1	Millwall	A	L	0-2		10,148
40	div1	West Ham	H	D	1-1	Branch 31	12,440
41	div1	Preston	H	D	1-1	Blake 19	15,837
42	div1	Coventry	A	L	0-4		12,953
43	div1	Nottm Forest	A	D	1-1	Chaplow 15	26,885
44	div1	Bradford	A	W	2-1	Blake 8; Moore, I 90	13,677
45	div1	Norwich	H	L	3-5	Wood 7; May 30; Blake 38	12,417
46	div1	Walsall	A	W	1-0	Blake 56 pen	7,769
47	div1	Watford	H	L	2-3	McGregor 29; Adebola 86	11,413
48	div1	Cardiff	A	L	0-2		13,525
49	div1	Wimbledon	H	W	2-0	Branch 26; Ntimban-Zeh 45 og	13,555
50	div1	Derby	H	W	1-0	Branch 42	16,189
51	div1	Rotherham	A	L	0-3		9,157
52	div1	Sunderland	H	L	1-2	Little 11	18,852

KEY PLAYERS - GOALSCORERS

Robbie Blake

Goals in the League	19
Goals in all competitions	22
Contribution to Attacking Power Average number of minutes between League team goals while on pitch	67
Player Strike Rate The total number of minutes he was on the pitch for every League goal scored	203
Club Strike Rate Average number of minutes between League goals scored by club	69

	PLAYER	GOALS LGE	GOALS ALL	POWER	S RATE
1	Robbie Blake	19	22	67	203 mins
2	Ian Moore	9	12	64	359 mins
3	Luke Chadwick	5	6	64	427 mins
4	Richard Chaplow	5	5	76	532 mins
5	David May	4	4	69	752 mins

KEY PLAYERS - MIDFIELDERS

Tony Grant

Goals in the League	0
Goals in all competitions	0
Defensive Rating Average number of mins between League goals conceded while on the pitch	61
Contribution to Attacking Power Average number of minutes between League team goals while on pitch	71
Scoring Difference Defensive Rating minus Contribution to Attacking Power	-10

	PLAYER	GOALS LGE	GOALS ALL	DEF RATE	ATT POWER	SCORE DIFF
1	Tony Grant	0	0	61	71	-10 mins
2	Luke Chadwick	5	6	53	65	-12 mins
3	Glen Little	3	3	54	67	-13 mins
4	Paul Weller	0	0	44	60	-16 mins
5	Richard Chaplow	5	5	52	76	-24 mins

KEY PLAYERS - DEFENDERS

Mark McGregor

Goals Conceded in League	30
Goals Conceded in all competitions	32
Clean Sheets In League games when he played at least 70 mins	6
Defensive Rating Ave number of mins between League goals conceded while on the pitch	61
Club Defensive Rating Average number of mins between League goals conceded by the club this season	54

	PLAYER	CON LGE	CON ALL	CLN SHEETS	DEF RATE
1	Mark McGregor	30	32	6	61 mins
2	David May	49	53	9	61 mins
3	Dean West	38	41	4	60 mins
4	Mohammed Camara	71	77	10	56 mins
5	Lee Roche	39	42	6	46 mins

MONTHLY POINTS TALLY

AUGUST	6	40%
SEPTEMBER	8	44%
OCTOBER	5	42%
NOVEMBER	6	33%
DECEMBER	3	20%
JANUARY	3	33%
FEBRUARY	7	58%
MARCH	6	40%
APRIL	9	50%
MAY	0	0%

LEAGUE GOALS

	PLAYER	LGE	FAC	LC	Oth	TOT
1	Blake	19	2	1	0	22
2	Moore, I	9	3	0	0	12
3	Facey	5	0	0	0	5
4	Chaplow	5	0	0	0	5
5	Chadwick	5	0	1	0	6
6	May	4	0	0	0	4
7	Branch	3	0	0	0	3
8	Little	3	0	0	0	3
9	Adebola	1	0	0	0	1
10	Gnohere	1	0	0	0	1
11	McGregor	1	0	0	0	1
	Other	4	0	1	0	5
	TOTAL	60	5	3	0	68

KEY GOALKEEPER

1 Brian Jensen

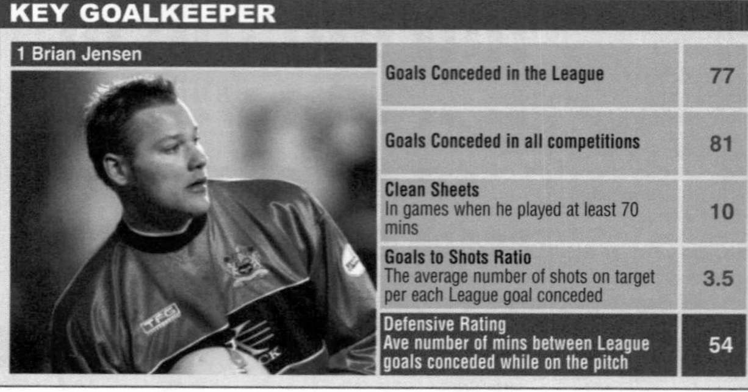

Goals Conceded in the League	77
Goals Conceded in all competitions	81
Clean Sheets In games when he played at least 70 mins	10
Goals to Shots Ratio The average number of shots on target per each League goal conceded	3.5
Defensive Rating Ave number of mins between League goals conceded while on the pitch	54

DISCIPLINARY RECORDS

	PLAYER	YELLOW	RED	AVE
1	Gnohere	6	2	137
2	May	10	1	273
3	Branch	9	0	301
4	Todd	2	0	315
5	Chaplow	7	0	380
6	West	6	0	382
7	Roche	4	0	451
8	Little	6	0	480
9	Grant	6	0	518
10	McGregor	3	0	610
11	Blake	6	0	643
12	Weller	3	0	699
13	Farrelly	1	0	736
	Other	13	0	
	TOTAL	82	3	

TOP POINT EARNERS

	PLAYER	GAMES	AV PTS
1	Mark McGregor	19	**1.32**
2	Lee Roche	17	**1.29**
3	Dean West	24	**1.25**
4	David May	32	**1.25**
5	Glen Little	32	**1.22**
6	Richard Chaplow	27	**1.22**
7	Mohammed Camara	44	**1.20**
8	Graham Branch	27	**1.19**
9	Brian Jensen	46	**1.15**
10	Tony Grant	33	**1.15**
	CLUB AVERAGE:		**1.15**

LEAGUE APPEARANCES AND BOOKINGS

	AGE (on 01/07/04)	IN NAMED 16	APPEARANCES	COUNTING GAMES	MINUTES ON PITCH	Yellow	Red
Goalkeepers							
Nathan Abbey	25	13	0	0	0	0	0
Brian Jensen	29	46	46	46	4140	2	0
Paul Rachubka	23	5	0	0	0	0	0
Defenders							
Mohammed Camara	29	45	45	44	3978	5	0
Arthur Gnohere	25	16	14	12	1101	6	2
David May	34	35	35	32	3008	10	1
James McEveley	18	4	4	0	77	1	0
Mark McGregor	27	29	23	19	1832	3	0
Lee Roche	23	36	25	17	1804	4	0
Paul Scott	19	10	2	0	26	0	0
Andy Todd	29	7	7	7	630	2	0
Ryan Townsend	2005	4	1	0	11	0	0
Dean West	31	38	32	24	2296	6	0
Midfielders							
Graham Branch	32	39	38	27	2716	9	0
Luke Chadwick	23	42	36	19	2133	2	0
Richard Chaplow	19	41	39	27	2662	7	0
Gareth Farrelly	28	12	12	7	736	1	0
Tony Grant	29	40	37	33	3112	6	0
Lenny Johnrose	34	7	7	5	470	0	0
Glen Little	28	34	34	32	2882	6	0
Alan Moore	29	24	14	5	610	0	0
Matthew O'Neill	20	26	4	0	50	0	0
Bradley Orr	21	5	4	1	154	0	0
Joel Pilkington	19	15	1	0	14	0	0
Danny Pugh	21	2	0	0	0	0	0
Paul Weller	29	36	33	19	2099	3	0
Neil Wood	21	10	10	7	669	0	0
Forwards							
Dele Adebola	29	6	3	0	127	0	0
Robbie Blake	28	45	45	42	3859	6	0
Delroy Facey	24	14	14	11	1082	0	0
Ian Moore	27	39	39	34	3229	3	0

TEAM OF THE SEASON

G
Brian Jensen
CG: 46 **DR:** 54

D
David May
CG: 32 **DR:** 61

D
Mark McGregor
CG: 19 **DR:** 61

D
Dean West
CG: 24 **DR:** 60

D
Mohammed Camara
CG: 44 **DR:** 56

M
Tony Grant
CG: 33 **SD:** -10

M
Luke Chadwick
CG: 19 **SD:** -12

M
Glen Little
CG: 32 **SD:** -13

M
Paul Weller
CG: 19 **SD:** -16

F
Robbie Blake
CG: 42 **SR:** 203

F
Ian Moore
CG: 34 **SR:** 359

SQUAD APPEARANCES

Match	1	2	3	4	5	6	7	8	9	10	11	12	13	14	15	16	17	18	19	20	21	22	23	24	25	26	27	28	29	30	31	32	33	34	35	36	37	38	39	40	41	42	43	44	45	46	47	48	49	50	51	52
Venue	H	A	A	H	A	H	A	A	H	H	A	A	A	H	A	A	H	A	H	A	A	H	H	A	H	H	A	A	H	A	A	H	H	A	H	A	H	A	A	H	H	A	A	A	H	A	H	A	H	H	A	H
Competition	L	W	L	L	L	L	L	L	L	L	W	L	L	L	L	L	L	W	L	L	L	L	L	L	L	L	L	L	L	F	L	L	F	L	L	F	L	L	L	L	L	L	L	L	L	L	L	L	L	L	L	L
Result	L	D	L	L	W	W	W	L	L	W	W	D	D	W	L	D	D	L	D	L	L	D	W	D	W	L	L	L	L	W	D	D	W	D	W	L	W	D	L	D	D	L	D	W	L	W	L	L	W	W	L	L

Goalkeepers
Nathan Abbey
Brian Jensen
Paul Rachubka

Defenders
Mohammed Camara
Arthur Gnohere
David May
James McEveley
Mark McGregor
Lee Roche
Paul Scott
Andy Todd
Ryan Townsend
Dean West

Midfielders
Graham Branch
Luke Chadwick
Richard Chaplow
Gareth Farrelly
Tony Grant
Lenny Johnrose
Glen Little
Alan Moore
Matthew O'Neill
Bradley Orr
Joel Pilkington
Danny Pugh
Paul Weller
Neil Wood

Forwards
Dele Adebola
Robbie Blake
Delroy Facey
Ian Moore

KEY: On all match | On bench | Subbed or sent off (Counting game) | Subbed or sent off (playing less than 70 minutes) | Subbed on from bench (Counting Game) | Subbed on (playing less than 70 minutes) | Subbed on and then subbed or sent off (Counting Game) | Subbed on and then subbed or sent off (playing less than 70 minutes) | Not in 16

DERBY COUNTY 20th

NICKNAME: THE RAMS KEY: Won Drawn Lost

							Attendance
1	div1	Stoke	H	L	0-3		21,517
2	ccR1	Huddersfield	A	L	1-2	Taylor 41	6,672
3	div1	Gillingham	A	D	0-0		7,850
4	div1	Reading	H	L	2-3	Taylor 7 pen; Svensson 81	18,970
5	div1	Cardiff	A	L	1-4	Svensson 48	15,091
6	div1	West Brom	H	L	0-1		21,499
7	div1	Walsall	A	W	1-0	Junior 80	8,726
8	div1	Watford	H	W	3-2	Taylor 18; Svensson 73; Junior 88	18,459
9	div1	Sunderland	H	D	1-1	Taylor 90	22,535
10	div1	Nottm Forest	A	D	1-1	Junior 25	29,059
11	div1	Bradford	A	W	2-1	Morris 45,79	10,143
12	div1	West Ham	H	L	0-1		22,810
13	div1	Wigan	H	D	2-2	Taylor 40 pen; Morris 62	19,151
14	div1	Crystal Palace	A	D	1-1	Zavagno 74	14,344
15	div1	Crewe	A	L	0-3		8,656
16	div1	Norwich	A	L	1-2	Taylor 61 pen	16,346
17	div1	Coventry	H	L	1-3	Holmes 52	21,641
18	div1	Preston	A	L	0-3		12,839
19	div1	Ipswich	H	D	2-2	Kennedy 45; Dichio 45	19,976
20	div1	Burnley	H	W	2-0	Morris 20; Taylor 90 pen	21,960
21	div1	Millwall	A	D	0-0		10,308
22	div1	Wimbledon	H	W	3-1	Herzig 13 og; Tudgay 52; Holmes 53	22,025
23	div1	Ipswich	A	L	1-2	Tudgay 73	25,018
24	div1	Rotherham	A	D	0-0		7,320
25	div1	West Brom	A	D	1-1	Candido Costa 86	26,412
26	div1	Norwich	H	L	0-4		23,783
27	facr3	Ipswich	A	L	0-3		16,159
28	div1	Stoke	A	L	1-2	Morris 1	16,402
29	div1	Gillingham	H	W	2-1	Vincent 14; Edwards 61	20,473
30	div1	Sheff Utd	H	W	2-0	Tudgay 70; McLeod 90	23,603
31	div1	Reading	A	L	1-3	Johnson 59	14,382
32	div1	Cardiff	H	D	2-2	Taylor 49; Osman 90	20,958
33	div1	Wigan	A	L	0-2		9,146
34	div1	Crystal Palace	H	W	2-1	Manel 70; Osman 76	21,856
35	div1	Coventry	A	L	0-2		16,042
36	div1	Crewe	H	D	0-0		19,861
37	div1	Rotherham	H	W	1-0	Peschisolido 61	21,741
38	div1	Watford	A	L	1-2	Peschisolido 16	13,931
39	div1	Nottm Forest	H	W	4-2	Taylor 4; Peschisolido 28,37; Tudgay 82	32,390
40	div1	Sheff Utd	A	D	1-1	Taylor 25 pen	21,351
41	div1	Sunderland	A	L	1-2	Taylor 64 pen	30,838
42	div1	Walsall	H	L	0-1		23,574
43	div1	West Ham	A	D	0-0		28,207
44	div1	Bradford	H	W	3-2	Osman 36; Taylor 64; Combe 84 og	21,593
45	div1	Preston	H	W	5-1	Manel 2,37; Tudgay 27,32; Junior 76 pen	24,162
46	div1	Burnley	A	L	0-1		16,189
47	div1	Millwall	H	W	2-0	Bolder 40; Reich 72	26,056
48	div1	Wimbledon	A	L	0-1		6,509

MONTHLY POINTS TALLY

Month	Points	%
AUGUST	1	7%
SEPTEMBER	11	73%
OCTOBER	2	11%
NOVEMBER	8	53%
DECEMBER	2	17%
JANUARY	6	50%
FEBRUARY	4	33%
MARCH	8	44%
APRIL	7	47%
MAY	3	50%

LEAGUE GOALS

	PLAYER	LGE	FAC	LC	Oth	TOT
1	Taylor	11	0	1	0	12
2	Tudgay	6	0	0	0	6
3	Morris	5	0	0	0	5
4	Junior	4	0	0	0	4
5	Peschisolido	4	0	0	0	4
6	Manel	3	0	0	0	3
7	Svensson	3	0	0	0	3
8	Osman	3	0	0	0	3
9	Holmes	2	0	0	0	2
10	Zavagno	1	0	0	0	1
11	Dichio	1	0	0	0	1
	Other	10	0	0	0	10
	TOTAL	53	0	1	0	54

KEY PLAYERS - GOALSCORERS

Marcus Tudgay

Goals in the League	6
Goals in all competitions	6
Contribution to Attacking Power Average number of minutes between League team goals while on pitch	63
Player Strike Rate The total number of minutes he was on the pitch for every League goal scored	315
Club Strike Rate Average number of minutes between League goals scored by club	78

	PLAYER	GOALS LGE	GOALS ALL	POWER	S RATE
1	Marcus Tudgay	6	6	63	315 mins
2	Lee Morris	5	5	89	340 mins
3	Ian Taylor	11	12	78	341 mins
4	Leon Osman	3	3	66	510 mins
5	Luciano Zavagno	1	1	113	1366 mins

KEY PLAYERS - MIDFIELDERS

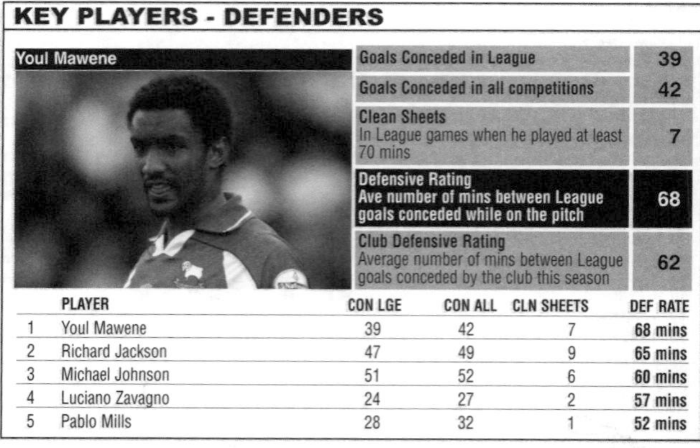

Leon Osman

Goals in the League	3
Goals in all competitions	3
Defensive Rating Average number of mins between League goals conceded while on the pitch	70
Contribution to Attacking Power Average number of minutes between League team goals while on pitch	67
Scoring Difference Defensive Rating minus Contribution to Attacking Power	3

	PLAYER	GOALS LGE	GOALS ALL	DEF RATE	ATT POWER	SCORE DIFF
1	Leon Osman	3	3	70	67	3 mins
2	Tom Huddlestone	0	0	65	78	-13 mins
3	Ian Taylor	11	12	65	78	-13 mins
4	Candido Costa	1	1	55	97	-42 mins

KEY PLAYERS - DEFENDERS

Youl Mawene

Goals Conceded in League	39
Goals Conceded in all competitions	42
Clean Sheets In League games when he played at least 70 mins	7
Defensive Rating Ave number of mins between League goals conceded while on the pitch	68
Club Defensive Rating Average number of mins between League goals conceded by the club this season	62

	PLAYER	CON LGE	CON ALL	CLN SHEETS	DEF RATE
1	Youl Mawene	39	42	7	68 mins
2	Richard Jackson	47	49	9	65 mins
3	Michael Johnson	51	52	6	60 mins
4	Luciano Zavagno	24	27	2	57 mins
5	Pablo Mills	28	32	1	52 mins

KEY GOALKEEPER

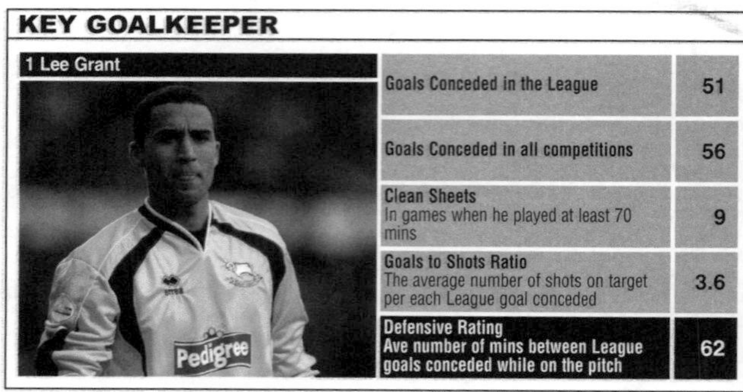
Pedigree

1 Lee Grant

Goals Conceded in the League	51
Goals Conceded in all competitions	56
Clean Sheets In games when he played at least 70 mins	9
Goals to Shots Ratio The average number of shots on target per each League goal conceded	3.6
Defensive Rating Ave number of mins between League goals conceded while on the pitch	62

DISCIPLINARY RECORDS

	PLAYER	YELLOW	RED	AVE
1	Bradbury	3	0	198
2	Manel	3	1	238
3	Taylor	14	1	249
4	Svensson	3	0	262
5	Reich	3	0	269
6	Dichio	2	0	270
7	Zavagno	5	0	273
8	Valakari	4	0	317
9	Johnson	6	1	436
10	Huddlestone	7	0	531
11	Caldwell	1	0	559
12	Vincent	1	0	574
13	Junior	1	0	605
	Other	21	1	
	TOTAL	74	4	

TOP POINT EARNERS

	PLAYER	GAMES	AV PTS
1	Marcus Tudgay	19	**1.53**
2	Leon Osman	17	**1.29**
3	Candido Costa	17	**1.24**
4	Richard Jackson	33	**1.21**
5	Youl Mawene	29	**1.21**
6	Tom Huddlestone	39	**1.15**
7	Ian Taylor	41	**1.12**
8	Lee Grant	35	**1.11**
9	Lee Morris	15	**1.07**
10	Michael Johnson	30	**1.07**
	CLUB AVERAGE:		**1.13**

LEAGUE APPEARANCES AND BOOKINGS

	AGE (on 01/07/04)	IN NAMED 16	APPEARANCES	COUNTING GAMES	MINUTES ON PITCH	Yellow	Red
Goalkeepers							
Lee Camp	19	21	0	0	0	0	0
Lee Grant	21	45	35	35	3150	2	0
Andy Oakes	27	25	10	10	900	0	0
Defenders							
Gary Caldwell	23	11	9	5	559	1	0
Nathan Doyle	17	3	2	1	93	0	0
Rob Edwards	21	12	11	8	850	0	0
Steve Elliott	25	11	5	3	315	1	0
Richard Jackson	24	38	36	33	3037	2	0
Michael Johnson	31	39	39	30	3058	6	1
Jeff Kenna	33	9	9	9	810	1	0
Peter Kennedy	30	5	5	5	434	0	0
Youl Mawene	24	30	30	29	2645	1	0
Pablo Mills	20	29	19	14	1469	0	0
Jamie Vincent	29	7	7	6	574	1	0
David Walton	31	7	5	3	344	0	0
Luciano Zavagno	26	18	17	14	1366	5	0
Midfielders							
Paul Boertien	25	29	18	9	1169	1	0
Adam Bolder	23	39	24	11	1377	2	0
Candido Costa	23	37	34	17	2029	1	1
Lee Holmes	17	28	23	12	1392	2	0
Tom Huddlestone	17	43	43	39	3721	7	0
Lewis Hunt	21	1	1	0	31	0	0
Barry Molloy	20	0	0	0	0	0	0
Leon Osman	23	17	17	17	1530	2	0
Ian Taylor	36	42	42	41	3749	14	1
Simo Valakari	31	23	20	10	1269	4	0
Forwards							
Lee Bradbury	29	7	7	7	596	3	0
Danny Dichio	29	6	6	6	540	2	0
Jose Luis Junior	27	13	12	6	605	1	0
Gianfranco Labarthe	19	4	2	0	66	0	0
Martinez Fernandez Manel	30	17	15	8	955	3	1
Izale McLeod	19	16	10	1	317	2	0
Lee Morris	24	23	23	15	1699	2	0
Paul Peschisolido	33	11	11	11	957	0	0
Marco Reich	26	13	13	8	807	3	0
Mathias Svensson	29	10	10	8	787	3	0
Gianfranco Tome	19	5	1	0	21	0	0
Marcus Tudgay	21	33	29	19	1890	1	0
Noel Whelan	29	9	8	2	346	1	0

TEAM OF THE SEASON

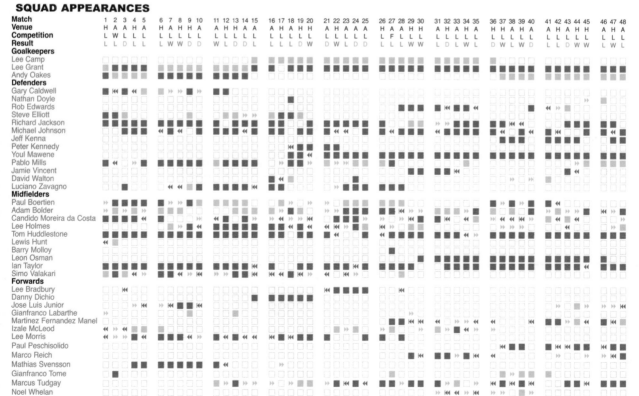

G
Lee Grant
CG: 35 **DR:** 62

D
Youl Mawene
CG: 29 **DR:** 68

D
Richard Jackson
CG: 33 **DR:** 65

D
Michael Johnson
CG: 30 **DR:** 60

D
Luciano Zavagno
CG: 14 **DR:** 57

M
Leon Osman
CG: 17 **SD:** 3

M
Tom Huddlestone
CG: 39 **SD:** -13

M
Ian Taylor
CG: 41 **SD:** -13

M
Candido Costa
CG: 17 **SD:** -42

F
Marcus Tudgay
CG: 19 **SR:** 315

F
Lee Morris
CG: 15 **SR:** 340

SQUAD APPEARANCES

Match	1	2	3	4	5	6	7	8	9	10	11	12	13	14	15	16	17	18	19	20	21	22	23	24	25	26	27	28	29	30	31	32	33	34	35	36	37	38	39	40	41	42	43	44	45	46	47	48
Venue	H	A	A	H	A	H	A	H	H	A	A	H	H	A	A	A	H	A	H	H	A	H	A	A	A	H	A	A	H	H	A	H	A	H	A	H	H	A	H	A	A	H	A	H	H	A	H	A
Competition	L	W	L	L	L	L	L	L	L	L	L	L	L	L	L	L	L	L	L	L	L	L	L	L	L	L	F	L	L	L	L	L	L	L	L	L	L	L	L	L	L	L	L	L	L	L	L	L
Result	L	L	D	L	L	L	W	W	D	D	W	L	D	D	L	L	L	L	D	W	D	W	L	D	D	L	L	L	W	W	L	D	L	W	L	D	W	L	W	D	L	L	D	W	W	L	W	L

Goalkeepers
Lee Camp
Lee Grant
Andy Oakes
Defenders
Gary Caldwell
Nathan Doyle
Rob Edwards
Steve Elliott
Richard Jackson
Michael Johnson
Jeff Kenna
Peter Kennedy
Youl Mawene
Pablo Mills
Jamie Vincent
David Walton
Luciano Zavagno
Midfielders
Paul Boertien
Adam Bolder
Candido Moreira da Costa
Lee Holmes
Tom Huddlestone
Lewis Hunt
Barry Molloy
Leon Osman
Ian Taylor
Simo Valakari
Forwards
Lee Bradbury
Danny Dichio
Jose Luis Junior
Gianfranco Labarthe
Martinez Fernandez Manel
Izale McLeod
Lee Morris
Paul Peschisolido
Marco Reich
Mathias Svensson
Gianfranco Tome
Marcus Tudgay
Noel Whelan

KEY: ■ On all match ■ On bench
⏮ Subbed or sent off (Counting game) « Subbed or sent off (playing less than 70 minutes)
⏭ Subbed on from bench (Counting Game) » Subbed on (playing less than 70 minutes)
⏭ Subbed on and then subbed or sent off (Counting Game) » Subbed on and then subbed or sent off (playing less than 70 minutes)
□ Not in 16

GILLINGHAM

Final Position: **21st**

NICKNAME: THE GILLS

KEY: ☐ Won ☐ Drawn ☐ Lost

#	Comp	Opponent	H/A	Res	Score	Scorers	Attendance
1	div1	Sheff Utd	A	D	0-0		21,569
2	ccR1	Cambridge	A	W	2-1	Hills 73; Nosworthy 86	3,044
3	div1	Derby	H	D	0-0		7,850
4	div1	Bradford	A	W	1-0	Hope 77	10,317
5	div1	Burnley	H	L	0-3		7,645
6	div1	Watford	A	D	2-2	Shaw 52; Spiller 63	12,793
7	div1	Millwall	H	W	4-3	Sidibe 28; Shaw 43; King 81; Nosworthy 87	8,237
8	div1	Cardiff	A	L	0-5		15,057
9	div1	Norwich	H	L	1-2	King 40	8,022
10	div1	West Ham	H	W	2-0	King 57; Benjamin 82	11,418
11	ccR2	Stoke	A	W	2-0	Saunders 24; King 52	4,607
12	div1	Rotherham	A	D	1-1	Spiller 36	5,501
13	div1	Walsall	A	L	1-2	Brown, W 48 pen	6,395
14	div1	West Brom	H	L	0-2		8,883
15	div1	Reading	A	L	1-2	King 73	13,011
16	div1	Wigan	A	L	0-1		6,696
17	div1	Crystal Palace	H	W	1-0	Perpetuini 83	8,889
18	ccR3	Bolton	A	L	0-2		5,258
19	div1	Ipswich	A	W	4-3	Wallace 14; Sidibe 45; Shaw 53; Saunders 90	24,788
20	div1	Sunderland	H	L	1-3	Shaw 37	9,066
21	div1	Crewe	H	W	2-0	Shaw 64; Spiller 70	6,923
22	div1	Wimbledon	H	L	1-2	Nosworthy 41	9,041
23	div1	Coventry	A	D	2-2	Johnson, T 66,85	13,432
24	div1	Stoke	H	W	3-1	Shaw 26; Hope 45; Sidibe 83	7,888
25	div1	Crewe	A	D	1-1	Perpetuini 49	6,271
26	div1	Preston	H	L	0-1		7,602
27	div1	Watford	H	W	1-0	Hills 56 pen	8,971
28	div1	Millwall	A	W	2-1	Hessenthaler 21; James 90	12,084
29	facr3	Charlton	H	W	3-2	Johnson, T 17; Sidibe 19; Smith 34	10,894
30	div1	Sheff Utd	H	L	0-3		8,353
31	div1	Derby	A	L	1-2	Johnson, T 69	20,473
32	facr4	Burnley	A	L	1-3	Henderson 71	9,735
33	div1	Bradford	H	W	1-0	Agyemang 16	7,836
34	div1	Burnley	A	L	0-1		10,400
35	div1	Reading	H	L	0-1		8,600
36	div1	Nottm Forest	A	D	0-0		26,473
37	div1	Crystal Palace	A	L	0-1		17,485
38	div1	Nottm Forest	H	W	2-1	Agyemang 34; Spiller 82	9,096
39	div1	Preston	A	D	0-0		13,111
40	div1	Norwich	A	L	0-3		23,198
41	div1	Rotherham	H	W	2-0	Ashby 15; Sidibe 19	8,047
42	div1	Sunderland	A	L	1-2	Agyemang 28	23,262
43	div1	West Ham	A	L	1-2	Spiller 32	34,551
44	div1	Cardiff	H	L	1-2	Hope 59	7,852
45	div1	Wigan	H	L	0-3		7,410
46	div1	West Brom	A	L	0-1		24,524
47	div1	Walsall	H	W	3-0	Agyemang 45,67; Spiller 90	8,244
48	div1	Ipswich	H	L	1-2	Hills 8 pen	9,641
49	div1	Wimbledon	A	W	2-1	Hessenthaler 62; Agyemang 79	5,049
50	div1	Coventry	H	L	2-5	Wales 64; Sidibe 72	10,388
51	div1	Stoke	A	D	0-0		19,240

KEY PLAYERS - GOALSCORERS

Patrick Agyemang

Goals in the League	6
Goals in all competitions	6
Contribution to Attacking Power Average number of minutes between League team goals while on pitch	103
Player Strike Rate The total number of minutes he was on the pitch for every League goal scored	276
Club Strike Rate Average number of minutes between League goals scored by club	86

	PLAYER	GOALS LGE	GOALS ALL	POWER	S RATE
1	Patrick Agyemang	6	6	103	276 mins
2	Paul Shaw	6	6	74	284 mins
3	Daniel Spiller	6	6	92	463 mins
4	Mamady Sidibe	5	6	78	611 mins
5	David Perpetuini	2	2	66	631 mins

KEY PLAYERS - MIDFIELDERS

David Perpetuini

Goals in the League	2
Goals in all competitions	2
Defensive Rating Average number of mins between League goals conceded while on the pitch	60
Contribution to Attacking Power Average number of minutes between League team goals while on pitch	66
Scoring Difference Defensive Rating minus Contribution to Attacking Power	-6

	PLAYER	GOALS LGE	GOALS ALL	DEF RATE	ATT POWER	SCORE DIFF
1	David Perpetuini	2	2	60	66	-6 mins
2	Andy Hessenthaler	2	2	72	82	-10 mins
3	Paul Smith	0	1	71	82	-11 mins
4	Nicky Southall	0	0	57	81	-24 mins
5	Leon Johnson	0	0	62	95	-33 mins

KEY PLAYERS - DEFENDERS

Barry Ashby

Goals Conceded in League	23
Goals Conceded in all competitions	29
Clean Sheets In League games when he played at least 70 mins	9
Defensive Rating Ave number of mins between League goals conceded while on the pitch	80
Club Defensive Rating Average number of mins between League goals conceded by the club this season	62

	PLAYER	CON LGE	CON ALL	CLN SHEETS	DEF RATE
1	Barry Ashby	23	29	9	80 mins
2	John Hills	36	44	8	64 mins
3	Nayron Nosworthy	36	44	8	64 mins
4	Richard Rose	20	20	3	60 mins
5	Ian Cox	50	55	8	57 mins

MONTHLY POINTS TALLY

Month	Points	%
AUGUST	6	40%
SEPTEMBER	7	39%
OCTOBER	3	25%
NOVEMBER	10	56%
DECEMBER	7	58%
JANUARY	3	33%
FEBRUARY	1	8%
MARCH	7	39%
APRIL	6	33%
MAY	1	17%

LEAGUE GOALS

	PLAYER	LGE	FAC	LC	Oth	TOT
1	Agyemang	6	0	0	0	6
2	Shaw	6	0	0	0	6
3	Spiller	6	0	0	0	6
4	Sidibe	5	1	0	0	6
5	King	4	0	1	0	5
6	Hope	3	0	0	0	3
7	Johnson, T	3	1	0	0	4
8	Hessenthaler	2	0	0	0	2
9	Hills	2	0	1	0	3
10	Nosworthy	2	0	1	0	3
11	Perpetuini	2	0	0	0	2
	Other	7	2	1	0	10
	TOTAL	48	4	4	0	56

KEY GOALKEEPER

1 Jason Brown

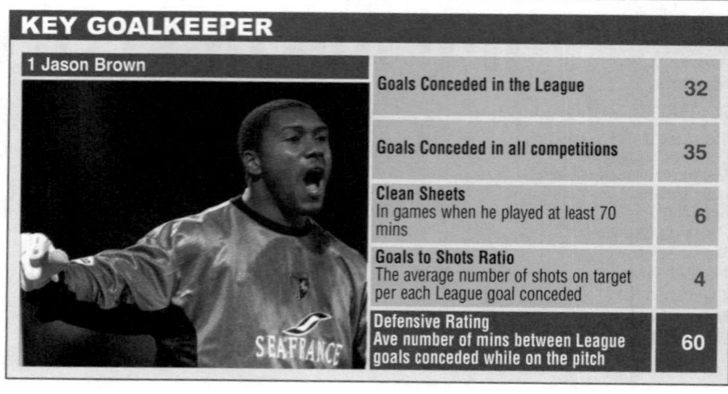

Goals Conceded in the League	32
Goals Conceded in all competitions	35
Clean Sheets In games when he played at least 70 mins	6
Goals to Shots Ratio The average number of shots on target per each League goal conceded	4
Defensive Rating Ave number of mins between League goals conceded while on the pitch	60

DISCIPLINARY RECORDS

	PLAYER	YELLOW	RED	AVE
1	Johnson, T	4	0	153
2	Hessenthaler	12	1	189
3	Pouton	5	0	245
4	Hills	8	1	255
5	Cox	6	1	408
6	Perpetuini	3	0	420
7	Ashby	3	1	458
8	James	2	0	558
9	Southall	5	0	602
10	Smith	4	0	714
11	Sidibe	4	0	764
12	Wallace	1	0	768
13	Nosworthy	3	0	771
	Other	10	1	
	TOTAL	70	5	

TOP POINT EARNERS

	PLAYER	GAMES	AV PTS
1	Paul Shaw	19	**1.47**
2	Barry Ashby	19	**1.37**
3	Andy Hessenthaler	22	**1.36**
4	Nayron Nosworthy	25	**1.28**
5	David Perpetuini	13	**1.23**
6	John Hills	23	**1.22**
7	Ian Cox	31	**1.19**
8	Mamady Sidibe	30	**1.17**
9	Nicky Southall	33	**1.15**
10	Jason Brown, J	21	**1.14**
	CLUB AVERAGE:		**1.11**

TEAM OF THE SEASON

- G — Jason Brown — CG: 21 DR: 60
- D — Barry Ashby — CG: 19 DR: 80
- D — John Hills — CG: 23 DR: 64
- D — Nayron Nosworthy — CG: 25 DR: 64
- D — Richard Rose — CG: 13 DR: 60
- M — David Perpetuini — CG: 13 SD: -6
- M — Andy Hessenthaler — CG: 22 SD: -10
- M — Paul Smith — CG: 31 SD: -11
- M — Nicky Southall — CG: 33 SD: -24
- F — Patrick Agyemang — CG: 18 SR: 276
- F — Paul Shaw — CG: 19 SR: 284

LEAGUE APPEARANCES AND BOOKINGS

	AGE (on 01/07/04)	IN NAMED 16	APPEARANCES	COUNTING GAMES	MINUTES ON PITCH	Yellow	Red
Goalkeepers							
Steve Banks	32	13	13	13	1170	0	0
Vince Bartram	35	6	1	1	90	0	0
Bertrand Bossu	23	23	4	3	315	0	0
Jason Brown	22	27	22	21	1935	0	0
Lars Hirschfeld	25	2	2	2	180	0	0
Danny Knowles	18	1	0	0	0	0	0
Nico Vaesen	34	5	5	5	450	0	0
Defenders							
Barry Ashby	33	34	23	19	1834	3	1
Dean Beckwith	20	12	0	0	0	0	0
Wayne Brown	26	6	4	4	346	1	0
Ian Cox	33	34	33	31	2859	6	1
Andrew Crofts	20	18	8	1	146	0	0
John Hills	26	32	29	23	2299	8	1
Chris Hope	31	37	37	36	3293	1	1
Nayron Nosworthy	23	27	27	25	2313	3	0
Richard Rose	21	28	17	13	1192	0	0
Midfielders							
Ashley Carew	18	1	0	0	0	0	0
Andy Hessenthaler	38	38	36	22	2458	12	1
Leon Johnson	23	28	21	17	1617	0	0
David Perpetuini	25	25	20	13	1261	3	0
Alan Pouton	27	19	19	12	1225	5	0
Mark Saunders	33	23	21	8	949	1	0
Paul Smith	32	33	33	31	2857	4	0
Nicky Southall	32	35	35	33	3013	5	0
Daniel Spiller	23	46	39	27	2776	3	0
John Wallis	18	2	0	0	0	0	0
Forwards							
Patrick Agyemang	23	20	20	18	1654	2	0
Jones Awuah	20	4	0	0	0	0	0
Trevor Benjamin	25	4	4	1	207	0	0
Darius Henderson	22	4	4	2	279	0	0
Kevin James	24	20	17	11	1116	2	0
Matthew Jarvis	18	17	10	1	285	0	0
Tommy Johnson	33	17	13	2	615	4	0
Marlon King	24	11	11	7	749	0	0
Paul Shaw	30	22	21	19	1705	1	0
Mamady Sidibe	24	41	41	30	3056	4	0
Gary Wales	25	6	6	3	339	1	0
Rod Wallace	34	15	14	5	768	1	0

SQUAD APPEARANCES

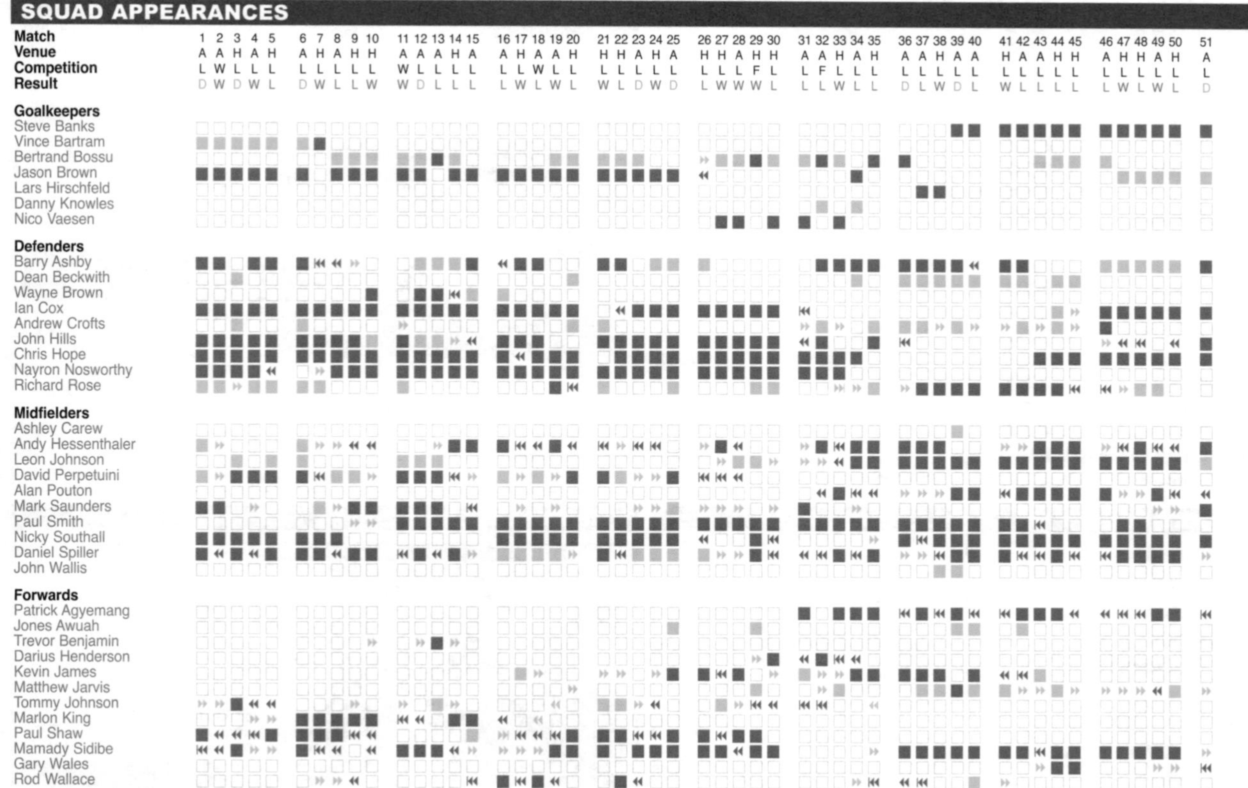

Match 1 2 3 4 5 6 7 8 9 10 11 12 13 14 15 16 17 18 19 20 21 22 23 24 25 26 27 28 29 30 31 32 33 34 35 36 37 38 39 40 41 42 43 44 45 46 47 48 49 50 51
Venue A A H A H A H A H H A A A H A A H A A H H H A H A H H A H H A A H A H A A H A A H A A H H A H H A H A
Competition L W L L L L L L L L W L L L L L L W L L L L L L L L L L F L L F L L L L L L L L L L L L L L L L L L L
Result D W D W L D W L L W W D L L L L W L W L W L D W D L W W W L L L W L L D L W D L W L L L L L W L W L D
Goalkeepers
Steve Banks
Vince Bartram
Bertrand Bossu
Jason Brown
Lars Hirschfeld
Danny Knowles
Nico Vaesen
Defenders
Barry Ashby
Dean Beckwith
Wayne Brown
Ian Cox
Andrew Crofts
John Hills
Chris Hope
Nayron Nosworthy
Richard Rose
Midfielders
Ashley Carew
Andy Hessenthaler
Leon Johnson
David Perpetuini
Alan Pouton
Mark Saunders
Paul Smith
Nicky Southall
Daniel Spiller
John Wallis
Forwards
Patrick Agyemang
Jones Awuah
Trevor Benjamin
Darius Henderson
Kevin James
Matthew Jarvis
Tommy Johnson
Marlon King
Paul Shaw
Mamady Sidibe
Gary Wales
Rod Wallace

KEY: On all match · On bench · Subbed or sent off (Counting game) · Subbed or sent off (playing less than 70 minutes) · Subbed on from bench (Counting Game) · Subbed on (playing less than 70 minutes) · Subbed on and then subbed or sent off (Counting Game) · Subbed on and then subbed or sent off (playing less than 70 minutes) · Not in 16

WALSALL

Final Position: **22nd**

NICKNAME: THE SADDLERS   KEY: Won Drawn Lost

							Attendance
1	div1	West Brom	H	W	4-1	Merson 18,39; Leitao 45; Corica 57	11,030
2	ccR1	Carlisle	H	W	2-1	Merson 35; Leitao 49	4,665
3	div1	Coventry	A	D	0-0		15,377
4	div1	Stoke	H	D	1-1	Merson 85	9,033
5	div1	Crewe	A	L	0-1		7,026
6	div1	Cardiff	H	D	1-1	Leitao 52	8,974
7	div1	Derby	H	L	0-1		8,726
8	div1	Ipswich	A	L	1-2	Birch 29	20,912
9	div1	Millwall	A	L	1-2	Corica 7 pen	9,262
10	ccR2	Bolton	A	L	1-3	Merson 74	5,229
11	div1	Preston	H	W	2-1	Emblen 50; Samways 59	6,981
12	div1	Gillingham	H	W	2-1	Matias 35; Hessenthaler 84 og	6,395
13	div1	Burnley	A	L	1-3	Merson 24	10,532
14	div1	Watford	A	D	1-1	Osborn 40	12,231
15	div1	Sunderland	A	L	0-1		36,278
16	div1	Reading	A	W	1-0	Samways 4	11,225
17	div1	Wigan	H	W	2-0	Wrack 50,66	7,041
18	div1	Norwich	H	L	1-3	Birch 10	8,331
19	div1	Nottm Forest	H	W	4-1	Wrack 30,64; Osborn 36; Birch 86	7,321
20	div1	Bradford	A	D	1-1	Wrack 35	9,629
21	div1	Crystal Palace	H	D	0-0		6,910
22	div1	Rotherham	A	L	0-2		6,101
23	div1	Bradford	H	W	1-0	Birch 77	6,876
24	div1	Sheff Utd	A	L	0-2		8,602
25	div1	Wimbledon	A	W	1-0	Emblen 72	3,315
26	div1	West Ham	H	D	1-1	Leitao 69	9,272
27	div1	Cardiff	A	W	1-0	Emblen 70	17,531
28	div1	Reading	H	D	1-1	Leitao 30	8,089
29	facr3	Millwall	A	L	1-2	Leitao 12	6,977
30	div1	West Brom	A	L	0-2		24,558
31	div1	Coventry	H	L	1-6	Wrack 45	8,264
32	div1	Stoke	A	L	2-3	Leitao 14; Taylor 42	18,035
33	div1	Crewe	H	D	1-1	Leitao 27	6,871
34	div1	Nottm Forest	A	D	3-3	Leitao 5; Lawrence 24; Wales 39	25,012
35	div1	Watford	H	L	0-1		6,684
36	div1	Wigan	A	L	0-1		7,593
37	div1	Sunderland	H	L	1-3	Emblen 53	7,185
38	div1	West Ham	A	D	0-0		33,177
39	div1	Wimbledon	H	W	1-0	Emblen 27	6,889
40	div1	Ipswich	H	L	1-3	Andrews 88	6,562
41	div1	Preston	A	W	2-1	Fryatt 2; Wright 65	11,551
42	div1	Millwall	H	D	1-1	Andrews 78	6,486
43	div1	Derby	A	W	1-0	Bradbury 86 pen	23,574
44	div1	Burnley	H	L	0-1		7,769
45	div1	Gillingham	A	L	0-3		8,244
46	div1	Norwich	A	L	0-5		23,558
47	div1	Sheff Utd	H	L	0-1		7,873
48	div1	Crystal Palace	A	L	0-1		21,518
49	div1	Rotherham	H	W	3-2	Osborn 49; Wright 69; Ritchie 90	11,049

MONTHLY POINTS TALLY

AUGUST	6	40%
SEPTEMBER	6	40%
OCTOBER	7	47%
NOVEMBER	5	33%
DECEMBER	11	61%
JANUARY	0	0%
FEBRUARY	2	17%
MARCH	8	44%
APRIL	3	20%
MAY	3	50%

LEAGUE GOALS

	PLAYER	LGE	FAC	LC	Oth	TOT
1	Leitao	7	1	1	0	9
2	Wrack	6	0	0	0	6
3	Emblen	5	0	0	0	5
4	Birch	4	0	0	0	4
5	Merson	4	0	2	0	6
6	Osborn	3	0	0	0	3
7	Andrews	2	0	0	0	2
8	Samways	2	0	0	0	2
9	Corica	2	0	0	0	2
10	Wright	2	0	0	0	2
11	Wales	1	0	0	0	1
	Other	7	0	0	0	7
	TOTAL	45	1	3	0	49

KEY PLAYERS - GOALSCORERS

Darren Wrack

Goals in the League	6
Goals in all competitions	6
Contribution to Attacking Power Average number of minutes between League team goals while on pitch	76
Player Strike Rate The total number of minutes he was on the pitch for every League goal scored	345
Club Strike Rate Average number of minutes between League goals scored by club	92

	PLAYER	GOALS LGE	GOALS ALL	POWER	S RATE
1	Darren Wrack	6	6	76	345 mins
2	Jorge Leitao	7	9	92	369 mins
3	Neil Emblen	5	5	89	502 mins
4	Gary Birch	4	4	87	566 mins
5	Steve Corica	2	2	105	688 mins

KEY PLAYERS - MIDFIELDERS

Vinny Samways

Goals in the League	2
Goals in all competitions	2
Defensive Rating Average number of mins between League goals conceded while on the pitch	69
Contribution to Attacking Power Average number of minutes between League team goals while on pitch	77
Scoring Difference Defensive Rating minus Contribution to Attacking Power	-8

	PLAYER	GOALS LGE	GOALS ALL	DEF RATE	ATT POWER	SCORE DIFF
1	Vinny Samways	2	2	69	77	-8 mins
2	Paul Merson	4	6	64	84	-20 mins
3	Steve Corica	2	2	76	106	-30 mins
4	Simon Osborn	3	3	67	105	-38 mins
5	Darren Bazeley	0	0	61	106	-45 mins

KEY PLAYERS - DEFENDERS

Danny Hay

Goals Conceded in League	16
Goals Conceded in all competitions	16
Clean Sheets In League games when he played at least 70 mins	2
Defensive Rating Ave number of mins between League goals conceded while on the pitch	80
Club Defensive Rating Average number of mins between League goals conceded by the club this season	64

	PLAYER	CON LGE	CON ALL	CLN SHEETS	DEF RATE
1	Danny Hay	16	16	2	80 mins
2	Ian Roper	34	37	9	78 mins
3	Paul Ritchie	44	49	6	67 mins
4	Zigor Aranalde	45	51	6	61 mins
5	Neil Emblen	43	49	6	58 mins

KEY GOALKEEPER

1 James Walker

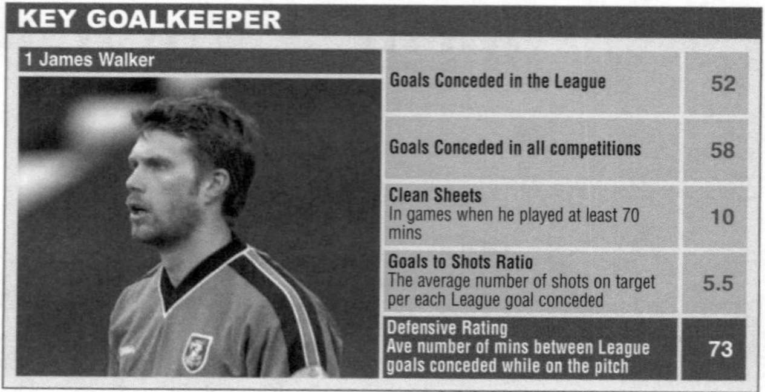

Goals Conceded in the League	52
Goals Conceded in all competitions	58
Clean Sheets In games when he played at least 70 mins	10
Goals to Shots Ratio The average number of shots on target per each League goal conceded	5.5
Defensive Rating Ave number of mins between League goals conceded while on the pitch	73

DISCIPLINARY RECORDS

	PLAYER	YELLOW	RED	AVE
1	Baird	3	2	169
2	Andrews	3	0	292
3	Ritchie	9	1	295
4	O'Neil	2	0	314
5	Osborn	9	1	337
6	Roper	6	0	442
7	Samways	4	0	617
8	Carbon	1	0	627
9	Taylor	1	0	634
10	Corica	2	0	687
11	Wrack	3	0	690
12	Matias	1	0	698
13	Vincent	1	0	910
	Other	16	2	
	TOTAL	61	6	

TOP POINT EARNERS

	PLAYER	GAMES	AV PTS
1	Darren Wrack	22	**1.32**
2	Ian Roper	28	**1.29**
3	Vinny Samways	27	**1.26**
4	Gary Birch	22	**1.23**
5	Paul Merson	29	**1.21**
6	James Walker	42	**1.19**
7	Paul Ritchie	33	**1.18**
8	Neil Emblen	25	**1.16**
9	Zigor Aranalde	29	**1.14**
10	Jorge Leitao	25	**1.08**
	CLUB AVERAGE:		**1.11**

LEAGUE APPEARANCES AND BOOKINGS

	AGE (on 01/07/04)	IN NAMED 16	APPEARANCES	COUNTING GAMES	MINUTES ON PITCH		
Goalkeepers							
Shaun Allaway	21	14	0	0	0	0	0
Aaron Kerr	21	15	0	0	0	0	0
Andy Petterson	34	16	3	3	270	0	0
James Walker	31	42	42	42	3780	1	0
Defenders							
Zigor Aranalde	31	38	36	29	2744	1	1
Chris Baird	22	10	10	9	847	3	2
Julian Bennett	19	2	1	0	21	0	0
Gavin Caines	20	2	0	0	0	0	0
Matthew Carbon	29	14	8	6	627	1	0
Neil Emblen	33	45	39	25	2510	2	0
Danny Hay	29	22	16	14	1285	1	0
Paul Ritchie	28	33	33	33	2959	9	1
Ian Roper	27	35	33	28	2655	6	0
Jamie Vincent	29	13	12	9	910	1	0
Midfielders							
Keith Andrews	23	12	11	9	877	3	0
Darren Bazeley	31	42	39	35	3178	3	0
Craig Burley	32	5	5	4	421	1	0
Steve Corica	31	26	19	13	1375	2	0
Tony Dinning	29	6	5	1	172	0	0
Matty Fryatt	18	15	11	3	409	0	0
Jamie Lawrence	34	18	17	7	859	0	0
Paul Merson	36	35	34	29	2761	0	0
Gary O'Neil	21	7	7	7	628	2	0
Stefan Oakes	25	10	5	0	106	1	1
Simon Osborn	32	44	42	37	3374	9	1
Vinny Samways	35	29	29	27	2470	4	0
Craig Stanley	21	1	0	0	0	0	0
Kris Taylor	20	18	12	5	634	1	0
Mark Wright	22	17	11	3	418	1	0
Forwards							
Gary Birch	22	35	35	22	2265	1	0
Lee Bradbury	29	8	8	5	585	0	0
Deon Burton	27	5	3	2	183	1	0
Karl Hawley	22	0	0	0	0	0	0
Jorge Leitao	30	40	39	25	2585	2	0
Pedro Miguel Matias	30	21	15	6	698	1	0
Jermaine McSporran	27	5	5	1	234	1	0
Gary Wales	25	7	7	5	468	0	0
Darren Wrack	28	29	27	22	2072	3	0

TEAM OF THE SEASON

G — James Walker, CG: 42 DR: 73

D — Danny Hay, CG: 14 DR: 80
D — Ian Roper, CG: 28 DR: 78
D — Paul Ritchie, CG: 33 DR: 67
D — Zigor Aranalde, CG: 29 DR: 61

M — Vinny Samways, CG: 27 SD: -8
M — Paul Merson, CG: 29 SD: -20
M — Steve Corica, CG: 13 SD: -30
M — Simon Osborn, CG: 37 SD: -38

F — Darren Wrack, CG: 22 SR: 345
F — Jorge Leitao, CG: 25 SR: 369

SQUAD APPEARANCES

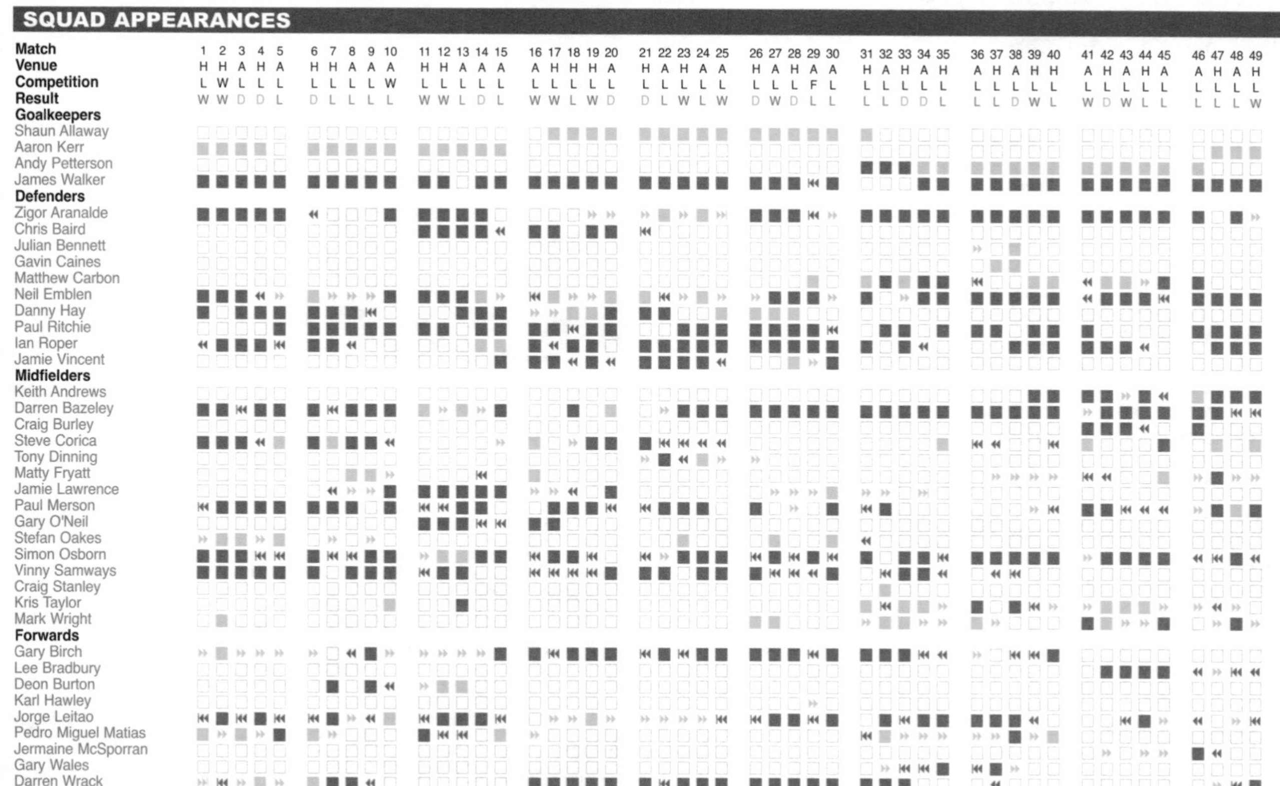

Match 1 2 3 4 5 6 7 8 9 10 11 12 13 14 15 16 17 18 19 20 21 22 23 24 25 26 27 28 29 30 31 32 33 34 35 36 37 38 39 40 41 42 43 44 45 46 47 48 49
Venue H H A H A H H A A A H H A A A A H H H A H A H A A H A H A A H A H A H A H A H H A H A H A A H A H
Competition L W L L L L L L L W L L L L L L L L L L L L L L L L L L F L L L L L L L L L L L L L L L L L L L L
Result W W D D L D L L L L W W L D L W W L W D D L W L W D W D L L L L D D L L L D W L W D W L L L L L W
Goalkeepers
Shaun Allaway
Aaron Kerr
Andy Petterson
James Walker
Defenders
Zigor Aranalde
Chris Baird
Julian Bennett
Gavin Caines
Matthew Carbon
Neil Emblen
Danny Hay
Paul Ritchie
Ian Roper
Jamie Vincent
Midfielders
Keith Andrews
Darren Bazeley
Craig Burley
Steve Corica
Tony Dinning
Matty Fryatt
Jamie Lawrence
Paul Merson
Gary O'Neil
Stefan Oakes
Simon Osborn
Vinny Samways
Craig Stanley
Kris Taylor
Mark Wright
Forwards
Gary Birch
Lee Bradbury
Deon Burton
Karl Hawley
Jorge Leitao
Pedro Miguel Matias
Jermaine McSporran
Gary Wales
Darren Wrack

KEY: ■ On all match ■ On bench | ⏮ Subbed or sent off (Counting game) « Subbed or sent off (playing less than 70 minutes) | » Subbed on from bench (Counting Game) » Subbed on (playing less than 70 minutes) | » Subbed on and then subbed or sent off (Counting Game) » Subbed on and then subbed or sent off (playing less than 70 minutes) | □ Not in 16

BRADFORD CITY

Final Position: **23rd**

NICKNAME: THE BANTAMS

KEY: Won / Drawn / Lost

							Attendance
1	div1	Norwich	H	D	2-2	Muirhead 84; Branch 90	13,159
2	ccR1	Darlington	H	D	3-5*	(*on penalties)	4,077
3	div1	Cardiff	A	W	2-0	Gray 6; Emanuel 69	16,421
4	div1	Gillingham	H	L	0-1		10,317
5	div1	West Ham	A	L	0-1		30,370
6	div1	Sunderland	H	L	0-4		14,116
7	div1	Preston	H	W	2-1	Branch 59; Summerbee 71	11,243
8	div1	Crystal Palace	A	W	1-0	Branch 42	13,514
9	div1	Burnley	A	L	0-4		12,719
10	div1	Sheff Utd	H	L	1-2	Windass 28	11,067
11	div1	Derby	H	L	1-2	Gray 59	10,143
12	div1	Reading	A	D	2-2	Evans 44; Gray 55	12,594
13	div1	Ipswich	H	L	0-1		10,229
14	div1	Crewe	A	D	2-2	Evans 55; Muirhead 87	5,867
15	div1	Watford	A	L	0-1		10,381
16	div1	Nottm Forest	H	L	1-2	Branch 5	11,654
17	div1	Wimbledon	A	L	1-2	Gray 34	3,334
18	div1	Coventry	A	D	0-0		11,862
19	div1	Walsall	H	D	1-1	Branch 5	9,629
20	div1	Stoke	A	L	0-1		11,661
21	div1	Millwall	H	W	3-2	Cadamarteri 52; Gray 69; Branch 90	10,107
22	div1	Walsall	A	L	0-1		6,876
23	div1	West Brom	H	L	0-1		11,198
24	div1	Wigan	A	L	0-1		7,256
25	div1	Rotherham	H	L	0-2		10,923
26	div1	Sunderland	A	L	0-3		29,639
27	div1	Coventry	H	W	1-0	Windass 33	11,432
28	facr3	Luton	H	L	1-2	Gray 83 pen	8,222
29	div1	Norwich	A	W	1-0	Armstrong 45	16,360
30	div1	Cardiff	H	L	0-1		11,132
31	div1	Crystal Palace	H	L	1-2	Wallwork 27	10,310
32	div1	Gillingham	A	L	0-1		7,836
33	div1	West Ham	H	L	1-2	Atherton 35	13,078
34	div1	Ipswich	A	L	1-3	Windass 45	21,478
35	div1	Crewe	H	W	2-1	Windass 51; Wallwork 79	9,935
36	div1	Nottm Forest	A	L	1-2	Windass 19	26,021
37	div1	Rotherham	A	W	2-1	Wallwork 40,45	6,796
38	div1	Watford	H	W	2-0	Evans 9; Windass 22	17,143
39	div1	Wigan	H	D	0-0		11,744
40	div1	Sheff Utd	A	L	0-2		20,052
41	div1	Burnley	H	L	1-2	Cadamarteri 18	13,677
42	div1	Preston	A	L	0-1		12,367
43	div1	Reading	H	W	2-1	Wetherall 12; Emanuel 53	10,287
44	div1	Derby	A	L	2-3	Atherton 67; Wolleaston 79	21,593
45	div1	Wimbledon	H	L	2-3	Sanasy 72; Cadamarteri 75	9,011
46	div1	West Brom	A	L	0-2		26,143
47	div1	Stoke	H	L	0-2		10,147
48	div1	Millwall	A	L	0-1		9,635

MONTHLY POINTS TALLY

AUGUST	4	27%
SEPTEMBER	6	40%
OCTOBER	2	13%
NOVEMBER	5	33%
DECEMBER	3	17%
JANUARY	3	25%
FEBRUARY	3	25%
MARCH	7	47%
APRIL	3	20%
MAY	0	0%

LEAGUE GOALS

	PLAYER	LGE	FAC	LC	Oth	TOT
1	Branch	6	0	0	0	6
2	Windass	6	0	0	0	6
3	Gray	5	1	0	0	6
4	Wallwork	4	0	0	0	4
5	Evans	3	0	0	0	3
6	Cadamarteri	3	0	0	0	3
7	Muirhead	2	0	0	0	2
8	Emanuel	2	0	0	0	2
9	Atherton	2	0	0	0	2
10	Summerbee	1	0	0	0	1
11	Wolleaston	1	0	0	0	1
	Other	3	0	0	0	3
	TOTAL	38	1	0	0	39

KEY PLAYERS - GOALSCORERS

Michael Branch

Goals in the League	6
Goals in all competitions	6
Contribution to Attacking Power Average number of minutes between League team goals while on pitch	133
Player Strike Rate The total number of minutes he was on the pitch for every League goal scored	401
Club Strike Rate Average number of minutes between League goals scored by club	109

	PLAYER	GOALS LGE	GOALS ALL	POWER	S RATE
1	Michael Branch	6	6	133	401 mins
2	Dean Windass	6	6	93	484 mins
3	Andy Gray	5	6	113	589 mins
4	Paul Evans	3	3	95	605 mins
5	Lewis Emanuel	2	2	127	891 mins

KEY PLAYERS - MIDFIELDERS

Paul Evans

Goals in the League	3
Goals in all competitions	3
Defensive Rating Average number of mins between League goals conceded while on the pitch	63
Contribution to Attacking Power Average number of minutes between League team goals while on pitch	95
Scoring Difference Defensive Rating minus Contribution to Attacking Power	-32

	PLAYER	GOALS LGE	GOALS ALL	DEF RATE	ATT POWER	SCORE DIFF
1	Paul Evans	3	3	63	95	-32 mins
2	Nicky Summerbee	1	1	59	97	-38 mins
3	Andy Gray	5	6	60	113	-53 mins
4	Lewis Emanuel	2	2	71	127	-56 mins
5	Gareth Farrelly	0	0	60	119	-59 mins

KEY PLAYERS - DEFENDERS

Simon Francis

Goals Conceded in League	35
Goals Conceded in all competitions	35
Clean Sheets In League games when he played at least 70 mins	5
Defensive Rating Ave number of mins between League goals conceded while on the pitch	67
Club Defensive Rating Average number of mins between League goals conceded by the club this season	60

	PLAYER	CON LGE	CON ALL	CLN SHEETS	DEF RATE
1	Simon Francis	35	35	5	67 mins
2	Paul Heckingbottom	62	64	7	61 mins
3	David Wetherall	49	51	6	61 mins
4	Jason Gavin	56	56	4	58 mins
5	Peter Atherton	40	42	4	58 mins

KEY GOALKEEPER

1 Alan Combe

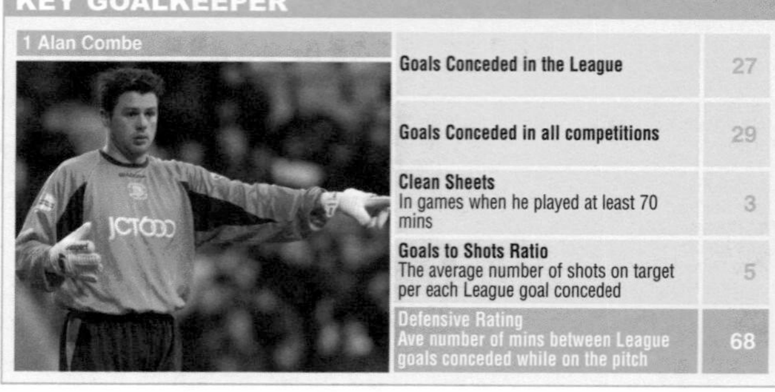

Goals Conceded in the League	27
Goals Conceded in all competitions	29
Clean Sheets In games when he played at least 70 mins	3
Goals to Shots Ratio The average number of shots on target per each League goal conceded	5
Defensive Rating Ave number of mins between League goals conceded while on the pitch	68

DISCIPLINARY RECORDS

	PLAYER	YELLOW	RED	AVE
1	Gavin	11	2	251
2	Evans	7	0	259
3	Atherton	8	0	290
4	Branch	7	1	301
5	Wallwork	2	0	315
6	Windass	8	1	322
7	Muirhead	4	0	329
8	Summerbee	6	0	453
9	Francis	5	0	469
10	Armstrong	1	0	537
11	Vaesen	1	0	540
12	Kearney	2	0	579
13	Edds	3	0	583
	Other	22	1	
	TOTAL	87	5	

TOP POINT EARNERS

	PLAYER	GAMES	AV PTS
1	Dean Windass	30	**1.07**
2	Paul Evans	19	**1.00**
3	David Wetherall	32	**0.97**
4	Peter Atherton	23	**0.96**
5	Simon Francis	25	**0.92**
6	Alan Combe	20	**0.85**
7	Paul Heckingbottom	42	**0.83**
8	Jason Gavin	35	**0.80**
9	Andy Gray	33	**0.79**
10	Nicky Summerbee	27	**0.70**
	CLUB AVERAGE:		**0.78**

TEAM OF THE SEASON

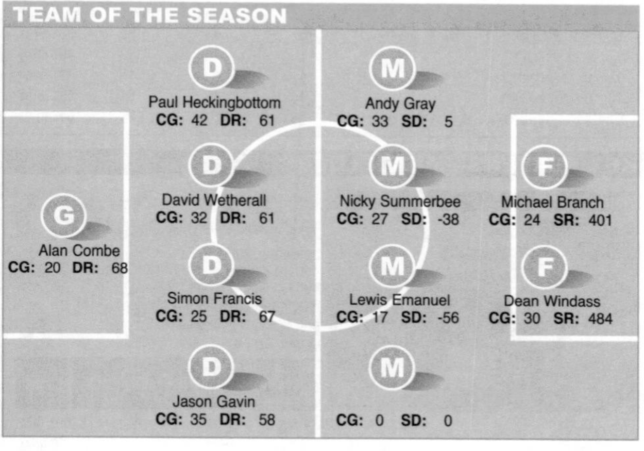
G
Alan Combe
CG: 20 DR: 68
D
Paul Heckingbottom
CG: 42 DR: 61
D
David Wetherall
CG: 32 DR: 61
D
Simon Francis
CG: 25 DR: 67
D
Jason Gavin
CG: 35 DR: 58
M
Andy Gray
CG: 33 SD: 5
M
Nicky Summerbee
CG: 27 SD: -38
M
Lewis Emanuel
CG: 17 SD: -56
M
CG: 0 SD: 0
F
Michael Branch
CG: 24 SR: 401
F
Dean Windass
CG: 30 SR: 484

LEAGUE APPEARANCES AND BOOKINGS

	AGE (on 01/07/04)	IN NAMED 16	APPEARANCES	COUNTING GAMES	MINUTES ON PITCH	Yellow	Red
Goalkeepers							
Marlon Beresford	34	7	5	5	450	0	0
Alan Combe	30	34	21	20	1845	0	1
Clint Davies	21	13	2	1	135	0	0
Mark Paston	27	23	13	13	1170	0	0
Andrew Rhodes	39	1	0	0	0	0	0
Nico Vaesen	34	6	6	6	540	1	0
Defenders							
Peter Atherton	34	27	27	23	2323	8	0
Mark Bower	24	24	14	11	1038	0	0
Gareth Edds	23	27	23	18	1751	3	0
Simon Francis	19	35	30	25	2349	5	0
Jason Gavin	24	38	38	35	3265	11	2
Paul Heckingbottom	26	43	43	42	3768	5	0
Wayne Jacobs	35	22	13	10	1008	1	0
Frazer McHugh	22	7	3	3	251	0	0
Ronnie Wallwork	26	7	7	7	630	2	0
David Wetherall	33	34	34	32	2979	5	0
Midfielders							
Lewis Emanuel	20	35	28	17	1781	0	0
Paul Evans	29	29	23	19	1814	7	0
Gareth Farrelly	28	14	14	13	1192	1	0
Andy Gray	26	33	33	33	2943	4	0
Thomas Kearney	22	30	17	10	1159	2	0
Thomas Penford	19	4	4	3	287	0	0
Michael Standing	23	14	6	1	248	1	0
Nicky Summerbee	32	36	35	27	2721	6	0
Forwards							
Alun Armstrong	29	6	6	6	537	1	0
Michael Branch	25	36	33	24	2408	7	1
Danny Cadamarteri	24	18	18	10	1219	1	0
Luke Cornwall	23	7	3	1	152	0	0
Danny Forrest	19	24	13	2	354	2	0
Ben Muirhead	21	39	28	8	1317	4	0
Kevin Sanasy	19	7	5	2	245	1	0
Dean Windass	35	36	36	30	2904	8	1
Robert Wolleaston	24	20	14	6	652	1	0

SQUAD APPEARANCES

KEY: ■ On all match ■ On bench | ⏮ Subbed or sent off (Counting game) « Subbed or sent off (playing less than 70 minutes) | ⏭ Subbed on from bench (Counting Game) » Subbed on (playing less than 70 minutes) | ⏭ Subbed on and then subbed or sent off (Counting Game) » Subbed on and then subbed or sent off (playing less than 70 minutes) | □ Not in 16

WIMBLEDON

Final Position: **24th**

NICKNAME: THE DONS/WOMBLES KEY: ☐ Won ☐ Drawn ☐ Lost

	Comp	Opponent	H/A	Res	Score	Scorers	Attendance
1	div1	Crewe	H	W	3-1	Agyemang 15; Tapp 54; Reo-Coker 62	1,145
2	ccR1	Wycombe	A	L	0-2		1,986
3	div1	Stoke	A	L	1-2	Agyemang 55	12,550
4	div1	Crystal Palace	H	L	1-3	Reo-Coker 34	6,113
5	div1	Norwich	A	L	2-3	Holdsworth 84; Leigertwood 90	16,082
6	div1	Reading	H	L	0-3		2,066
7	div1	Wigan	H	L	2-4	Agyemang 34; McAnuff 48	1,054
8	div1	Millwall	A	L	0-2		7,855
9	div1	Ipswich	A	L	1-4	Agyemang 45	23,428
10	div1	Burnley	H	D	2-2	Holdsworth 66; Agyemang 71	5,639
11	div1	Sheff Utd	H	L	1-2	Nowland 49	6,016
12	div1	Preston	A	L	0-1		13,801
13	div1	Coventry	A	L	0-1		10,872
14	div1	Nottm Forest	A	L	0-6		23,500
15	div1	West Brom	A	W	1-0	McAnuff 79	22,048
16	div1	Watford	H	L	1-3	Leigertwood 49	6,115
17	div1	Bradford	H	W	2-1	Small 62; Reo-Coker 66	3,334
18	div1	Rotherham	A	L	1-3	Nowland 68	5,777
19	div1	Gillingham	A	W	2-1	Nowland 22; Agyemang 66	9,041
20	div1	Cardiff	H	L	0-1		5,056
21	div1	West Ham	H	D	1-1	McAnuff 63	8,118
22	div1	Derby	A	L	1-3	Reo-Coker 20	22,025
23	div1	Rotherham	H	L	1-2	Holdsworth 78 pen	3,061
24	div1	Walsall	H	L	0-1		3,315
25	div1	Sunderland	A	L	1-2	Thirlwell 45 og	22,334
26	div1	Reading	A	W	3-0	Small 9; Lewington 23; McAnuff 81	14,486
27	div1	West Brom	H	D	0-0		6,376
28	facr3	Stoke	H	D	1-1	Nowland 73	3,609
29	div1	Crewe	A	L	0-1		6,234
30	facr3r	Stoke	A	W	1-0	Nowland 32	6,463
31	div1	Stoke	H	L	0-1		3,623
32	facr4	Birmingham	A	L	0-1		22,159
33	div1	Crystal Palace	A	L	1-3	McAnuff 50	20,552
34	div1	Norwich	H	L	0-1		7,368
35	div1	Coventry	H	L	0-3		5,905
36	div1	Watford	A	L	0-4		15,323
37	div1	Nottm Forest	H	L	0-1		6,317
38	div1	West Ham	A	L	0-5		29,818
39	div1	Walsall	A	L	0-1		6,889
40	div1	Millwall	H	L	0-1		3,037
41	div1	Ipswich	H	L	1-2	Smith 77	6,389
42	div1	Wigan	A	W	1-0	Chorley 5	7,622
43	div1	Sunderland	H	L	1-2	Kamara 67	4,800
44	div1	Preston	H	D	3-3	Gray 6,90; Chorley 65	2,866
45	div1	Sheff Utd	A	L	1-2	Gray 44 pen	19,391
46	div1	Bradford	A	W	3-2	Kamara 5; Smith 32; Gray 50	9,011
47	div1	Burnley	A	L	0-2		13,555
48	div1	Gillingham	H	L	1-2	Smith 52	5,049
49	div1	Cardiff	A	D	1-1	Williams 83	15,337
50	div1	Derby	H	W	1-0	Darlington 25	6,509

KEY PLAYERS - GOALSCORERS

Patrick Agyemang

Goals in the League	6
Goals in all competitions	6
Contribution to Attacking Power Average number of minutes between League team goals while on pitch	81
Player Strike Rate The total number of minutes he was on the pitch for every League goal scored	324
Club Strike Rate Average number of minutes between League goals scored by club	101

	PLAYER	GOALS LGE	GOALS ALL	POWER	S RATE
1	Patrick Agyemang	6	6	81	324 mins
2	Jobi McAnuff	5	5	120	457 mins
3	Wayne Gray	4	4	115	491 mins
4	Nigel Reo-Coker	4	4	84	551 mins
5	Adam Nowland	3	5	98	692 mins

KEY PLAYERS - MIDFIELDERS

Wade Small

Goals in the League	2
Goals in all competitions	2
Defensive Rating Average number of mins between League goals conceded while on the pitch	53
Contribution to Attacking Power Average number of minutes between League team goals while on pitch	89
Scoring Difference Defensive Rating minus Contribution to Attacking Power	-36

	PLAYER	GOALS LGE	GOALS ALL	DEF RATE	ATT POWER	SCORE DIFF
1	Wade Small	2	2	53	89	-36 mins
2	Nigel Reo-Coker	4	4	46	85	-39 mins
3	Ben Chorley	2	2	42	101	-59 mins
4	Malvin Kamara	2	2	45	120	-75 mins
5	Jobi McAnuff	5	5	43	120	-77 mins

KEY PLAYERS - DEFENDERS

Dean Lewington

Goals Conceded in League	42
Goals Conceded in all competitions	44
Clean Sheets In League games when he played at least 70 mins	4
Defensive Rating Ave number of mins between League goals conceded while on the pitch	57
Club Defensive Rating Average number of mins between League goals conceded by the club this season	47

	PLAYER	CON LGE	CON ALL	CLN SHEETS	DEF RATE
1	Dean Lewington	42	44	4	57 mins
2	Mikele Leigertwood	52	56	3	48 mins
3	Jermaine Darlington	78	82	4	47 mins
4	Peter Hawkins	34	36	1	43 mins
5	Nico Herzig	36	36	1	43 mins

MONTHLY POINTS TALLY

Month	Points	%
AUGUST	3	20%
SEPTEMBER	1	7%
OCTOBER	3	20%
NOVEMBER	7	39%
DECEMBER	4	27%
JANUARY	0	0%
FEBRUARY	0	0%
MARCH	0	0%
APRIL	7	33%
MAY	4	67%

LEAGUE GOALS

	PLAYER	LGE	FAC	LC	Oth	TOT
1	Agyemang	6	0	0	0	6
2	McAnuff	5	0	0	0	5
3	Reo-Coker	4	0	0	0	4
4	Gray	4	0	0	0	4
5	Nowland	3	2	0	0	5
6	Smith	3	0	0	0	3
7	Holdsworth	3	0	0	0	3
8	Leigertwood	2	0	0	0	2
9	Small	2	0	0	0	2
10	Chorley	2	0	0	0	2
11	Kamara	2	0	0	0	2
	Other	5	0	0	0	5
	TOTAL	41	2	0	0	43

KEY GOALKEEPER

1 Steve Banks

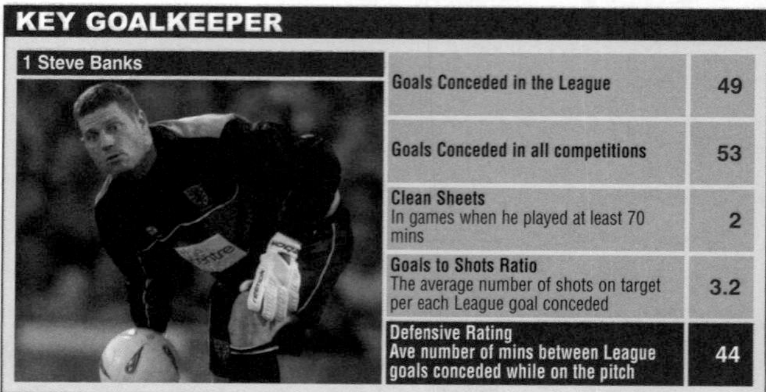

Goals Conceded in the League	49
Goals Conceded in all competitions	53
Clean Sheets In games when he played at least 70 mins	2
Goals to Shots Ratio The average number of shots on target per each League goal conceded	3.2
Defensive Rating Ave number of mins between League goals conceded while on the pitch	44

DISCIPLINARY RECORDS

	PLAYER	YELLOW	RED	AVE
1	Holloway	4	2	104
2	Kamara	7	0	222
3	Reo-Coker	7	0	314
4	Nowland	6	0	345
5	Mackie	2	0	353
6	Chorley	8	0	365
7	Hawkins	2	1	483
8	Tapp	2	0	487
9	Williams	1	1	491
10	Heald	1	0	751
11	McAnuff	3	0	762
12	Herzig	2	0	774
13	Leigertwood	3	0	824
	Other	14	3	
	TOTAL	62	7	

TOP POINT EARNERS

	PLAYER	GAMES	AV PTS
1	Wade Small	21	**1.00**
2	Dean Lewington	27	**0.81**
3	Nico Herzig	16	**0.81**
4	Nigel Reo-Coker	24	**0.75**
5	Malvin Kamara	14	**0.71**
6	Ben Chorley	31	**0.68**
7	Mikele Leigertwood	27	**0.67**
8	Patrick Agyemang	18	**0.67**
9	Jermaine Darlington	40	**0.65**
10	Wayne Gray	17	**0.65**
	CLUB AVERAGE:		**0.63**

TEAM OF THE SEASON

G Steve Banks — **CG:** 24 **DR:** 44

D Dean Lewington — **CG:** 27 **DR:** 57

D Mikele Leigertwood — **CG:** 27 **DR:** 48

D Jermaine Darlington — **CG:** 40 **DR:** 47

D Peter Hawkins — **CG:** 14 **DR:** 43

M Wade Small — **CG:** 21 **SD:** -36

M Nigel Reo-Coker — **CG:** 24 **SD:** -39

M Ben Chorley — **CG:** 31 **SD:** -59

M Malvin Kamara — **CG:** 14 **SD:** -75

F Patrick Agyemang — **CG:** 18 **SR:** 324

F Wayne Gray — **CG:** 17 **SR:** 491

LEAGUE APPEARANCES AND BOOKINGS

	AGE (on 01/07/04)	IN NAMED 16	APPEARANCES	COUNTING GAMES	MINUTES ON PITCH		
Goalkeepers							
Steve Banks	32	29	24	24	2152	0	1
Scott Bevan	24	10	10	10	900	0	0
Shane Gore	22	1	0	0	0	0	0
Paul Heald	35	16	9	7	751	1	0
David Martin	-	12	2	2	180	0	0
Lee Worgan	20	21	3	0	42	0	1
Defenders							
Warren Barton	35	5	5	4	394	1	0
Jermaine Darlington	30	41	41	40	3652	4	0
Robert Gier	23	36	25	22	2106	2	0
Peter Hawkins	25	24	19	14	1449	2	1
Nico Herzig	20	24	19	16	1548	2	0
Darren Holloway	26	18	13	6	628	4	2
Mikele Leigertwood	21	28	28	27	2472	3	0
Dean Lewington	20	27	27	27	2406	1	1
Harry Ntimban-Zeh	30	12	10	9	855	1	0
Shola Oyedele	-	13	9	7	750	0	0
Mark Williams	33	12	11	11	983	1	1
Midfielders							
Jamal Campbell-Ryce	21	4	4	2	258	0	0
Ben Chorley	21	43	34	31	2922	8	0
Michael Gordon	19	21	18	2	716	0	0
Ben Harding	19	24	15	9	954	0	0
Albert Jarrett	19	12	9	2	335	0	0
Malvin Kamara	20	32	27	14	1558	7	0
Jobi McAnuff	22	27	27	25	2286	3	0
Nick McKoy	-	7	3	0	78	0	0
Jason Puncheon	-	12	8	5	559	0	0
Nigel Reo-Coker	20	25	25	24	2204	7	0
Wade Small	20	27	27	21	2124	2	0
Gary Smith	20	11	11	9	909	0	0
Alex Tapp	22	17	14	10	974	2	0
Forwards							
Patrick Agyemang	23	26	26	18	1946	1	0
Wayne Gray	23	36	31	17	1963	1	0
Dean Holdsworth	35	33	28	11	1378	1	0
Jamie Mackie	-	16	13	4	707	2	0
Scott McDonald	20	4	1	0	24	0	0
Lionel Morgan	21	4	3	2	172	0	0
Adam Nowland	23	26	25	21	2075	6	0

SQUAD APPEARANCES

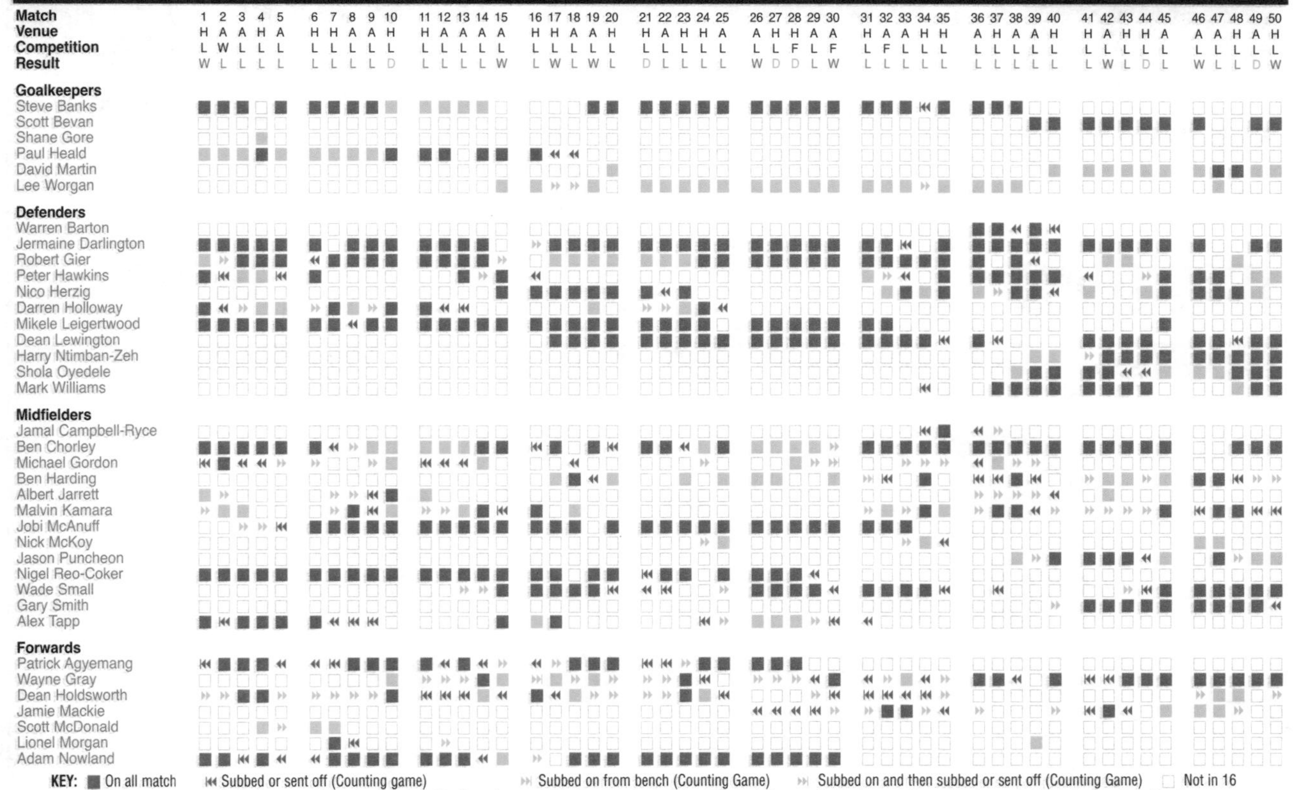

Match 1 2 3 4 5 6 7 8 9 10 11 12 13 14 15 16 17 18 19 20 21 22 23 24 25 26 27 28 29 30 31 32 33 34 35 36 37 38 39 40 41 42 43 44 45 46 47 48 49 50
Venue H A A H A H H A A H H A A A A H H A A H H A H H A A H H A A H A A H H A H A A H H A H H A A A H A H
Competition L W L L L L L L L L L L L L L L L L L L L L L L L L L F L F L F L L L L L L L L L L L L L L L L L L
Result W L L L L L L L L D L L L L W L W L W L D L L L L W D D L W L L L L L L L L L L L W L D L W L L D W
Goalkeepers
Steve Banks
Scott Bevan
Shane Gore
Paul Heald
David Martin
Lee Worgan
Defenders
Warren Barton
Jermaine Darlington
Robert Gier
Peter Hawkins
Nico Herzig
Darren Holloway
Mikele Leigertwood
Dean Lewington
Harry Ntimban-Zeh
Shola Oyedele
Mark Williams
Midfielders
Jamal Campbell-Ryce
Ben Chorley
Michael Gordon
Ben Harding
Albert Jarrett
Malvin Kamara
Jobi McAnuff
Nick McKoy
Jason Puncheon
Nigel Reo-Coker
Wade Small
Gary Smith
Alex Tapp
Forwards
Patrick Agyemang
Wayne Gray
Dean Holdsworth
Jamie Mackie
Scott McDonald
Lionel Morgan
Adam Nowland
KEY: On all match
On bench
Subbed or sent off (Counting game)
Subbed or sent off (playing less than 70 minutes)
Subbed on from bench (Counting Game)
Subbed on (playing less than 70 minutes)
Subbed on and then subbed or sent off (Counting Game)
Subbed on and then subbed or sent off (playing less than 70 minutes)
Not in 16

DIVISION TWO ROUND-UP

FINAL LEAGUE TABLE

	HOME						AWAY					TOTAL			
	P	W	D	L	F	A	W	D	L	F	A	F	A	DIF	PTS
Plymouth	46	17	5	1	52	13	9	7	7	33	28	85	41	44	90
QPR	46	16	7	0	47	12	6	10	7	33	33	80	45	35	83
Bristol City	46	15	6	2	34	12	8	7	8	24	25	58	37	21	82
Brighton	46	17	4	2	39	11	5	7	11	25	32	64	43	21	77
Swindon	46	12	7	4	41	23	8	6	9	35	35	76	58	18	73
Hartlepool	46	10	8	5	39	24	10	5	8	37	37	76	61	15	73
Port Vale	46	15	6	2	45	28	6	4	13	28	35	73	63	10	73
Tranmere	46	13	7	3	36	18	4	9	10	23	38	59	56	3	67
Bournemouth	46	11	8	4	35	25	6	7	10	21	26	56	51	5	66
Luton	46	14	6	3	44	27	3	9	11	25	39	69	66	3	66
Colchester	46	11	8	4	33	23	6	5	12	19	33	52	56	-4	64
Barnsley	46	7	12	4	25	19	8	5	10	29	39	54	58	-4	62
Wrexham	46	9	6	8	27	21	8	3	12	23	39	50	60	-10	60
Blackpool	46	9	5	9	31	28	7	6	10	27	37	58	65	-7	59
Oldham	46	9	8	6	37	25	3	13	7	29	35	66	60	6	57
Sheff Wed	46	7	9	7	25	26	6	5	12	23	38	48	64	-16	53
Brentford	46	9	5	9	34	38	5	6	12	18	31	52	69	-17	53
Peterborough	46	5	8	10	36	33	7	8	8	22	25	58	58	0	52
Stockport	46	6	8	9	31	36	5	11	7	31	34	62	70	-8	52
Chesterfield	46	9	7	7	34	31	3	8	12	15	40	49	71	-22	51
Grimsby	46	10	5	8	36	26	3	6	14	19	55	55	81	-26	50
Rushden & D	46	9	5	9	37	34	4	4	15	23	40	60	74	-14	48
Notts County	46	6	9	8	32	27	4	3	16	18	51	50	78	-28	42
Wycombe	46	5	7	11	31	39	1	12	10	19	36	50	75	-25	37

CLUB STRIKE FORCE

Norris of Plymouth on the ball v. QPR

1 Plymouth

Goals scored in the League	85
Goals scored in all competions	88
Club Strike Rate (CSR) Average number of minutes between League goals scored	49

	CLUB	LGE	ALL	CSR
1	Plymouth	85	88	49
2	QPR	80	84	52
3	Hartlepool	76	85	54
4	Swindon	76	84	54
5	Port Vale	73	77	57
6	Luton	69	85	60
7	Oldham	66	72	63
8	Brighton	64	69	65
9	Stockport	62	64	67
10	Rushden & D	60	61	69
11	Tranmere	59	71	70
12	Bristol City	58	69	71
13	Peterborough	58	64	71
14	Blackpool	57	71	73
15	Bournemouth	56	58	74
16	Grimsby	55	60	75
17	Barnsley	54	59	77
18	Brentford	52	59	80
19	Colchester	52	62	80
20	Notts County	50	63	83
21	Wrexham	50	51	83
22	Wycombe	50	59	83
23	Chesterfield	49	51	84
24	Sheff Wed	48	55	86

CLUB DISCIPLINARY RECORDS

Haining of Oldham enforcing

1 Oldham

League Yellow	90
League Red	6
All Competitions Yellow	94
All Competitions Red	8
Cards Average in League Average number of minutes between a card being shown	43

	CLUB	LEAGUE		TOTAL		AVE
1	Oldham	90Y	6R	94Y	8R	43
2	Chesterfield	90	4	93	4	44
3	QPR	91	3	99	4	44
4	Luton	86	6	100	6	45
5	Sheff Wed	82	7	91	7	47
6	Tranmere	81	4	97	4	49
7	Blackpool	75	7	84	9	50
8	Brighton	78	3	86	4	51
9	Barnsley	71	5	79	5	54
10	Swindon	69	6	76	7	55
11	Notts County	73	1	81	2	56
12	Colchester	68	5	81	5	57
13	Stockport	71	2	73	2	57
14	Wycombe	69	4	74	4	57
15	Wrexham	65	6	69	7	58
16	Peterborough	64	5	72	6	60
17	Bristol City	64	4	73	4	61
18	Brentford	62	4	68	6	63
19	Bournemouth	64	1	67	1	64
20	Grimsby	56	6	65	8	67
21	Plymouth	59	3	63	3	67
22	Port Vale	61	1	70	2	67
23	Rushden & D	57	4	60	4	68
24	Hartlepool	52	0	62	1	80

CLUB DEFENCES

	CLUB	LGE	ALL	CS	CDR
1	Bristol City	37	48	17	112
2	Plymouth	41	46	21	101
3	Brighton	43	49	20	96
4	QPR	45	50	18	92
5	Bournemouth	51	52	17	81
6	Colchester	56	62	11	74
7	Tranmere	56	63	15	74
8	Peterborough	57	63	11	73
9	Barnsley	58	64	13	71
10	Swindon	58	68	14	71
11	Oldham	60	67	9	69
12	Wrexham	60	66	14	69
13	Hartlepool	61	68	14	68
14	Port Vale	63	67	12	66
15	Sheff Wed	64	67	11	65
16	Blackpool	65	73	10	64
17	Luton	66	75	9	63
18	Brentford	69	77	6	60
19	Stockport	70	75	9	59
20	Chesterfield	71	74	10	58
21	Rushden & D	74	80	7	56
22	Wycombe	75	85	8	55
23	Notts County	78	88	8	53
24	Grimsby	81	87	12	51

Roberts defending for Bristol City

1 Bristol City

Goals conceded in the League	37
Goals conceded in all competitions	48
Clean Sheets (CS) Number of league games where no goals were conceded	17
Club Defensive Rate (CDR) Average number of minutes between League goals conceded	112

STADIUM CAPACITY AND HOME CROWDS

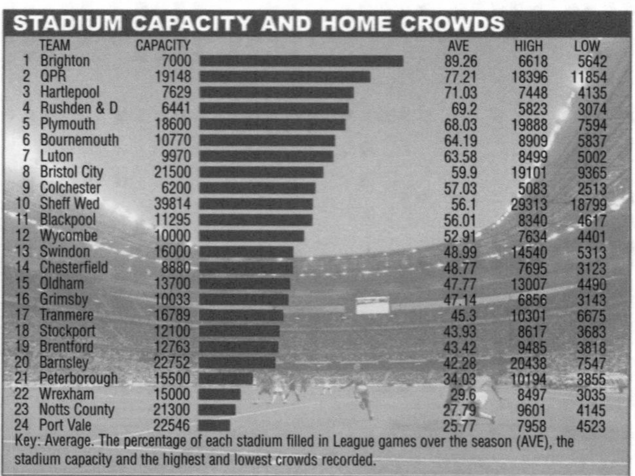

	TEAM	CAPACITY	AVE	HIGH	LOW
1	Brighton	7000	89.26	6618	5642
2	QPR	19148	77.21	18396	11854
3	Hartlepool	7629	71.03	7448	4135
4	Rushden & D	6441	69.2	5823	3074
5	Plymouth	18600	68.03	19888	7594
6	Bournemouth	10770	64.19	8909	5837
7	Luton	9970	63.58	8499	5002
8	Bristol City	21500	59.9	19101	9365
9	Colchester	6200	57.03	5083	2513
10	Sheff Wed	39814	56.1	29313	18799
11	Blackpool	11295	56.01	8340	4617
12	Wycombe	10000	52.91	7634	4401
13	Swindon	16000	48.99	14540	5313
14	Chesterfield	8880	48.77	7695	3123
15	Oldham	13700	47.77	13007	4490
16	Grimsby	10033	47.14	6856	3143
17	Tranmere	16789	45.3	10301	6675
18	Stockport	12100	43.93	8617	3683
19	Brentford	12763	43.42	9485	3818
20	Barnsley	22752	42.28	20438	7547
21	Peterborough	15500	34.03	10194	3855
22	Wrexham	15000	29.6	8497	3035
23	Notts County	21300	27.79	9601	4145
24	Port Vale	22546	25.77	7958	4523

Key: Average. The percentage of each stadium filled in League games over the season (AVE), the stadium capacity and the highest and lowest crowds recorded.

AWAY ATTENDANCE

	TEAM	AVE	HIGH	LOW
1	Sheff Wed	72.04	20438	5018
2	QPR	63.12	29313	3835
3	Plymouth	58.59	20090	3945
4	Bristol City	54.41	24154	3079
5	Brighton	53.39	19707	3673
6	Luton	53.27	21027	3143
7	Oldham	53.21	24630	2897
8	Swindon	52.87	22751	3339
9	Brentford	52.27	20004	3257
10	Grimsby	51.97	21918	2922
11	Barnsley	51.84	25664	3507
12	Bournemouth	51.6	18799	3131
13	Blackpool	51.53	21450	3265
14	Chesterfield	51.24	25296	3115
15	Stockport	51	22535	2513
16	Peterborough	50.7	21474	3035
17	Port Vale	50.6	24991	2539
18	Notts County	50.55	20354	3782
19	Wycombe	50.21	19596	3092
20	Rushden & D	50.03	22599	3680
21	Colchester	49.21	20464	3683
22	Hartlepool	48.99	20732	3348
23	Wrexham	48.91	24478	3077
24	Tranmere	47.7	21705	3074

Key: Average. How close each club has come to filling grounds in its away league matches (AVE) and the highest and lowest crowds recorded.

CHART-TOPPING MIDFIELDERS

DAS

1 Brown - Bristol City	
Goals scored in the League	5
Defensive Rating Av number of mins between League goals conceded while on the pitch	154
Contribution to Attacking Power Average number of minutes between League team goals while on pitch	66
Scoring Difference Defensive Rating minus Contribution to Attacking Power	88

	PLAYER	CLUB	GOALS	DEF RATE	POWER	S DIFF
1	Brown	Bristol City	5	154	66	88
2	Ainsworth	QPR	6	129	52	77
3	Jones	Brighton	0	135	62	73
4	Friio	Plymouth	14	112	44	68
5	Doherty	Bristol City	2	126	66	60
6	Bean	QPR	1	118	67	51
7	Evans	Plymouth	12	100	52	48
8	Bircham	QPR	2	96	50	46
9	Oatway	Brighton	1	110	67	43
10	Norris	Plymouth	5	94	52	42
11	Rowlands	QPR	11	96	54	42
12	Capaldi	Plymouth	7	93	54	39
13	Tinnion	Bristol City	2	109	75	34
14	Worrell	Plymouth	0	75	44	31
15	Harrison	Tranmere	2	95	64	31

CHART-TOPPING GOALSCORERS

1 Lowe - Rushden & Diamonds	
Goals scored in the League (GL)	15
Goals scored in all competitions (GA)	16
Contribution to Attacking Power (AP) Average number of minutes between League team goals while on pitch	55
Player Strike Rate Average number of minutes between League goals scored by player	146
Club Strike Rate (CSR) Average minutes between League goals scored by club	69

	PLAYER	CLUB	GOALS: LGE	ALL	POWER	CSR	S RATE
1	Lowe	Rushden & D.	15	16	55	69	146 mins
2	Heffernan	Notts County	19	20	75	83	148
3	Knight	Brighton	25	26	65	65	152
4	Dadi	Tranmere	16	19	73	70	157
5	Furlong	QPR	16	16	53	52	161
6	Taylor	Blackpool	16	25	70	73	168
7	McPhee	Port Vale	24	25	57	57	169
8	Jevons	Grimsby	12	13	78	75	170
9	McKenzie	Peterborough	10	10	74	71	171
10	Parkin	Swindon	18	22	48	54	190
11	N'dumbu	Sheff Wed	9	10	108	86	193
12	Mooney	Swindon	19	20	53	54	195
13	Boulding	Grimsby	12	13	81	75	196
14	Thorpe	QPR	10	10	45	52	201
15	Hurst	Chesterfield	12	12	73	84	202

CHART-TOPPING DEFENDERS

GINSTERS

1 Aljofree - Plymouth	
Goals Conceded in the League The number of League goals conceded while he was on the pitch	11
Goals Conceded in all competitions The number of goals conceded while he was on the pitch in all competitions	13
Clean Sheets In games when he played at least 70 mins	15
Defensive Rating Average number of minutes between League goals conceded while on pitch	168
Club Defensive Rating Average mins between League goals conceded by the club this season	101

	PLAYER	CLUB	CON: LGE	ALL	CS	CDR	DEF RATE
1	Aljofree	Plymouth	11	13	15	101	168 mins
2	Virgo	Brighton	14	16	10	96	127
3	Connolly	Plymouth	20	20	17	101	127
4	Harding	Brighton	13	16	10	96	123
5	Hill	Bristol City	28	39	15	112	122
6	Gilbert	Plymouth	30	35	21	101	119
7	Carey	Bristol City	33	39	16	112	111
8	Butler	Bristol City	30	39	15	112	111
9	Coles	Bristol City	36	47	15	112	110
10	Adams	Plymouth	22	24	9	101	109
11	Shittu	QPR	16	17	9	92	106
12	Coughlan	Plymouth	41	46	21	101	101
13	Padula	QPR	33	37	15	92	98
14	Butters	Brighton	40	46	20	96	97
15	Cullip	Brighton	35	41	17	96	96

CHART-TOPPING GOALKEEPERS

GINSTERS

1 McCormick - Plymouth	
Counting Games League games when he played at least 70 minutes	40
Goals Conceded in the League The number of League goals conceded while he was on the pitch	31
Goals Conceded in all competitions The number of goals conceded while he was on the pitch in all competitions	34
Clean Sheets In games when he played at least 70 mins	21
Defensive Rating Average number of minutes between League goals conceded while on pitch	116

	PLAYER	CLUB	CG	CONC LGE	CONC ALL	CS	DEF RATE
1	McCormick	Plymouth	40	31	34	21	116 mins
2	Phillips	Bristol City	46	37	48	17	112
3	Roberts	Brighton	32	28	30	14	100
4	Day	QPR	29	26	31	14	100
5	Lucas	Sheff Wed	17	18	18	4	84
6	Moss	Bournemouth	46	51	53	17	81
7	Dibble	Wrexham	34	37	43	13	81
8	Ilic	Barnsley	25	29	35	8	78
9	Brown	Colchester	40	48	55	10	75
10	Evans	Swindon	41	48	57	12	75
11	Achterberg	Tranmere	46	56	63	15	74
12	Tyler	Peterborough	43	53	59	11	73
13	Provett	Hartlepool	45	58	66	14	70
14	Brain	Port Vale	32	41	45	9	70
15	Pogliacomi	Oldham	46	60	67	9	69

PLAYER DISCIPLINARY RECORD

1 Killen - Oldham	
Cards Average mins between cards	119
League Yellow	4
League Red	2
TOTAL	6

	PLAYER		LY	LR	TOT	AVE
1	Killen	Oldham	4	2	6	119
2	Piercy	Brighton	6	1	7	125
3	Ellison	Stockport	6	0	6	132
4	Beckett	Stockport	3	1	4	135
5	Danns	Blackpool	5	2	7	146
6	Holt	Sheff Wed	4	1	5	149
7	Quinn	Sheff Wed	11	2	13	160
8	Scoffham	Notts County	3	0	3	162
9	Bayliss	Luton	3	0	3	165
10	Bignot	QPR	2	1	3	175
11	Robertson	Stockport	4	0	4	180
12	Taylor	Wycombe	3	0	3	180
13	Hillier	Luton	3	1	4	188
14	Fallon	Swindon	3	1	4	193
15	Kuqi	Sheff Wed	2	1	3	194
16	Branston	Wycombe	4	0	4	202
17	McMahon	Blackpool	3	0	3	204
18	Lita	Bristol City	3	0	3	209
19	Crane	Grimsby	13	2	15	212
20	N'dumbu	Sheff Wed	7	1	8	217
21	Wellens	Blackpool	13	2	15	230
22	Gabbiadini	Hartlepool	4	0	4	231
23	Burton	Peterborough	9	1	10	231
24	Fagan	Colchester	11	1	12	232

TEAM OF THE SEASON

G
McCormick : Plymouth
CG: 40 DR: 116

D
Aljofree : Plymouth
CG: 20 DR: 168

D
Virgo : Brighton
CG: 19 DR: 127

D
Hill : Bristol City
CG: 35 DR: 122

D
Shittu : QPR
CG: 18 DR: 106

M
Brown : Bristol City
CG: 25 SD: +88

M
Ainsworth : QPR
CG: 17 SD: +77

M
Jones : Brighton
CG: 28 SD: +73

M
Friio : Plymouth
CG: 30 SD: +68

F
Lowe : Rushden & D.
CG: 24 SR: 146

F
Thorpe : QPR
CG: 17 AP: 45

PLYMOUTH ARGYLE

Final Position: **1ST**

NICKNAME: THE PILGRIMS

KEY: Won, Drawn, Lost

							Attendance
1	div2	Grimsby	H	D	2-2	Keith 32; Coughlan 51	9,590
2	ccr1	Colchester	A	L	1-2	Evans 24	2,367
3	div2	Rushden & D	A	L	1-2	Capaldi 77	4,045
4	div2	Stockport	H	W	3-1	Keith 21; Hodges 23; Bent 28	7,594
5	div2	Chesterfield	A	D	1-1	Friio 66	4,089
6	div2	Brighton	H	D	3-3	Coughlan 19; Stonebridge 81; Friio 89	9,289
7	div2	Brentford	A	W	3-1	Stonebridge 9; Evans 58,84	5,688
8	div2	Luton	H	W	2-1	Evans 82; Friio 90	9,894
9	div2	Peterborough	A	D	2-2	Wotton 10 pen; Capaldi 84	4,183
10	div2	Wrexham	A	D	2-2	Norris 31; Capaldi 49	3,945
11	div2	Barnsley	H	W	2-0	Coughlan 38; Evans 75	8,695
12	div2	Bristol City	H	L	0-1		13,923
13	div2	Wycombe	A	D	0-0		5,708
14	div2	Tranmere	H	W	6-0	Friio 7; Wotton 38; Gilbert 45; Keith 49; Evans 56; Norris 79	7,610
15	div2	Port Vale	A	W	5-1	Keith 35; Friio 38,72; Adams 45; Wotton 46	5,786
16	div2	Sheff Wed	A	W	3-1	Friio 22,64; Wotton 62 pen	20,090
17	div2	Blackpool	H	W	1-0	Keith 42	12,372
18	div2	Oldham	H	D	2-2	Wotton 17; Evans 50	11,205
19	facr1	Northampton	A	L	2-3	Friio 32; Stonebridge 62	4,385
20	div2	QPR	A	L	0-3		17,049
21	div2	Hartlepool	H	W	2-0	Keith 45; Lowndes 48	9,000
22	div2	Colchester	A	W	2-0	Capaldi 4; Keith 11	4,332
23	div2	Swindon	A	W	3-2	Capaldi 13; Norris 76; Keith 90	9,374
24	div2	Notts County	H	W	3-0	Lowndes 28; Evans 79,82	9,923
25	div2	Bournemouth	A	W	2-0	Wotton 22; Norris 40	8,901
26	div2	Brentford	H	W	2-0	Capaldi 48; Lowndes 63	17,882
27	div2	Chesterfield	H	W	7-0	Hodges 4; Capaldi 11; Lowndes 12,18; Friio 15,36,88	13,109
28	div2	Grimsby	A	D	0-0		5,007
29	div2	Rushden & D	H	W	3-0	Coughlan 47; Stonebridge 58; Wotton 90	13,021
30	div2	Stockport	A	W	2-0	Friio 29; Coughlan 62	6,608
31	div2	Brighton	A	L	1-2	Lowndes 88	6,379
32	div2	Bournemouth	H	D	0-0		13,371
33	div2	Tranmere	A	L	0-3		7,948
34	div2	Port Vale	H	W	2-1	Phillips 80; Stonebridge 90	11,330
35	div2	Blackpool	A	W	1-0	Stonebridge 54	7,253
36	div2	Sheff Wed	H	W	2-0	Evans 7; Coughlan 77	17,218
37	div2	Notts County	A	D	0-0		8,057
38	div2	Swindon	H	W	2-1	Keith 11; Evans 84	16,080
39	div2	Peterborough	H	W	2-0	Lowndes 55; Wotton 79 pen	13,110
40	div2	Luton	A	D	1-1	Adams 90	8,499
41	div2	Wrexham	H	D	0-0		12,275
42	div2	Barnsley	A	L	0-1		9,266
43	div2	Wycombe	H	W	2-1	Coughlan 39; Evans 80	14,806
44	div2	Bristol City	A	L	0-1		19,045
45	div2	Oldham	A	L	1-4	Wotton 51	6,924
46	div2	QPR	H	W	2-0	Evans 81; Friio 86	19,888
47	div2	Hartlepool	A	W	3-1	Hodges 12; Lowndes 42; Tinkler 48 og	7,437
48	div2	Colchester	H	W	2-0	Friio 17; Norris 47	19,868

MONTHLY POINTS TALLY

Month	Points	%
AUGUST	6	40%
SEPTEMBER	11	61%
OCTOBER	13	87%
NOVEMBER	7	58%
DECEMBER	12	100%
JANUARY	10	67%
FEBRUARY	7	58%
MARCH	12	67%
APRIL	6	40%
MAY	6	100%

KEY PLAYERS - GOALSCORERS

Nathan Lowndes

Goals in the League	8	Player Strike Rate Average number of minutes between League goals scored by player	198
Contribution to Attacking Power Average number of minutes between League team goals while on pitch	47	Club Strike Rate Average number of minutes between League goals scored by club	49

	PLAYER	LGE GOALS	GOALS ALL	POWER	STRIKE RATE
1	Nathan Lowndes	8	8	47	198 mins
2	David Friio	14	15	43	207 mins
3	Marino Keith	9	9	44	265 mins
4	Micky Evans	12	13	51	267 mins

KEY PLAYERS - MIDFIELDERS

David Friio

Goals in the League	14	Contribution to Attacking Power Average number of minutes between League team goals while on pitch	44
Defensive Rating Average number of mins between League goals conceded while he was on the pitch	112	Scoring Difference Defensive Rating minus Contribution to Attacking Power	68

	PLAYER	LGE GOALS	GOALS ALL	DEF RATE	POWER	SCORE DIFF
1	David Friio	14	15	112	44	68 mins
2	Micky Evans	12	13	100	52	48 mins
3	David Norris	5	5	94	52	42 mins
4	Anthony Capaldi	7	7	93	54	39 mins

KEY PLAYERS - DEFENDERS

Hasney Aljofree

Goals Conceded (GC) The number of League goals conceded while he was on the pitch	11	Clean Sheets In games when he played at least 70 minutes	15
Defensive Rating Ave number of mins between League goals conceded while on the pitch	168	Club Defensive Rating Average number of mins between League goals conceded by the club this season	101

	PLAYER	CON LGE	CON ALL	CLEAN SHEETS	DEF RATE
1	Hasney Aljofree	11	13	15	168 mins
2	Paul Connolly	20	20	17	127 mins
3	Peter Gilbert	30	35	21	119 mins
4	Steve Adams	22	24	9	109 mins

KEY GOALKEEPER

Luke McCormick

Goals Conceded in the League	31	Counting Games Games when he played at least 70 mins	40
Defensive Rating Ave number of mins between League goals conceded while on the pitch	116	Clean Sheets In games when he played at least 70 mins	21

LEAGUE GOALS

David Friio

Minutes on the pitch	2901	Goals in the League	207
League average (mins between goals)	14		

	PLAYER	MINS	GOALS	AVE
1	Friio	2901	14	207
2	Evans	3201	12	267
3	Wotton	2897	9	322
4	Keith	2384	9	265
5	Lowndes	1580	8	198
6	Capaldi	2314	7	331
7	Coughlan	4140	7	591
8	Stonebridge	1833	5	367
9	Norris	3682	5	736
10	Hodges	2538	3	846
11	Adams	2399	2	1200
12	Bent	1188	1	1188
	Other		3	
	TOTAL		85	

DISCIPLINARY RECORDS

	PLAYER	YELLOW	RED	AVE
1	Aljofree	7	0	264
2	Friio	6	2	362
3	Wotton	6	1	413
4	Norris	8	0	460
5	Evans	6	0	533
6	Capaldi	4	0	578
7	Connolly	4	0	634
8	Hodges	4	0	634
9	Lowndes	2	0	790
10	Coughlan	5	0	828
11	Bent	1	0	1188
12	Adams	2	0	1199
13	Gilbert	2	0	1777
	Other	2	0	
	TOTAL	59	3	

TOP POINT EARNERS

	PLAYER	GAMES	AV PTS
1	Aljofree	20	2.40
2	Lowndes	13	2.23
3	Hodges	25	2.16
4	Friio	30	2.07
5	Capaldi	22	2.05
6	Gilbert	39	2.05
7	Connolly	28	2.04
8	McCormick	40	2.03
9	Keith	20	2.00
10	Coughlan	46	1.96
	CLUB AVERAGE:		**1.96**

TEAM OF THE SEASON

G
Luke McCormick
CG: 40 DR: 116

D
Hasney Aljofree
CG: 20 DR: 168

D
Paul Connolly
CG: 28 DR: 127

D
Peter Gilbert
CG: 39 DR: 119

D
Steve Adams
CG: 23 DR: 109

M
David Friio
CG: 30 SD: 68

M
Micky Evans
CG: 34 SD: 48

M
David Norris
CG: 39 SD: 42

M
Anthony Capaldi
CG: 22 SD: 39

F
Nathan Lowndes
CG: 13 SR: 198

F
Marino Keith
CG: 20 SR: 265

LEAGUE APPEARANCES AND BOOKINGS

	AGE (on 01/07/04)	IN NAMED 16	APPEARANCES	COUNTING GAMES	MINUTES ON PITCH	Yellow	Red
Goalkeepers							
Romain Larrieu	27	8	6	6	540	0	0
Luke McCormick	20	43	40	40	3600	1	0
Jani Viander	28	0	0	0	0	0	0
Defenders							
Steve Adams	23	39	36	23	2399	2	0
Hasney Aljofree	25	40	24	20	1852	7	0
Paul Connolly	20	31	29	28	2538	4	0
Graham Coughlan	29	46	46	46	4140	5	0
Peter Gilbert	20	42	40	39	3555	2	0
Eugene Kangulungu	28	3	0	0	0	0	0
Brian McGlinchey	26	1	0	0	0	0	0
Wayne O'Sullivan	30	1	0	0	0	0	0
Paul Wotton	26	44	38	30	2897	6	1
Midfielders							
Jason Bent	27	18	18	12	1188	1	0
David Beresford	27	9	1	0	11	0	0
Anthony Capaldi	22	42	33	22	2314	4	0
Ryan Dickson	-	1	0	0	0	0	0
Micky Evans	31	44	44	34	3201	6	0
David Friio	31	37	36	30	2901	6	2
David Norris	23	45	45	39	3682	8	0
Martin Phillips	28	23	9	2	396	0	0
David Worrell	26	20	18	17	1575	0	0
Forwards							
Lee Hodges	30	43	37	25	2538	4	0
Marino Keith	29	40	40	20	2384	1	0
Nathan Lowndes	27	36	33	13	1580	2	0
Marcus Martin	19	1	0	0	0	0	0
Ian Stonebridge	22	40	30	14	1833	0	0
Blair Sturrock	22	38	24	0	296	0	0
Stewart Yetton	18	1	1	0	8	0	0

SQUAD APPEARANCES

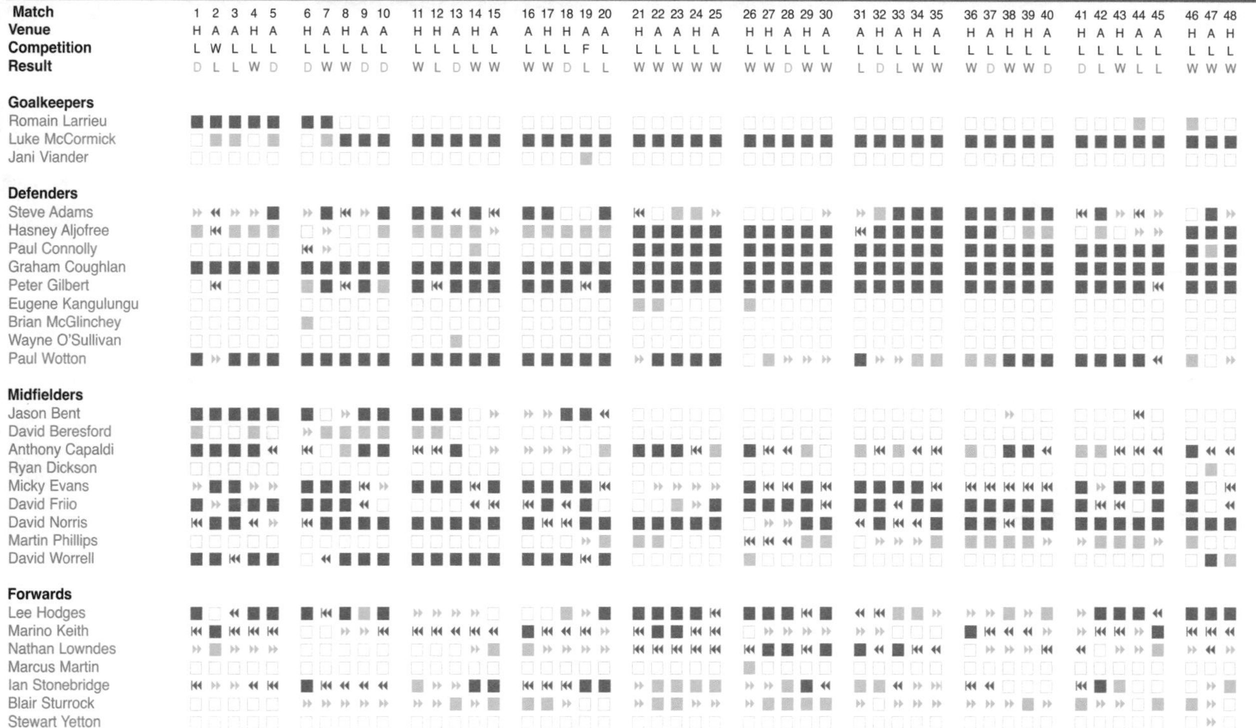

Match 1 2 3 4 5 6 7 8 9 10 11 12 13 14 15 16 17 18 19 20 21 22 23 24 25 26 27 28 29 30 31 32 33 34 35 36 37 38 39 40 41 42 43 44 45 46 47 48
Venue H A A H A H A H A A H H A H A A H H A A H A A H A H H A H A A H A H A H A H H A H A H A A H A H
Competition L W L L L L L L L L L L L L L L L L F L L L L L L L L L L L L L L L L L L L L L L L L L L L L L
Result D L L W D D W W D D W L D W W W W D L L W W W W W W W D W W L D L W W W D W W D D L W L L W W W
Goalkeepers
Romain Larrieu
Luke McCormick
Jani Viander
Defenders
Steve Adams
Hasney Aljofree
Paul Connolly
Graham Coughlan
Peter Gilbert
Eugene Kangulungu
Brian McGlinchey
Wayne O'Sullivan
Paul Wotton
Midfielders
Jason Bent
David Beresford
Anthony Capaldi
Ryan Dickson
Micky Evans
David Friio
David Norris
Martin Phillips
David Worrell
Forwards
Lee Hodges
Marino Keith
Nathan Lowndes
Marcus Martin
Ian Stonebridge
Blair Sturrock
Stewart Yetton

KEY: On all match · On bench · Subbed or sent off (Counting game) · Subbed or sent off (playing less than 70 minutes) · Subbed on from bench (Counting Game) · Subbed on (playing less than 70 minutes) · Subbed on and then subbed or sent off (Counting Game) · Subbed on and then subbed or sent off (playing less than 70 minutes) · Not in 16

QUEENS PARK RANGERS

Final Position: **2nd**

NICKNAME: RANGERS

KEY: Won Drawn Lost

							Attendance
1	div2	Blackpool	H	W	5-0	Ainsworth 4,69; Langley 43; Gallen 56; Palmer 90	14,581
2	ccr1	Cheltenham	A	W	2-1	Ainsworth 16; Langley 86	3,697
3	div2	Brighton	A	L	1-2	Padula 9	6,536
4	div2	Bournemouth	H	W	1-0	Furlong 63	13,065
5	div2	Rushden & D	A	D	3-3	Ainsworth 37,45; Furlong 53	5,544
6	div2	Chesterfield	H	W	3-0	Thorpe 29,67; Furlong 87	12,986
7	div2	Colchester	A	D	2-2	Furlong 49,66	3,835
8	div2	Wycombe	H	D	0-0		13,618
9	div2	Wrexham	A	W	2-0	Bean 7; Rowlands 90	4,539
10	div2	Luton	A	D	1-1	Furlong 90	8,339
11	ccr2	Sheff Utd	A	W	2-0	Rowlands 30,45	9,578
12	div2	Bristol City	H	D	1-1	Padula 73	14,913
13	div2	Barnsley	H	W	4-0	Gallen 60; Rowlands 61; Ainsworth 63; Thorpe 77	11,854
14	div2	Grimsby	A	W	1-0	Sabin 90	5,447
15	div2	Peterborough	A	D	0-0		7,247
16	div2	Port Vale	A	L	0-2		5,243
17	div2	Tranmere	H	D	1-1	Gallen 47	12,937
18	ccR3	Man City	H	L	0-3		16,773
19	div2	Stockport	A	W	2-1	Gallen 19; Rowlands 43	5,461
20	facr1	Grimsby	A	L	0-1		4,144
21	div2	Brentford	H	W	1-0	Thorpe 42	15,865
22	div2	Plymouth	H	W	3-0	Gallen 33,75; Thorpe 72	17,049
23	div2	Swindon	A	D	1-1	Rowlands 79	10,021
24	div2	Sheff Wed	H	W	3-0	Palmer 13; Thorpe 85; McLeod 90	17,393
25	div2	Hartlepool	H	W	4-1	Gallen 27,39; Padula 34; Ainsworth 50	15,003
26	div2	Oldham	A	L	1-2	Thorpe 31	5,603
27	div2	Notts County	A	D	3-3	Palmer 3; Richardson 10 og; Gallen 90	7,702
28	div2	Colchester	H	W	2-0	Gallen 12; Thorpe 57	15,720
29	div2	Rushden & D	H	W	1-0	Gallen 24	14,141
30	div2	Blackpool	A	W	1-0	Rowlands 38	7,329
31	div2	Brighton	H	W	2-1	Rowlands 20; Gallen 43	17,839
32	div2	Bournemouth	A	L	0-1		8,909
33	div2	Chesterfield	A	L	2-4	Thorpe 11; Palmer 63	4,567
34	div2	Notts County	H	W	3-2	McLeod 54; Thorpe 69; Furlong 83	14,412
35	div2	Brentford	A	D	1-1	Furlong 20	8,418
36	div2	Peterborough	H	D	1-1	Gallen 90	13,276
37	div2	Port Vale	H	W	3-2	Bircham 64; Cureton 77,90	12,593
38	div2	Oldham	H	D	1-1	Gallen 54 pen	13,696
39	div2	Hartlepool	A	W	4-1	Furlong 48,74; Gallen 52; Rowlands 76	6,519
40	div2	Wrexham	H	W	2-0	Carlisle 67; McLeod 88	13,363
41	div2	Wycombe	A	D	2-2	Gallen 46; Rowlands 68	7,634
42	div2	Luton	H	D	1-1	Furlong 45	17,695
43	div2	Bristol City	A	L	0-1		19,041
44	div2	Tranmere	A	D	0-0		7,699
45	div2	Grimsby	H	W	3-0	Furlong 42,86; Bircham 84	14,488
46	div2	Barnsley	A	D	3-3	Kay 32 og; Furlong 74,90	10,402
47	div2	Stockport	H	D	1-1	Rowlands 3	15,162
48	div2	Plymouth	A	L	0-2		19,888
49	div2	Swindon	H	W	1-0	Rowlands 2	18,396
50	div2	Sheff Wed	A	W	3-1	Gallen 35; Furlong 48; Carr 69 og	29,313

MONTHLY POINTS TALLY

Month	Points	%
AUGUST	10	67%
SEPTEMBER	10	56%
OCTOBER	5	42%
NOVEMBER	13	87%
DECEMBER	7	58%
JANUARY	9	60%
FEBRUARY	5	56%
MARCH	12	67%
APRIL	6	33%
MAY	6	100%

KEY PLAYERS - GOALSCORERS

Paul Furlong

Goals in the League	16	Player Strike Rate Average number of minutes between League goals scored by player	161
Contribution to Attacking Power Average number of minutes between League team goals while on pitch	53	Club Strike Rate Average number of minutes between League goals scored by club	52

	PLAYER	LGE GOALS	GOALS ALL	POWER	STRIKE RATE
1	Paul Furlong	16	16	53	161 mins
2	Tony Thorpe	10	10	45	201 mins
3	Kevin Gallen	17	17	51	233 mins
4	Gareth Ainsworth	6	7	52	322 mins

KEY PLAYERS - MIDFIELDERS

Gareth Ainsworth

Goals in the League	6	Contribution to Attacking Power Average number of minutes between League team goals while on pitch	52
Defensive Rating Average number of mins between League goals conceded while he was on the pitch	129	Scoring Difference Defensive Rating minus Contribution to Attacking Power	77

	PLAYER	LGE GOALS	GOALS ALL	DEF RATE	POWER	SCORE DIFF
1	Gareth Ainsworth	6	7	129	52	77 mins
2	Marcus Bean	1	1	118	67	51 mins
3	Marc Bircham	2	2	96	50	46 mins
4	Martin Rowlands	11	13	96	54	42 mins

KEY PLAYERS - DEFENDERS

Danny Shittu

Goals Conceded (GC) The number of League goals conceded while he was on the pitch	16	Clean Sheets In games when he played at least 70 minutes	9
Defensive Rating Ave number of mins between League goals conceded while on the pitch	106	Club Defensive Rating Average number of mins between League goals conceded by the club this season	92

	PLAYER	CON LGE	CON ALL	CLEAN SHEETS	DEF RATE
1	Danny Shittu	16	17	9	106 mins
2	Gino Padula	33	37	15	98 mins
3	Arthur Gnohere	17	17	6	93 mins
4	Clarke Carlisle	31	36	11	92 mins

KEY GOALKEEPER

Chris Day

Goals Conceded in the League	26	Counting Games Games when he played at least 70 mins	29
Defensive Rating Ave number of mins between League goals conceded while on the pitch	100	Clean Sheets In games when he played at least 70 mins	14

LEAGUE GOALS

Kevin Gallen

Minutes on the pitch	3961	Goals in the League	233
League average (mins between goals)	17		

	PLAYER	MINS	GOALS	AVE
1	Gallen	3961	17	233
2	Furlong	2579	16	161
3	Rowlands	3654	11	332
4	Thorpe	2012	10	201
5	Ainsworth	1929	6	322
6	Palmer	2429	4	607
7	McLeod	2332	3	777
8	Padula	3224	3	1075
9	Cureton	357	2	179
10	Bircham	3066	2	1533
11	Carlisle	2841	1	2841
12	Sabin	270	1	270
	Other		4	
	TOTAL		80	

DISCIPLINARY RECORDS

	PLAYER	YELLOW	RED	AVE
1	Bignot	2	1	175
2	Bean	8	0	250
3	Gnohere	6	0	262
4	Rowlands	12	0	304
5	Furlong	7	0	368
6	Bircham	8	0	383
7	Padula	8	0	403
8	Carlisle	7	0	405
9	Rose	3	0	436
10	McLeod	4	1	466
11	Palmer	5	0	485
12	Forbes	3	1	656
13	Gallen	6	0	660
	Other	12	0	
	TOTAL	91	3	

TOP POINT EARNERS

	PLAYER	GAMES	AV PTS
1	Ainsworth	17	2.18
2	Forbes	28	2.00
3	McLeod	23	2.00
4	Shittu	18	1.94
5	Thorpe	17	1.94
6	Carlisle	30	1.93
7	Bean	20	1.90
8	Padula	36	1.89
9	Bircham	33	1.88
10	Rowlands	39	1.87
	CLUB AVERAGE:		**1.80**

TEAM OF THE SEASON

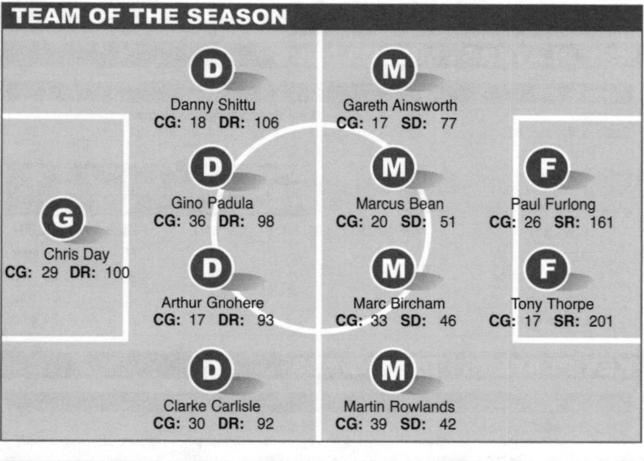

G
Chris Day
CG: 29 DR: 100
D
Danny Shittu
CG: 18 DR: 106
D
Gino Padula
CG: 36 DR: 98
D
Arthur Gnohere
CG: 17 DR: 93
D
Clarke Carlisle
CG: 30 DR: 92
M
Gareth Ainsworth
CG: 17 SD: 77
M
Marcus Bean
CG: 20 SD: 51
M
Marc Bircham
CG: 33 SD: 46
M
Martin Rowlands
CG: 39 SD: 42
F
Paul Furlong
CG: 26 SR: 161
F
Tony Thorpe
CG: 17 SR: 201

LEAGUE APPEARANCES AND BOOKINGS

	AGE (on 01/07/04)	IN NAMED 16	APPEARANCES	COUNTING GAMES	MINUTES ON PITCH	Yellow	Red
Goalkeepers							
Lee Camp	19	12	12	12	1080	0	0
Jake Cole	18	0	0	0	0	0	0
Nicky Culkin	26	32	5	5	450	1	0
Chris Day	28	41	29	29	2610	0	0
Defenders							
Warren Barton	35	3	3	1	157	0	0
Marcus Bignot	29	6	6	6	526	2	1
Clarke Carlisle	24	34	33	30	2841	7	0
Richard Edghill	29	25	20	12	1348	2	0
John Fletcher	17	0	0	0	0	0	0
Terell Forbes	22	32	30	28	2627	3	1
Arthur Gnohere	25	19	18	17	1575	6	0
Marien Ifura	19	1	0	0	0	0	0
Gino Padula	27	37	36	36	3224	8	0
Matthew Rose	28	24	20	13	1310	3	0
Danny Shittu	23	20	20	18	1689	2	0
Midfielders							
Gareth Ainsworth	31	32	29	17	1929	1	0
Marcus Bean	19	35	31	20	2004	8	0
Marc Bircham	26	39	38	33	3066	8	0
Wesley Daly	20	5	2	0	6	0	0
Richard Johnson	30	11	11	9	893	1	0
Richard Langley	24	1	1	1	90	0	0
Dean Marney	20	5	2	0	77	0	0
Kevin McLeod	23	35	35	23	2332	4	1
Steve Palmer	36	46	35	25	2429	5	0
Martin Rowlands	25	43	43	39	3654	12	0
Benjamin Walshe	21	1	0	0	0	0	0
Tommy Williams	23	6	5	4	332	0	0
Forwards							
Jamie Cureton	28	17	13	2	357	0	0
Paul Furlong	35	35	35	26	2579	7	0
Kevin Gallen	28	45	45	44	3961	6	0
Dennis Oli	20	14	3	0	32	0	0
Richard Pacquette	21	12	2	0	20	0	0
Eric Sabin	29	28	10	1	270	2	0
Tony Thorpe	30	38	31	17	2012	3	0

SQUAD APPEARANCES

Match	1	2	3	4	5	6	7	8	9	10	11	12	13	14	15	16	17	18	19	20	21	22	23	24	25	26	27	28	29	30	31	32	33	34	35	36	37	38	39	40	41	42	43	44	45	46	47	48	49	50
Venue	H	A	A	H	A	H	A	H	A	A	A	H	H	A	A	A	H	H	A	A	H	H	A	H	H	A	A	H	H	A	H	A	A	H	A	H	H	H	A	H	A	H	A	A	H	A	H	A	H	A
Competition	L	W	L	L	L	L	L	L	L	L	W	L	L	L	L	L	L	W	L	F	L	L	L	L	L	L	L	L	L	L	L	L	L	L	L	L	L	L	L	L	L	L	L	L	L	L	L	L	L	L
Result	W	W	L	W	D	W	D	D	W	D	W	D	W	W	D	L	D	L	W	L	W	W	D	W	W	L	D	W	W	W	W	L	L	W	D	D	W	D	W	W	D	D	L	D	W	D	D	L	W	W
Goalkeepers																																																		
Lee Camp																																																		
Jake Cole																																																		
Nicky Culkin																																																		
Chris Day																																																		
Defenders																																																		
Warren Barton																																																		
Marcus Bignot																																																		
Clarke Carlisle																																																		
Richard Edghill																																																		
John Fletcher																																																		
Terell Forbes																																																		
Arthur Gnohere																																																		
Marien Ifura																																																		
Gino Padula																																																		
Matthew Rose																																																		
Danny Shittu																																																		
Midfielders																																																		
Gareth Ainsworth																																																		
Marcus Bean																																																		
Marc Bircham																																																		
Wesley Daly																																																		
Richard Johnson																																																		
Richard Langley																																																		
Dean Marney																																																		
Kevin McLeod																																																		
Steve Palmer																																																		
Martin Rowlands																																																		
Benjamin Walshe																																																		
Tommy Williams																																																		
Forwards																																																		
Jamie Cureton																																																		
Paul Furlong																																																		
Kevin Gallen																																																		
Dennis Oli																																																		
Richard Pacquette																																																		
Eric Sabin																																																		
Tony Thorpe																																																		

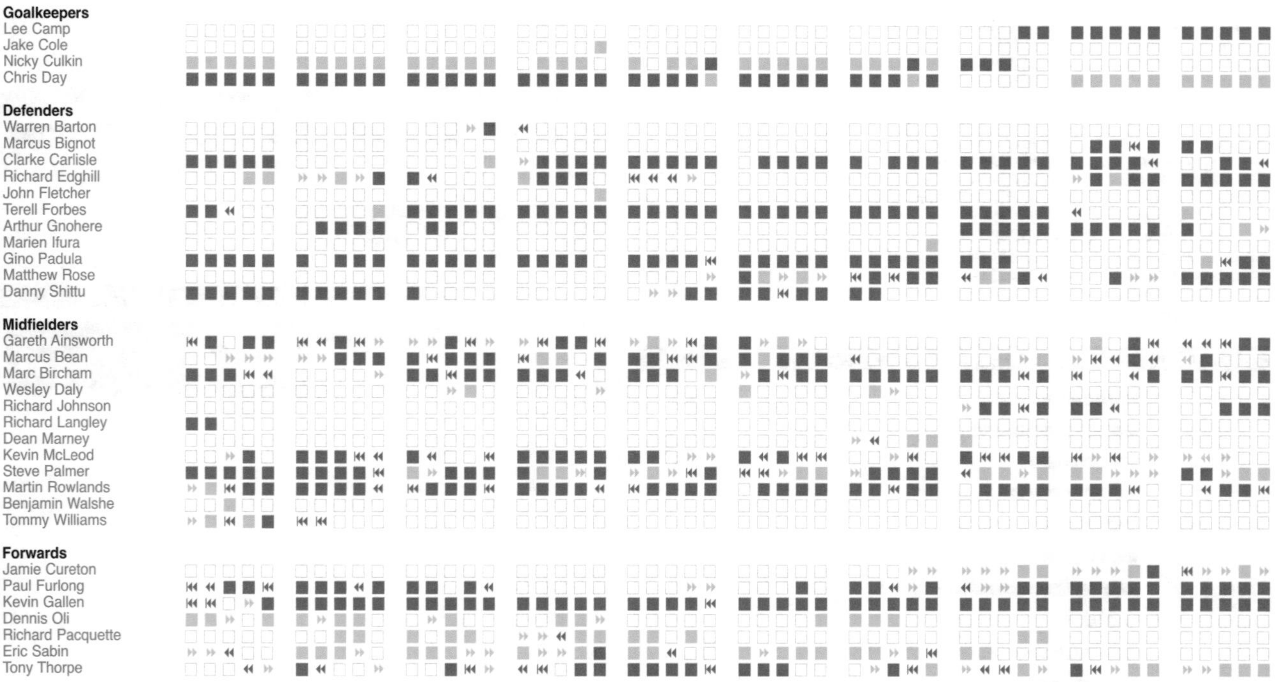

KEY: On all match | On bench | Subbed or sent off (Counting game) | Subbed or sent off (playing less than 70 minutes) | Subbed on from bench (Counting Game) | Subbed on (playing less than 70 minutes) | Subbed on and then subbed or sent off (Counting Game) | Subbed on and then subbed or sent off (playing less than 70 minutes) | Not in 16

BRISTOL CITY

Final Position: **3rd**

NICKNAME: THE ROBINS

KEY: ☐Won ☐Drawn ☐Lost

							Attendance
1	div2	**Notts County**	H	W	5-0	Peacock 12,37; Miller 50; Matthews 71,88	12,050
2	ccR1	**Swansea**	H	D	1-1	Peacock 14,108; Bell 96 pen; Coles 103	5,807
3	div2	**Chesterfield**	A	D	1-1	Coles 10	4,302
4	div2	**Hartlepool**	H	D	1-1	Peacock 56	10,730
5	div2	**Colchester**	A	L	1-2	Peacock 66	3,079
6	div2	**Grimsby**	H	W	1-0	Roberts 90	10,033
7	div2	**Bournemouth**	A	D	0-0		6,756
8	div2	**Oldham**	A	D	1-1	Butler 35	5,921
9	div2	**Tranmere**	H	W	2-0	Brown, A 23; Peacock 76	9,365
10	div2	**Port Vale**	H	L	0-1		11,369
11	ccR2	**Watford**	H	W	1-0	Miller 94	5,213
12	div2	**QPR**	A	D	1-1	Miller 76	14,913
13	div2	**Plymouth**	A	W	1-0	Peacock 27	13,923
14	div2	**Swindon**	H	W	2-1	Peacock 52; Brown, A 74	14,294
15	div2	**Peterborough**	H	D	1-1	Tinnion 24	11,053
16	div2	**Wrexham**	A	D	0-0		4,405
17	div2	**Wycombe**	A	L	0-3		4,613
18	div2	**Sheff Wed**	H	D	1-1	Peacock 70	13,668
19	ccR3	**Southampton**	H	L	0-3		17,408
20	div2	**Luton**	H	D	1-1	Burnell 2	9,735
21	facr1	**Bradford PA**	A	W	5-2	Amankwaah 6,8; Stansfield 55 og; Wilkshire 67; Matthews 83	1,945
22	div2	**Brighton**	A	W	4-1	Wilkshire 26; Miller 31; Brown, A 45; Hill 85	6,305
23	div2	**Barnsley**	H	W	2-1	Miller 38,90	10,031
24	div2	**Blackpool**	A	L	0-1		5,989
25	facr2	**Barnsley**	H	D	0-0		6,741
26	div2	**Rushden & D**	A	D	1-1	Miller 71	4,340
27	facr2r	**Barnsley**	A	L	1-2	Roberts 65	5,434
28	div2	**Stockport**	H	W	1-0	Peacock 69	10,478
29	div2	**Brentford**	A	W	2-1	Lita 77,82	5,912
30	div2	**Bournemouth**	H	W	2-0	Peacock 40; Brown, A 56	13,807
31	div2	**Notts County**	A	W	2-1	Peacock 11; Goodfellow 90	6,403
32	div2	**Chesterfield**	H	W	4-0	Doherty 44; Lita 84; Carey 86; Goodfellow 89	11,807
33	div2	**Hartlepool**	A	W	2-1	Peacock 54; Tinnion 76	5,375
34	div2	**Colchester**	H	W	1-0	Goodfellow 45	10,733
35	div2	**Brentford**	H	W	3-1	Miller 4; Hill 88; Lita 90	13,029
36	div2	**Peterborough**	A	W	1-0	Doherty 75	4,449
37	div2	**Grimsby**	A	W	2-1	Miller 10; Brown, A 88	5,272
38	div2	**Wrexham**	H	W	1-0	Wilkshire 3	13,871
39	div2	**Sheff Wed**	A	L	0-1		24,154
40	div2	**Wycombe**	H	D	1-1	Goodfellow 59	12,291
41	div2	**Stockport**	A	L	0-2		5,050
42	div2	**Rushden & D**	H	W	1-0	Lita 29	12,559
43	div2	**Oldham**	H	L	0-2		11,037
44	div2	**Tranmere**	A	L	0-1		6,712
45	div2	**Port Vale**	A	L	1-2	Peacock 90	6,724
46	div2	**QPR**	H	W	1-0	Roberts 40	19,041
47	div2	**Swindon**	A	D	1-1	Roberts 45	14,540
48	div2	**Plymouth**	H	W	1-0	Peacock 85	19,045
49	div2	**Luton**	A	L	2-3	Roberts 59; Coles 90	6,944
50	div2	**Brighton**	H	D	0-0		17,088
51	div2	**Barnsley**	A	W	1-0	Rougier 21	10,865
52	div2	**Blackpool**	H	W	2-1	Roberts 19,21	19,101
53	d2po1	**Hartlepool**	A	D	1-1	Rougier 5	7,211
54	d2po2	**Hartlepool**	H	W	2-1	Goodfellow 88; Roberts 90	18,434
55	d2pof	**Brighton**	H	L	0-1		65,167

MONTHLY POINTS TALLY

AUGUST	8	53%
SEPTEMBER	9	50%
OCTOBER	6	40%
NOVEMBER	7	58%
DECEMBER	10	83%
JANUARY	12	100%
FEBRUARY	12	80%
MARCH	4	22%
APRIL	8	53%
MAY	6	100%

KEY PLAYERS - GOALSCORERS

Lee Peacock

Goals in the League	14	**Player Strike Rate** Average number of minutes between League goals scored by player	249
Contribution to Attacking Power Average number of minutes between League team goals while on pitch	68	**Club Strike Rate** Average number of minutes between League goals scored by club	71

	PLAYER	LGE GOALS	GOALS ALL	POWER	STRIKE RATE
1	Lee Peacock	14	16	68	249 mins
2	Lee Miller	8	9	75	323 mins
3	Christian Roberts	6	8	82	387 mins
4	Aaron Brown	5	5	65	462 mins

KEY PLAYERS - MIDFIELDERS

Aaron Brown

Goals in the League	5	**Contribution to Attacking Power** Average number of minutes between League team goals while on pitch	66
Defensive Rating Average number of mins between League goals conceded while he was on the pitch	154	**Scoring Difference** Defensive Rating minus Contribution to Attacking Power	88

	PLAYER	LGE GOALS	GOALS ALL	DEF RATE	POWER	SCORE DIFF
1	Aaron Brown	5	5	154	66	88 mins
2	Tommy Doherty	2	2	126	66	60 mins
3	Brian Tinnion	2	2	109	75	34 mins
4	Luke Wilkshire	2	3	110	86	24 mins

KEY PLAYERS - DEFENDERS

Matthew Hill

Goals Conceded (GC) The number of League goals conceded while he was on the pitch	28	**Clean Sheets** In games when he played at least 70 minutes	15
Defensive Rating Ave number of mins between League goals conceded while on the pitch	122	**Club Defensive Rating** Average number of mins between League goals conceded by the club this season	112

	PLAYER	CON LGE	CON ALL	CLEAN SHEETS	DEF RATE
1	Matthew Hill	28	39	15	122 mins
2	Mick Bell	15	16	7	121 mins
3	Louis Carey	33	39	16	111 mins
4	Anthony Butler	30	39	15	111 mins

KEY GOALKEEPER

Steve Phillips

Goals Conceded in the League	37	**Counting Games** Games when he played at least 70 mins	46
Defensive Rating Ave number of mins between League goals conceded while on the pitch	112	**Clean Sheets** In games when he played at least 70 mins	17

LEAGUE GOALS

Lee Peacock

Minutes on the pitch	3491	**Goals in the League**	249
League average (mins between goals)	14		

	PLAYER	MINS	GOALS	AVE
1	Peacock	3491	14	249
2	Miller	2580	8	323
3	Roberts	2322	6	387
4	Lita	628	5	126
5	Brown, A	2308	5	462
6	Goodfellow	753	4	188
7	Matthews	173	2	87
8	Wilkshire	2739	2	1370
9	Coles	3967	2	1984
10	Hill	3418	2	1709
11	Doherty	2510	2	1255
12	Tinnion	3380	2	1690
	Other		4	
	TOTAL		58	

DISCIPLINARY RECORDS

	PLAYER	YELLOW	RED	AVE
1	Lita	3	0	209
2	Doherty	9	1	251
3	Roberts	8	0	290
4	Goodfellow	2	0	376
5	Coles	8	2	396
6	Burnell	3	0	411
7	Miller	4	1	516
8	Brown, A	3	0	769
9	Butler	4	0	828
10	Peacock	4	0	872
11	Carey	4	0	914
12	Tinnion	3	0	1126
13	Hill	3	0	1139
	Other	6	0	
	TOTAL	64	4	

TOP POINT EARNERS

	PLAYER	GAMES	AV PTS
1	Brown, A	25	2.16
2	Hill	35	2.03
3	Woodman	13	2.00
4	Peacock	38	1.95
5	Wilkshire	23	1.87
6	Doherty	27	1.85
7	Carey	40	1.80
8	Phillips	46	1.78
9	Miller	21	1.76
10	Roberts	20	1.75
	CLUB AVERAGE:		1.78

TEAM OF THE SEASON

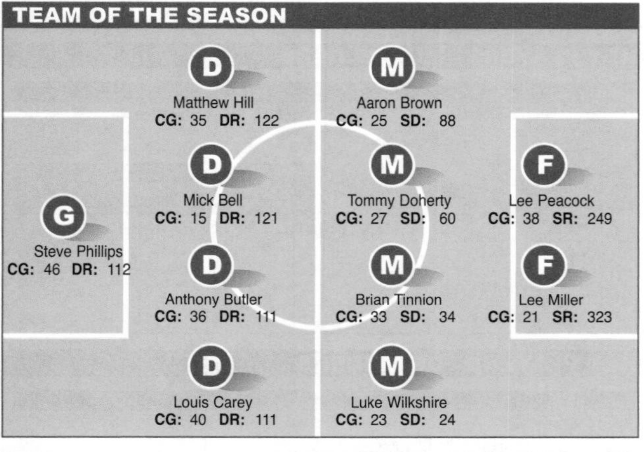

G
Steve Phillips
CG: 46 DR: 112
D
Matthew Hill
CG: 35 DR: 122
D
Mick Bell
CG: 15 DR: 121
D
Anthony Butler
CG: 36 DR: 111
D
Louis Carey
CG: 40 DR: 111
M
Aaron Brown
CG: 25 SD: 88
M
Tommy Doherty
CG: 27 SD: 60
M
Brian Tinnion
CG: 33 SD: 34
M
Luke Wilkshire
CG: 23 SD: 24
F
Lee Peacock
CG: 38 SR: 249
F
Lee Miller
CG: 21 SR: 323

LEAGUE APPEARANCES AND BOOKINGS

	AGE (on 01/07/04)	IN NAMED 16	APPEARANCES	COUNTING GAMES	MINUTES ON PITCH	Yellow	Red
Goalkeepers							
Steve Phillips	26	46	46	46	4140	0	0
Mike Stowell	39	29	0	0	0	0	0
Defenders							
Kevin Amankwaah	22	5	5	2	316	1	0
Mick Bell	32	32	27	15	1809	1	0
Anthony Butler	31	43	38	36	3315	4	0
Louis Carey	27	41	41	40	3656	4	0
Danny Coles	22	45	45	43	3967	8	2
Clayton Fortune	21	23	6	1	246	0	0
Matthew Hill	23	44	42	35	3418	3	0
Craig Woodman	21	31	21	13	1382	1	0
Midfielders							
Aaron Brown	24	28	28	25	2308	3	0
Joe Burnell	23	31	17	12	1233	3	0
Darren Caskey	29	1	0	0	0	0	0
Simon Clist	23	4	1	0	55	0	0
Tommy Doherty	25	34	33	27	2510	9	1
Marc Goodfellow	22	20	15	6	753	2	0
Robin Hulbert	24	4	0	0	0	0	0
Scott Murray	30	7	6	3	366	0	0
Anthony Rougier	32	8	6	3	441	2	0
Brian Tinnion	36	45	45	33	3380	3	0
Luke Wilkshire	22	39	37	23	2739	1	0
Forwards							
Marvin Brown	21	5	4	1	209	0	0
Leroy Lita	19	32	26	1	628	3	0
Lee Matthews	25	10	8	0	173	0	0
Lee Miller	21	46	42	21	2580	4	1
Lee Peacock	27	41	41	38	3491	4	0
Christian Roberts	24	42	38	20	2322	8	0

SQUAD APPEARANCES

Match	1 2 3 4 5	6 7 8 9 10	11 12 13 14 15	16 17 18 19 20	21 22 23 24 25	26 27 28 29 30	31 32 33 34 35	36 37 38 39 40	41 42 43 44 45	46 47 48 49 50	51 52 53 54 55
Match	1 2 3 4 5	6 7 8 9 10	11 12 13 14 15	16 17 18 19 20	21 22 23 24 25	26 27 28 29 30	31 32 33 34 35	36 37 38 39 40	41 42 43 44 45	46 47 48 49 50	51 52 53 54 55
Venue	H H A H A	H A A H H	H A A H H	A A H H H	A A H A H	A A H A H	A H A H H	A A H A H	A H H A A	H A H A H	A H A H H
Competition	L W L L L	L L L L L	W L L L L	L L L W L	F L L L F	L F L L L	L L L L L	L L L L L	L L L L L	L L L L L	L L O O O
Result	W D D D L	W D D W L	W D W W D	D L D L D	W W W L D	D L W W W	W W W W W	W W W L D	L W L L L	W D W L D	W W D W L

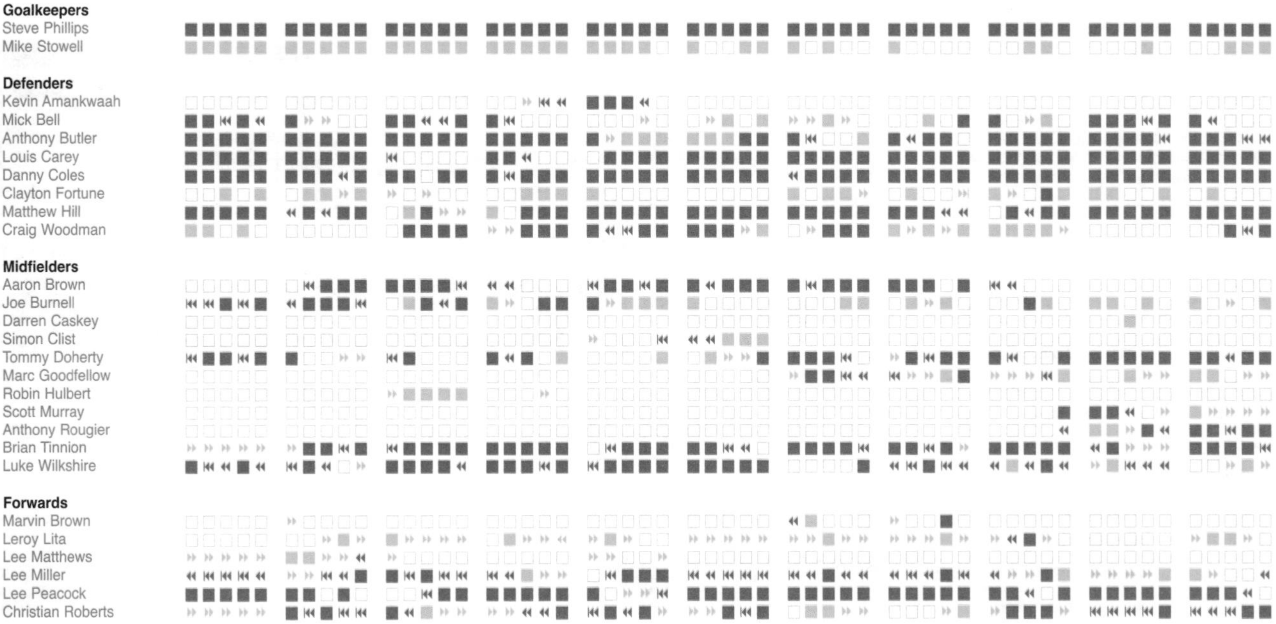

Goalkeepers
Steve Phillips
Mike Stowell

Defenders
Kevin Amankwaah
Mick Bell
Anthony Butler
Louis Carey
Danny Coles
Clayton Fortune
Matthew Hill
Craig Woodman

Midfielders
Aaron Brown
Joe Burnell
Darren Caskey
Simon Clist
Tommy Doherty
Marc Goodfellow
Robin Hulbert
Scott Murray
Anthony Rougier
Brian Tinnion
Luke Wilkshire

Forwards
Marvin Brown
Leroy Lita
Lee Matthews
Lee Miller
Lee Peacock
Christian Roberts

KEY: ■ On all match
■ On bench
⏮ Subbed or sent off (Counting game)
« Subbed or sent off (playing less than 70 minutes)
⏭ Subbed on from bench (Counting Game)
» Subbed on (playing less than 70 minutes)
» Subbed on and then subbed or sent off (Counting Game)
» Subbed on and then subbed or sent off (playing less than 70 minutes)
□ Not in 16

BRIGHTON & HOVE ALBION

Promoted via play-offs Final Position: **4th**

NICKNAME: THE SEAGULLS

KEY: ☐Won ☐Drawn ☐Lost

							Attendance
1	div2	Oldham	A	W	3-1	Henderson 23; Knight 44,62	6,522
2	ccR1	Bristol Rovers	A	W	1-0	McPhee 49	5,518
3	div2	QPR	H	W	2-1	Knight 12,68	6,536
4	div2	Barnsley	A	L	0-1		7,918
5	div2	Luton	H	W	2-0	Coyne 16 og; Oatway 85	6,604
6	div2	Plymouth	A	D	3-3	Connolly 14 og; Butters 36; Knight 73	9,289
7	div2	Swindon	H	D	2-2	Hart 15; Henderson 75 pen	6,534
8	div2	Colchester	A	L	0-1		4,169
9	div2	Chesterfield	H	W	1-0	Knight 33	6,054
10	div2	Sheff Wed	H	W	2-0	Knight 8; McPhee 84	6,602
11	ccR2	Middlesbrough	A	L	0-1		10,435
12	div2	Hartlepool	A	D	0-0		5,443
13	div2	Rushden & D	A	W	3-1	Butters 42; Knight 53; Rehman 77	4,634
14	div2	Blackpool	H	W	3-0	Coid 2 og; McPhee 38,73	6,483
15	div2	Grimsby	H	W	3-0	Rehman 53; Knight 55,90 pen	6,286
16	div2	Bournemouth	A	L	0-1		7,908
17	div2	Brentford	A	L	0-4		6,532
18	div2	Stockport	H	L	0-1		6,171
19	div2	Peterborough	A	D	2-2	Knight 26,69	5,929
20	facr1	Lincoln	A	L	1-3	McPhee 83	4,425
21	div2	Bristol City	H	L	1-4	Knight 45 pen	6,305
22	div2	Notts County	A	W	2-1	Knight 19,38	5,051
23	div2	Wrexham	H	W	2-0	Piercy 11; Carpenter 65	5,642
24	div2	Port Vale	H	D	1-1	Knight 16 pen	5,811
25	div2	Tranmere	A	L	0-1		7,616
26	div2	Wycombe	H	W	4-0	Carpenter 31; Piercy 42,63; McPhee 49	6,141
27	div2	Swindon	A	L	1-2	Knight 55	9,269
28	div2	Oldham	H	D	0-0		6,036
29	div2	QPR	A	L	1-2	Cullip 45	17,839
30	div2	Barnsley	H	W	1-0	Knight 32 pen	6,033
31	div2	Plymouth	H	W	2-1	Benjamin 12; Knight 34	6,379
32	div2	Wycombe	A	D	1-1	Benjamin 34	6,567
33	div2	Luton	A	L	0-2		6,846
34	div2	Grimsby	A	L	1-2	Benjamin 18	3,673
35	div2	Bournemouth	H	W	3-0	Harding 6; Benjamin 13; Knight 24 pen	6,441
36	div2	Stockport	A	D	1-1	Virgo 52	5,038
37	div2	Brentford	H	W	1-0	Carpenter 56	6,007
38	div2	Tranmere	H	W	3-0	Hart 7; Benjamin 18; Knight 31	5,994
39	div2	Port Vale	A	D	1-1	Knight 11 pen	5,646
40	div2	Chesterfield	A	W	2-0	Butters 49; Iwelumo 83	4,478
41	div2	Colchester	H	W	2-1	Iwelumo 30; Knight 87	6,156
42	div2	Sheff Wed	A	L	1-2	Carpenter 14	19,707
43	div2	Hartlepool	H	W	2-0	Knight 68; Iwelumo 90	6,257
44	div2	Blackpool	A	L	1-3	Piercy 83	6,194
45	div2	Rushden & D	H	D	0-0		6,320
46	div2	Peterborough	H	W	1-0	Knight 11 pen	6,285
47	div2	Bristol City	A	D	0-0		17,088
48	div2	Notts County	H	W	1-0	Wilson 74 og	6,618
49	div2	Wrexham	A	W	2-0	Iwelumo 8; Lawrence 50 og	4,542
50	d2po1	Swindon	A	W	1-0	Carpenter 72	14,034
51	d2po2	Swindon	H	W	4-3*	Virgo 120 (*on penalties)	6,876
52	d2pof	Bristol City	A	W	1-0	Knight 84 pen	65,167

MONTHLY POINTS TALLY

Month	Points	%
AUGUST	10	67%
SEPTEMBER	11	61%
OCTOBER	6	40%
NOVEMBER	7	58%
DECEMBER	4	33%
JANUARY	7	58%
FEBRUARY	5	33%
MARCH	13	72%
APRIL	8	53%
MAY	6	100%

KEY PLAYERS - GOALSCORERS

Leon Knight

Goals in the League	25	Player Strike Rate Average number of minutes between League goals scored by player	152
Contribution to Attacking Power Average number of minutes between League team goals while on pitch	65	Club Strike Rate Average number of minutes between League goals scored by club	65

	PLAYER	LGE GOALS	GOALS ALL	POWER	STRIKE RATE
1	Leon Knight	25	26	65	152 mins
2	Chris McPhee	4	6	59	387 mins
3	Richard Carpenter	4	5	62	881 mins
4	Guy Butters	3	3	65	1290 mins

KEY PLAYERS - MIDFIELDERS

Nathan Jones

Goals in the League	0	Contribution to Attacking Power Average number of minutes between League team goals while on pitch	62
Defensive Rating Average number of mins between League goals conceded while he was on the pitch	135	Scoring Difference Defensive Rating minus Contribution to Attacking Power	73

	PLAYER	LGE GOALS	GOALS ALL	DEF RATE	POWER	SCORE DIFF
1	Nathan Jones	0	0	135	62	73 mins
2	Charlie Oatway	1	1	110	67	43 mins
3	Gary Hart	2	2	92	66	26 mins
4	Richard Carpenter	4	5	88	63	25 mins

KEY PLAYERS - DEFENDERS

Adam Virgo

Goals Conceded (GC) The number of League goals conceded while he was on the pitch	14	Clean Sheets In games when he played at least 70 minutes	10
Defensive Rating Ave number of mins between League goals conceded while on the pitch	127	Club Defensive Rating Average number of mins between League goals conceded by the club this season	96

	PLAYER	CON LGE	CON ALL	CLEAN SHEETS	DEF RATE
1	Adam Virgo	14	16	10	127 mins
2	Daniel Harding	13	16	10	123 mins
3	Guy Butters	40	46	20	97 mins
4	Danny Cullip	35	41	17	96 mins

KEY GOALKEEPER

Ben Roberts

Goals Conceded in the League	28	Counting Games Games when he played at least 70 mins	32
Defensive Rating Ave number of mins between League goals conceded while on the pitch	100	Clean Sheets In games when he played at least 70 mins	14

LEAGUE GOALS

Leon Knight

Minutes on the pitch	3804	Goals in the League	152
League average (mins between goals)	25		

	PLAYER	MINS	GOALS	AVE
1	Knight	3804	25	152
2	Benjamin	849	5	170
3	Iwelumo	849	4	212
4	Carpenter	3522	4	881
5	Piercy	878	4	220
6	McPhee	1546	4	387
7	Butters	3870	3	1290
8	Henderson	842	2	421
9	Hart	3120	2	1560
10	Rehman	776	2	388
11	Oatway	2537	1	2537
12	Harding	1600	1	1600
	Other		7	
	TOTAL		64	

DISCIPLINARY RECORDS

	PLAYER	YELLOW	RED	AVE
1	Piercy	6	1	125
2	Yeates	3	0	256
3	Rehman	3	0	258
4	Henderson	3	0	280
5	El-Abd	2	0	334
6	Virgo	5	0	355
7	Knight	9	1	380
8	Watson	3	0	389
9	Hart	8	0	390
10	Carpenter	7	0	503
11	Harding	3	0	533
12	Cullip	6	0	557
13	Mayo	5	0	565
	Other	15	1	
	TOTAL	78	3	

TOP POINT EARNERS

	PLAYER	GAMES	AV PTS
1	Jones, N	28	2.07
2	Harding	17	1.88
3	Virgo	19	1.84
4	Roberts	30	1.77
5	Oatway	27	1.74
6	Hinshelwood	16	1.69
7	Knight	42	1.67
8	Cullip	37	1.65
9	Butters	43	1.65
10	Carpenter	37	1.59
	CLUB AVERAGE:		**1.67**

LEAGUE APPEARANCES AND BOOKINGS

	AGE (on 01/07/04)	IN NAMED 16	APPEARANCES	COUNTING GAMES	MINUTES ON PITCH	Yellow	Red
Goalkeepers							
Ross Flitney	20	16	3	3	270	0	0
Stuart Jones	26	10	3	2	225	0	0
John Keeley	42	9	0	0	0	0	0
Michel Kuipers	30	24	10	9	855	0	0
Ben Roberts	29	33	32	30	2790	3	0
Defenders							
Dean Blackwell	34	1	1	1	90	0	0
Nicky Bridle	20	1	1	1	90	0	0
Guy Butters	34	43	43	43	3870	2	0
Danny Cullip	27	39	39	37	3347	6	0
Adam El-Abd	19	26	11	6	668	2	0
Daniel Harding	20	39	23	17	1600	3	0
Adam Hinshelwood	20	20	17	16	1442	2	0
Kerry Mayo	26	40	33	31	2825	5	0
Robbie Pethick	33	22	14	7	680	0	0
Adam Virgo	21	23	22	19	1775	5	0
Paul Watson	29	17	15	13	1167	3	0
Midfielders							
Dan Beck	20	2	2	1	101	0	0
Richard Carpenter	31	43	41	37	3522	7	0
Gary Hart	27	43	42	32	3120	8	0
Nathan Jones	31	35	35	28	2832	2	1
David Lee	24	8	4	1	158	0	0
Charlie Oatway	30	33	31	27	2537	4	0
John Piercy	24	30	23	5	878	6	1
Zeshan Rehman	20	14	11	7	776	3	0
Paul Reid	25	7	5	4	366	0	0
Simon Rodger	32	7	7	6	581	1	0
Forwards							
Trevor Benjamin	25	10	10	9	849	0	0
Darius Henderson	22	11	10	8	842	3	0
Chris Iwelumo	25	10	10	9	849	0	0
Leon Knight	21	44	44	42	3804	9	1
Chris McPhee	21	40	28	13	1546	1	0
Jake Robinson	17	18	9	1	222	0	0
Mark Yeates	2005	9	9	9	769	3	0

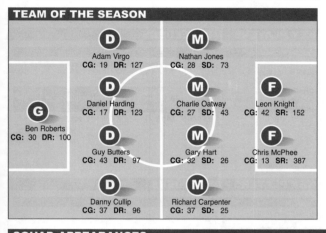

TEAM OF THE SEASON

G — Ben Roberts, CG: 30 DR: 100

D — Adam Virgo, CG: 19 DR: 127

D — Daniel Harding, CG: 17 DR: 123

D — Guy Butters, CG: 43 DR: 97

D — Danny Cullip, CG: 37 DR: 96

M — Nathan Jones, CG: 28 SD: 73

M — Charlie Oatway, CG: 27 SD: 43

M — Gary Hart, CG: 32 SD: 26

M — Richard Carpenter, CG: 37 SD: 25

F — Leon Knight, CG: 42 SR: 152

F — Chris McPhee, CG: 13 SR: 387

SQUAD APPEARANCES

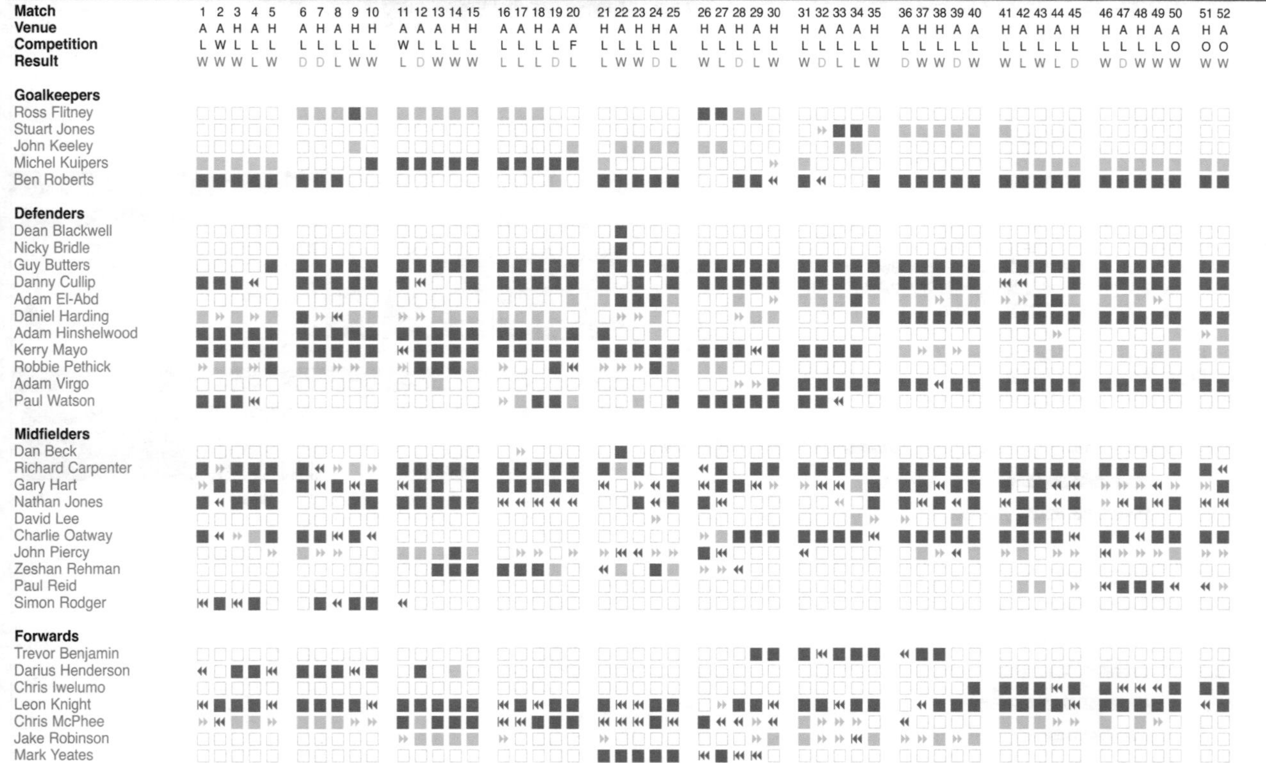

Match 1 2 3 4 5 6 7 8 9 10 11 12 13 14 15 16 17 18 19 20 21 22 23 24 25 26 27 28 29 30 31 32 33 34 35 36 37 38 39 40 41 42 43 44 45 46 47 48 49 50 51 52
Venue A A H A H A H A H H A A A H H A A H A A H A H H A H A H A H H A A A H A H H A A H A H A H H A H A A H A
Competition L W L L L L L L L L W L L L L L L L L F L L L L L L L L L L L L L L L L L L L L L L L L L L L L L O O O
Result W W W L W D D L W W L D W W W L L L D L L W W D L W L D L W W D L L W D W W D W W L W L D W D W W W W W
Goalkeepers
Ross Flitney
Stuart Jones
John Keeley
Michel Kuipers
Ben Roberts
Defenders
Dean Blackwell
Nicky Bridle
Guy Butters
Danny Cullip
Adam El-Abd
Daniel Harding
Adam Hinshelwood
Kerry Mayo
Robbie Pethick
Adam Virgo
Paul Watson
Midfielders
Dan Beck
Richard Carpenter
Gary Hart
Nathan Jones
David Lee
Charlie Oatway
John Piercy
Zeshan Rehman
Paul Reid
Simon Rodger
Forwards
Trevor Benjamin
Darius Henderson
Chris Iwelumo
Leon Knight
Chris McPhee
Jake Robinson
Mark Yeates

KEY: ■ On all match ■ On bench
⏮ Subbed or sent off (Counting game) « Subbed or sent off (playing less than 70 minutes)
⏭ Subbed on from bench (Counting Game) » Subbed on (playing less than 70 minutes)
Subbed on and then subbed or sent off (Counting Game) Subbed on and then subbed or sent off (playing less than 70 minutes)
□ Not in 16

SWINDON TOWN

Final Position: **5th**

NICKNAME: THE ROBINS

KEY: ☐Won ☐Drawn ☐Lost

							Attendance
1	div2	Sheff Wed	H	L	2-3	Miglioranzi 31; Igoe 57	10,573
2	ccR1	Southend	A	W	3-2	Parkin 34,48; Mooney 73	3,385
3	div2	Colchester	A	W	1-0	Mooney 87	3,339
4	div2	Notts County	H	W	4-0	Hewlett 8; Mooney 10; Parkin 47; Igoe 50	5,758
5	div2	Bournemouth	A	D	2-2	Mooney 18; Robinson 35	6,606
6	div2	Blackpool	H	D	2-2	Mooney 8,30	6,219
7	div2	Brighton	A	D	2-2	Parkin 14,67	6,534
8	div2	Wrexham	H	W	1-0	Gurney 79	6,160
9	div2	Grimsby	A	W	2-1	Gurney 53; Mooney 65	3,535
10	div2	Barnsley	A	D	1-1	Mooney 20	9,006
11	ccR2	Leeds	A	L	3-4*	Gurney 44; Parkin 74 (*on penalties)	29,211
12	div2	Peterborough	H	W	2-0	Parkin 84; Milner 90	6,767
13	div2	Luton	H	D	2-2	Milner 8; Howard 89	7,573
14	div2	Bristol City	A	L	1-2	Mooney 34	14,294
15	div2	Stockport	H	L	1-2	Mooney 45	7,060
16	div2	Chesterfield	A	L	0-3		3,506
17	div2	Tranmere	A	L	0-1		6,675
18	div2	Port Vale	H	D	0-0		5,313
19	div2	Wycombe	H	W	2-0	Burton 11; Miglioranzi 67	5,681
20	facr1	Wycombe	A	L	1-4	Gurney 71 pen	4,738
21	div2	Oldham	A	W	1-0	Parkin 61	5,282
22	div2	QPR	H	D	1-1	Parkin 40	10,021
23	div2	Hartlepool	A	L	0-2		4,493
24	div2	Plymouth	H	L	2-3	Fallon 80; Parkin 90	9,374
25	div2	Brentford	A	W	2-0	Howard 66; Parkin 82	5,077
26	div2	Rushden & D	A	L	0-2		4,845
27	div2	Brighton	H	W	2-1	Parkin 45; Miglioranzi 66	9,269
28	div2	Bournemouth	H	W	2-1	Mooney 15,80	7,158
29	div2	Sheff Wed	A	D	1-1	Mooney 52	22,751
30	div2	Colchester	H	W	2-0	Parkin 15; Mooney 46	6,014
31	div2	Notts County	A	W	2-1	Heywood 35; Miglioranzi 86	6,663
32	div2	Blackpool	A	D	2-2	Parkin 48; Gurney 83	6,463
33	div2	Rushden & D	H	W	4-2	Mooney 9; Gurney 17 pen; Duke 76; Hunter 90 og	7,023
34	div2	Stockport	A	W	4-2	Mooney 4,90; Howard 16; Nicholas 18	4,833
35	div2	Chesterfield	H	W	2-0	O'Hanlon 33; Parkin 86	6,814
36	div2	Tranmere	H	W	2-0	Parkin 31,82	6,928
37	div2	Brentford	H	W	2-1	Gurney 14; Igoe 82	7,649
38	div2	Plymouth	A	L	1-2	Mooney 90	16,080
39	div2	Grimsby	H	W	2-0	Mooney 34,45	6,954
40	div2	Wrexham	A	L	2-3	Igoe 49; Gurney 77	3,384
41	div2	Barnsley	H	D	1-1	Parkin 8	7,305
42	div2	Port Vale	A	D	3-3	Parkin 63; Hewlett 68; Fallon 83	5,702
43	div2	Peterborough	A	L	2-4	Heywood 4; Parkin 63	4,745
44	div2	Bristol City	H	D	1-1	Fallon 74	14,540
45	div2	Luton	A	W	3-0	Fallon 3,21; Hewlett 44	7,008
46	div2	Wycombe	A	W	3-0	Miglioranzi 7; Parkin 52; Gurney 75 pen	5,769
47	div2	Oldham	H	L	1-2	Fallon 79	8,506
48	div2	QPR	A	L	0-1		18,396
49	div2	Hartlepool	H	D	1-1	Igoe 7	11,627
50	d2po1	Brighton	H	L	0-1		14,034
51	d2po2	Brighton	A	L	3-4*	Parkin 81; Fallon 97 (*on penalties)	6,876

MONTHLY POINTS TALLY

AUGUST	8	53%
SEPTEMBER	11	73%
OCTOBER	2	11%
NOVEMBER	7	58%
DECEMBER	6	50%
JANUARY	11	73%
FEBRUARY	9	100%
MARCH	11	52%
APRIL	7	47%
MAY	1	17%

KEY PLAYERS - GOALSCORERS

Sam Parkin

Goals in the League	18	Player Strike Rate Average number of minutes between League goals scored by player	190
Contribution to Attacking Power Average number of minutes between League team goals while on pitch	48	Club Strike Rate Average number of minutes between League goals scored by club	54

	PLAYER	LGE GOALS	GOALS ALL	POWER	STRIKE RATE
1	Sam Parkin	18	22	48	190 mins
2	Tommy Mooney	19	20	53	195 mins
3	Andrew Gurney	7	9	53	538 mins
4	Sam Igoe	5	5	51	545 mins

KEY PLAYERS - MIDFIELDERS

Stefani Miglioranzi

Goals in the League	4	Contribution to Attacking Power Average number of minutes between League team goals while on pitch	50
Defensive Rating Average number of mins between League goals conceded while he was on the pitch	80	Scoring Difference Defensive Rating minus Contribution to Attacking Power	30

	PLAYER	LGE GOALS	GOALS ALL	DEF RATE	POWER	SCORE DIFF
1	Stefani Miglioranzi	4	4	80	50	30 mins
2	Matt Hewlett	3	3	78	55	23 mins
3	Sam Igoe	5	5	72	51	21 mins
4	Brian Howard	3	3	78	57	21 mins

KEY PLAYERS - DEFENDERS

Jerel Ifil

Goals Conceded (GC) The number of League goals conceded while he was on the pitch	17	Clean Sheets In games when he played at least 70 minutes	5
Defensive Rating Ave number of mins between League goals conceded while on the pitch	85	Club Defensive Rating Average number of mins between League goals conceded by the club this season	71

	PLAYER	CON LGE	CON ALL	CLEAN SHEETS	DEF RATE
1	Jerel Ifil	17	17	5	85 mins
2	Andrew Nicholas	35	41	9	71 mins
3	Matthew Heywood	50	60	12	68 mins
4	Andrew Gurney	55	63	12	68 mins

KEY GOALKEEPER

Rhys Evans

Goals Conceded in the League	48	Counting Games Games when he played at least 70 mins	41
Defensive Rating Ave number of mins between League goals conceded while on the pitch	75	Clean Sheets In games when he played at least 70 mins	12

LEAGUE GOALS

Tommy Mooney

Minutes on the pitch	3707	Goals in the League	195
League average (mins between goals)	19		

	PLAYER	MINS	GOALS	AVE
1	Mooney	3707	19	195
2	Parkin	3419	18	190
3	Gurney	3765	7	538
4	Fallon	775	6	129
5	Igoe	2724	5	545
6	Miglioranzi	2814	4	704
7	Howard	1954	3	651
8	Hewlett	3807	3	1269
9	Heywood	3408	2	1704
10	Milner	516	2	258
11	Nicholas	2495	1	2495
12	O'Hanlon	1563	1	1563
	Other		5	
	TOTAL		76	

DISCIPLINARY RECORDS

	PLAYER	YELLOW	RED	AVE
1	Fallon	3	1	193
2	Ifil	6	0	240
3	Milner	2	0	258
4	Gurney	12	1	289
5	Howard	4	1	390
6	Reeves	4	0	417
7	Igoe	5	1	454
8	Duke	5	0	616
9	Hewlett	6	0	634
10	Mooney	5	0	741
11	O'Hanlon	2	0	781
12	Robinson	2	0	822
13	Miglioranzi	2	1	938
	Other	11	1	
	TOTAL	69	6	

TOP POINT EARNERS

	PLAYER	GAMES	AV PTS
1	Nicholas	26	1.85
2	Ifil	16	1.81
3	Miglioranzi	30	1.80
4	Parkin	37	1.76
5	Howard	19	1.74
6	O'Hanlon	17	1.71
7	Hewlett	42	1.67
8	Evans	40	1.65
9	Mooney	40	1.63
10	Igoe	29	1.62
	CLUB AVERAGE:		**1.59**

TEAM OF THE SEASON

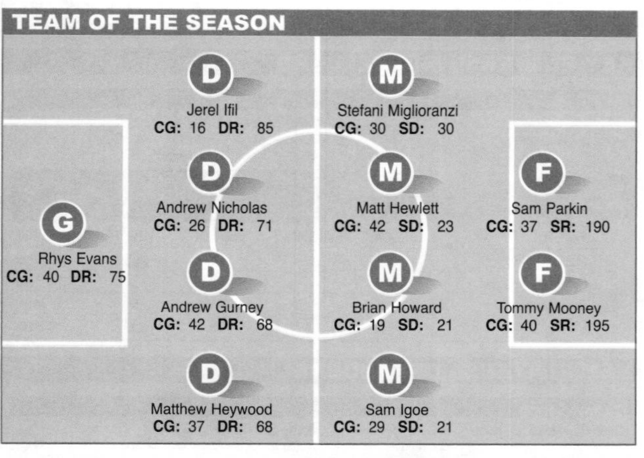

D
Jerel Ifil
CG: 16 DR: 85
M
Stefani Miglioranzi
CG: 30 SD: 30
D
Andrew Nicholas
CG: 26 DR: 71
M
Matt Hewlett
CG: 42 SD: 23
F
Sam Parkin
CG: 37 SR: 190
G
Rhys Evans
CG: 40 DR: 75
D
Andrew Gurney
CG: 42 DR: 68
M
Brian Howard
CG: 19 SD: 21
F
Tommy Mooney
CG: 40 SR: 195
D
Matthew Heywood
CG: 37 DR: 68
M
Sam Igoe
CG: 29 SD: 21

LEAGUE APPEARANCES AND BOOKINGS

	AGE (on 01/07/04)	IN NAMED 16	APPEARANCES	COUNTING GAMES	MINUTES ON PITCH	Yellow	Red
Goalkeepers							
Rhys Evans	22	46	41	40	3622	3	0
Bart Griemink	32	46	6	5	518	0	0
Steve Smith	20	1	0	0	0	0	0
Defenders							
Luke Garrard	19	4	1	0	14	0	0
Andrew Gurney	30	42	42	42	3765	12	1
Matthew Heywood	24	40	40	37	3408	2	1
Eddie Howe	26	1	0	0	0	0	0
Jerel Ifil	22	16	16	16	1440	6	0
Ben Martin	21	4	0	0	0	0	0
Andrew Nicholas	20	33	31	26	2495	2	0
Sean O'Hanlon	21	19	19	17	1563	2	0
Alan Reeves	36	46	27	16	1669	4	0
Adrian Viveash	34	20	15	12	1177	1	0
Midfielders							
David Duke	25	45	42	31	3080	5	0
Ian Herring	20	4	1	1	90	0	0
Matt Hewlett	28	45	43	42	3807	6	0
Brian Howard	21	41	34	19	1954	4	1
Sam Igoe	28	35	35	29	2724	5	1
Junior Lewis	30	5	5	5	446	1	0
Stefani Miglioranzi	26	35	35	30	2814	2	1
James Milner	18	6	6	6	516	2	0
Michael Pook	18	6	0	0	0	0	0
Steve Robinson	28	22	22	19	1644	2	0
Sebastien Ruster	21	7	2	0	71	0	0
John Stevenson	21	22	5	1	133	0	0
Forwards							
Deon Burton	27	4	4	3	315	0	0
Rory Fallon	22	25	19	5	775	3	1
Tommy Mooney	32	46	45	40	3707	5	0
Sam Parkin	23	40	40	37	3419	2	0
Grant Smith	24	29	7	0	149	0	0

SQUAD APPEARANCES

Match	1	2	3	4	5	6	7	8	9	10	11	12	13	14	15	16	17	18	19	20	21	22	23	24	25	26	27	28	29	30	31	32	33	34	35	36	37	38	39	40	41	42	43	44	45	46	47	48	49	50	51
Venue	H	A	A	H	A	H	A	H	A	A	A	H	H	A	H	A	A	H	H	A	A	H	A	H	A	A	H	H	A	H	A	A	H	A	H	H	H	A	H	A	H	A	A	H	A	A	H	A	H	H	A
Competition	L	W	L	L	L	L	L	L	L	L	W	L	L	L	L	L	L	L	L	F	L	L	L	L	L	L	L	L	L	L	L	L	L	L	L	L	L	L	L	L	L	L	L	L	L	L	L	L	L	O	O
Result	L	W	W	W	D	D	D	W	W	D	L	W	D	L	L	L	L	D	W	L	W	D	L	L	W	L	W	W	D	W	W	D	W	W	W	W	W	L	W	L	D	D	L	D	W	W	L	L	D	L	L

Goalkeepers
Rhys Evans
Bart Griemink
Steve Smith

Defenders
Luke Garrard
Andrew Gurney
Matthew Heywood
Eddie Howe
Jerel Ifil
Ben Martin
Andrew Nicholas
Sean O'Hanlon
Alan Reeves
Adrian Viveash

Midfielders
David Duke
Ian Herring
Matt Hewlett
Brian Howard
Sam Igoe
Junior Lewis
Stefani Miglioranzi
James Milner
Michael Pook
Steve Robinson
Sebastien Ruster
John Stevenson

Forwards
Deon Burton
Rory Fallon
Tommy Mooney
Sam Parkin
Grant Smith

KEY: On all match · On bench · Subbed or sent off (Counting game) · Subbed or sent off (playing less than 70 minutes) · Subbed on from bench (Counting Game) · Subbed on (playing less than 70 minutes) · Subbed on and then subbed or sent off (Counting Game) · Subbed on and then subbed or sent off (playing less than 70 minutes) · Not in 16

HARTLEPOOL

Final Position: **6th**

NICKNAME: THE POOL

KEY: ☐Won ☐Drawn ☐Lost

		Opponent			Score	Scorers	Attendance
1	div2	Peterborough	A	W	4-3	Strachan 38; Robinson 55; Robson 70; Nelson 85	5,965
2	ccR1	Sheff Wed	A	W	5-4*	Robson 56 pen; Istead 104 (*on penalties)	13,410
3	div2	Tranmere	H	D	0-0		5,357
4	div2	Bristol City	A	D	1-1	Gabbiadini 73	10,730
5	div2	Port Vale	H	W	2-0	Robinson 2; Gabbiadini 82 pen	5,314
6	div2	Luton	A	L	2-3	Clarke 40; Robinson 71 pen	5,515
7	div2	Oldham	H	D	0-0		5,728
8	div2	Grimsby	H	W	8-1	Groves 19 og; Robinson 20 pen,56,80; Strachan 28; Humphreys 31; Gabbiadini 60; Williams, E 66	5,528
9	div2	Stockport	A	W	2-1	Williams, E 8; Gabbiadini 54	4,021
10	div2	Brentford	A	L	1-2	Strachan 42	4,501
11	ccR2	West Brom	H	L	1-2	Robinson 45 pen	5,265
12	div2	Brighton	H	D	0-0		5,443
13	div2	Wrexham	H	W	2-0	Clarke 23,37	4,677
14	div2	Bournemouth	A	D	2-2	Tinkler 10; Strachan 90	6,342
15	div2	Sheff Wed	H	D	1-1	Gabbiadini 84	7,448
16	div2	Blackpool	A	L	0-4		6,871
17	div2	Chesterfield	A	W	2-1	Evatt 26 og; Robinson, P 76	3,411
18	div2	Wycombe	H	D	1-1	Barron 40	5,153
19	div2	Notts County	A	L	0-1		5,011
20	facr1	Whitby	H	W	4-0	Gabbiadini 25,30; Humphreys 51; Brackstone 68	5,294
21	div2	Rushden & D	H	W	2-1	Strachan 41 pen; Wilkinson 75	4,944
22	div2	Plymouth	A	L	0-2		9,000
23	div2	Swindon	H	W	2-0	Strachan 18 pen; Wilkinson 86	4,493
24	facr2	Burton	A	W	1-0	Porter 70	3,132
25	div2	QPR	A	L	1-4	Williams, A 72	15,003
26	div2	Colchester	H	D	0-0		4,135
27	div2	Barnsley	H	L	1-2	Williams, E 21	6,520
28	div2	Oldham	A	W	2-0	Williams, E 45; Porter 79	6,243
29	facr3	Sunderland	A	L	0-1		40,816
30	div2	Peterborough	H	W	1-0	Williams, E 37	4,855
31	div2	Tranmere	A	D	0-0		7,418
32	div2	Bristol City	H	L	1-2	Tinkler 70	5,375
33	div2	Port Vale	A	W	5-2	Shuker 6; Humphreys 31; Nelson 69; Williams, E 74; Clarke 83	4,845
34	div2	Barnsley	A	D	2-2	Williams, E 27; Tinkler 67	9,220
35	div2	Sheff Wed	A	L	0-1		20,732
36	div2	Blackpool	H	D	1-1	Robertson 51	5,497
37	div2	Wycombe	A	W	4-3	Williams, E 4,46; Robertson 10; Tinkler 39 pen	4,731
38	div2	Chesterfield	H	W	2-0	Williams, E 52; Tinkler 71	4,736
39	div2	Colchester	A	W	2-1	Nelson 17; Istead 78	3,348
40	div2	QPR	H	L	1-4	Porter 88	6,519
41	div2	Stockport	H	D	2-2	Williams, E 10; Porter 58	4,674
42	div2	Grimsby	A	W	2-0	Boyd 29,87	4,303
43	div2	Brentford	H	L	1-2	Boyd 38	5,206
44	div2	Brighton	A	L	0-2		6,257
45	div2	Luton	H	W	4-3	Sweeney 14; Boyd 53,90 pen; Robertson 55	4,434
46	div2	Bournemouth	H	W	2-1	Boyd 38,69	5,544
47	div2	Wrexham	A	W	2-1	Clarke 41; Danns 63	3,786
48	div2	Notts County	H	W	4-0	Humphreys 42; Boyd 55,56; Robertson 69	5,629
49	div2	Rushden & D	A	W	2-0	Williams, E 56; Boyd 79	4,568
50	div2	Plymouth	H	L	1-3	Boyd 11	7,437
51	div2	Swindon	A	D	1-1	Boyd 71	11,627
52	d2po1	Bristol City	H	D	1-1	Porter 74	7,211
53	d2po2	Bristol City	A	L	1-2	Sweeney 63	18,434

MONTHLY POINTS TALLY

Month	Points	%
AUGUST	8	53%
SEPTEMBER	11	61%
OCTOBER	6	40%
NOVEMBER	6	50%
DECEMBER	4	33%
JANUARY	7	58%
FEBRUARY	5	42%
MARCH	10	56%
APRIL	15	83%
MAY	1	17%

KEY PLAYERS - GOALSCORERS

Eifion Williams

Goals in the League	12	Player Strike Rate Average number of minutes between League goals scored by player	282
Contribution to Attacking Power Average number of minutes between League team goals while on pitch	52	Club Strike Rate Average number of minutes between League goals scored by club	54

	PLAYER	LGE GOALS	GOALS ALL	POWER	STRIKE RATE
1	Eifion Williams	12	12	52	282 mins
2	Darrell Clarke	5	5	54	379 mins
3	Hugh Robertson	4	4	48	401 mins
4	Gavin Strachan	6	6	59	496 mins

KEY PLAYERS - MIDFIELDERS

Mark Tinkler

Goals in the League	5	Contribution to Attacking Power Average number of minutes between League team goals while on pitch	56
Defensive Rating Average number of mins between League goals conceded while he was on the pitch	71	Scoring Difference Defensive Rating minus Contribution to Attacking Power	15

	PLAYER	LGE GOALS	GOALS ALL	DEF RATE	POWER	SCORE DIFF
1	Mark Tinkler	5	5	71	56	15 mins
2	Richie Humphreys	3	4	68	54	14 mins
3	Gavin Strachan	6	6	71	60	11 mins
4	Chris Shuker	1	1	69	69	0 mins

KEY PLAYERS - DEFENDERS

Michael Barron

Goals Conceded (GC) The number of League goals conceded while he was on the pitch	37	Clean Sheets In games when he played at least 70 minutes	11
Defensive Rating Ave number of mins between League goals conceded while on the pitch	76	Club Defensive Rating Average number of mins between League goals conceded by the club this season	68

	PLAYER	CON LGE	CON ALL	CLEAN SHEETS	DEF RATE
1	Michael Barron	37	43	11	76 mins
2	Micheal Nelson	47	55	12	72 mins
3	Matty Robson	23	26	5	69 mins
4	Chris Westwood	60	65	14	67 mins

KEY GOALKEEPER

Jim Provett

Goals Conceded in the League	58	Counting Games Games when he played at least 70 mins	45
Defensive Rating Ave number of mins between League goals conceded while on the pitch	70	Clean Sheets In games when he played at least 70 mins	14

LEAGUE GOALS

Adam Boyd

Minutes on the pitch	1080	Goals in the League	90
League average (mins between goals)	12		

	PLAYER	MINS	GOALS	AVE
1	Boyd	1080	12	90
2	Williams, E	3381	12	282
3	Strachan	2978	6	496
4	Robinson, M	911	6	152
5	Gabbiadini	926	5	185
6	Tinkler	3755	5	751
7	Clarke	1895	5	379
8	Robertson	1605	4	401
9	Nelson	3399	3	1133
10	Humphreys	4126	3	1375
11	Porter	1639	3	546
12	Wilkinson	177	2	89
	Other		10	
	TOTAL		76	

DISCIPLINARY RECORDS

	PLAYER	YELLOW	RED	AVE
1	Gabbiadini	4	0	231
2	Walker	2	0	235
3	Nelson	7	0	485
4	Barron	5	0	565
5	Istead	1	0	592
6	Tinkler	6	0	625
7	Clarke	3	0	631
8	Craddock	1	0	805
9	Robinson, M	1	0	911
10	Robinson, P	1	0	958
11	Strachan	3	0	992
12	Shuker	1	0	1173
13	Westwood	3	0	1337
	Other	14	0	
	TOTAL	52	0	

TOP POINT EARNERS

	PLAYER	GAMES	AV PTS
1	Clarke	17	1.88
2	Robertson	18	1.72
3	Tinkler	40	1.68
4	Westwood	44	1.64
5	Robson	14	1.64
6	Porter	15	1.60
7	Humphreys	46	1.59
8	Provett	45	1.56
9	Williams, E	35	1.54
10	Barron	31	1.52
	CLUB AVERAGE:		1,59

LEAGUE APPEARANCES AND BOOKINGS

	AGE (on 01/07/04)	IN NAMED 16	APPEARANCES	COUNTING GAMES	MINUTES ON PITCH	Yellow	Red
Goalkeepers							
Jim Provett	21	46	45	45	4050	0	0
Anthony Williams	26	14	1	1	90	0	0
Defenders							
Paul Arnison	26	6	4	1	153	1	0
Michael Barron	29	36	32	31	2829	5	0
John Brackstone	19	12	6	3	424	2	0
Darrell Clarke	26	46	33	17	1895	3	0
Darren Craddock	19	15	10	9	805	1	0
Andrew Jordan	24	10	5	4	354	2	0
Micheal Nelson	22	40	40	37	3399	7	0
Hugh Robertson	29	18	18	18	1605	1	0
Mark Robinson	22	13	13	9	911	1	0
Matty Robson	19	26	23	14	1580	1	0
Scott Walker	29	13	7	5	471	2	0
Chris Westwood	27	45	45	44	4013	3	0
Neil Wilkinson	18	5	4	1	177	0	0
Midfielders							
Steven Carson	23	4	3	0	120	0	0
Neil Danns	21	12	9	7	695	0	0
Richie Humphreys	26	46	46	46	4126	3	0
Steven Istead	18	33	30	1	592	1	0
Ryan McCann	22	6	3	0	44	1	0
Chris Shuker	22	14	14	12	1173	1	0
Gavin Strachan	25	38	36	31	2978	3	0
Anthony Sweeney	20	14	11	7	747	0	0
Mark Tinkler	29	44	44	40	3755	6	0
Forwards							
Adam Boyd	22	17	17	11	1080	0	0
Demitrios Donstantopoulos	25	32	0	0	0	0	0
Jermaine Easter	22	3	3	0	72	0	0
David Foley	16	1	1	0	9	0	0
Marco Gabbiadini	36	15	15	8	926	4	0
Kevin Henderson	30	4	3	1	131	0	0
Joel Porter	25	27	26	15	1639	1	0
Marcus Richardson	26	4	3	3	246	0	0
Paul Robinson	25	28	22	3	958	1	0
Eifion Williams	28	41	41	35	3381	2	0

TEAM OF THE SEASON

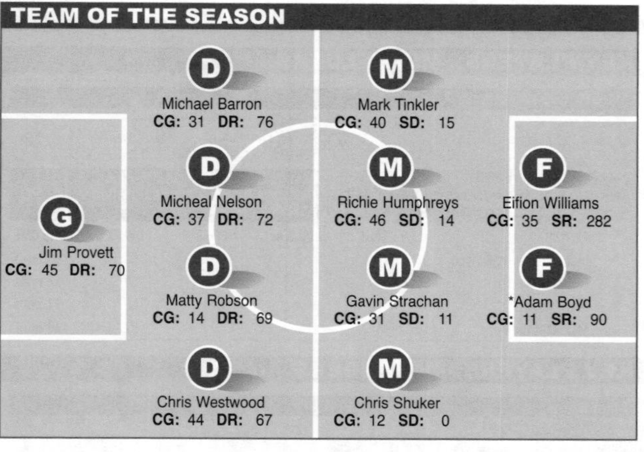

D
Michael Barron
CG: 31 DR: 76
M
Mark Tinkler
CG: 40 SD: 15
D
Micheal Nelson
CG: 37 DR: 72
M
Richie Humphreys
CG: 46 SD: 14
F
Eifion Williams
CG: 35 SR: 282
G
Jim Provett
CG: 45 DR: 70
D
Matty Robson
CG: 14 DR: 69
M
Gavin Strachan
CG: 31 SD: 11
F
*Adam Boyd
CG: 11 SR: 90
D
Chris Westwood
CG: 44 DR: 67
M
Chris Shuker
CG: 12 SD: 0

SQUAD APPEARANCES

Match	1	2	3	4	5	6	7	8	9	10	11	12	13	14	15	16	17	18	19	20	21	22	23	24	25	26	27	28	29	30	31	32	33	34	35	36	37	38	39	40	41	42	43	44	45	46	47	48	49	50	51	52	53
Venue	A	A	H	A	H	A	H	H	A	A	H	H	H	A	H	A	A	H	A	H	H	A	H	A	A	H	H	A	A	H	A	H	A	A	A	H	A	H	A	H	H	A	H	A	H	H	A	H	A	H	A	H	A
Competition	L	W	L	L	L	L	L	L	L	L	W	L	L	L	L	L	L	L	L	F	L	L	L	F	L	L	L	L	F	L	L	L	L	L	L	L	L	L	L	L	L	L	L	L	L	L	L	L	L	L	L	O	O
Result	W	W	D	D	W	L	D	W	W	L	L	D	W	D	D	L	W	D	L	W	W	L	W	W	L	D	L	W	L	W	D	L	W	D	L	D	W	W	W	L	D	W	L	L	W	W	W	W	W	L	D	D	L

Goalkeepers
Jim Provett
Anthony Williams

Defenders
Paul Arnison
Michael Barron
John Brackstone
Darrell Clarke
Darren Craddock
Andrew Jordan
Micheal Nelson
Hugh Robertson
Mark Robinson
Matty Robson
Scott Walker
Chris Westwood
Neil Wilkinson

Midfielders
Steven Carson
Neil Danns
Richie Humphreys
Steven Istead
Ryan McCann
Chris Shuker
Gavin Strachan
Anthony Sweeney
Mark Tinkler

Forwards
Adam Boyd
Demitrios Donstantopoulos
Jermaine Easter
David Foley
Marco Gabbiadini
Kevin Henderson
Joel Porter
Marcus Richardson
Paul Robinson
Eifion Williams

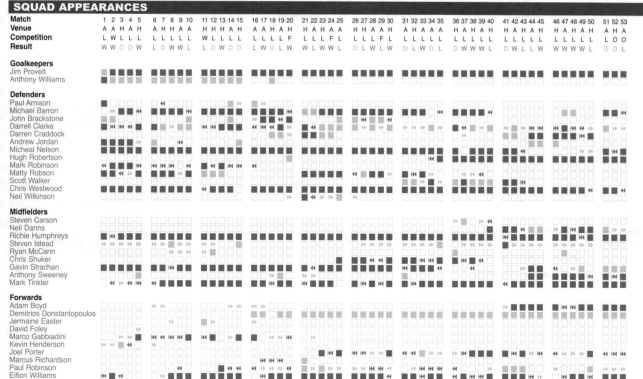

KEY: On all match · On bench · Subbed or sent off (Counting game) · Subbed or sent off (playing less than 70 minutes) · Subbed on from bench (Counting Game) · Subbed on (playing less than 70 minutes) · Subbed on and then subbed or sent off (Counting Game) · Subbed on and then subbed or sent off (playing less than 70 minutes) · Not in 16

PORT VALE

Final Position: **7th**

NICKNAME: THE VALIANTS

KEY: ☐Won ☐Drawn ☐Lost

	Comp	Opponent			Score	Scorers	Attendance
1	div2	Bournemouth	H	W	2-1	McPhee 67; Littlejohn 87	6,465
2	ccR1	Nottm Forest	H	L	2-3*	(*lost on penalties)	4,950
3	div2	Grimsby	A	W	2-1	McPhee 65; Paynter 68	4,816
4	div2	Colchester	H	W	4-3	Collins 34; Paynter 58; Armstrong 71; McPhee 73	5,133
5	div2	Hartlepool	A	L	0-2		5,314
6	div2	Brentford	H	W	1-0	Paynter 63	5,257
7	div2	Stockport	A	D	2-2	Paynter 82; Collins 90	5,316
8	div2	Barnsley	H	W	3-1	Lipa 23; Pilkington 55; Littlejohn 73	7,809
9	div2	Luton	A	L	0-2		5,079
10	div2	Bristol City	A	W	1-0	Paynter 71	11,369
11	div2	Wycombe	H	D	1-1	McPhee 44	6,822
12	div2	Peterborough	H	W	3-0	McPhee 12,67; Collins 86	5,495
13	div2	Wrexham	A	L	1-2	Paynter 20	5,822
14	div2	Oldham	A	L	1-2	Bridge-Wilkinson 78 pen	6,913
15	div2	Plymouth	H	L	1-5	McPhee 51	5,786
16	div2	QPR	H	W	2-0	Paynter 5; McPhee 9	5,243
17	div2	Swindon	A	D	0-0		5,313
18	div2	Chesterfield	A	L	0-1		4,088
19	facr1	Ford Utd	H	D	2-2	McPhee 60; Burns 64	4,016
20	div2	Notts County	H	W	1-0	McPhee 56	4,900
21	facr1r	Ford Utd	A	W	2-1	Paynter 38; Chandler 114 og	1,324
22	div2	Tranmere	A	L	0-1		7,081
23	div2	Rushden & D	H	D	1-1	Littlejohn 10	4,586
24	facr2	Scarborough	H	L	0-1		4,651
25	div2	Brighton	A	D	1-1	Littlejohn 50	5,811
26	div2	Sheff Wed	A	W	3-2	Littlejohn 25; Paynter 54; Brooker 89	24,991
27	div2	Stockport	H	D	2-2	McPhee 4,28	6,237
28	div2	Bournemouth	A	L	1-2	Boyd 23	5,926
29	div2	Blackpool	H	W	2-1	Brooker 8; Bridge-Wilkinson 29	4,523
30	div2	Grimsby	H	W	5-1	Lipa 18; Collins 20; Bridge-Wilkinson 33,74; Paynter 45	5,133
31	div2	Hartlepool	H	L	2-5	Brooker 8; Cummins 87	4,845
32	div2	Brentford	A	L	2-3	McPhee 30,90	4,306
33	div2	Sheff Wed	H	W	3-0	Littlejohn 42; McPhee 72; Brooker 90	7,958
34	div2	Oldham	H	W	1-0	McPhee 46	6,035
35	div2	Plymouth	A	L	1-2	McPhee 53	11,330
36	div2	Colchester	A	W	4-1	Brooker 13; Brown 24 og; Cummins 27; Bridge-Wilkinson 73	2,539
37	div2	QPR	A	L	2-3	Brooker 2; Littlejohn 90	12,593
38	div2	Blackpool	A	L	1-2	Paynter 4	6,878
39	div2	Brighton	H	D	1-1	Paynter 26	5,646
40	div2	Luton	H	W	1-0	Cummins 84	5,048
41	div2	Barnsley	A	D	0-0		8,267
42	div2	Bristol City	H	W	2-1	Brooker 66; Bridge-Wilkinson 77	6,724
43	div2	Swindon	H	D	3-3	Paynter 14; McPhee 41,58	5,702
44	div2	Wycombe	A	L	1-2	McPhee 7	4,738
45	div2	Wrexham	H	W	1-0	Cummins 52	5,892
46	div2	Peterborough	A	L	1-3	Bridge-Wilkinson 90	4,988
47	div2	Chesterfield	H	D	1-1	Paynter 74	5,582
48	div2	Notts County	A	W	2-1	McPhee 4; Brooker 34	5,834
49	div2	Tranmere	H	W	2-1	McPhee 10,90	6,806
50	div2	Rushden & D	A	W	2-0	McPhee 14,90	5,240

MONTHLY POINTS TALLY

Month	Points	%
AUGUST	12	80%
SEPTEMBER	11	61%
OCTOBER	4	27%
NOVEMBER	4	33%
DECEMBER	5	56%
JANUARY	6	40%
FEBRUARY	9	75%
MARCH	9	43%
APRIL	7	47%
MAY	6	100%

KEY PLAYERS - GOALSCORERS

Stephen McPhee

Goals in the League	24	Player Strike Rate Average number of minutes between League goals scored by player	169
Contribution to Attacking Power Average number of minutes between League team goals while on pitch	57	Club Strike Rate Average number of minutes between League goals scored by club	57

	PLAYER	LGE GOALS	GOALS ALL	POWER	STRIKE RATE
1	Stephen McPhee	24	25	57	169 mins
2	William Paynter	13	14	57	290 mins
3	Adrian Littlejohn	7	7	54	320 mins
4	Stephen Brooker	8	8	47	323 mins

KEY PLAYERS - MIDFIELDERS

Marc Bridge-Wilkinson

Goals in the League	7	Contribution to Attacking Power Average number of minutes between League team goals while on pitch	52
Defensive Rating Average number of mins between League goals conceded while he was on the pitch	72	Scoring Difference Defensive Rating minus Contribution to Attacking Power	20

	PLAYER	LGE GOALS	GOALS ALL	DEF RATE	POWER	SCORE DIFF
1	Marc Bridge -Wilkinson	7	7	72	52	20 mins
2	William Paynter	13	14	69	57	12 mins
3	Mark Boyd	1	1	64	53	11 mins
4	Michael Cummins	4	4	67	57	10 mins

KEY PLAYERS - DEFENDERS

Liam Burns

Goals Conceded (GC) The number of League goals conceded while he was on the pitch	25	Clean Sheets In games when he played at least 70 minutes	7
Defensive Rating Ave number of mins between League goals conceded while on the pitch	73	Club Defensive Rating Average number of mins between League goals conceded by the club this season	66

	PLAYER	CON LGE	CON ALL	CLEAN SHEETS	DEF RATE
1	Liam Burns	25	28	7	73 mins
2	Ryan Brown	20	20	4	69 mins
3	Sam Collins	55	59	11	68 mins
4	Steve Rowland	37	37	8	67 mins

KEY GOALKEEPER

Jonathan Brain

Goals Conceded in the League	41	Counting Games Games when he played at least 70 mins	32
Defensive Rating Ave number of mins between League goals conceded while on the pitch	70	Clean Sheets In games when he played at least 70 mins	9

LEAGUE GOALS

Stephen McPhee

Minutes on the pitch	4050	Goals in the League	169
League average (mins between goals)	24		

	PLAYER	MINS	GOALS	AVE
1	McPhee	4050	24	169
2	Paynter	3770	13	290
3	Brooker	2581	8	323
4	Bridge-Wilkinson	2361	7	337
5	Littlejohn	2239	7	320
6	Cummins	3624	4	906
7	Collins	3760	4	940
8	Lipa	2272	2	1136
9	Pilkington	3856	1	3856
10	Boyd	1735	1	1735
11	Armstrong	724	1	724
	Other		1	
	TOTAL		73	

DISCIPLINARY RECORDS

	PLAYER	YELLOW	RED	AVE
1	Brisco	6	0	318
2	Littlejohn	6	0	373
3	Paynter	9	0	418
4	Boyd	4	0	433
5	Collins	6	1	537
6	Burns	3	0	605
7	Rowland	4	0	623
8	Armstrong	1	0	724
9	Pilkington	5	0	771
10	Brooker	3	0	860
11	Walsh	1	0	916
12	Lipa	2	0	1136
13	Bridge-Wilkinson	2	0	1180
	Other	9	0	
	TOTAL	61	1	

TOP POINT EARNERS

	PLAYER	GAMES	AV PTS
1	Brown	14	2.07
2	Brooker	25	1.96
3	Bridge-Wilkinson	24	1.79
4	Cummins	39	1.67
5	Delaney	14	1.64
6	Collins	41	1.63
7	Pilkington	41	1.61
8	McPhee	44	1.57
9	Brain	32	1.56
10	Rowland	26	1.54
	CLUB AVERAGE:		**1.59**

TEAM OF THE SEASON

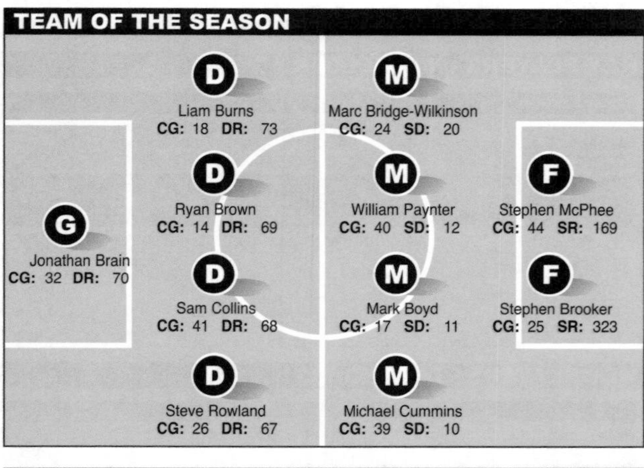
D
Liam Burns
CG: 18 DR: 73
M
Marc Bridge-Wilkinson
CG: 24 SD: 20
D
Ryan Brown
CG: 14 DR: 69
M
William Paynter
CG: 40 SD: 12
F
Stephen McPhee
CG: 44 SR: 169
G
Jonathan Brain
CG: 32 DR: 70
D
Sam Collins
CG: 41 DR: 68
M
Mark Boyd
CG: 17 SD: 11
F
Stephen Brooker
CG: 25 SR: 323
D
Steve Rowland
CG: 26 DR: 67
M
Michael Cummins
CG: 39 SD: 10

LEAGUE APPEARANCES AND BOOKINGS

	AGE (on 01/07/04)	IN NAMED 16	APPEARANCES	COUNTING GAMES	MINUTES ON PITCH	Yellow	Red
Goalkeepers							
Jonathan Brain	21	44	32	32	2880	1	0
Dean Delaney	23	41	15	14	1288	1	0
Mark Goodlad	24	5	0	0	0	0	0
Joe Molloy	19	2	0	0	0	0	0
Defenders							
Ryan Brown	19	19	17	14	1370	0	0
Liam Burns	25	43	26	18	1815	3	0
Sam Collins	27	43	43	41	3760	6	1
Craig James	21	9	8	8	720	0	0
Andreas Lipa	33	36	30	23	2272	2	0
George Pilkington	22	44	44	41	3856	5	0
Steve Rowland	26	37	30	26	2493	4	0
Michael Walsh	26	12	12	10	916	1	0
Midfielders							
Christopher Birchall	20	24	10	0	201	1	0
Mark Boyd	22	31	22	17	1735	4	0
Marc Bridge-Wilkinson	25	35	31	24	2361	2	0
Ian Brightwell	36	4	3	1	206	0	0
Neil Brisco	26	39	27	19	1912	6	0
Michael Cummins	26	42	42	39	3624	3	0
Adrian Littlejohn	33	39	36	21	2239	6	0
William Paynter	19	45	44	40	3770	9	0
Levi Reid	21	23	11	7	700	0	0
Forwards							
Ian Armstrong	22	38	20	2	724	1	0
Stephen Brooker	23	32	32	25	2581	3	0
Simon Eldershaw	20	3	0	0	0	0	0
Stephen McPhee	23	46	46	44	4050	3	0

SQUAD APPEARANCES

Match	1	2	3	4	5	6	7	8	9	10	11	12	13	14	15	16	17	18	19	20	21	22	23	24	25
Venue	H	H	A	H	A	H	A	H	A	A	H	H	A	A	H	H	A	A	H	H	A	A	H	H	A
Competition	L	W	L	L	L	L	L	L	L	L	L	L	L	L	L	L	L	L	F	L	F	L	L	F	L
Result	W	D	W	W	L	W	D	W	L	W	D	W	L	L	L	W	D	L	D	W	W	L	D	L	D

Match	26	27	28	29	30	31	32	33	34	35	36	37	38	39	40	41	42	43	44	45	46	47	48	49	50
Venue	A	H	A	H	H	H	A	H	H	A	A	A	A	H	H	A	H	H	A	H	A	H	A	H	A
Competition	L	L	L	L	L	L	L	L	L	L	L	L	L	L	L	L	L	L	L	L	L	L	L	L	L
Result	W	D	L	W	W	L	L	W	W	L	W	L	L	D	W	D	W	D	L	W	L	D	W	W	W

Goalkeepers
Jonathan Brain
Dean Delaney
Mark Goodlad
Joe Molloy

Defenders
Ryan Brown
Liam Burns
Sam Collins
Craig James
Andreas Lipa
George Pilkington
Steve Rowland
Michael Walsh

Midfielders
Christopher Birchall
Mark Boyd
Marc Bridge-Wilkinson
Ian Brightwell
Neil Brisco
Michael Cummins
Adrian Littlejohn
William Paynter
Levi Reid

Forwards
Ian Armstrong
Stephen Brooker
Simon Eldershaw
Stephen McPhee

KEY: On all match · On bench · Subbed or sent off (Counting game) · Subbed or sent off (playing less than 70 minutes) · Subbed on from bench (Counting Game) · Subbed on (playing less than 70 minutes) · Subbed on and then subbed or sent off (Counting Game) · Subbed on and then subbed or sent off (playing less than 70 minutes) · Not in 16

TRANMERE ROVERS

Final Position: **8th**

NICKNAME: ROVERS KEY: ☐Won ☐Drawn ☐Lost

							Attendance
1	div2	Brentford	H	W	4-1	Jones 23; Nicholson 39 pen,81 pen; Haworth 76	7,307
2	ccR1	Bury	H	W	1-0	Dadi 89	4,272
3	div2	Hartlepool	A	D	0-0		5,357
4	div2	Rushden & D	H	L	1-2	Jones 69	7,374
5	div2	Stockport	A	D	1-1	Dadi 45	4,886
6	div2	Colchester	H	D	1-1	Jones 14	6,745
7	div2	Sheff Wed	A	L	0-2		21,705
8	div2	Peterborough	H	D	0-0		6,726
9	div2	Bristol City	A	L	0-2		9,365
10	div2	Notts County	A	D	2-2	Haworth 7,57	4,215
11	ccR2	Nottm Forest	H	L	1-4*	(*on penalties)	4,477
12	div2	Wrexham	H	L	1-2	Haworth 19	8,230
13	div2	Wycombe	H	W	2-1	Dadi 41; Senda 82 og	6,847
14	div2	Luton	A	L	1-3	Dagnall 54	5,002
15	div2	Plymouth	A	L	0-6		7,610
16	div2	Oldham	H	W	2-1	Hume 70; Roberts 79	8,202
17	div2	Swindon	H	W	1-0	Jones 90	6,675
18	div2	QPR	A	D	1-1	Haworth, S 6	12,937
19	div2	Bournemouth	H	D	1-1	Allen 32	7,123
20	facr1	Chesterfield	H	W	3-2	Dadi 4; Hume 80; Mellon 87 pen	5,633
21	div2	Barnsley	A	L	0-2		9,663
22	div2	Port Vale	H	W	1-0	Hume 68	7,081
23	div2	Grimsby	A	W	1-0	Jones 71	4,406
24	facr2	Hornchurch	A	W	1-0	Jones 26	3,500
25	div2	Chesterfield	A	D	2-2	Dadi 1,54	3,123
26	div2	Brighton	H	W	1-0	Taylor 81 pen	7,616
27	div2	Blackpool	A	L	1-2	Haworth, S 82	8,340
28	div2	Sheff Wed	H	D	2-2	Jones 76; Taylor 85 pen	9,645
29	facr3	Bolton	H	D	1-1	Haworth, S 51	10,587
30	div2	Brentford	A	D	2-2	Dadi 9,60	4,105
31	facr3r	Bolton	A	W	2-1	Dadi 82; Hume 91	8,759
32	div2	Hartlepool	H	D	0-0		7,418
33	facr4	Luton	A	W	1-0	Mellon 81	8,767
34	div2	Stockport	H	W	3-2	Taylor 5 pen,87 pen; Goodwin 65 og	7,137
35	div2	Colchester	A	D	1-1	Dadi 27	3,099
36	div2	Blackpool	H	D	1-1	Hume 74	7,919
37	facr5	Swansea	H	W	2-1	Taylor 24 pen; Hume 59	12,215
38	div2	Plymouth	H	W	3-0	Dadi 19,52; Hume 23	7,948
39	div2	Oldham	A	D	1-1	Dadi 87	6,916
40	div2	Rushden & D	A	L	1-2	Harrison 55	3,074
41	div2	Swindon	A	L	0-2		6,928
42	facqf	Millwall	A	D	0-0		16,404
43	div2	Brighton	A	L	0-3		5,994
44	div2	Chesterfield	H	L	2-3	Hume 63,73	7,370
45	facqfr	Millwall	H	L	1-2	Jones 41	15,510
46	div2	Peterborough	A	D	0-0		4,185
47	div2	Bristol City	H	W	1-0	Dadi 82	6,712
48	div2	Notts County	H	W	4-0	Dadi 7,15 pen; Hume 69,74	7,308
49	div2	Wrexham	A	W	1-0	Sharps 78	4,496
50	div2	QPR	H	D	0-0		7,699
51	div2	Luton	H	W	1-0	Jones 30	7,937
52	div2	Wycombe	A	W	2-1	Dadi 11,45	5,256
53	div2	Bournemouth	A	W	5-1	Jones 42,58; Harrison 51; Hall 56; Beresford 81	7,063
54	div2	Barnsley	H	W	2-0	Hume 62; Taylor 88	7,612
55	div2	Port Vale	A	L	1-2	Hall 24	6,806
56	div2	Grimsby	H	W	2-1	Hume 57; Dadi 61	10,301

MONTHLY POINTS TALLY

AUGUST	6	40%
SEPTEMBER	5	28%
OCTOBER	7	47%
NOVEMBER	7	58%
DECEMBER	5	42%
JANUARY	6	50%
FEBRUARY	5	42%
MARCH	7	39%
APRIL	16	89%
MAY	3	50%

KEY PLAYERS - GOALSCORERS

Eugene Dadi

Goals in the League	16	Player Strike Rate Average number of minutes between League goals scored by player	157
Contribution to Attacking Power Average number of minutes between League team goals while on pitch	73	Club Strike Rate Average number of minutes between League goals scored by club	70

	PLAYER	LGE GOALS	GOALS ALL	POWER	STRIKE RATE
1	Eugene Dadi	16	19	73	157 mins
2	Iain Hume	10	13	73	287 mins
3	Simon Haworth	6	7	83	304 mins
4	Gary Jones	9	11	66	370 mins

KEY PLAYERS - MIDFIELDERS

Danny Harrison

Goals in the League	2	Contribution to Attacking Power Average number of minutes between League team goals while on pitch	64
Defensive Rating Average number of mins between League goals conceded while he was on the pitch	95	Scoring Difference Defensive Rating minus Contribution to Attacking Power	31

	PLAYER	LGE GOALS	GOALS ALL	DEF RATE	POWER	SCORE DIFF
1	Danny Harrison	2	2	95	64	31 mins
2	Gary Jones	9	11	79	67	12 mins
3	Micky Mellon	0	2	74	68	6 mins
4	Ryan Taylor	5	6	67	75	-8 mins

KEY PLAYERS - DEFENDERS

Ian Sharps

Goals Conceded (GC) The number of League goals conceded while he was on the pitch	28	Clean Sheets In games when he played at least 70 minutes	8
Defensive Rating Ave number of mins between League goals conceded while on the pitch	78	Club Defensive Rating Average number of mins between League goals conceded by the club this season	74

	PLAYER	CON LGE	CON ALL	CLEAN SHEETS	DEF RATE
1	Ian Sharps	28	29	8	78 mins
2	Graham Allen	46	53	15	78 mins
3	Gareth Roberts	54	61	13	72 mins
4	Paul Linwood	23	26	5	70 mins

KEY GOALKEEPER

John Achterberg

Goals Conceded in the League	56	Counting Games Games when he played at least 70 mins	46
Defensive Rating Ave number of mins between League goals conceded while on the pitch	74	Clean Sheets In games when he played at least 70 mins	15

LEAGUE GOALS

Eugene Dadi

Minutes on the pitch	2506	Goals in the League	157
League average (mins between goals)	16		

	PLAYER	MINS	GOALS	AVE
1	Dadi	2506	16	157
2	Hume	2873	10	287
3	Jones	3328	9	370
4	Haworth, S	1826	6	304
5	Taylor	1954	5	391
6	Hall	732	2	366
7	Nicholson	795	2	398
8	Harrison	2744	2	1372
9	Sharps	2194	1	2194
10	Dagnall	471	1	471
11	Roberts	3904	1	3904
12	Beresford	1363	1	1363
	Other		3	
	TOTAL		59	

DISCIPLINARY RECORDS

	PLAYER	YELLOW	RED	AVE
1	Dadi	10	0	250
2	Taylor	7	0	279
3	Connelly	10	0	301
4	Roberts	12	0	325
5	Mellon	7	1	426
6	Sharps	4	1	438
7	Hay	1	0	452
8	Loran	4	0	525
9	Allen	5	1	600
10	Haworth, S	3	0	608
11	Jones	5	0	665
12	Hume	4	0	718
13	Nicholson	1	0	795
	Other	8	1	
	TOTAL	81	4	

TOP POINT EARNERS

	PLAYER	GAMES	AV PTS
1	Harrison	30	1.83
2	Loran	20	1.80
3	Allen	39	1.56
4	Dadi	20	1.55
5	Mellon	34	1.53
6	Jones	35	1.51
7	Achterberg	46	1.46
8	Linwood	16	1.44
9	Hume	30	1.37
10	Sharps	23	1.35
	CLUB AVERAGE:		1.46

TEAM OF THE SEASON

G: John Achterberg — CG: 46 DR: 74

D: Graham Allen — CG: 39 DR: 78

D: Ian Sharps — CG: 23 DR: 78

D: Gareth Roberts — CG: 43 DR: 72

D: Paul Linwood — CG: 16 DR: 70

M: Danny Harrison — CG: 30 SD: 31

M: Gary Jones — CG: 35 SD: 12

M: Micky Mellon — CG: 34 SD: 6

M: Ryan Taylor — CG: 17 SD: -8

F: Eugene Dadi — CG: 20 SR: 157

F: Iain Hume — CG: 30 SR: 287

LEAGUE APPEARANCES AND BOOKINGS

	AGE (on 01/07/04)	IN NAMED 16	APPEARANCES	COUNTING GAMES	MINUTES ON PITCH	Yellow	Red
Goalkeepers							
John Achterberg	33	46	46	46	4140	1	0
Russell Howarth	22	46	0	0	0	0	0
Defenders							
Graham Allen	27	41	41	39	3601	5	1
Neil Ashton	19	3	1	0	1	0	0
Sean Connelly	34	40	37	32	3017	10	0
Ian Goodison	31	13	12	11	1030	1	0
Kevin Gray	32	12	2	2	180	1	0
Paul Linwood	20	24	20	16	1603	2	0
Shane Nicholson	34	22	16	7	795	1	0
James Olsen	22	1	0	0	0	0	0
Gareth Roberts	26	44	44	43	3904	12	0
Ian Sharps	23	29	27	23	2194	4	1
Carl Tremarco	-	2	0	0	0	0	0
Midfielders							
David Beresford	27	27	25	10	1363	0	0
Paul Hall	32	9	9	8	732	0	0
Danny Harrison	21	34	32	30	2744	2	1
Alex Hay	22	26	19	2	452	1	0
Stephen Jennings	19	9	4	0	91	1	0
Gary Jones	29	46	42	35	3328	5	0
Tyrone Loran	23	30	28	20	2103	4	0
Micky Mellon	32	44	43	34	3411	7	1
Alan Navarro	23	38	19	7	957	0	0
Ryan Taylor	19	34	30	17	1954	7	0
Forwards							
Eugene Dadi	30	38	38	20	2506	10	0
Chris Dagnall	19	10	10	4	471	0	0
Simon Haworth	27	22	22	20	1826	3	0
Iain Hume	20	40	40	30	2873	4	0
Iffy Onuora	36	5	3	0	110	0	0

SQUAD APPEARANCES

Match	1	2	3	4	5	6	7	8	9	10	11	12	13	14	15	16	17	18	19	20	21	22	23	24	25	26	27	28	29	30
Venue	H	H	A	H	A	H	A	H	A	A	H	H	H	A	A	H	H	A	H	H	A	H	A	A	A	H	A	H	H	A
Competition	L	W	L	L	L	L	L	L	L	L	W	L	L	L	L	L	L	L	L	F	L	L	L	F	L	L	L	L	F	L
Result	W	W	D	L	D	D	L	D	L	D	L	L	W	L	L	W	W	D	D	W	L	W	W	W	D	W	L	D	D	D

Match	31	32	33	34	35	36	37	38	39	40	41	42	43	44	45	46	47	48	49	50	51	52	53	54	55	56
Venue	A	H	A	H	A	H	H	H	A	A	A	A	A	H	H	A	H	H	A	H	H	A	A	H	A	H
Competition	F	L	F	L	L	L	F	L	L	L	L	F	L	L	F	L	L	L	L	L	L	L	L	L	L	L
Result	W	D	W	W	D	D	W	W	D	L	L	D	L	L	L	D	W	W	W	D	W	W	W	W	L	W

Goalkeepers
John Achterberg
Russell Howarth

Defenders
Graham Allen
Neil Ashton
Sean Connelly
Ian Goodison
Kevin Gray
Paul Linwood
Shane Nicholson
James Olsen
Gareth Roberts
Ian Sharps
Carl Tremarco

Midfielders
David Beresford
Paul Hall
Danny Harrison
Alex Hay
Stephen Jennings
Gary Jones
Tyrone Loran
Micky Mellon
Alan Navarro
Ryan Taylor

Forwards
Eugene Dadi
Chris Dagnall
Simon Haworth
Iain Hume
Iffy Onuora

KEY: On all match · On bench · Subbed or sent off (Counting game) · Subbed or sent off (playing less than 70 minutes) · Subbed on from bench (Counting Game) · Subbed on (playing less than 70 minutes) · Subbed on and then subbed or sent off (Counting Game) · Subbed on and then subbed or sent off (playing less than 70 minutes) · Not in 16

BOURNEMOUTH

Final Position: **9th**

NICKNAME: THE CHERRIES   KEY: ☐Won ☐Drawn ☐Lost

	Comp	Opponent	H/A	Res	Score	Scorers	Attendance
1	div2	Port Vale	A	L	1-2	Hayter 73	6,465
2	ccR1	Watford	A	D	0-0		9,561
3	div2	Barnsley	H	D	2-2	Fletcher, S 27,39	5,960
4	div2	QPR	A	L	0-1		13,065
5	div2	Swindon	H	D	2-2	Maher 21; Hayter 61	6,606
6	div2	Wrexham	A	W	1-0	Purches, S 8	4,929
7	div2	Bristol City	H	D	0-0		6,756
8	div2	Blackpool	A	W	2-1	Purches, S 49; Broadhurst 51	5,607
9	div2	Sheff Wed	H	W	1-0	Elliott 90	8,219
10	div2	Rushden & D	H	W	2-1	Feeney 69,71	6,464
11	div2	Colchester	A	L	0-1		3,602
12	div2	Chesterfield	A	D	1-1	Fletcher, S 80	3,131
13	div2	Hartlepool	H	D	2-2	Holmes 79; Feeney 81	6,342
14	div2	Notts County	A	W	1-0	Fletcher, S 54	4,419
15	div2	Brighton	H	W	1-0	Feeney 15	7,908
16	div2	Luton	H	W	6-3	Fletcher, S 7,45; Stock 34,62; O'Connor 42; Elliott 67	6,388
17	div2	Oldham	A	D	1-1	Feeney 45	5,850
18	div2	Tranmere	A	D	1-1	Feeney 72	7,123
19	facr1	Bristol Rovers	H	W	1-0	Elliott 37	7,200
20	div2	Peterborough	H	L	1-2	Feeney 73	6,963
21	div2	Stockport	A	L	2-3	Hayter 67; Feeney 75	4,622
22	div2	Brentford	H	W	1-0	Elliott 64	6,674
23	facr2	Accrington	H	D	1-1	Browning 56	7,551
24	div2	Grimsby	H	D	0-0		5,837
25	facr2r	Accrington	A	L	3-5*	(*on penalties)	2,585
26	div2	Wycombe	A	L	0-2		5,205
27	div2	Plymouth	H	L	0-2		8,901
28	div2	Bristol City	A	L	0-2		13,807
29	div2	Swindon	A	L	1-2	Hayter 5	7,158
30	div2	Port Vale	H	W	2-1	O'Connor 50 pen; Fletcher, S 55	5,926
31	div2	Barnsley	A	D	1-1	Hayter 31	7,934
32	div2	QPR	H	W	1-0	Feeney 58	8,909
33	div2	Plymouth	A	D	0-0		13,371
34	div2	Notts County	H	W	1-0	Hayter 83	6,332
35	div2	Brighton	A	L	0-3		6,441
36	div2	Wrexham	H	W	6-0	Purches, S 3; Cummings 45; Feeney 59; Hayter 85,86,88	5,899
37	div2	Oldham	H	W	1-0	Hayter 81	6,594
38	div2	Wycombe	H	W	1-0	Cummings 20	7,311
39	div2	Grimsby	A	D	1-1	Warhurst 73 og	5,015
40	div2	Sheff Wed	A	W	2-0	Fletcher, C 11; Fletcher, S 21	18,799
41	div2	Blackpool	H	L	1-2	Fletcher, S 51	6,436
42	div2	Rushden & D	A	W	3-0	Stock 37; Hayter 48; Feeney 62	4,500
43	div2	Colchester	H	D	1-1	Hayter 86	6,896
44	div2	Hartlepool	A	L	1-2	Hayter 31	5,544
45	div2	Chesterfield	H	D	2-2	Hayter 77; Holmes 80	7,081
46	div2	Tranmere	H	L	1-5	Allen 71 og	7,063
47	div2	Luton	A	D	1-1	Feeney 75	6,485
48	div2	Peterborough	A	W	1-0	Fletcher, C 81	4,831
49	div2	Stockport	H	D	0-0		7,541
50	div2	Brentford	A	L	0-1		9,485

MONTHLY POINTS TALLY

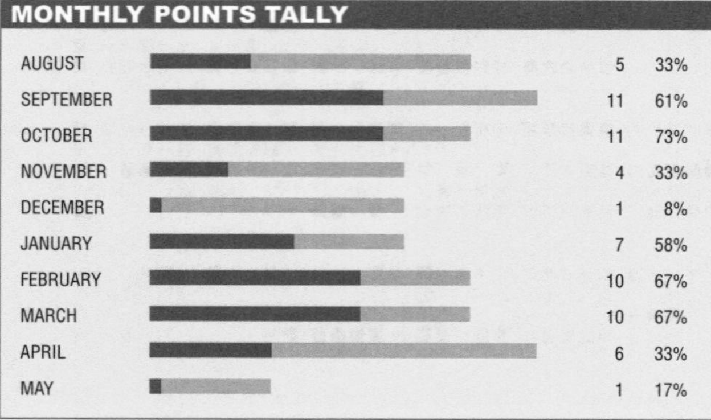
AUGUST 5 33%
SEPTEMBER 11 61%
OCTOBER 11 73%
NOVEMBER 4 33%
DECEMBER 1 8%
JANUARY 7 58%
FEBRUARY 10 67%
MARCH 10 67%
APRIL 6 33%
MAY 1 17%

KEY PLAYERS - GOALSCORERS

Warren Feeney

Goals in the League	12	Player Strike Rate Average number of minutes between League goals scored by player	237
Contribution to Attacking Power Average number of minutes between League team goals while on pitch	64	Club Strike Rate Average number of minutes between League goals scored by club	74

	PLAYER	LGE GOALS	GOALS ALL	POWER	STRIKE RATE
1	Warren Feeney	12	12	64	237 mins
2	James Hayter	14	14	72	239 mins
3	Steve Fletcher	9	9	74	391 mins
4	Wade Elliott	3	4	66	772 mins

KEY PLAYERS - MIDFIELDERS

James Hayter

Goals in the League	14	Contribution to Attacking Power Average number of minutes between League team goals while on pitch	73
Defensive Rating Average number of mins between League goals conceded while he was on the pitch	93	Scoring Difference Defensive Rating minus Contribution to Attacking Power	20

	PLAYER	LGE GOALS	GOALS ALL	DEF RATE	POWER	SCORE DIFF
1	James Hayter	14	14	93	73	20 mins
2	Garreth O'Connor	2	2	83	75	8 mins
3	Wade Elliott	3	4	68	66	2 mins
4	Marcus Browning	0	1	84	82	2 mins

KEY PLAYERS - DEFENDERS

Shaun Maher

Goals Conceded (GC) The number of League goals conceded while he was on the pitch	22	Clean Sheets In games when he played at least 70 minutes	9
Defensive Rating Ave number of mins between League goals conceded while on the pitch	90	Club Defensive Rating Average number of mins between League goals conceded by the club this season	81

	PLAYER	CON LGE	CON ALL	CLEAN SHEETS	DEF RATE
1	Shaun Maher	22	22	9	90 mins
2	Claus Jorgensen	16	16	8	88 mins
3	Carl Fletcher	42	44	15	84 mins
4	Karl Broadhurst	41	43	12	78 mins

KEY GOALKEEPER

Neil Moss

Goals Conceded in the League	51	Counting Games Games when he played at least 70 mins	46
Defensive Rating Ave number of mins between League goals conceded while on the pitch	81	Clean Sheets In games when he played at least 70 mins	17

LEAGUE GOALS

James Hayter

Minutes on the pitch	3352	Goals in the League	239
League average (mins between goals)	14		

	PLAYER	MINS	GOALS	AVE
1	Hayter	3352	14	239
2	Feeney	2839	12	237
3	Fletcher, S	3517	9	391
4	Elliott	2315	3	772
5	Stock	1046	3	349
6	Purches, S	3723	3	1241
7	O'Connor	2476	2	1238
8	Holmes	1100	2	550
9	Cummings	3725	2	1863
10	Fletcher, C	3543	2	1772
11	Maher	1970	1	1970
12	Broadhurst	3189	1	3189
	Other		2	
	TOTAL		56	

DISCIPLINARY RECORDS

	PLAYER	YELLOW	RED	AVE
1	O'Connor	8	0	309
2	Stock	2	1	348
3	Fletcher, C	9	0	393
4	Browning	8	0	442
5	Broadhurst	7	0	455
6	Young	1	0	485
7	Buxton	4	0	513
8	Holmes	2	0	550
9	Cummings	6	0	620
10	Fletcher, S	5	0	703
11	Feeney	4	0	709
12	Maher	2	0	985
13	Elliott	2	0	1157
	Other	4	0	
	TOTAL	64	1	

TOP POINT EARNERS

	PLAYER	GAMES	AV PTS
1	Buxton	20	1.65
2	Jorgensen	16	1.63
3	Elliott	22	1.59
4	Hayter	35	1.57
5	Fletcher, C	39	1.56
6	Fletcher, S	39	1.54
7	Maher	22	1.50
8	Browning	38	1.47
9	Moss	46	1.43
10	Cummings	41	1.41
	CLUB AVERAGE:		1.43

LEAGUE APPEARANCES AND BOOKINGS

	AGE (on 01/07/04)	IN NAMED 16	APPEARANCES	COUNTING GAMES	MINUTES ON PITCH	Yellow	Red
Goalkeepers							
Neil Moss	29	46	46	46	4140	0	0
Steve Scriven	-	6	0	0	0	0	0
Gareth Stewart	24	20	0	0	0	0	0
Defenders							
Karl Broadhurst	24	41	39	35	3189	7	0
Lewis Buxton	20	29	26	20	2054	4	0
Warren Cummings	23	42	42	41	3725	6	0
Carl Fletcher	24	40	40	39	3543	9	0
Claus Jorgensen	28	17	17	16	1406	1	0
Shaun Maher	26	36	29	22	1970	2	0
John Purches	21	0	0	0	0	0	0
Danny Thomas	23	24	10	0	248	0	0
Jason Tindall	26	25	19	3	441	1	0
Neil Young	30	14	10	4	485	1	0
Midfielders							
Marcus Browning	33	42	42	38	3543	8	0
Stephen Cooke	21	4	3	2	170	0	0
James Coutts	-	1	0	0	0	0	0
Wade Elliott	25	46	39	22	2315	2	0
James Hayter	25	45	43	35	3352	1	0
Garreth O'Connor	25	45	37	26	2476	8	0
Stephen Purches	24	42	42	42	3723	1	0
Fawzi Saadi	19	4	0	0	0	0	0
Brian Stock	22	34	19	10	1046	2	1
Forwards							
Alan Connell	21	14	7	1	173	0	0
Warren Feeney	23	40	40	30	2839	4	0
Steve Fletcher	32	42	41	39	3517	5	0
Derek Holmes	25	33	26	10	1100	2	0
Matthew Robinson	-	1	0	0	0	0	0
Gareth Williams	21	1	1	0	20	0	0

TEAM OF THE SEASON

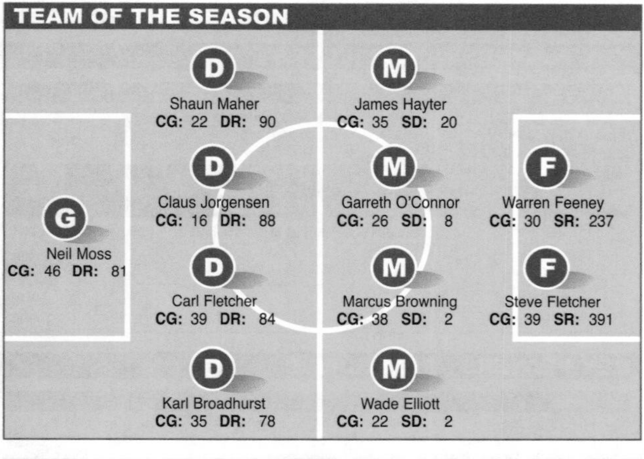

D
Shaun Maher
CG: 22 DR: 90
D
Claus Jorgensen
CG: 16 DR: 88
D
Carl Fletcher
CG: 39 DR: 84
D
Karl Broadhurst
CG: 35 DR: 78
G
Neil Moss
CG: 46 DR: 81
M
James Hayter
CG: 35 SD: 20
M
Garreth O'Connor
CG: 26 SD: 8
M
Marcus Browning
CG: 38 SD: 2
M
Wade Elliott
CG: 22 SD: 2
F
Warren Feeney
CG: 30 SR: 237
F
Steve Fletcher
CG: 39 SR: 391

SQUAD APPEARANCES

Match	1	2	3	4	5	6	7	8	9	10	11	12	13	14	15	16	17	18	19	20	21	22	23	24	25	26	27	28	29	30	31	32	33	34	35	36	37	38	39	40	41	42	43	44	45	46	47	48	49	50
Venue	A	A	H	A	H	A	H	A	H	H	A	A	H	A	H	H	A	A	H	H	A	H	H	H	A	A	H	A	A	H	A	H	A	H	A	H	H	H	A	A	H	A	H	A	H	H	A	A	H	A
Competition	L	W	L	L	L	L	L	L	L	L	L	L	L	L	L	L	L	L	F	L	L	L	F	L	F	L	L	L	L	L	L	L	L	L	L	L	L	L	L	L	L	L	L	L	L	L	L	L	L	L
Result	L	D	D	L	D	W	D	W	W	W	L	D	D	W	W	W	D	D	W	L	L	W	D	D	L	L	L	L	L	W	D	W	D	W	L	W	W	W	D	W	L	W	D	L	D	L	D	W	D	L

Goalkeepers
Neil Moss
Steve Scriven
Gareth Stewart

Defenders
Karl Broadhurst
Lewis Buxton
Warren Cummings
Carl Fletcher
Claus Jorgensen
Shaun Maher
John Purches
Danny Thomas
Jason Tindall
Neil Young

Midfielders
Marcus Browning
Stephen Cooke
James Coutts
Wade Elliott
James Hayter
Garreth O'Connor
Stephen Purches
Fawzi Saadi
Brian Stock

Forwards
Alan Connell
Warren Feeney
Steve Fletcher
Derek Holmes
Matthew Robinson
Gareth Williams

KEY: On all match · On bench · Subbed or sent off (Counting game) · Subbed or sent off (playing less than 70 minutes) · Subbed on from bench (Counting Game) · Subbed on (playing less than 70 minutes) · Subbed on and then subbed or sent off (Counting Game) · Subbed on and then subbed or sent off (playing less than 70 minutes) · Not in 16

LUTON TOWN

Final Position: **10th**

NICKNAME: THE HATTERS

KEY: Won / Drawn / Lost

							Attendance
1	div2	Rushden & D	H	W	3-1	Thorpe 50,59; Spring 90	6,878
2	ccR1	Yeovil	H	W	4-1	Foley 25; Thorpe 56; Pitt 64; Howard 68	4,337
3	div2	Stockport	A	W	2-1	Neilson 32; Howard 56	4,566
4	div2	Grimsby	H	L	1-2	Nicholls 85 pen	5,827
5	div2	Brighton	A	L	0-2		6,604
6	div2	Hartlepool	H	W	3-2	Howard 6,23; McSheffrey 14	5,515
7	div2	Notts County	A	D	1-1	Coyne 43	7,505
8	div2	Plymouth	A	L	1-2	McSheffrey 58	9,894
9	div2	Port Vale	H	W	2-0	McSheffrey 31; Foley 71	5,079
10	div2	QPR	H	D	1-1	McSheffrey 60	8,339
11	ccR2	Charlton	A	L	7-8*	Foley 30; Bayliss 32; McSheffrey 76; Coyne 110 (*on penalties)	10,905
12	div2	Oldham	A	L	0-3		6,077
13	div2	Swindon	A	D	2-2	McSheffrey 65; Forbes 67	7,573
14	div2	Tranmere	H	W	3-1	Perrett 45; McSheffrey 64; Forbes 72	5,002
15	div2	Wycombe	H	W	3-1	McSheffrey 76,89; Perrett 85	5,695
16	div2	Brentford	A	L	2-4	Forbes 48,88	5,579
17	div2	Bournemouth	A	L	3-6	Purches, S 10 og; Hughes 25; Forbes 60	6,388
18	div2	Peterborough	H	D	1-1	Forbes 29	6,067
19	div2	Bristol City	A	D	1-1	McSheffrey 18	9,735
20	facr1	Thurrock	A	D	1-1	Boyce 39	1,551
21	div2	Wrexham	H	W	3-2	Forbes 45; Robinson 52; Mansell 58	5,505
22	facr1r	Thurrock	H	W	3-1	Forbes 39,76,87 pen	3,667
23	div2	Sheff Wed	A	D	0-0		21,027
24	div2	Chesterfield	H	W	1-0	Howard 3	5,453
25	facr2	Rochdale	A	W	2-0	Robinson 20 pen; Mansell 77	2,807
26	div2	Blackpool	A	W	1-0	Robinson 35	5,739
27	div2	Barnsley	H	L	0-1		6,162
28	div2	Colchester	A	D	1-1	Mansell 28	5,083
29	div2	Notts County	H	W	2-0	Forbes 4; Boyce 79	7,181
30	facr3	Bradford	A	W	2-1	Forbes 22,48	8,222
31	div2	Rushden & D	A	D	2-2	Forbes 6; Hillier 39	5,823
32	div2	Stockport	H	D	2-2	Griffin 32 og; Howard 85	5,920
33	facr4	Tranmere	H	L	0-1		8,767
34	div2	Colchester	H	W	1-0	Showunmi 52	5,662
35	div2	Brighton	H	W	2-0	Holmes 27; Nicholls 77 pen	6,846
36	div2	Wycombe	A	D	0-0		6,407
37	div2	Brentford	H	W	4-1	Boyce 10; Showunmi 49,66,80	6,273
38	div2	Grimsby	A	L	2-3	Howard 19,80	3,143
39	div2	Peterborough	A	W	2-1	Howard 26; Brkovic 77	6,628
40	div2	Barnsley	A	D	0-0		8,656
41	div2	Blackpool	H	W	3-2	Boyce 25; Holmes 66; Showunmi 74	6,343
42	div2	Port Vale	A	L	0-1		5,048
43	div2	Plymouth	H	D	1-1	Coyne 42	8,499
44	div2	QPR	A	D	1-1	Showunmi 76	17,695
45	div2	Oldham	H	D	1-1	Showunmi 34	5,966
46	div2	Hartlepool	A	L	3-4	Howard 3; Leary 31,59	4,434
47	div2	Tranmere	A	L	0-1		7,937
48	div2	Swindon	H	L	0-3		7,008
49	div2	Bristol City	H	W	3-2	Howard 26; Boyce 56; Keane 90	6,944
50	div2	Bournemouth	H	D	1-1	Howard 15	6,485
51	div2	Wrexham	A	L	1-2	Howard 63	3,239
52	div2	Sheff Wed	H	W	3-2	Howard 54,90; O'Leary 78	7,157
53	div2	Chesterfield	A	L	0-1		6,285

MONTHLY POINTS TALLY

Month	Points	%
AUGUST	9	60%
SEPTEMBER	5	33%
OCTOBER	8	44%
NOVEMBER	8	67%
DECEMBER	7	58%
JANUARY	2	33%
FEBRUARY	13	72%
MARCH	6	40%
APRIL	5	24%
MAY	3	50%

KEY PLAYERS - GOALSCORERS

Gary McSheffrey

Goals in the League	9	Player Strike Rate Average number of minutes between League goals scored by player	172
Contribution to Attacking Power Average number of minutes between League team goals while on pitch	57	Club Strike Rate Average number of minutes between League goals scored by club	60

	PLAYER	LGE GOALS	GOALS ALL	POWER	STRIKE RATE
1	Gary McSheffrey	9	10	57	172 mins
2	Steven Howard	14	15	64	216 mins
3	Adrian Forbes	9	14	61	217 mins
4	Enoch Showunmi	7	7	61	245 mins

KEY PLAYERS - MIDFIELDERS

Matthew Spring

Goals in the League	1	Contribution to Attacking Power Average number of minutes between League team goals while on pitch	63
Defensive Rating Average number of mins between League goals conceded while he was on the pitch	74	Scoring Difference Defensive Rating minus Contribution to Attacking Power	11

	PLAYER	LGE GOALS	GOALS ALL	DEF RATE	POWER	SCORE DIFF
1	Matthew Spring	1	1	74	63	11 mins
2	Kevin Nicholls	2	2	73	63	10 mins
3	Steve Robinson	2	3	76	67	9 mins
4	Ahmet Brkovic	1	1	72	66	6 mins

KEY PLAYERS - DEFENDERS

Sol Davis

Goals Conceded (GC) The number of League goals conceded while he was on the pitch	43	Clean Sheets In games when he played at least 70 minutes	8
Defensive Rating Ave number of mins between League goals conceded while on the pitch	71	Club Defensive Rating Average number of mins between League goals conceded by the club this season	63

	PLAYER	CON LGE	CON ALL	CLEAN SHEETS	DEF RATE
1	Sol Davis	43	50	8	71 mins
2	Emmerson Boyce	55	64	9	67 mins
3	Chris Coyne	64	73	8	61 mins
4	Kevin Foley	52	57	5	56 mins

KEY GOALKEEPER

Morten Hyldgaard

Goals Conceded in the League	24	Counting Games Games when he played at least 70 mins	18
Defensive Rating Ave number of mins between League goals conceded while on the pitch	68	Clean Sheets In games when he played at least 70 mins	4

LEAGUE GOALS

Steven Howard

Minutes on the pitch	3026	Goals in the League	216
League average (mins between goals)	14		

	PLAYER	MINS	GOALS	AVE
1	Howard	3026	14	216
2	Forbes	1952	9	217
3	McSheffrey	1549	9	172
4	Showunmi	1713	7	245
5	Boyce	3704	4	926
6	Mansell	988	2	494
7	Coyne	3917	2	1959
8	Holmes	1036	2	518
9	Thorpe	180	2	90
10	Leary	768	2	384
11	Robinson	2875	2	1438
12	Nicholls	1816	2	908
	Other		12	
	TOTAL		69	

DISCIPLINARY RECORDS

	PLAYER	YELLOW	RED	AVE
1	Bayliss	3	0	165
2	Hillier	3	1	188
3	Davis	12	1	233
4	Davies	2	0	239
5	Hughes	6	1	250
6	Leary	3	0	256
7	Howard	9	1	302
8	Nicholls	4	1	363
9	Spring	5	0	427
10	Forbes	4	0	488
11	Mansell	2	0	494
12	McSheffrey	3	0	516
13	Boyce	6	0	617
	Other	24	1	
	TOTAL	86	6	

TOP POINT EARNERS

	PLAYER	GAMES	AV PTS
1	Spring	24	1.67
2	Forbes	19	1.63
3	Boyce	41	1.56
4	Nicholls	20	1.55
5	Robinson	32	1.53
6	Davis	33	1.52
7	Howard	33	1.52
8	McSheffrey	16	1.50
9	Hughes	19	1.47
10	Coyne	43	1.47
	CLUB AVERAGE:		**1.43**

TEAM OF THE SEASON

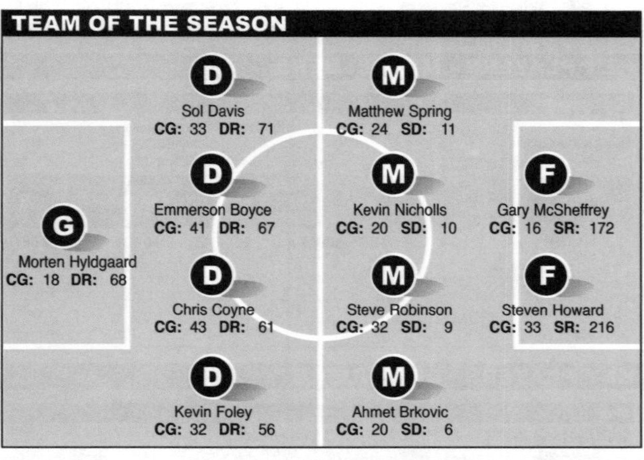

D
Sol Davis
CG: 33 DR: 71
M
Matthew Spring
CG: 24 SD: 11
D
Emmerson Boyce
CG: 41 DR: 67
M
Kevin Nicholls
CG: 20 SD: 10
F
Gary McSheffrey
CG: 16 SR: 172
G
Morten Hyldgaard
CG: 18 DR: 68
D
Chris Coyne
CG: 43 DR: 61
M
Steve Robinson
CG: 32 SD: 9
F
Steven Howard
CG: 33 SR: 216
D
Kevin Foley
CG: 32 DR: 56
M
Ahmet Brkovic
CG: 20 SD: 6

LEAGUE APPEARANCES AND BOOKINGS

	AGE (on 01/07/04)	IN NAMED 16	APPEARANCES	COUNTING GAMES	MINUTES ON PITCH	Yellow	Red
Goalkeepers							
Rob Beckwith	19	14	13	13	1150	0	1
Marlon Beresford	34	11	11	11	990	0	0
Dean Brill	17	45	4	4	360	0	0
Morten Hyldgaard	26	20	18	18	1620	0	0
Defenders							
Leon Barnet	19	1	0	0	0	0	0
David Bayliss	28	9	6	5	495	3	0
Emmerson Boyce	24	42	42	41	3704	6	0
Chris Coyne	25	44	44	43	3917	4	0
Curtis Davies	-	18	6	5	479	2	0
Sol Davis	24	39	36	33	3040	12	1
David Deeney	17	0	0	0	0	0	0
Kevin Foley	19	33	33	32	2903	4	0
Ian Hillier	24	25	12	6	753	3	1
Allan Neilson	31	20	14	10	1008	1	0
Russell Perrett	31	6	5	5	450	4	0
Midfielders							
Ahmet Brkovic	29	40	32	20	2101	3	0
Peter Holmes	23	19	16	11	1036	1	0
Paul Hughes	28	22	22	19	1750	6	1
Matthew Judge	19	2	1	0	13	0	0
Keith Keane	-	17	14	11	1137	0	0
Michael Leary	21	32	14	7	768	3	0
Lee Mansell	21	31	15	9	988	2	0
Kevin Nicholls	25	22	21	20	1816	4	1
Stephen O'Leary	18	9	5	3	295	2	0
Pary Okai	18	1	0	0	0	0	0
Courtney Pitt	22	12	12	11	976	0	0
Steve Robinson	29	35	34	32	2875	3	0
Matthew Spring	24	24	24	24	2136	5	0
Forwards							
Dean Crowe	25	20	8	0	157	0	0
Adrian Forbes	25	30	27	19	1952	4	0
Steven Howard	28	34	34	33	3026	9	1
Gary McSheffrey	22	18	18	16	1549	3	0
Enoch Showunmi	21	34	26	17	1713	2	0
Tony Thorpe	30	2	2	2	180	0	0

SQUAD APPEARANCES

Match	1	2	3	4	5	6	7	8	9	10	11	12	13	14	15	16	17	18	19	20	21	22	23	24	25	26	27	28	29	30	31	32	33	34	35	36	37	38	39	40	41	42	43	44	45	46	47	48	49	50	51	52	53
Venue	H	H	A	H	A	H	A	A	H	H	A	A	A	H	H	A	A	H	A	A	H	H	A	H	A	A	H	A	H	A	A	H	H	H	H	A	H	A	A	A	H	A	H	A	H	A	A	H	H	H	A	H	A
Competition	L	W	L	L	L	L	L	L	L	L	W	L	L	L	L	L	L	L	L	F	L	F	L	L	F	L	L	L	L	F	L	L	F	L	L	L	L	L	L	L	L	L	L	L	L	L	L	L	L	L	L	L	L
Result	W	W	W	L	L	W	D	L	W	D	L	L	D	W	W	L	L	D	D	D	W	W	D	W	W	W	L	D	W	W	D	D	L	W	W	D	W	L	W	D	W	L	D	D	D	L	L	L	W	D	L	W	L

Goalkeepers
Rob Beckwith
Marlon Beresford
Dean Brill
Morten Hyldgaard

Defenders
Leon Barnet
David Bayliss
Emmerson Boyce
Chris Coyne
Curtis Davies
Sol Davis
David Deeney
Kevin Foley
Ian Hillier
Allan Neilson
Russell Perrett

Midfielders
Ahmet Brkovic
Peter Holmes
Paul Hughes
Matthew Judge
Keith Keane
Michael Leary
Lee Mansell
Kevin Nicholls
Stephen O'Leary
Pary Okai
Courtney Pitt
Steve Robinson
Matthew Spring

Forwards
Dean Crowe
Adrian Forbes
Steven Howard
Gary McSheffrey
Enoch Showunmi
Tony Thorpe

KEY: On all match · On bench · Subbed or sent off (Counting game) · Subbed or sent off (playing less than 70 minutes) · Subbed on from bench (Counting Game) · Subbed on (playing less than 70 minutes) · Subbed on and then subbed or sent off (Counting Game) · Subbed on and then subbed or sent off (playing less than 70 minutes) · Not in 16

COLCHESTER UNITED

Final Position: **11th**

NICKNAME: THE U'S

KEY: Won / Drawn / Lost

							Attendance
1	div2	Barnsley	A	L	0-1		8,450
2	ccR1	Plymouth	H	W	2-1	Fagan 22; Pinault 40	2,367
3	div2	Swindon	H	L	0-1		3,339
4	div2	Port Vale	A	L	3-4	McGleish 26,38; Andrews 88	5,133
5	div2	Bristol City	H	W	2-1	McGleish 47,55	3,079
6	div2	Tranmere	A	D	1-1	Andrews 30	6,745
7	div2	QPR	H	D	2-2	Vine 10; McGleish 75 pen	3,835
8	div2	Brighton	H	W	1-0	Andrews 67	4,169
9	div2	Wycombe	A	W	2-1	Andrews 25; Vine 27	4,401
10	div2	Peterborough	A	W	2-1	Fagan 36; Keith 90	4,690
11	ccR2	Rotherham	A	L	0-1		2,474
12	div2	Bournemouth	H	W	1-0	Duguid 75	3,602
13	div2	Brentford	H	D	1-1	Vine 76	3,343
14	div2	Notts County	A	L	0-3		4,187
15	div2	Blackpool	H	D	1-1	Andrews 2	3,265
16	div2	Grimsby	A	L	0-2		5,021
17	div2	Stockport	A	W	3-1	Fagan 26; Andrews 34; Vine 47	3,683
18	div2	Chesterfield	H	W	1-0	Andrews 10	3,115
19	div2	Wrexham	A	W	1-0	Andrews 36	4,269
20	facr1	Oxford	H	W	1-0	McGleish 38	3,672
21	div2	Sheff Wed	H	W	3-1	McGleish 27; Andrews 81; Fagan 90	5,018
22	div2	Rushden & D	A	L	0-4		4,149
23	div2	Plymouth	H	L	0-2		4,332
24	facr2	Aldershot	H	W	1-0	Vine 83	4,255
25	div2	Oldham	H	W	2-1	Duguid 48; Vine 72	2,897
26	div2	Hartlepool	A	D	0-0		4,135
27	div2	Luton	H	D	1-1	McGleish 12	5,083
28	div2	QPR	A	L	0-2		15,720
29	facr3	Accrington	A	D	0-0		4,368
30	div2	Barnsley	H	D	1-1	Andrews 25	3,507
31	facr3r	Accrington	H	W	2-1	Keith 11,84	5,611
32	div2	Swindon	A	L	0-2		6,014
33	facr4	Coventry	A	D	1-1	Adebola 30 og	15,341
34	div2	Bristol City	A	L	0-1		10,733
35	div2	Tranmere	H	D	1-1	Izzet 89	3,099
36	facr4r	Coventry		W	3-1	Vine 12,43,57	5,530
37	div2	Luton	A	L	0-1		5,662
38	facr5	Sheff Utd	A	L	0-1		17,074
39	div2	Grimsby	H	W	2-0	Fagan 65; Izzet 90	2,922
40	div2	Port Vale	H	L	1-4	McGleish 10 pen	2,539
41	div2	Stockport	H	W	2-1	Vine 50; Andrews 60	2,513
42	div2	Hartlepool	H	L	1-2	Halford 35	3,348
43	div2	Oldham	A	D	0-0		5,937
44	div2	Wycombe	H	D	1-1	Fagan 8 pen	3,092
45	div2	Brighton	A	L	1-2	Izzet 69	6,156
46	div2	Chesterfield	A	W	2-1	Halford 31; Andrews 82	3,787
47	div2	Peterborough	H	D	0-0		3,754
48	div2	Blackpool	A	D	0-0		5,473
49	div2	Bournemouth	A	D	1-1	Halford 35	6,896
50	div2	Notts County	H	W	4-1	Fagan 9,17,53; Williams 78	3,782
51	div2	Brentford	A	L	2-3	White 53; Fagan 80	5,017
52	div2	Wrexham	H	W	3-1	Williams 16; Halford 45; McGleish 82	3,077
53	div2	Sheff Wed	A	W	1-0	Keith 48	20,464
54	div2	Rushden & D	H	W	2-0	McGleish 81 pen; Johnson, G 90	4,618
55	div2	Plymouth	A	L	0-2		19,868

MONTHLY POINTS TALLY

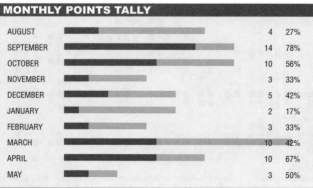

Month	Points	%
AUGUST	4	27%
SEPTEMBER	14	78%
OCTOBER	10	56%
NOVEMBER	3	33%
DECEMBER	5	42%
JANUARY	2	17%
FEBRUARY	3	33%
MARCH	10	42%
APRIL	10	67%
MAY	3	50%

KEY PLAYERS - GOALSCORERS

Scott McGleish

Goals in the League	10	Player Strike Rate Average number of minutes between League goals scored by player	221
Contribution to Attacking Power Average number of minutes between League team goals while on pitch	81	Club Strike Rate Average number of minutes between League goals scored by club	80

	PLAYER	LGE GOALS	GOALS ALL	POWER	STRIKE RATE
1	Scott McGleish	10	11	81	221 mins
2	Wayne Andrews	12	12	80	233 mins
3	Craig Fagan	9	10	79	310 mins
4	Greg Halford	4	4	77	350 mins

KEY PLAYERS - MIDFIELDERS

Bobby Bowry

Goals in the League	0	Contribution to Attacking Power Average number of minutes between League team goals while on pitch	61
Defensive Rating Average number of mins between League goals conceded while he was on the pitch	66	Scoring Difference Defensive Rating minus Contribution to Attacking Power	5

	PLAYER	LGE GOALS	GOALS ALL	DEF RATE	POWER	SCORE DIFF
1	Bobby Bowry	0	0	66	61	5 mins
2	Kemal Izzet	3	3	78	78	0 mins
3	Rowan Vine	6	7	79	81	-2 mins
4	Karl Duguid	2	2	69	79	-10 mins

KEY PLAYERS - DEFENDERS

Greg Halford

Goals Conceded (GC) The number of League goals conceded while he was on the pitch	17	Clean Sheets In games when he played at least 70 minutes	5
Defensive Rating Ave number of mins between League goals conceded while on the pitch	82	Club Defensive Rating Average number of mins between League goals conceded by the club this season	74

	PLAYER	CON LGE	CON ALL	CLEAN SHEETS	DEF RATE
1	Greg Halford	17	21	5	82 mins
2	Alan White	33	41	8	81 mins
3	Wayne Brown	18	18	6	80 mins
4	Sam Stockley	49	53	11	77 mins

KEY GOALKEEPER

Simon Brown

Goals Conceded in the League	48	Counting Games Games when he played at least 70 mins	40
Defensive Rating Ave number of mins between League goals conceded while on the pitch	75	Clean Sheets In games when he played at least 70 mins	10

LEAGUE GOALS

Wayne Andrews

Minutes on the pitch	2801	Goals in the League	233
League average (mins between goals)	12		

	PLAYER	MINS	GOALS	AVE
1	Andrews	2801	12	233
2	McGleish	2207	10	221
3	Fagan	2793	9	310
4	Vine	2688	6	448
5	Halford	1398	4	350
6	Izzet	3836	3	1279
7	Williams	410	2	205
8	Keith	1620	2	810
9	Duguid	2618	2	1309
10	White	2680	1	2680
11	Johnson, G	1170	1	1170
	Other		0	
	TOTAL		52	

DISCIPLINARY RECORDS

	PLAYER	YELLOW	RED	AVE
1	Fagan	11	1	232
2	Brown	5	1	240
3	Bowry	5	0	304
4	Andrews	6	1	400
5	Duguid	4	2	436
6	White	6	0	446
7	Vine	6	0	448
8	Myers	3	0	588
9	Chilvers	4	0	643
10	Izzet	5	0	767
11	Pinault	3	0	937
12	Stockley	4	0	945
13	McGleish	2	0	1103
	Other	4	0	
	TOTAL	68	5	

TOP POINT EARNERS

	PLAYER	GAMES	AV PTS
1	Bowry	14	1.71
2	Brown	16	1.56
3	Pinault	27	1.52
4	Fitzgerald	22	1.50
5	Stockley	41	1.49
6	Brown, S	40	1.48
7	Duguid	29	1.48
8	Myers	19	1.47
9	Halford	15	1.47
10	Vine	28	1.46
	CLUB AVERAGE:		1.39

LEAGUE APPEARANCES AND BOOKINGS

	AGE (on 01/07/04)	IN NAMED 16	APPEARANCES	COUNTING GAMES	MINUTES ON PITCH	Yellow	Red
Goalkeepers							
Simon Brown	27	43	40	40	3600	0	0
Dean Gerken	19	28	1	1	90	0	0
Richard McKinney	25	21	5	5	450	0	0
Defenders							
Wayne Brown	26	16	16	16	1440	5	1
Liam Chilvers	22	38	32	28	2572	4	0
Scott Fitzgerald	34	28	23	22	2028	1	0
Greg Halford	19	22	18	15	1398	1	0
Andy Myers	30	23	21	19	1765	3	0
Sam Stockley	26	44	43	41	3782	4	0
Alan White	28	39	33	28	2680	6	0
Midfielders							
Pat Baldwin	21	20	4	1	196	1	0
Bobby Bowry	33	39	24	14	1524	5	0
Karl Duguid	26	30	30	29	2618	4	2
Kemal Izzet	23	44	44	42	3836	5	0
Gavin Johnson	33	19	17	12	1170	0	0
Craig Johnston	18	2	1	1	80	0	0
Joe Keith	25	42	28	15	1620	1	0
Thomas Pinault	22	44	40	27	2812	3	0
Micky Stockwell	39	1	1	1	90	0	0
Paul Tierney	21	2	2	1	156	0	0
Tristan Toney	20	1	0	0	0	0	0
Rowan Vine	21	38	35	28	2688	6	0
Forwards							
Wayne Andrews	26	41	41	27	2801	6	1
Jamie Cade	20	25	15	5	625	0	0
Adrian Coote	25	0	0	0	0	0	0
Craig Fagan	21	39	37	29	2793	11	1
Phil Hadland	23	3	1	0	2	0	0
Scott McGleish	30	34	34	23	2207	2	0
Gareth Williams	21	10	7	3	410	0	0

TEAM OF THE SEASON

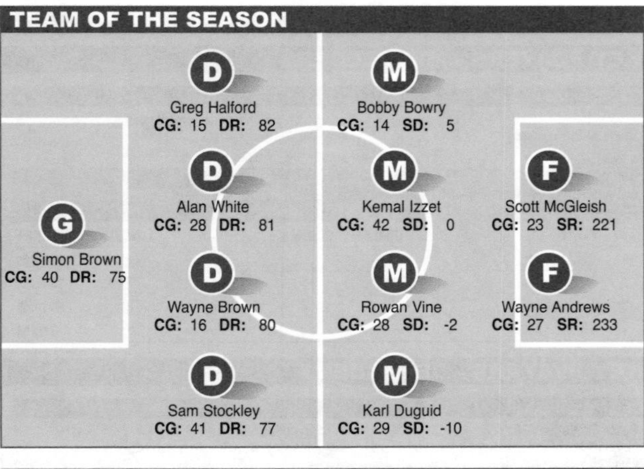
G
Simon Brown
CG: 40 DR: 75
D
Greg Halford
CG: 15 DR: 82
D
Alan White
CG: 28 DR: 81
D
Wayne Brown
CG: 16 DR: 80
D
Sam Stockley
CG: 41 DR: 77
M
Bobby Bowry
CG: 14 SD: 5
M
Kemal Izzet
CG: 42 SD: 0
M
Rowan Vine
CG: 28 SD: -2
M
Karl Duguid
CG: 29 SD: -10
F
Scott McGleish
CG: 23 SR: 221
F
Wayne Andrews
CG: 27 SR: 233

SQUAD APPEARANCES

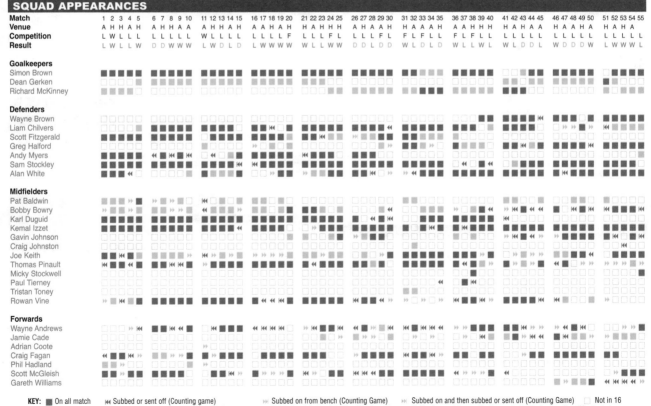

Match	1	2	3	4	5	6	7	8	9	10	11	12	13	14	15	16	17	18	19	20	21	22	23	24	25	26	27	28
Venue	A	H	H	A	H	A	H	H	A	A	A	H	H	A	H	A	A	H	A	H	H	A	H	H	H	A	H	A
Competition	L	W	L	L	L	L	L	L	L	L	W	L	L	L	L	L	L	L	L	F	L	L	L	F	L	L	L	L
Result	L	W	L	L	W	D	D	W	W	W	L	W	D	L	D	L	W	W	W	W	W	L	L	W	W	D	D	L

Match	29	30	31	32	33	34	35	36	37	38	39	40	41	42	43	44	45	46	47	48	49	50	51	52	53	54	55
Venue	A	H	H	A	A	A	H	A	A	H	H	H	H	A	H	A	A	H	A	A	H	A	H	A	H	A	
Competition	F	L	F	L	F	L	L	F	L	F	L	L	L	L	L	L	L	L	L	L	L	L	L	L	L	L	L
Result	D	D	W	L	D	L	D	W	L	L	W	L	W	L	D	D	L	W	D	D	D	W	L	W	W	W	L

Goalkeepers
Simon Brown
Dean Gerken
Richard McKinney

Defenders
Wayne Brown
Liam Chilvers
Scott Fitzgerald
Greg Halford
Andy Myers
Sam Stockley
Alan White

Midfielders
Pat Baldwin
Bobby Bowry
Karl Duguid
Kemal Izzet
Gavin Johnson
Craig Johnston
Joe Keith
Thomas Pinault
Micky Stockwell
Paul Tierney
Tristan Toney
Rowan Vine

Forwards
Wayne Andrews
Jamie Cade
Adrian Coote
Craig Fagan
Phil Hadland
Scott McGleish
Gareth Williams

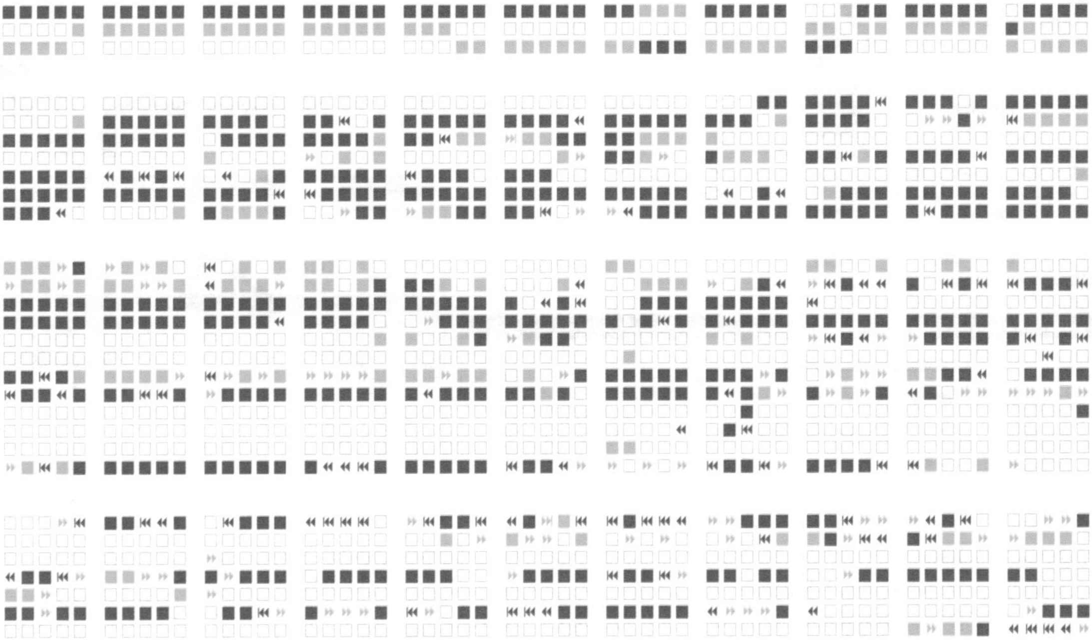

KEY: On all match | On bench | Subbed or sent off (Counting game) | Subbed or sent off (playing less than 70 minutes) | Subbed on from bench (Counting Game) | Subbed on (playing less than 70 minutes) | Subbed on and then subbed or sent off (Counting Game) | Subbed on and then subbed or sent off (playing less than 70 minutes) | Not in 16

BARNSLEY

Final Position: **12th**

NICKNAME: THE TYKES

KEY: Won / Drawn / Lost

No	Comp	Opponent	H/A	Res	Score	Scorers	Attendance
1	div2	Colchester	H	W	1-0	Gorre 47 pen	8,450
2	ccR1	Blackpool	H	L	1-2	Gorre 63 pen	5,378
3	div2	Bournemouth	A	D	2-2	Ireland 38; Gorre 57	5,960
4	div2	Brighton	H	W	1-0	Betsy 68	7,918
5	div2	Blackpool	A	W	2-0	Fallon 29; Lumsdon 51	6,039
6	div2	Notts County	H	D	1-1	Gorre 47	9,087
7	div2	Chesterfield	A	W	2-0	Kay 10; Ireland 67	5,605
8	div2	Port Vale	A	L	1-3	Fallon 8	7,809
9	div2	Oldham	H	D	1-1	Lumsdon 61	10,102
10	div2	Swindon	H	D	1-1	Fallon 77	9,006
11	div2	Plymouth	A	L	0-2		8,695
12	div2	QPR	A	L	0-4		11,854
13	div2	Rushden & D	H	W	2-0	Betsy 32; Gorre 57	8,461
14	div2	Wycombe	A	W	2-1	Rankin 29,33	4,446
15	div2	Peterborough	A	W	3-2	Betsy 35; Rankin 47; Carson 63	3,909
16	div2	Grimsby	H	D	0-0		10,092
17	div2	Wrexham	H	W	2-1	Gorre 24; Rankin 64	8,916
18	div2	Brentford	A	L	1-2	Fallon 90	4,789
19	facr1	York	A	W	2-1	Rankin 38; Betsy 82	5,658
20	div2	Tranmere	H	W	2-0	Rankin 23; Gorre 64 pen	9,663
21	div2	Bristol City	A	L	1-2	Burns 51	10,031
22	div2	Stockport	H	D	3-3	Betsy 5,76; Gorre 68	9,047
23	facr2	Bristol City	A	D	0-0		6,741
24	div2	Sheff Wed	H	D	1-1	Kay 26	20,438
25	facr2r	Bristol City	H	W	2-1	Kay 24; Monk 43	5,434
26	div2	Luton	A	W	1-0	Kay 90	6,162
27	div2	Hartlepool	A	W	2-1	Betsy 45,70	6,520
28	div2	Chesterfield	H	L	0-1		11,664
29	facr3	Scunthorpe	H	D	0-0		10,839
30	div2	Colchester	A	D	1-1	Betsy 79	3,507
31	facr3r	Scunthorpe	A	L	0-2		6,293
32	div2	Bournemouth	H	D	1-1	Lumsdon 80	7,934
33	div2	Brighton	A	L	0-1		6,033
34	div2	Blackpool	H	W	3-0	Nardiello 11,61; Stallard 54	7,918
35	div2	Notts County	A	D	1-1	Betsy 87 pen	7,355
36	div2	Hartlepool	H	D	2-2	Nardiello 56; Hayward 80	9,220
37	div2	Wrexham	A	L	0-1		4,086
38	div2	Wycombe	H	D	0-0		8,507
39	div2	Grimsby	A	L	1-6	Nardiello 47	5,603
40	div2	Peterborough	H	L	0-1		7,547
41	div2	Luton	H	D	0-0		8,656
42	div2	Sheff Wed	A	L	1-2	Williams 74 pen	25,664
43	div2	Oldham	A	D	1-1	Nardiello 34	5,837
44	div2	Port Vale	H	D	0-0		8,267
45	div2	Swindon	A	D	1-1	Nardiello 34 pen	7,305
46	div2	Plymouth	H	W	1-0	Birch 81	9,266
47	div2	Rushden & D	A	W	3-2	Murphy 10; Betsy 41; Neil 45	4,063
48	div2	QPR	H	D	3-3	Ireland 22; Nardiello 85; Murphy 89	10,402
49	div2	Brentford	H	L	0-2		9,824
50	div2	Tranmere	A	L	0-2		7,612
51	div2	Bristol City	H	L	0-1		10,865
52	div2	Stockport	A	W	3-2	Wroe 10; Birch 16; Neil 72	6,581

MONTHLY POINTS TALLY

Month	Points	%
AUGUST	11	73%
SEPTEMBER	5	28%
OCTOBER	13	87%
NOVEMBER	4	33%
DECEMBER	7	58%
JANUARY	6	40%
FEBRUARY	2	17%
MARCH	4	22%
APRIL	7	47%
MAY	3	50%

KEY PLAYERS - GOALSCORERS

Daniel Nardiello

Goals in the League	7	Player Strike Rate Average number of minutes between League goals scored by player	179
Contribution to Attacking Power Average number of minutes between League team goals while on pitch	104	Club Strike Rate Average number of minutes between League goals scored by club	77

	PLAYER	LGE GOALS	GOALS ALL	POWER	STRIKE RATE
1	Daniel Nardiello	7	7	104	179 mins
2	Kevin Betsy	10	11	74	390 mins
3	Chris Lumsdon	3	3	75	551 mins
4	Alex Neil	2	2	85	808 mins

KEY PLAYERS - MIDFIELDERS

Jacob Burns

Goals in the League	1	Contribution to Attacking Power Average number of minutes between League team goals while on pitch	71
Defensive Rating Average number of mins between League goals conceded while he was on the pitch	86	Scoring Difference Defensive Rating minus Contribution to Attacking Power	15

	PLAYER	LGE GOALS	GOALS ALL	DEF RATE	POWER	SCORE DIFF
1	Jacob Burns	1	1	86	71	15 mins
2	Steve Hayward	1	1	91	77	14 mins
3	Lee Crooks	0	0	69	72	-3 mins
4	Chris Lumsdon	3	3	69	75	-6 mins

KEY PLAYERS - DEFENDERS

Brian O'Callaghan

Goals Conceded (GC) The number of League goals conceded while he was on the pitch	25	Clean Sheets In games when he played at least 70 minutes	7
Defensive Rating Ave number of mins between League goals conceded while on the pitch	87	Club Defensive Rating Average number of mins between League goals conceded by the club this season	71

	PLAYER	CON LGE	CON ALL	CLEAN SHEETS	DEF RATE
1	Brian O'Callaghan	25	29	7	87 mins
2	Tony Gallimore	22	25	7	79 mins
3	Craig Ireland	53	59	12	72 mins
4	Peter Handyside	34	38	9	72 mins

KEY GOALKEEPER

1 Sasa Ilic

Goals Conceded in the League	29	Counting Games Games when he played at least 70 mins	25
Defensive Rating Ave number of mins between League goals conceded while on the pitch	78	Clean Sheets In games when he played at least 70 mins	8

LEAGUE GOALS

Kevin Betsy

Minutes on the pitch	3896	Goals in the League	390
League average (mins between goals)	10		

	PLAYER	MINS	GOALS	AVE
1	Betsy	3896	10	390
2	Gorre	1279	7	183
3	Nardiello	1254	7	179
4	Rankin	925	5	185
5	Fallon	1178	4	295
6	Lumsdon	1653	3	551
7	Kay	3415	3	1138
8	Ireland	3794	3	1265
9	Birch	715	2	358
10	Murphy	855	2	428
11	Neil	1615	2	808
12	Hayward	2000	1	2000
	Other		5	
	TOTAL		54	

DISCIPLINARY RECORDS

	PLAYER	YELLOW	RED	AVE
1	Hayward	8	0	250
2	Burns	6	0	259
3	Kay	11	2	262
4	Lumsdon	4	2	275
5	Fallon	3	0	392
6	Nardiello	3	0	418
7	Austin	5	0	573
8	Gallimore	3	0	578
9	Crooks	3	0	598
10	Ireland	6	0	632
11	Betsy	6	0	649
12	Birch	1	0	715
13	Shuker	1	0	745
	Other	11	1	
	TOTAL	71	5	

TOP POINT EARNERS

	PLAYER	GAMES	AV PTS
1	Gallimore	18	1.78
2	Crooks	18	1.72
3	O'Callaghan	20	1.70
4	Ilic	25	1.64
5	Fallon	12	1.58
6	Burns	16	1.44
7	Ireland	42	1.43
8	Betsy	42	1.38
9	Handyside	25	1.32
10	Kay	35	1.31
	CLUB AVERAGE:		1.35

LEAGUE APPEARANCES AND BOOKINGS

	AGE (on 01/07/04)	IN NAMED 16	APPEARANCES	COUNTING GAMES	MINUTES ON PITCH	Yellow	Red
Goalkeepers							
Danny Alcock	20	27	1	0	63	0	0
Marlon Beresford	34	15	14	13	1190	0	0
Tony Caig	30	3	3	3	270	0	0
Sasa Ilic	31	25	25	25	2250	0	0
Ross Turnbull	19	3	3	3	270	0	0
Gavin Ward	34	1	1	1	90	0	0
Defenders							
Neil Austin	21	43	37	29	2869	5	0
Tony Gallimore	32	21	20	18	1735	3	0
Paul Gibbs	31	8	3	0	37	0	0
Peter Handyside	29	34	28	25	2439	0	0
Craig Ireland	28	43	43	42	3794	6	0
Gary Monk	25	17	17	12	1203	1	0
Dave Mulligan	22	10	4	1	148	0	0
David Murphy	20	10	10	9	855	0	0
Brian O'Callaghan	23	33	29	20	2186	2	0
Paul Warhurst	34	4	4	2	290	2	1
Robbie Williams	20	6	4	3	269	2	0
Midfielders							
Jacob Burns	26	23	22	16	1556	6	0
Steven Carson	23	15	11	9	803	0	0
Lee Crooks	26	26	23	18	1796	3	0
Aaron Davies	20	8	4	1	149	0	0
Dean Gorre	33	20	19	11	1279	0	0
Steve Hayward	32	35	32	17	2000	8	0
Antony Kay	21	43	43	35	3415	11	2
Chris Lumsdon	24	35	28	16	1653	4	2
Alex Neil	23	35	31	14	1615	1	0
Craig Rocastle	22	7	5	3	325	1	0
Chris Shuker	22	9	9	8	745	1	0
Nicky Wroe	18	10	2	1	105	0	0
Forwards							
Kevin Betsy	26	45	45	42	3896	6	0
Gary Birch	22	8	8	8	715	1	0
Michael Boulding	28	6	6	5	448	0	0
Rory Fallon	22	16	16	12	1178	3	0
Daniel Nardiello	21	17	16	13	1254	3	0
Isaiah Rankin	26	26	20	9	925	1	0
Mark Stallard	29	10	10	10	888	1	0
Jonathan Walters	20	8	8	7	635	0	0

TEAM OF THE SEASON

G – Sasa Ilic – CG: 25 DR: 78

D – Brian O'Callaghan – CG: 20 DR: 87

D – Tony Gallimore – CG: 18 DR: 79

D – Peter Handyside – CG: 25 DR: 72

D – Craig Ireland – CG: 42 DR: 72

M – Jacob Burns – CG: 16 SD: 15

M – Steve Hayward – CG: 17 SD: 14

M – Lee Crooks – CG: 18 SD: -3

M – Chris Lumsdon – CG: 16 SD: -6

F – Daniel Nardiello – CG: 13 SR: 179

F – Kevin Betsy – CG: 42 SR: 390

SQUAD APPEARANCES

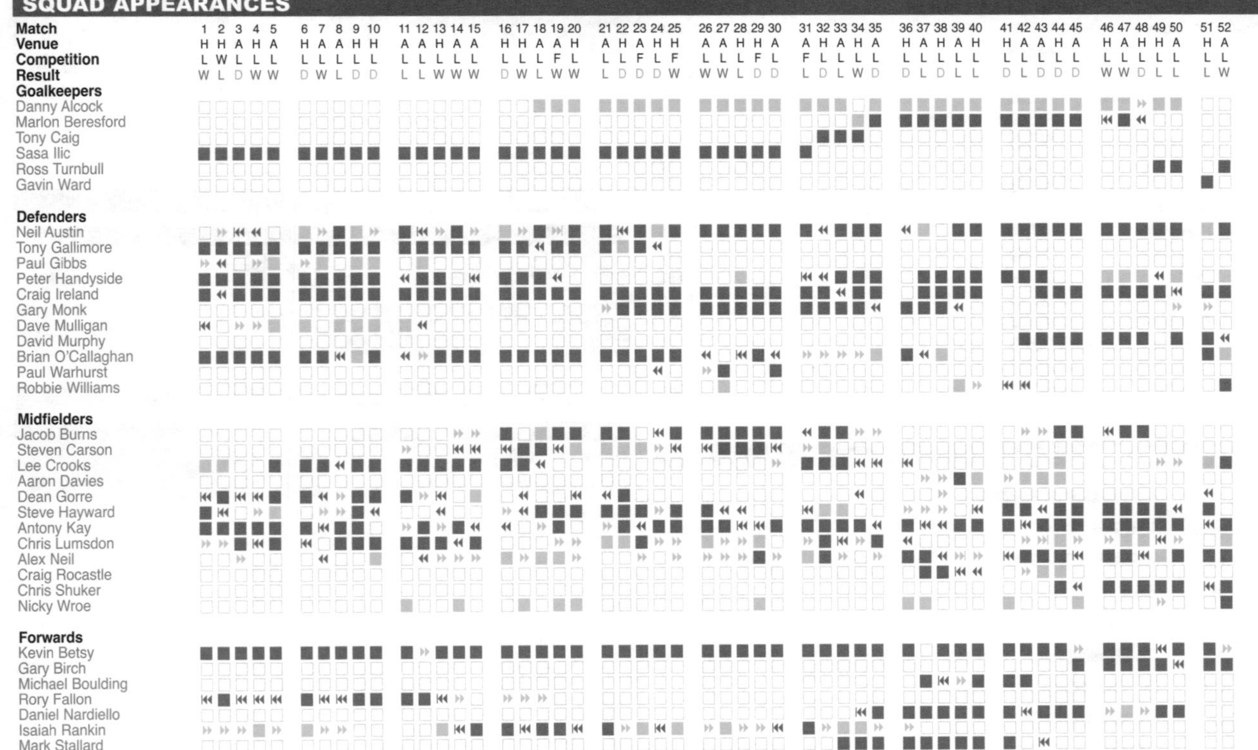

Match 1 2 3 4 5 6 7 8 9 10 11 12 13 14 15 16 17 18 19 20 21 22 23 24 25 26 27 28 29 30 31 32 33 34 35 36 37 38 39 40 41 42 43 44 45 46 47 48 49 50 51 52
Venue H H A H A H A A H H A A H A A H H A A H A H A H H A A H H A A H A H A H A H A H H A A H A H A H H A H A
Competition L W L L L L L L L L L L L L L L L L F L L L F L F L L L F L F L L L L L L L L L L L L L L L L L L L L L
Result W L D W W D W L D D L L W W W D W L W W L D D D W W W L D D L D L W D D L D L L D L D D D W W D L L L W
Goalkeepers
Danny Alcock
Marlon Beresford
Tony Caig
Sasa Ilic
Ross Turnbull
Gavin Ward
Defenders
Neil Austin
Tony Gallimore
Paul Gibbs
Peter Handyside
Craig Ireland
Gary Monk
Dave Mulligan
David Murphy
Brian O'Callaghan
Paul Warhurst
Robbie Williams
Midfielders
Jacob Burns
Steven Carson
Lee Crooks
Aaron Davies
Dean Gorre
Steve Hayward
Antony Kay
Chris Lumsdon
Alex Neil
Craig Rocastle
Chris Shuker
Nicky Wroe
Forwards
Kevin Betsy
Gary Birch
Michael Boulding
Rory Fallon
Daniel Nardiello
Isaiah Rankin
Mark Stallard
Jonathan Walters

KEY: On all match · On bench · Subbed or sent off (Counting game) · Subbed or sent off (playing less than 70 minutes) · Subbed on from bench (Counting Game) · Subbed on (playing less than 70 minutes) · Subbed on and then subbed or sent off (Counting Game) · Subbed on and then subbed or sent off (playing less than 70 minutes) · Not in 16

WREXHAM

Final Position: **13th**

NICKNAME: THE ROBINS

KEY: ☐ Won ☐ Drawn ☐ Lost

							Attendance
1	div2	Chesterfield	H	D	0-0		5,688
2	ccR1	Crewe	A	L	0-2		3,152
3	div2	Notts County	A	W	1-0	Sam 66	4,768
4	div2	Brentford	H	W	1-0	Lawrence 19	4,048
5	div2	Sheff Wed	A	W	3-2	Lawrence 40; Llewellyn 53; Edwards, C 64	24,478
6	div2	Bournemouth	H	L	0-1		4,929
7	div2	Swindon	A	L	0-1		6,160
8	div2	QPR	H	L	0-2		4,539
9	div2	Plymouth	H	D	2-2	Lawrence 28; Jones, L 42 pen	3,945
10	div2	Tranmere	A	W	2-1	Jones, L 64; Holmes 65	8,230
11	div2	Hartlepool	A	L	0-2		4,677
12	div2	Port Vale	H	W	2-1	Jones, L 33,78 pen	5,822
13	div2	Bristol City	H	D	0-0		4,405
14	div2	Oldham	H	W	4-0	Jones, L 32; Edwards, C 41; Lawrence 50; Jones, M 89	3,963
15	div2	Rushden & D	A	W	3-2	Edwards, C 10; Ferguson 35; Sam 56	4,117
16	div2	Barnsley	A	L	1-2	Holmes 74	8,916
17	div2	Colchester	H	L	0-1		4,269
18	facr1	Yeovil	A	L	1-4	Armstrong 88	5,049
19	div2	Blackpool	A	W	1-0	Lawrence 74	4,864
20	div2	Luton	A	L	2-3	Sam 19; Boyce 43 og	5,505
21	div2	Wycombe	H	D	0-0		3,208
22	div2	Brighton	A	L	0-2		5,642
23	div2	Peterborough	H	W	2-0	Carey 67; Sam 76	3,035
24	div2	Stockport	A	W	1-0	Barrett 88	6,256
25	div2	Blackpool	H	W	4-2	Llewellyn 15,21; Sam 33,44	6,171
26	div2	Sheff Wed	H	L	1-2	Carey 49	8,497
27	div2	Chesterfield	A	L	1-2	Armstrong 77	3,585
28	div2	Notts County	H	L	0-1		4,212
29	div2	Grimsby	A	W	3-1	Llewellyn 19; Thomas 24; Armstrong 63	3,572
30	div2	Brentford	A	W	1-0	Armstrong 58	4,567
31	div2	Stockport	H	D	0-0		5,046
32	div2	Barnsley	H	W	1-0	Llewellyn 24	4,086
33	div2	Bristol City	A	L	0-1		13,871
34	div2	Bournemouth	A	L	0-6		5,899
35	div2	Rushden & D	H	D	1-1	Edwards, C 20	3,680
36	div2	Grimsby	H	W	3-0	Crowell 34; Armstrong 36,36	3,127
37	div2	Peterborough	A	L	1-6	Llewellyn 21	4,323
38	div2	QPR	A	L	0-2		13,363
39	div2	Swindon	H	W	3-2	Llewellyn 25; Edwards, C 54; Thomas 68	3,384
40	div2	Plymouth	A	D	0-0		12,275
41	div2	Tranmere	H	L	0-1		4,496
42	div2	Port Vale	A	L	0-1		5,892
43	div2	Hartlepool	H	L	1-2	Barrett 71	3,786
44	div2	Colchester	A	L	1-3	Sam 18	3,077
45	div2	Oldham	A	D	1-1	Sam 19	5,646
46	div2	Luton	H	W	2-1	Sam 35,62	3,239
47	div2	Wycombe	A	D	1-1	Llewellyn 80	4,684
48	div2	Brighton	H	L	0-2		4,542

MONTHLY POINTS TALLY

Month	Points	%
AUGUST	10	67%
SEPTEMBER	4	27%
OCTOBER	10	56%
NOVEMBER	4	33%
DECEMBER	9	100%
JANUARY	6	40%
FEBRUARY	5	33%
MARCH	7	47%
APRIL	4	22%
MAY	1	17%

KEY PLAYERS - GOALSCORERS

Hector Sam

Goals in the League	10	Player Strike Rate Average number of minutes between League goals scored by player	226
Contribution to Attacking Power Average number of minutes between League team goals while on pitch	83	Club Strike Rate Average number of minutes between League goals scored by club	83

	PLAYER	LGE GOALS	GOALS ALL	POWER	STRIKE RATE
1	Hector Sam	10	10	83	226 mins
2	Chris Armstrong	5	6	113	364 mins
3	Chris Llewellyn	8	8	79	497 mins
4	Carlos Edwards	5	5	82	722 mins

KEY PLAYERS - MIDFIELDERS

Paul Edwards

Goals in the League	0	Contribution to Attacking Power Average number of minutes between League team goals while on pitch	81
Defensive Rating Average number of mins between League goals conceded while he was on the pitch	81	Scoring Difference Defensive Rating minus Contribution to Attacking Power	0

	PLAYER	LGE GOALS	GOALS ALL	DEF RATE	POWER	SCORE DIFF
1	Paul Edwards	0	0	81	81	0 mins
2	Stephen Thomas	2	2	77	82	-5 mins
3	Carlos Edwards	5	5	71	82	-11 mins
4	Darren Ferguson	1	1	68	81	-13 mins

KEY PLAYERS - DEFENDERS

Stephen Roberts

Goals Conceded (GC) The number of League goals conceded while he was on the pitch	27	Clean Sheets In games when he played at least 70 minutes	6
Defensive Rating Ave number of mins between League goals conceded while on the pitch	81	Club Defensive Rating Average number of mins between League goals conceded by the club this season	69

	PLAYER	CON LGE	CON ALL	CLEAN SHEETS	DEF RATE
1	Stephen Roberts	27	31	6	81 mins
2	Brian Carey	38	41	9	75 mins
3	Shaun Pejic	23	25	8	74 mins
4	Dennis Lawrence	59	65	13	68 mins

KEY GOALKEEPER

Andy Dibble

Goals Conceded in the League	37	Counting Games Games when he played at least 70 mins	34
Defensive Rating Ave number of mins between League goals conceded while on the pitch	81	Clean Sheets In games when he played at least 70 mins	13

LEAGUE GOALS

Hector Sam

Minutes on the pitch	2258	Goals in the League	226
League average (mins between goals)	10		

	PLAYER	MINS	GOALS	AVE
1	Sam	2258	10	226
2	Llewellyn	3973	8	497
3	Lawrence	4023	5	805
4	Edwards, C	3612	5	722
5	Jones, L	1237	5	247
6	Armstrong	1821	5	364
7	Carey	2848	2	1424
8	Thomas	2617	2	1309
9	Barrett	1747	2	874
10	Holmes	416	2	208
11	Jones, M	155	1	155
12	Ferguson	3488	1	3488
	Other		2	
	TOTAL		50	

DISCIPLINARY RECORDS

	PLAYER	YELLOW	RED	AVE
1	Morgan	4	1	240
2	Crowell	3	0	289
3	Carey	9	0	316
4	Thomas	8	0	327
5	Whitley	8	0	367
6	Ferguson	7	2	387
7	Jones, L	3	0	412
8	Edwards, P	7	1	436
9	Armstrong	4	0	455
10	Lawrence	4	1	804
11	Roberts	1	1	1090
12	Llewellyn	3	0	1324
13	Pejic	1	0	1706
	Other	3	0	
	TOTAL	65	6	

TOP POINT EARNERS

	PLAYER	GAMES	AV PTS
1	Thomas	26	1.65
2	Pejic	18	1.56
3	Dibble	33	1.45
4	Roberts	21	1.43
5	Edwards, C	39	1.41
6	Llewellyn	43	1.40
7	Barrett	16	1.38
8	Edwards, P	39	1.38
9	Ferguson	39	1.36
10	Sam	20	1.35
	CLUB AVERAGE:		**1.30**

TEAM OF THE SEASON

G — Andy Dibble — CG: 33 DR: 81

D — Stephen Roberts — CG: 21 DR: 81

D — Brian Carey — CG: 31 DR: 75

D — Shaun Pejic — CG: 18 DR: 74

D — Dennis Lawrence — CG: 44 DR: 68

M — Paul Edwards — CG: 39 SD: 0

M — Stephen Thomas — CG: 26 SD: -5

M — Carlos Edwards — CG: 39 SD: -11

M — Darren Ferguson — CG: 39 SD: -13

F — Hector Sam — CG: 20 SR: 226

F — Chris Armstrong — CG: 17 SR: 364

LEAGUE APPEARANCES AND BOOKINGS

	AGE (on 01/07/04)	IN NAMED 16	APPEARANCES	COUNTING GAMES	MINUTES ON PITCH	Yellow	Red
Goalkeepers							
Andy Dibble	39	35	35	33	2993	0	0
Michael Ingham	23	11	11	11	990	0	0
Paul Whitfield	22	44	3	2	176	0	0
Defenders							
Brian Carey	36	35	34	31	2848	9	0
Shaun Holmes	23	33	13	3	416	0	0
Mark Jones	20	23	12	0	155	0	0
Dennis Lawrence	30	45	45	44	4023	4	1
Jim McNulty	19	3	0	0	0	0	0
Craig Morgan	19	33	18	11	1203	4	1
Shaun Pejic	21	26	21	18	1706	1	0
Stephen Roberts	24	30	27	21	2181	1	1
Simon Spender	18	10	6	3	379	0	0
Midfielders							
Paul Barrett	26	31	27	16	1747	1	0
Matt Crowell	19	24	15	8	869	3	0
Carlos Edwards	25	42	42	39	3612	1	0
Paul Edwards	24	41	41	39	3494	7	1
Darren Ferguson	32	39	39	39	3488	7	2
Levi Macken	-	3	1	1	90	0	0
Stephen Thomas	25	43	39	26	2617	8	0
Jim Whitley	29	37	36	30	2936	8	0
Forwards							
Chris Armstrong	33	28	26	17	1821	4	0
Lee Jones	31	29	22	10	1237	3	0
Chris Llewellyn	24	46	46	43	3973	3	0
Armand One	21	3	3	0	128	0	0
Kevin Russell	37	1	1	1	89	0	0
Hector Sam	26	39	36	20	2258	1	0

SQUAD APPEARANCES

Match	1	2	3	4	5	6	7	8	9	10	11	12	13	14	15	16	17	18	19	20	21	22	23	24	25	26	27	28	29	30	31	32	33	34	35	36	37	38	39	40	41	42	43	44	45	46	47	48
Venue	H	A	A	H	A	H	A	H	H	A	A	H	H	H	A	A	H	A	A	A	H	A	H	A	H	H	A	H	A	A	H	H	A	A	H	H	A	A	H	A	H	A	H	A	A	H	A	H
Competition	L	W	L	L	L	L	L	L	L	L	L	L	L	L	L	L	L	F	L	L	L	L	L	L	L	L	L	L	L	L	L	L	L	L	L	L	L	L	L	L	L	L	L	L	L	L	L	L
Result	D	L	W	W	W	L	L	L	D	W	L	W	D	W	W	L	L	L	W	L	D	L	W	W	W	L	L	L	W	W	D	W	L	L	D	W	L	L	W	D	L	L	L	L	D	W	D	L

Goalkeepers
Andy Dibble
Michael Ingham
Paul Whitfield

Defenders
Brian Carey
Shaun Holmes
Mark Jones
Dennis Lawrence
Jim McNulty
Craig Morgan
Shaun Pejic
Stephen Roberts
Simon Spender

Midfielders
Paul Barrett
Matt Crowell
Carlos Edwards
Paul Edwards
Darren Ferguson
Levi Macken
Stephen Thomas
Jim Whitley

Forwards
Chris Armstrong
Lee Jones
Chris Llewellyn
Armand One
Kevin Russell
Hector Sam

KEY: On all match | On bench | Subbed or sent off (Counting game) | Subbed or sent off (playing less than 70 minutes) | Subbed on from bench (Counting Game) | Subbed on (playing less than 70 minutes) | Subbed on and then subbed or sent off (Counting Game) | Subbed on and then subbed or sent off (playing less than 70 minutes) | Not in 16

BLACKPOOL

Final Position: **14th**

NICKNAME: THE SEASIDERS

KEY: ☐ Won ☐ Drawn ☐ Lost

							Attendance
1	div2	QPR	A	L	0-5		14,581
2	ccR1	Barnsley	A	W	2-1	Taylor 5,22	5,378
3	div2	Wycombe	H	W	3-2	Taylor 45,45; Hilton 61	5,960
4	div2	Oldham	A	W	3-2	Danns 56; Douglas 69; Taylor 69	6,745
5	div2	Barnsley	H	L	0-2		6,039
6	div2	Swindon	A	D	2-2	Douglas 10; Taylor 27	6,219
7	div2	Bournemouth	H	L	1-2	Wellens 37	5,607
8	div2	Brentford	A	D	0-0		3,818
9	div2	Stockport	A	W	3-1	Grayson 56; Clarke 61; Murphy 69	5,420
10	ccR2	Birmingham	H	W	1-0	Taylor 6	7,370
11	div2	Notts County	H	W	2-1	Southern 11; Danns 43	6,206
12	div2	Grimsby	H	L	0-1		5,491
13	div2	Brighton	A	L	0-3		6,483
14	div2	Colchester	A	D	1-1	Taylor 52	3,265
15	div2	Hartlepool	H	W	4-0	Douglas 4; Taylor 20,40,72 pen	6,871
16	div2	Rushden & D	H	L	2-3	Murphy 4,62	5,234
17	div2	Plymouth	A	L	0-1		12,372
18	ccR3	Crystal Palace	H	L	1-3	Southern 88	6,010
19	div2	Sheff Wed	A	W	1-0	Taylor 80	21,450
20	facr1	Boreham W	H	W	4-0	Taylor 12,89; Coid 14; Burns 90	3,969
21	div2	Wrexham	H	L	0-1		4,864
22	div2	Chesterfield	H	W	1-0	Taylor 41	5,252
23	div2	Peterborough	A	W	1-0	Taylor 48	4,411
24	div2	Bristol City	H	W	1-0	Taylor 58	5,989
25	facr2	Oldham	A	W	5-2	Taylor 2,20,57; Southern 25; Richardson 73	6,143
26	div2	Luton	H	L	0-1		5,739
27	div2	Tranmere	H	W	2-1	Murphy 9; Jaszczun 79	8,340
28	div2	Wrexham	A	L	2-4	Taylor 23; Flynn 45	6,171
29	facr3	Portsmouth	A	L	1-2	Taylor 43	13,479
30	div2	QPR	H	L	0-1		7,329
31	div2	Port Vale	A	L	1-2	Sheron 73	4,523
32	div2	Wycombe	A	W	3-0	Coid 12; Taylor 27; Davis 67	4,834
33	div2	Oldham	H	D	1-1	Coid 25	7,508
34	div2	Barnsley	A	L	0-3		7,918
35	div2	Swindon	H	D	2-2	Taylor 14; Dinning 64	6,463
36	div2	Tranmere	A	D	1-1	Taylor 36	7,919
37	div2	Hartlepool	A	D	1-1	Sheron 74	5,497
38	div2	Plymouth	H	L	0-1		7,253
39	div2	Rushden & D	A	D	0-0		3,764
40	div2	Port Vale	H	W	2-1	Dinning 54 pen; Wellens 60	6,878
41	div2	Luton	A	L	2-3	Dinning 69 pen; Blinkhorn 79	6,343
42	div2	Brentford	H	D	1-1	Wellens 53	4,617
43	div2	Bournemouth	A	W	2-1	Sheron 45; Murphy 86	6,436
44	div2	Stockport	H	D	1-1	Sheron 62	7,604
45	div2	Colchester	H	D	0-0		5,473
46	div2	Notts County	A	L	1-4	Sheron 47	5,100
47	div2	Brighton	H	W	3-1	Sheron 24; Matias 58; Murphy 79	6,194
48	div2	Grimsby	A	W	2-0	Murphy 23; Coid 53	4,775
49	div2	Sheff Wed	H	W	4-1	Murphy 10,86; Sheron 26,79	7,388
50	div2	Chesterfield	A	L	0-1		4,117
51	div2	Peterborough	H	L	0-4		7,200
52	div2	Bristol City	A	L	1-2	Southern 78 pen	19,101

MONTHLY POINTS TALLY

Month	Points	%
AUGUST	7	47%
SEPTEMBER	7	47%
OCTOBER	4	27%
NOVEMBER	12	80%
DECEMBER	3	33%
JANUARY	5	28%
FEBRUARY	2	22%
MARCH	10	48%
APRIL	9	60%
MAY	0	0%

KEY PLAYERS - GOALSCORERS

Scott Taylor

Goals in the League	16	Player Strike Rate Average number of minutes between League goals scored by player	168
Contribution to Attacking Power Average number of minutes between League team goals while on pitch	70	Club Strike Rate Average number of minutes between League goals scored by club	73

	PLAYER	LGE GOALS	GOALS ALL	POWER	STRIKE RATE
1	Scott Taylor	16	25	70	168 mins
2	John Murphy	9	9	71	271 mins
3	Mike Sheron	8	8	68	315 mins
4	Jonathan Douglas	3	3	60	440 mins

KEY PLAYERS - MIDFIELDERS

Jonathan Douglas

Goals in the League	3	Contribution to Attacking Power Average number of minutes between League team goals while on pitch	60
Defensive Rating Average number of mins between League goals conceded while he was on the pitch	55	Scoring Difference Defensive Rating minus Contribution to Attacking Power	-5

	PLAYER	LGE GOALS	GOALS ALL	DEF RATE	POWER	SCORE DIFF
1	Jonathan Douglas	3	3	55	60	-5 mins
2	Richard Wellens	3	3	66	75	-9 mins
3	Martin Bullock	0	0	59	70	-11 mins
4	Keith Southern	2	4	95	116	-21 mins

KEY PLAYERS - DEFENDERS

Gareth Evans

Goals Conceded (GC) The number of League goals conceded while he was on the pitch	24	Clean Sheets In games when he played at least 70 minutes	4
Defensive Rating Ave number of mins between League goals conceded while on the pitch	74	Club Defensive Rating Average number of mins between League goals conceded by the club this season	64

	PLAYER	CON LGE	CON ALL	CLEAN SHEETS	DEF RATE
1	Gareth Evans	24	31	4	74 mins
2	Leam Richardson	30	33	6	72 mins
3	Steve Elliott	37	37	7	68 mins
4	Danny Coid	40	45	6	67 mins

KEY GOALKEEPER

Lee Jones

Goals Conceded in the League	30	Counting Games Games when he played at least 70 mins	22
Defensive Rating Ave number of mins between League goals conceded while on the pitch	66	Clean Sheets In games when he played at least 70 mins	3

LEAGUE GOALS

Scott Taylor

Minutes on the pitch	2686	Goals in the League	168
League average (mins between goals)	16		

	PLAYER	MINS	GOALS	AVE
1	Taylor	2686	16	168
2	Murphy	2442	9	271
3	Sheron	2522	8	315
4	Douglas	1320	3	440
5	Wellens	3450	3	1150
6	Coid	2681	3	894
7	Dinning	849	3	283
8	Danns	1028	2	514
9	Southern	1514	2	757
10	Matias	527	1	527
11	Davis	2014	1	2014
12	Blinkhorn	457	1	457
	Other		5	
	TOTAL		57	

DISCIPLINARY RECORDS

	PLAYER	YELLOW	RED	AVE
1	Danns	5	2	146
2	McMahon	3	0	204
3	Wellens	13	2	230
4	Douglas	3	1	330
5	Donnelly	2	0	358
6	Richardson	6	0	359
7	Davis	5	0	402
8	Coid	5	1	446
9	Elliott	5	0	504
10	Southern	3	0	504
11	Flynn	5	0	512
12	Jaszczun	1	0	513
13	Grayson	4	0	615
	Other	15	1	
	TOTAL	75	7	

TOP POINT EARNERS

	PLAYER	GAMES	AV PTS
1	Richardson	23	1.78
2	Douglas	13	1.62
3	Bullock	29	1.45
4	Southern	14	1.43
5	Flynn	28	1.36
6	Coid	25	1.36
7	Wellens	38	1.32
8	Taylor	29	1.28
9	Jones, L	22	1.27
10	Elliott	28	1.25
	CLUB AVERAGE:		**1.28**

LEAGUE APPEARANCES AND BOOKINGS

	AGE (on 01/07/04)	IN NAMED 16	APPEARANCES	COUNTING GAMES	MINUTES ON PITCH	Yellow	Red
Goalkeepers							
Philip Barnes	25	40	19	19	1708	0	1
Lewis Edge	17	5	1	1	90	0	0
Bradley Jones	22	3	3	3	270	1	0
Lee Jones	33	30	22	22	1980	3	0
Defenders							
Chris Clarke	30	19	19	11	1159	0	0
Danny Coid	22	36	35	25	2681	5	1
Steve Davis	35	34	29	22	2014	5	0
Steve Elliott	25	28	28	28	2520	5	0
Gareth Evans	23	24	23	18	1782	2	0
Mike Flynn	35	37	30	28	2560	5	0
Sean Hessey	25	8	6	2	248	0	0
Kirk Hilton	23	20	14	11	1040	1	0
Tommy Jaszczun	26	10	8	5	513	1	0
Leam Richardson	24	34	28	23	2154	6	0
Midfielders							
Martin Bullock	29	44	43	29	2950	3	0
Jamie Burns	20	19	11	4	507	0	0
Neil Danns	21	12	12	11	1028	5	2
Tony Dinning	29	10	10	9	849	1	0
Sean Doherty	19	2	1	0	3	0	0
Ciaran Donnelly	20	9	9	7	716	2	0
Jonathan Douglas	22	16	16	13	1320	3	1
Simon Grayson	34	39	33	25	2462	4	0
Simon Johnson	21	4	4	2	268	0	0
Steve McMahon	19	30	12	4	614	3	0
Keith Southern	20	29	28	14	1514	3	0
Richard Wellens	24	41	41	38	3450	13	2
Forwards							
Matthew Blinkhorn	19	15	12	3	457	0	0
Pedro Miguel Matias	30	7	7	6	527	0	0
John Murphy	27	30	30	25	2442	2	0
Mike Sheron	32	45	38	24	2522	1	0
Scott Taylor	28	31	31	29	2686	1	0
Richard Walker	26	14	9	2	296	0	0

TEAM OF THE SEASON

- **G** Lee Jones — CG: 22 DR: 66
- **D** Gareth Evans — CG: 18 DR: 74
- **D** Leam Richardson — CG: 23 DR: 72
- **D** Steve Elliott — CG: 28 DR: 68
- **D** Danny Coid — CG: 25 DR: 67
- **M** Jonathan Douglas — CG: 13 SD: -5
- **M** Richard Wellens — CG: 38 SD: -9
- **M** Martin Bullock — CG: 29 SD: -11
- **M** Keith Southern — CG: 14 SD: -21
- **F** Scott Taylor — CG: 29 SR: 168
- **F** John Murphy — CG: 25 SR: 271

SQUAD APPEARANCES

Match	1	2	3	4	5	6	7	8	9	10	11	12	13	14	15	16	17	18	19	20	21	22	23	24	25	26	27	28	29	30	31	32	33	34	35	36	37	38	39	40	41	42	43	44	45	46	47	48	49	50	51	52
Venue	A	A	H	A	H	A	H	A	A	H	H	H	A	A	H	H	A	H	A	H	H	H	A	H	A	H	H	A	A	H	A	A	H	A	H	A	A	H	A	H	A	H	A	H	H	A	H	A	H	A	H	A
Competition	L	W	L	L	L	L	L	L	L	W	L	L	L	L	L	L	L	W	L	F	L	L	L	L	F	L	L	L	F	L	L	L	L	L	L	L	L	L	L	L	L	L	L	L	L	L	L	L	L	L	L	L
Result	L	W	W	W	L	D	L	D	W	W	W	L	L	D	W	L	L	L	W	W	L	W	W	W	W	L	W	L	L	L	L	W	D	L	D	D	D	L	D	W	L	D	W	D	D	L	W	W	W	L	L	L

Goalkeepers
Philip Barnes
Lewis Edge
Bradley Jones
Lee Jones

Defenders
Chris Clarke
Danny Coid
Steve Davis
Steve Elliott
Gareth Evans
Mike Flynn
Sean Hessey
Kirk Hilton
Tommy Jaszczun
Leam Richardson

Midfielders
Martin Bullock
Jamie Burns
Neil Danns
Tony Dinning
Sean Doherty
Ciaran Donnelly
Jonathan Douglas
Simon Grayson
Simon Johnson
Steve McMahon
Keith Southern
Richard Wellens

Forwards
Matthew Blinkhorn
Pedro Miguel Matias
John Murphy
Mike Sheron
Scott Taylor
Richard Walker

KEY: On all match / On bench / Subbed or sent off (Counting game) / Subbed or sent off (playing less than 70 minutes) / Subbed on from bench (Counting Game) / Subbed on (playing less than 70 minutes) / Subbed on and then subbed or sent off (Counting Game) / Subbed on and then subbed or sent off (playing less than 70 minutes) / Not in 16

OLDHAM ATHLETIC

Final Position: **15th**

NICKNAME: THE LATICS

KEY: ☐ Won ☐ Drawn ☐ Lost

							Attendance
1	div2	Brighton	H	L	1-3	Murray 82	6,522
2	ccR1	Scunthorpe	A	L	1-2	Antoine-Curier 61	2,366
3	div2	Sheff Wed	A	D	2-2	Sheridan, J 6 pen; Antoine-Curier 55	24,630
4	div2	Blackpool	H	L	2-3	Eyre, J 1; Antoine-Curier 90	6,745
5	div2	Brentford	A	L	1-2	Holden 17	4,073
6	div2	Rushden & D	H	W	3-2	Sheridan, J 11 pen; Haining 75; O'Halloran 90	5,469
7	div2	Hartlepool	A	D	0-0		5,728
8	div2	Bristol City	H	D	1-1	Zola 54	5,921
9	div2	Barnsley	A	D	1-1	Vernon 65	10,102
10	div2	Wycombe	A	W	5-2	Murray 1,85; Hall, D 16; Zola 22; Killen 75 pen	4,725
11	div2	Luton	H	W	3-0	Sheridan, J 30 pen; Zola 45; Holden 47	6,077
12	div2	Stockport	H	W	2-0	Sheridan, J 11 pen; Vernon 46	7,015
13	div2	Peterborough	A	D	2-2	Cooksey 8; Sheridan, J 57 pen	4,465
14	div2	Port Vale	H	W	2-1	Killen 71; Eyres, D 87	6,913
15	div2	Tranmere	A	L	1-2	Eyre, J 30	8,202
16	div2	Wrexham	A	L	0-4		3,963
17	div2	Bournemouth	H	D	1-1	Vernon 30	5,850
18	div2	Plymouth	A	D	2-2	Beharall 10,63	11,205
19	facr1	Carlisle	H	W	3-0	Zola 35; Cooksey 37,78	4,391
20	div2	Swindon	H	L	0-1		5,282
21	div2	Chesterfield	A	D	1-1	Zola 55	3,565
22	div2	Notts County	H	L	0-1		5,190
23	facr2	Blackpool	H	L	2-5	Eyre, J 61; Johnson 90	6,143
24	div2	Colchester	A	L	1-2	Eyres, D 66	2,897
25	div2	QPR	H	W	2-1	Cooksey 67; Eyre, J 86	5,603
26	div2	Grimsby	A	D	3-3	Johnson 19; Cooksey 32; Vernon 73	6,172
27	div2	Hartlepool	H	L	0-2		6,243
28	div2	Brentford	H	D	1-1	Vernon 54	4,490
29	div2	Brighton	A	D	0-0		6,036
30	div2	Sheff Wed	H	W	1-0	Vernon 17	9,316
31	div2	Blackpool	A	D	1-1	Vernon 68	7,508
32	div2	Rushden & D	A	L	1-4	Johnson 55	4,591
33	div2	Grimsby	H	W	6-0	Vernon 9,16,45; Griffin 27; Johnson 34; Zola 85	13,007
34	div2	Port Vale	A	L	0-1		6,035
35	div2	Tranmere	H	D	1-1	Vernon 60	6,916
36	div2	Bournemouth	A	L	0-1		6,594
37	div2	QPR	A	D	1-1	Murray 45	13,696
38	div2	Colchester	H	D	0-0		5,937
39	div2	Barnsley	H	D	1-1	Murray 53	5,837
40	div2	Bristol City	A	W	2-0	Cooksey 26; Murray 36	11,037
41	div2	Wycombe	H	L	2-3	Murray 18; Eyre, J 44	5,758
42	div2	Luton	A	D	1-1	Crowe 33	5,966
43	div2	Peterborough	H	D	1-1	Vernon 90	5,688
44	div2	Stockport	A	D	1-1	Haining 1	8,617
45	div2	Plymouth	H	W	4-1	Johnson 34; Owen 42; Eyres, D 45; Murray 67	6,924
46	div2	Wrexham	H	D	1-1	Holden 45	5,646
47	div2	Swindon	A	W	2-1	Murray 8; Johnson 74	8,506
48	div2	Chesterfield	H	W	2-0	Eyre, J 50,81	8,177
49	div2	Notts County	A	D	1-1	Holden 61	6,715

MONTHLY POINTS TALLY

AUGUST	4	27%
SEPTEMBER	12	67%
OCTOBER	5	33%
NOVEMBER	2	17%
DECEMBER	4	33%
JANUARY	6	40%
FEBRUARY	4	33%
MARCH	6	40%
APRIL	10	56%
MAY	4	67%

KEY PLAYERS - GOALSCORERS

Scott Vernon

Goals in the League	12	Player Strike Rate Average number of minutes between League goals scored by player	209
Contribution to Attacking Power Average number of minutes between League team goals while on pitch	58	Club Strike Rate Average number of minutes between League goals scored by club	63

	PLAYER	LGE GOALS	GOALS ALL	POWER	STRIKE RATE
1	Scott Vernon	12	12	58	209 mins
2	John Sheridan	5	5	45	281 mins
3	Jermaine Johnson	5	6	67	322 mins
4	Calvin Makongo Zola	5	6	69	360 mins

KEY PLAYERS - MIDFIELDERS

John Sheridan

Goals in the League	5	Contribution to Attacking Power Average number of minutes between League team goals while on pitch	45
Defensive Rating Average number of mins between League goals conceded while he was on the pitch	74	Scoring Difference Defensive Rating minus Contribution to Attacking Power	29

	PLAYER	LGE GOALS	GOALS ALL	DEF RATE	POWER	SCORE DIFF
1	John Sheridan	5	5	74	45	29 mins
2	David Eyres	3	3	88	60	28 mins
3	Dean Holden	4	4	78	62	16 mins
4	Paul Murray	9	9	70	58	12 mins

KEY PLAYERS - DEFENDERS

Gareth Owen

Goals Conceded (GC) The number of League goals conceded while he was on the pitch	14	Clean Sheets In games when he played at least 70 minutes	3
Defensive Rating Ave number of mins between League goals conceded while on the pitch	90	Club Defensive Rating Average number of mins between League goals conceded by the club this season	69

	PLAYER	CON LGE	CON ALL	CLEAN SHEETS	DEF RATE
1	Gareth Owen	14	14	3	90 mins
2	Adam Griffin	28	30	6	80 mins
3	Daniel Hall	36	40	7	71 mins
4	Mark Hudson	19	19	3	71 mins

KEY GOALKEEPER

Leslie Pogliacomi

Goals Conceded in the League	60	Counting Games Games when he played at least 70 mins	46
Defensive Rating Ave number of mins between League goals conceded while on the pitch	69	Clean Sheets In games when he played at least 70 mins	9

LEAGUE GOALS

Scott Vernon

Minutes on the pitch	2512	Goals in the League	209
League average (mins between goals)	12		

	PLAYER	MINS	GOALS	AVE
1	Vernon	2512	12	209
2	Murray	3625	9	403
3	Eyre, J	3580	6	597
4	Zola	1800	5	360
5	Johnson	1612	5	322
6	Sheridan, J	1403	5	281
7	Holden	3267	4	817
8	Cooksey	2125	4	531
9	Eyres, D	1933	3	644
10	Killen	715	2	358
11	Antoine-Curier	481	2	241
12	Haining	2532	2	1266
	Other		7	
	TOTAL		66	

DISCIPLINARY RECORDS

	PLAYER	YELLOW	RED	AVE
1	Killen	4	2	119
2	Hudson	5	0	270
3	Holden	12	0	272
4	Sheridan, J	4	1	280
5	Hall, D	8	1	283
6	Johnson	4	1	322
7	Cooksey	6	0	354
8	Eyre, J	10	0	358
9	Sheridan, D	4	0	445
10	Antoine-Curier	1	0	481
11	Boshell	3	0	500
12	Haining	5	0	506
13	Bonner	1	0	585
	Other	23	1	
	TOTAL	90	6	

TOP POINT EARNERS

	PLAYER	GAMES	AV PTS
1	Sheridan, J	13	1.69
2	Eyres, D	20	1.55
3	Hudson	15	1.40
4	Holden	36	1.36
5	Griffin	25	1.36
6	Sheridan, D	17	1.35
7	Murray	40	1.35
8	Hall, D	27	1.33
9	Vernon	22	1.32
10	Eyre, J	38	1.32
	CLUB AVERAGE:		**1.24**

LEAGUE APPEARANCES AND BOOKINGS

	AGE (on 01/07/04)	IN NAMED 16	APPEARANCES	COUNTING GAMES	MINUTES ON PITCH	Yellow	Red
Goalkeepers							
Adam Collin	19	6	0	0	0	0	0
Steve Corry	22	4	0	0	0	0	0
Chris Grange	19	5	0	0	0	0	0
Leslie Pogliacomi	28	46	46	46	4140	2	0
Kieren Westwood	19	21	0	0	0	0	0
Defenders							
David Beharall	25	13	7	6	578	0	0
Michael Clegg	27	41	31	24	2438	3	0
Adam Griffin	19	27	26	25	2234	2	0
Will Haining	21	32	31	26	2532	5	0
Daniel Hall	20	36	31	27	2555	8	1
Mark Hudson	22	15	15	15	1350	5	0
Ndiwa Lord-Kangana	19	5	4	3	277	2	0
Gareth Owen	21	16	15	14	1266	1	0
Marc Tierney	18	15	2	0	9	0	0
Midfielders							
Mark Bonner	30	9	7	6	585	1	0
Danny Boshell	23	28	22	14	1500	3	0
David Carney	20	0	0	0	0	0	0
Ernie Cooksey	24	40	36	19	2125	6	0
John Eyre	29	43	43	38	3580	10	0
David Eyres	40	34	28	20	1933	3	0
Dean Holden	24	39	38	36	3267	12	0
Paul Murray	27	41	41	40	3625	5	1
Matt O'Halloran	21	16	13	2	398	2	0
Darren Sheridan	36	28	28	17	1780	4	0
John Sheridan	39	21	21	13	1403	4	1
Forwards							
Mickael Antoine-Curier	21	8	8	4	481	1	0
Dean Crowe	25	7	5	1	186	0	0
Jermaine Johnson	24	20	20	17	1612	4	1
Christopher Killen	22	13	13	5	715	4	2
Carlos Roca	19	13	7	0	145	0	0
Scott Vernon	20	46	45	22	2512	1	0
Rob Walker	18	2	1	1	90	0	0
Wes Wilkinson	20	6	5	2	271	0	0
Calvin Makongo Zola	19	27	25	17	1800	2	0

TEAM OF THE SEASON

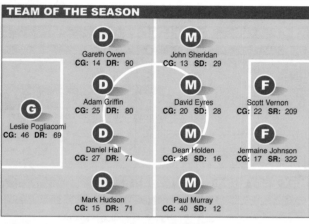

G – Leslie Pogliacomi – CG: 46 DR: 69

D – Gareth Owen – CG: 14 DR: 90

D – Adam Griffin – CG: 25 DR: 80

D – Daniel Hall – CG: 27 DR: 71

D – Mark Hudson – CG: 15 DR: 71

M – John Sheridan – CG: 13 SD: 29

M – David Eyres – CG: 20 SD: 28

M – Dean Holden – CG: 36 SD: 16

M – Paul Murray – CG: 40 SD: 12

F – Scott Vernon – CG: 22 SR: 209

F – Jermaine Johnson – CG: 17 SR: 322

SQUAD APPEARANCES

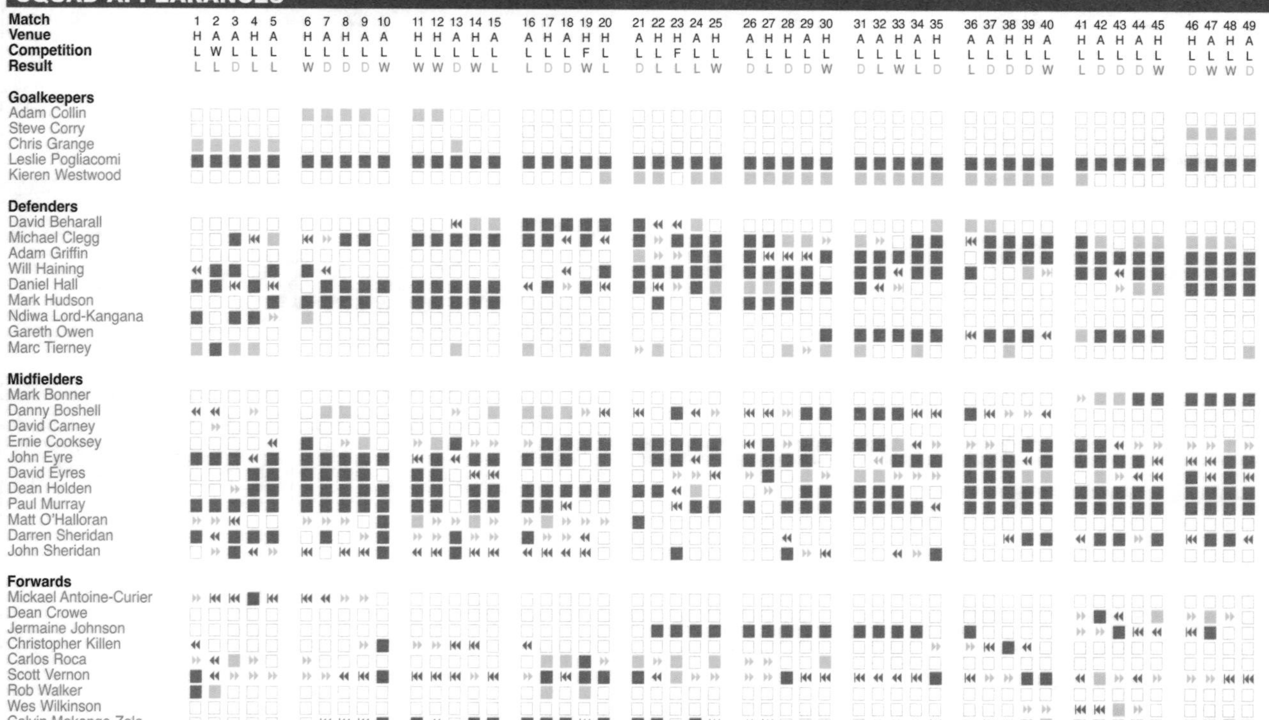

Match 1 2 3 4 5 6 7 8 9 10 11 12 13 14 15 16 17 18 19 20 21 22 23 24 25 26 27 28 29 30 31 32 33 34 35 36 37 38 39 40 41 42 43 44 45 46 47 48 49
Venue H A A H A H A H A A H H A H A A H A H H A H H A H A H H A H A A H A H A A H H A H A H A H H A H A
Competition L W L L L L L L L L L L L L L L L L F L L L F L L L L L L L L L L L L L L L L L L L L L L L L L L
Result L L D L L W D D D W W W D W L L D D W L D L L L W D L D D W D L W L D L D D D W L D D D W D W W D
Goalkeepers
Adam Collin
Steve Corry
Chris Grange
Leslie Pogliacomi
Kieren Westwood
Defenders
David Beharall
Michael Clegg
Adam Griffin
Will Haining
Daniel Hall
Mark Hudson
Ndiwa Lord-Kangana
Gareth Owen
Marc Tierney
Midfielders
Mark Bonner
Danny Boshell
David Carney
Ernie Cooksey
John Eyre
David Eyres
Dean Holden
Paul Murray
Matt O'Halloran
Darren Sheridan
John Sheridan
Forwards
Mickael Antoine-Curier
Dean Crowe
Jermaine Johnson
Christopher Killen
Carlos Roca
Scott Vernon
Rob Walker
Wes Wilkinson
Calvin Makongo Zola

KEY: On all match | On bench | Subbed or sent off (Counting game) | Subbed or sent off (playing less than 70 minutes) | Subbed on from bench (Counting Game) | Subbed on (playing less than 70 minutes) | Subbed on and then subbed or sent off (Counting Game) | Subbed on and then subbed or sent off (playing less than 70 minutes) | Not in 16

SHEFFIELD WEDNESDAY

Final Position: **16th**

NICKNAME: THE OWLS — KEY: Won / Drawn / Lost

							Attendance
1	div2	Swindon	A	W	3-2	Owusu 5,20; Kuqi 25	10,573
2	ccR1	Hartlepool	H	L	4-5*	Lee 50; Wood 115 (*on penalties)	13,410
3	div2	Oldham	H	D	2-2	Kuqi 26,53	24,630
4	div2	Peterborough	A	W	1-0	Kuqi 43	10,194
5	div2	Wrexham	H	L	2-3	Quinn 2; Smith, P 79	24,478
6	div2	Wycombe	A	W	2-1	Owusu 5; Quinn 8	6,444
7	div2	Tranmere	H	W	2-0	Smith, P 57; Cooke 61	21,705
8	div2	Stockport	H	D	2-2	Kuqi 17; Quinn 31	22,535
9	div2	Bournemouth	A	L	0-1		8,219
10	div2	Brighton	A	L	0-2		6,602
11	div2	Grimsby	H	D	0-0		21,918
12	div2	Notts County	H	W	2-1	McLaren 23,53	20,354
13	div2	Brentford	A	W	3-0	Holt 39,45; Owusu 75	8,631
14	div2	Hartlepool	A	D	1-1	Owusu 47	7,448
15	div2	Rushden & D	H	D	0-0		22,599
16	div2	Plymouth	H	L	1-3	Reddy 84	20,090
17	div2	Bristol City	A	D	1-1	Proudlock 25	13,668
18	div2	Blackpool	H	L	0-1		21,450
19	facr1	Salisbury	H	W	4-0	Proudlock 32 pen,47,64; Owusu 70	11,419
20	div2	Colchester	A	L	1-3	Bromby 58	5,018
21	div2	Luton	H	D	0-0		21,027
22	div2	QPR	A	L	0-3		17,393
23	facr2	Scunthorpe	A	D	2-2	N'dumbu 84; Holt 90	7,418
24	div2	Barnsley	A	D	1-1	N'dumbu 30	20,438
25	facr2r	Scunthorpe	H	L	1-3*	(*on penalties)	11,722
26	div2	Chesterfield	H	D	0-0		25,296
27	div2	Port Vale	H	L	2-3	Robins 21; Lee 30	24,991
28	div2	Tranmere	A	D	2-2	Lee 4; N'dumbu 21	9,645
29	div2	Wrexham	A	W	2-1	N'dumbu 39; Quinn 65	8,497
30	div2	Swindon	H	D	1-1	Robins 72	22,751
31	div2	Oldham	A	L	0-1		9,316
32	div2	Peterborough	H	W	2-0	Robins 55; Proudlock 90	21,474
33	div2	Wycombe	H	D	1-1	Proudlock 62	19,596
34	div2	Port Vale	A	L	0-3		7,958
35	div2	Hartlepool	H	W	1-0	N'dumbu 80 pen	20,732
36	div2	Rushden & D	A	W	2-1	N'dumbu 13 pen,55 pen	5,685
37	div2	Bristol City	H	W	1-0	Lee 90	24,154
38	div2	Plymouth	A	L	0-2		17,218
39	div2	Chesterfield	A	L	1-3	N'dumbu 66	7,695
40	div2	Barnsley	H	W	2-1	N'dumbu 36,56	25,664
41	div2	Bournemouth	H	L	0-2		18,799
42	div2	Stockport	A	L	0-1		8,011
43	div2	Brighton	H	W	2-1	Brunt 8; Mustoe 90	19,707
44	div2	Grimsby	A	L	0-2		6,641
45	div2	Brentford	H	D	1-1	Smith, D 90	20,004
46	div2	Notts County	A	D	0-0		9,601
47	div2	Blackpool	A	L	1-4	Brunt 37	7,388
48	div2	Colchester	H	L	0-1		20,464
49	div2	Luton	A	L	2-3	Shaw, J 23; Cooke 33	7,157
50	div2	QPR	H	L	1-3	Shaw, J 59	29,313

MONTHLY POINTS TALLY

Month	Points	%
AUGUST	7	58%
SEPTEMBER	8	44%
OCTOBER	9	50%
NOVEMBER	1	8%
DECEMBER	3	25%
JANUARY	8	53%
FEBRUARY	9	75%
MARCH	6	33%
APRIL	2	13%
MAY	0	0%

KEY PLAYERS - GOALSCORERS

Guylain Sungu N'dumbu

Goals in the League	9	Player Strike Rate Average number of minutes between League goals scored by player	193
Contribution to Attacking Power Average number of minutes between League team goals while on pitch	108	Club Strike Rate Average number of minutes between League goals scored by club	86

	PLAYER	LGE GOALS	GOALS ALL	POWER	STRIKE RATE
1	Guylain Sungu N'dumbu	9	10	108	193 mins
2	Mark Robins	3	3	93	407 mins
3	Alan Quinn	4	4	80	521 mins
4	Adam Proudlock	3	6	114	762 mins

KEY PLAYERS - MIDFIELDERS

Terry Cooke

Goals in the League	2	Contribution to Attacking Power Average number of minutes between League team goals while on pitch	65
Defensive Rating Average number of mins between League goals conceded while he was on the pitch	73	Scoring Difference Defensive Rating minus Contribution to Attacking Power	8

	PLAYER	LGE GOALS	GOALS ALL	DEF RATE	POWER	SCORE DIFF
1	Terry Cooke	2	2	73	65	8 mins
2	Alan Quinn	4	4	67	80	-13 mins
3	Paul McLaren	2	2	61	77	-16 mins
4	Steven Haslam	0	0	84	115	-31 mins

KEY PLAYERS - DEFENDERS

Guylain Sungu N'dumbu

Goals Conceded (GC) The number of League goals conceded while he was on the pitch	25	Clean Sheets In games when he played at least 70 minutes	4
Defensive Rating Ave number of mins between League goals conceded while on the pitch	70	Club Defensive Rating Average number of mins between League goals conceded by the club this season	65

	PLAYER	CON LGE	CON ALL	CLEAN SHEETS	DEF RATE
1	Guylain Sungu N'dumbu	25	26	4	70 mins
2	Graeme Lee	39	43	8	68 mins
3	Leigh Bromby	39	41	8	67 mins
4	Dean Smith	55	57	10	66 mins

KEY GOALKEEPER

David Lucas

Goals Conceded in the League	18	Counting Games Games when he played at least 70 mins	17
Defensive Rating Ave number of mins between League goals conceded while on the pitch	84	Clean Sheets In games when he played at least 70 mins	4

LEAGUE GOALS

Guylain Sungu N'dumbu

Minutes on the pitch	1738	Goals in the League	193
League average (mins between goals)	9		

	PLAYER	MINS	GOALS	AVE
1	N'dumbu	1738	9	193
2	Owusu	1143	5	229
3	Kuqi	584	5	117
4	Quinn	2083	4	521
5	Robins	1221	3	407
6	Lee	2655	3	885
7	Proudlock	2286	3	762
8	Cooke	1688	2	844
9	Holt	746	2	373
10	Shaw, J	721	2	361
11	Smith, P	1203	2	602
12	Brunt	726	2	363
	Other		6	
	TOTAL		48	

DISCIPLINARY RECORDS

	PLAYER	YELLOW	RED	AVE
1	Holt	4	1	149
2	Quinn	11	2	160
3	Kuqi	2	1	194
4	N'dumbu	7	1	217
5	Chambers, A	3	0	251
6	Geary	12	1	281
7	Smith, P	3	0	401
8	McMahon	2	0	420
9	Wood	2	0	464
10	McLaren	4	0	522
11	Haslam	3	0	535
12	Proudlock	3	1	571
13	Olsen	1	0	613
	Other	25	0	
	TOTAL	82	7	

TOP POINT EARNERS

	PLAYER	GAMES	AV PTS
1	Cooke	17	1.53
2	Haslam	17	1.41
3	N'dumbu	17	1.35
4	Quinn	22	1.32
5	Lee	29	1.28
6	Lucas	16	1.25
7	Barry-Murphy	37	1.24
8	Geary	40	1.23
9	Smith, D	39	1.23
10	Mustoe	18	1.11
	CLUB AVERAGE:		**1.15**

TEAM OF THE SEASON

G David Lucas — **CG:** 16 **DR:** 84

D Guylain Sungu N'dumbu — **CG:** 17 **DR:** 70

D Graeme Lee — **CG:** 29 **DR:** 68

D Leigh Bromby — **CG:** 29 **DR:** 67

D Dean Smith — **CG:** 39 **DR:** 66

M Terry Cooke — **CG:** 17 **SD:** 8

M Alan Quinn — **CG:** 22 **SD:** -13

M Paul McLaren — **CG:** 23 **SD:** -16

M Steven Haslam — **CG:** 17 **SD:** -31

F Mark Robins — **CG:** 13 **SR:** 407

F Adam Proudlock — **CG:** 20 **SR:** 762

LEAGUE APPEARANCES AND BOOKINGS

	AGE (on 01/07/04)	IN NAMED 16	APPEARANCES	COUNTING GAMES	MINUTES ON PITCH	Yellow	Red
Goalkeepers							
David Lucas	26	17	17	16	1507	0	0
Kevin Pressman	36	39	21	19	1761	0	0
Christopher Stringer	20	0	0	0	0	0	0
Ola Tidman	25	19	9	9	810	0	0
Defenders							
Craig Armstrong	29	11	10	2	418	3	0
Brian Barry-Murphy	25	43	41	37	3355	5	0
Jon Beswetherick	26	8	5	3	324	1	0
Leigh Bromby	24	33	29	29	2610	1	0
Chris Carr	19	3	2	0	46	0	0
Derek Geary	24	41	41	40	3655	12	1
Graeme Lee	26	30	30	29	2655	4	0
Guylain Sungu N'dumbu	21	30	24	17	1738	7	1
Dean Smith	33	45	41	39	3620	5	0
Richard Wood	19	34	12	10	929	2	0
Midfielders							
Chris Brunt	19	11	9	8	726	0	0
Adam Chambers	23	14	11	8	754	3	0
Terry Cooke	27	24	23	17	1688	2	0
Richard Evans	21	6	6	2	372	0	0
Steven Haslam	24	32	25	17	1605	3	0
Paul McLaren	27	25	25	23	2090	4	0
Lewis McMahon	19	15	10	9	841	2	0
Robbie Mustoe	36	27	25	18	1869	2	0
Robert Poulter	-	10	0	0	0	0	0
Alan Quinn	25	24	24	22	2083	11	2
Paul Smith	28	23	19	11	1203	3	0
Mark Wilson	25	9	3	3	254	0	0
Forwards							
Mark Burchill	23	5	5	2	316	0	0
Grant Holt	23	23	17	4	746	4	1
Shefki Kuqi	27	7	7	6	584	2	1
Liam Needham	18	3	0	0	0	0	0
Kim Olsen	25	13	10	5	613	1	0
Lloyd Owusu	27	21	20	11	1143	1	0
Adam Proudlock	23	30	30	20	2286	3	1
Michael Reddy	24	12	12	7	776	1	0
Mark Robins	34	15	15	13	1221	0	0
Jon Shaw	20	24	14	7	721	0	0

SQUAD APPEARANCES

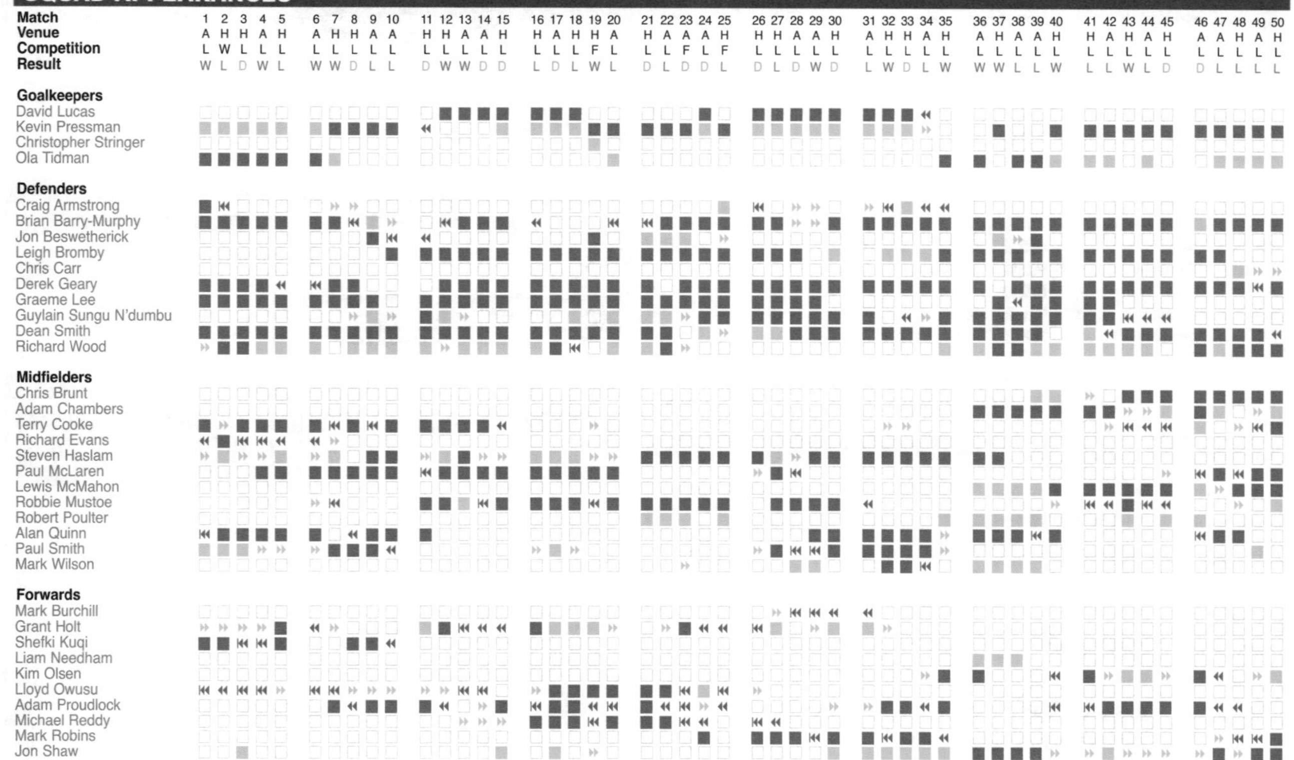

Match 1 2 3 4 5 6 7 8 9 10 11 12 13 14 15 16 17 18 19 20 21 22 23 24 25 26 27 28 29 30 31 32 33 34 35 36 37 38 39 40 41 42 43 44 45 46 47 48 49 50
Venue A H H A H A H H A A H H A A H H A H H A H A A A H H H A A H A H H A H A H A A H H A H A H A A H A H
Competition L W L L L L L L L L L L L L L L L L F L L L F L F L L L L L L L L L L L L L L L L L L L L L L L L L
Result W L D W L W W D L L D W W D D L D L W L D L D D L D L D W D L W D L W W W L L W L L W L D D L L L L
Goalkeepers
David Lucas
Kevin Pressman
Christopher Stringer
Ola Tidman
Defenders
Craig Armstrong
Brian Barry-Murphy
Jon Beswetherick
Leigh Bromby
Chris Carr
Derek Geary
Graeme Lee
Guylain Sungu N'dumbu
Dean Smith
Richard Wood
Midfielders
Chris Brunt
Adam Chambers
Terry Cooke
Richard Evans
Steven Haslam
Paul McLaren
Lewis McMahon
Robbie Mustoe
Robert Poulter
Alan Quinn
Paul Smith
Mark Wilson
Forwards
Mark Burchill
Grant Holt
Shefki Kuqi
Liam Needham
Kim Olsen
Lloyd Owusu
Adam Proudlock
Michael Reddy
Mark Robins
Jon Shaw
KEY: On all match
On bench
Subbed or sent off (Counting game)
Subbed or sent off (playing less than 70 minutes)
Subbed on from bench (Counting Game)
Subbed on (playing less than 70 minutes)
Subbed on and then subbed or sent off (Counting Game)
Subbed on and then subbed or sent off (playing less than 70 minutes)
Not in 16

BRENTFORD

Final Position: **17th**

NICKNAME: THE BEES

KEY: ☐ Won ☐ Drawn ☐ Lost

							Attendance
1	div2	Tranmere	A	L	1-4	Hunt 64 pen	7,307
2	ccR1	West Brom	A	L	0-4		10,440
3	div2	Peterborough	H	L	0-3		4,463
4	div2	Wrexham	A	L	0-1		4,048
5	div2	Oldham	H	W	2-1	Hutchinson 42; Rougier 58	4,073
6	div2	Port Vale	A	L	0-1		5,257
7	div2	Plymouth	H	L	1-3	May 27	5,688
8	div2	Rushden & D	A	W	1-0	Hunt 19	4,396
9	div2	Blackpool	H	D	0-0		3,818
10	div2	Hartlepool	H	W	2-1	Sonko 13; Wright 48	4,501
11	div2	Chesterfield	A	W	2-1	Hunt 63; Wright 82	3,257
12	div2	Colchester	A	D	1-1	Rougier 36	3,343
13	div2	Sheff Wed	H	L	0-3		8,631
14	div2	Luton	H	W	4-2	Hunt 12; Tabb 58,65; May 87	5,579
15	div2	Brighton	H	W	4-0	Hunt 8 pen,87 pen; Tabb 36; May 78	6,532
16	div2	Notts County	A	L	0-2		4,145
17	div2	Barnsley	H	W	2-1	Hutchinson 47; Rougier 58	4,789
18	facr1	Gainsborough	H	W	7-1	Harrold 45,65,86; Rougier 47; Purkiss 50 og; Frampton 55; O'Connor 76	3,041
19	div2	QPR	A	L	0-1		15,865
20	div2	Wycombe	A	W	2-1	Hutchinson 29; Tabb 90	6,445
21	div2	Grimsby	H	L	1-3	Hunt 10 pen	4,685
22	div2	Bournemouth	A	L	0-1		6,674
23	facr2	Telford	A	L	0-3		2,996
24	div2	Stockport	A	D	1-1	Jackman 66 og	4,081
25	div2	Swindon	H	L	0-2		5,077
26	div2	Bristol City	H	L	1-2	May 63	5,912
27	div2	Plymouth	A	L	0-2		17,882
28	div2	Oldham	A	D	1-1	May 13	4,490
29	div2	Tranmere	H	D	2-2	Hunt 18; May 62	4,105
30	div2	Peterborough	A	D	0-0		4,658
31	div2	Wrexham	H	L	0-1		4,567
32	div2	Port Vale	H	W	3-2	Tabb 2; Hunt 48; Rougier 56	4,306
33	div2	Bristol City	A	L	1-3	Hutchinson 77	13,029
34	div2	QPR	H	D	1-1	O'Connor 51	8,418
35	div2	Luton	A	L	1-4	Wright 63	6,273
36	div2	Notts County	H	L	2-3	Evans 16; Hutchinson 40	4,478
37	div2	Brighton	A	L	0-1		6,007
38	div2	Swindon	A	L	1-2	May 30	7,649
39	div2	Stockport	H	L	0-2		6,615
40	div2	Blackpool	A	D	1-1	Hunt 17 pen	4,617
41	div2	Rushden & D	H	W	3-2	Tabb 26; Hunt 27; Talbot 36	4,616
42	div2	Hartlepool	A	W	2-1	Tabb 2; Dobson 33	5,206
43	div2	Chesterfield	H	D	1-1	Evans 90	4,962
44	div2	Sheff Wed	A	D	1-1	Sonko 69	20,004
45	div2	Colchester	H	W	3-2	Tabb 45; Sonko 58; Harrold 78	5,017
46	div2	Barnsley	A	W	2-0	Talbot 2; Tabb 61	9,824
47	div2	Wycombe	H	D	1-1	Harrold 72	7,145
48	div2	Grimsby	A	L	0-1		6,856
49	div2	Bournemouth	H	W	1-0	Rhodes 83	9,485

MONTHLY POINTS TALLY

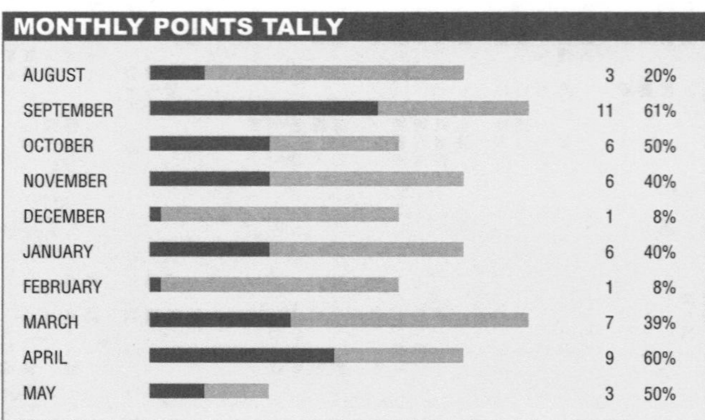

AUGUST 3 20%
SEPTEMBER 11 61%
OCTOBER 6 50%
NOVEMBER 6 40%
DECEMBER 1 8%
JANUARY 6 40%
FEBRUARY 1 8%
MARCH 7 39%
APRIL 9 60%
MAY 3 50%

KEY PLAYERS - GOALSCORERS

Jay Tabb

Goals in the League	9	Player Strike Rate Average number of minutes between League goals scored by player	243
Contribution to Attacking Power Average number of minutes between League team goals while on pitch	75	Club Strike Rate Average number of minutes between League goals scored by club	80

	PLAYER	LGE GOALS	GOALS ALL	POWER	STRIKE RATE
1	Jay Tabb	9	9	75	243 mins
2	Stephen Hunt	11	11	75	302 mins
3	Ben May	7	7	73	480 mins
4	Tommy Wright	3	3	94	533 mins

KEY PLAYERS - MIDFIELDERS

Stephen Hunt

Goals in the League	11	Contribution to Attacking Power Average number of minutes between League team goals while on pitch	75
Defensive Rating Average number of mins between League goals conceded while he was on the pitch	68	Scoring Difference Defensive Rating minus Contribution to Attacking Power	-7

	PLAYER	LGE GOALS	GOALS ALL	DEF RATE	POWER	SCORE DIFF
1	Stephen Hunt	11	11	68	75	-7 mins
2	Eddie Hutchinson	5	5	65	72	-7 mins
3	Anthony Rougier	4	5	61	79	-18 mins
4	Kevin O'Connor	1	2	59	80	-21 mins

KEY PLAYERS - DEFENDERS

Ibrahima Sonko

Goals Conceded (GC) The number of League goals conceded while he was on the pitch	62	Clean Sheets In games when he played at least 70 minutes	6
Defensive Rating Ave number of mins between League goals conceded while on the pitch	62	Club Defensive Rating Average number of mins between League goals conceded by the club this season	60

	PLAYED	CON LGE	CON ALL	CLEAN SHEETS	DEF RATE
1	Ibrahima Sonko	62	68	6	62 mins
2	Matt Somner	46	54	3	61 mins
3	Ronnie Bull	30	30	3	59 mins
4	Michael Dobson	65	72	4	57 mins

KEY GOALKEEPER

Paul Smith

Goals Conceded in the League	36	Counting Games Games when he played at least 70 mins	24
Defensive Rating Ave number of mins between League goals conceded while on the pitch	60	Clean Sheets In games when he played at least 70 mins	3

LEAGUE GOALS

Stephen Hunt

Minutes on the pitch	3318	Goals in the League	302
League average (mins between goals)	11		

	PLAYER	MINS	GOALS	AVE
1	Hunt	3318	11	302
2	Tabb	2187	9	243
3	May	3363	7	480
4	Hutchinson	3108	5	622
5	Rougier	2444	4	611
6	Sonko	3825	3	1275
7	Wright	1600	3	533
8	Evans	1280	2	640
9	Harrold	644	2	322
10	Talbot	1196	2	598
11	O'Connor	3219	1	3219
12	Rhodes	48	1	48
	Other		2	
	TOTAL		52	

DISCIPLINARY RECORDS

	PLAYER	YELLOW	RED	AVE
1	Roget	3	2	248
2	Evans	4	1	256
3	Wright	4	1	320
4	Frampton	2	0	436
5	Bull	4	0	444
6	Hunt	7	0	474
7	May	7	0	480
8	Somner	5	0	563
9	Julian	2	0	585
10	Talbot	2	0	598
11	Kitamirike	3	0	638
12	Fitzgerald	1	0	810
13	Rougier	3	0	814
	Other	15	0	
	TOTAL	62	4	

TOP POINT EARNERS

	PLAYER	GAMES	AV PTS
1	Hutchinson	34	1.35
2	Talbot	12	1.25
3	May	37	1.24
4	Bull	20	1.20
5	Sonko	42	1.19
6	Kitamirike	21	1.19
7	Rougier	27	1.19
8	Hunt	34	1.18
9	Tabb	19	1.16
10	Julian	13	1.15
	CLUB AVERAGE:		**1.15**

TEAM OF THE SEASON

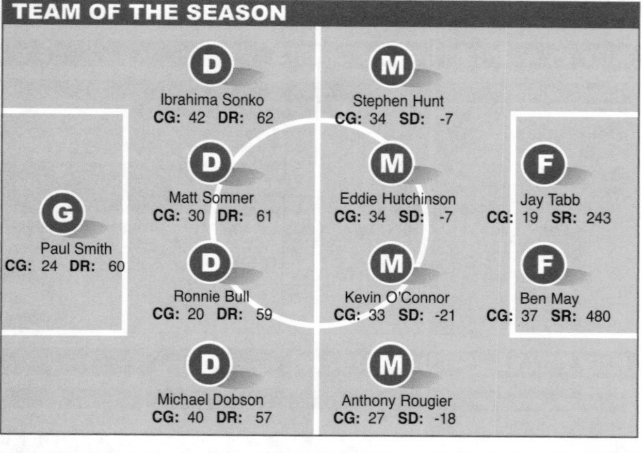

D
Ibrahima Sonko
CG: 42 DR: 62
D
Matt Somner
CG: 30 DR: 61
D
Ronnie Bull
CG: 20 DR: 59
D
Michael Dobson
CG: 40 DR: 57
G
Paul Smith
CG: 24 DR: 60
M
Stephen Hunt
CG: 34 SD: -7
M
Eddie Hutchinson
CG: 34 SD: -7
M
Kevin O'Connor
CG: 33 SD: -21
M
Anthony Rougier
CG: 27 SD: -18
F
Jay Tabb
CG: 19 SR: 243
F
Ben May
CG: 37 SR: 480

LEAGUE APPEARANCES AND BOOKINGS

	AGE (on 01/07/04)	IN NAMED 16	APPEARANCES	COUNTING GAMES	MINUTES ON PITCH	Yellow	Red
Goalkeepers							
Alan Julian	28	42	13	13	1170	2	0
Stuart Nelson	22	13	9	9	810	0	0
Paul Smith	24	25	24	24	2160	0	0
Jim Stannard	41	3	0	0	0	0	0
Jani Viander	28	2	0	0	0	0	0
Defenders							
Ronnie Bull	23	20	20	20	1778	4	0
Michael Dobson	23	42	42	40	3676	3	0
Scott Fitzgerald	34	9	9	9	810	1	0
Andrew Frampton	24	23	15	6	873	2	0
Joel Kitamirike	20	26	22	21	1916	3	0
Leo Roget	26	15	15	13	1243	3	2
Matt Somner	21	43	39	30	2817	5	0
Ibrahima Sonko	23	43	43	42	3825	1	0
Dean Wells	19	4	1	0	10	0	0
Midfielders							
Stephen Evans	23	37	25	12	1280	4	1
Lee Fieldwick	22	9	5	4	354	2	0
Stephen Hughes	20	23	9	1	209	1	0
Stephen Hunt	22	40	40	34	3318	7	0
Eddie Hutchinson	22	36	36	34	3108	2	0
Kevin O'Connor	22	44	43	33	3219	3	0
Anthony Rougier	32	32	31	27	2444	3	0
Jay Smith	22	28	17	8	972	1	0
Stewart Talbot	31	15	15	12	1196	2	0
Forwards							
Peter Beadle	32	2	1	1	90	1	0
Lloyd Blackman	20	5	3	0	36	0	0
Matt Harrold	20	14	14	5	644	0	0
Ben May	20	41	41	37	3363	7	0
Jide Olugbodi	26	2	2	0	48	0	0
Mark Peters	20	16	8	0	201	1	0
Alex Rhodes	2005	7	3	0	48	0	0
Jay Tabb	22	39	36	19	2187	0	0
Tommy Wright	19	28	25	16	1600	4	1

SQUAD APPEARANCES

Match	1	2	3	4	5	6	7	8	9	10	11	12	13	14	15	16	17	18	19	20	21	22	23	24	25	26	27	28	29	30	31	32	33	34	35	36	37	38	39	40	41	42	43	44	45	46	47	48	49
Venue	A	A	H	A	H	A	H	A	H	H	A	A	H	H	H	A	H	H	A	A	H	A	A	A	H	H	A	A	H	A	H	H	A	H	A	H	A	A	H	A	H	A	H	A	H	A	H	A	H
Competition	L	W	L	L	L	L	L	L	L	L	L	L	L	L	L	L	L	F	L	L	L	L	F	L	L	L	L	L	L	L	L	L	L	L	L	L	L	L	L	L	L	L	L	L	L	L	L	L	L
Result	L	L	L	L	W	L	L	W	D	W	W	D	L	W	W	L	W	W	L	W	L	L	L	D	L	L	L	D	D	D	L	W	L	D	L	L	L	L	L	D	W	W	D	D	W	W	D	L	W

Goalkeepers
Alan Julian
Stuart Nelson
Paul Smith
Jim Stannard
Jani Viander

Defenders
Ronnie Bull
Michael Dobson
Scott Fitzgerald
Andrew Frampton
Joel Kitamirike
Leo Roget
Matt Somner
Ibrahima Sonko
Dean Wells

Midfielders
Stephen Evans
Lee Fieldwick
Stephen Hughes
Stephen Hunt
Eddie Hutchinson
Kevin O'Connor
Anthony Rougier
Jay Smith
Stewart Talbot

Forwards
Peter Beadle
Lloyd Blackman
Matt Harrold
Ben May
Jide Olugbodi
Mark Peters
Alex Rhodes
Jay Tabb
Tommy Wright

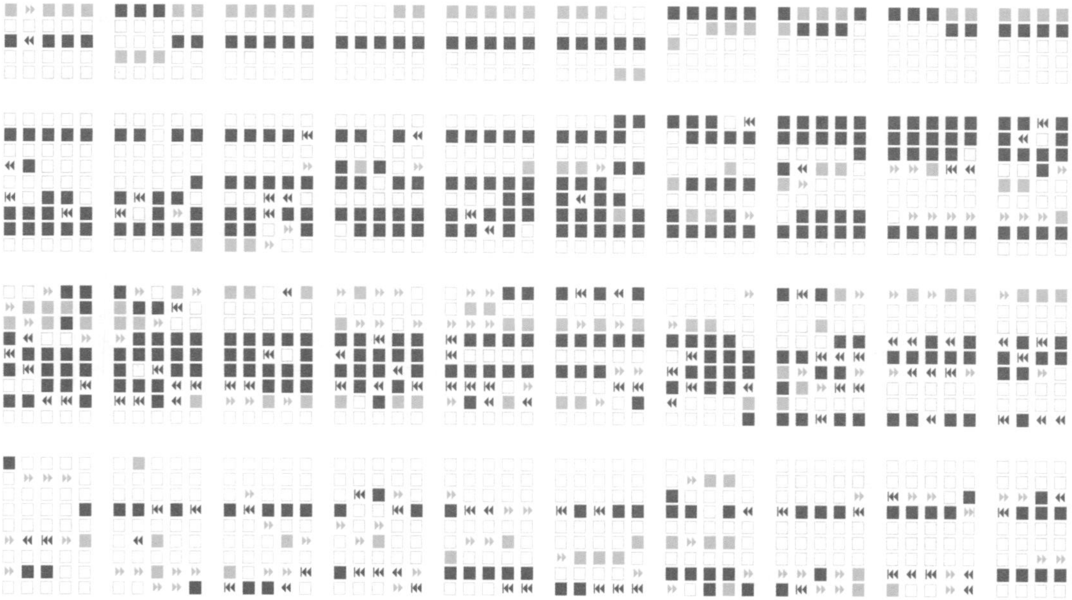

KEY: On all match · On bench · Subbed or sent off (Counting game) · Subbed or sent off (playing less than 70 minutes) · Subbed on from bench (Counting Game) · Subbed on (playing less than 70 minutes) · Subbed on and then subbed or sent off (Counting Game) · Subbed on and then subbed or sent off (playing less than 70 minutes) · Not in 16

PETERBOROUGH UNITED

Final Position: **18th**

NICKNAME: THE POSH

KEY: ☐ Won ☐ Drawn ☐ Lost

							Attendance
1	div2	Hartlepool	H	L	3-4	Arber 18 pen; Clarke, A 23,51	5,965
2	ccR1	Coventry	A	L	0-2		8,280
3	div2	Brentford	A	W	3-0	Clarke, A 3; Arber 48; Boucaud 90	4,463
4	div2	Sheff Wed	H	L	0-1		10,194
5	div2	Notts County	A	W	1-0	Clarke, A 39	5,177
6	div2	Stockport	H	L	1-2	McKenzie 90	4,395
7	div2	Grimsby	A	D	1-1	Newton 18	4,710
8	div2	Tranmere	A	D	0-0		6,726
9	div2	Plymouth	H	D	2-2	Arber 34 pen; Clarke, A 81	4,183
10	div2	Colchester	H	L	1-2	Wood 58	4,690
11	div2	Swindon	A	L	0-2		6,767
12	div2	Port Vale	A	L	0-3		5,495
13	div2	Oldham	H	D	2-2	McKenzie 21,50	4,465
14	div2	Bristol City	A	D	1-1	Logan 90	11,053
15	div2	QPR	H	D	0-0		7,247
16	div2	Barnsley	H	L	2-3	McKenzie 27,41	3,909
17	div2	Luton	A	D	1-1	McKenzie 65	6,067
18	div2	Brighton	H	D	2-2	McKenzie 15; Willock 29	5,929
19	facr1	Hereford	H	W	2-0	Willock 53; Logan 58	4,479
20	div2	Bournemouth	A	W	2-1	McKenzie 7; Woodhouse 21	6,963
21	div2	Blackpool	H	L	0-1		4,411
22	div2	Wycombe	A	W	2-1	McKenzie 34,90	4,669
23	facr2	Grimsby	H	W	3-2	Clarke, A 22; Thomson 47; Newton 65	4,836
24	div2	Wrexham	A	L	0-2		3,035
25	div2	Rushden & D	H	W	3-1	Willock 77; Woodhouse 84 pen; Farrell 86	6,167
26	div2	Chesterfield	A	L	1-2	Logan 13	4,376
27	div2	Grimsby	H	D	0-0		5,245
28	facr3	Coventry	A	L	1-2	Clarke, A 79	11,400
29	div2	Notts County	H	W	5-2	Woodhouse 10; Logan 28,80; Farrell 56; Clarke, A 83	3,855
30	div2	Hartlepool	A	L	0-1		4,855
31	div2	Brentford	H	D	0-0		4,658
32	div2	Sheff Wed	A	L	0-2		21,474
33	div2	Stockport	A	D	2-2	Woodhouse 5; Clarke, A 30	4,653
34	div2	Chesterfield	H	L	0-2		5,446
35	div2	Bristol City	H	L	0-1		4,449
36	div2	QPR	A	D	1-1	Platt 44	13,276
37	div2	Luton	H	L	1-2	Willock 79	6,628
38	div2	Barnsley	A	W	1-0	Willock 46	7,547
39	div2	Rushden & D	A	W	1-0	Willock 23	4,855
40	div2	Wrexham	H	W	6-1	Willock 24,54; Platt 32; Burton 60; Clarke, A 69; Farrell 76	4,323
41	div2	Plymouth	A	L	0-2		13,110
42	div2	Tranmere	H	D	0-0		4,185
43	div2	Colchester	A	D	0-0		3,754
44	div2	Swindon	H	W	4-2	Newton 3; Farrell 20; Logan 74; Thomson 89	4,745
45	div2	Oldham	A	D	1-1	Rea 37	5,688
46	div2	Port Vale	H	W	3-1	Logan 45; Williams 55; Clarke, A 67	4,988
47	div2	Brighton	A	L	0-1		6,285
48	div2	Bournemouth	H	L	0-1		4,831
49	div2	Blackpool	A	W	4-0	Woodhouse 19 pen,26; Willock 53; Farrell 58	7,200
50	div2	Wycombe	H	D	1-1	Woodhouse 64	6,398

MONTHLY POINTS TALLY

Month	Points	%
AUGUST	6	40%
SEPTEMBER	3	17%
OCTOBER	4	27%
NOVEMBER	7	58%
DECEMBER	4	33%
JANUARY	5	33%
FEBRUARY	1	8%
MARCH	11	61%
APRIL	7	47%
MAY	4	67%

KEY PLAYERS - GOALSCORERS

Leon McKenzie

Goals in the League	10	Player Strike Rate Average number of minutes between League goals scored by player	171
Contribution to Attacking Power Average number of minutes between League team goals while on pitch	74	Club Strike Rate Average number of minutes between League goals scored by club	71

	PLAYER	LGE GOALS	GOALS ALL	POWER	STRIKE RATE
1	Leon McKenzie	10	10	74	171 mins
2	Callum Willock	8	9	60	236 mins
3	Andy Clarke	9	11	77	266 mins
4	Curtis Woodhouse	7	7	62	322 mins

KEY PLAYERS - MIDFIELDERS

Tommy Williams

Goals in the League	1	Contribution to Attacking Power Average number of minutes between League team goals while on pitch	61
Defensive Rating Average number of mins between League goals conceded while he was on the pitch	85	Scoring Difference Defensive Rating minus Contribution to Attacking Power	24

	PLAYER	LGE GOALS	GOALS ALL	DEF RATE	POWER	SCORE DIFF
1	Tommy Williams	1	1	85	61	24 mins
2	Curtis Woodhouse	7	7	80	63	17 mins
3	Dave Farrell	5	5	74	64	10 mins
4	Adam Newton	2	3	77	74	3 mins

KEY PLAYERS - DEFENDERS

Guy Branston

Goals Conceded (GC) The number of League goals conceded while he was on the pitch	11	Clean Sheets In games when he played at least 70 minutes	5
Defensive Rating Ave number of mins between League goals conceded while on the pitch	111	Club Defensive Rating Average number of mins between League goals conceded by the club this season	73

	PLAYER	CON LGE	CON ALL	CLEAN SHEETS	DEF RATE
1	Guy Branston	11	11	5	111 mins
2	Andy Legg	42	46	10	78 mins
3	Simon Rea	29	35	6	76 mins
4	Mark Arber	54	60	11	72 mins

KEY GOALKEEPER

Mark Tyler

Goals Conceded in the League	53	Counting Games Games when he played at least 70 mins	43
Defensive Rating Ave number of mins between League goals conceded while on the pitch	73	Clean Sheets In games when he played at least 70 mins	11

LEAGUE GOALS

Leon McKenzie

Minutes on the pitch	1709	Goals in the League	171
League average (mins between goals)	10		

	PLAYER	MINS	GOALS	AVE
1	McKenzie	1709	10	171
2	Clarke, A	2397	9	266
3	Willock	1888	8	236
4	Woodhouse	2251	7	322
5	Logan	1262	6	210
6	Farrell	2816	5	563
7	Arber	3904	3	1301
8	Platt	1416	2	708
9	Newton	2529	2	1265
10	Burton	2314	1	2314
11	Thomson	2667	1	2667
12	Boucaud	618	1	618
	Other		3	
	TOTAL		58	

DISCIPLINARY RECORDS

	PLAYER	YELLOW	RED	AVE
1	Burton	9	1	231
2	Woodhouse	8	0	281
3	Boucaud	2	0	309
4	Rea	6	1	315
5	Gill	6	1	336
6	Shields	2	0	341
7	Legg	9	0	361
8	Kanu	2	1	500
9	Jenkins	0	1	531
10	Branston	2	0	613
11	Logan	2	0	631
12	Thomson	3	0	889
13	Williams	2	0	890
	Other	11	0	
	TOTAL	64	5	

TOP POINT EARNERS

	PLAYER	GAMES	AV PTS
1	Willock	17	1.71
2	Branston	13	1.62
3	Williams	18	1.50
4	Farrell	25	1.36
5	Rea	22	1.32
6	Woodhouse	24	1.25
7	Platt	15	1.20
8	Jelleyman	12	1.17
9	Burton	24	1.17
10	Newton	25	1.16
	CLUB AVERAGE:		1.13

LEAGUE APPEARANCES AND BOOKINGS

	AGE (on 01/07/04)	IN NAMED 16	APPEARANCES	COUNTING GAMES	MINUTES ON PITCH	Yellow	Red
Goalkeepers							
James Pullen	22	5	3	3	270	0	0
Mark Tyler	27	43	43	43	3870	1	0
Defenders							
Mark Arber	26	44	44	43	3904	4	0
Guy Branston	25	14	14	13	1226	2	0
Sagi Burton	26	32	30	24	2314	9	1
Mark Coulson	18	2	0	0	0	0	0
Gareth Jelleyman	23	27	17	12	1231	1	0
Stephen Jenkins	31	17	8	5	531	0	1
Christopher Kanu	24	30	21	14	1501	2	1
Andy Legg	37	44	42	33	3257	9	0
Dennis Pearce	29	6	3	1	113	1	0
Simon Rea	27	34	29	22	2207	6	1
Tony Shields	24	9	9	6	683	2	0
Sean St Ledger-Hall	19	9	2	1	123	0	0
Midfielders							
Andre Boucaud	19	12	8	6	618	2	0
Jamie Day	19	1	0	0	0	0	0
Dave Farrell	32	45	44	25	2816	1	0
Matthew Gill	23	40	32	24	2354	6	1
Adam Newton	23	43	37	25	2529	1	0
Richard Scott	29	11	0	0	0	0	0
Ryan Semple	19	2	2	1	127	0	0
Stephen Thomson	26	40	35	27	2667	3	0
Tommy Williams	23	22	21	18	1780	2	0
Neil Wood	21	6	3	0	172	1	0
Curtis Woodhouse	24	27	27	24	2251	8	0
Forwards							
Andy Clarke	36	46	43	16	2397	0	0
Andrew Fotiadis	26	12	8	0	126	0	0
Francis Green	24	6	3	0	21	0	0
Richard Logan	22	36	28	6	1262	2	0
Leon McKenzie	26	19	19	19	1709	0	0
Matt Nolan	22	1	1	1	77	0	0
Clive Platt	26	19	18	15	1416	0	0
Callum Willock	22	30	29	17	1888	1	0

TEAM OF THE SEASON

G — Mark Tyler — CG: 43 DR: 73

D — Andy Legg — CG: 33 DR: 78
D — Simon Rea — CG: 22 DR: 76
D — Mark Arber — CG: 43 DR: 72
D — Sagi Burton — CG: 24 DR: 66

M — Curtis Woodhouse — CG: 24 SD: 17
M — Dave Farrell — CG: 25 SD: 10
M — Adam Newton — CG: 25 SD: 3
M — Matthew Gill — CG: 24 SD: -14

F — Leon McKenzie — CG: 19 SR: 171
F — Callum Willock — CG: 17 SR: 236

SQUAD APPEARANCES

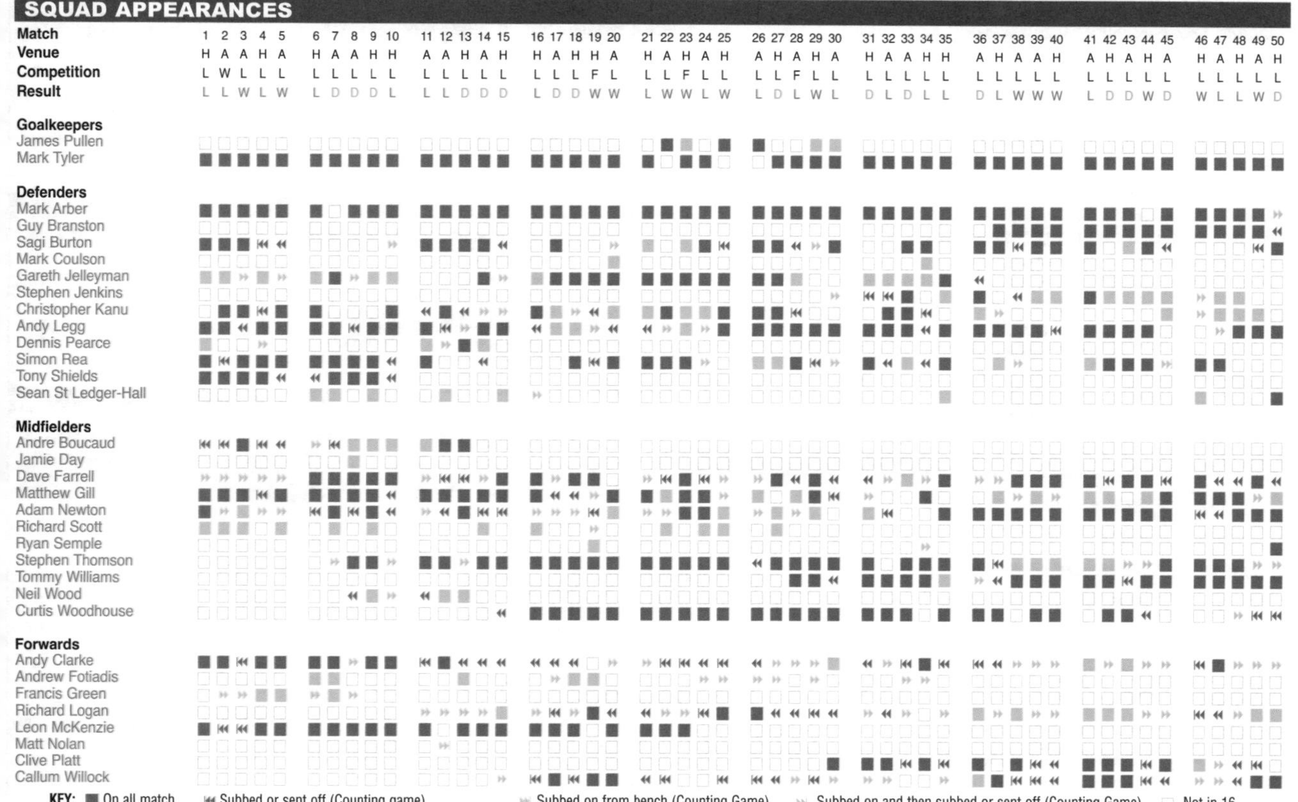

Match 1 2 3 4 5 6 7 8 9 10 11 12 13 14 15 16 17 18 19 20 21 22 23 24 25 26 27 28 29 30 31 32 33 34 35 36 37 38 39 40 41 42 43 44 45 46 47 48 49 50
Venue H A A H A H A A H H A A H A H H A H H A H A H A H A H A H A H A A H H A H A A H A H A H A H A H A H
Competition L W L L L L L L L L L L L L L L L L F L L L F L L L L F L L L L L L L L L L L L L L L L L L L L L L
Result L L W L W L D D D L L L D D D L D D W W L W W L W L D L W L D L D L L D L W W W L D D W D W L L W D
Goalkeepers
James Pullen
Mark Tyler
Defenders
Mark Arber
Guy Branston
Sagi Burton
Mark Coulson
Gareth Jelleyman
Stephen Jenkins
Christopher Kanu
Andy Legg
Dennis Pearce
Simon Rea
Tony Shields
Sean St Ledger-Hall
Midfielders
Andre Boucaud
Jamie Day
Dave Farrell
Matthew Gill
Adam Newton
Richard Scott
Ryan Semple
Stephen Thomson
Tommy Williams
Neil Wood
Curtis Woodhouse
Forwards
Andy Clarke
Andrew Fotiadis
Francis Green
Richard Logan
Leon McKenzie
Matt Nolan
Clive Platt
Callum Willock
KEY: On all match
On bench
Subbed or sent off (Counting game)
Subbed or sent off (playing less than 70 minutes)
Subbed on from bench (Counting Game)
Subbed on (playing less than 70 minutes)
Subbed on and then subbed or sent off (Counting Game)
Subbed on and then subbed or sent off (playing less than 70 minutes)
Not in 16

STOCKPORT COUNTY

Final Position: **19th**

NICKNAME: COUNTY   KEY: ☐Won ☐Drawn ☐Lost

							Attendance
1	div2	**Wycombe**	A	L	0-1		4,826
2	ccR1	**Lincoln**	A	W	1-0	Barlow 87	2,296
3	div2	**Luton**	H	L	1-2	Jones 72	4,566
4	div2	**Plymouth**	A	L	1-3	Beckett 43	7,594
5	div2	**Tranmere**	H	D	1-1	Beckett 90	4,886
6	div2	**Peterborough**	A	W	2-1	Beckett 38; Jones 58	4,395
7	div2	**Port Vale**	H	D	2-2	Beckett 2; Ellison 40	5,316
8	div2	**Sheff Wed**	A	D	2-2	Wilbraham 46,74	22,535
9	div2	**Hartlepool**	H	L	1-2	Wilbraham 43	4,021
10	div2	**Blackpool**	H	L	1-3	Lambert 26	5,420
11	ccR2	**Everton**	A	L	0-3		19,807
12	div2	**Rushden & D**	A	D	2-2	Barlow 6,54	4,049
13	div2	**Oldham**	A	L	0-2		7,015
14	div2	**Chesterfield**	H	D	0-0		4,764
15	div2	**Swindon**	A	W	2-1	Barlow 51; Wilbraham 87	7,060
16	div2	**Notts County**	H	D	2-2	Wilbraham 47; Goodwin 89	4,727
17	div2	**Colchester**	H	L	1-3	Goodwin 58 pen	3,683
18	div2	**Brighton**	A	W	1-0	Wilbraham 80	6,171
19	div2	**QPR**	H	L	1-2	Williams 85	5,461
20	facr1	**Stevenage**	A	L	1-2	Goodwin 69 pen	2,538
21	div2	**Grimsby**	A	D	1-1	Clare 67	4,014
22	div2	**Bournemouth**	H	W	3-2	Wilbraham 3; Lambert 41 pen; Barlow 81	4,622
23	div2	**Barnsley**	A	D	3-3	Goodwin 33; Welsh 36; Lambert 80	9,047
24	div2	**Brentford**	H	D	1-1	Barlow 82	4,081
25	div2	**Bristol City**	A	L	0-1		10,478
26	div2	**Wrexham**	H	L	0-1		6,256
27	div2	**Port Vale**	A	D	2-2	Barlow 6; Lynch 29	6,237
28	div2	**Wycombe**	H	W	2-0	Lambert 9 pen; Lynch 43	4,406
29	div2	**Luton**	A	D	2-2	Lynch 18; McLachlan 72	5,920
30	div2	**Plymouth**	H	L	0-2		6,608
31	div2	**Tranmere**	A	L	2-3	Griffin 34; McLachlan 73	7,137
32	div2	**Peterborough**	H	D	2-2	Platt 12 og; Lambert 26	4,653
33	div2	**Wrexham**	A	D	0-0		5,046
34	div2	**Swindon**	H	L	2-4	Robertson, M 21; Barlow 50	4,833
35	div2	**Notts County**	A	L	1-4	Byrne 58	5,168
36	div2	**Brighton**	H	D	1-1	McLachlan 41	5,038
37	div2	**Colchester**	A	L	1-2	Lambert 46	2,513
38	div2	**Bristol City**	H	W	2-0	Goodwin 11; Williams, C 88	5,050
39	div2	**Brentford**	A	W	2-0	Lambert 56 pen; Williams, C 85	6,615
40	div2	**Hartlepool**	A	D	2-2	Lambert 20 pen; Daly 21	4,674
41	div2	**Sheff Wed**	H	W	1-0	Lambert 25	8,011
42	div2	**Blackpool**	A	D	1-1	Wilbraham 74	7,604
43	div2	**Rushden & D**	H	W	2-1	Lambert 68,88 pen	4,717
44	div2	**Chesterfield**	A	W	3-0	Lambert 5; Daly 37; Jackman 53	5,901
45	div2	**Oldham**	H	D	1-1	Clare 33	8,617
46	div2	**QPR**	A	D	1-1	Clare 58	15,162
47	div2	**Grimsby**	H	W	2-1	Daly 6; Jackman 10	5,924
48	div2	**Bournemouth**	A	D	0-0		7,541
49	div2	**Barnsley**	H	L	2-3	Morrison 58; Barlow 90	6,581

MONTHLY POINTS TALLY

AUGUST	4	27%
SEPTEMBER	3	17%
OCTOBER	8	53%
NOVEMBER	5	42%
DECEMBER	2	17%
JANUARY	5	33%
FEBRUARY	2	17%
MARCH	11	61%
APRIL	11	73%
MAY	1	17%

KEY PLAYERS - GOALSCORERS

Stuart Barlow

Goals in the League	8	Player Strike Rate Average number of minutes between League goals scored by player	177
Contribution to Attacking Power Average number of minutes between League team goals while on pitch	61	Club Strike Rate Average number of minutes between League goals scored by club	67

	PLAYER	LGE GOALS	GOALS ALL	POWER	STRIKE RATE
1	Stuart Barlow	8	9	61	177 mins
2	Rickie Lambert	12	12	65	290 mins
3	Aaron Wilbraham	8	8	72	364 mins
4	Jon Daly	3	3	68	597 mins

KEY PLAYERS - MIDFIELDERS

Lee Cartwright

Goals in the League	0	Contribution to Attacking Power Average number of minutes between League team goals while on pitch	59
Defensive Rating Average number of mins between League goals conceded while he was on the pitch	96	Scoring Difference Defensive Rating minus Contribution to Attacking Power	37

	PLAYER	LGE GOALS	GOALS ALL	DEF RATE	POWER	SCORE DIFF
1	Lee Cartwright	0	0	96	59	37 mins
2	James Goodwin	4	5	72	74	-2 mins
3	Rickie Lambert	12	12	58	66	-8 mins
4	Alistair Gibb	0	0	46	59	-13 mins

KEY PLAYERS - DEFENDERS

Robert Clare

Goals Conceded (GC) The number of League goals conceded while he was on the pitch	46	Clean Sheets In games when he played at least 70 minutes	6
Defensive Rating Ave number of mins between League goals conceded while on the pitch	66	Club Defensive Rating Average number of mins between League goals conceded by the club this season	59

	PLAYER	CON LGE	CON ALL	CLEAN SHEETS	DEF RATE
1	Robert Clare	46	50	6	66 mins
2	Danny Jackman	39	39	7	60 mins
3	Daniel Griffin	22	22	5	59 mins
4	John Hardiker	62	67	6	56 mins

KEY GOALKEEPER

Anthony Williams

Goals Conceded in the League	17	Counting Games Games when he played at least 70 mins	15
Defensive Rating Ave number of mins between League goals conceded while on the pitch	79	Clean Sheets In games when he played at least 70 mins	51

LEAGUE GOALS

Rickie Lambert

Minutes on the pitch	3476	Goals in the League	290
League average (mins between goals)	12		

	PLAYER	MINS	GOALS	AVE
1	Lambert	3476	12	290
2	Barlow	1412	8	177
3	Wilbraham	2914	8	364
4	Goodwin	2807	4	702
5	Beckett	543	4	136
6	McLachlan	1168	3	389
7	Williams, C	442	3	147
8	Daly	1791	3	597
9	Clare	3016	3	1005
10	Lynch	747	3	249
11	Jones	1201	2	601
12	Jackman	2354	2	1177
	Other		7	
	TOTAL		62	

DISCIPLINARY RECORDS

	PLAYER	YELLOW	RED	AVE
1	Ellison	6	0	132
2	Beckett	3	1	135
3	Robertson, M	4	0	180
4	Goodwin	10	1	255
5	Lescott	3	0	363
6	Lynch	2	0	373
7	Hardiker	8	0	431
8	Daly	4	0	447
9	Morrison	2	0	538
10	Cartwright	2	0	621
11	Walton	1	0	630
12	Spencer	2	0	646
13	Gibb	3	0	648
	Other	21	0	
	TOTAL	71	2	

TOP POINT EARNERS

	PLAYER	GAMES	AV PTS
1	Adams	12	1.92
2	Cartwright	13	1.69
3	Williams, Anthony	15	1.60
4	Daly	18	1.50
5	Wilbraham	29	1.31
6	Clare	33	1.27
7	Jackman	25	1.24
8	Goodwin	28	1.21
9	Griffin	14	1.21
10	Lambert	38	1.11
	CLUB AVERAGE:		**1.13**

TEAM OF THE SEASON

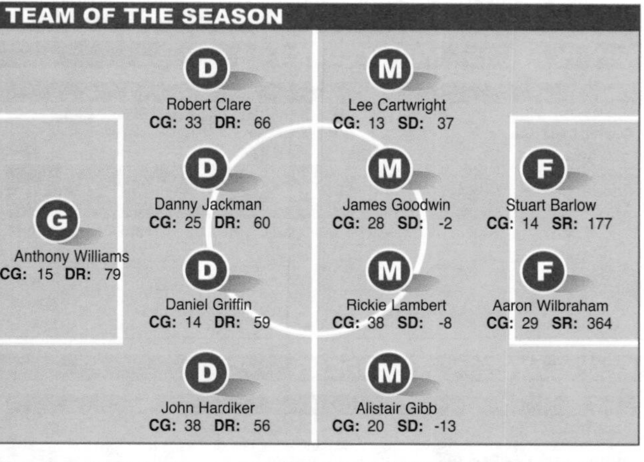

G
Anthony Williams
CG: 15 DR: 79
D
Robert Clare
CG: 33 DR: 66
D
Danny Jackman
CG: 25 DR: 60
D
Daniel Griffin
CG: 14 DR: 59
D
John Hardiker
CG: 38 DR: 56
M
Lee Cartwright
CG: 13 SD: 37
M
James Goodwin
CG: 28 SD: -2
M
Rickie Lambert
CG: 38 SD: -8
M
Alistair Gibb
CG: 20 SD: -13
F
Stuart Barlow
CG: 14 SR: 177
F
Aaron Wilbraham
CG: 29 SR: 364

LEAGUE APPEARANCES AND BOOKINGS

	AGE (on 01/07/04)	IN NAMED 16	APPEARANCES	COUNTING GAMES	MINUTES ON PITCH	Yellow	Red
Goalkeepers							
Nick Colgan	30	21	16	15	1407	0	0
Boaz Myhill	21	2	2	2	180	0	0
James Spencer	19	35	15	14	1293	2	0
Anthony Williams	26	21	15	15	1350	0	0
Defenders							
Daniel Adams	28	12	12	12	1080	1	0
David Challinor	28	24	17	14	1352	2	0
Robert Clare	21	38	35	33	3016	1	0
Daniel Griffin	26	15	15	14	1294	0	0
John Hardiker	22	41	39	38	3455	8	0
Matt Heath	23	8	8	8	720	0	0
Danny Jackman	21	28	27	25	2354	3	0
Robert Jones	24	19	16	11	1201	0	0
Martin Pemberton	28	7	6	4	417	1	0
Shaun Smith	33	6	5	2	247	0	0
David Walton	31	7	7	7	630	1	0
Ashley Williams	-	16	10	10	900	0	0
Midfielders							
Jamie Baguley	19	1	1	1	90	0	0
Lee Cartwright	31	16	15	13	1243	2	0
Wayne Collins	35	2	2	0	54	0	0
Alistair Gibb	28	27	25	20	1944	3	0
James Goodwin	22	41	35	28	2807	10	1
Rickie Lambert	22	44	40	38	3476	4	0
Aaron Lescott	25	21	14	12	1091	3	0
Fraser McLachlan	21	27	20	11	1168	1	0
Owen Morrison	22	29	22	9	1076	2	0
Mark Robertson	27	12	12	6	722	4	0
Andrew Welsh	20	39	34	23	2214	1	0
Forwards							
Stuart Barlow	35	43	30	14	1412	2	0
Luke Beckett	27	8	8	6	543	3	1
Mark Byrne	21	2	1	1	90	1	0
Jon Daly	21	25	25	18	1791	4	0
Kevin Ellison	25	20	14	7	794	6	0
Simon Lynch	22	9	9	8	747	2	0
Aaron Wilbraham	24	43	41	29	2914	3	0
Chris Williams	19	26	16	2	442	1	0

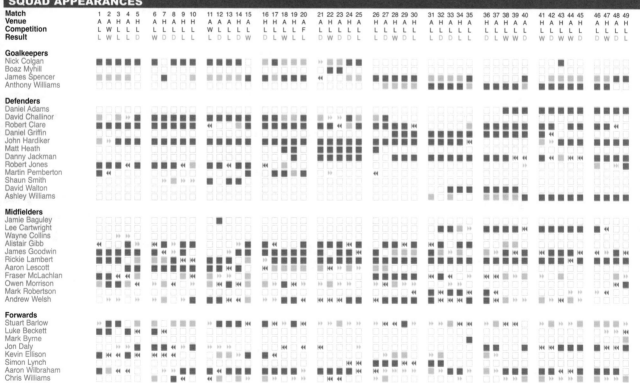

SQUAD APPEARANCES

Match	1	2	3	4	5	6	7	8	9	10	11	12	13	14	15	16	17	18	19	20	21	22	23	24	25
Venue	A	A	H	A	H	A	H	A	H	H	A	A	A	H	A	H	H	A	H	A	A	H	A	H	A
Competition	L	W	L	L	L	L	L	L	L	L	W	L	L	L	L	L	L	L	L	F	L	L	L	L	L
Result	L	W	L	L	D	W	D	D	L	L	L	D	L	D	W	D	L	W	L	L	D	W	D	D	L

Match	26	27	28	29	30	31	32	33	34	35	36	37	38	39	40	41	42	43	44	45	46	47	48	49
Venue	H	A	H	A	H	A	H	A	H	A	H	A	H	A	A	H	A	H	A	H	A	H	A	H
Competition	L	L	L	L	L	L	L	L	L	L	L	L	L	L	L	L	L	L	L	L	L	L	L	L
Result	L	D	W	D	L	L	D	D	L	L	D	L	W	W	D	W	D	W	W	D	D	W	D	L

Goalkeepers
Nick Colgan
Boaz Myhill
James Spencer
Anthony Williams

Defenders
Daniel Adams
David Challinor
Robert Clare
Daniel Griffin
John Hardiker
Matt Heath
Danny Jackman
Robert Jones
Martin Pemberton
Shaun Smith
David Walton
Ashley Williams

Midfielders
Jamie Baguley
Lee Cartwright
Wayne Collins
Alistair Gibb
James Goodwin
Rickie Lambert
Aaron Lescott
Fraser McLachlan
Owen Morrison
Mark Robertson
Andrew Welsh

Forwards
Stuart Barlow
Luke Beckett
Mark Byrne
Jon Daly
Kevin Ellison
Simon Lynch
Aaron Wilbraham
Chris Williams

KEY: On all match; On bench; Subbed or sent off (Counting game); Subbed or sent off (playing less than 70 minutes); Subbed on from bench (Counting Game); Subbed on (playing less than 70 minutes); Subbed on and then subbed or sent off (Counting Game); Subbed on and then subbed or sent off (playing less than 70 minutes); Not in 16

CHESTERFIELD

Final Position: **20th**

NICKNAME: THE SPIREITES

KEY: ☐Won ☐Drawn ☐Lost

							Attendance
1	div2	Wrexham	A	D	0-0		5,688
2	ccR1	Burnley	H	L	2-3*	(*lost on penalties)	2,928
3	div2	Bristol City	H	D	1-1	O'Hare 31	4,302
4	div2	Wycombe	A	D	3-3	Brandon 16; Hudson 45; Rushbury 90	4,529
5	div2	Plymouth	H	D	1-1	Brandon 50	4,089
6	div2	QPR	A	L	0-3		12,986
7	div2	Barnsley	H	L	0-2		5,605
8	div2	Notts County	H	L	0-1		4,367
9	div2	Brighton	A	L	0-1		6,054
10	div2	Grimsby	A	L	0-4		4,141
11	div2	Brentford	H	L	1-2	Payne 77 pen	3,257
12	div2	Bournemouth	H	D	1-1	Robinson 33	3,131
13	div2	Stockport	A	D	0-0		4,764
14	div2	Rushden & D	A	L	1-2	Robinson 14	3,817
15	div2	Swindon	H	W	3-0	Robinson 11,19; Cade 71	3,506
16	div2	Hartlepool	H	L	1-2	Cade 53	3,411
17	div2	Colchester	A	L	0-1		3,115
18	div2	Port Vale	H	W	1-0	Robinson 60	4,088
19	facr1	Tranmere	A	L	2-3	Davies 51; Evatt 83	5,633
20	div2	Blackpool	A	L	0-1		5,252
21	div2	Oldham	H	D	1-1	Blatherwick 30	3,565
22	div2	Luton	A	L	0-1		5,453
23	div2	Tranmere	H	D	2-2	Hurst 2; Allott 45	3,123
24	div2	Sheff Wed	A	D	0-0		25,296
25	div2	Peterborough	H	W	2-1	Robinson 48; Hudson 75	4,376
26	div2	Barnsley	A	W	1-0	Hurst 80	11,664
27	div2	Plymouth	A	L	0-7		13,109
28	div2	Wrexham	H	W	2-1	Blatherwick 70; Evatt 86	3,585
29	div2	Bristol City	A	L	0-4		11,807
30	div2	Wycombe	H	D	2-2	Brandon 75; Evatt 82	3,576
31	div2	QPR	H	W	4-2	McMaster 31; Evatt 50; Hurst 65; Hudson 79	4,567
32	div2	Peterborough	A	W	2-0	Hurst 47; McMaster 77	5,446
33	div2	Rushden & D	H	W	2-0	Hurst 2; Reeves 59 pen	4,361
34	div2	Swindon	A	L	0-2		6,814
35	div2	Hartlepool	A	L	0-2		4,736
36	div2	Sheff Wed	H	W	3-1	Hurst 45,59; Brandon 75	7,695
37	div2	Tranmere	A	W	3-2	Hurst 21,86; Jones 83 og	7,370
38	div2	Brighton	H	L	0-2		4,478
39	div2	Notts County	A	D	1-1	Richardson 77 og	7,808
40	div2	Colchester	H	L	1-2	Hurst 50	3,787
41	div2	Grimsby	H	D	4-4	Hurst 19; Reeves 66,73 pen,90 pen	4,444
42	div2	Brentford	A	D	1-1	Evatt 90	4,962
43	div2	Stockport	H	L	0-3		5,901
44	div2	Bournemouth	A	D	2-2	Allott 21; De Bolla 27	7,081
45	div2	Port Vale	A	D	1-1	Evatt 34	5,582
46	div2	Blackpool	H	W	1-0	Niven 20	4,117
47	div2	Oldham	A	L	0-2		8,177
48	div2	Luton	H	W	1-0	Hurst 88	6,285

MONTHLY POINTS TALLY

Month	Points	%
AUGUST	4	27%
SEPTEMBER	1	6%
OCTOBER	4	27%
NOVEMBER	4	33%
DECEMBER	8	67%
JANUARY	7	47%
FEBRUARY	6	67%
MARCH	8	38%
APRIL	6	40%
MAY	3	50%

KEY PLAYERS - GOALSCORERS

Glynn Hurst

Goals in the League	12	Player Strike Rate Average number of minutes between League goals scored by player	202
Contribution to Attacking Power Average number of minutes between League team goals while on pitch	73	Club Strike Rate Average number of minutes between League goals scored by club	84

	PLAYER	LGE GOALS	GOALS ALL	POWER	STRIKE RATE
1	Glynn Hurst	12	12	73	202 mins
2	Marvin Robinson	6	6	88	280 mins
3	David Reeves	4	4	69	415 mins
4	Ian Evatt	5	6	81	763 mins

KEY PLAYERS - MIDFIELDERS

Gareth Davies

Goals in the League	0	Contribution to Attacking Power Average number of minutes between League team goals while on pitch	88
Defensive Rating Average number of mins between League goals conceded while he was on the pitch	69	Scoring Difference Defensive Rating minus Contribution to Attacking Power	-19

	PLAYER	LGE GOALS	GOALS ALL	DEF RATE	POWER	SCORE DIFF
1	Gareth Davies	0	1	69	88	-19 mins
2	Derek Niven	1	1	50	71	-21 mins
3	Chris Brandon	4	4	60	85	-25 mins
4	Gus Uhlenbeek	0	0	55	80	-25 mins

KEY PLAYERS - DEFENDERS

Steve Payne

Goals Conceded (GC) The number of League goals conceded while he was on the pitch	25	Clean Sheets In games when he played at least 70 minutes	4
Defensive Rating Ave number of mins between League goals conceded while on the pitch	69	Club Defensive Rating Average number of mins between League goals conceded by the club this season	58

	PLAYER	CON LGE	CON ALL	CLEAN SHEETS	DEF RATE
1	Steve Payne	25	28	4	69 mins
2	Mark Innes	25	25	3	61 mins
3	Kevin Dawson	32	35	5	59 mins
4	Ian Evatt	65	68	8	59 mins

KEY GOALKEEPER

Carl Muggleton

Goals Conceded in the League	71	Counting Games Games when he played at least 70 mins	46
Defensive Rating Ave number of mins between League goals conceded while on the pitch	58	Clean Sheets In games when he played at least 70 mins	10

LEAGUE GOALS

Glynn Hurst

Minutes on the pitch	2429	Goals in the League	202
League average (mins between goals)	12		

	PLAYER	MINS	GOALS	AVE
1	Hurst	2429	12	202
2	Robinson	1680	6	280
3	Evatt	3817	5	763
4	Reeves	1659	4	415
5	Brandon	3500	4	875
6	Hudson	2903	3	968
7	Allott	3119	2	1560
8	McMaster	358	2	179
9	Cade	796	2	398
10	Blatherwick	3150	2	1575
11	Rushbury	129	1	129
12	O'Hare	3465	1	3465
	Other		5	
	TOTAL		49	

DISCIPLINARY RECORDS

	PLAYER	YELLOW	RED	AVE
1	Robinson	7	0	240
2	Uhlenbeek	10	2	267
3	Dawson	7	0	267
4	Innes	4	1	302
5	Davies	5	0	317
6	Blatherwick	9	0	350
7	Brandon	10	0	350
8	Niven	5	0	382
9	Evatt	9	0	424
10	Reeves	3	0	553
11	Hudson	4	0	725
12	Allott	4	0	779
13	Cade	1	0	796
	Other	12	1	
	TOTAL	90	4	

TOP POINT EARNERS

	PLAYER	GAMES	AV PTS
1	Innes	13	1.46
2	Niven	20	1.45
3	Hurst	26	1.38
4	Reeves	14	1.29
5	Robinson	13	1.23
6	Davies	14	1.21
7	Blatherwick	34	1.18
8	Hudson	31	1.16
9	Allott	34	1.12
10	Uhlenbeek	34	1.12
	CLUB AVERAGE:		1.11

LEAGUE APPEARANCES AND BOOKINGS

	AGE (on 01/07/04)	IN NAMED 16	APPEARANCES	COUNTING GAMES	MINUTES ON PITCH	Yellow	Red
Goalkeepers							
Carl Muggleton	35	46	46	46	4140	0	0
Andy Richmond	21	44	1	0	23	0	0
Defenders							
Steven Blatherwick	30	36	36	34	3150	9	0
Kevin Dawson	23	36	24	19	1872	7	0
Ian Evatt	22	43	43	42	3817	9	0
Steve Howson	22	25	9	5	564	0	0
Mark Innes	25	27	22	13	1513	4	1
Alan O'Hare	21	41	40	37	3465	3	0
Steve Payne	28	22	20	19	1731	1	0
Damon Searle	32	6	5	4	366	0	0
Paul Warhurst	34	4	4	3	283	1	0
Midfielders							
Mark Allott	26	41	40	34	3119	4	0
Chris Brandon	28	43	43	36	3500	10	0
Jamie Burt	24	2	1	0	1	0	0
Gareth Davies	21	39	28	14	1589	5	0
Jamie Fullarton	29	3	1	0	35	0	0
Mark Hudson	23	36	35	31	2903	4	0
Jamie McMaster	21	6	6	3	358	2	0
Derek Niven	20	22	22	20	1912	5	0
Matt O'Halloran	21	6	3	1	158	0	0
Lee Richardson	35	1	0	0	0	0	0
Andy Rushbury	21	13	5	0	129	0	0
Gus Uhlenbeek	33	37	37	34	3214	10	2
Stephen Warne	20	6	0	0	0	0	0
Forwards							
Jamie Cade	20	10	10	9	796	1	0
Mark De Bolla	21	12	8	2	325	0	0
Caleb Folan	18	7	7	4	424	2	0
Glynn Hurst	28	30	29	26	2429	2	1
Jez Mitchell	19	1	0	0	0	0	0
Tcham N'Toya	20	7	6	2	286	1	0
David Reeves	36	36	31	14	1659	3	0
Marvin Robinson	24	37	31	13	1680	7	0
Adam Smith	18	10	3	0	21	0	0

TEAM OF THE SEASON

G — Carl Muggleton CG: 46 DR: 58

D — Steve Payne CG: 19 DR: 69

D — Mark Innes CG: 13 DR: 61

D — Kevin Dawson CG: 19 DR: 59

D — Ian Evatt CG: 42 DR: 59

M — Gareth Davies CG: 14 SD: -19

M — Derek Niven CG: 20 SD: -21

M — Chris Brandon CG: 36 SD: -25

M — Gus Uhlenbeek CG: 34 SD: -25

F — Glynn Hurst CG: 26 SR: 202

F — Marvin Robinson CG: 13 SR: 280

SQUAD APPEARANCES

Match
Venue
Competition
Result
Goalkeepers
Carl Muggleton
Andy Richmond
Defenders
Steven Blatherwick
Kevin Dawson
Ian Evatt
Steve Howson
Mark Innes
Alan O'Hare
Steve Payne
Damon Searle
Paul Warhurst
Midfielders
Mark Allott
Chris Brandon
Jamie Burt
Gareth Davies
Jamie Fullarton
Mark Hudson
Jamie McMaster
Derek Niven
Matt O'Halloran
Lee Richardson
Andy Rushbury
Gus Uhlenbeek
Stephen Warne
Forwards
Jamie Cade
Mark De Bolla
Caleb Folan
Glynn Hurst
Jez Mitchell
Tcham N'Toya
David Reeves
Marvin Robinson
Adam Smith

KEY: On all match · On bench · Subbed or sent off (Counting game) · Subbed or sent off (playing less than 70 minutes) · Subbed on from bench (Counting Game) · Subbed on (playing less than 70 minutes) · Subbed on and then subbed or sent off (Counting Game) · Subbed on and then subbed or sent off (playing less than 70 minutes) · Not in 16

GRIMSBY TOWN

Final Position: **21st**

NICKNAME: THE MARINERS

KEY: ☐Won ☐Drawn ☐Lost

							Attendance
1	div2	Plymouth	A	D	2-2	Boulding 28; Anderson 64	9,590
2	ccR1	Doncaster	A	L	2-3	Campbell 38; Anderson 67 pen	6,057
3	div2	Port Vale	H	L	1-2	Boulding 39	4,816
4	div2	Luton	A	W	2-1	Anderson 34; Boulding 77	5,827
5	div2	Wycombe	H	W	3-1	Barnard 27; Boulding 52; Cas 79	4,512
6	div2	Bristol City	A	L	0-1		10,033
7	div2	Peterborough	H	D	1-1	Boulding 80	4,710
8	div2	Hartlepool	A	L	1-8	Rowan 48	5,528
9	div2	Swindon	H	L	1-2	Boulding 23	3,535
10	div2	Chesterfield	H	W	4-0	Campbell 23; Hockless 56; Cas 73; Edwards 80	4,141
11	div2	Sheff Wed	A	D	0-0		21,918
12	div2	Blackpool	A	W	1-0	Crane 72	5,491
13	div2	QPR	H	L	0-1		5,447
14	div2	Brighton	A	L	0-3		6,286
15	div2	Colchester	H	W	2-0	Onuora 41; Boulding 84	5,021
16	div2	Notts County	H	W	2-0	Boulding 23,63	4,274
17	div2	Barnsley	A	D	0-0		10,092
18	div2	Rushden & D	A	L	1-3	Anderson 40	4,185
19	facr1	QPR	H	W	1-0	Boulding 80	4,144
20	div2	Stockport	H	D	1-1	Mansaram 72	4,014
21	div2	Brentford	A	W	3-1	Onuora 45; Boulding 84,88	4,685
22	div2	Tranmere	H	L	0-1		4,406
23	facr2	Peterborough	A	L	2-3	Jevons 24; Cas 84	4,836
24	div2	Bournemouth	A	D	0-0		5,837
25	div2	Oldham	H	D	3-3	Jevons 9,76; Boulding 57	6,172
26	div2	Peterborough	A	D	0-0		5,245
27	div2	Wycombe	A	L	1-4	Onuora 8	4,519
28	div2	Plymouth	H	D	0-0		5,007
29	div2	Port Vale	A	L	1-5	Jevons 34	5,133
30	div2	Wrexham	H	L	1-3	Jevons 73	3,572
31	div2	Oldham	A	L	0-6		13,007
32	div2	Brighton	H	W	2-1	Rankin 5; Jevons 75	3,673
33	div2	Bristol City	H	L	1-2	Anderson 31 pen	5,272
34	div2	Colchester	A	L	0-2		2,922
35	div2	Luton	H	W	3-2	Jevons 55,69 pen; Ford 90	3,143
36	div2	Barnsley	H	W	6-1	Jevons 23,31,55 pen,75; Armstrong 27; Rankin 41	5,603
37	div2	Notts County	A	L	1-3	Crane 11	6,011
38	div2	Wrexham	A	L	0-3		3,127
39	div2	Bournemouth	H	D	1-1	Rowan 11	5,015
40	div2	Swindon	A	L	0-2		6,954
41	div2	Hartlepool	H	L	0-2		4,303
42	div2	Chesterfield	A	D	4-4	Anderson 35; Lawrence 42; Barnard 86; Rankin 87	4,444
43	div2	Sheff Wed	H	W	2-0	Mansaram 6; Crane 33	6,641
44	div2	QPR	A	L	0-3		14,488
45	div2	Blackpool	H	L	0-2		4,775
46	div2	Rushden & D	H	W	1-0	Jevons 80 pen	3,890
47	div2	Stockport	A	L	1-2	Hockless 70	5,924
48	div2	Brentford	H	W	1-0	Rankin 70	6,856
49	div2	Tranmere	A	L	1-2	Mansaram 24	10,301

MONTHLY POINTS TALLY

Month	Points	%
AUGUST	7	47%
SEPTEMBER	8	44%
OCTOBER	7	47%
NOVEMBER	4	33%
DECEMBER	3	33%
JANUARY	1	8%
FEBRUARY	9	50%
MARCH	2	11%
APRIL	6	40%
MAY	3	50%

KEY PLAYERS - GOALSCORERS

Phil Jevons

Goals in the League	12	Player Strike Rate Average number of minutes between League goals scored by player	170
Contribution to Attacking Power Average number of minutes between League team goals while on pitch	78	Club Strike Rate Average number of minutes between League goals scored by club	75

	PLAYER	LGE GOALS	GOALS ALL	POWER	STRIKE RATE
1	Phil Jevons	12	13	78	170 mins
2	Michael Boulding	12	13	81	196 mins
3	Iain Anderson	5	6	83	384 mins
4	Iffy Onuora	3	3	90	482 mins

KEY PLAYERS - MIDFIELDERS

Marcel Cas

Goals in the League	2	Contribution to Attacking Power Average number of minutes between League team goals while on pitch	58
Defensive Rating Average number of mins between League goals conceded while he was on the pitch	53	Scoring Difference Defensive Rating minus Contribution to Attacking Power	-5

	PLAYER	LGE GOALS	GOALS ALL	DEF RATE	POWER	SCORE DIFF
1	Marcel Cas	2	3	53	58	-5 mins
2	Nick Daws	0	0	49	63	-14 mins
3	Des Hamilton	0	0	61	75	-14 mins
4	Stuart Campbell	1	2	56	74	-18 mins

KEY PLAYERS - DEFENDERS

John McDermott

Goals Conceded (GC) The number of League goals conceded while he was on the pitch	28	Clean Sheets In games when he played at least 70 minutes	8
Defensive Rating Ave number of mins between League goals conceded while on the pitch	66	Club Defensive Rating Average number of mins between League goals conceded by the club this season	51

	PLAYER	CON LGE	CON ALL	CLEAN SHEETS	DEF RATE
1	John McDermott	28	31	8	66 mins
2	Tony Crane	55	61	11	58 mins
3	Darren Barnard	52	58	9	57 mins
4	Michael Edwards	50	53	9	55 mins

KEY GOALKEEPER

Aidan Davison

Goals Conceded in the League	56	Counting Games Games when he played at least 70 mins	32
Defensive Rating Ave number of mins between League goals conceded while on the pitch	51	Clean Sheets In games when he played at least 70 mins	9

LEAGUE GOALS

Michael Boulding

Minutes on the pitch	2355	Goals in the League	196
League average (mins between goals)	12		

	PLAYER	MINS	GOALS	AVE
1	Boulding	2355	12	196
2	Jevons	2045	12	170
3	Anderson	1918	5	384
4	Rankin	967	4	242
5	Onuora	1445	3	482
6	Mansaram	1117	3	372
7	Crane	3189	3	1063
8	Hockless	556	2	278
9	Rowan	724	2	362
10	Barnard	2975	2	1488
11	Cas	1276	2	638
12	Armstrong	735	1	735
	Other		4	
	TOTAL		55	

DISCIPLINARY RECORDS

	PLAYER	YELLOW	RED	AVE
1	Crane	13	2	212
2	Barnard	10	0	297
3	Rowan	2	0	362
4	Cas	3	0	425
5	Crowe	4	1	487
6	Bolder	1	0	510
7	Hockless	1	0	556
8	Mansaram	1	1	558
9	Young	2	0	560
10	Jevons	3	0	681
11	Onuora	2	0	722
12	Armstrong	1	0	735
13	Campbell	4	0	834
	Other	9	2	
	TOTAL	56	6	

TOP POINT EARNERS

	PLAYER	GAMES	AV PTS
1	Anderson	19	1.37
2	Onuora	14	1.36
3	Barnard	32	1.34
4	Daws	17	1.29
5	Crane	34	1.26
6	Campbell	36	1.22
7	Hamilton	20	1.20
8	Davison	32	1.13
9	Boulding	26	1.12
10	McDermott	21	1.05
	CLUB AVERAGE:		**1.09**

TEAM OF THE SEASON

G – Aidan Davison, CG: 32 DR: 51

D – John McDermott, CG: 21 DR: 66
D – Tony Crane, CG: 34 DR: 58
D – Darren Barnard, CG: 32 DR: 57
D – Michael Edwards, CG: 29 DR: 55

M – Marcel Cas, CG: 13 SD: -5
M – Nick Daws, CG: 17 SD: -14
M – Des Hamilton, CG: 20 SD: -14
M – Stuart Campbell, CG: 36 SD: -18

F – Phil Jevons, CG: 20 SR: 170
F – Michael Boulding, CG: 26 SR: 196

LEAGUE APPEARANCES AND BOOKINGS

	AGE (on 01/07/04)	IN NAMED 16	APPEARANCES	COUNTING GAMES	MINUTES ON PITCH	Yellow	Red
Goalkeepers							
Aidan Davison	36	32	32	32	2880	0	1
Alan Fettis	33	11	11	11	990	0	0
Andrew Pettinger	20	10	3	3	270	0	0
Defenders							
Craig Armstrong	29	9	9	8	735	1	0
Darren Barnard	32	34	34	32	2975	10	0
Tony Crane	21	37	37	34	3189	13	2
Jason Crowe	25	33	32	26	2438	4	1
Michael Edwards	24	41	33	29	2772	0	0
Simon Ford	22	32	26	20	1951	0	0
John McDermott	35	23	21	21	1858	0	0
Paul Warhurst	34	10	7	5	472	0	0
Greg Young	21	29	17	9	1121	2	0
Midfielders							
Iain Anderson	26	33	28	19	1918	1	1
Stuart Campbell	26	40	38	36	3338	4	0
Marcel Cas	32	21	21	13	1276	3	0
Stacy Coldicott	30	14	14	10	1062	0	0
Nick Daws	34	17	17	17	1509	1	0
Paul Groves	38	20	11	7	701	0	0
Des Hamilton	27	32	26	20	1961	2	0
Graham Hockless	21	24	13	4	556	1	0
Jamie Lawrence	34	5	5	4	374	1	0
Alan Pouton	27	5	5	5	450	0	0
John Thorrington	24	7	3	2	204	1	0
Forwards							
Mickael Antoine-Curier	21	6	5	1	254	1	0
Chris Bolder	21	14	7	5	510	1	0
Michael Boulding	28	27	27	26	2355	0	0
Phil Jevons	24	37	29	20	2045	3	0
Darren Mansaram	20	37	30	6	1117	1	1
Liam Nimmo	19	3	2	0	82	0	0
Iffy Onuora	36	20	19	14	1445	2	0
Isaiah Rankin	26	12	12	10	967	0	0
Jonathan Rowan	22	19	14	6	724	2	0
David Soames	19	16	10	0	165	0	0
Laurens Ten Heuvel	28	5	4	0	158	2	0
Lee Thorpe	28	6	6	4	419	0	0

SQUAD APPEARANCES

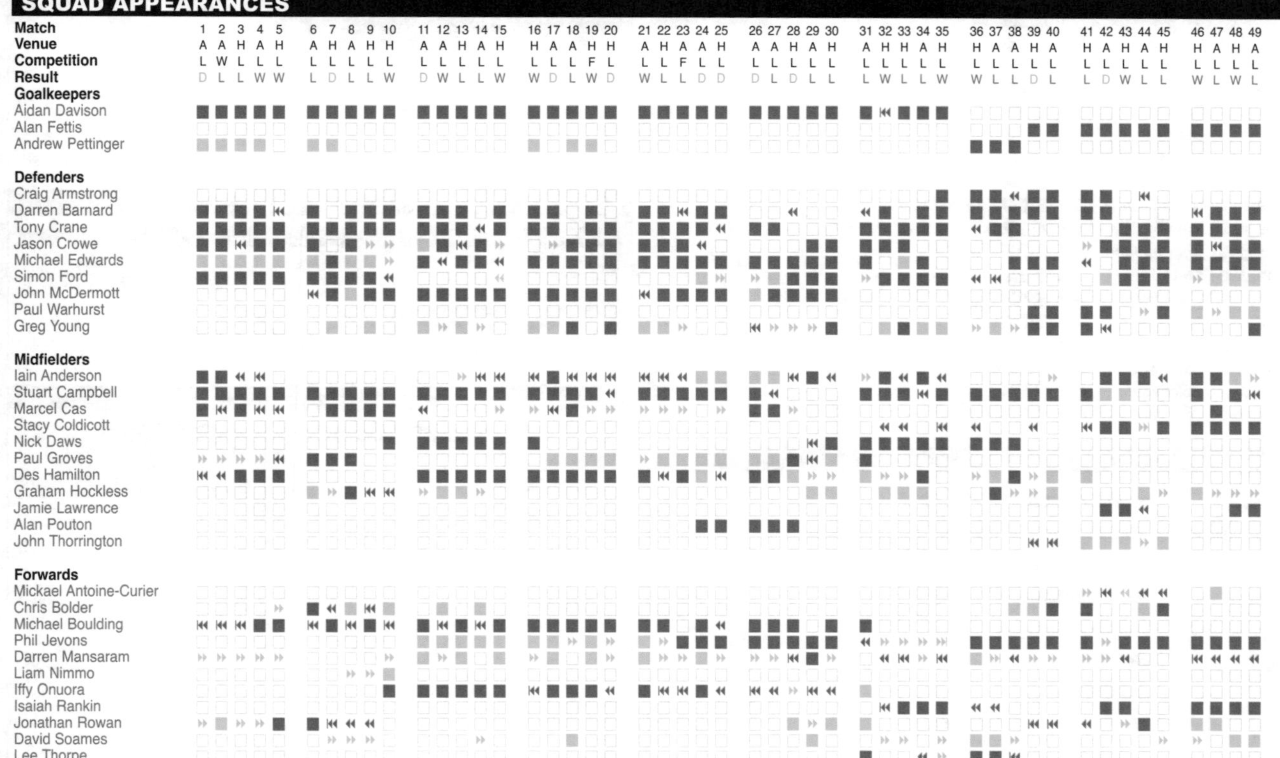

Match 1 2 3 4 5 6 7 8 9 10 11 12 13 14 15 16 17 18 19 20 21 22 23 24 25 26 27 28 29 30 31 32 33 34 35 36 37 38 39 40 41 42 43 44 45 46 47 48 49
Venue A A H A H A H A H H A A H A H H A A H H A H A A H A A H A H A H H A H H A A H A H A H A H H A H A
Competition L W L L L L L L L L L L L L L L L L F L L L F L L L L L L L L L L L L L L L L L L L L L L L L L L
Result D L L W W L D L L W D W L L W W D L W D W L L D D D L D L L L W L L W W L L D L L D W L L W L W L
Goalkeepers
Aidan Davison
Alan Fettis
Andrew Pettinger
Defenders
Craig Armstrong
Darren Barnard
Tony Crane
Jason Crowe
Michael Edwards
Simon Ford
John McDermott
Paul Warhurst
Greg Young
Midfielders
Iain Anderson
Stuart Campbell
Marcel Cas
Stacy Coldicott
Nick Daws
Paul Groves
Des Hamilton
Graham Hockless
Jamie Lawrence
Alan Pouton
John Thorrington
Forwards
Mickael Antoine-Curier
Chris Bolder
Michael Boulding
Phil Jevons
Darren Mansaram
Liam Nimmo
Iffy Onuora
Isaiah Rankin
Jonathan Rowan
David Soames
Lee Thorpe
KEY: On all match
On bench
Subbed or sent off (Counting game)
Subbed or sent off (playing less than 70 minutes)
Subbed on from bench (Counting Game)
Subbed on (playing less than 70 minutes)
Subbed on and then subbed or sent off (Counting Game)
Subbed on and then subbed or sent off (playing less than 70 minutes)
Not in 16

RUSHDEN & DIAMONDS

Final Position: **22nd**

NICKNAME: THE DIAMONDS — KEY: ☐Won ☐Drawn ☐Lost

							Attendance
1	div2	**Luton**	A	L	1-3	Lowe 37	6,878
2	ccR1	**West Ham**	A	L	1-3	Lowe 34	13,715
3	div2	**Plymouth**	H	W	2-1	Lowe 54; Jack 56	4,045
4	div2	**Tranmere**	A	W	2-1	Jack 6; Bell 33	7,374
5	div2	**QPR**	H	D	3-3	Darby 16; Hall 82; Lowe 90	5,544
6	div2	**Oldham**	A	L	2-3	Lowe 38; Bignot 83	5,469
7	div2	**Wycombe**	H	W	2-0	Jack 35; Lowe 85	4,192
8	div2	**Brentford**	H	L	0-1		4,396
9	div2	**Notts County**	A	W	3-1	Lowe 29; Gray 49 pen; Darby 81	4,250
10	div2	**Bournemouth**	A	L	1-2	Lowe 2	6,464
11	div2	**Stockport**	H	D	2-2	Gray 12; Edwards 86	4,049
12	div2	**Brighton**	H	L	1-3	Gray 50 pen	4,634
13	div2	**Barnsley**	A	L	0-2		8,461
14	div2	**Chesterfield**	H	W	2-1	Hunter 12; Jack 15	3,817
15	div2	**Sheff Wed**	A	D	0-0		22,599
16	div2	**Blackpool**	A	W	3-2	Burgess 45; Jack 46; Kitson 55	5,234
17	div2	**Wrexham**	H	L	2-3	Kitson 53,66	4,117
18	div2	**Grimsby**	H	W	3-1	Lowe 68,74; Hanlon 90	4,185
19	facr1	**Swansea**	A	L	0-3		5,031
20	div2	**Hartlepool**	A	L	1-2	Jack 57	4,944
21	div2	**Colchester**	H	W	4-0	Lowe 4; Gray 39; Burgess 58; Bignot 81	4,149
22	div2	**Port Vale**	A	D	1-1	Benjamin 31	4,586
23	div2	**Bristol City**	H	D	1-1	Talbot 4	4,340
24	div2	**Peterborough**	A	L	1-3	Kitson 49	6,167
25	div2	**Swindon**	H	W	2-0	Lowe 23,63	4,845
26	div2	**Wycombe**	A	W	2-0	Jack 4,35	5,421
27	div2	**QPR**	A	L	0-1		14,141
28	div2	**Luton**	H	D	2-2	Kitson 17; Hunter 65	5,823
29	div2	**Plymouth**	A	L	0-3		13,021
30	div2	**Oldham**	H	W	4-1	Jack 26; Lowe 36; Burgess 71; Hall 88	4,591
31	div2	**Swindon**	A	L	2-4	Reeves 53 og; Jack 77	7,023
32	div2	**Chesterfield**	A	L	0-2		4,361
33	div2	**Sheff Wed**	H	L	1-2	Jack 88	5,685
34	div2	**Tranmere**	H	W	2-1	Lowe 50; Mills 71	3,074
35	div2	**Wrexham**	A	D	1-1	Jack 30	3,680
36	div2	**Blackpool**	H	D	0-0		3,764
37	div2	**Peterborough**	H	L	0-1		4,855
38	div2	**Bristol City**	A	L	0-1		12,559
39	div2	**Notts County**	H	W	2-1	Edwards 12,36	4,030
40	div2	**Brentford**	A	L	2-3	Burgess 76; Lowe 88	4,616
41	div2	**Bournemouth**	H	L	0-3		4,500
42	div2	**Stockport**	A	L	1-2	Hunter 70	4,717
43	div2	**Barnsley**	H	L	2-3	Gray 27; Hunter 82	4,063
44	div2	**Brighton**	A	D	0-0		6,320
45	div2	**Grimsby**	A	L	0-1		3,890
46	div2	**Hartlepool**	H	L	0-2		4,568
47	div2	**Colchester**	A	L	0-2		4,618
48	div2	**Port Vale**	H	L	0-2		5,240

MONTHLY POINTS TALLY

Month	Points	%
AUGUST	7	47%
SEPTEMBER	7	39%
OCTOBER	7	47%
NOVEMBER	7	58%
DECEMBER	7	58%
JANUARY	4	33%
FEBRUARY	4	27%
MARCH	4	22%
APRIL	1	7%
MAY	0	0%

KEY PLAYERS - GOALSCORERS

Onandi Lowe

Goals in the League	15	**Player Strike Rate** Average number of minutes between League goals scored by player	146
Contribution to Attacking Power Average number of minutes between League team goals while on pitch	55	**Club Strike Rate** Average number of minutes between League goals scored by club	69

	PLAYER	LGE GOALS	GOALS ALL	POWER	STRIKE RATE
1	Onandi Lowe	15	16	55	146 mins
2	Rodney Jack	12	12	67	328 mins
3	Paul Kitson	5	5	77	342 mins
4	Stuart Gray	5	5	80	560 mins

KEY PLAYERS - MIDFIELDERS

Paul Hall

Goals in the League	2	**Contribution to Attacking Power** Average number of minutes between League team goals while on pitch	52
Defensive Rating Average number of mins between League goals conceded while he was on the pitch	56	**Scoring Difference** Defensive Rating minus Contribution to Attacking Power	4

	PLAYER	LGE GOALS	GOALS ALL	DEF RATE	POWER	SCORE DIFF
1	Paul Hall	2	2	56	52	4 mins
2	Andrew Burgess	4	4	57	64	-7 mins
3	David Bell	1	1	53	74	-21 mins
4	Gary Mills	1	1	50	73	-23 mins

KEY PLAYERS - DEFENDERS

Paul Underwood

Goals Conceded (GC) The number of League goals conceded while he was on the pitch	43	**Clean Sheets** In games when he played at least 70 minutes	4
Defensive Rating Ave number of mins between League goals conceded while on the pitch	62	**Club Defensive Rating** Average number of mins between League goals conceded by the club this season	56

	PLAYER	CON LGE	CON ALL	CLEAN SHEETS	DEF RATE
1	Paul Underwood	43	49	4	62 mins
2	Marcus Bignot	52	58	5	59 mins
3	Barry Hunter	67	73	6	56 mins
4	Leo Roget	26	26	2	56 mins

KEY GOALKEEPER

Jamie Ashdown

Goals Conceded in the League	26	**Counting Games** Games when he played at least 70 mins	19
Defensive Rating Ave number of mins between League goals conceded while on the pitch	66	**Clean Sheets** In games when he played at least 70 mins	4

LEAGUE GOALS

Onandi Lowe

Minutes on the pitch	2183	**Goals in the League**	146
League average (mins between goals)	15		

	PLAYER	MINS	GOALS	AVE
1	Lowe	2183	15	146
2	Jack	3934	12	328
3	Gray	2802	5	560
4	Kitson	1710	5	342
5	Burgess	2943	4	736
6	Hunter	3782	4	946
7	Edwards	2502	3	834
8	Darby	803	2	402
9	Hall	2443	2	1222
10	Bignot	3074	2	1537
11	Hanlon	1572	1	1572
12	Mills	2048	1	2048
	Other		4	
	TOTAL		60	

DISCIPLINARY RECORDS

	PLAYER	YELLOW	RED	AVE
1	Roget	5	0	290
2	Hunter	10	0	378
3	Mills	5	0	409
4	Kitson	4	0	427
5	Lowe	4	0	545
6	Dempster	1	1	608
7	Edwards	3	1	625
8	Underwood	4	0	669
9	Darby	1	0	803
10	Hall	2	1	814
11	Gray	3	0	934
12	Burgess	3	0	981
13	Bignot	3	0	1024
	Other	9	1	
	TOTAL	57	4	

TOP POINT EARNERS

	PLAYER	GAMES	AV PTS
1	Hall	22	1.50
2	Lowe	24	1.29
3	Edwards	27	1.26
4	Underwood	30	1.23
5	Bignot	34	1.21
6	Bell	27	1.15
7	Mills	20	1.15
8	Burgess	30	1.10
9	Ashdown	19	1.05
10	Jack	43	1.05
	CLUB AVERAGE:		**1.04**

LEAGUE APPEARANCES AND BOOKINGS

	AGE (on 01/07/04)	IN NAMED 16	APPEARANCES	COUNTING GAMES	MINUTES ON PITCH	Yellow	Red
Goalkeepers							
Jamie Ashdown	23	19	19	19	1710	0	0
Paul Evans	30	2	2	2	180	0	0
Stephen Gahan	19	5	0	0	0	0	0
Andy Petterson	34	2	0	0	0	0	0
Billy Turley	30	26	25	25	2250	1	0
Defenders							
Marcus Bignot	29	35	35	34	3074	3	0
John Dempster	21	41	19	12	1216	1	1
Andrew Edwards	32	33	29	27	2502	3	1
Barry Hunter	35	44	43	42	3782	10	0
Magnus Okounghae	18	11	1	0	3	0	0
Leo Roget	26	17	17	16	1452	5	0
Paul Underwood	30	30	30	30	2679	4	0
Midfielders							
David Bell	20	42	37	27	2756	1	0
Andrew Burgess	22	38	37	30	2943	3	0
Stuart Gray	30	37	35	27	2802	3	0
Paul Hall	32	37	33	22	2443	2	1
Richie Hanlon	26	29	27	13	1572	0	0
Marcus Kelly	2005	8	8	4	443	0	0
Gary Mills	23	33	30	20	2048	5	0
Barry Quinn	25	4	4	4	360	0	0
Andy Sambrook	24	40	20	14	1359	1	0
Daniel Talbot	20	36	8	1	250	0	0
Forwards							
Adebayo Akinfenwa	22	7	0	0	0	0	0
Trevor Benjamin	25	7	6	5	447	1	0
Duane Darby	30	13	12	6	803	1	0
Robert Duffy	21	14	7	3	378	3	1
Rodney Jack	31	45	45	43	3934	2	0
Paul Kitson	33	31	28	15	1710	4	0
Onandi Lowe	29	26	26	24	2183	4	0
Eric Manangu	2005	1	1	0	8	0	0
Owen Story	19	23	5	0	90	0	0

TEAM OF THE SEASON

G: Jamie Ashdown CG: 19 DR: 66

D: Paul Underwood CG: 30 DR: 62

D: Marcus Bignot CG: 34 DR: 59

D: Barry Hunter CG: 42 DR: 56

D: Leo Roget CG: 16 DR: 56

M: Andrew Burgess CG: 30 SD: -7

M: David Bell CG: 27 SD: -21

M: Gary Mills CG: 20 SD: -23

M: Paul Hall CG: 22 SD: 4

F: Onandi Lowe CG: 24 SR: 146

F: Rodney Jack CG: 43 SR: 328

SQUAD APPEARANCES

Match	1	2	3	4	5	6	7	8	9	10	11	12	13	14	15	16	17	18	19	20	21	22	23	24	25	26	27	28	29	30	31	32	33	34	35	36	37	38	39	40	41	42	43	44	45	46	47	48
Venue	A	A	H	A	H	A	H	H	A	A	H	H	A	H	A	A	H	H	A	A	H	A	H	A	H	A	A	H	A	H	A	A	H	H	A	H	H	A	H	A	H	A	H	A	A	H	A	H
Competition	L	W	L	L	L	L	L	L	L	L	L	L	L	L	L	L	L	L	F	L	L	L	L	L	L	L	L	L	L	L	L	L	L	L	L	L	L	L	L	L	L	L	L	L	L	L	L	L
Result	L	L	W	W	D	L	W	L	W	L	D	L	L	W	D	W	L	W	L	L	W	D	D	L	W	W	L	D	L	W	L	L	L	W	D	D	L	L	W	L	L	L	L	D	L	L	L	L

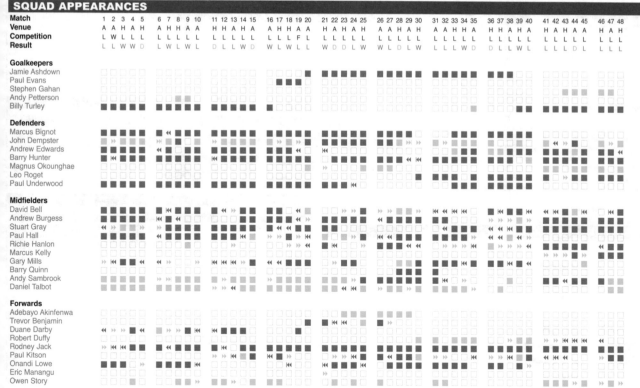

Goalkeepers
Jamie Ashdown
Paul Evans
Stephen Gahan
Andy Petterson
Billy Turley

Defenders
Marcus Bignot
John Dempster
Andrew Edwards
Barry Hunter
Magnus Okounghae
Leo Roget
Paul Underwood

Midfielders
David Bell
Andrew Burgess
Stuart Gray
Paul Hall
Richie Hanlon
Marcus Kelly
Gary Mills
Barry Quinn
Andy Sambrook
Daniel Talbot

Forwards
Adebayo Akinfenwa
Trevor Benjamin
Duane Darby
Robert Duffy
Rodney Jack
Paul Kitson
Onandi Lowe
Eric Manangu
Owen Story

KEY: On all match; On bench; Subbed or sent off (Counting game); Subbed or sent off (playing less than 70 minutes); Subbed on from bench (Counting Game); Subbed on (playing less than 70 minutes); Subbed on and then subbed or sent off (Counting Game); Subbed on and then subbed or sent off (playing less than 70 minutes); Not in 16

NOTTS COUNTY

Final Position: **23rd**

NICKNAME: THE MAGPIES

KEY: Won / Drawn / Lost

#	Comp	Opponent	H/A	Res	Score	Scorers	Attendance
1	div2	Bristol City	A	L	0-5		12,050
2	ccr1	Preston	A	W	7-6*	(*win on penalties)	5,016
3	div2	Wrexham	H	L	0-1		4,768
4	div2	Swindon	A	L	0-4		5,758
5	div2	Peterborough	H	L	0-1		5,177
6	div2	Barnsley	A	D	1-1	Heffernan 90	9,087
7	div2	Luton	H	D	1-1	Barras 60	7,505
8	div2	Chesterfield	A	W	1-0	Bolland 48	4,367
9	div2	Rushden & D	H	L	1-3	Stallard 27	4,250
10	div2	Tranmere	H	D	2-2	Stallard 4; Platt 72	4,215
11	ccr2	Ipswich	H	W	2-1	Baldry 2; Stallard 10 pen	4,059
12	div2	Blackpool	A	L	1-2	Stallard 21 pen	6,206
13	div2	Sheff Wed	A	L	1-2	Stallard 62	20,354
14	div2	Colchester	H	W	3-0	Heffernan 23,86; Riley 76	4,187
15	div2	Bournemouth	H	L	0-1		4,419
16	div2	Stockport	A	D	2-2	Caskey 59; Platt 85	4,727
17	div2	Grimsby	A	L	0-2		4,274
18	div2	Brentford	H	W	2-0	Platt 26; Caskey 90	4,145
19	ccR3	Chelsea	A	L	2-4	Barras 27; Stallard 85	35,997
20	div2	Hartlepool	H	W	1-0	Baldry 62	5,011
21	facr1	Shildon	H	W	7-2	Fenton 7; Platt 14,18; Nicholson 64; Richardson 69; Barras 84; Heffernan 88	4,016
22	div2	Port Vale	A	L	0-1		4,900
23	div2	Brighton	H	L	1-2	Heffernan 35 pen	5,051
24	div2	Oldham	A	W	1-0	Heffernan 4	5,190
25	facr2	Gravesend	A	W	2-1	Fenton 69; Platt 90	2,998
26	div2	Wycombe	H	D	1-1	Heffernan 74	5,014
27	div2	Plymouth	A	L	0-3		9,923
28	div2	QPR	H	D	3-3	Heffernan 6,28,72 pen	7,702
29	div2	Luton	A	L	0-2		7,181
30	facr3	Middlesbrough	A	L	0-2		15,061
31	div2	Peterborough	A	L	2-5	Riley 44,47	3,855
32	div2	Bristol City	H	L	1-2	Butler 42 og	6,403
33	div2	Wrexham	A	W	1-0	Parkinson 31	4,212
34	div2	Swindon	H	L	1-2	Harrad 66 pen	6,663
35	div2	Barnsley	H	D	1-1	Parkinson 26	7,355
36	div2	QPR	A	L	2-3	Parkinson 66; Richardson 90	14,412
37	div2	Bournemouth	A	L	0-1		6,332
38	div2	Stockport	H	W	4-1	Heffernan 2,27,73 pen,85	5,168
39	div2	Brentford	A	W	3-2	Richardson 12; Heffernan 72; Scully 82	4,478
40	div2	Grimsby	H	W	3-1	Antoine-Curier 17; Heffernan 28; Scoffham 83	6,011
41	div2	Plymouth	H	D	0-0		8,057
42	div2	Wycombe	A	D	1-1	Heffernan 17	5,125
43	div2	Rushden & D	A	L	1-2	Scully 62	4,030
44	div2	Chesterfield	H	D	1-1	Fenton 51	7,808
45	div2	Tranmere	A	L	0-4		7,308
46	div2	Blackpool	H	W	4-1	Scully 23; Heffernan 29,78; Scoffham 33	5,100
47	div2	Colchester	A	L	1-4	Richardson 88	3,782
48	div2	Sheff Wed	H	D	0-0		9,601
49	div2	Hartlepool	A	L	0-4		5,629
50	div2	Port Vale	H	L	1-2	Heffernan 90	5,834
51	div2	Brighton	A	L	0-1		6,618
52	div2	Oldham	H	D	1-1	Barras 90	6,715

MONTHLY POINTS TALLY

Month	Points	%
AUGUST	1	7%
SEPTEMBER	5	33%
OCTOBER	7	39%
NOVEMBER	6	50%
DECEMBER	2	17%
JANUARY	4	27%
FEBRUARY	6	50%
MARCH	6	33%
APRIL	4	27%
MAY	1	17%

KEY PLAYERS - GOALSCORERS

Paul Heffernan

Goals in the League	19	Player Strike Rate Average number of minutes between League goals scored by player	148
Contribution to Attacking Power Average number of minutes between League team goals while on pitch	75	Club Strike Rate Average number of minutes between League goals scored by club	83

	PLAYER	LGE GOALS	GOALS ALL	POWER	STRIKE RATE
1	Paul Heffernan	19	20	75	148 mins
2	Mark Stallard	4	6	110	413 mins
3	Clive Platt	3	6	92	553 mins
4	Ian Richardson	3	4	81	1144 mins

KEY PLAYERS - MIDFIELDERS

David Pipe

Goals in the League	0	Contribution to Attacking Power Average number of minutes between League team goals while on pitch	64
Defensive Rating Average number of mins between League goals conceded while he was on the pitch	61	Scoring Difference Defensive Rating minus Contribution to Attacking Power	-3

	PLAYER	LGE GOALS	GOALS ALL	DEF RATE	POWER	SCORE DIFF
1	David Pipe	0	0	61	64	-3 mins
2	Stefan Oakes	0	0	55	75	-20 mins
3	Darren Caskey	2	2	61	83	-22 mins
4	Simon Baldry	1	2	51	87	-36 mins

KEY PLAYERS - DEFENDERS

Stephen Jenkins

Goals Conceded (GC) The number of League goals conceded while he was on the pitch	25	Clean Sheets In games when he played at least 70 minutes	4
Defensive Rating Ave number of mins between League goals conceded while on the pitch	60	Club Defensive Rating Average number of mins between League goals conceded by the club this season	53

	PLAYER	CON LGE	CON ALL	CLEAN SHEETS	DEF RATE
1	Stephen Jenkins	25	33	4	60 mins
2	Ian Richardson	65	74	7	53 mins
3	Nicky Fenton	70	80	7	53 mins
4	Anthony Barras	68	76	6	50 mins

KEY GOALKEEPER

Steve Mildenhall

Goals Conceded in the League	43	Counting Games Games when he played at least 70 mins	28
Defensive Rating Ave number of mins between League goals conceded while on the pitch	58	Clean Sheets In games when he played at least 70 mins	6

LEAGUE GOALS

Paul Heffernan

Minutes on the pitch	2808	Goals in the League	148
League average (mins between goals)	19		

	PLAYER	MINS	GOALS	AVE
1	Heffernan	2808	19	148
2	Stallard	1651	4	413
3	Scully	591	3	197
4	Parkinson	1012	3	337
5	Platt	1659	3	553
6	Riley	1122	3	374
7	Richardson	3432	3	1144
8	Scoffham	487	2	244
9	Caskey	2562	2	1281
10	Barras	3418	2	1709
11	Antoine-Curier	303	1	303
12	Bolland	3015	1	3015
	Other		4	
	TOTAL		50	

DISCIPLINARY RECORDS

	PLAYER	YELLOW	RED	AVE
1	Scoffham	3	0	162
2	Caskey	9	0	284
3	Richardson	9	1	343
4	Baraclough	7	0	394
5	Stallard	4	0	412
6	Fenton	8	0	464
7	Brough	1	0	502
8	Nicholson	3	0	506
9	Pipe	3	0	512
10	Heffernan	5	0	561
11	Bolland	5	0	603
12	Barras	5	0	683
13	Platt	2	0	829
	Other	9	0	
	TOTAL	73	1	

TOP POINT EARNERS

	PLAYER	GAMES	AV PTS
1	Pipe	16	1.25
2	Garden	12	1.17
3	Caskey	25	1.12
4	Heffernan	29	1.03
5	Baldry	29	1.03
6	Richardson	36	1.00
7	Jenkins	16	1.00
8	Oakes	13	1.00
9	Platt	18	0.94
10	Fenton	40	0.93
	CLUB AVERAGE:		**0.91**

LEAGUE APPEARANCES AND BOOKINGS

	AGE (on 01/07/04)	IN NAMED 16	APPEARANCES	COUNTING GAMES	MINUTES ON PITCH	Yellow	Red
Goalkeepers							
Pegguy Arphexad	31	5	3	3	270	0	0
Ale Barcherini	2005	3	0	0	0	0	0
Saul Deeney	21	24	3	3	270	0	0
Stuart Garden	32	31	13	12	1097	1	0
Steve Mildenhall	26	29	28	28	2503	0	0
Defenders							
Anthony Barras	33	42	40	37	3418	5	0
Nicky Fenton	24	44	43	40	3712	8	0
Stephen Jenkins	31	17	17	16	1497	1	0
Danny Livesey	19	13	11	8	792	0	0
Shane McFaul	18	13	5	2	191	0	0
Frazer McHugh	22	17	13	6	768	0	0
Kevin Nicholson	23	29	23	15	1519	3	0
Ian Richardson	33	40	40	36	3432	9	1
Paul Riley	21	28	19	10	1122	0	0
Kelvin Wilson	-	4	3	2	204	0	0
Midfielders							
Simon Baldry	28	37	35	29	2857	1	0
Ian Baraclough	33	38	34	28	2758	7	0
Paul Boertien	25	5	5	5	450	1	0
Paul Bolland	24	42	39	28	3015	5	0
Michael Brough	22	11	10	5	502	1	0
Darren Caskey	29	35	33	25	2562	9	0
Willis Francis	18	9	3	0	38	0	0
Shaun Harrad	19	11	8	0	197	0	0
Adam Murray	22	3	3	1	143	0	0
Stefan Oakes	25	14	14	13	1205	1	0
David Pipe	20	18	18	16	1537	3	0
Tony Scully	28	11	10	5	591	0	0
Forwards							
Mickael Antoine-Curier	21	4	4	3	303	2	0
Tony Hackworth	24	21	12	2	394	0	0
Paul Heffernan	22	38	37	29	2808	5	0
David McGoldrick	16	8	4	1	173	0	0
Andy Parkinson	25	14	14	9	1012	1	0
Clive Platt	26	19	19	18	1659	2	0
Steve Scoffham	2005	15	15	2	487	3	0
Mark Stallard	29	24	22	17	1651	4	0
Matthew Williams	21	9	7	2	342	1	0

TEAM OF THE SEASON

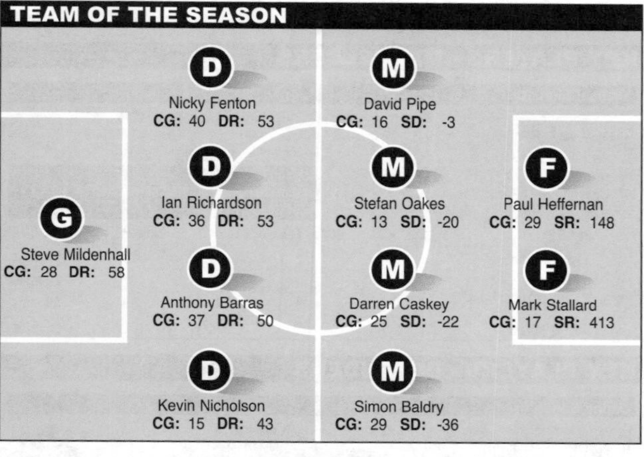

G
Steve Mildenhall
CG: 28 DR: 58
D
Nicky Fenton
CG: 40 DR: 53
D
Ian Richardson
CG: 36 DR: 53
D
Anthony Barras
CG: 37 DR: 50
D
Kevin Nicholson
CG: 15 DR: 43
M
David Pipe
CG: 16 SD: -3
M
Stefan Oakes
CG: 13 SD: -20
M
Darren Caskey
CG: 25 SD: -22
M
Simon Baldry
CG: 29 SD: -36
F
Paul Heffernan
CG: 29 SR: 148
F
Mark Stallard
CG: 17 SR: 413

SQUAD APPEARANCES

Match	1 2 3 4 5	6 7 8 9 10	11 12 13 14 15	16 17 18 19 20	21 22 23 24 25	26 27 28 29 30	31 32 33 34 35	36 37 38 39 40	41 42 43 44 45	46 47 48 49 50	51 52
Venue	A A H A H	A H A H H	H A A H H	A A H A H	H A H A A	H A H A A	A H A H H	A A H A H	H A A H A	H A H A H	A H
Competition	L W L L L	L L L L L	W L L L L	L L L W L	F L L L F	L L L L F	L L L L L	L L L L L	L L L L L	L L L L L	L L
Result	L D L L L	D D W L D	W L L W L	D L W L W	W L L W W	D L D L L	L L W L D	L L W W W	D D L D L	W L D L L	L D

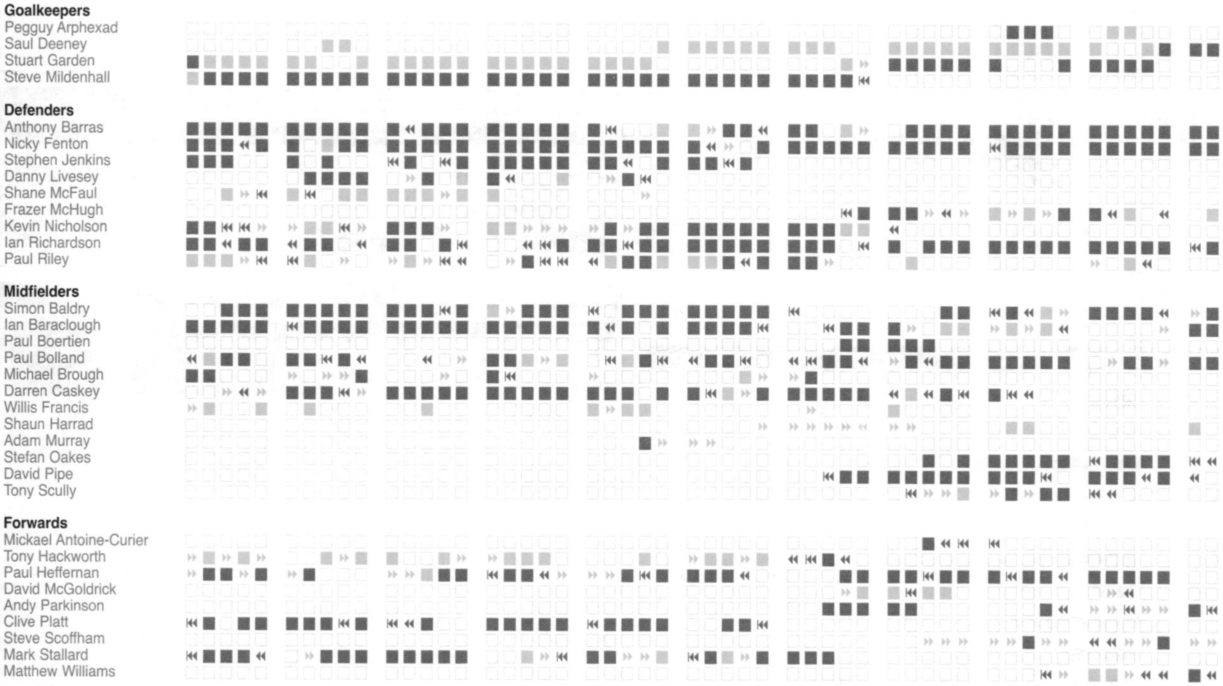

Goalkeepers
Pegguy Arphexad
Saul Deeney
Stuart Garden
Steve Mildenhall

Defenders
Anthony Barras
Nicky Fenton
Stephen Jenkins
Danny Livesey
Shane McFaul
Frazer McHugh
Kevin Nicholson
Ian Richardson
Paul Riley

Midfielders
Simon Baldry
Ian Baraclough
Paul Boertien
Paul Bolland
Michael Brough
Darren Caskey
Willis Francis
Shaun Harrad
Adam Murray
Stefan Oakes
David Pipe
Tony Scully

Forwards
Mickael Antoine-Curier
Tony Hackworth
Paul Heffernan
David McGoldrick
Andy Parkinson
Clive Platt
Steve Scoffham
Mark Stallard
Matthew Williams

KEY: On all match | On bench | Subbed or sent off (Counting game) | Subbed or sent off (playing less than 70 minutes) | Subbed on from bench (Counting Game) | Subbed on (playing less than 70 minutes) | Subbed on and then subbed or sent off (Counting Game) | Subbed on and then subbed or sent off (playing less than 70 minutes) | Not in 16

WYCOMBE WANDERERS

Final Position: **24th**

NICKNAME: THE CHAIRBOYS

KEY: ☐Won ☐Drawn ☐Lost

							Attendance
1	div2	Stockport	H	W	1-0	Mapes 16	4,826
2	ccR1	Wimbledon	H	W	2-0	Harris 3,57	1,986
3	div2	Blackpool	A	L	2-3	Patterson 24; Currie 31	5,960
4	div2	Chesterfield	H	D	3-3	Currie 4; McSporran 20; Patterson 61	4,529
5	div2	Grimsby	A	L	1-3	Mapes 90	4,512
6	div2	Sheff Wed	H	L	1-2	McSporran 42	6,444
7	div2	Rushden & D	A	L	0-2		4,192
8	div2	QPR	A	D	0-0		13,618
9	div2	Colchester	H	L	1-2	Currie 51 pen	4,401
10	div2	Oldham	H	L	2-5	Bell 49,76	4,725
11	ccR2	Aston Villa	H	L	0-5		6,072
12	div2	Port Vale	A	D	1-1	Mapes 64	6,822
13	div2	Tranmere	A	L	1-2	Bell 78	6,847
14	div2	Plymouth	H	D	0-0		5,708
15	div2	Luton	A	L	1-3	Brown 49 pen	5,695
16	div2	Barnsley	H	L	1-2	Thomson 63	4,446
17	div2	Bristol City	H	W	3-0	Holligan 40,70; McSporran 90	4,613
18	div2	Hartlepool	A	D	1-1	Currie 3	5,153
19	div2	Swindon	A	L	0-2		5,681
20	facr1	Swindon	H	W	4-1	Thomson 44; Currie 64,85; McSporran 87	4,738
21	div2	Brentford	H	L	1-2	McSporran 65	6,445
22	div2	Wrexham	A	D	0-0		3,208
23	div2	Peterborough	H	L	1-2	Currie 62	4,669
24	facr2	Mansfield	H	D	1-1	Holligan 53	3,212
25	div2	Notts County	A	D	1-1	Simpson 45	5,014
26	facr2r	Mansfield	A	L	2-3	McSporran 56,59	5,512
27	div2	Bournemouth	H	W	2-0	Ryan 45; Moore, L 75	5,205
28	div2	Brighton	A	L	0-4		6,141
29	div2	Rushden & D	H	L	0-2		5,421
30	div2	Grimsby	H	W	4-1	Moore, L 5,52,90; McSporran 28	4,519
31	div2	Stockport	A	L	0-2		4,406
32	div2	Blackpool	H	L	0-3		4,834
33	div2	Chesterfield	A	D	2-2	Tyson 8; Nethercott 51	3,576
34	div2	Sheff Wed	A	D	1-1	Simpemba 2	19,596
35	div2	Brighton	H	D	1-1	Tyson 45	6,567
36	div2	Luton	H	D	0-0		6,407
37	div2	Barnsley	A	D	0-0		8,507
38	div2	Hartlepool	H	L	3-4	Simpemba 8; McSporran 23; Tyson 64	4,731
39	div2	Bristol City	A	D	1-1	McSporran 72	12,291
40	div2	Bournemouth	A	L	0-1		7,311
41	div2	Notts County	H	D	1-1	Tyson 78	5,125
42	div2	Colchester	A	D	1-1	Simpson 38	3,092
43	div2	QPR	H	D	2-2	Bloomfield 27; Faulconbridge 30	7,634
44	div2	Oldham	A	W	3-2	Tyson 23,42; Faulconbridge 88	5,758
45	div2	Port Vale	H	W	2-1	Currie 42 pen,74	4,738
46	div2	Plymouth	A	L	1-2	Tyson 5	14,806
47	div2	Tranmere	H	L	1-2	Johnson 88	5,256
48	div2	Swindon	H	L	0-3		5,769
49	div2	Brentford	A	D	1-1	Tyson 54	7,145
50	div2	Wrexham	H	D	1-1	Johnson 79	4,684
51	div2	Peterborough	A	D	1-1	Tyson 90	6,398

MONTHLY POINTS TALLY

Month	Points	%
AUGUST	4	33%
SEPTEMBER	2	10%
OCTOBER	5	33%
NOVEMBER	1	8%
DECEMBER	4	33%
JANUARY	5	33%
FEBRUARY	3	25%
MARCH	7	39%
APRIL	4	27%
MAY	2	33%

KEY PLAYERS - GOALSCORERS

Nathan Tyson

Goals in the League	9	Player Strike Rate Average number of minutes between League goals scored by player	205
Contribution to Attacking Power Average number of minutes between League team goals while on pitch	76	Club Strike Rate Average number of minutes between League goals scored by club	83

	PLAYER	LGE GOALS	GOALS ALL	POWER	STRIKE RATE
1	Nathan Tyson	9	9	76	205 mins
2	Jermaine McSporran	7	10	81	373 mins
3	Darren Currie	7	9	81	510 mins
4	Ian Simpemba	2	2	85	774 mins

KEY PLAYERS - MIDFIELDERS

Michael Simpson

Goals in the League	2	Contribution to Attacking Power Average number of minutes between League team goals while on pitch	75
Defensive Rating Average number of mins between League goals conceded while he was on the pitch	54	Scoring Difference Defensive Rating minus Contribution to Attacking Power	-21

	PLAYER	LGE GOALS	GOALS ALL	DEF RATE	POWER	SCORE DIFF
1	Michael Simpson	2	2	54	75	-21 mins
2	Darren Currie	7	9	52	81	-29 mins
3	Ian Simpemba	2	2	47	86	-39 mins
4	Dannie Bulman	0	0	56	106	-50 mins

KEY PLAYERS - DEFENDERS

Danny Senda

Goals Conceded (GC) The number of League goals conceded while he was on the pitch	56	Clean Sheets In games when he played at least 70 minutes	7
Defensive Rating Ave number of mins between League goals conceded while on the pitch	60	Club Defensive Rating Average number of mins between League goals conceded by the club this season	55

	PLAYER	CON LGE	CON ALL	CLEAN SHEETS	DEF RATE
1	Danny Senda	56	63	7	60 mins
2	Chris Vinnicombe	52	62	8	60 mins
3	Stuart Nethercott	33	33	2	60 mins
4	Roger Jonhnson	42	52	5	58 mins

KEY GOALKEEPER

Frank Talia

Goals Conceded in the League	22	Counting Games Games when he played at least 70 mins	16
Defensive Rating Ave number of mins between League goals conceded while on the pitch	66	Clean Sheets In games when he played at least 70 mins	5

LEAGUE GOALS

1 Nathan Tyson

Minutes on the pitch	9	Goals in the League	0
League average (mins between goals)	0		

PLAYER MINS GOALS AVE

0

9

	PLAYER					
1	Tyson	9	0	0	0	9
2	Currie	7	2	0	0	9
3	McSporran	7	3	0	0	10
4	Moore, L	4	0	0	0	4
5	Bell	3	0	0	0	3
6	Mapes	3	0	0	0	3
7	Faulconbridge	2	0	0	0	2
8	Holligan	2	1	0	0	3
9	Patterson	2	0	0	0	2
10	Simpemba	2	0	0	0	2
11	Johnson	2	0	0	0	2
	Other	7	1	2	0	10
	TOTAL	50	7	2	0	59

DISCIPLINARY RECORDS

	PLAYER	YELLOW	RED	AVE
1	Taylor	3	0	180
2	Branston	4	0	202
3	Moore, L	2	0	259
4	Harris	2	0	268
5	Bloomfield	3	0	285
6	Ryan	3	0	287
7	Roberts	2	0	326
8	Brown	5	0	352
9	Marshall	2	0	360
10	Tyson	5	0	368
11	Johnson	5	1	407
12	McSporran	6	0	434
13	Vinnicombe	6	1	448
	Other	21	2	
	TOTAL	69	4	

TOP POINT EARNERS

	PLAYER	GAMES	AV PTS
1	Williams	19	1.11
2	Nethercott	22	0.95
3	Simpson	36	0.92
4	Tyson	20	0.90
5	McSporran	27	0.89
6	Johnson	27	0.89
7	Vinnicombe	34	0.88
8	Currie	38	0.87
9	Senda	37	0.78
10	Bulman	28	0.68
	CLUB AVERAGE:		**0.80**

LEAGUE APPEARANCES AND BOOKINGS

	AGE (on 01/07/04)	IN NAMED 16	APPEARANCES	COUNTING GAMES	MINUTES ON PITCH	Yellow	Red
Goalkeepers							
Scott Bevan	24	5	5	5	450	0	0
Wayne Henderson	20	3	3	3	270	0	0
Frank Talia	31	22	17	16	1445	0	1
Steve Williams	21	38	19	19	1703	0	0
Lee Worgan	20	2	2	2	180	0	0
Defenders							
Guy Branston	25	10	9	9	810	4	0
Steve Dell	24	6	4	3	320	1	0
Richard Harris	23	11	10	4	536	2	0
Roger Johnson	21	35	28	27	2446	5	1
Scott Marshall	31	8	8	8	720	2	0
Stuart Nethercott	31	22	22	22	1980	2	0
Luke Oliver	19	4	2	0	54	0	0
Andy Reilly	18	7	5	5	450	0	0
Mark Rogers	25	18	15	11	1157	1	1
Danny Senda	23	41	40	37	3371	4	0
Steven Taylor	18	6	6	6	540	3	0
Andrew Thomson	30	13	11	11	990	0	0
Chris Vinnicombe	33	38	36	34	3141	6	1
Midfielders							
Matt Bloomfield	20	19	12	8	855	3	0
Stephen Brown	38	33	25	15	1761	5	0
Dannie Bulman	25	45	38	28	2758	5	0
Lewis Cook	20	9	5	1	144	1	0
Darren Currie	29	45	42	38	3568	1	0
Charlie Mapes	18	27	15	4	782	0	0
Stuart Roberts	23	22	16	5	653	2	0
Keith Ryan	34	19	17	5	862	3	0
Ian Simpemba	21	26	19	17	1547	0	0
Michael Simpson	30	38	38	36	3372	6	0
Forwards							
Andrew Bell	20	13	11	2	355	0	0
Jonathan Dixon	20	18	8	1	220	0	0
Craig Faulconbridge	26	21	16	6	875	0	0
Gavin Holligan	24	15	13	5	762	0	0
Jermaine McSporran	27	33	33	27	2609	6	0
Luke Moore	18	6	6	6	519	2	0
Iffy Onuora	36	6	6	3	436	0	0
Simon Patterson	21	4	4	1	236	0	0
Nathan Tyson	22	21	21	20	1842	5	0

TEAM OF THE SEASON

G: Frank Talia — CG: 16 DR: 66

D: Stuart Nethercott — CG: 22 DR: 60

D: Danny Senda — CG: 37 DR: 60

D: Chris Vinnicombe — CG: 34 DR: 60

D: Roger Jonhnson — CG: 27 DR: 58

M: Michael Simpson — CG: 36 SD: -21

M: Darren Currie — CG: 38 SD: -29

M: Ian Simpemba — CG: 17 SD: -39

M: Dannie Bulman — CG: 28 SD: -50

F: Nathan Tyson — CG: 20 SR: 205

F: Jermaine McSporran — CG: 27 SR: 373

SQUAD APPEARANCES

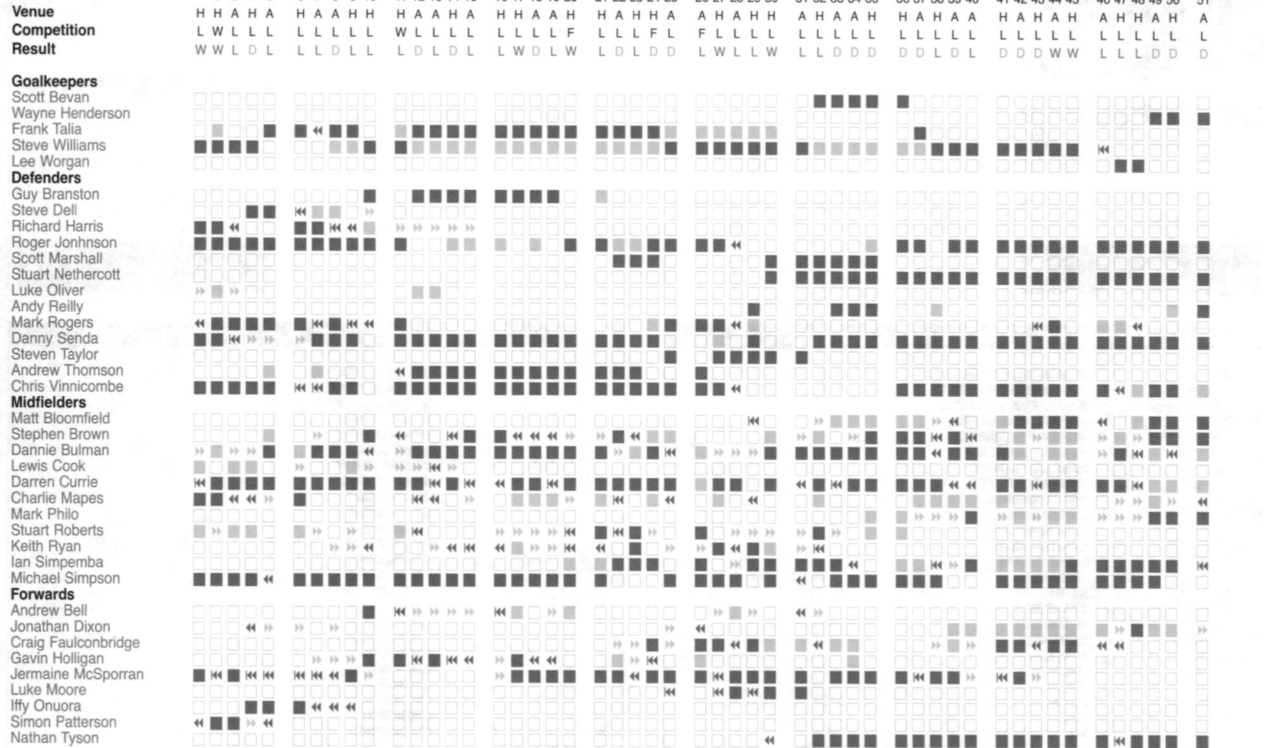
Match 1 2 3 4 5 6 7 8 9 10 11 12 13 14 15 16 17 18 19 20 21 22 23 24 25 26 27 28 29 30 31 32 33 34 35 36 37 38 39 40 41 42 43 44 45 46 47 48 49 50 51
Venue H H A H A H A A H H H A A H A H H A A H H A H H A A H A H H A H A A H H A H A A H A H A H A H H A H A
Competition L W L L L L L L L L W L L L L L L L L F L L L F L F L L L L L L L L L L L L L L L L L L L L L L L L L
Result W W L D L L L D L L L D L D L L W D L W L D L D D L W L L W L L D D D D D L D L D D D W W L L L D D D
Goalkeepers
Scott Bevan
Wayne Henderson
Frank Talia
Steve Williams
Lee Worgan
Defenders
Guy Branston
Steve Dell
Richard Harris
Roger Jonhnson
Scott Marshall
Stuart Nethercott
Luke Oliver
Andy Reilly
Mark Rogers
Danny Senda
Steven Taylor
Andrew Thomson
Chris Vinnicombe
Midfielders
Matt Bloomfield
Stephen Brown
Dannie Bulman
Lewis Cook
Darren Currie
Charlie Mapes
Mark Philo
Stuart Roberts
Keith Ryan
Ian Simpemba
Michael Simpson
Forwards
Andrew Bell
Jonathan Dixon
Craig Faulconbridge
Gavin Holligan
Jermaine McSporran
Luke Moore
Iffy Onuora
Simon Patterson
Nathan Tyson
KEY: On all match
On bench
Subbed or sent off (Counting game)
Subbed or sent off (playing less than 70 minutes)
Subbed on from bench (Counting Game)
Subbed on (playing less than 70 minutes)
Subbed on and then subbed or sent off (Counting Game)
Subbed on and then subbed or sent off (playing less than 70 minutes)
Not in 16

DIVISION THREE ROUND-UP

FINAL LEAGUE TABLE

	HOME						AWAY					TOTAL			
	P	W	D	L	F	A	W	D	L	F	A	F	A	DIF	PTS
Doncaster	46	17	4	2	47	13	10	7	6	32	24	79	37	42	92
Hull City	46	16	4	3	50	21	9	9	5	32	23	82	44	38	88
Torquay	46	15	6	2	44	18	8	6	9	24	26	68	44	24	81
Huddersfield	46	16	4	3	42	18	7	8	8	26	34	68	52	16	81
Mansfield	46	13	5	5	44	25	9	4	10	32	37	76	62	14	75
Northampton	46	13	4	6	30	23	9	5	9	28	28	58	51	7	75
Lincoln	46	9	11	3	36	23	10	6	7	32	24	68	47	21	74
Yeovil	46	14	3	6	40	19	9	2	12	30	38	70	57	13	74
Oxford	46	14	8	1	34	13	4	9	10	21	31	55	44	11	71
Swansea	46	9	8	6	36	26	6	6	11	22	35	58	61	-3	59
Boston	46	11	7	5	35	21	5	4	14	15	33	50	54	-4	59
Bury	46	10	7	6	29	26	5	4	14	25	38	54	64	-10	56
Cambridge	46	6	7	10	26	32	8	7	8	29	35	55	67	-12	56
Cheltenham	46	11	4	8	37	38	3	10	10	20	33	57	71	-14	56
Bristol Rovers	46	9	7	7	29	26	5	6	12	21	35	50	61	-11	55
Kidderminster	46	9	5	9	28	29	5	8	10	17	30	45	59	-14	55
Southend	46	8	4	11	27	29	6	8	9	24	34	51	63	-12	54
Darlington	46	10	4	9	30	28	4	7	12	23	33	53	61	-8	53
Leyton Orient	46	8	9	6	28	27	5	5	13	20	38	48	65	-17	53
Macclesfield	46	8	9	6	28	25	5	4	14	26	44	54	69	-15	52
Rochdale	46	7	8	8	28	26	5	6	12	21	32	49	58	-9	50
Scunthorpe	46	7	10	6	36	27	4	6	13	33	45	69	72	-3	49
Carlisle	46	8	5	10	23	27	4	4	15	23	42	46	69	-23	45
York	46	7	6	10	22	29	3	8	12	13	37	35	66	-31	44

CLUB STRIKE FORCE

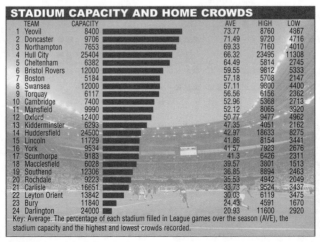

Ashbee strikes for Hull City

1 Hull City

Goals scored in the League	85
Goals scored in all competions	88
Club Strike Rate (CSR) Average number of minutes between League goals scored	49

	CLUB	LGE	ALL	CSR
1	Hull City	85	88	49
2	Doncaster	79	83	52
3	Mansfield	76	90	54
4	Scunthorpe	70	81	59
5	Yeovil	70	80	59
6	Huddersfield	68	78	61
7	Lincoln	68	74	61
8	Torquay	68	70	61
9	Northampton	58	74	71
10	Swansea	58	69	71
11	Cheltenham	57	65	73
12	Cambridge	55	61	75
13	Oxford	55	57	75
14	Bury	54	55	77
15	Macclesfield	54	62	77
16	Darlington	53	53	78
17	Southend	51	61	81
18	Boston	50	51	83
19	Bristol Rovers	50	50	83
20	Rochdale	49	52	84
21	Leyton Orient	48	52	86
22	Carlisle	46	47	90
23	Kidderminster	45	51	92
24	York	35	37	118

CLUB DISCIPLINARY RECORDS

Barber has a word with Scunthorpe's Beagrie

1 Scunthorpe

League Yellow	103
League Red	4
All Competitions Yellow	112
All Competitions Red	5
Cards Average in League Average number of minutes between a card being shown	39

	CLUB	LEAGUE		TOTAL		AVE
1	Scunthorpe	103 Y	4 R	112 Y	5 R	39
2	Boston	94	5	100	5	42
3	Leyton Orient	93	6	99	8	42
4	Carlisle	86	8	86	8	44
5	Huddersfield	80	12	91	13	45
6	Rochdale	86	7	93	7	45
7	Darlington	78	10	86	10	47
8	Bury	82	2	89	2	49
9	Swansea	79	6	91	8	49
10	Lincoln	78	3	82	3	51
11	Torquay	76	2	77	2	53
12	Doncaster	72	4	76	4	54
13	Cambridge	72	3	76	3	55
14	York	68	6	74	6	56
15	Bristol Rovers	66	7	71	8	57
16	Kidderminster	68	5	75	5	57
17	Yeovil	70	3	73	3	57
18	Southend	66	6	80	7	58
19	Macclesfield	63	6	77	9	60
20	Mansfield	63	4	80	6	62
21	Northampton	58	4	72	6	67
22	Oxford	58	4	62	4	67
23	Cheltenham	55	3	62	3	71
24	Hull City	50	1	52	1	81

CLUB DEFENCES

	CLUB	LGE	ALL	CS	CDR
1	Doncaster	37	42	19	112
2	Hull City	44	49	16	94
3	Oxford	44	48	17	94
4	Torquay	44	47	14	94
5	Lincoln	47	56	17	88
6	Northampton	51	67	15	81
7	Huddersfield	52	60	16	80
8	Boston	54	60	14	77
9	Rochdale	58	63	12	71
10	Yeovil	58	66	16	71
11	Kidderminster	59	63	11	70
12	Bristol Rovers	61	63	14	68
13	Darlington	61	65	12	68
14	Swansea	61	67	13	68
15	Mansfield	62	72	13	67
16	Southend	63	71	10	66
17	Bury	64	67	12	65
18	Leyton Orient	65	73	8	64
19	York	66	70	14	63
20	Cambridge	67	73	11	62
21	Carlisle	69	74	6	60
22	Macclesfield	69	76	10	60
23	Cheltenham	71	77	10	58
24	Scunthorpe	72	81	8	58

Ravenhill in action for Doncaster

1 Doncaster

Goals conceded in the League	37
Goals conceded in all competitions	42
Clean Sheets (CS) Number of league games where no goals were conceded	19
Club Defensive Rate (CDR) Average number of minutes between League goals conceded	112

STADIUM CAPACITY AND HOME CROWDS

	TEAM	CAPACITY	AVE	HIGH	LOW
1	Yeovil	8400	73.77	8760	4867
2	Doncaster	9706	71.49	9720	4716
3	Northampton	7653	69.33	7160	4010
4	Hull City	25404	66.32	23495	11308
5	Cheltenham	6382	64.49	5814	2745
6	Bristol Rovers	12000	59.55	9812	5333
7	Boston	5184	57.18	5708	2147
8	Swansea	12000	57.11	9800	4400
9	Torquay	6117	56.56	6156	2362
10	Cambridge	7400	52.96	5368	2713
11	Mansfield	9990	52.12	8065	3920
12	Oxford	12400	50.77	9477	4962
13	Kidderminster	6293	47.35	4051	2162
14	Huddersfield	24500	42.97	18633	8275
15	Lincoln	11729	41.86	8154	3441
16	York	9534	41.57	7923	2676
17	Scunthorpe	9183	41.3	6426	2311
18	Macclesfield	6028	39.57	3801	1513
19	Southend	12306	36.85	8894	2463
20	Rochdale	9223	35.53	4942	2049
21	Carlisle	16651	33.73	9524	3437
22	Leyton Orient	13842	30.03	6119	3475
23	Bury	11840	24.43	4591	1670
24	Darlington	24000	20.93	11600	2920

Key: Average. The percentage of each stadium filled in League games over the season (AVE), the stadium capacity and the highest and lowest crowds recorded.

AWAY ATTENDANCE

	TEAM	AVE	HIGH	LOW
1	Hull City	60.06	13893	3720
2	Doncaster	58.52	23006	2831
3	Huddersfield	57.52	23495	3059
4	Lincoln	53.53	17453	2016
5	Oxford	52.58	21491	2282
6	Yeovil	51.54	14367	2221
7	Mansfield	50.63	18633	2199
8	Carlisle	49.42	19050	2326
9	Bristol Rovers	47.71	22562	1542
10	Swansea	47.48	20903	1513
11	Northampton	47.41	18017	2585
12	Torquay	47.05	15222	1970
13	Kidderminster	46.65	13683	1988
14	York	46.02	19099	2282
15	Bury	45.99	11308	2260
16	Rochdale	45.67	16050	2152
17	Darlington	45.57	14675	2293
18	Scunthorpe	45.37	19076	2162
19	Cambridge	45.08	14271	2151
20	Boston	45	13091	2049
21	Southend	44.94	12545	1670
22	Cheltenham	44.86	12522	2061
23	Leyton Orient	44.67	15531	2156
24	Macclesfield	44.51	15053	2300

Key: Average. How close each club has come to filling grounds in its away league matches (AVE) and the highest and lowest crowds recorded.

CHART-TOPPING MIDFIELDERS

1 Green - Doncaster

Goals scored in the League	8
Defensive Rating Av number of mins between League goals conceded while on the pitch	124
Contribution to Attacking Power Average number of minutes between League team goals while on pitch	48
Scoring Difference Defensive Rating minus Contribution to Attacking Power	76

	PLAYER	CLUB	GOALS	DEF RATE	POWER	S DIFF
1	Green	Doncaster	8	124	48	76
2	Melligan	Doncaster	2	118	52	66
3	Doolan	Doncaster	0	112	51	61
4	McIndoe	Doncaster	10	110	52	58
5	Ashbee	Hull City	2	100	50	50
6	Green	Hull City	6	94	45	49
7	Price	Hull City	9	94	47	47
8	Elliott	Hull City	14	94	54	40
9	MacKenzie	Mansfield	2	84	44	40
10	Worthington	Huddersfield	3	95	59	36
11	Russell	Torquay	2	95	59	36
12	Bailey	Lincoln	1	102	67	35
13	Robinson	Oxford	1	105	71	34
14	Hockley	Torquay	5	93	59	34
15	Butcher	Lincoln	6	94	61	33

CHART-TOPPING GOALSCORERS

1 Trundle - Swansea

Goals scored in the League (GL)	17
Goals scored in all competitions (GA)	22
Contribution to Attacking Power (AP) Average number of minutes between League team goals while on pitch	57
Player Strike Rate Average number of minutes between League goals scored by player	141
Club Strike Rate (CSR) Average minutes between League goals scored by club	71

	PLAYER	CLUB	GOALS: LGE	ALL	POWER	CSR	S RATE
1	Trundle	Swansea	17	22	57	71	141
2	MacLean	Scunthorpe	23	23	54	59	143
3	Stead	Huddersfield	16	18	59	61	144
4	Constantine	Southend	21	21	81	81	170
5	Graham	Torquay	22	23	61	61	173
6	Allsopp	Hull City	15	15	46	50	177
7	Tipton	Macclesfield	16	19	69	77	183
8	Lawrence	Mansfield	19	22	50	54	190
9	Blundell	Doncaster	18	20	51	52	206
10	Beagrie	Scunthorpe	12	13	52	59	211
11	Burgess	Hull City	18	18	50	50	214
12	Basham	Oxford	14	15	69	75	215
13	Tait	Bristol Rovers	11	11	83	83	221
14	Fletcher	Lincoln	16	17	58	61	221
15	Fortune-West	Doncaster	11	12	64	52	228

CHART-TOPPING DEFENDERS

1 Albrighton - Doncaster

Goals Conceded in the League The number of League goals conceded while he was on the pitch	18
Goals Conceded in all competitions The number of goals conceded while he was on the pitch in all competitions	19
Clean Sheets In games when he played at least 70 mins	12
Defensive Rating Average number of minutes between League goals conceded while on pitch	137
Club Defensive Rating Average mins between League goals conceded by the club this season	112

	PLAYER	CLUB	CON: LGE	ALL	CS	CDR	DEF RATE
1	Albrighton	Doncaster	18	19	12	112	137
2	Foster	Doncaster	35	39	19	112	113
3	Bound	Oxford	26	30	14	94	111
4	Ryan	Doncaster	35	40	16	112	107
5	Dawson	Hull City	27	30	12	94	107
6	Price	Doncaster	15	17	8	112	106
7	Crittenden	Yeovil	17	21	10	71	105
8	Canoville	Torquay	25	28	9	94	103
9	Lloyd	Huddersfield	26	30	13	80	102
10	McNiven	Oxford	33	37	16	94	100
11	Mayo	Lincoln	28	33	13	88	98
12	Lyttle	Northampton	22	30	6	81	97
13	McGlinchey	Torquay	31	31	10	94	97
14	Delaney	Hull City	43	48	16	94	95
15	Futcher	Lincoln	40	49	16	88	95

CHART-TOPPING GOALKEEPERS

1 Musselwhite - Hull City

Counting Games League games when he played at least 70 minutes	18
Goals Conceded in the League The number of League goals conceded while he was on the pitch	13
Goals Conceded in all competitions The number of goals conceded while he was on the pitch in all competitions	16
Clean Sheets In games when he played at least 70 mins	8
Defensive Rating Average number of minutes between League goals conceded while on pitch	121

	PLAYER	CLUB	CG	CONC LGE	CONC ALL	CS	DEF RATE
1	Musselwhite	Hull City	18	13	16	8	121
2	Warrington	Doncaster	46	37	42	19	112
3	Van Heusden	Torquay	25	21	24	8	105
4	Woodman	Oxford	41	37	41	15	100
5	Myhill	Hull City	23	22	22	7	94
6	Marriott	Lincoln	46	47	56	17	88
7	Dearden	Torquay	22	23	23	6	84
8	Harper	Northampton	39	42	58	12	83
9	Edwards	Rochdale	34	38	40	11	81
10	Bastock	Boston	46	54	60	14	77
11	Price	Darlington	36	45	47	10	72
12	Flahavan	Southend	37	47	51	8	71
13	Freestone	Swansea	37	46	51	11	71
14	Weale	Yeovil	35	45	53	13	70
15	Brock	Kidderminster	37	49	54	9	68

PLAYER DISCIPLINARY RECORD

1 McCormack - Leyton Orient

Cards Average mins between cards	84
League Yellow	7
League Red	2
TOTAL	9

	PLAYER		LY	LR	TOT	AVE
1	McCormack	Leyton Orient	7	2	9	84
2	Sall	Kidderminster	3	1	4	132
3	Pearson	Darlington	5	2	7	137
4	Cozic	Cheltenham	3	0	3	154
5	Shaw	York	3	0	3	155
6	Thorpe	Leyton Orient	6	1	7	161
7	Twigg	Bristol Rovers	3	0	3	168
8	O'ghnessy	Bury	11	0	11	171
9	Simpkins	Rochdale	12	1	13	173
10	Featherstone	Scunthorpe	3	0	3	174
11	Foran	Carlisle	8	2	10	175
12	Fowler	Huddersfield	10	2	12	190
13	Kelly	Carlisle	4	0	4	193
14	Byrne	Carlisle	4	0	4	197
15	Scott	Huddersfield	6	1	7	199
16	Daly	Bury	2	1	3	200
17	Mackie	Leyton Orient	9	0	9	200
18	Odejayi	Cheltenham	7	0	7	203
19	Graham	Darlington	3	0	3	209
20	Rusk	Boston	7	0	7	210
21	Fullarton	Southend	3	0	3	210
22	Thorpe	Bristol Rovers	3	0	3	215
23	Willis	Kidderminster	4	1	5	215
24	Kell	Scunthorpe	7	1	8	220
25	Duffy	Swansea	4	2	6	220

TEAM OF THE SEASON

G — Musselwhite : Hull
CG: 18 DR: 121

D — Allbrighton : Doncaster
CG: 27 DR: 137

D — Bound : Oxford
CG: 31 DR: 111

D — Dawson : Hull
CG: 31 DR: 107

D — Crittenden : Yeovil
CG: 18 DR: 105

M — Green : Doncaster
CG: 36 SD: + 76

M — Ashbee : Hull
CG: 39 SD: + 50

M — MacKenzie : Mansfield
CG: 19 SD: + 40

M — Worthington : Huddersfield
CG: 37 SD: + 36

F — Trundle : Swansea
CG: 26 SR: 141

F — Allsopp : Hull
CG: 28 AP: 46

NATIONWIDE DIVISION THREE CHAMPIONS

DONCASTER ROVERS

Final Position: **1ST**

NICKNAME: ROVERS

KEY: ☐ Won ☐ Drawn ☐ Lost

							Attendance
1	div3	**Leyton Orient**	A	W	3-1	Blundell 45; Fortune-West 51,66	5,194
2	ccr1	**Grimsby**	H	W	3-2	Fortune-West 76; Barnes 81 pen; Blundell 90	6,057
3	div3	**Southend**	H	W	2-0	Foster 12; Green 55	5,592
4	div3	**Lincoln**	A	D	0-0		5,051
5	div3	**Huddersfield**	H	D	1-1	Fortune-West 47	7,367
6	div3	**Northampton**	A	L	0-1		4,933
7	div3	**Hull City**	H	D	0-0		7,132
8	div3	**Darlington**	A	L	1-2	Paterson 53 pen	5,518
9	div3	**Yeovil**	H	L	0-1		4,716
10	div3	**Oxford**	H	W	2-0	Ryan 39; Green 83	5,040
11	ccr2	**Crystal Palace**	A	L	1-2	Blundell 47	4,904
12	div3	**Bury**	A	W	3-1	Fortune-West 11; Blundell 35; McIndoe 53	3,606
13	div3	**Cambridge**	A	D	3-3	Tierney 57; Albrighton 64; Ryan 75	3,492
14	div3	**Bristol Rovers**	H	W	5-1	Tierney 12; Brown 41; McIndoe 45,57,82 pen	5,439
15	div3	**Macclesfield**	A	W	3-1	Blundell 45; Green 49; McIndoe 53 pen	2,831
16	div3	**Mansfield**	H	W	4-2	Blundell 38; Green 53; McIndoe 70 pen; Brown 77	8,500
17	div3	**Rochdale**	H	W	2-1	Tierney 2; Brown 75	5,890
18	div3	**Kidderminster**	A	W	2-0	Blundell 16; Brown 60	3,393
19	div3	**Torquay**	H	W	1-0	Green 21	6,863
20	facr1	**Scarborough**	A	L	0-1		3,497
21	div3	**York**	A	L	0-1		5,942
22	div3	**Boston**	H	W	3-0	Brown 31,55; Melligan 54	5,211
23	div3	**Carlisle**	A	W	1-0	Fortune-West 68	4,344
24	div3	**Cheltenham**	A	W	3-1	McIndoe 12 pen; Morley 24; Melligan 51	3,884
25	div3	**Swansea**	H	W	3-1	McIndoe 11 pen; Green 20; Blundell 90	6,566
26	div3	**Scunthorpe**	H	W	1-0	Blundell 67	8,961
27	div3	**Hull City**	A	L	1-3	Fortune-West 39	23,006
28	div3	**Huddersfield**	A	L	1-3	Blundell 73	13,044
29	div3	**Leyton Orient**	H	W	5-0	Fortune-West 6,14,18; Blundell 57; Hynes 80	6,293
30	div3	**Southend**	A	W	2-0	Fortune-West 4; McIndoe 7	4,308
31	div3	**Lincoln**	H	L	0-2		8,774
32	div3	**Northampton**	H	W	1-0	Green 9	6,017
33	div3	**Scunthorpe**	A	D	2-2	McIndoe 83 pen; Fortune-West 90	5,681
34	div3	**Macclesfield**	H	W	1-0	Blundell 45	5,525
35	div3	**Mansfield**	A	W	2-1	Blundell 60,67	7,724
36	div3	**Kidderminster**	H	W	5-0	Albrighton 5; Blundell 45,78; Ravenhill 56; Mulligan 90	7,594
37	div3	**Swansea**	A	D	1-1	Brown 56	8,045
38	div3	**Cheltenham**	H	D	1-1	Brown 90	7,510
39	div3	**Yeovil**	A	W	1-0	Ravenhill 72	7,587
40	div3	**Darlington**	H	D	1-1	Akinfenwa 86	7,178
41	div3	**Oxford**	A	D	0-0		8,483
42	div3	**Rochdale**	A	D	1-1	Albrighton 90	4,601
43	div3	**Bury**	H	W	3-1	Blundell 47,68; Akinfenwa 73	6,221
44	div3	**Bristol Rovers**	A	W	2-1	Ravenhill 51; Akinfenwa 61	8,571
45	div3	**Cambridge**	H	W	2-0	Akinfenwa 60; Green 65	9,644
46	div3	**Torquay**	A	L	0-1		5,808
47	div3	**York**	H	W	3-1	Blundell 5; Brown 8,57	7,843
48	div3	**Boston**	A	D	0-0		4,671
49	div3	**Carlisle**	H	W	1-0	Blundell 69	9,720

TEAM OF THE SEASON

G — Andy Warrington — CG: 46 DR: 112

D — Dave Mulligan — CG: 13 DR: 146

D — Mark Albrighton — CG: 27 DR: 137

D — Stephen Foster — CG: 44 DR: 113

D — Simon Marples — CG: 16 DR: 111

M — Paul Green — CG: 36 SD: 76

M — John Doolan — CG: 33 SD: 61

M — Michael McIndoe — CG: 44 SD: 58

M — John Melligan — CG: 18 SD: 66

F — Chris Brown — CG: 15 SR: 145

F — Greg Blundell — CG: 39 SR: 206

KEY PLAYER APPEARANCES

	PLAYER	POS	AGE	APP	MINS ON	GOALS	CARDS(Y/R)	
1	Andy Warrington	GK	28	46	4140	0	0	0
2	Michael McIndoe	MID	24	45	3973	10	2	0
3	Stephen Foster	DEF	29	44	3960	1	10	0
4	Tim Ryan	DEF	29	42	3733	2	10	0
5	Greg Blundell	ATT	28	44	3702	18	6	0
6	Paul Green	MID	21	43	3360	8	2	0
7	John Doolan	MID	30	39	3142	0	7	0
8	Leo Fortune-West	ATT	33	39	2513	11	6	1
9	Mark Albrighton	DEF	28	28	2463	3	7	0
10	John Melligan	MID	23	21	1654	2	2	0
11	Jamie Price	DEF	22	19	1586	0	0	1
12	Ricky Ravenhill	MID	23	36	1455	3	6	0
13	Chris Brown	ATT	19	22	1446	10	4	0
14	Simon Marples	DEF	28	16	1440	0	0	0
15	Dave Morley	DEF	26	21	1335	1	2	0
16	Dave Mulligan	DEF	22	14	1170	1	2	1
17	Chris Beech	DEF	28	11	920	0	0	0
18	Francis Tierney	MID	28	13	849	3	0	0

KEY PLAYERS - GOALSCORERS

Chris Brown

Goals in the League	10
Contribution to Attacking Power Average number of minutes between League team goals while on pitch	45
Player Strike Rate Average number of minutes between League goals scored by player	145
Club Strike Rate Average number of minutes between League goals scored by club	52

	PLAYER	LGE GOALS	POWER	STRIKE RATE
1	Chris Brown	10	45	145 mins
2	Greg Blundell	18	51	206 mins
3	Leo Fortune-West	11	64	228 mins
4	Michael McIndoe	10	51	397 mins
5	Paul Green	8	48	420 mins

KEY PLAYERS - MIDFIELDERS

Paul Green

Goals in the League	8
Defensive Rating Average number of mins between League goals conceded while he was on the pitch	124
Contribution to Attacking Power Average number of minutes between League team goals while on pitch	48
Scoring Difference Defensive Rating minus Contribution to Attacking Power	76

	PLAYER	LGE GOALS	DEF RATE	POWER	SCORE DIFF
1	Paul Green	8	124	48	76 mins
2	John Melligan	2	118	52	66 mins
3	John Doolan	0	112	51	61 mins
4	Michael McIndoe	10	110	52	58 mins
5	Ricky Ravenhill	3	112	73	39 mins

KEY PLAYERS - DEFENDERS

Dave Mulligan

Goals Conceded when he was on pitch	8
Defensive Rating Ave number of mins between League goals conceded while on the pitch	146
Clean Sheets In games when he played at least 70 minutes	5
Club Defensive Rating Average number of mins between League goals conceded by the club this season.	112

	PLAYER	CON LGE	CLN SHEETS	DEF RATE
1	Dave Mulligan	8	5	146 mins
2	Mark Albrighton	18	12	137 mins
3	Stephen Foster	35	19	113 mins
4	Simon Marples	13	7	111 mins
5	Tim Ryan	35	16	107 mins

KEY GOALKEEPER

Andy Warrington

Goals Conceded in the League	37
Defensive Rating Ave number of mins between League goals conceded while on the pitch.	112
Counting Games Games when he played at least 70 mins	46
Clean Sheets In games when he played at least 70 mins	19

TOP POINT EARNERS

	PLAYER	GAMES	AV PTS
1	Jamie Price	18	**2.28**
2	Chris Brown	15	**2.27**
3	Mark Albrighton	27	**2.26**
4	Dave Mulligan	13	**2.23**
5	John Melligan	18	**2.22**
6	John Doolan	33	**2.18**
7	Greg Blundell	39	**2.10**
8	Paul Green	36	**2.08**
9	Michael McIndoe	44	**2.02**
10	Dave Morley	14	**2.00**
	CLUB AVERAGE:		**2.00**

HULL CITY

Final Position: **2nd**

NICKNAME: THE TIGERS

KEY: Won / Drawn / Lost

							Attendance
1	div3	Darlington	H	W	4-1	Burgess 26; Price 49; Thelwell 50; Allsopp 82	14,675
2	ccr1	Wigan	A	L	0-2		3,295
3	div3	Oxford	A	L	1-2	Allsopp 77	6,618
4	div3	Cheltenham	H	D	3-3	Elliott 7; Price 42; Allsopp 51	12,522
5	div3	Cambridge	A	W	2-0	Price 5; Allsopp 21	4,571
6	div3	Boston	H	W	2-1	Elliott 34; Green 90	13,091
7	div3	Doncaster	A	D	0-0		7,132
8	div3	Southend	H	W	3-2	Allsopp 43; Dawson 59; Elliott 74	12,545
9	div3	Leyton Orient	A	D	1-1	Burgess 33	3,728
10	div3	Rochdale	A	W	2-0	Green 63; Burgess 67	4,215
11	div3	Kidderminster	H	W	6-1	Burgess 5,81; Allsopp 44; Dawson 57; France 84; Green 90	13,683
12	div3	Swansea	H	W	1-0	Elliott 27	20,903
13	div3	Northampton	A	W	5-1	Elliott 20; Allsopp 42; Price 67; Burgess 82; Forrester 90	6,011
14	div3	Carlisle	H	W	2-1	Burgess 13; Forrester 75	19,050
15	div3	Torquay	A	D	1-1	Elliott 79	3,720
16	div3	Bury	A	D	0-0		3,896
17	div3	Lincoln	H	W	3-0	Holt 45; Allsopp 52; Green 80	17,453
18	div3	Macclesfield	H	D	2-2	Hinds 8; Allsopp 57	15,053
19	facr1	Cheltenham	A	L	1-3	Price 46	3,624
20	div3	Huddersfield	A	L	1-3	Forrester 90	13,893
21	div3	Yeovil	H	D	0-0		14,367
22	div3	Bristol Rovers	A	L	1-2	Burgess 5	6,331
23	div3	Bury	H	W	2-0	Price 17; Burgess 47	11,308
24	div3	Scunthorpe	A	D	1-1	Elliott 70	6,426
25	div3	Mansfield	H	L	0-1		15,005
26	div3	York	A	W	2-0	Burgess 56; Forrester 69 pen	7,923
27	div3	Doncaster	H	W	3-1	Price 3,66,78	23,006
28	div3	Cambridge	H	W	2-0	Elliott 42,60	14,271
29	div3	Darlington	A	W	1-0	Elliott 30	6,847
30	div3	Oxford	H	W	4-2	Burgess 58; Allsopp 63,66; Crosby 80 og	21,491
31	div3	Cheltenham	A	W	2-0	Allsopp 58; Burgess 60	4,536
32	div3	York	H	W	2-1	Allsopp 56; Walters 74	19,099
33	div3	Carlisle	A	D	1-1	Green 82	7,176
34	div3	Torquay	H	L	0-1		15,222
35	div3	Lincoln	A	L	0-2		7,069
36	div3	Mansfield	A	L	0-1		6,859
37	div3	Scunthorpe	H	W	2-1	Burgess 12,30	19,076
38	div3	Leyton Orient	H	W	3-0	Elliott 20; Burgess 78; France 90	15,531
39	div3	Rochdale	H	W	1-0	Delaney 79	16,050
40	div3	Boston	A	W	2-1	Elliott 19; Allsopp 61	4,741
41	div3	Kidderminster	A	D	1-1	Burgess 68	3,853
42	div3	Northampton	H	L	2-3	Elliott 7; Dawson 69	18,017
43	div3	Swansea	A	W	3-2	Allsopp 10; Burgess 60,87	5,993
44	div3	Macclesfield	A	D	1-1	Joseph 6	3,801
45	div3	Southend	A	D	2-2	Lewis 42; Ashbee 67	5,389
46	div3	Huddersfield	H	D	0-0		23,495
47	div3	Yeovil	A	W	2-1	Green 11 pen; Ashbee 76	8,760
48	div3	Bristol Rovers	H	W	3-0	Price 58; Delaney 60; Elliott 73	22,562

TEAM OF THE SEASON

G	Paul Musselwhite	CG: 17 DR: 121
D	Justin Whittle	CG: 14 DR: 116
D	Andrew Dawson	CG: 31 DR: 107
D	Damien Delaney	CG: 45 DR: 95
D	Richard Hinds	CG: 30 DR: 86
M	Ian Ashbee	CG: 39 SD: 50
M	Stuart Green	CG: 37 SD: 49
M	Jason Price	CG: 26 SD: 47
M	Stuart Elliott	CG: 40 SD: 40
F	Daniel Allsopp	CG: 28 SR: 177
F	Ben Burgess	CG: 43 SR: 214

KEY PLAYER APPEARANCES

	PLAYER	POS	AGE	APP	MINS ON	GOALS	CARDS(Y/R)	
1	Damien Delaney	DEF	22	46	4095	2	1	0
2	Ben Burgess	ATT	22	44	3855	18	2	0
3	Ian Ashbee	MID	27	39	3510	2	11	1
4	Stuart Elliott	MID	25	42	3480	14	7	0
5	Stuart Green	MID	23	42	3366	6	4	0
6	Richard Hinds	DEF	23	39	2925	1	0	0
7	Andrew Dawson	DEF	25	33	2880	3	3	0
8	Marc Joseph	DEF	27	32	2880	1	3	0
9	Daniel Allsopp	ATT	25	36	2651	15	3	0
10	Jason Price	MID	27	33	2529	9	5	0
11	Boaz Myhill	GK	21	23	2070	0	0	0
12	Alton Thelwell	DEF	23	26	1913	1	2	0
13	Paul Musselwhite	GK	35	18	1576	0	0	0
14	Justin Whittle	DEF	33	18	1391	0	1	0
15	Junior Lewis	MID	30	13	1130	1	0	0
16	Ryan France	MID	23	28	947	2	1	0
17	Lee Marshall	DEF	25	11	820	0	3	0
18	Dean Keates	MID	26	14	761	0	1	0

KEY PLAYERS - GOALSCORERS

Daniel Allsopp

Goals in the League	15
Contribution to Attacking Power Average number of minutes between League team goals while on pitch	46
Player Strike Rate Average number of minutes between League goals scored by player	177
Club Strike Rate Average number of minutes between League goals scored by club	50

	PLAYER	LGE GOALS	POWER	STRIKE RATE
1	Daniel Allsopp	15	46	177 mins
2	Ben Burgess	18	50	214 mins
3	Stuart Elliott	14	54	249 mins
4	Jason Price	9	46	281 mins
5	Stuart Green	6	45	561 mins

KEY PLAYERS - MIDFIELDERS

Ian Ashbee

Goals in the League	2
Defensive Rating Average number of mins between League goals conceded while he was on the pitch	100
Contribution to Attacking Power Average number of minutes between League team goals while on pitch	50
Scoring Difference Defensive Rating minus Contribution to Attacking Power	50

	PLAYER	LGE GOALS	DEF RATE	POWER	SCORE DIFF
1	Ian Ashbee	2	100	50	50 mins
2	Stuart Green	6	94	45	49 mins
3	Jason Price	9	94	47	47 mins
4	Stuart Elliott	14	94	54	40 mins
5	Junior Lewis	1	94	66	28 mins

KEY PLAYERS - DEFENDERS

Justin Whittle

Goals Conceded when he was on pitch	12
Defensive Rating Ave number of mins between League goals conceded while on the pitch	116
Clean Sheets In games when he played at least 70 minutes	6
Club Defensive Rating Average number of mins between League goals conceded by the club this season.	94

	PLAYER	CON LGE	CLN SHEETS	DEF RATE
1	Justin Whittle	12	6	116 mins
2	Andrew Dawson	27	12	107 mins
3	Damien Delaney	43	16	95 mins
4	Richard Hinds	34	10	86 mins
5	Alton Thelwell	23	6	83 mins

KEY GOALKEEPER

Paul Musselwhite

Goals Conceded in the League	13
Defensive Rating Ave number of mins between League goals conceded while on the pitch.	121
Counting Games Games when he played at least 70 mins	18
Clean Sheets In games when he played at least 70 mins	8

TOP POINT EARNERS

	PLAYER	GAMES	AV PTS
1	Justin Whittle	14	2.29
2	Jason Price	26	2.23
3	Daniel Allsopp	28	2.21
4	Paul Musselwhite	17	2.12
5	Ian Ashbee	39	2.03
6	Andrew Dawson	31	2.00
7	Richard Hinds	30	1.97
8	Damien Delaney	45	1.96
9	Stuart Elliott	40	1.93
10	Stuart Green	37	1.92
	CLUB AVERAGE:		1.91

TORQUAY UNITED

Final Position: **3rd**

NICKNAME: THE GULLS

KEY: ☐ Won ☐ Drawn ☐ Lost

							Attendance
1	div3	Northampton	A	W	1-0	Fowler 62	5,675
2	ccR1	Crystal Palace	H	L	1-1	Graham 61 (*on penalties)	3,366
3	div3	Lincoln	H	W	1-0	Hockley 89	2,920
4	div3	Macclesfield	A	D	1-1	Wills 55	1,970
5	div3	Rochdale	H	L	1-3	Graham 75	3,003
6	div3	Scunthorpe	A	L	1-2	Gritton 15	3,080
7	div3	Leyton Orient	H	W	2-1	Graham 54,73	2,362
8	div3	Cambridge	A	D	1-1	Osei-Kuffour 36	3,723
9	div3	Bristol Rovers	H	W	2-1	Graham 31; Taylor 45	3,691
10	div3	Darlington	H	D	2-2	Woods 11; Graham 37	2,420
11	div3	Yeovil	A	W	2-0	Graham 15; Osei-Kuffour 67	7,718
12	div3	Oxford	A	L	0-1		5,479
13	div3	Bury	H	W	3-1	Graham 26; Osei-Kuffour 46; Russell 85	2,732
14	div3	Huddersfield	A	L	0-1		9,117
15	div3	Hull City	H	D	1-1	Graham 7	3,720
16	div3	Mansfield	H	W	1-0	Hockley 35	2,773
17	div3	Boston	A	L	0-4		2,431
18	div3	Doncaster	A	L	0-1		6,863
19	facr1	Burton	H	L	1-2	Benfield 55	2,790
20	div3	Cheltenham	H	W	3-1	Graham 51,68; Russell 86	2,653
21	div3	Kidderminster	A	W	2-1	Wills 7,58	2,725
22	div3	Southend	H	W	3-0	Bedeau 45; Hockley 52; Graham 54	2,631
23	div3	York	H	D	1-1	Parkin 57 og	2,564
24	div3	Carlisle	A	L	0-2		3,600
25	div3	Swansea	H	D	0-0		4,447
26	div3	Leyton Orient	A	D	0-0		4,288
27	div3	Rochdale	A	L	0-1		2,559
28	div3	Northampton	H	W	3-1	Osei-Kuffour 12; Canoville 40; Taylor 78	2,585
29	div3	Lincoln	A	W	3-1	Fowler 10; Hill 56; Osei-Kuffour 89	3,873
30	div3	Macclesfield	H	W	4-1	Hill 8; Graham 33; Taylor 41; Gritton 87	2,770
31	div3	Swansea	A	W	2-1	Graham 18; Osei-Kuffour 85	7,323
32	div3	Huddersfield	H	L	0-1		3,821
33	div3	Hull City	A	W	1-0	Gritton 45	15,222
34	div3	Scunthorpe	H	W	1-0	Hockley 13	2,561
35	div3	Boston	H	W	2-0	Graham 27; Woods 57 pen	3,000
36	div3	Carlisle	H	W	4-1	Hill 4,21; Graham 52; Woods 63 pen	3,366
37	div3	York	A	D	0-0		3,150
38	div3	Bristol Rovers	A	D	2-2	Osei-Kuffour 5,17	6,461
39	div3	Cambridge	H	W	3-0	Hockley 22; Graham 39,50	2,975
40	div3	Darlington	A	D	1-1	Graham 66	4,317
41	div3	Mansfield	A	L	1-2	Gritton 17	4,552
42	div3	Yeovil	H	D	2-2	Taylor 44; Woods 59	6,156
43	div3	Bury	A	L	1-2	Graham 30	2,770
44	div3	Oxford	H	W	3-0	Wanless 33 og; Hazell 63; Graham 75	5,114
45	div3	Doncaster	H	W	1-0	Hill 38	5,808
46	div3	Cheltenham	A	W	3-1	Osei-Kuffour 18,78; Woods 65	4,900
47	div3	Kidderminster	H	D	1-1	Graham 42	5,515
48	div3	Southend	A	W	2-1	Woods 3; Graham 11	8,894

TEAM OF THE SEASON

G — Arjan Van Heusden, CG: 24 DR: 105

D — Lee Canoville, CG: 27 DR: 103

D — Brian McGlinchey, CG: 34 DR: 97

D — Craig Taylor, CG: 43 DR: 94

D — *Reuben Hazell, CG: 12 DR: 119

M — Alex Russell, CG: 41 SD: 36

M — Matt Hockley, CG: 42 SD: 34

M — Kevin Hill, CG: 39 SD: 33

M — Jason Fowler, CG: 14 SD: 30

F — David Graham, CG: 42 SR: 173

F — Jo Osei-Kuffour, CG: 24 SR: 288

KEY PLAYER APPEARANCES

	PLAYER	POS	AGE	APP	MINS ON	GOALS	CARDS(Y/R)	
1	Stephen Woods	DEF	27	46	4140	6	5	0
2	Matt Hockley	MID	22	45	3926	5	8	1
3	Craig Taylor	DEF	30	43	3868	4	7	0
4	David Graham	ATT	25	45	3803	22	9	0
5	Kevin Hill	MID	28	45	3737	5	8	0
6	Alex Russell	MID	31	43	3721	2	6	0
7	Brian McGlinchey	DEF	26	34	3000	0	6	0
8	Jo Osei-Kuffour	ATT	22	41	2882	10	0	0
9	Lee Canoville	DEF	23	33	2579	1	5	0
10	Arjan Van Heusden	GK	31	25	2204	0	1	0
11	Jason Fowler	MID	29	31	1989	2	4	0
12	Kevin Dearden	GK	34	22	1936	0	2	0
13	Martin Gritton	ATT	26	31	1667	4	5	0
14	Anthony Bedeau	ATT	25	24	1204	1	3	1
15	Reuben Hazell	DEF	25	19	1188	1	2	0
16	Mike Williamson	DEF	20	11	833	0	2	0
17	Kevin Wills	ATT	23	23	829	3	2	0
18	Liam Rosenior	ATT	19	10	704	0	0	0

KEY PLAYERS - GOALSCORERS

David Graham

Goals in the League	22	Player Strike Rate Average number of minutes between League goals scored by player	173
Contribution to Attacking Power Average number of minutes between League team goals while on pitch	61	Club Strike Rate Average number of minutes between League goals scored by club	61

	PLAYER	LGE GOALS	POWER	STRIKE RATE
1	David Graham	22	61	173 mins
2	Jo Osei-Kuffour	10	58	288 mins
3	Martin Gritton	4	64	417 mins
4	Stephen Woods	6	60	690 mins
5	Kevin Hill	5	60	747 mins

KEY PLAYERS - MIDFIELDERS

Alex Russell

Goals in the League	2	Contribution to Attacking Power Average number of minutes between League team goals while on pitch	59
Defensive Rating Average number of mins between League goals conceded while he was on the pitch	95	Scoring Difference Defensive Rating minus Contribution to Attacking Power	36

	PLAYER	LGE GOALS	DEF RATE	POWER	SCORE DIFF
1	Alex Russell	2	95	59	36 mins
2	Matt Hockley	5	93	59	34 mins
3	Kevin Hill	5	93	60	33 mins
4	Jason Fowler	2	99	69	30 mins

KEY PLAYERS - DEFENDERS

Reuben Hazell

Goals Conceded when he was on pitch	10	Clean Sheets In games when he played at least 70 minutes	5
Defensive Rating Ave number of mins between League goals conceded while on the pitch	119	Club Defensive Rating Average number of mins between League goals conceded by the club this season.	94

	PLAYER	CON LGE	CLN SHEETS	DEF RATE
1	Reuben Hazell	10	5	119 mins
2	Lee Canoville	25	9	103 mins
3	Brian McGlinchey	31	10	97 mins
4	Craig Taylor	41	13	94 mins

KEY GOALKEEPER

Arjan Van Heusden

Goals Conceded in the League	21
Defensive Rating Ave number of mins between League goals conceded while on the pitch.	105
Counting Games Games when he played at least 70 mins	25
Clean Sheets In games when he played at least 70 mins	8

TOP POINT EARNERS

	PLAYER	GAMES	AV PTS
1	Reuben Hazell	12	**2.33**
2	Kevin Hill	39	**1.92**
3	Brian McGlinchey	34	**1.91**
4	Lee Canoville	27	**1.89**
5	Matt Hockley	42	**1.88**
6	Jo Osei-Kuffour	24	**1.88**
7	Jason Fowler	14	**1.86**
8	Alex Russell	41	**1.83**
9	Craig Taylor	43	**1.79**
10	Arjan Van Heusden	24	**1.79**
	CLUB AVERAGE:		**1.76**

HUDDERSFIELD TOWN

Promoted via play-offs Final Position: **4th**

NICKNAME: THE TERRIERS

KEY: Won / Drawn / Lost

No	Comp	Opponent	H/A	Res	Score	Scorers	Attendance
1	div3	**Cambridge**	H	D	2-2	Stead 30,59	10,319
2	ccR1	**Derby**	H	W	2-1	Stead 59; Thorrington 70	6,672
3	div3	**Boston**	A	D	2-2	Stead 55; Hughes 60	3,452
4	div3	**York**	H	L	0-1		9,850
5	div3	**Doncaster**	A	D	1-1	Booth 7	7,367
6	div3	**Bristol Rovers**	H	W	2-1	Edwards 32; Stead 78	8,486
7	div3	**Bury**	A	L	1-2	Scott 72	4,591
8	div3	**Northampton**	H	W	3-0	Stead 17,35; Carss 33 pen	8,285
9	div3	**Rochdale**	A	D	1-1	Worthington 22	4,626
10	div3	**Swansea**	A	L	0-2		8,048
11	ccR2	**Sunderland**	A	W	4-2	Carss 2; Stead 20; Holdsworth 54; Booth 87	13,516
12	div3	**Leyton Orient**	H	W	3-0	Yates 31; Scott 62; Booth 83	8,942
13	div3	**Kidderminster**	H	W	1-0	Stead 12	8,275
14	div3	**Southend**	A	W	2-1	Booth 45; Schofield 89	4,205
15	div3	**Torquay**	H	W	1-0	Carss 80	9,117
16	div3	**Lincoln**	A	L	1-3	Booth 6	5,718
17	div3	**Yeovil**	A	L	1-2	Stead 42	5,274
18	div3	**Carlisle**	H	W	2-1	Booth 38; Stead 45	9,059
19	ccR3	**Reading**	A	L	0-1		11,892
20	div3	**Scunthorpe**	A	L	2-6	Booth 46,72	4,715
21	facr1	**Accrington**	A	L	0-1		3,129
22	div3	**Hull City**	H	W	3-1	Stead 33; Booth 41; Schofield 80	13,893
23	div3	**Mansfield**	A	D	3-3	Schofield 15; Stead 32,64	5,828
24	div3	**Cheltenham**	H	D	0-0		8,442
25	div3	**Macclesfield**	A	L	0-4		3,059
26	div3	**Oxford**	H	D	1-1	Stead 38	9,368
27	div3	**Darlington**	A	W	1-0	Booth 28	6,205
28	div3	**Bury**	H	W	1-0	Swailes 32 og	10,217
29	div3	**Doncaster**	H	W	3-1	Stead 42,69; Worthington 82	13,044
30	div3	**Cambridge**	A	W	2-1	Stead 44 pen; Worthington 85	3,667
31	div3	**Boston**	H	W	2-0	Sodje 71; Lloyd 76	9,603
32	div3	**York**	A	W	2-0	Schofield 88; Mirfin 89	6,969
33	div3	**Darlington**	H	L	0-2		11,014
34	div3	**Torquay**	A	W	1-0	Clarke 71	3,821
35	div3	**Bristol Rovers**	A	D	1-1	Abbott 86	6,262
36	div3	**Lincoln**	H	W	2-1	Sodje 48; Abbott 67	11,553
37	div3	**Yeovil**	H	W	3-1	Abbott 40; Schofield 46,60	9,395
38	div3	**Oxford**	A	W	1-0	Sodje 41	7,278
39	div3	**Carlisle**	A	L	0-1		4,782
40	div3	**Macclesfield**	H	W	4-0	Booth 21; Abbott 47; Sodje 69; McAliskey 90	9,729
41	div3	**Rochdale**	H	D	1-1	Lloyd 49	10,884
42	div3	**Swansea**	H	W	3-0	Schofield 51,85; Lloyd 89	11,250
43	div3	**Leyton Orient**	A	D	1-1	Booth 9	4,137
44	div3	**Southend**	H	W	1-0	Abbott 30	10,680
45	div3	**Kidderminster**	A	L	1-2	Sall 84 og	4,051
46	div3	**Scunthorpe**	H	W	3-2	Mirfin 5; McAliskey 87,90	12,108
47	div3	**Northampton**	A	W	1-0	Booth 53	6,873
48	div3	**Hull City**	A	D	0-0		23,495
49	div3	**Mansfield**	H	L	1-3	McAliskey 14	18,633
50	div3	**Cheltenham**	A	D	1-1	Booth 16	5,814
51	d3po1	**Lincoln**	A	W	2-1	Onuora 5; Mirfin 72	9,202
52	d3po2	**Lincoln**	H	D	2-2	Schofield 60 pen; Edwards 83	19,467
53	d3pof	**Mansfield**	H	W	4-1*	(*on penalties)	37,298

TEAM OF THE SEASON

D Anthony Lloyd — **CG:** 29 **DR:** 102
D David Mirfin — **CG:** 15 **DR:** 99
D Steve Yates — **CG:** 30 **DR:** 94
D Efetobore Sodje — **CG:** 36 **DR:** 86

M John Worthington — **CG:** 37 **SD:** 36
M Andy Holdsworth — **CG:** 30 **SD:** 31
M Danny Schofield — **CG:** 36 **SD:** 20
M Lee Fowler — **CG:** 23 **SD:** 12

F John Stead — **CG:** 25 **SR:** 144
F Andy Booth — **CG:** 34 **SR:** 243

G Paul Rachubka — **CG:** 13 **DR:** 106

KEY PLAYER APPEARANCES

	PLAYER	POS	AGE	APP	MINS ON	GOALS	CARDS(Y)	CARDS(R)
1	Efetobore Sodje	DEF	31	39	3336	4	10	2
2	John Worthington	MID	21	39	3325	3	8	0
3	Danny Schofield	MID	24	40	3278	8	4	2
4	Andy Booth	ATT	30	37	3155	13	3	1
5	Anthony Carss	MID	28	36	3119	2	7	1
6	Steve Yates	DEF	34	35	2915	1	6	1
7	Andy Holdsworth	MID	20	36	2816	0	6	0
8	Anthony Lloyd	DEF	20	31	2659	3	1	0
9	John Stead	ATT	21	26	2310	16	6	0
10	Lee Fowler	MID	21	29	2280	0	10	2
11	Nathan Clarke	DEF	20	26	2200	1	3	0
12	Ian Gray	GK	29	17	1530	0	0	0
13	David Mirfin	DEF	19	21	1481	2	2	0
14	Paul Scott	DEF	24	19	1396	2	6	1
15	Phil Senior	GK	21	15	1350	0	0	0
16	Nathaniel Brown	DEF	23	21	1301	0	2	0
17	Paul Rachubka	GK	23	13	1170	0	0	0
18	Pawel Abbott	ATT	22	13	1045	5	2	1

KEY PLAYERS - GOALSCORERS

John Stead

Goals in the League	16
Contribution to Attacking Power Average number of minutes between League team goals while on pitch	59
Player Strike Rate Average number of minutes between League goals scored by player	144
Club Strike Rate Average number of minutes between League goals scored by club	61

	PLAYER	LGE GOALS	POWER	STRIKE RATE
1	John Stead	16	59	144 mins
2	Andy Booth	13	67	243 mins
3	Danny Schofield	8	57	410 mins
4	Paul Scott	2	58	698 mins

KEY PLAYERS - MIDFIELDERS

John Worthington

Goals in the League	3
Defensive Rating Average number of mins between League goals conceded while he was on the pitch	95
Contribution to Attacking Power Average number of minutes between League team goals while on pitch	59
Scoring Difference Defensive Rating minus Contribution to Attacking Power	36

	PLAYER	LGE GOALS	DEF RATE	POWER	SCORE DIFF
1	John Worthington	3	95	59	36 mins
2	Andy Holdsworth	0	88	57	31 mins
3	Danny Schofield	8	78	58	20 mins
4	Lee Fowler	0	81	69	12 mins

KEY PLAYERS - DEFENDERS

Anthony Lloyd

Goals Conceded when he was on pitch	26
Defensive Rating Ave number of mins between League goals conceded while on the pitch	102
Clean Sheets In games when he played at least 70 minutes	13
Club Defensive Rating Average number of mins between League goals conceded by the club this season.	80

	PLAYER	CON LGE	CLN SHEETS	DEF RATE
1	Anthony Lloyd	26	13	102 mins
2	David Mirfin	15	7	99 mins
3	Steve Yates	31	13	94 mins
4	Efetobore Sodje	39	13	86 mins

KEY GOALKEEPER

Paul Rachubka

Goals Conceded in the League	11
Defensive Rating Ave number of mins between League goals conceded while on the pitch.	106
Counting Games Games when he played at least 70 mins	13
Clean Sheets In games when he played at least 70 mins	6

TOP POINT EARNERS

	PLAYER	GAMES	AV PTS
1	Phil Senior	15	2.27
2	Steve Yates	30	2.03
3	Nathaniel Brown	12	2.00
4	John Worthington	37	1.97
5	Andy Holdsworth	30	1.97
6	Anthony Lloyd	29	1.93
7	Nathan Clarke	24	1.92
8	Danny Schofield	36	1.89
9	Lee Fowler	23	1.87
10	David Mirfin	15	1.87
	CLUB AVERAGE:		1.76

MANSFIELD TOWN

Final Position: **5th**

NICKNAME: THE STAGS

KEY: ☐ Won ☐ Drawn ☐ Lost

							Attendance
1	div3	Kidderminster	A	L	1-2	Corden 65	3,180
2	ccR1	Sunderland	H	L	1-2	Kyle 90 og	5,665
3	div3	Leyton Orient	H	D	1-1	Dimech 13	3,920
4	div3	Southend	A	W	3-0	Christie 42,51,90	3,837
5	div3	Scunthorpe	H	W	5-0	Day 9; Junior Mendes 18; Lawrence 65,90; Christie 72	5,142
6	div3	Swansea	A	L	1-4	Vaughan 44	6,991
7	div3	Macclesfield	H	W	3-2	Artell 7; Junior Mendes 52; Lawrence 69 pen	4,209
8	div3	Oxford	A	D	1-1	MacKenzie 79	5,625
9	div3	Bury	H	W	5-3	Junior Mendes 30; Corden 36,44; Lawrence 63,88	4,145
10	div3	Yeovil	H	L	0-1		5,270
11	div3	Cambridge	A	W	2-1	Disley 34; Lawrence 74 pen	4,068
12	div3	Bristol Rovers	A	W	3-1	Mendes 10; Disley 13,41	8,451
13	div3	Darlington	H	W	3-1	Vaughan 13; Christie 59; Corden 65	4,621
14	div3	York	H	W	2-0	Artell 31; Beardsley 76	4,914
15	div3	Doncaster	A	L	2-4	Lawrence 21; Corden 81	8,500
16	div3	Torquay	A	L	0-1		2,773
17	div3	Cheltenham	H	W	4-0	Lawrence 8 pen,86 pen; Larkin 45,53	4,095
18	div3	Boston	H	W	2-1	Junior Mendes 33,51	5,161
19	facr1	Bishops S	H	W	6-0	MacKenzie 12,43,51; Junior Mendes 15; Larkin 42; Curtis 78	4,679
20	div3	Carlisle	A	W	2-0	Corden 54; Junior Mendes 63	4,145
21	div3	Huddersfield	H	D	3-3	Day 45; Artell 62; Disley 90	5,828
22	div3	Northampton	A	W	3-0	Christie 5; Lawrence 66 pen; Disley 80	5,019
23	facr2	Wycombe	A	D	1-1	Christie 61	3,212
24	div3	Lincoln	H	L	1-2	Lawrence 34 pen	5,797
25	facr2r	Wycombe	H	W	3-2	Lawrence 14,72 pen,90 pen	5,512
26	div3	Hull City	A	W	1-0	MacKenzie 84	15,005
27	div3	Rochdale	H	W	1-0	Larkin 56	6,963
28	div3	Macclesfield	A	D	1-1	Christie 71	3,578
29	facr3	Burnley	H	L	0-2		8,290
30	div3	Kidderminster	H	W	1-0	Day 26	4,574
31	div3	Leyton Orient	A	L	1-3	Buxton 33	4,072
32	div3	Southend	H	W	1-0	Corden 15 pen	4,292
33	div3	Scunthorpe	A	D	0-0		3,113
34	div3	Rochdale	A	L	0-3		3,157
35	div3	York	A	W	2-1	Lawrence 29; Pacquette 53	4,068
36	div3	Doncaster	H	L	1-2	Lawrence 15 pen	7,724
37	div3	Cheltenham	A	L	2-4	Christie 64; Corden 83	3,818
38	div3	Hull City	H	W	1-0	D'Jaffo 69	6,859
39	div3	Lincoln	A	L	1-4	Lawrence 37 pen	6,034
40	div3	Bury	A	L	0-3		2,199
41	div3	Swansea	H	D	1-1	Lawrence 51 pen	4,058
42	div3	Yeovil	A	D	1-1	Day 79	6,002
43	div3	Torquay	H	W	2-1	Larkin 5; Mendes 10	4,552
44	div3	Cambridge	H	D	1-1	Mendes 61	4,342
45	div3	Oxford	H	W	3-1	Junior Mendes 16; Larkin 19; Day 37	5,132
46	div3	Darlington	A	L	0-1		4,946
47	div3	Bristol Rovers	H	D	0-0		4,735
48	div3	Boston	A	W	2-1	Larkin 50; Lawrence 59	3,826
49	div3	Carlisle	H	L	2-3	Lawrence 29 pen,45	5,361
50	div3	Huddersfield	A	W	3-1	Day 20; Mendes 38; Lawrence 76	18,633
51	div3	Northampton	H	L	1-2	Larkin 54	8,065
52	d3po1	Northampton	A	W	2-0	Day 40; Mendes 67	6,960
53	d3po2	Northampton	H	W	5-4*	Curtis 68 (*on penalties)	9,243
54	d3pof	Huddersfield	A	L	1-4*	(*on penalties)	37,298

TEAM OF THE SEASON

G — Kevin Pilkington CG: 46 DR: 67

D — Alex Baptiste CG: 13 DR: 81

D — Luke Dimech CG: 17 DR: 72

D — Rhys Day CG: 39 DR: 69

D — Tony Vaughan CG: 29 DR: 67

M — Neil MacKenzie CG: 19 SD: 40

M — Liam Lawrence CG: 39 SD: 16

M — Tom Curtis CG: 34 SD: 14

M — Wayne Corden CG: 32 SD: 11

F — Iyseden Christie CG: 19 SR: 245

F — Junior Mendes CG: 31 SR: 447

KEY PLAYER APPEARANCES

	PLAYER	POS	AGE	APP	MINS ON	GOALS	CARDS(Y/R)	
1	Kevin Pilkington	GK	30	46	4140	0	2	0
2	Liam Lawrence	MID	22	41	3615	19	6	0
3	Rhys Day	DEF	21	41	3579	6	1	1
4	Wayne Corden	MID	28	44	3229	8	3	0
5	Tom Curtis	MID	31	38	3149	0	7	0
6	Junior Mendes	ATT	27	39	3127	7	2	0
7	Bobby Hassell	DEF	24	34	2986	0	6	0
8	Lee Williamson	MID	22	35	2771	0	8	1
9	Tony Vaughan	DEF	28	31	2689	2	7	0
10	David Artell	DEF	23	26	2191	3	6	0
11	Neil MacKenzie	MID	28	32	2089	2	0	0
12	Iyseden Christie	ATT	27	27	1958	8	6	2
13	Colin Larkin	MID	22	37	1945	7	1	0
14	Luke Dimech	DEF	27	20	1586	1	3	0
15	Craig Disley	MID	22	34	1578	5	3	0
16	Alex Baptiste	DEF	18	17	1299	0	0	0
17	Jamie Clarke	MID	21	12	983	0	1	0
18	Jake Buxton	DEF	19	9	750	1	0	0

KEY PLAYERS - GOALSCORERS

Liam Lawrence

Goals in the League	19	**Player Strike Rate** Average number of minutes between League goals scored by player	190
Contribution to Attacking Power Average number of minutes between League team goals while on pitch	50	**Club Strike Rate** Average number of minutes between League goals scored by club	54

	PLAYER	LGE GOALS	POWER	STRIKE RATE
1	Liam Lawrence	19	50	190 mins
2	Iyseden Christie	8	55	245 mins
3	Colin Larkin	7	55	278 mins
4	Wayne Corden	8	53	404 mins

KEY PLAYERS - MIDFIELDERS

Neil MacKenzie

Goals in the League	2	**Contribution to Attacking Power** Average number of minutes between League team goals while on pitch	44
Defensive Rating Average number of mins between League goals conceded while he was on the pitch	84	**Scoring Difference** Defensive Rating minus Contribution to Attacking Power	40

	PLAYER	LGE GOALS	DEF RATE	POWER	SCORE DIFF
1	Neil MacKenzie	2	84	44	40 mins
2	Liam Lawrence	19	67	51	16 mins
3	Tom Curtis	0	72	58	14 mins
4	Wayne Corden	8	65	54	11 mins
5	Colin Larkin	7	65	56	9 mins

KEY PLAYERS - DEFENDERS

Alex Baptiste

Goals Conceded when he was on pitch	16	**Clean Sheets** In games when he played at least 70 minutes	2
Defensive Rating Ave number of mins between League goals conceded while on the pitch	81	**Club Defensive Rating** Average number of mins between League goals conceded by the club this season.	67

	PLAYER	CON LGE	CLN SHEETS	DEF RATE
1	Alex Baptiste	16	2	81 mins
2	Luke Dimech	22	7	72 mins
3	Rhys Day	52	12	69 mins
4	Tony Vaughan	40	9	67 mins

KEY GOALKEEPER

Kevin Pilkington

Goals Conceded in the League	62
Defensive Rating Ave number of mins between League goals conceded while on the pitch.	67
Counting Games Games when he played at least 70 mins	46
Clean Sheets In games when he played at least 70 mins	13

TOP POINT EARNERS

	PLAYER	GAMES	AV PTS
1	Colin Larkin	14	**2.07**
2	Neil MacKenzie	19	**1.95**
3	Tony Vaughan	29	**1.83**
4	Bobby Hassell	32	**1.75**
5	Junior Mendes	31	**1.74**
6	Rhys Day	39	**1.74**
7	Wayne Corden	32	**1.72**
8	Liam Lawrence	39	**1.67**
9	Kevin Pilkington	46	**1.63**
10	Alex Baptiste	13	**1.62**
	CLUB AVERAGE:		**1.63**

NORTHAMPTON TOWN

Final Position: **6th**

NICKNAME: THE COBBLERS KEY: ☐Won ☐Drawn ☐Lost

		Opponent			Score	Scorers	Attendance
1	div3	**Torquay**	H	L	0-1		5,675
2	ccR1	**Norwich**	H	W	1-0	Lowe 8	5,476
3	div3	**York**	A	L	0-1		3,870
4	div3	**Darlington**	H	W	1-0	Smith 43	5,020
5	div3	**Yeovil**	A	W	2-0	Reid 5; Low 41	6,105
6	div3	**Doncaster**	H	W	1-0	Dudfield 76	4,933
7	div3	**Cheltenham**	A	L	3-4	Dudfield 24,32; Smith 73 pen	5,002
8	div3	**Huddersfield**	A	L	0-3		8,285
9	div3	**Carlisle**	H	W	2-0	Smith, M 58 pen; Trollope 77	4,156
10	div3	**Macclesfield**	H	D	0-0		4,332
11	ccR2	**Portsmouth**	A	L	2-5	Hargreaves 77 pen; Dudfield 90	11,130
12	div3	**Oxford**	A	L	0-3		6,518
13	div3	**Lincoln**	A	D	0-0		3,928
14	div3	**Hull City**	H	L	1-5	Trollope 78	6,011
15	div3	**Rochdale**	A	D	1-1	Smith, M 52	2,710
16	div3	**Scunthorpe**	H	D	1-1	Smith, M 9	4,827
17	div3	**Kidderminster**	H	L	0-1		4,089
18	div3	**Leyton Orient**	A	D	1-1	Low 59	4,130
19	div3	**Southend**	A	W	1-0	Trollope 60	5,085
20	facr1	**Plymouth**	H	W	3-2	Walker 37; Hargreaves 60; Asamoah 83	4,385
21	div3	**Swansea**	H	W	2-1	Walker 44; Smith, M 58	4,010
22	div3	**Bury**	A	L	0-1		2,683
23	div3	**Mansfield**	H	L	0-3		5,019
24	facr2	**Weston SM**	H	W	4-1	Smith, M 36 pen; Low 64; Richards 77,90	3,948
25	div3	**Boston**	A	D	1-1	Lincoln 33	2,756
26	div3	**Cambridge**	H	L	1-2	Asamoah 72	4,910
27	div3	**Bristol Rovers**	A	W	2-1	Asamoah 75; Walker 86	7,695
28	div3	**Cheltenham**	H	W	1-0	Walker 10	5,118
29	facr3	**Rotherham**	H	D	1-1	Smith, M 63	5,741
30	div3	**Torquay**	A	L	1-3	Sampson 55	2,585
31	facr3r	**Rotherham**	A	W	2-1	Walker 36; Smith, M 54	9,405
32	div3	**York**	H	W	2-1	Walker 20; Parkin 45 og	5,003
33	facr4	**Man Utd**	H	L	0-3		7,356
34	div3	**Doncaster**	A	L	0-1		6,017
35	div3	**Yeovil**	H	W	2-0	Hargreaves 58; Smith, M 70	4,363
36	div3	**Bristol Rovers**	H	W	2-0	Vieira 31; Smith, M 77	5,068
37	div3	**Rochdale**	H	W	3-1	Hargreaves 68; Reid 80; Vieira 86	4,540
38	div3	**Darlington**	A	W	2-1	Smith, M 75 pen; Richards 76	4,764
39	div3	**Scunthorpe**	A	L	0-1		3,566
40	div3	**Leyton Orient**	H	W	1-0	Low 73	5,784
41	div3	**Kidderminster**	A	L	1-2	Hargreaves 56	2,699
42	div3	**Cambridge**	A	W	1-0	Willmott 90	4,298
43	div3	**Boston**	H	W	2-0	Morison 72; Sampson 86	6,243
44	div3	**Carlisle**	A	D	1-1	Trollope 83	6,269
45	div3	**Macclesfield**	A	W	4-0	Richards 18,23,26,39	2,634
46	div3	**Oxford**	H	W	2-1	Richards 63; Trollope 73	6,799
47	div3	**Hull City**	A	W	3-2	Richards 2; Sabin 20,31	18,017
48	div3	**Lincoln**	H	D	1-1	Trollope 44	7,160
49	div3	**Southend**	H	D	2-2	Smith, M 24 pen; Taylor, J 83	5,919
50	div3	**Huddersfield**	H	L	0-1		6,873
51	div3	**Swansea**	A	W	2-0	Sabin 34,43	4,985
52	div3	**Bury**	H	W	3-2	Smith, M 41; Richards 60; Asamoah 74	6,179
53	div3	**Mansfield**	A	W	2-1	Sabin 19; Ullathorne 70	8,065
54	d3po1	**Mansfield**	H	L	0-2		6,960
55	d3po2	**Mansfield**	A	L	4-5*	Richards 36; Hargreaves 42; Smith, M 46 (*on penalties)	9,243

TEAM OF THE SEASON

G Lee Harper CG: 39 DR: 83

D Des Lyttle CG: 23 DR: 97

D Christopher Willmott CG: 31 DR: 88

D Luke Chambers CG: 19 DR: 79

D Ian Sampson CG: 33 DR: 79

M Paul Trollope CG: 40 SD: 17

M Chris Hargreaves CG: 40 SD: 7

M Joshua Low CG: 24 SD: -4

M *Robert Ullathorne CG: 12 SD: 45

F Marc Richards CG: 18 SR: 292

F Martin Smith CG: 40 SR: 337

KEY PLAYER APPEARANCES

	PLAYER	POS	AGE	APP	MINS ON	GOALS	CARDS(Y/R)	
1	Paul Trollope	MID	32	43	3722	6	5	0
2	Martin Smith	ATT	29	44	3706	11	1	0
3	Chris Hargreaves	MID	32	42	3666	3	6	0
4	Lee Harper	GK	32	39	3490	0	0	1
5	Ian Sampson	DEF	35	37	3083	2	6	0
6	Christopher Willmott	DEF	26	36	2978	1	6	1
7	Paul Reid	DEF	22	33	2946	2	3	1
8	Joshua Low	MID	25	31	2338	3	4	0
9	Marc Richards	ATT	21	41	2336	8	5	0
10	Des Lyttle	DEF	32	27	2123	0	3	0
11	Luke Chambers	DEF	18	24	1818	0	2	0
12	Chris Carruthers	MID	20	24	1708	0	0	0
13	Robert Ullathorne	MID	32	13	1101	1	3	0
14	Lawrie Dudfield	ATT	24	19	1095	3	0	0
15	Derek Asamoah	ATT	23	31	938	3	1	0
16	Richard Walker	ATT	26	12	914	4	0	0
17	Chris Doig	DEF	23	9	790	0	1	0
18	Eric Sabin	ATT	29	11	671	5	2	1

KEY PLAYERS - GOALSCORERS

Marc Richards

Goals in the League	8
Contribution to Attacking Power Average number of minutes between League team goals while on pitch	68
Player Strike Rate Average number of minutes between League goals scored by player	292
Club Strike Rate Average number of minutes between League goals scored by club	71

	PLAYER	LGE GOALS	POWER	STRIKE RATE
1	Marc Richards	8	68	292 mins
2	Martin Smith	11	63	337 mins
3	Paul Trollope	6	71	620 mins
4	Joshua Low	3	73	779 mis

KEY PLAYERS - MIDFIELDERS

Robert Ullathorne

Goals in the League	1
Defensive Rating Average number of mins between League goals conceded while he was on the pitch	100
Contribution to Attacking Power Average number of minutes between League team goals while on pitch	55
Scoring Difference Defensive Rating minus Contribution to Attacking Power	45

	PLAYER	LGE GOALS	DEF RATE	POWER	SCORE DIFF
1	Robert Ullathorne	1	100	55	45 mins
2	Paul Trollope	6	89	72	17 mins
3	Chris Hargreaves	3	76	69	7 mins
4	Joshua Low	3	69	73	-4 mins
5	Chris Carruthers	0	71	81	-10 mins

KEY PLAYERS - DEFENDERS

Des Lyttle

Goals Conceded when he was on pitch	22
Defensive Rating Ave number of mins between League goals conceded while on the pitch	97
Clean Sheets In games when he played at least 70 minutes	6
Club Defensive Rating Average number of mins between League goals conceded by the club this season.	81

	PLAYER	CON LGE	CLN SHEETS	DEF RATE
1	Des Lyttle	22	6	97 mins
2	Christopher Willmott	34	9	88 mins
3	Ian Sampson	39	9	79 mins
4	Luke Chambers	23	9	79 mins
5	Paul Reid	38	11	78 mins

KEY GOALKEEPER

Lee Harper

Goals Conceded in the League	42
Defensive Rating Ave number of mins between League goals conceded while on the pitch.	83
Counting Games Games when he played at least 70 mins	39
Clean Sheets In games when he played at least 70 mins	12

TOP POINT EARNERS

	PLAYER	GAMES	AV PTS
1	Robert Ullathorne	12	**2.00**
2	Marc Richards	18	**1.94**
3	Ian Sampson	33	**1.82**
4	Des Lyttle	23	**1.78**
5	Paul Trollope	40	**1.73**
6	Martin Smith	40	**1.73**
7	Lee Harper	39	**1.69**
8	Chris Hargreaves	40	**1.68**
9	Christopher Willmott	31	**1.65**
10	Chris Carruthers	17	**1.65**
	CLUB AVERAGE:		**1.63**

LINCOLN CITY

Final Position: **7th**

NICKNAME: THE RED IMPS

KEY: ☐ Won ☐ Drawn ☐ Lost

							Attendance
1	div3	**Oxford**	H	L	0-1		4,543
2	ccR1	**Stockport**	H	L	0-1		2,296
3	div3	**Torquay**	A	L	0-1		2,920
4	div3	**Doncaster**	H	D	0-0		5,051
5	div3	**Bury**	A	L	1-2	Fletcher 25	2,576
6	div3	**York**	H	W	3-0	Fletcher 21; Butcher 72; Mayo 88 pen	3,892
7	div3	**Cambridge**	A	D	0-0		4,458
8	div3	**Leyton Orient**	H	D	0-0		3,940
9	div3	**Southend**	A	W	2-0	Richardson 10; Butcher 78	2,874
10	div3	**Kidderminster**	A	W	2-1	Richardson 32; Butcher 44	2,462
11	div3	**Rochdale**	H	D	1-1	Richardson 44	4,141
12	div3	**Northampton**	H	D	0-0		3,928
13	div3	**Swansea**	A	D	2-2	Butcher 11; Mayo 15 pen	7,914
14	div3	**Scunthorpe**	A	W	3-1	Futcher 5; Fletcher 31; Green 57	5,045
15	div3	**Huddersfield**	H	W	3-1	Fletcher 61; Richardson 65; Yeo 90	5,718
16	div3	**Macclesfield**	H	W	3-2	Gain 24; Butcher 56; Green 90	3,441
17	div3	**Hull City**	A	L	0-3		17,453
18	div3	**Carlisle**	H	W	2-0	Yeo 45; Fletcher 50	4,044
19	facr1	**Brighton**	H	W	3-1	Mayo 13 pen; Bloomer 37; Yeo 60	4,425
20	div3	**Darlington**	A	D	0-0		4,601
21	div3	**Bristol Rovers**	H	W	3-1	Yeo 11; Futcher 56; Fletcher 87	3,882
22	div3	**Yeovil**	A	L	1-3	Yeo 50	4,867
23	facr2	**Southend**	A	L	0-3		4,258
24	div3	**Mansfield**	A	W	2-1	Butcher 3; Gain 50	5,797
25	div3	**Boston**	A	W	1-0	Mayo 61 pen	5,708
26	div3	**Cambridge**	H	D	2-2	Fletcher 9,42	5,074
27	div3	**Bury**	H	W	2-1	Fletcher 4; Green 28	3,870
28	div3	**Oxford**	A	D	0-0		6,679
29	div3	**Cheltenham**	H	D	0-0		3,464
30	div3	**Torquay**	H	L	1-3	Mayo 39	3,873
31	div3	**Doncaster**	A	W	2-0	Ryan 12 og; Fletcher 58	8,774
32	div3	**Boston**	H	D	1-1	Richardson 40	7,114
33	div3	**Scunthorpe**	H	D	1-1	Gain 35	5,324
34	div3	**York**	A	W	4-1	Mayo 44 pen; Green 58; Gain 61; Yeo 76	3,396
35	div3	**Huddersfield**	A	L	1-2	Richardson 19	11,553
36	div3	**Hull City**	H	W	2-0	Gain 78; Mayo 85	7,069
37	div3	**Cheltenham**	A	L	2-3	Richardson 3,45 pen	3,783
38	div3	**Mansfield**	H	W	4-1	Fletcher 55,69; Green 71; Yeo 89	6,034
39	div3	**Southend**	H	D	2-2	Green 51; Yeo 90	3,943
40	div3	**Leyton Orient**	A	W	2-0	Fletcher 3,49	3,637
41	div3	**Kidderminster**	H	D	1-1	Richardson 89	4,797
42	div3	**Macclesfield**	A	D	0-0		2,016
43	div3	**Rochdale**	A	W	3-0	Fletcher 58,67; Yeo 66	4,224
44	div3	**Swansea**	H	W	2-1	Gain 57; Yeo 82	5,455
45	div3	**Northampton**	A	D	1-1	Yeo 84	7,160
46	div3	**Carlisle**	A	W	2-0	Gain 48; Bailey 90	7,875
47	div3	**Darlington**	H	D	1-1	Green 54	6,187
48	div3	**Bristol Rovers**	A	L	1-3	Futcher 24	8,562
49	div3	**Yeovil**	H	L	2-3	Wilford 82; Yeo 87	8,154
50	d3po1	**Huddersfield**	H	L	1-2	Fletcher 51	9,202
51	d3po2	**Huddersfield**	A	D	2-2	Butcher 38; Bailey 39	19,467

TEAM OF THE SEASON

G — Alan Marriott, CG: 46 DR: 88

D — Paul Mayo, CG: 31 DR: 98
D — Ben Futcher, CG: 42 DR: 95
D — Paul Morgan, CG: 40 DR: 90
D — Simon Weaver, CG: 36 DR: 83

M — Mark Bailey, CG: 31 SD: 35
M — Richard Butcher, CG: 25 SD: 33
M — Peter Gain, CG: 41 SD: 27
M — Ben Sedgemore, CG: 22 SD: 18

F — Gary Fletcher, CG: 40 SR: 221
F — Marcus Richardson, CG: 26 SR: 311

KEY PLAYER APPEARANCES

	PLAYER	POS	AGE	APP	MINS ON	GOALS	CARDS(Y/R)	
1	Alan Marriott	GK	25	46	4140	0	3	0
2	Ben Futcher	DEF	23	42	3780	3	11	0
3	Peter Gain	MID	27	42	3669	7	10	0
4	Paul Morgan	DEF	25	41	3599	0	3	0
5	Gary Fletcher	ATT	23	42	3534	16	2	0
6	Simon Weaver	DEF	26	39	3384	0	5	0
7	Mark Bailey	MID	27	35	2954	1	5	0
8	Marcus Richardson	ATT	26	38	2803	9	4	0
9	Paul Mayo	DEF	22	31	2754	6	8	1
10	Richard Butcher	MID	23	33	2453	6	3	0
11	Francis Green	ATT	24	35	2346	7	4	0
12	Ben Sedgemore	MID	28	27	2061	0	6	0
13	Simon Yeo	ATT	30	41	1664	11	5	1
14	Matthew Bloomer	DEF	25	27	1575	0	0	0
15	Richard Liburd	DEF	30	24	1499	0	3	1
16	Kevin Ellison	ATT	25	11	924	0	4	0
17	Jamie McCombe	DEF	21	8	693	0	1	0
18	Dean Cropper	ATT	21	21	564	0	0	0

KEY PLAYERS - GOALSCORERS

Gary Fletcher

Goals in the League	16
Contribution to Attacking Power Average number of minutes between League team goals while on pitch	58
Player Strike Rate Average number of minutes between League goals scored by player	221
Club Strike Rate Average number of minutes between League goals scored by club	61

	PLAYER	LGE GOALS	POWER	STRIKE RATE
1	Gary Fletcher	16	58	221 mins
2	Marcus Richardson	9	57	311 mins
3	Francis Green	7	57	335 mins
4	Richard Butcher	6	61	409 mins

KEY PLAYERS - MIDFIELDERS

Mark Bailey

Goals in the League	1
Defensive Rating Average number of mins between League goals conceded while he was on the pitch	102
Contribution to Attacking Power Average number of minutes between League team goals while on pitch	67
Scoring Difference Defensive Rating minus Contribution to Attacking Power	35

	PLAYER	LGE GOALS	DEF RATE	POWER	SCORE DIFF
1	Mark Bailey	1	102	67	35 mins
2	Richard Butcher	6	94	61	33 mins
3	Peter Gain	7	87	60	27 mins
4	Ben Sedgemore	0	82	64	18 mins

KEY PLAYERS - DEFENDERS

Paul Mayo

Goals Conceded when he was on pitch	28
Defensive Rating Ave number of mins between League goals conceded while on the pitch	98
Clean Sheets In games when he played at least 70 minutes	13
Club Defensive Rating Average number of mins between League goals conceded by the club this season.	88

	PLAYER	CON LGE	CLN SHEETS	DEF RATE
1	Paul Mayo	28	13	98 mins
2	Ben Futcher	40	16	95 mins
3	Paul Morgan	40	14	90 mins
4	Simon Weaver	41	13	83 mins
5	Matthew Bloomer	24	4	66 mins

KEY GOALKEEPER

Alan Marriott

Goals Conceded in the League	47
Defensive Rating Ave number of mins between League goals conceded while on the pitch.	88
Counting Games Games when he played at least 70 mins	46
Clean Sheets In games when he played at least 70 mins	17

TOP POINT EARNERS

	PLAYER	GAMES	AV PTS
1	Paul Morgan	40	**1.65**
2	Francis Green	22	**1.64**
3	Richard Butcher	25	**1.64**
4	Peter Gain	41	**1.63**
5	Gary Fletcher	40	**1.63**
6	Ben Futcher	42	**1.62**
7	Marcus Richardson	26	**1.62**
8	Alan Marriott	46	**1.61**
9	Paul Mayo	31	**1.61**
10	Mark Bailey	31	**1.61**
	CLUB AVERAGE:		**1.61**

YEOVIL

Final Position: **8th**

NICKNAME: THE GLOVERS

KEY: ☐Won ☐Drawn ☐Lost

							Attendance
1	div3	**Rochdale**	A	W	3-1	Gall 26,67; Johnson 55	4,611
2	ccR1	**Luton**	A	L	1-4	Boyce 47 og	4,337
3	div3	**Carlisle**	H	W	3-0	Gall 4,18; Jackson 79	6,347
4	div3	**Leyton Orient**	A	L	0-2		4,431
5	div3	**Northampton**	H	L	0-2		6,105
6	div3	**Macclesfield**	A	L	1-4	Lockwood 63	2,221
7	div3	**Swansea**	H	W	2-0	Stansfield 39; Jackson 55	6,655
8	div3	**York**	H	W	3-0	Jackson 21; Pluck 34; Stansfield 90	5,653
9	div3	**Doncaster**	A	W	1-0	Williams 35	4,716
10	div3	**Mansfield**	A	W	1-0	Jackson 42	5,270
11	div3	**Torquay**	H	L	0-2		7,718
12	div3	**Boston**	H	W	2-0	Williams 21 pen; Lockwood 38	5,093
13	div3	**Cheltenham**	A	L	1-3	Gall 40	4,960
14	div3	**Oxford**	A	L	0-1		6,301
15	div3	**Darlington**	H	W	1-0	Williams 5 pen	4,892
16	div3	**Huddersfield**	H	W	2-1	Skiverton 4; Johnson 51	5,274
17	div3	**Cambridge**	A	W	4-1	Edwards, J 16,59; Gall 61; Way 87	4,072
18	div3	**Bury**	A	L	1-2	Edwards, J 31	3,086
19	facr1	**Wrexham**	H	W	4-1	Gall 39; Williams 46; Pluck 59; Edwards, J 66	5,049
20	div3	**Southend**	H	W	4-0	Elam 33; Way 40; Johnson 43,56 pen	5,248
21	div3	**Hull City**	A	D	0-0		14,367
22	div3	**Lincoln**	H	W	3-1	Pluck 54; Stansfield 85; Gosling 90	4,867
23	facr2	**Barnet**	H	W	5-1	Pluck 9; Williams 18 pen,27; Crittenden 74; Edwards, J 78	5,973
24	div3	**Bristol Rovers**	A	W	1-0	Crittenden 43	9,812
25	div3	**Scunthorpe**	H	D	2-2	Jackson 71; Lindegaard 82	5,714
26	div3	**Kidderminster**	H	L	1-2	Gall 58	5,640
27	div3	**Swansea**	A	L	2-3	Williams 73; Gall 89	9,800
28	facr3	**Liverpool**	H	L	0-2		5,348
29	div3	**Rochdale**	H	W	1-0	Williams 14	5,806
30	div3	**Carlisle**	A	L	0-2		5,455
31	div3	**Leyton Orient**	H	L	1-2	Crittenden 76	6,299
32	div3	**Macclesfield**	H	D	2-2	Edwards 30; Way 60	5,257
33	div3	**Northampton**	A	L	0-2		4,363
34	div3	**Kidderminster**	A	W	1-0	Williams 65	3,255
35	div3	**Oxford**	H	W	1-0	Bent 29	7,404
36	div3	**Darlington**	A	L	2-3	Johnson 22; Lockwood 90	4,500
37	div3	**Cambridge**	H	W	4-1	Williams 18 pen; Bishop 19; Stansfield 27; Pluck 48	5,694
38	div3	**Huddersfield**	A	L	1-3	Way 78	9,395
39	div3	**Scunthorpe**	A	L	0-3		3,355
40	div3	**Bristol Rovers**	H	W	4-0	Lockwood 16; El Kholti 43; Williams 49; Pluck 72	8,726
41	div3	**Doncaster**	H	L	0-1		7,587
42	div3	**Mansfield**	H	D	1-1	Skiverton 61	6,002
43	div3	**Torquay**	A	D	2-2	Way 17; Edwards, J 27	6,156
44	div3	**Cheltenham**	H	D	0-0		6,613
45	div3	**Boston**	A	L	2-3	Weatherstone, S 4; Stansfield 51	2,848
46	div3	**Bury**	H	W	2-1	Rodrigues, D 55,59	5,172
47	div3	**York**	A	W	2-1	Terry 46; Lindegaard 70	2,802
48	div3	**Southend**	A	W	2-0	Rodrigues, D 21,32	5,676
49	div3	**Hull City**	H	L	1-2	Rodrigues, H 64	8,760
50	div3	**Lincoln**	A	W	3-2	Stansfield 47; Edwards, J 71; Williams 89	8,154

TEAM OF THE SEASON

G
Chris Weale
CG: 35 **DR:** 70

D
Nick Crittenden
CG: 18 **DR:** 105

D
Colin Pluck
CG: 30 **DR:** 83

D
Adam Lockwood
CG: 39 **DR:** 78

D
Terry Skiverton
CG: 21 **DR:** 75

M
Lee Johnson
CG: 44 **SD:** 15

M
Gavin Williams
CG: 41 **SD:** 15

M
Darren Way
CG: 35 **SD:** 12

M
*Andrew Lindegaard
CG: 12 **SD:** 3

F
Kirk Jackson
CG: 17 **SR:** 370

F
Kevin Gall
CG: 33 **SR:** 413

KEY PLAYER APPEARANCES

	PLAYER	POS	AGE	APP	MINS ON	GOALS	CARDS(Y/R)	
1	Lee Johnson	MID	23	44	3960	5	9	0
2	Gavin Williams	MID	23	43	3750	9	10	1
3	Adam Lockwood	DEF	22	43	3684	4	5	0
4	Darren Way	MID	24	39	3341	5	5	0
5	Kevin Gall	ATT	22	42	3306	8	3	0
6	Chris Weale	GK	22	35	3150	0	0	0
7	Colin Pluck	DEF	25	37	2983	4	8	0
8	Hugo Rodrigues	DEF	24	34	2318	1	6	0
9	Terry Skiverton	DEF	29	26	2175	2	7	0
10	Paul Terry	MID	25	33	1945	1	1	1
11	Kirk Jackson	ATT	30	31	1851	5	2	0
12	Nick Crittenden	DEF	25	29	1783	2	0	0
13	Abdelhalim El Kholti	DEF	23	23	1737	1	3	0
14	Jake Edwards	ATT	28	27	1538	5	1	0
15	Andrew Lindegaard	MID	23	23	1355	2	2	0
16	Roy O'Brien	DEF	29	13	1047	0	0	0
17	Stephen Collis	GK	23	11	990	0	0	0
18	Simon Weatherstone	ATT	24	15	950	1	1	0

KEY PLAYERS - GOALSCORERS

Kirk Jackson

Goals in the League	5
Contribution to Attacking Power Average number of minutes between League team goals while on pitch	56
Player Strike Rate Average number of minutes between League goals scored by player	370
Club Strike Rate Average number of minutes between League goals scored by club	59

	PLAYER	LGE GOALS	POWER	STRIKE RATE
1	Kirk Jackson	5	56	370 mins
2	Kevin Gall	8	71	413 mins
3	Gavin Williams	9	58	417 mins
4	Darren Way	5	57	668 mins

KEY PLAYERS - MIDFIELDERS

Gavin Williams

Goals in the League	9
Defensive Rating Average number of mins between League goals conceded while he was on the pitch	74
Contribution to Attacking Power Average number of minutes between League team goals while on pitch	59
Scoring Difference Defensive Rating minus Contribution to Attacking Power	15

	PLAYER	LGE GOALS	DEF RATE	POWER	SCORE DIFF
1	Gavin Williams	9	74	59	15 mins
2	Lee Johnson	5	73	58	15 mins
3	Darren Way	5	70	58	12 mins
4	Andrew Lindegaard	2	62	59	3 mins
5	Paul Terry	1	57	57	0 mins

KEY PLAYERS - DEFENDERS

Nick Crittenden

Goals Conceded when he was on pitch	17
Defensive Rating Ave number of mins between League goals conceded while on the pitch	105
Clean Sheets In games when he played at least 70 minutes	10
Club Defensive Rating Average number of mins between League goals conceded by the club this season.	71

	PLAYER	CON LGE	CLN SHEETS	DEF RATE
1	Nick Crittenden	17	10	105 mins
2	Colin Pluck	36	12	83 mins
3	Adam Lockwood	47	15	78 mins
4	Terry Skiverton	29	6	75 mins
5	Hugo Rodrigues	34	7	68 mins

KEY GOALKEEPER

Chris Weale

Goals Conceded in the League	45
Defensive Rating Ave number of mins between League goals conceded while on the pitch.	70
Counting Games Games when he played at least 70 mins	35
Clean Sheets In games when he played at least 70 mins	13

TOP POINT EARNERS

	PLAYER	GAMES	AV PTS
1	Nick Crittenden	18	**1.83**
2	Colin Pluck	30	**1.80**
3	Adam Lockwood	39	**1.69**
4	Kirk Jackson	17	**1.65**
5	Hugo Rodrigues	21	**1.62**
6	Kevin Gall	33	**1.61**
7	Lee Johnson	44	**1.61**
8	Gavin Williams	41	**1.59**
9	Darren Way	35	**1.57**
10	Chris Weale	35	**1.54**
	CLUB AVERAGE:		**1.57**

OXFORD UNITED

Final Position: **9th**

NICKNAME: THE U'S

KEY: ☐ Won ☐ Drawn ☐ Lost

							Attendance
1	div3	Lincoln	A	W	1-0	Basham 6	4,543
2	ccR1	Millwall	A	W	1-0	Basham 59	4,781
3	div3	Hull City	H	W	2-1	Basham 23,28	6,618
4	div3	Scunthorpe	A	D	1-1	Crosby 43 pen	3,617
5	div3	Swansea	H	W	3-0	Crosby 85 pen; Alsop 87; Rawle 89	6,725
6	div3	Kidderminster	A	D	1-1	Rawle 80	3,262
7	div3	Southend	H	W	2-0	Basham 26; Wanless 47	5,567
8	div3	Mansfield	H	D	1-1	Wanless 64	5,625
9	div3	Cheltenham	A	D	0-0		5,319
10	div3	Doncaster	A	L	0-2		5,040
11	ccR2	Reading	H	L	1-3	Louis 78	9,870
12	div3	Northampton	H	W	3-0	Basham 1,41; Whitehead 32	6,518
13	div3	Torquay	H	W	1-0	Alsop 70	5,479
14	div3	Boston	A	D	1-1	Louis 88	2,664
15	div3	Yeovil	H	W	1-0	Basham 13	6,301
16	div3	Bury	A	W	4-0	Whitehead 29,79; Basham 83,84	2,930
17	div3	York	A	D	2-2	Brass 5 og; Hackett 85	3,022
18	div3	Bristol Rovers	H	D	0-0		6,644
19	div3	Darlington	H	W	3-1	Rawle 52; Whitehead 74; Wanless 89	4,962
20	facr1	Colchester	A	L	0-1		3,672
21	div3	Cambridge	A	D	1-1	Rawle 90	4,430
22	div3	Macclesfield	H	W	3-1	Alsop 29; Hunt 45; Wanless 70	6,676
23	div3	Rochdale	A	W	2-1	Basham 30; Alsop 51	2,282
24	div3	Carlisle	H	W	2-1	Robinson 3; Crosby 31 pen	6,111
25	div3	Huddersfield	A	D	1-1	Rawle 72	9,368
26	div3	Leyton Orient	H	W	2-1	Crosby 33 pen; Alsop 90	9,477
27	div3	Southend	A	W	1-0	Rawle 68	6,449
28	div3	Swansea	A	D	0-0		8,896
29	div3	Lincoln	H	D	0-0		6,679
30	div3	Hull City	A	L	2-4	Basham 77; Bound 90	21,491
31	div3	Kidderminster	H	W	2-1	Basham 7; McCarthy 77	6,057
32	div3	Leyton Orient	A	L	0-1		5,433
33	div3	Scunthorpe	H	W	3-2	Wanless 30; Rawle 34; Steele 88	5,118
34	div3	Yeovil	A	L	0-1		7,404
35	div3	Bury	H	D	1-1	Whitehead 49	6,473
36	div3	Bristol Rovers	A	D	1-1	Rawle 13	6,556
37	div3	York	H	D	0-0		5,091
38	div3	Huddersfield	H	L	0-1		7,278
39	div3	Carlisle	A	L	0-2		5,492
40	div3	Cheltenham	H	W	1-0	Crosby 25 pen	5,916
41	div3	Doncaster	H	D	0-0		8,483
42	div3	Northampton	A	L	1-2	Basham 22	6,799
43	div3	Mansfield	A	L	1-3	Whitehead 34	5,132
44	div3	Boston	H	D	0-0		6,050
45	div3	Torquay	A	L	0-3		5,114
46	div3	Darlington	A	L	0-2		4,212
47	div3	Cambridge	H	D	2-2	McCarthy 75; Louis 86	5,830
48	div3	Macclesfield	A	L	1-2	Hunt 36	2,763
49	div3	Rochdale	H	W	2-0	Basham 33; Whitehead 39	5,134

TEAM OF THE SEASON

G — Andy Woodman — CG: 41 DR: 100

D — Matthew Bound — CG: 31 DR: 111

D — Scott McNiven — CG: 34 DR: 100

D — Andrew Crosby — CG: 39 DR: 95

D — Paul McCarthy — CG: 26 DR: 90

M — Matthew Robinson — CG: 39 SD: 34

M — Paul Wanless — CG: 33 SD: 26

M — Jon Ashton — CG: 30 SD: 21

M — James Hunt — CG: 36 SD: 15

F — Steve Basham — CG: 29 SR: 215

F — Julian Alsop — CG: 21 SR: 445

KEY PLAYER APPEARANCES

	PLAYER	POS	AGE	APP	MINS ON	GOALS	CARDS(Y/R)	
1	Andy Woodman	GK	32	41	3690	0	3	0
2	Andrew Crosby	DEF	31	42	3620	5	2	1
3	Matthew Robinson	MID	29	40	3574	1	8	0
4	Dean Whitehead	MID	22	44	3441	7	4	0
5	James Hunt	MID	27	41	3317	2	9	0
6	Scott McNiven	DEF	26	41	3308	0	4	0
7	Paul Wanless	MID	30	38	3230	5	3	0
8	Steve Basham	ATT	26	38	3007	14	0	0
9	Matthew Bound	DEF	31	36	2884	1	3	0
10	Jon Ashton	MID	21	35	2814	0	4	0
11	Paul McCarthy	DEF	32	29	2419	2	7	0
12	Julian Alsop	ATT	31	29	2224	5	6	3
13	Mark Rawle	ATT	25	31	1354	8	2	0
14	Danny Brown	MID	23	12	1021	0	0	0
15	Chris Hackett	MID	21	22	851	1	0	0
16	David Waterman	DEF	27	13	670	0	0	0
17	Jefferson Louis	ATT	25	20	664	2	2	0
18	Derek Townsley	MID	31	11	635	0	0	0

KEY PLAYERS - GOALSCORERS

Steve Basham

Goals in the League	14	Player Strike Rate Average number of minutes between League goals scored by player	215
Contribution to Attacking Power Average number of minutes between League team goals while on pitch	69	Club Strike Rate Average number of minutes between League goals scored by club	75

	PLAYER	LGE GOALS	POWER	STRIKE RATE
1	Steve Basham	14	69	215 mins
2	Julian Alsop	5	60	445 mins
3	Dean Whitehead	7	78	492 mins
4	Paul Wanless	5	68	646 mins

KEY PLAYERS - MIDFIELDERS

Matthew Robinson

Goals in the League	1	Contribution to Attacking Power Average number of minutes between League team goals while on pitch	71
Defensive Rating Average number of mins between League goals conceded while he was on the pitch	105	Scoring Difference Defensive Rating minus Contribution to Attacking Power	34

	PLAYER	LGE GOALS	DEF RATE	POWER	SCORE DIFF
1	Matthew Robinson	1	105	71	34 mins
2	Paul Wanless	5	95	69	26 mins
3	Jon Ashton	0	91	70	21 mins
4	James Hunt	2	90	75	15 mins

KEY PLAYERS - DEFENDERS

Matthew Bound

Goals Conceded when he was on pitch	26	Clean Sheets In games when he played at least 70 minutes	14
Defensive Rating Ave number of mins between League goals conceded while on the pitch	111	Club Defensive Rating Average number of mins between League goals conceded by the club this season.	94

	PLAYER	CON LGE	CLN SHEETS	DEF RATE
1	Matthew Bound	26	14	111 mins
2	Scott McNiven	33	16	100 mins
3	Andrew Crosby	38	14	95 mins
4	Paul McCarthy	27	8	90 mins

KEY GOALKEEPER

Andy Woodman

Goals Conceded in the League	37
Defensive Rating Ave number of mins between League goals conceded while on the pitch.	100
Counting Games Games when he played at least 70 mins	41
Clean Sheets In games when he played at least 70 mins	15

TOP POINT EARNERS

	PLAYER	GAMES	AV PTS
1	Julian Alsop	21	**2.00**
2	Paul Wanless	33	**1.88**
3	Steve Basham	29	**1.83**
4	Scott McNiven	34	**1.74**
5	Matthew Robinson	39	**1.69**
6	Matthew Bound	31	**1.68**
7	Andy Woodman	41	**1.63**
8	Jon Ashton	30	**1.63**
9	Andrew Crosby	39	**1.54**
10	Dean Whitehead	36	**1.47**
	CLUB AVERAGE:		**1.54**

SWANSEA

Final Position: **10th**

NICKNAME: THE SWANS

KEY: ☐Won ☐Drawn ☐Lost

							Attendance
1	div3	**Bury**	H	W	4-2	Maylett 5,79,90; Trundle 82	8,826
2	ccR1	**Bristol City**	A	L	1-1	Connolly 18 (lost on penalties)	5,807
3	div3	**Cheltenham**	A	W	4-3	Thomas 37; Trundle 63,79,90	4,660
4	div3	**Boston**	H	W	3-0	Trundle 49; Nugent 53; Robinson 87	9,041
5	div3	**Oxford**	A	L	0-3		6,725
6	div3	**Mansfield**	H	W	4-1	Durkan 16; Robinson 58; Trundle 70 pen; Nugent 71	6,991
7	div3	**Yeovil**	A	L	0-2		6,655
8	div3	**Scunthorpe**	A	D	2-2	Trundle 7,63	3,510
9	div3	**Macclesfield**	H	W	3-0	Britton 33; Duffy 45; Robinson 49	6,641
10	div3	**Huddersfield**	H	W	2-0	Trundle 33; Nugent 84	8,048
11	div3	**Carlisle**	A	W	2-1	Trundle 50 pen; Wilson 55	4,854
12	div3	**Hull City**	A	L	0-1		20,903
13	div3	**Lincoln**	H	D	2-2	Robinson 17; Trundle 74	7,914
14	div3	**Leyton Orient**	A	W	2-1	Trundle 10; Nugent 15	4,393
15	div3	**Kidderminster**	H	D	0-0		6,825
16	div3	**Cambridge**	H	L	0-2		6,211
17	div3	**Rochdale**	A	W	1-0	Wilson 16	2,646
18	div3	**Bristol Rovers**	H	D	0-0		7,536
19	facr1	**Rushden & D**	H	W	3-0	Trundle 38; Nugent 58; Durkan 88	5,031
20	div3	**Northampton**	A	L	1-2	Britton 48	4,010
21	div3	**Darlington**	H	W	1-0	Trundle 41	5,651
22	div3	**York**	A	D	0-0		3,209
23	facr2	**Stevenage**	H	W	2-1	Nugent 23; Trundle 51	6,125
24	div3	**Southend**	H	L	2-3	Thomas 14,90	5,439
25	div3	**Doncaster**	A	L	1-3	Robinson 74	6,566
26	div3	**Torquay**	A	D	0-0		4,447
27	div3	**Yeovil**	H	W	3-2	Trundle 29 pen,90; Connolly 67	9,800
28	facr3	**Macclesfield**	H	W	2-1	Trundle 44,70	8,112
29	div3	**Oxford**	H	D	0-0		8,896
30	div3	**Bury**	A	L	0-2		2,799
31	div3	**Cheltenham**	H	D	0-0		6,474
32	facr4	**Preston**	H	W	2-1	Robinson 80; Trundle 82	10,200
33	div3	**Torquay**	H	L	1-2	Nugent 81	7,323
34	facr5	**Tranmere**	A	L	1-2	Robinson 16	12,215
35	div3	**Boston**	A	D	1-1	Britton 14	2,573
36	div3	**Kidderminster**	A	L	0-2		3,407
37	div3	**Leyton Orient**	H	W	2-1	Trundle 12; Tate 81	4,727
38	div3	**Cambridge**	A	W	1-0	Iriekpen 5	2,713
39	div3	**Doncaster**	H	D	1-1	Roberts 39	8,045
40	div3	**Rochdale**	H	D	1-1	Maylett 78	5,819
41	div3	**Southend**	A	D	1-1	Nugent 62	4,753
42	div3	**Macclesfield**	A	L	1-2	Maylett 74	1,513
43	div3	**Scunthorpe**	H	W	4-2	Robinson 41 pen; Nugent 47; Connor 61,70	4,400
44	div3	**Mansfield**	A	D	1-1	Robinson 31	4,058
45	div3	**Huddersfield**	A	L	0-3		11,250
46	div3	**Carlisle**	H	L	1-2	Connor 15	5,238
47	div3	**Lincoln**	A	L	1-2	Rees 43	5,455
48	div3	**Hull City**	H	L	2-3	Robinson 45; Trundle 83	5,993
49	div3	**Bristol Rovers**	A	L	1-2	Connor 8	7,843
50	div3	**Northampton**	H	L	0-2		4,985
51	div3	**Darlington**	A	W	2-1	Connor 50; Nugent 80	5,487
52	div3	**York**	H	D	0-0		6,806

TEAM OF THE SEASON

G — Roger Freestone, CG: 36 DR: 71

D — Michael Howard, CG: 23 DR: 90
D — Ezomo Iriekpen, CG: 30 DR: 83
D — Alan Tate, CG: 23 DR: 70
D — Kristian O'Leary, CG: 25 DR: 65

M — Lenny Johnrose, CG: 18 SD: 12
M — Andy Robinson, CG: 32 SD: 5
M — Leon Britton, CG: 40 SD: 2
M — *Mark Wilson, CG: 12 SD: 26

F — Lee Trundle, CG: 26 SR: 141
F — Kevin Nugent, CG: 30 SR: 357

KEY PLAYER APPEARANCES

	PLAYER	POS	AGE	APP	MINS ON	GOALS	CARDS(Y)	CARDS(R)
1	Leon Britton	MID	21	41	3634	3	4	0
2	Roger Freestone	GK	35	37	3248	0	1	0
3	Andy Robinson	MID	20	37	3019	8	4	0
4	Ezomo Iriekpen	DEF	22	34	2889	1	10	1
5	Kevin Nugent	ATT	35	39	2858	8	8	0
6	Kristian O'Leary	DEF	26	34	2554	0	5	0
7	Lee Trundle	ATT	27	31	2398	17	3	1
8	Brad Maylett	MID	23	33	2369	5	4	0
9	Roberto Martinez	MID	30	27	2200	0	6	0
10	Alan Tate	DEF	21	26	2182	1	4	0
11	Michael Howard	DEF	25	25	2161	0	4	0
12	Lenny Johnrose	MID	34	25	1885	0	7	0
13	Stuart Jones	DEF	20	24	1656	0	2	0
14	Jonathan Coates	ATT	39	27	1410	0	3	0
15	Richard Duffy	DEF	18	18	1321	1	4	2
16	Mark Wilson	MID	25	12	1080	2	1	0
17	Paul Connor	ATT	25	12	1063	5	1	0
18	Leon Hilton	DEF	21	12	969	0	2	0

KEY PLAYERS - GOALSCORERS

Lee Trundle

Goals in the League	17
Contribution to Attacking Power Average number of minutes between League team goals while on pitch	57
Player Strike Rate Average number of minutes between League goals scored by player	141
Club Strike Rate Average number of minutes between League goals scored by club	71

	PLAYER	LGE GOALS	POWER	STRIKE RATE
1	Lee Trundle	17	57	141 mins
2	*Paul Connor	5	75	213 mins
3	Kevin Nugent	8	68	357 mins
4	Andy Robinson	8	67	377 mins
5	Brad Maylett	5	69	474 mins

KEY PLAYERS - MIDFIELDERS

Mark Wilson

Goals in the League	2
Defensive Rating Average number of mins between League goals conceded while he was on the pitch	98
Contribution to Attacking Power Average number of minutes between League team goals while on pitch	72
Scoring Difference Defensive Rating minus Contribution to Attacking Power	26

	PLAYER	LGE GOALS	DEF RATE	POWER	SCORE DIFF
1	Mark Wilson	2	98	72	26 mins
2	Lenny Johnrose	0	82	70	12 mins
3	Andy Robinson	8	72	67	5 mins
4	Leon Britton	3	73	71	2 mins
5	Brad Maylett	5	70	70	0 mins

KEY PLAYERS - DEFENDERS

Michael Howard

Goals Conceded when he was on pitch	24
Defensive Rating Ave number of mins between League goals conceded while on the pitch	90
Clean Sheets In games when he played at least 70 minutes	9
Club Defensive Rating Average number of mins between League goals conceded by the club this season.	68

	PLAYER	CON LGE	CLN SHEETS	DEF RATE
1	Michael Howard	24	9	90 mins
2	Ezomo Iriekpen	35	12	83 mins
3	Alan Tate	31	6	70 mins
4	Kristian O'Leary	39	7	65 mins
5	Stuart Jones	26	4	64 mins

KEY GOALKEEPER

Roger Freestone

Goals Conceded in the League	46
Defensive Rating Ave number of mins between League goals conceded while on the pitch.	71
Counting Games Games when he played at least 70 mins	37
Clean Sheets In games when he played at least 70 mins	11

TOP POINT EARNERS

	PLAYER	GAMES	AV PTS
1	Mark Wilson	12	**1.58**
2	Lenny Johnrose	18	**1.50**
3	Michael Howard	23	**1.43**
4	Leon Britton	40	**1.38**
5	Ezomo Iriekpen	30	**1.37**
6	Lee Trundle	26	**1.35**
7	Kristian O'Leary	25	**1.32**
8	Brad Maylett	22	**1.27**
9	Kevin Nugent	30	**1.23**
10	Roberto Martinez	23	**1.22**
	CLUB AVERAGE:		**1.28**

BOSTON UNITED

Final Position: **11th**

NICKNAME: THE PILGRIMS

KEY: ☐ Won ☐ Drawn ☐ Lost

							Attendance
1	div3	Macclesfield	A	D	0-0		2,222
2	ccR1	Reading	H	L	1-3	Redfearn 69 pen	2,055
3	div3	Huddersfield	H	D	2-2	Redfearn 22; Ellender 67	3,452
4	div3	Swansea	A	L	0-3		9,041
5	div3	Carlisle	H	W	1-0	Redfearn 30	2,527
6	div3	Hull City	A	L	1-2	Ellender 55	13,091
7	div3	Scunthorpe	H	D	1-1	Beevers 23	3,154
8	div3	Bristol Rovers	A	L	0-2		6,845
9	div3	Cambridge	H	L	1-2	Weatherstone, S 59	2,452
10	div3	Bury	H	W	1-0	Duffield 57	2,260
11	div3	Darlington	A	L	0-3		4,519
12	div3	Yeovil	A	L	0-2		5,093
13	div3	Oxford	H	D	1-1	Jones 35	2,664
14	div3	Cheltenham	H	W	3-1	Bennett 28; Balmer 33; Angel 57	2,283
15	div3	York	A	D	1-1	Weatherstone, S 59	3,190
16	div3	Southend	A	W	2-0	Thompson, L 59; Weatherstone, S 76	2,463
17	div3	Torquay	H	W	4-0	Redfearn 4; Thompson, L 61; Duffield 81,90	2,431
18	div3	Mansfield	A	L	1-2	Weatherstone, S 27	5,161
19	facr1	Macclesfield	A	L	0-3		2,059
20	div3	Leyton Orient	H	W	3-0	Jones 24; Redfearn 82,86	2,619
21	div3	Doncaster	A	L	0-3		5,211
22	div3	Kidderminster	H	D	2-2	Boyd 63,69	2,147
23	div3	Northampton	H	D	1-1	Thompson, L 38	2,756
24	div3	Rochdale	A	L	0-1		2,049
25	div3	Lincoln	H	L	0-1		5,708
26	div3	Scunthorpe	A	W	1-0	Duffield 12	4,346
27	div3	Carlisle	A	L	1-2	Jones 10	5,296
28	div3	Macclesfield	H	W	3-1	Jones 14; Boyd 40; Douglas 77	2,300
29	div3	Huddersfield	A	L	0-2		9,603
30	div3	Lincoln	A	D	1-1	Redfearn 6	7,114
31	div3	Cheltenham	A	L	0-1		3,434
32	div3	Swansea	H	D	1-1	Boyd 87	2,573
33	div3	York	H	W	2-0	Duffield 55; Jones 81	2,490
34	div3	Torquay	A	L	0-2		3,000
35	div3	Southend	H	L	0-2		2,780
36	div3	Rochdale	H	W	2-0	Ellender 20; Jones 76	2,466
37	div3	Northampton	A	L	0-2		6,243
38	div3	Cambridge	A	W	1-0	Balmer 6	3,294
39	div3	Bristol Rovers	H	W	1-0	Thomas 38	2,450
40	div3	Bury	A	W	3-1	Cropper 8; Thomas 25,88	2,693
41	div3	Hull City	H	L	1-2	Ellender 66	4,741
42	div3	Darlington	H	W	1-0	Melton 45	2,573
43	div3	Oxford	A	D	0-0		6,050
44	div3	Yeovil	H	W	3-2	Hurst 14; Noble, D 45; Thompson 90	2,848
45	div3	Mansfield	H	L	1-2	Balmer 69	3,826
46	div3	Leyton Orient	A	W	3-1	Beevers 67; Noble, D 90; Thompson, L 90	3,580
47	div3	Doncaster	H	D	0-0		4,671
48	div3	Kidderminster	A	L	0-2		3,047

TEAM OF THE SEASON

G — Paul Bastock CG: 46 DR: 77

D — Ben Chapman CG: 29 DR: 88

D — Lee Beevers CG: 38 DR: 80

D — Mark Greaves CG: 32 DR: 78

D — Paul Ellender CG: 40 DR: 77

M — Lee Thompson CG: 20 SD: 28

M — Tom Bennett CG: 34 SD: -4

M — David Noble CG: 14 SD: -5

M — Neil Redfearn CG: 16 SD: -23

F — Graeme Jones CG: 25 SR: 412

F — Adam Boyd CG: 12 SR: 294

KEY PLAYER APPEARANCES

	PLAYER	POS	AGE	APP	MINS ON	GOALS	CARDS(Y)	CARDS(R)
1	Paul Bastock	GK	34	46	4140	0	2	0
2	Paul Ellender	DEF	29	42	3711	4	13	0
3	Lee Beevers	DEF	20	40	3515	2	4	1
4	Tom Bennett	MID	34	35	3102	1	9	1
5	Mark Greaves	DEF	29	37	3037	0	10	0
6	Ben Chapman	DEF	25	37	2917	0	8	1
7	Graeme Jones	ATT	34	32	2469	6	6	0
8	Stuart Balmer	DEF	34	26	2200	3	4	1
9	Lee Thompson	MID	21	35	2121	4	3	0
10	Neil Redfearn	MID	39	23	1654	6	2	0
11	Matthew Hocking	DEF	26	22	1481	0	3	1
12	Simon Rusk	MID	22	19	1473	0	7	0
13	Stuart Douglas	ATT	26	29	1369	1	2	0
14	Peter Duffield	ATT	35	29	1241	5	1	0
15	David Noble	MID	22	14	1223	2	2	0
16	Simon Weatherstone	ATT	24	14	1181	4	4	0
17	Mark Angel	ATT	28	23	1177	1	3	0
18	Adam Boyd	ATT	22	14	1174	4	3	0

KEY PLAYERS - GOALSCORERS

Neil Redfearn

Goals in the League	6
Contribution to Attacking Power Average number of minutes between League team goals while on pitch	87
Player Strike Rate Average number of minutes between League goals scored by player	276
Club Strike Rate Average number of minutes between League goals scored by club	83

	PLAYER	LGE GOALS	POWER	STRIKE RATE
1	Neil Redfearn	6	87	276 mins
2	Adam Boyd	4	78	294 mins
3	*Simon Weatherstone	4	78	295 mins
4	Graeme Jones	6	72	412 mins
5	Lee Thompson	4	68	530 mins

KEY PLAYERS - MIDFIELDERS

Lee Thompson

Goals in the League	4
Defensive Rating Average number of mins between League goals conceded while he was on the pitch	96
Contribution to Attacking Power Average number of minutes between League team goals while on pitch	68
Scoring Difference Defensive Rating minus Contribution to Attacking Power	28

	PLAYER	LGE GOALS	DEF RATE	POWER	SCORE DIFF
1	Lee Thompson	4	96	68	28 mins
2	Tom Bennett	1	78	82	-4 mins
3	David Noble	2	82	87	-5 mins
4	Neil Redfearn	6	64	87	-23 mins
5	Simon Rusk	0	74	164	-90 mins

KEY PLAYERS - DEFENDERS

Ben Chapman

Goals Conceded when he was on pitch	33
Defensive Rating Ave number of mins between League goals conceded while on the pitch	88
Clean Sheets In games when he played at least 70 minutes	12
Club Defensive Rating Average number of mins between League goals conceded by the club this season.	77

	PLAYER	CON LGE	CLN SHEETS	DEF RATE
1	Ben Chapman	33	12	88 mins
2	Lee Beevers	44	12	80 mins
3	Mark Greaves	39	9	78 mins
4	Paul Ellender	48	14	77 mins
5	Stuart Balmer	31	6	71 mins

KEY GOALKEEPER

Paul Bastock

Goals Conceded in the League	54
Defensive Rating Ave number of mins between League goals conceded while on the pitch.	77
Counting Games Games when he played at least 70 mins	46
Clean Sheets In games when he played at least 70 mins	14

TOP POINT EARNERS

	PLAYER	GAMES	AV PTS
1	Lee Thompson	20	1.50
2	Ben Chapman	29	1.48
3	Tom Bennett	34	1.47
4	Graeme Jones	25	1.44
5	David Noble	14	1.43
6	Paul Ellender	40	1.43
7	Lee Beevers	38	1.39
8	Adam Boyd	12	1.33
9	Stuart Balmer	23	1.30
10	Paul Bastock	46	1.28
	CLUB AVERAGE:		1.28

BURY

Final Position: **12th**

NICKNAME: THE SHAKERS

KEY: ☐ Won ☐ Drawn ☐ Lost

	Comp	Opponent	H/A	Res	Score	Scorers	Attendance
1	div3	Swansea	A	L	2-4	Preece 20; Connell 85	8,826
2	ccR1	Tranmere	A	L	0-1		4,272
3	div3	Scunthorpe	H	L	2-3	Porter 45; Preece 76	2,761
4	div3	Kidderminster	A	W	2-0	Porter 28; Seddon 88	2,548
5	div3	Lincoln	H	W	2-1	Unsworth 81; Preece 90 pen	2,576
6	div3	Southend	A	L	0-1		3,172
7	div3	Huddersfield	H	W	2-1	Swailes 24; Connell 83	4,591
8	div3	Cheltenham	H	D	1-1	Preece 35 pen	2,753
9	div3	Mansfield	A	L	3-5	Connell 21,78; Seddon 58	4,145
10	div3	Boston	A	L	0-1		2,260
11	div3	Doncaster	H	L	1-3	Preece 28	3,606
12	div3	York	H	W	2-0	Porter 37; O'Neill, J 71	2,282
13	div3	Torquay	A	L	1-3	Porter 38	2,732
14	div3	Cambridge	A	W	2-1	Connell 33; Porter 39	5,106
15	div3	Oxford	H	L	0-4		2,930
16	div3	Hull City	H	D	0-0		3,896
17	div3	Darlington	A	W	3-1	Seddon 35; Connell 56; Singh 82	3,516
18	div3	Yeovil	H	W	2-1	O'Shaughnessy 35; Unsworth 88	3,086
19	facr1	Rochdale	H	L	1-2	Porter 71	5,464
20	div3	Bristol Rovers	A	W	2-1	Barrett 70 og; O'Neill, J 90	7,109
21	div3	Northampton	H	W	1-0	O'Neill, J 72	2,683
22	div3	Macclesfield	A	L	0-1		2,312
23	div3	Hull City	A	L	0-2		11,308
24	div3	Rochdale	H	L	1-2	Dunfield 49	3,646
25	div3	Leyton Orient	A	L	0-2		3,475
26	div3	Carlisle	H	L	1-3	Porter 30 pen	3,345
27	div3	Huddersfield	A	L	0-1		10,217
28	div3	Lincoln	A	L	1-2	Porter 90	3,870
29	div3	Swansea	H	W	2-0	Swailes 62; Daly 86	2,799
30	div3	Scunthorpe		D	0-0		3,869
31	div3	Kidderminster	H	D	0-0		2,526
32	div3	Carlisle	A	L	1-2	Seddon 25	4,954
33	div3	Cambridge	H	W	1-0	Seddon 2	2,322
34	div3	Oxford	A	D	1-1	Dunfield 47	6,473
35	div3	Southend	H	D	1-1	Seddon 90	1,670
36	div3	Darlington	H	D	1-1	Barrass 57	2,766
37	div3	Leyton Orient	H	D	1-1	Seddon 63	2,355
38	div3	Rochdale	A	D	0-0		4,225
39	div3	Mansfield	H	W	3-0	Seddon 26,60; Swailes 43 pen	2,199
40	div3	Cheltenham	A	W	2-1	Swailes 74; Porter 82	3,435
41	div3	Boston	H	L	1-3	Swailes 13 pen	2,693
42	div3	Doncaster	A	L	1-3	Singh 88	6,221
43	div3	Torquay	H	W	2-1	Seddon 35; Nugent 67	2,770
44	div3	York	A	D	1-1	Seddon 16	3,111
45	div3	Yeovil	A	L	1-2	Nugent 35	5,172
46	div3	Bristol Rovers	H	D	0-0		2,683
47	div3	Northampton	A	L	2-3	Cartledge 10; Nugent 45	6,179
48	div3	Macclesfield	H	W	2-0	Porter 85; Whaley 90	3,569

TEAM OF THE SEASON

G	Glyn Garner	CG: 46 DR: 65
D	David Challinor	CG: 15 DR: 96
D	Thomas Kennedy	CG: 22 DR: 78
D	Colin Woodthorpe	CG: 37 DR: 68
D	Danny Swailes	CG: 40 DR: 66
M	Harpal Singh	CG: 18 SD: -3
M	Lee Duxbury	CG: 32 SD: -8
M	Matthew Barrass	CG: 16 SD: -11
M	David Flitcroft	CG: 15 SD: -4
F	Chris Porter	CG: 15 SR: 214
F	Gareth Seddon	CG: 22 SR: 231

KEY PLAYER APPEARANCES

	PLAYER	POS	AGE	APP	MINS ON	GOALS	CARDS(Y)	CARDS(R)
1	Glyn Garner	GK	27	46	4140	0	3	0
2	Danny Swailes	DEF	25	41	3645	4	8	0
3	Colin Woodthorpe	DEF	35	39	3447	0	12	0
4	Lee Duxbury	MID	34	37	3069	0	2	0
5	Gareth Seddon	ATT	24	40	2537	11	8	0
6	Lee Unsworth	DEF	31	28	2444	2	5	1
7	Terry Dunfield	MID	22	30	2294	2	4	0
8	Thomas Kennedy	DEF	19	27	2114	0	1	0
9	Lee Connell	DEF	23	28	2087	6	1	0
10	Chris Porter	ATT	20	37	1922	9	1	0
11	Harpal Singh	MID	22	28	1897	2	4	0
12	Paul O'Shaughnessy	MID	18	27	1885	1	11	0
13	David Nugent	ATT	19	26	1834	3	4	0
14	Matthew Barrass	MID	24	21	1610	0	2	0
15	David Flitcroft	MID	30	17	1442	0	5	0
16	David Challinor	DEF	28	15	1350	0	1	0
17	Glenn Whelan	MID	20	13	1170	0	3	0
18	Joe O'Neill	ATT	21	23	1049	3	0	0

KEY PLAYERS - GOALSCORERS

Chris Porter

Goals in the League	9
Contribution to Attacking Power Average number of minutes between League team goals while on pitch	76
Player Strike Rate Average number of minutes between League goals scored by player	214
Club Strike Rate Average number of minutes between League goals scored by club	77

	PLAYER	LGE GOALS	POWER	STRIKE RATE
1	Chris Porter	9	76	214 mins
2	Gareth Seddon	11	76	231 mins
3	Lee Connell	6	80	348 mins
4	David Nugent	3	63	611 mins
5	Danny Swailes	4	77	911 mins

KEY PLAYERS - MIDFIELDERS

Harpal Singh

Goals in the League	2
Defensive Rating Average number of mins between League goals conceded while he was on the pitch	51
Contribution to Attacking Power Average number of minutes between League team goals while on pitch	54
Scoring Difference Defensive Rating minus Contribution to Attacking Power	-3

	PLAYER	LGE GOALS	DEF RATE	POWER	SCORE DIFF
1	Harpal Singh	2	51	54	-3 mins
2	David Flitcroft	0	72	76	-4 mins
3	Lee Duxbury	0	73	81	-8 mins
4	Glenn Whelan	0	73	84	-11 mins
5	Matthew Barrass	0	62	73	-11 mins

KEY PLAYERS - DEFENDERS

David Challinor

Goals Conceded when he was on pitch	14
Defensive Rating Ave number of mins between League goals conceded while on the pitch	96
Clean Sheets In games when he played at least 70 minutes	6
Club Defensive Rating Average number of mins between League goals conceded by the club this season.	65

	PLAYER	CON LGE	CLN SHEETS	DEF RATE
1	David Challinor	14	6	96 mins
2	Thomas Kennedy	27	8	78 mins
3	Colin Woodthorpe	51	10	68 mins
4	Danny Swailes	55	10	66 mins
5	Lee Unsworth	39	5	63 mins

KEY GOALKEEPER

Glyn Garner

Goals Conceded in the League	64
Defensive Rating Ave number of mins between League goals conceded while on the pitch.	65
Counting Games Games when he played at least 70 mins	46
Clean Sheets In games when he played at least 70 mins	12

TOP POINT EARNERS

	PLAYER	GAMES	AV PTS
1	Lee Duxbury	32	1.47
2	David Challinor	15	1.47
3	Chris Porter	15	1.47
4	Harpal Singh	18	1.44
5	Glenn Whelan	13	1.38
6	David Nugent	17	1.35
7	David Flitcroft	15	1.33
8	Gareth Seddon	22	1.32
9	Paul O'Shaughnessy	19	1.32
10	Colin Woodthorpe	37	1.24
	CLUB AVERAGE:		1.22

CAMBRIDGE UNITED

Final Position: **13th**

NICKNAME: THE U'S

KEY: ☐Won ☐Drawn ☐Lost

							Attendance
1	div3	Huddersfield	A	D	2-2	Chillingworth 18; Kitson 89	10,319
2	ccR1	Gillingham	H	L	1-2	Walker 28	3,044
3	div3	Macclesfield	H	W	3-1	Chillingworth 10,63; Revell 89	3,089
4	div3	Rochdale	A	D	2-2	Revell 32; Kitson 38	2,204
5	div3	Hull City	H	L	0-2		4,571
6	div3	Carlisle	A	D	0-0		4,571
7	div3	Lincoln	H	D	0-0		4,458
8	div3	Torquay	H	D	1-1	Guttridge 9	3,723
9	div3	Boston	A	W	2-1	Guttridge 41; Angus 88	2,452
10	div3	Cheltenham	A	W	3-0	Kitson 30,60; Opara 87	3,728
11	div3	Mansfield	H	L	1-2	Fleming 81	4,068
12	div3	Doncaster	H	D	3-3	Tudor 9; Kitson 36; Heathcote 55	3,492
13	div3	York	A	L	0-2		3,481
14	div3	Bury	H	L	1-2	Duncan 80	5,106
15	div3	Bristol Rovers	A	W	2-0	Turner 68; Walker 77	6,440
16	div3	Swansea	A	W	2-0	Kitson 1,59	6,211
17	div3	Yeovil	H	L	1-4	Kitson 44	4,072
18	div3	Kidderminster	A	D	2-2	Kitson 59; Williams 63	2,401
19	facr1	Lancaster	A	W	2-1	Kitson 16; Guttridge 90	1,864
20	div3	Oxford	H	D	1-1	Duncan 21	4,430
21	div3	Scunthorpe	A	L	0-4		3,397
22	div3	Leyton Orient	H	L	1-4	Turner 83	3,910
23	facr2	Macclesfield	A	D	1-1	Turner, J 23	2,182
24	div3	Darlington	H	W	1-0	Guttridge 45 pen	2,822
25	facr2r	Macclesfield	H	L	2-4*	Turner 66; Tann 119 (*on penalties)	2,545
26	div3	Northampton	A	W	2-1	Guttridge 28 pen; Tann 88	4,910
27	div3	Southend	H	L	0-1		5,368
28	div3	Lincoln	A	D	2-2	Guttridge 14; Webb 88	5,074
29	div3	Hull City	A	L	0-2		14,271
30	div3	Huddersfield	H	L	1-2	Tann 90	3,667
31	div3	Macclesfield	A	W	1-0	Guttridge 49	2,151
32	div3	Rochdale	H	D	0-0		3,221
33	div3	Southend	A	L	0-1		4,289
34	div3	Bury	A	L	0-1		2,322
35	div3	Carlisle	H	D	2-2	Bridges 53; Guttridge 56	3,280
36	div3	Bristol Rovers	H	W	3-1	Revell 13; Guttridge 25; Bridges 51	3,256
37	div3	Yeovil	A	L	1-4	Webb 45	5,694
38	div3	Swansea	H	L	0-1		2,713
39	div3	Northampton	H	L	0-1		4,298
40	div3	Darlington	A	W	4-3	Easter 30,65; Webb 41; Guttridge 81	5,056
41	div3	Boston	H	L	0-1		3,294
42	div3	Torquay	A	L	0-3		2,975
43	div3	Cheltenham	H	W	2-1	Turner, J 5; Tudor 10 pen	3,909
44	div3	Mansfield	A	D	1-1	Tudor 90	4,342
45	div3	York	H	W	2-0	Guttridge 24; Dunning 86 og	5,120
46	div3	Doncaster	A	L	0-2		9,644
47	div3	Kidderminster	H	D	0-0		3,765
48	div3	Oxford	A	D	2-2	Chillingworth 72,87	5,830
49	div3	Scunthorpe	H	W	3-2	Nicholls 37; Chillingworth 39,77	4,498
50	div3	Leyton Orient	A	W	1-0	Guttridge 8	5,482

TEAM OF THE SEASON

G — Shaun Marshall, CG: 45 DR: 60

D — Fred Murray, CG: 27 DR: 69

D — Mark Venus, CG: 20 DR: 66

D — Stevland Angus, CG: 37 DR: 64

D — Andrew Duncan, CG: 36 DR: 64

M — Luke Guttridge, CG: 44 SD: -12

M — Shane Tudor, CG: 29 SD: -13

M — Terry Fleming, CG: 17 SD: -14

M — Justine Walker, CG: 23 SD: 6

F — David Kitson, CG: 16 SR: 165

F — John Turner, CG: 13 SR: 824

KEY PLAYER APPEARANCES

	PLAYER	POS	AGE	APP	MINS ON	GOALS	CARDS(Y/R)	
1	Shaun Marshall	GK	25	45	4050	0	0	0
2	Luke Guttridge	MID	22	46	4016	11	3	0
3	Stevland Angus	DEF	23	40	3443	1	7	1
4	Andrew Duncan	DEF	26	37	3260	2	1	0
5	Adam Tann	DEF	22	34	2860	2	5	0
6	Fred Murray	DEF	22	38	2746	0	10	0
7	Shane Tudor	MID	22	36	2741	3	5	0
8	Warren Goodhind	DEF	26	26	2255	0	8	1
9	Justin Walker	MID	28	23	2039	1	5	0
10	Stuart Bimson	DEF	34	24	1896	0	0	0
11	Mark Venus	DEF	37	21	1858	0	2	0
12	Daniel Webb	ATT	21	21	1793	3	6	0
13	John Turner	ATT	18	35	1647	2	1	0
14	Terry Fleming	MID	31	18	1575	1	5	0
15	David Kitson	ATT	24	17	1482	9	4	1
16	Ashley Nicholls	MID	22	16	1341	1	2	0
17	David Bridges	MID	21	21	1058	2	0	0
18	Jermaine Easter	ATT	22	15	948	2	3	0

KEY PLAYERS - GOALSCORERS

David Kitson

Goals in the League	9
Contribution to Attacking Power Average number of minutes between League team goals while on pitch	70
Player Strike Rate Average number of minutes between League goals scored by player	165
Club Strike Rate Average number of minutes between League goals scored by club	75

	PLAYER	LGE GOALS	POWER	STRIKE RATE
1	David Kitson	9	70	165 mins
2	Luke Guttridge	11	73	365 mins
3	Daniel Webb	3	81	598 mins
4	John Turner	2	71	824 mins
5	Shane Tudor	3	78	914 mins

KEY PLAYERS - MIDFIELDERS

Justin Walker

Goals in the League	1
Defensive Rating Average number of mins between League goals conceded while he was on the pitch	68
Contribution to Attacking Power Average number of minutes between League team goals while on pitch	62
Scoring Difference Defensive Rating minus Contribution to Attacking Power	6

	PLAYER	LGE GOALS	DEF RATE	POWER	SCORE DIFF
1	Justin Walker	1	68	62	6 mins
2	Luke Guttridge	11	61	73	-12 mins
3	Shane Tudor	3	65	78	-13 mins
4	Terry Fleming	1	58	72	-14 mins
5	Ashley Nicholls	1	64	79	-15 mins

KEY PLAYERS - DEFENDERS

Fred Murray

Goals Conceded when he was on pitch	40
Defensive Rating Ave number of mins between League goals conceded while on the pitch	69
Clean Sheets In games when he played at least 70 minutes	7
Club Defensive Rating Average number of mins between League goals conceded by the club this season.	62

	PLAYER	CON LGE	CLN SHEETS	DEF RATE
1	Fred Murray	40	7	69 mins
2	Mark Venus	28	5	66 mins
3	Andrew Duncan	51	9	64 mins
4	Stevland Angus	54	11	64 mins
5	Warren Goodhind	38	5	59 mins

KEY GOALKEEPER

Shaun Marshall

Goals Conceded in the League	67
Defensive Rating Ave number of mins between League goals conceded while on the pitch.	60
Counting Games Games when he played at least 70 mins	45
Clean Sheets In games when he played at least 70 mins	10

TOP POINT EARNERS

	PLAYER	GAMES	AV PTS
1	John Turner	13	**1.62**
2	Justin Walker	23	**1.48**
3	Stuart Bimson	19	**1.37**
4	Stevland Angus	37	**1.32**
5	Andrew Duncan	36	**1.28**
6	Shane Tudor	29	**1.28**
7	Adam Tann	30	**1.27**
8	David Kitson	16	**1.25**
9	Luke Guttridge	44	**1.20**
10	Mark Venus	20	**1.20**
	CLUB AVERAGE:		**1.22**

CHELTENHAM

Final Position: **14th**

NICKNAME: THE ROBINS

KEY: ☐ Won ☐ Drawn ☐ Lost

							Attendance
1	div3	**Southend**	A	L	0-2		4,403
2	ccR1	**QPR**	H	L	1-2	McCann 4	3,697
3	div3	**Swansea**	H	L	3-4	Cozic 17; McCann 30,60 pen	4,660
4	div3	**Hull City**	A	D	3-3	Spencer 31,39,40	12,522
5	div3	**Kidderminster**	H	W	2-1	Victory 79; McCann 81	4,179
6	div3	**Leyton Orient**	A	W	4-1	Odejayi 23; Jones, D 32; Taylor 34,41	3,785
7	div3	**Northampton**	H	W	4-3	Taylor 56; Forsyth 76 pen,90 pen; Devaney 90	5,002
8	div3	**Bury**	A	D	1-1	Odejayi 71	2,753
9	div3	**Oxford**	H	D	0-0		5,319
10	div3	**Cambridge**	H	L	0-3		3,728
11	div3	**Bristol Rovers**	A	L	0-2		8,013
12	div3	**Scunthorpe**	A	L	2-5	Taylor 44; McCann 88 pen	2,857
13	div3	**Yeovil**	H	W	3-1	Devaney 4; Yates 15; Brayson 46	4,960
14	div3	**Boston**	A	L	1-3	McCann 23	2,283
15	div3	**Rochdale**	H	L	0-2		3,105
16	div3	**Darlington**	H	W	2-1	Victory 31; Devaney 90	2,745
17	div3	**Mansfield**	A	L	0-4		4,095
18	div3	**York**	H	D	1-1	Spencer 85	3,431
19	facr1	**Hull City**	H	W	3-1	Spencer 6; Yates 48; Brayson 90	3,624
20	div3	**Torquay**	A	L	1-3	Spencer 56	2,653
21	div3	**Carlisle**	H	W	2-1	Taylor 33; Spencer 51	3,414
22	div3	**Huddersfield**	A	D	0-0		8,442
23	facr2	**Leyton Orient**	H	W	3-1	McCann 18 pen,34; Taylor 60	3,959
24	div3	**Doncaster**	H	L	1-3	Yates 19	3,884
25	div3	**Macclesfield**	H	W	3-2	Spencer 30; Taylor 57; Devaney 73	4,237
26	div3	**Northampton**	A	L	0-1		5,118
27	facr3	**Fulham**	A	L	1-2	McCann 5	10,303
28	div3	**Southend**	H	D	1-1	Cort 87 og	4,451
29	div3	**Lincoln**	A	D	0-0		3,464
30	div3	**Swansea**	A	D	0-0		6,474
31	div3	**Hull City**	H	L	0-2		4,536
32	div3	**Leyton Orient**	H	W	1-0	Brayson 45	3,336
33	div3	**Macclesfield**	A	W	2-1	Whitaker 26 og; McCann 27	2,061
34	div3	**Kidderminster**	A	D	0-0		3,803
35	div3	**Boston**	H	W	1-0	Brough 62	3,434
36	div3	**Rochdale**	A	D	0-0		2,449
37	div3	**Mansfield**	H	W	4-2	Henry 42; Spencer 61; Brayson 70; Odejayi 90	3,818
38	div3	**Lincoln**	H	W	3-2	McCann 32; Finnigan 87; Odejayi 90	3,783
39	div3	**Darlington**	A	L	1-2	McCann 45	3,921
40	div3	**Doncaster**	A	D	1-1	Devaney 50	7,510
41	div3	**Oxford**	A	L	0-1		5,916
42	div3	**Bury**	H	L	1-2	Brayson 28	3,435
43	div3	**Cambridge**	A	L	1-2	Brayson 71	3,909
44	div3	**Bristol Rovers**	H	L	1-2	Brough 30	5,088
45	div3	**Yeovil**	A	D	0-0		6,613
46	div3	**Scunthorpe**	H	W	2-1	Brayson 45; Spencer 49	3,409
47	div3	**York**	A	W	2-0	Nogan 59 og; Brayson 90 pen	3,221
48	div3	**Torquay**	H	L	1-3	Spencer 81	4,900
49	div3	**Carlisle**	A	D	1-1	Odejayi 85	9,524
50	div3	**Huddersfield**	H	D	1-1	Duff, S 75	5,814

TEAM OF THE SEASON

G — Shane Higgs — CG: 41 DR: 64

D — Brian Wilson — CG: 14 DR: 74

D — Mike Duff — CG: 40 DR: 65

D — John Brough — CG: 20 DR: 63

D — Jamie Victory — CG: 44 DR: 59

M — Mark Yates — CG: 19 SD: -14

M — David Bird — CG: 15 SD: -6

M — Martin Devaney — CG: 31 SD: -16

M — Grant McCann — CG: 42 SD: -16

F — Damian Spencer — CG: 25 SR: 254

F — Paul Brayson — CG: 17 SR: 273

KEY PLAYER APPEARANCES

	PLAYER	POS	AGE	APP	MINS ON	GOALS	CARDS(Y/R)	
1	Jamie Victory	DEF	28	44	3960	2	1	0
2	Grant McCann	MID	24	43	3751	8	5	0
3	Shane Higgs	GK	27	41	3690	0	0	0
4	Mike Duff	DEF	26	42	3684	0	3	1
5	Martin Devaney	MID	24	40	3056	5	4	0
6	John Finnigan	MID	28	33	2855	1	7	0
7	Damian Spencer	ATT	22	36	2540	10	5	1
8	John Brough	DEF	31	26	2017	2	2	0
9	Paul Brayson	ATT	26	31	1909	7	0	0
10	Bob Taylor	ATT	37	28	1749	6	3	0
11	Mark Yates	MID	34	21	1743	2	6	0
12	David Bird	MID	19	24	1606	0	2	0
13	Kayode Odejayi	ATT	22	30	1427	5	7	0
14	Richard Forsyth	MID	33	27	1417	2	0	0
15	Brian Wilson	DEF	21	14	1260	0	1	0
16	Graham Fyfe	MID	21	20	1242	0	1	0
17	Shane Duff	DEF	22	15	1231	1	2	0
18	Darren Jones	DEF	20	14	1203	1	2	0

KEY PLAYERS - GOALSCORERS

Damian Spencer

Goals in the League	10
Contribution to Attacking Power Average number of minutes between League team goals while on pitch	74
Player Strike Rate Average number of minutes between League goals scored by player	254
Club Strike Rate Average number of minutes between League goals scored by club	73

	PLAYER	LGE GOALS	POWER	STRIKE RATE
1	Damian Spencer	10	74	254 mins
2	Paul Brayson	7	73	273 mins
3	Bob Taylor	6	67	292 mins
4	Grant McCann	8	76	469 mins
5	Martin Devaney	5	74	611 mins

KEY PLAYERS - MIDFIELDERS

Richard Forsyth

Goals in the League	2
Defensive Rating Average number of mins between League goals conceded while he was on the pitch	67
Contribution to Attacking Power Average number of minutes between League team goals while on pitch	67
Scoring Difference Defensive Rating minus Contribution to Attacking Power	0

	PLAYER	LGE GOALS	DEF RATE	POWER	SCORE DIFF
1	*Richard Forsyth	2	67	67	0 mins
2	David Bird	0	70	76	-6 mins
3	Mark Yates	2	44	58	-14 mins
4	Martin Devaney	5	59	75	-16 mins
5	Grant McCann	8	61	77	-16 mins

KEY PLAYERS - DEFENDERS

Brian Wilson

Goals Conceded when he was on pitch	17
Defensive Rating Ave number of mins between League goals conceded while on the pitch	74
Clean Sheets In games when he played at least 70 minutes	4
Club Defensive Rating Average number of mins between League goals conceded by the club this season.	58

	PLAYER	CON LGE	CLN SHEETS	DEF RATE
1	Brian Wilson	17	4	74 mins
2	Mike Duff	57	10	65 mins
3	John Brough	32	5	63 mins
4	Jamie Victory	67	10	59 mins
5	Shane Duff	21	4	59 mins

KEY GOALKEEPER

Shane Higgs

Goals Conceded in the League	58
Defensive Rating Ave number of mins between League goals conceded while on the pitch.	64
Counting Games Games when he played at least 70 mins	41
Clean Sheets In games when he played at least 70 mins	10

TOP POINT EARNERS

	PLAYER	GAMES	AV PTS
1	David Bird	15	**1.60**
2	Bob Taylor	15	**1.53**
3	Paul Brayson	17	**1.41**
4	Darren Jones	13	**1.38**
5	Shane Higgs	41	**1.34**
6	Martin Devaney	31	**1.32**
7	Mike Duff	40	**1.25**
8	Mark Yates	19	**1.21**
9	John Brough	20	**1.20**
10	Jamie Victory	44	**1.20**
	CLUB AVERAGE:		**1.22**

BRISTOL ROVERS

Final Position: **15th**

NICKNAME: THE PIRATES

KEY: ☐ Won ☐ Drawn ☐ Lost

							Attendance
1	div3	Scunthorpe	A	W	2-1	Barrett 13; Hodges 85	4,186
2	ccR1	Brighton	H	L	0-1		5,518
3	div3	Rochdale	H	D	0-0		7,575
4	div3	Carlisle	A	W	2-0	Carlisle 38,43	4,764
5	div3	Macclesfield	H	D	2-2	Tait 30; Quinn 33	7,064
6	div3	Huddersfield	A	L	1-2	Tait 90	8,486
7	div3	Kidderminster	H	W	1-0	Hodges 70	6,791
8	div3	Boston	H	W	2-0	Tait 67,80	6,845
9	div3	Torquay	A	L	1-2	Street 63	3,691
10	div3	York	A	L	1-2	Agogo 21	3,968
11	div3	Cheltenham	H	W	2-0	Tait 43; Carlisle 88 pen	8,013
12	div3	Mansfield	H	L	1-3	Tait 90 pen	8,451
13	div3	Doncaster	A	L	1-5	Haldene 61	5,439
14	div3	Darlington	A	W	4-0	Haldene 38; Savage 64; Rammell 78,90	4,268
15	div3	Cambridge	H	L	0-2		6,440
16	div3	Leyton Orient	H	D	1-1	Savage 34	5,333
17	div3	Oxford	A	D	0-0		6,644
18	div3	Swansea	A	D	0-0		7,536
19	facr1	Bournemouth	A	L	0-1		7,200
20	div3	Bury	H	L	1-2	Haldane 51	7,109
21	div3	Lincoln	A	L	1-3	Carlisle 19	3,882
22	div3	Hull City	H	W	2-1	Williams 33; Agogo 87	6,331
23	div3	Yeovil	H	L	0-1		9,812
24	div3	Southend	A	W	1-0	Savage 16	3,771
25	div3	Northampton	H	L	1-2	Carlisle 47 pen	7,695
26	div3	Kidderminster	A	L	0-1		3,411
27	div3	Scunthorpe	H	W	1-0	Carlisle 45 pen	5,789
28	div3	Macclesfield	A	L	1-2	Haldene 62	1,542
29	div3	Rochdale	A	D	2-2	Doughty 74 og; Agogo 83	2,497
30	div3	Carlisle	H	W	1-0	Carlisle 52 pen	8,485
31	div3	Northampton	A	L	0-2		5,068
32	div3	Darlington	H	L	0-3		6,011
33	div3	Huddersfield	H	D	1-1	Hyde 69	6,262
34	div3	Cambridge	A	L	1-3	Barrett 31	3,256
35	div3	Oxford	H	D	1-1	Haldane 82	6,556
36	div3	Leyton Orient	A	D	1-1	Tait 44	3,575
37	div3	Southend	H	D	1-1	Tait 15	5,625
38	div3	Yeovil	A	L	0-4		8,726
39	div3	Torquay	H	D	2-2	Tait 28; Parker 52	6,461
40	div3	Boston	A	L	0-1		2,450
41	div3	York	H	W	3-0	Williams, D 18; Barrett 20; Gibb 46	6,723
42	div3	Cheltenham	A	W	2-1	Barrett 34; Agogo 43	5,088
43	div3	Doncaster	H	L	1-2	Agogo 59	8,571
44	div3	Mansfield	A	D	0-0		4,735
45	div3	Swansea	H	W	2-1	Hyde 31; Agogo 82	7,843
46	div3	Bury	A	D	0-0		2,683
47	div3	Lincoln	H	W	3-1	Tait 7,64; Thorpe 80	8,562
48	div3	Hull City	A	L	0-3		22,562

TEAM OF THE SEASON

G — Kevin Miller — CG: 44 DR: 66

D — Sonny Parker — CG: 13 DR: 72

D — Kevin Austin — CG: 20 DR: 71

D — Robert Quinn — CG: 20 DR: 70

D — Ijah Anderson — CG: 32 DR: 69

M — Wayne Carlisle — CG: 21 SD: -2

M — Graham Hyde — CG: 31 SD: -17

M — Dave Savage — CG: 37 SD: -26

M — *Ryan Williams — CG: 19 SD: -42

F — Paul Tait — CG: 25 SR: 221

F — Lewis Haldane — CG: 14 SR: 370

KEY PLAYER APPEARANCES

	PLAYER	POS	AGE	APP	MINS ON	GOALS	CARDS(Y/R)	
1	Adam Barrett	DEF	24	45	4005	4	4	1
2	Kevin Miller	GK	35	44	3960	0	0	0
3	Christian Edwards	DEF	28	42	3644	0	4	1
4	Dave Savage	MID	30	38	3354	3	5	0
5	Ijah Anderson	DEF	28	39	3220	0	8	2
6	Graham Hyde	MID	33	37	2889	2	8	2
7	Junior Agogo	ATT	24	38	2470	6	1	0
8	Paul Tait	ATT	29	33	2426	11	5	0
9	Robert Quinn	DEF	27	36	2102	1	4	0
10	Daniel Boxall	DEF	26	24	2036	0	2	0
11	Kevin Austin	DEF	31	23	1923	0	3	0
12	Wayne Carlisle	MID	24	25	1907	7	1	0
13	Lewis Haldane	ATT	18	26	1479	4	5	0
14	Ryan Williams	MID	25	19	1353	1	0	0
15	Sonny Parker	DEF	21	15	1154	1	4	0
16	Lee Matthews	ATT	25	9	726	0	0	0
17	Aaron Lescott	MID	25	8	720	0	0	0
18	John Anderson	DEF	31	8	720	0	1	0

KEY PLAYERS - GOALSCORERS

Paul Tait

Goals in the League	11
Contribution to Attacking Power Average number of minutes between League team goals while on pitch	83
Player Strike Rate Average number of minutes between League goals scored by player	221
Club Strike Rate Average number of minutes between League goals scored by club	83

	PLAYER	LGE GOALS	POWER	STRIKE RATE
1	Paul Tait	11	83	221 mins
2	Wayne Carlisle	7	73	272 mins
3	Lewis Haldane	4	73	370 mins
4	Junior Agogo	6	85	412 mins
5	Adam Barrett	4	81	1001 mins

KEY PLAYERS - MIDFIELDERS

Wayne Carlisle

Goals in the League	7
Defensive Rating Average number of mins between League goals conceded while he was on the pitch	71
Contribution to Attacking Power Average number of minutes between League team goals while on pitch	73
Scoring Difference Defensive Rating minus Contribution to Attacking Power	-2

	PLAYER	LGE GOALS	DEF RATE	POWER	SCORE DIFF
1	Wayne Carlisle	7	71	73	-2 mins
2	Graham Hyde	2	76	93	-17 mins
3	Dave Savage	3	65	91	-26 mins
4	Ryan Williams	1	71	113	-42 mins

KEY PLAYERS - DEFENDERS

Sonny Parker

Goals Conceded when he was on pitch	16
Defensive Rating Ave number of mins between League goals conceded while on the pitch	72
Clean Sheets In games when he played at least 70 minutes	3
Club Defensive Rating Average number of mins between League goals conceded by the club this season.	68

	PLAYER	CON LGE	CLN SHEETS	DEF RATE
1	Sonny Parker	16	3	72 mins
2	Kevin Austin	27	5	71 mins
3	Robert Quinn	30	6	70 mins
4	Ijah Anderson	47	11	69 mins
5	Adam Barrett	59	13	68 mins

KEY GOALKEEPER

Kevin Miller

Goals Conceded in the League	60
Defensive Rating Ave number of mins between League goals conceded while on the pitch.	66
Counting Games Games when he played at least 70 mins	44
Clean Sheets In games when he played at least 70 mins	13

TOP POINT EARNERS

	PLAYER	GAMES	AV PTS
1	Junior Agogo	22	1.41
2	Lewis Haldane	14	1.36
3	Daniel Boxall	22	1.32
4	Christian Edwards	38	1.29
5	Wayne Carlisle	21	1.24
6	Adam Barrett	44	1.23
7	Robert Quinn	20	1.20
8	Kevin Miller	44	1.20
9	Ijah Anderson	32	1.19
10	Graham Hyde	31	1.19
	CLUB AVERAGE:		1.20

KIDDERMINSTER

Final Position: **16th**

NICKNAME: THE HARRIERS

KEY: ☐ Won ☐ Drawn ☐ Lost

	Comp	Opponent	H/A	W/D/L	Score	Scorers	Attendance
1	div3	Mansfield	H	W	2-1	Henriksen 15,74 pen	3,180
2	ccR1	Ipswich	A	L	0-0	(lost on penalties)	11,118
3	div3	Darlington	A	W	2-0	Williams, D 50; Bishop 57	11,600
4	div3	Bury	H	L	0-2		2,548
5	div3	Cheltenham	A	L	1-2	Williams, D 50	4,179
6	div3	Oxford	H	D	1-1	Willis 82	3,262
7	div3	Bristol Rovers	A	L	0-1		6,791
8	div3	Macclesfield	A	D	1-1	Williams, D 40	1,988
9	div3	Scunthorpe	H	L	0-2		2,162
10	div3	Lincoln	H	L	1-2	Dyer 11	2,462
11	div3	Hull City	A	L	1-6	Williams, J 21	13,683
12	div3	Huddersfield	A	L	0-1		8,275
13	div3	Carlisle	H	W	2-1	Bishop 56; Williams, D 83	2,488
14	div3	Southend	H	L	1-2	Melligan 84	2,429
15	div3	Swansea	A	D	0-0		6,825
16	div3	Northampton	A	W	1-0	Parrish 22	4,089
17	div3	Doncaster	H	L	0-2		3,393
18	div3	Cambridge	H	D	2-2	Parrish 41; Williams, J 80	2,401
19	facr1	Northwich	H	W	2-1	Bennett 39,84	2,052
20	div3	Rochdale	A	W	1-0	Gadsby 35	2,498
21	div3	Torquay	H	L	1-2	Williams, D 12	2,725
22	div3	Boston	A	D	2-2	Hinton 35 pen; White, A 54	2,147
23	facr2	Woking	A	W	3-0	Bennett 6,64; Burton 74	3,484
24	div3	Leyton Orient	H	W	2-1	Peters 31 og; Gadsby 66	2,605
25	div3	York	A	L	0-1		2,973
26	div3	Yeovil	A	W	2-1	Williams, J 45; Parrish 73	5,640
27	div3	Bristol Rovers	H	W	1-0	Bennett 47	3,411
28	facr3	Wolverhampton	H	D	1-1	Williams, J 77	6,005
29	div3	Mansfield	A	L	0-1		4,574
30	facr3r	Wolverhampton	A	L	0-2		25,808
31	div3	Darlington	H	D	1-1	Murray 8	2,550
32	div3	Bury	A	D	0-0		2,526
33	div3	Oxford	A	L	1-2	Murray 45	6,057
34	div3	Yeovil	H	L	0-1		3,255
35	div3	Cheltenham	H	D	0-0		3,803
36	div3	Southend	A	L	0-3		3,716
37	div3	Swansea	H	W	2-0	Foster 59; Christiansen 66	3,407
38	div3	Doncaster	A	L	0-5		7,594
39	div3	Northampton	H	W	2-1	Keates 29; Bennett 47	2,699
40	div3	York	H	W	4-1	Foster 10 pen; Bennett 35; Yates 45; Murray 67	2,569
41	div3	Leyton Orient	A	D	1-1	Yates 81 pen	3,764
42	div3	Scunthorpe	A	W	2-0	Foster 18; Keates 54	2,512
43	div3	Macclesfield	H	L	1-4	Rickards 84	2,666
44	div3	Lincoln	A	D	1-1	Brown 46	4,797
45	div3	Hull City	H	D	1-1	Brown 22	3,853
46	div3	Carlisle	A	L	0-1		7,296
47	div3	Huddersfield	H	W	2-1	Hatswell 30; Lloyd 54 og	4,051
48	div3	Cambridge	A	D	0-0		3,765
49	div3	Rochdale	H	L	0-1		3,580
50	div3	Torquay	A	D	1-1	Hatswell 73	5,515
51	div3	Boston	H	W	2-0	Bastock 22 og; Williams, J 73	3,047

TEAM OF THE SEASON

G — Stuart Brock — CG: 37 DR: 68

D — Wayne Hatswell — CG: 31 DR: 91

D — Matthew Gadsby — CG: 21 DR: 78

D — Craig Hinton — CG: 41 DR: 76

D — Scott Stamps — CG: 30 DR: 72

M — Mark Yates — CG: 14 SD: -5

M — Sean Parrish — CG: 13 SD: -9

M — Dean Bennett — CG: 32 SD: -20

M — Danny Williams — CG: 28 SD: -28

F — John Williams — CG: 20 SR: 626

F — Bo Henriksen — CG: 13 SR: 697

KEY PLAYER APPEARANCES

	PLAYER	POS	AGE	APP	MINS ON	GOALS	CARDS(Y/R)	
1	Craig Hinton	DEF	26	42	3722	1	4	0
2	Stuart Brock	GK	27	37	3330	0	3	0
3	Dean Bennett	MID	26	38	3105	3	5	0
4	Scott Stamps	DEF	29	35	2869	0	8	1
5	Wayne Hatswell	DEF	29	32	2816	2	7	0
6	Danny Williams	MID	24	28	2506	5	3	0
7	John Williams	ATT	36	44	2504	4	2	0
8	Matthew Gadsby	DEF	24	32	2183	2	3	0
9	Adam Murray	MID	22	22	1696	3	4	0
10	Adrian Smith	DEF	30	22	1639	0	0	0
11	Sean Parrish	MID	32	27	1581	3	4	0
12	Graham Ward	MID	21	21	1472	0	2	0
13	Bo Henriksen	ATT	29	22	1393	2	2	0
14	Mark Yates	MID	34	14	1250	2	3	0
15	Jesper Christiansen	ATT	24	21	1156	1	0	0
16	Adam Willis	DEF	27	12	1078	1	4	1
17	Steve Burton	DEF	21	12	896	0	1	0
18	Sam Shilton	MID	25	14	861	0	2	0

KEY PLAYERS - GOALSCORERS

Danny Williams

Goals in the League	5
Contribution to Attacking Power Average number of minutes between League team goals while on pitch	96
Player Strike Rate Average number of minutes between League goals scored by player	501
Club Strike Rate Average number of minutes between League goals scored by club	92

	PLAYER	LGE GOALS	POWER	STRIKE RATE
1	Danny Williams	5	96	501 mins
2	Sean Parrish	3	87	527 mins
3	Adam Murray	3	106	565 mins
4	Mark Yates	2	73	625 mins
5	John Williams	4	83	626 mins

KEY PLAYERS - MIDFIELDERS

Mark Yates

Goals in the League	2
Defensive Rating Average number of mins between League goals conceded while he was on the pitch	69
Contribution to Attacking Power Average number of minutes between League team goals while on pitch	74
Scoring Difference Defensive Rating minus Contribution to Attacking Power	-5

	PLAYER	LGE GOALS	DEF RATE	POWER	SCORE DIFF
1	Mark Yates	2	69	74	-5 mins
2	Sean Parrish	3	79	88	-9 mins
3	Dean Bennett	3	66	86	-20 mins
4	Danny Williams	5	68	96	-28 mins
5	Adam Murray	3	68	106	-38 mins

KEY PLAYERS - DEFENDERS

Wayne Hatswell

Goals Conceded when he was on pitch	31
Defensive Rating Ave number of mins between League goals conceded while on the pitch	91
Clean Sheets In games when he played at least 70 minutes	10
Club Defensive Rating Average number of mins between League goals conceded by the club this season.	70

	PLAYER	CON LGE	CLN SHEETS	DEF RATE
1	Wayne Hatswell	31	10	91 mins
2	Matthew Gadsby	28	7	78 mins
3	Craig Hinton	49	11	76 mins
4	Scott Stamps	40	7	72 mins
5	Adrian Smith	27	3	61 mins

KEY GOALKEEPER

Stuart Brock

Goals Conceded in the League	49
Defensive Rating Ave number of mins between League goals conceded while on the pitch.	68
Counting Games Games when he played at least 70 mins	37
Clean Sheets In games when he played at least 70 mins	9

TOP POINT EARNERS

	PLAYER	GAMES	AV PTS
1	Sean Parrish	13	**1.85**
2	John Williams	20	**1.55**
3	Mark Yates	14	**1.43**
4	Wayne Hatswell	31	**1.42**
5	Scott Stamps	30	**1.30**
6	Dean Bennett	32	**1.28**
7	Craig Hinton	41	**1.27**
8	Stuart Brock	37	**1.22**
9	Matthew Gadsby	21	**1.19**
10	Danny Williams	28	**1.11**
	CLUB AVERAGE:		**1.20**

SOUTHEND UNITED

Final Position: **17th**

NICKNAME: THE SHRIMPERS KEY: ☐ Won ☐ Drawn ☐ Lost

							Attendance
1	div3	Cheltenham	H	W	2-0	Gower 33,90 pen	4,403
2	ccR1	Swindon	H	L	2-3	Maher 11; Broughton 38	3,385
3	div3	Doncaster	A	L	0-2		5,592
4	div3	Mansfield	H	L	0-3		3,837
5	div3	York	A	L	0-2		4,202
6	div3	Bury	H	W	1-0	Constantine 89	3,172
7	div3	Oxford	A	L	0-2		5,567
8	div3	Hull City	A	L	2-3	Constantine 3; Bramble 82	12,545
9	div3	Lincoln	H	L	0-2		2,874
10	div3	Carlisle	H	D	2-2	McSweeney 23; Constantine 24	4,620
11	div3	Scunthorpe	A	D	1-1	Constantine 69	2,311
12	div3	Darlington	A	D	0-0		4,369
13	div3	Huddersfield	H	L	1-2	Odunsi 43	4,205
14	div3	Kidderminster	A	W	2-1	Warren 44; Bramble 90	2,429
15	div3	Leyton Orient	H	L	1-2	Constantine 90	6,077
16	div3	Boston	H	L	0-2		2,463
17	div3	Macclesfield	A	W	2-1	Constantine 51; Smith 59 pen	1,821
18	div3	Northampton	H	L	0-1		5,085
19	facr1	Canvey I	H	D	1-1	Gower 2	9,234
20	div3	Yeovil	A	L	0-4		5,248
21	facr1r	Canvey I	A	W	3-2	Bramble 23; Smith 46,90	2,731
22	div3	Rochdale	H	W	4-0	Bramble 34,36; Corbett 67 pen; Constantine 90	3,169
23	div3	Torquay	A	L	0-3		2,631
24	facr2	Lincoln	H	W	3-0	Bramble 39; Gower 64; Corbett 89	4,258
25	div3	Swansea	A	W	3-2	Constantine 17; Gower 45; Warren 90	5,439
26	div3	Bristol Rovers	H	L	0-1		3,771
27	div3	Cambridge	A	W	1-0	Constantine 38	5,368
28	div3	Oxford	H	L	0-1		6,449
29	facr3	Scarborough	H	D	1-1	Smith 9	6,902
30	div3	Cheltenham	A	D	1-1	Broughton 70	4,451
31	facr3r	Scarborough	A	L	0-1		4,859
32	div3	Doncaster	H	L	0-2		4,308
33	div3	Mansfield	A	L	0-1		4,292
34	div3	York	H	D	0-0		2,943
35	div3	Cambridge	H	W	1-0	Dudfield 43	4,289
36	div3	Kidderminster	H	W	3-0	Constantine 6 pen,54 pen; Hinton 79 og	3,716
37	div3	Leyton Orient	A	L	1-2	Dudfield 45	6,119
38	div3	Bury	A	D	1-1	Constantine 27	1,670
39	div3	Macclesfield	H	W	1-0	Dudfield 83	4,107
40	div3	Boston	A	W	2-0	Bentley 6; Jenkins 65	2,780
41	div3	Bristol Rovers	A	D	1-1	Gower 81	5,625
42	div3	Swansea	H	D	1-1	Dudfield 66	4,753
43	div3	Lincoln	A	D	2-2	Constantine 30,36	3,943
44	div3	Carlisle	A	W	2-1	Constantine 50,77 pen	6,173
45	div3	Scunthorpe	H	W	4-2	Constantine 26,86; Broughton 28; Cort 40	4,976
46	div3	Huddersfield	A	L	0-1		10,680
47	div3	Darlington	H	W	3-2	Bentley 46; Constantine 73 pen; Gower 85	5,132
48	div3	Northampton	A	D	2-2	Constantine 16 pen; Reid 45 og	5,919
49	div3	Hull City	H	D	2-2	Gower 34; Maher 45	5,389
50	div3	Yeovil	H	L	0-2		5,676
51	div3	Rochdale	A	D	1-1	Constantine 48	3,591
52	div3	Torquay	H	L	1-2	Dudfield 17	8,894

TEAM OF THE SEASON

G — Darryl Flahavan — CG: 37 DR: 71

D — Jamie Stuart — CG: 20 DR: 73
D — Duncan Jupp — CG: 38 DR: 69
D — Leon Cort — CG: 46 DR: 66
D — Mark Warren — CG: 24 DR: 65

M — Mark Bentley — CG: 13 SD: 0
M — Kevin Maher — CG: 42 SD: -9
M — Mark Gower — CG: 38 SD: -11
M — Lewis Hunt — CG: 20 SD: -11

F — Leon Constantine — CG: 37 SR: 170
F — Lawrie Dudfield — CG: 13 SR: 227

KEY PLAYER APPEARANCES

	PLAYER	POS	AGE	APP	MINS ON	GOALS	CARDS(Y/R)	
1	Leon Cort	DEF	24	46	4140	1	1	0
2	Kevin Maher	MID	27	42	3780	1	10	1
3	Leon Constantine	ATT	26	43	3577	21	0	0
4	Mark Gower	MID	25	40	3486	6	6	1
5	Duncan Jupp	DEF	29	40	3473	0	5	0
6	Darryl Flahavan	GK	25	37	3330	0	0	0
7	Mark Warren	DEF	29	33	2396	2	5	0
8	Drew Broughton	ATT	25	35	2352	2	7	1
9	Lewis Hunt	MID	21	26	2022	0	5	0
10	Jamie Stuart	DEF	27	25	1910	0	2	0
11	Tesfaye Bramble	ATT	23	34	1571	4	4	0
12	David McSweeney	DEF	22	21	1519	1	4	1
13	Mark Bentley	MID	26	21	1373	2	1	0
14	Jay Smith	MID	22	18	1312	1	3	1
15	Jim Corbett	ATT	24	17	1164	1	3	0
16	Lawrie Dudfield	ATT	24	13	1137	5	1	0
17	Che Wilson	MID	25	14	1040	0	1	0
18	Leke Odunsi	MID	23	12	1032	1	1	0

KEY PLAYERS - GOALSCORERS

Leon Constantine

Goals in the League	21
Contribution to Attacking Power Average number of minutes between League team goals while on pitch	81
Player Strike Rate Average number of minutes between League goals scored by player	170
Club Strike Rate Average number of minutes between League goals scored by club	81

	PLAYER	LGE GOALS	POWER	STRIKE RATE
1	Leon Constantine	21	81	170 mins
2	Lawrie Dudfield	5	66	227 mins
3	Tesfaye Bramble	4	65	393 mins
4	Mark Gower	6	81	581 mins
5	Mark Bentley	2	62	687 mins

KEY PLAYERS - MIDFIELDERS

Mark Bentley

Goals in the League	2
Defensive Rating Average number of mins between League goals conceded while he was on the pitch	62
Contribution to Attacking Power Average number of minutes between League team goals while on pitch	62
Scoring Difference Defensive Rating minus Contribution to Attacking Power	0

	PLAYER	LGE GOALS	DEF RATE	POWER	SCORE DIFF
1	Mark Bentley	2	62	62	0 mins
2	Kevin Maher	1	70	79	-9 mins
3	Lewis Hunt	0	61	72	-11 mins
4	Mark Gower	6	70	81	-11 mins
5	Jay Smith	1	66	101	-35 mins

KEY PLAYERS - DEFENDERS

Jamie Stuart

Goals Conceded when he was on pitch	26
Defensive Rating Ave number of mins between League goals conceded while on the pitch	73
Clean Sheets In games when he played at least 70 minutes	5
Club Defensive Rating Average number of mins between League goals conceded by the club this season.	66

	PLAYER	CON LGE	CLN SHEETS	DEF RATE
1	Jamie Stuart	26	5	73 mins
2	Duncan Jupp	50	8	69 mins
3	Leon Cort	63	10	66 mins
4	Mark Warren	37	6	65 mins
5	David McSweeney	30	4	51 mins

KEY GOALKEEPER

Darryl Flahavan

Goals Conceded in the League	47
Defensive Rating Ave number of mins between League goals conceded while on the pitch.	71
Counting Games Games when he played at least 70 mins	37
Clean Sheets In games when he played at least 70 mins	8

TOP POINT EARNERS

	PLAYER	GAMES	AV PTS
1	Lawrie Dudfield	13	**1.38**
2	Leon Constantine	37	**1.30**
3	Mark Warren	24	**1.29**
4	Darryl Flahavan	37	**1.27**
5	David McSweeney	15	**1.27**
6	Mark Gower	38	**1.26**
7	Drew Broughton	20	**1.25**
8	Jay Smith	13	**1.23**
9	Mark Bentley	13	**1.23**
10	Kevin Maher	42	**1.21**
	CLUB AVERAGE:		**1.17**

DARLINGTON

Final Position: **18th**

NICKNAME: THE QUAKERS

KEY: □ Won □ Drawn □ Lost

							Attendance
1	div3	**Hull City**	A	L	1-4	Conlon 41	14,675
2	ccR1	**Bradford**	A	W	0-0*	(*on penalties)	4,077
3	div3	**Kidderminster**	H	L	0-2		11,600
4	div3	**Northampton**	A	L	0-1		5,020
5	div3	**Leyton Orient**	H	W	2-1	Clarke, M 79; Hughes 90	4,660
6	div3	**Rochdale**	A	L	2-4	McGurk 30; Pearson 43	2,518
7	div3	**Carlisle**	H	W	2-0	Conlon 7,14	5,889
8	div3	**Doncaster**	H	W	2-1	Wainwright 59,67	5,518
9	div3	**York**	A	D	1-1	Conlon 45	3,867
10	div3	**Torquay**	A	D	2-2	Liddle, C 13; Clark 72	2,420
11	ccR2	**Wolverhampton**	A	L	0-2		10,232
12	div3	**Boston**	H	W	3-0	Liddle, C 65; Clarke, M 72; Clark 78	4,519
13	div3	**Southend**	H	D	0-0		4,369
14	div3	**Mansfield**	A	L	1-3	Clark 45	4,621
15	div3	**Bristol Rovers**	H	L	0-4		4,268
16	div3	**Yeovil**	A	L	0-1		4,892
17	div3	**Cheltenham**	A	L	1-2	Morgan 42	2,745
18	div3	**Bury**	H	L	1-3	Liddle, C 4	3,516
19	div3	**Oxford**	A	L	1-3	McGurk 23	4,962
20	facr1	**Hornchurch**	A	L	0-2		2,186
21	div3	**Lincoln**	H	D	0-0		4,601
22	div3	**Swansea**	A	L	0-1		5,651
23	div3	**Scunthorpe**	H	D	2-2	Conlon 39; Wainwright 59	3,606
24	div3	**York**	H	W	3-0	Conlon 11; Wainwright 35; James 78	4,115
25	div3	**Cambridge**	A	L	0-1		2,822
26	div3	**Macclesfield**	H	L	0-1		2,920
27	div3	**Huddersfield**	H	L	0-1		6,205
28	div3	**Carlisle**	A	D	1-1	Matthews 40	8,369
29	div3	**Leyton Orient**	A	L	0-1		3,737
30	div3	**Hull City**	H	L	0-1		6,847
31	div3	**Kidderminster**	A	D	1-1	McGurk 90	2,550
32	div3	**Rochdale**	H	W	1-0	Hughes 81	5,689
33	div3	**Huddersfield**	A	W	2-0	Clark, I 21 pen; Maddison 54	11,014
34	div3	**Bristol Rovers**	A	W	3-0	Liddle, C 74; Conlon 80,90	6,011
35	div3	**Northampton**	H	L	1-2	Willmott 47 og	4,764
36	div3	**Yeovil**	H	W	3-2	Conlon 20; Wainwright 33,80	4,500
37	div3	**Bury**	A	D	1-1	Conlon 19	2,766
38	div3	**Macclesfield**	A	W	1-0	Russell 53	2,293
39	div3	**Cheltenham**	H	W	2-1	McGurk 14; Conlon 39	3,921
40	div3	**Cambridge**	H	L	3-4	Convery 26; Keltie 86; Clarke, M 86	5,056
41	div3	**Doncaster**	A	D	1-1	Convery 59	7,178
42	div3	**Torquay**	H	D	1-1	Conlon 2	4,317
43	div3	**Boston**	A	L	0-1		2,573
44	div3	**Mansfield**	H	W	1-0	Clarke, M 48	4,946
45	div3	**Southend**	A	L	2-3	Graham 6; Valentine 33 pen	5,132
46	div3	**Oxford**	H	W	2-0	Valentine 26; Conlon 71	4,212
47	div3	**Lincoln**	A	D	1-1	Wainwright 37	6,187
48	div3	**Swansea**	H	L	1-2	Graham 65	5,487
49	div3	**Scunthorpe**	A	W	1-0	Conlon 5	4,801

TEAM OF THE SEASON

G — Michael Price, CG: 36 DR: 72

D — Matthew Clarke, CG: 42 DR: 69

D — Ryan Valentine, CG: 30 DR: 69

D — Craig Liddle, CG: 43 DR: 67

D — David McGurk, CG: 21 DR: 53

M — Neil Wainwright, CG: 26 SD: 7

M — Chris Hughes, CG: 21 SD: -3

M — Jonathan Hutchinson, CG: 36 SD: -3

M — Neil Maddison, CG: 27 SD: -19

F — Barry Conlon, CG: 36 SR: 238

F — Ian Clark, CG: 19 SR: 529

KEY PLAYER APPEARANCES

	PLAYER	POS	AGE	APP	MINS ON	GOALS	CARDS(Y/R)	
1	Matthew Clarke	DEF	23	45	3885	4	5	0
2	Craig Liddle	DEF	32	43	3870	4	7	0
3	Jonathan Hutchinson	MID	22	39	3384	0	6	1
4	Barry Conlon	ATT	25	39	3329	14	3	1
5	Michael Price	GK	21	36	3240	0	2	0
6	Ryan Valentine	DEF	21	40	2962	2	7	1
7	Neil Wainwright	MID	26	35	2612	7	4	0
8	Neil Maddison	MID	34	32	2516	1	1	0
9	Ashley Nicholls	MID	22	26	2146	0	3	0
10	Chris Hughes	MID	20	30	2142	2	6	0
11	Ian Clark	ATT	29	34	2114	4	1	0
12	David McGurk	DEF	21	27	2030	4	7	2
13	Clark Keltie	MID	20	30	2019	1	4	0
14	Mark Convery	ATT	23	25	1448	2	1	0
15	Gary Pearson	MID	27	18	962	1	5	2
16	Craig James	DEF	21	10	880	1	2	0
17	Brian Close	MID	22	12	824	0	3	0
18	Neil Teggart	ATT	19	15	813	0	1	1

KEY PLAYERS - GOALSCORERS

Barry Conlon

Goals in the League	14
Contribution to Attacking Power Average number of minutes between League team goals while on pitch	67
Player Strike Rate Average number of minutes between League goals scored by player	238
Club Strike Rate Average number of minutes between League goals scored by club	78

	PLAYER	LGE GOALS	POWER	STRIKE RATE
1	Barry Conlon	14	67	238 mins
2	Neil Wainwright	7	76	373 mins
3	David McGurk	4	67	508 mins
4	Ian Clark	4	75	529 mins
5	Mark Convery	2	62	724 mins

KEY PLAYERS - MIDFIELDERS

Neil Wainwright

Goals in the League	7
Defensive Rating Average number of mins between League goals conceded while he was on the pitch	84
Contribution to Attacking Power Average number of minutes between League team goals while on pitch	77
Scoring Difference Defensive Rating minus Contribution to Attacking Power	7

	PLAYER	LGE GOALS	DEF RATE	POWER	SCORE DIFF
1	Neil Wainwright	7	84	77	7 mins
2	Jonathan Hutchinson	0	72	75	-3 mins
3	Chris Hughes	2	71	74	-3 mins
4	Neil Maddison	1	74	93	-19 mins
5	Clark Keltie	1	58	78	-20 mins

KEY PLAYERS - DEFENDERS

Ryan Valentine

Goals Conceded when he was on pitch	43
Defensive Rating Ave number of mins between League goals conceded while on the pitch	69
Clean Sheets In games when he played at least 70 minutes	9
Club Defensive Rating Average number of mins between League goals conceded by the club this season.	68

	PLAYER	CON LGE	CLN SHEETS	DEF RATE
1	Ryan Valentine	43	9	69 mins
2	Matthew Clarke	56	12	69 mins
3	Craig Liddle	58	10	67 mins
4	David McGurk	38	5	53 mins

KEY GOALKEEPER

Michael Price

Goals Conceded in the League	45
Defensive Rating Ave number of mins between League goals conceded while on the pitch.	72
Counting Games Games when he played at least 70 mins	36
Clean Sheets In games when he played at least 70 mins	10

TOP POINT EARNERS

	PLAYER	GAMES	AV PTS
1	Mark Convery	13	**2.08**
2	Barry Conlon	36	**1.44**
3	Chris Hughes	21	**1.33**
4	Neil Wainwright	26	**1.27**
5	Matthew Clarke	42	**1.24**
6	Ryan Valentine	30	**1.23**
7	Ian Clark	19	**1.21**
8	Jonathan Hutchinson	36	**1.19**
9	David McGurk	21	**1.19**
10	Michael Price	36	**1.14**
	CLUB AVERAGE:		**1.15**

LEYTON ORIENT

Final Position: **19th**

NICKNAME: THE O'S

KEY: Won / Drawn / Lost

#	Comp	Opponent	H/A	Res	Score	Scorers	Attendance
1	div3	Doncaster	H	L	1-3	Lockwood 77 pen	5,194
2	ccR1	Cardiff	A	L	1-4	Ibehre 75	4,503
3	div3	Mansfield	A	D	1-1	Alexander 90	3,920
4	div3	Yeovil	H	W	2-0	Thorpe 4; Brazier 78	4,431
5	div3	Darlington	A	L	1-2	Thorpe 59	4,660
6	div3	Cheltenham	H	L	1-4	Purser 29	3,785
7	div3	Torquay	A	L	1-2	Newey 86	2,362
8	div3	Lincoln	A	D	0-0		3,940
9	div3	Hull City	H	D	1-1	Hunt 45	3,728
10	div3	Scunthorpe	H	D	1-1	Ibehre 90	3,663
11	div3	Huddersfield	A	L	0-3		8,942
12	div3	Carlisle	A	W	1-0	Ibehre 66	4,650
13	div3	Macclesfield	H	W	2-0	McGhee 14; Alexander 25	3,585
14	div3	Swansea	H	L	1-2	Tate 88	4,393
15	div3	Southend	A	W	2-1	Alexander 27; McSweeney 89 og	6,077
16	div3	Bristol Rovers	A	D	1-1	Ibehre 80	5,333
17	div3	Northampton	H	D	1-1	Alexander 89	4,130
18	div3	Rochdale	H	W	2-1	Lockwood 23 pen; Alexander 88	3,623
19	facr1	Grantham	A	W	2-1	Purser 17; Alexander 90	2,792
20	div3	Boston	A	L	0-3		2,619
21	div3	York	H	D	2-2	Miller 4; Thorpe 35	3,593
22	div3	Cambridge	A	W	4-1	Purser 17,45; Thorpe 34; Miller 54	3,910
23	facr2	Cheltenham	A	L	1-3	Lockwood 69	3,959
24	div3	Kidderminster	A	L	1-2	Zakauni 7	2,605
25	div3	Bury	H	W	2-0	Zakauni 60; Alexander 61	3,475
26	div3	Oxford	A	L	1-2	Alexander 26	9,477
27	div3	Torquay	H	D	0-0		4,288
28	div3	Darlington	H	W	1-0	Toner 9	3,737
29	div3	Doncaster	A	L	0-5		6,293
30	div3	Mansfield	H	W	3-1	Alexander 6,82; Newey 70	4,072
31	div3	Yeovil	A	W	2-1	Peters 25; Alexander 29	6,299
32	div3	Cheltenham	A	L	0-1		3,336
33	div3	Oxford	H	W	1-0	Alexander 64	5,433
34	div3	Southend	H	W	2-1	Broughton 67 og; Bramble 81 og	6,119
35	div3	Swansea	A	L	1-2	Purser 31	4,727
36	div3	Northampton	A	L	0-1		5,784
37	div3	Bristol Rovers	H	D	1-1	Ibehre 47	3,575
38	div3	Bury	A	D	1-1	Mackie 73	2,355
39	div3	Kidderminster	H	D	1-1	Alexander 24	3,764
40	div3	Hull City	A	L	0-3		15,531
41	div3	Lincoln	H	L	0-2		3,637
42	div3	Scunthorpe	A	D	1-1	Purser 80	2,822
43	div3	Huddersfield	H	D	1-1	Alexander 5	4,137
44	div3	Macclesfield	A	L	0-1		2,156
45	div3	Carlisle	H	D	1-1	Alexander 69	4,182
46	div3	Rochdale	A	L	0-3		2,417
47	div3	Boston	H	L	1-3	Scott 87	3,580
48	div3	York	A	W	2-1	Peters 28; Alexander 45	3,462
49	div3	Cambridge	H	L	0-1		5,482

TEAM OF THE SEASON

- G — Lee Harrison, CG: 19 DR: 65
- D — David Hunt, CG: 36 DR: 69
- D — John Mackie, CG: 20 DR: 67
- D — Mark Peters, CG: 38 DR: 67
- D — Matthew Joseph, CG: 21 DR: 64
- M — Tom Newey, CG: 24 SD: -5
- M — Jabo Ibehre, CG: 15 SD: -8
- M — Matthew Lockwood, CG: 22 SD: -12
- M — Justin Miller, CG: 24 SD: -24
- F — Gary Alexander, CG: 42 SR: 257
- F — Wayne Purser, CG: 25 SR: 517

KEY PLAYER APPEARANCES

	PLAYER	POS	AGE	APP	MINS ON	GOALS	CARDS(Y	/R)
1	Gary Alexander	ATT	24	44	3851	15	6	0
2	David Hunt	DEF	21	43	3502	1	14	1
3	Mark Peters	DEF	32	39	3435	2	5	0
4	Wayne Purser	ATT	24	40	2587	5	2	0
5	Tom Newey	MID	21	34	2524	2	4	0
6	Glenn Morris	GK	20	27	2384	0	2	1
7	Justin Miller	MID	23	34	2383	2	1	0
8	Billy Jones	DEF	21	31	2373	0	5	0
9	Matthew Lockwood	MID	27	25	2120	2	3	0
10	Matthew Joseph	DEF	31	24	1972	0	6	0
11	Ciaran Toner	MID	23	27	1834	1	1	1
12	Jabo Ibehre	MID	21	35	1810	4	4	0
13	John Mackie	DEF	28	20	1800	1	9	0
14	Lee Harrison	GK	32	20	1757	0	0	0
15	Donny Barnard	DEF	20	23	1600	0	3	0
16	Lee Thorpe	ATT	28	17	1129	4	6	1
17	Marcus Ebdon	MID	33	14	883	0	2	0
18	David McGhee	DEF	28	10	870	1	0	0

KEY PLAYERS - GOALSCORERS

Gary Alexander

Goals in the League	15
Contribution to Attacking Power Average number of minutes between League team goals while on pitch	87
Player Strike Rate Average number of minutes between League goals scored by player	257
Club Strike Rate Average number of minutes between League goals scored by club	86

	PLAYER	LGE GOALS	POWER	STRIKE RATE
1	Gary Alexander	15	87	257 mins
2	Jabo Ibehre	4	69	453 mins
3	Wayne Purser	5	86	517 mins
4	Matthew Lockwood	2	75	1060 mins
5	Justin Miller	2	76	1192 mins

KEY PLAYERS - MIDFIELDERS

Tom Newey

Goals in the League	2
Defensive Rating Average number of mins between League goals conceded while he was on the pitch	76
Contribution to Attacking Power Average number of minutes between League team goals while on pitch	81
Scoring Difference Defensive Rating minus Contribution to Attacking Power	-5

	PLAYER	LGE GOALS	DEF RATE	POWER	SCORE DIFF
1	Tom Newey	2	76	81	-5 mins
2	Jabo Ibehre	4	62	70	-8 mins
3	Matthew Lockwood	2	64	76	-12 mins
4	Justin Miller	2	53	77	-24 mins
5	Ciaran Toner	1	61	108	-47 mins

KEY PLAYERS - DEFENDERS

David Hunt

Goals Conceded when he was on pitch	51
Defensive Rating Ave number of mins between League goals conceded while on the pitch	69
Clean Sheets In games when he played at least 70 minutes	7
Club Defensive Rating Average number of mins between League goals conceded by the club this season.	64

	PLAYER	CON LGE	CLN SHEETS	DEF RATE
1	David Hunt	51	7	69 mins
2	John Mackie	27	1	67 mins
3	Mark Peters	51	7	67 mins
4	Matthew Joseph	31	5	64 mins

KEY GOALKEEPER

Lee Harrison

Goals Conceded in the League	27
Defensive Rating Ave number of mins between League goals conceded while on the pitch.	65
Counting Games Games when he played at least 70 mins	20
Clean Sheets In games when he played at least 70 mins	4

TOP POINT EARNERS

	PLAYER	GAMES	AV PTS
1	Tom Newey	24	1.58
2	Jabo Ibehre	15	1.33
3	Matthew Lockwood	22	1.32
4	Ciaran Toner	17	1.29
5	Billy Jones	23	1.26
6	Mark Peters	38	1.26
7	David Hunt	36	1.25
8	Matthew Joseph	21	1.24
9	Wayne Purser	25	1.20
10	Glenn Morris	26	1.19
	CLUB AVERAGE:		1.15

MACCLESFIELD

Final Position: **20th**

NICKNAME: THE SILKMEN

KEY: ☐ Won ☐ Drawn ☐ Lost

	Comp	Opponent	H/A	Res	Score	Scorers	Attendance
1	div3	**Boston**	H	D	0-0		2,222
2	ccR1	**Sheff Utd**	H	L	1-2	Whitaker 45	2,764
3	div3	**Cambridge**	A	L	1-3	Carruthers 61	3,089
4	div3	**Torquay**	H	D	1-1	Miles 8	1,970
5	div3	**Bristol Rovers**	A	D	2-2	Miles 2; Anderson 15 og	7,064
6	div3	**Yeovil**	H	W	4-1	Carruthers 8,78; Whitaker 21,90	2,221
7	div3	**Mansfield**	A	L	2-3	Tipton 14; Miles 38	4,209
8	div3	**Kidderminster**	H	D	1-1	Little 90	1,988
9	div3	**Swansea**	A	L	0-3		6,641
10	div3	**Northampton**	A	D	0-0		4,332
11	div3	**York**	H	D	0-0		2,311
12	div3	**Rochdale**	H	W	2-1	Burgess 67 og; Whitaker 74	2,152
13	div3	**Leyton Orient**	A	L	0-2		3,585
14	div3	**Doncaster**	H	L	1-3	Carruthers 17	2,831
15	div3	**Carlisle**	A	W	1-0	Tipton 68	4,366
16	div3	**Lincoln**	A	L	2-3	Tipton 55,79	3,441
17	div3	**Southend**	H	L	1-2	Little 90	1,821
18	div3	**Hull City**	A	D	2-2	Carruthers 6; Whitaker 90	15,053
19	facr1	**Boston**	H	W	3-0	Carruthers 20,61; Little 90	2,059
20	div3	**Scunthorpe**	H	D	2-2	Whitaker 39; Tipton 86	2,205
21	div3	**Oxford**	A	L	1-3	Priest 4	6,676
22	div3	**Bury**	H	W	1-0	Tipton 25	2,312
23	facr2	**Cambridge**	H	D	1-1	Tipton 22 pen	2,182
24	div3	**Huddersfield**	H	W	4-0	Tipton 13,76 pen; Miles 64; Priest 88	3,059
25	facr2r	**Cambridge**	A	W	4-2*	Miles 26; Tipton 101 (*on penalties)	2,545
26	div3	**Darlington**	A	W	1-0	Brackenridge 62	2,920
27	div3	**Cheltenham**	A	L	2-3	Brackenridge 83; Haddrell 86	4,237
28	div3	**Mansfield**	H	D	1-1	Tipton 90	3,578
29	facr3	**Swansea**	A	L	1-2	Tipton 65	8,112
30	div3	**Boston**	A	L	1-3	Little 61	2,300
31	div3	**Bristol Rovers**	H	W	2-1	Little 42; Miles 73	1,542
32	div3	**Cambridge**	H	L	0-1		2,151
33	div3	**Torquay**	A	L	1-4	Little 45	2,770
34	div3	**Yeovil**	A	D	2-2	Tipton 20 pen; Carruthers 39	5,257
35	div3	**Cheltenham**	H	L	1-2	Miles 10	2,061
36	div3	**Doncaster**	A	L	0-1		5,525
37	div3	**Carlisle**	H	D	1-1	Potter 29	3,256
38	div3	**Southend**	A	L	0-1		4,107
39	div3	**Darlington**	H	L	0-1		2,293
40	div3	**Huddersfield**	A	L	0-4		9,729
41	div3	**Swansea**	H	W	2-1	Tipton 8; Harsley 68	1,513
42	div3	**Kidderminster**	A	W	4-1	Tipton 5 pen,78; Carruthers 29; Harsley 37	2,666
43	div3	**Northampton**	H	L	0-4		2,634
44	div3	**Lincoln**	H	D	0-0		2,016
45	div3	**York**	A	W	2-0	Parkin 19; Potter 27	3,855
46	div3	**Leyton Orient**	H	W	1-0	Carruthers 60	2,156
47	div3	**Rochdale**	A	W	2-1	Tipton 62,82 pen	4,942
48	div3	**Hull City**	H	D	1-1	Tipton 64	3,801
49	div3	**Scunthorpe**	A	L	0-1		4,334
50	div3	**Oxford**	H	W	2-1	Ashton 17 og; Louis 44 og	2,763
51	div3	**Bury**	A	L	0-2		3,569

TEAM OF THE SEASON

G – Boaz Myhill CG: 15 DR: 61

D – George Abbey CG: 21 DR: 75

D – Matthew Carragher CG: 16 DR: 73

D – Graham Potter CG: 16 DR: 72

D – *Steve Payne CG: 12 DR: 75

M – Chris Priest CG: 26 SD: 4

M – Tommy Widdrington CG: 34 SD: -16

M – Karl Munroe CG: 35 SD: -21

M – Danny Whitaker CG: 33 SD: -21

F – Matthew Tipton CG: 29 SR: 183

F – Colin Little CG: 14 SR: 329

KEY PLAYER APPEARANCES

	PLAYER	POS	AGE	APP	MINS ON	GOALS	CARDS(Y	/R)
1	Karl Munroe	MID	24	36	3170	0	8	1
2	Michael Welch	DEF	22	38	3075	0	6	1
3	Tommy Widdrington	MID	32	35	3062	0	6	0
4	Danny Whitaker	MID	23	36	3032	5	1	0
5	Matthew Tipton	ATT	24	38	2930	16	5	1
6	Martin Carruthers	ATT	31	39	2907	8	6	0
7	Steve Wilson	GK	30	32	2791	0	1	0
8	Daniel Adams	DEF	28	27	2418	0	4	1
9	Chris Priest	MID	30	29	2358	2	6	1
10	John Miles	ATT	22	29	2057	6	1	0
11	George Abbey	DEF	25	25	2037	0	1	0
12	Colin Little	ATT	31	24	1644	5	1	0
13	Matthew Carragher	DEF	28	18	1528	0	2	1
14	Graham Potter	DEF	29	16	1440	2	1	0
15	Boaz Myhill	GK	21	15	1349	0	1	0
16	Paul Harsley	MID	26	16	1333	2	1	0
17	Steven Macauley	DEF	35	16	1331	0	2	0
18	David Flitcroft	MID	30	15	1174	0	2	0

KEY PLAYERS - GOALSCORERS

Matthew Tipton

Goals in the League	16
Contribution to Attacking Power Average number of minutes between League team goals while on pitch	69
Player Strike Rate Average number of minutes between League goals scored by player	183
Club Strike Rate Average number of minutes between League goals scored by club	77

	PLAYER	LGE GOALS	POWER	STRIKE RATE
1	Matthew Tipton	16	69	183 mins
2	Colin Little	5	74	329 mins
3	John Miles	6	73	343 mins
4	Martin Carruthers	8	74	363 mins

KEY PLAYERS - MIDFIELDERS

Chris Priest

Goals in the League	2
Defensive Rating Average number of mins between League goals conceded while he was on the pitch	66
Contribution to Attacking Power Average number of minutes between League team goals while on pitch	62
Scoring Difference Defensive Rating minus Contribution to Attacking Power	4

	PLAYER	LGE GOALS	DEF RATE	POWER	SCORE DIFF
1	Chris Priest	2	66	62	4 mins
2	Tommy Widdrington	0	65	81	-16 mins
3	Danny Whitaker	5	57	78	-21 mins
4	Karl Munroe	0	60	81	-21 mins

KEY PLAYERS - DEFENDERS

Steve Payne

Goals Conceded when he was on pitch	15
Defensive Rating Ave number of mins between League goals conceded while on the pitch	75
Clean Sheets In games when he played at least 70 minutes	3
Club Defensive Rating Average number of mins between League goals conceded by the club this season.	60

	PLAYER	CON LGE	CLN SHEETS	DEF RATE
1	Steve Payne	15	3	75 mins
2	George Abbey	27	7	75 mins
3	Matthew Carragher	21	4	73 mins
4	Graham Potter	20	3	72 mins
5	Michael Welch	47	9	65 mins

KEY GOALKEEPER

Boaz Myhill

Goals Conceded in the League	22
Defensive Rating Ave number of mins between League goals conceded while on the pitch.	61
Counting Games Games when he played at least 70 mins	15
Clean Sheets In games when he played at least 70 mins	4

TOP POINT EARNERS

	PLAYER	GAMES	AV PTS
1	Steve Payne	12	**1.67**
2	George Abbey	21	**1.43**
3	Chris Priest	26	**1.42**
4	Michael Welch	31	**1.32**
5	Paul Harsley	13	**1.31**
6	Matthew Carragher	16	**1.31**
7	Graham Potter	16	**1.31**
8	Matthew Tipton	29	**1.28**
9	Tommy Widdrington	34	**1.24**
10	Steve Wilson	31	**1.19**
	CLUB AVERAGE:		**1.13**

ROCHDALE

Final Position: **21st**

NICKNAME: THE DALE

KEY: ☐ Won ☐ Drawn ☐ Lost

	Comp	Opponent	H/A	Res	Score	Scorers	Attendance
1	div3	**Yeovil**	H	L	1-3	Connor 45	4,611
2	div3	**Bristol Rovers**	A	D	0-0		7,575
3	ccR1	**Stoke**	A	L	1-2	Townson 76	4,687
4	div3	**Cambridge**	H	D	2-2	McEvilly 67 pen; Connor 79	2,204
5	div3	**Torquay**	A	W	3-1	McEvilly 59 pen; Betts 63,78	3,003
6	div3	**Darlington**	H	W	4-2	McEvilly 37 pen,41; Connor 59; Bertos 65	2,518
7	div3	**York**	A	W	2-1	Townson 15; Bertos 19	3,982
8	div3	**Carlisle**	A	L	2-3	Connor 76; Townson 79	4,532
9	div3	**Huddersfield**	H	D	1-1	Connor 1	4,626
10	div3	**Hull City**	H	L	0-2		4,215
11	div3	**Lincoln**	A	D	1-1	Antoine-Curier 40	4,141
12	div3	**Macclesfield**	A	L	1-2	Shuker 51	2,152
13	div3	**Scunthorpe**	H	W	2-0	Bertos 82; Brannan 89 pen	2,838
14	div3	**Northampton**	H	D	1-1	Townson 72	2,710
15	div3	**Cheltenham**	A	W	2-0	Townson 32; Bertos 85	3,105
16	div3	**Doncaster**	A	L	1-2	Townson 4	5,890
17	div3	**Swansea**	H	L	0-1		2,646
18	div3	**Leyton Orient**	A	L	1-2	McEvilly 59 pen	3,623
19	facr1	**Bury**	A	W	2-1	Bertos 27; Townson 50	5,464
20	div3	**Kidderminster**	H	L	0-1		2,498
21	div3	**Southend**	A	L	0-4		3,169
22	div3	**Oxford**	H	L	1-2	Jones, Gary 54	2,282
23	facr2	**Luton**	H	L	0-2		2,807
24	div3	**Bury**	A	W	2-1	Bishop 18; Townson 83	3,646
25	div3	**Boston**	H	W	1-0	Griffiths 42	2,049
26	div3	**Mansfield**	A	L	0-1		6,963
27	div3	**York**	H	L	1-2	Townson 49 pen	2,764
28	div3	**Torquay**	H	W	1-0	Townson 36 pen	2,559
29	div3	**Yeovil**	A	L	0-1		5,806
30	div3	**Bristol Rovers**	H	D	2-2	McCourt 20; Townson 37	2,497
31	div3	**Cambridge**	A	D	0-0		3,221
32	div3	**Darlington**	A	L	0-1		5,689
33	div3	**Mansfield**	H	W	3-0	Jones, Gary 12 pen; Connor 27; Bertos 54	3,157
34	div3	**Northampton**	A	L	1-3	Townson 32	4,540
35	div3	**Cheltenham**	H	D	0-0		2,449
36	div3	**Boston**	A	L	0-2		2,466
37	div3	**Swansea**	A	D	1-1	Bertos 26	5,819
38	div3	**Bury**	H	D	0-0		4,225
39	div3	**Huddersfield**	A	D	1-1	Bertos 39	10,884
40	div3	**Carlisle**	H	W	2-0	Jones, Gary 34 pen; Holt 64	4,755
41	div3	**Hull City**	A	L	0-1		16,050
42	div3	**Doncaster**	H	D	1-1	McEvilly 73	4,601
43	div3	**Lincoln**	H	L	0-3		4,224
44	div3	**Scunthorpe**	A	D	2-2	Bertos 3; Warner 24	3,564
45	div3	**Macclesfield**	H	L	1-2	Heald 32	4,942
46	div3	**Leyton Orient**	H	W	3-0	Holt 23,58; McCourt 90	2,417
47	div3	**Kidderminster**	A	W	1-0	Bertos 38	3,580
48	div3	**Southend**	H	D	1-1	Jones, Gary 58	3,591
49	div3	**Oxford**	A	L	0-2		5,134

TEAM OF THE SEASON

G Neil Edwards — CG: 34 DR: 81

D Gareth Griffiths — CG: 28 DR: 84

D Michael Simpkins — CG: 24 DR: 75

D Wayne Evans — CG: 45 DR: 72

D *Shaun Smith — CG: 12 DR: 83

M Leo Bertos — CG: 40 SD: -10

M Gary Jones — CG: 24 SD: -14

M Sean McClare — CG: 31 SD: -16

M Chris Schuker — CG: 12 SD: -19

F Paul Connor — CG: 19 SR: 298

F Grant Holt — CG: 12 SR: 378

KEY PLAYER APPEARANCES

	PLAYER	POS	AGE	APP	MINS ON	GOALS	CARDS(Y	R)
1	Wayne Evans	DEF	32	45	4048	0	4	0
2	Leo Bertos	MID	22	40	3565	9	7	0
3	Neil Edwards	GK	33	34	3060	0	0	0
4	Sean McClare	MID	26	38	2855	0	5	1
5	Daryl Burgess	DEF	33	35	2841	0	11	0
6	Gareth Griffiths	DEF	34	33	2686	1	4	0
7	Michael Simpkins	DEF	25	27	2255	0	12	1
8	Gary Jones	MID	35	26	2239	4	5	1
9	Matt Doughty	DEF	22	31	2011	0	2	0
10	Paul Connor	ATT	25	24	1785	6	1	1
11	Kevin Townson	ATT	21	33	1775	10	4	0
12	Lee McEvilly	ATT	22	30	1435	6	2	1
13	Simon Grand	DEF	20	17	1159	0	4	0
14	Chris Shuker	MID	22	14	1158	1	4	1
15	Grant Holt	ATT	23	14	1133	3	5	0
16	Shaun Smith	DEF	33	12	1080	0	1	0
17	Mathew Gilkes	GK	22	12	1080	0	1	0
18	Danny Livesey	DEF	19	13	966	0	1	1

KEY PLAYERS - GOALSCORERS

Paul Connor

Goals in the League	6
Contribution to Attacking Power Average number of minutes between League team goals while on pitch	68
Player Strike Rate Average number of minutes between League goals scored by player	298
Club Strike Rate Average number of minutes between League goals scored by club	84

	PLAYER	LGE GOALS	POWER	STRIKE RATE
1	Paul Connor	6	68	298 mins
2	Grant Holt	3	87	378 mins
3	Leo Bertos	9	81	396 mins
4	Gary Jones	4	97	560 mins

KEY PLAYERS - MIDFIELDERS

Leo Bertos

Goals in the League	9
Defensive Rating Average number of mins between League goals conceded while he was on the pitch	71
Contribution to Attacking Power Average number of minutes between League team goals while on pitch	81
Scoring Difference Defensive Rating minus Contribution to Attacking Power	-10

	PLAYER	LGE GOALS	DEF RATE	POWER	SCORE DIFF
1	Leo Bertos	9	71	81	-10 mins
2	Gary Jones	4	83	97	-14 mins
3	Sean McClare	0	71	87	-16 mins
4	Chris Shuker	1	64	83	-19 mins

KEY PLAYERS - DEFENDERS

Gareth Griffiths

Goals Conceded when he was on pitch	32
Defensive Rating Ave number of mins between League goals conceded while on the pitch	84
Clean Sheets In games when he played at least 70 minutes	9
Club Defensive Rating Average number of mins between League goals conceded by the club this season.	71

	PLAYER	CON LGE	CLN SHEETS	DEF RATE
1	Gareth Griffiths	32	9	84 mins
2	Shaun Smith	13	4	83 mins
3	Michael Simpkins	30	6	75 mins
4	Wayne Evans	56	12	72 mins
5	Matt Doughty	30	4	67 mins

KEY GOALKEEPER

Neil Edwards

Goals Conceded in the League	38
Defensive Rating Ave number of mins between League goals conceded while on the pitch.	81
Counting Games Games when he played at least 70 mins	34
Clean Sheets In games when he played at least 70 mins	11

TOP POINT EARNERS

	PLAYER	GAMES	AV PTS
1	Paul Connor	19	**1.42**
2	Matt Doughty	16	**1.31**
3	Shaun Smith	12	**1.25**
4	Grant Holt	12	**1.25**
5	Leo Bertos	40	**1.15**
6	Daryl Burgess	30	**1.13**
7	Michael Simpkins	24	**1.13**
8	Gary Jones	24	**1.13**
9	Wayne Evans	45	**1.11**
10	Neil Edwards	34	**1.09**
	CLUB AVERAGE:		**1.09**

SCUNTHORPE UNITED

Final Position: **22nd**

NICKNAME: THE IRON

KEY: ☐ Won ☐ Drawn ☐ Lost

							Attendance
1	div3	Bristol Rovers	H	L	1-2	Beagrie 63 pen	4,186
2	ccR1	Oldham	H	W	2-1	Hayes 51,57	2,366
3	div3	Bury	A	W	3-2	Torpey 39,50; Beagrie 63	2,761
4	div3	Oxford	H	D	1-1	Beagrie 63	3,617
5	div3	Mansfield	A	L	0-5		5,142
6	div3	Torquay	H	W	2-1	MacLean 86; Calvo-Garcia 90	3,080
7	div3	Boston	A	D	1-1	Sharp 45 pen	3,154
8	div3	Swansea	H	D	2-2	Calvo-Garcia 9; MacLean 60 pen	3,510
9	div3	Kidderminster	A	W	2-0	Byrne 58; MacLean 77	2,162
10	div3	Leyton Orient	A	D	1-1	Kell 44	3,663
11	ccR2	Burnley	H	L	2-3	MacLean 32; Beagrie 85	2,915
12	div3	Southend	H	D	1-1	MacLean 6	2,311
13	div3	Cheltenham	H	W	5-2	MacLean 11,51,78 pen; Beagrie 28; Torpey 80	2,857
14	div3	Rochdale	A	L	0-2		2,838
15	div3	Lincoln	H	L	1-3	Hayes 72	5,045
16	div3	Northampton	A	D	1-1	Kell 52	4,827
17	div3	Carlisle	A	W	4-1	Taylor 23; MacLean 52; Sharp 64; Beagrie 83 pen	3,437
18	div3	York	H	D	0-0		3,807
19	div3	Huddersfield	H	W	6-2	Beagrie 17; Sparrow 24; Barwick 55; MacLean 59,68,87	4,715
20	facr1	Shrewsbury	H	W	2-1	Hayes 9,90	3,232
21	div3	Macclesfield	A	D	2-2	Beagrie 15; MacLean 54	2,205
22	div3	Cambridge	H	W	4-0	Hayes 13; MacLean 17,72,90	3,397
23	div3	Darlington	A	D	2-2	Torpey 70; Beagrie 82 pen	3,606
24	facr2	Sheff Wed	H	D	2-2	Torpey 33,71	7,418
25	div3	Hull City	H	D	1-1	Beagrie 65 pen	6,426
26	facr2r	Sheff Wed	A	W	3-1*	(*on penalties)	11,722
27	div3	Yeovil	A	D	2-2	Beagrie 38 pen,39	5,714
28	div3	Doncaster	A	L	0-1		8,961
29	div3	Boston	H	L	0-1		4,346
30	facr3	Barnsley	A	D	0-0		10,839
31	div3	Bristol Rovers	A	L	0-1		5,789
32	facr3r	Barnsley	H	W	2-0	Torpey 14; McCombe 74	6,293
33	div3	Bury	H	D	0-0		3,869
34	facr4	Portsmouth	A	L	1-2	Parton 88	17,508
35	div3	Mansfield	H	D	0-0		3,113
36	div3	Doncaster	H	D	2-2	Torpey 10; Butler 62	5,681
37	div3	Oxford	A	L	2-3	Torpey 37,44	5,118
38	div3	Lincoln	A	D	1-1	Taylor 82	5,324
39	div3	Northampton	H	W	1-0	Ridley, L 72	3,566
40	div3	Torquay	A	L	0-1		2,561
41	div3	Yeovil	H	W	3-0	MacLean 26,60; Holloway 45	3,355
42	div3	York	A	W	3-1	Groves 17,56; MacLean 33 pen	2,676
43	div3	Hull City	A	L	1-2	MacLean 73	19,076
44	div3	Kidderminster	H	L	0-2		2,512
45	div3	Swansea	A	L	2-4	Taylor 25,83	4,400
46	div3	Carlisle	H	L	2-3	MacLean 28,73 pen	2,326
47	div3	Leyton Orient	H	D	1-1	Sparrow 7	2,822
48	div3	Southend	A	L	2-4	Sparrow 30; Torpey 49	4,976
49	div3	Rochdale	H	D	2-2	MacLean 5; Butler 22	3,564
50	div3	Cheltenham	A	L	1-2	Groves 29	3,409
51	div3	Huddersfield	A	L	2-3	Sodje 8 og; MacLean 42	12,108
52	div3	Macclesfield	H	W	1-0	Torpey 55	4,334
53	div3	Cambridge	A	L	2-3	Beagrie 65; Torpey 90	4,498
54	div3	Darlington	H	L	0-1		4,801

TEAM OF THE SEASON

Pos	Player	CG	Rating
G	Tom Evans	36	DR: 55
D	Kevin Sharp	34	DR: 63
D	Clifford Byrne	38	DR: 59
D	Mark Jackson	14	DR: 58
D	Andy Butler	33	DR: 55
M	Peter Beagrie	26	SD: 7
M	Terry Barwick	22	SD: 0
M	Matthew Sparrow	34	SD: -4
M	Richard Kell	17	SD: -11
F	Steven MacLean	36	SR: 143
F	Steve Torpey	42	SR: 381

KEY PLAYER APPEARANCES

	PLAYER	POS	AGE	APP	MINS ON	GOALS	CARDS(Y)	CARDS(R)
1	Steve Torpey	ATT	33	43	3811	10	9	0
2	Clifford Byrne	DEF	22	39	3428	1	7	0
3	Steven MacLean	ATT	21	42	3298	23	8	0
4	Kevin Sharp	DEF	29	40	3277	2	10	1
5	Tom Evans	GK	27	36	3240	0	0	0
6	Matthew Sparrow	MID	20	38	3218	3	7	0
7	Andy Butler	DEF	20	34	3025	2	5	0
8	Nathan Stanton	DEF	23	33	2665	0	8	0
9	Peter Beagrie	MID	38	32	2531	12	5	0
10	Terry Barwick	MID	21	30	2241	1	8	0
11	Richard Kell	MID	24	24	1765	2	7	1
12	Cleveland Taylor	MID	20	20	1627	3	2	0
13	Paul Hayes	ATT	20	35	1391	2	3	0
14	Mark Jackson	DEF	26	17	1385	0	6	0
15	Lee Ridley	DEF	21	18	1350	1	3	0
16	Wayne Graves	MID	23	21	1266	0	3	1
17	Paul Groves	MID	38	13	1145	3	1	0
18	Ian Kilford	MID	30	18	1000	0	2	0

KEY PLAYERS - GOALSCORERS

Steven MacLean

Goals in the League	23
Contribution to Attacking Power Average number of minutes between League team goals while on pitch	54
Player Strike Rate Average number of minutes between League goals scored by player	143
Club Strike Rate Average number of minutes between League goals scored by club	59

	PLAYER	LGE GOALS	POWER	STRIKE RATE
1	Steven MacLean	23	54	143 mins
2	Peter Beagrie	12	52	211 mins
3	Steve Torpey	10	61	381 mins
4	Paul Groves	3	54	382 mins

KEY PLAYERS - MIDFIELDERS

Peter Beagrie

Goals in the League	12
Defensive Rating Average number of mins between League goals conceded while he was on the pitch	60
Contribution to Attacking Power Average number of minutes between League team goals while on pitch	53
Scoring Difference Defensive Rating minus Contribution to Attacking Power	7

	PLAYER	LGE GOALS	DEF RATE	POWER	SCORE DIFF
1	Peter Beagrie	12	60	53	7 mins
2	Terry Barwick	1	57	57	0 mins
3	Matthew Sparrow	3	55	59	-4 mins
4	Paul Groves	3	44	55	-11 mins
5	Richard Kell	2	57	68	-11 mins

KEY PLAYERS - DEFENDERS

Kevin Sharp

Goals Conceded when he was on pitch	52
Defensive Rating Ave number of mins between League goals conceded while on the pitch	63
Clean Sheets In games when he played at least 70 minutes	8
Club Defensive Rating Average number of mins between League goals conceded by the club this season.	58

	PLAYER	CON LGE	CLN SHEETS	DEF RATE
1	Kevin Sharp	52	8	63 mins
2	Clifford Byrne	58	7	59 mins
3	Mark Jackson	24	1	58 mins
4	Andy Butler	55	4	55 mins
5	Nathan Stanton	49	4	54 mins

KEY GOALKEEPER

Tom Evans

Goals Conceded in the League	59
Defensive Rating Ave number of mins between League goals conceded while on the pitch.	55
Counting Games Games when he played at least 70 mins	36
Clean Sheets In games when he played at least 70 mins	6

TOP POINT EARNERS

	PLAYER	GAMES	AV PTS
1	Mark Jackson	14	**1.57**
2	Kevin Sharp	34	**1.35**
3	Peter Beagrie	26	**1.19**
4	Richard Kell	17	**1.06**
5	Steven MacLean	36	**1.06**
6	Steve Torpey	42	**1.05**
7	Terry Barwick	22	**1.05**
8	Clifford Byrne	38	**1.05**
9	Matthew Sparrow	34	**1.00**
10	Andy Butler	33	**0.97**
	CLUB AVERAGE:		**1.09**

CARLISLE UNITED

Final Position: **23rd**

NICKNAME: THE FOXES

KEY: ☐ Won ☐ Drawn ☐ Lost

							Attendance
1	div3	York	H	L	1-2	Raven 4	7,261
2	ccR1	Walsall	A	L	1-2	Russell 32	4,665
3	div3	Yeovil	A	L	0-3		6,347
4	div3	Bristol Rovers	H	L	0-2		4,764
5	div3	Boston	A	L	0-1		2,527
6	div3	Cambridge	H	D	0-0		4,571
7	div3	Darlington	A	L	0-2		5,889
8	div3	Rochdale	H	W	3-2	Simpson 10; Foran 17; McGill 22	4,532
9	div3	Northampton	A	L	0-2		4,156
10	div3	Southend	A	D	2-2	Henderson 47; Foran 80	4,620
11	div3	Swansea	H	L	1-2	Foran 42 pen	4,854
12	div3	Leyton Orient	H	L	0-1		4,650
13	div3	Kidderminster	A	L	1-2	Murphy 63	2,488
14	div3	Hull City	A	L	1-2	McDonagh 59	19,050
15	div3	Macclesfield	H	L	0-1		4,366
16	div3	Scunthorpe	H	L	1-4	Farrell 88	3,437
17	div3	Huddersfield	A	L	1-2	Kelly 74	9,059
18	div3	Lincoln	A	L	0-2		4,044
19	facr1	Oldham	A	L	0-3		4,391
20	div3	Mansfield	H	L	0-2		4,145
21	div3	Cheltenham	A	L	1-2	Simpson 19	3,414
22	div3	Doncaster	H	L	0-1		4,344
23	div3	Oxford	A	L	1-2	Foran 78 pen	6,111
24	div3	Torquay	H	W	2-0	Preece 16; Arnison 53	3,600
25	div3	Bury	A	W	3-1	Gray 41; McGill 57; Henderson 69	3,345
26	div3	Darlington	H	D	1-1	McGill 10	8,369
27	div3	Boston	H	W	2-1	Chapman 15 og; Fryatt 62	5,296
28	div3	York	A	L	0-2		4,804
29	div3	Yeovil	H	W	2-0	Simpson 71; Farrell 75	5,455
30	div3	Bristol Rovers	A	L	0-1		8,485
31	div3	Bury	H	W	2-1	Simpson 31; Gray 35	4,954
32	div3	Hull City	H	D	1-1	Preece 56	7,176
33	div3	Cambridge	A	D	2-2	Simpson 7,83	3,280
34	div3	Macclesfield	A	D	1-1	McGill 24	3,256
35	div3	Torquay	A	L	1-4	McGill 73	3,366
36	div3	Huddersfield	H	W	1-0	Duffield 72	4,782
37	div3	Oxford	H	W	2-0	Cowan 52; Farrell 76	5,492
38	div3	Northampton	H	D	1-1	Farrell 82	6,269
39	div3	Rochdale	A	L	0-2		4,755
40	div3	Scunthorpe	A	W	3-2	Duffield 15; Boyd 55; Billy 77	2,326
41	div3	Southend	H	L	1-2	Farrell 87	6,173
42	div3	Swansea	A	W	2-1	Farrell 26 pen; Duffield 60	5,238
43	div3	Kidderminster	H	W	1-0	Farrell 78	7,296
44	div3	Leyton Orient	A	D	1-1	McGill 81	4,182
45	div3	Lincoln	H	L	0-2		7,875
46	div3	Mansfield	A	W	3-2	Gray 12; Preece 21; Langmead 66	5,361
47	div3	Cheltenham	H	D	1-1	McGill 9	9,524
48	div3	Doncaster	A	L	0-1		9,720

TEAM OF THE SEASON

G — Mathew Glennon — CG: 43 DR: 63

D — Thomas Cowan — CG: 20 DR: 74

D — Kevin Gray — CG: 22 DR: 72

D — Paul Arnison — CG: 19 DR: 71

D — Peter Murphy — CG: 33 DR: 62

M — Andy Preece — CG: 23 SD: 6

M — Paul Simpson — CG: 22 SD: -17

M — William McDonagh — CG: 21 SD: -26

M — Brendan McGill — CG: 37 SD: -27

F — Craig Farrell — CG: 16 SR: 278

F — Ritchie Foran — CG: 18 SR: 438

KEY PLAYER APPEARANCES

	PLAYER	POS	AGE	APP	MINS ON	GOALS	CARDS(Y	R)
1	Mathew Glennon	GK	25	44	3902	0	0	1
2	Brendan McGill	MID	23	44	3635	7	4	0
3	Chris Billy	MID	31	39	3341	1	8	0
4	Lee Andrews	DEF	21	37	3001	0	2	1
5	Peter Murphy	DEF	23	35	2999	1	6	0
6	Brian Shelley	DEF	22	31	2516	0	3	0
7	Kevin Gray	DEF	32	25	2151	3	3	1
8	William McDonagh	MID	21	27	2106	1	4	0
9	Paul Simpson	MID	37	25	2090	6	1	0
10	Andy Preece	MID	37	25	2041	3	3	0
11	Craig Farrell	ATT	21	30	1948	7	1	0
12	Paul Arnison	DEF	26	26	1923	1	5	0
13	Thomas Cowan	DEF	34	20	1778	1	6	0
14	Ritchie Foran	ATT	24	23	1753	4	8	2
15	Paul Raven	DEF	33	13	998	1	3	0
16	Kevin Henderson	ATT	30	19	934	2	1	0
17	Adam Rundle	ATT	19	23	829	0	0	0
18	Des Byrne	DEF	23	11	791	0	4	0

KEY PLAYERS - GOALSCORERS

Craig Farrell

Goals in the League	7
Contribution to Attacking Power Average number of minutes between League team goals while on pitch	88
Player Strike Rate Average number of minutes between League goals scored by player	278
Club Strike Rate Average number of minutes between League goals scored by club	90

	PLAYER	LGE GOALS	POWER	STRIKE RATE
1	Craig Farrell	7	88	278 mins
2	Paul Simpson	6	80	348 mins
3	Ritchie Foran	4	109	438 mins
4	Brendan McGill	7	84	519 mins
5	Andy Preece	3	70	680 mins

KEY PLAYERS - MIDFIELDERS

Andy Preece

Goals in the League	3
Defensive Rating Average number of mins between League goals conceded while he was on the pitch	76
Contribution to Attacking Power Average number of minutes between League team goals while on pitch	70
Scoring Difference Defensive Rating minus Contribution to Attacking Power	6

	PLAYER	LGE GOALS	DEF RATE	POWER	SCORE DIFF
1	Andy Preece	3	76	70	6 mins
2	Paul Simpson	6	63	80	-17 mins
3	William McDonagh	1	66	92	-26 mins
4	Brendan McGill	7	58	85	-27 mins

KEY PLAYERS - DEFENDERS

Thomas Cowan

Goals Conceded when he was on pitch	24
Defensive Rating Ave number of mins between League goals conceded while on the pitch	74
Clean Sheets In games when he played at least 70 minutes	3
Club Defensive Rating Average number of mins between League goals conceded by the club this season.	60

	PLAYER	CON LGE	CLN SHEETS	DEF RATE
1	Thomas Cowan	24	3	74 mins
2	Kevin Gray	30	4	72 mins
3	Paul Arnison	27	4	71 mins
4	Peter Murphy	48	5	62 mins
5	Lee Andrews	52	3	58 mins

KEY GOALKEEPER

Shaun Marshall

Goals Conceded in the League	67
Defensive Rating Ave number of mins between League goals conceded while on the pitch.	60
Counting Games Games when he played at least 70 mins	45
Clean Sheets In games when he played at least 70 mins	10

TOP POINT EARNERS

	PLAYER	GAMES	AV PTS
1	Andy Preece	23	1.61
2	Kevin Gray	22	1.59
3	Thomas Cowan	20	1.35
4	Paul Arnison	19	1.32
5	Paul Simpson	22	1.27
6	Peter Murphy	33	1.15
7	Craig Farrell	16	1.13
8	Brendan McGill	37	1.11
9	Mathew Glennon	43	0.98
10	Chris Billy	35	0.97
	CLUB AVERAGE:		0.98

YORK CITY

Final Position: **24th**

NICKNAME: THE MINSTERMEN

KEY: ☐ Won ☐ Drawn ☐ Lost

							Attendance
1	div3	Carlisle	A	W	2-1	Bullock 2; Nogan 13	7,261
2	ccR1	Rotherham	A	L	1-2	Merris 33	2,919
3	div3	Northampton	H	W	1-0	Nogan 44	3,870
4	div3	Huddersfield	A	W	1-0	Bullock 17	9,850
5	div3	Southend	H	W	2-0	Hope 36; George 49	4,202
6	div3	Lincoln	A	L	0-3		3,892
7	div3	Rochdale	H	L	1-2	Wilford 73	3,982
8	div3	Yeovil	A	L	0-3		5,653
9	div3	Darlington	H	D	1-1	George 16	3,867
10	div3	Bristol Rovers	H	W	2-1	Bullock 14; Wilford 35	3,968
11	div3	Macclesfield	A	D	0-0		2,311
12	div3	Bury	A	L	0-2		2,282
13	div3	Cambridge	H	W	2-0	Bullock 5; Brackstone 64	3,481
14	div3	Mansfield	A	L	0-2		4,914
15	div3	Boston	H	D	1-1	Parkin 45	3,190
16	div3	Oxford	H	D	2-2	Nogan 37; Hope 63	3,022
17	div3	Scunthorpe	A	D	0-0		3,807
18	div3	Cheltenham	A	D	1-1	Parkin 77	3,431
19	facr1	Barnsley	H	L	1-2	Nogan 36	5,658
20	div3	Doncaster	H	W	1-0	Dunning 60 pen	5,942
21	div3	Leyton Orient	A	D	2-2	Edmondson 59; Brackstone 64	3,593
22	div3	Swansea	H	D	0-0		3,209
23	div3	Darlington	A	L	0-3		4,115
24	div3	Torquay	A	D	1-1	Nogan 47	2,564
25	div3	Kidderminster	H	W	1-0	Bullock 52	2,973
26	div3	Hull City	H	L	0-2		7,923
27	div3	Rochdale	A	W	2-1	Nogan 28,76	2,764
28	div3	Carlisle	H	W	2-0	Brass 29; Cooper 50	4,804
29	div3	Northampton	A	L	1-2	Bullock 90	5,003
30	div3	Huddersfield	H	L	0-2		6,969
31	div3	Southend	A	D	0-0		2,943
32	div3	Hull City	A	L	1-2	Nogan 66	19,099
33	div3	Mansfield	H	L	1-2	Nogan 66	4,068
34	div3	Lincoln	H	L	1-4	Bullock 83	3,396
35	div3	Boston	A	L	0-2		2,490
36	div3	Oxford	A	D	0-0		5,091
37	div3	Kidderminster	A	L	1-4	Cooper 41	2,569
38	div3	Scunthorpe	H	L	1-3	Bell 76	2,676
39	div3	Torquay	H	D	0-0		3,150
40	div3	Bristol Rovers	A	L	0-3		6,723
41	div3	Macclesfield	H	L	0-2		3,855
42	div3	Cambridge	A	L	0-2		5,120
43	div3	Bury	H	D	1-1	George 24	3,111
44	div3	Cheltenham	H	L	0-2		3,221
45	div3	Yeovil	H	L	1-2	Dunning 8	2,802
46	div3	Doncaster	A	L	1-3	Dunning 49	7,843
47	div3	Leyton Orient	H	L	1-2	Wise 5	3,462
48	div3	Swansea	A	D	0-0		6,806

TEAM OF THE SEASON

G — Mark Ovendale — CG: 41 DR: 63

D — Darren Edmondson — CG: 24 DR: 71
D — Chris Brass — CG: 35 DR: 70
D — Richard Hope — CG: 32 DR: 68
D — Chris Smith — CG: 26 DR: 61

M — Mitch Ward — CG: 25 SD: -35
M — Darren Dunning — CG: 42 SD: -48
M — David Merris — CG: 40 SD: -53
M — Leigh Wood — CG: 21 SD: -84

F — Lee Nogan — CG: 32 SR: 379
F — Lee Bullock — CG: 33 SR: 434

KEY PLAYER APPEARANCES

	PLAYER	POS	AGE	APP	MINS ON	GOALS	CARDS(Y/R)	
1	Darren Dunning	MID	23	42	3776	3	12	1
2	David Merris	MID	2005	44	3705	0	2	0
3	Mark Ovendale	GK	30	41	3690	0	4	1
4	Chris Brass	DEF	28	39	3287	1	3	2
5	Lee Bullock	ATT	23	35	3040	7	1	0
6	Lee Nogan	ATT	35	39	3031	8	3	0
7	Richard Hope	DEF	26	35	3006	2	5	1
8	Richard Cooper	DEF	24	38	2609	2	8	0
9	Mitch Ward	MID	33	31	2404	0	1	0
10	Chris Smith	DEF	23	28	2382	0	5	0
11	Darren Edmondson	DEF	32	27	2265	1	7	0
12	Leigh Wood	MID	21	26	1978	0	2	0
13	Stuart Wise	DEF	20	19	1591	1	1	1
14	Liam George	ATT	25	21	1226	3	3	0
15	Jonathan Parkin	DEF	22	15	904	2	2	0
16	Justin Walker	MID	28	9	613	0	1	0
17	Jon Newby	ATT	25	7	560	0	0	0
18	Shaun Davies	DEF	19	8	531	0	0	0

KEY PLAYERS - GOALSCORERS

Lee Nogan

Goals in the League	8
Contribution to Attacking Power Average number of minutes between League team goals while on pitch	112
Player Strike Rate Average number of minutes between League goals scored by player	379
Club Strike Rate Average number of minutes between League goals scored by club	118

	PLAYER	LGE GOALS	POWER	STRIKE RATE
1	Lee Nogan	8	112	379 mins
2	Lee Bullock	7	98	434 mins
3	Darren Dunning	3	114	1259 mins
4	Richard Cooper	2	118	1305 mins
5	Richard Hope	2	111	1503 mins

KEY PLAYERS - MIDFIELDERS

Mitch Ward

Goals in the League	0
Defensive Rating Average number of mins between League goals conceded while he was on the pitch	65
Contribution to Attacking Power Average number of minutes between League team goals while on pitch	100
Scoring Difference Defensive Rating minus Contribution to Attacking Power	-35

	PLAYER	LGE GOALS	DEF RATE	POWER	SCORE DIFF
1	Mitch Ward	0	65	100	-35 mins
2	Darren Dunning	3	66	114	-48 mins
3	David Merris	0	63	116	-53 mins
4	Leigh Wood	0	57	141	-84 mins

KEY PLAYERS - DEFENDERS

Darren Edmondson

Goals Conceded when he was on pitch	32
Defensive Rating Ave number of mins between League goals conceded while on the pitch	71
Clean Sheets In games when he played at least 70 minutes	9
Club Defensive Rating Average number of mins between League goals conceded by the club this season.	63

	PLAYER	CON LGE	CLN SHEETS	DEF RATE
1	Darren Edmondson	32	9	71 mins
2	Chris Brass	47	11	70 mins
3	Richard Hope	44	10	68 mins
4	Chris Smith	39	7	61 mins
5	Richard Cooper	46	6	57 mins

KEY GOALKEEPER

Mark Ovendale

Goals Conceded in the League	59
Defensive Rating Ave number of mins between League goals conceded while on the pitch.	63
Counting Games Games when he played at least 70 mins	41
Clean Sheets In games when he played at least 70 mins	12

TOP POINT EARNERS

	PLAYER	GAMES	AV PTS
1	Darren Edmondson	24	**1.29**
2	Mitch Ward	25	**1.28**
3	Lee Bullock	33	**1.21**
4	David Merris	40	**1.08**
5	Lee Nogan	32	**1.06**
6	Mark Ovendale	41	**1.02**
7	Darren Dunning	42	**1.00**
8	Chris Brass	35	**0.97**
9	Richard Hope	32	**0.97**
10	Richard Cooper	25	**0.96**
	CLUB AVERAGE:		**0.96**

SCOTTISH PREMIERSHIP ROUND-UP

FINAL LEAGUE TABLE

		HOME					AWAY					TOTAL			
	P	W	D	L	F	A	W	D	L	F	A	F	A	DIF	PTS
Celtic	38	15	2	2	62	15	16	3	0	43	10	105	25	80	98
Rangers	38	16	0	3	48	11	9	6	4	28	22	76	33	43	81
Hearts	38	12	5	2	32	17	7	6	6	24	23	56	40	16	68
Dunfermline	38	9	7	3	28	19	5	4	10	17	33	45	52	-7	53
Dundee Utd	38	8	6	5	28	27	5	4	10	19	33	47	60	-13	49
Motherwell	38	7	7	5	25	22	5	3	11	17	27	42	49	-7	46
Dundee	38	8	3	8	21	20	4	7	8	27	37	48	57	-9	46
Hibernian	38	6	5	8	25	28	5	6	8	16	32	41	60	-19	44
Livingston	38	6	9	4	24	18	4	4	11	24	39	48	57	-9	43
Kilmarnock	38	8	3	8	29	31	4	3	12	22	43	51	74	-23	42
Aberdeen	38	5	3	11	22	29	4	4	11	17	34	39	63	-24	34
Partick	38	5	4	10	24	32	1	4	14	15	35	39	67	-28	26

CLUB STRIKE FORCE

Hartson and Larsson striking for Celtic

1 Celtic

Goals scored in the League	105
Club Strike Rate (CSR) Average number of minutes between League goals scored by club	33

	CLUB	LGE	CSR
1	Celtic	105	33
2	Rangers	76	45
3	Hearts	56	61
4	Kilmarnock	51	67
5	Dundee	48	71
6	Livingston	48	71
7	Dundee Utd	47	73
8	Dunfermline	45	76
9	Motherwell	42	81
10	Hibernian	41	83
11	Aberdeen	39	88
12	Partick	39	88

CLUB DISCIPLINARY RECORDS

Hibs get a talking to in Scottish League final

1 Livingston

League Yellow	72
League Red	1
League Total	73
Cards Average in League Average number of minutes between a card being shown of either colour	47

	CLUB	LEAGUE Y	LEAGUE R	TOTAL	AVE
1	Livingston	72 Y	1 R	73	47
2	Hearts	70	1	71	48
3	Hibernian	67	4	71	48
4	Dundee Utd	64	3	67	51
5	Dundee	61	1	62	55
6	Partick	59	3	62	55
7	Kilmarnock	54	3	57	60
8	Rangers	53	1	54	63
9	Motherwell	48	1	49	70
10	Celtic	42	2	44	78
11	Dunfermline	42	1	43	80
12	Aberdeen	36	3	39	88

CLUB DEFENCES

	CLUB	LGE	CS	CDR
1	Celtic	25	17	137
2	Rangers	33	16	104
3	Hearts	40	12	86
4	Motherwell	49	10	70
5	Dunfermline	52	13	66
6	Dundee	57	7	60
7	Livingston	57	11	60
8	Dundee Utd	60	11	57
9	Hibernian	60	9	57
10	Aberdeen	63	5	54
11	Partick	67	5	51
12	Kilmarnock	74	3	46

Balde of Celtic denies Bayern

1 Celtic

Goals conceded in the League	25
Clean Sheets (CS) Number of league games where no goals were conceded	17
Club Defensive Rate (CDR) Average number of minutes between League goals conceded by club	137

STADIUM CAPACITY AND HOME CROWDS

	TEAM	CAPACITY	AVE	HIGH	LOW
1	Rangers	50420	97.17	49962	46900
2	Celtic	60506	95.29	59739	47563
3	Hearts	18300	65.28	16632	9881
4	Dundee Utd	14200	54.32	12292	5421
5	Livingston	10016	51.09	9627	2677
6	Dundee	14000	50.64	10948	4942
7	Dunfermline	12510	49.85	11201	3914
8	Hibernian	18700	48.87	15060	5447
9	Aberdeen	22200	46.8	16452	6781
10	Motherwell	13742	45.3	10824	3920
11	Kilmarnock	18220	38.23	14576	4886
12	Partick	14538	32.4	9045	2727

Key: Average. The percentage of each stadium filled in League games over the season (AVE), the stadium capacity and the highest and lowest crowds recorded.

AWAY ATTENDANCE

	TEAM	AVE	HIGH	LOW
1	Celtic	74.02	49909	7749
2	Rangers	72.99	59087	6096
3	Hearts	57.97	59560	4043
4	Dundee Utd	55.21	58698	3082
5	Dunfermline	54.62	59739	3558
6	Aberdeen	53.91	59598	2839
7	Hibernian	53.4	59609	3155
8	Dundee	53	57573	2727
9	Motherwell	52.98	58013	3492
10	Partick	49.81	58202	3160
11	Kilmarnock	49.1	59138	2677
12	Livingston	48.24	57973	3011

Key: Average. How close each club has come to filling grounds in its away league matches (AVE) and the highest and lowest crowds recorded.

CHART-TOPPING MIDFIELDERS

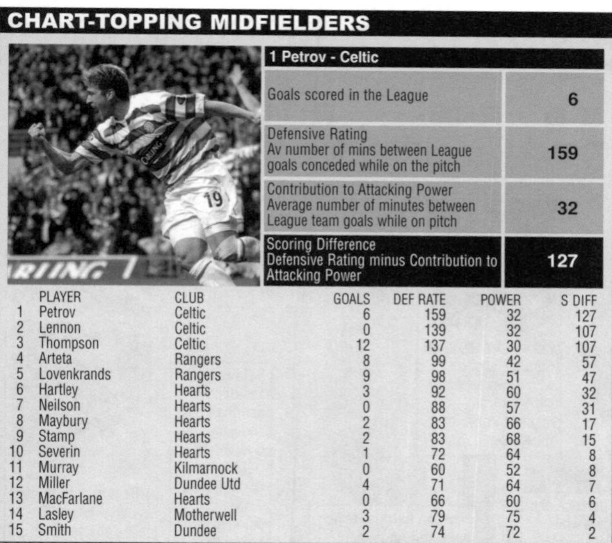

1 Petrov - Celtic	
Goals scored in the League	6
Defensive Rating Av number of mins between League goals conceded while on the pitch	159
Contribution to Attacking Power Average number of minutes between League team goals while on pitch	32
Scoring Difference Defensive Rating minus Contribution to Attacking Power	127

	PLAYER	CLUB	GOALS	DEF RATE	POWER	S DIFF
1	Petrov	Celtic	6	159	32	127
2	Lennon	Celtic	0	139	32	107
3	Thompson	Celtic	12	137	30	107
4	Arteta	Rangers	8	99	42	57
5	Lovenkrands	Rangers	9	98	51	47
6	Hartley	Hearts	3	92	60	32
7	Neilson	Hearts	0	88	57	31
8	Maybury	Hearts	2	83	66	17
9	Stamp	Hearts	2	83	68	15
10	Severin	Hearts	1	72	64	8
11	Murray	Kilmarnock	0	60	52	8
12	Miller	Dundee Utd	4	71	64	7
13	MacFarlane	Hearts	0	66	60	6
14	Lasley	Motherwell	3	79	75	4
15	Smith	Dundee	2	74	72	2

CHART-TOPPING GOALSCORERS

1 Larsson - Celtic	
Goals scored in the League (GL)	29
Goals scored in all competitions (GA)	40
Contribution to Attacking Power (AP) Average number of minutes between League team goals while on pitch	31
Player Strike Rate Average number of minutes between League goals scored by player	105
Club Strike Rate (CSR) Average minutes between League goals scored by club	33

	PLAYER	CLUB	GOALS: LGE	ALL	CSR	S RATE
1	Larsson	Celtic	29	40	33	105
2	Sutton	Celtic	19	29	33	117
3	Novo	Dundee	19	72	71	161
4	Riordan	Hibernian	15	76	83	162
5	de Vries	Hearts	13	58	61	172
6	Boyd	Kilmarnock	15	67	67	179
7	Thompson	Celtic	12	30	33	183
8	Grady	Partick	15	79	88	186
9	Booth	Aberdeen	8	58	88	204
10	Lovenkrands	Rangers	9	50	45	208
11	Dodds	Dundee Utd	10	72	73	210
12	Lilley	Livingston	12	66	71	215
13	Crawford	Dunfermline	13	72	76	229
14	Clarkson	Motherwell	12	88	81	235
15	Arteta	Rangers	8	41	45	236

CHART-TOPPING DEFENDERS

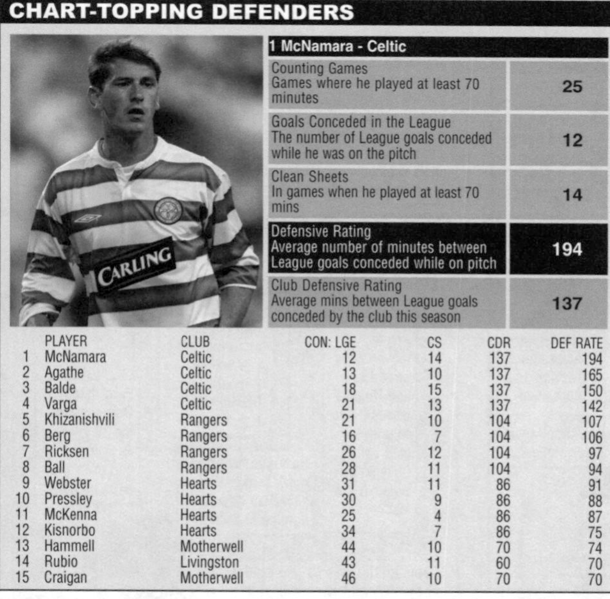

1 McNamara - Celtic	
Counting Games Games where he played at least 70 minutes	25
Goals Conceded in the League The number of League goals conceded while he was on the pitch	12
Clean Sheets In games when he played at least 70 mins	14
Defensive Rating Average number of minutes between League goals conceded while on pitch	194
Club Defensive Rating Average mins between League goals conceded by the club this season	137

	PLAYER	CLUB	CON: LGE	CS	CDR	DEF RATE
1	McNamara	Celtic	12	14	137	194
2	Agathe	Celtic	13	10	137	165
3	Balde	Celtic	18	15	137	150
4	Varga	Celtic	21	13	137	142
5	Khizanishvili	Rangers	21	10	104	107
6	Berg	Rangers	16	7	104	106
7	Ricksen	Rangers	26	12	104	97
8	Ball	Rangers	28	11	104	94
9	Webster	Hearts	31	11	86	91
10	Pressley	Hearts	30	9	86	88
11	McKenna	Hearts	25	4	86	87
12	Kisnorbo	Hearts	34	7	86	75
13	Hammell	Motherwell	44	10	70	74
14	Rubio	Livingston	43	11	60	70
15	Craigan	Motherwell	46	10	70	70

CHART-TOPPING GOALKEEPERS

1 Klos - Rangers	
Counting Games League games when he played at least 70 minutes	34
Goals Conceded in the League The number of League goals conceded while he was on the pitch	27
Goals Conceded in all competitions The number of goals conceded while he was on the pitch in all competitions	41
Clean Sheets In games when he played at least 70 mins	15
Defensive Rating Average number of minutes between League goals conceded while on pitch	113

	PLAYER	CLUB	CG	CONC LGE	CS	DEF RATE
1	Klos	Rangers	34	27	15	113
2	Gordon	Hearts	29	27	8	97
3	Marshall	Motherwell	34	42	9	73
4	Stillie	Dunfermline	37	51	13	65
5	McKenzie	Livingston	35	50	10	63
6	Speroni	Dundee	37	56	7	59
7	Andersson	Hibernian	38	60	9	57
8	Gallacher	Dundee Utd	33	54	9	55
9	Preece	Aberdeen	36	60	5	54
10	Meldrum	Kilmarnock	17	29	1	51
11	Arthur	Partick	22	44	3	45
12	Dubourdeau	Kilmarnock	18	39	1	42

PLAYER DISCIPLINARY RECORD

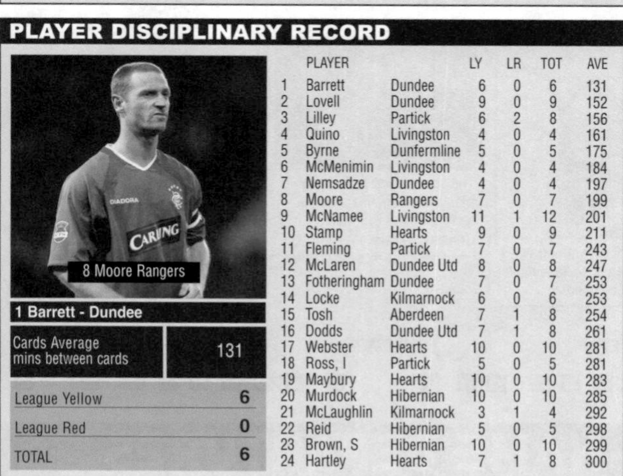
8 Moore Rangers

1 Barrett - Dundee	
Cards Average mins between cards	131
League Yellow	6
League Red	0
TOTAL	6

	PLAYER		LY	LR	TOT	AVE
1	Barrett	Dundee	6	0	6	131
2	Lovell	Dundee	9	0	9	152
3	Lilley	Partick	6	2	8	156
4	Quino	Livingston	4	0	4	161
5	Byrne	Dunfermline	5	0	5	175
6	McMenimin	Livingston	4	0	4	184
7	Nemsadze	Dundee	4	0	4	197
8	Moore	Rangers	7	0	7	199
9	McNamee	Livingston	11	1	12	201
10	Stamp	Hearts	9	0	9	211
11	Fleming	Partick	7	0	7	243
12	McLaren	Dundee Utd	8	0	8	247
13	Fotheringham	Dundee	7	0	7	253
14	Locke	Kilmarnock	6	0	6	253
15	Tosh	Aberdeen	7	1	8	254
16	Dodds	Dundee Utd	7	1	8	261
17	Webster	Hearts	10	0	10	281
18	Ross, I	Partick	5	0	5	281
19	Maybury	Hearts	10	0	10	283
20	Murdock	Hibernian	10	0	10	285
21	McLaughlin	Kilmarnock	3	1	4	292
22	Reid	Hibernian	5	0	5	298
23	Brown, S	Hibernian	10	0	10	299
24	Hartley	Hearts	7	1	8	300

TEAM OF THE SEASON

G
Klos : Rangers
CG: 34 DR: 97
D
McNamara : Celtic
CG: 25 DR: 194
D
Khizanishvili : Rangers
CG: 24 DR: 107
D
Webster : Hearts
CG: 30 DR: 91
D
Hammell : Motherwell
CG: 35 DR: 74
M
Petrov : Celtic
CG: 31 SD: + 107
M
Arteta : Rangers
CG: 19 SD: + 57
M
Hartley : Hearts
CG: 25 SD: + 32
M
Murray : Kilmarnock
CG: 18 SD: + 8
F
Larsson
CG: 31 SR: 105
F
Lovenkrands : Rangers
CG: 17 AP: 45

CELTIC RETAKE DOMESTIC CROWN

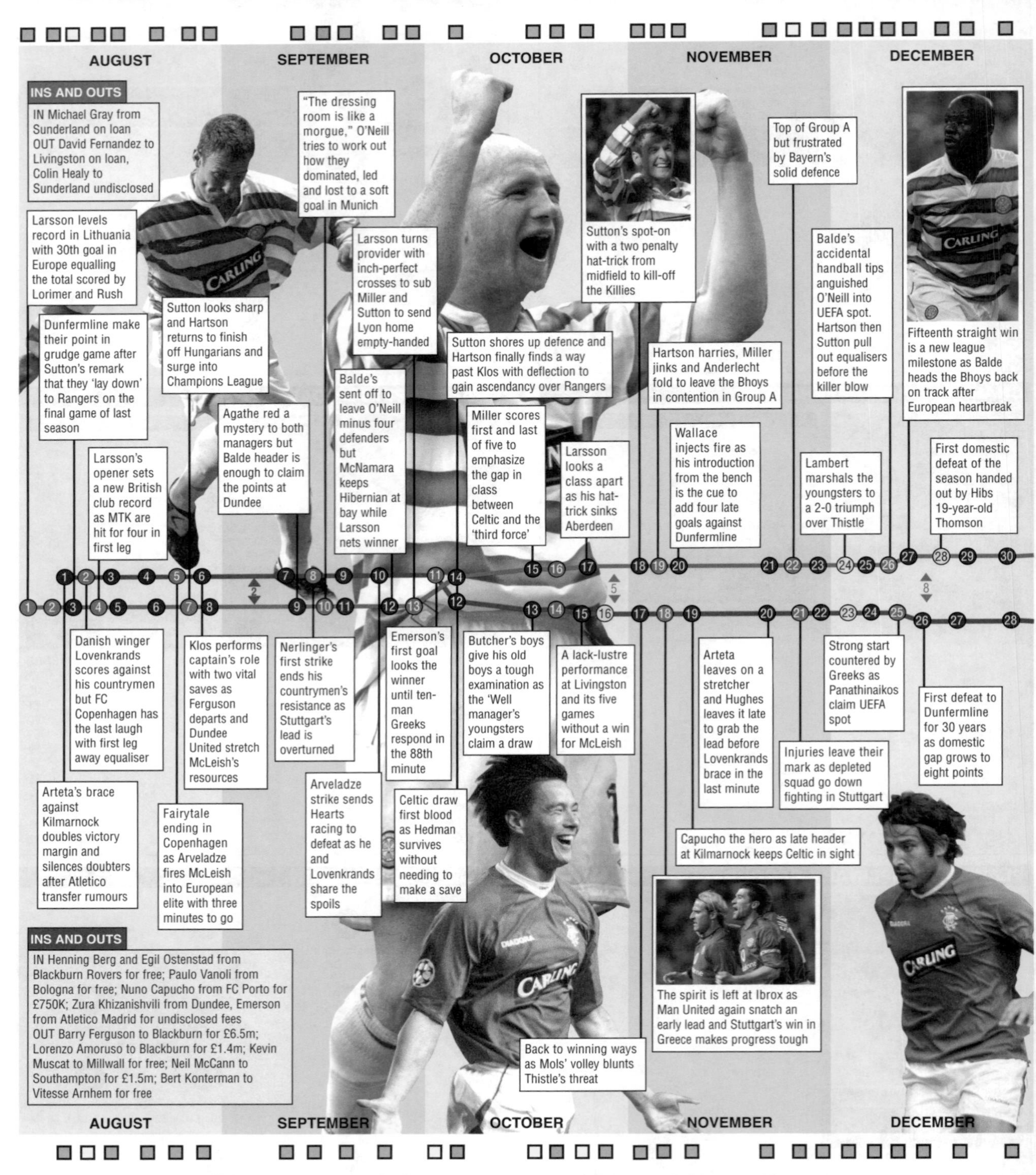

AUGUST
SEPTEMBER
OCTOBER
NOVEMBER
DECEMBER
INS AND OUTS
IN Michael Gray from Sunderland on loan
OUT David Fernandez to Livingston on loan, Colin Healy to Sunderland undisclosed
Larsson levels record in Lithuania with 30th goal in Europe equalling the total scored by Lorimer and Rush
Dunfermline make their point in grudge game after Sutton's remark that they 'lay down' to Rangers on the final game of last season
Larsson's opener sets a new British club record as MTK are hit for four in first leg
Sutton looks sharp and Hartson returns to finish off Hungarians and surge into Champions League
Agathe red a mystery to both managers but Balde header is enough to claim the points at Dundee
"The dressing room is like a morgue," O'Neill tries to work out how they dominated, led and lost to a soft goal in Munich
Larsson turns provider with inch-perfect crosses to sub Miller and Sutton to send Lyon home empty-handed
Balde's sent off to leave O'Neill minus four defenders but McNamara keeps Hibernian at bay while Larsson nets winner
Sutton shores up defence and Hartson finally finds a way past Klos with deflection to gain ascendancy over Rangers
Miller scores first and last of five to emphasize the gap in class between Celtic and the 'third force'
Larsson looks a class apart as his hat-trick sinks Aberdeen
Sutton's spot-on with a two penalty hat-trick from midfield to kill-off the Killies
Hartson harries, Miller jinks and Anderlecht fold to leave the Bhoys in contention in Group A
Wallace injects fire as his introduction from the bench is the cue to add four late goals against Dunfermline
Top of Group A but frustrated by Bayern's solid defence
Balde's accidental handball tips anguished O'Neill into UEFA spot. Hartson then Sutton pull out equalisers before the killer blow
Lambert marshals the youngsters to a 2-0 triumph over Thistle
Fifteenth straight win is a new league milestone as Balde heads the Bhoys back on track after European heartbreak
First domestic defeat of the season handed out by Hibs 19-year-old Thomson
Danish winger Lovenkrands scores against his countrymen but FC Copenhagen has the last laugh with first leg away equaliser
Arteta's brace against Kilmarnock doubles victory margin and silences doubters after Atletico transfer rumours
Klos performs captain's role with two vital saves as Ferguson departs and Dundee United stretch McLeish's resources
Fairytale ending in Copenhagen as Arveladze fires McLeish into European elite with three minutes to go
Nerlinger's first strike ends his countrymen's resistance as Stuttgart's lead is overturned
Arveladze strike sends Hearts racing to defeat as he and Lovenkrands share the spoils
Emerson's first goal looks the winner until ten-man Greeks respond in the 88th minute
Celtic draw first blood as Hedman survives without needing to make a save
Butcher's boys give his old boys a tough examination as the 'Well manager's youngsters claim a draw
A lack-lustre performance at Livingston and its five games without a win for McLeish
Back to winning ways as Mols' volley blunts Thistle's threat
Arteta leaves on a stretcher and Hughes leaves it late to grab the lead before Lovenkrands brace in the last minute
Capucho the hero as late header at Kilmarnock keeps Celtic in sight
The spirit is left at Ibrox as Man United again snatch an early lead and Stuttgart's win in Greece makes progress tough
Injuries leave their mark as depleted squad go down fighting in Stuttgart
Strong start countered by Greeks as Panathinaikos claim UEFA spot
First defeat to Dunfermline for 30 years as domestic gap grows to eight points
INS AND OUTS
IN Henning Berg and Egil Ostenstad from Blackburn Rovers for free; Paulo Vanoli from Bologna for free; Nuno Capucho from FC Porto for £750K; Zura Khizanishvili from Dundee, Emerson from Atletico Madrid for undisclosed fees
OUT Barry Ferguson to Blackburn for £6.5m; Lorenzo Amoruso to Blackburn for £1.4m; Kevin Muscat to Millwall for free; Neil McCann to Southampton for £1.5m; Bert Konterman to Vitesse Arnhem for free
AUGUST
SEPTEMBER
OCTOBER
NOVEMBER
DECEMBER

RANGERS ADJUST TO BIG-NAME DEPARTURES

Larsson finishes on seven year high

Final Position: **1st**

KEY: League, Champions Lge, UEFA Cup, Scottish FA Cup, Scottish League Cup, Other, Won, Drawn, Lost

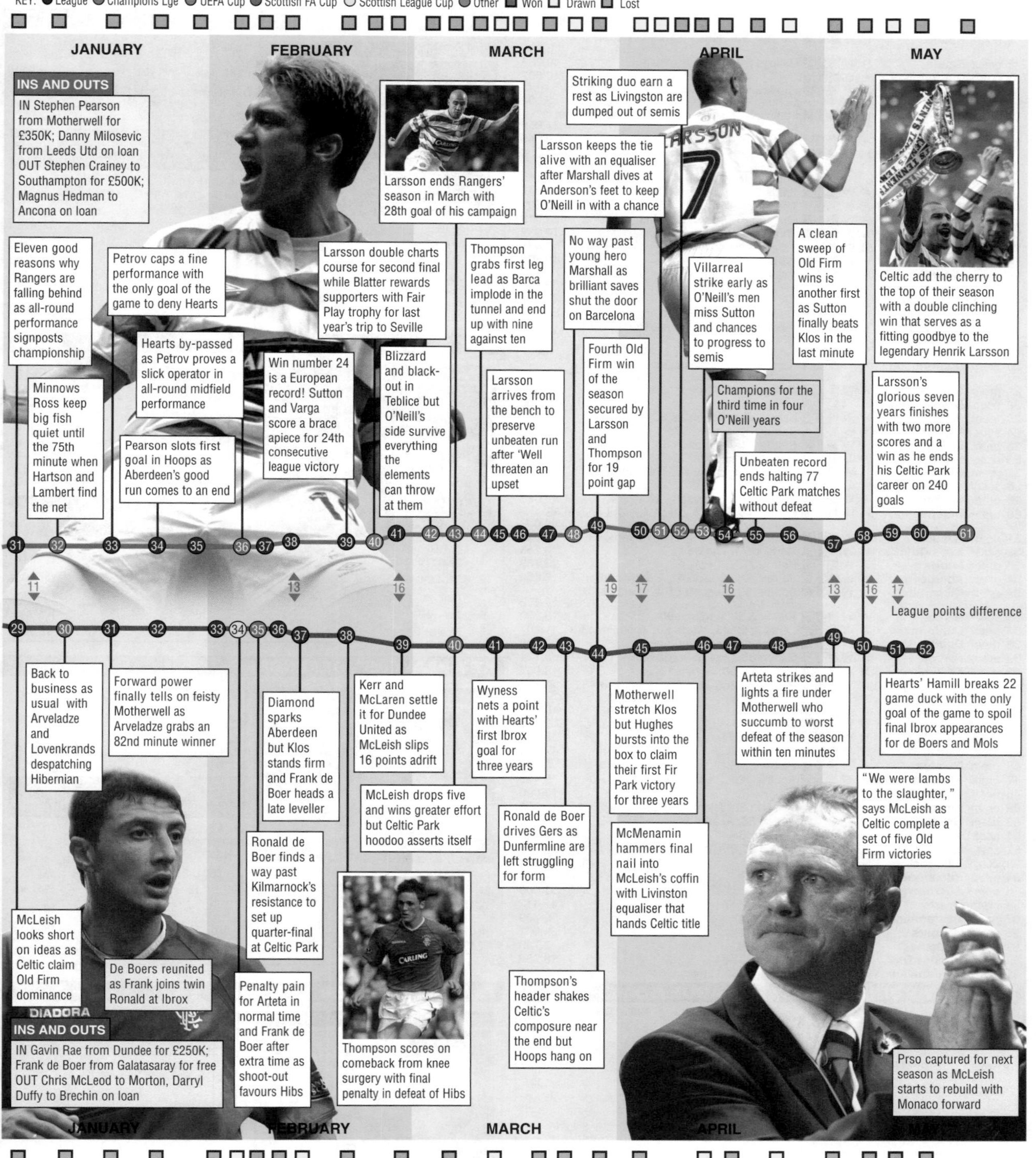

JANUARY
FEBRUARY
MARCH
APRIL
MAY
INS AND OUTS
IN Stephen Pearson from Motherwell for £350K; Danny Milosevic from Leeds Utd on loan OUT Stephen Crainey to Southampton for £500K; Magnus Hedman to Ancona on loan
Larsson ends Rangers' season in March with 28th goal of his campaign
Striking duo earn a rest as Livingston are dumped out of semis
Larsson keeps the tie alive with an equaliser after Marshall dives at Anderson's feet to keep O'Neill in with a chance
Celtic add the cherry to the top of their season with a double clinching win that serves as a fitting goodbye to the legendary Henrik Larsson
Eleven good reasons why Rangers are falling behind as all-round performance signposts championship
Petrov caps a fine performance with the only goal of the game to deny Hearts
Larsson double charts course for second final while Blatter rewards supporters with Fair Play trophy for last year's trip to Seville
Thompson grabs first leg lead as Barca implode in the tunnel and end up with nine against ten
No way past young hero Marshall as brilliant saves shut the door on Barcelona
Villarreal strike early as O'Neill's men miss Sutton and chances to progress to semis
A clean sweep of Old Firm wins is another first as Sutton finally beats Klos in the last minute
Minnows Ross keep big fish quiet until the 75th minute when Hartson and Lambert find the net
Hearts by-passed as Petrov proves a slick operator in all-round midfield performance
Win number 24 is a European record! Sutton and Varga score a brace apiece for 24th consecutive league victory
Blizzard and black-out in Teblice but O'Neill's side survive everything the elements can throw at them
Larsson arrives from the bench to preserve unbeaten run after 'Well threaten an upset
Fourth Old Firm win of the season secured by Larsson and Thompson for 19 point gap
Champions for the third time in four O'Neill years
Larsson's glorious seven years finishes with two more scores and a win as he ends his Celtic Park career on 240 goals
Pearson slots first goal in Hoops as Aberdeen's good run comes to an end
Unbeaten record ends halting 77 Celtic Park matches without defeat
31 32 33 34 35 36 37 38 39 40 41 42 43 44 45 46 47 48 49 50 51 52 53 54 55 56 57 58 59 60 61
11 13 16 19 17 16 13 16 17
League points difference
29 30 31 32 33 34 35 36 37 38 39 40 41 42 43 44 45 46 47 48 49 50 51 52
Back to business as usual with Arveladze and Lovenkrands despatching Hibernian
Forward power finally tells on feisty Motherwell as Arveladze grabs an 82nd minute winner
Diamond sparks Aberdeen but Klos stands firm and Frank de Boer heads a late leveller
Kerr and McLaren settle it for Dundee United as McLeish slips 16 points adrift
Wyness nets a point with Hearts' first Ibrox goal for three years
Motherwell stretch Klos but Hughes bursts into the box to claim their first Fir Park victory for three years
Arteta strikes and lights a fire under Motherwell who succumb to worst defeat of the season within ten minutes
Hearts' Hamill breaks 22 game duck with the only goal of the game to spoil final Ibrox appearances for de Boers and Mols
McLeish drops five and wins greater effort but Celtic Park hoodoo asserts itself
Ronald de Boer drives Gers as Dunfermline are left struggling for form
"We were lambs to the slaughter," says McLeish as Celtic complete a set of five Old Firm victories
Ronald de Boer finds a way past Kilmarnock's resistance to set up quarter-final at Celtic Park
McMenamin hammers final nail into McLeish's coffin with Livinston equaliser that hands Celtic title
McLeish looks short on ideas as Celtic claim Old Firm dominance
De Boers reunited as Frank joins twin Ronald at Ibrox
Penalty pain for Arteta in normal time and Frank de Boer after extra time as shoot-out favours Hibs
Thompson scores on comeback from knee surgery with final penalty in defeat of Hibs
Thompson's header shakes Celtic's composure near the end but Hoops hang on
Prso captured for next season as McLeish starts to rebuild with Monaco forward
INS AND OUTS
IN Gavin Rae from Dundee for £250K; Frank de Boer from Galatasaray for free OUT Chris McLeod to Morton, Darryl Duffy to Brechin on loan
JANUARY
FEBRUARY
MARCH
APRIL
MAY

Second! But from a long way out

Final Position: **2nd**

SCOTTISH PREMIER LEAGUE CHAMPIONS

CELTIC

Final Position: **1ST**

NICKNAME: THE BHOYS

KEY: Won / Drawn / Lost

	Comp	Opponent	H/A	Res	Score	Scorers	Attendance
1	ecql1	**Kaunas**	A	W	4-0	Larsson 13; Sutton 29; Maloney 54; Miller 85	3,000
2	ecql2	**Kaunas**	H	W	1-0	Gvildys 21 og	40,284
3	prem	**Dunfermline**	A	D	0-0		10,082
4	ecql1	**MTK Hungaria**	A	W	4-0	Larsson 16; Agathe 35; Petrov 68; Sutton 90	5,000
5	prem	**Dundee Utd**	H	W	5-0	Maloney 12; Agathe 27; Thompson 45 pen; McNamara 67; Larsson 84	57,658
6	prem	**Partick**	A	W	2-1	Lambert 8; Thompson 44 pen	9,045
7	ecql2	**MTK Budapest**	H	W	1-0	Sutton 13	41,720
8	prem	**Livingston**	H	W	5-1	Larsson 25,56,77; Maloney 39; Thompson 90	57,165
9	prem	**Dundee**	A	W	1-0	Balde 8	10,647
10	ecgpa	**Bayern Munich**	A	L	1-2	Thompson 56	48,500
11	prem	**Motherwell**	H	W	3-0	Larsson 47; Sutton 64; Maloney 70	58,013
12	prem	**Hibernian**	A	W	2-1	Thompson 40 pen; Larsson 51	12,032
13	ecgpa	**Lyon**	H	W	2-0	Miller 70; Sutton 78	57,475
14	prem	**Rangers**	A	W	1-0	Hartson 46	49,825
15	prem	**Hearts**	H	W	5-0	Miller 9,50; Stamp 12 og; Larsson 36; Varga 42	59,560
16	ecgpa	**Anderlecht**	A	L	0-1		27,000
17	prem	**Aberdeen**	H	W	4-0	Larsson 4,28,55; Sutton 45 pen	59,598
18	prem	**Kilmarnock**	A	W	5-0	Sutton 21 pen,76,90 pen; Hartson 70; Maloney 84	12,460
19	ecgpa	**Anderlecht**	H	W	3-1	Larsson 12; Miller 17; Sutton 29	59,057
20	prem	**Dunfermline**	H	W	5-0	Hartson 23,77; Wallace 81; Varga 83; Larsson 87	58,328
21	prem	**Dundee Utd**	A	W	5-1	Sutton 34,56,82 pen; Larsson 52,58	10,802
22	ecgpa	**Bayern Munich**	H	D	0-0		59,506
23	prem	**Partick**	H	W	3-1	Larsson 23; Sutton 36,60	58,202
24	sccc3	**Partick**	A	W	2-0	Beattie 31; Smith, J 75	5,700
25	prem	**Livingston**	A	W	2-0	Sutton 48; Thompson 85	9,523
26	ecgpa	**Lyon**	A	L	2-3	Hartson 24; Sutton 75	40,125
27	prem	**Dundee**	H	W	3-2	Larsson 15; Balde 69; Thompson 85	57,573
28	sccqf	**Hibernian**	A	L	1-2	Varga 56	9,246
29	prem	**Motherwell**	A	W	2-0	Hartson 3; Thompson 71	10,513
30	prem	**Hibernian**	H	W	6-0	Sutton 4,54 pen; Hartson 45,60; Larsson 66; Petrov 77	59,609
31	prem	**Rangers**	H	W	3-0	Petrov 19; Varga 60; Thompson 84	59,087
32	scr3	**Ross County**	H	W	2-0	Hartson 74; Lambert 79	30,565
33	prem	**Hearts**	A	W	1-0	Petrov 27	13,753
34	prem	**Aberdeen**	A	W	3-1	Petrov 30; Larsson 43; Pearson 58	16,452
35	prem	**Kilmarnock**	H	W	5-1	Agathe 55; Hartson 65,89; Larsson 76; Pearson 77	59,138
36	scr4	**Hearts**	A	W	3-0	Petrov 3,33; Larsson 90	15,372
37	prem	**Dunfermline**	A	W	4-1	Larsson 23,43; Varga 26; Thompson 68	11,201
38	prem	**Dundee Utd**	H	W	2-1	Maloney 81; Sutton 83 pen	58,698
39	prem	**Partick**	A	W	4-1	Sutton 35,52 pen; Varga 38,81	8,131
40	uc3rl1	**FK Teplice**	H	W	3-0	Larsson 3,90; Sutton 13	48,947
41	prem	**Livingston**	H	W	5-1	Pearson 12; Sutton 36; Thompson 48,80 pen; Larsson 55	57,973
42	uc3rl2	**FK Teplice**	A	L	0-1		10,000
43	Scpqf	**Rangers**	H	W	1-0	Larsson 53	58,735
44	uc4rl1	**Barcelona**	H	W	1-0	Thompson 59	59,539
45	prem	**Motherwell**	H	D	1-1	Larsson 70	47,563
46	prem	**Dundee**	A	W	2-1	Petrov 38; Larsson 68	8,593
47	prem	**Hibernian**	A	W	4-0	Agathe 18,81; Larsson 35,49	9,456
48	uc4rl2	**Barcelona**	A	D	0-0		78,000
49	prem	**Rangers**	A	W	2-1	Larsson 20; Thompson 52	49,909
50	prem	**Hearts**	H	D	2-2	Sutton 88; Agathe 90	59,348
51	ucqfl1	**Villarreal**	H	D	1-1	Larsson 64	58,493
52	scsf	**Livingston**	A	W	3-1	Sutton 37,65; Larsson 50	26,152
53	ucqfl2	**Villarreal**	A	L	0-2		15,964
54	prem	**Kilmarnock**	A	W	1-0	Petrov 32	14,576
55	prem	**Aberdeen**	H	L	1-2	Larsson 16	51,000
56	prem	**Hearts**	A	D	1-1	McGeady 17	12,112
57	prem	**Dunfermline**	H	L	1-2	Larsson 47	59,739
58	prem	**Rangers**	H	W	1-0	Sutton 90	58,851
59	prem	**Motherwell**	A	D	1-1	Beattie 79	7,749
60	prem	**Dundee Utd**	H	W	2-1	Larsson 81,84	58,386
61	scfin	**Dunfermline**	A	W	3-1	Larsson 58,71; Petrov 84	50,846

MONTHLY POINTS TALLY

Month	Points	%
AUGUST	10	83%
SEPTEMBER	9	100%
OCTOBER	9	100%
NOVEMBER	12	100%
DECEMBER	12	100%
JANUARY	12	100%
FEBRUARY	12	100%
MARCH	10	83%
APRIL	5	42%
MAY	7	58%

LEAGUE GOALS

	PLAYER	MINS	GOALS	AVE
1	Larsson	3059	29	105
2	Sutton	2218	19	117
3	Thompson	2194	12	183
4	Hartson	1181	9	131
5	Varga	2979	6	497
6	Petrov	2857	6	476
7	Maloney	784	5	157
8	Agathe	2150	5	430
9	Pearson	1380	3	460
10	Balde	2693	2	1347
11	Miller	1478	2	739
12	Beattie	332	1	332
13	Wallace	415	1	415
	Other		5	
	TOTAL		105	

KEY PLAYERS - GOALSCORERS

Henrik Larsson

Goals in the League	29
Goals in all competitions	40
Contribution to Attacking Power Average number of minutes between League team goals while on pitch	31
Player Strike Rate The total number of minutes he was on the pitch for every League goal scored	105
Club Strike Rate Average number of minutes between League goals scored by club	35

	PLAYER	GOALS LGE	GOALS ALL	POWER	S RATE
1	Henrik Larsson	29	40	31	105 mins
2	Chris Sutton	19	28	29	117 mins
3	Alan Thompson	12	14	30	183 mins
4	Didier Agathe	5	6	31	430 mins
5	Stephen Pearson	3	3	39	460 mins

KEY PLAYERS - MIDFIELDERS

Stilian Petrov

Goals in the League	6
Counting Games	31
Defensive Rating Average number of mins between League goals conceded while on the pitch	159
Contribution to Attacking Power Average number of minutes between League team goals while on pitch	32
Scoring Difference Defensive Rating minus Contribution to Attacking Power	127

	PLAYER	GOALS LGE	DEF RATE	ATT POWER	SCORE DIFF
1	Stilian Petrov	6	159	32	127 mins
2	Neil Lennon	0	139	32	107 mins
3	Alan Thompson	12	137	30	107 mins
4	Liam Miller	2	134	31	103 mins
5	Stephen Pearson	3	115	39	76 mins

KEY PLAYERS - DEFENDERS

Jackie McNamara

Goals Conceded in League	12
Counting Games	25
Clean Sheets In League games when he played at least 70 mins	14
Defensive Rating Ave number of mins between League goals conceded while on the pitch	194
Club Defensive Rating Average number of mins between League goals conceded by the club this season	137

	PLAYER	CON LGE	CLN SHEETS	DEF RATE
1	Jackie McNamara	12	14	194 mins
2	Didier Agathe	13	10	165 mins
3	Dianbobo Balde	18	15	150 mins
4	Stanislav Varga	21	13	142 mins

KEY GOALKEEPER

Robert Douglas

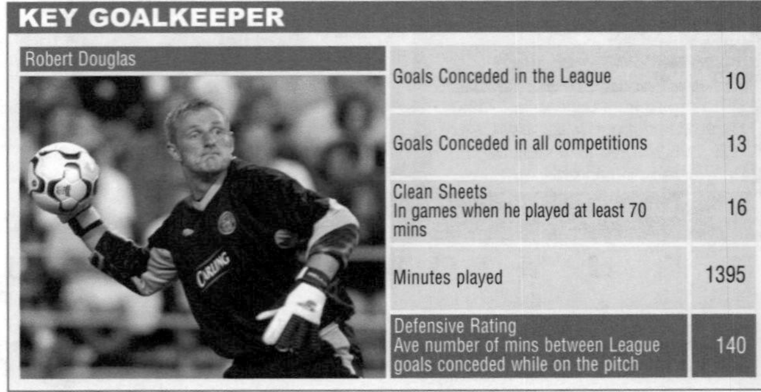

Goals Conceded in the League	10
Goals Conceded in all competitions	13
Clean Sheets In games when he played at least 70 mins	16
Minutes played	1395
Defensive Rating Ave number of mins between League goals conceded while on the pitch	140

DISCIPLINARY RECORDS

	PLAYER	YELLOW	RED	AVE
1	Thompson	6	0	365
2	Mjallby	2	0	443
3	Miller	3	0	492
4	Hartson	2	0	590
5	Varga	5	0	595
6	Pearson	2	0	690
7	Sutton	3	0	739
8	Lennon	4	0	762
9	McNamara	3	0	776
10	Maloney	1	0	784
11	Kennedy	1	0	843
12	Balde	2	1	897
13	Petrov	3	0	952
	Other	5	1	
	TOTAL	42	2	

TOP POINT EARNERS

	PLAYER	GAMES	AV PTS
1	McNamara	25	2.92
2	Douglas	15	2.87
3	Sutton	24	2.79
4	Agathe	23	2.74
5	Balde	29	2.72
6	Pearson	14	2.71
7	Petrov	31	2.71
8	Thompson	23	2.70
9	Miller	13	2.69
10	Lennon	34	2.65
	CLUB AVERAGE:		2.58

LEAGUE APPEARANCES, BOOKINGS AND CAPS

	AGE (on 01/07/04)	IN NAMED 16	APPEARANCES	COUNTING GAMES	MINUTES ON PITCH	YELLOW CARDS	RED CARDS	THIS SEASON	HOME COUNTRY
Goalkeepers									
Robert Douglas	32	30	16	15	1395	0	0	7	Scotland (63)
Magnus Hedman	31	18	12	11	1035	0	0	6	Sweden (21)
David Marshall	19	23	11	11	990	0	0	-	Scotland
Defenders									
Didier Agathe	28	27	26	23	2150	0	1	-	France
Dianbobo Balde	28	32	31	29	2693	2	1	-	France
Stephen Crainey	23	4	2	0	37	0	0	2	Scotland (63)
Michael Gray	29	10	7	2	333	0	0	-	England
John Kennedy	20	16	12	8	843	1	0	1	Scotland (63)
Ulrik Laursen	28	0	0	0	0	0	0	-	Denmark
Stephen McManus	21	7	5	2	353	2	0	-	Scotland
Jackie McNamara	30	29	27	25	2329	3	0	7	Scotland (63)
Johan Mjallby	33	16	13	8	886	2	0	3	Sweden (21)
Mohammed Sylla	27	22	14	4	576	0	0	-	Ivory coast
Joos Valgaeren	28	12	7	2	401	0	0	1	Belgium (17)
Stanislav Varga	31	37	35	31	2979	5	0	-	Slovakia
Midfielders									
Steve Guppy	35	0	0	0	0	0	0	-	England
Paul Lambert	34	22	13	8	809	0	0	2	Scotland (63)
Neil Lennon	33	36	35	34	3051	4	0	-	N Ireland
Kevin McBride	-	1	0	0	0	0	0	-	Scotland
Liam Miller	23	25	25	13	1478	3	0	-	Rep of Ireland
Stephen Pearson	21	17	17	14	1380	2	0	-	Scotland
Stilian Petrov	25	35	35	31	2857	3	0	-	Bulgaria
Bobby Petta	29	1	0	0	0	0	0	-	Holland
Jamie Smith	23	14	11	3	540	0	0	-	Scotland
Alan Thompson	30	26	26	23	2194	6	0	1	England (12)
Forwards									
Craig Beattie	20	19	10	2	332	1	0	-	Scotland
John Hartson	29	18	15	12	1181	2	0	5	Wales (66)
Henrik Larsson	32	37	36	31	3059	2	0	-	Sweden
Shaun Maloney	21	24	17	6	784	1	0	-	Scotland
Eiden McGeady	18	4	4	2	237	0	0	-	Rep or Ireland
Chris Sutton	31	25	25	24	2218	3	0	-	England
Ross Wallace	19	16	8	4	415	0	0	-	Scotland

TEAM OF THE SEASON

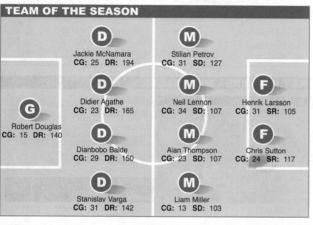

G — Robert Douglas — **CG:** 15 **DR:** 140

D — Jackie McNamara — **CG:** 25 **DR:** 194
D — Didier Agathe — **CG:** 23 **DR:** 165
D — Dianbobo Balde — **CG:** 29 **DR:** 150
D — Stanislav Varga — **CG:** 31 **DR:** 142

M — Stilian Petrov — **CG:** 31 **SD:** 127
M — Neil Lennon — **CG:** 34 **SD:** 107
M — Alan Thompson — **CG:** 23 **SD:** 107
M — Liam Miller — **CG:** 13 **SD:** 103

F — Henrik Larsson — **CG:** 31 **SR:** 105
F — Chris Sutton — **CG:** 24 **SR:** 117

SQUAD APPEARANCES

Match	Venue	Competition	Result
1	A	C	W
2	H	C	W
3	A	L	D
4	A	C	W
5	H	L	W
6	A	L	W
7	H	C	W
8	H	L	W
9	A	L	W
10	A	C	L
11	H	L	W
12	A	L	W
13	H	C	W
14	A	L	W
15	H	L	W
16	A	C	L
17	H	L	W
18	A	L	W
19	H	C	W
20	H	L	W
21	A	L	W
22	H	C	D
23	H	L	W
24	A	W	W
25	A	L	W
26	A	C	L
27	H	L	W
28	A	W	L
29	A	L	W
30	H	L	W
31	H	L	W
32	H	O	W
33	A	L	W
34	A	L	W
35	H	L	W
36	A	O	W
37	A	L	W
38	H	L	W
39	A	L	W
40	H	E	W
41	H	L	W
42	A	E	L
43	H	O	W
44	H	E	W
45	H	L	D
46	A	L	W
47	A	L	W
48	A	E	D
49	A	L	W
50	H	L	D
51	H	E	D
52	A	O	W
53	A	E	L
54	A	L	W
55	H	L	L
56	A	L	D
57	H	L	L
58	H	L	W
59	A	L	D
60	H	L	W
61	A	O	W

Goalkeepers
Robert Douglas
Magnus Hedman
David Marshall

Defenders
Didier Agathe
Dianbobo Balde
Stephen Crainey
Michael Gray
John Kennedy
Ulrik Laursen
Stephen McManus
Jackie McNamara
Johan Mjallby
Mohammed Sylla
Joos Valgaeren
Stanislav Varga

Midfielders
Steve Guppy
Paul Lambert
Neil Lennon
Kevin McBride
Liam Miller
Stephen Pearson
Stilian Petrov
Bobby Petta
Jamie Smith
Alan Thompson

Forwards
Craig Beattie
John Hartson
Henrik Larsson
Shaun Maloney
Eiden McGeady
Chris Sutton
Ross Wallace

KEY: On all match | On bench | Subbed or sent off (Counting game) | Subbed or sent off (playing less than 70 minutes) | Subbed on from bench (Counting Game) | Subbed on (playing less than 70 minutes) | Subbed on and then subbed or sent off (Counting Game) | Subbed on and then subbed or sent off (playing less than 70 minutes) | Not in 16

RANGERS

Final Position: **2nd**

NICKNAME: THE GERS

KEY: ☐Won ☐Drawn ☐Lost

#	Comp	Opponent	H/A	Res	Score	Scorers	Attendance
1	prem	**Kilmarnock**	H	W	4-0	Lovenkrands 14; Mols 38; Arteta 43 pen,72	49,108
2	ecql1	**Copenhagen**	H	D	1-1	Lovenkrands 7	47,401
3	prem	**Aberdeen**	A	W	3-2	de Boer 38; Arteta 43; Mols 58	16,348
4	prem	**Hibernian**	H	W	5-2	Mols 34,62; O'Connor 43 og; Arteta 67; Burke 84	49,642
5	ecql2	**Copenhagen**	A	W	2-1	Arteta 52 pen; Arveladze 86	35,519
6	prem	**Dundee Utd**	A	W	3-1	Capucho 14; Arveladze 85; Arteta 89 pen	9,752
7	prem	**Dunfermline**	H	W	4-0	Thompson 7; Mols 32; Arveladze 43; Capucho 66	49,072
8	ecge	**Stuttgart**	H	W	2-1	Nerlinger 72; Lovenkrands 79	47,957
9	prem	**Hearts**	A	W	4-0	Arveladze 45,73; Lovenkrands 51,89	14,732
10	prem	**Dundee**	H	W	3-1	Arveladze 60,89; Vanoli 86	49,548
11	ecge	**Panathinaikos**	A	D	1-1	Emerson 35	13,718
12	prem	**Celtic**	H	L	0-1		49,825
13	prem	**Motherwell**	A	D	1-1	Arveladze 15	10,824
14	ecgpe	**Man Utd**	H	L	0-1		48,730
15	prem	**Livingston**	A	D	0-0		9,627
16	sccc3	**Forfar**	H	W	6-0	Nerlinger 15,53,70; Lovenkrands 22; Capucho 50; Ostenstad 75	26,327
17	prem	**Partick**	H	W	3-1	Arteta 8,77 pen; Mols 40	49,551
18	ecge	**Man Utd**	A	L	0-3		66,707
19	prem	**Kilmarnock**	A	W	3-2	Arveladze 30,63; Capucho 87	12,204
20	prem	**Aberdeen**	H	W	3-0	Hughes 77; Lovenkrands 89,90	49,962
21	ecge	**Stuttgart**	A	L	0-1		50,348
22	prem	**Hibernian**	A	W	1-0	Hughes 90	11,160
23	sccqf	**St Johnstone**	H	W	3-0	Burke 16; Ostenstad 59; Mols 90	29,395
24	prem	**Dundee Utd**	H	W	2-1	Capucho 17; Lovenkrands 20	49,307
25	ecge	**Panathinaikos**	H	L	1-3	Mols 28	48,588
26	prem	**Dunfermline**	A	L	0-2		8,592
27	prem	**Hearts**	H	W	2-1	Arveladze 22; Burke 52	49,592
28	prem	**Dundee**	A	W	2-0	Capucho 6; Ball 35	10,948
29	prem	**Celtic**	A	L	0-3		59,087
30	scr3	**Hibernian**	A	W	2-0	Arveladze 35; Lovenkrands 49	11,392
31	prem	**Motherwell**	H	W	1-0	Arveladze 82	48,925
32	prem	**Livingston**	H	W	1-0	Nerlinger 13	48,628
33	prem	**Partick**	A	W	1-0	Lovenkrands 76	8,220
34	slc5	**Hibernian**	A	L	3-4*	Mols 40 (*on penalties)	27,954
35	scr4	**Kilmarnock**	A	W	2-0	de Boer, R 62; Arveladze 67 pen	10,993
36	prem	**Kilmarnock**	H	W	2-0	Moore 23; Namouchi 76	46,900
37	prem	**Aberdeen**	A	D	1-1	de Boer, F 87	15,815
38	prem	**Hibernian**	H	W	3-0	Arveladze 9 pen; Mols 60; Thompson 83 pen	49,698
39	prem	**Dundee Utd**	A	L	0-2		10,496
40	Scpqf	**Celtic**	A	L	0-1		58,735
41	prem	**Hearts**	A	D	1-1	Moore 55 pen	14,598
42	prem	**Dundee**	H	W	4-0	Lovenkrands 41; de Boer, F 47; Rae 81; Thompson 83	49,364
43	prem	**Dunfermline**	H	W	4-1	Hutton 2; Lovenkrands 11; de Boer, R 26; Mols 28	47,487
44	prem	**Celtic**	H	L	1-2	Thompson 82	49,909
45	prem	**Motherwell**	A	W	1-0	Hughes 44	8,967
46	prem	**Livingston**	A	D	1-1	Mols 25	6,096
47	prem	**Partick**	H	W	2-0	Thompson 40; Rae 49	49,279
48	prem	**Dundee Utd**	A	D	3-3	Thompson 6,14 pen; Namouchi 44	8,339
49	prem	**Motherwell**	H	W	4-0	Arteta 45; Ross 47; Namouchi 51; Thompson 55	47,579
50	prem	**Celtic**	A	L	0-1		58,851
51	prem	**Hearts**	H	L	0-1		47,467
52	prem	**Dunfermline**	A	W	3-2	Ricksen 42; Burke 45; McCormack 63 pen	6,798

KEY PLAYERS - GOALSCORERS

Shota Arveladze

Goals in the League	12
Goals in all competitions	15
Contribution to Attacking Power Average number of minutes between League team goals while on pitch	41
Player Strike Rate The total number of minutes he was on the pitch for every League goal scored	128
Club Strike Rate Average number of minutes between League goals scored by club	45

	PLAYER	GOALS LGE	GOALS ALL	POWER	S RATE
1	Shota Arveladze	12	15	41	128 mins
2	Peter Lovenkrands	9	13	50	208 mins
3	Mikel Arteta	8	9	41	236 mins
4	Michael Mols	9	12	41	279 mins

KEY PLAYERS - MIDFIELDERS

Nuno Fernando Capucho

CARLING

Goals in the League	5
Counting Games	13
Defensive Rating Average number of mins between League goals conceded while on the pitch	137
Contribution to Attacking Power Average number of minutes between League team goals while on pitch	52
Scoring Difference Defensive Rating minus Contribution to Attacking Power	85

	PLAYER	GOALS LGE	DEF RATE	ATT POWER	SCORE DIFF
1	Nuno Fernando Capucho	5	137	52	85 mins
2	Mikel Arteta	8	99	42	57 mins
3	Peter Lovenkrands	9	98	51	47 mins
4	Stephen Hughes	3	88	43	45 mins

KEY PLAYERS - DEFENDERS

Frank de Boer

CARLING

Goals Conceded in League	10
Counting Games	14
Clean Sheets In League games when he played at least 70 mins	7
Defensive Rating Ave number of mins between League goals conceded while on the pitch	131
Club Defensive Rating Average number of mins between League goals conceded by the club this season	104

	PLAYER	CON LGE	CLN SHEETS	DEF RATE
1	Frank de Boer	10	7	131 mins
2	Craig Moore	12	7	116 mins
3	Zurab Khizanishvili	21	10	107 mins
4	Henning Berg	16	7	106 mins
5	Fernando Ricksen	26	12	97 mins

MONTHLY POINTS TALLY

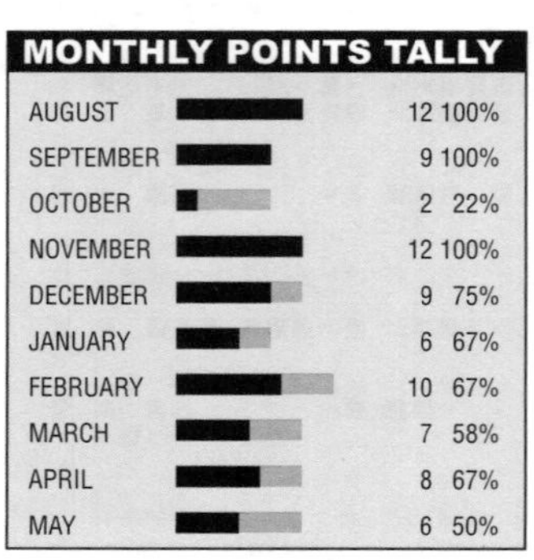
AUGUST 12 100%
SEPTEMBER 9 100%
OCTOBER 2 22%
NOVEMBER 12 100%
DECEMBER 9 75%
JANUARY 6 67%
FEBRUARY 10 67%
MARCH 7 58%
APRIL 8 67%
MAY 6 50%

LEAGUE GOALS

	PLAYER	MINS	GOALS	AVE
1	Arveladze	1532	12	128
2	Lovenkrands	1871	9	208
3	Mols	2514	9	279
4	Thompson	953	8	119
5	Arteta	1888	8	236
6	Capucho	1504	5	301
7	Namouchi	460	3	153
8	Burke	1210	3	403
9	Hughes	1592	3	531
10	Moore	1396	2	698
11	Rae	742	2	371
12	de Boer, F	1305	2	653
13	de Boer, R	952	2	476
	Other		8	
	TOTAL		76	

KEY GOALKEEPER

Stefan Klos

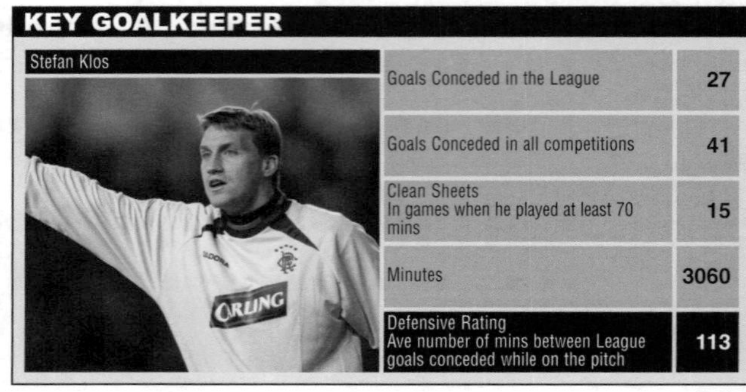
CARLING

Goals Conceded in the League	27
Goals Conceded in all competitions	41
Clean Sheets In games when he played at least 70 mins	15
Minutes	3060
Defensive Rating Ave number of mins between League goals conceded while on the pitch	113

DISCIPLINARY RECORDS

	PLAYER	YELLOW	RED	AVE
1	Moore	7	0	199
2	Hutton	3	0	300
3	Ball	7	0	375
4	Ricksen	6	0	421
5	Nerlinger	2	0	451
6	Namouchi	1	0	460
7	Thompson	2	0	476
8	Khizanishvili	4	0	563
9	Ross	2	0	591
10	Lovenkrands	3	0	623
11	Mols	3	1	628
12	de Boer, F	2	0	652
13	Capucho	2	0	752
	Other	9	0	
	TOTAL	53	1	

TOP POINT EARNERS

	PLAYER	GAMES	AV PTS
1	Capucho	13	2.46
2	Lovenkrands	17	2.35
3	Khizanishvili	24	2.29
4	Arveladze	14	2.29
5	Berg	18	2.28
6	Klos	34	2.18
7	Arteta	19	2.16
8	Ricksen	28	2.11
9	Ball	28	2.11
10	Mols	24	2.08
	CLUB AVERAGE:		2.13

TEAM OF THE SEASON

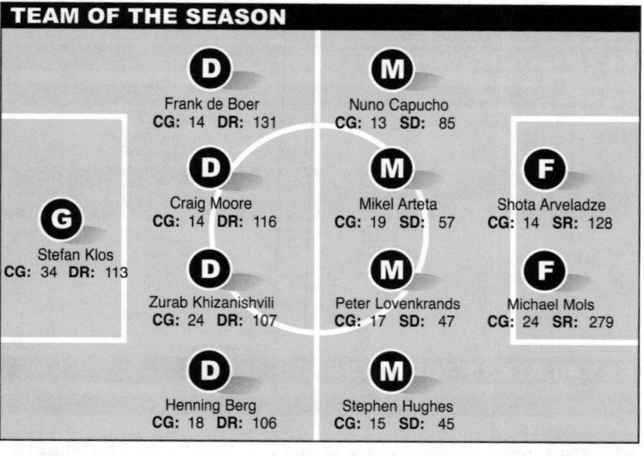

D
Frank de Boer
CG: 14 DR: 131
M
Nuno Capucho
CG: 13 SD: 85
D
Craig Moore
CG: 14 DR: 116
M
Mikel Arteta
CG: 19 SD: 57
F
Shota Arveladze
CG: 14 SR: 128
G
Stefan Klos
CG: 34 DR: 113
D
Zurab Khizanishvili
CG: 24 DR: 107
M
Peter Lovenkrands
CG: 17 SD: 47
F
Michael Mols
CG: 24 SR: 279
D
Henning Berg
CG: 18 DR: 106
M
Stephen Hughes
CG: 15 SD: 45

LEAGUE APPEARANCES, BOOKINGS AND CAPS

	AGE (on 01/07/04)	IN NAMED 16	APPEARANCES	COUNTING GAMES	MINUTES ON PITCH	YELLOW CARDS	RED CARDS	THIS SEASON	HOME COUNTRY
Goalkeepers									
Stefan Klos	32	34	34	34	3060	1	0	-	Germany
Allan McGregor	22	38	4	4	360	0	0	-	Scotland
Lee Robinson		4	0	0	0	0	0	-	Scotland
Defenders									
Michael Ball	24	34	32	28	2626	7	0	-	England
Henning Berg	34	22	20	18	1693	0	0	-	Norway
Frank de Boer	34	15	15	14	1305	2	0	9	Holland (4)
Zurab Khizanishvili	22	27	26	24	2254	4	0	-	Georgia
Gary MacKenzie	-	3	2	0	34	0	0	-	Scotland
Robert Malcolm	23	15	14	7	776	1	0	-	Scotland
Craig Moore	28	17	17	14	1396	7	0	2	Australia (89)
Fernando Ricksen	27	30	30	28	2527	6	0	-	Holland
Maurice Ross	23	30	20	10	1182	2	0	4	Scotland (63)
Steven Smith	-	1	0	0	0	0	0	-	Scotland
Paolo Vanoli	31	33	23	13	1466	0	0	-	Italy
Alex Walker	20	3	2	0	26	0	0	-	Scotland
Midfielders									
Charlie Adam	18	4	2	1	93	0	0	-	Scotland
Mikel Arteta	22	23	23	19	1888	2	0	-	Spain
Chris Burke	20	22	19	11	1210	0	0	-	Scotland
Nuno Capucho	32	23	22	13	1504	2	0	-	Portugal
Ronald de Boer	34	16	16	7	952	0	0	-	Holland
Moises Emerson	32	15	14	9	1012	1	0	-	Brazil
Barry Ferguson	26	3	3	3	270	1	0	6	Scotland (63)
Stephen Hughes	21	28	22	15	1592	1	0	-	Scotland
Alan Hutton	19	15	11	9	900	3	0	-	England
Peter Lovenkrands	24	25	25	17	1871	3	0	2	Denmark (14)
Hamed Namouchi	20	9	7	3	460	1	0	-	France
Christian Nerlinger	31	15	14	7	902	2	0	-	Germany
Gavin Rae	26	10	10	7	742	0	0	6	Scotland (63)
Forwards									
Shota Arveladze	31	19	19	14	1532	1	0	-	Georgia
Ross McCormack	17	6	2	0	93	0	0	-	Scotland
Michael Mols	33	35	34	24	2514	3	1	-	Holland
Egil Ostenstad	32	13	11	1	332	0	0	-	Norway
Steven Thompson	25	16	16	7	953	2	0	3	Scotland (63)

SQUAD APPEARANCES

Match	Venue	Competition	Result
1	H	L	W
2	H	C	D
3	A	L	W
4	H	L	W
5	A	C	W
6	A	L	W
7	H	L	W
8	H	C	W
9	A	L	W
10	H	L	W
11	A	C	D
12	H	L	L
13	A	L	D
14	H	C	L
15	A	L	D
16	H	W	W
17	H	L	W
18	A	C	L
19	A	L	W
20	H	L	W
21	A	C	L
22	A	L	W
23	H	W	W
24	H	L	W
25	H	C	L
26	A	L	L
27	H	L	W
28	A	L	W
29	A	L	L
30	A	O	W
31	H	L	W
32	H	L	W
33	A	L	W
34	A	W	L
35	A	O	W
36	H	L	W
37	A	L	D
38	H	L	W
39	A	L	L
40	A	O	L
41	A	L	D
42	H	L	W
43	H	L	W
44	H	L	L
45	A	L	W
46	A	L	D
47	H	L	W
48	A	L	D
49	H	L	W
50	A	L	L
51	H	L	L
52	A	L	W

Goalkeepers
Jesper Christiansen
Stefan Klos
Allan McGregor
Lee Robinson

Defenders
Michael Ball
Henning Berg
Frank de Boer
Zurab Khizanishvili
Gary MacKenzie
Robert Malcolm
Craig Moore
Fernando Ricksen
Maurice Ross
Steven Smith
Paolo Vanoli
Alex Walker

Midfielders
Charlie Adam
Mikel Arteta
Chris Burke
Nuno Fernando Capucho
Ronald de Boer
Moises Costa Emerson
Barry Ferguson
Stephen Hughes
Alan Hutton
Peter Lovenkrands
Hamed Namouchi
Christian Nerlinger
Gavin Rae

Forwards
Shota Arveladze
Ross McCormack
Michael Mols
Egil Ostenstad
Steven Thompson

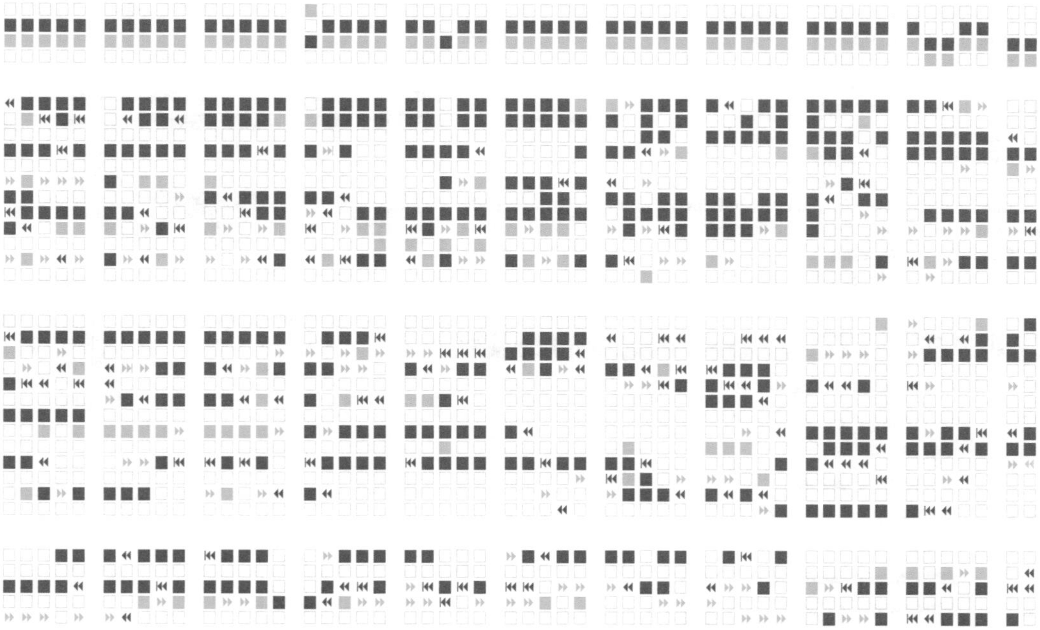

KEY: On all match / On bench
Subbed or sent off (Counting game) / Subbed or sent off (playing less than 70 minutes)
Subbed on from bench (Counting Game) / Subbed on (playing less than 70 minutes)
Subbed on and then subbed or sent off (Counting Game) / Subbed on and then subbed or sent off (playing less than 70 minutes)
Not in 16

HEART OF MIDLOTHIAN

Final Position: **3rd**

NICKNAME: THE JAM TARTS

KEY: Won / Drawn / Lost

							Attendance
1	prem	Aberdeen	H	W	2-0	de Vries 16; Kirk 90	14,260
2	prem	Hibernian	A	L	0-1		14,803
3	prem	Dundee Utd	H	W	3-0	Stamp 21; Wilson 22 og; de Vries 36	11,395
4	prem	Dunfermline	H	W	1-0	Wyness 62	11,934
5	prem	Kilmarnock	A	W	2-0	de Vries 14,41	6,925
6	prem	Rangers	H	L	0-4		14,732
7	uc1rl1	Zeljeznicar	H	W	2-0	de Vries 28; Webster 60	15,830
8	prem	Motherwell	A	D	1-1	Hartley 45	5,888
9	prem	Dundee	H	D	2-2	Weir 73; Pressley 81	11,348
10	uc1rl2	Zeljeznicar	A	D	0-0		20,000
11	prem	Celtic	A	L	0-5		59,560
12	prem	Partick	A	W	4-1	Kirk 13,30; de Vries 27; Simmons 74	4,814
13	sccc3	Falkirk	H	W	2-1	de Vries 54; Kirk 86	8,649
14	prem	Livingston	H	W	3-1	de Vries 67; Kirk 85; Pressley 90 pen	11,233
15	uc2rl1	Bordeaux	A	W	1-0	de Vries 78	15,536
16	prem	Aberdeen	A	W	1-0	Tosh 12 og	9,687
17	prem	Hibernian	H	W	2-0	Orman 9 og; Smith, G 67 og	16,632
18	uc2rl2	Bordeaux	H	L	0-2		17,587
19	prem	Dundee Utd	A	L	1-2	Severin 47	6,343
20	sccqf	Dundee	A	L	0-1		7,130
21	prem	Dunfermline	A	L	1-2	Maybury 41	6,199
22	prem	Kilmarnock	H	W	2-1	Kirk 64; Stamp 79	9,881
23	prem	Rangers	A	L	1-2	Kirk 11	49,592
24	prem	Motherwell	H	D	0-0		10,046
25	prem	Dundee	A	W	2-1	de Vries 47; Maybury 83	6,387
26	scr3	Berwick	H	W	2-0	Cowan 28 og; Hamill 66	8,428
27	prem	Celtic	H	L	0-1		13,753
28	prem	Partick	H	W	2-0	Wyness 42,78	10,264
29	scr4	Celtic	H	L	0-3		15,372
30	prem	Aberdeen	H	W	1-0	Pressley 81 pen	11,236
31	prem	Hibernian	A	D	1-1	Pressley 47 pen	15,060
32	prem	Dundee Utd	H	W	3-1	Hartley 16; Wilson 65 og; McKenna 72	10,265
33	prem	Livingston	A	W	3-2	de Vries 25; Kirk 47; McKenna 84	4,450
34	prem	Dunfermline	A	D	0-0		8,421
35	prem	Kilmarnock	A	D	1-1	Webster 60	5,297
36	prem	Rangers	H	D	1-1	Wyness 75	14,598
37	prem	Dundee	H	W	3-1	Hartley 52; Pressley 59 pen; Hamill 67	10,491
38	prem	Celtic	A	D	2-2	McKenna 21; de Vries 78	59,348
39	prem	Motherwell	A	D	1-1	Wyness 28	5,500
40	prem	Partick	A	L	0-1		4,043
41	prem	Livingston	H	D	1-1	McKenna 18	10,352
42	prem	Celtic	H	D	1-1	de Vries 74	12,112
43	prem	Dundee Utd	A	W	2-0	de Vries 4; Webster 72	6,620
44	prem	Dunfermline	H	W	2-1	de Vries 42,81	10,846
45	prem	Rangers	A	W	1-0	Hamill 50	47,467
46	prem	Motherwell	H	W	3-2	Wyness 5,68; McKenna 75	11,619

MONTHLY POINTS TALLY

Month	Points	%
AUGUST	9	75%
SEPTEMBER	4	44%
OCTOBER	4	44%
NOVEMBER	9	75%
DECEMBER	4	33%
JANUARY	6	67%
FEBRUARY	11	73%
MARCH	5	56%
APRIL	4	27%
MAY	12	100%

KEY PLAYERS - GOALSCORERS

Mark de Vries

Goals in the League	13	Player Strike Rate Average number of minutes between League goals scored by player	172
Contribution to Attacking Power Average number of minutes between League team goals while on pitch	58	Club Strike Rate Average number of minutes between League goals scored by club	61

	PLAYER	LGE GOALS	POWER	STRIKE RATE
1	Mark de Vries	13	58	172 mins
2	Andy Kirk	7	53	200 mins
3	Dennis Wyness	6	65	264 mins
4	Kevin McKenna	5	56	437 mins
5	Steven Pressley	5	58	530 mins

KEY PLAYERS - MIDFIELDERS

Paul Hartley

Goals in the League	3	Contribution to Attacking Power Average number of minutes between League team goals while on pitch	60
Defensive Rating Average number of mins between League goals conceded while he was on the pitch	92	Scoring Difference Defensive Rating minus Contribution to Attacking Power	32

	PLAYER	LGE GOALS	DEF RATE	POWER	SCORE DIFF
1	Paul Hartley	3	92	60	32 mins
2	Robbie Neilson	0	88	57	31 mins
3	Alan Maybury	2	83	66	17 mins
4	Phil Stamp	2	83	68	15 mins
5	Scott Severin	1	72	64	8 mins

KEY PLAYERS - DEFENDERS

Andy Webster

Goals Conceded (GC) The number of League goals conceded while he was on the pitch	31	Clean Sheets In games when he played at least 70 minutes	11
Defensive Rating Ave number of mins between League goals conceded while on the pitch	91	Club Defensive Rating Average number of mins between League goals conceded by the club this season	86

	PLAYER	CON LGE	CLEAN SHEETS	DEF RATE
1	Andy Webster	31	11	91 mins
2	Steven Pressley	30	9	88 mins
3	Kevin McKenna	25	4	87 mins
4	Patrick Kisnorbo	34	7	75 mins

KEY GOALKEEPER

Craig Gordon

Goals Conceded in the League	27	Counting Games Games when he played at least 70 mins	29
Defensive Rating Ave number of mins between League goals conceded while on the pitch	97	Clean Sheets In games when he played at least 70 mins	8

LEAGUE GOALS

Mark de Vries

Minutes on the pitch	2239	Goals in the League	13
League average (mins between goals)	172		

	PLAYER	MINS	GOALS	AVE
1	de Vries	2239	13	172
2	Kirk	1402	7	200
3	Wyness	1581	6	264
4	McKenna	2187	5	437
5	Pressley	2650	5	530
6	Hartley	2401	3	800
7	Webster	2812	2	1406
8	Hamill	1096	2	548
9	Maybury	2835	2	1418
10	Stamp	1903	2	952
11	Simmons	187	1	187
12	Weir	745	1	745
	Other		7	
	TOTAL		56	

DISCIPLINARY RECORDS

	PLAYER	YELLOW	RED	AVE
1	Stamp	9	0	211
2	Webster	10	0	281
3	Maybury	10	0	283
4	Hartley	7	1	300
5	Kisnorbo	8	0	320
6	de Vries	6	0	373
7	Severin	5	0	434
8	Neilson	4	0	573
9	Sloan	1	0	868
10	Pressley	3	0	883
11	Kirk	1	0	1402
12	Wyness	1	0	1581
13	MacFarlane	1	0	2107
	Other	4	0	
	TOTAL	70	1	

TOP POINT EARNERS

	PLAYER	GAMES	AV PTS
1	Wyness	13	2.08
2	de Vries	21	2.05
3	Hartley	25	2.00
4	Kirk	14	1.86
5	Pressley	29	1.86
6	Gordon	29	1.86
7	McKenna	22	1.82
8	Webster	30	1.80
9	Stamp	20	1.80
10	Maybury	31	1.68
	CLUB AVERAGE:		**1.79**

LEAGUE APPEARANCES, BOOKINGS AND CAPS

	AGE (on 01/07/04)	IN NAMED 16	APPEARANCES	COUNTING GAMES	MINUTES ON PITCH	YELLOW CARDS	RED CARDS	THIS SEASON	HOME COUNTRY
Goalkeepers									
Craig Gordon	21	38	29	29	2610	0	0	1	Scotland (63)
Teuvo Moilanen	30	38	9	9	810	0	0	-	Finland
Defenders									
Christophe Berra	-	9	6	2	236	0	0	-	Scotland
Patrick Kisnorbo	23	33	31	27	2562	8	0	-	Australia
Austin McCann	24	7	6	5	511	0	0	-	Scotland
Kevin McKenna	23	35	32	22	2187	1	0	-	Canada
Steven Pressley	30	31	31	29	2650	3	0	9	Scotland (63)
Gary Tierney	-	1	1	0	45	0	0	-	Scotland
Andy Webster	22	33	32	30	2812	10	0	7	Scotland (63)
Midfielders									
Steven Boyack	27	10	8	2	347	2	0	-	Scotland
Paul Hartley	27	32	30	25	2401	7	1	-	Scotland
Neil Janczyk	21	12	10	3	382	1	0	-	Scotland
Neil MacFarlane	26	35	30	21	2107	1	0	-	Scotland
Alan Maybury	25	34	33	31	2835	10	0	4	Rep of Ireland (15)
Paul McMullan	20	2	2	1	109	0	0	-	Scotland
Robbie Neilson	24	30	29	22	2295	4	0	-	Scotland
Scott Severin	25	26	26	23	2172	5	0	-	Scotland
Stephen Simmons	22	12	7	0	187	0	0	-	Scotland
Phil Stamp	28	25	25	20	1903	9	0	-	England
Forwards									
Mark de Vries	28	31	31	21	2239	6	0	-	Holland
Joe Hamill	20	20	18	7	1096	0	0	-	Scotland
Andy Kirk	25	29	23	14	1402	1	0	1	N Ireland (114)
Robert Sloan	20	14	13	9	868	1	0	-	Scotland
Jean Louis Valois	30	11	11	3	521	0	0	-	France
Gary Wales	25	1	1	0	4	0	0	-	Scotland
Graham Weir	19	23	18	6	745	0	0	-	Scotland
Dennis Wyness	27	34	27	13	1581	1	0	-	Scotland

TEAM OF THE SEASON

G – Craig Gordon CG: 29 DR: 97

D – Andy Webster CG: 30 DR: 91
D – Steven Pressley CG: 29 DR: 88
D – Kevin McKenna CG: 22 DR: 87
D – Patrick Kisnorbo CG: 27 DR: 75

M – Paul Hartley CG: 25 SD: 32
M – Robbie Neilson CG: 22 SD: 31
M – Alan Maybury CG: 31 SD: 17
M – Phil Stamp CG: 20 SD: 15

F – Mark de Vries CG: 21 SR: 172
F – Andy Kirk CG: 14 SR: 200

SQUAD APPEARANCES

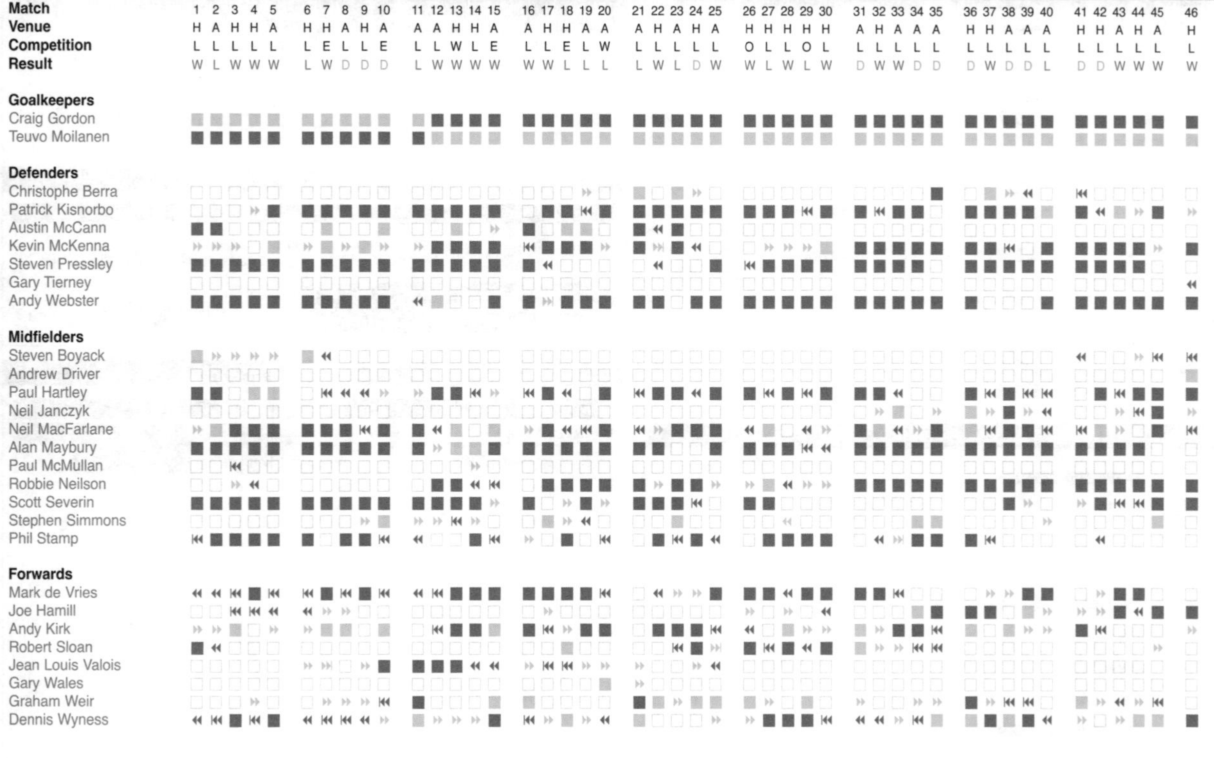
Match 1 2 3 4 5 6 7 8 9 10 11 12 13 14 15 16 17 18 19 20 21 22 23 24 25 26 27 28 29 30 31 32 33 34 35 36 37 38 39 40 41 42 43 44 45 46
Venue H A H H A H H A H A A A H H A A H H A A A H A H A H H H H H A H A A A H H A A A H H A H A H
Competition L L L L L L E L L E L L W L E L L E L W L L L L L O L L O L L L L L L L L L L L L L L L L L
Result W L W W W L W D D D L W W W W W W L L L L W L D W W L W L W D W W D D D W D D L D D W W W W
Goalkeepers
Craig Gordon
Teuvo Moilanen
Defenders
Christophe Berra
Patrick Kisnorbo
Austin McCann
Kevin McKenna
Steven Pressley
Gary Tierney
Andy Webster
Midfielders
Steven Boyack
Andrew Driver
Paul Hartley
Neil Janczyk
Neil MacFarlane
Alan Maybury
Paul McMullan
Robbie Neilson
Scott Severin
Stephen Simmons
Phil Stamp
Forwards
Mark de Vries
Joe Hamill
Andy Kirk
Robert Sloan
Jean Louis Valois
Gary Wales
Graham Weir
Dennis Wyness

KEY: On all match · On bench · Subbed or sent off (Counting game) · Subbed or sent off (playing less than 70 minutes) · Subbed on from bench (Counting Game) · Subbed on (playing less than 70 minutes) · Subbed on and then subbed or sent off (Counting Game) · Subbed on and then subbed or sent off (playing less than 70 minutes) · Not in 16

DUNFERMLINE

Final Position: **4th**

NICKNAME: THE PARS

KEY: ☐Won ☐Drawn ☐Lost

		Opponent			Score	Scorers	Attendance
1	prem	Celtic	H	D	0-0		10,082
2	prem	Dundee	A	W	2-0	Wilkie 45 og; Crawford 88	7,750
3	prem	Aberdeen	A	W	2-1	Brewster 30; Nicholson 56	10,870
4	prem	Hearts	A	L	0-1		11,934
5	prem	Rangers	A	L	0-4		49,072
6	prem	Hibernian	H	D	0-0		9,715
7	sccc2	Cowdenbeath	H	W	2-0	Crawford 54; Brewster 64	3,582
8	prem	Partick	H	W	2-1	Crawford 56,70	4,684
9	prem	Livingston	A	D	0-0		4,616
10	prem	Kilmarnock	H	L	2-3	Crawford 28,55	4,495
11	sccc3	St Johnstone	A	L	2-3	Crawford 80; Young, Darren 83	2,769
12	prem	Dundee Utd	H	W	2-0	Thomson, S M 59; Mehmet 90	5,078
13	prem	Celtic	A	L	0-5		58,328
14	prem	Dundee	H	W	2-0	Crawford 52,64	5,490
15	prem	Motherwell	A	D	2-2	Crawford 15; Brewster 39	4,220
16	prem	Aberdeen	H	D	2-2	Young, Derek 61; Bullen 74	5,294
17	prem	Hearts	H	W	2-1	Young, Derek 21; Wilson, S 62	6,199
18	prem	Rangers	H	W	2-0	Crawford 5; Vanoli 85 og	8,592
19	prem	Hibernian	A	W	2-1	Brewster 1,36	9,085
20	prem	Partick	A	L	1-4	Brewster 59	4,377
21	prem	Livingston	H	D	2-2	Nicholson 36 pen; Crawford 80	5,155
22	scr3	Dundee Utd	H	W	3-1	Crawford 16; Clark 36; Brewster 49	6,164
23	prem	Kilmarnock	A	D	1-1	Crawford 63	5,715
24	prem	Motherwell	H	W	1-0	Young, Derek 73	5,270
25	prem	Dundee Utd	A	L	0-1		5,564
26	prem	Celtic	H	L	1-4	Hunt 20	11,201
27	prem	Dundee	A	W	1-0	Hunt 32	5,643
28	prem	Aberdeen	A	L	0-2		11,035
29	scr4	Clyde	A	W	3-0	Nicholson 19 pen,38; Bullen 41	2,441
30	prem	Hearts	H	D	0-0		8,421
31	Scpqf	Partick	A	W	3-0	Byrne 11; Nicholson 36; Brewster 69	5,335
32	prem	Partick	H	W	1-0	Young, Darren 9	4,349
33	prem	Rangers	A	L	1-4	Tod 21	47,487
34	prem	Livingston	A	D	0-0		3,558
35	prem	Kilmarnock	H	W	2-1	Nicholson 40; Crawford 70	3,914
36	scsf	Inverness CT	A	D	1-1	Brewster 67	13,255
37	prem	Hibernian	H	D	1-1	Dempsey 78	5,041
38	prem	Motherwell	A	L	0-1		3,920
39	prem	Dundee Utd	H	D	1-1	Shields 45	4,409
40	scsf	Inverness CT	A	W	3-2	Young, Darren 25; Brewster 63; Nicholson 78	5,728
41	prem	Motherwell	H	W	3-0	Nicholson 36; Dempsey 52; Young, Derek 74	4,290
42	prem	Celtic	A	W	2-1	Nicholson 28; Dempsey 59	59,739
43	prem	Hearts	A	L	1-2	Tod 11	10,846
44	prem	Dundee Utd	A	L	2-3	Bullen 34; Crawford 46	5,998
45	prem	Rangers	H	L	2-3	Dempsey 27,66	6,798
46	scfin	Celtic	H	L	1-3	Skerla 40	50,846

MONTHLY POINTS TALLY

Month	Points	%
AUGUST	7	58%
SEPTEMBER	4	44%
OCTOBER	1	17%
NOVEMBER	8	53%
DECEMBER	9	75%
JANUARY	5	42%
FEBRUARY	4	33%
MARCH	4	44%
APRIL	8	53%
MAY	3	25%

KEY PLAYERS - GOALSCORERS

Stevie Crawford

Goals in the League	13	Player Strike Rate Average number of minutes between League goals scored by player	229
Contribution to Attacking Power Average number of minutes between League team goals while on pitch	72	Club Strike Rate Average number of minutes between League goals scored by club	76

	PLAYER	LGE GOALS	POWER	STRIKE RATE
1	Stevie Crawford	13	72	229 mins
2	Craig Brewster	5	70	383 mins
3	Derek Young	4	72	471 mins
4	Barry Nicholson	5	73	628 mins
5	Lee Bullen	2	67	950 mins

KEY PLAYERS - MIDFIELDERS

Gary Mason

Goals in the League	0	Contribution to Attacking Power Average number of minutes between League team goals while on pitch	71
Defensive Rating Average number of mins between League goals conceded while he was on the pitch	71	Scoring Difference Defensive Rating minus Contribution to Attacking Power	0

	PLAYER	LGE GOALS	DEF RATE	POWER	SCORE DIFF
1	Gary Mason	0	71	71	0 mins
2	Barry Nicholson	5	68	73	-5 mins
3	Darren Young	1	63	73	-10 mins
4	Lee Bullen	2	56	68	-12 mins

KEY PLAYERS - DEFENDERS

Greg Shields

Goals Conceded (GC) The number of League goals conceded while he was on the pitch	18	Clean Sheets In games when he played at least 70 minutes	5
Defensive Rating Ave number of mins between League goals conceded while on the pitch	79	Club Defensive Rating Average number of mins between League goals conceded by the club this season	66

	PLAYER	CON LGE	CLEAN SHEETS	DEF RATE
1	Greg Shields	18	5	79 mins
2	Scott Wilson	34	11	68 mins
3	Andrius Skerla	48	12	65 mins
4	Andy Tod	35	5	55 mins

KEY GOALKEEPER

Derek Stillie

Goals Conceded in the League	51	Counting Games Games when he played at least 70 mins	37
Defensive Rating Ave number of mins between League goals conceded while on the pitch	65	Clean Sheets In games when he played at least 70 mins	13

LEAGUE GOALS

Stevie Crawford

Minutes on the pitch	2981	Goals in the League	15
League average (mins between goals)	229		

	PLAYER	MINS	GOALS	AVE
1	Crawford	2981	13	229
2	Nicholson	3142	5	628
3	Dempsey	1540	5	308
4	Brewster	1916	5	383
5	Young, Derek	1884	4	471
6	Hunt	613	2	307
7	Bullen	1899	2	950
8	Tod	1929	2	965
9	Thomson, S M	1226	1	1226
10	Young, Darren	2900	1	2900
11	Wilson, S	2320	1	2320
12	Shields	1424	1	1424
	Other		3	
	TOTAL		45	

DISCIPLINARY RECORDS

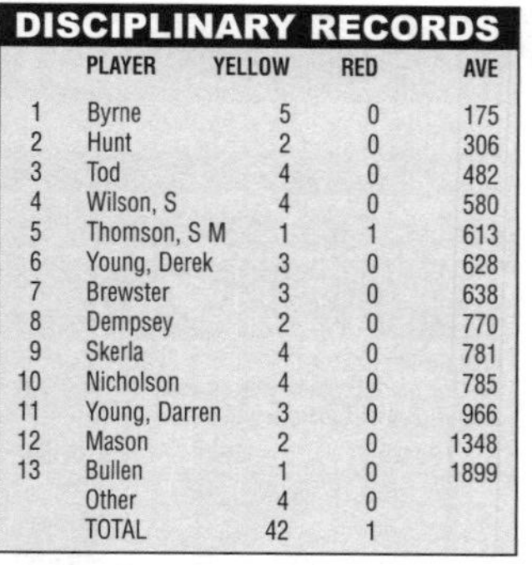

	PLAYER	YELLOW	RED	AVE
1	Byrne	5	0	175
2	Hunt	2	0	306
3	Tod	4	0	482
4	Wilson, S	4	0	580
5	Thomson, S M	1	1	613
6	Young, Derek	3	0	628
7	Brewster	3	0	638
8	Dempsey	2	0	770
9	Skerla	4	0	781
10	Nicholson	4	0	785
11	Young, Darren	3	0	966
12	Mason	2	0	1348
13	Bullen	1	0	1899
	Other	4	0	
	TOTAL	42	1	

TOP POINT EARNERS

	PLAYER	GAMES	AV PTS
1	Brewster	19	1.79
2	Mason	28	1.61
3	Young, Darren	33	1.48
4	Young, Derek	19	1.47
5	Crawford	33	1.45
6	Nicholson	34	1.44
7	Stillie	37	1.41
8	Skerla	34	1.41
9	Bullen	18	1.39
10	Tod	18	1.39
	CLUB AVERAGE:		1.39

LEAGUE APPEARANCES, BOOKINGS AND CAPS

	AGE (on 01/07/04)	IN NAMED 16	APPEARANCES	COUNTING GAMES	MINUTES ON PITCH	YELLOW CARDS	RED CARDS	THIS SEASON	HOME COUNTRY
Goalkeepers									
Marco Ruitenbeek	36	29	1	1	90	0	0	-	Holland
Derek Stillie	30	37	37	37	3330	1	0	-	Scotland
Scott Thomson	37	8	1	1	90	0	0	-	Scotland
Defenders									
Richie Byrne	22	20	13	7	876	5	0	-	Scotland
Aaron Labonte	20	31	21	6	834	0	0	-	England
Andrew McDermott	27	7	6	4	431	1	0	-	Australia
Greg Shields	27	17	17	15	1424	0	0	-	Scotland
Andrius Skerla	27	35	35	34	3126	4	0	-	Lithuania
Andy Tod	32	31	30	18	1929	4	0	-	Scotland
Scott Wilson	27	27	27	25	2320	4	0	-	Scotland
Midfielders									
Lee Bullen	33	27	27	18	1899	1	0	-	Scotland
Gary Dempsey	23	37	32	12	1540	2	0	-	Rep of Ireland
David Grondin	24	17	14	6	769	0	0	-	France
Noel Hunt	21	15	13	4	613	2	0	-	Rep of Ireland
Sean Kilgannon	23	12	11	4	446	0	0	-	Scotland
Gary Mason	24	33	32	28	2697	2	0	-	Scotland
Mark McGarty	21	2	1	0	2	0	0	-	Scotland
Chris McGroarty	23	2	2	1	135	0	0	-	Scotland
Barry Nicholson	25	37	36	34	3142	4	0	-	Scotland
Scott Thomson	32	18	15	12	1226	1	1	-	Scotland
Darren Wilson	19	4	3	3	270	1	0	-	Scotland
Darren Young	25	34	33	33	2900	3	0	-	Scotland
Forwards									
Craig Brewster	37	26	26	19	1916	3	0	-	Scotland
Patrick Clark	23	2	2	1	95	0	0	-	Scotland
Stevie Crawford	30	34	34	33	2981	1	0	8	Scotland (63)
Gary Greenhill	2005	2	1	0	45	0	0	-	Scotland
Billy Mehmet	20	24	18	2	529	0	0	-	England
Derek Young	24	26	26	19	1884	3	0	-	Scotland

TEAM OF THE SEASON

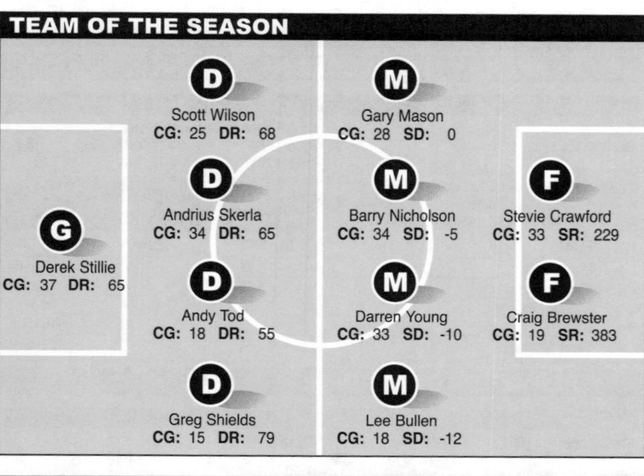
D
Scott Wilson
CG: 25 DR: 68
M
Gary Mason
CG: 28 SD: 0
D
Andrius Skerla
CG: 34 DR: 65
M
Barry Nicholson
CG: 34 SD: -5
F
Stevie Crawford
CG: 33 SR: 229
G
Derek Stillie
CG: 37 DR: 65
D
Andy Tod
CG: 18 DR: 55
M
Darren Young
CG: 33 SD: -10
F
Craig Brewster
CG: 19 SR: 383
D
Greg Shields
CG: 15 DR: 79
M
Lee Bullen
CG: 18 SD: -12

SQUAD APPEARANCES

Match	1	2	3	4	5	6	7	8	9	10	11	12	13	14	15	16	17	18	19	20	21	22	23	24	25	26	27	28	29	30	31	32	33	34	35	36	37	38	39	40	41	42	43	44	45	46
Venue	H	A	A	A	A	H	H	H	A	H	A	H	A	H	A	H	H	H	A	A	H	H	A	H	A	H	A	A	A	H	A	H	A	A	H	A	H	A	H	A	H	A	A	A	H	H
Competition	L	L	L	L	L	L	W	L	L	L	W	L	L	L	L	L	L	L	L	L	L	O	L	L	L	L	L	L	O	L	O	L	L	L	L	O	L	L	L	O	L	L	L	L	L	O
Result	D	W	W	L	L	D	W	W	D	L	L	W	L	W	D	D	W	W	W	L	D	W	D	W	L	L	W	L	W	D	W	W	L	D	W	D	D	L	D	W	W	W	L	L	L	L

Goalkeepers
Marco Ruitenbeek
Derek Stillie
Scott Thomson

Defenders
Richie Byrne
Aaron Labonte
Andrew McDermott
Scott McNicol
Greg Shields
Andrius Skerla
Andy Tod
Scott Walker
Scott Wilson

Midfielders
Lee Bullen
Gary Dempsey
David Grondin
Noel Hunt
Clark Kay
Sean Kilgannon
Gary Mason
Mark McGarty
Chris McGroarty
Keiran McGuire
Barry Nicholson
Anthony Storrie
Scott Thomson
Darren Wilson
Darren Young

Forwards
Craig Brewster
Patrick Clark
Stevie Crawford
Gary Greenhill
Billy Mehmet
Derek Young

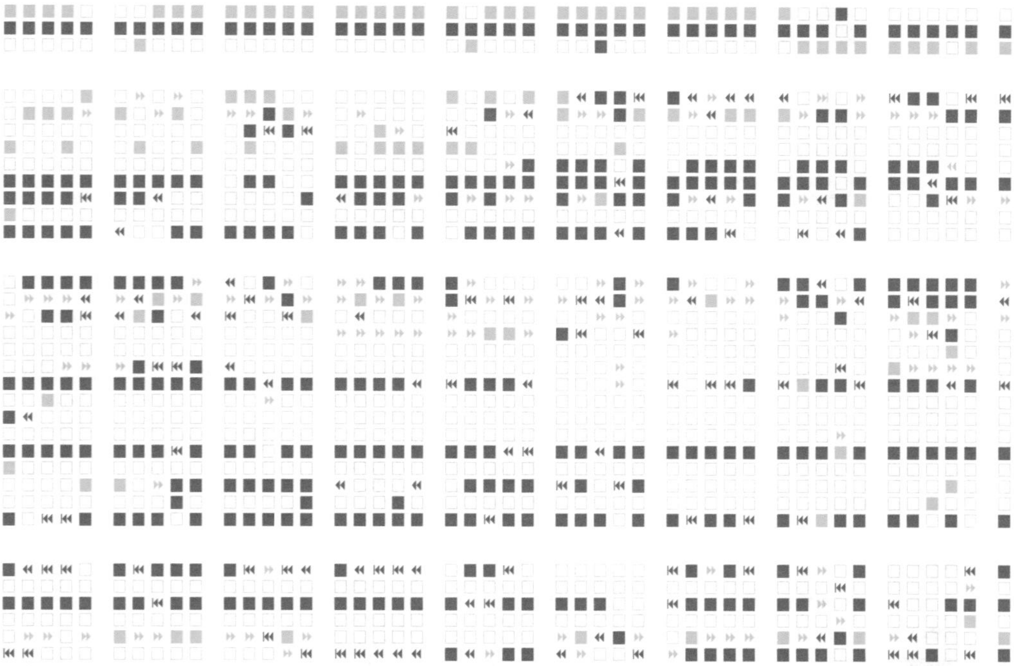

KEY: On all match; On bench; Subbed or sent off (Counting game); Subbed or sent off (playing less than 70 minutes); Subbed on from bench (Counting Game); Subbed on (playing less than 70 minutes); Subbed on and then subbed or sent off (Counting Game); Subbed on and then subbed or sent off (playing less than 70 minutes); Not in 16

DUNDEE UNITED

Final Position: **5th**

NICKNAME: THE DONS

KEY: ☐ Won ☐ Drawn ☐ Lost

							Attendance
1	prem	**Hearts**	A	L	0-2		14,260
2	prem	**Rangers**	H	L	2-3	Zdrilic 24; Deloumeaux 90	16,348
3	prem	**Dunfermline**	H	L	1-2	Zdrilic 23	10,870
4	prem	**Hibernian**	A	D	1-1	Anderson 6	10,682
5	prem	**Partick**	H	W	2-1	Booth 6; Anderson 76	10,597
6	prem	**Dundee**	A	L	0-2		7,887
7	sccc2	**Dumbarton**	H	W	3-1	Zdrilic 14,44; Hinds 48	3,944
8	prem	**Livingston**	H	L	0-3		10,307
9	prem	**Kilmarnock**	A	W	3-1	Zdrilic 3; Tosh 15; Booth 47	6,023
10	prem	**Dundee Utd**	H	L	0-1		11,244
11	prem	**Celtic**	A	L	0-4		59,598
12	sccc3	**Brechin**	H	W	5-0	Tosh 10; Booth 13; Muirhead 37; Sheerin 40; Hinds 85	3,631
13	prem	**Motherwell**	H	L	0-3		9,895
14	prem	**Hearts**	H	L	0-1		9,687
15	prem	**Rangers**	A	L	0-3		49,962
16	prem	**Dunfermline**	A	D	2-2	Deloumeaux 25; Booth 60	5,294
17	sccqf	**Livingston**	H	L	2-3	Tosh 34,59	6,090
18	prem	**Hibernian**	H	W	3-1	Hinds 26; Booth 85,90 pen	7,863
19	prem	**Partick**	A	W	3-0	Anderson 42,49; Clark 90	5,186
20	prem	**Dundee**	H	D	2-2	Anderson 42; Wilkie 59 og	10,354
21	prem	**Livingston**	A	D	1-1	Booth 23	7,115
22	prem	**Kilmarnock**	H	W	3-1	Diamond 7; Tosh 45; Hinds 60	11,698
23	scr3	**Dundee**	H	D	0-0		11,012
24	prem	**Dundee Utd**	A	L	2-3	Booth 55 pen; Archibald 65 og	6,666
25	scr3r	**Dundee**	A	W	3-2	Clark 5; Heikkinen 77; Zdrilic 89	5,857
26	prem	**Celtic**	H	L	1-3	Tosh 62	16,452
27	scr4	**Falkirk**	A	W	2-0	Zdrilic 60; Booth 64	4,747
28	prem	**Hearts**	A	L	0-1		11,236
29	prem	**Rangers**	H	D	1-1	Diamond 2	15,815
30	prem	**Dunfermline**	H	W	2-0	McGuire 36; Booth 52	11,035
31	prem	**Motherwell**	A	L	0-1		5,220
32	prem	**Hibernian**	A	W	1-0	Morrison 5	10,416
33	Scpqf	**Livingston**	H	D	1-1	Morrison 57	11,593
34	prem	**Partick**	H	D	0-0		7,395
35	prem	**Dundee**	A	D	1-1	Hinds 61	6,839
36	Scqfr	**Livingston**	A	L	0-1		4,485
37	prem	**Livingston**	H	L	1-2	Hinds 84	7,477
38	prem	**Kilmarnock**	A	L	1-3	Prunty 23	7,250
39	prem	**Dundee Utd**	H	W	3-0	Hinds 21; McGuire 24; Sheerin 43	8,448
40	prem	**Motherwell**	H	L	0-2		7,246
41	prem	**Celtic**	A	W	2-1	Prunty 56; Zdrilic 90	51,000
42	prem	**Livingston**	A	L	0-2		3,133
43	prem	**Partick**	A	L	0-2		2,839
44	prem	**Hibernian**	H	L	0-1		6,781
45	prem	**Kilmarnock**	A	L	0-4		4,987
46	prem	**Dundee**	H	L	1-2	Foster 6	7,878

MONTHLY POINTS TALLY

Month	Points	%
AUGUST	0	0%
SEPTEMBER	5	56%
OCTOBER	4	44%
NOVEMBER	4	33%
DECEMBER	7	58%
JANUARY	6	50%
FEBRUARY	4	33%
MARCH	10	83%
APRIL	3	25%
MAY	6	50%

KEY PLAYERS - GOALSCORERS

Billy Dodds

Goals in the League	10	**Player Strike Rate** Average number of minutes between League goals scored by player	210
Contribution to Attacking Power Average number of minutes between League team goals while on pitch	72	**Club Strike Rate** Average number of minutes between League goals scored by club	73

	PLAYER	LGE GOALS	POWER	STRIKE RATE
1	Billy Dodds	10	72	210 mins
2	James McIntyre	9	77	266 mins
3	Andrew McLaren	5	63	396 mins
4	Charlie Miller	4	63	477 mins
5	Barry Robson	3	67	716 mins

KEY PLAYERS - MIDFIELDERS

Charlie Miller

Goals in the League	4	**Contribution to Attacking Power** Average number of minutes between League team goals while on pitch	64
Defensive Rating Average number of mins between League goals conceded while he was on the pitch	71	**Scoring Difference** Defensive Rating minus Contribution to Attacking Power	7

	PLAYER	LGE GOALS	DEF RATE	POWER	SCORE DIFF
1	Charlie Miller	4	71	64	7 mins
2	Barry Robson	3	65	67	-2 mins
3	Andrew McLaren	5	60	64	-4 mins
4	Mark Kerr	1	57	73	-16 mins
5	Derek McInnes	1	56	77	-21 mins

KEY PLAYERS - DEFENDERS

Chris Innes

Goals Conceded (GC) The number of League goals conceded while he was on the pitch	38	**Clean Sheets** In games when he played at least 70 minutes	9
Defensive Rating Ave number of mins between League goals conceded while on the pitch	67	**Club Defensive Rating** Average number of mins between League goals conceded by the club this season	57

	PLAYER	CON LGE	CLEAN SHEETS	DEF RATE
1	Chris Innes	38	9	67 mins
2	Mark Wilson	47	9	58 mins
3	Alan Archibald	60	11	56 mins
4	David McCracken	52	9	55 mins

KEY GOALKEEPER

Paul Gallacher

Goals Conceded in the League	54	**Counting Games** Games when he played at least 70 mins	33
Defensive Rating Ave number of mins between League goals conceded while on the pitch	55	**Clean Sheets** In games when he played at least 70 mins	9

LEAGUE GOALS

Billy Dodds

Minutes on the pitch	2095	**Goals in the League**	10
League average (mins between goals)	210		

	PLAYER	MINS	GOALS	AVE
1	Dodds	2095	10	210
2	McIntyre	2391	9	266
3	Scotland	1067	5	213
4	McLaren	1981	5	396
5	Miller	1908	4	477
6	Wilson	2746	3	915
7	Robson	2149	3	716
8	Archibald	3388	2	1694
9	Samuel	1239	2	620
10	Kerr	2619	1	2619
11	McCracken	2862	1	2862
12	McInnes	2921	1	2921
	Other		1	
	TOTAL		47	

DISCIPLINARY RECORDS

	PLAYER	YELLOW	RED	AVE
1	McLaren	8	0	247
2	Dodds	7	1	261
3	Robson	6	1	307
4	Miller	6	0	318
5	McInnes	7	0	417
6	Innes	6	0	425
7	Kerr	5	0	523
8	Wilson	4	1	549
9	Duff	2	0	554
10	Easton	2	0	562
11	McIntyre	3	0	797
12	Griffin	1	0	829
13	Paterson, J	1	0	917
	Other	6	0	
	TOTAL	64	3	

TOP POINT EARNERS

	PLAYER	GAMES	AV PTS
1	McLaren	17	1.59
2	McIntyre	24	1.54
3	Innes	28	1.50
4	Wilson	30	1.47
5	Kerr	26	1.46
6	McCracken	32	1.38
7	Miller	17	1.35
8	Gallacher, P	33	1.33
9	Robson	23	1.30
10	Archibald	37	1.30
	CLUB AVERAGE:		**1.29**

LEAGUE APPEARANCES, BOOKINGS AND CAPS

	AGE (on 01/07/04)	IN NAMED 16	APPEARANCES	COUNTING GAMES	MINUTES ON PITCH	YELLOW CARDS	RED CARDS	THIS SEASON	HOME COUNTRY
Goalkeepers									
Tony Bullock	32	14	5	5	450	0	0	-	England
Paul Gallacher	24	38	33	33	2970	0	0	7	Scotland (63)
Paul Jarvie	22	24	0	0	0	0	0	-	Scotland
Defenders									
Steven Anderson	18	0	0	0	0	0	0	-	Scotland
Alan Archibald	26	38	38	37	3388	3	0	-	Scotland
Gary Bollan	31	2	2	0	71	0	0	-	Scotland
Daniel Griffin	26	16	13	8	829	1	0	4	N Ireland (114)
Chris Innes	27	29	29	28	2555	6	0	-	Scotland
Gary Kenneth	17	1	0	0	0	0	0	-	Scotland
David McCracken	22	37	32	32	2862	2	0	-	Scotland
Mark Wilson	20	33	32	30	2746	4	1	-	Scotland
Midfielders									
Stuart Duff	22	30	18	10	1109	2	0	-	Scotland
Craig Easton	25	30	21	10	1124	2	0	-	Scotland
Graeme Holmes	20	5	3	0	60	0	0	-	Scotland
Mark Kerr	22	37	33	26	2619	5	0	-	Scotland
Derek McInnes	33	35	35	31	2921	7	0	-	Scotland
Andrew McLaren	31	27	27	17	1981	8	0	-	Scotland
Charlie Miller	28	29	26	17	1908	6	0	-	Scotland
Jamie Paterson	24	20	16	7	917	1	0	-	Scotland
Scott Paterson	26	3	3	1	99	0	0	-	Scotland
Barry Robson	25	29	28	23	2149	6	1	-	Scotland
Forwards									
Aaron Conway	19	4	1	0	12	0	0	-	Scotland
Owen Coyle	37	4	3	0	55	0	0	-	Rep of Ireland
Billy Dodds	35	34	32	20	2095	7	1	-	Scotland
James McIntyre	32	30	30	24	2391	3	0	-	Scotland
Collin Samuel	22	30	26	10	1239	1	0	-	Trinidad & Tobago
Jason Scotland	25	29	20	8	1067	0	0	-	Trinidad & Tobago

TEAM OF THE SEASON

- **G** Paul Gallacher — CG: 33 DR: 55
- **D** Mark Wilson — CG: 30 DR: 58
- **D** Alan Archibald — CG: 37 DR: 56
- **D** David McCracken — CG: 32 DR: 55
- **D** Chris Innes — CG: 28 DR: 67
- **M** Charlie Miller — CG: 17 SD: 7
- **M** Barry Robson — CG: 23 SD: -2
- **M** Andrew McLaren — CG: 17 SD: -4
- **M** Mark Kerr — CG: 26 SD: -16
- **F** Billy Dodds — CG: 20 SR: 210
- **F** James McIntyre — CG: 24 SR: 266

SQUAD APPEARANCES

Match	1	2	3	4	5	6	7	8	9	10	11	12	13	14	15	16	17	18	19	20	21	22	23	24	25	26	27	28	29	30	31	32	33	34	35	36	37	38	39	40	41
Venue	H	A	A	H	A	A	H	H	H	A	H	H	A	A	H	H	A	H	H	A	A	A	H	A	H	H	A	A	H	A	H	A	H	A	H	A	H	H	A	H	A
Competition	L	L	L	L	L	L	W	L	L	L	L	W	L	L	L	L	L	L	L	L	L	O	L	L	L	L	L	L	L	L	L	L	L	L	L	L	L	L	L	L	L
Result	L	L	L	L	D	W	W	D	L	W	D	L	L	D	L	W	L	W	D	W	L	L	W	L	W	D	L	L	W	D	W	W	W	L	D	D	D	L	W	W	L

Goalkeepers
Tony Bullock
Paul Gallacher
Paul Jarvie

Defenders
Steven Anderson
Alan Archibald
Gary Bollan
Daniel Griffin
Chris Innes
Gary Kenneth
David McCracken
Mark Wilson

Midfielders
Stuart Duff
Craig Easton
Graeme Holmes
Mark Kerr
Derek McInnes
Andrew McLaren
Charlie Miller
Jamie Paterson
Scott Paterson
Barry Robson

Forwards
Aaron Conway
Owen Coyle
Billy Dodds
James McIntyre
Collin Samuel
Jason Scotland

KEY: On all match · On bench · Subbed or sent off (Counting game) · Subbed or sent off (playing less than 70 minutes) · Subbed on from bench (Counting Game) · Subbed on (playing less than 70 minutes) · Subbed on and then subbed or sent off (Counting Game) · Subbed on and then subbed or sent off (playing less than 70 minutes) · Not in 16

MOTHERWELL

Final Position: **6th**

NICKNAME: THE WELL

KEY: ☐Won ☐Drawn ☐Lost

#	Comp	Opponent	H/A	Res	Score	Scorers	Attendance
1	prem	**Dundee**	H	L	0-3		6,812
2	prem	**Livingston**	A	L	0-1		5,316
3	prem	**Kilmarnock**	H	W	2-1	McFadden 66 pen; Pearson 90	5,087
4	prem	**Partick**	H	D	2-2	McFadden 9,69	6,193
5	prem	**Hibernian**	A	W	2-0	Clarkson 45,75	8,387
6	prem	**Celtic**	A	L	0-3		58,013
7	sccc2	**Forfar**	A	L	2-4*	Craig 3; Lasley 55; Pearson 60 (*on penalties)	1,110
8	prem	**Hearts**	H	D	1-1	Adams 29	5,888
9	prem	**Dundee Utd**	A	W	2-0	Adams 22 pen,90	6,194
10	prem	**Rangers**	H	D	1-1	Pearson 25	10,824
11	prem	**Aberdeen**	A	W	3-0	Craig 10; Pearson 77; Lasley 90	9,895
12	prem	**Dundee**	A	W	1-0	Craig 52	6,374
13	prem	**Livingston**	H	D	1-1	Clarkson 28	6,357
14	prem	**Dunfermline**	H	D	2-2	Pearson 70; Corrigan 90	4,220
15	prem	**Kilmarnock**	A	L	0-2		6,320
16	prem	**Partick**	A	L	0-1		4,124
17	prem	**Hibernian**	H	L	0-1		4,533
18	prem	**Celtic**	H	L	0-2		10,513
19	prem	**Hearts**	A	D	0-0		10,046
20	prem	**Dundee Utd**	H	W	3-1	Clarkson 60,68,90	5,549
21	scr3	**St Johnstone**	A	W	3-0	Clarkson 24,32; McDonald 90	4,090
22	prem	**Rangers**	A	L	0-1		48,925
23	prem	**Dunfermline**	A	L	0-1		5,270
24	scr4	**Queen of South**	H	W	3-2	Adams 3 pen; Burns 18,45	8,101
25	prem	**Dundee**	H	W	5-3	Lasley 15; Dair 18,73; Clarkson 51; Burns 62	4,247
26	prem	**Livingston**	A	L	1-3	Adams 90	3,492
27	prem	**Kilmarnock**	H	W	1-0	Clarkson 15	5,163
28	prem	**Aberdeen**	H	W	1-0	Wright 84	5,220
29	prem	**Partick**	H	W	3-0	Hammell 11; Clarkson 52; Adams 80	5,814
30	scpqf	**Inverness CT**	H	L	0-1		7,930
31	prem	**Celtic**	A	D	1-1	Adams 26	47,563
32	prem	**Hibernian**	A	D	3-3	Lasley 46; Adams 60 pen; Doumbe 80 og	5,670
33	prem	**Dundee Utd**	A	L	0-1		7,585
34	prem	**Rangers**	H	L	0-1		8,967
35	prem	**Hearts**	H	D	1-1	Clarkson 61	5,500
36	prem	**Dunfermline**	H	W	1-0	Adams 10 pen	3,920
37	prem	**Aberdeen**	A	W	2-0	Burns 14; Craig 90	7,246
38	prem	**Dunfermline**	A	L	0-3		4,290
39	prem	**Rangers**	A	L	0-4		47,579
40	prem	**Dundee Utd**	H	L	0-1		5,722
41	prem	**Celtic**	H	D	1-1	Clarkson 64	7,749
42	prem	**Hearts**	A	L	2-3	McDonald 37; Clarkson 45	11,619

MONTHLY POINTS TALLY

Month	Points	%
AUGUST	4	33%
SEPTEMBER	4	44%
OCTOBER	4	67%
NOVEMBER	8	53%
DECEMBER	1	8%
JANUARY	3	33%
FEBRUARY	12	80%
MARCH	2	22%
APRIL	7	47%
MAY	1	8%

KEY PLAYERS - GOALSCORERS

David Clarkson

Goals in the League	12	**Player Strike Rate** Average number of minutes between League goals scored by player	235
Contribution to Attacking Power Average number of minutes between League team goals while on pitch	88	**Club Strike Rate** Average number of minutes between League goals scored by club	81

	PLAYER	LGE GOALS	POWER	STRIKE RATE
1	David Clarkson	12	88	235 mins
2	Derek Adams	8	73	349 mins
3	Stephen Pearson	4	92	369 mins
4	Steven Craig	3	89	446 mins
5	Jason Dair	2	75	944 mins

KEY PLAYERS - MIDFIELDERS

Keith Lasley

Goals in the League	3	**Contribution to Attacking Power** Average number of minutes between League team goals while on pitch	75
Defensive Rating Average number of mins between League goals conceded while he was on the pitch	79	**Scoring Difference** Defensive Rating minus Contribution to Attacking Power	4

	PLAYER	LGE GOALS	DEF RATE	POWER	SCORE DIFF
1	Keith Lasley	3	79	75	4 mins
2	Derek Adams	8	72	73	-1 mins
3	Jason Dair	2	73	76	-3 mins
4	David Partridge	0	75	79	-4 mins
5	Stephen Pearson	4	74	92	-18 mins

KEY PLAYERS - DEFENDERS

Steven Hammell

Goals Conceded (GC) The number of League goals conceded while he was on the pitch	44	**Clean Sheets** In games when he played at least 70 minutes	10
Defensive Rating Ave number of mins between League goals conceded while on the pitch	74	**Club Defensive Rating** Average number of mins between League goals conceded by the club this season	70

	PLAYER	CON LGE	CLEAN SHEETS	DEF RATE
1	Steven Hammell	44	10	74 mins
2	Stephen Craigan	46	10	70 mins
3	Martyn Corrigan	49	10	70 mins
4	Paul Quinn	34	6	65 mins

KEY GOALKEEPER

Gordon Marshall

Goals Conceded in the League	42	**Counting Games** Games when he played at least 70 mins	34
Defensive Rating Ave number of mins between League goals conceded while on the pitch	73	**Clean Sheets** In games when he played at least 70 mins	9

LEAGUE GOALS

David Clarkson

Minutes on the pitch	2822	Goals in the League	12
League average (mins between goals)	235		

	PLAYER	MINS	GOALS	AVE
1	Clarkson	2822	12	235
2	Adams	2790	8	349
3	Pearson	1476	4	369
4	Lasley	2907	3	969
5	McFadden	212	3	71
6	Craig	1338	3	446
7	Burns	2596	2	1298
8	Dair	1888	2	944
9	Wright	283	1	283
10	Hammell	3234	1	3234
11	Corrigan	3420	1	3420
	Other		2	
	TOTAL		42	

DISCIPLINARY RECORDS

	PLAYER	YELLOW	RED	AVE
1	Leitch	5	0	328
2	Fagan	2	0	407
3	Craig	3	0	446
4	Lasley	6	0	484
5	McDonald, S	1	0	494
6	O'Donnell	1	0	586
7	Hammell	5	0	646
8	Clarkson	4	0	705
9	Pearson	1	1	738
10	Craigan	4	0	810
11	Corrigan	4	0	855
12	Burns	3	0	865
13	Adams	3	0	930
	Other	6	0	
	TOTAL	48	1	

TOP POINT EARNERS

	PLAYER	GAMES	AV PTS
1	Adams	31	1.35
2	Partridge	15	1.33
3	Lasley	32	1.31
4	Hammell	35	1.29
5	Leitch	18	1.28
6	Pearson	15	1.27
7	Quinn	24	1.25
8	Marshall	34	1.24
9	Craig	13	1.23
10	Corrigan	38	1.21
	CLUB AVERAGE:		**1.21**

LEAGUE APPEARANCES, BOOKINGS AND CAPS

	AGE (on 01/07/04)	IN NAMED 16	APPEARANCES	COUNTING GAMES	MINUTES ON PITCH	YELLOW CARDS	RED CARDS	THIS SEASON	HOME COUNTRY
Goalkeepers									
Barry-John Corr	23	36	4	4	360	0	0	-	Scotland
Gordon Marshall	40	36	34	34	3060	0	0	-	Scotland
Defenders									
Gary Bollan	31	4	3	0	94	0	0	-	Scotland
Martyn Corrigan	26	38	38	38	3420	4	0	-	Scotland
David Cowan	22	1	1	0	5	0	0	-	England
Stephen Craigan	27	36	36	36	3240	4	0	3	N Ireland (114)
Steven Hammell	22	37	37	35	3234	5	0	-	Scotland
Chris Higgins	19	3	0	0	0	0	0	-	Scotland
Kevin McDonald	21	31	12	5	626	0	0	-	Scotland
Paul Quinn	19	37	26	24	2195	2	0	-	Scotland
Midfielders									
Derek Adams	29	31	31	31	2790	3	0	-	Scotland
Jason Dair	30	31	28	17	1888	2	0	-	Scotland
Shaun Fagan	20	25	13	8	815	2	0	-	Scotland
Mark Fitzpatrick	18	6	2	1	99	0	0	-	Scotland
William Kinniburgh	19	19	1	0	45	1	0	-	Scotland
Keith Lasley	24	33	33	32	2907	6	0	-	Scotland
Scott Leitch	34	20	20	18	1643	5	0	-	Scotland
Graeme Mathie	21	1	0	0	0	0	0	-	Scotland
James McFadden	21	3	3	2	212	1	0	10	Scotland (63)
Philip O'Donnell	32	11	9	5	586	1	0	-	Scotland
David Partridge	25	15	15	15	1350	0	0	-	Wales
Stephen Pearson	21	18	18	15	1476	1	1	-	Scotland
Forwards									
Alex Burns	30	33	33	28	2596	3	0	-	Scotland
David Clarkson	18	38	38	30	2822	4	0	-	Scotland
Steven Craig	23	25	24	13	1338	3	0	-	Scotland
Scott McDonald	20	7	7	5	494	1	0	-	Australia
Kenneth Wright	18	29	12	2	283	0	0	-	Scotland

TEAM OF THE SEASON

G
Gordon Marshall
CG: 34 DR: 73

D
Steven Hammell
CG: 35 DR: 74

D
Martyn Corrigan
CG: 38 DR: 70

D
Stephen Craigan
CG: 36 DR: 70

D
Paul Quinn
CG: 24 DR: 65

M
Keith Lasley
CG: 32 SD: 4

M
Derek Adams
CG: 31 SD: -1

M
Jason Dair
CG: 17 SD: -3

M
David Partridge
CG: 15 SD: -4

F
David Clarkson
CG: 30 SR: 235

F
Steven Craig
CG: 13 SR: 446

SQUAD APPEARANCES

Match	1	2	3	4	5	6	7	8	9	10	11	12	13	14	15	16	17	18	19	20	21	22	23	24	25	26	27	28	29	30	31	32	33	34	35	36	37	38	39	40	41	42
Venue	H	A	H	H	A	A	A	H	A	H	A	A	H	H	A	A	H	H	A	H	A	A	A	H	H	A	H	H	H	H	A	A	A	H	H	H	A	A	A	H	H	A
Competition	L	L	L	L	L	L	W	L	L	L	L	L	L	L	L	L	L	L	L	L	O	L	L	O	L	L	L	L	L	O	L	L	L	L	L	L	L	L	L	L	L	L
Result	L	L	W	D	W	L	L	D	W	D	W	W	D	D	L	L	L	L	D	W	W	L	L	W	W	L	W	W	W	L	D	D	L	L	D	W	W	L	L	L	D	L

Goalkeepers
Barry-John Corr
Jamie Ewings
Gordon Marshall
Andy Reid

Defenders
Gary Bollan
Martyn Corrigan
David Cowan
Stephen Craigan
Steven Hammell
Chris Higgins
Kevin McDonald
Paul Quinn

Midfielders
Derek Adams
Jason Dair
Shaun Fagan
Mark Fitzpatrick
William Kinniburgh
Keith Lasley
Scott Leitch
Graeme Mathie
James McFadden
Philip O'Donnell
David Partridge
Stephen Pearson

Forwards
Alex Burns
David Clarkson
Steven Craig
Scott McDonald
Kenneth Wright

KEY: On all match; On bench; Subbed or sent off (Counting game); Subbed or sent off (playing less than 70 minutes); Subbed on from bench (Counting Game); Subbed on (playing less than 70 minutes); Subbed on and then subbed or sent off (Counting Game); Subbed on and then subbed or sent off (playing less than 70 minutes); Not in 16

DUNDEE

Final Position: **7th**

NICKNAME: THE TERRORS/ ARABS   KEY: ☐Won ☐Drawn ☐Lost

							Attendance
1	prem	**Hibernian**	H	L	1-2	Samuel 46	9,809
2	prem	**Celtic**	A	L	0-5		57,658
3	prem	**Hearts**	A	L	0-3		11,395
4	prem	**Rangers**	H	L	1-3	Dodds 82	9,752
5	prem	**Livingston**	A	D	0-0		5,344
6	prem	**Partick**	A	W	2-0	Miller 41,63	4,711
7	sccc2	**G Morton**	H	W	3-1	McLaren 10; McIntyre 36,84 pen	5,638
8	prem	**Kilmarnock**	H	D	1-1	McLaren 74	6,529
9	prem	**Motherwell**	H	L	0-2		6,194
10	prem	**Aberdeen**	A	W	1-0	McLaren 11	11,244
11	prem	**Dundee**	H	D	1-1	McIntyre 56	12,292
12	sccc3	**Livingston**	H	L	0-1		2,899
13	prem	**Dunfermline**	A	L	0-2		5,078
14	prem	**Hibernian**	A	D	2-2	McLaren 28; Robson 83	8,756
15	prem	**Celtic**	H	L	1-5	McIntyre 76	10,802
16	prem	**Hearts**	H	W	2-1	Archibald 12; McInnes 44	6,343
17	prem	**Rangers**	A	L	1-2	Dodds 56	49,307
18	prem	**Livingston**	H	W	2-0	Dodds 41,80	5,421
19	prem	**Partick**	H	D	0-0		6,440
20	prem	**Kilmarnock**	A	W	2-0	Dodds 20; McIntyre 82 pen	6,062
21	prem	**Motherwell**	A	L	1-3	Wilson 15	5,549
22	scr3	**Dunfermline**	A	L	1-3	McInnes 38	6,164
23	prem	**Aberdeen**	H	W	3-2	Robson 20; McLaren 85; Dodds 90 pen	6,666
24	prem	**Dundee**	A	L	1-2	Dodds 44 pen	10,747
25	prem	**Dunfermline**	H	W	1-0	McIntyre 57	5,564
26	prem	**Hibernian**	H	D	0-0		6,389
27	prem	**Celtic**	A	L	1-2	Archibald 61	58,698
28	prem	**Hearts**	A	L	1-3	McIntyre 52	10,265
29	prem	**Rangers**	H	W	2-0	Kerr 31; McLaren 34	10,496
30	prem	**Partick**	A	D	1-1	Robson 68	3,510
31	prem	**Kilmarnock**	H	W	4-1	McIntyre 11,26,34; Miller 21	5,757
32	prem	**Livingston**	A	W	3-2	Scotland 13; Samuel 79; McIntyre 82	3,082
33	prem	**Motherwell**	H	W	1-0	Scotland 66	7,585
34	prem	**Aberdeen**	A	L	0-3		8,448
35	prem	**Dundee**	H	D	2-2	Dodds 56,85 pen	9,571
36	prem	**Dunfermline**	A	D	1-1	McCracken 64	4,409
37	prem	**Rangers**	H	D	3-3	Dodds 1; Scotland 59,90	8,339
38	prem	**Hearts**	H	L	0-2		6,620
39	prem	**Motherwell**	A	W	1-0	Wilson 52	5,722
40	prem	**Dunfermline**	H	W	3-2	Miller 8; Innes 23; Scotland 30	5,998
41	prem	**Celtic**	A	L	1-2	Wilson 87 pen	58,386

MONTHLY POINTS TALLY

Month	Points	%
AUGUST	7	58%
SEPTEMBER	3	33%
OCTOBER	5	56%
NOVEMBER	2	17%
DECEMBER	1	8%
JANUARY	7	58%
FEBRUARY	3	25%
MARCH	1	8%
APRIL	8	67%
MAY	9	75%

KEY PLAYERS - GOALSCORERS

Nacho Novo

Goals in the League	19	Player Strike Rate Average number of minutes between League goals scored by player	161
Contribution to Attacking Power Average number of minutes between League team goals while on pitch	72	Club Strike Rate Average number of minutes between League goals scored by club	71

	PLAYER	LGE GOALS	POWER	STRIKE RATE
1	Nacho Novo	19	72	161 mins
2	Steven Milne	8	56	170 mins
3	Steve Lovell	5	76	274 mins
4	Mark Fotheringham	4	63	443 mins
5	Barry Smith	2	72	1190 mins

KEY PLAYERS - MIDFIELDERS

Barry Smith

Goals in the League	2	Contribution to Attacking Power Average number of minutes between League team goals while on pitch	72
Defensive Rating Average number of mins between League goals conceded while he was on the pitch	74	Scoring Difference Defensive Rating minus Contribution to Attacking Power	2

	PLAYER	LGE GOALS	DEF RATE	POWER	SCORE DIFF
1	Barry Smith	2	74	72	2 mins
2	*Gavin Rae	2	68	68	0 mins
3	Garry Brady	0	63	70	-7 mins
4	Mark Fotheringham	4	45	63	-18 mins

KEY PLAYERS - DEFENDERS

Lee Wilkie

Goals Conceded (GC) The number of League goals conceded while he was on the pitch	28	Clean Sheets In games when he played at least 70 minutes	3
Defensive Rating Ave number of mins between League goals conceded while on the pitch	65	Club Defensive Rating Average number of mins between League goals conceded by the club this season	60

	PLAYER	CON LGE	CLEAN SHEETS	DEF RATE
1	Lee Wilkie	28	3	65 mins
2	Brent Sancho	30	3	59 mins
3	Lee Mair	54	6	59 mins
4	Dave Mackay	52	6	58 mins
5	Jonay Hernandez Santos	42	3	56 mins

KEY GOALKEEPER

Julian Speroni

Goals Conceded in the League	56	Counting Games Games when he played at least 70 mins	37
Defensive Rating Ave number of mins between League goals conceded while on the pitch	59	Clean Sheets In games when he played at least 70 mins	7

LEAGUE GOALS

Nacho Novo

Minutes on the pitch	3063	Goals in the League	19
League average (mins between goals)	161		

	PLAYER	MINS	GOALS	AVE
1	Novo	3063	19	161
2	Milne	1358	8	170
3	Lovell	1370	5	274
4	Fotheringham	1771	4	443
5	Barrett	791	2	396
6	Smith	2379	2	1190
7	Rae	945	2	473
8	McLean	245	1	245
9	Hutchinson	773	1	773
10	Kneissel	448	1	448
11	Mair	3160	1	3160
12	Wilkie	1826	1	1826
	Other		1	
	TOTAL		48	

DISCIPLINARY RECORDS

	PLAYER	YELLOW	RED	AVE
1	Barrett	6	0	131
2	Lovell	9	0	152
3	Nemsadze	4	0	197
4	Fotheringham	7	0	253
5	Wilkie	5	0	365
6	Novo	6	0	510
7	Cameron	1	0	622
8	Hutchinson	1	0	773
9	Mair	4	0	790
10	Rae	1	0	945
11	Hernandez Santos	2	0	1175
12	Milne	1	0	1358
13	Mackay	2	0	1519
	Other	12	1	
	TOTAL	61	1	

TOP POINT EARNERS

	PLAYER	GAMES	AV PTS
1	Lovell	14	1.50
2	Milne	14	1.36
3	Smith	26	1.31
4	Brady	35	1.31
5	Mackay	33	1.27
6	Sancho	17	1.24
7	Mair	35	1.20
8	Speroni	37	1.16
9	Hernandez Santos	24	1.13
10	Novo	34	1.12
	CLUB AVERAGE:		1.21

TEAM OF THE SEASON

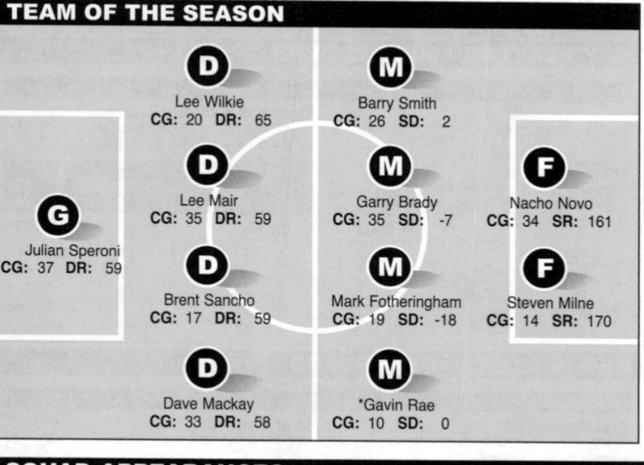
G
Julian Speroni
CG: 37 DR: 59
D
Lee Wilkie
CG: 20 DR: 65
D
Lee Mair
CG: 35 DR: 59
D
Brent Sancho
CG: 17 DR: 59
D
Dave Mackay
CG: 33 DR: 58
M
Barry Smith
CG: 26 SD: 2
M
Garry Brady
CG: 35 SD: -7
M
Mark Fotheringham
CG: 19 SD: -18
M
*Gavin Rae
CG: 10 SD: 0
F
Nacho Novo
CG: 34 SR: 161
F
Steven Milne
CG: 14 SR: 170

LEAGUE APPEARANCES, BOOKINGS AND CAPS

	AGE (on 01/07/04)	IN NAMED 16	APPEARANCES	COUNTING GAMES	MINUTES ON PITCH	YELLOW CARDS	RED CARDS	THIS SEASON	HOME COUNTRY
Goalkeepers									
James Langfield	24	12	0	0	0	0	0	-	Scotland
Derek Soutar	23	18	1	1	90	0	0	-	Scotland
Julian Speroni	25	38	37	37	3330	1	0	-	Argentina
Defenders									
Thomas Cowan	34	5	5	4	340	1	0	-	Scotland
Hernandez Santos	25	31	29	24	2351	2	0	-	Spain
Tom Hutchinson	22	17	12	8	773	1	0	-	England
Calum MacDonald	21	16	6	5	490	0	0	-	Scotland
Dave Mackay	23	36	35	33	3038	2	0	-	Scotland
Lee Mair	23	36	36	35	3160	4	0	-	Scotland
Brent Sancho	27	23	21	17	1774	1	0	-	Trinidad & Tobago
Lee Wilkie	24	21	21	20	1826	5	0	6	Scotland (63)
Midfielders									
Neil Barrett	22	12	12	6	791	6	0	-	England
Garry Brady	27	37	37	35	3143	0	0	-	Scotland
Craig Burley	32	2	2	0	64	0	1	-	Scotland
Douglas Cameron	-	19	10	6	622	1	0	-	Scotland
Beto Caranza	32	4	2	0	33	0	0	-	Argentina
Mark Fotheringham	20	29	23	19	1771	7	0	-	Scotland
Chris Hegarty	-	7	4	0	92	1	0	-	Scotland
Neil Jablonski	21	15	11	2	362	2	0	-	Scotland
Georghi Nemsadze	32	9	9	9	791	4	0	-	Georgia
Gavin Rae	26	13	13	10	945	1	0	6	Scotland (63)
Stephen Robb	22	16	15	6	764	0	0	-	Scotland
Juan Sara	25	11	10	3	436	1	0	-	Argentina
Barry Smith	30	29	29	26	2379	1	0	-	Scotland
Forwards									
Fabian Caballero	26	13	13	9	865	0	0	-	Argentina
Sebastian Kneissel	21	12	11	0	448	0	0	-	Germany
Bobby Linn	18	15	12	1	305	1	0	-	Scotland
Steve Lovell	23	21	20	14	1370	9	0	-	England
Duncan McLean	-	5	4	2	245	0	0	-	Scotland
Steven McNally	-	7	1	1	90	0	0	-	Scotland
Steven Milne	24	20	20	14	1358	1	0	-	Scotland
Nacho Novo	25	35	35	34	3063	6	0	-	Spain
Fabrizio Ravanelli	35	5	5	5	425	3	0	-	Italy

SQUAD APPEARANCES

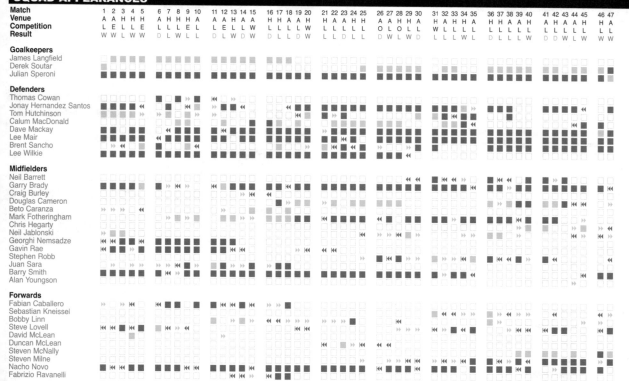

Match	1	2	3	4	5	6	7	8	9	10	11	12	13	14	15	16	17	18	19	20	21	22	23	24	25	26	27	28	29	30	31	32	33	34	35	36	37	38	39	40	41	42	43	44	45	46	47
Venue	A	A	H	H	H	A	H	H	H	A	A	A	H	A	A	H	H	A	A	H	H	A	A	H	H	A	A	H	H	A	H	A	H	H	A	H	H	A	A	H	A	H	A	A	H	H	A
Competition	L	E	L	L	E	L	L	L	E	L	L	E	L	L	W	L	L	L	L	W	L	L	L	L	L	O	L	O	L	L	W	L	L	L	L	L	L	L	L	L	L	L	L	L	L	L	L
Result	W	W	L	W	W	D	L	W	L	L	D	L	W	D	W	D	L	L	D	W	L	L	D	L	L	D	W	L	W	D	L	L	L	W	L	D	L	L	L	W	D	D	W	L	W	W	W

Goalkeepers
James Langfield
Derek Soutar
Julian Speroni

Defenders
Thomas Cowan
Jonay Hernandez Santos
Tom Hutchinson
Calum MacDonald
Dave Mackay
Lee Mair
Brent Sancho
Lee Wilkie

Midfielders
Neil Barrett
Garry Brady
Craig Burley
Douglas Cameron
Beto Caranza
Mark Fotheringham
Chris Hegarty
Neil Jablonski
Georghi Nemsadze
Gavin Rae
Stephen Robb
Juan Sara
Barry Smith
Alan Youngson

Forwards
Fabian Caballero
Sebastian Kneissel
Bobby Linn
Steve Lovell
David McLean
Duncan McLean
Steven McNally
Steven Milne
Nacho Novo
Fabrizio Ravanelli

KEY: On all match; On bench; Subbed or sent off (Counting game); Subbed or sent off (playing less than 70 minutes); Subbed on from bench (Counting Game); Subbed on (playing less than 70 minutes); Subbed on and then subbed or sent off (Counting Game); Subbed on and then subbed or sent off (playing less than 70 minutes); Not in 16

HIBERNIAN

Final Position: **8th**

NICKNAME: THE HIBEES

KEY: ☐ Won ☐ Drawn ☐ Lost

							Attendance
1	prem	Dundee Utd	A	W	2-1	Riordan 74; McManus 88 pen	9,809
2	prem	Hearts	H	W	1-0	O'Connor 90	14,803
3	prem	Rangers	A	L	2-5	Murray 29; McManus 36	49,642
4	prem	Aberdeen	H	D	1-1	Brown, S 69	10,682
5	prem	Motherwell	H	L	0-2		8,387
6	prem	Dunfermline	A	D	0-0		9,715
7	sccc2	Montrose	H	W	9-0	Dobbie 1,29,31 pen; O'Connor 18,85; Murray 66; Kerrigan 70 og; Riordan 78; Brown, S 86	5,032
8	prem	Celtic	H	L	1-2	Doumbe 38	12,032
9	prem	Partick	A	W	1-0	Brebner 90	4,125
10	prem	Livingston	H	L	0-2		8,562
11	prem	Kilmarnock	H	W	3-1	Murdock 13; Riordan 16; O'Connor 90	7,191
12	sccc3	Queen of South	H	W	2-1	Riordan 11,23	7,613
13	prem	Dundee	A	D	1-1	Riordan 81	7,032
14	prem	Dundee Utd	H	D	2-2	Brown, S 15; McCracken 90 og	8,756
15	prem	Hearts	A	L	0-2		16,632
16	prem	Rangers	H	L	0-1		11,160
17	prem	Aberdeen	A	L	1-3	Dobbie 57	7,863
18	prem	Motherwell	A	W	1-0	Riordan 90	4,533
19	sccqf	Celtic	H	W	2-1	Brebner 64 pen; Thomson 82	9,246
20	prem	Dunfermline	H	L	1-2	Riordan 64	9,085
21	prem	Celtic	A	L	0-6		59,609
22	prem	Partick	H	W	3-2	O'Connor 9; Dobbie 35; Whittaker 84	8,875
23	scr3	Rangers	H	L	0-2		11,392
24	prem	Livingston	A	L	0-1		5,621
25	prem	Kilmarnock	A	W	2-0	Brown, S 48; O'Connor 50	5,571
26	prem	Dundee	H	D	1-1	Riordan 69 pen	8,023
27	slc5	Rangers	H	W	4-3*	Dobbie 79 (*on penalties)	27,954
28	prem	Dundee Utd	A	D	0-0		6,389
29	prem	Hearts	H	D	1-1	Riordan 24	15,060
30	prem	Rangers	A	L	0-3		49,698
31	prem	Aberdeen	H	L	0-1		10,416
32	scccf	Livingston	H	L	0-2		45,500
33	prem	Celtic	H	L	0-4		9,456
34	prem	Motherwell	H	D	3-3	Nicol 6; Reid 37; Riordan 62 pen	5,670
35	prem	Partick	A	D	1-1	Murdock 68	3,155
36	prem	Livingston	H	W	3-1	McManus 39; Riordan 54,82	6,507
37	prem	Kilmarnock	H	W	3-0	Caldwell 22; Thomson 45; Riordan 64 pen	7,326
38	prem	Dunfermline	A	D	1-1	Riordan 5	5,041
39	prem	Dundee	A	D	2-2	Riordan 45,50 pen	5,508
40	prem	Kilmarnock	A	L	0-2		4,886
41	prem	Dundee	H	W	1-0	Riordan 42	6,180
42	prem	Partick	H	L	1-2	Murdock 33	5,447
43	prem	Aberdeen	A	W	1-0	O'Connor 90	6,781
44	prem	Livingston	A	L	1-4	Doumbe 75	4,409

MONTHLY POINTS TALLY

Month	Points	%
AUGUST	7	58%
SEPTEMBER	1	11%
OCTOBER	6	67%
NOVEMBER	2	17%
DECEMBER	3	25%
JANUARY	7	58%
FEBRUARY	2	17%
MARCH	2	22%
APRIL	8	53%
MAY	6	50%

KEY PLAYERS - GOALSCORERS

Derek Riordan

Goals in the League	15	Player Strike Rate Average number of minutes between League goals scored by player	162
Contribution to Attacking Power Average number of minutes between League team goals while on pitch	76	Club Strike Rate Average number of minutes between League goals scored by club	83

	PLAYER	LGE GOALS	POWER	STRIKE RATE
1	Derek Riordan	15	76	162 mins
2	Garry O'Connor	5	89	463 mins
3	Tom McManus	3	72	533 mins
4	Colin Murdock	3	81	951 mins
5	Scott Brown	3	88	1000 mins

KEY PLAYERS - MIDFIELDERS

Alan Reid

Goals in the League	1	Contribution to Attacking Power Average number of minutes between League team goals while on pitch	65
Defensive Rating Average number of mins between League goals conceded while he was on the pitch	55	Scoring Difference Defensive Rating minus Contribution to Attacking Power	-10

	PLAYER	LGE GOALS	DEF RATE	POWER	SCORE DIFF
1	Alan Reid	1	55	65	-10 mins
2	Kevin Thomson	1	64	86	-22 mins
3	Ian Murray	1	64	88	-24 mins
4	Steven Whittaker	1	47	78	-31 mins
5	Grant Brebner	1	48	87	-39 mins

KEY PLAYERS - DEFENDERS

Colin Murdock

Goals Conceded (GC) The number of League goals conceded while he was on the pitch	42	Clean Sheets In games when he played at least 70 minutes	8
Defensive Rating Ave number of mins between League goals conceded while on the pitch	68	Club Defensive Rating Average number of mins between League goals conceded by the club this season	57

	PLAYER	CON LGE	CLEAN SHEETS	DEF RATE
1	Colin Murdock	42	8	68 mins
2	Roland Edge	25	4	64 mins
3	Mathias Doumbe	51	8	58 mins
4	Gary Caldwell	26	4	58 mins
5	Gary Smith	33	3	48 mins

KEY GOALKEEPER

Daniel Andersson

Goals Conceded in the League	60	Counting Games Games when he played at least 70 mins	38
Defensive Rating Ave number of mins between League goals conceded while on the pitch	57	Clean Sheets In games when he played at least 70 mins	9

LEAGUE GOALS

Derek Riordan

Minutes on the pitch	2434	Goals in the League	15
League average (mins between goals)	162		

	PLAYER	MINS	GOALS	AVE
1	Riordan	2434	15	162
2	O'Connor	2315	5	463
3	Murdock	2852	3	951
4	Brown, S	2999	3	1000
5	McManus	1599	3	533
6	Doumbe	2970	2	1485
7	Dobbie	896	2	448
8	Nicol	1092	1	1092
9	Murray	1225	1	1225
10	Reid	1493	1	1493
11	Thomson	1803	1	1803
12	Whittaker	1560	1	1560
	Other		3	
	TOTAL		41	

DISCIPLINARY RECORDS

	PLAYER	YELLOW	RED	AVE
1	Murdock	10	0	285
2	Reid	5	0	298
3	Brown, S	10	0	299
4	Thomson	5	1	300
5	McManus	5	0	319
6	Nicol	3	0	364
7	Glass	2	0	399
8	Brebner	3	1	455
9	Caldwell	3	0	501
10	Whittaker	3	0	520
11	Edge	3	0	536
12	Doumbe	5	0	594
13	Murray	2	0	612
	Other	8	2	
	TOTAL	67	4	

TOP POINT EARNERS

	PLAYER	GAMES	AV PTS
1	Reid	15	1.33
2	Riordan	24	1.25
3	Edge	16	1.25
4	O'Connor	21	1.24
5	Murdock	31	1.23
6	Murray	13	1.23
7	Brown, S	32	1.19
8	Andersson	38	1.16
9	Whittaker	13	1.15
10	Doumbe	33	1.15
	CLUB AVERAGE:		**1.16**

TEAM OF THE SEASON

G — Daniel Andersson, CG: 38 DR: 57

D — Colin Murdock, CG: 31 DR: 68
D — Roland Edge, CG: 16 DR: 64
D — Gary Caldwell, CG: 16 DR: 58
D — Mathias Doumbe, CG: 33 DR: 58

M — Alan Reid, CG: 15 SD: -10
M — Kevin Thomson, CG: 19 SD: -22
M — Ian Murray, CG: 13 SD: -24
M — Steven Whittaker, CG: 13 SD: -31

F — Derek Riordan, CG: 24 SR: 162
F — Garry O'Connor, CG: 21 SR: 463

LEAGUE APPEARANCES, BOOKINGS AND CAPS

	AGE (on 01/07/04)	IN NAMED 16	APPEARANCES	COUNTING GAMES	MINUTES ON PITCH	YELLOW CARDS	RED CARDS	THIS SEASON	HOME COUNTRY
Goalkeepers									
Daniel Andersson	31	38	38	38	3420	1	0	-	Sweden
Alistair Brown	2005	16	0	0	0	0	0	-	Scotland
Defenders									
Jonathan Baillie	2005	10	2	2	178	0	1	-	Scotland
Gary Caldwell	23	17	17	16	1504	3	0	5	Scotland (63)
Mathias Doumbe	24	33	33	33	2970	5	0	-	France
Roland Edge	25	20	20	16	1610	3	0	-	England
Colin Murdock	29	32	32	31	2852	10	0	3	N Ireland (114)
Alen Orman	26	24	18	12	1255	2	0	-	Austria
Gary Smith	33	19	19	17	1579	1	0	-	Scotland
Midfielders									
Frederic Arpinon	35	1	1	1	90	0	0	-	France
Grant Brebner	26	21	21	20	1820	3	1	-	Scotland
Stephen Dobbie	21	29	28	6	896	0	0	-	Scotland
Stephen Glass	28	14	12	9	799	2	0	-	Scotland
Jamie McCluskey	2005	4	1	0	7	0	0	-	Scotland
Kevin McDonald	2005	2	1	0	45	0	0	-	Scotland
Ian Murray	23	14	14	13	1225	2	0	-	Scotland
Kevin Nicol	22	21	15	10	1092	3	0	-	Scotland
Steven Notman	2005	1	0	0	0	0	0	-	Scotland
Alan Reid	23	25	20	15	1493	5	0	-	Scotland
Jay Shields	2005	3	2	1	135	0	0	-	Scotland
Kevin Thomson	19	25	23	19	1803	5	1	-	Scotland
Steven Whittaker	20	36	28	13	1560	3	0	-	Scotland
Jarkko Wiss	32	15	13	10	1011	1	0	-	Finland
Yannick Zambernardi	26	14	8	7	648	1	0	-	France
Forwards									
Scott Brown	19	36	36	32	2999	10	0	-	Scotland
Steven Fletcher	2005	8	5	1	142	0	0	-	Scotland
Tom McManus	23	35	32	13	1599	5	0	-	Scotland
Garry O'Connor	21	34	33	21	2315	2	0	-	Scotland
Derek Riordan	21	34	34	24	2434	0	1	-	Scotland

SQUAD APPEARANCES

Match 1 2 3 4 5 6 7 8 9 10 11 12 13 14 15 16 17 18 19 20 21 22 23 24 25 26 27 28 29 30 31 32 33 34 35 36 37 38 39 40 41 42 43 44
Venue A H A H H A H H A H H H A H A H A A H H A H H A A H H A H A H H H H A H H A A A H H A A
Competition L L L L L L W L L L L W L L L L L L W L L L O L L L W L L L L W L L L L L L L L L L L L
Result W W L D L D W L W L W W D D L L L W W L L W L L W D W D D L L L L D D W W D D L W L W L
Goalkeepers
Daniel Andersson
Alistair Brown
Morten Hyldgaard
Defenders
Jonathan Baillie
Gary Caldwell
Mathias Doumbe
Roland Edge
Dermot McCaffrey
Colin Murdock
Alen Orman
Gary Smith
Midfielders
Frederic Arpinon
Grant Brebner
Stephen Dobbie
Stephen Glass
John Kane
Jamie McCluskey
Kevin McDonald
Ian Murray
Kevin Nicol
Steven Notman
Alan Reid
Jay Shields
Kevin Thomson
Steven Whittaker
Jarkko Wiss
Yannick Zambernardi
Forwards
Scott Brown
Steven Fletcher
Tom McManus
Garry O'Connor
Derek Riordan
KEY: On all match
On bench
Subbed or sent off (Counting game)
Subbed or sent off (playing less than 70 minutes)
Subbed on from bench (Counting Game)
Subbed on (playing less than 70 minutes)
Subbed on and then subbed or sent off (Counting Game)
Subbed on and then subbed or sent off (playing less than 70 minutes)
Not in 16

LIVINGSTON

Final Position: **9th**

NICKNAME: THE LIVI' LIONS

KEY: ☐Won ☐Drawn ☐Lost

							Attendance
1	prem	Partick	A	D	1-1	Pasquinelli 77	4,220
2	prem	Motherwell	H	W	1-0	Lilley 78	5,316
3	prem	Dundee	A	L	1-2	O'Brien 37	5,815
4	prem	Celtic	A	L	1-5	Lilley 85	57,165
5	prem	Dundee Utd	H	D	0-0		5,344
6	prem	Kilmarnock	H	L	1-2	Makel 18	6,150
7	sccc2	Queens Park	A	W	3-1	Makel 9 pen,79 pen; Quino 40	1,011
8	prem	Aberdeen	A	W	3-0	Quino 45; Rubio 65; Pasquinelli 70	10,307
9	prem	Dunfermline	H	D	0-0		4,616
10	prem	Hibernian	A	W	2-0	Lilley 38,83	8,562
11	prem	Rangers	H	D	0-0		9,627
12	sccc3	Dundee Utd	A	W	1-0	Gallacher, P 19 og	2,899
13	prem	Hearts	A	L	1-3	Lilley 52	11,233
14	prem	Partick	H	W	2-0	Lilley 26 pen; Makel 45	5,226
15	prem	Motherwell	A	D	1-1	Lilley 39	6,357
16	prem	Dundee	H	D	1-1	Lilley 71 pen	4,625
17	sccqf	Aberdeen	A	W	3-2	Lilley 15; Pasquinelli 50; Makel 99	6,090
18	prem	Celtic	H	L	0-2		9,523
19	prem	Dundee Utd	A	L	0-2		5,421
20	prem	Kilmarnock	A	W	3-0	Camacho 50; Pasquinelli 80; O'Brien 90	5,035
21	prem	Aberdeen	H	D	1-1	O'Brien 90	7,115
22	prem	Dunfermline	A	D	2-2	McLaughlin, S 15; Makel 62	5,155
23	scr3	Montrose	H	W	1-0	Fernandez 17	2,675
24	prem	Hibernian	H	W	1-0	Makel 26	5,621
25	prem	Rangers	A	L	0-1		48,628
26	slc5	Dundee	A	W	1-0	Lilley 90 pen	6,600
27	scr4	Spartans	A	W	4-0	Lilley 53,61,70; Fernandez 59	2,364
28	prem	Partick	A	L	2-5	Makel 85; McMenimin 90	3,011
29	prem	Motherwell	H	W	3-1	McAllister 3; Lilley 29; Fernandez 45	3,492
30	prem	Dundee	A	L	0-1		6,108
31	prem	Hearts	H	L	2-3	Makel 5; McMenimin 56	4,450
32	prem	Celtic	A	L	1-5	Lilley 41	57,973
33	scpqf	Aberdeen	A	D	1-1	Anderson 51 og	11,593
34	scccf	Hibernian	A	W	2-0	Lilley 50; McAllister 52	45,500
35	scqfr	Aberdeen	H	W	1-0	O'Brien 26	4,485
36	prem	Aberdeen	A	W	2-1	McMenimin 14; O'Brien 87	7,477
37	prem	Dundee Utd	H	L	2-3	McNamee 38; McLaughlin, S 72	3,082
38	prem	Dunfermline	H	D	0-0		3,558
39	prem	Hibernian	A	L	1-3	Lilley 50	6,507
40	prem	Kilmarnock	H	D	1-1	Fernandez 83	2,677
41	scsf	Celtic	H	L	1-3	McMenimin 79	26,152
42	prem	Rangers	H	D	1-1	McMenimin 79	6,096
43	prem	Hearts	A	D	1-1	McMenimin 73	10,352
44	prem	Aberdeen	H	W	2-0	McNamee 24; McMenimin 63	3,133
45	prem	Kilmarnock	A	L	2-4	Makel 13; O'Brien 23	5,023
46	prem	Partick	H	D	2-2	O'Brien 22; McMenimin 68	3,160
47	prem	Dundee	A	L	0-2		4,954
48	prem	Hibernian	H	W	4-1	Lovell 8; Lilley 64; Fernandez 78; Makel 89	4,409

MONTHLY POINTS TALLY

AUGUST	4	33%
SEPTEMBER	4	44%
OCTOBER	5	56%
NOVEMBER	5	42%
DECEMBER	4	33%
JANUARY	4	44%
FEBRUARY	3	20%
MARCH	4	44%
APRIL	6	40%
MAY	4	33%

KEY PLAYERS - GOALSCORERS

Derek Lilley

Goals in the League	12	**Player Strike Rate** Average number of minutes between League goals scored by player	215
Contribution to Attacking Power Average number of minutes between League team goals while on pitch	66	**Club Strike Rate** Average number of minutes between League goals scored by club	71

	PLAYER	LGE GOALS	POWER	STRIKE RATE
1	Derek Lilley	12	66	215 mins
2	Lee Makel	8	67	390 mins
3	Burton O'Brien	6	67	430 mins
4	Fernando Pasquinelli	3	86	492 mins
5	David Fernandez	3	65	742 mins

KEY PLAYERS - MIDFIELDERS

Stuart Lovell

Goals in the League	1	**Contribution to Attacking Power** Average number of minutes between League team goals while on pitch	67
Defensive Rating Average number of mins between League goals conceded while he was on the pitch	60	**Scoring Difference** Defensive Rating minus Contribution to Attacking Power	-7

	PLAYER	LGE GOALS	DEF RATE	POWER	SCORE DIFF
1	Stuart Lovell	1	60	67	-7 mins
2	Lee Makel	8	60	68	-8 mins
3	Burton O'Brien	6	56	68	-12 mins
4	John-Paul McGovern	0	53	74	-21 mins

KEY PLAYERS - DEFENDERS

Oscar Rubio

Goals Conceded (GC) The number of League goals conceded while he was on the pitch	43	**Clean Sheets** In games when he played at least 70 minutes	11
Defensive Rating Ave number of mins between League goals conceded while on the pitch	70	**Club Defensive Rating** Average number of mins between League goals conceded by the club this season	60

	PLAYER	CON LGE	CLEAN SHEETS	DEF RATE
1	Oscar Rubio	43	11	70 mins
2	Emmanuel Dorado	35	7	65 mins
3	James McAllister	46	10	64 mins
4	Marvin Andrews	54	11	61 mins
5	David McNamee	42	6	58 mins

KEY GOALKEEPER

Roddy McKenzie

Goals Conceded in the League	50	**Counting Games** Games when he played at least 70 mins	35
Defensive Rating Ave number of mins between League goals conceded while on the pitch	63	**Clean Sheets** In games when he played at least 70 mins	10

LEAGUE GOALS

Derek Lilley

Minutes on the pitch	2585	**Goals in the League**	12
League average (mins between goals)	215		

	PLAYER	MINS	GOALS	AVE
1	Lilley	2585	12	215
2	Makel	3122	8	390
3	McMenimin	737	7	105
4	O'Brien	2578	6	430
5	Pasquinelli	1477	3	492
6	Fernandez	2227	3	742
7	McNamee	2423	2	1212
8	Rubio	2995	1	2995
9	Quino	645	1	645
10	Lovell	1935	1	1935
11	McLaughlin, S	943	1	943
12	McAllister	2942	1	2942
	Other		2	
	TOTAL		48	

DISCIPLINARY RECORDS

	PLAYER	YELLOW	RED	AVE
1	Quino	4	0	161
2	McMenimin	4	0	184
3	McNamee	11	1	201
4	Makel	10	0	312
5	Pasquinelli	4	0	369
6	Dorado	6	0	381
7	Lilley	6	0	430
8	Fernandez	5	0	445
9	Kerr	2	0	483
10	Lovell	4	0	483
11	McAllister	6	0	490
12	Rubio	6	0	499
13	McGovern	1	0	1471
	Other	3	0	
	TOTAL	72	1	

TOP POINT EARNERS

	PLAYER	GAMES	AV PTS
1	McGovern	13	1.38
2	Lovell	18	1.33
3	Rubio	31	1.26
4	Makel	33	1.18
5	Andrews	36	1.17
6	Fernandez	24	1.17
7	McAllister	31	1.16
8	McKenzie	35	1.14
9	Dorado	24	1.13
10	McNamee	26	1.08
	CLUB AVERAGE:		**1.13**

LEAGUE APPEARANCES, BOOKINGS AND CAPS

	AGE (on 01/07/04)	IN NAMED 16	APPEARANCES	COUNTING GAMES	MINUTES ON PITCH	YELLOW CARDS	RED CARDS	THIS SEASON	HOME COUNTRY
Goalkeepers									
Alan Main	36	22	3	3	270	0	0	-	Scotland
Roddy McKenzie	28	38	35	35	3150	1	0	-	Scotland
Kevin Montgomery	18	8	0	0	0	0	0	-	England
Defenders									
Marvin Andrews	28	38	38	36	3314	1	0	-	Trinidad & Tobago
Emmanuel Dorado	31	29	28	24	2286	6	0	-	Argentina
Jim Lauchlan	27	1	0	0	0	0	0	-	Scotland
James McAllister	26	34	34	31	2942	6	0	1	Scotland (63)
David McNamee	23	30	30	26	2423	11	1	2	Scotland (63)
Oscar Rubio	28	37	37	31	2995	6	0	-	Portugal
William Snowdon	21	11	3	1	118	0	0	-	England
Midfielders									
Richard Brittain	20	20	12	4	521	0	0	-	Scotland
Juan Jose Camacho	23	7	6	0	190	0	0	-	Spain
Salvadore Capin	28	2	2	2	167	1	0	-	Spain
Brian Kerr	22	13	13	10	967	2	0	3	Scotland (63)
Stuart Lovell	32	25	25	18	1935	4	0	-	Australia
Lee Makel	31	36	36	33	3122	10	0	-	England
John-Paul McGovern	23	30	27	13	1471	1	0	-	Scotland
Scott McLaughlin	20	33	16	9	943	0	0	-	Scotland
Steven Miller	20	5	0	0	0	0	0	-	Scotland
Burton O'Brien	23	34	33	27	2578	0	0	-	Scotland
Francisco Guinovart	33	13	12	6	645	4	0	-	Spain
Cherif Toure-Maman	23	1	1	0	45	0	0	-	Togo
Allan Walker	17	3	0	0	0	0	0	-	Scotland
Barry Wilson	32	4	4	1	278	0	0	-	Scotland
Forwards									
Robbie Arthur	17	3	0	0	0	0	0	-	Scotland
David Fernandez	28	27	27	24	2227	5	0	-	Spain
Guy Ipoua	28	1	1	0	30	0	0	-	Cameroon
Derek Lilley	30	36	35	27	2585	6	0	-	Scotland
Paul McLaughlin	2005	3	1	0	44	0	0	-	Scotland
Colin McMenamin	23	17	15	5	737	4	0	-	Scotland
James McPake	20	1	1	0	3	0	0	-	Scotland
Fernando Pasquinelli	24	22	22	14	1477	4	0	-	Argentina
Theodore Whitmore	31	3	3	1	136	0	0	-	Jamaica
Davide Xausa	28	1	1	0	21	0	0	-	Canada

TEAM OF THE SEASON

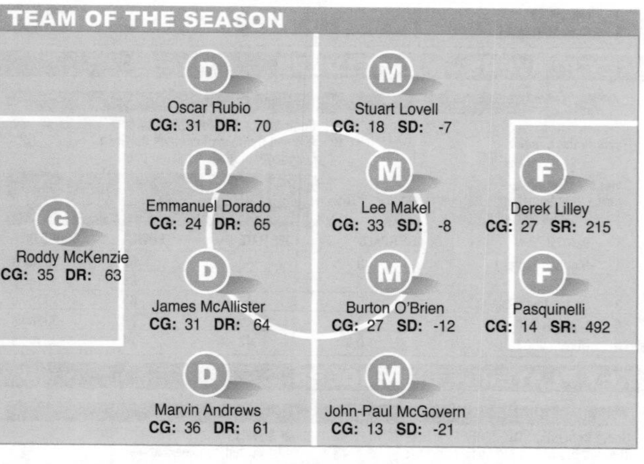

D
Oscar Rubio
CG: 31 DR: 70
D
Emmanuel Dorado
CG: 24 DR: 65
D
James McAllister
CG: 31 DR: 64
D
Marvin Andrews
CG: 36 DR: 61
G
Roddy McKenzie
CG: 35 DR: 63
M
Stuart Lovell
CG: 18 SD: -7
M
Lee Makel
CG: 33 SD: -8
M
Burton O'Brien
CG: 27 SD: -12
M
John-Paul McGovern
CG: 13 SD: -21
F
Derek Lilley
CG: 27 SR: 215
F
Pasquinelli
CG: 14 SR: 492

SQUAD APPEARANCES

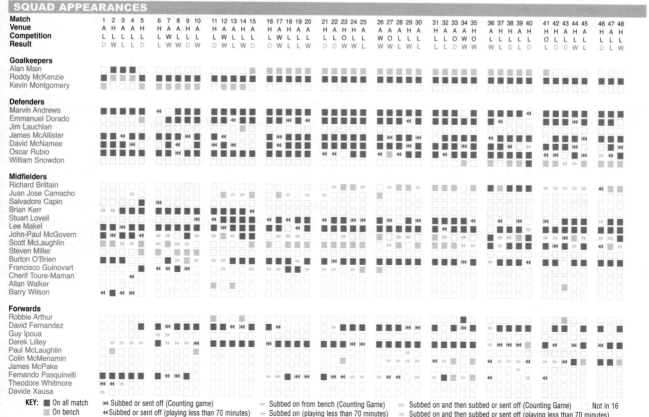

Match	1	2	3	4	5	6	7	8	9	10	11	12	13	14	15	16	17	18	19	20	21	22	23	24	25	26	27	28	29	30	31	32	33	34	35	36	37	38	39	40	41	42	43	44	45	46	47	48
Venue	A	H	A	A	H	H	A	A	H	A	H	A	A	H	A	H	A	H	A	A	H	A	H	H	A	A	A	A	H	A	H	A	A	A	H	A	H	H	A	H	H	H	A	H	A	H	A	H
Competition	L	L	L	L	L	L	W	L	L	L	L	W	L	L	L	L	W	L	L	L	L	L	O	L	L	W	O	L	L	L	L	L	O	W	O	L	L	L	L	L	O	L	L	L	L	L	L	L
Result	D	W	L	L	D	L	W	W	D	W	D	W	L	W	D	D	W	L	L	W	D	D	W	W	L	W	W	L	W	L	L	L	D	W	W	W	L	D	L	D	L	D	D	W	L	D	L	W

Goalkeepers
Alan Main
Roddy McKenzie
Kevin Montgomery

Defenders
Marvin Andrews
Emmanuel Dorado
Jim Lauchlan
James McAllister
David McNamee
Oscar Rubio
William Snowdon

Midfielders
Richard Brittain
Juan Jose Camacho
Salvadore Capin
Brian Kerr
Stuart Lovell
Lee Makel
John-Paul McGovern
Scott McLaughlin
Steven Miller
Burton O'Brien
Francisco Guinovart
Cherif Toure-Maman
Allan Walker
Barry Wilson

Forwards
Robbie Arthur
David Fernandez
Guy Ipoua
Derek Lilley
Paul McLaughlin
Colin McMenamin
James McPake
Fernando Pasquinelli
Theodore Whitmore
Davide Xausa

KEY: On all match · On bench · Subbed or sent off (Counting game) · Subbed or sent off (playing less than 70 minutes) · Subbed on from bench (Counting Game) · Subbed on (playing less than 70 minutes) · Subbed on and then subbed or sent off (Counting Game) · Subbed on and then subbed or sent off (playing less than 70 minutes) · Not in 16

KILMARNOCK

Final Position: **10th**

NICKNAME: KILLIE

KEY: ☐ Won ☐ Drawn ☐ Lost

							Attendance
1	prem	Rangers	A	L	0-4		49,108
2	prem	Partick	H	W	2-1	Hardie 47; Boyd 61	6,778
3	prem	Motherwell	A	L	1-2	Dindeleux 76	5,087
4	prem	Dundee	H	D	1-1	Boyd 79	5,973
5	prem	Hearts	H	L	0-2		6,925
6	prem	Livingston	A	W	2-1	Hessey 15; Boyd 22	6,150
7	sccc2	Brechin	A	L	0-1		829
8	prem	Dundee Utd	A	D	1-1	Boyd 72	6,529
9	prem	Aberdeen	H	L	1-3	Nish 67	6,023
10	prem	Dunfermline	A	W	3-2	McSwegan 24,84; Shields 69	4,495
11	prem	Hibernian	A	L	1-3	Nish 80	7,191
12	prem	Celtic	H	L	0-5		12,460
13	prem	Rangers	H	L	2-3	McDonald 39; Canero 50	12,204
14	prem	Partick	A	W	4-2	Nish 26,90; McDonald 61,66	4,445
15	prem	Motherwell	H	W	2-0	Canero 13; Boyd 60	6,320
16	prem	Dundee	A	W	2-1	Nish 8; Boyd 37	6,954
17	prem	Hearts	A	L	1-2	McSwegan 90	9,881
18	prem	Livingston	H	L	0-3		5,035
19	prem	Dundee Utd	H	L	0-2		6,062
20	prem	Aberdeen	A	L	1-3	Nish 82	11,698
21	scr3	Raith	A	W	3-1	McSwegan 28; McDonald 32; Nish 35	3,610
22	prem	Dunfermline	H	D	1-1	McSwegan 29 pen	5,715
23	prem	Hibernian	H	L	0-2		5,571
24	prem	Celtic	A	L	1-5	Skora 84	59,138
25	scr4	Rangers	H	L	0-2		10,993
26	prem	Rangers	A	L	0-2		46,900
27	prem	Partick	H	W	2-1	Lilley 55; Boyd 58	5,818
28	prem	Motherwell	A	L	0-1		5,163
29	prem	Dundee	H	W	4-2	Skora 32; Invincible 34,64; Boyd 54 pen	5,454
30	prem	Hearts	H	D	1-1	Invincible 87	5,297
31	prem	Dundee Utd	A	L	1-4	Invincible 61	5,757
32	prem	Aberdeen	H	W	3-1	Dargo 3; Boyd 28,76	7,250
33	prem	Dunfermline	A	L	1-2	Invincible 9	3,914
34	prem	Livingston	A	D	1-1	Dargo 85	2,677
35	prem	Hibernian	A	L	0-3		7,326
36	prem	Celtic	H	L	0-1		14,576
37	prem	Hibernian	H	W	2-0	Boyd 28,85	4,886
38	prem	Livingston	H	W	4-2	Nish 54,79; Canning 74; McSwegan 87	5,023
39	prem	Dundee	A	L	0-2		4,942
40	prem	Aberdeen	H	W	4-0	Skora 24; Boyd 36,58; Nish 61	4,987
41	prem	Partick	A	D	2-2	Boyd 6; Dargo 68	4,124

MONTHLY POINTS TALLY

Month	Points	%
AUGUST	4	33%
SEPTEMBER	4	44%
OCTOBER	3	33%
NOVEMBER	6	50%
DECEMBER	3	25%
JANUARY	1	8%
FEBRUARY	6	50%
MARCH	4	44%
APRIL	4	27%
MAY	7	58%

KEY PLAYERS - GOALSCORERS

Colin Nish

Goals in the League	9	Player Strike Rate Average number of minutes between League goals scored by player	172
Contribution to Attacking Power Average number of minutes between League team goals while on pitch	51	Club Strike Rate Average number of minutes between League goals scored by club	67

	PLAYER	LGE GOALS	POWER	STRIKE RATE
1	Colin Nish	9	51	172 mins
2	Kris Boyd	15	67	179 mins
3	Danny Invincible	5	65	312 mins
4	Eric Skora	3	60	485 mins
5	Gary McDonald	3	69	490 mins

KEY PLAYERS - MIDFIELDERS

Stephen Murray

Goals in the League	0	Contribution to Attacking Power Average number of minutes between League team goals while on pitch	52
Defensive Rating Average number of mins between League goals conceded while he was on the pitch	60	Scoring Difference Defensive Rating minus Contribution to Attacking Power	8

	PLAYER	LGE GOALS	DEF RATE	POWER	SCORE DIFF
1	Stephen Murray	0	60	52	8 mins
2	Eric Skora	3	52	61	-9 mins
3	Danny Invincible	5	45	65	-20 mins
4	Gary McDonald	3	40	70	-30 mins
5	Steve Fulton	0	42	74	-32 mins

KEY PLAYERS - DEFENDERS

James Fowler

Goals Conceded (GC) The number of League goals conceded while he was on the pitch	43	Clean Sheets In games when he played at least 70 minutes	2
Defensive Rating Ave number of mins between League goals conceded while on the pitch	51	Club Defensive Rating Average number of mins between League goals conceded by the club this season	46

	PLAYER	CON LGE	CLEAN SHEETS	DEF RATE
1	James Fowler	43	2	51 mins
2	Garry Hay	52	3	49 mins
3	Frederic Dindeleux	63	3	47 mins
4	Gordon Greer	47	2	45 mins
5	Greg Shields	38	1	42 mins

KEY GOALKEEPER

Colin Meldrum

Goals Conceded in the League	29	Counting Games Games when he played at least 70 mins	17
Defensive Rating Ave number of mins between League goals conceded while on the pitch	51	Clean Sheets In games when he played at least 70 mins	1

LEAGUE GOALS

Kris Boyd

Minutes on the pitch	2691	Goals in the League	15
League average (mins between goals)	179		

	PLAYER	MINS	GOALS	AVE
1	Boyd	2691	15	179
2	Nish	1550	9	172
3	Invincible	1562	5	312
4	McSwegan	1300	5	260
5	Skora	1455	3	485
6	Dargo	425	3	142
7	McDonald	1469	3	490
8	Canero	1125	2	563
9	Lilley	1151	1	1151
10	Hessey	630	1	630
11	Canning	314	1	314
12	Dindeleux	2970	1	2970
	Other		2	
	TOTAL		51	

DISCIPLINARY RECORDS

	PLAYER	YELLOW	RED	AVE
1	Locke	6	0	253
2	McLaughlin	3	1	292
3	Hessey	2	0	315
4	Lilley	3	0	383
5	Shields	4	0	401
6	Greer	5	0	427
7	Hardie	2	0	458
8	Nish	3	0	516
9	Fowler	3	1	549
10	Canero	2	0	562
11	Fulton	3	0	616
12	McSwegan	2	0	650
13	Dindeleux	4	0	742
	Other	12	1	
	TOTAL	54	3	

TOP POINT EARNERS

	PLAYER	GAMES	AV PTS
1	Murray	18	1.67
2	Fowler	21	1.38
3	Meldrum	16	1.25
4	Skora	16	1.25
5	Shields	17	1.24
6	Hay	28	1.21
7	Boyd	26	1.19
8	Dindeleux	33	1.09
9	Fulton	20	1.05
10	Invincible	14	1.00
	CLUB AVERAGE:		**1.11**

TEAM OF THE SEASON

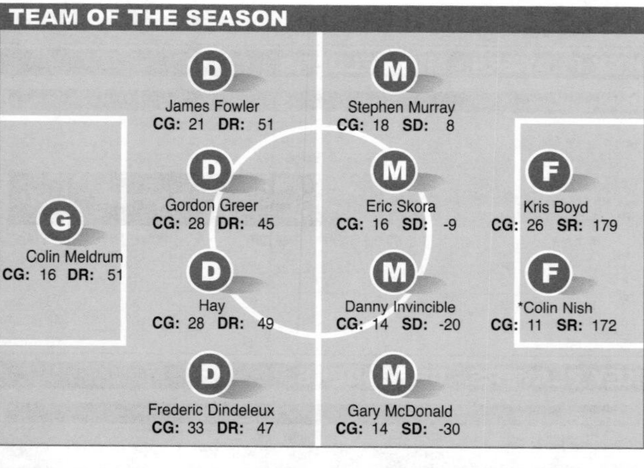

D
James Fowler
CG: 21 DR: 51
D
Gordon Greer
CG: 28 DR: 45
D
Hay
CG: 28 DR: 49
D
Frederic Dindeleux
CG: 33 DR: 47
G
Colin Meldrum
CG: 16 DR: 51
M
Stephen Murray
CG: 18 SD: 8
M
Eric Skora
CG: 16 SD: -9
M
Danny Invincible
CG: 14 SD: -20
M
Gary McDonald
CG: 14 SD: -30
F
Kris Boyd
CG: 26 SR: 179
F
*Colin Nish
CG: 11 SR: 172

LEAGUE APPEARANCES, BOOKINGS AND CAPS

	AGE (on 01/07/04)	IN NAMED 16	APPEARANCES	COUNTING GAMES	MINUTES ON PITCH	YELLOW CARDS	RED CARDS	THIS SEASON	HOME COUNTRY
Goalkeepers									
Francais Dubourdeau	23	25	18	18	1620	1	0	-	France
Colin Meldrum	28	32	17	16	1486	0	0	-	Scotland
Craig Samson	-	6	1	1	90	0	0	-	Scotland
Graeme Smith	21	13	3	2	224	0	0	-	Scotland
Defenders									
Peter Canero	23	13	13	12	1125	2	0	-	Scotland
Shaun Dillon	19	5	2	2	180	0	0	-	Scotland
Frederic Dindeleux	30	35	33	33	2970	4	0	-	France
James Fowler	23	34	31	21	2198	3	1	-	Scotland
Gordon Greer	23	27	25	22	2136	5	0	-	Scotland
Garry Hay	26	32	30	28	2539	2	0	-	Scotland
Sean Hessey	25	10	7	7	630	2	0	-	England
Chris Innes	27	1	1	0	35	2	1	-	Scotland
David Lilley	26	14	14	12	1151	3	0	-	Scotland
Barry McLaughlin	31	23	17	10	1168	3	1	-	Scotland
Greg Shields	27	19	19	17	1605	4	0	-	Scotland
Midfielders									
Mark Canning	20	5	5	3	314	0	0	-	Scotland
Rhian Dodds	2005	18	11	7	739	0	0	-	England
Steve Fulton	33	21	21	20	1849	3	0	-	Scotland
Martin Hardie	28	20	16	7	917	2	0	-	Scotland
Danny Invincible	25	23	22	14	1562	0	0	-	Australia
Gary Locke	29	20	20	14	1521	6	0	-	Scotland
Alan Mahood	31	5	5	1	213	1	0	-	Scotland
Gary McDonald	22	29	23	14	1469	1	0	-	Scotland
Stephen Murray	21	30	29	18	1982	0	0	-	Scotland
Eric Skora	22	17	17	16	1455	0	0	-	France
Forwards									
Kris Boyd	20	37	37	26	2691	3	0	-	Scotland
Craig Dargo	26	13	12	2	425	1	0	-	Scotland
Paul Di Giacomo	22	7	7	2	353	1	0	-	Scotland
Gary McSwegan	33	36	31	9	1300	2	0	-	Scotland
Steven Naysmith	2005	2	1	0	15	0	0	-	Scotland
Colin Nish	23	35	30	11	1550	3	0	-	Scotland

SQUAD APPEARANCES

Match	1	2	3	4	5	6	7	8	9	10	11	12	13	14	15	16	17	18	19	20	21	22	23	24	25	26	27	28	29	30	31	32	33	34	35	36	37	38	39	40	41
Venue	A	H	A	H	H	A	A	A	H	A	A	H	H	A	H	A	A	H	H	A	A	H	H	A	H	A	H	A	H	H	A	H	A	A	A	H	H	H	A	H	A
Competition	L	L	L	L	L	L	W	L	L	L	L	L	L	L	L	L	L	L	L	L	O	L	L	L	O	L	L	L	L	L	L	L	L	L	L	L	L	L	L	L	L
Result	L	W	L	D	L	W	L	D	L	W	L	L	L	W	W	W	L	L	L	L	W	D	L	L	L	L	W	L	W	D	L	W	L	D	L	L	W	W	L	W	D

Goalkeepers
Francais Dubourdeau
Colin Meldrum
Craig Samson
Graeme Smith

Defenders
Peter Canero
Shaun Dillon
Frederic Dindeleux
James Fowler
Gordon Greer
Garry Hay
Sean Hessey
Chris Innes
David Lilley
Barry McLaughlin
Greg Shields

Midfielders
Mark Canning
Rhian Dodds
Steve Fulton
Martin Hardie
Danny Invincible
Gary Locke
Alan Mahood
Gary McDonald
Stephen Murray
Eric Skora

Forwards
Kris Boyd
Craig Dargo
Paul Di Giacomo
Gary McSwegan
Steven Naysmith
Colin Nish

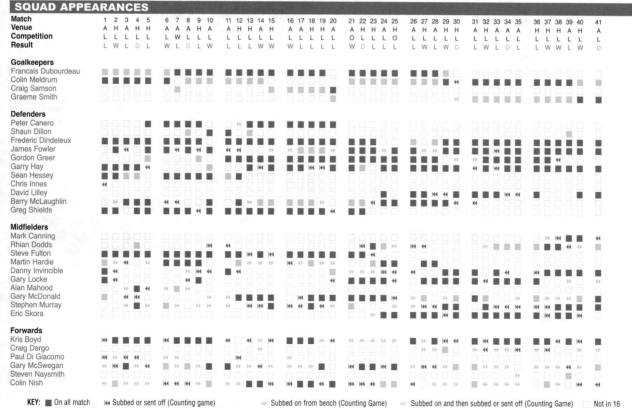

KEY: ■ On all match | ■ On bench | ⏮ Subbed or sent off (Counting game) | « Subbed or sent off (playing less than 70 minutes) | ⏭ Subbed on from bench (Counting Game) | » Subbed on (playing less than 70 minutes) | Subbed on and then subbed or sent off (Counting Game) | Subbed on and then subbed or sent off (playing less than 70 minutes) | □ Not in 16

ABERDEEN

Final Position: **11th**

NICKNAME: THE DONS

KEY: Won / Drawn / Lost

							Attendance
1	prem	Hearts	A	L	0-2		14,260
2	prem	Rangers	H	L	2-3	Zdrilic 24; Deloumeaux 90	16,348
3	prem	Dunfermline	H	L	1-2	Zdrilic 23	10,870
4	prem	Hibernian	A	D	1-1	Anderson 6	10,682
5	prem	Partick	H	W	2-1	Booth 6; Anderson 76	10,597
6	prem	Dundee	A	L	0-2		7,887
7	sccc2	Dumbarton	H	W	3-1	Zdrilic 14,44; Hinds 48	3,944
8	prem	Livingston	H	L	0-3		10,307
9	prem	Kilmarnock	A	W	3-1	Zdrilic 3; Tosh 15; Booth 47	6,023
10	prem	Dundee Utd	H	L	0-1		11,244
11	prem	Celtic	A	L	0-4		59,598
12	sccc3	Brechin	H	W	5-0	Tosh 10; Booth 13; Muirhead 37; Sheerin 40; Hinds 85	3,631
13	prem	Motherwell	H	L	0-3		9,895
14	prem	Hearts	H	L	0-1		9,687
15	prem	Rangers	A	L	0-3		49,962
16	prem	Dunfermline	A	D	2-2	Deloumeaux 25; Booth 60	5,294
17	sccqf	Livingston	H	L	2-3	Tosh 34,59	6,090
18	prem	Hibernian	H	W	3-1	Hinds 26; Booth 85,90 pen	7,863
19	prem	Partick	A	W	3-0	Anderson 42,49; Clark 90	5,186
20	prem	Dundee	H	D	2-2	Anderson 42; Wilkie 59 og	10,354
21	prem	Livingston	A	D	1-1	Booth 23	7,115
22	prem	Kilmarnock	H	W	3-1	Diamond 7; Tosh 45; Hinds 60	11,698
23	scr3	Dundee	H	D	0-0		11,012
24	prem	Dundee Utd	A	L	2-3	Booth 55 pen; Archibald 65 og	6,666
25	scr3r	Dundee	A	W	3-2	Clark 5; Heikkinen 77; Zdrilic 89	5,857
26	prem	Celtic	H	L	1-3	Tosh 62	16,452
27	scr4	Falkirk	A	W	2-0	Zdrilic 60; Booth 64	4,747
28	prem	Hearts	A	L	0-1		11,236
29	prem	Rangers	H	D	1-1	Diamond 2	15,815
30	prem	Dunfermline	H	W	2-0	McGuire 36; Booth 52	11,035
31	prem	Motherwell	A	L	0-1		5,220
32	prem	Hibernian	A	W	1-0	Morrison 5	10,416
33	scpqf	Livingston	H	D	1-1	Morrison 57	11,593
34	prem	Partick	H	D	0-0		7,395
35	prem	Dundee	A	D	1-1	Hinds 61	6,839
36	scqfr	Livingston	A	L	0-1		4,485
37	prem	Livingston	H	L	1-2	Hinds 84	7,477
38	prem	Kilmarnock	A	L	1-3	Prunty 23	7,250
39	prem	Dundee Utd	H	W	3-0	Hinds 21; McGuire 24; Sheerin 43	8,448
40	prem	Motherwell	H	L	0-2		7,246
41	prem	Celtic	A	W	2-1	Prunty 56; Zdrilic 90	51,000
42	prem	Livingston	A	L	0-2		3,133
43	prem	Partick	A	L	0-2		2,839
44	prem	Hibernian	H	L	0-1		6,781
45	prem	Kilmarnock	A	L	0-4		4,987
46	prem	Dundee	H	L	1-2	Foster 6	7,878

MONTHLY POINTS TALLY

AUGUST	1	8%
SEPTEMBER	3	33%
OCTOBER	3	33%
NOVEMBER	1	8%
DECEMBER	8	67%
JANUARY	3	33%
FEBRUARY	7	47%
MARCH	2	17%
APRIL	6	50%
MAY	0	0%

KEY PLAYERS - GOALSCORERS

Scott Booth

Goals in the League	8	Player Strike Rate Average number of minutes between League goals scored by player	204
Contribution to Attacking Power Average number of minutes between League team goals while on pitch	58	Club Strike Rate Average number of minutes between League goals scored by club	88

	PLAYER	LGE GOALS	POWER	STRIKE RATE
1	Scott Booth	8	58	204 mins
2	Leigh Hinds	5	82	395 mins
3	Russell Anderson	5	75	440 mins
4	David Zdrilic	4	84	508 mins
5	Steven Tosh	3	72	679 mins

KEY PLAYERS - MIDFIELDERS

Christopher Clark

Goals in the League	1	Contribution to Attacking Power Average number of minutes between League team goals while on pitch	75
Defensive Rating Average number of mins between League goals conceded while he was on the pitch	64	Scoring Difference Defensive Rating minus Contribution to Attacking Power	-11

	PLAYER	LGE GOALS	DEF RATE	POWER	SCORE DIFF
1	Christopher Clark	1	64	75	-11 mins
2	Steven Tosh	3	50	73	-23 mins
3	Markus Heikkinen	0	60	88	-28 mins
4	Paul Sheerin	1	54	102	-48 mins
5	Scott Muirhead	0	49	115	-66 mins

KEY PLAYERS - DEFENDERS

Alexander Diamond

Goals Conceded (GC) The number of League goals conceded while he was on the pitch	21	Clean Sheets In games when he played at least 70 minutes	4
Defensive Rating Ave number of mins between League goals conceded while on the pitch	71	Club Defensive Rating Average number of mins between League goals conceded by the club this season	54

	PLAYER	CON LGE	CLEAN SHEETS	DEF RATE
1	Alexander Diamond	21	4	71 mins
2	Scott Morrison	39	5	62 mins
3	Russell Anderson	38	3	58 mins
4	Kevin McNaughton	22	1	56 mins
5	Kevin Rutkiewicz	26	2	55 mins

KEY GOALKEEPER

David Preece

Goals Conceded in the League	60	Counting Games Games when he played at least 70 mins	36
Defensive Rating Ave number of mins between League goals conceded while on the pitch	54	Clean Sheets In games when he played at least 70 mins	5

LEAGUE GOALS

Scott Booth

Minutes on the pitch	1635	Goals in the League	8
League average (mins between goals)	204		

	PLAYER	MINS	GOALS	AVE
1	Booth	1635	8	204
2	Anderson	2200	5	440
3	Hinds	1973	5	395
4	Zdrilic	2030	4	508
5	Tosh	2038	3	679
6	Diamond	1498	2	749
7	Prunty	765	2	383
8	Deloumeaux	761	2	381
9	McGuire	1444	2	722
10	Clark	1729	1	1729
11	Foster	947	1	947
12	Sheerin	2443	1	2443
	Other		3	
	TOTAL		39	

DISCIPLINARY RECORDS

	PLAYER	YELLOW	RED	AVE
1	Tosh	7	1	254
2	Anderson	6	0	366
3	Diamond	3	1	374
4	Deloumeaux	2	0	380
5	Zdrilic	3	1	507
6	Rutkiewicz	2	0	711
7	McGuire	2	0	722
8	Booth	2	0	817
9	Clark	2	0	864
10	Sheerin	2	0	1221
11	Heikkinen	2	0	1633
12	Muirhead	1	0	2294
13	Morrison	1	0	2407
	Other	1	0	
	TOTAL	36	3	

TOP POINT EARNERS

	PLAYER	GAMES	AV PTS
1	Diamond	15	1.33
2	Booth	17	1.29
3	Clark	18	1.17
4	Hinds	21	1.14
5	Rutkiewicz	16	1.13
6	Morrison	26	1.04
7	Tosh	22	1.00
8	Heikkinen	35	0.97
9	Anderson	24	0.96
10	Preece	36	0.94
	CLUB AVERAGE:		0.89

LEAGUE APPEARANCES, BOOKINGS AND CAPS

	AGE (on 01/07/04)	IN NAMED 16	APPEARANCES	COUNTING GAMES	MINUTES ON PITCH	YELLOW CARDS	RED CARDS	THIS SEASON	HOME COUNTRY
Goalkeepers									
Ryan Esson	24	29	2	2	180	0	0	-	Scotland
David Preece	27	37	36	36	3240	0	0	-	England
Defenders									
Russell Anderson	25	25	25	24	2200	6	0	-	Scotland
Richard Buckley	19	8	8	5	498	0	0	-	Scotland
Andrew Considine		4	1	1	90	0	0	-	Scotland
Eric Deloumeaux	31	15	11	8	761	2	0	-	France
Alexander Diamond	19	21	19	15	1498	3	1	-	Scotland
Craig Higgins	18	4	4	4	360	1	0	-	Scotland
Murray McCulloch	20	3	3	2	173	0	0	-	Scotland
Philip McGuire	24	21	17	16	1444	2	0	-	Scotland
Kevin McNaughton	21	18	17	13	1228	0	0	-	Scotland
James McQuilken	29	7	7	7	616	0	0	-	Scotland
Scott Morrison	19	27	27	26	2407	1	0	-	Scotland
Ryan O'Leary	16	4	2	2	180	0	0	-	Rep or Ireland
Kevin Rutkiewicz	24	19	16	16	1423	2	0	-	Scotland
Midfielders									
Christopher Clark	23	24	23	18	1729	2	0	-	Scotland
Richard Foster	18	23	18	8	947	0	0	-	Scotland
Markus Heikkinen	25	38	38	35	3266	2	0	3	Finland (42)
Scott Muirhead	20	35	32	23	2294	1	0	-	Scotland
Paul Sheerin	29	37	33	24	2443	2	0	-	Scotland
Kevin Souter	20	8	3	1	105	0	0	-	Scotland
Fergus Tiernan	22	11	6	3	313	0	0	-	Scotland
Steven Tosh	31	26	26	22	2038	7	1	-	Scotland
Forwards									
Michael Bird	20	3	2	0	30	0	0	-	England
Scott Booth	32	21	21	17	1635	2	0	-	Scotland
Michael Hart	24	11	10	10	887	0	0	-	Scotland
Leigh Hinds	25	34	30	21	1973	0	0	-	England
Michele Lombardi	18	1	1	0	14	0	0	-	Scotland
Darren Mackie	22	16	16	3	453	0	0	-	Scotland
Bryan Prunty	21	19	17	6	765	0	0	-	Scotland
John Stewart	18	10	7	2	294	0	0	-	Scotland
Stephen Tarditi	19	2	1	0	16	0	0	-	England
David Zdrilic	30	32	31	21	2030	3	1	4	Australia (89)

TEAM OF THE SEASON

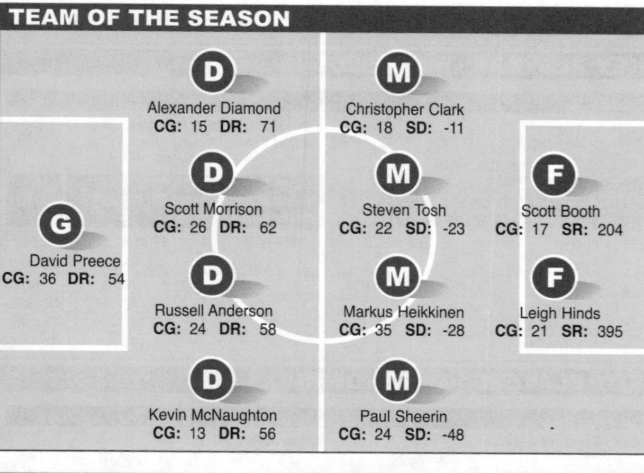
G
David Preece
CG: 36 DR: 54
D
Alexander Diamond
CG: 15 DR: 71
D
Scott Morrison
CG: 26 DR: 62
D
Russell Anderson
CG: 24 DR: 58
D
Kevin McNaughton
CG: 13 DR: 56
M
Christopher Clark
CG: 18 SD: -11
M
Steven Tosh
CG: 22 SD: -23
M
Markus Heikkinen
CG: 35 SD: -28
M
Paul Sheerin
CG: 24 SD: -48
F
Scott Booth
CG: 17 SR: 204
F
Leigh Hinds
CG: 21 SR: 395

SQUAD APPEARANCES

Match	1	2	3	4	5	6	7	8	9	10	11	12	13	14	15	16	17	18	19	20	21	22	23	24	25	26	27	28	29	30	31	32	33	34	35	36	37	38	39	40	41	42	43	44	45	46
Venue	A	H	H	A	H	A	H	H	A	H	A	H	H	H	A	A	H	H	A	H	A	H	H	A	A	H	A	A	H	H	A	A	H	H	A	A	H	A	H	H	A	A	A	H	A	H
Competition	L	L	L	L	L	L	W	L	L	L	L	W	L	L	L	L	W	L	L	L	L	L	O	L	O	L	O	L	L	L	L	L	O	L	L	O	L	L	L	L	L	L	L	L	L	L
Result	L	L	L	D	W	L	W	L	W	L	L	W	L	L	L	D	L	W	W	D	D	W	D	L	W	L	W	L	D	W	L	W	D	D	D	L	L	L	W	L	W	L	L	L	L	L

Goalkeepers
Ryan Esson
David Preece

Defenders
Russell Anderson
Richard Buckley
Andrew Considine
Eric Deloumeaux
Alexander Diamond
Craig Higgins
Murray McCulloch
Philip McGuire
Kevin McNaughton
James McQuilken
Scott Morrison
Ryan O'Leary
Kevin Rutkiewicz

Midfielders
Christopher Clark
Richard Foster
Markus Heikkinen
Scott Muirhead
Paul Sheerin
Kevin Souter
Fergus Tiernan
Steven Tosh

Forwards
Michael Bird
Scott Booth
Michael Hart
Leigh Hinds
Michele Lombardi
Darren Mackie
Bryan Prunty
John Stewart
Stephen Tarditi
David Zdrilic

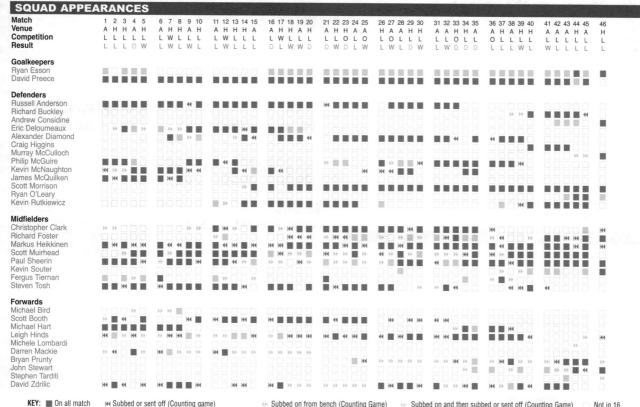

KEY: On all match | On bench | Subbed or sent off (Counting game) | Subbed or sent off (playing less than 70 minutes) | Subbed on from bench (Counting Game) | Subbed on (playing less than 70 minutes) | Subbed on and then subbed or sent off (Counting Game) | Subbed on and then subbed or sent off (playing less than 70 minutes) | Not in 16

PARTICK THISTLE

Final Position: **12th**

NICKNAME: THE JAGS

KEY: ☐ Won ☐ Drawn ☐ Lost

No	Comp	Opponent	H/A	Res	Score	Scorers	Attendance
1	prem	**Livingston**	H	D	1-1	Milne 31	4,220
2	prem	**Kilmarnock**	A	L	1-2	Grady 39	6,778
3	prem	**Celtic**	H	L	1-2	Grady 26	9,045
4	prem	**Motherwell**	A	D	2-2	Britton 26; Taylor 82	6,193
5	prem	**Aberdeen**	A	L	1-2	Mitchell 52	10,597
6	prem	**Dundee Utd**	H	L	0-2		4,711
7	sccc2	**Peterhead**	A	W	4-3*	Grady 2; Milne 108 (*on penalties)	1,350
8	prem	**Dunfermline**	A	L	1-2	Grady 50	4,684
9	prem	**Hibernian**	H	L	0-1		4,125
10	prem	**Dundee**	A	L	0-1		6,497
11	prem	**Hearts**	H	L	1-4	Waddell 63	4,814
12	prem	**Rangers**	A	L	1-3	Grady 82	49,551
13	prem	**Livingston**	A	L	0-2		5,226
14	prem	**Kilmarnock**	H	L	2-4	Mitchell 19; Grady 81	4,445
15	prem	**Celtic**	A	L	1-3	Grady 12	58,202
16	sccc3	**Celtic**	H	L	0-2		5,700
17	prem	**Motherwell**	H	W	1-0	McBride 59	4,124
18	prem	**Aberdeen**	H	L	0-3		5,186
19	prem	**Dundee Utd**	A	D	0-0		6,440
20	prem	**Dunfermline**	H	W	4-1	Thomson 38; Grady 56 pen,90; Ross, A 89	4,377
21	prem	**Hibernian**	A	L	2-3	Grady 53; Madaschi 78	8,875
22	scr3	**G Morton**	A	W	3-0	Rowson 35; Grady 53 pen,90 pen	6,613
23	prem	**Dundee**	H	L	1-2	Rowson 31	4,690
24	prem	**Hearts**	A	L	0-2		10,264
25	prem	**Rangers**	H	L	0-1		8,220
26	scr4	**Hamilton**	H	W	5-1	Mitchell 40; Britton 54,62; McBride 81; Bonnes 84	4,004
27	prem	**Livingston**	H	W	5-2	Grady 10; Britton 41,73; McNamee 68 og; Thomson 82	3,011
28	prem	**Kilmarnock**	A	L	1-2	Bonnes 52	5,818
29	prem	**Celtic**	H	L	1-4	Britton 55	8,131
30	prem	**Motherwell**	A	L	0-3		5,814
31	scpqf	**Dunfermline**	H	L	0-3		5,335
32	prem	**Aberdeen**	A	D	0-0		7,395
33	prem	**Dundee Utd**	H	D	1-1	Rowson 65	3,510
34	prem	**Dunfermline**	A	L	0-1		4,349
35	prem	**Hibernian**	H	D	1-1	Thomson 70 pen	3,155
36	prem	**Dundee**	A	L	1-2	Thomson 14	5,084
37	prem	**Hearts**	H	W	1-0	Thomson 49	4,043
38	prem	**Rangers**	A	L	0-2		49,279
39	prem	**Dundee**	H	L	0-1		2,727
40	prem	**Aberdeen**	H	W	2-0	Grady 10; Mitchell 80	2,839
41	prem	**Hibernian**	A	W	2-1	Grady 38; Murdock 60 og	5,447
42	prem	**Livingston**	A	D	2-2	Madaschi 5; Grady 63	3,160
43	prem	**Kilmarnock**	H	D	2-2	Grady 19,90 pen	4,124

MONTHLY POINTS TALLY

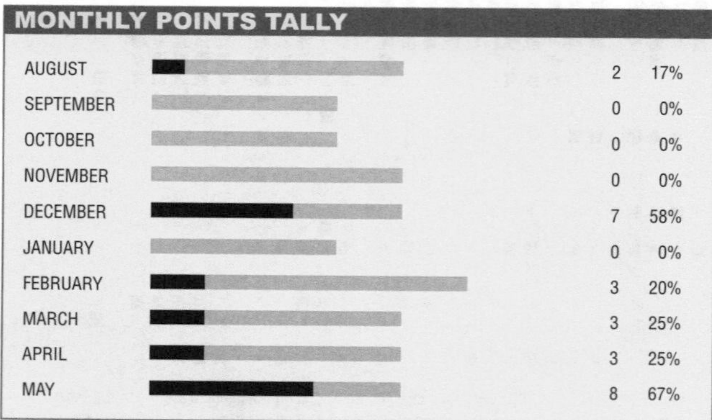

AUGUST 2 17%
SEPTEMBER 0 0%
OCTOBER 0 0%
NOVEMBER 0 0%
DECEMBER 7 58%
JANUARY 0 0%
FEBRUARY 3 20%
MARCH 3 25%
APRIL 3 25%
MAY 8 67%

KEY PLAYERS - GOALSCORERS

James Grady

Goals in the League	15	Player Strike Rate Average number of minutes between League goals scored by player	186
Contribution to Attacking Power Average number of minutes between League team goals while on pitch	79	Club Strike Rate Average number of minutes between League goals scored by club	88

	PLAYER	LGE GOALS	POWER	STRIKE RATE
1	James Grady	15	79	186 mins
2	Gerry Britton	4	100	378 mins
3	Jamie Mitchell	3	100	871 mins
4	Adrian Madaschi	2	73	1024 mins
5	John-Paul McBride	1	100	1509 mins

KEY PLAYERS - MIDFIELDERS

Billy Gibson

Goals in the League	0	Contribution to Attacking Power Average number of minutes between League team goals while on pitch	75
Defensive Rating Average number of mins between League goals conceded while he was on the pitch	65	Scoring Difference Defensive Rating minus Contribution to Attacking Power	-10

	PLAYER	LGE GOALS	DEF RATE	POWER	SCORE DIFF
1	Billy Gibson	0	65	75	-10 mins
2	Ian Ross	0	50	78	-28 mins
3	David Rowson	2	53	87	-34 mins
4	Jamie Mitchell	3	49	100	-51 mins
5	John-Paul McBride	1	50	101	-51 mins

KEY PLAYERS - DEFENDERS

Jean Yves Anis

Goals Conceded (GC) The number of League goals conceded while he was on the pitch	29	Clean Sheets In games when he played at least 70 minutes	3
Defensive Rating Ave number of mins between League goals conceded while on the pitch	62	Club Defensive Rating Average number of mins between League goals conceded by the club this season	51

	PLAYER	CON LGE	CLEAN SHEETS	DEF RATE
1	Jean Yves Anis	29	3	62 mins
2	Derek Fleming	28	4	61 mins
3	Grant Murray	64	5	51 mins
4	David Lilley	25	2	50 mins
5	Adrian Madaschi	43	4	48 mins

KEY GOALKEEPER

Kenny Arthur

Goals Conceded in the League	44	Counting Games Games when he played at least 70 mins	22
Defensive Rating Ave number of mins between League goals conceded while on the pitch	45	Clean Sheets In games when he played at least 70 mins	3

LEAGUE GOALS

James Grady

Minutes on the pitch	2790	Goals in the League	15
League average (mins between goals)	186		

	PLAYER	MINS	GOALS	AVE
1	Grady	2790	15	186
2	Thomson	1099	5	220
3	Britton	1512	4	378
4	Mitchell	2612	3	871
5	Madaschi	2047	2	1024
6	Rowson	3040	2	1520
7	Ross, A	933	1	933
8	Waddell	388	1	388
9	Bonnes	963	1	963
10	Milne	2111	1	2111
11	Taylor	657	1	657
	Other		4	
	TOTAL		39	

DISCIPLINARY RECORDS

	PLAYER	YELLOW	RED	AVE
1	Lilley	6	2	156
2	Fleming	7	0	243
3	Ross, I	5	0	281
4	Mitchell	6	1	373
5	McBride	4	0	377
6	Milne	5	0	422
7	Gibson, A	1	0	484
8	Whyte	2	0	576
9	Murray	5	0	648
10	Taylor	1	0	657
11	Britton	2	0	756
12	Anis	2	0	901
13	Ross, A	1	0	933
	Other	12	0	
	TOTAL	59	3	

TOP POINT EARNERS

	PLAYER	GAMES	AV PTS
1	Fleming	16	1.13
2	Gibson, B	16	1.06
3	Madaschi	21	1.00
4	Anis	19	0.79
5	Arthur	22	0.77
6	McBride	13	0.77
7	Grady	31	0.74
8	Murray	36	0.72
9	Rowson	34	0.68
10	Mitchell	26	0.65
	CLUB AVERAGE:		**0.68**

TEAM OF THE SEASON

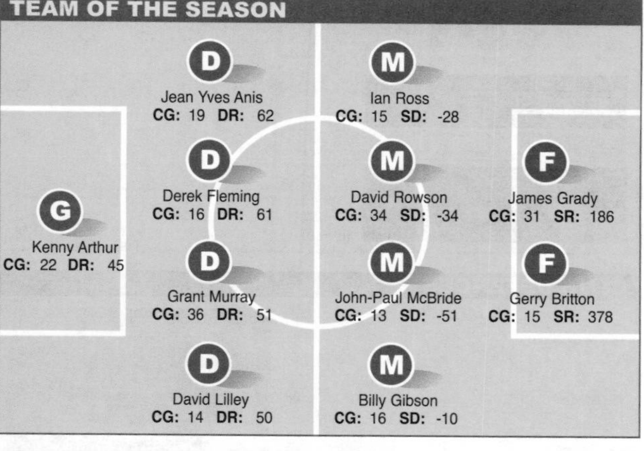

D
Jean Yves Anis
CG: 19 DR: 62
M
Ian Ross
CG: 15 SD: -28
D
Derek Fleming
CG: 16 DR: 61
M
David Rowson
CG: 34 SD: -34
F
James Grady
CG: 31 SR: 186
G
Kenny Arthur
CG: 22 DR: 45
D
Grant Murray
CG: 36 DR: 51
M
John-Paul McBride
CG: 13 SD: -51
F
Gerry Britton
CG: 15 SR: 378
D
David Lilley
CG: 14 DR: 50
M
Billy Gibson
CG: 16 SD: -10

LEAGUE APPEARANCES, BOOKINGS AND CAPS

	AGE (on 01/07/04)	IN NAMED 16	APPEARANCES	COUNTING GAMES	MINUTES ON PITCH	YELLOW CARDS	RED CARDS	THIS SEASON	HOME COUNTRY
Goalkeepers									
Kenny Arthur	25	35	22	22	1980	1	0	-	Scotland
James Langfield	24	15	10	10	900	0	0	-	Scotland
Jakup Mikkelsen	33	13	5	5	450	0	0	-	Faroe Islands
Steven Pinkowski	21	6	1	1	90	0	0	-	Scotland
Defenders									
Jean Yves Anis	23	25	24	19	1802	2	0	-	France
Daniele Chiarini	25	15	6	5	495	0	0	-	Italy
Derek Fleming	30	24	23	16	1702	7	0	-	Scotland
Edward Forrest	25	8	5	3	281	0	0	-	Scotland
David Lilley	26	15	15	14	1250	6	2	-	Scotland
Adrian Madaschi	21	29	24	21	2047	2	0	-	Australia
Grant Murray	28	36	36	36	3240	5	0	-	Scotland
Derek Whyte	35	14	14	12	1152	2	0	-	Scotland
Midfielders									
Tommy English	20	2	2	0	53	0	0	-	England
Andy Gibson	22	13	10	4	484	1	0	-	Scotland
Billy Gibson	22	16	16	16	1430	1	0	-	Scotland
Willie Howie	21	13	10	4	492	0	0	-	Scotland
John-Paul McBride	25	22	21	13	1509	4	0	-	Scotland
Ken Milne	24	25	25	21	2111	5	0	-	Scotland
Jamie Mitchell	28	32	32	26	2612	6	1	-	Scotland
Emmanuel Panther	19	12	8	0	182	0	0	-	Scotland
Andy Ross	21	22	18	8	933	1	0	-	Scotland
Ian Ross	29	18	18	15	1405	5	0	-	Scotland
David Rowson	27	35	35	34	3040	3	0	-	Scotland
Adam Strachan	17	4	4	1	200	0	0	-	Scotland
Stuart Taylor	29	15	13	5	657	1	0	-	Scotland
Forwards									
Stephane Bonnes	26	22	19	7	963	1	0	-	France
Gerry Britton	33	28	27	15	1512	2	0	-	Scotland
Jorge Cadete	35	5	4	1	179	0	0	-	Mozambique
John Gemmell	19	11	5	0	82	0	0	-	Scotland
James Grady	33	33	33	31	2790	2	0	-	Scotland
Andy Thomson	33	22	21	11	1099	0	0	-	Scotland
Richard Waddell	23	9	8	2	388	2	0	-	Scotland

SQUAD APPEARANCES

Match	1	2	3	4	5	6	7	8	9	10	11	12	13	14	15	16	17	18	19	20	21	22
Venue	H	A	H	A	A	H	A	A	H	A	H	A	A	H	A	H	H	H	A	H	A	A
Competition	L	L	L	L	L	L	W	L	L	L	L	L	L	L	L	W	L	L	L	L	L	O
Result	D	L	L	D	L	L	W	L	L	L	L	L	L	L	L	L	W	L	D	W	L	W

Match	23	24	25	26	27	28	29	30	31	32	33	34	35	36	37	38	39	40	41	42	43
Venue	H	A	H	H	H	A	H	A	H	A	H	A	H	A	H	A	H	H	A	A	H
Competition	L	L	L	O	L	L	L	L	O	L	L	L	L	L	L	L	L	L	L	L	L
Result	L	L	L	W	W	L	L	L	L	D	D	L	D	L	W	L	L	W	W	D	D

Goalkeepers
Kenny Arthur
James Langfield
Jakup Mikkelsen
Steven Pinkowski

Defenders
Jean Yves Anis
Daniele Chiarini
Derek Fleming
Edward Forrest
David Lilley
Adrian Madaschi
Grant Murray
Derek Whyte

Midfielders
Tommy English
Andy Gibson
Billy Gibson
Willie Howie
John-Paul McBride
Ken Milne
Jamie Mitchell
Emmanuel Panther
Andy Ross
Ian Ross
David Rowson
Adam Strachan
Stuart Taylor

Forwards
Stephane Bonnes
Gerry Britton
Jorge Cadete
John Gemmell
James Grady
Andy Thomson
Richard Waddell

KEY: ■ On all match ■ On bench | ◄◄ Subbed or sent off (Counting game) ◄◄ Subbed or sent off (playing less than 70 minutes) | ►► Subbed on from bench (Counting Game) ►► Subbed on (playing less than 70 minutes) | ►► Subbed on and then subbed or sent off (Counting Game) ►► Subbed on and then subbed or sent off (playing less than 70 minutes) | □ Not in 16

SCOTTISH DIVISION ONE ROUND-UP

FINAL LEAGUE TABLE

	HOME						AWAY					TOTAL			
	P	W	D	L	F	A	W	D	L	F	A	F	A	DIF	PTS
Inverness CT	36	13	4	1	37	12	8	3	7	30	21	67	33	34	70
Clyde	36	11	4	3	34	17	9	5	4	30	23	64	40	24	69
St Johnstone	36	8	5	5	34	27	7	7	4	25	18	59	45	14	57
Falkirk	36	8	4	6	20	16	7	6	5	23	21	43	37	6	55
Queen of South	36	9	6	3	24	16	6	3	9	22	32	46	48	-2	54
Ross County	36	8	6	4	24	17	4	7	7	25	24	49	41	8	49
St Mirren	36	6	9	3	27	23	3	5	10	12	23	39	46	-7	41
Raith	36	5	5	8	18	28	3	5	10	19	29	37	57	-20	34
Ayr	36	4	7	7	21	29	2	6	10	16	29	37	58	-21	31
Brechin	36	5	3	10	21	33	1	6	11	16	40	37	73	-36	27

CLUB STRIKE FORCE

Wilson scores for Inverness

1 Inverness CT

Goals scored in the League	67
Club Strike Rate (CSR) Average number of minutes between League goals scored by club	48

	CLUB	LGE	ALL	CSR
1	Inverness CT	67	85	48
2	Clyde	64	73	51
3	St Johnstone	59	71	55
4	Ross County	49	54	66
5	Queen of South	46	56	70
6	Falkirk	43	50	75
7	St Mirren	39	46	83
8	Ayr	37	40	88
9	Brechin	37	44	88
10	Raith	37	43	88

CLUB DISCIPLINARY RECORDS

Hughes of Falkirk listens to the ref

1 Raith

League Yellow	64
League Red	4
League Total	68
Cards Average in League Average number of minutes between a card being shown of either colour	46

	CLUB	LEAGUE		TOTAL		AVE
1	Raith	64 Y	4 R	66 Y	4 R	46
2	Falkirk	63	3	67	3	49
3	Brechin	58	4	61	4	52
4	St Mirren	53	2	54	2	59
5	Ayr	43	3	48	4	70
6	Clyde	42	2	44	3	74
7	Inverness CT	42	2	46	2	74
8	St Johnstone	39	4	48	4	75
9	Ross County	38	2	39	2	81
10	Queen of South	30	4	34	4	95

CLUB DEFENCES

	CLUB	LGE	ALL	CS	CDR
1	Inverness CT	33	41	14	98
2	Falkirk	37	46	13	88
3	Clyde	40	51	14	81
4	Ross County	41	48	9	79
5	St Johnstone	45	57	8	72
6	St Mirren	46	52	6	70
7	Queen of South	48	56	11	68
8	Raith	57	63	7	57
9	Ayr	58	63	7	56
10	Brechin	73	83	4	44

Inverness's Duncan defending

1 Inverness CT

Goals conceded in the League	33
Clean Sheets (CS) Number of league games where no goals were conceded	14
Club Defensive Rate (CDR) Average number of minutes between League goals conceded by club	98

STADIUM CAPACITY AND HOME CROWDS

	TEAM	CAPACITY	AVE	HIGH	LOW
1	Ross County	5800	55.22	6120	2413
2	Queen of South	6412	36.81	4075	1352
3	Inverness CT	6500	36.54	6092	1248
4	Falkirk	7550	34.85	3887	2060
5	St Mirren	10800	25.78	3613	2180
6	St Johnstone	10620	24.64	4185	2026
7	Raith	10100	21.69	4232	1432
8	Clyde	8030	20.82	4850	765
9	Brechin	3960	20.53	1502	463
10	Ayr	10250	16.65	2519	997

Key: Average. The percentage of each stadium filled in League games over the season (AVE), the stadium capacity and the highest and lowest crowds recorded.

AWAY ATTENDANCE

	TEAM	AVE	HIGH	LOW
1	Falkirk	35.62	4232	768
2	St Johnstone	34.93	6092	822
3	Inverness CT	33.42	6120	652
4	Clyde	30.27	3512	808
5	St Mirren	29.63	3086	887
6	Raith	27.83	3237	925
7	Ayr	26.52	3555	508
8	Queen of South	25.73	3064	621
9	Ross County	25.72	4019	463
10	Brechin	23.85	3161	1035

Key: Average. How close each club has come to filling grounds in its away league matches (AVE) and the highest and lowest crowds recorded.

CHART-TOPPING MIDFIELDERS

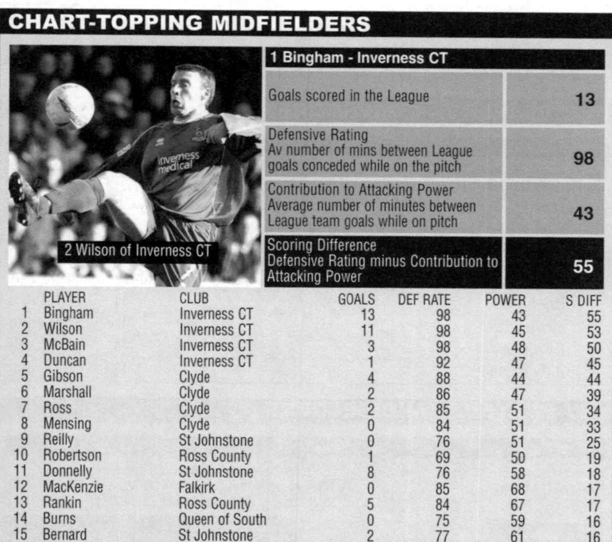
2 Wilson of Inverness CT

1 Bingham - Inverness CT	
Goals scored in the League	13
Defensive Rating Av number of mins between League goals conceded while on the pitch	98
Contribution to Attacking Power Average number of minutes between League team goals while on pitch	43
Scoring Difference Defensive Rating minus Contribution to Attacking Power	55

	PLAYER	CLUB	GOALS	DEF RATE	POWER	S DIFF
1	Bingham	Inverness CT	13	98	43	55
2	Wilson	Inverness CT	11	98	45	53
3	McBain	Inverness CT	3	98	48	50
4	Duncan	Inverness CT	1	92	47	45
5	Gibson	Clyde	4	88	44	44
6	Marshall	Clyde	2	86	47	39
7	Ross	Clyde	2	85	51	34
8	Mensing	Clyde	0	84	51	33
9	Reilly	St Johnstone	0	76	51	25
10	Robertson	Ross County	1	69	50	19
11	Donnelly	St Johnstone	8	76	58	18
12	MacKenzie	Falkirk	0	85	68	17
13	Rankin	Ross County	5	84	67	17
14	Burns	Queen of South	0	75	59	16
15	Bernard	St Johnstone	2	77	61	16

CHART-TOPPING GOALSCORERS

3 Ritchie of Inverness CT

1 Sutton - Raith	
Goals scored in the League (GL)	13
Goals scored in all competitions (GA)	13
Contribution to Attacking Power (AP) Average number of minutes between League team goals while on pitch	74
Player Strike Rate Average number of minutes between League goals scored by player	138
Club Strike Rate (CSR) Average minutes between League goals scored by club	85

	PLAYER	CLUB	GOALS: LGE	ALL	POWER	CSR	S RATE
1	Sutton	Raith	13	13	74	85	138
2	O'Connor	Queen of South	12	15	65	70	147
3	Ritchie	Inverness CT	14	20	54	48	151
4	Harty	Clyde	15	15	53	51	168
5	Hislop	Inverness CT	9	9	46	48	188
6	Burke	Queen of South	13	16	64	70	192
7	Bingham	Inverness CT	13	15	43	48	195
8	Wilson	Inverness CT	11	12	44	48	215
9	Paatelainen	St Johnstone	11	13	55	55	223
10	Lee	Falkirk	8	9	71	75	295
11	McGinty	St Mirren	6	6	69	83	322
12	Kean	Ayr	9	9	89	88	357
13	Gillies	St Mirren	8	8	76	83	373
14	Donnelly	St Johnstone	8	10	57	55	382
15	Latapy	Falkirk	7	8	74	75	383

CHART-TOPPING DEFENDERS

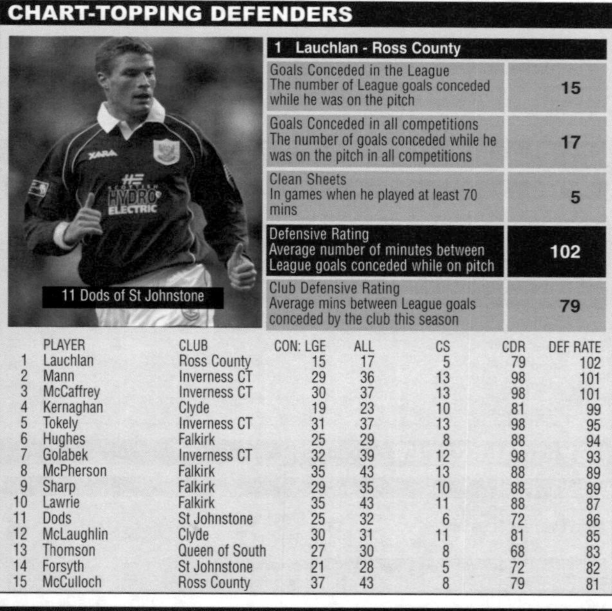
11 Dods of St Johnstone

1 Lauchlan - Ross County	
Goals Conceded in the League The number of League goals conceded while he was on the pitch	15
Goals Conceded in all competitions The number of goals conceded while he was on the pitch in all competitions	17
Clean Sheets In games when he played at least 70 mins	5
Defensive Rating Average number of minutes between League goals conceded while on pitch	102
Club Defensive Rating Average mins between League goals conceded by the club this season	79

	PLAYER	CLUB	CON: LGE	ALL	CS	CDR	DEF RATE
1	Lauchlan	Ross County	15	17	5	79	102
2	Mann	Inverness CT	29	36	13	98	101
3	McCaffrey	Inverness CT	30	37	13	98	101
4	Kernaghan	Clyde	19	23	10	81	99
5	Tokely	Inverness CT	31	37	13	98	95
6	Hughes	Falkirk	25	29	8	88	94
7	Golabek	Inverness CT	32	39	12	98	93
8	McPherson	Falkirk	35	43	13	88	89
9	Sharp	Falkirk	29	35	10	88	89
10	Lawrie	Falkirk	35	43	11	88	87
11	Dods	St Johnstone	25	32	6	72	86
12	McLaughlin	Clyde	30	31	11	81	85
13	Thomson	Queen of South	27	30	8	68	83
14	Forsyth	St Johnstone	21	28	5	72	82
15	McCulloch	Ross County	37	43	8	79	81

CHART-TOPPING GOALKEEPERS

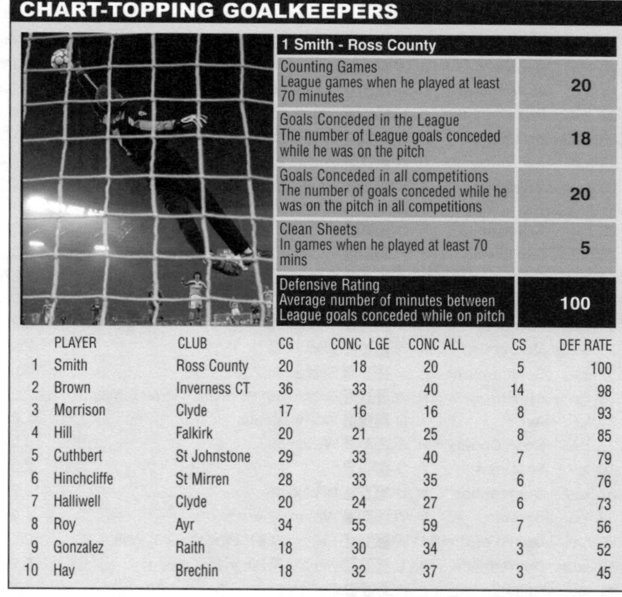

1 Smith - Ross County	
Counting Games League games when he played at least 70 minutes	20
Goals Conceded in the League The number of League goals conceded while he was on the pitch	18
Goals Conceded in all competitions The number of goals conceded while he was on the pitch in all competitions	20
Clean Sheets In games when he played at least 70 mins	5
Defensive Rating Average number of minutes between League goals conceded while on pitch	100

	PLAYER	CLUB	CG	CONC LGE	CONC ALL	CS	DEF RATE
1	Smith	Ross County	20	18	20	5	100
2	Brown	Inverness CT	36	33	40	14	98
3	Morrison	Clyde	17	16	16	8	93
4	Hill	Falkirk	20	21	25	8	85
5	Cuthbert	St Johnstone	29	33	40	7	79
6	Hinchcliffe	St Mirren	28	33	35	6	76
7	Halliwell	Clyde	20	24	27	6	73
8	Roy	Ayr	34	55	59	7	56
9	Gonzalez	Raith	18	30	34	3	52
10	Hay	Brechin	18	32	37	3	45

PLAYER DISCIPLINARY RECORD

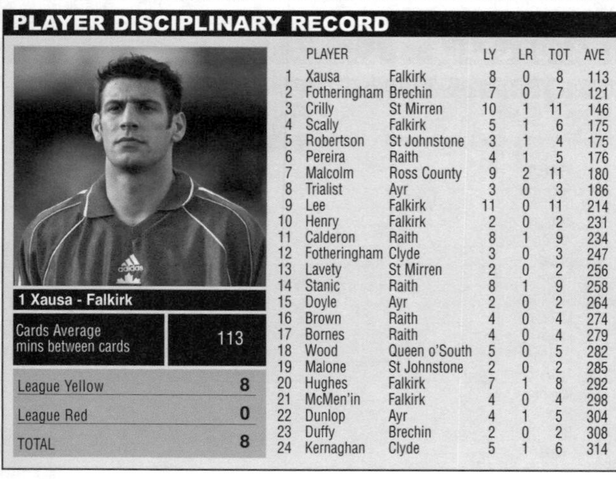
1 Xausa - Falkirk

Cards Average mins between cards	113
League Yellow	8
League Red	0
TOTAL	8

	PLAYER		LY	LR	TOT	AVE
1	Xausa	Falkirk	8	0	8	113
2	Fotheringham	Brechin	7	0	7	121
3	Crilly	St Mirren	10	1	11	146
4	Scally	Falkirk	5	1	6	175
5	Robertson	St Johnstone	3	1	4	175
6	Pereira	Raith	4	1	5	176
7	Malcolm	Ross County	9	2	11	180
8	Trialist	Ayr	3	0	3	186
9	Lee	Falkirk	11	0	11	214
10	Henry	Falkirk	2	0	2	231
11	Calderon	Raith	8	1	9	234
12	Fotheringham	Clyde	3	0	3	247
13	Lavety	St Mirren	2	0	2	256
14	Stanic	Raith	8	1	9	258
15	Doyle	Ayr	2	0	2	264
16	Brown	Raith	4	0	4	274
17	Bornes	Raith	4	0	4	279
18	Wood	Queen o'South	5	0	5	282
19	Malone	St Johnstone	2	0	2	285
20	Hughes	Falkirk	7	1	8	292
21	McMen'in	Falkirk	4	0	4	298
22	Dunlop	Ayr	4	1	5	304
23	Duffy	Brechin	2	0	2	308
24	Kernaghan	Clyde	5	1	6	314

TEAM OF THE SEASON

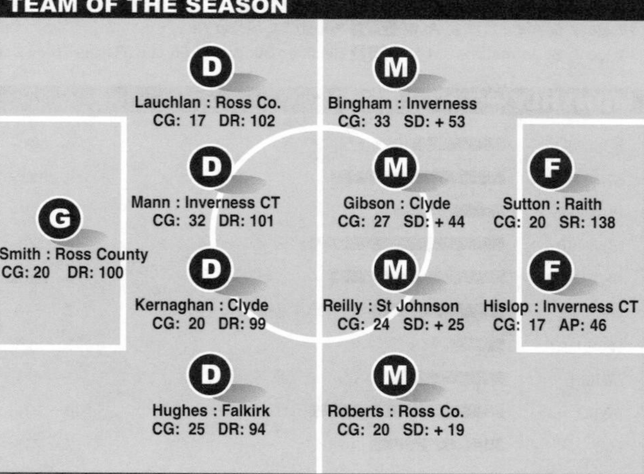
G
Smith : Ross County
CG: 20 DR: 100
D
Lauchlan : Ross Co.
CG: 17 DR: 102
D
Mann : Inverness CT
CG: 32 DR: 101
D
Kernaghan : Clyde
CG: 20 DR: 99
D
Hughes : Falkirk
CG: 25 DR: 94
M
Bingham : Inverness
CG: 33 SD: + 53
M
Gibson : Clyde
CG: 27 SD: + 44
M
Reilly : St Johnson
CG: 24 SD: + 25
M
Roberts : Ross Co.
CG: 20 SD: + 19
F
Sutton : Raith
CG: 20 SR: 138
F
Hislop : Inverness CT
CG: 17 AP: 46

SCOTTISH DIVISION ONE CHAMPIONS

INVERNESS CT

Not promoted to the Premier Division

Final Position: **1ST**

NICKNAME: CALEY THISTLE

KEY: ☐Won ☐Drawn ☐ Lost

							Attendance
1	slcc1	Gretna	A	W	5-0	Bingham 22; Hislop 54; Ritchie 55; Hart 60,81	
2	lge	Falkirk	A	L	1-2	McCaffrey 13	2,596
3	slcc2	Peterhead	A	W	2-1	Hislop 14	
4	lge	Clyde	H	D	0-0		1,839
5	lge	St Johnstone	A	W	2-1	Bingham 53; Hislop 74	3,031
6	lge	Ross County	A	D	1-1	Mann 22	5,020
7	sccc1	Queens Park	H	L	1-2	Ritchie 26	968
8	lge	Ayr	H	W	1-0	Ritchie 23	1,476
9	lge	Brechin	A	W	2-0	McBain 60; Ritchie 77	652
10	lge	St Mirren	H	W	2-0	Ritchie 21; McCaffrey 36	1,896
11	lge	Raith	H	W	2-1	Tokely 36; McCaffrey 72	1,707
12	lge	Queen of South	A	L	2-3	Ritchie 54; Bingham 89	3,547
13	lge	Falkirk	H	L	1-2	Hughes 80 og	2,223
14	lge	Clyde	A	L	0-1		765
15	lge	Ayr	A	W	3-0	Golabek 17; Hart 38; Hislop 61	1,464
16	lge	Ross County	H	D	3-3	Bingham 30; Hislop 31; Wilson 34	3,523
17	lge	St Mirren	A	W	4-0	Bingham 30,66; McBain 34,57	2,204
18	lge	Brechin	H	W	5-0	Hislop 1; Tokely 36,76; Keogh 45; Wilson 85	1,393
19	lge	Queen of South	H	W	4-1	Hislop 49,76; Tokely 55; Wilson 84	1,745
20	lge	Raith	A	W	3-1	Munro 68; Bingham 83; Ritchie 90	1,432
21	lge	St Johnstone	H	W	1-0	Wilson 80 pen	2,949
22	lge	Ross County	A	L	0-1		6,120
23	scr3	Brechin	H	W	5-1	Ritchie 8,9,68; Bingham 23; McBain 56	1,412
24	lge	Ayr	H	W	2-1	Ritchie 22; Bingham 81	1,443
25	lge	Brechin	A	W	4-2	Thomson 10; Ritchie 41; Bingham 47; Duncan 83	667
26	lge	St Mirren	H	D	1-1	Bingham 88	1,913
27	scr4	St Mirren	A	W	1-0	Thomson 78	3,859
28	lge	Raith	H	W	3-0	Bingham 44; Keogh 81; Wilson 86	1,879
29	lge	Queen of South	A	L	1-2	Ritchie 77	2,021
30	lge	Falkirk	A	L	1-2	Ritchie 35	2,268
31	scpqf	Motherwell	A	W	1-0	Wilson 10	7,930
32	lge	St Johnstone	A	L	2-3	Ritchie 64,73	2,913
33	lge	Clyde	H	W	3-1	Ritchie 35; Bingham 41; Wilson 88 pen	2,645
34	lge	Ayr	A	D	1-1	Wilson 42 pen	1,207
35	lge	Ross County	H	W	1-0	Wilson 60	4,019
36	lge	St Mirren	A	D	0-0		2,272
37	scsf	Dunfermline	H	D	1-1	Ritchie 45	13,255
38	lge	Brechin	H	W	1-0	Wilson 67 pen	1,248
39	lge	Queen of South	H	W	4-1	Hislop 39,81; Bingham 40; Wilson 65	2,126
40	scsfr	Dunfermline	H	L	2-3	Ritchie 7; Bingham 90 pen	5,728
41	lge	Raith	A	W	1-0	Ritchie 2	1,748
42	lge	Falkirk	H	D	0-0		2,631
43	lge	Clyde	A	W	2-1	Keogh 54; Hislop 79	4,850
44	lge	St Johnstone	H	W	3-1	Bingham 30; Wilson 55 pen; Ritchie 76	6,092

MONTHLY POINTS TALLY

Month	Points	%
AUGUST	5	42%
SEPTEMBER	9	100%
OCTOBER	3	50%
NOVEMBER	10	56%
DECEMBER	9	100%
JANUARY	7	58%
FEBRUARY	3	50%
MARCH	7	47%
APRIL	10	83%
MAY	7	78%

KEY PLAYERS - GOALSCORERS

Paul Ritchie

Goals in the League	14	Player Strike Rate Average number of minutes between League goals scored by player	151
Contribution to Attacking Power Average number of minutes between League team goals while on pitch	54	Club Strike Rate Average number of minutes between League goals scored by club	48

	PLAYER	LGE GOALS	POWER	STRIKE RATE
1	Paul Ritchie	14	54	151 mins
2	Stephen Hislop	9	46	188 mins
3	David Bingham	13	43	195 mins
4	Barry Wilson	11	44	215 mins

KEY PLAYERS - MIDFIELDERS

Richard Hart

Goals in the League	1	Contribution to Attacking Power Average number of minutes between League team goals while on pitch	64
Defensive Rating Average number of mins between League goals conceded while he was on the pitch	127	Scoring Difference Defensive Rating minus Contribution to Attacking Power	63

	PLAYER	LGE GOALS	DEF RATE	POWER	SCORE DIFF
1	Richard Hart	1	127	64	63 mins
2	David Bingham	13	98	43	55 mins
3	Barry Wilson	11	98	45	53 mins
4	Roy McBain	3	98	48	50 mins

KEY PLAYERS - DEFENDERS

Robert Mann

Goals Conceded (GC) The number of League goals conceded while he was on the pitch	29	Clean Sheets In games when he played at least 70 minutes	13
Defensive Rating Ave number of mins between League goals conceded while on the pitch	101	Club Defensive Rating Average number of mins between League goals conceded by the club this season	98

	PLAYER	CON LGE	CLEAN SHEETS	DEF RATE
1	Robert Mann	29	13	101 mins
2	Stuart McCaffrey	30	13	101 mins
3	Ross Tokely	31	13	95 mins
4	Stuart Golabek	32	12	93 mins

KEY GOALKEEPER

1 Mark Brown

Goals Conceded in the League	33	Counting Games Games when he played at least 70 mins	36
Defensive Rating Ave number of mins between League goals conceded while on the pitch	98	Clean Sheets In games when he played at least 70 mins	14

LEAGUE GOALS

Paul Ritchie

Minutes on the pitch	2108	Goals in the League	151
League average (mins between goals)	14		

	PLAYER	MINS	GOALS	AVE
1	Ritchie	2108	14	151
2	Bingham	2539	13	195
3	Wilson	2360	11	215
4	Hislop	1691	9	188
5	Tokely	2943	4	736
6	McCaffrey	3028	3	1009
7	McBain	2843	3	948
8	Keogh	1815	3	605
9	Duncan	2849	1	2849
10	Thomson	737	1	737
11	Munro	840	1	840
12	Mann	2921	1	2921
	Other		3	
	TOTAL		67	

DISCIPLINARY RECORDS

	PLAYER	YELLOW	RED	AVE
1	McCaffrey	6	1	432
2	Hislop	3	0	563
3	McBain	4	1	568
4	Mann	5	0	584
5	Tokely	5	0	588
6	Wilson	4	0	590
7	Keogh	3	0	605
8	Duncan	3	0	949
9	Ritchie	2	0	1054
10	Bingham	2	0	1269
11	Golabek	2	0	1482
12	Hart	1	0	1528
	Other	2	0	
	TOTAL	42	2	

TOP POINT EARNERS

	PLAYER	GAMES	AV PTS
1	Proctor	3	3.00
2	Mackie	4	2.50
3	Thomson	4	2.25
4	Bingham	26	2.19
5	Tokely	32	1.97
6	McCaffrey	34	1.97
7	Golabek	33	1.97
8	Mann	32	1.97
9	Brown	36	1.94
10	Hislop	17	1.94
	CLUB AVERAGE:		**1.94**

TEAM OF THE SEASON

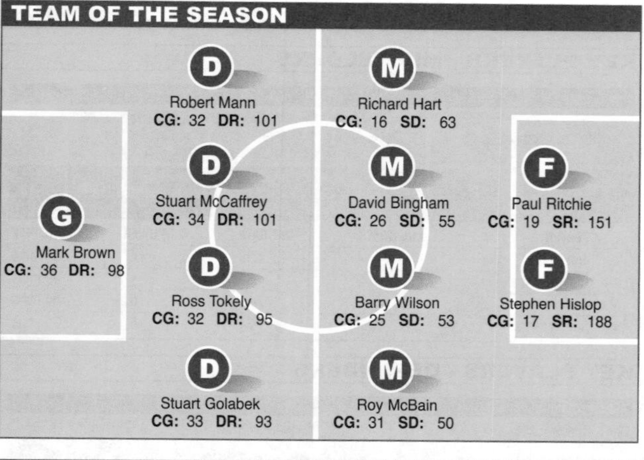
D
Robert Mann
CG: 32 DR: 101
M
Richard Hart
CG: 16 SD: 63
D
Stuart McCaffrey
CG: 34 DR: 101
M
David Bingham
CG: 26 SD: 55
F
Paul Ritchie
CG: 19 SR: 151
G
Mark Brown
CG: 36 DR: 98
D
Ross Tokely
CG: 32 DR: 95
M
Barry Wilson
CG: 25 SD: 53
F
Stephen Hislop
CG: 17 SR: 188
D
Stuart Golabek
CG: 33 DR: 93
M
Roy McBain
CG: 31 SD: 50

LEAGUE APPEARANCES AND BOOKINGS

	AGE (on 01/07/04)	IN NAMED 16	APPEARANCES	COUNTING GAMES	MINUTES ON PITCH	Yellow	Red
Goalkeepers							
Mark Brown	23	36	36	36	3240	0	0
Mike Fraser	-	27	0	0	0	0	0
Ali Ridgers	24	6	0	0	0	0	0
Defenders							
Brian Gilfillan	19	1	1	1	90	0	0
Stuart Golabek	29	33	33	33	2964	2	0
Robert Mann	30	33	33	32	2921	5	0
Stuart McCaffrey	25	36	34	34	3028	6	1
Lewis McKinnon	-	1	1	0	5	0	0
Grant Munro	23	36	15	8	840	0	0
Mark Smith	-	1	0	0	0	0	0
Darren Thomson	-	35	21	4	737	0	0
Ross Tokely	25	35	34	32	2943	5	0
Midfielders							
David Bingham	33	33	33	26	2539	2	0
Charles Christie	38	4	3	0	113	0	0
Russell Duncan	23	32	32	32	2849	3	0
Richard Hart	26	22	21	16	1528	1	0
Anthony Low	20	1	1	0	28	0	0
David Macrae	-	7	2	0	39	0	0
Roy McBain	29	32	32	31	2843	4	1
Gary McGowan	-	1	0	0	0	0	0
Craig McMillan	22	17	10	0	107	0	0
David Proctor	-	17	11	3	366	0	0
Barry Wilson	32	29	29	25	2360	4	0
Forwards							
Stephen Hislop	26	27	26	17	1691	3	0
Liam Keogh	22	30	29	18	1815	3	0
Darren Mackie	22	6	6	4	437	2	0
Paul Ritchie	35	34	34	19	2108	2	0

SQUAD APPEARANCES

Match	1	2	3	4	5	6	7	8	9	10	11	12	13	14	15	16	17	18	19	20	21	22	23	24	25	26	27	28	29	30	31	32	33	34	35	36	37	38	39	40	41	42	43	44
Venue	A	A	A	H	A	A	H	H	A	H	H	A	H	A	A	H	A	H	H	A	H	A	H	H	A	H	A	H	A	A	A	A	H	A	H	A	H	H	H	H	A	H	A	H
Competition	O	L	O	L	L	L	W	L	L	L	L	L	L	L	L	L	L	L	L	L	L	L	O	L	L	L	O	L	L	L	O	L	L	L	L	L	O	L	L	O	L	L	L	L
Result	W	L	W	D	W	D	L	W	W	W	W	L	L	L	W	D	W	W	W	W	W	L	W	W	W	D	W	W	L	L	W	L	W	D	W	D	D	W	W	L	W	D	W	W

Goalkeepers
Mark Brown
Mike Fraser
Ali Ridgers

Defenders
Brian Gilfillan
Stuart Golabek
Robert Mann
Stuart McCaffrey
Lewis McKinnon
Grant Munro
Mark Smith
Darren Thomson
Ross Tokely

Midfielders
David Bingham
Charles Christie
Russell Duncan
Richard Hart
Anthony Low
David Macrae
Roy McBain
Gary McGowan
Craig McMillan
David Proctor
Barry Wilson

Forwards
Stephen Hislop
Liam Keogh
Darren Mackie
Paul Ritchie

KEY: ■ On all match ■ On bench
⏮ Subbed or sent off (Counting game)
« Subbed or sent off (playing less than 70 minutes)
⏭ Subbed on from bench (Counting Game)
» Subbed on (playing less than 70 minutes)
⏭ Subbed on and then subbed or sent off (Counting Game)
» Subbed on and then subbed or sent off (playing less than 70 minutes)
□ Not in 16

CLYDE

Final Position: **2nd**

NICKNAME: THE BULLY WEE

KEY: Won / Drawn / Lost

							Attendance
1	slcc1	Alloa	A	W	2-1	McConalogue 44; Fraser 89	
2	lge	Ayr	H	W	3-0	Keogh 56,70; McLaughlin 60	1,067
3	slcc2	St Johnstone	H	L	0-1		
4	lge	Inverness CT	A	D	0-0		1,839
5	lge	Brechin	H	W	2-1	Harty 32; Hagen 90	1,102
6	lge	St Mirren	A	L	1-2	Gilhaney 52	3,010
7	lge	St Johnstone	H	W	2-0	Harty 42; McConalogue 61	1,469
8	lge	Falkirk	H	L	1-2	McConalogue 29	2,803
9	sccc2	Airdrie Utd	H	W	2-1	Millen 55; Gilhaney 70	1,381
10	lge	Queen of South	A	L	1-4	McConalogue 42	1,953
11	lge	Ross County	H	D	2-2	McConalogue 29; McCunnie 90 og	1,056
12	lge	Raith	A	W	1-0	Gibson 8	1,765
13	sccc3	Dundee	H	L	2-5	Keogh 2; Gilhaney 78	1,701
14	lge	Ayr	A	D	2-2	Keogh 4,53	1,653
15	lge	Inverness CT	H	W	1-0	McConalogue 60	765
16	lge	St Johnstone	A	L	0-3		2,474
17	lge	St Mirren	H	W	2-0	Keogh 41; Gilhaney 90	1,861
18	lge	Queen of South	H	W	3-1	Smith 53,60; Harty 56	1,271
19	lge	Falkirk	A	W	2-0	McLaughlin 51; Smith 61	2,898
20	lge	Raith	H	D	0-0		1,375
21	lge	Ross County	A	W	1-0	Harty 44	2,721
22	lge	Ayr	H	W	2-1	McLaughlin 49; Harty 61	1,102
23	lge	Brechin	A	W	3-1	Smith 54; Gibson 59; Harty 66	808
24	lge	St Mirren	A	W	3-2	Harty 14; Smith 25; McLaughlin 58	3,355
25	scr3	Gretna	H	W	3-0	Smith 57,64; Ross 88	1,056
26	lge	Falkirk	H	W	4-2	Marshall 57; Harty 59; McLaughlin 77; Keogh 90	3,161
27	lge	Ross County	H	W	1-0	Harty 43 pen	1,139
28	lge	Raith	A	W	3-0	Harty 25,70; Marshall 60	1,871
29	scr4	Dunfermline	H	L	0-3		2,441
30	lge	St Johnstone	H	L	2-3	Smith 29; Keogh 78	1,518
31	lge	Queen of South	A	W	2-1	Fotheringham 7; Harty 46	2,169
32	lge	Brechin	H	D	0-0		1,035
33	lge	Inverness CT	A	L	1-3	Fotheringham 36	2,645
34	lge	St Johnstone	A	W	3-1	McConalogue 10; Smith 35; Harty 69	3,512
35	lge	St Mirren	H	D	2-2	Harty 10 pen; Ross 84	1,788
36	lge	Queen of South	H	W	2-0	McConalogue 46; Ross 73	1,207
37	lge	Falkirk	A	D	1-1	Smith 73	2,536
38	lge	Raith	H	W	4-1	Gibson 21,75; McCluskey 73; Keogh 84	1,533
39	lge	Ross County	A	D	0-0		3,220
40	lge	Ayr	A	D	1-1	Keogh 15	1,816
41	lge	Inverness CT	H	L	1-2	Harty 72 pen	4,850
42	lge	Brechin	A	W	5-2	Keogh 2,20,79; Smith 25,57	1,254

MONTHLY POINTS TALLY

Month	Points	%
AUGUST	7	58%
SEPTEMBER	3	33%
OCTOBER	4	67%
NOVEMBER	13	72%
DECEMBER	10	83%
JANUARY	6	100%
FEBRUARY	6	100%
MARCH	8	44%
APRIL	8	67%
MAY	4	44%
JUNE	0	%

KEY PLAYERS - GOALSCORERS

Ian Harty

Goals in the League	15	Player Strike Rate Average number of minutes between League goals scored by player	168
Contribution to Attacking Power Average number of minutes between League team goals while on pitch	53	Club Strike Rate Average number of minutes between League goals scored by club	51

	PLAYER	LGE GOALS	POWER	STRIKE RATE
1	Ian Harty	15	53	168 mins
2	Brian Smith	8	48	237 mins
3	Mark McLaughlin	5	47	512 mins
4	Jim Gibson	4	44	550 mins

KEY PLAYERS - MIDFIELDERS

Jim Gibson

Goals in the League	4	Contribution to Attacking Power Average number of minutes between League team goals while on pitch	44
Defensive Rating Average number of mins between League goals conceded while he was on the pitch	88	Scoring Difference Defensive Rating minus Contribution to Attacking Power	44

	PLAYER	LGE GOALS	DEF RATE	POWER	SCORE DIFF
1	Jim Gibson	4	88	44	44 mins
2	Colin Marshall	2	86	47	39 mins
3	Jack Ross	2	85	51	34 mins
4	Simon Mensing	0	84	51	33 mins

KEY PLAYERS - DEFENDERS

Alan Kernaghan

Goals Conceded (GC) The number of League goals conceded while he was on the pitch	19	Clean Sheets In games when he played at least 70 minutes	10
Defensive Rating Ave number of mins between League goals conceded while on the pitch	99	Club Defensive Rating Average number of mins between League goals conceded by the club this season	81

	PLAYER	CON LGE	CLEAN SHEETS	DEF RATE
1	Alan Kernaghan	19	10	99 mins
2	Brian Smith	22	4	86 mins
3	Mark McLaughlin	30	11	85 mins
4	Stuart McCluskey	19	3	75 mins

KEY GOALKEEPER

Alan Morrison

Goals Conceded in the League	16	Counting Games Games when he played at least 70 mins	17
Defensive Rating Ave number of mins between League goals conceded while on the pitch	93	Clean Sheets In games when he played at least 70 mins	8

LEAGUE GOALS

Ian Harty

Minutes on the pitch	2514	Goals in the League	168
League average (mins between goals)	15		

	PLAYER	MINS	GOALS	AVE
1	Harty	2514	15	168
2	Keogh	1252	12	104
3	Smith	1899	8	237
4	McConalogue	1258	7	180
5	McLaughlin	2561	5	512
6	Gibson	2200	4	550
7	Gilhaney	1036	2	518
8	Ross	3141	2	1571
9	Marshall	2146	2	1073
10	Fotheringham	741	2	371
11	Hagen	2088	1	2088
12	McCluskey	1421	1	1421
	Other		3	
	TOTAL		64	

DISCIPLINARY

	PLAYER	YELLOW	RED	AVE
1	Fotheringham	3	0	247
2	Kernaghan	5	1	314
3	Fraser	3	1	333
4	Mensing	6	0	448
5	Potter	2	0	507
6	Gibson	4	0	550
7	McConalogue	2	0	629
8	McLaughlin	4	0	640
9	McCluskey	2	0	710
10	Harty	3	0	838
11	Smith	2	0	949
12	McGroarty	1	0	1025
13	Gilhaney	1	0	1036
	Other	4	0	
	TOTAL	42	2	

TOP POINT EARNERS

	PLAYER	GAMES	AV PTS
1	Smith	15	2.47
2	Morrison	16	2.38
3	Hagen	19	2.26
4	McCluskey	14	2.14
5	Keogh	8	2.13
6	Gibson	23	2.13
7	Harty	25	2.04
8	McLaughlin	27	2.04
9	Fotheringham	7	2.00
10	Kernaghan	20	2.00
	CLUB AVERAGE:		1.92

LEAGUE APPEARANCES AND BOOKINGS

	AGE (on 01/07/04)	IN NAMED 16	APPEARANCES	COUNTING GAMES	MINUTES ON PITCH	Yellow	Red
Goalkeepers							
Robert Halliday	-	2	0	0	0	0	0
Bryn Halliwell	23	30	20	19	1751	0	0
Alan Morrison	-	33	17	16	1489	0	0
Defenders							
Paul Doyle	-	19	7	1	257	1	0
Pat Keogh	28	26	26	8	1252	1	0
Alan Kernaghan	37	23	22	20	1885	5	1
Austin McCann	-	7	7	7	615	0	0
Stuart McCluskey	26	17	17	14	1421	2	0
Mark McLaughlin	28	31	31	27	2561	4	0
Andy Millen	39	18	17	13	1257	0	0
John-Paul Potter	24	13	12	11	1014	2	0
Brian Smith	27	33	32	15	1899	2	0
Midfielders							
John Baird	18	1	0	0	0	0	0
Charlie Clark	-	8	0	0	0	0	0
John Fraser	26	20	18	12	1332	3	1
Jim Gibson	24	29	27	23	2200	4	0
David Greenhill	-	2	0	0	0	0	0
Colin Marshall	19	31	26	23	2146	2	0
Chris McGroarty	23	12	12	11	1025	1	0
Simon Mensing	22	32	31	30	2688	6	0
William Reid	-	2	0	0	0	0	0
Jack Ross	28	35	35	35	3141	0	0
Forwards							
Kevin Fotheringham	28	13	12	7	741	3	0
Mark Gilhaney	19	36	33	3	1036	1	0
David Hagen	31	32	30	19	2088	0	0
Ian Harty	26	34	34	25	2514	3	0
Stephen McConalogue	23	33	24	9	1258	2	0

TEAM OF THE SEASON

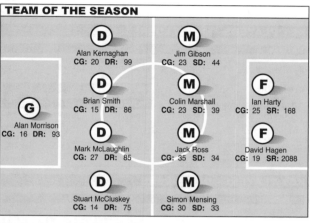

G — Alan Morrison — CG: 16 DR: 93

D — Alan Kernaghan — CG: 20 DR: 99
D — Brian Smith — CG: 15 DR: 86
D — Mark McLaughlin — CG: 27 DR: 85
D — Stuart McCluskey — CG: 14 DR: 75

M — Jim Gibson — CG: 23 SD: 44
M — Colin Marshall — CG: 23 SD: 39
M — Jack Ross — CG: 35 SD: 34
M — Simon Mensing — CG: 30 SD: 33

F — Ian Harty — CG: 25 SR: 168
F — David Hagen — CG: 19 SR: 2088

SQUAD APPEARANCES

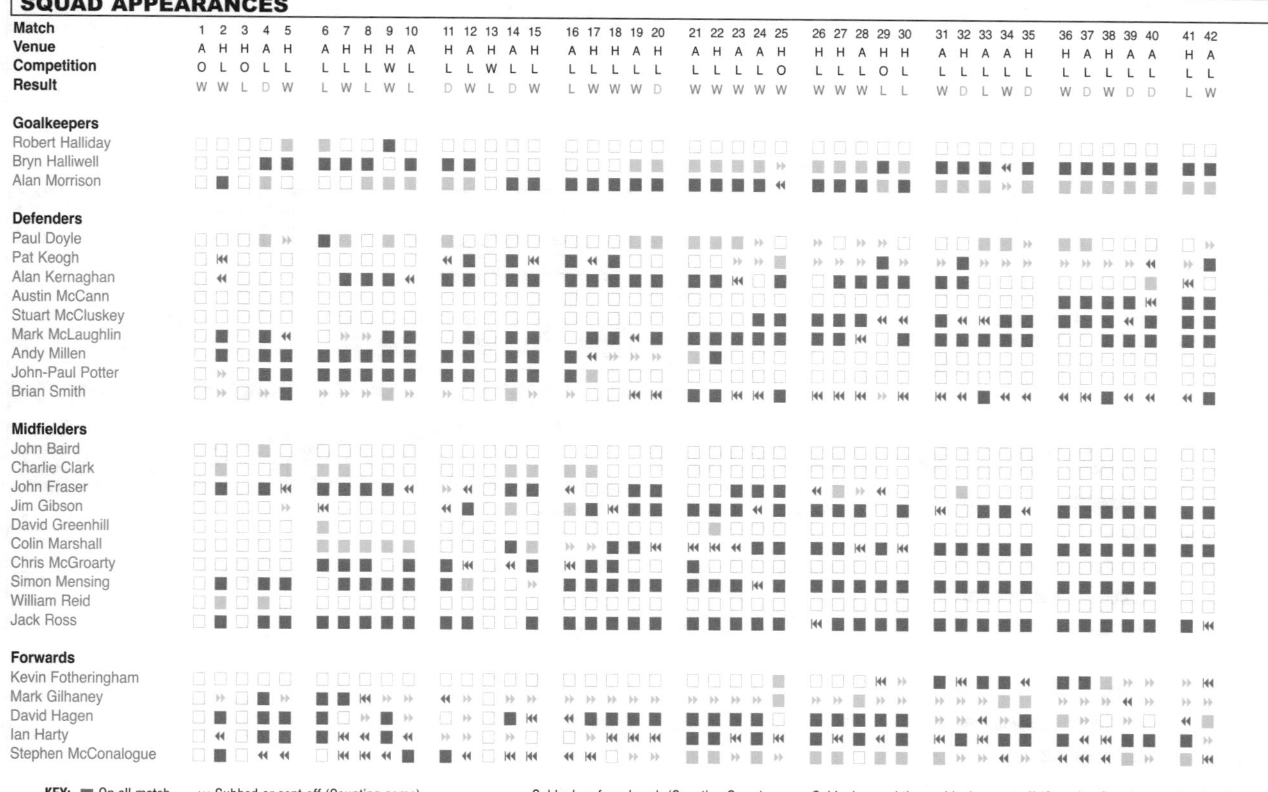
Match 1 2 3 4 5 6 7 8 9 10 11 12 13 14 15 16 17 18 19 20 21 22 23 24 25 26 27 28 29 30 31 32 33 34 35 36 37 38 39 40 41 42
Venue A H H A H A H H H A H A H A H A H H A H A H A A H H H A H H A H A A H H A H A A H A
Competition O L O L L L L L W L L L W L L L L L L L L L L L O L L L O L L L L L L L L L L L L L
Result W W L D W L W L W L D W L D W L W W W D W W W W W W W W L L W D L W D W D W D D L W
Goalkeepers
Robert Halliday
Bryn Halliwell
Alan Morrison
Defenders
Paul Doyle
Pat Keogh
Alan Kernaghan
Austin McCann
Stuart McCluskey
Mark McLaughlin
Andy Millen
John-Paul Potter
Brian Smith
Midfielders
John Baird
Charlie Clark
John Fraser
Jim Gibson
David Greenhill
Colin Marshall
Chris McGroarty
Simon Mensing
William Reid
Jack Ross
Forwards
Kevin Fotheringham
Mark Gilhaney
David Hagen
Ian Harty
Stephen McConalogue
KEY: On all match
On bench
Subbed or sent off (Counting game)
Subbed or sent off (playing less than 70 minutes)
Subbed on from bench (Counting Game)
Subbed on (playing less than 70 minutes)
Subbed on and then subbed or sent off (Counting Game)
Subbed on and then subbed or sent off (playing less than 70 minutes)
Not in 16

ST JOHNSTONE

Final Position: **3rd**

NICKNAME: THE SAINTS

KEY: Won / Drawn / Lost

							Attendance
1	slcc1	Hamilton	A	W	3-2	Paatelainen 59; Parker 65; Donnelly 103	
2	lge	Queen of South	H	W	4-1	Fotheringham 17; Parker 22,59; Malone 86	2,939
3	slcc2	Clyde	A	W	1-0		
4	lge	St Mirren	A	D	1-1	Parker 61	3,613
5	lge	Inverness CT	H	L	1-2	Parker 67	3,031
6	lge	Brechin	H	W	3-1	Paatelainen 49,71; Dods 76	2,219
7	sccc1	St Mirren	A	W	2-0	Dods 98; Paatelainen 102 pen	3,100
8	lge	Clyde	A	L	0-2		1,469
9	lge	Raith	H	L	0-1		2,681
10	sccc2	Hamilton	H	W	3-2	Donnelly 58; McLaughlin 90; Paatelainen 107	1,471
11	lge	Falkirk	A	W	3-0	MacDonald 30,45; Paatelainen 46	3,887
12	lge	Ayr	H	D	1-1	MacDonald 72	2,026
13	lge	Ross County	A	W	3-0	Paatelainen 7,38,40	3,195
14	lge	St Mirren	H	W	1-0	Robertson, M 33	2,677
15	sccc3	Dunfermline	H	W	3-2	Donnelly 9; Dods 70; MacDonald 73	2,769
16	lge	Queen of South	A	D	1-1	McLaughlin 70	3,159
17	lge	Clyde	H	W	3-0	MacDonald 8; Donnelly 43,71	2,474
18	lge	Brechin	A	W	1-0	MacDonald 42	1,502
19	lge	Falkirk	H	L	0-4		4,185
20	lge	Raith	A	W	4-1	McLaughlin 41; Hay 52; Paatelainen 76; MacDonald 90	1,996
21	sccqf	Rangers	A	L	0-3		29,395
22	lge	Ross County	H	D	1-1	Paatelainen 12	2,478
23	lge	Ayr	A	D	1-1	Bernard 65	1,203
24	lge	Queen of South	H	D	2-2	Thomson 33 og; Paatelainen 90	2,029
25	lge	Inverness CT	A	L	0-1		2,949
26	lge	Brechin	H	D	2-2	MacDonald 22; Paatelainen 28	2,171
27	scr3	Motherwell	H	L	0-3		4,090
28	lge	Raith	H	W	5-2	Hay 2,62; McLaughlin 13; Taylor 23; MacDonald 81	2,636
29	lge	Ayr	H	W	3-0	Maxwell 7; McQuilken 42; Donnelly 61	2,067
30	lge	Ross County	A	L	0-2		3,072
31	lge	Clyde	A	W	3-2	Donnelly 18,64; Bernard 89	1,518
32	lge	Falkirk	A	W	1-0	Hay 86	2,786
33	lge	Inverness CT	H	W	3-2	Donnelly 13; Paatelainen 21; Parker 90	2,913
34	lge	St Mirren	A	D	1-1	Robertson, J 62	2,180
35	lge	Clyde	H	L	1-3	Parker 90	3,512
36	lge	Brechin	A	W	2-0	Hay 18; Baxter 59	822
37	lge	Falkirk	H	W	2-1	Hay 45,84	2,532
38	lge	Raith	A	D	1-1	Donnelly 53 pen	2,676
39	lge	Ross County	H	D	1-1	Hay 3	2,169
40	lge	Ayr	A	D	1-1	Hay 66	1,119
41	lge	Queen of South	A	D	1-1	Donnelly 62 pen	1,629
42	lge	St Mirren	H	L	1-3	Parker 72	2,363
43	lge	Inverness CT	A	L	1-3	Parker 44	6,092

MONTHLY POINTS TALLY

Month	Points	%
AUGUST	7	58%
SEPTEMBER	3	33%
OCTOBER	7	78%
NOVEMBER	10	67%
DECEMBER	3	25%
JANUARY	4	67%
FEBRUARY	3	50%
MARCH	13	72%
APRIL	6	50%
MAY	1	11%

KEY PLAYERS - GOALSCORERS

Keigan Parker

Goals in the League	8	Player Strike Rate Average number of minutes between League goals scored by player	187
Contribution to Attacking Power Average number of minutes between League team goals while on pitch	59	Club Strike Rate Average number of minutes between League goals scored by club	55

	PLAYER	LGE GOALS	POWER	STRIKE RATE
1	Keigan Parker	8	59	187 mins
2	Mixu Paatelainen	11	55	223 mins
3	Simon Donnelly	8	57	382 mins
4	Brian McLaughlin	3	57	651 mins

KEY PLAYERS - MIDFIELDERS

Mark Reilly

Goals in the League	0	Contribution to Attacking Power Average number of minutes between League team goals while on pitch	51
Defensive Rating Average number of mins between League goals conceded while he was on the pitch	76	Scoring Difference Defensive Rating minus Contribution to Attacking Power	25

	PLAYER	LGE GOALS	DEF RATE	POWER	SCORE DIFF
1	Mark Reilly	0	76	51	25 mins
2	Simon Donnelly	8	76	58	18 mins
3	Paul Bernard	2	77	61	16 mins
4	Brian McLaughlin	3	65	57	8 mins

KEY PLAYERS - DEFENDERS

Darren Dods

Goals Conceded (GC) The number of League goals conceded while he was on the pitch	25	Clean Sheets In games when he played at least 70 minutes	6
Defensive Rating Ave number of mins between League goals conceded while on the pitch	86	Club Defensive Rating Average number of mins between League goals conceded by the club this season	72

	PLAYER	CON LGE	CLEAN SHEETS	DEF RATE
1	Darren Dods	25	6	86 mins
2	Ross Forsyth	21	5	82 mins
3	John Robertson	32	6	74 mins
4	Ian Maxwell	39	7	73 mins

KEY GOALKEEPER

Kevin Cuthbert

Goals Conceded in the League	33	Counting Games Games when he played at least 70 mins	29
Defensive Rating Ave number of mins between League goals conceded while on the pitch	79	Clean Sheets In games when he played at least 70 mins	7

LEAGUE GOALS

Mixu Paatelainen

Minutes on the pitch	2458	Goals in the League	223
League average (mins between goals)	11		

	PLAYER	MINS	GOALS	AVE
1	Paatelainen	2458	11	223
2	Hay	1058	9	118
3	MacDonald	859	8	107
4	Parker	1494	8	187
5	Donnelly	3056	8	382
6	McLaughlin	1953	3	651
7	Bernard	2078	2	1039
8	Robertson, J	2376	1	2376
9	Robertson, M	702	1	702
10	Fotheringham	270	1	270
11	Maxwell	2865	1	2865
12	Malone	571	1	571
	Other		5	
	TOTAL		59	

DISCIPLINARY RECORDS

	PLAYER	YELLOW	RED	AVE
1	Robertson, M	3	1	175
2	Malone	2	0	285
3	Weir	2	0	370
4	Parker	4	0	373
5	Bernard	3	2	415
6	McLaughlin	4	0	488
7	Reilly	4	0	550
8	Forsyth	3	0	575
9	Maxwell	4	0	716
10	Paatelainen	3	0	819
11	Robertson, J	2	0	1188
12	Vata	1	0	1305
13	Donnelly	2	0	1528
	Other	2	1	
	TOTAL	39	4	

TOP POINT EARNERS

	PLAYER	GAMES	AV PTS
1	Weir	8	2.00
2	Baxter	9	2.00
3	Taylor	8	2.00
4	Vata	14	1.86
5	Reilly	24	1.79
6	Hay	9	1.78
7	Paatelainen	25	1.76
8	Robertson, M	8	1.75
9	Forsyth	17	1.71
10	Robertson, J	26	1.69
	CLUB AVERAGE:		**1.58**

LEAGUE APPEARANCES AND BOOKINGS

	AGE (on 01/07/04)	IN NAMED 16	APPEARANCES	COUNTING GAMES	MINUTES ON PITCH	Yellow	Red
Goalkeepers							
Kevin Cuthbert	21	36	29	29	2610	0	0
Craig Nelson	33	35	7	7	630	0	0
Defenders							
Mark Baxter	19	20	16	9	1077	0	0
Darren Dods	39	35	26	23	2159	0	1
Mark Ferry	20	2	1	0	60	0	0
Ross Forsyth	21	32	23	17	1726	3	0
Stephen Fraser	-	3	2	2	180	1	0
Paul Lovering	28	5	5	4	354	1	0
Ian Maxwell	29	33	33	31	2865	4	0
Stuart McCluskey	26	2	0	0	0	0	0
James McQuilken	29	15	15	15	1350	0	0
John Robertson	28	27	27	26	2376	2	0
Rudi Vata	35	15	15	14	1305	1	0
James Weir	35	9	9	8	740	2	0
Midfielders							
Paul Bernard	31	25	24	23	2078	3	2
Simon Donnelly	29	36	36	33	3056	2	0
Mark Ferry	20	1	0	0	0	0	0
Edward Malone	19	22	9	4	571	2	0
Brian McLaughlin	30	31	29	18	1953	4	0
Mark Reilly	35	27	27	24	2202	4	0
Mark Robertson	27	9	9	8	702	3	1
Ryan Stevenson	19	19	13	5	698	0	0
Stuart Taylor	29	9	9	8	645	0	0
Forwards							
Martyn Fotheringham	21	17	7	2	270	0	0
Chris Hay	29	27	24	9	1058	0	0
Peter MacDonald	23	15	15	5	859	0	0
Mixu Paatelainen	37	33	33	25	2458	3	0
Keigan Parker	22	34	31	13	1494	4	0

TEAM OF THE SEASON

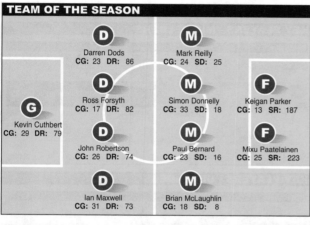

G Kevin Cuthbert — **CG:** 29 **DR:** 79

D Darren Dods — **CG:** 23 **DR:** 86

D Ross Forsyth — **CG:** 17 **DR:** 82

D John Robertson — **CG:** 26 **DR:** 74

D Ian Maxwell — **CG:** 31 **DR:** 73

M Mark Reilly — **CG:** 24 **SD:** 25

M Simon Donnelly — **CG:** 33 **SD:** 18

M Paul Bernard — **CG:** 23 **SD:** 16

M Brian McLaughlin — **CG:** 18 **SD:** 8

F Keigan Parker — **CG:** 13 **SR:** 187

F Mixu Paatelainen — **CG:** 25 **SR:** 223

SQUAD APPEARANCES

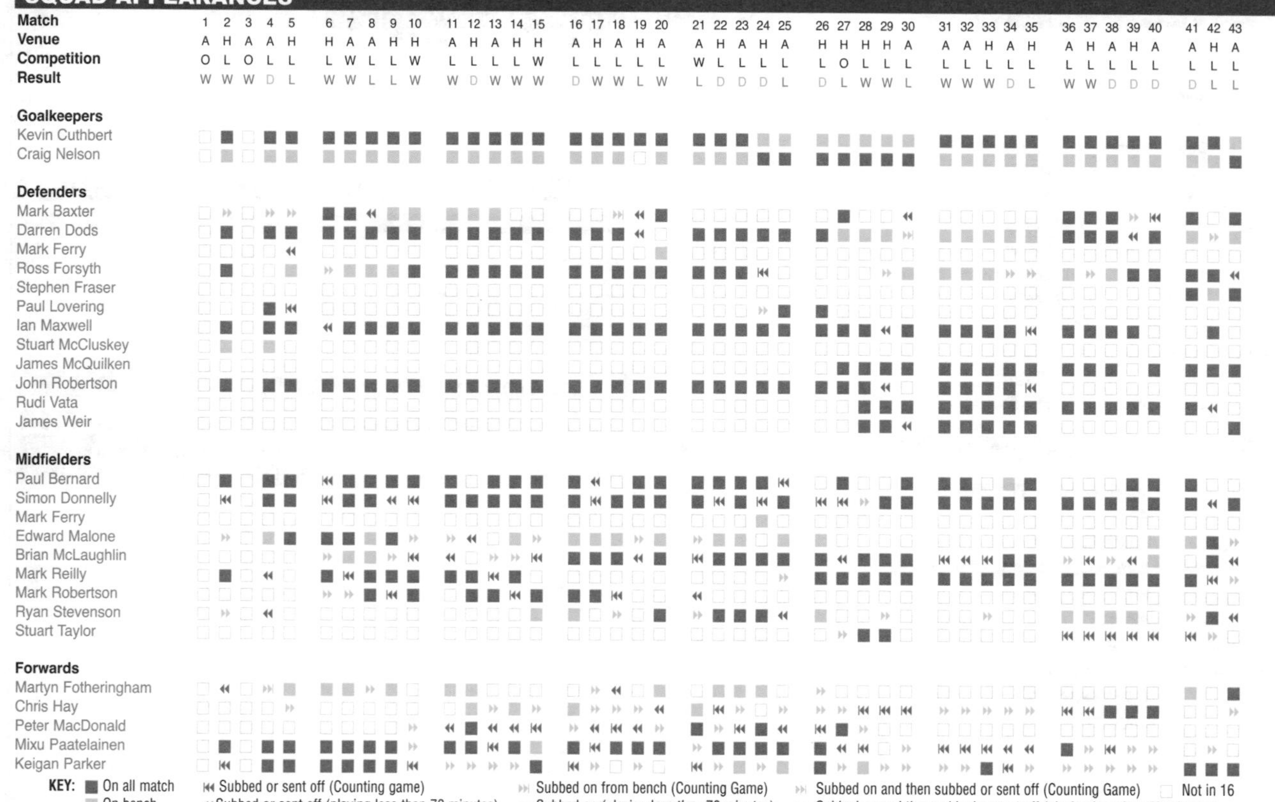

Match 1 2 3 4 5 6 7 8 9 10 11 12 13 14 15 16 17 18 19 20 21 22 23 24 25 26 27 28 29 30 31 32 33 34 35 36 37 38 39 40 41 42 43
Venue A H A A H H A A H H A H A H H A H A H A A H A H A H H H H A A A H A H A H A H A A H A
Competition O L O L L L W L L W L L L L W L L L L L W L L L L L O L L L L L L L L L L L L L L L L
Result W W W D L W W L L W W D W W W D W W L W L D D D L D L W W L W W W D L W W D D D D L L
Goalkeepers
Kevin Cuthbert
Craig Nelson
Defenders
Mark Baxter
Darren Dods
Mark Ferry
Ross Forsyth
Stephen Fraser
Paul Lovering
Ian Maxwell
Stuart McCluskey
James McQuilken
John Robertson
Rudi Vata
James Weir
Midfielders
Paul Bernard
Simon Donnelly
Mark Ferry
Edward Malone
Brian McLaughlin
Mark Reilly
Mark Robertson
Ryan Stevenson
Stuart Taylor
Forwards
Martyn Fotheringham
Chris Hay
Peter MacDonald
Mixu Paatelainen
Keigan Parker
KEY: On all match
On bench
Subbed or sent off (Counting game)
Subbed or sent off (playing less than 70 minutes)
Subbed on from bench (Counting Game)
Subbed on (playing less than 70 minutes)
Subbed on and then subbed or sent off (Counting Game)
Subbed on and then subbed or sent off (playing less than 70 minutes)
Not in 16

FALKIRK

Final Position: **4th**

NICKNAME: THE BAIRNS

KEY: ☐Won ☐Drawn ☐Lost

							Attendance
1	slcc1	Brechin	A	L	0-1		
2	lge	Inverness CT	H	W	2-1	McMenimin 36; Lee 83	2,596
3	lge	Ayr	A	D	1-1	Lee 18	2,519
4	lge	Queen of South	H	D	0-0		3,064
5	lge	Raith	A	W	1-0	O'Neil 68 pen	4,232
6	lge	Ross County	H	L	0-2		2,970
7	lge	Clyde	A	W	2-1	Henry 3,64	2,803
8	sccc2	Arbroath	A	W	4-3	McMenimin 36; Rodgers 83; Nicholls 108,119	923
9	lge	St Johnstone	H	L	0-3		3,887
10	lge	St Mirren	A	D	0-0		3,105
11	lge	Brechin	H	W	3-0	Henry 8,25; O'Neil 64 pen	2,442
12	lge	Ayr	H	L	0-1		2,609
13	sccc3	Hearts	A	L	1-2	Latapy 58	8,649
14	lge	Inverness CT	A	W	2-1	Lawrie 69; Lee 83	2,223
15	lge	Ross County	A	W	2-1	Lawrie 8; Lee 17	3,204
16	lge	Raith	H	W	3-2	Sharp 4; McMenimin 24,60	3,237
17	lge	St Johnstone	A	W	4-0	Latapy 10; James 35; McMenimin 62; McAnespie 85	4,185
18	lge	Clyde	H	L	0-2		2,898
19	lge	Brechin	A	D	2-2	White 69 og; Lee 82	1,043
20	lge	St Mirren	H	D	0-0		2,581
21	lge	Queen of South	A	L	0-2		4,075
22	lge	Raith	A	L	0-2		2,885
23	scr3	Ayr	A	W	2-1	Lee 20; Xausa 75	2,632
24	lge	Ross County	H	W	2-0	Latapy 25; Colquhoun 49	2,482
25	lge	Clyde	A	L	2-4	McAnespie 25 pen; Colquhoun 44	3,161
26	scr4	Aberdeen	H	L	0-2		4,747
27	lge	St Mirren	A	D	1-1	Hughes 56	2,944
28	lge	Brechin	H	W	5-0	Hughes 3; Latapy 10,25; Scally 37; Lee 77	2,060
29	lge	Inverness CT	H	W	2-1	Lee 9; McAnespie 76	2,268
30	lge	Ayr	A	W	3-2	Lee 52; Scally 57 pen; Nicholls 81	2,048
31	lge	St Johnstone	H	L	0-1		2,786
32	lge	Queen of South	H	L	0-2		2,098
33	lge	Ross County	A	D	1-1	McPherson 67	2,931
34	lge	Raith	H	W	1-0	O'Neil 38	2,386
35	lge	St Johnstone	A	L	1-2	Latapy 9	2,532
36	lge	Clyde	H	D	1-1	Latapy 79 pen	2,536
37	lge	Brechin	A	W	1-0	Latapy 68	768
38	lge	St Mirren	H	W	1-0	O'Neil 25	2,386
39	lge	Inverness CT	A	D	0-0		2,631
40	lge	Ayr	H	D	0-0		2,077
41	lge	Queen of South	A	L	0-1		2,751

MONTHLY POINTS TALLY

Month	Points	%
AUGUST	8	67%
SEPTEMBER	3	33%
OCTOBER	4	44%
NOVEMBER	12	80%
DECEMBER	2	22%
JANUARY	3	33%
FEBRUARY	4	67%
MARCH	10	56%
APRIL	7	58%
MAY	2	22%
JUNE	0	%

KEY PLAYERS - GOALSCORERS

Jason Lee

Goals in the League	8	Player Strike Rate Average number of minutes between League goals scored by player	295
Contribution to Attacking Power Average number of minutes between League team goals while on pitch	71	Club Strike Rate Average number of minutes between League goals scored by club	75

	PLAYER	LGE GOALS	POWER	STRIKE RATE
1	Jason Lee	8	71	295 mins
2	Colin McMenamin	4	59	298 mins
3	Russell Latapy	7	74	383 mins
4	John O'Neil	4	66	649 mins

KEY PLAYERS - MIDFIELDERS

Brent Rahim

Goals in the League	0	Contribution to Attacking Power Average number of minutes between League team goals while on pitch	62
Defensive Rating Average number of mins between League goals conceded while he was on the pitch	97	Scoring Difference Defensive Rating minus Contribution to Attacking Power	35

	PLAYER	LGE GOALS	DEF RATE	POWER	SCORE DIFF
1	Brent Rahim	0	97	62	35 mins
2	Scott MacKenzie	0	85	68	17 mins
3	John O'Neil	4	81	67	14 mins
4	Russell Latapy	7	86	74	12 mins

KEY PLAYERS - DEFENDERS

John Hughes

Goals Conceded (GC) The number of League goals conceded while he was on the pitch	25	Clean Sheets In games when he played at least 70 minutes	8
Defensive Rating Ave number of mins between League goals conceded while on the pitch	94	Club Defensive Rating Average number of mins between League goals conceded by the club this season	88

	PLAYER	CON LGE	CLEAN SHEETS	DEF RATE
1	John Hughes	25	8	94 mins
2	Craig McPherson	35	13	89 mins
3	James Sharp	29	10	89 mins
4	Andy Lawrie	35	11	87 mins

KEY GOALKEEPER

Allan Ferguson

Goals Conceded in the League	17	Counting Games Games when he played at least 70 mins	16
Defensive Rating Ave number of mins between League goals conceded while on the pitch	85	Clean Sheets In games when he played at least 70 mins	5

LEAGUE GOALS

Jason Lee

Minutes on the pitch	2356	Goals in the League	295
League average (mins between goals)	8		

	PLAYER	MINS	GOALS	AVE
Lee	2356	8	295	
2	Latapy	2679	7	383
3	McMenimin	1193	4	298
4	O'Neil	2596	4	649
5	Henry	463	4	116
6	McAnespie	1319	3	440
7	Hughes	2342	2	1171
8	Lawrie	3048	2	1524
9	Colquhoun	637	2	319
10	Scally	1052	2	526
11	James	1104	1	1104
12	Sharp	2585	1	2585
	Other		3	
	TOTAL		43	

DISCIPLINARY RECORDS

	PLAYER	YELLOW	RED	AVE
1	Xausa	8	0	113
2	Scally	5	1	175
3	Lee	11	0	214
4	Henry	2	0	231
5	Hughes	7	1	292
6	McMenimin	4	0	298
7	Nicholls	4	0	334
8	Sharp	4	0	646
9	McAnespie	2	0	659
10	O'Neil	3	0	865
11	Ferguson	0	1	1448
12	Lawrie	2	0	1524
13	Rahim	1	0	1546
	Other	10	0	
	TOTAL	63	3	

TOP POINT EARNERS

	PLAYER	GAMES	AV PTS
1	McSween	4	2.00
2	McMenimin	10	1.80
3	MacKenzie	24	1.75
4	Colquhoun	4	1.75
5	Hughes	25	1.68
6	Sharp	27	1.63
7	Ferguson	16	1.63
8	Lee	25	1.60
9	McPherson	34	1.59
10	Latapy	28	1.57
	CLUB AVERAGE:		1.53

TEAM OF THE SEASON

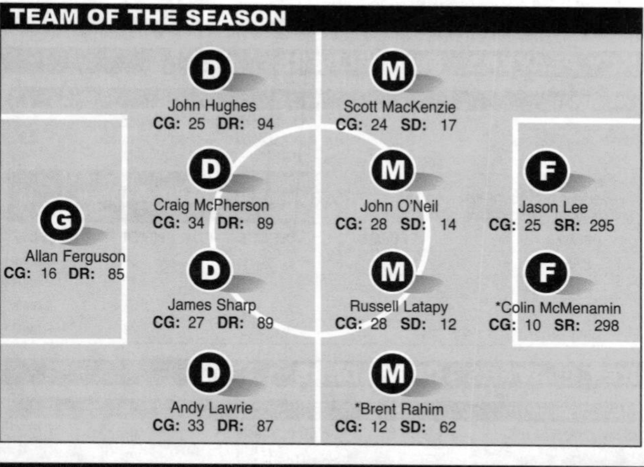
D
John Hughes
CG: 25 DR: 94
M
Scott MacKenzie
CG: 24 SD: 17
D
Craig McPherson
CG: 34 DR: 89
M
John O'Neil
CG: 28 SD: 14
F
Jason Lee
CG: 25 SR: 295
G
Allan Ferguson
CG: 16 DR: 85
D
James Sharp
CG: 27 DR: 89
M
Russell Latapy
CG: 28 SD: 12
F
*Colin McMenamin
CG: 10 SR: 298
D
Andy Lawrie
CG: 33 DR: 87
M
*Brent Rahim
CG: 12 SD: 62

LEAGUE APPEARANCES AND BOOKINGS

	AGE (on 01/07/04)	IN NAMED 16	APPEARANCES	COUNTING GAMES	MINUTES ON PITCH	Yellow	Red
Goalkeepers							
Allan Ferguson	35	23	17	16	1448	0	1
Darren Hill	22	34	20	20	1793	0	0
John Hutchison	-	13	0	0	0	0	0
Defenders							
Kevin Christie	28	2	2	2	180	2	0
John Henry	32	7	7	5	463	2	0
John Hughes	39	27	27	25	2342	7	1
Kevin James	28	13	13	12	1104	0	0
Andy Lawrie	25	36	35	33	3048	2	0
Eddie May	36	4	4	1	185	1	0
Kieran McAnespie	24	27	25	9	1319	2	0
Craig McPherson	32	35	35	34	3106	1	0
James Sharp	28	36	30	27	2585	4	0
Mark Twaddle	-	4	3	1	115	1	0
Midfielders							
Darren Barr	-	3	1	0	3	0	0
Phil Creaney	21	8	1	0	34	0	0
Russell Latapy	35	34	32	28	2679	1	0
Scott MacKenzie	34	31	28	24	2308	0	0
Stephen Manson	-	2	1	0	28	0	0
Art Neilson	-	3	0	0	0	0	0
David Nicholls	32	24	22	11	1336	4	0
John O'Neil	33	30	30	28	2596	3	0
Brent Rahim	25	26	26	12	1546	1	0
Andrew Rodgers	-	1	1	0	55	0	0
Neil Scally	25	27	20	9	1052	5	1
Forwards							
Derek Colquhoun	19	19	15	4	637	0	0
Jason Lee	33	29	29	25	2356	11	0
Colin McMenamin	23	18	17	10	1193	4	0
Ryan McStay	-	9	6	2	213	1	0
Iain McSween	-	17	10	4	453	0	0
Mark Ramsay	-	4	2	0	36	0	0
Andy Rodgers	20	6	5	1	176	2	0
Davide Xausa	28	16	15	7	910	8	0

SQUAD APPEARANCES

Match	1	2	3	4	5	6	7	8	9	10	11	12	13	14	15	16	17	18	19	20	21	22	23	24	25	26	27	28	29	30	31	32	33	34	35	36	37	38	39	40	41
Match	1	2	3	4	5	6	7	8	9	10	11	12	13	14	15	16	17	18	19	20	21	22	23	24	25	26	27	28	29	30	31	32	33	34	35	36	37	38	39	40	41
Venue	A	H	A	H	A	H	A	A	H	A	H	H	A	A	A	H	A	H	A	H	A	A	A	H	A	H	A	H	H	A	H	H	A	H	A	H	A	H	A	H	A
Competition	O	L	L	L	L	L	L	W	L	L	L	L	W	L	L	L	L	L	L	L	L	L	O	L	L	O	L	L	L	L	L	L	L	L	L	L	L	L	L	L	L
Result	L	W	D	D	W	L	W	W	L	D	W	L	L	W	W	W	W	L	D	D	L	L	W	W	L	L	D	W	W	W	L	L	D	W	L	D	W	W	D	D	L

Goalkeepers
Allan Ferguson
Darren Hill
John Hutchison

Defenders
Kevin Christie
John Henry
John Hughes
Kevin James
Andy Lawrie
Eddie May
Kieran McAnespie
Craig McPherson
James Sharp
Mark Twaddle

Midfielders
Darren Barr
Phil Creaney
Russell Latapy
Scott MacKenzie
Stephen Manson
Art Neilson
David Nicholls
John O'Neil
Brent Rahim
Andrew Rodgers
Neil Scally
A Trialist

Forwards
Derek Colquhoun
Jason Lee
Colin McMenamin
Ryan McStay
Iain McSween
Mark Ramsay
Andy Rodgers
Davide Xausa

KEY: On all match · On bench · Subbed or sent off (Counting game) · Subbed or sent off (playing less than 70 minutes) · Subbed on from bench (Counting Game) · Subbed on (playing less than 70 minutes) · Subbed on and then subbed or sent off (Counting Game) · Subbed on and then subbed or sent off (playing less than 70 minutes) · Not in 16

QUEEN OF THE SOUTH

Final Position: **5th**

NICKNAME: THE DOONHAMMER'S KEY: ☐Won ☐Drawn ☐Lost

	Comp	Opponent	H/A	Res	Score	Scorers	Attendance
1	slcc1	Stranraer	A	L	1-2	Lyle 80	
2	lge	St Johnstone	A	L	1-4	Bowey 63	2,939
3	lge	Ross County	H	W	1-0	Lyle 11	1,734
4	lge	Falkirk	A	D	0-0		3,064
5	lge	Ayr	A	W	4-1	Paton 16; O'Connor 59,84; Burke 76	2,143
6	sccc1	Stenhousemuir	A	W	2-1	Wood 4; Bagan 85	424
7	lge	Raith	H	L	0-2		2,142
8	lge	St Mirren	A	W	2-1	O'Connor 36; Burke 45	2,681
9	sccc2	Ross County	A	W	3-0	Burke 5,38; Burns 51	959
10	lge	Clyde	H	W	4-1	Paton 12; O'Connor 38; Burke 64,69	1,953
11	lge	Brechin	A	W	1-0	O'Connor 54	621
12	lge	Inverness CT	H	W	3-2	Bagan 65; O'Connor 68,74	3,547
13	lge	Ross County	A	L	0-1		2,962
14	sccc3	Hibernian	A	L	1-2	Burke 90 pen	7,613
15	lge	St Johnstone	H	D	1-1	McColligan 10	3,159
16	lge	Raith	A	W	1-0	Burke 48	1,944
17	lge	Ayr	H	W	1-0	Burke 46	3,555
18	lge	Clyde	A	L	1-3	Wood 45	1,271
19	lge	St Mirren	H	L	1-2	Burke 56 pen	2,473
20	lge	Inverness CT	A	L	1-4	Wood 5	1,745
21	lge	Brechin	H	W	1-0	Wood 85	1,736
22	lge	St Johnstone	A	D	2-2	O'Connor 36; Reid 82	2,029
23	lge	Falkirk	H	W	2-0	O'Connor 49; Wood 68	4,075
24	lge	Ayr	A	D	1-1	Bowey 20	2,303
25	scr3	East Fife	A	W	1-0	O'Connor 75	1,063
26	lge	Raith	H	D	1-1	O'Connor 50	2,098
27	lge	St Mirren	A	L	1-3	Bagan 56	2,540
28	scr4	Motherwell	A	L	2-3	O'Connor 65,69	8,101
29	lge	Brechin	A	L	1-2	Bowey 55	644
30	lge	Inverness CT	H	W	2-1	O'Connor 9; Bowey 29	2,021
31	lge	Ross County	H	D	1-1	Bowey 7	2,047
32	lge	Clyde	H	L	1-2	Burke 71 pen	2,169
33	lge	Falkirk	A	W	2-0	Burke 10,23	2,098
34	lge	Raith	A	L	1-3	O'Connor 12	1,482
35	lge	Ayr	H	D	0-0		1,831
36	lge	Clyde	A	L	0-2		1,207
37	lge	St Mirren	H	W	1-0	Bowey 8	2,211
38	lge	Inverness CT	A	L	1-4	Burke 78	2,126
39	lge	Brechin	H	D	2-2	Jaconelli 15; Burke 46	1,352
40	lge	St Johnstone	H	D	1-1	Jaconelli 74	1,629
41	lge	Ross County	A	W	2-1	Bowey 43; Burke 66	2,842
42	lge	Falkirk	H	W	1-0	Jaconelli 18	2,751

MONTHLY POINTS TALLY

Month	Points	%
AUGUST	7	58%
SEPTEMBER	6	67%
OCTOBER	6	67%
NOVEMBER	7	58%
DECEMBER	7	47%
JANUARY	2	22%
FEBRUARY	3	50%
MARCH	5	33%
APRIL	4	33%
MAY	7	78%

KEY PLAYERS - GOALSCORERS

Sean O'Connor

Goals in the League	12	Player Strike Rate Average number of minutes between League goals scored by player	147
Contribution to Attacking Power Average number of minutes between League team goals while on pitch	65	Club Strike Rate Average number of minutes between League goals scored by club	70

	PLAYER	LGE GOALS	POWER	STRIKE RATE
1	Sean O'Connor	12	65	147 mins
2	Alex Burke	13	64	192 mins
3	Garry Wood	4	74	354 mins
4	Steve Bowey	7	68	422 mins

KEY PLAYERS - MIDFIELDERS

Paul Burns

Goals in the League	0	Contribution to Attacking Power Average number of minutes between League team goals while on pitch	59
Defensive Rating Average number of mins between League goals conceded while he was on the pitch	75	Scoring Difference Defensive Rating minus Contribution to Attacking Power	16

	PLAYER	LGE GOALS	DEF RATE	POWER	SCORE DIFF
1	Paul Burns	0	75	59	16 mins
2	David Bagan	2	72	70	2 mins
3	Joe McAlpine	0	69	67	2 mins
4	Eric Paton	2	70	72	-2 mins

KEY PLAYERS - DEFENDERS

James Thomson

Goals Conceded (GC) The number of League goals conceded while he was on the pitch	27	Clean Sheets In games when he played at least 70 minutes	8
Defensive Rating Ave number of mins between League goals conceded while on the pitch	83	Club Defensive Rating Average number of mins between League goals conceded by the club this season	68

	PLAYER	CON LGE	CLEAN SHEETS	DEF RATE
1	James Thomson	27	8	83 mins
2	Brian Reid	39	10	74 mins
3	Brian McColligan	25	5	71 mins
4	Derek Allan	22	5	63 mins

KEY GOALKEEPER

John Dodds

Goals Conceded in the League	19	Counting Games Games when he played at least 70 mins	13
Defensive Rating Ave number of mins between League goals conceded while on the pitch	61	Clean Sheets In games when he played at least 70 mins	4

LEAGUE GOALS

Alex Burke

Minutes on the pitch	2501	Goals in the League	192
League average (mins between goals)	13		

	PLAYER	MINS	GOALS	AVE
1	Burke	2501	13	192
2	O'Connor	1763	12	147
3	Bowey	2957	7	422
4	Wood	1414	4	354
5	Jaconelli	1027	3	342
6	Bagan	2517	2	1259
7	Paton	3100	2	1550
8	Lyle	689	1	689
9	Reid	2875	1	2875
10	McColligan	1780	1	1780
	Other		0	
	TOTAL		46	

DISCIPLINARY RECORDS

	PLAYER	YELLOW	RED	AVE
1	Wood	5	0	282
2	Thomson	5	2	318
3	McColligan	4	1	356
4	Payne	1	0	456
5	Reid	3	1	718
6	Aitken	3	0	777
7	McAlpine	2	0	833
8	Jaconelli	1	0	1027
9	Gibson	1	0	1105
10	O'Connor	1	0	1763
11	Bagan	1	0	2517
12	Bowey	1	0	2957
13	Paton	1	0	3100
	Other	1	0	
	TOTAL	30	4	

TOP POINT EARNERS

	PLAYER	GAMES	AV PTS
1	Scott	10	2.50
2	Burns	17	1.76
3	Thomson	23	1.74
4	Burke	26	1.69
5	Reid	31	1.68
6	McAlpine	18	1.67
7	Bagan	28	1.61
8	Paton	33	1.52
9	Bowey	33	1.52
10	Gibson	11	1.45
	CLUB AVERAGE:		1.50

LEAGUE APPEARANCES AND BOOKINGS

	AGE (on 01/07/04)	IN NAMED 16	APPEARANCES	COUNTING GAMES	MINUTES ON PITCH	Yellow	Red
Goalkeepers							
John Dodds	22	30	13	13	1164	0	0
Stuart Robertson	19	7	0	0	0	0	0
Craig Samson	19	13	11	11	990	0	0
Colin Scott	34	19	11	10	906	0	0
Defenders							
Andrew Aitken	26	35	31	24	2331	3	0
Derek Allan	29	25	18	15	1376	0	0
Patrick Atkinson	34	2	0	0	0	0	0
Sandy Hodge	23	1	0	0	0	0	0
Brian McColligan	23	28	24	18	1780	4	1
Stephen Payne	20	15	10	1	456	1	0
Brian Reid	34	33	33	31	2875	3	1
Steven Sloan	-	1	0	0	0	0	0
Paul Talbot	24	5	4	1	202	0	0
James Thomson	33	30	27	23	2232	5	2
Midfielders							
David Bagan	27	33	31	28	2517	1	0
Steve Bowey	29	34	33	33	2957	1	0
Paul Burns	20	35	29	17	1942	0	0
William Gibson	19	24	15	11	1105	1	0
Richard Maxwell	2005	1	0	0	0	0	0
Joe McAlpine	22	25	21	18	1667	2	0
Paul McMullan	20	15	12	1	334	1	0
Eric Paton	25	35	35	33	3100	1	0
Forwards							
Alex Burke	26	35	33	26	2501	0	0
Emilo Jaconelli	21	21	16	10	1027	1	0
Derek Lyle	23	16	14	7	689	0	0
Sean O'Connor	23	28	27	18	1763	1	0
Garry Wood	27	22	21	15	1414	5	0

TEAM OF THE SEASON

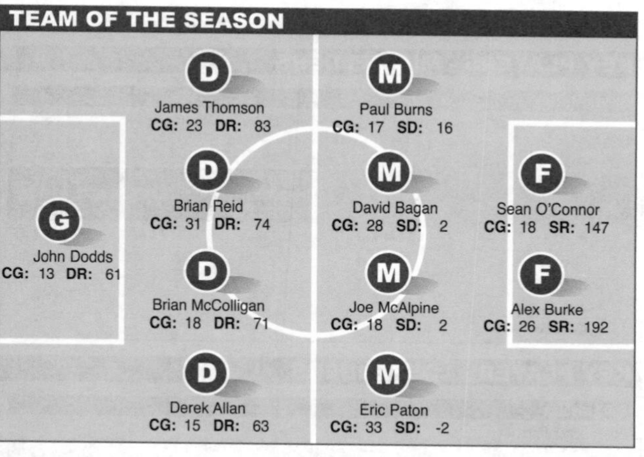

D
James Thomson
CG: 23 DR: 83
M
Paul Burns
CG: 17 SD: 16
D
Brian Reid
CG: 31 DR: 74
M
David Bagan
CG: 28 SD: 2
F
Sean O'Connor
CG: 18 SR: 147
G
John Dodds
CG: 13 DR: 61
D
Brian McColligan
CG: 18 DR: 71
M
Joe McAlpine
CG: 18 SD: 2
F
Alex Burke
CG: 26 SR: 192
D
Derek Allan
CG: 15 DR: 63
M
Eric Paton
CG: 33 SD: -2

SQUAD APPEARANCES

Match	Venue	Competition	Result
1	A	O	L
2	A	L	L
3	H	L	W
4	A	L	D
5	A	L	W
6	A	W	W
7	H	L	L
8	A	L	W
9	A	W	W
10	H	L	W
11	A	L	W
12	H	L	W
13	A	L	L
14	A	W	L
15	H	L	D
16	A	L	W
17	H	L	W
18	A	L	L
19	H	L	L
20	A	L	L
21	H	L	W
22	A	L	D
23	H	L	W
24	A	L	D
25	A	O	W
26	H	L	D
27	A	L	L
28	A	O	L
29	A	L	L
30	H	L	W
31	H	L	D
32	H	L	L
33	A	L	W
34	A	L	L
35	H	L	D
36	A	L	L
37	H	L	W
38	A	L	L
39	H	L	D
40	H	L	D
41	A	L	W
42	H	L	W

Goalkeepers
John Dodds
Stuart Robertson
Craig Samson
Colin Scott

Defenders
Andrew Aitken
Derek Allan
Patrick Atkinson
Sandy Hodge
Brian McColligan
Stephen Payne
Brian Reid
Steven Sloan
Paul Talbot
James Thomson

Midfielders
David Bagan
Steve Bowey
Paul Burns
William Gibson
Richard Maxwell
Joe McAlpine
Paul McMullan
Eric Paton
A Trialist

Forwards
Alex Burke
Emilo Jaconelli
Derek Lyle
Sean O'Connor
Garry Wood

KEY: On all match; On bench; Subbed or sent off (Counting game); Subbed or sent off (playing less than 70 minutes); Subbed on from bench (Counting Game); Subbed on (playing less than 70 minutes); Subbed on and then subbed or sent off (Counting Game); Subbed on and then subbed or sent off (playing less than 70 minutes); Not in 16

ROSS COUNTY

Final Position: **6th**

NICKNAME: THE HIGHLANDERS

KEY: Won Drawn Lost

							Attendance
1	slcc1	Cowdenbeath	A	W	2-1	Campbell 22 og; Rankin 80	
2	lge	Brechin	H	W	4-0	MacKay 17; Higgins 20; Hamilton 66 pen; Tait 89	3,161
3	slcc2	Dumbarton	H	D	1-0	Winters 29	
4	lge	Queen of South	A	L	0-1		1,734
5	lge	St Mirren	H	W	2-0	Winters 67 pen; Gemmill 88 og	3,053
6	lge	Inverness CT	H	D	1-1	Hamilton 2 pen	5,020
7	sccc1	East Stirling	A	W	2-1	Cowie 69; McGarry 73	208
8	lge	Falkirk	A	W	2-0	Winters 11 pen; Rankin 88	2,970
9	lge	Ayr	H	D	2-2	Higgins 3,14	2,832
10	sccc2	Queen of South	H	L	0-3		959
11	lge	Raith	A	W	7-1	McGarry 7; Higgins 38; Winters 45,86,88; Bayne 74; O'Donnell 79	2,292
12	lge	Clyde	A	D	2-2	Rankin 22; O'Donnell 31	1,056
13	lge	St Johnstone	H	L	0-3		3,195
14	lge	Queen of South	H	W	1-0	Webb 58	2,962
15	lge	Brechin	A	L	2-4	Bayne 1,44	565
16	lge	Falkirk	H	L	1-2	Robertson 30	3,204
17	lge	Inverness CT	A	D	3-3	Winters 36; Bayne 70; McGarry 90	3,523
18	lge	Raith	H	W	3-2	Winters 43,49; Gethins 60	2,803
19	lge	Ayr	A	W	3-1	O'Donnell 25; Rankin 27,82	997
20	lge	St Johnstone	A	D	1-1	Hamilton 46	2,478
21	lge	Clyde	H	L	0-1		2,721
22	lge	Brechin	H	W	2-1	McGarry 22; Higgins 51	2,545
23	lge	St Mirren	A	D	1-1	Rankin 90	3,550
24	lge	Inverness CT	H	W	1-0	Golabek 83 og	6,120
25	scr3	Celtic	A	L	0-2		30,565
26	lge	Falkirk	A	L	0-2		2,482
27	lge	Ayr	H	D	1-1	Bayne 39	2,732
28	lge	Raith	A	D	0-0		1,562
29	lge	Clyde	A	L	0-1		1,139
30	lge	St Johnstone	H	W	2-0	Higgins 42; Winters 90	3,072
31	lge	Queen of South	A	D	1-1	McGarry 82	2,047
32	lge	St Mirren	H	W	1-0	Winters 76	2,819
33	lge	Falkirk	H	D	1-1	Bayne 72	2,931
34	lge	Inverness CT	A	L	0-1		4,019
35	lge	Raith	H	D	1-1	Hamilton 22	2,413
36	lge	Ayr	A	W	2-1	McGarry 19; Hamilton 37	1,535
37	lge	St Johnstone	A	D	1-1	Dods 35 og	2,169
38	lge	Clyde	H	D	0-0		3,220
39	lge	Brechin	A	L	0-1		463
40	lge	Queen of South	H	L	1-2	Hamilton 35	2,842
41	lge	St Mirren	A	L	0-2		2,491

MONTHLY POINTS TALLY

Month	Points	%
AUGUST	7	58%
SEPTEMBER	7	78%
OCTOBER	4	44%
NOVEMBER	7	47%
DECEMBER	5	42%
JANUARY	4	44%
FEBRUARY	4	44%
MARCH	5	42%
APRIL	6	50%
MAY	0	0%

KEY PLAYERS - GOALSCORERS

David Winters

Goals in the League	10	Player Strike Rate: Average number of minutes between League goals scored by player	189
Contribution to Attacking Power: Average number of minutes between League team goals while on pitch	57	Club Strike Rate: Average number of minutes between League goals scored by club	66

	PLAYER	LGE GOALS	POWER	STRIKE RATE
1	David Winters	10	57	189 mins
2	Graeme Bayne	6	60	250 mins
3	John Rankin	5	67	619 mins
4	Steven MacKay	1	60	1625 mins

KEY PLAYERS - MIDFIELDERS

Steven MacKay

Goals in the League	1	Contribution to Attacking Power: Average number of minutes between League team goals while on pitch	60
Defensive Rating: Average number of mins between League goals conceded while he was on the pitch	86	Scoring Difference: Defensive Rating minus Contribution to Attacking Power	26

	PLAYER	LGE GOALS	DEF RATE	POWER	SCORE DIFF
1	Steven MacKay	1	86	60	26 mins
2	Hugh Robertson	1	69	50	19 mins
3	John Rankin	5	84	67	17 mins
4	David Hannah	0	84	77	7 mins

KEY PLAYERS - DEFENDERS

Jim Lauchlan

Goals Conceded (GC): The number of League goals conceded while he was on the pitch	15	Clean Sheets: In games when he played at least 70 minutes	5
Defensive Rating: Ave number of mins between League goals conceded while on the pitch	102	Club Defensive Rating: Average number of mins between League goals conceded by the club this season	79

	PLAYER	CON LGE	CLEAN SHEETS	DEF RATE
1	Jim Lauchlan	15	5	102 mins
2	Martin Canning	13	3	95 mins
3	Mark McCulloch	37	8	81 mins
4	Jamie McCunnie	38	8	80 mins

KEY GOALKEEPER

Graeme Smith

Goals Conceded in the League	18	Counting Games: Games when he played at least 70 mins	20
Defensive Rating: Ave number of mins between League goals conceded while on the pitch	100	Clean Sheets: In games when he played at least 70 mins	5

LEAGUE GOALS

David Winters

Minutes on the pitch	1890	Goals in the League	189
League average (mins between goals)	10		

	PLAYER	MINS	GOALS	AVE
	Winters	1890	10	189
2	Hamilton	1244	6	207
3	Bayne	1501	6	250
4	Higgins	1149	6	192
5	McGarry	1691	5	338
6	Rankin	3095	5	619
7	O'Donnell	1312	3	437
8	Tait	709	1	709
9	Webb	982	1	982
10	Gethins	686	1	686
11	MacKay	1625	1	1625
12	Robertson	1660	1	1660
	Other		3	
	TOTAL		49	

DISCIPLINARY RECORDS

	PLAYER	YELLOW	RED	AVE
1	Malcolm	9	2	180
2	MacKay	5	0	325
3	Lauchlan	3	0	510
4	Hamilton	2	0	622
5	Hannah	4	0	710
6	Bayne	2	0	750
7	McGarry	2	0	845
8	Winters	2	0	945
9	Rankin	3	0	1031
10	Higgins	1	0	1149
11	O'Donnell	1	0	1312
12	Stewart	1	0	1420
13	McCunnie	2	0	1524
	Other	1	0	
	TOTAL	38	2	

TOP POINT EARNERS

	PLAYER	GAMES	AV PTS
1	Higgins	4	2.50
2	Tait	6	1.83
3	Webb	10	1.70
4	Stewart	16	1.63
5	O'Donnell	10	1.60
6	MacKay	16	1.56
7	Gethins	2	1.50
8	Robertson	17	1.47
9	Winters	13	1.46
10	McGarry	11	1.45
	CLUB AVERAGE:		**1.36**

LEAGUE APPEARANCES AND BOOKINGS

	AGE (on 01/07/04)	IN NAMED 16	APPEARANCES	COUNTING GAMES	MINUTES ON PITCH	Yellow	Red
Goalkeepers							
Leslie Fridge	35	25	1	0	20	0	0
Kevin Miller	2005	9	0	0	0	0	0
Graeme Smith	21	20	20	20	1800	0	0
Colin Stewart	24	16	16	16	1420	1	0
Defenders							
Martin Canning	22	15	15	13	1234	0	0
Jim Lauchlan	27	17	17	17	1530	3	0
Stuart Malcolm	24	32	24	21	1981	9	2
Mark McCulloch	29	36	36	32	2987	0	0
Jamie McCunnie	21	35	35	33	3049	2	0
Jordan Tait	24	11	9	6	709	0	0
Sean Webb	21	18	14	10	982	0	0
Midfielders							
Don Cowie	21	29	21	7	999	0	0
David Hannah	30	32	32	31	2842	4	0
Steven MacKay	23	24	21	16	1625	5	0
John McDonald	-	3	1	1	79	0	0
Stephen O'Donnell	20	29	25	10	1312	1	0
Daniel Ogunmade	20	5	4	0	67	0	0
John Rankin	21	35	35	34	3095	3	0
Hugh Robertson	29	20	20	17	1660	1	0
Forwards							
Graeme Bayne	24	26	25	12	1501	2	0
Connor Gethins	20	22	19	2	686	0	0
Jim Hamilton	28	22	21	11	1244	2	0
Sean Higgins	19	28	26	4	1149	1	0
Steven McGarry	24	30	28	11	1691	2	0
David Winters	21	33	33	13	1890	2	0

TEAM OF THE SEASON

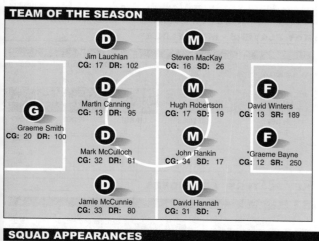

G – Graeme Smith CG: 20 DR: 100

D – Jim Lauchlan CG: 17 DR: 102

D – Martin Canning CG: 13 DR: 95

D – Mark McCulloch CG: 32 DR: 81

D – Jamie McCunnie CG: 33 DR: 80

M – Steven MacKay CG: 16 SD: 26

M – Hugh Robertson CG: 17 SD: 19

M – John Rankin CG: 34 SD: 17

M – David Hannah CG: 31 SD: 7

F – David Winters CG: 13 SR: 189

F – *Graeme Bayne CG: 12 SR: 250

SQUAD APPEARANCES

Match	1	2	3	4	5	6	7	8	9	10	11	12	13	14	15	16	17	18	19	20	21	22	23	24	25	26	27	28	29	30	31	32	33	34	35	36	37	38	39	40	41
Venue	A	H	H	A	H	H	A	A	H	H	A	A	H	H	A	H	A	H	A	A	H	H	A	H	A	A	H	A	A	H	A	H	H	A	H	A	A	H	A	H	A
Competition	O	L	O	L	L	L	W	L	L	W	L	L	L	L	L	L	L	L	L	L	L	L	L	L	O	L	L	L	L	L	L	L	L	L	L	L	L	L	L	L	L
Result	W	W	D	L	W	D	W	W	D	L	W	D	L	W	L	L	D	W	W	D	L	W	D	W	L	L	D	D	L	W	D	W	D	L	D	W	D	D	L	L	L

Goalkeepers: Leslie Fridge, Kevin Miller, Graeme Smith, Colin Stewart

Defenders: Martin Canning, Jim Lauchlan, Stuart Malcolm, Mark McCulloch, Jamie McCunnie, Jordan Tait, Sean Webb

Midfielders: Don Cowie, David Hannah, Steven MacKay, John McDonald, Stephen O'Donnell, Daniel Ogunmade, John Rankin, Hugh Robertson

Forwards: Graeme Bayne, Connor Gethins, Jim Hamilton, Sean Higgins, Steven McGarry, David Winters

KEY: On all match; On bench; Subbed or sent off (Counting game); Subbed or sent off (playing less than 70 minutes); Subbed on from bench (Counting Game); Subbed on (playing less than 70 minutes); Subbed on and then subbed or sent off (Counting Game); Subbed on and then subbed or sent off (playing less than 70 minutes); Not in 16

ST MIRREN

Final Position: **7th**

NICKNAME: BUDDIES/SAINTS

KEY: ☐ Won ☐ Drawn ☐ Lost

							Attendance
1	slcc1	Queens Park	H	W	3-2	Crilly 63; McGinty 88 pen; O'Neill 90	
2	lge	Raith	A	D	1-1	Gillies 51 pen	3,086
3	slcc2	Berwick	H	W	2-1	O'Neill 32	
4	lge	St Johnstone	H	D	1-1	O'Neill 63	3,613
5	lge	Ross County	A	L	0-2		3,053
6	lge	Clyde	H	W	2-1	Russell 66,86	3,010
7	sccc1	St Johnstone	H	L	0-2		3,100
8	lge	Brechin	A	D	1-1	Gillies 13	965
9	lge	Queen of South	H	L	1-2	Gillies 45 pen	2,681
10	lge	Inverness CT	A	L	0-2		1,896
11	lge	Falkirk	H	D	0-0		3,105
12	lge	Ayr	A	W	2-0	Broadfoot 12,68	2,447
13	lge	St Johnstone	A	L	0-1		2,677
14	lge	Raith	H	W	2-1	O'Neill 5; Gillies 81	3,005
15	lge	Brechin	H	D	0-0		2,801
16	lge	Clyde	A	L	0-2		1,861
17	lge	Inverness CT	H	L	0-4		2,204
18	lge	Queen of South	A	W	2-1	Gillies 12; Russell 54	2,473
19	lge	Ayr	H	W	3-2	Lappin 14; Gillies 75,90	2,567
20	lge	Falkirk	A	D	0-0		2,581
21	lge	Ross County	H	D	1-1	Gillies 23	3,550
22	lge	Clyde	H	L	2-3	Dunn 16; Millen 52 pen	3,355
23	scr3	Airdrie Utd	H	W	2-0	Lavety 83; McKenna 90	3,490
24	lge	Brechin	A	L	0-2		887
25	lge	Queen of South	H	W	3-1	O'Neill 29,50; McGinty 49	2,540
26	lge	Inverness CT	A	D	1-1	Lappin 17	1,913
27	scr4	Inverness CT	H	L	0-1		3,859
28	lge	Falkirk	H	D	1-1	Murray 28	2,944
29	lge	Ayr	A	L	0-2		2,252
30	lge	Raith	A	L	0-2		1,882
31	lge	Ross County	A	L	0-1		2,819
32	lge	St Johnstone	H	D	1-1	Murray 42	2,180
33	lge	Brechin	H	D	3-3	Dunn 7; Millar, M 12 og; Crilly 55	2,209
34	lge	Clyde	A	D	2-2	Lappin 61; Russell 67	1,788
35	lge	Inverness CT	H	D	0-0		2,272
36	lge	Queen of South	A	L	0-1		2,211
37	lge	Ayr	H	W	4-1	van Zanten 70,84; McGinty 77; Lappin 85	3,211
38	lge	Falkirk	A	L	0-1		2,386
39	lge	Raith	H	D	1-1	Broadfoot 23	2,372
40	lge	St Johnstone	A	W	3-1	McGinty 10 pen,62,76 pen	2,363
41	lge	Ross County	H	W	2-0	McGowne 45; McGinty 77	2,491

MONTHLY POINTS TALLY

Month	Points	%
AUGUST	5	42%
SEPTEMBER	1	11%
OCTOBER	4	44%
NOVEMBER	4	33%
DECEMBER	8	67%
JANUARY	4	33%
FEBRUARY	1	17%
MARCH	3	20%
APRIL	4	33%
MAY	7	78%

KEY PLAYERS - GOALSCORERS

Brian McGinty

Goals in the League	6	Player Strike Rate Average number of minutes between League goals scored by player	322
Contribution to Attacking Power Average number of minutes between League team goals while on pitch	69	Club Strike Rate Average number of minutes between League goals scored by club	83

	PLAYER	LGE GOALS	POWER	STRIKE RATE
1	Brian McGinty	6	69	322 mins
2	Ricky Gillies	8	76	373 mins
3	Jon O'Neill	4	87	479 mins
4	Simon Lappin	4	74	504 mins

KEY PLAYERS - MIDFIELDERS

Simon Lappin

Goals in the League	4	Contribution to Attacking Power Average number of minutes between League team goals while on pitch	75
Defensive Rating Average number of mins between League goals conceded while he was on the pitch	65	Scoring Difference Defensive Rating minus Contribution to Attacking Power	-10

	PLAYER	LGE GOALS	DEF RATE	POWER	SCORE DIFF
1	Simon Lappin	4	65	75	-10 mins
2	Mark Crilly	1	77	90	-13 mins
3	Hugh Murray	2	63	77	-14 mins
4	Mark Dempsie	0	65	83	-18 mins

KEY PLAYERS - DEFENDERS

Laurence Ellis

Goals Conceded (GC) The number of League goals conceded while he was on the pitch	24	Clean Sheets In games when he played at least 70 minutes	5
Defensive Rating Ave number of mins between League goals conceded while on the pitch	76	Club Defensive Rating Average number of mins between League goals conceded by the club this season	70

	PLAYER	CON LGE	CLEAN SHEETS	DEF RATE
1	Laurence Ellis	24	5	76 mins
2	David van Zanten	39	5	72 mins
3	Kirk Broadfoot	36	5	71 mins
4	Andy Millen	23	2	70 mins

KEY GOALKEEPER

Craig Hinchcliffe

Goals Conceded in the League	33	Counting Games Games when he played at least 70 mins	28
Defensive Rating Ave number of mins between League goals conceded while on the pitch	76	Clean Sheets In games when he played at least 70 mins	6

LEAGUE GOALS

Ricky Gillies

Minutes on the pitch	2983	Goals in the League	373
League average (mins between goals)	8		

	PLAYER	MINS	GOALS	AVE
1	Gillies	2983	8	373
2	McGinty	1933	6	322
3	Russell	1549	4	387
4	Lappin	2014	4	504
5	O'Neill	1914	4	479
6	Broadfoot	2540	3	847
7	Dunn	1214	2	607
8	van Zanten	2817	2	1409
9	Murray	2380	2	1190
10	Crilly	1612	1	1612
11	McGowne	2415	1	2415
12	Millen	1605	1	1605
	Other		1	
	TOTAL		39	

DISCIPLINARY

	PLAYER	YELLOW	RED	AVE
1	Crilly	10	1	146
2	Lavety	2	0	256
3	O'Neill	4	1	382
4	McGinty	5	0	386
5	Dunn	3	0	404
6	Millen	3	0	535
7	McGroarty	2	0	553
8	Murray	4	0	595
9	Dempsie	3	0	607
10	Broadfoot	4	0	635
11	Lappin	3	0	671
12	MacPherson	1	0	745
13	van Zanten	2	0	1408
	Other	7	0	
	TOTAL	53	2	

TOP POINT EARNERS

	PLAYER	GAMES	AV PTS
1	McGowan	2	1.50
2	Ellis	19	1.42
3	McGinty	18	1.39
4	Hinchcliffe	28	1.29
5	O'Neill	17	1.29
6	Gillies	32	1.28
7	Russell	12	1.25
8	Crilly	16	1.19
9	Broadfoot	26	1.19
10	Murray	24	1.17
	CLUB AVERAGE:		**1.14**

LEAGUE APPEARANCES AND BOOKINGS

	AGE (on 01/07/04)	IN NAMED 16	APPEARANCES	COUNTING GAMES	MINUTES ON PITCH	Yellow	Red
Goalkeepers							
Craig Hinchcliffe	32	35	28	28	2520	1	0
Chris Smith	18	1	0	0	0	0	0
Stephen Woods	34	35	8	8	720	0	0
Defenders							
Kirk Broadfoot	19	31	31	26	2540	4	0
Laurence Ellis	24	26	23	19	1832	1	0
Brian Gordon	18	2	0	0	0	0	0
Angus MacPherson	35	10	9	8	745	1	0
Jamie McGowan	33	2	2	2	180	0	0
Kevin McGowne	34	31	28	26	2415	1	0
Andy Millen	39	18	18	18	1605	3	0
David van Zanten	22	36	35	30	2817	2	0
Scott Walker	29	1	1	1	90	0	0
Midfielders							
Mark Crilly	24	28	25	16	1612	10	1
Mark Dempsie	23	27	23	19	1823	3	0
Simon Lappin	21	24	24	22	2014	3	0
Ryan McCay	-	1	1	0	68	0	0
Chris McGroarty	23	15	13	12	1106	2	0
Tom McHard	17	2	0	0	0	0	0
Graham McWilliam	18	0	0	0	0	0	0
Craig Molloy	18	6	2	1	84	0	0
Alan Muir	17	7	3	0	40	0	0
Hugh Murray	25	31	30	24	2380	4	0
Jon O'Neill	30	29	29	17	1914	4	1
Allan Russell	23	26	26	12	1549	1	0
Forwards							
Eddie Annand	31	10	6	1	301	0	0
Edward Annand	31	3	3	0	162	1	0
Robert Dunn	25	28	27	9	1214	3	0
Scott Gemmill	17	5	3	0	25	0	0
Ricky Gillies	27	36	36	32	2983	2	0
Barry Lavety	29	16	13	2	512	2	0
Brian McGinty	27	28	28	18	1933	5	0
David McKenna	17	14	9	0	176	0	0
Paul McKnight	27	6	4	0	96	0	0
Kevin Twaddle	32	3	3	0	74	0	0

TEAM OF THE SEASON

G — Craig Hinchcliffe — CG: 28 DR: 76

D — Laurence Ellis — CG: 19 DR: 76

D — David van Zanten — CG: 30 DR: 72

D — Kirk Broadfoot — CG: 26 DR: 71

D — Andy Millen — CG: 18 DR: 70

M — Simon Lappin — CG: 22 SD: -10

M — Mark Crilly — CG: 16 SD: -13

M — Hugh Murray — CG: 24 SD: -14

M — Mark Dempsie — CG: 19 SD: -18

F — Brian McGinty — CG: 18 SR: 322

F — Ricky Gillies — CG: 32 SR: 373

SQUAD APPEARANCES

Match	1	2	3	4	5	6	7	8	9	10	11	12	13	14	15	16	17	18	19	20	21	22	23	24	25	26	27	28	29	30	31	32	33	34	35	36	37	38	39	40	41
Venue	H	A	H	H	A	H	H	A	H	A	H	A	A	H	H	A	H	A	H	A	H	H	H	A	H	A	H	H	A	A	A	H	H	A	H	A	H	A	H	A	H
Competition	O	L	O	L	L	L	W	L	L	L	L	L	L	L	L	L	L	L	L	L	L	L	O	L	L	L	O	L	L	L	L	L	L	L	L	L	L	L	L	L	L
Result	W	D	W	D	L	W	L	D	L	L	D	W	L	W	D	L	L	W	W	D	D	L	W	L	W	D	L	D	L	L	L	D	D	D	D	L	W	L	D	W	W

Goalkeepers
Craig Hinchcliffe
Chris Smith
Stephen Woods

Defenders
Kirk Broadfoot
Laurence Ellis
Brian Gordon
Angus MacPherson
Jamie McGowan
Kevin McGowne
Andy Millen
David van Zanten
Scott Walker

Midfielders
Mark Crilly
Mark Dempsie
Simon Lappin
Ryan McCay
Chris McGroarty
Tom McHard
Graham McWilliam
Craig Molloy
Alan Muir
Hugh Murray
Jon O'Neill
Allan Russell

Forwards
Edward Annand
Eddie Annand
Robert Dunn
Scott Gemmill
Ricky Gillies
Barry Lavety
Brian McGinty
David McKenna
Paul McKnight
Kevin Twaddle

KEY: On all match — On bench — Subbed or sent off (Counting game) — Subbed or sent off (playing less than 70 minutes) — Subbed on from bench (Counting Game) — Subbed on (playing less than 70 minutes) — Subbed on and then subbed or sent off (Counting Game) — Subbed on and then subbed or sent off (playing less than 70 minutes) — Not in 16

RAITH ROVERS

Final Position: **8th**

NICKNAME: ROVERS

KEY: ☐ Won ☐ Drawn ☐ Lost

							Attendance
1	slcc1	East Stirling	A	W	5-2	Sutton 24,69; Peers 49; Prest 65; Stanley 88	
2	lge	St Mirren	H	D	1-1	Brittain 28	3,086
3	slcc2	Stranraer	H	D	2-0		
4	lge	Brechin	A	W	3-0	Sutton 12,75 pen,84	1,021
5	lge	Ayr	H	D	1-1	Dennis 70	2,364
6	lge	Falkirk	H	L	0-1		4,232
7	sccc1	Arbroath	A	L	0-1		879
8	lge	Queen of South	A	W	2-0	Sutton 25,78	2,142
9	lge	St Johnstone	A	W	1-0	Calderon 28	2,681
10	lge	Ross County	H	L	1-7	Brown 11	2,292
11	lge	Inverness CT	A	L	1-2	Sutton 88	1,707
12	lge	Clyde	H	L	0-1		1,765
13	lge	Brechin	H	W	2-1	Hawley 28; Sutton 36	1,685
14	lge	St Mirren	A	L	1-2	Paquito 43	3,005
15	lge	Queen of South	H	L	0-1		1,944
16	lge	Falkirk	A	L	2-3	Sutton 35; Blackadder 80	3,237
17	lge	Ross County	A	L	2-3	Sutton 60; Calderon 78	2,803
18	lge	St Johnstone	H	L	1-4	Hawley 62	1,996
19	lge	Clyde	A	D	0-0		1,375
20	lge	Inverness CT	H	L	1-3	Sutton 45	1,432
21	lge	Ayr	A	L	0-1		1,791
22	lge	Falkirk	H	W	2-0	Sutton 8 pen; Stanley 72	2,885
23	scr3	Kilmarnock	H	L	1-3	Talio 55	3,610
24	lge	Queen of South	A	D	1-1	Sutton 77	2,098
25	lge	St Johnstone	A	L	2-5	Sutton 12; Patino 68	2,636
26	lge	Ross County	H	D	0-0		1,562
27	lge	Inverness CT	A	L	0-3		1,879
28	lge	Clyde	H	L	0-3		1,871
29	lge	St Mirren	H	W	2-0	Ferrero 15; Pereira 71	1,882
30	lge	Brechin	A	D	1-1	Calderon 21	925
31	lge	Ayr	H	W	2-1	Pereira 30 pen; Ferrero 67	2,231
32	lge	Queen of South	H	W	3-1	Pereira 1; Paquito 6; Thomson 90 og	1,482
33	lge	Falkirk	A	L	0-1		2,386
34	lge	Ross County	A	D	1-1	Pereira 61	2,413
35	lge	St Johnstone	H	D	1-1	Pereira 39	2,676
36	lge	Clyde	A	L	1-4	Ferrero 2	1,533
37	lge	Inverness CT	H	L	0-1		1,748
38	lge	St Mirren	A	D	1-1	Ferrero 63	2,372
39	lge	Brechin	H	D	1-1	O'Reilly 52	2,311
40	lge	Ayr	A	L	0-1		1,283

MONTHLY POINTS TALLY

Month	Points	%
AUGUST	5	42%
SEPTEMBER	6	67%
OCTOBER	3	33%
NOVEMBER	0	0%
DECEMBER	1	11%
JANUARY	4	44%
FEBRUARY	1	11%
MARCH	10	67%
APRIL	2	17%
MAY	2	22%

KEY PLAYERS - GOALSCORERS

John Sutton

Goals in the League	13	Player Strike Rate Average number of minutes between League goals scored by player	138
Contribution to Attacking Power Average number of minutes between League team goals while on pitch	74	Club Strike Rate Average number of minutes between League goals scored by club	85

	PLAYER	LGE GOALS	POWER	STRIKE RATE
1	John Sutton	13	74	138 mins
2	Sebastien Ferrero	4	88	243 mins
3	Antonio Calderon	2	78	1055 mins
4	Francisco Ortiz Rivas Paquito	2	85	1326 mins

KEY PLAYERS - MIDFIELDERS

Antonio Calderon

Goals in the League	2	Contribution to Attacking Power Average number of minutes between League team goals while on pitch	78
Defensive Rating Average number of mins between League goals conceded while he was on the pitch	57	Scoring Difference Defensive Rating minus Contribution to Attacking Power	-21

	PLAYER	LGE GOALS	DEF RATE	POWER	SCORE DIFF
1	Antonio Calderon	2	57	78	-21 mins
2	Darren Brady	0	56	79	-23 mins
3	Craig Stanley	0	53	81	-28 mins
4	Goran Stanic	0	51	93	-42 mins

KEY PLAYERS - DEFENDERS

Christian Patino

Goals Conceded (GC) The number of League goals conceded while he was on the pitch	23	Clean Sheets In games when he played at least 70 minutes	4
Defensive Rating Ave number of mins between League goals conceded while on the pitch	72	Club Defensive Rating Average number of mins between League goals conceded by the club this season	56

	PLAYER	CON LGE	CLEAN SHEETS	DEF RATE
1	Christian Patino	23	4	72 mins
2	Shaun Dennis	32	6	62 mins
3	Joaquin Bornes	18	2	62 mins
4	Francisco Ortiz Rivas Paquito	50	6	53 mins

KEY GOALKEEPER

David Berthelot

Goals Conceded in the League	18	Counting Games Games when he played at least 70 mins	13
Defensive Rating Ave number of mins between League goals conceded while on the pitch	64	Clean Sheets In games when he played at least 70 mins	2

LEAGUE GOALS

John Sutton

Minutes on the pitch	1799	Goals in the League	138
League average (mins between goals)	13		

	PLAYER	MINS	GOALS	AVE
	Sutton 1799	13	138	
2	Pereira	880	5	176
3	Ferrero	973	4	243
4	Paquito	2651	2	1326
5	Hawley	612	2	306
6	Calderon	2109	2	1055
7	Brown	1099	1	1099
8	Brittain	884	1	884
9	Blackadder	852	1	852
10	Patino	1665	1	1665
11	Stanley	1655	1	1655
12	O'Reilly	255	1	255
	Other		3	
	TOTAL		37	

DISCIPLINARY RECORDS

	PLAYER	YELLOW	RED	AVE
1	Pereira	4	1	176
2	Calderon	8	1	234
3	Stanic	8	1	258
4	Brown	4	0	274
5	Bornes	4	0	279
6	Capin	3	0	315
7	Blackadder	2	0	426
8	Brittain	2	0	442
9	Boyle	1	0	486
10	Dennis	3	1	495
11	Jack	1	0	514
12	Gonzalez	3	0	519
13	Paquito	5	0	530
	Other	16	0	
	TOTAL	64	4	

TOP POINT EARNERS

	PLAYER	GAMES	AV PTS
1	Boyle	2	1.50
2	Nieto	6	1.50
3	Pereira	10	1.40
4	Capin	10	1.40
5	Brittain	8	1.38
6	Brady	17	1.35
7	Stanley	3	1.33
8	Bornes	12	1.25
9	Brown	9	1.22
10	Dennis	22	1.18
	CLUB AVERAGE:		0.94

TEAM OF THE SEASON

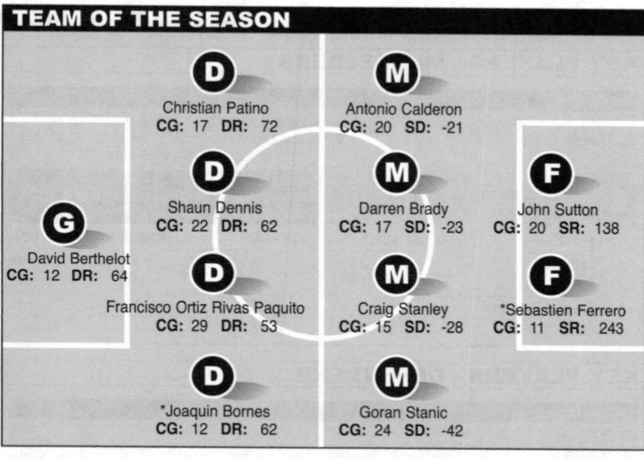

D
Christian Patino
CG: 17 DR: 72
M
Antonio Calderon
CG: 20 SD: -21
D
Shaun Dennis
CG: 22 DR: 62
M
Darren Brady
CG: 17 SD: -23
F
John Sutton
CG: 20 SR: 138
G
David Berthelot
CG: 12 DR: 64
D
Francisco Ortiz Rivas Paquito
CG: 29 DR: 53
M
Craig Stanley
CG: 15 SD: -28
F
*Sebastien Ferrero
CG: 11 SR: 243
D
*Joaquin Bornes
CG: 12 DR: 62
M
Goran Stanic
CG: 24 SD: -42

LEAGUE APPEARANCES AND BOOKINGS

	AGE (on 01/07/04)	IN NAMED 16	APPEARANCES	COUNTING GAMES	MINUTES ON PITCH	Yellow	Red
Goalkeepers							
David Berthelot	-	13	13	12	1143	0	0
Ramiro Gonzalez	23	32	18	17	1557	3	0
James Langfield	24	5	5	5	450	0	0
Defenders							
Joaquin Bornes	29	13	13	12	1119	4	0
Iain Brown	20	19	16	9	1099	4	0
Salvador Capin	28	11	11	10	945	3	0
Shaun Dennis	34	22	22	22	1980	3	1
Andy Dow	31	9	8	4	517	0	0
Danny Glynn	17	1	1	1	90	0	0
Matthias Jack	35	6	6	5	514	1	0
Juan Nieto	-	10	10	6	724	0	0
Francisco Ortiz Rivas Paquito	34	31	31	29	2651	5	0
Christian Patino	24	21	20	17	1665	3	0
Jonathan Smart	-	13	10	8	813	1	0
Vincent Talio	23	13	10	7	685	1	0
Midfielders							
Ryan Blackadder	20	19	17	8	852	2	0
Darren Brady	22	32	28	17	2066	2	0
Richard Brittain	20	14	13	8	884	2	0
Antonio Calderon	37	28	27	20	2109	8	1
Beto Carranza	32	3	3	1	127	0	0
James Henry	29	3	2	0	52	0	0
Craig Malcolm	17	8	5	1	138	0	0
Ryan Maxwell	21	10	6	2	262	3	0
Paul Miller	-	3	2	1	119	0	0
Wilfred Nanou	-	1	1	1	90	0	0
Stephen Robb	22	11	10	4	574	0	0
Goran Stanic	31	28	28	24	2324	8	1
Craig Stanley	21	20	20	18	1655	1	0
Forwards							
John Boyle	17	15	14	2	486	1	0
David Evans	22	10	8	1	252	0	0
Sebastien Ferrero	22	11	11	11	973	1	0
Karl Hawley	22	13	10	4	567	1	0
Karl Hawley	22	1	1	0	45	0	0
John Martin	19	9	5	1	132	0	0
Craig O'Reilly	16	4	4	2	255	0	0
Mark Peers	20	5	5	0	185	0	0
Ramon Pereira	25	10	10	10	880	4	1
Martin Prest	25	16	11	6	725	0	0
Steven Robb	-	1	1	1	90	0	0
John Sutton	20	21	21	20	1799	3	0
Lloyd Young	-	14	12	8	809	0	0

SQUAD APPEARANCES

Match	1	2	3	4	5	6	7	8	9	10	11	12	13	14	15	16	17	18	19	20	21	22	23	24	25	26	27	28	29	30	31	32	33	34	35	36	37	38	39	40
Venue	A	H	H	A	H	H	A	A	A	H	A	H	H	A	H	A	A	H	A	H	A	H	H	A	A	H	A	H	H	A	H	H	A	A	H	A	H	A	H	A
Competition	O	L	O	L	L	L	W	L	L	L	L	L	L	L	L	L	L	L	L	L	L	L	O	L	L	L	L	L	L	L	L	L	L	L	L	L	L	L	L	L
Result	W	D	D	W	D	L	L	W	W	L	L	L	W	L	L	L	L	L	D	L	L	W	L	D	L	D	L	L	W	D	W	W	L	D	D	L	L	D	D	L

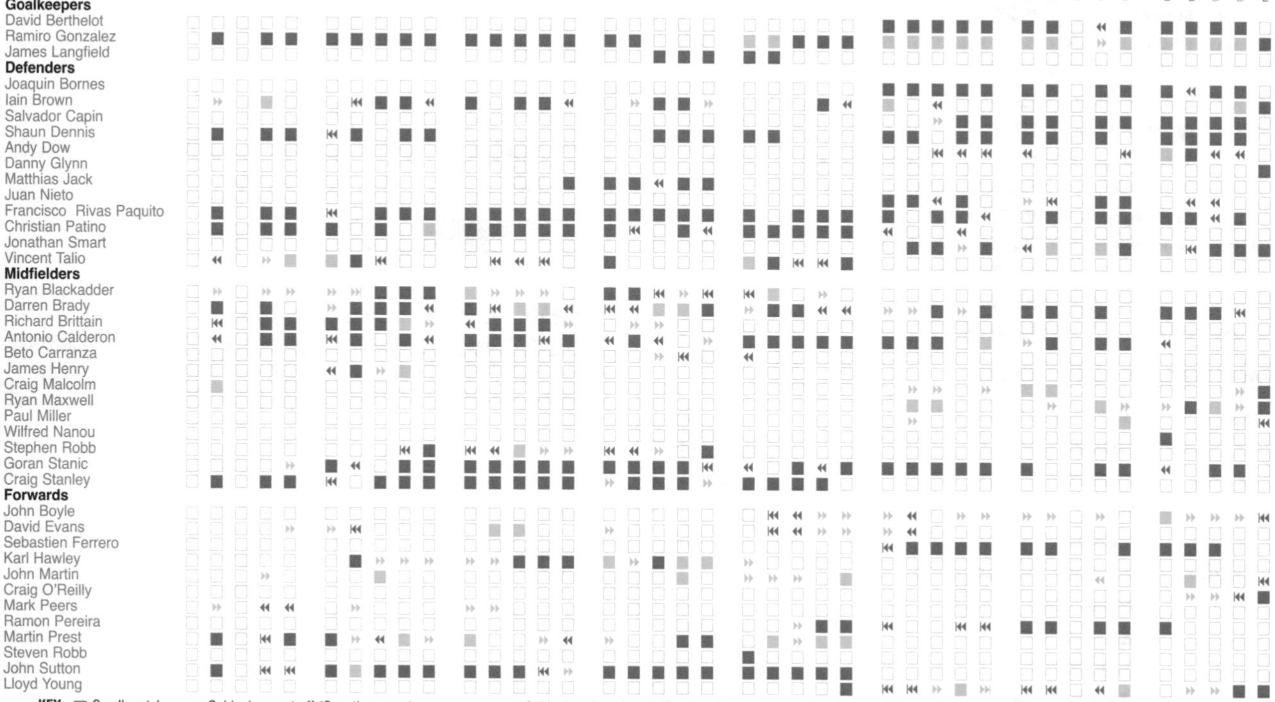

Goalkeepers
David Berthelot
Ramiro Gonzalez
James Langfield
Defenders
Joaquin Bornes
Iain Brown
Salvador Capin
Shaun Dennis
Andy Dow
Danny Glynn
Matthias Jack
Juan Nieto
Francisco Rivas Paquito
Christian Patino
Jonathan Smart
Vincent Talio
Midfielders
Ryan Blackadder
Darren Brady
Richard Brittain
Antonio Calderon
Beto Carranza
James Henry
Craig Malcolm
Ryan Maxwell
Paul Miller
Wilfred Nanou
Stephen Robb
Goran Stanic
Craig Stanley
Forwards
John Boyle
David Evans
Sebastien Ferrero
Karl Hawley
John Martin
Craig O'Reilly
Mark Peers
Ramon Pereira
Martin Prest
Steven Robb
John Sutton
Lloyd Young

KEY: On all match · On bench · Subbed or sent off (Counting game) · Subbed or sent off (playing less than 70 minutes) · Subbed on from bench (Counting Game) · Subbed on (playing less than 70 minutes) · Subbed on and then subbed or sent off (Counting Game) · Subbed on and then subbed or sent off (playing less than 70 minutes) · Not in 16

AYR UNITED

Final Position: **9th**

NICKNAME: THE HONEST MEN

KEY: Won / Drawn / Lost

							Attendance
1	slcc1	Stirling	H	D	1-1	Kean 57	
2	lge	Clyde	A	L	0-3		1,067
3	lge	Falkirk	H	D	1-1	Kean 88	2,519
4	lge	Raith	A	D	1-1	Ferguson 17	2,364
5	lge	Queen of South	H	L	1-4	Campbell 82	2,143
6	sccc1	Dumbarton	H	L	1-2	Smyth 75	1,048
7	lge	Inverness CT	A	L	0-1		1,476
8	lge	Ross County	A	D	2-2	Whalen 18; Chaplain 40	2,832
9	lge	Brechin	H	W	3-2	Craig 3; Chaplain 15; Dunlop 90	1,427
10	lge	St Johnstone	A	D	1-1	Kean 88	2,026
11	lge	St Mirren	H	L	0-2		2,447
12	lge	Falkirk	A	W	1-0	Ferguson, A 9	2,609
13	lge	Clyde	H	D	2-2	Chaplain 52; Kean 75	1,653
14	lge	Inverness CT	H	L	0-3		1,464
15	lge	Queen of South	A	L	0-1		3,555
16	lge	Brechin	A	L	1-3	Dunlop 50	508
17	lge	Ross County	H	L	1-3	Trialist 35	997
18	lge	St Mirren	A	L	2-3	Kean 47; Ferguson, A 85	2,567
19	lge	St Johnstone	H	D	1-1	Ramsey 90	1,203
20	lge	Clyde	A	L	1-2	Chaplain 78	1,102
21	lge	Raith	H	W	1-0	Ferguson, A 23	1,791
22	lge	Queen of South	H	D	1-1	Ferguson, A 80	2,303
23	scr3	Falkirk	H	L	1-2	Craig 28	2,632
24	lge	Inverness CT	A	L	1-2	Doyle 62	1,443
25	lge	Ross County	A	D	1-1	Kean 72	2,732
26	lge	Brechin	H	L	1-2	Brown 39	1,512
27	lge	St Johnstone	A	L	0-3		2,067
28	lge	St Mirren	H	W	2-0	Ferguson, A 9; Kean 66	2,252
29	lge	Falkirk	H	L	2-3	Kean 32; Hardy 80 pen	2,048
30	lge	Raith	A	L	1-2	Hardy 13	2,231
31	lge	Inverness CT	H	D	1-1	Hardy 1	1,207
32	lge	Queen of South	A	D	0-0		1,831
33	lge	Brechin	A	W	3-0	Black 54; Smyth 58; Kean 61	519
34	lge	Ross County	H	L	1-2	Brown 90	1,535
35	lge	St Mirren	A	L	1-4	Kean 64	3,211
36	lge	St Johnstone	H	D	1-1	Forsyth 7 og	1,119
37	lge	Clyde	H	D	1-1	Campbell 72	1,816
38	lge	Falkirk	A	D	0-0		2,077
39	lge	Raith	H	W	1-0	Ferguson, A 40	1,283

MONTHLY POINTS TALLY

Month	Points	%
AUGUST	2	17%
SEPTEMBER	4	44%
OCTOBER	4	44%
NOVEMBER	1	7%
DECEMBER	4	33%
JANUARY	2	17%
FEBRUARY	3	50%
MARCH	2	17%
APRIL	4	33%
MAY	5	56%

KEY PLAYERS - GOALSCORERS

Andrew Ferguson

Goals in the League	6	Player Strike Rate Average number of minutes between League goals scored by player	264
Contribution to Attacking Power Average number of minutes between League team goals while on pitch	93	Club Strike Rate Average number of minutes between League goals scored by club	88

	PLAYER	LGE GOALS	POWER	STRIKE RATE
1	Andrew Ferguson	6	93	264 mins
2	Stuart Kean	9	89	357 mins
3	Lee Hardy	3	84	591 mins
4	Scott Chaplain	4	98	614 mins

KEY PLAYERS - MIDFIELDERS

Lee Hardy

Goals in the League	3	Contribution to Attacking Power Average number of minutes between League team goals while on pitch	84
Defensive Rating Average number of mins between League goals conceded while he was on the pitch	63	Scoring Difference Defensive Rating minus Contribution to Attacking Power	-21

	PLAYER	LGE GOALS	DEF RATE	POWER	SCORE DIFF
1	Lee Hardy	3	63	84	-21 mins
2	Aaron Black	1	65	90	-25 mins
3	Douglas Ramsey	1	58	86	-28 mins
4	Scott Chaplain	4	51	98	-47 mins

KEY PLAYERS - DEFENDERS

Michael Dunlop

Goals Conceded (GC) The number of League goals conceded while he was on the pitch	23	Clean Sheets In games when he played at least 70 minutes	3
Defensive Rating Ave number of mins between League goals conceded while on the pitch	66	Club Defensive Rating Average number of mins between League goals conceded by the club this season	56

	PLAYER	CON LGE	CLEAN SHEETS	DEF RATE
1	Michael Dunlop	23	3	66 mins
2	Mark Campbell	38	6	59 mins
3	Willie Lyle	42	6	57 mins
4	David Craig	50	5	55 mins

KEY GOALKEEPER

Ludovic Roy

Goals Conceded in the League	55	Counting Games Games when he played at least 70 mins	34
Defensive Rating Ave number of mins between League goals conceded while on the pitch	56	Clean Sheets In games when he played at least 70 mins	7

LEAGUE GOALS

Stuart Kean

Minutes on the pitch	3212	Goals in the League	357
League average (mins between goals)	9		

	PLAYER	MINS	GOALS	AVE
1	Kean	3212	9	357
2	Ferguson, A	1585	6	264
3	Chaplain	2455	4	614
4	Hardy	1772	3	591
5	Dunlop	1520	2	760
6	Campbell	2243	2	1122
7	Brown	1022	2	511
8	Doyle	528	1	528
9	Trialist	560	1	560
10	Smyth	2809	1	2809
11	Black	1438	1	1438
12	Ramsey	2328	1	2328
	Other		4	
	TOTAL		37	

DISCIPLINARY

	PLAYER	YELLOW	RED	AVE
1	Trialist	3	0	186
2	Doyle	2	0	264
3	Dunlop	4	1	304
4	Campbell	6	1	320
5	Lyle	7	0	344
6	Smyth	8	0	351
7	Ferguson, S	2	0	361
8	Whalen	1	0	556
9	Black	2	0	719
10	Ramsey	3	0	776
11	Ferguson, A	2	0	792
12	McGrady	1	0	1040
13	Chaplain	1	1	1227
	Other	1	0	
	TOTAL	43	3	

TOP POINT EARNERS

	PLAYER	GAMES	AV PTS
1	Doyle	5	1.40
2	Tait	8	1.25
3	Ferguson, A	10	1.20
4	Ferguson, S	7	1.14
5	McGrady	8	1.13
6	Black	14	1.07
7	Whalen	4	1.00
8	Campbell	25	1.00
9	Ramsey	25	0.96
10	Lyle	25	0.92
	CLUB AVERAGE:		**0.86**

LEAGUE APPEARANCES AND BOOKINGS

	AGE (on 01/07/04)	IN NAMED 16	APPEARANCES	COUNTING GAMES	MINUTES ON PITCH	Yellow	Red
Goalkeepers							
John Hillcoat	33	34	2	2	176	0	0
Darren Johnson	18	1	0	0	0	0	0
Ludovic Roy	26	35	35	34	3064	0	0
Defenders							
Robert Burgess	19	26	8	4	403	0	0
Mark Campbell	26	26	25	25	2243	6	1
David Craig	35	31	31	30	2745	0	0
Michael Dunlop	21	26	23	15	1520	4	1
Chris Kerr	25	11	9	4	473	0	0
Willie Lyle	20	32	31	25	2414	7	0
Stewart McGrady	18	22	20	8	1040	1	0
Marc Smyth	21	35	35	29	2809	8	0
Jordan Tait	24	10	10	8	805	0	0
Midfielders							
Aaron Black	20	22	19	14	1438	2	0
Scott Chaplain	20	35	34	23	2455	1	1
Steven Crawford	17	2	2	1	146	0	0
Jamie Doyle	19	8	7	5	528	2	0
Steve Ferguson, S	27	9	9	7	722	2	0
Lee Hardy	22	21	21	19	1772	1	0
William Kinniburgh	19	8	7	7	630	0	0
James Latta	19	8	3	1	129	0	0
Steven Miller	20	5	5	1	182	0	0
Boyd Mullen	18	8	5	0	115	0	0
Douglas Ramsey	25	27	27	25	2328	3	0
Forwards							
Graeme Brown	23	16	15	8	1022	0	0
Craig Conway	19	14	8	0	151	0	0
Andrew Ferguson	19	32	31	10	1585	2	0
Stuart Kean	21	36	36	36	3212	0	0
Mark McColl	19	15	14	0	337	0	0
Stephen Whalen	22	10	9	4	556	1	0

TEAM OF THE SEASON

G — Ludovic Roy, CG: 34 DR: 56

D — Michael Dunlop, CG: 15 DR: 66
D — Mark Campbell, CG: 25 DR: 59
D — Willie Lyle, CG: 25 DR: 57
D — David Craig, CG: 30 DR: 55

M — Lee Hardy, CG: 19 SD: -21
M — Aaron Black, CG: 14 SD: -25
M — Douglas Ramsey, CG: 25 SD: -28
M — Scott Chaplain, CG: 23 SD: -47

F — Stuart Kean, CG: 36 SR: 357
F — *Andrew Ferguson, CG: 10 SR: 264

SQUAD APPEARANCES

Match	1	2	3	4	5	6	7	8	9	10	11	12	13	14	15	16	17	18	19	20	21	22	23	24	25	26	27	28	29	30	31	32	33	34	35	36	37	38	39
Venue	H	A	H	A	H	H	A	A	H	A	H	A	H	H	A	A	H	A	H	A	H	H	H	A	A	H	A	H	H	A	H	A	A	H	A	H	H	A	H
Competition	O	L	L	L	L	W	L	L	L	L	L	L	L	L	L	L	L	L	L	L	L	L	O	L	L	L	L	L	L	L	L	L	L	L	L	L	L	L	L
Result	D	L	D	D	L	L	L	D	W	D	L	W	D	L	L	L	L	L	D	L	W	D	L	L	D	L	L	W	L	L	D	D	W	L	L	D	D	D	W

Goalkeepers
John Hillcoat
Darren Johnson
Ludovic Roy

Defenders
Robert Burgess
Mark Campbell
David Craig
Michael Dunlop
Chris Kerr
Willie Lyle
Stewart McGrady
Marc Smyth
Jordan Tait

Midfielders
Aaron Black
Scott Chaplain
Steven Crawford
Jamie Doyle
Steve Ferguson, S
Lee Hardy
William Kinniburgh
James Latta
Steven Miller
Boyd Mullen
Douglas Ramsey

Forwards
Graeme Brown
Craig Conway
Andrew Ferguson
Stuart Kean
Mark McColl
Stephen Whalen

KEY: On all match · On bench · Subbed or sent off (Counting game) · Subbed or sent off (playing less than 70 minutes) · Subbed on from bench (Counting Game) · Subbed on (playing less than 70 minutes) · Subbed on and then subbed or sent off (Counting Game) · Subbed on and then subbed or sent off (playing less than 70 minutes) · Not in 16

BRECHIN

Final Position: **10th**

NICKNAME: CITY

KEY: Won Drawn Lost

							Attendance
1	slcc1	Falkirk	H	W	1-0	King 75	
2	lge	Ross County	A	L	0-4		3,161
3	slcc2	Stirling	H	D	3-1	Templeman 5; Johnson 42	
4	lge	Raith	H	L	0-3		1,021
5	lge	Clyde	A	L	1-2	Jablonski 4	1,102
6	lge	St Johnstone	A	L	1-3	Gibson 90	2,219
7	sccc1	Elgin City	A	W	4-0	Fotheringham, K 33; White 55; Gibson 80; Templeman 87	486
8	lge	St Mirren	H	D	1-1	Fotheringham, K 11 pen	965
9	lge	Inverness CT	H	L	0-2		652
10	sccc2	Kilmarnock	H	W	1-0	Hampshire 18	829
11	lge	Ayr	A	L	2-3	King 40; Hampshire 60	1,427
12	lge	Queen of South	H	L	0-1		621
13	lge	Falkirk	A	L	0-3		2,442
14	lge	Raith	A	L	1-2	Fotheringham, K 73 pen	1,685
15	sccc3	Aberdeen	A	L	0-5		3,631
16	lge	Ross County	H	W	4-2	White 39,54; Smith, J 63; McLeish 83	565
17	lge	St Mirren	A	D	0-0		2,801
18	lge	St Johnstone	H	L	0-1		1,502
19	lge	Ayr	H	W	3-1	Templeman 10; Hampshire 39; McLeish 57	508
20	lge	Inverness CT	A	L	0-5		1,393
21	lge	Falkirk	H	D	2-2	Mitchell 6; Millar, M 18 pen	1,043
22	lge	Queen of South	A	L	0-1		1,736
23	lge	Ross County	A	L	1-2	Templeman 67	2,545
24	lge	Clyde	H	L	1-3	Hampshire 73	808
25	lge	St Johnstone	A	D	2-2	Mitchell 46; Hampshire 69	2,171
26	scr3	Inverness CT	A	L	1-5	King 51	1,412
27	lge	St Mirren	H	W	2-0	McCulloch, S 54; Smith, J 78	887
28	lge	Inverness CT	H	L	2-4	Duffy 14,61	667
29	lge	Ayr	A	W	2-1	Millar, M 25 pen; King 33	1,512
30	lge	Queen of South	H	W	2-1	King 72; Beith 79	644
31	lge	Falkirk	A	L	0-5		2,060
32	lge	Raith	H	D	1-1	Duffy 70	925
33	lge	Clyde	A	D	0-0		1,035
34	lge	St Mirren	A	D	3-3	McCulloch, S 27; Templeman 49; Winter 61	2,209
35	lge	St Johnstone	H	L	0-2		822
36	lge	Ayr	H	L	0-3		519
37	lge	Inverness CT	A	L	0-1		1,248
38	lge	Falkirk	H	L	0-1		768
39	lge	Queen of South	A	D	2-2	Winter 68; Gibson 74	1,352
40	lge	Ross County	H	W	1-0	Gibson 90	463
41	lge	Raith	A	D	1-1	Gibson 4	2,311
42	lge	Clyde	H	L	2-5	Templeman 80 pen,88	1,254

MONTHLY POINTS TALLY

Month	Points	%
AUGUST	0	0%
SEPTEMBER	1	11%
OCTOBER	0	0%
NOVEMBER	7	47%
DECEMBER	1	8%
JANUARY	7	58%
FEBRUARY	3	50%
MARCH	3	25%
APRIL	1	8%
MAY	4	44%

KEY PLAYERS - GOALSCORERS

Christopher Templeman

Goals in the League	5	Player Strike Rate Average number of minutes between League goals scored by player	408
Contribution to Attacking Power Average number of minutes between League team goals while on pitch	97	Club Strike Rate Average number of minutes between League goals scored by club	88

	PLAYER	LGE GOALS	POWER	STRIKE RATE
1	Christopher Templeman	5	97	408 mins
2	Steven Hampshire	4	83	566 mins
3	Charles King	3	82	741 mins
4	Scott McCulloch	2	116	1045 mins

KEY PLAYERS - MIDFIELDERS

Grant Johnson

Goals in the League	0	Contribution to Attacking Power Average number of minutes between League team goals while on pitch	68
Defensive Rating Average number of mins between League goals conceded while he was on the pitch	44	Scoring Difference Defensive Rating minus Contribution to Attacking Power	-24

	PLAYER	LGE GOALS	DEF RATE	POWER	SCORE DIFF
1	Grant Johnson	0	44	68	-24 mins
2	Marc Millar	2	49	85	-36 mins
3	Charles King	3	45	82	-37 mins
4	Ally Mitchell	2	46	89	-43 mins

KEY PLAYERS - DEFENDERS

Paul Deas

Goals Conceded (GC) The number of League goals conceded while he was on the pitch	56	Clean Sheets In games when he played at least 70 minutes	4
Defensive Rating Ave number of mins between League goals conceded while on the pitch	49	Club Defensive Rating Average number of mins between League goals conceded by the club this season	44

	PLAYER	CON LGE	CLEAN SHEETS	DEF RATE
1	Paul Deas	56	4	49 mins
2	James Smith	49	3	49 mins
3	Andrew Dowie	30	2	45 mins
4	Scott McCulloch	47	3	44 mins

KEY GOALKEEPER

David Hay

Goals Conceded in the League	32	Counting Games Games when he played at least 70 mins	18
Defensive Rating Ave number of mins between League goals conceded while on the pitch	45	Clean Sheets In games when he played at least 70 mins	3

LEAGUE GOALS

Christopher Templeman

Minutes on the pitch	2039	Goals in the League	408
League average (mins between goals)	5		

	PLAYER	MINS	GOALS	AVE
1	Templeman	2039	5	408
2	Gibson	1106	4	277
3	Hampshire	2264	4	566
4	Duffy	617	3	206
5	King	2224	3	741
6	Millar, M	2125	2	1063
7	Fotheringham	847	2	424
8	Winter	811	2	406
9	Mitchell	2407	2	1204
10	White	2352	2	1176
11	Smith, J	2404	2	1202
12	McLeish	1073	2	537
	Other		4	
	TOTAL		37	

DISCIPLINARY RECORDS

	PLAYER	YELLOW	RED	AVE
1	Fotheringham	7	0	121
2	Duffy	2	0	308
3	Johnson	6	0	330
4	McLeish	2	1	357
5	White	5	1	392
6	Mitchell	5	1	401
7	McCulloch, S	5	0	418
8	Gibson	1	1	553
9	Deas	5	0	554
10	Jablonski	2	0	567
11	Templeman	3	0	679
12	Millar, M	3	0	708
13	Budinauckas	1	0	761
	Other	11	0	
	TOTAL	58	4	

TOP POINT EARNERS

	PLAYER	GAMES	AV PTS
1	Duffy	6	1.83
2	Gibson	5	1.20
3	King	21	1.10
4	Smith, J	25	1.00
5	Hay	15	1.00
6	McLeish	9	1.00
7	Johnson	22	0.95
8	Dowie	15	0.93
9	Deas	29	0.83
10	Millar, M	23	0.83
	CLUB AVERAGE:		0.75

TEAM OF THE SEASON

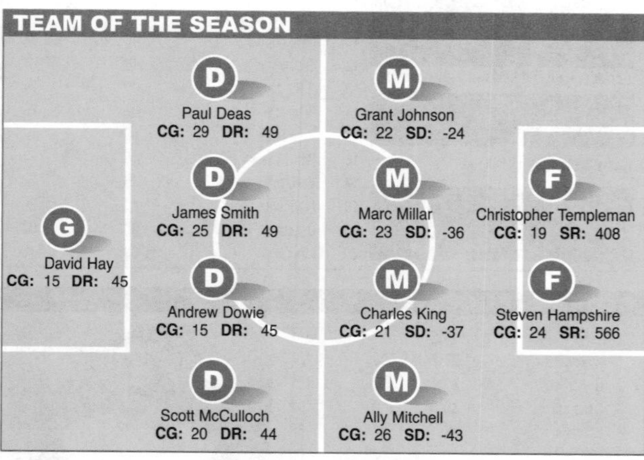
D
Paul Deas
CG: 29 DR: 49
M
Grant Johnson
CG: 22 SD: -24
D
James Smith
CG: 25 DR: 49
M
Marc Millar
CG: 23 SD: -36
F
Christopher Templeman
CG: 19 SR: 408
G
David Hay
CG: 15 DR: 45
D
Andrew Dowie
CG: 15 DR: 45
M
Charles King
CG: 21 SD: -37
F
Steven Hampshire
CG: 24 SR: 566
D
Scott McCulloch
CG: 20 DR: 44
M
Ally Mitchell
CG: 26 SD: -43

LEAGUE APPEARANCES AND BOOKINGS

	AGE (on 01/07/04)	IN NAMED 16	APPEARANCES	COUNTING GAMES	MINUTES ON PITCH	Yellow	Red
Goalkeepers							
Kevin Budinauckas	29	17	9	8	761	1	0
David Hay	24	32	18	15	1431	0	0
Derek Soutar	23	12	12	11	1048	0	0
Stephen Vanderdeyl	-	7	0	0	0	0	0
Defenders							
Gavin Beith	22	7	4	0	155	1	0
Iain Davidson	-	4	4	3	273	0	0
Paul Deas	32	34	32	29	2770	5	0
Andrew Dowie	21	15	15	15	1350	0	0
Marc McCulloch	24	10	7	3	330	1	0
Scott McCulloch	28	35	30	20	2090	5	0
James Smith	25	28	28	25	2404	2	0
David White	36	30	28	25	2352	5	1
Midfielders							
Roddy Black	26	13	9	3	470	0	0
Colin Boylan	20	16	13	1	287	0	0
Derek Clark	27	16	7	2	316	2	0
Neil Jablonski	21	15	15	12	1135	2	0
Chris Jackson	30	1	1	1	90	1	0
Grant Johnson	32	25	25	22	1984	6	0
Charles King	24	33	33	21	2224	1	0
Kevin McLeish	23	24	20	9	1073	2	1
Marc Millar	35	24	24	23	2125	3	0
Greg Miller	28	14	13	2	404	1	0
Ally Mitchell	35	30	29	26	2407	5	1
Jay Stein	25	9	4	0	193	0	0
Craig Winter	28	10	10	9	811	1	0
Forwards							
Darryl Duffy	-	8	8	6	617	2	0
Kevin Fotheringham	28	12	12	9	847	7	0
Graham Gibson	-	28	27	5	1106	1	1
Steven Hampshire	24	27	27	24	2264	1	0
Dene Shields	21	2	2	0	57	0	0
Christopher Templeman	24	33	33	19	2039	3	0

SQUAD APPEARANCES

Match	1	2	3	4	5	6	7	8	9	10	11	12	13	14	15	16	17	18	19	20	21	22	23	24	25	26	27	28	29	30	31	32	33	34	35	36	37	38	39	40	41	42
Venue	H	A	H	H	A	A	A	H	H	H	A	H	A	A	A	H	A	H	H	A	H	A	A	H	A	A	H	H	A	H	A	H	A	A	H	H	A	H	A	H	A	H
Competition	O	L	O	L	L	L	W	L	L	W	L	L	L	L	W	L	L	L	L	L	L	L	L	L	L	O	L	L	L	L	L	L	L	L	L	L	L	L	L	L	L	L
Result	W	L	D	L	L	L	W	D	L	W	L	L	L	L	L	W	D	L	W	L	D	L	L	L	D	L	W	L	W	W	L	D	D	D	L	L	L	L	D	W	D	L

Goalkeepers
Kevin Budinauckas
David Hay
Derek Soutar
Stephen Vanderdeyl

Defenders
Gavin Beith
Iain Davidson
Paul Deas
Andrew Dowie
Marc McCulloch
Scott McCulloch
James Smith
David White

Midfielders
Roddy Black
Colin Boylan
Derek Clark
Neil Jablonski
Chris Jackson
Grant Johnson
Charles King
Kevin McLeish
Marc Millar
Greg Miller
Ally Mitchell
Jay Stein
Craig Winter

Forwards
Darryl Duffy
Kevin Fotheringham
Graham Gibson
Steven Hampshire
Dene Shields
Christopher Templeman

KEY: On all match · On bench · Subbed or sent off (Counting game) · Subbed or sent off (playing less than 70 minutes) · Subbed on from bench (Counting Game) · Subbed on (playing less than 70 minutes) · Subbed on and then subbed or sent off (Counting Game) · Subbed on and then subbed or sent off (playing less than 70 minutes) · Not in 16

SPANISH LEAGUE ROUND-UP

FINAL LEAGUE TABLE

		HOME					AWAY					TOTAL			
	P	W	D	L	F	A	W	D	L	F	A	F	A	DIF	PTS
Valencia	38	12	3	4	38	16	11	5	3	33	11	71	27	44	77
Barcelona	38	10	6	3	33	14	11	3	5	30	25	63	39	24	72
Deportivo	38	13	3	3	36	15	8	5	6	24	19	60	34	26	71
Real Madrid	38	13	2	4	43	26	8	5	6	29	28	72	54	18	70
Athl Bilbao	38	10	5	4	32	20	5	6	8	21	29	53	49	4	56
Seville	38	12	2	5	30	15	3	8	8	26	30	56	45	11	55
Atl Madrid	38	11	5	3	30	17	4	5	10	21	36	51	53	-2	55
Villarreal	38	10	5	4	28	19	5	4	10	19	30	47	49	-2	54
Real Betis	38	6	9	4	22	20	7	4	8	24	23	46	43	3	52
Malaga	38	10	4	5	35	27	5	2	12	15	28	50	55	-5	51
Mallorca	38	7	5	7	29	32	8	1	10	25	34	54	66	-12	51
Osasuna	38	6	7	6	24	24	5	8	6	14	13	38	37	1	48
Real Zaragoza	38	7	7	5	25	20	6	2	11	21	35	46	55	-9	48
Albacete	38	9	2	8	25	21	4	6	9	15	27	40	48	-8	47
Real Sociedad	38	7	7	5	24	22	4	6	9	25	31	49	53	-4	46
R Santander	38	5	4	10	23	32	6	6	7	25	31	48	63	-15	43
Espanyol	38	8	2	9	24	26	5	2	12	24	38	48	64	-16	43
Valladolid	38	7	6	6	25	23	3	5	11	21	33	46	56	-10	41
Celta Vigo	38	4	4	11	16	38	5	8	6	32	30	48	68	-20	39
Murcia	38	5	7	7	21	25	0	4	15	8	32	29	57	-28	26

CLUB STRIKE FORCE

RONALDO
9
SIEMENS
mobile

Ronaldo, Raul and Beckham -top scorers

1 Real Madrid

Goals scored in the League	72
Club Strike Rate (CSR) Average number of minutes between League goals scored by club	48

	CLUB	GOALS	CSR
1	Real Madrid	72	48
2	Valencia	71	48
3	Barcelona	63	54
4	Deportivo	60	57
5	Seville	56	61
6	Mallorca	54	63
7	Athl Bilbao	53	65
8	Atl Madrid	51	67
9	Malaga	50	68
10	Real Sociedad	49	70
11	Celta Vigo	48	71
12	Espanyol	48	71
13	R Santander	48	71
14	Villarreal	47	73
15	Real Betis	46	74
16	Real Zaragoza	46	74
17	Valladolid	46	74
18	Albacete	40	86
19	Osasuna	38	90
20	Murcia	29	118

CLUB DISCIPLINARY RECORDS

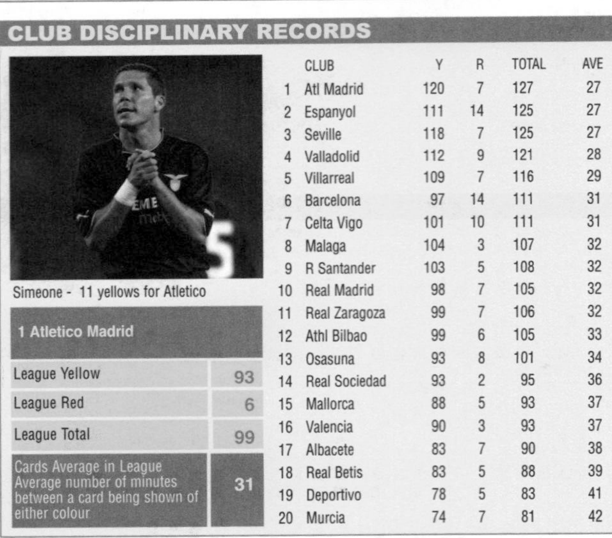

Simeone - 11 yellows for Atletico

1 Atletico Madrid

League Yellow	93
League Red	6
League Total	99
Cards Average in League Average number of minutes between a card being shown of either colour	31

	CLUB	Y	R	TOTAL	AVE
1	Atl Madrid	120	7	127	27
2	Espanyol	111	14	125	27
3	Seville	118	7	125	27
4	Valladolid	112	9	121	28
5	Villarreal	109	7	116	29
6	Barcelona	97	14	111	31
7	Celta Vigo	101	10	111	31
8	Malaga	104	3	107	32
9	R Santander	103	5	108	32
10	Real Madrid	98	7	105	32
11	Real Zaragoza	99	7	106	32
12	Athl Bilbao	99	6	105	33
13	Osasuna	93	8	101	34
14	Real Sociedad	93	2	95	36
15	Mallorca	88	5	93	37
16	Valencia	90	3	93	37
17	Albacete	83	7	90	38
18	Real Betis	83	5	88	39
19	Deportivo	78	5	83	41
20	Murcia	74	7	81	42

CLUB DEFENCES

	CLUB	LGE	CS	CDR
1	Valencia	27	20	127
2	Deportivo	34	17	101
3	Osasuna	37	9	92
4	Barcelona	39	13	88
5	Real Betis	43	10	80
6	Seville	45	11	76
7	Albacete	48	11	71
8	Athl Bilbao	49	9	70
9	Villarreal	49	10	70
10	Atl Madrid	53	11	65
11	Real Sociedad	53	7	65
12	Real Madrid	54	5	63
13	Malaga	55	8	62
14	Real Zaragoza	55	9	62
15	Valladolid	56	9	61
16	Murcia	57	5	60
17	R Santander	63	7	54
18	Espanyol	64	8	53
19	Mallorca	66	7	52
20	Celta Vigo	68	8	50

Carboni defending for Valencia

1 Valencia

Goals conceded in the League	27
Clean Sheets (CS) Number of league games where no goals were conceded	20
Club Defensive Rate (CDR) Average number of minutes between League goals conceded by club	127

PLAYER NATIONALITIES

Overseas country with the most player appearances in the Spanish League - Argentina — 1229 league appearances by Argentinean players

	COUNTRY	PLAYERS	IN SQUAD	LGE APP	% LGE ACT	CAPS	MOST APP	APP
1	Spain	429	9026	6666	63.4	129	Jose Reina	100.0
2	Argentina	56	1483	1229	12.1	30	Albano Bizzarri	98.7
3	Brazil	29	703	615	5.9	29	Alvaro	92.7
4	Uruguay	18	417	317	2.8	28	G De Los Santos	78.1
5	Holland	11	310	269	2.5	56	Phillip Cocu	88.8
6	France	10	227	209	2.2	6	Cyril Domoraud	88.7
7	Portugal	7	216	197	2.0	16	Jorge Andrade	97.4
8	Serbia & M'tenegro	9	194	161	1.4	8	Savo Milosevic	86.3
9	Italy	3	98	82	0.9	0	Amadeo Carboni	85.8
10	Cameroon	3	68	59	0.6	5	Samuel Eto'o	83.4
11	Russia	2	64	62	0.6		Valeri Karpin	93.7
12	Turkey	3	91	57	0.6		Kahveci Nihat	75.7
13	Israel	3	102	63	0.5		Yossi Benayoun	76.3
14	England	1	31	31	0.4	7	David Beckham	78.6
15	Morocco	2	34	32	0.3		Noureddine Naybet	41.1
16	Belgium	1	30	29	0.3	2	Erwin Lemmens	75.9
17	Norway	1	34	29	0.3		Bjorn Tore Kvarme	75.0
18	Australia	1	33	33	0.3	0	John Aloisi	70.8
19	Paraguay	2	36	31	0.3		Delio Cesar Toledo	53.5
20	Romania	3	50	32	0.3		Catalin Munteanu	41.1

CLUB MAKE-UP – HOME AND OVERSEAS PLAYERS

1 Celta Vigo — 64.2% of appearances by overseas players

	CLUB	OVERSEAS	HOME	% OVERSEAS	% LGE ACT	MOST APP	APP
1	Celta Vigo	16	15	51.6	64.2	Savo Milosevic	86.3
2	Espanyol	14	21	40.0	56.9	Cyril Domoraud	88.7
3	Barcelona	13	20	39.4	56.2	Phillip Cocu	88.8
4	Real Zaragoza	8	21	27.6	48.3	Luiz Maior Alvaro	92.7
5	Real Sociedad	8	24	25.0	47.9	Valeri Karpin	93.7
6	Atl Madrid	13	21	38.2	44.8	Matias Lequi	89.5
7	Mallorca	11	19	36.7	43.6	Leonardo Franco	84.8
8	Real Madrid	7	25	21.9	43.3	Luis Figo	85.2
9	Villarreal	7	24	22.6	37.7	M Arruabarrena	85.7
10	Valladolid	11	16	40.7	37.0	Benjamin Bizzarri	98.7
11	Murcia	11	26	29.7	36.1	Jose Luis Acciari	85.0
12	R Santander	10	15	40.0	33.1	Mehdi Nafti	76.5
13	Deportivo	9	19	32.1	33.0	Jorge Andrade	97.4
14	Malaga	7	20	25.9	30.3	Carlos Litos	83.1
15	Valencia	9	20	31.0	30.1	Amadeo Carboni	85.8
16	Albacete	8	26	23.5	25.5	Laurent Viaud	80.6
17	Seville	8	26	23.5	23.3	Julio Baptista	74.0
18	Osasuna	7	18	28.0	21.2	John Aloisi	70.8
19	Real Betis	5	23	17.9	19.4	Alejandro Lembo	75.0
20	Athl Bilbao	0	30	0.0	0.0	N/A	N/A

CHART-TOPPING MIDFIELDERS

3 Albelda of Valencia

1 Jorge Lopez - Valencia	
Goals scored in the League	4
Defensive Rating Av number of mins between League goals conceded while on the pitch	148
Contribution to Attacking Power Average number of minutes between League team goals while on pitch	52
Scoring Difference Defensive Rating minus Contribution to Attacking Power	96

	PLAYER	CLUB	GOALS	DEF RATE	POWER	S DIFF
1	Jorge Lopez	Valencia	4	148	52	96
2	Mauro Silva	Deportivo	0	141	51	90
3	Albelda	Valencia	1	130	45	85
4	Baraja	Valencia	8	125	44	81
5	Victor	Deportivo	7	97	55	42
6	Xavi	Barcelona	4	91	53	38
7	Sergio	Deportivo	3	100	63	37
8	Valeron	Deportivo	3	90	58	32
9	Cocu	Barcelona	5	82	51	31
10	Van Bronckhorst	Barcelona	1	86	55	31
11	Alkiza	Real Sociedad	0	81	51	30
12	Baptista	Seville	20	84	56	28
13	Zidane	Real Madrid	6	72	46	26
14	Moha	Osasuna	2	100	80	20
15	Beckham	Real Madrid	3	66	47	19

CHART-TOPPING GOALSCORERS

1 Ronaldo - Real Madrid	
Goals scored in the League	24
Contribution to Attacking Power (AP) Average number of minutes between League team goals while on pitch	43
Club Strike Rate (CSR) Average minutes between League goals scored by club	46
Player Strike Rate Average number of minutes between League goals scored by player	127

	PLAYER	CLUB	GOALS: LGE	POWER	CSR	S RATE
1	Ronaldo	Real Madrid	24	43	46	127
2	Baptista	Seville	20	56	61	127
3	Mista	Valencia	19	49	48	127
4	Tamudo	Espanyol	19	65	71	131
5	Torres	Atl Madrid	19	66	67	157
6	Salva	Malaga	18	66	68	159
7	Saviola	Barcelona	14	49	54	162
8	Eto'o	Mallorca	17	63	63	168
9	Ronaldinho	Barcelona	15	52	54	178
10	Anderson	Villarreal	12	64	73	183
11	Nihat	Real Sociedad	14	68	70	185
12	Yeste	Athl Bilbao	11	62	65	187
13	Villa	Real Zaragoza	17	75	74	194
14	Guerrero	R Santander	11	80	71	219
15	Milosevic	Celta Vigo	13	70	71	227

CHART-TOPPING DEFENDERS

1 Marchena - Valencia	
Goals Conceded in the League The number of League goals conceded while he was on the pitch	15
Clean Sheets In games when he played at least 70 mins	17
Club Defensive Rating Average mins between League goals conceded by the club this season	127
Defensive Rating Average number of minutes between League goals conceded while on pitch	170

	PLAYER	CLUB	CON: LGE	CS	CDR	DEF RATE
1	Marchena	Valencia	15	17	127	170
2	Carboni	Valencia	21	18	127	140
3	Oleguer	Barcelona	12	8	88	130
4	Curro Torres	Valencia	20	14	127	122
5	Capdevila	Deportivo	20	13	101	117
6	Ayala	Valencia	24	14	127	112
7	Reiziger	Barcelona	24	11	88	104
8	Andrade	Deportivo	34	16	101	98
9	Cruchaga	Osasuna	31	9	92	98
10	Lopez	Osasuna	32	8	92	97
11	Izquierdo	Osasuna	33	9	92	95
12	Josetxo	Osasuna	31	7	92	91
13	Puyol	Barcelona	26	8	88	90
14	Luis Fernandez	Real Betis	20	7	80	88
15	Baudes	Albacete	24	8	71	83

CHART-TOPPING GOALKEEPERS

1 Canizares - Valencia	
Counting Games Games where he played at least 70 minutes	37
Goals Conceded The number of League goals conceded while he was on the pitch	25
Clean Sheets In games when he played at least 70 mins	15
Defensive Rating Average number of minutes between League goals conceded while on pitch	133

	PLAYER	CLUB	CG	Conc	CS	DEF RATE
1	Canizares	Valencia	33	25	15	133
2	Molina	Deportivo	33	30	15	99
3	Sanzol	Osasuna	34	32	9	96
4	Victor	Barcelona	33	31	13	94
5	Contreras	Real Betis	22	25	8	79
6	Esteban	Seville	30	34	9	79
7	Almunia	Albacete	24	28	8	77
8	Aranzubia	Athl Bilbao	34	43	8	71
9	Reina	Villarreal	38	49	10	70
10	Casillas	Real Madrid	36	48	5	68
11	Arnau	Malaga	22	29	5	66
12	Alberto	Real Sociedad	18	25	2	65
13	Westerveld	Real Sociedad	20	28	5	64
14	Bizzarri	Valladolid	38	53	9	64
15	Juanmi	Murcia	18	26	4	62

PLAYER DISCIPLINARY RECORD

1 Motta - Barcelona	
Cards Average mins between cards	85
League Yellow	9
League Red	3
TOTAL	12

	PLAYER		LY	LR	TOT	AVE
1	Motta	Barcelona	9	3	12	85
2	Torrado	Seville	4	1	5	105
3	Generelo	Real Zaragoza	7	1	8	106
4	Lopo	Espanyol	19	3	22	123
5	Alfredo	Osasuna	5	1	6	124
6	Guti	Real Madrid	11	1	12	130
7	Alex	Espanyol	9	0	9	133
8	Battaglia	Villarreal	7	1	8	137
9	Quaresma	Barcelona	6	1	7	145
10	Alvarez	Villarreal	15	2	17	147
11	Mejia	Real Madrid	4	1	5	148
12	Carreras	Murcia	6	1	7	152
13	Jose Mari	Villarreal	14	2	16	152
14	Gerard	Barcelona	7	1	8	154
15	Mendez	Celta Vigo	6	0	6	157
16	Alkiza	Real Sociedad	11	0	11	161
17	DSantos	Atl Madrid	16	0	16	166
18	Nagore	Mallorca	7	0	7	168
19	Solari	Real Madrid	8	1	9	168
20	Juanfran	Celta Vigo	10	0	10	169
21	Giovanella	Celta Vigo	5	0	5	171
22	Tais	Real Betis	3	1	4	172
23	Alves	Seville	14	0	14	172
24	Simeone	Atl Madrid	11	0	11	173

TEAM OF THE SEASON

G
Canizares : Valencia
CG: 33 DR: 133

D
Marchena : Valencia
CG: 26 DR: 127

D
Oleguer : Barcelona
CG: 17 DR: 130

D
Capdevila : Deportivo
CG: 26 DR: 117

D
Cruchago : Osasuna
CG: 33 DR: 98

M
Jorge Lopez : Valencia
CG: 20 SD: + 96

M
Mauro Silva : Deportivo
CG: 23 SD: + 90

M
Xavi : Barcelona
CG: 32 SD: + 38

M
Akiza : Real Sociedad
CG: 17 SD: + 30

F
Ronaldo : R Madrid
CG: 29 SR: 127

F
Mista : Valencia
CG: 24 AP: 49

SPANISH PRIMEIRA LIGA CHAMPIONS

VALENCIA

Final Position: **1st**

KEY: Won / Drawn / Lost

							Attendance
1	lge	Valladolid	H	D	1-1	Aimar 77	45,000
2	lge	Osasuna	A	W	1-0	Baraja 50	14,195
3	lge	Malaga	H	W	1-0	Marchena 44	45,000
4	lge	Atl Madrid	A	W	3-0	Vicente 69; Mista 77,90	55,000
5	uc1rl1	AIK Solna	A	W	1-0	Oliveira 64	25,433
6	lge	Real Madrid	H	W	2-0	Mista 5; Oliveira 71	53,000
7	lge	Barcelona	A	W	1-0	Oliveira 15	98,000
8	uc1rl2	AIK Solna	H	W	1-0	Mista 70	20,000
9	lge	Espanyol	H	W	4-0	Mista 9,45; Baraja 45; Vicente 80	44,000
10	lge	Deportivo	A	L	1-2	Mista 73	27,500
11	lge	Celta Vigo	H	D	2-2	Aimar 42; Canobbio 68	50,000
12	lge	Mallorca	A	W	5-0	Jorge Lopez 3 pen; Oliveira 7,45,77; Xisco 89	21,500
13	uc2rl1	Maccabi Haifa	H	D	0-0		53,000
14	lge	R Santander	H	L	1-2	Baraja 25	52,500
15	lge	Murcia	A	D	2-2	Mista 12,54	11,500
16	lge	Real Zaragoza	H	W	3-2	Jorge Lopez 20; Vicente 27; Aimar 45	48,000
17	lge	Real Sociedad	A	D	0-0		21,500
18	lge	Athl Bilbao	H	W	2-1	Vicente 18,65	50,000
19	uc2rl2	Maccabi Haifa	A	W	4-0	Mista 11; Baraja 24; Albelda 90; Angulo 90	2,333
20	lge	Real Betis	A	W	1-0	Juanito 19 og	40,000
21	lge	Seville	H	W	1-0	Mista 61	48,000
22	lge	Villarreal	H	W	4-2	Baraja 57,73; Aimar 58; Mista 88	52,000
23	lge	Albacete	A	W	1-0	Jorge Lopez 9 pen	12,500
24	lge	Valladolid	A	D	0-0		13,000
25	lge	Osasuna	H	L	0-1		47,500
26	lge	Malaga	A	W	6-1	Mista 5; Oliveira 13,59,66; Marchena 48; Albelda 73	23,000
27	lge	Atl Madrid	H	W	3-0	Mista 31,70; Vicente 67	50,000
28	lge	Real Madrid	A	D	1-1	Ayala 74	78,000
29	lge	Barcelona	H	L	0-1		48,000
30	uc3rl1	Besiktas	H	W	3-2	Sissoko 25; Canobbio 43; Navarro 90	34,450
31	lge	Espanyol	A	L	1-2	Mista 78	16,500
32	uc3rl2	Besiktas	A	W	2-0	Angulo 12; Sanchez 57	20,800
33	lge	Deportivo	H	W	3-0	Vicente 22 pen,90; Sanchez 90	44,000
34	uc4rl1	Genclerbirligi	A	L	0-1		30,000
35	lge	Celta Vigo	A	W	2-0	Rufete 39,90	26,076
36	lge	Mallorca	H	W	5-1	Mista 45,68,69; Baraja 57; Angulo 61	47,700
37	uc4rl2	Genclerbirligi	H	W	2-0	Mista 63; Vicente 94	37,100
38	lge	R Santander	A	W	3-0	Ayoze 8 og; Albiol 45; Vicente 75	13,781
39	lge	Murcia	H	W	2-0	Pellegrino 73; Mista 82	40,000
40	ucqfl1	Bordeaux	A	W	2-1	Baraja 75; Rufete 88	29,108
41	lge	Real Zaragoza	A	W	1-0	Angulo 71	34,000
42	ucqfl2	Bordeaux	H	W	2-1	Pellegrino 52; Rufete 60	42,400
43	lge	Real Sociedad	H	D	2-2	Vicente 72; Mista 90	45,000
44	ucsfl1	Villarreal	A	D	0-0		16,800
45	lge	Athl Bilbao	A	D	1-1	Jorge Lopez 13 pen	36,000
46	lge	Real Betis	H	W	2-0	Curro Torres 36; Baraja 49	45,000
47	ucsfl2	Villarreal	H	W	1-0	Mista 16 pen	53,000
48	lge	Seville	A	W	2-0	Vicente 12; Baraja 89	38,000
49	lge	Villarreal	A	L	1-2	Pellegrino 35	12,000
50	ucfin	Marseille	A	W	2-0	Vicente 45 pen; Mista 57	40,000
51	lge	Albacete	H	L	0-1		49,000

MONTHLY POINTS TALLY

Month	Points	%
AUGUST	1	33%
SEPTEMBER	12	100%
OCTOBER	7	58%
NOVEMBER	7	58%
DECEMBER	10	83%
JANUARY	10	67%
FEBRUARY	4	33%
MARCH	12	100%
APRIL	8	67%
MAY	6	50%

LEAGUE GOALS

	PLAYER	MINS	GOALS	AVE
1	Mista	2411	19	127
2	Vicente	2624	11	239
3	Baraja	2615	8	327
4	Oliveira	1143	8	143
5	Jorge Lopez	1930	4	483
6	Aimar	1628	4	407
7	Rufete	1437	2	719
8	Marchena	2556	2	1278
9	Pellegrino	1476	2	738
10	Angulo	1181	2	591
11	Xisco	722	1	722
12	Canobbio	432	1	432
13	Curro Torres	2435	1	2435
	Other		6	
	TOTAL		71	

KEY PLAYERS - GOALSCORERS

Miguel Angel Ferrer 'Mista'

Goals in the League	19
Contribution to Attacking Power Average number of minutes between League team goals while on pitch	49
Player Strike Rate The total number of minutes he was on the pitch for every League goal scored	127
Club Strike Rate Average number of minutes between League goals scored by club	48

	PLAYER	GOALS LGE	POWER	S RATE
1	Miguel Angel Ferrer 'Mista'	19	49	127 mins
2	Rodriguez Guillen Vicente	11	52	239 mins
3	Ruben Vegas Baraja	8	44	327 mins
4	Pablo Aimar	4	54	407 mins

KEY PLAYERS - MIDFIELDERS

Montana Jorge Lopez

2 David Aliques Albelda

Goals in the League	4
Defensive Rating Average number of mins between League goals conceded while on the pitch	148
Contribution to Attacking Power Average number of minutes between League team goals while on pitch	52
Scoring Difference Defensive Rating minus Contribution to Attacking Power	96

	PLAYER	GOALS LGE	DEF RATE	ATT POWER	SCORE DIFF
1	Montana Jorge Lopez	4	148	52	96 mins
2	David Aliques Albelda	1	130	45	85 mins
3	Ruben Vegas Baraja	8	125	44	81 mins
4	Francisco Joaquin Perez Rufete	2	111	48	63 mins

KEY PLAYERS - DEFENDERS

Carlos Marchena

Goals Conceded in League	15
Clean Sheets In League games when he played at least 70 mins	17
Defensive Rating Ave number of mins between League goals conceded while on the pitch	170
Club Defensive Rating Average number of mins between League goals conceded by the club this season	127

	PLAYER	CON LGE	CLEAN SHEETS	DEF RATE
1	Carlos Marchena	15	17	170 mins
2	Amadeo Carboni	21	18	140 mins
3	Cristobal Emilio Curro Torres	20	14	122 mins
4	Roberto Fabian Ayala	24	14	112 mins

KEY GOALKEEPER

Santiago Ruiz Canizares

Goals Conceded in the League	25
Counting Games Games when he played at least 70 minutes	37
Clean Sheets In games when he played at least 70 mins	20
League minutes played Number of minutes played in league matches	3330
Defensive Rating Ave number of mins between League goals conceded while on the pitch	133

DISCIPLINARY RECORDS

	PLAYER	YELLOW	RED	AVE
1	Carboni	11	2	225
2	Xisco	3	0	240
3	Albelda	11	0	247
4	Garrido	4	0	278
5	Baraja	9	0	290
6	Marchena	8	0	319
7	Aimar	5	0	325
8	Navarro	2	0	369
9	Vicente	7	0	374
10	Ayala	6	1	383
11	Mista	5	0	482
12	Jorge Lopez	4	0	482
13	Sissoko	2	0	488
	Other	13	0	
	TOTAL	90	3	

TOP POINT EARNERS

	PLAYER	GAMES	AV PTS
1	Marchena	26	2.31
2	Jorge Lopez	20	2.30
3	Albelda	29	2.24
4	Mista	24	2.13
5	Carboni	33	2.12
6	Curro Torres	25	2.12
7	Canizares	37	2.08
8	Vicente	25	2.08
9	Baraja	25	2.04
10	Ayala	30	1.93
	CLUB AVERAGE:		2.03

LEAGUE APPEARANCES AND BOOKINGS

	AGE (on 01/07/04)	IN NAMED 18	APPEARANCES	COUNTING GAMES	MINUTES ON PITCH	YELLOW CARDS	RED CARDS	THIS SEASON	HOME COUNTRY
Goalkeepers									
Santiago Canizares	34	38	37	37	3330	3	0	7	Spain (3)
Andres Palop	30	28	0	0	0	0	0	-	Spain
David Rangel Pastor	24	10	1	1	90	0	0	-	Spain
Defenders									
Fabio Aurelio	24	3	2	0	40	0	0	-	Brazil
Roberto Ayala	31	31	30	30	2686	6	1	7	Argentina (5)
Amadeo Carboni	39	34	33	33	2936	11	2	-	Italy
Curro Torres	27	34	29	25	2435	4	0	-	Spain
Javier Garrido	25	29	15	10	1113	4	0	-	Spain
Carlos Marchena	25	36	31	26	2556	8	0	6	Spain (3)
David Navarro	24	24	12	7	739	2	0	-	Spain
Mauricio Pellegrino	32	33	21	14	1476	2	0	-	Argentina
Midfielders									
Pablo Aimar	24	26	25	15	1628	5	0	6	Argentina (5)
David Albelda	26	34	33	29	2727	11	0	6	Spain (3)
Ruben Baraja	28	36	35	25	2615	9	0	8	Spain (3)
Fabian Canobbio	24	25	11	2	432	0	0	-	Uruguay
Jaime Gavilan	20	1	0	0	0	0	0	-	Spain
Jorge Lopez	25	31	26	20	1930	4	0	-	Spain
Francisco Rufete	27	28	27	13	1437	2	0	-	Spain
Cesar Soriano	21	1	0	0	0	0	0	-	Spain
Forwards									
Miguel Albiol	22	0	0	0	0	0	0	-	Spain
Miguel Angulo	27	23	22	11	1181	2	0	-	Spain
Eduardo Borja	22	2	0	0	0	0	0	-	Spain
Angel Ferrer Mista	25	36	33	24	2411	5	0	-	Spain
Ricardo Oliveira	24	32	21	6	1143	0	0	-	Brazil
Juan Sanchez	32	18	10	1	363	0	0	-	Spain
Mohamed Sissoko	19	27	20	8	992	2	0	-	France
Rodriguez Vicente	22	36	33	25	2624	7	0	8	Spain (3)
Munoz Xisco	23	29	22	4	722	3	0	-	Spain

TEAM OF THE SEASON

G: Canizares — CG: 37 DR: 133

D: Marchena — CG: 26 DR: 170
D: Carboni — CG: 33 DR: 140
D: Curro Torres — CG: 25 DR: 122
D: Ayala — CG: 30 DR: 112

M: Jorge Lopez — CG: 20 SD: 96
M: Albelda — CG: 29 SD: 85
M: Baraja — CG: 25 SD: 81
M: Rufete — CG: 13 SD: 63

F: Mista — CG: 24 SR: 127
F: Vicente — CG: 25 SR: 239

SQUAD APPEARANCES

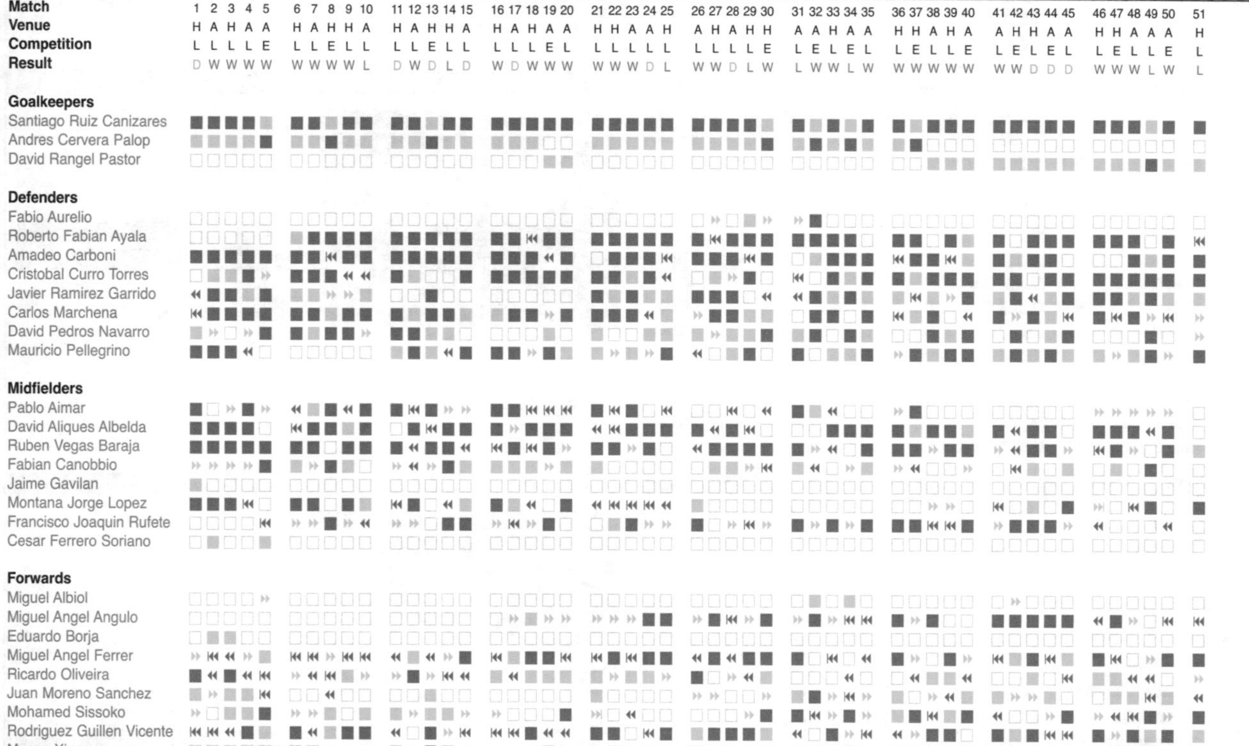

Match 1 2 3 4 5 6 7 8 9 10 11 12 13 14 15 16 17 18 19 20 21 22 23 24 25 26 27 28 29 30 31 32 33 34 35 36 37 38 39 40 41 42 43 44 45 46 47 48 49 50 51
Venue H A H A A H A H H A H A H H A H A H A A H H A A H A H A H H A A H A A H H A H A A H H A A H H A A A H
Competition L L L L E L L E L L L L E L L L L L E L L L L L L L L L L E L E L E L L E L L E L E L E L L E L L E L
Result D W W W W W W W W L D W D L D W D W W W W W W D L W W D L W L W W L W W W W W W W W D D D W W W L W L
Goalkeepers
Santiago Ruiz Canizares
Andres Cervera Palop
David Rangel Pastor
Defenders
Fabio Aurelio
Roberto Fabian Ayala
Amadeo Carboni
Cristobal Curro Torres
Javier Ramirez Garrido
Carlos Marchena
David Pedros Navarro
Mauricio Pellegrino
Midfielders
Pablo Aimar
David Aliques Albelda
Ruben Vegas Baraja
Fabian Canobbio
Jaime Gavilan
Montana Jorge Lopez
Francisco Joaquin Rufete
Cesar Ferrero Soriano
Forwards
Miguel Albiol
Miguel Angel Angulo
Eduardo Borja
Miguel Angel Ferrer
Ricardo Oliveira
Juan Moreno Sanchez
Mohamed Sissoko
Rodriguez Guillen Vicente
Munoz Xisco
KEY: On all match
On bench
Subbed or sent off (Counting game)
Subbed or sent off (playing less than 70 minutes)
Subbed on from bench (Counting Game)
Subbed on (playing less than 70 minutes)
Subbed on and then subbed or sent off (Counting Game)
Subbed on and then subbed or sent off (playing less than 70 minutes)
Not in 16

BARCELONA

Final Position: **2nd**

KEY: ☐ Won ☐ Drawn ☐ Lost

							Attendance
1	lge	Athl Bilbao	A	W	1-0	Cocu, P 12	41,000
2	lge	Seville	H	D	1-1	Ronaldinho 58	80,237
3	lge	Albacete	A	W	2-1	Cocu, P 2; Luis Enrique 69	17,000
4	lge	Osasuna	H	D	1-1	Ronaldinho 70	83,000
5	uc1rl1	Puchov	A	D	1-1	Kluivert 49	6,468
6	lge	Atl Madrid	A	D	0-0		56,000
7	lge	Valencia	H	L	0-1		98,000
8	uc1rl2	Puchov	H	W	8-0	Ronaldinho 6,20,57; Motta 40; Luis Enrique 63,75; Saviola 71,89	29,000
9	lge	Deportivo	H	L	0-2		68,000
10	lge	Mallorca	A	W	3-1	Saviola 10; Ronaldinho 21; Cocu, P 52	22,500
11	lge	Murcia	H	W	3-0	Saviola 38; Xavi 56; Ronaldinho 65	51,000
12	lge	Real Sociedad	A	D	3-3	Motta 34; Overmars 72; Gabri 81	29,000
13	uc2rl1	Panionios	A	W	3-0	Luis Garcia 43; Kluivert 47; Xavi 90	15,960
14	lge	Real Betis	H	W	2-1	Kluivert 42; Marquez 83	88,000
15	lge	Villarreal	A	L	1-2	Kluivert 72	20,000
16	uc2rl2	Panionios	H	W	2-0	Saviola 33; Luis Garcia 43	25,321
17	lge	Valladolid	H	D	0-0		91,000
18	lge	Malaga	A	L	1-5	Fernando Sanz 79 og	20,000
19	lge	Real Madrid	H	L	1-2	Kluivert 82	93,000
20	lge	Espanyol	A	W	3-1	Ronaldinho 10; Kluivert 20,35	35,000
21	lge	Celta Vigo	H	D	1-1	Cocu, P 70	78,000
22	lge	R Santander	A	L	0-3		22,000
23	lge	Real Zaragoza	H	W	3-0	Saviola 23; Ronaldinho 45 pen; Xavi 66	56,000
24	lge	Athl Bilbao	H	D	1-1	Kluivert 62	68,000
25	lge	Seville	A	W	1-0	Kluivert 31	43,000
26	lge	Albacete	H	W	5-0	Xavi 17; Saviola 50; Quaresma 53; Davids 55; Luis Enrique 90	78,000
27	lge	Osasuna	A	W	2-1	Saviola 44; Ronaldinho 76	19,000
28	lge	Atl Madrid	H	W	3-1	Saviola 11; Ronaldinho 24; Luis Garcia 43	95,000
29	lge	Valencia	A	W	1-0	Gerard 77	48,000
30	uc3rl1	Brondby	A	W	1-0	Ronaldinho 63	29,925
31	lge	Deportivo	A	W	3-2	Ronaldinho 25,48; Saviola 29	34,532
32	uc3rl2	Brondby	H	W	2-1	Luis Garcia 31; Cocu, P 43	44,100
33	lge	Mallorca	H	W	3-2	Luis Garcia 2,57; Luis Enrique 15	93,000
34	uc4rl1	Celtic	A	L	0-1		59,539
35	lge	Murcia	A	W	2-0	Saviola 5; Ronaldinho 62	17,000
36	lge	Real Sociedad	H	W	1-0	Ronaldinho 88	84,280
37	uc4rl2	Celtic	H	D	0-0		78,000
38	lge	Villarreal	H	D	0-0		50,000
39	lge	Valladolid	A	W	3-1	Saviola 2; Ronaldinho 31; Iniesta 85	17,000
40	lge	Real Betis	A	D	1-1	Saviola 5	48,825
41	lge	Malaga	H	W	3-0	Saviola 19; Luis Garcia 24; Cocu, P 35	48,000
42	lge	Real Madrid	A	W	2-1	Kluivert 59; Xavi 86	78,000
43	lge	Espanyol	H	W	4-1	Ronaldinho 35; Saviola 44,58; Van Bronckhorst 55	89,000
44	lge	Celta Vigo	A	L	0-1		27,000
45	lge	R Santander	H	W	1-0	Ronaldinho 15 pen	88,000
46	lge	Real Zaragoza	A	L	1-2	Saviola 10	34,500

MONTHLY POINTS TALLY

Month	Points	%
AUGUST	3	100%
SEPTEMBER	6	50%
OCTOBER	6	50%
NOVEMBER	5	42%
DECEMBER	4	33%
JANUARY	7	58%
FEBRUARY	15	100%
MARCH	9	100%
APRIL	11	73%
MAY	6	50%

LEAGUE GOALS

	PLAYER	MINS	GOALS	AVE
1	Ronaldinho	2673	15	178
2	Saviola	2262	14	162
3	Kluivert	1290	8	161
4	Cocu, P	3038	5	608
5	Xavi	3012	4	753
6	Luis Garcia	1637	4	409
7	Luis Enrique	1018	3	339
8	V Bronckhorst	3002	1	3002
9	Overmars	807	1	807
10	Gabri	1095	1	1095
11	Iniesta	500	1	500
12	Motta	1020	1	1020
13	Quaresma	1016	1	1016
	Other		4	
	TOTAL		63	

KEY PLAYERS - GOALSCORERS

Javier Saviola

Goals in the League	14
Contribution to Attacking Power Average number of minutes between League team goals while on pitch	49
Player Strike Rate The total number of minutes he was on the pitch for every League goal scored	162
Club Strike Rate Average number of minutes between League goals scored by club	54

	PLAYER	GOALS LGE	POWER	S RATE
1	Javier Saviola	14	49	162 mins
2	De Assis Moreira Ronaldinho	15	52	178 mins
3	Javier Sanz Luis Garcia	4	45	409 mins
4	Phillip Cocu	5	51	608 mins

KEY PLAYERS - MIDFIELDERS

Edgar Davids

Goals in the League	1
Defensive Rating Average number of mins between League goals conceded while on the pitch	120
Contribution to Attacking Power Average number of minutes between League team goals while on pitch	42
Scoring Difference Defensive Rating minus Contribution to Attacking Power	78

	PLAYER	GOALS LGE	DEF RATE	ATT POWER	SCORE DIFF
1	Edgar Davids	1	120	42	78 mins
2	Javier Sanz Luis Garcia	4	102	45	57 mins
3	Xavi Hernandez	4	91	53	38 mins
4	Giovanni Van Bronckhorst	1	86	55	31 mins

KEY PLAYERS - DEFENDERS

Presas Oleguer

Goals Conceded in League	12
Clean Sheets In League games when he played at least 70 mins	8
Defensive Rating Ave number of mins between League goals conceded while on the pitch	130
Club Defensive Rating Average number of mins between League goals conceded by the club this season	88

	PLAYER	CON LGE	CLEAN SHEETS	DEF RATE
1	Presas Oleguer	12	8	130 mins
2	Rafael Marquez	12	4	116 mins
3	Michael Reiziger	24	11	104 mins
4	Carlos Puyol	26	8	90 mins

KEY GOALKEEPER

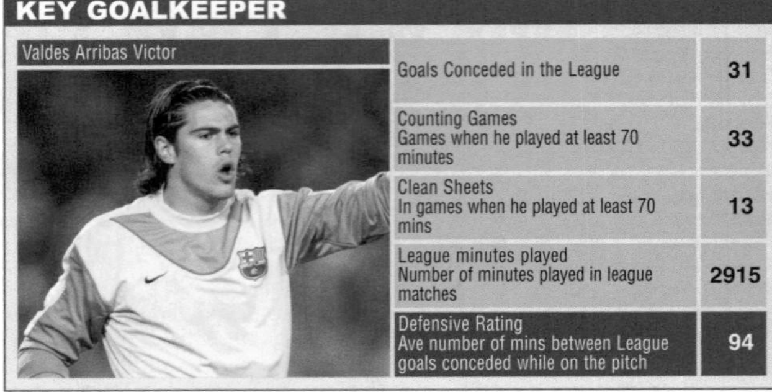

Valdes Arribas Victor

Goals Conceded in the League	31
Counting Games Games when he played at least 70 minutes	33
Clean Sheets In games when he played at least 70 mins	13
League minutes played Number of minutes played in league matches	2915
Defensive Rating Ave number of mins between League goals conceded while on the pitch	94

DISCIPLINARY RECORDS

	PLAYER	YELLOW	RED	AVE
1	Motta	9	3	85
2	Quaresma	6	1	145
3	Gerard	7	1	154
4	Davids	7	1	180
5	Gabri	5	1	182
6	Puyol	9	1	234
7	Ronaldinho	10	1	243
8	Luis Enrique	3	1	254
9	Marquez	4	1	278
10	Reiziger	6	0	415
11	Saviola	5	0	452
12	Van Bronckhorst	6	0	500
13	Cocu, P	4	2	506
	Other	16	1	
	TOTAL	97	14	

TOP POINT EARNERS

	PLAYER	GAMES	AV PTS
1	Davids	14	2.29
2	Oleguer	17	2.29
3	Luis Garcia	13	2.23
4	Reiziger	26	2.08
5	Xavi	32	1.97
6	Victor	32	1.97
7	Ronaldinho	28	1.96
8	Puyol	25	1.92
9	Cocu, P	32	1.91
10	Saviola	20	1.90
	CLUB AVERAGE:		1.89

TEAM OF THE SEASON

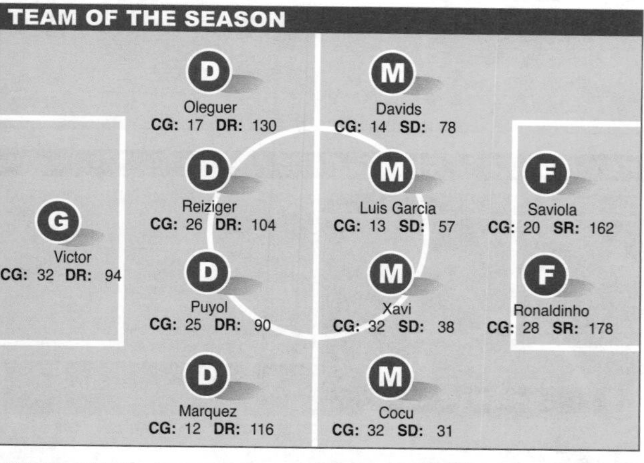

G
Victor
CG: 32 DR: 94
D
Oleguer
CG: 17 DR: 130
D
Reiziger
CG: 26 DR: 104
D
Puyol
CG: 25 DR: 90
D
Marquez
CG: 12 DR: 116
M
Davids
CG: 14 SD: 78
M
Luis Garcia
CG: 13 SD: 57
M
Xavi
CG: 32 SD: 38
M
Cocu
CG: 32 SD: 31
F
Saviola
CG: 20 SR: 162
F
Ronaldinho
CG: 28 SR: 178

LEAGUE APPEARANCES AND BOOKINGS

	AGE (on 01/07/04)	IN NAMED 18	APPEARANCES	COUNTING GAMES	MINUTES ON PITCH	YELLOW CARDS	RED CARDS	THIS SEASON	HOME COUNTRY
Goalkeepers									
Albert Jorquera	25	5	2	2	180	0	0	-	Spain
Ivan Martinez	-	1	0	0	0	0	0	-	Spain
Recber Rustu	31	34	4	3	326	1	0	-	Turkey
Valdes Victor	22	36	33	32	2915	3	1	-	Spain
Defenders									
Patrik Andersson	32	8	4	2	211	0	0	-	Sweden
Haro David Garcia	24	0	0	0	0	0	0	-	Spain
Rafael Marquez	25	32	22	12	1392	4	1	-	Mexico
Fernando Navarro	22	3	0	0	0	0	0	-	Spain
Presas Oleguer	24	20	18	17	1558	3	0	-	Spain
Oscar Lopez	24	23	7	3	402	1	0	-	Spain
Carlos Puyol	26	27	27	25	2343	9	1	6	Spain (3)
Michael Reiziger	31	35	30	26	2490	6	0	10	Holland (4)
Sergio Rodri	19	2	0	0	0	0	0	-	Spain
Midfielders									
Phillip Cocu	33	35	35	32	3038	4	2	10	Holland (4)
Edgar Davids	31	18	18	14	1442	7	1	9	Holland (4)
de la Torre Gabri	25	17	16	10	1095	5	1	1	Spain (3)
Lopez Segu Gerard	25	29	19	11	1232	7	1	-	Spain
Andres Lujan	20	24	10	3	500	0	0	-	Spain
Luis Enrique	34	33	24	6	1018	3	1	-	Spain
Javier Luis Garcia	26	28	25	13	1637	1	0	-	Spain
Pedro Mario	22	9	1	1	90	0	0	-	Spain
Thiago Motta	21	25	20	8	1020	9	3	3	Brazil (1)
Marc Overmars	31	28	20	5	807	0	0	10	Holland (4)
Ramon Ros	20	6	1	0	7	0	0	-	Spain
Sergio Garcia	21	6	4	2	209	0	0	-	Spain
Van Bronckhorst	29	34	34	32	3002	6	0	7	Holland (4)
Xavi Hernandez	24	38	36	32	3012	5	0	4	Spain (3)
Forwards									
Patrick Kluivert	28	25	21	12	1290	2	0	9	Holland (4)
Ricardo Quaresma	20	26	22	7	1016	6	1	-	Portugal
Oriol Riera	-	1	0	0	0	0	0	-	Spain
Ronaldinho	24	32	32	28	2673	10	1	5	Brazil (1)
Sergio Santamaria	23	5	4	0	146	0	0	-	Spain
Javier Saviola	22	36	33	20	2262	5	0	4	Argentina (5)

SQUAD APPEARANCES

Match	1	2	3	4	5	6	7	8	9	10	11	12	13	14	15	16	17	18	19	20	21	22	23	24	25	26	27	28	29	30	31	32	33	34	35	36	37	38	39	40	41	42	43	44	45	46
Venue	A	H	A	H	A	A	H	H	H	A	H	A	A	H	A	H	H	A	H	A	H	A	H	H	A	H	A	H	A	A	A	H	H	A	A	H	H	H	A	A	H	A	H	A	H	A
Competition	L	L	L	L	E	L	L	E	L	L	L	L	E	L	L	E	L	L	L	L	L	L	L	L	L	L	L	L	L	E	L	E	L	E	L	L	E	L	L	L	L	L	L	L	L	L
Result	W	D	W	D	D	D	L	W	L	W	W	D	W	W	L	W	D	L	L	W	D	L	W	D	W	W	W	W	W	W	W	W	W	L	W	W	D	D	W	D	W	W	W	L	W	L

Goalkeepers
Albert Jorquera
Ivan Ruben Martinez
Recber Rustu
Valdes Arribas Victor

Defenders
Patrik Andersson
Haro David Garcia
Rafael Marquez
Fernando Navarro
Presas Oleguer
Hernandez Oscar Lopez
Carlos Puyol
Michael Reiziger
Sergio Rodri

Midfielders
Phillip Cocu
Edgar Davids
Garcia de la Torre Gabri
Lopez Segu Gerard
Andres Iniesta Lujan
Martinez Luis Enrique
Javier Sanz Luis Garcia
Pedro Alvarez Mario
Thiago Motta
Marc Overmars
Ramon Ros
Sergio Garcia
Giovanni Van Bronckhorst
Xavi Hernandez

Forwards
Patrick Kluivert
Ricardo Quaresma
Oriol Riera
Ronaldinho
Sergio Santamaria
Javier Saviola

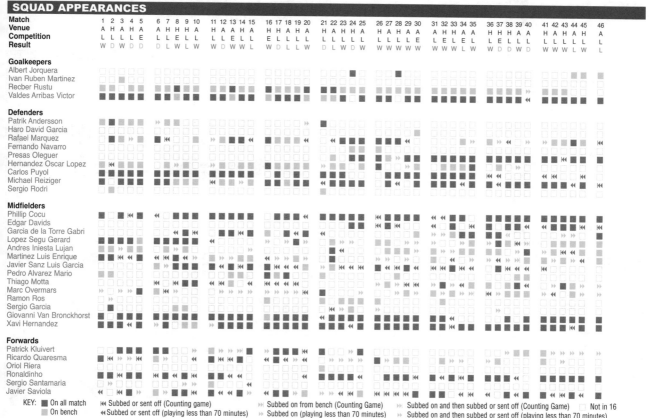

KEY: On all match | On bench | Subbed or sent off (Counting game) | Subbed or sent off (playing less than 70 minutes) | Subbed on from bench (Counting Game) | Subbed on (playing less than 70 minutes) | Subbed on and then subbed or sent off (Counting Game) | Subbed on and then subbed or sent off (playing less than 70 minutes) | Not in 16

DEPORTIVO LA CORUNA

Final Position: **3rd**

KEY: Won Drawn Lost

							Attendance
1	clql1	**Rosenborg BK**	A	D	0-0		21,100
2	clql2	**Rosenborg BK**	H	W	1-0		
3	lge	**Real Zaragoza**	A	W	1-0	Pandiani 66	32,000
4	lge	**Athl Bilbao**	H	W	2-0	Valeron 15; Pandiani 63	34,532
5	lge	**Seville**	A	W	2-1	Pandiani 39; Tristan 79	35,000
6	cl gc	**AEK Athens**	A	D	1-1	Pandiani 12	16,000
7	lge	**Albacete**	H	W	3-0	Naybet 50; Luque 52; Pandiani 90	25,000
8	lge	**Osasuna**	A	L	2-3	Luque 28; Pandiani 90	15,000
9	cl gc	**PSV Eindhoven**	H	W	2-0	Sergio 20; Pandiani 51 pen	28,480
10	lge	**Atl Madrid**	H	W	5-1	Fran 7; Romero 35; Sergio 52; Pandiani 57; Scaloni 90	28,000
11	lge	**Barcelona**	A	W	2-0	Luque 41; Sergio 71	68,000
12	cl gc	**Monaco**	H	W	1-0	Tristan 83	22,000
13	lge	**Valencia**	H	W	2-1	Valeron 15; Tristan 80	27,500
14	lge	**Mallorca**	H	L	0-2		23,000
15	lge	**Murcia**	A	D	0-0		10,500
16	cl gc	**Monaco**	A	L	3-8	Tristan 39,52; Scaloni 45	60,000
17	lge	**Real Sociedad**	H	W	2-1	Jauregui 72 og; Pandiani 87	29,000
18	lge	**Real Betis**	A	D	0-0		26,000
19	cl gc	**AEK Athens**	H	W	3-0	Hector 22; Valeron 51; Luque 71	30,260
20	lge	**Villarreal**	H	L	0-1		32,000
21	lge	**Valladolid**	A	D	1-1	Jonathan 50 og	20,000
22	lge	**Malaga**	H	W	1-0	Capdevila 59	24,000
23	cl gc	**PSV Eindhoven**	A	L	2-3	Luque 58; Pandiani 83	32,000
24	lge	**Real Madrid**	A	L	1-2	Pandiani 63	78,000
25	lge	**Espanyol**	H	W	2-1	Luque 45; Torricelli 65 og	27,000
26	lge	**Celta Vigo**	A	W	5-0	Luque 16; Victor 42,71,79; Tristan 86	25,000
27	lge	**R Santander**	H	D	1-1	Luque 41	28,000
28	lge	**Real Zaragoza**	H	W	4-1	Tristan 23,75; Valeron 50; Sergio 86	24,000
29	lge	**Athl Bilbao**	A	L	0-1		33,000
30	lge	**Seville**	H	W	1-0	Tristan 29 pen	31,000
31	lge	**Albacete**	A	W	2-0	Scaloni 60; Luque 62	12,500
32	lge	**Osasuna**	H	W	2-0	Victor 22,36	26,000
33	lge	**Atl Madrid**	A	D	0-0		40,000
34	clr1l1	**Juventus**	H	W	1-0	Luque 37	30,000
35	lge	**Barcelona**	H	L	2-3	Pandiani 51,56	34,532
36	lge	**Valencia**	A	L	0-3		44,000
37	clr1l2	**Juventus**	A	W	1-0	Pandiani 12	24,680
38	lge	**Mallorca**	A	L	2-4	Munitis 22; Djalminha 81	18,486
39	lge	**Murcia**	H	W	1-0	Capdevila 40	24,920
40	clqfl1	**AC Milan**	A	L	1-4	Pandiani 11	60,335
41	lge	**Real Sociedad**	A	W	2-1	Pandiani 10; Lopez Rekarte 90 og	25,600
42	lge	**Real Betis**	H	D	2-2	Luque 14; Victor 19	24,000
43	clqfl2	**AC Milan**	H	W	4-0	Pandiani 5; Valeron 35; Luque 44; Fran 76	30,260
44	lge	**Villarreal**	A	W	2-0	Pandiani 39; Tristan 90	15,000
45	lge	**Valladolid**	H	D	1-1	Djalminha 56 pen	27,000
46	clsfl1	**Porto**	A	D	0-0		50,818
47	lge	**Malaga**	A	D	1-1	Victor 21	21,000
48	lge	**Real Madrid**	H	W	2-0	Tristan 29; Capdevila 69	24,600
49	clsfl2	**Porto**	H	L	0-1		34,611
50	lge	**Espanyol**	A	L	0-2		40,300
51	lge	**Celta Vigo**	H	W	3-0	Silvinho 12 og; Pandiani 23; Munitis 24	29,000
52	lge	**R Santander**	A	W	1-0	Pandiani 23	17,000

MONTHLY POINTS TALLY

AUGUST	3	100%
SEPTEMBER	9	75%
OCTOBER	9	75%
NOVEMBER	5	42%
DECEMBER	7	58%
JANUARY	7	58%
FEBRUARY	10	67%
MARCH	6	50%
APRIL	6	50%
MAY	9	75%

LEAGUE GOALS

	PLAYER	MINS	GOALS	AVE
1	Pandiani	1535	12	128
2	Tristan	1854	8	232
3	Luque	2098	8	262
4	Victor	2128	7	304
5	Valeron	2602	3	867
6	Capdevila	2335	3	778
7	Sergio	2700	3	900
8	Scaloni	1438	2	719
9	Munitis	878	2	439
10	Djalminha	374	2	187
11	Fran	1399	1	1399
12	Naybet	1406	1	1406
13	Romero	1326	1	1326
	Other		7	
	TOTAL		60	

KEY PLAYERS - GOALSCORERS

Walter Gerardo Pandiani

Goals in the League	12
Contribution to Attacking Power Average number of minutes between League team goals while on pitch	42
Player Strike Rate The total number of minutes he was on the pitch for every League goal scored	128
Club Strike Rate Average number of minutes between League goals scored by club	57

	PLAYER	GOALS LGE	POWER	S RATE
1	Walter Gerardo Pandiani	12	42	128 mins
2	Herrera Diego Tristan	8	63	232 mins
3	Alberto Martos Luque	8	58	262 mins
4	Sanchez del Amo Victor	7	54	304 mins

KEY PLAYERS - MIDFIELDERS

Mauro Gomes da Silva

2 Sanchez del Amo Victor

Goals in the League	0
Defensive Rating Average number of mins between League goals conceded while on the pitch	141
Contribution to Attacking Power Average number of minutes between League team goals while on pitch	51
Scoring Difference Defensive Rating minus Contribution to Attacking Power	90

	PLAYER	GOALS LGE	DEF RATE	ATT POWER	SCORE DIFF
1	Mauro Gomes da Silva	0	141	51	90 mins
2	Sanchez del Amo Victor	7	97	55	42 mins
3	Gonzalez Soriano Sergio	3	100	63	37 mins
4	Juan Carlos Valeron	3	90	58	32 mins

KEY PLAYERS - DEFENDERS

Hector Berenguel Del Pino

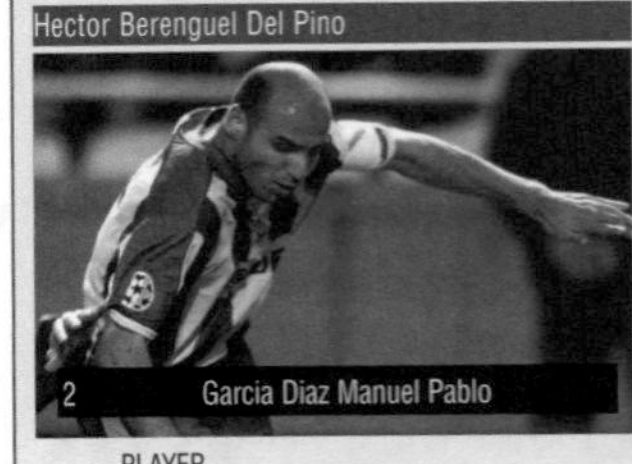

2 Garcia Diaz Manuel Pablo

Goals Conceded in League	11
Clean Sheets In League games when he played at least 70 mins	7
Defensive Rating Ave number of mins between League goals conceded while on the pitch	130
Club Defensive Rating Average number of mins between League goals conceded by the club this season	101

	PLAYER	CON LGE	CLEAN SHEETS	DEF RATE
1	Hector Berenguel Del Pino	11	7	130 mins
2	Garcia Diaz Manuel Pablo	11	6	128 mins
3	Joan Mendez Capdevila	20	13	117 mins
4	Enrique Fernandez Romero	13	6	102 mins

KEY GOALKEEPER

Francisco Molina

FADESA

Goals Conceded in the League	30
Counting Games Games when he played at least 70 minutes	33
Clean Sheets In games when he played at least 70 mins	15
League minutes played Number of minutes played in league matches	2970
Defensive Rating Ave number of mins between League goals conceded while on the pitch	99

DISCIPLINARY RECORDS

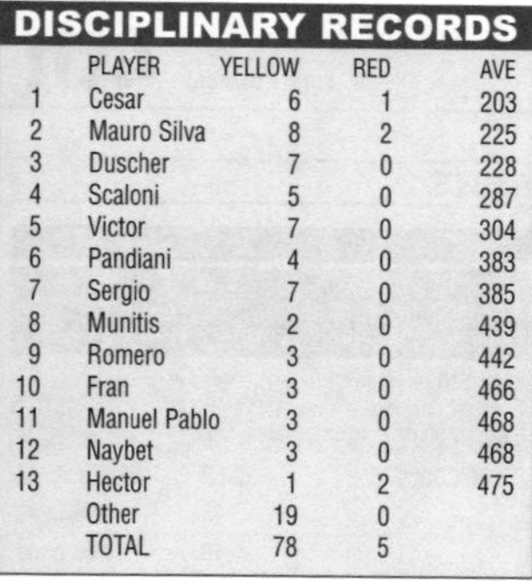

	PLAYER	YELLOW	RED	AVE
1	Cesar	6	1	203
2	Mauro Silva	8	2	225
3	Duscher	7	0	228
4	Scaloni	5	0	287
5	Victor	7	0	304
6	Pandiani	4	0	383
7	Sergio	7	0	385
8	Munitis	2	0	439
9	Romero	3	0	442
10	Fran	3	0	466
11	Manuel Pablo	3	0	468
12	Naybet	3	0	468
13	Hector	1	2	475
	Other	19	0	
	TOTAL	78	5	

TOP POINT EARNERS

	PLAYER	GAMES	AV PTS
1	Victor	19	2.21
2	Mauro Silva	23	2.09
3	Manuel Pablo	14	2.07
4	Pandiani	13	2.00
5	Romero	14	2.00
6	Naybet	16	1.94
7	Molina	33	1.91
8	Sergio	25	1.88
9	Duscher	15	1.87
10	Hector	15	1.87
	CLUB AVERAGE:		1.87

LEAGUE APPEARANCES AND BOOKINGS

	AGE (on 01/07/04)	IN NAMED 18	APPEARANCES	COUNTING GAMES	MINUTES ON PITCH	YELLOW CARDS	RED CARDS	THIS SEASON	HOME COUNTRY
Goalkeepers									
Miguel Garcia	33	0	0	0	0	0	0	-	Spain
Francisco Molina	33	35	33	33	2970	4	0	-	Spain
Gustavo Munua	26	36	5	5	444	1	0	7	Uruguay (25)
Jacques Songo'o	40	4	1	0	6	0	0	-	Cameroon
David Yanez	21	1	0	0	0	0	0	-	Spain
Defenders									
Jorge Andrade	26	37	37	37	3330	5	0	8	Portugal (20)
Joan Capdevila	26	35	27	26	2335	2	0	1	Spain (3)
Martin Villar Cesar	27	28	16	16	1424	6	1	3	Spain (3)
Hector Del Pino	29	25	17	15	1426	1	2	-	Spain
Manuel Pablo	28	34	18	14	1406	3	0	-	Spain
Noureddine Naybet	34	18	16	16	1406	3	0	-	Morocco
Pablo Amo	26	14	5	5	450	0	0	-	Spain
Enrique Romero	33	24	17	14	1326	3	0	1	Spain (3)
Lionel Scaloni	26	29	23	13	1438	5	0	-	Argentina
Midfielders									
Jose Amavisca	33	12	3	0	76	0	0	-	Spain
Djalminha	33	19	11	2	374	2	0	-	Brazil
Pedro Duscher	25	33	26	15	1596	7	0	-	Argentina
Javier Gonazales	34	34	31	7	1399	3	0	-	Spain
Fernandez Jaime	31	3	0	0	0	0	0	-	Spain
Mauro Silva	36	29	27	23	2252	8	2	-	Brazil
Gonzalez Sergio	27	37	37	25	2700	7	0	-	Spain
Juan Valeron	29	35	34	23	2602	1	0	7	Spain (3)
Sanchez Victor	28	32	31	19	2128	7	0	-	Spain
Forwards									
Munoz Ivan Perez	28	4	1	0	26	0	0	-	Spain
Alberto Luque	26	34	32	17	2098	3	0	4	Spain (3)
Pedro Munitis	29	27	21	6	878	2	0	-	Spain
Walter Pandiani	28	29	28	13	1535	4	0	-	Uruguay
Diego Tristan	28	35	33	14	1854	1	0	1	Spain (3)

TEAM OF THE SEASON

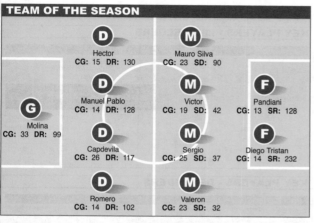

G Molina CG: 33 DR: 99

D Hector CG: 15 DR: 130

D Manuel Pablo CG: 14 DR: 128

D Capdevila CG: 26 DR: 117

D Romero CG: 14 DR: 102

M Mauro Silva CG: 23 SD: 90

M Victor CG: 19 SD: 42

M Sergio CG: 25 SD: 37

M Valeron CG: 23 SD: 32

F Pandiani CG: 13 SR: 128

F Diego Tristan CG: 14 SR: 232

SQUAD APPEARANCES

Match	1	2	3	4	5	6	7	8	9	10	11	12	13	14	15	16	17	18	19	20	21	22	23	24	25	26
Venue	A	H	A	H	A	A	H	A	H	H	A	H	H	H	A	A	H	A	H	H	A	H	A	A	H	A
Competition	C	C	L	L	L	C	L	L	C	L	L	C	L	L	L	C	L	L	C	L	L	L	C	L	L	L
Result	D	W	W	W	W	D	W	L	W	W	W	W	W	L	D	L	W	D	W	L	D	W	L	L	W	W

Match	27	28	29	30	31	32	33	34	35	36	37	38	39	40	41	42	43	44	45	46	47	48	49	50	51	52
Venue	H	H	A	H	A	H	A	H	H	A	A	A	H	A	A	H	H	A	H	A	A	H	H	A	H	A
Competition	L	L	L	L	L	L	L	C	L	L	C	L	L	C	L	L	C	L	L	C	L	L	C	L	L	L
Result	D	W	L	W	W	W	D	W	L	L	W	L	W	L	W	D	W	W	D	D	D	W	L	L	W	W

Goalkeepers
Juan Miguel Garcia Ingles
Francisco Molina
Gustavo Munua
Jacques Celestin Songo'o
David Lacorzana Yanez

Defenders
Jorge Manuel Andrade
Joan Mendez Capdevila
Martin Villar Cesar
Hector Del Pino
Garcia Diaz Manuel Pablo
Noureddine Naybet
Aguado Pablo Amo
Enrique Romero
Lionel Scaloni

Midfielders
Jose Emilio Amavisca
Djalma Dias Djalminha
Aldo Pedro Duscher
Javier Gonazales Fran
Sanchez Fernandez Jaime
Mauro Gomes da Silva
Gonzalez Soriano Sergio
Juan Carlos Valeron
Sanchez del Amo Victor

Forwards
Munoz Ivan Perez
Alberto Martos Luque
Pedro Munitis
Walter Gerardo Pandiani
Herrera Diego Tristan

KEY: On all match · On bench · Subbed or sent off (Counting game) · Subbed or sent off (playing less than 70 minutes) · Subbed on from bench (Counting Game) · Subbed on (playing less than 70 minutes) · Subbed on and then subbed or sent off (Counting Game) · Subbed on and then subbed or sent off (playing less than 70 minutes) · Not in 16

REAL MADRID

Final Position: **4th**

KEY: Won Drawn Lost

							Attendance
1	lge	Real Betis	H	W	2-1	Beckham 2; Ronaldo 61	76,000
2	lge	Villarreal	A	D	1-1	Nunez 85	21,000
3	lge	Valladolid	H	W	7-2	Julio Cesar 24 og; Raul 31,34,75; Zidane 54; Figo 58 pen; Ronaldo 69	70,000
4	cl gf	Marseille	H	W	4-2	Roberto Carlos 29; Ronaldo 34,57; Figo 61 pen	65,000
5	lge	Malaga	A	W	3-1	Ronaldo 14; Beckham 74; Guti 87	23,000
6	lge	Valencia	A	L	0-2		53,000
7	cl gf	Porto	A	W	3-1	Helguera 28; Solari 37; Zidane 67	37,506
8	lge	Espanyol	H	W	2-1	Ronaldo 53,83	76,000
9	lge	Celta Vigo	A	W	2-0	Ronaldo 25; Roberto Carlos 66	26,000
10	cl gf	Partizan	H	W	1-0	Raul 38	72,485
11	lge	R Santander	H	W	3-1	Zidane 28; Raul 80,90	68,000
12	lge	Real Zaragoza	A	D	0-0		33,000
13	lge	Athl Bilbao	H	W	3-0	Ronaldo 34,55; Figo 71	76,000
14	cl gf	Partizan	A	D	0-0		32,700
15	lge	Seville	A	L	1-4	Ronaldo 54	45,000
16	lge	Albacete	H	W	2-1	Beckham 37; Zidane 81	76,000
17	cl gf	Marseille	A	W	2-1	Beckham 35; Ronaldo 73	59,000
18	lge	Osasuna	A	D	1-1	Ronaldo 74	20,000
19	lge	Atl Madrid	H	W	2-0	Ronaldo 1; Raul 20	78,000
20	lge	Barcelona	A	W	2-1	Roberto Carlos 37; Ronaldo 74	93,000
21	cl gf	Porto	H	D	1-1	Solari 9	49,595
22	lge	Deportivo	H	W	2-1	Ronaldo 45; Raul 85	78,000
23	lge	Mallorca	A	W	3-1	Raul 45; Ronaldo 55; Figo 68 pen	23,000
24	lge	Murcia	H	W	1-0	Raul 8	75,000
25	lge	Real Sociedad	A	L	0-1		32,000
26	lge	Real Betis	A	D	1-1	Ronaldo 59	49,000
27	lge	Villarreal	H	W	2-1	Solari 14; Ronaldo 54	70,000
28	lge	Valladolid	A	W	3-2	Ronaldo 48,90; Figo 62 pen	25,000
29	lge	Malaga	H	W	2-1	Ronaldo 24; Roberto Carlos 59	35,000
30	lge	Valencia	H	D	1-1	Figo 90 pen	78,000
31	lge	Espanyol	A	W	4-2	Ronaldo 26 pen,69; Roberto Carlos 52; Raul Bravo 66	46,000
32	clr1l1	Bayern Munich	A	D	1-1	Roberto Carlos 83	59,000
33	lge	Celta Vigo	H	W	4-2	Ronaldo 54; Zidane 64,90; Figo 71	72,000
34	lge	R Santander	A	D	1-1	Solari 29	22,000
35	clr1l2	Bayern Munich	H	W	1-0	Zidane 32	75,000
36	lge	Real Zaragoza	H	D	1-1	Portillo 28	90,000
37	lge	Athl Bilbao	A	L	2-4	Raul 46,61	30,000
38	clqfl1	Monaco	H	W	4-2	Helguera 52; Zidane 70; Figo 77; Ronaldo 81	70,000
39	lge	Seville	H	W	5-1	Solari 6; Ronaldo 45,90; Zidane 64; Salgado 75	65,000
40	lge	Albacete	A	W	2-1	Roberto Carlos 20,71	17,000
41	clqfl2	Monaco	A	L	1-3	Raul 36	18,000
42	lge	Osasuna	H	L	0-3		55,000
43	lge	Atl Madrid	A	W	2-1	Solari 5; Helguera 78	55,000
44	lge	Barcelona	H	L	1-2	Solari 54	78,000
45	lge	Deportivo	A	L	0-2		24,600
46	lge	Mallorca	H	L	2-3	Pavon 17; Figo 51 pen	55,000
47	lge	Murcia	A	L	1-2	Guti 89	15,668
48	lge	Real Sociedad	H	L	1-4	Figo 40 pen	50,000

MONTHLY POINTS TALLY

AUGUST	3	100%
SEPTEMBER	7	58%
OCTOBER	10	83%
NOVEMBER	7	58%
DECEMBER	12	100%
JANUARY	7	58%
FEBRUARY	13	87%
MARCH	5	42%
APRIL	6	50%
MAY	0	0%

KEY PLAYERS - GOALSCORERS

Ronaldo Luiz Nazario de Lima

Goals in the League	24	Player Strike Rate Average number of minutes between League goals scored by player	106
Contribution to Attacking Power Average number of minutes between League team goals while on pitch	43	Club Strike Rate Average number of minutes between League goals scored by club	46

	PLAYER	LGE GOALS	POWER	STRIKE RATE
1	Ronaldo Luiz Nazario de Lima	24	43	106 mins
2	Raul Gonzalez Blanco	11	43	265 mins
3	Luis Madeira Caeira Figo	8	47	364 mins
4	Zinedine Zidane	6	45	442 mins

KEY PLAYERS - MIDFIELDERS

Zinedine Zidane

Goals in the League	6	Contribution to Attacking Power Average number of minutes between League team goals while on pitch	46
Defensive Rating Average number of mins between League goals conceded while he was on the pitch	72	Scoring Difference Defensive Rating minus Contribution to Attacking Power	26

	PLAYER	LGE GOALS	DEF RATE	POWER	SCORE DIFF
1	Zinedine Zidane	6	72	46	26 mins
2	David Beckham	3	66	47	19 mins
3	Luis Madeira Caeira Figo	8	66	48	18 mins
4	Jose Maria Guti	2	63	47	16 mins

KEY PLAYERS - DEFENDERS

Sanfelix Raul Bravo

Goals Conceded (GC) The number of League goals conceded while he was on the pitch	37	Clean Sheets In games when he played at least 70 minutes	5
Defensive Rating Ave number of mins between League goals conceded while on the pitch	75	Club Defensive Rating Average number of mins between League goals conceded by the club this season	64

	PLAYER	CON LGE	CLEAN SHEETS	DEF RATE
1	Sanfelix Raul Bravo	37	5	75 mins
2	Michel Fernandez Salgado	43	5	71 mins
3	Roberto Carlos Da Silva	40	5	69 mins
4	Ivan Bujia Helguera	38	5	67 mins

KEY GOALKEEPER

Iker Fernandez Casillas

Goals Conceded in the League	48	Counting Games Games when he played at least 70 mins	36
Defensive Rating Ave number of mins between League goals conceded while on the pitch	68	Clean Sheets In games when he played at least 70 mins	5

LEAGUE GOALS

Ronaldo Luiz Nazario de Lima

Minutes on the pitch	2548	Goals in the League	24
League average (mins between goals)	106		

	PLAYER	MINS	GOALS	AVE
1	Ronaldo	2548	24	106
2	Raul	2919	11	265
3	Figo	2915	8	364
4	Roberto Carlos	2752	6	459
5	Zidane	2653	6	442
6	Solari	1518	5	304
7	Beckham	2688	3	896
8	Guti	1567	2	784
9	Raul Bravo	2769	1	2769
10	Portillo	389	1	389
11	Pavon	2138	1	2138
12	Salgado	3060	1	3060
	Other		3	
	TOTAL		72	

DISCIPLINARY

	PLAYER	YELLOW	RED	AVE
1	Guti	11	1	130
2	Mejia	4	1	148
3	Solari	8	1	168
4	Pavon	9	2	194
5	Helguera	10	0	255
6	Salgado	12	0	255
7	Figo	10	1	265
8	Cambiasso	2	0	362
9	Beckham	6	1	384
10	Raul Bravo	6	0	461
11	Ronaldo	5	0	509
12	Zidane	5	0	530
13	Roberto Carlos	5	0	550
	Other	5	0	
	TOTAL	98	7	

TOP POINT EARNERS

	PLAYER	GAMES	AV PTS
1	Ronaldo	29	2.14
2	Salgado	34	2.03
3	Zidane	29	2.00
4	Beckham	30	2.00
5	Raul	33	1.97
6	Raul Bravo	31	1.97
7	Roberto Carlos	30	1.97
8	Casillas	36	1.94
9	Helguera	28	1.82
10	Pavon	22	1.82
	CLUB AVERAGE:		1.84

LEAGUE APPEARANCES, BOOKINGS AND CAPS

	AGE (on 01/07/04)	IN NAMED 18	APPEARANCES	COUNTING GAMES	MINUTES ON PITCH	YELLOW CARDS	RED CARDS	THIS SEASON	HOME COUNTRY
Goalkeepers									
Iker Casillas	23	37	36	36	3240	2	0	8	Spain (3)
Dominguez Cesar	32	31	1	1	90	0	0	-	Spain
Lopez Diego	22	3	0	0	0	0	0	-	Spain
Garcia Sanchez	26	3	0	0	0	0	0	-	Spain
Defenders									
Coca Alvaro	21	1	0	0	0	0	0	-	Spain
Ivan Helguera	29	31	29	28	2550	10	0	5	Spain (3)
Alvaro Perez Mejia	22	18	9	8	742	4	1	-	Spain
Oscar Minambres	23	5	2	0	73	0	0	-	Spain
Juan Olalla	24	2	0	0	0	0	0	-	Spain
Javier Paredes	22	5	0	0	0	0	0	-	Spain
Francisco Pavon	24	33	28	22	2138	9	2	-	Spain
Sanfelix Raul Bravo	23	35	31	31	2769	6	0	4	Spain (3)
Roberto Carlos	31	31	31	30	2752	5	0	7	Brazil (1)
Gonzalez Ruben	22	13	2	1	115	1	0	-	Spain
Michel Salgado	28	34	34	34	3060	12	0	8	Spain (3)
Midfielders									
David Beckham	29	31	31	30	2688	6	1	7	England (12)
Borja Fernandez	23	35	15	5	642	0	0	-	Spain
Esteban Cambiasso	23	33	16	6	724	2	0	2	Argentina (5)
Luis Figo	31	35	35	31	2915	10	1	8	Portugal (20)
Jose Maria Guti	27	28	26	14	1567	11	1	4	Spain (3)
Jordi Lopez	23	6	2	1	91	0	0	-	Spain
Juan Juanfran	19	15	5	0	127	0	0	-	Spain
Jose Jurado	18	1	0	0	0	0	0	-	Spain
Antonio Nunez	25	31	10	0	149	0	0	-	Spain
Santiago Solari	27	35	33	12	1518	8	1	1	Argentina (5)
Roberto Soldado	19	1	0	0	0	0	0	-	Spain
Zinedine Zidane	32	32	32	29	2653	5	0	6	France (2)
Forwards									
Morientes	28	1	1	0	5	0	0	2	Spain (3)
Javier Portillo	22	34	17	2	389	1	0	-	Spain
Raul Blanco	27	34	34	33	2919	1	0	8	Spain (3)
Ivan Riki	23	1	0	0	0	0	0	-	Spain
Ronaldo	27	31	31	29	2548	5	0	8	Brazil (1)

TEAM OF THE SEASON

G — Casillas — CG: 36 DR: 68

D — Raul Bravo — CG: 31 DR: 75

D — Salgado — CG: 34 DR: 71

D — Roberto Carlos — CG: 30 DR: 69

D — Helguera — CG: 28 DR: 67

M — Zidane — CG: 29 SD: 26

M — Beckham — CG: 30 SD: 19

M — Figo — CG: 31 SD: 18

M — Guti — CG: 14 SD: 16

F — Ronaldo — CG: 29 SR: 106

F — Raul — CG: 33 SR: 265

SQUAD APPEARANCES

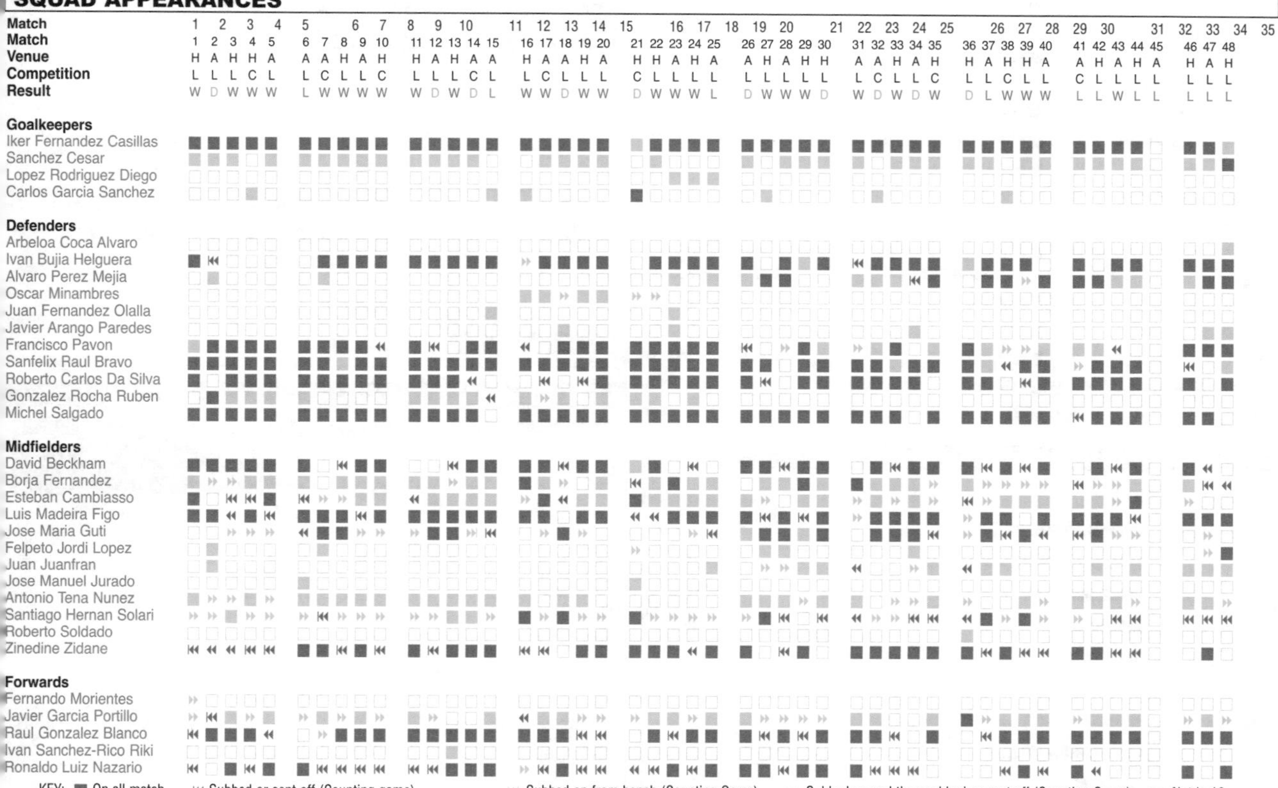

Match
Match
Venue
Competition
Result
Goalkeepers
Iker Fernandez Casillas
Sanchez Cesar
Lopez Rodriguez Diego
Carlos Garcia Sanchez
Defenders
Arbeloa Coca Alvaro
Ivan Bujia Helguera
Alvaro Perez Mejia
Oscar Minambres
Juan Fernandez Olalla
Javier Arango Paredes
Francisco Pavon
Sanfelix Raul Bravo
Roberto Carlos Da Silva
Gonzalez Rocha Ruben
Michel Salgado
Midfielders
David Beckham
Borja Fernandez
Esteban Cambiasso
Luis Madeira Figo
Jose Maria Guti
Felpeto Jordi Lopez
Juan Juanfran
Jose Manuel Jurado
Antonio Tena Nunez
Santiago Hernan Solari
Roberto Soldado
Zinedine Zidane
Forwards
Fernando Morientes
Javier Garcia Portillo
Raul Gonzalez Blanco
Ivan Sanchez-Rico Riki
Ronaldo Luiz Nazario
KEY: On all match
On bench
Subbed or sent off (Counting game)
Subbed or sent off (playing less than 70 minutes)
Subbed on from bench (Counting Game)
Subbed on (playing less than 70 minutes)
Subbed on and then subbed or sent off (Counting Game)
Subbed on and then subbed or sent off (playing less than 70 minutes)
Not in 16

ATHLETIC BILBAO

Final Position: **5th**

KEY: Won Drawn Lost

							Attendance
1	lge	Barcelona	H	L	0-1		41,000
2	lge	Deportivo	A	L	0-2		34,532
3	lge	Mallorca	H	W	4-0	Urzaiz 38,44; Joseba Etxeberria 76,89 pen	36,000
4	lge	Murcia	A	D	2-2	Joseba Etxeberria 40; Tiko 62	14,000
5	lge	Real Sociedad	H	W	1-0	Tiko 82	40,000
6	lge	Real Betis	A	D	1-1	Tiko 46	28,000
7	lge	Villarreal	H	W	2-0	Urzaiz 51; Joseba Etxeberria 83	38,000
8	lge	Valladolid	A	L	0-2		15,500
9	lge	Malaga	H	W	2-1	Urzaiz 62; Tiko 72	28,000
10	lge	Real Madrid	A	L	0-3		76,000
11	lge	Espanyol	H	W	1-0	Iraola 14	35,000
12	lge	Celta Vigo	A	W	2-0	Lacruz Gomez 58; Iraola 90	16,000
13	lge	R Santander	H	L	1-2	Jonan 8	38,000
14	lge	Real Zaragoza	A	D	2-2	Yeste 16; Tiko 26	29,000
15	lge	Valencia	A	L	1-2	Ezquerro 53	50,000
16	lge	Seville	H	W	2-1	Urzaiz 5; Yeste 24	30,000
17	lge	Albacete	A	D	1-1	Ezquerro 41	15,500
18	lge	Osasuna	H	D	1-1	Del Horno 45	37,000
19	lge	Atl Madrid	A	L	0-3		45,000
20	lge	Barcelona	A	D	1-1	Gurpegui 85	68,000
21	lge	Deportivo	H	W	1-0	Yeste 50	33,000
22	lge	Mallorca	A	W	3-1	Yeste 18; Joseba Etxeberria 61; Franco 85 og	19,500
23	lge	Murcia	H	W	2-1	Urzaiz 12; Yeste 45 pen	30,000
24	lge	Real Sociedad	A	D	1-1	Yeste 15	29,000
25	lge	Real Betis	H	D	1-1	Ezquerro 54	35,000
26	lge	Villarreal	A	W	1-0	Jonan 45	11,928
27	lge	Valladolid	H	L	1-4	Guerrero 81	36,000
28	lge	Malaga	A	L	1-2	Larrazabal 38	23,744
29	lge	Real Madrid	H	W	4-2	Yeste 41; Urzaiz 43; Del Horno 73,76	30,000
30	lge	Espanyol	A	L	1-2	Pocchettino 90 og	22,000
31	lge	Celta Vigo	H	D	0-0		28,000
32	lge	R Santander	A	W	2-1	Iraola 41; Yeste 90	15,000
33	lge	Real Zaragoza	H	W	4-0	Joseba Etxeberria 34; Del Horno 59; Yeste 76,90	35,000
34	lge	Valencia	H	D	1-1	Del Horno 30	36,000
35	lge	Seville	A	L	0-2		29,568
36	lge	Albacete	H	D	1-1	Iraola 88	35,000
37	lge	Osasuna	A	W	2-1	Yeste 47; Urzaiz 61	17,000
38	lge	Atl Madrid	H	L	3-4	Iraola 19; Arriaga 53,89	25,000

MONTHLY POINTS TALLY

AUGUST	0	0%
SEPTEMBER	7	58%
OCTOBER	7	58%
NOVEMBER	6	50%
DECEMBER	5	42%
JANUARY	5	42%
FEBRUARY	11	73%
MARCH	3	25%
APRIL	8	67%
MAY	4	33%

KEY PLAYERS - GOALSCORERS

Francisco Navaro Yeste

Goals in the League	11	Player Strike Rate Average number of minutes between League goals scored by player	187
Contribution to Attacking Power Average number of minutes between League team goals while on pitch	62	Club Strike Rate Average number of minutes between League goals scored by club	65

	PLAYER	LGE GOALS	POWER	STRIKE RATE
1	Francisco Navaro Yeste	11	62	187 mins
2	Ismael Urzaiz	8	56	335 mins
3	Roberto Martinez Tiko	5	70	478 mins
4	Joseba Etxeberria Lizardi	6	66	501 mins

KEY PLAYERS - MIDFIELDERS

Carlos Nausia Gurpegui

Goals in the League	1	Contribution to Attacking Power Average number of minutes between League team goals while on pitch	65
Defensive Rating Average number of mins between League goals conceded while he was on the pitch	74	Scoring Difference Defensive Rating minus Contribution to Attacking Power	9

	PLAYER	LGE GOALS	DEF RATE	POWER	SCORE DIFF
1	Carlos Nausia Gurpegui	1	74	65	9 mins
2	Roberto Martinez Tiko	5	77	70	7 mins
3	Luis Prieto	0	65	63	2 mins
4	Francisco Navaro Yeste	11	61	62	-1 mins

KEY PLAYERS - DEFENDERS

Jesus Maria Lacruz Gomez

Goals Conceded (GC) The number of League goals conceded while he was on the pitch	23	Clean Sheets In games when he played at least 70 minutes	5
Defensive Rating Ave number of mins between League goals conceded while on the pitch	78	Club Defensive Rating Average number of mins between League goals conceded by the club this season	70

	PLAYER	CON LGE	CLEAN SHEETS	DEF RATE
1	Jesus Maria Lacruz Gomez	23	5	78 mins
2	Aitor de la Hoz Karanka	38	8	77 mins
3	Asier Del Horno	35	8	73 mins
4	Pablo Orbaiz Lesaca	27	4	64 mins

KEY GOALKEEPER

Daniel Aranzubia Aguado

Goals Conceded in the League	43	Counting Games Games when he played at least 70 mins	34
Defensive Rating Ave number of mins between League goals conceded while on the pitch	71	Clean Sheets In games when he played at least 70 mins	8

LEAGUE GOALS

Francisco Navaro Yeste

Minutes on the pitch	2060	Goals in the League	11
League average (mins between goals)	187		

	PLAYER	MINS	GOALS	AVE
1	Yeste	2060	11	187
2	Urzaiz	2677	8	335
3	Joseba Etxeberria	3004	6	501
4	Del Horno	2546	5	509
5	Tiko	2392	5	478
6	Iraola	1772	5	354
7	Ezquerro	2563	3	854
8	Arriaga	456	2	228
9	Jonan	819	2	410
10	Larrazabal	851	1	851
11	Lacruz Gomez	1784	1	1784
12	Gurpegui	2522	1	2522
13	Guerrero	322	1	322
	Other		2	
	TOTAL		53	

DISCIPLINARY RECORDS

	PLAYER	YELLOW	RED	AVE
1	Lacruz Gomez	7	2	198
2	Prieto	10	1	229
3	Del Horno	10	1	231
4	Gurpegui	9	1	252
5	Yeste	8	0	257
6	Larrazabal	3	0	283
7	Tiko	8	0	299
8	Cesar	2	0	320
9	Joseba Etxeberria	8	0	375
10	Urzaiz	7	0	382
11	Jonan	2	0	409
12	Karanka	6	1	415
13	Arriaga	1	0	456
	Other	18	0	
	TOTAL	99	6	

TOP POINT EARNERS

	PLAYER	GAMES	AV PTS
1	Urzaiz	24	1.92
2	Del Horno	27	1.81
3	Ezquerro	25	1.60
4	Tiko	24	1.58
5	Joseba Etxeberria	34	1.56
6	Gurpegui	27	1.52
7	Orbaiz	17	1.47
8	Prieto	27	1.44
9	Lacruz Gomez	19	1.42
10	Karanka	31	1.42
	CLUB AVERAGE:		1.47

TEAM OF THE SEASON

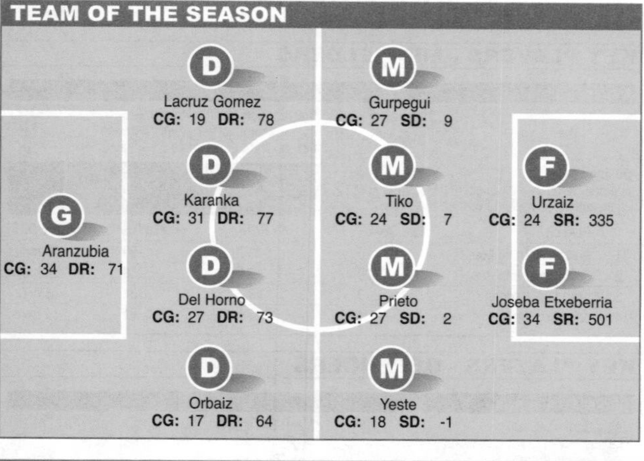
G
Aranzubia
CG: 34 DR: 71
D
Lacruz Gomez
CG: 19 DR: 78
D
Karanka
CG: 31 DR: 77
D
Del Horno
CG: 27 DR: 73
D
Orbaiz
CG: 17 DR: 64
M
Gurpegui
CG: 27 SD: 9
M
Tiko
CG: 24 SD: 7
M
Prieto
CG: 27 SD: 2
M
Yeste
CG: 18 SD: -1
F
Urzaiz
CG: 24 SR: 335
F
Joseba Etxeberria
CG: 34 SR: 501

LEAGUE APPEARANCES, BOOKINGS AND CAPS

	AGE (on 01/07/04)	IN NAMED 18	APPEARANCES	COUNTING GAMES	MINUTES ON PITCH	YELLOW CARDS	RED CARDS	THIS SEASON	HOME COUNTRY
Goalkeepers									
Daniel Aranzubia	24	36	34	34	3060	2	0	-	Spain
Oinatz Aulestia	23	1	0	0	0	0	0	-	Spain
Miguel Escalona	20	1	0	0	0	0	0	-	Spain
Inaki Lafuente	28	38	4	4	360	0	0	-	Spain
Defenders									
Gorka Azkorra	21	1	0	0	0	0	0	-	Spain
Javier Casas	22	5	0	0	0	0	0	-	Spain
Fernandez Cesar	26	15	10	6	641	2	0	-	Spain
Cesar Caneda	30	1	0	0	0	0	0	-	
Asier Del Horno	23	31	31	27	2546	10	1	-	Spain
Aitor Karanka	30	34	34	31	2911	6	1	-	Spain
Lacruz Gomez	26	29	25	19	1784	7	2	-	Spain
Aitor Larrazabal	33	30	15	8	851	3	0	-	Spain
Ander Murillo	20	9	4	2	234	0	0	-	Spain
Pablo Orbaiz	25	30	26	17	1727	3	0	-	Spain
Oscar Vales Varela	29	8	2	2	170	2	0	-	Spain
Midfielders									
Endika Bordas	22	21	7	1	215	2	0	-	Spain
Gurendez Felipe	28	11	2	0	33	0	0	-	Spain
Guerrero Lopez	30	25	15	2	322	1	0	-	Spain
Carlos Gurpegui	23	32	29	27	2522	9	1	-	Spain
Andoni Iraola	22	36	30	10	1772	3	0	-	Spain
Carlos Gonzalez	24	3	1	0	45	0	0	-	Spain
Luis Prieto	25	33	29	27	2525	10	1	-	Spain
Roberto Tiko	27	31	29	24	2392	8	0	-	Spain
Francisco Yeste	24	30	30	18	2060	8	0	-	Spain
Forwards									
Joseba Arriaga	21	26	13	2	456	1	0	-	Spain
Santiago Ezquerro	27	35	35	25	2563	3	0	-	Spain
Javi Gonzalez	30	28	25	17	1866	2	0	-	Spain
Garcia Jonan	21	33	23	3	819	2	0	-	Spain
Joseba Exteberria	26	34	34	34	3004	8	0	2	Spain (3)
Ismael Urzaiz	32	37	37	24	2677	7	0	-	Spain

SQUAD APPEARANCES

Match	1	2	3	4	5	6	7	8	9	10	11	12	13	14	15	16	17	18	19	20	21	22	23	24	25	26	27	28	29	30	31	32	33	34	35	36	37	38
Venue	H	A	H	A	H	A	H	A	H	A	H	A	H	A	A	H	A	H	A	A	H	A	H	A	H	A	H	A	H	A	H	A	H	H	A	H	A	H
Competition	L	L	L	L	L	L	L	L	L	L	L	L	L	L	L	L	L	L	L	L	L	L	L	L	L	L	L	L	L	L	L	L	L	L	L	L	L	L
Result	L	L	W	D	W	D	W	L	W	L	W	W	L	D	L	W	D	D	L	D	W	W	W	D	D	W	L	L	W	L	D	W	W	D	L	D	W	L

Goalkeepers
Daniel Aranzubia Aguado
Oinatz Aulestia
Miguel Escalona
Inaki Lafuente Sancha

Defenders
Gorka Azkorra
Javier Casas
Cesar Heras Caneda
Fernandez Cesar
Asier Del Horno
Aitor de la Hoz Karanka
Jesus Lacruz Gomez
Aitor Larrazabal
Ander Murillo
Pablo Orbaiz Lesaca
Oscar Vales Varela

Midfielders
Endika Bordas
Gurendez Felipe
Julen Guerrero Lopez
Carlos Nausia Gurpegui
Andoni Sagarra Iraola
Carlos Merino Gonzalez
Luis Prieto
Roberto Martinez Tiko
Francisco Navaro Yeste

Forwards
Joseba Arriaga
Santiago Ezquerro Marin
Gomez Javi Gonzalez
Garcia Jonan
Joseba Etxeberria Lizardi
Ismael Urzaiz

KEY: On all match · On bench · Subbed or sent off (Counting game) · Subbed or sent off (playing less than 70 minutes) · Subbed on from bench (Counting Game) · Subbed on (playing less than 70 minutes) · Subbed on and then subbed or sent off (Counting Game) · Subbed on and then subbed or sent off (playing less than 70 minutes) · Not in 16

FC SEVILLE

Final Position: **6th**

KEY: Won Drawn Lost

						Attendance
1 lge	Atl Madrid	H	W	1-0	Baptista 26	36,000
2 lge	Barcelona	A	D	1-1	Reyes 8 pen	80,237
3 lge	Deportivo	H	L	1-2	Dario Silva 52	35,000
4 lge	Mallorca	A	D	1-1	Dario Silva 20	12,000
5 lge	Murcia	H	W	1-0	Antonito 90	36,000
6 lge	Real Sociedad	A	D	1-1	Dario Silva 14	25,500
7 lge	Real Betis	H	D	2-2	Reyes 51; Antonito 81	44,000
8 lge	Villarreal	A	D	3-3	Casquero 3; Reyes 30 pen; Carlos 86	15,000
9 lge	Valladolid	H	D	1-1	Dario Silva 17	31,000
10 lge	Malaga	A	L	0-2		35,000
11 lge	Real Madrid	H	W	4-1	Helguera 5 og; Dario Silva 7; Daniel Alves 14; Casquero 38	45,000
12 lge	Espanyol	A	L	0-1		32,000
13 lge	Celta Vigo	H	L	0-1		35,500
14 lge	R Santander	A	W	4-0	Baptista 12,45; Dario Silva 22; Reyes 46	11,000
15 lge	Real Zaragoza	H	W	3-2	Podesta 33,47; Antonito 72	20,000
16 lge	Athl Bilbao	A	L	1-2	Baptista 2	30,000
17 lge	Valencia	A	L	0-1		48,000
18 lge	Albacete	H	W	2-0	Baptista 40; Antonito 90	45,000
19 lge	Osasuna	A	D	1-1	Baptista 47	19,500
20 lge	Atl Madrid	A	L	1-2	Reyes 76 pen	52,000
21 lge	Barcelona	H	L	0-1		43,000
22 lge	Deportivo	A	L	0-1		31,000
23 lge	Mallorca	H	W	3-0	Baptista 50; Gallardo 55; Marti 85	27,500
24 lge	Murcia	A	W	3-1	Baptista 4 pen,72 pen,90	10,000
25 lge	Real Sociedad	H	W	1-0	Hornos 90	25,000
26 lge	Real Betis	A	D	1-1	Navarro 27	48,000
27 lge	Villarreal	H	W	2-0	Carlos 57,76	37,000
28 lge	Valladolid	A	L	0-2		23,850
29 lge	Malaga	H	L	0-1		28,350
30 lge	Real Madrid	A	L	1-5	Baptista 59 pen	65,000
31 lge	Espanyol	H	W	1-0	Antonito 51	25,000
32 lge	Celta Vigo	A	D	0-0		20,000
33 lge	R Santander	H	W	5-2	Baptista 4,7,47,59 pen; Magallanes 90	35,000
34 lge	Real Zaragoza	A	D	4-4	Casquero 5,47; Baptista 67 pen; Carlos 90	34,000
35 lge	Athl Bilbao	H	W	2-0	Baptista 39,63 pen	29,568
36 lge	Valencia	H	L	0-2		38,000
37 lge	Albacete	A	W	4-1	Dario Silva 39; Baptista 51 pen; Casquero 52; Hornos 89	16,000
38 lge	Osasuna	H	W	1-0	Baptista 55	46,000

MONTHLY POINTS TALLY

Month	Points	%
AUGUST	3	100%
SEPTEMBER	5	42%
OCTOBER	4	33%
NOVEMBER	3	25%
DECEMBER	6	50%
JANUARY	4	33%
FEBRUARY	10	67%
MARCH	3	25%
APRIL	8	67%
MAY	9	75%

KEY PLAYERS - GOALSCORERS

Julio Cesar Baptista

Goals in the League	20	Player Strike Rate Average number of minutes between League goals scored by player	127
Contribution to Attacking Power Average number of minutes between League team goals while on pitch	56	Club Strike Rate Average number of minutes between League goals scored by club	61

	PLAYER	LGE GOALS	POWER	STRIKE RATE
1	Julio Cesar Baptista	20	56	127 mins
2	Debray Dario Silva	7	63	299 mins
3	Jose Antonio Reyes	5	66	345 mins
4	Francisco Casquero	5	56	350 mins

KEY PLAYERS - MIDFIELDERS

Alvarez Antonio Lopez

Goals in the League	0	Contribution to Attacking Power Average number of minutes between League team goals while on pitch	59
Defensive Rating Average number of mins between League goals conceded while he was on the pitch	112	Scoring Difference Defensive Rating minus Contribution to Attacking Power	53

	PLAYER	LGE GOALS	DEF RATE	POWER	SCORE DIFF
1	Alvarez Antonio Lopez	0	112	59	53 mins
2	Julio Cesar Baptista	20	84	56	28 mins
3	Jean Luis Redondo	0	72	54	18 mins
4	Jose Luis Marti	1	75	61	14 mins

KEY PLAYERS - DEFENDERS

Pablo Alfaro Armengot

Goals Conceded (GC) The number of League goals conceded while he was on the pitch	42	Clean Sheets In games when he played at least 70 minutes	10
Defensive Rating Ave number of mins between League goals conceded while on the pitch	78	Club Defensive Rating Average number of mins between League goals conceded by the club this season	76

	PLAYER	CON LGE	CLEAN SHEETS	DEF RATE
1	Pablo Alfaro Armengot	42	10	78 mins
2	Da Silva Daniel Alves	31	8	78 mins
3	Francisco Javi Navarro	41	10	77 mins
4	David Castedo Escudero	42	11	75 mins

KEY GOALKEEPER

Andres Suarez Esteban

Goals Conceded in the League	34	Counting Games Games when he played at least 70 mins	30
Defensive Rating Ave number of mins between League goals conceded while on the pitch	79	Clean Sheets In games when he played at least 70 mins	9

LEAGUE GOALS

Julio Cesar Baptista

Minutes on the pitch	2532	Goals in the League	20
League average (mins between goals)	127		

	PLAYER	MINS	GOALS	AVE
1	Baptista	2532	20	127
2	Dario Silva	2092	7	299
3	Reyes	1725	5	345
4	Casquero	1751	5	350
5	Carlos	800	4	200
6	Antonito	1546	4	387
7	Hornos	650	2	325
8	Podesta	368	2	184
9	Gallardo	1100	1	1100
10	Magallanes	47	1	47
11	Navarro	3156	1	3156
12	Marti	3211	1	3211
13	Daniel Alves	2418	1	2418
	Other		2	
	TOTAL		56	

DISCIPLINARY

	PLAYER	YELLOW	RED	AVE
1	Torrado	4	1	105
2	Daniel Alves	14	0	172
3	Antonio Lopez	6	0	224
4	Navarro	13	0	242
5	Redondo	8	0	262
6	Gallardo	4	0	275
7	Casquero	6	0	291
8	Dario Silva	6	1	298
9	Hornos	1	1	325
10	Marti	8	1	356
11	Antonito	3	1	386
12	Pablo Alfaro	7	1	408
13	Baptista	6	0	422
	Other	32	1	
	TOTAL	118	7	

TOP POINT EARNERS

	PLAYER	GAMES	AV PTS
1	Antonio Lopez	13	1.85
2	Baptista	26	1.73
3	Redondo	21	1.62
4	Daniel Alves	25	1.60
5	Esteban	30	1.50
6	Casquero	15	1.47
7	Navarro	34	1.47
8	Marti	36	1.44
9	Pablo Alfaro	36	1.44
10	David Castedo	35	1.40
	CLUB AVERAGE:		1.45

LEAGUE APPEARANCES, BOOKINGS AND CAPS

	AGE (on 01/07/04)	IN NAMED 18	APPEARANCES	COUNTING GAMES	MINUTES ON PITCH	YELLOW CARDS	RED CARDS	THIS SEASON	HOME COUNTRY
Goalkeepers									
Juan Caballero	25	8	0	0	0	0	0	-	Spain
Andres Esteban	29	37	30	30	2695	3	0	-	Spain
Antonio Notario	31	29	9	8	725	1	0	-	Spain
Defenders									
Carrion Aitor Ocio	27	19	7	1	157	0	0	-	Spain
Daniel Alves	21	29	29	25	2418	14	0	-	Brazil
David Castedo	30	35	35	35	3150	5	0	-	Spain
Alejandro Maranon	24	15	5	3	283	3	0	-	Spain
Marcos Vales	29	11	9	2	368	2	0	-	Spain
Javi Navarro	30	36	36	34	3156	13	0	-	Spain
Rodriguez Oscar	24	25	8	4	445	4	0	-	Spain
Pablo Alfaro	35	37	37	36	3265	7	1	-	Spain
Ramos Sergio	23	10	6	3	361	1	0	-	Spain
Midfielders									
Jurado Alvaro	22	1	0	0	0	0	0	-	Spain
Antonio Lopez	24	32	20	13	1347	6	0	-	Spain
Julio Cesar Baptista	22	30	30	26	2532	6	0	6	Brazil (1)
Juan Bezares	23	3	1	0	52	0	0	-	Spain
Francisco Casquero	27	29	25	15	1751	6	0	-	Spain
Jose Luis Marti	29	36	36	36	3211	8	1	-	Spain
Jesus Navas	18	11	8	1	263	0	0	-	Spain
Marco Navas	21	1	0	0	0	0	0	-	Spain
Zoran Njegus	31	6	3	1	119	2	0	-	Serbia & Montenegro
Inti Podesta	26	8	6	3	368	5	1	-	Uruguay
Antonio Puerta	19	4	1	1	70	0	0	-	Spain
Jean Redondo	27	35	29	21	2101	8	0	-	Spain
Gerardo Torrado	25	16	9	4	526	4	1	-	Mexico
Victor Salas Banos	24	6	2	0	35	0	0	-	Spain
Forwards									
Ramiro Antonito	26	32	26	9	1546	3	1	-	Spain
Dominguez Carlos	27	28	24	1	800	1	0	-	Spain
Debray Dario Silva	31	28	27	21	2092	6	1	-	Uruguay
Francisco Gallardo	24	29	20	8	1100	4	0	-	Spain
German Hornos	21	22	16	3	650	1	1	3	Uruguay (25)
Torres Luis Gil	28	7	4	1	183	1	0	-	Spain
Federico Magallanes	27	7	4	0	47	0	0	-	Uruguay
Jose Antonio Reyes	20	21	21	18	1725	4	0	5	Spain (3)

TEAM OF THE SEASON

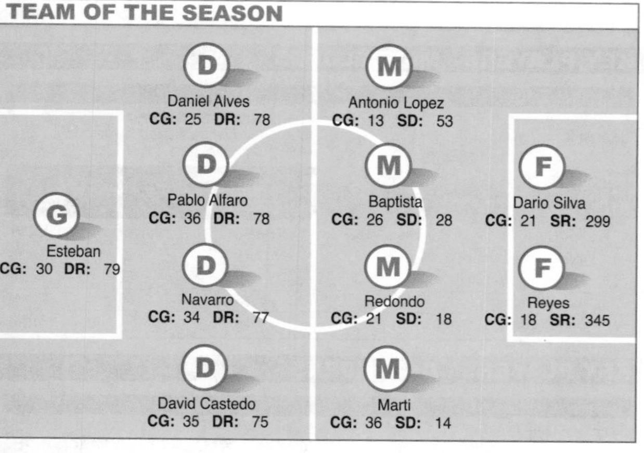

G
Esteban
CG: 30 DR: 79
D
Daniel Alves
CG: 25 DR: 78
D
Pablo Alfaro
CG: 36 DR: 78
D
Navarro
CG: 34 DR: 77
D
David Castedo
CG: 35 DR: 75
M
Antonio Lopez
CG: 13 SD: 53
M
Baptista
CG: 26 SD: 28
M
Redondo
CG: 21 SD: 18
M
Marti
CG: 36 SD: 14
F
Dario Silva
CG: 21 SR: 299
F
Reyes
CG: 18 SR: 345

SQUAD APPEARANCES

Match	1	2	3	4	5	6	7	8	9	10	11	12	13	14	15	16	17	18	19	20	21	22	23	24	25	26	27	28	29	30	31	32	33	34	35	36	37	38
Venue	H	A	H	A	H	A	H	A	H	A	H	A	H	A	H	A	A	H	H	A	H	A	H	A	H	A	H	A	H	A	H	A	H	A	H	H	A	H
Competition	L	L	L	L	L	L	L	L	L	L	L	L	L	L	L	L	L	L	L	L	L	L	L	L	L	L	L	L	L	L	L	L	L	L	L	L	L	L
Result	W	D	L	D	W	D	D	D	D	L	W	L	L	W	W	L	L	W	D	L	L	L	W	W	W	D	W	L	L	L	W	D	W	D	W	L	W	W

Goalkeepers
Juan Carlos Caballero
Andres Suarez Esteban
Antonio Notario Caro

Defenders
Carrion Aitor Ocio
Da Silva Daniel Alves
David Castedo Escudero
Alejandro Maranon
Llanes Marcos Vales
Francisco Javi Navarro
Rodriguez Oscar
Pablo Alfaro Armengot
Ramos Sergio

Midfielders
Jurado Espinosa Alvaro
Alvarez Antonio Lopez
Julio Cesar Baptista
Juan Jose Bezares
Francisco Casquero
Jose Luis Marti
Jesus Navas
Marco Gonzalez Navas
Zoran Njegus
Inti Podesta
Antonio Puerta
Jean Luis Redondo
Gerardo Torrado
Victor Salas Banos

Forwards
Ramiro Perez Antonito
Dominguez Carlos
Debray Dario Silva
Francisco Gallardo
German Hornos
Torres Luis Gil
Federico Magallanes
Jose Antonio Reyes

KEY: On all match · On bench · Subbed or sent off (Counting game) · Subbed or sent off (playing less than 70 minutes) · Subbed on from bench (Counting Game) · Subbed on (playing less than 70 minutes) · Subbed on and then subbed or sent off (Counting Game) · Subbed on and then subbed or sent off (playing less than 70 minutes) · Not in 16

ATLETICO MADRID

Final Position: **7th**

KEY: ☐Won ☐Drawn ☐Lost

							Attendance
1	lge	Seville	A	L	0-1		36,000
2	lge	Albacete	H	W	1-0	Jorge 50	54,150
3	lge	Osasuna	A	L	0-1		20,000
4	lge	Valencia	H	L	0-3		55,000
5	lge	Barcelona	H	D	0-0		56,000
6	lge	Deportivo	A	L	1-5	Lequi 11	28,000
7	lge	Mallorca	H	W	2-1	Torres 27; Jorge 90	57,000
8	lge	Murcia	A	W	3-1	Torres 14 pen,84; Nikolaidis 38	16,000
9	lge	Real Sociedad	H	W	4-0	Nikolaidis 19; Torres 56 pen,64; Simeone 80	34,000
10	lge	Real Betis	A	W	2-1	Torres 39,50 pen	50,000
11	lge	Villarreal	H	W	1-0	Novo 55	45,500
12	lge	Valladolid	A	L	1-3	Musampa 14	15,500
13	lge	Malaga	H	W	2-0	De Los Santos 6; Nikolaidis 71	45,500
14	lge	Real Madrid	A	L	0-2		78,000
15	lge	Espanyol	H	W	2-0	Torres 21,75 pen	40,000
16	lge	Celta Vigo	A	D	2-2	Simeone 17; Lequi 83	16,000
17	lge	R Santander	H	D	2-2	Paunovic 62; Musampa 70	45,000
18	lge	Real Zaragoza	A	D	0-0		23,000
19	lge	Athl Bilbao	H	W	3-0	Torres 73,83 pen; Paunovic 90	45,000
20	lge	Seville	H	W	2-1	Torres 42; Nikolaidis 70	52,000
21	lge	Albacete	A	D	1-1	Nano 32	14,000
22	lge	Osasuna	H	D	1-1	Nikolaidis 90	40,000
23	lge	Valencia	A	L	0-3		50,000
24	lge	Barcelona	A	L	1-3	Nikolaidis 22	95,000
25	lge	Deportivo	H	D	0-0		40,000
26	lge	Mallorca	A	W	1-0	Torres 90	16,500
27	lge	Murcia	H	D	1-1	Nano 90	35,000
28	lge	Real Sociedad	A	L	1-2	Paunovic 72	21,865
29	lge	Real Betis	H	W	2-1	Paunovic 51; Torres 68	45,587
30	lge	Villarreal	A	D	0-0		9,000
31	lge	Valladolid	H	W	2-1	Torres 24; Paunovic 45	50,000
32	lge	Malaga	A	L	1-3	Nano 45	22,000
33	lge	Real Madrid	H	L	1-2	Paunovic 48 pen	55,000
34	lge	Espanyol	A	L	1-3	Torres 90	34,200
35	lge	Celta Vigo	H	W	3-2	Nano 2; Torres 6; Garcia Calvo 38	40,000
36	lge	R Santander	A	D	2-2	Ibagaza 27; De Los Santos 59	14,000
37	lge	Real Zaragoza	H	L	1-2	Nano 65	52,000
38	lge	Athl Bilbao	A	W	4-3	Ibagaza 25; De Los Santos 32; Torres 34,84	25,000

MONTHLY POINTS TALLY

Month	Points	%
AUGUST	0	0%
SEPTEMBER	4	33%
OCTOBER	9	75%
NOVEMBER	9	75%
DECEMBER	5	42%
JANUARY	9	60%
FEBRUARY	4	33%
MARCH	5	42%
APRIL	3	25%
MAY	7	58%

KEY PLAYERS - GOALSCORERS

Fernando Torres

Goals in the League	19	Player Strike Rate Average number of minutes between League goals scored by player	157
Contribution to Attacking Power Average number of minutes between League team goals while on pitch	66	Club Strike Rate Average number of minutes between League goals scored by club	67

	PLAYER	LGE GOALS	POWER	STRIKE RATE
1	Fernando Torres	19	66	157 mins
2	Veljko Paunovic	6	56	243 mins
3	Gonzalo De Los Santos	3	62	890 mins
4	Diego Simeone	2	65	952 mins

KEY PLAYERS - MIDFIELDERS

Alvaro Ramirez Novo

Goals in the League	1	Contribution to Attacking Power Average number of minutes between League team goals while on pitch	66
Defensive Rating Average number of mins between League goals conceded while he was on the pitch	75	Scoring Difference Defensive Rating minus Contribution to Attacking Power	9

	PLAYER	LGE GOALS	DEF RATE	POWER	SCORE DIFF
1	Alvaro Ramirez Novo	1	75	66	9 mins
2	Gonzalo De Los Santos	3	70	62	8 mins
3	Diego Simeone	2	68	66	2 mins
4	Carlos Aguilera	0	56	74	-18 mins

KEY PLAYERS - DEFENDERS

Jose Antonio Garcia Calvo

Goals Conceded (GC) The number of League goals conceded while he was on the pitch	24	Clean Sheets In games when he played at least 70 minutes	6
Defensive Rating Ave number of mins between League goals conceded while on the pitch	78	Club Defensive Rating Average number of mins between League goals conceded by the club this season	65

	PLAYER	CON LGE	CLEAN SHEETS	DEF RATE
1	Jose Antonio Garcia Calvo	24	6	78 mins
2	Sergi Barjuan	38	10	72 mins
3	Galvez Burgos Gaspar	36	6	66 mins
4	Matias Lequi	48	10	64 mins

KEY GOALKEEPER

German Adrian Burgos

Goals Conceded in the League	20	Counting Games Games when he played at least 70 mins	15
Defensive Rating Ave number of mins between League goals conceded while on the pitch	65	Clean Sheets In games when he played at least 70 mins	5

LEAGUE GOALS

Fernando Torres

Minutes on the pitch	2974	Goals in the League	19
League average (mins between goals)	157		

	PLAYER	MINS	GOALS	AVE
1	Torres	2974	19	157
2	Paunovic	1456	6	243
3	Nikolaidis	1452	6	242
4	Nano	1522	5	304
5	De Los Santos	2671	3	890
6	Jorge	1297	2	649
7	Ibagaza	2347	2	1174
8	Lequi	3060	2	1530
9	Simeone	1903	2	952
10	Musampa	1271	2	636
11	Novo	2181	1	2181
12	Garcia Calvo	1883	1	1883
	Other		0	
	TOTAL		51	

DISCIPLINARY RECORDS

	PLAYER	YELLOW	RED	AVE
1	De Los Santos	16	0	166
2	Simeone	11	0	173
3	Santi	5	0	182
4	Sergi	12	1	210
5	Gaspar	10	0	238
6	Torres	9	1	297
7	Novo	6	1	311
8	Garcia Calvo	6	0	313
9	Musampa	4	0	317
10	Jorge	3	1	324
11	Aguilera	4	1	325
12	Lequi	9	0	340
13	Juanma	2	0	472
	Other	23	2	
	TOTAL	120	7	

TOP POINT EARNERS

	PLAYER	GAMES	AV PTS
1	Nikolaidis	12	2.00
2	Nano	12	1.75
3	Novo	22	1.73
4	Sergi	29	1.66
5	De Los Santos	29	1.62
6	Torres	33	1.58
7	Burgos	14	1.57
8	Gaspar	26	1.50
9	Simeone	18	1.50
10	Ibagaza	23	1.48
	CLUB AVERAGE:		1.45

TEAM OF THE SEASON

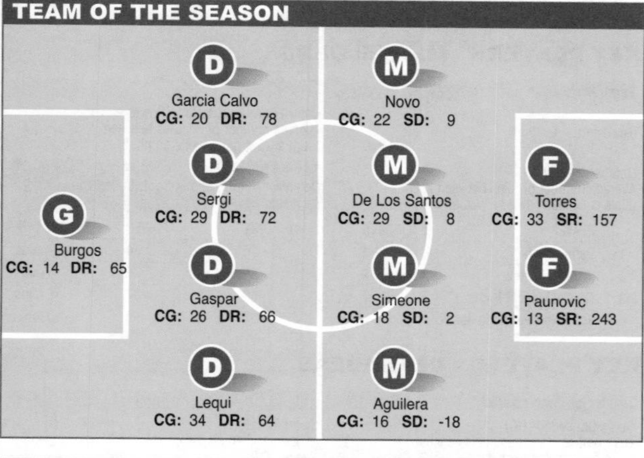

D
Garcia Calvo
CG: 20 DR: 78
M
Novo
CG: 22 SD: 9
D
Sergi
CG: 29 DR: 72
M
De Los Santos
CG: 29 SD: 8
F
Torres
CG: 33 SR: 157
G
Burgos
CG: 14 DR: 65
D
Gaspar
CG: 26 DR: 66
M
Simeone
CG: 18 SD: 2
F
Paunovic
CG: 13 SR: 243
D
Lequi
CG: 34 DR: 64
M
Aguilera
CG: 16 SD: -18

LEAGUE APPEARANCES, BOOKINGS AND CAPS

	AGE (on 01/07/04)	IN NAMED 18	APPEARANCES	COUNTING GAMES	MINUTES ON PITCH	YELLOW CARDS	RED CARDS	THIS SEASON	HOME COUNTRY
Goalkeepers									
German Burgos	35	17	15	14	1305	0	0	-	Argentina
Ivan Cuellar	-	2	0	0	0	0	0	-	Spain
Juanma Barrero	24	36	11	10	945	2	0	-	Spain
Sergio Sanchez	27	5	0	0	0	0	0	-	Spain
Aragoneses Sergio	27	16	13	13	1170	2	0	-	Spain
Defenders									
Cosmin Contra	28	11	4	2	284	0	0	-	Romania
Jose Garcia Calvo	29	23	22	20	1883	6	0	1	Spain (3)
Burgos Gaspar	25	28	27	26	2385	10	0	-	Spain
Mirsad Hibic	30	1	1	1	71	0	0	-	Bosnia
Miguel Ibagaza	27	31	30	23	2347	4	0	-	Argentina
Matias Lequi	23	34	34	34	3060	9	0	-	Argentina
Juan Manuel Ortiz	22	12	5	1	220	2	1	-	Spain
Javier Pinola	21	2	2	2	180	0	0	-	Argentina
Ivan Romero	23	1	1	1	72	1	0	-	Spain
Denia Santi	30	30	14	9	913	5	0	-	Spain
Sergi Barjuan	32	32	32	29	2734	12	1	-	Spain
Midfielders									
Carlos Aguilera	35	29	23	16	1629	4	1	-	Spain
De Los Santos	27	32	32	29	2671	16	0	-	Uruguay
Diego Rivas	24	10	3	1	193	3	0	-	Spain
Fernandez Gabi	20	11	6	1	226	2	0	-	Spain
Avellaneda Jorge	22	33	29	10	1297	3	1	-	Spain
Jose Maria Movilla	29	8	2	0	45	0	0	-	Spain
Kiki Musampa	26	33	26	7	1271	4	0	-	Holland
Alvaro Novo	26	33	32	22	2181	6	1	-	Spain
Ruben Olivera	21	4	2	0	26	0	0	3	Uruguay (25)
Diego Simeone	34	34	28	18	1903	11	0	-	Argentina
Forwards									
Angel Arizmendi	20	7	4	1	202	0	0	-	Spain
Javi Moreno	29	10	5	0	81	3	1	-	Spain
Fernando Nano	22	37	28	12	1522	1	0	-	Spain
Nikolaidis	30	29	22	12	1452	3	0	-	Greece
Veljko Paunovic	26	31	25	13	1456	2	0	1	Serbia & M,negro (45)
Fabri Rodrigo	28	27	16	6	727	0	0	-	Portugal
Jose Toche	-	1	1	0	9	0	0	-	Spain
Fernando Torres	20	35	35	33	2974	9	1	-	Spain

SQUAD APPEARANCES

Match	1	2	3	4	5	6	7	8	9	10	11	12	13	14	15	16	17	18	19	20	21	22	23	24	25	26	27	28	29	30	31	32	33	34	35	36	37	38
Venue	A	H	A	H	H	A	H	A	H	A	H	A	H	A	H	A	H	A	H	H	A	H	A	A	H	A	H	A	H	A	H	A	H	A	H	A	H	A
Competition	L	L	L	L	L	L	L	L	L	L	L	L	L	L	L	L	L	L	L	L	L	L	L	L	L	L	L	L	L	L	L	L	L	L	L	L	L	L
Result	L	W	L	L	D	L	W	W	W	W	W	L	W	L	W	D	D	D	W	W	D	D	L	L	D	W	D	L	W	D	W	L	L	L	W	D	L	W

Goalkeepers
German Adrian Burgos
Ivan Cuellar
Juan Manuel Barrero
Sergio Sanchez
Aragoneses Sergio

Defenders
Cosmin Marius Contra
Jose Antonio Garcia Calvo
Galvez Burgos Gaspar
Mirsad Hibic
Miguel Santiago Ibagaza
Matias Lequi
Juan Manuel Ortiz
Javier Horacio Pinola
Ivan Mingo Romero
Denia Santi
Sergi Barjuan

Midfielders
Carlos Aguilera
Gonzalo De Los Santos
Gutierrez Diego Rivas
Fernandez Gabi
Larena-Avellaneda Jorge
Jose Maria Movilla
Kiki Musampa
Alvaro Ramirez Novo
Ruben Olivera
Diego Simeone

Forwards
Angel Javier Arizmendi
Javi Moreno
Fernando Nano
Themistoklis Nikolaidis
Veljko Paunovic
Fabri Rodrigo
Jose Verdu Toche
Fernando Torres

KEY: ■ On all match | ■ On bench | ◂◂ Subbed or sent off (Counting game) | ◂◂ Subbed or sent off (playing less than 70 minutes) | ▸▸ Subbed on from bench (Counting Game) | ▸▸ Subbed on (playing less than 70 minutes) | ▸▸ Subbed on and then subbed or sent off (Counting Game) | ▸▸ Subbed on and then subbed or sent off (playing less than 70 minutes) | □ Not in 16

VILLARREAL

Final Position: **8th**

KEY: Won Drawn Lost

							Attendance
1	etfl2	**Heerenveen**	H	D	0-0		23,000
2	lge	**Malaga**	A	D	0-0		18,000
3	lge	**Real Madrid**	H	D	1-1	Anderson 71	21,000
4	lge	**Espanyol**	A	W	2-1	Victor 25; Riquelme 90 pen	20,000
5	lge	**Celta Vigo**	H	D	1-1	Berizzo 78 og	14,000
6	uc1rl1	**Trabzonspor**	H	D	0-0		17,000
7	lge	**R Santander**	A	W	2-0	Anderson 70; Riquelme 89	19,000
8	lge	**Real Zaragoza**	H	D	1-1	Victor 5	16,000
9	uc1rl2	**Trabzonspor**	A	W	3-2	Anderson 60; Jose Mari 65,90	21,000
10	lge	**Athl Bilbao**	A	L	0-2		38,000
11	lge	**Seville**	H	D	3-3	Anderson 10,69; Arruabarrena 90	15,000
12	lge	**Albacete**	A	L	0-2		13,000
13	lge	**Osasuna**	H	W	1-0	Guayre 23	11,000
14	uc2rl1	**T Moscow**	H	W	2-0	Riquelme 51,68	23,000
15	lge	**Atl Madrid**	A	L	0-1		45,500
16	lge	**Barcelona**	H	W	2-1	Jose Mari 40; Anderson 90	20,000
17	uc2rl2	**T Moscow**	A	L	0-1		4,000
18	lge	**Deportivo**	A	W	1-0	Roger 88	32,000
19	lge	**Mallorca**	H	L	0-2		16,000
20	lge	**Murcia**	A	D	1-1	Nadal 90	9,900
21	lge	**Real Sociedad**	H	W	2-0	Riquelme 12; Anderson 33	17,000
22	lge	**Real Betis**	A	W	3-1	Anderson 74; Guayre 88,90	40,000
23	lge	**Valencia**	A	L	2-4	Riquelme 15; Belletti 78	52,000
24	lge	**Valladolid**	H	W	3-1	Jose Mari 39; Victor 73; Roger 84	17,000
25	lge	**Malaga**	H	W	2-0	Arruabarrena 67; Anderson 83	11,000
26	lge	**Real Madrid**	A	L	1-2	Ballesteros 87	70,000
27	lge	**Espanyol**	H	L	0-1		14,000
28	lge	**Celta Vigo**	A	L	1-2	Anderson 85	22,000
29	lge	**R Santander**	H	W	6-3	Belletti 6,35; Riquelme 32; Jose Mari 68; Anderson 72; Juanma 90 og	17,000
30	lge	**Real Zaragoza**	A	L	1-4	Riquelme 62 pen	32,000
31	uc3rl1	**Galatasaray**	A	D	2-2	Anderson 7; Riquelme 22	40,000
32	lge	**Athl Bilbao**	H	L	0-1		11,928
33	uc3rl2	**Galatasaray**	H	W	3-0	Anderson 48; Roger 52; Riquelme 88	15,960
34	lge	**Seville**	A	L	0-2		37,000
35	uc4rl1	**Roma**	H	W	2-0	Anderson 29; Jose Mari 35	23,000
36	lge	**Albacete**	H	W	2-1	Coloccini 50; Anderson 58	16,000
37	lge	**Osasuna**	A	L	1-2	Riquelme 77 pen	16,915
38	uc4rl2	**Roma**	A	L	1-2	Anderson 66	29,088
39	lge	**Atl Madrid**	H	D	0-0		9,000
40	lge	**Barcelona**	A	D	0-0		50,000
41	ucqfl1	**Celtic**	A	D	1-1	Josico 9	58,493
42	lge	**Deportivo**	H	L	0-2		15,000
43	ucqfl2	**Celtic**	H	W	2-0	Anderson 6; Roger 68	15,964
44	lge	**Mallorca**	A	W	2-1	Alvarez 38; Marti 78	22,000
45	ucsfl1	**Valencia**	H	D	0-0		16,800
46	lge	**Murcia**	H	W	1-0	Alvarez 68	9,000
47	lge	**Real Sociedad**	A	D	2-2	Jose Mari 11,47	26,143
48	ucsfl2	**Valencia**	A	L	0-1		53,000
49	lge	**Real Betis**	H	W	1-0	Jose Mari 66	15,000
50	lge	**Valencia**	H	W	2-1	Anderson 13; Riquelme 26	12,000
51	lge	**Valladolid**	A	L	0-3		15,000

MONTHLY POINTS TALLY

AUGUST	1	33%
SEPTEMBER	8	67%
OCTOBER	2	17%
NOVEMBER	9	75%
DECEMBER	7	58%
JANUARY	6	50%
FEBRUARY	3	20%
MARCH	4	33%
APRIL	7	58%
MAY	7	58%

KEY PLAYERS - GOALSCORERS

Sonny Anderson

Goals in the League	12	Player Strike Rate Average number of minutes between League goals scored by player	183
Contribution to Attacking Power Average number of minutes between League team goals while on pitch	64	Club Strike Rate Average number of minutes between League goals scored by club	73

	PLAYER	LGE GOALS	POWER	STRIKE RATE
1	Sonny Anderson	12	64	183 mins
2	Juan Riquelme	8	71	347 mins
3	Romero Jose Mari	6	66	407 mins
4	Antonio Guayre	3	70	653 mins

KEY PLAYERS - MIDFIELDERS

Pedro Marti

Goals in the League	1	Contribution to Attacking Power Average number of minutes between League team goals while on pitch	74
Defensive Rating Average number of mins between League goals conceded while he was on the pitch	76	Scoring Difference Defensive Rating minus Contribution to Attacking Power	2

	PLAYER	LGE GOALS	DEF RATE	POWER	SCORE DIFF
1	Pedro Marti	1	76	74	2 mins
2	Juan Riquelme	8	65	71	-6 mins
3	Garcia Junyent Roger	2	80	87	-7 mins
4	Jose Moreno Verdu Josico	0	58	68	-10 mins

KEY PLAYERS - DEFENDERS

Quique San Juan Alvarez

Goals Conceded (GC) The number of League goals conceded while he was on the pitch	32	Clean Sheets In games when he played at least 70 minutes	8
Defensive Rating Ave number of mins between League goals conceded while on the pitch	78	Club Defensive Rating Average number of mins between League goals conceded by the club this season	70

	PLAYER	CON LGE	CLEAN SHEETS	DEF RATE
1	Quique San Juan Alvarez	32	8	78 mins
2	Fabricio Coloccini	32	6	73 mins
3	Sergio Martinez Ballesteros	37	8	72 mins
4	Rodolfo Martin Arruabarrena	41	9	71 mins

KEY GOALKEEPER

Jose Manuel Perez Reina

Goals Conceded in the League	**49**	Counting Games Games when he played at least 70 mins	**38**
Defensive Rating Ave number of mins between League goals conceded while on the pitch	**70**	Clean Sheets In games when he played at least 70 mins	**10**

LEAGUE GOALS

Sonny Anderson

Minutes on the pitch	2191	Goals in the League	12
League average (mins between goals)	183		

	PLAYER	MINS	GOALS	AVE
1	Anderson	2191	12	183
2	Riquelme	2778	8	347
3	Jose Mari	2442	6	407
4	Victor	1522	3	507
5	Belletti	2287	3	762
6	Guayre	1960	3	653
7	Roger	1917	2	959
8	Alvarez	2503	2	1252
9	Arruabarrena	2930	2	1465
10	Ballesteros	2678	1	2678
11	Marti	2661	1	2661
12	Coloccini	2348	1	2348
	Other		3	
	TOTAL		47	

DISCIPLINARY RECORDS

	PLAYER	YELLOW	RED	AVE
1	Battaglia	7	1	137
2	Alvarez	15	2	147
3	Jose Mari	14	2	152
4	Belletti	10	0	228
5	Coloccini	8	1	260
6	Marti	10	0	266
7	Arruabarrena	11	0	266
8	Ballesteros	9	1	267
9	Josico	4	0	460
10	Riquelme	6	0	463
11	Senna	1	0	484
12	Roger	3	0	639
13	Guayre	3	0	653
	Other	8	0	
	TOTAL	109	7	

TOP POINT EARNERS

	PLAYER	GAMES	AV PTS
1	Alvarez	28	1.71
2	Guayre	19	1.68
3	Roger	14	1.50
4	Arruabarrena	32	1.47
5	Jose Mari	26	1.46
6	Josico	18	1.44
7	Coloccini	23	1.43
8	Riquelme	30	1.43
9	Reina	38	1.42
10	Marti	27	1.41
	CLUB AVERAGE:		1.42

TEAM OF THE SEASON

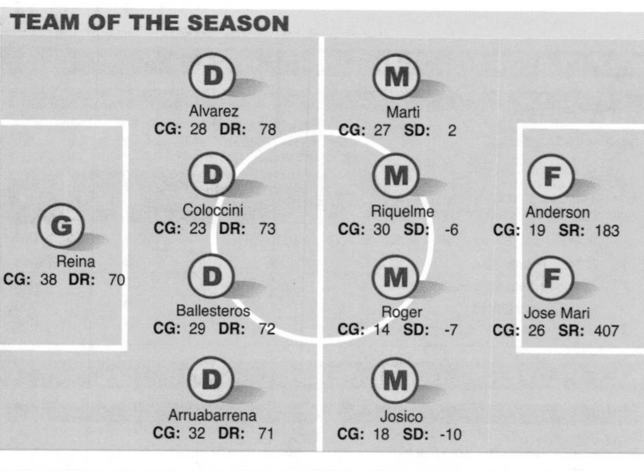

G
Reina
CG: 38 DR: 70
D
Alvarez
CG: 28 DR: 78
D
Coloccini
CG: 23 DR: 73
D
Ballesteros
CG: 29 DR: 72
D
Arruabarrena
CG: 32 DR: 71
M
Marti
CG: 27 SD: 2
M
Riquelme
CG: 30 SD: -6
M
Roger
CG: 14 SD: -7
M
Josico
CG: 18 SD: -10
F
Anderson
CG: 19 SR: 183
F
Jose Mari
CG: 26 SR: 407

LEAGUE APPEARANCES, BOOKINGS AND CAPS

	AGE (on 01/07/04)	IN NAMED 18	APPEARANCES	COUNTING GAMES	MINUTES ON PITCH	YELLOW CARDS	RED CARDS	THIS SEASON	HOME COUNTRY
Goalkeepers									
Javier Lopez Vallejo	28	38	0	0	0	0	0	-	Spain
Antonio Reguero	22	0	0	0	0	0	0	-	Spain
Jose Manuel Reina	21	38	38	38	3420	2	0	-	Spain
Defenders									
Carlos Alcantara	19	2	0	0	0	0	0	-	Spain
Quique Alvarez	28	30	29	28	2503	15	2	-	Spain
Martin Arruabarrena	28	34	34	32	2930	11	0	-	Argentina
Sergio Ballesteros	28	34	30	29	2678	9	1	-	Spain
Juliano Belletti	28	30	28	23	2287	10	0	-	Brazil
Fabricio Coloccini	22	36	31	23	2348	8	1	-	Argentina
Bel Edu Caballer	22	1	0	0	0	0	0	-	Spain
Javier Javi Venta	28	33	23	11	1426	2	0	-	Spain
Miguel Angel Tena	22	9	2	1	151	0	0	-	Spain
Midfielders									
Sebastian Battaglia	23	20	14	9	1103	7	1	-	Argentina
Javier Revilla Calleja	26	13	9	1	409	0	0	-	Spain
Jose Maria Cases	17	3	0	0	0	0	0	-	Spain
Amposta Cesar Arzo	18	18	10	0	140	2	0	-	Spain
David Galindo	21	1	0	0	0	0	0	-	Spain
Jose Moreno Josico	29	28	26	18	1843	4	0	-	Spain
Pedro Marti	22	36	34	27	2661	10	0	-	Spain
Juan Riquelme	26	34	33	30	2778	6	0	2	Argentina (5)
Garcia Roger	27	33	31	14	1917	3	0	-	Spain
Gonzalez Ruben	18	2	0	0	0	0	0	-	Spain
Gonzalez Santi	19	3	2	0	67	0	0	-	Spain
Marcos Senna	27	8	8	4	484	1	0	-	Brazil
Jose Teo	-	2	0	0	0	0	0	-	Spain
Jose Antonio Verza	17	14	3	1	102	0	0	-	Spain
Xisco Nada	18	13	7	0	71	0	0	-	Spain
Forwards									
Sonny Anderson	33	35	35	19	2191	1	0	-	Brazil
Antonio Guayre	24	33	31	19	1960	3	0	-	Spain
Romero Jose Mari	25	33	32	26	2442	14	2	-	Spain
Manuel Victor	30	30	27	8	1522	1	0	-	Spain

SQUAD APPEARANCES

Match	1 2 3 4 5	6 7 8 9 10	11 12 13 14 15	16 17 18 19 20	21 22 23 24 25	26 27 28 29 30	31 32 33 34 35	36 37 38 39 40	41 42 43 44 45	46 47 48 49 50	51
Venue	H A H A H	H A H A A	H A H H A	H A A H A	H A A H H	A H A H A	A H H A H	H A A H A	A H H A H	H A A H H	A
Competition	L L L L L	E L L E L	L L L E L	L E L L L	L L L L L	L L L L L	E L E L E	L L E L L	E L E L E	L L E L L	L
Result	D D D W D	D W D W L	D L W W L	W L W L D	W W L W W	L L L W L	D L W L W	W L L D D	D L W W D	W D L W W	L

Goalkeepers
Javier Lopez Vallejo
Antonio Chapinal Reguero
Jose Manuel Perez Reina

Defenders
Carlos Alcantara
Quique San Juan Alvarez
Martin Arruabarrena
Sergio Ballesteros
Juliano Haus Belletti
Fabricio Coloccini
Bel Edu Caballer
Rodriguez Javi Venta
Miguel Angel Tena

Midfielders
Sebastian Battaglia
Javier Revilla Calleja
Jose Maria Cases
Amposta Cesar Arzo
David Gallego Galindo
Jose Moreno Verdu Josico
Pedro Marti
Juan Riquelme
Garcia Junyent Roger
Gonzalez Ruben
Gonzalez Cazorla Santi
Marcos Antonio Senna
Jose Teodoro Teo
Jose Antonio Garcia Verza
Sebastian Xisco Nada

Forwards
Sonny Anderson
Antonio Guayre
Romero Jose Mari
Manuel Fernandez Victor

KEY: ■ On all match | ■ On bench | ⏮ Subbed or sent off (Counting game) | ◀◀ Subbed or sent off (playing less than 70 minutes) | ▶▶ Subbed on from bench (Counting Game) | ▶▶ Subbed on (playing less than 70 minutes) | ▶▶ Subbed on and then subbed or sent off (Counting Game) | ▶▶ Subbed on and then subbed or sent off (playing less than 70 minutes) | □ Not in 16

REAL BETIS

Final Position: **9th**

KEY: Won Drawn Lost

							Attendance
1	lge	Real Madrid	A	L	1-2	Juanito 33	76,000
2	lge	Espanyol	H	D	2-2	Joaquin 30; Palermo 42	33,600
3	lge	Celta Vigo	A	W	2-0	Assuncao 37; Fernando 86 pen	18,000
4	lge	R Santander	H	D	0-0		42,000
5	lge	Real Zaragoza	A	W	1-0	Assuncao 83	17,500
6	lge	Athl Bilbao	H	D	1-1	Assuncao 90	28,000
7	lge	Seville	A	D	2-2	Denilson 53; Tote 61	44,000
8	lge	Albacete	H	W	3-2	Tote 42; Fernando 45; Capi 51	42,000
9	lge	Osasuna	A	L	0-2		14,000
10	lge	Atl Madrid	H	L	1-2	Assuncao 20	50,000
11	lge	Barcelona	A	L	1-2	Fernando 53	88,000
12	lge	Deportivo	H	D	0-0		26,000
13	lge	Mallorca	A	L	1-2	Palermo 38	12,000
14	lge	Murcia	H	D	1-1	Ismael 49	19,000
15	lge	Real Sociedad	A	W	4-0	Capi 5; Joaquin 15,59; Juanito 49	25,000
16	lge	Valencia	H	L	0-1		40,000
17	lge	Villarreal	H	L	1-3	Juanito 81	40,000
18	lge	Valladolid	A	D	0-0		18,500
19	lge	Malaga	H	W	3-0	Alfonso 7; Joaquin 48,59	35,000
20	lge	Real Madrid	H	D	1-1	Joaquin 32	49,000
21	lge	Espanyol	A	W	2-1	Mingo 9; Fernando 30 pen	38,500
22	lge	Celta Vigo	H	W	1-0	Lembo 36	35,000
23	lge	R Santander	A	W	2-1	Benjamin 32; Joaquin 90	21,000
24	lge	Real Zaragoza	H	W	2-1	Denilson 33; Alfonso 38	40,000
25	lge	Athl Bilbao	A	D	1-1	Benjamin 52	35,000
26	lge	Seville	H	D	1-1	Alfonso 2 pen	48,000
27	lge	Albacete	A	L	0-1		16,000
28	lge	Osasuna	H	D	1-1	Benjamin 42	36,750
29	lge	Atl Madrid	A	L	1-2	Joaquin 67	45,587
30	lge	Deportivo	A	D	2-2	Assuncao 31; Dani 77	24,000
31	lge	Mallorca	H	L	0-2		17,000
32	lge	Barcelona	H	D	1-1	Alfonso 36 pen	48,825
33	lge	Murcia	A	W	1-0	Assuncao 4	8,943
34	lge	Real Sociedad	H	W	2-1	Benjamin 15; Dani 20	25,000
35	lge	Valencia	A	L	0-2		45,000
36	lge	Villarreal	A	L	0-1		15,000
37	lge	Valladolid	H	W	1-0	Assuncao 74	25,000
38	lge	Malaga	A	W	3-2	Dani 62,90; Juanito 70	20,000

MONTHLY POINTS TALLY

AUGUST	0	0%
SEPTEMBER	8	67%
OCTOBER	5	42%
NOVEMBER	1	8%
DECEMBER	4	33%
JANUARY	11	73%
FEBRUARY	8	67%
MARCH	1	11%
APRIL	8	53%
MAY	6	50%

KEY PLAYERS - GOALSCORERS

Zacarias Marcos Assuncao

Goals in the League	7	Player Strike Rate Average number of minutes between League goals scored by player	219
Contribution to Attacking Power Average number of minutes between League team goals while on pitch	80	Club Strike Rate Average number of minutes between League goals scored by club	74

	PLAYER	LGE GOALS	POWER	STRIKE RATE
1	Zacarias Marcos Assuncao	7	80	219 mins
2	Joaquin Sanchez Rodriguez	8	73	397 mins
3	Benjamin Zarandona Esono	4	71	413 mins
4	Fernandez Escribano Fernando	4	72	451 mins

KEY PLAYERS - MIDFIELDERS

Antonio Alvarez Ito

Goals in the League	0	Contribution to Attacking Power Average number of minutes between League team goals while on pitch	72
Defensive Rating Average number of mins between League goals conceded while he was on the pitch	81	Scoring Difference Defensive Rating minus Contribution to Attacking Power	9

	PLAYER	LGE GOALS	DEF RATE	POWER	SCORE DIFF
1	Antonio Alvarez Ito	0	81	72	9 mins
2	Benjamin Zarandona Esono	4	79	72	7 mins
3	Arturo Garcia Munoz	0	81	78	3 mins
4	Joaquin Sanchez Rodriguez	8	77	74	3 mins

KEY PLAYERS - DEFENDERS

Gutierrez Luis Fernandez

Goals Conceded (GC) The number of League goals conceded while he was on the pitch	20	Clean Sheets In games when he played at least 70 minutes	7
Defensive Rating Ave number of mins between League goals conceded while on the pitch	88	Club Defensive Rating Average number of mins between League goals conceded by the club this season	80

	PLAYER	CON LGE	CLEAN SHEETS	DEF RATE
1	Gutierrez Luis Fernandez	20	7	88 mins
2	Daniel Alejandro Lembo	32	8	80 mins
3	Juan Jesus Juanito	39	8	79 mins
4	David Rivas Rodriguez	23	6	79 mins

KEY GOALKEEPER

Antonio Prats

Goals Conceded in the League	18	Counting Games Games when he played at least 70 mins	16
Defensive Rating Ave number of mins between League goals conceded while on the pitch	80	Clean Sheets In games when he played at least 70 mins	2

LEAGUE GOALS

Joaquin Sanchez Rodriguez

Minutes on the pitch	3176	Goals in the League	8
League average (mins between goals)	397		

	PLAYER	MINS	GOALS	AVE
1	Joaquin	3176	8	397
2	Assuncao	1530	7	219
3	Alfonso	1310	4	328
4	Benjamin	1652	4	413
5	Dani	1097	4	274
6	Juanito	3081	4	770
7	Fernando	1804	4	451
8	Tote	828	2	414
9	Palermo	615	2	308
10	Capi	1311	2	656
11	Denilson	1884	2	942
12	Mingo	1046	1	1046
13	Ismael	1493	1	1493
	Other		1	
	TOTAL		46	

DISCIPLINARY RECORDS

	PLAYER	YELLOW	RED	AVE
1	Tais	3	1	172
2	Lembo	13	1	183
3	Capi	6	0	218
4	Rivas	7	0	259
5	Ito	6	1	266
6	Varela	8	0	277
7	Arzu	7	0	279
8	Luis Fernandez	5	0	351
9	Mingo	2	0	523
10	Dani	2	0	548
11	Fernando	3	0	601
12	Palermo	1	0	615
13	Denilson	3	0	628
	Other	17	2	
	TOTAL	83	5	

TOP POINT EARNERS

	PLAYER	GAMES	AV PTS
1	Fernando	12	2.08
2	Mingo	12	1.75
3	Benjamin	18	1.67
4	Lembo	27	1.59
5	Denilson	15	1.53
6	Varela	23	1.52
7	Prats	16	1.44
8	Juanito	33	1.39
9	Contreras	22	1.32
10	Joaquin	34	1.32
	CLUB AVERAGE:		1.37

TEAM OF THE SEASON

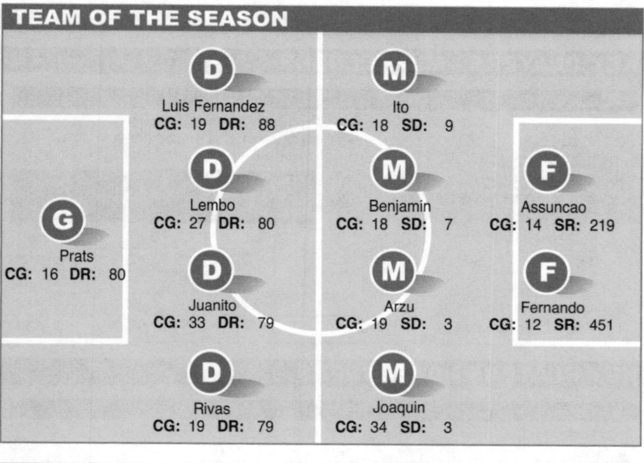

G
Prats
CG: 16 DR: 80
D
Luis Fernandez
CG: 19 DR: 88
D
Lembo
CG: 27 DR: 80
D
Juanito
CG: 33 DR: 79
D
Rivas
CG: 19 DR: 79
M
Ito
CG: 18 SD: 9
M
Benjamin
CG: 18 SD: 7
M
Arzu
CG: 19 SD: 3
M
Joaquin
CG: 34 SD: 3
F
Assuncao
CG: 14 SR: 219
F
Fernando
CG: 12 SR: 451

LEAGUE APPEARANCES, BOOKINGS AND CAPS

	AGE (on 01/07/04)	IN NAMED 18	APPEARANCES	COUNTING GAMES	MINUTES ON PITCH	YELLOW CARDS	RED CARDS	THIS SEASON	HOME COUNTRY
Goalkeepers									
Pedro Contreras	32	33	22	22	1980	1	0	-	Spain
Antonio Prats	32	34	16	16	1440	1	0	-	Spain
Pablo Vargas	20	9	0	0	0	0	0	-	Spain
Defenders									
David Belenguer	31	6	0	0	0	0	0	-	Spain
Juan Jesus Juanito	27	35	35	33	3081	3	0	2	Spain (3)
Daniel Lembo	26	35	30	27	2565	13	1	1	Uruguay (25)
Luis Fernandez	31	25	20	19	1758	5	0	-	Spain
Carles Mingo	27	17	12	12	1046	2	0	-	Spain
David Rivas	25	36	26	19	1819	7	0	-	Spain
Washington Tais	31	11	8	7	690	3	1	-	Uruguay
Midfielders									
Arturo Munoz Arzu	23	37	30	19	1953	7	0	-	Spain
Benjamin Esono	28	31	22	18	1652	1	1	-	Spain
Juan Jose Canas	32	19	7	1	149	0	0	-	Spain
Jesus Prada	27	26	24	11	1311	6	0	-	Spain
Denilson	26	30	29	15	1884	3	0	-	Brazil
Antonio Alvarez Ito	29	36	29	18	1866	6	1	-	Spain
Joaquin	23	36	36	34	3176	4	1	6	Spain (3)
Juan Alvarado Melli	20	11	4	2	285	2	0	-	Spain
Fernando Varela	24	32	28	23	2223	8	0	-	Spain
Forwards									
Perez Alfonso	31	22	20	11	1310	1	0	-	Spain
Navarro Antonito	23	3	0	0	0	0	0	-	Spain
Zacarias Assuncao	27	20	19	14	1530	2	0	-	Brazil
Daniel Martin Dani	22	24	17	9	1097	2	0	-	Spain
Fernandez Fernando	30	38	31	12	1804	3	0	-	Spain
Lopez Ismael	26	38	30	9	1493	1	0	-	Spain
Jose Maldonado	23	1	1	0	18	0	0	-	Spain
Martin Palermo	30	17	11	4	615	1	0	-	Argentina
Jorge Lopez Marco Tote	25	20	17	3	828	1	0	-	Spain

SQUAD APPEARANCES

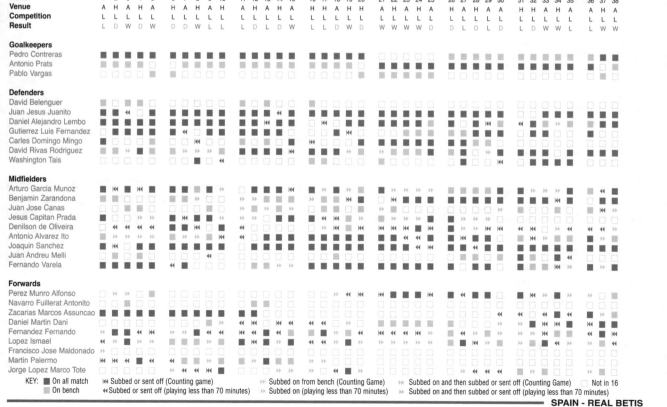

Match	1	2	3	4	5	6	7	8	9	10	11	12	13	14	15	16	17	18	19	20	21	22	23	24	25	26	27	28	29	30	31	32	33	34	35	36	37	38
Venue	A	H	A	H	A	H	A	H	A	H	A	H	A	H	A	H	H	A	H	H	A	H	A	H	A	H	A	H	A	A	H	H	A	H	A	A	H	A
Competition	L	L	L	L	L	L	L	L	L	L	L	L	L	L	L	L	L	L	L	L	L	L	L	L	L	L	L	L	L	L	L	L	L	L	L	L	L	L
Result	L	D	W	D	W	D	D	W	L	L	L	D	L	D	W	L	L	D	W	D	W	W	W	W	D	D	L	D	L	D	L	D	W	W	L	L	W	W

Goalkeepers
Pedro Contreras
Antonio Prats
Pablo Vargas

Defenders
David Belenguer
Juan Jesus Juanito
Daniel Alejandro Lembo
Gutierrez Luis Fernandez
Carles Domingo Mingo
David Rivas Rodriguez
Washington Tais

Midfielders
Arturo Garcia Munoz
Benjamin Zarandona
Juan Jose Canas
Jesus Capitan Prada
Denilson de Oliveira
Antonio Alvarez Ito
Joaquin Sanchez
Juan Andreu Melli
Fernando Varela

Forwards
Perez Munro Alfonso
Navarro Fuillerat Antonito
Zacarias Marcos Assuncao
Daniel Martin Dani
Fernandez Fernando
Lopez Ismael
Francisco Jose Maldonado
Martin Palermo
Jorge Lopez Marco Tote

KEY: ■ On all match ■ On bench ⏮ Subbed or sent off (Counting game) ◀◀ Subbed or sent off (playing less than 70 minutes) ⏭ Subbed on from bench (Counting Game) ▶▶ Subbed on (playing less than 70 minutes) ⏭ Subbed on and then subbed or sent off (Counting Game) ▶▶ Subbed on and then subbed or sent off (playing less than 70 minutes) □ Not in 16

MALAGA

Final Position: **10th**

KEY: ☐ Won ☐ Drawn ☐ Lost

							Attendance
1	lge	Villarreal	H	D	0-0		18,000
2	lge	Valladolid	A	L	0-1		11,000
3	lge	Valencia	A	L	0-1		45,000
4	lge	Real Madrid	H	L	1-3	Edgar 79	23,000
5	lge	Espanyol	A	W	2-1	Romero 38; Salva 86	19,000
6	lge	Celta Vigo	H	W	2-1	Fernando Sanz 14; Miguel Angel 75	28,000
7	lge	R Santander	A	L	2-4	Salva 20; Leko 90	21,500
8	lge	Real Zaragoza	H	W	2-1	Litos 29; Salva 45 pen	19,000
9	lge	Athl Bilbao	A	L	1-2	Diego Alonso 3	28,000
10	lge	Seville	H	W	2-0	Duda 2; Salva 22 pen	35,000
11	lge	Albacete	A	W	1-0	Salva 63	12,500
12	lge	Osasuna	H	D	0-0		35,500
13	lge	Atl Madrid	A	L	0-2		45,500
14	lge	Barcelona	H	W	5-1	Salva 9,15,69; Diego Alonso 73; Canabal 87	20,000
15	lge	Deportivo	A	L	0-1		24,000
16	lge	Mallorca	H	W	3-1	Fernando Sanz 12; Duda 71; Salva 90 pen	20,000
17	lge	Murcia	A	W	2-1	Insua 16; Canabal 90	16,500
18	lge	Real Sociedad	H	L	1-2	Litos 25	27,454
19	lge	Real Betis	A	L	0-3		35,000
20	lge	Villarreal	A	L	0-2		11,000
21	lge	Valladolid	H	L	2-3	Salva 23,80	22,000
22	lge	Valencia	H	L	1-6	Salva 74	23,000
23	lge	Real Madrid	A	L	1-2	Luque 74	35,000
24	lge	Espanyol	H	W	5-2	Miguel Angel 36; Manu 43; Juanito 45; Salva 61; Insua 84	20,000
25	lge	Celta Vigo	A	W	2-0	Salva 15 pen; Diego Alonso 90	20,000
26	lge	R Santander	H	W	1-0	Salva 37	35,245
27	lge	Real Zaragoza	A	L	0-1		27,000
28	lge	Athl Bilbao	H	W	2-1	Luque 47; Salva 90	23,744
29	lge	Seville	A	W	1-0	Salva 77	28,350
30	lge	Albacete	H	D	1-1	Diego Alonso 82	8,000
31	lge	Osasuna	A	D	1-1	Insua 89	14,800
32	lge	Atl Madrid	H	W	3-1	Leko 31; Diego Alonso 45,48	22,000
33	lge	Barcelona	A	L	0-3		48,000
34	lge	Deportivo	H	D	1-1	Canabal 42	21,000
35	lge	Mallorca	A	L	1-2	Salva 60	20,000
36	lge	Murcia	H	W	1-0	Miguel Angel 66	20,000
37	lge	Real Sociedad	A	D	1-1	Duda 63	28,713
38	lge	Real Betis	H	L	2-3	Salva 21; Canabal 45	20,000

MONTHLY POINTS TALLY

Month	Points	%
AUGUST	1	33%
SEPTEMBER	3	25%
OCTOBER	6	50%
NOVEMBER	7	58%
DECEMBER	9	75%
JANUARY	0	0%
FEBRUARY	9	75%
MARCH	7	58%
APRIL	5	42%
MAY	4	33%

KEY PLAYERS - GOALSCORERS

Ioan Ballesta Salva

Goals in the League	18	Player Strike Rate Average number of minutes between League goals scored by player	159
Contribution to Attacking Power Average number of minutes between League team goals while on pitch	66	Club Strike Rate Average number of minutes between League goals scored by club	68

	PLAYER	LGE GOALS	POWER	STRIKE RATE
1	Ioan Ballesta Salva	18	66	159 mins
2	Ivan Leko	2	63	757 mins
3	Sergio Paulo Ouda	3	79	931 mins
4	Lozano Ayala Miguel Angel	3	61	1001 mins

KEY PLAYERS - MIDFIELDERS

Ivan Leko

Goals in the League	2	Contribution to Attacking Power Average number of minutes between League team goals while on pitch	63
Defensive Rating Average number of mins between League goals conceded while he was on the pitch	69	Scoring Difference Defensive Rating minus Contribution to Attacking Power	6

	PLAYER	LGE GOALS	DEF RATE	POWER	SCORE DIFF
1	Ivan Leko	2	69	63	6 mins
2	Patricio Edgar	1	68	65	3 mins
3	Lozano Ayala Miguel Angel	3	64	61	3 mins
4	Sergio Paulo Barbosa Duda	3	65	80	-15 mins

KEY PLAYERS - DEFENDERS

Garcia Moreno Leon Gerardo

Goals Conceded (GC) The number of League goals conceded while he was on the pitch	32	Clean Sheets In games when he played at least 70 minutes	5
Defensive Rating Ave number of mins between League goals conceded while on the pitch	71	Club Defensive Rating Average number of mins between League goals conceded by the club this season	62

	PLAYER	CON LGE	CLEAN SHEETS	DEF RATE
1	Garcia Moreno Leon Gerardo	32	5	71 mins
2	Carlos Litos	40	8	71 mins
3	Vicente Cano Valcarce	39	5	69 mins
4	Miguel Gonzalez Rey Josemi	50	8	64 mins

KEY GOALKEEPER

Francesc Arnau Grabalosa

Goals Conceded in the League	29	Counting Games Games when he played at least 70 mins	22
Defensive Rating Ave number of mins between League goals conceded while on the pitch	66	Clean Sheets In games when he played at least 70 mins	5

LEAGUE GOALS

Ioan Ballesta Salva

Minutes on the pitch	2860	Goals in the League	18
League average (mins between goals)	159		

	PLAYER	MINS	GOALS	AVE
1	Salva	2860	18	159
2	Diego Alonso	745	6	124
3	Duda	2793	3	931
4	Miguel Angel	3002	3	1001
5	Canabal	665	3	222
6	Litos	2842	2	1421
7	Insua	1365	2	683
8	Leko	1514	2	757
9	Luque	300	2	150
10	Fernando Sanz	2174	2	1087
11	Manu	1348	1	1348
12	Romero	2031	1	2031
13	Juanito	614	1	614
	Other		4	
	TOTAL		50	

DISCIPLINARY RECORDS

	PLAYER	YELLOW	RED	AVE
1	Rojas	3	0	186
2	Romero	10	0	203
3	Fernando Sanz	10	0	217
4	Manu	6	0	224
5	Valcarce	11	1	225
6	Duda	11	1	232
7	Litos	12	0	236
8	Josemi	12	0	266
9	Juanito	2	0	307
10	Canabal	2	0	332
11	Leko	4	0	378
12	Gerardo	6	0	380
13	Arnau	3	1	478
	Other	12	0	
	TOTAL	104	3	

TOP POINT EARNERS

	PLAYER	GAMES	AV PTS
1	Leko	14	1.57
2	Miguel Angel	32	1.56
3	Litos	29	1.52
4	Valcarce	28	1.50
5	Edgar	27	1.48
6	Arnau	21	1.48
7	Gerardo	20	1.40
8	Salva	32	1.38
9	Josemi	36	1.33
10	Fernando Sanz	23	1.26
	CLUB AVERAGE:		1.34

LEAGUE APPEARANCES, BOOKINGS AND CAPS

	AGE (on 01/07/04)	IN NAMED 18	APPEARANCES	COUNTING GAMES	MINUTES ON PITCH	YELLOW CARDS	RED CARDS	THIS SEASON	HOME COUNTRY
Goalkeepers									
Francesc Arnau	29	26	22	21	1914	3	1	-	Spain
Juan Calatayud	25	35	17	16	1505	0	0	-	Spain
Inaki Pena Goitia	-	15	0	0	0	0	0	-	Spain
Defenders									
Delgado Alexis	18	8	2	0	41	0	0	-	Spain
Fernando Sanz	30	36	26	23	2174	10	0	-	Spain
Garcia Gerardo	29	35	33	20	2283	6	0	-	Spain
Raul Zabala Iznata	26	2	1	0	18	0	0	-	Spain
Miguel Rey Josemi	24	37	37	36	3202	12	0	-	Spain
Carlos Litos	30	36	34	29	2842	12	0	-	Portugal
Roberto Rojas	29	22	10	4	558	3	0	-	Spain
Vicente Valcarce	29	36	32	28	2700	11	1	-	Spain
Midfielders									
Aguilar Alberto	19	2	2	2	180	0	0	-	Spain
Sergio Duda	24	36	35	29	2793	11	1	-	Portugal
Patricio Edgar	26	35	34	27	2660	2	0	-	Spain
Juan Rodriguez	22	11	2	0	79	0	0	-	Spain
Ivan Leko	26	33	22	14	1514	4	0	-	Croatia
Jose Juan Luque	26	22	11	1	300	0	0	-	Spain
Sanchez Manu	25	36	27	6	1348	6	0	-	Spain
Miguel Angel	25	37	35	32	3002	6	0	-	Spain
Insua Pocho	24	2	2	0	47	0	0	-	Argentina
Marcelo Romero	28	29	26	21	2031	10	0	3	Uruguay (25)
Forwards									
Manuel Canabal	29	31	19	2	665	2	0	-	Spain
Diego Alonso	29	35	22	4	745	0	0	-	Uruguay
Alexandre Geijo	22	1	1	0	37	0	0	-	Spain
Federico Insua	24	36	28	7	1365	0	0	-	Argentina
Jesus Juanito	24	14	8	6	614	2	0	2	Spain (3)
Ioan Ballesta Salva	29	34	33	32	2860	4	0	-	Spain

TEAM OF THE SEASON

G — Arnau — CG: 21 DR: 66

D — Gerardo — CG: 20 DR: 71

D — Litos — CG: 29 DR: 71

D — Valcarce — CG: 28 DR: 69

D — Josemi — CG: 36 DR: 64

M — Romero — CG: 21 SD: -30

M — Edgar — CG: 27 SD: 3

M — Miguel Angel — CG: 32 SD: 3

M — Duda — CG: 29 SD: -15

F — Salva — CG: 32 SR: 159

F — *Leko — CG: 14 SR: 75

SQUAD APPEARANCES

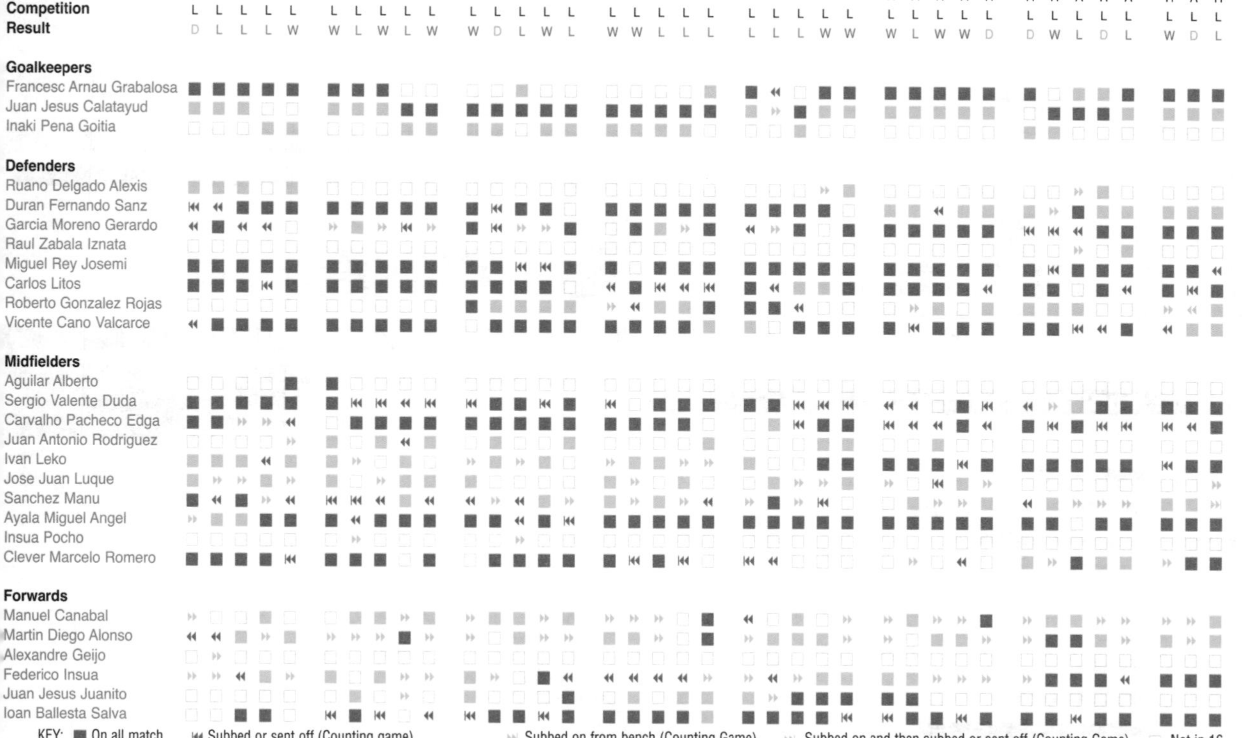

Match 1 2 3 4 5 6 7 8 9 10 11 12 13 14 15 16 17 18 19 20 21 22 23 24 25 26 27 28 29 30 31 32 33 34 35 36 37 38
Venue H A A H A H A H A H A H A H A H A H A A H H A H A H A H A H A H A H A H A H
Competition L L L L L L L L L L L L L L L L L L L L L L L L L L L L L L L L L L L L L L
Result D L L L W W L W L W W D L W L W W L L L L L L W W W L W W D D W L D L W D L
Goalkeepers
Francesc Arnau Grabalosa
Juan Jesus Calatayud
Inaki Pena Goitia
Defenders
Ruano Delgado Alexis
Duran Fernando Sanz
Garcia Moreno Gerardo
Raul Zabala Iznata
Miguel Rey Josemi
Carlos Litos
Roberto Gonzalez Rojas
Vicente Cano Valcarce
Midfielders
Aguilar Alberto
Sergio Valente Duda
Carvalho Pacheco Edga
Juan Antonio Rodriguez
Ivan Leko
Jose Juan Luque
Sanchez Manu
Ayala Miguel Angel
Insua Pocho
Clever Marcelo Romero
Forwards
Manuel Canabal
Martin Diego Alonso
Alexandre Geijo
Federico Insua
Juan Jesus Juanito
Ioan Ballesta Salva
KEY: On all match
On bench
Subbed or sent off (Counting game)
Subbed or sent off (playing less than 70 minutes)
Subbed on from bench (Counting Game)
Subbed on (playing less than 70 minutes)
Subbed on and then subbed or sent off (Counting Game)
Subbed on and then subbed or sent off (playing less than 70 minutes)
Not in 16

MALLORCA

Final Position: **11th**

KEY: Won Drawn Lost

							Attendance
1	lge	R Santander	A	L	1-2	Eto'o 89 pen	11,517
2	lge	Real Zaragoza	H	W	2-0	Bruggink 43; Eto'o 55 pen	22,515
3	lge	Athl Bilbao	A	L	0-4		36,000
4	lge	Seville	H	D	1-1	Bruggink 40	12,000
5	uc1rl1	Apoel Nicosia	A	W	2-1	Toni Gonzalez 20; Bruggink 60	7,000
6	lge	Albacete	A	L	0-2		13,000
7	lge	Osasuna	H	D	1-1	Nadal 85	22,500
8	uc1rl2	Apoel Nicosia	H	W	4-2	Eto'o 28,61,70; Correa 89	7,000
9	lge	Atl Madrid	A	L	1-2	Eto'o 39	57,000
10	lge	Barcelona	H	L	1-3	Correa 87	22,500
11	lge	Deportivo	A	W	2-0	Eto'o 76 pen; Bruggink 88	23,000
12	lge	Valencia	H	L	0-5		21,500
13	uc2rl1	Copenhagen	A	W	2-1	Albrechtsen 27 og; Nagore 73	41,781
14	lge	Murcia	H	W	4-1	Colsa 8; Correa 40,43; Eto'o 69	14,000
15	lge	Real Sociedad	A	W	1-0	Eto'o 18	29,000
16	uc2rl2	Copenhagen	H	D	1-1	Campano 69	9,000
17	lge	Real Betis	H	W	2-1	Campano 25; Raul Martin 82	12,000
18	lge	Villarreal	A	W	2-0	Eto'o 54; Campano 60	16,000
19	lge	Valladolid	H	W	1-0	Correa 15	14,500
20	lge	Malaga	A	L	1-3	Eto'o 31	20,000
21	lge	Real Madrid	H	L	1-3	Correa 11	23,000
22	lge	Espanyol	A	L	0-2		36,000
23	lge	Celta Vigo	H	L	2-4	Bruggink 13 pen,45	15,500
24	lge	R Santander	H	D	1-1	Colsa 48	15,500
25	lge	Real Zaragoza	A	W	3-1	Delibasic 41; Bruggink 43; Nene 90	28,000
26	lge	Athl Bilbao	H	L	1-3	Gurpegui 38 og	19,500
27	lge	Seville	A	L	0-3		27,500
28	lge	Albacete	H	D	0-0		16,000
29	lge	Osasuna	A	D	1-1	Delibasic 6	14,000
30	uc3rl1	Sp Moscow	A	W	3-0	Eto'o 67; Toni Gonzalez 81; Perera 85	30,000
31	lge	Atl Madrid	H	L	0-1		16,500
32	uc3rl2	Sp Moscow	H	L	0-1		5,000
33	lge	Barcelona	A	L	2-3	Eto'o 89; Delibasic 90	93,000
34	uc4rl1	Newcastle	A	L	1-4	Correa 57	38,012
35	lge	Deportivo	H	W	4-2	Correa 7; Ramis 35; Eto'o 59 pen; Perera 84	18,486
36	lge	Valencia	A	L	1-5	Eto'o 84 pen	47,700
37	uc4rl2	Newcastle	H	L	0-3		11,500
38	lge	Murcia	A	L	0-2		2,500
39	lge	Real Sociedad	H	D	1-1	Perera 57	20,000
40	lge	Real Betis	A	W	2-0	Eto'o 15; Perera 51	17,000
41	lge	Villarreal	H	L	1-2	Eto'o 45 pen	22,000
42	lge	Valladolid	A	W	3-1	Delibasic 16; Correa 68,84	21,000
43	lge	Malaga	H	W	2-1	Eto'o 25,67	20,000
44	lge	Real Madrid	A	W	3-2	Eto'o 11,37; Campano 43	55,000
45	lge	Espanyol	H	W	4-2	Perera 64; Bruggink 73; Pereyra 89; Colsa 90	18,000
46	lge	Celta Vigo	A	W	2-1	Nene 90; Perera 90	27,000

MONTHLY POINTS TALLY

Month	Points	%
AUGUST	0	0%
SEPTEMBER	4	33%
OCTOBER	4	33%
NOVEMBER	9	75%
DECEMBER	6	50%
JANUARY	4	33%
FEBRUARY	2	13%
MARCH	3	25%
APRIL	7	58%
MAY	12	100%

KEY PLAYERS - GOALSCORERS

Samuel Fils Eto'o

Goals in the League	17	Player Strike Rate Average number of minutes between League goals scored by player	168
Contribution to Attacking Power Average number of minutes between League team goals while on pitch	63	Club Strike Rate Average number of minutes between League goals scored by club	63

	PLAYER	LGE GOALS	POWER	STRIKE RATE
1	Samuel Fils Eto'o	17	63	168 mins
2	Fernando Correa	8	51	199 mins
3	Alejandro Hernando Campano	3	59	651 mins
4	Gonzalo Ruiz Abendea Colsa	3	70	841 mins

KEY PLAYERS - MIDFIELDERS

Martin de la Fuente Marcos

Goals in the League	0	Contribution to Attacking Power Average number of minutes between League team goals while on pitch	63
Defensive Rating Average number of mins between League goals conceded while he was on the pitch	54	Scoring Difference Defensive Rating minus Contribution to Attacking Power	-9

	PLAYER	LGE GOALS	DEF RATE	POWER	SCORE DIFF
1	Martin de la Fuente Marcos	0	54	63	-9 mins
2	Alejandro Hernando Campano	3	48	59	-11 mins
3	Gonzalo Ruiz Abendea Colsa	3	55	70	-15 mins
4	Anderson Nene	2	50	67	-17 mins

KEY PLAYERS - DEFENDERS

Fernandez Poli

Goals Conceded (GC) The number of League goals conceded while he was on the pitch	36	Clean Sheets In games when he played at least 70 minutes	5
Defensive Rating Ave number of mins between League goals conceded while on the pitch	62	Club Defensive Rating Average number of mins between League goals conceded by the club this season	52

	PLAYER	CON LGE	CLEAN SHEETS	DEF RATE
1	Fernandez Poli	36	5	62 mins
2	David Cortez	44	7	62 mins
3	Federico Lussenhof	40	4	56 mins
4	Fernando Bejarano Nino	45	5	52 mins

KEY GOALKEEPER

Leonardo Franco

Goals Conceded in the League	57	Counting Games Games when he played at least 70 mins	33
Defensive Rating Ave number of mins between League goals conceded while on the pitch	51	Clean Sheets In games when he played at least 70 mins	6

LEAGUE GOALS

Samuel Fils Eto'o

Minutes on the pitch	2851	Goals in the League	17
League average (mins between goals)	168		

	PLAYER	MINS	GOALS	AVE
1	Eto'o	2851	17	168
2	Correa	1588	8	199
3	Bruggink	1318	6	220
4	Perera	769	5	154
5	Delibasic	1126	4	282
6	Campano	1952	3	651
7	Colsa	2524	3	841
8	Nene	1799	2	900
9	Nadal	1747	1	1747
10	Ramis	679	1	679
11	Raul Martin	365	1	365
12	Pereyra	1205	1	1205
	Other		2	
	TOTAL		54	

DISCIPLINARY RECORDS

	PLAYER	YELLOW	RED	AVE
1	Nagore	7	0	168
2	Nino	10	1	214
3	Poli	8	0	277
4	Lussenhof	8	0	280
5	Pereyra	4	0	301
6	Edu Moya	2	0	320
7	Marcos	5	0	325
8	Perera	2	0	384
9	Campano	5	0	390
10	Correa	4	0	397
11	Franco	5	2	414
12	Nadal	4	0	436
13	Cortez	6	0	453
	Other	18	2	
	TOTAL	88	5	

TOP POINT EARNERS

	PLAYER	GAMES	AV PTS
1	Campano	15	1.87
2	Correa	12	1.83
3	Nene	12	1.67
4	Marcos	14	1.57
5	Lussenhof	25	1.56
6	Cortez	29	1.52
7	Poli	23	1.39
8	Franco	32	1.38
9	Eto'o	32	1.38
10	Nino	25	1.32
	CLUB AVERAGE:		1.34

LEAGUE APPEARANCES, BOOKINGS AND CAPS

	AGE (on 01/07/04)	IN NAMED 18	APPEARANCES	COUNTING GAMES	MINUTES ON PITCH	YELLOW CARDS	RED CARDS	THIS SEASON	HOME COUNTRY
Goalkeepers									
Martinez Alberto	25	3	0	0	0	0	0	-	Spain
Leonardo Franco	27	33	33	32	2899	5	2	-	Argentina
Miguel Garo Miki	28	37	6	6	519	0	0	-	Spain
Defenders									
David Cortez	24	34	32	29	2720	6	0	-	Spain
Castillo Edu Moya	23	18	9	6	640	2	0	-	Spain
Federico Lussenhof	30	30	26	25	2240	8	0	-	Argentina
Miguel Angel Nadal	37	28	24	18	1747	4	0	-	Spain
Fernando Nino	29	28	28	25	2358	10	1	-	Spain
Xavier Olaizola	34	25	14	9	1027	0	0	-	Spain
Fernandez Poli	27	27	27	23	2216	8	0	-	Spain
Rafael Rafita	21	0	0	0	0	0	0	-	Spain
Ivan Ramis	19	16	9	7	679	1	0	-	Spain
Midfielders									
Alejandro Campano	25	32	30	15	1952	5	0	-	Spain
Gonzalo Colsa	25	33	32	23	2524	3	0	-	Spain
Sola Enric Pi	21	1	0	0	0	0	0	-	Spain
Martin Liguera	23	9	1	0	11	0	0	7	Uruguay (25)
de la Fuente Marcos	35	32	25	14	1627	5	0	-	Spain
Arbizu Nagore	29	29	22	8	1179	7	0	-	Spain
Anderson Nene	22	35	28	12	1799	1	1	-	Brazil
Guillermo Pereyra	24	16	16	11	1205	4	0	-	Argentina
Raul Martin	24	9	7	3	365	1	0	-	Spain
Jovan Stankovic	33	15	11	1	323	2	0	-	Serbia & Montenegro
Toni Gonzalez	22	27	14	5	788	1	0	-	Spain
Fernandez Vicente	28	1	0	0	0	0	0	-	Spain
Forwards									
Arnold Bruggink	26	32	26	8	1318	2	0	-	Holland
Fernando Correa	30	30	27	12	1588	4	0	2	Uruguay (25)
Andrija Delibasic	23	17	17	9	1126	1	0	-	Serbia & Montenegro
Samuel Fils Eto'o	23	32	32	32	2851	5	1	4	Cameroon (12)
Finidi George	33	16	14	7	957	1	0	-	Nigeria
Jose Jesus Perera	24	34	19	4	769	2	0	-	Spain

TEAM OF THE SEASON

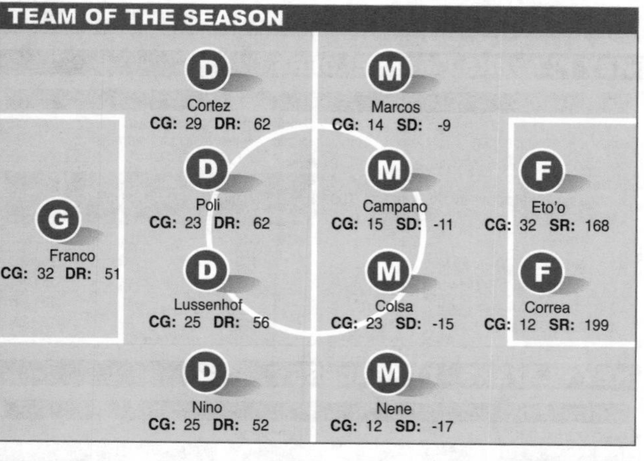

D
Cortez
CG: 29 DR: 62
M
Marcos
CG: 14 SD: -9
D
Poli
CG: 23 DR: 62
M
Campano
CG: 15 SD: -11
F
Eto'o
CG: 32 SR: 168
G
Franco
CG: 32 DR: 51
D
Lussenhof
CG: 25 DR: 56
M
Colsa
CG: 23 SD: -15
F
Correa
CG: 12 SR: 199
D
Nino
CG: 25 DR: 52
M
Nene
CG: 12 SD: -17

SQUAD APPEARANCES

Match	1	2	3	4	5	6	7	8	9	10	11	12	13	14	15	16	17	18	19	20	21	22	23	24	25	26	27	28	29	30	31	32	33	34	35	36	37	38	39	40	41	42	43	44	45	46
Venue	A	H	A	H	A	A	H	H	A	H	A	H	A	H	A	H	H	A	H	A	H	A	H	H	A	H	A	H	A	A	H	H	A	A	H	A	H	A	H	A	H	A	H	A	H	A
Competition	L	L	L	L	E	L	L	E	L	L	L	L	E	L	L	E	L	L	L	L	L	L	L	L	L	L	L	L	L	E	L	E	L	E	L	L	E	L	L	L	L	L	L	L	L	L
Result	L	W	L	D	W	L	D	W	L	L	W	L	W	W	W	D	W	W	W	L	L	L	L	D	W	L	L	D	D	W	L	L	L	L	W	L	L	L	D	W	L	W	W	W	W	W

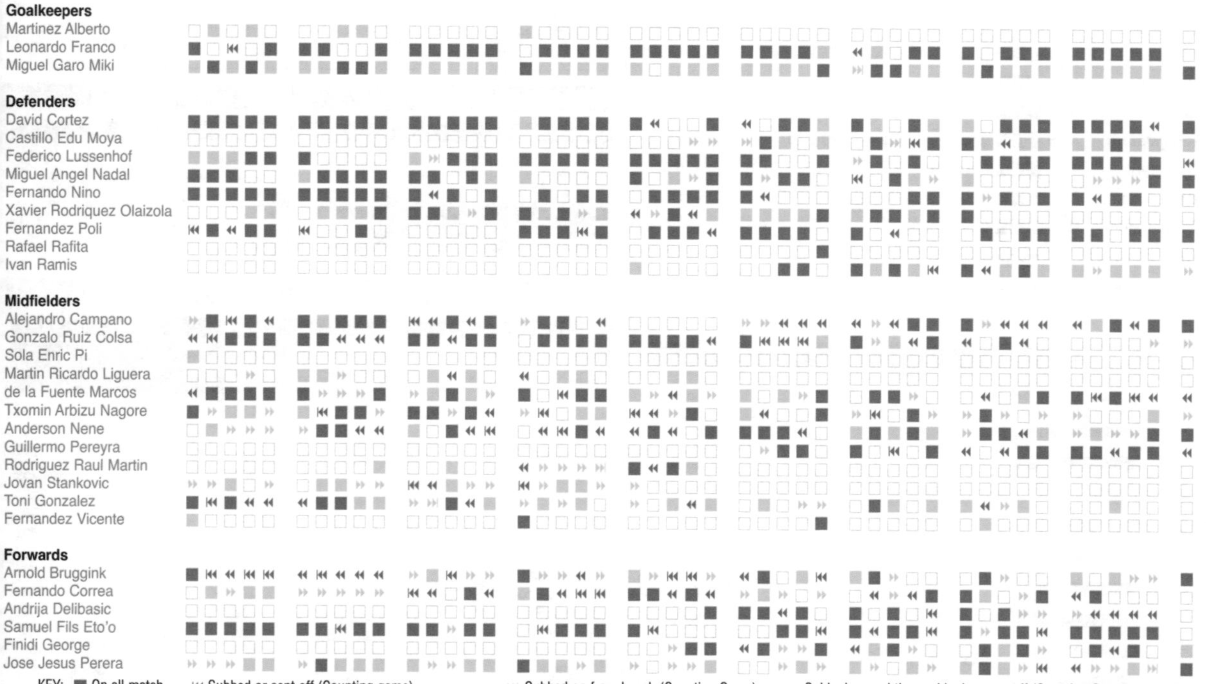

Goalkeepers
Martinez Alberto
Leonardo Franco
Miguel Garo Miki

Defenders
David Cortez
Castillo Edu Moya
Federico Lussenhof
Miguel Angel Nadal
Fernando Nino
Xavier Rodriquez Olaizola
Fernandez Poli
Rafael Rafita
Ivan Ramis

Midfielders
Alejandro Campano
Gonzalo Ruiz Colsa
Sola Enric Pi
Martin Ricardo Liguera
de la Fuente Marcos
Txomin Arbizu Nagore
Anderson Nene
Guillermo Pereyra
Rodriguez Raul Martin
Jovan Stankovic
Toni Gonzalez
Fernandez Vicente

Forwards
Arnold Bruggink
Fernando Correa
Andrija Delibasic
Samuel Fils Eto'o
Finidi George
Jose Jesus Perera

KEY: ■ On all match · On bench · ⏮ Subbed or sent off (Counting game) · ◀◀ Subbed or sent off (playing less than 70 minutes) · ▶▶ Subbed on from bench (Counting Game) · ▶▶ Subbed on (playing less than 70 minutes) · ⏭ Subbed on and then subbed or sent off (Counting Game) · ▶▶ Subbed on and then subbed or sent off (playing less than 70 minutes) · □ Not in 16

OSASUNA

Final Position: **12th**

KEY: Won Drawn Lost

							Attendance
1	lge	Albacete	A	W	2-0	Valdo 43; Punal 90 pen	15,000
2	lge	Valencia	H	L	0-1		14,195
3	lge	Atl Madrid	H	W	1-0	Garcia 36	20,000
4	lge	Barcelona	A	D	1-1	Cruchaga 54	83,000
5	lge	Deportivo	H	W	3-2	Punal 21 pen; Ivan Rosado 23; Hector 25 og	15,000
6	lge	Mallorca	A	D	1-1	Webo 86	22,500
7	lge	Murcia	H	W	2-1	Bakayoko 12,85	13,930
8	lge	Real Sociedad	A	L	0-1		28,000
9	lge	Real Betis	H	W	2-0	Moha 51; Munoz 81	14,000
10	lge	Villarreal	A	L	0-1		11,000
11	lge	Valladolid	H	D	1-1	Valdo 45	19,000
12	lge	Malaga	A	D	0-0		35,500
13	lge	Real Madrid	H	D	1-1	Bakayoko 10	20,000
14	lge	Espanyol	A	W	1-0	Webo 87	11,000
15	lge	Celta Vigo	H	W	3-2	Aloisi 28,49; Bakayoko 74	14,000
16	lge	R Santander	A	D	0-0		11,500
17	lge	Real Zaragoza	H	L	0-1		18,500
18	lge	Athl Bilbao	A	D	1-1	Izquierdo 35	37,000
19	lge	Seville	H	D	1-1	Garcia 83	19,500
20	lge	Albacete	H	D	1-1	Aloisi 33	16,000
21	lge	Valencia	A	W	1-0	Pellegrino 45 og	47,500
22	lge	Atl Madrid	A	D	1-1	Valdo 23	40,000
23	lge	Barcelona	H	L	1-2	Punal 67 pen	19,000
24	lge	Deportivo	A	L	0-2		26,000
25	lge	Mallorca	H	D	1-1	Aloisi 16	14,000
26	lge	Murcia	A	W	1-0	Webo 30	13,500
27	lge	Real Sociedad	H	D	1-1	Webo 13	17,000
28	lge	Real Betis	A	D	1-1	Aloisi 45	36,750
29	lge	Villarreal	H	W	2-1	Reina 33 og; Alvarez 72 og	16,915
30	lge	Valladolid	A	D	1-1	Morales 74	12,000
31	lge	Malaga	H	D	1-1	Morales 23	14,800
32	lge	Real Madrid	A	W	3-0	Valdo 2; Garcia 44; Moha 61	55,000
33	lge	Espanyol	H	L	1-3	Garcia 46	15,000
34	lge	Celta Vigo	A	L	0-1		18,000
35	lge	R Santander	H	L	1-2	Punal 55 pen	17,000
36	lge	Real Zaragoza	A	L	0-1		34,000
37	lge	Athl Bilbao	H	L	1-2	Valdo 88	17,000
38	lge	Seville	A	L	0-1		46,000

MONTHLY POINTS TALLY

Month	Points	%
AUGUST	3	100%
SEPTEMBER	7	58%
OCTOBER	7	58%
NOVEMBER	3	25%
DECEMBER	7	58%
JANUARY	7	47%
FEBRUARY	4	33%
MARCH	6	50%
APRIL	4	33%
MAY	0	0%

KEY PLAYERS - GOALSCORERS

Ibrahim Bakayoko

Goals in the League	4	Player Strike Rate Average number of minutes between League goals scored by player	432
Contribution to Attacking Power Average number of minutes between League team goals while on pitch	95	Club Strike Rate Average number of minutes between League goals scored by club	90

	PLAYER	LGE GOALS	POWER	STRIKE RATE
1	Ibrahim Bakayoko	4	95	432 mins
2	John Aloisi	5	86	484 mins
3	Valmiro Lopes Rocha Valdo	5	82	546 mins
4	Pablo Garcia	4	82	598 mins

KEY PLAYERS - MIDFIELDERS

Mohamed El Yaagoubi Moha

Goals in the League	2	Contribution to Attacking Power Average number of minutes between League team goals while on pitch	80
Defensive Rating Average number of mins between League goals conceded while he was on the pitch	100	Scoring Difference Defensive Rating minus Contribution to Attacking Power	20

	PLAYER	LGE GOALS	DEF RATE	POWER	SCORE DIFF
1	Mohamed El Yaagoubi Moha	2	100	80	20 mins
2	Valmiro Lopes Rocha Valdo	5	98	83	15 mins
3	Francisco Martinez Punal	4	92	82	10 mins
4	Pablo Garcia	4	92	82	10 mins

KEY PLAYERS - DEFENDERS

Cesar Lasa Cruchaga

Goals Conceded (GC) The number of League goals conceded while he was on the pitch	31	Clean Sheets In games when he played at least 70 minutes	9
Defensive Rating Ave number of mins between League goals conceded while on the pitch	98	Club Defensive Rating Average number of mins between League goals conceded by the club this season	92

	PLAYER	CON LGE	CLEAN SHEETS	DEF RATE
1	Cesar Lasa Cruchaga	31	9	98 mins
2	Antonio Lopez	32	8	97 mins
3	Jose Martinez Izquierdo	33	9	95 mins
4	Jose Romero Urtasun Josetxo	31	7	91 mins

KEY GOALKEEPER

Ricardo Goni Sanzol

Goals Conceded in the League	32	Counting Games Games when he played at least 70 mins	34
Defensive Rating Ave number of mins between League goals conceded while on the pitch	96	Clean Sheets In games when he played at least 70 mins	9

LEAGUE GOALS

Valmiro Lopes Rocha Valdo

Minutes on the pitch	2732	Goals in the League	5
League average (mins between goals)	546		

	PLAYER	MINS	GOALS	AVE
1	Valdo	2732	5	546
2	Aloisi	2422	5	484
3	Punal	3034	4	759
4	Garcia	2391	4	598
5	Webo	1142	4	286
6	Bakayoko	1727	4	432
7	Moha	2400	2	1200
8	Morales	532	2	266
9	Izquierdo	3129	1	3129
10	Ivan Rosado	482	1	482
11	Cruchaga	3032	1	3032
12	Munoz	1604	1	1604
	Other		4	
	TOTAL		38	

DISCIPLINARY RECORDS

	PLAYER	YELLOW	RED	AVE
1	Alfredo	5	1	124
2	Morales	3	0	177
3	Garcia	12	1	183
4	Punal	13	0	233
5	Moha	6	2	300
6	Lopez	9	1	309
7	Izquierdo	10	0	312
8	Josetxo	8	0	353
9	Bakayoko	3	1	431
10	Aloisi	5	0	484
11	Cruchaga	4	1	606
12	Mateo	1	0	645
13	Valdo	4	0	683
	Other	10	1	
	TOTAL	93	8	

TOP POINT EARNERS

	PLAYER	GAMES	AV PTS
1	Aloisi	23	1.52
2	Punal	31	1.48
3	Garcia	26	1.38
4	Izquierdo	35	1.34
5	Moha	24	1.33
6	Sanzol	34	1.32
7	Valdo	26	1.31
8	Josetxo	31	1.26
9	Bakayoko	14	1.21
10	Lopez	34	1.21
	CLUB AVERAGE:		1.26

TEAM OF THE SEASON

G
Sanzol
CG: 34 DR: 96
D
Cruchaga
CG: 33 DR: 98
D
Lopez
CG: 34 DR: 97
D
Izquierdo
CG: 35 DR: 95
D
Josetxo
CG: 31 DR: 91
M
Moha
CG: 24 SD: 20
M
Valdo
CG: 26 SD: 15
M
Garcia
CG: 26 SD: 10
M
Punal
CG: 31 SD: 10
F
Bakayoko
CG: 14 SR: 432
F
Aloisi
CG: 23 SR: 484

LEAGUE APPEARANCES, BOOKINGS AND CAPS

	AGE (on 01/07/04)	IN NAMED 18	APPEARANCES	COUNTING GAMES	MINUTES ON PITCH	YELLOW CARDS	RED CARDS	THIS SEASON	HOME COUNTRY
Goalkeepers									
Juantxo Elia	34	37	4	4	360	0	0	-	Spain
Ricardo Sanzol	28	37	34	34	3060	3	0	-	Spain
Defenders									
Cesar Cruchaga	30	34	34	33	3032	4	1	-	Spain
Carlos Cuellar	32	13	5	4	369	1	0	-	Spain
Unai Exposito	24	5	3	2	205	0	0	-	Spain
Gorka Garcia	29	21	10	4	450	1	0	-	Spain
Jose Izquierdo	23	35	35	35	3129	10	0	-	Spain
Romero Josetxo	29	34	32	31	2829	8	0	-	Spain
Antonio Lopez	22	35	35	34	3097	9	1	-	Spain
Jose Mateo	29	32	9	6	645	1	0	-	Spain
Midfielders									
Sanchez Alfredo	31	27	14	6	744	5	1	-	Spain
Pablo Garcia	27	29	27	26	2391	12	1	-	Uruguay
El Yaagoubi Moha	26	30	30	24	2400	6	2	-	Spain
Inaki Oroz Munoz	26	34	29	14	1604	2	0	-	Spain
Cesar Palacios	29	24	14	1	186	0	0	-	Spain
Cesar Pinhiero	27	10	6	1	173	2	1	-	Brazil
Francisco Punal	28	35	35	31	3034	13	0	-	Spain
Gerald Rivero	29	32	15	3	667	0	0	-	Argentina
Juan Angel Seguro	20	2	2	0	30	0	0	-	Mexico
Lopes Valdo	23	35	35	26	2732	4	0	-	Spain
Forwards									
John Aloisi	28	33	33	23	2422	5	0	-	Australia
Ibrahim Bakayoko	27	29	26	14	1727	3	1	-	Ivory Coast
Ivan Rosado	30	24	14	3	482	0	0	-	Spain
Richard Morales	29	15	12	2	532	3	0	-	Uruguay
Pierre Webo	22	32	27	7	1142	1	0	-	Spain

SQUAD APPEARANCES

Match	1	2	3	4	5	6	7	8	9	10	11	12	13	14	15	16	17	18	19	20	21	22	23	24	25	26	27	28	29	30	31	32	33	34	35	36	37	38
Venue	A	H	H	A	H	A	H	A	H	A	H	A	H	A	H	A	H	A	H	H	A	A	H	A	H	A	H	A	H	A	H	A	H	A	H	A	H	A
Competition	L	L	L	L	L	L	L	L	L	L	L	L	L	L	L	L	L	L	L	L	L	L	L	L	L	L	L	L	L	L	L	L	L	L	L	L	L	L
Result	W	L	W	D	W	D	W	L	W	L	D	D	D	W	W	D	L	D	D	D	W	D	L	L	D	W	D	D	W	D	D	W	L	L	L	L	L	L

Goalkeepers
Juantxo Vallejo Elia
Ricardo Goni Sanzol

Defenders
Cesar Lasa Cruchaga
Carlos Javier Cuellar
Unai Medina Exposito
Zubikaray Gorka Garcia
Jose Martinez Izquierdo
Romero Urtasun Josetxo
Antonio Lopez
Jose Manuel Mateo

Midfielders
Sanchez Benito Alfredo
Pablo Garcia
El Yaagoubi Moha
Inaki Oroz Munoz
Cesar Chocarro Palacios
Julio Cesar Pinhiero
Francisco Martinez Punal
Gerald Damian Rivero
Juan Angel Seguro
Valmiro Lopes Valdo

Forwards
John Aloisi
Ibrahim Bakayoko
Mojarro Ivan Rosado
Richard Morales
Pierre Achille Webo

KEY: ■ On all match ■ On bench ⏮ Subbed or sent off (Counting game) ⏪ Subbed or sent off (playing less than 70 minutes) ⏭ Subbed on from bench (Counting Game) ⏩ Subbed on (playing less than 70 minutes) ⏭ Subbed on and then subbed or sent off (Counting Game) ⏩ Subbed on and then subbed or sent off (playing less than 70 minutes) □ Not in 16

REAL ZARAGOZA

Final Position: **13th**

KEY: Won Drawn Lost

					Score	Scorers	Attendance
1	lge	Deportivo	H	L	0-1		32,000
2	lge	Mallorca	A	L	0-2		22,515
3	lge	Murcia	H	W	3-0	Savio 2; Villa 9 pen; Galletti 33	30,000
4	lge	Real Sociedad	A	L	0-3		25,000
5	lge	Real Betis	H	L	0-1		17,500
6	lge	Villarreal	A	D	1-1	Villa 23	16,000
7	lge	Valladolid	H	W	1-0	Savio 16	29,000
8	lge	Malaga	A	L	1-2	Drulic 89	19,000
9	lge	Real Madrid	H	D	0-0		33,000
10	lge	Espanyol	A	W	2-0	Galletti 11; Alvaro 23	41,500
11	lge	Celta Vigo	H	D	1-1	Ponzio 8	31,000
12	lge	R Santander	A	W	2-1	Alvaro 45; Soriano 85	13,500
13	lge	Valencia	A	L	2-3	Villa 49; Cani 79	48,000
14	lge	Athl Bilbao	H	D	2-2	Villa 28,46	29,000
15	lge	Seville	A	L	2-3	David Castedo 22 og; Villa 30 pen	20,000
16	lge	Albacete	H	L	0-1		28,500
17	lge	Osasuna	A	W	1-0	Villa 35 pen	18,500
18	lge	Atl Madrid	H	D	0-0		23,000
19	lge	Barcelona	A	L	0-3		56,000
20	lge	Deportivo	A	L	1-4	Generelo 4	24,000
21	lge	Mallorca	H	L	1-3	Ponzio 66	28,000
22	lge	Murcia	A	L	0-1		15,000
23	lge	Real Sociedad	H	W	2-1	Villa 6,90 pen	30,500
24	lge	Real Betis	A	L	1-2	Cani 3	40,000
25	lge	Villarreal	H	W	4-1	Ponzio 3; Cani 20; Dani 38; Villa 79	32,000
26	lge	Valladolid	A	W	2-1	Generelo 9; Galletti 82	9,000
27	lge	Malaga	H	W	1-0	Villa 72	27,000
28	lge	Real Madrid	A	D	1-1	Toledo 32	90,000
29	lge	Espanyol	H	D	1-1	Villa 20	34,650
30	lge	Celta Vigo	A	W	2-0	Alvaro 75; Yordi 90	17,000
31	lge	R Santander	H	D	2-2	Dani 38; Villa 50	34,000
32	lge	Valencia	H	L	0-1		34,000
33	lge	Athl Bilbao	A	L	0-4		35,000
34	lge	Seville	H	D	4-4	Villa 26,43,54,58 pen	34,000
35	lge	Albacete	A	L	1-3	Rebosio 75	15,000
36	lge	Osasuna	H	W	1-0	Alvaro 90	34,000
37	lge	Atl Madrid	A	W	2-1	Toledo 90,90	52,000
38	lge	Barcelona	H	W	2-1	Cani 42; Soriano 60	34,500

MONTHLY POINTS TALLY

Month	Points	%
AUGUST	0	0%
SEPTEMBER	3	25%
OCTOBER	5	42%
NOVEMBER	7	58%
DECEMBER	4	33%
JANUARY	1	8%
FEBRUARY	9	60%
MARCH	8	67%
APRIL	2	17%
MAY	9	75%

KEY PLAYERS - GOALSCORERS

David Sanchez Villa

Goals in the League	17	Player Strike Rate Average number of minutes between League goals scored by player	194
Contribution to Attacking Power Average number of minutes between League team goals while on pitch	75	Club Strike Rate Average number of minutes between League goals scored by club	74

	PLAYER	LGE GOALS	POWER	STRIKE RATE
1	David Sanchez Villa	17	75	194 mins
2	Cani	4	62	467 mins
3	Delio Cesar Toledo	3	57	610 mins
4	Luiz Maior De Aquino Alvaro	4	77	793 mins

KEY PLAYERS - MIDFIELDERS

Jose Maria Cubero Movilla

Goals in the League	0	Contribution to Attacking Power Average number of minutes between League team goals while on pitch	56
Defensive Rating Average number of mins between League goals conceded while he was on the pitch	61	Scoring Difference Defensive Rating minus Contribution to Attacking Power	5

	PLAYER	LGE GOALS	DEF RATE	POWER	SCORE DIFF
1	Jose Maria Cubero Movilla	0	61	56	5 mins
2	Cani	4	60	62	-2 mins
3	Fernando Soriano	2	77	81	-4 mins
4	Leonardo Ponzio	3	62	74	-12 mins

KEY PLAYERS - DEFENDERS

Delio Cesar Toledo

Goals Conceded (GC) The number of League goals conceded while he was on the pitch	23	Clean Sheets In games when he played at least 70 minutes	6
Defensive Rating Ave number of mins between League goals conceded while on the pitch	80	Club Defensive Rating Average number of mins between League goals conceded by the club this season	62

	PLAYER	CON LGE	CLEAN SHEETS	DEF RATE
1	Delio Cesar Toledo	23	6	80 mins
2	Luis Carlos Laporga Cuartero	25	5	71 mins
3	Luiz Maior De Aquino Alvaro	48	9	66 mins
4	Gabriel Alejandro Milito	48	8	65 mins

KEY GOALKEEPER

Cesar Sanjuan Lainez

Goals Conceded in the League	45	Counting Games Games when he played at least 70 mins	31
Defensive Rating Ave number of mins between League goals conceded while on the pitch	62	Clean Sheets In games when he played at least 70 mins	8

LEAGUE GOALS

David Sanchez Villa

Minutes on the pitch	3300	Goals in the League	17
League average (mins between goals)	194		

	PLAYER	MINS	GOALS	AVE
1	Villa	3300	17	194
2	Cani	1869	4	467
3	Alvaro	3170	4	793
4	Galletti	2459	3	820
5	Toledo	1831	3	610
6	Ponzio	2905	3	968
7	Generelo	851	2	426
8	Savio	2314	2	1157
9	Dani	1200	2	600
10	Soriano	1701	2	851
11	Rebosio	2021	1	2021
12	Drulic	280	1	280
13	Yordi	398	1	398
	Other		1	
	TOTAL		46	

DISCIPLINARY

	PLAYER	YELLOW	RED	AVE
1	Generelo	7	1	106
2	Galletti	12	0	204
3	Ponzio	13	1	207
4	Toledo	7	1	228
5	Soriano	7	0	243
6	Cuartero	5	2	255
7	Pirri	6	0	271
8	Milito	10	1	281
9	Movilla	4	0	337
10	Alvaro	8	1	352
11	Corona	2	0	450
12	Cani	4	0	467
13	Rebosio	4	0	505
	Other	10	0	
	TOTAL	99	7	

TOP POINT EARNERS

	PLAYER	GAMES	AV PTS
1	Dani	12	2.00
2	Toledo	17	1.88
3	Movilla	15	1.67
4	Soriano	14	1.57
5	Cuartero	16	1.38
6	Galletti	20	1.35
7	Alvaro	34	1.32
8	Villa	37	1.30
9	Rebosio	19	1.26
10	Ponzio	29	1.21
	CLUB AVERAGE:		1.26

LEAGUE APPEARANCES, BOOKINGS AND CAPS

	AGE (on 01/07/04)	IN NAMED 18	APPEARANCES	COUNTING GAMES	MINUTES ON PITCH	YELLOW CARDS	RED CARDS	THIS SEASON	HOME COUNTRY
Goalkeepers									
Cesar Lainez	27	32	32	31	2794	3	0	-	Spain
Raul Valbuena	29	36	6	6	536	0	0	-	Spain
Jorge Zapa	20	8	1	1	90	0	0	-	Spain
Defenders									
Luiz Maior Alvaro	27	36	36	34	3170	8	1	-	Brazil
Manuel Capi	23	1	1	0	24	0	0	-	Spain
Luis Cuartero	29	34	24	16	1786	5	2	-	Spain
Jordi Ferron	25	13	3	0	81	1	0	-	Spain
Gabriel Milito	23	35	35	33	3097	10	1	1	Argentina (5)
Martin Paco	34	1	1	0	45	0	0	-	Spain
Cesar Rebosio	27	34	27	19	2021	4	0	-	Peru
Cesar Toledo	27	25	23	17	1831	7	1	-	Paraguay
Midfielders									
Ruben Cani	22	38	32	15	1869	4	0	-	Spain
Miguel Corona	23	24	17	7	900	2	0	-	Spain
David Generelo	21	29	18	6	851	7	1	-	Spain
Munoz Jesus	28	10	5	2	215	1	0	-	Spain
Jose Maria Movilla	29	15	15	15	1350	4	0	-	Spain
David Pirri	30	32	23	17	1631	6	0	-	Spain
Leonardo Ponzio	22	36	35	29	2905	13	1	-	Argentina
Fernando Soriano	24	33	24	14	1701	7	0	-	Spain
Martin Vellisca	33	10	4	0	131	0	0	-	Spain
Forwards									
Daniel Garcia Dani	29	15	15	12	1200	0	0	-	Spain
Goran Drulic	27	21	11	0	280	1	0	-	Serbia & Montenegro
Iban Espadas	25	15	7	0	121	0	0	-	Spain
Luciano Galletti	23	34	34	20	2459	12	0	-	Argentina
Jose Ignacio Inaki	32	18	9	0	195	0	0	-	Spain
Juan Juanele	33	11	6	0	139	1	0	-	Spain
Bortolini Savio	30	29	29	24	2314	1	0	-	Brazil
David Sanchez Villa	22	38	38	37	3300	2	0	-	Spain
Gonzalez Yordi	29	22	12	1	398	0	0	-	Spain

TEAM OF THE SEASON

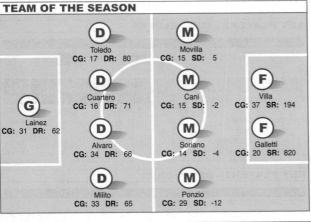

- **G** Lainez — CG: 31 DR: 62
- **D** Toledo — CG: 17 DR: 80
- **D** Cuartero — CG: 16 DR: 71
- **D** Alvaro — CG: 34 DR: 66
- **D** Milito — CG: 33 DR: 65
- **M** Movilla — CG: 15 SD: 5
- **M** Cani — CG: 15 SD: -2
- **M** Soriano — CG: 14 SD: -4
- **M** Ponzio — CG: 29 SD: -12
- **F** Villa — CG: 37 SR: 194
- **F** Galletti — CG: 20 SR: 820

SQUAD APPEARANCES

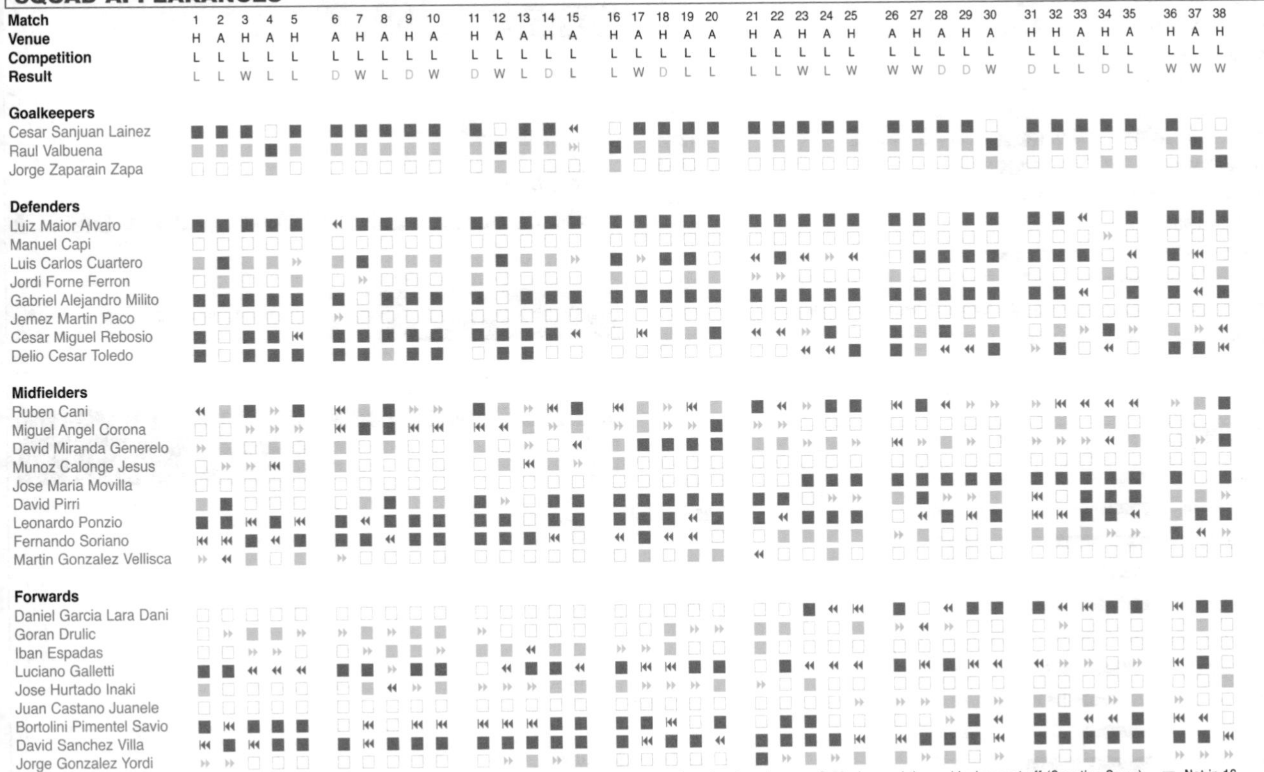

Match 1 2 3 4 5 6 7 8 9 10 11 12 13 14 15 16 17 18 19 20 21 22 23 24 25 26 27 28 29 30 31 32 33 34 35 36 37 38
Venue H A H A H A H A H A H A A H A H A H A A H A H A H A H A H A H H A H A H A H
Competition L L L L L L L L L L L L L L L L L L L L L L L L L L L L L L L L L L L L L L
Result L L W L L D W L D W D W L D L L W D L L L L W L W W W D D W D L L D L W W W
Goalkeepers
Cesar Sanjuan Lainez
Raul Valbuena
Jorge Zaparain Zapa
Defenders
Luiz Maior Alvaro
Manuel Capi
Luis Carlos Cuartero
Jordi Forne Ferron
Gabriel Alejandro Milito
Jemez Martin Paco
Cesar Miguel Rebosio
Delio Cesar Toledo
Midfielders
Ruben Cani
Miguel Angel Corona
David Miranda Generelo
Munoz Calonge Jesus
Jose Maria Movilla
David Pirri
Leonardo Ponzio
Fernando Soriano
Martin Gonzalez Vellisca
Forwards
Daniel Garcia Lara Dani
Goran Drulic
Iban Espadas
Luciano Galletti
Jose Hurtado Inaki
Juan Castano Juanele
Bortolini Pimentel Savio
David Sanchez Villa
Jorge Gonzalez Yordi
KEY: On all match
On bench
Subbed or sent off (Counting game)
Subbed or sent off (playing less than 70 minutes)
Subbed on from bench (Counting Game)
Subbed on (playing less than 70 minutes)
Subbed on and then subbed or sent off (Counting Game)
Subbed on and then subbed or sent off (playing less than 70 minutes)
Not in 16

ALBACETE

Final Position: **14th**

KEY: Won / Drawn / Lost

							Attendance
1	lge	Osasuna	H	L	0-2		15,000
2	lge	Atl Madrid	A	L	0-1		54,150
3	lge	Barcelona	H	L	1-2	Ibanez 90	17,000
4	lge	Deportivo	A	L	0-3		25,000
5	lge	Mallorca	H	W	2-0	Parri 17; Mikel 81	13,000
6	lge	Murcia	A	L	0-1		16,500
7	lge	Real Sociedad	H	W	3-1	Delporte 68; David Sanchez 77; Aranda 82	15,000
8	lge	Real Betis	A	L	2-3	Mikel 12; Parri 66	42,000
9	lge	Villarreal	H	W	2-0	Parri 67; Basti 71	13,000
10	lge	Valladolid	A	L	0-2		21,000
11	lge	Malaga	H	L	0-1		12,500
12	lge	Real Madrid	A	L	1-2	Parri 38	76,000
13	lge	Espanyol	H	W	2-1	Aranda 45 pen,68	12,000
14	lge	Celta Vigo	A	D	2-2	Pacheco 45; Aranda 53	15,000
15	lge	R Santander	H	W	4-0	Aranda 42 pen; Pacheco 59; Delporte 73; Juanma 88 og	14,000
16	lge	Real Zaragoza	A	W	1-0	Mikel 78	28,500
17	lge	Athl Bilbao	H	D	1-1	Aranda 10	15,500
18	lge	Seville	A	L	0-2		45,000
19	lge	Valencia	H	L	0-1		12,500
20	lge	Osasuna	A	D	1-1	Viaud 5	16,000
21	lge	Atl Madrid	H	D	1-1	Lequi 59 og	14,000
22	lge	Barcelona	A	L	0-5		78,000
23	lge	Deportivo	H	L	0-2		12,500
24	lge	Mallorca	A	D	0-0		16,000
25	lge	Murcia	H	W	1-0	Cuadrado 8 og	15,000
26	lge	Real Sociedad	A	W	1-0	Redondo 48	24,000
27	lge	Real Betis	H	W	1-0	Pacheco 27	16,000
28	lge	Villarreal	A	L	1-2	Pacheco 5	16,000
29	lge	Valladolid	H	W	2-0	Aranda 10; Mikel 56	14,685
30	lge	Malaga	A	D	1-1	Fabiano 28	8,000
31	lge	Real Madrid	H	L	1-2	Parri 82	17,000
32	lge	Espanyol	A	D	1-1	Redondo 22	25,000
33	lge	Celta Vigo	H	L	0-2		16,000
34	lge	R Santander	A	W	2-0	Pacheco 42; Redondo 54	15,500
35	lge	Real Zaragoza	H	W	3-1	Aranda 3; Pacheco 55; Mikel 78	15,000
36	lge	Athl Bilbao	A	D	1-1	Pacheco 55 pen	35,000
37	lge	Seville	H	L	1-4	Parri 68	16,000
38	lge	Valencia	A	W	1-0	Aranda 66	49,000

MONTHLY POINTS TALLY

AUGUST	0	0%
SEPTEMBER	3	25%
OCTOBER	6	50%
NOVEMBER	3	25%
DECEMBER	8	67%
JANUARY	2	17%
FEBRUARY	7	47%
MARCH	7	58%
APRIL	4	33%
MAY	7	58%

KEY PLAYERS - GOALSCORERS

Carlos Reina Aranda

Goals in the League	9	Player Strike Rate Average number of minutes between League goals scored by player	179
Contribution to Attacking Power Average number of minutes between League team goals while on pitch	76	Club Strike Rate Average number of minutes between League goals scored by club	86

	PLAYER	LGE GOALS	POWER	STRIKE RATE
1	Carlos Reina Aranda	9	76	179 mins
2	Libero Romero Parri	6	86	317 mins
3	Antonio Pacheco	7	82	319 mins
4	Pablo Redondo Martinez	3	77	439 mins

KEY PLAYERS - MIDFIELDERS

Catalin Munteanu

Goals in the League	0	Contribution to Attacking Power Average number of minutes between League team goals while on pitch	94
Defensive Rating Average number of mins between League goals conceded while he was on the pitch	88	Scoring Difference Defensive Rating minus Contribution to Attacking Power	-6

	PLAYER	LGE GOALS	DEF RATE	POWER	SCORE DIFF
1	Catalin Munteanu	0	88	94	-6 mins
2	Ludovic Delporte	2	66	78	-12 mins
3	Pablo Redondo Martinez	3	66	78	-12 mins
4	Libero Romero Parri	6	68	86	-18 mins

KEY PLAYERS - DEFENDERS

Miguel Baudes

Goals Conceded (GC) The number of League goals conceded while he was on the pitch	24	Clean Sheets In games when he played at least 70 minutes	8
Defensive Rating Ave number of mins between League goals conceded while on the pitch	83	Club Defensive Rating Average number of mins between League goals conceded by the club this season	71

	PLAYER	CON LGE	CLEAN SHEETS	DEF RATE
1	Miguel Baudes	24	8	83 mins
2	Luis Marin Oscar Montiel	43	11	75 mins
3	Francisco Paco Pena	37	9	73 mins
4	Ibanez Tebar Pablo	36	8	71 mins

KEY GOALKEEPER

Manuel Rivero Almunia

Goals Conceded in the League	28	Counting Games Games when he played at least 70 mins	24
Defensive Rating Ave number of mins between League goals conceded while on the pitch	77	Clean Sheets In games when he played at least 70 mins	8

LEAGUE GOALS

Carlos Reina Aranda

Minutes on the pitch	1609	Goals in the League	9
League average (mins between goals)	179		

	PLAYER	MINS	GOALS	AVE
1	Aranda	1609	9	179
2	Pacheco	2236	7	319
3	Parri	1902	6	317
4	Mikel	1213	5	243
5	Redondo	1318	3	439
6	Delporte	1648	2	824
7	Fabiano	594	1	594
8	Viaud	2757	1	2757
9	David Sanchez	1424	1	1424
10	Basti	431	1	431
	Other		4	
	TOTAL		40	

DISCIPLINARY

	PLAYER	YELLOW	RED	AVE
1	Unai	5	1	179
2	Aranda	7	1	201
3	Delporte	7	1	206
4	Viaud	13	0	212
5	Pablo Garcia	4	0	281
6	David Sanchez	4	1	284
7	Parri	5	1	317
8	Ivan Diaz	3	0	326
9	Redondo	4	0	329
10	Cristian Diaz	1	0	495
11	Baudes	4	0	495
12	Navarro	1	0	496
13	Fabiano	1	0	594
	Other	24	2	
	TOTAL	83	7	

TOP POINT EARNERS

	PLAYER	GAMES	AV PTS
1	Redondo	13	1.54
2	Munteanu	15	1.53
3	Pacheco	18	1.50
4	Baudes	21	1.43
5	Pablo	28	1.32
6	Oscar Montiel	35	1.31
7	Aranda	13	1.31
8	Almunia	24	1.29
9	Delporte	17	1.24
10	Paco Pena	30	1.23
	CLUB AVERAGE:		1.24

LEAGUE APPEARANCES, BOOKINGS AND CAPS

	AGE (on 01/07/04)	IN NAMED 18	APPEARANCES	COUNTING GAMES	MINUTES ON PITCH	YELLOW CARDS	RED CARDS	THIS SEASON	HOME COUNTRY
Goalkeepers									
Manuel Almunia	27	37	24	24	2160	2	0	-	Spain
Joaquin Moso	25	19	1	0	12	0	0	-	Spain
Nunez Raul	22	6	0	0	0	0	0	-	Spain
Carlos Angel Roa	34	14	14	14	1260	0	1	-	Argentina
Defenders									
Miguel Baudes	24	30	23	21	1980	4	0	-	Spain
Antonio Pou Coll	-	1	0	0	0	0	0	-	Spain
Lionel Cristian Diaz	28	12	7	5	495	1	0	-	Argentina
Fernando Navarro	22	16	7	5	496	1	0	-	Spain
Luis Oscar Montiel	34	36	36	35	3214	4	0	-	Spain
Ibanez Tebar Pablo	22	30	29	28	2546	2	0	-	Spain
Paco Pena	25	35	31	30	2702	3	1	-	Spain
Hernandez Pedro	25	10	2	2	180	1	0	-	Spain
Gustavo Siviero	34	8	5	3	369	0	0	-	Argentina
Vergara Unai	27	18	14	10	1074	5	1	-	Spain
Midfielders									
Rubio Alvaro	25	26	23	8	1300	2	0	-	Spain
David Sanchez	21	30	27	9	1424	4	1	-	Spain
Ludovic Delporte	24	30	22	17	1648	7	1	-	Spain
Ruiz Ivan Diaz	25	17	15	8	980	3	0	-	Spain
Abass Lawal	23	6	5	5	450	2	0	-	Nigeria
Catalin Munteanu	25	22	17	15	1405	2	0	-	Romania
Pablo Garcia	19	30	21	8	1126	4	0	-	Spain
Libero Parri	22	32	29	16	1902	5	1	-	Spain
Pablo Redondo	22	27	18	13	1318	4	0	-	Spain
Pedro Santana	23	1	0	0	0	0	0	-	Spain
Jose Simeon	30	6	2	0	42	0	0	-	Spain
Laurent Viaud	34	34	33	28	2757	13	0	-	France
Forwards									
Gabriel Amato	33	8	8	2	426	0	0	-	Spain
Reina Aranda	23	26	25	13	1609	7	1	-	Spain
Sebastian Basti	30	23	14	2	431	3	0	-	Spain
Carlos Caca	25	3	2	0	81	0	0	-	Spain
David Alvarez	18	2	2	0	111	0	0	-	Spain
Pereira Fabiano	26	17	12	3	594	1	0	-	Brazil
Larrea Mikel	29	34	28	7	1213	1	0	-	Spain
Antonio Pacheco	28	36	33	18	2236	2	0	-	Italy

TEAM OF THE SEASON

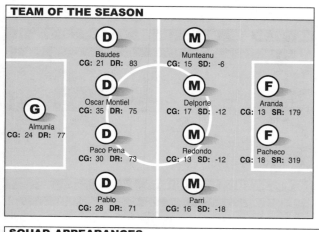

G Almunia CG: 24 DR: 77

D Baudes CG: 21 DR: 83

D Oscar Montiel CG: 35 DR: 75

D Paco Pena CG: 30 DR: 73

D Pablo CG: 28 DR: 71

M Munteanu CG: 15 SD: -6

M Delporte CG: 17 SD: -12

M Redondo CG: 13 SD: -12

M Parri CG: 16 SD: -18

F Aranda CG: 13 SR: 179

F Pacheco CG: 18 SR: 319

SQUAD APPEARANCES

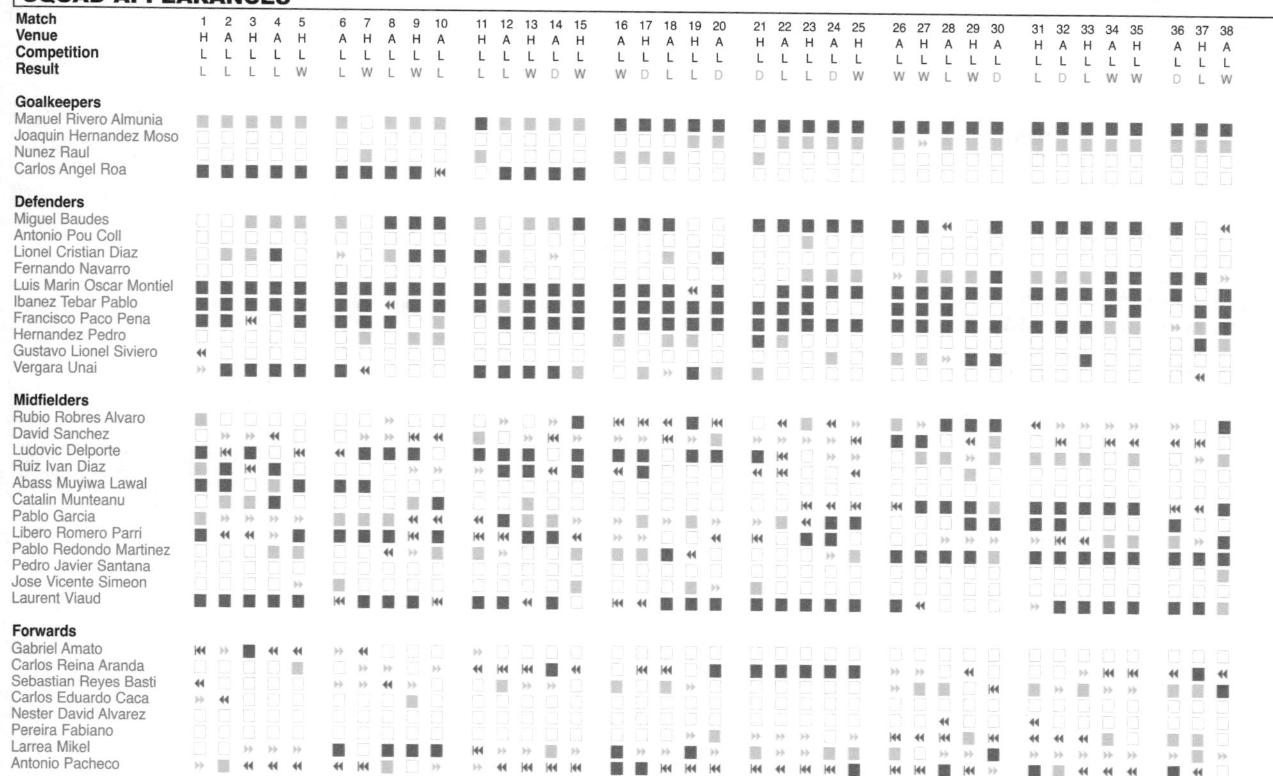
Match 1 2 3 4 5 6 7 8 9 10 11 12 13 14 15 16 17 18 19 20 21 22 23 24 25 26 27 28 29 30 31 32 33 34 35 36 37 38
Venue H A H A H A H A H A H A H A H A H A H A H A H A H A H A H A H A H A H A H A
Competition L L L L L L L L L L L L L L L L L L L L L L L L L L L L L L L L L L L L L L
Result L L L L W L W L W L L L W D W W D L L D D L L D W W W L W D L D L W W D L W
Goalkeepers
Manuel Rivero Almunia
Joaquin Hernandez Moso
Nunez Raul
Carlos Angel Roa
Defenders
Miguel Baudes
Antonio Pou Coll
Lionel Cristian Diaz
Fernando Navarro
Luis Marin Oscar Montiel
Ibanez Tebar Pablo
Francisco Paco Pena
Hernandez Pedro
Gustavo Lionel Siviero
Vergara Unai
Midfielders
Rubio Robres Alvaro
David Sanchez
Ludovic Delporte
Ruiz Ivan Diaz
Abass Muyiwa Lawal
Catalin Munteanu
Pablo Garcia
Libero Romero Parri
Pablo Redondo Martinez
Pedro Javier Santana
Jose Vicente Simeon
Laurent Viaud
Forwards
Gabriel Amato
Carlos Reina Aranda
Sebastian Reyes Basti
Carlos Eduardo Caca
Nester David Alvarez
Pereira Fabiano
Larrea Mikel
Antonio Pacheco
KEY: On all match
On bench
Subbed or sent off (Counting game)
Subbed or sent off (playing less than 70 minutes)
Subbed on from bench (Counting Game)
Subbed on (playing less than 70 minutes)
Subbed on and then subbed or sent off (Counting Game)
Subbed on and then subbed or sent off (playing less than 70 minutes)
Not in 16

REAL SOCIEDAD

Final Position: **15th**

KEY: ☐ Won ☐ Drawn ☐ Lost

						Scorers	Attendance
1	lge	Espanyol	A	D	1-1	Kovacevic 56	17,800
2	lge	Celta Vigo	H	D	1-1	Kovacevic 37	23,000
3	lge	R Santander	A	W	1-0	De Paula 32	11,396
4	cl gd	Olympiakos	H	W	1-0	Kovacevic 80 pen	29,000
5	lge	Real Zaragoza	H	W	3-0	Nihat 58; De Paula 84,89	25,000
6	lge	Athl Bilbao	A	L	0-1		40,000
7	cl gd	Galatasaray	A	W	2-1	Kovacevic 3; Xabier Alonso 72	17,600
8	lge	Seville	H	D	1-1	Kovacevic 5	25,500
9	lge	Albacete	A	L	1-3	Nihat 73	15,000
10	cl gd	Juventus	A	L	2-4	Tudor 67 og; De Pedro 80	17,246
11	lge	Osasuna	H	W	1-0	Kovacevic 78	28,000
12	lge	Atl Madrid	A	L	0-4		34,000
13	lge	Barcelona	H	D	3-3	Jauregui 56; De Pedro 59; Karpin 76	29,000
14	cl gd	Juventus	H	D	0-0		29,000
15	lge	Deportivo	A	L	1-2	Nihat 29	29,000
16	lge	Mallorca	H	L	0-1		29,000
17	cl gd	Olympiakos	A	D	2-2	Gabilondo 31; Schurrer 74	14,000
18	lge	Murcia	A	D	2-2	Gabilondo 30; De Paula 48	16,000
19	lge	Valencia	H	D	0-0		21,500
20	lge	Real Betis	H	L	0-4		25,000
21	cl gd	Galatasaray	H	D	1-1	De Paula 51	29,000
22	lge	Villarreal	A	L	0-2		17,000
23	lge	Valladolid	H	L	1-3	Nihat 6	24,000
24	lge	Malaga	A	W	2-1	Karpin 37; Nihat 45	27,454
25	lge	Real Madrid	H	W	1-0	Karpin 63	32,000
26	lge	Espanyol	H	W	3-1	Karpin 8; Gabilondo 84; Nihat 88	21,000
27	lge	Celta Vigo	A	W	5-2	Kovacevic 23; Milosevic 45 og; Xabier Alonso 60; Nihat 70,72	24,000
28	lge	R Santander	H	W	1-0	Karpin 63 pen	24,000
29	lge	Real Zaragoza	A	L	1-2	Xabier Alonso 37	30,500
30	lge	Athl Bilbao	H	D	1-1	Nihat 40	29,000
31	lge	Seville	A	L	0-1		25,000
32	clr1l1	Lyon	H	L	0-1		29,000
33	lge	Albacete	H	L	0-1		24,000
34	lge	Osasuna	A	D	1-1	Kovacevic 87	17,000
35	clr1l2	Lyon	A	L	0-1		38,914
36	lge	Atl Madrid	H	W	2-1	Karpin 34; Simeone 41 og	21,865
37	lge	Barcelona	A	L	0-1		84,280
38	lge	Deportivo	H	L	1-2	Nihat 42	25,600
39	lge	Mallorca	A	D	1-1	Gabilondo 33	20,000
40	lge	Murcia	H	W	2-0	Nihat 65,89	22,723
41	lge	Valencia	A	D	2-2	Xabier Alonso 65; Karpin 70 pen	45,000
42	lge	Real Betis	A	L	1-2	Nihat 45	25,000
43	lge	Villarreal	H	D	2-2	Schurrer 42; Gabilondo 61	26,143
44	lge	Valladolid	A	D	2-2	Gabilondo 19; Nihat 42	17,000
45	lge	Malaga	H	D	1-1	Kovacevic 71	28,713
46	lge	Real Madrid	A	W	4-1	Kovacevic 18; Prieto 29,61 pen; De Paula 32	50,000

MONTHLY POINTS TALLY

Month	Points	%
AUGUST	1	33%
SEPTEMBER	7	58%
OCTOBER	4	33%
NOVEMBER	2	17%
DECEMBER	1	8%
JANUARY	12	100%
FEBRUARY	4	27%
MARCH	4	33%
APRIL	5	42%
MAY	6	50%

KEY PLAYERS - GOALSCORERS

Kahveci Nihat

Goals in the League	14	Player Strike Rate Average number of minutes between League goals scored by player	185
Contribution to Attacking Power Average number of minutes between League team goals while on pitch	68	Club Strike Rate Average number of minutes between League goals scored by club	70

	PLAYER	LGE GOALS	POWER	STRIKE RATE
1	Kahveci Nihat	14	68	185 mins
2	Darko Kovacevic	8	75	349 mins
3	Igor del Campo Gabilondo	5	68	438 mins
4	Valeri Karpin	7	69	458 mins

KEY PLAYERS - MIDFIELDERS

Bittor Alkiza Fernandez

Goals in the League	0	Contribution to Attacking Power Average number of minutes between League team goals while on pitch	51
Defensive Rating Average number of mins between League goals conceded while he was on the pitch	81	Scoring Difference Defensive Rating minus Contribution to Attacking Power	30

	PLAYER	LGE GOALS	DEF RATE	POWER	SCORE DIFF
1	Bittor Alkiza Fernandez	0	81	51	30 mins
2	Igor del Campo Gabilondo	5	71	68	3 mins
3	Valeri Karpin	7	62	70	-8 mins
4	Olano Xabier Alonso	3	63	76	-13 mins

KEY PLAYERS - DEFENDERS

Gabriel Peralta Schurrer

Goals Conceded (GC) The number of League goals conceded while he was on the pitch	42	Clean Sheets In games when he played at least 70 minutes	7
Defensive Rating Ave number of mins between League goals conceded while on the pitch	71	Club Defensive Rating Average number of mins between League goals conceded by the club this season	65

	PLAYER	CON LGE	CLEAN SHEETS	DEF RATE
1	Gabriel Peralta Schurrer	42	7	71 mins
2	Aitor Lopez Rekarte	46	7	68 mins
3	Bjorn Tore Kvarme	38	6	68 mins
4	Lionel Potillon	27	2	62 mins

KEY GOALKEEPER

Lopez Fernandez Alberto

Goals Conceded in the League	25	Counting Games Games when he played at least 70 mins	18
Defensive Rating Ave number of mins between League goals conceded while on the pitch	65	Clean Sheets In games when he played at least 70 mins	2

LEAGUE GOALS

Kahveci Nihat

Minutes on the pitch	2589	Goals in the League	14
League average (mins between goals)	185		

	PLAYER	MINS	GOALS	AVE
1	Nihat	2589	14	185
2	Kovacevic	2792	8	349
3	Karpin	3206	7	458
4	De Paula	1038	5	208
5	Gabilondo	2191	5	438
6	Xabier Alonso	2513	3	838
7	Prieto	292	2	146
8	Jauregui	1292	1	1292
9	Schurrer	2962	1	2962
10	De Pedro	832	1	832
	Other		2	
	TOTAL		49	

DISCIPLINARY RECORDS

	PLAYER	YELLOW	RED	AVE
1	Alkiza	11	0	161
2	Schurrer	12	0	246
3	Xabier Alonso	10	0	251
4	Aramburu	7	1	253
5	Kvarme	10	0	256
6	De Paula	3	0	346
7	Lopez Rekarte	9	0	350
8	Aranzabal	4	1	415
9	Kovacevic	6	0	465
10	Nihat	5	0	517
11	Potillon	3	0	559
12	Jauregui	2	0	646
13	Gabilondo	3	0	730
	Other	8	0	
	TOTAL	93	2	

TOP POINT EARNERS

	PLAYER	GAMES	AV PTS
1	Alkiza	17	1.76
2	Gabilondo	22	1.50
3	Potillon	18	1.39
4	Alberto	18	1.33
5	Kovacevic	31	1.29
6	Schurrer	33	1.27
7	Kvarme	28	1.25
8	Lopez Rekarte	35	1.23
9	Nihat	29	1.21
10	Karpin	33	1.18
	CLUB AVERAGE:		1.21

TEAM OF THE SEASON

G Alberto CG: 18 DR: 65

D Schurrer CG: 33 DR: 71

D Kvarme CG: 28 DR: 68

D Lopez Rekarte CG: 35 DR: 68

D Potillon CG: 18 DR: 62

M Alkiza CG: 17 SD: 30

M Gabilondo CG: 22 SD: 3

M Karpin CG: 33 SD: -8

M Xabier Alonso CG: 26 SD: -13

F Nihat CG: 29 SR: 185

F Kovacevic CG: 31 SR: 349

LEAGUE APPEARANCES, BOOKINGS AND CAPS

	AGE (on 01/07/04)	IN NAMED 18	APPEARANCES	COUNTING GAMES	MINUTES ON PITCH	YELLOW CARDS	RED CARDS	THIS SEASON	HOME COUNTRY
Goalkeepers									
Lopez Alberto	35	37	18	18	1620	1	0	-	Spain
Asier Riesgo	20	5	0	0	0	0	0	-	Spain
Mikel Saizar	21	7	0	0	0	0	0	-	Spain
Sander Westerveld	29	26	20	20	1800	1	0	1	Holland (4)
Defenders									
Agustin Aranzabal	31	33	24	23	2079	4	1	-	Spain
Mikel Azparren	-	2	0	0	0	0	0	-	Spain
Ignacio Azpilicueta	22	6	1	1	90	0	0	-	Spain
Sergio Boris	24	17	7	2	246	0	0	-	Spain
Javier Garrido	19	8	0	0	0	0	0	-	Spain
Zuhaitz Gurrutxaga	23	5	0	0	0	0	0	-	Spain
Bjorn Tore Kvarme	31	34	29	28	2565	10	0	-	Norway
Aitor Lopez Rekarte	28	35	35	35	3150	9	0	-	Spain
Lionel Potillon	30	27	20	18	1678	3	0	-	France
Gabriel Schurrer	32	35	33	33	2962	12	0	-	Argentina
Iban Zubiaurre	21	4	0	0	0	0	0	-	Spain
Midfielders									
Alkiza Fernandez	33	34	27	17	1781	11	0	-	Spain
Miguel Aramburu	25	36	33	20	2027	7	1	-	Spain
Jose Javier Barkero	25	10	3	0	65	0	0	-	Spain
Francisco De Pedro	30	18	14	8	832	1	0	-	Spain
Campo Gabilondo	25	34	32	22	2191	3	0	-	Spain
Igor Iraola Jauregui	30	28	17	14	1292	2	0	-	Spain
Valeri Karpin	35	38	38	33	3206	4	0	-	Russia
Gorka Larrea	20	1	1	0	21	0	0	-	Spain
Bergara Markel	18	2	0	0	0	0	0	-	Spain
Mikel Alonso Olano	24	9	6	3	337	0	0	-	Spain
Xavier Prieto	20	23	11	2	292	1	0	-	Spain
Xabier Alonso	22	32	31	26	2513	10	0	8	Spain (3)
Forwards									
Oscar De Paula	29	38	26	7	1038	3	0	-	Spain
Darko Kovacevic	30	36	36	31	2792	6	0	3	Serbia & M'negro (45)
Chun-Soo Lee	22	24	12	3	415	0	0	-	South Korea
Kahveci Nihat	24	33	32	29	2589	5	0	-	Turkey
Gil Oskitz	17	2	1	0	17	0	0	-	Spain

SQUAD APPEARANCES

Match	1	2	3	4	5	6	7	8	9	10	11	12	13	14	15	16	17	18	19	20	21	22	23	24	25	26	27	28	29	30	31	32	33	34	35	36	37	38	39	40	41	42	43	44	45	46
Venue	A	H	A	H	H	A	A	H	A	A	H	A	H	H	A	H	A	A	H	H	H	A	H	A	H	H	A	H	A	H	A	H	H	A	A	H	A	H	A	H	A	A	H	A	H	A
Competition	L	L	L	C	L	L	C	L	L	C	L	L	L	C	L	L	C	L	L	L	C	L	L	L	L	L	L	L	L	L	L	C	L	L	C	L	L	L	L	L	L	L	L	L	L	L
Result	D	D	W	W	W	L	W	D	L	L	W	L	D	D	L	L	D	D	D	L	D	L	L	W	W	W	W	W	L	D	L	L	L	D	L	W	L	L	D	W	D	L	D	D	D	W

Goalkeepers
Lopez Fernandez Alberto
Asier Unamuno Riesgo
Mikel Saizar
Sander Westerveld

Defenders
Agustin Alkorta Aranzabal
Mikel Azparren
Ignacio Azpilicueta
Sergio Monteagudo Boris
Javier Garrido
Zuhaitz Loiola Gurrutxaga
Bjorn Tore Kvarme
Aitor Lopez Rekarte
Lionel Potillon
Gabriel Peralta Schurrer
Iban Zubiaurre

Midfielders
Bittor Alkiza Fernandez
Miguel Aramburu
Jose Javier Barkero
Francisco Javier De Pedro
Igor Campo Gabilondo
Igor Iraola Jauregui
Valeri Karpin
Gorka Larrea
Bergara Markel
Mikel Alonso Olano
Xavier Argarate Prieto
Olano Xabier Alonso

Forwards
Oscar Gamero De Paula
Darko Kovacevic
Chun-Soo Lee
Kahveci Nihat
Estefania Gil Oskitz

KEY: On all match · On bench · Subbed or sent off (Counting game) · Subbed or sent off (playing less than 70 minutes) · Subbed on from bench (Counting Game) · Subbed on (playing less than 70 minutes) · Subbed on and then subbed or sent off (Counting Game) · Subbed on and then subbed or sent off (playing less than 70 minutes) · Not in 16

ESPANYOL

Final Position: **16th**

KEY: ☐Won ☐Drawn ☐Lost

							Attendance
1	lge	Real Sociedad	H	D	1-1	Wome 22	17,800
2	lge	Real Betis	A	D	2-2	Raul Molina 70; Lopo 90	33,600
3	lge	Villarreal	H	L	1-2	Maxi 14	20,000
4	lge	Valladolid	A	L	1-3	Bobson 35	12,000
5	lge	Malaga	H	L	1-2	Tamudo 58	19,000
6	lge	Real Madrid	A	L	1-2	Fernandez 90	76,000
7	lge	Valencia	A	L	0-4		44,000
8	lge	Celta Vigo	H	L	0-4		45,500
9	lge	R Santander	A	W	1-0	Oscar 84	10,000
10	lge	Real Zaragoza	H	L	0-2		41,500
11	lge	Athl Bilbao	A	L	0-1		35,000
12	lge	Seville	H	W	1-0	Domoraud 90	32,000
13	lge	Albacete	A	L	1-2	Tamudo 15	12,000
14	lge	Osasuna	H	L	0-1		11,000
15	lge	Atl Madrid	A	L	0-2		40,000
16	lge	Barcelona	H	L	1-3	Jordi 8	35,000
17	lge	Deportivo	A	L	1-2	Jordi 16	27,000
18	lge	Mallorca	H	W	2-0	Tamudo 1,74	36,000
19	lge	Murcia	A	W	1-0	Maxi 10	12,000
20	lge	Real Sociedad	A	L	1-3	Jordi 90	21,000
21	lge	Real Betis	H	L	1-2	Tamudo 63 pen	38,500
22	lge	Villarreal	A	W	1-0	Raducanu 89	14,000
23	lge	Valladolid	H	W	2-0	Tamudo 56; Fredson 58	33,000
24	lge	Malaga	A	L	2-5	Lopo 45; Tamudo 77	20,000
25	lge	Real Madrid	H	L	2-4	Tamudo 32 pen; Lopo 84	46,000
26	lge	Valencia	H	W	2-1	Tamudo 38,75	16,500
27	lge	Celta Vigo	A	W	5-1	Tamudo 30,64 pen; Hadji 43; Sergio 82 og; Maxi 86	17,000
28	lge	R Santander	H	L	0-1		45,100
29	lge	Real Zaragoza	A	D	1-1	Fredson 29	34,650
30	lge	Athl Bilbao	H	W	2-1	Tamudo 2,83 pen	22,000
31	lge	Seville	A	L	0-1		25,000
32	lge	Albacete	H	D	1-1	Maxi 71	25,000
33	lge	Osasuna	A	W	3-1	Tamudo 42; Alex 62; Maxi 71	15,000
34	lge	Atl Madrid	H	W	3-1	Fredson 63; Raducanu 82,88	34,200
35	lge	Barcelona	A	L	1-4	Tamudo 19 pen	89,000
36	lge	Deportivo	H	W	2-0	Pocchettino 8; De La Pena 74	40,300
37	lge	Mallorca	A	L	2-4	Tamudo 7 pen,26	18,000
38	lge	Murcia	H	W	2-0	Tamudo 72; Lopo 81	51,700

MONTHLY POINTS TALLY

Month	Points	%
AUGUST	1	33%
SEPTEMBER	1	8%
OCTOBER	3	25%
NOVEMBER	3	25%
DECEMBER	0	0%
JANUARY	6	50%
FEBRUARY	9	60%
MARCH	7	58%
APRIL	7	58%
MAY	6	50%

KEY PLAYERS - GOALSCORERS

Raul Tamudo

Goals in the League	19	Player Strike Rate Average number of minutes between League goals scored by player	131
Contribution to Attacking Power Average number of minutes between League team goals while on pitch	65	Club Strike Rate Average number of minutes between League goals scored by club	71

	PLAYER	LGE GOALS	POWER	STRIKE RATE
1	Raul Tamudo	19	65	131 mins
2	Maximilliano Rodriguez Maxi	5	80	518 mins
3	Jordi Cruyff	3	86	579 mins
4	Camara Pereira Fredson	3	55	613 mins

KEY PLAYERS - MIDFIELDERS

Camara Pereira Fredson

Goals in the League	3	Contribution to Attacking Power Average number of minutes between League team goals while on pitch	56
Defensive Rating Average number of mins between League goals conceded while he was on the pitch	74	Scoring Difference Defensive Rating minus Contribution to Attacking Power	18

	PLAYER	LGE GOALS	DEF RATE	POWER	SCORE DIFF
1	Camara Pereira Fredson	3	74	56	18 mins
2	Ivan De La Pena	1	60	58	2 mins
3	David Garcia	0	59	81	-22 mins
4	Maximilliano Rodriguez Maxi	5	52	81	-29 mins

KEY PLAYERS - DEFENDERS

Mauricio Pocchettino

Goals Conceded (GC) The number of League goals conceded while he was on the pitch	31	Clean Sheets In games when he played at least 70 minutes	6
Defensive Rating Ave number of mins between League goals conceded while on the pitch	61	Club Defensive Rating Average number of mins between League goals conceded by the club this season	53

	PLAYER	CON LGE	CLEAN SHEETS	DEF RATE
1	Mauricio Pocchettino	31	6	61 mins
2	Cyril Domoraud	53	7	57 mins
3	Pierre Nlend Wome	36	2	53 mins
4	Alberto Lopo	52	6	52 mins

KEY GOALKEEPER

Erwin Lemmens

Goals Conceded in the League	47	Counting Games Games when he played at least 70 mins	29
Defensive Rating Ave number of mins between League goals conceded while on the pitch	55	Clean Sheets In games when he played at least 70 mins	6

LEAGUE GOALS

Raul Tamudo

Minutes on the pitch	2485	Goals in the League	19
League average (mins between goals)	131		

	PLAYER	MINS	GOALS	AVE
1	Tamudo	2485	19	131
2	Maxi	2590	5	518
3	Lopo	2718	4	680
4	Fredson	1838	3	613
5	Raducanu	351	3	117
6	Jordi	1736	3	579
7	Bobson	384	1	384
8	Oscar	161	1	161
9	Raul Molina	771	1	771
10	Wome	1905	1	1905
11	Pocchettino	1890	1	1890
12	Alex	1201	1	1201
13	Hadji	1197	1	1197
	Other		4	
	TOTAL		48	

DISCIPLINARY RECORDS

	PLAYER	YELLOW	RED	AVE
1	Lopo	19	3	123
2	Alex	9	0	133
3	Torricelli	6	1	176
4	Wome	8	2	190
5	Jarque	3	0	202
6	Bastia	3	0	207
7	De La Pena	6	1	274
8	Fredson	6	0	306
9	Morales	5	1	308
10	Tamudo	7	0	355
11	Maxi	6	0	431
12	Tayfun	3	0	474
13	Jordi	3	0	578
	Other	27	6	
	TOTAL	111	14	

TOP POINT EARNERS

	PLAYER	GAMES	AV PTS
1	Fredson	18	1.94
2	Pocchettino	21	1.67
3	De La Pena	19	1.53
4	Garcia	17	1.47
5	Morales	14	1.36
6	Lopo	29	1.28
7	Lemmens	29	1.28
8	Domoraud	32	1.25
9	Jordi	14	1.21
10	Tamudo	26	1.12
	CLUB AVERAGE:		1.13

TEAM OF THE SEASON

G Lemmens CG: 29 DR: 55

D Pocchettino CG: 21 DR: 61

D Domoraud CG: 32 DR: 57

D Wome CG: 18 DR: 53

D Lopo CG: 29 DR: 52

M Fredson CG: 18 SD: 18

M De La Pena CG: 19 SD: 2

M Garcia CG: 17 SD: -22

M Maxi CG: 25 SD: -29

F Tamudo CG: 26 SR: 131

F *Jordi CG: 14 SR: 579

LEAGUE APPEARANCES, BOOKINGS AND CAPS

	AGE (on 01/07/04)	IN NAMED 18	APPEARANCES	COUNTING GAMES	MINUTES ON PITCH	YELLOW CARDS	RED CARDS	THIS SEASON	HOME COUNTRY
Goalkeepers									
Gorka Iraioz	23	9	0	0	0	0	0	-	Spain
Erwin Lemmens	28	30	29	29	2596	1	1	2	Belgium (17)
Antonio Toni	33	35	9	9	810	0	0	-	Spain
Defenders									
Marc Bertran	22	13	6	4	465	0	0	-	Spain
Carlos Garcia	20	5	3	2	232	1	0	-	Spain
Cyril Domoraud	32	36	36	32	3033	5	0	-	France
Daniel Jarque	21	16	8	5	607	3	0	-	Spain
Alberto Lopo	25	31	31	29	2718	19	3	-	Spain
Pocchettino	32	21	21	21	1890	3	0	-	Argentina
Antoni Soldevilla	25	6	4	2	286	3	2	-	Spain
Moreno Torricelli	34	28	16	12	1236	6	1	-	Italy
Gregory Vignal	22	10	8	4	402	2	1	-	France
Pierre Nlend Wome	25	32	26	18	1905	8	2	1	Cameroon (12)
Midfielders									
Adrian Bastia	25	13	8	6	621	3	0	-	Argentina
Ivan De La Pena	28	25	25	19	1924	6	1	-	Spain
Camara Fredson	23	26	24	18	1838	6	0	-	Brazil
David Garcia	23	38	24	17	1781	3	0	-	Spain
Moustapha Hadji	32	16	16	11	1197	2	0	-	Morocco
Simon Hector	20	17	8	1	251	1	0	-	Spain
Jordi Cruyff	30	33	30	14	1736	3	0	-	Holland
Enric Maureta	-	1	0	0	0	0	0	-	Spain
Rodriguez Maxi	23	36	35	25	2590	6	0	-	Argentina
Angel Morales	28	37	31	14	1850	5	1	-	Spain
Francisco Punal	28	1	1	1	90	0	0	-	Spain
Korkut Tayfun	30	24	21	12	1424	3	0	-	Turkey
Velamanzan	27	20	12	0	393	1	0	-	Spain
Forwards									
Alex	30	26	23	8	1201	9	0	-	Spain
Kevin Bobson	23	11	9	1	384	0	0	-	Holland
Ferran Corominas	21	2	2	0	52	0	0	-	Spain
Soriano Jonathan	18	1	0	0	0	0	0	-	Spain
Gracia Luismi	20	3	1	0	7	0	0	-	Spain
Garcia Oscar	31	10	7	0	161	2	1	-	Spain
Claudiu Raducanu	27	17	11	0	351	2	1	-	Romania
Raul Molina	27	16	13	5	771	1	0	-	Spain
Raul Tamudo	26	32	31	26	2485	7	0	1	Spain (3)

SQUAD APPEARANCES

Match	1	2	3	4	5	6	7	8	9	10	11	12	13	14	15	16	17	18	19	20	21	22	23	24	25	26	27	28	29	30	31	32	33	34	35	36	37	38
Venue	H	A	H	A	H	A	A	H	A	H	A	H	A	H	A	H	A	H	A	A	H	A	H	A	H	H	A	H	A	H	A	H	A	H	A	H	A	H
Competition	L	L	L	L	L	L	L	L	L	L	L	L	L	L	L	L	L	L	L	L	L	L	L	L	L	L	L	L	L	L	L	L	L	L	L	L	L	L
Result	D	D	L	L	L	L	L	L	W	L	L	W	L	L	L	L	L	W	W	L	L	W	W	L	L	W	W	L	D	W	L	D	W	W	L	W	L	W

Goalkeepers
Gorka Iraioz
Erwin Lemmens
Antonio Jimenez Toni

Defenders
Marc Bertran
Badias Carlos Garcia
Cyril Domoraud
Daniel Jarque
Alberto Lopo
Mauricio Pocchettino
Antoni Soldevilla
Moreno Torricelli
Gregory Vignal
Pierre Nlend Wome

Midfielders
Adrian Jesus Bastia
Ivan De La Pena
Camara Pereira Fredson
David Garcia
Moustapha Hadji
Simon Hector
Jordi Cruyff
Enric Maureta
Rodriguez Maxi
Angel Morales
Francisco Punal
Korkut Tayfun
Antonio Velamanzan

Forwards
Fernandez Sanchez Alex
Kevin Bobson
Ferran Corominas
Soriano Jonathan
Gracia Luismi
Garcia Junyent Oscar
Claudiu Nicu Raducanu
Alcocer Raul Molina
Raul Tamudo

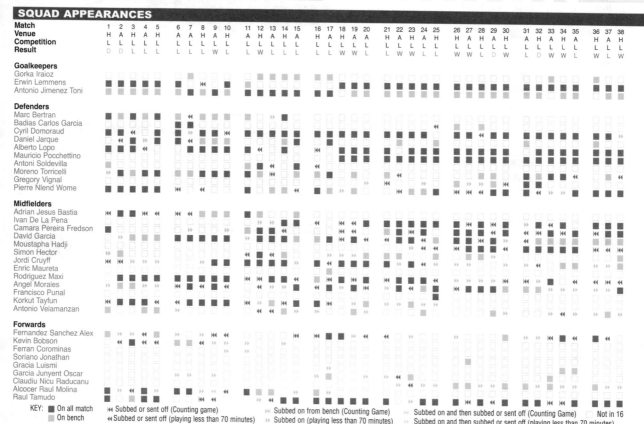

KEY: On all match; On bench; Subbed or sent off (Counting game); Subbed or sent off (playing less than 70 minutes); Subbed on from bench (Counting Game); Subbed on (playing less than 70 minutes); Subbed on and then subbed or sent off (Counting Game); Subbed on and then subbed or sent off (playing less than 70 minutes); Not in 16

RACING SANTANDER 17th

KEY: ☐ Won ☐ Drawn ☐ Lost

							Attendance
1	lge	Mallorca	H	W	2-1	Benayoun 12; Guerrero 69	11,517
2	lge	Murcia	A	D	1-1	Guerrero 44	17,000
3	lge	Real Sociedad	H	L	0-1		11,396
4	lge	Real Betis	A	D	0-0		42,000
5	lge	Villarreal	H	L	0-2		19,000
6	lge	Valladolid	A	W	4-0	Bodipo 15,84; Regueiro 59; Nafti 85	24,000
7	lge	Malaga	H	W	4-2	Moran 56; Benayoun 59; Johnatan 70; Bodipo 82	21,500
8	lge	Real Madrid	A	L	1-3	Benayoun 16	68,000
9	lge	Espanyol	H	L	0-1		10,000
10	lge	Celta Vigo	A	W	1-0	Benayoun 2	17,000
11	lge	Valencia	A	W	2-1	Bodipo 23,49	52,500
12	lge	Real Zaragoza	H	L	1-2	Rebosio 40 og	13,500
13	lge	Athl Bilbao	A	W	2-1	Bodipo 42; Regueiro 66	38,000
14	lge	Seville	H	L	0-4		11,000
15	lge	Albacete	A	L	0-4		14,000
16	lge	Osasuna	H	D	0-0		11,500
17	lge	Atl Madrid	A	D	2-2	Mata Buena 52; Johnatan 80	45,000
18	lge	Barcelona	H	W	3-0	Juanma 52; Regueiro 80; Guerrero 84	22,000
19	lge	Deportivo	A	D	1-1	Guerrero 79	28,000
20	lge	Mallorca	A	D	1-1	Regueiro 74	15,500
21	lge	Murcia	H	W	3-2	Guerrero 33,72,90	16,000
22	lge	Real Sociedad	A	L	0-1		24,000
23	lge	Real Betis	H	L	1-2	Benjamin 6 og	21,000
24	lge	Villarreal	A	L	3-6	Benayoun 33,84; Alvarez 56 pen	17,000
25	lge	Valladolid	H	W	1-0	Bodipo 67	17,000
26	lge	Malaga	A	L	0-1		35,245
27	lge	Real Madrid	H	D	1-1	Benayoun 31	22,000
28	lge	Espanyol	A	W	1-0	Moran 57	45,100
29	lge	Celta Vigo	H	D	4-4	Alvarez 17 pen,83 pen; Guerrero 38,86	21,375
30	lge	Valencia	H	L	0-3		13,781
31	lge	Real Zaragoza	A	D	2-2	Casar 53; Moran 81	34,000
32	lge	Athl Bilbao	H	L	1-2	Guerrero 77	15,000
33	lge	Seville	A	L	2-5	Guerrero 71 pen; Mata Buena 84	35,000
34	lge	Albacete	H	L	0-2		15,500
35	lge	Osasuna	A	W	2-1	Alvarez 64; Afek 90	17,000
36	lge	Atl Madrid	H	D	2-2	Alvarez 57; Afek 89	14,000
37	lge	Barcelona	A	L	0-1		88,000
38	lge	Deportivo	H	L	0-1		17,000

MONTHLY POINTS TALLY

Month	Points	%
AUGUST	3	100%
SEPTEMBER	2	17%
OCTOBER	6	50%
NOVEMBER	9	75%
DECEMBER	2	17%
JANUARY	8	67%
FEBRUARY	3	20%
MARCH	5	42%
APRIL	1	8%
MAY	4	33%

KEY PLAYERS - GOALSCORERS

Javier Garcia Guerrero

Goals in the League	11	Player Strike Rate Average number of minutes between League goals scored by player	219
Contribution to Attacking Power Average number of minutes between League team goals while on pitch	80	Club Strike Rate Average number of minutes between League goals scored by club	71

	PLAYER	LGE GOALS	POWER	STRIKE RATE
1	Javier Garcia Guerrero	11	80	219 mins
2	Cristian Alvarez	5	70	255 mins
3	Rodolfo Diaz Bodipo	7	61	282 mins
4	Yossi Benayoun	7	72	373 mins

KEY PLAYERS - MIDFIELDERS

Fernando Escudero Moran

Goals in the League	3	Contribution to Attacking Power Average number of minutes between League team goals while on pitch	69
Defensive Rating Average number of mins between League goals conceded while he was on the pitch	57	Scoring Difference Defensive Rating minus Contribution to Attacking Power	-12

	PLAYER	LGE GOALS	DEF RATE	POWER	SCORE DIFF
1	Fernando Escudero Moran	3	57	69	-12 mins
2	Mario Regueiro	4	64	77	-13 mins
3	Yossi Benayoun	7	58	72	-14 mins
4	Diaz Ayoze	0	45	66	-21 mins

KEY PLAYERS - DEFENDERS

Borja Enrique Ayensa Neru

Goals Conceded (GC) The number of League goals conceded while he was on the pitch	24	Clean Sheets In games when he played at least 70 minutes	6
Defensive Rating Ave number of mins between League goals conceded while on the pitch	71	Club Defensive Rating Average number of mins between League goals conceded by the club this season	54

	PLAYER	CON LGE	CLEAN SHEETS	DEF RATE
1	Borja Enrique Ayensa Neru	24	6	71 mins
2	Jose Taeno Moraton	22	2	68 mins
3	David Pararols Coromina	21	3	60 mins
4	Mehdi Nafti	46	5	57 mins

KEY GOALKEEPER

Ricardo Lopez Felipe

Goals Conceded in the League	58	Counting Games Games when he played at least 70 mins	34
Defensive Rating Ave number of mins between League goals conceded while on the pitch	53	Clean Sheets In games when he played at least 70 mins	7

LEAGUE GOALS

Javier Garcia Guerrero

Minutes on the pitch	2408	Goals in the League	11
League average (mins between goals)	219		

	PLAYER	MINS	GOALS	AVE
1	Guerrero	2408	11	219
2	Benayoun	2609	7	373
3	Bodipo	1973	7	282
4	Alvarez	1276	5	255
5	Regueiro	2378	4	595
6	Moran	2673	3	891
7	Afek	947	2	474
8	Johnatan	846	2	423
9	Mata Buena	1233	2	617
10	Juanma	3004	1	3004
11	Casar	2794	1	2794
12	Nafti	2615	1	2615
	Other		2	
	TOTAL		48	

DISCIPLINARY

	PLAYER	YELLOW	RED	AVE
1	Juanma	14	1	200
2	Coromina	6	0	210
3	Regueiro	10	1	216
4	Mateo	7	2	216
5	Afek	4	0	236
6	Nafti	9	1	261
7	Bodipo	7	0	281
8	Moran	9	0	297
9	Casar	7	0	399
10	Guerrero	6	0	401
11	Neru	4	0	427
12	Benayoun	6	0	434
13	Moraton	3	0	495
	Other	11	0	
	TOTAL	103	5	

TOP POINT EARNERS

	PLAYER	GAMES	AV PTS
1	Regueiro	23	1.48
2	Coromina	14	1.43
3	Mateo	15	1.33
4	Benayoun	25	1.32
5	Juanma	32	1.28
6	Moran	28	1.21
7	Nafti	29	1.21
8	Neru	19	1.21
9	Ricardo	34	1.15
10	Casar	31	1.13
	CLUB AVERAGE:		1.13

LEAGUE APPEARANCES, BOOKINGS AND CAPS

	AGE (on 01/07/04)	IN NAMED 18	APPEARANCES	COUNTING GAMES	MINUTES ON PITCH	YELLOW CARDS	RED CARDS	THIS SEASON	HOME COUNTRY
Goalkeepers									
Dudu Aouate	26	38	5	4	379	0	0	-	Israel
Ricardo Lopez	32	38	34	34	3060	0	0	-	Spain
Defenders									
Cristian Alvarez	26	16	15	13	1276	2	0	-	Argentina
Franz Bertin	21	1	0	0	0	0	0	-	France
Pablo Casar	25	37	32	31	2794	7	0	-	Spain
David Coromina	29	28	14	14	1260	6	0	-	Spain
Sanchez Juanma	27	34	34	32	3004	14	1	-	Spain
Jose Moraton	24	27	19	16	1486	3	0	-	Spain
Mehdi Nafti	25	31	31	29	2615	9	1	-	France
Borja Enrique Neru	30	34	20	19	1711	4	0	-	Spain
Midfielders									
Omri Afek	25	30	24	5	947	4	0	-	Israel
Anderson Silva	21	18	7	0	247	1	0	-	Brazil
Enrique Arturo	21	1	0	0	0	0	0	-	Brazil
Diaz Ayoze	22	33	27	22	2117	4	0	-	Spain
Yossi Benayoun	24	34	34	25	2609	6	0	-	Israel
Sergio Mata Buena	25	36	25	11	1233	2	0	-	Spain
Diego Mateo	25	34	30	15	1945	7	2	-	Argentina
Fernando Moran	28	36	36	28	2673	9	0	-	Spain
Pablo Lago	29	21	7	1	247	0	0	-	Spain
Martin Raul	21	10	4	0	78	1	0	-	Spain
Mario Regueiro	25	33	33	23	2378	10	1	2	Uruguay (25)
Daniel Perez Txiki	27	14	4	0	139	0	0	-	Spain
Forwards									
Rodolfo Bodipo	26	30	30	17	1973	7	0	-	Spain
Javier Guerrero	27	36	36	21	2408	6	0	-	Spain
Valle Johnatan	19	36	25	2	846	1	0	-	Spain

TEAM OF THE SEASON

G — Ricardo CG: 34 DR: 53

D — Neru CG: 19 DR: 71

D — Moraton CG: 16 DR: 68

D — Coromina CG: 14 DR: 60

D — Nafti CG: 29 DR: 57

M — Moran CG: 28 SD: -12

M — Regueiro CG: 23 SD: -13

M — Benayoun CG: 25 SD: -14

M — Ayoze CG: 22 SD: -21

F — Guerrero CG: 21 SR: 219

F — Bodipo CG: 17 SR: 282

SQUAD APPEARANCES

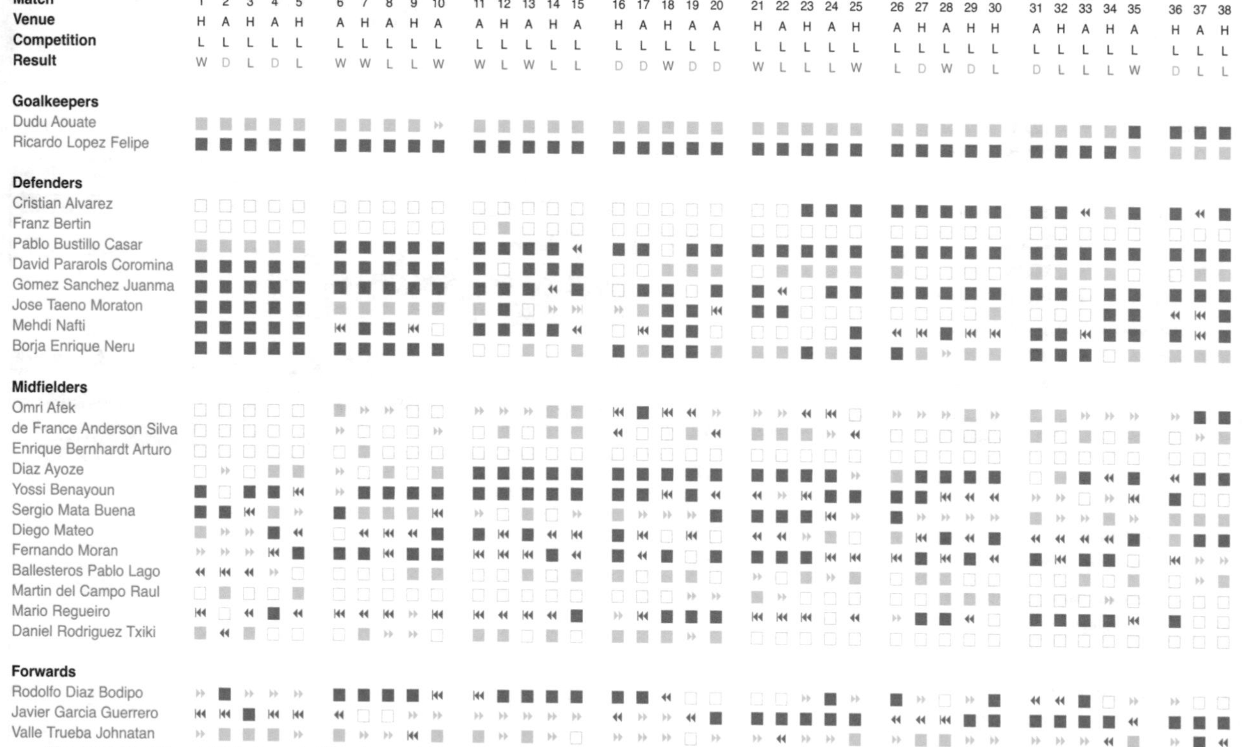

Match 1 2 3 4 5 6 7 8 9 10 11 12 13 14 15 16 17 18 19 20 21 22 23 24 25 26 27 28 29 30 31 32 33 34 35 36 37 38
Venue H A H A H A H A H A A H A H A H A H A A H A H A H A H A H H A H A H A H A H
Competition L L L L L L L L L L L L L L L L L L L L L L L L L L L L L L L L L L L L L L
Result W D L D L W W L L W W L W L L D D W D D W L L L W L D W D L D L L L W D L L
Goalkeepers
Dudu Aouate
Ricardo Lopez Felipe
Defenders
Cristian Alvarez
Franz Bertin
Pablo Bustillo Casar
David Pararols Coromina
Gomez Sanchez Juanma
Jose Taeno Moraton
Mehdi Nafti
Borja Enrique Neru
Midfielders
Omri Afek
de France Anderson Silva
Enrique Bernhardt Arturo
Diaz Ayoze
Yossi Benayoun
Sergio Mata Buena
Diego Mateo
Fernando Moran
Ballesteros Pablo Lago
Martin del Campo Raul
Mario Regueiro
Daniel Rodriguez Txiki
Forwards
Rodolfo Diaz Bodipo
Javier Garcia Guerrero
Valle Trueba Johnatan

KEY: On all match; On bench; Subbed or sent off (Counting game); Subbed or sent off (playing less than 70 minutes); Subbed on from bench (Counting Game); Subbed on (playing less than 70 minutes); Subbed on and then subbed or sent off (Counting Game); Subbed on and then subbed or sent off (playing less than 70 minutes); Not in 16

VALLADOLID

Final Position: **18th**

KEY: Won Drawn Lost

							Attendance
1	lge	Valencia	A	D	1-1	Sousa 26	45,000
2	lge	Malaga	H	W	1-0	Jesus 43 pen	11,000
3	lge	Real Madrid	A	L	2-7	Losada 55 pen; Chema 59	70,000
4	lge	Espanyol	H	W	3-1	Zapata 5; Jesus 10; Ciric 83 pen	12,000
5	lge	Celta Vigo	A	L	2-3	Makukula 6,50	18,000
6	lge	R Santander	H	L	0-4		24,000
7	lge	Real Zaragoza	A	L	0-1		29,000
8	lge	Athl Bilbao	H	W	2-0	Sousa 17; Makukula 55	15,500
9	lge	Seville	A	D	1-1	Makukula 51	31,000
10	lge	Albacete	H	W	2-0	Makukula 34; Losada 90 pen	21,000
11	lge	Osasuna	A	D	1-1	Sales 29	19,000
12	lge	Atl Madrid	H	W	3-1	Makukula 21; Zapata 37; Sousa 66	15,500
13	lge	Barcelona	A	D	0-0		91,000
14	lge	Deportivo	H	D	1-1	Oscar 65	20,000
15	lge	Mallorca	A	L	0-1		14,500
16	lge	Murcia	H	D	0-0		11,500
17	lge	Real Sociedad	A	W	3-1	Makukula 30; Oscar 74; Losada 86	24,000
18	lge	Real Betis	H	D	0-0		18,500
19	lge	Villarreal	A	L	1-3	Makukula 65	17,000
20	lge	Valencia	H	D	0-0		13,000
21	lge	Malaga	A	W	3-2	Oscar 41,68; Julio Cesar 78	22,000
22	lge	Real Madrid	H	L	2-3	Oscar 33,41	25,000
23	lge	Espanyol	A	L	0-2		33,000
24	lge	Celta Vigo	H	L	0-2		12,000
25	lge	R Santander	A	L	0-1		17,000
26	lge	Real Zaragoza	H	L	1-2	Oscar 33	9,000
27	lge	Athl Bilbao	A	W	4-1	Losada 2,75; Oscar 14; Jesus 37	36,000
28	lge	Seville	H	W	2-0	Jonathan 52; Jesus 63 pen	23,850
29	lge	Albacete	A	L	0-2		14,685
30	lge	Osasuna	H	D	1-1	Losada 23	12,000
31	lge	Atl Madrid	A	L	1-2	Richetti 66	50,000
32	lge	Barcelona	H	L	1-3	Oscar 66	17,000
33	lge	Deportivo	A	D	1-1	Oscar 45	27,000
34	lge	Mallorca	H	L	1-3	Chema 59	21,000
35	lge	Murcia	A	L	1-2	Jonathan 31	5,900
36	lge	Real Sociedad	H	D	2-2	Sales 22,72	17,000
37	lge	Real Betis	A	L	0-1		25,000
38	lge	Villarreal	H	W	3-0	Losada 33,83; Caminero 87	15,000

MONTHLY POINTS TALLY

Month	Points	%
AUGUST	1	33%
SEPTEMBER	6	50%
OCTOBER	4	33%
NOVEMBER	8	67%
DECEMBER	5	42%
JANUARY	5	42%
FEBRUARY	0	0%
MARCH	7	58%
APRIL	1	8%
MAY	4	33%

KEY PLAYERS - GOALSCORERS

Ariza Makukula

Goals in the League	8	Player Strike Rate Average number of minutes between League goals scored by player	184
Contribution to Attacking Power Average number of minutes between League team goals while on pitch	77	Club Strike Rate Average number of minutes between League goals scored by club	74

	PLAYER	LGE GOALS	POWER	STRIKE RATE
1	Ariza Makukula	8	77	184 mins
2	Roberto Losada	8	66	232 mins
3	Gonzalez Marcos Oscar	10	78	283 mins
4	Sanchez Japon Jesus	4	73	567 mins

KEY PLAYERS - MIDFIELDERS

Francisco David Sousa

Goals in the League	3	Contribution to Attacking Power Average number of minutes between League team goals while on pitch	64
Defensive Rating Average number of mins between League goals conceded while he was on the pitch	83	Scoring Difference Defensive Rating minus Contribution to Attacking Power	19

	PLAYER	LGE GOALS	DEF RATE	POWER	SCORE DIFF
1	Francisco David Sousa	3	83	64	19 mins
2	Sanchez Japon Jesus	4	71	73	-2 mins
3	Jose Luis Perez Caminero	1	63	76	-13 mins
4	Gonzalez Marcos Oscar	10	57	79	-22 mins

KEY PLAYERS - DEFENDERS

Juan Manuel Montano Pena

Goals Conceded (GC) The number of League goals conceded while he was on the pitch	25	Clean Sheets In games when he played at least 70 minutes	4
Defensive Rating Ave number of mins between League goals conceded while on the pitch	67	Club Defensive Rating Average number of mins between League goals conceded by the club this season	61

	PLAYER	CON LGE	CLEAN SHEETS	DEF RATE
1	Juan Manuel Montano Pena	25	4	67 mins
2	Martin Carabias Jonathan	35	7	65 mins
3	Julio Cesar	38	6	61 mins
4	Javier Torres Gomez	51	7	59 mins

KEY GOALKEEPER

Albano Benjamin Bizzarri

Goals Conceded in the League	53	Counting Games Games when he played at least 70 mins	38
Defensive Rating Ave number of mins between League goals conceded while on the pitch	64	Clean Sheets In games when he played at least 70 mins	9

LEAGUE GOALS

Gonzalez Marcos Oscar

Minutes on the pitch	2834	Goals in the League	10
League average (mins between goals)	283		

	PLAYER	MINS	GOALS	AVE
1	Oscar	2834	10	283
2	Losada	1854	8	232
3	Makukula	1470	8	184
4	Jesus	2269	4	567
5	Sales	3007	3	1002
6	Sousa	1733	3	578
7	Zapata	1455	2	728
8	Chema	1079	2	540
9	Jonathan	2284	2	1142
10	Caminero	1832	1	1832
11	Julio Cesar	2308	1	2308
12	Ciric	169	1	169
13	Richetti	2297	1	2297
	Other		0	
	TOTAL		46	

DISCIPLINARY RECORDS

	PLAYER	YELLOW	RED	AVE
1	Sousa	10	0	173
2	Richetti	11	2	176
3	Chema	5	1	179
4	Jesus	9	1	226
5	Pena	5	2	239
6	Makukula	6	0	245
7	Pablo Paz	2	0	258
8	Torres Gomez	10	1	274
9	Julio Cesar	7	1	288
10	Caminero	6	0	305
11	Marcos	9	0	318
12	Sales	8	0	375
13	Jonathan	6	0	380
	Other	18	1	
	TOTAL	112	9	

TOP POINT EARNERS

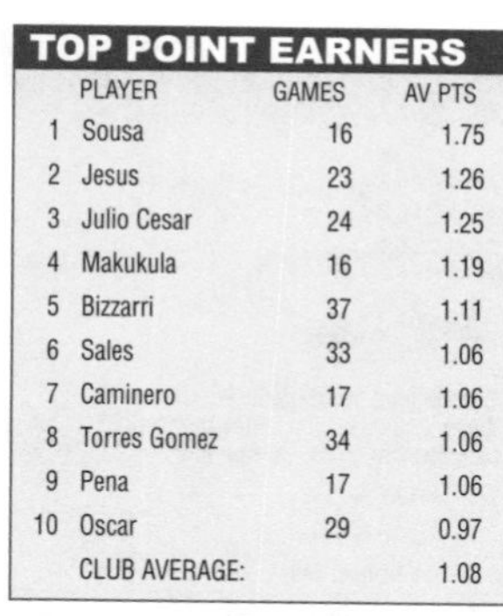

	PLAYER	GAMES	AV PTS
1	Sousa	16	1.75
2	Jesus	23	1.26
3	Julio Cesar	24	1.25
4	Makukula	16	1.19
5	Bizzarri	37	1.11
6	Sales	33	1.06
7	Caminero	17	1.06
8	Torres Gomez	34	1.06
9	Pena	17	1.06
10	Oscar	29	0.97
	CLUB AVERAGE:		1.08

TEAM OF THE SEASON

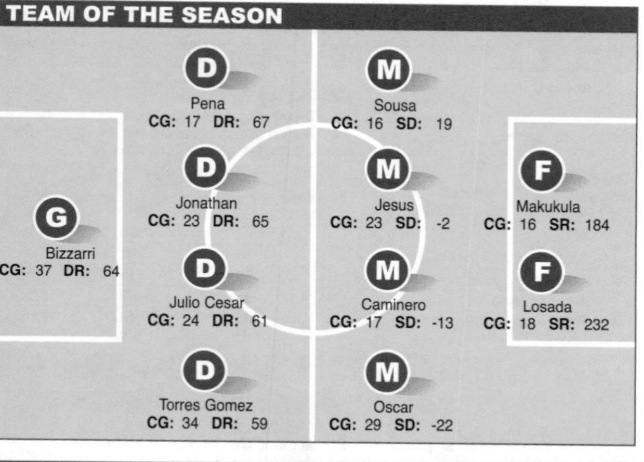
D
Pena
CG: 17 DR: 67
D
Jonathan
CG: 23 DR: 65
D
Julio Cesar
CG: 24 DR: 61
D
Torres Gomez
CG: 34 DR: 59
G
Bizzarri
CG: 37 DR: 64
M
Sousa
CG: 16 SD: 19
M
Jesus
CG: 23 SD: -2
M
Caminero
CG: 17 SD: -13
M
Oscar
CG: 29 SD: -22
F
Makukula
CG: 16 SR: 184
F
Losada
CG: 18 SR: 232

LEAGUE APPEARANCES, BOOKINGS AND CAPS

	AGE (on 01/07/04)	IN NAMED 18	APPEARANCES	COUNTING GAMES	MINUTES ON PITCH	YELLOW CARDS	RED CARDS	THIS SEASON	HOME COUNTRY
Goalkeepers									
Benjamin Bizzarri	26	38	38	37	3375	5	1	-	Argentina
Catriel Orcellet	26	38	1	0	45	0	0	-	Argentina
Defenders									
Antonio Ayala	-	1	0	0	0	0	0	-	Spain
Martin Jonathan	23	36	31	23	2284	6	0	-	Spain
Julio Cesar	28	30	28	24	2308	7	1	-	Brazil
Alberto Marcos	30	34	33	31	2870	9	0	-	Spain
Oscar Sanchez	24	23	10	2	368	2	0	-	Spain
Ariel Pablo Paz	31	16	9	4	517	2	0	-	Argentina
Juan Manuel Pena	31	23	21	17	1673	5	2	-	Bolivia
Pablo Richetti	27	33	30	24	2297	11	2	-	Argentina
Torres Gomez	34	34	34	34	3022	10	1	-	Spain
Midfielders									
Jose Caminero	36	33	27	17	1832	6	0	-	Spain
Jose Chema	28	33	23	5	1079	5	1	-	Spain
Diego Figueredo	22	11	8	1	302	2	0	-	Paraguay
Pozo Javi Jimenez	28	14	4	0	56	1	0	-	Spain
Sanchez Jesus	29	27	27	23	2269	9	1	-	Spain
Javier Roca More	22	9	4	0	154	0	0	-	Spain
Gonzalez Oscar	21	37	37	29	2834	4	0	-	Spain
Lopez Rafa	19	13	3	0	99	0	0	-	Spain
David Sousa	24	24	24	16	1733	10	0	-	Spain
Victor Zapata	25	33	25	11	1455	3	0	-	Argentina
Forwards									
Martin Cardetti	28	25	11	0	206	0	0	-	Argentina
Dragan Ciric	29	15	8	0	169	0	0	-	Serbia & Montenegro
Roberto Losada	27	37	27	18	1854	1	0	-	Spain
Ariza Makukula	23	19	18	16	1470	6	0	-	Portugal
Valentin Pachon	27	12	3	1	99	0	0	-	Spain
Fernando Sales	26	35	35	33	3007	8	0	-	Spain

SQUAD APPEARANCES

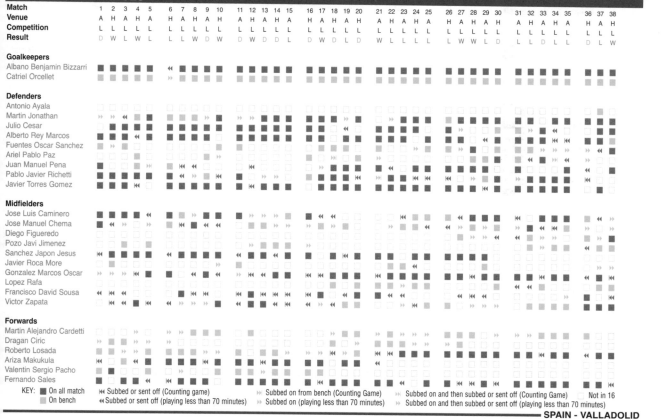

Match	1	2	3	4	5	6	7	8	9	10	11	12	13	14	15	16	17	18	19	20	21	22	23	24	25	26	27	28	29	30	31	32	33	34	35	36	37	38
Venue	A	H	A	H	A	H	A	H	A	H	A	H	A	H	A	H	A	H	A	H	A	H	A	H	A	H	A	H	A	H	A	H	A	H	A	H	A	H
Competition	L	L	L	L	L	L	L	L	L	L	L	L	L	L	L	L	L	L	L	L	L	L	L	L	L	L	L	L	L	L	L	L	L	L	L	L	L	L
Result	D	W	L	W	L	L	L	W	D	W	D	W	D	D	L	D	W	D	L	D	W	L	L	L	L	L	W	W	L	D	L	L	D	L	L	D	L	W

Goalkeepers
Albano Benjamin Bizzarri
Catriel Orcellet

Defenders
Antonio Ayala
Martin Jonathan
Julio Cesar
Alberto Rey Marcos
Fuentes Oscar Sanchez
Ariel Pablo Paz
Juan Manuel Pena
Pablo Javier Richetti
Javier Torres Gomez

Midfielders
Jose Luis Caminero
Jose Manuel Chema
Diego Figueredo
Pozo Javi Jimenez
Sanchez Japon Jesus
Javier Roca More
Gonzalez Marcos Oscar
Lopez Rafa
Francisco David Sousa
Victor Zapata

Forwards
Martin Alejandro Cardetti
Dragan Ciric
Roberto Losada
Ariza Makukula
Valentin Sergio Pacho
Fernando Sales

KEY: On all match | On bench | Subbed or sent off (Counting game) | Subbed or sent off (playing less than 70 minutes) | Subbed on from bench (Counting Game) | Subbed on (playing less than 70 minutes) | Subbed on and then subbed or sent off (Counting Game) | Subbed on and then subbed or sent off (playing less than 70 minutes) | Not in 16

CELTA VIGO

Final Position: **19th**

KEY: Won Drawn Lost

		Opponent			Score	Scorers	Attendance
1	clql1	Slavia Prague	H	W	3-0	Mostovoi 17; Jesuli 50; Edu 54	25,000
2	clql2	Slavia Prague	A	L	0-2		
3	lge	Murcia	H	D	1-1	Milosevic 29	18,000
4	lge	Real Sociedad	A	D	1-1	Milosevic 68	23,000
5	lge	Real Betis	H	L	0-2		18,000
6	cl gh	Club Brugge	A	D	1-1	Juanfran 50	26,639
7	lge	Villarreal	A	D	1-1	Mostovoi 75	14,000
8	lge	Valladolid	H	W	3-2	Jesuli 57; Milosevic 73; Mostovoi 83	18,000
9	cl gh	AC Milan	H	D	0-0		27,000
10	lge	Malaga	A	L	1-2	Milosevic 71	28,000
11	lge	Real Madrid	H	L	0-2		26,000
12	cl gh	Ajax	A	L	0-1		48,514
13	lge	Espanyol	A	W	4-0	Luccin 16 pen; Milosevic 59; Mostovoi 77; Jandro 89	45,500
14	lge	Valencia	A	D	2-2	Berizzo 57; Jesuli 66	50,000
15	lge	R Santander	H	L	0-1		17,000
16	cl gh	Ajax	H	W	3-2	Luccin 25 pen; Milosevic 39; Vagner 63	20,000
17	lge	Real Zaragoza	A	D	1-1	Jose Ignacio 4	31,000
18	lge	Athl Bilbao	H	L	0-2		16,000
19	cl gh	Club Brugge	H	D	1-1	Mostovoi 74	22,000
20	lge	Seville	A	W	1-0	Jesuli 35	35,500
21	lge	Albacete	H	D	2-2	Jose Ignacio 19; Contreras 60	15,000
22	lge	Osasuna	A	L	2-3	Jose Ignacio 37; Catanha 90	14,000
23	cl gh	AC Milan	A	W	2-1	Jesuli 42; Jose Ignacio 71	55,510
24	lge	Atl Madrid	H	D	2-2	Luccin 37; Milosevic 40	16,000
25	lge	Barcelona	A	D	1-1	Jesuli 17	78,000
26	lge	Deportivo	H	L	0-5		25,000
27	lge	Mallorca	A	W	4-2	Jose Ignacio 15; Jesuli 71; Luccin 85 pen; Milosevic 90	15,500
28	lge	Murcia	A	D	2-2	Luccin 7; Milosevic 45	10,000
29	lge	Real Sociedad	H	L	2-5	Gustavo Lopez 1; Luccin 51 pen	24,000
30	lge	Real Betis	A	L	0-1		35,000
31	lge	Villarreal	H	W	2-1	Milosevic 18,48	22,000
32	lge	Valladolid	A	W	2-0	Mostovoi 47; Jesuli 87	12,000
33	lge	Malaga	H	L	0-2		20,000
34	clr1l1	Arsenal	H	L	2-3	Edu 27; Jose Ignacio 64	21,000
35	lge	Real Madrid	A	L	2-4	Ilic 18; Milosevic 90	72,000
36	lge	Espanyol	H	L	1-5	Edu 90	17,000
37	clr1l2	Arsenal	A	L	0-2		35,402
38	lge	Valencia	H	L	0-2		26,076
39	lge	R Santander	A	D	4-4	Milosevic 28,72 pen; Mostovoi 46,61	21,375
40	lge	Real Zaragoza	H	L	0-2		17,000
41	lge	Athl Bilbao	A	D	0-0		28,000
42	lge	Seville	H	D	0-0		20,000
43	lge	Albacete	A	W	2-0	Juanfran 21; Gustavo Lopez 47	16,000
44	lge	Osasuna	H	W	1-0	Munoz 49 og	18,000
45	lge	Atl Madrid	A	L	2-3	Milosevic 32; Edu 69	40,000
46	lge	Barcelona	H	W	1-0	Edu 43	27,000
47	lge	Deportivo	A	L	0-3		29,000
48	lge	Mallorca	H	L	1-2	Jandro 90	27,000

MONTHY POINTS TALLY

Month	Points	%
AUGUST	1	33%
SEPTEMBER	5	42%
OCTOBER	4	33%
NOVEMBER	4	33%
DECEMBER	3	25%
JANUARY	4	27%
FEBRUARY	6	50%
MARCH	1	8%
APRIL	8	67%
MAY	3	25%

KEY PLAYERS - GOALSCORERS

Savo Milosevic

Goals in the League	13	Player Strike Rate Average number of minutes between League goals scored by player	227
Contribution to Attacking Power Average number of minutes between League team goals while on pitch	70	Club Strike Rate Average number of minutes between League goals scored by club	71

	PLAYER	LGE GOALS	POWER	STRIKE RATE
1	Savo Milosevic	13	70	227 mins
2	Alexander Mostovoi	6	72	254 mins
3	Jesus Antonio Jesuli	6	65	315 mins
4	Luis Eduardo Schmidt Edu	3	115	425 mins

KEY PLAYERS - MIDFIELDERS

Saenz Marin Jose Ignacio

Goals in the League	4	Contribution to Attacking Power Average number of minutes between League team goals while on pitch	61
Defensive Rating Average number of mins between League goals conceded while he was on the pitch	53	Scoring Difference Defensive Rating minus Contribution to Attacking Power	-8

	PLAYER	LGE GOALS	DEF RATE	POWER	SCORE DIFF
1	Saenz Marin Jose Ignacio	4	53	61	-8 mins
2	Jesus Antonio Jesuli	6	52	65	-13 mins
3	Alexander Mostovoi	6	55	73	-18 mins
4	Peter Luccin	5	45	64	-19 mins

KEY PLAYERS - DEFENDERS

Juan Francisco Garcia

Goals Conceded (GC) The number of League goals conceded while he was on the pitch	21	Clean Sheets In games when he played at least 70 minutes	7
Defensive Rating Ave number of mins between League goals conceded while on the pitch	81	Club Defensive Rating Average number of mins between League goals conceded by the club this season	50

	PLAYER	CON LGE	CLEAN SHEETS	DEF RATE
1	Juan Francisco Garcia	21	7	81 mins
2	Juan Velasco Damas	42	7	53 mins
3	Fernando Gabriel Caceres	40	3	50 mins
4	Eduardo Berizzo	45	6	50 mins

KEY GOALKEEPER

Pablo Rodriguez Cavallero

Goals Conceded in the League	53	Counting Games Games when he played at least 70 mins	32
Defensive Rating Ave number of mins between League goals conceded while on the pitch	54	Clean Sheets In games when he played at least 70 mins	8

LEAGUE GOALS

Savo Milosevic

Minutes on the pitch	2950	Goals in the League	13
League average (mins between goals)	227		

	PLAYER	MINS	GOALS	AVE
1	Milosevic	2950	13	227
2	Jesuli	1887	6	315
3	Mostovoi	1526	6	254
4	Luccin	2545	5	509
5	Jose Ignacio	2016	4	504
6	Edu	1275	3	425
7	Gustavo Lopez	1824	2	912
8	Jandro	244	2	122
9	Berizzo	2232	1	2232
10	Contreras	471	1	471
11	Catanha	315	1	315
12	Ilic	896	1	896
13	Juanfran	1692	1	1692
	Other		2	
	TOTAL		48	

DISCIPLINARY RECORDS

	PLAYER	YELLOW	RED	AVE
1	Mendez	6	0	157
2	Juanfran	10	0	169
3	Giovanella	5	0	171
4	Berizzo	7	4	202
5	Ilic	4	0	224
6	Gustavo Lopez	8	0	228
7	Sergio	4	1	291
8	Mostovoi	5	0	305
9	Jesuli	6	0	314
10	Luccin	7	1	318
11	Silvinho	6	1	330
12	Milosevic	8	0	368
13	Jose Ignacio	4	1	403
	Other	21	2	
	TOTAL	101	10	

TOP POINT EARNERS

	PLAYER	GAMES	AV PTS
1	Mostovoi	14	1.50
2	Juanfran	18	1.22
3	Cavallero	32	1.19
4	Jose Ignacio	18	1.17
5	Velasco	25	1.08
6	Jesuli	18	1.06
7	Berizzo	22	1.05
8	Luccin	28	1.04
9	Edu	13	1.00
10	Milosevic	30	1.00
	CLUB AVERAGE:		1.03

TEAM OF THE SEASON

G — Cavallero CG: 32 DR: 54

D — Juanfran CG: 18 DR: 81

D — Velasco CG: 25 DR: 53

D — Berizzo CG: 22 DR: 50

D — Caceres CG: 22 DR: 50

M — Jose Ignacio CG: 18 SD: -8

M — Jesuli CG: 18 SD: -13

M — Mostovoi CG: 14 SD: -18

M — Luccin CG: 28 SD: -19

F — Milosevic CG: 30 SR: 227

F — Edu CG: 13 SR: 425

LEAGUE APPEARANCES, BOOKINGS AND CAPS

	AGE (on 01/07/04)	IN NAMED 18	APPEARANCES	COUNTING GAMES	MINUTES ON PITCH	YELLOW CARDS	RED CARDS	THIS SEASON	HOME COUNTRY
Goalkeepers									
Pablo Cavallero	30	33	32	32	2880	2	0	7	Argentina (5)
Garcia Jose Juan	24	8	0	0	0	0	0	-	Spain
Jose Colorado	28	36	6	6	540	0	0	-	Spain
Defenders									
Eduardo Berizzo	34	30	27	22	2232	7	4	-	Argentina
Amoedo Bouzon	21	4	2	0	56	1	0	-	Spain
Fernando Caceres	35	35	24	22	2015	2	1	-	Argentina
Pablo Contreras	25	15	6	5	471	1	0	-	Chile
Israel Delgado	25	8	2	1	152	0	0	-	Spain
Garcia Juanfran	27	22	21	18	1692	10	0	-	Spain
Sanchez Manolo	28	2	1	0	36	1	0	-	Spain
Sebastien Mendez	27	23	12	10	942	6	0	-	Argentina
Fernandez Sergio	27	29	19	15	1456	4	1	-	Spain
Silvinho	30	33	29	25	2313	6	1	-	Brazil
Juan Velasco	27	26	25	25	2237	4	1	-	Spain
Midfielders									
Everton Giovanella	33	25	16	7	855	5	0	-	Brazil
Gustavo Lopez	31	30	30	13	1824	8	0	-	Argentina
Sasa Ilic	26	16	13	8	896	4	0	-	Serbia & Montenegro
Castro Jandro	25	23	12	1	244	0	0	-	Spain
Antonio Jesuli	26	30	30	18	1887	6	0	-	Spain
Aspas Jonathan	22	3	3	0	78	0	0	-	Spain
Jose Ignacio	30	36	29	18	2016	4	1	-	Spain
Peter Luccin	25	29	29	28	2545	7	1	-	France
Alexander Mostovoi	35	26	24	14	1526	5	0	-	Russia
Borja Oubina	22	14	12	8	861	2	0	-	Spain
Rogerio Vagner	25	25	19	6	834	2	0	-	Brazil
Forwards									
Lopez Ruano Angel	23	34	30	18	2132	4	0	-	Spain
Henrique Catanha	32	14	10	1	315	2	0	-	Brazil
Luis Schmidt Edu	25	20	18	13	1275	0	0	-	Brazil
Zumeta Franco	23	4	2	0	15	0	0	-	Spain
Savo Milosevic	30	37	37	30	2950	8	0	4	Serbia & M,negro (45)
Mauricio Pinilla	20	15	6	0	151	0	0	-	Chile

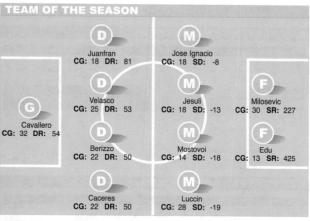

SQUAD APPEARANCES

åMatch	1	2	3	4	5	6	7	8	9	10	11	12	13	14	15	16	17	18	19	20	21	22	23	24	25	26	27	28	29	30	31	32	33	34	35	36	37	38	39	40	41	42	43	44	45	46	47	48
Venue	H	A	H	A	H	A	A	H	H	A	H	A	A	A	H	H	A	H	H	A	H	A	A	H	A	H	A	A	H	A	H	A	H	H	A	H	A	H	A	H	A	H	A	H	A	H	A	H
Competition	C	C	L	L	L	C	L	L	C	L	L	C	L	L	L	C	L	L	C	L	L	L	C	L	L	L	L	L	L	L	L	L	L	C	L	L	C	L	L	L	L	L	L	L	L	L	L	L
Result	W	L	D	D	L	D	D	W	D	L	L	L	W	D	L	W	D	L	D	W	D	L	W	D	D	L	W	D	L	L	W	W	L	L	L	L	L	L	D	L	D	D	W	W	L	W	L	L
Goalkeepers																																																
Pablo Rodriguez Cavallero																																																
Garcia Jose Juan																																																
Jose Manuel Colorado																																																
Defenders																																																
Eduardo Berizzo																																																
Iago Amoedo Bouzon																																																
Fernando Gabriel Caceres																																																
Pablo Andres Contreras																																																
Israel Delgado																																																
Juan Francisco Garcia																																																
Sanchez Murias Manolo																																																
Sebastien Ariel Mendez																																																
Fernandez Sergio																																																
Mendes Silvinho																																																
Juan Velasco Damas																																																
Midfielders																																																
Everton Giovanella																																																
Pablo Gustavo Lopez																																																
Sasa Ilic																																																
Fernandez Jandro																																																
Jesus Antonio Jesuli																																																
Aspas Juncal Jonathan																																																
Marin Jose Ignacio																																																
Peter Luccin																																																
Alexander Mostovoi																																																
Borja Melendez Oubina																																																
Rogerio Nunes Vagner																																																
Forwards																																																
Lopez Ruano Angel																																																
Henrique Catanha																																																
Luis Schmidt Edu																																																
Zumeta Nacho Franco																																																
Savo Milosevic																																																
Mauricio Pinilla																																																

KEY: ■ On all match · ■ On bench · ⏮ Subbed or sent off (Counting game) · « Subbed or sent off (playing less than 70 minutes) · ⏭ Subbed on from bench (Counting Game) · » Subbed on (playing less than 70 minutes) · Subbed on and then subbed or sent off (Counting Game) · Subbed on and then subbed or sent off (playing less than 70 minutes) · □ Not in 16

MURCIA

Final Position: **20th**

KEY: Won Drawn Lost

						Attendance
1 lge	Celta Vigo	A	D	1-1	Luis Garcia 72 pen	18,000
2 lge	R Santander	H	D	1-1	Richi 8	17,000
3 lge	Real Zaragoza	A	L	0-3		30,000
4 lge	Athl Bilbao	H	D	2-2	Michel 16; Luis Garcia 69	14,000
5 lge	Seville	A	L	0-1		36,000
6 lge	Albacete	H	W	1-0	Michel 7	16,500
7 lge	Osasuna	A	L	1-2	Luis Garcia 19	13,930
8 lge	Atl Madrid	H	L	1-3	Karanka 71	16,000
9 lge	Barcelona	A	L	0-3		51,000
10 lge	Deportivo	H	D	0-0		10,500
11 lge	Mallorca	A	L	1-4	Karanka 31	14,000
12 lge	Valencia	H	D	2-2	Richi 38; Michel 47	11,500
13 lge	Real Sociedad	H	D	2-2	Luis Garcia 47; Karanka 69	16,000
14 lge	Real Betis	A	D	1-1	Luis Garcia 90	19,000
15 lge	Villarreal	H	D	1-1	Karanka 13	9,900
16 lge	Valladolid	A	D	0-0		11,500
17 lge	Malaga	H	L	1-2	Karanka 23	16,500
18 lge	Real Madrid	A	L	0-1		75,000
19 lge	Espanyol	H	L	0-1		12,000
20 lge	Celta Vigo	H	D	2-2	Quintana 68; Karanka 81	10,000
21 lge	R Santander	A	L	2-3	Esnaider 43; Karanka 90	16,000
22 lge	Real Zaragoza	H	W	1-0	Richi 35	15,000
23 lge	Athl Bilbao	A	L	1-2	Luis Garcia 15	30,000
24 lge	Seville	H	L	1-3	Luis Garcia 89 pen	10,000
25 lge	Albacete	A	L	0-1		15,000
26 lge	Osasuna	H	L	0-1		13,500
27 lge	Atl Madrid	A	D	1-1	Luis Garcia 55 pen	35,000
28 lge	Barcelona	H	L	0-2		17,000
29 lge	Deportivo	A	L	0-1		24,920
30 lge	Mallorca	H	W	2-0	Acciari 17; Michel 50	2,500
31 lge	Valencia	A	L	0-2		40,000
32 lge	Real Sociedad	A	L	0-2		22,723
33 lge	Real Betis	H	L	0-1		8,943
34 lge	Villarreal	A	L	0-1		9,000
35 lge	Valladolid	H	W	2-1	Acciari 33; Luis Garcia 89	5,900
36 lge	Malaga	A	L	0-1		20,000
37 lge	Real Madrid	H	W	2-1	Luis Garcia 3,33 pen	15,668
38 lge	Espanyol	A	L	0-2		51,700

MONTHLY POINTS TALLY

Month	Points	%
AUGUST	1	33%
SEPTEMBER	2	17%
OCTOBER	3	25%
NOVEMBER	3	25%
DECEMBER	3	25%
JANUARY	1	8%
FEBRUARY	3	20%
MARCH	4	33%
APRIL	0	0%
MAY	6	50%

KEY PLAYERS - GOALSCORERS

David Karanka de la Hoz

Goals in the League	7	Player Strike Rate Average number of minutes between League goals scored by player	261
Contribution to Attacking Power Average number of minutes between League team goals while on pitch	121	Club Strike Rate Average number of minutes between League goals scored by club	118

	PLAYER	LGE GOALS	POWER	STRIKE RATE
1	David Karanka de la Hoz	7	121	261 mins
2	Luis Garcia Fernandez	11	112	297 mins
3	Miguel Angel Sanchez Michel	4	95	524 mins
4	Ricardo Perez de Zabalza Richi	3	119	794 mins

KEY PLAYERS - MIDFIELDERS

Miguel Angel Sanchez Michel

Goals in the League	4	Contribution to Attacking Power Average number of minutes between League team goals while on pitch	95
Defensive Rating Average number of mins between League goals conceded while he was on the pitch	57	Scoring Difference Defensive Rating minus Contribution to Attacking Power	-38

	PLAYER	LGE GOALS	DEF RATE	POWER	SCORE DIFF
1	Miguel Angel Sanchez Michel	4	57	95	-38 mins
2	Daniel Jensen	0	70	126	-56 mins
3	Ricardo Perez de Zabalza Richi	3	61	119	-58 mins
4	Jose Luis Acciari	2	57	116	-59 mins

KEY PLAYERS - DEFENDERS

Rafael Prados Clavero

Goals Conceded (GC) The number of League goals conceded while he was on the pitch	28	Clean Sheets In games when he played at least 70 minutes	3
Defensive Rating Ave number of mins between League goals conceded while on the pitch	65	Club Defensive Rating Average number of mins between League goals conceded by the club this season	60

	PLAYER	CON LGE	CLEAN SHEETS	DEF RATE
1	Rafael Prados Clavero	28	3	65 mins
2	Ivan Angulo Hurtado	20	1	63 mins
3	Ivan Javier Alonso Cuadrado	48	5	61 mins
4	Juan Manuel Valero Mart'nez Ju	44	5	60 mins

KEY GOALKEEPER

Juan Miguel Garcia Ingles

Goals Conceded in the League	26	Counting Games Games when he played at least 70 mins	18
Defensive Rating Ave number of mins between League goals conceded while on the pitch	62	Clean Sheets In games when he played at least 70 mins	4

LEAGUE GOALS

Luis Garcia Fernandez

Minutes on the pitch	3271	Goals in the League	11
League average (mins between goals)	297		

	PLAYER	MINS	GOALS	AVE
1	Luis Garcia	3271	11	297
2	Karanka	1826	7	261
3	Michel	2095	4	524
4	Richi	2382	3	794
5	Acciari	2908	2	1454
6	Quintana	230	1	230
7	Esnaider	889	1	889
	Other		0	
	TOTAL		29	

DISCIPLINARY RECORDS

	PLAYER	YELLOW	RED	AVE
1	Carreras	6	1	152
2	Jensen	5	3	219
3	Acciari	10	1	264
4	Gancedo	4	0	288
5	Cuadrado	10	0	294
6	Esnaider	2	1	296
7	Loeschbor	4	0	312
8	Michel	5	0	419
9	Roteta	2	0	421
10	Clavero	4	0	456
11	Valera	1	0	620
12	Hurtado	1	1	633
13	Luis Garcia	5	0	654
	Other	15	0	
	TOTAL	74	7	

TOP POINT EARNERS

	PLAYER	GAMES	AV PTS
1	Jensen	14	1.21
2	Juanma	28	0.89
3	Richi	21	0.81
4	Clavero	18	0.78
5	Acciari	30	0.77
6	Hurtado	13	0.77
7	Michel	19	0.74
8	Juanmi	18	0.72
9	Cuadrado	32	0.69
10	Loeschbor	12	0.67
	CLUB AVERAGE:		0.68

TEAM OF THE SEASON

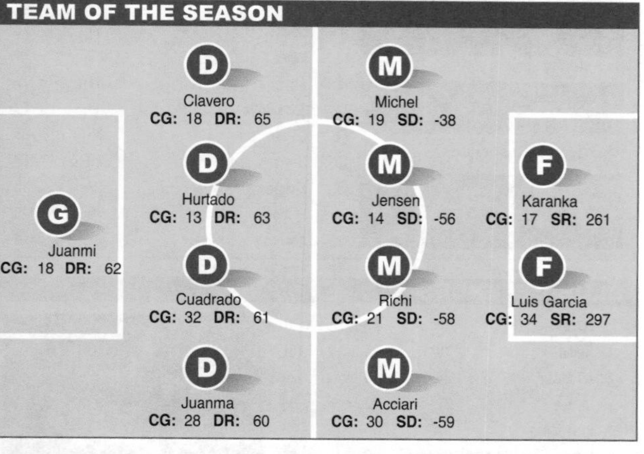

G
Juanmi
CG: 18 DR: 62
D
Clavero
CG: 18 DR: 65
D
Hurtado
CG: 13 DR: 63
D
Cuadrado
CG: 32 DR: 61
D
Juanma
CG: 28 DR: 60
M
Michel
CG: 19 SD: -38
M
Jensen
CG: 14 SD: -56
M
Richi
CG: 21 SD: -58
M
Acciari
CG: 30 SD: -59
F
Karanka
CG: 17 SR: 261
F
Luis Garcia
CG: 34 SR: 297

LEAGUE APPEARANCES, BOOKINGS AND CAPS

	AGE (on 01/07/04)	IN NAMED 18	APPEARANCES	COUNTING GAMES	MINUTES ON PITCH	YELLOW CARDS	RED CARDS	THIS SEASON	HOME COUNTRY
Goalkeepers									
Roberto Bonano	34	15	11	11	990	1	0	-	Argentina
Sanchez Broto	32	23	9	9	810	0	0	-	Spain
Jose Emilio	19	2	0	0	0	0	0	-	Spain
Juanmi Ingles	33	33	18	18	1620	0	0	-	Spain
Defenders									
Frederico Azcarate	20	12	8	7	611	0	0	-	Spain
Ricardo Carrero	32	2	0	0	0	0	0	-	Spain
Rafael Clavero	27	28	24	18	1827	4	0	-	Spain
Ivan Cuadrado	25	36	34	32	2946	10	0	-	Spain
Ivan Hurtado	29	16	15	13	1267	1	1	-	Ecuador
Juanma Valero	26	34	31	28	2626	4	0	-	Spain
Gabriel Loeschbor	27	26	17	12	1251	4	0	-	Argentina
Francisco Maciel	26	17	16	10	1100	1	0	-	Argentina
Pedro Largo Carazo	32	24	16	9	967	1	0	-	Spain
Mikel Roteta	34	13	11	8	842	2	0	-	Spain
Esparza Sebas	20	5	2	0	85	0	0	-	Spain
Juan Zamora	21	4	2	2	180	1	0	-	Spain
Midfielders									
Jose Luis Acciari	25	35	35	30	2908	10	1	-	Argentina
Luis Carreras	31	25	15	10	1066	6	1	-	Spain
Alfredo Sanchez	30	19	14	4	791	1	0	-	Spain
Pipa Gancedo	33	18	17	10	1153	4	0	-	Argentina
Jose Casado	24	3	0	0	0	0	0	-	Spain
Carlos Ramos	25	1	0	0	0	0	0	-	Spain
Daniel Jensen	25	31	28	14	1758	5	3	5	Denmark (14)
Julio Alvarez	23	21	12	2	413	1	0	-	Spain
Angel Michel	28	31	30	19	2095	5	0	-	Spain
Ricardo Richi	27	35	34	21	2382	2	0	-	Spain
Roberto Luis Prieto	31	12	8	3	431	0	0	-	Spain
Joseph Setvalls	29	5	1	1	90	0	0	-	Spain
Juan Valera	19	16	10	5	620	1	0	-	Spain
Forwards									
Juan Esnaider	31	18	17	4	889	2	1	-	Argentina
Carlos Juarez	32	9	4	1	145	0	0	-	Argentina
David Karanka	26	35	31	17	1826	1	0	-	Argentina
Luis Garcia	23	38	38	34	3271	5	0	-	Spain
Jesus Quintana	26	18	11	0	230	1	0	-	Argentina
Jesus Tato	20	10	7	0	203	1	0	-	Spain

SQUAD APPEARANCES

Match	1	2	3	4	5	6	7	8	9	10	11	12	13	14	15	16	17	18	19	20	21	22	23	24	25	26	27	28	29	30	31	32	33	34	35	36	37	38
Venue	A	H	A	H	A	H	A	H	A	H	A	H	H	A	H	A	H	A	H	H	A	H	A	H	A	H	A	H	A	H	A	A	H	A	H	A	H	A
Competition	L	L	L	L	L	L	L	L	L	L	L	L	L	L	L	L	L	L	L	L	L	L	L	L	L	L	L	L	L	L	L	L	L	L	L	L	L	L
Result	D	D	L	D	L	W	L	L	L	D	L	D	D	D	D	D	L	L	L	D	L	W	L	L	L	L	D	L	L	W	L	L	L	L	W	L	W	L

Goalkeepers
Roberto Bonano
Javier Sanchez Broto
Jose Emilio
Juan Miguel Garcia Ingles

Defenders
Frederico Xavier Azcarate
Ricardo Carrero Gomez
Rafael Prados Clavero
Javier Alonso Cuadrado
Ivan Angulo Hurtado
Juanma Valero
Gabriel Loeschbor
Francisco Maciel
Pedro Largo Carazo
Mikel Roteta
Esparza Sebas
Juan Antonio Zamora

Midfielders
Jose Luis Acciari
Luis Ferrer Carreras
Alfredo Lobeiras Sanchez
Fernando Pipa Gancedo
Jose Antonio Casado
Carlos Isach Ramos
Daniel Jensen
Mosquera Julio Alvarez
Miguel Angel Michel
Ricardo Perez Richi
Roberto Luis Prieto
Joseph Morera Setvalls
Juan Valera

Forwards
Juan Eduardo Esnaider
Carlos Alberto Juarez
David Karanka de la Hoz
Luis Garcia Fernandez
Jesus Quintana
Jesus Rodriguez Tato

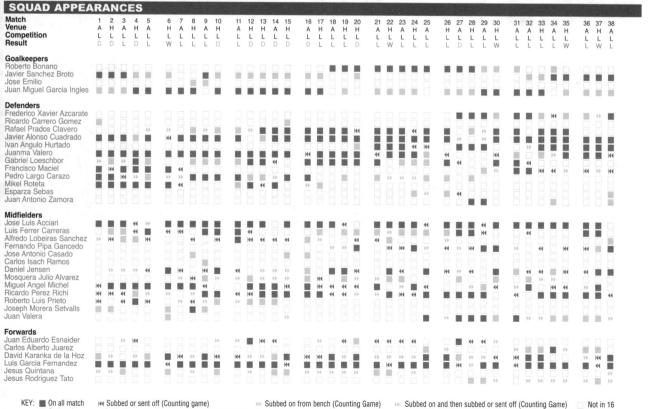

KEY: On all match; On bench; Subbed or sent off (Counting game); Subbed or sent off (playing less than 70 minutes); Subbed on from bench (Counting Game); Subbed on (playing less than 70 minutes); Subbed on and then subbed or sent off (Counting Game); Subbed on and then subbed or sent off (playing less than 70 minutes); Not in 16

ITALIAN LEAGUE ROUND-UP

FINAL LEAGUE TABLE

	HOME						AWAY					TOTAL			
	P	W	D	L	F	A	W	D	L	F	A	F	A	DIF	PTS
AC Milan	34	14	2	1	39	15	11	5	1	26	9	65	24	41	82
Roma	34	13	1	3	45	12	8	7	2	23	7	68	19	49	71
Juventus	34	13	1	3	40	18	8	5	4	27	24	67	42	25	69
Inter Milan	34	9	4	4	31	15	8	4	5	28	22	59	37	22	59
Parma	34	9	5	3	32	20	7	5	5	25	26	57	46	11	58
Lazio	34	10	4	3	35	19	6	4	7	17	19	52	38	14	56
Udinese	34	6	7	4	19	15	7	4	6	25	25	44	40	4	50
Sampdoria	34	8	4	5	26	23	3	9	5	14	19	40	42	-2	46
Chievo	34	5	6	6	17	19	6	5	6	19	18	36	37	-1	44
Lecce	34	6	4	7	19	23	5	4	8	24	33	43	56	-13	41
Brescia	34	5	7	5	29	25	4	6	7	23	32	52	57	-5	40
Bologna	34	7	5	5	26	24	3	4	10	19	29	45	53	-8	39
Siena	34	7	4	6	23	15	1	6	10	18	39	41	54	-13	34
Reggina	34	4	8	5	14	17	2	8	7	15	28	29	45	-16	34
Perugia	34	3	10	4	26	27	3	4	10	18	29	44	56	-12	32
Modena	34	5	6	6	17	20	1	6	10	10	26	27	46	-19	30
Empoli	34	6	6	5	19	18	1	3	13	7	36	26	54	-28	30
Ancona	34	2	6	9	10	24	0	1	16	11	46	21	70	-49	13

CLUB STRIKE FORCE

Totti, helping Roma to strike

1 Roma

Goals scored in the League	68
Club Strike Rate (CSR) Average number of minutes between League goals scored by club	45

	CLUB	GOALS	CSR
1	Roma	68	45
2	Juventus	67	46
3	AC Milan	65	47
4	Inter Milan	59	52
5	Parma	57	54
6	Brescia	52	59
7	Lazio	52	59
8	Bologna	45	68
9	Perugia	44	70
10	Udinese	44	70
11	Lecce	43	71
12	Siena	41	75
13	Sampdoria	40	77
14	Chievo	36	85
15	Reggina	29	106
16	Modena	27	113
17	Empoli	26	118
18	Ancona	21	146

CLUB DISCIPLINARY RECORDS

Roberto D'aversa of Siena

1 Siena

League Yellow	93
League Red	6
League Total	99
Cards Average in League Average number of minutes between a card being shown of either colour	31

	CLUB	Y	R	TOTAL	AVE
1	Siena	93	6	99	31
2	Bologna	83	4	87	35
3	Perugia	77	8	85	36
4	Lecce	79	4	83	37
5	Ancona	75	5	80	38
6	Sampdoria	77	3	80	38
7	Parma	70	6	76	40
8	Brescia	63	10	73	42
9	Modena	68	5	73	42
10	Chievo	66	5	71	43
11	Lazio	64	6	70	44
12	Roma	61	3	64	48
13	Empoli	55	6	61	50
14	Inter Milan	57	4	61	50
15	Reggina	57	4	61	50
16	Udinese	50	5	55	56
17	Juventus	49	4	53	58
18	AC Milan	39	4	43	71

CLUB DEFENCES

	CLUB	LGE	CS	CDR
1	Roma	19	20	161
2	AC Milan	24	15	128
3	Chievo	37	12	83
4	Inter Milan	37	15	83
5	Lazio	38	8	81
6	Udinese	40	12	77
7	Juventus	42	12	73
8	Sampdoria	42	11	73
9	Reggina	45	9	68
10	Modena	46	6	67
11	Parma	46	9	67
12	Bologna	53	6	58
13	Empoli	54	9	57
14	Siena	54	10	57
15	Lecce	56	5	55
16	Perugia	56	4	55
17	Brescia	57	7	54
18	Ancona	70	4	44

Chrsitian Panucci of Roma

1 Roma

Goals conceded in the League	19
Clean Sheets (CS) Number of league games where no goals were conceded	20
Club Defensive Rate (CDR) Average number of minutes between League goals conceded by club	161

PLAYER NATIONALITIES

Overseas country with the most player appearances in the Italian League - Brazil — **567 league appearances by Brazilian players**

	COUNTRY	PLAYERS	IN SQUAD	LGE APP	% LGE ACT	CAPS	MOST APP	APP
1	Italy	403	7355	5628	67.8	160	Gianluca Pagliuca	89.5
2	Brazil	33	657	567	7.0	61	Alessandro Mancini	86.8
3	Argentina	22	442	370	4.6	21	Javier Zanetti	88.7
4	France	15	319	243	2.8	26	Sebastian Frey	86.8
5	Uruguay	9	167	137	1.5	17	Gianni Guigou	78.0
6	Denmark	5	146	123	1.5	32	Martin Jorgensen	86.3
7	Serbia & M'tenegro	10	187	132	1.5	4	Sinisa Mihajlovic	61.1
8	Czech Republic	5	121	94	1.2	19	Marek Jankulovski	80.6
9	Australia	3	89	87	1.1	14	Zeljko Kalac	71.9
10	Holland	5	94	77	0.9	32	Jaap Stam	71.8
11	Nigeria	8	104	80	0.9		Christian Obodo	78.5
12	Colombia	4	72	63	0.8		Ivan Cordoba	78.0
13	Ghana	6	93	63	0.7		Stephen Appiah	65.8
14	Croatia	4	86	55	0.6	21	Milan Rapaic	32.1
15	Norway	2	63	53	0.6		Tore Andre Flo	78.0
16	Portugal	3	75	57	0.6	17	Fernando Couto	47.0
17	Japan	4	79	60	0.6		Hidetoshi Nakata	44.7
18	Chile	4	49	43	0.5		David Pizarro	47.4

CLUB MAKE-UP – HOME AND OVERSEAS PLAYERS

1 Inter Milan — **63.2% of appearances by overseas players**

	CLUB	OVERSEAS	HOME	% OVERSEAS	% LGE ACT	MOST APP	APP
1	Inter Milan	21	12	63.6	63.2	Javier Zanetti	99.1
2	Roma	12	19	38.7	59.4	A Mancini	97.0
3	AC Milan	13	16	44.8	52.6	Nelson Dida	94.1
4	Udinese	18	13	58.1	51.4	Martin Jorgensen	96.4
5	Perugia	18	31	36.7	45.2	Christian Obodo	87.7
6	Siena	11	20	35.5	42.5	Leandro Cufre	89.9
7	Juventus	11	19	36.7	39.7	Pavel Nedved	77.3
8	Lazio	10	17	37.0	35.3	Jaap Stam	80.2
9	Lecce	14	20	41.2	34.0	Cristian Ledesma	85.4
10	Parma	11	26	29.7	26.9	Sebastian Frey	97.1
11	Ancona	11	40	21.6	26.6	Daniel Andersson	64.4
12	Brescia	8	24	25.0	22.6	F Matuzalem	85.7
13	Reggina	7	19	26.9	21.0	Martin Jiranek	68.9
14	Empoli	3	25	10.7	18.7	Emilson Cribari	89.4
15	Bologna	6	25	19.4	18.4	Igli Tare	68.3
16	Modena	6	28	17.6	11.8	D Kamara	68.3
17	Chievo	6	24	20.0	8.8	Mario Santana	66.6
18	Sampdoria	4	25	13.8	2.4	A Yanagisawa	13.6

CHART-TOPPING MIDFIELDERS

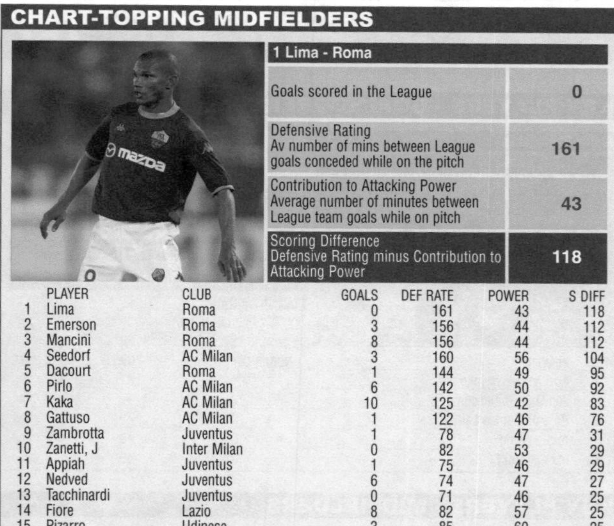

1 Lima - Roma

Goals scored in the League	0
Defensive Rating Av number of mins between League goals conceded while on the pitch	161
Contribution to Attacking Power Average number of minutes between League team goals while on pitch	43
Scoring Difference Defensive Rating minus Contribution to Attacking Power	118

	PLAYER	CLUB	GOALS	DEF RATE	POWER	S DIFF
1	Lima	Roma	0	161	43	118
2	Emerson	Roma	3	156	44	112
3	Mancini	Roma	8	156	44	112
4	Seedorf	AC Milan	3	160	56	104
5	Dacourt	Roma	1	144	49	95
6	Pirlo	AC Milan	6	142	50	92
7	Kaka	AC Milan	10	125	42	83
8	Gattuso	AC Milan	1	122	46	76
9	Zambrotta	Juventus	1	78	47	31
10	Zanetti, J	Inter Milan	0	82	53	29
11	Appiah	Juventus	1	75	46	29
12	Nedved	Juventus	6	74	47	27
13	Tacchinardi	Juventus	0	71	46	25
14	Fiore	Lazio	8	82	57	25
15	Pizarro	Udinese	3	85	60	25

CHART-TOPPING GOALSCORERS

1 Gilardino - Parma

Goals scored in the League	23
Contribution to Attacking Power (AP) Average number of minutes between League team goals while on pitch	51
Club Strike Rate (CSR) Average minutes between League goals scored by club	54
Player Strike Rate Average number of minutes between League goals scored by player	108

	PLAYER	CLUB	GOALS: LGE	POWER	CSR	S RATE
1	Gilardino	Parma	23	51	54	108
2	Shevchenko	AC Milan	24	47	47	112
3	Trezeguet	Juventus	16	45	46	126
4	Vieri	Inter Milan	13	51	52	127
5	Chevanton	Lecce	19	68	71	137
6	Totti	Roma	20	44	45	138
7	Iaquinta	Udinese	11	57	70	173
8	Baggio	Brescia	12	57	59	186
9	Cassano	Roma	14	48	45	191
10	Chiesa	Siena	10	75	75	195
11	Fava	Udinese	12	68	70	195
12	Bazzani	Sampdoria	13	73	77	221
13	Caracciolo	Brescia	11	62	59	222
14	Kaka	AC Milan	10	42	47	224
15	Corradi	Lazio	10	57	59	252

CHART-TOPPING DEFENDERS

1 Zebina - Roma

Goals Conceded in the League The number of League goals conceded while he was on the pitch	7
Clean Sheets In games when he played at least 70 mins	13
Club Defensive Rating Average mins between League goals conceded by the club this season	161
Defensive Rating Average number of minutes between League goals conceded while on pitch	261

	PLAYER	CLUB	CON: LGE	CS	CDR	DEF RATE
1	Zebina	Roma	7	13	161	261
2	Chivu	Roma	10	14	161	192
3	Nesta	AC Milan	14	14	128	160
4	Samuel	Roma	17	18	161	159
5	Cafu	AC Milan	16	10	128	135
6	Maldini	AC Milan	20	12	128	132
7	Panucci	Roma	17	10	161	123
8	Costacurta	AC Milan	15	8	128	115
9	Cannavaro	Inter Milan	18	11	83	107
10	Stam	Lazio	27	8	81	91
11	Bertotto	Udinese	28	11	77	89
12	Lanna	Chievo	31	11	83	88
13	D'Anna	Chievo	25	9	83	87
14	Mihajlovic	Lazio	24	5	81	87
15	Favalli	Lazio	27	4	81	86

CHART-TOPPING GOALKEEPERS

1 Pellizzoli - Roma

Counting Games Games in which he played at least 70 minutes	31
Goals Conceded in the League The number of League goals conceded while he was on the pitch	14
Clean Sheets In games when he played at least 70 mins	20
Defensive Rating Average number of minutes between League goals conceded while on pitch	199

	PLAYER	CLUB	CG	CONC	CS	DEF RATE
1	Pellizzoli	Roma	31	14	20	199
2	Dida	AC Milan	32	20	15	144
3	Marchegiani	Chievo	30	25	11	102
4	Peruzzi	Lazio	28	29	7	84
5	Toldo	Inter Milan	32	35	14	82
6	De Sanctis	Udinese	34	40	12	77
7	Belardi	Reggina	31	38	9	73
8	Zancope	Modena	17	21	4	72
9	Antonioli	Sampdoria	29	36	8	71
10	Buffon	Juventus	31	40	11	70
11	Sicignano	Lecce	17	22	4	69
12	Agliardi	Brescia	18	24	6	65
13	Frey	Parma	33	46	8	65
14	Rossi	Siena	21	30	6	63
15	Ballotta	Modena	18	25	3	62

PLAYER DISCIPLINARY RECORD

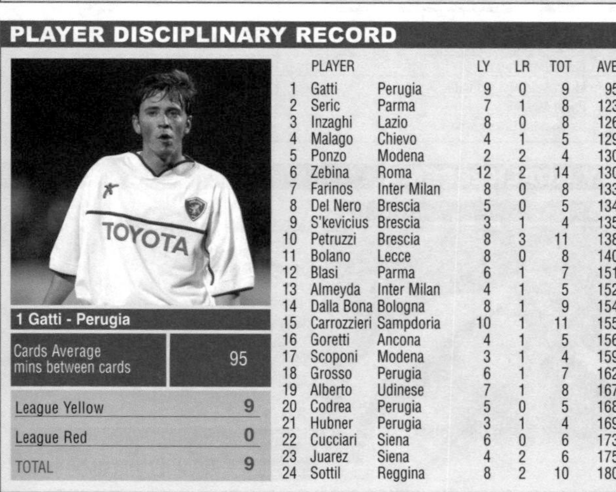

1 Gatti - Perugia

Cards Average mins between cards	95
League Yellow	9
League Red	0
TOTAL	9

	PLAYER		LY	LR	TOT	AVE
1	Gatti	Perugia	9	0	9	95
2	Seric	Parma	7	1	8	123
3	Inzaghi	Lazio	8	0	8	126
4	Malago	Chievo	4	1	5	129
5	Ponzo	Modena	2	2	4	130
6	Zebina	Roma	12	2	14	130
7	Farinos	Inter Milan	8	0	8	133
8	Del Nero	Brescia	5	0	5	134
9	S'kevicius	Brescia	3	1	4	135
10	Petruzzi	Brescia	8	3	11	138
11	Bolano	Lecce	8	0	8	140
12	Blasi	Parma	6	1	7	151
13	Almeyda	Inter Milan	4	1	5	152
14	Dalla Bona	Bologna	8	1	9	154
15	Carrozzieri	Sampdoria	10	1	11	155
16	Goretti	Ancona	4	1	5	156
17	Scoponi	Modena	3	1	4	159
18	Grosso	Perugia	6	1	7	162
19	Alberto	Udinese	7	1	8	167
20	Codrea	Perugia	5	0	5	168
21	Hubner	Perugia	3	1	4	169
22	Cucciari	Siena	6	0	6	173
23	Juarez	Siena	4	2	6	175
24	Sottil	Reggina	8	2	10	180

TEAM OF THE SEASON

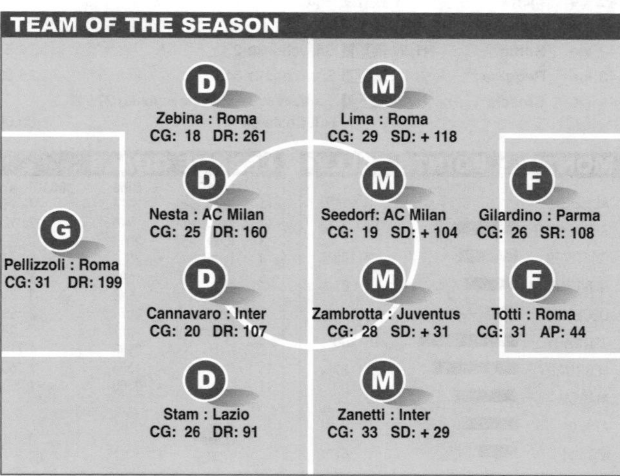
G
Pellizzoli : Roma
CG: 31 DR: 199
D
Zebina : Roma
CG: 18 DR: 261
D
Nesta : AC Milan
CG: 25 DR: 160
D
Cannavaro : Inter
CG: 20 DR: 107
D
Stam : Lazio
CG: 26 DR: 91
M
Lima : Roma
CG: 29 SD: + 118
M
Seedorf: AC Milan
CG: 19 SD: + 104
M
Zambrotta : Juventus
CG: 28 SD: + 31
M
Zanetti : Inter
CG: 33 SD: + 29
F
Gilardino : Parma
CG: 26 SR: 108
F
Totti : Roma
CG: 31 AP: 44

ITALIAN SERIE A CHAMPIONS

AC MILAN

Final Position: **1st**

KEY: Won Drawn Lost

							Attendance
1	lge	Ancona	A	W	2-0	Shevchenko 30,76	22,000
2	lge	Bologna	H	W	2-1	Shevchenko 10; Inzaghi 85	55,000
3	cl gh	Ajax	H	W	1-0	Inzaghi 67	48,000
4	lge	Perugia	A	D	1-1	Gattuso 19	18,000
5	lge	Lecce	H	W	3-0	Shevchenko 21,69; Tomasson 90	64,000
6	cl gh	Celta Vigo	A	D	0-0		27,000
7	lge	Inter Milan	A	W	3-1	Inzaghi 39; Kaka 46; Shevchenko 77	75,831
8	lge	Lazio	H	W	1-0	Pirlo 37	62,000
9	cl gh	Club Brugge	H	L	0-1		85,400
10	lge	Sampdoria	A	W	3-0	Tomasson 38; Shevchenko 59,90	35,000
11	lge	Juventus	H	D	1-1	Tomasson 68	80,000
12	cl gh	Club Brugge	A	W	1-0	Kaka 86	28,000
13	lge	Parma	A	D	0-0		25,000
14	lge	Chievo	A	W	2-0	Shevchenko 45,50	45,000
15	cl gh	Ajax	A	W	1-0	Shevchenko 51	51,324
16	lge	Modena	H	W	2-0	Shevchenko 24,67	55,000
17	lge	Empoli	A	W	1-0	Kaka 81	13,000
18	cl gh	Celta Vigo	H	L	1-2	Kaka 41	55,510
19	lge	Udinese	H	L	1-2	Cafu 70	60,000
20	lge	Roma	A	W	2-1	Shevchenko 24,63	73,383
21	lge	Reggina	H	W	3-1	Kaka 8,55; Pirlo 71 pen	62,000
22	lge	Brescia	A	W	1-0	Pancaro 80	26,000
23	lge	Ancona	H	W	5-0	Shevchenko 64 pen; Rui Costa 71; Tomasson 78; Kaka 84,89	55,000
24	lge	Siena	H	W	2-1	Kaka 38; Tomasson 54	54,428
25	lge	Bologna	A	W	2-0	Shevchenko 19; Tomasson 89	36,000
26	lge	Perugia	H	W	2-1	Rui Costa 73; Pirlo 77 pen	60,000
27	lge	Lecce	A	D	1-1	Shevchenko 53	31,427
28	lge	Inter Milan	H	W	3-2	Tomasson 56; Kaka 57; Seedorf 85	80,000
29	clr1l1	Sparta Prague	A	D	0-0		21,000
30	lge	Lazio	A	W	1-0	Ambrosini 75	55,000
31	lge	Sampdoria	H	W	3-1	Pirlo 17; Inzaghi 35; Kaka 49	60,000
32	clr1l2	Sparta Prague	H	W	4-1	Inzaghi 45; Shevchenko 66,79; Gattuso 85	55,000
33	lge	Juventus	A	W	3-1	Shevchenko 25; Seedorf 63,75	52,300
34	lge	Parma	H	W	3-1	Tomasson 33,52; Shevchenko 65	60,000
35	clr2l1	Deportivo	H	W	4-1	Kaka 45,49; Shevchenko 46; Pirlo 53 fk	60,335
36	lge	Chievo	H	D	2-2	Pirlo 80; Shevchenko 90	65,000
37	lge	Modena	A	D	1-1	Tomasson 42	16,000
38	clr2l1	Deportivo	A	L	0-4		30,260
39	lge	Empoli	H	W	1-0	Pirlo 86 pen	
40	lge	Siena	A	W	2-1	Shevchenko 26; Kaka 80	
41	lge	Udinese	A	D	0-0		24,000
42	lge	Roma	H	W	1-0	Shevchenko 2	76,647
43	lge	Reggina	A	L	1-2	Shevchenko 51	28,000
44	lge	Brescia	H	W	4-2	Tomasson 36,59; Shevchenko 37; Rui Costa 66	80,000

MONTHLY POINTS TALLY

AUGUST	0	%
SEPTEMBER	10	83%
OCTOBER	9	100%
NOVEMBER	8	67%
DECEMBER	3	50%
JANUARY	15	100%
FEBRUARY	13	87%
MARCH	10	83%
APRIL	8	67%
MAY	6	67%

LEAGUE GOALS

	PLAYER	MINS	GOALS	AVE
1	Shevchenko	2676	24	112
2	Tomasson	1546	12	129
3	Kaka	2242	10	224
4	Pirlo	2693	6	449
5	Rui Costa	1585	3	528
6	Inzaghi	949	3	316
7	Seedorf	2074	3	691
8	Ambrosini	987	1	987
9	Cafu	2163	1	2163
10	Pancaro	1565	1	1565
11	Gattuso	2560	1	2560
	Other		0	
	TOTAL		65	

KEY PLAYERS - GOALSCORERS

Andriy Shevchenko

Goals in the League	24
Contribution to Attacking Power Average number of minutes between League team goals while on pitch	47
Player Strike Rate The total number of minutes he was on the pitch for every League goal scored	112
Club Strike Rate Average number of minutes between League goals scored by club	47

	PLAYER	GOALS LGE	POWER	S RATE
1	Andriy Shevchenko	24	47	112 mins
2	Jon Dahl Tomasson	12	44	129 mins
3	Ricardo Santos Laite Kaka	10	42	224 mins
4	Andrea Pirlo	6	49	449 mins
5	Manuel Rui Costa	3	49	528 mins

KEY PLAYERS - MIDFIELDERS

Clarence Seedorf

Goals in the League	3
Defensive Rating Average number of mins between League goals conceded while on the pitch	160
Contribution to Attacking Power Average number of minutes between League team goals while on pitch	56
Scoring Difference Defensive Rating minus Contribution to Attacking Power	104

	PLAYER	GOALS LGE	DEF RATE	ATT POWER	SCORE DIFF
1	Clarence Seedorf	3	160	56	104 mins
2	Andrea Pirlo	6	142	50	92 mins
3	Ricardo Santos Laite Kaka	10	125	42	83 mins
4	Gennaro Gattuso	1	122	46	76 mins
5	Manuel Rui Costa	3	122	50	72 mins

KEY PLAYERS - DEFENDERS

Guiseppe Pancaro

Goals Conceded in League	9
Clean Sheets In League games when he played at least 70 mins	8
Defensive Rating Ave number of mins between League goals conceded while on the pitch	174
Club Defensive Rating Average number of mins between League goals conceded by the club this season	128

	PLAYER	CON LGE	CLEAN SHEETS	DEF RATE
1	Guiseppe Pancaro	9	8	174 mins
2	Alessandro Nesta	14	14	160 mins
3	Marcos de Moraes Cafu	16	10	135 mins
4	Paolo Maldini	20	12	132 mins
5	Alessandro Costacurta	15	8	115 mins

KEY GOALKEEPER

Nelson Dida

Goals Conceded in the League	20
Counting Games Games when he played at least 70 minutes	32
Clean Sheets In games when he played at least 70 mins	15
League minutes played Number of minutes played in league matches	2880
Defensive Rating Ave number of mins between League goals conceded while on the pitch	144

DISCIPLINARY RECORDS

	PLAYER	YELLOW	RED	AVE
1	Ambrosini	4	1	197
2	Nesta	6	0	374
3	Maldini	5	1	439
4	Kaka	5	0	448
5	Pancaro	2	1	521
6	Simic	1	0	577
7	Cafu	3	0	721
8	Serginho	1	0	778
9	Costacurta	2	0	864
10	Seedorf	2	0	1037
11	Gattuso	2	0	1280
12	Shevchenko	2	0	1338
13	Pirlo	2	0	1346
	Other	2	1	
	TOTAL	39	4	

TOP POINT EARNERS

	PLAYER	GAMES	AV PTS
1	Seedorf	19	2.68
2	Pancaro	16	2.63
3	Cafu	23	2.61
4	Gattuso	23	2.61
5	Shevchenko	30	2.57
6	Costacurta	18	2.56
7	Pirlo	27	2.56
8	Rui Costa	13	2.54
9	Kaka	23	2.52
10	Nesta	25	2.48
	CLUB AVERAGE:		2.41

TEAM OF THE SEASON

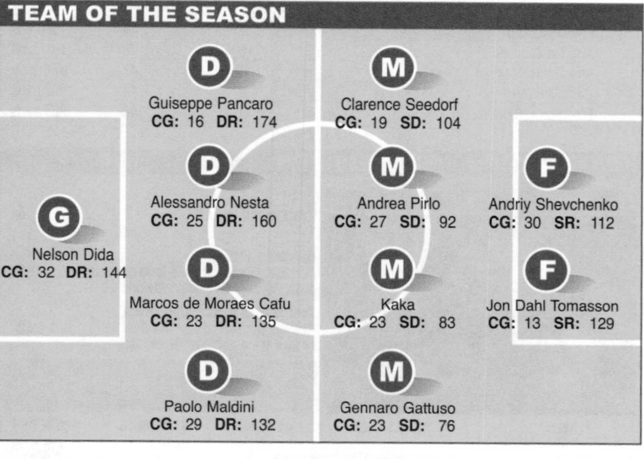
D
Guiseppe Pancaro
CG: 16 DR: 174
M
Clarence Seedorf
CG: 19 SD: 104
D
Alessandro Nesta
CG: 25 DR: 160
M
Andrea Pirlo
CG: 27 SD: 92
F
Andriy Shevchenko
CG: 30 SR: 112
G
Nelson Dida
CG: 32 DR: 144
D
Marcos de Moraes Cafu
CG: 23 DR: 135
M
Kaka
CG: 23 SD: 83
F
Jon Dahl Tomasson
CG: 13 SR: 129
D
Paolo Maldini
CG: 29 DR: 132
M
Gennaro Gattuso
CG: 23 SD: 76

LEAGUE APPEARANCES AND BOOKINGS

	AGE (on 01/07/04)	IN NAMED 18	APPEARANCES	COUNTING GAMES	MINUTES ON PITCH	YELLOW CARDS	RED CARDS	THIS SEASON	HOME COUNTRY
Goalkeepers									
Christian Abbiati	27	23	2	2	180	0	0	1	Italy (11)
Nelson Dida	30	32	32	32	2880	0	0	9	Brazil (1)
Valerio Fiori	35	11	0	0	0	0	0	-	Italy
Defenders									
Cafu	34	32	27	23	2163	3	0	9	Brazil (1)
A Costacurta	38	29	22	18	1729	2	0	-	Italy
Kakha Kaladze	26	9	6	5	442	0	1	-	Georgia
Martin Laursen	26	23	10	3	422	0	0	7	Denmark (14)
Elia Legati	18	0	0	0	0	0	0	-	Italy
Paolo Maldini	36	30	30	29	2637	5	1	-	Italy
Alessandro Nesta	28	26	26	25	2246	6	0	6	Italy (11)
Guiseppe Pancaro	32	24	21	16	1565	2	1	5	Italy (11)
Dario Simic	28	21	10	4	577	1	0	8	Croatia (25)
Midfielders									
Ignazio Abate	17	1	0	0	0	0	0	-	Italy
Massimo Ambrosini	27	24	20	8	987	4	1	4	Italy (11)
Christian Brocchi	28	21	11	1	225	0	0	-	Italy
Davide Canini	19	1	1	1	90	0	0	-	Italy
Gennaro Gattuso	26	34	33	23	2560	2	0	5	Italy (11)
Kaka	22	32	30	23	2242	5	0	12	Brazil (1)
Andrea Pirlo	25	33	32	27	2693	2	0	4	Italy (11)
Fernando Redondo	35	17	8	2	274	0	0	-	Argentina
Manuel Rui Costa	32	33	27	13	1585	1	0	8	Portugal (20)
Clarence Seedorf	28	31	29	19	2074	2	0	6	Holland (4)
Serginho	33	30	20	6	778	1	0	-	Brazil
Forwards									
Marco Borriello	22	15	4	0	71	1	0	-	Italy
Filippo Inzaghi	30	18	14	7	949	0	0	4	Italy (11)
Allessandro Matri	19	0	0	0	0	0	0	-	Italy
Rivaldo	32	2	0	0	0	0	0	5	Brazil (1)
Andriy Shevchenko	27	32	32	30	2676	2	0	-	Ukraine
Jon Dahl Tomasson	27	30	26	13	1546	0	0	7	Denmark (14)

SQUAD APPEARANCES

Match	1	2	3	4	5	6	7	8	9	10	11	12	13	14	15	16	17	18	19	20	21	22	23	24	25	26	27	28	29	30	31	32	33	34	35	36	37	38	39	40	41	42	43	44
Venue	A	H	H	A	H	A	A	H	H	A	H	A	A	A	A	H	A	H	H	A	H	A	H	H	A	H	A	H	A	A	H	H	A	H	H	H	A	A	H	A	A	H	A	H
Competition	L	L	C	L	L	C	L	L	C	L	L	C	L	L	C	L	L	C	L	L	L	L	L	L	L	L	L	L	C	L	L	C	L	L	C	L	L	C	L	L	L	L	L	L
Result	W	W	W	D	W	D	W	W	L	W	D	W	D	W	W	W	W	L	L	W	W	W	W	W	W	W	D	W	D	W	W	W	W	W	W	D	D	L	W	W	D	W	L	W

Goalkeepers
Christian Abbiati
Nelson Dida
Valerio Fiori

Defenders
Marcos de Moraes Cafu
Alessandro Costacurta
Kakha Kaladze
Martin Laursen
Elia Legati
Paolo Maldini
Alessandro Nesta
Guiseppe Pancaro
Dario Simic

Midfielders
Ignazio Abate
Massimo Ambrosini
Christian Brocchi
Davide Canini
Gennaro Gattuso
Ricardo Santos Laite Kaka
Andrea Pirlo
Fernando Redondo
Manuel Rui Costa
Clarence Seedorf
Serginho

Forwards
Marco Borriello
Filippo Inzaghi
Allessandro Matri
Rivaldo Vitor Borba Ferreira
Andriy Shevchenko
Jon Dahl Tomasson

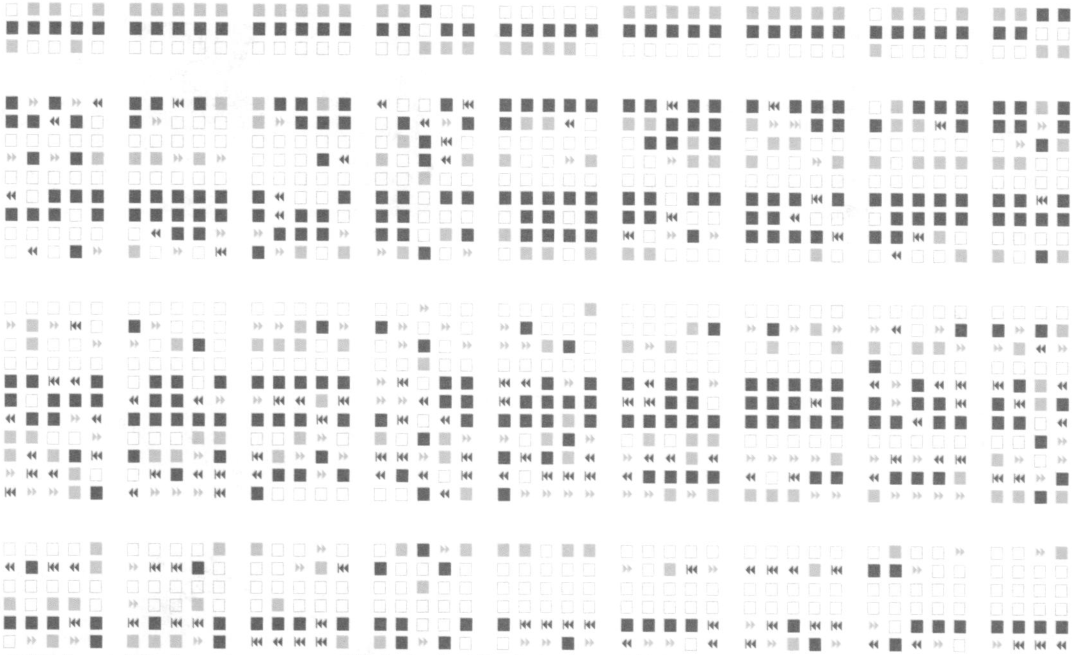

KEY: On all match | On bench | Subbed or sent off (Counting game) | Subbed or sent off (playing less than 70 minutes) | Subbed on from bench (Counting Game) | Subbed on (playing less than 70 minutes) | Subbed on and then subbed or sent off (Counting Game) | Subbed on and then subbed or sent off (playing less than 70 minutes) | Not in 16

ROMA

Final Position: **2nd**

KEY: ☐ Won ☐ Drawn ☐ Lost

							Attendance
1	lge	Udinese	A	W	2-1	Delvecchio 13; Montella 70	22,000
2	lge	Brescia	H	W	5-0	Montella 11; Chivu 16; Totti 23,58; Carew 90 pen	50,000
3	lge	Juventus	A	D	2-2	Chivu 23; Zebina 87	43,402
4	uc1rl1	Vardar Skopje	H	W	4-0	Dellas 12; De Rossi 20; Carew 54; Delvecchio 90	17,082
5	lge	Ancona	H	W	3-0	Montella 47; Totti 78; Delvecchio 86	49,150
6	lge	Siena	A	D	0-0		13,400
7	uc1rl2	Vardar Skopje	A	D	1-1	Mancini 63	5,000
8	lge	Parma	H	W	2-0	Samuel 30; Cassano 62	54,000
9	lge	Inter Milan	A	D	0-0		68,641
10	lge	Reggina	H	W	2-0	Montella 18; Carew 81	50,000
11	uc2rl1	Hajduk Split	H	W	1-0	Cassano 90	16,709
12	lge	Lazio	H	W	2-0	Mancini 81; Emerson 86	80,000
13	lge	Bologna	A	W	4-0	Totti 15; Montella 33; Panucci 39; Cassano 49	34,000
14	uc2rl2	Hajduk Split	A	D	1-1	Cassano 85	35,000
15	lge	Lecce	H	W	3-1	Mancini 19; Carew 45; Totti 77	50,000
16	lge	Chievo	A	W	3-0	Totti 67; Mancini 70; Cassano 72	19,000
17	lge	Modena	H	W	1-0	Totti 8 pen	48,000
18	lge	Empoli	A	W	2-0	Totti 24,45	15,000
19	lge	AC Milan	H	L	1-2	Cassano 45	73,383
20	lge	Perugia	A	W	1-0	Mancini 3	22,000
21	lge	Sampdoria	H	W	3-1	Carew 10; Totti 61,67	52,000
22	lge	Udinese	H	D	1-1	Panucci 16	44,882
23	lge	Brescia	A	L	0-1		18,000
24	lge	Juventus	H	W	4-0	Dacourt 13; Totti 53 pen; Cassano 70,85	70,000
25	lge	Ancona	A	D	0-0		20,000
26	lge	Siena	H	W	6-0	Cassano 20,25,71; Mancini 31; Delvecchio 82; Totti 87	45,000
27	uc3rl1	Gaziantepspor	A	L	0-1		18,000
28	lge	Parma	A	W	4-1	Cassano 45; Emerson 52; Totti 70; Mancini 78	21,000
29	uc3rl2	Gaziantepspor	H	W	2-0	Emerson 23; Cassano 43	11,191
30	lge	Inter Milan	H	W	4-1	Cassano 45; Mancini 63,90; Totti 90 pen	66,000
31	uc4rl1	Villarreal	A	L	0-2		23,000
32	lge	Reggina	A	D	0-0		21,000
33	uc4rl2	Villarreal	H	W	2-1	Emerson 10; Cassano 50	29,088
34	lge	Bologna	H	L	1-2	Cassano 32	44,123
35	lge	Lecce	A	W	3-0	Emerson 50; Bovo 54 og; Totti 90 pen	12,000
36	lge	Chievo	H	W	3-1	Carew 29; Cassano 60; Barzagli 78 og	23,000
37	lge	Modena	A	W	1-0	Totti 55	17,000
38	lge	Lazio	A	D	1-1	Totti 62 pen	44,000
39	lge	Empoli	H	W	3-0	Totti 41,89; Carew 65	15,000
40	lge	AC Milan	A	L	0-1		76,647
41	lge	Perugia	H	L	1-3	Cassano 12	3,000
42	lge	Sampdoria	A	D	0-0		12,500

MONTHLY POINTS TALLY

AUGUST	3	100%
SEPTEMBER	7	78%
OCTOBER	5	56%
NOVEMBER	12	100%
DECEMBER	9	100%
JANUARY	7	47%
FEBRUARY	10	83%
MARCH	4	44%
APRIL	13	87%
MAY	1	11%

LEAGUE GOALS

	PLAYER	MINS	GOALS	AVE
1	Totti	2765	20	138
2	Cassano	2669	14	191
3	Mancini	2967	8	371
4	Carew	880	5	176
5	Montella	496	5	99
6	Delvecchio	421	3	140
7	Emerson	2965	3	988
8	Panucci	2083	2	1042
9	Chivu	1923	2	962
10	Samuel	2697	1	2697
11	Zebina	1825	1	1825
12	Dacourt	2301	1	2301
	Other		3	
	TOTAL		68	

KEY PLAYERS - GOALSCORERS

Francesco Totti

Goals in the League	20
Contribution to Attacking Power Average number of minutes between League team goals while on pitch	44
Player Strike Rate The total number of minutes he was on the pitch for every League goal scored	138
Club Strike Rate Average number of minutes between League goals scored by club	45

	PLAYER	GOALS LGE	POWER	S RATE
1	Francesco Totti	20	44	138 mins
2	Antonio Cassano	14	48	191 mins
3	Alessandro Mancini	8	43	371 mins
4	Christian Chivu	2	44	962 mins
5	Emerson Ferreira da Rosa	3	44	988 mins

KEY PLAYERS - MIDFIELDERS

Francisco Lima

Goals in the League	0
Defensive Rating Average number of mins between League goals conceded while on the pitch	161
Contribution to Attacking Power Average number of minutes between League team goals while on pitch	43
Scoring Difference Defensive Rating minus Contribution to Attacking Power	118

	PLAYER	GOALS LGE	DEF RATE	ATT POWER	SCORE DIFF
1	Francisco Lima	0	161	43	118 mins
2	Emerson Ferreira da Rosa	3	156	44	112 mins
3	Alessandro Mancini	8	156	44	112 mins
4	Olivier Dacourt	1	144	49	95 mins

KEY PLAYERS - DEFENDERS

Jonathan Zebina

Goals Conceded in League	7
Clean Sheets In League games when he played at least 70 mins	13
Defensive Rating Ave number of mins between League goals conceded while on the pitch	261
Club Defensive Rating Average number of mins between League goals conceded by the club this season	161

	PLAYER	CON LGE	CLEAN SHEETS	DEF RATE
1	Jonathan Zebina	7	13	261 mins
2	Christian Chivu	10	14	192 mins
3	Walter Adrian Samuel	17	18	159 mins
4	Christian Panucci	17	10	123 mins

KEY GOALKEEPER

Ivan Pellizzoli

Goals Conceded in the League	14
Counting Games Games when he played at least 70 minutes	31
Clean Sheets In games when he played at least 70 mins	20
League minutes played Number of minutes played in league matches	2790
Defensive Rating Ave number of mins between League goals conceded while on the pitch	199

DISCIPLINARY RECORDS

	PLAYER	YELLOW	RED	AVE
1	Zebina	12	2	130
2	Dacourt	11	0	209
3	Montella	2	0	248
4	D'Agostino	2	0	325
5	Dellas	2	0	425
6	Carew	1	1	440
7	Samuel	6	0	449
8	De Rossi	1	0	530
9	Totti	5	0	553
10	Chivu	3	0	641
11	Candela	1	0	708
12	Emerson	4	0	741
13	Tommasi	1	0	767
	Other	10	0	
	TOTAL	61	3	

TOP POINT EARNERS

	PLAYER	GAMES	AV PTS
1	Zebina	18	2.28
2	Pellizzoli	31	2.16
3	Mancini	33	2.12
4	Chivu	21	2.10
5	Lima	29	2.10
6	Emerson	33	2.06
7	Totti	31	2.06
8	Cassano	30	2.03
9	Samuel	30	2.03
10	Panucci	23	2.00
	CLUB AVERAGE:		**2.09**

TEAM OF THE SEASON

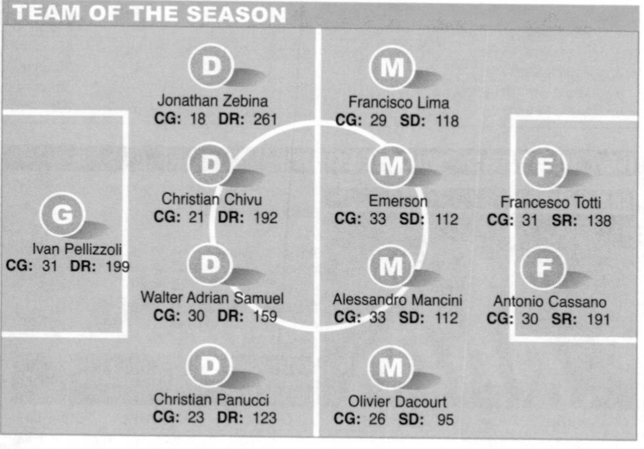

G
Ivan Pellizzoli
CG: 31 DR: 199
D
Jonathan Zebina
CG: 18 DR: 261
D
Christian Chivu
CG: 21 DR: 192
D
Walter Adrian Samuel
CG: 30 DR: 159
D
Christian Panucci
CG: 23 DR: 123
M
Francisco Lima
CG: 29 SD: 118
M
Emerson
CG: 33 SD: 112
M
Alessandro Mancini
CG: 33 SD: 112
M
Olivier Dacourt
CG: 26 SD: 95
F
Francesco Totti
CG: 31 SR: 138
F
Antonio Cassano
CG: 30 SR: 191

LEAGUE APPEARANCES AND BOOKINGS

	AGE (on 01/07/04)	IN NAMED 18	APPEARANCES	COUNTING GAMES	MINUTES ON PITCH	YELLOW CARDS	RED CARDS	THIS SEASON	HOME COUNTRY
Goalkeepers									
Gianluca Curci	18	4	1	0	15	0	0	-	Italy
Cristiano Lupatelli	26	9	0	0	0	0	0	-	Italy
Ivan Pellizzoli	23	32	31	31	2790	0	0	-	Italy
Carlo Zotti	21	24	3	3	270	1	0	-	Italy
Defenders									
Vincent Candela	30	21	12	4	708	1	0	-	France
Christian Chivu	23	24	22	21	1923	3	0	-	Romania
Daniele De Rossi	19	26	17	4	530	1	0	-	Italy
Traianos Dellas	28	32	14	7	850	2	0	-	Greece
Christian Panucci	31	30	24	23	2083	1	0	9	Italy (11)
Walter Samuel	26	30	30	30	2697	6	0	5	Argentina (5)
Luigi Sartor	29	4	0	0	0	0	0	-	Italy
Giuseppe Scurto	20	3	0	0	0	0	0	-	Italy
Andrea Servi	20	2	0	0	0	0	0	-	Italy
Jonathan Zebina	25	25	23	18	1825	12	2	-	France
Midfielders									
Akande Ajide	18	3	1	0	3	0	0	-	Nigeria
Gaetano D'Agostino	22	30	16	5	650	2	0	-	Italy
Olivier Dacourt	29	28	27	26	2301	11	0	7	France (2)
Raffaele De Martino	18	2	0	0	0	0	0	-	Italy
Emerson	28	33	33	33	2965	4	0	4	Brazil (1)
Gianluca Galasso	20	3	1	1	90	0	0	-	Italy
Francisco Lima	33	33	32	29	2731	2	0	-	Brazil
Alessandro Mancini	23	33	33	33	2967	3	0	1	Brazil (1)
Damiano Tommasi	30	31	20	6	767	1	0	1	Italy (11)
Adewale Wahab	20	10	1	1	87	0	0	-	Nigeria
Forwards									
John Alieu Carew	24	30	20	4	880	1	1	-	Norway
Antonio Cassano	21	33	33	30	2669	2	0	-	Italy
Daniele Corvia	19	7	3	1	103	0	0	-	Italy
Marco Delvecchio	31	24	16	1	421	1	0	3	Italy (11)
Vincenzo Montella	30	12	11	2	496	2	0	-	Italy
Francesco Totti	27	31	31	31	2765	5	0	6	Italy (11)

SQUAD APPEARANCES

Match	1	2	3	4	5	6	7	8	9	10	11	12	13	14	15	16	17	18	19	20	21	22	23	24	25	26	27	28	29	30	31	32	33	34	35	36	37	38	39	40	41	42
Venue	A	H	A	H	H	A	A	H	A	H	H	H	A	A	H	A	H	A	H	A	H	H	A	H	A	H	A	A	H	H	A	A	H	H	A	H	A	A	H	A	H	A
Competition	L	L	L	E	L	L	E	L	L	L	E	L	L	E	L	L	L	L	L	L	L	L	L	L	L	L	E	L	E	L	E	L	E	L	L	L	L	L	L	L	L	L
Result	W	W	D	W	W	D	D	W	D	W	W	W	W	D	W	W	W	W	L	W	W	D	L	W	D	W	L	W	W	W	L	D	W	L	W	W	W	D	W	L	L	D

Goalkeepers
Gianluca Curci
Cristiano Lupatelli
Ivan Pellizzoli
Carlo Zotti

Defenders
Vincent Candela
Christian Chivu
Daniele De Rossi
Traianos Dellas
Christian Panucci
Walter Adrian Samuel
Luigi Sartor
Giuseppe Scurto
Andrea Servi
Jonathan Zebina

Midfielders
Olasunkanmi Akande Ajide
Gaetano D'Agostino
Olivier Dacourt
Raffaele De Martino
Emerson Ferreira da Rosa
Gianluca Galasso
Francisco Lima
Alessandro Mancini
Damiano Tommasi
Adewale Dauda Wahab

Forwards
John Alieu Carew
Antonio Cassano
Daniele Corvia
Marco Delvecchio
Vincenzo Montella
Francesco Totti

KEY: ■ On all match ■ On bench ⏮ Subbed or sent off (Counting game) « Subbed or sent off (playing less than 70 minutes) ⏭ Subbed on from bench (Counting Game) » Subbed on (playing less than 70 minutes) Subbed on and then subbed or sent off (Counting Game) Subbed on and then subbed or sent off (playing less than 70 minutes) □ Not in 16

JUVENTUS

Final Position: **3rd**

KEY: Won / Drawn / Lost

		Opponent	H/A	Res	Score	Scorers	Attendance
1	lge	**Empoli**	H	W	5-1	Del Piero 16,51; Trezeguet 61,74; Di Vaio 85 pen	40,000
2	lge	**Chievo**	A	W	2-1	Legrottaglie 26; Trezeguet 49	34,600
3	cl gd	**Galatasaray**	H	W	2-1	Del Piero 5; Ferrara 73	14,420
4	lge	**Roma**	H	D	2-2	Di Vaio 21,35	43,402
5	lge	**Reggina**	A	W	2-0	Di Vaio 13; Nedved 50	30,000
6	cl gd	**Olympiakos**	A	W	2-1	Nedved 21,79	77,400
7	lge	**Bologna**	H	W	2-1	Iuliano 23; Trezeguet 79 pen	31,493
8	lge	**Ancona**	A	W	3-2	Miccoli 30,51; Zambrotta 45	24,000
9	cl gd	**Real Sociedad**	H	W	4-2	Trezeguet 3,63; Di Vaio 7,45	17,246
10	lge	**Brescia**	H	W	2-0	Nedved 6; Trezeguet 44	32,360
11	lge	**AC Milan**	A	D	1-1	Di Vaio 83	80,000
12	cl gd	**Real Sociedad**	A	D	0-0		29,000
13	lge	**Udinese**	H	W	4-1	Di Vaio 79,88; Miccoli 85; Trezeguet 90	31,418
14	lge	**Modena**	A	W	2-0	Trezeguet 42; Nedved 50	17,000
15	lge	**Inter Milan**	H	L	1-3	Montero 89	53,883
16	cl gd	**Galatasaray**	A	L	0-2		60,000
17	lge	**Lazio**	A	L	0-2		60,000
18	cl gd	**Olympiakos**	H	W	7-0	Trezeguet 14,25; Miccoli 19; Maresca 28; Di Vaio 62; Del Piero 67; Zalayeta 79	12,500
19	lge	**Parma**	H	W	4-0	Miccoli 10,32; Del Piero 71; Nedved 73	31,738
20	lge	**Lecce**	A	D	1-1	Trezeguet 87	30,325
21	lge	**Perugia**	H	W	1-0	Nedved 29	41,500
22	lge	**Sampdoria**	A	W	2-1	Camoranesi 23; Conte 64	38,000
23	lge	**Siena**	H	W	4-2	Del Piero 15 pen,59 pen,64; Trezeguet 37	31,000
24	lge	**Empoli**	A	D	3-3	Trezeguet 30,50,75	22,000
25	lge	**Chievo**	H	W	1-0	Camoranesi 10	30,100
26	lge	**Roma**	A	L	0-4		70,000
27	lge	**Reggina**	H	W	1-0	Maresca 51	30,000
28	lge	**Bologna**	A	W	1-0	Iuliano 56	36,000
29	clr1l1	**Deportivo**	A	L	0-1		30,000
30	lge	**Ancona**	H	W	3-0	Camoranesi 7; Miccoli 41; Del Piero 45	29,000
31	lge	**Brescia**	A	W	3-2	Miccoli 53 pen; Di Vaio 54; Nedved 75	22,000
32	clr1l2	**Deportivo**	H	L	0-1		24,680
33	lge	**AC Milan**	H	L	1-3	Ferrara 81	52,300
34	lge	**Udinese**	A	D	0-0		25,000
35	lge	**Modena**	H	W	3-1	Maresca 57; Trezeguet 64,84	30,666
36	lge	**Inter Milan**	A	L	2-3	Kily Gonzalez 25 og; Di Vaio 90	
37	lge	**Lazio**	H	W	1-0	Trezeguet 88	31,190
38	lge	**Parma**	A	D	2-2	Di Vaio 78; Tudor 90	26,678
39	lge	**Lecce**	H	L	3-4	Trezeguet 3; Maresca 56; Del Piero 79	20,000
40	lge	**Perugia**	A	L	0-1		15,000
41	lge	**Sampdoria**	H	W	2-0	Legrottaglie 37; Appiah 43	31,866
42	lge	**Siena**	A	W	3-1	Tudor 32; Miccoli 42; Di Vaio 60	13,500

MONTHLY POINTS TALLY

Month	Points	%
AUGUST	3	100%
SEPTEMBER	7	78%
OCTOBER	9	100%
NOVEMBER	7	58%
DECEMBER	4	44%
JANUARY	10	83%
FEBRUARY	12	80%
MARCH	7	58%
APRIL	4	33%
MAY	6	67%

LEAGUE GOALS

	PLAYER	MINS	GOALS	AVE
1	Trezeguet	2008	16	126
2	Di Vaio	1517	11	138
3	Miccoli	1118	8	140
4	Del Piero	1462	8	183
5	Nedved	2365	6	394
6	Maresca	1128	3	376
7	Camoranesi	1762	3	587
8	Iuliano	1180	2	590
9	Tudor	969	2	485
10	Legrottaglie	1746	2	873
11	Zambrotta	2585	1	2585
12	Montero	1449	1	1449
13	Ferrara	1326	1	1326
	Other		3	
	TOTAL		67	

KEY PLAYERS - GOALSCORERS

David Trezeguet

Goals in the League	16
Contribution to Attacking Power Average number of minutes between League team goals while on pitch	45
Player Strike Rate The total number of minutes he was on the pitch for every League goal scored	126
Club Strike Rate Average number of minutes between League goals scored by club	46

	PLAYER	GOALS LGE	POWER	S RATE
1	David Trezeguet	16	45	126 mins
2	Alessandro Del Piero	8	48	183 mins
3	Pavel Nedved	6	47	394 mins
4	Mauro German Camoranesi	3	50	587 mins
5	Nicola Legrottaglie	2	52	873 mins

KEY PLAYERS - MIDFIELDERS

Gianluca Zambrotta

Goals in the League	1
Defensive Rating Average number of mins between League goals conceded while on the pitch	78
Contribution to Attacking Power Average number of minutes between League team goals while on pitch	47
Scoring Difference Defensive Rating minus Contribution to Attacking Power	31

	PLAYER	GOALS LGE	DEF RATE	ATT POWER	SCORE DIFF
1	Gianluca Zambrotta	1	78	47	31 mins
2	Stephen Appiah	1	75	46	29 mins
3	Pavel Nedved	6	74	47	27 mins
4	Alessio Tacchinardi	0	71	46	25 mins
5	Mauro German Camoranesi	3	70	50	20 mins

KEY PLAYERS - DEFENDERS

Ciro Ferrara

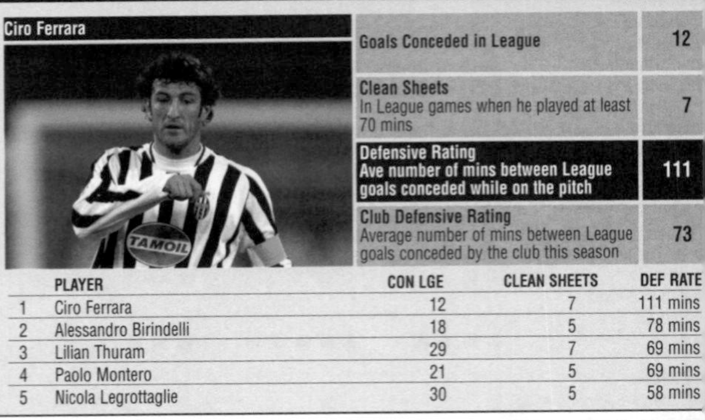
TAMOIL

Goals Conceded in League	12
Clean Sheets In League games when he played at least 70 mins	7
Defensive Rating Ave number of mins between League goals conceded while on the pitch	111
Club Defensive Rating Average number of mins between League goals conceded by the club this season	73

	PLAYER	CON LGE	CLEAN SHEETS	DEF RATE
1	Ciro Ferrara	12	7	111 mins
2	Alessandro Birindelli	18	5	78 mins
3	Lilian Thuram	29	7	69 mins
4	Paolo Montero	21	5	69 mins
5	Nicola Legrottaglie	30	5	58 mins

KEY GOALKEEPER

Gianluigi Buffon

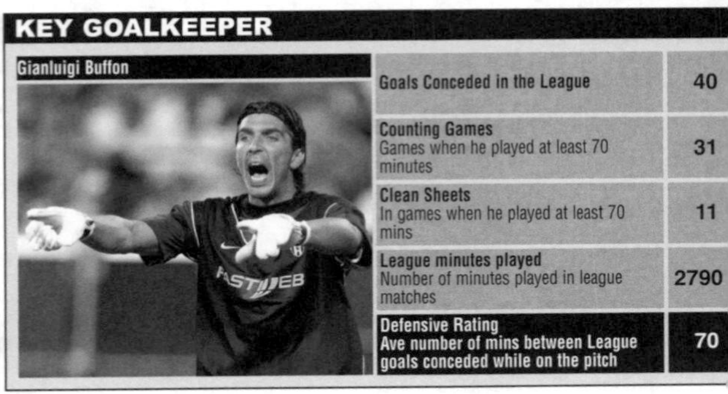

Goals Conceded in the League	40
Counting Games Games when he played at least 70 minutes	31
Clean Sheets In games when he played at least 70 mins	11
League minutes played Number of minutes played in league matches	2790
Defensive Rating Ave number of mins between League goals conceded while on the pitch	70

DISCIPLINARY RECORDS

	PLAYER	YELLOW	RED	AVE
1	Montero	6	2	181
2	Conte	5	0	207
3	Ferrara	4	1	265
4	Birindelli	4	0	351
5	Iuliano	2	1	393
6	Nedved	5	0	473
7	Camoranesi	3	0	587
8	Tacchinardi	3	0	638
9	Del Piero	2	0	731
10	Appiah	3	0	749
11	Zambrotta	3	0	861
12	Legrottaglie	2	0	873
13	Tudor	1	0	969
	Other	6	0	
	TOTAL	49	4	

TOP POINT EARNERS

	PLAYER	GAMES	AV PTS
1	Montero	13	2.46
2	Ferrara	14	2.29
3	Camoranesi	15	2.20
4	Zambrotta	28	2.11
5	Del Piero	12	2.08
6	Birindelli	14	2.07
7	Nedved	24	2.04
8	Buffon	31	2.00
9	Appiah	21	1.95
10	Tacchinardi	20	1.95
	CLUB AVERAGE:		**2.03**

LEAGUE APPEARANCES AND BOOKINGS

	AGE (on 01/07/04)	IN NAMED 18	APPEARANCES	COUNTING GAMES	MINUTES ON PITCH	YELLOW CARDS	RED CARDS	THIS SEASON	HOME COUNTRY
Goalkeepers									
Gianluigi Buffon	26	33	31	31	2790	1	0	8	Italy (11)
Antonio Chimenti	34	27	2	2	180	0	0	-	Italy
Antonio Mirante	20	6	0	0	0	0	0	-	Italy
Defenders									
Giovanni Bartolucci	20	3	0	0	0	0	0	-	Italy
A Birindelli	29	24	20	14	1406	4	0	1	Italy (11)
Ciro Ferrara	37	27	17	14	1326	4	1	-	Italy
Mark Iuliano	30	25	18	11	1180	2	1	-	Italy
Nicola Legrottaglie	27	25	21	18	1746	2	0	4	Italy (11)
Andrea Masiello	18	1	0	0	0	0	0	-	Italy
Paolo Montero	32	23	19	13	1449	6	2	-	Uruguay
Gianluca Pessotto	33	24	18	5	812	0	0	-	Italy
Lilian Thuram	32	25	23	22	2009	1	0	9	France (2)
Igor Tudor	26	25	15	8	969	1	0	6	Croatia (25)
Midfielders									
Stephen Appiah	23	32	30	21	2249	3	0	-	Ghana
Viktor Boudianski	20	6	2	0	93	0	0	-	Ukraine
Mauro Camoranesi	27	27	26	15	1762	3	0	-	Argentina
Davide Chiumiento	19	6	1	0	31	0	0	-	Italy
Antonio Conte	34	21	16	10	1036	5	0	-	Italy
Edgar Davids	31	11	5	3	332	2	0	9	Holland (4)
Enzo Maresca	24	26	20	7	1128	0	0	-	Italy
Pavel Nedved	31	30	30	24	2365	5	0	7	Czech Republic (10)
Ruben Olivera	21	0	0	0	0	0	0	3	Uruguay (25)
Raffaele Padalino	20	5	0	0	0	0	0	-	Italy
Alessio Tacchinardi	28	24	24	20	1915	3	0	-	Italy
Gianluca Zambrotta	27	30	30	28	2585	3	0	7	Italy (11)
Forwards									
Alessandro Del Piero	29	23	22	12	1462	2	0	5	Italy (11)
Marco Di Vaio	27	34	29	9	1517	0	0	4	Italy (11)
Fabrizio Miccoli	25	31	25	4	1118	1	0	3	Italy (11)
David Trezeguet	26	27	25	20	2008	1	0	8	France (2)
Marcelo Zalayeta	25	5	2	0	82	0	0	-	Uruguay

TEAM OF THE SEASON

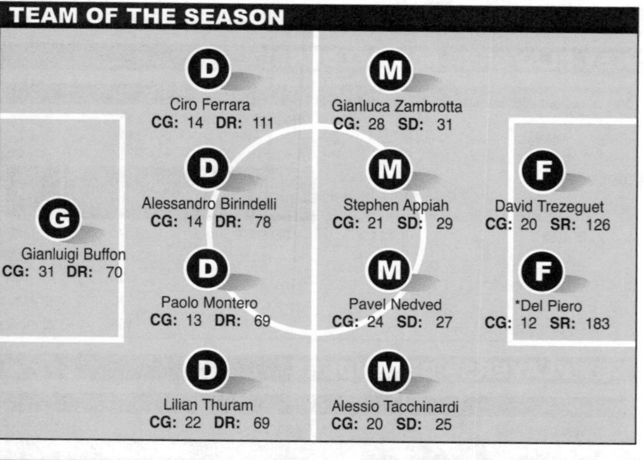

D
Ciro Ferrara
CG: 14 DR: 111
M
Gianluca Zambrotta
CG: 28 SD: 31
D
Alessandro Birindelli
CG: 14 DR: 78
M
Stephen Appiah
CG: 21 SD: 29
F
David Trezeguet
CG: 20 SR: 126
G
Gianluigi Buffon
CG: 31 DR: 70
D
Paolo Montero
CG: 13 DR: 69
M
Pavel Nedved
CG: 24 SD: 27
F
*Del Piero
CG: 12 SR: 183
D
Lilian Thuram
CG: 22 DR: 69
M
Alessio Tacchinardi
CG: 20 SD: 25

SQUAD APPEARANCES

Match	1	2	3	4	5	6	7	8	9	10	11	12	13	14	15	16	17	18	19	20	21	22	23	24	25	26	27	28	29	30	31	32	33	34	35	36	37	38	39	40	41	42
Venue	H	A	H	H	A	A	H	A	H	H	A	A	H	A	H	A	A	H	H	A	H	A	H	A	H	A	H	A	A	H	A	H	H	A	H	A	H	A	H	A	H	A
Competition	L	L	C	L	L	C	L	L	C	L	L	C	L	L	L	C	L	C	L	L	L	L	L	L	L	L	L	L	C	L	L	C	L	L	L	L	L	L	L	L	L	L
Result	W	W	W	D	W	W	W	W	W	W	D	D	W	W	L	L	L	W	W	D	W	W	W	D	W	L	W	W	L	W	W	L	L	D	W	L	W	D	L	L	W	W

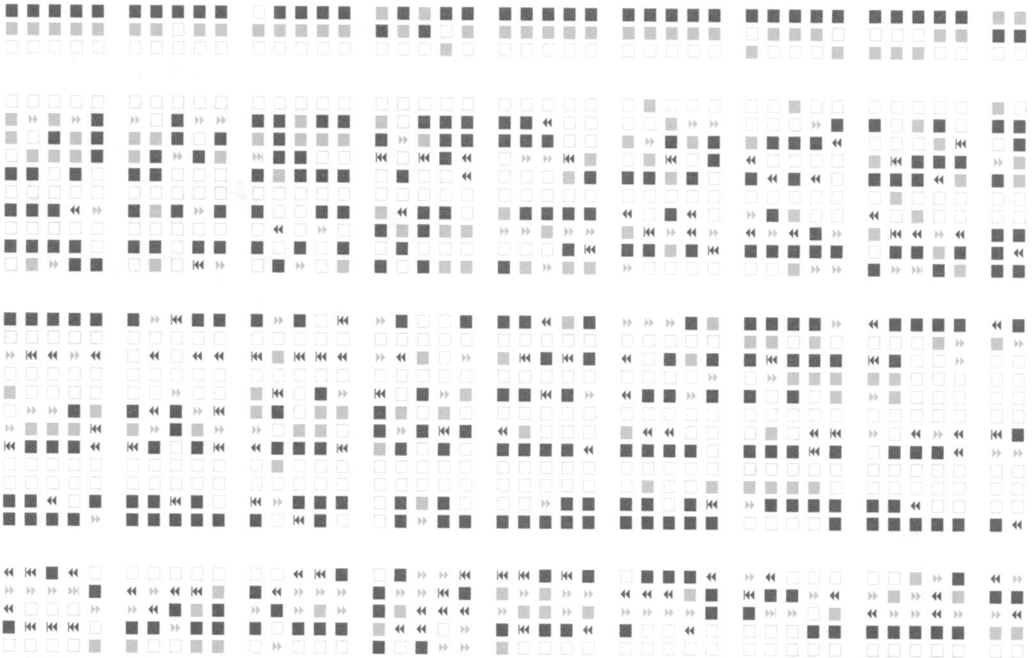

Goalkeepers
Gianluigi Buffon
Antonio Chimenti
Antonio Mirante

Defenders
Giovanni Bartolucci
Alessandro Birindelli
Ciro Ferrara
Mark Iuliano
Nicola Legrottaglie
Andrea Masiello
Paolo Montero
Gianluca Pessotto
Lilian Thuram
Igor Tudor

Midfielders
Stephen Appiah
Viktor Boudianski
Mauro German Camoranesi
Davide Chiumiento
Antonio Conte
Edgar Davids
Enzo Maresca
Pavel Nedved
Ruben Olivera
Raffaele Padalino
Alessio Tacchinardi
Gianluca Zambrotta

Forwards
Alessandro Del Piero
Marco Di Vaio
Fabrizio Miccoli
David Trezeguet
Marcelo Zalayeta

KEY: On all match | On bench | Subbed or sent off (Counting game) | Subbed or sent off (playing less than 70 minutes) | Subbed on from bench (Counting Game) | Subbed on (playing less than 70 minutes) | Subbed on and then subbed or sent off (Counting Game) | Subbed on and then subbed or sent off (playing less than 70 minutes) | Not in 16

INTER MILAN

Final Position: **4th**

KEY: ☐ Won ☐ Drawn ☐ Lost

#	Comp	Opponent	H/A	Res	Score	Scorers	Attendance
1	lge	Modena	H	W	2-0	Vieri 86; Materazzi 90	51,000
2	lge	Siena	A	W	1-0	Cufre 29 og	12,100
3	cl gb	Arsenal	A	W	3-0	Cruz 22; van der Meyde 24; Martins 41	34,393
4	lge	Sampdoria	H	D	0-0		65,000
5	lge	Udinese	A	D	0-0		18,000
6	cl gb	Dinamo Kiev	H	W	2-1	Adani 23; Vieri 90	70,882
7	lge	AC Milan	H	L	1-3	Martins 78	75,831
8	lge	Brescia	A	D	2-2	Cruz 62; Vieri 87 pen	25,000
9	cl gb	Lokomotiv M.	A	L	0-3		25,000
10	lge	Roma	H	D	0-0		68,641
11	lge	Chievo	A	W	2-0	Vieri 65; Recoba 69	25,000
12	cl gb	Lokomotiv M.	H	D	1-1	Recoba 14	25,000
13	lge	Ancona	H	W	3-0	Cruz 25; Materazzi 50; Vieri 79	45,000
14	lge	Reggina	H	W	6-0	Cannavaro 34; Martins 43; van der Meyde 50; Farinos 60; Cruz 65; Vieri 75	55,000
15	cl gb	Arsenal	H	L	1-5	Vieri 32	85,400
16	lge	Juventus	A	W	3-1	Cruz 12,69; Martins 75	53,883
17	lge	Perugia	H	W	2-1	Vieri 25,81	50,000
18	cl gb	Dinamo Kiev	A	D	1-1	Adani 68	30,000
19	lge	Bologna	A	W	2-0	Martins 30; Recoba 39	32,000
20	lge	Lazio	A	L	1-2	Vieri 30	55,000
21	lge	Lecce	H	W	3-1	Vieri 44; Cruz 51; Cordoba 60	55,000
22	lge	Parma	A	L	0-1		22,300
23	lge	Empoli	H	L	0-1		60,000
24	lge	Modena	A	D	1-1	Recoba 11	19,000
25	lge	Siena	H	W	4-0	Recoba 22,67 pen; Adriano 49,79	50,732
26	lge	Sampdoria	A	D	2-2	Vieri 31,79	38,000
27	lge	Udinese	H	L	1-2	Cruz 72	55,000
28	lge	AC Milan	A	L	2-3	Stankovic 15; Zanetti, C 40	80,000
29	uc3rl1	Sochaux	A	D	2-2	Vieri 18; Recoba 61	20,000
30	lge	Brescia	H	L	1-3	Stankevicius 48 og	45,000
31	uc3rl2	Sochaux	H	D	0-0		30,000
32	lge	Roma	A	L	1-4	Vieri 75	66,000
33	uc4rl1	Benfica	A	D	0-0		64,569
34	lge	Chievo	H	D	0-0		40,000
35	lge	Ancona	A	W	2-0	Recoba 61; Adani 70	20,000
36	uc4rl2	Benfica	H	W	4-3	Martins 45,70; Recoba 60; Vieri 64	27,638
37	lge	Reggina	A	W	2-0	Bonazzoli 41 og; Adriano 90	28,000
38	lge	Juventus	H	W	3-2	Martins 6; Vieri 45 pen; Stankovic 47	
39	ucqfl1	Marseille	A	L	0-1		60,000
40	lge	Perugia	A	W	3-2	Adriano 24,86; Martins 88	13,000
41	ucqfl2	Marseille	H	L	0-1		36,044
42	lge	Bologna	H	W	4-2	Recoba 32; Cannavaro 52; Stankovic 54; Martins 70	40,000
43	lge	Lazio	H	D	0-0		35,000
44	lge	Lecce	A	L	1-2	Adriano 36 pen	21,296
45	lge	Parma	H	W	1-0	Adriano 62	75,000
46	lge	Empoli	A	W	3-2	Adriano 45,69; Recoba 65	11,000

MONTHLY POINTS TALLY

Month	Points	%
AUGUST	3	100%
SEPTEMBER	5	56%
OCTOBER	2	22%
NOVEMBER	12	100%
DECEMBER	6	67%
JANUARY	4	33%
FEBRUARY	4	27%
MARCH	7	58%
APRIL	10	83%
MAY	6	67%

KEY PLAYERS - GOALSCORERS

Christian Vieri

Goals in the League	13	Player Strike Rate Average number of minutes between League goals scored by player	127
Contribution to Attacking Power Average number of minutes between League team goals while on pitch	51	Club Strike Rate Average number of minutes between League goals scored by club	52

	PLAYER	LGE GOALS	POWER	STRIKE RATE
1	Christian Vieri	13	51	127 mins
2	Julio Cruz	7	54	193 mins
3	Dejan Stankovic	3	48	391 mins
4	Marco Materazzi	2	57	607 mins

KEY PLAYERS - MIDFIELDERS

Emre Belozoglu

Goals in the League	0	Contribution to Attacking Power Average number of minutes between League team goals while on pitch	57
Defensive Rating Average number of mins between League goals conceded while he was on the pitch	105	Scoring Difference Defensive Rating minus Contribution to Attacking Power	48

	PLAYER	LGE GOALS	DEF RATE	POWER	SCORE DIFF
1	Emre Belozoglu	0	105	57	48 mins
2	Dejan Stankovic	3	78	49	29 mins
3	Javier Zanetti	0	82	53	29 mins
4	Cristiano Zanetti	1	75	49	26 mins

KEY PLAYERS - DEFENDERS

Marco Materazzi

Goals Conceded (GC) The number of League goals conceded while he was on the pitch	10	Clean Sheets In games when he played at least 70 minutes	8
Defensive Rating Ave number of mins between League goals conceded while on the pitch	121	Club Defensive Rating Average number of mins between League goals conceded by the club this season	83

	PLAYER	CON LGE	CLEAN SHEETS	DEF RATE
1	Marco Materazzi	10	8	121 mins
2	Fabio Cannavaro	18	11	107 mins
3	Ivan Cordoba	33	12	81 mins
4	Daniele Adani	24	5	74 mins

KEY GOALKEEPER

1 Francesco Toldo

Goals Conceded in the League	35	Counting Games Games when he played at least 70 mins	32
Defensive Rating Ave number of mins between League goals conceded while on the pitch	82	Clean Sheets In games when he played at least 70 mins	14

LEAGUE GOALS

Christian Vieri

Minutes on the pitch	1652	Goals in the League	13
League average (mins between goals)	127		

	PLAYER	MINS	GOALS	AVE
1	Vieri	1652	13	127
2	Adriano	1185	9	132
3	Recoba	921	8	115
4	Cruz	1351	7	193
5	Martins	1298	7	185
6	Stankovic	1172	3	391
7	Cannavaro	1925	2	963
8	Materazzi	1213	2	607
9	van der Meyde	751	1	751
10	Cordoba	2667	1	2667
11	Adani	1784	1	1784
12	Zanetti, C	1576	1	1576
	Other		4	
	TOTAL		59	

DISCIPLINARY RECORDS

	PLAYER	YELLOW	RED	AVE
1	Farinos	8	0	133
2	Almeyda	4	1	152
3	Zanetti, C	8	0	197
4	Emre Belozoglu	5	1	227
5	Pasquale	3	0	298
6	Helveg	4	0	343
7	Cordoba	7	0	381
8	Vieri	4	0	413
9	Kily Gonzalez	3	0	492
10	Stankovic	1	1	586
11	Materazzi	2	0	606
12	Adani	2	0	892
13	Cannavaro	2	0	962
	Other	4	1	
	TOTAL	57	4	

TOP POINT EARNERS

	PLAYER	GAMES	AV PTS
1	Materazzi	13	2.15
2	Zanetti, C	15	1.93
3	Emre Belozoglu	13	1.92
4	Kily Gonzalez	14	1.79
5	Toldo	32	1.72
6	Zanetti, J	33	1.70
7	Cordoba	29	1.69
8	Helveg	12	1.67
9	Cannavaro	20	1.65
10	Vieri	17	1.65
	CLUB AVERAGE:		**1.74**

LEAGUE APPEARANCES, BOOKINGS AND CAPS

	AGE (on 01/07/04)	IN NAMED 18	APPEARANCES	COUNTING GAMES	MINUTES ON PITCH	YELLOW CARDS	RED CARDS	THIS SEASON	HOME COUNTRY
Goalkeepers									
Alex Cordaz	21	4	0	0	0	0	0	-	Italy
Alberto Fontana	37	30	2	2	180	0	0	-	Italy
Francesco Toldo	32	33	32	32	2880	0	0	5	Italy (11)
Defenders									
Daniele Adani	29	29	23	17	1784	2	0	2	Italy (11)
Jeremie Brechet	24	11	9	3	370	0	0	-	France
Fabio Cannavaro	30	23	22	20	1925	2	0	8	Italy (11)
Ivan Cordoba	27	32	31	29	2667	7	0	-	Colombia
Carlos Gamarra	33	19	10	10	900	0	0	-	Paraguay
Marco Materazzi	30	14	14	13	1213	2	0	2	Italy (11)
Giovanni Pasquale	22	22	13	9	896	3	0	-	Italy
Midfielders									
Matias Almeyda	30	16	11	7	763	4	1	5	Argentina (5)
Francesco Coco	27	3	3	3	244	0	0	-	Italy
Emre Belozoglu	23	21	21	13	1366	5	1	-	Turkey
Javier Farinos	26	21	16	9	1071	8	0	-	Spain
Thomas Helveg	33	28	23	12	1372	4	0	7	Denmark (14)
G Karagounis	27	16	9	2	336	0	0	-	Greece
Kily Gonzalez	29	28	21	14	1476	3	0	4	Argentina (5)
Sabri Lamouchi	32	20	15	4	654	0	0	-	France
Luciano	28	9	6	0	197	0	1	-	Brazil
Buruk Okan	30	12	3	0	50	0	0	-	Turkey
Dejan Stankovic	25	14	14	13	1172	1	1	2	Serbia & Mont (45)
Andy van der Meyde	24	21	14	4	751	0	0	8	Holland (4)
Cristiano Zanetti	27	20	19	15	1576	8	0	4	Italy (11)
Javier Zanetti	30	34	34	33	3033	1	0	6	Argentina (5)
Forwards									
Leite Ribeiro Adriano	22	17	16	11	1185	0	0	2	Brazil (1)
Julio Cruz	29	28	21	13	1351	1	0	-	Argentina
Abdulahi Isah Eliakwu	18	1	0	0	0	0	0	-	Nigeria
Mohammed Kallon	24	7	5	1	252	1	0	-	Sierra Leone
Obafemi Martins	19	27	24	8	1298	1	0	-	Nigeria
Alvaro Recoba	28	22	19	7	921	0	0	6	Uruguay (25)
Christian Vieri	30	24	22	17	1652	4	0	9	Italy (11)

TEAM OF THE SEASON

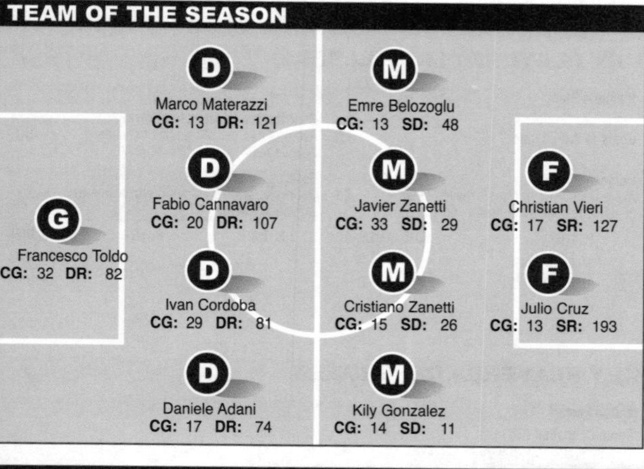

G
Francesco Toldo
CG: 32 DR: 82
D
Marco Materazzi
CG: 13 DR: 121
D
Fabio Cannavaro
CG: 20 DR: 107
D
Ivan Cordoba
CG: 29 DR: 81
D
Daniele Adani
CG: 17 DR: 74
M
Emre Belozoglu
CG: 13 SD: 48
M
Javier Zanetti
CG: 33 SD: 29
M
Cristiano Zanetti
CG: 15 SD: 26
M
Kily Gonzalez
CG: 14 SD: 11
F
Christian Vieri
CG: 17 SR: 127
F
Julio Cruz
CG: 13 SR: 193

SQUAD APPEARANCES

Match	1	2	3	4	5	6	7	8	9	10	11	12	13	14	15	16	17	18	19	20	21	22	23	24	25	26	27	28	29	30	31	32	33	34	35	36	37	38	39	40	41	42	43	44	45	46
Venue	H	A	A	H	A	H	H	A	A	H	A	H	H	H	H	A	H	A	A	A	H	A	H	A	H	A	H	A	A	H	H	A	A	H	A	H	A	H	A	A	H	H	H	A	H	A
Competition	L	L	C	L	L	C	L	L	C	L	L	C	L	L	C	L	L	C	L	L	L	L	L	L	L	L	L	L	E	L	E	L	E	L	L	E	L	L	E	L	E	L	L	L	L	L
Result	W	W	W	D	D	W	L	D	L	D	W	D	W	W	L	W	W	D	W	L	W	L	L	D	W	D	L	L	D	L	D	L	D	D	W	W	W	W	L	W	L	W	D	L	W	W

Goalkeepers
Alex Cordaz
Alberto Fontana
Francesco Toldo

Defenders
Daniele Adani
Jeremie Brechet
Fabio Cannavaro
Ivan Cordoba
Carlos Alberto Gamarra
Marco Materazzi
Giovanni Pasquale

Midfielders
Matias Almeyda
Francesco Coco
Emre Belozoglu
Javier Zampata Farinos
Thomas Helveg
Georgios Karagounis
Kily Gonzalez
Sabri Lamouchi
Siqueira Luciano
Buruk Okan
Dejan Stankovic
Andy van der Meyde
Cristiano Zanetti
Javier Zanetti

Forwards
Leite Ribeiro Adriano
Julio Cruz
Abdulahi Isah Eliakwu
Mohammed Kallon
Obafemi Martins
Alvaro Recoba
Christian Vieri

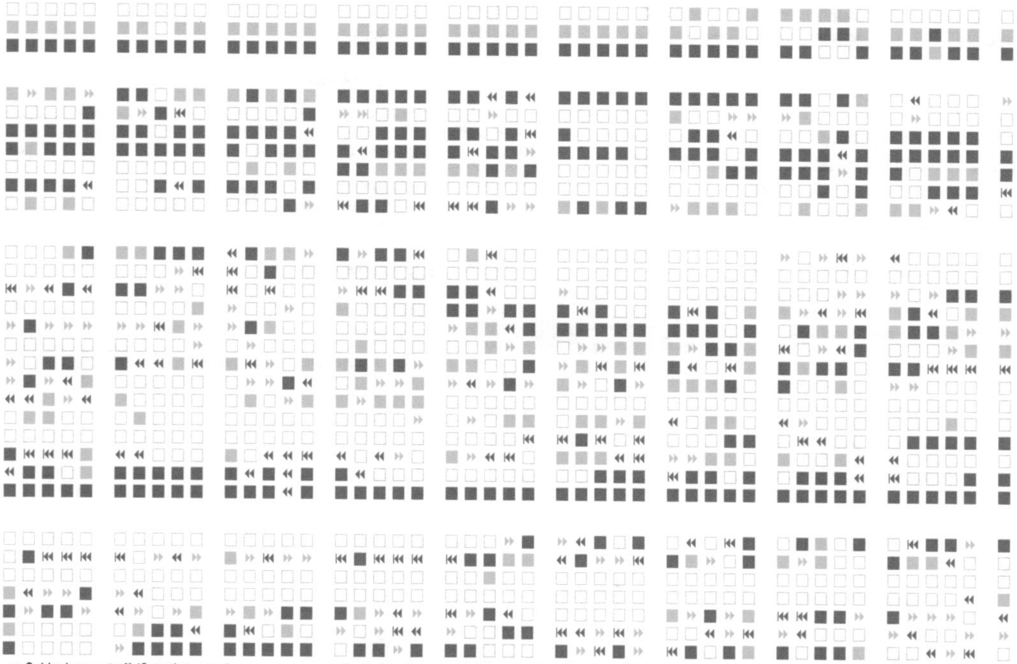

KEY: ■ On all match ■ On bench ⏮ Subbed or sent off (Counting game) « Subbed or sent off (playing less than 70 minutes) ⏭ Subbed on from bench (Counting Game) » Subbed on (playing less than 70 minutes) ⏭ Subbed on and then subbed or sent off (Counting Game) » Subbed on and then subbed or sent off (playing less than 70 minutes) □ Not in 16

PARMA

Final Position: **5th**

KEY: Won Drawn Lost

							Attendance
1	lge	Bologna	A	D	2-2	Adriano 20,87	18,000
2	lge	Perugia	H	W	3-0	Bresciano 27; Adriano 50 pen; Gilardino 83	22,000
3	lge	Lazio	A	W	3-2	Bresciano 1,89; Adriano 62	45,000
4	uc1rl1	Met. Donetsk	A	D	1-1	Adriano 67	30,000
5	lge	Siena	H	D	1-1	Adriano 80	15,408
6	lge	Sampdoria	H	W	1-0	Adriano 20	18,000
7	uc1rl2	Met. Donetsk	H	W	3-0	Gilardino 43,46; Marchionni 73	8,308
8	lge	Roma	A	L	0-2		54,000
9	lge	Modena	H	W	3-0	Morfeo 28; Adriano 86; Marchionni 88	18,000
10	lge	Brescia	A	W	3-2	Morfeo 12; Marchionni 43; Gilardino 70	16,000
11	uc2rl1	Salzburg	A	W	4-0	Filippini 50; Gilardino 65; Ferrari 84; Rosina 86	4,500
12	lge	AC Milan	H	D	0-0		25,000
13	lge	Empoli	A	L	0-1		4,645
14	uc2rl2	Salzburg	H	W	5-0	Carbone 1,7; Filippini 43; Sorrentino 47,86	6,000
15	lge	Chievo	H	W	3-1	Morfeo 52; Marchionni 70; Gilardino 81 pen	12,000
16	lge	Lecce	A	W	2-1	Gilardino 47,78	10,633
17	lge	Juventus	A	L	0-4		31,738
18	lge	Reggina	H	L	1-2	Gilardino 85	17,000
19	lge	Ancona	A	W	2-0	Barone 27,64	10,000
20	lge	Inter Milan	H	W	1-0	Filippini 41	22,300
21	lge	Udinese	A	D	1-1	Adriano 80	12,000
22	lge	Bologna	H	D	0-0		13,000
23	lge	Perugia	A	D	2-2	Gilardino 35; Morfeo 38	10,000
24	lge	Lazio	H	L	0-3		18,000
25	lge	Siena	A	W	2-1	Gilardino 58; Bresciano 90	10,000
26	lge	Sampdoria	A	W	2-1	Gilardino 59; Bresciano 74	23,000
27	uc3rl1	Genclerbirligi	H	L	0-1		3,598
28	lge	Roma	H	L	1-4	Gilardino 30	21,000
29	uc3rl2	Genclerbirligi	A	L	0-3		19,000
30	lge	Modena	A	D	2-2	Gilardino 45; Ferrari 87	14,000
31	lge	Brescia	H	D	2-2	Carbone 5; Marchionni 60	15,000
32	lge	AC Milan	A	L	1-3	Gilardino 82	60,000
33	lge	Empoli	H	W	4-0	Barone 37; Gilardino 60 pen,64; Bresciano 80	13,000
34	lge	Chievo	A	W	2-0	Marchionni 31; Gilardino 71	16,000
35	lge	Lecce	H	W	3-1	Carbone 1; Gilardino 42,83	24,000
36	lge	Juventus	H	D	2-2	Carbone 35; Gilardino 80	26,678
37	lge	Reggina	A	D	1-1	Bresciano 9	20,000
38	lge	Ancona	H	W	3-1	Gilardino 9; Carbone 16; Bresciano 30	11,500
39	lge	Inter Milan	A	L	0-1		75,000
40	lge	Udinese	H	W	4-3	Gilardino 60,72,78,86	27,000

MONTHLY POINTS TALLY

Month	Points	%
AUGUST	1	33%
SEPTEMBER	7	78%
OCTOBER	6	67%
NOVEMBER	7	58%
DECEMBER	3	33%
JANUARY	8	67%
FEBRUARY	7	47%
MARCH	5	42%
APRIL	8	67%
MAY	6	67%

KEY PLAYERS - GOALSCORERS

Alberto Gilardino

Goals in the League	23	Player Strike Rate Average number of minutes between League goals scored by player	108
Contribution to Attacking Power Average number of minutes between League team goals while on pitch	51	Club Strike Rate Average number of minutes between League goals scored by club	54

	PLAYER	LGE GOALS	POWER	STRIKE RATE
1	Alberto Gilardino	23	51	108 mins
2	Mark Bresciano	8	60	302 mins
3	Domenico Morfeo	4	54	370 mins
4	Marco Marchionni	5	57	498 mins

KEY PLAYERS - MIDFIELDERS

Manuele Blasi

Goals in the League	0	Contribution to Attacking Power Average number of minutes between League team goals while on pitch	50
Defensive Rating Average number of mins between League goals conceded while he was on the pitch	81	Scoring Difference Defensive Rating minus Contribution to Attacking Power	31

	PLAYER	LGE GOALS	DEF RATE	POWER	SCORE DIFF
1	Manuele Blasi	0	81	50	31 mins
2	Marco Donadel	0	62	48	14 mins
3	Domenico Morfeo	4	67	55	12 mins
4	Simone Barone	3	66	54	12 mins

KEY PLAYERS - DEFENDERS

Matteo Ferrari

Goals Conceded (GC) The number of League goals conceded while he was on the pitch	43	Clean Sheets In games when he played at least 70 minutes	9
Defensive Rating Ave number of mins between League goals conceded while on the pitch	69	Club Defensive Rating Average number of mins between League goals conceded by the club this season	67

	PLAYER	CON LGE	CLEAN SHEETS	DEF RATE
1	Matteo Ferrari	43	9	69 mins
2	Daniele Bonera	32	5	66 mins
3	Paolo Cannavaro	21	5	63 mins
4	Marcello Castellini	45	8	63 mins

KEY GOALKEEPER

1 Sebastian Frey

Goals Conceded in the League	46	Counting Games Games when he played at least 70 mins	33
Defensive Rating Ave number of mins between League goals conceded while on the pitch	65	Clean Sheets In games when he played at least 70 mins	8

LEAGUE GOALS

Alberto Gilardino

Minutes on the pitch	2490	Goals in the League	23
League average (mins between goals)	108		

	PLAYER	MINS	GOALS	AVE
1	Gilardino	2490	23	108
2	Bresciano	2416	8	302
3	Adriano	720	8	90
4	Marchionni	2489	5	498
5	Morfeo	1479	4	370
6	Carbone	990	4	248
7	Barone	2925	3	975
8	Ferrari	2970	1	2970
9	Filippini	584	1	584
	Other		0	
	TOTAL		57	

DISCIPLINARY RECORDS

	PLAYER	YELLOW	RED	AVE
P 1	Seric	7	1	123
2	Blasi	6	1	151
3	Cannavaro	4	1	266
4	Donadel	5	1	289
5	Filippini	2	0	292
6	Bonera	6	0	350
7	Ferrari	8	0	371
8	Castellini	7	0	408
9	Barone	7	0	417
10	Marchionni	4	1	497
11	Junior Jenilson	2	0	565
12	Morfeo	2	0	739
13	Carbone	1	0	990
	Other	9	1	
	TOTAL	70	6	

TOP POINT EARNERS

	PLAYER	GAMES	AV PTS
1	Morfeo	14	2.07
2	Bonera	23	2.00
3	Donadel	17	2.00
4	Blasi	12	1.83
5	Barone	32	1.78
6	Ferrari	33	1.76
7	Junior Jenilson	12	1.75
8	Bresciano	19	1.74
9	Frey	33	1.73
10	Castellini	31	1.68
	CLUB AVERAGE:		1.71

LEAGUE APPEARANCES, BOOKINGS AND CAPS

	AGE (on 01/07/04)	IN NAMED 18	APPEARANCES	COUNTING GAMES	MINUTES ON PITCH	YELLOW CARDS	RED CARDS	THIS SEASON	HOME COUNTRY
Goalkeepers									
Marco Amelia	22	18	0	0	0	0	0	-	Italy
Sebastian Frey	24	33	33	33	2970	1	0	-	France
Vincenzo Sicignano	30	16	1	1	90	0	0	-	Italy
Defenders									
Antonio Benarrivo	35	20	5	0	145	0	0	-	Italy
Daniele Bonera	23	25	24	23	2101	6	0	-	Italy
Paolo Cannavaro	23	26	16	14	1332	4	1	-	Italy
Giuseppe Cardone	30	6	3	1	139	2	1	-	Italy
Marcello Castellini	31	32	32	31	2856	7	0	1	Italy (11)
Matteo Ferrari	24	33	33	33	2970	8	0	7	Italy (11)
Angelo Junior	31	16	14	12	1130	2	0	3	Brazil (1)
Alessandro Potenza	20	15	13	5	691	0	0	-	Italy
Mirko Stefani	20	4	0	0	0	0	0	-	Italy
Midfielders									
Simone Barone	26	33	33	32	2925	7	0	1	Italy (11)
Manuele Blasi	23	12	12	12	1057	6	1	-	Italy
Jorge Bolano	27	7	2	0	8	0	0	-	Colombia
Sory Camara	19	5	0	0	0	0	0	-	Guinea
Marco Donadel	21	29	23	17	1735	5	1	-	Italy
Emanuele Filippini	31	15	12	5	584	2	0	-	Italy
Domenico Morfeo	28	24	23	14	1479	2	0	-	Italy
Hidetoshi Nakata	27	14	12	5	616	0	0	-	Japan
Gabriel Oyola	21	5	0	0	0	0	0	-	Argentina
Alessandro Rosina	19	17	7	0	164	1	0	-	Italy
Anthony Seric	25	26	16	7	991	7	1	1	Croatia (25)
Forwards									
Adriano	22	9	9	7	720	0	0	2	Brazil (1)
Mark Bresciano	24	34	33	19	2416	1	0	6	Australia (89)
Fabrizio Cammarata	28	15	8	0	205	0	0	-	Italy
Benito Carbone	32	24	17	6	990	1	0	-	Italy
Daniele Degano	21	8	4	0	104	1	0	-	Italy
Alberto Gilardino	22	34	34	26	2490	1	0	-	Italy
Gaetano Grieco	21	8	2	0	13	0	0	-	Italy
Marco Marchionni	23	33	32	28	2489	4	1	-	Italy
Ianis Zicu	18	12	6	0	198	2	0	-	Nigeria

TEAM OF THE SEASON

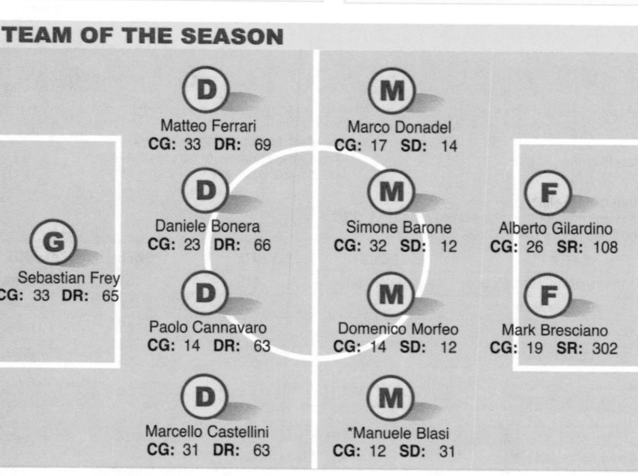

G
Sebastian Frey
CG: 33 DR: 65
D
Matteo Ferrari
CG: 33 DR: 69
D
Daniele Bonera
CG: 23 DR: 66
D
Paolo Cannavaro
CG: 14 DR: 63
D
Marcello Castellini
CG: 31 DR: 63
M
Marco Donadel
CG: 17 SD: 14
M
Simone Barone
CG: 32 SD: 12
M
Domenico Morfeo
CG: 14 SD: 12
M
*Manuele Blasi
CG: 12 SD: 31
F
Alberto Gilardino
CG: 26 SR: 108
F
Mark Bresciano
CG: 19 SR: 302

SQUAD APPEARANCES

Match	1	2	3	4	5	6	7	8	9	10	11	12	13	14	15	16	17	18	19	20	21	22	23	24	25	26	27	28	29	30	31	32	33	34	35	36	37	38	39	40
Venue	A	H	A	A	H	H	H	A	H	A	A	H	A	H	H	A	A	H	A	H	A	H	A	H	A	A	H	H	A	A	H	A	H	A	H	H	A	H	A	H
Competition	L	L	L	E	L	L	E	L	L	L	E	L	L	E	L	L	L	L	L	L	L	L	L	L	L	L	E	L	E	L	L	L	L	L	L	L	L	L	L	L
Result	D	W	W	D	D	W	W	L	W	W	W	D	L	W	W	W	L	L	W	W	D	D	D	L	W	W	L	L	L	D	D	L	W	W	W	D	D	W	L	W

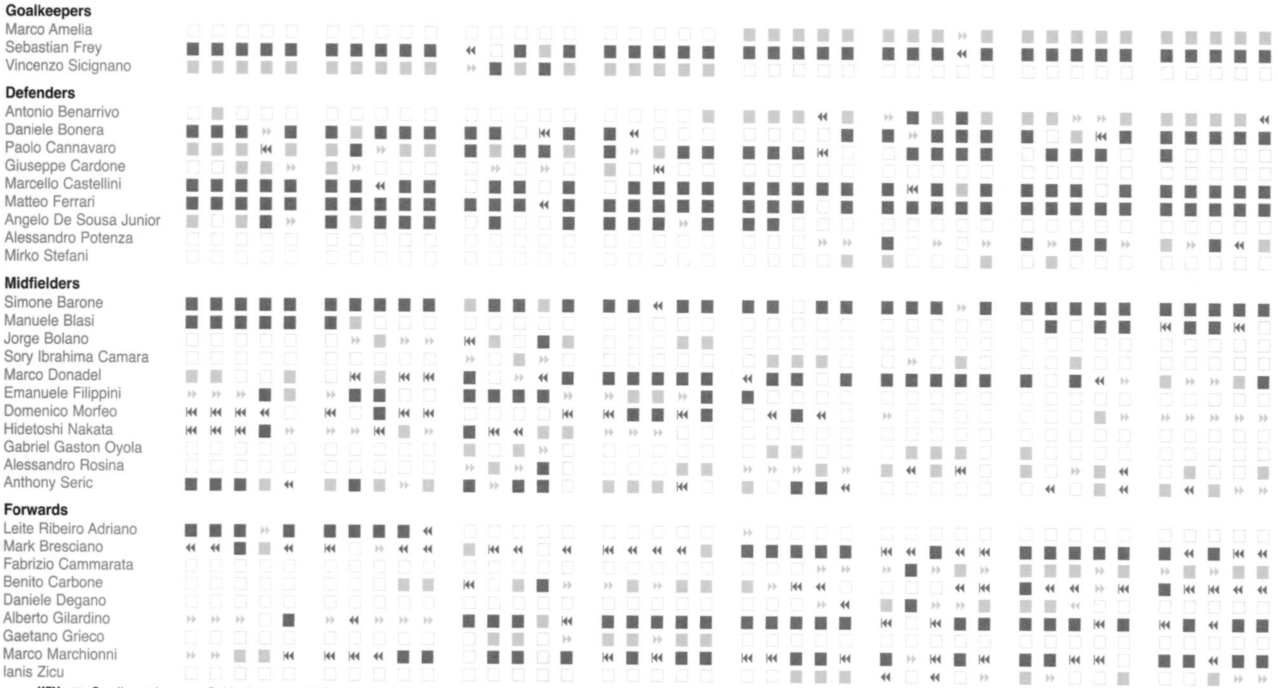

Goalkeepers
Marco Amelia
Sebastian Frey
Vincenzo Sicignano

Defenders
Antonio Benarrivo
Daniele Bonera
Paolo Cannavaro
Giuseppe Cardone
Marcello Castellini
Matteo Ferrari
Angelo De Sousa Junior
Alessandro Potenza
Mirko Stefani

Midfielders
Simone Barone
Manuele Blasi
Jorge Bolano
Sory Ibrahima Camara
Marco Donadel
Emanuele Filippini
Domenico Morfeo
Hidetoshi Nakata
Gabriel Gaston Oyola
Alessandro Rosina
Anthony Seric

Forwards
Leite Ribeiro Adriano
Mark Bresciano
Fabrizio Cammarata
Benito Carbone
Daniele Degano
Alberto Gilardino
Gaetano Grieco
Marco Marchionni
Ianis Zicu

KEY: On all match · On bench · Subbed or sent off (Counting game) · Subbed or sent off (playing less than 70 minutes) · Subbed on from bench (Counting Game) · Subbed on (playing less than 70 minutes) · Subbed on and then subbed or sent off (Counting Game) · Subbed on and then subbed or sent off (playing less than 70 minutes) · Not in 16

LAZIO

Final Position: **6th**

KEY: ☐ Won ☐ Drawn ☐ Lost

No	Comp	Opponent	H/A	Res	Score	Scorers	Attendance
1	clql1	Benfica	H	W	3-1	Corradi 16; Fiore 50; Mihajlovic 80	50,000
2	clql2	Benfica	A	W	1-0	Cesar 28	18,000
3	lge	Lecce	H	W	4-1	Albertini 20; Corradi 25; Fiore 36; Oddo 84	44,000
4	lge	Sampdoria	A	W	2-1	Inzaghi 9; Albertini 64 pen	35,000
5	cg gg	Besiktas	A	W	2-0	Stam 37; Fiore 77	28,000
6	lge	Parma	H	L	2-3	Stam 33; Inzaghi 79	45,000
7	lge	Empoli	A	D	2-2	Stankovic 38; Fiore 87	5,818
8	cg gg	Sparta Prague	H	D	2-2	Inzaghi 46,61 pen	30,000
9	lge	Chievo	H	W	1-0	Mihajlovic 64	45,000
10	lge	AC Milan	A	L	0-1		62,000
11	cg gg	Chelsea	A	L	1-2	Inzaghi 38	40,405
12	lge	Bologna	H	W	2-1	Inzaghi 83; Corradi 90	45,300
13	lge	Udinese	A	W	2-1	Corradi 16; Inzaghi 33	25,000
14	cg gg	Chelsea	H	L	0-4		50,000
15	lge	Roma	A	L	0-2		80,000
16	lge	Perugia	H	W	3-1	Stankovic 45; Corradi 87; Inzaghi 90	40,000
17	cg gg	Besiktas	H	D	1-1	Muzzi 56	40,000
18	lge	Siena	A	L	0-3		10,000
19	lge	Juventus	H	W	2-0	Corradi 21; Fiore 48	60,000
20	cg gg	Sparta Prague	A	L	0-1		17,825
21	lge	Ancona	A	W	1-0	Liverani 76	12,000
22	lge	Inter Milan	H	W	2-1	Corradi 43; Zauri 82	55,000
23	lge	Reggina	A	L	1-2	Liverani 16	25,000
24	lge	Brescia	H	L	0-1		45,000
25	lge	Modena	A	D	1-1	Lopez 24	14,000
26	lge	Lecce	A	W	1-0	Cesar 56	10,834
27	lge	Sampdoria	H	D	1-1	Fiore 10	45,000
28	lge	Parma	A	W	3-0	Lopez 40 pen,57; Corradi 66	18,000
29	lge	Empoli	H	W	3-0	Couto 5; Zauri 45; Stam 71	40,000
30	lge	Chievo	A	D	0-0		11,706
31	lge	AC Milan	H	L	0-1		55,000
32	lge	Udinese	H	D	2-2	Muzzi 4; Inzaghi 5	40,000
33	lge	Bologna	A	L	1-2	Fiore 38	15,000
34	lge	Perugia	A	W	2-1	Fiore 29; Giannichedda 58	12,000
35	lge	Siena	H	W	5-2	Cesar 3,45,50; Fiore 29; Corradi 78	42,000
36	lge	Juventus	A	L	0-1		31,190
37	lge	Ancona	H	W	4-2	Couto 12,81; Fiore 73; Zauri 89	40,000
38	lge	Roma	H	D	1-1	Corradi 40	44,000
39	lge	Inter Milan	A	D	0-0		35,000
40	lge	Reggina	H	D	1-1	Lopez 23	46,000
41	lge	Brescia	A	L	1-2	Cesar 90	20,000
42	lge	Modena	H	W	2-1	Corradi 17; Cesar 49	50,000

MONTHLY POINTS TALLY

Month	Points	%
AUGUST	3	100%
SEPTEMBER	4	44%
OCTOBER	6	67%
NOVEMBER	6	50%
DECEMBER	9	100%
JANUARY	4	33%
FEBRUARY	8	53%
MARCH	4	44%
APRIL	8	53%
MAY	4	44%

KEY PLAYERS - GOALSCORERS

Bernardo Corradi

Goals in the League	10	**Player Strike Rate** Average number of minutes between League goals scored by player	252
Contribution to Attacking Power Average number of minutes between League team goals while on pitch	57	**Club Strike Rate** Average number of minutes between League goals scored by club	59

	PLAYER	LGE GOALS	POWER	STRIKE RATE
1	Bernardo Corradi	10	57	252 mins
2	Stefano Fiore	8	57	338 mins
3	Luciano Zauri	3	52	422 mins
4	Claudio Lopez	4	55	430 mins

KEY PLAYERS - MIDFIELDERS

Guiliano Giannichedda

Goals in the League	1	**Contribution to Attacking Power** Average number of minutes between League team goals while on pitch	81
Defensive Rating Average number of mins between League goals conceded while he was on the pitch	110	**Scoring Difference** Defensive Rating minus Contribution to Attacking Power	29

	PLAYER	LGE GOALS	DEF RATE	POWER	SCORE DIFF
1	Guiliano Giannichedda	1	110	81	29 mins
2	Stefano Fiore	8	82	57	25 mins
3	Fabio Liverani	2	84	65	19 mins
4	Luciano Zauri	3	70	53	17 mins

KEY PLAYERS - DEFENDERS

Jaap Stam

Goals Conceded (GC) The number of League goals conceded while he was on the pitch	27	**Clean Sheets** In games when he played at least 70 minutes	8
Defensive Rating Ave number of mins between League goals conceded while on the pitch	91	**Club Defensive Rating** Average number of mins between League goals conceded by the club this season	81

	PLAYER	CON LGE	CLEAN SHEETS	DEF RATE
1	Jaap Stam	27	8	91 mins
2	Sinisa Mihajlovic	24	5	87 mins
3	Giuseppe Favalli	27	4	86 mins
4	Manuel Silva Fernando Couto	19	4	85 mins

KEY GOALKEEPER

1 Angelo Peruzzi

Goals Conceded in the League	29	**Counting Games** Games when he played at least 70 mins	28
Defensive Rating Ave number of mins between League goals conceded while on the pitch	84	**Clean Sheets** In games when he played at least 70 mins	7

LEAGUE GOALS

Bernardo Corradi

Minutes on the pitch	2516	Goals in the League	10
League average (mins between goals)	252		

	PLAYER	MINS	GOALS	AVE
1	Corradi	2516	10	252
2	Fiore	2700	8	338
3	Inzaghi	1010	6	168
4	Cesar	962	6	160
5	Lopez	1720	4	430
6	Couto	1606	3	535
7	Zauri	1267	3	422
8	Albertini	1232	2	616
9	Liverani	1939	2	970
10	Stankovic	1301	2	651
11	Stam	2455	2	1228
12	Mihajlovic	2091	1	2091
	Other		3	
	TOTAL		52	

DISCIPLINARY RECORDS

	PLAYER	YELLOW	RED	AVE
1	Inzaghi	8	0	126
2	Liverani	8	2	193
3	Muzzi	4	1	196
4	Negro	4	0	202
5	Mihajlovic	9	1	209
6	Giannichedda	6	0	256
7	Stankovic	2	1	433
8	Dabo	3	0	443
9	Cesar	2	0	481
10	Corradi	5	0	503
11	Favalli	3	0	775
12	Stam	3	0	818
13	Albertini	1	0	1232
	Other	6	1	
	TOTAL	64	6	

TOP POINT EARNERS

	PLAYER	GAMES	AV PTS
1	Stankovic	14	1.86
2	Zauri	13	1.77
3	Couto	15	1.67
4	Liverani	19	1.63
5	Lopez	16	1.63
6	Stam	26	1.62
7	Oddo	22	1.59
8	Fiore	29	1.59
9	Corradi	27	1.56
10	Peruzzi	26	1.54
	CLUB AVERAGE:		**1.65**

TEAM OF THE SEASON

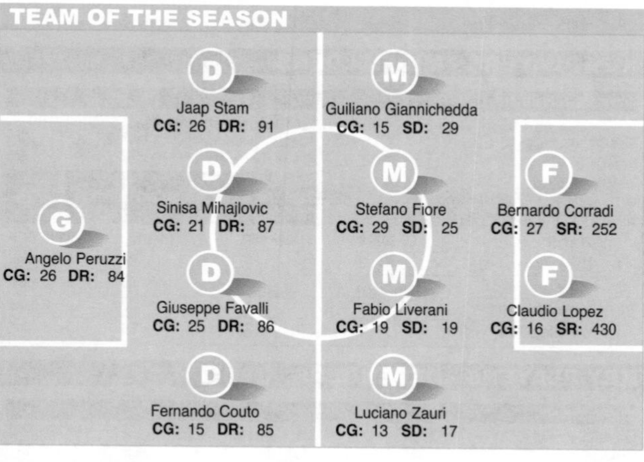

G
Angelo Peruzzi
CG: 26 DR: 84
D
Jaap Stam
CG: 26 DR: 91
D
Sinisa Mihajlovic
CG: 21 DR: 87
D
Giuseppe Favalli
CG: 25 DR: 86
D
Fernando Couto
CG: 15 DR: 85
M
Guiliano Giannichedda
CG: 15 SD: 29
M
Stefano Fiore
CG: 29 SD: 25
M
Fabio Liverani
CG: 19 SD: 19
M
Luciano Zauri
CG: 13 SD: 17
F
Bernardo Corradi
CG: 27 SR: 252
F
Claudio Lopez
CG: 16 SR: 430

LEAGUE APPEARANCES, BOOKINGS AND CAPS

	AGE (on 01/07/04)	IN NAMED 18	APPEARANCES	COUNTING GAMES	MINUTES ON PITCH	YELLOW CARDS	RED CARDS	THIS SEASON	HOME COUNTRY
Goalkeepers									
Fabrizio Casazza	33	9	0	0	0	0	0	-	Italy
Angelo Peruzzi	34	29	28	26	2438	0	0	-	Italy
Matteo Sereni	29	30	8	6	622	0	0	-	Italy
Defenders									
Rodriguez Cesar	29	17	13	9	962	2	0	-	Brazil
F Colonnese	32	8	0	0	0	0	0	-	Italy
Fernando Couto	34	33	23	15	1606	0	0	8	Portugal (20)
Giuseppe Favalli	32	31	29	25	2327	3	0	-	Italy
Sinisa Mihajlovic	35	28	25	21	2091	9	1	-	Serbia & Montenegro
Paolo Negro	32	21	13	6	810	4	0	-	Italy
Massimo Oddo	28	33	31	22	2303	1	0	7	Italy (11)
Jaap Stam	31	30	29	26	2455	3	0	9	Holland (4)
Midfielders									
Demetrio Albertini	32	29	23	9	1232	1	0	-	Italy
Sergio Conceicao	29	9	7	2	275	0	1	1	Portugal (20)
Ousmane Dabo	27	33	19	11	1330	3	0	2	France (2)
Stefano Fiore	29	32	32	29	2700	2	0	7	Italy (11)
G Giannichedda	29	29	21	15	1540	6	0	-	Italy
Guerino Gottardi	33	7	0	0	0	0	0	-	Italy
Fabio Liverani	28	30	25	19	1939	8	2	-	Italy
Fabrizio Melara	18	3	0	0	0	0	0	-	Italy
Gaizka Mendieta	30	0	0	0	0	0	0	-	Spain
Dejan Stankovic	25	15	15	14	1301	2	1	2	Serbia & Mont (45)
Luciano Zauri	26	33	19	13	1267	1	0	-	Italy
Forwards									
Bernardo Corradi	28	33	31	27	2516	5	0	7	Italy (11)
Alfonso Delgado	18	8	4	0	88	1	0	-	Spain
Simone Inzaghi	28	27	24	5	1010	8	0	-	Italy
Claudio Lopez	29	27	27	16	1720	1	0	1	Argentina (5)
Roberto Muzzi	32	27	22	5	982	4	1	-	Italy

SQUAD APPEARANCES

Match	1	2	3	4	5	6	7	8	9	10	11	12	13	14	15	16	17	18	19	20	21	22	23	24	25	26	27	28	29	30	31	32	33	34	35	36	37	38	39	40	41	42
Venue	H	A	H	A	A	H	A	H	H	A	A	H	A	H	A	H	H	A	H	A	A	H	A	H	A	A	H	A	H	A	H	H	A	A	H	A	H	H	A	H	A	H
Competition	C	C	L	L	C	L	L	C	L	L	C	L	L	C	L	L	C	L	L	C	L	L	L	L	L	L	L	L	L	L	L	L	L	L	L	L	L	L	L	L	L	L
Result	W	W	W	W	W	L	D	D	W	L	L	W	W	L	L	W	D	L	W	L	W	W	L	L	D	W	D	W	W	D	L	D	L	W	W	L	W	D	D	D	L	W

Goalkeepers
Fabrizio Casazza
Angelo Peruzzi
Matteo Sereni

Defenders
Rodriguez Cesar
Francesco Colonnese
Fernando Couto
Giuseppe Favalli
Sinisa Mihajlovic
Paolo Negro
Massimo Oddo
Jaap Stam

Midfielders
Demetrio Albertini
Sergio Conceicao
Ousmane Dabo
Stefano Fiore
Guiliano Giannichedda
Guerino Gottardi
Fabio Liverani
Fabrizio Melara
Gaizka Mendieta
Dejan Stankovic
Luciano Zauri

Forwards
Bernardo Corradi
Alfonso Delgado
Simone Inzaghi
Claudio Lopez
Roberto Muzzi

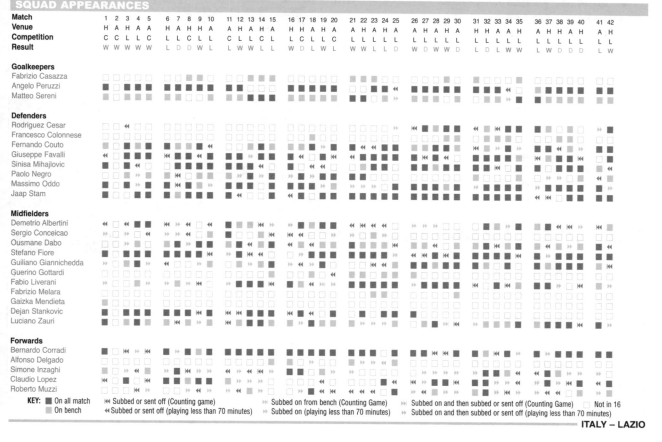

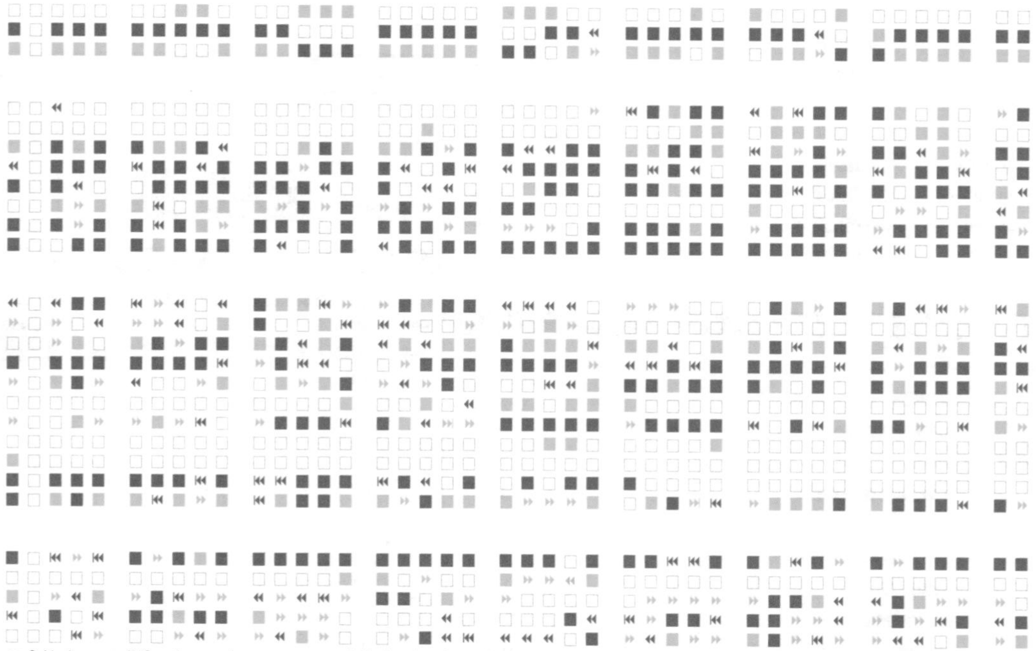

KEY: ■ On all match
■ On bench
⏮ Subbed or sent off (Counting game)
« Subbed or sent off (playing less than 70 minutes)
» Subbed on from bench (Counting Game)
» Subbed on (playing less than 70 minutes)
» Subbed on and then subbed or sent off (Counting Game)
» Subbed on and then subbed or sent off (playing less than 70 minutes)
□ Not in 16

UDINESE

Final Position: **7th**

NICKNAME:

KEY: ☐Won ☐Drawn ☐Lost

							Attendance
1	lge	Roma	H	L	1-2	Kroldrup 26	22,000
2	lge	Modena	A	W	1-0	Pizarro 82 pen	15,000
3	lge	Bologna	A	L	0-2		20,000
4	uc1rl1	Salzburg	A	W	1-0	Fava 36	10,000
5	lge	Inter Milan	H	D	0-0		18,000
6	lge	Ancona	A	W	3-0	Fava 12,47; Iaquinta 31	10,740
7	uc1rl2	Salzburg	H	L	1-2	Bertotto 15	15,000
8	lge	Empoli	H	W	2-0	Sensini 31; Iaquinta 32	16,000
9	lge	Perugia	A	D	3-3	Fava 36,62,77	8,000
10	lge	Lazio	H	L	1-2	Iaquinta 27	25,000
11	lge	Juventus	A	L	1-4	Jankulovski 65 pen	31,418
12	lge	Siena	H	D	1-1	Fava 42	16,000
13	lge	Brescia	A	W	2-1	Jorgensen 48; Fava 56	14,000
14	lge	Reggina	H	W	1-0	Jancker 87	17,000
15	lge	Lecce	H	W	1-0	Pinzi 31	17,000
16	lge	AC Milan	A	W	2-1	Fava 2; Bertotto 51	60,000
17	lge	Sampdoria	H	L	0-1		13,000
18	lge	Chievo	A	D	0-0		10,200
19	lge	Parma	H	D	1-1	Ferrari 23 og	12,000
20	lge	Roma	A	D	1-1	Jankulovski 89	44,882
21	lge	Modena	H	W	1-0	Iaquinta 90	15,000
22	lge	Bologna	H	L	1-3	Jankulovski 45	13,000
23	lge	Inter Milan	A	W	2-1	Pinzi 53; Fava 66	55,000
24	lge	Ancona	H	W	3-0	Fava 58; Jankulovski 83; Pizarro 86	13,000
25	lge	Empoli	A	L	0-2		4,000
26	lge	Perugia	H	D	1-1	Iaquinta 46	12,500
27	lge	Lazio	A	D	2-2	Castroman 11; Iaquinta 90	40,000
28	lge	Juventus	H	D	0-0		25,000
29	lge	Siena	A	L	0-1		
30	lge	Brescia	H	W	4-3	Iaquinta 5,30; Fava 15,82	16,000
31	lge	Reggina	A	W	1-0	Iaquinta 77	25,000
32	lge	Lecce	A	L	1-2	Jorgensen 23	
33	lge	AC Milan	H	D	0-0		24,000
34	lge	Sampdoria	A	W	3-1	Jankulovski 29; Pizarro 58; Iaquinta 87	28,000
35	lge	Chievo	H	D	1-1	Iaquinta 45	13,000
36	lge	Parma	A	L	3-4	Kroldrup 56; Jorgensen 75; Jankulovski 90	27,000

MONTHLY POINTS TALLY

Month	Points	%
AUGUST	0	0%
SEPTEMBER	4	44%
OCTOBER	7	78%
NOVEMBER	4	33%
DECEMBER	9	100%
JANUARY	3	25%
FEBRUARY	9	60%
MARCH	3	25%
APRIL	7	58%
MAY	4	44%

KEY PLAYERS - GOALSCORERS

Vincenzo Iaquinta

Goals in the League	11	Player Strike Rate Average number of minutes between League goals scored by player	173
Contribution to Attacking Power Average number of minutes between League team goals while on pitch	57	Club Strike Rate Average number of minutes between League goals scored by club	70

	PLAYER	LGE GOALS	POWER	STRIKE RATE
1	Vincenzo Iaquinta	11	57	173 mins
2	Dino Fava	12	68	195 mins
3	David Marcelo Pizarro	3	60	540 mins
4	Marek Jankulovski	5	65	551 mins

KEY PLAYERS - MIDFIELDERS

David Marcelo Pizarro

Goals in the League	3	Contribution to Attacking Power Average number of minutes between League team goals while on pitch	60
Defensive Rating Average number of mins between League goals conceded while he was on the pitch	85	Scoring Difference Defensive Rating minus Contribution to Attacking Power	25

	PLAYER	LGE GOALS	DEF RATE	POWER	SCORE DIFF
1	David Marcelo Pizarro	3	85	60	25 mins
2	Marek Jankulovski	5	79	66	13 mins
3	Martin Jorgensen	3	76	70	6 mins
4	Giampiero Pinzi	2	73	69	4 mins

KEY PLAYERS - DEFENDERS

Valerio Bertotto

Goals Conceded (GC) The number of League goals conceded while he was on the pitch	28	Clean Sheets In games when he played at least 70 minutes	11
Defensive Rating Ave number of mins between League goals conceded while on the pitch	89	Club Defensive Rating Average number of mins between League goals conceded by the club this season	77

	PLAYER	CON LGE	CLEAN SHEETS	DEF RATE
1	Valerio Bertotto	28	11	89 mins
2	Roberto Nester Sensini	27	9	81 mins
3	Valentin Do Carmo Alberto	17	2	79 mins
4	Per Kroldrup	35	9	76 mins

KEY GOALKEEPER

1 Morgan De Sanctis

Goals Conceded in the League	40	Counting Games Games when he played at least 70 mins	34
Defensive Rating Ave number of mins between League goals conceded while on the pitch	77	Clean Sheets In games when he played at least 70 mins	12

LEAGUE GOALS

Dino Fava

Minutes on the pitch	2341	Goals in the League	12
League average (mins between goals)	195		

	PLAYER	MINS	GOALS	AVE
1	Fava	2341	12	195
2	Iaquinta	1905	11	173
3	Jankulovski	2756	5	551
4	Pizarro	1621	3	540
5	Jorgensen	2951	3	984
6	Pinzi	2194	2	1097
7	Kroldrup	2653	2	1327
8	Jancker	314	1	314
9	Castroman	848	1	848
10	Sensini	2197	1	2197
11	Bertotto	2480	1	2480
	Other		2	
	TOTAL		44	

DISCIPLINARY RECORDS

	PLAYER	YELLOW	RED	AVE
1	Alberto	7	1	167
2	Pinzi	9	1	219
3	Manfredini	2	0	274
4	Pazienza	4	0	350
5	Bertotto	6	1	354
6	Castroman	2	0	424
7	Pizarro	2	1	540
8	Jankulovski	5	0	551
9	Muntari	2	0	738
10	Felipe Dal Belo	1	0	789
11	Kroldrup	2	1	884
12	Pierini	1	0	972
13	Pieri	1	0	1052
	Other	6	0	
	TOTAL	50	5	

TOP POINT EARNERS

	PLAYER	GAMES	AV PTS
1	Muntari	12	1.67
2	Pinzi	23	1.65
3	Pizarro	17	1.65
4	Sensini	24	1.63
5	Fava	24	1.58
6	Bertotto	27	1.56
7	Jankulovski	31	1.52
8	De Sanctis	34	1.47
9	Jorgensen	33	1.42
10	Kroldrup	29	1.38
	CLUB AVERAGE:		1.47

TEAM OF THE SEASON

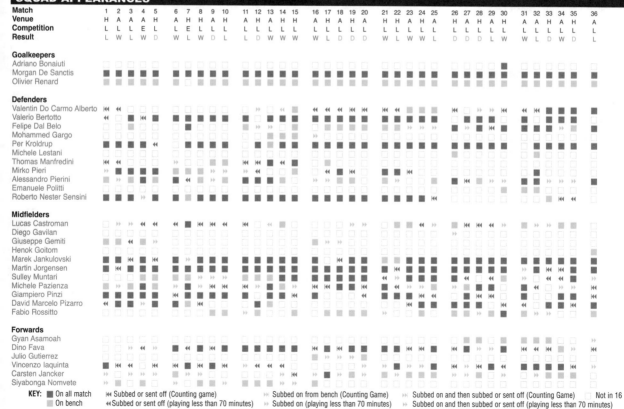

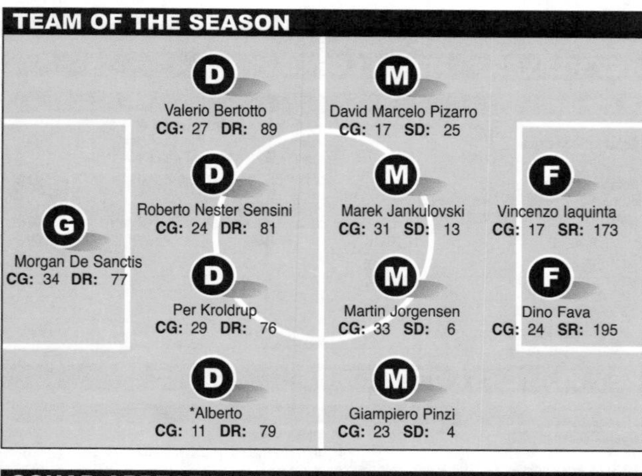
G
Morgan De Sanctis
CG: 34 DR: 77
D
Valerio Bertotto
CG: 27 DR: 89
D
Roberto Nester Sensini
CG: 24 DR: 81
D
Per Kroldrup
CG: 29 DR: 76
D
*Alberto
CG: 11 DR: 79
M
David Marcelo Pizarro
CG: 17 SD: 25
M
Marek Jankulovski
CG: 31 SD: 13
M
Martin Jorgensen
CG: 33 SD: 6
M
Giampiero Pinzi
CG: 23 SD: 4
F
Vincenzo Iaquinta
CG: 17 SR: 173
F
Dino Fava
CG: 24 SR: 195

LEAGUE APPEARANCES, BOOKINGS AND CAPS

	AGE (on 01/07/04)	IN NAMED 18	APPEARANCES	COUNTING GAMES	MINUTES ON PITCH	YELLOW CARDS	RED CARDS	THIS SEASON	HOME COUNTRY
Goalkeepers									
Adriano Bonaiuti	37	1	1	1	90	0	0	-	Italy
Morgan De Sanctis	27	34	34	34	3060	0	0	-	Italy
Olivier Renard	25	34	0	0	0	0	0	-	Belgium
Defenders									
Valentin Alberto	29	25	21	11	1336	7	1	-	Brazil
Valerio Bertotto	31	28	28	27	2480	6	1	-	Italy
Felipe Dal Belo	19	25	15	8	789	1	0	-	Brazil
Mohammed Gargo	29	4	1	0	12	0	0	-	Ghana
Per Kroldrup	24	31	30	29	2653	2	1	4	Denmark (14)
Michele Lestani	18	2	0	0	0	0	0	-	Italy
Thomas Manfredini	24	11	8	5	548	2	0	-	Italy
Mirko Pieri	25	18	15	9	1052	1	0	-	Italy
Alessandro Pierini	31	30	19	9	972	1	0	-	Italy
Emanuele Politti	16	3	0	0	0	0	0	-	Italy
Roberto N Sensini	37	26	25	24	2197	1	0	-	Argentina
Midfielders									
Lucas Castroman	23	26	19	5	848	2	0	-	Argentina
Diego Gavilan	24	1	1	0	17	0	0	-	Paraguay
Giuseppe Gemiti	23	7	4	0	145	0	0	-	Germany
Henok Goitom	20	1	0	0	0	0	0	-	Sierra Leone
Marek Jankulovski	27	33	31	31	2756	5	0	6	Czech Republic (10)
Martin Jorgensen	28	34	34	33	2951	1	0	7	Denmark (14)
Sulley Muntari	19	29	23	12	1477	2	0	-	Ghana
Michele Pazienza	21	32	26	14	1403	4	0	-	Italy
Giampiero Pinzi	23	26	26	23	2194	9	1	-	Italy
David Pizarro	24	20	19	17	1621	2	1	-	Chile
Fabio Rossitto	24	20	6	1	215	0	0	-	Italy
Forwards									
Gyan Asamoah	18	7	1	0	8	0	0	-	Ghana
Dino Fava	27	32	31	24	2341	1	0	-	Italy
Julio Gutierrez	24	5	3	0	28	0	0	-	Chile
Vincenzo Iaquinta	24	29	29	17	1905	1	0	-	Italy
Carsten Jancker	29	25	15	2	314	2	0	-	Germany
Siyabonga Nomvete	26	12	5	0	74	0	0	-	South Africa

SQUAD APPEARANCES

Match	1	2	3	4	5	6	7	8	9	10	11	12	13	14	15	16	17	18	19	20	21	22	23	24	25	26	27	28	29	30	31	32	33	34	35	36
Venue	H	A	A	A	H	A	H	H	A	H	A	H	A	H	H	A	H	A	H	A	H	H	A	H	A	H	A	H	A	H	A	A	H	A	H	A
Competition	L	L	L	E	L	L	E	L	L	L	L	L	L	L	L	L	L	L	L	L	L	L	L	L	L	L	L	L	L	L	L	L	L	L	L	L
Result	L	W	L	W	D	W	L	W	D	L	L	D	W	W	W	W	L	D	D	D	W	L	W	W	L	D	D	D	L	W	W	L	D	W	D	L

Goalkeepers
Adriano Bonaiuti
Morgan De Sanctis
Olivier Renard

Defenders
Valentin Do Carmo Alberto
Valerio Bertotto
Felipe Dal Belo
Mohammed Gargo
Per Kroldrup
Michele Lestani
Thomas Manfredini
Mirko Pieri
Alessandro Pierini
Emanuele Politti
Roberto Nester Sensini

Midfielders
Lucas Castroman
Diego Gavilan
Giuseppe Gemiti
Henok Goitom
Marek Jankulovski
Martin Jorgensen
Sulley Muntari
Michele Pazienza
Giampiero Pinzi
David Marcelo Pizarro
Fabio Rossitto

Forwards
Gyan Asamoah
Dino Fava
Julio Gutierrez
Vincenzo Iaquinta
Carsten Jancker
Siyabonga Nomvete

KEY: ■ On all match ■ On bench | ⏮ Subbed or sent off (Counting game) ⏪ Subbed or sent off (playing less than 70 minutes) | ⏭ Subbed on from bench (Counting Game) ⏩ Subbed on (playing less than 70 minutes) | Subbed on and then subbed or sent off (Counting Game) Subbed on and then subbed or sent off (playing less than 70 minutes) | □ Not in 16

SAMPDORIA

Final Position: **8th**

KEY: Won / Drawn / Lost

							Attendance
1	lge	Reggina	A	D	2-2	Bazzani 64; Diana 73	26,000
2	lge	Lazio	H	L	1-2	Bazzani 73	35,000
3	lge	Inter Milan	A	D	0-0		65,000
4	lge	Brescia	H	W	2-1	Bazzani 88; Flachi 90 pen	27,000
5	lge	Parma	A	L	0-1		18,000
6	lge	Chievo	A	D	1-1	Diana 60	13,890
7	lge	AC Milan	H	L	0-3		35,000
8	lge	Bologna	A	W	1-0	Doni 33	22,000
9	lge	Empoli	H	W	2-0	Bazzani 21; Doni 27	25,000
10	lge	Lecce	A	D	0-0		13,760
11	lge	Ancona	H	W	2-0	Bazzani 66; Flachi 89	25,000
12	lge	Siena	H	W	2-1	Flachi 1; Bazzani 73	25,000
13	lge	Perugia	A	D	3-3	Flachi 16,88; Doni 59	15,000
14	lge	Modena	H	D	1-1	Bazzani 50	26,000
15	lge	Udinese	A	W	1-0	Flachi 58	13,000
16	lge	Juventus	H	L	1-2	Flachi 56	38,000
17	lge	Roma	A	L	1-3	Bazzani 6	52,000
18	lge	Reggina	H	W	2-0	Bazzani 45,47	
19	lge	Lazio	A	D	1-1	Bazzani 49	45,000
20	lge	Inter Milan	H	D	2-2	Cipriani 57; Doni 85 pen	38,000
21	lge	Brescia	A	D	1-1	Doni 57	13,000
22	lge	Parma	H	L	1-2	Flores 82	23,000
23	lge	Chievo	H	W	1-0	Diana 50	22,000
24	lge	AC Milan	A	L	1-3	Doni 27	60,000
25	lge	Bologna	H	W	3-2	Volpi 9 pen; Diana 28; Cipriani 49	25,000
26	lge	Empoli	A	D	1-1	Belleri 18 og	6,500
27	lge	Lecce	H	D	2-2	Flachi 8,42	24,000
28	lge	Ancona	A	W	1-0	Bazzani 19	8,000
29	lge	Siena	A	D	0-0		18,500
30	lge	Perugia	H	W	3-2	Diana 38; Flachi 45,87	25,000
31	lge	Modena	A	L	0-1		18,000
32	lge	Udinese	H	L	1-3	Bazzani 52	28,000
33	lge	Juventus	A	L	0-2		31,866
34	lge	Roma	H	D	0-0		12,500

MONTHLY POINTS TALLY

Month	Points	%
AUGUST	1	33%
SEPTEMBER	4	44%
OCTOBER	1	11%
NOVEMBER	10	83%
DECEMBER	5	56%
JANUARY	6	50%
FEBRUARY	6	40%
MARCH	5	42%
APRIL	7	58%
MAY	1	11%

KEY PLAYERS - GOALSCORERS

Francesco Flachi

Goals in the League	11	Player Strike Rate Average number of minutes between League goals scored by player	153
Contribution to Attacking Power Average number of minutes between League team goals while on pitch	64	Club Strike Rate Average number of minutes between League goals scored by club	77

	PLAYER	LGE GOALS	POWER	STRIKE RATE
1	Francesco Flachi	11	64	153 mins
2	Fabio Bazzani	13	73	221 mins
3	Cristiano Doni	6	66	289 mins
4	Stefano Aimo Diana	5	77	560 mins

KEY PLAYERS - MIDFIELDERS

Massimo Donati

Goals in the League	0	Contribution to Attacking Power Average number of minutes between League team goals while on pitch	71
Defensive Rating Average number of mins between League goals conceded while he was on the pitch	90	Scoring Difference Defensive Rating minus Contribution to Attacking Power	19

	PLAYER	LGE GOALS	DEF RATE	POWER	SCORE DIFF
1	Massimo Donati	0	90	71	19 mins
2	Sergio Volpi	1	68	72	-4 mins
3	Cristiano Doni	6	60	67	-7 mins
4	Angelo Palombo	0	70	100	-30 mins

KEY PLAYERS - DEFENDERS

Morris Carrozzieri

Goals Conceded (GC) The number of League goals conceded while he was on the pitch	19	Clean Sheets In games when he played at least 70 minutes	6
Defensive Rating Ave number of mins between League goals conceded while on the pitch	90	Club Defensive Rating Average number of mins between League goals conceded by the club this season	73

	PLAYER	CON LGE	CLEAN SHEETS	DEF RATE
1	Morris Carrozzieri	19	6	90 mins
2	Stefano Sacchetti	18	6	84 mins
3	Stefano Bettarini	32	9	80 mins
4	Stefano Aimo Diana	37	9	76 mins

KEY GOALKEEPER

1 Francesco Antonioli

Goals Conceded in the League	36	Counting Games Games when he played at least 70 mins	29
Defensive Rating Ave number of mins between League goals conceded while on the pitch	71	Clean Sheets In games when he played at least 70 mins	8

LEAGUE GOALS

Fabio Bazzani

Minutes on the pitch	2877	Goals in the League	13
League average (mins between goals)	221		

	PLAYER	MINS	GOALS	AVE
1	Bazzani	2877	13	221
2	Flachi	1685	11	153
3	Doni	1733	6	289
4	Diana	2798	5	560
5	Flores	109	1	109
6	Volpi	2719	1	2719
	Other		3	
	TOTAL		40	

DISCIPLINARY RECORDS

	PLAYER	YELLOW	RED	AVE
1	Carrozzieri	10	1	155
2	Doni	8	0	216
3	Conte	7	1	225
4	Donati	5	1	226
5	Volpi	9	0	302
6	Sacchetti	5	0	303
7	Bettarini	8	0	320
8	Flachi	5	0	337
9	Falcone	4	0	593
10	Diana	4	0	699
11	Bazzani	4	0	719
12	Zenoni	2	0	887
13	Cipriani	1	0	915
	Other	5	0	
	TOTAL	77	3	

TOP POINT EARNERS

	PLAYER	GAMES	AV PTS
1	Donati	13	1.69
2	Zenoni	17	1.59
3	Falcone	25	1.52
4	Conte	20	1.50
5	Volpi	29	1.45
6	Antonioli	28	1.43
7	Bettarini	28	1.39
8	Bazzani	32	1.34
9	Flachi	13	1.31
10	Doni	17	1.29
	CLUB AVERAGE:		**1.35**

LEAGUE APPEARANCES, BOOKINGS AND CAPS

	AGE (on 01/07/04)	IN NAMED 18	APPEARANCES	COUNTING GAMES	MINUTES ON PITCH	YELLOW CARDS	RED CARDS	THIS SEASON	HOME COUNTRY
Goalkeepers									
Francesco Antonioli	34	31	29	28	2565	0	0	-	Italy
Luigi Turci	34	33	3	2	225	0	0	-	Italy
Defenders									
Stefano Bettarini	32	32	30	28	2565	8	0	1	Italy (11)
Morris Carrozzieri	23	28	25	16	1709	10	1	-	Italy
Mirko Conte	29	25	22	20	1806	7	1	-	Italy
Stefano Aimo Diana	26	33	33	29	2798	4	0	1	Italy (11)
Maurizio Domizzi	24	8	5	2	196	2	0	-	Italy
Guilio Falcone	30	28	28	25	2373	4	0	-	Italy
A Grandoni	26	3	2	2	180	0	0	-	Italy
Stefano Sacchetti	31	29	18	17	1519	5	0	-	Italy
Nenad Sakic	33	5	0	0	0	0	0	-	Serbia & Montenegro
Cristiano Zenoni	27	30	24	17	1774	2	0	-	Italy
Midfielders									
Luca Antonini	22	10	6	3	367	0	0	-	Italy
Massimo Donati	23	26	19	13	1356	5	1	-	Italy
Cristiano Doni	31	22	22	17	1733	8	0	-	Italy
Biagio Pagano	21	7	5	2	332	0	0	-	Italy
Angelo Palombo	22	33	31	20	2100	2	0	-	Italy
Francesco Pedone	36	22	10	1	309	1	0	-	Italy
Fabian Valtolina	33	10	5	0	70	0	0	-	Italy
Sergio Volpi	30	31	31	29	2719	9	0	1	Italy (11)
Bratislav Zivkovic	33	22	9	1	266	0	0	-	Serbia & Montenegro
Forwards									
Fabio Bazzani	27	32	32	32	2877	4	0	2	Italy (11)
Giacomo Cipriani	23	18	18	6	915	1	0	-	Italy
Corrado Colombo	24	5	2	0	40	0	0	-	Italy
Francesco Flachi	29	28	28	13	1685	5	0	-	Italy
Antonio Floro Flores	21	13	4	0	109	0	0	-	Italy
Herve Job Iyock	19	5	3	0	125	0	0	-	Cameroon
Massimo Marazzina	29	13	12	1	529	0	0	-	Italy
Atsushi Yanagisawa	27	25	15	0	417	0	0	-	Japan

TEAM OF THE SEASON

G Francesco Antonioli — **CG:** 28 **DR:** 71

D Morris Carrozzieri — **CG:** 16 **DR:** 90

D Stefano Sacchetti — **CG:** 17 **DR:** 84

D Stefano Bettarini — **CG:** 28 **DR:** 80

D Stefano Aimo Diana — **CG:** 29 **DR:** 76

M Massimo Donati — **CG:** 13 **SD:** 19

M Sergio Volpi — **CG:** 29 **SD:** -4

M Cristiano Doni — **CG:** 17 **SD:** -7

M Angelo Palombo — **CG:** 20 **SD:** -30

F Francesco Flachi — **CG:** 13 **SR:** 153

F Fabio Bazzani — **CG:** 32 **SR:** 221

SQUAD APPEARANCES

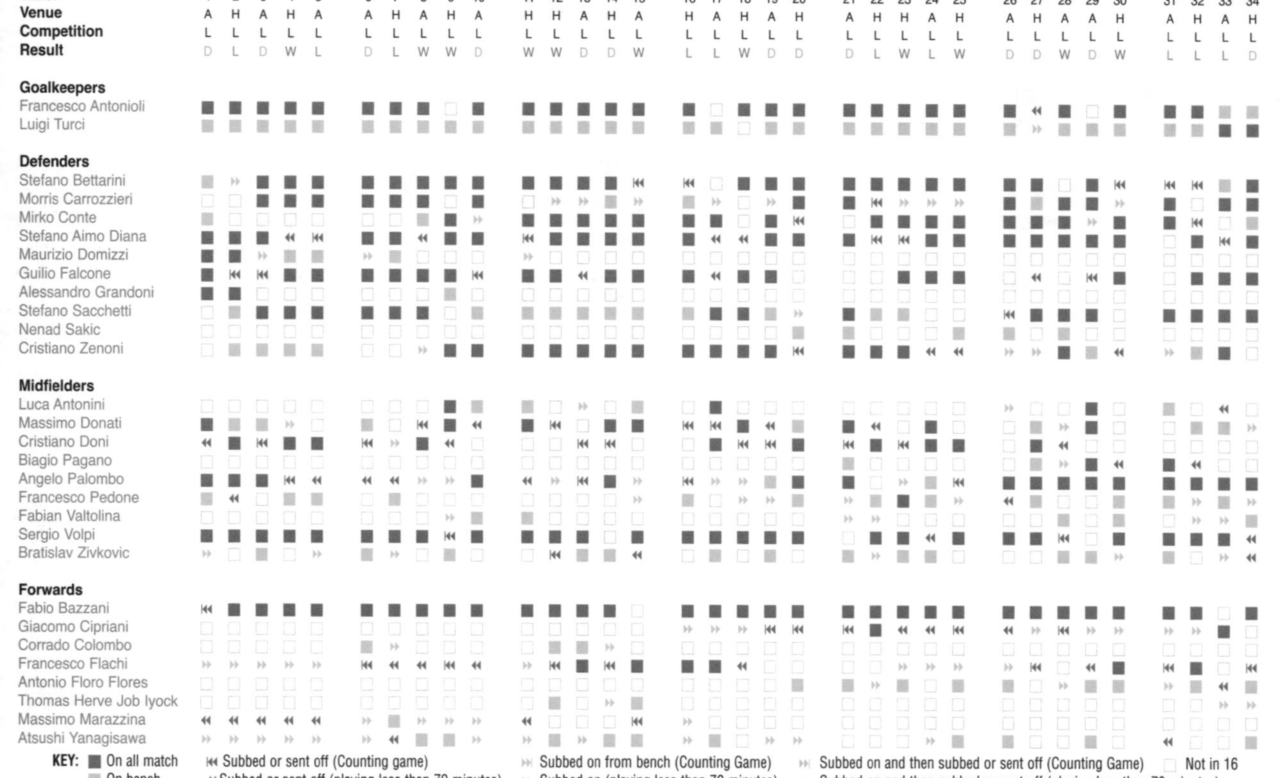

Match	1	2	3	4	5	6	7	8	9	10	11	12	13	14	15	16	17	18	19	20	21	22	23	24	25	26	27	28	29	30	31	32	33	34
Venue	A	H	A	H	A	A	H	A	H	A	H	H	A	H	A	H	A	H	A	H	A	H	H	A	H	A	H	A	A	H	A	H	A	H
Competition	L	L	L	L	L	L	L	L	L	L	L	L	L	L	L	L	L	L	L	L	L	L	L	L	L	L	L	L	L	L	L	L	L	L
Result	D	L	D	W	L	D	L	W	W	D	W	W	D	D	W	L	L	W	D	D	D	L	W	L	W	D	D	W	D	W	L	L	L	D

Goalkeepers
Francesco Antonioli
Luigi Turci

Defenders
Stefano Bettarini
Morris Carrozzieri
Mirko Conte
Stefano Aimo Diana
Maurizio Domizzi
Guilio Falcone
Alessandro Grandoni
Stefano Sacchetti
Nenad Sakic
Cristiano Zenoni

Midfielders
Luca Antonini
Massimo Donati
Cristiano Doni
Biagio Pagano
Angelo Palombo
Francesco Pedone
Fabian Valtolina
Sergio Volpi
Bratislav Zivkovic

Forwards
Fabio Bazzani
Giacomo Cipriani
Corrado Colombo
Francesco Flachi
Antonio Floro Flores
Thomas Herve Job Iyock
Massimo Marazzina
Atsushi Yanagisawa

KEY: On all match · On bench · Subbed or sent off (Counting game) · Subbed or sent off (playing less than 70 minutes) · Subbed on from bench (Counting Game) · Subbed on (playing less than 70 minutes) · Subbed on and then subbed or sent off (Counting Game) · Subbed on and then subbed or sent off (playing less than 70 minutes) · Not in 16

CHIEVO VERONA

Final Position: **9th**

KEY: ☐ Won ☐ Drawn ☐ Lost

							Attendance
1	lge	Brescia	A	D	1-1	Lanna 12	12,000
2	lge	Juventus	H	L	1-2	D'Anna 21 pen	34,600
3	lge	Lecce	A	W	2-1	Lanna 52; Cossato 71	16,140
4	lge	Perugia	H	W	4-1	Zanchetta 40,52 pen; Semioli 65; Santana 80	11,000
5	lge	Lazio	A	L	0-1		45,000
6	lge	Sampdoria	H	D	1-1	Amauri 25	13,890
7	lge	Empoli	A	W	1-0	Amauri 60	4,000
8	lge	Inter Milan	H	L	0-2		25,000
9	lge	Siena	A	W	2-1	Pellissier 28,48	11,000
10	lge	AC Milan	H	L	0-2		45,000
11	lge	Parma	A	L	1-3	Pellissier 74	12,000
12	lge	Roma	H	L	0-3		19,000
13	lge	Reggina	A	D	0-0		20,000
14	lge	Ancona	H	W	1-0	Cossato 42	11,000
15	lge	Modena	A	W	3-0	Cossato 41; Lanna 67; Barzagli 78	14,000
16	lge	Udinese	H	D	0-0		10,200
17	lge	Bologna	A	L	1-3	Santana 33	18,000
18	lge	Brescia	H	W	3-1	Barzagli 53; Santana 73; Sculli 84	11,594
19	lge	Juventus	A	L	0-1		30,100
20	lge	Lecce	H	L	2-3	Luciano 45; D'Anna 88 pen	10,137
21	lge	Perugia	A	W	2-0	Barzagli 67; Cossato 90	7,000
22	lge	Lazio	H	D	0-0		11,706
23	lge	Sampdoria	A	L	0-1		22,000
24	lge	Empoli	H	D	0-0		12,000
25	lge	Inter Milan	A	D	0-0		40,000
26	lge	Siena	H	D	1-1	D'Anna 69 pen	10,145
27	lge	AC Milan	A	D	2-2	Sculli 22; Perrotta 39	65,000
28	lge	Parma	H	L	0-2		16,000
29	lge	Roma	A	L	1-3	Cossato 32	23,000
30	lge	Reggina	H	D	0-0		9,964
31	lge	Ancona	A	W	2-0	Sala 58; Semioli 79	5,000
32	lge	Modena	H	W	2-0	Sala 70; Amauri 90	13,798
33	lge	Udinese	A	D	1-1	Amauri 33	13,000
34	lge	Bologna	H	W	2-1	Amauri 17; Zanchetta 22	13,338

MONTHLY POINTS TALLY

AUGUST	1	33%
SEPTEMBER	6	67%
OCTOBER	4	44%
NOVEMBER	3	25%
DECEMBER	4	44%
JANUARY	7	58%
FEBRUARY	4	27%
MARCH	4	33%
APRIL	4	33%
MAY	7	78%

KEY PLAYERS - GOALSCORERS

Carvalho De Oliveira Amauri

Goals in the League	6	Player Strike Rate Average number of minutes between League goals scored by player	323
Contribution to Attacking Power Average number of minutes between League team goals while on pitch	80	Club Strike Rate Average number of minutes between League goals scored by club	85

	PLAYER	LGE GOALS	POWER	STRIKE RATE
1	Carvalho De Oliveira Amauri	6	80	323 mins
2	Federico Cossato	5	81	490 mins
3	Mario Santana	3	78	679 mins
4	Luigi Sala	2	73	701 mins

KEY PLAYERS - MIDFIELDERS

Franco Semioli

Goals in the League	2	Contribution to Attacking Power Average number of minutes between League team goals while on pitch	75
Defensive Rating Average number of mins between League goals conceded while he was on the pitch	113	Scoring Difference Defensive Rating minus Contribution to Attacking Power	38

	PLAYER	LGE GOALS	DEF RATE	POWER	SCORE DIFF
1	Franco Semioli	2	113	75	38 mins
2	Mario Santana	3	102	78	24 mins
3	Simone Perrotta	1	83	91	-8 mins
4	Roberto Baronio	0	97	111	-14 mins

KEY PLAYERS - DEFENDERS

Salvatore Lanna

Goals Conceded (GC) The number of League goals conceded while he was on the pitch	31	Clean Sheets In games when he played at least 70 minutes	11
Defensive Rating Ave number of mins between League goals conceded while on the pitch	88	Club Defensive Rating Average number of mins between League goals conceded by the club this season	83

	PLAYER	CON LGE	CLEAN SHEETS	DEF RATE
1	Salvatore Lanna	31	11	88 mins
2	Lorenzo D'Anna	25	9	87 mins
3	Luigi Sala	17	4	82 mins
4	Andrea Barzagli	30	11	82 mins

KEY GOALKEEPER

1 Luca Marchegiani

Goals Conceded in the League	25	Counting Games Games when he played at least 70 mins	30
Defensive Rating Ave number of mins between League goals conceded while on the pitch	102	Clean Sheets In games when he played at least 70 mins	11

LEAGUE GOALS

Carvalho De Oliveira Amauri

Minutes on the pitch	1937	Goals in the League	6
League average (mins between goals)	323		

	PLAYER	MINS	GOALS	AVE
1	Amauri	1937	6	323
2	Cossato	2449	5	490
3	D'Anna	2169	3	723
4	Barzagli	2464	3	821
5	Lanna	2734	3	911
6	Pellissier	1046	3	349
7	Santana	2038	3	679
8	Sculli	831	2	416
9	Semioli	2034	2	1017
10	Sala	1401	2	701
11	Luciano	645	1	645
12	Perrotta	2728	1	2728
	Other		2	
	TOTAL		36	

DISCIPLINARY RECORDS

	PLAYER	YELLOW	RED	AVE
1	Malago	4	1	129
2	D'Anna	8	1	241
3	Perrotta	10	0	272
4	Morrone	3	0	279
5	Zanchetta	4	0	310
6	Amauri	5	0	387
7	Lanna	7	0	390
8	Moro	7	0	411
9	Sculli	2	0	415
10	Semioli	3	1	508
11	Baronio	2	1	516
12	Luciano	1	0	645
13	Sala	2	0	700
	Other	8	1	
	TOTAL	66	5	

TOP POINT EARNERS

	PLAYER	GAMES	AV PTS
1	Semioli	15	1.80
2	Santana	18	1.56
3	Amauri	15	1.53
4	Marchegiani	27	1.48
5	Sala	15	1.47
6	Cossato	25	1.40
7	Moro	32	1.31
8	Lanna	29	1.28
9	Barzagli	27	1.26
10	Perrotta	30	1.23
	CLUB AVERAGE:		1.29

LEAGUE APPEARANCES, BOOKINGS AND CAPS

	AGE (on 01/07/04)	IN NAMED 18	APPEARANCES	COUNTING GAMES	MINUTES ON PITCH	YELLOW CARDS	RED CARDS	THIS SEASON	HOME COUNTRY
Goalkeepers									
Giorgio Frezzolini	28	34	7	4	521	0	0	-	Italy
Guido Lippi	22	4	0	0	0	0	0	-	Italy
Luca Marchegiani	38	30	30	27	2540	1	1	-	Italy
Defenders									
Andrea Barzagli	23	34	29	27	2464	2	0	-	Italy
Simone Bonomi	23	8	2	0	65	0	0	-	Italy
Vinicio Cesar	25	6	1	1	90	0	0	-	Brazil
Maurizio D'Angelo	34	1	1	0	27	0	0	-	Italy
Lorenzo D'Anna	32	25	25	23	2169	8	1	-	Italy
Daniele Gastaldello	21	2	0	0	0	0	0	-	Italy
Salvatore Lanna	27	32	32	29	2734	7	0	-	Italy
Marco Malago	25	25	13	4	645	4	1	-	Italy
John Mensah	21	11	2	1	109	0	0	-	Ghana
Fabio Moro	28	33	32	32	2880	7	0	-	Italy
Emanuele Pesaresi	27	1	1	0	45	0	0	-	Italy
Luigi Sala	30	32	17	15	1401	2	0	-	Italy
Midfielders									
Roberto Baronio	26	26	21	14	1549	2	1	-	Italy
I De Franceschi	30	10	2	0	100	0	0	-	Italy
D Franceschini	28	10	8	1	300	0	0	-	Italy
Siqueira Luciano	28	12	12	3	645	1	0	-	Brazil
Stefano Morrone	25	30	20	6	837	3	0	-	Italy
Simone Perrotta	26	31	31	30	2728	10	0	10	Italy (11)
Mario Santana	22	28	28	18	2038	2	0	-	Argentina
Franco Semioli	24	31	31	15	2034	3	1	-	Italy
Andrea Zanchetta	29	23	19	8	1241	4	0	-	Italy
Forwards									
Carvalho Amauri	24	35	30	15	1937	5	0	-	Italy
Federico Cossato	31	31	31	25	2449	2	0	-	Italy
Sergio Pellissier	25	30	25	3	1046	1	0	-	Italy
Mauricio Pinilla	20	7	4	0	73	0	0	-	Chile
Diego Silva Reis	22	2	0	0	0	0	0	-	Brazil
Giuseppe Sculli	23	29	17	5	831	2	0	-	Italy

TEAM OF THE SEASON

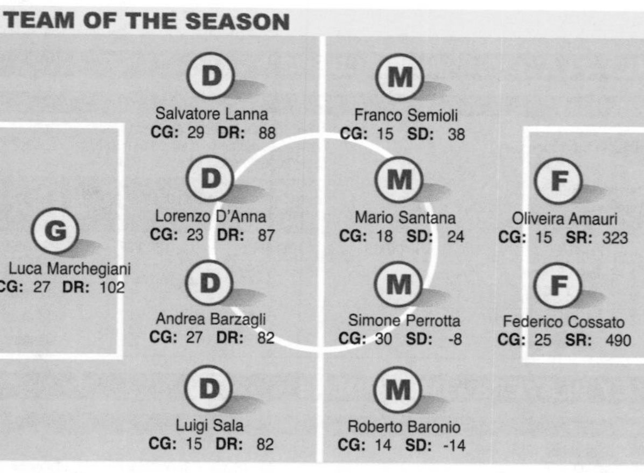

G
Luca Marchegiani
CG: 27 DR: 102
D
Salvatore Lanna
CG: 29 DR: 88
D
Lorenzo D'Anna
CG: 23 DR: 87
D
Andrea Barzagli
CG: 27 DR: 82
D
Luigi Sala
CG: 15 DR: 82
M
Franco Semioli
CG: 15 SD: 38
M
Mario Santana
CG: 18 SD: 24
M
Simone Perrotta
CG: 30 SD: -8
M
Roberto Baronio
CG: 14 SD: -14
F
Oliveira Amauri
CG: 15 SR: 323
F
Federico Cossato
CG: 25 SR: 490

SQUAD APPEARANCES

Match	1	2	3	4	5	6	7	8	9	10	11	12	13	14	15	16	17	18	19	20	21	22	23	24	25	26	27	28	29	30	31	32	33	34
Venue	A	H	A	H	A	H	A	H	A	H	A	H	A	H	A	H	A	H	A	H	A	H	A	H	A	H	A	H	A	H	A	H	A	H
Competition	L	L	L	L	L	L	L	L	L	L	L	L	L	L	L	L	L	L	L	L	L	L	L	L	L	L	L	L	L	L	L	L	L	L
Result	D	L	W	W	L	D	W	L	W	L	L	L	D	W	W	D	L	W	L	L	W	D	L	D	D	D	D	L	L	D	W	W	D	W

Goalkeepers
Giorgio Frezzolini
Guido Lippi
Luca Marchegiani

Defenders
Andrea Barzagli
Simone Bonomi
Vinicio Cesar
Maurizio D'Angelo
Lorenzo D'Anna
Daniele Gastaldello
Salvatore Lanna
Marco Malago
John Mensah
Fabio Moro
Emanuele Pesaresi
Luigi Sala

Midfielders
Roberto Baronio
Ivone De Franceschi
Daniele Franceschini
Siqueira de Oliveira Luciano
Stefano Morrone
Simone Perrotta
Mario Santana
Franco Semioli
Andrea Zanchetta

Forwards
Carvalho De Oliveira Amauri
Federico Cossato
Sergio Pellissier
Mauricio Pinilla
Diego Silva Reis
Giuseppe Sculli

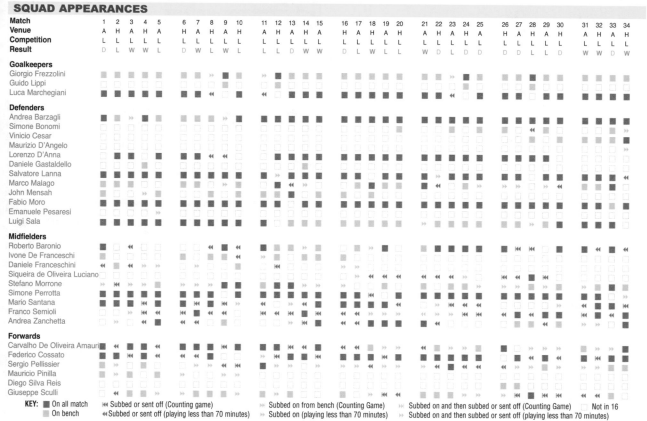

KEY: On all match; On bench; Subbed or sent off (Counting game); Subbed or sent off (playing less than 70 minutes); Subbed on from bench (Counting Game); Subbed on (playing less than 70 minutes); Subbed on and then subbed or sent off (Counting Game); Subbed on and then subbed or sent off (playing less than 70 minutes); Not in 16

LECCE

Final Position: **10th**

KEY: Won Drawn Lost

							Attendance
1	lge	**Lazio**	A	L	1-4	Konan 50	44,000
2	lge	**Ancona**	H	W	3-1	Siviglia 34; Vucinic 79; Cassetti 84	13,780
3	lge	**Chievo**	H	L	1-2	Chevanton 57	16,140
4	lge	**AC Milan**	A	L	0-3		64,000
5	lge	**Brescia**	H	L	1-4	Cassetti 33	13,081
6	lge	**Modena**	A	L	0-2		15,850
7	lge	**Siena**	A	L	1-2	Chevanton 9	11,000
8	lge	**Empoli**	H	W	2-1	Chevanton 2 pen,43	9,462
9	lge	**Perugia**	A	D	2-2	Chevanton 6; Ledesma 56	10,000
10	lge	**Sampdoria**	H	D	0-0		13,760
11	lge	**Roma**	A	L	1-3	Chevanton 88	50,000
12	lge	**Parma**	H	L	1-2	Chevanton 70 pen	10,633
13	lge	**Udinese**	A	L	0-1		17,000
14	lge	**Juventus**	H	D	1-1	Konan 24	30,325
15	lge	**Inter Milan**	A	L	1-3	Bovo 3	55,000
16	lge	**Bologna**	H	L	1-2	Bojinov 22	12,000
17	lge	**Reggina**	A	W	3-1	Bojinov 2,59; Chevanton 4	20,000
18	lge	**Lazio**	H	L	0-1		10,834
19	lge	**Ancona**	A	W	2-0	Chevanton 1; Konan 61	13,000
20	lge	**Chievo**	A	W	3-2	Barzagli 17 og; Chevanton 21; Cassetti 57	10,137
21	lge	**AC Milan**	H	D	1-1	Chevanton 19	31,427
22	lge	**Brescia**	A	W	2-1	Chevanton 13; Cassetti 88	13,000
23	lge	**Modena**	H	W	1-0	Chevanton 22 pen	14,500
24	lge	**Siena**	H	D	0-0		12,500
25	lge	**Empoli**	A	D	0-0		5,000
26	lge	**Perugia**	H	L	1-2	Dalmat 86	7,092
27	lge	**Sampdoria**	A	D	2-2	Chevanton 37 pen; Konan 90	24,000
28	lge	**Roma**	H	L	0-3		12,000
29	lge	**Parma**	A	L	1-3	Chevanton 63	24,000
30	lge	**Udinese**	H	W	2-1	Cassetti 44; Chevanton 85	
31	lge	**Juventus**	A	W	4-3	Franceschini 24; Konan 30,44; Chevanton 52	20,000
32	lge	**Inter Milan**	H	W	2-1	Tonetto 48; Bovo 71	21,296
33	lge	**Bologna**	A	D	1-1	Chevanton 90	28,000
34	lge	**Reggina**	H	W	2-1	Chevanton 11; Franceschini 38	16,125

MONTHLY POINTS TALLY

AUGUST	0	0%
SEPTEMBER	3	33%
OCTOBER	0	0%
NOVEMBER	5	42%
DECEMBER	1	11%
JANUARY	3	25%
FEBRUARY	13	87%
MARCH	3	25%
APRIL	6	50%
MAY	7	78%

KEY PLAYERS - GOALSCORERS

Ernesto Javier Chevanton

Goals in the League	19	**Player Strike Rate** Average number of minutes between League goals scored by player	137
Contribution to Attacking Power Average number of minutes between League team goals while on pitch	68	**Club Strike Rate** Average number of minutes between League goals scored by club	71

	PLAYER	LGE GOALS	POWER	STRIKE RATE
1	Ernesto Javier Chevanton	19	68	137 mins
2	Marco Cassetti	5	67	472 mins
3	Cesare Bovo	2	70	850 mins
4	Cristian Daniel Ledesma	1	67	2613 mins

KEY PLAYERS - MIDFIELDERS

Jorge Bolano

Goals in the League	0	**Contribution to Attacking Power** Average number of minutes between League team goals while on pitch	62
Defensive Rating Average number of mins between League goals conceded while he was on the pitch	59	**Scoring Difference** Defensive Rating minus Contribution to Attacking Power	-3

	PLAYER	LGE GOALS	DEF RATE	POWER	SCORE DIFF
1	Jorge Bolano	0	59	62	-3 mins
2	Marco Cassetti	5	55	67	-12 mins
3	Cristian Daniel Ledesma	1	54	67	-13 mins
4	Luigi Piangarelli	0	50	106	-56 mins

KEY PLAYERS - DEFENDERS

Cesare Bovo

Goals Conceded (GC) The number of League goals conceded while he was on the pitch	28	**Clean Sheets** In games when he played at least 70 minutes	4
Defensive Rating Ave number of mins between League goals conceded while on the pitch	61	**Club Defensive Rating** Average number of mins between League goals conceded by the club this season	55

	PLAYER	CON LGE	CLEAN SHEETS	DEF RATE
1	Cesare Bovo	28	4	61 mins
2	Sebastiano Siviglia	48	4	57 mins
3	Lorenzo Stovini	54	5	56 mins
4	Giuseppe Abruzzese	34	4	56 mins

KEY GOALKEEPER

1 Vincenzo Sicignano

Goals Conceded in the League	22	**Counting Games** Games when he played at least 70 mins	17
Defensive Rating Ave number of mins between League goals conceded while on the pitch	69	**Clean Sheets** In games when he played at least 70 mins	4

LEAGUE GOALS

Ernesto Javier Chevanton

Minutes on the pitch	2597	Goals in the League	19
League average (mins between goals)	137		

	PLAYER	MINS	GOALS	AVE
1	Chevanton	2597	19	137
2	Konan	1771	6	295
3	Cassetti	2362	5	472
4	Bojinov	1267	3	422
5	Bovo	1699	2	850
6	Franceschini	1168	2	584
7	Vucinic	486	1	486
8	Tonetto	2953	1	2953
9	Ledesma	2613	1	2613
10	Dalmat	146	1	146
11	Siviglia	2728	1	2728
	Other		1	
	TOTAL		43	

DISCIPLINARY RECORDS

	PLAYER	YELLOW	RED	AVE
1	Bolano	8	0	140
2	Piangarelli	5	0	211
3	Chevanton	9	0	288
4	Konan	5	1	295
5	Abruzzese	6	0	315
6	Bovo	5	0	339
7	Ledesma	6	1	373
8	Siviglia	7	0	389
9	Tonetto	7	0	421
10	Silvestri	3	0	452
11	Cassetti	4	1	472
12	Vucinic	1	0	486
13	Giacomazzi	2	0	492
	Other	11	1	
	TOTAL	79	4	

TOP POINT EARNERS

	PLAYER	GAMES	AV PTS
1	Sicignano	17	1.88
2	Bovo	19	1.37
3	Cassetti	25	1.32
4	Abruzzese	19	1.21
5	Stovini	34	1.21
6	Chevanton	27	1.19
7	Konan	12	1.17
8	Siviglia	30	1.17
9	Ledesma	29	1.17
10	Tonetto	33	1.15
	CLUB AVERAGE:		1.21

TEAM OF THE SEASON

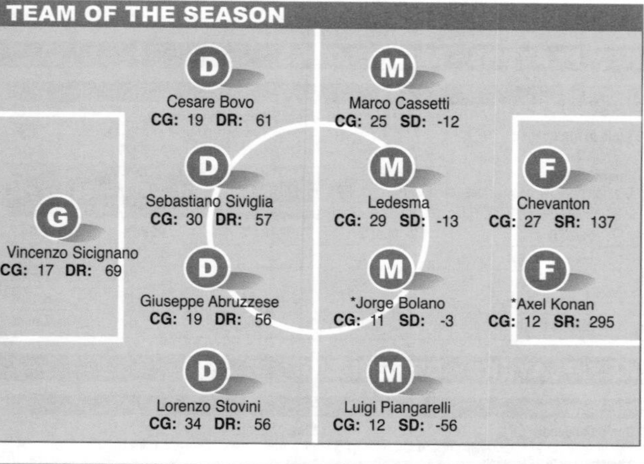

D
Cesare Bovo
CG: 19 DR: 61
M
Marco Cassetti
CG: 25 SD: -12
D
Sebastiano Siviglia
CG: 30 DR: 57
M
Ledesma
CG: 29 SD: -13
F
Chevanton
CG: 27 SR: 137
G
Vincenzo Sicignano
CG: 17 DR: 69
D
Giuseppe Abruzzese
CG: 19 DR: 56
M
*Jorge Bolano
CG: 11 SD: -3
F
*Axel Konan
CG: 12 SR: 295
D
Lorenzo Stovini
CG: 34 DR: 56
M
Luigi Piangarelli
CG: 12 SD: -56

LEAGUE APPEARANCES, BOOKINGS AND CAPS

	AGE (on 01/07/04)	IN NAMED 18	APPEARANCES	COUNTING GAMES	MINUTES ON PITCH	YELLOW CARDS	RED CARDS	THIS SEASON	HOME COUNTRY
Goalkeepers									
Marco Amelia	22	17	14	13	1230	1	0	-	Italy
Andrea Panico	25	1	0	0	0	0	0	-	Italy
Vukasin Poleksic	21	33	5	3	319	0	1	-	Serbia & Montenegro
Vincenzo Sicignano	30	17	17	17	1511	2	0	-	Italy
Defenders									
G Abruzzese	23	33	26	19	1892	6	0	-	Italy
Cesare Bovo	21	31	19	19	1699	5	0	-	Italy
Andrea Esposito	18	1	1	0	40	0	0	-	Italy
Arnaud Kouyo	20	10	1	0	1	0	0	-	Ivory Coast
Erminio Rullo	20	17	11	2	395	0	0	-	Italy
Alberto Savino	30	7	0	0	0	0	0	-	Italy
Cristian Silvestri	29	34	16	15	1357	3	0	-	Italy
Sebastiano Siviglia	31	31	31	30	2728	7	0	-	Italy
M Stendardo	-	1	0	0	0	0	0	-	Italy
Lorenzo Stovini	27	34	34	34	3041	4	0	-	Italy
Midfielders									
Philippe Billy	22	17	3	0	42	0	0	-	France
Jorge Bolano	27	16	16	11	1121	8	0	-	Colombia
Alessandro Budel	23	14	7	2	325	0	0	-	Italy
Marco Cassetti	27	30	30	25	2362	4	1	-	Italy
Drissa Diarra	18	4	3	0	49	0	0	-	Ivory Coast
D Franceschini	28	15	15	10	1168	2	0	-	Italy
G Giacomazzi	26	31	23	9	984	2	0	-	Uruguay
Cristian Ledesma	25	31	30	29	2613	6	1	-	Argentina
Nicola Mariniello	27	10	6	2	328	0	0	-	Italy
Luigi Piangarelli	30	12	12	12	1055	5	0	-	Italy
Marco Testa	21	2	0	0	0	0	0	-	Italy
Mirko Vucinic	20	14	13	2	486	1	0	-	Serbia & Montenegro
Djuric Winklaar	22	1	0	0	0	0	0	-	Holland
Forwards									
Emilov Bojinov	18	32	27	5	1267	2	0	-	Bulgaria
Ernesto Chevanton	23	31	31	27	2597	9	0	7	Uruguay (25)
Sebastjan Cimirotic	29	2	0	0	0	0	0	-	Slovenia
Wilfried Dalmat	21	14	7	0	146	0	0	-	France
Axel Cedric Konan	21	32	32	12	1771	5	1	-	Ivory Coast
Graziano Pelle	18	3	2	0	37	0	0	-	Italy
Max Tonetto	29	33	33	33	2953	7	0	-	Italy

SQUAD APPEARANCES

Match	1	2	3	4	5	6	7	8	9	10	11	12	13	14	15	16	17	18	19	20	21	22	23	24	25	26	27	28	29	30	31	32	33	34
Venue	A	H	H	A	H	A	A	H	A	H	A	H	A	H	A	H	A	H	A	A	H	A	H	H	A	H	A	H	A	H	A	H	A	H
Competition	L	L	L	L	L	L	L	L	L	L	L	L	L	L	L	L	L	L	L	L	L	L	L	L	L	L	L	L	L	L	L	L	L	L
Result	L	W	L	L	L	L	L	W	D	D	L	L	L	D	L	L	W	L	W	W	D	W	W	D	D	L	D	L	L	W	W	W	D	W

Goalkeepers
Marco Amelia
Andrea Panico
Vukasin Rodomir Poleksic
Vincenzo Sicignano

Defenders
Giuseppe Abruzzese
Cesare Bovo
Andrea Esposito
Arnaud Kouyo
Erminio Rullo
Alberto Savino
Cristian Silvestri
Sebastiano Siviglia
Mariano Stendardo
Lorenzo Stovini

Midfielders
Philippe Billy
Jorge Bolano
Alessandro Budel
Marco Cassetti
Drissa Diarra
Daniele Franceschini
Guillermo Giacomazzi
Cristian Daniel Ledesma
Nicola Mariniello
Luigi Piangarelli
Marco Testa
Mirko Vucinic
Djuric Winklaar

Forwards
Emilov Valeri Bojinov
Ernesto Javier Chevanton
Sebastjan Cimirotic
Wilfried Dalmat
Hauillas Axel Cedric Konan
Graziano Pelle
Max Tonetto

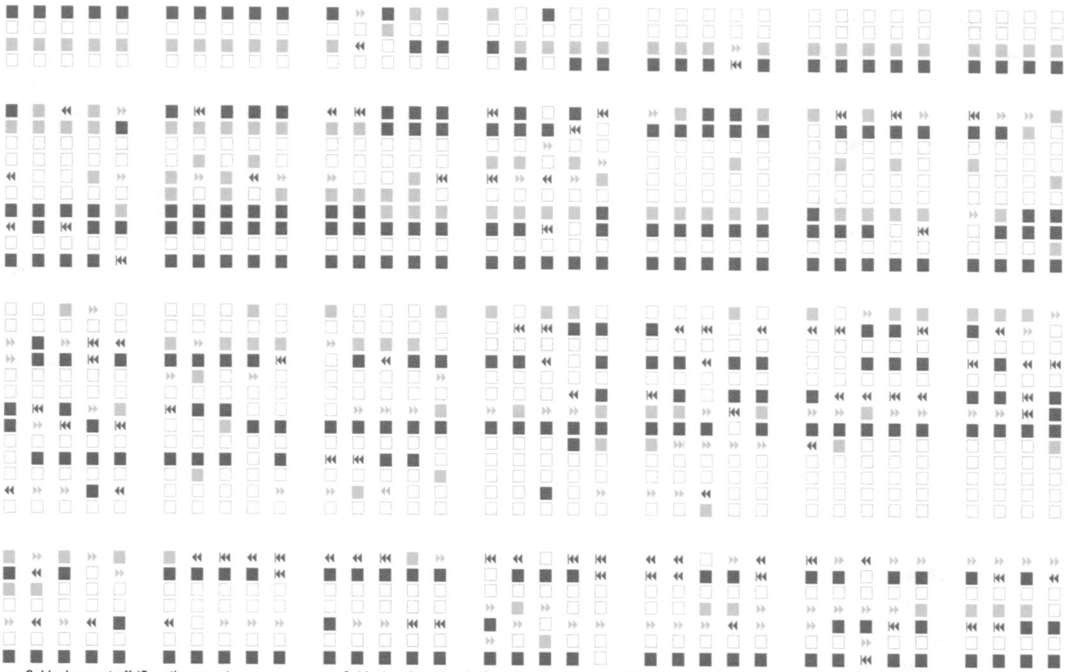

KEY: ■ On all match; ■ On bench; ⏮ Subbed or sent off (Counting game); « Subbed or sent off (playing less than 70 minutes); ⏭ Subbed on from bench (Counting Game); » Subbed on (playing less than 70 minutes); ⏯ Subbed on and then subbed or sent off (Counting Game); ⏯ Subbed on and then subbed or sent off (playing less than 70 minutes); □ Not in 16

BRESCIA

Final Position: **11th**

KEY: Won Drawn Lost

							Attendance
1	lge	Chievo	H	D	1-1	Filippini 57 pen	12,000
2	lge	Roma	A	L	0-5		50,000
3	lge	Reggina	H	D	4-4	di Biagio 10; Caracciolo 52; Filippini 54; Petruzzi 87	16,000
4	lge	Sampdoria	A	L	1-2	Mauri 68	27,000
5	lge	Lecce	A	W	4-1	Caracciolo 7,69,84; Baggio 86	13,081
6	lge	Inter Milan	H	D	2-2	Baggio 21; Caracciolo 47	25,000
7	lge	Juventus	A	L	0-2		32,360
8	lge	Parma	H	L	2-3	Matuzalem 4; Di Biagio 37	16,000
9	lge	Bologna	H	D	0-0		15,000
10	lge	Ancona	A	D	1-1	Baggio 5	11,703
11	lge	Udinese	H	L	1-2	Caracciolo 66	14,000
12	lge	Modena	A	D	1-1	Bachini 84	14,000
13	lge	Empoli	H	W	2-0	Mauri 15; di Biagio 20	13,000
14	lge	Perugia	A	D	2-2	Di Biagio 10; Filippini 77	12,000
15	lge	Siena	H	W	4-2	Mauri 16,87; Baggio 21,52	20,000
16	lge	Lazio	A	W	1-0	Di Biagio 4	45,000
17	lge	AC Milan	H	L	0-1		26,000
18	lge	Chievo	A	L	1-3	Caracciolo 10	11,594
19	lge	Roma	H	W	1-0	Bachini 43 pen	18,000
20	lge	Reggina	A	D	0-0		19,783
21	lge	Sampdoria	H	D	1-1	Caracciolo 5	13,000
22	lge	Lecce	H	L	1-2	Baggio 90	13,000
23	lge	Inter Milan	A	W	3-1	Caracciolo 69; Del Nero 73; Helveg 82 og	45,000
24	lge	Juventus	H	L	2-3	Mauri 3; Caracciolo 39	22,000
25	lge	Parma	A	D	2-2	Di Biagio 31; Baggio 74	15,000
26	lge	Bologna	A	L	0-3		22,000
27	lge	Ancona	H	W	5-2	Baggio 23,83; Mauri 30; Colucci 45; Caracciolo 75	10,000
28	lge	Udinese	A	L	3-4	Baggio 45; Di Biagio 46; Maniero 59	16,000
29	lge	Modena	H	D	0-0		9,000
30	lge	Empoli	A	D	1-1	Ficini 37 og	5,000
31	lge	Perugia	H	D	1-1	Baggio 45	10,000
32	lge	Siena	A	W	1-0	Brighi 62	11,000
33	lge	Lazio	H	W	2-1	Mauri 80; Baggio 89	20,000
34	lge	AC Milan	A	L	2-4	Matuzalem 53,69	80,000

MONTHLY POINTS TALLY

Month	Points	%
AUGUST	1	33%
SEPTEMBER	1	11%
OCTOBER	4	44%
NOVEMBER	2	17%
DECEMBER	5	56%
JANUARY	9	60%
FEBRUARY	5	42%
MARCH	4	33%
APRIL	3	25%
MAY	6	67%

KEY PLAYERS - GOALSCORERS

Roberto Baggio

Goals in the League	12	Player Strike Rate Average number of minutes between League goals scored by player	186
Contribution to Attacking Power Average number of minutes between League team goals while on pitch	57	Club Strike Rate Average number of minutes between League goals scored by club	59

	PLAYER	LGE GOALS	POWER	STRIKE RATE
1	Roberto Baggio	12	57	186 mins
2	Andrea Caracciolo	11	62	222 mins
3	Stefano Mauri	7	64	339 mins
4	Luigi Di Biagio	6	58	436 mins

KEY PLAYERS - MIDFIELDERS

Luigi Di Biagio

Goals in the League	6	Contribution to Attacking Power Average number of minutes between League team goals while on pitch	58
Defensive Rating Average number of mins between League goals conceded while he was on the pitch	57	Scoring Difference Defensive Rating minus Contribution to Attacking Power	-1

	PLAYER	LGE GOALS	DEF RATE	POWER	SCORE DIFF
1	Luigi Di Biagio	6	57	58	-1 mins
2	Antonio Filippini	3	53	55	-2 mins
3	Jonathan Bachini	2	60	66	-6 mins
4	Matteo Brighi	1	59	66	-7 mins

KEY PLAYERS - DEFENDERS

Paoli Castellini

Goals Conceded (GC) The number of League goals conceded while he was on the pitch	25	Clean Sheets In games when he played at least 70 minutes	4
Defensive Rating Ave number of mins between League goals conceded while on the pitch	58	Club Defensive Rating Average number of mins between League goals conceded by the club this season	54

	PLAYER	CON LGE	CLEAN SHEETS	DEF RATE
1	Paoli Castellini	25	4	58 mins
2	Dario Dainelli	52	6	54 mins
3	Gilberto Martinez	47	4	54 mins
4	Fabio Petruzzi	34	2	45 mins

KEY GOALKEEPER

1 Federico Agliardi

Goals Conceded in the League	24	Counting Games Games when he played at least 70 mins	18
Defensive Rating Ave number of mins between League goals conceded while on the pitch	65	Clean Sheets In games when he played at least 70 mins	6

LEAGUE GOALS

Roberto Baggio

Minutes on the pitch	2227	Goals in the League	12
League average (mins between goals)	186		

	PLAYER	MINS	GOALS	AVE
1	Baggio	2227	12	186
2	Caracciolo	2441	11	222
3	Mauri	2375	7	339
4	Di Biagio	2613	6	436
5	Filippini	1313	3	438
6	Matuzalem	2621	3	874
7	Bachini	1511	2	756
8	Del Nero	673	1	673
9	Brighi	2188	1	2188
10	Colucci	640	1	640
11	Petruzzi	1520	1	1520
12	Maniero	637	1	637
	Other		3	
	TOTAL		52	

DISCIPLINARY RECORDS

	PLAYER	YELLOW	RED	AVE
1	Del Nero	5	0	134
2	Stankevicius	3	1	135
3	Petruzzi	8	3	138
4	Brighi	9	1	218
5	Schopp	3	0	249
6	Di Biagio	9	0	290
7	Colucci	1	1	320
8	Matuzalem	5	2	374
9	Mauri	5	0	475
10	Caracciolo	4	1	488
11	Dainelli	3	1	697
12	Castellini	2	0	720
13	Castellazzi	1	0	1219
	Other	5	0	
	TOTAL	63	10	

TOP POINT EARNERS

	PLAYER	GAMES	AV PTS
1	Bachini	14	1.43
2	Brighi	23	1.35
3	Filippini	13	1.31
4	Caracciolo	26	1.31
5	Castellini	16	1.31
6	Di Biagio	28	1.25
7	Mauri	24	1.25
8	Castellazzi	13	1.23
9	Dainelli	31	1.16
10	Martinez	27	1.15
	CLUB AVERAGE:		**1.18**

TEAM OF THE SEASON

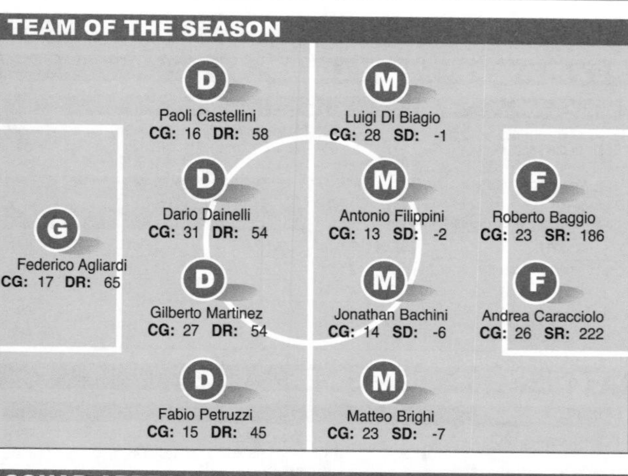
D
Paoli Castellini
CG: 16 DR: 58
D
Dario Dainelli
CG: 31 DR: 54
D
Gilberto Martinez
CG: 27 DR: 54
D
Fabio Petruzzi
CG: 15 DR: 45
M
Luigi Di Biagio
CG: 28 SD: -1
M
Antonio Filippini
CG: 13 SD: -2
M
Jonathan Bachini
CG: 14 SD: -6
M
Matteo Brighi
CG: 23 SD: -7
G
Federico Agliardi
CG: 17 DR: 65
F
Roberto Baggio
CG: 23 SR: 186
F
Andrea Caracciolo
CG: 26 SR: 222

LEAGUE APPEARANCES, BOOKINGS AND CAPS

	AGE (on 01/07/04)	IN NAMED 18	APPEARANCES	COUNTING GAMES	MINUTES ON PITCH	YELLOW CARDS	RED CARDS	THIS SEASON	HOME COUNTRY
Goalkeepers									
Federico Agliardi	21	27	18	17	1571	1	0	-	Italy
Luca Castellazzi	28	29	14	13	1219	1	0	-	Italy
Diego Saja	25	9	4	4	360	0	0	-	Argentina
Emliano Viviano	18	2	0	0	0	0	0	-	Italy
Defenders									
Paoli Castellini	25	16	16	16	1440	2	0	-	Italy
Dario Dainelli	25	31	31	31	2790	3	1	-	Italy
Victor Mareco	20	20	10	7	714	0	0	-	Paraguay
Gilberto Martinez	25	30	30	27	2547	2	0	-	Costa Rica
G Paganotto	19	1	0	0	0	0	0	-	Italy
Fabio Petruzzi	33	24	20	15	1520	8	3	-	Italy
Marco Pisano	22	9	8	7	640	0	0	-	Italy
M Stankevicius	22	30	15	3	540	3	1	-	Lithuania
Midfielders									
Jonathan Bachini	29	31	25	14	1511	0	0	-	Italy
Matteo Brighi	23	29	28	23	2188	9	1	-	Italy
Giuseppe Colucci	23	20	16	3	640	1	1	-	Italy
A Rodriguez	24	17	5	0	51	0	0	-	Uruguay
Luigi Di Biagio	33	30	30	28	2613	9	0	-	Italy
Antonio Filippini	31	16	16	13	1313	1	0	-	Italy
Roberto Guana	23	23	5	1	122	0	0	-	Italy
F Matuzalem	24	30	30	29	2621	5	2	-	Brazil
Stefano Mauri	24	31	30	24	2375	5	0	-	Italy
Diego Pedrocca	20	1	0	0	0	0	0	-	Italy
Markus Schopp	30	28	20	3	748	3	0	-	Austria
Andres Yllana	29	1	0	0	0	0	0	-	italy
Forwards									
Andrea Alberti	19	3	0	0	0	0	0	-	Italy
Roberto Baggio	37	27	27	23	2227	1	0	-	Italy
Andrea Caracciolo	22	31	31	26	2441	4	1	-	Italy
Simone Del Nero	22	26	21	2	673	5	0	-	Italy
Raul Gonzales	28	4	2	0	13	0	0	-	Italy
Abderrazak Jadid	21	1	0	0	0	0	0	-	Morocco
Filippo Maniero	31	26	17	3	637	0	0	-	Italy
Mattia Turetta	20	2	0	0	0	0	0	-	Italy

SQUAD APPEARANCES

Match	1	2	3	4	5	6	7	8	9	10	11	12	13	14	15	16	17	18	19	20	21	22	23	24	25	26	27	28	29	30	31	32	33	34
Venue	H	A	H	A	A	H	A	H	H	A	H	A	H	A	H	A	H	A	H	A	H	H	A	H	A	A	H	A	H	A	H	A	H	A
Competition	L	L	L	L	L	L	L	L	L	L	L	L	L	L	L	L	L	L	L	L	L	L	L	L	L	L	L	L	L	L	L	L	L	L
Result	D	L	D	L	W	D	L	L	D	D	L	D	W	D	W	W	L	L	W	D	D	L	W	L	D	L	W	L	D	D	D	W	W	L

Goalkeepers
Federico Agliardi
Luca Castellazzi
Diego Sebastian Saja
Emliano Viviano

Defenders
Paoli Castellini
Dario Dainelli
Victor Hugo Mareco
Gilberto Martinez
Giordano Paganotto
Fabio Petruzzi
Marco Pisano
Marius Stankevicius

Midfielders
Jonathan Bachini
Matteo Brighi
Giuseppe Colucci
Alejandro Rodriguez
Luigi Di Biagio
Antonio Filippini
Roberto Guana
Francelino Matuzalem
Stefano Mauri
Diego Pedrocca
Markus Schopp
Andres Yllana

Forwards
Andrea Alberti
Roberto Baggio
Andrea Caracciolo
Simone Del Nero
Raul Gonzales
Abderrazak Jadid
Filippo Maniero
Mattia Turetta

KEY: On all match | On bench | Subbed or sent off (Counting game) | Subbed or sent off (playing less than 70 minutes) | Subbed on from bench (Counting Game) | Subbed on (playing less than 70 minutes) | Subbed on and then subbed or sent off (Counting Game) | Subbed on and then subbed or sent off (playing less than 70 minutes) | Not in 16

BOLOGNA

Final Position: **12th**

KEY: Won Drawn Lost

							Attendance
1	lge	Parma	H	D	2-2	Guly 8; Locatelli 78	18,000
2	lge	AC Milan	A	L	1-2	Nervo 32	55,000
3	lge	Udinese	H	W	2-0	Guly 63; Dalla Bona 90 pen	20,000
4	lge	Modena	A	L	0-2		19,000
5	lge	Juventus	A	L	1-2	Signori 25 pen	31,493
6	lge	Perugia	H	D	2-2	Dalla Bona 72; Rossini 77	17,000
7	lge	Lazio	A	L	1-2	Dabo 87 og	45,300
8	lge	Sampdoria	H	L	0-1		22,000
9	lge	Brescia	A	D	0-0		15,000
10	lge	Roma	H	L	0-4		34,000
11	lge	Reggina	A	D	0-0		20,000
12	lge	Ancona	H	W	3-2	Bilica 2 og; Nervo 28; Signori 48	20,000
13	lge	Inter Milan	H	L	0-2		32,000
14	lge	Siena	A	D	0-0		9,000
15	lge	Empoli	H	W	2-1	Bellucci 30; Pecchia 75	20,000
16	lge	Lecce	A	W	2-1	Pecchia 12; Tare 76	12,000
17	lge	Chievo	H	W	3-1	Signori 2; Tare 17; Nervo 44	18,000
18	lge	Parma	A	D	0-0		13,000
19	lge	AC Milan	H	L	0-2		36,000
20	lge	Udinese	A	W	3-1	Locatelli 22; Nakata 48; Colucci 89	13,000
21	lge	Modena	H	D	1-1	Locatelli 35	29,000
22	lge	Juventus	H	L	0-1		36,000
23	lge	Perugia	A	L	2-4	Bellucci 61,86	7,000
24	lge	Sampdoria	A	L	2-3	Signori 10; Nervo 69	25,000
25	lge	Brescia	H	W	3-0	Tare 40; Nervo 70; Signori 80	22,000
26	lge	Lazio	H	W	2-1	Signori 34; Amoroso 64	15,000
27	lge	Roma	A	W	2-1	Pecchia 25; Tare 78	44,123
28	lge	Reggina	H	D	2-2	Locatelli 43; Bellucci 68	25,000
29	lge	Ancona	A	L	2-3	Nakata 12; Tare 64	11,000
30	lge	Inter Milan	A	L	2-4	Bellucci 67,76	40,000
31	lge	Siena	H	W	3-1	Dalla Bona 32; Bellucci 63; Nervo 83	20,000
32	lge	Empoli	A	L	0-2		10,000
33	lge	Lecce	H	D	1-1	Tare 34	28,000
34	lge	Chievo	A	L	1-2	Pecchia 12	13,338

MONTHLY POINTS TALLY

Month	Points	%
AUGUST	1	33%
SEPTEMBER	3	33%
OCTOBER	1	11%
NOVEMBER	2	17%
DECEMBER	4	44%
JANUARY	10	83%
FEBRUARY	4	27%
MARCH	9	75%
APRIL	4	33%
MAY	1	11%

KEY PLAYERS - GOALSCORERS

Guiseppe Signori

Goals in the League	6	Player Strike Rate: Average number of minutes between League goals scored by player	302
Contribution to Attacking Power: Average number of minutes between League team goals while on pitch	67	Club Strike Rate: Average number of minutes between League goals scored by club	68

	PLAYER	LGE GOALS	POWER	STRIKE RATE
1	Guiseppe Signori	6	67	302 mins
2	Igli Tare	6	67	349 mins
3	Carlo Nervo	6	67	371 mins
4	Fabio Pecchia	4	65	412 mins

KEY PLAYERS - MIDFIELDERS

Hidetoshi Nakata

Goals in the League	2	Contribution to Attacking Power: Average number of minutes between League team goals while on pitch	51
Defensive Rating: Average number of mins between League goals conceded while he was on the pitch	57	Scoring Difference: Defensive Rating minus Contribution to Attacking Power	6

	PLAYER	LGE GOALS	DEF RATE	POWER	SCORE DIFF
1	Hidetoshi Nakata	2	57	51	6 mins
2	Fabio Pecchia	4	61	66	-5 mins
3	Carlo Nervo	6	62	67	-5 mins
4	Sam Dalla Bona	3	54	100	-46 mins

KEY PLAYERS - DEFENDERS

Juarez De Souza Texeira

Goals Conceded (GC): The number of League goals conceded while he was on the pitch	16	Clean Sheets: In games when he played at least 70 minutes	4
Defensive Rating: Ave number of mins between League goals conceded while on the pitch	65	Club Defensive Rating: Average number of mins between League goals conceded by the club this season	58

	PLAYER	CON LGE	CLEAN SHEETS	DEF RATE
1	Juarez De Souza Texeira	16	4	65 mins
2	Cesare Natali	49	6	57 mins
3	Cristian Zaccardo	41	4	54 mins
4	Andrea Sussi	25	0	50 mins

KEY GOALKEEPER

1 Emiliano Moretti

Goals Conceded in the League	47	Counting Games: Games when he played at least 70 mins	32
Defensive Rating: Ave number of mins between League goals conceded while on the pitch	59	Clean Sheets: In games when he played at least 70 mins	6

LEAGUE GOALS

Claudio Bellucci

Minutes on the pitch	1478	Goals in the League	7
League average (mins between goals)	211		

	PLAYER	MINS	GOALS	AVE
1	Bellucci	1478	7	211
2	Signori	1813	6	302
3	Nervo	2227	6	371
4	Tare	2091	6	349
5	Pecchia	1649	4	412
6	Locatelli	1028	4	257
7	Dalla Bona	1393	3	464
8	Nakata	1530	2	765
9	Guly	1038	2	519
10	Rossini	879	1	879
11	Colucci	1540	1	1540
12	Amoroso	642	1	642
	Other		2	
	TOTAL		45	

DISCIPLINARY RECORDS

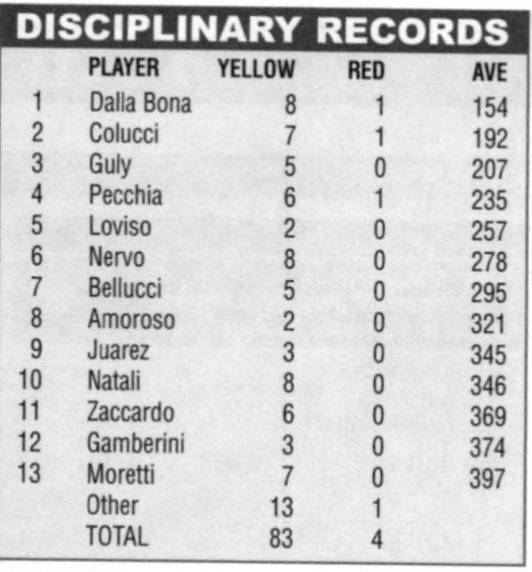

	PLAYER	YELLOW	RED	AVE
1	Dalla Bona	8	1	154
2	Colucci	7	1	192
3	Guly	5	0	207
4	Pecchia	6	1	235
5	Loviso	2	0	257
6	Nervo	8	0	278
7	Bellucci	5	0	295
8	Amoroso	2	0	321
9	Juarez	3	0	345
10	Natali	8	0	346
11	Zaccardo	6	0	369
12	Gamberini	3	0	374
13	Moretti	7	0	397
	Other	13	1	
	TOTAL	83	4	

TOP POINT EARNERS

	PLAYER	GAMES	AV PTS
1	Nakata	17	1.47
2	Signori	18	1.44
3	Nervo	24	1.33
4	Moretti	29	1.17
5	Zaccardo	23	1.17
6	Sussi	13	1.15
7	Pagliuca	34	1.15
8	Pecchia	14	1.14
9	Natali	31	1.13
10	Tare	19	1.11
	CLUB AVERAGE:		**1.15**

TEAM OF THE SEASON

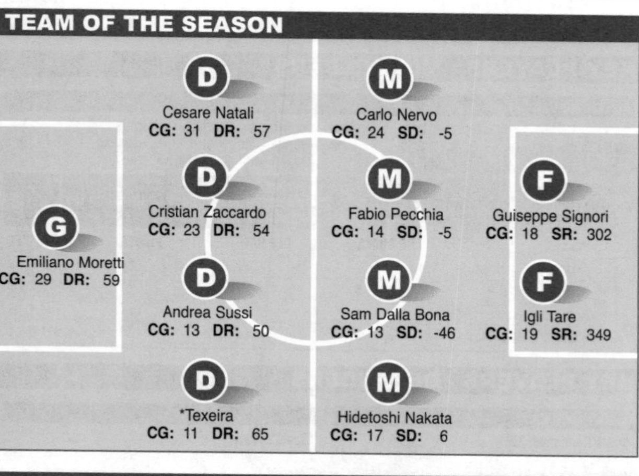
D
Cesare Natali
CG: 31 DR: 57
D
Cristian Zaccardo
CG: 23 DR: 54
D
Andrea Sussi
CG: 13 DR: 50
D
*Texeira
CG: 11 DR: 65
G
Emiliano Moretti
CG: 29 DR: 59
M
Carlo Nervo
CG: 24 SD: -5
M
Fabio Pecchia
CG: 14 SD: -5
M
Sam Dalla Bona
CG: 13 SD: -46
M
Hidetoshi Nakata
CG: 17 SD: 6
F
Guiseppe Signori
CG: 18 SR: 302
F
Igli Tare
CG: 19 SR: 349

LEAGUE APPEARANCES, BOOKINGS AND CAPS

	AGE (on 01/07/04)	IN NAMED 18	APPEARANCES	COUNTING GAMES	MINUTES ON PITCH	YELLOW CARDS	RED CARDS	THIS SEASON	HOME COUNTRY
Goalkeepers									
Alex Manninger	27	29	0	0	0	0	0	-	Austria
Emiliano Moretti	23	32	32	29	2779	7	0	-	Italy
Gianluca Pagliuca	37	34	34	34	3060	2	0	-	Italy
Andrea Pansera	24	5	0	0	0	0	0	-	Italy
Defenders									
Pasquale D'Aniello	18	1	0	0	0	0	0	-	Italy
Luca Ferrari	21	1	0	0	0	0	0	-	Italy
A Gamberini	22	25	16	10	1123	3	0	-	Italy
Juarez Texeira	29	17	13	11	1037	3	0	-	Brazil
Cesare Natali	25	31	31	31	2772	8	0	-	Italy
Andrea Sussi	30	16	15	13	1261	1	0	-	Italy
Claudio Terzi	19	10	6	0	119	0	0	-	Italy
Emanuele Troise	25	18	10	3	439	1	0	-	Italy
Cristian Zaccardo	22	28	28	23	2219	6	0	-	Italy
Marco Zanchi	27	8	5	4	356	1	1	-	Italy
Midfielders									
Christian Amoroso	27	21	12	3	642	2	0	-	Italy
Leonardo Colucci	31	31	25	11	1540	7	1	-	Italy
Nicolo Consolini	19	2	0	0	0	0	0	-	Italy
Sam Dalla Bona	23	20	19	13	1393	8	1	-	Italy
Gennaro Fragiello	-	1	1	0	15	0	0	-	Italy
A Guglielminpietro	30	23	18	8	1038	5	0	-	Argentina
Tomas Locatelli	28	21	20	8	1028	1	0	-	Italy
Massimo Loviso	20	27	11	4	514	2	0	-	Italy
Mourad Meghni	20	23	12	3	479	0	0	-	France
Hidetoshi Nakata	27	17	17	17	1530	0	0	-	Japan
Carlo Nervo	32	28	28	24	2227	8	0	3	Italy (11)
Fabio Pecchia	30	31	27	14	1649	6	1	-	Italy
Forwards									
Claudio Bellucci	29	30	24	11	1478	5	0	-	Italy
Francesco Cataldi	19	2	1	1	90	0	0	-	Italy
Fausto Rossini	26	18	13	8	879	2	0	-	Italy
Guiseppe Signori	36	26	23	18	1813	3	0	-	Italy
Igli Tare	30	34	29	19	2091	2	0	-	Albania

SQUAD APPEARANCES

Match	1	2	3	4	5	6	7	8	9	10	11	12	13	14	15	16	17	18	19	20	21	22	23	24	25	26	27	28	29	30	31	32	33	34
Venue	H	A	H	A	A	H	A	H	A	H	A	H	H	A	H	A	H	A	H	A	H	H	A	A	H	H	A	H	A	A	H	A	H	A
Competition	L	L	L	L	L	L	L	L	L	L	L	L	L	L	L	L	L	L	L	L	L	L	L	L	L	L	L	L	L	L	L	L	L	L
Result	D	L	W	L	L	D	L	L	D	L	D	W	L	D	W	W	W	D	L	W	D	L	L	L	W	W	W	D	L	L	W	L	D	L

Goalkeepers
Alex Manninger
Emiliano Moretti
Gianluca Pagliuca
Andrea Pansera

Defenders
Pasquale D'Aniello
Luca Ferrari
Alessandro Gamberini
Juarez De Souza Texeira
Cesare Natali
Andrea Sussi
Claudio Terzi
Emanuele Troise
Cristian Zaccardo
Marco Zanchi

Midfielders
Christian Amoroso
Leonardo Colucci
Nicolo Consolini
Sam Dalla Bona
Gennaro Fragiello
Andreas Guglielminpietro
Tomas Locatelli
Massimo Loviso
Mourad Meghni
Hidetoshi Nakata
Carlo Nervo
Fabio Pecchia

Forwards
Claudio Bellucci
Francesco Cataldi
Fausto Rossini
Guiseppe Signori
Igli Tare

KEY: ■ On all match ■ On bench
⏮ Subbed or sent off (Counting game)
« Subbed or sent off (playing less than 70 minutes)
⏭ Subbed on from bench (Counting Game)
» Subbed on (playing less than 70 minutes)
Subbed on and then subbed or sent off (Counting Game)
Subbed on and then subbed or sent off (playing less than 70 minutes)
□ Not in 16

SIENA

Final Position: **13th**

NICKNAME:

KEY: ☐ Won ☐ Drawn ☐ Lost

							Attendance
1	lge	Perugia	A	D	2-2	Ardito 19; Taddei 49	12,000
2	lge	Inter Milan	H	L	0-1		12,100
3	lge	Empoli	H	W	4-0	Chiesa 25 pen,48 pen,61; Flo 67	12,000
4	lge	Parma	A	D	1-1	Lazetic 41	15,408
5	lge	Roma	H	D	0-0		13,400
6	lge	Reggina	A	L	1-2	Flo 90	20,190
7	lge	Lecce	H	W	2-1	Taddei 12; Chiesa 76	11,000
8	lge	Ancona	A	D	0-0		15,000
9	lge	Chievo	H	L	1-2	Chiesa 77 pen	11,000
10	lge	Udinese	A	D	1-1	Flo 79	16,000
11	lge	Lazio	H	W	3-0	Taddei 41,43; Menegazzo 45	10,000
12	lge	Sampdoria	A	L	1-2	D'aversa 39	25,000
13	lge	Bologna	H	D	0-0		9,000
14	lge	Brescia	A	L	2-4	Argilli 45; Flo 46	20,000
15	lge	Modena	H	W	4-0	Lazetic 5; Chiesa 44; Ventola 71; Morello 82	15,000
16	lge	Juventus	A	L	2-4	Ventola 70 pen,81	31,000
17	lge	Perugia	H	W	2-1	Flo 87; Menegazzo 90	12,000
18	lge	AC Milan	A	L	1-2	Flo 87	54,428
19	lge	Inter Milan	A	L	0-4		50,732
20	lge	Empoli	A	L	0-1		7,047
21	lge	Parma	H	L	1-2	Chiesa 43	10,000
22	lge	Roma	A	L	0-6		45,000
23	lge	Reggina	H	D	0-0		9,000
24	lge	Lecce	A	D	0-0		12,500
25	lge	Ancona	H	W	3-2	Chiesa 22; Vergassola 44; Taddei 45	9,500
26	lge	Chievo	A	D	1-1	Ventola 87	10,145
27	lge	Udinese	H	W	1-0	Flo 6	
28	lge	Lazio	A	L	2-5	Guigou 9; Taddei 24	42,000
29	lge	Sampdoria	H	D	0-0		18,500
30	lge	AC Milan	H	L	1-2	Chiesa 38 pen	
31	lge	Bologna	A	L	1-3	Mignani 68	20,000
32	lge	Brescia	H	L	0-1		11,000
33	lge	Modena	A	W	3-1	Taddei 42,81; Chiesa 90	15,000
34	lge	Juventus	H	L	1-3	Flo 38	13,500

MONTHLY POINTS TALLY

Month	Points	%
AUGUST	1	33%
SEPTEMBER	4	44%
OCTOBER	4	44%
NOVEMBER	5	42%
DECEMBER	1	17%
JANUARY	6	40%
FEBRUARY	1	7%
MARCH	8	67%
APRIL	1	8%
MAY	3	33%

KEY PLAYERS - GOALSCORERS

Enrico Chiesa

Goals in the League	10	Player Strike Rate Average number of minutes between League goals scored by player	195
Contribution to Attacking Power Average number of minutes between League team goals while on pitch	75	Club Strike Rate Average number of minutes between League goals scored by club	75

	PLAYER	LGE GOALS	POWER	STRIKE RATE
1	Enrico Chiesa	10	75	195 mins
2	Rodrigo Taddei	8	70	283 mins
3	Tore Andre Flo	8	74	333 mins
4	Simone Vergassola	1	89	1428 mins

KEY PLAYERS - MIDFIELDERS

Alessandro Cucciari

Goals in the League	0	Contribution to Attacking Power Average number of minutes between League team goals while on pitch	58
Defensive Rating Average number of mins between League goals conceded while he was on the pitch	61	Scoring Difference Defensive Rating minus Contribution to Attacking Power	3

	PLAYER	LGE GOALS	DEF RATE	POWER	SCORE DIFF
1	Alessandro Cucciari	0	61	58	3 mins
2	Rodrigo Taddei	8	59	71	-12 mins
3	Roberto D'aversa	1	54	77	-23 mins
4	Simone Vergassola	1	48	89	-41 mins

KEY PLAYERS - DEFENDERS

Daniele Delli Carri

Goals Conceded (GC) The number of League goals conceded while he was on the pitch	18	Clean Sheets In games when he played at least 70 minutes	5
Defensive Rating Ave number of mins between League goals conceded while on the pitch	69	Club Defensive Rating Average number of mins between League goals conceded by the club this season	57

	PLAYER	CON LGE	CLEAN SHEETS	DEF RATE
1	Daniele Delli Carri	18	5	69 mins
2	Leandro Damian Cufre	45	9	61 mins
3	Michele Mignani	46	9	60 mins
4	Bruno Cirillo	30	7	59 mins

KEY GOALKEEPER

1 Francesco Rossi

Goals Conceded in the League	30	Counting Games Games when he played at least 70 mins	21
Defensive Rating Ave number of mins between League goals conceded while on the pitch	63	Clean Sheets In games when he played at least 70 mins	6

LEAGUE GOALS

Enrico Chiesa

Minutes on the pitch	1951	Goals in the League	10
League average (mins between goals)	195		

	PLAYER	MINS	GOALS	AVE
1	Chiesa	1951	10	195
2	Taddei	2260	8	283
3	Flo	2666	8	333
4	Ventola	1192	4	298
5	Lazetic	1648	2	824
6	Menegazzo	411	2	206
7	D'aversa	2531	1	2531
8	Ardito	865	1	865
9	Mignani	2756	1	2756
10	Argilli	825	1	825
11	Guigou	2666	1	2666
12	Vergassola	1428	1	1428
	Other		1	
	TOTAL		41	

DISCIPLINARY RECORDS

	PLAYER	YELLOW	RED	AVE
1	Cucciari	6	0	173
2	Juarez	4	2	175
3	Vergassola	6	1	204
4	Delli Carri	6	0	206
5	D'aversa	11	1	210
6	Cirillo	8	0	219
7	Lazetic	7	0	235
8	Mignani	11	0	250
9	Cufre	10	0	275
10	Ventola	3	0	397
11	Argilli	2	0	412
12	Ardito	2	0	432
13	Taddei	4	1	452
	Other	13	1	
	TOTAL	93	6	

TOP POINT EARNERS

	PLAYER	GAMES	AV PTS
1	Delli Carri	13	1.31
2	Cirillo	18	1.17
3	Taddei	22	1.14
4	Mignani	30	1.10
5	Rossi	21	1.00
6	Fortin	13	1.00
7	D'aversa	27	0.96
8	Vergassola	16	0.94
9	Cufre	30	0.93
10	Chiesa	17	0.88
	CLUB AVERAGE:		1.00

LEAGUE APPEARANCES, BOOKINGS AND CAPS

	AGE (on 01/07/04)	IN NAMED 18	APPEARANCES	COUNTING GAMES	MINUTES ON PITCH	YELLOW CARDS	RED CARDS	THIS SEASON	HOME COUNTRY
Goalkeepers									
Simone Farelli	21	6	0	0	0	0	0	-	Italy
Marco Fortin	30	34	13	13	1170	0	0	-	Italy
Francesco Rossi	26	28	21	21	1890	0	0	-	Italy
Defenders									
Carlos Arano	24	2	0	0	0	0	0	-	Argentina
Stefano Argilli	31	33	13	7	825	2	0	-	Italy
Simone Bonomi	23	13	5	2	268	1	0	-	Italy
Bruno Cirillo	27	31	23	18	1758	8	0	-	Italy
Leandro Cufre	26	31	31	30	2750	10	0	-	Argentina
Daniele Delli Carri	32	15	15	13	1240	6	0	-	Italy
Paolo Foglio	28	12	7	2	320	2	0	-	Italy
Gianni Guigou	29	32	32	26	2666	4	1	1	Uruguay (25)
Duccio Innocenti	28	4	0	0	0	0	0	-	Italy
Juarez Texeira	29	13	13	11	1054	4	2	-	Brazil
Angelo Junior	31	16	12	3	503	0	0	3	Brazil (1)
Michele Mignani	32	31	31	30	2756	11	0	-	Italy
Roque Junior	27	6	4	3	279	0	0	8	Brazil (1)
Midfielders									
Fabio Alleruzzo	18	2	0	0	0	0	0	-	Italy
Andrea Ardito	27	13	10	10	865	2	0	-	Italy
Matteo Berretti	19	3	0	0	0	0	0	-	Italy
Alessandro Cucciari	34	27	18	11	1042	6	0	-	Italy
Roberto D'aversa	28	29	29	27	2531	11	1	-	Italy
Nikola Lazetic	26	32	31	8	1648	7	0	-	Serbia & Montenegro
K Loumpoutis	25	13	2	0	31	0	0	-	Greece
F Menegazzo	23	34	18	1	411	1	0	-	Brazil
Rodrigo Taddei	24	28	27	22	2260	4	1	-	Brazil
Simone Vergassola	28	16	16	16	1428	6	1	-	Italy
Forwards									
Enrico Chiesa	33	31	30	17	1951	3	0	-	Italy
Tore Andre Flo	31	33	33	28	2666	1	0	-	Norway
Antonio Morello	27	2	1	0	11	0	0	-	Italy
Raffaele Rubino	26	12	5	0	95	1	0	-	Italy
Nicola Ventola	26	28	28	7	1192	3	0	-	Italy

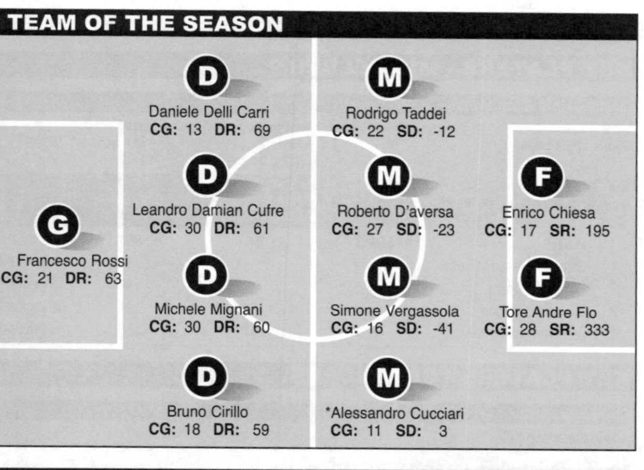

TEAM OF THE SEASON

D
Daniele Delli Carri
CG: 13 DR: 69
M
Rodrigo Taddei
CG: 22 SD: -12
D
Leandro Damian Cufre
CG: 30 DR: 61
M
Roberto D'aversa
CG: 27 SD: -23
F
Enrico Chiesa
CG: 17 SR: 195
G
Francesco Rossi
CG: 21 DR: 63
D
Michele Mignani
CG: 30 DR: 60
M
Simone Vergassola
CG: 16 SD: -41
F
Tore Andre Flo
CG: 28 SR: 333
D
Bruno Cirillo
CG: 18 DR: 59
M
*Alessandro Cucciari
CG: 11 SD: 3

SQUAD APPEARANCES

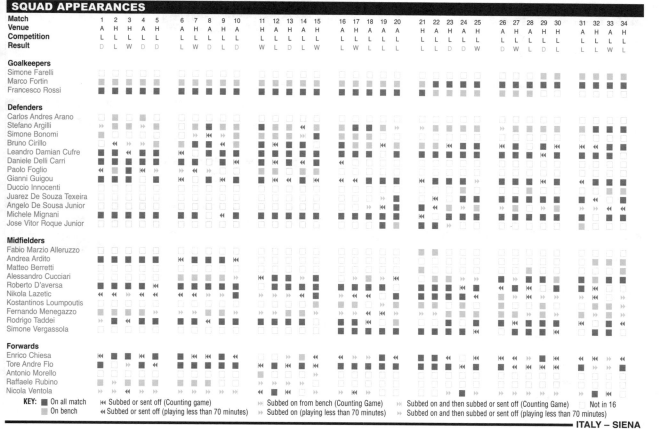

Match	1	2	3	4	5	6	7	8	9	10	11	12	13	14	15	16	17	18	19	20	21	22	23	24	25	26	27	28	29	30	31	32	33	34
Venue	A	H	H	A	H	A	H	A	H	A	H	A	H	A	H	A	H	A	A	A	H	A	H	A	H	A	H	A	H	H	A	H	A	H
Competition	L	L	L	L	L	L	L	L	L	L	L	L	L	L	L	L	L	L	L	L	L	L	L	L	L	L	L	L	L	L	L	L	L	L
Result	D	L	W	D	D	L	W	D	L	D	W	L	D	L	W	L	W	L	L	L	L	L	D	D	W	D	W	L	D	L	L	L	W	L

Goalkeepers
Simone Farelli
Marco Fortin
Francesco Rossi

Defenders
Carlos Andres Arano
Stefano Argilli
Simone Bonomi
Bruno Cirillo
Leandro Damian Cufre
Daniele Delli Carri
Paolo Foglio
Gianni Guigou
Duccio Innocenti
Juarez De Souza Texeira
Angelo De Sousa Junior
Michele Mignani
Jose Vitor Roque Junior

Midfielders
Fabio Marzio Alleruzzo
Andrea Ardito
Matteo Berretti
Alessandro Cucciari
Roberto D'aversa
Nikola Lazetic
Kostantinos Loumpoutis
Fernando Menegazzo
Rodrigo Taddei
Simone Vergassola

Forwards
Enrico Chiesa
Tore Andre Flo
Antonio Morello
Raffaele Rubino
Nicola Ventola

KEY: On all match · On bench · Subbed or sent off (Counting game) · Subbed or sent off (playing less than 70 minutes) · Subbed on from bench (Counting Game) · Subbed on (playing less than 70 minutes) · Subbed on and then subbed or sent off (Counting Game) · Subbed on and then subbed or sent off (playing less than 70 minutes) · Not in 16

REGGINA

Final Position: **14th**

KEY: ☐ Won ☐ Drawn ☐ Lost

							Attendance
1	lge	Sampdoria	H	D	2-2	Cozza 5; Di Michele 41	26,000
2	lge	Empoli	A	D	1-1	Mozart 29	4,500
3	lge	Brescia	A	D	4-4	Nakamura 24 pen,74; Bonazzoli 40; Sottil 67	16,000
4	lge	Juventus	H	L	0-2		30,000
5	lge	Perugia	A	D	0-0		8,000
6	lge	Siena	H	W	2-1	Mozart 22; Leon 90	20,190
7	lge	Ancona	H	D	0-0		19,600
8	lge	Roma	A	L	0-2		50,000
9	lge	Modena	H	D	1-1	Dall' Acqua 31	22,335
10	lge	Inter Milan	A	L	0-6		55,000
11	lge	Bologna	H	D	0-0		20,000
12	lge	Udinese	A	L	0-1		17,000
13	lge	Chievo	H	D	0-0		20,000
14	lge	Parma	A	W	2-1	Di Michele 27; Cozza 45	17,000
15	lge	Lazio	H	W	2-1	Di Michele 60; Cozza 69	25,000
16	lge	AC Milan	A	L	1-3	Torrisi 2	62,000
17	lge	Lecce	H	L	1-3	Cozza 25	20,000
18	lge	Sampdoria	A	L	0-2		
19	lge	Empoli	H	W	2-0	Cozza 50; Di Michele 89	18,000
20	lge	Brescia	H	D	0-0		19,783
21	lge	Juventus	A	L	0-1		30,000
22	lge	Perugia	H	L	1-2	Cozza 53 pen	18,000
23	lge	Siena	A	D	0-0		9,000
24	lge	Ancona	A	D	1-1	Di Michele 42	6,000
25	lge	Roma	H	D	0-0		21,000
26	lge	Modena	A	W	2-1	Bonazzoli 16; Di Michele 45	14,000
27	lge	Inter Milan	H	L	0-2		28,000
28	lge	Bologna	A	D	2-2	Di Michele 8; Stellone 30	25,000
29	lge	Udinese	H	L	0-1		25,000
30	lge	Chievo	A	D	0-0		9,964
31	lge	Parma	H	D	1-1	Torrisi 48	20,000
32	lge	Lazio	A	D	1-1	Cozza 54 pen	46,000
33	lge	AC Milan	H	W	2-1	Di Michele 8; Cozza 29 pen	28,000
34	lge	Lecce	A	L	1-2	Dall' Acqua 31	16,125

MONTHLY POINTS TALLY

AUGUST	1	33%
SEPTEMBER	2	22%
OCTOBER	5	56%
NOVEMBER	2	17%
DECEMBER	4	44%
JANUARY	6	40%
FEBRUARY	2	17%
MARCH	5	42%
APRIL	3	25%
MAY	4	44%

KEY PLAYERS - GOALSCORERS

Francesco Cozza

Goals in the League	8	Player Strike Rate Average number of minutes between League goals scored by player	272
Contribution to Attacking Power Average number of minutes between League team goals while on pitch	103	Club Strike Rate Average number of minutes between League goals scored by club	106

	PLAYER	LGE GOALS	POWER	STRIKE RATE
1	Francesco Cozza	8	103	272 mins
2	David Di Michele	8	90	284 mins
3	Stefano Torrisi	2	126	949 mins
4	Santos Batista Junior Mozart	2	91	957 mins

KEY PLAYERS - MIDFIELDERS

Santos Batista Junior Mozart

Goals in the League	2	Contribution to Attacking Power Average number of minutes between League team goals while on pitch	91
Defensive Rating Average number of mins between League goals conceded while he was on the pitch	83	Scoring Difference Defensive Rating minus Contribution to Attacking Power	-8

	PLAYER	LGE GOALS	DEF RATE	POWER	SCORE DIFF
1	Santos Batista Junior Mozart	2	83	91	-8 mins
2	Francesco Cozza	8	72	103	-31 mins
3	Giacomo Tedesco	0	65	96	-31 mins
4	Giandomenico Mesto	0	70	127	-57 mins

KEY PLAYERS - DEFENDERS

Gianluca Comotto

Goals Conceded (GC) The number of League goals conceded while he was on the pitch	10	Clean Sheets In games when he played at least 70 minutes	5
Defensive Rating Ave number of mins between League goals conceded while on the pitch	121	Club Defensive Rating Average number of mins between League goals conceded by the club this season	68

	PLAYER	CON LGE	CLEAN SHEETS	DEF RATE
1	Gianluca Comotto	10	5	121 mins
2	Stefano Torrisi	26	6	73 mins
3	Ivan Franceschini	34	8	70 mins
4	Andrea Sottil	26	4	69 mins

KEY GOALKEEPER

1 Emanuele Belardi

Goals Conceded in the League	38	Counting Games Games when he played at least 70 mins	31
Defensive Rating Ave number of mins between League goals conceded while on the pitch	73	Clean Sheets In games when he played at least 70 mins	9

LEAGUE GOALS

Francesco Cozza

Minutes on the pitch	2173	Goals in the League	8
League average (mins between goals)	272		

	PLAYER	MINS	GOALS	AVE
1	Cozza	2173	8	272
2	Di Michele	2273	8	284
3	Dall' Acqua	575	2	288
4	Bonazzoli	1998	2	999
5	Torrisi	1898	2	949
6	Mozart	1914	2	957
7	Nakamura	793	2	397
8	Leon	344	1	344
9	Sottil	1806	1	1806
10	Stellone	740	1	740
	Other		0	
	TOTAL		29	

DISCIPLINARY RECORDS

	PLAYER	YELLOW	RED	AVE
1	Sottil	8	2	180
2	Martinez	3	0	248
3	Tedesco	6	0	302
4	Franceschini	7	0	342
5	Di Michele	3	2	454
6	Mozart	4	0	478
7	Paredes	2	0	488
8	Dall' Acqua	1	0	575
9	Torrisi	3	0	632
10	Bonazzoli	3	0	666
11	Baiocco	3	0	674
12	Cozza	3	0	724
13	Stellone	1	0	740
	Other	10	0	
	TOTAL	57	4	

TOP POINT EARNERS

	PLAYER	GAMES	AV PTS
1	Tedesco	17	1.24
2	Comotto	13	1.23
3	Sottil	18	1.17
4	Di Michele	25	1.08
5	Cozza	22	1.05
6	Torrisi	19	1.05
7	Falsini	23	1.04
8	Franceschini	25	1.04
9	Belardi	31	1.03
10	Mozart	19	1.00
	CLUB AVERAGE:		**1.00**

TEAM OF THE SEASON

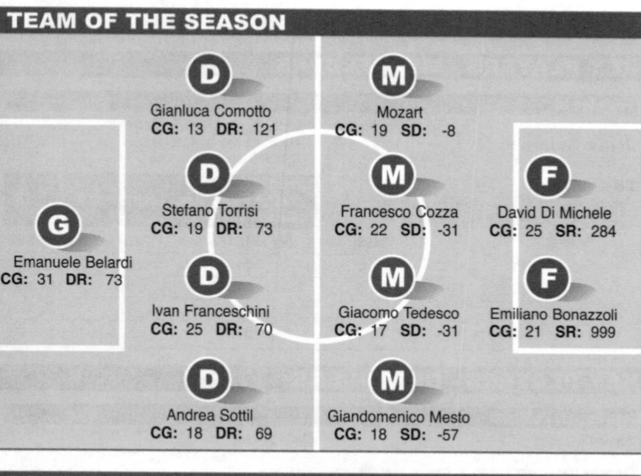
D
Gianluca Comotto
CG: 13 DR: 121
M
Mozart
CG: 19 SD: -8
D
Stefano Torrisi
CG: 19 DR: 73
M
Francesco Cozza
CG: 22 SD: -31
F
David Di Michele
CG: 25 SR: 284
G
Emanuele Belardi
CG: 31 DR: 73
D
Ivan Franceschini
CG: 25 DR: 70
M
Giacomo Tedesco
CG: 17 SD: -31
F
Emiliano Bonazzoli
CG: 21 SR: 999
D
Andrea Sottil
CG: 18 DR: 69
M
Giandomenico Mesto
CG: 18 SD: -57

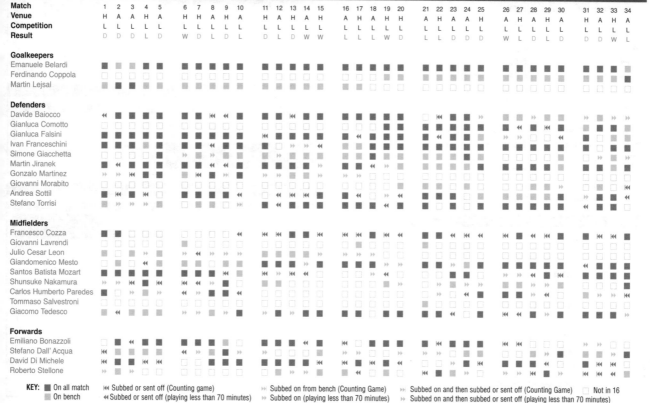

LEAGUE APPEARANCES, BOOKINGS AND CAPS

	AGE (on 01/07/04)	IN NAMED 18	APPEARANCES	COUNTING GAMES	MINUTES ON PITCH	YELLOW CARDS	RED CARDS	THIS SEASON	HOME COUNTRY
Goalkeepers									
Emanuele Belardi	26	34	31	31	2790	2	0	-	Italy
Ferdinando Coppola	26	16	1	1	90	0	0	-	Italy
Martin Lejsal	21	17	2	2	180	0	0	-	Czech Republic
Defenders									
Davide Baiocco	29	33	28	21	2023	3	0	-	Italy
Gianluca Comotto	25	16	14	13	1207	1	0	-	Italy
Gianluca Falsini	28	31	28	23	2302	3	0	-	Italy
Ivan Franceschini	27	32	29	25	2394	7	0	-	Italy
Simone Giacchetta	34	25	8	3	417	0	0	-	Italy
Martin Jiranek	25	34	27	21	2107	1	0	6	Czech Republic (10)
Gonzalo Martinez	28	17	14	7	744	3	0	-	Colombia
Giovanni Morabito	25	9	2	0	93	0	0	-	Italy
Andrea Sottil	30	30	25	18	1806	8	2	-	Italy
Stefano Torrisi	33	29	25	19	1898	3	0	-	Italy
Midfielders									
Francesco Cozza	30	27	27	22	2173	3	0	-	Italy
Giovanni Lavrendi	18	3	0	0	0	0	0	-	Italy
Julio Cesar Leon	24	17	10	0	344	0	0	-	Honduras
G Mesto	22	31	24	18	1900	2	0	-	Italy
Mozart	24	27	26	19	1914	4	0	-	Brazil
S Nakamura	26	23	16	5	793	1	0	-	Japan
Carlos Paredes	27	20	18	7	977	2	0	-	Paraguay
T Salvestroni	19	1	0	0	0	0	0	-	Italy
Giacomo Tedesco	28	32	27	17	1817	6	0	-	Italy
Forwards									
Emiliano Bonazzoli	25	26	25	21	1998	3	0	-	Italy
Stefano Dall' Acqua	22	26	15	4	575	1	0	-	Italy
David Di Michele	28	28	28	25	2273	3	2	-	Italy
Roberto Stellone	26	23	16	6	740	1	0	-	Italy

SQUAD APPEARANCES

Match	1	2	3	4	5	6	7	8	9	10	11	12	13	14	15	16	17	18	19	20	21	22	23	24	25	26	27	28	29	30	31	32	33	34
Venue	H	A	A	H	A	H	H	A	H	A	H	A	H	A	H	A	H	A	H	H	A	H	A	A	H	A	H	A	H	A	H	A	H	A
Competition	L	L	L	L	L	L	L	L	L	L	L	L	L	L	L	L	L	L	L	L	L	L	L	L	L	L	L	L	L	L	L	L	L	L
Result	D	D	D	L	D	W	D	L	D	L	D	L	D	W	W	L	L	L	W	D	L	L	D	D	D	W	L	D	L	D	D	D	W	L

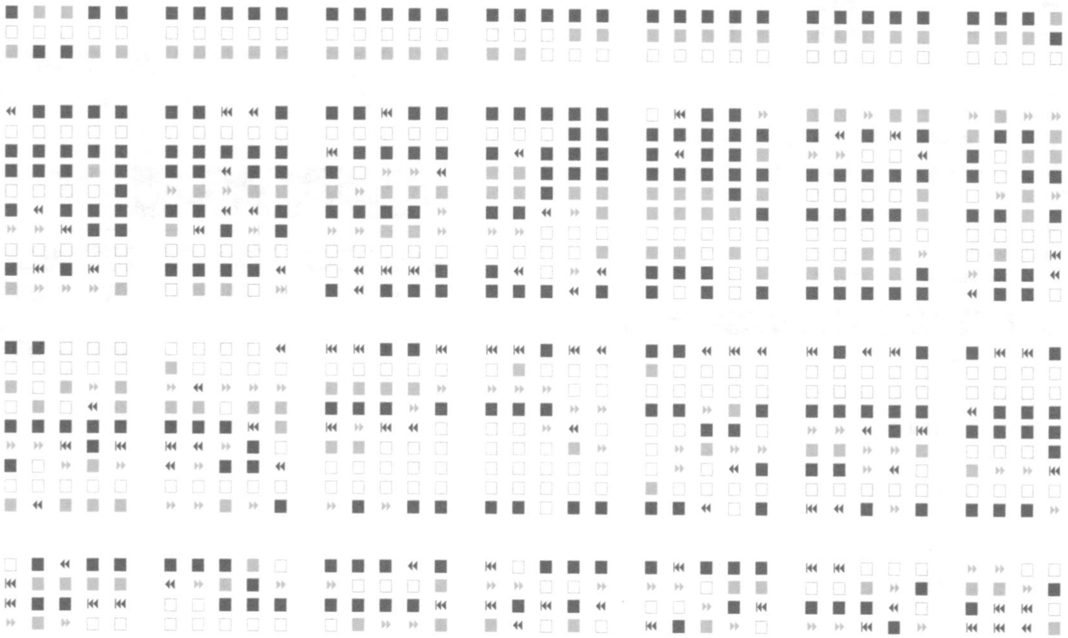

Goalkeepers
Emanuele Belardi
Ferdinando Coppola
Martin Lejsal

Defenders
Davide Baiocco
Gianluca Comotto
Gianluca Falsini
Ivan Franceschini
Simone Giacchetta
Martin Jiranek
Gonzalo Martinez
Giovanni Morabito
Andrea Sottil
Stefano Torrisi

Midfielders
Francesco Cozza
Giovanni Lavrendi
Julio Cesar Leon
Giandomenico Mesto
Santos Batista Mozart
Shunsuke Nakamura
Carlos Humberto Paredes
Tommaso Salvestroni
Giacomo Tedesco

Forwards
Emiliano Bonazzoli
Stefano Dall' Acqua
David Di Michele
Roberto Stellone

KEY: On all match / On bench / Subbed or sent off (Counting game) / Subbed or sent off (playing less than 70 minutes) / Subbed on from bench (Counting Game) / Subbed on (playing less than 70 minutes) / Subbed on and then subbed or sent off (Counting Game) / Subbed on and then subbed or sent off (playing less than 70 minutes) / Not in 16

PERUGIA

Final Position: **15th**

NICKNAME:

KEY: Won Drawn Lost

							Attendance
1	lge	Siena	H	D	2-2	Vryzas 9; Bothroyd 27	12,000
2	lge	Parma	A	L	0-3		22,000
3	lge	AC Milan	H	D	1-1	Vryzas 31	18,000
4	uc1rl1	Dundee	A	W	2-1	Di Loreto 49; Fusani 82	9,911
5	lge	Chievo	A	L	1-4	Di Loreto 50	11,000
6	lge	Reggina	H	D	0-0		8,000
7	uc1rl2	Dundee	H	W	1-0	Margiotta 71	10,000
8	lge	Bologna	A	D	2-2	Rossini 50 og; Bothroyd 70	17,000
9	lge	Udinese	H	D	3-3	Di Loreto 42; Bothroyd 44; Margiotta 89	8,000
10	lge	Modena	A	L	0-1		14,000
11	uc2rl1	Aris	H	W	2-0	Margiotta 47,90 pen	10,000
12	lge	Lecce	H	D	2-2	Margiotta 45; Grosso 82	10,000
13	lge	Lazio	A	L	1-3	Grosso 62	40,000
14	uc2rl2	Aris	A	D	1-1	Margiotta 28	20,000
15	lge	Empoli	H	D	1-1	Vryzas 40	18,000
16	lge	Inter Milan	A	L	1-2	Tedesco 87	50,000
17	lge	Sampdoria	H	D	3-3	Ignoffo 39; Margiotta 54; Tedesco 57	15,000
18	lge	Brescia	H	D	2-2	Margiotta 5; Dainelli 72	12,000
19	lge	Juventus	A	L	0-1		41,500
20	lge	Roma	H	L	0-1		22,000
21	lge	Ancona	A	D	0-0		11,000
22	lge	Siena	A	L	1-2	Ravanelli 6	12,000
23	lge	Parma	H	D	2-2	Hubner 8; Ze Maria 42 pen	10,000
24	lge	AC Milan	A	L	1-2	Fresi 83 pen	60,000
25	lge	Chievo	H	L	0-2		7,000
26	lge	Reggina	A	W	2-1	Ze Maria 20; Hubner 90	18,000
27	uc3rl1	PSV Eindhoven	H	D	0-0		10,000
28	lge	Bologna	H	W	4-2	Ravanelli 32; Codrea 68; Ze Maria 75 pen; Fresi 84 pen	7,000
29	uc3rl2	PSV Eindhoven	A	L	1-3	Ze Maria 88	25,000
30	lge	Udinese	A	D	1-1	Di Loreto 57	12,500
31	lge	Modena	H	D	1-1	Ze Maria 75 pen	10,000
32	lge	Lecce	A	W	2-1	Brienza 14; Di Loreto 60	7,092
33	lge	Lazio	H	L	1-2	Brienza 49	12,000
34	lge	Empoli	A	L	0-1		7,500
35	lge	Inter Milan	H	L	2-3	Di Francesco 50; Hubner 58	13,000
36	lge	Sampdoria	A	L	2-3	Ze Maria 47; Ravanelli 85	25,000
37	lge	Brescia	A	D	1-1	Ravanelli 37	10,000
38	lge	Juventus	H	W	1-0	Ravanelli 50	15,000
39	lge	Roma	A	W	3-1	Ze Maria 19,24; Ravanelli 83	3,000
40	lge	Ancona	H	W	1-0	Bothroyd 65	13,000

MONTHLY POINTS TALLY

Month	Points	%
AUGUST	1	33%
SEPTEMBER	1	11%
OCTOBER	3	33%
NOVEMBER	2	17%
DECEMBER	2	22%
JANUARY	1	8%
FEBRUARY	7	47%
MARCH	5	42%
APRIL	1	8%
MAY	9	100%

KEY PLAYERS - GOALSCORERS

Fabrizio Ravanelli

Goals in the League	6	Player Strike Rate Average number of minutes between League goals scored by player	187
Contribution to Attacking Power Average number of minutes between League team goals while on pitch	62	Club Strike Rate Average number of minutes between League goals scored by club	70

	PLAYER	LGE GOALS	POWER	STRIKE RATE
1	Fabrizio Ravanelli	6	62	187 mins
2	Jose Ferriera Ze Maria	7	76	371 mins
3	Jay Bothroyd	4	78	372 mins
4	Fabio Grosso	2	66	569 mins

KEY PLAYERS - MIDFIELDERS

Fabio Grosso

Goals in the League	2	Contribution to Attacking Power Average number of minutes between League team goals while on pitch	67
Defensive Rating Average number of mins between League goals conceded while he was on the pitch	54	Scoring Difference Defensive Rating minus Contribution to Attacking Power	-13

	PLAYER	LGE GOALS	DEF RATE	POWER	SCORE DIFF
1	Fabio Grosso	2	54	67	-13 mins
2	Christian Obodo	0	50	64	-14 mins
3	Giovanni Tedesco	2	54	80	-26 mins
4	Massimilano Fusani	0	51	82	-31 mins

KEY PLAYERS - DEFENDERS

Jose Ferriera Ze Maria

Goals Conceded (GC) The number of League goals conceded while he was on the pitch	45	Clean Sheets In games when he played at least 70 minutes	3
Defensive Rating Ave number of mins between League goals conceded while on the pitch	58	Club Defensive Rating Average number of mins between League goals conceded by the club this season	55

	PLAYER	CON LGE	CLEAN SHEETS	DEF RATE
1	Jose Ferriera Ze Maria	45	3	58 mins
2	Giovanni Ignoffo	23	2	54 mins
3	Marco Di Loreto	53	3	53 mins
4	Souleymane Diamoutene	42	1	49 mins

KEY GOALKEEPER

1 Zeljko Kalac

Goals Conceded in the League	42	Counting Games Games when he played at least 70 mins	28
Defensive Rating Ave number of mins between League goals conceded while on the pitch	59	Clean Sheets In games when he played at least 70 mins	4

LEAGUE GOALS

Jose Ferriera Ze Maria

Minutes on the pitch	2599	Goals in the League	7
League average (mins between goals)	371		

	PLAYER	MINS	GOALS	AVE
1	Ze Maria	2599	7	371
2	Ravanelli	1122	6	187
3	Bothroyd	1486	4	372
4	Di Loreto	2790	4	698
5	Margiotta	913	4	228
6	Vryzas	646	3	215
7	Hubner	679	3	226
8	Tedesco	1513	2	757
9	Grosso	1138	2	569
10	Brienza	711	2	356
11	Di Francesco	922	1	922
12	Ignoffo	1242	1	1242
	Other		5	
	TOTAL		44	

DISCIPLINARY RECORDS

	PLAYER	YELLOW	RED	AVE
1	Gatti	9	0	95
2	Grosso	6	1	162
3	Codrea	5	0	168
4	Hubner	3	1	169
5	Vryzas	2	1	215
6	Fusani	6	0	231
7	Ignoffo	4	1	248
8	Diamoutene	6	2	257
9	Manfredini	3	0	268
10	Fresi	3	0	330
11	Do Prado	2	0	339
12	Obodo	7	0	383
13	Di Loreto	5	1	465
	Other	16	1	
	TOTAL	77	8	

TOP POINT EARNERS

	PLAYER	GAMES	AV PTS
1	Fabiano	12	1.75
2	Kalac	27	1.04
3	Obodo	29	0.93
4	Ze Maria	28	0.93
5	Di Loreto	31	0.90
6	Bothroyd	13	0.85
7	Diamoutene	21	0.81
8	Grosso	12	0.67
9	Tedesco	17	0.59
10	Fusani	12	0.58
	CLUB AVERAGE:		0.94

TEAM OF THE SEASON

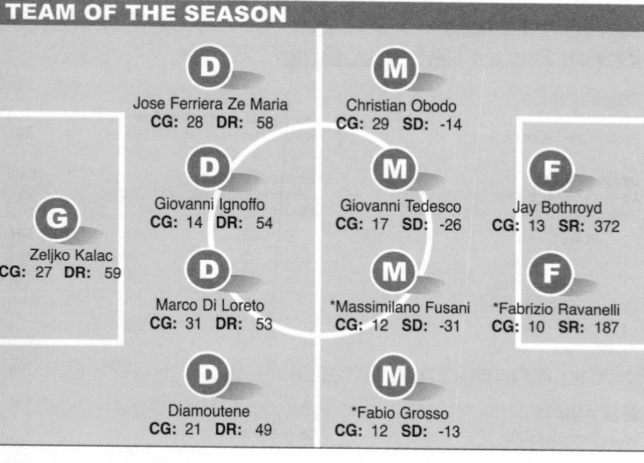
D
Jose Ferriera Ze Maria
CG: 28 DR: 58
M
Christian Obodo
CG: 29 SD: -14
D
Giovanni Ignoffo
CG: 14 DR: 54
M
Giovanni Tedesco
CG: 17 SD: -26
F
Jay Bothroyd
CG: 13 SR: 372
G
Zeljko Kalac
CG: 27 DR: 59
D
Marco Di Loreto
CG: 31 DR: 53
M
*Massimilano Fusani
CG: 12 SD: -31
F
*Fabrizio Ravanelli
CG: 10 SR: 187
D
Diamoutene
CG: 21 DR: 49
M
*Fabio Grosso
CG: 12 SD: -13

LEAGUE APPEARANCES, BOOKINGS AND CAPS

	AGE (on 01/07/04)	IN NAMED 18	APPEARANCES	COUNTING GAMES	MINUTES ON PITCH	YELLOW CARDS	RED CARDS	THIS SEASON	HOME COUNTRY
Goalkeepers									
Zeljko Kalac	31	29	29	27	2458	2	0	4	Australia (89)
Stefano Pardini	29	24	2	1	155	0	0	-	Italy
Michele Tardioli	29	14	6	6	537	0	0	-	Italy
Defenders									
Jamal Alioui	22	8	5	4	405	0	0	-	Morocco
Roberto Cardinale	23	3	1	0	29	0	0	-	Italy
Ferdinand Coly	30	16	11	7	802	1	0	2	Senegal (31)
Marco Di Loreto	29	31	31	31	2790	5	1	-	Italy
S Diamoutene	21	24	24	21	2061	6	2	-	Italy
Salvatore Fresi	31	12	11	11	990	3	0	-	Italy
Giovanni Ignoffo	27	30	14	14	1242	4	1	-	Italy
Vangelis Nastos	23	18	8	6	535	0	1	-	Greece
Jose Ze Maria	30	31	31	28	2599	1	0	-	Brazil
Midfielders									
Franco Brienza	25	12	12	6	711	0	0	-	Italy
Paul Codrea	23	13	12	7	841	5	0	-	Romania
E Di Francesco	34	13	12	9	922	1	0	-	Italy
G Do Prado	22	22	17	4	678	2	0	-	Brazil
Massimilano Fusani	24	32	22	12	1389	6	0	-	Italy
Fabio Gatti	22	32	22	5	858	9	0	-	Italy
Gael Genevier	22	9	4	0	85	0	0	-	France
Al-Saadi Gheddafi	31	5	1	0	16	0	0	-	Libya
Fabio Grosso	26	13	13	12	1138	6	1	1	Italy (11)
K Loumpoutis	25	11	8	3	491	0	0	-	Greece
C Manfredini	29	15	12	7	806	3	0	-	Italy
Christian Obodo	20	32	31	29	2684	7	0	-	Nigeria
Giovanni Tedesco	32	17	17	17	1513	2	0	-	Italy
Forwards									
Emanuele Berrettoni	23	12	8	0	200	1	0	-	Italy
Jay Bothroyd	22	31	26	13	1486	3	0	-	England
Luis Fabiano	23	13	12	12	1080	2	0	3	Brazil (1)
Luigi Giandomenico	25	9	5	2	293	0	0	-	Italy
Dario Hubner	37	13	13	5	679	3	1	-	Italy
Massimo Margiotta	26	17	16	8	913	1	0	-	Italy
Fabrizio Ravanelli	35	15	15	10	1122	2	0	-	Italy
Gabriele Scandurra	25	2	2	0	44	0	0	-	Italy
Juan Martin Turchi	28	2	0	0	0	0	0	-	Argentina
Zisis Vryzas	30	9	9	6	646	2	1	-	Greece
Marcelo Zalayeta	25	6	6	4	370	0	0	-	Uruguay
Francesco Zerbini	24	3	2	0	31	0	0	-	Italy

SQUAD APPEARANCES

Match	1	2	3	4	5	6	7	8	9	10	11	12	13	14	15	16	17	18	19	20	21	22	23	24	25	26	27	28	29	30	31	32	33	34	35	36	37	38	39	40
Venue	H	A	H	A	A	H	H	A	H	A	H	H	A	A	H	A	H	H	A	H	A	A	H	A	H	A	H	H	A	A	H	A	H	A	H	A	A	H	A	H
Competition	L	L	L	E	L	L	E	L	L	L	E	L	L	E	L	L	L	L	L	L	L	L	L	L	L	L	E	L	E	L	L	L	L	L	L	L	L	L	L	L
Result	D	L	D	W	L	D	W	D	D	L	W	D	L	D	D	L	D	D	L	L	D	L	D	L	L	W	D	W	L	D	D	W	L	L	L	L	D	W	W	W

Goalkeepers
Zeljko Kalac
Stefano Pardini
Michele Tardioli

Defenders
Jamal Alioui
Roberto Cardinale
Ferdinand Colya
Marco Di Loreto
Souleymane Diamoutene
Salvatore Fresi
Giovanni Ignoffo
Vangelis Nastos
Jose Ferriera Ze Maria

Midfielders
Franco Brienza
Paul Codrea
Eusebio Di Francesco
Guilherme Do Prado
Massimilano Fusani
Fabio Gatti
Gael Genevier
Al-Saadi Gheddafi
Fabio Grosso
Kostantinos Loumpoutis
Christian Manfredini
Christian Obodo
Giovanni Tedesco

Forwards
Emanuele Berrettoni
Jay Bothroyd
Luis Fabiano
Luigi Giandomenico
Dario Hubner
Massimo Margiotta
Fabrizio Ravanelli
Gabriele Scandurra
Juan Martin Turchi
Zisis Vryzas
Marcelo Zalayeta
Francesco Zerbini

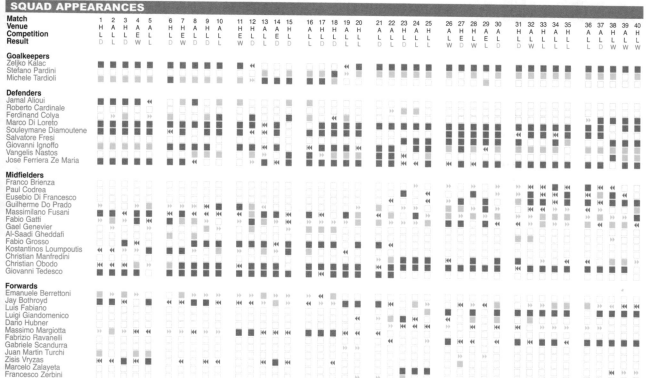

KEY: On all match | On bench | Subbed or sent off (Counting game) | Subbed or sent off (playing less than 70 minutes) | Subbed on from bench (Counting Game) | Subbed on (playing less than 70 minutes) | Subbed on and then subbed or sent off (Counting Game) | Subbed on and then subbed or sent off (playing less than 70 minutes) | Not in 16

MODENA

Final Position: **16th**

KEY: Won Drawn Lost

							Attendance
1	lge	Inter Milan	A	L	0-2		51,000
2	lge	Udinese	H	L	0-1		15,000
3	lge	Ancona	A	D	1-1	Kamara 54	11,472
4	lge	Bologna	H	W	2-0	Amoruso 16; Kamara 40	19,000
5	lge	Empoli	A	W	3-0	Cevoli 54; Ungari 69; Milanetto 75 pen	5,200
6	lge	Lecce	H	W	2-0	Vignaroli 66; Kamara 90	15,850
7	lge	Parma	A	L	0-3		18,000
8	lge	Perugia	H	W	1-0	Allegretti 49	14,000
9	lge	Reggina	A	D	1-1	Campedelli 45	22,335
10	lge	Juventus	H	L	0-2		17,000
11	lge	AC Milan	A	L	0-2		55,000
12	lge	Brescia	H	D	1-1	Taldo 81	14,000
13	lge	Roma	A	L	0-1		48,000
14	lge	Sampdoria	A	D	1-1	Kamara 22	26,000
15	lge	Chievo	H	L	0-3		14,000
16	lge	Siena	A	L	0-4		15,000
17	lge	Lazio	H	D	1-1	Campedelli 60	14,000
18	lge	Inter Milan	H	D	1-1	Makinwa 41	19,000
19	lge	Udinese	A	L	0-1		15,000
20	lge	Ancona	H	W	2-1	Marazzina 37; Milanetto 61	14,000
21	lge	Bologna	A	D	1-1	Amoruso 64	29,000
22	lge	Empoli	H	D	1-1	Amoruso 38	13,500
23	lge	Lecce	A	L	0-1		14,500
24	lge	Parma	H	D	2-2	Pivotto 42; Domizzi 60	14,000
25	lge	Perugia	A	D	1-1	Vignaroli 18	10,000
26	lge	Reggina	H	L	1-2	Kamara 50 pen	14,000
27	lge	Juventus	A	L	1-3	Marazzina 67	30,666
28	lge	AC Milan	H	D	1-1	Amoruso 52	16,000
29	lge	Brescia	A	D	0-0		9,000
30	lge	Roma	H	L	0-1		17,000
31	lge	Sampdoria	H	W	1-0	Kamara 59	18,000
32	lge	Chievo	A	L	0-2		13,798
33	lge	Siena	H	L	1-3	Marazzina 84	15,000
34	lge	Lazio	A	L	1-2	Amoruso 84 pen	50,000

MONTHLY POINTS TALLY

Month	Points	%
AUGUST	0	0%
SEPTEMBER	4	44%
OCTOBER	6	67%
NOVEMBER	4	33%
DECEMBER	2	22%
JANUARY	2	17%
FEBRUARY	5	33%
MARCH	2	17%
APRIL	5	42%
MAY	0	0%

KEY PLAYERS - GOALSCORERS

Diomansy Mehdi Kamara

Goals in the League	6	Player Strike Rate Average number of minutes between League goals scored by player	349
Contribution to Attacking Power Average number of minutes between League team goals while on pitch	104	Club Strike Rate Average number of minutes between League goals scored by club	113

	PLAYER	LGE GOALS	POWER	STRIKE RATE
1	Diomansy Mehdi Kamara	6	104	349 mins
2	Nicola Amoruso	4	114	488 mins
3	Nicola Campedelli	2	107	1017 mins
4	Omar Milanetto	2	99	1041 mins

KEY PLAYERS - MIDFIELDERS

Omar Milanetto

Goals in the League	2	Contribution to Attacking Power Average number of minutes between League team goals while on pitch	99
Defensive Rating Average number of mins between League goals conceded while he was on the pitch	72	Scoring Difference Defensive Rating minus Contribution to Attacking Power	-27

	PLAYER	LGE GOALS	DEF RATE	POWER	SCORE DIFF
1	Omar Milanetto	2	72	99	-27 mins
2	Antonio Marasco	0	75	104	-29 mins
3	Nicola Campedelli	2	70	107	-37 mins
4	Jacopo Balestri	0	67	121	-54 mins

KEY PLAYERS - DEFENDERS

Mauro Mayer

Goals Conceded (GC) The number of League goals conceded while he was on the pitch	16	Clean Sheets In games when he played at least 70 minutes	5
Defensive Rating Ave number of mins between League goals conceded while on the pitch	96	Club Defensive Rating Average number of mins between League goals conceded by the club this season	67

	PLAYER	CON LGE	CLEAN SHEETS	DEF RATE
1	Mauro Mayer	16	5	96 mins
2	Luca Ungari	17	4	80 mins
3	Roberto Cevoli	34	5	69 mins
4	Maurizio Domizzi	23	0	60 mins

KEY GOALKEEPER

1 Adriano Zancope

Goals Conceded in the League	21	Counting Games Games when he played at least 70 mins	17
Defensive Rating Ave number of mins between League goals conceded while on the pitch	72	Clean Sheets In games when he played at least 70 mins	4

LEAGUE GOALS

Diomansy Mehdi Kamara

Minutes on the pitch	2091	Goals in the League	6
League average (mins between goals)	349		

	PLAYER	MINS	GOALS	AVE
1	Kamara	2091	6	349
2	Amoruso	1950	4	488
3	Marazzina	593	2	297
4	Milanetto	2082	2	1041
5	Campedelli	2034	2	1017
6	Pivotto	1027	1	1027
7	Cevoli	2347	1	2347
8	Taldo	159	1	159
9	Allegretti	1049	1	1049
10	Vignaroli	1839	1	1839
11	Makinwa	1129	1	1129
12	Domizzi	1380	1	1380
	Other		4	
	TOTAL		27	

DISCIPLINARY RECORDS

	PLAYER	YELLOW	RED	AVE
1	Ponzo	2	2	130
2	Scoponi	3	1	159
3	Mayer	4	1	308
4	Marasco	8	0	326
5	Campedelli	6	0	339
6	Ungari	4	0	341
7	Milanetto	6	0	347
8	Kamara	6	0	348
9	Allegretti	3	0	349
10	Vignaroli	4	0	459
11	Domizzi	3	0	460
12	Cevoli	5	0	469
13	Grandoni	3	0	502
	Other	11	1	
	TOTAL	68	5	

TOP POINT EARNERS

	PLAYER	GAMES	AV PTS
1	Mayer	16	1.13
2	Milanetto	23	1.09
3	Ungari	15	1.07
4	Zancope	17	1.06
5	Kamara	19	1.05
6	Marasco	27	1.04
7	Cevoli	26	1.00
8	Amoruso	21	1.00
9	Balestri	31	0.94
10	Vignaroli	16	0.81
	CLUB AVERAGE:		**0.88**

LEAGUE APPEARANCES, BOOKINGS AND CAPS

	AGE (on 01/07/04)	IN NAMED 18	APPEARANCES	COUNTING GAMES	MINUTES ON PITCH	YELLOW CARDS	RED CARDS	THIS SEASON	HOME COUNTRY
Goalkeepers									
Mathias Altamirano	19	1	0	0	0	0	0	-	Italy
Marco Ballotta	40	31	18	17	1545	1	1	-	Italy
Andrea Sentimenti	19	3	0	0	0	0	0	-	Italy
Adriano Zancope	32	34	17	17	1514	1	0	-	Italy
Defenders									
Marco Bernardi	18	6	0	0	0	0	0	-	Italy
Roberto Cevoli	35	29	27	26	2347	5	0	-	Italy
Maurizio Domizzi	24	17	17	14	1380	3	0	-	Italy
A Grandoni	26	18	17	16	1507	3	0	-	Italy
Mauro Mayer	33	19	18	16	1540	4	1	-	Italy
John Mensah	21	10	6	3	372	0	0	-	Ghana
Simone Pavan	30	19	12	7	829	1	0	-	Italy
Matteo Pivotto	29	19	13	11	1027	1	0	-	Italy
Cristian Stellini	30	7	2	0	46	0	0	-	Italy
Luca Ungari	29	18	16	15	1364	4	0	-	Italy
Vincenzo Vado	20	2	0	0	0	0	0	-	Italy
A Zago	34	1	0	0	0	0	0	-	Brazil
Midfielders									
Riccardo Allegretti	26	20	18	7	1049	3	0	-	Italy
Jacopo Balestri	29	33	33	31	2892	5	0	-	Italy
Nicola Campedelli	25	31	27	20	2034	6	0	-	Italy
Nicola Corrent	25	13	4	0	47	0	0	-	Italy
David Limbersky	20	7	4	0	67	1	0	-	Czech Republic
Antonio Marasco	34	31	31	27	2610	8	0	-	Italy
Omar Milanetto	28	25	25	23	2082	6	0	-	Italy
Vedin Music	31	20	8	2	296	0	0	-	Bosnia
Marco Nicoletti	18	1	0	0	0	0	0	-	Italy
Paulo Ponzo	32	25	13	2	520	2	2	-	Italy
Massimo Scoponi	30	32	16	3	638	3	1	-	Italy
Forwards									
Nicola Amoruso	29	28	25	21	1950	0	0	-	Italy
Manuel De Luca	20	2	0	0	0	0	0	-	Italy
Diomansy Kamara	23	29	29	19	2091	6	0	-	France
Stephen Makinwa	20	18	17	11	1129	0	0	-	Nigeria
Massimo Marazzina	29	16	12	5	593	1	0	-	Italy
Carlo Taldo	32	13	10	0	159	0	0	-	Italy
Fabio Vignaroli	28	32	30	16	1839	4	0	-	Italy

TEAM OF THE SEASON

G: Adriano Zancope — CG: 17 DR: 72

D: Mauro Mayer — CG: 16 DR: 96

D: Luca Ungari — CG: 15 DR: 80

D: Roberto Cevoli — CG: 26 DR: 69

D: Maurizio Domizzi — CG: 14 DR: 60

M: Omar Milanetto — CG: 23 SD: -27

M: Antonio Marasco — CG: 27 SD: -29

M: Nicola Campedelli — CG: 20 SD: -37

M: Jacopo Balestri — CG: 31 SD: -54

F: Kamara — CG: 19 SR: 349

F: Nicola Amoruso — CG: 21 SR: 488

SQUAD APPEARANCES

Match	1	2	3	4	5	6	7	8	9	10	11	12	13	14	15	16	17	18	19	20	21	22	23	24	25	26	27	28	29	30	31	32	33	34
Venue	A	H	A	H	A	H	A	H	A	H	A	H	A	A	H	A	H	H	A	H	A	H	A	H	A	H	A	H	A	H	H	A	H	A
Competition	L	L	L	L	L	L	L	L	L	L	L	L	L	L	L	L	L	L	L	L	L	L	L	L	L	L	L	L	L	L	L	L	L	L
Result	L	L	D	W	W	W	L	W	D	L	L	D	L	D	L	L	D	D	L	W	D	D	L	D	D	L	L	D	D	L	W	L	L	L

Goalkeepers
Mathias Altamirano
Marco Ballotta
Andrea Sentimenti
Adriano Zancope

Defenders
Marco Bernardi
Roberto Cevoli
Maurizio Domizzi
Alessandro Grandoni
Mauro Mayer
John Mensah
Simone Pavan
Matteo Pivotto
Cristian Stellini
Luca Ungari
Vincenzo Vado
Antonio Carlos Zago

Midfielders
Riccardo Allegretti
Jacopo Balestri
Nicola Campedelli
Nicola Corrent
David Limbersky
Antonio Marasco
Omar Milanetto
Vedin Music
Marco Nicoletti
Paulo Ponzo
Massimo Scoponi

Forwards
Nicola Amoruso
Manuel De Luca
Diomansy Mehdi Kamara
Stephen Ayodele Makinwa
Massimo Marazzina
Carlo Taldo
Fabio Vignaroli

KEY: On all match · On bench · Subbed or sent off (Counting game) · Subbed or sent off (playing less than 70 minutes) · Subbed on from bench (Counting Game) · Subbed on (playing less than 70 minutes) · Subbed on and then subbed or sent off (Counting Game) · Subbed on and then subbed or sent off (playing less than 70 minutes) · Not in 16

EMPOLI

Final Position: **17th**

KEY: Won Drawn Lost

							Attendance
1	lge	Juventus	A	L	1-5	Di Natale 87	40,000
2	lge	Reggina	H	D	1-1	Di Natale 41	4,500
3	lge	Siena	A	L	0-4		12,000
4	lge	Lazio	H	D	2-2	Di Natale 75; Tavano 79	5,818
5	lge	Modena	H	L	0-3		5,200
6	lge	Udinese	A	L	0-2		16,000
7	lge	Chievo	H	L	0-1		4,000
8	lge	Lecce	A	L	1-2	Rocchi 60	9,462
9	lge	Sampdoria	A	L	0-2		25,000
10	lge	Parma	H	W	1-0	Foggia 90	4,645
11	lge	Perugia	A	D	1-1	Rocchi 3	18,000
12	lge	AC Milan	H	L	0-1		13,000
13	lge	Brescia	A	L	0-2		13,000
14	lge	Roma	H	L	0-2		15,000
15	lge	Bologna	A	L	1-2	Di Natale 18	20,000
16	lge	Ancona	H	W	2-0	Di Natale 47; Vannucchi 50	4,000
17	lge	Inter Milan	A	W	1-0	Rocchi 90	60,000
18	lge	Juventus	H	D	3-3	Rocchi 21,55,62	22,000
19	lge	Reggina	A	L	0-2		18,000
20	lge	Siena	H	W	1-0	Rocchi 70	7,047
21	lge	Lazio	A	L	0-3		40,000
22	lge	Modena	A	D	1-1	Rocchi 50	13,500
23	lge	Udinese	H	W	2-0	Busce 22; Cribari 41	4,000
24	lge	Chievo	A	D	0-0		12,000
25	lge	Lecce	H	D	0-0		5,000
26	lge	Sampdoria	H	D	1-1	Rocchi 90	6,500
27	lge	Parma	A	L	0-4		13,000
28	lge	Perugia	H	W	1-0	Rocchi 64	7,500
29	lge	AC Milan	A	L	0-1		
30	lge	Brescia	H	D	1-1	Gasparetto 78	5,000
31	lge	Roma	A	L	0-3		15,000
32	lge	Bologna	H	W	2-0	Belleri 40; Vannucchi 75	10,000
33	lge	Ancona	A	L	1-2	Vannucchi 68	4,000
34	lge	Inter Milan	H	L	2-3	Lucchini 18; Rocchi 83	11,000

MONTHLY POINTS TALLY

AUGUST	0	0%
SEPTEMBER	2	22%
OCTOBER	0	0%
NOVEMBER	4	33%
DECEMBER	0	0%
JANUARY	7	47%
FEBRUARY	7	58%
MARCH	3	25%
APRIL	4	33%
MAY	3	33%

KEY PLAYERS - GOALSCORERS

Tommaso Rocchi

Goals in the League	11	Player Strike Rate Average number of minutes between League goals scored by player	259
Contribution to Attacking Power Average number of minutes between League team goals while on pitch	118	Club Strike Rate Average number of minutes between League goals scored by club	118

	PLAYER	LGE GOALS	POWER	STRIKE RATE
1	Tommaso Rocchi	11	118	259 mins
2	Antonio Di Natale	5	108	543 mins
3	Ighli Vannucchi	3	100	569 mins
4	Stefano Lucchini	1	102	1432 mins

KEY PLAYERS - MIDFIELDERS

Jorge Vargas

Goals in the League	0	Contribution to Attacking Power Average number of minutes between League team goals while on pitch	87
Defensive Rating Average number of mins between League goals conceded while he was on the pitch	82	Scoring Difference Defensive Rating minus Contribution to Attacking Power	-5

	PLAYER	LGE GOALS	DEF RATE	POWER	SCORE DIFF
1	Jorge Vargas	0	82	87	-5 mins
2	Ighli Vannucchi	3	74	100	-26 mins
3	Vincenzo Grella	0	62	102	-40 mins
4	Fabrizio Ficini	0	56	120	-64 mins

KEY PLAYERS - DEFENDERS

Andrea Cupi

Goals Conceded (GC) The number of League goals conceded while he was on the pitch	26	Clean Sheets In games when he played at least 70 minutes	5
Defensive Rating Ave number of mins between League goals conceded while on the pitch	66	Club Defensive Rating Average number of mins between League goals conceded by the club this season	57

	PLAYER	CON LGE	CLEAN SHEETS	DEF RATE
1	Andrea Cupi	26	5	66 mins
2	Emilson Sanchez Cribari	46	9	59 mins
3	Stefano Lucchini	28	2	51 mins
4	Manuel Belleri	50	5	50 mins

KEY GOALKEEPER

1 Adriano Zancope

Goals Conceded in the League	21	Counting Games Games when he played at least 70 mins	17
Defensive Rating Ave number of mins between League goals conceded while on the pitch	72	Clean Sheets In games when he played at least 70 mins	4

LEAGUE GOALS

Tommaso Rocchi

Minutes on the pitch	2846	Goals in the League	11
League average (mins between goals)	259		

	PLAYER	MINS	GOALS	AVE
1	Rocchi	2846	11	259
2	Di Natale	2713	5	543
3	Vannucchi	1706	3	569
4	Lucchini	1432	1	1432
5	Belleri	2521	1	2521
6	Busce	2733	1	2733
7	Foggia	576	1	576
8	Cribari	2735	1	2735
9	Tavano	645	1	645
10	Gasparetto	431	1	431
	Other		0	
	TOTAL		26	

DISCIPLINARY RECORDS

	PLAYER	YELLOW	RED	AVE
1	Zanetti	3	0	218
2	Cappellini	2	0	255
3	Lucchini	4	1	286
4	Pratali	4	0	315
5	Giampieretti	3	0	317
6	Vargas	3	1	370
7	Ficini	6	0	380
8	Grella	5	0	407
9	Agostini	1	0	497
10	Cupi	3	0	569
11	Foggia	1	0	576
12	Balli	1	1	627
13	Cribari	4	0	683
	Other	15	3	
	TOTAL	55	6	

TOP POINT EARNERS

	PLAYER	GAMES	AV PTS
1	Vargas	15	1.40
2	Vannucchi	17	1.35
3	Balli	14	1.14
4	Grella	20	1.10
5	Cupi	17	1.06
6	Ficini	20	1.00
7	Cribari	30	1.00
8	Di Natale	27	0.96
9	Rocchi	32	0.91
10	Busce	31	0.84
	CLUB AVERAGE:		**0.88**

LEAGUE APPEARANCES, BOOKINGS AND CAPS

	AGE (on 01/07/04)	IN NAMED 18	APPEARANCES	COUNTING GAMES	MINUTES ON PITCH	YELLOW CARDS	RED CARDS	THIS SEASON	HOME COUNTRY
Goalkeepers									
Daniele Balli	36	16	14	14	1254	1	1	-	Italy
Luca Bucci	35	19	17	16	1487	0	1	-	Italy
Mario Cassano	20	30	4	3	316	0	0	-	Italy
Gabriele Paoletti	26	2	0	0	0	0	0	-	Italy
Defenders									
A Agostini	24	16	9	3	497	1	0	-	Italy
Manuel Belleri	26	30	30	26	2521	2	0	-	Italy
Andrea Coda	19	3	0	0	0	0	0	-	Italy
Emilson Cribari	24	31	31	30	2735	4	0	-	Brazil
Andrea Cupi	28	26	23	17	1707	3	0	-	Italy
Maurizio Lanzaro	22	18	8	2	409	0	2	-	Italy
Stefano Lucchini	23	29	21	13	1432	4	1	-	Italy
Roberto Mirri	25	1	0	0	0	0	0	-	Italy
Francesco Pratali	25	31	19	12	1260	4	0	-	Italy
Midfielders									
Antonio Busce	28	31	31	31	2733	3	0	-	Italy
Fabrizio Ficini	30	33	30	20	2285	6	0	-	Italy
Flavio Giampieretti	30	24	13	8	953	3	0	-	Italy
Vincenzo Grella	24	26	25	20	2035	5	0	4	Australia (89)
Francesco Lodi	20	5	1	0	45	0	0	-	Italy
Ighli Vannucchi	27	20	20	17	1706	2	0	-	Italy
Jorge Vargas	28	17	17	15	1480	3	1	-	Chile
Paolo Zanetti	21	27	13	5	654	3	0	-	Italy
Forwards									
M Cappellini	33	27	17	2	510	2	0	-	Italy
Marco Carparelli	28	9	7	1	271	0	0	-	Italy
Antonio Di Natale	26	33	32	27	2713	2	0	1	Italy (11)
Pasquuale Foggia	21	27	18	0	576	1	0	-	Italy
Mirco Gasparetto	24	21	13	1	431	2	0	-	Italy
Tommaso Rocchi	26	33	33	32	2846	4	0	-	Italy
Francesco Tavano	25	25	17	2	645	0	0	-	Italy

TEAM OF THE SEASON

G — Daniele Balli CG: 14 DR: 74

D — Andrea Cupi CG: 17 DR: 66

D — Cribari CG: 30 DR: 59

D — Stefano Lucchini CG: 13 DR: 51

D — Manuel Belleri CG: 26 DR: 50

M — Jorge Vargas CG: 15 SD: -5

M — Ighli Vannucchi CG: 17 SD: -26

M — Vincenzo Grella CG: 20 SD: -40

M — Fabrizio Ficini CG: 20 SD: -64

F — Tommaso Rocchi CG: 32 SR: 259

F — Antonio Di Natale CG: 27 SR: 543

SQUAD APPEARANCES

Match	1	2	3	4	5	6	7	8	9	10	11	12	13	14	15	16	17	18	19	20	21	22	23	24	25	26	27	28	29	30	31	32	33	34
Venue	A	H	A	H	H	A	H	A	A	H	A	H	A	H	A	H	A	H	A	H	A	A	H	A	H	H	A	H	A	H	A	H	A	H
Competition	L	L	L	L	L	L	L	L	L	L	L	L	L	L	L	L	L	L	L	L	L	L	L	L	L	L	L	L	L	L	L	L	L	L
Result	L	D	L	D	L	L	L	L	L	W	D	L	L	L	L	W	W	D	L	W	L	D	W	D	D	D	L	W	L	D	L	W	L	L

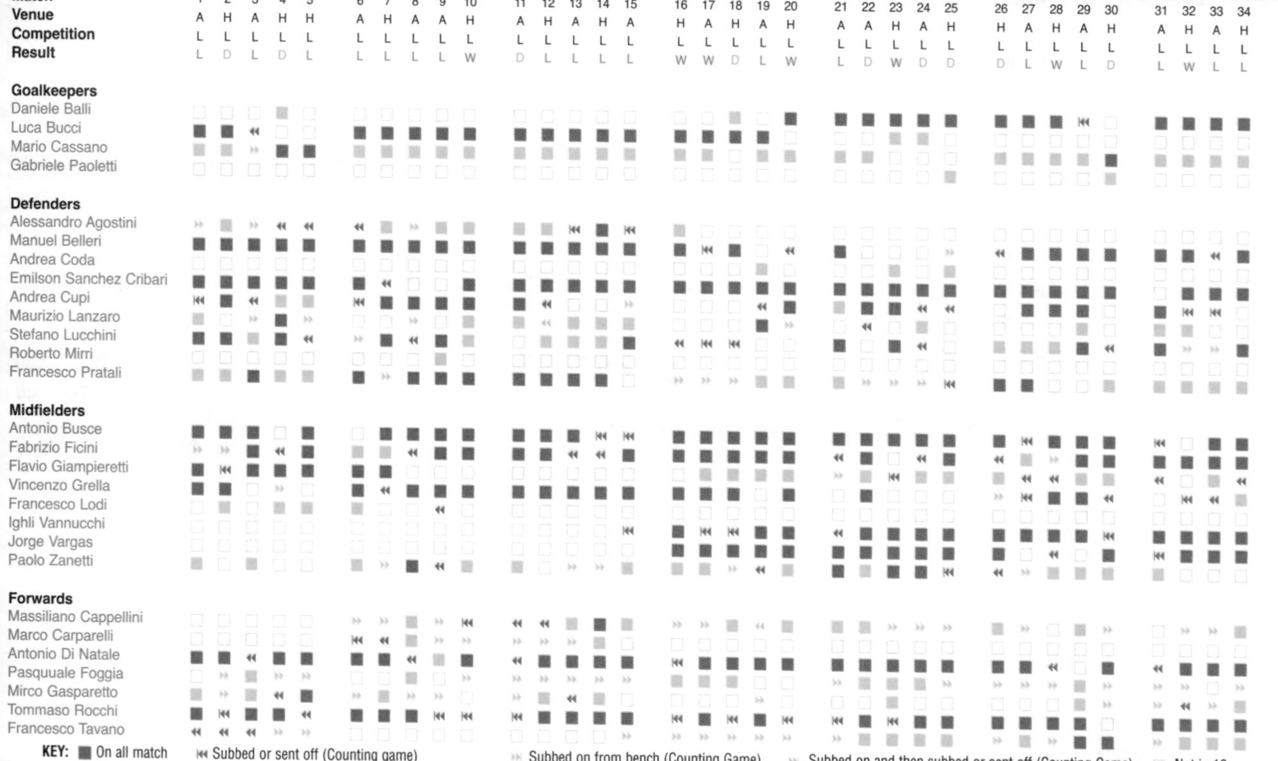

Goalkeepers
Daniele Balli
Luca Bucci
Mario Cassano
Gabriele Paoletti
Defenders
Alessandro Agostini
Manuel Belleri
Andrea Coda
Emilson Sanchez Cribari
Andrea Cupi
Maurizio Lanzaro
Stefano Lucchini
Roberto Mirri
Francesco Pratali
Midfielders
Antonio Busce
Fabrizio Ficini
Flavio Giampieretti
Vincenzo Grella
Francesco Lodi
Ighli Vannucchi
Jorge Vargas
Paolo Zanetti
Forwards
Massiliano Cappellini
Marco Carparelli
Antonio Di Natale
Pasquuale Foggia
Mirco Gasparetto
Tommaso Rocchi
Francesco Tavano

KEY: On all match · On bench · Subbed or sent off (Counting game) · Subbed or sent off (playing less than 70 minutes) · Subbed on from bench (Counting Game) · Subbed on (playing less than 70 minutes) · Subbed on and then subbed or sent off (Counting Game) · Subbed on and then subbed or sent off (playing less than 70 minutes) · Not in 16

ANCONA

Final Position: **18th**

KEY: Won Drawn Lost

							Attendance
1	lge	AC Milan	H	L	0-2		22,000
2	lge	Lecce	A	L	1-3	Ganz 68 pen	13,780
3	lge	Modena	H	D	1-1	Bilica 63	11,472
4	lge	Roma	A	L	0-3		49,150
5	lge	Udinese	H	L	0-3		10,740
6	lge	Juventus	H	L	2-3	Viali 56; Ganz 89	24,000
7	lge	Reggina	A	D	0-0		19,600
8	lge	Siena	H	D	0-0		15,000
9	lge	Inter Milan	A	L	0-3		45,000
10	lge	Brescia	H	D	1-1	Berretta 60	11,703
11	lge	Sampdoria	A	L	0-2		25,000
12	lge	Bologna	A	L	2-3	Viali 70; Pandev 79	20,000
13	lge	Lazio	H	L	0-1		12,000
14	lge	Chievo	A	L	0-1		11,000
15	lge	Parma	H	L	0-2		10,000
16	lge	Empoli	A	L	0-2		4,000
17	lge	Perugia	H	D	0-0		11,000
18	lge	AC Milan	A	L	0-5		55,000
19	lge	Lecce	H	L	0-2		13,000
20	lge	Modena	A	L	1-2	Bucchi 6	14,000
21	lge	Roma	H	D	0-0		20,000
22	lge	Udinese	A	L	0-3		13,000
23	lge	Juventus	A	L	0-3		29,000
24	lge	Reggina	H	D	1-1	Ganz 10	6,000
25	lge	Siena	A	L	2-3	Bucchi 30; Rapaic 58	9,500
26	lge	Inter Milan	H	L	0-2		20,000
27	lge	Brescia	A	L	2-5	Rapaic 32; Maini 39 og	10,000
28	lge	Sampdoria	H	L	0-1		8,000
29	lge	Bologna	H	W	3-2	Rapaic 26,56; Bucchi 51	11,000
30	lge	Lazio	A	L	2-4	Bucchi 11; Andersson 64	40,000
31	lge	Chievo	H	L	0-2		5,000
32	lge	Parma	A	L	1-3	Bucchi 34	11,500
33	lge	Empoli	H	W	2-1	Milanese 19; Sommese 73	4,000
34	lge	Perugia	A	L	0-1		13,000

MONTHLY POINTS TALLY

Month	Points	%
AUGUST	0	%
SEPTEMBER	1	8%
OCTOBER	1	11%
NOVEMBER	2	17%
DECEMBER	0	0%
JANUARY	1	8%
FEBRUARY	1	7%
MARCH	1	8%
APRIL	3	25%
MAY	3	33%

KEY PLAYERS - GOALSCORERS

Milan Rapaic

Goals in the League	4	Player Strike Rate Average number of minutes between League goals scored by player	274
Contribution to Attacking Power Average number of minutes between League team goals while on pitch	121	Club Strike Rate Average number of minutes between League goals scored by club	146

	PLAYER	LGE GOALS	POWER	STRIKE RATE
1	Milan Rapaic	4	121	274 mins
2	William Viali	2	195	585 mins
3	Goran Pandev	1	126	1134 mins
4	Fabio Da Silva Bilica	1	252	1264 mins

KEY PLAYERS - MIDFIELDERS

Daniel Andersson

Goals in the League	1	Contribution to Attacking Power Average number of minutes between League team goals while on pitch	110
Defensive Rating Average number of mins between League goals conceded while he was on the pitch	41	Scoring Difference Defensive Rating minus Contribution to Attacking Power	-69

	PLAYER	LGE GOALS	DEF RATE	POWER	SCORE DIFF
1	Daniel Andersson	1	41	110	-69 mins
2	Vincenzo Sommese	1	42	146	-104 mins
3	Daniele Berretta	1	50	214	-164 mins
4	Davide Carrus	0	53	263	-210 mins

KEY PLAYERS - DEFENDERS

Mauro Milanese

Goals Conceded (GC) The number of League goals conceded while he was on the pitch	45	Clean Sheets In games when he played at least 70 minutes	4
Defensive Rating Ave number of mins between League goals conceded while on the pitch	50	Club Defensive Rating Average number of mins between League goals conceded by the club this season	44

	PLAYER	CON LGE	CLEAN SHEETS	DEF RATE
1	Mauro Milanese	45	4	50 mins
2	William Viali	25	2	47 mins
3	Fabio Da Silva Bilica	28	2	45 mins
4	Drazen Bolic	34	1	40 mins

KEY GOALKEEPER

1 Alessio Scarpi

Goals Conceded in the League	25	Counting Games Games when he played at least 70 mins	13
Defensive Rating Ave number of mins between League goals conceded while on the pitch	47	Clean Sheets In games when he played at least 70 mins	2

LEAGUE GOALS

Christian Bucchi

Minutes on the pitch	767	Goals in the League	5
League average (mins between goals)	153		

	PLAYER	MINS	GOALS	AVE
1	Bucchi	767	5	153
2	Rapaic	1097	4	274
3	Ganz	1298	3	433
4	Viali	1170	2	585
5	Berretta	1714	1	1714
6	Bilica	1264	1	1264
7	Pandev	1134	1	1134
8	Sommese	1756	1	1756
9	Andersson	1971	1	1971
10	Milanese	2245	1	2245
	Other		1	
	TOTAL		21	

DISCIPLINARY RECORDS

	PLAYER	YELLOW	RED	AVE
1	Goretti	4	1	156
2	Ganz	5	1	216
3	Russo	3	0	227
4	Viali	5	0	234
5	Zavagno	2	0	244
6	Milanese	8	0	280
7	Pandev	4	0	283
8	Sartor	2	0	326
9	Carrus	4	0	328
10	Esposito	3	0	330
11	Baggio	3	0	336
12	Berretta	5	0	342
13	Bucchi	1	1	383
	Other	26	2	
	TOTAL	75	5	

TOP POINT EARNERS

	PLAYER	GAMES	AV PTS
1	Sommese	13	0.54
2	Marcon	18	0.50
3	Andersson	19	0.47
4	Milanese	23	0.43
5	Bolic	14	0.36
6	Bilica	12	0.33
7	Carrus	13	0.31
8	Scarpi	13	0.31
9	Berretta	17	0.29
10	Viali	13	0.23
	CLUB AVERAGE:		**0.38**

LEAGUE APPEARANCES, BOOKINGS AND CAPS

	AGE (on 01/07/04)	IN NAMED 18	APPEARANCES	COUNTING GAMES	MINUTES ON PITCH	YELLOW CARDS	RED CARDS	THIS SEASON	HOME COUNTRY
Goalkeepers									
Sergio Marcon	33	32	18	18	1620	1	0	-	Italy
Alessio Scarpi	31	14	13	13	1170	0	0	-	Italy
Defenders									
Dario Baccin	27	8	5	2	324	0	0	-	Italy
Fabio Da Silva Bilica	25	20	16	12	1264	2	1	-	Brazil
Drazen Bolic	32	20	16	14	1350	2	0	-	Serbia & Montenegro
Daniele Daino	24	8	7	4	486	0	0	-	Italy
Ginaluca Esposito	27	21	12	10	990	3	0	-	Italy
Roberto Maltagliati	35	6	5	3	332	0	1	-	Italy
Mauro Milanese	32	28	27	23	2245	8	0	-	Italy
Luigi Sartor	29	10	9	7	652	2	0	-	Italy
Sean Sogliano	33	13	11	7	787	2	0	-	Italy
Andrea Sussi	30	11	4	4	360	0	0	-	Italy
William Viali	29	13	13	13	1170	5	0	-	Italian
Luciano Zavagno	26	15	8	3	488	2	0	-	Argentina
Midfielders									
Daniel Andersson	26	32	25	19	1971	3	0	-	Sweden
Dino Baggio	32	13	13	10	1010	3	0	-	Italy
Daniele Berretta	32	24	22	17	1714	5	0	-	Italy
Davide Carrus	25	16	16	13	1313	4	0	-	Italy
Andrea De Falco	18	8	7	3	382	0	0	-	Italy
E Di Francesco	34	12	10	4	552	1	0	-	Italy
M Giacobbo	29	8	4	3	306	0	0	-	Italy
Roberto Goretti	28	13	13	6	780	4	1	-	Italy
Luis Helguera	28	14	13	7	913	2	0	-	Spain
Stefano Lombardi	27	6	4	3	311	0	0	-	Italy
Giampiero Maini	32	19	17	7	1009	1	0	-	Italy
Pietro Parente	32	7	5	2	297	0	0	-	Italy
Salvatore Russo	32	12	9	5	681	3	0	-	Italy
Vincenzo Sommese	25	26	26	13	1756	3	0	-	Italy
Forwards									
Salvatore Bruno	24	11	8	2	382	1	0	-	Italy
Christian Bucchi	27	14	12	7	767	1	1	-	Italy
Maurizio Ganz	35	31	25	7	1298	5	1	-	Italy
Corrado Grabbi	28	8	7	4	453	0	0	-	Italy
Dario Hubner	37	9	9	2	514	1	0	-	Italy
Goran Pandev	20	21	20	10	1134	4	0	-	Macedonia
Paolo Poggi	33	13	9	2	445	2	0	-	Italy
Milan Rapaic	30	14	14	10	1097	0	0	6	Croatia (25)

Also appeared: D Degano; D Fortuato; G Goracci; M Hedman; M Jardel; P Luiso; B Pungu; M Rossi

TEAM OF THE SEASON

G — Alessio Scarpi — CG: 13 DR: 47

D — Mauro Milanese — CG: 23 DR: 50

D — William Viali — CG: 13 DR: 47

D — Drazen Bolic — CG: 14 DR: 40

D — *Fabio Da Silva Bilica — CG: 12 DR: 45

M — Daniel Andersson — CG: 19 SD: -69

M — Vincenzo Sommese — CG: 13 SD: -104

M — Daniele Berretta — CG: 17 SD: -164

M — Davide Carrus — CG: 13 SD: -210

F — *Milan Rapaic — CG: 10 SR: 274

F — *Goran Pandev — CG: 10 SR: 1134

SQUAD APPEARANCES

Match	1	2	3	4	5	6	7	8	9	10	11	12	13	14	15	16	17	18	19	20	21	22	23	24	25	26	27	28	29	30	31	32	33	34
Venue	H	A	H	A	H	H	A	H	A	H	A	A	H	A	H	A	H	A	H	A	H	A	A	H	A	H	A	H	H	A	H	A	H	A
Competition	L	L	L	L	L	L	L	L	L	L	L	L	L	L	L	L	L	L	L	L	L	L	L	L	L	L	L	L	L	L	L	L	L	L
Result	L	L	D	L	L	L	D	D	L	D	L	L	L	L	L	L	D	L	L	L	D	L	L	D	L	L	L	L	W	L	L	L	W	L

Goalkeepers
Sergio Marcon
Alessio Scarpi
Defenders
Dario Baccin
Fabio Da Silva Bilica
Drazen Bolic
Daniele Daino
Ginaluca Esposito
Roberto Maltagliati
Mauro Milanese
Luigi Sartor
Sean Sogliano
Andrea Sussi
William Viali
Luciano Zavagno
Midfielders
Daniel Andersson
Dino Baggio
Daniele Berretta
Davide Carrus
Marco Cerioni
Andrea De Falco
Eusebio Di Francesco
Massimiliano Giacobbo
Roberto Goretti
Luis Helguera
Stefano Lombardi
Giampiero Maini
Pietro Parente
Salvatore Russo
Vincenzo Sommese
Forwards
Salvatore Bruno
Christian Bucchi
Maurizio Ganz
Corrado Grabbi
Dario Hubner
Goran Pandev
Paolo Poggi
Milan Rapaic

KEY: ■ On all match ■ On bench ⏮ Subbed or sent off (Counting game) « Subbed or sent off (playing less than 70 minutes) ⏭ Subbed on from bench (Counting Game) » Subbed on (playing less than 70 minutes) ⏭ Subbed on and then subbed or sent off (Counting Game) » Subbed on and then subbed or sent off (playing less than 70 minutes) □ Not in 16

DUTCH LEAGUE ROUND-UP

FINAL LEAGUE TABLE

		HOME					AWAY					TOTAL			
	P	W	D	L	F	A	W	D	L	F	A	F	A	DIF	PTS
Ajax	34	16	1	0	47	10	9	4	4	32	21	79	31	48	80
PSV Eindhoven	34	11	3	3	45	14	12	2	3	47	16	92	30	62	74
Feyenoord	34	12	2	3	39	20	8	6	3	32	18	71	38	33	68
Heerenveen	34	12	3	2	31	13	5	4	8	14	22	45	35	10	58
AZ Alkmaar	34	9	4	4	37	21	8	2	7	28	21	65	42	23	57
Roda JC Kerk	34	8	6	3	33	17	6	5	6	27	24	60	41	19	53
Willem II Tilb	34	10	2	5	33	20	3	8	6	14	34	47	54	-7	49
Twente	34	11	2	4	38	22	4	1	12	18	31	56	53	3	48
NAC Breda	34	8	3	6	33	28	4	7	6	25	27	58	55	3	46
Utrecht	34	9	1	7	24	24	4	6	7	18	28	42	52	-10	46
RKC Waalwijk	34	5	8	4	20	18	5	2	10	27	37	47	55	-8	40
Roosendaal	34	3	8	6	13	23	7	2	8	21	24	34	47	-13	40
Groningen	34	6	6	5	22	20	3	4	10	16	33	38	53	-15	37
NEC Nijmegen	34	5	3	9	24	25	5	1	11	20	37	44	62	-18	34
Den Haag	34	5	6	6	22	26	4	1	12	14	35	36	61	-25	34
Vitesse Arnhem	34	3	8	6	28	28	1	8	8	11	28	39	56	-17	28
Volendam	34	5	2	10	19	35	2	4	11	12	44	31	79	-48	27
Zwolle	34	5	5	7	13	26	0	6	11	14	41	27	67	-40	26

CLUB STRIKE FORCE

PSV hitting the most goals in Europe

1 PSV Eindhoven

Goals scored in the League	92
Club Strike Rate (CSR) Average number of minutes between League goals scored by club	33

	CLUB	LGE	CSR
1	PSV Eindhoven	92	33
2	Ajax	79	39
3	Feyenoord	71	43
4	AZ Alkmaar	65	47
5	Roda JC Kerk	60	51
6	NAC Breda	58	53
7	Twente	56	55
8	RKC Waalwijk	47	65
9	Willem II Tilb	47	65
10	Heerenveen	45	68
11	NEC Nijmegen	44	70
12	Utrecht	42	73
13	Vitesse Arnhem	39	78
14	Groningen	38	81
15	Den Haag	36	85
16	Roosendaal	34	90
17	Volendam	31	99
18	Zwolle	27	113

CLUB DISCIPLINARY RECORDS

Utrecht's Vreven upsets Bridge

1 Utrecht

League Yellow	60
League Red	4
League Total	64
Cards Average in League Average number of minutes between a card being shown of either colour	48

	CLUB	LEAGUE		TOTAL	AVE
1	Utrecht	60Y	4R	64	48
2	Den Haag	55	3	58	53
3	Groningen	55	3	58	53
4	Vitesse Arnhem	52	6	58	53
5	NAC Breda	53	1	54	57
6	NEC Nijmegen	49	2	51	60
7	Roosendaal	49	1	50	61
8	Willem II Tilb	48	1	49	62
9	Feyenoord	46	2	48	64
10	Roda JC Kerk	44	4	48	64
11	Twente	45	2	47	65
12	PSV Eindhoven	42	3	45	68
13	RKC Waalwijk	42	2	44	70
14	Volendam	41	3	44	70
15	Zwolle	42	2	44	70
16	AZ Alkmaar	37	2	39	78
17	Heerenveen	37	1	38	81
18	Ajax	25	2	27	113

CLUB DEFENCES

PSV's Bouma thwarts Jenas of Newcastle

1 PSV Eindhoven

Goals conceded in the League	30
Clean Sheets (CS) Number of league games where no goals were conceded	15
Club Defensive Rate (CDR) Average number of minutes between League goals conceded by club	102

	CLUB	LGE	CS	CDR
1	PSV Eindhoven	30	15	102
2	Ajax	31	14	99
3	Heerenveen	35	14	87
4	Feyenoord	38	12	81
5	Roda JC Kerk	41	7	75
6	AZ Alkmaar	42	11	73
7	Roosendaal	47	8	65
8	Utrecht	52	7	59
9	Groningen	53	7	58
10	Twente	53	7	58
11	Willem II Tilb	54	12	57
12	NAC Breda	55	5	56
13	RKC Waalwijk	55	9	56
14	Vitesse Arnhem	56	7	55
15	Den Haag	61	6	50
16	NEC Nijmegen	62	6	49
17	Zwolle	67	6	46
18	Volendam	79	4	39

PLAYER NATIONALITIES

Overseas country with the most player appearances in the Dutch League - Belgium

435 league appearances by Belgian players

	COUNTRY	PLAYERS	IN SQUAD	LGE APP	% LGE ACT	CAPS	MOST APP	APP
1	Holland	353	6885	5260	63.6	52	Four players	100.0
2	Belgium	33	624	435	5.2	28	Sidney Lammens	97.1
3	Serbia & Montenegro	11	299	274	3.6	7	Vladan Kujovic	100.0
4	Sweden	8	196	188	2.5	17	Petter Hansson	97.1
5	Morocco	10	219	182	2.2		Khalid Sinouh	96.5
6	Denmark	9	201	186	2.1	13	Kenneth Perez	82.5
7	Brazil	13	208	167	1.8	0	Maxwell	89.3
8	Nigeria	4	112	98	1.2		Azubuike Oliseh	81.9
9	South Korea	3	94	85	1.1		Young-Pyo Lee	93.3
10	Finland	8	131	94	1.1	6	Mika Vayrynen	90.3
11	South Africa	3	75	75	1.0		Hans Vonk	97.1
12	Czech Republic	3	78	74	1.0	9	Tomas Galasek	82.9
13	Hungary	4	78	68	0.9		Gabor Babos	72.8
14	Burkino Faso	4	101	80	0.9		Rahim Ouedraogo	74.6
15	Spain	3	76	66	0.8	0	Juan Castellano	60.5
16	Poland	4	75	60	0.8		Arek Radomski	81.8
17	Portugal	3	60	59	0.8	0	Virgilio Teixeira	74.4
18	Switzerland	3	84	69	0.7		Blaise N'Kufo	73.7

CLUB MAKE-UP – HOME AND OVERSEAS PLAYERS

1 Roda JC Kerk

65.6% of appearances by overseas players

	CLUB	OVERSEAS	HOME	% OVERSEAS	% LGE ACT	MOST APP	APP
1	Roda JC Kerk	19	10	65.5	68.6	Vladan Kujovic	100.0
2	Ajax	23	10	69.7	64.6	Maxwell	89.3
3	Heerenveen	12	21	36.4	60.0	Petter Hansson	97.1
4	Roosendaal	9	16	36.0	50.4	S Lammens	97.1
5	Feyenoord	17	13	56.7	44.4	Thomas Buffel	96.7
6	NAC Breda	9	22	29.0	43.6	Gabor Babos	72.8
7	Twente	9	19	32.1	39.2	Adil Ramzi	86.5
8	Groningen	8	22	26.7	37.1	Mathias Floren	91.1
9	Vitesse Arnhem	12	19	38.7	36.9	A Rankovic	72.5
10	PSV Eindhoven	13	17	43.3	35.1	Young-Pyo Lee	93.3
11	Willem II Tilb	12	18	40.0	33.4	Tom Caluwe	77.6
12	Zwolle	8	21	27.6	30.8	Jasar Takak	96.2
13	AZ Alkmaar	7	20	25.9	29.1	Kenneth Perez	82.5
14	RKC Waalwijk	7	21	25.0	27.3	Khalid Sinouh	96.5
15	NEC Nijmegen	5	22	18.5	17.8	Jarda Simr	61.5
16	Den Haag	5	30	14.3	13.1	Alberto Saavedra	52.3
17	Utrecht	4	26	13.3	11.1	Stefaan Tanghe	87.1
18	Volendam	2	25	7.4	9.2	Lindsay Wilson	73.2

CHART-TOPPING MIDFIELDERS

1 van Bommel - PSV Eindhoven

Goals scored in the League	6
Defensive Rating Av number of mins between League goals conceded while on the pitch	120
Contribution to Attacking Power Average number of minutes between League team goals while on pitch	33
Scoring Difference Defensive Rating minus Contribution to Attacking Power	87

	PLAYER	CLUB	GOALS	DEF RATE	POWER	S DIFF
1	van Bonnel	PSV Eindhoven	6	120	33	87
2	Sneijder	Ajax	9	126	46	80
3	Lee	PSV Eindhoven	0	114	34	80
4	de Jong	PSV Eindhoven	8	107	32	75
5	Lucius	PSV Eindhoven	4	100	33	67
6	van der Vaart	Ajax	7	109	47	62
7	Ono	Feyenoord	2	101	39	62
8	Galasek	Ajax	4	91	36	55
9	Vogel	PSV Eindhoven	1	86	34	52
10	Lindenbergh	AZ Alkmaar	1	81	39	42
11	Buffel	Feyenoord	14	80	44	36
12	Sergio	Roda JC Kerk	2	77	51	26
13	van Dessel	Roda JC Kerk	4	74	50	24
14	Victoria	Willem II Tilb	2	79	55	24
15	van Dijk	Roda JC Kerk	2	77	54	23

CHART-TOPPING GOALSCORERS

1 Kezman - PSV Eindhoven

Goals scored in the League	31
Contribution to Attacking Power (AP) Average number of minutes between League team goals while on pitch	32
Club Strike Rate (CSR) Average minutes between League goals scored by club	33
Player Strike Rate Average number of minutes between League goals scored by player	74

	PLAYER	CLUB	GOALS: LGE	POWER	CSR	S RATE
1	Kezman	PSV Eindhoven	31	32	33	74
2	Sibon	Heerenveen	15	74	68	128
3	Elkhattabi	AZ Alkmaar	14	46	47	148
4	Kuijt	Feyenoord	20	42	43	152
5	N'Kufo	Twente	14	49	55	161
6	Vennegoor	PSV Eindhoven	12	39	33	180
7	Sonck	Ajax	9	34	39	195
8	Anastasiou	Roda JC Kerk	8	48	51	196
9	Stroeve	Den Haag	10	72	85	203
10	Kone	Roda JC Kerk	11	49	51	203
11	Buffel	Feyenoord	14	43	43	211
12	Caluwe	Willem II Tilb	10	55	65	238
13	Hersi	NEC Nijmegen	10	67	70	242
14	Perez	AZ Alkmaar	10	46	47	253
15	Engelaar	NAC Breda	9	53	53	260

CHART-TOPPING DEFENDERS

1 Bakkati - Heerenveen

Goals Conceded in the League The number of League goals conceded while he was on the pitch	18
Clean Sheets In games when he played at least 70 mins	10
Club Defensive Rating Average mins between League goals conceded by the club this season	87
Defensive Rating Average number of minutes between League goals conceded while on pitch	115

	PLAYER	CLUB	CON: LGE	CS	CDR	DEF RATE
1	Bakkati	Heerenveen	18	10	87	115
2	de Jong	Ajax	20	11	99	113
3	Heitinga	Ajax	22	11	99	101
4	Escude	Ajax	27	12	99	100
5	Maxwell	Ajax	28	12	99	98
6	Seip	Heerenveen	22	11	87	96
7	Edman	Heerenveen	27	11	87	91
8	van den Berg	Feyenoord	24	9	81	89
9	Molenaar	Roosendaal	28	8	65	88
10	Hansson	Heerenveen	35	13	87	85
11	Paauwe	Feyenoord	31	9	81	82
12	Song	Feyenoord	25	8	81	80
13	Buskermolen	AZ Alkmaar	32	10	73	79
14	van Hintum	RKC Waalwijk	23	6	56	78
15	Luijpers	Roda JC Kerk	35	5	75	75

CHART-TOPPING GOALKEEPERS

1 Waterreus - PSV Eindhoven

Goals Conceded in the League The number of League goals conceded while he was on the pitch	33
Clean Sheets In games when he played at least 70 mins	28
Club Defensive Rating Average mins between League goals conceded by the club this season	15
Defensive Rating Average number of minutes between League goals conceded while on pitch	106

	PLAYER	CLUB	CG	CONC	CS	DEF RATE
1	Waterreus	PSV Eindhoven	33	22	9	106
2	Lobont	Ajax	24	22	9	98
3	Zoetebier	Feyenoord	20	19	7	93
4	Vonk	Heerenveen	33	34	14	87
5	Kujovic	Roda JC Kerk	34	41	7	75
6	Timmer	AZ Alkmaar	34	42	11	73
7	De Vlieger	Willem II Tilb	27	34	11	68
8	Aerts	Roosendaal	34	47	8	65
9	Paauwe	Twente	22	28	6	64
10	Ponk	Utrecht	29	41	6	62
11	Beukenkamp	Groningen	28	42	5	60
12	Babos	NAC Breda	25	39	3	57
13	de Vries	Den Haag	18	29	6	56
14	Sinouh	RKC Waalwijk	33	55	8	54
15	van Fessem	Vitesse Arnhem	22	36	5	54

PLAYER DISCIPLINARY RECORD

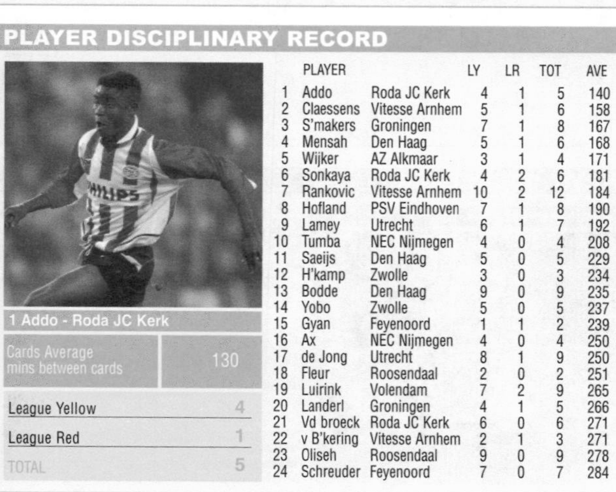

1 Addo - Roda JC Kerk

Cards Average mins between cards	130
League Yellow	4
League Red	1
TOTAL	5

	PLAYER		LY	LR	TOT	AVE
1	Addo	Roda JC Kerk	4	1	5	140
2	Claessens	Vitesse Arnhem	5	1	6	158
3	S'makers	Groningen	7	1	8	167
4	Mensah	Den Haag	5	1	6	168
5	Wijker	AZ Alkmaar	3	1	4	171
6	Sonkaya	Roda JC Kerk	4	2	6	181
7	Rankovic	Vitesse Arnhem	10	2	12	184
8	Hofland	PSV Eindhoven	7	1	8	190
9	Lamey	Utrecht	6	1	7	192
10	Tumba	NEC Nijmegen	4	0	4	208
11	Saeijs	Den Haag	5	0	5	229
12	H'kamp	Zwolle	3	0	3	234
13	Bodde	Den Haag	9	0	9	235
14	Yobo	Zwolle	5	0	5	237
15	Gyan	Feyenoord	1	1	2	239
16	Ax	NEC Nijmegen	4	0	4	250
17	de Jong	Utrecht	8	1	9	250
18	Fleur	Roosendaal	2	0	2	251
19	Luirink	Volendam	7	2	9	265
20	Landerl	Groningen	4	1	5	266
21	Vd broeck	Roda JC Kerk	6	0	6	271
22	v B'kering	Vitesse Arnhem	2	1	3	271
23	Oliseh	Roosendaal	9	0	9	278
24	Schreuder	Feyenoord	7	0	7	284

TEAM OF THE SEASON

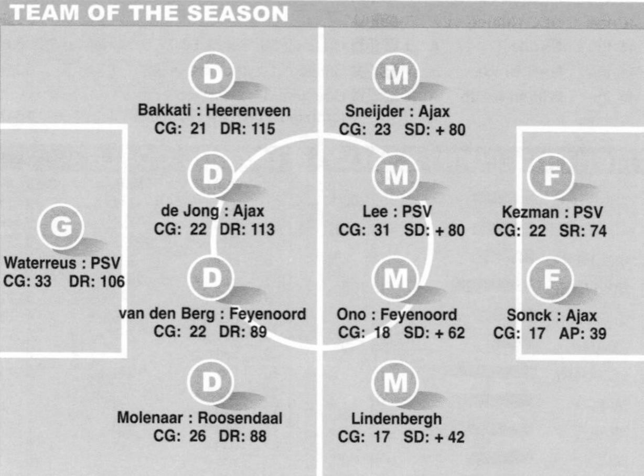

D
Bakkati : Heerenveen
CG: 21 DR: 115
M
Sneijder : Ajax
CG: 23 SD: + 80
D
de Jong : Ajax
CG: 22 DR: 113
M
Lee : PSV
CG: 31 SD: + 80
F
Kezman : PSV
CG: 22 SR: 74
G
Waterreus : PSV
CG: 33 DR: 106
D
van den Berg : Feyenoord
CG: 22 DR: 89
M
Ono : Feyenoord
CG: 18 SD: + 62
F
Sonck : Ajax
CG: 17 AP: 39
D
Molenaar : Roosendaal
CG: 26 DR: 88
M
Lindenbergh
CG: 17 SD: + 42

AJAX

Final Position: **1st**

KEY: □ Won □ Drawn □ Lost

							Attendance
1	clql1	Grazer AK	A	D	1-1	Sneijder 79 fk	15,428
2	lge	V Arnhem	A	W	2-1	Frankel 21 og; Sneijder 87	22,000
3	lge	Roosendaal	A	W	1-0	Soetaers 35	5,000
4	clql2	Grazer AK	H	W	2-1	Ibrahimovic 16; Galasek 104 pen	48,000
5	lge	Zwolle	H	W	1-0	Pienaar 32	47,880
6	lge	RKC Waalwijk	H	W	4-1	Maxwell 21; Ibrahimovic 27; Galasek 47 pen; Sonck 61	48,121
7	cl gh	AC Milan	A	L	0-1		48,000
8	lge	NAC Breda	A	L	2-4	Sikora 70; Ibrahimovic 72	16,000
9	lge	Willem II Tilb	H	W	6-0	Sonck 13; Ibrahimovic 29; Sneijder 49; Sikora 57; Soetaers 68; Pienaar 81	47,728
10	cl gh	Club Brugge	H	W	2-0	Sonck 11,54	49,731
11	lge	Groningen	A	W	3-1	Ibrahimovic 27; Sonck 82; Mitea 90	12,400
12	lge	Volendam	H	W	5-1	Sonck 5; van der Vaart 32,38; Mitea 78; Trabelsi 85	49,521
13	cl gh	Celta Vigo	H	W	1-0	Ibrahimovic 54	48,514
14	lge	PSV Eindhoven	A	D	2-2	Sonck 58; Ibrahimovic 72	35,000
15	lge	AZ Alkmaar	H	W	3-2	Ibrahimovic 21; de Jong 77; Galasek 90	50,222
16	cl gh	Celta Vigo	A	L	2-3	Sonck 53; van der Vaart 82	20,000
17	lge	Den Haag	A	W	4-1	Heitinga 33; Sneijder 47; Ibrahimovic 62; Sikora 80	9,420
18	lge	Heerenveen	H	W	3-1	Sneijder 36; Mitea 37; Ibrahimovic 58	49,331
19	cl gh	AC Milan	H	L	0-1		51,324
20	lge	Feyenoord	H	W	2-0	van der Vaart 4,11	50,344
21	cl gh	Club Brugge	A	L	1-2	Sonck 42 pen	28,041
22	lge	Utrecht	H	W	1-0	van der Vaart 76	48,972
23	hocr3	NAC Breda	H	L	0-1		19,910
24	lge	Twente	A	L	0-2		13,250
25	lge	Roda JC Kerk	A	W	2-1	Sikora 48; Soetaers 62	18,222
26	lge	NEC Nijmegen	H	W	1-0	Sonck 61	49,018
27	lge	Den Haag	H	W	4-0	de Jong 4; Sikora 19; Sneijder 38; Mitea 78	47,264
28	lge	PSV Eindhoven	H	W	2-1	Sneijder 51; Mitea 61	50,406
29	lge	Volendam	A	W	2-0	Anastasiou 11; Galasek 88 pen	6,199
30	lge	Twente	H	W	1-0	Escude 12	48,979
31	lge	Heerenveen	A	L	1-4	Hansson 87 og	13,500
32	lge	Utrecht	A	L	0-1		18,000
33	lge	RKC Waalwijk	A	W	1-0	Olfers 39 og	7,500
34	lge	Roda JC Kerk	H	W	4-2	Mitea 26; Anastasiou 37,45; Pienaar 82	49,553
35	lge	Vitesse Arnhem	H	W	5-0	Maxwell 17; Sneijder 26; Mitea 29; Heitinga 73; Ibrahimovic 80	49,265
36	lge	AZ Alkmaar	A	D	1-1	Ibrahimovic 64	8,241
37	lge	Groningen	H	W	2-1	van der Vaart 57; Heitinga 84	49,212
38	lge	Feyenoord	A	D	1-1	Ibrahimovic 68	51,000
39	lge	Roosendaal	H	D	1-1	van der Vaart 30	49,112
40	lge	NEC Nijmegen	A	D	0-0		12,500
41	lge	Zwolle	A	W	5-0	Galasek 36; Sonck 56,77,81; Sneijder 79	6,800
42	lge	NAC Breda	H	W	2-0	Sneijder 11; Ibrahimovic 43	50,000
43	lge	Willem II Tilb	A	W	5-2	Soetaers 37; Obodai 53,73; Ibrahimovic 82; de Ridder 90	13,000

MONTHLY POINTS TALLY

AUGUST	9	100%
SEPTEMBER	6	67%
OCTOBER	7	78%
NOVEMBER	12	100%
DECEMBER	3	50%
JANUARY	6	100%
FEBRUARY	12	67%
MARCH	10	83%
APRIL	6	50%
MAY	9	100%

LEAGUE GOALS

	PLAYER	MINS	GOALS	AVE
1	Ibrahimovic	1432	13	110
2	Sonck	1756	9	195
3	Sneijder	2387	9	265
4	Mitea	977	7	140
5	van der Vaart	2074	7	296
6	Sikora	1102	5	220
7	Galasek	2538	4	635
8	Soetaers	1092	4	273
9	Heitinga	2225	3	742
10	Pienaar	1244	3	415
11	Anastasiou	760	3	253
12	Maxwell	2734	2	1367
13	Obodai	450	2	225
	Other		8	
	TOTAL		79	

KEY PLAYERS - GOALSCORERS

Zlatan Ibrahimovic

Goals in the League	13
Contribution to Attacking Power Average number of minutes between League team goals while on pitch	32
Player Strike Rate The total number of minutes he was on the pitch for every League goal scored	110
Club Strike Rate Average number of minutes between League goals scored by club	39

	PLAYER	GOALS LGE	POWER	S RATE
1	Zlatan Ibrahimovic	13	32	110 mins
2	Wesley Sonck	9	34	195 mins
3	Wesley Sneijder	9	45	265 mins
4	Rafael van der Vaart	7	47	296 mins

KEY PLAYERS - MIDFIELDERS

Wesley Sneijder

Goals in the League	9
Defensive Rating Average number of mins between League goals conceded while on the pitch	126
Contribution to Attacking Power Average number of minutes between League team goals while on pitch	46
Scoring Difference Defensive Rating minus Contribution to Attacking Power	80

	PLAYER	GOALS LGE	DEF RATE	ATT POWER	SCORE DIFF
1	Wesley Sneijder	9	126	46	80 mins
2	Steven Pienaar	3	113	36	77 mins
3	Rafael van der Vaart	7	109	47	62 mins
4	Tomas Galasek	4	91	36	55 mins

KEY PLAYERS - DEFENDERS

Nigel de Jong

Goals Conceded in League	20
Clean Sheets In League games when he played at least 70 mins	11
Defensive Rating Ave number of mins between League goals conceded while on the pitch	113
Club Defensive Rating Average number of mins between League goals conceded by the club this season	99

	PLAYER	CON LGE	CLEAN SHEETS	DEF RATE
1	Nigel de Jong	20	11	113 mins
2	John Heitinga	22	11	101 mins
3	Julien Escude	27	12	100 mins
4	Scherrer Cabelino Andrade Maxw	28	12	98 mins

KEY GOALKEEPER

Bogdan Lonut Lobont

Goals Conceded in the League	22
Counting Games Games when he played at least 70 minutes	24
Clean Sheets In games when he played at least 70 mins	9
League minutes played Number of minutes played in league matches	2160
Defensive Rating Ave number of mins between League goals conceded while on the pitch	98

DISCIPLINARY RECORDS

	PLAYER	YELLOW	RED	AVE
1	Heitinga	4	1	445
2	Galasek	5	0	507
3	Trabelsi	1	0	565
4	van der Vaart	2	1	691
5	Grygera	2	0	699
6	Ibrahimovic	2	0	716
7	de Jong	3	0	756
8	Sneijder	3	0	795
9	Soetaers	1	0	1092
10	Pienaar	1	0	1244
11	Sonck	1	0	1756
	Other	0	0	
	TOTAL	25	2	

TOP POINT EARNERS

	PLAYER	GAMES	AV PTS
1	Grygera	12	2.67
2	Sonck	17	2.53
3	Maxwell	29	2.45
4	Sneijder	23	2.35
5	Escude	29	2.34
6	van der Vaart	21	2.33
7	Lobont	24	2.33
8	Galasek	28	2.32
9	de Jong	22	2.32
10	Pienaar	13	2.31
	CLUB AVERAGE:		**2.35**

TEAM OF THE SEASON

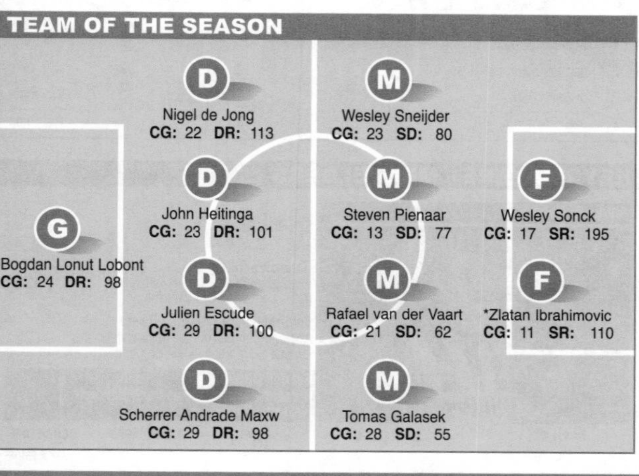
D
Nigel de Jong
CG: 22 DR: 113
M
Wesley Sneijder
CG: 23 SD: 80
D
John Heitinga
CG: 23 DR: 101
M
Steven Pienaar
CG: 13 SD: 77
F
Wesley Sonck
CG: 17 SR: 195
G
Bogdan Lonut Lobont
CG: 24 DR: 98
D
Julien Escude
CG: 29 DR: 100
M
Rafael van der Vaart
CG: 21 SD: 62
F
*Zlatan Ibrahimovic
CG: 11 SR: 110
D
Scherrer Andrade Maxw
CG: 29 DR: 98
M
Tomas Galasek
CG: 28 SD: 55

LEAGUE APPEARANCES, BOOKINGS AND CAPS

	AGE (on 01/07/04)	IN NAMED 18	APPEARANCES	COUNTING GAMES	MINUTES ON PITCH	YELLOW CARDS	RED CARDS	THIS SEASON	HOME COUNTRY
Goalkeepers									
Sander Boschker	33	10	0	0	0	0	0	-	Holland
Bogdan Lobont	26	25	24	24	2160	0	0	-	Romania
M Stekelenburg	21	30	10	10	900	0	0	-	Holland
Kenneth Vermeer	-	1	0	0	0	0	0	-	Holland
Defenders									
Nigel de Jong	19	33	32	22	2268	3	0	2	Holland (4)
Julien Escude	24	31	31	29	2699	0	0	-	France
Zdenek Grygera	24	22	20	12	1398	2	0	3	Czech Republic (10)
John Heitinga	20	27	26	23	2225	4	1	-	Holland
Maxwell	22	31	31	29	2734	0	0	-	Brazil
John O'Brien	26	4	4	3	321	0	0	-	United States
Petri Pasanen	23	11	6	4	437	0	0	-	Finland
Hatem Trabelsi	25	10	8	5	565	1	0	-	Tunisia
Jelle van Damme	20	23	6	2	206	0	0	6	Belgium (17)
Thomas Vermaelen	18	7	1	1	90	0	0	-	Belgium
Abubakarl Yakubu	22	23	11	3	461	0	0	-	Ghana
Midfielders									
Jason Culina	23	5	2	0	52	0	0	-	Australia
Tomas Galasek	31	29	29	28	2538	5	0	6	Czech Republic (10)
Anthony Obodai	21	16	8	4	450	0	0	-	Ghana
Steven Pienaar	22	16	16	13	1244	1	0	-	South Africa
Victor Sikora	26	32	27	2	1102	0	0	-	Holland
Wesley Sneijder	20	33	30	23	2387	3	0	8	Holland (4)
Rafael van der Vaart	21	27	26	21	2074	2	1	10	Holland (4)
Forwards									
Ioannis Anastasiou	31	16	13	4	760	0	0	-	Greece
Ryan Babel	18	3	1	1	90	0	0	-	Holland
Nordin Boukhari	24	0	0	0	0	0	0	-	Morocco
Tom De Mul	18	2	2	0	65	0	0	-	Belgium
Daniel de Ridder	20	18	14	8	838	0	0	-	Holland
Zlatan Ibrahimovic	22	23	22	11	1432	2	0	6	Sweden (21)
Jari Litmanen	33	7	6	0	151	0	0	2	Finland (42)
Nicolae Mitea	19	26	23	4	977	0	0	-	Romania
Tom Soetaers	23	20	17	7	1092	1	0	5	Belgium (17)
Wesley Sonck	25	26	25	17	1756	1	0	5	Belgium (17)
Wamberto	29	8	4	0	112	0	0	-	Brazil

SQUAD APPEARANCES

Match	1	2	3	4	5	6	7	8	9	10	11	12	13	14	15	16	17	18	19	20	21	22	23	24	25	26	27	28	29	30	31	32	33	34	35	36	37	38	39	40	41	42	43
Venue	A	A	A	H	H	H	A	A	H	H	A	H	H	A	H	A	A	H	H	H	A	H	H	A	A	H	H	H	A	H	A	A	A	H	H	A	H	A	H	A	A	H	A
Competition	C	L	L	C	L	L	C	L	L	C	L	L	C	L	L	C	L	L	C	L	C	L	L	L	L	L	L	L	L	L	L	L	L	L	L	L	L	L	L	L	L	L	L
Result	D	W	W	W	W	W	L	L	W	W	W	W	W	D	W	L	W	W	L	W	L	W	L	L	W	W	W	W	W	W	L	L	W	W	W	D	W	D	D	D	W	W	W

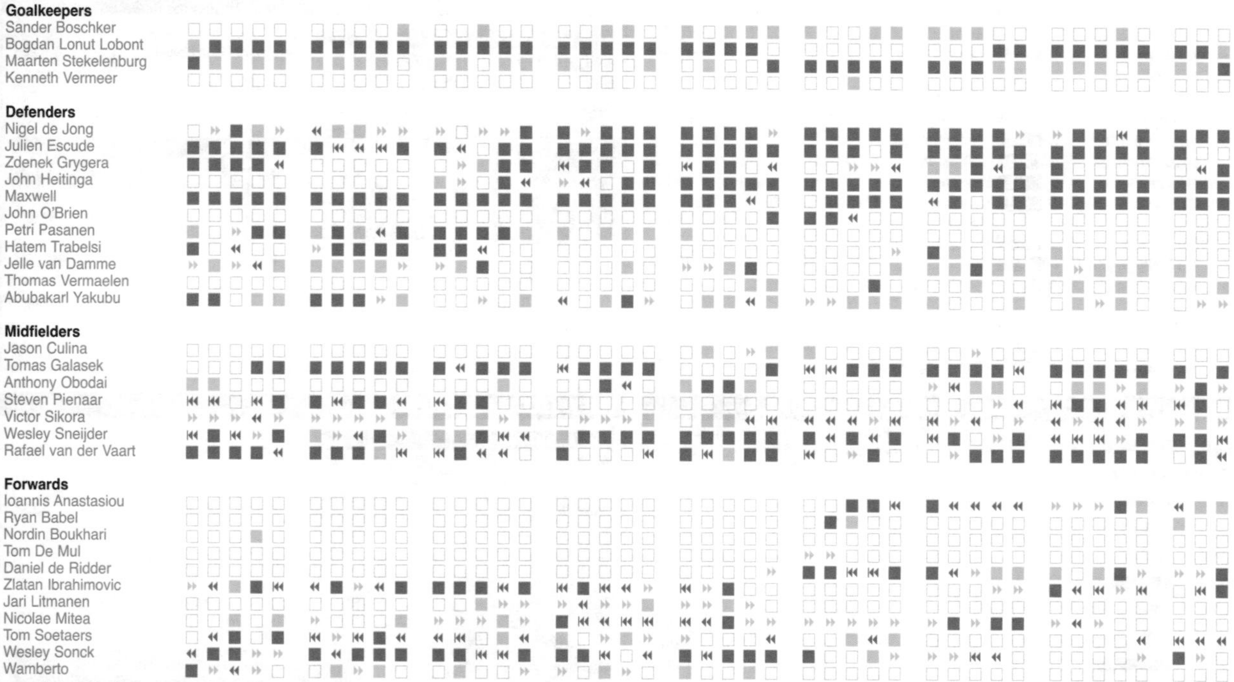

Goalkeepers
Sander Boschker
Bogdan Lonut Lobont
Maarten Stekelenburg
Kenneth Vermeer

Defenders
Nigel de Jong
Julien Escude
Zdenek Grygera
John Heitinga
Maxwell
John O'Brien
Petri Pasanen
Hatem Trabelsi
Jelle van Damme
Thomas Vermaelen
Abubakarl Yakubu

Midfielders
Jason Culina
Tomas Galasek
Anthony Obodai
Steven Pienaar
Victor Sikora
Wesley Sneijder
Rafael van der Vaart

Forwards
Ioannis Anastasiou
Ryan Babel
Nordin Boukhari
Tom De Mul
Daniel de Ridder
Zlatan Ibrahimovic
Jari Litmanen
Nicolae Mitea
Tom Soetaers
Wesley Sonck
Wamberto

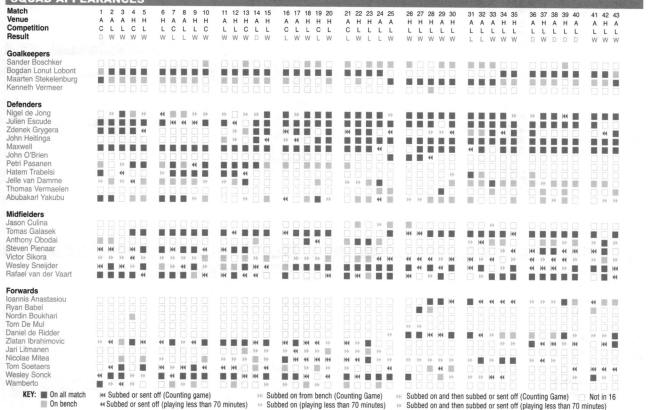

KEY: On all match · On bench · Subbed or sent off (Counting game) · Subbed or sent off (playing less than 70 minutes) · Subbed on from bench (Counting Game) · Subbed on (playing less than 70 minutes) · Subbed on and then subbed or sent off (Counting Game) · Subbed on and then subbed or sent off (playing less than 70 minutes) · Not in 16

PSV EINDHOVEN

Final Position: **2nd**

KEY: Won Drawn Lost

							Attendance
1	JCS	**Utrecht**	H	W	3-1	Robben 14; van Bommel 47; Kezman 88	
2	lge	**Roda JC Kerk**	A	D	2-2	Kezman 13,56	14,000
3	lge	**Willem II Tilb**	H	W	6-1	Ooijer 10; Rommedahl 32; van Bommel 36; Kezman 39,58; Park 63	32,000
4	lge	**Twente**	A	W	2-0	Kezman 18; Rommedahl 31	13,000
5	lge	**Utrecht**	H	W	2-1	Kezman 16; van Bommel 72	32,000
6	cl gc	**Monaco**	H	L	1-2	Bouma 65 fk	30,000
7	lge	**Feyenoord**	A	W	3-1	Kezman 7,55; Vennegoor 74	44,000
8	lge	**AZ Alkmaar**	H	L	0-1		33,500
9	cl gc	**Deportivo**	A	L	0-2		28,480
10	lge	**Den Haag**	A	W	4-0	Bouma 2; de Jong 54; Rommedahl 65; Robben 83	7,500
11	lge	**Heerenveen**	H	W	2-0	Robben 40; Kezman 79	32,500
12	cl gc	**AEK Athens**	A	W	1-0	Lucius 36	10,000
13	lge	**Ajax**	H	D	2-2	van Bommel 47; de Jong 69	35,000
14	lge	**NAC Breda**	A	W	3-1	Lucius 4; Park 32,40	14,749
15	cl gc	**AEK Athens**	H	W	2-0	Bouma 51; Robben 63	28,000
16	lge	**Roosendaal**	H	D	1-1	Molenaar 5 og	33,000
17	lge	**NEC Nijmegen**	A	W	3-2	de Jong 13; Kezman 71,73	12,500
18	cl gc	**Monaco**	A	D	1-1	Vennegoor 84	12,175
19	lge	**Zwolle**	A	W	4-0	Park 23; Vogel 34; Yobo 48 og; Robben 62	6,800
20	lge	**Volendam**	H	W	7-0	Kezman 12,50,55,57; Vennegoor 19,67; de Jong 78	32,500
21	cl gc	**Deportivo**	H	W	3-2	de Jong 14,90; Robben 48	32,000
22	lge	**RKC Waalwijk**	H	W	3-1	Lucius 2,75; Robben 55	33,500
23	hocr3	**Willem II Tilb**	H	W	2-0	Vennegoor 19,30	24,000
24	lge	**Vitesse Arnhem**	A	D	0-0		21,500
25	lge	**Groningen**	A	W	2-0	Bouma 32; Vennegoor 36	12,334
26	lge	**Zwolle**	H	W	5-1	Colin 16; de Jong 22; Vennegoor 25,75; Vonlanthen 86	31,000
27	lge	**Vitesse Arnhem**	H	W	3-0	de Jong 45; Vennegoor 77; Robben 86	32,500
28	hocqf	**NAC Breda**	H	L	0-1		20,000
29	lge	**Ajax**	A	L	1-2	Vennegoor 42	50,406
30	lge	**Twente**	H	W	1-0	Kezman 90	33,000
31	lge	**Heerenveen**	A	L	2-3	Lucius 45; Bouma 74	15,000
32	uc3rl1	**Perugia**	A	D	0-0		10,000
33	lge	**Roda JC Kerk**	H	L	1-2	Vennegoor 35	33,000
34	uc3rl2	**Perugia**	H	W	3-1	Hofland 22; Kezman 44,48	25,000
35	lge	**Utrecht**	A	W	4-0	Bouma 43; van Bommel 45; Park 85; Kezman 90	20,000
36	uc4rl1	**Auxerre**	A	D	1-1	Lucius 72	17,850
37	lge	**Feyenoord**	H	L	0-1		36,500
38	lge	**NAC Breda**	H	D	1-1	Vennegoor 17	33,000
39	uc4rl2	**Auxerre**	H	W	3-0	Kezman 4,27; van Bommel 73	25,000
40	lge	**Willem II Tilb**	A	L	1-3	Vonlanthen 80	13,330
41	lge	**RKC Waalwijk**	A	W	4-0	Vennegoor 8; Kezman 52,84; Park 59	7,200
42	ucqfl1	**Newcastle**	H	D	1-1	Kezman 15	35,000
43	lge	**Groningen**	H	W	5-0	Kezman 6,32,56; Vennegoor 76; Vonlanthen 90	32,000
44	ucqfl2	**Newcastle**	A	L	1-2	Kezman 52 pen	50,083
45	lge	**NEC Nijmegen**	H	W	3-0	Kezman 38 pen,85; van Bommel 89	33,500
46	lge	**Roosendaal**	A	W	3-0	van Bommel 13; Kezman 22 pen; Rommedahl 88	5,000
47	lge	**Volendam**	A	W	5-0	Ooijer 12; de Jong 51,58; Kezman 60,89	4,807
48	lge	**Den Haag**	H	W	3-2	Park 30; Kezman 56; Bouma 81	34,000
49	lge	**AZ Alkmaar**	A	W	4-2	Reini 2 og; Kezman 52,81,89	8,000

MONTHLY POINTS TALLY

AUGUST	7	78%
SEPTEMBER	6	67%
OCTOBER	7	78%
NOVEMBER	10	83%
DECEMBER	7	78%
JANUARY	9	100%
FEBRUARY	3	25%
MARCH	4	33%
APRIL	12	100%
MAY	9	100%

LEAGUE GOALS

	PLAYER	MINS	GOALS	AVE
1	Kezman	2282	31	74
2	Vennegoor	2164	12	180
3	de Jong	2135	8	267
4	Park	1788	7	255
5	van Bommel	2044	6	341
6	Bouma	2816	5	563
7	Robben	1751	5	350
8	Lucius	1698	4	425
9	Rommedahl	1301	4	325
10	Vonlanthen	377	3	126
11	Ooijer	1270	2	635
12	Vogel	1814	1	1814
13	Colin	1532	1	1532
	Other		3	
	TOTAL		92	

KEY PLAYERS - GOALSCORERS

Mateja Kezman

Goals in the League	31
Contribution to Attacking Power Average number of minutes between League team goals while on pitch	32
Player Strike Rate The total number of minutes he was on the pitch for every League goal scored	74
Club Strike Rate Average number of minutes between League goals scored by club	33

	PLAYER	GOALS LGE	POWER	S RATE
1	Mateja Kezman	31	32	74 mins
2	Jan Vennegoor of Hesselink	12	39	180 mins
3	Ji-Sung Park	7	30	255 mins
4	John de Jong	8	31	267 mins

KEY PLAYERS - MIDFIELDERS

Mark van Bommel

Goals in the League	6
Defensive Rating Average number of mins between League goals conceded while on the pitch	120
Contribution to Attacking Power Average number of minutes between League team goals while on pitch	33
Scoring Difference Defensive Rating minus Contribution to Attacking Power	87

	PLAYER	GOALS LGE	DEF RATE	ATT POWER	SCORE DIFF
1	Mark van Bommel	6	120	33	87 mins
2	Young-Pyo Lee	0	114	34	80 mins
3	John de Jong	8	107	32	75 mins
4	Theo Lucius	4	100	33	67 mins

KEY PLAYERS - DEFENDERS

Kevin Hofland

Goals Conceded in League	10
Clean Sheets In League games when he played at least 70 mins	7
Defensive Rating Ave number of mins between League goals conceded while on the pitch	152
Club Defensive Rating Average number of mins between League goals conceded by the club this season	102

	PLAYER	CON LGE	CLEAN SHEETS	DEF RATE
1	Kevin Hofland	10	7	152 mins
2	Kasper Bogelund	10	7	123 mins
3	Andre Ooijer	13	5	98 mins
4	Jurgen Colin	19	5	81 mins

KEY GOALKEEPER

Ronald Waterreus

Goals Conceded in the League	28
Counting Games Games when he played at least 70 minutes	33
Clean Sheets In games when he played at least 70 mins	15
League minutes played Number of minutes played in league matches	2970
Defensive Rating Ave number of mins between League goals conceded while on the pitch	106

DISCIPLINARY RECORDS

	PLAYER	YELLOW	RED	AVE
1	Hofland	7	1	190
2	Kezman	5	1	380
3	Colin	4	0	383
4	van Bommel	4	1	408
5	de Jong	4	0	533
6	Vogel	3	0	604
7	Bouma	3	0	938
8	Lee	3	0	952
9	van der Schaaf	1	0	1059
10	Bogelund	1	0	1226
11	Ooijer	1	0	1270
12	Rommedahl	1	0	1301
13	Robben	1	0	1751
	Other	4	0	
	TOTAL	42	3	

TOP POINT EARNERS

	PLAYER	GAMES	AV PTS
1	van der Schaaf	9	2.56
2	Ooijer	14	2.50
3	Rommedahl	11	2.36
4	Robben	18	2.33
5	van Bommel	22	2.27
6	Lucius	17	2.24
7	Bouma	30	2.20
8	Lee	31	2.19
9	Park	16	2.19
10	de Jong	19	2.16
	CLUB AVERAGE:		**2.18**

LEAGUE APPEARANCES, BOOKINGS AND CAPS

	AGE (on 01/07/04)	IN NAMED 18	APPEARANCES	COUNTING GAMES	MINUTES ON PITCH	YELLOW CARDS	RED CARDS	THIS SEASON	HOME COUNTRY
Goalkeepers									
Rob van Dijk	35	33	1	1	90	0	0	-	Holland
Ronald Waterreus	33	34	33	33	2970	1	0	10	Holland (4)
Defenders									
Erik Addo	25	15	8	3	379	0	0	-	Holland
Kasper Bogelund	23	17	15	13	1226	1	0	2	Denmark (14)
Jurgen Colin	23	30	20	14	1532	4	0	-	Holland
Ernest Faber	32	5	2	0	52	0	0	-	Holland
Daniel Velasco	20	12	2	0	39	0	0	-	Belgium
Kevin Hofland	25	25	20	15	1521	7	1	-	Holland
Michael Jacobsen	18	2	1	0	7	0	0	-	Denmark
Andre Ooijer	29	15	15	14	1270	1	0	6	Holland (4)
Jan Wuytens	19	3	0	0	0	0	0	-	Belgium
Midfielders									
Ibrahim Afellay	18	6	1	0	43	0	0	-	Holland
Otman Bakkal	19	6	2	0	70	1	0	-	Holland
John de Jong	27	30	29	19	2135	4	0	-	Holland
Jordi Hoogstrate	21	10	5	1	187	1	0	-	Holland
Leandro do Bomfim	20	5	1	0	23	0	0	-	Brazil
Young-Pyo Lee	27	32	32	31	2856	3	0	-	South Korea
Theo Lucius	27	24	22	17	1698	0	0	-	Holland
Ji-Sung Park	23	32	28	16	1788	0	0	-	South Korea
Mark van Bommel	27	23	23	22	2044	4	1	6	Holland (4)
van der Schaaf	25	33	18	9	1059	1	0	-	Holland
Johann Vogel	27	24	24	17	1814	3	0	-	Switzerland
Johann Vonlanthen	18	32	17	0	377	0	0	-	Switzerland
Forwards									
Wilfred Bouma	26	33	32	30	2816	3	0	5	Holland (4)
Sepp de Roover	-	5	0	0	0	0	0	-	Belgium
RolandoEdson Silva	20	4	2	1	89	0	0	-	Cape Verde
Mateja Kezman	25	29	29	22	2282	5	1	4	Serbia & Mont (45)
Argen Robben	20	23	23	18	1751	1	0	5	Holland (4)
Dennis Rommedahl	25	20	19	11	1301	1	0	6	Denmark (14)
Jan Vennegoor	25	33	30	21	2164	1	0	-	Holland

TEAM OF THE SEASON

G – Ronald Waterreus CG: 33 DR: 106

D – Kevin Hofland CG: 15 DR: 152

D – Kasper Bogelund CG: 13 DR: 123

D – Andre Ooijer CG: 14 DR: 98

D – Jurgen Colin CG: 14 DR: 81

M – Mark van Bommel CG: 22 SD: 87

M – Young-Pyo Lee CG: 31 SD: 80

M – John de Jong CG: 19 SD: 75

M – Theo Lucius CG: 17 SD: 67

F – Mateja Kezman CG: 22 SR: 74

F – Jan Vennegoor CG: 21 SR: 180

SQUAD APPEARANCES

Match	1	2	3	4	5	6	7	8	9	10	11	12	13	14	15	16	17	18	19	20	21	22	23	24	25
Venue	H	A	H	A	H	H	A	H	A	A	H	A	H	A	H	H	A	A	A	H	H	H	H	A	A
Competition	L	L	L	L	L	C	L	L	C	L	L	C	L	L	C	L	L	C	L	L	C	L	L	L	L
Result	W	D	W	W	W	L	W	L	L	W	W	W	D	W	W	D	W	D	W	W	W	W	W	D	W

Match	26	27	28	29	30	31	32	33	34	35	36	37	38	39	40	41	42	43	44	45	46	47	48	49
Venue	H	H	H	A	H	A	A	H	H	A	A	H	H	H	A	A	H	H	A	H	A	A	H	A
Competition	L	L	L	L	L	L	E	L	E	L	E	L	L	E	L	L	E	L	E	L	L	L	L	L
Result	W	W	L	L	W	L	D	L	W	W	D	L	D	W	L	W	D	W	L	W	W	W	W	W

Goalkeepers
Rob van Dijk
Ronald Waterreus

Defenders
Erik Addo
Kasper Bogelund
Jurgen Colin
Ernest Faber
Daniel Guijo Velasco
Kevin Hofland
Michael Jacobsen
Andre Ooijer
Jan Wuytens

Midfielders
Ibrahim Afellay
Otman Bakkal
John de Jong
Jordi Hoogstrate
Leandro do Bomfim
Young-Pyo Lee
Theo Lucius
Ji-Sung Park
Mark van Bommel
Remco van der Schaaf
Johann Vogel
Johann Vonlanthen

Forwards
Wilfred Bouma
Sepp de Roover
Rolando Edson Silva
Mateja Kezman
Argen Robben
Dennis Rommedahl
Jan Vennegoor

KEY: On all match | On bench | Subbed or sent off (Counting game) | Subbed or sent off (playing less than 70 minutes) | Subbed on from bench (Counting Game) | Subbed on (playing less than 70 minutes) | Subbed on and then subbed or sent off (Counting Game) | Subbed on and then subbed or sent off (playing less than 70 minutes) | Not in 16

FEYENOORD

Final Position: **3rd**

KEY: ☐ Won ☐ Drawn ☐ Lost

							Attendance
1	lge	NEC Nijmegen	H	W	2-1	Lazovic 53; Buffel 74	42,000
2	lge	Heerenveen	A	L	0-1		14,600
3	lge	NAC Breda	H	W	2-1	Bombarda 83; Buffel 90	42,000
4	lge	AZ Alkmaar	A	D	2-2	Kuijt 9 pen,80	7,821
5	lge	PSV Eindhoven	H	L	1-3	Buffel 20	44,000
6	uc1rl1	Karnten	H	W	2-1	Kuijt 63; Buffel 77	25,000
7	lge	Zwolle	A	W	3-0	Ono 53,71; Lurling 69	6,600
8	lge	Roosendaal	H	W	2-0	van Persie 14; Lurling 90	41,000
9	uc1rl2	Karnten	A	W	1-0	Buffel 15	7,000
10	lge	Roda JC Kerk	A	D	1-1	Kuijt 3	13,000
11	lge	Willem II Tilb	H	W	2-1	Lurling 31; Buffel 90	44,000
12	lge	Groningen	A	D	3-3	Lurling 5; Kuijt 35; Paauwe 45	12,500
13	uc2rl1	FK Teplice	H	L	0-2		27,000
14	lge	Volendam	A	W	3-1	Kuijt 4 pen,86; van Persie 81	6,113
15	lge	Vitesse Arnhem	H	W	3-0	van Persie 22; Paauwe 33; Kuijt 80	40,500
16	uc2rl2	FK Teplice	A	D	1-1	Snojil 37	17,054
17	lge	Ajax	A	L	0-2		50,344
18	lge	Den Haag	H	W	4-1	van Persie 24,47; van Wonderen 45; Pardo 58	40,800
19	lge	Twente	A	L	2-4	Kuijt 44; Pardo 86	13,250
20	hocr3	Vitesse Arnhem	H	W	1-0	Lurling 36	13,054
21	lge	RKC Waalwijk	A	D	0-0		6,500
22	lge	Utrecht	H	W	3-2	Buffel 28; Lazovic 79,81	39,800
23	lge	NEC Nijmegen	A	W	2-1	Kuijt 46; Buffel 57	12,500
24	lge	Twente	H	W	3-2	Buffel 10,68; Kuijt 36	40,000
25	hocqf	Twente	A	L	1-3	Kuijt 29	11,250
26	lge	Vitesse Arnhem	A	D	0-0		18,750
27	lge	AZ Alkmaar	H	L	0-3		41,500
28	lge	Den Haag	A	D	2-2	van Persie 37; Buffel 45	8,083
29	lge	Willem II Tilb	A	W	3-0	Lurling 60; Song 71; Smolarek 84	14,000
30	lge	Heerenveen	H	D	2-2	Buffel 75,82	45,000
31	lge	PSV Eindhoven	A	W	1-0	Smolarek 13	36,500
32	lge	RKC Waalwijk	H	W	1-0	Kuijt 6	38,000
33	lge	Roda JC Kerk	H	W	3-0	Buffel 17; Kuijt 58 pen; Smolarek 75	43,500
34	lge	NAC Breda	A	W	3-0	van den Berg 51; Buffel 66; Barakat 73 og	15,900
35	lge	Ajax	H	D	1-1	Kuijt 89	51,000
36	lge	Utrecht	A	W	3-0	Smolarek 52,76; Kuijt 63	21,000
37	lge	Volendam	H	W	2-0	Smolarek 43; Kuijt 75 pen	42,000
38	lge	Groningen	H	L	1-2	Kuijt 55	39,600
39	lge	Roosendaal	A	W	4-1	Kuijt 18; Buffel 36; Paauwe 74; Smolarek 80	5,000
40	lge	Zwolle	H	W	7-1	Lazovic 2,8,81; Kuijt 16,28,79; Paauwe 50	44,000

KEY PLAYERS - GOALSCORERS

Dirk Kuijt

Goals in the League	**20**
Contribution to Attacking Power Average number of minutes between League team goals while on pitch	**42**
Player Strike Rate The total number of minutes he was on the pitch for every League goal scored	**152**
Club Strike Rate Average number of minutes between League goals scored by club	**43**

	PLAYER	GOALS LGE	POWER	S RATE
1	Dirk Kuijt	20	42	152 mins
2	Thomas Buffel	14	43	211 mins
3	Robin van Persie	6	51	248 mins
4	Anthony Lurling	5	38	346 mins

KEY PLAYERS - MIDFIELDERS

Anthony Lurling

Goals in the League	**5**
Defensive Rating Average number of mins between League goals conceded while on the pitch	**115**
Contribution to Attacking Power Average number of minutes between League team goals while on pitch	**38**
Scoring Difference Defensive Rating minus Contribution to Attacking Power	**77**

	PLAYER	GOALS LGE	DEF RATE	ATT POWER	SCORE DIFF
1	Anthony Lurling	5	115	38	77 mins
2	Shinji Ono	2	101	39	62 mins
3	Thomas Buffel	14	80	44	36 mins
4	Alfred Schreuder	0	64	49	15 mins

KEY PLAYERS - DEFENDERS

Peter van den Berg

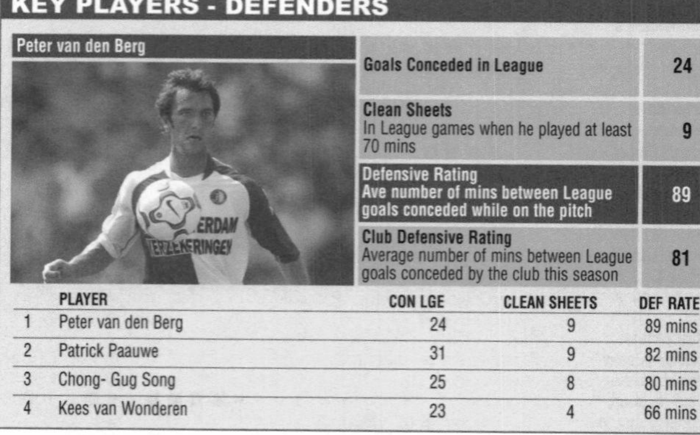

Goals Conceded in League	**24**
Clean Sheets In League games when he played at least 70 mins	**9**
Defensive Rating Ave number of mins between League goals conceded while on the pitch	**89**
Club Defensive Rating Average number of mins between League goals conceded by the club this season	**81**

	PLAYER	CON LGE	CLEAN SHEETS	DEF RATE
1	Peter van den Berg	24	9	89 mins
2	Patrick Paauwe	31	9	82 mins
3	Chong- Gug Song	25	8	80 mins
4	Kees van Wonderen	23	4	66 mins

MONTHLY POINTS TALLY

AUGUST	6	67%
SEPTEMBER	4	44%
OCTOBER	7	78%
NOVEMBER	7	58%
DECEMBER	4	44%
JANUARY	6	100%
FEBRUARY	8	53%
MARCH	10	83%
APRIL	10	83%
MAY	6	67%

LEAGUE GOALS

	PLAYER	MINS	GOALS	AVE
1	Kuijt	3044	20	152
2	Buffel	2958	14	211
3	Smolarek	1376	7	197
4	Lazovic	784	6	131
5	van Persie	1485	6	248
6	Lurling	1731	5	346
7	Paauwe	2543	4	636
8	Pardo	1048	2	524
9	Ono	1825	2	913
10	Bombarda	66	1	66
11	Song	1992	1	1992
12	van Wonderen	1526	1	1526
13	van den Berg	2127	1	2127
	Other		1	
	TOTAL		71	

KEY GOALKEEPER

Edwin Zoetebier

Goals Conceded in the League	**19**
Counting Games Games when he played at least 70 minutes	**20**
Clean Sheets In games when he played at least 70 mins	**7**
League minutes played Number of minutes played in league matches	**1768**
Defensive Rating Ave number of mins between League goals conceded while on the pitch	**93**

DISCIPLINARY RECORDS

	PLAYER	YELLOW	RED	AVE
1	Gyan	1	1	239
2	Schreuder	7	0	284
3	Paauwe	6	0	423
4	Mtiliga	2	0	495
5	Pardo	2	0	524
6	van den Berg	4	0	531
7	de Nooijer	1	0	538
8	Lurling	3	0	577
9	Song	2	1	664
10	Smolarek	2	0	688
11	van Persie	2	0	742
12	van Wonderen	2	0	763
13	Lazovic	1	0	784
	Other	11	0	
	TOTAL	46	2	

TOP POINT EARNERS

	PLAYER	GAMES	AV PTS
1	Smolarek	10	2.60
2	Ghali	12	2.42
3	de Nooijer	5	2.40
4	Mtiliga	11	2.36
5	Lurling	16	2.31
6	Lazovic	4	2.25
7	Ono	18	2.22
8	Snojil	6	2.17
9	van den Berg	22	2.14
10	Zoetebier	19	2.11
	CLUB AVERAGE:		2.00

TEAM OF THE SEASON

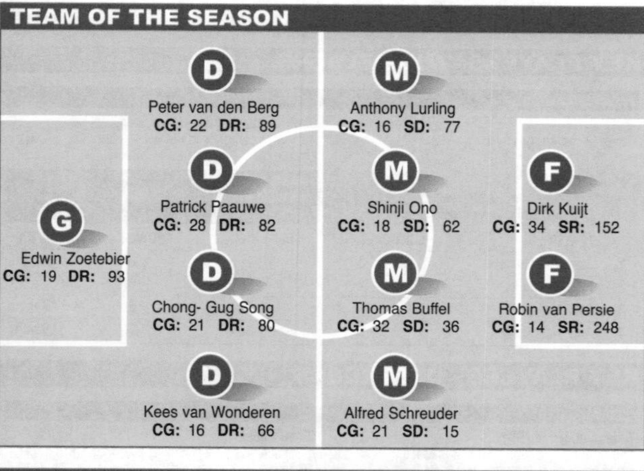

G
Edwin Zoetebier
CG: 19 DR: 93
D
Peter van den Berg
CG: 22 DR: 89
D
Patrick Paauwe
CG: 28 DR: 82
D
Chong- Gug Song
CG: 21 DR: 80
D
Kees van Wonderen
CG: 16 DR: 66
M
Anthony Lurling
CG: 16 SD: 77
M
Shinji Ono
CG: 18 SD: 62
M
Thomas Buffel
CG: 32 SD: 36
M
Alfred Schreuder
CG: 21 SD: 15
F
Dirk Kuijt
CG: 34 SR: 152
F
Robin van Persie
CG: 14 SR: 248

LEAGUE APPEARANCES, BOOKINGS AND CAPS

	AGE (on 01/07/04)	IN NAMED 18	APPEARANCES	COUNTING GAMES	MINUTES ON PITCH	YELLOW CARDS	RED CARDS	THIS SEASON	HOME COUNTRY
Goalkeepers									
Patrick Lodewijks	37	22	15	14	1292	0	0	-	Holland
Zbigniew Malkowski	26	15	0	0	0	0	0	-	Poland
Edwin Zoetebier	34	28	20	19	1768	0	0	-	Holland
Defenders									
Reinhard Breinburg	-	2	0	0	0	0	0	-	Holland
Gerard de Nooijer	35	11	7	5	538	1	0	-	Holland
Christian Gyan	25	16	6	5	478	1	1	-	Ghana
Carlos Donde Jean	20	4	1	0	10	0	0	-	Brazil
Glenn Loovens	20	2	0	0	0	0	0	-	Holland
Patrick Paauwe	28	29	29	28	2543	6	0	-	Holland
Ferne Snojil	19	11	8	6	576	0	0	-	China
Chong- Gug Song	25	30	25	21	1992	2	1	-	South Korea
Peter van den Berg	32	31	25	22	2127	4	0	-	Holland
Ramon van Haaren	31	10	8	7	648	0	0	-	Holland
Kees van Wonderen	35	19	18	16	1526	2	0	-	Holland
Midfielders									
Jorge Acuna	25	21	5	5	419	2	0	-	Chile
Thomas Buffel	23	34	34	32	2958	3	0	7	Belgium (17)
Hossam Ghali	22	16	13	12	1125	1	0	-	Egypt
Anthony Lurling	27	28	27	16	1731	3	0	-	Holland
Shinji Ono	24	24	24	18	1825	2	0	-	Japan
Sebastien Pardo	22	20	15	10	1048	2	0	-	Chile
Alfred Schreuder	31	29	24	21	1990	7	0	-	Holland
Gill Swerts	21	32	17	12	1168	1	0	-	Belgium
Forwards									
Mariano Bombarda	31	21	4	0	66	0	0	-	Argentina
Salomon Kalou	18	3	1	0	23	0	0	-	Ivory Coast
Dirk Kuijt	23	34	34	34	3044	2	0	-	Holland
Danko Lazovic	21	29	23	4	784	1	0	-	Serbia & Montenegro
Leonardo Santiago	21	3	3	0	64	0	0	-	Brazil
Patrick Mtiliga	23	11	11	11	990	2	0	-	Denmark
Euzebiusz Smolarek	23	21	21	10	1376	2	0	-	Poland
Robin van Persie	20	31	28	14	1485	2	0	-	Holland

SQUAD APPEARANCES

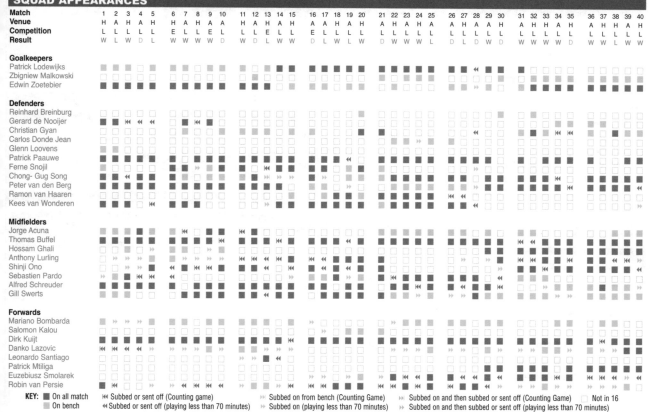

Match	1	2	3	4	5	6	7	8	9	10	11	12	13	14	15	16	17	18	19	20	21	22	23	24	25	26	27	28	29	30	31	32	33	34	35	36	37	38	39	40
Venue	H	A	H	A	H	H	A	H	A	A	H	A	H	A	H	A	A	H	A	H	A	H	A	H	A	A	H	A	A	H	A	H	H	A	H	A	H	H	A	H
Competition	L	L	L	L	L	E	L	L	E	L	L	L	E	L	L	E	L	L	L	L	L	L	L	L	L	L	L	L	L	L	L	L	L	L	L	L	L	L	L	L
Result	W	L	W	D	L	W	W	W	W	D	W	D	L	W	W	D	L	W	L	W	D	W	W	W	L	D	L	D	W	D	W	W	W	W	D	W	W	L	W	W

Goalkeepers
Patrick Lodewijks
Zbigniew Malkowski
Edwin Zoetebier

Defenders
Reinhard Breinburg
Gerard de Nooijer
Christian Gyan
Carlos Donde Jean
Glenn Loovens
Patrick Paauwe
Ferne Snojil
Chong- Gug Song
Peter van den Berg
Ramon van Haaren
Kees van Wonderen

Midfielders
Jorge Acuna
Thomas Buffel
Hossam Ghali
Anthony Lurling
Shinji Ono
Sebastien Pardo
Alfred Schreuder
Gill Swerts

Forwards
Mariano Bombarda
Salomon Kalou
Dirk Kuijt
Danko Lazovic
Leonardo Santiago
Patrick Mtiliga
Euzebiusz Smolarek
Robin van Persie

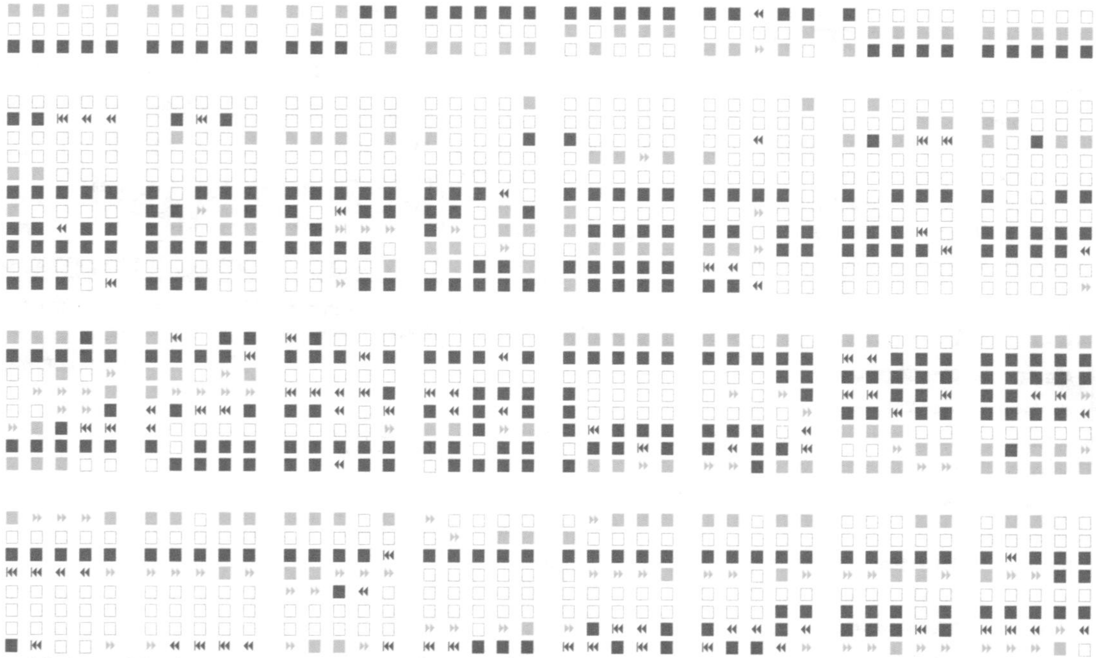

KEY: On all match · On bench · Subbed or sent off (Counting game) · Subbed or sent off (playing less than 70 minutes) · Subbed on from bench (Counting Game) · Subbed on (playing less than 70 minutes) · Subbed on and then subbed or sent off (Counting Game) · Subbed on and then subbed or sent off (playing less than 70 minutes) · Not in 16

HEERENVEEN

Final Position: **4th**

KEY: Won Drawn Lost

#	Comp	Opponent	H/A	Res	Score	Scorers	Attendance
1	lge	Volendam	A	W	1-0	Selakovic 29 pen	5,037
2	lge	Feyenoord	H	W	1-0	Sibon 19	14,600
3	etfl2	Villarreal	A	D	0-0		23,000
4	lge	Willem II Tilb	A	L	0-2		11,500
5	hocr1	SDC Putten	A	W	4-0	Vayrynen 41; Selakovic 57,73,86	
6	lge	Groningen	H	W	1-0	Hansson 38	14,000
7	lge	AZ Alkmaar	A	L	1-3	Knopper 42	7,636
8	hocr2	AZ Alkmaar	H	W	3-1	Sibon 22; Selakovic 58 pen; Correia 60	
9	lge	Twente	H	W	3-0	Knopper 11; Sibon 15,61	14,500
10	lge	RKC Waalwijk	H	W	1-0	Knopper 45	14,300
11	lge	PSV Eindhoven	A	L	0-2		32,500
12	lge	NEC Nijmegen	H	L	1-2	Samaras 87	14,500
13	hocr3	Telstar	H	W	3-1	Sibon 31; Knopper 41,70	6,200
14	lge	Utrecht	A	L	1-2	Knopper 88	18,000
15	lge	Zwolle	H	D	1-1	Sibon 60	12,500
16	lge	Ajax	A	L	1-3	Sibon 18	49,331
17	lge	Den Haag	H	W	2-0	Sibon 33; Samaras 79	14,200
18	lge	NAC Breda	A	W	3-2	Sibon 6,16; de Lange 45	12,100
19	lge	Roosendaal	A	D	1-1	Samaras 75	5,000
20	hocr3	NEC Nijmegen	H	L	0-1		9,000
21	lge	Roda JC Kerk	H	W	2-1	Samaras 7; Selakovic 78	10,400
22	lge	Vitesse Arnhem	A	W	1-0	Knopper 6	20,864
23	lge	NAC Breda	H	L	3-4	Selakovic 16; Knopper 37; Sibon 40	14,300
24	lge	RKC Waalwijk	A	D	0-0		6,500
25	lge	Willem II Tilb	H	D	1-1	Seip 18	14,300
26	lge	PSV Eindhoven	H	W	3-2	Vayrynen 45; Knopper 77; Hansson 87	15,000
27	lge	Ajax	H	W	4-1	Vayrynen 44,74; Knopper 59; Hakansson 83	13,500
28	lge	NEC Nijmegen	A	W	2-1	Vayrynen 62,80	12,000
29	lge	Feyenoord	A	D	2-2	Selakovic 12 pen; Knopper 66	45,000
30	lge	Volendam	H	W	2-1	Sibon 7; Hakansson 88	15,000
31	lge	Groningen	A	D	0-0		12,500
32	lge	Roosendaal	H	W	1-0	Sibon 45	14,500
33	lge	Roda JC Kerk	A	W	1-0	Vayrynen 88	12,318
34	lge	Utrecht	H	W	4-0	Sibon 27,30,33; Hakansson 58	15,050
35	lge	Zwolle	A	L	0-1		6,500
36	lge	Vitesse Arnhem	H	D	0-0		15,150
37	lge	Den Haag	A	L	0-1		13,501
38	lge	AZ Alkmaar	H	W	1-0	Sibon 80	15,000
39	lge	Twente	A	L	0-2		13,250

MONTHLY POINTS TALLY

Month	Points	%
AUGUST	6	67%
SEPTEMBER	6	67%
OCTOBER	3	33%
NOVEMBER	1	11%
DECEMBER	10	83%
JANUARY	3	100%
FEBRUARY	11	61%
MARCH	8	67%
APRIL	7	58%
MAY	3	33%

KEY PLAYERS - GOALSCORERS

Gerald Sibon

Goals in the League	15	Player Strike Rate Average number of minutes between League goals scored by player	128
Contribution to Attacking Power Average number of minutes between League team goals while on pitch	74	Club Strike Rate Average number of minutes between League goals scored by club	68

	PLAYER	LGE GOALS	POWER	STRIKE RATE
1	Gerald Sibon	15	74	128 mins
2	Richard Knopper	9	72	296 mins
3	Mika Vayrynen	6	64	460 mins
4	Jesper Hakansson	3	61	494 mins

KEY PLAYERS - MIDFIELDERS

Jesper Hakansson

Goals in the League	3	Contribution to Attacking Power Average number of minutes between League team goals while on pitch	62
Defensive Rating Average number of mins between League goals conceded while he was on the pitch	114	Scoring Difference Defensive Rating minus Contribution to Attacking Power	52

	PLAYER	LGE GOALS	DEF RATE	POWER	SCORE DIFF
1	Jesper Hakansson	3	114	62	52 mins
2	Paul de Lange	1	88	67	21 mins
3	Mika Vayrynen	6	81	64	17 mins
4	Arek Radomski	0	86	70	16 mins

KEY PLAYERS - DEFENDERS

Said Bakkati

Goals Conceded (GC) The number of League goals conceded while he was on the pitch	18	Clean Sheets In games when he played at least 70 minutes	10
Defensive Rating Ave number of mins between League goals conceded while on the pitch	115	Club Defensive Rating Average number of mins between League goals conceded by the club this season	87

	PLAYER	CON LGE	CLEAN SHEETS	DEF RATE
1	Said Bakkati	18	10	115 mins
2	Marcel Seip	22	11	96 mins
3	Erik Edman	27	11	91 mins
4	Petter Hansson	35	13	85 mins

KEY GOALKEEPER

Hans Vonk

Goals Conceded in the League	34	Counting Games Games when he played at least 70 mins	33
Defensive Rating Ave number of mins between League goals conceded while on the pitch	87	Clean Sheets In games when he played at least 70 mins	14

LEAGUE GOALS

Gerald Sibon

Minutes on the pitch	1927	Goals in the League	15
League average (mins between goals)	128		

	PLAYER	MINS	GOALS	AVE
1	Sibon	1927	15	128
2	Knopper	2667	9	296
3	Vayrynen	2762	6	460
4	Selakovic	2782	4	696
5	Samaras	1070	4	268
6	Hakansson	1481	3	494
7	Hansson	2970	2	1485
8	Seip	2105	1	2105
9	de Lange	1408	1	1408
	Other		0	
	TOTAL		45	

DISCIPLINARY RECORDS

	PLAYER	YELLOW	RED	AVE
1	Haarala	2	0	290
2	Edman	6	1	349
3	de Lange	3	0	469
4	Bakkati	4	0	519
5	Vayrynen	5	0	552
6	Radomski	4	0	625
7	Sibon	2	0	963
8	Seip	2	0	1052
9	Selakovic	2	0	1391
10	Hakansson	1	0	1481
11	Hansson	2	0	1485
12	Knopper	1	0	2667
13	Vonk	1	0	2970
	Other	2	0	
	TOTAL	37	1	

TOP POINT EARNERS

	PLAYER	GAMES	AV PTS
1	Venema	2	3.00
2	Sijp	6	2.17
3	Hooiveld	5	2.00
4	Hakansson	14	1.93
5	Samaras	7	1.86
6	Sibon	19	1.84
7	Selakovic	31	1.81
8	Seip	23	1.78
9	Edman	27	1.78
10	Bakkati	21	1.76
	CLUB AVERAGE:		1.71

LEAGUE APPEARANCES, BOOKINGS AND CAPS

	AGE (on 01/07/04)	IN NAMED 18	APPEARANCES	COUNTING GAMES	MINUTES ON PITCH	YELLOW CARDS	RED CARDS	THIS SEASON	HOME COUNTRY
Goalkeepers									
Jacob De Vries	24	3	0	0	0	0	0	-	Holland
Hans Vonk	34	33	33	33	2970	1	0	-	South Africa
Boy Waterman	20	32	1	1	90	0	0	-	Holland
Defenders									
Said Bakkati	22	25	25	21	2078	4	0	-	Holland
Jeroen Drost	17	1	0	0	0	0	0	-	Holland
Erik Edman	25	28	28	27	2447	6	1	8	Sweden (21)
Johan Hansma	35	6	1	1	85	0	0	-	Holland
Petter Hansson	27	33	33	33	2970	2	0	3	Sweden (21)
Marcel Seip	22	27	25	23	2105	2	0	-	Holland
Stephan van Hoving	21	8	4	3	311	1	0	-	Holland
Ronnie Venema	29	18	8	2	296	1	0	-	Holland
Spencer Verbiest	20	14	1	0	24	0	0	-	Belgium
Midfielders									
Abgar Barsom	26	1	0	0	0	0	0	-	Sweden
Paul de Lange	23	33	26	11	1408	3	0	-	Holland
Mark Jan Fledderus	19	14	3	0	59	0	0	-	Holland
Hannu Haarala	22	15	9	5	581	2	0	-	Finland
Jesper Hakansson	23	30	23	14	1481	1	0	-	Denmark
Daniel Berg Hestad	28	18	15	9	965	0	0	-	Norway
Jos Hooiveld	21	25	11	5	495	0	0	-	Holland
Thomas Prager	18	17	2	0	39	0	0	-	Holland
Arek Radomski	27	28	28	28	2502	4	0	-	Poland
Georgios Samaras	19	28	27	7	1070	0	0	-	Holland
Marcel Sijp	22	6	6	6	540	0	0	-	Holland
Mika Vayrynen	22	32	32	30	2762	5	0	-	Finland
Jerrel Wolfgang	-	11	0	0	0	0	0	-	Holland
Forwards									
Antonio Correia	20	16	13	5	701	0	0	-	Angola
R Denneboom	23	2	1	1	69	0	0	-	Holland
Richard Knopper	26	32	32	29	2667	1	0	-	Holland
Santi Kolk	22	4	3	1	126	0	0	-	Holland
Maceo Rigters	20	5	2	1	102	0	0	-	Holland
Stefan Selakovic	27	33	33	31	2782	2	0	-	Sweden
Gerald Sibon	30	25	25	19	1927	2	0	-	Holland
Mark van Eijk	22	1	0	0	0	0	0	-	Holland

TEAM OF THE SEASON

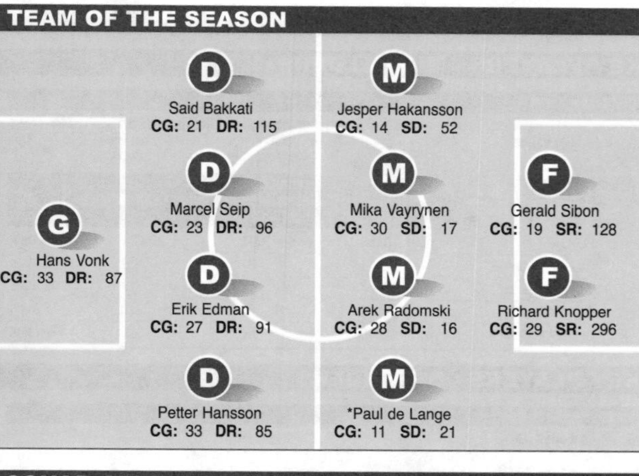

D
Said Bakkati
CG: 21 DR: 115
D
Marcel Seip
CG: 23 DR: 96
D
Erik Edman
CG: 27 DR: 91
D
Petter Hansson
CG: 33 DR: 85
G
Hans Vonk
CG: 33 DR: 87
M
Jesper Hakansson
CG: 14 SD: 52
M
Mika Vayrynen
CG: 30 SD: 17
M
Arek Radomski
CG: 28 SD: 16
M
*Paul de Lange
CG: 11 SD: 21
F
Gerald Sibon
CG: 19 SR: 128
F
Richard Knopper
CG: 29 SR: 296

SQUAD APPEARANCES

Match	1	2	3	4	5	6	7	8	9	10	11	12	13	14	15	16	17	18	19	20	21	22	23	24	25	26	27	28	29	30	31	32	33	34	35	36	37	38	39
Venue	A	H	A	A	A	H	A	H	H	H	A	H	H	A	H	A	H	A	A	H	H	A	H	A	H	H	H	A	A	H	A	H	A	H	A	H	A	H	A
Competition	L	L	L	L	L	L	L	L	L	L	L	L	L	L	L	L	L	L	L	L	L	L	L	L	L	L	L	L	L	L	L	L	L	L	L	L	L	L	L
Result	W	W	D	L	W	W	L	W	W	W	L	L	W	L	D	L	W	W	D	L	W	W	L	D	D	W	W	W	D	W	D	W	W	W	L	D	L	W	L

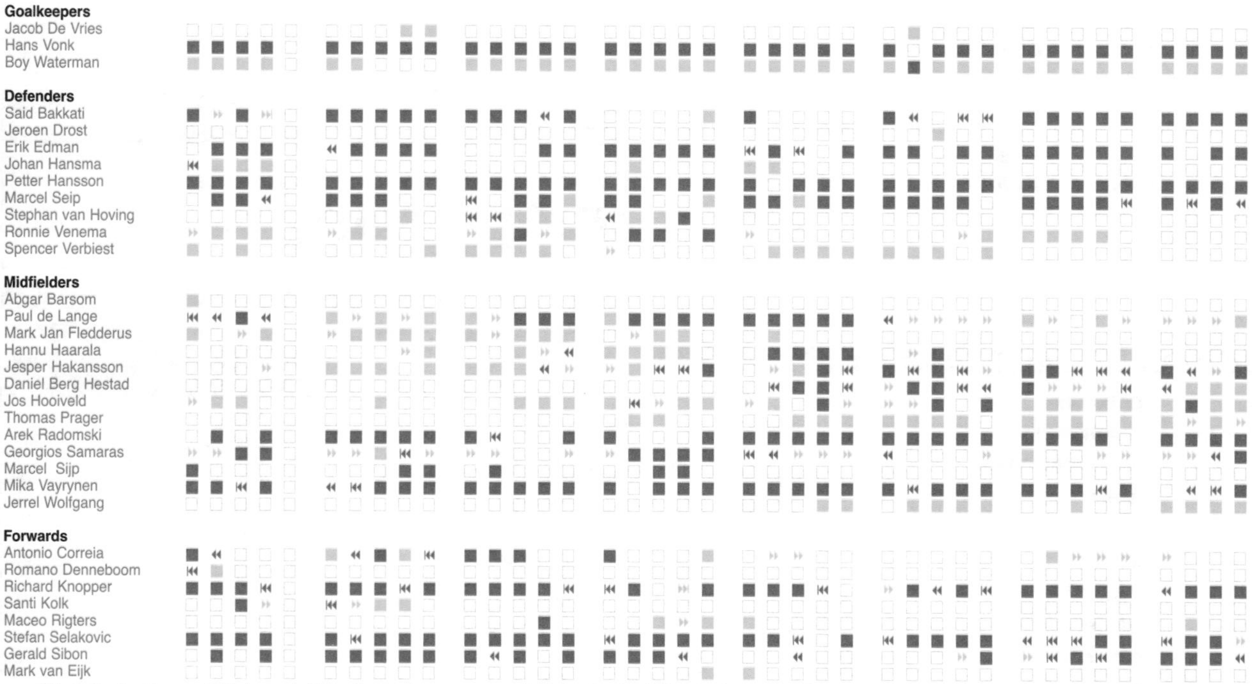

Goalkeepers
Jacob De Vries
Hans Vonk
Boy Waterman

Defenders
Said Bakkati
Jeroen Drost
Erik Edman
Johan Hansma
Petter Hansson
Marcel Seip
Stephan van Hoving
Ronnie Venema
Spencer Verbiest

Midfielders
Abgar Barsom
Paul de Lange
Mark Jan Fledderus
Hannu Haarala
Jesper Hakansson
Daniel Berg Hestad
Jos Hooiveld
Thomas Prager
Arek Radomski
Georgios Samaras
Marcel Sijp
Mika Vayrynen
Jerrel Wolfgang

Forwards
Antonio Correia
Romano Denneboom
Richard Knopper
Santi Kolk
Maceo Rigters
Stefan Selakovic
Gerald Sibon
Mark van Eijk

KEY: On all match | On bench | Subbed or sent off (Counting game) | Subbed or sent off (playing less than 70 minutes) | Subbed on from bench (Counting Game) | Subbed on (playing less than 70 minutes) | Subbed on and then subbed or sent off (Counting Game) | Subbed on and then subbed or sent off (playing less than 70 minutes) | Not in 16

AZ ALKMAAR

Final Position: **5th**

KEY: Won Drawn Lost

No.	Comp	Opponent	H/A	Res	Score	Scorers	Attendance
1	lge	Willem II Tilb	A	L	0-1		10,700
2	lge	Twente	H	W	3-0	Reini 19; Nelisse 66; Elkhattabi 87	6,776
3	lge	Vitesse Arnhem	A	W	2-1	Buskermolen 41; Meerdink 86	17,500
4	hocr1	J Heerenveen	A	W	3-1	de Cler 23; van Galen 58,76 pen	
5	lge	Feyenoord	H	D	2-2	van Galen 14; Elkhattabi 43	7,821
6	lge	Heerenveen	H	W	3-1	Elkhattabi 11; van Galen 44 pen; Perez 56	7,636
7	hocr2	Heerenveen	A	L	1-3	Huysegems 67	
8	lge	PSV Eindhoven	A	W	1-0	Nelisse 72	33,500
9	lge	NEC Nijmegen	H	W	2-0	Wijker 1; Elkhattabi 90 pen	7,700
10	lge	Utrecht	A	W	3-0	Elkhattabi 2,4; Perez 5	17,000
11	lge	Zwolle	H	W	4-0	Elkhattabi 4; Perez 38; Huysegems 40; van Galen 46	7,892
12	lge	Ajax	A	L	2-3	Perez 5,23	50,222
13	lge	NAC Breda	A	W	2-1	Huysegems 40; Perez 62	13,197
14	lge	Roda JC Kerk	H	L	1-5	Elkhattabi 66	8,275
15	lge	RKC Waalwijk	A	D	1-1	Fortes Rodriguez 90	6,000
16	lge	Groningen	H	W	2-1	Elkhattabi 17,82	7,329
17	lge	Roosendaal	A	L	0-1		5,000
18	lge	Volendam	A	W	6-0	Huysegems 28; Buskermolen 43; Elkhattabi 59,76; Perez 68,78	6,051
19	lge	Den Haag	H	L	0-1		7,069
20	lge	Willem II Tilb	H	D	0-0		7,065
21	lge	Roda JC Kerk	A	L	1-3	Wisse 70	12,000
22	lge	Volendam	H	W	3-0	van Galen 5; Huysegems 14; Elkhattabi 80	8,080
23	lge	Feyenoord	A	W	3-0	Perez 23; Elkhattabi 47; Landzaat 68 pen	41,500
24	lge	Roosendaal	H	W	2-1	van Galen 1; Buskermolen 52	7,357
25	lge	Twente	A	L	1-4	Huysegems 20	13,000
26	lge	Den Haag	A	W	3-2	van Galen 31; Wijker 81; Meerdink 90	9,049
27	lge	Utrecht	H	L	1-2	Buskermolen 47	7,577
28	lge	NEC Nijmegen	A	W	2-0	Nelisse 44; Opdam 63	12,250
29	lge	Ajax	H	D	1-1	Lindenbergh 89	8,241
30	lge	Vitesse Arnhem	H	W	2-1	Meerdink 52; Nelisse 57	7,971
31	lge	Zwolle	A	L	0-2		6,500
32	lge	Groningen	A	D	1-1	Wijker 89	11,618
33	lge	RKC Waalwijk	H	W	7-0	Meerdink 21,28,59; Perez 49; Landzaat 51; Nelisse 55,65	7,713
34	lge	NAC Breda	H	D	2-2	Meerdink 35; Landzaat 38	7,732
35	lge	Heerenveen	A	L	0-1		15,000
36	lge	PSV Eindhoven	H	L	2-4	Meerdink 16; van Galen 49	8,000

MONTHLY POINTS TALLY

Month	Points	%
AUGUST	6	67%
SEPTEMBER	7	78%
OCTOBER	9	100%
NOVEMBER	4	33%
DECEMBER	6	67%
JANUARY	1	11%
FEBRUARY	9	75%
MARCH	7	58%
APRIL	7	58%
MAY	1	11%

KEY PLAYERS - GOALSCORERS

Ali Elkhattabi

Goals in the League	14	Player Strike Rate — Average number of minutes between League goals scored by player	148
Contribution to Attacking Power — Average number of minutes between League team goals while on pitch	46	Club Strike Rate — Average number of minutes between League goals scored by club	47

	PLAYER	LGE GOALS	POWER	STRIKE RATE
1	Ali Elkhattabi	14	46	148 mins
2	Kenneth Perez	10	46	253 mins
3	Robin Nelisse	6	51	256 mins
4	Barry van Galen	7	48	313 mins

KEY PLAYERS - MIDFIELDERS

Olaf Lindenbergh

Goals in the League	1	Contribution to Attacking Power — Average number of minutes between League team goals while on pitch	39
Defensive Rating — Average number of mins between League goals conceded while he was on the pitch	81	Scoring Difference — Defensive Rating minus Contribution to Attacking Power	42

	PLAYER	LGE GOALS	DEF RATE	POWER	SCORE DIFF
1	Olaf Lindenbergh	1	81	39	42 mins
2	Barry van Galen	7	71	49	22 mins
3	Barry Opdam	1	68	51	17 mins
4	Denny Landzaat	3	66	51	15 mins

KEY PLAYERS - DEFENDERS

Michael Buskermolen

Goals Conceded (GC) — The number of League goals conceded while he was on the pitch	32	Clean Sheets — In games when he played at least 70 minutes	10
Defensive Rating — Ave number of mins between League goals conceded while on the pitch	79	Club Defensive Rating — Average number of mins between League goals conceded by the club this season	73

	PLAYER	CON LGE	CLEAN SHEETS	DEF RATE
1	Michael Buskermolen	32	10	79 mins
2	Tim de Cler	41	11	72 mins
3	Jan Kromkamp	42	11	72 mins
4	Jose Fortes Rodriguez	21	5	69 mins

KEY GOALKEEPER

Henk Timmer

Goals Conceded in the League	42	Counting Games — Games when he played at least 70 mins	34
Defensive Rating — Ave number of mins between League goals conceded while on the pitch	73	Clean Sheets — In games when he played at least 70 mins	11

LEAGUE GOALS

Ali Elkhattabi

Minutes on the pitch	2072	Goals in the League	14
League average (mins between goals)	148		

	PLAYER	MINS	GOALS	AVE
1	Elkhattabi	2072	14	148
2	Perez	2525	10	253
3	Meerdink	1030	8	129
4	van Galen	2193	7	313
5	Nelisse	1538	6	256
6	Huysegems	2121	5	424
7	Buskermolen	2530	4	633
8	Landzaat	1524	3	508
9	Wijker	685	3	228
10	Opdam	2254	1	2254
11	Fortes Rodriguez	1458	1	1458
12	Wisse	195	1	195
	Other		2	
	TOTAL		65	

DISCIPLINARY RECORDS

	PLAYER	YELLOW	RED	AVE
1	Wijker	3	1	171
2	Fortes Rodriguez	5	0	291
3	Landzaat	3	0	508
4	Perez	4	0	631
5	Buskermolen	4	0	632
6	Mans	1	0	648
7	van Galen	3	0	731
8	de Cler	3	1	742
9	Opdam	3	0	751
10	Nelisse	2	0	769
11	Lindenbergh	2	0	926
12	Elkhattabi	2	0	1036
13	Huysegems	1	0	2121
	Other	1	0	
	TOTAL	37	2	

TOP POINT EARNERS

	PLAYER	GAMES	AV PTS
1	Wijker	4	3.00
2	Mans	4	2.50
3	Huysegems	21	1.90
4	Lindenbergh	17	1.88
5	Elkhattabi	23	1.83
6	Fortes Rodriguez	15	1.80
7	Kromkamp	33	1.73
8	Timmer	34	1.68
9	Reini	15	1.67
10	Meerdink	9	1.67
	CLUB AVERAGE:		**1.68**

LEAGUE APPEARANCES, BOOKINGS AND CAPS

	AGE (on 01/07/04)	IN NAMED 18	APPEARANCES	COUNTING GAMES	MINUTES ON PITCH	YELLOW CARDS	RED CARDS	THIS SEASON	HOME COUNTRY
Goalkeepers									
Henk Timmer	32	34	34	34	3060	0	0	-	Holland
Theo Zwarthoed	21	30	0	0	0	0	0	-	Holland
Defenders									
M Buskermolen	32	31	30	25	2530	4	0	-	Holland
Tim de Cler	25	33	33	33	2970	3	1	-	Holland
Jose Rodriguez	32	25	18	15	1458	5	0	-	Spain
Jan Kromkamp	23	34	34	33	3035	1	0	-	Holland
Miel Mans	26	28	13	4	648	1	0	-	Holland
Juha Reini	29	21	19	15	1463	0	0	4	Finland (42)
Ron Vlaar	-	5	0	0	0	0	0	-	Holland
Peter Wijker	32	29	17	4	685	3	1	-	Holland
Tom Zoontjes	19	9	0	0	0	0	0	-	Holland
Midfielders									
Alair Cruz Vicente	23	12	4	1	130	0	0	-	Brazil
Christy Janga	18	4	1	0	4	0	0	-	Holland
Denny Landzaat	28	17	17	17	1524	3	0	-	Holland
Olaf Lindenbergh	30	30	29	17	1852	2	0	-	Holland
Martijn Meerdink	27	23	18	9	1030	0	0	-	Holland
Barry Opdam	28	29	28	23	2254	3	0	-	Holland
Reinier Robbemond	32	17	12	1	300	0	0	-	Holland
H van der Woude	24	6	0	0	0	0	0	-	Holland
Barry van Galen	34	33	31	16	2193	3	0	-	Holland
Forwards									
Nascimento Canigia	25	2	1	0	4	0	0	-	Brazil
Jamal Dibi	24	11	3	0	38	0	0	-	Holland
Ali Elkhattabi	27	26	25	23	2072	2	0	-	Morocco
Stein Huysegems	22	29	29	21	2121	1	0	-	Belgium
Robin Nelisse	26	33	30	13	1538	2	0	-	Holland
Kenneth Perez	29	32	32	26	2525	4	0	5	Denmark (14)
Arjan Wisse	19	11	5	2	195	0	0	-	Holland

TEAM OF THE SEASON

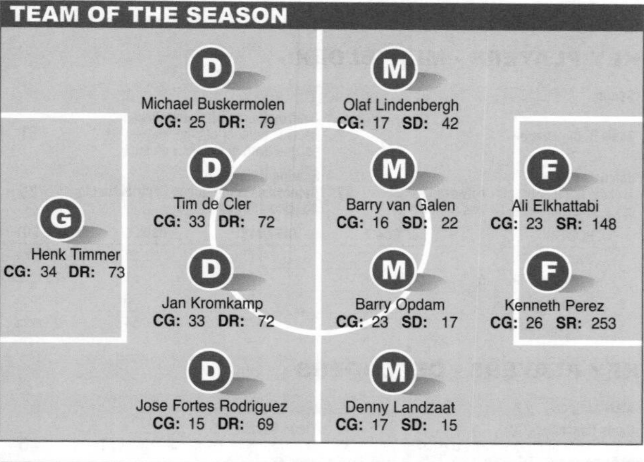

G
Henk Timmer
CG: 34 DR: 73
D
Michael Buskermolen
CG: 25 DR: 79
D
Tim de Cler
CG: 33 DR: 72
D
Jan Kromkamp
CG: 33 DR: 72
D
Jose Fortes Rodriguez
CG: 15 DR: 69
M
Olaf Lindenbergh
CG: 17 SD: 42
M
Barry van Galen
CG: 16 SD: 22
M
Barry Opdam
CG: 23 SD: 17
M
Denny Landzaat
CG: 17 SD: 15
F
Ali Elkhattabi
CG: 23 SR: 148
F
Kenneth Perez
CG: 26 SR: 253

SQUAD APPEARANCES

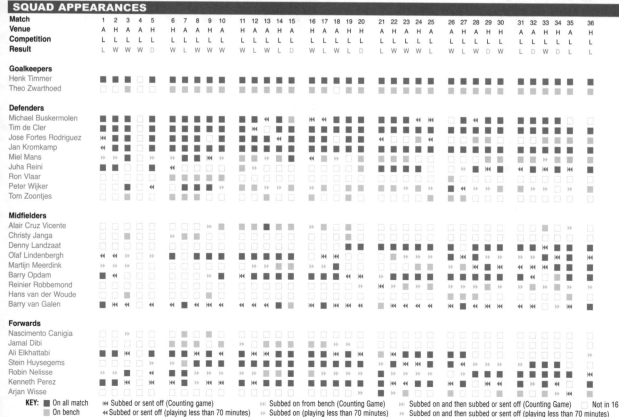

Match	1	2	3	4	5	6	7	8	9	10	11	12	13	14	15	16	17	18	19	20	21	22	23	24	25	26	27	28	29	30	31	32	33	34	35	36
Venue	A	H	A	A	H	H	A	A	H	A	H	A	A	H	A	H	A	A	H	H	A	H	A	H	A	A	H	A	H	H	A	A	H	H	A	H
Competition	L	L	L	L	L	L	L	L	L	L	L	L	L	L	L	L	L	L	L	L	L	L	L	L	L	L	L	L	L	L	L	L	L	L	L	L
Result	L	W	W	W	D	W	L	W	W	W	W	L	W	L	D	W	L	W	L	D	L	W	W	W	L	W	L	W	D	W	L	D	W	D	L	L

Goalkeepers
Henk Timmer
Theo Zwarthoed

Defenders
Michael Buskermolen
Tim de Cler
Jose Fortes Rodriguez
Jan Kromkamp
Miel Mans
Juha Reini
Ron Vlaar
Peter Wijker
Tom Zoontjes

Midfielders
Alair Cruz Vicente
Christy Janga
Denny Landzaat
Olaf Lindenbergh
Martijn Meerdink
Barry Opdam
Reinier Robbemond
Hans van der Woude
Barry van Galen

Forwards
Nascimento Canigia
Jamal Dibi
Ali Elkhattabi
Stein Huysegems
Robin Nelisse
Kenneth Perez
Arjan Wisse

KEY: On all match · On bench · Subbed or sent off (Counting game) · Subbed or sent off (playing less than 70 minutes) · Subbed on from bench (Counting Game) · Subbed on (playing less than 70 minutes) · Subbed on and then subbed or sent off (Counting Game) · Subbed on and then subbed or sent off (playing less than 70 minutes) · Not in 16

RODA JC KERK

Final Position: **6th**

KEY: ☐ Won ☐ Drawn ☐ Lost

No	Comp	Opponent	H/A	Res	Score	Scorers	Attendance
1	hocr1	Babberich	A	W	3-1	Cristiano 50, Sergio 60, Vicelich 89	
2	lge	PSV Eindhoven	H	D	2-2	Anastasiou 38 pen; van Dessel 43	14,000
3	lge	NEC Nijmegen	A	W	3-1	Cristiano 40,70; Anastasiou 61	12,250
4	lge	Roosendaal	H	L	0-2		12,500
5	lge	Zwolle	A	D	0-0		6,000
6	lge	Vitesse Arnhem	A	D	1-1	Kone 40	16,500
7	hocr2	De Baronie	A	L	0-1		
8	lge	Groningen	H	D	0-0		12,000
9	lge	Willem II Tilb	A	W	2-0	Sonko 36; Kone 88	12,300
10	lge	Feyenoord	H	D	1-1	Sergio 34	13,000
11	lge	Volendam	A	L	1-2	Senden 18	4,541
12	lge	Den Haag	H	W	5-1	Vicelich 17,43,89; Sonko 71; Kone 82	13,068
13	lge	Twente	H	W	2-1	Senden 25; Anastasiou 89	12,524
14	lge	AZ Alkmaar	A	W	5-1	Senden 44; Anastasiou 50,64; Vicelich 51; Kone 75	8,275
15	lge	Utrecht	A	L	1-3	Cristiano 69	17,100
16	lge	NAC Breda	H	D	2-2	Cristiano 7,19	12,500
17	lge	Heerenveen	A	L	1-2	Cristiano 89	10,400
18	lge	Ajax	H	L	1-2	Anastasiou 14	18,222
19	lge	RKC Waalwijk	H	W	2-1	Anastasiou 16; Kone 33	12,850
20	lge	AZ Alkmaar	H	W	3-1	Anastasiou 24; Kone 26,45	12,000
21	lge	Roosendaal	A	W	4-1	Sergio 43; Kone 69; van Dessel 86; Vicelich 89	5,000
22	lge	NAC Breda	A	D	0-0		11,580
23	lge	Volendam	H	W	1-0	Cristiano 60	12,387
24	lge	Den Haag	A	L	0-1		7,381
25	lge	PSV Eindhoven	A	W	2-1	Kone 12; Cristiano 18	33,000
26	lge	Zwolle	H	D	1-1	Redan 51	13,000
27	lge	Ajax	A	L	2-4	Redan 45; Luijpers 46	49,553
28	lge	Willem II Tilb	H	W	6-1	Kone 30; van Dijk 39; Senden 45; Redan 53; van Dessel 73; Elberkani 86	12,000
29	lge	Feyenoord	A	L	0-3		43,500
30	lge	Heerenveen	H	L	0-1		12,318
31	lge	NEC Nijmegen	H	W	4-0	Redan 31,87; Filipovic 53; Kone 55	26,226
32	lge	RKC Waalwijk	A	D	1-1	Luijpers 90	6,000
33	lge	Utrecht	H	D	1-1	Cristiano 90	13,230
34	lge	Twente	A	W	2-1	Vicelich 13; Cristiano 82	13,000
35	lge	Vitesse Arnhem	H	W	2-0	van Dessel 6; Cristiano 28	13,813
36	lge	Groningen	A	D	2-2	Cristiano 20; van Dijk 83	12,490

MONTHLY POINTS TALLY

Month	Points	%
AUGUST	4	44%
SEPTEMBER	3	33%
OCTOBER	7	58%
NOVEMBER	6	67%
DECEMBER	1	17%
JANUARY	6	67%
FEBRUARY	10	67%
MARCH	4	33%
APRIL	5	42%
MAY	7	78%

KEY PLAYERS - GOALSCORERS

Dos Santos Rodriquez Cristiano

Goals in the League	12	**Player Strike Rate** Average number of minutes between League goals scored by player	106
Contribution to Attacking Power Average number of minutes between League team goals while on pitch	49	**Club Strike Rate** Average number of minutes between League goals scored by club	51

	PLAYER	LGE GOALS	POWER	STRIKE RATE
1	Dos Santos Rodriquez Cristiano	12	49	106 mins
2	Ioannis Anastasiou	8	48	196 mins
3	Arouna Kone	11	49	203 mins
4	Ivan Vicelich	6	45	343 mins

KEY PLAYERS - MIDFIELDERS

Sergio

Goals in the League	2	**Contribution to Attacking Power** Average number of minutes between League team goals while on pitch	51
Defensive Rating Average number of mins between League goals conceded while he was on the pitch	77	**Scoring Difference** Defensive Rating minus Contribution to Attacking Power	26

	PLAYER	LGE GOALS	DEF RATE	POWER	SCORE DIFF
1	Sergio	2	77	51	26 mins
2	Sven Vandenbroeck	0	77	51	26 mins
3	Kevin van Dessel	4	74	50	24 mins
4	Gregoor van Dijk	2	77	54	23 mins

KEY PLAYERS - DEFENDERS

Mark Luijpers

Goals Conceded (GC) The number of League goals conceded while he was on the pitch	35	**Clean Sheets** In games when he played at least 70 minutes	5
Defensive Rating Ave number of mins between League goals conceded while on the pitch	75	**Club Defensive Rating** Average number of mins between League goals conceded by the club this season	75

	PLAYER	CON LGE	CLEAN SHEETS	DEF RATE
1	Mark Luijpers	35	5	75 mins
2	Roel Brouwers	19	2	73 mins
3	Predrag Filipovic	41	6	73 mins
4	Ger Senden	34	5	72 mins

KEY GOALKEEPER

Vladan Kujovic

Goals Conceded in the League	41	**Counting Games** Games when he played at least 70 mins	34
Defensive Rating Ave number of mins between League goals conceded while on the pitch	75	**Clean Sheets** In games when he played at least 70 mins	7

LEAGUE GOALS

Dos Santos Rodriquez Cristiano

Minutes on the pitch	1275	Goals in the League	12
League average (mins between goals)	106		

	PLAYER	MINS	GOALS	AVE
1	Cristiano	1275	12	106
2	Kone	2238	11	203
3	Anastasiou	1566	8	196
4	Vicelich	2060	6	343
5	van Dessel	2808	4	702
6	Redan	719	4	180
7	Senden	2454	4	614
8	Sergio	1924	2	962
9	Luijpers	2615	2	1308
10	Sonko	1049	2	525
11	van Dijk	1847	2	924
12	Filipovic	3005	1	3005
	Other		2	
	TOTAL		60	

DISCIPLINARY RECORDS

	PLAYER	YELLOW	RED	AVE
1	Addo	4	1	130
2	Sonkaya, F	4	2	181
3	Vandenbroeck	6	0	271
4	Brouwers	3	1	347
5	Senden	6	0	409
6	Berglund	1	0	462
7	van Dessel	6	0	468
8	van Hoogdalem	1	0	664
9	van Dijk	2	0	923
10	Sergio	2	0	962
11	Sonko	1	0	1049
12	Luijpers	2	0	1307
13	Filipovic	2	0	1502
	Other	4	0	
	TOTAL	44	4	

TOP POINT EARNERS

	PLAYER	GAMES	AV PTS
1	Rudge	6	2.17
2	Brouwers	13	1.85
3	Cristiano	13	1.77
4	Sergio	22	1.73
5	Senden	27	1.67
6	Kone	24	1.67
7	Luijpers	27	1.67
8	Vicelich	21	1.62
9	van Dijk	19	1.58
10	van Dessel	32	1.56
	CLUB AVERAGE:		**1.56**

LEAGUE APPEARANCES, BOOKINGS AND CAPS

	AGE (on 01/07/04)	IN NAMED 18	APPEARANCES	COUNTING GAMES	MINUTES ON PITCH	YELLOW CARDS	RED CARDS	THIS SEASON	HOME COUNTRY
Goalkeepers									
Taylan Aydagan	21	22	0	0	0	0	0	-	Turkey
Vladan Kujovic	25	34	34	34	3060	0	0	-	Serbia & Montenegro
Bas Roorda	31	9	0	0	0	0	0	-	Holland
Defenders									
Eric Addo	25	14	11	5	652	4	1	-	Ghana
Roel Brouwers	22	30	20	13	1390	3	1	-	Holland
Predrag Filipovic	29	34	34	33	3005	2	0	-	Serbia & Montenegro
Vincent Lachambre	23	13	1	0	34	0	0	-	Belgium
Mark Luijpers	33	31	31	27	2615	2	0	-	Holland
Dave Roemgens	21	7	1	0	24	1	0	-	Belgium
Humphrey Rudge	26	17	10	6	636	0	0	-	Holland
Ger Senden	33	28	28	27	2454	6	0	-	Holland
Fatih Sonkaya	23	28	14	12	1091	4	2	-	Turkey
M van Hoogdalem	32	13	10	6	664	1	0	-	Holland
Midfielders									
Seydihan Baslanti	20	11	3	0	54	0	0	-	Holland
Jerome Collinet	21	17	4	1	172	1	0	-	Belgium
Cristiano	23	25	23	13	1275	0	0	-	Brazil
Faton Popova	-	4	0	0	0	0	0	-	Turkey
Sergio	23	28	23	22	1924	2	0	-	Brazil
Edrissa Sonko	24	17	17	8	1049	1	0	-	Gambia
Kevin van Dessel	25	32	32	32	2808	6	0	-	Belgium
Gregoor van Dijk	22	31	24	19	1847	2	0	-	Holland
Alain van Mieghem	22	2	0	0	0	0	0	-	Belgium
Sven Vandenbroeck	24	31	22	15	1626	6	0	-	Belgium
Ivan Vicelich	28	34	32	21	2060	1	0	-	New Zealand
Forwards									
Ioannis Anastasiou	31	18	18	17	1566	1	0	-	Greece
Fredrik Berglund	25	14	9	3	462	1	0	-	Sweden
M Elberkani	-	13	8	1	171	0	0	-	Holland
Arouna Kone	20	28	28	24	2238	0	0	-	Ivory Coast
Iwan Redan	23	11	11	6	719	0	0	-	Holland

TEAM OF THE SEASON

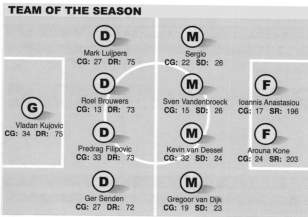

G – Vladan Kujovic CG: 34 DR: 75

D – Mark Luijpers CG: 27 DR: 75

D – Roel Brouwers CG: 13 DR: 73

D – Predrag Filipovic CG: 33 DR: 73

D – Ger Senden CG: 27 DR: 72

M – Sergio CG: 22 SD: 26

M – Sven Vandenbroeck CG: 15 SD: 26

M – Kevin van Dessel CG: 32 SD: 24

M – Gregoor van Dijk CG: 19 SD: 23

F – Ioannis Anastasiou CG: 17 SR: 196

F – Arouna Kone CG: 24 SR: 203

SQUAD APPEARANCES

Match	1	2	3	4	5	6	7	8	9	10	11	12	13	14	15	16	17	18	19	20	21	22	23	24	25	26	27	28	29	30	31	32	33	34	35	36
Venue	A	H	A	H	A	A	A	H	A	H	A	H	H	A	A	H	A	H	H	H	A	A	H	A	A	H	A	H	A	H	H	A	H	A	H	A
Competition	L	L	L	L	L	L	L	L	L	L	L	L	L	L	L	L	L	L	L	L	L	L	L	L	L	L	L	L	L	L	L	L	L	L	L	L
Result	D	D	W	L	D	D	L	D	W	D	L	W	W	W	L	D	L	L	W	W	W	D	W	L	W	D	L	W	L	L	W	D	D	W	W	D

Goalkeepers
Taylan Aydagan
Vladan Kujovic
Bas Roorda

Defenders
Eric Addo
Roel Brouwers
Predrag Filipovic
Vincent Lachambre
Mark Luijpers
Dave Roemgens
Humphrey Rudge
Ger Senden
Fatih Sonkaya
Marco van Hoogdalem

Midfielders
Seydihan Baslanti
Jerome Collinet
Dos Santos Cristiano
Faton Popova
Sergio
Edrissa Sonko
Kevin van Dessel
Gregoor van Dijk
Alain van Mieghem
Sven Vandenbroeck
Ivan Vicelich

Forwards
Ioannis Anastasiou
Fredrik Berglund
Mohammed Elberkani
Arouna Kone
Iwan Redan

KEY: On all match · On bench · Subbed or sent off (Counting game) · Subbed or sent off (playing less than 70 minutes) · Subbed on from bench (Counting Game) · Subbed on (playing less than 70 minutes) · Subbed on and then subbed or sent off (Counting Game) · Subbed on and then subbed or sent off (playing less than 70 minutes) · Not in 16

WILLEM II TILB

Final Position: **7th**

KEY: Won Drawn Lost

No	Comp	Opponent	H/A	Res	Score	Scorers	Attendance
1	hocr1	**Meersen**	A	W	0-6		
2	lge	**AZ Alkmaar**	H	W	1-0	Mathijsen, J 8	10,700
3	lge	**PSV Eindhoven**	A	L	1-6	Sektioui 18	32,000
4	lge	**Heerenveen**	H	W	2-0	Hadouir 2; Shoukov 31	11,500
5	lge	**NAC Breda**	A	D	1-1	Landzaat 7	14,500
6	lge	**Zwolle**	H	W	2-1	Shoukov 43; Mathijsen, J 89	12,050
7	hocr2	**Bennekom**	A	W	8-2	Landzaat 17; Van den Eede 34 pen,41,55; Shoukov 50; Mathijssen, D 77; Quinn 82; Caluwe 84	
8	lge	**Ajax**	A	L	0-6		47,728
9	lge	**Roda JC Kerk**	H	L	0-2		12,300
10	lge	**Roosendaal**	A	D	0-0		5,000
11	lge	**Feyenoord**	A	L	1-2	Quinn 88	44,000
12	hocr3	**FC Eindhoven**	A	W	2-0	Caluwe 58,64	830
13	lge	**RKC Waalwijk**	H	W	4-1	Caluwe 27; Quinn 32 pen; Denneboom 72; Van Den Eede 90	12,900
14	lge	**Vitesse Arnhem**	A	D	2-2	Quinn 10 pen; Caluwe 24	16,501
15	lge	**Volendam**	H	W	6-0	Quinn 34; Jaliens 36; Caluwe 41; Shoukov 56; Koning 61 og; Landzaat 90	12,300
16	lge	**NEC Nijmegen**	H	W	3-0	Denneboom 55; Caluwe 66; Van Den Eede 89	12,300
17	lge	**Utrecht**	H	L	0-2		12,900
18	lge	**Den Haag**	A	W	1-0	Quinn 35	5,211
19	hocr3	**PSV Eindhoven**	A	L	0-2		24,000
20	lge	**Groningen**	A	W	2-1	Hadouir 63,81	12,054
21	lge	**Twente**	H	L	2-3	Quinn 77; Victoria 90	13,000
22	lge	**AZ Alkmaar**	A	D	0-0		7,065
23	lge	**NAC Breda**	H	D	1-1	Caluwe 90	13,200
24	lge	**Den Haag**	H	W	1-0	Hadouir 50	12,800
25	lge	**Utrecht**	A	D	2-2	Victoria 36; Denneboom 80	17,128
26	lge	**Heerenveen**	A	D	1-1	Caluwe 90	14,300
27	lge	**Feyenoord**	H	L	0-3		14,000
28	lge	**Groningen**	H	W	2-0	Denneboom 81; Hadouir 90	13,200
29	lge	**RKC Waalwijk**	A	D	1-1	Mathijsen, J 65	5,511
30	lge	**Roda JC Kerk**	A	L	1-6	Mathijssen, D 56	12,000
31	lge	**PSV Eindhoven**	H	W	3-1	Caluwe 56; Van Den Eede 74,90	13,330
32	lge	**NEC Nijmegen**	A	L	0-4		11,500
33	lge	**Volendam**	A	W	1-0	Denissen 87	5,000
34	lge	**Vitesse Arnhem**	H	D	1-1	Van Den Eede 48	13,400
35	lge	**Twente**	A	L	0-2		13,011
36	lge	**Roosendaal**	H	W	3-0	Caluwe 30,65; Denneboom 82	8,000
37	lge	**Zwolle**	A	D	0-0		6,500
38	lge	**Ajax**	H	L	2-5	Caluwe 45; Van den Eede 71	13,000

MONTHLY POINTS TALLY

Month	Points	%
AUGUST	6	67%
SEPTEMBER	4	44%
OCTOBER	1	11%
NOVEMBER	10	83%
DECEMBER	6	67%
JANUARY	1	17%
FEBRUARY	6	40%
MARCH	7	58%
APRIL	4	33%
MAY	4	44%

KEY PLAYERS - GOALSCORERS

Tom Caluwe

Goals in the League	10	Player Strike Rate Average number of minutes between League goals scored by player	238
Contribution to Attacking Power Average number of minutes between League team goals while on pitch	55	Club Strike Rate Average number of minutes between League goals scored by club	65

	PLAYER	LGE GOALS	POWER	STRIKE RATE
1	Tom Caluwe	10	55	238 mins
2	Romano Denneboom	5	57	414 mins
3	Anouar Hadouir	5	67	420 mins
4	Dmitri Shoukov	3	76	559 mins

KEY PLAYERS - MIDFIELDERS

Raymond Victoria

Goals in the League	2	Contribution to Attacking Power Average number of minutes between League team goals while on pitch	55
Defensive Rating Average number of mins between League goals conceded while he was on the pitch	79	Scoring Difference Defensive Rating minus Contribution to Attacking Power	24

	PLAYER	LGE GOALS	DEF RATE	POWER	SCORE DIFF
1	Raymond Victoria	2	79	55	24 mins
2	Tom Caluwe	10	58	55	3 mins
3	Danny Mathijssen	1	52	61	-9 mins
4	Dmitri Shoukov	3	60	76	-16 mins

KEY PLAYERS - DEFENDERS

Joris Mathijsen

Goals Conceded (GC) The number of League goals conceded while he was on the pitch	49	Clean Sheets In games when he played at least 70 minutes	11
Defensive Rating Ave number of mins between League goals conceded while on the pitch	59	Club Defensive Rating Average number of mins between League goals conceded by the club this season	57

	PLAYER	CON LGE	CLEAN SHEETS	DEF RATE
1	Joris Mathijsen	49	11	59 mins
2	Frank van Mosselveld	42	10	59 mins
3	Jos van Nieuwstadt	32	9	58 mins
4	Kew Jaliens	54	11	54 mins

KEY GOALKEEPER

Geert De Vlieger

Goals Conceded in the League	34	Counting Games Games when he played at least 70 mins	27
Defensive Rating Ave number of mins between League goals conceded while on the pitch	68	Clean Sheets In games when he played at least 70 mins	11

LEAGUE GOALS

Tom Caluwe

Minutes on the pitch	2376	Goals in the League	10
League average (mins between goals)	238		

	PLAYER	MINS	GOALS	AVE
1	Caluwe	2376	10	238
2	Van den Eede	1485	6	248
3	Quinn	983	6	164
4	Denneboom	2071	5	414
5	Hadouir	2100	5	420
6	Mathijsen, J	2880	3	960
7	Shoukov	1677	3	559
8	Victoria	1827	2	914
9	Denissen	46	1	46
10	Sektioui	653	1	653
11	Mathijssen, D	2512	1	2512
12	Jaliens	2928	1	2928
	Other		3	
	TOTAL		47	

DISCIPLINARY RECORDS

	PLAYER	YELLOW	RED	AVE
1	Quinn	3	0	327
2	van Mosselveld	6	0	413
3	Denneboom	4	1	414
4	van Nieuwstadt	4	0	463
5	Mathijsen, J	6	0	480
6	Jaliens	5	0	585
7	Victoria	3	0	609
8	Sektioui	1	0	653
9	Wau	3	0	697
10	Shoukov	2	0	838
11	Landzaat	1	0	1024
12	Hadouir	2	0	1050
13	De Vlieger	2	0	1155
	Other	6	0	
	TOTAL	48	1	

TOP POINT EARNERS

	PLAYER	GAMES	AV PTS
1	De Vlieger	25	1.68
2	Quinn	6	1.67
3	Landzaat	10	1.60
4	van Mosselveld	28	1.57
5	Caluwe	24	1.54
6	Mathijssen, D	26	1.54
7	Denneboom	23	1.52
8	Van den Eede	12	1.50
9	Van der Struijk	2	1.50
10	Mathijsen, J	32	1.50
	CLUB AVERAGE:		1.44

TEAM OF THE SEASON

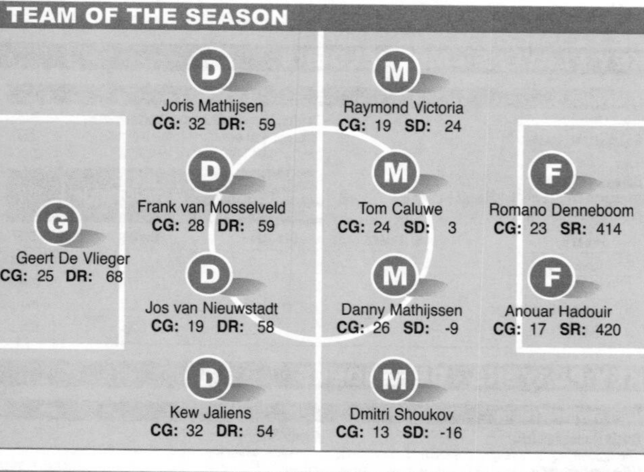
G
Geert De Vlieger
CG: 25 DR: 68
D
Joris Mathijsen
CG: 32 DR: 59
D
Frank van Mosselveld
CG: 28 DR: 59
D
Jos van Nieuwstadt
CG: 19 DR: 58
D
Kew Jaliens
CG: 32 DR: 54
M
Raymond Victoria
CG: 19 SD: 24
M
Tom Caluwe
CG: 24 SD: 3
M
Danny Mathijssen
CG: 26 SD: -9
M
Dmitri Shoukov
CG: 13 SD: -16
F
Romano Denneboom
CG: 23 SR: 414
F
Anouar Hadouir
CG: 17 SR: 420

LEAGUE APPEARANCES, BOOKINGS AND CAPS

	AGE (on 01/07/04)	IN NAMED 18	APPEARANCES	COUNTING GAMES	MINUTES ON PITCH	YELLOW CARDS	RED CARDS	THIS SEASON	HOME COUNTRY
Goalkeepers									
Ahmet Altin	18	6	0	0	0	0	0	-	Turkey
Geert De Vlieger	32	27	27	25	2311	2	0	5	Belgium (17)
Joost Peijnenburg	21	1	0	0	0	0	0	-	Holland
Peter Zois	26	32	9	8	749	0	0	-	Australia
Defenders									
Kew Jaliens	25	33	33	32	2928	5	0	-	Holland
Joris Mathijsen	24	32	32	32	2880	6	0	-	Holland
Ricardo Smits	22	9	1	0	16	0	0	-	Holland
F Van der Struijk	19	16	6	2	318	0	0	-	Holland
F van Mosselveld	20	31	29	28	2480	6	0	-	Holland
Jos van Nieuwstadt	24	31	23	19	1852	4	0	-	Holland
Nuelson Wau	23	33	28	19	2093	3	0	-	Holland
Midfielders									
Tom Caluwe	29	33	29	24	2376	2	0	-	Belgium
Sven Delanoy	20	18	4	2	235	0	0	-	Belgium
Denny Landzaat	28	13	12	10	1024	1	0	-	Holland
Youssef Mariana	30	31	7	3	379	1	0	-	Morocco
Danny Mathijssen	21	32	31	26	2512	2	0	-	Holland
Mourad Mghizrat	29	4	2	0	36	0	0	-	Morocco
Ozcan Ozkaya	23	4	2	0	34	0	0	-	Holland
Tarik Sektioui	27	12	11	6	653	1	0	-	Morocco
Dmitri Shoukov	28	25	25	13	1677	2	0	-	Russia
Stefan Van Dam	21	7	1	0	12	0	0	-	Holland
E Van der Meerakker	23	12	0	0	0	0	0	-	Holland
Raymond Victoria	31	21	21	19	1827	3	0	-	Holland
Forwards									
Jattoo Ceesay	29	6	6	1	346	0	0	-	Gambia
Erik de Kruijk	19	11	9	1	220	0	0	-	Holland
Hans Denissen	20	7	4	0	46	0	0	-	Holland
R Denneboom	23	25	25	23	2071	4	1	-	Holland
Anouar Hadouir	21	34	32	17	2100	2	0	-	Holland
James Quinn	29	27	19	6	983	3	0	2	N Ireland (114)
Bart Van den Eede	30	27	26	12	1485	1	0	-	Belgium

SQUAD APPEARANCES

Match	1	2	3	4	5	6	7	8	9	10	11	12	13	14	15	16	17	18	19	20	21	22	23	24	25	26	27	28	29	30	31	32	33	34	35	36	37	38
Venue	A	H	A	H	A	H	A	A	H	A	A	A	H	A	H	H	H	A	A	A	H	A	H	H	A	A	H	H	A	A	H	A	A	H	A	H	A	H
Competition	L	L	L	L	L	L	L	L	L	L	L	L	L	L	L	L	L	L	L	L	L	L	L	L	L	L	L	L	L	L	L	L	L	L	L	L	L	L
Result	D	W	L	W	D	W	W	L	L	D	L	W	W	D	W	W	L	W	L	W	L	D	D	W	D	D	L	W	D	L	W	L	W	D	L	W	D	L

Goalkeepers
Ahmet Altin
Geert De Vlieger
Joost Peijnenburg
Peter Zois

Defenders
Kew Jaliens
Joris Mathijsen
Ricardo Smits
Frank Van der Struijk
Frank van Mosselveld
Jos van Nieuwstadt
Nuelson Wau

Midfielders
Tom Caluwe
Sven Delanoy
Denny Landzaat
Youssef Mariana
Danny Mathijssen
Mourad Mghizrat
Ozcan Ozkaya
Tarik Sektioui
Dmitri Shoukov
Stefan Van Dam
Emile Van der Meerakker
Raymond Victoria

Forwards
Jattoo Ceesay
Erik de Kruijk
Hans Denissen
Romano Denneboom
Anouar Hadouir
James Quinn
Bart Van den Eede

KEY: ■ On all match | ■ On bench | ⏮ Subbed or sent off (Counting game) | « Subbed or sent off (playing less than 70 minutes) | » Subbed on from bench (Counting Game) | » Subbed on (playing less than 70 minutes) | » Subbed on and then subbed or sent off (Counting Game) | » Subbed on and then subbed or sent off (playing less than 70 minutes) | □ Not in 16

TWENTE ENSCHEDE

Final Position: **8th**

KEY: Won / Drawn / Lost

							Attendance
1	hocr1	VVOG	A	W	0-7		
2	lge	Roosendaal	H	W	3-1	Polak 52 fk; Christensen 75; N'Kufo 90	13,000
3	lge	AZ Alkmaar	A	L	0-3		6,776
4	lge	PSV Eindhoven	H	L	0-2		13,000
5	lge	NEC Nijmegen	A	L	1-2	John 16	12,350
6	lge	RKC Waalwijk	H	W	2-1	Sinouh 2 og; Christensen 83	13,000
7	hocr2	Kloetinge	A	W	3-0	Ramzi 5; Polak 58 pen; Gakhokidze 89	
8	lge	Heerenveen	A	L	0-3		14,500
9	lge	Vitesse Arnhem	A	W	5-3	Frankel 1 og; John 9,39; Ramzi 56; N'Kufo 72	18,437
10	lge	Groningen	H	W	5-3	John 2,38,76; N'Kufo 29; van der Weerden 82	13,200
11	lge	Utrecht	H	D	2-2	Christensen 74; Ramzi 86	13,300
12	hocr3	Cambuur	A	W	3-1	N'Kufo 45; Sibum 96; Christensen 100	2,500
13	lge	Zwolle	A	L	0-1		6,200
14	lge	Roda JC Kerk	A	L	1-2	van der Weerden 16	12,524
15	lge	Den Haag	H	W	4-0	Niemeyer 3; N'Kufo 13,64; Polak 90 pen	13,000
16	lge	NAC Breda	H	W	2-1	John 50; Christensen 86	13,150
17	lge	Volendam	A	L	0-2		4,574
18	lge	Feyenoord	H	W	4-2	N'Kufo 10,30; John 56; Polak 67 pen	13,250
19	hocr3	Jong Ajax	H	W	1-0	John 73	8,000
20	lge	Ajax	H	W	2-0	N'Kufo 38,60	13,250
21	lge	Willem II Tilb	A	W	3-2	John 19; Victoria 24 og; N'Kufo 76	13,000
22	lge	Vitesse Arnhem	H	D	0-0		13,000
23	lge	Feyenoord	A	L	2-3	Polak 77; Zomer 90	40,000
24	hocqf	Feyenoord	H	W	3-1	N'Kufo 20; Sibum 110; Christensen 111	11,250
25	lge	Zwolle	H	W	2-0	N'Kufo 63; Gakhokidze 87	13,450
26	lge	PSV Eindhoven	A	L	0-1		33,000
27	lge	Ajax	A	L	0-1		48,979
28	lge	AZ Alkmaar	H	W	4-1	Cziommer 11,59; Gakhokidze 32 pen; Ramzi 43	13,000
29	lge	NAC Breda	A	W	1-0	N'Kufo 6	11,303
30	lge	NEC Nijmegen	H	L	2-5	Ramzi 14; De Visscher 66	13,145
31	hocsf	NAC Breda	H	W	6-5*	Niemeyer 69; N'Kufo 77 (*on penalties)	13,200
32	lge	Utrecht	A	L	0-2		20,000
33	lge	Groningen	A	L	0-1		12,000
34	lge	Volendam	H	L	1-2	Ramzi 53	12,800
35	lge	Roosendaal	A	W	2-1	Cziommer 52,62	5,000
36	lge	Den Haag	A	L	0-1		7,000
37	lge	Willem II Tilb	H	W	2-0	Gakhokidze 55; N'Kufo 88	13,011
38	lge	Roda JC Kerk	H	L	1-2	Ramzi 34	13,000
39	lge	RKC Waalwijk	A	D	3-3	N'Kufo 41; Ramzi 61; Christensen 86	5,500
40	lge	Heerenveen	H	W	2-0	Christensen 15,20	13,250

MONTHLY POINTS TALLY

Month	Points	%
AUGUST	3	33%
SEPTEMBER	3	33%
OCTOBER	7	78%
NOVEMBER	6	50%
DECEMBER	6	67%
JANUARY	4	67%
FEBRUARY	6	40%
MARCH	3	25%
APRIL	6	50%
MAY	4	44%

KEY PLAYERS - GOALSCORERS

Blaise N'Kufo

Goals in the League	14	Player Strike Rate Average number of minutes between League goals scored by player	161
Contribution to Attacking Power Average number of minutes between League team goals while on pitch	49	Club Strike Rate Average number of minutes between League goals scored by club	55

	PLAYER	LGE GOALS	POWER	STRIKE RATE
1	Blaise N'Kufo	14	49	161 mins
2	Adil Ramzi	7	51	378 mins
3	Sjaak Polak	4	53	492 mins
4	Georgi Gakhokidze	3	51	731 mins

KEY PLAYERS - MIDFIELDERS

Sjaak Polak

Goals in the League	4	Contribution to Attacking Power Average number of minutes between League team goals while on pitch	53
Defensive Rating Average number of mins between League goals conceded while he was on the pitch	60	Scoring Difference Defensive Rating minus Contribution to Attacking Power	7

	PLAYER	LGE GOALS	DEF RATE	POWER	SCORE DIFF
1	Sjaak Polak	4	60	53	7 mins
2	Peter Niemeyer	1	60	60	0 mins
3	Rahim Ouedraogo	0	51	51	0 mins
4	Bas Sibum	0	62	78	-16 mins

KEY PLAYERS - DEFENDERS

Chris van der Weerden

Goals Conceded (GC) The number of League goals conceded while he was on the pitch	46	Clean Sheets In games when he played at least 70 minutes	7
Defensive Rating Ave number of mins between League goals conceded while on the pitch	58	Club Defensive Rating Average number of mins between League goals conceded by the club this season	58

	PLAYER	CON LGE	CLEAN SHEETS	DEF RATE
1	Chris van der Weerden	46	7	58 mins
2	Jeroen Heubach	46	4	55 mins
3	Patrick Pothuizen	49	4	55 mins
4	Spira Grujic	28	2	52 mins

KEY GOALKEEPER

Cees Paauwe

Goals Conceded in the League	28	Counting Games Games when he played at least 70 mins	22
Defensive Rating Ave number of mins between League goals conceded while on the pitch	64	Clean Sheets In games when he played at least 70 mins	6

LEAGUE GOALS

Blaise N'Kufo

Minutes on the pitch	2254	Goals in the League	14
League average (mins between goals)	161		

	PLAYER	MINS	GOALS	AVE
1	N'Kufo	2254	14	161
2	John	1222	9	136
3	Ramzi	2647	7	378
4	Christensen	1096	7	157
5	Polak	1966	4	492
6	Cziommer	1114	4	279
7	Gakhokidze	2193	3	731
8	van der Weerden	2677	2	1339
9	Zomer	1026	1	1026
10	Niemeyer	2654	1	2654
11	De Visscher	110	1	110
	Other		3	
	TOTAL		56	

DISCIPLINARY RECORDS

	PLAYER	YELLOW	RED	AVE
1	Heubach	8	0	318
2	Ouedraogo	5	0	456
3	Zomer	2	0	513
4	van der Weerden	5	0	535
5	Pothuizen	5	0	538
6	Gakhokidze	4	0	548
7	Cziommer	2	0	557
8	Grujic	2	0	734
9	N'Kufo	2	1	751
10	Sibum	2	0	777
11	Ramzi	2	1	882
12	ten Rouwelaar	1	0	921
13	Polak	2	0	983
	Other	3	0	
	TOTAL	45	2	

TOP POINT EARNERS

	PLAYER	GAMES	AV PTS
1	John	12	1.92
2	Ramzi	28	1.71
3	Paauwe	19	1.68
4	Polak	19	1.63
5	Zomer	10	1.60
6	N'Kufo	25	1.56
7	Gakhokidze	23	1.52
8	Allach	2	1.50
9	Heubach	28	1.46
10	van der Weerden	29	1.45
	CLUB AVERAGE:		1.41

LEAGUE APPEARANCES, BOOKINGS AND CAPS

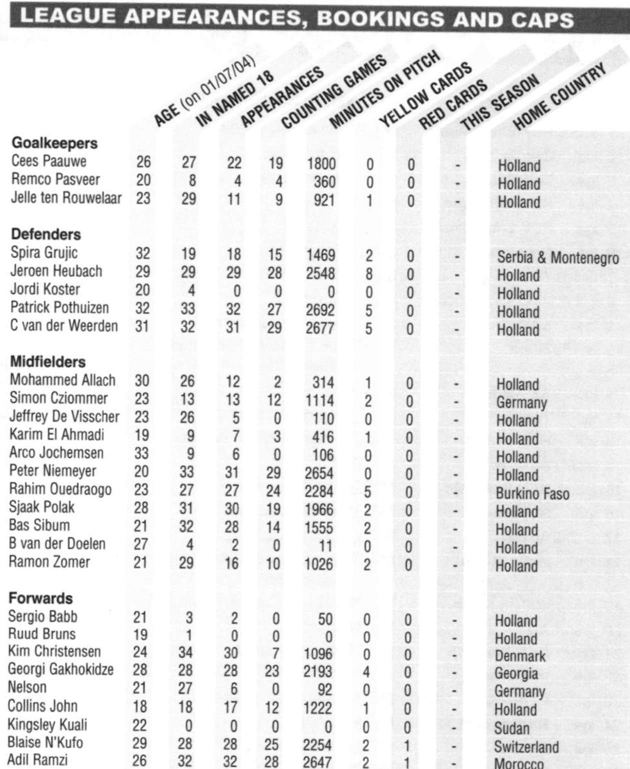

	AGE (on 01/07/04)	IN NAMED 18	APPEARANCES	COUNTING GAMES	MINUTES ON PITCH	YELLOW CARDS	RED CARDS	THIS SEASON	HOME COUNTRY
Goalkeepers									
Cees Paauwe	26	27	22	19	1800	0	0	-	Holland
Remco Pasveer	20	8	4	4	360	0	0	-	Holland
Jelle ten Rouwelaar	23	29	11	9	921	1	0	-	Holland
Defenders									
Spira Grujic	32	19	18	15	1469	2	0	-	Serbia & Montenegro
Jeroen Heubach	29	29	29	28	2548	8	0	-	Holland
Jordi Koster	20	4	0	0	0	0	0	-	Holland
Patrick Pothuizen	32	33	32	27	2692	5	0	-	Holland
C van der Weerden	31	32	31	29	2677	5	0	-	Holland
Midfielders									
Mohammed Allach	30	26	12	2	314	1	0	-	Holland
Simon Cziommer	23	13	13	12	1114	2	0	-	Germany
Jeffrey De Visscher	23	26	5	0	110	0	0	-	Holland
Karim El Ahmadi	19	9	7	3	416	1	0	-	Holland
Arco Jochemsen	33	9	6	0	106	0	0	-	Holland
Peter Niemeyer	20	33	31	29	2654	0	0	-	Holland
Rahim Ouedraogo	23	27	27	24	2284	5	0	-	Burkino Faso
Sjaak Polak	28	31	30	19	1966	2	0	-	Holland
Bas Sibum	21	32	28	14	1555	2	0	-	Holland
B van der Doelen	27	4	2	0	11	0	0	-	Holland
Ramon Zomer	21	29	16	10	1026	2	0	-	Holland
Forwards									
Sergio Babb	21	3	2	0	50	0	0	-	Holland
Ruud Bruns	19	1	0	0	0	0	0	-	Holland
Kim Christensen	24	34	30	7	1096	0	0	-	Denmark
Georgi Gakhokidze	28	28	28	23	2193	4	0	-	Georgia
Nelson	21	27	6	0	92	0	0	-	Germany
Collins John	18	18	17	12	1222	1	0	-	Holland
Kingsley Kuali	22	0	0	0	0	0	0	-	Sudan
Blaise N'Kufo	29	28	28	25	2254	2	1	-	Switzerland
Adil Ramzi	26	32	32	28	2647	2	1	-	Morocco

TEAM OF THE SEASON

D
Chris van der Weerden
CG: 29 DR: 58
M
Sjaak Polak
CG: 19 SD: 7
D
Jeroen Heubach
CG: 28 DR: 55
M
Peter Niemeyer
CG: 29 SD: 0
F
Blaise N'Kufo
CG: 25 SR: 161
G
Cees Paauwe
CG: 19 DR: 64
D
Patrick Pothuizen
CG: 27 DR: 55
M
Rahim Ouedraogo
CG: 24 SD: 0
F
Adil Ramzi
CG: 28 SR: 378
D
Spira Grujic
CG: 15 DR: 52
M
Bas Sibum
CG: 14 SD: -16

SQUAD APPEARANCES

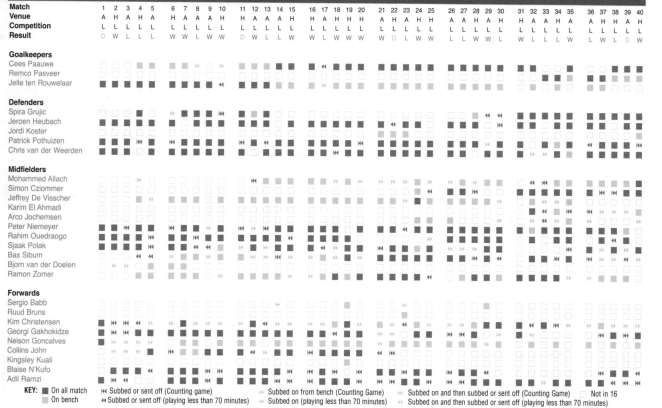

Match	1	2	3	4	5	6	7	8	9	10	11	12	13	14	15	16	17	18	19	20	21	22	23	24	25	26	27	28	29	30	31	32	33	34	35	36	37	38	39	40
Venue	A	H	A	H	A	H	A	A	A	H	H	A	A	A	H	H	A	H	H	H	A	H	A	H	H	A	A	H	A	H	H	A	A	H	A	A	H	H	A	H
Competition	L	L	L	L	L	L	L	L	L	L	L	L	L	L	L	L	L	L	L	L	L	L	L	L	L	L	L	L	L	L	L	L	L	L	L	L	L	L	L	L
Result	D	W	L	L	L	W	W	L	W	W	D	W	L	L	W	W	L	W	W	W	W	D	L	W	W	L	L	W	W	L	W	L	L	L	W	L	W	L	D	W

Goalkeepers
Cees Paauwe
Remco Pasveer
Jelle ten Rouwelaar

Defenders
Spira Grujic
Jeroen Heubach
Jordi Koster
Patrick Pothuizen
Chris van der Weerden

Midfielders
Mohammed Allach
Simon Cziommer
Jeffrey De Visscher
Karim El Ahmadi
Arco Jochemsen
Peter Niemeyer
Rahim Ouedraogo
Sjaak Polak
Bas Sibum
Bjorn van der Doelen
Ramon Zomer

Forwards
Sergio Babb
Ruud Bruns
Kim Christensen
Georgi Gakhokidze
Nelson Goncalves
Collins John
Kingsley Kuali
Blaise N'Kufo
Adil Ramzi

KEY: On all match | On bench | Subbed or sent off (Counting game) | Subbed or sent off (playing less than 70 minutes) | Subbed on from bench (Counting Game) | Subbed on (playing less than 70 minutes) | Subbed on and then subbed or sent off (Counting Game) | Subbed on and then subbed or sent off (playing less than 70 minutes) | Not in 16

UTRECHT

Final Position: **9th**

KEY: Won Drawn Lost

							Attendance
1	JCS	PSV Eindhoven	A	L	1-3	van der Haar 22	
2	lge	Zwolle	H	W	1-0	Zwaanswijk 19	15,000
3	lge	Den Haag	A	D	1-1	de Groot 19	6,135
4	lge	NEC Nijmegen	H	L	0-1		18,000
5	lge	PSV Eindhoven	A	L	1-2	Fujita 90	32,000
6	lge	Groningen	A	D	1-1	Tanghe 2	11,743
7	uc1rl1	Zilina	H	W	2-0	van der Haar 44; Tanghe 85	14,000
8	lge	Vitesse Arnhem	H	L	1-3	Tanghe 37	18,000
9	lge	NAC Breda	A	W	2-1	de Groot 79; Koning 81 og	12,684
10	uc1rl2	Zilina	A	W	4-0	van der Haar 29,66; Lamey 80; Tanghe 83	6,673
11	lge	AZ Alkmaar	H	L	0-3		17,000
12	lge	Twente	A	D	2-2	van der Haar 37,70	13,300
13	lge	Heerenveen	H	W	2-1	Tanghe 53; Van den Brink 68	18,000
14	uc2rl1	Auxerre	H	D	0-0		20,000
15	lge	RKC Waalwijk	H	W	1-0	van de Haar 69	16,500
16	lge	Roosendaal	A	D	1-1	van der Haar 75	5,000
17	uc2rl2	Auxerre	A	L	0-4		18,000
18	lge	Roda JC Kerk	H	W	3-1	Vandenbroeck 29 og; de Groot 61; Leitoe 77	17,100
19	lge	Willem II Tilb	A	W	2-0	Keller 60; van de Haar 72	12,900
20	lge	Ajax	A	L	0-1		48,972
21	hocr3	RKC Waalwijk	H	W	3-1	van de Haar 28; Tanghe 45,90	11,000
22	lge	Volendam	H	W	3-0	Zwaanswijk 14,31; Tanghe 23 pen	11,448
23	lge	Feyenoord	A	L	2-3	Tanghe 22; Leitoe 26	39,800
24	lge	Roosendaal	H	L	0-1		12,000
25	lge	Zwolle	A	D	1-1	Chaiat 36	5,600
26	hocqf	Heracles	H	W	3-2	van den Bergh 29; van der Haar 60; Tanghe 82	15,000
27	lge	Willem II Tilb	H	D	2-2	Tanghe 37; de Groot 90	17,128
28	lge	NEC Nijmegen	A	L	0-4		12,000
29	lge	NAC Breda	H	L	1-2	van de Haar 11	18,500
30	lge	Ajax	H	W	1-0	Tanghe 75	18,000
31	lge	PSV Eindhoven	H	L	0-4		20,000
32	lge	AZ Alkmaar	A	W	2-1	van de Haar 56; Calabro 82	7,577
33	hocsf	S Rotterdam	A	W	4-3*	de Groot 10; van den Bergh 77; Broerse 104 (*on penalties)	
34	lge	Twente	H	W	2-0	Tanghe 3; Broerse 72	20,000
35	lge	Volendam	A	W	2-1	Keller 61; Kras 73 og	5,000
36	lge	Den Haag	H	W	5-3	Zwaanswijk 5,35; van den Bergh 18,63; de Groot 71	18,500
37	lge	Heerenveen	A	L	0-4		15,050
38	lge	Feyenoord	H	L	0-3		21,000
39	lge	Roda JC Kerk	A	D	1-1	Tanghe 13	13,230
40	lge	RKC Waalwijk	A	L	0-1		5,300
41	lge	Groningen	H	W	2-0	Zwaanswijk 43; Calabro 51	18,000
42	lge	Vitesse Arnhem	A	L	0-3		20,000

MONTHLY POINTS TALLY

Month	Points	%
AUGUST	4	44%
SEPTEMBER	1	11%
OCTOBER	4	44%
NOVEMBER	10	83%
DECEMBER	6	67%
JANUARY	0	0%
FEBRUARY	5	33%
MARCH	9	75%
APRIL	4	33%
MAY	3	33%

KEY PLAYERS - GOALSCORERS

Stefaan Tanghe

Goals in the League	9	Player Strike Rate — Average number of minutes between League goals scored by player	296
Contribution to Attacking Power — Average number of minutes between League team goals while on pitch	76	Club Strike Rate — Average number of minutes between League goals scored by club	73

	PLAYER	LGE GOALS	POWER	STRIKE RATE
1	Stefaan Tanghe	9	76	296 mins
2	Hans van de Haar	7	72	321 mins
3	Patrick Zwaanswijk	6	68	455 mins
4	Sander Keller	2	66	734 mins

KEY PLAYERS - MIDFIELDERS

Jean-Paul de Jong

Goals in the League	0	Contribution to Attacking Power — Average number of minutes between League team goals while on pitch	73
Defensive Rating — Average number of mins between League goals conceded while he was on the pitch	64	Scoring Difference — Defensive Rating minus Contribution to Attacking Power	-9

	PLAYER	LGE GOALS	DEF RATE	POWER	SCORE DIFF
1	Jean-Paul de Jong	0	64	73	-9 mins
2	Pascal Bosschaart	0	59	75	-16 mins
3	Stefaan Tanghe	9	58	76	-18 mins
4	Joost Broerse	1	61	87	-26 mins

KEY PLAYERS - DEFENDERS

Sander Keller

Goals Conceded (GC) — The number of League goals conceded while he was on the pitch	19	Clean Sheets — In games when he played at least 70 minutes	4
Defensive Rating — Ave number of mins between League goals conceded while on the pitch	77	Club Defensive Rating — Average number of mins between League goals conceded by the club this season	59

	PLAYER	CON LGE	CLEAN SHEETS	DEF RATE
1	Sander Keller	19	4	77 mins
2	Michael Lamey	18	2	75 mins
3	Patrick Zwaanswijk	46	7	59 mins
4	Ettiene Shew-Atjon	30	5	59 mins

KEY GOALKEEPER

Rene Ponk

Goals Conceded in the League	41	Counting Games — Games when he played at least 70 mins	29
Defensive Rating — Ave number of mins between League goals conceded while on the pitch	62	Clean Sheets — In games when he played at least 70 mins	6

LEAGUE GOALS

Stefaan Tanghe

Minutes on the pitch	2666	Goals in the League	9
League average (mins between goals)	296		

	PLAYER	MINS	GOALS	AVE
1	Tanghe	2666	9	296
2	van de Haar	2245	7	321
3	Zwaanswijk	2730	6	455
4	de Groot	1133	5	227
5	Leitoe	901	2	451
6	Keller	1467	2	734
7	van den Bergh	2578	2	1289
8	Broerse	1825	1	1825
9	Fujita	989	1	989
10	Calabro	485	1	485
11	Chaiat	365	1	365
12	Van den Brink	886	1	886
	Other		4	
	TOTAL		42	

DISCIPLINARY RECORDS

	PLAYER	YELLOW	RED	AVE
1	Lamey	6	1	192
2	de Jong	8	1	250
3	van de Haar	6	1	320
4	Schut	3	0	349
5	Zuidam	4	0	445
6	Zwaanswijk	5	0	546
7	de Groot	2	0	566
8	Bosschaart	4	0	603
9	van den Bergh	4	0	644
10	Keller	2	0	733
11	Braafheid	1	0	861
12	Tanghe	3	0	888
13	Shew-Atjon	2	0	889
	Other	10	1	
	TOTAL	60	4	

TOP POINT EARNERS

	PLAYER	GAMES	AV PTS
1	de Groot	9	2.11
2	Shew-Atjon	19	1.89
3	Fujita	9	1.78
4	Van den Brink	9	1.67
5	Zwaanswijk	30	1.50
6	de Jong	24	1.46
7	Keller	14	1.43
8	Terol	5	1.40
9	Ponk	28	1.36
10	Schut	12	1.33
	CLUB AVERAGE:		**1.35**

TEAM OF THE SEASON

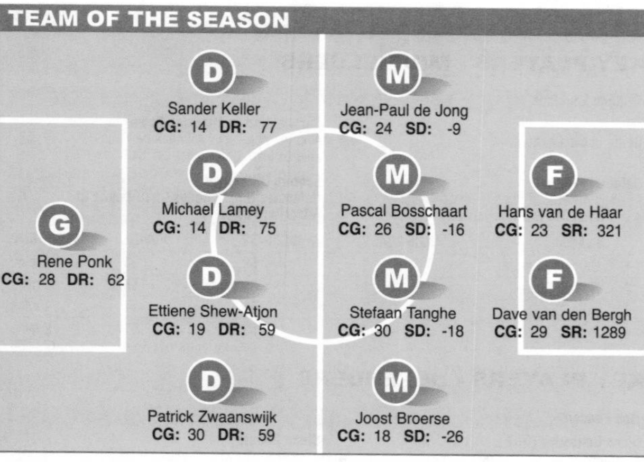
G
Rene Ponk
CG: 28 DR: 62
D
Sander Keller
CG: 14 DR: 77
D
Michael Lamey
CG: 14 DR: 75
D
Ettiene Shew-Atjon
CG: 19 DR: 59
D
Patrick Zwaanswijk
CG: 30 DR: 59
M
Jean-Paul de Jong
CG: 24 SD: -9
M
Pascal Bosschaart
CG: 26 SD: -16
M
Stefaan Tanghe
CG: 30 SD: -18
M
Joost Broerse
CG: 18 SD: -26
F
Hans van de Haar
CG: 23 SR: 321
F
Dave van den Bergh
CG: 29 SR: 1289

LEAGUE APPEARANCES, BOOKINGS AND CAPS

	AGE (on 01/07/04)	IN NAMED 18	APPEARANCES	COUNTING GAMES	MINUTES ON PITCH	YELLOW CARDS	RED CARDS	THIS SEASON	HOME COUNTRY
Goalkeepers									
Rene Ponk	32	29	29	28	2560	0	0	-	Holland
Joost Terol	24	31	6	5	500	0	0	-	Holland
Michel Vorm	20	5	0	0	0	0	0	-	Holland
Defenders									
Iwan Axwijk	21	1	0	0	0	0	0	-	Holland
Edson Braafheid	21	25	14	9	861	1	0	-	Holland
Sander Keller	24	30	23	14	1467	2	0	-	Holland
Michael Lamey	24	18	17	14	1350	6	1	-	Holland
Alje Schut	23	14	12	12	1049	3	0	-	Holland
Ettiene Shew-Atjon	24	27	22	19	1778	2	0	-	Holland
Bas Van den Brink	21	22	13	9	886	0	0	-	Holland
L van Steensel	20	1	1	0	40	0	0	-	Holland
Patrick Zwaanswijk	29	31	31	30	2730	5	0	-	Holland
Midfielders									
Pascal Bosschaart	24	28	28	26	2413	4	0	-	Holland
Joost Broerse	25	33	28	18	1825	2	0	-	Holland
Abdelhali Chaiat	20	16	11	3	365	3	0	-	Holland
Jean-Paul de Jong	33	29	28	24	2254	8	1	-	Holland
Toshiya Fujita	32	16	14	9	989	1	0	-	Japan
Rick Kruys	18	24	10	1	223	1	0	-	Holland
Stefaan Tanghe	32	30	30	30	2666	3	0	-	Belgium
Karim Touzani	23	6	5	3	330	2	1	-	Holland
Tom van Mol	31	1	1	0	28	0	0	-	Belgium
Jordy Zuidam	23	23	22	20	1783	4	0	-	Holland
Forwards									
Adnan Alesic	20	5	2	0	46	0	0	-	Holland
Sandro Calabro	21	30	16	2	485	0	0	-	Holland
Donny de Groot	24	26	22	9	1133	2	0	-	Holland
Richal Leitoe	21	23	20	5	901	1	0	-	Holland
Paulus Roiha	23	3	3	0	34	0	0	-	Finland
Kevin van Baarlen	19	2	0	0	0	0	0	-	Holland
Hans van de Haar	29	30	28	23	2245	6	1	-	Holland
Dave van den Bergh	28	30	30	29	2578	4	0	-	Holland

SQUAD APPEARANCES

Match	1	2	3	4	5	6	7	8	9	10	11	12	13	14	15	16	17	18	19	20	21	22	23	24	25	26	27	28	29	30	31	32	33	34	35	36	37	38	39	40	41	42
Venue	A	H	A	H	A	A	H	H	A	A	H	A	H	H	H	A	A	H	A	A	H	H	A	H	A	H	H	A	H	H	H	A	A	H	A	H	A	H	A	A	H	A
Competition	L	L	L	L	L	L	E	L	L	E	L	L	L	E	L	L	E	L	L	L	L	L	L	L	L	L	L	L	L	L	L	L	L	L	L	L	L	L	L	L	L	L
Result	L	W	D	L	L	D	W	L	W	W	L	D	W	D	W	D	L	W	W	L	W	W	L	L	D	W	D	L	L	W	L	W	W	W	W	W	L	L	D	L	W	L

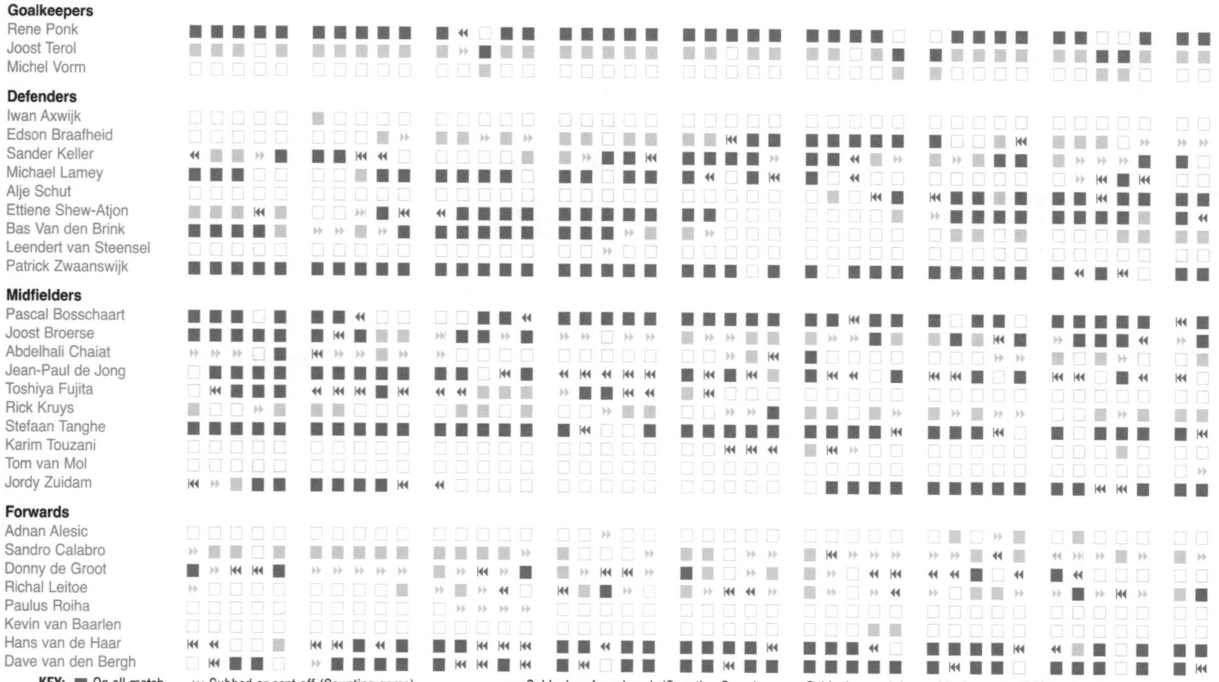

Goalkeepers
Rene Ponk
Joost Terol
Michel Vorm

Defenders
Iwan Axwijk
Edson Braafheid
Sander Keller
Michael Lamey
Alje Schut
Ettiene Shew-Atjon
Bas Van den Brink
Leendert van Steensel
Patrick Zwaanswijk

Midfielders
Pascal Bosschaart
Joost Broerse
Abdelhali Chaiat
Jean-Paul de Jong
Toshiya Fujita
Rick Kruys
Stefaan Tanghe
Karim Touzani
Tom van Mol
Jordy Zuidam

Forwards
Adnan Alesic
Sandro Calabro
Donny de Groot
Richal Leitoe
Paulus Roiha
Kevin van Baarlen
Hans van de Haar
Dave van den Bergh

KEY: On all match · On bench · Subbed or sent off (Counting game) · Subbed or sent off (playing less than 70 minutes) · Subbed on from bench (Counting Game) · Subbed on (playing less than 70 minutes) · Subbed on and then subbed or sent off (Counting Game) · Subbed on and then subbed or sent off (playing less than 70 minutes) · Not in 16

NAC BREDA

Final Position: **10th**

KEY: Won / Drawn / Lost

							Attendance
1	lge	Groningen	A	L	0-1		11,483
2	lge	Vitesse Arnhem	H	W	2-0	Stam 67; Peto 75	13,000
3	lge	Feyenoord	A	L	1-2	Diba 24	42,000
4	lge	Willem II Tilb	H	D	1-1	Seedorf 89	14,500
5	lge	Ajax	H	W	4-2	Boukhari 7; Elmander 46,57; Seedorf 90	16,000
6	uc1rl1	Newcastle	A	L	0-5		36,007
7	lge	RKC Waalwijk	A	L	0-2		6,200
8	lge	Utrecht	H	L	1-2	Elmander 44	12,684
9	uc1rl2	Newcastle	H	L	0-1		15,060
10	lge	NEC Nijmegen	A	W	3-0	Seedorf 6; Elmander 10; Engelaar 64 pen	12,000
11	lge	Den Haag	A	D	1-1	Penders 89	6,548
12	lge	PSV Eindhoven	H	L	1-3	Engelaar 90 pen	14,749
13	lge	AZ Alkmaar	H	L	1-2	Boussaboun 39	13,197
14	lge	Zwolle	A	W	2-0	Boukhari 28; Vos 90	
15	lge	Twente	A	L	1-2	Slot 68	13,150
16	lge	Heerenveen	H	L	2-3	Venema 7 og; Slot 90	12,100
17	lge	Roda JC Kerk	A	D	2-2	Elmander 57; Engelaar 90 pen	12,500
18	hocr3	Ajax	A	W	1-0	Boussaboun 54	19,910
19	lge	Roosendaal	H	W	3-2	Engelaar 5,44; Boussaboun 29	12,238
20	lge	Volendam	H	W	3-2	Engelaar 32; Penders 49; Slot 52	11,019
21	lge	Willem II Tilb	A	D	1-1	Elmander 62	13,200
22	hocqf	PSV Eindhoven	A	W	1-0	Boukhari 24	20,000
23	lge	Heerenveen	A	W	4-3	Vos 27,83 pen; Diba 47; Feher 73	14,300
24	lge	Roda JC Kerk	H	D	0-0		11,580
25	lge	Utrecht	A	W	2-1	Vos 64; Boukhari 83	18,500
26	lge	Groningen	H	D	1-1	Feher 33	10,315
27	lge	Roosendaal	A	D	1-1	Diba 53	5,000
28	lge	Twente	H	L	0-1		11,303
29	lge	Zwolle	H	W	3-1	Boussaboun 18; Boukhari 22; Diba 61	11,704
30	hocsf	Twente	A	L	5-6*	Boukhari 35; Collen 88 (*on penalties)	13,200
31	lge	PSV Eindhoven	A	D	1-1	Seedorf 54	33,000
32	lge	NEC Nijmegen	H	W	5-2	Seedorf 2,14,44; Engelaar 9,23	12,800
33	lge	Feyenoord	H	L	0-3		15,900
34	lge	Vitesse Arnhem	A	D	2-2	Diba 16; Engelaar 41	20,000
35	lge	Volendam	A	L	2-4	Boukhari 10; Boussaboun 12	4,552
36	lge	Den Haag	H	W	1-0	Feher 2	11,500
37	lge	AZ Alkmaar	A	D	2-2	Boussaboun 57; Diba 72	7,732
38	lge	Ajax	A	L	0-2		50,000
39	lge	RKC Waalwijk	H	W	5-3	Feher 5; Elmander 25; Vos 47,85; Boussaboun 84	12,000

MONTHLY POINTS TALLY

AUGUST	3	33%
SEPTEMBER	4	44%
OCTOBER	4	44%
NOVEMBER	3	25%
DECEMBER	4	44%
JANUARY	3	100%
FEBRUARY	10	56%
MARCH	7	58%
APRIL	4	33%
MAY	4	44%

KEY PLAYERS - GOALSCORERS

Ali Boussaboun

Goals in the League	6	Player Strike Rate Average number of minutes between League goals scored by player	258
Contribution to Attacking Power Average number of minutes between League team goals while on pitch	49	Club Strike Rate Average number of minutes between League goals scored by club	53

	PLAYER	LGE GOALS	POWER	STRIKE RATE
1	Ali Boussaboun	6	49	258 mins
2	Orlando Engelaar	9	53	260 mins
3	Johan Elmander	7	63	291 mins
4	Stefano Seedorf	7	50	311 mins

KEY PLAYERS - MIDFIELDERS

Orlando Engelaar

Goals in the League	9	Contribution to Attacking Power Average number of minutes between League team goals while on pitch	53
Defensive Rating Average number of mins between League goals conceded while he was on the pitch	59	Scoring Difference Defensive Rating minus Contribution to Attacking Power	6

	PLAYER	LGE GOALS	DEF RATE	POWER	SCORE DIFF
1	Orlando Engelaar	9	59	53	6 mins
2	Ronnie Stam	1	63	58	5 mins
3	Arne Slot	3	58	54	4 mins
4	Stefano Seedorf	7	53	51	2 mins

KEY PLAYERS - DEFENDERS

Rob Penders

Goals Conceded (GC) The number of League goals conceded while he was on the pitch	34	Clean Sheets In games when he played at least 70 minutes	4
Defensive Rating Ave number of mins between League goals conceded while on the pitch	63	Club Defensive Rating Average number of mins between League goals conceded by the club this season	56

	PLAYER	CON LGE	CLEAN SHEETS	DEF RATE
1	Rob Penders	34	4	63 mins
2	Csaba Feher	31	4	63 mins
3	Pieter Collen	29	2	56 mins
4	Adnan Barakat	27	2	53 mins

KEY GOALKEEPER

Gabor Babos

Goals Conceded in the League	39	Counting Games Games when he played at least 70 mins	25
Defensive Rating Ave number of mins between League goals conceded while on the pitch	57	Clean Sheets In games when he played at least 70 mins	3

LEAGUE GOALS

Orlando Engelaar

Minutes on the pitch	2340	Goals in the League	9
League average (mins between goals)	260		

	PLAYER	MINS	GOALS	AVE
1	Engelaar	2340	9	260
2	Seedorf	2178	7	311
3	Elmander	2040	7	291
4	Boussaboun	1548	6	258
5	Vos	858	6	143
6	Diba	1893	6	316
7	Boukhari	2202	5	440
8	Feher	1949	4	487
9	Slot	2761	3	920
10	Penders	2137	2	1069
11	Stam	1503	1	1503
12	Peto	875	1	875
	Other		1	
	TOTAL		58	

DISCIPLINARY RECORDS

	PLAYER	YELLOW	RED	AVE
1	Peto	3	0	291
2	Barakat	4	0	355
3	Boukhari	6	0	367
4	Feher	5	0	389
5	Collen	4	0	409
6	Vos	2	0	429
7	Boussaboun	3	0	516
8	Seedorf	4	0	544
9	Engelaar	4	0	585
10	Diba	2	1	631
11	Elmander	3	0	680
12	Slot	4	0	690
13	Kerstens	2	0	707
	Other	7	0	
	TOTAL	53	1	

TOP POINT EARNERS

	PLAYER	GAMES	AV PTS
1	Barakat	13	1.85
2	Vos	5	1.60
3	Boukhari	22	1.59
4	Seedorf	22	1.55
5	Diba	19	1.53
6	Bobson	2	1.50
7	Schenning	11	1.45
8	Boussaboun	14	1.43
9	Kerstens	14	1.43
10	Feher	22	1.41
	CLUB AVERAGE:		**1.35**

LEAGUE APPEARANCES, BOOKINGS AND CAPS

	AGE (on 01/07/04)	IN NAMED 18	APPEARANCES	COUNTING GAMES	MINUTES ON PITCH	YELLOW CARDS	RED CARDS	THIS SEASON	HOME COUNTRY
Goalkeepers									
Gabor Babos	29	25	25	24	2228	0	0	-	Hungary
Gino Coutinho	21	15	3	3	270	0	0	-	Holland
Arjan Cristianen	21	1	0	0	0	0	0	-	Holland
Arno van Zwam	34	26	7	6	562	0	0	-	Holland
Defenders									
Eric Atuahene	-	1	1	1	90	0	0	-	Holland
Adnan Barakat	21	32	23	13	1420	4	0	-	Holland
Pieter Collen	24	24	19	17	1637	4	0	-	Belgium
Csaba Feher	28	22	22	22	1949	5	0	-	Hungary
Benny Kerstens	21	31	19	14	1414	2	0	-	Holland
W Kousemaker	-	12	2	0	66	0	0	-	Holland
Rob Penders	28	25	25	22	2137	2	0	-	Holland
Levi Risamasu	21	14	1	1	90	0	0	-	Holland
Mark Schenning	33	12	12	11	1025	1	0	-	Holland
Midfielders									
Orlando Engelaar	24	30	29	24	2340	4	0	-	Holland
Nebosja Gudelj	34	25	25	22	2122	1	0	-	Serbia & Montenegro
Rob Haemhouts	20	26	2	0	50	0	0	-	Belgium
Marcel Koning	29	5	4	2	216	1	0	-	Holland
Tamas Peto	30	14	14	7	875	3	0	-	Hungary
Niek Ripson	-	6	1	0	2	0	0	-	Holland
Stefano Seedorf	22	29	29	22	2178	4	0	-	Holland
Arne Slot	25	32	32	30	2761	4	0	-	Holland
Ronnie Stam	20	26	21	15	1503	2	0	-	Holland
J van Housselt	16	1	0	0	0	0	0	-	Holland
Forwards									
Kevin Bobson	23	2	2	2	156	0	0	-	Holland
Nordin Boukhari	24	29	28	22	2202	6	0	-	Morocco
Ali Boussaboun	25	30	28	14	1548	3	0	-	Morocco
Anouar Diba	21	31	29	19	1893	2	1	-	Holland
Johan Elmander	23	32	31	20	2040	3	0	-	Sweden
Faysal Houba	21	1	0	0	0	0	0	-	Holland
Julian Jenner	-	1	1	0	7	0	0	-	Holland
Henk Vos	36	31	25	5	858	2	0	-	Holland

TEAM OF THE SEASON

D
Csaba Feher
CG: 22 DR: 63
D
Rob Penders
CG: 22 DR: 63
D
Pieter Collen
CG: 17 DR: 56
D
Adnan Barakat
CG: 13 DR: 53
G
Gabor Babos
CG: 24 DR: 57
M
Orlando Engelaar
CG: 24 SD: 6
M
Ronnie Stam
CG: 15 SD: 5
M
Arne Slot
CG: 30 SD: 4
M
Stefano Seedorf
CG: 22 SD: 2
F
Ali Boussaboun
CG: 14 SR: 258
F
Johan Elmander
CG: 20 SR: 291

SQUAD APPEARANCES

Match	1	2	3	4	5	6	7	8	9	10	11	12	13	14	15	16	17	18	19	20	21	22	23	24	25	26	27	28	29	30	31	32	33	34	35	36	37	38	39
Venue	A	H	A	H	H	A	A	H	H	A	A	H	H	A	A	H	A	A	H	H	A	A	A	H	A	H	A	H	H	A	A	H	H	A	A	H	A	A	H
Competition	L	L	L	L	L	E	L	L	E	L	L	L	L	L	L	L	L	L	L	L	L	L	L	L	L	L	L	L	L	L	L	L	L	L	L	L	L	L	L
Result	L	W	L	D	W	L	L	L	L	W	D	L	L	W	L	L	D	W	W	W	D	W	W	D	W	D	D	L	W	L	D	W	L	D	L	W	D	L	W

Goalkeepers
Gabor Babos
Gino Coutinho
Arjan Cristianen
Arno van Zwam

Defenders
Eric Atuahene
Adnan Barakat
Pieter Collen
Csaba Feher
Benny Kerstens
Wilmer Kousemaker
Rob Penders
Levi Risamasu
Mark Schenning

Midfielders
Orlando Engelaar
Nebosja Gudelj
Rob Haemhouts
Marcel Koning
Tamas Peto
Niek Ripson
Stefano Seedorf
Arne Slot
Ronnie Stam
Julian van Housselt

Forwards
Kevin Bobson
Nordin Boukhari
Ali Boussaboun
Anouar Diba
Johan Elmander
Faysal Houba
Julian Jenner
Henk Vos

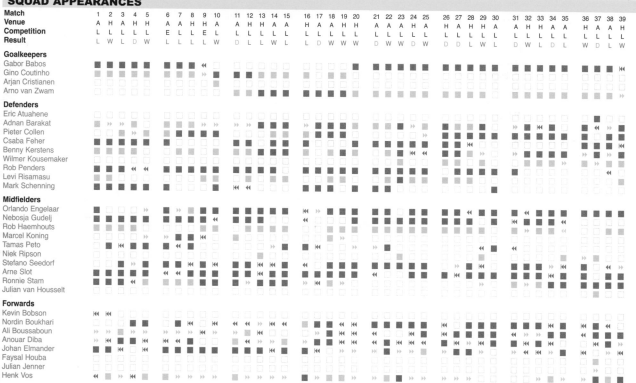

KEY: ■ On all match
■ On bench
⏮ Subbed or sent off (Counting game)
« Subbed or sent off (playing less than 70 minutes)
» Subbed on from bench (Counting Game)
» Subbed on (playing less than 70 minutes)
» Subbed on and then subbed or sent off (Counting Game)
» Subbed on and then subbed or sent off (playing less than 70 minutes)
□ Not in 16

RKC WAALWIJK

Final Position: **11th**

KEY: ☐Won ☐Drawn ☐Lost

							Attendance
1	hocr1	**Tonegido**	A	W	0-8		
2	lge	**Den Haag**	H	W	1-0	Redan 62	6,000
3	lge	**Zwolle**	A	W	3-0	Redan 24,28; Petrovic 90	6,150
4	lge	**Volendam**	H	W	3-0	Hoogendorp 7 pen,17; Redan 27	5,000
5	lge	**Ajax**	A	L	1-4	Boulahrouz 63	48,121
6	lge	**Twente**	A	L	1-2	Boutahar 48	13,000
7	hocr2	**AGOVV**	A	W	2-0	Hoogendorp 65,74 pen	
8	lge	**NAC Breda**	H	W	2-0	Greene 5; Redan 85	6,200
9	lge	**Heerenveen**	A	L	0-1		14,300
10	lge	**Vitesse Arnhem**	H	D	2-2	Redan 11; Oost 82	6,500
11	lge	**Roosendaal**	H	L	1-2	Boutahar 39	5,000
12	hocr3	**FC Omniworld**	A	W	4-2	Boulahrouz 7; Olfers 86; Hoogendorp 97 pen,100	2,500
13	lge	**Willem II Tilb**	A	L	1-4	Greene 26	12,900
14	lge	**Utrecht**	A	L	0-1		16,500
15	lge	**Groningen**	H	D	1-1	Teixeira 8	6,000
16	lge	**AZ Alkmaar**	H	D	1-1	Boulahrouz 51	6,000
17	lge	**NEC Nijmegen**	A	D	1-1	Greene 88	
18	lge	**PSV Eindhoven**	A	L	1-3	Teixeira 38	33,500
19	hocr3	**Utrecht**	A	L	1-3	Fuchs 10	11,000
20	lge	**Feyenoord**	H	D	0-0		6,500
21	lge	**Roda JC Kerk**	A	L	1-2	Hoogendorp 85	12,850
22	lge	**Volendam**	A	W	4-0	Cornelisse 49; Boutahar 55; Fuchs 87; Redan 90	4,057
23	lge	**NEC Nijmegen**	H	L	1-2	Redan 74	6,500
24	lge	**Roosendaal**	A	W	3-1	Cornelisse 4; Hoogendorp 25; Boutahar 83	5,000
25	lge	**Heerenveen**	H	D	0-0		6,500
26	lge	**Zwolle**	H	W	2-0	Boulahrouz 20; Molhoek 32	5,000
27	lge	**Groningen**	A	W	2-1	Boutahar 68; Cornelisse 76	12,500
28	lge	**Ajax**	H	L	0-1		7,500
29	lge	**Willem II Tilb**	H	D	1-1	Boutahar 59	5,511
30	lge	**Feyenoord**	A	L	0-1		38,000
31	lge	**Vitesse Arnhem**	A	D	3-3	Hoogendorp 55,75; Boulahrouz 64	20,500
32	lge	**PSV Eindhoven**	H	L	0-4		7,200
33	lge	**Den Haag**	A	W	3-1	Oost 25; Fuchs 68; Vasconcelos 85	8,000
34	lge	**Roda JC Kerk**	H	D	1-1	Boutahar 41	6,000
35	lge	**AZ Alkmaar**	A	L	0-7		7,713
36	lge	**Utrecht**	H	W	1-0	Hoogendorp 62	5,300
37	lge	**Twente**	H	D	3-3	Vasconcelos 25; van Diemen 67; Petrovic 90	5,500
38	lge	**NAC Breda**	A	L	3-5	Olfers 6; Vasconcelos 32,90	12,000

MONTHLY POINTS TALLY

AUGUST	9	100%
SEPTEMBER	3	33%
OCTOBER	1	11%
NOVEMBER	2	17%
DECEMBER	2	22%
JANUARY	3	33%
FEBRUARY	10	83%
MARCH	2	17%
APRIL	4	33%
MAY	4	44%

KEY PLAYERS - GOALSCORERS

Rick Hoogendorp

Goals in the League	7	**Player Strike Rate** Average number of minutes between League goals scored by player	355
Contribution to Attacking Power Average number of minutes between League team goals while on pitch	67	**Club Strike Rate** Average number of minutes between League goals scored by club	65

	PLAYER	LGE GOALS	POWER	STRIKE RATE
1	Rick Hoogendorp	7	67	355 mins
2	Said Boutahar	7	77	365 mins
3	Khalid Boulahrouz	4	66	516 mins
4	Robert Fuchs	2	58	705 mins

KEY PLAYERS - MIDFIELDERS

Zeljko Petrovic

Goals in the League	2	**Contribution to Attacking Power** Average number of minutes between League team goals while on pitch	63
Defensive Rating Average number of mins between League goals conceded while he was on the pitch	61	**Scoring Difference** Defensive Rating minus Contribution to Attacking Power	2

	PLAYER	LGE GOALS	DEF RATE	POWER	SCORE DIFF
1	Zeljko Petrovic	2	61	63	-2 mins
2	Patrick van Diemen	1	55	64	-9 mins
3	Robert Fuchs	2	43	59	-16 mins
4	Said Boutahar	7	57	78	-21 mins

KEY PLAYERS - DEFENDERS

Marc van Hintum

Goals Conceded (GC) The number of League goals conceded while he was on the pitch	23	**Clean Sheets** In games when he played at least 70 minutes	6
Defensive Rating Ave number of mins between League goals conceded while on the pitch	78	**Club Defensive Rating** Average number of mins between League goals conceded by the club this season	56

	PLAYER	CON LGE	CLEAN SHEETS	DEF RATE
1	Marc van Hintum	23	6	78 mins
2	Virgilio Teixeira	37	7	62 mins
3	Serginho Greene	48	7	58 mins
4	Steve Olfers	45	9	55 mins

KEY GOALKEEPER

Khalid Sinouh

Goals Conceded in the League	55	**Counting Games** Games when he played at least 70 mins	33
Defensive Rating Ave number of mins between League goals conceded while on the pitch	54	**Clean Sheets** In games when he played at least 70 mins	8

LEAGUE GOALS

Iwan Redan

Minutes on the pitch	872	**Goals in the League**	8
League average (mins between goals)	109		

	PLAYER	MINS	GOALS	AVE
1	Redan	872	8	109
2	Boutahar	2558	7	365
3	Hoogendorp	2482	7	355
4	Boulahrouz	2062	4	516
5	Vasconcelos	985	4	246
6	Greene	2785	3	928
7	Cornelisse	2670	3	890
8	Teixeira	2277	2	1139
9	Oost	947	2	474
10	Fuchs	1410	2	705
11	Petrovic	2766	2	1383
12	Molhoek	820	1	820
	Other		2	
	TOTAL		47	

DISCIPLINARY RECORDS

	PLAYER	YELLOW	RED	AVE
1	van Hintum	6	0	299
2	Teixeira	6	1	325
3	Petrovic	6	0	461
4	Hoogendorp	3	1	620
5	Fuchs	2	0	705
6	Olfers	3	0	824
7	Redan	1	0	872
8	Cornelisse	3	0	890
9	Greene	3	0	928
10	Oost	1	0	947
11	Boulahrouz	2	0	1031
12	Sinouh	2	0	1476
13	van Diemen	2	0	1507
	Other	2	0	
	TOTAL	42	2	

TOP POINT EARNERS

	PLAYER	GAMES	AV PTS
1	Vasconcelos	8	1.38
2	Peppinck	3	1.33
3	Teixeira	25	1.32
4	Cornelisse	29	1.31
5	Petrovic	31	1.29
6	Olfers	25	1.28
7	van Hintum	20	1.25
8	Hoogendorp	25	1.20
9	van Diemen	33	1.18
10	Boutahar	26	1.15
	CLUB AVERAGE:		1.18

LEAGUE APPEARANCES, BOOKINGS AND CAPS

	AGE (on 01/07/04)	IN NAMED 18	APPEARANCES	COUNTING GAMES	MINUTES ON PITCH	YELLOW CARDS	RED CARDS	THIS SEASON	HOME COUNTRY
Goalkeepers									
Wilko de Vogt	28	10	1	0	17	0	0	-	Holland
Khalid Sinouh	29	34	33	33	2953	2	0	-	Morocco
R van der Gouw	41	19	1	1	90	0	0	-	Holland
Defenders									
Khalid Boulahrouz	22	29	29	21	2062	2	0	-	Holland
Serginho Greene	22	34	34	29	2785	3	0	-	Holland
Steve Olfers	22	33	32	25	2472	3	0	-	Holland
Virgilio Teixeira	30	26	26	25	2277	6	1	-	Portugal
K Van der Geest	22	3	0	0	0	0	0	-	Holland
Marc van Hintum	37	21	21	20	1798	6	0	-	Holland
Midfielders									
Said Boutahar	21	34	33	26	2558	1	0	-	Holland
Robert Fuchs	29	28	23	13	1410	2	0	-	Holland
Rogier Molhoek	22	18	13	7	820	0	0	-	Holland
Kris Ottoy	19	1	0	0	0	0	0	-	Belgium
Fabian Peppinck	26	29	7	3	331	0	0	-	Holland
Zeljko Petrovic	38	31	31	31	2766	6	0	-	Serbia & Montenegro
M Van der Heijden	22	1	1	0	45	1	0	-	Holland
Patrick van Diemen	32	34	34	33	3014	2	0	-	Holland
Forwards									
Tim Aelbrecht	22	21	3	0	25	0	0	-	Belgium
Biko Brazil	20	2	0	0	0	0	0	-	Holland
Yori Cornelisse	29	32	32	29	2670	3	0	-	Holland
Rick Hoogendorp	29	31	31	25	2482	3	1	-	Holland
Jason Oost	21	26	21	7	947	1	0	-	Holland
Tim Peters	-	5	0	0	0	0	0	-	Holland
Iwan Redan	23	20	18	7	872	1	0	-	Holland
Gabor Torma	27	17	7	0	151	0	0	-	Hungary
N van der Velden	19	19	4	0	48	0	0	-	Holland
B Vasconcelos	-	18	17	8	985	0	0	-	Portugal
Chakib Zbayri	-	5	1	0	3	0	0	-	Holland

TEAM OF THE SEASON

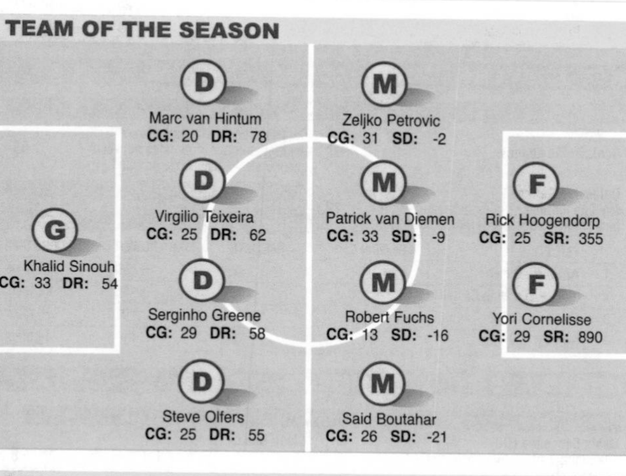

G
Khalid Sinouh
CG: 33 DR: 54
D
Marc van Hintum
CG: 20 DR: 78
D
Virgilio Teixeira
CG: 25 DR: 62
D
Serginho Greene
CG: 29 DR: 58
D
Steve Olfers
CG: 25 DR: 55
M
Zeljko Petrovic
CG: 31 SD: -2
M
Patrick van Diemen
CG: 33 SD: -9
M
Robert Fuchs
CG: 13 SD: -16
M
Said Boutahar
CG: 26 SD: -21
F
Rick Hoogendorp
CG: 25 SR: 355
F
Yori Cornelisse
CG: 29 SR: 890

SQUAD APPEARANCES

Match	1	2	3	4	5	6	7	8	9	10	11	12	13	14	15	16	17	18	19	20	21	22	23	24	25	26	27	28	29	30	31	32	33	34	35	36	37	38
Venue	A	H	A	H	A	A	A	H	A	H	H	A	A	A	H	H	A	A	A	H	A	A	H	A	H	H	A	H	H	A	A	H	A	H	A	H	H	A
Competition	L	L	L	L	L	L	L	L	L	L	L	L	L	L	L	L	L	L	L	L	L	L	L	L	L	L	L	L	L	L	L	L	L	L	L	L	L	L
Result	D	W	W	W	L	L	W	W	L	D	L	W	L	L	D	D	D	L	L	D	L	W	L	W	D	W	W	L	D	L	D	L	W	D	L	W	D	L

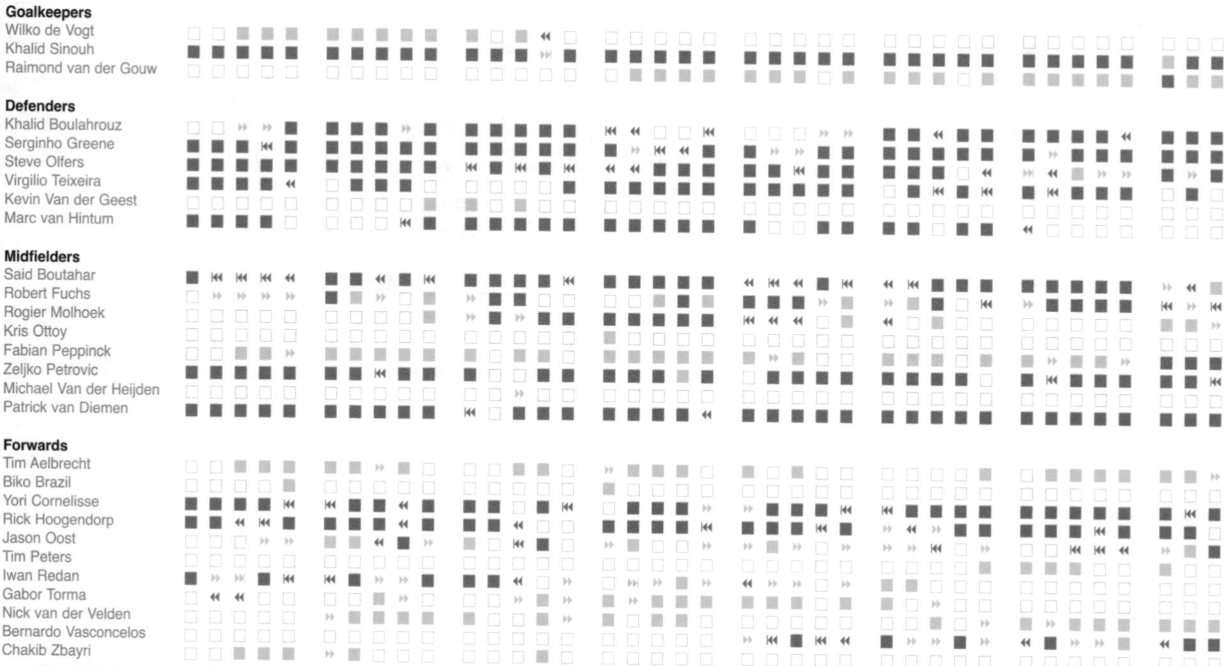

Goalkeepers
Wilko de Vogt
Khalid Sinouh
Raimond van der Gouw

Defenders
Khalid Boulahrouz
Serginho Greene
Steve Olfers
Virgilio Teixeira
Kevin Van der Geest
Marc van Hintum

Midfielders
Said Boutahar
Robert Fuchs
Rogier Molhoek
Kris Ottoy
Fabian Peppinck
Zeljko Petrovic
Michael Van der Heijden
Patrick van Diemen

Forwards
Tim Aelbrecht
Biko Brazil
Yori Cornelisse
Rick Hoogendorp
Jason Oost
Tim Peters
Iwan Redan
Gabor Torma
Nick van der Velden
Bernardo Vasconcelos
Chakib Zbayri

KEY: On all match · On bench · Subbed or sent off (Counting game) · Subbed or sent off (playing less than 70 minutes) · Subbed on from bench (Counting Game) · Subbed on (playing less than 70 minutes) · Subbed on and then subbed or sent off (Counting Game) · Subbed on and then subbed or sent off (playing less than 70 minutes) · Not in 16

RBC ROOSENDAAL

Final Position: **12th**

KEY: Won Drawn Lost

							Attendance
1	hocr1	Elinkwijk	A	W	1-4		
2	lge	Twente	A	L	1-3	Tininho 24 fk	13,000
3	lge	Ajax	H	L	0-1		5,000
4	lge	Roda JC Kerk	A	W	2-0	Youssouf 18; Daelemans 89	12,500
5	lge	Vitesse Arnhem	H	D	1-1	Hesp 56	5,000
6	lge	Den Haag	A	W	2-1	Youssouf 32; Molenaar 77	6,200
7	hocr2	MVV Maastricht	H	W	4-0	Daelemans 13; de Graaf 39; Maseland 57; Hertog 64	
8	lge	Volendam	H	D	1-1	Youssouf 64	5,000
9	lge	Feyenoord	A	L	0-2		41,000
10	lge	Willem II Tilb	H	D	0-0		5,000
11	lge	RKC Waalwijk	A	W	2-1	Lammens 56; Razic 63	5,000
12	hocr3	Groningen	H	W	1-0	Thompson 105	
13	lge	NEC Nijmegen	H	W	1-0	Hesp 55 pen	5,000
14	lge	PSV Eindhoven	A	D	1-1	Thompson 73	33,000
15	lge	Utrecht	H	D	1-1	Youssouf 49	5,000
16	lge	Groningen	A	L	0-2		12,500
17	lge	AZ Alkmaar	H	W	1-0	de Graaf 63	5,000
18	lge	Heerenveen	H	D	1-1	Youssouf 38	5,000
19	hocr3	S Rotterdam	A	L	0-2		2,540
20	lge	NAC Breda	A	L	2-3	Ikedia 32; de Graaf 61	12,238
21	lge	Zwolle	A	W	3-0	Lammens 22; de Graaf 70; Luijten 83	6,150
22	lge	Utrecht	A	W	1-0	Molenaar 83	12,000
23	lge	RKC Waalwijk	H	L	1-3	Daelemans 26	5,000
24	lge	Roda JC Kerk	H	L	1-4	Luijten 84	5,000
25	lge	Vitesse Arnhem	A	W	2-1	de Graaf 45; Hesp 67	19,000
26	lge	AZ Alkmaar	A	L	1-2	de Graaf 53	7,357
27	lge	NAC Breda	H	D	1-1	de Graaf 20	5,000
28	lge	NEC Nijmegen	A	W	2-1	Molenaar 56; Daelemans 60	12,050
29	lge	Groningen	H	W	1-0	Youssouf 7	5,000
30	lge	Den Haag	H	D	0-0		5,000
31	lge	Heerenveen	A	L	0-1		14,500
32	lge	Zwolle	H	D	1-1	de Graaf 1	5,000
33	lge	Twente	H	L	1-2	Pothuizen 1 og	5,000
34	lge	Ajax	A	D	1-1	Hellemons 3	49,112
35	lge	PSV Eindhoven	H	L	0-3		5,000
36	lge	Willem II Tilb	A	L	0-3		8,000
37	lge	Feyenoord	H	L	1-4	Youssouf 19	5,000
38	lge	Volendam	A	L	1-2	Cas 81	5,000

MONTHLY POINTS TALLY

AUGUST	3	33%
SEPTEMBER	5	56%
OCTOBER	4	44%
NOVEMBER	5	42%
DECEMBER	4	44%
JANUARY	6	100%
FEBRUARY	4	27%
MARCH	7	58%
APRIL	2	17%
MAY	0	0%

KEY PLAYERS - GOALSCORERS

Sammy Youssouf

Goals in the League	7	**Player Strike Rate** Average number of minutes between League goals scored by player	304
Contribution to Attacking Power Average number of minutes between League team goals while on pitch	96	**Club Strike Rate** Average number of minutes between League goals scored by club	90

	PLAYER	LGE GOALS	POWER	STRIKE RATE
1	Sammy Youssouf	7	96	304 mins
2	Edwin de Graaf	7	91	418 mins
3	Bjorn Daelemans	3	85	514 mins
4	Robert Molenaar	3	84	818 mins

KEY PLAYERS - MIDFIELDERS

Azubuike Oliseh

Goals in the League	0	**Contribution to Attacking Power** Average number of minutes between League team goals while on pitch	90
Defensive Rating Average number of mins between League goals conceded while he was on the pitch	72	**Scoring Difference** Defensive Rating minus Contribution to Attacking Power	-18

	PLAYER	LGE GOALS	DEF RATE	POWER	SCORE DIFF
1	Azubuike Oliseh	0	72	90	-18 mins
2	Juan Pablo Nino Castellano	0	66	88	-22 mins
3	Edwin de Graaf	7	65	91	-26 mins
4	Ronildo Tininho	1	72	116	-44 mins

KEY PLAYERS - DEFENDERS

Robert Molenaar

Goals Conceded (GC) The number of League goals conceded while he was on the pitch	28	**Clean Sheets** In games when he played at least 70 minutes	8
Defensive Rating Ave number of mins between League goals conceded while on the pitch	88	**Club Defensive Rating** Average number of mins between League goals conceded by the club this season	65

	PLAYER	CON LGE	CLEAN SHEETS	DEF RATE
1	Robert Molenaar	28	8	88 mins
2	Eric Hellemons	32	6	67 mins
3	Danny Hesp	45	8	66 mins
4	Sidney Lammens	46	8	65 mins

KEY GOALKEEPER

Maikel Aerts

Goals Conceded in the League	47	**Counting Games** Games when he played at least 70 mins	34
Defensive Rating Ave number of mins between League goals conceded while on the pitch	65	**Clean Sheets** In games when he played at least 70 mins	8

LEAGUE GOALS

Edwin de Graaf

Minutes on the pitch	2923	Goals in the League	7
League average (mins between goals)	418		

	PLAYER	MINS	GOALS	AVE
1	de Graaf	2923	7	418
2	Youssouf	2126	7	304
3	Hesp	2961	3	987
4	Molenaar	2453	3	818
5	Daelemans	1541	3	514
6	Lammens	2970	2	1485
7	Luijten	163	2	82
8	Ikedia	2327	1	2327
9	Razic	210	1	210
10	Cas	508	1	508
11	Thompson	995	1	995
12	Tininho	2444	1	2444
	Other		2	
	TOTAL		34	

DISCIPLINARY RECORDS

	PLAYER	YELLOW	RED	AVE
1	Fleur	2	0	251
2	Oliseh	9	0	278
3	Viedma	2	0	383
4	Daelemans	4	0	385
5	Tininho	4	1	488
6	Youssouf	4	0	531
7	Hellemons	4	0	534
8	Hesp	5	0	592
9	Molenaar	4	0	613
10	de Graaf	3	0	974
11	Lammens	3	0	990
12	Thompson	1	0	995
13	Pablo Nino	1	0	1851
	Other	3	0	
	TOTAL	49	1	

TOP POINT EARNERS

	PLAYER	GAMES	AV PTS
1	Pablo Nino	16	1.56
2	Hertog	10	1.50
3	Molenaar	26	1.50
4	Oliseh	25	1.40
5	Daelemans	14	1.29
6	Youssouf	22	1.27
7	Fleur	4	1.25
8	Hesp	33	1.18
9	Aerts	34	1.18
10	Lammens	33	1.18
	CLUB AVERAGE:		**1.18**

LEAGUE APPEARANCES, BOOKINGS AND CAPS

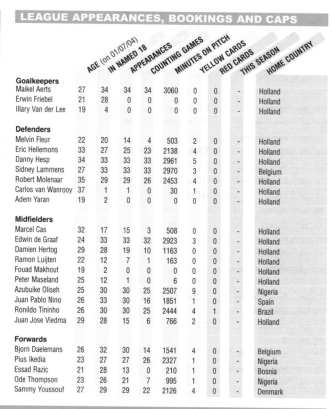

	AGE (on 01/07/04)	IN NAMED 18	APPEARANCES	COUNTING GAMES	MINUTES ON PITCH	YELLOW CARDS	RED CARDS	THIS SEASON	HOME COUNTRY
Goalkeepers									
Maikel Aerts	27	34	34	34	3060	0	0	-	Holland
Erwin Friebel	21	28	0	0	0	0	0	-	Holland
Illary Van der Lee	19	4	0	0	0	0	0	-	Holland
Defenders									
Melvin Fleur	22	20	14	4	503	2	0	-	Holland
Eric Hellemons	33	27	25	23	2138	4	0	-	Holland
Danny Hesp	34	33	33	33	2961	5	0	-	Holland
Sidney Lammens	27	33	33	33	2970	3	0	-	Belgium
Robert Molenaar	35	29	29	26	2453	4	0	-	Holland
Carlos van Wanrooy	37	1	1	0	30	1	0	-	Holland
Adem Yaran	19	2	0	0	0	0	0	-	Holland
Midfielders									
Marcel Cas	32	17	15	3	508	0	0	-	Holland
Edwin de Graaf	24	33	33	32	2923	3	0	-	Holland
Damien Hertog	29	28	19	10	1163	0	0	-	Holland
Ramon Luijten	22	12	7	1	163	0	0	-	Holland
Fouad Makhout	19	2	0	0	0	0	0	-	Holland
Peter Maseland	25	12	1	0	6	0	0	-	Holland
Azubuike Oliseh	25	30	30	25	2507	9	0	-	Nigeria
Juan Pablo Nino	26	33	30	16	1851	1	0	-	Spain
Ronildo Tininho	26	30	30	25	2444	4	1	-	Brazil
Juan Jose Viedma	29	28	15	6	766	2	0	-	Holland
Forwards									
Bjorn Daelemans	26	32	30	14	1541	4	0	-	Belgium
Pius Ikedia	23	27	27	26	2327	1	0	-	Nigeria
Essad Razic	21	28	13	0	210	1	0	-	Bosnia
Ode Thompson	23	26	21	7	995	1	0	-	Nigeria
Sammy Youssouf	27	29	29	22	2126	4	0	-	Denmark

TEAM OF THE SEASON

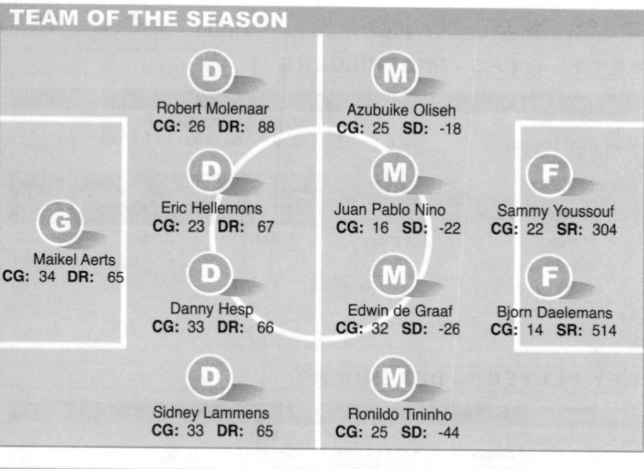

G
Maikel Aerts
CG: 34 DR: 65
D
Robert Molenaar
CG: 26 DR: 88
D
Eric Hellemons
CG: 23 DR: 67
D
Danny Hesp
CG: 33 DR: 66
D
Sidney Lammens
CG: 33 DR: 65
M
Azubuike Oliseh
CG: 25 SD: -18
M
Juan Pablo Nino
CG: 16 SD: -22
M
Edwin de Graaf
CG: 32 SD: -26
M
Ronildo Tininho
CG: 25 SD: -44
F
Sammy Youssouf
CG: 22 SR: 304
F
Bjorn Daelemans
CG: 14 SR: 514

SQUAD APPEARANCES

Match	1	2	3	4	5	6	7	8	9	10	11	12	13	14	15	16	17	18	19	20	21	22	23	24	25	26	27	28	29	30	31	32	33	34	35	36	37	38
Venue	A	A	H	A	H	A	H	H	A	H	A	H	H	A	H	A	H	H	A	A	A	A	H	H	A	A	H	A	H	H	A	H	H	A	H	A	H	A
Competition	L	L	L	L	L	L	L	L	L	L	L	L	L	L	L	L	L	L	L	L	L	L	L	L	L	L	L	L	L	L	L	L	L	L	L	L	L	L
Result	D	L	L	W	D	W	W	D	L	D	W	W	W	D	D	L	W	D	L	L	W	W	L	L	W	L	D	W	W	D	L	D	L	D	L	L	L	L

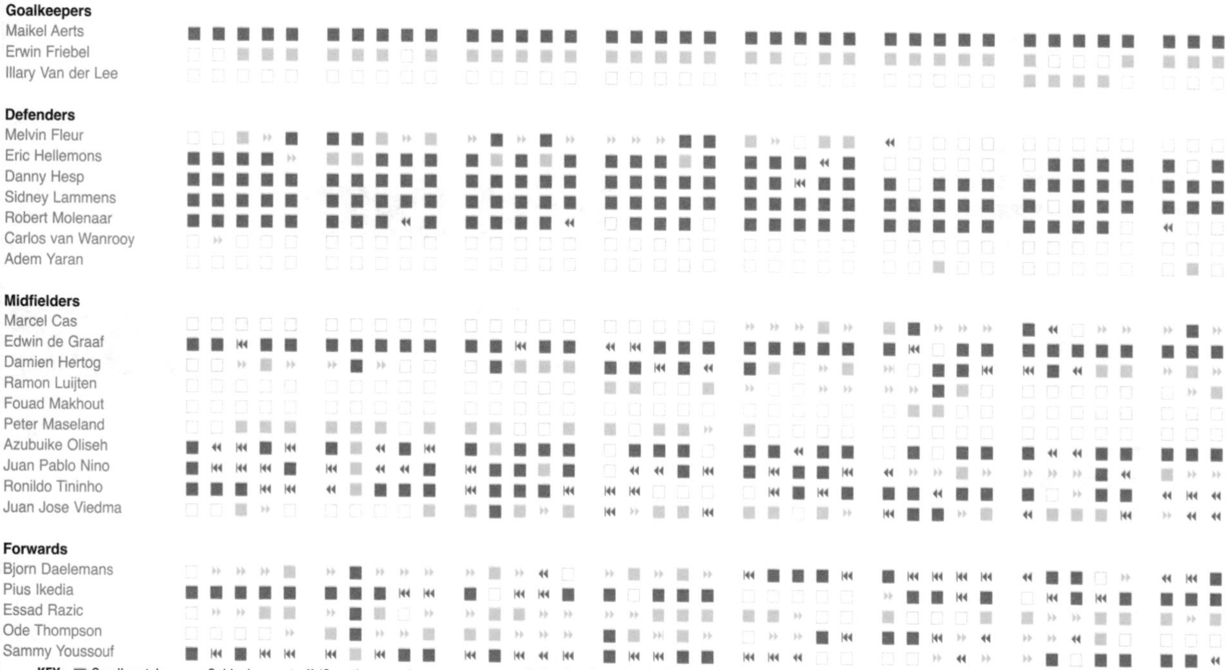

Goalkeepers
Maikel Aerts
Erwin Friebel
Illary Van der Lee

Defenders
Melvin Fleur
Eric Hellemons
Danny Hesp
Sidney Lammens
Robert Molenaar
Carlos van Wanrooy
Adem Yaran

Midfielders
Marcel Cas
Edwin de Graaf
Damien Hertog
Ramon Luijten
Fouad Makhout
Peter Maseland
Azubuike Oliseh
Juan Pablo Nino
Ronildo Tininho
Juan Jose Viedma

Forwards
Bjorn Daelemans
Pius Ikedia
Essad Razic
Ode Thompson
Sammy Youssouf

KEY: On all match · On bench · Subbed or sent off (Counting game) · Subbed or sent off (playing less than 70 minutes) · Subbed on from bench (Counting Game) · Subbed on (playing less than 70 minutes) · Subbed on and then subbed or sent off (Counting Game) · Subbed on and then subbed or sent off (playing less than 70 minutes) · Not in 16

FC GRONINGEN

Final Position: **13th**

KEY: ☐ Won ☐ Drawn ☐ Lost

							Attendance
1	hocr1	HSC '21	A	W	1-4		
2	lge	NAC Breda	H	W	1-0	Vrede 4	11,483
3	lge	Volendam	A	L	0-3		5,000
4	lge	Den Haag	H	W	2-0	Matthijs 14; Salmon 87	11,000
5	lge	Heerenveen	A	L	0-1		14,000
6	lge	Utrecht	H	D	1-1	Salmon 22	11,743
7	hocr2	WHC	A	W	0-1		
8	lge	Roda JC Kerk	A	D	0-0		12,000
9	lge	Ajax	H	L	1-3	Smit 21	12,400
10	lge	Twente	A	L	3-5	Tuhuteru 42; Pinas 45; Salmon 90	13,200
11	lge	Vitesse Arnhem	H	W	2-1	Smit 85; Drent 88	12,500
12	hocr3	Roosendaal	A	L	0-1		
13	lge	Feyenoord	H	D	3-3	Drent 53; Hugo 77; van Gessel 89	12,500
14	lge	NEC Nijmegen	A	W	3-2	van Gessel 47; Pinas 50; van der Linden 63	12,000
15	lge	RKC Waalwijk	A	D	1-1	Smit 57	6,000
16	lge	Roosendaal	H	W	2-0	Salmon 46; van Gessel 80	12,500
17	lge	AZ Alkmaar	A	L	1-2	Salmon 83	7,329
18	lge	Zwolle	A	D	1-1	Hugo 50	6,650
19	lge	Willem II Tilb	H	L	1-2	van Gessel 25	12,054
20	lge	PSV Eindhoven	H	L	0-2		12,334
21	lge	Volendam	H	L	0-1		11,034
22	lge	NEC Nijmegen	H	W	2-0	Smit 60; de Witte 90	11,024
23	lge	Den Haag	A	L	1-3	van Gessel 25	5,721
24	lge	Vitesse Arnhem	A	W	2-1	Krstev 48; van Gessel 90	19,010
25	lge	NAC Breda	A	D	1-1	de Witte 45	10,315
26	lge	RKC Waalwijk	H	L	1-2	Vrede 82	12,500
27	lge	Willem II Tilb	A	L	0-2		13,200
28	lge	Roosendaal	A	L	0-1		5,000
29	lge	Heerenveen	H	D	0-0		12,500
30	lge	Twente	H	W	1-0	Krstev 30	12,000
31	lge	Ajax	A	L	1-2	Salmon 75	49,212
32	lge	PSV Eindhoven	A	L	0-5		32,000
33	lge	AZ Alkmaar	H	D	1-1	Smit 56	11,618
34	lge	Zwolle	H	D	2-2	van Gessel 25; Matthijs 45	12,000
35	lge	Feyenoord	A	W	2-1	Drent 86,90	39,600
36	lge	Utrecht	A	L	0-2		18,000
37	lge	Roda JC Kerk	H	D	2-2	Tuhuteru 61; van Gessel 88	12,490

MONTHLY POINTS TALLY

AUGUST	6	67%
SEPTEMBER	2	22%
OCTOBER	3	33%
NOVEMBER	8	67%
DECEMBER	1	11%
JANUARY	0	0%
FEBRUARY	7	39%
MARCH	4	33%
APRIL	2	17%
MAY	4	44%

KEY PLAYERS - GOALSCORERS

Glen Salmon

Goals in the League	6	Player Strike Rate Average number of minutes between League goals scored by player	331
Contribution to Attacking Power Average number of minutes between League team goals while on pitch	82	Club Strike Rate Average number of minutes between League goals scored by club	81

	PLAYER	LGE GOALS	POWER	STRIKE RATE
1	Glen Salmon	6	82	331 mins
2	Sander van Gessel	8	80	331 mins
3	Arvid Smit	5	76	445 mins
4	Brian Pinas	2	84	848 mins

KEY PLAYERS - MIDFIELDERS

Alves Velame Hugo

Goals in the League	2	Contribution to Attacking Power Average number of minutes between League team goals while on pitch	61
Defensive Rating Average number of mins between League goals conceded while he was on the pitch	51	Scoring Difference Defensive Rating minus Contribution to Attacking Power	-10

	PLAYER	LGE GOALS	DEF RATE	POWER	SCORE DIFF
1	Alves Velame Hugo	2	51	61	-10 mins
2	Sander van Gessel	8	63	80	-17 mins
3	Paul Matthijs	2	60	80	-20 mins
4	Arvid Smit	5	56	77	-21 mins

KEY PLAYERS - DEFENDERS

Arnold Kruiswijk

Goals Conceded (GC) The number of League goals conceded while he was on the pitch	38	Clean Sheets In games when he played at least 70 minutes	7
Defensive Rating Ave number of mins between League goals conceded while on the pitch	65	Club Defensive Rating Average number of mins between League goals conceded by the club this season	58

	PLAYER	CON LGE	CLEAN SHEETS	DEF RATE
1	Arnold Kruiswijk	38	7	65 mins
2	Melchior Schoenmakers	21	2	64 mins
3	Kurt Elshot	48	7	58 mins
4	Antoine van der Linden	39	3	54 mins

KEY GOALKEEPER

Roy Beukenkamp

Goals Conceded in the League	42	Counting Games Games when he played at least 70 mins	28
Defensive Rating Ave number of mins between League goals conceded while on the pitch	60	Clean Sheets In games when he played at least 70 mins	5

LEAGUE GOALS

Sander van Gessel

Minutes on the pitch	2647	Goals in the League	8
League average (mins between goals)	331		

	PLAYER	MINS	GOALS	AVE
1	van Gessel	2647	8	331
2	Salmon	1988	6	331
3	Smit	2227	5	445
4	Drent	1359	4	340
5	Hugo	1217	2	609
6	Pinas	1695	2	848
7	Tuhuteru	661	2	331
8	Krstev	1098	2	549
9	de Witte	1153	2	577
10	Matthijs	2325	2	1163
11	van der Linden	2096	1	2096
12	Vrede	915	1	915
	Other		1	
	TOTAL		38	

DISCIPLINARY

	PLAYER	YELLOW	RED	AVE
1	Schoenmakers	7	1	167
2	Landerl	4	1	266
3	Krstev	3	0	366
4	de Witte	3	0	384
5	Matthijs	6	0	387
6	Salmon	5	0	397
7	Elshot	7	0	397
8	van der Linden	5	0	419
9	Vrede	2	0	457
10	Smit	3	0	742
11	Kruiswijk	3	0	821
12	van Gessel	3	0	882
13	Floren	2	1	929
	Other	2	0	
	TOTAL	55	3	

TOP POINT EARNERS

	PLAYER	GAMES	AV PTS
1	Hugo	11	1.64
2	Krstev	10	1.60
3	Schoenmakers	13	1.46
4	Landerl	10	1.30
5	Salmon	19	1.21
6	Beukenkamp	28	1.18
7	Elshot	31	1.13
8	Matthijs	25	1.12
9	Kruiswijk	27	1.07
10	Floren	30	1.03
	CLUB AVERAGE:		**1.09**

TEAM OF THE SEASON

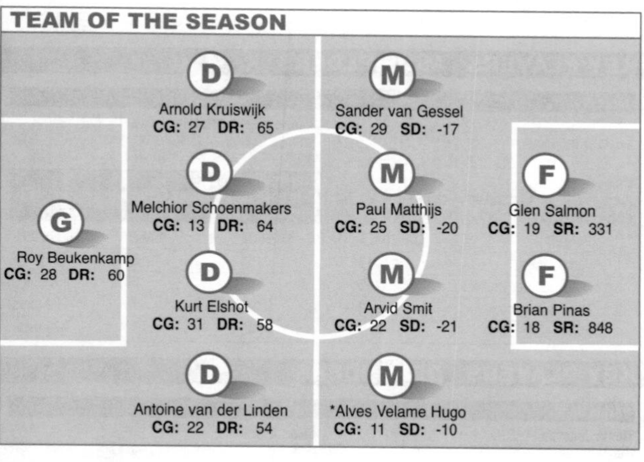
D
Arnold Kruiswijk
CG: 27 DR: 65
M
Sander van Gessel
CG: 29 SD: -17
D
Melchior Schoenmakers
CG: 13 DR: 64
M
Paul Matthijs
CG: 25 SD: -20
F
Glen Salmon
CG: 19 SR: 331
G
Roy Beukenkamp
CG: 28 DR: 60
D
Kurt Elshot
CG: 31 DR: 58
M
Arvid Smit
CG: 22 SD: -21
F
Brian Pinas
CG: 18 SR: 848
D
Antoine van der Linden
CG: 22 DR: 54
M
*Alves Velame Hugo
CG: 11 SD: -10

LEAGUE APPEARANCES, BOOKINGS AND CAPS

	AGE (on 01/07/04)	IN NAMED 18	APPEARANCES	COUNTING GAMES	MINUTES ON PITCH	YELLOW CARDS	RED CARDS	THIS SEASON	HOME COUNTRY
Goalkeepers									
Roy Beukenkamp	36	28	28	28	2504	0	0	-	Holland
Egbert Darwinkel	38	1	0	0	0	0	0	-	Holland
Jeroen Lambers	23	30	7	6	556	0	0	-	Holland
Mike Romer	-	5	0	0	0	0	0	-	Holland
Defenders									
Kurt Elshot	27	31	31	31	2785	7	0	-	Surinam
Mathias Floren	27	32	32	30	2788	2	1	-	Sweden
Ray Frankel	21	15	5	1	156	0	0	-	Holland
Mile Krstev	25	25	18	10	1098	3	0	-	Macedonia
Arnold Kruiswijk	19	28	28	27	2463	3	0	-	Holland
M Schoenmakers	28	24	18	13	1342	7	1	-	Holland
A van der Linden	28	31	26	22	2096	5	0	-	Holland
Regillio Vrede	31	18	15	8	915	2	0	-	Holland
R Zimmerman	20	2	0	0	0	0	0	-	Holland
Midfielders									
R Bronkhorst	25	4	1	0	8	0	0	-	Holland
J Hardarson	27	11	2	1	111	0	0	-	Iceland
Alves Velame Hugo	29	31	23	11	1217	0	0	-	Brazil
Rolf Landerl	28	24	23	10	1331	4	1	-	Austria
Paul Matthijs	27	27	27	25	2325	6	0	-	Holland
Arvid Smit	23	29	29	22	2227	3	0	-	Holland
S van Gessel	27	32	31	29	2647	3	0	-	Holland
Mark Veldmate	19	4	1	0	68	0	0	-	Holland
K Westerveld	20	8	1	0	5	0	0	-	Holland
Forwards									
Shutlan Axwijk	-	6	2	0	67	0	0	-	Holland
Soeres Baidjoe	-	6	0	0	0	0	0	-	Holland
Chris de Witte	26	29	24	8	1153	3	0	-	Belgium
Martin Drent	34	30	26	10	1359	1	0	-	Holland
Brian Pinas	25	23	23	18	1695	1	0	-	Holland
Glen Salmon	26	26	26	19	1988	5	0	-	South Africa
Valery Sedoc	18	2	2	0	83	0	0	-	Holland
Ignacio Tuhuteru	30	24	15	3	661	0	0	-	Holland

SQUAD APPEARANCES

Match	1	2	3	4	5	6	7	8	9	10	11	12	13	14	15	16	17	18	19	20	21	22	23	24	25	26	27	28	29	30	31	32	33	34	35	36	37
Venue	A	H	A	H	A	H	A	A	H	A	H	A	H	A	A	H	A	A	H	H	H	H	A	A	A	H	A	A	H	H	A	A	H	H	A	A	H
Competition	L	L	L	L	L	L	L	L	L	L	L	L	L	L	L	L	L	L	L	L	L	L	L	L	L	L	L	L	L	L	L	L	L	L	L	L	L
Result	D	W	L	W	L	D	D	D	L	L	W	L	D	W	D	W	L	D	L	L	L	W	L	W	D	L	L	L	D	W	L	L	D	D	W	L	D

Goalkeepers
Roy Beukenkamp
Egbert Darwinkel
Jeroen Lambers
Mike Romer

Defenders
Kurt Elshot
Mathias Floren
Ray Frankel
Mile Krstev
Arnold Kruiswijk
Melchior Schoenmakers
Antoine van der Linden
Regillio Vrede
Roberto Zimmerman

Midfielders
Raymond Bronkhorst
Johannes Hardarson
Alves Velame Hugo
Rolf Landerl
Paul Matthijs
Arvid Smit
Sander van Gessel
Mark Veldmate
Kristian Westerveld

Forwards
Shutlan Axwijk
Soeres Baidjoe
Chris de Witte
Martin Drent
Brian Pinas
Glen Salmon
Valery Sedoc
Ignacio Tuhuteru

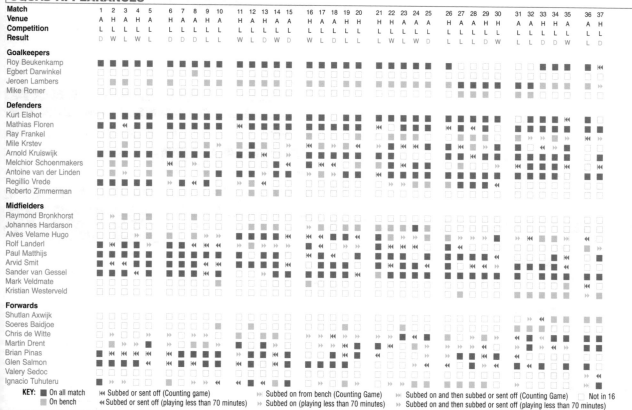

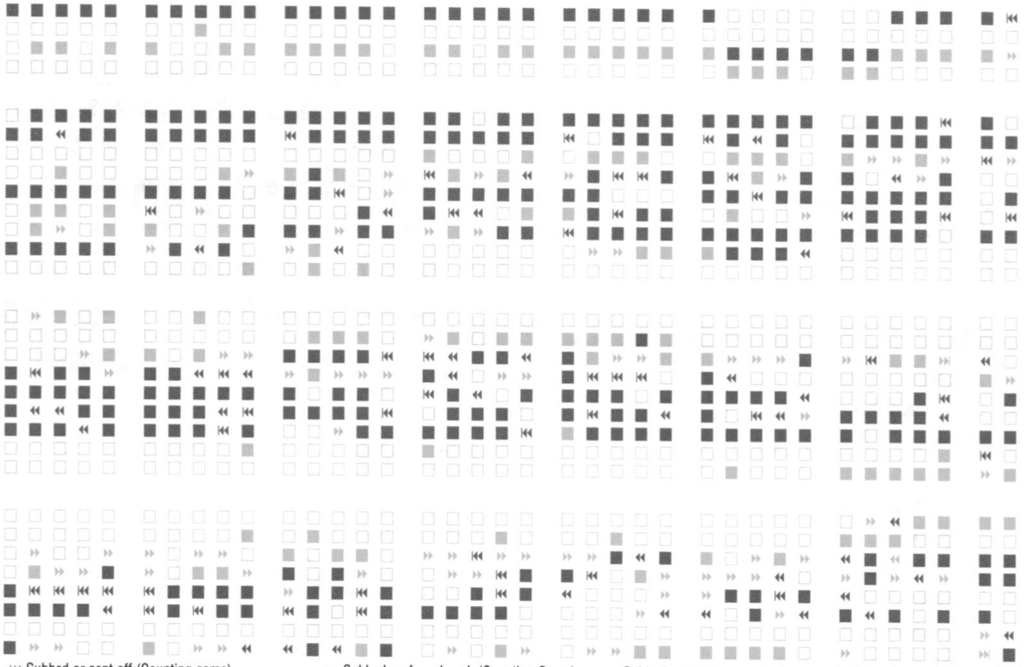

KEY: ■ On all match | On bench | ⏮ Subbed or sent off (Counting game) | « Subbed or sent off (playing less than 70 minutes) | Subbed on from bench (Counting Game) | » Subbed on (playing less than 70 minutes) | Subbed on and then subbed or sent off (Counting Game) | Subbed on and then subbed or sent off (playing less than 70 minutes) | □ Not in 16

NEC NIJMEGEN

Final Position: **14th**

KEY: ☐Won ☐Drawn ☐Lost

							Attendance
1	lge	Feyenoord	A	L	1-2	Wielaert 90 pen	42,000
2	lge	Roda JC Kerk	H	L	1-3	De Freitas 90	12,250
3	lge	Utrecht	A	W	1-0	Schuurmen 42	18,000
4	lge	Twente	H	W	2-1	De Freitas 47; de Nooijer 50	12,350
5	lge	Volendam	A	W	3-2	Schuurmen 13; Hersi 20; Ax 71	4,631
6	uc1rl1	Wisla Krakow	A	L	1-2	Wielaert 65 pen	6,000
7	lge	Den Haag	H	L	1-2	van As 38 og	12,350
8	lge	AZ Alkmaar	A	L	0-2		7,700
9	uc1rl2	Wisla Krakow	H	L	1-2	Zonneveld 33	4,500
10	lge	NAC Breda	H	L	0-3		12,000
11	lge	Heerenveen	A	W	2-1	de Nooijer 43; Hersi 62	14,500
12	lge	Roosendaal	A	L	0-1		5,000
13	lge	Groningen	H	L	2-3	Demouge 26; Hersi 31	12,000
14	lge	PSV Eindhoven	H	L	2-3	van der Doelen 5; Demouge 8	12,500
15	lge	Willem II Tilb	A	L	0-3		12,300
16	lge	RKC Waalwijk	H	D	1-1	Wielaert 57 pen	
17	lge	Vitesse Arnhem	H	W	2-0	Ebbinge 30; Govedarica 43	12,500
18	hocr3	Heerenveen	A	W	1-0	Hersi 82	9,000
19	lge	Zwolle	H	W	1-0	Hersi 44	11,250
20	lge	Ajax	A	L	0-1		49,018
21	lge	Feyenoord	H	L	1-2	Niedzielan 22	12,500
22	lge	RKC Waalwijk	A	W	2-1	Simr 15; Demouge 35	6,500
23	hocqf	S Rotterdam	A	L	2-3*	(*on penalties)	
24	lge	Groningen	A	L	0-2		11,024
25	lge	Utrecht	H	W	4-0	Niedzielan 13,72; Simr 32; van der Doelen 63	12,000
26	lge	Zwolle	A	L	1-2	van der Doelen 28	5,960
27	lge	Heerenveen	H	L	1-2	Hersi 13	12,000
28	lge	Roosendaal	H	L	1-2	Zonneveld 45	12,050
29	lge	Twente	A	W	5-2	Wielaert 5; Wisgerhof 50; Tumba 52; De Freitas 88; van Rijswijk 90	13,145
30	lge	AZ Alkmaar	H	L	0-2		12,250
31	lge	NAC Breda	A	L	2-5	Tumba 66; van Rijswijk 80	12,800
32	lge	Willem II Tilb	H	W	4-0	Wielaert 5 pen; Tumba 15; Hersi 60,79	11,500
33	lge	Roda JC Kerk	A	L	0-4		26,226
34	lge	PSV Eindhoven	A	L	0-3		33,500
35	lge	Ajax	H	D	0-0		12,500
36	lge	Vitesse Arnhem	A	D	2-2	Hersi 77,84	22,500
37	lge	Volendam	H	D	1-1	Hersi 58	12,250
38	lge	Den Haag	A	L	1-4	Demouge 18	9,783

MONTHLY POINTS TALLY

AUGUST	3	33%
SEPTEMBER	6	67%
OCTOBER	3	33%
NOVEMBER	0	0%
DECEMBER	7	78%
JANUARY	3	33%
FEBRUARY	3	25%
MARCH	3	25%
APRIL	4	33%
MAY	2	22%

KEY PLAYERS - GOALSCORERS

Youssef Hersi

Goals in the League	10	Player Strike Rate Average number of minutes between League goals scored by player	242
Contribution to Attacking Power Average number of minutes between League team goals while on pitch	67	Club Strike Rate Average number of minutes between League goals scored by club	70

	PLAYER	LGE GOALS	POWER	STRIKE RATE
1	Youssef Hersi	10	67	242 mins
2	Frank Demouge	4	78	394 mins
3	Bjorn van der Doelen	3	63	611 mins
4	Rob Wielaert	4	68	719 mins

KEY PLAYERS - MIDFIELDERS

Jarda Simr

Goals in the League	2	Contribution to Attacking Power Average number of minutes between League team goals while on pitch	67
Defensive Rating Average number of mins between League goals conceded while he was on the pitch	54	Scoring Difference Defensive Rating minus Contribution to Attacking Power	-13

	PLAYER	LGE GOALS	DEF RATE	POWER	SCORE DIFF
1	Jarda Simr	2	54	67	-13 mins
2	Bjorn van der Doelen	3	50	63	-13 mins
3	Resit Schuurmen	2	48	70	-22 mins
4	Mike Zonneveld	1	46	69	-23 mins

KEY PLAYERS - DEFENDERS

Pascal Heije

Goals Conceded (GC) The number of League goals conceded while he was on the pitch	23	Clean Sheets In games when he played at least 70 minutes	4
Defensive Rating Ave number of mins between League goals conceded while on the pitch	56	Club Defensive Rating Average number of mins between League goals conceded by the club this season	49

	PLAYER	CON LGE	CLEAN SHEETS	DEF RATE
1	Pascal Heije	23	4	56 mins
2	Jeffrey Leiwakabessy	35	3	56 mins
3	Arjan Ebbinge	46	5	56 mins
4	Rob Wielaert	61	5	47 mins

KEY GOALKEEPER

Dennis Gentenaar

Goals Conceded in the League	62	Counting Games Games when he played at least 70 mins	34
Defensive Rating Ave number of mins between League goals conceded while on the pitch	49	Clean Sheets In games when he played at least 70 mins	6

LEAGUE GOALS

Youssef Hersi

Minutes on the pitch	2423	Goals in the League	10
League average (mins between goals)	242		

	PLAYER	MINS	GOALS	AVE
1	Hersi	2423	10	242
2	Demouge	1577	4	394
3	Wielaert	2877	4	719
4	van der Doelen	1834	3	611
5	De Freitas	564	3	188
6	Niedzielan	905	3	302
7	Tumba	832	3	277
8	Simr	1883	2	942
9	Schuurmen	2602	2	1301
10	de Nooijer	978	2	489
11	van Rijswijk	327	2	164
12	Ax	1002	1	1002
	Other		5	
	TOTAL		44	

DISCIPLINARY RECORDS

	PLAYER	YELLOW	RED	AVE
1	Tumba	4	0	208
2	Ax	4	0	250
3	Zonneveld	6	0	285
4	van der Doelen	5	0	366
5	Wielaert	6	1	411
6	Ebbinge	6	0	428
7	Simr	4	0	470
8	Govedarica	2	1	518
9	Wisgerhof	5	0	556
10	Demouge	2	0	788
11	Niedzielan	1	0	905
12	Schuurmen	2	0	1301
13	Leiwakabessy	1	0	1954
	Other	1	0	
	TOTAL	49	2	

TOP POINT EARNERS

	PLAYER	GAMES	AV PTS
1	De Freitas	2	3.00
2	Ax	5	1.80
3	Tumba	7	1.43
4	Hersi	26	1.15
5	Ebbinge	27	1.15
6	Leiwakabessy	20	1.10
7	Zonneveld	17	1.06
8	van der Doelen	20	1.05
9	Schuurmen	28	1.04
10	Wisgerhof	29	1.03
	CLUB AVERAGE:		**1.00**

TEAM OF THE SEASON

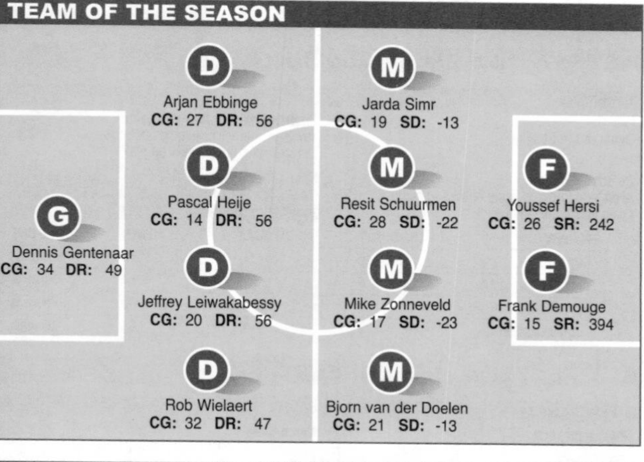
D
Arjan Ebbinge
CG: 27 DR: 56
D
Pascal Heije
CG: 14 DR: 56
D
Jeffrey Leiwakabessy
CG: 20 DR: 56
D
Rob Wielaert
CG: 32 DR: 47
G
Dennis Gentenaar
CG: 34 DR: 49
M
Jarda Simr
CG: 19 SD: -13
M
Resit Schuurmen
CG: 28 SD: -22
M
Mike Zonneveld
CG: 17 SD: -23
M
Bjorn van der Doelen
CG: 21 SD: -13
F
Youssef Hersi
CG: 26 SR: 242
F
Frank Demouge
CG: 15 SR: 394

LEAGUE APPEARANCES, BOOKINGS AND CAPS

	AGE (on 01/07/04)	IN NAMED 18	APPEARANCES	COUNTING GAMES	MINUTES ON PITCH	YELLOW CARDS	RED CARDS	THIS SEASON	HOME COUNTRY
Goalkeepers									
Dennis Gentenaar	28	34	34	34	3060	0	0	-	Holland
Matheus Hoop	23	1	0	0	0	0	0	-	Holland
A Van der Sleen	41	30	1	0	10	0	0	-	Holland
Defenders									
Arjan Ebbinge	29	31	31	27	2570	6	0	-	Holland
Pascal Heije	24	19	17	14	1280	0	0	-	Holland
J Leiwakabessy	23	25	24	20	1954	1	0	-	Holland
Mark Otten	18	21	3	0	22	0	0	-	Holland
Nick Raymans	19	2	0	0	0	0	0	-	Holland
Rob Wielaert	25	32	32	32	2877	6	1	-	Holland
Peter Wisgerhof	24	33	33	29	2780	5	0	-	Holland
Midfielders									
Patrick Ax	24	27	25	5	1002	4	0	-	Holland
Edgar Barreto	19	9	9	9	790	0	0	-	Paraguay
Ralf de Haan	20	11	1	0	19	0	0	-	Holland
Dejan Govedarica	34	30	23	15	1554	2	1	-	Serbia & Montenegro
Michael Hendriks	24	3	1	0	33	0	0	-	Holland
Alexander Prent	21	2	0	0	0	0	0	-	Holland
Resit Schuurmen	25	34	32	28	2602	2	0	-	Holland
Jarda Simr	25	27	25	19	1883	4	0	-	Czech Republic
B van der Doelen	27	21	21	20	1834	5	0	-	Holland
Mike Zonneveld	23	21	21	17	1713	6	0	-	Holland
Forwards									
Fabian De Freitas	30	26	19	2	564	0	0	-	Holland
Dennis de Nooijer	35	14	14	10	978	0	0	-	Holland
Frank Demouge	22	23	23	15	1577	2	0	-	Holland
Youssef Hersi	21	31	31	26	2423	1	0	-	Holland
Andrzej Niedzielan	25	11	11	9	905	1	0	-	Poland
Zico Tumba	27	27	21	7	832	4	0	-	Congo
Rene van Rijswijk	33	26	11	2	327	0	0	-	Holland

SQUAD APPEARANCES

Match	1	2	3	4	5	6	7	8	9	10	11	12	13	14	15	16	17	18	19	20	21	22	23	24	25	26	27	28	29	30	31	32	33	34	35	36	37	38
Venue	A	H	A	H	A	A	H	A	H	H	A	A	H	H	A	H	H	A	H	A	H	A	A	A	H	A	H	H	A	H	A	H	A	A	H	A	H	A
Competition	L	L	L	L	L	E	L	L	E	L	L	L	L	L	L	L	L	L	L	L	L	L	L	L	L	L	L	L	L	L	L	L	L	L	L	L	L	L
Result	L	L	W	W	W	L	L	L	L	L	W	L	L	L	L	D	W	W	W	L	L	W	L	L	W	L	L	L	W	L	L	W	L	L	D	D	D	L

Goalkeepers
Dennis Gentenaar
Matheus Hoop
Albert Van der Sleen

Defenders
Arjan Ebbinge
Pascal Heije
Jeffrey Leiwakabessy
Mark Otten
Nick Raymans
Rob Wielaert
Peter Wisgerhof

Midfielders
Patrick Ax
Edgar Barreto
Ralf de Haan
Dejan Govedarica
Michael Hendriks
Alexander Prent
Resit Schuurmen
Jarda Simr
Bjorn van der Doelen
Mike Zonneveld

Forwards
Fabian De Freitas
Dennis de Nooijer
Frank Demouge
Youssef Hersi
Andrzej Niedzielan
Zico Tumba
Rene van Rijswijk

KEY: On all match; On bench; Subbed or sent off (Counting game); Subbed or sent off (playing less than 70 minutes); Subbed on from bench (Counting Game); Subbed on (playing less than 70 minutes); Subbed on and then subbed or sent off (Counting Game); Subbed on and then subbed or sent off (playing less than 70 minutes); Not in 16

ADO DEN HAAG

Final Position: **15th**

KEY: Won Drawn Lost

							Attendance
1	hocr1	Schijndel	A	W	1-2		
2	lge	RKC Waalwijk	A	L	0-1		6,000
3	lge	Utrecht	H	D	1-1	Pronk 87	6,135
4	lge	Groningen	A	L	0-2		11,000
5	lge	Volendam	H	D	1-1	Bodde 20 fk	6,335
6	lge	Roosendaal	H	L	1-2	Hofstede 48	6,200
7	hocr2	Heracles	A	L	0-4		
8	lge	NEC Nijmegen	A	W	2-1	Van der Gun 54; Stroeve 79	12,350
9	lge	PSV Eindhoven	H	L	0-4		7,500
10	lge	Zwolle	A	W	2-1	Hofstede 10,75	6,000
11	lge	NAC Breda	H	D	1-1	Cales 20	6,548
12	lge	Roda JC Kerk	A	L	1-5	Cales 20 fk	13,068
13	lge	Ajax	H	L	1-4	Stroeve 17	9,420
14	lge	Twente	A	L	0-4		13,000
15	lge	Vitesse Arnhem	H	D	1-1	Hofstede 28	6,500
16	lge	Heerenveen	A	L	0-2		14,200
17	lge	Feyenoord	A	L	1-4	Van der Gun 14	40,800
18	lge	Willem II Tilb	H	L	0-1		5,211
19	lge	AZ Alkmaar	A	W	1-0	Kromkamp 59 og	7,069
20	lge	Ajax	A	L	0-4		47,264
21	lge	Willem II Tilb	A	L	0-1		12,800
22	lge	Groningen	H	W	3-1	Simons 52,89 pen; Stroeve 57	5,721
23	lge	Feyenoord	H	D	2-2	Castelen 19; van der Gun 83	8,083
24	lge	Roda JC Kerk	H	W	1-0	van der Gun 18	7,381
25	lge	Volendam	A	W	2-0	van der Gun 50; Stroeve 87	5,000
26	lge	AZ Alkmaar	H	L	2-3	Stroeve 10; Castelen 51	9,049
27	lge	Vitesse Arnhem	A	L	0-1		18,990
28	lge	Roosendaal	A	D	0-0		5,000
29	lge	Zwolle	H	D	1-1	Van der Gun 45	8,566
30	lge	Utrecht	A	L	3-5	El-Akchaoui 1; Stroeve 16; Castelen 44	18,500
31	lge	RKC Waalwijk	H	L	1-3	Saeijs 80 pen	8,000
32	lge	Twente	H	W	1-0	Stroeve 21	7,000
33	lge	NAC Breda	A	L	0-1		11,500
34	lge	Heerenveen	H	W	1-0	Hofstede 48	13,501
35	lge	PSV Eindhoven	A	L	2-3	Castelen 63; Stroeve 75	34,000
36	lge	NEC Nijmegen	H	W	4-1	Stroeve 10,84; Saeijs 42; Simons 64	9,783

MONTHLY POINTS TALLY

Month	Points	%
AUGUST	1	11%
SEPTEMBER	4	44%
OCTOBER	4	33%
NOVEMBER	1	11%
DECEMBER	0	0%
JANUARY	3	100%
FEBRUARY	10	56%
MARCH	2	17%
APRIL	3	25%
MAY	6	67%

KEY PLAYERS - GOALSCORERS

Roy Stroeve

Goals in the League	10	Player Strike Rate Average number of minutes between League goals scored by player	203
Contribution to Attacking Power Average number of minutes between League team goals while on pitch	72	Club Strike Rate Average number of minutes between League goals scored by club	85

	PLAYER	LGE GOALS	POWER	STRIKE RATE
1	Roy Stroeve	10	72	203 mins
2	Cedric van der Gun	6	71	359 mins
3	Jean Paul Saeijs	2	60	575 mins
4	Romeo Castelen	4	94	589 mins

KEY PLAYERS - MIDFIELDERS

Roy Stroeve

Goals in the League	10	Contribution to Attacking Power Average number of minutes between League team goals while on pitch	73
Defensive Rating Average number of mins between League goals conceded while he was on the pitch	55	Scoring Difference Defensive Rating minus Contribution to Attacking Power	-18

	PLAYER	LGE GOALS	DEF RATE	POWER	SCORE DIFF
1	Roy Stroeve	10	55	73	-18 mins
2	Tom van der Leegte	0	46	84	-38 mins
3	Ferrie Bodde	1	47	92	-45 mins
4	Romeo Castelen	4	48	94	-46 mins

KEY PLAYERS - DEFENDERS

Alberto Saavedra

Goals Conceded (GC) The number of League goals conceded while he was on the pitch	25	Clean Sheets In games when he played at least 70 minutes	6
Defensive Rating Ave number of mins between League goals conceded while on the pitch	64	Club Defensive Rating Average number of mins between League goals conceded by the club this season	50

	PLAYER	CON LGE	CLEAN SHEETS	DEF RATE
1	Alberto Saavedra	25	6	64 mins
2	Jean Paul Saeijs	20	4	57 mins
3	Youssef El-Akchaoui	32	6	55 mins
4	Daniel Rijaard	38	5	52 mins

KEY GOALKEEPER

Dorus de Vries

Goals Conceded in the League	29	Counting Games Games when he played at least 70 mins	18
Defensive Rating Ave number of mins between League goals conceded while on the pitch	56	Clean Sheets In games when he played at least 70 mins	6

LEAGUE GOALS

Roy Stroeve

Minutes on the pitch	2031	Goals in the League	10
League average (mins between goals)	203		

	PLAYER	MINS	GOALS	AVE
1	Stroeve	2031	10	203
2	van der Gun	2153	6	359
3	Hofstede	1261	5	252
4	Castelen	2354	4	589
5	Simons	832	3	277
6	Saeijs	1149	2	575
7	Cales	982	2	491
8	Pronk	485	1	485
9	El-Akchaoui	1751	1	1751
10	Bodde	2122	1	2122
	Other		1	
	TOTAL		36	

DISCIPLINARY RECORDS

	PLAYER	YELLOW	RED	AVE
1	Mensah	5	1	168
2	Saeijs	5	0	229
3	Bodde	9	0	235
4	van der Gun	6	0	358
5	van As	5	0	360
6	Rijaard	5	0	397
7	Toda	2	0	433
8	van Boxel	2	0	444
9	Oulida	1	0	456
10	Ros	1	0	473
11	van der Leegte	5	0	504
12	Saavedra	2	1	533
13	Carrilho	2	0	684
	Other	5	1	
	TOTAL	55	3	

TOP POINT EARNERS

	PLAYER	GAMES	AV PTS
1	Toda	7	2.14
2	Leonardo	4	1.75
3	Platvoet	5	1.40
4	Saavedra	18	1.33
5	Cales	6	1.33
6	El-Akchaoui	19	1.26
7	van der Gun	23	1.17
8	Stroeve	19	1.16
9	Saeijs	13	1.15
10	Rijaard	20	1.10
	CLUB AVERAGE:		1.00

TEAM OF THE SEASON

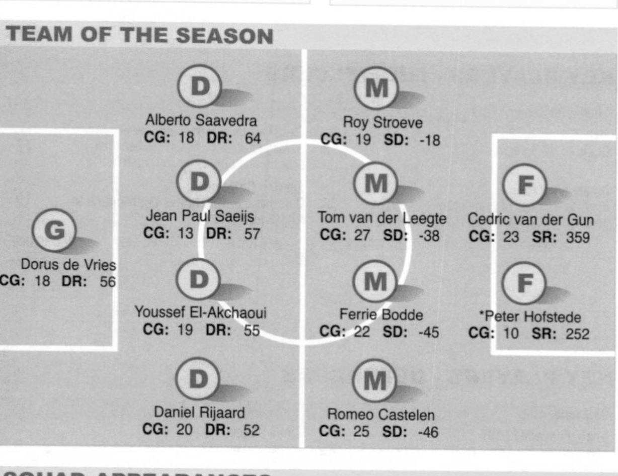

G
Dorus de Vries
CG: 18 DR: 56
D
Alberto Saavedra
CG: 18 DR: 64
D
Jean Paul Saeijs
CG: 13 DR: 57
D
Youssef El-Akchaoui
CG: 19 DR: 55
D
Daniel Rijaard
CG: 20 DR: 52
M
Roy Stroeve
CG: 19 SD: -18
M
Tom van der Leegte
CG: 27 SD: -38
M
Ferrie Bodde
CG: 22 SD: -45
M
Romeo Castelen
CG: 25 SD: -46
F
Cedric van der Gun
CG: 23 SR: 359
F
*Peter Hofstede
CG: 10 SR: 252

LEAGUE APPEARANCES, BOOKINGS AND CAPS

	AGE (on 01/07/04)	IN NAMED 18	APPEARANCES	COUNTING GAMES	MINUTES ON PITCH	YELLOW CARDS	RED CARDS	THIS SEASON	HOME COUNTRY
Goalkeepers									
Patrick de Groot	26	4	0	0	0	0	0	-	Holland
Dorus de Vries	23	29	18	18	1620	0	0	-	Holland
Roland Jansen	36	28	17	16	1474	0	0	-	Holland
Defenders									
Mirano Carrilho	28	31	19	13	1368	2	0	-	Holland
Y El-Akchaoui	23	29	22	19	1751	2	0	-	Holland
Kofi Mensah	26	21	13	10	1010	5	1	-	Ghana
Daniel Rijaard	27	30	26	20	1989	5	0	-	Holland
Michael Ros	22	12	9	3	473	1	0	-	Holland
Alberto Saavedra	22	18	18	18	1600	2	1	-	Spain
Jean Paul Saeijs	26	14	13	13	1149	5	0	-	Holland
Eelco Tigchelar	22	1	0	0	0	0	0	-	Holland
Jeffrey van As	32	28	22	19	1804	5	0	-	Holland
Robert van Boxel	21	20	12	9	888	2	0	-	Holland
Maurice Verberne	33	5	4	2	278	0	0	-	Holland
Wesley Zandstra	20	1	0	0	0	0	0	-	Holland
Midfielders									
Ferrie Bodde	22	30	28	22	2122	9	0	-	Holland
Romeo Castelen	21	28	28	25	2354	1	0	-	Holland
Leonardo	27	7	5	1	204	0	0	-	Brazil
Stefan Huisman	20	3	0	0	0	0	0	-	Holland
Leonardo	27	22	18	4	726	0	0	-	Brazil
Tarik Oulida	30	16	8	4	456	1	0	-	Holland
Marcel Pronk	20	13	8	4	485	0	0	-	Holland
Roy Stroeve	27	30	29	19	2031	1	0	-	Holland
Kazuyuki Toda	26	15	15	7	866	2	0	-	Japan
Arjan van der Laan	34	15	9	4	504	0	0	-	Holland
T van der Leegte	27	30	30	27	2524	5	0	-	Holland
Forwards									
Gijs Cales	27	16	14	6	982	0	0	-	Holland
Rachidi Gilkes	-	1	0	0	0	0	0	-	Holland
Peter Hofstede	37	19	19	10	1261	1	0	-	Holland
G Knijnenburg	21	3	0	0	0	0	0	-	Holland
Daniel Koegler	22	2	1	0	10	0	0	-	Holland
Imro Nurse	-	2	1	0	24	0	0	-	Holland
Rik Platvoet	28	13	12	5	694	0	0	-	Holland
Regillio Simons	31	15	15	6	832	0	1	-	Holland
C van der Gun	25	26	26	23	2153	6	0	-	Holland

SQUAD APPEARANCES

Match	1	2	3	4	5	6	7	8	9	10	11	12	13	14	15	16	17	18	19	20	21	22	23	24	25	26	27	28	29	30	31	32	33	34	35	36
Venue	A	A	H	A	H	H	A	A	H	A	H	A	H	A	H	A	A	H	A	A	A	H	H	H	A	H	A	A	H	A	H	H	A	H	A	H
Competition	L	L	L	L	L	L	L	L	L	L	L	L	L	L	L	L	L	L	L	L	L	L	L	L	L	L	L	L	L	L	L	L	L	L	L	L
Result	D	L	D	L	D	L	L	W	L	W	D	L	L	L	D	L	L	L	W	L	L	W	D	W	W	L	L	D	D	L	L	W	L	W	L	W

Goalkeepers
Patrick de Groot
Dorus de Vries
Roland Jansen

Defenders
Mirano Carrilho
Youssef El-Akchaoui
Kofi Mensah
Daniel Rijaard
Michael Ros
Alberto Saavedra
Jean Paul Saeijs
Eelco Tigchelar
Jeffrey van As
Robert van Boxel
Maurice Verberne
Wesley Zandstra

Midfielders
Ferrie Bodde
Romeo Castelen
Leonardo Dos Santos
Stefan Huisman
Leonardo
Tarik Oulida
Marcel Pronk
Roy Stroeve
Kazuyuki Toda
Arjan van der Laan
Tom van der Leegte

Forwards
Gijs Cales
Rachidi Gilkes
Peter Hofstede
Geoffrey Knijnenburg
Daniel Koegler
Imro Nurse
Rik Platvoet
Regillio Simons
Cedric van der Gun

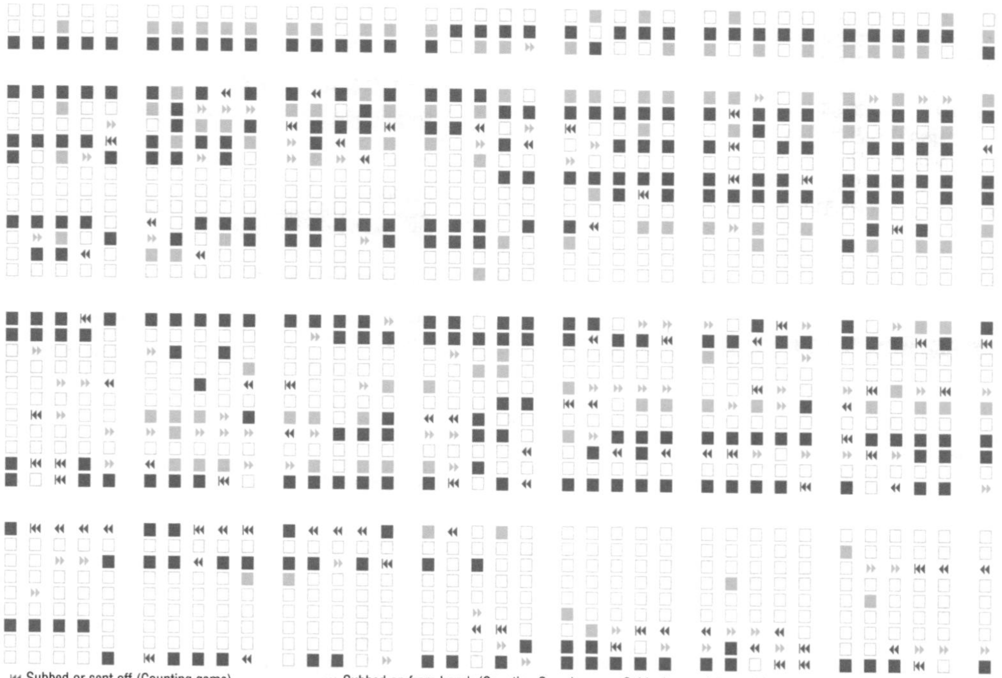

KEY: ■ On all match ■ On bench
⏮ Subbed or sent off (Counting game)
« Subbed or sent off (playing less than 70 minutes)
» Subbed on from bench (Counting Game)
» Subbed on (playing less than 70 minutes)
» Subbed on and then subbed or sent off (Counting Game)
» Subbed on and then subbed or sent off (playing less than 70 minutes)
□ Not in 16

VITESSE ARNHEM

Final Position: **16th**

KEY: ☐ Won ☐ Drawn ☐ Lost

No	Comp	Opponent	H/A	Res	Score	Scorers	Attendance
1	hocr1	UDI '19	A	W	0-4		
2	lge	Ajax	H	L	1-2	Amoah 14	22,000
3	lge	NAC Breda	A	L	0-2		13,000
4	lge	AZ Alkmaar	H	L	1-2	Bochem 66	17,500
5	lge	Roosendaal	A	D	1-1	Amoah 30	5,000
6	lge	Roda JC Kerk	H	D	1-1	Mbamba 27	16,500
7	hocr2	Fortuna S	H	W	4-0	Cornelisse 16; Mbamba 48; Claessens 53; Martel 62	
8	lge	Utrecht	A	W	3-1	Hofs 12; Zongo 81; Claessens 86	18,000
9	lge	Twente	H	L	3-5	Dingsdag 34; Cornelisse 36; van Beukering 83	18,437
10	lge	RKC Waalwijk	A	D	2-2	Rojer 77,81	6,500
11	lge	Groningen	A	L	1-2	Martel 62	12,500
12	hocr3	Volendam	H	W	4-0	Jansen, M 6; van Beukering 24; Bochem 72; Rojer 88	5,500
13	lge	Volendam	H	D	2-2	Claessens 57; Mbamba 69	17,500
14	lge	Willem II Tilb	H	D	2-2	Mbamba 7; van Beukering 58 pen	16,501
15	lge	Feyenoord	A	L	0-3		40,500
16	lge	Den Haag	A	D	1-1	Mbamba 73	6,500
17	lge	Zwolle	H	W	5-2	Mbamba 2; Hofs 17,74; Claessens 20; van Beukering 55	16,020
18	lge	NEC Nijmegen	A	L	0-2		12,500
19	hocr3	Feyenoord	A	L	0-1		13,054
20	lge	PSV Eindhoven	H	D	0-0		21,500
21	lge	Heerenveen	H	L	0-1		20,864
22	lge	Twente	A	D	0-0		13,000
23	lge	PSV Eindhoven	A	L	0-3		32,500
24	lge	Feyenoord	H	D	0-0		18,750
25	lge	Roosendaal	H	L	1-2	Rink 80	19,000
26	lge	Groningen	H	L	1-2	Rink 50	19,010
27	lge	Zwolle	A	D	1-1	Knol 68	6,500
28	lge	Volendam	A	D	0-0		5,000
29	lge	Den Haag	H	W	1-0	Knol 86 pen	18,990
30	lge	Ajax	A	L	0-5		49,265
31	lge	RKC Waalwijk	H	D	3-3	Rankovic 5; Mbamba 61; Rink 88	20,500
32	lge	AZ Alkmaar	A	L	1-2	Amoah 74	7,971
33	lge	NAC Breda	H	D	2-2	Janssen 68; Zongo 70	20,000
34	lge	Willem II Tilb	A	D	1-1	Amoah 78	13,400
35	lge	Heerenveen	A	D	0-0		15,150
36	lge	NEC Nijmegen	H	D	2-2	Hofs 53,90	22,500
37	lge	Roda JC Kerk	A	L	0-2		13,813
38	lge	Utrecht	H	W	3-0	Rink 31,34; Fafiani 64	20,000
39	honac	VVV	H	W	5-0	Janssen 41; Rankovic 53; Amoah 70; Hofs 81; Schaars 87	12,000
40	honac	Helmond Sport	A	D	2-2	Amoah 13; Hofs 24	3,111
41	honac	Helmond Sport	H	W	1-0	Knol 15 pen	18,000
42	honac	VVV	A	D	1-1	Amoah 29	4,500

MONTHLY POINTS TALLY

Month	Points	%
AUGUST	0	0%
SEPTEMBER	5	56%
OCTOBER	1	11%
NOVEMBER	3	25%
DECEMBER	4	44%
JANUARY	1	11%
FEBRUARY	2	17%
MARCH	5	42%
APRIL	3	25%
MAY	4	44%

KEY PLAYERS - GOALSCORERS

Paolo Roberto Rink

Goals in the League	5	Player Strike Rate Average number of minutes between League goals scored by player	270
Contribution to Attacking Power Average number of minutes between League team goals while on pitch	112	Club Strike Rate Average number of minutes between League goals scored by club	78

	PLAYER	LGE GOALS	POWER	STRIKE RATE
1	Paolo Roberto Rink	5	112	270 mins
2	Emile Mbamba	6	61	288 mins
3	Nick Hofs	5	121	364 mins
4	Mamadou Zongo	2	77	695 mins

KEY PLAYERS - MIDFIELDERS

Mamadou Zongo

Goals in the League	2	Contribution to Attacking Power Average number of minutes between League team goals while on pitch	77
Defensive Rating Average number of mins between League goals conceded while he was on the pitch	58	Scoring Difference Defensive Rating minus Contribution to Attacking Power	19

	PLAYER	LGE GOALS	DEF RATE	POWER	SCORE DIFF
1	Mamadou Zongo	2	58	77	-19 mins
2	Aleksandar Rankovic	1	54	76	-22 mins
3	Theo Janssen	1	56	113	-57 mins
4	Nick Hofs	5	55	121	-66 mins

KEY PLAYERS - DEFENDERS

Aleksander Ilic

Goals Conceded (GC) The number of League goals conceded while he was on the pitch	25	Clean Sheets In games when he played at least 70 minutes	6
Defensive Rating Ave number of mins between League goals conceded while on the pitch	64	Club Defensive Rating Average number of mins between League goals conceded by the club this season	55

	PLAYER	CON LGE	CLEAN SHEETS	DEF RATE
1	Aleksander Ilic	25	6	64 mins
2	Bert Konterman	48	7	57 mins
3	Tim Cornelisse	56	5	51 mins
4	Purrel Frankel	48	4	49 mins

KEY GOALKEEPER

Dragoslav Jevric

Goals Conceded in the League	20	Counting Games Games when he played at least 70 mins	13
Defensive Rating Ave number of mins between League goals conceded while on the pitch	56	Clean Sheets In games when he played at least 70 mins	2

LEAGUE GOALS

Emile Mbamba

Minutes on the pitch	1728	Goals in the League	6
League average (mins between goals)	288		

	PLAYER	MINS	GOALS	AVE
1	Mbamba	1728	6	288
2	Rink	1348	5	270
3	Hofs	1822	5	364
4	Amoah	897	4	224
5	Claessens	950	3	317
6	van Beukering	815	3	272
7	Knol	970	2	485
8	Zongo	1390	2	695
9	Rojer	1062	2	531
10	Janssen	1352	1	1352
11	Rankovic	2217	1	2217
12	Dingsdag	1006	1	1006
	Other		4	
	TOTAL		39	

DISCIPLINARY RECORDS

	PLAYER	YELLOW	RED	AVE
1	Claessens	5	1	158
2	Rankovic	10	2	184
3	van Beukering	2	1	271
4	Knol	2	1	323
5	Frankel	7	0	335
6	Hofs	5	0	364
7	Cornelisse	7	0	411
8	Mbamba	3	0	576
9	Janssen	2	0	676
10	Bochem	1	0	684
11	Ilic	2	0	804
12	Amoah	1	0	897
13	Dingsdag	1	0	1006
	Other	4	1	
	TOTAL	52	6	

TOP POINT EARNERS

	PLAYER	GAMES	AV PTS
1	Bochem	6	1.17
2	Jansen, M	12	1.08
3	Claessens	10	1.00
4	Knol	10	1.00
5	Jevric	12	1.00
6	Zongo	13	0.92
7	Rankovic	25	0.88
8	Rink	14	0.86
9	Ilic	18	0.83
10	Cornelisse	32	0.81
	CLUB AVERAGE:		**0.82**

LEAGUE APPEARANCES, BOOKINGS AND CAPS

	AGE (on 01/07/04)	IN NAMED 18	APPEARANCES	COUNTING GAMES	MINUTES ON PITCH	YELLOW CARDS	RED CARDS	THIS SEASON	HOME COUNTRY
Goalkeepers									
Dragoslav Jevric	30	23	13	12	1113	0	0	3	Serbia & Mont (45)
Sjoerd Rensen	20	7	0	0	0	0	0	-	Holland
Raymond Van Driel	20	1	0	0	0	0	0	-	Holland
Jimmy van Fessem	28	33	22	21	1947	0	0	-	Holland
Defenders									
Tim Cornelisse	26	32	32	32	2880	7	0	-	Holland
Jaap Davids	19	1	0	0	0	0	0	-	Holland
Michael Dingsdag	21	29	13	10	1006	1	0	-	Holland
Purrel Frankel	27	32	27	25	2351	7	0	-	Holland
Aleksander Ilic	35	18	18	18	1609	2	0	-	Serbia & Montenegro
Michael Jansen	20	29	18	12	1220	0	0	-	Holland
Ruud Knol	23	13	12	10	970	2	1	-	Holland
Bert Konterman	33	31	31	30	2745	2	0	-	Holland
Midfielders									
Ricky Bochem	21	20	15	6	684	1	0	-	Holland
Gert Claessens	32	12	12	10	950	5	1	-	Belgium
Lucien Dors	-	0	0	0	0	0	0	-	
Theo Groeneveld	21	1	0	0	0	0	0	-	Holland
Nick Hofs	21	30	27	17	1822	5	0	-	Holland
Theo Janssen	22	18	16	14	1352	2	0	-	Holland
Didier Martel	32	15	13	11	1070	1	0	-	France
A Rankovic	25	27	26	25	2217	10	2	-	Serbia & Montenegro
Stijn Schaars	20	33	21	12	1286	0	0	-	Holland
Mamadou Zongo	23	30	21	13	1390	0	0	-	Burkino Faso
Forwards									
Matthew Amoah	23	11	11	10	897	1	0	-	Ghana
Raymond Fafiani	20	30	13	7	794	0	0	-	Holland
Emile Mbamba	21	28	26	15	1728	3	0	-	Cameroon
Bob Peeters	30	1	1	0	57	0	0	-	Belgium
Paolo Roberto Rink	31	17	17	14	1348	1	0	-	Germany
Eldridge Rojer	20	30	25	7	1062	0	0	-	Holland
Kalle Sone	21	2	0	0	0	0	0	-	Cameroon
J van Beukering	20	21	14	6	815	2	1	-	Holland
Peter Van Vossen	36	7	6	0	211	0	1	-	Holland

TEAM OF THE SEASON

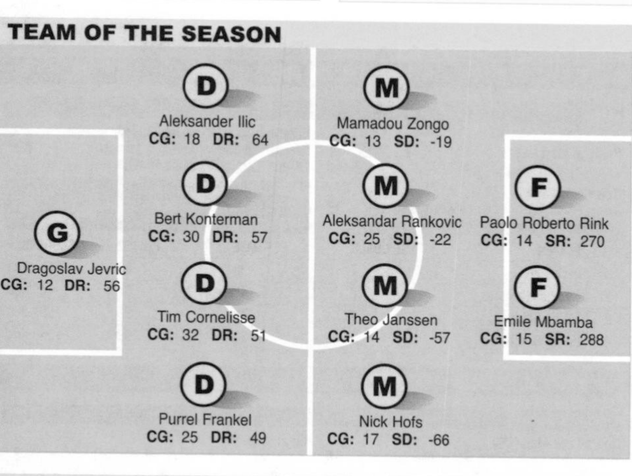
D
Aleksander Ilic
CG: 18 DR: 64
M
Mamadou Zongo
CG: 13 SD: -19
D
Bert Konterman
CG: 30 DR: 57
M
Aleksandar Rankovic
CG: 25 SD: -22
F
Paolo Roberto Rink
CG: 14 SR: 270
G
Dragoslav Jevric
CG: 12 DR: 56
D
Tim Cornelisse
CG: 32 DR: 51
M
Theo Janssen
CG: 14 SD: -57
F
Emile Mbamba
CG: 15 SR: 288
D
Purrel Frankel
CG: 25 DR: 49
M
Nick Hofs
CG: 17 SD: -66

SQUAD APPEARANCES

Match	1	2	3	4	5	6	7	8	9	10	11	12	13	14	15	16	17	18	19	20	21	22	23	24	25	26	27	28	29	30	31	32	33	34	35	36	37	38	39	40	41	42	43
Venue	A	H	A	H	A	H	H	A	H	A	A	H	H	H	A	A	H	A	A	H	H	A	A	H	H	H	A	A	H	A	H	A	H	A	A	H	A	H	H	A	H	A	H
Competition	L	L	L	L	L	L	L	L	L	L	L	L	L	L	L	L	L	L	L	L	L	L	L	L	L	L	L	L	L	L	L	L	L	L	L	L	L	L	L	L	L	L	L
Result	D	L	L	L	D	D	W	W	L	D	L	W	D	D	L	D	W	L	L	D	L	D	L	D	L	L	D	D	W	L	D	L	D	D	D	D	L	W	W	D	W	D	W

Goalkeepers
Dragoslav Jevric
Sjoerd Rensen
Raymond Van Driel
Jimmy van Fessem

Defenders
Tim Cornelisse
Jaap Davids
Michael Dingsdag
Purrel Frankel
Aleksander Ilic
Michael Jansen
Ruud Knol
Bert Konterman

Midfielders
Ricky Bochem
Gert Claessens
Lucien Dors
Theo Groeneveld
Nick Hofs
Theo Janssen
Didier Martel
Aleksandar Rankovic
Stijn Schaars
Mamadou Zongo

Forwards
Matthew Amoah
Raymond Fafiani
Emile Mbamba
Bob Peeters
Paolo Roberto Rink
Eldridge Rojer
Kalle Sone
Jhonny van Beukering
Peter Van Vossen

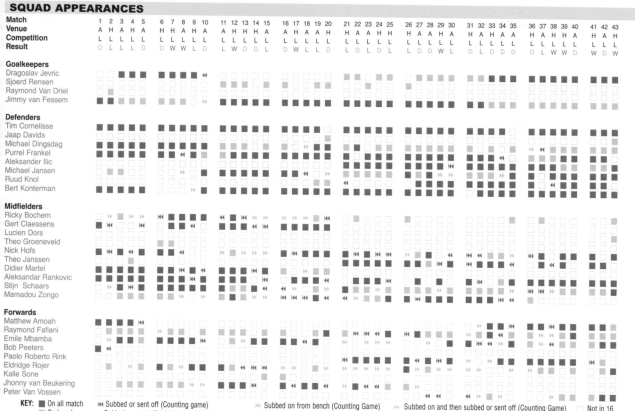

KEY: ■ On all match ■ On bench ⏮ Subbed or sent off (Counting game) ◀◀ Subbed or sent off (playing less than 70 minutes) ▶▶ Subbed on from bench (Counting Game) ▶▶ Subbed on (playing less than 70 minutes) ▶▶ Subbed on and then subbed or sent off (Counting Game) ▶▶ Subbed on and then subbed or sent off (playing less than 70 minutes) □ Not in 16

FC VOLENDAM

Final Position: **17th**

KEY: ☐ Won ☐ Drawn ☐ Lost

#	Comp	Opponent	H/A	Res	Score	Scorers	Attendance
1	hocr1	Spakenburg	A	W	0-2		
2	lge	Heerenveen	H	L	0-1		5,037
3	lge	Groningen	H	W	3-0	Putter 16; Buys 19 pen; Esajas 55	5,000
4	lge	RKC Waalwijk	A	L	0-3		5,000
5	lge	Den Haag	A	D	1-1	Tuyp 10	6,335
6	lge	NEC Nijmegen	H	L	2-3	Buys 36 pen,61 pen	4,631
7	hocr2	Argon	A	W	4-3	Putter 31; Buys 32 fk,61; Tuyp 55	
8	lge	Roosendaal	A	D	1-1	Tuyp 40	5,000
9	lge	Zwolle	H	D	2-2	Tuyp 27; Bridji 73	4,810
10	lge	Ajax	A	L	1-5	Esajas 13	49,521
11	lge	Roda JC Kerk	H	W	2-1	Ouhsaine 57; Salden 85	4,541
12	hocr3	Vitesse Arnhem	A	L	0-4		5,500
13	lge	Vitesse Arnhem	A	D	2-2	Faria 27; Tuyp 29	17,500
14	lge	Feyenoord	H	L	1-3	Ouhsaine 7	6,113
15	lge	Willem II Tilb	A	L	0-6		12,300
16	lge	Twente	H	W	2-0	Esajas 12,74	4,574
17	lge	PSV Eindhoven	A	L	0-7		32,500
18	lge	AZ Alkmaar	H	L	0-6		6,051
19	lge	Utrecht	A	L	0-3		11,448
20	lge	NAC Breda	A	L	2-3	Putter 73; Ouhsaine 82	11,019
21	lge	RKC Waalwijk	H	L	0-4		4,057
22	lge	Groningen	A	W	1-0	Buys 76 pen	11,034
23	lge	AZ Alkmaar	A	L	0-3		8,080
24	lge	Ajax	H	L	0-2		6,199
25	lge	Roda JC Kerk	A	L	0-1		12,387
26	lge	Den Haag	H	L	0-2		5,000
27	lge	Vitesse Arnhem	H	D	0-0		5,000
28	lge	Heerenveen	A	L	1-2	van Zaanen 74	15,000
29	lge	Zwolle	A	L	0-3		6,500
30	lge	Utrecht	H	L	1-2	Tuyp 51	5,000
31	lge	Twente	A	W	2-1	Buys 66 pen; Esajas 88	12,800
32	lge	Willem II Tilb	H	L	0-1		5,000
33	lge	NAC Breda	H	W	4-2	Buys 17; Bridji 44,74; Steur 70	4,552
34	lge	Feyenoord	A	L	0-2		42,000
35	lge	PSV Eindhoven	H	L	0-5		4,807
36	lge	NEC Nijmegen	A	D	1-1	Esajas 44	12,250
37	lge	Roosendaal	H	W	2-1	Tuyp 30,65	5,000
38	honac	De Graafschap	H	L	0-1		3,563
39	honac	Excelsior	A	L	1-2	Woudenberg 69	2,158
40	honac	Excelsior	H	L	1-2	Tuyp 40	2,681
41	honac	De Graafschap	A	L	0-4		10,500

MONTHLY POINTS TALLY

Month	Points	%
AUGUST	3	33%
SEPTEMBER	2	22%
OCTOBER	4	44%
NOVEMBER	1	11%
DECEMBER	3	25%
JANUARY	0	0%
FEBRUARY	3	20%
MARCH	1	8%
APRIL	6	50%
MAY	4	44%

KEY PLAYERS - GOALSCORERS

Jack Tuyp

Goals in the League	7	Player Strike Rate Average number of minutes between League goals scored by player	274
Contribution to Attacking Power Average number of minutes between League team goals while on pitch	83	Club Strike Rate Average number of minutes between League goals scored by club	99

	PLAYER	LGE GOALS	POWER	STRIKE RATE
1	Jack Tuyp	7	83	274 mins
2	Dion Esajas	6	94	317 mins
3	Karim Bridji	3	92	433 mins
4	Maurice Buys	6	86	433 mins

KEY PLAYERS - MIDFIELDERS

Jack Tuyp

Goals in the League	7	Contribution to Attacking Power Average number of minutes between League team goals while on pitch	83
Defensive Rating Average number of mins between League goals conceded while he was on the pitch	38	Scoring Difference Defensive Rating minus Contribution to Attacking Power	-45

	PLAYER	LGE GOALS	DEF RATE	POWER	SCORE DIFF
1	Jack Tuyp	7	38	83	-45 mins
2	Maurice Buys	6	40	87	-47 mins
3	Misha Salden	1	42	92	-50 mins
4	Karim Bridji	3	38	93	-55 mins

KEY PLAYERS - DEFENDERS

Lindsay Wilson

Goals Conceded (GC) The number of League goals conceded while he was on the pitch	56	Clean Sheets In games when he played at least 70 minutes	2
Defensive Rating Ave number of mins between League goals conceded while on the pitch	40	Club Defensive Rating Average number of mins between League goals conceded by the club this season	39

	PLAYER	CON LGE	CLEAN SHEETS	DEF RATE
1	Lindsay Wilson	56	2	40 mins
2	Gerry Koning	73	4	39 mins
3	Ruud Kras	70	4	38 mins
4	Ronald Breinburg	54	2	37 mins

KEY GOALKEEPER

Jeroen Verhoeven

Goals Conceded in the League	28	Counting Games Games when he played at least 70 mins	16
Defensive Rating Ave number of mins between League goals conceded while on the pitch	51	Clean Sheets In games when he played at least 70 mins	2

LEAGUE GOALS

Jack Tuyp

Minutes on the pitch	1919	Goals in the League	7
League average (mins between goals)	274		

	PLAYER	MINS	GOALS	AVE
1	Tuyp	1919	7	274
2	Esajas	1899	6	317
3	Buys	2600	6	433
4	Ouhsaine	848	3	283
5	Bridji	1298	3	433
6	Putter	1190	2	595
7	Faria	1002	1	1002
8	Salden	2383	1	2383
9	Steur	1499	1	1499
10	van Zaanen	261	1	261
	Other		0	
	TOTAL		31	

DISCIPLINARY RECORDS

	PLAYER	YELLOW	RED	AVE
1	Luirink	7	2	265
2	Tevreden	3	0	349
3	Bridji	3	0	432
4	Wing	2	0	461
5	Koning	5	0	571
6	Putter	2	0	595
7	Salden	4	0	595
8	Steur	2	0	749
9	Ouhsaine	1	0	848
10	Kras	3	0	894
11	Tuyp	2	0	959
12	Faria	1	0	1002
13	Wilson	2	0	1120
	Other	4	1	
	TOTAL	41	3	

TOP POINT EARNERS

	PLAYER	GAMES	AV PTS
1	Woudenberg	4	1.00
2	Tuyp	19	1.00
3	Wing	9	1.00
4	Ouhsaine	6	1.00
5	Esajas	17	1.00
6	Bridji	13	0.92
7	Buys	29	0.90
8	Verhoeven	16	0.88
9	Koning	32	0.84
10	Salden	25	0.84
	CLUB AVERAGE:		0.79

LEAGUE APPEARANCES, BOOKINGS AND CAPS

	AGE (on 01/07/04)	IN NAMED 18	APPEARANCES	COUNTING GAMES	MINUTES ON PITCH	YELLOW CARDS	RED CARDS	THIS SEASON	HOME COUNTRY
Goalkeepers									
R van Westerop	25	34	18	18	1620	0	0	-	Holland
Jeroen Verhoeven	24	29	16	16	1440	1	0	-	Holland
Defenders									
Ronald Breinburg	23	29	26	21	1996	0	1	-	Holland
Patrick Huisman	24	8	1	0	1	0	0	-	Holland
Gerry Koning	24	32	32	32	2857	5	0	-	Holland
Ruud Kras	22	30	30	30	2682	3	0	-	Holland
Rowin van Zaanen	19	18	6	2	261	2	0	-	Holland
Lindsay Wilson	25	34	26	24	2240	2	0	-	Australia
Midfielders									
Carel Bartele	30	16	10	7	771	0	0	-	Holland
Karim Bridji	22	23	18	13	1298	3	0	-	Holland
Maurice Buys	24	33	33	29	2600	1	0	-	Holland
Charles Dissels	19	2	1	0	17	0	0	-	Holland
Reginald Faria	22	23	23	8	1002	1	0	-	Holland
Kees Kwakman	21	9	0	0	0	0	0	-	Holland
Gijs Luirink	20	28	28	26	2385	7	2	-	Holland
Misha Salden	30	32	29	25	2383	4	0	-	Holland
Orlando Smeekes	22	2	1	0	12	0	0	-	Holland
Brian Tevreden	22	23	15	10	1048	3	0	-	Holland
Jack Tuyp	20	31	27	19	1919	2	0	-	Holland
M Woudenberg	20	27	14	4	540	0	0	-	Holland
Forwards									
Dion Esajas	23	29	27	17	1899	0	0	-	Holland
Raoul Henar	31	6	3	0	100	0	0	-	Holland
Houssein Ouhsaine	24	21	16	6	848	1	0	-	Morocco
Eddy Putter	22	17	17	13	1190	2	0	-	Holland
Sebastiaan Steur	20	27	25	14	1499	2	0	-	Holland
C Fung A Wing	20	23	16	10	1012	2	0	-	Holland

TEAM OF THE SEASON

G
Jeroen Verhoeven
CG: 16 DR: 51
D
Lindsay Wilson
CG: 24 DR: 40
D
Gerry Koning
CG: 32 DR: 39
D
Ruud Kras
CG: 30 DR: 38
D
Ronald Breinburg
CG: 21 DR: 37
M
Jack Tuyp
CG: 19 SD: -45
M
Maurice Buys
CG: 29 SD: -47
M
Misha Salden
CG: 25 SD: -50
M
Karim Bridji
CG: 13 SD: -55
F
Dion Esajas
CG: 17 SR: 317
F
Eddy Putter
CG: 13 SR: 595

SQUAD APPEARANCES

Match	1	2	3	4	5	6	7	8	9	10	11	12	13	14	15	16	17	18	19	20	21	22	23	24	25	26	27	28	29	30	31	32	33	34	35	36	37	38	39	40	41	42
Venue	A	H	H	A	A	H	A	A	H	A	H	A	A	H	A	H	A	H	A	A	H	A	A	H	A	H	H	A	A	H	A	H	H	A	H	A	H	H	A	H	A	H
Competition	L	L	L	L	L	L	L	L	L	L	L	L	L	L	L	L	L	L	L	L	L	L	L	L	L	L	L	L	L	L	L	L	L	L	L	L	L	L	L	L	L	L
Result	D	L	W	L	D	L	W	D	D	L	W	L	D	L	L	W	L	L	L	L	L	W	L	L	L	L	D	L	L	L	W	L	W	L	L	D	W	L	L	L	L	D

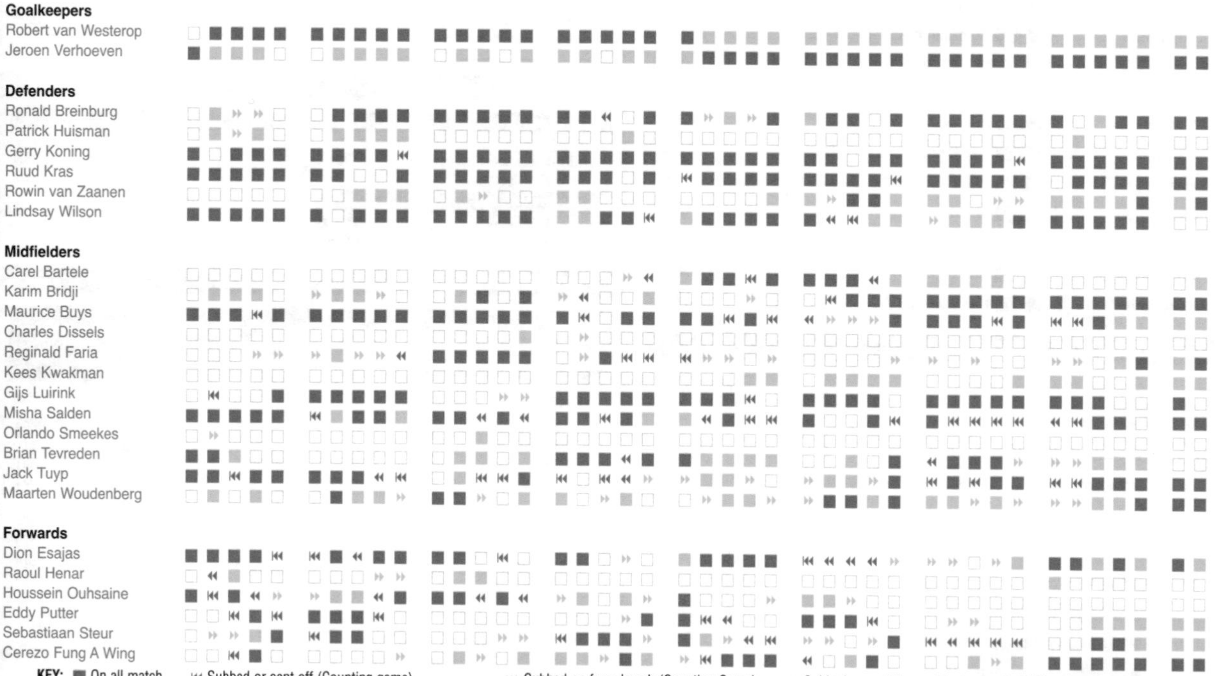

Goalkeepers
Robert van Westerop
Jeroen Verhoeven

Defenders
Ronald Breinburg
Patrick Huisman
Gerry Koning
Ruud Kras
Rowin van Zaanen
Lindsay Wilson

Midfielders
Carel Bartele
Karim Bridji
Maurice Buys
Charles Dissels
Reginald Faria
Kees Kwakman
Gijs Luirink
Misha Salden
Orlando Smeekes
Brian Tevreden
Jack Tuyp
Maarten Woudenberg

Forwards
Dion Esajas
Raoul Henar
Houssein Ouhsaine
Eddy Putter
Sebastiaan Steur
Cerezo Fung A Wing

KEY: On all match; On bench; Subbed or sent off (Counting game); Subbed or sent off (playing less than 70 minutes); Subbed on from bench (Counting Game); Subbed on (playing less than 70 minutes); Subbed on and then subbed or sent off (Counting Game); Subbed on and then subbed or sent off (playing less than 70 minutes); Not in 16

FC ZWOLLE

Final Position: **18th**

KEY: Won Drawn Lost

							Attendance
1	hocr1	Noordwijk	A	W	0-7		
2	lge	Utrecht	A	L	0-1		15,000
3	lge	RKC Waalwijk	H	L	0-3		6,150
4	lge	Ajax	A	L	0-1		47,880
5	lge	Roda JC Kerk	H	D	0-0		6,000
6	lge	Willem II Tilb	A	L	1-2	Hristov 68	12,050
7	hocr2	Den Bosch	A	L	1-2	Hristov 19	
8	lge	Feyenoord	H	L	0-3		6,600
9	lge	Volendam	A	D	2-2	Takak 30; Hristov 45	4,810
10	lge	Den Haag	H	L	1-2	Hristov 45	6,000
11	lge	AZ Alkmaar	A	L	0-4		7,892
12	lge	Twente	H	W	1-0	Takak 52	6,200
13	lge	Heerenveen	A	D	1-1	Zuurman 90	12,500
14	lge	NAC Breda	H	L	0-2		
15	lge	PSV Eindhoven	H	L	0-4		6,800
16	lge	Vitesse Arnhem	A	L	2-5	Takak 40; Hristov 58	16,020
17	lge	Groningen	H	D	1-1	Lim-Duan 32	6,650
18	lge	NEC Nijmegen	A	L	0-1		11,250
19	lge	Roosendaal	H	L	0-3		6,150
20	lge	PSV Eindhoven	A	L	1-5	de Ridder 28	31,000
21	lge	Utrecht	H	D	1-1	Takak 9	5,600
22	lge	Twente	A	L	0-2		13,450
23	lge	RKC Waalwijk	A	L	0-2		5,000
24	lge	NEC Nijmegen	H	W	2-1	Takak 73,79	5,960
25	lge	Vitesse Arnhem	H	D	1-1	van der Haar 89 pen	6,500
26	lge	Roda JC Kerk	A	D	1-1	van Dinteren 63	13,000
27	lge	NAC Breda	A	L	1-3	Takak 25	11,704
28	lge	Volendam	H	W	3-0	Zuurman 4; Lim-Duan 43; van Dinteren 61	6,500
29	lge	Den Haag	A	D	1-1	Takak 15	8,566
30	lge	Roosendaal	A	D	1-1	Zuurman 27	5,000
31	lge	AZ Alkmaar	H	W	2-0	van Dinteren 18; Lim-Duan 61	6,500
32	lge	Heerenveen	H	W	1-0	Zuurman 45	6,500
33	lge	Groningen	A	D	2-2	van der Haar 70; Almeida 86	12,000
34	lge	Ajax	H	L	0-5		6,800
35	lge	Willem II Tilb	H	D	0-0		6,500
36	lge	Feyenoord	A	L	1-7	Lim-Duan 63	44,000

MONTHLY POINTS TALLY

Month	Points	%
AUGUST	0	0%
SEPTEMBER	1	11%
OCTOBER	1	11%
NOVEMBER	4	33%
DECEMBER	1	11%
JANUARY	0	0%
FEBRUARY	5	33%
MARCH	5	42%
APRIL	8	67%
MAY	1	11%

KEY PLAYERS - GOALSCORERS

Jasar Takak

Goals in the League	8	Player Strike Rate Average number of minutes between League goals scored by player	368
Contribution to Attacking Power Average number of minutes between League team goals while on pitch	113	Club Strike Rate Average number of minutes between League goals scored by club	113

	PLAYER	LGE GOALS	POWER	STRIKE RATE
1	Jasar Takak	8	113	368 mins
2	Bert Zuurman	4	88	441 mins
3	Dominggus Lim-Duan	4	107	617 mins
4	Ivar van Dinteren	3	113	681 mins

KEY PLAYERS - MIDFIELDERS

Andre de Ridder

Goals in the League	1	Contribution to Attacking Power Average number of minutes between League team goals while on pitch	99
Defensive Rating Average number of mins between League goals conceded while he was on the pitch	45	Scoring Difference Defensive Rating minus Contribution to Attacking Power	-54

	PLAYER	LGE GOALS	DEF RATE	POWER	SCORE DIFF
1	Andre de Ridder	1	45	99	-54 mins
2	Morten Karlsen	0	49	111	-62 mins
3	Jasar Takak	8	47	113	-66 mins
4	Ivar van Dinteren	3	46	113	-67 mins

KEY PLAYERS - DEFENDERS

Mauro Almeida

Goals Conceded (GC) The number of League goals conceded while he was on the pitch	21	Clean Sheets In games when he played at least 70 minutes	4
Defensive Rating Ave number of mins between League goals conceded while on the pitch	66	Club Defensive Rating Average number of mins between League goals conceded by the club this season	46

	PLAYER	CON LGE	CLEAN SHEETS	DEF RATE
1	Mauro Almeida	21	4	66 mins
2	Robert-Jan Ravensbergen	58	6	47 mins
3	Albert van der Haar	67	6	46 mins
4	Marco Roelofsen	52	4	44 mins

KEY GOALKEEPER

Johan van der Werff

Goals Conceded in the League	61	Counting Games Games when he played at least 70 mins	33
Defensive Rating Ave number of mins between League goals conceded while on the pitch	48	Clean Sheets In games when he played at least 70 mins	6

LEAGUE GOALS

Jasar Takak

Minutes on the pitch	2945	Goals in the League	8
League average (mins between goals)	368		

	PLAYER	MINS	GOALS	AVE
1	Takak	2945	8	368
2	Lim-Duan	2468	4	617
3	Zuurman	1765	4	441
4	Hristov	977	4	244
5	van Dinteren	2042	3	681
6	van der Haar	3060	2	1530
7	Almeida	1379	1	1379
8	de Ridder	2374	1	2374
	Other		0	
	TOTAL		27	

DISCIPLINARY RECORDS

	PLAYER	YELLOW	RED	AVE
1	Hoogenkamp	3	0	234
2	Yobo	5	0	237
3	Hristov	3	0	325
4	Almeida	4	0	344
5	Karlsen	5	0	420
6	Roelofsen, M	3	1	577
7	Zuurman	3	0	588
8	van Dinteren	3	0	680
9	Ravensbergen	4	0	682
10	Cvetkov	1	0	749
11	Promes	1	0	799
12	de Ridder	2	0	1187
13	Lim-Duan	1	0	2468
	Other	4	1	
	TOTAL	42	2	

TOP POINT EARNERS

	PLAYER	GAMES	AV PTS
1	Almeida	15	1.27
2	Zuurman	18	1.22
3	de Ridder	25	0.96
4	Karlsen	21	0.86
5	Lim-Duan	27	0.85
6	Ravensbergen	30	0.83
7	van Dinteren	18	0.83
8	van der Werff	32	0.81
9	Takak	32	0.81
10	van der Haar	34	0.76
	CLUB AVERAGE:		0.76

LEAGUE APPEARANCES, BOOKINGS AND CAPS

	AGE (on 01/07/04)	IN NAMED 18	APPEARANCES	COUNTING GAMES	MINUTES ON PITCH	YELLOW CARDS	RED CARDS	THIS SEASON	HOME COUNTRY
Goalkeepers									
Diederik Boer	23	30	2	1	136	0	0	-	Holland
D Van der Kraan	20	1	0	0	0	0	0	-	Holland
J van der Werff	29	34	33	32	2924	1	0	-	Holland
Defenders									
Mauro Almeida	22	16	16	15	1379	4	0	-	Portugal
Martijn Jansen	19	7	1	0	12	0	0	-	Holland
Marco Parnela	23	25	8	5	529	0	0	-	Finland
R J Ravensbergen	25	32	31	30	2728	4	0	-	Holland
Marco Roelofsen	35	32	30	21	2309	3	1	-	Holland
Remco Snippe	19	1	1	0	11	0	0	-	Holland
J Van den Bosch	20	1	0	0	0	0	0	-	Holland
Albert van der Haar	28	34	34	34	3060	1	0	-	Holland
J Vosselman	20	2	0	0	0	0	0	-	Holland
A M Yobo	25	29	20	11	1187	5	0	-	Nigeria
Midfielders									
Andre de Ridder	30	33	29	25	2374	2	0	-	Holland
H Hoogenkamp	19	23	13	6	702	3	0	-	Holland
Morten Karlsen	25	26	26	21	2101	5	0	-	Denmark
Tjeerd Korf	21	30	19	8	946	0	0	-	Holland
Remco Schol	31	13	8	3	430	1	1	-	Holland
Jasar Takak	22	34	34	32	2945	1	0	-	Turkey
Ivar van Dinteren	27	33	30	18	2042	3	0	-	Holland
Harry Vollema	-	1	0	0	0	0	0	-	Holland
Forwards									
Arjan Bosschaart	32	11	10	4	516	0	0	-	Holland
Ivan Cvetkov	24	22	16	6	749	1	0	-	Bulgaria
Thijs Heuvink	19	1	0	0	0	0	0	-	Holland
Georgi Hristov	28	13	13	9	977	3	0	-	Macedonia
D Lim-Duan	21	33	32	27	2468	1	0	-	Holland
Marino Promes	27	24	18	6	799	1	0	-	Holland
Paulus Roiha	23	17	11	3	486	0	0	-	Finland
Bert Zuurman	31	29	25	18	1765	3	0	-	Holland

TEAM OF THE SEASON

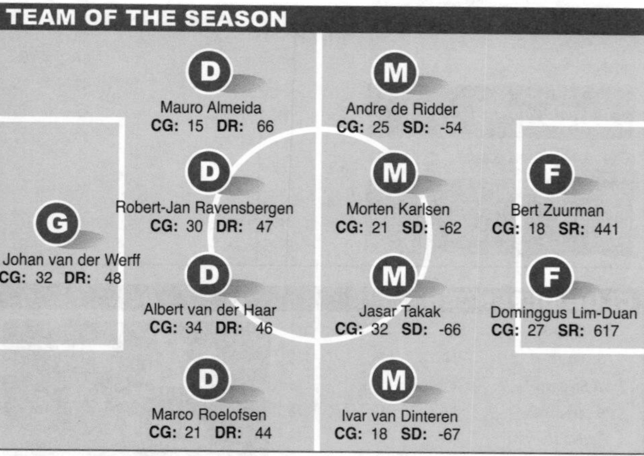
D
Mauro Almeida
CG: 15 DR: 66
M
Andre de Ridder
CG: 25 SD: -54
D
Robert-Jan Ravensbergen
CG: 30 DR: 47
M
Morten Karlsen
CG: 21 SD: -62
F
Bert Zuurman
CG: 18 SR: 441
G
Johan van der Werff
CG: 32 DR: 48
D
Albert van der Haar
CG: 34 DR: 46
M
Jasar Takak
CG: 32 SD: -66
F
Dominggus Lim-Duan
CG: 27 SR: 617
D
Marco Roelofsen
CG: 21 DR: 44
M
Ivar van Dinteren
CG: 18 SD: -67

SQUAD APPEARANCES

Match	1	2	3	4	5	6	7	8	9	10	11	12	13	14	15	16	17	18	19	20	21	22	23	24	25	26	27	28	29	30	31	32	33	34	35	36
Venue	A	A	H	A	H	A	A	H	A	H	A	H	A	H	H	A	H	A	H	A	H	A	A	H	H	A	A	H	A	A	H	H	A	H	H	A
Competition	L	L	L	L	L	L	L	L	L	L	L	L	L	L	L	L	L	L	L	L	L	L	L	L	L	L	L	L	L	L	L	L	L	L	L	L
Result	D	L	L	L	D	L	L	L	D	L	L	W	D	L	L	L	D	L	L	L	D	L	L	W	D	D	L	W	D	D	W	W	D	L	D	L

Goalkeepers
Diederik Boer
Dennis Van der Kraan
Johan van der Werff

Defenders
Mauro Almeida
Martijn Jansen
Marco Parnela
Robert-Jan Ravensbergen
Marco Roelofsen
Remco Snippe
Jeroen Van den Bosch
Albert van der Haar
Jonathan Vosselman
Albert-Michael Yobo

Midfielders
Andre de Ridder
Hermen Hoogenkamp
Morten Karlsen
Tjeerd Korf
Remco Schol
Jasar Takak
Ivar van Dinteren
Harry Vollema

Forwards
Arjan Bosschaart
Ivan Cvetkov
Thijs Heuvink
Georgi Hristov
Dominggus Lim-Duan
Marino Promes
Paulus Roiha
Bert Zuurman

KEY: On all match | On bench | Subbed or sent off (Counting game) | Subbed or sent off (playing less than 70 minutes) | Subbed on from bench (Counting Game) | Subbed on (playing less than 70 minutes) | Subbed on and then subbed or sent off (Counting Game) | Subbed on and then subbed or sent off (playing less than 70 minutes) | Not in 16

GERMAN LEAGUE ROUND-UP

FINAL LEAGUE TABLE

		HOME					AWAY					TOTAL			
	P	W	D	L	F	A	W	D	L	F	A	F	A	DIF	PTS
W Bremen	34	11	4	2	42	21	11	4	2	37	17	79	38	41	74
Bayern Munich	34	13	3	1	43	19	7	5	5	27	20	70	39	31	68
B Leverkusen	34	12	1	4	43	18	7	7	3	30	21	73	39	34	65
Stuttgart	34	9	7	1	29	13	9	3	5	23	11	52	24	28	64
Bochum	34	11	5	1	30	6	4	6	7	27	33	57	39	18	56
B Dortmund	34	12	3	2	39	16	4	4	9	20	32	59	48	11	55
Schalke	34	7	7	3	28	16	6	4	7	21	26	49	42	7	50
Hamburg	34	11	3	3	33	22	3	4	10	14	38	47	60	-13	49
Hansa Rostock	34	10	1	6	34	18	2	7	8	21	36	55	54	1	44
Wolfsburg	34	11	1	5	38	25	2	2	13	18	36	56	61	-5	42
B M'gladbach	34	7	6	4	21	16	3	3	11	19	33	40	49	-9	39
Hertha Berlin	34	6	6	5	26	24	3	6	8	16	35	42	59	-17	39
Freiburg	34	10	3	4	32	25	0	5	12	10	42	42	67	-25	38
Hannover 96	34	5	7	5	27	26	4	3	10	22	37	49	63	-14	37
Kaiserslautern	34	8	5	4	25	19	3	1	13	14	43	39	62	-23	*36
Eintr Frankfurt	34	6	4	7	25	24	3	1	13	11	29	36	53	-17	32
1860 Munich	34	5	4	8	16	25	3	4	10	16	30	32	55	-23	32
Cologne	34	6	2	9	22	23	0	3	14	10	34	32	57	-25	23

*Kaiserslautern docked three points for financial irregularities

CLUB STRIKE FORCE

Bremen's Tim Borowski and Paul Stalteri

1 Werder Bremen

Goals scored in the League	79
Club Strike Rate (CSR) Average number of minutes between League goals scored by club	39

	CLUB	GOALS	CSR
1	W Bremen	79	39
2	B Leverkusen	73	42
3	Bayern Munich	70	44
4	B Dortmund	59	52
5	Bochum	57	54
6	Wolfsburg	56	55
7	Hansa Rostock	55	56
8	Stuttgart	52	59
9	Hannover 96	49	62
10	Schalke	49	62
11	Hamburg	47	65
12	Freiburg	42	73
13	Hertha Berlin	42	73
14	B M'gladbach	40	77
15	Kaiserslautern	39	78
16	Eintr Frankfurt	36	85
17	1860 Munich	32	96
18	Cologne	32	96

CLUB DISCIPLINARY RECORDS

Yellow for Neuendorf of Hertha Berlin

1 Kaiserslautern

League Yellow	96
League Red	7
League Total	103
Cards Average in League Average number of minutes between a card being shown of either colour	30

	CLUB	Y	R	TOTAL	AVE
1	Kaiserslautern	96	7	103	30
2	Wolfsburg	92	4	96	32
3	Hertha Berlin	85	8	93	33
4	1860 Munich	83	7	90	34
5	Hamburg	78	3	81	38
6	Hannover 96	73	7	80	38
7	Hansa Rostock	75	5	80	38
8	B Leverkusen	70	4	74	41
9	B M'gladbach	69	4	73	42
10	Eintr Frankfurt	69	4	73	42
11	Cologne	67	4	71	43
12	Schalke	67	5	72	43
13	B Dortmund	66	3	69	44
14	Bayern Munich	65	5	70	44
15	Stuttgart	65	3	68	45
16	Freiburg	56	4	60	51
17	W Bremen	56	4	60	51
18	Bochum	58	0	58	53

CLUB DEFENCES

	CLUB	LGE	CS	CDR
1	Stuttgart	24	18	128
2	W Bremen	38	13	81
3	B Leverkusen	39	13	78
4	Bayern Munich	39	11	78
5	Bochum	39	15	78
6	Schalke	42	10	73
7	B Dortmund	48	8	64
8	B M'gladbach	49	6	62
9	Eintr Frankfurt	53	5	58
10	Hansa Rostock	54	6	57
11	1860 Munich	55	5	56
12	Cologne	57	8	54
13	Hertha Berlin	59	7	52
14	Hamburg	60	5	51
15	Wolfsburg	61	6	50
16	Kaiserslautern	62	7	49
17	Hannover 96	63	8	49
18	Freiburg	67	7	46

Hinkel battles to keep Chelsea at bay

1 Stuttgart

Goals conceded in the League	24
Clean Sheets (CS) Number of league games where no goals were conceded	18
Club Defensive Rate (CDR) Average number of minutes between League goals conceded by club	128

PLAYER NATIONALITIES

Overseas country with the most player appearances in the German League - Brazil — **484 league appearances by Brazilian players**

	COUNTRY	PLAYERS	IN SQUAD	LGE APP	% LGE ACT	CAPS	MOST APP	APP
1	Germany	269	4978	3574	43.0	137	Two Players	100.0
2	Brazil	29	541	484	6.2	17	Rodrigo Costa	88.2
3	Croatia	15	354	279	3.3	36	Zvonimir Soldo	88.9
4	Czech Republic	13	314	262	3.3	34	Jan Koller	91.3
5	Holland	10	253	235	3.1	8	R Van Duijnhoven	100.0
6	Denmark	11	249	225	2.9	22	Soren Colding	96.0
7	Argentina	40	297	247	2.5	37	Diego Klimowicz	93.9
8	France	9	181	155	2.1	15	Valerien Ismael	93.4
9	Poland	10	227	154	1.8		Tomasz Zdebel	92.7
10	Switzerland	9	187	150	1.8		Jorg Stiel	82.0
11	Bosnia	6	164	141	1.6		Sergei Barbarez	91.1
12	Austria	8	179	146	1.5		Martin Stranzl	63.1
13	Hungary	4	125	103	1.4		Krisztian Lisztes	81.0
14	Sweden	5	155	123	1.3	8	Marcus Lantz	93.1
15	Cameroon	6	140	119	1.3	13	Raymond Kalla	76.7
16	Belgium	7	136	110	1.3	7	N van Kerckhoven	74.5
17	Bulgaria	5	121	104	1.3		Marian Hristov	87.0
18	Georgia	3	89	88	1.2		Alexander Iaschvili	85.3

CLUB MAKE-UP – HOME AND OVERSEAS PLAYERS

1 Borussia Monchengladbach — **70.9% of appearances by overseas players**

	CLUB	OVERSEAS	HOME	% OVERSEAS	% LGE ACT	MOST APP	APP
1	B M'gladbach	18	16	52.9	70.9	Jeff Strasser	89.6
2	Schalke	20	12	62.5	68.3	Hamit Altintop	81.5
3	Bochum	16	10	61.5	68.3	Van Duijnhoven	100.0
4	Hannover 96	19	15	55.9	66.4	S Cherundolo	77.5
5	W Bremen	15	11	57.7	66.3	Paul Stalteri	94.9
6	Bayern Munich	15	16	48.4	65.6	Roy Makaay	90.6
7	Freiburg	13	14	48.1	62.9	Boubacar Diarra	88.9
8	Wolfsburg	17	13	56.7	61.7	Diego Klimowicz	93.9
9	B Dortmund	20	15	57.1	61.4	Jan Koller	91.3
10	Hamburg	13	14	48.1	61.4	Sergei Barbarez	91.1
11	Hansa Rostock	14	11	56.0	59.3	Delano Hill	97.1
12	Kaiserslautern	18	17	51.4	59.0	Marian Hristov	87.0
13	Stuttgart	16	12	57.1	56.9	Kevin Kuranyi	95.1
14	B Leverkusen	12	16	42.9	51.8	Silveira Juan	87.2
15	Hertha Berlin	14	15	48.3	51.6	Pal Dardai	79.7
16	1860 Munich	14	17	45.2	47.3	Rodrigo Costa	88.2
17	Eintr Frankfurt	10	20	33.3	37.2	Ervin Skela	88.2
18	Cologne	8	24	25.0	17.2	Moses Sichone	60.5

CHART-TOPPING MIDFIELDERS

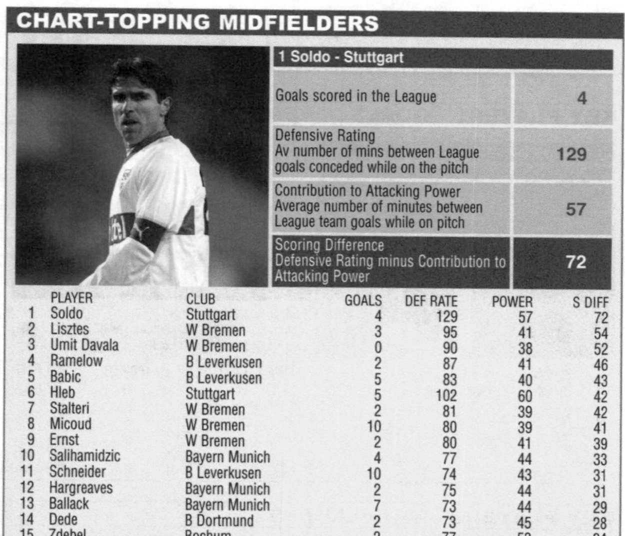

1 Soldo - Stuttgart	
Goals scored in the League	4
Defensive Rating Av number of mins between League goals conceded while on the pitch	129
Contribution to Attacking Power Average number of minutes between League team goals while on pitch	57
Scoring Difference Defensive Rating minus Contribution to Attacking Power	72

	PLAYER	CLUB	GOALS	DEF RATE	POWER	S DIFF
1	Soldo	Stuttgart	4	129	57	72
2	Lisztes	W Bremen	3	95	41	54
3	Umit Davala	W Bremen	0	90	38	52
4	Ramelow	B Leverkusen	2	87	41	46
5	Babic	B Leverkusen	5	83	40	43
6	Hleb	Stuttgart	5	102	60	42
7	Stalteri	W Bremen	2	81	39	42
8	Micoud	W Bremen	10	80	39	41
9	Ernst	W Bremen	2	80	41	39
10	Salihamidzic	Bayern Munich	4	77	44	33
11	Schneider	B Leverkusen	10	74	43	31
12	Hargreaves	Bayern Munich	2	75	44	31
13	Ballack	Bayern Munich	7	73	44	29
14	Dede	B Dortmund	2	73	45	28
15	Zdebel	Bochum	2	77	53	24

CHART-TOPPING GOALSCORERS

1 Ailton - Werders Bremen	
Goals scored in the League	28
Contribution to Attacking Power (AP) Average number of minutes between League team goals while on pitch	41
Club Strike Rate (CSR) Average minutes between League goals scored by club	39
Player Strike Rate Average number of minutes between League goals scored by player	92

	PLAYER	CLUB	GOALS: LGE	POWER	CSR	S RATE
1	Ailton	W Bremen	28	41	39	92 mins
2	Makaay	Bayern Munich	23	43	44	120
3	Berbatov	B Leverkusen	16	41	42	142
4	Max	Hansa Rostock	20	58	56	143
5	Ewerthon	B Dortmund	14	51	52	158
6	Hashemian	Bochum	16	53	54	162
7	Franca	B Leverkusen	14	37	42	167
8	Klasnic	W Bremen	13	38	39	167
9	Romeo	Hamburg	11	56	65	171
10	Koller	B Dortmund	16	50	52	175
11	Brdaric	Hannover 96	12	64	62	178
12	Klimowicz	Wolfsburg	15	55	55	191
13	Sverkos	B M'gladbach	9	69	77	192
14	Madsen	Bochum	13	48	54	205
15	Lauth	1860 Munich	9	89	96	238

CHART-TOPPING DEFENDERS

1 Hinkel - Stuttgart	
Goals Conceded in the League The number of League goals conceded while he was on the pitch	13
Clean Sheets In games when he played at least 70 mins	16
Club Defensive Rating Average mins between League goals conceded by the club this season	128
Defensive Rating Average number of minutes between League goals conceded while on pitch	181

	PLAYER	CLUB	CON: LGE	CS	CDR	DEF RATE
1	Hinkel	Stuttgart	13	16	128	181
2	Bordon	Stuttgart	15	14	128	144
3	Fernando Meira	Stuttgart	22	17	128	130
4	Lahm	Stuttgart	23	12	128	109
5	Kuffour	Bayern Munich	20	8	78	101
6	Lizarazu	Bayern Munich	25	9	78	90
7	Nowotny	B Leverkusen	23	9	78	84
8	Baumann	W Bremen	35	12	81	82
9	Ismael	W Bremen	35	12	81	82
10	Fahrenhorst	Bochum	36	15	78	80
11	Lucio	B Leverkusen	29	9	78	79
12	Juan	B Leverkusen	34	11	78	78
13	Kovac, R	Bayern Munich	21	5	78	78
14	Placente	B Leverkusen	29	9	78	77
15	Colding	Bochum	38	14	78	77

CHART-TOPPING GOALKEEPERS

1 Hildebrand - Stuttgart	
Counting Games Games where he played at least 70 minutes	34
Goals Conceded in the League The number of League goals conceded while he was on the pitch	24
Clean Sheets In games when he played at least 70 mins	18
Defensive Rating Average number of minutes between League goals conceded while on pitch	128

	PLAYER	CLUB	CG	CONC	CS	DEF RATE
1	Hildebrand	Stuttgart	32	30	9	81
2	Rost	Schalke	27	30	9	81
3	Reinke	W Bremen	34	38	13	79
4	Butt	B Leverkusen	34	39	13	78
5	Van Duijnhoven	Bochum	34	39	15	78
6	Kahn	Bayern Munich	33	39	10	75
7	Warmuz	B Dortmund	17	23	5	67
8	Stiel	B M'gladbach	28	39	4	64
9	Weidenfeller	B Dortmund	17	25	3	61
10	Nikolov	Eintr Frankfurt	31	46	5	61
11	Wachter	Hamburg	24	35	5	61
12	Fiedler	Hertha Berlin	17	26	3	58
13	Hofmann, M	1860 Munich	31	50	5	55
14	Schober	Hansa Rostock	33	54	5	55
15	Wessels	Cologne	32	53	7	54

PLAYER DISCIPLINARY RECORD

2 Hollerbach 10 cards for Hamburg

1 Obradovic - B M'gladbach	
Cards Average mins between cards	96
League Yellow	4
League Red	1
TOTAL	5

	PLAYER		LY	LR	TOT	AVE
1	Obradovic	B M'gladbach	4	1	5	96
2	Hollerbach	Hamburg	10	0	10	106
3	Benjamin	Hamburg	6	1	7	107
4	Rafael	Hertha Berlin	6	1	7	127
5	Agali	Schalke	6	0	6	130
6	Matellan	Schalke	3	2	5	131
7	Schulz	W Bremen	6	1	7	136
8	Vreven	Kaiserslautern	4	0	4	143
9	Riedl	Kaiserslautern	11	0	11	143
10	Basturk	B Leverkusen	5	0	5	146
11	Malz	Kaiserslautern	7	1	8	146
12	Hajto	Schalke	9	0	9	153
13	Klos	Cologne	3	0	3	156
14	Plassnegger	Hansa Rostock	4	2	6	157
15	Bjelica	Kaiserslautern	9	0	9	162
16	Kovac	Hertha Berlin	8	0	8	166
17	Davids	1860 Munich	3	0	3	167
18	De Guzman	Hannover 96	12	2	14	167
19	Hengen	Kaiserslautern	5	0	5	167
20	Santos	1860 Munich	3	1	4	168
21	Mettomo	Kaiserslautern	5	1	6	169
22	Neuendorf	Hertha Berlin	8	0	8	170
23	Demichelis	Bayern Munich	5	0	5	171
24	Freund	Kaiserslautern	3	0	3	171

TEAM OF THE SEASON

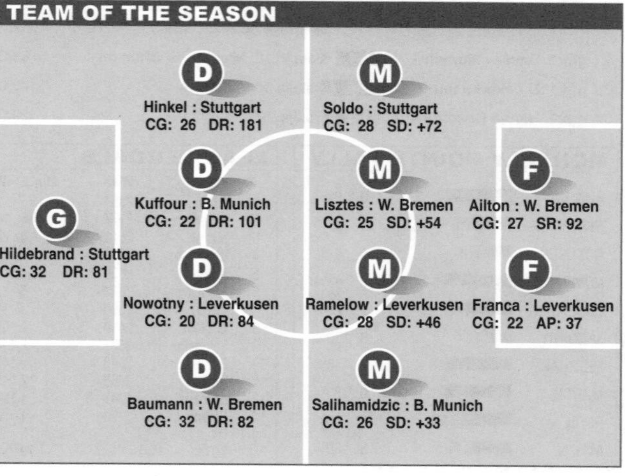
D
Hinkel : Stuttgart
CG: 26 DR: 181
M
Soldo : Stuttgart
CG: 28 SD: +72
D
Kuffour : B. Munich
CG: 22 DR: 101
M
Lisztes : W. Bremen
CG: 25 SD: +54
F
Ailton : W. Bremen
CG: 27 SR: 92
G
Hildebrand : Stuttgart
CG: 32 DR: 81
D
Nowotny : Leverkusen
CG: 20 DR: 84
M
Ramelow : Leverkusen
CG: 28 SD: +46
F
Franca : Leverkusen
CG: 22 AP: 37
D
Baumann : W. Bremen
CG: 32 DR: 82
M
Salihamidzic : B. Munich
CG: 26 SD: +33

GERMAN BUNDESLIGA CHAMPIONS

WERDER BREMEN

Final Position: **1st**

KEY: Won Drawn Lost

							Attendance
1	grpr1	**Hertha Berlin**	A	W	3-0	Ailton 18,65; Micoud 21	38,000
2	grpr1	**B M'gladbach**	H	D	1-1	Ailton 64 pen	30,100
3	grpr1	**Kaiserslautern**	A	W	1-0	Micoud 66	33,000
4	grpr1	**Schalke**	H	W	4-1	Charisteas 13; Borowski 28; Ailton 35; Haedo Valdez 81	36,000
5	grpr1	**B Dortmund**	A	L	1-2	Lisztes 41	81,000
6	grpr1	**1860 Munich**	H	W	2-1	Ailton 48 pen; Micoud 67	32,000
7	grpr1	**Cologne**	A	W	4-1	Micoud 10; Klasnic 40; Stalteri 70; Charisteas 90	33,000
8	grpr1	**Wolfsburg**	H	W	5-3	Ailton 2,21; Stalteri 41; Micoud 57; Klasnic 58	33,000
9	grpr1	**Stuttgart**	H	L	1-3	Charisteas 60	41,100
10	grpr1	**Freiburg**	A	W	4-2	Ailton 14,28; Micoud 37; Klasnic 65	23,000
11	grpr1	**Eintr Frankfurt**	H	W	3-1	Ailton 18; Baumann 25; Klasnic 71	32,000
12	grpr1	**Hannover 96**	A	W	5-1	Haedo Valdez 8,37; Klasnic 40,79; Ernst 87	25,000
13	grpr1	**Bochum**	H	W	3-1	Ailton 6,14,50 pen	34,000
14	grpr1	**Hamburg**	A	D	1-1	Ernst 27	55,000
15	grpr1	**Bayern Munich**	H	D	1-1	Ailton 58 pen	43,000
16	grpr1	**B Leverkusen**	A	W	3-1	Ailton 42; Krstajic 44; Lisztes 90	22,500
17	grpr1	**Hansa Rostock**	H	W	3-0	Ailton 3; Ismael 78; Lisztes 89	36,000
18	grpr1	**Hertha Berlin**	H	W	4-0	Ailton 17,30; Micoud 35; Haedo Valdez 90	35,000
19	grpr1	**B M'gladbach**	A	W	2-1	Klasnic 53; Baumann 90	30,000
20	grpr1	**Kaiserslautern**	H	W	1-0	Ailton 90 pen	37,000
21	grpr1	**Schalke**	A	D	0-0		61,000
22	grpr1	**B Dortmund**	H	W	2-0	Ismael 57; Ailton 86	43,000
23	grpr1	**1860 Munich**	A	W	2-0	Klasnic 38; Charisteas 79	25,000
24	grpr1	**Cologne**	H	W	3-2	Micoud 16; Ailton 37,43	41,000
25	grpr1	**Wolfsburg**	A	W	2-0	Klasnic 76; Micoud 85	30,000
26	grpr1	**Stuttgart**	A	D	4-4	Klasnic 12,35; Ailton 44,70	48,000
27	grpr1	**Freiburg**	H	D	1-1	Ailton 17	42,500
28	grpr1	**Eintr Frankfurt**	A	W	1-0	Ismael 80 pen	33,400
29	grpr1	**Hannover 96**	H	D	0-0		42,500
30	grpr1	**Bochum**	A	D	0-0		32,645
31	grpr1	**Hamburg**	H	W	6-0	Barbarez 17 og; Ismael 22; Klasnic 40; Ailton 48; Haedo Valdez 81; Skrypnyk 85 pen	42,500
32	grpr1	**Bayern Munich**	A	W	3-1	Klasnic 18; Micoud 26; Ailton 35	63,000
33	grpr1	**B Leverkusen**	H	L	2-6	Krstajic 50; Ailton 53	42,500
34	grpr1	**Hansa Rostock**	A	L	1-3	Krstajic 37	29,000

KEY PLAYERS - GOALSCORERS

Da Silva Gonclaves Ailton

Goals in the League	**28**
Contribution to Attacking Power Average number of minutes between League team goals while on pitch	**41**
Player Strike Rate The total number of minutes he was on the pitch for every League goal scored	**92**
Club Strike Rate Average number of minutes between League goals scored by club	**39**

	PLAYER	GOALS LGE	POWER	S RATE
1	Da Silva Gonclaves Ailton	28	41	92 mins
2	Ivan Klasnic	13	38	167 mins
3	Johan Micoud	10	38	281 mins
4	Valerien Ismael	4	36	715 mins

KEY PLAYERS - MIDFIELDERS

Krisztian Lisztes

Goals in the League	**3**
Defensive Rating Average number of mins between League goals conceded while on the pitch	**95**
Contribution to Attacking Power Average number of minutes between League team goals while on pitch	**41**
Scoring Difference Defensive Rating minus Contribution to Attacking Power	**54**

	PLAYER	GOALS LGE	DEF RATE	ATT POWER	SCORE DIFF
1	Krisztian Lisztes	3	95	41	54 mins
2	Umit Davala	0	90	38	52 mins
3	Paul Stalteri	2	81	39	42 mins
4	Johan Micoud	10	80	39	41 mins

KEY PLAYERS - DEFENDERS

Valerien Ismael

Goals Conceded in League	**35**
Clean Sheets In League games when he played at least 70 mins	**12**
Defensive Rating Ave number of mins between League goals conceded while on the pitch	**82**
Club Defensive Rating Average number of mins between League goals conceded by the club this season	**81**

	PLAYER	CON LGE	CLEAN SHEETS	DEF RATE
1	Valerien Ismael	35	12	82 mins
2	Frank Baumann	35	12	82 mins
3	Mladen Krstajic	36	9	73 mins
4	Tim Borowski	18	4	69 mins

MONTHLY POINTS TALLY

AUGUST	10	83%
SEPTEMBER	6	67%
OCTOBER	6	67%
NOVEMBER	10	83%
DECEMBER	7	78%
JANUARY	3	100%
FEBRUARY	10	83%
MARCH	10	83%
APRIL	6	50%
MAY	6	50%

LEAGUE GOALS

	PLAYER	MINS	GOALS	AVE
1	Ailton	2584	28	92
2	Klasnic	2177	13	167
3	Micoud	2811	10	281
4	Charisteas	862	4	216
5	Ismael	2859	4	715
6	Krstajic	2627	3	876
7	Valdez	350	3	117
8	Lisztes	2480	3	827
9	Baumann	2871	2	1436
10	Ernst	2948	2	1474
11	Stalteri	2905	2	1453
12	Borowski	1247	1	1247
13	Skrypnyk	99	1	99
	Other		3	
	TOTAL		79	

KEY GOALKEEPER

Andreas Reinke

Goals Conceded in the League	**38**
Counting Games Games when he played at least 70 minutes	**34**
Clean Sheets In games when he played at least 70 mins	**13**
League minutes played Number of minutes played in league matches	**3015**
Defensive Rating Ave number of mins between League goals conceded while on the pitch	**79**

DISCIPLINARY RECORDS

	PLAYER	YELLOW	RED	AVE
1	Schulz	6	1	136
2	Krstajic	6	1	375
3	Micoud	5	1	468
4	Umit Davala	3	1	474
5	Ismael	5	0	571
6	Baumann	5	0	574
7	Stalteri	5	0	581
8	Ailton	4	0	646
9	Ernst	4	0	737
10	Lisztes	3	0	826
11	Klasnic	2	0	1088
12	Borowski	1	0	1247
	Other	7	0	
	TOTAL	56	4	

TOP POINT EARNERS

	PLAYER	GAMES	AV PTS
1	Lagerblom	2	3.00
2	Umit Davala	21	2.33
3	Lisztes	25	2.28
4	Ismael	32	2.28
5	Stalteri	32	2.22
6	Krstajic	28	2.21
7	Micoud	30	2.17
8	Klasnic	24	2.17
9	Ailton	27	2.15
10	Ernst	33	2.15
	CLUB AVERAGE:		**2.18**

LEAGUE APPEARANCES, BOOKINGS AND CAPS

	AGE (on 01/07/04)	IN NAMED 18	APPEARANCES	COUNTING GAMES	MINUTES ON PITCH	YELLOW CARDS	RED CARDS	THIS SEASON	HOME COUNTRY
Goalkeepers									
Pascal Borel	24	32	1	0	45	0	0	-	Germany
Andreas Reinke	43	34	34	33	3015	0	0	-	Germany
Defenders									
Frank Baumann	28	32	32	32	2871	5	0	6	Germany (9)
Tim Borowski	24	32	25	10	1247	1	0	-	Germany
Valerien Ismael	28	32	32	32	2859	5	0	-	France
Mladen Krstajic	30	30	30	28	2627	6	1	4	Serbia & Mont (45)
Victor Skrypnyk	34	13	6	0	99	1	0	-	Ukraine
Midfielders									
Ivica Banovic	23	14	3	0	45	1	0	-	Croatia
Fabian Ernst	25	33	33	33	2948	4	0	4	Germany (9)
Manuel Friedrich	24	3	1	0	9	0	0	-	Germany
Pekka Lagerblom	22	15	7	2	299	0	0	-	Finland
Krisztian Lisztes	28	30	30	25	2480	3	0	-	Hungary
Ludovic Magnin	25	9	4	0	112	1	0	-	Switzerland
Johan Micoud	30	32	32	30	2811	5	1	1	France (2)
Simon Rolfes	22	2	0	0	0	0	0	-	Germany
Christian Schulz	21	28	17	10	956	6	1	-	Germany
Paul Stalteri	26	33	33	32	2905	5	0	-	Canada
Umit Davala	30	23	22	21	1898	3	1	-	Turkey
Holger Wehlage	28	23	4	0	110	1	0	-	Germany
Forwards									
Ailton	30	33	33	27	2584	4	0	-	Brazil
Angelos Charisteas	24	31	24	5	862	0	0	-	Greece
Markus Daun	23	25	5	0	88	0	0	-	Germany
Ivan Klasnic	24	30	29	24	2177	2	0	2	Croatia (25)
Marco Reich	26	6	2	0	18	0	0	-	Germany
Nelson Haedo Valdez	20	27	21	1	494	3	0	-	Paraguay

TEAM OF THE SEASON

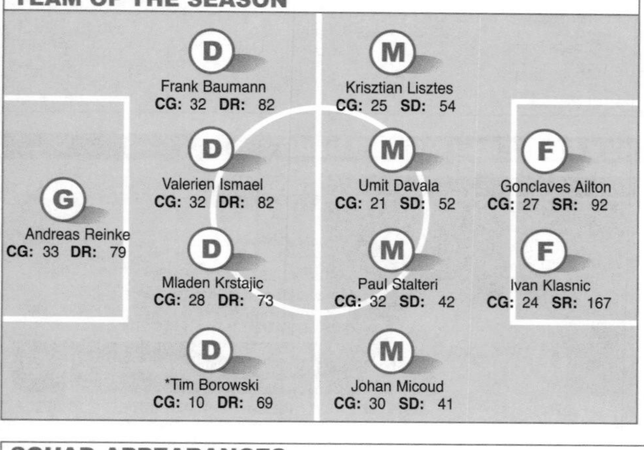
D
Frank Baumann
CG: 32 DR: 82
M
Krisztian Lisztes
CG: 25 SD: 54
D
Valerien Ismael
CG: 32 DR: 82
M
Umit Davala
CG: 21 SD: 52
F
Gonclaves Ailton
CG: 27 SR: 92
G
Andreas Reinke
CG: 33 DR: 79
D
Mladen Krstajic
CG: 28 DR: 73
M
Paul Stalteri
CG: 32 SD: 42
F
Ivan Klasnic
CG: 24 SR: 167
D
*Tim Borowski
CG: 10 DR: 69
M
Johan Micoud
CG: 30 SD: 41

SQUAD APPEARANCES

Match	1	2	3	4	5	6	7	8	9	10	11	12	13	14	15	16	17	18	19	20	21	22	23	24	25	26	27	28	29	30	31	32	33	34
Venue	A	H	A	H	A	H	A	H	H	A	H	A	H	A	H	A	H	H	A	H	A	H	A	H	A	A	H	A	H	A	H	A	H	A
Competition	L	L	L	L	L	L	L	L	L	L	L	L	L	L	L	L	L	L	L	L	L	L	L	L	L	L	L	L	L	L	L	L	L	L
Result	W	D	W	W	L	W	W	W	L	W	W	W	W	D	D	W	W	W	W	W	D	W	W	W	W	D	D	W	D	D	W	W	L	L

Goalkeepers
Pascal Borel
Andreas Reinke

Defenders
Frank Baumann
Tim Borowski
Valerien Ismael
Mladen Krstajic
Victor Skrypnyk

Midfielders
Ivica Banovic
Fabian Ernst
Manuel Friedrich
Pekka Lagerblom
Krisztian Lisztes
Ludovic Magnin
Johan Micoud
Simon Rolfes
Christian Schulz
Paul Stalteri
Umit Davala
Holger Wehlage

Forwards
Da Silva Gonclaves Ailton
Angelos Charisteas
Markus Daun
Ivan Klasnic
Marco Reich
Nelson Haedo Valdez

KEY: ■ On all match
■ On bench
⏮ Subbed or sent off (Counting game)
« Subbed or sent off (playing less than 70 minutes)
» Subbed on from bench (Counting Game)
» Subbed on (playing less than 70 minutes)
» Subbed on and then subbed or sent off (Counting Game)
» Subbed on and then subbed or sent off (playing less than 70 minutes)
□ Not in 16

BAYERN MUNICH

Final Position: **2nd**

KEY: Won Drawn Lost

							Attendance
1	grpr1	**Eintr Frankfurt**	H	W	3-1	Ze Reberto 16; Salihamidzic 20; Pizarro 42	63,000
2	grpr1	**Hannover 96**	A	D	3-3	Ballack 39; Pizarro 49; Hargreaves 90	23,217
3	grpr1	**Bochum**	H	W	2-0	Pizarro 21; Deisler 26	63,000
4	grpr1	**Hamburg**	A	W	2-0	Pizarro 14; Elber 78	55,000
5	grpr1	**Wolfsburg**	A	L	2-3	Schweinsteiger 49; Makaay 60	30,000
6	cl ga	**Celtic**	H	W	2-1	Makaay 73,86	48,500
7	grpr1	**B Leverkusen**	H	D	3-3	Makaay 25; Santa Cruz 64; Ballack 69	63,000
8	grpr1	**Hansa Rostock**	A	W	2-1	Santa Cruz 30; Makaay 86	29,000
9	cl ga	**Anderlecht**	A	D	1-1	Santa Cruz 74	23,328
10	grpr1	**Hertha Berlin**	H	W	4-1	Makaay 22; Ballack 45; Schweinsteiger 58; Salihamidzic 88	63,000
11	grpr1	**B M'gladbach**	A	D	0-0		34,500
12	cl ga	**Lyon**	A	D	1-1	Makaay 25	38,145
13	grpr1	**Kaiserslautern**	H	W	4-1	Deisler 2,69; Makaay 27,80	42,000
14	grpr1	**Schalke**	A	L	0-2		61,000
15	cl ga	**Lyon**	H	L	1-2	Makaay 14	59,000
16	grpr1	**B Dortmund**	H	W	4-1	Ballack 27; Sagnol 50; Salihamidzic 72; Pizarro 90	63,000
17	grpr1	**1860 Munich**	A	W	1-0	Makaay 34	69,000
18	cl ga	**Celtic**	A	D	0-0		59,506
19	grpr1	**Cologne**	H	D	2-2	Pizarro 42,49	45,000
20	grpr1	**W Bremen**	A	D	1-1	Pizarro 79	43,000
21	cl ga	**Anderlecht**	H	W	1-0	Makaay 41 pen	52,000
22	grpr1	**Stuttgart**	H	W	1-0	Makaay 75	63,000
23	grpr1	**Freiburg**	A	W	6-0	Demichelis 5; Salihamidzic 22; Makaay 32,67; Pizarro 60; Trochowski 87	25,000
24	grpr1	**Eintr Frankfurt**	A	D	1-1	Makaay 1	37,500
25	grpr1	**Hannover 96**	H	W	3-1	Ballack 10; Ze Roberto 66; Makaay 78	32,000
26	grpr1	**Bochum**	A	L	0-1		33,000
27	grpr1	**Hamburg**	H	W	1-0	Demichelis 87	38,000
28	clr1l1	**Real Madrid**	H	D	1-1	Makaay 75	59,000
29	grpr1	**Wolfsburg**	H	W	2-0	Makaay 11; Schweinsteiger 76	30,000
30	grpr1	**B Leverkusen**	A	W	3-1	Makaay 39,77; Ballack 58	22,500
31	clr1l2	**Real Madrid**	A	L	0-1		75,000
32	grpr1	**Hansa Rostock**	H	D	3-3	Jeremies 3; Makaay 9,76 pen	35,000
33	grpr1	**Hertha Berlin**	A	D	1-1	Makaay 8	60,000
34	grpr1	**B M'gladbach**	H	W	5-2	Kuffour 20; Santa Cruz 39; Makaay 48 pen; Hargreaves 88; Ballack 90	56,000
35	grpr1	**Kaiserslautern**	A	W	2-0	Makaay 47; Santa Cruz 76	47,315
36	grpr1	**Schalke**	H	W	2-1	Makaay 8,64	63,000
37	grpr1	**B Dortmund**	A	L	0-2		83,000
38	grpr1	**1860 Munich**	H	W	1-0	Santa Cruz 51	71,000
39	grpr1	**Cologne**	A	W	2-1	Pizarro 40; Schweinsteiger 75	50,200
40	grpr1	**W Bremen**	H	L	1-3	Makaay 56	63,000
41	grpr1	**Stuttgart**	A	L	1-3	Pizarro 77	48,000
42	grpr1	**Freiburg**	H	W	2-0	Deisler 18; Lizarazu 73 pen	63,000

KEY PLAYERS - GOALSCORERS

Roy Makaay

Goals in the League	23
Contribution to Attacking Power Average number of minutes between League team goals while on pitch	43
Player Strike Rate The total number of minutes he was on the pitch for every League goal scored	120
Club Strike Rate Average number of minutes between League goals scored by club	44

	PLAYER	GOALS LGE	POWER	S RATE
1	Roy Makaay	23	43	120 mins
2	Claudio Pizarro	11	43	154 mins
3	Michael Ballack	7	44	353 mins
4	Roque Santa Cruz	5	51	373 mins

KEY PLAYERS - MIDFIELDERS

Hazan Salihamidzic

Goals in the League	4
Defensive Rating Average number of mins between League goals conceded while on the pitch	77
Contribution to Attacking Power Average number of minutes between League team goals while on pitch	44
Scoring Difference Defensive Rating minus Contribution to Attacking Power	33

	PLAYER	GOALS LGE	DEF RATE	ATT POWER	SCORE DIFF
1	Hazan Salihamidzic	4	77	44	33 mins
2	Owen Hargreaves	2	75	44	31 mins
3	Jens Jeremies	1	74	44	30 mins
4	Michael Ballack	7	73	44	29 mins

KEY PLAYERS - DEFENDERS

Willy Sagnol

Goals Conceded in League	13
Clean Sheets In League games when he played at least 70 mins	7
Defensive Rating Ave number of mins between League goals conceded while on the pitch	113
Club Defensive Rating Average number of mins between League goals conceded by the club this season	78

	PLAYER	CON LGE	CLEAN SHEETS	DEF RATE
1	Willy Sagnol	13	7	113 mins
2	Samuel Osei Kuffour	20	8	101 mins
3	Bixente Lizarazu	25	9	90 mins
4	Robert Kovac	21	5	78 mins

MONTHLY POINTS TALLY

AUGUST	10	83%
SEPTEMBER	4	44%
OCTOBER	7	78%
NOVEMBER	7	58%
DECEMBER	7	78%
JANUARY	1	33%
FEBRUARY	9	75%
MARCH	8	67%
APRIL	9	75%
MAY	6	50%

LEAGUE GOALS

	PLAYER	MINS	GOALS	AVE
1	Makaay	2771	23	120
2	Pizarro	1697	11	154
3	Ballack	2468	7	353
4	Santa Cruz	1863	5	373
5	Deisler	587	4	147
6	Salihamidzic	2552	4	638
7	Schweinsteiger	1482	3	494
8	Demichelis	855	2	428
9	Hargreaves	2332	2	1166
10	Trochowski	155	1	155
11	Sagnol	1473	1	1473
12	Kuffour	2011	1	2011
13	Ze Roberto	2321	1	2321
	Other		5	
	TOTAL		70	

KEY GOALKEEPER

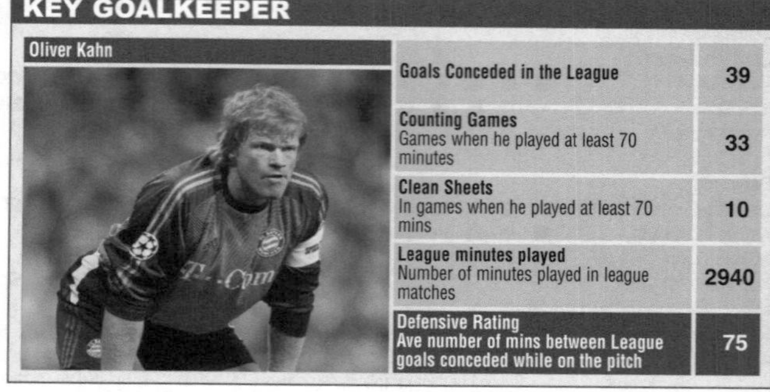

Oliver Kahn

Goals Conceded in the League	39
Counting Games Games when he played at least 70 minutes	33
Clean Sheets In games when he played at least 70 mins	10
League minutes played Number of minutes played in league matches	2940
Defensive Rating Ave number of mins between League goals conceded while on the pitch	75

DISCIPLINARY RECORDS

	PLAYER	YELLOW	RED	AVE
1	Demichelis	5	0	171
2	Ballack	12	2	176
3	Jeremies	5	0	296
4	Schweinsteiger	4	0	370
5	Linke	3	1	405
6	Salihamidzic	5	1	425
7	Lizarazu	5	0	450
8	Hargreaves	5	0	466
9	Sagnol	3	0	491
10	Kuffour	4	0	502
11	Kovac, R	3	0	547
12	Ze Roberto	3	1	580
13	Pizarro	2	0	848
	Other	6	0	
	TOTAL	65	5	

TOP POINT EARNERS

	PLAYER	GAMES	AV PTS
1	Deisler	4	2.50
2	Sagnol	14	2.36
3	Rau	3	2.33
4	Jeremies	14	2.21
5	Schweinsteiger	12	2.17
6	Kuffour	22	2.14
7	Lizarazu	24	2.13
8	Santa Cruz	17	2.12
9	Ballack	27	2.07
10	Makaay	31	2.03
	CLUB AVERAGE:		**2.00**

TEAM OF THE SEASON

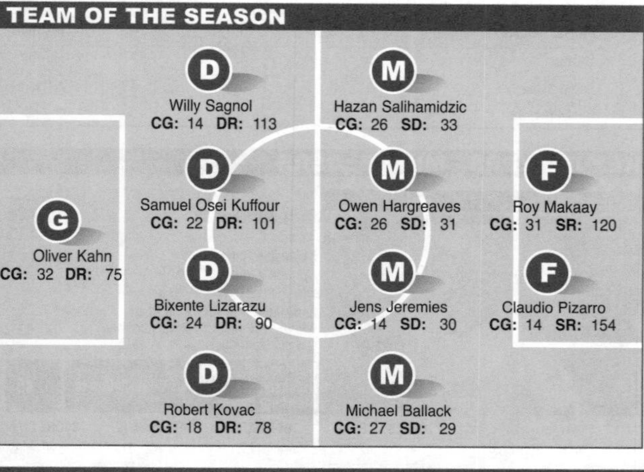

D
Willy Sagnol
CG: 14 DR: 113
M
Hazan Salihamidzic
CG: 26 SD: 33
D
Samuel Osei Kuffour
CG: 22 DR: 101
M
Owen Hargreaves
CG: 26 SD: 31
F
Roy Makaay
CG: 31 SR: 120
G
Oliver Kahn
CG: 32 DR: 75
D
Bixente Lizarazu
CG: 24 DR: 90
M
Jens Jeremies
CG: 14 SD: 30
F
Claudio Pizarro
CG: 14 SR: 154
D
Robert Kovac
CG: 18 DR: 78
M
Michael Ballack
CG: 27 SD: 29

LEAGUE APPEARANCES, BOOKINGS AND CAPS

	AGE (on 01/07/04)	IN NAMED 18	APPEARANCES	COUNTING GAMES	MINUTES ON PITCH	YELLOW CARDS	RED CARDS	THIS SEASON	HOME COUNTRY
Goalkeepers									
Oliver Kahn	35	33	33	32	2940	2	0	7	Germany (9)
Michael Rensing	20	30	2	1	120	0	0	-	Germany
Jan Schlosser	21	4	0	0	0	0	0	-	Germany
Defenders									
Martin Demichelis	23	24	14	7	855	5	0	-	Argentina
Robert Kovac	30	22	19	18	1642	3	0	7	Croatia (25)
S Osei Kuffour	27	29	23	22	2011	4	0	-	Ghana
Christian Lell	19	11	4	0	79	0	0	-	Germany
Thomas Linke	34	28	21	17	1622	3	1	-	Germany
Bixente Lizarazu	34	26	26	24	2250	5	0	8	France (2)
Christian Saba	25	1	0	0	0	0	0	-	Ghana
Willy Sagnol	27	23	21	14	1473	3	0	6	France (2)
Midfielders									
Michael Ballack	27	28	28	27	2468	12	2	6	Germany (9)
Sebastian Deisler	24	12	11	4	587	0	0	1	Germany (9)
Markus Feulner	22	5	1	0	14	0	0	-	Germany
Thorsten Fink	36	7	1	0	19	0	0	-	Germany
M Grunberger	-	1	0	0	0	0	0	-	Germany
Owen Hargreaves	23	27	26	26	2332	5	0	5	England (12)
Jens Jeremies	30	28	23	14	1480	5	0	6	Germany (9)
Zvjezdan Misimovic	22	8	2	0	3	0	0	-	Serbia & Montenegro
Tobias Rau	22	16	8	3	408	2	0	2	Germany (9)
Hazan Salihamidzic	27	33	33	26	2552	5	1	-	Bosnia
Mehmet Scholl	33	6	5	1	149	0	0	-	Germany
B Schweinsteiger	19	29	25	12	1482	4	0	-	Germany
Piotr Trochowski	20	29	10	0	155	0	0	-	Germany
Forwards									
Giovane Elber	31	4	4	2	210	1	0	-	Brazil
Jose Paolo Guerrero	20	1	0	0	0	0	0	-	Peru
Roy Makaay	29	32	32	31	2771	1	0	8	Holland (4)
Claudio Pizarro	25	30	29	14	1697	2	0	-	Peru
Roque Santa Cruz	22	29	29	17	1863	0	0	-	Paraguay
Jose Ze Roberto	30	30	30	24	2321	3	1	9	Brazil (1)
Alexander Zickler	30	1	0	0	0	0	0	-	Germany

SQUAD APPEARANCES

Match	1	2	3	4	5	6	7	8	9	10	11	12	13	14	15	16	17	18	19	20	21	22	23	24	25	26	27	28	29	30	31	32	33	34	35	36	37	38	39	40	41	42
Venue	H	A	H	A	A	H	H	A	A	H	A	A	H	A	H	H	A	A	H	A	H	H	A	A	H	A	H	H	H	A	A	H	A	H	A	H	A	H	A	H	A	H
Competition	L	L	L	L	L	C	L	L	C	L	L	C	L	L	C	L	L	C	L	L	C	L	L	L	L	L	L	C	L	L	C	L	L	L	L	L	L	L	L	L	L	L
Result	W	D	W	W	L	W	D	W	D	W	D	D	W	L	L	W	W	D	D	D	W	W	W	D	W	L	W	D	W	W	L	D	D	W	W	W	L	W	W	L	L	W

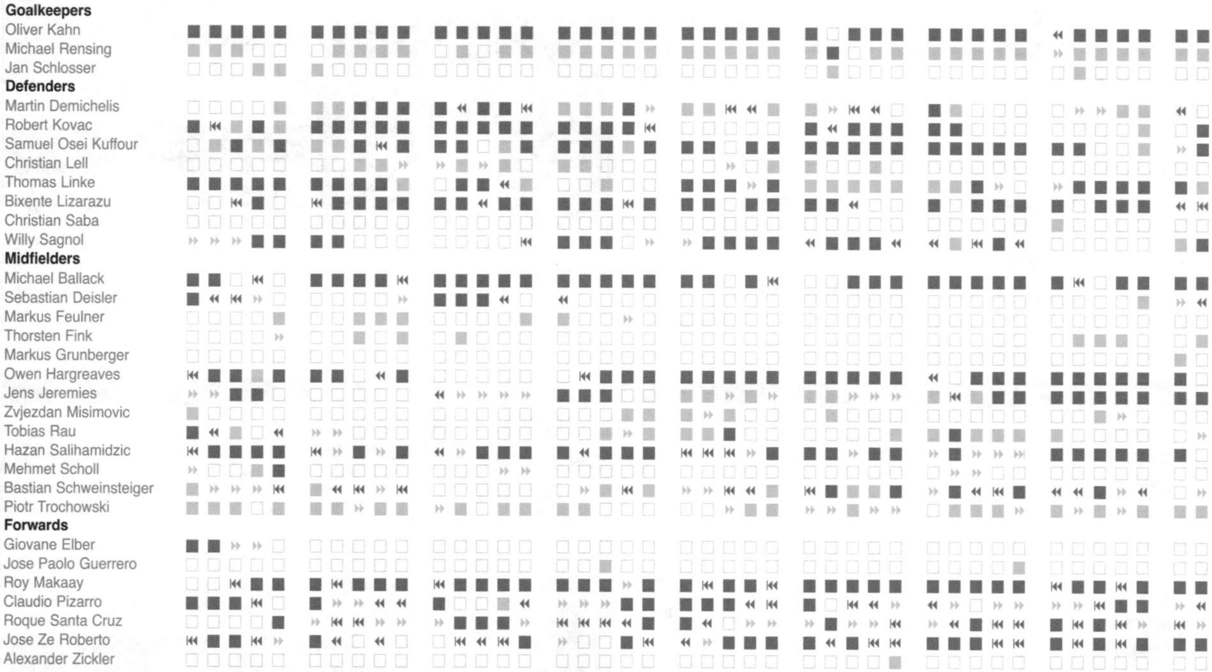

Goalkeepers
Oliver Kahn
Michael Rensing
Jan Schlosser
Defenders
Martin Demichelis
Robert Kovac
Samuel Osei Kuffour
Christian Lell
Thomas Linke
Bixente Lizarazu
Christian Saba
Willy Sagnol
Midfielders
Michael Ballack
Sebastian Deisler
Markus Feulner
Thorsten Fink
Markus Grunberger
Owen Hargreaves
Jens Jeremies
Zvjezdan Misimovic
Tobias Rau
Hazan Salihamidzic
Mehmet Scholl
Bastian Schweinsteiger
Piotr Trochowski
Forwards
Giovane Elber
Jose Paolo Guerrero
Roy Makaay
Claudio Pizarro
Roque Santa Cruz
Jose Ze Roberto
Alexander Zickler

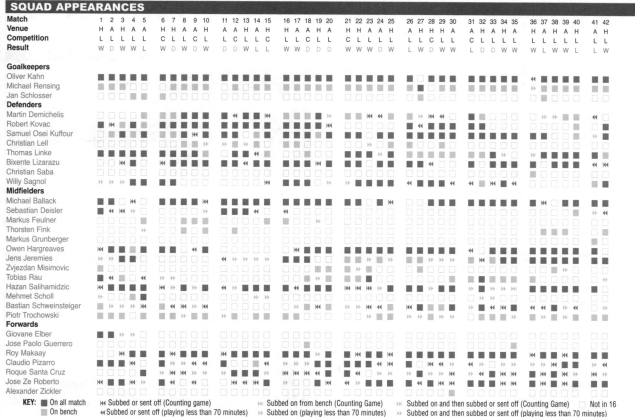

KEY: ■ On all match · ■ On bench · ⏮ Subbed or sent off (Counting game) · ⏪ Subbed or sent off (playing less than 70 minutes) · ⏭ Subbed on from bench (Counting Game) · ⏩ Subbed on (playing less than 70 minutes) · Subbed on and then subbed or sent off (Counting Game) · Subbed on and then subbed or sent off (playing less than 70 minutes) · □ Not in 16

BAYER LEVERKUSEN

Final Position: **3rd**

KEY: ☐Won ☐Drawn ☐Lost

							Attendance
1	grpr1	**Freiburg**	H	W	4-1	Ponte 17; Lucio 28; Juan 41; Neuville 61	22,500
2	grpr1	**Eintr Frankfurt**	A	W	2-1	Schneider 51; Cipi 84 og	22,500
3	grpr1	**Hannover 96**	H	W	4-0	Franca 2; Neuville 9,52; Bierofka 73	22,500
4	grpr1	**Bochum**	A	L	0-1		20,000
5	grpr1	**Hamburg**	H	W	1-0	Juan 28	22,500
6	grpr1	**Bayern Munich**	A	D	3-3	Ramelow 10; Franca 34; Basturk 81	63,000
7	grpr1	**Wolfsburg**	A	W	1-0	Schneider 57	24,000
8	grpr1	**Hansa Rostock**	H	W	3-0	Placente 70; Berbatov 75; Bierofka 79	22,500
9	grpr1	**Hertha Berlin**	A	W	4-1	Franca 11; Berbatov 54; Schneider 72; Babic 86	36,638
10	grpr1	**B M'gladbach**	H	W	1-0	Schneider 49	22,500
11	grpr1	**Kaiserslautern**	A	D	0-0		39,000
12	grpr1	**Schalke**	H	W	3-1	Berbatov 3; Lucio 27; Bierofka 57	22,500
13	grpr1	**B Dortmund**	A	D	2-2	Neuville 35; Babic 78	82,000
14	grpr1	**1860 Munich**	H	D	2-2	Ponte 60; Lucio 78	23,000
15	grpr1	**Cologne**	A	D	0-0		40,000
16	grpr1	**W Bremen**	H	L	1-3	Nowotny 72	22,500
17	grpr1	**Stuttgart**	A	W	3-2	Ramelow 24; Berbatov 44,62	47,000
18	grpr1	**Freiburg**	A	L	0-1		24,500
19	grpr1	**Eintr Frankfurt**	H	L	1-2	Neuville 61	22,500
20	grpr1	**Hannover 96**	A	D	2-2	Berbatov 65; Franca 71	22,000
21	grpr1	**Bochum**	H	L	1-3	Berbatov 60	22,500
22	grpr1	**Hamburg**	A	L	1-3	Schneider 40	43,000
23	grpr1	**Bayern Munich**	H	L	1-3	Schneider 90	22,500
24	grpr1	**Wolfsburg**	H	W	4-2	Berbatov 1; Babic 13 ; Schneider 33; Franca 63	22,500
25	grpr1	**Hansa Rostock**	A	W	2-0	Berbatov 58; Babic 75	22,000
26	grpr1	**Hertha Berlin**	H	W	4-1	Berbatov 29,73; Franca 34,55	20,500
27	grpr1	**B M'gladbach**	A	D	0-0		32,000
28	grpr1	**Kaiserslautern**	H	W	6-0	Wenzel 2 og; Berbatov 22; Lucio 34; Franca 38,55; Basturk 48	22,500
29	grpr1	**Schalke**	A	W	3-2	Berbatov 30; Schneider 72; Butt 77 pen	61,266
30	grpr1	**B Dortmund**	H	W	3-0	Babic 6; Franca 22; Berbatov 54	22,500
31	grpr1	**1860 Munich**	A	D	1-1	Schneider 48	25,000
32	grpr1	**Cologne**	H	W	2-0	Fritz 20; Franca 74	22,500
33	grpr1	**W Bremen**	A	W	6-2	Franca 7,21,61; Bierofka 12; Berbatov 65; Neuville 80	42,500
34	grpr1	**Stuttgart**	H	W	2-0	Berbatov 63; Schneider 86 pen	22,500

MONTHLY POINTS TALLY

AUGUST	9	75%
SEPTEMBER	7	78%
OCTOBER	9	100%
NOVEMBER	6	50%
DECEMBER	4	44%
JANUARY	0	0%
FEBRUARY	1	7%
MARCH	9	75%
APRIL	10	83%
MAY	10	83%

LEAGUE GOALS

	PLAYER	MINS	GOALS	AVE
1	Berbatov	2268	16	142
2	Franca	2332	14	167
3	Schneider	2802	10	280
4	Neuville	1429	6	238
5	Babic	2578	5	516
6	Bierofka	1816	4	454
7	Lucio	2279	3	760
8	Ramelow	2688	2	1344
9	Ponte	1493	2	747
10	Juan	2668	2	1334
11	Basturk	734	2	367
12	Placente	2220	1	2220
13	Fritz	910	1	910
	Other		5	
	TOTAL		73	

KEY PLAYERS - GOALSCORERS

Dimitar Berbatov

Goals in the League	16
Contribution to Attacking Power Average number of minutes between League team goals while on pitch	41
Player Strike Rate The total number of minutes he was on the pitch for every League goal scored	142
Club Strike Rate Average number of minutes between League goals scored by club	42

	PLAYER	GOALS LGE	POWER	S RATE
1	Dimitar Berbatov	16	41	142 mins
2	Franca	14	37	167 mins
3	Bernd Schneider	10	43	280 mins
4	Daniel Bierofka	4	39	454 mins

KEY PLAYERS - MIDFIELDERS

Carsten Ramelow

Goals in the League	2
Defensive Rating Average number of mins between League goals conceded while on the pitch	87
Contribution to Attacking Power Average number of minutes between League team goals while on pitch	41
Scoring Difference Defensive Rating minus Contribution to Attacking Power	46

	PLAYER	GOALS LGE	DEF RATE	ATT POWER	SCORE DIFF
1	Carsten Ramelow	2	87	41	46 mins
2	Marko Babic	5	83	40	43 mins
3	Daniel Bierofka	4	73	39	34 mins
4	Bernd Schneider	10	74	43	31 mins

KEY PLAYERS - DEFENDERS

Jens Nowotny

Goals Conceded in League	23
Clean Sheets In League games when he played at least 70 mins	9
Defensive Rating Ave number of mins between League goals conceded while on the pitch	84
Club Defensive Rating Average number of mins between League goals conceded by the club this season	78

	PLAYER	CON LGE	CLEAN SHEETS	DEF RATE
1	Jens Nowotny	23	9	84 mins
2	Lucimar da Silva Lucio	29	9	79 mins
3	Silveira dos Santos Juan	34	11	78 mins
4	Diego Placente	29	9	77 mins

KEY GOALKEEPER

Hans-Jorg Butt

Goals Conceded in the League	39
Counting Games Games when he played at least 70 minutes	34
Clean Sheets In games when he played at least 70 mins	13
League minutes played Number of minutes played in league matches	3060
Defensive Rating Ave number of mins between League goals conceded while on the pitch	78

DISCIPLINARY RECORDS

	PLAYER	YELLOW	RED	AVE
1	Basturk	5	0	146
2	Lucic	3	0	209
3	Ramelow	10	0	268
4	Placente	6	2	277
5	Balitsch	5	0	294
6	Bierofka	6	0	302
7	Juan	7	1	333
8	Ponte	4	0	373
9	Nowotny	4	1	385
10	Neuville	3	0	476
11	Babic	5	0	515
12	Schneider	4	0	700
13	Berbatov	3	0	756
	Other	5	0	
	TOTAL	70	4	

TOP POINT EARNERS

	PLAYER	GAMES	AV PTS
1	Basturk	5	2.60
2	Franca	22	2.27
3	Babic	25	2.16
4	Ramelow	28	2.14
5	Lucio	24	2.00
6	Ponte	16	2.00
7	Lucic	5	2.00
8	Schneider	30	1.93
9	Juan	30	1.93
10	Butt	34	1.91
	CLUB AVERAGE:		**1.91**

TEAM OF THE SEASON

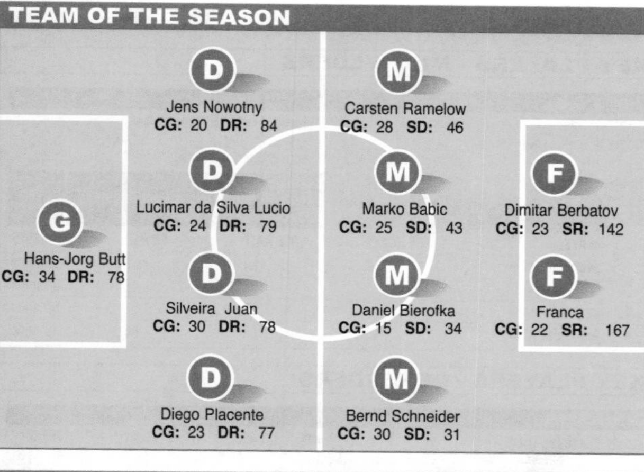
G
Hans-Jorg Butt
CG: 34 DR: 78
D
Jens Nowotny
CG: 20 DR: 84
D
Lucimar da Silva Lucio
CG: 24 DR: 79
D
Silveira Juan
CG: 30 DR: 78
D
Diego Placente
CG: 23 DR: 77
M
Carsten Ramelow
CG: 28 SD: 46
M
Marko Babic
CG: 25 SD: 43
M
Daniel Bierofka
CG: 15 SD: 34
M
Bernd Schneider
CG: 30 SD: 31
F
Dimitar Berbatov
CG: 23 SR: 142
F
Franca
CG: 22 SR: 167

LEAGUE APPEARANCES, BOOKINGS AND CAPS

	AGE (on 01/07/04)	IN NAMED 18	APPEARANCES	COUNTING GAMES	MINUTES ON PITCH	YELLOW CARDS	RED CARDS	THIS SEASON	HOME COUNTRY
Goalkeepers									
Hans-Jorg Butt	30	34	34	34	3060	1	0	-	Germany
Frank Juric	30	18	0	0	0	0	0	-	Australia
Tom Starke	23	14	0	0	0	0	0	-	Germany
Defenders									
J Callsen-Bracker	19	9	1	0	12	0	0	-	Germany
Ingo Hertzsch	26	12	3	0	45	0	0	-	Germany
Silveira Juan	25	30	30	30	2668	7	1	1	Brazil (1)
Teddy Lucic	31	28	11	5	629	3	0	8	Sweden (21)
Lucimar Lucio	26	26	26	24	2279	2	0	7	Brazil (1)
Jens Nowotny	30	29	23	20	1925	4	1	-	Germany
Diego Placente	27	30	27	23	2220	6	2	4	Argentina (5)
Midfielders									
Marko Babic	23	33	32	25	2578	5	0	7	Croatia (25)
Hanno Balitsch	23	28	25	14	1473	5	0	-	Germany
Yildiray Basturk	25	17	17	5	734	5	0	-	Turkey
Daniel Bierofka	25	32	31	15	1816	6	0	-	Germany
Radoslaw Kaluzny	30	22	5	1	163	0	0	-	Poland
Christoph Preuss	23	1	0	0	0	0	0	-	Germany
Carsten Ramelow	30	31	31	28	2688	10	0	5	Germany (9)
Bernd Schneider	30	33	33	30	2802	4	0	9	Germany (9)
Zoltan Sebescen	28	3	0	0	0	0	0	-	Germany
Forwards									
Dimitar Berbatov	23	32	32	23	2268	3	0	-	Bulgaria
Franca	28	34	33	22	2332	1	0	-	Brazil
Clemens Fritz	23	27	15	8	910	1	0	-	Germany
Jermaine Jones	22	2	0	0	0	0	0	-	Germany
Ioannis Masmanidis	21	8	1	0	21	0	0	-	Germany
Oliver Neuville	31	32	32	8	1429	3	0	5	Germany (9)
Robson Ponte	27	21	20	16	1493	4	0	-	Brazil
Kenan Sahin	19	13	5	0	53	0	0	-	Turkey
Sebastian Schoof	24	4	0	0	0	0	0	-	Germany

SQUAD APPEARANCES

Match	1	2	3	4	5	6	7	8	9	10	11	12	13	14	15	16	17	18	19	20	21	22	23	24	25	26	27	28	29	30	31	32	33	34
Venue	H	A	H	A	H	A	A	H	A	H	A	H	A	H	A	H	A	A	H	A	H	A	H	H	A	H	A	H	A	H	A	H	A	H
Competition	L	L	L	L	L	L	L	L	L	L	L	L	L	L	L	L	L	L	L	L	L	L	L	L	L	L	L	L	L	L	L	L	L	L
Result	W	W	W	L	W	D	W	W	W	W	D	W	D	D	D	L	W	L	L	D	L	L	L	W	W	W	D	W	W	W	D	W	W	W

Goalkeepers
Hans-Jorg Butt
Frank Juric
Tom Starke

Defenders
Jan-Ingwar Callsen-Bracker
Ingo Hertzsch
Silveira dos Santos Juan
Teddy Lucic
Lucimar da Silva Lucio
Jens Nowotny
Diego Placente

Midfielders
Marko Babic
Hanno Balitsch
Yildiray Basturk
Daniel Bierofka
Radoslaw Kaluzny
Christoph Preuss
Carsten Ramelow
Bernd Schneider
Zoltan Sebescen

Forwards
Dimitar Berbatov
Franca
Clemens Fritz
Jermaine Jones
Ioannis Masmanidis
Oliver Neuville
Robson Ponte
Kenan Sahin
Sebastian Schoof

KEY: ■ On all match ■ On bench
⏮ Subbed or sent off (Counting game) ⏪ Subbed or sent off (playing less than 70 minutes)
⏭ Subbed on from bench (Counting Game) ⏩ Subbed on (playing less than 70 minutes)
⏭ Subbed on and then subbed or sent off (Counting Game) ⏩ Subbed on and then subbed or sent off (playing less than 70 minutes)
□ Not in 16

VFB STUTTGART

4th

KEY: Won / Drawn / Lost

							Attendance
1	grpr1	Hansa Rostock	A	W	2-0	Szabics 75,78	26,000
2	grpr1	Hertha Berlin	H	D	0-0		37,000
3	grpr1	B M'gladbach	A	W	1-0	Cacau 33	32,000
4	grpr1	Kaiserslautern	H	W	2-0	Cacau 8; Soldo 14	27,000
5	grpr1	Schalke	A	D	0-0		61,000
6	cl ge	Rangers	A	L	1-2	Kuranyi 45	47,957
7	grpr1	B Dortmund	H	W	1-0	Kuranyi 67	48,000
8	grpr1	1860 Munich	A	W	3-0	Soldo 12; Fernando Meira 18 pen; Hleb 50	38,000
9	cl ge	Man Utd	H	W	2-1	Szabics 50; Kuranyi 52	53,000
10	grpr1	Cologne	H	D	0-0		52,000
11	grpr1	W Bremen	A	W	3-1	Szabics 31; Kuranyi 34; Tiffert 90	41,100
12	cl ge	Panathinaikos	H	W	2-0	Szabics 13; Soldo 25	50,348
13	grpr1	Wolfsburg	H	W	1-0	Amanatidis 74	40,000
14	grpr1	Freiburg	H	W	4-1	Kuranyi 33,65; Tiffert 62; Hleb 64	51,000
15	cl ge	Panathinaikos	A	W	3-1	Fissas 68 og; Kuranyi 75; Hinkel 77	6,015
16	grpr1	Eintr Frankfurt	A	W	2-0	Szabics 8; Kuranyi 69	27,000
17	grpr1	Hannover 96	H	W	3-1	Szabics 30; Meissner 78,90	35,000
18	cl ge	Rangers	H	W	1-0	Wenzel 45	50,348
19	grpr1	Bochum	A	D	0-0		28,000
20	grpr1	Hamburg	H	D	0-0		38,000
21	cl ge	Man Utd	A	L	0-2		67,141
22	grpr1	Bayern Munich	A	L	0-1		63,000
23	grpr1	B Leverkusen	H	L	2-3	Kuranyi 56; Soldo 68	47,000
24	grpr1	Hansa Rostock	H	W	2-0	Hleb 60; Kuranyi 75	42,000
25	grpr1	Hertha Berlin	A	L	0-1		39,000
26	grpr1	B M'gladbach	H	D	1-1	Szabics 5	32,000
27	grpr1	Kaiserslautern	A	L	0-1		40,000
28	clr1l1	Chelsea	H	L	0-1		50,000
29	grpr1	Schalke	H	D	0-0		42,000
30	grpr1	B Dortmund	A	W	2-0	Hleb 5; Heldt 82 pen	83,000
31	clr1l2	Chelsea	A	D	0-0		36,657
32	grpr1	1860 Munich	H	W	2-0	Soldo 32; Streller 35	41,000
33	grpr1	Cologne	A	D	2-2	Meissner 28; Scherz 72 og	50,000
34	grpr1	W Bremen	H	D	4-4	Bordon 4,24,51; Streller 69	48,000
35	grpr1	Wolfsburg	A	W	5-1	Gerber 6; Streller 26; Lahm 43; Kuranyi 75; Szabics 87	25,000
36	grpr1	Freiburg	A	W	1-0	Kuranyi 11	25,000
37	grpr1	Eintr Frankfurt	H	W	3-1	Kuranyi 44; Hleb 50; Bordon 80	48,000
38	grpr1	Hannover 96	A	W	1-0	Meissner 10	27,537
39	grpr1	Bochum	H	D	1-1	Cacau 31	47,000
40	grpr1	Hamburg	A	L	1-2	Cacau 85	54,500
41	grpr1	Bayern Munich	H	W	3-1	Szabics 19,52; Kuranyi 54	48,000
42	grpr1	B Leverkusen	A	L	0-2		22,500

MONTHLY POINTS TALLY

Month	Points	%
AUGUST	10	83%
SEPTEMBER	7	78%
OCTOBER	7	78%
NOVEMBER	10	83%
DECEMBER	1	11%
JANUARY	3	100%
FEBRUARY	2	17%
MARCH	8	67%
APRIL	12	100%
MAY	4	33%

KEY PLAYERS - GOALSCORERS

Imre Szabics

Goals in the League	9	Player Strike Rate Average number of minutes between League goals scored by player	192
Contribution to Attacking Power Average number of minutes between League team goals while on pitch	57	Club Strike Rate Average number of minutes between League goals scored by club	59

	PLAYER	LGE GOALS	POWER	STRIKE RATE
1	Imre Szabics	9	57	192 mins
2	Kevin Kuranyi	11	59	264 mins
3	Silvio Meissner	4	57	402 mins
4	Alexander Hleb	5	59	467 mins

KEY PLAYERS - MIDFIELDERS

Zvonimir Soldo

Goals in the League	4	Contribution to Attacking Power Average number of minutes between League team goals while on pitch	57
Defensive Rating Average number of mins between League goals conceded while he was on the pitch	129	Scoring Difference Defensive Rating minus Contribution to Attacking Power	72

	PLAYER	LGE GOALS	DEF RATE	POWER	SCORE DIFF
1	Zvonimir Soldo	4	129	57	72 mins
2	Heiko Gerber	1	107	47	60 mins
3	Silvio Meissner	4	107	57	50 mins
4	Alexander Hleb	5	102	60	42 mins

KEY PLAYERS - DEFENDERS

Andreas Hinkel

Goals Conceded (GC) The number of League goals conceded while he was on the pitch	13	Clean Sheets In games when he played at least 70 minutes	16
Defensive Rating Ave number of mins between League goals conceded while on the pitch	181	Club Defensive Rating Average number of mins between League goals conceded by the club this season	128

	PLAYER	CON LGE	CLEAN SHEETS	DEF RATE
1	Andreas Hinkel	13	16	181 mins
2	Marcelo Jose Bordon	15	14	144 mins
3	Jose da Silva Fernando Meira	22	17	130 mins
4	Philip Lahm	23	12	109 mins

KEY GOALKEEPER

Timo Hildebrand

Goals Conceded in the League	24	Counting Games Games when he played at least 70 mins	34
Defensive Rating Ave number of mins between League goals conceded while on the pitch	128	Clean Sheets In games when he played at least 70 mins	18

LEAGUE GOALS

Kevin Kuranyi

Minutes on the pitch	2909	Goals in the League	11
League average (mins between goals)	264		

	PLAYER	MINS	GOALS	AVE
1	Kuranyi	2909	11	264
2	Szabics	1727	9	192
3	Hleb	2335	5	467
4	Bordon	2158	4	540
5	Soldo	2719	4	680
6	Meissner	1606	4	402
7	Cacau	839	4	210
8	Streller	606	3	202
9	Tiffert	1329	2	665
10	Heldt	1753	1	1753
11	Lahm	2509	1	2509
12	Fernando Meira	2858	1	2858
	Other		3	
	TOTAL		52	

DISCIPLINARY

	PLAYER	YELLOW	RED	AVE
1	Tiffert	5	0	265
2	Meissner	6	0	267
3	Bordon	7	1	269
4	Cacau	3	0	279
5	Zivkovic	2	1	291
6	Soldo	8	0	339
7	Vranjes	4	0	358
8	Gerber	3	0	391
9	Heldt	4	0	438
10	Hinkel	5	0	471
11	Fernando Meira	4	1	571
12	Szabics	3	0	575
13	Kuranyi	5	0	581
	Other	6	0	
	TOTAL	65	3	

TOP POINT EARNERS

	PLAYER	GAMES	AV PTS
1	Heldt	8	2.13
2	Tiffert	9	2.11
3	Gerber	12	2.08
4	Bordon	24	2.08
5	Vranjes	11	2.00
6	Meissner	15	2.00
7	Streller	2	2.00
8	Kuranyi	33	1.94
9	Szabics	14	1.93
10	Hildebrand	34	1.88
	CLUB AVERAGE:		1.88

LEAGUE APPEARANCES, BOOKINGS AND CAPS

	AGE (on 01/07/04)	IN NAMED 18	APPEARANCES	COUNTING GAMES	MINUTES ON PITCH	YELLOW CARDS	RED CARDS	THIS SEASON	HOME COUNTRY
Goalkeepers									
Diego Benaglio	20	4	0	0	0	0	0	-	Switzerland
Dirk Heinen	33	28	0	0	0	0	0	-	Germany
Timo Hildebrand	25	34	34	34	3060	1	0	3	Germany (9)
Defenders									
Marcelo Bordon	28	24	24	24	2158	7	1	-	Brazil
Serge Branco	23	3	2	0	5	0	0	-	Cameroon
Steffen Dangelmayr	25	1	0	0	0	0	0	-	Germany
J Fernando Meira	26	32	32	32	2858	4	1	3	Portugal (20)
Andreas Hinkel	22	28	27	26	2358	5	0	6	Germany (9)
Markus Husterer	21	5	2	0	21	0	0	-	Germany
Philip Lahm	20	33	31	27	2509	2	0	4	Germany (9)
R Manuel Marques	26	3	0	0	0	0	0	-	Angola
Timo Wenzel	26	14	8	7	675	0	0	-	Germany
Boris Zivkovic	28	16	12	9	873	2	1	9	Croatia (25)
Midfielders									
Heiko Gerber	31	33	18	12	1175	3	0	-	Germany
Horst Heldt	34	34	30	8	1753	4	0	-	Germany
Alexander Hleb	23	32	31	23	2335	2	0	-	Belarus
Silvio Meissner	31	31	27	15	1606	6	0	-	Germany
Zvonimir Soldo	36	33	33	28	2719	8	0	1	Croatia (25)
Jurica Vranjes	24	31	22	11	1433	4	0	2	Croatia (25)
Forwards									
Ioannis Amanatidis	22	16	8	0	181	1	0	-	Greece
Jeronimo Baretto	23	31	15	5	839	3	0	-	Brazil
Emanuel Centurion	21	9	5	0	116	0	0	-	Argentina
Mario Gomez	18	1	0	0	0	0	0	-	Germany
Kevin Kuranyi	22	33	33	33	2909	5	0	-	Brazil
Marco Streller	23	14	13	2	606	0	0	-	Switzerland
Imre Szabics	23	34	26	14	1727	3	0	-	Hungary
Christian Tiffert	22	33	27	9	1329	5	0	-	Germany
Hakan Yakin	27	12	8	1	356	0	0	-	Switzerland

TEAM OF THE SEASON

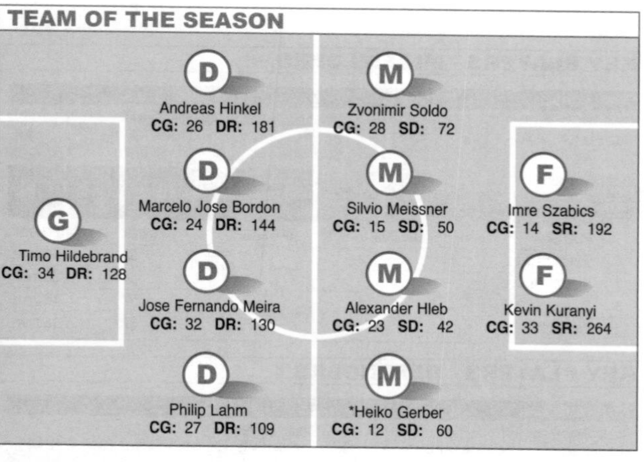
D
Andreas Hinkel
CG: 26 DR: 181
D
Marcelo Jose Bordon
CG: 24 DR: 144
D
Jose Fernando Meira
CG: 32 DR: 130
D
Philip Lahm
CG: 27 DR: 109
G
Timo Hildebrand
CG: 34 DR: 128
M
Zvonimir Soldo
CG: 28 SD: 72
M
Silvio Meissner
CG: 15 SD: 50
M
Alexander Hleb
CG: 23 SD: 42
M
*Heiko Gerber
CG: 12 SD: 60
F
Imre Szabics
CG: 14 SR: 192
F
Kevin Kuranyi
CG: 33 SR: 264

SQUAD APPEARANCES

Match	1	2	3	4	5	6	7	8	9	10	11	12	13	14	15	16	17	18	19	20	21	22	23	24	25	26	27	28	29	30	31	32	33	34	35	36	37	38	39	40	41	42
Venue	A	H	A	H	A	A	H	H	H	H	A	H	H	H	A	A	H	H	A	H	A	A	H	H	A	H	A	H	H	A	A	H	A	H	A	A	H	A	H	A	H	A
Competition	L	L	L	L	L	C	L	L	C	L	L	C	L	L	C	L	L	C	L	L	C	L	L	L	L	L	L	C	L	L	C	L	L	L	L	L	L	L	L	L	L	L
Result	W	D	W	W	D	L	W	W	W	D	W	W	W	W	W	W	W	W	D	D	L	L	L	W	L	D	L	L	D	W	D	W	D	D	W	W	W	W	D	L	W	L

Goalkeepers
Diego Benaglio
Dirk Heinen
Timo Hildebrand

Defenders
Marcelo Jose Bordon
Serge Branco
Steffen Dangelmayr
Jose da Silva Fernando Meira
Andreas Hinkel
Markus Husterer
Philip Lahm
Rui Manuel Marques
Timo Wenzel
Boris Zivkovic

Midfielders
Heiko Gerber
Horst Heldt
Alexander Hleb
Silvio Meissner
Zvonimir Soldo
Jurica Vranjes

Forwards
Ioannis Amanatidis
Jeronimo Cacau Baretto
Emanuel Centurion
Mario Gomez
Kevin Kuranyi
Marco Streller
Imre Szabics
Christian Tiffert
Hakan Yakin

KEY: On all match; On bench; Subbed or sent off (Counting game); Subbed or sent off (playing less than 70 minutes); Subbed on from bench (Counting Game); Subbed on (playing less than 70 minutes); Subbed on and then subbed or sent off (Counting Game); Subbed on and then subbed or sent off (playing less than 70 minutes); Not in 16

VFL BOCHUM

5th

KEY: ☐ Won ☐ Drawn ☐ Lost

#	Comp	Opponent	Venue	Result	Score	Scorers	Attendance
1	grpr1	Wolfsburg	A	L	2-3	Madsen 37; Fahrenhorst 44	15,976
2	grpr1	Hamburg	H	D	1-1	Madsen 31	20,400
3	grpr1	Bayern Munich	A	L	0-2		63,000
4	grpr1	B Leverkusen	H	W	1-0	Zdebel 64	20,000
5	grpr1	Hansa Rostock	A	W	2-0	Hashemian 46; Gudjonsson, B 90	15,000
6	grpr1	Hertha Berlin	H	D	2-2	Zdebel 45; Hashemian 72	21,000
7	grpr1	B M'gladbach	A	D	2-2	Diabang 60; Madsen 89	29,000
8	lge	Kaiserslautern	H	W	4-0	Hashemian 49,83; Madsen 60,90	20,000
9	lge	Schalke	A	W	2-0	Fahrenhorst 66; Diabang 79	61,178
10	lge	B Dortmund	H	W	3-0	Hashemian 8,56; Oliseh 79	33,000
11	lge	1860 Munich	A	L	1-3	Hashemian 35	18,000
12	lge	Cologne	H	W	4-0	Hashemian 7; Madsen 15; Kalla 45; Stevic 87	31,000
13	lge	W Bremen	A	L	1-3	Fahrenhorst 75	34,000
14	lge	Stuttgart	H	D	0-0		28,000
15	lge	Freiburg	A	L	2-4	Hashemian 15; Madsen 24	24,500
16	lge	Eintr Frankfurt	H	W	1-0	Hashemian 21	21,000
17	lge	Hannover 96	A	D	2-2	Madsen 53; Hashemian 75	20,000
18	lge	Wolfsburg	H	W	1-0	Fahrenhorst 36	21,000
19	lge	Hamburg	A	D	1-1	Colding 70	38,000
20	lge	Bayern Munich	H	W	1-0	Madsen 8	33,000
21	lge	B Leverkusen	A	W	3-1	Meichelbeck 52; Wosz 54; Diabang 73	22,500
22	lge	Hansa Rostock	H	D	0-0		21,000
23	lge	Hertha Berlin	A	D	1-1	Fahrenhorst 57	35,000
24	lge	B M'gladbach	H	W	1-0	Asanin 88 og	32,645
25	lge	Kaiserslautern	A	D	2-2	Hashemian 15; Wosz 45	35,000
26	lge	Schalke	H	L	1-2	Meichelbeck 24	32,645
27	lge	B Dortmund	A	L	1-4	Madsen 14	83,000
28	lge	1860 Munich	H	W	4-0	Hashemian 26,40; Madsen 61; Diabang 81	21,000
29	lge	Cologne	A	W	2-1	Wosz 31; Fahrenhorst 64	43,500
30	lge	W Bremen	H	D	0-0		32,645
31	lge	Stuttgart	A	D	1-1	Meichelbeck 58	47,000
32	lge	Freiburg	H	W	3-0	Madsen 2; Hashemian 53; Cairo 68 og	29,474
33	lge	Eintr Frankfurt	A	L	2-3	Hashemian 30; Wosz 49	32,000
34	lge	Hannover 96	H	W	3-1	Madsen 26; Freier 76; Fahrenhorst 87	32,645

MONTHLY POINTS TALLY

Month	Points	%
AUGUST	4	33%
SEPTEMBER	5	56%
OCTOBER	9	100%
NOVEMBER	4	33%
DECEMBER	4	44%
JANUARY	3	100%
FEBRUARY	8	67%
MARCH	5	42%
APRIL	7	58%
MAY	7	58%

KEY PLAYERS - GOALSCORERS

Vahid Hashemian

Goals in the League	16	Player Strike Rate Average number of minutes between League goals scored by player	162
Contribution to Attacking Power Average number of minutes between League team goals while on pitch	53	Club Strike Rate Average number of minutes between League goals scored by club	54

	PLAYER	LGE GOALS	POWER	STRIKE RATE
1	Vahid Hashemian	16	53	162 mins
2	Peter Madsen	13	48	205 mins
3	Frank Fahrenhorst	7	53	413 mins
4	Dariusz Wosz	4	57	603 mins

KEY PLAYERS - MIDFIELDERS

Tomasz Zdebel

Goals in the League	2	Contribution to Attacking Power Average number of minutes between League team goals while on pitch	53
Defensive Rating Average number of mins between League goals conceded while he was on the pitch	77	Scoring Difference Defensive Rating minus Contribution to Attacking Power	24

	PLAYER	LGE GOALS	DEF RATE	POWER	SCORE DIFF
1	Tomasz Zdebel	2	77	53	24 mins
2	Sunday Oliseh	1	76	54	22 mins
3	Dariusz Wosz	4	75	57	18 mins
4	Paul Freier	1	75	57	18 mins

KEY PLAYERS - DEFENDERS

Frank Fahrenhorst

Goals Conceded (GC) The number of League goals conceded while he was on the pitch	36	Clean Sheets In games when he played at least 70 minutes	15
Defensive Rating Ave number of mins between League goals conceded while on the pitch	80	Club Defensive Rating Average number of mins between League goals conceded by the club this season	78

	PLAYER	CON LGE	CLEAN SHEETS	DEF RATE
1	Frank Fahrenhorst	36	15	80 mins
2	Soren Colding	38	14	77 mins
3	Raymond Kalla	33	11	71 mins
4	Phillip Bonig	34	11	68 mins

KEY GOALKEEPER

Rein Van Duijnhoven

Goals Conceded in the League	39	Counting Games Games when he played at least 70 mins	34
Defensive Rating Ave number of mins between League goals conceded while on the pitch	78	Clean Sheets In games when he played at least 70 mins	15

LEAGUE GOALS

Vahid Hashemian

Minutes on the pitch	2586	Goals in the League	16
League average (mins between goals)	162		

	PLAYER	MINS	GOALS	AVE
1	Hashemian	2586	16	162
2	Madsen	2667	13	205
3	Fahrenhorst	2893	7	413
4	Diabang	967	4	242
5	Wosz	2411	4	603
6	Meichelbeck	636	3	212
7	Zdebel	2837	2	1419
8	Freier	2180	1	2180
9	Gudjonsson, B	125	1	125
10	Kalla	2346	1	2346
11	Oliseh	1822	1	1822
12	Stevic	1115	1	1115
	Other		3	
	TOTAL		57	

DISCIPLINARY

	PLAYER	YELLOW	RED	AVE
1	Vriesde	2	0	261
2	Meichelbeck	2	0	318
3	Kalla	7	0	335
4	Stevic	3	0	371
5	Colding	7	0	419
6	Freier	5	0	436
7	Oliseh	4	0	455
8	Wosz	4	0	602
9	Madsen	4	0	666
10	Zdebel	4	0	709
11	Bonig	3	0	769
12	Buckley	1	0	776
13	Diabang	1	0	967
	Other	11	0	
	TOTAL	58	0	

TOP POINT EARNERS

	PLAYER	GAMES	AV PTS
1	Edu	2	2.00
2	Vriesde	5	1.80
3	Fahrenhorst	32	1.72
4	Hashemian	28	1.71
5	Madsen	27	1.70
6	Colding	32	1.69
7	Wosz	22	1.68
8	Tapalovic, F	3	1.67
9	Zdebel	29	1.66
10	Van Duijnhoven	34	1.65
	CLUB AVERAGE:		**1.65**

TEAM OF THE SEASON

G — Rein Van Duijnhoven **CG:** 34 **DR:** 78

D — Frank Fahrenhorst **CG:** 32 **DR:** 80

D — Soren Colding **CG:** 32 **DR:** 77

D — Raymond Kalla **CG:** 25 **DR:** 71

D — Phillip Bonig **CG:** 25 **DR:** 68

M — Tomasz Zdebel **CG:** 29 **SD:** 24

M — Sunday Oliseh **CG:** 19 **SD:** 22

M — Paul Freier **CG:** 22 **SD:** 18

M — Dariusz Wosz **CG:** 22 **SD:** 18

F — Vahid Hashemian **CG:** 28 **SR:** 162

F — Peter Madsen **CG:** 27 **SR:** 205

LEAGUE APPEARANCES, BOOKINGS AND CAPS

	AGE (on 01/07/04)	IN NAMED 18	APPEARANCES	COUNTING GAMES	MINUTES ON PITCH	YELLOW CARDS	RED CARDS	THIS SEASON	HOME COUNTRY
Goalkeepers									
Bastian Gorrissin	20	3	0	0	0	0	0	-	Germany
R Van Duijnhoven	36	34	34	34	3060	2	0	-	Holland
Christian Vander	23	30	0	0	0	0	0	-	Germany
Defenders									
Phillip Bonig	24	28	28	25	2307	3	0	-	Germany
Soren Colding	31	33	33	32	2938	7	0	-	Denmark
Goncalves Edu	22	21	12	2	445	3	0	-	Brazil
Frank Fahrenhorst	26	33	33	32	2893	2	0	-	Germany
Raymond Kalla	29	28	28	25	2346	7	0	-	Cameroon
Martin Meichelbeck	27	19	12	5	636	2	0	-	Germany
Filip Tapalovic	27	18	12	3	424	0	0	-	Croatia
Midfielders									
Michael Bemben	28	34	10	1	247	0	0	-	Germany
Paul Freier	24	27	27	22	2180	5	0	7	Germany (9)
Bjarni Gudjonsson	25	8	5	0	125	1	0	-	Iceland
T Gudjonsson	30	28	11	1	356	1	0	-	Iceland
Sasche Hohle	21	1	0	0	0	0	0	-	Germany
Sunday Oliseh	29	21	21	19	1822	4	0	-	Nigeria
Miroslav Stevic	34	26	21	8	1115	3	0	-	Serbia & Montenegro
Ersan Tekkan	19	1	0	0	0	0	0	-	Germany
Luciano Velardi	22	1	0	0	0	0	0	-	Italy
Anton Vriesde	35	21	10	5	522	2	0	-	Holland
Dariusz Wosz	35	33	33	22	2411	4	0	-	Germany
Tomasz Zdebel	30	34	34	29	2837	4	0	-	Poland
Forwards									
Delron Buckley	26	27	20	3	776	1	0	-	South Africa
Mamadou Diabang	25	31	24	5	967	1	0	1	Senegal (31)
Vahid Hashemian	27	33	32	28	2586	2	0	-	Iran
Peter Madsen	26	32	32	27	2667	4	0	4	Denmark (14)

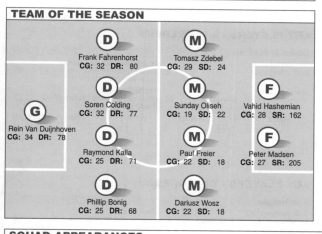

SQUAD APPEARANCES

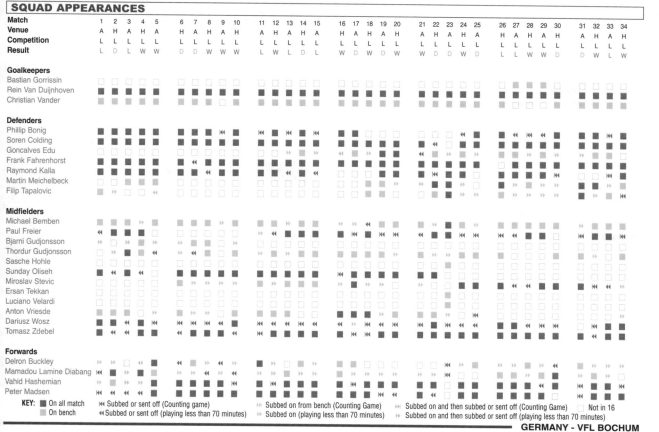

Match	1	2	3	4	5	6	7	8	9	10	11	12	13	14	15	16	17	18	19	20	21	22	23	24	25	26	27	28	29	30	31	32	33	34
Venue	A	H	A	H	A	H	A	H	A	H	A	H	A	H	A	H	A	H	A	H	A	H	A	H	A	H	A	H	A	H	A	H	A	H
Competition	L	L	L	L	L	L	L	L	L	L	L	L	L	L	L	L	L	L	L	L	L	L	L	L	L	L	L	L	L	L	L	L	L	L
Result	L	D	L	W	W	D	D	W	W	W	L	W	L	D	L	W	D	W	D	W	W	D	D	W	D	L	L	W	W	D	D	W	L	W

Goalkeepers
Bastian Gorrissin
Rein Van Duijnhoven
Christian Vander

Defenders
Phillip Bonig
Soren Colding
Goncalves Edu
Frank Fahrenhorst
Raymond Kalla
Martin Meichelbeck
Filip Tapalovic

Midfielders
Michael Bemben
Paul Freier
Bjarni Gudjonsson
Thordur Gudjonsson
Sasche Hohle
Sunday Oliseh
Miroslav Stevic
Ersan Tekkan
Luciano Velardi
Anton Vriesde
Dariusz Wosz
Tomasz Zdebel

Forwards
Delron Buckley
Mamadou Lamine Diabang
Vahid Hashemian
Peter Madsen

KEY: On all match · On bench · Subbed or sent off (Counting game) · Subbed or sent off (playing less than 70 minutes) · Subbed on from bench (Counting Game) · Subbed on (playing less than 70 minutes) · Subbed on and then subbed or sent off (Counting Game) · Subbed on and then subbed or sent off (playing less than 70 minutes) · Not in 16

BORUSSIA DORTMUND

Final Position: **6th**

KEY: Won / Drawn / Lost

							Attendance
1	lge	**Schalke**	A	D	2-2	Conceicao 65; Amoroso 90	61,014
2	lge	**Wolfsburg**	H	W	4-0	Rosicky 25,50; Amoroso 74; Koller 87	72,500
3	clql1	**Club Brugge**	A	L	1-2	Amoroso 53	18,559
4	lge	**1860 Munich**	H	W	3-1	Amoroso 46,56 pen; Koller 61	74,000
5	lge	**Cologne**	A	L	0-1		33,500
6	clql2	**Club Brugge**	H	L	2-4*	Amoroso 3; Ewerthon 86 (*on penalties)	62,000
7	lge	**W Bremen**	H	W	2-1	Ewerthon 17; Ismael 69 og	81,000
8	lge	**Stuttgart**	A	L	0-1		48,000
9	uc1rl1	**Austria Vienna**	A	W	2-1	Addo 38; Ricken 68	30,500
10	lge	**Freiburg**	H	W	1-0	Ewerthon 68	78,000
11	lge	**Eintr Frankfurt**	A	W	1-0	Reina 10	23,000
12	uc1rl2	**Austria Vienna**	H	W	1-0	Ricken 17	50,500
13	lge	**Hannover 96**	H	W	6-2	Ewerthon 35,76; Ricken 42; Kehl 57; Koller 65,77	78,000
14	lge	**Bochum**	A	L	0-3		33,000
15	lge	**Hamburg**	H	W	3-2	Koller 63,66 pen; Ewerthon 69	78,000
16	uc2rl1	**Sochaux**	H	D	2-2	Senesie 68; Ewerthon 76	40,500
17	lge	**Bayern Munich**	A	L	1-4	Koller 49	63,000
18	lge	**B Leverkusen**	H	D	2-2	Gambino 29,32	82,000
19	uc2rl2	**Sochaux**	A	L	0-4		22,000
20	lge	**Hansa Rostock**	A	L	1-2	Ewerthon 66	24,000
21	lge	**Hertha Berlin**	H	D	1-1	Leandro 67	77,000
22	lge	**B M'gladbach**	A	L	1-2	Koller 12	34,500
23	lge	**Kaiserslautern**	H	D	1-1	Koller 45	73,000
24	lge	**Schalke**	H	L	0-1		83,000
25	lge	**Wolfsburg**	A	W	4-2	Jensen 42 ; Koller 45; Frings 53; Ricken 78	26,000
26	lge	**1860 Munich**	A	W	2-0	Ewerthon 43 pen,60	25,000
27	lge	**Cologne**	H	W	1-0	Ewerthon 26	80,000
28	lge	**W Bremen**	A	L	0-2		43,000
29	lge	**Stuttgart**	H	L	0-2		83,000
30	lge	**Freiburg**	A	D	2-2	Dede 45; Hermel 59 og	25,000
31	lge	**Eintr Frankfurt**	H	W	2-0	Ewerthon 23; Koller 80	80,000
32	lge	**Hannover 96**	A	D	1-1	Frings 13	27,504
33	lge	**Bochum**	H	W	4-1	Koller 9; Gambino 31; Frings 45; Ewerthon 53	83,000
34	lge	**Hamburg**	A	W	2-0	Frings 8; Koller 28	53,000
35	lge	**Bayern Munich**	H	W	2-0	Ewerthon 56 pen; Worns 62	83,000
36	lge	**B Leverkusen**	A	L	0-3		22,500
37	lge	**Hansa Rostock**	H	W	4-1	Madouni 11; Ewerthon 35; Koller 37; Odonkor 77	82,500
38	lge	**Hertha Berlin**	A	L	2-6	Ewerthon 52,79	60,000
39	lge	**B M'gladbach**	H	W	3-1	Ewerthon 15; Dede 45; Koller 83	82,500
40	lge	**Kaiserslautern**	A	D	1-1	Koller 71	47,315

MONTHLY POINTS TALLY

Month	Points	%
AUGUST	7	58%
SEPTEMBER	6	67%
OCTOBER	6	67%
NOVEMBER	4	33%
DECEMBER	2	22%
JANUARY	0	0%
FEBRUARY	9	75%
MARCH	5	42%
APRIL	9	75%
MAY	7	58%

KEY PLAYERS - GOALSCORERS

Henrique da Souza Ewerthon

Goals in the League	14	**Player Strike Rate** Average number of minutes between League goals scored by player	158
Contribution to Attacking Power Average number of minutes between League team goals while on pitch	51	**Club Strike Rate** Average number of minutes between League goals scored by club	52

	PLAYER	LGE GOALS	POWER	STRIKE RATE
1	Henrique da Souza Ewerthon	14	51	158 mins
2	Jan Koller	16	50	175 mins
3	Torsten Frings	4	50	353 mins
4	Salvatore Gambino	3	45	471 mins

KEY PLAYERS - MIDFIELDERS

Leonardo De Deus Santos

Goals in the League	2	**Contribution to Attacking Power** Average number of minutes between League team goals while on pitch	45
Defensive Rating Average number of mins between League goals conceded while he was on the pitch	73	**Scoring Difference** Defensive Rating minus Contribution to Attacking Power	28

	PLAYER	LGE GOALS	DEF RATE	POWER	SCORE DIFF
1	Leonardo De Deus Santos	2	73	45	28 mins
2	Niclas Jensen	1	62	49	13 mins
3	Torsten Frings	4	61	50	11 mins
4	Tomas Rosicky	2	64	67	-3 mins

KEY PLAYERS - DEFENDERS

Andre Bergdolmo

Goals Conceded (GC) The number of League goals conceded while he was on the pitch	15	**Clean Sheets** In games when he played at least 70 minutes	4
Defensive Rating Ave number of mins between League goals conceded while on the pitch	80	**Club Defensive Rating** Average number of mins between League goals conceded by the club this season	64

	PLAYER	CON LGE	CLEAN SHEETS	DEF RATE
1	Andre Bergdolmo	15	4	80 mins
2	Christian Worns	39	8	71 mins
3	Sebastian Kehl	28	7	70 mins
4	Stefan Reuter	43	5	59 mins

KEY GOALKEEPER

Guillaume Warmuz

Goals Conceded in the League	23	**Counting Games** Games when he played at least 70 mins	17
Defensive Rating Ave number of mins between League goals conceded while on the pitch	67	**Clean Sheets** In games when he played at least 70 mins	5

LEAGUE GOALS

Jan Koller

Minutes on the pitch	2793	**Goals in the League**	16
League average (mins between goals)	175		

	PLAYER	MINS	GOALS	AVE
1	Koller	2793	16	175
2	Ewerthon	2209	14	158
3	Amoroso	344	4	86
4	Frings	1412	4	353
5	Gambino	1414	3	471
6	Ricken	1150	2	575
7	Rosicky	1540	2	770
8	Dede	1907	2	954
9	Worns	2769	1	2769
10	Leandro	255	1	255
11	Madouni	938	1	938
12	Kehl	1967	1	1967
	Other		8	
	TOTAL		5	

DISCIPLINARY RECORDS

	PLAYER	YELLOW	RED	AVE
1	Ricken	6	0	191
2	Dede	8	0	238
3	Rosicky	4	1	308
4	Odonkor	2	0	351
5	Frings	4	0	353
6	Evanilson	2	0	357
7	Reuter	7	0	360
8	Conceicao	2	0	455
9	Madouni	2	0	469
10	Kehl	3	1	491
11	Jensen	4	0	542
12	Demel	2	0	547
13	Worns	5	0	553
	Other	15	1	
	TOTAL	66	3	

TOP POINT EARNERS

	PLAYER	GAMES	AV PTS
1	Bergdolmo	13	1.92
2	Dede	21	1.90
3	Madouni	10	1.90
4	Addo	5	1.80
5	Jensen	24	1.79
6	Ewerthon	24	1.79
7	Warmuz	17	1.76
8	Conceicao	8	1.75
9	Amoroso	4	1.75
10	Demel	11	1.73
	CLUB AVERAGE:		1.62

LEAGUE APPEARANCES, BOOKINGS AND CAPS

	AGE (on 01/07/04)	IN NAMED 18	APPEARANCES	COUNTING GAMES	MINUTES ON PITCH	YELLOW CARDS	RED CARDS	THIS SEASON	HOME COUNTRY
Goalkeepers									
Guillaume Warmuz	33	33	17	17	1530	1	0	-	France
Roman Weidenfeller	23	34	17	17	1530	1	0	-	Germany
Defenders									
Andre Bergdolmo	32	21	16	13	1206	1	0	-	Norway
Markus Brzenska	20	18	5	0	49	2	1	-	Germany
Juan Fernandez	24	3	2	1	95	0	0	-	Argentina
Sebastian Kehl	24	23	23	21	1967	3	1	7	Germany (9)
Benjamin Knoche	25	3	0	0	0	0	0	-	Germany
Ahmed Madouni	23	14	13	10	938	2	0	-	France
Christoph Metzelder	23	0	0	0	0	0	0	-	Germany
Malte Metzelder	22	12	9	5	540	0	0	-	Germany
Stefan Reuter	37	33	31	24	2523	7	0	-	Germany
Deniz Sahin	26	2	0	0	0	0	0	-	Germany
Christian Worns	32	31	31	31	2769	5	0	7	Germany (9)
Midfielders									
Otto Addo	29	6	6	5	431	1	0	-	Ghana
Flavio Conceicao	30	18	14	8	911	2	0	-	Brazil
Leonardo	26	24	23	21	1907	8	0	-	Brazil
Guy Demel	23	14	13	11	1095	2	0	-	France
Ferreira Evanilson	28	12	10	7	715	2	0	-	Brazil
Juan Fernandez	24	8	8	6	650	1	0	-	Argentina
Torsten Frings	27	16	16	16	1412	4	0	4	Germany (9)
Stefan Hoffmann	20	7	0	0	0	0	0	-	Germany
Niclas Jensen	29	34	25	24	2170	4	0	8	Denmark (14)
Santos Leandro	27	11	6	2	255	0	0	-	Brazil
Lars Ricken	27	26	21	9	1150	6	0	-	Germany
Tomas Rosicky	23	20	19	17	1540	4	1	4	Czech Republic (10)
Amos Sasy	25	2	0	0	0	0	0	-	Israel
Sahr Senesie	19	24	11	3	387	0	0	-	Sierra Leone
Forwards									
Marcio Amoroso	30	4	4	4	344	1	0	-	Brazil
HenriqueEwerthon	23	31	29	24	2209	3	0	-	Brazil
Salvatore Gambino	20	26	20	14	1414	1	0	-	Italy
Heiko Herrlich	32	2	0	0	0	0	0	-	Germany
Jan Koller	31	32	32	31	2793	2	0	7	Czech Republic (10)
David Odonkor	20	31	23	3	703	2	0	-	Germany
Giuseppe Reina	32	16	11	1	275	1	0	-	Germany
Anderson Thiago	19	1	0	0	0	0	0	-	Brazil

TEAM OF THE SEASON

G
Guillaume Warmuz
CG: 17 DR: 67
D
Andre Bergdolmo
CG: 13 DR: 80
D
Christian Worns
CG: 31 DR: 71
D
Sebastian Kehl
CG: 21 DR: 70
D
Stefan Reuter
CG: 24 DR: 59
M
Leonardo De Santos
CG: 21 SD: 28
M
Niclas Jensen
CG: 24 SD: 13
M
Torsten Frings
CG: 16 SD: 11
M
Tomas Rosicky
CG: 17 SD: -3
F
Henrique Ewerthon
CG: 24 SR: 158
F
Jan Koller
CG: 31 SR: 175

SQUAD APPEARANCES

Match	1	2	3	4	5	6	7	8	9	10	11	12	13	14	15	16	17	18	19	20	21	22	23	24	25	26	27	28	29	30	31	32	33	34	35	36	37	38	39	40
Venue	A	H	A	H	A	H	H	A	A	H	A	H	H	A	H	H	A	H	A	A	H	A	H	H	A	A	H	A	H	A	H	A	H	A	H	A	H	A	H	A
Competition	L	L	C	L	L	C	L	L	E	L	L	E	L	L	L	E	L	L	E	L	L	L	L	L	L	L	L	L	L	L	L	L	L	L	L	L	L	L	L	L
Result	D	W	L	W	L	L	W	L	W	W	W	W	W	L	W	D	L	D	L	L	D	L	D	L	W	W	W	L	L	D	W	D	W	W	W	L	W	L	W	D

Goalkeepers
Guillaume Warmuz
Roman Weidenfeller
Defenders
Andre Bergdolmo
Markus Brzenska
Juan Ramon Fernandez
Sebastian Kehl
Benjamin Knoche
Ahmed Reda Madouni
Christoph Metzelder
Malte Metzelder
Stefan Reuter
Deniz Sahin
Christian Worns
Midfielders
Otto Addo
Flavio Conceicao
Leonardo De Deus Santos
Guy Demel
Ferreira Evanilson
Juan Ramon Fernandez
Torsten Frings
Stefan Hoffmann
Niclas Jensen
De Deus Santos Leandro
Lars Ricken
Tomas Rosicky
Amos Sasy
Sahr Senesie
Forwards
Marcio Amoroso
Henrique Ewerthon
Salvatore Gambino
Heiko Herrlich
Jan Koller
avid Odonkor
Giuseppe Reina
Anderson de Souza Thiago

KEY: ■ On all match ■ On bench | ⏮ Subbed or sent off (Counting game) « Subbed or sent off (playing less than 70 minutes) | ⏭ Subbed on from bench (Counting Game) » Subbed on (playing less than 70 minutes) | Subbed on and then subbed or sent off (Counting Game) Subbed on and then subbed or sent off (playing less than 70 minutes) | □ Not in 16

SCHALKE 04

Final Position: **7th**

KEY: Won Drawn Lost

							Attendance
1	lge	B Dortmund	H	D	2-2	Altintop 39,58	61,014
2	lge	1860 Munich	A	D	1-1	Rodriguez 56	33,000
3	lge	Cologne	H	W	2-1	Agali 42; Altintop 90	61,000
4	lge	W Bremen	A	L	1-4	Agali 82	36,000
5	lge	Stuttgart	H	D	0-0		61,000
6	lge	Freiburg	A	L	1-2	Rodriguez 13	25,000
7	uc1rl1	NK Kamen Veli	A	D	0-0		9,000
8	lge	Eintr Frankfurt	H	D	1-1	Rodriguez 33	61,000
9	lge	Hannover 96	A	W	2-1	Asamoah 27; Rodriguez 41	22,000
10	uc1rl2	NK Kamen Veli	H	W	1-0	Hanke 76	52,600
11	lge	Bochum	H	L	0-2		61,178
12	lge	Hamburg	A	D	2-2	Matellan 73; Glieder 90	55,500
13	lge	Bayern Munich	H	W	2-0	Hajto 16 pen; Oude Kamphuis 79	61,000
14	uc2rl1	Brondby	H	W	2-1	Hanke 60,72	50,000
15	lge	B Leverkusen	A	L	1-3	Hanke 14	22,500
16	lge	Hansa Rostock	H	L	0-1		61,000
17	uc2rl2	Brondby	A	L	1-3*	Agali 55 (*on penalties)	26,000
18	lge	Hertha Berlin	A	W	3-1	Oude Kamphuis 59; Waldoch 68; Asamoah 81	37,000
19	lge	B M'gladbach	H	W	2-1	Seitz 2,55	61,000
20	lge	Kaiserslautern	A	W	2-0	Asamoah 6; Agali 85	40,000
21	lge	Wolfsburg	H	D	1-1	Altintop 26	60,000
22	lge	B Dortmund	A	W	1-0	Sand 89	83,000
23	lge	1860 Munich	H	D	0-0		61,000
24	lge	Cologne	A	W	2-0	van Kerckhoven 25; Delura 81	51,000
25	lge	W Bremen	H	D	0-0		61,000
26	lge	Stuttgart	A	D	0-0		42,000
27	lge	Freiburg	H	W	3-0	Sand 43,52; Glieder 62	61,000
28	lge	Eintr Frankfurt	A	L	0-3		35,255
29	lge	Hannover 96	H	D	2-2	Mertesacker 63 og; Sand 84	61,266
30	lge	Bochum	A	W	2-1	Klasener 79; Delura 83	32,645
31	lge	Hamburg	H	W	4-1	Waldoch 10; Sand 29; Lamotte 43; Delura 55	61,000
32	lge	Bayern Munich	A	L	1-2	Vermant 4 pen	63,000
33	lge	B Leverkusen	H	L	2-3	Delura 56; Hanke 77	61,266
34	lge	Hansa Rostock	A	L	1-3	Asamoah 10	26,000
35	lge	Hertha Berlin	H	W	3-0	Altintop 19; Bohme 52; Sand 58	61,266
36	lge	B M'gladbach	A	L	0-2		34,500
37	lge	Kaiserslautern	H	W	4-1	Reuter 2 og; Sand 24,67; Vermant 34 pen	61,266
38	lge	Wolfsburg	A	D	1-1	Franz 20 og	30,000

MONTHLY POINTS TALLY

Month	Points	%
AUGUST	5	42%
SEPTEMBER	2	22%
OCTOBER	4	44%
NOVEMBER	6	50%
DECEMBER	7	78%
JANUARY	3	100%
FEBRUARY	6	50%
MARCH	7	58%
APRIL	3	25%
MAY	7	58%

KEY PLAYERS - GOALSCORERS

Ebbe Sand

Goals in the League	8	Player Strike Rate Average number of minutes between League goals scored by player	278
Contribution to Attacking Power Average number of minutes between League team goals while on pitch	61	Club Strike Rate Average number of minutes between League goals scored by club	62

	PLAYER	LGE GOALS	POWER	STRIKE RATE
1	Ebbe Sand	8	61	278 mins
2	Gerald Asamoah	4	67	419 mins
3	Hamit Altintop	5	60	499 mins
4	Tomasz Waldoch	2	54	818 mins

KEY PLAYERS - MIDFIELDERS

Sven Vermant

Goals in the League	2	Contribution to Attacking Power Average number of minutes between League team goals while on pitch	57
Defensive Rating Average number of mins between League goals conceded while he was on the pitch	79	Scoring Difference Defensive Rating minus Contribution to Attacking Power	22

	PLAYER	LGE GOALS	DEF RATE	POWER	SCORE DIFF
1	Sven Vermant	2	79	57	22 mins
2	Hamit Altintop	5	78	61	17 mins
3	Christian Poulsen	0	84	73	11 mins
4	Levan Kobiashvili	0	73	68	5 mins

KEY PLAYERS - DEFENDERS

Thomas Klasener

Goals Conceded (GC) The number of League goals conceded while he was on the pitch	28	Clean Sheets In games when he played at least 70 minutes	6
Defensive Rating Ave number of mins between League goals conceded while on the pitch	75	Club Defensive Rating Average number of mins between League goals conceded by the club this season	73

	PLAYER	CON LGE	CLEAN SHEETS	DEF RATE
1	Thomas Klasener	28	6	75 mins
2	Nico van Kerckhoven	31	7	74 mins
3	Tomasz Hajto	19	3	73 mins
4	Tomasz Waldoch	23	4	71 mins

KEY GOALKEEPER

Frank Rost

Goals Conceded in the League	30	Counting Games Games when he played at least 70 mins	27
Defensive Rating Ave number of mins between League goals conceded while on the pitch	81	Clean Sheets In games when he played at least 70 mins	9

LEAGUE GOALS

Ebbe Sand

Minutes on the pitch	2221	Goals in the League	8
League average (mins between goals)	278		

	PLAYER	MINS	GOALS	AVE
1	Sand	2221	8	278
2	Altintop	2495	5	499
3	Delura	840	4	210
4	Asamoah	1675	4	419
5	Rodriguez	1397	4	349
6	Agali	785	3	262
7	Glieder	697	2	349
8	Seitz	992	2	496
9	Hanke	873	2	437
10	Oude Kamphuis	1093	2	547
11	Vermant	2062	2	1031
12	Waldoch	1635	2	818
	Other		9	
	TOTAL		49	

DISCIPLINARY RECORDS

	PLAYER	YELLOW	RED	AVE
1	Agali	6	0	130
2	Matellan	3	2	131
3	Hajto	9	0	153
4	Bohme	3	0	310
5	Pinto	2	0	321
6	Seitz	2	1	330
7	Rodriguez	4	0	349
8	Oude Kamphuis	3	0	364
9	Asamoah	3	1	418
10	Kobiashvili	5	0	478
11	Altintop	5	0	499
12	Klasener	3	1	526
13	Poulsen	4	0	527
	Other	15	0	
	TOTAL	67	5	

TOP POINT EARNERS

	PLAYER	GAMES	AV PTS
1	Hanke	4	2.25
2	Glieder	6	2.17
3	Bohme	8	2.13
4	Oude Kamphuis	11	1.91
5	Seitz	9	1.78
6	Unlu	4	1.75
7	Vermant	21	1.71
8	Hajto	13	1.69
9	Waldoch	18	1.67
10	Pinto	5	1.60
	CLUB AVERAGE:		**1.47**

TEAM OF THE SEASON

D
Thomas Klasener
CG: 22 DR: 75
M
Sven Vermant
CG: 21 SD: 22
D
Nico van Kerckhoven
CG: 25 DR: 74
M
Hamit Altintop
CG: 27 SD: 17
F
Ebbe Sand
CG: 23 SR: 278
G
Frank Rost
CG: 27 DR: 81
D
Tomasz Hajto
CG: 13 DR: 73
M
Christian Poulsen
CG: 22 SD: 11
F
Gerald Asamoah
CG: 14 SR: 419
D
Tomasz Waldoch
CG: 18 DR: 71
M
Levan Kobiashvili
CG: 26 SD: 5

LEAGUE APPEARANCES, BOOKINGS AND CAPS

	AGE (on 01/07/04)	IN NAMED 18	APPEARANCES	COUNTING GAMES	MINUTES ON PITCH	YELLOW CARDS	RED CARDS	THIS SEASON	HOME COUNTRY
Goalkeepers									
C Heimeroth	22	19	3	3	270	0	0	-	Germany
Oliver Reck	39	5	0	0	0	0	0	-	Germany
Frank Rost	31	27	27	27	2430	3	0	-	Germany
Volkan Unlu	20	15	4	4	360	0	0	-	Turkey
Defenders									
Alcides Eduardo	19	4	3	1	162	0	0	-	Brazil
Tomasz Hajto	31	24	19	13	1382	9	0	-	Poland
Thomas Klasener	27	27	26	22	2104	3	1	-	Germany
Fabian Lamotte	21	10	7	5	487	0	0	-	Germany
Anibal Matellan	27	13	10	6	658	3	2	-	Argentina
Dario Rodriguez	29	25	22	12	1397	4	0	1	Uruguay (25)
M van Hoogdalem	32	2	1	1	90	0	0	-	Holland
Nico van Kerckhoven	33	28	27	25	2279	1	0	-	Belgium
Tomasz Waldoch	33	32	20	18	1635	2	0	-	Poland
Midfielders									
Hamit Altintop	21	30	30	27	2495	5	0	-	Turkey
Jorg Bohme	30	15	14	8	932	3	0	-	Germany
Simon Cziommer	23	9	2	0	25	1	0	-	Germany
Levan Kobiashvili	26	29	29	26	2394	5	0	-	Georgia
N Oude Kamphuis	26	14	14	11	1093	3	0	-	Holland
Christian Pander	20	0	0	0	0	0	0	-	Germany
Christian Poulsen	24	27	27	22	2109	4	0	4	Denmark (14)
Filip Trojan	21	25	8	0	209	1	0	-	Czech Republic
Gustavo Varela	26	6	1	0	19	0	0	-	Uruguay
Sven Vermant	31	28	25	21	2062	3	0	2	Belgium (17)
Forwards									
Victor Agali	25	17	12	7	785	6	0	-	Nigeria
Eduardo Alcides	19	3	3	1	209	0	0	-	Brazil
Gerald Asamoah	25	25	24	14	1675	3	1	-	Germany
Michael Delura	19	16	15	6	840	0	0	-	Germany
Eduard Glieder	35	20	15	6	697	0	0	-	Austria
Michael Hanke	20	29	23	4	873	0	0	-	Germany
Sergio Pinto	23	19	13	5	642	2	0	-	Portugal
Ebbe Sand	31	31	30	23	2221	4	0	6	Denmark (14)
Jochen Seitz	27	26	18	9	992	2	1	-	Germany

SQUAD APPEARANCES

Match	1	2	3	4	5	6	7	8	9	10	11	12	13	14	15	16	17	18	19	20	21	22	23	24	25	26	27	28	29	30	31	32	33	34	35	36	37	38
Venue	H	A	H	A	H	A	A	H	A	H	H	A	H	H	A	H	A	A	H	A	H	A	H	A	H	A	H	A	H	A	H	A	H	A	H	A	H	A
Competition	L	L	L	L	L	L	E	L	L	E	L	L	L	E	L	L	E	L	L	L	L	L	L	L	L	L	L	L	L	L	L	L	L	L	L	L	L	L
Result	D	D	W	L	D	L	D	D	W	W	L	D	W	W	L	L	L	W	W	W	D	W	D	W	D	D	W	L	D	W	W	L	L	L	W	L	W	D

Goalkeepers
Christofer Heimeroth
Oliver Reck
Frank Rost
Volkan Unlu

Defenders
Alcides Eduardo
Tomasz Hajto
Thomas Klasener
Fabian Lamotte
Anibal Matellan
Dario Rodriguez
Marco van Hoogdalem
Nico van Kerckhoven
Tomasz Waldoch

Midfielders
Hamit Altintop
Jorg Bohme
Simon Cziommer
Levan Kobiashvili
Niels Oude Kamphuis
Christian Pander
Christian Poulsen
Filip Trojan
Gustavo Antonio Varela
Sven Vermant

Forwards
Victor Agali
Eduardo Alcides
Gerald Asamoah
Michael Delura
Eduard Glieder
Michael Hanke
Sergio Pinto
Ebbe Sand
Jochen Seitz

KEY: ■ On all match | ■ On bench | ⏮ Subbed or sent off (Counting game) | ◀◀ Subbed or sent off (playing less than 70 minutes) | ▶▶ Subbed on from bench (Counting Game) | ▶▶ Subbed on (playing less than 70 minutes) | ▶▶ Subbed on and then subbed or sent off (Counting Game) | ▶▶ Subbed on and then subbed or sent off (playing less than 70 minutes) | □ Not in 16

HAMBURG SV

8th

KEY: Won Drawn Lost

							Attendance
1	lge	Hannover 96	H	L	0-3		53,224
2	lge	Bochum	A	D	1-1	Takahara 18	20,400
3	lge	Wolfsburg	A	L	1-5	Barbarez 48	28,000
4	lge	Bayern Munich	H	L	0-2		55,000
5	lge	B Leverkusen	A	L	0-1		22,500
6	lge	Hansa Rostock	H	W	2-1	Romeo 68; Reinhardt 86	44,000
7	uc1rl1	Dnipro	H	W	2-1	Hoogma 49 pen; Romeo 81	26,839
8	lge	Hertha Berlin	A	D	1-1	Ujfalusi 90	37,000
9	lge	B M'gladbach	H	W	2-1	Barbarez 59,74	51,000
10	uc1rl2	Dnipro	A	L	0-3		25,700
11	lge	Kaiserslautern	A	L	0-4		38,016
12	lge	Schalke	H	D	2-2	Romeo 29,68	55,500
13	lge	B Dortmund	A	L	2-3	Reinhardt 14; Romeo 60	78,000
14	lge	1860 Munich	H	W	3-1	Romeo 54,76; Mahdavikia 79 pen	48,000
15	lge	Cologne	A	W	1-0	Barbarez 42	40,000
16	lge	W Bremen	H	D	1-1	Rahn 50	55,000
17	lge	Stuttgart	A	D	0-0		38,000
18	lge	Freiburg	H	W	4-1	Reinhardt 8; Barbarez 19; Maltritz 66; Rahn 87	42,000
19	lge	Eintr Frankfurt	A	W	3-2	Beinlich 16; Takahara 52; Barbarez 85	19,000
20	lge	Hannover 96	A	L	2-3	Barbarez 7; Romeo 77	23,000
21	lge	Bochum	H	D	1-1	Romeo 82	38,000
22	lge	Wolfsburg	H	W	2-0	Barbarez 18; Rahn 88	36,000
23	lge	Bayern Munich	A	L	0-1		38,000
24	lge	B Leverkusen	H	W	3-1	Hoogma 11; Mahdavikia 17 pen; Romeo 37	43,000
25	lge	Hansa Rostock	A	L	0-3		25,000
26	lge	Hertha Berlin	H	W	2-0	Rahn 33; Romeo 71	42,000
27	lge	B M'gladbach	A	L	0-3		31,000
28	lge	Kaiserslautern	H	W	3-2	Rahn 30,70; Romeo 47	41,020
29	lge	Schalke	A	L	1-4	Mahdavikia 35 pen	61,000
30	lge	B Dortmund	H	L	0-2		53,000
31	lge	1860 Munich	A	W	2-1	Santos 65 og; Mahdavikia 79	20,000
32	lge	Cologne	H	W	4-2	Rahn 41; Barbarez 52; Jarolim 64; Fukal 68	48,413
33	lge	W Bremen	A	L	0-6		42,500
34	lge	Stuttgart	H	W	2-1	Beinlich 38; Hoogma 47	54,500
35	lge	Freiburg	A	D	0-0		25,000
36	lge	Eintr Frankfurt	H	W	2-1	Mahdavikia 27; Barbarez 57	53,000

MONTHLY POINTS TALLY

Month	Points	%
AUGUST	1	8%
SEPTEMBER	4	44%
OCTOBER	4	44%
NOVEMBER	7	58%
DECEMBER	7	78%
JANUARY	0	0%
FEBRUARY	7	47%
MARCH	6	50%
APRIL	6	50%
MAY	7	58%

KEY PLAYERS - GOALSCORERS

Bernardo Romeo

Goals in the League	11	Player Strike Rate Average number of minutes between League goals scored by player	171
Contribution to Attacking Power Average number of minutes between League team goals while on pitch	56	Club Strike Rate Average number of minutes between League goals scored by club	65

	PLAYER	LGE GOALS	POWER	STRIKE RATE
1	Bernardo Romeo	11	56	171 mins
2	Sergei Barbarez	10	63	279 mins
3	Mehdi Mahdavikia	5	60	534 mins
4	Bastian Reinhardt	3	67	606 mins

KEY PLAYERS - MIDFIELDERS

David Jarolim

Goals in the League	1	Contribution to Attacking Power Average number of minutes between League team goals while on pitch	58
Defensive Rating Average number of mins between League goals conceded while he was on the pitch	58	Scoring Difference Defensive Rating minus Contribution to Attacking Power	0

	PLAYER	LGE GOALS	DEF RATE	POWER	SCORE DIFF
1	David Jarolim	1	58	58	0 mins
2	Sergei Barbarez	10	57	63	-6 mins
3	Raphael Wicky	0	52	63	-11 mins
4	Stefan Beinlich	2	57	73	-16 mins

KEY PLAYERS - DEFENDERS

Marcel Maltritz

Goals Conceded (GC) The number of League goals conceded while he was on the pitch	25	Clean Sheets In games when he played at least 70 minutes	2
Defensive Rating Ave number of mins between League goals conceded while on the pitch	60	Club Defensive Rating Average number of mins between League goals conceded by the club this season	51

	PLAYER	CON LGE	CLEAN SHEETS	DEF RATE
1	Marcel Maltritz	25	2	60 mins
2	Nico Hoogma	49	5	52 mins
3	Bastian Reinhardt	36	2	51 mins
4	Tomas Ujfalusi	48	4	49 mins

KEY GOALKEEPER

Stefan Wachter

Goals Conceded in the League	35	Counting Games Games when he played at least 70 mins	24
Defensive Rating Ave number of mins between League goals conceded while on the pitch	61	Clean Sheets In games when he played at least 70 mins	5

LEAGUE GOALS

Bernardo Romeo

Minutes on the pitch	1880	Goals in the League	11
League average (mins between goals)	171		

	PLAYER	MINS	GOALS	AVE
1	Romeo	1880	11	171
2	Barbarez	2789	10	279
3	Rahn	1254	7	179
4	Mahdavikia	2672	5	534
5	Reinhardt	1818	3	606
6	Hoogma	2553	2	1277
7	Takahara	1646	2	823
8	Beinlich	1815	2	908
9	Maltritz	1509	1	1509
10	Jarolim	2199	1	2199
11	Ujfalusi	2329	1	2329
12	Fukal	434	1	434
	Other		1	
	TOTAL		47	

DISCIPLINARY

	PLAYER	YELLOW	RED	AVE
1	Hollerbach	10	0	106
2	Benjamin	6	1	107
3	Reinhardt	6	0	303
4	Rahn	4	0	313
5	Wicky	7	0	335
6	Barbarez	8	0	348
7	Schlicke	4	0	353
8	Hoogma	6	1	364
9	Jarolim	6	0	366
10	Maltritz	3	0	503
11	Jacobsen	1	0	531
12	Takahara	3	0	548
13	Beinlich	3	0	605
	Other	11	1	
	TOTAL	78	3	

TOP POINT EARNERS

	PLAYER	GAMES	AV PTS
1	Benjamin	3	3.00
2	Kling	7	1.86
3	Romeo	17	1.71
4	Jarolim	24	1.67
5	Wachter	23	1.65
6	Wicky	24	1.63
7	Hoogma	27	1.56
8	Rahn	11	1.55
9	Barbarez	30	1.50
10	Mahdavikia	29	1.48
	CLUB AVERAGE:		1.44

LEAGUE APPEARANCES, BOOKINGS AND CAPS

	AGE (on 01/07/04)	IN NAMED 18	APPEARANCES	COUNTING GAMES	MINUTES ON PITCH	YELLOW CARDS	RED CARDS	THIS SEASON	HOME COUNTRY
Goalkeepers									
Michael Frech	28	6	0	0	0	0	0	-	Germany
M Pieckenhagen	32	9	9	9	810	1	0	-	Germany
Tom Starke	23	17	2	1	129	0	0	-	Germany
Stefan Wachter	26	33	24	23	2121	0	0	-	Germany
Defenders									
Milan Fukal	29	13	7	5	434	2	1	-	Czech Republic
Nico Hoogma	35	29	29	27	2553	6	1	-	Holland
Lars Jacobsen	24	14	9	5	531	1	0	-	Denmark
Stephan Kling	23	30	15	7	927	1	0	-	Germany
Marcel Maltritz	25	18	18	15	1509	3	0	-	Germany
Bastian Reinhardt	28	31	26	18	1818	6	0	-	Germany
Bjorn Schlicke	23	27	20	13	1414	4	0	-	Germany
Tomas Ujfalusi	26	26	26	26	2329	3	0	5	Czech Republic (10)
Midfielders									
Sergei Barbarez	32	32	32	30	2789	8	0	-	Bosnia
Stefan Beinlich	32	29	23	20	1815	3	0	-	Germany
Collin Benjamin	25	24	16	3	755	6	1	-	Namibia
Fabian Brocker	21	3	0	0	0	0	0	-	Germany
Rodolfo Cardoso	35	21	9	0	242	0	0	-	Argentina
Vjatscheslaw Hleb	21	16	7	0	221	0	0	-	Belarus
Bernd Hollerbach	34	16	14	9	1060	10	0	-	Germany
David Jarolim	25	27	26	24	2199	6	0	-	Czech Republic
Alexander Meier	21	10	4	0	100	0	0	-	Germany
Christian Rahn	25	25	22	11	1254	4	0	4	Germany (9)
Naohiro Takahara	25	30	29	10	1646	3	0	-	Japan
Raphael Wicky	27	32	29	24	2347	7	0	-	Switzerland
Forwards									
Mehdi Mahdavikia	26	32	32	29	2672	1	0	-	Iran
Bernardo Romeo	26	29	29	17	1880	3	0	-	Argentina
Eren Sen	19	8	1	0	15	0	0	-	Germany

TEAM OF THE SEASON

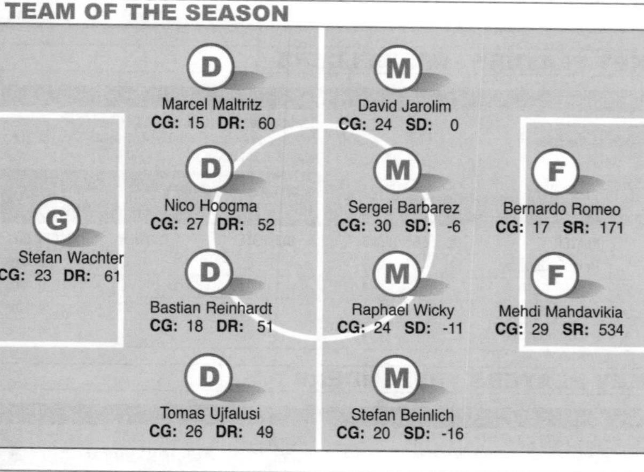

D
Marcel Maltritz
CG: 15 DR: 60
M
David Jarolim
CG: 24 SD: 0
D
Nico Hoogma
CG: 27 DR: 52
M
Sergei Barbarez
CG: 30 SD: -6
F
Bernardo Romeo
CG: 17 SR: 171
G
Stefan Wachter
CG: 23 DR: 61
D
Bastian Reinhardt
CG: 18 DR: 51
M
Raphael Wicky
CG: 24 SD: -11
F
Mehdi Mahdavikia
CG: 29 SR: 534
D
Tomas Ujfalusi
CG: 26 DR: 49
M
Stefan Beinlich
CG: 20 SD: -16

SQUAD APPEARANCES

Match	1	2	3	4	5	6	7	8	9	10	11	12	13	14	15	16	17	18	19	20	21	22	23	24	25	26	27	28	29	30	31	32	33	34	35	36
Venue	H	A	A	H	A	H	H	A	H	A	A	H	A	H	A	H	A	H	A	A	H	H	A	H	A	H	A	H	A	H	A	H	A	H	A	H
Competition	L	L	L	L	L	L	E	L	L	E	L	L	L	L	L	L	L	L	L	L	L	L	L	L	L	L	L	L	L	L	L	L	L	L	L	L
Result	L	D	L	L	L	W	W	D	W	L	L	D	L	W	W	D	D	W	W	L	D	W	L	W	L	W	L	W	L	L	W	W	L	W	D	W

Goalkeepers
Michael Frech
Martin Pieckenhagen
Tom Starke
Stefan Wachter

Defenders
Milan Fukal
Nico Hoogma
Lars Jacobsen
Stephan Kling
Marcel Maltritz
Bastian Reinhardt
Bjorn Schlicke
Tomas Ujfalusi

Midfielders
Sergei Barbarez
Stefan Beinlich
Collin Benjamin
Fabian Brocker
Rodolfo Esteban Cardoso
Vjatscheslaw Hleb
Bernd Hollerbach
David Jarolim
Alexander Meier
Christian Rahn
Naohiro Takahara
Raphael Wicky

Forwards
Mehdi Mahdavikia
Bernardo Romeo
Eren Sen

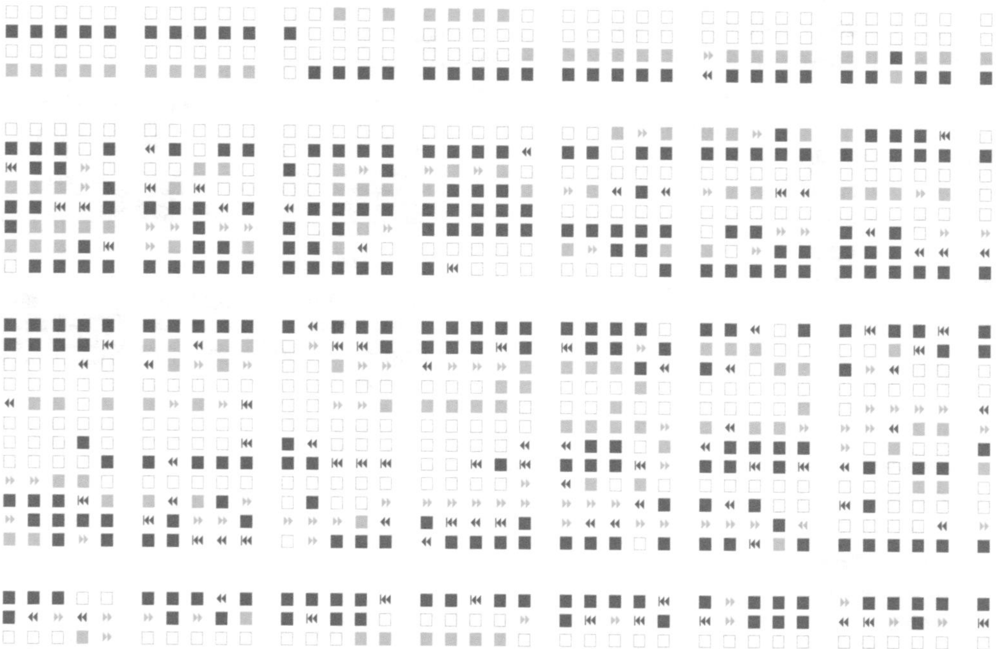

KEY: ■ On all match
■ On bench
⏮ Subbed or sent off (Counting game)
« Subbed or sent off (playing less than 70 minutes)
⏭ Subbed on from bench (Counting Game)
» Subbed on (playing less than 70 minutes)
⏭ Subbed on and then subbed or sent off (Counting Game)
» Subbed on and then subbed or sent off (playing less than 70 minutes)
□ Not in 16

HANSA ROSTOCK 9th

KEY: Won Drawn Lost

							Attendance
1	lge	Stuttgart	H	L	0-2		26,000
2	lge	Freiburg	A	D	2-2	Prica 11; Max 45	24,000
3	lge	Eintr Frankfurt	H	W	3-0	Max 21,54,66	20,000
4	lge	Hannover 96	A	D	3-3	Max 44,63; Vorbeck 90	21,000
5	lge	Bochum	H	L	0-2		15,000
6	lge	Hamburg	A	L	1-2	Max 10	44,000
7	lge	Bayern Munich	H	L	1-2	Linke 47 og	29,000
8	lge	B Leverkusen	A	L	0-3		22,500
9	lge	Wolfsburg	A	L	1-3	Rydlewicz 43	19,846
10	lge	Hertha Berlin	H	L	0-1		20,000
11	lge	B M'gladbach	A	D	1-1	Persson 33	29,000
12	lge	Kaiserslautern	H	W	4-0	Rydlewicz 15 ; Di Salvo 22,33; Max 79	12,000
13	lge	Schalke	A	W	1-0	Tjikuzu 52	61,000
14	lge	B Dortmund	H	W	2-1	Max 54,87	24,000
15	lge	1860 Munich	A	W	4-1	Rydlewicz 9; Max 17 pen,80; Shultz 68	13,000
16	lge	Cologne	H	D	1-1	Prica 64 pen	20,000
17	lge	W Bremen	A	L	0-3		36,000
18	lge	Stuttgart	A	L	0-2		42,000
19	lge	Freiburg	H	W	4-1	Di Salvo 8; Arvidsson 77; Plassnegger 81; Tjikuzu 90	20,000
20	lge	Eintr Frankfurt	A	D	1-1	Arvidsson 82	23,000
21	lge	Hannover 96	H	W	3-1	Arvidsson 12; Max 33,39	12,000
22	lge	Bochum	A	D	0-0		21,000
23	lge	Hamburg	H	W	3-0	Melkam 5; Arvidsson 19; Di Salvo 79	25,000
24	lge	Bayern Munich	A	D	3-3	Max 53; Arvidsson 65; Rasmussen 71	35,000
25	lge	B Leverkusen	H	L	0-2		22,000
26	lge	Wolfsburg	H	W	3-1	Arvidsson 10; Max 34; Mohrle 37	19,800
27	lge	Hertha Berlin	A	D	1-1	Rasmussen 65	43,000
28	lge	B M'gladbach	H	L	1-2	Rydlewicz 28	25,800
29	lge	Kaiserslautern	A	L	2-3	Rydlewicz 37,71 pen	35,000
30	lge	Schalke	H	W	3-1	Tjikuzu 35; Max 62,68	26,000
31	lge	B Dortmund	A	L	1-4	Max 67	82,500
32	lge	1860 Munich	H	W	3-0	Max 15; Rydlewicz 48 pen; Tjikuzu 82	23,000
33	lge	Cologne	A	L	0-4		40,000
34	lge	W Bremen	H	W	3-1	Prica 29; Krstajic 47 og; Lantz 74 pen	29,000

MONTHLY POINTS TALLY

Month	Points	%
AUGUST	5	42%
SEPTEMBER	0	0%
OCTOBER	0	0%
NOVEMBER	10	83%
DECEMBER	4	44%
JANUARY	0	0%
FEBRUARY	8	67%
MARCH	7	58%
APRIL	4	33%
MAY	6	50%

KEY PLAYERS - GOALSCORERS

Martin Max

Goals in the League	20	Player Strike Rate Average number of minutes between League goals scored by player	143
Contribution to Attacking Power Average number of minutes between League team goals while on pitch	58	Club Strike Rate Average number of minutes between League goals scored by club	56

	PLAYER	LGE GOALS	POWER	STRIKE RATE
1	Martin Max	20	58	143 mins
2	Rene Rydlewicz	7	51	304 mins
3	Razundara Tjikuzu	4	53	719 mins
4	Thomas Shultz	1	52	2222 mins

KEY PLAYERS - MIDFIELDERS

Rene Rydlewicz

Goals in the League	7	Contribution to Attacking Power Average number of minutes between League team goals while on pitch	52
Defensive Rating Average number of mins between League goals conceded while he was on the pitch	61	Scoring Difference Defensive Rating minus Contribution to Attacking Power	9

	PLAYER	LGE GOALS	DEF RATE	POWER	SCORE DIFF
1	Rene Rydlewicz	7	61	52	9 mins
2	Marcus Lantz	1	61	52	9 mins
3	Thomas Shultz	1	57	53	4 mins
4	Joakim Persson	1	55	59	-4 mins

KEY PLAYERS - DEFENDERS

Uwe Mohrle

Goals Conceded (GC) The number of League goals conceded while he was on the pitch	35	Clean Sheets In games when he played at least 70 minutes	5
Defensive Rating Ave number of mins between League goals conceded while on the pitch	64	Club Defensive Rating Average number of mins between League goals conceded by the club this season	57

	PLAYER	CON LGE	CLEAN SHEETS	DEF RATE
1	Uwe Mohrle	35	5	64 mins
2	Razundara Tjikuzu	46	6	63 mins
3	Ronald Maul	32	5	60 mins
4	Delano Hill	51	6	58 mins

KEY GOALKEEPER

Matthias Schober

Goals Conceded in the League	54	Counting Games Games when he played at least 70 mins	33
Defensive Rating Ave number of mins between League goals conceded while on the pitch	55	Clean Sheets In games when he played at least 70 mins	5

LEAGUE GOALS

Martin Max

Minutes on the pitch	2866	Goals in the League	20
League average (mins between goals)	143		

	PLAYER	MINS	GOALS	AVE
1	Max	2866	20	143
2	Rydlewicz	2126	7	304
3	Arvidsson	1159	6	193
4	Tjikuzu	2877	4	719
5	Di Salvo	771	4	193
6	Prica	1061	3	354
7	Mohrle	2250	1	2250
8	Lantz	2850	1	2850
9	Vorbeck	215	1	215
10	Shultz	2222	1	2222
11	Melkam	1073	1	1073
12	Plassnegger	945	1	945
	Other		5	
	TOTAL		55	

DISCIPLINARY

	PLAYER	YELLOW	RED	AVE
1	Plassnegger	4	2	157
2	Aduobe	4	0	176
3	Di Salvo	4	0	192
4	Kientz	4	0	202
5	Rydlewicz	7	1	265
6	Maul	7	0	272
7	Lantz	9	0	316
8	Shultz	6	1	317
9	Prica	3	0	353
10	Max	7	0	409
11	Melkam	2	0	536
12	Arvidsson	2	0	579
13	Hill	5	0	594
	Other	11	1	
	TOTAL	75	5	

TOP POINT EARNERS

	PLAYER	GAMES	AV PTS
1	Di Salvo	5	3.00
2	Arvidsson	10	1.80
3	Madsen	4	1.75
4	Maul	20	1.75
5	Rydlewicz	22	1.59
6	Mohrle	25	1.56
7	Shultz	23	1.48
8	Persson	25	1.44
9	Tjikuzu	31	1.42
10	Lantz	32	1.38
	CLUB AVERAGE:		**1.29**

LEAGUE APPEARANCES, BOOKINGS AND CAPS

	AGE (on 01/07/04)	IN NAMED 18	APPEARANCES	COUNTING GAMES	MINUTES ON PITCH	YELLOW CARDS	RED CARDS	THIS SEASON	HOME COUNTRY
Goalkeepers									
Perry Brautigam	35	1	0	0	0	0	0	-	Germany
Daniel Klewer	27	32	2	1	95	0	0	-	Germany
Matthias Schober	28	33	33	33	2965	2	0	-	Germany
Defenders									
Delano Hill	29	33	33	33	2970	5	0	-	Holland
Jochen Kientz	31	10	9	9	810	4	0	-	Germany
Michal Kovar	30	25	3	1	164	0	0	-	Czech Republic
Kim Madsen	30	15	13	4	612	0	1	-	Denmark
Ronald Maul	31	31	24	20	1904	7	0	-	Germany
Uwe Mohrle	24	25	25	25	2250	3	0	-	Germany
Tim Sebastian	20	1	0	0	0	0	0	-	Germany
Razundara Tjikuzu	24	34	34	31	2877	3	0	-	Namibia
Midfielders									
Godfried Aduobe	28	24	12	6	705	4	0	-	Ghana
Marcus Lantz	28	32	32	32	2850	9	0	-	Sweden
Thomas Meggle	29	21	11	3	372	0	0	-	Germany
Gabriel Melkam	24	24	18	11	1073	2	0	-	Nigeria
Joakim Persson	29	33	28	25	2316	3	0	-	Sweden
Gernot Plassnegger	26	24	19	8	945	4	2	-	Austria
Rene Rydlewicz	30	32	28	22	2126	7	1	-	Germany
Thomas Shultz	27	30	28	23	2222	6	1	-	Denmark
Gerd Wimmer	27	14	4	1	127	0	0	-	Austria
Forwards									
Magnus Arvidsson	30	30	24	10	1159	2	0	-	Sweden
Antonio Di Salvo	25	30	21	5	771	4	0	-	Italy
Martin Max	35	33	33	32	2866	7	0	-	Germany
Rade Prica	24	32	28	7	1061	3	0	-	Sweden
Marco Vorbeck	23	5	5	1	215	0	0	-	Germany

TEAM OF THE SEASON

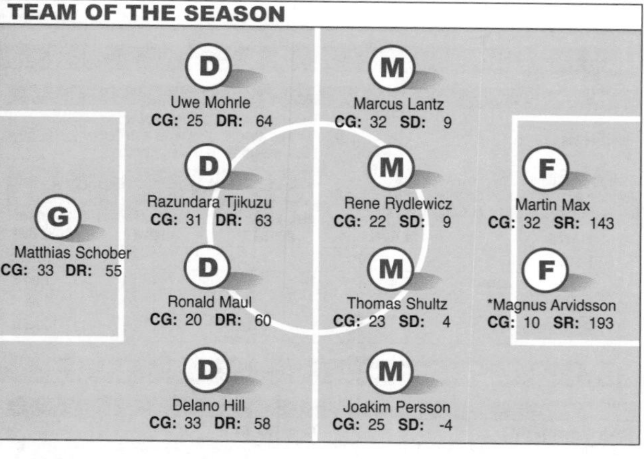
D
Uwe Mohrle
CG: 25 DR: 64
M
Marcus Lantz
CG: 32 SD: 9
D
Razundara Tjikuzu
CG: 31 DR: 63
M
Rene Rydlewicz
CG: 22 SD: 9
F
Martin Max
CG: 32 SR: 143
G
Matthias Schober
CG: 33 DR: 55
D
Ronald Maul
CG: 20 DR: 60
M
Thomas Shultz
CG: 23 SD: 4
F
*Magnus Arvidsson
CG: 10 SR: 193
D
Delano Hill
CG: 33 DR: 58
M
Joakim Persson
CG: 25 SD: -4

SQUAD APPEARANCES

Match	1	2	3	4	5	6	7	8	9	10	11	12	13	14	15	16	17	18	19	20	21	22	23	24	25	26	27	28	29	30	31	32	33	34
Venue	H	A	H	A	H	A	H	A	A	H	A	H	A	H	A	H	A	A	H	A	H	A	H	A	H	H	A	H	A	H	A	H	A	H
Competition	L	L	L	L	L	L	L	L	L	L	L	L	L	L	L	L	L	L	L	L	L	L	L	L	L	L	L	L	L	L	L	L	L	L
Result	L	D	W	D	L	L	L	L	L	L	D	W	W	W	W	D	L	L	W	D	W	D	W	D	L	W	D	L	L	W	L	W	L	W

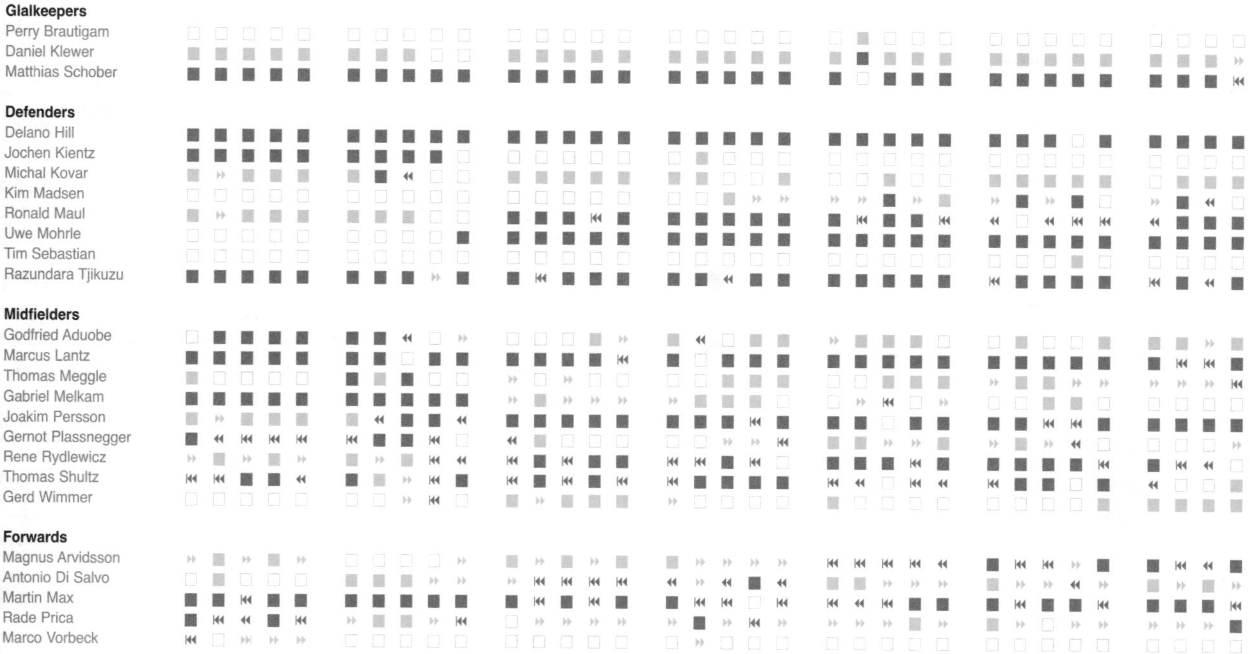

Glalkeepers
Perry Brautigam
Daniel Klewer
Matthias Schober

Defenders
Delano Hill
Jochen Kientz
Michal Kovar
Kim Madsen
Ronald Maul
Uwe Mohrle
Tim Sebastian
Razundara Tjikuzu

Midfielders
Godfried Aduobe
Marcus Lantz
Thomas Meggle
Gabriel Melkam
Joakim Persson
Gernot Plassnegger
Rene Rydlewicz
Thomas Shultz
Gerd Wimmer

Forwards
Magnus Arvidsson
Antonio Di Salvo
Martin Max
Rade Prica
Marco Vorbeck

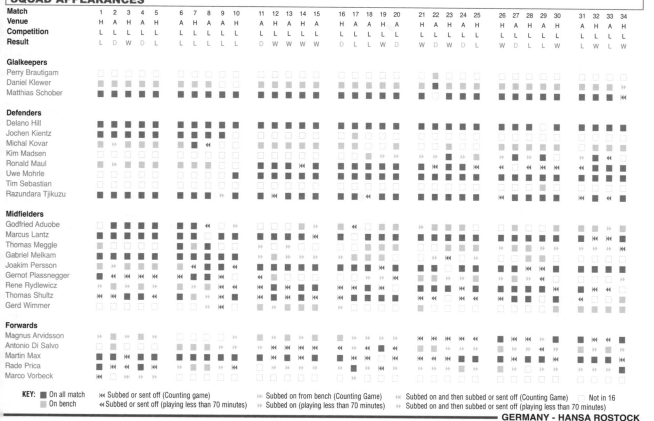

KEY: ■ On all match | ■ On bench | ⏮ Subbed or sent off (Counting game) | « Subbed or sent off (playing less than 70 minutes) | ⏭ Subbed on from bench (Counting Game) | » Subbed on (playing less than 70 minutes) | ⏭ Subbed on and then subbed or sent off (Counting Game) | » Subbed on and then subbed or sent off (playing less than 70 minutes) | □ Not in 16

VFL WOLFSBURG

Final Position: **10th**

KEY: ☐ Won ☐ Drawn ☐ Lost

							Attendance
1	lge	**Bochum**	H	W	3-2	Thiam 9; Klimowicz 14; Petrov 75	15,976
2	lge	**B Dortmund**	A	L	0-4		72,500
3	lge	**Hamburg**	H	W	5-1	Klimowicz 50,86; Petrov 60; Muller 70; D'Alessandro 75	28,000
4	lge	**1860 Munich**	A	L	0-1		24,000
5	lge	**Bayern Munich**	H	W	3-2	Baiano 11,83; Klimowicz 89	30,000
6	lge	**Cologne**	A	W	3-2	Biliskov 3; Petrov 26; Klimowicz 73	33,000
7	lge	**B Leverkusen**	H	L	0-1		24,000
8	lge	**W Bremen**	A	L	3-5	Biliskov 40; Streit 54; Karhan 65	33,000
9	lge	**Hansa Rostock**	H	W	3-1	Klimowicz 32; Baiano 40,68	19,846
10	lge	**Stuttgart**	A	L	0-1		40,000
11	lge	**Hertha Berlin**	H	W	3-0	D'Alessandro 24; Klimowicz 47,71	25,000
12	lge	**Freiburg**	A	L	2-3	Topic 62; Franz 90	23,500
13	lge	**B M'gladbach**	H	L	1-3	Schnoor 32	22,000
14	lge	**Eintr Frankfurt**	A	L	2-3	Karhan 13; Klimowicz 27	20,000
15	lge	**Kaiserslautern**	H	W	4-1	Baiano 23,54,56; Schnoor 90 pen	21,000
16	lge	**Hannover 96**	H	W	2-1	Baiano 29; Petrov 78	30,000
17	lge	**Schalke**	A	D	1-1	Petrov 40	60,000
18	lge	**Bochum**	A	L	0-1		21,000
19	lge	**B Dortmund**	H	L	2-4	Petrov 36 pen; Baiano 88	26,000
20	lge	**Hamburg**	A	L	0-2		36,000
21	lge	**1860 Munich**	H	W	3-1	Biliskov 9; D'Alessandro 19; Klimowicz 62	13,000
22	lge	**Bayern Munich**	A	L	0-2		30,000
23	lge	**Cologne**	H	W	2-0	Klimowicz 30; Topic 84	18,246
24	lge	**B Leverkusen**	A	L	2-4	Topic 21; Klimowicz 82	22,500
25	lge	**W Bremen**	H	L	0-2		30,000
26	lge	**Hansa Rostock**	A	L	1-3	Quattrocchi 26	19,800
27	lge	**Stuttgart**	H	L	1-5	Petrov 30	25,000
28	lge	**Hertha Berlin**	A	L	0-1		33,970
29	lge	**Freiburg**	H	W	4-0	Franz 10; Baiano 20; Sarpei 47; Klimowicz 68	25,000
30	lge	**B M'gladbach**	A	W	2-0	Baiano 44; Karhan 65	33,600
31	lge	**Eintr Frankfurt**	H	W	1-0	Klimowicz 18	22,000
32	lge	**Kaiserslautern**	A	L	2-3	Klimowicz 65; Petrov 66	40,000
33	lge	**Hannover 96**	A	D	0-0		27,537
34	lge	**Schalke**	H	D	1-1	Karhan 3	30,000

MONTHLY POINTS TALLY

AUGUST	6	50%
SEPTEMBER	6	67%
OCTOBER	3	33%
NOVEMBER	3	25%
DECEMBER	7	78%
JANUARY	0	0%
FEBRUARY	3	25%
MARCH	3	25%
APRIL	6	50%
MAY	5	42%

KEY PLAYERS - GOALSCORERS

Diego Fernando Klimowicz

Goals in the League	15	Player Strike Rate Average number of minutes between League goals scored by player	191
Contribution to Attacking Power Average number of minutes between League team goals while on pitch	55	Club Strike Rate Average number of minutes between League goals scored by club	55

	PLAYER	LGE GOALS	POWER	STRIKE RATE
1	Diego Fernando Klimowicz	15	55	191 mins
2	Martin Petrov	8	63	268 mins
3	Marko Topic	3	68	480 mins
4	Marino Biliskov	3	52	547 mins

KEY PLAYERS - MIDFIELDERS

Patrick Weiser

Goals in the League	0	Contribution to Attacking Power Average number of minutes between League team goals while on pitch	51
Defensive Rating Average number of mins between League goals conceded while he was on the pitch	53	Scoring Difference Defensive Rating minus Contribution to Attacking Power	2

	PLAYER	LGE GOALS	DEF RATE	POWER	SCORE DIFF
1	Patrick Weiser	0	53	51	2 mins
2	Andres D'Alessandro	3	53	54	-1 mins
3	Hans Sarpei	1	50	51	-1 mins
4	Pablo Thiam	1	45	59	-14 mins

KEY PLAYERS - DEFENDERS

Thomas Rytter

Goals Conceded (GC) The number of League goals conceded while he was on the pitch	26	Clean Sheets In games when he played at least 70 minutes	4
Defensive Rating Ave number of mins between League goals conceded while on the pitch	68	Club Defensive Rating Average number of mins between League goals conceded by the club this season	50

	PLAYER	CON LGE	CLEAN SHEETS	DEF RATE
1	Thomas Rytter	26	4	68 mins
2	Maik Franz	33	4	55 mins
3	Miroslav Karhan	45	6	54 mins
4	Stefan Schnoor	57	5	48 mins

KEY GOALKEEPER

Simon Jentzsch

Goals Conceded in the League	43	Counting Games Games when he played at least 70 mins	26
Defensive Rating Ave number of mins between League goals conceded while on the pitch	54	Clean Sheets In games when he played at least 70 mins	5

LEAGUE GOALS

Diego Fernando Klimowicz

Minutes on the pitch	2872	Goals in the League	15
League average (mins between goals)	191		

	PLAYER	MINS	GOALS	AVE
1	Klimowicz	2872	15	191
2	Baiano	1268	11	115
3	Petrov	2142	8	268
4	Karhan	2429	4	607
5	Biliskov	1641	3	547
6	Topic	1441	3	480
7	D'Alessandro	2431	3	810
8	Schnoor	2749	2	1375
9	Franz	1822	2	911
10	Streit	205	1	205
11	Sarpei	2110	1	2110
12	Quattrocchi	341	1	341
	Other		2	
	TOTAL		56	

DISCIPLINARY RECORDS

	PLAYER	YELLOW	RED	AVE
1	Schnoor	13	1	196
2	Franz	8	1	202
3	Biliskov	8	0	205
4	D'Alessandro	10	1	221
5	Klimowicz	10	0	287
6	Thiam	6	1	303
7	Petrov	6	0	357
8	Rytter	4	0	438
9	Topic	3	0	480
10	Sarpei	4	0	527
11	Menseguez	3	0	576
12	Baiano	2	0	634
13	Ramovic	1	0	720
	Other	14	0	
	TOTAL	92	4	

TOP POINT EARNERS

	PLAYER	GAMES	AV PTS
1	Baiano	12	1.75
2	Rytter	19	1.68
3	Weiser	26	1.46
4	D'Alessandro	27	1.41
5	Sarpei	20	1.40
6	Franz	18	1.33
7	Karhan	25	1.32
8	Menseguez	16	1.31
9	Petrov	23	1.30
10	Jentzsch	26	1.27
	CLUB AVERAGE:		1.24

LEAGUE APPEARANCES, BOOKINGS AND CAPS

	AGE (on 01/07/04)	IN NAMED 18	APPEARANCES	COUNTING GAMES	MINUTES ON PITCH	YELLOW CARDS	RED CARDS	THIS SEASON	HOME COUNTRY
Goalkeepers									
Simon Jentzsch	28	33	26	26	2340	0	0	-	Germany
Fabian Lucas	23	1	0	0	0	0	0	-	Germany
Sead Ramovic	25	32	8	8	720	1	0	-	Germany
Defenders									
Marino Biliskov	28	31	23	16	1641	8	0	-	Croatia
Karsten Fischer	20	4	1	0	8	0	0	-	Germany
Maik Franz	22	27	23	18	1822	8	1	-	Germany
Mirko Hrgovic	25	30	15	2	431	4	0	-	Bosnia
Miroslav Karhan	28	34	31	25	2429	3	0	-	Slovakia
Nenad Lalatovic	26	6	0	0	0	0	0	-	Serbia & Montenegro
Kim Madsen	30	2	0	0	0	0	0	-	Denmark
Sven Muller	24	13	9	1	319	1	0	-	Germany
Waldo Ponce	21	24	4	0	36	0	0	-	Chile
Pablo Quattrocchi	30	14	5	3	341	2	0	-	Argentina
Thomas Rytter	30	23	21	19	1755	4	0	-	Denmark
Stefan Schnoor	33	31	31	30	2749	13	1	-	Germany
Midfielders									
A D'Alessandro	23	29	29	27	2431	10	1	7	Argentina (5)
Dorinel Munteanu	36	8	3	0	82	0	0	-	Romania
Nderim Nedzipi	20	1	0	0	0	0	0	-	Macedonia
Hans Sarpei	28	33	31	20	2110	4	0	-	Germany
Benjamin Siegert	23	1	0	0	0	0	0	-	Germany
Albert Streit	24	9	5	1	205	0	0	-	Germany
Pablo Thiam	30	28	27	21	2122	6	1	-	Guinea
Patrick Weiser	32	31	30	26	2494	3	0	-	Germany
Forwards									
Francesco Baiano	36	25	22	12	1268	2	0	-	Italy
Diego Klimowicz	30	33	33	31	2872	10	0	-	Argentina
Juan Menseguez	20	30	27	16	1730	3	0	-	Argentina
Martin Petrov	25	28	28	23	2142	6	0	-	Bulgaria
Roy Prager	32	9	2	0	68	1	0	-	Germany
Christian Ritter	19	1	1	0	2	0	0	-	Germany
Marko Topic	28	27	24	13	1441	3	0	-	Bosnia

TEAM OF THE SEASON

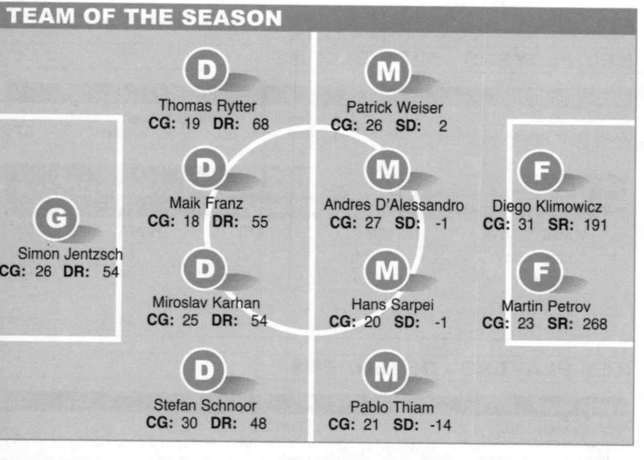

G
Simon Jentzsch
CG: 26 DR: 54
D
Thomas Rytter
CG: 19 DR: 68
D
Maik Franz
CG: 18 DR: 55
D
Miroslav Karhan
CG: 25 DR: 54
D
Stefan Schnoor
CG: 30 DR: 48
M
Patrick Weiser
CG: 26 SD: 2
M
Andres D'Alessandro
CG: 27 SD: -1
M
Hans Sarpei
CG: 20 SD: -1
M
Pablo Thiam
CG: 21 SD: -14
F
Diego Klimowicz
CG: 31 SR: 191
F
Martin Petrov
CG: 23 SR: 268

SQUAD APPEARANCES

Match	1	2	3	4	5	6	7	8	9	10	11	12	13	14	15	16	17	18	19	20	21	22	23	24	25	26	27	28	29	30	31	32	33	34
Venue	H	A	H	A	H	A	H	A	H	A	H	A	H	A	H	H	A	A	H	A	H	A	H	A	H	A	H	A	H	A	H	A	A	H
Competition	L	L	L	L	L	L	L	L	L	L	L	L	L	L	L	L	L	L	L	L	L	L	L	L	L	L	L	L	L	L	L	L	L	L
Result	W	L	W	L	W	W	L	L	W	L	W	L	L	L	W	W	D	L	L	L	W	L	W	L	L	L	L	L	W	W	W	L	D	D

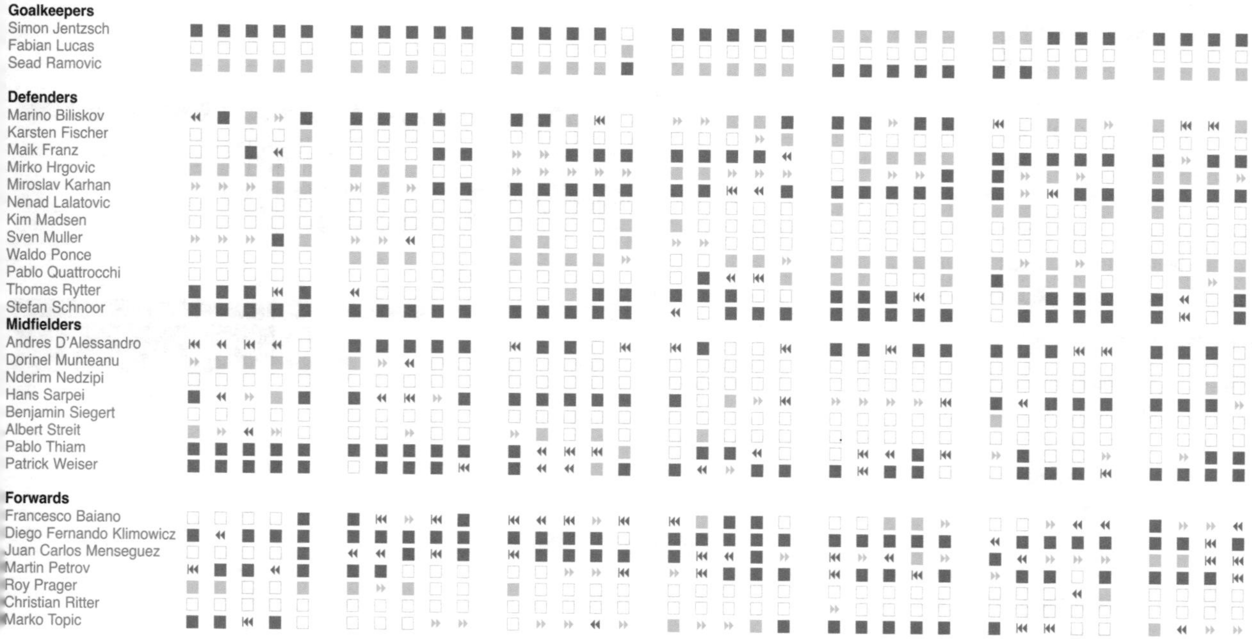

Goalkeepers
Simon Jentzsch
Fabian Lucas
Sead Ramovic

Defenders
Marino Biliskov
Karsten Fischer
Maik Franz
Mirko Hrgovic
Miroslav Karhan
Nenad Lalatovic
Kim Madsen
Sven Muller
Waldo Ponce
Pablo Quattrocchi
Thomas Rytter
Stefan Schnoor

Midfielders
Andres D'Alessandro
Dorinel Munteanu
Nderim Nedzipi
Hans Sarpei
Benjamin Siegert
Albert Streit
Pablo Thiam
Patrick Weiser

Forwards
Francesco Baiano
Diego Fernando Klimowicz
Juan Carlos Menseguez
Martin Petrov
Roy Prager
Christian Ritter
Marko Topic

KEY: ■ On all match ■ On bench ⏮ Subbed or sent off (Counting game) « Subbed or sent off (playing less than 70 minutes) ⏭ Subbed on from bench (Counting Game) » Subbed on (playing less than 70 minutes) Subbed on and then subbed or sent off (Counting Game) Subbed on and then subbed or sent off (playing less than 70 minutes) □ Not in 16

BORUSSIA MONCHENGLADBACH 11th

KEY: Won / Drawn / Lost

		Opponent	H/A	Result	Score	Scorers	Attendance
1	lge	Cologne	H	W	1-0	Scherz 63 og	34,500
2	lge	W Bremen	A	D	1-1	Van Hout 81	30,100
3	lge	Stuttgart	H	L	0-1		32,000
4	lge	Freiburg	A	L	1-4	Van Lent 68	25,000
5	lge	Eintr Frankfurt	H	L	0-2		34,000
6	lge	Hannover 96	A	L	0-2		22,000
7	lge	Bochum	H	D	2-2	Van Lent 5 pen,90	29,000
8	lge	Hamburg	A	L	1-2	Van Lent 18	51,000
9	lge	Bayern Munich	H	D	0-0		34,500
10	lge	B Leverkusen	A	L	0-1		22,500
11	lge	Hansa Rostock	H	D	1-1	Sverkos 30	29,000
12	lge	Hertha Berlin	A	L	1-2	Sverkos 7	28,000
13	lge	Wolfsburg	A	W	3-1	Van Hout 13; Van Lent 69; Kolkka 77	22,000
14	lge	Kaiserslautern	H	W	2-1	Carnell 46; Van Lent 69	31,000
15	lge	Schalke	A	L	1-2	Ulich 44	61,000
16	lge	B Dortmund	H	W	2-1	Demo 11; Asanin 83	34,500
17	lge	1860 Munich	A	W	2-1	Ulich 15; Van Lent 83	15,000
18	lge	Cologne	A	L	0-1		51,000
19	lge	W Bremen	H	L	1-2	Sverkos 51	30,000
20	lge	Stuttgart	A	D	1-1	Sverkos 84	32,000
21	lge	Freiburg	H	D	2-2	Maric 57 pen; Kolkka 60	29,000
22	lge	Eintr Frankfurt	A	L	1-3	Van Lent 74	32,000
23	lge	Hannover 96	H	W	1-0	Demo 24	32,000
24	lge	Bochum	A	L	0-1		32,645
25	lge	Hamburg	H	W	3-0	Strasser 61; Sverkos 79; Broich 81	31,000
26	lge	Bayern Munich	A	L	2-5	Sverkos 54,65	56,000
27	lge	B Leverkusen	H	D	0-0		32,000
28	lge	Hansa Rostock	A	W	2-1	Ulich 30; Van Hout 84	25,800
29	lge	Hertha Berlin	H	D	1-1	Ulich 86	34,000
30	lge	Wolfsburg	H	L	0-2		33,600
31	lge	Kaiserslautern	A	D	2-2	Broich 50; Demo 90	45,000
32	lge	Schalke	H	W	2-0	Hausweiler 1; Sverkos 44 pen	34,500
33	lge	B Dortmund	A	L	1-3	Ulich 10	82,500
34	lge	1860 Munich	H	W	3-1	Sverkos 23; Demo 35; Van Lent 74	34,500

MONTHLY POINTS TALLY

Month	Points	%
AUGUST	4	33%
SEPTEMBER	1	11%
OCTOBER	1	11%
NOVEMBER	7	58%
DECEMBER	6	67%
JANUARY	0	0%
FEBRUARY	2	17%
MARCH	6	50%
APRIL	5	42%
MAY	7	58%

KEY PLAYERS - GOALSCORERS

Vaclav Sverkos

Goals in the League	9	Player Strike Rate Average number of minutes between League goals scored by player	192
Contribution to Attacking Power Average number of minutes between League team goals while on pitch	69	Club Strike Rate Average number of minutes between League goals scored by club	77

	PLAYER	LGE GOALS	POWER	STRIKE RATE
1	Vaclav Sverkos	9	69	192 mins
2	Ari Van Lent	9	74	288 mins
3	Ivo Ulich	5	79	526 mins
4	Joonas Kolkka	2	78	982 mins

KEY PLAYERS - MIDFIELDERS

Bradley Carnell

Goals in the League	1	Contribution to Attacking Power Average number of minutes between League team goals while on pitch	67
Defensive Rating Average number of mins between League goals conceded while he was on the pitch	67	Scoring Difference Defensive Rating minus Contribution to Attacking Power	0

	PLAYER	LGE GOALS	DEF RATE	POWER	SCORE DIFF
1	Bradley Carnell	1	67	67	0 mins
2	Bernd Korzynietz	0	64	76	-12 mins
3	Ivo Ulich	5	60	80	-20 mins
4	Peer Kluge	0	57	90	-33 mins

KEY PLAYERS - DEFENDERS

Slajdan Asanin

Goals Conceded (GC) The number of League goals conceded while he was on the pitch	34	Clean Sheets In games when he played at least 70 minutes	5
Defensive Rating Ave number of mins between League goals conceded while on the pitch	68	Club Defensive Rating Average number of mins between League goals conceded by the club this season	62

	PLAYER	CON LGE	CLEAN SHEETS	DEF RATE
1	Slajdan Asanin	34	5	68 mins
2	Enrico Gaede	31	4	63 mins
3	Jeff Strasser	46	6	60 mins
4	Marcello Pletsch	22	3	56 mins

KEY GOALKEEPER

Jorg Stiel

Goals Conceded in the League	39	Counting Games Games when he played at least 70 mins	28
Defensive Rating Ave number of mins between League goals conceded while on the pitch	64	Clean Sheets In games when he played at least 70 mins	4

LEAGUE GOALS

Ari Van Lent

Minutes on the pitch	2592	Goals in the League	9
League average (mins between goals)	288		

	PLAYER	MINS	GOALS	AVE
1	Van Lent	2592	9	288
2	Sverkos	1728	9	192
3	Ulich	2628	5	526
4	Demo	1428	4	357
5	Van Hout	1156	3	385
6	Kolkka	1964	2	982
7	Broich	948	2	474
8	Carnell	1536	1	1536
9	Maric	231	1	231
10	Asanin	2322	1	2322
11	Hausweiler	786	1	786
12	Strasser	2741	1	2741
	Other		1	
	TOTAL		40	

DISCIPLINARY

	PLAYER	YELLOW	RED	AVE
1	Obradovic	4	1	96
2	Hausweiler	4	0	196
3	Gaede	7	2	218
4	Broich	4	0	237
5	Strasser	10	0	274
6	Korzynietz	8	0	359
7	Pletsch	3	0	409
8	Sverkos	4	0	432
9	Van Hout	2	0	578
10	Kolkka	3	0	654
11	Kluge	2	0	716
12	Carnell	2	0	768
13	Ulich	3	0	876
	Other	13	1	
	TOTAL	69	4	

TOP POINT EARNERS

	PLAYER	GAMES	AV PTS
1	Demo	12	1.58
2	Hausweiler	6	1.50
3	Obradovic	5	1.40
4	Carnell	16	1.38
5	Gaede	21	1.33
6	Asanin	25	1.32
7	Sverkos	17	1.29
8	Pletsch	13	1.23
9	Reitmaier	5	1.20
10	Stiel	28	1.18
	CLUB AVERAGE:		**1.15**

LEAGUE APPEARANCES, BOOKINGS AND CAPS

	AGE (on 01/07/04)	IN NAMED 18	APPEARANCES	COUNTING GAMES	MINUTES ON PITCH	YELLOW CARDS	RED CARDS	THIS SEASON	HOME COUNTRY
Goalkeepers									
Uwe Kamps	40	1	1	0	11	0	0	-	Germany
Michael Melka	25	6	1	1	90	0	0	-	Germany
Claus Reitmaier	40	29	5	5	450	0	0	-	Germany
Jorg Stiel	36	32	28	28	2509	0	0	-	Switzerland
Defenders									
Slajdan Asanin	32	29	27	25	2322	2	0	-	Croatia
Max Eberl	30	22	4	2	296	1	0	-	Germany
Enrico Gaede	22	27	25	21	1963	7	2	-	Germany
Markus Hausweiler	28	14	12	6	786	4	0	-	Germany
Steffan Korell	32	3	1	0	24	0	0	-	Germany
Milan Obradovic	26	19	8	5	484	4	1	-	Serbia & Montenegro
Marcello Pletsch	28	18	16	13	1227	3	0	-	Brazil
G Rocha Ruben	22	4	3	1	186	0	0	-	Spain
S Schulz-Winge	29	6	2	0	2	0	0	-	Germany
Jeff Strasser	29	31	31	30	2741	10	0	-	Luxembourg
Midfielders									
Thomas Broich	23	15	13	10	948	4	0	-	Germany
Bradley Carnell	27	19	18	16	1536	2	0	-	South Africa
Igor Demo	28	29	27	12	1428	1	0	-	Slovakia
Marcel Jansen	18	1	0	0	0	0	0	-	Germany
Oliver Kirch	21	15	8	3	380	2	0	-	Germany
Peer Kluge	23	30	22	13	1432	2	0	-	Germany
Bernd Korzynietz	24	33	33	31	2872	8	0	-	Germany
Pascal Ojigwe	27	13	7	4	496	0	0	-	Nigeria
Andreas Spann	20	1	0	0	0	0	0	-	Germany
Ivo Ulich	29	34	34	24	2628	3	0	-	Czech Republic
Forwards									
Lawrence Aidoo	22	7	5	1	193	0	1	-	Ghana
Marcel Ketelaer	26	8	7	4	488	0	0	-	Germany
Joonas Kolkka	29	33	28	18	1964	3	0	5	Finland (42)
Tomislav Maric	31	9	7	1	231	3	0	-	Croatia
Marcel Podszus	27	13	4	0	25	0	0	-	Germany
Morten Skoubo	24	8	7	2	348	1	0	-	Denmark
Vaclav Sverkos	20	32	31	17	1728	4	0	-	Czech Republic
Peter van Houdt	27	6	2	0	53	1	0	-	Belgium
Joris Van Hout	27	26	23	9	1156	2	0	-	Belgium
Ari Van Lent	32	34	34	27	2592	2	0	-	Holland

TEAM OF THE SEASON

G Jorg Stiel — CG: 28 DR: 64

D Slajdan Asanin — CG: 25 DR: 68

D Enrico Gaede — CG: 21 DR: 63

D Jeff Strasser — CG: 30 DR: 60

D Marcello Pletsch — CG: 13 DR: 56

M Bradley Carnell — CG: 16 SD: 0

M Bernd Korzynietz — CG: 31 SD: -12

M Ivo Ulich — CG: 24 SD: -20

M Peer Kluge — CG: 13 SD: -33

F Vaclav Sverkos — CG: 17 SR: 192

F Ari Van Lent — CG: 27 SR: 288

SQUAD APPEARANCES

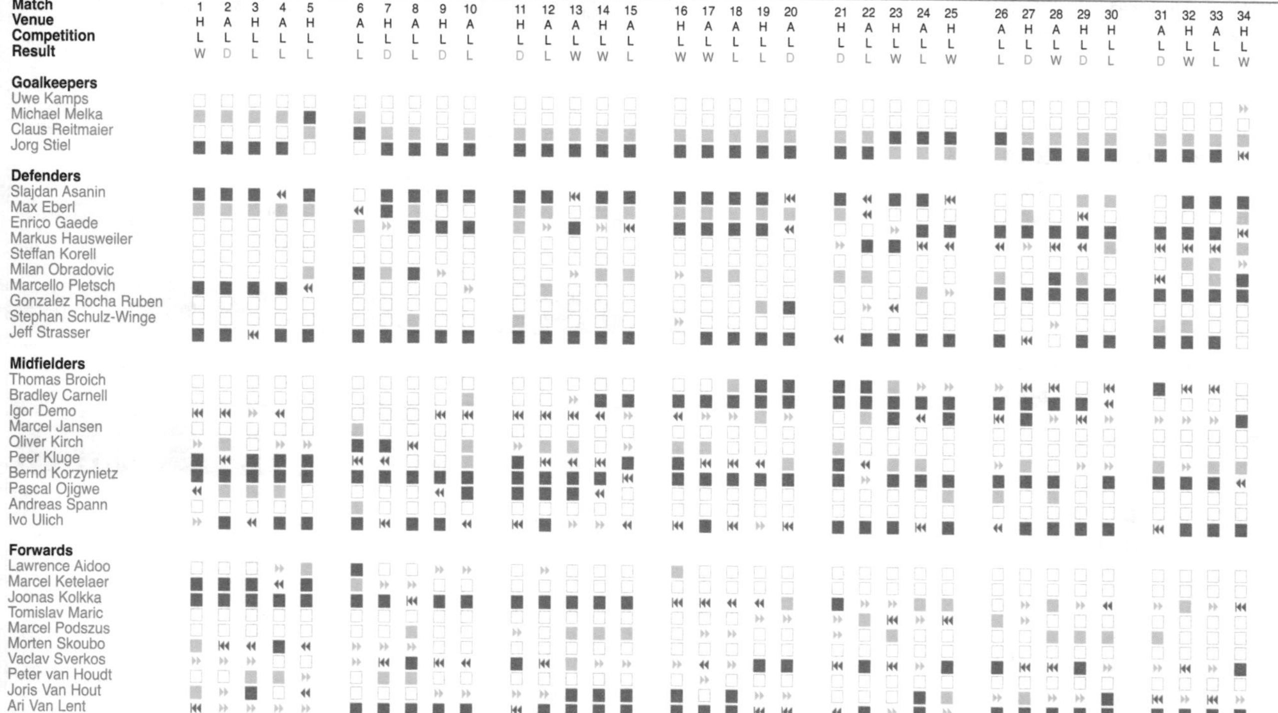

Match 1 2 3 4 5 6 7 8 9 10 11 12 13 14 15 16 17 18 19 20 21 22 23 24 25 26 27 28 29 30 31 32 33 34
Venue H A H A H A H A H A H A A H A H A A H A H A H A H A H A H H A H A H
Competition L L L L L L L L L L L L L L L L L L L L L L L L L L L L L L L L L L
Result W D L L L L D L D L D L W W L W W L L D D L W L W L D W D L D W L W
Goalkeepers
Uwe Kamps
Michael Melka
Claus Reitmaier
Jorg Stiel
Defenders
Slajdan Asanin
Max Eberl
Enrico Gaede
Markus Hausweiler
Steffan Korell
Milan Obradovic
Marcello Pletsch
Gonzalez Rocha Ruben
Stephan Schulz-Winge
Jeff Strasser
Midfielders
Thomas Broich
Bradley Carnell
Igor Demo
Marcel Jansen
Oliver Kirch
Peer Kluge
Bernd Korzynietz
Pascal Ojigwe
Andreas Spann
Ivo Ulich
Forwards
Lawrence Aidoo
Marcel Ketelaer
Joonas Kolkka
Tomislav Maric
Marcel Podszus
Morten Skoubo
Vaclav Sverkos
Peter van Houdt
Joris Van Hout
Ari Van Lent

KEY: On all match; On bench; Subbed or sent off (Counting game); Subbed or sent off (playing less than 70 minutes); Subbed on from bench (Counting Game); Subbed on (playing less than 70 minutes); Subbed on and then subbed or sent off (Counting Game); Subbed on and then subbed or sent off (playing less than 70 minutes); Not in 16

HERTHA BERLIN 12th

KEY: Won Drawn Lost

						Attendance
1	lge	W Bremen	H	L	0-3		38,000
2	lge	Stuttgart	A	D	0-0		37,000
3	lge	Freiburg	H	D	0-0		28,000
4	lge	Eintr Frankfurt	A	D	0-0		17,000
5	lge	Hannover 96	H	L	2-3	Bobic 4,21	30,000
6	lge	Bochum	A	D	2-2	Neuendorf 7,66	21,000
7	uc1rl1	Groclin	H	D	0-0		23,142
8	lge	Hamburg	H	D	1-1	Friedrich 33	37,000
9	lge	Bayern Munich	A	L	1-4	Kovac 65	63,000
10	uc1rl2	Groclin	A	L	0-1		4,450
11	lge	B Leverkusen	H	L	1-4	Bobic 47	36,638
12	lge	Hansa Rostock	A	W	1-0	Luizao 31	20,000
13	lge	Wolfsburg	A	L	0-3		25,000
14	lge	B M'gladbach	H	W	2-1	Luizao 15; Madlung 87	28,000
15	lge	Kaiserslautern	A	L	2-4	Rafael 37; Knavs 45 og	33,000
16	lge	Schalke	H	L	1-3	Lapaczinski 37	37,000
17	lge	B Dortmund	A	D	1-1	Madlung 79	77,000
18	lge	1860 Munich	H	D	1-1	Costa 53	20,000
19	lge	Cologne	A	L	0-3		30,000
20	lge	W Bremen	A	L	0-4		35,000
21	lge	Stuttgart	H	W	1-0	Bobic 88	39,000
22	lge	Freiburg	A	W	3-2	Friedrich 24; Neuendorf 44; Rehmer 63	24,000
23	lge	Eintr Frankfurt	H	L	1-2	Rafael 62	27,000
24	lge	Hannover 96	A	W	3-1	Marcelinho 42,81; Reina 78	22,000
25	lge	Bochum	H	D	1-1	Marcelinho 20	35,000
26	lge	Hamburg	A	L	0-2		42,000
27	lge	Bayern Munich	H	D	1-1	Marcelinho 43 pen	60,000
28	lge	B Leverkusen	A	L	1-4	Marcelinho 7	20,500
29	lge	Hansa Rostock	H	D	1-1	Pinto 59	43,000
30	lge	Wolfsburg	H	W	1-0	Rafael 22	33,970
31	lge	B M'gladbach	A	D	1-1	Pinto 9	34,000
32	lge	Kaiserslautern	H	W	3-0	Marcelinho 2; Wichinarek 16; Bobic 25	45,292
33	lge	Schalke	A	L	0-3		61,266
34	lge	B Dortmund	H	W	6-2	Kehl 7 og; Marcelinho 20; Bobic 37; Wichinarek 57; Neuendorf 86; Rafael 90	60,000
35	lge	1860 Munich	A	D	1-1	Madlung 82	48,000
36	lge	Cologne	H	W	3-1	Marcelinho 51; Bobic 63; Rafael 78	50,000

MONTHLY POINTS TALLY

Month	Points	%
AUGUST	3	25%
SEPTEMBER	2	22%
OCTOBER	3	33%
NOVEMBER	3	25%
DECEMBER	2	22%
JANUARY	0	0%
FEBRUARY	9	75%
MARCH	2	17%
APRIL	8	67%
MAY	7	58%

KEY PLAYERS - GOALSCORERS

Marcelo dos Santos Marcelinho

Goals in the League	8	Player Strike Rate Average number of minutes between League goals scored by player	265
Contribution to Attacking Power Average number of minutes between League team goals while on pitch	68	Club Strike Rate Average number of minutes between League goals scored by club	73

	PLAYER	LGE GOALS	POWER	STRIKE RATE
1	Marcelo dos Santos Marcelinho	8	68	265 mins
2	Fredi Bobic	7	73	349 mins
3	Alexander Madlung	3	52	546 mins
4	Arne Friedrich	2	66	1287 mins

KEY PLAYERS - MIDFIELDERS

Roberto Pinto

Goals in the League	2	Contribution to Attacking Power Average number of minutes between League team goals while on pitch	52
Defensive Rating Average number of mins between League goals conceded while he was on the pitch	58	Scoring Difference Defensive Rating minus Contribution to Attacking Power	6

	PLAYER	LGE GOALS	DEF RATE	POWER	SCORE DIFF
1	Roberto Pinto	2	58	52	6 mins
2	Pal Dardai	0	58	79	-21 mins
3	Nico Kovac	1	47	102	-55 mins
4	Bart Goor	0	44	112	-68 mins

KEY PLAYERS - DEFENDERS

Arne Friedrich

Goals Conceded (GC) The number of League goals conceded while he was on the pitch	44	Clean Sheets In games when he played at least 70 minutes	6
Defensive Rating Ave number of mins between League goals conceded while on the pitch	59	Club Defensive Rating Average number of mins between League goals conceded by the club this season	52

	PLAYER	CON LGE	CLEAN SHEETS	DEF RATE
1	Arne Friedrich	44	6	59 mins
2	Dick Van Burik	27	3	58 mins
3	Josip Simunic	47	5	52 mins
4	Marko Rehmer	34	4	49 mins
5	Alexander Madlung	36	1	45 mins

KEY GOALKEEPER

Christian Fiedler

Goals Conceded in the League	26	Counting Games Games when he played at least 70 mins	17
Defensive Rating Ave number of mins between League goals conceded while on the pitch	58	Clean Sheets In games when he played at least 70 mins	3

LEAGUE GOALS

Marcelo dos Santos Marcelinho

Minutes on the pitch	2118	Goals in the League	8
League average (mins between goals)	266		

	PLAYER	MINS	GOALS	AVE
1	Marcelinho	2118	8	265
2	Bobic	2440	7	349
3	Rafael	893	5	179
4	Neuendorf	1363	4	341
5	Madlung	1637	3	546
6	Friedrich	2574	2	1287
7	Wichinarek	1065	2	533
8	Luizao	490	2	245
9	Pinto	1040	2	520
10	Kovac	1329	1	1329
11	Lapaczinski	321	1	321
12	Reina	613	1	613
	Other		4	
	TOTAL		42	

DISCIPLINARY

	PLAYER	YELLOW	RED	AVE
1	Rafael	6	1	127
2	Kovac	8	0	166
3	Neuendorf	8	0	170
4	Fathi	4	1	220
5	Dardai	10	0	244
6	Luizao	2	0	245
7	Rehmer	5	1	280
8	Reina	2	0	306
9	Hartmann	2	0	310
10	Wichinarek	2	1	355
11	Friedrich	6	1	367
12	Simunic	6	0	404
13	Goor	4	0	419
	Other	20	3	
	TOTAL	85	8	

TOP POINT EARNERS

	PLAYER	GAMES	AV PTS
1	Cagara	5	2.60
2	Schmidt	8	2.00
3	Chahed	5	1.60
4	Reina	7	1.57
5	Fiedler	17	1.53
6	Marcelinho	23	1.48
7	Pinto	11	1.45
8	Luizao	5	1.40
9	Simunic	25	1.36
10	Dardai	26	1.31
	CLUB AVERAGE:		**1.15**

TEAM OF THE SEASON

G — Christian Fiedler, CG: 17 DR: 58

D — Arne Friedrich, CG: 27 DR: 59
D — Dick Van Burik, CG: 14 DR: 58
D — Josip Simunic, CG: 25 DR: 52
D — Marko Rehmer, CG: 17 DR: 49

M — Pal Dardai, CG: 26 SD: -21
M — Nico Kovac, CG: 14 SD: -55
M — Bart Goor, CG: 17 SD: -68
M — *Roberto Pinto, CG: 11 SD: 6

F — Marcelo Marcelinho, CG: 23 SR: 265
F — Fredi Bobic, CG: 25 SR: 349

LEAGUE APPEARANCES, BOOKINGS AND CAPS

	AGE (on 01/07/04)	IN NAMED 18	APPEARANCES	COUNTING GAMES	MINUTES ON PITCH	YELLOW CARDS	RED CARDS	THIS SEASON	HOME COUNTRY
Goalkeepers									
Christian Fiedler	29	31	17	17	1516	0	0	-	Germany
Gabor Kiraly	28	30	18	17	1544	1	0	-	Hungary
Tomasz Kuszczak	22	5	0	0	0	0	0	-	Poland
Defenders									
Dennis Cagara	19	9	8	5	524	0	0	-	Germany
Sofian Chahed	21	11	8	5	569	0	0	-	Germany
Malik Fathi	20	20	14	11	1102	4	1	-	Germany
Arne Friedrich	25	30	30	27	2574	6	1	8	Germany (9)
Denis Lapaczinski	22	19	6	3	321	1	1	-	Germany
Alexander Madlung	21	32	25	17	1637	3	0	-	Germany
Marko Rehmer	32	26	24	17	1681	5	1	5	Germany (9)
Josip Simunic	26	28	28	25	2428	6	0	-	Australia
Dick Van Burik	30	21	20	14	1559	2	1	-	Holland
Midfielders									
Pal Dardai	28	31	29	26	2440	10	0	-	Hungary
Bart Goor	31	26	24	17	1679	4	0	5	Belgium (17)
Michael Hartmann	29	14	9	5	621	2	0	3	Germany (9)
Bartosz Karwan	28	14	7	2	262	1	0	-	Poland
Nico Kovac	32	22	17	14	1329	8	0	8	Croatia (25)
Alexander Ludwig	20	11	4	0	149	0	0	-	Germany
Thorben Marx	23	8	5	1	188	1	0	-	Germany
Alexander Mladenov	22	21	8	3	406	3	0	-	Bulgaria
Andreas Neuendorf	29	26	23	9	1363	8	0	-	Germany
Roberto Pinto	25	23	19	11	1040	2	0	-	Portugal
Andreas Schmidt	30	20	12	8	902	0	0	-	Germany
Forwards									
Fredi Bobic	32	33	32	25	2440	3	0	9	Germany (9)
Luiz Carlos Goulart	28	9	7	5	490	2	0	-	Brazil
Marcelinho	29	25	25	23	2118	3	1	-	Brazil
Nando Rafael	20	25	23	7	893	6	1	-	Angola
Giuseppe Reina	32	7	7	7	613	2	0	-	Germany
Artur Wichinarek	27	25	18	8	1065	2	1	-	Poland

SQUAD APPEARANCES

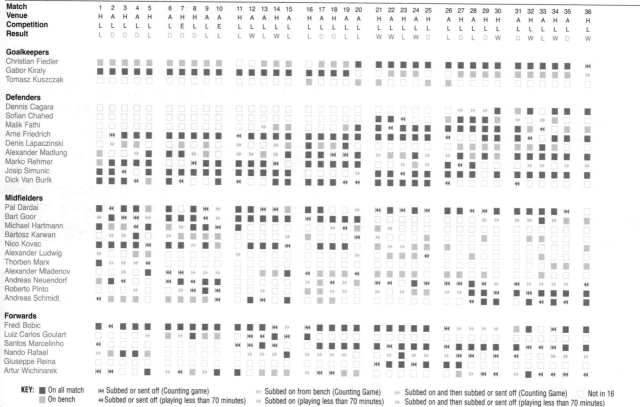

Match	1	2	3	4	5	6	7	8	9	10	11	12	13	14	15	16	17	18	19	20	21	22	23	24	25	26	27	28	29	30	31	32	33	34	35	36
Venue	H	A	H	A	H	A	H	H	A	A	H	A	A	H	A	H	A	H	A	A	H	A	H	A	H	A	H	A	H	H	A	H	A	H	A	H
Competition	L	L	L	L	L	L	E	L	L	E	L	L	L	L	L	L	L	L	L	L	L	L	L	L	L	L	L	L	L	L	L	L	L	L	L	L
Result	L	D	D	D	L	D	D	D	L	L	L	W	L	W	L	L	D	D	L	L	W	W	L	W	D	L	D	L	D	W	D	W	L	W	D	W

Goalkeepers
Christian Fiedler
Gabor Kiraly
Tomasz Kuszczak

Defenders
Dennis Cagara
Sofian Chahed
Malik Fathi
Arne Friedrich
Denis Lapaczinski
Alexander Madlung
Marko Rehmer
Josip Simunic
Dick Van Burik

Midfielders
Pal Dardai
Bart Goor
Michael Hartmann
Bartosz Karwan
Nico Kovac
Alexander Ludwig
Thorben Marx
Alexander Mladenov
Andreas Neuendorf
Roberto Pinto
Andreas Schmidt

Forwards
Fredi Bobic
Luiz Carlos Goulart
Santos Marcelinho
Nando Rafael
Giuseppe Reina
Artur Wichinarek

KEY: On all match | On bench | Subbed or sent off (Counting game) | Subbed or sent off (playing less than 70 minutes) | Subbed on from bench (Counting Game) | Subbed on (playing less than 70 minutes) | Subbed on and then subbed or sent off (Counting Game) | Subbed on and then subbed or sent off (playing less than 70 minutes) | Not in 16

FC FREIBURG

Final Position: **13th**

KEY: Won Drawn Lost

							Attendance
1	lge	B Leverkusen	A	L	1-4	Riether 20	22,500
2	lge	Hansa Rostock	H	D	2-2	Coulibaly 56 pen; Bajramovic 87	24,000
3	lge	Hertha Berlin	A	D	0-0		28,000
4	lge	B M'gladbach	H	W	4-1	Bajramovic 13,28; Zeyer 33; Iaschvili 80	25,000
5	lge	Kaiserslautern	A	D	2-2	Coulibaly 23; Zeyer 35	36,000
6	lge	Schalke	H	W	2-1	Bajramovic 3; Tskitishvilli 39	25,000
7	lge	B Dortmund	A	L	0-1		78,000
8	lge	1860 Munich	H	W	1-0	Bajramovic 77	25,000
9	lge	Cologne	A	L	0-1		33,000
10	lge	W Bremen	H	L	2-4	Iaschvili 60,90	23,000
11	lge	Stuttgart	A	L	1-4	Coulibaly 45 pen	51,000
12	lge	Wolfsburg	H	W	3-2	Iaschvili 31,34,76	23,500
13	lge	Eintr Frankfurt	H	W	1-0	Sanou 82	24,000
14	lge	Hannover 96	A	L	0-3		22,000
15	lge	Bochum	H	W	4-2	Antar 3,11,79; Sanou 22	24,500
16	lge	Hamburg	A	L	1-4	Antar 50	42,000
17	lge	Bayern Munich	H	L	0-6		25,000
18	lge	B Leverkusen	H	W	1-0	Antar 55	24,500
19	lge	Hansa Rostock	A	L	1-4	Sanou 65	20,000
20	lge	Hertha Berlin	H	L	2-3	Hartmann 76 og; Tskitishvilli 87 pen	24,000
21	lge	B M'gladbach	A	D	2-2	Cairo 19; Berner 50	29,000
22	lge	Kaiserslautern	H	W	1-0	Tskitishvilli 83	24,500
23	lge	Schalke	A	L	0-3		61,000
24	lge	B Dortmund	H	D	2-2	Antar 16; Tskitishvilli 67 pen	25,000
25	lge	1860 Munich	A	D	1-1	Coulibaly 10	19,500
26	lge	Cologne	H	W	3-0	Iaschvili 15; Riether 77; Antar 81	25,000
27	lge	W Bremen	A	D	1-1	Krupke 1	42,500
28	lge	Stuttgart	H	L	0-1		25,000
29	lge	Wolfsburg	A	L	0-4		25,000
30	lge	Eintr Frankfurt	A	L	0-3		55,300
31	lge	Hannover 96	H	W	4-1	Riether 14; Bajramovic 51; Iaschvili 69,78	24,000
32	lge	Bochum	A	L	0-3		29,474
33	lge	Hamburg	H	D	0-0		25,000
34	lge	Bayern Munich	A	L	0-2		63,000

MONTHLY POINTS TALLY

AUGUST	5	42%
SEPTEMBER	4	44%
OCTOBER	3	33%
NOVEMBER	6	50%
DECEMBER	3	33%
JANUARY	0	0%
FEBRUARY	7	47%
MARCH	5	42%
APRIL	1	8%
MAY	4	33%

KEY PLAYERS - GOALSCORERS

Roda Antar

Goals in the League	7	Player Strike Rate Average number of minutes between League goals scored by player	203
Contribution to Attacking Power Average number of minutes between League team goals while on pitch	78	Club Strike Rate Average number of minutes between League goals scored by club	73

	PLAYER	LGE GOALS	POWER	STRIKE RATE
1	Roda Antar	7	78	203 mins
2	Alexander Iaschvili	9	66	290 mins
3	Zlatan Bajramovic	6	68	310 mins
4	Wilfried Sanou	3	81	516 mins

KEY PLAYERS - MIDFIELDERS

Ismael Soumaila Coulibaly

Goals in the League	4	Contribution to Attacking Power Average number of minutes between League team goals while on pitch	73
Defensive Rating Average number of mins between League goals conceded while he was on the pitch	50	Scoring Difference Defensive Rating minus Contribution to Attacking Power	-23

	PLAYER	LGE GOALS	DEF RATE	POWER	SCORE DIFF
1	Ismael Soumaila Coulibaly	4	50	73	-23 mins
2	Levan Tskitishvilli	4	53	77	-24 mins
3	Zlatan Bajramovic	6	43	69	-26 mins
4	Sascha Riether	3	45	75	-30 mins

KEY PLAYERS - DEFENDERS

Boubacar Diarra

Goals Conceded (GC) The number of League goals conceded while he was on the pitch	54	Clean Sheets In games when he played at least 70 minutes	7
Defensive Rating Ave number of mins between League goals conceded while on the pitch	50	Club Defensive Rating Average number of mins between League goals conceded by the club this season	46

	PLAYER	CON LGE	CLEAN SHEETS	DEF RATE
1	Boubacar Diarra	54	7	50 mins
2	Bruno Berner	48	6	46 mins
3	Stefan Muller	32	2	45 mins
4	Oumar Konde	38	4	43 mins

KEY GOALKEEPER

Richard Golz

Goals Conceded in the League	48	Counting Games Games when he played at least 70 mins	23
Defensive Rating Ave number of mins between League goals conceded while on the pitch	43	Clean Sheets In games when he played at least 70 mins	4

LEAGUE GOALS

Alexander Iaschvili

Minutes on the pitch	2609	Goals in the League	9
League average (mins between goals)	290		

	PLAYER	MINS	GOALS	AVE
1	Iaschvili	2609	9	290
2	Antar	1419	7	203
3	Bajramovic	1859	6	310
4	Coulibaly	2341	4	585
5	Tskitishvilli	2297	4	574
6	Riether	2906	3	969
7	Sanou	1549	3	516
8	Zeyer	1249	2	625
9	Berner	2207	1	2207
10	Cairo	1598	1	1598
	Other		2	
	TOTAL		42	

DISCIPLINARY RECORDS

	PLAYER	YELLOW	RED	AVE
1	Kruppke	8	0	244
2	Bajramovic	6	1	265
3	Zeyer	3	1	312
4	Tskitishvili	6	0	382
5	Diarra	7	0	388
6	Coulibaly	5	1	390
7	Hermel	2	0	456
8	Willi	1	0	524
9	Riether	5	0	581
10	Antar	1	1	709
11	Berner	3	0	735
12	Cairo	2	0	799
13	Konde	2	0	819
	Other	5	0	
	TOTAL	56	4	

TOP POINT EARNERS

	PLAYER	GAMES	AV PTS
1	Reus	2	1.50
2	Sanou	13	1.38
3	Konde	16	1.31
4	Iaschvili	28	1.29
5	Cairo	11	1.27
6	Diarra	30	1.27
7	Berner	19	1.26
8	Kruppke	17	1.24
9	Coulibaly	25	1.24
10	Golz	23	1.17
	CLUB AVERAGE:		1.12

TEAM OF THE SEASON

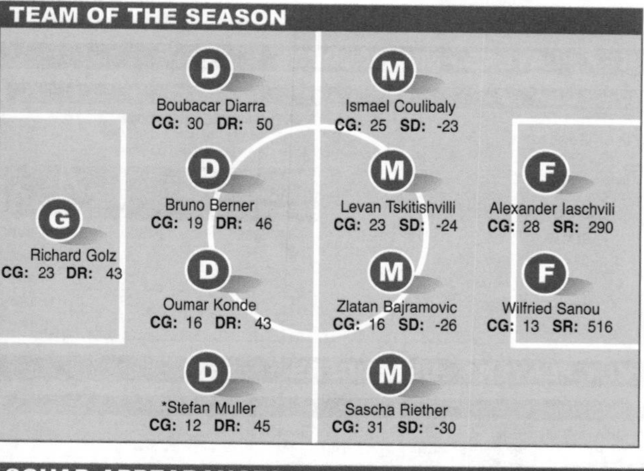

G
Richard Golz
CG: 23 DR: 43
D
Boubacar Diarra
CG: 30 DR: 50
D
Bruno Berner
CG: 19 DR: 46
D
Oumar Konde
CG: 16 DR: 43
D
*Stefan Muller
CG: 12 DR: 45
M
Ismael Coulibaly
CG: 25 SD: -23
M
Levan Tskitishvili
CG: 23 SD: -24
M
Zlatan Bajramovic
CG: 16 SD: -26
M
Sascha Riether
CG: 31 SD: -30
F
Alexander Iaschvili
CG: 28 SR: 290
F
Wilfried Sanou
CG: 13 SR: 516

LEAGUE APPEARANCES, BOOKINGS AND CAPS

	AGE (on 01/07/04)	IN NAMED 18	APPEARANCES	COUNTING GAMES	MINUTES ON PITCH	YELLOW CARDS	RED CARDS	THIS SEASON	HOME COUNTRY
Goalkeepers									
Richard Golz	36	23	23	23	2070	0	0	-	Germany
Julian Reinard	21	16	9	9	810	0	0	-	Germany
Timo Reus	30	26	2	2	180	0	0	-	Germany
Dominik Wohlfarth	26	1	0	0	0	0	0	-	Germany
Defenders									
Bruno Berner	26	34	33	19	2207	3	0	-	Switzerland
Boubacar Diarra	24	32	32	30	2720	7	0	-	Mali
Lars Hermel	33	27	13	9	913	2	0	-	Germany
Oumar Konde	31	27	21	16	1639	2	0	-	Switzerland
Stefan Muller	30	29	27	12	1437	1	0	-	Germany
Seyi Olajengbesi	23	9	3	0	68	1	0	-	Nigeria
Daniel Schumann	27	10	5	2	303	1	0	-	Germany
Midfielders									
Roda Antar	23	18	17	15	1419	1	1	-	Lebanon
Zlatan Bajramovic	24	27	26	16	1859	6	1	-	Bosnia
Ismael Coulibaly	26	29	29	25	2341	5	1	-	Mali
Jurgen Gjasula	18	4	0	0	0	0	0	-	Germany
Rolf Guie-Mien	26	26	10	0	113	0	0	-	Congo DR
Torge Hollmann	22	2	0	0	0	0	0	-	Germany
Sascha Riether	21	33	33	31	2906	5	0	-	Germany
Levan Tskitishvili	27	29	29	23	2297	6	0	-	Georgia
Iobias Willi	24	27	10	3	524	1	0	-	Germany
Andreas Zeyer	36	29	23	10	1249	3	1	-	Germany
Forwards									
Ellery Cairo	25	33	28	11	1598	2	0	-	Holland
Alexander Iaschvili	26	31	30	28	2609	1	0	-	Georgia
Dennis Krupke	24	1	1	1	83	0	0	-	Germany
Dennis Kruppke	24	31	27	17	1957	8	0	-	Germany
Wilfried Sanou	20	24	24	13	1549	1	0	-	Burkino Faso
Ibrahim Tanko	26	23	16	3	684	0	0	-	Ghana

SQUAD APPEARANCES

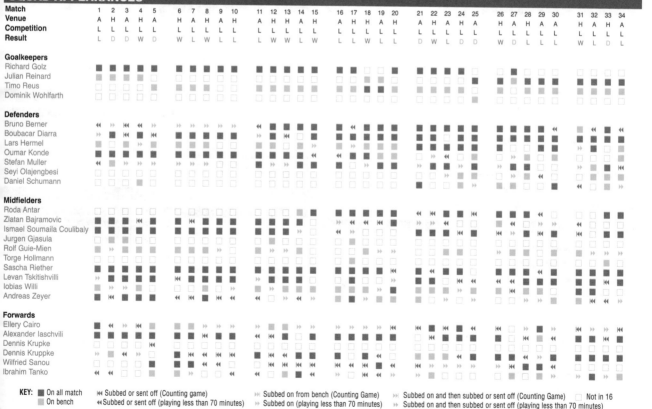

Match	1	2	3	4	5	6	7	8	9	10	11	12	13	14	15	16	17	18	19	20	21	22	23	24	25	26	27	28	29	30	31	32	33	34
Venue	A	H	A	H	A	H	A	H	A	H	A	H	H	A	H	A	H	H	A	H	A	H	A	H	A	H	A	H	A	A	H	A	H	A
Competition	L	L	L	L	L	L	L	L	L	L	L	L	L	L	L	L	L	L	L	L	L	L	L	L	L	L	L	L	L	L	L	L	L	L
Result	L	D	D	W	D	W	L	W	L	L	L	W	W	L	W	L	L	W	L	L	D	W	L	D	D	W	D	L	L	L	W	L	D	L

Goalkeepers
Richard Golz
Julian Reinard
Timo Reus
Dominik Wohlfarth

Defenders
Bruno Berner
Boubacar Diarra
Lars Hermel
Oumar Konde
Stefan Muller
Seyi Olajengbesi
Daniel Schumann

Midfielders
Roda Antar
Zlatan Bajramovic
Ismael Soumaila Coulibaly
Jurgen Gjasula
Rolf Guie-Mien
Torge Hollmann
Sascha Riether
Levan Tskitishvili
Iobias Willi
Andreas Zeyer

Forwards
Ellery Cairo
Alexander Iaschvili
Dennis Krupke
Dennis Kruppke
Wilfried Sanou
Ibrahim Tanko

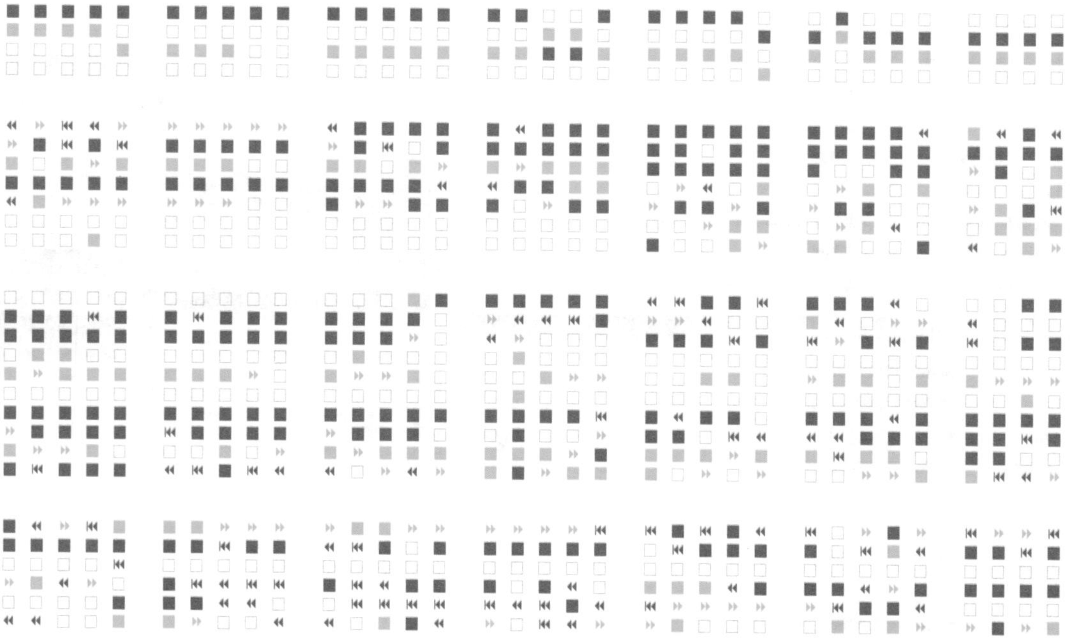

KEY: On all match · On bench · Subbed or sent off (Counting game) · Subbed or sent off (playing less than 70 minutes) · Subbed on from bench (Counting Game) · Subbed on (playing less than 70 minutes) · Subbed on and then subbed or sent off (Counting Game) · Subbed on and then subbed or sent off (playing less than 70 minutes) · Not in 16

HANNOVER 96

Final Position: **14th**

KEY: Won Drawn Lost

						Attendance
1	lge	Hamburg	A W	3-0	Stajner 11; Brdaric 76; Idrissou 79	53,224
2	lge	Bayern Munich	H D	3-3	Krupnikovic 9; Stajner 27; Christiansen 43	23,217
3	lge	B Leverkusen	A L	0-4		22,500
4	lge	Hansa Rostock	H D	3-3	Christiansen 16,66; Simak 71	21,000
5	lge	Hertha Berlin	A W	3-2	Simak 25; Kleber 69; De Guzman 80	30,000
6	lge	B M'gladbach	H W	2-0	Christiansen 18; Idrissou 83	22,000
7	lge	Kaiserslautern	A L	0-1		32,361
8	lge	Schalke	H L	1-2	Christiansen 17	22,000
9	lge	B Dortmund	A L	2-6	Vinicius 58; Wolf 85	78,000
10	lge	1860 Munich	H D	1-1	Idrissou 34	19,754
11	lge	Cologne	A W	2-1	Brdaric 33; Stendel 80	33,000
12	lge	W Bremen	H L	1-5	Stajner 55	25,000
13	lge	Stuttgart	A L	1-3	Brdaric 82	35,000
14	lge	Freiburg	H W	3-0	Brdaric 43; Stendel 66; Christiansen 85	22,000
15	lge	Eintr Frankfurt	A D	2-2	Stendel 18; Christiansen 88 pen	20,000
16	lge	Wolfsburg	A L	1-2	Stendel 15	30,000
17	lge	Bochum	H D	2-2	Brdaric 18; De Guzman 61	20,000
18	lge	Hamburg	H W	3-2	Krupnikovic 14; Mathis 27; Jaime 76	23,000
19	lge	Bayern Munich	A L	1-3	Svitlica 83	32,000
20	lge	B Leverkusen	H D	2-2	Mathis 40; Konstantinidis 48	22,000
21	lge	Hansa Rostock	A L	1-3	Mathis 38	12,000
22	lge	Hertha Berlin	H L	1-3	Mathis 67	22,000
23	lge	B M'gladbach	A L	0-1		32,000
24	lge	Kaiserslautern	H L	0-1		22,000
25	lge	Schalke	A D	2-2	Brdaric 14,71	61,266
26	lge	B Dortmund	H D	1-1	Christiansen 84	27,504
27	lge	1860 Munich	A W	2-0	Zuraw 71; Brdaric 74	22,000
28	lge	Cologne	H W	1-0	Brdaric 35	27,200
29	lge	W Bremen	A D	0-0		42,500
30	lge	Stuttgart	H L	0-1		27,537
31	lge	Freiburg	A L	1-4	Brdaric 52	24,000
32	lge	Eintr Frankfurt	H W	3-0	Brdaric 42,75; Idrissou 89	27,500
33	lge	Wolfsburg	H D	0-0		27,537
34	lge	Bochum	A L	1-3	Christiansen 41	32,645

MONTHLY POINTS TALLY

AUGUST	5	42%
SEPTEMBER	6	67%
OCTOBER	1	11%
NOVEMBER	6	50%
DECEMBER	2	22%
JANUARY	0	0%
FEBRUARY	4	27%
MARCH	2	17%
APRIL	7	58%
MAY	4	33%

KEY PLAYERS - GOALSCORERS

Thomas Brdaric

Goals in the League	12	Player Strike Rate Average number of minutes between League goals scored by player	178
Contribution to Attacking Power Average number of minutes between League team goals while on pitch	64	Club Strike Rate Average number of minutes between League goals scored by club	62

	PLAYER	LGE GOALS	POWER	STRIKE RATE
1	Thomas Brdaric	12	64	178 mins
2	Thomas Christiansen	8	61	214 mins
3	Clint Mathis	4	90	317 mins
4	Mohamadou Idrissou	4	70	492 mins

KEY PLAYERS - MIDFIELDERS

Christophe Dabrowski

Goals in the League	0	Contribution to Attacking Power Average number of minutes between League team goals while on pitch	64
Defensive Rating Average number of mins between League goals conceded while he was on the pitch	60	Scoring Difference Defensive Rating minus Contribution to Attacking Power	-4

	PLAYER	LGE GOALS	DEF RATE	POWER	SCORE DIFF
1	Christophe Dabrowski	0	60	64	-4 mins
2	Nebosja Krupnikovic	2	44	52	-8 mins
3	Julian De Guzman	2	49	59	-10 mins
4	Altin Lala	0	47	71	-24 mins

KEY PLAYERS - DEFENDERS

Dariusz Zuraw

Goals Conceded (GC) The number of League goals conceded while he was on the pitch	24	Clean Sheets In games when he played at least 70 minutes	5
Defensive Rating Ave number of mins between League goals conceded while on the pitch	68	Club Defensive Rating Average number of mins between League goals conceded by the club this season	49

	PLAYER	CON LGE	CLEAN SHEETS	DEF RATE
1	Dariusz Zuraw	24	5	68 mins
2	Steve Cherundolo	43	7	55 mins
3	Kleber de Carvalho Correia	39	4	46 mins
4	Bergantin Vinicius	46	3	40 mins

KEY GOALKEEPER

Marc Ziegler

Goals Conceded in the League	49	Counting Games Games when he played at least 70 mins	29
Defensive Rating Ave number of mins between League goals conceded while on the pitch	52	Clean Sheets In games when he played at least 70 mins	7

LEAGUE GOALS

Thomas Brdaric

Minutes on the pitch	2139	Goals in the League	12
League average (mins between goals)	178		

	PLAYER	MINS	GOALS	AVE
1	Brdaric	2139	12	178
2	Christiansen	1714	8	214
3	Idrissou	1966	4	492
4	Mathis	1266	4	317
5	Stendel	1360	4	340
6	Stajner	979	3	326
7	Simak	472	2	236
8	De Guzman	2350	2	1175
9	Krupnikovic	1550	2	775
10	Jaime	522	1	522
11	Zuraw	1630	1	1630
12	Konstantinidis	1918	1	1918
	Other		5	
	TOTAL		49	

DISCIPLINARY RECORDS

	PLAYER	YELLOW	RED	AVE
1	De Guzman	12	2	167
2	Simak	2	0	236
3	Brdaric	8	1	237
4	Jaime	2	0	261
5	Idrissou	5	2	280
6	Cherundolo	7	1	296
7	Christiansen	4	1	342
8	Konstantinidis	5	0	383
9	Krupnikovic	4	0	387
10	Zuraw	4	0	407
11	Mathis	3	0	422
12	Dabrowski	4	0	447
13	Stajner	2	0	489
	Other	11	0	
	TOTAL	73	7	

TOP POINT EARNERS

	PLAYER	GAMES	AV PTS
1	Simak	4	1.75
2	Tremmel	5	1.60
3	Schuler	8	1.50
4	Stajner	7	1.43
5	Christiansen	15	1.33
6	Dabrowski	17	1.29
7	Jaime	5	1.20
8	Cherundolo	25	1.20
9	Krupnikovic	17	1.18
10	Konstantinidis	20	1.15
	CLUB AVERAGE:		1.09

TEAM OF THE SEASON

G
Marc Ziegler
CG: 28 DR: 52
D
Dariusz Zuraw
CG: 17 DR: 68
D
Steve Cherundolo
CG: 25 DR: 55
D
Kleber Correia
CG: 19 DR: 46
D
Kostas Konstantinidis
CG: 20 DR: 40
M
Christophe Dabrowski
CG: 17 SD: -4
M
Nebosja Krupnikovic
CG: 17 SD: -8
M
Julian De Guzman
CG: 24 SD: -10
M
*Altin Lala
CG: 12 SD: -24
F
Thomas Brdaric
CG: 22 SR: 178
F
Thomas Christiansen
CG: 15 SR: 214

LEAGUE APPEARANCES, BOOKINGS AND CAPS

	AGE (on 01/07/04)	IN NAMED 18	APPEARANCES	COUNTING GAMES	MINUTES ON PITCH	YELLOW CARDS	RED CARDS	THIS SEASON	HOME COUNTRY
Goalkeepers									
Daniel Hass	20	6	1	0	45	0	0	-	Germany
Gerd Tremmel	25	26	5	5	450	0	0	-	Germany
Marc Ziegler	28	34	29	28	2565	1	0	-	Germany
Defenders									
Abel Xavier	31	6	5	4	410	0	0	-	Portugal
Gurman Agac	21	1	0	0	0	0	0	-	Germany
Steve Cherundolo	25	30	29	25	2372	7	1	-	United States
Kleber Correia	24	25	23	19	1785	3	0	-	Brazil
K Konstantinidis	31	22	22	20	1918	5	0	-	Greece
Per Mertesacker	19	21	13	12	1113	0	0	-	Germany
Nils Pfingsten	22	1	0	0	0	0	0	-	Germany
Thomas Schneider	31	11	3	0	59	0	0	-	Germany
Markus Schuler	26	31	19	8	997	1	0	-	Germany
Bergantin Vinicius	23	23	22	18	1820	3	0	-	Brazil
Dariusz Zuraw	31	34	24	17	1630	4	0	-	Poland
Midfielders									
Vladimir But	26	10	3	0	103	0	0	-	Russia
C Dabrowski	26	31	25	17	1788	4	0	-	Germany
Julian De Guzman	23	30	29	24	2350	12	2	-	Canada
Salim Djefaflia	25	2	1	0	7	0	0	-	France
Sanchez Jaime	31	13	10	5	522	2	0	-	Spain
N Krupnikovic	30	24	19	17	1550	4	0	-	Serbia & Montenegro
Altin Lala	28	14	13	12	1070	0	0	-	Albania
Markus Schinner	23	2	0	0	0	0	0	-	Germany
Silvio Schroter	25	14	12	5	691	1	0	-	Germany
Jan Simak	25	6	6	4	472	2	0	-	Czech Republic
Danijel Stefulj	31	14	8	1	233	0	0	-	Croatia
Forwards									
Thomas Brdaric	29	29	29	22	2139	8	1	-	Germany
T Christiansen	31	27	26	15	1714	4	1	-	Spain
Mu Idrissou	24	28	26	20	1966	5	2	5	Cameroon (12)
Clint Mathis	27	16	16	13	1266	3	0	-	United States
Fabian Montabell	19	2	1	0	13	0	0	-	Germany
Jiri Stajner	28	18	16	7	979	2	0	6	Czech Republic (10)
Daniel Stendel	30	34	28	11	1360	2	0	-	Germany
Stanko Svitlica	28	8	3	0	114	0	0	-	Serbia & Montenegro
Denis Wolf	21	9	4	0	49	0	0	-	Germany

SQUAD APPEARANCES

Match	1	2	3	4	5	6	7	8	9	10	11	12	13	14	15	16	17	18	19	20	21	22	23	24	25	26	27	28	29	30	31	32	33	34
Venue	A	H	A	H	A	H	A	H	A	H	A	H	A	H	A	A	H	H	A	H	A	H	A	H	A	H	A	H	A	H	A	H	H	A
Competition	L	L	L	L	L	L	L	L	L	L	L	L	L	L	L	L	L	L	L	L	L	L	L	L	L	L	L	L	L	L	L	L	L	L
Result	W	D	L	D	W	W	L	L	L	D	W	L	L	W	D	L	D	W	L	D	L	L	L	L	D	D	W	W	D	L	L	W	D	L

Goalkeepers
Daniel Hass
Gerd Tremmel
Marc Ziegler

Defenders
Luis Silva Abel Xavier
Gurman Agac
Steve Cherundolo
Kleber de Carvalho Correia
Kostas Konstantinidis
Per Mertesacker
Nils Pfingsten
Thomas Schneider
Markus Schuler
Bergantin Vinicius
Dariusz Zuraw

Midfielders
Vladimir But
Christophe Dabrowski
Julian De Guzman
Salim Djefaflia
Sanchez Fernandez Jaime
Nebosja Krupnikovic
Altin Lala
Markus Schinner
Silvio Schroter
Jan Simak
Danijel Stefulj

Forwards
Thomas Brdaric
Thomas Christiansen
Mohamadou Idrissou
Clint Mathis
Fabian Montabell
Jiri Stajner
Daniel Stendel
Stanko Svitlica
Denis Wolf

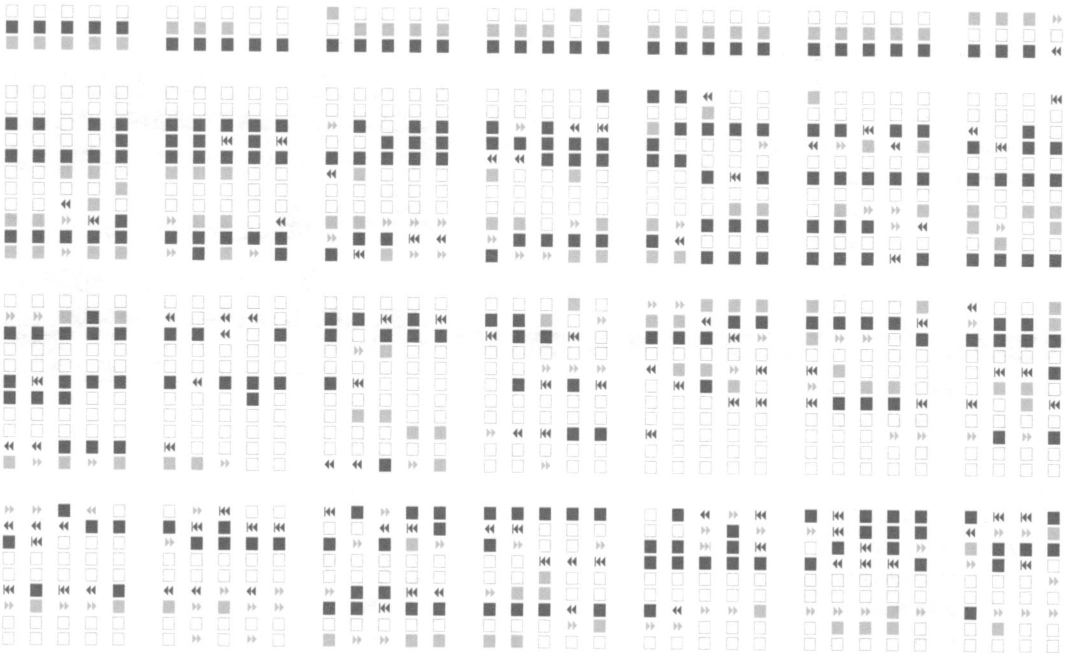

KEY: On all match; On bench; Subbed or sent off (Counting game); Subbed or sent off (playing less than 70 minutes); Subbed on from bench (Counting Game); Subbed on (playing less than 70 minutes); Subbed on and then subbed or sent off (Counting Game); Subbed on and then subbed or sent off (playing less than 70 minutes); Not in 16

KAISERSLAUTERN

Final Position: **15th**

KEY: ☐ Won ☐ Drawn ☐ Lost

								Attendance
1	lge	1860 Munich	H	L	0-1			35,000
2	lge	Cologne	A	W	2-1	Klose, M 39; Grammozis 76		33,000
3	lge	W Bremen	H	L	0-1			33,000
4	lge	Stuttgart	A	L	0-2			27,000
5	lge	Freiburg	H	D	2-2	Hristov 32,38		36,000
6	lge	Eintr Frankfurt	A	W	3-1	Hristov 6,52; Klose, M 48		23,000
7	uc1rl1	FK Teplice	H	L	1-2	Klose 58		18,011
8	lge	Hannover 96	H	W	1-0	Klose, M 90		32,361
9	lge	Bochum	A	L	0-4			20,000
10	uc1rl2	FK Teplice	A	L	0-1			14,300
11	lge	Hamburg	H	W	4-0	Mettomo 37; Klose, M 63,75; Timm 74		38,016
12	lge	Bayern Munich	A	L	1-4	Klose, M 78		42,000
13	lge	B Leverkusen	H	D	0-0			39,000
14	lge	Hansa Rostock	A	L	0-4			12,000
15	lge	Hertha Berlin	H	W	4-2	Klose 47,69,79; Tchato 77		33,000
16	lge	B M'gladbach	A	L	1-2	Lincoln 23		31,000
17	lge	Wolfsburg	A	L	1-4	Knavs 14		21,000
18	lge	Schalke	H	L	0-2			40,000
19	lge	B Dortmund	A	D	1-1	Lincoln 77		73,000
20	lge	1860 Munich	A	L	1-2	Lokvenc 25		20,000
21	lge	Cologne	H	W	1-0	Lokvenc 23		38,000
22	lge	W Bremen	A	L	0-1			37,000
23	lge	Stuttgart	H	W	1-0	Dominguez 4		40,000
24	lge	Freiburg	A	L	0-1			24,500
25	lge	Eintr Frankfurt	H	W	1-0	Malz 90		40,952
26	lge	Hannover 96	A	W	1-0	Hristov 63		22,000
27	lge	Bochum	H	D	2-2	Lokvenc 55,64		35,000
28	lge	Hamburg	A	L	2-3	Klose 52; Hristov 81		41,020
29	lge	Bayern Munich	H	L	0-2			47,315
30	lge	B Leverkusen	A	L	0-6			22,500
31	lge	Hansa Rostock	H	W	3-2	Bjelica 32; Hristov 36; Lokvenc 75		35,000
32	lge	Hertha Berlin	A	L	0-3			45,292
33	lge	B M'gladbach	H	D	2-2	Altintop 3; Hristov 47		45,000
34	lge	Wolfsburg	H	W	3-2	Lokvenc 57; Klose 72; Bjelica 75		40,000
35	lge	Schalke	A	L	1-4	Altintop 55		61,266
36	lge	B Dortmund	H	D	1-1	Lokvenc 6		47,315

MONTHLY POINTS TALLY

AUGUST	3	25%
SEPTEMBER	7	78%
OCTOBER	3	33%
NOVEMBER	4	33%
DECEMBER	1	11%
JANUARY	0	0%
FEBRUARY	6	50%
MARCH	7	58%
APRIL	3	25%
MAY	5	42%

KEY PLAYERS - GOALSCORERS

Miroslav Klose

Goals in the League	8	Player Strike Rate Average number of minutes between League goals scored by player	272
Contribution to Attacking Power Average number of minutes between League team goals while on pitch	75	Club Strike Rate Average number of minutes between League goals scored by club	78

	PLAYER	LGE GOALS	POWER	STRIKE RATE
1	Miroslav Klose	8	75	272 mins
2	Vratislav Lokvenc	7	77	298 mins
3	Marian Hristov	8	83	333 mins
4	Nenad Bjelica	2	73	732 mins

KEY PLAYERS - MIDFIELDERS

Stefan Malz

Goals in the League	1	Contribution to Attacking Power Average number of minutes between League team goals while on pitch	84
Defensive Rating Average number of mins between League goals conceded while he was on the pitch	73	Scoring Difference Defensive Rating minus Contribution to Attacking Power	-11

	PLAYER	LGE GOALS	DEF RATE	POWER	SCORE DIFF
1	Stefan Malz	1	73	84	-11 mins
2	Nenad Bjelica	2	54	73	-19 mins
3	Marian Hristov	8	51	83	-32 mins
4	Thomas Riedl	0	45	83	-38 mins

KEY PLAYERS - DEFENDERS

Hervi Nzelo Lembi

Goals Conceded (GC) The number of League goals conceded while he was on the pitch	21	Clean Sheets In games when he played at least 70 minutes	3
Defensive Rating Ave number of mins between League goals conceded while on the pitch	52	Club Defensive Rating Average number of mins between League goals conceded by the club this season	49

	PLAYER	CON LGE	CLEAN SHEETS	DEF RATE
1	Hervi Nzelo Lembi	21	3	52 mins
2	Timo Wenzel	31	4	49 mins
3	Aleksander Knavs	44	4	48 mins
4	Bill Tchato	35	3	47 mins

KEY GOALKEEPER

Tim Wiese

Goals Conceded in the League	50	Counting Games Games when he played at least 70 mins	30
Defensive Rating Ave number of mins between League goals conceded while on the pitch	52	Clean Sheets In games when he played at least 70 mins	7

LEAGUE GOALS

Marian Hristov

Minutes on the pitch	2663	Goals in the League	8
League average (mins between goals)	333		

	PLAYER	MINS	GOALS	AVE
1	Hristov	2663	8	333
2	Klose	2177	8	272
3	Lokvenc	2088	7	298
4	Altintop	1302	2	651
5	Bjelica	1463	2	732
6	Lincoln	535	2	268
7	Knavs	2132	1	2132
8	Grammozis	1037	1	1037
9	Timm	289	1	289
10	Malz	1172	1	1172
11	Dominguez	1363	1	1363
12	Mettomo	1019	1	1019
	Other		3	
	TOTAL		39	

DISCIPLINARY RECORDS

	PLAYER	YELLOW	RED	AVE
1	Vreven	4	0	143
2	Riedl	11	0	143
3	Malz	7	1	146
4	Bjelica	9	0	162
5	Hengen	5	0	167
6	Mettomo	5	1	169
7	Freund	3	0	171
8	Hristov	11	1	221
9	Tchato	5	1	274
10	Lehmann	2	0	329
11	Dominguez	3	1	340
12	Knavs	4	1	426
13	Klose	5	0	435
	Other	22	1	
	TOTAL	96	7	

TOP POINT EARNERS

	PLAYER	GAMES	AV PTS
1	Nurmela	9	1.78
2	Freund	4	1.75
3	Dominguez	8	1.75
4	Grammozis	11	1.55
5	Timm	2	1.50
6	Bjelica	15	1.40
7	Malz	13	1.38
8	Lokvenc	21	1.33
9	Knavs	23	1.30
10	Wenzel	17	1.24
	CLUB AVERAGE:		1.15

LEAGUE APPEARANCES, BOOKINGS AND CAPS

	AGE (on 01/07/04)	IN NAMED 18	APPEARANCES	COUNTING GAMES	MINUTES ON PITCH	YELLOW CARDS	RED CARDS	THIS SEASON	HOME COUNTRY
Goalkeepers									
Thomas Ernst	36	30	6	5	464	0	0	-	Germany
Jens Kern	21	4	0	0	0	0	0	-	Germany
Tim Wiese	22	30	30	28	2599	4	1	-	Germany
Defenders									
Kristjan Glibo	22	7	1	0	8	0	0	-	Germany
Thomas Hengen	29	14	10	9	839	5	0	-	Germany
Aleksander Knavs	28	26	25	23	2132	4	1	-	Slovenia
Hervi Nzelo Lembi	28	13	13	12	1091	1	0	-	Congo DR
Lucien Mettomo	32	23	16	10	1019	5	1	4	Cameroon (12)
Hany Ramzy	35	1	1	0	43	0	0	-	Egypt
Torsten Reuter	21	19	7	5	492	1	0	-	Germany
Bill Tchato	29	25	22	17	1649	5	1	4	Cameroon (12)
Stijn Vreven	30	21	8	6	575	4	0	-	Belgium
Timo Wenzel	26	17	17	17	1530	3	0	-	Germany
Midfielders									
Markus Anfang	30	11	8	4	441	2	0	-	Germany
Michael Berndt	25	2	0	0	0	0	0	-	Germany
Nenad Bjelica	32	23	19	15	1463	9	0	-	Croatia
Jose Dominguez	30	30	26	8	1363	3	1	-	Portugal
Thomas Drescher	25	15	11	9	919	0	0	-	Germany
Steffen Freund	34	10	8	4	513	3	0	-	Germany
D Grammozis	26	12	12	11	1037	2	0	-	Greece
Marian Hristov	30	31	31	29	2663	11	1	-	Bulgaria
Kamil Kosowski	26	25	21	12	1479	1	0	-	Poland
Mathias Lehmann	21	17	12	5	658	2	0	-	Germany
Cassio Lincoln	25	8	6	6	535	1	0	-	Brazil
Nicolas Loison	23	5	0	0	0	0	0	-	France
Stefan Malz	32	19	16	13	1172	7	1	-	Germany
Thomas Riedl	28	25	21	15	1577	11	0	-	Germany
Patrick Wittich	22	2	1	0	7	0	0	-	Germany
Forwards									
Halil Altintop	21	31	26	9	1302	1	0	-	Turkey
Danko Boskovic (45)	22	1	1	0	16	0	0	4	Serbia & M'tenegro
Miroslav Klose	26	27	26	22	2177	5	0	8	Germany (9)
Vratislav Lokvenc	30	27	25	21	2088	5	3	6	Czech Republic (10)
Michael Mifsud	23	1	0	0	0	0	0	-	Malta
Mike Nurmela	32	30	20	9	1207	2	0	-	Finland
Christian Timm	25	8	6	2	289	1	0	-	Germany

TEAM OF THE SEASON

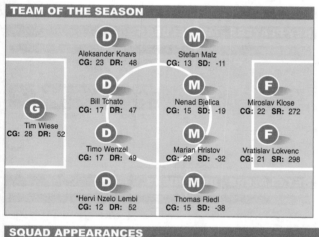

G Tim Wiese CG: 28 DR: 52

D Aleksander Knavs CG: 23 DR: 48

D Bill Tchato CG: 17 DR: 47

D Timo Wenzel CG: 17 DR: 49

D *Hervi Nzelo Lembi CG: 12 DR: 52

M Stefan Malz CG: 13 SD: -11

M Nenad Bjelica CG: 15 SD: -19

M Marian Hristov CG: 29 SD: -32

M Thomas Riedl CG: 15 SD: -38

F Miroslav Klose CG: 22 SR: 272

F Vratislav Lokvenc CG: 21 SR: 298

SQUAD APPEARANCES

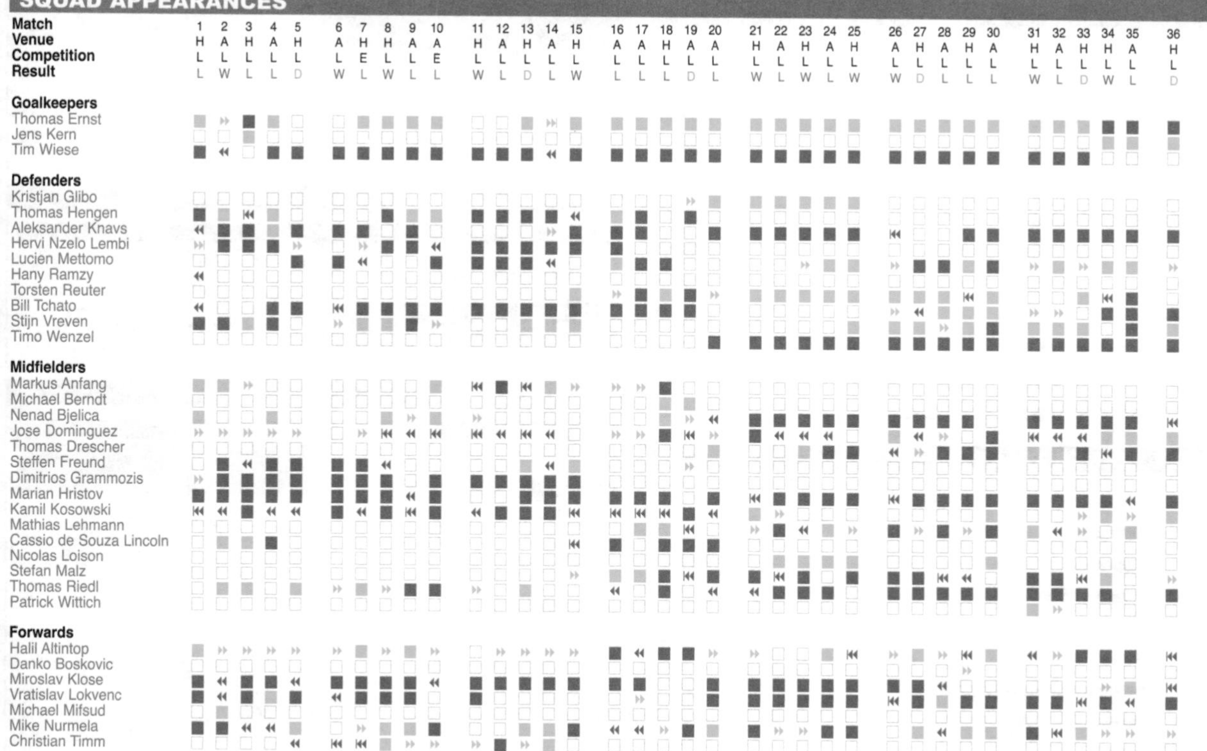

Match 1 2 3 4 5 6 7 8 9 10 11 12 13 14 15 16 17 18 19 20 21 22 23 24 25 26 27 28 29 30 31 32 33 34 35 36
Venue H A H A H A H H A A H A H A H A A H A A H A H A H A H A H A H A H H A H
Competition L L L L L L E L L E L L L L L L L L L L L L L L L L L L L L L L L L L L
Result L W L L D W L W L L W L D L W L L L D L W L W L W W D L L L W L D W L D
Goalkeepers
Thomas Ernst
Jens Kern
Tim Wiese
Defenders
Kristjan Glibo
Thomas Hengen
Aleksander Knavs
Hervi Nzelo Lembi
Lucien Mettomo
Hany Ramzy
Torsten Reuter
Bill Tchato
Stijn Vreven
Timo Wenzel
Midfielders
Markus Anfang
Michael Berndt
Nenad Bjelica
Jose Dominguez
Thomas Drescher
Steffen Freund
Dimitrios Grammozis
Marian Hristov
Kamil Kosowski
Mathias Lehmann
Cassio de Souza Lincoln
Nicolas Loison
Stefan Malz
Thomas Riedl
Patrick Wittich
Forwards
Halil Altintop
Danko Boskovic
Miroslav Klose
Vratislav Lokvenc
Michael Mifsud
Mike Nurmela
Christian Timm

KEY: ■ On all match ■ On bench | ⏮ Subbed or sent off (Counting game) « Subbed or sent off (playing less than 70 minutes) | ⏭ Subbed on from bench (Counting Game) » Subbed on (playing less than 70 minutes) | ⏭ Subbed on and then subbed or sent off (Counting Game) » Subbed on and then subbed or sent off (playing less than 70 minutes) | □ Not in 16

EINTRACHT FRANKFURT

Final Position: **16th**

KEY: Won Drawn Lost

							Attendance
1	lge	Bayern Munich	A	L	1-3	Skela 68	63,000
2	lge	B Leverkusen	H	L	1-2	Frommer 42	22,500
3	lge	Hansa Rostock	A	L	0-3		20,000
4	lge	Hertha Berlin	H	D	0-0		17,000
5	lge	B M'gladbach	A	W	2-0	Kreuz 17; Burger 90	34,000
6	lge	Kaiserslautern	H	L	1-3	Beierle 90	23,000
7	lge	Schalke	A	D	1-1	Chris 38	61,000
8	lge	B Dortmund	H	L	0-1		23,000
9	lge	1860 Munich	A	L	0-1		20,000
10	lge	Cologne	H	W	2-0	Frommer 63; Dragusha 81	20,000
11	lge	W Bremen	A	L	1-3	Reinke 66 og	32,000
12	lge	Stuttgart	H	L	0-2		27,000
13	lge	Freiburg	A	L	0-1		24,000
14	lge	Wolfsburg	H	W	3-2	Preuss 33; Skela 55 pen; Beierle 73	20,000
15	lge	Hannover 96	H	D	2-2	Schur 18; Skela 64 pen	20,000
16	lge	Bochum	A	L	0-1		21,000
17	lge	Hamburg	H	L	2-3	Skela 54; Beierle 66	19,000
18	lge	Bayern Munich	H	D	1-1	Skela 45 pen	37,500
19	lge	B Leverkusen	A	W	2-1	Hertzsch 20; Amanatidis 77	22,500
20	lge	Hansa Rostock	H	D	1-1	Chris 40	23,000
21	lge	Hertha Berlin	A	W	2-1	Cha 18; Amanatidis 66	27,000
22	lge	B M'gladbach	H	W	3-1	Skela 16; Amanatidis 17; Schur 55	32,000
23	lge	Kaiserslautern	A	L	0-1		40,952
24	lge	Schalke	H	W	3-0	Amanatidis 57; Skela 76; Schur 80	35,255
25	lge	B Dortmund	A	L	0-2		80,000
26	lge	1860 Munich	H	L	0-3		30,000
27	lge	Cologne	A	L	0-2		44,000
28	lge	W Bremen	H	L	0-1		33,400
29	lge	Stuttgart	A	L	1-3	Schur 85	48,000
30	lge	Freiburg	H	W	3-0	Skela 29; Preuss 45; Beierle 72	55,300
31	lge	Wolfsburg	A	L	0-1		22,000
32	lge	Hannover 96	A	L	0-3		27,500
33	lge	Bochum	H	W	3-2	Preuss 13; Puljiz 19; Amanatidis 51	32,000
34	lge	Hamburg	A	L	1-2	Amanatidis 26	53,000

MONTHLY POINTS TALLY

Month	Points	%
AUGUST	1	8%
SEPTEMBER	4	44%
OCTOBER	3	33%
NOVEMBER	3	25%
DECEMBER	1	11%
JANUARY	1	33%
FEBRUARY	10	83%
MARCH	3	25%
APRIL	3	25%
MAY	3	25%

KEY PLAYERS - GOALSCORERS

Ioannis Amanatidis

Goals in the League	6	Player Strike Rate Average number of minutes between League goals scored by player	214
Contribution to Attacking Power Average number of minutes between League team goals while on pitch	80	Club Strike Rate Average number of minutes between League goals scored by club	85

	PLAYER	LGE GOALS	POWER	STRIKE RATE
1	Ioannis Amanatidis	6	80	214 mins
2	Ervin Skela	8	81	338 mins
3	Alexander Schur	4	77	679 mins
4	Christoph Preuss	3	76	844 mins

KEY PLAYERS - MIDFIELDERS

Henning Burger

Goals in the League	1	Contribution to Attacking Power Average number of minutes between League team goals while on pitch	69
Defensive Rating Average number of mins between League goals conceded while he was on the pitch	56	Scoring Difference Defensive Rating minus Contribution to Attacking Power	-13

	PLAYER	LGE GOALS	DEF RATE	POWER	SCORE DIFF
1	Henning Burger	1	56	69	-13 mins
2	Sven Gunther	0	66	82	-16 mins
3	Christoph Preuss	3	59	77	-18 mins
4	Markus Kreuz	1	59	81	-22 mins

KEY PLAYERS - DEFENDERS

Ingo Hertzsch

Goals Conceded (GC) The number of League goals conceded while he was on the pitch	18	Clean Sheets In games when he played at least 70 minutes	2
Defensive Rating Ave number of mins between League goals conceded while on the pitch	71	Club Defensive Rating Average number of mins between League goals conceded by the club this season	58

	PLAYER	CON LGE	CLEAN SHEETS	DEF RATE
1	Ingo Hertzsch	18	2	71 mins
2	Christian Maicon Hening Chris	34	1	59 mins
3	Uwe Bindewald	27	2	57 mins
4	Andre Weidener	27	3	54 mins

KEY GOALKEEPER

Oka Nikolov

Goals Conceded in the League	46	Counting Games Games when he played at least 70 mins	31
Defensive Rating Ave number of mins between League goals conceded while on the pitch	61	Clean Sheets In games when he played at least 70 mins	5

LEAGUE GOALS

Ervin Skela

Minutes on the pitch	2700	Goals in the League	8
League average (mins between goals)	338		

	PLAYER	MINS	GOALS	AVE
1	Skela	2700	8	338
2	Amanatidis	1286	6	214
3	Schur	2717	4	679
4	Beierle	1175	4	294
5	Preuss	2533	3	844
6	Chris	2015	2	1008
7	Frommer	785	2	393
8	Dragusha	343	1	343
9	Kreuz	2260	1	2260
10	Cha	1903	1	1903
11	Puljiz	1077	1	1077
12	Burger	1518	1	1518
	Other		2	
	TOTAL		36	

DISCIPLINARY RECORDS

	PLAYER	YELLOW	RED	AVE
1	Burger	7	1	189
2	Schur	11	0	247
3	Chris	7	0	287
4	Lexa	4	0	318
5	Hertzsch	4	0	319
6	Puljiz	3	0	359
7	Kreuz	6	0	376
8	Frommer	2	0	392
9	Amanatidis	2	1	428
10	Gunther	4	0	429
11	Bindewald	3	0	512
12	Cipi	1	1	562
13	Moller	1	0	599
	Other	14	1	
	TOTAL	69	4	

TOP POINT EARNERS

	PLAYER	GAMES	AV PTS
1	Burger	14	1.43
2	Hertzsch	14	1.21
3	Amanatidis	14	1.21
4	Frommer	5	1.20
5	Kreuz	24	1.17
6	Preuss	28	1.11
7	Gunther	17	1.06
8	Proll	3	1.00
9	Puljiz	10	1.00
10	Beierle	11	1.00
	CLUB AVERAGE:		0.94

TEAM OF THE SEASON

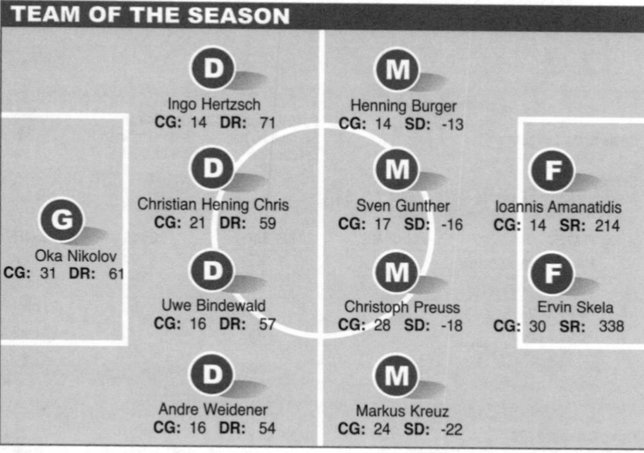

D
Ingo Hertzsch
CG: 14 DR: 71
M
Henning Burger
CG: 14 SD: -13
D
Christian Hening Chris
CG: 21 DR: 59
M
Sven Gunther
CG: 17 SD: -16
F
Ioannis Amanatidis
CG: 14 SR: 214
G
Oka Nikolov
CG: 31 DR: 61
D
Uwe Bindewald
CG: 16 DR: 57
M
Christoph Preuss
CG: 28 SD: -18
F
Ervin Skela
CG: 30 SR: 338
D
Andre Weidener
CG: 16 DR: 54
M
Markus Kreuz
CG: 24 SD: -22

LEAGUE APPEARANCES, BOOKINGS AND CAPS

	AGE (on 01/07/04)	IN NAMED 18	APPEARANCES	COUNTING GAMES	MINUTES ON PITCH	YELLOW CARDS	RED CARDS	THIS SEASON	HOME COUNTRY
Goalkeepers									
Andreas Menger	31	2	0	0	0	0	0	-	Germany
Oka Nikolov	30	33	31	31	2790	1	0	-	Germany
Markus Proll	24	29	3	3	270	0	0	-	Germany
Defenders									
Uwe Bindewald	35	27	20	16	1538	3	0	-	Germany
Chris	25	24	24	21	2015	7	0	-	Brazil
Daniyel Cimen	19	1	0	0	0	0	0	-	Germany
Geri Cipi	28	14	13	12	1124	1	1	-	Albania
Baldo di Gregorio	20	1	0	0	0	0	0	-	Germany
Mehmet Dragusha	26	28	13	1	343	0	0	-	Albania
Ingo Hertzsch	26	15	15	14	1276	4	0	-	Germany
Jens Keller	33	3	2	1	96	0	0	-	Germany
Jurica Puljiz	24	29	16	10	1077	3	0	-	Croatia
J Tsoumou-Madza	29	9	8	8	709	1	0	-	Congo
Nascimento Vivaldo	24	5	2	0	65	0	0	-	Brazil
Andre Weidener	34	26	17	16	1459	2	0	-	Germany
Midfielders									
Henning Burger	34	27	21	14	1518	7	1	-	Germany
Sven Gunther	28	31	25	17	1718	4	0	-	Germany
Markus Kreuz	27	32	30	24	2260	6	0	-	Germany
Stefan Lexa	27	33	30	9	1272	4	0	-	Austria
Andreas Moller	34	12	11	5	599	1	0	-	Germany
David Montero	28	2	1	1	76	0	0	-	Germany
Christoph Preuss	23	29	29	28	2533	3	0	-	Germany
Alexander Schur	32	31	31	30	2717	11	0	-	Germany
Ervin Skela	27	30	30	30	2700	3	1	-	Albania
Lars Weissenfeldt	24	9	1	0	31	0	0	-	Germany
Forwards									
Ioannis Amanatidis	22	15	15	14	1286	2	1	-	Greece
Markus Beierle	32	31	19	11	1175	1	0	-	Germany
Doo-Ri Cha	23	32	29	17	1903	3	0	-	South Korea
Nico Frommer	26	32	18	5	785	2	0	-	Germany
Jermaine Jones	22	5	5	0	225	0	0	-	Germany

SQUAD APPEARANCES

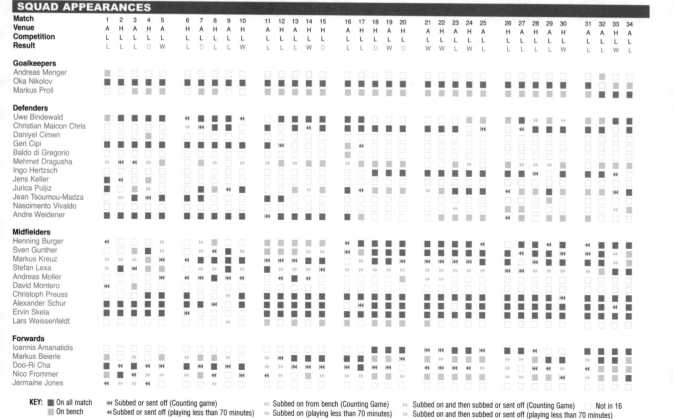

Match	1	2	3	4	5	6	7	8	9	10	11	12	13	14	15	16	17	18	19	20	21	22	23	24	25	26	27	28	29	30	31	32	33	34
Venue	A	H	A	H	A	H	A	H	A	H	A	H	A	H	H	A	H	H	A	H	A	H	A	H	A	H	A	H	A	H	A	A	H	A
Competition	L	L	L	L	L	L	L	L	L	L	L	L	L	L	L	L	L	L	L	L	L	L	L	L	L	L	L	L	L	L	L	L	L	L
Result	L	L	L	D	W	L	D	L	L	W	L	L	L	W	D	L	L	D	W	D	W	W	L	W	L	L	L	L	L	W	L	L	W	L

Goalkeepers
Andreas Menger
Oka Nikolov
Markus Proll

Defenders
Uwe Bindewald
Christian Maicon Chris
Daniyel Cimen
Geri Cipi
Baldo di Gregorio
Mehmet Dragusha
Ingo Hertzsch
Jens Keller
Jurica Puljiz
Jean Tsoumou-Madza
Nascimento Vivaldo
Andre Weidener

Midfielders
Henning Burger
Sven Gunther
Markus Kreuz
Stefan Lexa
Andreas Moller
David Montero
Christoph Preuss
Alexander Schur
Ervin Skela
Lars Weissenfeldt

Forwards
Ioannis Amanatidis
Markus Beierle
Doo-Ri Cha
Nico Frommer
Jermaine Jones

KEY: On all match · On bench · Subbed or sent off (Counting game) · Subbed or sent off (playing less than 70 minutes) · Subbed on from bench (Counting Game) · Subbed on (playing less than 70 minutes) · Subbed on and then subbed or sent off (Counting Game) · Subbed on and then subbed or sent off (playing less than 70 minutes) · Not in 16

TSV 1860 MUNICH

Final Position: **17th**

KEY: ☐ Won ☐ Drawn ☐ Lost

							Attendance
1	lge	Kaiserslautern	A	W	1-0	Schroth 44	35,000
2	lge	Schalke	H	D	1-1	Schroth 19	33,000
3	lge	B Dortmund	A	L	1-3	Kioyo 87	74,000
4	lge	Wolfsburg	H	W	1-0	Schwarz 60	24,000
5	lge	Cologne	H	W	2-1	Kioyo 7; Agostino 83	25,000
6	lge	W Bremen	A	L	1-2	Schroth 57	32,000
7	lge	Stuttgart	H	L	0-3		38,000
8	lge	Freiburg	A	L	0-1		25,000
9	lge	Eintr Frankfurt	H	W	1-0	Lauth 90 pen	20,000
10	lge	Hannover 96	A	D	1-1	Weissenberger 35	19,754
11	lge	Bochum	H	W	3-1	Lauth 50,67,78	18,000
12	lge	Hamburg	A	L	1-3	Schwarz 58	48,000
13	lge	Bayern Munich	H	L	0-1		69,000
14	lge	B Leverkusen	A	D	2-2	Schwarz 36; Schroth 56	23,000
15	lge	Hansa Rostock	H	L	1-4	Weissenberger 3	13,000
16	lge	Hertha Berlin	A	D	1-1	Lauth 57	20,000
17	lge	B M'gladbach	H	L	1-2	Lauth 62	15,000
18	lge	Kaiserslautern	H	W	2-1	Lauth 18,39	20,000
19	lge	Schalke	A	D	0-0		61,000
20	lge	B Dortmund	H	L	0-2		25,000
21	lge	Wolfsburg	A	L	1-3	Weissenberger 27	13,000
22	lge	Cologne	A	W	3-1	Schroth 14,39; Lauth 36 pen	35,000
23	lge	W Bremen	H	L	0-2		25,000
24	lge	Stuttgart	A	L	0-2		41,000
25	lge	Freiburg	H	D	1-1	Agostino 58	19,500
26	lge	Eintr Frankfurt	A	W	3-0	Gorlitz 9; Lehmann 17; Agostino 59	30,000
27	lge	Hannover 96	H	L	0-2		22,000
28	lge	Bochum	A	L	0-4		21,000
29	lge	Hamburg	H	L	1-2	Agostino 87	20,000
30	lge	Bayern Munich	A	L	0-1		71,000
31	lge	B Leverkusen	H	D	1-1	Agostino 4	25,000
32	lge	Hansa Rostock	A	L	0-3		23,000
33	lge	Hertha Berlin	H	D	1-1	Costa 6	48,000
34	lge	B M'gladbach	A	L	1-3	Hoffmann, T 21 pen	34,500

MONTHLY POINTS TALLY

AUGUST	7	58%
SEPTEMBER	3	33%
OCTOBER	4	44%
NOVEMBER	4	33%
DECEMBER	1	11%
JANUARY	3	100%
FEBRUARY	4	33%
MARCH	4	33%
APRIL	0	0%
MAY	2	17%

KEY PLAYERS - GOALSCORERS

Benjamin Lauth

Goals in the League	9	**Player Strike Rate** Average number of minutes between League goals scored by player	238
Contribution to Attacking Power Average number of minutes between League team goals while on pitch	89	**Club Strike Rate** Average number of minutes between League goals scored by club	96

	PLAYER	LGE GOALS	POWER	STRIKE RATE
1	Benjamin Lauth	9	89	238 mins
2	Markus Schroth	6	93	389 mins
3	Danny Schwarz	3	79	477 mins
4	Markus Weissenberger	3	73	493 mins

KEY PLAYERS - MIDFIELDERS

Markus Weissenberger

Goals in the League	3	**Contribution to Attacking Power** Average number of minutes between League team goals while on pitch	74
Defensive Rating Average number of mins between League goals conceded while he was on the pitch	53	**Scoring Difference** Defensive Rating minus Contribution to Attacking Power	-21

	PLAYER	LGE GOALS	DEF RATE	POWER	SCORE DIFF
1	Markus Weissenberger	3	53	74	-21 mins
2	Danny Schwarz	3	57	79	-22 mins
3	Harald Cerny	0	54	87	-33 mins
4	Rodrigo Costa	1	59	96	-37 mins

KEY PLAYERS - DEFENDERS

Martin Stranzl

Goals Conceded (GC) The number of League goals conceded while he was on the pitch	28	**Clean Sheets** In games when he played at least 70 minutes	3
Defensive Rating Ave number of mins between League goals conceded while on the pitch	69	**Club Defensive Rating** Average number of mins between League goals conceded by the club this season	56

	PLAYER	CON LGE	CLEAN SHEETS	DEF RATE
1	Martin Stranzl	28	3	69 mins
2	Janne Saarinen	21	4	66 mins
3	Torben Hoffmann	48	4	57 mins
4	Roman Tyce	43	2	50 mins

KEY GOALKEEPER

Michael Hofmann

Goals Conceded in the League	50	**Counting Games** Games when he played at least 70 mins	31
Defensive Rating Ave number of mins between League goals conceded while on the pitch	55	**Clean Sheets** In games when he played at least 70 mins	5

LEAGUE GOALS

Benjamin Lauth

Minutes on the pitch	2142	Goals in the League	9
League average (mins between goals)	238		

	PLAYER	MINS	GOALS	AVE
1	Lauth	2142	9	238
2	Schroth	2333	6	389
3	Agostino	1039	5	208
4	Weissenberger	1478	3	493
5	Schwarz	1430	3	477
6	Kioyo	972	2	486
7	Gorlitz	2560	1	2560
8	Lehmann	1189	1	1189
9	Costa	2700	1	2700
10	Hoffmann, T	2731	1	2731
	Other		0	
	TOTAL		32	

DISCIPLINARY RECORDS

	PLAYER	YELLOW	RED	AVE
1	Davids	3	0	167
2	Santos	3	1	168
3	Tyce	10	1	195
4	Costa	12	0	225
5	Saarinen	6	0	231
6	Baier	2	0	245
7	Stranzl	6	1	275
8	Meyer	2	1	283
9	Kurz	3	0	295
10	Cerny	6	0	304
11	Schwarz	4	0	357
12	Gorlitz	5	1	426
13	Hoffmann, T	6	0	455
	Other	15	2	
	TOTAL	83	7	

TOP POINT EARNERS

	PLAYER	GAMES	AV PTS
1	Purk	4	1.50
2	Poschner	3	1.33
3	Saarinen	15	1.33
4	Schwarz	14	1.29
5	Weissenberger	14	1.14
6	Stranzl	19	1.11
7	Lehmann	11	1.09
8	Lauth	22	1.09
9	Gorlitz	26	1.08
10	Hoffmann, T	30	1.03
	CLUB AVERAGE:		**0.94**

TEAM OF THE SEASON

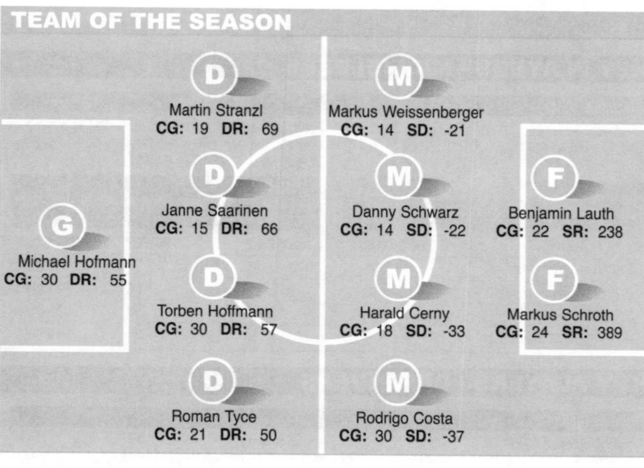

D
Martin Stranzl
CG: 19 DR: 69
M
Markus Weissenberger
CG: 14 SD: -21
D
Janne Saarinen
CG: 15 DR: 66
M
Danny Schwarz
CG: 14 SD: -22
F
Benjamin Lauth
CG: 22 SR: 238
G
Michael Hofmann
CG: 30 DR: 55
D
Torben Hoffmann
CG: 30 DR: 57
M
Harald Cerny
CG: 18 SD: -33
F
Markus Schroth
CG: 24 SR: 389
D
Roman Tyce
CG: 21 DR: 50
M
Rodrigo Costa
CG: 30 SD: -37

LEAGUE APPEARANCES, BOOKINGS AND CAPS

	AGE (on 01/07/04)	IN NAMED 18	APPEARANCES	COUNTING GAMES	MINUTES ON PITCH	YELLOW CARDS	RED CARDS	THIS SEASON	HOME COUNTRY
Goalkeepers									
Michael Hofmann	31	32	31	30	2760	5	0	-	Germany
Christian Horn	21	1	0	0	0	0	0	-	Germany
Matthias Kufner	23	1	0	0	0	0	0	-	Germany
Andre Lenz	30	31	3	2	210	0	0	-	Germany
Defenders									
Daniel Baier	20	24	11	2	491	2	0	-	Germany
Torben Hoffmann	29	31	31	30	2731	6	0	-	Germany
Christoph Janker	19	1	0	0	0	0	0	-	Germany
Marco Kurz	35	29	16	7	885	3	0	-	Germany
Janne Saarinen	27	21	17	15	1389	6	0	-	Finland
Fernando Santos	24	12	10	6	675	3	1	-	Brazil
Martin Stranzl	24	25	24	19	1930	6	1	-	Austria
Roman Tyce	27	29	29	21	2155	10	1	6	Czech Republic (10)
Midfielders									
Daniel Borimirov	34	9	5	1	127	1	1	-	Bulgaria
Harald Cerny	30	27	24	18	1825	6	0	-	Austria
Rodrigo Costa	28	30	30	30	2700	12	0	-	Brazil
Lance Davids	19	15	12	3	501	3	0	-	Germany
Andreas Gorlitz	22	32	32	26	2560	5	1	-	Germany
Mathias Lehmann	21	21	16	11	1189	1	0	-	Germany
Remo Meyer	23	23	14	7	851	2	1	-	Switzerland
Gerhard Poschner	34	8	4	3	299	0	0	-	Germany
Marcus Purk	29	11	9	4	548	1	0	-	Austria
Marcel Schafer	-	5	1	0	2	0	0	-	Germany
Danny Schwarz	29	18	18	14	1430	4	0	-	Germany
Jiayi Shao	24	10	4	0	122	0	0	-	China
M Weissenberger	29	25	21	14	1478	2	0	-	Austria
Micheal Wiesinger	31	8	2	0	70	0	0	-	Germany
Forwards									
Paul Agostino	29	28	22	9	1039	1	0	1	Australia (89)
Francis Kioyo	24	33	25	7	972	0	0	-	Cameroon
Benjamin Lauth	22	28	28	22	2142	3	1	3	Germany (9)
Christophe Lepoint	22	1	1	0	19	0	0	-	Belgium
Markus Schroth	29	33	29	24	2333	1	0	-	Germany

SQUAD APPEARANCES

Match	1	2	3	4	5	6	7	8	9	10	11	12	13	14	15	16	17	18	19	20	21	22	23	24	25	26	27	28	29	30	31	32	33	34
Venue	A	H	A	H	H	A	H	A	H	A	H	A	H	A	H	A	H	H	A	H	A	A	H	A	H	A	H	A	H	A	H	A	H	A
Competition	L	L	L	L	L	L	L	L	L	L	L	L	L	L	L	L	L	L	L	L	L	L	L	L	L	L	L	L	L	L	L	L	L	L
Result	W	D	L	W	W	L	L	L	W	D	W	L	L	D	L	D	L	W	D	L	L	W	L	L	D	W	L	L	L	L	D	L	D	L

Goalkeepers
Michael Hofmann
Christian Horn
Matthias Kufner
Andre Lenz

Defenders
Daniel Baier
Torben Hoffmann
Christoph Janker
Marco Kurz
Janne Saarinen
Fernando Santos
Martin Stranzl
Roman Tyce

Midfielders
Daniel Borimirov
Harald Cerny
Rodrigo Costa
Lance Davids
Andreas Gorlitz
Mathias Lehmann
Remo Meyer
Gerhard Poschner
Marcus Purk
Marcel Schafer
Danny Schwarz
Jiayi Shao
Markus Weissenberger
Micheal Wiesinger

Forwards
Paul Agostino
Francis Kioyo
Benjamin Lauth
Christophe Lepoint
Markus Schroth

KEY: ■ On all match ■ On bench
⏮ Subbed or sent off (Counting game)
« Subbed or sent off (playing less than 70 minutes)
» Subbed on from bench (Counting Game)
» Subbed on (playing less than 70 minutes)
» Subbed on and then subbed or sent off (Counting Game)
» Subbed on and then subbed or sent off (playing less than 70 minutes)
□ Not in 16

COLOGNE

Final Position: **18th**

KEY: ☐ Won ☐ Drawn ☐ Lost

		Opponent	H/A	Result	Score	Scorers	Attendance
1	lge	B M'gladbach	A	L	0-1		34,500
2	lge	Kaiserslautern	H	L	1-2	Ebbers 37	33,000
3	lge	Schalke	A	L	1-2	Lottner 51	61,000
4	lge	B Dortmund	H	W	1-0	Lottner 58	33,500
5	lge	1860 Munich	A	L	1-2	Springer 62	25,000
6	lge	Wolfsburg	H	L	2-3	Scherz 36; Voronin 60	33,000
7	lge	W Bremen	H	L	1-4	Scherz 79	33,000
8	lge	Stuttgart	A	D	0-0		52,000
9	lge	Freiburg	H	W	1-0	Dogan 70	33,000
10	lge	Eintr Frankfurt	A	L	0-2		20,000
11	lge	Hannover 96	H	L	1-2	Scherz 37	33,000
12	lge	Bochum	A	L	0-4		31,000
13	lge	Hamburg	H	L	0-1		40,000
14	lge	Bayern Munich	A	D	2-2	Voronin 35; Voigt 60	45,000
15	lge	B Leverkusen	H	D	0-0		40,000
16	lge	Hansa Rostock	A	D	1-1	Podolski 34	20,000
17	lge	Hertha Berlin	H	W	3-0	Voronin 47; Podolski 75; Scherz 87	30,000
18	lge	B M'gladbach	H	W	1-0	Podolski 52	51,000
19	lge	Kaiserslautern	A	L	0-1		38,000
20	lge	Schalke	H	L	0-2		51,000
21	lge	B Dortmund	A	L	0-1		80,000
22	lge	1860 Munich	H	L	1-3	Voronin 50	35,000
23	lge	Wolfsburg	A	L	0-2		18,246
24	lge	W Bremen	A	L	2-3	Schroder 57; Lottner 70	41,000
25	lge	Stuttgart	H	D	2-2	Kringe 45; Feulner 71	50,000
26	lge	Freiburg	A	L	0-3		25,000
27	lge	Eintr Frankfurt	H	W	2-0	Hertzsch 5 og; Podolski 35	44,000
28	lge	Hannover 96	A	L	0-1		27,200
29	lge	Bochum	H	L	1-2	Podolski 54	43,500
30	lge	Hamburg	A	L	2-4	Podolski 44; Springer 83	48,413
31	lge	Bayern Munich	H	L	1-2	Podolski 24	50,200
32	lge	B Leverkusen	A	L	0-2		22,500
33	lge	Hansa Rostock	H	W	4-0	Podolski 45 pen,58; Sinkala 56; Lottner 89	40,000
34	lge	Hertha Berlin	A	L	1-3	Podolski 54	50,000

MONTHLY POINTS TALLY

Month	Points	%
AUGUST	3	25%
SEPTEMBER	0	0%
OCTOBER	4	44%
NOVEMBER	1	8%
DECEMBER	5	56%
JANUARY	3	100%
FEBRUARY	0	0%
MARCH	1	8%
APRIL	3	25%
MAY	3	25%

KEY PLAYERS - GOALSCORERS

Lukas Podolski

Goals in the League	10	Player Strike Rate Average number of minutes between League goals scored by player	146
Contribution to Attacking Power Average number of minutes between League team goals while on pitch	76	Club Strike Rate Average number of minutes between League goals scored by club	96

	PLAYER	LGE GOALS	POWER	STRIKE RATE
1	Lukas Podolski	10	76	146 mins
2	Andriy Voronin	4	111	417 mins
3	Dirk Lottner	4	105	450 mins
4	Matthias Scherz	4	94	519 mins

KEY PLAYERS - MIDFIELDERS

Alexander Voigt

Goals in the League	1	Contribution to Attacking Power Average number of minutes between League team goals while on pitch	84
Defensive Rating Average number of mins between League goals conceded while he was on the pitch	65	Scoring Difference Defensive Rating minus Contribution to Attacking Power	-19

	PLAYER	LGE GOALS	DEF RATE	POWER	SCORE DIFF
1	Alexander Voigt	1	65	84	-19 mins
2	Christian Springer	2	53	86	-33 mins
3	Oliver Schroder	1	58	93	-35 mins
4	Matthias Scherz	4	48	94	-46 mins

KEY PLAYERS - DEFENDERS

Thomas Cichon

Goals Conceded (GC) The number of League goals conceded while he was on the pitch	23	Clean Sheets In games when he played at least 70 minutes	6
Defensive Rating Ave number of mins between League goals conceded while on the pitch	74	Club Defensive Rating Average number of mins between League goals conceded by the club this season	54

	PLAYER	CON LGE	CLEAN SHEETS	DEF RATE
1	Thomas Cichon	23	6	74 mins
2	Mustafa Dogan	36	6	60 mins
3	Moses Sichone	36	4	51 mins
4	Carsten Cullman	27	3	50 mins

KEY GOALKEEPER

Stefan Wessels

Goals Conceded in the League	53	Counting Games Games when he played at least 70 mins	32
Defensive Rating Ave number of mins between League goals conceded while on the pitch	54	Clean Sheets In games when he played at least 70 mins	7

LEAGUE GOALS

Lukas Podolski

Minutes on the pitch	1456	Goals in the League	10
League average (mins between goals)	146		

	PLAYER	MINS	GOALS	AVE
1	Podolski	1456	10	146
2	Scherz	2074	4	519
3	Voronin	1667	4	417
4	Lottner	1801	4	450
5	Springer	2330	2	1165
6	Voigt	1936	1	1936
7	Schroder	2315	1	2315
8	Kringe	1934	1	1934
9	Sinkala	959	1	959
10	Ebbers	723	1	723
11	Dogan	2144	1	2144
12	Feulner	775	1	775
	Other		1	
	TOTAL		32	

DISCIPLINARY RECORDS

	PLAYER	YELLOW	RED	AVE
1	Klos	3	0	156
2	Sichone	7	1	231
3	Ebbers	2	1	241
4	Voigt	7	1	242
5	Streit	4	0	249
6	Dogan	7	0	306
7	Grujic	2	0	393
8	Cichon	4	0	425
9	Cullman	3	0	450
10	Lottner	4	0	450
11	Springer	5	0	466
12	Sinkala	2	0	479
13	Kringe	4	0	483
	Other	13	1	
	TOTAL	67	4	

TOP POINT EARNERS

	PLAYER	GAMES	AV PTS
1	Bade	2	1.50
2	Federico	2	1.50
3	Helbig	5	1.40
4	Streit	9	1.11
5	Cichon	17	1.00
6	Podolski	16	0.94
7	Voigt	20	0.90
8	Springer	25	0.80
9	Schroder	24	0.75
10	Sinkiebicz	4	0.75
	CLUB AVERAGE:		**0.68**

TEAM OF THE SEASON

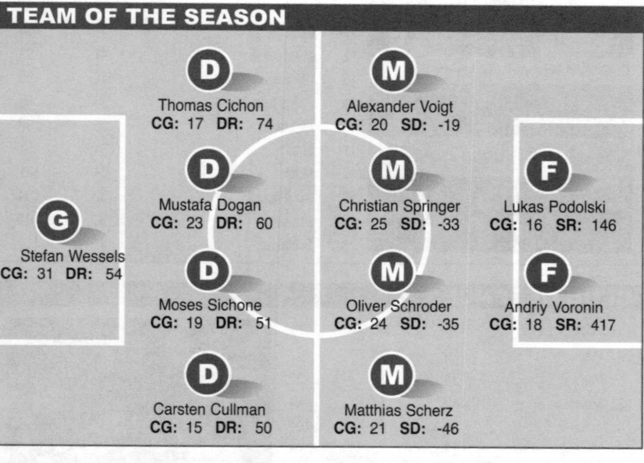

G
Stefan Wessels
CG: 31 DR: 54
D
Thomas Cichon
CG: 17 DR: 74
D
Mustafa Dogan
CG: 23 DR: 60
D
Moses Sichone
CG: 19 DR: 51
D
Carsten Cullman
CG: 15 DR: 50
M
Alexander Voigt
CG: 20 SD: -19
M
Christian Springer
CG: 25 SD: -33
M
Oliver Schroder
CG: 24 SD: -35
M
Matthias Scherz
CG: 21 SD: -46
F
Lukas Podolski
CG: 16 SR: 146
F
Andriy Voronin
CG: 18 SR: 417

LEAGUE APPEARANCES, BOOKINGS AND CAPS

	AGE (on 01/07/04)	IN NAMED 18	APPEARANCES	COUNTING GAMES	MINUTES ON PITCH	YELLOW CARDS	RED CARDS	THIS SEASON	HOME COUNTRY
Goalkeepers									
Alexander Bade	33	32	3	2	221	0	0	-	Germany
Vjaceslav Sokolov	25	2	0	0	0	0	0	-	Russia
Stefan Wessels	25	32	32	31	2839	0	0	-	Germany
Defenders									
Thomas Cichon	27	24	22	17	1700	4	0	-	Germany
Carsten Cullman	28	16	15	15	1350	3	0	-	Germany
Mustafa Dogan	28	26	25	23	2144	7	0	-	Germany
Markus Happe	32	5	2	0	67	1	0	-	Germany
Tomasz Klos	31	12	6	5	468	3	0	-	Poland
Efangelos Nessou	24	7	0	0	0	0	0	-	Greece
Moses Sichone	27	25	23	19	1852	7	1	-	Zambia
Andrew Sinkala	25	24	13	10	959	2	0	-	Zambia
Lukas Sinkiebicz	18	5	4	4	360	2	0	-	Germany
Midfielders									
Giovanni Federico	23	23	12	2	405	0	0	-	Germany
Markus Feulner	22	15	12	7	775	1	0	-	Germany
Vladan Grujic	23	15	11	8	787	2	0	-	Bosnia
Jorg Heinrich	34	22	19	16	1498	2	1	-	Germany
Florian Kringe	21	31	29	18	1934	4	0	-	Germany
Michael Lejan	21	8	2	0	30	0	0	-	Germany
Dirk Lottner	32	27	25	19	1801	4	0	-	Germany
Michael Niedrig	24	12	1	0	45	1	0	-	Germany
Matthias Scherz	32	33	30	21	2074	0	0	-	Germany
S Schindzielorz	25	3	3	2	180	0	0	-	Germany
Oliver Schroder	24	33	28	24	2315	1	0	-	Germany
Christian Springer	32	30	28	25	2330	5	0	-	Germany
Albert Streit	24	17	15	9	996	4	0	-	Germany
Alexander Voigt	26	28	25	20	1936	7	1	-	Germany
Forwards									
Markus Dworrak	26	8	2	0	39	0	0	-	Germany
Markus Ebbers	26	24	17	7	723	2	1	-	Germany
Sebastian Helbig	27	13	12	5	585	1	0	-	Germany
Joshua Kennedy	21	8	4	0	55	0	0	-	Australia
Lukas Podolski	19	19	18	16	1456	2	0	-	Germany
Andriy Voronin	24	19	19	18	1667	2	0	-	Ukraine

SQUAD APPEARANCES

Match	1	2	3	4	5	6	7	8	9	10	11	12	13	14	15	16	17	18	19	20	21	22	23	24	25	26	27	28	29	30	31	32	33	34
Venue	A	H	A	H	A	H	H	A	H	A	H	A	H	A	H	A	H	H	A	H	A	H	A	A	H	A	H	A	H	A	H	A	H	A
Competition	L	L	L	L	L	L	L	L	L	L	L	L	L	L	L	L	L	L	L	L	L	L	L	L	L	L	L	L	L	L	L	L	L	L
Result	L	L	L	W	L	L	L	D	W	L	L	L	L	D	D	D	W	W	L	L	L	L	L	L	D	L	W	L	L	L	L	L	W	L

Goalkeepers
Alexander Bade
Vjaceslav Sokolov
Stefan Wessels

Defenders
Thomas Cichon
Carsten Cullman
Mustafa Dogan
Markus Happe
Tomasz Klos
Efangelos Nessou
Moses Sichone
Andrew Sinkala
Lukas Sinkiebicz

Midfielders
Giovanni Federico
Markus Feulner
Vladan Grujic
Jorg Heinrich
Florian Kringe
Michael Lejan
Dirk Lottner
Michael Niedrig
Matthias Scherz
Sebastian Schindzielorz
Oliver Schroder
Christian Springer
Albert Streit
Alexander Voigt

Forwards
Markus Dworrak
Markus Ebbers
Sebastian Helbig
Joshua Kennedy
Lukas Podolski
Andriy Voronin

KEY: On all match / On bench / Subbed or sent off (Counting game) / Subbed or sent off (playing less than 70 minutes) / Subbed on from bench (Counting Game) / Subbed on (playing less than 70 minutes) / Subbed on and then subbed or sent off (Counting Game) / Subbed on and then subbed or sent off (playing less than 70 minutes) / Not in 16

FRENCH LEAGUE ROUND-UP

FINAL LEAGUE TABLE

	HOME						AWAY					TOTAL			
	P	W	D	L	F	A	W	D	L	F	A	F	A	DIF	PTS
Lyon	38	13	4	2	39	8	11	3	5	25	18	64	26	38	79
Paris SG	38	13	4	2	33	15	9	6	4	17	13	50	28	22	76
Monaco	38	11	5	3	35	16	10	7	2	24	14	59	30	29	75
Auxerre	38	13	3	3	38	15	6	5	8	22	19	60	34	26	65
Sochaux	38	12	4	3	33	17	6	5	8	21	25	54	42	12	63
Nantes	38	10	6	3	26	12	7	3	9	21	23	47	35	12	60
Marseille	38	12	3	4	34	18	5	3	11	17	27	51	45	6	57
Lens	38	10	6	3	21	17	5	2	12	13	31	34	48	-14	53
Rennes	38	11	6	2	36	15	3	4	12	20	29	56	44	12	52
Lille	38	8	6	5	19	15	6	3	10	22	26	41	41	0	51
Nice	38	8	7	4	24	13	3	10	6	18	26	42	39	3	50
Bordeaux	38	10	5	4	26	15	3	6	10	14	28	40	43	-3	50
Strasbourg	38	7	6	6	26	23	3	7	9	17	27	43	50	-7	43
Metz	38	6	3	10	18	22	5	6	8	16	20	34	42	-8	42
AC Ajaccio	38	8	5	6	18	17	2	5	12	15	38	33	55	-22	40
Toulouse	38	5	7	7	16	21	4	5	10	15	23	31	44	-13	39
Bastia	38	8	6	5	22	18	1	6	12	11	31	33	49	-16	39
Guingamp	38	8	3	8	26	28	2	5	12	10	30	36	58	-22	38
Le Mans	38	6	7	6	22	18	3	4	12	13	39	35	57	-22	38
Montpellier	38	6	3	10	22	27	2	4	13	19	47	41	74	-33	31

CLUB STRIKE FORCE

Lyon celebrate a goal against Rennes

1 Lyon

Goals scored in the League	64
Club Strike Rate (CSR) Average number of minutes between League goals scored by club	53

	CLUB	GOALS	CSR
1	Lyon	64	53
2	Auxerre	60	57
3	Monaco	59	58
4	Rennes	56	61
5	Sochaux	54	63
6	Marseille	51	67
7	Paris SG	50	68
8	Nantes	47	73
9	Strasbourg	43	80
10	Nice	42	81
11	Lille	41	83
12	Montpellier	41	83
13	Bordeaux	40	86
14	Guingamp	36	95
15	Le Mans	35	98
16	Lens	34	101
17	Metz	34	101
18	AC Ajaccio	33	104
19	Bastia	33	104
20	Toulouse	31	110

CLUB DISCIPLINARY RECORDS

Habib Beye of Marseille being booked

1 Bastia

League Yellow	87
League Red	7
League Total	94
Cards Average in League Average number of minutes between a card being shown of either colour	36

	CLUB	Y	R	TOTAL	AVE
1	Bastia	87	7	94	36
2	Lens	81	13	94	36
3	Montpellier	86	7	93	37
4	Toulouse	89	4	93	37
5	Nice	84	5	89	38
6	Paris SG	83	5	88	39
7	AC Ajaccio	78	5	83	41
8	Bordeaux	76	7	83	41
9	Nantes	74	5	79	43
10	Marseille	71	5	76	45
11	Rennes	71	5	76	45
12	Guingamp	69	2	71	48
13	Lille	66	5	71	48
14	Strasbourg	64	4	68	50
15	Sochaux	59	4	63	54
16	Le Mans	58	3	61	56
17	Lyon	55	5	60	57
18	Metz	56	4	60	57
19	Monaco	57	2	59	58
20	Auxerre	43	1	44	78

CLUB DEFENCES

	CLUB	LGE	CS	CDR
1	Lyon	26	19	132
2	Paris SG	28	19	122
3	Monaco	30	17	114
4	Auxerre	34	13	101
5	Nantes	35	14	98
6	Nice	39	12	88
7	Lille	41	14	83
8	Metz	42	11	81
9	Sochaux	42	10	81
10	Bordeaux	43	13	80
11	Rennes	44	12	78
12	Toulouse	44	10	78
13	Marseille	45	12	76
14	Lens	48	13	71
15	Bastia	49	11	70
16	Strasbourg	50	11	68
17	AC Ajaccio	55	13	62
18	Le Mans	57	10	60
19	Guingamp	58	10	59
20	Montpellier	74	6	46

Dhorasoo defending for Lyon

1 Lyon

Goals conceded in the League	26
Clean Sheets (CS) Number of league games where no goals were conceded	19
Club Defensive Rate (CDR) Average number of minutes between League goals conceded by club	132

PLAYER NATIONALITIES

Overseas country with the most player appearances in the French League - Brazil — 402 league appearances by Brazilian players

	COUNTRY	PLAYERS	IN SQUAD	LGE APP	% LGE ACT	CAPS	MOST APP	APP
1	France	423	8108	6784	66.8	50	Four Players	100.0
2	Brazil	21	446	402	3.7	9	Edmilson	92.8
3	Senegal	20	426	352	3.3	38	Lamine Diatta	83.9
4	Argentina	11	219	203	2.1	4	Gabriel Ivan Heinze	86.8
5	Cameroon	12	221	185	2.0	22	Achille Emana	80.0
6	Ivory Coast	15	273	220	1.9		Didier Drogba	76.2
7	Serbia & M'tenegro	11	214	190	1.9	5	Predrag Ocokoljic	88.6
8	Portugal	7	184	161	1.6	9	Pauleta	91.4
9	Switzerland	7	182	156	1.5		Patrick Muller	80.4
10	Czech Republic	6	158	144	1.3	15	Petr Cech	84.9
11	Morocco	7	151	136	1.2		Abdeslam Ouaddou	73.8
12	Mali	5	114	106	1.1		Mamadou Bagayoko	88.9
13	Spain	4	98	97	1.0	2	Albert Ortega Riera	76.9
14	Sweden	4	92	86	0.8	5	Pontus Farnerud	74.0
15	Nigeria	4	86	84	0.8		John Utaka	69.3
16	Gabon	3	81	76	0.7		Daniel Cousin	79.7
17	Belgium	3	67	57	0.6	11	Eric Deflandre	54.1
18	Guinea	2	63	60	0.5		Pascal Feindouno	66.4
19	Columbia	2	48	46	0.5		Tressor Moreno	40.1
20	Greece	2	48	46	0.5		Vassilis Zikos	72.6

CLUB MAKE-UP – HOME AND OVERSEAS PLAYERS

1 Bordeaux — 57.4% of appearances by overseas players

	CLUB	OVERSEAS	HOME	% OVERSEAS	% LGE ACT	MOST APP	APP
1	Bordeaux	13	19	40.6	57.4	Marco Caneira	89.5
2	Paris SG	13	14	48.1	54.6	Pedro Pauleta	91.4
3	Monaco	14	17	45.2	48.5	Flavio Roma	86.8
4	Lyon	11	19	36.7	47.1	Edmilson	92.8
5	Marseille	13	26	33.3	44.3	Didier Drogba	76.2
6	Lens	11	19	36.7	43.6	Rigobert Song	71.2
7	Sochaux	9	16	36.0	38.7	S Diawara	73.4
8	Strasbourg	14	19	42.4	38.0	Pontus Farnerud	74.0
9	Rennes	10	22	31.3	36.2	Petr Cech	84.9
10	Lille	9	22	29.0	29.2	Jean Makoun	79.1
11	Le Mans	10	18	35.7	28.2	Daniel Cousin	79.7
12	Guingamp	11	26	29.7	26.6	BM Dagano	69.8
13	Toulouse	6	23	20.7	25.5	Predrag Ocokoljic	88.6
14	Montpellier	9	26	25.7	22.2	Nenad Dzodic	54.4
15	Auxerre	8	23	25.8	22.1	B Kalou	75.1
16	Bastia	9	23	28.1	22.0	Youssouf Hadji	60.7
17	Nice	10	23	30.3	21.6	Pereira Everson	70.0
18	AC Ajaccio	8	25	24.2	19.9	M Bagayoko	88.9
19	Metz	11	22	33.3	19.2	Tressor Moreno	40.1
20	Nantes	8	21	27.6	18.1	Mario Yepes	74.6

CHART-TOPPING MIDFIELDERS

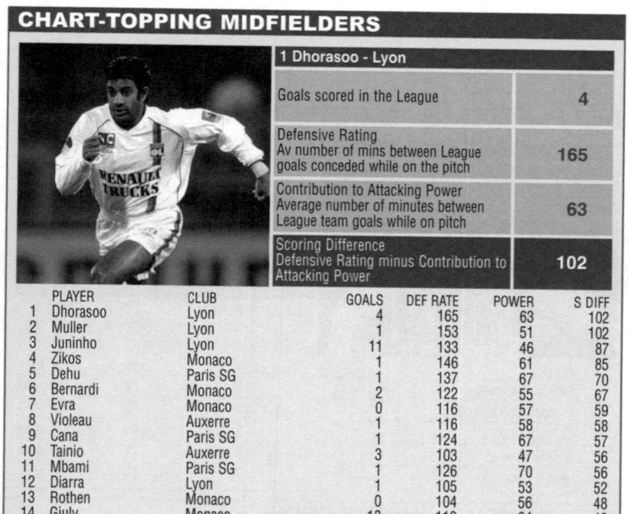

1 Dhorasoo - Lyon	
Goals scored in the League	4
Defensive Rating Av number of mins between League goals conceded while on the pitch	165
Contribution to Attacking Power Average number of minutes between League team goals while on pitch	63
Scoring Difference Defensive Rating minus Contribution to Attacking Power	102

	PLAYER	CLUB	GOALS	DEF RATE	POWER	S DIFF
1	Dhorasoo	Lyon	4	165	63	102
2	Muller	Lyon	1	153	51	102
3	Juninho	Lyon	11	133	46	87
4	Zikos	Monaco	1	146	61	85
5	Dehu	Paris SG	1	137	67	70
6	Bernardi	Monaco	2	122	55	67
7	Evra	Monaco	0	116	57	59
8	Violeau	Auxerre	1	116	58	58
9	Cana	Paris SG	1	124	67	57
10	Tainio	Auxerre	3	103	47	56
11	Mbami	Paris SG	1	126	70	56
12	Diarra	Lyon	1	105	53	52
13	Rothen	Monaco	0	104	56	48
14	Giuly	Monaco	13	110	64	46
15	Lachuer	Auxerre	3	101	56	45

CHART-TOPPING GOALSCORERS

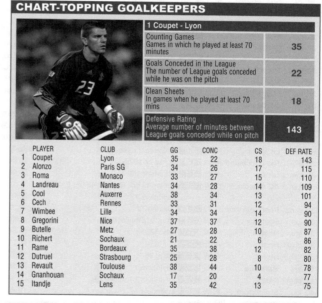

1 Frei - Rennes	
Goals scored in the League	20
Contribution to Attacking Power (AP) Average number of minutes between League team goals while on pitch	50
Club Strike Rate (CSR) Average minutes between League goals scored by club	61
Player Strike Rate Average number of minutes between League goals scored by player	98

	PLAYER	CLUB	GOALS: LGE	POWER	CSR	S RATE
1	Frei	Rennes	20	50	61	98
2	Cisse	Auxerre	26	54	57	125
3	Drogba	Marseille	19	68	67	137
4	Manchev	Lille	13	92	83	157
5	Santos	Sochaux	14	53	63	160
6	Pauleta	Paris SG	18	67	68	174
7	Giuly	Monaco	13	64	58	178
8	Frau	Sochaux	16	59	63	179
9	Luyindula	Lyon	16	54	53	184
10	Bamago	Montpellier	16	82	83	201
11	Morientes	Monaco	10	56	58	202
12	Niang	Strasbourg	9	73	80	203
13	Juninho	Lyon	11	45	53	230
14	Maoulida	Metz	12	98	101	230
15	Cousin	Le Mans	11	87	98	248

CHART-TOPPING DEFENDERS

1 Sorin - Paris SG	
Goals Conceded in the League The number of League goals conceded while he was on the pitch	9
Clean Sheets In games when he played at least 70 mins	11
Club Defensive Rating Average mins between League goals conceded by the club this season	122
Defensive Rating Average number of minutes between League goals conceded while on pitch	198

	PLAYER	CLUB	CON: LGE	CS	CDR	DEF RATE
1	Sorin	Paris SG	9	11	122	198
2	Berthod	Lyon	13	13	132	162
3	Essien	Lyon	15	11	132	155
4	Ibarra	Monaco	13	9	114	145
5	Deflandre	Lyon	13	9	132	142
6	Squillaci	Monaco	17	12	114	133
7	Heinze	Paris SG	23	18	122	129
8	Pierre-Fanfan	Paris SG	23	17	122	128
9	Edmilson	Lyon	25	16	132	127
10	Rodriguez	Monaco	25	16	114	126
11	Pichot	Lille	21	14	83	123
12	Mendy	Paris SG	23	16	122	120
13	Givet	Monaco	19	9	114	117
14	Reveillere	Lyon	22	11	132	111
15	Yepes	Nantes	24	11	98	106

CHART-TOPPING GOALKEEPERS

1 Coupet - Lyon	
Counting Games Games in which he played at least 70 minutes	35
Goals Conceded in the League The number of League goals conceded while he was on the pitch	22
Clean Sheets In games when he played at least 70 mins	18
Defensive Rating Average number of minutes between League goals conceded while on pitch	143

	PLAYER	CLUB	GG	CONC	CS	DEF RATE
1	Coupet	Lyon	35	22	18	143
2	Alonzo	Paris SG	34	26	17	115
3	Roma	Monaco	33	27	15	110
4	Landreau	Nantes	34	28	14	109
5	Cool	Auxerre	38	34	13	101
6	Cech	Rennes	33	31	12	94
7	Wimbee	Lille	34	34	14	90
8	Gregorini	Nice	37	37	12	90
9	Butelle	Metz	27	28	10	87
10	Richert	Sochaux	21	22	6	86
11	Rame	Bordeaux	35	38	12	82
12	Dutruel	Strasbourg	25	28	8	80
13	Revault	Toulouse	38	44	10	78
14	Gnanhouan	Sochaux	17	20	4	77
15	Itandje	Lens	35	42	13	75

PLAYER DISCIPLINARY RECORD

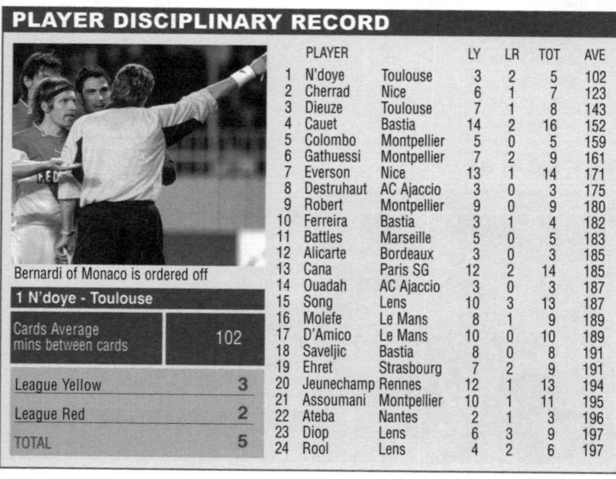

Bernardi of Monaco is ordered off

1 N'doye - Toulouse	
Cards Average mins between cards	102
League Yellow	3
League Red	2
TOTAL	5

	PLAYER		LY	LR	TOT	AVE
1	N'doye	Toulouse	3	2	5	102
2	Cherrad	Nice	6	1	7	123
3	Dieuze	Toulouse	7	1	8	143
4	Cauet	Bastia	14	2	16	152
5	Colombo	Montpellier	5	0	5	159
6	Gathuessi	Montpellier	7	2	9	161
7	Everson	Nice	13	1	14	171
8	Destruhaut	AC Ajaccio	3	0	3	175
9	Robert	Montpellier	9	0	9	180
10	Ferreira	Bastia	3	1	4	182
11	Battles	Marseille	5	0	5	183
12	Alicarte	Bordeaux	3	0	3	185
13	Cana	Paris SG	12	2	14	185
14	Ouadah	AC Ajaccio	3	0	3	187
15	Song	Lens	10	3	13	187
16	Molefe	Le Mans	8	1	9	189
17	D'Amico	Le Mans	10	0	10	189
18	Saveljic	Bastia	8	0	8	191
19	Ehret	Strasbourg	7	2	9	191
20	Jeunechamp	Rennes	12	1	13	194
21	Assoumani	Montpellier	10	1	11	195
22	Ateba	Nantes	2	1	3	196
23	Diop	Lens	6	3	9	197
24	Rool	Lens	4	2	6	197

TEAM OF THE SEASON

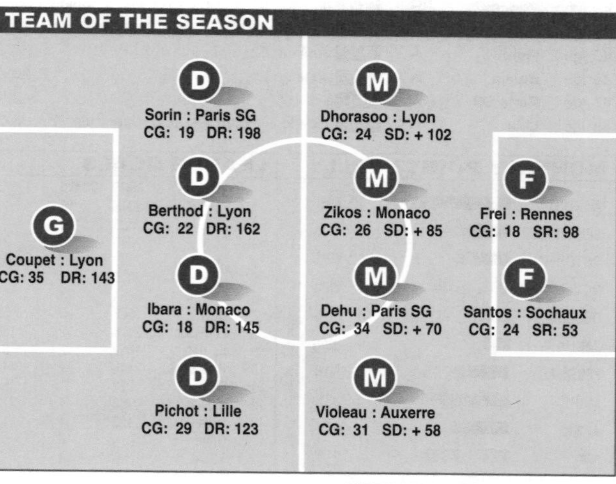
D
Sorin : Paris SG
CG: 19 DR: 198
M
Dhorasoo : Lyon
CG: 24 SD: + 102
D
Berthod : Lyon
CG: 22 DR: 162
M
Zikos : Monaco
CG: 26 SD: + 85
F
Frei : Rennes
CG: 18 SR: 98
G
Coupet : Lyon
CG: 35 DR: 143
D
Ibara : Monaco
CG: 18 DR: 145
M
Dehu : Paris SG
CG: 34 SD: + 70
F
Santos : Sochaux
CG: 24 SR: 53
D
Pichot : Lille
CG: 29 DR: 123
M
Violeau : Auxerre
CG: 31 SD: + 58

FRANCE LIGUE 1 CHAMPIONS

LYON

Final Position: **1st**

KEY: Won Drawn Lost

							Attendance
1	lge	Lille	A	L	0-1		17,000
2	lge	Monaco	H	W	3-1	Squillaci 15 og; Essien 25; Luyindula 44	37,246
3	lge	Montpellier	A	W	2-0	Cacapa 11; Carriere 26	20,850
4	lge	Toulouse	H	D	0-0		35,192
5	lge	Guingamp	A	L	0-2		11,610
6	lge	Auxerre	H	D	1-1	Elber 43	38,000
7	cl ga	Anderlecht	H	W	1-0	Juninho 25 pen	32,000
8	lge	Le Mans	A	W	2-0	Elber 14,88	12,000
9	lge	Lens	H	W	4-0	Juninho 9,43,57; Reveillere 25	33,695
10	cl ga	Celtic	A	L	0-2		57,475
11	lge	AC Ajaccio	A	W	4-2	Luyindula 15,70,87; Malouda 66	6,625
12	lge	Sochaux	H	D	1-1	Luyindula 66	37,029
13	cl ga	Bayern Munich	H	D	1-1	Luyindula 88	38,145
14	lge	Nantes	A	W	1-0	Juninho 66	32,000
15	lge	Nice	H	W	5-0	Juninho 24,74; Malouda 27; Elber 39; Govou 45	34,034
16	cl ga	Bayern Munich	A	W	2-1	Juninho 6; Elber 53	59,000
17	lge	Marseille	A	W	4-1	Elber 20; Juninho 38,90; Luyindula 58	56,207
18	lge	Strasbourg	H	W	1-0	Luyindula 90 pen	45,366
19	cl ga	Anderlecht	A	L	0-1		26,208
20	lge	Rennes	A	L	1-3	Malouda 21	15,511
21	lge	Metz	H	W	2-1	Luyindula 26; Edmilson 47	39,500
22	cl ga	Celtic	H	W	3-2	Elber 6; Juninho 52,86 pen	40,125
23	lge	Bastia	A	D	0-0		5,500
24	lge	Paris SG	H	D	1-1	Carriere 84	36,720
25	lge	Monaco	A	L	0-3		15,674
26	lge	Montpellier	H	W	3-0	Dhorasoo 9; Luyindula 35; Viale 90	32,658
27	lge	Bordeaux	H	W	3-0	Muller 65; Luyindula 67; Essien 81	32,363
28	lge	Toulouse	A	W	1-0	Dhorasoo 60	26,297
29	lge	Guingamp	H	L	0-1		34,523
30	lge	Auxerre	A	W	2-1	Violeau 9 og; Luyindula 67	15,000
31	lge	Le Mans	H	W	2-0	Malouda 21; Govou 60	32,000
32	cl rl1	Real Sociedad	A	W	1-0	Schurrer 18 og	29,000
33	lge	Lens	A	D	1-1	Dhorasoo 33	39,000
34	lge	AC Ajaccio	H	W	4-0	Terrier 43 og; Rodrigo 48 og; Elber 50; Luyindula 73	30,000
35	cl rl2	Real Sociedad	H	W	1-0	Juninho 77	38,914
36	lge	Sochaux	A	W	2-1	Elber 3; Edmilson 65	19,500
37	lge	Nantes	H	W	1-0	Elber 26	35,643
38	cl qf1	Porto	A	L	0-2		46,910
39	lge	Nice	A	W	1-0	Elber 16	12,784
40	lge	Marseille	H	L	1-2	Luyindula 17	38,602
41	cl qf2	Porto	H	D	2-2	Luyindula 14; Elber 89	39,547
42	lge	Strasbourg	A	W	1-0	Luyindula 47	19,400
43	lge	Rennes	H	W	3-0	Juninho 57 pen; Essien 62; Luyindula 71	39,869
44	lge	Bordeaux	A	D	1-1	Dhorasoo 87	23,637
45	lge	Metz	A	W	2-1	Juninho 22; Elber 74	24,778
46	lge	Bastia	H	W	1-0	Juninho 25	38,723
47	lge	Paris SG	A	L	0-1		42,502
48	lge	Lille	H	W	3-0	Govou 39; Diarra 51 pen; Luyindula 77	36,000

MONTHLY POINTS TALLY

AUGUST	12	80%
SEPTEMBER	6	67%
OCTOBER	6	67%
NOVEMBER	3	25%
DECEMBER	3	50%
JANUARY	4	33%
FEBRUARY	9	60%
MARCH	4	33%
APRIL	6	67%
MAY	4	27%

LEAGUE GOALS

	PLAYER	MINS	GOALS	AVE
1	Luyindula	2946	16	184
2	Juninho	2525	11	230
3	Elber	2030	8	254
4	Malouda	2689	4	672
5	Dhorasoo	2316	4	579
6	Essien	2324	3	775
7	Govou	1688	3	563
8	Edmilson	3175	2	1588
9	Carriere	1632	2	816
10	Reveillere	2446	1	2446
11	Cacapa	922	1	922
12	Muller	2750	1	2750
13	Viale	123	1	123
	Other		7	
	TOTAL		64	

KEY PLAYERS - GOALSCORERS

Pegguy Luyindula

Goals in the League	16
Contribution to Attacking Power Average number of minutes between League team goals while on pitch	54
Player Strike Rate The total number of minutes he was on the pitch for every League goal scored	184
Club Strike Rate Average number of minutes between League goals scored by club	53

	PLAYER	GOALS LGE	POWER	S RATE
1	Pegguy Luyindula	16	54	184 mins
2	Pernambucano Juninho	11	45	230 mins
3	Giovane Elber	8	49	254 mins
4	Sydney Govou	3	51	563 mins
5	Vikash Dhorasoo	4	62	579 mins

KEY PLAYERS - MIDFIELDERS

Vikash Dhorasoo

Goals in the League	4
Defensive Rating Average number of mins between League goals conceded while on the pitch	165
Contribution to Attacking Power Average number of minutes between League team goals while on pitch	63
Scoring Difference Defensive Rating minus Contribution to Attacking Power	102

	PLAYER	GOALS LGE	DEF RATE	ATT POWER	SCORE DIFF
1	Vikash Dhorasoo	4	165	63	102 mins
2	Patrick Muller	1	153	51	102 mins
3	Eric Carriere	2	148	51	97 mins
4	Pernambucano Juninho	11	133	46	87 mins
5	Mahamadou Diarra	1	105	53	52 mins

KEY PLAYERS - DEFENDERS

Jeremie Berthod

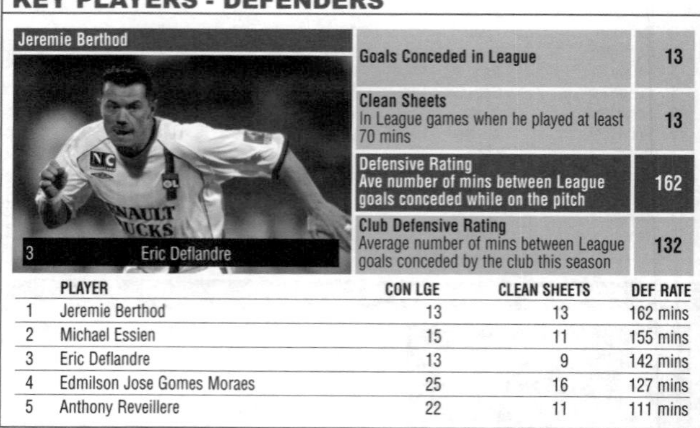
3 Eric Deflandre

Goals Conceded in League	13
Clean Sheets In League games when he played at least 70 mins	13
Defensive Rating Ave number of mins between League goals conceded while on the pitch	162
Club Defensive Rating Average number of mins between League goals conceded by the club this season	132

	PLAYER	CON LGE	CLEAN SHEETS	DEF RATE
1	Jeremie Berthod	13	13	162 mins
2	Michael Essien	15	11	155 mins
3	Eric Deflandre	13	9	142 mins
4	Edmilson Jose Gomes Moraes	25	16	127 mins
5	Anthony Reveillere	22	11	111 mins

KEY GOALKEEPER

Gregory Coupet

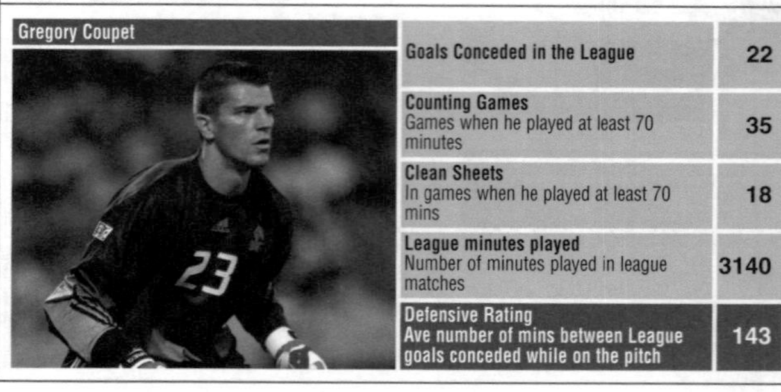

Goals Conceded in the League	22
Counting Games Games when he played at least 70 minutes	35
Clean Sheets In games when he played at least 70 mins	18
League minutes played Number of minutes played in league matches	3140
Defensive Rating Ave number of mins between League goals conceded while on the pitch	143

DISCIPLINARY RECORDS

	PLAYER	YELLOW	RED	AVE
1	Diarra	8	1	233
2	Essien	7	1	290
3	Govou	4	1	337
4	Malouda	6	1	384
5	Cacapa	2	0	461
6	Reveillere	5	0	489
7	Berthod	4	0	525
8	Deflandre	3	0	617
9	Edmilson	4	0	793
10	Juninho	3	0	841
11	Muller	2	1	916
12	Elber	2	0	1015
13	Luyindula	2	0	1473
	Other	3	0	
	TOTAL	55	5	

TOP POINT EARNERS

	PLAYER	GAMES	AV PTS
1	Carriere	13	2.46
2	Deflandre	19	2.26
3	Muller	29	2.24
4	Coupet	35	2.09
5	Elber	22	2.09
6	Berthod	22	2.09
7	Essien	22	2.09
8	Luyindula	32	2.09
9	Malouda	27	2.07
10	Govou	16	2.06
	CLUB AVERAGE:		**2.08**

TEAM OF THE SEASON

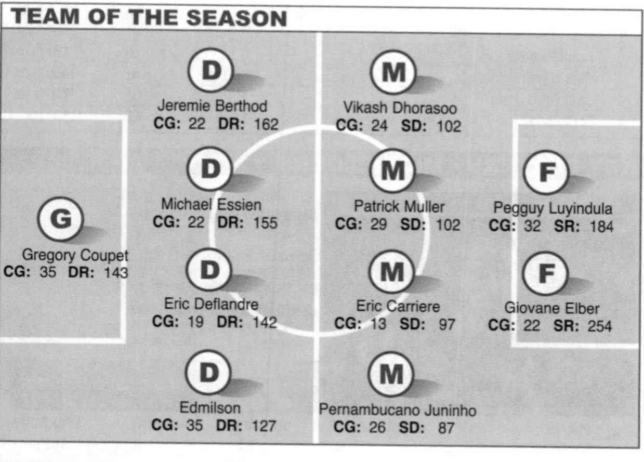
D
Jeremie Berthod
CG: 22 DR: 162
M
Vikash Dhorasoo
CG: 24 SD: 102
D
Michael Essien
CG: 22 DR: 155
M
Patrick Muller
CG: 29 SD: 102
F
Pegguy Luyindula
CG: 32 SR: 184
G
Gregory Coupet
CG: 35 DR: 143
D
Eric Deflandre
CG: 19 DR: 142
M
Eric Carriere
CG: 13 SD: 97
F
Giovane Elber
CG: 22 SR: 254
D
Edmilson
CG: 35 DR: 127
M
Pernambucano Juninho
CG: 26 SD: 87

LEAGUE APPEARANCES AND BOOKINGS

	AGE (on 01/07/04)	IN NAMED 16	APPEARANCES	COUNTING GAMES	MINUTES ON PITCH	YELLOW CARDS	RED CARDS	THIS SEASON	HOME COUNTRY
Goalkeepers									
Fabien Caballero	20	2	0	0	0	0	0	-	France
Gregory Coupet	31	35	35	35	3140	0	0	7	France (2)
Nicolas Puydebois	23	8	2	2	180	0	0	-	France
Remi Vercoutre	24	29	2	1	100	0	0	-	France
Defenders									
Jeremie Berthod	20	30	26	22	2100	4	0	-	France
Claudio Cacapa	28	18	15	8	922	2	0	-	Brazil
Francois Clerc	21	0	0	0	0	0	0	-	France
Eric Deflandre	30	32	26	19	1851	3	0	7	Belgium (17)
Edmilson	27	36	36	35	3175	4	0	4	Brazil (1)
Michael Essien	21	34	34	22	2324	7	1	-	Ghana
Yohann Gomez	22	13	6	0	78	0	0	-	France
Anthony Reveillere	24	32	31	24	2446	5	0	-	France
Pierre Sartre	21	5	2	0	34	0	0	-	France
Midfielders									
Eric Carriere	31	29	28	13	1632	0	0	-	France
Jeremie Clement	19	4	2	0	14	0	0	-	France
Christophe Delmotte	35	2	1	1	90	0	0	-	France
Vikash Dhorasoo	30	32	31	24	2316	1	0	-	France
Mahamadou Diarra	23	27	27	22	2100	8	1	-	Mali
Juninho	29	32	32	26	2525	3	0	5	Brazil (1)
Patrick Muller	27	37	36	29	2750	2	1	-	Switzerland
Philippe Violeau	33	4	2	0	58	1	0	-	France
Forwards									
Bryan Bergougnoux	21	17	12	0	186	1	0	-	France
Giovane Elber	31	28	27	22	2030	2	0	-	Brazil
Sydney Govou	24	26	26	16	1688	4	1	4	France (2)
Pegguy Luyindula	25	38	37	32	2946	2	0	-	France
Florent Malouda	24	36	35	27	2689	6	1	-	France
Julien Viale	22	20	12	0	123	0	0	-	France

SQUAD APPEARANCES

Match	1	2	3	4	5	6	7	8	9	10	11	12	13	14	15	16	17	18	19	20	21	22	23	24
Venue	A	H	A	H	A	H	H	A	H	A	A	H	H	A	H	A	A	H	A	A	H	H	A	H
Competition	L	L	L	L	L	L	C	L	L	C	L	L	C	L	L	C	L	L	C	L	L	C	L	L
Result	L	W	W	D	L	D	W	W	W	L	W	D	D	W	W	W	W	W	L	L	W	W	D	D

Match	25	26	27	28	29	30	31	32	33	34	35	36	37	38	39	40	41	42	43	44	45	46	47	48
Venue	A	H	H	A	H	A	H	A	A	H	H	A	H	A	A	H	H	A	H	A	A	H	A	H
Competition	L	L	L	L	L	L	L	C	L	L	C	L	L	C	L	L	C	L	L	L	L	L	L	L
Result	L	W	W	W	L	W	W	W	D	W	W	W	W	L	W	L	D	W	W	D	W	W	L	W

Goalkeepers
Fabien Caballero
Gregory Coupet
Nicolas Puydebois
Remi Vercoutre

Defenders
Jeremie Berthod
Claudio Roberto Cacapa
Francois Clerc
Eric Deflandre
Edmilson Jose Moraes
Michael Essien
Yohann Gomez
Anthony Reveillere
Pierre Sartre

Midfielders
Eric Carriere
Jeremie Clement
Christophe Delmotte
Vikash Dhorasoo
Mahamadou Diarra
Pernambucano Juninho
Patrick Muller
Philippe Violeau

Forwards
Bryan Bergougnoux
Giovane Elber
Sydney Govou
Pegguy Luyindula
Florent Malouda
Julien Viale

KEY: ■ On all match
■ On bench
⏮ Subbed or sent off (Counting game)
« Subbed or sent off (playing less than 70 minutes)
» Subbed on from bench (Counting Game)
» Subbed on (playing less than 70 minutes)
» Subbed on and then subbed or sent off (Counting Game)
» Subbed on and then subbed or sent off (playing less than 70 minutes)
□ Not in 16

PARIS St GERMAIN

Final Position: **2nd**

KEY: ☐ Won ☐ Drawn ☐ Lost

							Attendance
1	lge	Bastia	H	D	0-0		43,500
2	lge	Lille	A	L	0-1		18,455
3	lge	Metz	A	W	1-0	Leroy 64	15,547
4	lge	Monaco	H	L	2-4	Pauleta 15; Reinaldo 49	36,417
5	lge	Montpellier	A	L	2-3	Reinaldo 17,73	13,893
6	lge	Toulouse	H	W	2-1	Dieuze 43 og; Heinze 67	35,651
7	lge	Guingamp	A	W	2-0	Fiorese 65; Pauleta 70 pen	14,500
8	lge	Auxerre	H	W	1-0	Pauleta 9	39,777
9	lge	Sochaux	A	W	1-0	Pauleta 20	19,561
10	lge	Le Mans	H	W	5-1	Pauleta 28,62; Fiorese 40,61; Reinaldo 90	41,409
11	lge	AC Ajaccio	A	D	0-0		3,500
12	lge	Lens	H	L	0-1		39,366
13	lge	Nantes	A	W	1-0	Fiorese 62	34,510
14	lge	Nice	H	D	0-0		35,000
15	lge	Marseille	A	W	1-0	Fiorese 89	59,000
16	lge	Strasbourg	H	W	3-2	Boskovic 20; Reinaldo 61; Pauleta 66	34,175
17	lge	Rennes	A	D	1-1	Fiorese 48	18,003
18	lge	Bordeaux	H	W	2-1	Reinaldo 35; Pauleta 47	41,000
19	lge	Lyon	A	D	1-1	Pauleta 40	36,720
20	lge	Lille	H	W	1-0	Tavlaridis 14 og	38,620
21	lge	Metz	H	D	0-0		40,601
22	lge	Monaco	A	D	1-1	Heinze 31	14,147
23	lge	Montpellier	H	W	6-1	Ljuboja 6,55; Pauleta 19,49; Boskovic 75; Reinaldo 76	38,952
24	lge	Toulouse	A	W	1-0	Ljuboja 28	24,000
25	lge	Guingamp	H	W	2-0	Mbami 23; Ljuboja 82	41,000
26	lge	Auxerre	A	D	1-1	Cana 79	21,500
27	lge	Sochaux	H	D	1-1	Pauleta 49 pen	41,500
28	lge	Le Mans	A	W	1-0	Ljuboja 66	15,000
29	lge	AC Ajaccio	H	W	1-0	Pauleta 67 pen	38,580
30	lge	Lens	A	L	0-1		37,775
31	lge	Nantes	H	W	3-2	Armand 34 og; Boskovic 68; Pauleta 76	40,000
32	lge	Nice	A	W	2-1	Pierre-Fanfan 80; Sorin 87	12,661
33	lge	Marseille	H	W	2-1	Pauleta 12,61	41,978
34	lge	Strasbourg	A	D	0-0		26,000
35	lge	Rennes	H	W	1-0	Dehu 61	42,000
36	lge	Bordeaux	A	L	0-3		30,527
37	lge	Lyon	H	W	1-0	Pauleta 5	42,502
38	lge	Bastia	A	W	1-0	Pauleta 52	7,500

KEY PLAYERS - GOALSCORERS

Pedro Resendes Pauleta

Goals in the League	18
Contribution to Attacking Power Average number of minutes between League team goals while on pitch	67
Player Strike Rate The total number of minutes he was on the pitch for every League goal scored	174
Club Strike Rate Average number of minutes between League goals scored by club	68

	PLAYER	GOALS LGE	POWER	S RATE
1	Pedro Resendes Pauleta	18	67	174 mins
2	Fabrice Fiorese	6	68	491 mins
3	Gabriel Ivan Heinze	2	67	1485 mins
4	Juan Pablo Sorin	1	55	1786 mins
5	Lorik Cana	1	66	2594 mins

KEY PLAYERS - MIDFIELDERS

Danijel Ljuboja

2 Frederic Dehu

Goals in the League	5
Defensive Rating Average number of mins between League goals conceded while on the pitch	165
Contribution to Attacking Power Average number of minutes between League team goals while on pitch	64
Scoring Difference Defensive Rating minus Contribution to Attacking Power	101

	PLAYER	GOALS LGE	DEF RATE	ATT POWER	SCORE DIFF
1	Danijel Ljuboja	5	165	64	101 mins
2	Frederic Dehu	1	137	67	70 mins
3	Lorik Cana	1	124	67	57 mins
4	Modeste Mbami	1	126	70	56 mins

KEY PLAYERS - DEFENDERS

Juan Pablo Sorin

Goals Conceded in League	9
Clean Sheets In League games when he played at least 70 mins	11
Defensive Rating Ave number of mins between League goals conceded while on the pitch	198
Club Defensive Rating Average number of mins between League goals conceded by the club this season	122

	PLAYER	CON LGE	CLEAN SHEETS	DEF RATE
1	Juan Pablo Sorin	9	11	198 mins
2	Gabriel Ivan Heinze	23	18	129 mins
3	Jose Karl Pierre-Fanfan	23	17	128 mins
4	Talal El Karkouri	13	7	121 mins
5	Bernard Mendy	23	16	120 mins

MONTHLY POINTS TALLY

AUGUST	4	27%
SEPTEMBER	9	100%
OCTOBER	7	78%
NOVEMBER	7	58%
DECEMBER	8	67%
JANUARY	5	56%
FEBRUARY	10	83%
MARCH	7	58%
APRIL	9	100%
MAY	10	67%

LEAGUE GOALS

	PLAYER	MINS	GOALS	AVE
1	Pauleta	3127	18	174
2	Reinaldo	1257	7	180
3	Fiorese	2943	6	491
4	Ljuboja	1157	5	231
5	Boskovic	1303	3	434
6	Heinze	2970	2	1485
7	Mbami	2651	1	2651
8	Cana	2594	1	2594
9	Sorin	1786	1	1786
10	Dehu	3156	1	3156
11	Pierre-Fanfan	2946	1	2946
12	Leroy	299	1	299
	Other		3	
	TOTAL		50	

KEY GOALKEEPER

Jerome Alonzo

Goals Conceded in the League	26
Counting Games Games when he played at least 70 minutes	34
Clean Sheets In games when he played at least 70 mins	17
League minutes played Number of minutes played in league matches	2979
Defensive Rating Ave number of mins between League goals conceded while on the pitch	115

DISCIPLINARY RECORDS

	PLAYER	YELLOW	RED	AVE
1	Cana	12	2	185
2	Cubilier	3	0	218
3	Mendy	12	0	230
4	Reinaldo	4	0	314
5	Boskovic	3	1	325
6	Mbami	7	1	331
7	Leal	2	0	454
8	Rocchi	1	0	470
9	Fiorese	6	0	490
10	Pierre-Fanfan	6	0	491
11	Heinze	6	0	495
12	Dehu	6	0	526
13	Ljuboja	2	0	578
	Other	13	1	
	TOTAL	83	5	

TOP POINT EARNERS

	PLAYER	GAMES	AV PTS
1	Sorin	19	2.47
2	Cana	28	2.18
3	Pierre-Fanfan	32	2.13
4	Mbami	29	2.10
5	Dehu	34	2.09
6	Fiorese	33	2.09
7	Heinze	33	2.06
8	Mendy	29	2.00
9	Pauleta	35	1.97
10	Alonzo	32	1.88
	CLUB AVERAGE:		2.00

LEAGUE APPEARANCES AND BOOKINGS

	AGE (on 01/07/04)	IN NAMED 16	APPEARANCES	COUNTING GAMES	MINUTES ON PITCH	YELLOW CARDS	RED CARDS	THIS SEASON	HOME COUNTRY
Goalkeepers									
Jerome Alonzo	31	36	34	32	2979	1	1	-	France
Mohamed Benhamou	24	14	0	0	0	0	0	-	France
Lionel Letizi	31	25	6	4	441	0	0	-	France
Defenders									
Jean-Michel Badiane	21	1	0	0	0	0	0	-	France
Eric Cubilier	25	20	15	6	654	3	0	-	France
Talal El Karkouri	28	31	26	14	1573	1	0	-	Morocco
Gabriel Ivan Heinze	26	33	33	33	2970	6	0	2	Argentina (5)
Bernard Mendy	22	33	33	29	2762	12	0	1	France (2)
Arruda Paulo Cesar	31	12	9	3	320	0	0	-	Brazil
Jose Pierre-Fanfan	28	35	34	32	2946	6	0	-	France
Lionel Potillon	30	2	2	2	180	0	0	-	France
Juan Pablo Sorin	28	21	21	19	1786	3	0	2	Argentina (5)
Midfielders									
Lorik Cana	20	32	32	28	2594	12	2	-	Bosnia
Frederic Dehu	31	36	36	34	3156	6	0	-	France
Hugo Leal	24	17	14	9	908	2	0	-	Portugal
Jerome Leroy	29	5	4	3	299	0	0	-	France
Danijel Ljuboja	26	17	17	12	1157	2	0	2	Serbia & M'negro (45)
Modeste Mbami	21	30	30	29	2651	7	1	4	Cameroon (12)
Romain Rocchi	22	19	18	3	470	1	0	-	France
Forwards									
Selim Benachour	22	14	8	3	285	2	0	-	Tunisia
Branco Boskovic	24	28	24	12	1303	3	1	-	Serbia & Montenegro
Kaba Diawara	28	3	3	1	88	0	0	-	France
Francke Dja Dje Dje	18	2	2	0	20	1	0	-	Ivory Coast
Fabrice Fiorese	28	34	34	33	2943	6	0	-	France
Chigury Lucau	19	1	1	1	90	0	0	-	Congo
Bart Ogbeche	19	14	13	4	422	2	0	-	Nigeria
Pauleta	31	37	37	35	3127	3	0	7	Portugal (20)
Cruz Reinaldo	25	35	31	11	1257	4	0	-	Brazil
Alioune Toure	25	19	9	0	87	0	0	-	France

TEAM OF THE SEASON

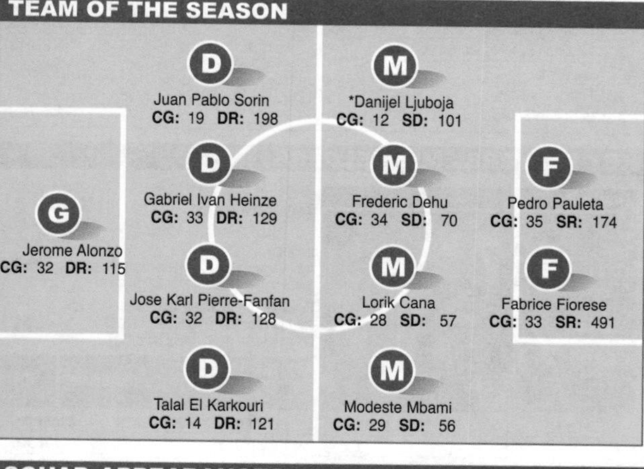

G
Jerome Alonzo
CG: 32 DR: 115
D
Juan Pablo Sorin
CG: 19 DR: 198
D
Gabriel Ivan Heinze
CG: 33 DR: 129
D
Jose Karl Pierre-Fanfan
CG: 32 DR: 128
D
Talal El Karkouri
CG: 14 DR: 121
M
*Danijel Ljuboja
CG: 12 SD: 101
M
Frederic Dehu
CG: 34 SD: 70
M
Lorik Cana
CG: 28 SD: 57
M
Modeste Mbami
CG: 29 SD: 56
F
Pedro Pauleta
CG: 35 SR: 174
F
Fabrice Fiorese
CG: 33 SR: 491

SQUAD APPEARANCES

Match	1	2	3	4	5	6	7	8	9	10	11	12	13	14	15	16	17	18	19	20	21	22	23	24	25	26	27	28	29	30	31	32	33	34	35	36	37	38
Venue	H	A	A	H	A	H	A	H	A	H	A	H	A	H	A	H	A	H	A	H	H	A	H	A	H	A	H	A	H	A	H	A	H	A	H	A	H	A
Competition	L	L	L	L	L	L	L	L	L	L	L	L	L	L	L	L	L	L	L	L	L	L	L	L	L	L	L	L	L	L	L	L	L	L	L	L	L	L
Result	D	L	W	L	L	W	W	W	W	W	D	L	W	D	W	W	D	W	D	W	D	D	W	W	W	D	D	W	W	L	W	W	W	D	W	L	W	W

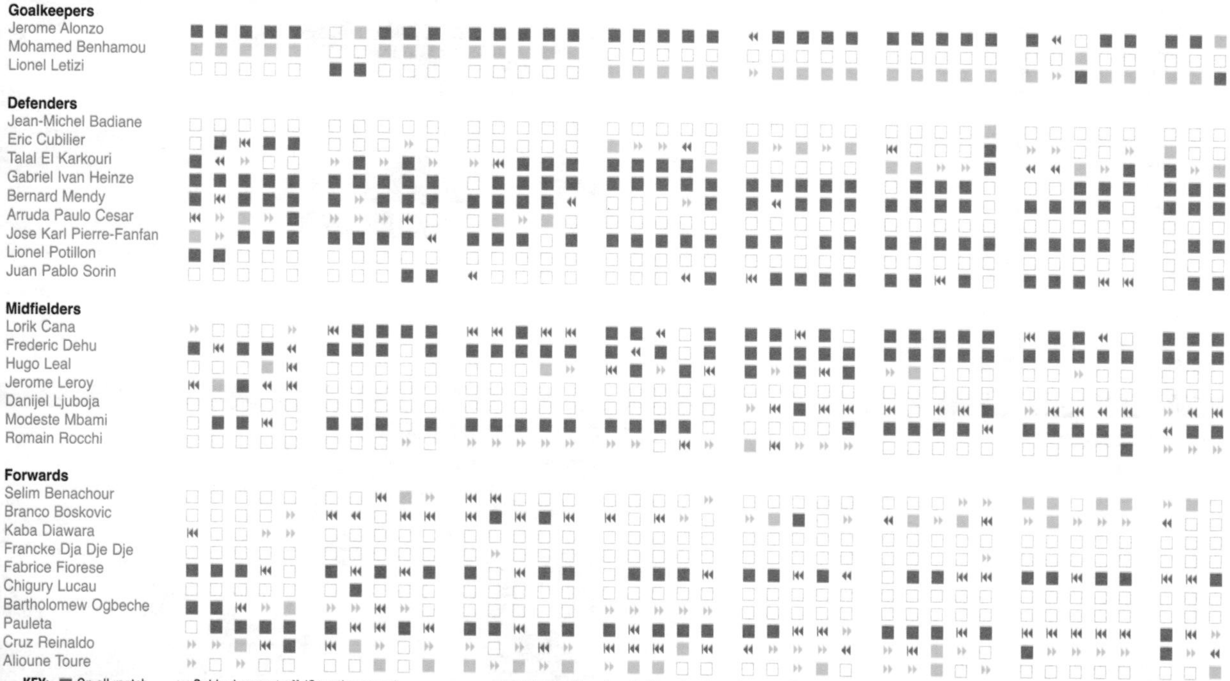

Goalkeepers
Jerome Alonzo
Mohamed Benhamou
Lionel Letizi

Defenders
Jean-Michel Badiane
Eric Cubilier
Talal El Karkouri
Gabriel Ivan Heinze
Bernard Mendy
Arruda Paulo Cesar
Jose Karl Pierre-Fanfan
Lionel Potillon
Juan Pablo Sorin

Midfielders
Lorik Cana
Frederic Dehu
Hugo Leal
Jerome Leroy
Danijel Ljuboja
Modeste Mbami
Romain Rocchi

Forwards
Selim Benachour
Branco Boskovic
Kaba Diawara
Francke Dja Dje Dje
Fabrice Fiorese
Chigury Lucau
Bartholomew Ogbeche
Pauleta
Cruz Reinaldo
Alioune Toure

KEY: ■ On all match ■ On bench ⏮ Subbed or sent off (Counting game) ◀◀ Subbed or sent off (playing less than 70 minutes) ⏭ Subbed on from bench (Counting Game) ▶▶ Subbed on (playing less than 70 minutes) ⏭ Subbed on and then subbed or sent off (Counting Game) ▶▶ Subbed on and then subbed or sent off (playing less than 70 minutes) □ Not in 16

MONACO

Final Position: **3rd**

KEY: Won / Drawn / Lost

		Opponent			Score	Scorers	Attendance
1	lge	**Bordeaux**	H	W	2-0	Nonda 31,56 pen	13,448
2	lge	**Lyon**	A	L	1-3	Nonda 55	37,246
3	lge	**Bastia**	H	W	2-0	Adebayor 38; Zikos 45	11,000
4	lge	**Paris SG**	A	W	4-2	Giuly 35,90; Adebayor 37; Squillaci 56	36,417
5	lge	**Metz**	H	W	1-0	Squillaci 37	6,000
6	lge	**Lille**	A	D	1-1	Giuly 45	16,000
7	cl gc	**PSV Eindhoven**	A	W	2-1	Morientes 31; Cisse 56	30,000
8	lge	**Montpellier**	A	W	2-1	Adebayor 18; Giuly 73	13,870
9	lge	**Toulouse**	H	W	3-0	Adebayor 11; Cisse 29; Prso 49	6,000
10	cl gc	**AEK Athens**	H	W	4-0	Giuly 23; Morientes 27,56; Prso 86	15,000
11	lge	**Guingamp**	A	W	2-1	Giuly 17,26	13,261
12	lge	**Auxerre**	H	D	1-1	Giuly 76	7,000
13	cl gc	**Deportivo**	A	L	0-1		22,000
14	lge	**Sochaux**	A	D	1-1	Morientes 21	19,326
15	lge	**Le Mans**	H	W	4-2	Morientes 5; Cousin 21 og; Squillaci 65; Molefe 84 og	4,000
16	cl gc	**Deportivo**	H	W	8-3	Rothen 2; Giuly 11; Porato 26; Prso 30,45,49; Plasil 47; Cisse 67	60,000
17	lge	**AC Ajaccio**	A	W	1-0	Prso 81	3,886
18	lge	**Lens**	H	W	2-0	Giuly 57; Morientes 67	9,042
19	cl gc	**PSV Eindhoven**	H	D	1-1	Morientes 35	12,175
20	lge	**Nantes**	A	W	1-0	Bernardi 75	36,465
21	lge	**Marseille**	A	W	2-1	Squillaci 57; Giuly 65	59,366
22	cl gc	**AEK Athens**	A	D	0-0		4,000
23	lge	**Strasbourg**	H	W	2-0	Prso 42,75	7,549
24	lge	**Rennes**	A	L	0-1		18,633
25	lge	**Lyon**	H	W	3-0	Giuly 34,90 pen; Morientes 47	15,674
26	lge	**Bastia**	A	D	0-0		6,068
27	lge	**Nice**	H	D	1-1	Morientes 40	19,000
28	lge	**Paris SG**	H	D	1-1	Squillaci 26	14,147
29	lge	**Metz**	A	W	2-0	Plasil 38; Givet 51	18,891
30	lge	**Lille**	H	L	0-1		5,000
31	lge	**Montpellier**	H	W	4-0	Adebayor 47,55,75; Morientes 48	6,000
32	cl rl1	**Lokomotiv**	A	L	1-2	Morientes 69	28,000
33	lge	**Toulouse**	A	D	1-1	Givet 72	24,000
34	lge	**Guingamp**	H	W	3-1	Morientes 24,37; Prso 27	5,000
35	cl rl2	**Lokomotiv**	H	W	1-0	Prso 60	18,000
36	lge	**Auxerre**	A	D	0-0		20,000
37	lge	**Sochaux**	H	D	1-1	Morientes 57	7,500
38	cl qfl1	**Real Madrid**	A	L	2-4	Squillaci 43; Morientes 83	70,000
39	lge	**Le Mans**	A	W	1-0	Prso 49	14,440
40	lge	**AC Ajaccio**	H	D	3-3	Nonda 50; Plasil 65; Prso 90	6,208
41	cl qf2	**Real Madrid**	H	W	3-1	Giuly 45,66; Morientes 49	18,000
42	lge	**Lens**	A	D	0-0		40,011
43	cl sfl1	**Chelsea**	H	W	3-1	Prso 17; Morientes 78; Nonda 83	15,000
44	lge	**Nantes**	H	L	0-1		11,000
45	lge	**Nice**	A	W	2-1	Prso 33; Giuly 43	13,000
46	cl sfl2	**Chelsea**	A	D	2-2	Ibarra 45; Morientes 60	37,132
47	lge	**Marseille**	H	W	1-0	Giuly 90	17,000
48	lge	**Strasbourg**	A	D	0-0		25,590
49	lge	**Rennes**	H	L	1-4	Morientes 10	10,000
50	lge	**Bordeaux**	A	W	3-1	Adebayor 24; Bernardi 76; Nonda 78	32,397
51	ecfin	**Porto**	A	L	0-3		52,000

MONTHLY POINTS TALLY

Month	Points	%
AUGUST	12	80%
SEPTEMBER	7	78%
OCTOBER	5	56%
NOVEMBER	12	100%
DECEMBER	6	67%
JANUARY	6	50%
FEBRUARY	7	58%
MARCH	8	67%
APRIL	5	42%
MAY	7	58%

LEAGUE GOALS

	PLAYER	MINS	GOALS	AVE
1	Giuly	2316	13	178
2	Morientes	2016	10	202
3	Prso	1651	8	206
4	Adebayor	1872	6	312
5	Nonda	738	5	148
6	Squillaci	2263	5	453
7	Plasil	1753	2	877
8	Givet	2230	2	1115
9	Bernardi	2798	2	1399
10	Zikos	2483	1	2483
11	Cisse	1819	1	1819
	Other		4	
	TOTAL		59	

KEY PLAYERS - GOALSCORERS

Ludovic Giuly

Goals in the League	13
Contribution to Attacking Power Average number of minutes between League team goals while on pitch	64
Player Strike Rate The total number of minutes he was on the pitch for every League goal scored	178
Club Strike Rate Average number of minutes between League goals scored by club	58

	PLAYER	GOALS LGE	POWER	S RATE
1	Ludovic Giuly	13	64	178 mins
2	Fernando Sanchez Morientes	10	56	202 mins
3	Dado Prso	8	58	206 mins
4	Emmanuel Adebayor	6	53	312 mins
5	Sebastien Squillaci	5	55	453 mins

KEY PLAYERS - MIDFIELDERS

Jaroslav Plasil

Goals in the League	2
Defensive Rating Average number of mins between League goals conceded while on the pitch	159
Contribution to Attacking Power Average number of minutes between League team goals while on pitch	58
Scoring Difference Defensive Rating minus Contribution to Attacking Power	101

	PLAYER	GOALS LGE	DEF RATE	ATT POWER	SCORE DIFF
1	Jaroslav Plasil	2	159	58	101 mins
2	Vassilis Zikos	1	146	61	85 mins
3	Lucas Ademar Bernardi	2	122	55	67 mins
4	Patrice Evra	0	116	57	59 mins
5	Jerome Rothen	0	104	56	48 mins

KEY PLAYERS - DEFENDERS

Hugo Benjamin Ibarra

Goals Conceded in League	13
Clean Sheets In League games when he played at least 70 mins	9
Defensive Rating Ave number of mins between League goals conceded while on the pitch	145
Club Defensive Rating Average number of mins between League goals conceded by the club this season	114

	PLAYER	CON LGE	CLEAN SHEETS	DEF RATE
1	Hugo Benjamin Ibarra	13	9	145 mins
2	Sebastien Squillaci	17	12	133 mins
3	Julien Rodriguez	25	16	126 mins
4	Gael Givet	19	9	117 mins

KEY GOALKEEPER

Flavio Roma

Goals Conceded in the League	27
Counting Games Games when he played at least 70 minutes	33
Clean Sheets In games when he played at least 70 mins	15
League minutes played Number of minutes played in league matches	2970
Defensive Rating Ave number of mins between League goals conceded while on the pitch	110

DISCIPLINARY RECORDS

	PLAYER	YELLOW	RED	AVE
1	Bernardi	9	0	310
2	Evra	7	1	361
3	Cisse	5	0	363
4	Zikos	6	0	413
5	Ibarra	4	0	472
6	Prso	3	0	550
7	Givet	3	1	557
8	Plasil	3	0	584
9	Rodriguez	4	0	787
10	Adebayor	2	0	936
11	Squillaci	2	0	1131
12	Giuly	2	0	1158
13	Rothen	2	0	1349
	Other	5	0	
	TOTAL	57	2	

TOP POINT EARNERS

	PLAYER	GAMES	AV PTS
1	Squillaci	24	2.25
2	Bernardi	31	2.16
3	Prso	14	2.14
4	Zikos	26	2.12
5	Plasil	13	2.08
6	Rothen	27	2.04
7	Rodriguez	35	2.03
8	Ibarra	18	2.00
9	Roma	33	2.00
10	Evra	31	2.00
	CLUB AVERAGE:		1.83

LEAGUE APPEARANCES AND BOOKINGS

	AGE (on 01/07/04)	IN NAMED 16	APPEARANCES	COUNTING GAMES	MINUTES ON PITCH	YELLOW CARDS	RED CARDS	THIS SEASON	HOME COUNTRY
Goalkeepers									
Andre Biancarelli	34	9	1	1	90	0	0	-	France
Flavio Roma	30	34	33	33	2970	2	0	-	Italy
Tony Mario Sylva	29	32	5	4	370	0	0	6	Senegal (31)
Defenders									
Jim Ablancourt	21	6	3	1	147	0	0	-	France
Gael Givet	22	34	33	21	2230	3	1	-	France
Hugo Ibarra	30	29	25	18	1891	4	0	-	Argentina
Arnaud Lescure	18	0	0	0	0	0	0	-	France
Joseph Oshadogan	28	5	3	1	146	1	0	-	Switzerland
Julien Rodriguez	26	35	35	35	3150	4	0	-	France
Sebastien Squillaci	23	29	27	24	2263	2	0	1	France (2)
Midfielders									
Ademar Bernardi	26	33	33	31	2798	9	0	-	Argentina
Edouard Cisse	26	34	31	17	1819	5	0	-	France
Hassan El Fakiri	27	27	17	6	873	0	0	-	Norway
Patrice Evra	23	33	33	31	2892	7	1	-	France
Ludovic Giuly	27	30	30	24	2316	2	0	4	France (2)
Nicolas Hislen	21	7	2	0	22	0	0	-	France
Jimmy Juan	21	2	1	0	30	0	0	-	France
Laurent Lanteri	19	1	1	0	15	0	0	-	France
Jaroslav Plasil	22	36	33	13	1753	3	0	1	Czech Republic (10)
Jerome Rothen	26	34	34	27	2698	2	0	1	France (2)
Vassilis Zikos	30	32	30	26	2483	6	0	-	Greece
Forwards									
Emmanuel Adebayor	20	36	31	16	1872	2	0	-	Togo
Souleymane Camara	21	7	4	1	174	1	0	1	Senegal (31)
Sebastien Grax	20	2	1	0	11	0	0	-	France
Fernando Morientes	28	28	28	17	2016	1	0	2	Spain (3)
Shabani Nonda	27	12	12	6	738	0	0	-	Burundi
Dado Prso	29	28	27	14	1651	3	0	-	France
Marco Ramos	21	4	2	1	118	0	0	-	Portugal
Nicolas Raynier	20	1	1	0	6	0	0	-	France

TEAM OF THE SEASON

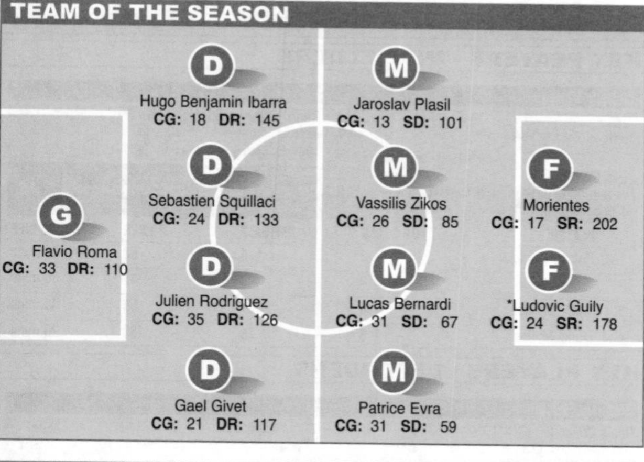

G
Flavio Roma
CG: 33 DR: 110
D
Hugo Benjamin Ibarra
CG: 18 DR: 145
D
Sebastien Squillaci
CG: 24 DR: 133
D
Julien Rodriguez
CG: 35 DR: 126
D
Gael Givet
CG: 21 DR: 117
M
Jaroslav Plasil
CG: 13 SD: 101
M
Vassilis Zikos
CG: 26 SD: 85
M
Lucas Bernardi
CG: 31 SD: 67
M
Patrice Evra
CG: 31 SD: 59
F
Morientes
CG: 17 SR: 202
F
*Ludovic Guily
CG: 24 SR: 178

SQUAD APPEARANCES

Match	1 2 3 4 5	6 7 8 9 10	11 12 13 14 15	16 17 18 19 20	21 22 23 24 25	26 27 28 29 30	31 32 33 34 35	36 37 38 39 40	41 42 43 44 45	46 47 48 49 50	51
Venue	H A H A H	A A A H H	A H A A H	H A H H A	A A H A H	A H H A H	H A A H H	A H A A H	H A H H A	A H A H A	A
Competition	L L L L L	L C L L C	L L C L L	C L L C L	L C L L L	L L L L L	L C L L C	L L C L L	C L C L L	C L L L L	C
Result	W L W W W	D W W W W	W D L D W	W W W D W	W D W L W	D D D W L	W L D W W	D D L W D	W D W L W	D W D L W	L

Goalkeepers
Andre Biancarelli
Flavio Roma
Tony Mario Sylva

Defenders
Jim Ablancourt
Gael Givet
Hugo Benjamin Ibarra
Arnaud Lescure
Joseph Dayo Oshadogan
Julien Rodriguez
Sebastien Squillaci

Midfielders
Lucas Ademar Bernardi
Edouard Cisse
Hassan El Fakiri
Patrice Evra
Ludovic Giuly
Nicolas Hislen
Jimmy Juan
Laurent Lanteri
Jaroslav Plasil
Jerome Rothen
Vassilis Zikos

Forwards
Emmanuel Adebayor
Souleymane Camara
Sebastien Grax
Morientes
Shabani Nonda
Dado Prso
Marco Ramos
Nicolas Raynier

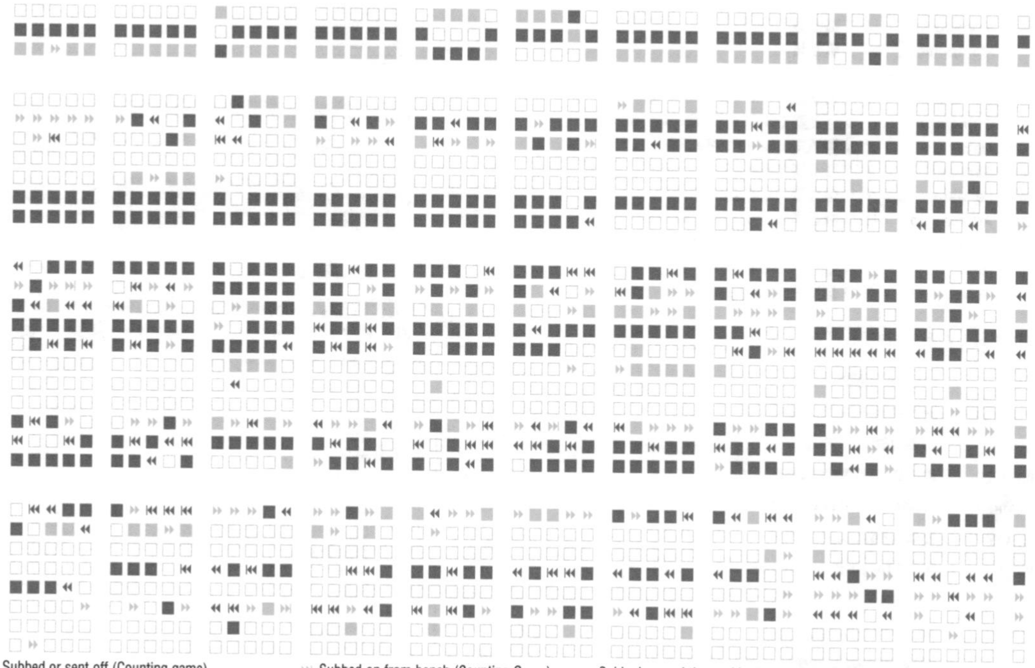

KEY: On all match; On bench; Subbed or sent off (Counting game); Subbed or sent off (playing less than 70 minutes); Subbed on from bench (Counting Game); Subbed on (playing less than 70 minutes); Subbed on and then subbed or sent off (Counting Game); Subbed on and then subbed or sent off (playing less than 70 minutes); Not in 16

AUXERRE — 4th

KEY: Won Drawn Lost

							Attendance
1	lge	Nice	H	L	1-2	Jaures 90 pen	16,673
2	lge	Marseille	A	L	0-1		60,000
3	lge	Strasbourg	H	W	3-2	Akale 10; Kalou 31; Mathis 86	12,750
4	lge	Bordeaux	A	L	0-2		27,848
5	lge	Rennes	H	W	2-1	Cisse 25; Kalou 74	8,000
6	lge	Lyon	A	D	1-1	Cisse 28	38,000
7	lge	Bastia	H	W	4-1	Cisse 24,60; Lachuer 35; Mexes 45	8,000
8	ucr1l1	Neuchatel	H	W	1-0	Kalou 7	8,000
9	lge	Paris SG	A	L	0-1		39,777
10	lge	Lille	H	W	3-0	Cisse 43,45,63	
11	ucr1l2	Neuchatel	A	W	1-0	Lachuer 53	5,585
12	lge	Monaco	A	D	1-1	Kalou 5	7,000
13	lge	Montpellier	H	L	0-1		7,000
14	lge	Toulouse	A	W	3-0	Eduardo 7 og; Kalou 24; Violeau 90	28,721
15	ucr2l1	Utrecht	A	D	0-0		20,000
16	lge	Guingamp	H	W	3-0	Cisse 32,83; Tainio 39	9,103
17	lge	Metz	A	W	2-0	Lachuer 56; Cisse 90	20,106
18	ucr2l2	Utrecht	H	W	4-0	Cisse 22,49; Kapo Obou 29; Kalou 57	18,000
19	lge	Sochaux	A	L	2-3	Cisse 69,74	17,796
20	lge	Le Mans	H	W	1-0	Fischer 18 og	9,000
21	lge	AC Ajaccio	A	W	2-1	Mexes 15; Cisse 63	3,000
22	lge	Lens	H	W	2-0	Kalou 17; Cisse 83	12,000
23	lge	Nantes	A	L	0-1		29,446
24	lge	Marseille	H	W	2-0	Tainio 3; Kalou 16	21,112
25	lge	Strasbourg	A	W	2-0	Kapo Obou 18; Cisse 90	14,894
26	lge	Bordeaux	H	W	5-0	Cisse 7,44 pen; Akale 11,59; Tainio 27	9,500
27	lge	Rennes	A	W	2-0	Mexes 14; Kalou 53	18,484
28	lge	Lyon	H	L	1-2	Boumsong 75	15,000
29	lge	Bastia	A	D	0-0		5,500
30	ucr3l1	Panathinaikos	H	D	0-0		19,000
31	lge	Paris SG	H	D	1-1	Cisse 45	21,500
32	ucr3l2	Panathinaikos	A	W	1-0	Kalou 72	14,500
33	lge	Lille	A	L	0-1		14,000
34	ucr4l1	PSV Eindhoven	H	D	1-1	Tainio 36	17,850
35	lge	Monaco	H	D	0-0		20,000
36	lge	Montpellier	A	L	0-1		13,179
37	ucr4l2	PSV Eindhoven	A	L	0-3		25,000
38	lge	Toulouse	H	W	3-2	Akale 14; Cisse 43,66	7,000
39	lge	Guingamp	A	D	2-2	Sirieix 52; Kapo Obou 90	15,774
40	lge	Metz	H	W	2-1	Cisse 51; Kalou 64	7,000
41	lge	Sochaux	H	W	2-1	Kalou 49; Cisse 56	15,000
42	lge	Le Mans	A	L	1-2	Cisse 46	14,000
43	lge	AC Ajaccio	H	D	1-1	Kalou 1	8,000
44	lge	Lens	A	W	3-1	Lachuer 22; Mathis 74; Cisse 89	25,000
45	lge	Nantes	H	W	2-0	Cisse 2,13	17,000
46	lge	Nice	A	D	1-1	Mathis 81	10,850

MONTHLY POINTS TALLY

AUGUST	6	40%
SEPTEMBER	4	44%
OCTOBER	4	44%
NOVEMBER	9	75%
DECEMBER	9	75%
JANUARY	9	100%
FEBRUARY	5	42%
MARCH	4	33%
APRIL	7	78%
MAY	8	53%

KEY PLAYERS - GOALSCORERS

Djibril Cisse

Goals in the League	26	Player Strike Rate Average number of minutes between League goals scored by player	125
Contribution to Attacking Power Average number of minutes between League team goals while on pitch	54	Club Strike Rate Average number of minutes between League goals scored by club	57

	PLAYER	LGE GOALS	POWER	STRIKE RATE
1	Djibril Cisse	26	54	125 mins
2	Bonaventure Kalou	10	64	257 mins
3	Lionel Mathis	3	53	495 mins
4	Teemu Tainio	3	47	585 mins
5	Philippe Mexes	3	57	960 mins

KEY PLAYERS - MIDFIELDERS

Philippe Violeau

Goals in the League	1	Contribution to Attacking Power Average number of minutes between League team goals while on pitch	58
Defensive Rating Average number of mins between League goals conceded while he was on the pitch	116	Scoring Difference Defensive Rating minus Contribution to Attacking Power	58

	PLAYER	LGE GOALS	DEF RATE	POWER	SCORE DIFF
1	Philippe Violeau	1	116	58	58 mins
2	Teemu Tainio	3	103	47	56 mins
3	Yann Lachuer	3	101	56	45 mins
4	Lionel Mathis	3	78	53	25 mins

KEY PLAYERS - DEFENDERS

Stephane Grichting

Goals Conceded (GC) The number of League goals conceded while he was on the pitch	12	Clean Sheets In games when he played at least 70 minutes	7
Defensive Rating Ave number of mins between League goals conceded while on the pitch	120	Club Defensive Rating Average number of mins between League goals conceded by the club this season	101

	PLAYER	CON LGE	CLEAN SHEETS	DEF RATE
1	Stephane Grichting	12	7	120 mins
2	Philippe Mexes	28	11	103 mins
3	Johan Radet	27	11	102 mins
4	Jean-Alain Boumsong	31	9	90 mins
5	Jean-Sebastien Jaures	23	5	81 mins

KEY GOALKEEPER

Fabien Cool

Goals Conceded in the League	34	Counting Games Games when he played at least 70 mins	38
Defensive Rating Ave number of mins between League goals conceded while on the pitch	101	Clean Sheets In games when he played at least 70 mins	13

LEAGUE GOALS

Djibril Cisse

Minutes on the pitch	3244	Goals in the League	26
League average (mins between goals)	125		

	PLAYER	MINS	GOALS	AVE
1	Cisse	3244	26	125
2	Kalou	2569	10	257
3	Akale	1343	4	336
4	Tainio	1756	3	585
5	Mathis	1484	3	495
6	Mexes	2880	3	960
7	Lachuer	3330	3	1110
8	Kapo Obou	2043	2	1022
9	Jaures	1861	1	1861
10	Violeau	2774	1	2774
11	Sirieix	1350	1	1350
12	Boumsong	2801	1	2801
	Other		2	
	TOTAL		60	

DISCIPLINARY

	PLAYER	YELLOW	RED	AVE
1	Sirieix	5	1	225
2	Kalou	7	0	367
3	Grichting	3	0	478
4	Tainio	3	0	585
5	Jaures	3	0	620
6	Akale	2	0	671
7	Kapo Obou	3	0	681
8	Violeau	4	0	693
9	Mignot	1	0	758
10	Radet	3	0	920
11	Mexes	3	0	960
12	Mathis	1	0	1484
13	Cisse	2	0	1622
	Other	3	0	
	TOTAL	43	1	

TOP POINT EARNERS

	PLAYER	GAMES	AV PTS
1	Mathis	14	1.86
2	Kalou	27	1.85
3	Tainio	17	1.82
4	Boumsong	31	1.81
5	Radet	31	1.81
6	Cisse	36	1.78
7	Mexes	32	1.78
8	Lachuer	37	1.76
9	Grichting	16	1.75
10	Violeau	31	1.71
	CLUB AVERAGE:		1.71

TEAM OF THE SEASON

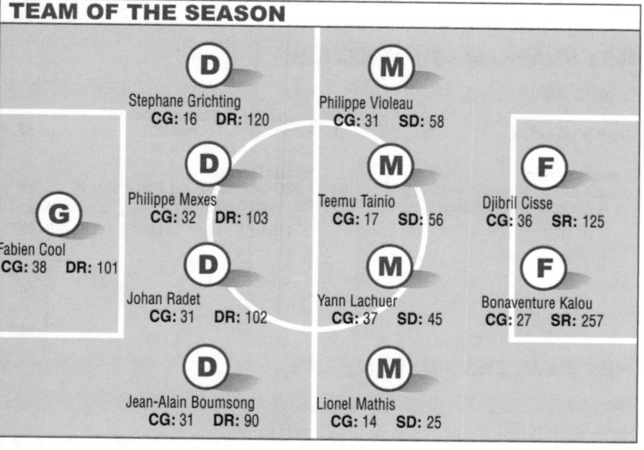

G
Fabien Cool
CG: 38 DR: 101
D
Stephane Grichting
CG: 16 DR: 120
D
Philippe Mexes
CG: 32 DR: 103
D
Johan Radet
CG: 31 DR: 102
D
Jean-Alain Boumsong
CG: 31 DR: 90
M
Philippe Violeau
CG: 31 SD: 58
M
Teemu Tainio
CG: 17 SD: 56
M
Yann Lachuer
CG: 37 SD: 45
M
Lionel Mathis
CG: 14 SD: 25
F
Djibril Cisse
CG: 36 SR: 125
F
Bonaventure Kalou
CG: 27 SR: 257

LEAGUE APPEARANCES, BOOKINGS AND CAPS

	AGE (on 01/07/04)	IN NAMED 16	APPEARANCES	COUNTING GAMES	MINUTES ON PITCH	YELLOW CARDS	RED CARDS	THIS SEASON	HOME COUNTRY
Goalkeepers									
Fabien Cool	31	38	38	38	3420	0	0	-	France
Sebastien Hamel	28	31	0	0	0	0	0	-	France
Christophe Langlois	-	2	0	0	0	0	0	-	France
Defenders									
Jean-Alain Boumsong	24	32	32	31	2801	1	0	7	France (2)
Mamoutou Coulibaly	20	1	0	0	0	0	0	-	Mali
Stephane Grichting	25	30	17	16	1435	3	0	-	Switzerland
Jean-Sebastien Jaures	26	26	24	20	1861	3	0	-	France
Younes Kabul	-	1	0	0	0	0	0	-	France
Philippe Mexes	22	32	32	32	2880	3	0	2	France (2)
Jean Pascal Mignot	23	14	10	7	758	1	0	-	France
Jean-Noel Doumbe	25	29	17	12	1142	0	0	5	Cameroon (12)
Johan Radet	27	31	31	31	2760	3	0	-	France
David Recorbet	27	3	1	0	34	0	0	-	France
Bacary Sagna	21	2	0	0	0	0	0	-	France
Midfielders									
Kanga Akale	23	31	23	12	1343	2	0	-	Ivory Coast
Pierre Deblock	31	5	1	0	23	0	0	-	France
Yann Lachuer	32	37	37	37	3330	1	0	-	France
Lionel Mathis	22	31	25	14	1484	1	0	-	France
Francois Sirieix	23	33	22	12	1350	5	1	-	France
Teemu Tainio	24	23	22	17	1756	3	0	-	Finland
Philippe Violeau	33	31	31	31	2774	4	0	-	France
Hassan Yebda	20	3	0	0	0	0	0	-	France
Forwards									
Djibril Cisse	22	38	38	36	3244	2	0	3	France (2)
Arnaud Gonzalez	26	18	13	3	432	1	0	-	France
Bonaventure Kalou	26	32	32	27	2569	7	0	-	Ivory Coast
Narcisse Kapo Obou	23	30	29	21	2043	3	0	2	France (2)
Benjamin Mwaruwari	25	3	3	1	79	0	0	-	Zimbabwe
Romain Poyet	23	8	6	0	55	0	0	-	France
David Vandenbossche	23	4	2	0	19	0	0	-	France

SQUAD APPEARANCES

Match	1	2	3	4	5	6	7	8	9	10	11	12	13	14	15	16	17	18	19	20	21	22	23	24	25	26	27	28	29	30	31	32	33	34	35	36	37	38	39	40	41	42	43	44	45	46
Venue	H	A	H	A	H	A	H	H	A	H	A	A	H	A	A	H	A	H	A	H	A	H	A	H	A	H	A	H	A	H	H	A	A	H	H	A	A	H	A	H	H	A	H	A	H	A
Competition	L	L	L	L	L	L	L	E	L	L	E	L	L	L	E	L	L	E	L	L	L	L	L	L	L	L	L	L	L	E	L	E	L	E	L	L	E	L	L	L	L	L	L	L	L	L
Result	L	L	W	L	W	D	W	W	L	W	W	D	L	W	D	W	W	W	L	W	W	W	L	W	W	W	W	L	D	D	D	W	L	D	D	L	L	W	D	W	W	L	D	W	W	D

Goalkeepers
Fabien Cool
Sebastien Hamel
Christophe Langlois

Defenders
Jean-Alain Boumsong
Mamoutou Coulibaly
Stephane Grichting
Jean-Sebastien Jaures
Younes Kabul
Philippe Mexes
Jean Pascal Mignot
Jean-Noel Perrier Doumbe
Johan Radet
David Recorbet
Bacary Sagna

Midfielders
Kanga Akale
Pierre Deblock
Yann Lachuer
Lionel Mathis
Francois Sirieix
Teemu Tainio
Philippe Violeau
Hassan Yebda

Forwards
Djibril Cisse
Arnaud Gonzalez
Bonaventure Kalou
Narcisse Olivier Kapo Obou
Benjamin Mwaruwari
Romain Poyet
David Vandenbossche

KEY: ■ On all match ■ On bench ⏮ Subbed or sent off (Counting game) ◀◀ Subbed or sent off (playing less than 70 minutes) ⏭ Subbed on from bench (Counting Game) ▶▶ Subbed on (playing less than 70 minutes) ⏭ Subbed on and then subbed or sent off (Counting Game) ▶▶ Subbed on and then subbed or sent off (playing less than 70 minutes) □ Not in 16

SOCHAUX

Final Position: **5th**

KEY: ☐ Won ☐ Drawn ☐ Lost

							Attendance
1	lge	**Nantes**	H	W	2-1	Frau 22 pen; Zairi 90	15,258
2	lge	**Nice**	A	L	0-1		13,946
3	lge	**Rennes**	H	D	1-1	Diawara 55	14,069
4	lge	**Marseille**	A	L	0-2		58,000
5	lge	**Lille**	H	W	2-1	Santos 9; Abidal 21	14,643
6	lge	**Bordeaux**	A	W	3-1	Frau 22; Isabey 76; Flachez 79 pen	22,000
7	lge	**Strasbourg**	H	W	3-0	Isabey 10; Santos 25; Pagis 90	15,000
8	ucr1l1	**MyPa-47**	A	W	1-0	Diawara 45	2,275
9	lge	**Bastia**	A	L	0-2		6,000
10	lge	**Paris SG**	H	L	0-1		19,561
11	ucr1l2	**MyPa-47**	H	W	2-0	Monsoreau 58; Santos 80	8,885
12	lge	**Lyon**	A	D	1-1	Isabey 63	37,029
13	lge	**Monaco**	H	D	1-1	Frau 68	19,326
14	lge	**Metz**	A	W	1-0	Frau 11	16,834
15	ucr2l1	**B Dortmund**	A	D	2-2	Santos 12; Frau 26	40,500
16	lge	**Toulouse**	H	W	3-1	Frau 9; Santos 64; Pedretti 90	15,526
17	lge	**Guingamp**	A	W	2-1	Frau 10; Santos 62	14,458
18	ucr2l2	**B Dortmund**	H	W	4-0	Frau 5 pen; Santos 67; Oruma 76; Mathieu 89	22,000
19	lge	**Auxerre**	H	W	3-2	Frau 6; Santos 18,43	17,796
20	lge	**Lens**	A	W	3-0	Santos 15,77; Mathieu 74	34,340
21	lge	**AC Ajaccio**	H	W	2-0	Frau 36; Santos 66	13,699
22	lge	**Le Mans**	A	D	2-2	Santos 49; Zairi 65	12,579
23	lge	**Nice**	H	D	0-0		11,265
24	lge	**Rennes**	A	L	0-4		15,225
25	lge	**Montpellier**	A	W	3-1	Frau 13,28,43	10,755
26	lge	**Marseille**	H	W	2-1	Mathieu 29; Frau 70 pen	19,754
27	lge	**Lille**	A	L	0-2		14,426
28	lge	**Bordeaux**	H	D	1-1	Oruma 90	15,000
29	lge	**Strasbourg**	A	W	2-0	Frau 6; Isabey 23	18,000
30	ucr3l1	**Inter Milan**	H	D	2-2	Frau 59,81	20,000
31	lge	**Bastia**	H	W	2-1	Lonfat 34; Frau 59	12,000
32	ucr3l2	**Inter Milan**	A	D	0-0		30,000
33	lge	**Paris SG**	A	D	1-1	Santos 54	41,500
34	lge	**Lyon**	H	L	1-2	Santos 29	19,500
35	lge	**Monaco**	A	D	1-1	Pagis 90	7,500
36	lge	**Metz**	H	W	2-0	Beria 51 og; Pagis 90	14,372
37	lge	**Toulouse**	A	D	0-0		21,120
38	lge	**Guingamp**	H	W	2-0	Pedretti 57; Ferrier 82 og	15,144
39	lge	**Auxerre**	A	L	1-2	Mexes 55 og	15,000
40	lge	**Montpellier**	H	W	3-1	Zairi 6; Frau 22; Santos 68	16,352
41	lge	**Lens**	H	L	0-3		19,791
42	lge	**AC Ajaccio**	A	L	0-1		5,000
43	lge	**Le Mans**	H	W	3-0	Mathieu 38; Santos 87; Frau 89	17,387
44	lge	**Nantes**	A	L	1-3	Diawara 63	25,600

MONTHLY POINTS TALLY

AUGUST	7	47%
SEPTEMBER	6	67%
OCTOBER	2	22%
NOVEMBER	12	100%
DECEMBER	7	78%
JANUARY	7	58%
FEBRUARY	7	58%
MARCH	5	42%
APRIL	4	44%
MAY	6	40%

KEY PLAYERS - GOALSCORERS

Francileudo Santos

Goals in the League	14	**Player Strike Rate** Average number of minutes between League goals scored by player	160
Contribution to Attacking Power Average number of minutes between League team goals while on pitch	53	**Club Strike Rate** Average number of minutes between League goals scored by club	63

	PLAYER	LGE GOALS	POWER	STRIKE RATE
1	Francileudo Santos	14	53	160 mins
2	Pierre-Alain Frau	16	59	179 mins
3	Mickael Isabey	4	61	630 mins
4	Jeremy Mathieu	3	72	698 mins
5	Souleymane Diawara	2	61	1256 mins

KEY PLAYERS - MIDFIELDERS

Wilson Oruma

Goals in the League	1	**Contribution to Attacking Power** Average number of minutes between League team goals while on pitch	56
Defensive Rating Average number of mins between League goals conceded while he was on the pitch	84	**Scoring Difference** Defensive Rating minus Contribution to Attacking Power	28

	PLAYER	LGE GOALS	DEF RATE	POWER	SCORE DIFF
1	Wilson Oruma	1	84	56	28 mins
2	Mickael Isabey	4	84	61	23 mins
3	Benoit Pedretti	2	80	60	20 mins
4	Jeremy Mathieu	3	87	72	15 mins
5	Ibrahim Tall	0	67	83	-16 mins

KEY PLAYERS - DEFENDERS

Omar Daf

Goals Conceded (GC) The number of League goals conceded while he was on the pitch	14	**Clean Sheets** In games when he played at least 70 minutes	5
Defensive Rating Ave number of mins between League goals conceded while on the pitch	100	**Club Defensive Rating** Average number of mins between League goals conceded by the club this season	81

	PLAYER	CON LGE	CLEAN SHEETS	DEF RATE
1	Omar Daf	14	5	100 mins
2	Gregory Paisley	18	6	91 mins
3	Souleymane Diawara	30	8	84 mins
4	Sylvain Monsoreau	31	6	84 mins
5	Maxence Flachez	36	8	79 mins

KEY GOALKEEPER

Teddy Richert

Goals Conceded in the League	22	**Counting Games** Games when he played at least 70 mins	21
Defensive Rating Ave number of mins between League goals conceded while on the pitch	86	**Clean Sheets** In games when he played at least 70 mins	6

LEAGUE GOALS

Pierre-Alain Frau

Minutes on the pitch	2858	**Goals in the League**	16
League average (mins between goals)	179		

	PLAYER	MINS	GOALS	AVE
1	Frau	2858	16	179
2	Santos	2233	14	160
3	Isabey	2519	4	630
4	Pagis	1273	3	424
5	Zairi	736	3	245
6	Mathieu	2094	3	698
7	Pedretti	2946	2	1473
8	Diawara	2511	2	1256
9	Oruma	1850	1	1850
10	Flachez	2837	1	2837
11	Lonfat	1873	1	1873
	Other		4	
	TOTAL		54	

DISCIPLINARY RECORDS

	PLAYER	YELLOW	RED	AVE
1	Zairi	3	0	245
2	Boudarene	4	1	250
3	Pagis	5	0	254
4	Daf	4	0	349
5	Oruma	4	1	370
6	Gnanhouan	4	0	382
7	Paisley	3	1	408
8	Mathieu	5	0	418
9	Diawara	6	0	418
10	Flachez	6	0	472
11	Tall	3	0	582
12	Pedretti	5	0	589
13	Monsoreau	2	0	1295
	Other	5	1	
	TOTAL	59	4	

TOP POINT EARNERS

	PLAYER	GAMES	AV PTS
1	Paisley	14	2.07
2	Gnanhouan	17	2.00
3	Isabey	23	1.96
4	Santos	24	1.92
5	Oruma	18	1.78
6	Monsoreau	28	1.75
7	Flachez	31	1.74
8	Daf	15	1.73
9	Pedretti	32	1.72
10	Mathieu	20	1.70
	CLUB AVERAGE:		**1.66**

TEAM OF THE SEASON

G
Teddy Richert
CG: 21 DR: 86
D
Omar Daf
CG: 15 DR: 100
D
Gregory Paisley
CG: 14 DR: 91
D
Souleymane Diawara
CG: 28 DR: 84
D
Sylvain Monsoreau
CG: 28 DR: 84
M
Wilson Oruma
CG: 18 SD: 28
M
Mickael Isabey
CG: 23 SD: 23
M
Benoit Pedretti
CG: 32 SD: 20
M
Jeremy Mathieu
CG: 20 SD: 15
F
Francileudo Santos
CG: 24 SR: 160
F
Pierre-Alain Frau
CG: 29 SR: 179

LEAGUE APPEARANCES, BOOKINGS AND CAPS

	AGE (on 01/07/04)	IN NAMED 16	APPEARANCES	COUNTING GAMES	MINUTES ON PITCH	YELLOW CARDS	RED CARDS	THIS SEASON	HOME COUNTRY
Goalkeepers									
Gerard Gnanhouan	25	36	17	17	1530	4	0	-	Ivory Coast
Alexandre Martinovic	29	12	0	0	0	0	0	-	France
Teddy Richert	29	26	21	21	1890	0	0	-	France
Defenders									
Omar Daf	27	17	17	15	1396	4	0	4	Senegal (31)
Diawara	25	29	29	28	2511	6	0	3	Senegal (31)
Maxence Flachez	31	32	32	31	2837	6	0	-	France
Aime Lavie	-	3	1	1	90	0	0	-	France
Johan Lonfat	30	31	29	18	1873	0	0	-	Switzerland
Sylvain Monsoreau	23	30	30	28	2591	2	0	-	France
Gregory Paisley	27	27	24	14	1633	3	1	-	France
Phillipe Raschke	36	23	18	5	784	0	0	-	France
Midfielders									
Fabien Boudarene	25	26	21	10	1250	4	1	-	France
Boumelaha	20	4	0	0	0	0	0	-	France
Adel Chedli	27	7	4	2	256	1	0	-	France
Mickael Isabey	29	37	36	23	2519	1	0	-	France
Jeremy Mathieu	20	29	29	20	2094	5	0	-	France
Guirane N'Daw	20	13	8	1	126	0	1	-	Senegal
Wilson Oruma	27	25	24	18	1850	4	1	-	Nigeria
Benoit Pedretti	23	33	33	32	2946	5	0	5	France (2)
Ibrahim Tall	28	31	22	18	1748	3	0	-	Senegal
Forwards									
Sigamary Diarra	20	2	1	0	9	0	0	-	France
Pierre-Alain Frau	24	36	36	29	2858	2	0	-	France
Michael Pagis	30	27	24	10	1273	5	0	-	France
Francileudo Santos	25	29	29	24	2233	1	0	-	Brazil
Marcelo Trapasso	28	18	16	4	560	0	0	-	Argentina
Jaouad Zairi	22	19	17	5	736	3	0	-	Morocco

SQUAD APPEARANCES

Match	1	2	3	4	5	6	7	8	9	10	11	12	13	14	15	16	17	18	19	20	21	22	23	24	25	26	27	28	29	30	31	32	33	34	35	36	37	38	39	40	41	42	43	44
Venue	H	A	H	A	H	A	H	A	A	H	H	A	H	A	A	H	A	H	H	A	H	A	H	A	A	H	A	H	A	H	H	A	A	H	A	H	A	H	A	H	H	A	H	A
Competition	L	L	L	L	L	L	L	E	L	L	E	L	L	L	E	L	L	E	L	L	L	L	L	L	L	L	L	L	L	E	L	E	L	L	L	L	L	L	L	L	L	L	L	L
Result	W	L	D	L	W	W	W	W	L	L	W	D	D	W	D	W	W	W	W	W	W	D	D	L	W	W	L	D	W	D	W	D	D	L	D	W	D	W	L	W	L	L	W	L

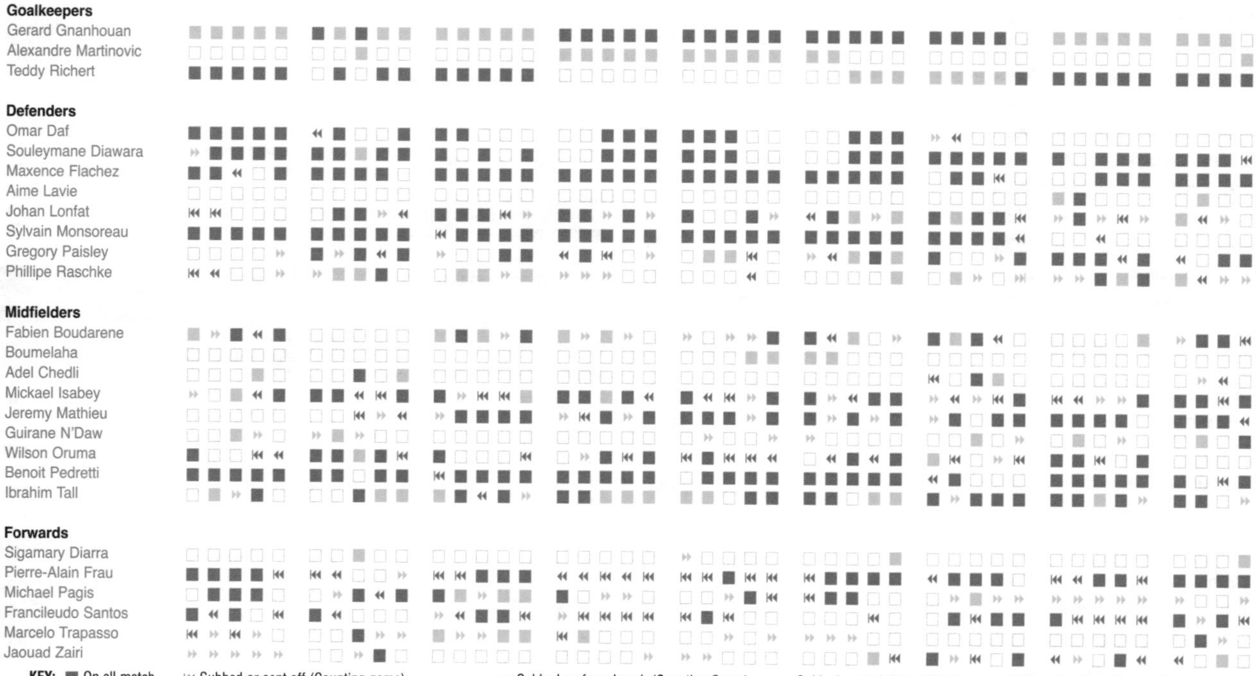

Goalkeepers
Gerard Gnanhouan
Alexandre Martinovic
Teddy Richert

Defenders
Omar Daf
Souleymane Diawara
Maxence Flachez
Aime Lavie
Johan Lonfat
Sylvain Monsoreau
Gregory Paisley
Phillipe Raschke

Midfielders
Fabien Boudarene
Boumelaha
Adel Chedli
Mickael Isabey
Jeremy Mathieu
Guirane N'Daw
Wilson Oruma
Benoit Pedretti
Ibrahim Tall

Forwards
Sigamary Diarra
Pierre-Alain Frau
Michael Pagis
Francileudo Santos
Marcelo Trapasso
Jaouad Zairi

KEY: On all match · On bench · Subbed or sent off (Counting game) · Subbed or sent off (playing less than 70 minutes) · Subbed on from bench (Counting Game) · Subbed on (playing less than 70 minutes) · Subbed on and then subbed or sent off (Counting Game) · Subbed on and then subbed or sent off (playing less than 70 minutes) · Not in 16

NANTES

Final Position: **6th**

KEY: Won / Drawn / Lost

							Attendance
1	lge	Sochaux	A	L	1-2	Vahirua 11	15,258
2	lge	Lens	H	W	2-0	Vahirua 47; Pujol 55	32,333
3	lge	AC Ajaccio	A	W	3-1	Da Rocha 23; Armand 43; Pujol 51	10,000
4	lge	Le Mans	H	W	1-0	N'Zigou 79	33,000
5	lge	Bordeaux	H	D	0-0		33,346
6	lge	Nice	A	L	0-1		12,373
7	lge	Marseille	H	W	1-0	Vahirua 3	35,500
8	lge	Strasbourg	A	L	0-1		15,000
9	lge	Rennes	H	W	1-0	Hadjadj 22	32,400
10	lge	Metz	A	W	3-1	Berson 6; Glombard 61; Pujol 72	15,903
11	lge	Lyon	H	L	0-1		32,000
12	lge	Montpellier	A	L	1-4	Armand 62	10,641
13	lge	Paris SG	H	L	0-1		34,510
14	lge	Bastia	A	W	3-1	Vahirua 41; Fae 59; Ziani 86	5,488
15	lge	Monaco	H	L	0-1		36,465
16	lge	Lille	A	L	0-2		11,000
17	lge	Toulouse	H	D	1-1	Gillet 19 pen	28,521
18	lge	Guingamp	A	D	1-1	Vahirua 26	15,069
19	lge	Auxerre	H	W	1-0	Da Rocha 2	29,446
20	lge	Lens	A	D	0-0		32,251
21	lge	AC Ajaccio	H	W	4-0	Vahirua 10; Berson 14; Moldovan 53; N'Zigou 82	26,817
22	lge	Le Mans	A	W	1-0	Moldovan 12	14,121
23	lge	Bordeaux	A	L	0-2		22,145
24	lge	Nice	H	W	3-1	Pujol 6; Moldovan 29,83 pen	30,000
25	lge	Marseille	A	D	1-1	Moldovan 41	48,000
26	lge	Strasbourg	H	D	1-1	Da Rocha 24	31,000
27	lge	Rennes	A	W	3-0	Moldovan 50,74; Quint 52	18,500
28	lge	Metz	H	D	2-2	Moldovan 12; Armand 38	27,400
29	lge	Lyon	A	L	0-1		35,643
30	lge	Montpellier	H	W	3-2	Moldovan 27,48,89	28,510
31	lge	Paris SG	A	L	2-3	Pujol 16; Ziani 90	40,000
32	lge	Bastia	H	D	1-1	Gillet 88	24,569
33	lge	Monaco	A	W	1-0	Vahirua 78	11,000
34	lge	Lille	H	W	2-0	Da Rocha 23,43	27,814
35	lge	Toulouse	A	W	1-0	Pujol 73	21,195
36	lge	Guingamp	H	D	0-0		28,000
37	lge	Auxerre	A	L	0-2		17,000
38	lge	Sochaux	H	W	3-1	Da Rocha 6; Yapi 33; Savinaud 70	25,600

MONTHLY POINTS TALLY

Month	Points	%
AUGUST	10	67%
SEPTEMBER	3	33%
OCTOBER	6	67%
NOVEMBER	3	25%
DECEMBER	5	42%
JANUARY	7	78%
FEBRUARY	5	42%
MARCH	7	58%
APRIL	4	44%
MAY	10	67%

KEY PLAYERS - GOALSCORERS

Marama Vahirua

Goals in the League	7	**Player Strike Rate** Average number of minutes between League goals scored by player	229
Contribution to Attacking Power Average number of minutes between League team goals while on pitch	69	**Club Strike Rate** Average number of minutes between League goals scored by club	73

	PLAYER	LGE GOALS	POWER	STRIKE RATE
1	Marama Vahirua	7	69	229 mins
2	Gregory Pujol	6	73	329 mins
3	Frederic Da Rocha	6	65	505 mins
4	Nicholas Gillet	2	53	863 mins
5	Stephane Ziani	2	69	898 mins

KEY PLAYERS - MIDFIELDERS

Jeremy Toulalan

Goals in the League	0	**Contribution to Attacking Power** Average number of minutes between League team goals while on pitch	69
Defensive Rating Average number of mins between League goals conceded while he was on the pitch	206	**Scoring Difference** Defensive Rating minus Contribution to Attacking Power	137

	PLAYER	LGE GOALS	DEF RATE	POWER	SCORE DIFF
1	Jeremy Toulalan	0	206	69	137 mins
2	Loic Guillon	0	123	98	25 mins
3	Mathieu Berson	2	105	84	21 mins
4	Nicholas Gillet	2	96	53	96 mins

KEY PLAYERS - DEFENDERS

Mario Yepes

Goals Conceded (GC) The number of League goals conceded while he was on the pitch	24	**Clean Sheets** In games when he played at least 70 minutes	11
Defensive Rating Ave number of mins between League goals conceded while on the pitch	106	**Club Defensive Rating** Average number of mins between League goals conceded by the club this season	98

	PLAYER	CON LGE	CLEAN SHEETS	DEF RATE
1	Mario Yepes	24	11	106 mins
2	Sylvain Armand	29	13	101 mins
3	Nicolas Savinaud	21	7	100 mins
4	Emerse Fae	18	6	95 mins

KEY GOALKEEPER

Mickael Landreau

Goals Conceded in the League	28	**Counting Games** Games when he played at least 70 mins	34
Defensive Rating Ave number of mins between League goals conceded while on the pitch	109	**Clean Sheets** In games when he played at least 70 mins	14

LEAGUE GOALS

Dinu Viorel Moldovan

Minutes on the pitch	934	Goals in the League	11
League average (mins between goals)	85		

	PLAYER	MINS	GOALS	AVE
1	Moldovan	934	11	85
2	Vahirua	1605	7	229
3	Pujol	1976	6	329
4	Da Rocha	3032	6	505
5	Armand	2943	3	981
6	Berson	2102	2	1051
7	Gillet	1725	2	863
8	N'Zigou	738	2	369
9	Ziani	1796	2	898
10	Savinaud	2107	1	2107
11	Glombard	206	1	206
12	Quint	1101	1	1101
	Other		3	
	TOTAL		47	

DISCIPLINARY RECORDS

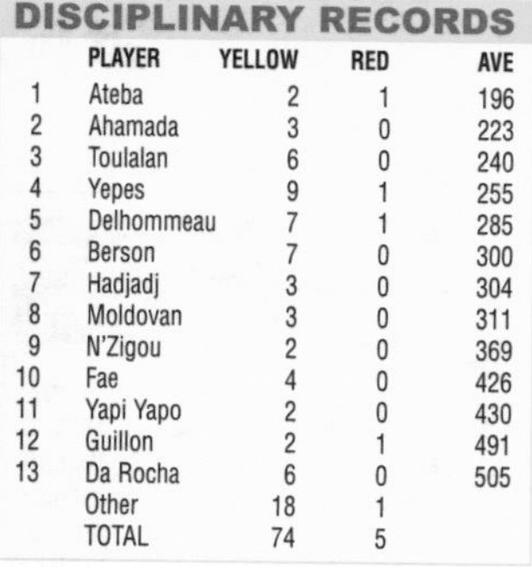

	PLAYER	YELLOW	RED	AVE
1	Ateba	2	1	196
2	Ahamada	3	0	223
3	Toulalan	6	0	240
4	Yepes	9	1	255
5	Delhommeau	7	1	285
6	Berson	7	0	300
7	Hadjadj	3	0	304
8	Moldovan	3	0	311
9	N'Zigou	2	0	369
10	Fae	4	0	426
11	Yapi Yapo	2	0	430
12	Guillon	2	1	491
13	Da Rocha	6	0	505
	Other	18	1	
	TOTAL	74	5	

TOP POINT EARNERS

	PLAYER	GAMES	AV PTS
1	Toulalan	15	2.07
2	Vahirua	13	1.92
3	Gillet	18	1.72
4	Armand	32	1.72
5	Yepes	28	1.71
6	Landreau	34	1.68
7	Da Rocha	33	1.64
8	Savinaud	23	1.57
9	Berson	23	1.57
10	Ziani	18	1.56
	CLUB AVERAGE:		**1.58**

TEAM OF THE SEASON

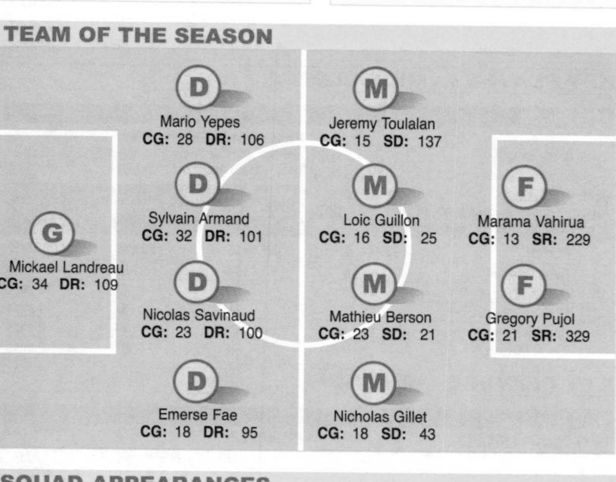
D
Mario Yepes
CG: 28 DR: 106
M
Jeremy Toulalan
CG: 15 SD: 137
D
Sylvain Armand
CG: 32 DR: 101
M
Loic Guillon
CG: 16 SD: 25
F
Marama Vahirua
CG: 13 SR: 229
G
Mickael Landreau
CG: 34 DR: 109
D
Nicolas Savinaud
CG: 23 DR: 100
M
Mathieu Berson
CG: 23 SD: 21
F
Gregory Pujol
CG: 21 SR: 329
D
Emerse Fae
CG: 18 DR: 95
M
Nicholas Gillet
CG: 18 SD: 43

LEAGUE APPEARANCES, BOOKINGS AND CAPS

	AGE (on 01/07/04)	IN NAMED 16	APPEARANCES	COUNTING GAMES	MINUTES ON PITCH	YELLOW CARDS	RED CARDS	THIS SEASON	HOME COUNTRY
Goalkeepers									
Willy Grondin	29	36	4	4	360	0	0	-	France
Mickael Landreau	25	34	34	34	3060	0	0	1	France (2)
Perica Radic	20	4	0	0	0	0	0	-	Serbia & Montenegro
Defenders									
Sylvain Armand	23	34	34	32	2943	4	1	1	France (2)
Jean-Hughes Ateba	22	19	10	5	588	2	1	-	Cameroon
Marc Boucher	21	3	3	1	103	0	0	-	France
Mauro Cetto	22	6	3	2	206	1	0	-	Argentina
Pascal Delhommeau	25	27	27	24	2283	7	1	-	France
Stephen Drouin	20	15	9	6	603	1	0	-	France
Emerse Fae	20	27	25	18	1707	4	0	-	France
Nicolas Savinaud	28	26	25	23	2107	3	0	-	France
Mario Yepes	28	30	29	28	2550	9	1	-	Columbia
Midfielders									
Mathieu Berson	24	24	24	23	2102	7	0	-	France
Nicholas Gillet	27	21	20	18	1725	1	0	-	France
Luigi Glombard	19	9	7	1	206	0	0	-	France
Loic Guillon	22	24	18	16	1473	2	1	-	France
Fodil Hadjadj	21	26	18	8	912	3	0	-	Algeria
Loic Pailleres	24	5	5	2	238	1	0	-	France
Olivier Quint	32	26	25	8	1101	1	0	-	France
Jeremy Toulalan	20	20	19	15	1442	6	0	-	France
Forwards									
Hassan Ahamada	23	12	11	6	669	3	0	-	France
Pierre Aristouy	24	5	4	1	112	0	0	-	France
Frederic Da Rocha	29	35	35	33	3032	6	0	-	France
Dinu Moldovan	32	12	12	9	934	3	0	-	Romania
Shiva N'Zigou	20	22	20	4	738	2	0	-	Gambia
Gregory Pujol	24	28	28	21	1976	2	0	-	France
Marama Vahirua	24	30	28	13	1605	2	0	-	France
Gilles Yapi Yapo	22	15	15	8	860	2	0	-	Ivory Coast
Stephane Ziani	31	31	28	18	1796	2	0	-	France

SQUAD APPEARANCES

Match	1	2	3	4	5	6	7	8	9	10	11	12	13	14	15	16	17	18	19	20	21	22	23	24	25	26	27	28	29	30	31	32	33	34	35	36	37	38
Venue	A	H	A	H	H	A	H	A	H	A	H	A	H	A	H	A	H	A	H	A	H	A	A	H	A	H	A	H	A	H	A	H	A	H	A	H	A	H
Competition	L	L	L	L	L	L	L	L	L	L	L	L	L	L	L	L	L	L	L	L	L	L	L	L	L	L	L	L	L	L	L	L	L	L	L	L	L	L
Result	L	W	W	W	D	L	W	L	W	W	L	L	L	W	L	L	D	D	W	D	W	W	L	W	D	D	W	D	L	W	L	D	W	W	W	D	L	W

Goalkeepers
Willy Grondin
Mickael Landreau
Perica Radic

Defenders
Sylvain Armand
Jean-Hughes Ateba
Marc Boucher
Mauro Cetto
Pascal Delhommeau
Stephen Drouin
Emerse Fae
Nicolas Savinaud
Mario Yepes

Midfielders
Mathieu Berson
Nicholas Gillet
Luigi Glombard
Loic Guillon
Fodil Hadjadj
Loic Pailleres
Olivier Quint
Jeremy Toulalan

Forwards
Hassan Ahamada
Pierre Aristouy
Frederic Da Rocha
Dinu Viorel Moldovan
Shiva N'Zigou
Gregory Pujol
Marama Vahirua
Gilles Yapi Yapo
Stephane Ziani

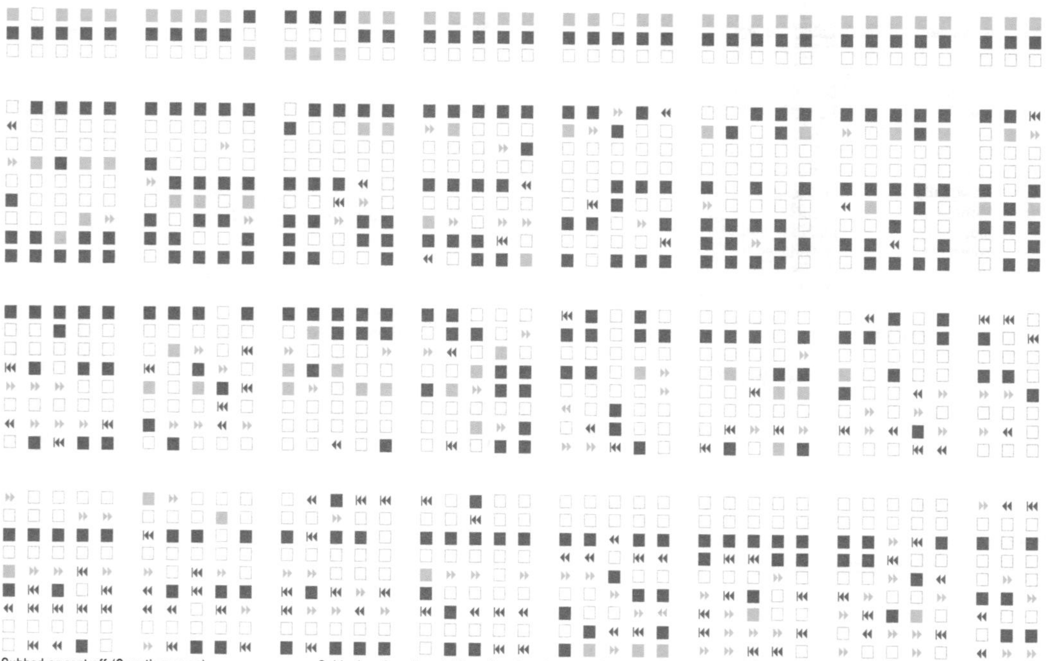

KEY: On all match; On bench; Subbed or sent off (Counting game); Subbed or sent off (playing less than 70 minutes); Subbed on from bench (Counting Game); Subbed on (playing less than 70 minutes); Subbed on and then subbed or sent off (Counting Game); Subbed on and then subbed or sent off (playing less than 70 minutes); Not in 16

MARSEILLE

7th

KEY: ☐ Won ☐ Drawn ☐ Lost

							Attendance
1	lge	Guingamp	A	W	1-0	Bakayoko 90	18,040
2	lge	Auxerre	H	W	1-0	Mido 58	60,000
3	cl ql1	Austria Vienna	A	W	1-0	Sychev 4	28,300
4	lge	Lens	A	L	1-2	Drogba 11	40,465
5	lge	Sochaux	H	W	2-0	Drogba 34; Hemdani 85	58,000
6	cl ql2	Austria Vienna	H	D	0-0		
7	lge	AC Ajaccio	A	W	1-0	Meriem 65	9,144
8	lge	Le Mans	H	W	5-0	Drogba 13; Marlet 24; Mido 54,85; Sychev 68	54,445
9	cl gf	Real Madrid	A	L	2-4	Drogba 26; Van Buyten 83	65,000
10	lge	Nantes	A	L	0-1		35,500
11	lge	Nice	H	W	2-1	Drogba 58,90 pen	
12	cl gf	Partizan	H	W	3-0	Drogba 62,68,85	56,825
13	lge	Bastia	H	W	3-1	Drogba 15; Marlet 19; Skacel 65	52,923
14	lge	Strasbourg	A	L	1-4	Marlet 33	27,000
15	cl gf	Porto	H	L	2-3	Drogba 24; Marlet 84	59,000
16	lge	Rennes	H	W	2-0	Van Buyten 45; Drogba 76	53,000
17	lge	Bordeaux	A	L	0-1		32,500
18	cl gf	Porto	A	L	0-1		33,215
19	lge	Lyon	H	L	1-4	Van Buyten 21	56,207
20	lge	Lille	A	W	2-0	Drogba 21; Mido 46	20,480
21	cl gf	Real Madrid	H	L	1-2	Mido 63	59,000
22	lge	Paris SG	H	L	0-1		59,000
23	lge	Monaco	H	L	1-2	Mido 43	59,366
24	cl gf	Partizan	A	D	1-1	Mido 61	35,000
25	lge	Toulouse	H	W	1-0	Drogba 62	50,838
26	lge	Auxerre	A	L	0-2		21,112
27	lge	Lens	H	W	3-2	Drogba 9,48; Sychev 87	48,638
28	lge	Metz	A	D	1-1	Drogba 76	25,811
29	lge	Sochaux	A	L	1-2	Drogba 5	19,754
30	lge	Montpellier	A	W	1-0	Drogba 64	21,085
31	lge	AC Ajaccio	H	W	2-1	Mido 10; Marlet 90	47,000
32	lge	Le Mans	A	D	0-0		16,000
33	lge	Nantes	H	D	1-1	Drogba 29	48,000
34	uc3rl1	Dnipro	H	W	1-0	Drogba 54 pen	25,000
35	lge	Nice	A	D	0-0		15,000
36	uc3rl2	Dnipro	A	D	0-0		25,000
37	lge	Bastia	A	L	1-4	Drogba 78 pen	7,000
38	uc4rl1	Liverpool	A	D	1-1	Drogba 78	41,270
39	lge	Strasbourg	H	W	4-0	Drogba 21 pen; Marlet 38; Ferreira 46,90	38,900
40	lge	Rennes	A	L	3-4	Battles 30; Drogba 45; Mido 72	18,979
41	uc4rl2	Liverpool	H	W	2-1	Drogba 38 pen; Meite 58	50,000
42	lge	Bordeaux	H	D	1-1	Meriem 50	51,573
43	lge	Lyon	A	W	2-1	Drogba 5; Meriem 85	38,602
44	ucqfl1	Inter Milan	H	W	1-0	Drogba 46	60,000
45	ucqfl2	Inter Milan	A	W	1-0	Meriem 74	36,044
46	lge	Lille	H	W	2-1	Marlet 45; Battles 79	48,000
47	ucsfl1	Newcastle	A	D	0-0		52,004
48	lge	Paris SG	A	L	1-2	Battles 89	41,978
49	lge	Metz	H	L	0-1		44,000
50	ucsfl2	Newcastle	H	W	2-0	Drogba 18,82	57,500
51	lge	Monaco	A	L	0-1		17,000
52	lge	Montpellier	H	D	1-1	Marlet 31	44,000
53	lge	Toulouse	A	L	1-2	Dao 5	36,000
54	ucf	Valencia	H	L	0-2		40,000
55	lge	Guingamp	H	W	2-1	Marlet 13,40	43,000

MONTHLY POINTS TALLY

AUGUST	12	80%
SEPTEMBER	6	67%
OCTOBER	6	67%
NOVEMBER	3	25%
DECEMBER	3	50%
JANUARY	4	33%
FEBRUARY	9	60%
MARCH	4	33%
APRIL	6	67%
MAY	4	27%

KEY PLAYERS - GOALSCORERS

Didier Drogba

Goals in the League	19	Player Strike Rate Average number of minutes between League goals scored by player	137
Contribution to Attacking Power Average number of minutes between League team goals while on pitch	68	Club Strike Rate Average number of minutes between League goals scored by club	67

	PLAYER	LGE GOALS	POWER	STRIKE RATE
1	Didier Drogba	19	68	137 mins
2	Ahmed Hossam Mido	7	67	221 mins
3	Camel Meriem	2	67	1147 mins
4	Rudolf Skacel	1	56	1641 mins
5	Ibrahim Hemdani	1	73	2289 mins

KEY PLAYERS - MIDFIELDERS

Fabio Celestini

Goals in the League	0	Contribution to Attacking Power Average number of minutes between League team goals while on pitch	58
Defensive Rating Average number of mins between League goals conceded while he was on the pitch	100	Scoring Difference Defensive Rating minus Contribution to Attacking Power	42

	PLAYER	LGE GOALS	DEF RATE	POWER	SCORE DIFF
1	Fabio Celestini	0	100	58	42 mins
2	Sylvain N'Diaye	0	76	61	15 mins
3	Rudolf Skacel	1	71	57	14 mins
4	Ibrahim Hemdani	1	82	74	8 mins
5	Camel Meriem	2	69	67	2 mins

KEY PLAYERS - DEFENDERS

Habib Beye

Goals Conceded (GC) The number of League goals conceded while he was on the pitch	17	Clean Sheets In games when he played at least 70 minutes	7
Defensive Rating Ave number of mins between League goals conceded while on the pitch	97	Club Defensive Rating Average number of mins between League goals conceded by the club this season	76

	PLAYER	CON LGE	CLEAN SHEETS	DEF RATE
1	Habib Beye	17	7	97 mins
2	Daniel van Buyten	23	8	75 mins
3	David Sommeil	16	4	72 mins
4	Abdoulaye Meite	35	8	71 mins
5	Philippe Christanval	16	2	71 mins

KEY GOALKEEPER

Vedran Runje

Goals Conceded in the League	17	Counting Games Games when he played at least 70 mins	16
Defensive Rating Ave number of mins between League goals conceded while on the pitch	85	Clean Sheets In games when he played at least 70 mins	7

LEAGUE GOALS

Didier Drogba

Minutes on the pitch	2607	Goals in the League	19
League average (mins between goals)	137		

	PLAYER	MINS	GOALS	AVE
1	Drogba	2607	19	137
2	Marlet	1396	9	155
3	Mido	1544	7	221
4	Battles	919	3	306
5	Van Buyten	1572	2	786
6	Sychev	785	2	393
7	Meriem	2293	2	1147
8	Ferreira	1068	2	534
9	Hemdani	2289	1	2289
10	Skacel	1641	1	1641
11	Bakayoko	48	1	48
	Other		2	
	TOTAL		51	

DISCIPLINARY

	PLAYER	YELLOW	RED	AVE
1	Battles	5	0	183
2	Flamini	4	1	210
3	Sommeil	4	1	229
4	Vachousek	6	0	244
5	Meite	10	0	248
6	Beye	5	0	330
7	Johansen	3	0	352
8	Ferreira	3	0	356
9	Christanval	2	1	377
10	Mido	3	0	514
11	Van Buyten	3	0	524
12	Skacel	3	0	547
13	Koke	1	0	549
	Other	19	2	
	TOTAL	71	5	

TOP POINT EARNERS

	PLAYER	GAMES	AV PTS
1	Skacel	16	1.81
2	Vachousek	15	1.80
3	Celestini	19	1.74
4	Runje	16	1.69
5	Hemdani	24	1.67
6	Van Buyten	17	1.65
7	Beye	17	1.53
8	Meite	27	1.52
9	Drogba	26	1.46
10	N'Diaye	14	1.43
	CLUB AVERAGE:		**1.50**

LEAGUE APPEARANCES, BOOKINGS AND CAPS

	AGE (on 01/07/04)	IN NAMED 16	APPEARANCES	COUNTING GAMES	MINUTES ON PITCH	YELLOW CARDS	RED CARDS	THIS SEASON	HOME COUNTRY
Goalkeepers									
Fabien Barthez	33	21	20	20	1800	3	0	6	France (2)
Cedric Carasso	22	9	0	0	0	0	0	-	France
Jeremy Gavanon	-	28	2	2	180	0	0	-	France
Vedran Runje	29	16	16	16	1440	0	0	-	Croatia
Defenders									
Elhadji Khalifa Ba	-	3	1	0	55	2	1	-	Senegal
Habib Beye	27	23	23	17	1653	5	0	-	France
Philippe Christanval	25	13	13	13	1132	2	1	-	France
Manuel Dos Santos	30	13	12	10	1003	0	0	-	France
Johnny Ecker	31	29	22	16	1530	2	0	-	France
Demetrius Ferreira	30	16	13	11	1068	3	0	-	Brazil
Fabien Laurenti	21	4	2	1	158	0	0	-	France
Abdoulaye Meite	23	31	30	27	2483	10	0	-	France
Sebastien Perez	30	10	8	7	603	1	0	-	France
David Sommeil	29	15	13	13	1149	4	1	-	France
Daniel Van Buyten	26	19	18	17	1572	3	0	4	Belgium (17)
Midfielders									
Laurent Battles	28	15	15	6	919	5	0	-	France
Fabien Camus	19	2	2	0	36	0	0	-	France
Fabio Celestini	28	30	26	19	1900	3	0	-	Switzerland
Mathieu Flamini	20	16	14	10	1050	4	1	-	France
Ibrahim Hemdani	26	30	29	24	2289	2	0	-	France
Pascal Johansen	25	20	16	8	1056	3	0	-	France
Camel Meriem	24	32	31	22	2293	0	0	-	France
Laurent Merlin	19	3	1	0	54	0	0	-	France
Sylvain N'Diaye	28	27	21	14	1516	1	0	3	Senegal (31)
Salomon Olembe	23	2	1	1	90	0	0	1	Cameroon (12)
Thierry Racon	20	3	1	0	45	0	0	-	France
Lamine Sahko	26	1	1	0	12	0	0	-	France
Rudolf Skacel	24	24	21	16	1641	3	0	2	Czech Republic (10)
Dmitri Sychev	20	17	16	3	785	1	0	-	Russia
Forwards									
Ibrahim Bakayoko	27	2	2	0	48	0	0	-	Ivory Coast
Rakhmane Barry	17	3	3	0	38	0	0	-	France
Didier Drogba	26	35	35	26	2607	3	1	-	Ivory Coast
Lucio Fernandao	26	11	10	1	357	0	0	-	Brazil
Sergio Pardo Koke	21	10	10	4	549	1	0	-	Spain
Steve Marlet	30	24	23	11	1396	1	0	5	France (2)
Ahmed Hossam Mido	21	22	21	15	1544	3	0	-	Egypt
Stepan Vachousek	24	22	20	15	1464	6	0	5	Czech Republic (10)

TEAM OF THE SEASON

G: Vedran Runje, CG: 16 DR: 85

D: Daniel Van Buyten, CG: 17 DR: 75

D: David Sommeil, CG: 13 DR: 72

D: Habib Beye, CG: 17 DR: 97

D: Abdoulaye Meite, CG: 27 DR: 71

M: Fabio Celestini, CG: 19 SD: 42

M: Sylvain N'Diaye, CG: 14 SD: 15

M: Rudolf Skacel, CG: 16 SD: 14

M: Ibrahim Hemdani, CG: 24 SD: 8

F: Didier Drogba, CG: 26 SR: 137

F: Ahmed Hossam Mido, CG: 15 SR: 221

SQUAD APPEARANCES

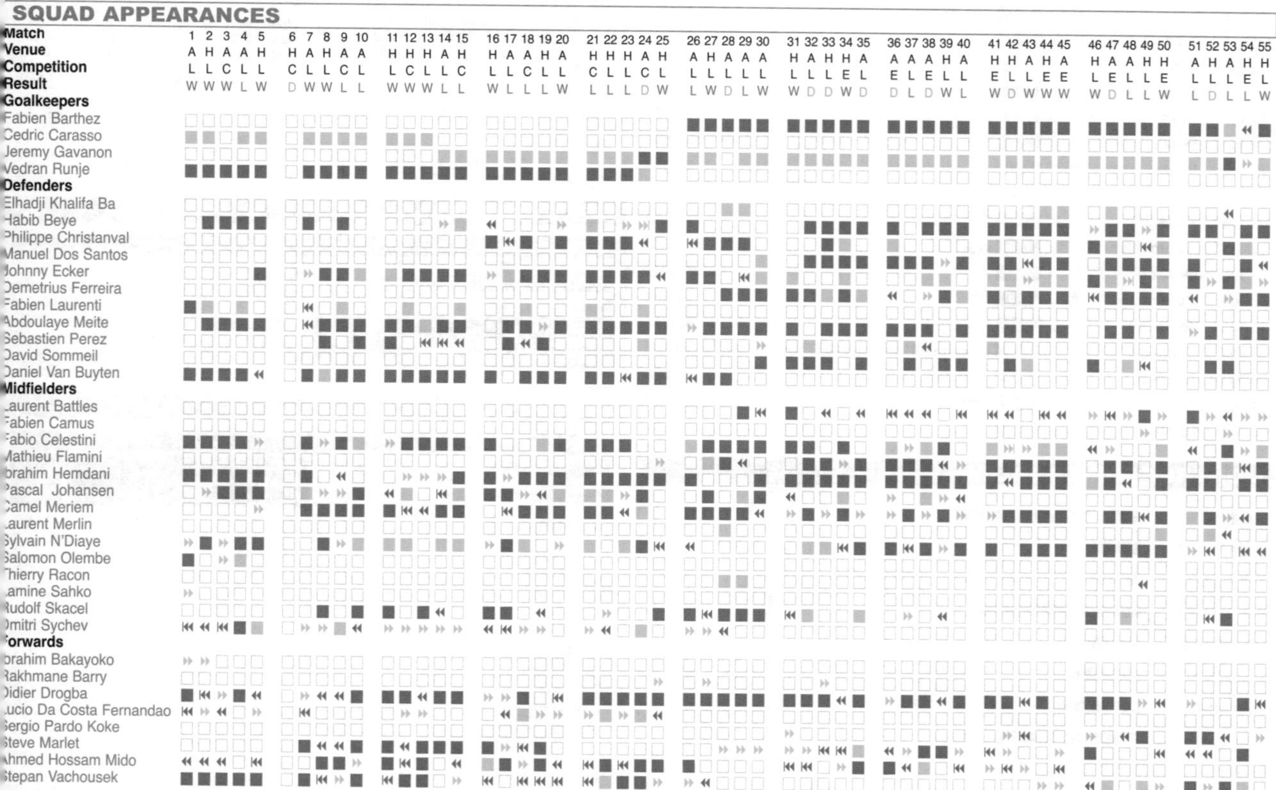

Match 1 2 3 4 5 6 7 8 9 10 11 12 13 14 15 16 17 18 19 20 21 22 23 24 25 26 27 28 29 30 31 32 33 34 35 36 37 38 39 40 41 42 43 44 45 46 47 48 49 50 51 52 53 54 55
Venue A H A A H H A H A A H H H A H H A A H A H H H A H A H A A A H A H H A A A A H A H H A H A H A A H H A H A H H
Competition L L C L L C L L C L L C L L C L L C L L C L L C L L L L L L L L L E L E L E L L E L L E E L E L L E L L L E L
Result W W W L W D W W L L W W W L L W L L L W L L L D W L W D L W W D D W D D L D W L W D W W W W D L L W L D L L W
Goalkeepers
Fabien Barthez
Cedric Carasso
Jeremy Gavanon
Vedran Runje
Defenders
Elhadji Khalifa Ba
Habib Beye
Philippe Christanval
Manuel Dos Santos
Johnny Ecker
Demetrius Ferreira
Fabien Laurenti
Abdoulaye Meite
Sebastien Perez
David Sommeil
Daniel Van Buyten
Midfielders
Laurent Battles
Fabien Camus
Fabio Celestini
Mathieu Flamini
Ibrahim Hemdani
Pascal Johansen
Camel Meriem
Laurent Merlin
Sylvain N'Diaye
Salomon Olembe
Thierry Racon
Lamine Sahko
Rudolf Skacel
Dmitri Sychev
Forwards
Ibrahim Bakayoko
Rakhmane Barry
Didier Drogba
Lucio Da Costa Fernandao
Sergio Pardo Koke
Steve Marlet
Ahmed Hossam Mido
Stepan Vachousek

KEY: On all match; On bench; Subbed or sent off (Counting game); Subbed or sent off (playing less than 70 minutes); Subbed on from bench (Counting Game); Subbed on (playing less than 70 minutes); Subbed on and then subbed or sent off (Counting Game); Subbed on and then subbed or sent off (playing less than 70 minutes); Not in 16

LENS

Final Position: **8th**

:

KEY: ☐ Won ☐ Drawn ☐ Lost

					Score	Scorers	Attendance
1	lge	Le Mans	H	D	0-0		36,500
2	lge	Nantes	A	L	0-2		32,333
3	lge	Marseille	H	W	2-1	Diop 20; Thomert 90	40,465
4	lge	Strasbourg	A	W	1-0	Moreira 15	19,690
5	lge	Nice	H	W	1-0	Bakari 71	35,500
6	lge	Rennes	A	L	0-2		15,035
7	lge	Bordeaux	H	W	1-0	Thomert 25	38,000
8	uc1rl1	Cementarnica	A	W	1-0	Diop 90	8,000
9	lge	Lyon	A	L	0-4		33,695
10	lge	Metz	H	L	0-2		36,083
11	uc1rl2	Cementarnica	H	W	5-0	Coridon 14; Moreira 45; Utaka 52 pen; Coulibaly 55; Bakari 90	22,671
12	lge	Bastia	A	L	1-3	Coridon 46	10,000
13	lge	Lille	H	W	2-1	Utaka 72; Bakari 74	37,646
14	lge	Paris SG	A	W	1-0	Moreira 77	39,366
15	uc2rl1	Gaziantepspor	A	L	0-3		12,000
16	lge	Montpellier	H	W	3-2	Utaka 32; Moreira 51; Bakari 53	34,301
17	lge	Monaco	A	L	0-2		9,042
18	uc2rl2	Gaziantepspor	H	L	1-3	Fanni 73	37,372
19	lge	Guingamp	H	W	2-1	Utaka 31; Moreira 56	33,430
20	lge	Toulouse	A	W	2-1	Moreira 56; Diane 58	13,660
21	lge	Sochaux	H	L	0-3		34,340
22	lge	Auxerre	A	L	0-2		12,000
23	lge	AC Ajaccio	A	L	0-2		3,500
24	lge	Nantes	H	D	0-0		32,251
25	lge	Marseille	A	L	2-3	Moreira 13; Thomert 62	48,638
26	lge	Strasbourg	H	W	2-1	Ekani 69; Bakari 72	30,093
27	lge	Nice	A	L	0-4		13,000
28	lge	Rennes	H	W	2-1	Thomert 24; Coridon 84	31,000
29	lge	Bordeaux	A	D	0-0		23,000
30	lge	Lyon	H	D	1-1	Eloi 70	39,000
31	lge	Metz	A	W	2-0	Utaka 26; Diop 67 pen	11,600
32	lge	Bastia	H	D	0-0		35,000
33	lge	Lille	A	D	1-1	Coridon 6	22,000
34	lge	Paris SG	H	W	1-0	Coridon 32	37,775
35	lge	Montpellier	A	L	0-1		8,000
36	lge	Monaco	H	D	0-0		40,011
37	lge	Guingamp	A	L	0-1		15,094
38	lge	Toulouse	H	D	1-1	Moreira 22	32,047
39	lge	Sochaux	A	W	3-0	Coridon 29; Moreira 40; Thomert 61	19,791
40	lge	Auxerre	H	L	1-3	Coulibaly 34	25,000
41	lge	AC Ajaccio	H	W	2-0	Diop 41; Coridon 90	34,642
42	lge	Le Mans	A	L	0-3		14,000

MONTHLY POINTS TALLY

Month	Points	%
AUGUST	10	67%
SEPTEMBER	3	33%
OCTOBER	3	33%
NOVEMBER	9	75%
DECEMBER	3	25%
JANUARY	4	44%
FEBRUARY	5	42%
MARCH	8	67%
APRIL	1	11%
MAY	7	47%

KEY PLAYERS - GOALSCORERS

Daniel Moreira

Goals in the League	8	Player Strike Rate Average number of minutes between League goals scored by player	355
Contribution to Attacking Power Average number of minutes between League team goals while on pitch	97	Club Strike Rate Average number of minutes between League goals scored by club	101

	PLAYER	LGE GOALS	POWER	STRIKE RATE
1	Daniel Moreira	8	97	355 mins
2	Charles-Edouard Coridon	6	104	451 mins
3	Olivier Thomert	5	91	510 mins
4	John Utaka	4	107	592 mins
5	Papa Bouba Diop	3	98	593 mins

KEY PLAYERS - MIDFIELDERS

Papa Bouba Diop

Goals in the League	3	Contribution to Attacking Power Average number of minutes between League team goals while on pitch	99
Defensive Rating Average number of mins between League goals conceded while he was on the pitch	99	Scoring Difference Defensive Rating minus Contribution to Attacking Power	0

	PLAYER	LGE GOALS	DEF RATE	POWER	SCORE DIFF
1	Papa Bouba Diop	3	99	99	0 mins
2	Abdoulaye Diagne Faye	0	104	112	-8 mins
3	Pape Sarr	0	78	107	-29 mins
4	Daniel Moreira	8	63	98	-35 mins
5	Charles-Edouard Coridon	6	66	104	-38 mins

KEY PLAYERS - DEFENDERS

Rigobert Bahanag Song

Goals Conceded (GC) The number of League goals conceded while he was on the pitch	28	Clean Sheets In games when he played at least 70 minutes	10
Defensive Rating Ave number of mins between League goals conceded while on the pitch	87	Club Defensive Rating Average number of mins between League goals conceded by the club this season	71

	PLAYER	CON LGE	CLEAN SHEETS	DEF RATE
1	Rigobert Bahanag Song	28	10	87 mins
2	Patrick Barul	18	7	85 mins
3	Jacek Bak	26	7	80 mins
4	Yoan Lachor	29	8	75 mins
5	Adama Coulibaly	27	7	71 mins

KEY GOALKEEPER

Charles-Hubert Itandje

Goals Conceded in the League	42	Counting Games Games when he played at least 70 mins	35
Defensive Rating Ave number of mins between League goals conceded while on the pitch	75	Clean Sheets In games when he played at least 70 mins	13

LEAGUE GOALS

Daniel Moreira

Minutes on the pitch	2838	Goals in the League	8
League average (mins between goals)	355		

	PLAYER	MINS	GOALS	AVE
1	Moreira	2838	8	355
2	Coridon	2704	6	451
3	Thomert	2549	5	510
4	Bakari	1394	4	349
5	Utaka	2369	4	592
6	Diop	1778	3	593
7	Coulibaly	1917	1	1917
8	Diane	796	1	796
9	Ekani	212	1	212
10	Eloi	96	1	96
	Other		0	
	TOTAL		34	

DISCIPLINARY RECORDS

	PLAYER	YELLOW	RED	AVE
1	Song	10	3	187
2	Diop	6	3	197
3	Rool	4	2	197
4	Diane	4	0	199
5	Keita	6	1	202
6	Bakari	5	1	232
7	Lachor	8	0	270
8	Barul	2	2	381
9	Coridon	6	1	386
10	Jabi	3	0	400
11	Thomert	6	0	424
12	Faye	3	0	486
13	Fanni	2	0	501
	Other	16	0	
	TOTAL	81	13	

TOP POINT EARNERS

	PLAYER	GAMES	AV PTS
1	Utaka	25	1.72
2	Song	27	1.63
3	Diop	18	1.61
4	Bak	21	1.52
5	Sarr	18	1.50
6	Faye	14	1.50
7	Itandje	35	1.43
8	Barul	17	1.41
9	Thomert	23	1.39
10	Moreira	32	1.34
	CLUB AVERAGE:		**1.39**

TEAM OF THE SEASON

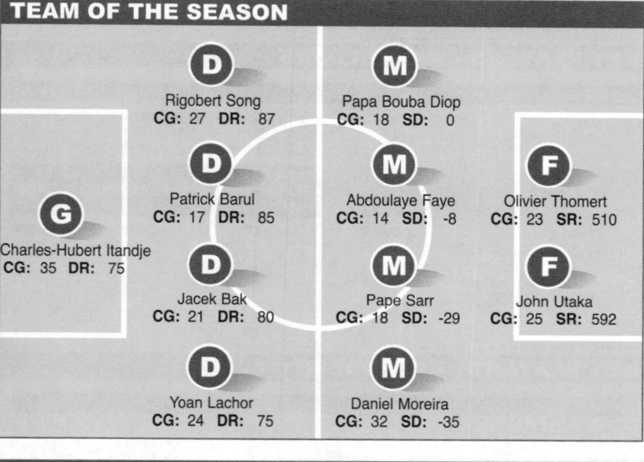
D
Rigobert Song
CG: 27 DR: 87
M
Papa Bouba Diop
CG: 18 SD: 0
D
Patrick Barul
CG: 17 DR: 85
M
Abdoulaye Faye
CG: 14 SD: -8
F
Olivier Thomert
CG: 23 SR: 510
G
Charles-Hubert Itandje
CG: 35 DR: 75
D
Jacek Bak
CG: 21 DR: 80
M
Pape Sarr
CG: 18 SD: -29
F
John Utaka
CG: 25 SR: 592
D
Yoan Lachor
CG: 24 DR: 75
M
Daniel Moreira
CG: 32 SD: -35

LEAGUE APPEARANCES, BOOKINGS AND CAPS

	AGE (on 01/07/04)	IN NAMED 16	APPEARANCES	COUNTING GAMES	MINUTES ON PITCH	YELLOW CARDS	RED CARDS	THIS SEASON	HOME COUNTRY
Goalkeepers									
Sebastien Chabbert	25	35	3	3	270	0	0	-	France
Guillaume Cherreau	21	6	0	0	0	0	0	-	France
Charles-Hubert Itandje	21	35	35	35	3150	2	0	-	France
Defenders									
Benoit Assou-Ekotto	20	5	3	3	270	0	0	-	France
Jacek Bak	31	28	26	21	2067	4	0	-	Poland
Patrick Barul	26	19	19	17	1527	2	2	-	France
Stephane Besle	20	5	1	0	15	0	0	-	France
Adama Coulibaly	23	26	22	21	1917	1	0	-	Mali
Martin Ekani	20	5	4	2	212	1	0	-	France
Rod Fanni	22	23	22	8	1003	2	0	-	France
Daouda Jabi	22	25	18	11	1201	3	0	-	France
Yoan Lachor	28	33	26	24	2161	8	0	-	France
Ibrahima N'Diaye	29	2	1	0	14	0	0	-	Senegal
Eric Sikora	36	7	5	4	396	2	0	-	France
Rigobert Song	28	28	28	27	2434	10	3	5	Cameroon (12)
Midfielders									
Charles-Ed'd Coridon	31	34	32	29	2704	6	1	-	France
Mounir Diane	22	20	18	3	796	4	0	-	Morocco
Papa Bouba Diop	26	27	25	18	1778	6	3	5	Senegal (31)
Abdoulaye Faye	26	23	19	14	1458	3	0	1	Senegal (31)
Yazid Kaissi	23	1	0	0	0	0	0	-	France
Seyadou Keita	24	26	23	13	1418	6	1	-	Mali
Daniel Moreira	26	34	33	32	2838	2	0	-	France
Cyril Rool	29	16	15	12	1187	4	2	-	France
Pape Sarr	26	34	27	18	2034	3	0	-	Senegal
Forwards									
Dagui Bakari	29	29	27	11	1394	5	1	-	France
Wagneau Eloi	30	7	4	0	96	0	0	-	France
Bruno Rodriguez	31	4	4	0	110	0	0	-	France
Olivier Thomert	24	37	36	23	2549	6	0	-	France
John Utaka	22	32	32	25	2369	1	0	-	Nigeria

SQUAD APPEARANCES

Match	1	2	3	4	5	6	7	8	9	10	11	12	13	14	15	16	17	18	19	20	21	22	23	24	25	26	27	28	29	30	31	32	33	34	35	36	37	38	39	40	41	42
Venue	H	A	H	A	H	A	H	A	A	H	H	A	H	A	A	H	A	H	H	A	H	A	A	H	A	H	A	H	A	H	A	H	A	H	A	H	A	H	A	H	H	A
Competition	L	L	L	L	L	L	L	E	L	L	E	L	L	L	E	L	L	E	L	L	L	L	L	L	L	L	L	L	L	L	L	L	L	L	L	L	L	L	L	L	L	L
Result	D	L	W	W	W	L	W	W	L	L	W	L	W	W	L	W	L	L	W	W	L	L	L	D	L	W	L	W	D	D	W	D	D	W	L	D	L	D	W	L	W	L

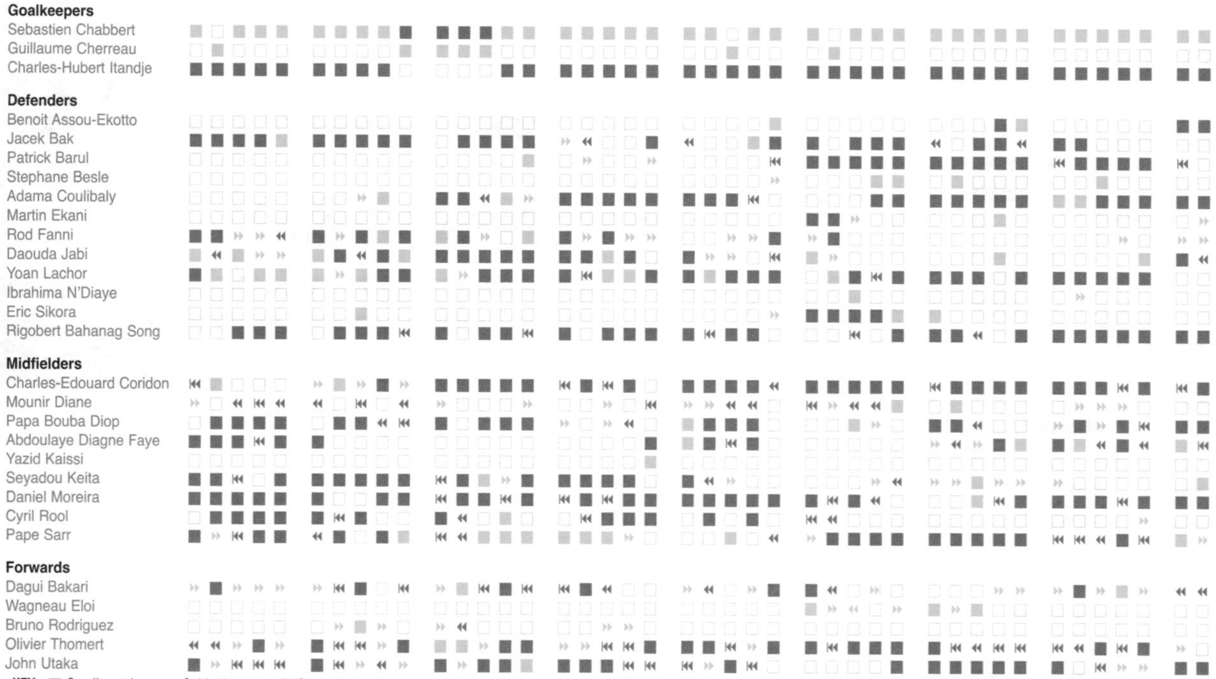

Goalkeepers
Sebastien Chabbert
Guillaume Cherreau
Charles-Hubert Itandje

Defenders
Benoit Assou-Ekotto
Jacek Bak
Patrick Barul
Stephane Besle
Adama Coulibaly
Martin Ekani
Rod Fanni
Daouda Jabi
Yoan Lachor
Ibrahima N'Diaye
Eric Sikora
Rigobert Bahanag Song

Midfielders
Charles-Edouard Coridon
Mounir Diane
Papa Bouba Diop
Abdoulaye Diagne Faye
Yazid Kaissi
Seyadou Keita
Daniel Moreira
Cyril Rool
Pape Sarr

Forwards
Dagui Bakari
Wagneau Eloi
Bruno Rodriguez
Olivier Thomert
John Utaka

KEY: On all match · On bench · ⏮ Subbed or sent off (Counting game) · ◀◀ Subbed or sent off (playing less than 70 minutes) · ⏭ Subbed on from bench (Counting Game) · ▶▶ Subbed on (playing less than 70 minutes) · Subbed on and then subbed or sent off (Counting Game) · Subbed on and then subbed or sent off (playing less than 70 minutes) · Not in 16

RENNES

Final Position: **9th**

KEY: Won Drawn Lost

						Attendance
1 lge	Montpellier	A	D	1-1	Ouaddou 24	20,418
2 lge	Toulouse	H	W	1-0	N'Guema 3	16,286
3 lge	Sochaux	A	D	1-1	Frei 79	14,069
4 lge	Guingamp	H	D	0-0		18,428
5 lge	Auxerre	A	L	1-2	N'Guema 56	8,000
6 lge	Lens	H	W	2-0	Sorlin 22; Monterrubio 76	15,035
7 lge	AC Ajaccio	A	L	0-1		8,500
8 lge	Le Mans	H	W	2-0	Ouaddou 35; Jeunechamp 90	15,245
9 lge	Nantes	A	L	0-1		32,400
10 lge	Nice	H	D	0-0		14,047
11 lge	Marseille	A	L	0-2		53,000
12 lge	Strasbourg	H	D	1-1	Frei 26	15,007
13 lge	Lille	H	D	2-2	Frei 53; N'Guema 61	14,028
14 lge	Bordeaux	A	L	1-2	Diatta 24	20,805
15 lge	Lyon	H	W	3-1	Reveillere 24 og; Puydebois 39 og; Frei 74	15,511
16 lge	Bastia	A	L	2-3	Ouaddou 8; Piquionne 59	3,500
17 lge	Paris SG	H	D	1-1	Frei 73	18,003
18 lge	Metz	A	D	1-1	Monterrubio 90	13,272
19 lge	Monaco	H	W	1-0	Barbosa 47	18,633
20 lge	Toulouse	A	L	0-2		13,310
21 lge	Sochaux	H	W	4-0	Frei 39,64; Flachez 71 og; Kallstrom 85	15,225
22 lge	Guingamp	A	W	2-0	Arribage 70; Barbosa 78	15,723
23 lge	Auxerre	H	L	0-2		18,484
24 lge	Lens	A	L	1-2	Piquionne 79	31,000
25 lge	AC Ajaccio	H	W	4-1	Frei 51; Vairelles 51; Kallstrom 74,87	15,500
26 lge	Le Mans	A	D	2-2	Piquionne 13; Diatta 90	16,000
27 lge	Nantes	H	L	0-3		18,500
28 lge	Nice	A	L	1-3	Piquionne 54	11,200
29 lge	Marseille	H	W	4-3	Frei 34,38,60,74	18,979
30 lge	Strasbourg	A	W	3-0	Frei 60,62; Monterrubio 83	15,000
31 lge	Lille	A	L	0-1		13,829
32 lge	Bordeaux	H	W	3-1	Sorlin 4; Kallstrom 57; Frei 68	17,537
33 lge	Lyon	A	L	0-3		39,869
34 lge	Bastia	H	W	4-0	Kallstrom 12; Frei 17,63; Sorlin 35	20,634
35 lge	Paris SG	A	L	0-1		42,000
36 lge	Metz	H	D	0-0		22,143
37 lge	Monaco	A	W	4-1	Frei 9; Monterrubio 59; Kallstrom 71,90	10,000
38 lge	Montpellier	H	W	4-0	Frei 13,63; Diatta 27; Briand 87	21,309

MONTHLY POINTS TALLY

Month	Points	%
AUGUST	6	40%
SEPTEMBER	6	67%
OCTOBER	1	11%
NOVEMBER	5	42%
DECEMBER	5	42%
JANUARY	6	67%
FEBRUARY	4	33%
MARCH	6	50%
APRIL	3	33%
MAY	10	67

KEY PLAYERS - GOALSCORERS

Alexander Frei

Goals in the League	20	Player Strike Rate Average number of minutes between League goals scored by player	98
Contribution to Attacking Power Average number of minutes between League team goals while on pitch	50	Club Strike Rate Average number of minutes between League goals scored by club	61

	PLAYER	LGE GOALS	POWER	STRIKE RATE
1	Alexander Frei	20	50	98 mins
2	Kim Kallstrom	7	46	211 mins
3	Frederic Piquionne	4	95	479 mins
4	Oliver Sorlin	3	47	510 mins
5	Abdeslam Ouaddou	3	64	841 mins

KEY PLAYERS - MIDFIELDERS

Kim Kallstrom

Goals in the League	7	Contribution to Attacking Power Average number of minutes between League team goals while on pitch	46
Defensive Rating Average number of mins between League goals conceded while he was on the pitch	70	Scoring Difference Defensive Rating minus Contribution to Attacking Power	24

	PLAYER	LGE GOALS	DEF RATE	POWER	SCORE DIFF
1	Kim Kallstrom	7	70	46	24 mins
2	Oliver Sorlin	3	67	48	19 mins
3	Cyril Jeunechamp	1	70	52	18 mins
4	Cedric Barbosa	2	77	61	16 mins
5	Etienne Didot	0	73	59	14 mins

KEY PLAYERS - DEFENDERS

Arnaud le Lan

Goals Conceded (GC) The number of League goals conceded while he was on the pitch	15	Clean Sheets In games when he played at least 70 minutes	7
Defensive Rating Ave number of mins between League goals conceded while on the pitch	104	Club Defensive Rating Average number of mins between League goals conceded by the club this season	76

	PLAYER	CON LGE	CLEAN SHEETS	DEF RATE
1	Arnaud le Lan	15	7	104 mins
2	Dominique Arribage	31	7	80 mins
3	Jacques Faty	33	7	75 mins
4	Abdeslam Ouaddou	35	8	72 mins
5	Lamine Diatta	41	8	70 mins

KEY GOALKEEPER

Petr Cech

Goals Conceded in the League	32	Counting Games Games when he played at least 70 mins	33
Defensive Rating Ave number of mins between League goals conceded while on the pitch	91	Clean Sheets In games when he played at least 70 mins	11

LEAGUE GOALS

Alexander Frei

Minutes on the pitch	1962	Goals in the League	20
League average (mins between goals)	98		

	PLAYER	MINS	GOALS	AVE
1	Frei	1962	20	98
2	Kallstrom	1475	7	211
3	Piquionne	1916	4	479
4	N'Guema	1250	3	417
5	Ouaddou	2523	3	841
6	Sorlin	1531	3	510
7	Monterrubio	2586	3	862
8	Diatta	2870	3	957
9	Barbosa	2541	2	1271
10	Jeunechamp	2532	1	2532
11	Vairelles	599	1	599
12	Arribage	2466	1	2466
	Other		5	
	TOTAL		56	

DISCIPLINARY RECORDS

	PLAYER	YELLOW	RED	AVE
1	Jeunechamp	12	1	194
2	N'Guema	5	0	250
3	Bourillon	3	1	256
4	Didot	7	1	273
5	Lucas	2	0	282
6	Arribage	8	0	308
7	Ouaddou	8	0	315
8	Frei	4	0	490
9	Faty	5	0	493
10	Barbosa	4	1	508
11	Diatta	4	0	717
12	Kallstrom	2	0	737
13	Piquionne	1	1	958
	Other	6	0	
	TOTAL	71	5	

TOP POINT EARNERS

	PLAYER	GAMES	AV PTS
1	Sorlin	13	1.85
2	Kallstrom	15	1.67
3	Frei	18	1.61
4	Jeunechamp	26	1.58
5	Monterrubio	26	1.58
6	Didot	23	1.48
7	Barbosa	28	1.43
8	Cech	32	1.41
9	Faty	23	1.35
10	le Lan	17	1.35
	CLUB AVERAGE:		**1.37**

TEAM OF THE SEASON

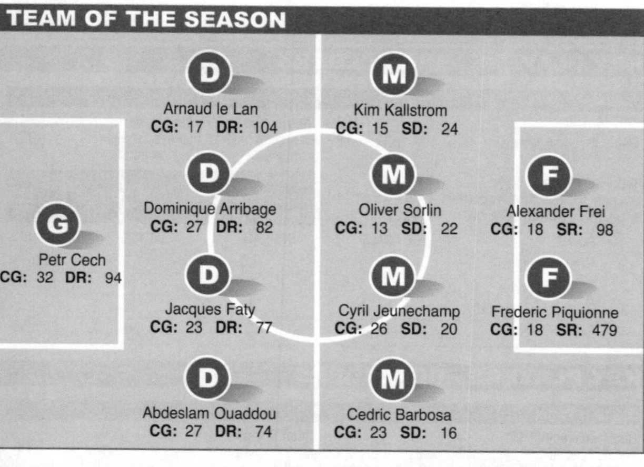
D
Arnaud le Lan
CG: 17 DR: 104
M
Kim Kallstrom
CG: 15 SD: 24
D
Dominique Arribage
CG: 27 DR: 82
M
Oliver Sorlin
CG: 13 SD: 22
F
Alexander Frei
CG: 18 SR: 98
G
Petr Cech
CG: 32 DR: 94
D
Jacques Faty
CG: 23 DR: 77
M
Cyril Jeunechamp
CG: 26 SD: 20
F
Frederic Piquionne
CG: 18 SR: 479
D
Abdeslam Ouaddou
CG: 27 DR: 74
M
Cedric Barbosa
CG: 23 SD: 16

LEAGUE APPEARANCES, BOOKINGS AND CAPS

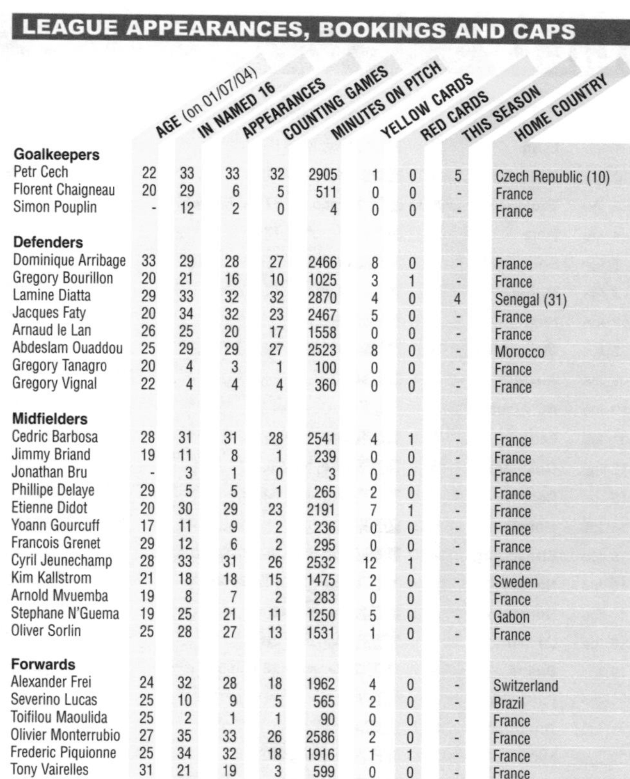

	AGE (on 01/07/04)	IN NAMED 16	APPEARANCES	COUNTING GAMES	MINUTES ON PITCH	YELLOW CARDS	RED CARDS	THIS SEASON	HOME COUNTRY
Goalkeepers									
Petr Cech	22	33	33	32	2905	1	0	5	Czech Republic (10)
Florent Chaigneau	20	29	6	5	511	0	0	-	France
Simon Pouplin	-	12	2	0	4	0	0	-	France
Defenders									
Dominique Arribage	33	29	28	27	2466	8	0	-	France
Gregory Bourillon	20	21	16	10	1025	3	1	-	France
Lamine Diatta	29	33	32	32	2870	4	0	4	Senegal (31)
Jacques Faty	20	34	32	23	2467	5	0	-	France
Arnaud le Lan	26	25	20	17	1558	0	0	-	France
Abdeslam Ouaddou	25	29	29	27	2523	8	0	-	Morocco
Gregory Tanagro	20	4	3	1	100	0	0	-	France
Gregory Vignal	22	4	4	4	360	0	0	-	France
Midfielders									
Cedric Barbosa	28	31	31	28	2541	4	1	-	France
Jimmy Briand	19	11	8	1	239	0	0	-	France
Jonathan Bru	-	3	1	0	3	0	0	-	France
Phillipe Delaye	29	5	5	1	265	2	0	-	France
Etienne Didot	20	30	29	23	2191	7	1	-	France
Yoann Gourcuff	17	11	9	2	236	0	0	-	France
Francois Grenet	29	12	6	2	295	0	0	-	France
Cyril Jeunechamp	28	33	31	26	2532	12	1	-	France
Kim Kallstrom	21	18	18	15	1475	2	0	-	Sweden
Arnold Mvuemba	19	8	7	2	283	0	0	-	France
Stephane N'Guema	19	25	21	11	1250	5	0	-	Gabon
Oliver Sorlin	25	28	27	13	1531	1	0	-	France
Forwards									
Alexander Frei	24	32	28	18	1962	4	0	-	Switzerland
Severino Lucas	25	10	9	5	565	2	0	-	Brazil
Toifilou Maoulida	25	2	1	1	90	0	0	-	France
Olivier Monterrubio	27	35	33	26	2586	2	0	-	France
Frederic Piquionne	25	34	32	18	1916	1	1	-	France
Tony Vairelles	31	21	19	3	599	0	0	-	France

SQUAD APPEARANCES

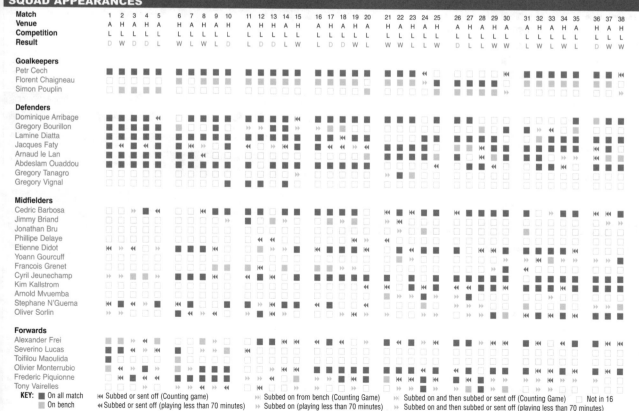

Match	1	2	3	4	5	6	7	8	9	10	11	12	13	14	15	16	17	18	19	20	21	22	23	24	25	26	27	28	29	30	31	32	33	34	35	36	37	38
Venue	A	H	A	H	A	H	A	H	A	H	A	H	H	A	H	A	H	A	H	A	H	A	H	A	H	A	H	A	H	A	A	H	A	H	A	H	A	H
Competition	L	L	L	L	L	L	L	L	L	L	L	L	L	L	L	L	L	L	L	L	L	L	L	L	L	L	L	L	L	L	L	L	L	L	L	L	L	L
Result	D	W	D	D	L	W	L	W	L	D	L	D	D	L	W	L	D	D	W	L	W	W	L	L	W	D	L	L	W	W	L	W	L	W	L	D	W	W

Goalkeepers
Petr Cech
Florent Chaigneau
Simon Pouplin

Defenders
Dominique Arribage
Gregory Bourillon
Lamine Diatta
Jacques Faty
Arnaud le Lan
Abdeslam Ouaddou
Gregory Tanagro
Gregory Vignal

Midfielders
Cedric Barbosa
Jimmy Briand
Jonathan Bru
Phillipe Delaye
Etienne Didot
Yoann Gourcuff
Francois Grenet
Cyril Jeunechamp
Kim Kallstrom
Arnold Mvuemba
Stephane N'Guema
Oliver Sorlin

Forwards
Alexander Frei
Severino Lucas
Toifilou Maoulida
Olivier Monterrubio
Frederic Piquionne
Tony Vairelles

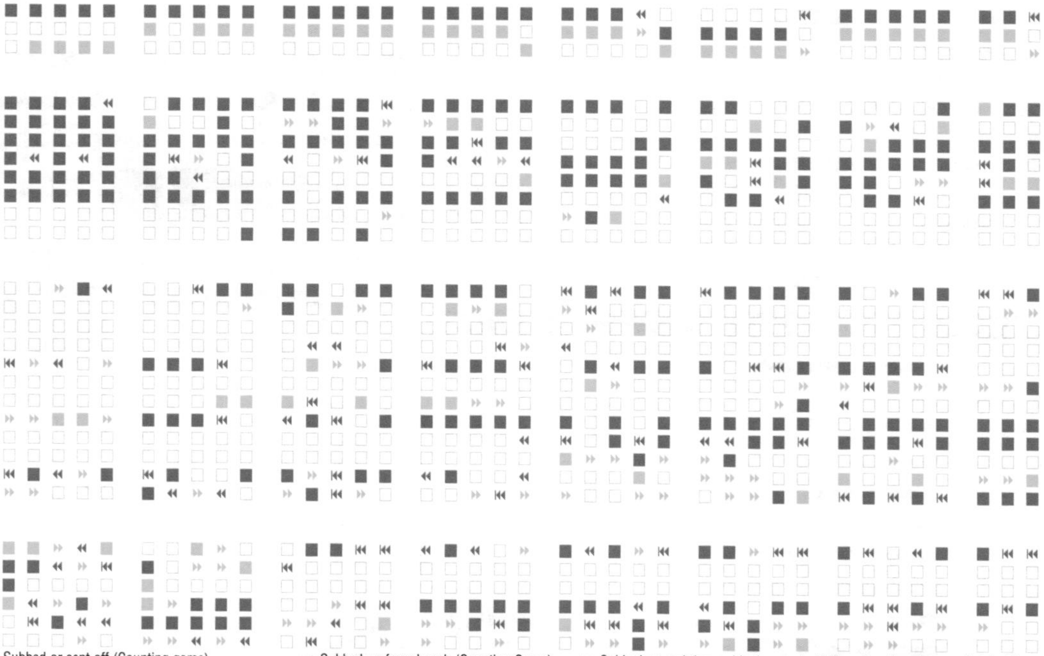

KEY: ■ On all match ■ On bench
⏮ Subbed or sent off (Counting game) ◀◀ Subbed or sent off (playing less than 70 minutes)
⏭ Subbed on from bench (Counting Game) ▶▶ Subbed on (playing less than 70 minutes)
Subbed on and then subbed or sent off (Counting Game) Subbed on and then subbed or sent off (playing less than 70 minutes)
□ Not in 16

LILLE

Final Position: **10th**

KEY: Won / Drawn / Lost

							Attendance
1	lge	Lyon	H	W	1-0	Makoun 11	17,000
2	lge	Paris SG	H	W	1-0	Tapia 45	18,455
3	lge	Toulouse	A	W	3-0	Manchev 37,64; Brunel 70	36,982
4	lge	Metz	H	D	1-1	Manchev 47	15,651
5	lge	Sochaux	A	L	1-2	Brunel 6	14,643
6	lge	Monaco	H	D	1-1	Manchev 74	16,000
7	lge	Nice	A	L	0-2		14,000
8	lge	Montpellier	H	D	1-1	Manchev 26	20,000
9	lge	Auxerre	A	L	0-3		
10	lge	AC Ajaccio	H	D	0-0		14,298
11	lge	Lens	A	L	1-2	Manchev 31	37,646
12	lge	Guingamp	H	L	1-3	Cheyrou 90	12,151
13	lge	Rennes	A	D	2-2	Manchev 32,71	14,028
14	lge	Marseille	H	L	0-2		20,480
15	lge	Strasbourg	A	D	2-2	Manchev 35; Baciu 90	10,915
16	lge	Nantes	H	W	2-0	Brunel 42; Tapia 90	11,000
17	lge	Bordeaux	A	L	1-2	Caneira 48 og	20,688
18	lge	Le Mans	H	D	1-1	Manchev 76	11,994
19	lge	Bastia	A	W	2-0	Manchev 28 pen,51	4,921
20	lge	Paris SG	A	L	0-1		38,620
21	lge	Toulouse	H	L	0-1		12,560
22	lge	Metz	A	W	1-0	Acimovic 40	12,712
23	lge	Sochaux	H	W	2-0	Dernis 45; Moussilou 52	14,426
24	lge	Monaco	A	W	1-0	Moussilou 77	5,000
25	lge	Nice	H	L	1-2	Acimovic 74 pen	15,000
26	lge	Montpellier	A	W	2-0	Moussilou 13,69	10,000
27	lge	Auxerre	H	W	1-0	Moussilou 53	14,000
28	lge	AC Ajaccio	A	W	3-0	Chalme 45,61,68	5,000
29	lge	Lens	H	D	1-1	Moussilou 29	22,000
30	lge	Guingamp	A	L	1-2	Bodmer 23	14,240
31	lge	Rennes	H	W	1-0	Acimovic 55	13,829
32	lge	Marseille	A	L	1-2	Bodmer 11	48,000
33	lge	Strasbourg	H	L	0-1		13,456
34	lge	Nantes	A	L	0-2		27,814
35	lge	Bordeaux	H	W	2-1	Acimovic 32 pen; Manchev 48	14,611
36	lge	Le Mans	A	D	1-1	Acimovic 34	14,072
37	lge	Bastia	H	W	2-0	Acimovic 69; Moussilou 90	15,000
38	lge	Lyon	A	L	0-3		36,000

MONTHLY POINTS TALLY

Month	Points	%
AUGUST	10	67%
SEPTEMBER	2	22%
OCTOBER	1	11%
NOVEMBER	2	17%
DECEMBER	7	58%
JANUARY	3	33%
FEBRUARY	9	75%
MARCH	7	58%
APRIL	3	33%
MAY	7	47%

KEY PLAYERS - GOALSCORERS

Vladimir Manchev

Goals in the League	13	Player Strike Rate Average number of minutes between League goals scored by player	157
Contribution to Attacking Power Average number of minutes between League team goals while on pitch	92	Club Strike Rate Average number of minutes between League goals scored by club	83

	PLAYER	LGE GOALS	POWER	STRIKE RATE
1	Vladimir Manchev	13	92	157 mins
2	Milenko Acimovic	6	76	217 mins
3	Mathieu Chalme	3	62	460 mins
4	Phillipe Brunel	3	92	866 mins
5	Mathieu Bodmer	2	103	928 mins

KEY PLAYERS - MIDFIELDERS

Milenko Acimovic

Goals in the League	6	Contribution to Attacking Power Average number of minutes between League team goals while on pitch	77
Defensive Rating Average number of mins between League goals conceded while he was on the pitch	100	Scoring Difference Defensive Rating minus Contribution to Attacking Power	23

	PLAYER	LGE GOALS	DEF RATE	POWER	SCORE DIFF
1	Milenko Acimovic	6	100	77	23 mins
2	Mathieu Chalme	3	81	63	18 mins
3	Christophe Landrin	0	74	78	-4 mins
4	Benoit Cheyrou	1	70	92	-22 mins

KEY PLAYERS - DEFENDERS

Stephane Pichot

Goals Conceded (GC) The number of League goals conceded while he was on the pitch	21	Clean Sheets In games when he played at least 70 minutes	14
Defensive Rating Ave number of mins between League goals conceded while on the pitch	123	Club Defensive Rating Average number of mins between League goals conceded by the club this season	83

	PLAYER	CON LGE	CLEAN SHEETS	DEF RATE
1	Stephane Pichot	21	14	123 mins
2	Efstathios Tavlaridis	13	7	110 mins
3	Gregory Tafforeau	28	12	92 mins
4	Eric Abidal	37	12	85 mins
5	Mathieu Bodmer	23	8	81 mins

KEY GOALKEEPER

Gregory Wimbee

Goals Conceded in the League	34	Counting Games Games when he played at least 70 mins	34
Defensive Rating Ave number of mins between League goals conceded while on the pitch	90	Clean Sheets In games when he played at least 70 mins	14

LEAGUE GOALS

Vladimir Manchev

Minutes on the pitch	2042	Goals in the League	13
League average (mins between goals)	157		

	PLAYER	MINS	GOALS	AVE
1	Manchev	2042	13	157
2	Moussilou	1357	6	226
3	Acimovic	1303	6	217
4	Brunel	2599	3	866
5	Chalme	1381	3	460
6	Tapia	655	2	328
7	Bodmer	1856	2	928
8	Cheyrou	2109	1	2109
9	Dernis	925	1	925
10	Makoun	2706	1	2706
11	Baciu	1086	1	1086
	Other		2	
	TOTAL		41	

DISCIPLINARY RECORDS

	PLAYER	YELLOW	RED	AVE
1	Chalme	4	2	230
2	Makoun	10	0	270
3	Baciu	4	0	271
4	Landrin	5	1	272
5	Tavlaridis	3	1	357
6	Cheyrou	5	0	421
7	Acimovic	3	0	434
8	Dernis	2	0	462
9	Delpierre	3	0	503
10	Dante	1	0	549
11	Bodmer	3	0	618
12	Pichot	4	0	645
13	Brunel	4	0	649
	Other	15	1	
	TOTAL	66	5	

TOP POINT EARNERS

	PLAYER	GAMES	AV PTS
1	Chalme	14	1.71
2	Acimovic	14	1.64
3	Tafforeau	28	1.64
4	Pichot	29	1.59
5	Tavlaridis	16	1.44
6	Wimbee	34	1.38
7	Makoun	30	1.33
8	Bodmer	18	1.33
9	Cheyrou	22	1.27
10	Abidal	35	1.26
	CLUB AVERAGE:		**1.34**

LEAGUE APPEARANCES, BOOKINGS AND CAPS

	AGE (on 01/07/04)	IN NAMED 16	APPEARANCES	COUNTING GAMES	MINUTES ON PITCH	YELLOW CARDS	RED CARDS	THIS SEASON	HOME COUNTRY
Goalkeepers									
Gregory Malicki	30	31	4	4	360	1	0	-	France
Laurent Pichon	23	8	0	0	0	0	0	-	France
Gregory Wimbee	32	37	34	34	3060	2	0	-	France
Defenders									
Eric Abidal	24	35	35	35	3130	2	0	-	France
Marius Achim Baciu	29	16	14	10	1086	4	0	-	Romania
Mathieu Bodmer	21	36	33	18	1856	3	0	-	France
Dante Bonfim Santos	20	12	9	5	549	1	0	-	Brazil
Mathieu Delpierre	23	18	17	17	1511	3	0	-	France
Stephane Pichot	27	30	29	29	2581	4	0	-	France
Nicolas Plestan	23	9	8	3	349	0	1	-	France
Rafael Schmitz	23	11	5	4	380	1	0	-	Brazil
Gregory Tafforeau	27	31	31	28	2584	3	0	-	France
Efstathios Tavlaridis	24	16	16	16	1430	3	1	-	Greece
Midfielders									
Milenko Acimovic	27	16	16	14	1303	3	0	-	Slovenia
Mathieu Chalme	23	26	20	14	1381	4	2	-	France
Benoit Cheyrou	23	27	27	22	2109	5	0	-	France
Mathieu Debuchy	18	8	5	2	224	1	0	-	France
Stephane Dumont	21	8	6	2	238	0	0	-	France
Peter Franquart	19	3	0	0	0	0	0	-	France
Christophe Landrin	27	20	20	18	1637	5	1	-	France
Forwards									
Djezon Boutoille	28	11	9	1	333	0	0	-	France
Phillipe Brunel	31	34	34	27	2599	4	0	-	France
Geoffrey Dernis	23	21	19	10	925	2	0	-	France
Nicolas Fauverge	19	1	1	0	22	0	0	-	France
Ali Mabula Lukunku	28	4	1	1	80	0	0	-	France
Jean Makoun	21	33	32	30	2706	10	0	3	Cameroon (12)
Vladimir Manchev	26	30	30	19	2042	3	0	-	Bulgaria
Matt Moussilou	22	22	21	11	1357	1	0	-	France
Youssef Sofiane	19	3	3	0	95	0	0	-	France
Mike Sterjovski	25	24	21	5	802	1	0	4	Australia (89)
Hector Tapia	26	24	21	2	655	0	0	-	Chile

TEAM OF THE SEASON

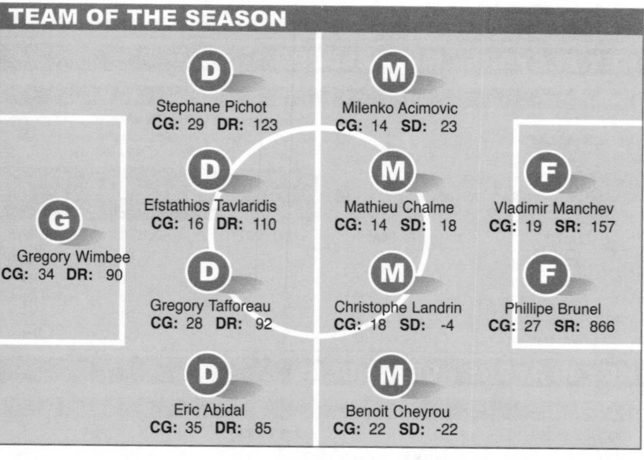

G
Gregory Wimbee
CG: 34 DR: 90
D
Stephane Pichot
CG: 29 DR: 123
D
Efstathios Tavlaridis
CG: 16 DR: 110
D
Gregory Tafforeau
CG: 28 DR: 92
D
Eric Abidal
CG: 35 DR: 85
M
Milenko Acimovic
CG: 14 SD: 23
M
Mathieu Chalme
CG: 14 SD: 18
M
Christophe Landrin
CG: 18 SD: -4
M
Benoit Cheyrou
CG: 22 SD: -22
F
Vladimir Manchev
CG: 19 SR: 157
F
Phillipe Brunel
CG: 27 SR: 866

SQUAD APPEARANCES

Match	1	2	3	4	5	6	7	8	9	10	11	12	13	14	15	16	17	18	19	20	21	22	23	24	25	26	27	28	29	30	31	32	33	34	35	36	37	38
Venue	H	H	A	H	A	H	A	H	A	H	A	H	A	H	A	H	A	H	A	A	H	A	H	A	H	A	H	A	H	A	H	A	H	A	H	A	H	A
Competition	L	L	L	L	L	L	L	L	L	L	L	L	L	L	L	L	L	L	L	L	L	L	L	L	L	L	L	L	L	L	L	L	L	L	L	L	L	L
Result	W	W	W	D	L	D	L	D	L	D	L	L	D	L	D	W	L	D	W	L	L	W	W	W	L	W	W	W	D	L	W	L	L	L	W	D	W	L

Goalkeepers
Gregory Malicki
Laurent Pichon
Gregory Wimbee

Defenders
Eric Abidal
Marius Achim Baciu
Mathieu Bodmer
Dante Bonfim Costa Santos
Mathieu Delpierre
Stephane Pichot
Nicolas Plestan
Rafael Schmitz
Gregory Tafforeau
Efstathios Tavlaridis

Midfielders
Milenko Acimovic
Mathieu Chalme
Benoit Cheyrou
Mathieu Debuchy
Stephane Dumont
Peter Franquart
Christophe Landrin

Forwards
Djezon Boutoille
Phillipe Brunel
Geoffrey Dernis
Nicolas Fauverge
Ali Mabula Lukunku
Jean Makoun
Vladimir Manchev
Matt Moussilou
Youssef Sofiane
Mike Sterjovski
Hector Tapia

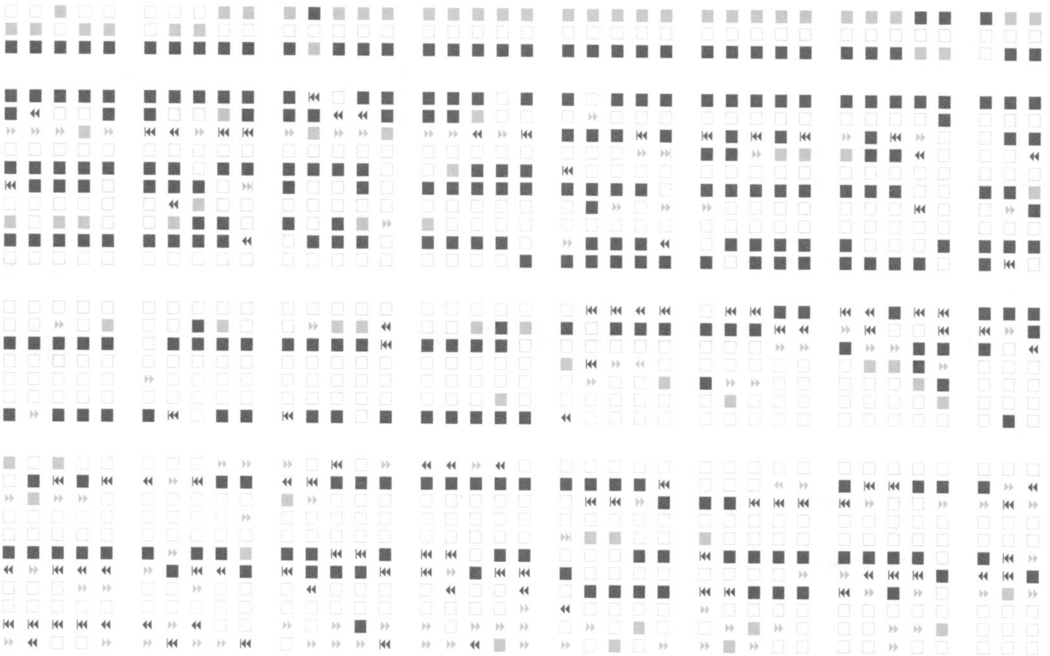

KEY: On all match · On bench · Subbed or sent off (Counting game) · Subbed or sent off (playing less than 70 minutes) · Subbed on from bench (Counting Game) · Subbed on (playing less than 70 minutes) · Subbed on and then subbed or sent off (Counting Game) · Subbed on and then subbed or sent off (playing less than 70 minutes) · Not in 16

NICE

Final Position: **11th**

KEY: Won Drawn Lost

							Attendance
1	lge	**Auxerre**	A	W	2-1	Laslandes 7; Pitau 46	16,673
2	lge	**Sochaux**	H	W	1-0	Everson 74	13,946
3	lge	**Le Mans**	A	D	1-1	Everson 43	12,127
4	lge	**AC Ajaccio**	H	D	2-2	Laslandes 13,67	12,610
5	lge	**Lens**	A	L	0-1		35,500
6	lge	**Nantes**	H	W	1-0	Cherrad 10	12,373
7	lge	**Lille**	H	W	2-0	Cherrad 32,42	14,000
8	lge	**Marseille**	A	L	1-2	Laslandes 35	
9	lge	**Strasbourg**	H	D	0-0		12,527
10	lge	**Rennes**	A	D	0-0		14,047
11	lge	**Bordeaux**	H	D	0-0		12,658
12	lge	**Lyon**	A	L	0-5		34,034
13	lge	**Bastia**	H	W	2-0	Meslin 31,64	10,000
14	lge	**Paris SG**	A	D	0-0		35,000
15	lge	**Metz**	H	D	1-1	Meslin 43 pen	10,445
16	lge	**Montpellier**	H	W	2-1	Everson 22; Laslandes 35	10,422
17	lge	**Toulouse**	A	D	1-1	Echouafni 57	13,441
18	lge	**Guingamp**	H	W	2-0	Traore 35; Laslandes 87	10,215
19	lge	**Sochaux**	A	D	0-0		11,265
20	lge	**Le Mans**	H	L	0-1		11,261
21	lge	**Monaco**	A	D	1-1	Meslin 90 pen	19,000
22	lge	**AC Ajaccio**	A	D	1-1	Ba 74	5,000
23	lge	**Lens**	H	W	4-0	Meslin 8; Pamarot 16; Everson 31; Diakite 77	13,000
24	lge	**Nantes**	A	L	1-3	Meslin 38	30,000
25	lge	**Lille**	A	W	2-1	Pamarot 33; Echouafni 82	15,000
26	lge	**Marseille**	H	D	0-0		15,000
27	lge	**Strasbourg**	A	D	2-2	Pitau 33; Echouafni 39	12,000
28	lge	**Rennes**	H	W	3-1	Meslin 41; Laslandes 49; Everson 90	11,200
29	lge	**Bordeaux**	A	D	1-1	Laslandes 10	22,435
30	lge	**Lyon**	H	L	0-1		12,784
31	lge	**Bastia**	A	L	1-2	Meslin 39	5,500
32	lge	**Paris SG**	H	L	1-2	Laslandes 15	12,661
33	lge	**Metz**	A	L	0-1		17,679
34	lge	**Monaco**	H	L	1-2	Varrault 10	13,000
35	lge	**Montpellier**	A	D	2-2	Ba 23; Godemeche 81 og	8,900
36	lge	**Toulouse**	H	D	1-1	Ba 62	9,663
37	lge	**Guingamp**	A	W	2-1	Traore 85; Laslandes 90	16,003
38	lge	**Auxerre**	H	D	1-1	Larbi 68	10,850

MONTHLY POINTS TALLY

Month	Points	%
AUGUST	8	53%
SEPTEMBER	6	67%
OCTOBER	3	33%
NOVEMBER	5	42%
DECEMBER	7	78%
JANUARY	3	25%
FEBRUARY	7	58%
MARCH	5	42%
APRIL	0	0%
MAY	6	50%

KEY PLAYERS - GOALSCORERS

Christophe Meslin

Goals in the League	8	Player Strike Rate Average number of minutes between League goals scored by player	190
Contribution to Attacking Power Average number of minutes between League team goals while on pitch	65	Club Strike Rate Average number of minutes between League goals scored by club	81

	PLAYER	LGE GOALS	POWER	STRIKE RATE
1	Christophe Meslin	8	65	190 mins
2	Lilian Laslandes	10	81	286 mins
3	Pereira da Silva Everson	5	92	479 mins
4	Olivier Echouafni	3	71	788 mins
5	Sammy Traore	2	84	889 mins

KEY PLAYERS - MIDFIELDERS

Sammy Traore

Goals in the League	2	Contribution to Attacking Power Average number of minutes between League team goals while on pitch	85
Defensive Rating Average number of mins between League goals conceded while he was on the pitch	99	Scoring Difference Defensive Rating minus Contribution to Attacking Power	14

	PLAYER	LGE GOALS	DEF RATE	POWER	SCORE DIFF
1	Sammy Traore	2	99	85	14 mins
2	Olivier Echouafni	3	81	72	9 mins
3	Pereira da Silva Everson	5	96	92	4 mins
4	Romain Pitau	2	83	81	2 mins
5	Yohann Bigne	0	84	88	-4 mins

KEY PLAYERS - DEFENDERS

Louis Pamarot

Goals Conceded (GC) The number of League goals conceded while he was on the pitch	32	Clean Sheets In games when he played at least 70 minutes	12
Defensive Rating Ave number of mins between League goals conceded while on the pitch	90	Club Defensive Rating Average number of mins between League goals conceded by the club this season	88

	PLAYER	CON LGE	CLEAN SHEETS	DEF RATE
1	Louis Pamarot	32	12	90 mins
2	Jose Cobos	31	11	89 mins
3	Jacques Abardonado	35	10	85 mins
4	Cedric Varrault	37	9	81 mins

KEY GOALKEEPER

Damien Gregorini

Goals Conceded in the League	37	Counting Games Games when he played at least 70 mins	37
Defensive Rating Ave number of mins between League goals conceded while on the pitch	90	Clean Sheets In games when he played at least 70 mins	12

LEAGUE GOALS

Lilian Laslandes

Minutes on the pitch	2861	Goals in the League	10
League average (mins between goals)	286		

	PLAYER	MINS	GOALS	AVE
1	Laslandes	2861	10	286
2	Meslin	1516	8	190
3	Everson	2394	5	479
4	Echouafni	2363	3	788
5	Cherrad	861	3	287
6	Ba	733	3	244
7	Traore	1777	2	889
8	Pamarot	2889	2	1445
9	Pitau	2738	2	1369
10	Varrault	3004	1	3004
11	Diakite	99	1	99
	Other		2	
	TOTAL		42	

DISCIPLINARY RECORDS

	PLAYER	YELLOW	RED	AVE
1	Cherrad	6	1	123
2	Everson	13	1	171
3	Die	4	0	224
4	Pamarot	10	1	262
5	Roy	3	0	290
6	Traore	4	1	355
7	Bigne	5	0	403
8	Scotto Di Porfirio	3	0	421
9	Pitau	5	1	456
10	Cobos	6	0	460
11	Laslandes	6	0	476
12	Varrault	6	0	500
13	Echouafni	4	0	590
	Other	9	0	
	TOTAL	84	5	

TOP POINT EARNERS

	PLAYER	GAMES	AV PTS
1	Meslin	15	1.67
2	Bigne	20	1.40
3	Cobos	30	1.40
4	Laslandes	31	1.39
5	Traore	16	1.38
6	Echouafni	24	1.38
7	Pitau	28	1.36
8	Gregorini	37	1.32
9	Everson	24	1.29
10	Abardonado	33	1.27
	CLUB AVERAGE:		**1.32**

TEAM OF THE SEASON

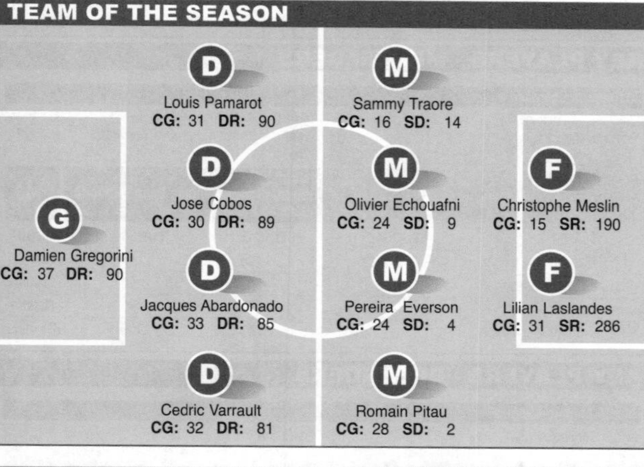
D
Louis Pamarot
CG: 31 DR: 90
M
Sammy Traore
CG: 16 SD: 14
D
Jose Cobos
CG: 30 DR: 89
M
Olivier Echouafni
CG: 24 SD: 9
F
Christophe Meslin
CG: 15 SR: 190
G
Damien Gregorini
CG: 37 DR: 90
D
Jacques Abardonado
CG: 33 DR: 85
M
Pereira Everson
CG: 24 SD: 4
F
Lilian Laslandes
CG: 31 SR: 286
D
Cedric Varrault
CG: 32 DR: 81
M
Romain Pitau
CG: 28 SD: 2

LEAGUE APPEARANCES, BOOKINGS AND CAPS

	AGE (on 01/07/04)	IN NAMED 16	APPEARANCES	COUNTING GAMES	MINUTES ON PITCH	YELLOW CARDS	RED CARDS	THIS SEASON	HOME COUNTRY
Goalkeepers									
Madjid Ben Haddou	28	3	0	0	0	0	0	-	Algeria
Damien Gregorini	25	38	37	37	3330	0	0	-	France
Hilaire Munoz	21	4	0	0	0	0	0	-	France
Bruno Valencony	36	31	1	1	90	0	0	-	France
Defenders									
Jacques Abardonado	26	34	34	33	2987	3	0	-	France
Jose Cobos	36	33	33	30	2763	6	0	-	France
Serge Die	26	14	13	6	897	4	0	-	Ivory Coast
Philippe Leonard	30	16	13	10	973	1	0	-	Belgium
Louis Pamarot	25	33	33	31	2889	10	1	-	France
Cedric Varrault	24	37	36	32	3004	6	0	-	France
Midfielders									
Oumar Bakari	24	5	3	0	36	0	0	-	France
Yohann Bigne	26	31	27	20	2019	5	0	-	France
Olivier Echouafni	31	31	31	24	2363	4	0	-	France
Pereira Everson	28	29	29	24	2394	13	1	-	Brazil
J-P Kamudimba	22	2	2	0	20	0	0	-	France
Franck Padovani	-	5	4	0	108	0	0	-	France
Romain Pitau	26	34	33	28	2738	5	1	-	France
Eric Roy	36	21	15	8	871	3	0	-	France
Tony Scaramozzino	-	4	4	2	264	1	0	-	France
Thibault Di Porfirio	25	26	20	12	1265	3	0	-	France
Sammy Traore	22	30	27	16	1777	4	1	-	Ivory Coast
Forwards									
Georges Ba	25	30	21	7	733	1	0	-	Ivory Coast
Abdelmalek Cherrad	23	19	19	6	861	6	1	-	Algeria
Bakary Diakite	23	14	8	0	99	0	0	-	Germany
Pablo Franco Dolci	-	6	4	2	216	0	0	-	France
Kamel Larbi	-	3	3	0	56	1	0	-	France
Lilian Laslandes	32	33	33	31	2861	6	0	-	France
Christophe Meslin	26	29	25	15	1516	2	0	-	France
Cedric Mionnet	30	1	0	0	0	0	0	-	France
Marco Simone	35	7	7	1	365	0	0	-	Italy

SQUAD APPEARANCES

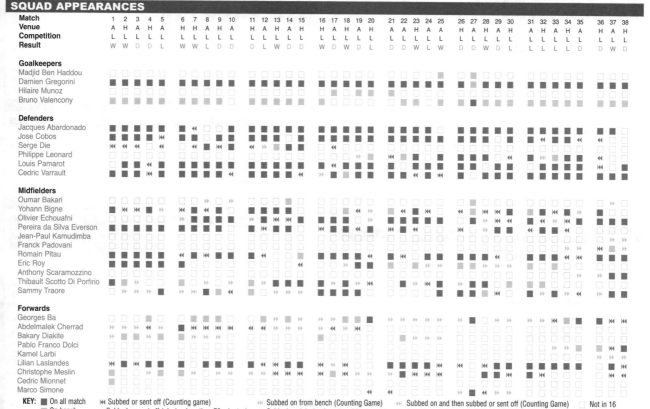

Match	1	2	3	4	5	6	7	8	9	10	11	12	13	14	15	16	17	18	19	20	21	22	23	24	25	26	27	28	29	30	31	32	33	34	35	36	37	38
Venue	A	H	A	H	A	H	H	A	H	A	H	A	H	A	H	H	A	H	A	H	A	A	H	A	A	H	A	H	A	H	A	H	A	H	A	H	A	H
Competition	L	L	L	L	L	L	L	L	L	L	L	L	L	L	L	L	L	L	L	L	L	L	L	L	L	L	L	L	L	L	L	L	L	L	L	L	L	L
Result	W	W	D	D	L	W	W	L	D	D	D	L	W	D	D	W	D	W	D	L	D	D	W	L	W	D	D	W	D	L	L	L	L	L	D	D	W	D

Goalkeepers
Madjid Ben Haddou
Damien Gregorini
Hilaire Munoz
Bruno Valencony

Defenders
Jacques Abardonado
Jose Cobos
Serge Die
Philippe Leonard
Louis Pamarot
Cedric Varrault

Midfielders
Oumar Bakari
Yohann Bigne
Olivier Echouafni
Pereira da Silva Everson
Jean-Paul Kamudimba
Franck Padovani
Romain Pitau
Eric Roy
Anthony Scaramozzino
Thibault Scotto Di Porfirio
Sammy Traore

Forwards
Georges Ba
Abdelmalek Cherrad
Bakary Diakite
Pablo Franco Dolci
Kamel Larbi
Lilian Laslandes
Christophe Meslin
Cedric Mionnet
Marco Simone

KEY: ■ On all match ■ On bench ⏮ Subbed or sent off (Counting game) « Subbed or sent off (playing less than 70 minutes) ⏭ Subbed on from bench (Counting Game) » Subbed on (playing less than 70 minutes) ⏭ Subbed on and then subbed or sent off (Counting Game) » Subbed on and then subbed or sent off (playing less than 70 minutes) □ Not in 16

BORDEAUX

Final Position: **12th**

KEY: Won Drawn Lost

						Attendance
1	lge	Monaco	A	L	0-2		13,448
2	lge	Montpellier	H	L	0-1		24,876
3	lge	Guingamp	A	W	3-1	Deivid 5; Darcheville 32,54	15,907
4	lge	Auxerre	H	W	2-0	Deivid 12; Pocchettino 27	27,848
5	lge	Nantes	A	D	0-0		33,346
6	lge	Sochaux	H	L	1-3	Darcheville 20 pen	22,000
7	lge	Lens	A	L	0-1		38,000
8	uc1rl1	A Petrzalka	H	W	2-1	Riera 6; Darcheville 36	18,000
9	lge	AC Ajaccio	H	W	1-0	Darcheville 78	19,945
10	lge	Le Mans	A	D	0-0		14,127
11	uc1rl2	A Petrzalka	A	D	1-1	Basto 86	3,300
12	lge	Toulouse	H	L	1-2	Darcheville 63	22,097
13	lge	Nice	A	D	0-0		12,658
14	lge	Marseille	H	W	1-0	Darcheville 45	32,500
15	uc2rl1	Hearts	H	L	0-1		15,536
16	lge	Strasbourg	A	D	1-1	Chamakh 45	15,817
17	lge	Rennes	H	W	2-1	Darcheville 45 pen; Feindouno 82	20,805
18	uc2rl2	Hearts	A	W	2-0	Riera 8; Feindouno 66	17,587
19	lge	Bastia	H	D	1-1	Deivid 5	20,378
20	lge	Lille	H	W	2-1	Pichot 7 og; Francia 13	20,688
21	lge	Paris SG	A	L	1-2	Celades 17	41,000
22	lge	Metz	H	W	2-0	Francia 45; Chamakh 60	19,693
23	lge	Montpellier	A	W	2-1	Chamakh 9; Mavuba 52	10,436
24	lge	Guingamp	H	W	2-0	Francia 16; Franco 84	18,312
25	lge	Lyon	A	L	0-3		32,363
26	lge	Auxerre	A	L	0-5		9,500
27	lge	Nantes	H	W	2-0	Francia 19; Riera 23	22,145
28	lge	Sochaux	A	D	1-1	Francia 85	15,000
29	lge	Lens	H	D	0-0		23,000
30	uc3rl1	G Grodzisk	A	W	1-0	Chamakh 90	5,000
31	lge	AC Ajaccio	A	L	0-1		3,000
32	uc3rl2	G Grodzisk	H	W	4-1	Planus 41; Chamakh 42,65; Riera 74 pen	9,197
33	lge	Le Mans	H	W	2-0	Celades 28; Beda 58	18,000
34	uc4rl1	Club Brugge	H	W	3-1	Celades 59,71; Riera 87	14,398
35	lge	Toulouse	A	L	0-1		25,000
36	lge	Nice	H	D	1-1	Jemmali 39	22,435
37	uc4rl2	Club Brugge	A	W	1-0	Chamakh 84	27,000
38	lge	Marseille	A	D	1-1	Francia 8	51,573
39	lge	Strasbourg	H	D	1-1	Costa 89	22,643
40	ucqfl1	Valencia	H	L	1-2	Riera 18	29,108
41	ucqfl2	Valencia	A	L	1-2	Costa 77	42,400
42	lge	Rennes	A	L	1-3	Chamakh 75	17,537
43	lge	Bastia	A	W	2-0	Celades 37; Feindouno 48	3,000
44	lge	Lyon	H	D	1-1	Chamakh 59	23,637
45	lge	Lille	A	L	1-2	Alicarte 74 pen	14,611
46	lge	Paris SG	H	W	3-0	Feindouno 21,49; Chamakh 73	30,527
47	lge	Metz	A	L	1-3	Francia 25	22,059
48	lge	Monaco	H	L	1-3	Riera 14	32,397

MONTHLY POINTS TALLY

Month	Points	%
AUGUST	7	47%
SEPTEMBER	3	33%
OCTOBER	2	22%
NOVEMBER	8	67%
DECEMBER	6	67%
JANUARY	6	50%
FEBRUARY	5	42%
MARCH	5	42%
APRIL	4	44%
MAY	4	27%

KEY PLAYERS - GOALSCORERS

Jean-Claude Darcheville

Goals in the League	7	Player Strike Rate Average number of minutes between League goals scored by player	217
Contribution to Attacking Power Average number of minutes between League team goals while on pitch	101	Club Strike Rate Average number of minutes between League goals scored by club	86

	PLAYER	LGE GOALS	POWER	STRIKE RATE
1	Jean-Claude Darcheville	7	101	217 mins
2	Pablo Francia	7	70	253 mins
3	Maromane Chamakh	6	68	273 mins
4	Deivid de Souza	3	122	449 mins
5	Pascal Feindouno	4	75	568 mins

KEY PLAYERS - MIDFIELDERS

Maromane Chamakh

Goals in the League	6	Contribution to Attacking Power Average number of minutes between League team goals while on pitch	68
Defensive Rating Average number of mins between League goals conceded while he was on the pitch	86	Scoring Difference Defensive Rating minus Contribution to Attacking Power	18

	PLAYER	LGE GOALS	DEF RATE	POWER	SCORE DIFF
1	Maromane Chamakh	6	86	68	18 mins
2	Albert Celades	3	83	94	-11 mins
3	Eduardo Costa	1	78	90	-12 mins
4	Antonio Rio Mavuba	1	88	109	-21 mins

KEY PLAYERS - DEFENDERS

Marco Antonio Caneira

Goals Conceded (GC) The number of League goals conceded while he was on the pitch	33	Clean Sheets In games when he played at least 70 minutes	12
Defensive Rating Ave number of mins between League goals conceded while on the pitch	93	Club Defensive Rating Average number of mins between League goals conceded by the club this season	80

	PLAYER	CON LGE	CLEAN SHEETS	DEF RATE
1	Marco Antonio Caneira	33	12	93 mins
2	Franck Jurietti	33	12	89 mins
3	David Jemmali	25	8	83 mins
4	Bruno Basto	35	9	66 mins
5	Marc Planus	31	6	66 mins

KEY GOALKEEPER

Ulrich Rame

Goals Conceded in the League	38	Counting Games Games when he played at least 70 mins	35
Defensive Rating Ave number of mins between League goals conceded while on the pitch	82	Clean Sheets In games when he played at least 70 mins	12

LEAGUE GOALS

Jean-Claude Darcheville

Minutes on the pitch	1522	Goals in the League	7
League average (mins between goals)	217		

	PLAYER	MINS	GOALS	AVE
1	Darcheville	1522	7	217
2	Francia	1768	7	253
3	Chamakh	1640	6	273
4	Feindouno	2272	4	568
5	Celades	2071	3	690
6	Deivid	1348	3	449
7	Riera	2630	2	1315
8	Mavuba	1505	1	1505
9	Beda	323	1	323
10	Franco	295	1	295
11	Jemmali	2068	1	2068
12	Costa	2258	1	2258
	Other		3	
	TOTAL		40	

DISCIPLINARY RECORDS

	PLAYER	YELLOW	RED	AVE
1	Alicarte	3	0	185
2	Celades	7	1	258
3	Paulo Costa	2	0	260
4	Jurietti	9	1	294
5	Costa	6	1	322
6	Chamakh	4	1	328
7	Riera	7	0	375
8	Basto	6	0	386
9	Jemmali	4	1	413
10	Caneira	7	0	437
11	Planus	2	2	512
12	Rame	5	0	625
13	Deivid	2	0	674
	Other	12	0	
	TOTAL	76	7	

TOP POINT EARNERS

	PLAYER	GAMES	AV PTS
1	Jemmali	23	1.61
2	Chamakh	17	1.59
3	Basto	24	1.46
4	Costa	24	1.46
5	Riera	30	1.43
6	Feindouno	24	1.42
7	Caneira	34	1.38
8	Jurietti	32	1.38
9	Darcheville	16	1.38
10	Francia	19	1.37
	CLUB AVERAGE:		**1.32**

LEAGUE APPEARANCES, BOOKINGS AND CAPS

	AGE (on 01/07/04)	IN NAMED 16	APPEARANCES	COUNTING GAMES	MINUTES ON PITCH	YELLOW CARDS	RED CARDS	THIS SEASON	HOME COUNTRY
Goalkeepers									
Fabien Farnolle	-	2	0	0	0	0	0	-	France
Ulrich Rame	31	35	35	34	3127	5	0	-	France
Frederick Roux	31	26	3	2	203	0	0	-	France
Mathieu Valverde	21	9	1	1	90	0	0	-	France
Defenders									
Anicet Adjamossi	20	0	0	0	0	0	0	-	Benin
Kodjo Afanou	32	7	5	3	382	0	0	-	France
Herve Alicarte	29	13	9	5	556	3	0	-	France
Bruno Basto	26	35	32	24	2321	6	0	-	Portugal
Mathieu Beda	22	8	5	3	323	2	0	-	France
Marco Caneira	25	34	34	34	3060	7	0	2	Portugal (20)
David Jemmali	29	24	24	23	2068	4	1	-	France
Franck Jurietti	29	35	34	32	2944	9	1	-	France
Marc Planus	22	30	26	22	2051	2	2	-	France
Mauricio Pocchettino	32	14	11	11	982	1	0	-	Argentina
Nicolas Sahnoun	23	7	6	3	395	2	0	-	France
Midfielders									
Albert Celades	28	28	27	22	2071	7	1	-	Spain
Maromane Chamakh	20	28	25	17	1640	4	1	-	France
Gerald Cid	-	3	1	1	90	0	0	-	France
Eduardo Costa	21	27	27	24	2258	6	1	-	Brazil
Ted Lavie	-	1	1	0	8	0	0	-	France
Antonio Rio Mavuba	20	19	19	16	1505	1	0	-	Angola
Camel Meriem	24	3	3	1	163	1	0	-	France
Paulo Miranda	30	26	18	6	639	0	0	-	Brazil
Jonathan Sarrade	21	2	0	0	0	0	0	-	France
Alexei Smertin	29	2	2	2	180	0	0	-	Russia
Forwards									
Jean-C Darcheville	28	19	18	16	1522	2	0	-	France
Deivid de Souza	24	29	22	13	1348	2	0	-	Brazil
Pascal Feindouno	23	32	31	24	2272	3	0	-	Guinea
Pablo Francia	19	23	23	19	1768	0	0	-	Argentina
Sylvain Franco	-	15	11	2	295	0	0	-	France
Paulo da Costa	24	30	15	4	520	2	0	-	Portugal
Erwan Quintin	20	1	1	0	19	0	0	-	France
Albert Ortega Riera	22	32	32	30	2630	7	0	-	Spain

TEAM OF THE SEASON

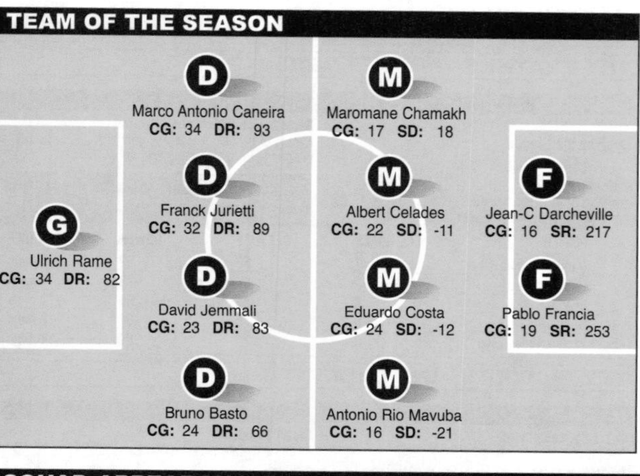
D
Marco Antonio Caneira
CG: 34 DR: 93
M
Maromane Chamakh
CG: 17 SD: 18
D
Franck Jurietti
CG: 32 DR: 89
M
Albert Celades
CG: 22 SD: -11
F
Jean-C Darcheville
CG: 16 SR: 217
G
Ulrich Rame
CG: 34 DR: 82
D
David Jemmali
CG: 23 DR: 83
M
Eduardo Costa
CG: 24 SD: -12
F
Pablo Francia
CG: 19 SR: 253
D
Bruno Basto
CG: 24 DR: 66
M
Antonio Rio Mavuba
CG: 16 SD: -21

SQUAD APPEARANCES

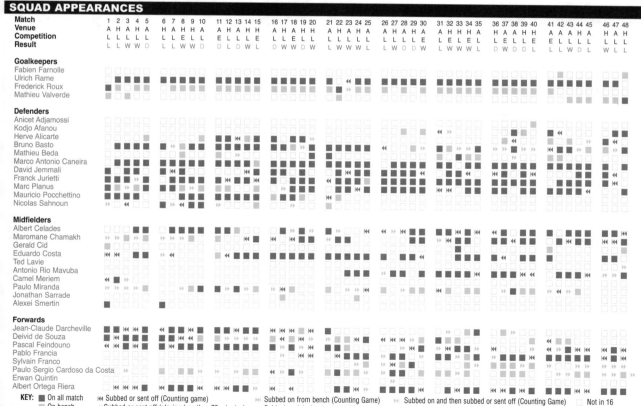

Match	1	2	3	4	5	6	7	8	9	10	11	12	13	14	15	16	17	18	19	20	21	22	23	24	25
Venue	A	H	A	H	A	H	A	H	H	A	A	H	A	H	H	A	H	A	H	H	A	H	A	H	A
Competition	L	L	L	L	L	L	L	E	L	L	E	L	L	L	E	L	L	E	L	L	L	L	L	L	L
Result	L	L	W	W	D	L	L	W	W	D	D	L	D	W	L	D	W	W	D	W	L	W	W	W	L

Match	26	27	28	29	30	31	32	33	34	35	36	37	38	39	40	41	42	43	44	45	46	47	48
Venue	A	H	A	H	A	A	H	H	H	A	H	A	A	H	H	A	A	A	H	A	H	A	H
Competition	L	L	L	L	E	L	E	L	E	L	L	E	L	L	E	E	L	L	L	L	L	L	L
Result	L	W	D	D	W	L	W	W	W	L	D	W	D	D	L	L	L	W	D	L	W	L	L

Goalkeepers
Fabien Farnolle
Ulrich Rame
Frederick Roux
Mathieu Valverde

Defenders
Anicet Adjamossi
Kodjo Afanou
Herve Alicarte
Bruno Basto
Mathieu Beda
Marco Antonio Caneira
David Jemmali
Franck Jurietti
Marc Planus
Mauricio Pocchettino
Nicolas Sahnoun

Midfielders
Albert Celades
Maromane Chamakh
Gerald Cid
Eduardo Costa
Ted Lavie
Antonio Rio Mavuba
Camel Meriem
Paulo Miranda
Jonathan Sarrade
Alexei Smertin

Forwards
Jean-Claude Darcheville
Deivid de Souza
Pascal Feindouno
Pablo Francia
Sylvain Franco
Paulo Sergio Cardoso da Costa
Erwan Quintin
Albert Ortega Riera

KEY: On all match · On bench · Subbed or sent off (Counting game) · Subbed or sent off (playing less than 70 minutes) · Subbed on from bench (Counting Game) · Subbed on (playing less than 70 minutes) · Subbed on and then subbed or sent off (Counting Game) · Subbed on and then subbed or sent off (playing less than 70 minutes) · Not in 16

STRASBOURG

13th

KEY: Won Drawn Lost

							Attendance
1	lge	Toulouse	A	D	1-1	Bassila 75	18,080
2	lge	Guingamp	H	W	2-0	Niang 18; Ljuboja 47	15,000
3	lge	Auxerre	A	L	2-3	Ljuboja 41; Mouloungui 88	12,750
4	lge	Lens	H	L	0-1		19,690
5	lge	Le Mans	A	W	3-0	Niang 33,57; Ljuboja 87	11,711
6	lge	AC Ajaccio	H	W	3-2	Ljuboja 4 pen; Niang 21,27	12,000
7	lge	Sochaux	A	L	0-3		15,000
8	lge	Nantes	H	W	1-0	Kobylik 90	15,000
9	lge	Nice	A	D	0-0		12,527
10	lge	Marseille	H	W	4-1	Martins 20; Niang 37; Ljuboja 45; Ehret 88	27,000
11	lge	Metz	H	L	0-2		24,000
12	lge	Rennes	A	D	1-1	Niang 71	15,007
13	lge	Bordeaux	H	D	1-1	Martins 82	15,817
14	lge	Lyon	A	L	0-1		45,366
15	lge	Lille	H	D	2-2	Bassila 54,88	10,915
16	lge	Paris SG	A	L	2-3	Ljuboja 13; Fahmi 78	34,175
17	lge	Bastia	H	W	4-2	Ljuboja 14; Le Pen 38; Niang 44; Ehret 53	11,000
18	lge	Monaco	A	L	0-2		7,549
19	lge	Montpellier	H	W	4-2	Le Pen 31 pen,63; Mouloungui 40; Bassila 54	11,643
20	lge	Guingamp	A	L	2-3	Le Pen 38; Niang 45	11,791
21	lge	Auxerre	H	L	0-2		14,894
22	lge	Lens	A	L	1-2	Mouloungui 58	30,093
23	lge	Le Mans	H	W	3-0	Le Pen 52,80; Chapuis 71	12,327
24	lge	AC Ajaccio	A	D	0-0		3,000
25	lge	Sochaux	H	L	0-2		18,000
26	lge	Nantes	A	D	1-1	Yepes 90 og	31,000
27	lge	Nice	H	D	2-2	Le Pen 61,63	12,000
28	lge	Marseille	A	L	0-4		38,900
29	lge	Metz	A	L	0-1		15,000
30	lge	Rennes	H	L	0-3		15,000
31	lge	Bordeaux	A	D	1-1	Le Pen 80 pen	22,643
32	lge	Lyon	H	L	0-1		19,400
33	lge	Lille	A	W	1-0	Makoun 30 og	13,456
34	lge	Paris SG	H	D	0-0		26,000
35	lge	Bastia	A	D	0-0		3,000
36	lge	Monaco	H	D	0-0		25,590
37	lge	Montpellier	A	W	2-1	Fahmi 48; Camadini 73	10,000
38	lge	Toulouse	H	D	0-0		12,453

MONTHLY POINTS TALLY

AUGUST	7	47%
SEPTEMBER	6	67%
OCTOBER	4	44%
NOVEMBER	3	25%
DECEMBER	6	50%
JANUARY	0	0%
FEBRUARY	5	42%
MARCH	1	8%
APRIL	4	44%
MAY	7	47%

KEY PLAYERS - GOALSCORERS

Mamadou Niang

Goals in the League	9	Player Strike Rate Average number of minutes between League goals scored by player	203
Contribution to Attacking Power Average number of minutes between League team goals while on pitch	73	Club Strike Rate Average number of minutes between League goals scored by club	80

	PLAYER	LGE GOALS	POWER	STRIKE RATE
1	Mamadou Niang	9	73	203 mins
2	Danijel Ljuboja	7	52	203 mins
3	Ulrich Le Pen	9	76	313 mins
4	Abdelilah Fahmi	2	77	694 mins
5	Christian Bassila	4	72	760 mins

KEY PLAYERS - MIDFIELDERS

Danijel Ljuboja

Goals in the League	7	Contribution to Attacking Power Average number of minutes between League team goals while on pitch	53
Defensive Rating Average number of mins between League goals conceded while he was on the pitch	62	Scoring Difference Defensive Rating minus Contribution to Attacking Power	9

	PLAYER	LGE GOALS	DEF RATE	POWER	SCORE DIFF
1	Danijel Ljuboja	7	62	53	9 mins
2	Ulrich Le Pen	9	67	76	-9 mins
3	Yves Deroff	0	58	69	-11 mins
4	Guillaume Lacour	0	76	88	-12 mins
5	Yacine Abdessadki	0	75	89	-14 mins

KEY PLAYERS - DEFENDERS

Cedric Kante

Goals Conceded (GC) The number of League goals conceded while he was on the pitch	28	Clean Sheets In games when he played at least 70 minutes	8
Defensive Rating Ave number of mins between League goals conceded while on the pitch	78	Club Defensive Rating Average number of mins between League goals conceded by the club this season	68

	PLAYER	CON LGE	CLEAN SHEETS	DEF RATE
1	Cedric Kante	28	8	78 mins
2	Abdelilah Fahmi	18	6	77 mins
3	Jean-Christophe Devaux	27	6	74 mins
4	Christian Bassila	43	10	71 mins
5	Vaclav Drobny	29	5	68 mins

KEY GOALKEEPER

Richard Dutruel

Goals Conceded in the League	28	Counting Games Games when he played at least 70 mins	25
Defensive Rating Ave number of mins between League goals conceded while on the pitch	80	Clean Sheets In games when he played at least 70 mins	8

LEAGUE GOALS

Mamadou Niang

Minutes on the pitch	1827	Goals in the League	9
League average (mins between goals)	203		

	PLAYER	MINS	GOALS	AVE
1	Niang	1827	9	203
2	Le Pen	2821	9	313
3	Ljuboja	1418	7	203
4	Bassila	3041	4	760
5	Mouloungui	1294	3	431
6	Ehret	1723	2	862
7	Martins	1362	2	681
8	Fahmi	1388	2	694
9	Kobylik	349	1	349
10	Chapuis	756	1	756
11	Camadini	981	1	981
	Other		2	
	TOTAL		43	

DISCIPLINARY

	PLAYER	YELLOW	RED	AVE
1	Ehret	7	2	191
2	Bassila	9	1	304
3	Camadini	2	1	327
4	Abdessadki	4	0	357
5	Lacour	5	0	423
6	Dorsin	3	0	453
7	Niang	4	0	456
8	Drobny	4	0	490
9	Farnerud, P	5	0	506
10	Devaux	3	0	662
11	Fahmi	2	0	694
12	Le Pen	4	0	705
13	Ljuboja	2	0	709
	Other	10	0	
	TOTAL	64	4	

TOP POINT EARNERS

	PLAYER	GAMES	AV PTS
1	Ljuboja	16	1.50
2	Fahmi	15	1.40
3	Kante	24	1.29
4	Bassila	34	1.24
5	Dutruel	25	1.24
6	Abdessadki	13	1.23
7	Deroff	24	1.17
8	Le Pen	29	1.14
9	Farnerud, P	27	1.11
10	Drobny	20	1.05
	CLUB AVERAGE:		**1.13**

LEAGUE APPEARANCES, BOOKINGS AND CAPS

	AGE (on 01/07/04)	IN NAMED 16	APPEARANCES	COUNTING GAMES	MINUTES ON PITCH	YELLOW CARDS	RED CARDS	THIS SEASON	HOME COUNTRY
Goalkeepers									
Nicolas Bonis	22	25	2	2	180	0	0	-	France
Benjamin Delin	21	4	0	0	0	0	0	-	France
Richard Dutruel	31	25	25	25	2250	1	0	-	France
Vincent Fernandez	29	21	11	11	990	1	0	-	France
Defenders									
Christian Bassila	26	34	34	34	3041	9	1	-	France
Habib Beye	27	1	1	1	90	0	0	-	France
Jean-C'ophe Devaux	29	26	26	20	1988	3	0	-	France
Vaclav Drobny	23	26	25	20	1961	4	0	2	Czech Republic (10)
Abdelilah Fahmi	30	21	17	15	1388	2	0	-	Morocco
Cedric Kante	24	26	25	24	2172	3	0	-	France
Jacques Momha	21	1	0	0	0	0	0	-	Cameroon
Midfielders									
Yacine Abdessadki	23	27	22	13	1430	4	0	-	Algeria
Pascal Camadini	32	24	19	8	981	2	1	-	France
Yves Deroff	25	31	31	24	2362	3	0	-	France
Mikael Dorsin	22	25	20	12	1359	3	0	-	Sweden
Alexander Farnerud	20	16	16	6	685	0	0	-	Sweden
Pontus Farnerud	24	33	32	27	2530	5	0	5	Sweden (21)
Yannick Fischer	29	6	3	0	59	0	0	-	France
David Kobylik	23	17	12	1	349	0	0	-	Czech Republic
Guillaume Lacour	23	28	26	23	2118	5	0	-	France
Ulrich Le Pen	30	36	36	29	2821	4	0	-	France
Danijel Ljuboja	26	16	16	16	1418	2	0	2	Serbia & M'negro (45)
Corentin Martins	34	24	21	9	1362	0	0	-	France
Cedric Moukouri	24	11	10	0	103	0	0	-	France
Forwards									
Salim Arrache	21	16	12	1	281	1	0	-	France
Cyril Chapuis	25	9	9	8	756	0	0	-	France
Fabrice Ehret	24	29	27	16	1723	7	2	-	France
Yannick Kamanan	21	1	0	0	0	0	0	-	France
Katlego M'Phela	19	2	2	0	13	0	0	-	South Africa
Eric Mouloungui	20	23	22	11	1294	1	0	-	Gabon
Mamadou Niang	24	24	23	19	1827	4	0	6	Senegal (31)

TEAM OF THE SEASON

G
Richard Dutruel
CG: 25 DR: 80

D
Cedric Kante
CG: 24 DR: 78

D
Abdelilah Fahmi
CG: 15 DR: 77

D
Jean-C'ophe Devaux
CG: 20 DR: 74

D
Christian Bassila
CG: 34 DR: 71

M
Danijel Ljuboja
CG: 16 SD: 9

M
Ulrich Le Pen
CG: 29 SD: -9

M
Yves Deroff
CG: 24 SD: -11

M
Guillaume Lacour
CG: 23 SD: -12

F
Mamadou Niang
CG: 19 SR: 203

F
Fabrice Ehret
CG: 16 SR: 862

SQUAD APPEARANCES

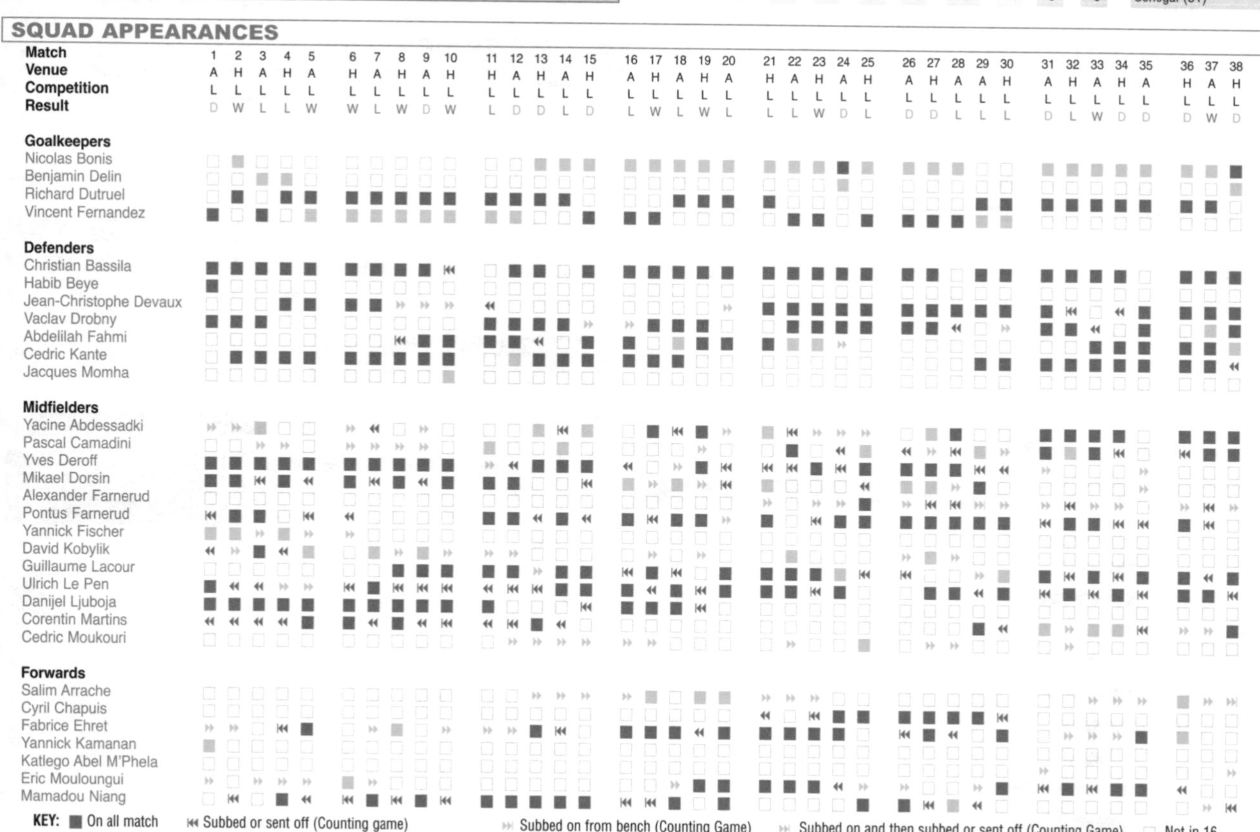

Match 1 2 3 4 5 6 7 8 9 10 11 12 13 14 15 16 17 18 19 20 21 22 23 24 25 26 27 28 29 30 31 32 33 34 35 36 37 38
Venue A H A H A H A H A H H A H A H A H A H A H A H A H A H A A H A H A H A H A H
Competition L L L L L L L L L L L L L L L L L L L L L L L L L L L L L L L L L L L L L L
Result D W L L W W L W D W L D D L D L W L W L L L W D L D D L L L D L W D D D W D
Goalkeepers
Nicolas Bonis
Benjamin Delin
Richard Dutruel
Vincent Fernandez
Defenders
Christian Bassila
Habib Beye
Jean-Christophe Devaux
Vaclav Drobny
Abdelilah Fahmi
Cedric Kante
Jacques Momha
Midfielders
Yacine Abdessadki
Pascal Camadini
Yves Deroff
Mikael Dorsin
Alexander Farnerud
Pontus Farnerud
Yannick Fischer
David Kobylik
Guillaume Lacour
Ulrich Le Pen
Danijel Ljuboja
Corentin Martins
Cedric Moukouri
Forwards
Salim Arrache
Cyril Chapuis
Fabrice Ehret
Yannick Kamanan
Katlego Abel M'Phela
Eric Mouloungui
Mamadou Niang
KEY: On all match
On bench
Subbed or sent off (Counting game)
Subbed or sent off (playing less than 70 minutes)
Subbed on from bench (Counting Game)
Subbed on (playing less than 70 minutes)
Subbed on and then subbed or sent off (Counting Game)
Subbed on and then subbed or sent off (playing less than 70 minutes)
Not in 16

METZ

Final Position: **14th**

KEY: ☐ Won ☐ Drawn ☐ Lost

							Attendance
1	lge	AC Ajaccio	H	L	0-1		15,000
2	lge	Bastia	A	W	2-0	Saki 45; Thiaw 54	6,000
3	lge	Paris SG	H	L	0-1		15,547
4	lge	Lille	A	D	1-1	Thiaw 3	15,651
5	lge	Monaco	A	L	0-1		6,000
6	lge	Montpellier	H	W	2-1	Borbiconi 5; Thiaw 90	15,000
7	lge	Toulouse	A	L	0-1		13,620
8	lge	Guingamp	H	D	1-1	Gueye 90	15,603
9	lge	Lens	A	W	2-0	Maoulida 56,90	36,083
10	lge	Nantes	H	L	1-3	Thiaw 22 pen	15,903
11	lge	Strasbourg	A	W	2-0	Maoulida 32,71	24,000
12	lge	Sochaux	H	L	0-1		16,834
13	lge	Le Mans	A	L	0-2		10,786
14	lge	Auxerre	H	L	0-2		20,106
15	lge	Nice	A	D	1-1	Maoulida 18	10,445
16	lge	Lyon	A	L	1-2	Jager 21	39,500
17	lge	Rennes	H	D	1-1	Jager 35	13,272
18	lge	Bordeaux	A	L	0-2		19,693
19	lge	Bastia	H	W	1-0	Thiaw 64	12,428
20	lge	Paris SG	A	D	0-0		40,601
21	lge	Marseille	H	D	1-1	Rodriguez 47	25,811
22	lge	Lille	H	L	0-1		12,712
23	lge	Monaco	H	L	0-2		18,891
24	lge	Montpellier	A	W	1-0	Leca 5	7,000
25	lge	Toulouse	H	L	0-2		7,000
26	lge	Lens	H	L	0-2		11,600
27	lge	Nantes	A	D	2-2	Meniri 49; Maoulida 73	27,400
28	lge	Strasbourg	H	W	1-0	Meniri 17	15,000
29	lge	Sochaux	A	L	0-2		14,372
30	lge	Le Mans	H	W	5-0	Borbiconi 5; Maoulida 18,51,66; Thiaw 88	13,802
31	lge	Auxerre	A	L	1-2	Maoulida 59	7,000
32	lge	Guingamp	A	D	1-1	Le Crom 8 og	15,569
33	lge	Nice	H	W	1-0	Proment 61	17,679
34	lge	Marseille	A	W	1-0	Meniri 26	44,000
35	lge	Lyon	H	L	1-2	Maoulida 9	24,778
36	lge	Rennes	A	D	0-0		22,143
37	lge	Bordeaux	H	W	3-1	Proment 53; Meniri 66; Renouard 73	22,059
38	lge	AC Ajaccio	A	L	1-3	Maoulida 31	5,000

MONTHLY POINTS TALLY

Month	Points	%
AUGUST	4	27%
SEPTEMBER	4	44%
OCTOBER	6	67%
NOVEMBER	1	8%
DECEMBER	1	11%
JANUARY	5	42%
FEBRUARY	3	33%
MARCH	4	33%
APRIL	7	58%
MAY	7	47%

KEY PLAYERS - GOALSCORERS

Toifilou Maoulida

Goals in the League	12	Player Strike Rate Average number of minutes between League goals scored by player	230
Contribution to Attacking Power Average number of minutes between League team goals while on pitch	98	Club Strike Rate Average number of minutes between League goals scored by club	101

	PLAYER	LGE GOALS	POWER	STRIKE RATE
1	Toifilou Maoulida	12	98	230 mins
2	Papa Thaiw	4	83	376 mins
3	Gregory Proment	2	82	906 mins
4	Stephane Borbiconi	2	93	1497 mins
5	Gregory Leca	1	92	2774 mins

KEY PLAYERS - MIDFIELDERS

Gregory Proment

Goals in the League	2	Contribution to Attacking Power Average number of minutes between League team goals while on pitch	82
Defensive Rating Average number of mins between League goals conceded while he was on the pitch	86	Scoring Difference Defensive Rating minus Contribution to Attacking Power	4

	PLAYER	LGE GOALS	DEF RATE	POWER	SCORE DIFF
1	Gregory Proment	2	86	82	4 mins
2	Gregory Leca	1	82	92	-10 mins
3	Alexandre Frutos	0	92	105	-13 mins
4	Dino Djiba	0	85	150	-65 mins

KEY PLAYERS - DEFENDERS

Mehdi Meniri

Goals Conceded (GC) The number of League goals conceded while he was on the pitch	6	Clean Sheets In games when he played at least 70 minutes	6
Defensive Rating Ave number of mins between League goals conceded while on the pitch	100	Club Defensive Rating Average number of mins between League goals conceded by the club this season	81

	PLAYER	CON LGE	CLEAN SHEETS	DEF RATE
1	Mehdi Meniri	13	6	100 mins
2	Stephane Morisot	22	6	89 mins
3	Franck Signorino	36	10	80 mins
4	Stephane Borbiconi	38	9	79 mins
5	Sylvain Marchal	23	4	79 mins

KEY GOALKEEPER

Ludovic Butelle

Goals Conceded in the League	28	Counting Games Games when he played at least 70 mins	27
Defensive Rating Ave number of mins between League goals conceded while on the pitch	87	Clean Sheets In games when he played at least 70 mins	10

LEAGUE GOALS

Toifilou Maoulida

Minutes on the pitch	2764	Goals in the League	12
League average (mins between goals)	230		

	PLAYER	MINS	GOALS	AVE
1	Maoulida	2764	12	230
2	Meniri	1503	4	376
3	Thiaw	1295	4	324
4	Proment	1811	2	906
5	Borbiconi	2994	2	1497
6	Jager	600	2	300
7	Leca	2774	1	2774
8	Rodriguez	691	1	691
9	Gueye	1208	1	1208
10	Renouard	1065	1	1065
	Other		4	
	TOTAL		34	

DISCIPLINARY RECORDS

	PLAYER	YELLOW	RED	AVE
1	Thiaw	5	1	215
2	Beria	3	1	244
3	Proment	7	0	258
4	Die	1	1	294
5	Rodriguez	2	0	345
6	Moreno	3	0	457
7	Maoulida	6	0	460
8	Meniri	3	0	501
9	Renouard	2	0	532
10	Marchal	3	0	604
11	Morisot	2	1	649
12	Djiba	2	0	677
13	Signorino	3	0	955
	Other	14	0	
	TOTAL	56	4	

TOP POINT EARNERS

	PLAYER	GAMES	AV PTS
1	Meniri	16	1.44
2	Butelle	27	1.33
3	Proment	19	1.32
4	Signorino	31	1.19
5	Leca	28	1.18
6	Maoulida	30	1.17
7	Frutos	13	1.15
8	Morisot	20	1.15
9	Borbiconi	33	1.12
10	Marchal	18	1.06
	CLUB AVERAGE:		**1.11**

TEAM OF THE SEASON

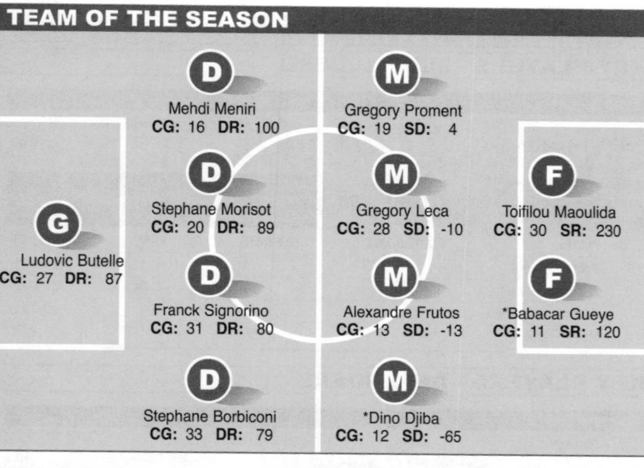

D
Mehdi Meniri
CG: 16 DR: 100
M
Gregory Proment
CG: 19 SD: 4
D
Stephane Morisot
CG: 20 DR: 89
M
Gregory Leca
CG: 28 SD: -10
F
Toifilou Maoulida
CG: 30 SR: 230
G
Ludovic Butelle
CG: 27 DR: 87
D
Franck Signorino
CG: 31 DR: 80
M
Alexandre Frutos
CG: 13 SD: -13
F
*Babacar Gueye
CG: 11 SR: 120
D
Stephane Borbiconi
CG: 33 DR: 79
M
*Dino Djiba
CG: 12 SD: -65

LEAGUE APPEARANCES, BOOKINGS AND CAPS

	AGE (on 01/07/04)	IN NAMED 16	APPEARANCES	COUNTING GAMES	MINUTES ON PITCH	YELLOW CARDS	RED CARDS	THIS SEASON	HOME COUNTRY
Goalkeepers									
Kossi Agassa	-	26	11	10	990	1	0	-	Togo
Ludovic Butelle	21	37	27	27	2430	1	0	-	France
Johan Liebus	25	13	0	0	0	0	0	-	France
Defenders									
Samuel Allegro	-	34	31	27	2511	1	0	-	France
Schumann Bah	29	9	5	4	422	1	0	-	France
Frank Beria	21	15	11	11	978	3	1	-	France
Stephane Borbiconi	25	34	34	33	2994	2	0	-	France
Aimen Demai	21	6	4	3	274	0	0	-	France.
Serge Die	26	10	8	4	589	1	1	-	Ivory Coast
Sylvain Marchal	24	27	24	18	1812	3	0	-	France
Mehdi Meniri	27	20	18	16	1503	3	0	-	France
Stephane Morisot	26	23	23	20	1948	2	1	-	France
Oguchi Onyewu	21	2	2	1	94	1	0	-	United States
Franck Signorino	22	37	34	31	2867	3	0	-	France
Midfielders									
Jeferson De Souza	22	2	1	0	13	0	0	-	Togo
Dino Djiba	18	22	22	12	1354	2	0	-	Senegal
Alexandre Frutos	22	29	27	13	1469	1	0	-	France
Gregory Leca	23	37	36	28	2774	1	0	-	France
Stephane Noro	24	9	7	2	357	3	0	-	France
Ludovic Obraniak	19	14	9	6	559	0	0	-	France
Gregory Proment	25	21	21	19	1811	7	0	-	France
Sebastien Renouard	20	20	18	10	1065	2	0	-	France
Christophe Walter	21	20	12	3	514	0	0	-	France
Forwards									
Babacar Gueye	18	26	23	11	1208	1	0	-	Senegal
Jonathan Jager	26	12	11	5	600	0	0	-	France
Toifilou Maoulida	25	33	33	30	2764	6	0	-	France
Tressor Moreno	25	18	17	14	1373	3	0	-	Colombia
Bruno Rodriguez	31	8	8	7	691	2	0	-	France
Hakim Saci	27	14	10	2	299	1	0	-	Algeria
Pape Thiaw	23	28	26	10	1295	5	1	-	Senegalese

SQUAD APPEARANCES

Match	1	2	3	4	5	6	7	8	9	10	11	12	13	14	15	16	17	18	19
Venue	H	A	H	A	A	H	A	H	A	H	A	H	A	H	A	A	H	A	H
Competition	L	L	L	L	L	L	L	L	L	L	L	L	L	L	L	L	L	L	L
Result	L	W	L	D	L	W	L	D	W	L	W	L	L	L	D	L	D	L	W

Match	20	21	22	23	24	25	26	27	28	29	30	31	32	33	34	35	36	37	38
Venue	A	H	H	H	A	H	H	A	H	A	H	A	A	H	A	H	A	H	A
Competition	L	L	L	L	L	L	L	L	L	L	L	L	L	L	L	L	L	L	L
Result	D	D	L	L	W	L	L	D	W	L	W	L	D	W	W	L	D	W	L

Goalkeepers
Kossi Agassa
Ludovic Butelle
Johan Liebus

Defenders
Samuel Allegro
Schumann Bah
Frank Beria
Stephane Borbiconi
Aimen Demai
Serge Die
Sylvain Marchal
Mehdi Meniri
Stephane Morisot
Oguchi Onyewu
Franck Signorino

Midfielders
Jeferson De Souza
Dino Djiba
Alexandre Frutos
Gregory Leca
Stephane Noro
Ludovic Obraniak
Gregory Proment
Sebastien Renouard
Christophe Walter

Forwards
Babacar Gueye
Jonathan Jager
Toifilou Maoulida
Tressor Moreno
Bruno Rodriguez
Hakim Saci
Pape Thiaw

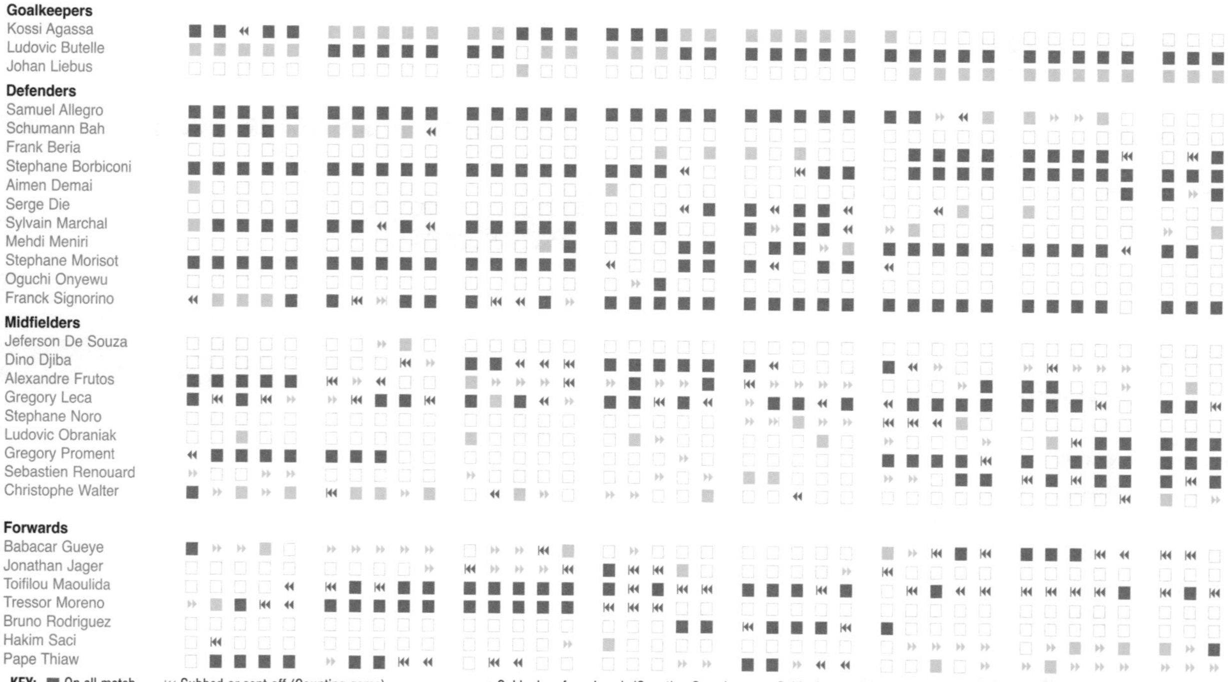

KEY: ■ On all match ■ On bench
⏮ Subbed or sent off (Counting game) ⏪ Subbed or sent off (playing less than 70 minutes)
⏭ Subbed on from bench (Counting Game) ⏩ Subbed on (playing less than 70 minutes)
Subbed on and then subbed or sent off (Counting Game) Subbed on and then subbed or sent off (playing less than 70 minutes)
□ Not in 16

AC AJACCIO

15th

KEY: Won / Drawn / Lost

							Attendance
1	lge	Metz	A	W	1-0	Regragui 41	15,000
2	lge	Le Mans	A	W	1-0	Bagayoko 28	13,500
3	lge	Nantes	H	L	1-3	Bagayoko 87	10,000
4	lge	Nice	A	D	2-2	Bigne 24 og; Laslandes 59 og	12,610
5	lge	Marseille	H	L	0-1		9,144
6	lge	Strasbourg	A	L	2-3	Bagayoko 18; Ouadah 33	12,000
7	lge	Rennes	H	W	1-0	Mitrovic 44	8,500
8	lge	Bordeaux	A	L	0-1		19,945
9	lge	Lyon	H	L	2-4	Diomede 45; Mitrovic 90	6,625
10	lge	Lille	A	D	0-0		14,298
11	lge	Paris SG	H	D	0-0		3,500
12	lge	Bastia	A	D	1-1	Regragui 62	8,000
13	lge	Monaco	H	L	0-1		3,886
14	lge	Montpellier	A	L	1-3	Bagayoko 44	11,542
15	lge	Toulouse	H	W	2-1	Diomede 27; Bagayoko 85	2,536
16	lge	Guingamp	A	L	0-2		15,314
17	lge	Auxerre	H	L	1-2	Bagayoko 50	3,000
18	lge	Sochaux	A	L	0-2		13,699
19	lge	Lens	H	W	2-0	Bonnal 12; Demont 83	3,500
20	lge	Le Mans	H	W	2-0	Lacombe 10,76	2,135
21	lge	Nantes	A	L	0-4		26,817
22	lge	Nice	H	D	1-1	Danjou 6	5,000
23	lge	Marseille	A	L	1-2	Seck 74	47,000
24	lge	Strasbourg	H	D	0-0		3,000
25	lge	Rennes	A	L	1-4	Diomede 15 pen	15,500
26	lge	Bordeaux	H	W	1-0	Bagayoko 19	3,000
27	lge	Lyon	A	L	0-4		30,000
28	lge	Lille	H	L	0-3		5,000
29	lge	Paris SG	A	L	0-1		38,580
30	lge	Bastia	H	W	1-0	Diomede 22	4,500
31	lge	Monaco	A	D	3-3	Loko 25; Robin 36,42	6,208
32	lge	Montpellier	H	D	0-0		4,000
33	lge	Toulouse	A	L	1-3	Bagayoko 90	16,149
34	lge	Guingamp	H	D	0-0		2,321
35	lge	Auxerre	A	D	1-1	Demont 88	8,000
36	lge	Sochaux	H	W	1-0	Demont 14	5,000
37	lge	Lens	A	L	0-2		34,642
38	lge	Metz	H	W	3-1	Diomede 38,44,54	5,000

MONTHLY POINTS TALLY

Month	Points	%
AUGUST	7	47%
SEPTEMBER	3	33%
OCTOBER	2	22%
NOVEMBER	4	33%
DECEMBER	3	25%
JANUARY	4	44%
FEBRUARY	4	33%
MARCH	3	25%
APRIL	2	22%
MAY	8	53%

KEY PLAYERS - GOALSCORERS

Bernard Diomede

Goals in the League	6	Player Strike Rate Average number of minutes between League goals scored by player	345
Contribution to Attacking Power Average number of minutes between League team goals while on pitch	115	Club Strike Rate Average number of minutes between League goals scored by club	104

	PLAYER	LGE GOALS	POWER	STRIKE RATE
1	Bernard Diomede	6	115	345 mins
2	Mamadou Bagayoko	8	101	380 mins
3	Yohan Demont	3	95	444 mins
4	Hoalid Regragui	2	79	879 mins
5	Martial Robin	2	122	922 mins

KEY PLAYERS - MIDFIELDERS

Yohan Demont

Goals in the League	3	Contribution to Attacking Power Average number of minutes between League team goals while on pitch	95
Defensive Rating Average number of mins between League goals conceded while he was on the pitch	74	Scoring Difference Defensive Rating minus Contribution to Attacking Power	-21

	PLAYER	LGE GOALS	DEF RATE	POWER	SCORE DIFF
1	Yohan Demont	3	74	95	-21 mins
2	Stephane Gregoire	0	71	102	-31 mins
3	Bernard Diomede	6	65	115	-50 mins
4	Martial Robin	2	64	123	-59 mins

KEY PLAYERS - DEFENDERS

Mamadou Seck

Goals Conceded (GC) The number of League goals conceded while he was on the pitch	32	Clean Sheets In games when he played at least 70 minutes	8
Defensive Rating Ave number of mins between League goals conceded while on the pitch	64	Club Defensive Rating Average number of mins between League goals conceded by the club this season	62

	PLAYER	CON LGE	CLEAN SHEETS	DEF RATE
1	Mamadou Seck	32	8	64 mins
2	Frederic Danjou	51	12	64 mins
3	David Terrier	46	10	63 mins
4	Xavier Collin	49	11	61 mins

KEY GOALKEEPER

Stephane Trevisan

Goals Conceded in the League	55	Counting Games Games when he played at least 70 mins	38
Defensive Rating Ave number of mins between League goals conceded while on the pitch	62	Clean Sheets In games when he played at least 70 mins	13

LEAGUE GOALS

Mamadou Bagayoko

Minutes on the pitch	3042	Goals in the League	8
League average (mins between goals)	380		

	PLAYER	MINS	GOALS	AVE
1	Bagayoko	3042	8	380
2	Diomede	2071	6	345
3	Demont	1331	3	444
4	Regragui	1758	2	879
5	Robin	1843	2	922
6	Lacombe	868	2	434
7	Bonnal	1387	1	1387
8	Seck	2037	1	2037
9	Mitrovic	567	1	567
10	Loko	603	1	603
11	Ouadah	563	1	563
12	Danjou	3262	1	3262
	Other		4	
	TOTAL		33	

DISCIPLINARY

	PLAYER	YELLOW	RED	AVE
1	Destruhaut	3	0	175
2	Ouadah	3	0	187
3	Bonnal	6	1	198
4	Lacombe	3	1	217
5	Terrier	12	1	221
6	Regragui	7	0	251
7	Bagayoko	10	1	276
8	Demont	4	0	332
9	Diomede	5	1	345
10	Diabate	2	0	386
11	Moracchini	2	0	388
12	Connen	2	0	463
13	Mitrovic	1	0	567
	Other	18	0	
	TOTAL	78	5	

TOP POINT EARNERS

	PLAYER	GAMES	AV PTS
1	Regragui	17	1.47
2	Demont	13	1.23
3	Bonnal	15	1.13
4	Bagayoko	34	1.12
5	Gregoire	33	1.12
6	Terrier	31	1.06
7	Trevisan	38	1.05
8	Danjou	36	1.03
9	Robin	20	1.00
10	Collin	32	1.00
	CLUB AVERAGE:		**1.05**

LEAGUE APPEARANCES, BOOKINGS AND CAPS

	AGE (on 01/07/04)	IN NAMED 16	APPEARANCES	COUNTING GAMES	MINUTES ON PITCH	YELLOW CARDS	RED CARDS	THIS SEASON	HOME COUNTRY
Goalkeepers									
Florian Lucchini	23	11	0	0	0	0	0	-	France
Herve Sekli	26	24	0	0	0	0	0	-	France
Stephane Trevisan	31	38	38	38	3420	1	0	-	France
Defenders									
Xavier Collin	29	34	34	32	2980	3	0	-	France
Frederic Danjou	29	37	37	36	3262	4	0	-	France
C'"tophe Destruhaut	31	19	13	3	525	3	0	-	France
Lassina Diabate	29	15	13	7	772	2	0	-	Ivory Coast
David Jaureguiberry	28	1	1	1	90	0	0	-	France
Fabien Laurenti	21	14	10	6	673	0	0	-	France
Milan Martinovic	24	2	1	1	90	0	0	-	Serbia & Montenegro
Stephane Maurel	23	2	1	1	90	0	0	-	France
Mamadou Seck	24	26	26	22	2037	2	0	-	Senegal
David Terrier	30	33	33	31	2876	12	1	-	France
Abderaouf Zarabi	25	1	1	0	29	1	0	-	Algeria
Midfielders									
Yacine Bezzaz	22	5	5	0	161	0	0	-	Algeria
Renaud Connen	24	12	12	10	926	2	0	-	France
Yohan Demont	26	21	20	13	1331	4	0	-	France
Bernard Diomede	30	31	30	20	2071	5	1	-	France
Cyril Granon	32	25	22	5	924	1	0	-	France
Stephane Gregoire	36	34	33	33	2970	2	0	-	France
Laurent Moracchini	36	12	11	7	776	2	0	-	France
Abdelnasser Ouadah	28	16	12	3	563	3	0	-	France
Martial Robin	26	32	26	20	1843	2	0	-	France
Lacerba Rodrigo	23	13	10	8	750	1	0	-	Brazil
Forwards									
Djamel Abdoun	-	1	1	0	11	0	0	-	France
Mamadou Bagayoko	25	34	34	34	3042	10	1	-	Mali
Nicolas Bonnal	27	22	20	15	1387	6	1	-	France
David Faderne	34	3	2	0	30	0	0	-	France
Gregory Lacombe	22	23	21	7	868	3	1	-	France
Patrice Loko	34	15	12	6	603	1	0	-	France
Dalibor Mitrovic	26	20	14	3	567	1	0	-	Serbia & Montenegro
Hoalid Regragui	28	24	24	17	1758	7	0	-	France

TEAM OF THE SEASON

G — Stephane Trevisan — CG: 38 DR: 62

D — Frederic Danjou — CG: 36 DR: 64

D — Mamadou Seck — CG: 22 DR: 64

D — David Terrier — CG: 31 DR: 63

D — Xavier Collin — CG: 32 DR: 61

M — Yohan Demont — CG: 13 SD: -21

M — Stephane Gregoire — CG: 33 SD: -31

M — Bernard Diomede — CG: 20 SD: -50

M — Martial Robin — CG: 20 SD: -59

F — Mamadou Bagayoko — CG: 34 SR: 380

F — Hoalid Regragui — CG: 17 SR: 879

SQUAD APPEARANCES

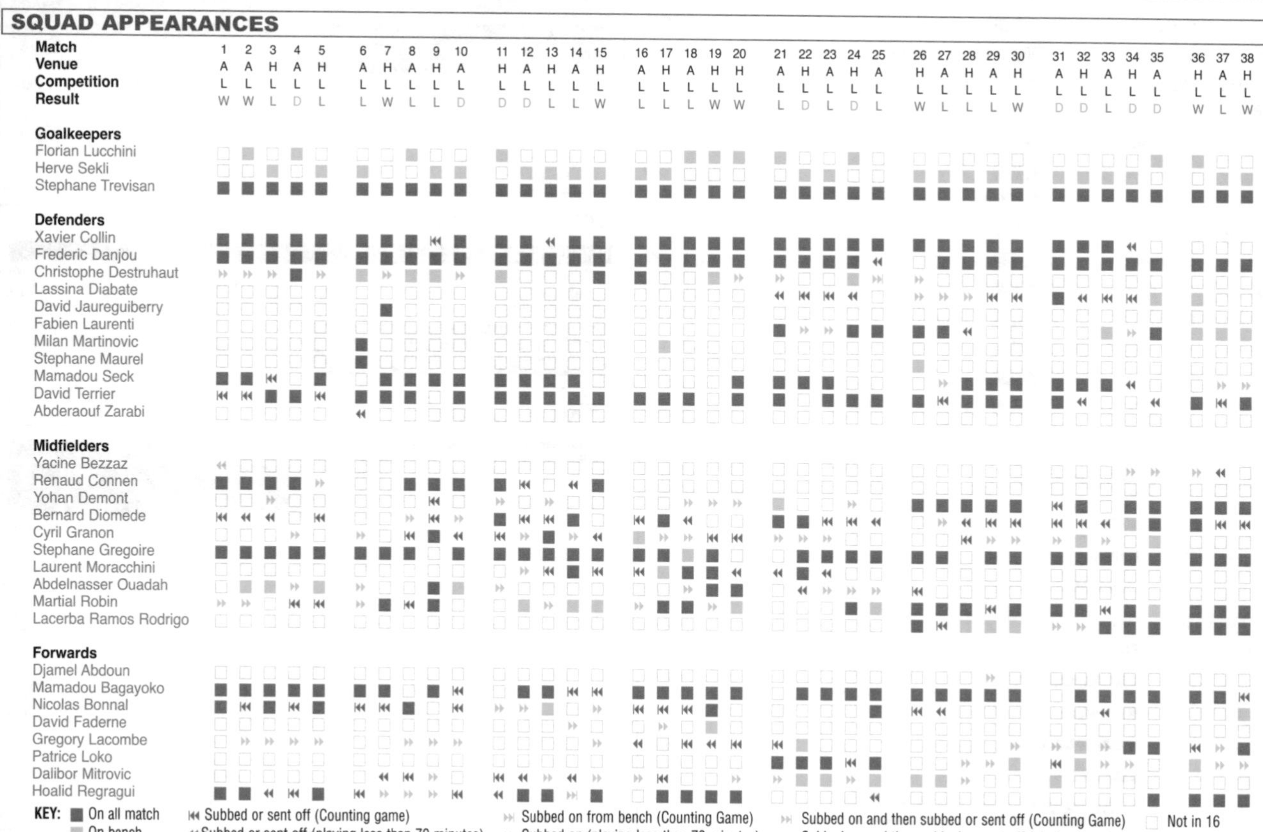
Match 1 2 3 4 5 6 7 8 9 10 11 12 13 14 15 16 17 18 19 20 21 22 23 24 25 26 27 28 29 30 31 32 33 34 35 36 37 38
Venue A A H A H A H A H A H A H A H A H A H H A H A H A H A H A H A H A H A H A H
Competition L L L L L L L L L L L L L L L L L L L L L L L L L L L L L L L L L L L L L L
Result W W L D L L W L L D D D L L W L L L W W L D L D L W L L L W D D L D D W L W
Goalkeepers
Florian Lucchini
Herve Sekli
Stephane Trevisan
Defenders
Xavier Collin
Frederic Danjou
Christophe Destruhaut
Lassina Diabate
David Jaureguiberry
Fabien Laurenti
Milan Martinovic
Stephane Maurel
Mamadou Seck
David Terrier
Abderaouf Zarabi
Midfielders
Yacine Bezzaz
Renaud Connen
Yohan Demont
Bernard Diomede
Cyril Granon
Stephane Gregoire
Laurent Moracchini
Abdelnasser Ouadah
Martial Robin
Lacerba Ramos Rodrigo
Forwards
Djamel Abdoun
Mamadou Bagayoko
Nicolas Bonnal
David Faderne
Gregory Lacombe
Patrice Loko
Dalibor Mitrovic
Hoalid Regragui
KEY: On all match
On bench
Subbed or sent off (Counting game)
Subbed or sent off (playing less than 70 minutes)
Subbed on from bench (Counting Game)
Subbed on (playing less than 70 minutes)
Subbed on and then subbed or sent off (Counting Game)
Subbed on and then subbed or sent off (playing less than 70 minutes)
Not in 16

TOULOUSE

16th

KEY: Won / Drawn / Lost

							Attendance
1	lge	Strasbourg	H	D	1-1	Faure 59	18,080
2	lge	Rennes	A	L	0-1		16,286
3	lge	Lille	H	L	0-3		36,982
4	lge	Lyon	A	D	0-0		35,192
5	lge	Bastia	H	L	0-2		14,052
6	lge	Paris SG	A	L	1-2	Dieuze 58	35,651
7	lge	Metz	H	W	1-0	Avezac 72	13,620
8	lge	Monaco	A	L	0-3		6,000
9	lge	Montpellier	H	D	2-2	Emana 12; Faure 75	
10	lge	Bordeaux	A	W	2-1	Faure 15,66 pen	22,097
11	lge	Guingamp	A	L	0-1		12,738
12	lge	Auxerre	H	L	0-3		28,721
13	lge	Sochaux	A	L	1-3	Braizat 70	15,526
14	lge	Le Mans	H	D	1-1	Eduardo 89	14,519
15	lge	AC Ajaccio	A	L	1-2	N'doye 76	2,536
16	lge	Lens	H	L	1-2	N'doye 77	13,660
17	lge	Nantes	A	D	1-1	Dieuze 45 pen	28,521
18	lge	Nice	H	D	1-1	Eduardo 8	13,441
19	lge	Marseille	A	L	0-1		50,838
20	lge	Rennes	H	W	2-0	Faure 5; Dieuze 82	13,310
21	lge	Lille	A	W	1-0	Faure 36	12,560
22	lge	Lyon	H	L	0-1		26,297
23	lge	Bastia	A	L	0-1		5,320
24	lge	Paris SG	H	L	0-1		24,000
25	lge	Metz	A	W	2-0	Faure 8; Fernandao 72	7,000
26	lge	Monaco	H	D	1-1	Didot 47	24,000
27	lge	Montpellier	A	W	1-0	Emana 14	5,000
28	lge	Bordeaux	H	W	1-0	Avezac 74	25,000
29	lge	Guingamp	H	D	0-0		19,200
30	lge	Auxerre	A	L	2-3	Faure 8; Eduardo 83	7,000
31	lge	Sochaux	H	D	0-0		21,120
32	lge	Le Mans	A	L	1-2	Faure 76	11,071
33	lge	AC Ajaccio	H	W	3-1	Emana 41; Faure 64 pen; Avezac 88	16,149
34	lge	Lens	A	D	1-1	Cardy 49	32,047
35	lge	Nantes	H	L	0-1		21,195
36	lge	Nice	A	D	1-1	Fernandao 4	9,663
37	lge	Marseille	H	W	2-1	Fernandao 45 pen; Eduardo 87	36,000
38	lge	Strasbourg	A	D	0-0		12,453

MONTHLY POINTS TALLY

Month	Points	%
AUGUST	2	13%
SEPTEMBER	3	33%
OCTOBER	4	44%
NOVEMBER	1	8%
DECEMBER	2	17%
JANUARY	6	67%
FEBRUARY	4	33%
MARCH	7	58%
APRIL	4	44%
MAY	6	40%

KEY PLAYERS - GOALSCORERS

Cedric Faure

Goals in the League	9	Player Strike Rate Average number of minutes between League goals scored by player	264
Contribution to Attacking Power Average number of minutes between League team goals while on pitch	95	Club Strike Rate Average number of minutes between League goals scored by club	110

	PLAYER	LGE GOALS	POWER	STRIKE RATE
1	Cedric Faure	9	95	264 mins
2	Lucio Fernandao	3	103	414 mins
3	Adelino Eduardo	4	109	508 mins
4	Christophe Avezac	3	98	723 mins
5	Achille Emana	3	105	912 mins

KEY PLAYERS - MIDFIELDERS

Julien Cardy

Goals in the League	1	Contribution to Attacking Power Average number of minutes between League team goals while on pitch	108
Defensive Rating Average number of mins between League goals conceded while he was on the pitch	88	Scoring Difference Defensive Rating minus Contribution to Attacking Power	-20

	PLAYER	LGE GOALS	DEF RATE	POWER	SCORE DIFF
1	Julien Cardy	1	88	108	-20 mins
2	Issou Malia Dao	0	80	101	-21 mins
3	Florent Balmont	0	73	109	-36 mins
4	Nabil Taider	0	71	107	-36 mins

KEY PLAYERS - DEFENDERS

Clement

Goals Conceded (GC) The number of League goals conceded while he was on the pitch	14	Clean Sheets In games when he played at least 70 minutes	4
Defensive Rating Ave number of mins between League goals conceded while on the pitch	94	Club Defensive Rating Average number of mins between League goals conceded by the club this season	78

	PLAYER	CON LGE	CLEAN SHEETS	DEF RATE
1	Clement	14	4	94 mins
2	Predrag Ocokoljic	36	10	84 mins
3	Lucien Aubey	40	9	74 mins
4	Stephane Lievre	33	4	65 mins

KEY GOALKEEPER

Christophe Revault

Goals Conceded in the League	44	Counting Games Games when he played at least 70 mins	38
Defensive Rating Ave number of mins between League goals conceded while on the pitch	78	Clean Sheets In games when he played at least 70 mins	10

LEAGUE GOALS

Cedric Faure

Minutes on the pitch	2380	Goals in the League	9
League average (mins between goals)	264		

	PLAYER	MINS	GOALS	AVE
1	Faure	2380	9	264
2	Eduardo	2031	4	508
3	Fernandao	1243	3	414
4	Dieuze	1144	3	381
5	Avezac	2168	3	723
6	Emana	2735	3	912
7	N'doye	510	2	255
8	Braizat	283	1	283
9	Cardy	1946	1	1946
10	Didot	1054	1	1054
	Other		1	
	TOTAL		31	

DISCIPLINARY

	PLAYER	YELLOW	RED	AVE
1	N'doye	3	2	102
2	Dieuze	7	1	143
3	Cardy	9	0	216
4	Avezac	8	1	240
5	Emana	9	0	303
6	Clement	4	0	328
7	Didot	3	0	351
8	Lievre	5	0	431
9	Dao	6	0	437
10	Balmont	6	0	462
11	Taider	4	0	480
12	Eduardo	4	0	507
13	Faure	4	0	595
	Other	17	0	
	TOTAL	89	4	

TOP POINT EARNERS

	PLAYER	GAMES	AV PTS
1	Fernandao	14	1.43
2	Cardy	20	1.35
3	Clement	14	1.21
4	Faure	21	1.19
5	Dao	29	1.14
6	Emana	29	1.10
7	Ocokoljic	33	1.06
8	Revault	38	1.03
9	Aubey	32	1.00
10	Avezac	20	1.00
	CLUB AVERAGE:		**1.03**

LEAGUE APPEARANCES, BOOKINGS AND CAPS

	AGE (on 01/07/04)	IN NAMED 16	APPEARANCES	COUNTING GAMES	MINUTES ON PITCH	YELLOW CARDS	RED CARDS	THIS SEASON	HOME COUNTRY
Goalkeepers									
Benoit Benvegnu	19	12	0	0	0	0	0	-	France
Jeremie Moreau	23	23	0	0	0	0	0	-	France
Christophe Revault	32	38	38	38	3420	3	0	-	France
Defenders									
Lucien Aubey	20	36	36	32	3061	3	0	-	France
Julien Baudet	25	1	0	0	0	0	0	-	France
Clement	27	19	17	14	1313	4	0	-	France
Albin Ebondo	20	8	3	1	124	0	0	-	France
Stephane Lievre	31	32	28	21	2158	5	0	-	France
Aurelien Mazel	21	14	4	3	281	0	0	-	France
Predrag Ocokoljic	26	36	35	33	3029	5	0	1	Serbia & M'negro (45)
William Prunier	36	9	8	8	720	1	0	-	France
Mathieu Puig	26	3	1	1	90	0	0	-	France
Midfielders									
Florent Balmont	24	35	34	30	2777	6	0	-	France
Henri Bedimo Nsame	20	2	0	0	0	0	0	-	Cameroon
Anthony Braizat	26	17	9	0	283	3	0	-	France
Julien Cardy	22	29	27	20	1946	9	0	-	France
Issou Malia Dao	20	34	30	29	2624	6	0	-	France
Sylvian Didot	28	25	22	6	1054	3	0	-	France
Thibault Giresse	23	9	5	1	233	0	0	-	France
Nabil Taider	21	34	28	20	1922	4	0	-	France
Forwards									
Christophe Avezac	27	33	32	20	2168	8	1	-	France
Jeremy Blayac	21	2	2	0	18	0	0	-	France
Nicolas Dieuze	25	27	26	5	1144	7	1	-	France
AdelinoEduardo	24	33	32	18	2031	4	0	-	Brazil
Achille Emana	22	32	32	29	2735	9	0	1	Cameroon (12)
Cedric Faure	25	36	36	21	2380	4	0	-	France
Lucio Fernandao	26	16	16	14	1243	2	0	-	Brazil
Othmane Hamama	22	2	2	2	180	0	0	-	France
Oussmane N'doye	26	9	8	5	510	3	2	4	Senegal (31)

TEAM OF THE SEASON

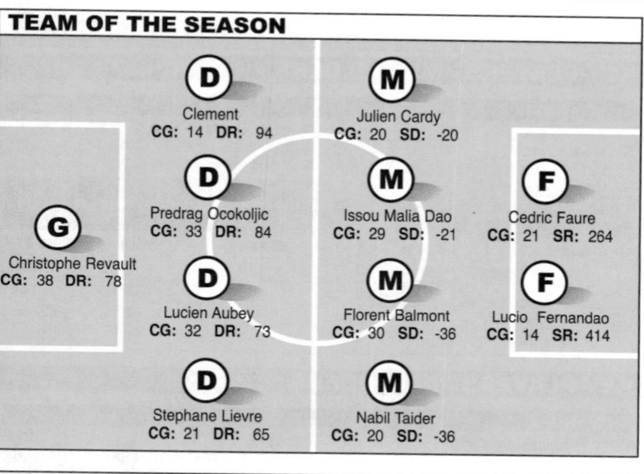
G
Christophe Revault
CG: 38 DR: 78
D
Clement
CG: 14 DR: 94
D
Predrag Ocokoljic
CG: 33 DR: 84
D
Lucien Aubey
CG: 32 DR: 73
D
Stephane Lievre
CG: 21 DR: 65
M
Julien Cardy
CG: 20 SD: -20
M
Issou Malia Dao
CG: 29 SD: -21
M
Florent Balmont
CG: 30 SD: -36
M
Nabil Taider
CG: 20 SD: -36
F
Cedric Faure
CG: 21 SR: 264
F
Lucio Fernandao
CG: 14 SR: 414

SQUAD APPEARANCES

Match	1	2	3	4	5	6	7	8	9	10	11	12	13	14	15	16	17	18	19	20	21	22	23	24	25	26	27	28	29	30	31	32	33	34	35	36	37	38
Venue	H	A	H	A	H	A	H	A	H	A	A	H	A	H	A	H	A	H	A	H	A	H	A	H	A	H	A	H	H	A	H	A	H	A	H	A	H	A
Competition	L	L	L	L	L	L	L	L	L	L	L	L	L	L	L	L	L	L	L	L	L	L	L	L	L	L	L	L	L	L	L	L	L	L	L	L	L	L
Result	D	L	L	D	L	L	W	L	D	W	L	L	L	D	L	L	D	D	L	W	W	L	L	L	W	D	W	W	D	L	D	L	W	D	L	D	W	D
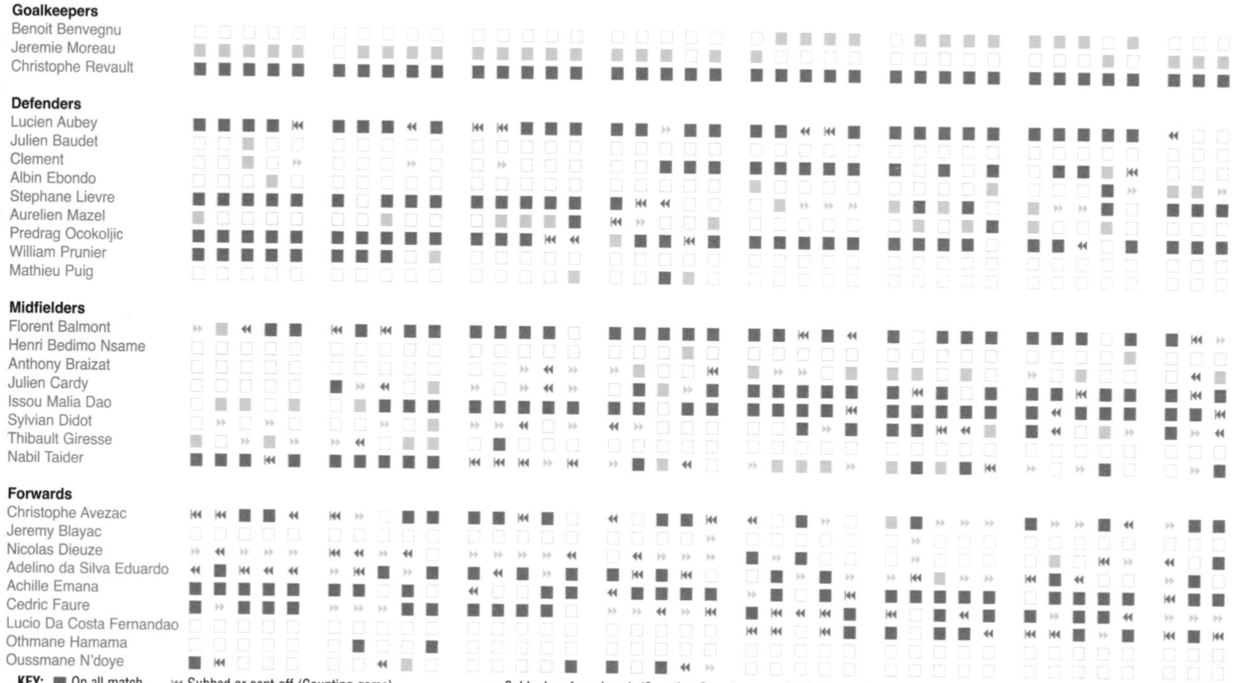 **Goalkeepers**																																						
Benoit Benvegnu																																						
Jeremie Moreau																																						
Christophe Revault																																						
Defenders																																						
Lucien Aubey																																						
Julien Baudet																																						
Clement																																						
Albin Ebondo																																						
Stephane Lievre																																						
Aurelien Mazel																																						
Predrag Ocokoljic																																						
William Prunier																																						
Mathieu Puig																																						
Midfielders																																						
Florent Balmont																																						
Henri Bedimo Nsame																																						
Anthony Braizat																																						
Julien Cardy																																						
Issou Malia Dao																																						
Sylvian Didot																																						
Thibault Giresse																																						
Nabil Taider																																						
Forwards																																						
Christophe Avezac																																						
Jeremy Blayac																																						
Nicolas Dieuze																																						
Adelino da Silva Eduardo																																						
Achille Emana																																						
Cedric Faure																																						
Lucio Da Costa Fernandao																																						
Othmane Hamama																																						
Oussmane N'doye																																						

KEY: ■ On all match | ■ On bench | ⏮ Subbed or sent off (Counting game) | ⏪ Subbed or sent off (playing less than 70 minutes) | ⏩ Subbed on from bench (Counting Game) | ⏩ Subbed on (playing less than 70 minutes) | ⏩ Subbed on and then subbed or sent off (Counting Game) | ⏩ Subbed on and then subbed or sent off (playing less than 70 minutes) | □ Not in 16

BASTIA

Final Position: **17th**

KEY: Won Drawn Lost

						Scorers	Attendance
1	lge	Paris SG	A	D	0-0		43,500
2	lge	Metz	H	L	0-2		6,000
3	lge	Monaco	A	L	0-2		11,000
4	lge	Montpellier	H	W	1-0	Maurice 88	9,000
5	lge	Toulouse	A	W	2-0	Maurice 34; Ben Saada 39	14,052
6	lge	Guingamp	H	W	4-2	Diarra 15; Ben Saada 37; Nee 51,86	8,000
7	lge	Auxerre	A	L	1-4	Diarra 29	8,000
8	lge	Sochaux	H	W	2-0	Hadji 7; Flachez 20 og	6,000
9	lge	Marseille	A	L	1-3	Nee 49	52,923
10	lge	Lens	H	W	3-1	Saveljic 8; Hadji 24; Nee 48	10,000
11	lge	Le Mans	A	D	1-1	Maurice 19	10,000
12	lge	AC Ajaccio	H	D	1-1	Maurice 45	8,000
13	lge	Nice	A	L	0-2		10,000
14	lge	Nantes	H	L	1-3	Chimbonda 5	5,488
15	lge	Bordeaux	A	D	1-1	Hadji 90	20,378
16	lge	Rennes	H	W	3-2	Maurice 34; Cauet 61; Hadji 80	3,500
17	lge	Strasbourg	A	L	2-4	Hadji 39,70	11,000
18	lge	Lyon	H	D	0-0		5,500
19	lge	Lille	H	L	0-2		4,921
20	lge	Metz	A	L	0-1		12,428
21	lge	Monaco	H	D	0-0		6,068
22	lge	Montpellier	A	D	1-1	Cauet 63	13,799
23	lge	Toulouse	H	W	1-0	Ogbeche 29	5,320
24	lge	Guingamp	A	L	0-1		13,000
25	lge	Auxerre	H	D	0-0		5,500
26	lge	Sochaux	A	L	1-2	Maurice 51 pen	12,000
27	lge	Marseille	H	W	4-1	Maurice 21; Diarra 27; Ben Saada 49; Ogbeche 55	7,000
28	lge	Lens	A	D	0-0		35,000
29	lge	Le Mans	H	D	0-0		5,565
30	lge	AC Ajaccio	A	L	0-1		4,500
31	lge	Nice	H	W	2-1	Diarra 27; Maurice 36	5,500
32	lge	Nantes	A	D	1-1	Gourvennec 79	24,569
33	lge	Bordeaux	H	L	0-2		3,000
34	lge	Rennes	A	L	0-4		20,634
35	lge	Strasbourg	H	D	0-0		3,000
36	lge	Lyon	A	L	0-1		38,723
37	lge	Lille	A	L	0-2		15,000
38	lge	Paris SG	H	L	0-1		7,500

MONTHLY POINTS TALLY

Month	Points	%
AUGUST	7	47%
SEPTEMBER	6	67%
OCTOBER	4	44%
NOVEMBER	2	17%
DECEMBER	4	33%
JANUARY	2	22%
FEBRUARY	4	33%
MARCH	5	42%
APRIL	4	44%
MAY	1	7%

KEY PLAYERS - GOALSCORERS

Youssouf Hadji

Goals in the League	6	Player Strike Rate Average number of minutes between League goals scored by player	346
Contribution to Attacking Power Average number of minutes between League team goals while on pitch	129	Club Strike Rate Average number of minutes between League goals scored by club	104

	PLAYER	LGE GOALS	POWER	STRIKE RATE
1	Youssouf Hadji	6	129	346 mins
2	Florian Maurice	8	98	368 mins
3	Frederic Nee	4	75	380 mins
4	Chaouki Ben Saada	3	103	619 mins
5	Alou Diarra	4	99	693 mins

KEY PLAYERS - MIDFIELDERS

Sebastien Piocelle

Goals in the League	0	Contribution to Attacking Power Average number of minutes between League team goals while on pitch	81
Defensive Rating Average number of mins between League goals conceded while he was on the pitch	64	Scoring Difference Defensive Rating minus Contribution to Attacking Power	-17

	PLAYER	LGE GOALS	DEF RATE	POWER	SCORE DIFF
1	Sebastien Piocelle	0	64	81	-17 mins
2	Laurent Battles	0	103	120	-17 mins
3	Benoit Cauet	2	84	106	-22 mins
4	Frederic Mendy	0	78	142	-64 mins

KEY PLAYERS - DEFENDERS

Anthar Yahia

Goals Conceded (GC) The number of League goals conceded while he was on the pitch	18	Clean Sheets In games when he played at least 70 minutes	6
Defensive Rating Ave number of mins between League goals conceded while on the pitch	89	Club Defensive Rating Average number of mins between League goals conceded by the club this season	70

	PLAYER	CON LGE	CLEAN SHEETS	DEF RATE
1	Anthar Yahia	18	6	89 mins
2	Greg Vanney	16	6	84 mins
3	Da Silva Hilton	15	4	83 mins
4	Pascal Chimbonda	41	8	64 mins
5	Alou Diarra	44	7	63 mins

KEY GOALKEEPER

Nicolas Penneteau

Goals Conceded in the League	48	Counting Games Games when he played at least 70 mins	37
Defensive Rating Ave number of mins between League goals conceded while on the pitch	69	Clean Sheets In games when he played at least 70 mins	11

LEAGUE GOALS

Florian Maurice

Minutes on the pitch	2946	Goals in the League	8
League average (mins between goals)	368		

	PLAYER	MINS	GOALS	AVE
1	Maurice	2946	8	368
2	Hadji	2075	6	346
3	Nee	1518	4	380
4	Diarra	2772	4	693
5	Ben Saada	1857	3	619
6	Cauet	2442	2	1221
7	Ogbeche	1146	2	573
8	Saveljic	1530	1	1530
9	Gourvennec	953	1	953
10	Chimbonda	2622	1	2622
	Other		1	
	TOTAL		33	

DISCIPLINARY RECORDS

	PLAYER	YELLOW	RED	AVE
1	Cauet	14	2	152
2	Ferreira	3	1	182
3	Saveljic	8	0	191
4	Gourvennec	4	0	238
5	Uras	8	2	244
6	Diarra	10	0	277
7	Mendy	5	0	312
8	Battles	5	0	326
9	Yahia	4	0	398
10	Hadji	5	0	415
11	Delaye	1	1	531
12	Ben Saada	3	0	619
13	Hilton	1	1	622
	Other	16	0	
	TOTAL	87	7	

TOP POINT EARNERS

	PLAYER	GAMES	AV PTS
1	Piocelle	13	1.38
2	Vanney	14	1.36
3	Nee	13	1.31
4	Battles	19	1.26
5	Cauet	24	1.21
6	Ben Saada	15	1.20
7	Maurice	31	1.13
8	Chimbonda	28	1.07
9	Yahia	16	1.06
10	Penneteau	37	1.05
	CLUB AVERAGE:		**1.03**

TEAM OF THE SEASON

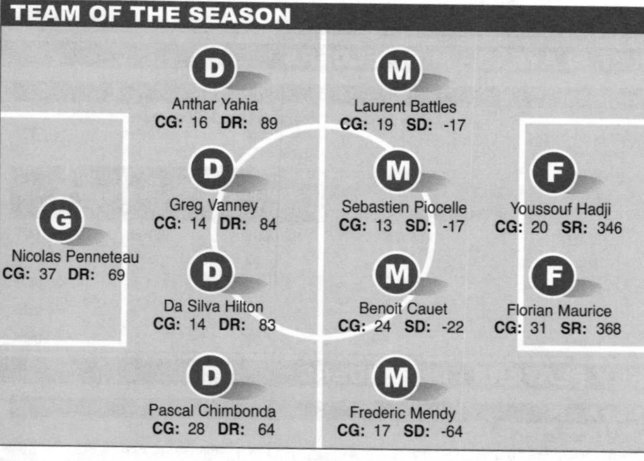
G
Nicolas Penneteau
CG: 37 DR: 69
D
Anthar Yahia
CG: 16 DR: 89
D
Greg Vanney
CG: 14 DR: 84
D
Da Silva Hilton
CG: 14 DR: 83
D
Pascal Chimbonda
CG: 28 DR: 64
M
Laurent Battles
CG: 19 SD: -17
M
Sebastien Piocelle
CG: 13 SD: -17
M
Benoit Cauet
CG: 24 SD: -22
M
Frederic Mendy
CG: 17 SD: -64
F
Youssouf Hadji
CG: 20 SR: 346
F
Florian Maurice
CG: 31 SR: 368

LEAGUE APPEARANCES, BOOKINGS AND CAPS

	AGE (on 01/07/04)	IN NAMED 16	APPEARANCES	COUNTING GAMES	MINUTES ON PITCH	YELLOW CARDS	RED CARDS	THIS SEASON	HOME COUNTRY
Goalkeepers									
Angelo Hugues	37	28	0	0	0	0	0	-	France
Nicolas Penneteau	23	37	37	37	3330	1	0	-	France
Julien Vanni	18	1	1	1	90	0	0	-	France
Daniel Yeboah	19	7	0	0	0	0	0	-	Ivory Coast
Defenders									
Pascal Chimbonda	25	32	32	28	2622	4	0	-	France
Alou Diarra	22	36	34	29	2772	10	0	-	France
Demetrius Ferreira	30	9	9	8	730	3	1	-	Brazil
Florent Ghisolfi	19	6	0	0	0	0	0	-	France
Da Silva Hilton	26	14	14	14	1244	1	1	-	Brazil
Franck Matingou	24	10	6	4	404	1	0	-	France
Nisa Saveljic	34	17	17	17	1530	8	0	-	Serbia & Montenegro
Patrice Sorbara	18	1	1	1	90	0	0	-	France
Cedric Uras	26	29	29	26	2448	8	2	-	France
Greg Vanney	30	24	16	14	1347	1	0	-	United States
Anthar Yahia	22	25	20	16	1593	4	0	-	France
Midfielders									
Laurent Battles	28	19	19	19	1633	5	0	-	France
Benoit Cauet	35	32	32	24	2442	14	2	-	France
Phillipe Delaye	29	13	13	10	1062	1	1	-	France
Paul Essola	22	9	2	1	103	0	0	-	Cameroon
Jocelyn Gourvennec	32	26	24	5	953	4	0	-	France
Frederic Mendy	30	24	18	17	1564	5	0	-	France
Sebastien Piocelle	25	23	18	13	1288	2	0	-	France
Forwards									
Chaouki Ben Saada	20	34	33	15	1857	3	0	-	France
Samir D'Avesnes	-	13	7	0	113	0	0	-	France
Cyril Eboki-Poh	24	1	0	0	0	0	0	-	France
Herve Guy	-	1	1	1	90	0	0	-	Ivory Coast
Youssouf Hadji	24	29	29	20	2075	5	0	-	Morocco
Kevin Jacmot	20	7	5	1	164	0	0	-	France
Florian Maurice	30	37	37	31	2946	3	0	-	France
Frederic Nee	29	27	27	13	1518	2	0	-	France
Barth Ogbeche	19	15	15	10	1146	1	0	-	Nigeria
Jonathan Tehoue	20	9	7	1	188	1	0	-	France

SQUAD APPEARANCES

Match	1	2	3	4	5	6	7	8	9	10	11	12	13	14	15	16	17	18	19	20	21	22	23	24	25	26	27	28	29	30	31	32	33	34	35	36	37	38
Venue	A	H	A	H	A	H	A	H	A	H	A	H	A	H	A	H	A	H	H	A	H	A	H	A	H	A	H	A	H	A	H	A	H	A	H	A	A	H
Competition	L	L	L	L	L	L	L	L	L	L	L	L	L	L	L	L	L	L	L	L	L	L	L	L	L	L	L	L	L	L	L	L	L	L	L	L	L	L
Result	D	L	L	W	W	W	L	W	L	W	D	D	L	L	D	W	L	D	L	L	D	D	W	L	D	L	W	D	D	L	W	D	L	L	D	L	L	L

Goalkeepers
Angelo Hugues
Nicolas Penneteau
Julien Vanni
Daniel Yeboah

Defenders
Pascal Chimbonda
Alou Diarra
Demetrius Ferreira
Florent Ghisolfi
Da Silva Hilton
Franck Matingou
Nisa Saveljic
Patrice Sorbara
Cedric Uras
Greg Vanney
Anthar Yahia

Midfielders
Laurent Battles
Benoit Cauet
Phillipe Delaye
Paul Essola
Jocelyn Gourvennec
Frederic Mendy
Sebastien Piocelle

Forwards
Chaouki Ben Saada
Samir Bertin D'Avesnes
Cyril Eboki-Poh
Herve Guy
Youssouf Hadji
Kevin Jacmot
Florian Maurice
Frederic Nee
Bartholomew Ogbeche
Jonathan Tehoue

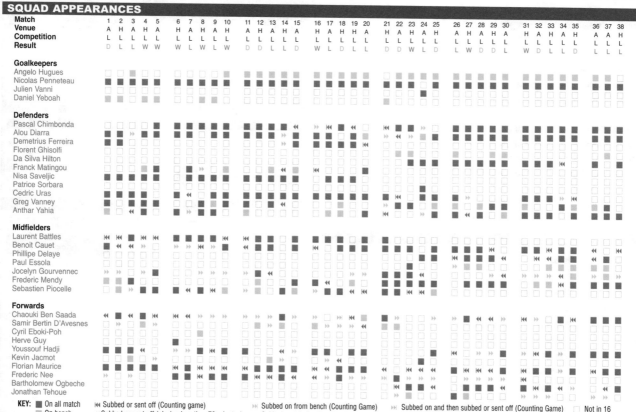

KEY: On all match · On bench · Subbed or sent off (Counting game) · Subbed or sent off (playing less than 70 minutes) · Subbed on from bench (Counting Game) · Subbed on (playing less than 70 minutes) · Subbed on and then subbed or sent off (Counting Game) · Subbed on and then subbed or sent off (playing less than 70 minutes) · Not in 16

GUINGAMP

Final Position: **18th**

KEY: Won Drawn Lost

#		Opponent			Score	Scorers	Attendance
1	lge	**Marseille**	H	L	0-1		18,040
2	lge	**Strasbourg**	A	L	0-2		15,000
3	lge	**Bordeaux**	H	L	1-3	Gousse 23	15,907
4	lge	**Rennes**	A	D	0-0		18,428
5	lge	**Lyon**	H	W	2-0	Dagano 32; Fuentes 38	11,610
6	lge	**Bastia**	A	L	2-4	Gousse 46; Le Roux 65 pen	8,000
7	lge	**Paris SG**	H	L	0-2		14,500
8	lge	**Metz**	A	D	1-1	Le Roux 45	15,603
9	lge	**Monaco**	H	L	1-2	Gousse 53	13,261
10	lge	**Montpellier**	A	L	0-2		9,874
11	lge	**Toulouse**	H	W	1-0	Sikimic 64	12,738
12	lge	**Lille**	A	W	3-1	Bourhani 69,88; Gousse 84	12,151
13	lge	**Auxerre**	A	L	0-3		9,103
14	lge	**Sochaux**	H	L	1-2	Sikimic 77	14,458
15	lge	**Lens**	A	L	1-2	Dagano 88	33,430
16	lge	**AC Ajaccio**	H	W	2-0	Yahia 64; Andre 71	15,314
17	lge	**Le Mans**	A	L	0-2		12,058
18	lge	**Nantes**	H	D	1-1	Bourhani 68	15,069
19	lge	**Nice**	A	L	0-2		10,215
20	lge	**Strasbourg**	H	W	3-2	Dagano 30,34,62	11,791
21	lge	**Bordeaux**	A	L	0-2		18,312
22	lge	**Rennes**	H	L	0-2		15,723
23	lge	**Lyon**	A	W	1-0	Saveljic 90	34,523
24	lge	**Bastia**	H	W	1-0	Shereni 16	13,000
25	lge	**Paris SG**	A	L	0-2		41,000
26	lge	**Monaco**	A	L	1-3	Dagano 18	5,000
27	lge	**Montpellier**	H	W	4-3	Leroy 45,60,78; Tchomogo 54	13,700
28	lge	**Toulouse**	A	D	0-0		19,200
29	lge	**Lille**	H	W	2-1	Camara 12,32	14,240
30	lge	**Auxerre**	H	D	2-2	Dagano 33; Colleau 75	15,774
31	lge	**Sochaux**	A	L	0-2		15,144
32	lge	**Metz**	H	D	1-1	Shereni 23	15,569
33	lge	**Lens**	H	W	1-0	Leroy 5	15,094
34	lge	**AC Ajaccio**	A	D	0-0		2,321
35	lge	**Le Mans**	H	L	2-4	Shereni 66; Leroy 69	15,414
36	lge	**Nantes**	A	D	0-0		28,000
37	lge	**Nice**	H	L	1-2	Dagano 25	16,003
38	lge	**Marseille**	A	L	1-2	Talhaoui 75	43,000

MONTHLY POINTS TALLY

Month	Points	%
AUGUST	4	27%
SEPTEMBER	1	11%
OCTOBER	3	33%
NOVEMBER	3	25%
DECEMBER	4	33%
JANUARY	3	33%
FEBRUARY	6	67%
MARCH	7	58%
APRIL	5	42%
MAY	2	13%

KEY PLAYERS - GOALSCORERS

Bell-Moumouni Dagano

Goals in the League	8	Player Strike Rate Average number of minutes between League goals scored by player	298
Contribution to Attacking Power Average number of minutes between League team goals while on pitch	82	Club Strike Rate Average number of minutes between League goals scored by club	95

	PLAYER	LGE GOALS	POWER	STRIKE RATE
1	Bell-Moumouni Dagano	8	82	298 mins
2	Jerome Leroy	5	80	484 mins
3	Milovan Sikimic	2	79	915 mins
4	Christophe Le Roux	2	106	1115 mins

KEY PLAYERS - MIDFIELDERS

Jerome Leroy

Goals in the League	5	Contribution to Attacking Power Average number of minutes between League team goals while on pitch	81
Defensive Rating Average number of mins between League goals conceded while he was on the pitch	62	Scoring Difference Defensive Rating minus Contribution to Attacking Power	-19

	PLAYER	LGE GOALS	DEF RATE	POWER	SCORE DIFF
1	Jerome Leroy	5	62	81	-19 mins
2	Claude Michel	0	60	99	-39 mins
3	Christophe Le Roux	2	62	106	-44 mins
4	Fabrice Colleau	1	70	150	-80 mins

KEY PLAYERS - DEFENDERS

Blaise Kouassi

Goals Conceded (GC) The number of League goals conceded while he was on the pitch	47	Clean Sheets In games when he played at least 70 minutes	10
Defensive Rating Ave number of mins between League goals conceded while on the pitch	65	Club Defensive Rating Average number of mins between League goals conceded by the club this season	59

	PLAYER	CON LGE	CLEAN SHEETS	DEF RATE
1	Blaise Kouassi	47	10	65 mins
2	Auriol Guillaume	20	4	62 mins
3	Nicolas Laspalles	41	8	61 mins
4	Romain Ferrier	21	3	59 mins
5	Milovan Sikimic	33	5	55 mins

KEY GOALKEEPER

Ronan Le Crom

Goals Conceded in the League	58	Counting Games Games when he played at least 70 mins	38
Defensive Rating Ave number of mins between League goals conceded while on the pitch	59	Clean Sheets In games when he played at least 70 mins	10

LEAGUE GOALS

Bell-Moumouni Dagano

Minutes on the pitch	2386	Goals in the League	8
League average (mins between goals)	298		

	PLAYER	MINS	GOALS	AVE
1	Dagano	2386	8	298
2	Leroy	2421	5	484
3	Gousse	1322	4	331
4	Bourhani	979	3	326
5	Shereni	1241	3	414
6	Camara	803	2	402
7	Sikimic	1830	2	915
8	Le Roux	2229	2	1115
9	Saveljic	1530	1	1530
10	Fuentes	1027	1	1027
11	Colleau	1197	1	1197
12	Yahia	949	1	949
	Other		3	
	TOTAL		36	

DISCIPLINARY RECORDS

	PLAYER	YELLOW	RED	AVE
1	Guillaume	5	1	206
2	Laspalles	10	0	248
3	Kouassi	11	1	253
4	Cabanas	3	0	289
5	Fuentes	3	0	342
6	Saveljic	4	0	382
7	Leroy	6	0	403
8	Shereni	3	0	413
9	Yahia	2	0	474
10	Bourhani	2	0	489
11	Carnot	1	0	606
12	Sikimic	3	0	610
13	Le Roux	3	0	743
	Other	13	0	
	TOTAL	69	2	

TOP POINT EARNERS

	PLAYER	GAMES	AV PTS
1	Dagano	24	1.21
2	Leroy	26	1.19
3	Le Roux	24	1.17
4	Kouassi	34	1.12
5	Saveljic	17	1.12
6	Ferrier	13	1.08
7	Sikimic	18	1.06
8	Guillaume	13	1.00
9	Le Crom	38	1.00
10	Laspalles	26	0.96
	CLUB AVERAGE:		**1.00**

TEAM OF THE SEASON

G Ronan Le Crom CG: 38 DR: 59

D Blaise Kouassi CG: 34 DR: 65
D Auriol Guillaume CG: 13 DR: 62
D Nicolas Laspalles CG: 26 DR: 61
D Romain Ferrier CG: 13 DR: 59

M Jerome Leroy CG: 26 SD: -19
M Claude Michel CG: 32 SD: -39
M Christophe Le Roux CG: 24 SD: -44
M Fabrice Colleau CG: 13 SD: -80

F Bell-M'uni Dagano CG: 24 SR: 298
F Pierre-Yves Andre CG: 25 SR: 2317

LEAGUE APPEARANCES, BOOKINGS AND CAPS

	AGE (on 01/07/04)	IN NAMED 16	APPEARANCES	COUNTING GAMES	MINUTES ON PITCH	YELLOW CARDS	RED CARDS	THIS SEASON	HOME COUNTRY
Goalkeepers									
Guillaume Gauclin	23	18	0	0	0	0	0	-	France
Ronan Le Crom	29	38	38	38	3420	0	0	-	France
Eric Loussouarn	29	6	0	0	0	0	0	-	France
Clement Rigaud	19	14	0	0	0	0	0	-	France
Defenders									
Romain Ferrier	28	19	16	13	1246	0	0	-	France
Fabricio Fuentes	27	13	12	11	1027	3	0	-	Argentina
Auriol Guillaume	24	19	16	13	1236	5	1	-	France
Steve Joseph-Reinette	20	11	7	3	406	2	0	-	France
Blaise Kouassi	29	34	34	34	3041	11	1	-	France
Nicolas Laspalles	32	32	31	26	2483	10	0	-	France
Nisa Saveljic	34	17	17	17	1530	4	0	-	Serbia & Montenegro
Milovan Sikimic	23	32	25	18	1830	3	0	-	Serbia & Montenegro
Benjamin Tholmer	2005	1	1	0	23	0	0	-	France
Alledine Yahia	22	20	14	10	949	2	0	-	France
Midfielders									
Lionel Bah	24	5	5	2	223	0	0	-	France
Ricardo Cabanas	25	17	17	5	867	3	0	-	Switzerland
Stephane Carnot	31	16	13	3	606	1	0	-	France
Fabrice Colleau	27	20	18	13	1197	1	0	-	France
Yann Jouffre	19	8	5	0	91	0	0	-	France
J-B Le Bescond	24	3	1	0	2	0	0	-	France
Christophe Le Roux	35	28	27	24	2229	3	0	-	France
Jerome Leroy	29	28	28	26	2421	6	0	-	France
Claude Michel	33	33	33	32	2868	2	0	-	France
Yohan Riviere	19	4	2	0	77	1	0	-	France
Harlington Shereni	29	15	15	12	1241	3	0	-	Zimbabwe
Guillame Stephan	21	1	0	0	0	0	0	-	France
Farid Talhaoui	22	7	4	1	166	0	0	-	France
Forwards									
Pierre-Yves Andre	30	34	34	25	2317	3	0	-	France
Cedric Bardon	27	8	6	1	188	0	0	-	France
Kemal Bourhani	22	22	19	8	979	2	0	-	France
Souleymane Camara	21	13	13	6	803	1	0	1	Senegal (31)
Bell-M'uni Dagano	23	32	31	24	2386	2	0	-	Burkina Faso
Nicolas Gousse	28	24	21	12	1322	1	0	-	France
Oumar Tchomogo	26	15	12	0	324	0	0	-	Benin

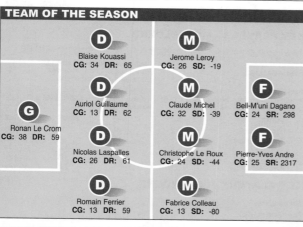

SQUAD APPEARANCES

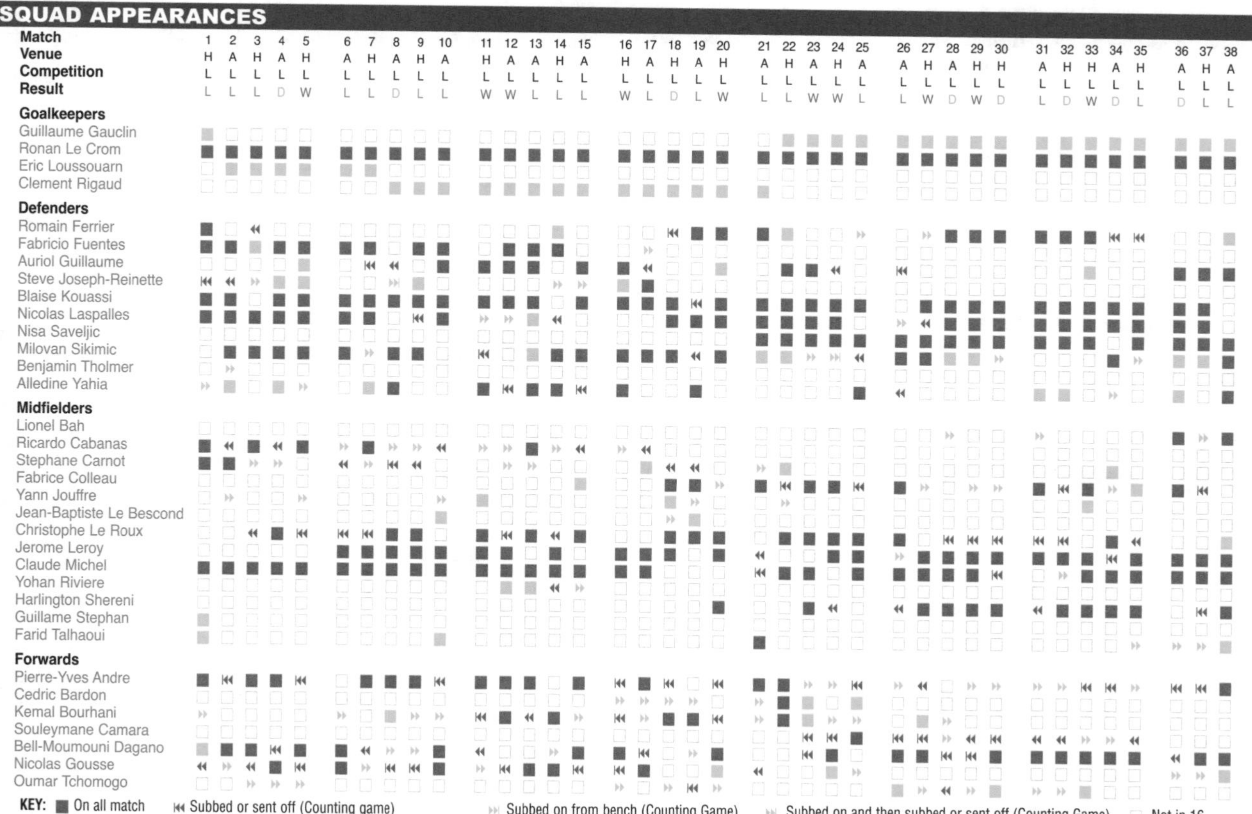
Match 1 2 3 4 5 6 7 8 9 10 11 12 13 14 15 16 17 18 19 20 21 22 23 24 25 26 27 28 29 30 31 32 33 34 35 36 37 38
Venue H A H A H A H A H A H A A H A H A H A H A H A H A A H A H H A H H A H A H A
Competition L L L L L L L L L L L L L L L L L L L L L L L L L L L L L L L L L L L L L L
Result L L L D W L L D L L W W L L L W L D L W L L W W L L W D W D L D W D L D L L
Goalkeepers
Guillaume Gauclin
Ronan Le Crom
Eric Loussouarn
Clement Rigaud
Defenders
Romain Ferrier
Fabricio Fuentes
Auriol Guillaume
Steve Joseph-Reinette
Blaise Kouassi
Nicolas Laspalles
Nisa Saveljic
Milovan Sikimic
Benjamin Tholmer
Alledine Yahia
Midfielders
Lionel Bah
Ricardo Cabanas
Stephane Carnot
Fabrice Colleau
Yann Jouffre
Jean-Baptiste Le Bescond
Christophe Le Roux
Jerome Leroy
Claude Michel
Yohan Riviere
Harlington Shereni
Guillame Stephan
Farid Talhaoui
Forwards
Pierre-Yves Andre
Cedric Bardon
Kemal Bourhani
Souleymane Camara
Bell-Moumouni Dagano
Nicolas Gousse
Oumar Tchomogo
KEY: On all match
On bench
Subbed or sent off (Counting game)
Subbed or sent off (playing less than 70 minutes)
Subbed on from bench (Counting Game)
Subbed on (playing less than 70 minutes)
Subbed on and then subbed or sent off (Counting Game)
Subbed on and then subbed or sent off (playing less than 70 minutes)
Not in 16

LE MANS

Final Position: **19th**

KEY: Won Drawn Lost

						Attendance
1	lge	Lens	A	D	0-0		36,500
2	lge	AC Ajaccio	H	L	0-1		13,500
3	lge	Nice	H	D	1-1	D'Amico 22	12,127
4	lge	Nantes	A	L	0-1		33,000
5	lge	Strasbourg	H	L	0-3		11,711
6	lge	Marseille	A	L	0-5		54,445
7	lge	Lyon	H	L	0-2		12,000
8	lge	Rennes	A	L	0-2		15,245
9	lge	Bordeaux	H	D	0-0		14,127
10	lge	Paris SG	A	L	1-5	Molefe 12	41,409
11	lge	Bastia	H	D	1-1	Hautcoeur 18	10,000
12	lge	Monaco	A	L	2-4	Cousin 8; Peyrelade 10	4,000
13	lge	Metz	H	W	2-0	Peyrelade 33; Cousin 80	10,786
14	lge	Toulouse	A	D	1-1	Cousin 44	14,519
15	lge	Montpellier	H	W	4-0	Pancrate 12; Peyrelade 24; Cousin 29; Fanchone 85	10,480
16	lge	Auxerre	A	L	0-1		9,000
17	lge	Guingamp	H	W	2-0	Cousin 33; Celdran 77	12,058
18	lge	Lille	A	D	1-1	Fischer 41	11,994
19	lge	Sochaux	H	D	2-2	Cousin 27,56	12,579
20	lge	AC Ajaccio	A	L	0-2		2,135
21	lge	Nice	A	W	1-0	Cousin 40	11,261
22	lge	Nantes	H	L	0-1		14,121
23	lge	Strasbourg	A	L	0-3		12,327
24	lge	Marseille	H	D	0-0		16,000
25	lge	Lyon	A	L	0-2		32,000
26	lge	Rennes	H	D	2-2	Peyrelade 41,77	16,000
27	lge	Bordeaux	A	L	0-2		18,000
28	lge	Paris SG	H	L	0-1		15,000
29	lge	Bastia	A	D	0-0		5,565
30	lge	Monaco	H	L	0-1		14,440
31	lge	Metz	A	L	0-5		13,802
32	lge	Toulouse	H	W	2-1	Dao 12 og; Pancrate 55	11,071
33	lge	Montpellier	A	W	3-0	D'Amico 16; Cousin 29; Pancrate 32	11,165
34	lge	Auxerre	H	W	2-1	Boumsong 5 og; Cousin 30	14,000
35	lge	Guingamp	A	W	4-2	Cousin 18; Pancrate 25; Eggen 57; Hautcoeur 90	15,414
36	lge	Lille	H	D	1-1	Fanchone 43 pen	14,072
37	lge	Sochaux	A	L	0-3		17,387
38	lge	Lens	H	W	3-0	Bonnart 19; Thomas, F 53; Pancrate 71	14,000

MONTHLY POINTS TALLY

AUGUST	2	13%
SEPTEMBER	0	0%
OCTOBER	2	22%
NOVEMBER	7	58%
DECEMBER	5	42%
JANUARY	3	33%
FEBRUARY	2	17%
MARCH	1	8%
APRIL	6	67%
MAY	10	67%

KEY PLAYERS - GOALSCORERS

Daniel Cousin

Goals in the League	11	Player Strike Rate Average number of minutes between League goals scored by player	248
Contribution to Attacking Power Average number of minutes between League team goals while on pitch	87	**Club Strike Rate** Average number of minutes between League goals scored by club	98

	PLAYER	LGE GOALS	POWER	STRIKE RATE
1	Daniel Cousin	11	87	248 mins
2	Laurent Peyrelade	5	75	407 mins
3	Fabrice Pancrate	5	75	423 mins
4	James Fanchone	2	224	897 mins
5	Fernando D'Amico	2	146	949 mins

KEY PLAYERS - MIDFIELDERS

Yohan Hautcoeur

Goals in the League	2	**Contribution to Attacking Power** Average number of minutes between League team goals while on pitch	79
Defensive Rating Average number of mins between League goals conceded while he was on the pitch	64	Scoring Difference Defensive Rating minus Contribution to Attacking Power	-15

	PLAYER	LGE GOALS	DEF RATE	POWER	SCORE DIFF
1	Yohan Hautcoeur	2	64	79	-15 mins
2	Frederic Thomas	1	66	91	-25 mins
3	Periatambee	0	55	102	-47 mins
4	Yannick Fischer	1	60	111	-51 mins
5	Fernando D'Amico	2	51	146	-95 mins

KEY PLAYERS - DEFENDERS

Laurent Bonnart

Goals Conceded (GC) The number of League goals conceded while he was on the pitch	33	**Clean Sheets** In games when he played at least 70 minutes	7
Defensive Rating Ave number of mins between League goals conceded while on the pitch	69	**Club Defensive Rating** Average number of mins between League goals conceded by the club this season	60

	PLAYER	CON LGE	CLEAN SHEETS	DEF RATE
1	Laurent Bonnart	33	7	69 mins
2	Dan Eggen	22	4	65 mins
3	Yohann Poulard	20	4	63 mins
4	Olivier Thomas	44	6	56 mins
5	Thabang Molefe	31	6	55 mins

KEY GOALKEEPER

Jean-Francois Bedenik

Goals Conceded in the League	44	**Counting Games** Games when he played at least 70 mins	28
Defensive Rating Ave number of mins between League goals conceded while on the pitch	57	**Clean Sheets** In games when he played at least 70 mins	7

LEAGUE GOALS

Daniel Cousin

Minutes on the pitch	2726	Goals in the League	11
League average (mins between goals)	248		

	PLAYER	MINS	GOALS	AVE
1	Cousin	2726	11	248
2	Pancrate	2116	5	423
3	Peyrelade	2036	5	407
4	Fanchone	1794	2	897
5	Hautcoeur	2292	2	1146
6	D'Amico	1898	2	949
7	Bonnart	2282	1	2282
8	Thomas, F	3099	1	3099
9	Molefe	1702	1	1702
10	Fischer	2216	1	2216
11	Celdran	1700	1	1700
12	Eggen	1439	1	1439
	Other		2	
	TOTAL		35	

DISCIPLINARY RECORDS

	PLAYER	YELLOW	RED	AVE
1	D'Amico	10	0	189
2	Molefe	8	1	189
3	Domoraud	3	0	248
4	Periatambee	5	0	327
5	Capron	3	0	405
6	Fischer	5	0	443
7	Cousin	4	1	545
8	Thomas, O	4	0	618
9	Peyrelade	3	0	678
10	Eggen	2	0	719
11	Hautcoeur	3	0	764
12	Poulard	1	0	1260
13	Thomas, F	1	1	1549
	Other	6	0	
	TOTAL	58	3	

TOP POINT EARNERS

	PLAYER	GAMES	AV PTS
1	Pancrate	18	1.67
2	Hautcoeur	22	1.41
3	Poulard	14	1.36
4	Eggen	16	1.31
5	Peyrelade	18	1.28
6	Thomas, O	24	1.21
7	Cousin	29	1.14
8	Thomas, F	34	1.09
9	Bonnart	25	1.04
10	Celdran	17	1.00
	CLUB AVERAGE:		**1.00**

LEAGUE APPEARANCES, BOOKINGS AND CAPS

	AGE (on 01/07/04)	IN NAMED 16	APPEARANCES	COUNTING GAMES	MINUTES ON PITCH	YELLOW CARDS	RED CARDS	THIS SEASON	HOME COUNTRY
Goalkeepers									
Jean-Fr'cois Bedenik	25	35	28	28	2520	0	0	-	France
Vincent Demarconnay	21	10	0	0	0	0	0	-	France
Yohann Pele	21	29	10	10	900	0	0	-	France
Defenders									
Laurent Bonnart	24	26	26	25	2282	1	0	-	France
Eddy Capron	33	18	17	12	1217	3	0	-	France
J-J Domoraud	23	13	11	8	744	3	0	-	Ivory Coast
Dan Eggen	34	22	21	16	1439	2	0	-	Norway
Ulick Lupede	20	4	3	2	185	0	0	-	France
Thabang Molefe	25	21	21	17	1702	8	1	-	South Africa
Yohann Poulard	28	16	14	14	1260	1	0	-	France
Olivier Thomas	29	37	34	24	2472	4	0	-	France
Midfielders									
Sekou Baradji	20	4	2	2	180	0	0	-	Argentina
Fernando D'Amico	29	25	24	19	1898	10	0	-	Argentina
Jerome Drouin	26	6	5	4	397	2	0	-	France
Yannick Fischer	29	30	28	23	2216	5	0	-	France
Yohan Hautcoeur	22	35	32	22	2292	3	0	-	France
Cedric Liabeuf	24	20	12	4	441	0	0	-	France
Periatambee	28	32	31	15	1636	5	0	-	Mauritius
Frederic Thomas	23	36	36	34	3099	1	1	-	France
Forwards									
Philippe Celdran	30	29	28	17	1700	1	0	-	France
Daniel Cousin	27	33	33	29	2726	4	1	-	Gabon
James Fanchone	24	28	27	16	1794	1	0	-	France
Fabrice Pancrate	24	38	36	18	2116	1	0	-	France
Laurent Peyrelade	34	35	34	18	2036	3	0	-	France
Sergiu Radu	26	19	12	0	270	0	0	-	Romania
Yannick Yenga	19	3	1	0	26	0	0	-	France

TEAM OF THE SEASON

- G — Jean-Fr'cois Bedenik — CG: 28 DR: 57
- D — Laurent Bonnart — CG: 25 DR: 69
- D — Dan Eggen — CG: 16 DR: 65
- D — Yohann Poulard — CG: 14 DR: 63
- D — Olivier Thomas — CG: 24 DR: 56
- M — Yohan Hautcoeur — CG: 22 SD: -15
- M — Frederic Thomas — CG: 34 SD: -25
- M — Periatambee — CG: 15 SD: -47
- M — Yannick Fischer — CG: 23 SD: -51
- F — Daniel Cousin — CG: 29 SR: 248
- F — Laurent Peyrelade — CG: 18 SR: 407

SQUAD APPEARANCES

Match	1	2	3	4	5	6	7	8	9	10	11	12	13	14	15	16	17	18	19	20	21	22	23	24	25	26	27	28	29	30	31	32	33	34	35	36	37	38
Venue	A	H	H	A	H	A	H	A	H	A	H	A	H	A	H	A	H	A	H	A	A	H	A	H	A	H	A	H	A	H	A	H	A	H	A	H	A	H
Competition	L	L	L	L	L	L	L	L	L	L	L	L	L	L	L	L	L	L	L	L	L	L	L	L	L	L	L	L	L	L	L	L	L	L	L	L	L	L
Result	D	L	D	L	L	L	L	L	D	L	D	L	W	D	W	L	W	D	D	L	W	L	L	D	L	D	L	L	D	L	L	W	W	W	W	D	L	W

Goalkeepers
Jean-Francois Bedenik
Vincent Demarconnay
Yohann Pele

Defenders
Laurent Bonnart
Eddy Capron
Jean-Jacques Domoraud
Dan Eggen
Ulick Lupede
Thabang Molefe
Yohann Poulard
Olivier Thomas

Midfielders
Sekou Baradji
Fernando D'Amico
Jerome Drouin
Yannick Fischer
Yohan Hautcoeur
Cedric Liabeuf
Periatambee
Frederic Thomas

Forwards
Philippe Celdran
Daniel Cousin
James Fanchone
Fabrice Pancrate
Laurent Peyrelade
Sergiu Radu
Yannick Yenga

KEY: ■ On all match ■ On bench | ⏮ Subbed or sent off (Counting game) ◀◀ Subbed or sent off (playing less than 70 minutes) | ⏭ Subbed on from bench (Counting Game) ▶▶ Subbed on (playing less than 70 minutes) | ⏭ Subbed on and then subbed or sent off (Counting Game) ▶▶ Subbed on and then subbed or sent off (playing less than 70 minutes) | □ Not in 16

MONTPELLIER

Final Position: **20th**

KEY: Won Drawn Lost

							Attendance
1	lge	**Rennes**	H	D	1-1	Mansare 88 pen	20,418
2	lge	**Bordeaux**	A	W	1-0	Bamago 46	24,876
3	lge	**Lyon**	H	L	0-2		20,850
4	lge	**Bastia**	A	L	0-1		9,000
5	lge	**Paris SG**	H	W	3-2	Bamago 58,68; Rui Pataca 84	13,893
6	lge	**Metz**	A	L	1-2	Bamago 61	15,000
7	lge	**Monaco**	H	L	1-2	Laigle 26	13,870
8	lge	**Lille**	A	D	1-1	Carotti 88	20,000
9	lge	**Toulouse**	A	D	2-2	Bamago 42 pen,58	
10	lge	**Guingamp**	H	W	2-0	Rui Pataca 2,65	9,874
11	lge	**Auxerre**	A	W	1-0	Rouviere 40	7,000
12	lge	**Nantes**	H	W	4-1	Rui Pataca 10,19; Assoumani 31; Bamago 80	10,641
13	lge	**Lens**	A	L	2-3	Carotti 9; Rouviere 14	34,301
14	lge	**AC Ajaccio**	H	W	3-1	Bamago 28; Rui Pataca 78,86	11,542
15	lge	**Le Mans**	A	L	0-4		10,480
16	lge	**Nice**	A	L	1-2	Bamago 86	10,422
17	lge	**Strasbourg**	A	L	2-4	Carotti 27; Lafourcade 38	11,643
18	lge	**Bordeaux**	H	L	1-2	Rui Pataca 55	10,436
19	lge	**Lyon**	A	L	0-3		32,658
20	lge	**Sochaux**	H	L	1-3	Bamago 20 pen	10,755
21	lge	**Bastia**	H	D	1-1	Bamago 20	13,799
22	lge	**Marseille**	H	L	0-1		21,085
23	lge	**Paris SG**	A	L	1-6	Dzodic 53	38,952
24	lge	**Metz**	H	L	0-1		7,000
25	lge	**Monaco**	A	L	0-4		6,000
26	lge	**Lille**	H	L	0-2		10,000
27	lge	**Toulouse**	H	L	0-1		5,000
28	lge	**Guingamp**	A	L	3-4	Moullec 31; Bamago 45 pen; Lafourcade 88	13,700
29	lge	**Auxerre**	H	W	1-0	Mezague 46 pen	13,179
30	lge	**Nantes**	A	L	2-3	Delhommeau 2 og; Moullec 58	28,510
31	lge	**Lens**	H	W	1-0	Bamago 31	8,000
32	lge	**AC Ajaccio**	A	D	0-0		4,000
33	lge	**Le Mans**	H	L	0-3		11,165
34	lge	**Sochaux**	A	L	1-3	Bamago 15	16,352
35	lge	**Nice**	H	D	2-2	Bamago 36; Lafourcade 69	8,900
36	lge	**Marseille**	A	D	1-1	Mansare 65	44,000
37	lge	**Strasbourg**	H	L	1-2	Bamago 52 pen	10,000
38	lge	**Rennes**	A	L	0-4		21,309

MONTHLY POINTS TALLY

Month	Points	%
AUGUST	7	47%
SEPTEMBER	1	11%
OCTOBER	7	78%
NOVEMBER	6	50%
DECEMBER	0	0%
JANUARY	1	8%
FEBRUARY	0	0%
MARCH	3	25%
APRIL	4	44%
MAY	2	13%

KEY PLAYERS - GOALSCORERS

Habib Bamago

Goals in the League	16	Player Strike Rate Average number of minutes between League goals scored by player	201
Contribution to Attacking Power Average number of minutes between League team goals while on pitch	82	Club Strike Rate Average number of minutes between League goals scored by club	83

	PLAYER	LGE GOALS	POWER	STRIKE RATE
1	Habib Bamago	16	82	201 mins
2	Carlos Jorge Rui Pataca	8	81	224 mins
3	Bruno Carotti	3	76	760 mins
4	Fode Mansare	2	88	890 mins
5	Jean Christophe Rouviere	2	71	1257 mins

KEY PLAYERS - MIDFIELDERS

Bruno Carotti

Goals in the League	3	Contribution to Attacking Power Average number of minutes between League team goals while on pitch	76
Defensive Rating Average number of mins between League goals conceded while he was on the pitch	53	Scoring Difference Defensive Rating minus Contribution to Attacking Power	-23

	PLAYER	LGE GOALS	DEF RATE	POWER	SCORE DIFF
1	Bruno Carotti	3	53	76	-23 mins
2	Jean Christophe Rouviere	2	47	72	-25 mins
3	Pierre Laigle	1	48	88	-40 mins
4	Guillaume Moullec	2	46	86	-40 mins

KEY PLAYERS - DEFENDERS

Nenad Dzodic

Goals Conceded (GC) The number of League goals conceded while he was on the pitch	38	Clean Sheets In games when he played at least 70 minutes	3
Defensive Rating Ave number of mins between League goals conceded while on the pitch	49	Club Defensive Rating Average number of mins between League goals conceded by the club this season	46

	PLAYER	CON LGE	CLEAN SHEETS	DEF RATE
1	Nenad Dzodic	38	3	49 mins
2	Mansour Assoumani	47	4	46 mins
3	Sebastien Michalowski	42	3	45 mins
4	Theirry Gathuessi	33	2	44 mins

KEY GOALKEEPER

Rudy Riou

Goals Conceded in the League	57	Counting Games Games when he played at least 70 mins	31
Defensive Rating Ave number of mins between League goals conceded while on the pitch	49	Clean Sheets In games when he played at least 70 mins	6

LEAGUE GOALS

Habib Bamago

Minutes on the pitch	3219	Goals in the League	16
League average (mins between goals)	201		

	PLAYER	MINS	GOALS	AVE
1	Bamago	3219	16	201
2	Rui Pataca	1792	8	224
3	Lafourcade	1135	3	378
4	Carotti	2281	3	760
5	Moullec	2651	2	1326
6	Rouviere	2514	2	1257
7	Mansare	1779	2	890
8	Dzodic	1860	1	1860
9	Laigle	1759	1	1759
10	Mezague	1024	1	1024
11	Assoumani	2151	1	2151
	Other		1	
	TOTAL		41	

DISCIPLINARY RECORDS

	PLAYER	YELLOW	RED	AVE
1	Colombo	5	0	159
2	Gathuessi	7	2	161
3	Robert	9	0	180
4	Assoumani	10	1	195
5	Dzodic	7	2	206
6	Blanc	5	0	217
7	Mezague	3	1	256
8	Ramond	2	0	290
9	Mainfroi	3	0	325
10	Carotti	7	0	325
11	Lafourcade	3	0	378
12	Doumeng	3	0	429
13	Rouviere	5	0	502
	Other	17	1	
	TOTAL	86	7	

TOP POINT EARNERS

	PLAYER	GAMES	AV PTS
1	Rouviere	25	1.16
2	Carotti	25	1.04
3	Gathuessi	14	1.00
4	Riou	31	0.94
5	Michalowski	18	0.94
6	Dzodic	18	0.89
7	Rui Pataca	16	0.88
8	Laigle	17	0.88
9	Assoumani	23	0.87
10	Moullec	27	0.85
	CLUB AVERAGE:		0.82

TEAM OF THE SEASON

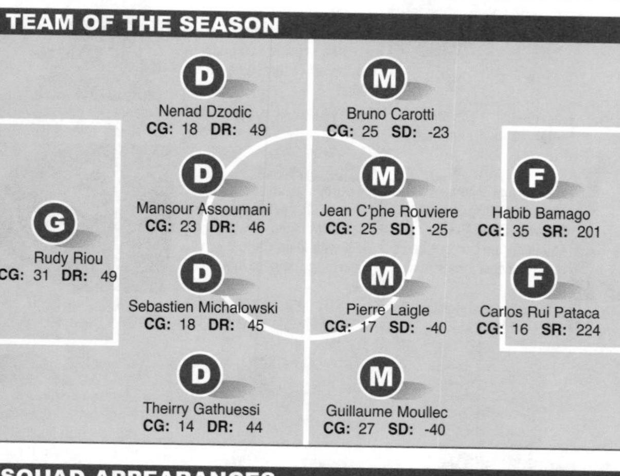

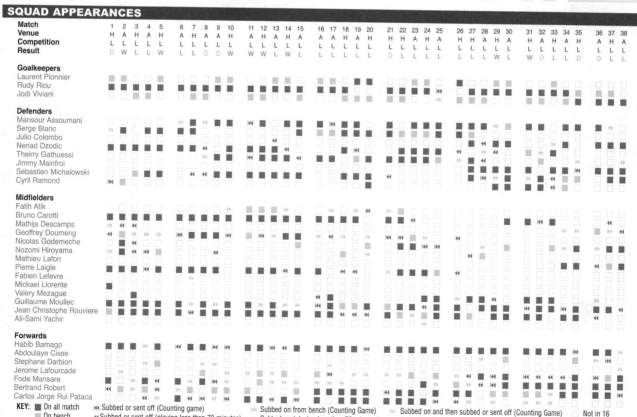

D
Nenad Dzodic
CG: 18 DR: 49
M
Bruno Carotti
CG: 25 SD: -23
D
Mansour Assoumani
CG: 23 DR: 46
M
Jean C'phe Rouviere
CG: 25 SD: -25
F
Habib Bamago
CG: 35 SR: 201
G
Rudy Riou
CG: 31 DR: 49
D
Sebastien Michalowski
CG: 18 DR: 45
M
Pierre Laigle
CG: 17 SD: -40
F
Carlos Rui Pataca
CG: 16 SR: 224
D
Theirry Gathuessi
CG: 14 DR: 44
M
Guillaume Moullec
CG: 27 SD: -40

LEAGUE APPEARANCES, BOOKINGS AND CAPS

	AGE (on 01/07/04)	IN NAMED 16	APPEARANCES	COUNTING GAMES	MINUTES ON PITCH	YELLOW CARDS	RED CARDS	THIS SEASON	HOME COUNTRY
Goalkeepers									
Laurent Pionnier	22	17	3	3	270	0	0	-	France
Rudy Riou	24	34	31	31	2785	1	1	-	France
Jodi Viviani	22	23	5	4	365	0	0	-	France
Defenders									
Mansour Assoumani	21	28	27	23	2151	10	1	-	France
Serge Blanc	31	19	13	12	1085	5	0	-	France
Julio Colombo	20	10	10	7	799	5	0	-	France
Nenad Dzodic	27	25	24	18	1860	7	2	-	Serbia & Montenegro
Theirry Gathuessi	22	23	20	14	1449	7	2	1	Cameroon (12)
Jimmy Mainfroi	-	11	11	11	977	3	0	-	France
Seb Michalowski	26	27	24	18	1871	3	0	-	France
Cyril Ramond	24	9	7	6	580	2	0	-	France
Midfielders									
Fatih Atik	20	10	6	0	178	1	0	-	France
Bruno Carotti	31	27	27	25	2281	7	0	-	France
Mathijs Descamps	21	8	7	0	225	0	0	-	France
Geoffrey Doumeng	23	24	21	10	1287	3	0	-	France
Nicolas Godemeche	20	16	12	8	815	1	0	-	France
Nozomi Hiroyama	27	10	7	2	402	0	0	-	Japan
Mathieu Lafon	-	5	4	3	315	0	0	-	France
Pierre Laigle	33	23	22	17	1759	2	0	-	France
Fabien Lefevre	32	1	1	0	21	0	0	-	France
Mickael Llorente	21	1	1	1	90	0	0	-	France
Valery Mezague	20	13	13	9	1024	3	1	2	Cameroon (12)
Guillaume Moullec	24	37	34	27	2651	3	0	-	France
Jean C'phe Rouviere	29	34	30	25	2514	5	0	-	France
Ali-Sami Yachir	-	1	1	0	16	0	0	-	France
Forwards									
Habib Bamago	22	38	38	35	3219	3	0	-	France
Abdoulaye Cisse	20	5	3	1	93	0	0	-	France
Stephane Darbion	20	6	5	0	38	0	0	-	France
Jerome Lafourcade	21	28	21	8	1135	3	0	-	France
Fode Mansare	22	31	29	16	1779	2	0	-	Guinea
Bertrand Robert	20	32	21	17	1627	9	0	-	France
Carlos Rui Pataca	31	27	27	16	1792	1	0	-	Portugal

SQUAD APPEARANCES

Match	1	2	3	4	5	6	7	8	9	10	11	12	13	14	15	16	17	18	19	20	21	22	23	24	25	26	27	28	29	30	31	32	33	34	35	36	37	38
Venue	H	A	H	A	H	A	H	A	A	H	A	H	A	H	A	A	A	H	A	H	H	H	A	H	A	H	H	A	H	A	H	A	H	A	H	A	H	A
Competition	L	L	L	L	L	L	L	L	L	L	L	L	L	L	L	L	L	L	L	L	L	L	L	L	L	L	L	L	L	L	L	L	L	L	L	L	L	L
Result	D	W	L	L	W	L	L	D	D	W	W	W	L	W	L	L	L	L	L	L	D	L	L	L	L	L	L	L	W	L	W	D	L	L	D	D	L	L

Goalkeepers
Laurent Pionnier
Rudy Riou
Jodi Viviani

Defenders
Mansour Assoumani
Serge Blanc
Julio Colombo
Nenad Dzodic
Theirry Gathuessi
Jimmy Mainfroi
Sebastien Michalowski
Cyril Ramond

Midfielders
Fatih Atik
Bruno Carotti
Mathijs Descamps
Geoffrey Doumeng
Nicolas Godemeche
Nozomi Hiroyama
Mathieu Lafon
Pierre Laigle
Fabien Lefevre
Mickael Llorente
Valery Mezague
Guillaume Moullec
Jean Christophe Rouviere
Ali-Sami Yachir

Forwards
Habib Bamago
Abdoulaye Cisse
Stephane Darbion
Jerome Lafourcade
Fode Mansare
Bertrand Robert
Carlos Jorge Rui Pataca

KEY: ■ On all match ■ On bench
⏮ Subbed or sent off (Counting game)
« Subbed or sent off (playing less than 70 minutes)
⏭ Subbed on from bench (Counting Game)
» Subbed on (playing less than 70 minutes)
⏭ Subbed on and then subbed or sent off (Counting Game)
» Subbed on and then subbed or sent off (playing less than 70 minutes)
□ Not in 16

THE CHAMPIONS LEAGUE

GROUPS

GROUP A
Anderlecht
Bayern Munich
Celtic
Lyon

MATCHDAY 1
Two late goals from Bayern's Roy Makaay see his side overturn an Alan Thompson lead and leave Celtic cursing defensive slip-ups
B Munich 2 Celtic 1
Lyon 1 Anderlecht 0

MATCHDAY 2

Anderlecht 1 B Munich 1
Celtic 2 Lyon 0

MATCHDAY 3
Giovane Elber scores the vital goal against his old club Bayern Munich which makes Lyon favourites to qualify ahead of the Germans
Anderlecht 1 Celtic 0
Lyon 1 B Munich 1

MATCHDAY 4
B Munich 1 Lyon 2
Celtic 3 Anderlecht 1

MATCHDAY 5

Anderlecht 1 Lyon 0
Celtic 0 B Munich 0

MATCHDAY 6
Last-gasp Lyon squeeze past Celtic in a heart-breaking finale with Juninho converting from the spot after a Bobo Balde handball
B Munich 1 Anderlecht 0
Lyon 3 Celtic 2

GROUP B
Arsenal
Dinamo Kiev
Inter Milan
Lokomotiv Moscow

MATCHDAY 1
Julio Cruz and Andy van der Meyde score twice in two minutes as Inter humiliate Arsenal with three before half-time
Arsenal 0 Inter Milan 3
Dinamo 2 Lokomotiv 0

MATCHDAY 2
Inter Milan 2 Dinamo 1
Lokomotiv 0 Arsenal 0

MATCHDAY 3
Dmitri Loskov strikes after only two minutes as Lokomotiv Moscow steam past an Inter side still recovering from the sacking of coach Héctor Cúper
Dinamo 2 Arsenal 1
Lokomotiv 3 Inter Milan 0

MATCHDAY 4
Arsenal 1 Dinamo 0
Inter Milan 1 Lokomotiv 1

MATCHDAY 5
Level at halftime, Arsenal gain complete revenge over Inter with a rampant Thierry Henry leading the line and scoring two goals during a 5-1 thrashing for Milan
Inter Milan 1 Arsenal 5
Lokomotiv 3 Dinamo 2

MATCHDAY 6

Arsenal 2 Lokomotiv 0
Dinamo 1 Inter Milan 1

GROUP C
AEK Athens
Deportivo
Monaco
PSV Eindhoven

MATCHDAY 1

AEK 1 Deportivo 1
PSV 1 Monaco 2

MATCHDAY 2
On loan Fernando Morientes shows his Champions League pedigree with two goals as Monaco trounce AEK hitting four without reply
Deportivo 2 PSV 0
Monaco 4 AEK 0

MATCHDAY 3

AEK 0 PSV 1
Deportivo 1 Monaco 0

MATCHDAY 4
Eleven goal madness as Monaco thump Deportivo 8-3 with Dado Prso equalling the competition's record of four goals in one game
Monaco 8 Deportivo 3
PSV 2 AEK 0

MATCHDAY 5
Deportivo exercise the demons of their eight-goal loss to Monaco, beating AEK with Juan Carlos Valerón prominent in a 3-0 win
Deportivo 3 AEK 0
Monaco 1 PSV 1

MATCHDAY 6

AEK 0 Monaco 0
PSV 3 Deportivo 2

GROUP D
Galatasaray
Juventus
Olympiakos
Real Sociedad

MATCHDAY 1

Juventus 2 Galatasaray 1
Sociedad 1 Olympiakos 0

MATCHDAY 2
Pavel Nedved shows his determination after missing out on last year's final, leading Juvé to overturn OlympiaKos' early lead in Athens
Galatasaray 1 Sociedad 2
Olympiakos 1 Juventus 2

MATCHDAY 3
David Trezeguet and Marco Di Vaio both score twice as Juvé race into a four goal lead in Turin before Real Sociedad reply twice
Galatasaray 1 Olympiakos 0
Juventus 4 Sociedad 2

MATCHDAY 4

Olympiakos 3 Galatasaray 0
Sociedad 0 Juventus 0

MATCHDAY 5

Olympiakos 2 Sociedad 2
Galatasaray 2 Juventus 0

MATCHDAY 6
Enzo Maresca inspires a record-breaking 7-0 win as Juvé sail through against Olympiakos, sharing the goals around
Juventus 7 Olympiakos 0
Sociedad 1 Galatasaray 1

GROUP E
Manchester United
Panathinaikos
Rangers
Stuttgart

MATCHDAY 1
Peter Lovenkrands comes off the bench at halftime to turn the game around for Rangers. He hits a winner against Stuttgart after Christian Nerlinger's equaliser.
Man Utd 5 Panathinaikos 0
Rangers 2 Stuttgart 1

MATCHDAY 2
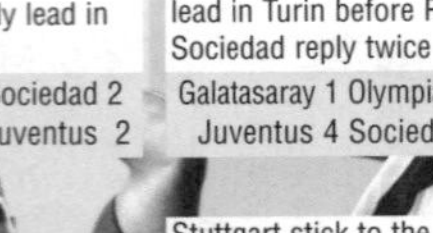
Panathinaikos 1 Rangers 1
Stuttgart 2 Man Utd 1

MATCHDAY 3
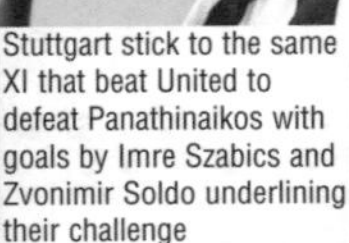
Stuttgart stick to the same XI that beat United to defeat Panathinaikos with goals by Imre Szabics and Zvonimir Soldo underlining their challenge
Rangers 0 Man Utd 1
Stuttgart 2 Panathinaikos 0

MATCHDAY 4
Man Utd 3 Rangers 0
Panathinaikos 1 Stuttgart 3

MATCHDAY 5

Rangers need a win in Germany to progress but Felix Magath out-thinks Alex McLeish for Stuttgart to make it a two-horse race in Group E
Panathinaikos 0 Man Utd 1
Stuttgart 1 Rangers 0

MATCHDAY 6

Man Utd 2 Stuttgart 0
Rangers 1 Panathinaikos 3

GROUP F
Marseille
Partizan Belgrade
Porto
Real Madrid

MATCHDAY 1

Partizan 1 Porto 1
Real Madrid 4 Marseille 2

MATCHDAY 2
UEFA Cup winners Porto are given a reminder of their step up in class as countryman Luis Figo orchestrates Madrid's calm away win
Porto 1 Real Madrid 3
Marseille 3 Partizan 0

MATCHDAY 3
Marseille 2 Porto 3
Real Madrid 1 Partizan 0

MATCHDAY 4
Porto made themselves favourites to qualify with Madrid from Group F with Dmitri Alenichev scoring to beat Marseille
Porto 1 Marseille 0
Partizan 0 Real Madrid 0

MATCHDAY 5

Porto 2 Partizan 1
Marseille 1 Real Madrid 2

MATCHDAY 6
Vital draw sends Porto through in Madrid with Derlei equalising a goal by Argentinean midfielder Santiago Solari for the home side
Partizan 1 Marseille 1
Real Madrid 1 Porto 1

GROUP G
Besiktas
Chelsea
Lazio
Sparta Prague

MATCHDAY 1
Besiktas 0 Lazio 2
Sparta Prague 0 Chelsea 1

MATCHDAY 2
Roman Abramovich sees his Chelsea side lose for the first time as Sergen Yalçin scores twice and Besiktas hang on with ten men
Chelsea 0 Besiktas 2
Lazio 2 Sparta Prague 2

MATCHDAY 3

Chelsea 2 Lazio 1
Sparta Prague 2 Besiktas 1

MATCHDAY 4
Hernán Crespo scored against former club Lazio in Rome to open the floodgates for new teammates Duff, Lampard and Gudjohnsen to take advantage
Besiktas 1 Sparta Prague 0
Lazio 0 Chelsea 4

MATCHDAY 5
Chelsea collect the point they need but are frustrated by Sparta's defensive formation with Jaromir Blazek ensuring it remains goalless
Chelsea 0 Sparta 0
Lazio 1 Besiktas 1

MATCHDAY 6

Besiktas 0 Chelsea 2
Sparta Prague 1 Lazio 0

GROUP H
AC Milan
Ajax
Celta Vigo
Club Brugge

MATCHDAY 1
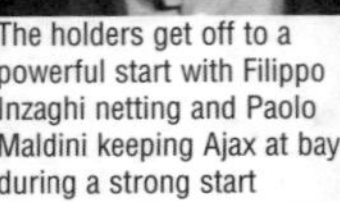
The holders get off to a powerful start with Filippo Inzaghi netting and Paolo Maldini keeping Ajax at bay during a strong start
AC Milan 1 Ajax 0
Club Brugge 1 Celta Vigo 1

MATCHDAY 2

Ajax 2 Club Brugge 0
Celta Vigo 0 AC Milan 0

MATCHDAY 3
Andrés Mendoza gives Andrei Shevchenko a lesson in finishing as Club Brugge pull off a great result with a shock win in Milan
AC Milan 0 Club Brugge 1
Ajax 1 Celta Vigo 0

MATCHDAY 4

Celta Vigo 3 Ajax 2
Club Brugge 0 AC Milan 1

MATCHDAY 5

Ajax 0 AC Milan 1
Celta Vigo 1 Club Brugge 1

MATCHDAY 6
Celta spring a surprise to progress from Group H, with hosts AC Milan, after winning 2-1. Kaka and Jesuli trade goals before Jose Ignacio hits the winner
AC Milan 1 Celta Vigo 2
Club Brugge 2 Ajax 1

LEAGUE TABLES AFTER GROUP STAGES

A	P	W	D	L	DIF	PTS
Lyon	6	3	1	2	0	10
B Munich	6	2	3	1	1	9
Celtic	6	2	1	3	1	7
Anderlecht	6	2	1	3	-2	7

B	P	W	D	L	DIF	PTS
Arsenal	6	3	1	2	3	10
Lokomotiv	6	2	2	2	0	8
Inter Milan	6	2	2	2	-3	8
Dinamo	6	2	1	3	0	7

C	P	W	D	L	DIF	PTS
Monaco	6	3	2	1	9	11
Deportivo	6	3	1	2	0	10
PSV	6	3	1	2	1	10
AEK	6	0	2	4	-10	2

D	P	W	D	L	DIF	PTS
Juventus	6	4	1	1	9	13
Sociedad	6	2	3	1	0	9
Galatasaray	6	2	1	3	-2	7
Olympiakos	6	1	1	4	-7	4

E	P	W	D	L	DIF	PTS
Man Utd	6	5	0	1	11	15
Stuttgart	6	4	0	2	3	12
Panathinaikos	6	1	1	4	-8	4
Rangers	6	1	1	4	-6	4

F	P	W	D	L	DIF	PTS
RealMadrid	6	4	2	0	6	14
Porto	6	3	2	1	1	11
Marseille	6	1	1	4	-2	4
Partizan	6	0	3	3	-5	3

G	P	W	D	L	DIF	PTS
Chelsea	6	4	1	1	6	13
Sparta Prague	6	2	2	2	0	8
Besiktas	6	2	1	3	-2	7
Lazio	6	1	2	3	-4	5

H	P	W	D	L	DIF	PTS
AC Milan	6	3	1	2	1	10
Celta Vigo	6	2	3	1	1	9
Club Brugge	6	2	2	2	-1	8
Ajax	6	2	0	4	-1	6

Last 16 Leg 1

Bayern Munich (0) 1 Real Madrid (0) 1
Makaay 75 — Roberto Carlos 83
59,000

Celta Vigo (1) 2 Arsenal (1) 3
Edu 27, Jose Ignacio 64 — Edu 18,58, Pires 80
21,000

Edu to Edu stuff as Arsenal's Brazilian hits two sweet goals while Celta's version heads one of his own but Londoners go through

Deportivo (1) 1 Juventus (0) 0
Luque 37
30,000

Lokomotiv M (1) 2 Monaco (0) 1
Izmailov 32, Maminov 59 — Morientes 69
28,000

Porto (1) 2 Man Utd (1) 1
McCarthy 29,78 — Fortune 14
49,977

Real Sociedad (0) 0 Lyon (1) 1
29,000 — Schurrer 18 og

Sparta Prague (0) 0 AC Milan (0) 0
21,000

Stuttgart (0) 0 Chelsea (1) 1
50,000 — Meira 12 og

Last 16 Leg 2

Chelsea (0) 0 Stuttgart (0) 0
36,657

A stuttering display is enough for Chelsea to despatch Stuttgart but they have to rely on a first leg own goal by Meira

Juventus (0) 0 Deportivo (1) 1
24,680 — Pandiani 12

Lyon (0) 1 Real Sociedad (0) 0
Juninho 77 — 38,914

Man Utd (1) 1 Porto (0) 1
Scholes 32 — Costinha 90
67,029

Costinha costs United as his late goal ends their long run of last eight appearances despite Scholes' strike and linesman's wrongly disallowed 'goal'

AC Milan (1) 4 Sparta Prague (0) 1
Inzaghi 45, Shevchenko 66,79, Gattuso 85 — Jun 59
55,000

Arsenal (2) 2 Celta Vigo (0) 0
Henry 14,34
35,402

Monaco (0) 1 Lokomotiv M (0) 0
Prso 60
18,000
Monaco win on away goals rule

Real Madrid (1) 1 Bayern Munich (0) 0
Zidane 32
75,000

Salgado sets up winner for Zidane and then adds a vital goal-line clearance to steer Real through against Bayern

Quarter-finals Leg 1

AC Milan (1) 4 Deportivo (1) 1
Kaka 45,49, Shevchenko 46, Pirlo 53 fk — Pandiani 11
60,335

Chelsea (0) 1 Arsenal (0) 1
Gudjohnsen 53 — Pires 59
40,778

Porto (1) 2 Lyon (0) 0
Deco 44, Ricardo Carvalho 71
46,910

Deco deals a blow to Lyons' hopes with a goal and an assist for Carvalho in a confident 2-0 home win in Porto and Maniche makes sure, netting twice in the away leg

Real Madrid (0) 4 Monaco (1) 2
Helguera 52, Zidane 70, Figo 77, Ronaldo 81 — Squillaci 43, Morientes 83
70,000

Quarter-finals Leg 2

Arsenal (1) 1 Chelsea (0) 2
Reyes 45 — Lampard 51, Bridge 87
35,486

Tinkerman triumphs at last as Ranieri changes it at halftime to claim Champions League semi-final spot, coming from behind with goals from Lampard and Bridge after Reyes gave Arsenal a lead

Deportivo (3) 4 AC Milan (0) 0
Pandiani 5, Valeron 35, Luque 44, Fran 76
30,260

Lyon (1) 2 Porto (1) 2
Luyindula 14, Elber 89 — Maniche 6,47
39,547

Monaco (1) 3 Real Madrid (1) 1
Giuly 45,66, Morientes 49 — Raul 36
18,000
Monaco win on away goals rule

Giuly nets twice to overturn a Madrid lead on the night and claim the tie for Monaco on the away goal scored by Morientes – on loan from Real!

SEMI-FINALS

Monaco (1) 3 Chelsea (1) 1
Prso 17, Morientes 78, Nonda 83 — Crespo 23
15,000

Ten-man Monaco delight Deschamps, who tinkers more effectively than Ranieri. Chelsea fritter away a strong first half performance with poor substitutions despite having an extra man after Zikos is dismissed

Chelsea (2) 2 Monaco (1) 2
Gronkjaer 22, Lampard 44 — Ibarra 45, Morientes 60
37,132

Chelsea start with a rocket from Gronkjaer and a Lampard strike but end with a whimper after Ibarra's arm intervenes and Morientes' skill engineers the draw

Porto (0) 0 Deportivo (0) 0
50,818

Deportivo keep it tight in Porto but defender Andrade is sent off and Mauro Silva also misses the second leg after a booking

Deportivo (0) 0 Porto (0) 1
34,611 — Derlei 59 pen

Coach Mourinho shows Chelsea the way to final with Derlei (straight back in the side after a four month lay-off) scoring the only goal for Porto. Deco taunts Deportivo after Naybet is sent off

FINAL

Porto (1) 3 Monaco (0) 0
Alberto 39, Deco 71, Alenitchev 75
52,000

Deco destroys Monaco's hopes with a breakaway second strike in the 71st minute to confirm Porto as Champions League winners.
The Portuguese champions looked likely to add to their UEFA win of last year as soon as Carlos Alberto hooked in a vital first goal on the 39th minute.
However, it was as the French pressed for an equaliser that Deco led a breakout from his own half. A one-two left him with time to thread the ball past Roma in the Monaco goal.
Monaco lost their skipper Giuly to an injury early on. Two goals down and with the Porto defence well marshalled by veteran captain Costa, they were a well-beaten side. Four minutes after the second goal, Porto sub Alenitchev scored a third and the Portuguese champions' 41-year-old coach Mourinho was awaiting offers.

STADIUM CAPACITY AND HOME CROWDS

	TEAM	CAPACITY	AVE (%)	HIGH	LOW
1	B Leverkusen	22500	100.00	22500	22500
2	Man Utd	67750	97.67	67014	63439
3	Basel	31539	94.61	31500	29031
4	Ajax	51324	91.99	51025	37455
5	Arsenal	38500	91.38	35472	34793
6	Newcastle	52200	86.72	51883	40185
7	Valencia	53000	79.66	50000	34980
8	AC Milan	85700	79.29	78175	45000
9	Real Madrid	87000	73.26	78000	40000
10	Barcelona	98800	68.93	98000	42928
11	Deportivo	35800	67.4	33000	7120
12	Roma	82307	62.62	80000	23734
13	Lokomotiv Mos	30000	62.61	20000	17000
14	B Dortmund	83100	60.17	52000	48000
15	Inter Milan	85700	60.15	83679	31448
16	Juventus	69041	59.37	60253	22639

Key: Average. The percentage of each stadium filled in League games over the season (AVE), the stadium capacity and the highest and lowest crowds recorded.

AWAY ATTENDANCE

	TEAM	AVE (%)	HIGH	LOW
1	Inter Milan	91.26	82717	21040
2	Roma	89.85	71722	22989
3	Barcelona	85.94	71740	18000
4	Juventus	85.87	98000	27500
5	AC Milan	85.79	83679	20000
6	Arsenal	84.13	70000	23000
7	Real Madrid	83.63	80000	18000
8	Man Utd	82.25	66708	7120
9	Lokomotiv Moscow	79.38	72028	23000
10	Ajax	77.52	76079	21300
11	Valencia	73.8	52623	15000
12	Deportivo	72.43	67014	25070
13	B Dortmund	70.74	50000	17000
14	Newcastle	69.84	53459	22500
15	B Leverkusen	67.86	66185	5000
16	Basel	63.64	66870	5000

Key: Average. How close each club has come to filling grounds in its away league matches (AVE) and the highest and lowest crowds recorded.

CLUB STRIKE FORCE

	CLUB	GOALS	CSR
1	Monaco	27	43
2	Juventus	15	48
3	Man Utd	15	48
4	Real Madrid	18	50
5	Arsenal	16	56
6	Porto	20	59
7	Chelsea	21	60
8	Deportivo	20	63
9	AC Milan	12	75
10	Celta Vigo	12	75
11	Lokomotiv Moscow	12	75
12	Stuttgart	9	80
13	Lyon	11	82
14	Sparta Prague	11	82
15	Real Sociedad	8	90
16	Bayern Munich	7	103

Morientes and Plasil of Monaco celebrate

1 Monaco

Goals in the Champions League: 27

Club Strike Rate (CSR) Average number of minutes between League goals scored by club: 43

CLUB DEFENCE

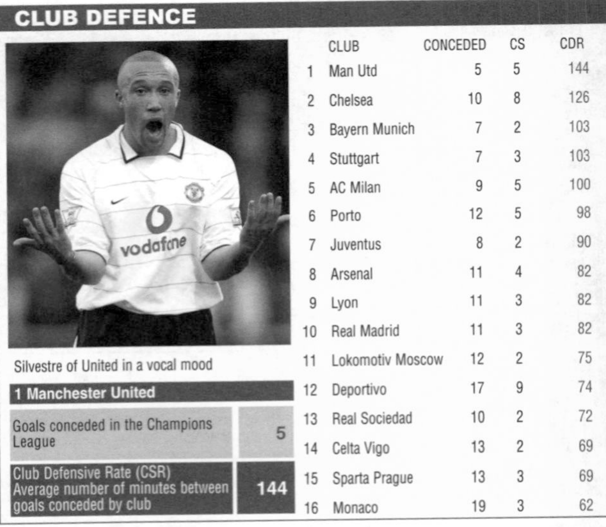

Silvestre of United in a vocal mood

1 Manchester United

Goals conceded in the Champions League: 5

Club Defensive Rate (CSR) Average number of minutes between goals conceded by club: 144

	CLUB	CONCEDED	CS	CDR
1	Man Utd	5	5	144
2	Chelsea	10	8	126
3	Bayern Munich	7	2	103
4	Stuttgart	7	3	103
5	AC Milan	9	5	100
6	Porto	12	5	98
7	Juventus	8	2	90
8	Arsenal	11	4	82
9	Lyon	11	3	82
10	Real Madrid	11	3	82
11	Lokomotiv Moscow	12	2	75
12	Deportivo	17	9	74
13	Real Sociedad	10	2	72
14	Celta Vigo	13	2	69
15	Sparta Prague	13	3	69
16	Monaco	19	3	62

CLUB DISCIPLINARY RECORD

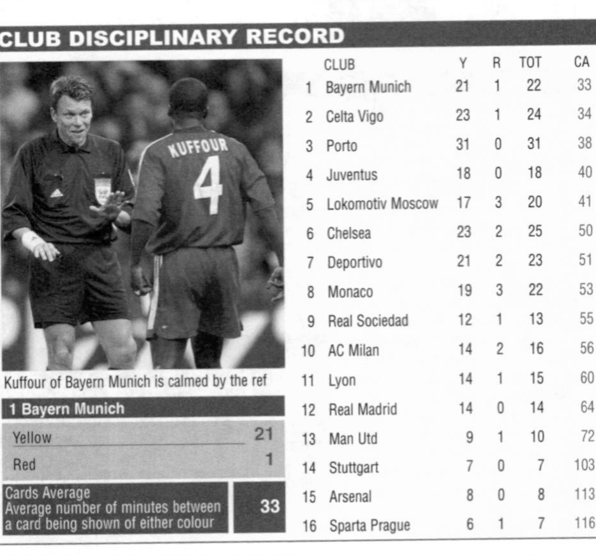
KUFFOUR
4

Kuffour of Bayern Munich is calmed by the ref

1 Bayern Munich

Yellow: 21

Red: 1

Cards Average Average number of minutes between a card being shown of either colour: 33

	CLUB	Y	R	TOT	CA
1	Bayern Munich	21	1	22	33
2	Celta Vigo	23	1	24	34
3	Porto	31	0	31	38
4	Juventus	18	0	18	40
5	Lokomotiv Moscow	17	3	20	41
6	Chelsea	23	2	25	50
7	Deportivo	21	2	23	51
8	Monaco	19	3	22	53
9	Real Sociedad	12	1	13	55
10	AC Milan	14	2	16	56
11	Lyon	14	1	15	60
12	Real Madrid	14	0	14	64
13	Man Utd	9	1	10	72
14	Stuttgart	7	0	7	103
15	Arsenal	8	0	8	113
16	Sparta Prague	6	1	7	116

PLAYER DISCIPLINARY RECORD

	PLAYER	CLUB	Y	R	TOT	CA
1	Lekseto	Lokomotiv	5	1	6	82
2	Johnson	Chelsea	4	1	5	137
3	Zikos	Monaco	3	2	5	140
4	Loskov	Lokomotiv	4	1	5	143
5	Carlos Alberto	Porto	3	0	3	151
6	Nesta	AC Milan	2	1	3	162
7	Jorge Costa	Porto	5	0	5	169
8	Kovacevic	R Sociedad	2	1	3	192
9	Victor	Deportivo	4	0	4	201
10	Schurrer	R Sociedad	3	0	3	208
11	Gattuso	AC Milan	2	1	3	210
12	Beckham	Real Madrid	3	0	3	210
13	Naybet	Deportivo	4	1	5	212
14	Lizarazu	B Munich	3	0	3	219
15	Desailly	Chelsea	2	1	3	219
16	Edmilson	Lyon	3	1	4	221
17	Tristan	Deportivo	2	0	2	233
18	Johana	S Prague	3	0	3	240
19	Costinha	Porto	4	0	4	255
20	Silvinho	Celta Vigo	2	0	2	262
21	Angel	Celta Vigo	2	0	2	264
22	Deco	Porto	4	0	4	264
23	Juanfran	Celta Vigo	2	0	2	270
24	Mauro Silva	Deportivo	3	0	3	270
25	Scaloni	Deportivo	2	0	2	270

Monaco's Zikos is dismissed against Chelsea

1 Jacob Lekseto- Lokomotiv Moscow

Yellow: 5

Red: 1

Cards Average Average number of minutes between a card being shown of either colour: 82

CHART-TOPPING GOALSCORERS

1 Dado Prso - Monaco

Goals in Chapions League	6
Contribution to Attacking Power (AP) Average number of minutes between League team goals while on pitch	36
Player Strike Rate (SR) Average number of minutes between League goals scored by player	86

	PLAYER	TEAM	G	AP	SR
1	Prso	Monaco	6	36	86
2	Morientes	Monaco	9	56	114
3	Makaay	Bayern Munich	6	102	120
4	McCarthy	Porto	5	58	129
5	Pandiani	Deportivo	6	57	134
6	van Nistelrooy	Man Utd	4	42	149
7	Luque	Deportivo	4	58	160
8	Juninho	Lyon	5	79	160
9	Henry	Arsenal	5	59	178
10	Ronaldo	Real Madrid	4	42	182

CHART-TOPPING MIDFIELDERS

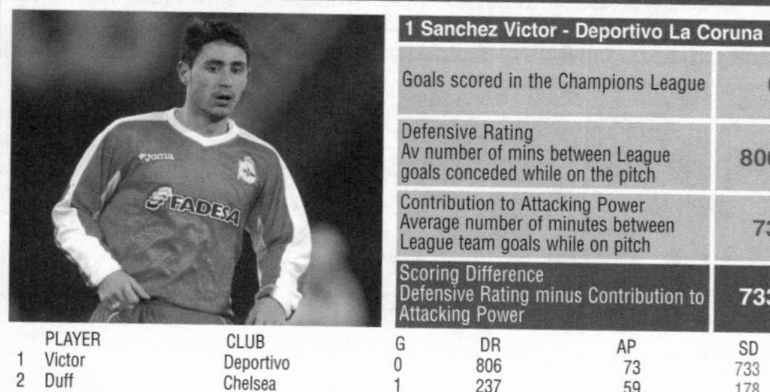

1 Sanchez Victor - Deportivo La Coruna

Goals scored in the Champions League	0
Defensive Rating Av number of mins between League goals conceded while on the pitch	806
Contribution to Attacking Power Average number of minutes between League team goals while on pitch	73
Scoring Difference Defensive Rating minus Contribution to Attacking Power	733

	PLAYER	CLUB	G	DR	AP	SD
1	Victor	Deportivo	0	806	73	733
2	Duff	Chelsea	1	237	59	178
3	Gronkjaer	Chelsea	1	189	44	145
4	P Neville	Man Utd	1	151	43	108
5	Geremi	Chelsea	0	167	61	106

CHART-TOPPING DEFENDERS

1 Glen Johnson- Chelsea

Goals Conceded in the League The number of League goals conceded while he was on the pitch	1
Clean Sheets In games when he played at least 70 mins	6
Defensive Rating Average number of minutes between League goals conceded while on pitch	685
Club Defensive Rating Average mins between League goals conceded by the club this season	126

	PLAYER	CLUB	Conc	CS	CDR	DR
1	Johnson	Chelsea	1	6	126	685
2	Silvestre	Man Utd	2	5	144	270
3	Ferdinand	Man Utd	2	5	144	266
4	Costacurta	AC Milan	2	3	100	260
5	Gallas	Chelsea	7	6	126	141

CHART-TOPPING GOALKEEPERS

1 Cudicini - Chelsea

Goals conceded in the Champions League	5
Counting Games League games when he played at least 70 minutes	11
Clean Sheets In games when he played at least 70 mins	8
Defensive Rating Average number of minutes between League goals conceded while on pitch	198

	PLAYER	CLUB	CG	Conc	CS	DR
1	Cudicini	Chelsea	11	5	8	198
2	Howard	Man Utd	7	5	4	126
3	Dida	AC Milan	9	7	5	116
4	Kahn	Bayern Munich	8	7	2	103
5	Hildebrand	Stuttgart	8	7	3	103

TEAM OF THE SEASON

CUDICINI
Chelsea
M 990 DR 198
JOHNSON
Chelsea
M 685 DR 685
COSTACURTA
AC Milan
M 1229 DR 260
SILVESTRE
Man Utd
M 540 DR 270
RAUL BRAVO
Real Madrid
M 981 DR 123
VICTOR
Deportivo
M 806 SD 733
PHIL NEVILLE
Man Utd
M 603 SD 108
JESULI
Celta Vigo
M 663 SD 67
DUFF
Chelsea
M 712 SD 178
VAN NISTELROOY
Man Utd
M 596 AP 42
PRSO
Monaco
M 514 SR 86

KEY: DR = Defensive Rate, SD = Scoring Difference AP = Attacking Power SR = Strike Rate, M = Minutes played in Champions League proper.

The Champions League Team of the Season shows a 4-4-2 of the best players in the competition based upon the selection criteria used for the chart-toppers. The players selected are taken from the lists for each 'last 16' club except that to get into the Team of the Season you must have played at least 500 minutes in the competition. The other restriction is that we are only allowing one player from each club in each position. So the maximum number of players one club can have in the divisional team is four.

- **The Champions League team's goalkeeper** is the player with the highest Defensive Rating
- **The Champions League team's defenders** are also tested by Defensive Rating, i.e. the average number of minutes between league goals conceded while on the pitch.
- **The Champions League team's midfield** are selected on their Scoring Difference, i.e.their Defensive Rating minus their Contribution to Attacking Power (average number of minutes between league goals scored while on the pitch. It takes no account of assists.
- **The Champions League team strikeforce** is made up of the striker with the highest Strike Rate (his average number of minutes between league goals scored while on the pitch) together with the striker with the highest Contribution to Attacking Power.

CHART-TOPPING POINT EARNERS

	PLAYER	TEAM	GAMES	POINTS	AVE
1	Fortune	Man Utd	5	15	3
2	Johnson	Chelsea	4	12	3
3	Szabics	Stuttgart	4	12	3
4	Gattuso	AC Milan	3	9	3
5	Kaka	AC Milan	3	9	3
6	Sergio	Deportivo	3	9	3
7	Thuram	Juventus	3	9	3
8	Montero	Juventus	3	9	3
9	Trezeguet	Juventus	3	9	3
10	Zambrotta	Juventus	3	9	3
11	Appiah	Juventus	3	9	3
12	O'Shea	Man Utd	3	9	3
13	Seedorf	AC Milan	2	6	3
14	Bergkamp	Arsenal	2	6	3
15	Cygan	Arsenal	2	6	3
16	Pizarro	Bayern Munich	2	6	3
17	Manuel Pablo	Deportivo	2	6	3
18	Tacchinardi	Juventus	2	6	3
19	Fletcher	Man Utd	2	6	3
20	Aramburu	Real Sociedad	2	6	3

1 Fortune - Man United

Counting Games League games where he played at least 70 minutes	5
Total League Points Taken in Counting Games	15
Average League Points Taken in Counting Games	3.00

PORTO

PORTUGAL
Winners

1	gpf	Partizan	A	D	1-1	Costinha 22	32,000
2	gpf	Real Madrid	H	L	1-3	Costinha 7	37,506
3	gpf	Marseille	A	W	3-2	Maniche 31; Derlei 35; Alenitchev 81	59,000
4	gpf	Marseille	H	W	1-0	McCarthy 21	33,215
5	gpf	Partizan	H	W	2-1	McCarthy 25,50	22,177
6	gpf	Real Madrid	A	D	1-1	Derlei 35 pen	49,595
7	koL1	Man Utd	H	W	2-1	McCarthy 29,78	49,977
8	koL2	Man Utd	A	D	1-1	Costinha 90	67,029
9	qfL1	Lyon	H	W	2-0	Deco 44; Ricardo Carvalho 71	46,910
10	qfL2	Lyon	A	D	2-2	Maniche 6,47	39,547
11	sfL1	Deportivo	H	D	0-0		50,818
12	sfL2	Deportivo	A	W	1-0	Derlei 59 pen	34,611
13	ecfin	Monaco	H	W	3-0	Alberto 39; Deco 71; Alenitchev 75	52,000

SECOND GROUP F

	P	W	D	L	F	A	DIF	PTS
Real Madrid	6	4	2	0	11	5	6	14
Porto	6	3	2	1	9	8	1	11
Marseille	6	1	1	4	9	11	-2	4
Partizan	6	0	3	3	3	8	-5	3

PLAYER APPEARANCES

5 Anderson Deco — Midfield

Age (on 01/07/04)	26
Appearances in Champions league	12
Total minutes on the pitch	1056
Goals	1
Yellow cards	2
Red cards	0
Home Country	Portugal

	PLAYER	POS	AGE	APP	MINS ON	GOALS	CARDS(Y/R)		HOME COUNTRY
1	Vitor Manuel Baia	GK	34	13	1170	0	2	0	Portugal
2	Ricardo Alberto Carvalho	DEF	26	13	1170	1	2	0	Portugal
3	Paulo Ferreira	DEF	25	13	1170	0	0	0	Portugal
4	Maniche	MID	26	12	1067	3	3	0	Portugal
5	Anderson Deco	MID	26	12	1056	2	4	0	Portugal
6	Francisco Rodrigu Costa	MID	29	12	1022	3	4	0	Portugal
7	Nuno Valente	DEF	29	11	959	0	2	0	Portugal
8	Jorge Costa	DEF	32	10	845	0	5	0	Portugal
9	Derlei	ATT	28	8	692	3	0	0	Brazil
10	Benni McCarthy	ATT	26	11	644	5	1	0	South Africa
11	Pedro M da Silva Mendes	MID	25	10	604	0	2	0	Portugal
12	Dmitri Alenitchev	MID	31	9	576	2	0	0	Russia
13	Carlos Alberto	ATT	19	7	453	1	3	0	Brazil
14	Pedro Emanuel	DEF	29	7	377	0	0	0	Portugal
15	Edgaras Jankauskas	ATT	29	10	297	0	0	0	Lithuania
16	Bosingwa	MID	21	8	238	0	2	0	Portugal
17	Ricardo Costa	DEF	23	2	121	0	0	0	Portugal
18	Marco Ferreira	ATT	26	3	121	0	1	0	Portugal
19	Mario Silva	DEF	27	1	90	0	0	0	Portugal
20	Ricardo Fernandes	MID	26	5	84	0	0	0	Portugal
21	Cesar Peixoto	ATT	24	1	64	0	0	0	Portugal
22	Miguel Hugo Almeida	ATT	20	2	41	0	0	0	Portugal
23	Bruno Vale	GK	21	2	9	0	0	0	Portugal

KEY PLAYERS - GOALSCORERS

Benni McCarthy

Goals in the Champions League	5
Contribution to Attacking Power Average number of minutes between team goals while on pitch	58
Player Strike Rate The total number of minutes he was on the pitch for every goal scored	129
Club Strike Rate Average number of minutes between goals scored by club	59

	PLAYER	GOALS	ATT POWER	STRIKE RATE
1	Benni McCarthy	5	58	129 mins
2	Derlei	3	53	231 mins
3	Dmitri Alenitchev	2	57	288 mins
4	Francisco Rodrigues Costa	3	56	341 mins
5	Maniche	3	56	356 mins

KEY PLAYERS - MIDFIELDERS

Maniche

Goals in the Champions League	3
Defensive Rating Average number of mins between goals conceded while on the pitch	97
Contribution to Attacking Power Average number of minutes between team goals while on pitch	56
Scoring Difference Defensive Rating minus Contribution to attacking power	41

	PLAYER	GOALS	DEF RATE	ATT POWER	SCORE DIFF
1	Maniche	3	97	56	41 mins
2	Anderson Deco	2	96	56	40 mins
3	Dmitri Alenitchev	2	96	58	38 mins
4	Francisco Rodrigues Costa	3	93	57	36 mins
5	Pedro Miguel da Silva Mendes	0	86	60	26 mins

KEY PLAYERS - DEFENDERS

Jorge Costa

Goals Conceded in Champions League	8
Clean Sheets In League games when he played at least than 70 mins	4
Defensive Rating Ave number of mins between goals conceded while on the pitch	106
Club Defensive Rating Average number of mins between goals conceded by the club this season	98

	PLAYER	CONCEDED	CLEAN SHEETS	DEF RATE
1	Jorge Costa	8	4	106 mins
2	Ricardo Alberto Carvalho	12	5	98 mins
3	Paulo Ferreira	12	5	98 mins
4	Nuno Valente	10	4	96 mins

KEY GOALKEEPER

Vitor Manuel Baia

Goals Conceded	12
Clean Sheets	5
Counting Games (at least 70mins)	13
Defensive Rating Ave number of mins between goals conceded while on the pitch	98

TOP POINT EARNERS

	PLAYER	GAMES	AV PTS
1	Jorge Costa	4	2.50
2	Maniche	5	2.00
3	Dmitri Alenitchev	2	2.00
4	Ricardo Carvalho	6	1.83
5	Derlei	6	1.83
6	Paulo Ferreira	6	1.83
7	Vitor Manuel Baia	6	1.83
8	Francisco Rodrigu Costa	6	1.83
9	Anderson Deco	5	1.60
10	Nuno Valente	3	1.33
	CLUB AVERAGE:		1.83

Note: Points awarded for knock-out section

MONACO

FRANCE
Final

1	gc	PSV Eindhoven	A	W	2-1	Morientes 31; Cisse 56	30,000
2	gc	AEK Athens	H	W	4-0	Giuly 23; Morientes 27,56; Prso 86	15,000
3	gc	Deportivo	A	L	0-1		22,000
4	gc	Deportivo	H	W	8-3	Rothen 2; Giuly 11; Porato 26; Prso 30,45,49; Plasil 47; Cisse 67	60,000
5	gc	PSV Eindhoven	H	D	1-1	Morientes 35	12,175
6	gc	AEK Athens	A	D	0-0		4,000
7	koL1	Lok Moscow	A	L	1-2	Morientes 69	28,000
8	koL2	Lok Moscow	H	W	1-0	Prso 60	18,000
9	qfL1	Real Madrid	A	L	2-4	Squillaci 43; Morientes 83	70,000
10	qfL2	Real Madrid	H	W	3-1	Giuly 45,66; Morientes 49	18,000
11	sfL1	Chelsea	H	W	3-1	Prso 17; Morientes 78; Nonda 83	15,000
12	sfL2	Chelsea	A	D	2-2	Ibarra 45; Morientes 60	37,132
13	fin	Porto	A	L	0-3		52,000

FIRST GROUP C

	P	W	D	L	F	A	DIF	PTS
Monaco	6	3	2	1	15	6	9	11
Deportivo	6	3	1	2	12	12	0	10
PSV	6	3	1	2	8	7	1	10
AEK	6	0	2	4	1	11	-10	2

PLAYER APPEARANCES

1 Julien Rodriguez — Defence

Age (on 01/07/04)	26
Appearances in Champions league	13
Total minutes on the pitch	1170
Goals	0
Yellow cards	1
Red cards	0
Home Country	France

	PLAYER	POS	AGE	APP	MINS ON	GOALS	CARDS(Y)	CARDS(R)	HOME COUNTRY
1	Julien Rodriguez	MID	26	13	1170	0	1	0	France
2	Patrice Evra	MID	23	13	1144	0	2	0	France
3	Gael Givet	DEF	22	13	1143	0	1	0	France
4	Flavio Roma	GK	30	12	1080	0	1	0	Italy
5	Lucas Ademar Bernardi	MID	26	12	1080	0	4	0	Argentina
6	Jerome Rothen	MID	26	12	1070	1	2	0	France
7	Fernando Morientes	ATT	28	12	1025	9	0	0	Spain
8	Edouard Cisse	MID	26	13	843	2	1	0	France
9	Ludovic Giuly	MID	27	10	785	4	0	1	France
10	Vassilis Zikos	MID	30	9	701	0	3	2	Greece
11	Sebastien Squillaci	DEF	23	9	694	1	1	0	France
12	Hugo Benjamin Ibarra	DEF	30	10	644	1	1	0	Argentina
13	Dado Prso	ATT	29	11	514	6	1	0	France
14	Jaroslav Plasil	MID	22	10	429	1	1	0	Czech Republic
15	Emmanuel Adebayor	ATT	20	9	279	0	0	0	Togo
16	Tony Mario Sylva	GK	29	1	90	0	0	0	Senegal
17	Shabani Nonda	ATT	27	4	72	1	0	0	Burundi
18	Souleymane Camara	ATT	21	1	32	0	0	0	Senegal
19	Sebastien Carole	MID	21	1	18	0	0	0	France
20	Hassan El Fakiri	MID	27	2	11	0	0	0	Norway

KEY PLAYERS - GOALSCORERS

Dado Prso

Goals in the Champions League	6
Contribution to Attacking Power Average number of minutes between team goals while on pitch	36
Player Strike Rate The total number of minutes he was on the pitch for every goal scored	86
Club Strike Rate Average number of minutes between goals scored by club	43

	PLAYER	GOALS	ATT POWER	STRIKE RATE
1	Dado Prso	6	36	86 mins
2	Fernando Sanchez Morientes	9	56	114 mins
3	Ludovic Giuly	4	32	196 mins
4	Edouard Cisse	2	42	422 mins
5	Hugo Benjamin Ibarra	1	58	644 mins

KEY PLAYERS - MIDFIELDERS

Edouard Cisse

Goals in the Champions League	2
Defensive Rating Average number of mins between goals conceded while on the pitch	65
Contribution to Attacking Power Average number of minutes between team goals while on pitch	42
Scoring Difference Defensive Rating minus Contribution to attacking power	23

	PLAYER	GOALS	DEF RATE	ATT POWER	SCORE DIFF
1	Edouard Cisse	2	65	42	23 mins
2	Ludovic Giuly	4	56	33	23 mins
3	Patrice Evra	0	64	42	22 mins
4	Jerome Rothen	1	56	41	15 mins
5	Lucas Ademar Bernardi	0	60	45	15 mins

KEY PLAYERS - DEFENDERS

Hugo Benjamin Ibarra

Goals Conceded in Champions League	10
Clean Sheets In League games when he played at least than 70 mins	2
Defensive Rating Ave number of mins between goals conceded while on the pitch	64
Club Defensive Rating Average number of mins between goals conceded by the club this season	62

	PLAYER	CONCEDED	CLEAN SHEETS	DEF RATE
1	Hugo Benjamin Ibarra	10	2	64 mins
2	Gael Givet	18	3	64 mins
3	Julien Rodriguez	19	3	62 mins
4	Sebastien Squillaci	13	2	53 mins

KEY GOALKEEPER

Ravio Roma

Goals Conceded	19
Clean Sheets	2
Counting Games (at least 70mins)	12
Defensive Rating Ave number of mins between goals conceded while on the pitch	57

TOP POINT EARNERS

	PLAYER	GAMES	AV PTS
1	Vassilis Zikos	3	2.33
2	Jerome Rothen	5	2.00
3	Ludovic Giuly	5	2.00
4	Flavio Roma	5	2.00
5	Gael Givet	6	1.83
6	Lucas Ademar Bernardi	6	1.83
7	Julien Rodriguez	6	1.83
8	Sebastien Squillaci	6	1.83
9	Patrice Evra	6	1.83
10	Edouard Cisse	4	1.75
	CLUB AVERAGE:		1.83

Note: Points awarded for knock-out section

CHELSEA

ENGLAND
Semi-Final

	Round	Opponent	Venue	Result	Score	Scorers	Attendance
1	3ql1	**Zilina**	A	W	2-0	Gudjohnsen 42; Drahno 75 og	6,160
2	3ql2	**Zilina**	H	W	3-0	Johnson 32; Huth 67; Hasselbaink 78	23,408
3	gg	**Sparta Prague**	A	W	1-0	Gallas 85	18,997
4	gg	**Besiktas**	H	L	0-2		32,957
5	gg	**Lazio**	H	W	2-1	Lampard 57; Mutu 65	40,405
6	gg	**Lazio**	A	W	4-0	Crespo 15; Gudjohnsen 70; Duff 75; Lampard 80	50,000
7	gg	**Sparta Prague**	H	D	0-0		40,152
8	gg	**Besiktas**	A	W	2-0	Hasselbaink 77; Bridge 85	55,350
9	koL1	**Stuttgart**	A	W	1-0	Fernando Meira 12 og	50,000
10	koL2	**Stuttgart**	H	D	0-0		36,657
11	qfL1	**Arsenal**	H	D	1-1	Gudjohnsen 53	40,778
12	qfL2	**Arsenal**	A	W	2-1	Lampard 51; Bridge 87	35,486
13	sfL1	**Monaco**	A	L	1-3	Crespo 23	15,000
14	sfL2	**Monaco**	H	D	2-2	Gronkjaer 22; Lampard 44	37,132

FIRST GROUP G

	P	W	D	L	F	A	DIF	PTS
Chelsea	6	4	1	1	9	3	6	13
Sparta	6	2	2	2	5	5	0	8
Besiktas	6	2	1	3	5	7	-2	7
Lazio	6	1	2	3	6	10	-4	5

PLAYER APPEARANCES

1 John Terry Defence

Age (on 01/07/04)	23
Appearances in Champions league	13
Total minutes on the pitch	1170
Goals	0
Yellow cards	2
Red cards	0
Home Country	England

	PLAYER	POS	AGE	APP	MINS ON	GOALS	CARDS(Y)	CARDS(R)	HOME COUNTRY
1	John Terry	DEF	23	13	1170	0	2	0	England
2	Frank Lampard	MID	26	14	1170	4	1	0	England
3	Wayne Bridge	DEF	23	13	1066	2	0	0	England
4	Claude Makelele	MID	31	11	990	0	3	0	France
5	Carlo Cudicini	GK	30	11	990	0	2	0	Italy
6	William Gallas	DEF	26	11	990	1	1	0	France
7	Eidur Gudjohnsen	ATT	25	10	739	3	0	0	Iceland
8	Damien Duff	MID	25	11	712	1	0	0	Rep of Ireland
9	Glen Johnson	DEF	19	9	685	1	4	1	England
10	Geremi	MID	25	10	669	0	0	0	Cameroon
11	Marcel Desailly	DEF	35	8	658	0	2	1	France
12	Hernan Crespo	ATT	29	10	572	2	0	0	Argentina
13	Jesper Gronkjaer	MID	26	10	567	1	1	0	Holland
14	Juan Sebastian Veron	MID	29	6	453	0	1	0	Argentina
15	Jimmy-Floyd Hasselbaink	ATT	32	8	440	2	1	0	Holland
16	Adrian Mutu	ATT	25	7	402	1	2	0	Romania
17	Joe Cole	MID	22	9	322	0	2	0	England
18	Mario Melchiot	DEF	27	5	309	0	1	0	Holland
19	Marco Ambrosio	GK	31	3	270	0	0	0	Italy
20	Scott Parker	MID	23	5	266	0	0	0	England
21	Celestine Babayaro	DEF	25	3	194	0	0	0	Nigeria
22	Emmanuel Petit	MID	33	2	90	0	0	0	France
23	Mikael Forssell	ATT	23	1	57	0	0	0	Finland
24	Robert Huth	DEF	19	2	49	1	0	0	Germany
25	Mario Stanic	MID	32	1	23	0	0	0	Croatia

KEY PLAYERS - GOALSCORERS

Eidur Gudjohnsen

Goals in the Champions League	3
Contribution to Attacking Power Average number of minutes between team goals while on pitch	43
Player Strike Rate The total number of minutes he was on the pitch for every goal scored	246
Club Strike Rate Average number of minutes between goals scored by club	60

	PLAYER	GOALS	ATT POWER	STRIKE RATE
1	Eidur Gudjohnsen	3	43	246 mins
2	Hernan Crespo	2	143	286 mins
3	Frank Lampard	4	61	293 mins
4	Wayne Bridge	2	62	533 mins
5	Jesper Gronkjaer	1	43	567 mins

KEY PLAYERS - MIDFIELDERS

Damien Duff

Goals in the Champions League	1
Defensive Rating Average number of mins between goals conceded while on the pitch	237
Contribution to Attacking Power Average number of minutes between team goals while on pitch	59
Scoring Difference Defensive Rating minus Contribution to attacking power	178

	PLAYER	GOALS	DEF RATE	ATT POWER	SCORE DIFF
1	Damien Duff	1	237	59	178 mins
2	Jesper Gronkjaer	1	189	44	145 mins
3	Geremi Sorele Nitjap Fotso	0	167	61	106 mins
4	Frank Lampard	4	117	62	55 mins
5	Claude Makelele	0	124	71	53 mins

KEY PLAYERS - DEFENDERS

Glen Johnson

Goals Conceded in Champions League	1
Clean Sheets In League games when he played at least than 70 mins	6
Defensive Rating Ave number of mins between goals conceded while on the pitch	685
Club Defensive Rating Average number of mins between goals conceded by the club this season	126

	PLAYER	CONCEDED	CLEAN SHEETS	DEF RATE
1	Glen Johnson	1	6	685 mins
2	William Gallas	7	6	141 mins
3	John Terry	10	7	117 mins
4	Marcel Desailly	6	3	110 mins
5	Wayne Bridge	10	6	107 mins

KEY GOALKEEPER

Carlo Cudicini

Goals Conceded	5
Clean Sheets	8
Counting Games (at least 70mins)	11
Defensive Rating Ave number of mins between goals conceded while on the pitch	198

TOP POINT EARNERS

	PLAYER	GAMES	AV PTS
1	Glen Johnson	4	3.00
2	Wayne Bridge	4	2.50
3	Damien Duff	3	2.33
4	Claude Makelele	6	2.17
5	Carlo Cudicini	6	2.17
6	William Gallas	6	2.17
7	Marcel Desailly	3	2.00
8	Adrian Mutu	2	2.00
9	Geremi	3	2.00
10	Juan Sebastian Veron	3	2.00
	CLUB AVERAGE:		2.17

Note: Points awarded for knock-out section

DEPORTIVO LA CORUNA

SPAIN
Semi-Final

	Round	Opponent	H/A	Res	Score	Scorers	Att
1	3ql1	**Rosenborg BK**	A	D	0-0		21,100
2	3ql2	**Rosenborg BK**	H	W	1-0		
3	gc	**AEK Athens**	A	D	1-1	Pandiani 12	16,000
4	gc	**PSV Eindhoven**	H	W	2-0	Sergio 20; Pandiani 51 pen	28,480
5	gc	**Monaco**	H	W	1-0	Tristan 83	22,000
6	gc	**Monaco**	A	L	3-8	Tristan 39,52; Scaloni 45	60,000
7	gc	**AEK Athens**	H	W	3-0	Hector 22; Valeron 51; Luque 71	30,260
8	gc	**PSV Eindhoven**	A	L	2-3	Luque 58 fk; Pandiani 83	32,000
9	koL1	**Juventus**	H	W	1-0	Luque 37	30,000
10	koL2	**Juventus**	A	W	1-0	Pandiani 12	24,680
11	qfL1	**AC Milan**	A	L	1-4	Pandiani 11	60,335
12	qfL2	**AC Milan**	H	W	4-0	Pandiani 5; Valeron 35; Luque 44; Fran 76	30,260
13	sfL1	**Porto**	A	D	0-0		50,818
14	sfL2	**Porto**	H	L	0-1		34,611

SECOND GROUP C

	P	W	D	L	F	A	DIF	PTS
Monaco	6	3	2	1	15	6	9	11
Deportivo	6	3	1	2	12	12	0	10
PSV	6	3	1	2	8	7	1	10
AEK	6	0	2	4	1	11	-10	2

PLAYER APPEARANCES

2 Juan Carlos Valeron — Midfield

Age (on 01/07/04)	29
Appearances in Champions league	13
Total minutes on the pitch	1086
Goals	2
Yellow cards	0
Red cards	0
Home Country	Spain

	PLAYER	POS	AGE	APP	MINS ON	GOALS	CARDS(Y/R)		HOME COUNTRY
1	Fransisco Molina	GK	33	13	1125	0	0	0	Spain
2	Juan Carlos Valeron	MID	29	13	1086	2	0	0	Spain
3	Jorge Manuel Andrade	DEF	26	12	1077	0	0	1	Portugal
4	Noureddine Naybet	DEF	34	12	1060	0	4	1	Morocco
5	Gonzalez Soriano Sergio	MID	27	13	1030	1	1	0	Spain
6	Mauro Silva	MID	36	9	810	0	3	0	Brazil
7	Sanchez del Amo Victor	MID	28	10	806	0	4	0	Spain
8	Walter Pandiani	ATT	28	13	801	6	2	0	Uruguay
9	Enrique Romero	DEF	33	9	726	0	0	0	Spain
10	Alberto Martos Luque	ATT	26	11	639	4	0	0	Spain
11	Lionel Scaloni	DEF	26	10	541	1	2	0	Argentina
12	Garcia Diaz Manuel Pablo	DEF	28	8	512	0	0	0	Spain
13	Aldo Pedro Duscher	MID	25	9	480	0	0	0	Argentina
14	Diego Tristan	ATT	28	10	467	3	2	0	Spain
15	Joan Mendez Capdevila	DEF	26	6	463	0	0	0	Spain
16	Javier Gonazales	MID	34	10	413	1	0	0	Spain
17	Hector Del Pino	DEF	29	4	360	1	1	0	Spain
18	Jose Emilio Amavisca	MID	33	2	180	0	2	0	Spain
19	Martin Villar Cesar	DEF	27	4	170	0	0	0	Spain
20	Pedro Munitis	ATT	29	2	55	0	0	0	Spain
21	Gustavo Munua	GK	26	1	45	0	0	0	Uruguay
22	Djalma Dias Djalminha	MID	33	1	1	0	0	0	Brazil

KEY PLAYERS - GOALSCORERS

Walter Gerardo Pandiani

Goals in the Champions League	6
Contribution to Attacking Power Average number of minutes between team goals while on pitch	57
Player Strike Rate The total number of minutes he was on the pitch for every goal scored	134
Club Strike Rate Average number of minutes between goals scored by club	62

	PLAYER	GOALS	ATT POWER	STRIKE RATE
1	Walter Gerardo Pandiani	6	57	134 mins
2	Alberto Martos Luque	4	58	160 mins
3	Lionel Scaloni	1	54	541 mins
4	Juan Carlos Valeron	2	63	543 mins
5	Gonzalez Soriano Sergio	1	60	1030 mins

KEY PLAYERS - MIDFIELDERS

Sanchez del Amo Victor

Goals in the Champions League	0
Defensive Rating Average number of mins between goals conceded while on the pitch	806
Contribution to Attacking Power Average number of minutes between team goals while on pitch	73
Scoring Difference Defensive Rating minus Contribution to attacking power	733

	PLAYER	GOALS	DEF RATE	ATT POWER	SCORE DIFF
1	Sanchez del Amo Victor	0	806	73	733 mins
2	Gonzalez Soriano Sergio	1	74	61	13 mins
3	Mauro Gomes da Silva	0	62	62	0 mins
4	Juan Carlos Valeron	2	64	64	0 mins

KEY PLAYERS - DEFENDERS

Garcia Diaz Manuel Pablo

Goals Conceded in Champions League	6
Clean Sheets In League games when he played at least than 70 mins	4
Defensive Rating Ave number of mins between goals conceded while on the pitch	85
Club Defensive Rating Average number of mins between goals conceded by the club this season	69

	PLAYER	CONCEDED	CLEAN SHEETS	DEF RATE
1	Garcia Diaz Manuel Pablo	6	4	85 mins
2	Enrique Fernandez Romero	10	5	73 mins
3	Jorge Manuel Gomes Andrade	16	8	67 mins
4	Noureddine Naybet	17	7	62 mins
5	Lionel Scaloni	16	2	34 mins

KEY GOALKEEPER

Fransisco Molina

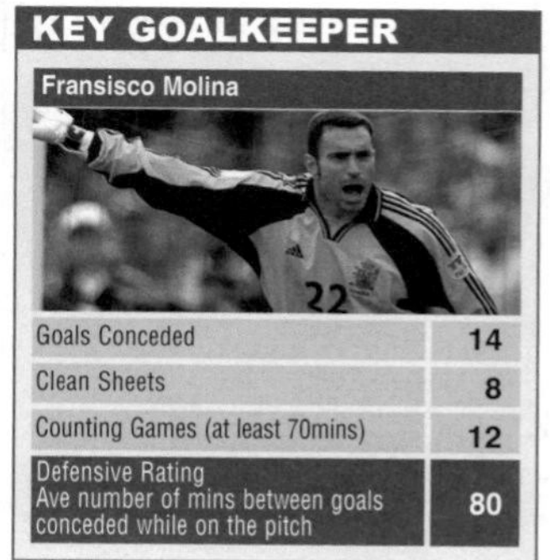

Goals Conceded	14
Clean Sheets	8
Counting Games (at least 70mins)	12
Defensive Rating Ave number of mins between goals conceded while on the pitch	80

TOP POINT EARNERS

	PLAYER	GAMES	AV PTS
1	Gonzalez Soriano Sergio	3	3.00
2	Garcia Diaz Manuel Pablo	2	3.00
3	Sanchez del Amo Victor	3	2.33
4	Francisco Molina	5	2.00
5	Aldo Pedro Duscher	3	2.00
6	Joan Mendez Capdevila	3	2.00
7	Walter Gerardo Pandiani	2	2.00
8	Jorge Andrade	6	1.67
9	Herrera Diego Tristan	2	1.50
10	Javier Gonazales	2	1.50
	CLUB AVERAGE:		1.87

Note: Points awarded for knock-out section

LYON

FRANCE
Quarter-Final

1 ga	Anderlecht	H W	1-0	Juninho 25 pen	32,000
2 ga	Celtic	A L	0-2		57,475
3 ga	Bayern Munich	H D	1-1	Luyindula 88	38,145
4 ga	Bayern Munich	A W	2-1	Juninho 6; Elber 53	59,000
5 ga	Anderlecht	A L	0-1		26,208
6 ga	Celtic	H W	3-2	Elber 6; Juninho 52,86 pen	40,125
7 koL1	Real Sociedad	A W	1-0	Schurrer 18 og	29,000
8 koL2	Real Sociedad	H W	1-0	Juninho 77	38,914
9 qfL1	Porto	A L	0-2		46,910
10 qfL2	Porto	H D	2-2	Luyindula 14; Elber 89	39,547

FIRST GROUP A

	P	W	D	L	F	A	DIF	PTS
Lyon	6	3	1	2	7	7	0	10
Bayern	6	2	3	1	6	5	1	9
Celtic	6	2	1	3	8	7	1	7
Anderlecht	6	2	1	3	4	6	-2	7

KEY PLAYERS - GOALSCORERS

Pernambucano Juninho

2 Giovane Elber

Goals in the Champions League	5
Contribution to Attacking Power Average number of minutes between team goals while on pitch	79
Player Strike Rate The total number of minutes he was on the pitch for every goal scored	160
Club Strike Rate Average number of minutes between goals scored by club	82

	PLAYER	GOALS	ATT POWER	STRIKE RATE
1	Pernambucano Juninho	5	79	160 mins
2	Giovane Elber	3	78	236 mins
3	Pegguy Luyindula	2	66	332 mins

KEY PLAYERS - MIDFIELDERS

Pernambucano Juninho

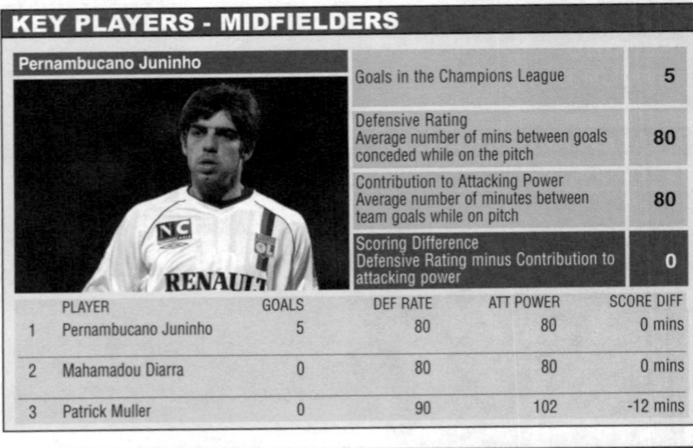

Goals in the Champions League	5
Defensive Rating Average number of mins between goals conceded while on the pitch	80
Contribution to Attacking Power Average number of minutes between team goals while on pitch	80
Scoring Difference Defensive Rating minus Contribution to attacking power	0

	PLAYER	GOALS	DEF RATE	ATT POWER	SCORE DIFF
1	Pernambucano Juninho	5	80	80	0 mins
2	Mahamadou Diarra	0	80	80	0 mins
3	Patrick Muller	0	90	102	-12 mins

PLAYER APPEARANCES

1 Edmilson Defence

Age (on 01/07/04)	27
Appearances in Champions league	10
Total minutes on the pitch	884
Goals	0
Yellow cards	1
Red cards	0
Home Country	Brazil

	PLAYER	POS	AGE	APP	MINS ON	GOALS	CARDS(Y/R)		HOME COUNTRY
1	Edmilson	DEF	27	10	884	0	1	0	Brazil
2	Mahamadou Diarra	MID	23	10	883	0	1	0	Mali
3	Patrick Muller	MID	27	10	812	0	1	0	Switzerland
4	Pernambucano Juninho	MID	29	10	798	5	2	0	Brazil
5	Gregory Coupet	GK	31	9	735	0	1	0	France
6	Giovane Elber	ATT	31	9	709	3	0	0	Brazil
7	Florent Malouda	ATT	24	10	708	0	2	0	France
8	Sydney Govou	ATT	24	9	666	0	1	0	France
9	Pegguy Luyindula	ATT	25	10	664	2	0	0	France
10	Michael Essien	DEF	21	8	613	0	0	0	Ghana
11	Anthony Reveillere	DEF	24	8	588	0	2	0	France
12	Eric Deflandre	DEF	30	7	493	0	0	0	Belgium
13	Vikash Dhorasoo	MID	30	8	454	0	0	0	France
14	Jeremie Berthod	DEF	20	6	365	0	1	0	France
15	Eric Carriere	MID	31	6	139	0	0	0	France
16	Claudio Roberto Cacapa	DEF	28	3	113	0	0	0	Brazil
17	Nicolas Puydebois	GK	23	1	90	0	0	0	France
18	Remi Vercoutre	GK	24	1	75	0	0	0	France
19	Pierre Sartre	DEF	21	1	64	0	0	0	France
20	Bryan Bergougnoux	ATT	21	1	31	0	0	0	France

KEY PLAYERS - DEFENDERS

Anthony Reveillere

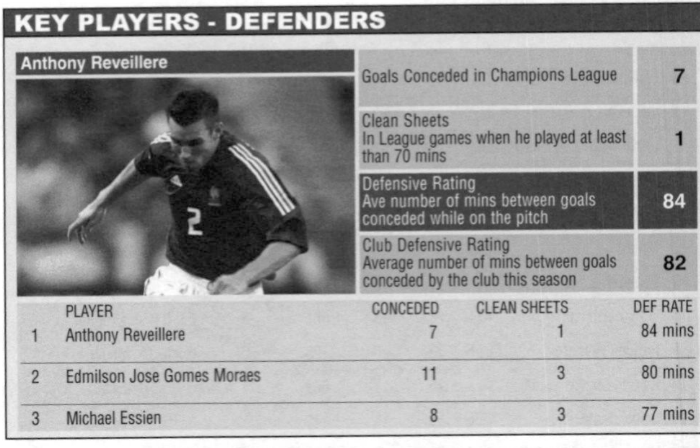

Goals Conceded in Champions League	7
Clean Sheets In League games when he played at least than 70 mins	1
Defensive Rating Ave number of mins between goals conceded while on the pitch	84
Club Defensive Rating Average number of mins between goals conceded by the club this season	82

	PLAYER	CONCEDED	CLEAN SHEETS	DEF RATE
1	Anthony Reveillere	7	1	84 mins
2	Edmilson Jose Gomes Moraes	11	3	80 mins
3	Michael Essien	8	3	77 mins

KEY GOALKEEPER

Gregory Coupet

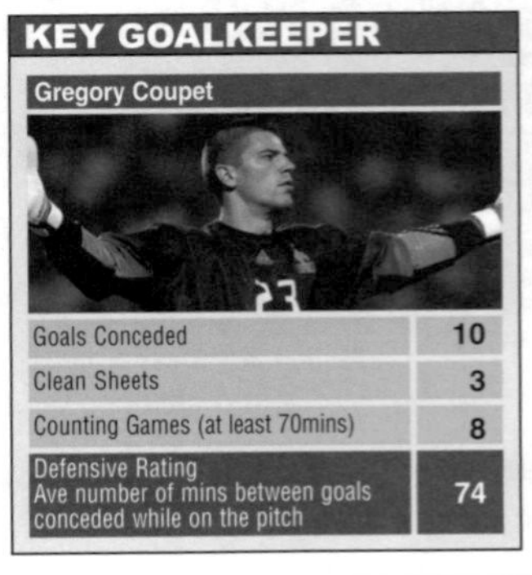

Goals Conceded	10
Clean Sheets	3
Counting Games (at least 70mins)	8
Defensive Rating Ave number of mins between goals conceded while on the pitch	74

TOP POINT EARNERS

	PLAYER	GAMES	AV PTS
1	Michael Essien	3	2.33
2	Florent Malouda	3	2.00
3	Gregory Coupet	5	2.00
4	Jeremie Berthod	3	2.00
5	Pegguy Luyindula	3	2.00
6	Giovane Elber	6	1.67
7	Edmilson	6	1.67
8	Anthony Reveillere	6	1.67
9	Mahamadou Diarra	6	1.67
10	Sydney Govou	4	1.50
	CLUB AVERAGE:		2.08

Note: Points awarded for knock-out section

REAL MADRID

SPAIN
Quarter-Final

1	gf	Marseille	H	W	4-2	Roberto Carlos 29; Ronaldo 34,57; Figo 61 pen	65,000
2	gf	**Porto**	A	W	3-1	Helguera 28; Solari 37; Zidane 67	37,506
3	gf	**Partizan**	H	W	1-0	Raul 38	72,485
4	gf	**Partizan**	A	D	0-0		32,700
5	gf	**Marseille**	A	W	2-1	Beckham 35 fk; Ronaldo 73	59,000
6	gf	**Porto**	H	D	1-1	Solari 9	49,595
7	kl1	**Bayern Munich**	A	D	1-1	Roberto Carlos 83	59,000
8	kl2	**Bayern Munich**	H	W	1-0	Zidane 32	75,000
9	ql1	**Monaco**	H	W	4-2	Helguera 52; Zidane 70; Figo 77; Ronaldo 81	70,000
10	ql2	**Monaco**	A	L	1-3	Raul 36	18,000

FIRST GROUP F

	P	W	D	L	F	A	DIF	PTS
Real Madrid	6	4	2	0	11	5	6	14
Porto	6	3	2	1	9	8	1	11
Marseille	6	1	1	4	9	11	-2	4
Partizan	6	0	3	3	3	8	-5	3

PLAYER APPEARANCES

1 Michel Salgado — Defence

Age (on 01/07/04)	28
Appearances in Champions league	10
Total minutes on the pitch	894
Goals	0
Yellow cards	1
Red cards	0
Home Country	Spain

	PLAYER	POS	AGE	APP	MINS ON	GOALS	CARDS(Y)	CARDS(R)	HOME COUNTRY
1	Michel Salgado	DEF	28	10	894	0	1	0	Spain
2	Zinedine Zidane	MID	32	10	878	3	1	0	France
3	Luis Figo	MID	31	10	855	2	1	0	Portugal
4	Iker Fernandez Casillas	GK	23	9	810	0	0	0	Spain
5	Sanfelix Raul Bravo	DEF	23	10	753	0	1	0	Spain
6	Raul Gonzalez Blanco	ATT	27	9	728	2	1	0	Spain
7	Ronaldo	ATT	27	9	728	4	0	0	Brazil
8	Ivan Bujia Helguera	DEF	29	8	720	2	2	0	Spain
9	Roberto Carlos	DEF	31	8	632	2	1	0	Brazil
10	David Beckham	MID	29	7	630	1	3	0	England
11	Jose Maria Guti	MID	27	9	578	0	1	0	Spain
12	Francisco Pavon	DEF	24	6	468	0	1	0	Spain
13	Santiago Hernan Solari	MID	27	9	324	2	0	0	Argentina
14	Alvaro Perez Mejia	DEF	22	3	270	0	0	0	Spain
15	Esteban Cambiasso	MID	23	5	254	0	0	0	Argentina
16	Fernandez Borja	MID	23	4	174	0	1	0	Spain
17	Carlos Garcia Sanchez	GK	26	1	90	0	0	0	Spain
18	Javier Garcia Portillo	ATT	22	4	66	0	0	0	Spain
19	Oscar Minambres	DEF	23	1	45	0	0	0	Spain
20	Felpeto Jordi Lopez	MID	23	1	2	0	0	0	Spain
21	Gonzalez Rocha Ruben	DEF	22	1	1	0	0	0	Spain

KEY PLAYERS - GOALSCORERS

Ronaldo Luiz Nazario de Lima

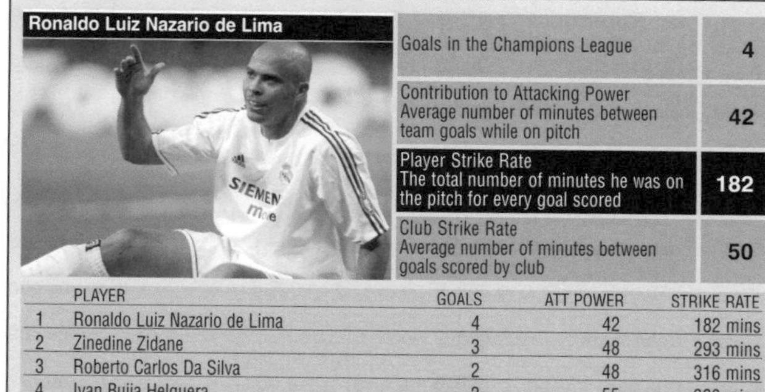

Goals in the Champions League	4
Contribution to Attacking Power Average number of minutes between team goals while on pitch	42
Player Strike Rate The total number of minutes he was on the pitch for every goal scored	182
Club Strike Rate Average number of minutes between goals scored by club	50

	PLAYER	GOALS	ATT POWER	STRIKE RATE
1	Ronaldo Luiz Nazario de Lima	4	42	182 mins
2	Zinedine Zidane	3	48	293 mins
3	Roberto Carlos Da Silva	2	48	316 mins
4	Ivan Bujia Helguera	2	55	360 mins
5	Raul Gonzalez Blanco	2	52	364 mins

KEY PLAYERS - MIDFIELDERS

David Beckham

Goals in the Champions League	1
Defensive Rating Average number of mins between goals conceded while on the pitch	105
Contribution to Attacking Power Average number of minutes between team goals while on pitch	48
Scoring Difference Defensive Rating minus Contribution to attacking power	57

	PLAYER	GOALS	DEF RATE	ATT POWER	SCORE DIFF
1	David Beckham	1	105	48	57 mins
2	Zinedine Zidane	3	80	49	31 mins
3	Luis Madeira Caeira Figo	2	78	48	30 mins
4	Jose Maria Guti	0	83	72	11 mins

KEY PLAYERS - DEFENDERS

Sanfelix Raul Bravo

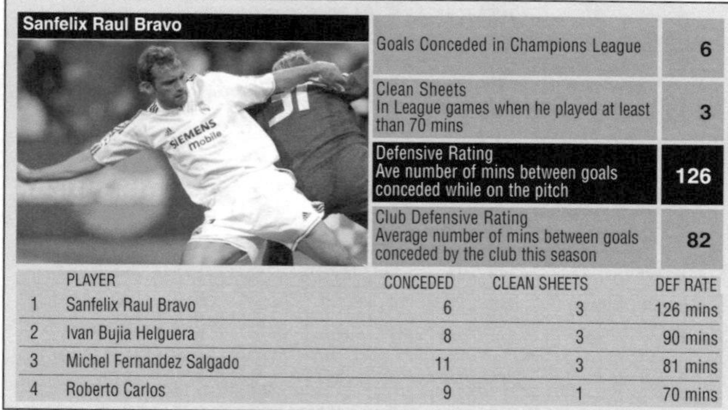

Goals Conceded in Champions League	6
Clean Sheets In League games when he played at least than 70 mins	3
Defensive Rating Ave number of mins between goals conceded while on the pitch	126
Club Defensive Rating Average number of mins between goals conceded by the club this season	82

	PLAYER	CONCEDED	CLEAN SHEETS	DEF RATE
1	Sanfelix Raul Bravo	6	3	126 mins
2	Ivan Bujia Helguera	8	3	90 mins
3	Michel Fernandez Salgado	11	3	81 mins
4	Roberto Carlos	9	1	70 mins

KEY GOALKEEPER

Iker Fernandez Casillas

Goals Conceded	10
Clean Sheets	3
Counting Games (at least 70mins)	9
Defensive Rating Ave number of mins between goals conceded while on the pitch	81

TOP POINT EARNERS

	PLAYER	GAMES	AV PTS
1	Luis Figo	5	2.60
2	Roberto Carlos	5	2.60
3	Iker Fernandez Casillas	5	2.60
4	Ronaldo	5	2.60
5	Raul Gonzalez Blanco	4	2.50
6	David Beckham	4	2.50
7	Ivan Bujia Helguera	4	2.50
8	Esteban Cambiasso	3	2.33
9	Sanfelix Raul Bravo	6	2.33
10	Zinedine Zidane	6	2.33
	CLUB AVERAGE:		1.84

Note: Points awarded for knock-out section

ARSENAL

ENGLAND
Quarter-Final

1	gb	Inter Milan	H	L	0-3		34,393
2	gb	Lok Moscow	A	D	0-0		24,000
3	gb	Dinamo Kiev	A	L	1-2	Henry 80	80,000
4	gb	Dinamo Kiev	H	W	1-0	Cole 88	34,419
5	gb	Inter Milan	A	W	5-1	Henry 25,85; Ljungberg 49; Edu 87; Pires 89	85,400
6	gb	Loko Moscow	H	W	2-0	Pires 12; Ljungberg 67	35,343
7	koL1	Celta Vigo	A	W	3-2	Edu 18,58; Pires 80	21,000
8	koL2	Celta Vigo	H	W	2-0	Henry 14,34	35,402
9	qfL1	Chelsea	A	D	1-1	Pires 59	40,778
10	qfL2	Chelsea	H	L	1-2	Reyes 45	35,486

FIRST GROUP B

	P	W	D	L	F	A	DIF	PTS
Arsenal	6	3	1	2	9	6	3	10
Lokomotiv Moskva	6	2	2	2	7	7	0	8
Internazionale	6	2	2	2	8	11	-3	8
Dynamo Kyiv	6	2	1	3	8	8	0	7

PLAYER APPEARANCES

2 Kolo Toure — Defence

Age (on 01/07/04)	23
Appearances in Champions league	10
Total minutes on the pitch	900
Goals	0
Yellow cards	1
Red cards	0
Home Country	Ivory Coast

	PLAYER	POS	AGE	APP	MINS ON	GOALS	CARDS(Y)	CARDS(R)	HOME COUNTRY
1	Jens Lehman	GK	34	10	900	0	0	0	Germany
2	Habib Kolo Toure	DEF	23	10	900	0	1	0	Ivory Coast
3	Thierry Henry	ATT	26	10	888	5	1	0	France
4	Robert Pires	MID	30	10	852	4	0	0	France
5	Sol Campbell	DEF	29	9	810	0	0	0	England
6	Ashley Cole	DEF	23	9	810	1	0	0	England
7	Lauren	DEF	27	8	720	0	1	0	Cameroon
8	Fredrik Ljungberg	MID	27	9	701	2	0	0	Sweden
9	Edu	MID	26	8	580	3	2	0	Brazil
10	Patrick Vieira	MID	28	7	570	0	1	0	France
11	Gilberto Silva	MID	27	8	464	0	1	0	Brazil
12	Dennis Bergkamp	ATT	35	6	347	0	0	0	Holland
13	Ray Parlour	MID	31	5	340	0	0	0	England
14	Sylvain Wiltord	ATT	30	4	279	0	0	0	France
15	Jose Antonio Reyes	ATT	20	3	188	1	0	0	Spain
16	Pascal Cygan	DEF	30	3	181	0	1	0	France
17	Nwankwo Kanu	ATT	27	7	175	0	0	0	Nigeria
18	Martin Keown	DEF	37	2	103	0	0	0	England
19	Gael Clichy	DEF	18	1	88	0	0	0	France
20	Jeremie Aliadiere	ATT	21	1	2	0	0	0	France
21	David Bentley	MID	19	1	2	0	0	0	England

KEY PLAYERS - GOALSCORERS

Thierry Henry

O2

Goals in the Champions League	5
Contribution to Attacking Power Average number of minutes between team goals while on pitch	59
Player Strike Rate The total number of minutes he was on the pitch for every goal scored	178
Club Strike Rate Average number of minutes between goals scored by club	56

	PLAYER	GOALS	ATT POWER	STRIKE RATE
1	Thierry Henry	5	59	178 mins
2	Edu	3	48	193 mins
3	Robert Pires	4	53	213 mins
4	Fredrik Ljungberg	2	46	351 mins
5	Ashley Cole	1	62	810 mins

KEY PLAYERS - MIDFIELDERS

Edu

Goals in the Champions League	3
Defensive Rating Average number of mins between goals conceded while on the pitch	83
Contribution to Attacking Power Average number of minutes between team goals while on pitch	48
Scoring Difference Defensive Rating minus Contribution to attacking power	35

	PLAYER	GOALS	DEF RATE	ATT POWER	SCORE DIFF
1	Edu	3	83	48	35 mins
2	Fredrik Ljungberg	2	78	47	31 mins
3	Robert Pires	4	77	53	24 mins
4	Patrick Vieira	0	63	57	6 mins

KEY PLAYERS - DEFENDERS

Ashley Cole

O2

Goals Conceded in Champions League	9
Clean Sheets In League games when he played at least than 70 mins	4
Defensive Rating Ave number of mins between goals conceded while on the pitch	90
Club Defensive Rating Average number of mins between goals conceded by the club this season	82

	PLAYER	CONCEDED	CLEAN SHEETS	DEF RATE
1	Ashley Cole	9	4	90 mins
2	Habib Kolo Toure	11	4	82 mins
3	Sol Campbell	11	3	74 mins
4	Bisan Etame Mayer Lauren	10	3	72 mins

KEY GOALKEEPER

Jens Lehmann

Goals Conceded	11
Clean Sheets	4
Counting Games (at least 70mins)	10
Defensive Rating Ave number of mins between goals conceded while on the pitch	82

TOP POINT EARNERS

	PLAYER	GAMES	AV PTS
1	Dennis Bergkamp	2	3.00
2	Pascal Cygan	2	3.00
3	Fredrik Ljungberg	3	2.00
4	Robert Pires	5	2.00
5	Edu	2	2.00
6	Sol Campbell	5	1.80
7	Ray Parlour	4	1.75
8	Gilberto Silva	4	1.75
9	Thierry Henry	6	1.67
10	Ashley Cole	6	1.67
	CLUB AVERAGE:		1.67

Note: Points awarded for knock-out section

AC MILAN

ITALY
Quarter-Final

1 gh	Ajax	H W	1-0	Inzaghi 67	48,000
2 gh	Celta Vigo	A D	0-0		27,000
3 gh	Club Brugge	H L	0-1		85,400
4 gh	Club Brugge	A W	1-0	Kaka 86	28,000
5 gh	Ajax	A W	1-0	Shevchenko 51	51,324
6 gh	Celta Vigo	H L	1-2	Kaka 41	55,510
7 koL1	Sparta Prague	A D	0-0		21,000
8 ekoL2	Sparta Prague	H W	4-1	Inzaghi 45; Shevchenko 66,79; Gattuso 85	55,000
9 qfL1	Deportivo	H W	4-1	Kaka 45,49; Shevchenko 46; Pirlo 53	60,335
10 qfL2	Deportivo	A L	0-4		30,260

FIRST GROUP H

	P	W	D	L	F	A	DIF	PTS
Milan	6	3	1	2	4	3	1	10
Celta	6	2	3	1	7	6	1	9
Club Brugge	6	2	2	2	5	6	-1	8
Ajax	6	2	0	4	6	7	-1	6

PLAYER APPEARANCES

2 Cafu — Defence

Age (on 01/07/04)	34
Appearances in Champions league	9
Total minutes on the pitch	807
Goals	0
Yellow cards	2
Red cards	0
Home Country	Brazil

	PLAYER	POS	AGE	APP	MINS ON	GOALS	CARDS(Y/R)		HOME COUNTRY
1	Nelson Dida	GK	30	9	810	0	0	0	Brazil
2	Cafu	DEF	34	9	807	0	2	0	Brazil
3	Ricardo Kaka	MID	22	10	778	4	0	0	Brazil
4	Andrea Pirlo	MID	25	9	778	1	2	0	Italy
5	Andriy Shevchenko	ATT	27	9	765	4	0	0	Ukraine
6	Paolo Maldini	DEF	36	9	753	0	1	0	Italy
7	Gennaro Gattuso	MID	26	7	630	1	2	1	Italy
8	Clarence Seedorf	MID	28	8	618	0	0	0	Holland
9	Guiseppe Pancaro	DEF	32	7	552	0	1	0	Italy
10	Filippo Inzaghi	ATT	30	8	525	2	1	0	Italy
11	Alessandro Costacurta	DEF	38	8	519	0	1	0	Italy
12	Alessandro Nesta	DEF	28	6	487	0	2	1	Italy
13	Serginho	MID	33	7	264	0	0	0	Brazil
14	Massimo Ambrosini	MID	27	6	233	0	1	0	Italy
15	Christian Brocchi	MID	28	3	198	0	1	0	Italy
16	Manuel Rui Costa	MID	32	6	198	0	0	0	Portugal
17	Martin Laursen	DEF	26	3	193	0	0	0	Denmark
18	Jon Dahl Tomasson	ATT	27	6	188	0	0	0	Denmark
19	Dario Simic	DEF	28	2	140	0	0	0	Croatia
20	Christian Abbiati	GK	27	1	90	0	0	0	Italy
21	Kakha Kaladze	DEF	26	1	90	0	0	0	Georgia
22	Fernando Redondo	MID	35	1	90	0	0	0	Argentina
23	Marco Borriello	ATT	22	1	90	0	0	0	Italy
24	Rivaldo	ATT	32	1	28	0	0	0	Brazil
25	Ignazio Abate	MID	17	1	23	0	0	0	Italy

KEY PLAYERS - GOALSCORERS

Andriy Shevchenko

Goals in the Champions League	4
Contribution to Attacking Power Average number of minutes between team goals while on pitch	69
Player Strike Rate The total number of minutes he was on the pitch for every goal scored	191
Club Strike Rate Average number of minutes between goals scored by club	75

	PLAYER	GOALS	ATT POWER	STRIKE RATE
1	Andriy Shevchenko	4	69	191 mins
2	Ricardo Santos Laite Kaka	4	70	195 mins
3	Filippo Inzaghi	2	65	263 mins
4	Gennaro Gattuso	1	57	630 mins
5	Andrea Pirlo	1	70	778 mins

KEY PLAYERS - MIDFIELDERS

Andrea Pirlo

Goals in the Champions League	1
Defensive Rating Average number of mins between goals conceded while on the pitch	130
Contribution to Attacking Power Average number of minutes between team goals while on pitch	71
Scoring Difference Defensive Rating minus Contribution to attacking power	59

	PLAYER	GOALS	DEF RATE	ATT POWER	SCORE DIFF
1	Andrea Pirlo	1	130	71	59 mins
2	Gennaro Gattuso	1	105	57	48 mins
3	Ricardo Santos Laite Kaka	4	97	71	26 mins
4	Clarence Seedorf	0	88	88	0 mins

KEY PLAYERS - DEFENDERS

Alessandro Costacurta

Goals Conceded in Champions League	2
Clean Sheets In League games when he played at least than 70 mins	3
Defensive Rating Ave number of mins between goals conceded while on the pitch	260
Club Defensive Rating Average number of mins between goals conceded by the club this season	100

	PLAYER	CONCEDED	CLEAN SHEETS	DEF RATE
1	Alessandro Costacurta	2	3	260 mins
2	Marcos de Moraes Cafu	7	5	115 mins
3	Paolo Maldini	7	4	108 mins
4	Guiseppe Pancaro	7	2	79 mins

KEY GOALKEEPER

Nelson Dida

Goals Conceded	7
Clean Sheets	5
Counting Games (at least 70mins)	9
Defensive Rating Ave number of mins between goals conceded while on the pitch	116

TOP POINT EARNERS

	PLAYER	GAMES	AV PTS
1	Clarence Seedorf	2	3.00
2	Gennaro Gattuso	3	3.00
3	Ricardo Santos Laite Kaka	3	3.00
4	Andrea Pirlo	5	2.00
5	Filippo Inzaghi	3	2.00
6	Nelson Dida	5	2.00
7	Andriy Shevchenko	5	2.00
8	Marcos de Moraes Cafu	5	2.00
9	Alessandro Costacurta	2	2.00
10	Paolo Maldini	4	1.75
	CLUB AVERAGE:		2.41

Note: Points awarded for knock-out section

MANCHESTER UNITED

ENGLAND
Last 16

						Scorers	Att
1	ge	Panathinaikos	H	W	5-0	Silvestre 14; Fortune 15; Solskjaer 33; Butt 40; Djemba-Djemba 83	66,520
2	ge	Stuttgart	A	L	1-2	van Nistelrooy 67 pen	53,000
3	ge	Rangers	A	W	1-0	Neville, P 5	48,730
4	ge	Rangers	H	W	3-0	Forlan 6; van Nistelrooy 43,60	66,707
5	ge	Panathinaikos	A	W	1-0	Forlan 85	16,000
6	ge	Stuttgart	H	W	2-0	van Nistelrooy 45; Giggs 58	67,141
7	koL1	Porto	A	L	1-2	Fortune 14	49,977
8	koL2	Porto	H	D	1-1	Scholes 32	67,029

KEY PLAYERS - GOALSCORERS

Ruud van Nistelrooy

Goals in the Champions League	4
Contribution to Attacking Power Average number of minutes between team goals while on pitch	42
Player Strike Rate The total number of minutes he was on the pitch for every goal scored	149
Club Strike Rate Average number of minutes between goals scored by club	48

	PLAYER	GOALS	ATT POWER	STRIKE RATE
1	Ruud van Nistelrooy	4	42	149 mins
2	Quinton Fortune	2	40	283 mins
3	Mikael Silvestre	1	41	540 mins
4	Phil Neville	1	43	603 mins
5	Ryan Giggs	1	45	676 mins

FIRST GROUP E

	P	W	D	L	F	A	DIF	PTS
Man. United	6	5	0	1	13	2	11	15
Stuttgart	6	4	0	2	9	6	3	12
Panathinaikos	6	1	1	4	5	13	-8	4
Rangers	6	1	1	4	4	10	-6	4

PLAYER APPEARANCES

1 Ryan Giggs Midfield

Age (on 01/07/04)	30
Appearances in Champions league	8
Total minutes on the pitch	676
Goals	1
Yellow cards	0
Red cards	0
Home Country	Wales

	PLAYER	POS	AGE	APP	MINS ON	GOALS	CARDS(Y/R)		HOME COUNTRY
1	Ryan Giggs	MID	30	8	676	1	0	0	Wales
2	Gary Neville	DEF	29	7	630	0	0	0	England
3	Tim Howard	GK	25	7	630	0	0	0	United States
4	Phil Neville	MID	27	7	603	1	1	0	England
5	Ruud van Nistelrooy	ATT	28	7	596	4	0	0	Holland
6	Quinton Fortune	MID	27	7	565	2	2	0	South Africa
7	Mikael Silvestre	DEF	26	6	540	1	0	0	France
8	Rio Ferdinand	DEF	25	6	531	0	1	0	England
9	John O'Shea	DEF	23	7	501	0	1	0	Rep of Ireland
10	Paul Scholes	MID	29	5	438	1	3	0	England
11	Roy Keane	MID	32	4	357	0	0	1	Rep of Ireland
12	Nicky Butt	MID	29	5	332	1	1	0	England
13	Christiano Ronaldo	MID	19	5	292	0	0	0	Portugal
14	Darren Fletcher	MID	20	6	286	0	0	0	Scotland
15	Diego Forlan	ATT	25	4	186	2	0	0	Uruguay
16	Wes Brown	DEF	24	2	180	0	0	0	England
17	Louis Saha	ATT	25	2	120	0	0	0	France
18	Jose Pereira Kleberson	MID	25	2	113	0	0	0	Brazil
19	David Bellion	ATT	21	4	106	0	0	0	France
20	Eric Djemba-Djemba	MID	23	4	92	1	0	0	Cameroon
21	Roy Carroll	GK	26	1	90	0	0	0	N Ireland
22	Ole Gunnar Solskjaer	ATT	31	2	53	1	0	0	Norway

LOKOMOTIV MOSCOW

RUSSIA
Last 16

						Scorers	Att
1	3ql1	Shak Donetsk	A	L	0-1		
2	3ql2	Shak Donetsk	H	W	3-2		
3	gb	Dinamo Kiev	A	L	0-2		79,500
4	gb	Arsenal	H	D	0-0		24,000
5	gb	Inter Milan	H	W	3-0	Loskov 2; Ashvetia 50; Khokhlov 57	25,000
6	gb	Inter Milan	A	D	1-1	Loskov 54	25,000
7	gb	Dinamo Kiev	H	W	3-2	Buznikin 28; Ignashevitch 45 pen; Parks 89	24,000
8	gb	Arsenal	A	L	0-2		35,343
9	koL1	Monaco	H	W	2-1	Izmailov 32; Maminov 59	28,000
10	koL2	Monaco	A	L	0-1		18,000

KEY PLAYERS - GOALSCORERS

Dmitri Loskov

Goals in the Champions League	2
Contribution to Attacking Power Average number of minutes between team goals while on pitch	79
Player Strike Rate The total number of minutes he was on the pitch for every goal scored	359
Club Strike Rate Average number of minutes between goals scored by club	90

	PLAYER	GOALS	ATT POWER	STRIKE RATE
1	Dmitri Loskov	2	79	359 mins
2	Marat Izmailov	1	95	573 mins
3	Mikheil Ashvetia	1	75	602 mins
4	Sergei Ignashevitch	1	90	630 mins
5	Dmitri Khokhlov	1	79	712 mins

SECOND GROUP B

	P	W	D	L	F	A	DIF	PTS
Arsenal	6	3	1	2	9	6	3	10
Lokomotiv Moskva	6	2	2	2	7	7	0	8
Internazionale	6	2	2	2	8	11	-3	8
Dynamo Kyiv	6	2	1	3	8	8	0	7

PLAYER APPEARANCES

2 Dimitri Sennikov Midfield

Age (on 01/07/04)	28
Appearances in Champions league	9
Total minutes on the pitch	784
Goals	0
Yellow cards	0
Red cards	0
Home Country	Russia

	PLAYER	POS	AGE	APP	MINS ON	GOALS	CARDS(Y/R)		HOME COUNTRY
1	Vladimir Maminov	MID	29	9	810	1	0	0	Russia
2	Dmitri Sennikov	MID	28	9	784	0	0	0	Russia
3	Oleg Pashinin	DEF	29	9	762	0	1	1	Russia
4	Sergei Ovchinnikov	GK	33	8	720	0	0	0	Russia
5	Dmitri Loskov	MID	30	9	718	2	4	1	Russia
6	Dmitri Khokhlov	MID	28	8	712	1	0	0	Russia
7	Sergei Ignashevitch	DEF	24	7	630	1	1	0	Russia
8	Mikheil Ashvetia	ATT	26	9	602	1	0	0	Georgia
9	Vadim Evseev	MID	28	7	596	0	2	0	Russia
10	Marat Izmailov	MID	21	7	573	1	0	0	Russia
11	Jacob Lekseto	DEF	30	6	495	0	5	1	South Africa
12	Gennadi Nizhergorodov	DEF	27	7	298	0	1	0	Russia
13	Sergei Gurenko	MID	31	5	267	0	0	0	Belarus
14	Maxim Buznikin	ATT	27	5	194	1	0	0	Russia
15	Malkhaz Asatiani	MID	22	2	180	0	1	0	Georgia
16	Winston Parks	ATT	22	5	178	1	1	0	Costa Rica
17	James Obiorah	ATT	25	2	135	0	1	0	Nigeria
18	Serguei Ovtchinnikov	ATT	19	1	90	0	0	0	Russia
19	Rouslan Pimenov	ATT	22	2	29	0	0	0	Russia
20	Jorge Wagner	ATT	25	1	17	0	0	0	Brazil
21	Leandro	ATT	23	1	4	0	0	0	Brazil

STUTTGART

GERMANY
Last 16

1	ge	Rangers	A	L	1-2	Kuranyi 45	47,957
2	ge	Man Utd	H	W	2-1	Szabics 50; Kuranyi 52	53,000
3	ge	Panathinaikos	H	W	2-0	Szabics 13; Soldo 25	50,348
4	ge	Panathinaikos	A	W	3-1	Fissas 68 og; Kuranyi 75; Hinkel 77	6,015
5	ge	Rangers	H	W	1-0	Wenzel 45	50,348
6	ge	Man Utd	A	L	0-2		67,141
7	koL1	Chelsea	H	L	0-1		50,000
8	koL2	Chelsea	A	D	0-0		36,657

KEY PLAYERS - GOALSCORERS

Kevin Kuranyi

Goals in the Champions League	3
Contribution to Attacking Power Average number of minutes between team goals while on pitch	80
Player Strike Rate The total number of minutes he was on the pitch for every goal scored	240
Club Strike Rate Average number of minutes between goals scored by club	80

	PLAYER	GOALS	ATT POWER	STRIKE RATE
1	Kevin Kuranyi	3	80	240 mins
2	Imre Szabics	2	66	268 mins
3	Andreas Hinkel	1	78	710 mins
4	Zvonimir Soldo	1	80	720 mins

SECOND GROUP E

	P	W	D	L	F	A	DIF	PTS
Man. United	6	5	0	1	13	2	11	15
Stuttgart	6	4	0	2	9	6	3	12
Panathinaikos	6	1	1	4	5	13	-8	4
Rangers	6	1	1	4	4	10	-6	4

PLAYER APPEARANCES

2 Jose Fernando Meira — Defence

Age (on 01/07/04)	26
Appearances in Champions league	8
Total minutes on the pitch	720
Goals	0
Yellow cards	1
Red cards	0
Home Country	Portugal

	PLAYER	POS	AGE	APP	MINS ON	GOALS	CARDS(Y)	CARDS(R)	HOME COUNTRY
1	Timo Hildebrand	GK	25	8	720	0	0	0	Germany
2	Jose Fernando Meira	DEF	26	8	720	0	1	0	Portugal
3	Zvonimir Soldo	MID	36	8	720	1	0	0	Croatia
4	Kevin Kuranyi	ATT	22	8	720	3	0	0	Germany
5	Andreas Hinkel	DEF	22	8	710	1	1	0	Germany
6	Alexander Hleb	MID	23	8	638	0	1	0	Belarus
7	Philip Lahm	DEF	20	7	610	0	0	0	Germany
8	Imre Szabics	ATT	23	8	535	2	0	0	Hungary
9	Horst Heldt	MID	34	7	467	0	1	0	Germany
10	Marcelo Jose Bordon	DEF	28	5	450	0	1	0	Brazil
11	Christian Tiffert	ATT	22	8	343	0	1	0	Germany
12	Timo Wenzel	DEF	26	3	270	1	0	0	Germany
13	Silvio Meissner	MID	31	7	249	0	1	0	Germany
14	Jurica Vranjes	MID	24	4	238	0	0	0	Croatia
15	Jeronimo Cacau Baretto	ATT	23	4	154	0	0	0	Brazil
16	Ioannis Amanatidis	ATT	22	3	141	0	0	0	Greece
17	Heiko Gerber	MID	31	2	100	0	0	0	Germany
18	Boris Zivkovic	DEF	28	1	90	0	0	0	Croatia
19	Emanuel Centurion	ATT	21	2	33	0	0	0	Argentina
20	Mario Gomez	ATT	18	1	10	0	0	0	Germany
21	Serge Branco	DEF	23	1	2	0	0	0	Cameroon

JUVENTUS

ITALY
Last 16

1	gd	Galatasaray	H	W	2-1	Del Piero 5; Ferrara 73	14,420
2	gd	Olympiakos	A	W	2-1	Nedved 21,79	77,400
3	gd	Real Sociedad	H	W	4-2	Trezeguet 3,63; Di Vaio 7,45	17,246
4	gd	Real Sociedad	A	D	0-0		29,000
5	gd	Galatasaray	A	L	0-2		60,000
6	gd	Olympiakos	H	W	7-0	Trezeguet 14,25; Miccoli 19; Maresca 28; Di Vaio 62; Del Piero 67; Zalayeta 79	12,500
7	koL1	Deportivo	A	L	0-1		30,000
8	koL2	Deportivo	H	L	0-1		24,680

KEY PLAYERS - GOALSCORERS

Pavel Nedved

2 David Trezeguet

Goals in the Champions League	2
Contribution to Attacking Power Average number of minutes between team goals while on pitch	67
Player Strike Rate The total number of minutes he was on the pitch for every goal scored	269
Club Strike Rate Average number of minutes between goals scored by club	48

	PLAYER	GOALS	ATT POWER	STRIKE RATE
1	Pavel Nedved	2	67	269 mins
2	David Trezeguet	4	30	
3	Marco Di Vaio	3	51	
4	Alessandro Del Piero	2	53	

FIRST GROUP D

	P	W	D	L	F	A	DIF	PTS
Juventus	6	4	1	1	15	6	9	13
Real Sociedad	6	2	3	1	8	8	0	9
Galatasaray	6	2	1	3	6	8	-2	7
Olympiacos	6	1	1	4	6	13	-7	4

PLAYER APPEARANCES

2 Pavel Nedved — Midfield

Age (on 01/07/04)	31
Appearances in Champions league	6
Total minutes on the pitch	538
Goals	2
Yellow cards	0
Red cards	0
Home Country	Czech Republic

	PLAYER	POS	AGE	APP	MINS ON	GOALS	CARDS(Y)	CARDS(R)	HOME COUNTRY
1	Gianluigi Buffon	GK	26	6	540	0	0	0	Italy
2	Pavel Nedved	MID	31	6	538	2	0	0	Czech Republic
3	Stephen Appiah	MID	23	7	489	0	0	0	Ghana
4	Lilian Thuram	DEF	32	5	450	0	0	0	France
5	Paolo Montero	DEF	32	6	431	0	1	0	Uruguay
6	Alessio Tacchinardi	MID	28	6	415	0	2	0	Italy
7	Marco Di Vaio	ATT	27	7	408	3	1	0	Italy
8	Fabrizio Miccoli	ATT	25	6	408	1	1	0	Italy
9	Igor Tudor	DEF	26	5	370	0	2	0	Croatia
10	Gianluca Zambrotta	MID	27	5	367	0	0	0	Italy
11	David Trezeguet	ATT	26	5	360	4	0	0	France
12	Ciro Ferrara	DEF	37	4	360	1	2	0	Italy
13	Gianluca Pessotto	DEF	33	5	354	0	0	0	Italy
14	Edgar Davids	MID	31	5	341	0	3	0	Holland
15	Mark Iuliano	DEF	30	4	337	0	1	0	Italy
16	Antonio Conte	MID	34	4	283	0	3	0	Italy
17	Nicola Legrottaglie	DEF	27	3	225	0	0	0	Italy
18	Marcelo Zalayeta	ATT	25	3	225	1	1	0	Uruguay
19	Alessandro Birindelli	DEF	29	5	224	0	0	0	Italy
20	Alessandro Del Piero	ATT	29	4	212	2	0	0	Italy
21	Mauro Camoranesi	MID	27	4	202	0	0	0	Argentina

REAL SOCIEDAD

SPAIN
Last 16

1 gd	Olympiakos	H	W	1-0	Kovacevic 80 pen	29,000
2 gd	Galatasaray	A	W	2-1	Kovacevic 3; Xabier Alonso 72	17,600
3 gd	Juventus	A	L	2-4	Tudor 67 og; De Pedro 80	17,246
4 gd	Juventus	H	D	0-0		29,000
5 gd	Olympiakos	A	D	2-2	Gabilondo 31; Schurrer 74	14,000
6 gd	Galatasaray	H	D	1-1	De Paula 51	29,000
7 kl1	Lyon	H	L	0-1		29,000
8 kl2	Lyon	A	L	0-1		38,914

KEY PLAYERS - GOALSCORERS

Darko Kovacevic

Goals in the Champions League	2
Contribution to Attacking Power Average number of minutes between team goals while on pitch	115
Player Strike Rate The total number of minutes he was on the pitch for every goal scored	289
Club Strike Rate Average number of minutes between goals scored by club	90

	PLAYER	GOALS	ATT POWER	STRIKE RATE
1	Darko Kovacevic	2	115	289 mins
2	Gabriel Peralta Schurrer	1	104	624 mins
3	Olano Xabier Alonso	1	86	690 mins

SECOND GROUP D

	P	W	D	L	F	A	DIF	PTS
Juventus	6	4	1	1	15	6	9	13
Real Sociedad	6	2	3	1	8	8	0	9
Galatasaray	6	2	1	3	6	8	-2	7
Olympiacos	6	1	1	4	6	13	-7	4

PLAYER APPEARANCES

1 Valeri Karpin Midield

Age (on 01/07/04)	35
Appearances in Champions league	8
Total minutes on the pitch	711
Goals	0
Yellow cards	1
Red cards	0
Home Country	Russia

	PLAYER	POS	AGE	APP	MINS ON	GOALS	CARDS(Y/R)		HOME COUNTRY
1	Valeri Karpin	MID	35	8	711	0	1	0	Russia
2	Olano Xabier Alonso	MID	22	8	690	1	2	0	Spain
3	Igor Iraola Jauregui	MID	30	8	632	0	1	0	Spain
4	Agustin Alkorta Aranzabal	DEF	31	7	630	0	0	0	Spain
5	Gabriel Peralta Schurrer	DEF	32	7	624	1	3	0	Argentina
6	Darko Kovacevic	ATT	30	7	578	2	2	1	Serbia & Mont.
7	Bittor Alkiza Fernandez	MID	33	7	560	0	1	0	Spain
8	Aitor Lopez Rekarte	DEF	28	6	540	0	1	0	Spain
9	Sander Westerveld	GK	29	6	540	0	0	0	Holland
10	Kahveci Nihat	ATT	24	8	471	0	0	0	Turkey
11	Campo Gabilondo	MID	25	6	457	1	0	0	Spain
12	Miguel Aramburu	MID	25	7	297	0	1	0	Spain
13	Lionel Potillon	DEF	30	3	270	0	0	0	France
14	Bjorn Tore Kvarme	DEF	31	2	180	0	0	0	Norway
15	Lopez Fernandez Alberto	GK	35	2	180	0	0	0	Spain
16	Chun-Soo Lee	ATT	22	6	176	0	0	0	South Korea
17	Oscar Gamero De Paula	ATT	29	5	162	1	0	0	Spain
18	Francisco de Pedro	MID	30	3	130	1	0	0	Spain
19	Jose Javier Barkero	MID	25	1	62	0	0	0	Spain
20	Sergio Bor	DEF	24	2	8	0	0	0	Spain

BAYERN MUNICH

GERMANY
Last 16

1 ga	Celtic	H	W	2-1	Makaay 73,86	48,500
2 ga	Anderlecht	A	D	1-1	Santa Cruz 74	23,328
3 ga	Lyon	A	D	1-1	Makaay 25	38,145
4 ga	Lyon	H	L	1-2	Makaay 14	59,000
5 ga	Celtic	A	D	0-0		59,506
6 ga	Anderlecht	H	W	1-0	Makaay 41 pen	52,000
7 eckl1	Real Madrid	H	D	1-1	Makaay 75	59,000
8 eckl2	Real Madrid	A	L	0-1		75,000

KEY PLAYERS - GOALSCORERS

Roy Makaay

Goals in the Champions League	6
Contribution to Attacking Power Average number of minutes between team goals while on pitch	102
Player Strike Rate The total number of minutes he was on the pitch for every goal scored	120
Club Strike Rate Average number of minutes between goals scored by club	103

	PLAYER	GOALS	ATT POWER	STRIKE RATE
1	Roy Makaay	6	102	120 mins

Roque Santa Cruz, the only other scorer did not play sufficient minutes to Chart a Strike Rate

SECOND GROUP A

	P	W	D	L	F	A	DIF	PTS
Lyon	6	3	1	2	7	7	0	10
Bayern	6	2	3	1	6	5	1	9
Celtic	6	2	1	3	8	7	1	7
Anderlecht	6	2	1	3	4	6	-2	7

PLAYER APPEARANCES

4 Bixente Lizarazu Defence

Age (on 01/07/04)	34
Appearances in Champions league	8
Total minutes on the pitch	668
Goals	0
Yellow cards	3
Red cards	0
Home Country	France

	PLAYER	POS	AGE	APP	MINS ON	GOALS	CARDS(Y/R)		HOME COUNTRY
1	Roy Makaay	ATT	29	8	720	6	1	0	Holland
2	Michael Ballack	MID	27	8	720	0	2	0	Germany
3	Oliver Kahn	GK	35	8	720	0	1	0	Germany
4	Bixente Lizarazu	DEF	34	8	658	0	3	0	France
5	Robert Kovac	DEF	30	7	630	0	2	0	Croatia
6	Samuel Osei Kuffour	DEF	27	7	612	0	2	0	Ghana
7	Jose Ze Roberto	ATT	30	7	576	0	1	0	Brazil
8	Owen Hargreaves	MID	23	6	467	0	0	0	England
9	Claudio Pizarro	ATT	25	7	442	0	2	1	Peru
10	Willy Sagnol	DEF	27	6	432	0	2	0	France
11	Hazan Salihamidzic	MID	27	8	418	0	1	0	Bosnia
12	Martin Demichelis	DEF	23	5	385	0	2	0	Argentina
13	Thomas Linke	DEF	34	4	360	0	0	0	Germany
14	Roque Santa Cruz	ATT	22	8	359	1	1	0	Paraguay
15	Jens Jeremies	MID	30	4	155	0	1	0	Germany
16	Sebastian Deisler	MID	24	1	90	0	0	0	Germany
17	Bastian Schweinsteiger	MID	19	3	86	0	0	0	Germany
18	Mehmet Scholl	MID	33	1	19	0	0	0	Germany
19	Tobias Rau	MID	22	1	17	0	0	0	Germany

CELTA VIGO

SPAIN
Last 16

1	ql1	Slavia Prague	H	W	3-0	Mostovoi 17; Jesuli 50; Edu 54	25,000
2	ql2	Slavia Prague	A	L	0-2		
3	gh	Club Brugge	A	D	1-1	Juanfran 50	26,639
4	gh	AC Milan	H	D	0-0		27,000
5	gh	Ajax	A	L	0-1		48,514
6	gh	Ajax	H	W	3-2	Luccin 25 pen; Milosevic 39; Vagner 63	20,000
7	gh	Club Brugge	H	D	1-1	Mostovoi 74	22,000
8	gh	AC Milan	A	W	2-1	Jesuli 42; Jose Ignacio 71	55,510
9	kl1	Arsenal	H	L	2-3	Edu 27; Jose Ignacio 64	21,000
10	kl2	Arsenal	A	L	0-2		35,402

KEY PLAYERS - GOALSCORERS

Saenz Marin Jose Ignacio

Goals in the Champions League	2
Contribution to Attacking Power Average number of minutes between team goals while on pitch	58
Player Strike Rate The total number of minutes he was on the pitch for every goal scored	265
Club Strike Rate Average number of minutes between goals scored by club	68

	PLAYER	GOALS	ATT POWER	STRIKE RATE
1	Saenz Marin Jose Ignacio	2	58	265 mins
2	Alexander Mostovoi	2	68	308 mins
3	Jesus Antonio Jesuli	2	66	332 mins
4	Juan Francisco Garcia	1	77	540 mins
5	Savo Milosevic	1	52	629 mins

SECOND GROUP H

	P	W	D	L	F	A	DIF	PTS
Milan	6	3	1	2	4	3	1	10
Celta	6	2	3	1	7	6	1	9
Club Brugge	6	2	2	2	5	6	-1	8
Ajax	6	2	0	4	6	7	-1	6

PLAYER APPEARANCES

2 Savo Milosevic — Attack

Age (on 01/07/04)	30
Appearances in Champions league	8
Total minutes on the pitch	663
Goals	2
Yellow cards	1
Red cards	0
Home Country	Serbia & Mont.

	PLAYER	POS	AGE	APP	MINS ON	GOALS	CARDS(Y)	CARDS(R)	HOME COUNTRY
1	Jesus Antonio Jesuli	MID	26	8	663	2	1	0	Spain
2	Savo Milosevic	ATT	30	8	629	1	1	0	Serbia & Mont.
3	Alexander Mostovoi	MID	35	7	616	2	1	0	Russia
4	Juan Francisco Garcia	DEF	27	6	540	1	2	0	Spain
5	Fernando Gabriel Caceres	DEF	35	6	534	0	1	0	Argentina
6	Jose Ignacio	MID	30	6	529	2	1	0	Spain
7	Lopez Ruano Angel	ATT	23	8	528	0	2	0	Spain
8	Sylvinho	DEF	30	8	525	0	2	0	Brazil
9	Fernandez Sergio	DEF	27	6	495	0	1	0	Spain
10	Peter Luccin	MID	25	6	478	1	1	0	France
11	Juan Velasco Damas	DEF	27	6	464	0	0	0	Spain
12	Eduardo Berizzo	DEF	34	5	450	0	2	0	Argentina
13	Pablo Cavallero	GK	30	5	422	0	0	0	Argentina
14	Jose Colorado	GK	28	5	388	0	1	0	Spain
15	Pablo Gustavo Lopez	MID	31	6	332	0	0	0	Argentina
16	Rogerio Nunes Vagner	MID	25	5	311	1	1	0	Brazil
17	Pablo Contreras	DEF	25	6	287	0	3	1	Chile
18	Everton Giovanella	MID	33	4	271	0	2	0	Brazil
19	Luis Schmidt Edu	ATT	25	2	141	2	1	0	Brazil
20	Mauricio Pinilla	ATT	20	2	106	0	0	0	Chile
21	Borja Melendez Oubina	MID	22	2	91	0	0	0	Spain

SPARTA PRAGUE

CZECH REPUBLIC
Last 16

1	ql1	Vardar Skopje	A	W	3-2	Poborsky 36,89; Gluscevic 40	
2	ql2	Vardar Skopje	H	D	2-2		
3	gg	Chelsea	H	L	0-1		18,997
4	gg	Lazio	A	D	2-2	Sionko 27; Poborsky 35	30,000
5	gg	Besiktas	H	W	2-1	Zelenka, L 58; Poborsky 84	14,512
6	gg	Besiktas	A	L	0-1		25,000
7	gg	Chelsea	A	D	0-0		40,152
8	gg	Lazio	H	W	1-0	Kincl 90	17,825
9	kl1	AC Milan	H	D	0-0		21,000
10	kl2	AC Milan	A	L	1-4	Jun 59	55,000

KEY PLAYERS - GOALSCORERS

Karel Poborsky

Goals in the Champions League	4
Contribution to Attacking Power Average number of minutes between team goals while on pitch	90
Player Strike Rate The total number of minutes he was on the pitch for every goal scored	203
Club Strike Rate Average number of minutes between goals scored by club	90

	PLAYER	GOALS	ATT POWER	STRIKE RATE
1	Karel Poborsky	4	90	203 mins
2	Lukas Zelenka	1	117	589 mins

Other scorers did not play sufficient minutes to chart

SECOND GROUP G

	P	W	D	L	F	A	DIF	PTS
Chelsea	6	4	1	1	9	3	6	13
Sparta	6	2	2	2	5	5	0	8
Besiktas	6	2	1	3	5	7	-2	7
Lazio	6	1	2	3	6	10	-4	5

PLAYER APPEARANCES

2 Radoslav Kovac — Midfield

Age (on 01/07/04)	24
Appearances in Champions league	9
Total minutes on the pitch	810
Goals	0
Yellow cards	1
Red cards	0
Home Country	Czech Republic

	PLAYER	POS	AGE	APP	MINS ON	GOALS	CARDS(Y)	CARDS(R)	HOME COUNTRY
1	Jaromir Blazek	GK	31	9	810	0	0	0	Czech Republic
2	Radoslav Kovac	MID	24	9	810	0	1	0	Czech Republic
3	Tomas Hubschmann	DEF	22	9	810	0	0	0	Czech Republic
4	Karel Poborsky	MID	32	9	810	4	0	0	Czech Republic
5	Petr Johana	DEF	27	8	720	0	3	0	Czech Republic
6	Vladimir Labant	DEF	30	8	716	0	0	0	Slovakia
7	Pavel Pergl	MID	26	7	630	0	1	0	Czech Republic
8	Lukas Zelenka	MID	24	7	589	1	0	0	Midfield
9	Libor Sionko	MID	27	6	468	1	0	0	Czech Republic
10	Ratislav Michalik	MID	30	9	398	0	0	0	Slovenia
11	Igor Gluscevic	ATT	30	8	360	1	0	0	Serbia & Mont.
12	Jiri Nemec	MID	38	3	270	0	0	0	Czech Republic
13	Marek Kincl	ATT	31	4	260	1	0	0	Czech Republic
14	Tomas Jun	ATT	21	6	191	1	0	0	Czech Republic
15	Martin Petras	DEF	24	2	180	0	0	0	Slovakia
16	Pavel Krmas	MID	24	3	174	0	0	0	Czech Republic
17	Jiri Stajner	ATT	28	2	171	0	0	0	Czech Republic
18	Jan Flachbart	ATT	26	3	111	0	0	0	Czech Republic
19	Tomas Sivok	MID	20	2	91	0	1	0	Czech Republic
20	Jiri Homola	DEF	24	1	90	0	0	0	Czech Republic
21	Patrik Jezek	DEF	27	4	79	0	0	0	Czech Republic
22	Mirko Poledica	DEF	25	2	75	0	0	1	Serbia & M'negro

CELTIC

SCOTLAND
3rd in Group A

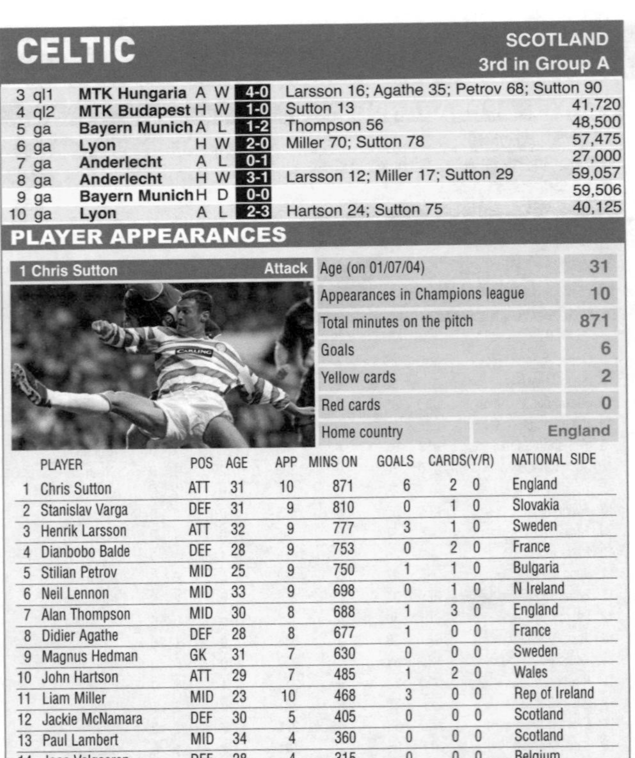

3	ql1	MTK Hungaria	A	W	4-0	Larsson 16; Agathe 35; Petrov 68; Sutton 90	
4	ql2	MTK Budapest	H	W	1-0	Sutton 13	41,720
5	ga	Bayern Munich	A	L	1-2	Thompson 56	48,500
6	ga	Lyon	H	W	2-0	Miller 70; Sutton 78	57,475
7	ga	Anderlecht	A	L	0-1		27,000
8	ga	Anderlecht	H	W	3-1	Larsson 12; Miller 17; Sutton 29	59,057
9	ga	Bayern Munich	H	D	0-0		59,506
10	ga	Lyon	A	L	2-3	Hartson 24; Sutton 75	40,125

PLAYER APPEARANCES

1 Chris Sutton — Attack	
Age (on 01/07/04)	31
Appearances in Champions league	10
Total minutes on the pitch	871
Goals	6
Yellow cards	2
Red cards	0
Home country	England

	PLAYER	POS	AGE	APP	MINS ON	GOALS	CARDS(Y)	CARDS(R)	NATIONAL SIDE
1	Chris Sutton	ATT	31	10	871	6	2	0	England
2	Stanislav Varga	DEF	31	9	810	0	1	0	Slovakia
3	Henrik Larsson	ATT	32	9	777	3	1	0	Sweden
4	Dianbobo Balde	DEF	28	9	753	0	2	0	France
5	Stilian Petrov	MID	25	9	750	1	1	0	Bulgaria
6	Neil Lennon	MID	33	9	698	0	1	0	N Ireland
7	Alan Thompson	MID	30	8	688	1	3	0	England
8	Didier Agathe	DEF	28	8	677	1	0	0	France
9	Magnus Hedman	GK	31	7	630	0	0	0	Sweden
10	John Hartson	ATT	29	7	485	1	2	0	Wales
11	Liam Miller	MID	23	10	468	3	0	0	Rep of Ireland
12	Jackie McNamara	DEF	30	5	405	0	0	0	Scotland
13	Paul Lambert	MID	34	4	360	0	0	0	Scotland
14	Joos Valgaeren	DEF	28	4	315	0	0	0	Belgium
15	Robert Douglas	GK	32	3	270	0	0	0	Scotland
16	Johan Mjallby	DEF	33	3	270	0	0	0	Sweden

INTER MILAN

ITALY
3rd in Group B

1	gb	Arsenal	A	W	3-0	Cruz 22; van der Meyde 24; Martins 41	34,393
2	gb	Dinamo Kiev	H	W	2-1	Adani 23; Vieri 90	70,882
3	gb	Lokomotiv M.	A	L	0-3		25,000
4	gb	Lokomotiv M.	H	D	1-1	Recoba 14	25,000
5	gb	Arsenal	H	L	1-5	Vieri 32	85,400
6	gb	Dinamo Kiev	A	D	1-1	Adani 68	30,000

PLAYER APPEARANCES

6. Christian Vieri — Attack	
Age (on 01/07/04)	30
Appearances in Champions league	6
Total minutes on the pitch	540
Goals	2
Yellow cards	0
Red cards	0
Home country	Italy

	PLAYER	POS	AGE	APP	MINS ON	GOALS	CARDS(Y)	CARDS(R)	NATIONAL SIDE
1	Javier Zanetti	MID	30	6	540	0	0	0	Argentina
2	Francesco Toldo	GK	32	6	540	0	0	0	Italy
3	Fabio Cannavaro	DEF	30	6	508	0	1	0	Italy
4	Ivan Cordoba	DEF	27	5	450	0	0	0	Colombia
5	Cristiano Zanetti	MID	27	5	426	0	1	0	Italy
6	Christian Vieri	ATT	30	5	392	2	0	0	Italy
7	Julio Cruz	ATT	29	6	339	1	0	0	Argentina
8	Marco Materazzi	DEF	30	4	330	0	1	0	Italy
9	Obafemi Martins	ATT	19	5	310	1	0	0	Nigeria
10	Matias Almeyda	MID	30	4	304	0	0	0	Argentina
11	Emre Belozoglu	MID	23	4	273	0	1	0	Turkey
12	Daniele Adani	DEF	29	3	270	2	0	0	Italy
13	Kily Gonzalez	MID	29	3	269	0	1	0	Argentina
14	Andy van der Meyde	MID	24	4	244	1	0	0	Holland
15	Alvaro Recoba	ATT	28	3	167	1	1	0	Uruguay
16	Jeremie Brechet	DEF	24	2	161	0	1	0	France

PSV EINDHOVEN

HOLLAND
3rd in Group C

1	gpc	Monaco	H	L	1-2	Bouma 65	30,000
2	gpc	Deportivo	A	L	0-2		28,480
3	gpc	AEK Athens	A	W	1-0	Lucius 36	10,000
4	gpc	AEK Athens	H	W	2-0	Bouma 51; Robben 63	28,000
5	gpc	Monaco	A	D	1-1	Vennegoor 84	12,175
6	gpc	Deportivo	H	W	3-2	de Jong 14,90; Robben 48	32,000

PLAYER APPEARANCES

5 Argen Robben — Attack	
Age (on 01/07/04)	20
Appearances in Champions league	6
Total minutes on the pitch	478
Goals	2
Yellow cards	2
Red cards	0
Home country	Holland

	PLAYER	POS	AGE	APP	MINS ON	GOALS	CARDS(Y)	CARDS(R)	NATIONAL SIDE
1	Mateja Kezman	ATT	25	6	540	0	1	0	Serbia & Mont.
2	Wilfred Bouma	ATT	26	6	540	2	0	0	Holland
3	Ronald Waterreus	GK	33	6	540	0	0	0	Holland
4	Young-Pyo Lee	MID	27	6	527	0	0	0	South Korea
5	Argen Robben	ATT	20	6	478	2	2	0	Holland
6	Andre Ooijer	DEF	29	5	450	0	1	0	Holland
7	Ji-Sung Park	MID	23	5	405	0	1	0	South Korea
8	Johann Vogel	MID	27	4	346	0	1	0	Switzerland
9	Dennis Rommedahl	ATT	25	4	315	0	0	0	Denmark
10	John de Jong	MID	27	5	291	2	0	0	Holland
11	Kevin Hofland	DEF	25	3	242	0	3	0	Holland
12	Theo Lucius	MID	27	3	230	1	2	1	Holland
13	Jurgen Colin	DEF	23	4	227	0	0	0	Holland
14	Mark van Bommel	MID	27	2	180	0	0	0	Holland
15	Jan Vennegoor of Hess.	ATT	25	4	176	1	0	0	Holland
16	Kasper Bogelund	DEF	23	2	161	0	1	0	Denmark

GALATASARAY

TURKEY
3rd in Group D

3	gd	Juventus	A	L	1-2	Sukur 19	14,420
4	gd	Real Sociedad	H	L	1-2	Sukur 60	17,600
5	gd	Olympiakos	H	W	1-0	Cihan 9	41,000
6	gd	Olympiakos	A	L	0-3		14,000
7	gd	Juventus	H	W	2-0	Sukur 47,90	60,000
8	gd	Real Sociedad	A	D	1-1	Sukur 27	29,000

PLAYER APPEARANCES

2 Hakan Suker — Attack	
Age (on 01/07/04)	32
Appearances in Champions league	7
Total minutes on the pitch	628
Goals	6
Yellow cards	1
Red cards	0
Home country	Turkey

	PLAYER	POS	AGE	APP	MINS ON	GOALS	CARDS(Y)	CARDS(R)	NATIONAL SIDE
1	Faryd Mondragon	GK	33	7	630	0	1	0	Colombia
2	Hakan Sukur	ATT	32	7	628	6	1	0	Turkey
3	Frank de Boer	DEF	34	7	618	0	0	0	Holland
4	Penbe Ergun	MID	32	7	605	0	0	0	Turkey
5	Bulent Korkmaz	DEF	35	7	547	0	1	0	Turkey
6	Sarioglu Sabri	MID	19	6	460	0	1	0	Turkey
7	Gokhan Hasan Sas	MID	27	6	435	1	2	1	Turkey
8	Cesar Prates	DEF	29	6	411	0	1	0	Brazil
9	Hakan Unsal	DEF	31	5	360	0	2	0	Turkey
10	Joao Batista	MID	29	4	320	0	0	0	Brazil
11	Akman Ayhan	MID	27	4	288	0	2	0	Turkey
12	Ovidiu Petre	MID	22	3	270	0	1	0	Romania
13	Haspolati Cihan	MID	24	6	254	1	1	0	Turkey
14	Erden Arif	ATT	32	5	234	1	0	0	Turkey
15	Sebastian Tamas	DEF	20	4	232	0	1	0	Romania
16	Goktan Berkant	ATT	23	2	180	0	1	0	Turkey

PANATHINAIKOS

GREECE
3rd in Group E

1	ge	Man Utd	A	L	0-5		66,520
2	ge	Rangers	H	D	1-1	Konstanindis 88	13,718
3	ge	Stuttgart	A	L	0-2		50,348
4	ge	Stuttgart	H	L	1-3	Konstantinou 60	6,015
5	ge	Man Utd	H	L	0-1		16,000
6	ge	Rangers	A	W	3-1	Zutautas 32; Basinas 62; Konstantinou 80	48,588

PLAYER APPEARANCES

3 Michael Konstantinou — Attack

Age (on 01/07/04)	26
Appearances in Champions league	6
Total minutes on the pitch	479
Goals	2
Yellow cards	1
Red cards	0
Home country	Cyprus

	PLAYER	POS	AGE	APP	MINS ON	GOALS	CARDS(Y)	CARDS(R)	NATIONAL SIDE
1	Georgios Seitaridis	DEF	23	6	540	0	0	0	Greece
2	Raimondas Zutautas	MID	31	6	540	1	0	0	Lithuania
3	Michael Konstantinou	ATT	26	6	479	2	1	0	Cyprus
4	Rene Henriksen	DEF	34	5	450	0	0	0	Denmark
5	Silvio Maric	MID	29	5	437	0	1	0	Coatia
6	Antonias Nikopolidis	GK	32	5	405	0	0	0	Greece
7	Panagiotis Fissas	DEF	31	4	360	0	1	0	Greece
8	Angelis Basinas	MID	28	4	360	1	0	0	Greece
9	Yannis Goumas	DEF	29	5	326	0	3	1	Greece
10	Dimitrios Papadopoulos	ATT	22	5	306	0	0	0	Greece
11	Nasief Morris	DEF	23	3	270	0	0	0	South Africa
12	Jan Michaelsen	MID	33	3	250	0	1	0	Denmark
13	Markus Munch	DEF	31	3	248	0	2	0	Germany
14	Joel Epalle	MID	26	4	213	0	1	0	Cameroon
15	Lucian Sanmartean	MID	24	4	200	0	1	0	Romania

MARSEILLE

FRANCE
3rd in Group F

3	gf	Real Madrid	A	L	2-4	Drogba 26; Van Buyten 83	65,000
4	gf	Partizan	H	W	3-0	Drogba 62,68,85	56,825
5	gf	Porto	H	L	2-3	Drogba 24; Marlet 84	59,000
6	gf	Porto	A	L	0-1		33,215
7	gf	Real Madrid	H	L	1-2	Mido 63	59,000
8	gf	Partizan	A	D	1-1	Mido 61	35,000

PLAYER APPEARANCES

5. Didier Drogba — Attack

Age (on 01/07/04)	26
Appearances in Champions league	7
Total minutes on the pitch	537
Goals	5
Yellow cards	1
Red cards	0
Home country	Ivory Coast

	PLAYER	POS	AGE	APP	MINS ON	GOALS	CARDS(Y)	CARDS(R)	NATIONAL SIDE
1	Abdoulaye Meite	DEF	23	7	630	0	1	0	France
2	Daniel Van Buyten	DEF	26	7	630	1	1	0	Belgium
3	Vedran Runje	GK	29	6	540	0	1	0	Croatia
4	Johnny Ecker	DEF	31	6	540	0	0	0	France
5	Didier Drogba	ATT	26	7	537	5	1	0	Ivory Coast
6	Ibrahim Hemdani	MID	26	7	528	0	0	0	France
7	Ahmed Hossam Mido	ATT	21	7	509	2	2	0	Egypt
8	Stepan Vachousek	ATT	24	7	472	0	2	0	Czech Republic
9	Fabio Celestini	MID	28	5	450	0	0	0	Switzerland
10	Camel Meriem	MID	24	5	432	0	0	0	France
11	Steve Marlet	ATT	30	4	265	1	1	0	France
12	Habib Beye	DEF	27	3	255	0	0	0	France
13	Pascal Johansen	MID	25	4	246	0	0	0	France
14	Philippe Christanval	DEF	25	3	195	0	0	0	France
15	Dmitri Sychev	MID	20	5	153	1	0	0	Russia
16	Sylvain N'Diaye	MID	28	3	139	0	0	0	Senegal

BESIKTAS

TURKEY
3rd in Group G

1	gpg	Lazio	H	L	0-2		28,000
2	gpg	Chelsea	A	W	2-0	Yalcin 24,29	32,957
3	gpg	Sparta Prague	A	L	1-2	Pancu 60 pen	14,512
4	gpg	Sparta Prague	H	W	1-0	Ronaldo 82	25,000
5	gpg	Lazio	A	D	1-1	Pancu 45 pen	40,000
6	gpg	Chelsea	H	L	0-2		55,350

PLAYER APPEARANCES

1 Oscar Cordoba — Goalkeeper

Age (on 01/07/04)	34
Appearances in Champions league	6
Total minutes on the pitch	540
Goals	0
Yellow cards	0
Red cards	0
Home country	Columbia

	PLAYER	POS	AGE	APP	MINS ON	GOALS	CARDS(Y)	CARDS(R)	NATIONAL SIDE
1	Oscar Cordoba	GK	34	6	540	0	0	0	Columbia
2	Guiaro Ronaldo	DEF	30	6	540	1	1	0	Brazil
3	Havutcu Tayfur	MID	34	6	540	0	1	0	Turkey
4	Daniel Pancu	ATT	26	6	540	2	1	0	Romania
5	Antonio Carlos Zago	DEF	34	6	540	0	1	0	Brazil
6	Uzulmez Ibrahim	MID	30	6	516	0	0	0	Turkey
7	Sergen Yalcin	MID	31	6	437	2	1	0	Turkey
8	Federico Giunti	MID	32	5	406	0	3	0	Italy
9	Ilhan Mansiz	ATT	28	5	375	0	2	1	Turkey
10	Emre Asik	DEF	30	4	360	0	2	0	Turkey
11	Kaan Dopra	MID	32	5	341	0	0	0	Poland
12	Ahmet Yildirim	MID	30	3	181	0	0	0	Turkey
13	Okan Koc	MID	22	3	171	0	0	0	Turkey
14	Metin Tumer	MID	29	4	107	0	0	0	Turkey
15	Yasin Sulun	MID	26	2	103	0	0	0	Turkey
16	Ahmed Hassan	MID	29	5	93	0	0	0	Egypt

CLUB BRUGGE

BELGIUM
3rd in Group H

3	gh	Celta Vigo	H	D	1-1	Saeternes 84	26,639
4	gh	Ajax	A	L	0-2		49,731
5	gh	AC Milan	A	W	1-0	Mendoza 33	85,400
6	gh	AC Milan	H	L	0-1		28,000
7	gh	Celta Vigo	A	D	1-1	Lange 90	22,000
8	gh	Ajax	H	W	2-1	Lange 27; Saeternes 84	28,041

PLAYER APPEARANCES

3. Philippe Clement — Midfield

Age (on 01/07/04)	28
Appearances in Champions league	7
Total minutes on the pitch	615
Goals	0
Yellow cards	1
Red cards	0
Home country	Belgium

	PLAYER	POS	AGE	APP	MINS ON	GOALS	CARDS(Y)	CARDS(R)	NATIONAL SIDE
1	Olivier De Cock	DEF	28	7	630	0	1	0	Belgium
2	Timmy Simons	MID	28	7	630	0	0	0	Belgium
3	Philippe Clement	MID	30	7	615	0	0	0	Belgium
4	Gert Verheyen	ATT	33	7	552	1	2	0	Belgium
5	Peter van der Heyden	DEF	27	6	540	0	1	0	Belgium
6	David Rozehnal	DEF	24	6	528	0	1	0	Czech Republic
7	Nastja Ceh	ATT	26	7	516	1	0	0	Slovenia
8	Dany Verlinden	GK	40	5	450	0	1	0	Belgium
9	Sandy Martens	MID	31	5	395	0	2	1	Belgium
10	Ivan Gvozdenovic	MID	25	6	367	0	0	0	Serbia & Mont.
11	Gaetan Englebert	MID	28	4	303	0	2	0	Belgium
12	Andres Mendoza	ATT	26	4	297	1	0	1	Peru
13	Bierger Maertens	MID	24	3	270	0	0	0	Belgium
14	Bengt Saeternes	ATT	29	7	259	2	1	0	Norway
15	Tomislav Butina	GK	29	2	180	0	0	0	Croatia
16	Alin Stoica	MID	24	4	145	0	0	0	Romania

ANDERLECHT

BELGIUM
4th in Group A

1	ql1	Wisla Krakow	H W	3-1	Jestrovic 12; Lovre 39; Dindane 59	
2	ql2	Wisla Krakow	A W	1-0		
3	gpa	Lyon	A L	0-1		32,000
4	gpa	Bayern Munich	H D	1-1	Mornar 53	23,328
5	gpa	Celtic	H W	1-0	Dindane 72	27,000
6	gpa	Celtic	A L	1-3	Dindane 77	59,057
7	gpa	Lyon	H W	1-0	Tihinen 71	26,208
8	gpa	Bayern Munich	A L	0-1		52,000

PLAYER APPEARANCES

6 Aruna Dindane — Midfield

Age (on 01/07/04)	23
Appearances in Champions league	6
Total minutes on the pitch	540
Goals	3
Yellow cards	2
Red cards	0
Home country	Ivory Coast

	PLAYER	POS	AGE	APP	MINS ON	GOALS	CARDS(Y/R)		NATIONAL SIDE
1	Walter Baseggio	MID	25	7	630	0	1	0	Belgium
2	Daniel Zitka	GK	29	7	630	0	1	0	Czech Republic
3	Oliver Deschacht	DEF	23	7	630	0	1	0	Belgium
4	Besnik Hasi	MID	32	7	590	0	2	0	Albania
5	Hannu Tihinen	DEF	28	7	541	1	1	0	Finland
6	Aruna Dindane	MID	23	6	540	3	2	0	Ivory Coast
7	Vincent Kompany	DEF	18	6	540	0	0	0	Belgium
8	Michal Zewlakow	DEF	28	6	489	0	2	0	Poland
9	Ivica Mornar	ATT	30	6	473	1	0	0	Croatia
10	Christian Wilhelmsson	MID	24	6	437	0	1	0	Sweden
11	Par Zetterberg	MID	33	5	275	0	1	0	Sweden
12	Ki-Hyeun Seol	ATT	25	3	270	0	0	0	South Korea
13	Marc Hendrikx	DEF	30	5	254	0	2	0	Belgium
14	Martin Kolar	MID	20	5	219	0	0	0	Czech Republic
15	Glen De Boeck	DEF	32	2	116	0	2	1	Belgium
16	Oliver Doll	DEF	31	1	90	0	0	0	Belgium

DINAMO KIEV

UKRAINE
4th in Group B

1	3ql1	Din Zagreb	H W	3-1	Fedorov 32; Leko 38; Gusev 82	
2	3ql2	Din Zagreb	A W	2-0		
3	gpb	Loko Moscow	H W	2-0	Rincon 83,90	79,500
4	gpb	Inter Milan	A L	1-2	Fedorov 34	70,882
5	gpb	Arsenal	H W	2-1	Shatskikh 27; Belkevich 64	80,000
6	gpb	Arsenal	A L	0-1		34,419
7	gpb	Loko Moscow	A L	2-3	Belkevich 37; Shatskikh 65	24,000
8	gpb	Inter Milan	H D	1-1	Rincon 85	30,000

PLAYER APPEARANCES

5 Jerko Leko — Midfield

Age (on 01/07/04)	24
Appearances in Champions league	6
Total minutes on the pitch	540
Goals	1
Yellow cards	2
Red cards	0
Home country	Croatia

	PLAYER	POS	AGE	APP	MINS ON	GOALS	CARDS(Y/R)		NATIONAL SIDE
1	Valentin Belkevich	ATT	31	7	630	2	0	0	Belarus
2	Andrii Nesmachnyi	DEF	25	7	630	0	1	0	Ukraine
3	Olexandr Shovkovskiy	GK	29	7	630	0	0	0	Ukraine
4	Maksim Shatskikh	ATT	25	7	605	2	0	0	Uzbekistan
5	Jerko Leko	MID	24	6	540	1	2	0	Croatia
6	Goran Gavrancic	DEF	25	6	540	0	0	0	Serbia & Mont.
7	Georgi Pejev	ATT	25	6	468	0	0	0	Bulgaria
8	Tiberiu Ghioane	MID	23	6	466	0	0	0	Romania
9	Sergeiy Fedorov	DEF	29	5	450	2	0	0	Ukraine
10	Diogo Rincon	ATT	24	7	447	3	1	0	Brazil
11	Goran Sablic	DEF	24	5	398	0	2	0	Ukraine
12	Yuri Dmitrulin	DEF	29	6	342	0	1	0	Ukraine
13	Oleg Gusev	MID	21	6	313	1	0	0	Ukraine
14	Alexandre Khatskevitch	MID	30	5	171	0	0	0	Belarus
15	Andriy Husin	MID	31	1	90	0	0	0	Ukraine
16	Denys Onischenko	MID	25	2	85	0	0	0	Ukraine

AEK ATHENS

GREECE
4th in Group C

3	gc	Deportivo	H D	1-1	Tsartas 85	16,000
4	gc	Monaco	A L	0-4		15,000
5	gc	PSV Eindhoven	H L	0-1		10,000
6	gc	PSV Eindhoven	A L	0-2		28,000
7	gc	Deportivo	A L	0-3		30,260
8	gc	Monaco	H D	0-0		4,000

PLAYER APPEARANCES

5 Nikolaos Georgeas — Defence

Age (on 01/07/04)	27
Appearances in Champions league	5
Total minutes on the pitch	450
Goals	0
Yellow cards	1
Red cards	0
Home country	Greece

	PLAYER	POS	AGE	APP	MINS ON	GOALS	CARDS(Y/R)		NATIONAL SIDE
1	Konstantinos Katsouranis	MID	25	7	630	0	1	0	Greece
2	Theodoros Zagorakis	MID	32	7	615	0	0	0	Greece
3	Vassilios Tsartas	MID	31	7	539	1	2	0	Greece
4	Yiannis Okkas	ATT	27	7	531	0	2	0	Cyprus
5	Nikolaos Georgeas	DEF	27	5	450	0	1	0	Greece
6	Michalis Kapsis	DEF	30	5	379	0	1	0	Greece
7	Vassilios Borbokis	DEF	35	5	375	0	0	0	Greece
8	Nikos Kostenoglou	DEF	33	5	368	0	1	0	Greece
9	Nikos Liberopoulos	ATT	28	5	366	0	0	0	Greece
10	Chrisostomos Mihailidis	GK	29	4	360	0	0	0	Greece
11	Evangelos Moras	DEF	22	5	315	0	0	0	Greece
12	Mihalis Kassapis	DEF	33	5	313	0	1	0	Greece
13	Dionisios Chiotis	GK	27	3	270	0	0	0	Greece
14	Kofi Amponsah	DEF	26	3	245	0	2	1	Ghana
15	Vassilios Lakis	MID	27	4	223	0	0	0	Greece
16	Christos Maladenis	MID	30	3	202	0	0	0	Greece

OLYMPIAKOS

GREECE
4th in Group D

1	gd	Real Sociedad	A L	0-1		29,000
2	gd	Juventus	H L	1-2	Stoltidis 11	77,400
3	gd	Galatasaray	A L	0-1		41,000
4	gd	Galatasaray	H W	3-0	Mavrogenidis 6; Castillo 34; Giovanni 90	14,000
5	gd	Real Sociedad	H D	2-2	Stoltidis 59; Castillo 71	14,000
6	gd	Juventus	A L	0-7		12,500

PLAYER APPEARANCES

1 Christian Karembeu — Midfield

Age (on 01/07/04)	33
Appearances in Champions league	6
Total minutes on the pitch	540
Goals	0
Yellow cards	0
Red cards	0
Home country	France

	PLAYER	POS	AGE	APP	MINS ON	GOALS	CARDS(Y/R)		NATIONAL SIDE
1	Christian Karembeu	MID	33	6	540	0	0	0	France
2	Stelios Venetidis	DEF	27	6	535	0	2	0	Greece
3	Silva Giovanni	MID	31	6	471	1	1	0	Brazil
4	Anastasios Pantos	DEF	28	6	467	0	1	0	Greece
5	Dimitrios Mavrogenidis	DEF	27	6	456	1	0	0	Greece
6	Predrag Djordjevic	MID	31	5	450	0	3	1	Serbia & Mont.
7	Georgios Anatolakis	DEF	30	5	427	0	2	0	Greece
8	Ieroklis Stoltidis	MID	29	5	421	2	2	0	Greece
9	Nery Castillo	MID	20	5	395	2	2	0	Uruguay
10	Theofanis Katergiannakis	GK	30	4	360	0	0	0	Greece
11	Pareskevas Antzas	MID	27	4	315	0	0	0	Greece
12	Athanasios Kostoulas	DEF	28	4	271	0	0	0	Greece
13	Pantelis Kafes	MID	26	5	242	0	0	0	Greece
14	Georgios Georgiadis	MID	32	5	242	0	0	0	Greece
15	Juraj Bucek	GK	30	1	90	0	0	0	Slovakia
16	Dimitrios Eleftheropoulos	GK	27	1	90	0	0	0	Greece

RANGERS

SCOTLAND
4th in Group E

1 ql1	FC Copenhag.	H D	1-1	Lovenkrands 7	47,401
2 ql2	FC Copenhag.	A W	2-1	Arteta 52 pen; Arveladze 86	35,519
3 ge	Stuttgart	H W	2-1	Nerlinger 72; Lovenkrands 79	47,957
4 ge	Panathinaikos	A D	1-1	Emerson 35	13,718
5 ge	Man Utd	H L	0-1		48,730
6 ge	Man Utd	A L	0-3		66,707
7 ge	Stuttgart	A L	0-1		50,348
8 ge	Panathinaikos	H L	1-3	Mols 28	48,588

PLAYER APPEARANCES

7 Mikel Arteta — Midfield

Age (on 01/07/04)	22
Appearances in Champions league	6
Total minutes on the pitch	540
Goals	1
Yellow cards	1
Red cards	0
Home country	Spain

	PLAYER	POS	AGE	APP	MINS ON	GOALS	CARDS(Y	/R)	NATIONAL SIDE
1	Stefan Klos	GK	32	8	720	0	0	0	Germany
2	Michael Ball	DEF	24	8	720	0	0	0	England
3	Zurab Khizanishvili	DEF	22	8	690	0	1	0	Georgia
4	Henning Berg	DEF	34	7	611	0	0	0	Norway
5	Michael Mols	ATT	33	8	604	1	0	0	Holland
6	Peter Lovenkrands	MID	24	7	559	2	1	0	Denmark
7	Mikel Arteta	MID	22	6	540	1	1	0	Spain
8	Shota Arveladze	ATT	31	6	534	1	1	0	Georgia
9	Fernando Ricksen	DEF	27	6	481	0	2	0	Holland
10	Nuno Fernando Capucho	MID	32	6	354	0	0	0	Portugal
11	Craig Moore	DEF	28	4	337	0	0	0	Australia
12	Maurice Ross	DEF	23	6	306	0	0	0	Scotland
13	Paolo Vanoli	DEF	31	7	303	0	0	0	Italy
14	Stephen Hughes	MID	21	3	270	0	1	0	Scotland
15	Christian Nerlinger	MID	31	4	210	1	1	0	Germany
16	Barry Ferguson	MID	26	2	180	0	1	0	Scotland

PARTIZAN

SERBIA & MONTENEGRO
4th in Group F

1 ql1	Newcastle	H L	0-1		32,500
2 ql2	Newcastle	A W	4-3*	Iliev 50 (*on penalties)	37,293
3 gf	Porto	H D	1-1	Delibasic 54	32,000
4 gf	Marseille	A L	0-3		56,825
5 gf	Real Madrid	A L	0-1		72,485
6 gf	Real Madrid	H D	0-0		32,700
7 gf	Porto	A L	1-2	Delibasic 90	22,177
8 gf	Marseille	H D	1-1	Delibasic 61	35,000

PLAYER APPEARANCES

2 Sasa Ilic — Midfield

Age (on 01/07/04)	26
Appearances in Champions league	7
Total minutes on the pitch	581
Goals	0
Yellow cards	0
Red cards	0
Home country	Serbia & Montenegro

	PLAYER	POS	AGE	APP	MINS ON	GOALS	CARDS(Y	/R)	NATIONAL SIDE
1	Ivica Iliev	ATT	24	7	611	0	0	0	Serbia & Mont.
2	Sasa Ilic	MID	26	7	585	0	0	0	Serbia & Mont.
3	Igor Duljaj	MID	24	7	585	0	0	0	Serbia & Mont.
4	Nikola Malbasa	DEF	26	6	468	0	1	0	Serbia & Mont.
5	Nenad Djordjevic	MID	-	5	449	0	1	0	Serbia & Mont.
6	Branko Savic	DEF	31	6	409	0	0	0	Serbia & Mont.
7	Andrija Delibasic	ATT	23	5	405	3	2	0	Serbia & Mont.
8	Taribo West	DEF	30	4	360	0	1	0	Nigeria
9	Djordje Pantic	GK	24	4	360	0	0	0	Serbia & Mont.
10	Milwoje Cirkovic	DEF	27	5	348	0	0	0	Serbia & Mont.
11	Albert Nadj	MID	29	4	335	0	1	0	Serbia & Mont.
12	Milan Stojanoski	DEF	30	6	324	0	0	0	Macedonia
13	Tomasz Rzasa	DEF	31	4	272	0	1	0	Poland
14	Ljubinko Drulovic	ATT	35	7	251	0	0	0	Serbia & Mont.
15	Branimir Bajic	DEF	24	2	180	0	0	0	Serbia & Mont.
16	Dejan Ognjanovic	DEF	26	2	180	0	0	0	Serbia & Mont.

LAZIO

ITALY
4th in Group G

1 ql1	Benfica	H W	3-1	Corradi 16; Fiore 50; Mihajlovic 80	50,000
2 ql2	Benfica	A W	1-0	Cesar 28	18,000
3 gg	Besiktas	A W	2-0	Stam 37; Fiore 77	28,000
4 gg	Sparta Prague	H D	2-2	Inzaghi 46,61 pen	30,000
5 gg	Chelsea	A L	1-2	Inzaghi 38	40,405
6 gg	Chelsea	H L	0-4		50,000
7 gg	Besiktas	H D	1-1	Muzzi 56	40,000
8 gg	Sparta Prague	A L	0-1		17,825

PLAYER APPEARANCES

1 Dejan Stankovic — Midfield

Age (on 01/07/04)	25
Appearances in Champions league	7
Total minutes on the pitch	623
Goals	0
Yellow cards	1
Red cards	0
Home country	Serbia & Mont.

	PLAYER	POS	AGE	APP	MINS ON	GOALS	CARDS(Y	/R)	NATIONAL SIDE
1	Dejan Stankovic	MID	25	7	623	0	1	0	Serbia & Mont.
2	Bernardo Corradi	ATT	28	7	622	1	2	0	Italy
3	Giuseppe Favalli	DEF	32	7	567	0	0	0	Italy
4	Demetrio Albertini	MID	32	7	542	0	0	0	Italy
5	Jaap Stam	DEF	31	6	540	1	0	0	Holland
6	Angelo Peruzzi	GK	34	6	540	0	0	0	Italy
7	Stefano Fiore	MID	29	7	478	2	1	0	Italy
8	Massimo Oddo	DEF	28	5	450	0	2	0	Italy
9	Simone Inzaghi	ATT	28	5	325	3	1	0	Italy
10	Sinisa Mihajlovic	DEF	35	4	322	1	3	1	Serbia & Mont.
11	Luciano Zauri	MID	26	4	292	0	0	0	Italy
12	Sergio Conceicao	MID	29	6	277	0	0	0	Portugal
13	Fernando Couto	DEF	34	3	270	0	0	0	Portugal
14	Roberto Muzzi	ATT	32	6	213	1	1	0	Italy
15	Paolo Negro	DEF	32	3	213	0	0	0	Italy
16	Fabio Liverani	MID	28	6	211	0	1	0	Italy

AJAX

HOLLAND
4th in Group H

1 ql1	Grazer AK	A D	1-1	Sneijder 79 fk	15,428
2 ql2	Grazer AK	H W	2-1	Ibrahimovic 16; Galasek 104 pen	48,000
3 gh	AC Milan	A L	0-1		48,000
4 gh	Club Brugge	H W	2-0	Sonck 11,54	49,731
5 gh	Celta Vigo	H W	1-0	Ibrahimovic 54	48,514
6 gh	Celta Vigo	A L	2-3	Sonck 53; van der Vaart 82	20,000
7 gh	AC Milan	H L	0-1		51,324
8 gh	Club Brugge	A L	1-2	Sonck 42 pen	28,041

PLAYER APPEARANCES

7 Wesley Sneijder — Midfield

Age (on 01/07/04)	20
Appearances in Champions league	7
Total minutes on the pitch	505
Goals	1
Yellow cards	1
Red cards	0
Home country	Holland

	PLAYER	POS	AGE	APP	MINS ON	GOALS	CARDS(Y	/R)	NATIONAL SIDE
1	Scherrer Maxwell	DEF	22	8	750	0	1	0	Brazil
2	Bogdan Lonut Lobont	GK	26	7	660	0	0	0	Romania
3	Julien Escude	DEF	24	7	639	0	1	0	France
4	Zlatan Ibrahimovic	ATT	22	8	595	2	2	0	Sweden
5	Rafael van der Vaart	MID	21	7	593	1	3	0	Holland
6	Tomas Galasek	MID	31	6	557	1	2	0	Czech Republic
7	Wesley Sneijder	MID	20	7	505	1	1	0	Holland
8	Wesley Sonck	ATT	25	7	492	4	0	0	Belgium
9	Petri Pasanen	DEF	23	4	390	0	1	0	Finland
10	Steven Pienaar	MID	22	5	389	0	0	0	South Africa
11	Zdenek Grygera	DEF	24	4	383	0	2	1	Czech Republic
12	Abubakarl Yakubu	DEF	22	5	345	0	1	0	Ghana
13	Hatem Trabelsi	DEF	25	4	333	0	0	0	Tunisia
14	Nigel de Jong	DEF	19	5	328	0	2	0	Holland
15	Nicolae Mitea	ATT	19	4	295	0	0	0	Romania
16	John Heitinga	DEF	20	3	207	0	1	0	Holland

THE UEFA CUP

1ST ROUND

	AGG		1ST	2ND
AIK Solna	0-2	Valencia	0-1	0-1
Apoel Nicosia	3-6	Mallorca	1-2	2-4
Austria Vienna	1-3	B Dortmund	1-2	0-1
Auxerre	2-0	Neuchatel	1-0	1-0
Bordeaux	3-2	Artmedia Pet	2-1	1-1
Brondby	2-0	Zizkov	1-0	1-0
Cementarnica	0-6	Lens	0-1	0-5
CSKA Sofia	2-2	Torpedo Moscow	1-1	1-1
		Torpedo Moscow win on penalties		
D Bucharest	5-2	Shakhtar Donetsk	2-0	3-2
D Zagreb	3-1	MTK Hungaria	3-1	0-0
Dundee	1-3	Perugia	1-2	0-1
Ferencvaros	2-2	FC Copenhagen	1-1	1-1
		FC Copenhagen win on penalties		
Feyenoord	3-1	Karnten	2-1	1-0
FK Sartid	2-4	Slavia Prague	1-2	1-2
FK Ventspils	1-10	Rosenborg BK	1-4	0-6
Gaziantepspor	1-0	Hapoel Tel-Aviv	1-0	0-0
Genclerbirligi	4-2	Blackburn	3-1	1-1
Grasshoppers	1-1	Hajduk Split	1-1	0-0
		Hajduk Split win on away goals rule		
Hamburg	2-4	Dnipro	2-1	0-3
Hapoel R-Gan	0-5	Levski Sofia	0-1	0-4
Hearts	2-0	Zeljeznicar	2-0	0-0
Hertha Berlin	0-1	Groclin Grodzisk	0-0	0-1
Kaiserslautern	1-3	FK Teplice	1-2	0-1
Kamen I Veli	0-1	Schalke	0-0	0-1
La Louviere	1-2	Benfica	1-1	0-1
Leiria	2-3	Molde	1-0	1-3
Maccabi Haifa	4-3	NK Publikum	2-1	2-2
Malatyaspor	2-3	Basel	0-2	2-1
		After Extra Time		
Man City	4-2	Lokeren	3-2	1-0
Met Donetsk	1-4	Parma	1-1	0-3
MyPa-47	0-3	Sochaux	0-1	0-2
Newcastle	6-0	NAC Breda	5-0	1-0
Odense	5-6	Crvena Zvezda	2-2	3-4
O Ljubljana	1-4	Liverpool	1-1	0-3
Panionios	3-1	Nordsjaelland	2-1	1-0
PAOK Salonika	3-1	SFK Lyn	0-1	3-0
Puchov	1-9	Barcelona	1-1	0-8
Roma	5-1	Vardar Skopje	4-0	1-1
Salzburg	2-2	Udinese	0-1	2-1
		Salzburg win on away goals rule		
Southampton	1-2	Steaua Bucharest	1-1	0-1
Sp Lisbon	3-0	Malmo	2-0	1-0
Spartak M	3-1	Esbjerg	2-0	1-1
Utrecht	6-0	Zilina	2-0	4-0
Valerenga	1-1	Grazer AK	0-0	1-1
		Valerenga win on away goals rule		
Varteks	3-6	Debreceni	1-3	2-3
Villarreal	3-2	Trabzonspor	0-0	3-2
Wisla Krakow	4-2	NEC Nijmegen	2-1	2-1
Zimbru	2-3	Aris	1-1	1-2

2ND ROUND

	AGG		1ST	2ND
B Dortmund	2-6	Sochaux	2-2	0-4
Basel	2-4	Newcastle	2-3	0-1
Benfica	5-1	Molde	3-1	2-0
Bordeaux	2-1	Hearts	0-1	2-0
D Zagreb	1-3	Dnipro	0-2	1-1
FC Copenhagen	2-3	Mallorca	1-2	1-1
Feyenoord	1-3	FK Teplice	0-2	1-1
Gaziantepspor	6-1	Lens	3-0	3-1
Genclerbirligi	4-1	Sp Lisbon	1-1	3-0
Man City	1-1	Groclin Grodzisk	1-1	0-0
		Groclin Grodzisk win on away goals rule		
Panionios	0-5	Barcelona	0-3	0-2
PAOK Salonika	1-1	Debreceni	1-1	0-0
		Debreceni win on away goals rule		
Perugia	3-1	Aris	2-0	1-1
Roma	2-1	Hajduk Split	1-0	1-1
Rosenborg BK	1-0	Crvena Zvezda	0-0	1-0
Salzburg	0-9	Parma	0-4	0-5
Schalke	3-3	Brondby	2-1	1-2
		Brondby win on penalties		
Slavia Prague	2-2	Levski Sofia	2-2	0-0
		Levski Sofia win on away goals		
Spartak M	5-3	D Bucharest	4-0	1-3
S Bucharest	1-2	Liverpool	1-1	0-1
Utrecht	0-4	Auxerre	0-0	0-4
Valencia	4-0	Maccabi Haifa	0-0	4-0
Valerenga	0-0	Wisla Krakow	0-0	0-0
		Valerenga win on penalties		
Villarreal	2-1	Torpedo Moscow	2-0	0-1

3RD ROUND

Auxerre (0) 0 Panathinaikos (0) 0
19,000

Panathinaikos (0) 0 Auxerre (0) 1
14,500
Kalou 72

Benfica (0) 1 Rosenborg BK (0) 0
Zahovic 59

Rosenborg BK (2) 2 Benfica (1) 1
Berg 8
Karadas 16
Nuno Gomes 21
18,200
Benfica win on away goals

Brondby (0) 0 Barcelona (0) 1
29,925
Ronaldinho 63

Barcelona (2) 2 Brondby (0) 1
Luis Garcia 31
Cocu, P 43
Nielsen 84
44,100

Celtic (2) 3 FK Teplice (0) 0
Larsson 3,90
Sutton 13
48,947

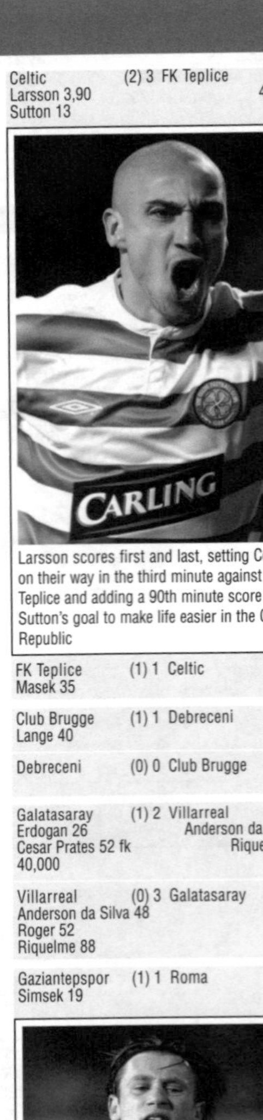
CARLING

Larsson scores first and last, setting Celtic on their way in the third minute against Teplice and adding a 90th minute score to Sutton's goal to make life easier in the Czech Republic

FK Teplice (1) 1 Celtic (0) 0
Masek 35
10,000

Club Brugge (1) 1 Debreceni (0) 0
Lange 40
20,586

Debreceni (0) 0 Club Brugge (0) 0
7,000

Galatasaray (1) 2 Villarreal (2) 2
Erdogan 26
Cesar Prates 52 fk
Anderson da Silva 7
Riquelme 22
40,000

Villarreal (0) 3 Galatasaray (0) 0
Anderson da Silva 48
Roger 52
Riquelme 88
15,960

Gaziantepspor (1) 1 Roma (0) 0
Simsek 19
18,000

DIADORA
mazda

Cassano puts Roma through with a vital second goal in a tough tie against Gaziantepspor after Emerson levels the Turks' goal from their home leg

Roma (2) 2 Gaziantepspor (0) 0
Emerson 23
Cassano 43
11,191

Groclin Grodzisk (0) 0 Bordeaux (0) 1
5,000
Chamakh 90

Bordeaux (2) 4 Groclin Grodzisk (0) 1
Planus 41
Chamakh 42,65
Riera 74 pen
Wieszczycki 90
9,197

Liverpool (0) 2 Levski Sofia (0) 0
Gerrard 67
Kewell 70
39,149

Cracking strikes by Gerrard and Kewell put Liverpool on track against Levski Sofia and they add early goals in the away leg in Bulgaria to make sure

Reebok

Levski Sofia (2) 2 Liverpool (3) 4
Ivanov, G 27
Simonovich 40
Gerrard 7
Owen 11
Hamann 43
Hyypia 67
40,281

Marseille (0) 1 Dnipro (0) 0
Drogba 54 pen
25,000

Dnipro (0) 0 Marseille (0) 0
25,000

Parma (0) 0 Genclerbirligi (0) 1
3,598
Skoko 59

Genclerbirligi (1) 3 Parma (0) 0
Daems 37 pen
Ferrari 81 og
Tandogan 90
19,000

Perugia (0) 0 PSV Eindhoven (0) 0
10,000

PSV Eindhoven (2) 3 Perugia (0) 1
Hofland 22
Kezman 44,48
Ze Maria 88
25,000

Sochaux (0) 2 Inter Milan (1) 2
Frau 59,81
Vieri 18
Recoba 61
20,000

Inter Milan (0) 0 Sochaux (0) 0
30,000
Inter Milan win on away goals

Spartak Moscow (0) 0 Mallorca (0) 3
30,000
Eto'o 67
Gonzalez 81, Perera 85

Mallorca (0) 0 Spartak Moscow (1) 1
5,000
Samedov 44

Valencia (2) 3 Besiktas (2) 2
Sissoko 25
Canobbio 43, Navarro 90
Pancu 17,39
34,450

Besiktas (0) 0 Valencia (1) 2
20,800
Angulo 12
Sanchez 57

Valerenga (0) 1 Newcastle (1) 1
Normann 54
Bellamy 39
25,000

Newcastle (1) 3 Valerenga (1) 1
Shearer 19
Ameobi 47,89
Hagen 25
38,531

4TH ROUND

Auxerre Tainio 36 17,850	(1) 1	PSV Eindhoven Lucius 72	(0) 1
PSV Eindhoven Kezman 4,27 Van Bommel 73	(2) 3	Auxerre 25,000	(0) 0
Benfica	(0) 0	Inter Milan 64,569	(0) 0
Inter Milan Martins 45,70 Recoba 60 Vieri 64	(1) 4	Benfica Nuno Gomes 36,67 Tiago 77 27,638	(1) 3
Bordeaux Celades 59,71 Riera 87	(0) 3	Club Brugge Verheyen 58 14,398	(0) 1
Club Brugge 27,000	(0) 0	Bordeaux Chamakh 84	(0) 1
Celtic Thompson 59	(0) 1	Barcelona 59,539	(0) 0
Barcelona	(0) 0	Celtic 78,000	(0) 0
Genclerbirligi Daems 12 pen	(1) 1	Valencia 30,000	(0) 0
Valencia Mista 63 Vicente 94	(0) 2	Genclerbirligi 37,100	(0) 0

Inter Milan win on away goals

Liverpool Baros 55 41,270	(0) 1	Marseille Drogba 78	(0) 1
Marseille Drogba 38 pen Meite 58	(1) 2	Liverpool Heskey 15 50,000	(1) 1
Newcastle Bellamy 67 Shearer 71 Robert 74 Bramble 84	(0) 4	Mallorca Correa 57 38,012	(0) 1
Mallorca 11,500	(0) 0	Newcastle Shearer 46,89 Bellamy 78	(0) 3
Villarreal Anderson da Silva 29 José Mari 35	(2) 2	Roma 23,000	(0) 0
Roma Emerson 10 Cassano 50	(1) 2	Villarreal Anderson da Silva 66 29,088	(0) 1

Kezman adds to reputation with a brace against Auxerre that puts PSV in control at home after an away draw in France

Inter find no way past Barthez as the well-marshalled Marseilles defence defies the Italians over both legs and secures a win with Meriem adding to Drogba's first leg goal

Martins edges best of seven thriller against Benfica who refuse to give way after a 0-0 draw in Portugal. Gomes scores twice for the visitors to ensure a tense finish but Martins' second proves enough for Inter

Josico's glancing header is enough to knock-out last year's finalists Celtic with the 1-1 draw in Scotland putting Villarreal in the driving seat for the return leg which they win 2-0

Barca blow up in the tunnel with Motta and Celtic's keeper Douglas not coming out after a halftime scuffle. Saviola is also sent off and after Thompson scores it is 18-year-old replacement goalie Marshall who eclipses stars like Ronaldinho and Larsson over the two legs

Valencia ring the changes after a goalless first leg, coach Benítez leaves Aimar out and triumphs in the second leg of this all-Spanish semi-final.
With the Spanish league title in their grasp, Valencia were always likely to be top dogs in this domestic dispute and a Mista penalty settled the tie.

Drogba shows his threat by volleying onto the post in a tight first leg at St James' Park.
Then the French League's footballer of the year hits a brace in the second leg tormenting a Newcastle defence which lacks Woodgate's pace, while Marseille comfortably contain Shearer and Co.

QUARTER FINALS

Marseille Drogba 46	(0) 1	Inter Milan 60,000	(0) 0
Inter Milan 36,044	(0) 0	Marseille Meriem 74	(0) 1
Celtic Larsson 64 58,493	(0) 1	Villarreal Josico 9	(1) 1
Villarreal Anderson 6 Roger 68	(1) 2	Celtic 15,964	(0) 0
Bordeaux Riera 18 29,108	(1) 1	Valencia Baraja 75 Rufete 88	(0) 2
Valencia Pellegrino 52 Rufete 60	(0) 2	Bordeaux Costa 77 42,400	(0) 1
PSV Eindhoven Kezman 15 35,000	(1) 1	Newcastle Jenas 45	(1) 1
Newcastle Shearer 9 Speed 66	(1) 2	PSV Eindhoven Kezman 52 pen 50,083	(0) 1

SEMI FINALS

Villarreal	(0) 0	Valencia 16,800	(0) 0
Valencia Mista 16 pen	(1) 1	Villarreal 53,000	(0) 0
Newcastle	(0) 0	Marseille 52,004	(0) 0
Marseille Drogba 18,82	(1) 2	Newcastle 57,500	(0) 0

THE FINAL

Marseille 40,000	(0) 0	Valencia Vicente 45 pen Mista 57	(1) 2

VICENTE
14
UEFA CUP

Barthez's moment of madness sends the final Valencia's way.
The Spanish champions made it two trophies in as many weeks, capitalising on the ex-Man United keeper's rash challenge in first half stoppage time.
Referee Collina correctly showed the Marseille goalie a red card for bringing down striker Mista on the edge of the six-yard box with Vicente converting the resulting penalty. Valencia controlled the second half, dominating possession and scoring the second goal with Vicente sweeping a pass for Mista to score his fifth goal of the competition giving reserve keeper Gavanon no chance.
Drogba never quite found a way past the last line of defence and Valencia claimed their first European trophy for 24 years.

UEFA Cup Winners
Göteborg 2004

EUROPEAN LEAGUES ROUND-UP

FINAL PREMIERSHIP LEAGUE TABLE - TOP THREE

		HOME					AWAY					TOTAL			
	P	W	D	L	F	A	W	D	L	F	A	F	A	DIF	PTS
Arsenal	38	15	4	0	40	14	11	8	0	33	12	73	26	47	90
Chelsea	38	12	4	3	34	13	12	3	4	33	17	67	30	37	79
Man Utd	38	12	4	3	37	15	11	2	6	27	20	64	35	29	75

FINAL DUTCH LEAGUE TABLE - TOP THREE

		HOME					AWAY					TOTAL			
	P	W	D	L	F	A	W	D	L	F	A	F	A	DIF	PTS
Ajax	34	16	1	0	47	10	9	4	4	32	21	79	31	48	80
PSV Eindhoven	34	11	3	3	45	14	12	2	3	47	16	92	30	62	74
Feyenoord	34	12	2	3	39	20	8	6	3	32	18	71	38	33	68

FINAL FRENCH LEAGUE TABLE - TOP THREE

		HOME					AWAY					TOTAL			
	P	W	D	L	F	A	W	D	L	F	A	F	A	DIF	PTS
Lyon	38	13	4	2	39	8	11	3	5	25	18	64	26	38	79
Paris SG	38	13	4	2	33	15	9	6	4	17	13	50	28	22	76
Monaco	38	11	5	3	35	16	10	7	2	24	14	59	30	29	75

FINAL GERMAN LEAGUE TABLE - TOP THREE

		HOME					AWAY					TOTAL			
	P	W	D	L	F	A	W	D	L	F	A	F	A	DIF	PTS
W Bremen	34	11	4	2	42	21	11	4	2	37	17	79	38	41	74
Bayern Munich	34	13	3	1	43	19	7	5	5	27	20	70	39	31	68
B Leverkusen	34	12	1	4	43	18	7	7	3	30	21	73	39	34	65

FINAL ITALIAN LEAGUE TABLE - TOP THREE

		HOME					AWAY					TOTAL			
	P	W	D	L	F	A	W	D	L	F	A	F	A	DIF	PTS
AC Milan	34	14	2	1	39	15	11	5	1	26	9	65	24	41	82
Roma	34	13	1	3	45	12	8	7	2	23	7	68	19	49	71
Juventus	34	13	1	3	40	18	8	5	4	27	24	67	42	25	69

FINAL SPANISH LEAGUE TABLE - TOP THREE

		HOME					AWAY					TOTAL			
	P	W	D	L	F	A	W	D	L	F	A	F	A	DIF	PTS
Valencia	38	12	3	4	38	16	11	5	3	33	11	71	27	44	77
Barcelona	38	10	6	3	33	14	11	3	5	30	25	63	39	24	72
Deportivo	38	13	3	3	36	15	8	5	6	24	19	60	34	26	71

CLUB STRIKE FORCE

PHILI

De Jong and team-mates celebrate a goal

Goals scored in the League	92

1 PSV Eindhoven

Club Strike Rate (CSR) Average number of minutes between League goals scored by club	33

	CLUB	LEAGUE GOALS	CSR
1	PSV Eindhoven	92	33
2	W Bremen	79	39
3	Ajax	79	39
4	B Leverkusen	73	42
5	Feyenoord	71	43
6	Bayern Munich	70	44
7	Roma	68	45
8	Juventus	67	46
9	AZ Alkmaar	65	47
10	AC Milan	65	47
11	Arsenal	73	47
12	Real Madrid	72	48
13	Valencia	71	48
14	Roda JC Kerk	60	51
15	Chelsea	67	51
16	B Dortmund	59	52
17	Inter Milan	59	52
18	Lyon	64	53
19	NAC Breda	58	53
20	Man Utd	64	53

CLUB DEFENCES

1 Roma

Club Defensive Rate (CDR) Average number of minutes between League goals conceded by club	161

	CLUB	CONCEDED	CLEAN SH	CDR
1	Roma	19	20	161
2	Lyon	26	19	132
3	Arsenal	26	15	132
4	Stuttgart	24	18	128
5	AC Milan	24	15	128
6	Valencia	27	20	127
7	Paris SG	28	19	122
8	Monaco	30	17	114
9	Chelsea	30	21	114
10	PSV Eindhoven	30	15	102
11	Auxerre	34	13	101
12	Deportivo	34	17	101
13	Ajax	31	14	99
14	Nantes	35	14	98
15	Man Utd	35	14	98
16	Osasuna	37	9	92
17	Liverpool	37	15	92
18	Nice	39	12	88
19	Barcelona	39	13	88
20	Heerenveen	35	14	87

DIADORA
mazda

Panucci of Roma

Goals conceded Number of goals conceded in League games	19
Clean Sheets (CS) Number of league games where no goals were conceded	20

PLAYER NATIONALITIES

1 Country with the most player representation across major European leagues - France

Number of players	512	International appearances 03-04	162
Number of occasions in squad	9983	Total minutes played	622633
Actual League appearances	8397	% of European League action	15.28

COUNTRY	NO OF PLAYERS	CAPS	IN SQUAD	LGE APP	MINS PLAYED	% LGE ACT
1 France	512	162	9983	8397	622633	15.28
2 Spain	448	136	9386	6991	498041	12.22
3 Holland	396	190	7967	6173	454398	11.15
4 Italy	421	160	7747	5948	431497	10.59
5 England	287	163	4960	4088	305188	7.49
6 Germany	283	139	5288	3827	278155	6.83
7 Brazil	135	133	2783	2432	177312	4.35
8 Argentina	107	77	2454	2041	150425	3.69
9 Serbia & M'tenegro	51	36	1067	881	64276	1.58
10 Rep of Ireland	36	104	769	686	55229	1.36
11 Denmark	34	93	816	731	53335	1.31
12 Portugal	33	54	793	676	47460	1.16
13 Belgium	49	54	900	637	46945	1.15
14 Czech Republic	32	84	740	630	46881	1.15
15 Sweden	29	71	704	608	44099	1.08
16 Cameroon	29	49	584	500	37281	0.91
17 Senegal	28	65	612	505	34960	0.86
18 Nigeria	29	0	548	465	33864	0.83
19 Australia	20	45	521	445	33860	0.83
20 Uruguay	31	53	668	520	33763	0.83
Others (74 countries)	543		10868	8723	612150	15.02
Mins lost through red cards					13088	0.32

CLUB MAKE-UP – HOME AND OVERSEAS PLAYERS

1 Club which used the most overseas players in league action - Arsenal

Overseas players in named 16s	24	Home country players in named 16s	13
Percent of overseas players	64.9	Percent of League action	78.9
Most appearances	Jens Lehmann	% of match time played	100

	CLUB	OVERSEAS	HOME	% OVERSEAS	% LGE ACT	MOST APP	% APP
1	Arsenal	24	13	64.9	78.9	Jens Lehmann	100
2	Fulham	19	15	55.9	71.9	Edwin Van der Sar	97.4
3	B M'gladbach	18	16	52.9	70.9	Jeff Strasser	89.6
4	Roda JC Kerk	19	10	65.5	68.6	Vladan Kujovic	100
5	Schalke	20	12	62.5	68.3	Hamit Altintop	81.5
6	Bochum	16	10	61.5	68.3	Rein Van Duijnhoven	100
7	Portsmouth	21	17	55.3	68.2	Arjan De Zeeuw	94.7
8	Hannover 96	19	15	55.9	66.4	Steve Cherundolo	77.5
9	W Bremen	15	11	57.7	66.3	Paul Stalteri	94.9
10	Bolton	18	16	52.9	65.9	Jussi Jaaskelainen	100
11	Bayern Munich	15	16	48.4	65.6	Roy Makaay	90.6
12	Ajax	23	10	69.7	64.6	Maxwell	89.3
13	Celta Vigo	16	15	51.6	64.2	Savo Milosevic	86.3
14	Inter Milan	21	12	63.6	63.2	Javier Zanetti	99.1
15	Freiburg	13	14	48.1	62.9	Boubacar Diarra	88.9
16	Wolfsburg	17	13	56.7	61.7	Diego Klimowicz	93.9
17	Liverpool	17	12	58.6	61.6	Sami Hyypia	100
18	B Dortmund	20	15	57.1	61.4	Jan Koller	91.3
19	Hamburg	13	14	48.1	61.4	Sergei Barbarez	91.1
20	Middlesbrough	13	19	40.6	60.2	George Boateng	91.2

CLUB DISCIPLINARY RECORDS

Simeone pleads Atletico's case

Yellow cards	120
Red cards	7
Total	127

1 Atletico Madrid

Cards Average in League Average number of minutes between a card being shown of either colour	27

	CLUB	Y	R	TOTAL	AVE
1	Atl Madrid	120	7	127	27
2	Espanyol	111	14	125	27
3	Seville	118	7	125	27
4	Valladolid	112	9	121	28
5	Villarreal	109	7	116	29
6	Kaiserslautern	96	7	103	30
7	Siena	93	6	99	31
8	Barcelona	97	14	111	31
9	Celta Vigo	101	10	111	31
10	Wolfsburg	92	4	96	32
11	Malaga	104	3	107	32
12	R Santander	103	5	108	32
13	Real Madrid	98	7	105	32
14	Real Zaragoza	99	7	106	32
15	Hertha Berlin	85	8	93	33
16	Athl Bilbao	99	6	105	33
17	1860 Munich	83	7	90	34
18	Osasuna	93	8	101	34
19	Bologna	83	4	87	35
20	Bastia	87	7	94	36

PLAYER DISCIPLINARY RECORD

1 Motta - Barcelona

Cards Average mins between cards	85
League Yellow	9
League Red	3
TOTAL	12

	PLAYER	LEAGUE	Y	R	TOTAL	AVE
1	Motta	Barcelona	9	3	12	85
2	Huth	Chelsea	8	1	9	88
3	Gatti	Perugia	9	0	9	95
4	Obradovic	B M'gladbach	4	1	5	96
5	N'doye	Toulouse	3	2	5	102
6	Torrado	Seville	4	1	5	105
7	Hollerbach	Hamburg	10	0	10	106
8	Generelo	Real Zaragoza	7	1	8	106
9	Benjamin	Hamburg	6	1	7	107
10	Cisse	Birmingham	5	0	5	108
11	Sherwood	Portsmouth	6	0	6	108
12	Cherrad	Nice	6	1	7	123
13	Seric	Parma	7	1	8	123
14	Lopo	Espanyol	19	3	22	123
15	Alfredo	Osasuna	5	1	6	124
16	Inzaghi	Lazio	8	0	8	126
17	Rafael	Hertha Berlin	6	1	7	127
18	Malago	Chievo	4	1	5	129
19	Agali	Schalke	6	0	6	130
20	Addo	Roda JC Kerk	4	1	5	130

TEAM OF THE SEASON

PELLIZZOLI – ROMA – CG 31 DR 199

ZEBINA – ROMA – CG 18 DR 261
SORIN – PARIS SG – CG 19 DR 198
GALLAS – CHELSEA – CG 22 DR 191
HINKEL – STUTTGART – CG 26 DR 181

LJUNGBERG – ARSENAL – CG 26 SD +111
SEEDORF – AC MILAN – CG 19 SD +104
DHORASOO – LYON – CG 24 SD +102
LIMA – ROMA – CG 29 SD +118

AILTON – W BREMEN – CG 27 AP 39
KEZMAN – PSV EINDHOVEN – CG 22 SR 74

The European Team of the Season shows a 4-4-2 of the best players in the major European Leagues based upon the selection criteria used for the chart-toppers. The players selected are taken from the lists for each club except that to get into this Team of the Season you must have played at least 17 Counting Games in league matches (roughly half the league season) and not 12 as is the case in the club lists. The other restriction is that we are only allowing one player from each club in each position.

- **The Top team's goalkeeper** is the player with the highest Defensive Rating
- **The Top team's defenders** are also tested by Defensive Rating, i.e. the average number of minutes between league goals conceded while on the pitch.
- **The Top team's midfield** are selected on their Scoring Difference, i.e.their Defensive Rating minus their Contribution to Attacking Power (average number of minutes between league goals scored while on the pitch). It takes no account of assists.
- **The Top team strikeforce** is made up of the striker with the highest Strike Rate (his average number of minutes between league goals scored while on the pitch) together with the striker with the highest Contribution to Attacking Power.

CHART-TOPPING POINT EARNERS

	PLAYER	TEAM	GAMES	POINTS	AVE
1	Seedorf	AC Milan	19	51	2.68
2	Gattuso	AC Milan	23	60	2.61
3	Cafu	AC Milan	23	60	2.61
4	Shevchenko	AC Milan	30	77	2.57
5	Costacurta	AC Milan	18	46	2.56
6	Pirlo	AC Milan	27	69	2.56
7	Sonck	Ajax	17	43	2.53
8	Kaka	AC Milan	23	58	2.52
9	Pires	Arsenal	32	80	2.50
10	Nesta	AC Milan	25	62	2.48
11	Sorin	Paris SG	19	47	2.47
12	Dida	AC Milan	32	79	2.47
13	Ferdinand	Man Utd	19	47	2.47
14	Maxwell	Ajax	29	71	2.45
15	Gallas	Chelsea	22	54	2.45
16	Toure	Arsenal	34	82	2.41
17	Henry	Arsenal	37	89	2.41
18	Maldini	AC Milan	29	69	2.38
19	Lehmann	Arsenal	38	90	2.37
20	Sneijder	Ajax	23	54	2.35

MERIVA

1 Seedord - AC Milan

Counting Games Played at least 70mins.	19
Total Points Taken in Counting Games	51
Average points per game Taken in Counting Games	2.68

MOST MISSED PLAYERS

	PLAYER	TEAM	AVERAGE	CLUB	DIFF
1	Ferdinand	Man Utd	2.47	1.97	0.50
2	Sorin	Paris SG	2.47	2.00	0.47
3	Oleguer	Barcelona	2.29	1.89	0.40
4	Gallas	Chelsea	2.45	2.08	0.37
5	Franca	B Leverkusen	2.27	1.91	0.36
6	Victor	Deportivo	2.21	1.87	0.34
7	Marchena	Valencia	2.31	2.03	0.28
8	Squillaci	Monaco	2.25	1.97	0.28
9	Jorge Lopez	Valencia	2.3	2.03	0.27
10	Seedorf	AC Milan	2.68	2.41	0.27
11	Ono	Feyenoord	2.22	2.00	0.22
12	Albelda	Valencia	2.24	2.03	0.21
13	Gattuso	AC Milan	2.61	2.41	0.20
14	Cafu	AC Milan	2.61	2.41	0.20
15	Zebina	Roma	2.28	2.09	0.19
16	Deflandre	Lyon	2.26	2.08	0.18
17	Cana	Paris SG	2.18	2.00	0.18
18	Sonck	Ajax	2.53	2.35	0.18
19	Muller	Lyon	2.24	2.08	0.16
20	Shevchenko	AC Milan	2.57	2.41	0.16

vodafone

1 Ferdinand - Man Utd

Average pionts	2.47
Club average	1.97
Difference	0.50

CHART-TOPPING GOALSCORERS

1 Kezman - PSV Eindhoven	
Goals scored in the League	31
Contribution to Attacking Power Average number of minutes between League team goals while on pitch	32
Player Strike Rate Average number of minutes between League goals scored by player	74
Club Strike Rate (CSR) Average minutes between League goals scored by club	33

	PLAYER	CLUB	GOALS	POWER	CSR	S RATE
1	Kezman	PSV Eindhoven	31	32	33	74
2	Ailton	W Bremen	28	41	39	92
3	Frei	Rennes	20	50	61	98
4	Ronaldo	Real Madrid	24	43	46	106
5	Gilardino	Parma	23	51	54	108
6	Henry	Arsenal	30	46	47	111
7	Shevchenko	AC Milan	24	47	47	112
8	Makaay	Bayern Munich	23	43	44	120
9	Cisse	Auxerre	26	54	57	125
10	Trezeguet	Juventus	16	45	46	126
11	Vieri	Inter Milan	13	51	52	127
12	Baptista	Seville	20	56	61	127
13	Mista	Valencia	19	49	48	127
14	Sibon	Heerenveen	15	74	68	128
15	Tamudo	Espanyol	19	65	71	131
16	Saha	Fulham	13	60	66	131
17	Drogba	Marseille	19	68	67	137
18	Chevanton	Lecce	19	68	71	137
19	Totti	Roma	20	44	45	138
20	van Nistelrooy	Man Utd	20	50	53	138

The Chart-topping Goalscorers measures the players by Strike Rate. They are most likely to be Forwards but Midfield players and even Defenders do come through the club tables. It is not a measure of the number of League goals scored - although that is also noted - but how often on average they have scored.

CHART-TOPPING MIDFIELDERS

1 Lima - Roma	
Goals scored in the League	0
Defensive Rating Av number of mins between League goals conceded while on the pitch	161
Contribution to Attacking Power Average number of minutes between League team goals while on pitch	43
Scoring Difference Defensive Rating minus Contribution to Attacking Power	118

	PLAYER	CLUB	GOALS	DEF R	POWER	SCORE DIFF
1	Lima	Roma	0	161	43	118
2	Emerson	Roma	3	156	44	112
3	Mancini	Roma	8	156	44	112
4	Ljungberg	Arsenal	4	158	47	111
5	Seedorf	AC Milan	3	160	56	104
6	Dhorasoo	Lyon	4	165	63	102
7	Muller	Lyon	1	153	51	102
8	Vieira	Arsenal	4	149	47	102
9	Pires	Arsenal	14	142	42	100
10	Jorge Lopez	Valencia	4	148	52	96
11	Dacourt	Roma	1	144	49	95
12	Pirlo	AC Milan	6	142	50	92
13	Mauro Silva	Deportivo	0	141	51	90
14	Juninho	Lyon	11	133	46	87
15	van Bommel	PSV Eindhoven	6	120	33	87
16	Zikos	Monaco	1	146	61	85
17	Albelda	Valencia	1	130	45	85
18	Kaka	AC Milan	10	125	42	83
19	Baraja	Valencia	8	125	44	81
20	Sneijder	Ajax	9	126	46	80

The Divisional Round-up charts combine the records of chart-topping keepers, defenders, midfield players and forwards, from every club in the division.. The one above is for **the Chart-topping Midfielders**. The players are ranked by their Scoring Difference although other attributes are shown for you to compare.

TOP LEAGUES IN EUROPE –

	UEFA 2nd Round	Pts	Champions League 1st Phase	Pts	UEFA 3rd Round	Pts	Champions League last 16	Pts
Spain	Mallorca, Villarreal, Barcelona, Valencia	4	Deportivo, R. Soc, R Madrid, C Vigo	8	Barcelona, Valencia, Villarreal, Mallorca	4	Deportivo, R Madrid, C Vigo, R. Soc	8
France	Auxerre, Sochaux, Bordeaux, Lens	4	Lyon, Monaco, Marseille (U)	6	Marseille, Bordeaux, Sochaux, Auxerre	4	Lyon, Monaco	4
England	Man City, Liverpool, Newcastle	3	Arsenal, Chelsea, Man Utd	6	Liverpool, Newcastle	2	Chelsea, Arsenal, Man U	6
Italy	Perugia, Roma, Parma	3	Juventus, Lazio, AC Milan, Inter (U)	8	Parma, Perugia, Inter Milan, Roma	4	Juventus, AC Milan	4
Portugal	Benfica, Sporting	2	Porto	2	Benfica	1	Porto	2
Turkey	Gaziantepspor, Genclerbirligi	2	Galatasaray (U), Besiktas (U)	4	Genclerbirligi, Besiktas, Gala', Gaziantepspor	4		
Germany	Dortmund, Schalke	2	Bayern (U), Stuttgart (U)	4	Bayern, Stuttgart	2		
Greece	Aris, Poak, Panionios	3	AEK, Olympiacos, Panathinaikos (U)	6	Panathinaikos	1		
Holland	Utrecht, Feyenoord	2	PSV (U), Ajax	4	PSV	1		
Scotland	Hearts	1	Celtic (U), Rangers	4	Celtic	1		
Russia	Spartak Mos., Torpedo Mos.	2	Lokomotiv	2	Spartak Mos.	1	Lokomotiv	2
Czech Rep.	Slavia, Teplice	2	Sparta Prague	2	Teplice	1	Sparta Prague	2
Belgium		0	Anderlecht, Club Brugge (U)	4	Club Brugge	1		
Norway	Rosenborg, Molde, Valerenga	3			Rosenborg, Valerenga	2		
Ukraine	Dnipro	1	Dynamo Kiev	2	Dnipro	1		
Serbia & Mont	Crvena Zvezde	1	Partizan Belg.	2				
Poland	Groclin, Wisla	2			Groclin	1		
Denmark	Brondby, Copenhagen	2			Brondby	1		
Croatia	Din'o Zagreb, Hajduk Split	2						
Bulgaria	Levski Sofia	1			Levski Sofia	1		
Romania	Dinamo Buc., Steaua Buc.	2						
Hungary	Debrecen	1			Debrecen	1		

(U) shows club has dropped from Champions League into the 3rd round of UEFA Cup

Key to abbreviations: Gaz'spor = Gaziantespor; Crvena Z. = Crvena Zvezde; Genc'ligi = Genclerbirligi; Gal'saray = Galatasaray; Pan'aikos = Panathinaikos; Din'o Zagreb = Dinamo Zagreb; Dinamo Buc. = Dinamo Bucharest; Steaua Buc. = Steaua Bucharest.

CHART-TOPPING DEFENDERS

1 Zebina - Roma	
Goals conceded in the League	7
Clean Sheets In games when he played at least 70 mins	13
Defensive Rating Average number of minutes between League goals conceded while on pitch	261
Club Defensive Rating Average mins between League goals conceded by the club this season	161

	PLAYER	CLUB	CON: LGE	CS	CDR	DEF RATE
1	Zebina	Roma	7	13	161	261
2	Sorin	Paris SG	9	11	122	198
3	Chivu	Roma	10	14	161	192
4	Gallas	Chelsea	11	16	114	191
5	Hinkel	Stuttgart	13	16	128	181
6	Marchena	Valencia	15	17	127	170
7	Berthod	Lyon	13	13	132	162
8	Nesta	AC Milan	14	14	128	160
9	Samuel	Roma	17	18	161	159
10	Essien	Lyon	15	11	132	155
11	Ibarra	Monaco	13	9	114	145
12	Bordon	Stuttgart	15	14	128	144
13	Deflandre	Lyon	13	9	132	142
14	Carboni	Valencia	21	18	127	140
15	Campbell	Arsenal	22	14	132	140
16	Cafu	AC Milan	16	10	128	135
17	Toure	Arsenal	23	14	132	135
18	Ferdinand	Man Utd	13	9	98	135
19	Cole	Arsenal	21	12	132	134
20	Squillaci	Monaco	17	12	114	133

The Chart-topping Defenders are resolved by their Defensive Rating, how often their team concedes a goal while they are playing. All these rightly favour players at the best performing clubs because good players win matches. However, good players in lower-table clubs will chart where they have lifted the team's performance.

CHART-TOPPING GOALKEEPERS

1 Pellizzoli - Roma	
Counting Games Games where he played at least 70 minutes	31
Goals Conceded in the League The number of League goals conceded while he was on the pitch	14
Clean Sheets In games when he played at least 70 mins	20
Defensive Rating Average number of minutes between League goals conceded while on pitch	199

	PLAYER	CLUB	CG	CONC	CS	DEF RATE
1	Pellizzoli	Roma	31	14	20	199
2	Dida	AC Milan	32	20	15	144
3	Coupet	Lyon	35	22	18	143
4	Canizares	Valencia	37	25	20	133
5	Hildebrand	Stuttgart	34	24	18	128
6	Alonzo	Paris SG	34	26	17	115
7	Roma	Monaco	33	27	15	110
8	Landreau	Nantes	34	28	14	109
9	Waterreus	PSV Eindhoven	33	28	15	106
10	Marchegiani	Chievo	30	25	11	102
11	Cool	Auxerre	38	34	13	101
12	Molina	Deportivo	33	30	15	99
13	Lobont	Ajax	24	22	9	98
14	Sanzol	Osasuna	34	32	9	96
15	Cech	Rennes	33	31	12	94
16	Victor	Barcelona	33	31	13	94
17	Zoetebier	Feyenoord	20	19	7	93
18	Wimbee	Lille	34	34	14	90
19	Gregorini	Nice	37	37	12	90
20	Butelle	Metz	27	28	10	87

The Chart-topping Goalkeepers are positioned by their Defensive Rating. We also show Clean Sheets where the team has not conceded and the Keeper has played all or most (at least 70 minutes) of the game. Now teams use several keepers in a season, not every team will necessarily chart on this page.

UEFA 4th round	Pts	Champ's L. Q-finals	Pts	UEFA Q. finals	Pts	Champ's L.S-finals	Pts	UEFA Semi-finals	Pts	Champ's L.Final	Winners	Pts	UEFA Final	Winners	Pts	TOTAL
Barcelona Valencia Mallorca Villarreal	4	Deportivo R Madrid	4	Valencia Villarreal	2	Deportivo	2	Valencia Villarreal	2				Valencia	Valencia	2	40 Spain
Bordeaux Auxerre Marseille	3	Lyon Monaco	4	Marseille Bordeaux	2	Monaco	2	Marseille	1	Monaco		2	Marseille		1	33 France
Newcastle Liverpool	2	Chelsea Arsenal	4	Newcastle	1	Chelsea	2	Newcastle	1							27 England
Inter Milan Roma	2	AC Milan	2	Inter Milan	1											24 Italy
Benfica	1	Porto	2			Porto	2			Porto	Porto	4				16 Portugal
Genclerbirligi	1															11 Turkey
																8 Germany
																10 Greece
PSV	1			PSV	1											9 Holland
Celtic	1			Celtic	1											8 Scotland
																7 Russia
																7 Czech Rep.
Club Brugge	1															6 Belgium
																5 Norway
																4 Ukraine
																3 Serbia & Mont
																3 Poland
																3 Denmark
																2 Croatia
																2 Bulgaria
																2 Romania
																2 Hungary
																Switzerland
																Austria
																Israel

Top Leagues in Europe

This chart sees how different country's leagues fared in cross-border rivalries. Picking up from the Champions League Group Phase and the UEFA Cup Second Round we've noted every surviving club. 25 leagues feature initially and it's gradually whittled down to two winners.

Each league wins a point for every survivor in the UEFA Cup each round and two points in the Champions League.

The resulting points total gives an indication of where European dominance resides and this year it is definitely with Spanish clubs. The French show a marked improvement to take second and Germany and Holland will both feel they have under-performed. Porto flew a lone but very successful flag for Portugal and Turkish and Greek leagues also fared well.

International Football

Where tournament stars play

Van Nistelrooy, Henry, Henry... the last few years have seen overseas stars taking the English title PFA Player of the Year. High-level football is the most multinational big business. The clubs visiting our grounds and appearing in our living rooms feature a whole host of different nationalities. Familiar faces from the Premiership increasingly turn up in unfamiliar strips in European Championships and World Cups. And if an opponent catches the eye you want to know what country he's eligible for and whether he's been capped.

We've tracked the 20 nationalities providing most players to the top divisions of Europe. And to these we've added the four home countries.

For all top division clubs we show the nationalities of the players and, if they play for one of these 24 international teams, how often they have been capped this season. The following pages provide the other side of the coin, showing where these international sides' stars are playing their club football. They give their results and caps, and highlight their stars over the 2003/4 season.

The 20 national teams from which the big European leagues draw most of their players inevitably include the big-hitting international sides from Europe and South America, plus top sides from Africa.

HOW OUR 24 COUNTRY TEAMS HAVE FARED

	RANKING 2003	RANKING 2004	DIFFERENCE
Cameroon	18	12	+6
Czech Republic	13	10	+3
Uruguay	28	25	+3
Finland	45	42	+3
Netherlands	6	4	+2
Italy	12	11	+1
Croatia	26	25	+1
Scotland	64	63	+1
Brazil	1	1	no change
France	2	2	no change
Argentina	5	5	no change
Republic of Ireland	15	15	no change
Spain	2	3	-1
Belgium	16	17	-1
Sweden	20	21	-1
Senegal	29	31	-2
Northern Ireland	111	114	-3
Denmark	10	14	-4
Germany	4	9	-5
England	7	12	-5
Portugal	14	20	-6
Wales	50	66	-16
Serbia and Montenegro	22	45	-23
Australia	49	89	-40

FIFA Rankings

Here are the top 80 teams from the 205 countries ranked in the Coca-Cola-sponsored FIFA World Rankings.

The table shows how teams have fared over the 12 months to May 31st. The vagaries of world football don't make the rankings a definitive guide to team performance or quality, but they give a rough guide to how football power ebbs and flows within each individual continent.

Mexico may be flying high in the chart, but they rarely play far afield, and few of their players are plying their trade in Europe. The small chart above focuses on the teams whose players dominate European club football and shows how their rankings have risen or fallen over the year.

FIFA RANKINGS

RANK JUNE 04	COUNTRY	POINTS JUNE 04	RANK JUNE 03	RANK DIFF	POINTS JUNE 03	POINTS DIFF
1	Brazil	838	1	0	843	-5
2	France	819	2	0	784	35
3	Spain	784	2	-1	784	0
4	Netherlands	744	6	2	746	-2
5	Argentina	741	5	0	753	-12
6	Mexico	738	9	3	720	18
7	Turkey	737	8	1	722	15
8	USA	724	10	2	715	9
9	Germany	723	4	-5	757	-34
10	Czech Republic	720	13	3	707	13
11	Italy	717	12	1	709	8
12	Cameroon	714	18	6	666	48
12	England	714	7	-5	739	-25
14	Denmark	700	10	-4	715	-15
15	Republic of Ireland	697	15	0	704	-7
16	Nigeria	683	32	16	621	62
17	Belgium	674	16	-1	681	-7
18	Iran	666	34	16	614	52
19	Korea Republic	665	21	2	656	9
20	Portugal	662	14	-6	706	-44
21	Sweden	660	20	-1	660	0
22	Costa Rica	659	17	-5	671	-12
23	Romania	658	27	4	631	27
23	Saudi Arabia	658	42	19	594	64
25	Croatia	655	26	1	640	15
25	Japan	655	23	-2	645	10
25	Paraguay	655	19	-6	664	-9
25	Uruguay	655	28	3	629	26
29	Poland	653	29	0	627	26
30	Russia	652	25	-5	641	11
31	Senegal	651	29	-2	627	24
32	Morocco	642	38	6	604	38
33	Tunisia	639	40	7	596	43
34	Egypt	638	44	10	587	51
34	Greece	638	45	11	577	61
36	Colombia	619	39	3	601	18
36	Norway	619	24	-12	643	-24
38	Bulgaria	618	35	-3	611	7
39	Slovenia	617	36	-3	610	7
40	South Africa	610	31	-9	624	-14
41	Ecuador	598	33	-8	620	-22
42	Finland	594	45	3	577	17
43	Jordan	588	75	32	492	96
44	Iraq	584	56	12	535	49
45	Mali	583	74	29	493	90
45	Serbia and Montenegro	583	22	-23	650	-67
47	Switzerland	578	43	-4	588	-10
48	Zimbabwe	563	55	7	538	25
49	Venezuela	562	63	14	527	35
50	Jamaica	560	48	-2	570	-10
51	Honduras	552	37	-14	608	-56
52	Latvia	551	79	27	483	68
53	Algeria	550	66	13	517	33
54	Kuwait	548	87	33	464	84
54	Slovakia	548	53	-1	548	0
56	Iceland	547	70	14	509	38
57	Israel	545	40	-17	596	-51
57	Qatar	545	71	14	506	39
59	Thailand	544	59	0	533	11
60	Bahrain	542	100	40	427	115
61	Bosnia-Herzegovina	535	72	11	503	32
61	Oman	535	106	45	418	117
63	Congo DR	534	65	2	520	14
63	Scotland	534	64	1	524	10
65	Ukraine	528	47	-18	570	-42
66	Wales	527	50	-16	558	-31
67	China PR	525	68	1	513	12
68	Hungary	522	54	-14	544	-22
68	Libya	522	97	29	439	83
70	United Arab Emirates	519	90	20	448	71
71	Estonia	518	61	-10	528	-10
72	Burkina Faso	517	83	11	472	45
73	Austria	516	61	-12	528	-12
74	Kenya	514	78	4	486	28
75	Ivory Coast	512	59	-16	533	-21
75	Trinidad and Tobago	512	52	-23	553	-41
77	Chile	510	73	-4	494	16
77	Cuba	510	56	-21	535	-25
77	Uzbekistan	510	104	27	422	88
80	Zambia	507	69	-11	512	-5

FRANCE

FIFA/COCA COLA WORLD RANKING: **2nd**

MANAGER: JACQUES SANTINI

1	intnls	**Switzerland**	A	W	2-0	Wiltord 13; Marlet 55	30,000
2	eq1	**Cyprus**	H	W	5-0	Trezeguet 8,80; Wiltord 18,40; Henry 58	60,000
3	eq1	**Slovenia**	A	W	2-0	Trezeguet 11; Dacourt 73	7,556
4	eq1	**Israel**	H	W	3-0	Henry 8; Trezeguet 25; Boumsong 42	56,000
5	intnls	**Germany**	A	W	3-0	Henry 21; Trezeguet 55,82	
6	intnls	**Belgium**	A	W	2-0	Govou 45; Saha 82	
7	intnls	**Holland**	A	D	0-0		
8	intnls	**Brazil**	H	D	0-0		75,000
9	intnls	**Andorra**	H	W	4-0	Wiltord 45,55; Saha 68; Marlet 74	27,750

KEY PLAYERS - GOALSCORERS

Sylvain Wiltord

Goals in Internationals	5
Contribution to Attacking Power Average number of minutes between team goals while on pitch	27
Player Strike Rate The total number of minutes he was on the pitch for every goal scored	77
Team Strike Rate Average number of minutes between goals scored by club	39

	PLAYER	GOALS	ATT POWER	STRIKE RATE
1	Sylvain Wiltord	5	27	77 mins
2	Louis Saha	2	31	78 mins
3	Steve Marlet	2	25	90 mins
4	David Trezeguet	6	40	94 mins
5	Thierry Henry	3	39	171 mins

TOP PLAYER APPEARANCES

8 Zinedine Zidane — Midfield

Age (on 01/07/04)	32
Caps this season	6
Total minutes on the pitch	477
Goals	0
Yellow Cards	1
Red Cards	0
Club Side	Real Madrid

	PLAYER	POS	AGE	CAPS	MINS	GOALS	CARDS(Y)	CARDS(R)	CLUB SIDE
1	Lilian Thuram	DEF	31	9	663	0	0	0	Juventus
2	Bixente Lizarazu	DEF	34	8	597	0	0	0	Bayern Munich
3	David Trezeguet	ATT	26	8	564	6	0	0	Juventus
4	Marcel Desailly	DEF	35	7	552	0	0	0	Chelsea
5	Fabien Barthez	GK	33	6	540	0	0	0	Marseille
6	Mikael Silvestre	DEF	26	7	529	0	0	0	Man Utd
7	Thierry Henry	ATT	26	7	513	3	0	0	Arsenal
8	Zinedine Zidane	MID	32	6	477	0	1	0	Real Madrid
9	Claude Makelele	MID	31	6	468	0	2	1	Chelsea
10	Robert Pires	MID	30	8	464	0	0	0	Arsenal
11	Olivier Dacourt	MID	29	7	410	1	0	0	Roma
12	Patrick Vieira	MID	28	6	393	0	1	0	Arsenal
13	Sylvain Wiltord	ATT	30	6	386	5	0	0	Arsenal
14	William Gallas	MID	26	5	320	0	0	0	Chelsea
15	Willy Sagnol	MID	27	6	309	0	0	0	Bayern Munich
16	Gregory Coupet	GK	31	3	270	0	0	0	Lyon
17	Benoit Pedretti	MID	23	4	258	0	0	0	Sochaux
18	Jean-Alain Boumsong	DEF	24	5	208	1	0	0	Auxerre
19	Steve Marlet	ATT	30	5	179	2	0	0	Marseille
20	Louis Saha	ATT	25	2	155	2	0	0	Man Utd
21	Sydney Govou	ATT	24	3	99	1	0	0	Lyon

SPAIN

FIFA/COCA COLA WORLD RANKING: **3rd**

MANAGER: INAKI SAEZ

1	intnls	**Portugal**	A	W	3-0	Joseba Etxeberria 12; Joaquin 63; Tristan 76	29,500
2	c6	**Ukraine**	H	W	2-1	Raul 61,72	38,000
3	eq6	**Armenia**	A	W	4-0	Valeron 7; Raul 78; Reyes 89,90	15,000
4	eqpl1	**Norway**	H	W	2-1	Raul 21; Baraja 85	53,000
5	eqpl2	**Norway**	A	W	3-0	Raul 34; Valeron 49; Joseba Etxeberria 56	25,500
6	intnls	**Peru**	H	W	2-1	Joseba Etxeberria 30; Baraja 32	22,580
7	intnls	**Denmark**	H	W	2-0	Morientes 23; Raul 60	22,000
8	intnls	**Italy**	A	D	1-1	Torres 53	36,000

KEY PLAYERS - GOALSCORERS

Jose Antonio Reyes

Goals in Internationals	2
Contribution to Attacking Power Average number of minutes between team goals while on pitch	25
Player Strike Rate The total number of minutes he was on the pitch for every goal scored	90
Team Strike Rate Average number of minutes between goals scored by club	38

	PLAYER	GOALS	ATT POWER	STRIKE RATE
1	Jose Antonio Reyes	2	25	90 mins
2	Raul Gonzalez Blanco	5	43	105 mins
3	Joaquin Sanchez Rodriguez	1	40	162 mins
4	Ruben Vegas Baraja	2	43	196 mins
5	Juan Carlos Valeron	2	27	196 mins

TOP PLAYER APPEARANCES

10 Rodriguez Vicente — Attack

Age (on 01/07/04)	22
Caps this season	8
Total minutes on the pitch	406
Goals	0
Yellow Cards	1
Red Cards	0
Club Side	Valencia

	PLAYER	POS	AGE	CAPS	MINS	GOALS	CARDS(Y)	CARDS(R)	CLUB SIDE
1	Michel Salgado	DEF	28	8	568	0	1	0	Real Madrid
2	Iker Fernandez Casillas	GK	23	8	543	0	0	0	Real Madrid
3	Carlos Marchena	DEF	25	6	540	0	1	0	Valencia
4	Raul Gonzalez Blanco	ATT	27	8	527	5	0	0	Real Madrid
5	Carlos Puyol	DEF	26	6	495	0	0	0	Barcelona
7	Olano Xabier Alonso	MID	22	7	448	0	0	0	Real Sociedad
8	Ivan Bujia Helguera	MID	29	5	423	0	0	0	Real Madrid
9	David Aliques Albelda	MID	26	6	413	0	1	0	Valencia
10	Rodriguez Vicente	ATT	22	8	406	0	1	0	Valencia
11	Ruben Vegas Baraja	MID	28	8	392	2	0	0	Valencia
12	Juan Carlos Valeron	MID	29	7	391	2	0	0	Deportivo
14	Martin Villar Cesar	DEF	27	3	207	0	0	0	Deportivo
15	Juan Jesus Juanito	DEF	27	2	180	0	0	0	Real Betis
16	Jose Antonio Reyes	ATT	20	4	179	2	0	0	Spain
17	Santiago Canizares	GK	34	4	177	0	0	0	Valencia
18	Joaquin	MID	23	5	162	1	0	0	Real Betis
19	Jose Maria Guti	MID	27	3	153	0	0	0	Real Madrid
20	Xavi Hernandez	MID	24	4	142	0	0	0	Barcelona
21	Joseba Etxeberria	ATT	26	2	135	1	0	0	Athl Bilbao
22	Sanfelix Raul Bravo	MID	23	2	135	0	0	0	Real Madrid
23	Alberto Martos Luque	ATT	26	3	103	0	0	0	Deportivo

HOLLAND

FIFA/COCA COLA WORLD RANKING: **4th**

MANAGER: DICK ADVOCAAT

1	intnls	**Belgium**	A	D	1-1	Makaay 54	35,000
2	eq3	**Austria**	H	W	3-1	van der Vaart 30; Kluivert 60; Cocu 64	47,000
3	eq3	**Czech Republic**	A	L	1-3	van der Vaart 61	18,365
4	eq3	**Moldova**	H	W	5-0	Kluivert 43; Sneijder 51; van Hooijdonk 74 pen; van der Vaart 80; Robben 89	30,995
5	eqpl1	**Scotland**	A	L	0-1		50,670
6	eqpl2	**Scotland**	H	W	6-0	Sneijder 14; Ooijer 32; van Nistelrooy 37,51,67; de Boer, F 65	52,000
7	intnls	**United States**	H	W	1-0	Robben 57	27,000
8	intnls	**France**	H	D	0-0		
9	intnls	**Greece**	H	W	4-0	Makaay 50; Zenden 58; Heitinga 61; van Hooijdonk 89	25,000
10	intnls	**Belgium**	H	L	0-1		34,000

KEY PLAYERS - GOALSCORERS

Pierre van Hooijdonk

Goals in Internationals	2
Contribution to Attacking Power Average number of minutes between team goals while on pitch	38
Player Strike Rate The total number of minutes he was on the pitch for every goal scored	117
Team Strike Rate Average number of minutes between goals scored by club	41

	PLAYER	GOALS	ATT POWER	STRIKE RATE
1	Pierre van Hooijdonk	2	38	117 mins
2	Ruud van Nistelrooy	3	41	150 mins
3	Roy Makaay	2	29	161 mins
4	Rafael van der Vaart	4	34	198 mins
5	Wesley Sneijder	2	27	248 mins

TOP PLAYER APPEARANCES

3 Rafael van der Vaart — Midfield

Age (on 01/07/04)	21
Caps this season	10
Total minutes on the pitch	792
Goals	4
Yellow Cards	0
Red Cards	0
Club Side	Ajax

	PLAYER	POS	AGE	CAPS	MINS	GOALS	CARDS(Y/R)		CLUB SIDE
1	Edwin van der Sar	GK	33	11	990	0	0	0	Fulham
2	Phillip Cocu	MID	33	10	869	1	2	1	Barcelona
3	Rafael van der Vaart	MID	21	10	792	4	0	0	Ajax
4	Jaap Stam	DEF	31	9	721	0	2	0	Lazio
5	Patrick Kluivert	ATT	28	9	683	2	0	0	Barcelona
6	Michael Reiziger	DEF	31	7	526	0	0	0	Barcelona
7	Wesley Sneijder	MID	20	7	495	2	0	0	Ajax
8	Edgar Davids	MID	31	8	478	0	3	1	Barcelona
9	Andy van der Meyde	MID	24	6	474	0	0	0	Inter Milan
10	Ruud van Nistelrooy	ATT	28	6	451	3	2	0	Man Utd
11	Giov. Van Bronckhorst	MID	29	6	450	0	0	0	Barcelona
12	Marc Overmars	ATT	31	7	446	0	0	0	Barcelona
13	Wilfred Bouma	MID	26	5	418	0	0	0	PSV Eindhoven
14	Boudewijn Zenden	MID	27	6	379	1	0	0	Middlesbrough
15	Frank de Boer	DEF	34	6	369	1	0	0	Rangers
16	Mark Van Bommel	MID	27	6	360	0	1	0	PSV Eindhoven
17	Johnny Heitinga	DEF	20	4	360	1	0	0	Ajax
18	Clarence Seedorf	MID	28	6	338	0	0	0	AC Milan
19	Roy Makaay	ATT	29	6	321	2	0	0	Bayern Munich
20	Andre Ooijer	MID	29	5	314	1	1	0	PSV Eindhoven
21	Pierre van Hooijdonk	ATT	34	7	233	2	0	0	Fenerbahce

ITALY

FIFA/COCA COLA WORLD RANKING: **11th**

MANAGER: GIOVANNI TRAPATTONI

1	intnls	**Germany**	A	W	1-0	Vieri 17	50,328
2	eq9	**Wales**	H	W	4-0	Inzaghi 59,63,70; Del Piero 76 pen	70,000
3	eq9	**Serbia & Mont.**	A	D	1-1	Inzaghi 22	30,000
4	eq9	**Azerbaijan**	H	W	4-0	Vieri 15; Inzaghi 24,88; Di Vaio 65	30,000
5	intnls	**Poland**	A	L	1-3	Cassano 18	
6	intnls	**Romania**	H	W	1-0	Di Vaio 57	11,700
7	intnls	**Czech Republic**	H	D	2-2	Vieri 13; Di Natale 85	25,000
8	intnls	**Portugal**	A	W	2-1	Vieri 39; Miccoli 75	35,000
9	intnls	**Spain**	H	D	1-1	Vieri 56	36,000
10	intnls	**Tunisia**	A	W	4-0	Bouazizi 15 og; Cannavaro 27; Pirlo 85 fk; Zambrotta 90	

KEY PLAYERS - GOALSCORERS

Filippo Inzaghi

Goals in Internationals	6
Contribution to Attacking Power Average number of minutes between team goals while on pitch	29
Player Strike Rate The total number of minutes he was on the pitch for every goal scored	44
Team Strike Rate Average number of minutes between goals scored by club	39

	PLAYER	GOALS	ATT POWER	STRIKE RATE
1	Filippo Inzaghi	6	29	44 mins
2	Marco Di Vaio	2	42	107 mins
3	Christian Vieri	5	40	130 mins
4	Alessandro Del Piero	1	35	386 mins
5	Fabio Cannavaro	1	39	595 mins

TOP PLAYER APPEARANCES

3 Gianluca Zambrotta — Midfield

Age (on 01/07/04)	27
Caps this season	7
Total minutes on the pitch	630
Goals	1
Yellow Cards	1
Red Cards	0
Club Side	Juventus

	PLAYER	POS	AGE	CAPS	MINS	GOALS	CARDS(Y/R)		CLUB SIDE
1	Simone Perrotta	MID	26	10	795	0	0	0	Chievo
2	Christian Vieri	ATT	30	9	649	5	0	0	Inter Milan
3	Gianluca Zambrotta	MID	27	7	630	1	1	0	Juventus
4	Gianluigi Buffon	GK	26	8	630	0	1	0	Juventus
5	Christian Panucci	DEF	31	9	626	0	1	0	Roma
6	Fabio Cannavaro	DEF	30	8	595	1	1	0	Inter Milan
7	Alessandro Nesta	DEF	28	6	480	0	0	0	AC Milan
8	Francesco Totti	ATT	27	6	414	0	0	0	Roma
9	Mauro Camoranesi	MID	27	6	409	0	0	0	Juventus
10	Alessandro Del Piero	ATT	29	5	386	1	1	0	Juventus
11	Cristiano Zanetti	MID	27	4	360	0	0	0	Inter Milan
12	Massimo Oddo	DEF	28	6	329	0	0	0	Lazio
13	Matteo Ferrari	DEF	24	7	299	0	0	0	Parma
14	Filippo Inzaghi	ATT	30	4	262	6	0	0	AC Milan
15	Stefano Fiore	MID	29	6	245	0	0	0	Lazio
16	Marco Di Vaio	ATT	27	4	213	2	0	0	Juventus
17	Andrea Pirlo	MID	25	4	184	0	0	0	AC Milan
19	Francesco Toldo	GK	32	3	180	0	0	0	Inter Milan
20	Massimo Ambrosini	MID	27	4	157	0	0	0	AC Milan
21	Gennaro Gattuso	MID	35	5	143	0	0	0	AC Milan
22	Daniele Adani	DEF	29	2	135	0	0	0	Inter Milan

ENGLAND

FIFA/COCA COLA WORLD RANKING: **12th**

MANAGER: SVEN GORAN ERIKSSON

1	intnls	Croatia	H	W	3-1	Beckham 10 pen; Owen 51; Lampard 80	27,000
2	eq7	Macedonia	A	W	2-1	Rooney 53; Beckham 63 pen	20,500
3	eq7	Liechtenstein	H	W	2-0	Owen 46; Rooney 52	64,931
4	eq7	Turkey	A	D	0-0		42,000
5	intnls	Denmark	H	L	2-3	Rooney 5; Cole, J 9	64,159
6	intnls	Portugal	A	D	1-1	King 47	27,000
7	intnls	Sweden	A	L	0-1		

KEY PLAYERS - GOALSCORERS

Michael Owen

Goals in Internationals	3
Contribution to Attacking Power Average number of minutes between team goals while on pitch	47
Player Strike Rate The total number of minutes he was on the pitch for every goal scored	127
Team Strike Rate Average number of minutes between goals scored by club	65

	PLAYER	GOALS	ATT POWER	STRIKE RATE
1	Michael Owen	3	47	127 mins
2	Wayne Rooney	3	60	161 mins
3	Joe Cole	1	52	211 mins
4	David Beckham	2	52	264 mins
5	Frank Lampard	1	59	416 mins

TOP PLAYER APPEARANCES

3 David Beckham Midfield

Age (on 01/07/04)	29
Caps this season	7
Total minutes on the pitch	528
Goals	2
Yellow Cards	1
Red Cards	0
Club Side	Real Madrid

	PLAYER	POS	AGE	CAPS	MINS	GOALS	CARDS(Y)	CARDS(R)	CLUB SIDE
1	David James	GK	33	8	630	0	1	0	Man City
2	John Terry	DEF	23	7	582	0	0	0	Chelsea
3	David Beckham	MID	29	7	528	2	1	0	Real Madrid
4	Wayne Rooney	ATT	18	7	484	3	0	0	Everton
5	Nicky Butt	MID	29	7	422	0	1	0	Man Utd
6	Frank Lampard	MID	26	7	416	1	0	0	Chelsea
7	Ashley Cole	DEF	23	6	390	0	0	0	Arsenal
8	Michael Owen	ATT	24	5	380	3	0	0	Liverpool
9	Gary Neville	DEF	29	5	370	0	0	0	Man Utd
10	Steven Gerrard	MID	24	5	367	0	1	0	Liverpool
11	Phil Neville	DEF	27	7	315	0	0	0	Man Utd
12	Emile Heskey	ATT	26	7	297	0	0	0	Liverpool
13	Paul Scholes	MID	29	4	273	0	0	0	Man Utd
14	Sol Campbell	DEF	29	3	270	0	1	0	Arsenal
15	Wayne Bridge	DEF	23	4	234	0	1	0	Chelsea
16	Matthew Upson	DEF	25	3	211	0	0	0	Birmingham
17	Joe Cole	MID	22	6	211	1	0	0	Chelsea
18	Owen Hargreaves	MID	23	5	196	0	0	0	Bayern Munich
19	James Beattie	ATT	26	3	150	0	0	0	Southampton
20	Gareth Southgate	DEF	33	2	135	0	0	0	Middlesbrough
21	Kieron Dyer	MID	25	5	110	0	0	0	Newcastle

GERMANY

FIFA/COCA COLA WORLD RANKING: **9th**

MANAGER: RUDI VOLLER

1	intnls	Italy	H	L	0-1		50,328
2	eq5	Iceland	A	D	0-0		
3	eq5	Scotland	H	W	2-1	Bobic 25; Ballack 50	67,000
4	eq5	Iceland	H	W	3-0	Ballack 9; Bobic 59; Kuranyi 79	50,785
5	intnls	France	H	L	0-3		
6	intnls	Croatia	A	W	2-1	Klose 34; Ramelow 89	
7	intnls	Belgium	H	W	3-0	Kuranyi 45; Hamann 55; Ballack 81	
8	intnls	Romania	A	L	1-5	Lahm 88	12,000
9	intnls	Malta	H	W	7-0	Ballack 15,17,59,86; Nowotny 33; Frings 42; Bobic 90	23,000

KEY PLAYERS - GOALSCORERS

Michael Ballack

Goals in Internationals	7
Contribution to Attacking Power Average number of minutes between team goals while on pitch	35
Player Strike Rate The total number of minutes he was on the pitch for every goal scored	76
Club Strike Rate Average number of minutes between goals scored by club	45

	PLAYER	GOALS	ATT POWER	STRIKE RATE
1	Michael Ballack	7	35	76 mins
2	Fredi Bobic	3	35	153 mins
3	Torsten Frings	1	25	255 mins
4	Kevin Kuranyi	2	45	293 mins
5	Miroslav Klose	1	61	305 mins

TOP PLAYER APPEARANCES

5 Kevin Kuranyi Attack

Age (on 01/07/04)	22
Caps this season	8
Total minutes on the pitch	565
Goals	2
Yellow Cards	0
Red Cards	0
Club Side	Stuttgart

	PLAYER	POS	AGE	CAPS	MINS	GOALS	CARDS(Y)	CARDS(R)	CLUB SIDE
1	Arne Friedrich	DEF	25	8	720	0	1	0	Hertha Berlin
2	Bernd Schneider	MID	30	9	650	0	0	0	B Leverkusen
3	Christian Worns	DEF	32	7	585	0	1	0	B Dortmund
4	Oliver Kahn	GK	35	7	585	0	0	0	Bayern Munich
5	Kevin Kuranyi	ATT	22	8	585	2	0	0	Stuttgart
6	Michael Ballack	MID	27	6	531	7	0	0	Bayern Munich
7	Frank Baumann	DEF	28	6	520	0	0	0	W Bremen
8	Fredi Bobic	ATT	32	8	459	3	0	0	Hertha Berlin
9	Carsten Ramelow	MID	30	5	344	1	1	0	B Leverkusen
10	Dietmar Hamann	MID	30	4	338	1	0	0	Liverpool
11	Philip Lahm	MID	20	4	338	1	0	0	Stuttgart
12	Paul Freier	MID	24	6	317	0	0	0	Bochum
13	Andreas Hinkel	MID	22	4	315	0	0	0	Stuttgart
14	Jens Jeremies	MID	30	5	314	0	0	0	Bayern Munich
15	Miroslav Klose	ATT	26	7	305	1	1	0	Kaiserslautern
16	Torsten Frings	MID	27	4	255	1	0	0	B Dortmund
17	Sebastian Kehl	DEF	24	5	190	0	1	0	B Dortmund
18	Tobias Rau	MID	22	2	180	0	0	0	Bayern Munich
19	Oliver Neuville	ATT	31	5	180	0	0	0	B Leverkusen
20	Jens Lehmann	GK	34	2	180	0	0	0	Arsenal
21	Christian Rahn	MID	25	3	159	0	1	0	Hamburg

BRAZIL

FIFA/COCA COLA WORLD RANKING: **1st**

MANAGER: CARLOS ALBERTO PARREIRA

1	gcgp	**Honduras**	H	W	2-1	Maicon 16; Diego 84	
2	gcqf	**Colombia**	A	W	2-0	Kaka 42,67	23,425
3	gcsf	**United States**	A	D	1-1	Kaka 90; Diego 100 pen	35,211
4	gcf	**Mexico**	H	D	0-0		80,000
5	wcq1	**Colombia**	A	W	2-1	Ronaldo 22; Kaka 61	47,600
6	wcq1	**Ecuador**	H	W	1-0	Ronaldinho 12	36,601
7	intnls	**Jamaica**	A	W	1-0	Roberto Carlos 15	32,000
8	wcq1	**Peru**	A	D	1-1	Rivaldo 21 pen	80,000
9	wcq1	**Uruguay**	H	D	3-3	Kaka 20; Ronaldo 28,86	30,000
10	intnls	**Rep of Ireland**	A	D	0-0		44,000
11	wcq1	**Paraguay**	A	D	0-0		43,000
12	intnls	**Hungary**	A	W	4-1	Kaka 33; Fabiano 36,45; Ronaldinho 76	45,000
13	intnls	**France**	A	D	0-0		75,000

KEY PLAYERS - GOALSCORERS

Ricardo Santos Laite Kaka

Goals in Internationals	6
Contribution to Attacking Power Average number of minutes between team goals while on pitch	72
Player Strike Rate The total number of minutes he was on the pitch for every goal scored	145
Team Strike Rate Average number of minutes between goals scored by club	71

	PLAYER	GOALS	ATT POWER	STRIKE RATE
1	Ricardo Santos Laite Kaka	6	72	145 mins
2	De Assis Moreira Ronaldinho	2	82	207 mins
3	Ronaldo Luiz Nazario de Lima	3	90	240 mins
4	Diego Ribas da Cunha Santos	1	83	334 mins
5	Rivaldo Vitor Borba Ferreira	1	53	376 mins

TOP PLAYER APPEARANCES

13 Ronaldinho — Attack

Age (on 01/07/04)	24
Caps this season	5
Total minutes on the pitch	413
Goals	2
Yellow Cards	0
Red Cards	0
Club Side	Barcelona

	PLAYER	POS	AGE	CAPS	MINS	GOALS	CARDS(Y)	CARDS(R)	CLUB SIDE
1	Ricardo Kaka	MID	22	12	871	6	0	0	Ac Milan
2	Nelson Dida	GK	30	9	810	0	0	0	AC Milan
3	Marcos Cafu	DEF	34	9	765	0	0	0	AC Milan
4	Jose Ze Roberto	MID	30	9	721	0	0	0	Bayern Munich
5	Roque Junior	DEF	27	8	720	0	0	0	Siena
6	Ronaldo	ATT	27	8	720	3	0	0	Real Madrid
7	Lucio	DEF	26	7	607	0	0	0	B Leverkusen
8	Roberto Carlos da Silva	DEF	31	7	585	1	0	0	Real Madrid
9	Gilberto Silva	MID	27	7	553	0	0	0	Arsenal
10	Pinho Alex	MID	32	9	502	0	0	0	Vasco da Gama
11	Anderson Luisao da Silva	MID	23	4	420	0	1	0	Cruzeiro
12	Julio Cesar Baptista	MID	22	6	417	0	1	0	Seville
13	Ronaldinho	ATT	24	5	413	2	0	0	Barcelona
14	Rivaldo	MID	32	5	376	1	0	0	AC Milan
15	Diego Santos	MID	19	4	334	1	1	0	Santos
16	Paulo Almeida Santos	MID	23	3	330	0	1	0	Santos
17	Maicon Sisenando	DEF	22	3	330	0	1	0	Cruzeiro
18	Heurelhio Gomes	GK	23	3	330	0	0	0	Cruzeiro
19	Edmilson	DEF	27	4	280	0	0	0	Lyon
20	Honorato Nilmar	ATT	19	3	259	0	1	0	Internacional
21	Emerson Ferreira	MID	28	4	247	0	0	0	Roma

ARGENTINA

FIFA/COCA COLA WORLD RANKING: **5th**

MANAGER: MARCELO BIELSA

1	intnls	**Uruguay**	A	W	3-2	Veron 45; Samuel 81; D'Alessandro 85	8,000
2	wcq1	**Chile**	H	D	2-2	Kily Gonzalez 31; Aimar 3535,372	
3	wcq1	**Venezuela**	A	W	3-0	Aimar 7; Crespo 25; Cesar Delgado 32	24,783
4	wcq1	**Bolivia**	H	W	3-0	D'Alessandro 55; Crespo 61; Aimar 63	25,000
5	wcq1	**Colombia**	A	D	1-1	Crespo 26	30,000
6	wcq1	**Ecuador**	H	W	1-0	Crespo 60	
7	intnls	**Morocco**	A	W	1-0	Kily Gonzalez 52	

KEY PLAYERS - GOALSCORERS

Hernan Crespo

Goals in Internationals	4
Contribution to Attacking Power Average number of minutes between team goals while on pitch	43
Player Strike Rate The total number of minutes he was on the pitch for every goal scored	142
Team Strike Rate Average number of minutes between goals scored by club	45

	PLAYER	GOALS	ATT POWER	STRIKE RATE
1	Hernan Crespo	4	43	142 mins
2	Pablo Aimar	3	38	152 mins
3	Andres D'Alessandro	2	40	243 mins
4	Juan Sebastian Veron	1	44	266 mins

TOP PLAYER APPEARANCES

7 Pablo Aimar — Midfield

Age (on 01/07/04)	24
Caps this season	6
Total minutes on the pitch	457
Goals	3
Yellow Cards	0
Red Cards	0
Club Side	Valencia

	PLAYER	POS	AGE	CAPS	MINS	GOALS	CARDS(Y)	CARDS(R)	CLUB SIDE
1	Pablo Cavallero	GK	30	7	630	0	0	0	Celta Vigo
2	Roberto Fabian Ayala	DEF	31	7	630	0	0	0	Valencia
3	Hernan Crespo	ATT	29	7	567	4	0	0	Chelsea
4	Javier Zanetti	MID	30	6	540	0	0	0	Inter Milan
5	Andres D'Alessandro	MID	23	7	485	2	0	0	Wolfsburg
6	Cesar Delgado	ATT	22	6	459	1	0	0	Cruz Azul
7	Pablo Aimar	MID	24	6	457	3	0	0	Valencia
8	Walter Adrian Samuel	DEF	26	5	447	1	0	1	Roma
9	Kily Gonzalez	MID	29	4	315	1	0	0	Inter Milan
10	Matias Almeyda	MID	30	5	300	0	0	0	Parma
11	Diego Placente	DEF	26	4	274	0	0	0	B Leverkusen
12	Facundo Quiroga	DEF	26	3	270	0	0	0	SP Lisbon
13	Juan Sebastian Veron	MID	29	4	266	1	0	0	Chelsea
14	Gabriel Ivan Heinze	DEF	26	2	118	0	0	0	Paris SG
15	Luis Gonzalez	MID	23	3	104	0	0	0	River Plate
16	Juan Pablo Sorin	MID	28	2	96	0	0	0	Paris SG
17	Esteban Cambiasso	MID	23	2	92	0	0	0	Real Madrid
18	Clemente Rodriguez	DEF	22	1	90	0	0	0	Boca Juniors
19	Juan Riquelme	MID	26	2	80	0	0	0	Barcelona
20	Javier Saviola	ATT	22	4	78	0	0	0	Barcelona
21	Claudio Lopez	ATT	29	1	63	0	0	0	Lazio

BELGIUM

FIFA/COCA COLA WORLD RANKING: **17th**

MANAGER: AIME ANTHUENIS

1	intnls	**Holland**	H	D	1-1	Sonck 38	35,000
2	eq8	**Croatia**	H	W	2-1	Sonck 34,42	3,500
3	eq8	**Estonia**	H	W	2-0	Reinumae 44 og; Buffel 60	26,000
4	intnls	**France**	H	L	0-2		
5	intnls	**Germany**	A	L	0-3		
6	intnls	**Turkey**	H	L	2-3	Sonck 33; Dufer 86	25,000
7	intnls	**Holland**	A	W	1-0	Goor 78 pen 34,000	

KEY PLAYERS - GOALSCORERS

Wesley Sonck

Goals in Internationals	4
Contribution to Attacking Power Average number of minutes between team goals while on pitch	66
Player Strike Rate The total number of minutes he was on the pitch for every goal scored	100
Team Strike Rate Average number of minutes between goals scored by club	79

	PLAYER	GOALS	ATT POWER	STRIKE RATE
1	Wesley Sonck	4	66	100 mins
2	Bart Goor	1	55	446 mins
3	Thomas Buffel	1	80	564 mins

TOP PLAYER APPEARANCES

3 Thomas Buffel — Midfield

Age (on 01/07/04)	23
Caps this season	7
Total minutes on the pitch	564
Goals	1
Yellow Cards	0
Red Cards	0
Club Side	Feyenoord

	PLAYER	POS	AGE	CAPS	MINS	GOALS	CARDS(Y)	CARDS(R)	CLUB SIDE
1	Philippe Clement	DEF	30	7	607	0	0	0	Club Brugge
2	Eric Deflandre	DEF	30	7	574	0	0	0	Lyon
3	Thomas Buffel	MID	23	7	564	1	0	0	Feyenoord
4	Timmy Simons	MID	28	6	540	0	0	0	Club Brugge
5	Bart Goor	MID	31	5	446	1	0	0	Hertha Berlin
6	Jelle Van Damme	DEF	20	6	432	0	1	0	Ajax
7	Geert De Vlieger	GK	32	5	405	0	0	0	Willem II Tilb
8	Wesley Sonck	ATT	25	5	400	4	0	0	Ajax
9	Walter Baseggio	MID	25	6	387	0	0	0	Anderlecht
10	Mbo Mpenza	ATT	27	5	381	0	0	0	Mouscron
11	Vincent Kompany	DEF	18	4	360	0	0	0	Anderlecht
12	Daniel Van Buyten	DEF	26	3	270	0	1	0	Marseille
13	Didier Dheedene	DEF	32	2	180	0	0	0	1860 Munich
14	Sven Vermant	MID	31	2	158	0	0	0	Schalke
15	Oliver Deschacht	DEF	23	4	154	0	0	0	Anderlecht
16	Luigi Pieroni	ATT	23	3	115	0	0	0	Mouscron
17	Frederic Herpoel	GK	29	2	100	0	0	0	Gent
18	Jonathan Walasiak	MID	21	1	90	0	0	0	Standard Liege
19	Tristan Peersman	GK	24	1	90	0	0	0	Anderlecht
20	Emile Mpenza	ATT	26	3	84	0	0	0	Schalke
21	Roberto Bisconti	MID	30	3	63	0	0	0	Standard Liege

SERBIA & MONTENEGRO

FIFA/COCA COLA WORLD RANKING: **45th**

MANAGER: ILIJA PETKOVIC

1	eq9	**Wales**	H	W	1-0	Mladenovic 72	30,000
2	eq9	**Italy**	H	D	1-1	Ilic 81	30,000
3	eq9	**Wales**	A	W	3-2	Vukic 4; Milosevic 82; Ljuboja 87	72,514
4	intnls	**Poland**	A	L	3-4	Boskovic 70; Vukic 79; Iliev 89	9,000
5	intnls	**N Ireland**	A	D	1-1	Paunovic 7	

KEY PLAYERS - GOALSCORERS

Zvonimir Vukic

Goals in Internationals	2
Contribution to Attacking Power Average number of minutes between team goals while on pitch	44
Player Strike Rate The total number of minutes he was on the pitch for every goal scored	133
Team Strike Rate Average number of minutes between goals scored by club	50

	PLAYER	GOALS	ATT POWER	STRIKE RATE
1	Zvonimir Vukic	2	44	133 mins
2	Danko Boskovic	1	21	153 mins
3	Sasa Ilic	1	81	163 mins

TOP PLAYER APPEARANCES

Mateja Kezman — Attack

Age (on 01/07/04)	25
Caps this season	4
Total minutes on the pitch	329
Goals	0
Yellow Cards	1
Red Cards	0
Club Side	PSV Eindhoven

	PLAYER	POS	AGE	CAPS	MINS	GOALS	CARDS(Y)	CARDS(R)	CLUB SIDE
1	Goran Gavrancic	DEF	25	4	360	0	0	0	Dinamo Kiev
2	Milwoje Cirkovic	DEF	27	4	352	0	0	0	Partizan
3	Mateja Kezman	ATT	25	4	329	0	1	0	PSV Eindhoven
4	Dragoslav Jevric	GK	30	3	270	0	1	0	Vitesse Arnhem
5	Mladen Krstajic	DEF	30	3	270	0	1	0	W Bremen
6	Zvonimir Vukic	MID	24	4	265	2	1	0	Shakhtar Donetsk
7	Dragan Mladenovic	MID	28	3	251	0	1	0	Crvena Zvezda
8	Darko Kovacevic	ATT	30	3	243	0	1	0	Real Sociedad
9	Ivica Dragutinovic	DEF	28	3	203	0	0	0	Standard Liege
10	Savo Milosevic	ATT	30	3	180	0	1	0	Celta Vigo
11	Dragan Sarac	MID	28	2	180	0	0	0	SV Pasching
12	Dejan Stefanovic	DEF	29	2	180	0	2	0	Portsmouth
13	Nenad Djordjevic	DEF	24	3	168	0	1	0	Partizan
14	Dejan Stankovic	MID	25	2	166	0	0	0	Inter Milan
15	Sasa Ilic	MID	26	3	163	1	0	0	Partizan
16	Danko Boskovic	ATT	24	3	153	1	0	0	Kaiserslauten
17	Slobodan Markovic	DEF	25	2	126	0	0	0	Zeleznik
19	Ivan Dudic	DEF	32	1	90	0	0	0	Crvena Zvezda
20	Goran Bunjevcevic	MID	31	1	90	0	1	0	Tottenham
21	Dragan Zilic	GK	29	1	90	0	0	0	Sartid
22	Predrag Djordjevic	MID	31	1	90	0	0	0	Olympiakos

DENMARK

FIFA/COCA COLA WORLD RANKING: **14th**

MANAGER: MORTEN OLSEN

1 intnls	**Finland**	H	D	1-1	Gronkjaer 42 14,882	
2 e2kq2	**Romania**	H	D	2-2	Tomasson 34 pen; Laursen 90	42,049
3 e2kq2	**Bosnia**	A	D	1-1	Jorgensen 12	35,500
4 intnls	**England**	A	W	3-2	Jorgensen 8,30 pen; Tomasson 82	64,159
5 intnls	**Turkey**	A	W	1-0	Jorgensen 32	
6 intnls	**Spain**	A	L	0-2		22,000
7 intnls	**Scotland**	H	W	1-0	Sand 60	22,885
8 intnls	**Estonia**	A	D	2-2	Tomasson 27; Perez 79	

KEY PLAYERS - GOALSCORERS

Martin Jorgensen

Goals in Internationals	4
Contribution to Attacking Power Average number of minutes between team goals while on pitch	53
Player Strike Rate The total number of minutes he was on the pitch for every goal scored	121
Team Strike Rate Average number of minutes between goals scored by club	65

	PLAYER	GOALS	ATT POWER	STRIKE RATE
1	Martin Jorgensen	4	53	121 mins
2	Jon Dahl Tomasson	2	91	183 mins
3	Kenneth Perez	1	52	211 mins
4	Ebbe Sand	1	42	297 mins
5	Martin Laursen	1	77	541 mins

TOP PLAYER APPEARANCES

7 Thomas Gravesen — Midfield

Age (on 01/07/04)	28
Caps this season	6
Total minutes on the pitch	489
Goals	0
Yellow Cards	2
Red Cards	1
Club Side	Everton

	PLAYER	POS	AGE	CAPS	MINS	GOALS	CARDS(Y)	CARDS(R)	CLUB SIDE
1	Thomas Sorensen	GK	28	8	675	0	0	0	Aston Villa
2	Niclas Jensen	DEF	29	8	656	0	2	0	B Dortmund
3	Rene Henriksen	DEF	34	8	600	0	0	0	Panathinaikos
4	Jesper Gronkjaer	ATT	27	8	573	1	2	0	Chelsea
5	Thomas Helveg	DEF	33	7	567	0	0	0	Inter Milan
6	Martin Laursen	DEF	32	7	541	1	0	0	AC Milan
7	Thomas Gravesen	MID	28	6	489	0	2	1	Everton
8	Martin Jorgensen	MID	28	7	484	4	0	0	Udinese
9	Claus Jensen	ATT	26	6	406	0	0	0	Charlton
10	Jon Dahl Tomasson	ATT	27	7	366	2	0	0	AC Milan
11	Daniel Jensen	MID	25	5	356	0	1	0	Murcia
12	Morten Wieghorst	MID	33	5	305	0	0	0	Brondby
13	Ebbe Sand	ATT	31	6	297	1	0	0	Schalke
14	Christian Poulsen	MID	24	4	258	0	0	0	Schalke
15	Dennis Rommedahl	ATT	25	6	223	0	0	0	PSV Eindhoven
16	Kenneth Perez	ATT	29	5	211	1	0	0	AZ Alkmaar
17	Per Kroldrup	DEF	24	4	181	0	0	0	Udinese
18	Brian Priske	DEF	27	3	128	0	0	0	Genk
19	Peter Madsen	ATT	26	3	85	0	0	0	Bochum
20	Per Nielsen	ATT	30	2	71	0	0	0	Brondby
21	Kasper Bogelund	DEF	23	2	62	0	0	0	PSV Eindhoven

PORTUGAL

FIFA/COCA COLA WORLD RANKING: **20th**

MANAGER: LUIZ FELIPE SCOLARI

1 intnls	**Kazakhstan**	H	W	1-0	Simao Sabrosa 65	14,000
2 intnls	**Spain**	H	L	0-3	29,500	
3 intnls	**Greece**	H	D	1-1	Pauleta 60	
4 intnls	**Kuwait**	H	W	8-0	Pauleta 10, 20, 45, 52; Figo 33;	
					Nuno Gomes 69, 75, 87	
5 intnls	**England**	H	D	1-1	Pauleta 70 27,000	
6 intnls	**Italy**	H	L	1-2	Nuno Valente 5	35,000
7 intnls	**Sweden**	H	D	2-2	Pauleta 33; Nuno Gomes 90	
8 intnls	**Luxembourg**	H	W	3-0	Figo 15; Nuno Gomes 28; Rui Costa 36	9,000

KEY PLAYERS - GOALSCORERS

Pedro Resendes Pauleta

Goals in Internationals	7
Contribution to Attacking Power Average number of minutes between team goals while on pitch	53
Player Strike Rate The total number of minutes he was on the pitch for every goal scored	77
Team Strike Rate Average number of minutes between goals scored by club	42

	PLAYER	GOALS	ATT POWER	STRIKE RATE
1	Pedro Resendes Pauleta	7	53	77 mins
2	Nuno Jorge Pereira Valente	1	55	165 mins
3	Luis Figo	2	51	258 mins
4	Pedro Fonseca Simao Sabrosa	1	26	404 mins
5	Manuel Rui Costa	1	52	526 mins

TOP PLAYER APPEARANCES

5 Luis Figo — Midfield

Age (on 01/07/04)	31
Caps this season	8
Total minutes on the pitch	515
Goals	2
Yellow Cards	0
Red Cards	0
Club Side	Real Madrid

	PLAYER	POS	AGE	CAPS	MINS	GOALS	CARDS(Y)	CARDS(R)	CLUB SIDE
1	Fernando Couto	DEF	34	8	615	0	1	0	Lazio
2	Jorge Andrade	DEF	26	8	554	0	0	0	Deportivo
3	Pedro Pauleta	ATT	31	7	536	7	0	0	Paris SG
4	Manuel Rui Costa	MID	32	8	526	1	0	0	AC Milan
5	Luis Figo	MID	31	8	515	2	0	0	Real Madrid
6	Costinha	MID	29	7	473	0	0	0	Porto
7	Pereira Ricardo	GK	28	6	471	0	0	0	Boavista
8	Rui Jorge	DEF	31	7	462	0	0	0	Sp Lisbon
9	Pedro Fonseca	MID	24	7	404	1	0	0	Benfica
10	Anderson Deco	MID	26	7	384	0	0	0	Porto
11	Joaquim Man. Sampaio	GK	28	4	240	0	0	0	Braga
12	Luis Boa Morte	ATT	26	6	231	0	0	0	Fulham
13	Monteiro Miguel	DEF	24	4	218	0	0	0	Benfica
14	Armando Teixeira Petit	MID	27	3	214	0	1	0	Benfica
15	Tiago Cardoso Mendes	MID	23	4	177	0	0	0	Benfica
16	Nuno Jorge	DEF	29	4	165	1	0	0	Porto
17	Maniche	MID	26	3	146	0	0	0	Porto
18	Paulo Ferreira	DEF	25	3	145	0	0	0	Porto
21	Hugo Viana	MID	21	3	122	0	0	0	Newcastle
22	Fernando Meira	DEF	26	3	116	0	0	0	Stuttgart
23	Nuno Gomes	ATT	28	4	114	5	0	0	Benfica

CZECH REPUBLIC

FIFA/COCA COLA WORLD RANKING: **10th**

MANAGER: KAREL BRUCKNER

1	eq3	**Belarus**	A	W	3-1	Nedved 37; Baros 54; Smicer 85	11,000
2	eq3	**Holland**	H	W	3-1	Koller 15 pen; Poborsky 38; Baros 90	18,365
3	eq3	**Austria**	A	W	3-2	Jankulovski 26; Vachousek 79; Koller 90	32,300
4	intnls	**Canada**	H	W	5-1	Jankulovski 26 pen; Heinz 49; Poborsky 55; Sionko 63; Skacel 82	
5	intnls	**Italy**	A	D	2-2	Stajner 42; Rosicky 88	25,000
6	intnls	**Rep of Ireland**	A	L	1-2	Baros 81	42,000
7	intnls	**Japan**	H	L	0-1		11,802

KEY PLAYERS - GOALSCORERS

Milan Baros

Goals in Internationals	3
Contribution to Attacking Power Average number of minutes between team goals while on pitch	57
Player Strike Rate The total number of minutes he was on the pitch for every goal scored	76
Team Strike Rate Average number of minutes between goals scored by club	37

	PLAYER	GOALS	ATT POWER	STRIKE RATE
1	Milan Baros	3	57	76 mins
2	Karel Poborsky	2	36	166 mins
3	Vladimir Smicer	1	36	184 mins
4	Jan Koller	2	31	207 mins
5	Jiri Stajner	1	37	223 mins

TOP PLAYER APPEARANCES

7 Petr Cech Goalkeeper

Age (on 01/07/04)	22
Caps this season	5
Total minutes on the pitch	360
Goals	0
Yellow Cards	0
Red Cards	0
Club Side	Rennes

	PLAYER	POS	AGE	CAPS	MINS	GOALS	CARDS(Y)	CARDS(R)	CLUB SIDE
1	Pavel Nedved	MID	31	7	524	1	1	0	Juventus
2	Rene Bolf	DEF	30	7	505	0	1	0	Sparta Prague
3	Marek Jankulovski	MID	27	6	489	2	1	0	Udinese
4	Tomas Ujfalusi	DEF	26	5	450	0	1	0	Hamburg
5	Tomas Galasek	DEF	31	6	436	0	0	0	Ajax
6	Jan Koller	ATT	31	7	414	2	0	0	B Dortmund
7	Petr Cech	GK	22	5	360	0	0	0	Rennes
8	Roman Tyce	MID	27	6	354	0	0	0	1860 Munich
9	Karel Poborsky	MID	32	5	331	2	2	0	Sparta Prague
10	Tomas Rosicky	MID	23	4	312	1	0	0	B Dortmund
11	Martin Jiranek	DEF	25	5	286	0	0	0	Reggina
13	Stepan Vachousek	ATT	24	5	238	1	0	0	Marseille
14	Milan Baros	ATT	22	4	228	3	0	0	Liverpool
15	Jiri Stajner	ATT	28	4	223	1	0	0	Sparta Prague
16	Vratislav Lokvenc	ATT	30	4	220	0	0	0	Kaiserslautern
17	Vladimir Smicer	ATT	31	3	184	1	0	0	Liverpool
18	Jaromir Blazek	GK	31	3	180	0	0	0	Sparta Prague
19	Zdenek Grygera	DEF	24	3	159	0	0	0	Ajax
20	Tomas Hubschmann	DEF	22	3	127	0	0	0	Sparta Prague
22	Adam Petrous	DEF	26	1	90	0	0	0	Slavia Prague
23	Libor Sionko	MID	27	2	80	1	0	0	Sparta Prague

AUSTRALIA

FIFA/COCA COLA WORLD RANKING: **89th**

MANAGER: FRANK FARINA

1	intnls	**Rep of Ireland**	A	L	1-2	Viduka 49	40,000
2	intnls	**Jamaica**	H	W	2-1	Bresciano 20; Kewell 59	
3	intnls	**Venezuela**	A	D	1-1	Agostino 18	12,000
4	intnls	**South Africa**	H	W	1-0	Bresciano 19	
5	intnls	**Turkey**	H	L	1-3	Bresciano 50 pen	
6	intnls	**Turkey**	H	L	0-1		28,953

KEY PLAYERS - GOALSCORERS

Harry Kewell

Goals in Internationals	1
Contribution to Attacking Power Average number of minutes between team goals while on pitch	51
Player Strike Rate The total number of minutes he was on the pitch for every goal scored	153
Team Strike Rate Average number of minutes between goals scored by club	90

	PLAYER	GOALS	ATT POWER	STRIKE RATE
1	Harry Kewell	1	51	153 mins
2	Mark Bresciano	3	86	173 mins
3	Mark Viduka	1	56	224 mins

TOP PLAYER APPEARANCES

2 Mark Schwarzer Goalkeeper

Age (on 01/07/04)	31
Caps this season	5
Total minutes on the pitch	396
Goals	0
Yellow Cards	0
Red Cards	0
Club Side	Middlesbrough

	PLAYER	POS	AGE	CAPS	MINS	GOALS	CARDS(Y)	CARDS(R)	CLUB SIDE
1	Mark Bresciano	ATT	24	6	518	3	0	0	Parma
2	Mark Schwarzer	GK	31	5	396	0	0	0	Middlesbrough
3	Stan Lazaridis	MID	31	5	387	0	0	0	Birmingham
4	Lucas Neill	DEF	26	4	360	0	0	0	Blackburn
5	Brett Emerton	MID	25	4	346	0	0	0	Blackburn
6	Josip Skoko	MID	28	4	335	0	0	0	Genclerbirligi
7	Tony Vidmar	DEF	34	5	322	0	0	0	Cardiff
8	Scott Chipperfield	MID	28	5	321	0	0	0	Basel
9	Tony Popovic	DEF	31	3	270	0	0	0	Crystal Palace
10	Stephen Laybutt	DEF	26	3	270	0	0	0	Mouscron
11	Kevin Muscat	DEF	30	3	270	0	0	0	Millwall
12	Simon Colosimo	DEF	25	3	256	0	0	0	Antwerp
13	David Zdrilic	ATT	30	4	235	0	0	0	Aberdeen
14	Mark Viduka	ATT	28	3	224	1	0	0	Leeds
15	Vincenzo Grella	MID	24	4	213	0	0	0	Empoli
16	Craig Moore	DEF	28	2	180	0	0	0	Rangers
17	Paul Okon	MID	32	2	156	0	1	0	Oostende
18	Harry Kewell	MID	25	2	153	1	0	0	Liverpool
19	Mike Sterjovski	ATT	25	4	149	0	0	0	Lille
20	Zeljko Kalac	GK	31	3	144	0	0	0	Perugia
21	Max Vieri	ATT	25	2	107	0	0	0	Verona

SENEGAL

FIFA/COCA COLA WORLD RANKING: **31st**

MANAGER: GUY STEPHAN

1	intnls	Japan	A	W	1-0	Diop Papa, B 6	40,000
2	intnls	Egypt	A	L	0-1		
3	intnls	Ivory Coast	H	W	1-0	Diouf 89	
4	intnls	South Africa	H	W	2-1	Diop 29; Mabizela 83 og	50,000
5	anc	Burkina Faso	H	D	0-0		
6	anc	Kenya	H	W	3-0	Niang 4,31; Diop Papa, B 19	
7	anc	Mali	H	D	1-1	Beye 45	
8	anc	Tunisia	A	L	0-1		

KEY PLAYERS - GOALSCORERS

Mamadou Niang

Goals in Internationals	2
Contribution to Attacking Power Average number of minutes between team goals while on pitch	61
Player Strike Rate The total number of minutes he was on the pitch for every goal scored	186
Team Strike Rate Average number of minutes between goals scored by club	77

2 Papa Bouba Diop

	PLAYER	GOALS	ATT POWER	STRIKE RATE
1	Mamadou Niang	2	61	186 mins
2	Papa Bouba Diop	2	70	213 mins
3	Malick Diop Papa	1	77	540 mins

TOP PLAYER APPEARANCES

3 Henri Camara Attack

Age (on 01/07/04)	27
Caps this season	6
Total minutes on the pitch	535
Goals	0
Yellow Cards	0
Red Cards	0
Club Side	Wolverhampton

	PLAYER	POS	AGE	CAPS	MINS	GOALS	CARDS(Y/R)		CLUB SIDE
1	Tony Mario Sylva	GK	29	6	540	0	0	0	Monaco
2	Malick Diop Papa	DEF	29	6	540	1	0	0	Lorient
3	Henri Camara	ATT	27	6	535	0	0	0	Wolverhampton
4	Salif Diao	MID	27	6	508	0	0	0	Liverpool
5	El Hadji Diouf	ATT	23	5	427	0	0	0	Liverpool
6	Papa Bouba Diop	MID	26	5	425	2	0	0	Lens
7	Mamadou Niang	ATT	24	6	371	2	0	0	Strasbourg
8	Omar Daf	DEF	27	4	354	0	0	0	Sochaux
9	Lamine Diatta	DEF	29	4	331	0	0	0	Rennes
10	Aliou Cisse	DEF	29	4	295	0	0	0	Birmingham
11	Souleymane Diawara	DEF	25	3	270	0	0	0	Sochaux
12	Ibrahima Faye, I	DEF	24	3	270	0	0	0	Gent
13	Oussmane N'Doye	ATT	26	4	197	0	0	0	Toulouse
14	Ferdinand Coly	DEF	30	2	171	0	0	0	Perugia
15	Diomansy Mehdi Kamara	ATT	23	4	135	0	0	0	Modena
16	Habib Beye	DEF	26	4	134	1	0	0	Marseille
17	Sylvain N'Diaye	MID	28	3	125	0	0	0	Marseille
18	Lamine Sakho	MID	2005	2	105	0	0	0	Leeds
19	Abdoulaye Diagne Faye	DEF	26	1	90	0	0	0	Lens
20	Amdy Faye	MID	26	1	52	0	0	0	Portsmouth
21	Frederic Mendy	MID	30	2	31	0	0	0	Bastia

SWEDEN

FIFA/COCA COLA WORLD RANKING: **21st**

MANAGER: LARS LAGERBACK and TOMMY SODERBERG

1	intnls	Greece	H	L	1-2	Svensson, A 16	19,000
2	e2kq4	San Marino	H	W	5-0	Jonson 32; Jakobsson 48; Ibrahimovic 53,81; Kallstrom 66 pen	31,098
3	e2kq4	Poland	A	W	2-0	Nilsson, M 2; Mellberg 36	20,000
4	e2kq4	Latvia	H	L	0-1		32,095
5	intnls	Egypt	A	L	0-1		15,000
6	intnls	Albania	A	D	1-1	Selakovic 50	
7	intnls	England	H	W	1-0	Ibrahimovic 54	
8	intnls	Portugal	A	D	2-2	Kallstrom 17; Rui Jorge 85 og	
9	intnls	Finland	A	W	3-1	Andersson, Anders 30; Allback 45,82	16,000

KEY PLAYERS - GOALSCORERS

Zlatan Ibrahimovic

Goals in Internationals	3
Contribution to Attacking Power Average number of minutes between team goals while on pitch	36
Player Strike Rate The total number of minutes he was on the pitch for every goal scored	120
Team Strike Rate Average number of minutes between goals scored by club	54

	PLAYER	GOALS	ATT POWER	STRIKE RATE
1	Zlatan Ibrahimovic	3	36	120 mins
3	Marcus Allback	2	54	190 mins
4	Kim Kallstrom	2	47	213 mins
5	Anders Andersson	1	60	241 mins

TOP PLAYER APPEARANCES

4 Olof Mellburg Defence

Age (on 01/07/04)	26
Caps this season	7
Total minutes on the pitch	505
Goals	1
Yellow Cards	0
Red Cards	0
Club Side	Aston Villa

	PLAYER	POS	AGE	CAPS	MINS	GOALS	CARDS(Y/R)		CLUB SIDE
1	Teddy Lucic	DEF	31	8	631	0	0	0	B Leverkusen
2	Erik Edman	DEF	25	8	612	0	0	0	Heerenveen
3	Anders Svensson	MID	27	8	547	1	0	0	Southampton
4	Olof Mellberg	DEF	26	7	505	1	0	0	Aston Villa
5	Tobias Linderoth	MID	25	7	502	0	0	0	Everton
6	Andreas Isaksson	GK	22	7	495	0	0	0	Djurgarden
7	Michael Nilsson	MID	26	6	495	1	0	0	IFK Gothenburg
8	Michael Svensson	DEF	28	5	450	0	2	0	Southampton
9	Kim Kallstrom	MID	21	6	425	2	0	0	Rennes
10	Andreas Jakobsson	DEF	31	6	398	1	0	0	Brondby
11	Marcus Allback	ATT	30	6	380	2	0	0	Aston Villa
12	Zlatan Ibrahimovic	ATT	22	6	361	3	0	0	Ajax
13	Christian Wilhelmsson	MID	24	4	344	0	0	0	Anderlecht
14	Mattias Jonson	ATT	30	5	335	1	0	0	Brondby
15	Magnus Hedman	GK	31	4	270	0	0	0	Ancona
16	Anders Andersson	MID	30	6	241	1	0	0	Benfica
17	Johan Mjallby	DEF	33	3	231	0	0	0	Celtic
18	Petter Hansson	MID	27	3	219	0	0	0	Heerenveen
19	Pontus Farnerud	MID	24	4	187	0	0	0	Strasbourg
20	Andreas Johansson	MID	26	5	171	0	0	0	AIK Solna
21	Niklas Skoog	ATT	30	3	132	0	0	0	Malmo

URUGUAY

FIFA/COCA COLA WORLD RANKING: **25th**

MANAGER: JUAN RAKON CARRASCO

1	intnls	**Argentina**	H	L	2-3	Forlan 2; Liguera 57	8,000
2	wcq1	**Bolivia**	H	W	5-0	Forlan 19; Chevanton 41,61; Abeijon 83; Bueno 87	39,253
3	wcq1	**Paraguay**	A	L	1-4	Chevanton 24	15,000
4	intnls	**Mexico**	H	W	2-0	Perrone 27,65	41,587
5	wcq1	**Chile**	H	W	2-1	Chevanton 30; Romero 48	60,000
6	wcq1	**Brazil**	A	D	3-3	Forlan 57,75; Silva 77 og	30,000
7	intnls	**Jamaica**	A	L	0-2		
8	wcq1	**Venezuela**	H	L	0-3		

KEY PLAYERS - GOALSCORERS

Diego Forlan

Goals in Internationals	4
Contribution to Attacking Power Average number of minutes between team goals while on pitch	48
Player Strike Rate The total number of minutes he was on the pitch for every goal scored	121
Team Strike Rate Average number of minutes between goals scored by club	48

	PLAYER	GOALS	ATT POWER	STRIKE RATE
1	Diego Forlan	4	48	121 mins
2	Ernesto Javier Chevanton	4	44	134 mins
3	Clever Marcelo Romero	1	57	172 mins
4	Nelson Abeijon	1	45	183 mins
5	Carlos Bueno	1	34	277 mins

TOP PLAYER APPEARANCES

7 Dario Silva — Attack

Age (on 01/07/04)	28
Caps this season	6
Total minutes on the pitch	429
Goals	0
Yellow Cards	0
Red Cards	0
Club Side	Grasshoppers

	PLAYER	POS	AGE	CAPS	MINS	GOALS	CARDS(Y)	CARDS(R)	CLUB SIDE
1	Gustavo Munua	GK	26	7	630	0	0	0	Deportivo
2	Ernesto Javier Chevanton	ATT	23	7	534	4	0	0	Lecce
3	Martin Ricardo Liguera	ATT	23	7	502	1	0	0	Mallorca
4	Diego Forlan	ATT	25	7	485	4	0	0	Man Utd
5	Marcelo Sosa	MID	26	6	482	0	0	0	Colon
6	Luis Diego Lopez	DEF	29	5	450	0	0	0	Cagliari
7	Dario Silva	ATT	28	6	429	0	0	0	Grasshoppers
8	Alvaro Recoba	MID	28	6	370	0	0	0	Inter Milan
9	Alejandro Lago	DEF	25	4	360	0	0	0	Fenix
10	Carlos Bueno	ATT	24	5	277	1	0	0	Penarol
11	Mauricio Gonzalez	ATT	26	3	270	0	0	0	Aguada
12	Nelson Abeijon	MID	30	4	183	1	0	0	Como
13	Joe Bizera	DEF	24	2	180	0	0	0	Penarol
14	Gonzalo Sorondo	DEF	24	2	180	0	0	0	Inter Milan
15	Clever Marcelo Romero	MID	28	3	172	1	0	0	Malaga
16	Mario Regueiro	ATT	25	2	166	0	0	0	R Santander
17	German Hornos	ATT	21	3	157	0	0	0	Seville
18	Ruben Olivera	MID	21	3	149	0	0	0	Atl Madrid
19	Alejandro Mello	MID	25	2	101	0	0	0	Nacional
20	Gianni Guigou	MID	29	1	90	0	0	0	Siena
21	Luis Alberto Barbat	GK	28	1	90	0	0	0	Danubio

CAMEROON

FIFA/COCA COLA WORLD RANKING: **12th**

MANAGER: WINFRIED SCHAFER

1	anc	**Algeria**	H	D	1-1	Mboma 43	
2	anc	**Zimbabwe**	H	W	5-3	Mboma 30,44,64; Mbami 40,66	
3	anc	**Egypt**	H	D	0-0		
4	anc	**Nigeria**	H	L	1-2	Eto'o 42	
5	intnls	**Bulgaria**	A	L	0-3		13,987

KEY PLAYERS - GOALSCORERS

Patrick Mboma

Goals in Internationals	4
Contribution to Attacking Power Average number of minutes between team goals while on pitch	42
Player Strike Rate The total number of minutes he was on the pitch for every goal scored	75
'TeamStrike Rate Average number of minutes between goals scored by club	64

	PLAYER	GOALS	ATT POWER	STRIKE RATE
1	Patrick Mboma	4	42	75 mins
2	Modeste Mbami	2	51	180 mins
3	Samuel Fils Eto'o	1	50	350 mins

TOP PLAYER APPEARANCES

8 Samuel Fils Eto'o — Attack

Age (on 01/07/04)	23
Caps this season	4
Total minutes on the pitch	350
Goals	1
Yellow Cards	0
Red Cards	0
Club Side	Mallorca

	PLAYER	POS	AGE	CAPS	MINS	GOALS	CARDS(Y)	CARDS(R)	CLUB SIDE
1	Perrier Doumbe	DEF	25	5	450	0	0	0	Auxerre
2	Rigobert Song	DEF	28	5	446	0	0	0	Lens
3	Idriss Carlos Kameni	GK	20	5	405	0	0	0	Le Havre
4	Modeste Mbami	MID	21	4	360	2	0	0	Paris SG
5	Eric Djemba-Djemba	MID	23	4	360	0	0	0	Man Utd
6	Lucien Mettomo	DEF	27	4	360	0	0	0	Kaiserslautern
7	Geremi	MID	25	4	353	0	0	0	Chelsea
8	Samuel Fils Eto'o	ATT	23	4	350	1	0	0	Mallorca
9	Timothee Atouba	MID	22	5	334	0	0	0	Basle
10	Bill Tchato	MID	29	4	303	0	0	0	Kaiserslautern
11	Patrick Mboma	ATT	33	4	299	4	0	0	Al-Ittihad
12	Mohamadou Idrissou	ATT	24	5	251	0	0	0	Hannover 96
13	Jean Makoun	ATT	21	3	180	0	0	0	Lille
14	Valery Mezague	MID	20	2	106	0	0	0	Montpellier
15	Pierre Nlend Wome	DEF	25	1	90	0	0	0	Espanyol
16	Achille Emana	ATT	22	1	77	0	0	0	Toulouse
17	Albert Meyong Ze	ATT	23	1	46	0	0	0	Vitoria Setubal
18	Herve Tum	ATT	25	1	44	0	0	0	Basel
19	Salomon Olembe	MID	30	1	38	0	0	0	Marseille
20	Pius Ndiefi	ATT	29	2	23	0	0	0	Sedan
21	Daniel Ngom Kome	MID	24	2	13	0	0	0	Numancia

CROATIA

FIFA/COCA COLA WORLD RANKING: **25th**

MANAGER: OTTO BARIC

1	intnls	**England**	A	L	1-3	Mornar 78	27,000
2	eq8	**Andorra**	A	W	3-0	Kovac, N 5; Simunic 16; Rosso 71	800
3	eq8	**Belgium**	A	L	1-2	Simic 35	3,500
4	eq8	**Bulgaria**	H	W	1-0	Olic 48	37,000
5	eqpl1	**Slovenia**	H	D	1-1	Prso 5	35,000
6	eqpl2	**Slovenia**	A	W	1-0	Prso 60	10,000
7	intnls	**Germany**	H	L	1-2	Neretljak 86	
8	intnls	**Turkey**	H	D	2-2	Sokota 2; Srna 76	
9	intnls	**Macedonia**	A	W	1-0	Klasnic 29	
10	intnls	**Slovakia**	H	W	1-0	Olic 29	5,500

KEY PLAYERS - GOALSCORERS

Tomislav Sokota

Goals in Internationals	1
Contribution to Attacking Power Average number of minutes between team goals while on pitch	53
Player Strike Rate The total number of minutes he was on the pitch for every goal scored	160
Team Strike Rate Average number of minutes between goals scored by club	69

	PLAYER	GOALS	ATT POWER	STRIKE RATE
1	Tomislav Sokota	1	53	163 mins
2	Dado Prso	2	80	240 mins
3	Ivica Olic	2	58	263 mins
4	Darijo Srna	1	106	424 mins
5	Ivica Mornar	1	55	502 mins

TOP PLAYER APPEARANCES

13 Igor Tudor — Defence

Age (on 01/07/04)	26
Caps this season	6
Total minutes on the pitch	418
Goals	0
Yellow Cards	2
Red Cards	0
Club Side	Juventus

	PLAYER	POS	AGE	CAPS	MINS	GOALS	CARDS(Y)	CARDS(R)	CLUB SIDE
1	Boris Zivkovic	DEF	28	9	759	0	1	0	Stuttgart
2	Stipe Pletikosa	GK	25	9	744	0	0	0	Shakhtar Donetsk
3	Josip Simunic	DEF	26	8	598	1	2	1	Hertha Berlin
4	Stjepan Tomas	DEF	28	8	578	0	2	0	Como
5	Nico Kovac	MID	32	8	571	1	1	0	Hertha Berlin
6	Robert Kovac	DEF	30	7	546	0	4	0	Bayern Munich
7	Dario Simic	DEF	28	8	540	1	0	0	AC Milan
8	Ivica Olic	ATT	24	9	525	2	0	0	Dinamo Zagreb
9	Dovani Rosso	MID	31	10	524	1	0	0	Maccabi Haifa
10	Ivica Mornar	ATT	30	7	502	1	1	0	Portsmouth
11	Dado Prso	ATT	29	7	480	2	1	0	Monaco
12	Darijo Srna	MID	22	8	424	1	1	0	Hajduk Split
13	Igor Tudor	DEF	26	6	418	0	2	0	Juventus
14	Jerko Leko	MID	24	9	412	0	3	0	Dinamo Kiev
15	Milan Rapaic	MID	30	6	374	0	0	0	Ancona
16	Marko Babic	MID	23	5	236	0	0	0	B Leverkusen
17	Mario Tokic	DEF	28	3	219	0	0	0	Grazer AK
18	Tomislav Sokota	ATT	27	3	163	1	0	0	Benfica
19	Jurica Vranjes	MID	24	2	149	0	0	0	Stuttgart
20	Ivan Klasnic	ATT	24	2	138	1	0	0	W Bremen
21	Marijo Maric	ATT	27	3	123	0	0	0	Karnten

FINLAND

FIFA/COCA COLA WORLD RANKING: **42nd**

MANAGER: ANTTI MUURINEN

1	intnls	**Denmark**	A	D	1-1	Riihilahti 88	14,882
2	eq9	**Azerbaijan**	A	W	2-1	Tainio 52; Nurmela 74	7,500
3	eq9	**Wales**	A	D	1-1	Forssell 80	70,000
4	intnls	**Costa Rica**	A	L	1-2	Nurmela 62	
5	intnls	**Bosnia**	A	L	0-1	20,000	
6	intnls	**Sweden**	H	L	1-3	Litmanen 8	16,000

KEY PLAYERS - GOALSCORERS

Jari Litmanen

Goals in Internationals	1
Contribution to Attacking Power Average number of minutes between team goals while on pitch	159
Player Strike Rate The total number of minutes he was on the pitch for every goal scored	159
Team Strike Rate Average number of minutes between goals scored by club	90

	PLAYER	GOALS	ATT POWER	STRIKE RATE
1	Jari Litmanen	1	159	159 mins
2	Mika Nurmela	2	100	252 mins
3		1	66	264 mins
4	Mikael Forssell	1	72	360 mins

TOP PLAYER APPEARANCES

6 Antti Niemi — Goalkeeper

Age (on 01/07/04)	32
Caps this season	4
Total minutes on the pitch	319
Goals	0
Yellow Cards	0
Red Cards	0
Club Side	Southampton

	PLAYER	POS	AGE	CAPS	MINS	GOALS	CARDS(Y)	CARDS(R)	CLUB SIDE
1	Mika Nurmela	ATT	32	6	503	2	0	1	Kaiserslautern
2	Joonas Kolkka	ATT	29	5	392	0	0	0	B M'gladbach
3	Mika Vayrynen	ATT	22	5	206	0	0	0	Heerenveen
4	Mikael Forssell	ATT	23	4	360	1	0	0	Birmingham
5	Hannu Tihinen	DEF	28	4	360	0	0	0	Anderlecht
6	Antti Niemi	GK	32	4	319	0	0	0	Southampton
7	Petri Pasanen	DEF	23	4	314	0	1	0	Portsmouth
8	Sami Hyypia	DEF	30	4	289	0	0	0	Liverpool
9	Janne Saariinen	DEF	27	4	271	0	0	0	1860 Munich
10	Juha Reini	DEF	29	4	270	0	0	0	AZ Alkmaar
11	Teemu Tainio	MID	-	3	264	1	0	0	
12	Toni Kuivasto	DEF	-	4	251	0	0	0	
13	Aleksei Eremenko jr	ATT	21	3	234	0	0	0	HJK Helsinki
14	Peter Kopteff	MID	25	5	381	0	0	0	Viking23
15	Jonatan Johansson	ATT	28	4	171	0	0	0	Charlton
16	Jari Litmanen	ATT	33	2	159	1	0	0	Ajax
17	Aki Riihilahti	MID	27	3	140	1	0	0	Crystal Palace
18	Mikko Kaven	GK	29	2	131	0	0	0	Valerenga
19	Markus Heikkinen	MID	-	3	111	0	0	0	
20	Jari Niemi	MID	27	2	101	0	0	0	Mons
21	Ville Kaj Nylund	DEF	32	1	90	0	0	0	HJK Helsinki

SCOTLAND

FIFA/COCA COLA WORLD RANKING: **63rd**

MANAGER: BERTI VOGTS

1 intnls	**Norway**	A	D	0-0		12,858
2 eq5	**Faroe Islands**	H	W	3-1	McCann 8; Dickov 45; McFadden 74	40,109
3 eq5	**Germany**	A	L	1-2	McCann 60	67,000
4 eq5	**Lithuania**	H	W	1-0	Fletcher 70	50,343
5 eqpl1	**Holland**	H	W	1-0	McFadden 22	50,670
6 eqpl2	**Holland**	A	L	0-6		52,000
7 intnls	**Wales**	A	L	0-4		47,124
8 intnls	**Romania**	H	L	1-2	McFadden 57	20,433
9 intnls	**Denmark**	A	L	0-1		22,885
10 intnls	**Estonia**	A	W	1-0	McFadden 76	
11 intnls	**Trinidad & Tob.**	H	W	4-1	Fletcher 6; Holt 14; Caldwell, G 23; Quashie 34	16,187

KEY PLAYERS - GOALSCORERS

James McFadden

Goals in Internationals	4
Contribution to Attacking Power Average number of minutes between team goals while on pitch	77
Player Strike Rate The total number of minutes he was on the pitch for every goal scored	175
Team Strike Rate Average number of minutes between goals scored by club	83

	PLAYER	GOALS	ATT POWER	STRIKE RATE
1	James McFadden	4	77	175 mins
2	Neil McCann	2	74	224 mins
3	Paul Dickov	1	89	267 mins
4	Darren Fletcher	2	74	296 mins

TOP PLAYER APPEARANCES

6 Darren Fletcher — Midfield

Age (on 01/07/04)	20
Caps this season	8
Total minutes on the pitch	592
Goals	2
Yellow Cards	0
Red Cards	0
Club Side	Manchester United

	PLAYER	POS	AGE	CAPS	MINS	GOALS	CARDS(Y)	CARDS(R)	CLUB SIDE
1	Steven Pressley	DEF	30	9	765	0	2	0	Hearts
2	James McFadden	MID	21	10	699	4	1	0	Everton
3	Robert Douglas	GK	32	7	630	0	0	0	Celtic
4	Christian Dailly	DEF	30	7	630	0	2	0	West Ham
5	Jackie McNamara	MID	30	7	630	0	1	0	Celtic
6	Darren Fletcher	MID	20	8	592	2	0	0	Scotland
7	Gary Naysmith	DEF	25	7	540	0	2	0	Everton
8	Barry Ferguson	MID	26	6	540	0	1	0	Blackburn
9	Colin Cameron	MID	31	7	529	0	0	0	Wolverhampton
10	Neil McCann	ATT	29	6	448	2	0	0	Southampton
11	Stevie Crawford	ATT	30	7	394	0	1	0	Dunfermline
12	Kenny Miller	ATT	24	7	358	0	0	0	Wolverhampton
13	Gary Caldwell	DEF	23	4	348	1	0	0	Hibernian
14	Gavin Rae	DEF	26	6	337	0	0	0	Rangers
15	Paul Gallacher	GK	24	4	294	0	0	0	Dundee Utd
16	Lee Wilkie	DEF	24	3	270	0	0	0	Dundee
17	Paul Dickov	ATT	31	4	267	1	1	0	Leicester
18	Malcolm Mackay	DEF	32	3	264	0	0	0	Norwich
19	Andy Webster	DEF	22	5	236	0	0	0	Hearts
20	Paul Lambert	MID	34	2	180	0	0	0	Celtic
21	Steven Thompson	ATT	25	3	169	0	0	0	Rangers

REPUBLIC OF IRELAND

FIFA/COCA COLA WORLD RANKING: **15th**

MANAGER: BRIAN KERR

1 intnls	**Australia**	H	W	2-1	O'Shea 74; Morrison 81	40,000
2 eq10	**Russia**	H	D	1-1	Duff 35	36,000
3 intnls	**Turkey**	H	D	2-2	Connolly 35; Dunne 90	27,200
4 eq10	**Switzerland**	A	L	0-2		31,006
5 intnls	**Canada**	H	W	3-0	Duff 23; Keane, Robbie 60,84	30,000
6 intnls	**Brazil**	H	D	0-0		44,000
7 intnls	**Czech Rep.**	H	W	2-1	Harte 52; Keane, Robbie 90	42,000
8 intnls	**Poland**	A	D	0-0		18,000
9 intnls	**Romania**	H	W	1-0	Holland 85	42,356
10 intnls	**Nigeria**	H	L	0-3		

KEY PLAYERS - GOALSCORERS

Robbie Keane

Goals in Internationals	3
Contribution to Attacking Power Average number of minutes between team goals while on pitch	78
Player Strike Rate The total number of minutes he was on the pitch for every goal scored	210
Team Strike Rate Average number of minutes between goals scored by club	82

	PLAYER	GOALS	ATT POWER	STRIKE RATE
1	Robbie Keane	3	78	210 mins
2	Damien Duff	2	66	233 mins
3	John O'Shea	1	94	472 mins
4	Ian Harte	1	59	476 mins
5	Clinton Morrison	1	66	532 mins

TOP PLAYER APPEARANCES

3 Matt Holland — Midfield

Age (on 01/07/04)	30
Caps this season	8
Total minutes on the pitch	622
Goals	1
Yellow Cards	0
Red Cards	0
Club Side	Charlton

	PLAYER	POS	AGE	CAPS	MINS	GOALS	CARDS(Y)	CARDS(R)	CLUB SIDE
1	Kenny Cunningham	DEF	33	8	713	0	1	0	Birmingham
2	Robbie Keane	ATT	23	7	630	3	0	0	Tottenham
3	Matt Holland	MID	30	8	622	1	0	0	Charlton
4	Shay Given	GK	28	7	591	0	0	0	Newcastle
5	Clinton Morrison	ATT	25	9	532	1	0	0	Birmingham
6	Kevin Kilbane	MID	27	7	477	0	1	0	Everton
7	Ian Harte	DEF	26	7	476	1	0	0	Leeds
8	John O'Shea	DEF	23	6	472	1	0	0	Man Utd
9	Damien Duff	ATT	25	6	466	2	0	0	Chelsea
10	Gary Doherty	DEF	2005	7	448	0	0	0	Tottenham
11	Steve Finnan	DEF	28	6	440	0	0	0	Liverpool
12	Mark Kinsella	MID	31	6	391	0	1	0	West Brom
13	Andrew Reid	MID	21	5	356	0	0	0	Nott'm Forest
14	Colin Healy	MID	24	4	324	0	0	0	Sunderland
15	Gary Breen	DEF	30	4	312	0	0	0	Sunderland
16	Andy O'Brien	DEF	25	5	309	0	0	0	Newcastle
17	Alan Maybury	DEF	25	4	297	0	0	0	Hearts
18	Liam Miller	MID	23	4	291	0	0	0	Celtic
19	Nick Colgan	GK	30	5	284	0	0	0	Stockport
20	Stephen Carr	DEF	27	5	282	0	1	0	Tottenham
21	Steven Reid	MID	23	4	240	0	0	0	Blackburn

WALES

FIFA/COCA COLA WORLD RANKING: **66th**

MANAGER: MARK HUGHES

1	eq9	**Serbia & Mont.**	A	L	0-1		30,000
2	eq9	**Italy**	A	L	0-4		70,000
3	eq9	**Finland**	H	D	1-1	Davies 3	70,000
4	eq9	**Serbia & Mont.**	H	L	2-3	Hartson 24 pen; Earnshaw 90	72,514
5	eqpl1	**Russia**	A	D	0-0		29,000
6	eqpl2	**Russia**	H	L	0-1		73,062
7	intnls	**Scotland**	H	W	4-0	Earnshaw 1,35,58; Taylor 78	47,124
8	intnls	**Hungary**	A	W	2-1	Koumas 20; Earnshaw 81	15,000
9	intnls	**Norway**	A	D	0-0		14,137
10	intnls	**Canada**	H	W	1-0	Parry 21	10,805

KEY PLAYERS - GOALSCORERS

Robert Earnshaw

Goals in Internationals	5
Contribution to Attacking Power Average number of minutes between team goals while on pitch	60
Player Strike Rate The total number of minutes he was on the pitch for every goal scored	108
Club Strike Rate Average number of minutes between goals scored by club	90

	PLAYER	GOALS	ATT POWER	STRIKE RATE
1	Robert Earnshaw	5	60	108 mins
2	Simon Davies	1	151	302 mins
3	Jason Koumas	1	129	387 mins
4	John Hartson	1	141	424 mins

TOP PLAYER APPEARANCES

7 Robbie Savage — Midfield

Age (on 01/07/04)	29
Caps this season	6
Total minutes on the pitch	521
Goals	5
Yellow Cards	0
Red Cards	0
Club Side	Cardiff

	PLAYER	POS	AGE	CAPS	MINS	GOALS	CARDS(Y)	CARDS(R)	CLUB SIDE
1	Daniel Gabbidon	DEF	24	8	720	0	0	0	Cardiff
2	Ryan Giggs	MID	30	8	674	0	0	0	Man Utd
3	Mark Delaney	DEF	28	7	630	0	3	0	Aston Villa
4	Gary Speed	MID	34	7	611	0	0	0	Newcastle
5	Paul Jones	GK	37	7	585	0	0	0	Wolverhampton
6	Robert Earnshaw	ATT	23	9	540	5	0	0	Cardiff
7	Robbie Savage	MID	29	6	521	0	3	0	Birmingham
8	Robert Page	DEF	29	5	450	0	0	0	Sheff Utd
9	Andy Melville	DEF	35	5	446	0	1	0	West Ham
10	Craig Bellamy	ATT	24	5	444	0	2	0	Newcastle
11	John Hartson	ATT	29	5	424	1	0	0	Celtic
12	Jason Koumas	ATT	24	5	387	1	3	1	West Brom
13	Carl Robinson	MID	27	5	349	0	0	0	Portsmouth
14	Simon Davies	MID	24	4	302	1	0	0	Tottenham
15	Darren Barnard	DEF	32	4	271	0	1	0	Grimsby
16	John Oster	MID	25	3	269	0	0	0	Sunderland
17	Mark Pembridge	MID	33	3	257	0	0	0	Fulham
18	Ben Thatcher	DEF	28	3	233	0	0	0	Leicester
19	Carl Fletcher	MID	24	4	201	0	0	0	Bournemouth
20	Danny Coyne	GK	31	3	180	0	0	0	Leicester
21	Andy Johnson	MID	30	4	178	0	1	0	West Brom

NORTHERN IRELAND

FIFA/COCA COLA WORLD RANKING: **114th**

MANAGER: LAWRIE SANCHEZ

1	eq6	**Ukraine**	A	D	0-0		24,000
2	eq6	**Armenia**	H	L	0-1		8,616
3	eq6	**Greece**	A	L	0-1		12,500
4	intnls	**Norway**	H	L	1-4	Healy, D 56	
5	intnls	**Estonia**	A	W	1-0	Healy, D 45	
6	intnls	**Serbia & Mont.**	H	D	1-1	Quinn, Ja 18	
7	intnls	**Barbados**	A	D	1-1	Healy, D 71	8,000

KEY PLAYERS - GOALSCORERS

James Quinn

Goals in Internationals	1
Contribution to Attacking Power Average number of minutes between team goals while on pitch	84
Player Strike Rate The total number of minutes he was on the pitch for every goal scored	169
Club Strike Rate Average number of minutes between goals scored by club	158

	PLAYER	GOALS	ATT POWER	STRIKE RATE
1	James Quinn	1	84	169 mins
2	David Healy	3	133	178 mins

TOP PLAYER APPEARANCES

2 Maik Taylor — Goalkeeper

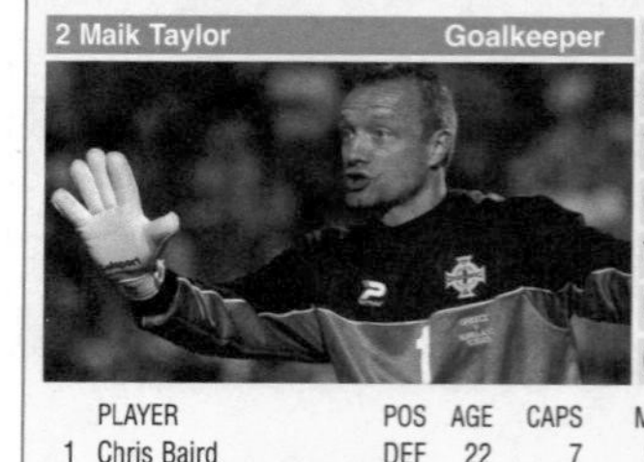

Age (on 01/07/04)	32
Caps this season	7
Total minutes on the pitch	585
Goals	0
Yellow Cards	1
Red Cards	0
Club Side	Birmingham

	PLAYER	POS	AGE	CAPS	MINS	GOALS	CARDS(Y)	CARDS(R)	CLUB SIDE
1	Chris Baird	DEF	22	7	606	0	0	0	Southampton
2	Maik Taylor	GK	32	7	585	0	1	0	Birmingham
3	David Healy	ATT	24	7	534	3	0	0	Preston
4	Andrew Smith	ATT	23	7	383	0	0	0	Glentoran
5	Aaron Hughes	DEF	24	4	360	0	0	0	Newcastle
6	Damien Johnson	MID	25	4	360	0	1	0	Birmingham
7	Keith Gillespie	MID	29	6	343	0	1	0	Leicester
8	George McCartney	DEF	23	4	339	0	2	1	Sunderland
9	Daniel Griffin	DEF	26	4	312	0	1	0	Stockport
10	Michael Hughes	MID	32	4	273	0	2	0	Crystal Palace
11	Stephen Craigan	DEF	27	3	270	0	0	0	Motherwell
12	Phillip Mulryne	MID	26	5	266	0	0	0	Norwich
13	Peter Kennedy	MID	30	3	256	0	0	0	Wigan
14	Mark Williams	DEF	33	4	255	0	0	1	Wimbledon
15	Anthony Capaldi	MID	22	3	246	0	0	0	Plymouth
16	Steve Jones	ATT	27	6	210	0	0	0	Crewe
17	Tommy Doherty	MID	25	3	172	0	1	0	Bristol City
18	James Quinn	ATT	29	2	169	1	0	0	Willem II Tilb
19	Danny Sonner	MID	32	3	155	0	0	0	Nott'm Forest
20	Grant McCann	MID	24	2	113	0	0	0	Cheltenham
21	Stuart Elliott	MID	25	3	107	0	0	0	Hull City